1 MONTH OF
FREE
READING

at
www.ForgottenBooks.com

By purchasing this book you are eligible for one month membership to ForgottenBooks.com, giving you unlimited access to our entire collection of over 1,000,000 titles via our web site and mobile apps.

To claim your free month visit:

www.forgottenbooks.com/free733598

ISBN 978-0-483-39941-9
PIBN 10733598

This book is a reproduction of an important historical work. Forgotten Books uses
state-of-the-art technology to digitally reconstruct the work, preserving the original format
whilst repairing imperfections present in the aged copy. In rare cases, an imperfection in
the original, such as a blemish or missing page, may be replicated in our edition. We do,
however, repair the vast majority of imperfections successfully; any imperfections that
remain are intentionally left to preserve the state of such historical works.

Dr. Wellons was licensed in 1854 and ordained to the Gospel ministry by the North Carolina and Virginia Christian Conference in 1856, and during sixty-four years that have since elapsed he has missed only two sessions of his Conference—one due to his being behind the Federal lines during the Civil War, the other due to serious illness—a record that we doubt can be matched. He has never missed a session of the Southern Christian Convention since 1854, and but one session of the American Christian Convention, and then on account of sickness. His strict attendance on his Conference sessions and his Church Conventions, has not been perfunctory, but arose out of the vital response of a devoted heart to duty, and no man has exercised a more powerful influence nor proven a worthier counselor than he. The beauty of his life is now seen in the sweet and gracious spirit in which he rejoices to see younger men taking the place of leadership so long conceded to him—sweet and gracious beyond the portrayal of language, because so sublimely sincere and absolutely unaffected.

Dr. Wellons had preached as a local preacher by the authority of Barrett's church, Southampton County, Virginia, for two years before he came to North Carolina and accepted license by his present Conference, but up to his twenty-sixth year was an interested layman, being a deacon, and also secretary and treasurer of the church. It was at the earnest solicitation of his fellow-laymen that he first gave serious thought to the ministry. They recognized his rare gift for that important calling, and sixty-six years of devoted service has given abundant proof of his divine appointment to this work.

When Elon College was being agitated and initiated, he was an uncompromising advocate of the idea. He was a member of the Provisional Board that located the college where it is, and offered the first prayer, for its growth and progress, on the present campus. From that day to this, he has been a member of the Board of Trustees and of the Executive Board and has never missed a session of either. He is now one of its wisest and most trusted members.

Uncle Wellons has little of this world's goods, but he has left what he has to the permanent funds of the college that is in a very real sense the wife of his heart. He has been too busy in the King's business to establish a home and take a wife. Elon is his bride, and he is as fond of her as a gallant knight ever was or could be of his fair lady.

It is an honor to know an love this noble man.

W. A. HARPER.

HE IS MY FRIEND

It has been my good fortune to know Rev. J. W. Wellons, D. D., all of my life. He was one of the first preachers I ever knew, and he has influenced my life in many ways. I never caught him indulging in melancholy, sitting around grumbling, but he went about cheerful and happy, and made me feel how blessed it is to be a Christian. His life has been an open book, and many young preachers have been inspired to high and holy things by his exemplary life.

On this, his ninety-third birthday, thousands will call him blessed because of the fact that he helped them to get rid of the shackels of sin. It was said that William Wilberforce would go to God with the shackels of eight hundred thousand West India slaves in his hands, and we believe that our Brother has filled his hands with many shackels he has removed from lives bounds in the shackels of sin. He is leading many to heaven because he has heaven's sunlight on his face. He is my friend.

C. H. ROWLAND.

NEW YEAR GREETINGS FOR REV. J. W. WELLONS

May Brother Wellons live many more years to work for his Lord. Thousands have been converted to Christ through his ministry. I have been with him in many good meetings, one being in Norfolk, Virginia, after which he reorganized the first Christian church. He is truly a great and good man. May the richest blessings of Heaven continue with Brother Wellons.

H. H. BUTLER.

A TRIBUTE TO "UNCLE WELLONS"

A life full of years, lived maintaining high ideals, serving faithfully in the highest calling, the gospel ministry, contending for the faith once delivered to the saints. I pen these lines in appreciation of his long life of service in the Church that he loves; because he has been preserved to this good age. May his last days be bright and full of joy in view of the welcome by the Master to the joys on high.

W. D. HARWARD.

RE-EMPLOYMENT OF SOLDIERS AND SAILORS

The United States Government, through its Labor Department, is initiating a plan by which the returning soldiers and sailors shall find opportunity for employment immediately upon their return home. Organizations are being set up in every community throughout the land under the auspices of the Government. These organizations will be Employment Bureaus for the discharged troops.

The churches can serve this excellent cause by appointing committees to co-operate with these bureaus in behalf of their respective groups of soldiers and sailors as they return.

One hundred and thirty-one judges in the United States are to get a fifteen hundred dollar raise each in salary.

The Reformed Church has launched a "Forward Movement." So has the Friends' Church.

The measure of a man is his doings and not his capacity to do.

God can use men that men cannot use—and men are using men that God wants to use.

Give us the man who can laugh—who can really laugh. There are enough of clouds without cloudy faces.

PASTOR AND PEOPLE

GREENSBORO

I arrived in this city to take charge of the work November 15, 1918. On my arrival I found things in a rather peculiar shape. The city was closed against all services for the public, and of course all church doors were closed. The cause being a second epidemic of influenza. I had nothing to do but wait for the opening which within itself was a big job. I had often wondered how a man would feel if he went on a new field and the folks would not let him preach; now I know. Yet with closed doors the church furnished plenty of work to do, since it had been hard hit by the first and second epidemic. Our doors remained closed until Sunday, December 8, at which time we held our first service which was well attended, considering the great amount of sickness among the members of the church.

In spite of the scare and many other difficulties, I have held two Sunday services, morning and evening. These services have been well attended and the congregations are on the increase each Sunday. All church work of the city has been completely demoralized. The loss by death has been great. The city has lost some of its most prominent business men. The loss in our own particular field has been very great.

There are some advantages and disadvantages here. First of all, the work is badly disorganized. Not having a regular pastor since July, and the two epidemics have completely disorganized the working forces of the church. I am conscious of the fact that the work, (like all other city work) will be difficult for a while. Yet there is nothing too difficult for our Christ who is able to do more for us than we are able to think, or ask. Then in the death toll we have lost some of the leaders in the work, and it takes time to fill these vacancies in the church, Sunday school, and Christian Endeavor Society.

In the second place, there are several advantages. The church is located near the center of possibly one of the cleanest cities of the South. The people with whom you come in contact are, generally speaking, clean, clever, kind, and very generous in many ways. I have been from home to home since I came, and at no time have I failed to receive the most courteous replies when asking for information.

Then the church folks, though compelled to remain most of the time at home, have given me a very hearty welcome. I find among our people a longing to return to the church services again. Even some who did not go to church much are anxious to get in. There is a spirit of anxiousness that we are very glad to see. It inspires me to forget my trials, difficulties, and press on into the work. I am conscious of the fact that this church had been under the leadership of some of the very best men of our church. Of all these men, the church speaks very highly.

Brother minister, do you have a member of your church in this city who has not united with the church here? If so, won't you please send his or her name and address to me? Better still, send their church letters along, and write them that you have done so. It is a shame that so many of our church folks move to the city, and are completely lost from the church. Give me their names and they will have a hard time if they do not line up with our work.

J. VINCENT KNIGHT.

A CHURCH SECRETARY WITH A RECORD

In the month of January, 1889, or just twenty-nine years ago, Brother M. W. Hollowell of Deep Creek, Va., was elected secretary of Berea Christian church of Norfolk county, Va., of which church the writer now has the pleasure of being pastor. During the twenty-nine years that Brother Hollowell has served as secretary of his church, one hundred and forty-four business sessions have been held. Only seventeen times in twenty-nine years has he been absent from the business meetings of the church. In other words, he has attended one hundred and twenty-seven times out of the one hundred and forty-four meetings that have occurred. The seventeen absences that he has recorded against himself represent seventeen impossibilities; for each time he has not been present there was an unavoidable cause.

Thus it is seen that our brother is faithful in that which has been committed to him. But he is more than faithful; he is efficient. Just as his record of attendance speaks of his faithfulness to duty, so does the work he has done give evidence of his efficiency. Through faithfulness he has become efficient. As a result, he now has recorded in one large volume an accurate account of all the meetings that have been held during the time he has served as secretary. In fact he has in this one volume the records of the church since its organization in 1871. Forty-seven years since the church was organized with an account of every business session neatly and accurately kept, and now recorded, these facts speak in no uncertain way as to the type of church secretary who makes such a thing possible.

Brother Hollowell deserves very high commendation for his faithfulness and efficiency, but the facts here given and the statements here made are not intended merely as a compliment to our good friend, but are passed on in the hope of calling attention to the need in many of our churches of arousing those who are in the various offices to do their work and do it well. Every office in the church from sexton to pastor is important enough to demand not good service, but the very best, highest service which it is possible to render. It will help our church forward in a wonderful way when the officers in our local churches learn to do their work definitely, accurately, and without needless delay.

G. O. LANKFORD.

Berkley, Va.

FIRST CHURCH, NORFOLK

This has been a splendid year for this church. Interest has been very good in all departments of our church life, and the outlook for the coming year is hopeful.

During the past year we have paid off a large part of the debt on our Sunday school room, overaid our apportionments to Conference, given more than $375.00 to the mission fund in the interest of which Dr. J. O. Atkinson has been working, even though we have not had a visit from him. We have given the Christian Orphanage aside from our regular monthly offering of the Sunday school, $300.00, or probably a little more. In addition to these we have received into our church 35 new members, and splendid work has been done along spiritual lines in all the auxiliaries of the church.

We begin the New Year with a prayer and an earnest desire that we may be enabled to do more for our Master than we have ever done before, and we desire the prayers of the brotherhood in our behalf.

J. F. MORGAN.

SOCIAL SERVICE AT ATLANTIC CITY

The Commission on the Church and Social Service of the Federal Council met in connection with the Executive Committee, December 10 and 11. The Executive Secretary, Dr. Worth M. Tippy, reported the work of the year, which was largely done in co-operation with other organizations, such as the Red Cross, the Joint Committee on Social Hygiene, the Joint Committee on War Production Communities, and others. This feature of co-operation is increasingly characteristic of Federal Council methods, thus avoiding duplication of effort, and adding greatly to the efficiency of all the agencies.

A Committee on Rural Fields has been formed, with Rev. E. DeS. Brunner as Secretary. He has also become the Executive Secretary of the Commission on the Church and Country life, thus bringing that Commission into active relations with the Social Service Commission. The staff of the Commission has also been increased by adding a "Research Secretary" who has done much valuable work.

The plans of the Commission for the coming year include three lines of educational effort. There will be an endeavor to promote the application of the principles of Christianity to society, with emphasis upon the problems of industrial democracy and social reconstruction. Churches will be given assistance in social organization, with especial reference to community service. And an attempt will be made to relate the churches more closely to the social activities of the national, state and municipal government. As far as possible use will be made of the existing denominational agencies for this educational work.

The Commission urged full freedom of discussion and service in the churches. Recognizing the necessity in war-time of the limitation of certain rights of speech and action, it was urged that with the coming of peace these must be fully restored, and that especially in the churches there should be no restriction upon the advocacy of the claims of social and economic justice.

The Church Forum, or popular meetings under the auspices of the churches for the free discussion of current social and religious questions was recommended, both for community purposes, and as a valuable variation of the Sunday night service. The Commission hopes to co-operate with the Christian Educational Association and other agencies in working out proper Forum programs, and in making available information concerning Forum methods.

The immense amount of social effort made necessary by war conditions has given the churches a new impulse toward this form of service. As the special agencies are discontinued, their tasks will be taken up by the regular organizations of the churches. The various social groups will find their field greatly enlarged, and they should be prepared to meet their new responsibility.

O. W. POWERS.

Dayton, Ohio.

A WAR LESSON
By Rev. F. G. Coffin, D. D.

Now that we can "rest arms" for a time, war lessons are myriad. These should never be forgotten. They are of a kind not growing out of philosophies but clinically produced by ample demonstration. Industrial, political, social and religious life may share alike in their benefits.

None is more prominent than the necessity in all matters of absolute dependence upon God. It is doubtful if the world has ever been more general in the practice of prayer or more intense in its spirit. Men not previously noted for a devotional spirit have freely confessed that apart from God no victory was possible, or even if possible, it would be undesirable. Days, seasons, and objects were designated sacred to prayer. The daily stopping of all activities at our national capital for a brief petition at the whistle of the prayer siren expressed the prevalent national spirit.

Another example of this spirit is found in a prayer movement known as The National Women's Prayer Battalion. Its founder and executive secretary, the Rev. Eva Ryerson Ludgate, was so impressed during a visit to England by the attitude of English women toward prayer, that when this country entered the war she felt she could do no greater things for her country than to "strengthen the third line of defense," by reminding the women that God would comfort their need. The call of this organization for prayer in behalf of the new world order is as follows:

1. That the kingdom of God may be established among the nations.

2. That the divine spirit may guide the deliberations of the peace conference.

3. That the nations may enact laws that will afford no less protection to our youth in times of peace than in times of war.

4. That the Church, in this day of opportunity, may more perfectly represent the spirit of our Lord Jesus Christ, in its life and service.

5. That the ministers may have inspiration and courage for the great tasks which lie before them.

6. That the young men and women of the world may enlist for Christ's service with the same eager devotion that led them to answer the call for the preservation of the world's liberty. Its covenant reads:

I covenant with God and the members of the International Prayer Battalion to pray for the peoples of the world, that they may be worthy of the victory for Democracy which has been achieved at so great cost.

I will pray for the soldiers and sailors who are guarding the peace for which they and their immortal comrades fought, and for all those engaged in the service of reconstruction.

Not only will I pray for the world, but I will do all in my power by my daily life and example to bring in a newer and brighter day.

From many sources have come calls for prayer and testimonies of benefits derived from the movement. Miss Ludgate says:

"As I write, I have before me letters from women of three different nationalities; the first is from a woman of noble birth who lives in Holland. She writes: 'Do pray for us; situated as we are, we see daily such terrible suffering; indeed we could not live it if we did not believe we were in the hands of God.'

"The second letter is from an English woman who has worked for years in the Young Women's Christian Association in London: 'We must pray. Prayer has sustained us through the dark years of this war. And whatever may be before us in the reconstruction period, we will find strength and wisdom as we need it, if we only pray.'

"The last letter is from a woman who is neither educated nor of noble birth; her story is very briefly told. She is a young wife and mother whose husband has been overseas for a year. She is working very hard to make ends meet. She says: 'I never thought I would pray in my kitchen, but I do. Sometimes when my heart is so heavy I cannot bear it another moment, I kneel down and just talk to the Heavenly Father, and soon I receive the strength I need to go on.' That is what the world needs more than any other one thing: 'Strength to go on.' We cannot generate this power within ourselves—it must be God-given.

"'I brought home from England one year a motto which reads. 'Prayer Changes Things:' The Church needs to reaffirm this. The war has brought the world to believe there is power in prayer, and if we at this time lay the emphasis on prayer, we can make religion not a thing apart but the very heart and soul of the great world reconstruction movement.'"

While the first Battalion was organized for women only and was to last for the duration of the war, the name has been changed and the movement is developing a world construction program. It is now called the International Prayer Battalion and will in the future work in a spirit of helpful co-operation with the churches.
Albany, N. Y.

MEETING OF COMMISSIONERS OF CONFERENCE UNION

The commissioners representing the three Christian conferences in North Carolina met here today to discuss the preliminary basis of the union of the three conferences into one, to be known as the North Carolina Christian Conference.

The commissioners from the North Carolina-Virginia Christian Conference were Revs. P. H. Fleming, J. O. Atkinson and W. A. Harper; from the Eastern North Carolina Conference, Hon. K. B. Johnson, Dr. W. C.

Wicker, Rev. A. T. Banks; from the Western North Carolina Conference Rev. T. E. White, Dr. E. L. Moffitt, Rev. L. I. Cox.

Rev. J. W. Wellons, Dr. N. G. Newman, and J. Dolph Long, Esq., attorney, sat with the commissioners throughout their deliberations. The move for the union of the three conferences began on November 22, 1917, in the North Carolina-Virginia Christian Conference in its session at Haw River, N. C., where a resolution was passed inviting the other two conferences to join with it, and created its three commissioners to present the matter to the other two conferences and secure the approval of the Southern Christian Conference for the merger.

The Southern Christian Conference gave its consent to the measure on May 3, of the recent year. On November 27, the Western North Carolina Conference voted to unite, and on December 4, the Eastern North Carolina Conference took similar action, and the meeting held here today composed of the nine commissioners from the three conferences was the first united step in the progress of a united conference for the State.

Rev. J. O. Atkinson, Rev. W. C. Wicker, and Rev. L. I. Cox, with Attorney Long, were appointed to draft the charter for final approval at a later meeting, and the nine commissioners were constituted incorporators for the new conference.

The officers for the purpose of incorporation are President, Rev. T. E. White, Sanford, N. C.; Vice-President; Rev. W. C. Wicker, Elon College, N. C.; Secretary, President W. A. Harper, Elon College, N. C.; Treasurer, Hon. K. B. Johnson, Cardenas, N. C.; Executive Secretary, Rev. L. I. Cox, Elon College, N. C.

As soon as the charter has been granted by the Secretary of State the temporary officers will call the incorporators together and a permanent organization will be affected. It is hoped this can be done quite speedily.

One of the problems facing the conference was as to the standing committees and boards of the conferences, and it was decided to constitute the boards for the first session of the new conference out of all the members of the corresponding boards in the three conferences.

W. A. HARPER, *Secretary.*

Elon College, N. C.
December 27, 1918.

REV. H. JENNINGS FLEMING ORDAINED

Rev. H. Jennings Fleming, son of Dr. P. H. Fleming, was ordained at the Burlington Christian church last Sunday. The ordination sermon was preached by Dr. J. O. Atkinson, who used as a theme: "A Man, a Message and a Mission." The candidate was presented, after the sermon, by Pastor J. W. Harrell, the charge was delivered by Dr. Atkinson, the scripture read by Dr. Fleming, the Bible presented by Rev. P. T. Klapp, the certificate of ordination presented by the candidate's father and the prayer offered by Rev. J. W. Wellons. The service was sacred, sweet and solemn.

The Church conducts all kinds of surveys. Why not a survey to find out how much money the people have that has been dedicated to God?

MISSIONARY

MISSION BOARD RECORDS

The Mission Board of the Christian church met in annual session Tuesday forenoon, December 17, 1918, at Dayton, Ohio, in the Christian Mission rooms with all members present except Chaplain Carlyle Summerbell, Departments represented as follows: *Home Department*—Rev. O. S. Thomas, Rev. C. B. Kershner, M. S. Campbell, Mrs. J. F. Burnett; *Foreign Department*—Rev. M. T. Morrill, Rev. W. P. Fletcher, Rev. J. W. Harrell, Mr. J. O. Winters, Rev. W. H. Denison. The following message was sent to Chaplain Summerbell:

"The Mission Board of which you have been for these four years a faithful and efficient member convened this morning. All the members are present except yourself and your absence was at once felt. We are very glad that you are having the opportunity of extending the Kingdom as Chaplain and feel that we are honored in having one of our members thus serving our boys at the front and also the cause of liberty and democracy.

Your brethren of the Mission Board wish you God-speed in your great work and express the hope that when your work is over with our soldier boys you will return to us all the better equipped for hardship in redemption work in the home land."

The Board met several times in conference with the Executive Board of the American Christian Convention and, the Sunday School Board. The Board made the following memorial to the Executive Board of the American Christian Convention:

"That a definite date be set for an Every-Member-Canvass in all the churches of the denomination, and that we adopt the slogan 'As much for others as for ourselves; and that all the departments of the American Christian Convention co-operate in the organization and campaign for this canvass.'"

Committees:

Nominations—Members Campbell, Harrell, Mrs. Burnett.

Literature and Publicity—Members Fletcher, Winters, Kershner.

Greetings—Members Fletcher, Kershner.

The correspondence proceedings for the year were read and approved. The Home Mission Secretary, Rev. O. S. Thomas; The Foreign Mission Secretary; Rev. M. T. Morrill; the Financial gent; Rev. J. G. Bishop; the Publisher of the Christian Missionary, Rev. M. T. Morrill, and the Treasurer, Rev. O. S. Thomas, and the Auditors, S. O. Albaugh, A. F. Chase, all made their reports and they were referred to the proper committees and departments.

Officers

Honorary President—Rev. J. G. Bishop, D. D.; *President*—Rev. M. T. Morrill, D. D.; *Secretary*—Rev. W. H. Denison, D. D.; *Treasurer*—Rev. O. S. Thomas; *Financial Agent*—Rev. J. G. Bishop, D. D.; *Mission Council*—Members Morrill, Denison, Winters, Thomas, Kershner, Mrs. Burnett; *Investment Committee*—Members Thomas, Winters, Denison.

Salaries Beginning January 1, 1919

Home Mission Secretary, at rate of $1,800 per year. Foreign Mission Secretary, $50 per month. (This contemplates only supervision of the work, but not of service in the office, until the Quadrennial Convention meets. Financial Agent, at rate of $600 per year.

Appropriations

The Missionary Education Movement, $50; For the Secretary's clerical expense, $10; Board meeting expenses.

The Treasurer's, Auditor's and Financial Agent's report were adopted. It was voted that the Foreign Mission Secretary be authorized to secure necessary office assistance. The following action was taken:

"We rejoice with our brethren of the Southern Christian Convention that they have so splendidly achieved their goal of raising $100,000 for missions, home and foreign.

"We wish to congratulate them on their move for greater efficiency in the Kingdom by incorporation of the Mission Board of the Southern Christian Convention, and express our appreciation of the enlarged objective of $50,000 act before them. We hope and believe that they will be blessed in their unselfish and sacrificing service, and that the Christian church and the Kingdom will be enlarged by this increased bounty and efficiency of service."

The Christian Missionary

We especially commend the Christian Missionary for its very efficient service. We are pleased to note the increase in the subscription list in these days when so many papers and magazines have found it necessary to discontinue publication. In view of the special service rendered by the Christian Missionary in the field of publicity we recommend that the price of the subscription be continued at fifty cents per year.

That the size of the Christian Missionary conform to the government requirement but in no case the amount of space for matter be lessened.

That Dr. M. T. Morrill be asked to continue as Editor-in-chief of the Christian Missionary and that he be asked to nominate to the Mission Board such persons as he desires to have co-oerate with him as departmental assistants.

That we especially commend the book of Dr. J. G. Bishop, "The Christians and the Great Commission," and ask our people everywhere to further its circulatin believing that our future work will be helped by knowing the way we have come.

Believing that nothing is so valuable in publicity as the personal touch, we recommend that the Secretary of each department do as much field work as his time will allow.

The Home Mission and Foreign Mission departments considered all matters pertaining to their respective departments, and made reports of their actions to this board which on motion were adopted.

All unfinished business was referred to the Mission Council. After reading and approving the minutes the Board adjourned Thursday night, December 19, 1918 with prayer by Dr. J. G. Bishop.

WARREN H. DENISON, *Sec'y.*

(Minutes of the Foreign Mission Department will appear next week.)

M. W. Hollowell—This is my 39th renewal. I have been reading THE SUN for forty years, and should the Lord let me live so long as dear Dr. Wellons, I expect to read it forty more.

THE CHRISTIAN ORPHANAGE

SUPERINTENDENT'S LETTER

Dear Friends:—Our financial report still climbs upward and we are glad. We pass the $13,000.00 mile post in this report, but we have not reached our goal for the Thanksgiving offering.

Ninety-seven churches have responded to the call and with the individual offerings have raised $4,342.33. Oh! where are the 165 churches that have not fallen in line? It is our earnest prayer that each church will make this offering this year. I have been hoping and praying that we could be able to report each one on the banner list when we close our report for this year's work.

If these churches could know just how hard I have worked this year and the many sacrifices I have made in order to pull this Institution out of debt I feel sure I would have their sympathy and they would be glad to make this offering to give me the joy and happiness it would bring to just have them on the banner list. Will some one in each one of these churches make himself or herself a committee to see to it that this offering is made and send it in by at least the middle of January? Perhaps the pastor or the Sunday school superintendent will be glad to see that this is done. It would be the joy of my heart to see each church on the banner list this year. Friends, pastors, Sunday school superintendents, will you see that this thing happens? Then I will have some good news to tell you when I close my report for this year's work.

Our little folks have had a real happy Christmas and have been filled with joy and happiness by the many presents sent in by a number of churches. It is our happiness to see them happy and our joy to see their hearts full of gladness.

Now, my friends we just lack $657.67 being at our goal of $5,000.00 for our Thanksgivinw offering. *We must reach it. You must see that we do reach it.* As your superintendent, I have given you a faithful year's work and I do ask that you see to it that I reach this goal. I have reached each one set since I have been in this work and have gone over the top. *I must not fail in this one.*

You have been loyal indeed and I am very grateful to you and you have all the credit for what has been accomplished during the two years past. I have just been the servant of the church and have tried to be faithful in discharging the duties entrusted to me and the good Lord has been good to me and has caused you to rally to our support in the work.

LETTERS

Dear Uncle Charley:—As we are expecting old Santa to be good to us we enclose one dollar to help him a little at the Orphanage. Wishing you and all the orphans a happy Christmas.—*Virginia, Elinor, Annie and Robert Wells.*

We are glad you remembered us at Christmas time.

It was real good of you. We trust old Santa was good to you.—*"Uncle Charley."*

Dear Uncle Charley:—Our grandmother Iseley gave us a nickle a piece to give the orphans for Christmas. Best wishes for a Merry Christmas to all.—*Edward, Rena Maud, Earl, Virginia Frances Isley, Virginia Isley, Margaret and Annie Lee Green.*

It is fortunate for little folks to have grandmas. I spent many pleasant hours with mine when I was a little boy and she would give me good things to eat and tell me stories of her girlhood days. Those were great days to me and they are to you.—*"Uncle Charley."*

REPORT FOR DECEMBER 25—Continued

Amount brought forward—$11,991.71.

Children's Offerings

Edward Isley, 5 cents; Rena Maud Isley, 5 cents; Earl Isley, 5 cents; Virgie Francis Isley, 5 cents; Virginia Isley, 5 cents; Margaret Green, 5 cents; Annie Lee Green, 5 cents; Virginia, Elinor, Annie and Robert Wells, $1.00; Total, $1.35.

Sunday School Monthly Offerings

Columbus, Ga., $2.00; Wadley, Ala., $1.02; Antioch, (Va.), $2.00; Palm Street, Greensboro, N. C., $6.00; Holy Neck, $5.00; Shallow Ford, $2.00; First Christian, (Norfolk), $2.24; Auburn, $3.00; Total, $23.36.

Special Offerings

Woman's Home and Foreign Board of the S. C. C., $197.16.

Miscellaneous

J. H. Jones, Newport News, Va., on support of children, $30.00; County Board of Education, Alamance County, N. C., $12.65; Total, $42.65.

Thanksgiving and Christmas Offerings

Graham Christian church, $18.03; Washington St. church, Portsmouth, Va., $80.00; Dr. J. H. Brooks, $100.00; Mrs. J. W. Boon, $1.00; Centerville church, $8.07; Mr. J. H. Massey, $2.00; Sarem church, $6.01; Henderson church, $47.00; Noon Day, $5.01; Mrs. A. Maxton, $1.00; East End Christian Sunday school, $100.00; Mrs. Reta Thomas, $1.00; Progressive Bible Class, Suffolk, Va., $5.00; Shallow Ford church, $2.00; E. B. Atkinson, $1.00; E. Jones Philipps, $10.00; People's church, Dover, Del., $50.00; Asheboro church, $11.65; Zion church, $8.90; Memorial Christian Temple, $31.00; Aiming High Class, Suffolk, Va., $5.00; J. W. Knight and family, $5.00; Little Nollie Washburn, 40 cents; J. H. Jones, $1.00; First Christian church, Norfolk, Va., $103.41; Mrs. L. M. Pierce, $1.00; Earl Pierce, 25 cents; Ernest Pierce, Jr., 25 cents; Waverly S. S., Va., $55.45; Berea, Va., S. S., $37.00; Mrs. L. F. Brickhouse, $5.00; Berta Isley, $1.25; Margaret Isley, $1.25; Mrs. Rosa Keeves, $1.00; D. J. Mood, $5.00; Third Christian church, $66.25; New Hope, Ala., $6.15; G. W. Nelson and wife, $5.00; Total for the week, $1,051.85; Grand total, $13,043.56.

The following contributions have been sent in for Thanksgiving and Christmas:

Revolution Cotton Mills, Greensboro, N. C., 300 yards outing goods; Jas. N. Williamson & Sons, Burlington, N. C., 100 yards onting goods; Elmira Cotton Mills, Burlington, N. C., 408 yards Ginghams; Glencoe Cotton Mills, Burlington, N. C., 200 yards outing goods; E. M. Holt Plaid Mills, Burlington, N. C., 75 yards Ginghams; Lake Side Cotton Mills, Burlington, N. C., 40 yards Cheviots; White Oak Mills, Greensboro, N. C., 150 Denims; Pilot Cotton Mills, Raleigh, N. C., 65½ yards Chambra; Salisbury Cotton Mills, 135 yards Chambras; L. Banks Holt Manufacturing Co., Graham, N. C., 100 yards Chambras; Saxapahaw Cotton Mills, 100 yards Ginghams.

Union Seed & Fertilizer Co., 5 bags cotton seed meal; Farmers Cotton Oil Co., Wilson, N. C., 5 bags cotton seed meal; Farmville Oil and Fertilizer Co., 5 bags cotton seed meal; Clayton Oil Mills, 5 bags cotton seed meal.

Mr. C. W. Cather, Winchester, Va., 5 barrels apples; Mr. A. B. Richards, Winchester, Va., 2 barrels apples; Mr. A. C. Richards, Winchester, Va., 2 barrels apples; Mr. T. E. Brickhouse, Norfolk, Va., 1 barrel apples.

Mrs. C. V. Dunn, Paces, Va., 1 white table cloth; Capt. J. A. Turrentine, Burlington, N. C., 5 bushels corn, 5 pumpkins, 1 crate rape, Irish potatoes.

Hico Milling Co., Burlington, N. C., 1 barrel flour; W. H. Turrentine, Burlington, N. C., 2 bushel sweet potatoes, 1 bushel Irish potatoes.

Durham Hosiery Mills, 5 dozens hose; Miss Nettie Simpson, one-half dozen napkins; Mr. J. I. Branch, Auburn, N. C., 2 bushels sweet potatoes.

Mrs. Duke Eason, Sunbury, N. C., 21 half gallons fruit; Mrs. Dunn, Paces, Va., 13 half gallon cans fruits; Mrs. J. Pearl Long, Hertford, N. C., dried fruit.

Missionary Society Christian church, Eaton, Ill., box clothing; B. A. Sellars & Sons, Burlington, N. C., one box goods.

Mrs. C. D. Johnston, Graham, N. C. 10 pounds sausage; "A Friend," Cardenas, N C., 8 sheets; Ladies' Aid Society Ramseur church, 6 dozen can fruit, 2 quilts; W. H. Freeman, Ether, N. C., 8 gallons beans, 1 dozen cans tomatoes.

Ladies' Aid Society, Graham Christian church, 2 bushel potatoes; 1 bushel peas, 2 bushels Irish potatoes, 3 table cloths.

Mrs. Lizzie Sipe, News Ferry, Va., 1 barrel flour; Rev. P. T. Clapp, 1 barrel corn, 2 bushels potatoes; Ladies's Missionary Society, Antioch church, Frankfort, Ind., 1 box dresses; Mrs. Fannie W. Brickhouse, Norfolk, Va., one magic lantern; Rev, A. F. Isley, Burlington, N. C., 36 half gallon cans fruit; 4 chickens, 1 bushel sweet potatoes, ½ bushel Irish potatoes; Sunday school class, Christian church, Goshen, Ind., one box clothing for little girl.

NOTES

Write it 1919.

If you are going to make a New Year's resolution, make one that you can keep.

Are we moving forward in the Forward Movement, or are we "just talking" it? Which?

Elon College opens January 7. Will your family be represented in the enrollment?

Dr. D. A. Long writes from Dover, Delaware, that he is liking and having plenty of work to do.

Superintendent Johnston gives us a fine report this week. Note that it is to be continued.

Mr. Jobe Walker, father of Mrs. W. A. Harper, died at his home near Burlington, December 28.

The holidays put us one day late with THE SUN this week. That explains the delay of one day in your paper, kind reader.

Help us to make THE CHRISTIAN SUN for 1919 all that it should be and can be. All together financially and in other ways.

How do you like the new headings in THE SUN. See reasons on editorial pages why departments were discontinued.

We have been too busy during the last few months to send out statements to many of our subscribers, but we will have to do it in a week or so. Why not let your renewal come along without a reminder?

Editor Barrett of The Herald of Gospel Liberty has just taken a short vacation. Dr. Barrett, we do not know how to rejoice with you for such has never come our way since taking hold of the quill driving business.

Remember that we have Tarbell's Guide, also Peloubet's Select Notes and can send either by return mail. The price is $1.35 delivered. This has been the price of each for years.

Rev. H. Jennings Fleming, a student in Vanderbilt University, spent the holidays with his parents, Dr. and Mrs. P. H. Fleming of Burlington. They also had their sons, J. Sipe and J. Holt, who are in the navy, with them during the holidays.

Brother J. V. Knight calls attention to an important matter in his letter. All too many people move from the rural sections to the city and cease their church activity. They seem to feel that when they leave their home church their obligation ceases. Let all of us look well into this matter of importance.

Mrs. T. A. Jones, Norfolk, Va., one of THE SUN's truest friends, sends $5.00 as an offering to the Worthy Aid Fund to send THE SUN to those who are not able to take it. That is the real Christmas spirit—the spirit of giving that others may be blessed and benefitted. Mrs. Jones adds her appreciation of the paper.

Last week we failed to mention the passing of Mrs. J. N. H. Clendennin of Graham. Mrs. Clendennin was a most loyal member of her denomination. She was the only sister of Dr. D. A. and W. S. Long. The burial service was conducted by Drs. Staley and J. U. Newman as reported by Pastor F. C. Lester in his obituary note of the deceased.

Brother J. M. Darden writes Superintendent Chas. D. Johnston as follows:

"I am in receipt of the photograph of the Southern Car No. 34640, which was shipped from Suffolk loaded with supplies for the Orphanage, with the children, the matrons and yourself grouped in front of the car.

"This picture is worth all of the trouble and work I did in loading this car as I can look into the faces of these dear little orphans and tell how happy they were over the car. Then it is a good sight to see behind them a car of food for them to use during the cold winter.

"I shall have this picture enlarged, framed and presented to each one of the churches that donated towards loading the car. I would like for you to give Mr. Riddle one of these ictures and ask him to print it in THE CHRISTIAN SUN." If there will be any charge for the cut I will pay same,"

See Feb 5, 1919, p. 13

CHRISTIAN EDUCATION

BOOKS ARE NEEDED FOR OUR MEN IN HOSPITALS AND OVERSEAS

The Library War Service of the American Library Association, which is charged with the duty of providing books for soldiers, sailors and marines and for civilian war workers, authorizes the following appeal.—Herbert Putnam, General Director.

To the Superintendent, Board of Education, President, Professor, Trustees, or Custodian of Books:

This is an appeal to you to send books to the men of our Army and Navy and to all who are working with and for them.

You have many books you no longer need, books discarded or set aside. Please gather these up and send them to your nearest public library, which will send them at once where they are needed.

Do not delay. The need is pressing. The war has taken from their homes, their occupations, their friends, recreations and all familiar things, millions of our boys and young men. They need books for recreation. These have been furnished by the millions through our public libraries by gifts from thousands of homes. Still more are needed and are being gathered daily. Do not think that because hostilities have ceased the need for books for our soldiers overseas is ended. On the contrary, it is even greater than when they were keyed up by the stimulus of active warfare. Thousands of our armed forces abroad will have to remain there for a long time to come. The time of the men must be filled with other activities if the morale of this great body of troops is to be maintained. Part of their time will be occupied by the schools which the Government, in co-operation with various welfare agencies, is establishing. They will need books for recreation and diversion in their leisure hours.

Besides these special books which the American Library Association must furnish in large quanities for the use of the trade and technical schools for our men in France—books that must be bought with the funds which the public has subscribed for the maintenance of Library War Service—at least five million more books of all kinds are needed at once.

Many of these boys, millions of them in fact, are without even the rudiments of an education. Many cannot speak English, much less read it. Many have had only a few years of schooling. They are aroused and stimulated by their new life. They want to be better educated when they leave the Army and Navy than they were when they entered. And so they need books. They need grammars, dictionaries and books on English and books of literature and books on literature. They need geometries, trigonometries, and books on chemistry, botany, biology and all the sciences. They need books on drawing, painting and all the arts.

In many cases the old books are just as good for their purposes as the newest ones.

Books on logic, ethics, mechanics, sociology, plumbing, agriculture, roadmaking, the Ancient Romans, the climate of Patagonia, spavin in horses, metaphysics, or any other subject of possible practical or theoretic interest to any kind of person at any point in his career, are of possible value.

If you have such books, unused, you know that you cannot sell them for any sum that will pay for the book-keeping and correspondence connected with the transaction. Yet are they not a load on your conscience?

Then give them to your country. Ask your Board for a blanket instruction to dispose of them. Cut red tape. Present them to the American Library Association, now collaborating with the United States Bureau of Education in an effort to meet the educational needs of the Great Army engaged in the Great War.

By a careful survey and an illuminating experience the A. L. A. Committee has discovered that, while the book that amuses, refreshes and inspires is undoubtedly needed, the book that informs and instructs is no less desired.

It seeks to provide the book for every soldier's need, and it expects to find a need for almost every discarded book you may be able to provide.

Therefore, send all you can spare. This is a pressing need. All the librarians in the country have been at work gathering books for nearly two years. They know how to sort them out and where to send them. The national organization of librarians has raised money and built library buildings in cantonments, and sent books into hospitals, shipyards, munition works and into Y. M. C. A. huts and Salvation Army quarters and Naval Bases and Aviation Schools, and in fact to hundreds of Army and Navy centres of work and training of every kind. It has a picked body of men and women at work in the selection and distribution of books, and knows how to do it.

More than fifty ship tons of books go every month. They go in boxes which, when their lids are unscrewed, become units in shelved books cases. They are labeled and pocketed and ready for circulation. Instructions for amateur librarians accompany them. And a card surmounting each overseas case says:

"These books came to us overseas from home, To read them is a privilege; To restore them promptly unabused a duty.
                   —"John J. Pershing."

To get the books you have available into the hands of soldiers promptly, first gather your books together and find out how many there are that can be turned over for this purpose. Then notify your nearest public library. Every public library in the United States is a receiving station for books for Library War Service. If there is no public library in your community, send a notification of the number of books you have to contribute to Library War Service Headquarters, The Library of Congress, Washington, D. C., and instructions will be sent you how and where to ship the books by Quartermaster freight to the nearest A. L. A. dispatch office.

                   JOHN COTTON DANA

THE FORWARD MOVEMENT

Warren H. Denison, D. D., Superintendent

The Women's Mission Boards Heartily Behind the Forward Movement

The Woman's Home and Foreign Mission Boards of the Christian Church have undertaken a worthy task in connection with the Forward Movement. The Boards in annual session after consultation with the Superintendent of the Forward Movement voted unanimously to undertake the following goals for the present quadrennium:

1. *Devotion*—600 new pledged intercessors.

2. *Evangelism*—(a) 100 new Missionary Societies; (b) 2,000 new members in the Missionary Societies.

3. *Religious Education*—(a) 150 Missionary Societies studying the Women's and Foreign Mission Study Books each year; (b) 600 increase in number of Christian missionaries taken; (c) a Woman's Mission Board thoroughly organized in every Conference.

4. *Missions*—$80,000.00 for the Quadrennium.

5. *Benevolence*—(a) Teach tithing and principles of stewardship; (b) Urge individuals and churches to support missionaries and mission stations.

Our new Forward Movement song was sung for the first time at the Forward Movement rally at Dayton, Ohio, December 18. A splendid audience made it ring. There were thirty Christian ministers present and many of our strong laymen from a distance of thirty miles. The members of the Executive Board of the American Christian Convention, the Mission Board, and the Sun-School Board were present too. Of course you will recognize that it is to be sung to the familiar tune of "Onward, Christian Soldiers." Its six verses bring out "Forward" and the five points of the Forward Movement.

Our Forward Movement

By Nora Van Zant Thayer, Dayton, Ohio

Forward, Christian Churches, to the world wide call,
Hold aloft your banner, Brotherhood for all,
Get in line for service, join the mighty throng;
Forward, now, together, with a courage strong.

CHORUS—
Forward, Christian people, with the Truth unfurled,
'Till the name of Jesus, sounds through all the world.

Forward, Christians, trusting in your Father's care,
Read His Word so precious, lift your hearts in prayer,
For He marketh ever, e'en the sparrow's fall;
Take to Him your burdens, He will share them all.

Forward, Christian workers, there is much to do,
Here are fields now ready, laborers are few,
Souls are waiting, longing, for the story old;
Christians, lift your voices, until all are told.

Hear the trumpet sounding, hear the call for men,
Go ye forth as leaders; to the church proclaim,
That her task, unfinished, waits for teachers, true,
Ready with their talents, God's great work to do.

"Unto every creature"—the glad tidings send,
"I am with you always, e'en unto the end."
Glory, hallelujah, praise the Lord and King,
Through the countless ages, Christian voices ring.

Forward, then, ye people, for our cause now plead,
Only one-half million will supply the need,
Heart and mind and treasure, they belong to Him,
He'll restore full measure, give to you again.

Have you started that Christian Endeavor Expert Class? Now is the time. Start it with the New Year.

Has your pastor begun the series of sermons yet on "The Forward Movement?"

Will you start the New Year with the Family Altar in your home?

Are you reading the Forward Movement articles in *The Sunday School Herald?*

Why not join the "Quiet Hour" with the opening of the New Year? Will you?

You will never regret it if you start the New Year by tithing. It will be one of the great blessings of your life. Do you take *The Tither*, published at Burlington, N. C.? It will pay you to do so.

Are you and your church after a net gain of ten per cent in your church membership this year?

The Forward Movement asks for an active Evangelistic Committee in each church and conference. We regard this as very important.

What methods are you using to train your church membership in soul-winning?

THE CHURCH'S DUTY TO THE RETURNING SOLDIERS AND SAILORS

In the midst of the demobilization of the army and navy and the return of the soldiers and sailors to their homes, the pastors are asking themselves what they can do for the boys. The General War-Time Commission of the Churches, anticipating this anxiety on the part of the ministers, has prepared a statement in which many proposals are offered to the pastors and the churches throughout the country. This statement has been sent out from the office of the General War-Time Commission directly to the ministers throughout the nation.

YOUR SUNDAY-SCHOOL WORK FOR NEXT YEAR

What about your Sunday school work for another year, Brother Sunday School Teacher? Are you going to go along the same way or are you going to get something that will give you a larger vision of your work?

That copy of Peloubet's Notes is what you need. Or its equal is a copy of Tarbell's Guide. Peloubet's Notes is a production of two men; Tarbell's is the production of a woman—Martha Tarbell, Ph. D. THE CHRISTIAN SUN office has both. $1.25 will bring you a copy by return mail. Get ready for 1919.

Mrs. S. J. Moore—I am sending my renewal. I am eighty-one years old and can read without glasses.

Jas. B. Morris—Mark me up as a member of THE SUN family for another year.

Sunday School and Christian Endeavor

HELP REFERENCES

Sunday School—Officers and Teachers Journal and Christian Bible Class Quarterly by Christian Association, Dayton, Ohio; also Tarbell's Guide or Peloubet's Select Notes from any book dealer.

For Christian Endeavor—The Christian Endeavor World, Boston, Mass., and the Dixie Endeavorer, Chattanooga, Tenn.

PHARAOH OPPRESSES ISRAEL

(Exodus 1:1-14; 2:1-25)

Golden Text: He will save the children of the needy, and will break in pieces the oppressor. Ps. 72:4.

This is the first lesson for a New Year. What are you going to do with it? Are you going to study it in the same haphazard way in which you have done it in times past? Are you going to read the lesson responsively in your class, and ask the printed questions, and feel that you have done your duty as a teacher? Will you take the larger portion of the time discussing the historical and geographical questions, and allowing a few hasty moments for summing up the great spiritual truths? God forbid! "We are living, we are dwelling in a grand, an awful time" and you and I, as co-workers with God must take advantage of that fact. We must prepare ourselves to meet the responsibilities of our class. We must study in order that we may win the divine approval of God, and show ourselves workmen that need not to be ashamed. You will find suggestive thoughts for each grade in the quarterlies, while the *Teachers* and *Officers Journal* contains teaching thoughts for all grades. If you love your local church, your denomination, and your work; if you believe that this business of working together with God is the finest and grandest business in the world, then shall we not plan to make this year a splendid Forward Movement of all our Sunday school forces for Christ and His Church?

IMPORTANT NOTICE TO SUNDAY SCHOOLS AND CHRISTIAN ENDEAVOR SOCIETIES

I heartily thank my friend and brother, Dr. Atkinson, for his most flattering lines in THE SUN of December 18, introducing me as corresponding secretary and treasurer of the Board of Religious Education of the Southern Christian Convention. Now, the Doctor is a mighty good man and means well, but is liable to make mistakes, sometimes. When the tenth man appointed by the Convention could not be located, and the time for organization could not continue to be postponed, I was appointed to take his place, and a meeting was called and held in Raleigh, at which time Rev. J. W. Harrell was elected president; I. A. Luke, vice-president and Dr. J. O. Atkinson, secretary-treasurer. Later, when Dr. Atkinson tendered his resignation, I agreed to assist him and act as secretary-treasurer, but not as corresponding secretary, inasmuch as the seal and home office of this Board is to be at Elon College.

For several days now I have considered the work, thought of its possibilities and endeavored to outline a plan of action. These are my conclusions: We all must get in line. Dr. Harrell is president of this Board and head of this procession. He is entitled to some consideration, hard work and a reasonable portion of the criticism that is soon to come our way. Therefore, if you have any bills against this Board, send them direct to Dr. Harrell who will O. K. them and your treasurer will promptly pay them with borrowed money. If you wish inside information of any kind or desire to do some real Sunday school work, see or write the president and he will direct you into the right channel. If you have anything for publication or anything that should come under the various duties of corresponding secretary, do not fail to see or get in direct touch with Dr. Atkinson, for he, too is entitled to some of the honors, misfortunes, etc., of this organization. Keep him busy. And again, if you have any money, however small the amount, that you want to put in a live, wide-a-wake proposition that will be of real service to the present and future generation, by all means send it direct to your humble treasurer who will promptly give you credit and send you receipt for same.

We cannot afford to have a treasury containing only borrowed money—a word to the wise.

What do you think of a company of soldiers having only a captain; corporal and sergeant marching and the private loitering along or resting by the wayside? This cannot be seen in army life and it must not be so in our Sunday school work. It is important that all of us get in line. This means you, and you and you.

Since the three Conferences of North Carolina are about to consolidate why not the Sunday school and Christian Endeavor Conventions consolidate? We should put on record next July the biggest Sunday school and Christian Endeavor Convention in our denomination. We can do it. Are you willing to help now and help then? It does not matter how small your school or society is, we want every school and society represented. Let us know where you are so we can locate you. All that we are asking of you is that you do your duty. Think it over, talk it over in your Sunday school and society and volunteer your services.

I shall keep a record of all persons and Sunday schools who report their names and addresses, and who will agree to make a donation or appropriate one Sunday's offering in each month toward this general work. Every cent of the money will be spent to organize, keep alive, and promote Sunday schools and Christian Endeavor societies in the bounds of the Southern Christian Convention until we have sufficient funds to expand our work. You will be proud of the fact next July if your Sunday school, yourself, or both, get on the honor roll. Get in line and let me hear from you and I will whisper the good news to our president and other officers. Don't put this off until to-morrow. Follow the impulse of the heart and follow it now. If the cause appeals to you, say so and if it does not, say nothing. Get in line and do your duty.

C. H. STEPHENSON.

Raleigh, N. C.

 **MARRIAGES**

 **OBITUARIES**

FRANKS-JONES

A quiet, but very pretty, marriage took place in the balcony of the Hotel Guilford, Thursday night, December 19, 1918, when Miss Anna F. Jones became the bride of Mr. Willie S. Franks, of Alamance County. The young couple, accompanied by Mr. and Mrs. D. W. Kernodle, of Gibsonville, Mr. and Mrs. L. D. Ross, of Altamahaw, and the bride's brother, Marvin Jones, motored to Greensboro where the words that made them man and wife were read by the writer.

Immediately after the marriage, the parties returned to their home in Alamance County. Both are members of Berea Christian church, and among the leaders in the work there. They played together in early childhood, and have always been intimately associated with each other. Their many friends will rejoice to know they are locating in the old home community, and will continue their work in the community circles. The very best wishes and prayers of their former pastor and many friends follow them to their new home.

J. VINCENT KNIGHT.

LYTTON-ALEXANDER

A second marriage immediately following the Franks-Jones, took place in the Hotel Guilford, Thursday night, December 19, 1918, when Miss Eula B. Alexander, became the bride of Mr. M. H. Lytton. The young couple came over from Statesville, N. C., where each were prominent in the business and social life of that town.

Mr. and Mrs. Lytton returned to Statesville on the morning of the 20th and will make their home there where Mr. Lytton has a very thriving business. Their many friends were agreeably surprised when they reached their former home. Success and happiness follow them wherever they may go.

J. VINCENT KNIGHT.

The New Year is yours. How are you going to use it?

MITCHELL

On December 4, 1918 G. W. Mitchell departed this life at the age of 77 years. For many years he held his church membership with one of our churches in Chatham county. He leaves a wife, one daughter, and two brothers. The funeral was conducted from the home in West Durham and the interment was made in a community cemetery just out of Durham. May God's richest blessings attend those who mourn.

R. F. BROWN.

WILSON

Jacob Wilson, one of the deacons at Woods' Chapel Christian church, died December 14, 1918 at the age of 60 years, 8 months, and 5 days. Brother Wilson was a good man and held in high esteem by all who knew him. His death came rather suddenly, and was a shock to his many friends. Surviving him are his widow, one son, and three daughters. Funeral services were held at Cedar Grove church of the Brethren, on Sunday, December 15, 1918. May our Heavenly Father comfort the bereaved.

A. W. ANDES.

TATE

Miss Luna Catherine Tate was born February 8, 1891, and died December 13, 1918 at the age of 27 years, 10 months, and 5 days. In this death a splendid young woman has gone from her earthly afflictions to her heavenly reward. She possessed many noble traits of character, and was a general favorite among all who knew her. It seems a pity that such a life could not have been spared longer to be a blessing to those about her, but it becomes our humble duty to say, not our will but Thine be done. Miss Luna was a faithful member of the Antioch Christian church. She is survived by her mother and two brothers. Funeral services were held at Antioch, December 15, and the remains laid to rest by the side of her father in the church cemetery.

A. W. ANDES.

RESOLUTIONS

Whereas, William Walter Wicker, a faithful and much beloved member of Sanford Christian church and Sunday school, has bravely fallen upon the field of battle in France, fighting for the cause of freedom, Therefore be it resolved by the joint committee of the Sanford Christian church and Sunday school,

First, That in the death of Brother Wicker we have lost a faithful and true member.

Second, That while we keenly feel our loss, we bow submissively to the will of God, who doeth all things well.

Third, That we will cherish his memory, and that we will extend unto his family our sympathy, and for them, offer our sincere prayers.

Fourth, That these resolutions be spread upon our minutes, a copy sent to the family, and that copies be offered to The Christian Sun and Sanford Express for publication.

J. N. STOUT,
MISS EMMA HEART,
J. D. GUNTER, Sr.,
J. T. PHILLIPS,
Committee.

PROGRESS OF CHRISTIAN EDUCATION

The Commission on Christian Education held a meeting at Atlantic City, December 10th and 11th, in connection with the meeting of the Executive Committee of the Council. Forty-three persons were present—the largest number in attendance at any recent meeting of the Commission.

The purpose of the meeting was to effect a reorganization by which the work of the Commission may be brought into closer relationship to that of the various educational agencies of the churches. According to this plan of reorganization, the Commission now is made up of representatives chosen by the Commission of Church Boards, the Missionary Education Movement, the Sunday School Council, and the World Sunday School Association together with members appointed at large by the Federal Council, representatives of the Theological Seminaries, Christian Associations, International Sunday School Association, the Young People's Societies, the Sunday School Union and other similar bodies.

FOR SALE OR RENT

I have two good houses and lots at Elon College that I will rent or sell. Attractive proposition. Write me.

J. L. FOSTER, *Waverly, Va.*

Peloubets Select Notes can also be secured at THE CHRISTIAN SUN Office, Burlington, North Carolina.

The Christian Sun

"IN ESSENTIALS UNITY, IN NON-ESSENTIALS LIBERTY, IN ALL THINGS CHARITY"

The Mission of the Church

THE mission of the Church is to carry out that command of the Master, "Go ye into all the world and preach the Gospel," and when the Church ceases to do that, or even falls short of that task and undertaking, it needs a new baptism of the Holy Spirit and a restoration to the faith once delivered to the saints. The command is to *go* and not to parley over trivial matters; the territory is *all* and not a little section where proselyting may be carried on; the injunction is to *preach* and not to scheme, and that which is to be preached is the *Gospel* and not sectarianism.

Volume LXXI   WEDNESDAY, JANUARY 8, 1919   Number 2

BURLINGTON · · · NORTH CAROLINA

THE CHRISTIAN SUN

Founded 1844 by Rev. Daniel W. Kerr

C. B. RIDDLE   - - -   Editor

Entered at the Burlington, N. C. Post Office as second class matter.

Subscription Rates

One year .... $ 2.00
Six months 1.00

In Advance

Give both your old and new postoffice when asking that your address be changed.

The change of your label is your receipt for money. Written receipts sent upon request.

Marriage and obituary notices not exceeding 150 words printed free if received within 60 days from date of event, all over this at the rate of one-half cent a word.

Original poetry not accepted for publication.

Principles of the Christian Church

(1) The Lord Jesus Christ is the only Head of the Church.
(2) Christian is a sufficient name of the Church.
(3) The Holy Bible is a sufficient rule of faith and practice.
(4) Christian character is a sufficient test of fellowship, and of church membership.
(5) The right of private judgment and the liberty of conscience is a right and a privilege that should be accorded to, and exercised by all.

EDITORIAL

THE Y. M. C. A. AND ITS WORK

Recognition of the self-sacrifice and willingness to face death on the part of men who put aside their business to serve in the war zone, under fire if necessary, as Y. M. C. A. workers is being given by the Red Triangle organization in the form of certificates of honorable discharge to those volunteers who were not sent overseas. In a statement announcing this, the personnel division of the National War Work Council Y. M. C. A. sets forth the particular need of specialists instead of general hut secretaries, developed by the War Department's speed in returning the American Expeditionary Forces. The statement follows:

"The Young Men's Christian Association as one of the larger organizations that have been serving our military forces overseas finds itself confronted, following cessation of hostilities, with the necessity for a radical revision of its program. The character of much of the wok required under present condition is quite different from that called for while men were entering, leaving or in the trenches.

"Immediately following the armistice it was thought that a large increased force would be needed, and a call was made for more men. Later when the return of the arm from Great Britain was put into effect immediately, and the early demobilization of the American forces in France was begun, it was found that entire classes of men heretofore needed in considerable numbers by the Y. M. C. A. would not be required.

"The 'Y' now has over 5,000 workers in France alone. Hereafter the requirements will be limited to certain specialists and experienced leaders. This change of program will assist very materially in conserving the gifts of the nation. Educational work will be largely increased for the armies of occupation, and to an even greater extent than before an all round Red Triangle program will be maintained. This will limit recruiting to specialists.

"Many men, some of whom already had reached New York on their way overseas, have had to be returned to their homes because the particular form of work for which they were chosen will not now be needed. They will add to the number of men in every community disappointed because they did not get overseas but entitled to equal honor with those whose unselfish and patriotic desire has not been thwarted. All will receive certificate of honorable discharge in recognition of their patriotism."

COLD CHURCHES

This is a season of the year when the matter of church warming is a part of the worship. No one can worship best who is cold and uncomfortable. "Fires from the altar" will not keep your feet warm. A cold church building is dangerous to health as well as uninviting to worshippers. Keep the house of God comfortable.

AN ESSENTIAL AT THE PEACE CONFERENCE

The Peace Conference is to undertake great things. We consider it the greatest gathering in political history. We have nothing against the men who are to represent the nations of the earth. We believe that they are men of fine character and splendid conduct such that will greatly reflect upon the future world history.

The one essential thing for the Conference to consider is that the defeating of Germany alone will not bring world peace. The obedience of all nations to the principle of brotherly love is the one thing very necessary toward a world peace.

THE DEAD LINER AND THE WORN OUT

There is a great difference between the minister who is worn out and the one who has reached "the dead line" because he has ceased to study, or followed some hobby until he can no longer attract people with it. Not every minister who retires is worn out; it may be that he has rusted out. There is a difference.

EDITORIAL NOTES

When storm and strain and stress bear down upon a man he prays.

All of us agree that the Christian life is a *growth*, but few seem to believe in the cultivation of it.

It is the thinking that really makes us old. Years alone will not humble and quench the young spirit.

We have no patience with the chronic grumbler who is always telling how some one has treated him unfair.

Signing a card is not a *conversion*. Conversion is its own definition—it changes us from one life to another.

Christian unity cannot come until men can agree that the business of a denomination is to save the world and not itself.

The world is finding out that there is more in the right kind of a leader than in the success of any one party. Can the Church not profit by this. God is the leader. Let *all* follow.

You can talk all your life about your creed, but the world looks for the deed.

If the author who wrote the song "Let the lower lights be burning" had said, "I'll keep the lower lights burning," he would have changed a *command* to *action* —and that is what the world needs.

The church that keeps its minister's nose on the financial grindstone can never hope to have the souls of its members lifted up very near to a throne of grace.

A LEAGUE OF NATIONS

(A Statement Issued by the Executive Cmmittee of The Federal Council of Churches of Christ in America)

The war crisis of the world has passed, but a world crisis is upon us. "Are we to lapse back," asks Lloyd George, "into the old national rivalries, animosities and competitive armaments, or are we to initiate the reign on earth of the Prince of Peace?"

"Shall there be a common standard of right and privilege for all peoples and nations," President Wilson inquires, or shall the strong do as they will and the weak suffer without redress?"

The time has come to organize the world for truth and right, justice and humanity. To this end as Chistians we urge the establishment of a League of Free Nations at the coming Peace Conference. Such a League is not a mere political expedient; it is rather the political manifestation of the Kingdom of God on earth.

The Church of the Living God rightfully calls for the creation of agencies adequate to enforce law, to keep order throughout the world and to preserve the rights of the weak and helpless. Selfish and lawless nations must be restrained. Security and fair economic opportunity must be guaranteed to each by the united power of all. "The impartial justice meted out must involve no discrimination between those to whom we wish to be just and those to whom we do not wish to be just," These are matters fundamental to the rule of the Prince of Peace.

The world is now so small, the life of nations so intertwined, the mastery of nature's titanic forces so complete, and the power of selfish, economic or nationalistic groups to enslave whole peoples and to bring tragedy to the entire world so dangerous, that the re-establishment of the old world-order of irresponsible states has become intolerable.

We must have a governed world in which the security and rights of each shall rest upon the combined strength of all. Humanity must be organized on a basis of justice and fair dealing. The law of brotherhood must supersede the law of the jungle.

A League to attain these results must be democratic in spirit and in form. It must be capable of continuous adjustment to the advancing life of separate nations and also of the world. It must be directed by the

enlightened conscience of mankind. The heroic dead will have died in vain unless out of victory shall come a new earth wherein dwelleth righteousness.

The Church has much to give and much to gain. It can give a powerful sanction by imparting to the new international order something of the prophetic glory of the Kingdom of God, if it be not the triumph of God's will in the affairs of men, "righteousness and peace and joy in the Holy Spirit?" And what is this vision of a world-federation of humanity organized on a basis of justice and fair-dealing, for the effective and impartial maintenance of peace, if it be not an international expression of the Kingdom of God?

The Church can give a spirit of good-will, without which no League of Nations can endure. Nations have been held together by the vivid perils and gigantic tasks of war. New bonds must be forged that will still hold them together. This is the special function of the Church.

The Church can give the driving wer of Faith, without which no great ideal can be realized. To doubt is to fail; to believe is to conquer.

The Church can give the driving power of Faith, without counter less opposition from selfish nationalism. Its missionary enterprise will prosper as never before, freed from the blight of un-Christian conduct of the nations of Christendom.

The Church will, moreover, recover its international character and consciousness. National churches will find themselves linked in a world brotherhood. A new era of fellowship and co-operation will dawn.

The League of Nations is rooted in the Gospel. Like its objective is "peace on earth good-will toward men." Like the Gospel its appeal is universal.

Let us implore our Heavenly Father, God Almighty that the Peace Delegates of the Nations may be guided by the Divine Spirit and enlightened by the Divine Wisdom to the end that they may embody in the new fabric of the world's life His righteousness, loving and holy will.

We call upon all Christians and upon all believers in God and lovers of man, to work and pray with whole souls, that out of the ashes of the old civilization may rise the fair outlines of a new world, based on the Christ ideal of justice, co-operation, brotherhood and service.

FROM OTHER SANCTUMS

The Macedonian Call

(Christian Advocate)

If we will listen, we can hear many Macedonian cries coming from across the seas: "Come over and help us." These cries come from cold, hungry, distressed brothers and sisters of ours in the larger sense, living in lands where only a few years ago sweet flowers bloomed; where fruit blossoms in thousands of orchards in the springtime sent out their fragrant odors foretelling the coming of luscious fruits to be gathered in late summer and early fall; where fertile fields brought forth their plentiful increase as a result of the diligent toil of industrious farmers; where sleek cattle grazed in green meadows and fat hogs fed on the broad fields of growing clover; where the hum and rattle of industry were ever to be heard in forge, factory, and shop; where happy and prosperous people dwelt in picturesque villages, thriving towns, and splendid cities. To-day these people need our help, need what we can do for them in a physical way, and need and want what we can do for their souls. Shall we answer the calls, be a blessing and receive a blessing?

Qualified For Christ
(Sunday School Times)

God's "favorites" are those who let Him do the most for them. It is a distinction open to any of us. A Christian man who enjoys an unusually intimate fellowship with God recently wrote to a friend: "If, as some one has said, our wants qualify us for Christ, then my qualification are unsurpassed." Each of us is eligible to enter the class of the debtor of the parable who owed his Lord ten million dollars and was forgiven. If we will but see it our sins were as geart as those of the sinful woman who anointed Jesus in the Pharisee's house. And Christ has cleansed them! But more than that: Having shared not His own Son, but delivered Him up for us, God stands ready with Him to give us freely all things. The richest Christians are the poorest, those with greatest needs, those with largest capacity for receiving free gifts of grace.

Safe Only On Your Knees
(Pittsburgh Christian Advocate)

Principal George Adam Smith tells a tale of how, in his early Alpine-climbing days, he was climbing one of the Swiss Alps on the sheltered side. Though they did not know it, a great wind was blowing, and as they climbed to the topmost crag, the guide, who had been leading the way upwards, stepped back, as his wont, that the traveler might have his foot upon the top. Dr. Smith sprang to the top of the peak and was almost blown back over the edge by the wind. The guide seized him and brought him down to his knees, crying in his ear: "Down! Here, on the summit, you are safe only on your knees." So with the heights of our gladness, when life is splendid, and the world is full of glory, we are safe only upon our knees.

A Great Temptation
(Christian Observer)

There is a temptation to preachers at the present time to make their message from the pulpits savor more of current events than to sound forth clearly and convincingly the call of the glorious Gospel of Jesus Christ to men everywhere to repent and turn to God. The principles that animated our nation in entering the war were undoubtedly founded upon truth and righteousness as set forth in the Word of God, but when the people gather in God's House to worship Him, they desire to hear the soul-stirring truths of the Gospel presented in all their power. The ministers, as well as the members of the churches, have been loyal in their support of the government in the present war. There must be, however, a constant recognition that the greatest need of the human soul is to hear and know and obey the Word of God.

PREACHING THE DOCTRINE OF HELL
(Lutheran Church Work and Observer)

The preaching of the doctrine of the punishment of sin has unquestionably fallen into disuse, as compared with its prominence in the preaching of a half century ago. But there is a hell prepared for the devil and his angels and it ought to be affirmed that all those who follow the devil and walk in the ways of ungodliness, adding iniquity to iniquity, will find that the broad way upon which they are walking leads inevitably to that very place. Men, accordingly, should be instructed, warned, and admonished on this subject. More and more it seems that scientific men are preaching this doctrine in their own way. Said one of these scientific men recently, "If the preachers quit preaching the consequences of sin the doctors will have to take it up." Physicians stand aghast when they are brought face to face, as they are in their professional work, with the direful physical ravages of sin. They are not disinclined to speak of the fearful ravages wrought by man's depravity. These men see the necessity of placing every safeguard around the youth of our land especially, and warning them of what is certain to ensue as the fruits of sin.

At a meeting of one of the American Medical Associations a few months ago one of the leading physicians present, in an address on the subject of "Health as a Moral Issue," said: "If there is no hell it is an oversight." If this is the attitude of physicians, who deal with the bodies of men, what ought to be the attitude of preachers who deal with the souls of men? This awful doctrine ought to be preached, but preached in the right way. It is not surprising to us that some reaction followed against the old-time method of presenting this doctrine and the crudities of some modern evangelists. God is not guilty of an oversight. There is a hell and it ought to be preached in all of its awfulness. But there is a right way and a wrong way to preach on this subject. The right way, in our judgment, is indicated in a paragraph taken from the late Dr. Archibald Hodge's "Popular Lectures on Theological Themes." In his treatment of the subject of final rewards and punishment, Dr. Hodge says this:

"There is nothing on earth more outrageously vulgar and profane than the coarse and careless shouting out of threats of damnation against heedless sinners by an orthodox ranter. When we declare the terrible judgment of our Lord against our fellow sinners of our own flesh and blood, who by nature are no worse than we are, we should do it tremblingly and with tears."

During the year ended July 31, 1918, the mills of the United States consumed 6,566,489 running bales of cotton. This consumption comprised 6,296,756 bales of domestic upland cotton, 85,939 bales of sea-island cotton, and 183,794 bales of foreign cotton. In addition, 1,118,840 bales of linters were consumed. The stocks held in the country on July 31, 1918, aggregated 3,450,188 bales of lint cotton and 439,917 bales of linters.

Russia lost 9,150,000 men in the recent war, according to a statement just issued.

EVENTS OF THE PAST YEAR

Outstanding Landmarks in the Political and Economic History of 1918

January 29—Secretary of the treasury takes over control of exchange markets.

February 12—Announcement officially made that Russia has withdrawn from the war.

February 15—Official announcement made that all imports and exports will be licensed.

February 23—President Wilson fixes price of wheat at $2.20 per bushel.

March 4—Rumania accepts German peace terms.

March 7—Senate passes war finance corporation bill.

March 14—All-Russian congress of soviets ratify German peace treaty.

March 15—Interstate Commerce commission grants eastern railroads 15 per cent increase in rates.

March 21—President Wilson signs railroad control bill.

March 27—United States Steel corporation grants 15 per cent increase in wages.

April 15—Count Czernin, Austro-Hungarian premier, resigns.

April 18—Senate passes bill to melt 350,000,000 silver dollars.

May 4—Third liberty loan campaign ends.

May 6 —Peace treaty between center power and Rumania signed.

May 14—Overman bill passes house, 295 to 2.

May 21—Director General McAdoo removes all railroad presidents.

May 27—President Wilson addresses Congress on taxation—Railway administration announces 25 per cent increase in freight rates; also increase in passenger rates; wage increases also granted.

May 28—Secretary McAdoo merges express companies.

June 3—German submarines make raids on American coast; sink many ships.

June 6—Secretary McAdoo advises doubling war taxes—War industry board commandeers all steel for war.

June 17—Government plans to pool war resources with allies.

June 25—German government makes new peace statement.

June 26—Czar of Russia reported slain.

July 1—President Wilson recommends taking over telephone and telegraph systems.

July 3—Government increases price of copper from 23½ to 26 cents.

July 15—American troops break German attacks and advance, the movement later proving the turning point of the war.

July 16—President Wilson signs wire control bill.

July 18—Allied troops launch great counter-offensive; advance on 25-mile front.

August 15—Maximum silver price fixed by treasury at $1.01½.

August 29—Chairman of "money committee" warns against excessive speculation with borrowed money.

September 6—"Money committee" asks stock exchange for data on call loans.

September 11—Secretary McAdoo favors higher exemption of liberty bonds from income tax.

September 13—Americans wipe out St. Mihiel salient.

September 18—President Wilson rejects Austrian peace proposal.

September 23—Turkish armies in Palestine wiped out.

September 27—Bulgaria seeks peace; request armistice terms.

September 30—Bulgaria yields all points; allies grant armistice.

October 6—Germany sends another appeal for peace.

October 8—President Wilson replies to German peace note.

October 11—Kaiser summons German sovereigns to council.

October 13—Germany's request for an armistice reaches this country.

October 15—President Wilson's answer to Germany's armistice request published.

October 19—Fourth liberty loan campaign ends.

October 21—German reply to Wilson's note received; again asks armistice terms.

October 24—Wilson in note to Germany demands surrender of autocracy.

October 25—President Wilson asks nation to elect Democratic Congress.

October 28—Austria ready for separate peace; accepts Wilson's terms.

October 30—Another note from Germany requests terms of armistice.

October 31—Turkey surrenders unconditionally to allies—Austrian commander asks Italy for armistice.

November 1—Versailles conference on armistice terms begins.

Novomer 4—Austria officially out of war.

November 6—Peace and armistice commission leaves Berlin for France.

November 7—German armistice commission reaches French line—Revolution breaks out in Germany.

November 9—Emperor William and crown prince abdicate; flee to Holland.

November 11—Germany signs armistice; world war officially comes to an end.

November 12—Austrian emperor abdicates.

November 20—Twenty German submarines surrender.

November 22—Senate committee cuts $1,000,000,000 from 1919 revenue bill.

December 2—President Wilson addresses Congress on railroad control.

December 4—President Wilson sails for France to attend peace conference.

December 11—Director McAdoo recommends government operation of railroads for fifive years.

The American cotton crop of 1917 fell below that of 1916 by 147,555 equivalent 500-pound bales, or 1.3 per cent, but exceeded that of 1915 by 110,555 bales, or 1 per cent. Each of these three crops was smaller than that of any year from 1910 to 1914, inclusive.

REASONS FOR TITHING
By Rev. W. A. Ayres

ONE-TENTH of the income of God's people consecrated to the service of Christ would effectually solve the financial problems in all our churches, and in the work of his kingdom throughout the world. It would not only relieve the great and constant strain, but would actually double if not quadruple, the work now being done.

Some are giving a tenth, and a few even more. We rejoice that the number of such givers is increasing. But many tithers having small incomes, and millions of others giving but a small fraction of a tithe, brings the average down to one-fortieth instead of one-tenth for God. If all gave the tenth we might build four times as many churches and parsonages and schoolhouses annually, and support four times as many pastors and missionaries.

With such tremendous possibilities before us, why do we not all give a tenth? Do we love money more than we love Christ and the souls and we might help to save? Many surely do not clearly understand the principle of tithing nor the teaching of the Scriptures concerning it; they have never thought it through for themselves. Prayerful attention is therefore called to the following reasons for tithing:

1 The Old Testament Teaches It

This teaching is very clear and positive. For the first voluntary (gospel spirit) instances of it we have these records: Abraham gave tithes to Melchizedek (Gen. 14:20). Jacob pledged tithes to God, (Gen. 28:22). These are clear instances of tithing before the law was given or the Jewish nation had an existence.

As Dr. O. P. Gifford says: "The law did not create tithes; it recognized them." Also: "Before law commanded tithes, tithing was wrought into the nature of things."

For the law of the tithes, see Lev. 27:30-32; for its purpose, see Num. 18:20, 21. "But," some one may say, "that old Mosaic or Levitical law has been abrogated." No! the tithes has no more been abolished than the Sabbath. Both existed before the Mosaic law.

Mr. J. P. Hobson, a lawyer, says: "If the tithe, therefore, was the law before Moses, the fact that it was incorporated in the Levitical law, and that this law has expired, would not abrogate the tithe, but the expiring of this law would leave it as obligatory as it was before the latter was promulgated at Sinai."

WOMAN AND HER WORK

The foreign department of the Y. W. C. A. needs forty-nine secretaries who will be sent to China, Japan, South America and India during the year 1919.

Nine women, representing nine nationalities, sat down to a tea together in an International Institute recently. These Institutes conducted by the Young Women's Christian Association, are bringing all the women of different tongues together and uniting them in a common language, in common interests.

This is an age of specialization. The Y. W. C. A. is the only organization that specializes in girls regardless of race, country or color. It is extending a charm string all around the belt of Old Mother Earth, every button on the string being represented by a girl, and girls standing side by side, with the same hope, interests and ambition, from every civilized country on the map, and some that we might, perhaps, think are not civilized.

A speaker had told eloquently of what the women had done in France, England and America in winning the war. Then she passed on to what they are doing now in the work of reconstruction, paying eloquent tribute, to the nurses who served side by side with the men, regardless of difficulties and danger, and who are remaining at their posts. She sat down. Then the preacher prayed, and in his prayer he asked God's blessing on all the men who had served at the front, and were still serving. He did not mention the women! The Y. W. C. A. secretary who had made the speech was dazed. Doesn't the world know this was also a woman's war?

GREETINGS TO THE WOMAN'S MISSIONARY WORKERS

I have great pleasure in sending this word of greeting for the New Year to the workers in our Woman's Missionary Societies, and with this greeting I send sincere appreciation for the good accomplishments of 1918, handicapped as we were on every side.

And 1919—what challenge it offers us! The new era of enlarged missionary work is before us. We must do more this year than ever before. Shortly we will announce the goals for the various Conferences and in true womanly style we shall expect each Conference to go happily "over the top."

I send my very best wishes for a fruitful and serviceable year in Christian effort to every worker and each Society.

MRS. W. A. HARPER,
Pres. Woman's Board S. C. C.

THE CHRISTIAN ANNUAL

The final copy for the *Christian Annual* reached me January 3, 1919 and by the time this note reaches the public the type matter on the publication will be completed. Practically all the press work has been done. The printers hope to have the *Annual* ready by the latter part of next week.

As voted by the last session of the Southern Christian Convention, the price of the *Annual* is 25c the copy, delivered. Conference secretaries will do me a favor by sending at once a mailing list showing distribution of the number of copies taken. Each Conference has already voted to take a certain number of copies and it is not necessary that bill be sent to each secretary. If each secretary will send with his mailing list an order on the treasurer of his Conference for the number of copies taken by his Conference it will save me unnecessary work and will be appreciated.

C. B. RIDDLE, *Editor.*

January 4, 1919.

THE CHRISTIAN ORPHANAGE

SUPERINTENDENT'S LETTER

Dear Friends:—

This report brings us within $496.74 of our goal of five thousand dollars for our Thanksgiving offering. Less than five hundred dollars to raise and two more weeks to reach it. Just one hundred churches have responded to our call. One hundred and twenty-two to hear from yet. Will the 122 churches respond in the next three weeks? I will close this year's work on January 22, and trust we will have gone over the top by that date and all the churches have in their reports. I would be delighted to get each church on the Banner list this time. It would be a joy to me and would do the church good to make this offering. See to it that your church gets on the Banner list.

Our children have had a very happy Christmas and the churches have been real kind to them.

The First Christian church of Norfolk sent a box containing two presents for each child which delighted each one. Also a box of oranges and a 25-pound box of candy.

The Burlington church sent a box containing towels, hose, handkerchiefs, and many things that are useful to us in this work.

The Portsmouth church sent a box containing many useful things for the children.

Mrs. Bowden's Sunday school class sent a box containing one-half dollar for each child. When we gave them the money all the little children wanted to go to the store right away, so Mrs. Wicker (one of the Matrons) went with them and it was a busy day for the merchants and it was very gratifying to see the wise selections many of them made in buying little articles that were real useful to them.

Mr. and Mrs. R. A. Thompson, of the Bethlehem church, sent a box containing thread, ginghams, percale, toboggans, etc.; Mr. L. D. Rippy, two pumpkins; Mrs. C. M. McCray, can fruit; Lottie McRay, 2 pair hose, 5 cans fruit, bunch lace; Mrs. J. H. Massey, Durham, N. C., 4 books; W. N. Goodwin, New Hill, N. C., 5 pair shoes, 1 pair pants, 4 dozen boxes matches; Concord Christian church, Va., one barrell containing can fruit, syrup, sack of butter beans, sack of cabbage, a peck of apples, etc.

For all these contributions we are profoundly grateful.

REPORT FOR DECEMBER 1918—Continued

Amount brought forward, $13,043.56.

Children's Offerings

Leon Wesley Newman, 10 cents; Ralph Rain Newman, 10 cents; Total, 20 cents.

Sunday School Offerings

Spring Hill, $2.00; New Hope, (Valley Conference) $1.00; Pleasant Grove, (Va.), $4.00; Morrisville, N. C., $2.00; Bethlehem, $1.00; Raleigh, $4.00; Total, $14.00.

Special Offerings

Rev. B. F. Black, $10.00.

Thanksgiving and Christmas Offerings

Rev. A. F. Isley, $5.00; Burlington, S. S. special Christmas offering, $58.32; Burlington church, (Additional), $1.00; Spring Hill, Sunday school, $15.45; Concord church and friends, $5.00; M. W. Hollowell, $5.00; Mrs. C. G. Sharpe, $1.00; Wadley, Ala., Sunday school, $8.00; Concord Christian church, $4.20; Carter Boyd, 50 cents; C. A. Richardson, $5.00; Mrs. Rebecca Watkins, $5.00; Miss Mary Rawles, $5.00; Raleigh Sunday school, special Christmas offering, $22.50; Mrs. C. A. High, $1.00; A Friend, 50 cents; Wentworth church, $17.46; Mrs. J. H. Pierce, $1.00; Total, $160.93;

Total for the week, $185.10; Grand total, $13,228.66.

LETTERS

Dear Uncle Charley: I am sending you the first dime I ever earned. I am four years old and I made my dime piling up wood for Mrs. Nicholas next door. I did not know I would make any money, I saw the wood needed to be piled, so I just piled it. I was surprised when she paid me.—*Ralph Bain Newman.*

"He that hath pity pon the poor lendeth unto the Lord; and that which he hath given will he pay again." I see you have loaned the first money you ever earned to the Lord and I truly hope it will come back to you in future years with a big interest.—*"Uncle Charley."*

Dear Uncle Charley: I have to do everything that Ralph does, so mamma will give me a dime to send. I love to work, too, but no one ever pays me. I love the work so well that I sometimes haul the wood back to the wood pile after my brothers have put it on the porch. I am jealous of Oliver Young. I was Uncle Johnny's baby before he came. Maybe Helen and George will write next time.—*Leon Wesley Newman.*

You are a working boy. I am fond of little boys who are always busy. I have a litle boy at home who is so busy that he keeps me busy when I am at home.—*"Uncle Charley."*

Thousands of our returning boys will spend many weeks, perhaps months, in camp before they are returned to their homes. It will interest the mothers and fathers to learn that these boys have had the first pangs of home-sickness alleviated by the sight of the hostess in the Hostess House who was the last to whom they waved good-bye when they marched away, and who was still on the job to welcome them when they returned. "Felt tough to think I couldn't go on home," said one boy, "but this place comes so near to it, I'm not kicking. Looks just like it did when we went away, and you don't look a day older." The hostess laughed; she was receiving many of such compliments, and she knew what they meant. So much had been crowded into the boys' lives since they left that they fully expected every one they met on returning to look years and years older.

J. W. Winfree—THE SUN has been shining in the Winfree home since Rev. W. B. Wellons was publisher and I want it to shine as long as I live.

PASTOR AND PEOPLE

POUNDED! POUNDED! !

On the night of December 17, 1918 the door bell of the Graham Christian church parsonage rang and the pastor opened it to be greeted by little Chas. D. Johnston, Jr., who said that Santa Claus had told him to leave some things at the home of F. C. Lester. He was invited in and following him came a large number of the good people of Graham and New Providence Christian churches. They were led not to the parlor, but to the kitchen. When they were through presenting, our pantry was supplied with more than twenty-five dollars worth of good things to eat, such as meal, flour, ham, chicken, eggs, potatoes, jelly, canned fruits, etc. The Ladies' Aid Society also presented a quilt. After a brief stay the visitors all retired leaving the pastor and his family both happy and grateful.

But this seemed to not be enough for there was another church to be heard from. It was Thursday of Christmas that I attended a Christmas tree at Haw River Christian church. After a nice little program given by the small children and the presentation of the gifts and treat to the members of the Sunday school, some of the brethren led me to one corner of the church where they presented me with more than a barrel full of nice things for the pantry that had been brought in by the members and friends of that church. This came as an absolute surprise. There was about twenty-five dollars worth of this "pounding." I should like to give the name of each one who contributed, but that would be a list too long.

To one and all who had a part in either of these "poundings" I express my grateful appreciation.

F. C. LESTER.

POUNDED

Just before Christmas Mrs. Arthur McIver called me over the telephone and asked me to come to their home that evening. On my arrival I found a number of the Shallow Well people had gathered to enjoy seeing me stare at a table covered with cans, jars, boxes, packages, and paper bags filled with all sorts of good things. No one but a preacher who has had a similar experience can imagine the joy that came to us as we unloaded the packages, spelled out the givers, and put them away. To the good people of Shallow Well, we thank you.

We are also grateful to Mr. S. H. McDuffie and others of Grace's Chapel and to members of Sanford church for kindness, expressed in useful gifts.

MR. & MRS. T. E. WHITE.

ANOTHER POUNDING

Our Saviour said that it was more blessed to give than to receive. Since it is God-like to give freely and human-like to desire to receive, we mortals often feel that we are happier when we receive gifts than the givers could possibly be. Truly has this writer felt, many times, that he was exceedingly happier because of having received many gracious gifts for himself and fam-

ily during the past year than his many good friends— members of his churches and others— who gave them, could be. For instance, after the hail storm had destroyed our garden at Holly Springs last July, several of the members and friends of Plymouth Christian church gave us three dozen cans of tomatoes and other vegetables.

Of course, the "pounding" the Pleasant Union people gave us some time ago has already been mentioned in THE SUN; but the fact that those kind people promised a salary of one hundred dollars and gave one hundred and fifty has not heretofore been published.

Besides these things, individual members of Plymouth, Pleasant Union, Center Grove and Antioch (Chatham) churches and others in those communities, have made their pastor's heart glad various times during the past year by giving him butter, fruit, vegetables and other good things to take home.

However, the last time the writer was made to feel that it was more "happy" to *receive* than to *give*, was the fourth Sunday morning in December, 1918. It happened at Youngsville, N. C. As it was a rainy day, had only a congregation of seventeen, besides the janitor, that morning. The writer tried to preach to that little company about Heaven's richest gift to man—the gift of a Saviour. As he talked of the Heavenly Gift, he could see in front of the pulpit, a table loaded with packages containing such things as sugar, salt, soda, raisins, butter; and canned peaches, pears, pine apple, cherries, blackberries (white) and snap beans. When, after the services, two of the members informed their pastor that the abundance of good things on that table was intended as a "pounding" for him from his Youngsville members, he couldn't command words capable of expressing the gratitude and happiness that were his. Certainly, it is more blessed to give than it is to receive; but when such things happen to one as have been mentioned above, we frail creatures of the dust can scarcely understand how human givers can be any happier than human recipients. If those who have been so kind to this writer the past year were any happier in the giving than he was in the receiving, they must have been mighty happy people.

May the Giver of all good gifts richly reward each and all of them; and may He enable His humble servant to be of some real Christian service to those whom he endeavors to serve as their pastor.

R. P. CRUMPLER.

Varina, N. C.

A GOOD BEGINNING

The Mission Secretary of the Western North Carolina Christian Conference, Rev. L. I. Cox, has sent in his first month's report to the Home Mission Board, and it is full of encouragement. It has taken considerable work to get started. The report shows nine active memberships, seven at $10.00, and two at $5.00 per member, secured for the Christian Missionary Association. Also $10.00 for Home Missions.

Ten individuals and one local church have agreed to pay the salary and all necessary expense of the Secretary for one-fourth of his time during this year. I take this opportunity of saying to those generous givers who are making it possible for us to have a Secretary for a part of his time, that the expense is necessarily more for the first month than we may expect for any other. Yet our Secretary has, in his first month, secured more in cash and membership pledges than twice his salary and the expense of stationery and printing.

I trust that every pastor in the Western Conference or every pastor who has a church within our bounds, will arrange with our Secretary and have him to visit the churches. The Secretary has a message that the churches need, and the churches have a presence that the Secretary needs. Let both come together and each help the other.

T. E. WHITE,
Ch'm. H. M. B., W. N. C. C. C.

Sanford, N. C.

HENDERSON LETTER

Since we came here on November 13, 1918, there has not been much to report in the way of public services. We found the influenza still raging, and the churches of city and county closed by order of the Health Board. On the first Sunday of December the closing ban was lifted as to the morning services, but the Sunday schools are still closed, and no night services are yet allowed.

While the members were not permitted to assemble in a reception meeting, we have met quite a number of our people, at church and in their homes; and if we are to judge from the acquaintance thus formed, we anticipate pleasant relations with the people here, and expect much good to be accomplished in the Master's name and cause.

I also serve as pastor at Fuller's Chapel, about five miles from Henderson. It has not been our privilege to go there, but hope soon to do so.

A number of the members of Henderson and Fuller's Chapel have remembered us with part of the good things with which they are blessed. These acts of kindness were received with deep appreciation, and made a substantial contribution to our pleasure.

There is not as much sickness here as when we came, and we hope that soon the church activities will become normal.

R. L. WILLIAMSON.

THE RAMSEUR PASTORATE

We left the good people of Henderson and Fuller's Chapel November 13, 1918, with whom we had labored for six years, to enter upon the duties of the Ramseur pastorate, which includes the churches at Ramseur, Park's Cross Roads, Pleasant Ridge and Shiloh. We arrived at Ramseur November 21, 1918 receiving a welcome that is hard to express.

We were met at the station by Brother Herbert Brady with his automobile and brought to our home, which had been arranged by a committee appointed by the churches. We were received by three young ladies with smiling faces, giving a welcome that would make a king feel good and honored. On coming in the house behold, we found our furniture all unpacked and put up as if we had done it ourselves. After a few minutes we were escorted to the dining room and there we found a most sumptuous supper already prepared and hot on our own dining room table. Those three young ladies dined with us and it was a pleasure to have them. After supper several of the members here came in. We had a good social time till 10 o'clock when they left us alone for the night.

On account of the epidemic of Influenza we have not been able to have services at all the churches. We have been to Pleasant Ridge and Shiloh one Sunday each and here last Sunday night. We have not been to Park's Cross Roads yet. We hope to have regular services after this and to get things lined up for a great year's work.

We have installed the envelope system in the Ramseur church, and expect to lay plans to use them in all the churches next year. We are expecting great things for missions, devotion, evangelism, education and benevolences.

A. T. BANKS.

Ramseur, N. C.

SUFFOLK LETTER

The routine of life affords a field of study as well as a field for work. Universal experience keeps routine ever before us, for most of daily toil is of that kind of service. The clerk in the store with yardstick and scissors, and the opening and folding of goods, runs one constant round; but the variety in customers and the constant change in faces and voices relieves the monotory of the daily task. The cook in the kitchen with pots and pans, wood and ashes, water and grease, dishes and spoons, cloths and soaps, to say nothing of meal and meat, cereals and eggs, soda and salt, turnips and potatoes, furnishs ample chance for routine duties. It is not one day, but every day. There is little Sunday in the kitchen. The parlor is the Sunday-room. Few kitchens keep Sunday. We forget that the ignorant Jews gathered enough manna on the sixth day to last the seventh day. It does no credit to this day to say, that the Israelites in the desert kept the Lord's day better than the great cities of Christian civilization. Goodness is not necessarily learned; it is the obedience of the life of the word and will of God.

When Naaman came to Elisha and was directed by the prophet to, "Go and wash in Jordan seven times, and thy flesh shall come again to thee and thou shalt be clean," Naaman was wrath, and went away, and said, "Behold, I thought He will surely come out to me, and stand and call upon the name of the Lord." So he went away in a rage. Then his servants spake unto him, and said, "If the prophet had bid thee do some *great* thing, wouldst thou not have done it?" Then he went and dipped himself seven times in Jordan and he was clean. So many people want to do the big things and not the little things; but it is the little things that count. It is one thing to play the piano in the parlor; it is quite another thing to clean the pot in the kitchen. It is one thing to dine with a deacon; it is another thing to sup with a sinner; but Jesus did both. He took upon Himself the *form* of a servant; and He rendered the help of a servant.

Some Christians are prominent at the great meetings of the Church; but those who maintain the regular services by faithful attendance and systematic contributions perform the routine duties of the Kingdom, and wash their robes in the blood of the Lamb. All garments are made by a stitch at a time, whether the stitch is made by steel fingers or human hands. It is the drop of water added to drops of water that makes the flood; the roaring river is the chorus of the rivulets whose hidden beauty creeps along the path of the mountain and among the willows in the meadow. It is the constant flow of the tide that carves its artistic lines on the beach and builds mountains of sand. Do not think your place in the home or the church too small. Think of what the Psalmist says: "I had rather be a doorkeeper in the house of my God, than to dwell in the tents of wickedness." It is equivalent to saying, "I had rather be an obscure Christian than a prominent worldling." How many would thus choose? We want to do the big things; but it is the little things that cleanses the leper and feeds the world.

It is better to be a good sexton than a poor preacher; and it is better to be a good member than a poor official. Jesus made Himself of no reputation, though He could have made a reputation by doing great things. His work was little and simple. He labored among the poor and needy. He went about doing good. His teachings were greater than His works. The nations will never be free till they know Him and the power of His resurrection. "Ye shall know the truth, and the truth shall make you free." "If the Son therefore shall make you free, ye shall be free indeed." Truth always builds up great things from small things, as oaks from acorns; and great people are not above the routine of daily life in all the spheres where human service helps to save the world.

W. W. STALEY.

DR. ATKINSON AT SALEM CHAPEL

The little country church at Salem Chapel stands in an open grove of majestic oaks; the cemetery near by. The pastor had prepared the little band of worshippers some time before the coming of the great apostle of missions. He came as teacher, editor and orator. Atkinson has the art of saying the right thing in the best English. He is tall and graceful. He is always bright and happy as a May morning. He faced our little congregation with the same degree of satisfaction as he did a large and rich one. Missions, missions, his heart was in every word and every sentence was filled with sincerity. What he said was always to the point and just enough. It was not the traditional way of begging for money and passing the plate for a few paltry dollars. His facts from the Bible and history made the logical climax plain as the stars of Heaven, that it was our Christian duty and glorious privilege to give and to labor for the cause of missions.

With the exception, perhaps of service, there is no more expressive word in the English language than *missions*. The loftiest matter that ever blazed upon a warrior's shield, or glittered upon a nation's arms, is the word *service*. Before Brother Atkinson left the good people of Salem Chapel gave in cash and pledges about $1,000.00 to the cause of missions.

DANIEL ALBRIGHT LONG.

UNITED CONFERENCES

THE CHRISTIAN SUN of January 1, 1919, brings the news that the three Christian Conferences in North Carolina have united. United and for what? It will eliminate two-thirds of the officials of the three separate Conferences. As these officers serve without salaries or nearly so, but little will be saved. Additional cost in attending the sessions of Conference will be greatly increased. The representation will be reduced owing to longer distance to travel. A larger body will be more efficient, it is claimed. Why not for the same reasons unite all the families, all the farms and all kindred enterprises, all the counties, all the states, into one county, state and nation? Yet nearly every session of the State Legislature creates new counties; new families are being established continually. The federation of Germany gave us the world war. The federation of states tends to work autocracy which is the bone of evil and religious freedom, and the more so when the measures by which it is accomplished are clandestinly executed. The original paper which inaugurated this union movement was carried by a vote of eight or nine with only one majority just an hour or two before the final adjournment in November, 1917 at Haw River, N. C. Why was not the matter allowed to come before the Conference at Reidsville, N. C., in November, 1918? I do not question the right of the Conferences to unite, but I do not think fair play has been shown. Why not let the people—the local churches—speak after a full presentation of the matter has been given them? I would not charge the manner in which this matter has been handled to ambition for ambition is sure to make or break something. The poet says, "By it the angels fell," and Ceasar lost his crown, and an emperor has lost his. Then I say with the poet, "Fling away ambition." I enter my protest against the manner by which this union has been effected.

JEREMIAH W. HOLT.

Burlington, N. C.

COLUMBUS, GEORGIA

Our Rose Hill church held a very interesting and helful Watch Night Social, with a good attendance. The Duplex Envelope system is being introduced, which means the Every Member canvass too; the floors of the social rooms and the floor of the auditorium have been stained; new carpet placed in the aisles and on the platform. A very interesting Christmas entertainment was enjoyed by all present.

In December the Georgia and Alabama Conference held a short, hurried session in the North Highland church, this city. It has been postponed on account of the influenza epidemic.

HENRY CRAMPTON.

NOTES

We regret to learn that Dr. J. H. Wilson, Dover, Delaware, is in feeble health.

Peloubet's Notes and Tarbell's Guide. We have them and can send by return mail.

A letter from Chaplain B. F. Black says: "I have written to 87 preachers and two of them have replied. They seem interested."

We chronicle with sadness the passing of Mrs. T. A. Jones, Norfolk, Va. Possibly the last letter she wrote was one to Dr. Atkinson in which she said: "Kindly hand the enclosed $5.00 to the editor of THE CHRISTIAN SUN to send the paper to some worthy persons who are not able to pay for it." THE SUN never had a more constant reader or truer friend.

City Attorney, John H. Vernon, Burlington, N. C., died January 5, 1919, following an attack of Influenza and pneumonia. He was sick for several weeks and was, it seemed, on the road to recovery when a change came and he soon passed away. Mr. Vernon was a public spirited citizen, a man deeply interested in the work of his Church (the Baptist) and will be greatly missed. And for nearly three dozen times, from the effects of the "Flu," the hearse has moved slowly up the long street to the "city of the dead" taking of our best citizens.

Among the boys recently dying in France as members of our Church were Mr. Herbert H. Barber, a member of Shallow Ford church, and Mr. W. F. Odom, son of Mr. R. B. Odom, Bennett Creek, Va. Both these young men attended school at Elon College and their decease will be mourned by their many friends. Brother Barber graduated in the Class of '18 and Odom was scheduled to graduate this year, but left college to join the Colors. He will be remembered by former students as "Happy" Odom—a name rightly bestowed by his fellow students on account of his sunny disposition. To the parents we extend much sympathy.

COLONEL ROOSEVELT DEAD!

As we close our forms this (Monday) morning, news is received that Colonel Roosevelt was found dead in the bed this morning.

Theodore Roosevelt was born in New York, October 27, 1858 and was the twenty-sixth president of the United States. He graduated from Harvard in 1880; he also held degrees from notable institutions. He was a member of the New York Legislature in 1882-1884; resident of New York Police Board 1895, 1897; Assistant Secretary of the Navy 1897-1898 and resigned to organize the Rough Riders; Governor of New York January 1, 1899 to December 31, 1900; elected Vice-President of the United States March 4, 1900 and became president upon the death of William McKinley,

September 14, 1901, and was elected president November 8, 1904 by the largest majority ever accorded a candidate up to that time. In 1906 he won the Nobel Peace prize of $40,000. Roosevelt was the author of many books, and a great politician, being in the last year or so a critic of the present administration.

NORTH CAROLINA ANTI-SALOON LEAGUE MEETING

The Tenth Biennial Convention of the State Anti-Saloon League will be held in Raleigh January 16-17, 1919, beginning at 10:00 A. M. Thursday.

The Headquarters Committee, who have in charge the arranging of the program, are preparing a feast of oratory and other good things for the prohibitionists of the State. Among the out-of-state speakers are Dr. P. A. Baker, General Superintendent of the Anti-Saloon League of America; Bishop James Cannon, Jr., of the M. E. Church South; the inimitable George R. Stewart of Birmingham, Alabama; Hon. Wayne B. Wheeler, General Counsel of the Anti-Saloon League of America; and Hon. Wm. H. Anderson of New York City.

Among prominent men of the State on the program are W. B. Cooper, State Senator from Wilmington; W. L. Poteat, LL. D., President of Wake Forest College; W. T. Shaw, manufacturer of Weldon; Hon. O. M. Mull, representative from Cleveland and the law partner of Congressman E. Y. Webb; William Allen Harper, LL. D., President of Elon College; Hon. W. O. Saunders, representative from Pasquotank; Hon. J. D. Eckles of Buncombe; Judge John A. Oates of Fayetteville; Rev. R. L. Davis, Superintendent of the Anti-Saloon League; Rev. L. S. Massey, Editor of the Raleigh Christian Advocate and Dr. W. S. Rankin, Secretary of State Board of Health.

It is expected that many churches, Sunday schools and other organizations will send delegates to this Convention, and that hundreds of citizens throughout the State who want to break up the blind tiger and blockade business will attend. All who attend have the rights and privileges of the floor as well as those sent as delegates.

DR. WELLONS SENDS THANKS

My dear Brother Riddle:—

I was never more surprised than I was on New Year's morning (my 93rd birthday) when Dr. Harper came to my room, before I had got up, and brought six or eight copies of THE CHRISTIAN SUN to me. I do not know how to express my surprise and gratification for that issue being dedicated to me, for I was not thinking of such a thing.

The issue contained articles from yourself and six other ministers, but I feel that all of you said more than was due me. I only wish that I was worthy of such such compliments. I try to live keeping my spiritual life and physical condition in readiness to meet the Master at His coming to take me to my spiritual home.

J. W. WELLONS,

Elon College, N. C.
January 3, 1919.

CHRISTIAN EDUCATION

THE NEED FOR CHRISTIAN COLLEGES

A small Christian college in New England, which, recently celebrated the centennial of its birth, has never had, in the one hundred years of its existence, an attendance that exceeded one hundred students, yet its record of graduates shows 542 clergymen, 70 foreign missionaries, 102 college professors, 32 college presidents, 9 governors of states, and 15 members of congress.

De Pauw University, a Methodist institution, also numbers among its graduates 448 ministers and missionaries, 107 editors and journalists, 146 college professors, 57 college presidents, 5 governors, 15 members of congress, 2 cabinet officers, and a host of other public servants and useful citizens. These two illustrations, cited by the Methodist Episcopal Board of Education, are typical of what Christian colleges have been doing for civilization in the United States and foreign lands.

Careful tabulation shows that one Christian university sent more men and women into the foreign field than all the state universities of the country put together. The Student Volunteer Movement reports for a period of five years: foreign missionaries from Christian schools and colleges, 82 per cent; from state and city universities and schools, 13 per cent; miscellaneous, 5 per cent. From "hay-stack prayer-meeting" even until now the Christian college has been the dynamic of the missionary enterprise.—*From The Missionary Review of The World for December.*

ITEMS FROM ELON COLLEGE

The work of the winter and spring terms is to be resumed on Wednesday the 8th. The registration books will be open on Monday and Tuesday but the real rush, as is always the case after Christmas will be on the 8th.

As far as information reaching the registrar's office is concerned the prospect for the return of the students is quite bright. Sickness in a few homes will prevent some from returning, and one student, Miss Blanche Lee, has died during the holidays.

The greatest drop off will be in the S. A. T. C. men. It is expected that about fifty per cent of these men will return and resume their studies. The College would be glad for all of them to return and has agreed to give them credit for academic studies for the year's work if they should return after Christmas and pass their studies in the winter and spring terms. However, the prospect is that not more than fifty per cent of these men will resume their studies after Christmas.

The young men of the civilian population last fall and the young ladies seem to be planning to return in about the normal proportion of previous years, and withal the enrollment looks encouraging in view of all the circumstances.

The college has just published a forty-eight page bulletin which is styled "The S. A. T. C. Number." It is printed in the national colors and dedicated to "The

Elon patriots in the world war with grateful esteem and honorable pride." This bulletin has before it the following purpose as quoted from the introductory paragraphs: "This bulletin is printed for its historical significance. The story of the Elon Students' Army Training Corps is told within, without veneer or garnishment of any sort."

Careful examination of the bulletin reveals the fact that the thrilling tale of the S. A. T. C. is here told with strict fidelity to facts. It gives the complete history of the unit including the courses of study, and every detail of the work during the sixty-eight days of the unit's life.

Appended are two addresses by President Harper as interpreting the spirit of the college in entering into the S. A. T. C. arrangement.

On the concluding page of the bulletin is found this paragraph: "Students who were in the government service last fall will receive the same credit on the fall term's work they missed as they shall make on the winter term's work. This will enable them to complete the year in college. This applies to those who would have entered the Freshman class as well as those who have been students here before."

There will be no military training at Elon College this spring. The College was asked to apply for all R. O. T. C. and did, but today the application was withdrawn. Elon is glad as an S. A. T. C. College to have done her part toward breaking the Kaiser's spirit.

C. M. CANNON.

The crops of Alabama, Arkansas, Florida, Missouri, North Carolina, Tennessee, Texas, and Virginia were smaller in 1917 than in 1916; but Arizona, California, Georgia, Louisiana, Mississippi, Oklahoma, and South Carolina showed increases.

Dr. J. Y. Joyner has resigned as superintendent of public instruction of North Carolina and has been succeeded by Dr. E. C. Brooks of Trinity College, Durham, N. C.

1,400,000 French soldiers were killed during the recent world war.

T. J. Simpson—This makes twenty-two years that I have taken THE SUN. I would not feel right without it.

Mrs. M. S. Coles—Am sending check for THE SUN. I do not want to miss a number.

Mrs. H. E. Pearce—I cannot do without THE SUN, as it has been in my home for eighteen years.

Mrs. E. T. Holland—May THE SUN shine in more homes in the year of 1919 than in any previous year.

Mrs. Mary E. Williams—I have been a subscriber to THE SUN for thirteen years and feel that I can't do without it; it has been a welcome visitor for so long.

MISSIONARY

MISSION BOARD MINUTES—THE FOREIGN DEPARTMENT

The Foreign Mission Department of the Mission Board of the Christian Church met Wednesday morning and adjourned Thursday afternoon, December 18-19, 1918. All members were present. The following persons were present with the Board at various times: Rev. E. A. Watkins, Rev. O. P. Furnas, Mr. John H. Kilworth, Rev. William Williams, Mrs. M. T. Morrill, President of the Woman's Foreign Missionary Board, Mrs. Emily K. Bishop, President of the Woman's Home Mission Board; Miss Martha Stacy, Haverhill, Mass., Rev. William Q. McKnight, Princeton, N. J.; Mr. Hermon Eldredge, Rev. Edwin B. Flory, Covington, Ohio; Rév. E. K. McCord, Missionary.

The Board requested the Executive Board of the American Christian Convention not to accept the resignation of Rev. M. T. Morrill as Mission Secretary, and also requested Dr. Morrill to withdraw such resignation.

Officers

President, Rev. M. T. Morrill; Secretary, Rev. W. H. Denison; Treasurer, Rev. O. S. Thomas; Council, Members Morrill, Denison and Winters.

Made an appropriation of the $45.00 to the Committee on Reference and Counsel for Headquarters Building expense; also appropriated $200 to the work of the Committee on Co-operation to Latin-America.

Japan

The minutes of the Japan Mission for the past year were approved.

The Christian Missionary was ordered sent to our English reading Japanese pastors.

That as soon as $600 is on hand for the purpose of building the Kannari chapel that the Mission be instructed to proceed to erect the same.

That the Foreign Mission Secretary be authorized to visit Japan within the next eighteen months.

That Rev. and Mrs. E. K. McCord be returned to Japan not later than the summer of 1919.

Inasmuch as another mission home is vitally needed at this time in Japan and that we have already on hand $4,000 for that purpose, we ask our brotherhood to raise at once the needed balance of $6,000 for that purpose.

That our Foreign Mission Secretary assist in working up a delegation to the World's Sunday School Convention in Tokyo, and that said delegation be a deputation to visit our Japan fields.

That we express our appreciation to the Japan Mission for their thoughtfulness in furnishing each member of the Foreign Department of the Board with a copy of The Christian Movement in Japan.

The salaries of the Japan missionaries for 1919 were scheduled as follows: $1200 per family for those who have been in the service from one to five years; $1300 per family for those who have been in the service from six to fifteen years; $1400 per family for those who have been in the service from sixteen to twenty years;

$1500 per family for those who have been in the service from twenty-one years upward; and that children's allowances be as per manual.

Appropriation for the Japan work budget $11,500; and for furlough salaries and travel $3,700; and rental for missionaries on furlough.

That the Foreign Mission Secretary be requested to reply to the splendid letter from the Japanese conference expressing our appreciation of their message, their plans for their Forward Movement, and their Evangelistic campaign, this splendid keeping in harmony with the spirit of the times.

Porto Rico

That we adopt the policy of remitting funds to Porto Rico a month in advance.

That the Foreign Secretary be authorized to visit Porto Rico the coming spring.

The Board approve the proposals of the Evangelical Seminary of Porto Rico for training of Ministers and other Evangelical workers; also the Evangelical School for Young Women in Porto Rico; that the Foreign Secretary be Trustee representing our denomination; that Rev. D. P. Barrett and Miss Olive G. Williams be nominated as members of the Boards of Managers in Porto Rico.

That the salaries of Rev. D. P. Barrett and family be $1300 and children's allowances as per manual; and that of Miss Olive G. Williams be $720 and rental and that the total budget for Porto Rico be $5,600.

The Foreign Secretary was authorized to have necessary repairs made on the Porto Rico properties.

Missionaries Appointed

Miss Martha Stacy, Haverhill, Mass., and Rev. William Q. McKnight were before the Board as applicants for appointment as missionaries.

It was voted that Rev. William Q. McKnight, Princeton, N. J., be placed under appointment as missionary to Porto Rico and that he be sent to the field as soon as possible.

Whereas, this Board has placed under appointment Rev. William Q. McKnight, as missionary to Porto Rico, we hereby request the Western Indiana Christian Conference, within whose bounds Mr. McKnight was born and reared, to assume his support as soon as he goes to the field.

It was voted that Miss Martha R. Stacy, Haverhill, Mass., be placed under appointment as missionary to Japan and that she be sent to the field as soon as arrangements can be made.

It was voted that the opportunity to support Miss Stacy is offered to individuals, churches or groups of churches.

It was voted to ask the Woman's Foreign Mission Board this year to support the Sendai, Japan field and to assist in securing funds to complete the mission homes in Naka Shibuya, Tokyo, and in Ponce, Porto Rico.

The Foreign Secretary was authorized to purchase five hundred copies (cloth) of "The Call of a World Task" to use in the foreign mission campaign of 1919.

WARREN H. DENISON, Sec'y.

Sunday School and Christian Endeavor

HELP REFERENCES

Sunday School—Officers and Teachers Journal and Christian Bible Class Quarterly by Christian Association, Dayton, Ohio; also Tarbell's Guide or Peloubet's Select Notes from any book dealer.

For Christian Endeavor—The Christian Endeavor World, Boston, Mass., and the Dixie Endeavorer, Chattanooga, Tenn.

MOSES THE LEADER OF ISRAEL
Exodus 3:1-4:117.

Golden Text—Moses, indeed, was faithful in all his house. Heb. 3:5.

Additional Material For Teachers—Ex. 12:37-42; Num. 12:3-8; Deut. 34:10-12; Acts 7:17-36.

Primary Topic—God speaks to Moses.

Junior Topic—Moses called to be a leader.

Intermediate Topic—A champion of the oppressed.

Senior and Adult Topic—The World's Call for Leadership.

Additional Material—Same as for teachers.

God took eighty years to make Moses a leader. He sent him to school in his mother's house, and in the court of Pharaoh for forty years. Then He gave him forty years of wilderness life, solitude and silence, uncongenial surroundings and heartaches. But with it all Moses remained keenly alive to the happenings around him. He did not draw into a shell because his endeavor to help his brethren was misunderstood. He saw and aided the Midianitish maidens at the well, and forty years later a burning bush attracts his immediate attention. He lived to see, to help and to learn. What about your work as a teacher? Did you take up the Teacher Training work during that "drive" last fall? What books have you read, what observation work have you done, what Teachers Helps do you take? God wants leaders today. The call for leadership has never been so loud and so insistent as now. Are you hearing it, and are you heeding?

Has your hymn book a selection of "Opening Exercise" in the back? Has it a number of selected Psalms for responsive reading? If so, do you ever use them? The responsive reading in the quarterly is very good, but it was never intended for use through the entire Quarter. Select your responsive reading and your hymns with care and thought in order that you may have one complete and perfect lesson, every part directed toward the same thought.

CHRISTIAN ENDEAVOR WORK

Rev. C. M. Dollar used to say the way to manage our young people in the church was to give them something to do and encourage them to do it. This opinion was shared by most of us. Many efforts were made to employ and encourage our young people. Sometimes they were asked to fill places on important committees. Sometimes to represent the church at important gathering when older and more experienced persons should have gone. All this was done mainly to encourage them, to make them feel they were a part of the church and that the church was interested in them and wanted to lead them into service for the Master. This was all an effort in the right direction but failed in many instances because backed up by no system upheld by no organized effort and in many instances the young were asked to do things beyond their ability. Consequently they sometimes became discouraged at the very things they were asked to do as an encouragement. Now no doubt the venerable Dr. Clark wrestled with these same problems as most pastors have. One day a bright idea came to him, it was the vision of the Christian Endeavor Society. This Society helps to solve the problem of giving employment to our young people of learning them to work in the Master's Kingdom. Dr. Clark's argument that there was no way to learn an individual to work so well as by giving him work to do for he says that you cannot teach a man to swim out of water. So this movement has grown from one little society nearly thirty-eight years ago to more than one hundred thousand societies at present. It has found a home in all Christian lands. It has even pushed its way with the church into the benighted heathen lands and wherever it has gone has carried sunshine and joy. Yet notwithstanding this fact many of our churches are still without Endeavor Societies. Many of our people are still strangers to this movement. Now comes the announcement, "A Board of Religious Education," has been incorporated to promote Sunday school and Christian Endeavor work. A part of their first year's program is a Christian Endeavor Society in every church of the Southern Christian Convention. I am proud of this Board and glad of its program. I am especially anxious to see a Christian Endeavor Society in all our churches. I believe the young people of our country churches are entitled to the best. I pray God's blessing upon this Board and their work.

J. H. HUGHES.

R. 4, Roanoke, Ala.

A WORD TO TEACHERS

Why not have some special help on your Sunday school work? Send $1.35 to THE CHRISTIAN SUN office and get a copy of Peloubet's Select Notes.

MARRIAGES

HORNE-BRIDGER

Mr. Fletcher H. Horne of Southhampton County, Virginia, and Miss Annie Maude Bridger, daughter of Mr. and Mrs. J. H. W. Bridger of Antioch Christian church, Zuni, Virginia, were married at 207 Chestnut Street, Suffolk, Virginia, December 24 1918. The young and happy couple have the congratulations of their many friends.

H. H. BUTLER.

KING-WALKER

A very quiet marriage took place at the parsonage in Graham at 3:30 o'clock Christmas eve when Mr. Joe Henry King and Miss Eva Francis Walker were united by the writer. There were only two friends of the couple present. The groom is from Union Ridge, Alamance County and the bride from Corbett, Caswell County. May happiness and good success attend them.

F. C. LESTER.

RIDDICK-CAYTON

At 4:30 P. M., December 24, 1918, Miss Tinnie May Cayton became the bride of Mr. Luther A. Riddick. Mr. Riddick lived at Elon College before he came to Durham about four years ago. Miss Cayton lived on Eva street, Durham, N. C., where the two happy hearts were united in marriage. The writer gave the sanction of the church to their love, using the Merrell ring ceremony. Their vows were witnessed by only a few friends and relatives. The contracting parties are very popular in the social circles of Durham and are very useful members of the Christian church. We wish them long lives of usefulness and prosperity.

R. F. BROWN.

OBITUARIES

VUNCANNON

Hattie Louise Vuncannon, the daughter of Mr. and Mrs. C. A. Vuncannon, was born May 6, 1887, Randolph County, N.

C. She was married to Madison M. Martin, August 26, 1906. To this union were born three children, William Charlie, Carl Alexander, and Colon Page. She is survived by her husband, Madison M. Martin, father and mother, five sisters, four brothers and children, William Charlie, and Colon Page, one child, Carl Alexander, having departed this life on July 23, 1916. She was 31 years, 6 months and four days old when she departed this life. During her life she was a devoted wife and mother. In young womanhood she made profession of faith in her Savior, and wherever opportunity afforded she pointed others to the Way.

"She's left this world and gone on before
To welcome her loved ones on the other shore.
She eagerly watches and waits each day,
To beckon them on the upward way.
And when this life on earth shall cease,
May all her loved ones meet her in peace."

A FRIEND.

SPIVEY

Captain James W. Spivey died at his home at Exit, Virginia, November 24, 1918, aged forty-three years, nine months and two days. He leaves a devoted wife, five children, three brothers and one sister. Funeral services conducted at Cedar Hill cemetery, Suffolk, Virginia. The Lord bless and comfort the dear bereaved ones.

H. H. BUTLER.

HAYES

William F. Hayes, son of Mr. and Mrs. John C. Hayes, aged five weeks, died December 4, 1918. Funeral services conducted at the grave at Bethlehem Christian church. The dear parents have the sympathy of their many friends.

H. H. BUTLER.

RAWLES

December 15, 1918, Hersey E. Rawles, son of Mr. and Mrs. W. E. Rawles, aged 10 years, two months and three days, departed this life. Funeral services were conducted at the grave near Nurney, Virginia, in the Rawles. cemetery.

H. H. BUTLER.

RAWLES

Wiley Edward Rawles, son of Mr. and Mrs. W. E. Rawles, Norfolk, Virginia, died December 18, 1918, aged three years, ten months and twenty-eight days. There were but a few days difference in the death of the two children. The remains were laid to rest beside the older brother

in the Rawles cemetery, funeral services being conducted at the grave. They will not return to us but we can go to them where we shall live again. God bless and comfort the bereaved parents.

H. H. BUTLER.

WHITESELL

Mrs. Malinda Phillipps Whitesell was born September 28, 1860 and died December 23, 1918. She was a member of the Methodist Episcopal church of Haw River for about twenty-three years. When the end came she was happy. She was the mother of Mrs. J. A. Hall of Burlington, Mrs. W. G. James, Messrs. J. H. and Mack Whitesell of Haw River She was making her home with Mrs. James at the time of her death. A short service was held in the home, conducted by the writer.

F. C. LESTER.

LISKEY

Avis Harrison Liskey, son of Mr. and Mrs. Joseph Liskey, died at the home of his parents, near Harrisonburg, Virginia, December 11, 1918, at the age of 30 years. He was a faithful, active member of New Hope Christian church, where his presence and loyal service will be greatly missed. He was a young man of amiable disposition and sterling Christian character and his death is a severe loss to the community in which he was held in high esteem. He is survived by his father and mother and three brothers and four sisters. Funeral services were conducted by the writer. May the Lord comfort and bless the bereaved.

W. T. WALTERS.

RESOLUTIONS OF RESPECT

Whereas, God in His all-wise providence, has seen fit to call from labor to reward Brother Anis Harrison Liskey, our vice-president and active co-worker; therefore, we, the members of the New Hope Christian Endeavor Society wish to express our gratitude for the service he rendered while with us, and while we shall miss him in our meetings and deplore the loss to our services, yet we pray that our Heavenly Father will help us to bow in humble submission to His Divine will and to strive more earnestly to emulate the example of our deceased brother in faithful attendance and active service. Therefore be it resolved:

1. That in his death the Society has lost a consecrated worker, the church and Sunday school a faithful member and the community a worthy citizen.

2. That we extend to the bereaved family our deepest sympathy and, in we would commend them to the God of love and mercy.

3. That a copy of these resolutions be sent to the family, a copy spread on the records of the Society, and a copy be sent to The Christian Sun and the Harrisonburg papers for publication.

N. M. HASLER, President,
MATTIE LISKEY, Sec. Protem.

UNDERWOOD

During the mist and rain on December 24, 1918 in the city of the dead at Concord Christian church, the infant of Rev. I. T. Underwood and wife was laid to rest in Mother earth. May the Lord, wise and good comfort and bless in the time of need.

"How brief the stay, as beautiful as fleeting.
The time that baby came with us to dwell;
Just long enough to give a happy greeting,
Just long enough to bid us all farewell!
Death travels down the thickly settled highway,
At shining marks they say he loves to aim;
How did he find, far down our lonely by-way,
Our little one who died without a name."

L. L. WYRICK.

WHITE

Charles Nyack White, physical director of the Y. M. C. A., at Wilmington, N. C., died of pneumonia October 28, 1918, at 3 o'clock P. M., at Jas. Walker Memorial Hospital. The announcement of his death came as a distinct shock to his friends and cast a deep sense of sadness among the many people in the city who knew him and held him in high esteem because of his excellent character and, for the magnificent service rendered by him during the epidemic of influenza.

From the beginning of the scourge he worked faithfully and untiringly to relieve the suffering patients stricken with influenza and pneumonia. As volunteer ambulance driver of the above named hospital, he carried numberless people to the hospital and was without doubt the means of saving the lives of many patients who would not have been able to reach the hospital had he not worked so relentlessly up until the very day he was forced to go to bed, himself stricken with influenza.

Mr. White was only twenty years old, a boy in years but a man in discretion and in the amount of service rendered the community. Although almost a stranger in the city, he did not hesitate to give his service in behalf of the people whom he had never seen before, and his memory will ever be kept green in the hearts of all who knew him. He devoted his time to relief work, rendering invaluable aid to the Red Cross and the hospitals.

Mindful of the unselfish devotion to duty and the embodiment of the true Red Cross spirit, his was the supreme sacrifice as truly as if his life blood had been poured upon the battle fields of France. "Greater love hath no man than this— that he lay down his life for his friends."

The above is a clipping from the Wilmington Daily paper, and in our judgment pictures most beautifully the life and character of our noble young brother.

When we stand over the lifeless form of a dear young friend taken all too soon, as we think, we wonder at the mysterious workings of an all wise Providence. We cannot understand why one so gentle, unselfish and good, and in the midst of his usefulness should be removed from the scene of his earthly labors, but we must remember that God is too wise to err and too good to be unkind and that He calls those whom He loveth. Why should not His jewels shine in His own home, even though ours be made dreary? These sentiments express the emotions of our hearts as we meditate upon the unselfish and beautiful life of our noble young brother.

The memory of his noble and unselfish young life in sacrificing his life blood for others, will linger with us as we make the pilgrimage of life, and inspire us to emulate the beautiful Christian virtures that adorn his character.

Resolved, that we extend our heartfelt sympathy, to the bereaved parents, brothers and sisters and his many friends in their great loss.

Resolved, that a copy of these resolutions be spread upon the records of our school, a copy be sent the family of our young brother and a copy to The Christian Sun for publication.

T. EDWIN BAIRD,
MRS. ERL K. HENLEY,
Committee from Memorial Christian Temple Sunday School.

1919	JANUARY				1919	
Su	Mo	Tu	We	Th	Fr	Sa
			1	2	3	4
5	6	7	8	9	10	11
12	13	14	15	16	17	18
19	20	21	22	23	24	25
26	27	28	29	30	31	

THE CHRISTIAN SUN

"IN ESSENTIALS UNITY, IN NON-ESSENTIALS LIBERTY, IN ALL THINGS CHARITY"

Citizenship

CITIZENSHIP is a term that world builders and world thinkers and reformers must study. All too long it has been confined to strict observance of the laws of the land without respect to the laws eternal and abiding. The things of earth and the things of heaven are so connected that *citizenship* in the full and true meanmeaning of the word must embrace a loyal connection with both worlds. True citizenship not only prompts a man to defend his country but prompts him to help enlarge the Kingdom's work, for the kingdoms of earth shall become the kingdoms of our God.

Volume LXXI WEDNESDAY, JANUARY 15, 1919 Number 3

BURLINGTON - - - NORTH CAROLINA

THE CHRISTIAN SUN

Founded 1844 by Rev. Daniel W. Kerr

C. B. RIDDLE - - - Editor

Entered at the Burlington, N. C. Post Office as second class matter.

Subscription Rates

One year .... $ 2.00
Six months 1.00

In Advance

Give both your old and new postoffice when asking that your address be changed.

The change of your label is your receipt for money. Written receipts sent upon request.

Marriage and obituary notices not exceeding 150 words printed free if received within 60 days from date of event, all over this at the rate of one-half cent a word.

Original poetry not accepted for publication.

Principles of the Christian Church

(1) The Lord Jesus Christ is the only Head of the Church.
(2) Christian is a sufficient name of the Church.
(3) The Holy Bible is a sufficient rule of faith and practice.
(4) Christian character is a sufficient test of fellowship, and of church membership.
(5) The right of private judgment and the liberty of conscience is a right and a privilege that should be accorded to, and exercised by all.

EDITORIAL

BEATING THE PASTOR

"The janitor can beat the pastor any time," said a man in THE SUN office last week as he read the short editorial on "Cold Churches." He went his way and we went ours.

Again and again the words of our visitor come to us. Did he mean it? And so again we pondered and began to analyze it. The janitor can beat the pastor in the preparation for the service. He can have the house warm and comfortable, or if in summer, he can have the house well ventilated and arranged so that fresh air can be had. It is the poor ventilation that puts people to sleep—when it is not poor preaching.

So the janitor serves God in his work and as well as he does in his worship. "It is better to be a door keeper in the house of the Lord than to dwell in the tents of the wicked."

THE MINISTERIAL STUDENT AND THE CHURCH PAPER

We have noticed for years a certain thing in the Church that has to us become interesting and ought to concern every member. Our love and appreciation for the Church paper dates back to boyhood. Well do we remember the time and place where THE CHRISTIAN SUN used to come. We look back to a few years ago when we looked forward to the coming of THE CHRISTIAN SUN with the greatest delight.

We have always *loved* THE SUN. We say *loved* because that is what we mean; we more than like it. When in college, and when the paper was edited and printed at Elon College, we became accustomed to the mailing day of the paper and knew about the time it was carried to the post office. We confess with no apology that at least two or three times have been the trips to the post office in one afternoon with the hope of finding THE CHRISTIAN SUN in our box. It was a delight, a joy—and it is yet. After reading the "copy" one or more times, reading the proofs from one to three times and standing by the printers until the last page is made up, we do with delight go to the mailing room and get two copies for our files and a copy for private use with almost the same delight as if the pages were new.

And we say all this that you, dear reader, may understand why that we have noticed *a certain thing of* which we started out to speak about. That thing is this: The ministerial students who have stood by THE CHRISTIAN SUN during their college days have been the men who have graduated from college, ordained to the sacred office of an elder in the Church, and have since that time been making good. These are facts that are not fiction. They can be backed up by proof after proof. It is a temptation not to call names. We can name them by the half dozen of our acquaintance who have entered Elon College, joined the ministerial class, and are today not to be located. These facts have been brought to our mind recently in a more emphatic way because of our recent reading the "copy" and proof of the *Christian Annual.* Young men whom we once knew as fellow ministerial students in college are reported by the Educational Committee of the various conferences as being unconcerned about their work, and in many cases their whereabouts not even known. In practically every instance we recall that these young men had very little interest in their Church papers while in college. When a young man offers his services to his Church he ought to show with that offer an interest in the various enterprises of his denomination, and especially the publications of his denomination, because these things keep him in vital touch with the issues of his Church. We believe, and do hereby recommend, that the Educational Committee of each conference make this one important question in the examination for entrance to the Biblical class and for license: "Do you read your Church papers regularly?" It is high time that the Church awake from its slumber and cease to throw down its requirements so low that most any fellow can join the ministerial ranks.

A young man in training for the ministry ought to read every issue of as many of his denomination's papers as he can. There is no excuse why he should not because they are at his disposal in the college library. A course on Religious Journalism would not be a thing amiss in our colleges. (And certain elements in the course would lighten the burdens of an editor).

Let us bestir ourselves in seeing that young men who are offering themselves to the Church as preachers and teachers have an abiding interest in the publicity enterprises of their denomination. Those under whose control they are had better put them to a test than to have the world do it. The diseases are many an dthere are remedies sufficient. May our doctors prescribe.

AN APPRECIATED LETTER

Among the good letters received during the last few days is the following which we very much appreciate:

Dear Brother Riddle:—

I have just returned from a visit to Ramseur, N. C., and during my stay there I was talking over some things that were religious and some that were not with my grandmother, Mrs. A. J. Elliott, who is now eighty years old. During our conversation she asked for THE SUN, after receiving it she said: "This is the first paper that I read when a child, and it has been in our home each year since. I count the days from one issue until the next, and if I am to make any more sacrifices in order to have THE SUN I am willing to do so."

It gives me great pleasure, old college mate, to send you a check for my subscription if for no other purpose than to be a pleasure to my dear grandmother and a partial help to you. I wish you all the success that is possible for an editor to have, and should you ever venture within the boundaries of Franklin County, I extend to you and yours a sincere greeting.

Yours truly,
W. C. POE.

Louisburg, N. C.

NATIONAL JUNIOR CHRISTIAN ENDEAVOR WORKER COMING

Miss Grace Hooper of Nebraska, National Superintendent of Junior Christian Endeavor, will be in Burlington and Graham on January 21.

Miss Hooper is a brilliant young woman and an exceptionally fine speaker. She has traveled extensively and is the best authority in North America on religious work for children in Junior Christian Endeavor Societies, Mission Bands, Epworth Leagues and B. Y. P. U's. It is hoped that she will get a great hearing in our cities.

Miss Hooper's schedules of meetings in these cities include a Junior Rally for all the boys and girls at 4:00 P. M., in the Burlington Christian church, a conference with the Junior leaders after this rally and a great Young People's Rally at 7:45 P. M., in the Graham Presbyterian church. To these meetings everybody is cordially invited.

We ought to make this day a memorable one in our cities for religious work for the children.

Miss Hooper comes to us with the endorsement of the World's Christian Endeavor Union, the All-South Christian Endeavor Extension Committee, the State Christian Endeavor Union and the personal commendation of many religious workers of world-wide and national reputation.

An offering will be received at the evening rally for the work of the State Christian Endeavor Union.

Brother W. E. McClenny, Suffolk, Va., seems to be pleased with THE SUN from this note in a recent letter to the Editor: "I must congratulate you upon your paper for the past few weeks. You are doing your part, and if the preachers will give you the news from the field, it will be an excellent paper, and by so doing the interest of the local churches will be greatly increased."

Brother Alva H. Morrill, Woodstock, Vermont, writes: "Here is my check for THE CHRISTIAN SUN. Your new heading arrangement is an improvement. You Southern brethren are outdistancing us of the North."

WHY OCCASIONALLY?

So many of the brethren do not write to THE SUN except occasionally. Why not often, even if the note be short, for that is the kind that is read? No pastor should mind spending a few dollars for postage and stationery in order that his people may be represented in the Church organ. But why write about local matters all the time? Why not let the readers of THE SUN have a few quotations from some of your sermons? And why not a sermon occasionally? A sermon does not have to be long enough to fill half the paper. If this be the case the Sermon on the Mount was not a *sermon.* Let us have the news so that what is in THE SUN cannot be found elsewhere until it is reprinted from it. Readers like a paper that gives them something that they cannot find elsewhere.

RANDOM PARAGRAPHS

The last time that I wrote "Random Paragraphs" dates back to a time beyond the "Flu," and since that has hindered so many of you from doing what you had hoped to. I am sure that you will understand my silence.

* *

In college days I read of a man—one of the great poets—who carried his pencil and paper in his hand and jotted down all his best thoughts. That is a good idea and should be followed by many of us lest we have the gems of thought that come to us.

* *

There is a man who sweeps the streets in my town. I meet him each morning on my way to the office. His happy "good morning" gives me cheer and I have the greatest respect for him. The sound of his scrape on the pavement is a song of no mean sound.

* *

And there is another man whom I often meet. He is never well and the day is too—well something, first one thing and then another. Excuse me, Mr. Grumbler, I pity you.

* *

I asked a man the other day if he believed in tithing and he replied that he had been *thinking* about it. That is a good step in the direction of doing anything. *Thinking* precedes action.

* *

It is a pleasure to edit a paper when friends are so kind and loyal. Thank you, good friends, for such loyal support.

C. B. R.

WORSHIP AND MEDITATION

FAMILY WORSHIP

In things social, as well as in things individual, God calls upon men to have faith in him, and in His wisdom appoints a way in which those who do trust Him may give outward and tangible expression to their faith. No man lives to himself alone. The blessing and progress of the world are inseparable from the united experience and co-operation of groups of men and women. The unit of these groups is the family. Accordingly when God proclaimed through Moses the Ten Commandments of His moral law, He gave orders that they should be faithfully observed and promulgated in every household, saying: ''These words, which I command thee this day, shall be in thine heart; and thou shalt teach them diligently unto thy children, and shalt talk of them when thou sittest in thine house, and when thou walkest by the way, and when thou liest down, and when thou risest up. And thou shalt bind them for a sign upon thine hand, and they shall be as frontlets between thine eyes. And thou shalt write them upon the posts of thine house and on thy gates.''

Abraham was called the ''friend of God,'' and Jehovah himself thus defined the strong bond of friendship of friendship between them: ''I know him, that he will command his children and his household after him, and they shall keep the way of the Lord.''. Joshua, the great commander, who brought God's people into the land of promise, revealed the secret of his greatness in his challenge to them toward the close of his life: ''Choose you in this day whom you will serve; ......as for me and my house, we will serve the Lord.''.

In the New Testament especial care is taken to make mention of the fact that the noble tradeswoman, Lydia of Thyatira, was a believer in family religion, for upon hearing the precious news of the gospel of Christ, she was baptized, with all her household. It is also recorded of Cornelius, the Roman centurion, that he feared God, with all his house. Moreover, where can the assurance of our Lord, that where two or three are gathered together in his name he is in the midst of them, find more frequent or more natural fulfillment than when father and mother and children come together at the family altar day by day to meet with God?

Loud and insistent have been the complaints of a lack of young men for the ministry, of a disregard for the sacredness of the Lord's Day, of the meager attendance of worshipers in the Lord's house, of the conspicuous silence of elders and deacons, and of the other men who are sometimes found in the week day meetings of God's people, when there is a call for prayer. The humble, faithful setting up of the family altar in every Christian home and beginning the day there with God would revolutionize the moral and spiritual condition of the world in both Church and State. All history will verify the truth of this statement.

God has promised, ''Them that honor me I will honor;'' and the pages of history show with perfect distinctness that the world's greatest men and women, the world's greatest benefactors, the world's truest, purest, best spirits have come from homes in which the family altar was reared and honored. Students for the ministry may be reaped in schools and colleges; but they are sown in Christian homes; and where, because of lack of family devotion, there is a meager sowing of the seed, it is hopeless to expect, no matter how great an effort may be put forth, to reap large and satisfactory harvets of workers after home has been left behind.

God's order for a prosperous and happy people is, first, prayer in secret, then the prayer of two or three united; first, the praying Christian, then the praying family, then the praying Church, then the outpoured blessing on the Church and family and community. That grand old missionary, John G. Paton, speaking of his father, says: ''In his seventeenth year began that blessed custom of family prayer, morning and evening, which my father practiced probably without one single omission until he lay on his deathbed, seventy-seven years of age; when, even to the last day of his life, a portion of Scripture was read and his voice was heard softly joining in the Psalm, and his lips breathed the morning and evening prayer, falling in sweet benediction on the heads of all his children, far away, many of them over all the earth, but all meeting him there at the throne of grace. None of us can ever remember that any day ever passed unhallowed thus. No hurry for market, no rush to business, no arrival of friends or guests, no trouble or sorrow, no joy or excitement ever prevented at least our kneeling around the family altar, while the high priest led our prayers to God and offered himself and his children there. And blessed to others as well as to ourselves was the light of such an example.''

It was good in God's eyes that Abraham should bring up his household to know and fear him; that Joshua should serve the Lord himself and lead his household in that service; that the father of this glorious missionary should worship God in the bosom of his family for sixty years, every single day; and it is good in God's sight for all Christian parents to do likewise.

Two principal objections are urged. The first is the lack of time. Some family prayers may take a long time, but the best are brief. Ideal family prayers do not call for the reading of long chapters or the making of long prayers. ''I remember,'' wrote a devoted and gifted Christian woman, ''being very much impressed by a scene in a home where I chanced to be a guest. The father was a business man with large interests depending on him, and at least four of the family daily had to take an early train to the city. When I heard the hour announced for breakfast and saw the

(Continued on page 10)

MISSIONARY

"HOLDING THE ROPES"

I did not know till the other day where we got "Holding the Ropes" from. Here is its derivation, I am told, "We saw there was a gold mine in India," said Andrew Fuller, in 1793, after listening to the stirring words of John Thomas, who had been pleading for India, "but it seemed almost as deep as the center of the earth. Who will venture to go and explore it?" we asked. "I will go down," responded William Cary, "but remember that you must *hold the ropes.*" We who are at home are the rope holders. Our missionaries have gone down for us. Their safety and their efficiency are with us. I wonder if we pray for our missionaries as we should, and do all we can to hold the ropes while they go down?

WHAT IS BEING DONE?

I wonder what is being done to reach the three objectives set for ourselves by the Southern Christian Convention at Franklin, Va., last May? Unless something is done, it will have been of little or no use for the Convention to have debated and adopted the matter. And the closing of the war has made the attainment of these objectives more essential than has been realized.
Briefly stated the three goals are these:
1. The securing of one hundred new recruits giving all their time and strength as ministers and missionaries to advance the kingdom of our blessed Christ in the world.
2. Along with these we have set out to improve our financial system by adopting in every church, the Every-Member Canvass with the envelope system of collections.
3. That to make the envelope system easy and the financial problem a pleasure and not a burden, we are to teach Church members the law by tithing and get them to adopt the same.
As to the first goal: Are we taking this matter seriously? Have we realized that we *must* have workers to take the place of those who have gone out from us or who by age or death can no longer prosecute the work of the Church? God will give us the needed workers to carry forward the kingdom when we human beings lay the matter upon our hearts and beg Him to supply the same. One of the mightiest religious and even evangelical factors in the recent war was the Y. M. C. A. This organization secured its recruits by well-planned and persistent efforts. The Church will secure its recruits when it likewise adopts well-planned and persistent efforts. We may not reach the matter as rapidly as did the Y. M. C. A. but we may do so as effectually. There must, however, be effort and prayer and the expression of the real need before the response will come. It is doubtful if God ever supplies any human want until the need thereof has been felt and expressed. All through the ministry of Christ while here on earth, individuals and situations were relieved and made fit and proper only when human beings realized and expressed the need. A notable example of this was when Christ was asleep upon a pillow in the ship that was likely to sink. The winds were furious and the waves boisterous and the ship was filling. But the Master of men and waves moved not to relieve the situation until appealed to by human beings who sorely felt the distress of their direful situation. I am wondering what is to hinder every pastor in the Christian Church from announcing to his congregation the need of ministers and missionaries and then ask the people of the congregation, after the need has been set forth, to unite in prayer with him to God that He will give the workers. This kind cometh but prayer. If we meant what we did at Franklin, it is certainly time we were proving the same by our deeds.

The second objective is certainly a necessity. There is abundance of money in the hands of Christian people with which to carry forward the Lord's work. And the only reason why that money is not available is because of the poor or indifferent management in securing the funds. The Every-Member-Canvass and the envelope system have been tried out and they have not been found wanting. They have solved the financial problem so far as I have learned in every Church where they have been tried. Give them a good trial in your Church and you will, I believe, see a revolution there in the financial situation.

And then the third objective is by no means to be neglected. The real joy of giving is never realized until adopted for oneself the law of the tithe. God never had any law enacted or taught in His Word for the cramping, the harm, or the impoverishment of His people. The law of the tithe is no exception, and the people who have practiced it through the years have not become poorer, but richer. There is a reason for this. Any individual who adopts this law will keep a closer accounting with himself for funds received and expended and will know at the end of the year what he is doing. When the time of giving comes he is not pinched or strained as those are who have not adopted the law but simply gives from the tenth that he has laid aside for this purpose. If Christian people generally would adopt the law of the tithe, there would be enough money in the Lord's treasury with which to send the gospel to every nation, community and peoples on earth within ten years. We are not going to have permanent peace in the world until it is made and kept in the name of the Prince of Peace. And if Christian peoples will give of their men and money in the next ten years one-half of what they have had to give for our war the past two years, this world will be taken for Christ and the kingdoms of this earth shall become the kingdoms of our Lord. Can't we, Brethren and Beloved, pull together and pray together and strive together for the carrying out of the plan so wisely adopted by our Convention and the achievement of the objectives which the Convention so timely set? May our Father's wisdom help us, and His blessings be upon us as we go about His work as becometh faithful servants.

J. O. ATKINSON,
Field Secretary of Missions.

PASTOR AND PEOPLE

THANKS, THANKS

To my many friends:

I thank you all for your kind remembrances of more than fifty Christmas and New Year cards and letters on my ninety-third birthday. Also for the many nice presents, among which was fifteen dollars in money. I wish I could write to each separately but there are too many. At this writing I am in my usual good health but cannot walk very much because of the lack of strength in my lower limbs.

J. W. WELLONS.

Elon College, N. C.

A POUNDING AND A PURSE

Just two or three days before Thanksgiving, this writer received a telephone message ordering him to stay at home for the afternoon, this message stating that "company" was coming. Not knowing what else to do, the coming of the "company" was awaited with all the patience it was possible to summon under the circumstances. By and by the ringing of the door bell announced the arrival of the short while expected guests, whose names, whose number, and whose mission in coming were not revealed until the door swung back its welcome to five ladies who had come to represent Berea church in charging upon the pastor's pantry with a generous quantity of good things for our table. This was a genuine, good old-fashioned country pounding, such as the Berea people like to "pull off" on their pastor.

On Sunday before Christmas two friends at Rosemont, representing other friends of this church and Sunday school, sprung another surprise for the pastor and his family when a purse amounting to $58.50 was handed the undersigned. Accompanying this remembrance, or rather as a large part of it, was a written statement expressing the church's appreciation for the relationship that exists between pastor and people,' which statement can not be forgotten soon.

For these evidences of love and good-will towards us, on the part of the people whom we are trying to serve, we fail to find any words sufficiently strong to express our appreciation. Such kindness and consideration moves our hearts with the desire to do our utmost in the interest of the pastorate where we labor.

G. O. LANKFORD.

Berkley, Va.

NO LONGER IN NEWPORT NEWS

More than a year ago an announcement was made concerning my willingness to assist the boys in uniform who were stationed in Newport News, Virginia. This I did on condition that pastors, parent and church secretaries would notify me of the arrival of their friends in that city. It is the present need of that work that calls forth this note.

While in that city I did all I could to find the boys and render any assistance possible to them. While doing so I was amply paid for all the service I rendered by the many friends made among men from all sections of our Church. Some of the letters from mothers of these men expressing their appreciation of my service, would make the heart of any man leap for joy. God bless every one of them and bring their boys back home again. Thanks to every one who sent a name.

Since the boys are returning, letters are again flooding my office concerning these men. I am using the Church papers to notify all parties concerned that since I have taken charge of the First Christian church, Greensboro, N. C., I am more than 200 miles from Newport News, and can no longer give any time to that face of the work. This will save expense of correspondence to both you and my office work.

J. VINCENT KNIGHT.

SUFFOLK LETTER

(A letter from Chaplain Rev. B. F. Black)

My dear Doctor Staley:—

I am settled down at last and am happy in my new found task, though I had to search for it. After covering five hundred miles of rail, seeing something of Brest Tours, Le Mons, Angers, Nautes, am now here. I have walked where Caesar's legions trod two thousand years ago, seen the hand-work of the slaves in the days B. C.—walls, towers, catacombs. I have slept in a place erected in the tenth century. Have seen the chateau which was begun in Caesar's day, also the lookout tower and fortifications made in those days and during one hundred years were walls and motes.

I have spent nearly ten days in a Chaplain school in Chateau, where the gates now stand ajar and the motes forever dry. The sound of the bugle announcing the coming of God and Master has long since died away.

The lake, a part of defense, is no longer the lounging place for sweet maidens; lillies no longer perfume the air. Every peasant will tell you the love of the country. Today the remnant of departed glory is held together by a Count—who married a Chicago lady and with $40,000.00 of her father's money bought "all this I have said." Poor deluded—no undeluded lass. Yet a countess to be of fourteen is quite American.

The school of Chaplains covers from Seattle, Washington, to New York. Chaplains from the front rest here, some gassed and some crippled, many of whom will have to stay at some base hospital or camp for further service. They have done their bit and the gas will from two to five years do its deadly bit. Yet it is all in the big game we are playing.

I am nicely fixed here. Happy in the service of my country and in His name. I move from 7:00 A. M. to 11:00 P. M., doing my bit. I walk from five to eight miles daily. Have the best of health now. Go days without water—only coffee or tea at meals. How would you like a funeral every day? Suppose you had fifty, or suppose you were called to assist in a procession of one hundred and fifty? Would you enjoy going in and out of a meningitis ward, or pneumonia, or scarlet fever or diptheria? Oh, well what is the use to ask the ques-

tion? "Stand not upon the ordinary going, but go."
You leave your nerves and fear of death in the hotel
before you sail.

I think of you all daily and look on the wall at the
"Bonnie lasses" and count not the days to my embark-
ing but rather steel myself for each new day's task with
but a single thought. You are too far off to know;
your newspaper is but a scrap of paper.

The U. S. A. is here two million strong. Cities grow
up in a day. There is everything here except a cotton
mill. Plenty to eat and wear. Our boys are delivering
the goods and "going west" without a murmur. I have
not had a line from the United States, but hope to get
letters now as I am settled and Uncle Sam can put his
finger on me. I know my dear ones are in good hands
so why should I worry? Regards to all.

                        B. F. Black,
                Camp Hospital No. 11, Camp No. 1
                        A. E. F.—A. P. O. 701.
October 30, 1918.

DEATHS FROM DIPHTHERIA TO BE INVESTIGATED

The State Board of Health of North Carolina has
centered its guns, to use the figure of the day, upon another disease—diphtheria. For several years typhoid
fever, tuberculosis, malaria and other easily preventable diseases have been objects of the Board's attack.
As a result of a continued warfare on the causes of
these diseases the State's death rate has been reduced
till now it one of the lowest in the Union. Deaths from
typhoid fever alone have decreased from 839 in 1914
to 502 in 1918. In other words, 337 lives during the
year 1918 were saved as a result of the Board's war
fare on typhoid fever.

The Board has decided that 400 deaths from diphtheria a year, particularly since the prevention of this
disease has been made so easy and put within reach of
all the people, are entirely too many and should not
be. Therefore, it proposes to adopt a new policy in
dealing with this disease. The plan to make a careful
investigation by a trained epidemic ologist of each
death from diphtheria for the purpose of placing the
responsibility of the death. The Board holds that
whenever a death occurs from this disease, some one has
blundered, some one failed to give the antitoxin in time.

Before inaugurating this new policy of dealing with
deaths from diphtheria, the Board made provision
whereby the people of the State are to be furnished
diphtheria antitoxin practically free of cost. The
charge for the package, irrespective of its size, whether
it contains 1,000 units or 10,000 units, is twenty-five
cens, which is the cost of the syringes and the package
and not the antitoxin.

UNCLE SAM'S INSURANCE

To the Soldiers and Sailors of America:—

Approximately four million officers and men of the
Army and Navy are now insured with the United
States for a grand total of almost thirty-seven billion
dollars.

You owe it to yourself and to your family to hold
on to Uncle Sam's insurance. It is the strongest, safest,
and cheapest life insurance ever written.

For your protection Uncle Sam has established the
greatest life insurance company in the world—a company as mighty, as generous, and as democratic as the
United States Government itself. Just as Uncle Sam
protected you and your loved ones during the war, so
he stands ready to continue this protection through the
days of readjustment and peace.

The privilege of continuing your Government insurance is a valuable right given to you as part of the
compensation for your heroic and triumphant services.
If you permit the insurance to lapse, you lose that
right, and you will never be able to regain it. But if
you keep your present insurance—by the regular payment of premiums—you will be able to change it into
a standard Government policy *without medical examination.* Meantime you can keep up your present insurance at substantially the same low rate. The Government will write ordinary life insurance, twenty-pay-
ment life, endowment maturing at age 62, and other
usual forms of insurance. This will be Government insurance—at Government rates.

The United States Government—through the Bureau
of War Risk Insurance of the Treasury Department—
will safeguard you and your loved ones with the spirit
and purpose of a Republic grateful to its gallant de-
fenders. To avail yourself of this protection, you must
keep up your present insurance. Carry back with you
to civil life, as an aid and an asset, the continued insurance protection of the United States Government.

Hold on to Uncle Sam's insurance. -
                        W. G. McAdoo, *Sec'y.*

THE RAINBOW FAIRIES

Two little clouds one summer's day
    Went flying through the sky;
They went so fast they bumped their heads,
And both began to cry.

Old Father Sun looked out and said,
    "Oh, never mind, my dears;
I'll send the little fairy folk
    To dry your falling tears."

One fairy came in violet,
    And one in indigo;
In blue, green, yellow, orange, red—
    They made a pretty row.

They wiped the cloud tears all away,
    And then, from out the sky,
Upon a line the sunbeam made,
    They hung their gowns to dry.
                —*Lizzie M. Hadley.*

Burlington's new Christian church is about enclosed
and the work continues.

It looks as if we are not about to have a "winterless"
winter. We have had so many things during the last
year with the *less* on them.

THE FORWARD MOVEMENT

The Forward Movement Rally

As soon as it was decided that the Executive Board of the American Christian Convention, the Mission Board, and the Sunday School Board would be holding meetings at the same time in Dayton, Ohio, we planned for a Forward Movement rally at the First Christian church, December 8. The banquet took place at 7 o'clock and some seventy-five sat down to the splendid dinner provided by the ladies of the church. The orchestra, the male quartett, rendered splendid music. The Forward Movement song was led by Rev. Pressley E. Zartmann; Rev. R. H. McDaniel, the author of "Since Jesus Came Into My Heart," sang that song that has been sung in almost every church. There were thirty ministers from the Christian Church, and a large number of churches within a radius of thirty miles were represented. Rev. E. D. Hammond brought fourteen of his laymen from his pastorate thirty miles away. Rev. Hiley Baker brought fourteen from Eaton church some twenty-five miles away. The auditorium was decorated with Forward Movement mottoes and slogans. A committee from the United Brethren Forward Movement and another from the Methodist church interested in the Centenary were present to get suggestions and learn of our program.

The speakers were Rev. Dr. F. G. Coffin, the President of the Forward Movement Committee who brought the opening message of the evening and set forth the imperative need of the Movement in these wonderful times in which we are living and briefly outlined the Movement. President W. A. Harper sent a message on the first point of the campaign—Devotion—which paper was read by Dr. W. C. Wicker, Elon College, N. C.; Mr. Hermon Eldredge, our Religious Education Secretary, came from Camp Upton and spoke on "Religious Education." Mrs. M. T. Morrill spoke on "Missions" in a most telling way. The Superintendent closed the evening messages and showed how we just must meet our goal of a half million dollars for the work of the Church and the Kingdom, and expressed his confidence that our people are ready to go forward together in this plan which seems to be surely Providential in its plan and time. We believe that our Forward Movement program is the answer of the Christian Church to the Divine call of God. He urged the thirty ministers to build church programs around these points, and to see that their conference and institute programs were so constructed, and asked them to hold similar rallies in their churches with groups from several churches present. We hope our pastors will plan for just such rallies in many sections. Pastor Howsare and his people did everything possible to make the meeting a splendid success. The spirit was fine, the attendance large and many pledged themselves to the Forward Movement work.

We expect soon to have a Sunday school Forward Movement program ready to announce. We are now working it out with the Sunday School Board and we

are already asking our Sunday School Superintendents and their Sunday School Councils to prepare to take it up at the very announcement of the program.

We are thoroughly convinced that one of our great needs in the Forward Movement work is to work out a definite church program in each congregation. We would urge every pastor with his church officials to work out a definite program for his congregation. Make out a tentative program, work to it, center the minds of the Church on it, prepare for it. It will greatly help. Some of our workers are doing that very thing with great profit. We are expecting to tell you about it soon. Incorporate all five of the Forward Movement fundaments.

Have you realized that the Christian Church of which you are a part is responsible for no less than one million souls who have no Christian light as yet? All this aside from those who have not found Christ but know about Him in our many fields at home and abroad. We are responsible for giving the light to a million who have never yet heard. Have you ever felt your responsibility in the sight of God? Has not God called you to go? Has He not called you to give? Has He not called you to pray? Yes, to pray, that is the hardest of all.

Things Are Being Done

Rev. Fred Cooper, Clemons, Iowa, says: "I have been giving my people sermons on the Forward Movement, and have been working to get the church better organized for work. I have gotten the official board to agree to the budget system. Am making the Every-Member canvass."

Rev. Raymond G. Clark, Neb., says: "I want to tell you what a joy it was to preach a series of five sermons on the Forward Movement. The points seem so logically arranged, the goals set forth are within the reach of every willing church. They are inspiring to ambitious people. Mine are pleased. Am sending you Member canvass this year. All bills are paid, pastor paid in advance, and money in the treasury."

The First Church, Dayton, Ohio, observed "Religion in the Home" Sunday in December and the Superintendent preached a sermon on that theme. He also presented the Sunday school Forward Movement program to the Sunday School Council meeting of teachers and officers and church officers.

Rev. A. W. Sparks, Argos, Indiana, asks, "As Secretary of Sunday Schools both of the Northwestern Indiana, and the Indiana State Conference, I would like to know how I can best use my office to further the Forward Movement? I want to do my utmost to make the Movement win in Indiana as elsewhere. I am now preaching a series of sermons on the Forward Movement." With that kind of a spirit the Forward Movement cannot but be a great help to the churches and accomplish its purpose.

WARREN H. DENISON, Supt.

Mrs. W. K. Wagner—Find check for two dollars for my renewal to THE SUN for I do not want to miss a number.

THE CHRISTIAN ORPHANAGE

SUPERINTENDENT'S LETTER

Dear Friends:—We are still climbing toward our goal of five thousand dollars for our Thanksgiving offering. We now just lack $279.40 being at the mark. We must reach it. Too near now to give up. We believe our people are too much interested now to fail in this undertaking. We must close up the books for the year and have from now till the 22nd, to reach this goal; my next letter could not reach you before that date, so this will be my last appeal for the Thanksgiving offering for the year 1918.

I have a little secret I am very anxious to tell you and want to reach this goal first. If you will push me up to it by the 22nd I will let you know the secret.

We have more than one hundred churches that have not made this offering. It is my earnest desire that each church take a part.

Now to make sure we reach the goal I am going to ask that ten men mail me a check for $10.00 each. Twenty men mail me a check for $5.00 each and seventy-nine women mail me check for $1.00 each. Let these checks be mailed on January 20 so they will reach me by the 22nd. When you read this letter and you are anxious to reach this goal, and I know you are, make up your mind which one of these amounts you feel that you want to give and then call up your neighbors and ask them to join in with you and mail their checks too and by this earnest co-operation right at this critical time—right at the end of the race when we want to reach the goal. I feel sure we can get enough friends of the Institution interested to put us across the line.

I received a letter from a good sister this week enclosing check for $10.00 saying that we must reach the goal. How encouraging those words were! They put spice and energy in our being to not give up but to put forth greater efforts not only to reach the goal set but go over the top.

Now my friends, let us all make one more effort. All make one hard pull for the next week. All pull together with earnest co-operation and make this undertaking a success.

I have faith in your earnest co-operation. I believe you want to see me reach this goal. I know it will bring you happiness as well as myself to see that our church can do things.

Now for our final effort to go over the top.

C. D. J.

REPORT FOR DECEMBER 25, 1918—Continued

Amount brought forward, $13,228.66.

Sunday School Monthly Offerings

Timber Ridge, $1.30; Columbus, Ga., $2.50; Lanett, Ala., $3.80; Pleasant Hill, $2.10; Total, $9.70.

Special Offerings

Dr. J. F. Burnett, Sec. A. C. C., Dayton, Ohio, $6.00; Mrs. Coleman, $1.50; Total, $7.50.

Thanksgiving Offering

C. A. Shoop, $100.00; Mrs. W. C. Whitaker, $10.00; W. J. Ballentine, $25.00; Timber Ridge, Sunday school, $14.02; First

Christian Church Sunday school, Ravena, N. Y., "white Gifts for the King," $32.00; J. T. Lambert, $5.00; Mrs. F. A. Jones, Norfolk, Va., $10.00; Rev and Mrs L. I. Cox, $5.00; Oak Grove church, Chipley, Ga., $8.78; Antioch church, Valley of Virginia, viz.: Miss Sophia R. Byrd, $1.00; Miss Maggie R. Byrd, $1.00; R. A. Henton, $1.00; Mrs. R. A. Hinton, $1.00; Barretts Christian church, Va., $3.54; Total, $217.34.

Total for the week, $234.54; Grand total, $13,463.20.

MONEY—SPENT OR MISSPENT?

The "Baptist Commonwealth" points out that according to Dr. W. E. Biederwolf, of the Federal Council of the Church of Christ in America, in a report made last year, we spend our money for various objects, as follows: All missions, twelve million dollars; chewing gum, twenty-one millions; millinery, ninety millions; soft drinks, one hundred and twenty millions; candy, two hundred millions; theatres, seven hundred and fifty millions; jewelry, eight hundred millions; tobacco, one billion, two hundred millions; intoxicating liquors, two billions. About $450 for luxury and appetite for every dollar given to missions.

The importance of Sunday schools, churches and all other organizations working with the North Carolina State Board of Health in its efforts to save baby lives is seen from the fact that . 11,745 infants under five years of age die in North Carolina every year; over 2,600 of these result from diarrheal diseases, while over 2,000 result from congenital debility, lack of care, and other conditions due to the ignorance of the mother during the first month of the baby's life. These diseases and conditions are for the most part preventable.

WITH EYES OF FAITH

By Frances M'Kinnon Morton

O young New Year, just come today
To lead us out an unknown way!
A strange new path before you lies,
And hidden dreams are in your eyes.

The way you go you will not tell,
And what you bring is hidden well.
But keep your secrets, brave New Year;
The heart that trusts shall know no fear.

With eyes of faith we calmly look
Upon your new, unopened book;
Since God, who holds almighty power,
Is guardian of its every hour.

In ten months of 1918 the Ballard School of the Young Women's Christian Association in New York gave 1,856 business courses; 1,155 volunteers passed through its volunteer clearing house; it enrolled 9,636 in war work; served 202,792 in its cafeteria; there were 20,039 registrations in its employment department, and 10,120 in physical education.

Mrs. K. B. Way—I have been taking THE SUN for eighteen years, and it gets better all the time. Let THE SUN shine on.

WORSHIP AND MEDITATION

(Continued from page 4)

scurrying about in the rooms upstairs to be ready at the appointed minute, I said to myself: 'There will evidently be no family worship in this home, yet this is one of the best men in the world.' I was mistaken. The moment the bell sounded through the house—and it sounded on the second—the large family came trooping in; even the baby was there. But instead of seating themselves at the table, they knelt, the servant in waiting kneeling with the rest. The father, on his knees, read from a pocket Bible this verse: 'Blessed is every one that feareth the Lord, that walketh in his ways.' Then he prayed: 'Father, we thank thee for the rest of the night and the peace and promise of the morning. As we each go on our appointed ways, may we go in the fear of the Lord and in the confidence that He will guide our steps. May we be faithful in our work, doing it always with the thought of thine eyes upon us and with the love of the Master whom we serve strong in our hearts. And this we ask for Jesus' sake. Amen!' This is not the highest ideal of family prayer. God's mercies are too rich to be properly acknowledged in two minutes, with only one verse of Scripture and no song of praise. But acceptable and blessed worship may go up to God in two minutes.''

There is an old-fashioned but fearfully true warning in the ninth Psalm about the fate of those nations that forget God. Let us have a nation-wide rearing of family altars, lest we forget. This is God's own antidote to forgetfulness, and it is infallible.—*John G. Gebhard, D. D., in the Mission Field.*

NOTES

President Harper is, we understand, to be in Dover, Delaware, next Sunday.

Elon College has had a good opening. About 250 students were expected, but 292 have registered to date.

The Baptist State Convention is in session at Greensboro this week.

The French losses in the recent war amounts to 1,028,000.

William Jennings Bryan spoke in Raleigh one day last week.

The peace program seems to be under proper construction and is soon to be discussed.

Poland has declared her independence from Germany.

United States Attorney, General Gregory, has resigned to take effect March 4. His resignation was accepted by President Wilson by cable,

The General Assembly of North Carolina convened last week.

General outbreaks in Germany are occurring frequently but are not likely to amount to very much.

The epidemic of Spanish Influenza seems to be getting a new hold in many sections of the country.

Rev. J. H. Dixon, Pastor of the Pegram Street Presbyterian church, Charlotte, N. C., dropped dead in his church last Sunday.

Thomas Settle, former congressman for Greensboro district, and leading Republican, is critically ill in a hospital in Asheville.

The fraternity house at the University of North Carolina, Chapel Hill, was destroyed by fire January 9. The loss is estimated at $20,000.00 with $2,500.00 insurance.

The Methodist Protestants of North Carolina are meeting with splendid success in raising a special fund to begin their college in this State.

Dr. D. A. Long speaks in highest terms of the People's Christian church, Dover, Delaware, and regrets that sickness in his family called him back to North Carolina, before his month was out.

Dr. Kemp P. Battle, ex-president of the university of North Carolina, is ill at his home in Chapel Hill.

By order of the Railroad Administration, several hundreds of thousands of pounds of high explosive material have been dumped out into the sea from South Amboy, New Jersey. About 228 car loads were destroyed. The United States Government reports a loss of one hundred and fifty million dollars through the operation of the railroads.

Dr. D. A. Long returned from Dover, Delaware, sooner than he anticipated, on account of the sickness of his wife. She is convalescing and he will fill his appointment at Salem Chapel the third Sunday in this month.

Mrs. S. J. Rollings—I cannot do without my church paper.

W. H. Joyner—Find check for $2 to keep THE SUN shining in my home. The last issue is worth the $2.

J. P. Morgan—I have been taking THE SUN for a good while and don't like to live without my church paper.

Does your label read 2-1-9? If so why not renew today?

LITTLE RED CROSS WORKERS

Not long ago the Red Cross chapter in Bay City, Mich., received a hurry-up call for one hundred and fifty·dunnage bags. Troops were about to move and, through an oversight, their equipment was not complete. The bags had to be made and sent within forty-eight hours. A request for help was sent over the town, and the stores were searched successfully for the right materials.

Among those who quickly responded and came to the chapter work-rooms to help were two little girls, sisters, about ten and twelve years of age, each eager to lend a hand and do something for the boys who were going to the front. All day long the fingers of the women and the little girls were fairly flying. Bag after bag received the last stitch, until scores were piled up, ready for shipment.

Closing time came, and the woman· superintending the making of the bags counted those completed and announced that if every one of the workers would come early the next morning and work all·day the bags would surely be finished in time for shipping by evening. Two crestfallen little girls, the little sisters, were waiting for her at the door as she departed.

"We are awfully sorry, ma'am," said the older of the two, "but we can't come back tomorrow. You see tomorrow we have to—" And, without finishing the sentence, she looked back wistfully at the pile of bags.

"It is too bad you can't come back," said the superintendent, "but I want to thank you, and we all thank you, for the work you've done today. You two have been a wonderful help, and that pile of bags wouldn't be nearly so big if you hadn't been here. Good-night."

The next morning, when the superintendent came down to unlock the work-rooms for the day, she was astonished to see the two little girls standing in the cold by the locked door.

"Oh, I'm so glad to see you!" she said. "I thought you said you couldn't come."

"Oh, we know those Red Cross bags just had to be finished for the soldiers," exclaimed the little one, with glistening eyes, "and we got up at three o'clock this morning and got the washing done early!"

A SOLDIER'S STOCKING

Rosabel had knit almost around before she discovered it; then her brow puckered into an impatient frown. What was one dropped stitch, anyhow? She kept right on knitting stubbornly. Isabel's stocking was an inch longer than hers already. She couldn't afford to ravel any out. One little stitch way up in the leg wouldn't matter much; no one could see it.

Perhaps it wouldn't matter at first, but Rosabel knew that it would matter a very great deal after a while,

when the stocking was being worn—that the tiny hole would eat its way clear to the top.

But click, click, click her needles went on keeping time with Isabel's, and every moment it seemed harder to ravel back to the dropped stitch.

The twins were each knitting a pair of stockings for the soldiers. Grandmother, who had come to visit them, was showing them how. They were very proud of being able to do something to help their country in time of need. Already they had finished one stocking and were well started upon the second. They knit an hour each day, and it was surprising how fast the stockings grew; but the longer they got the more miserable Rosabel became.

"Won't the soldier who gets these be glad? Won't his toes be nice and warm? I wonder if it is very cold in the trenches?" Isabel said. They had been chatting merrily, but now Rosabel was strangely silent.

"I'm going to write my name on a little slip of paper and put it in the toe of mine," Isabel said proudly. 'Isabel Blair; age, twelve years.' Don't you think the soldiers would like to know who made them? I'll be so proud of mine."

Rosabel hung her head miserably. Pride in her work was marred by the knowledge of the dropped stitch. When they were finished she pined her pair together, so the droped stitch would not be discovered, and went away where she could not hear grandmother's praises. It seemed almost like telling a lie to accept praise when she did not deserve it.

That night father read to them about the sufferings of the soldiers, of the cold, wet trenches and of the long, frozen marches when their feet left bloody stains upon the snow.

After·they had gone to bed Rosabel lay and thought and thought until she could stand it no longer. She got up and went into the sewing-room and found her stocking; then she sat down and unravelled it round by round until it came to the dropped stitch; then, after she had knit a little, just to know that she had started right, she went back to bed and went to sleep.

When grandmother knew, she said that that stocking was worth more to Rosabel than it would be to the soldier who was to wear it, for it gave her the opportunity to prove that she had the courage to acknowledge her mistakes and to rectify them, too.—*The Child's Gem.*

Rev. M. W. Butler, Conshohocken, Pa., sends greetings for the New Year.

Remember that THE SUN does not print original poetry.

We congratulate our neighbor, *The Burlington Falcon*, on its recent improvements.

Have you sent for a copy of Peloubet's Notes, or Tarbell's Guide?

CHRISTIAN EDUCATION

OFFICIAL REPORT OF THE STUDENTS' ARMY
TRAINING CORPS

Letter of Transmittal

Major Ralph Barton Perry,
Committee on Education and Special Training,
 Mills Building,
  Washington, D. C.
Dear Major Perry:—
 I am greatly pleased to hand you herewith three copies of our estimate of the S. A. T. C. here as requested, and I am mailing under separate cover three copies of a bulletin we have issued in commemoration of the S. A. T. C. on our campus.
 If there is any further service I can render you in this connection, or in any other, it will be a pleasure.
 With every good wish to you, I am
    Yours sincerely,
     W. A. HARPER, *President.*

Report

Name of Institution—Elon College.
Type of Institution—Denomination Co-educational.
Location of Institution—Elon College, N. C.
Report made by—W. A. Harper, President.
 1. We enrolled the same numer of students in 1917-18 as in 1916-17; it is possible that we should have enrolled our full 400 students in 1918-19.
 2. During 1917-18 201 men enrolled at Elon College and 112 were inducted into the S. A. T. C.
 3. I suspect that 85 per cent of the S. A. T. C. men would have enrolled at Elon under normal conditions. Perhaps the estimate should be higher than this.
 4. I suspect that we will lose 50 per cent of the S. A. T. C. men. This loss will come from the Freshmen. It was their first experience in college and not liking the military discipline they thought this was the spirit of the college, and so, as I have said about 50 per cent of them will not return.
 5. (a) We were among the first colleges in this section to have the influenza epidemic; a few over 300 cases were reported with only three deaths. We did not even stop our recitation work for half a day because of it. However, the epidemic, of course, interfered with our work somewhat.
  (b) Late inductions did not interfere with the work because the men were here and in classes even though they were not inducted.
  (c) No students were withdrawn from the unit here for officers' training camps.
  (d) Extra military duties during the month of October greatly interferred with the academic work, but this was the fault of the Commanding Officer and not of the system.
 6. We found no difficulty in meeting the suggestions of the Committee in respect to the academic program.
 7. We could detect no difference in interest on the part of the students in their academic work as compared with peace times after Captain Lord reached Elon, but

during the time that Lieutenant Wilson was in charge the S. A. T. C. men were given to understand that the academic work did not count for much and there was a notable dropping off.
 8. Our faculty was thoroughly sympathetic toward the combination of military interests with the academic work, and we found the combination worked out well in practice.
 9. The academic work done by the members of the S. A. T. C. was of sufficient value to warrant credit for a degree here. Of course, some of the men failed to make their work for one reason or another, but for the most part the work was satisfactory and credit will be given.
 10. "Supervised study" made us all its friends.
 11. The course on the issues of the war was highly satisfactory. It was a capital idea to require this course.
 12. The relations between the academic and military authorities here were strained and unsatisfactory to us during the time that Lieutenant Robert I. Wilson was Commanding Officer. He seemed to think we were a camp, that the college traditions counted for nothing and we were constantly in conflict with him. When Captain Franklin T. Lord came a new spirit reached the campus and from that time on military training became popular here.
 13. The effect of military discipline upon the general morale and conduct of the student body was salutary.
 14. The same is true with reference to its effect upon the physical condition of the men.
 15. It is difficult to say just what effect the S. A. T. C. will have upon the future educational policy of Elon. The "Y" hut is here to stay, and the weekly movies that go with it. There will also undoubtedly be a course that will make history practical and modern, and a larger emphasis on science. Entrance requirements too will be modified but to what extent it is unsafe to predict at this time.
 16. In case of a similar national emergency I feel sure the S. A. T. C. will be found helpful, but the military authorities who are sent to command at colleges should be given to understand that they must co-operate with the college authorities and assist in maintaining the traditions and ideals of the institutions. This is the only criticism that we could possibly make on the S. A. T. C. during its short stay here.
 17. In case of universal military training I feel sure that colleges would give full credit for the men who are in their course when the year for military training arrives. I know this college would be glad to do it.
 18. There were 112 men in the S. A. T. C. here. In the Army and Navy in addition to this we supplied about 600 men, and a few of our women went to the Red Cross service and as yeomanettes. I am not able to say how many of the Elon men were commissioned, though the highest rank of any commissioned officer from our college was that of major.
 19. I am sending under separate cover three copies of the S. A. T. C. bulletin which we issued on com-

memoration of the S. A. T. C's. presence on our campus.

In conclusion permit me to say that this college was glad to have been able to serve the country through the S. A. T. C., and we shall always look back to the S. A. T. C. here with satisfaction.

W. A. HARPER, *President.*

FROM OVER THE SEAS

NOTES FROM THE MIDDLE FIELD
By E. C. Fry, Utsunomiya, Japan
(Reprinted from The Christian Missionary)

Our Southern District Conference (held twice a year) met at Utsunomiya October 8 and 9. Eleven ministerial members were in attendance. The reports from the different fields mentioned baptisms nearly everywhere and other indications of general progress. Dr. Woodworth gave a lecture on the Book of Leviticus. A new member, Brother Kimura, was received, and farewell words were spoken to Dr. Woodworth, soon to leave for America on furlough. We closed with a communion service conducted by Brother Garman, the sermon being by Brother Takahashi.

Our Japanese brethren have a Forward Movement, somewhat like the one in America in some ways. It was arranged for its special meetings at Utsunomiya to be held on the two evenings of the District Conference. Col. Iijima, a member of our Naka Shibuya Church, was one of the speakers. There was a very large attendance, bringing out many not in the habit of coming and more or less difficult to reach.

In general, the occasion was another milestone of progress.

Ninomiya was a famous Japanese sage of the last century, noted for his ability to improve the moral and economic conditions of apparently hopeless communities. He once lived at Moka, in the house we now hire for our preaching place. Pastor Irokawa's study is the very room similarly occupied by that great man.

At the close of the sermon at Moka, Sunday, Sept. 16, Rev. Irokawa baptized two of his sons, Makoto and Heishiro. The service was naturally a most impressive one, the father's heart being full. Makoto, the older of the boys, was on the point of leaving home for the first time, to enter the employ of wholesalers of fertilizers at Tokyo.

Pastor Abe, of Ichinoseki, has specialized quite a little in Sunday school work and recently made a round of our churches in that interest. I had the pleasure of attending the meeting he held in our Utsunomiya church.

Christianity has promise of the life that now is as well as of that which is to come, developing man's ability, reliability, and desirability. This is especially shown

in the recent history of our Yaita Church, which was composed mainly of a fine group of young men. They have been called to various positions of responsibility, Tokyo, the Philippines, and elsewhere, and within a short space of time that entire group has scattered. Just now the Yaita Church has but two resident members aside from the pastor and his family. Our success has become our temporary ruin. However, there is a good Sunday school, street preaching is continued, and enquirers and others come to church. Brother Muraoka has the grit and grace to "do it all over again." Pretty much the same thing, including a good recovery from the setback, happened at Moka a few years ago.

Brother Kimura has organized a Young Men's Christian Society, meeting monthly at our Utsunohiya church. It has about twenty members, students in the Commercial School, who also attend a weekly English Bible Class. Mr. Takita, a Christian teacher in that school, has been very helpful about both. Four have already received baptism and two more are ready for it.

At the October meeting of the Utsunomiya Christian workers (six different denominations), the subject of Christian union was mentioned. It is a live question in Japan, a large Laymen's Conference, perhaps the first ever held in this land, having put it emphatically at the front. However, in the governing general bodies of various Japanese Churches opposition to radical measures has developed, and not much is to be expected immediately.

There were baptisms at both Utsunomiya and Otawara on September 22, the candidate at Otawara being the wife of a member of the national parliament (the equivalent of an American congressman). Seven students in the Government and Girls' High School, and the wife of a Middle School teacher were the candidates at Utsunomiya.

We have hired a new preaching place at Otawara, but neither location nor building is altogether ideal. At Kurobane an average of about one hundred come to our meetings, advertised to be held in a room twelve feet square. It has an open front, but the approaching winter will increase the difficulties. It should be a part of our general plan to buy land and erect a building in every town where we propose to work permanently.

H. P. Hilliard—I don't see how I could do without THE SUN. I enclose renewal.

Celestia L. Penny—We enjoy every number of THE SUN and are anxious not to miss a single copy.

L. N. Kimball—I hope and pray that this may be the best year you have ever had.

R. H. Utley—I have been a subscriber to THE SUN for several years and my hope is that I shall continue to be.

Mrs. J. Paul Long—Please continue THE SUN for it affords me much pleasure. It gets better all the time.

OBITUARIES

MARTIN

Joseph Edward Martin, son of John W. and Sallie Martin, of Eclipse, Va., was Born December 27, 1901, and died December 22, 1918. He was ill only a few days. Pneumonia was the cause of his death. His parents and four brothers and three sisters survive him. "Eddie," as he was called by his friends, was a bright, cheerful young man. During his illness he realied that the end was near, and assured his family that he was ready to go. The funeral service was conducted by the writer. He was a faithful member of the M. E. church. Peace to his soul. The comfort of the Lord be with the family.

I. W. JOHNSON.

WILBOURN

Sister Cynthia Wilbourn passed out of this world of toil into that of rest just a few days before Christmas, 1918. She had been blessed of the Lord to see many days upon the earth, being at the time of her death, ninety-four years of age. Sister Wilbourn was one of the charter members of Wake Chapel Christian church, where she was a member at her decease. She was was the oldest member at her death. In all her long life there was never a blot against her as a consisant church member that I know. I wonder if she did not, in great measure, fulfill the figth Commandment. May the blessings of our Father rest upon those of her friends and loved ones remaining.

J. LEE JOHNSON.

RESOLUTION OF RESPECT—YOUNG

Whereas, it has pleased our Heavenly Father to remove from the ministerial ranks of our Conference, our much beloved and highly esteemed brother, Rev. B. F. Young; and, whereas in the removal of Brother Young from labor to reward, our Conference has lost a consecrated preacher, his churches a tender sympathetic shepherd and his family a loving and devoted husband and father.

Therefore, be it resolved by this Conference assembled:

1. That, we bow in humble submission to the supreme will of God.

2. That, we commend to his wife and child; also his churches, to our gracious

Heavenly Father, who is able to comfort and console in this dark hour.

3. That, we strive to emulate his virtues and cherish his good deeds and loving disposition among men.

4. That, a copy of these resolutions be spread upon our minutes; a copy presented to his dear wife and a copy printed in The Christian Sun.

G. D. HUNT,
C. W. CARTER,
Committee.

By order of the Alabama Christian Conference.

OUR NATIONAL PRINTING

Uncle Sam is the world's greatest printer and publisher. An article by Henry Litchfield West in The Bookman contains so much information concerning this important branch of our Government that we give a summary of it.

This enormous business has been only about two decades in developing.

During Washington's Presidency, Congress set aside $10,000 for "firewood, stationery, and printing." A national printing office was suggested in 1818, when the cost of the public printing had risen to $65,000 a year, but nothing came of the idea at the time.

In 1840, when again a Federal printing office was proposed, the Senate opposed it vigorously as a method "abhorrent to the genius of our free institutions." So Congress kept on electing "official printers" from time to time.

When the work became most unsatisfactory, Congress tried giving the job to the lowest bidder. That failing, in 1852 Congress established the office of superintendent of printing, and among the unsuccessful candidates for the post was Horace Greeley.

The Civil War greatly increased the Government's printing, and Congress bought for $135,000 the four-story printing office of Cornelius Wendell, with twenty-six presses and twenty-six tons of type.

Now the Government Printing Office represents an investment of more than $10,000,000.

It is by far the greatest establishment of the kind in the world, either public or private.

Among the nations only three others—France, Austria, and Holland—carry on government publications. Even Great Britain hires private printers.

The Government Printing Office has thirteen and a half acres of buildings. It keeps busy more than 5,000 employees.

It works all day and all night. Its hundreds of typesetting machines set about 2,000,000,000 "ems" of type every year—more than any six of the largest book publishers in the country turn out

It spends more than $2,000,000 every year for paper alone. It buys every year thousands of rolls and packets of gold leaf for lettering. Its office pay roll is more than $34,500.000.

It electrotypes or stereotypes more than 15,000,000 square inches a year. It turned out in a recent year 48,647,371 wire stitched publications, 9,633,524 paper-backed and 2,600,938 bound books.

The bound books it published last year, if placed end to end, would reach 400 miles.

It can receive, set in type, proofread, stereotype, print, bind, and deliver a book of more than 2,000 pages within twenty-four hours.

The great war placed unprecedented burdens upon the Government Printing Office, but it bore them nobly. For instance, when the selective draft law was enacted, the Government had to have immediately—and received—25,000,000 registration cards. When it became necessary to advertise the Liberty Loan, the Printing Office delivered in three days one million posters printed in two colors.

And all this extra work was done in addition to the regular task of printing the thousands of publications of the Government departments, including the large legislative daily, The Congressional Record, which alone requires 3,000,000 pounds of paper a year.

Surely the Government Printing Office, though little is said about it, is one of the institutions of which every American has a right to be proud.—*Christian Endeavor World.*

A LITTLE FUN

Seeing is Believing

Average Father (showing his prodigy's drawings).—''Would you believe that he never took a lesson in his life?''

Art Editor.—''Seeing is believing.''—*Buffalo Express.*

Well Named

"I don't see why you call your place a bungalow," said Smith to his neighbor.

"Well, if it isn't a bungalow, what is it?" said the neighbor. "The job was a bungle, and I still owe for it."—*Ladies' Home Journal.*

Cash

Corporal Bilkins had arrived in France after a few days in England. "How much money have you got left?" asked Corporal Wilkins. "Well, I've got four shillings, a quid, two farthings, nine pennies, a franc, half a pound, four sous, and fifty centimes; but 've only got two dollars in cash."—*Camp Dodger.*

They Were Acquaintances

"Yes, sir," boasted the hotel proprietor, "that dog's the best rat-catchin' dog in the country."

Even as he spoke two big rats scurried across the office door. The dog merely wrinkled his nose.

"Rat dog!" scoffed the traveling man. "Look at that, will you?"

"Huh," snorted the landlord, "he knows them. But you just let a strange rat come in here once!"

Proxy Giving

Bessie had a new dime to invest in ice cream soda.

"Why don't you give your dime to missions?" said the minister, who was calling.

"I thought about that," said Bessie, "but I think I'll buy the ice cream and let the druggist give it to the missions."—*Christian Herald.*

The School Board Should Furnish It

Johnny handed the following note from his mother to the teacher one morning:

"Dere Teecher:—You keep tellin' my boy to brethe with his diafram. Maybe rich children has got diaframs, but how about when there father only makes one dollar and fifty

cents a day and has got five children to keep? First, it's one thing, then it's another, and now it's diaframs. That's the worst yet.''—*Selected.*

That Boy!

For four consecutive nights the hotel man had watched his fair, timid guest fill her pitcher at the water-cooler. "Madame," he said on the fifth night, "if you would ring, this would be done for you." "But where is my bell?" asked the lady. "The bell is beside your bed," replied the proprietor. "That the bell!" she exclaimed. "Why, the boy told me that was the fire alarm, and that I was not to touch it on any account!"

In The Code

The letter from the front read: "I traveled six hours from Paris, and am twelve miles west of Baby Sparks. Plumbers always forget to bring them. Carpenters carry them in a wooden box. But none of these are as singular as my headquarters." After a bit of reflection the wife guessed her husband was in Toul. "Baby Sparks" puzzled her till a friend asked if she knew a family named Sparks. She did; the baby was named Nancy, and upon examining a map she found Nancy to be exactly twelve miles from Toul.—*Life.*

LET'S BOTHER

Let's bother ourselves a little bit
  With the troubles of other folk;
Let's bother ourselves to help them
    bear
  The weight of their daily yoke.
Let's bother ourselves to help them
  · sing
  And help them laugh and smile;
Let's bother ourselves with how they.
    live
  If just for a little while.

Let's bother ourselves, though oft we
    say;
  We haven't time to do it;
Let's bother ourselves for our fellow-
    men
  I'm sure we'll never rue it.
Let's bother ourselves to help them
    out
  When they're in distress and
    trouble;

Let's bother ourselves to make their
    care
  Blow by like an airy bubble.

Let's bother ourselves; it may not
    count
  But the fact that we took some
    thought
For the way they lived and the way
    they strove
  And the battle of life they fought,
Will have its bearing on our own lives
  And make it finer and sweet
To face the storms that sometimes
    round
  Our own bared temples beat.

Let's bother ourselves a little bit
  To be as true and kind
As ever we can to the weary heart,
  The troubled body and mind.
Let's bother ourselves to utter a word
  Of kindly cheer each day
As down through the toil and trust
    of life
We struggle along our way.
          —*Selected.*

A WORD TO TEACHERS

Why not have some special help on your Sunday school work? Send $1.35 to THE CHRISTIAN SUN office and get a copy of Peloubet's Select Notes.

Money the Acid Test.

After all, isn't money the real test? It is doubtful if anything else on earth measures a man (or a woman), as does his (or her) money.

Once upon a time I asked a man for some money for missions—money with which to reach and to save this ruined world for Christ. "Not a penny," was the reply. "May I inuire why you will not give a penny?" "Well, because I believe God will save the heathen in His own good time." I asked that man if he really had the faith to believe God would save the heathen in His own good time. He said that he had such faith. I asked him then if he was willing to pray that God would save the heathen in His own good time. He said he was, and that he did so pray. "Now, how much money are you going to give that God will save the heathen and the rest of the world in His own good time?" "Not a dollar," was the ready reply. "Then," said I, "your talk is mockery of God." Your faith does not cost you much. You can have that in your easy chair at night when your day's hard work is done. Your prayer does not cost you much. You can offer up that on Sunday when the week's work is over. But when you are asked to give that which really costs you something—your money for which you toiled hard in the heat and cold and that which stands for effort, energy, sacrifice, self-denial—when you are called upon to give that, then you say, No. God will have the best, or He will have nothing. The man who will not back up his praying with his paying cannot expect God to hear him, for he offers God that which costs him little or nothing but withholds from God that which really costs him something.

Your money is your coined character. When you cast your money into the Kingdom you cast that there which stands for something and is something, namely, your strength and your self-denial. This is why Christ took note of the poor widow—she cast into the treasury her living. And that is why Christ said, "Where your treasure is, there will your heart be also." (Matt. 19:6).

You may back up an enterprise with your words; but words are cheap and often do not mean much. But when you put money in, does it not show that you have put your mind, strength, heart in also? After all isn't money the real, the acid test? I think so.

J. O. ATKINSON

WILL YOU?

Will *you* join me in praying daily that the Lord will give from your community, your church, your home a worker as minister or missionary to help win this wicked world to Christ, and so hasten the day of that permanent peace through the coming into the world of the Prince of Peace? Please do.

Our Southern Christian Convention is now calling for 100 life recruits who will give their whole time as ministers or missionaries. "This kind cometh not but by prayer." Your church, or community, gave was it half dozen or a dozen young men, to make the world safe for democracy? How many will it *now* give to help make the world safe for Christ? If we gave so many in love of country try to fight and to kill, can we not now give *some* to help fight the battle of the Cross, and to make alive in the name of the Prince of Peace?

God will call them to His service if we really feel the need and ask Him to do so.

God never supplies a human want until there is felt and expressed a human need. Christ was asleep on a pillow in a ship that was likely to sink. He arose, rebuked the wind, and made the whole sea safe for sailing, only when human beings realized the danger and prayed for help. And even now the same Christ is ready to supply all needed power to save this world, when we human beings realize the need and go to Him for help. Will *you* join me in praying daily that God give us the hundred ministers and missionaries? Please do.

J. O. ATKINSON.

Peloubets Select Notes can also be secured at THE CHRISTIAN SUN Office, Burlington, North Carolina.

THE CHRISTIAN SUN

"IN ESSENTIALS UNITY, IN NON-ESSENTIALS LIBERTY, IN ALL THINGS CHARITY"

The Fireside

THE fireside is a place where friendship grows, where the family forms its real circle and where each member receives equal welcome; the fireside is a place where the cares of the day are rehearsed, the burdens shared and the joys and sorrows entered into; a place where the chatter of children is sweet music to the ears of mother and father, and where children return and find a welcome that can be found in no other place. The poets have the fireside praised and millions of men and women find there a wholesome recreation from their toil. God bless the home and its fireside, for it is the beacon light to every one who thinks of home, sweet home.

Volume LXXI   WEDNESDAY, JANUARY 22, 1919   Number 4

BURLINGTON   ·   ·   ·   NORTH CAROLINA

THE CHRISTIAN SUN

Founded 1844 by Rev. Daniel W. Kerr

C. B. RIDDLE - - - Editor

Entered at the Burlington, N. C. Post Office as second class matter.

Subscription Rates

One year ....$ 2.00
Six months 1.00

In Advance

Give both your old and new postoffice when asking that your address be changed.

The change of your label is your receipt for money. Written receipts sent upon request.

Marriage and obituary notices not exceeding 150 words printed free if received within 60 days from date of event, all over this at the rate of one-half cent a word.

Original poetry not accepted for publication.

Principles of the Christian Church

(1) The Lord Jesus Christ is the only Head of the Church.
(2) Christian is a sufficient name of the Church.
(3) The Holy Bible is a sufficient rule of faith and practice.
(4) Christian character is a sufficient test of fellowship, and of church membership.
(5) The right of private judgment and the liberty of conscience is a right and a privilege that should be accorded to, and exercised by all.

EDITORIAL

PROHIBITION MEASURE GOES OVER THE TOP

The National Prohibition Bill has been ratified by thirty-eight states and the manufacture, sale and importation of liquors must cease. The thirty-eight ratifications seal the prohibition amendment to the Federal Constitution. More than half the territory of the United States is already dry through state and local action and now the whole United States is to go dry.

We consider this measure one of the greatest in this age. Had there been no dry territory until this time the applause would have been as great as it was when the recent armistice was signed. But gradually prohibition has cleared the way and the rejoicing has been gradually in one state and then another.

There will be those who will continue to say that prohibition does not prohibit and that the ratification of the amendment to the Federal Constitution will be of no avail. This is what a few characters have been saying all these years, but in spite of what they have said prohibition has marched on; bar-rooms have left; the grog shops have been pushed out into the far distance, and the man with his liquor appetite has been, by necessity forced to eliminate the awful habit. Yes, prohibition does prohibit and the greatest testimony to this statement is given by the police forces in all the cities where whisky was once sold. The policemen will tell you that where one arrest is made now for drunken-

ness ten to twenty arrests were made when whisky was sold in the open bar. Those who claim that prohibition does not prohibit do not believe their own statement, and if they do, their statement is denied so fast by public proof that the only escape that they have from public sentiment is to join the ranks of decent men and women, and ask for forgiveness of their evil.

BROTHER HINES MAKES A PROTEST

Brother Charles A. Hines, city attorney for Greensboro, and a member of our First church at that place, enters a protest against a protest sent up by the Baptist Convention in session in Greensboro last week. We consider Brother Hines' article pertinent and to the point and take pleasure in reproducing it below as it appeared in the *Greensboro Daily News*:

To the Editor of The Daily News:

The author of the resolution adopted by the state Baptist convention today "denouncing" the war department for permitting the Knights of Columbus homes in army camps is in an indefensible position, it seems to me. He demands that persons of all religious beliefs and all denominations be treated alike, and yet criticises the war department for doing this very thing.

It is true that the Y. M. C. A. is interdenominational, but it is certainly Protestant. No Catholic or Jew can be a voting member of the association, and, as I understand, none but Protestants were accepted as secretaries or war workers by it. When the war department permitted the Protestant Y. M. C. A. to go into camps, it could not in justice deny equal privileges to non-Protestant men's religious organizations.

Because the President and secretary of war are Protestants, and because a majority of those affiliated with churches in the United States are Protestants, we are not justified in law or morals in denying equal privileges to those of other faiths. If the history of the last four years (and six thousand years before) teaches us anything, one of the things it does teach is that no faith, religion or creed can override and persecute those of a different faith and escape the punishment it so richly deserves for its bigotry. May the Protestants of the United States never have visited upon the world scorn and infamy that have come to nations and peoples both in ancient and very recent times on account of religious intolerance.
January 15, 1919.

NEWS-FROM THE PEACE TABLE

At the time we write this note the public press gives out the news that there is a movement among a few that the doings of the Peace Conference be kept secret. Mr. Wilson is not in favor of such a policy and we do not believe that Mr. Lloyd George is. This has been a question of consideration since the Conference was proposed, and the average citizen has considered that the peace parliament would be an open forum to the newspaper men of the world. That is the crystalized sentiment of the American people—and Mr. Wilson knew it before he left this country. We believe that Mr. Wilson will stand by his convictions and contend for a conference that the citizens of the world can know about.

We believe that what the average citizen wants to be assured of is that there will be no more war. We believe that it is the desire and the hope of every true American that justice will be done to every nation at the Peace Conference. If we correctly understand and interpret the American spirit, the spirit of democracy, we understand it to be that the world shall know exactly what takes place at the Peace Conference.

We have sent our boys to the front and accepted sad intelligence in many cases for their return; we have purchased Liberty Bonds that the Government may have financial backing to carry out its program and prosecute the war; of our means we have contributed to the Red Cross to alleviate the suffering and minister to the wounded; we have shared in our homes our every dish with the allied nations, and in brief, the American people became a unit to stamp out autocracy and to establish democracy. It was fifty men behind closed doors between the days of June 24 and July 5, 1914—fifty men in secret session—that threw the entire world into the greatest war that was ever known. The average man fears secrecy, secret councils, and the League of Nations will never mean to the people what it should mean, if it is formed behind closed doors and under guard. The rank and file of the peoples of the world will not follow their leaders with the same eagerness if those leaders do not stand ready and willing to let the world know what they are doing.

DETERMINATION

There was once a man in the State of Massachusetts who ran for governor sixteen times and was defeated. Unfaltering in his purpose, never flagging in his efforts, the seventeenth time he ran he was elected by a majority of one vote in a total of over two hundred and fifty. Can you equal such determination anywhere? Destroy the nest of a sparrow every few days if you will and see how she builds it again. Every time that you destroy that down cradle that mother bird works with renewed energy to remake a nestling home for her young. Do you call that *determination?* Have you ever seen the little ant diligently and determinedly rebuilding its subteranean palace when day after day it was destroyed? That little creature knows not the word *failure.* Where is there a better illustration of *determination?* Have you ever watched the determined waves beat and break upon the solid rock day after day, year in and year out? Slowly, but surely, does that Gibralter yield before those uncompromising billows of storm and calm.

It is *determination* that turns the wheels of progress. It founds beautiful cities, erects majestic temples, spans yawning chasms, tunnels solid rock and opens up lines of commerce and communication. The essential and comforts of life are the fruits of *determination.* All of our great inventions must render homage to her shrine.

It was *determination* alone that raised the great and incomparable Napoleon from the rank and file and placed crowns upon his head and nations at his feet. *Determination* was the sword with which Hannibal of Carthage carved his name high upon the table of fame. *Determination,* fired by ambition, bade the mighty Ceasar cross the Rubicon and become the master of Rome, and later the whole civilized world. It was *determination* to stick to principles which they believed that were just and right that caused the Pilgrims and Hugenots to seek a new land, forsaking home, and leaving friends and loved ones behind them. It was that self-same *determination,* infused into the blood of succeeding generations, that won the American Revolution of 1776. In the early sixties it was *determination* that enabled those men and boys in tattered garments of gray to hold another gallant army many times stronger than itself at bay for four long years and challenge the admiration of a cold and sullen world. *Determination* to sacrifice everything to right and duty lost to John C. Calhoun, the presidency of the United States, but it crowned him the greatest of American statesmen. It was *determination* that impelled James A. Garfield, a poor country boy, to burn the mid-night oil night after night in order to lead his class at college, and in after years it placed him in the President's chair. All of Thomas A. Edison's great inventions, in his own words, "are the results of *perspiration* and *determination.* Do you remember that heart breaking Bible scene where Christ prayed in the garden of Gethsemane for strength with which to endure that trying ordeal? It was *determination* which caused Him to yield His life on the Cross.

To young men and women everywhere our plea is that you have a determination; one that is filled with a zeal for work and baptized with a spirit of the times and love of Christ. Without a goal and a determination to reach that goal the youth drifts into a realm where he goes with the tide and lands into the land of failure.

SOURCE OF LIFE

The other day President Wilson visited the little town of Carlisle, England. It was there where his mother was born and where his father was once pastor of the village church. In an address in the old church Mr. Wilson said, among other things: "It is from quiet places like this all over the world that forces are accumulated that presently will empower any attempt to accomplish evil on a great scale."

In the President's words we find one great truth—that in the common places, the quiet places, are found the sources that furnish the moral backing for every great issue. In the little communities and hamlets men have gathered for rest and worship and meditation for centuries, and from these places great men have gone out to bless and benefit the world. It is in such places, and by such people, that the whisky traffic has been overthrown, autocracy stamped out and democracy enthroned.

GETTING MEMBERS OUT OF THE CHURCH

Did you ever hear such a thing? Perhaps you have not *heard* of such, but you have *seen* it. So eager are all of us to get men and women *into* the Church, but little do we think that we oftimes get them *out* of the Church.

The lives we live may get our fellowman out of the Church. Some business deal with our neighbor may cause him to stumble and leave the Church.

Let us not only insist upon men becoming Christians and joining the Church, but let us help to keep them Christians and in the Church.

WORSHIP AND MEDITATION

"I WAS SICK, AND YE VISITED ME"
By Edward W. Rushton
(In New York Christian Advocate)

It was during my stay at one of our great military camps that the Spanish Influenza swept among the soldiers. The vast base hospital became crowded and I was called to serve as chaplain to the sick, and for the days and nights that followed those hospital wards were as truly front line trenches as were the lines in France.

Boys, brave hearted and true, gave their young lives heroically while they fought death to the very last breath. To these soldiers the Word of God brought the story of the Great Physician, and He spoke peace to tired minds and weary hearts. It was a joy to read them and to place the Testament by their pillow with a lesson marked to be read on the morrow. From the many incidents that thronged the hours, let us pass to the crowded wards, walk among the cots and tarry by the bedside while the sick and lonely lads speak to us.

In The Pneumonia Ward

The pneumonia wards were the scene of our night watches, for there the boys were slipping away so swiftly and the cry of delirium, as the sick soldier stared wild-eyed and spoke with struggling breath, was for "Mother, mother, why don't you come, my mother!" And your heart nearly broke as you tried in your rough way to speak in the place of the one he wanted. Yes, the names of mother and home were the words that burdened their burning minds.

I stood by the side of one who labored so hard and suggested a bit of Scripture and a prayer. Almost too far gone for words, he nodded his appreciation. After the prayer, amid pauses and heavy breathing, he said courageously, "Chaplain, I'm a Christian. I'm going soon, but I'm ready and it is all right." As I, with eyes none too steady, turned away to the next cot, I saw the sick boy pull the sheet over his face and then the cot quivered as he quietly and alone sobbed his loneliness. Before leaving the ward I returned to him and said, "Good night, my boy. Perhaps you will sleep better now." Poor lad! That courageous heart! "Chaplain," said he, "I don't mind going—only it is hard—so far—from home." Then he said, "Are you going away?" I told him that I would be on duty all night. "I'm glad," he added, and then with eyes lifted toward me—eyes that burned a message more than words could express—he continued, "Will you stand by me, chaplain?" I have a lad at home, and I thought what might be in the years ahead for my boy, and I answered that homesick dying soldier just as you would have answered—and a few hours later I "stood by" as he went out.

In response to a suggestion of prayer, another boy said, "I don't know anything about religion, for my folks did not believe in it. But I married a Lutheran girl two years ago and she kept on going to church, and I went with her after a while. Since I joined the army and now in the hospital I have thought much about it, and when the war is over, I'm going back home and join her church. See that letter?" he added, pointing to the foot of his bed. "The orderly wrote it for me today, and in it I told my wife that when I come home I'll join with her."

I took up the letter and said, "This is fine, my boy, but do you want to do something even better? Will you permit me to tear open this letter and write one more page, and tell that good wife of yours that here, this night, in the base hospital, you found and accepted her Lord and Saviour as your Saviour too?" After explaining the way by faith to salvation, he found Jesus, and I wrote the few lines for him and mailed the letter. As I left, his lips and eyes were as near a smile as the fever and pain would permit, and he said, "I'll—sleep, —better—now." Yes, dear boy, he did, for the next morning the nurse told me that an hour before dawn he fell into that sleep of perfect peace. It was worth while to take that Testament to him.

Going from cot to cot was hard, and when the pressure became too great, I would slip out onto the open-air porch to gather myself together, and to look into the face of the stars and ask God for just the kind of message the men needed. Returning from such a trip, I passed a cot by the side of which sat the "nearest relative"—a half sister. She said, "He is just like a baby to me, see, he is only eighteen years of age, just a baby to me, for I brought him up from childhood. Perhaps your prayer will not do him much good, now, he is so near the end, but O sir, it will help me so much." May God bless every heart that has gone down to the water's edge with a loved one and then returned alone.

"Hold on Tight"

In the semi-darkness of the ward during the early hours of the night, the captain turned away from a boy and said that the lad had a fighting chance if a home message could be obtained to help pull him out of his deepening loneliness; for in fighting pneumonia so far from home and alone, he was about to let go. Word was wired to his home, and far off in the Southland, as the father was rushing North, the message caught him in time for a reply. What a joy it was to that boy, alone, lonely, sick unto death, and discouraged, when the words were read to him, "Hold on tight, Bob, I am coming. Dad." The boy opened his weary eyes and as though he heard in a dream, whispered to read it again. How he followed it, "Hold on tight, Bob. I am coming. Dad." Then he awoke to its meaning and cried, "If he said that then he will be here sure, for I know Dad." And Bob held on tight all night, all the next day, and all the next night until his father held him in his arms; and the two fought on together and won. A few days later the captain said that the message from home had accomplished more than medicine to lure the boy back toward health; and the father, whose eyes gleamed with the flashes of a hidden fire that had burned deep on the sacrificial altar of his heart, thanked God that the supreme offering had not been asked.

A father and mother had journeyed from the hills of Arkansas, and had reached their soldier boy three hours before the end. They told how they sold, in order to make the journey, their mountain patch, their cabin, even the old family mule. They had six dollars left, and the return journey ahead of them. But they said it was all they had in the world to be by his side as he fell alseep, for their boy was their only treasure. I am glad that there is a Book that tells of a Land where death, heartache and war never come, and where those whom we have loved and lost for awhile shall be joined in the family circle never to be taken away. No wonder that every boy in the army says that his mother is the best mother in all the world; and that is just as it should be.

The wards are dotted with patients who were brought over from the stockade, that cluster of barracks hedged by a ten-foot barbed wire barrier under the patrol of sentries whose guns flash their glistening bayonets. These prisoner boys have brought upon themselves penal discipline because of violated regulations and misdemeanors; but in the hospital they are simply soldier lads who are sick and with no token of sentence other than the presence of the guard who seems out of place as he stands day and night with gun and bayonet at the foot of the cot. When that last sickness comes prisoner and guard are just boys, so human, and with souls so alike.

As one prisoner boy went on through the last hours of his life, his guard stood by the bedside and in his boy-like way, somewhat crudely, helped the sick soldier to make up his decision to accept Christ's hand for the dark journey ahead. Later, when the delirium came, that guard placed his gun against the cot, and with touch as gentle as the trained orderly and nurse, held and comforted that boy who was slipping away as prisoner to a life free and good. With roles reversed I thought of him as a Saint Paul in khaki.

The Blood on The New Testament

I returned to that camp when the overseas wounded men were brought back, and in that same hospital I met a convalescent hero who was interested as I went among them distributing the Word of God. This soldier slipped his hand under his pillow and brought out a Testament that he had carried through action. He said, "Look here.' 'And I saw the edges were stained a sticky crimson. "This is my blood," he added, as he told of his wound and of how his blood had colored the Testament. How proud he was of it, and would not give it up for anything. I said, "Of course, you are a Christian boy," but he replied, "No, I am not a Christian, but I will not give up this Book because this is my blood on it."

I took the prized Book in my hand, and as I fingered those red edged pages, I said, "This is truly a treasure. Think of it! The Word of God dyed with your blood!" In the meantime I had turned to the nineteenth chapter of John and read the story of the Cross to the close of the thirty-fourth verse, where "a sword pierced His side and forthwith there came out blood." Said I to my soldier, "Your blood is on the page edge, but on the inside these pages are crimson with the blood of Jesus the Son of God, slain on Calvary for each of us. Think of it, boy, your blood and His blood together on these pages!" He said, "I never saw it that way. I'd better take Christ." And he did. For him that Testament stained on the battlefield of France with his own blood took on the eternal value.

What would you say to the desperately wounded men who say, "No, we are not the heroes, for the heroes are over there sleeping under the crude wooden crosses in the soil of France. They had wounds like these—and more—and then gave their life. No, we are not the heroes; they are, sir." And you never cease to marvel at the humility of heroism.

That blind soldier who turns so restlessly on his cot, what of him? He thinks and dreams of home and loved ones, and cries out in the midnight that shrouds his every hour, "My God! To think that I shall never see their faces again!" Thank God that the long trail awinding into the land of his dreams may lead, through His grace and mercy, his stumbling steps to that Land where dreams shall melt into reality, where blind eyes shall see the joys of an endless life, and where broken bodies, weary minds, and heavy hearts shall be revealed in glory like unto the son of God.
Wayne, Pa.

EDITORIAL BREVITIES

Thank God for the things that money cannot buy.

If the Peace Conference fails to protect the rights of the individual it will be a *piece* Conference.

Our disappointments may be God's appointments.

Blessed is the man who loves his church for her influence will save his children from ruin.

Those who fall into a ditch do not have hold of God's hand.

Law is love to a man when he desires to obey the law.

If all the heartaches that whisky have caused were joys this world would be a Paradise.

This is a good world in which to live. Some may not agree with us, but when it comes to experience with other worlds we are all equal. The world is sinful, but that gives us a task that the Master left for us. It is, after all, a good world in which to live. Don't you think so?

PASTOR AND PEOPLE

FROM BROTHER PATTON'S FIELD

Influenza and inclement weather have, of late, militated much against my church work.

Last Sunday I was at Mt. Auburn. We had a good service. It was Communion day.

The day before, Brother John A. Wilson made me a present of $15.00 in cash. He and his family are faithful member of Mt. Auburn. Brother Wilson is a liberal payer on the pastor's salary and other purposes. The $15.00 was not on pastor's salary.

Next Sunday I go to Shallow Ford, near Elon College. I am expecting a good meeting. This is my old home church where I made a profession and first joined the Church.

I have been to Hines' Chapel twice since Conference. I go there on the first Sunday. I served this church some twenty-five years ago. This is a good people with great possibilities.

I go to Hank's Chapel on the fourth Sundays. At my last appointment, Brother R. N. Farrell of Pittsboro, took me to the church. It rained, but with chains on the car we made it. Brother Farrell, his wife, and myself composed the congregation. We held a service.

May Heaven's richest blessings attend all these congregations and may much and lasting good be accomplished.

J. W. PATTON.

Greensboro, N. C.
January 16, 1919.

REIDSVILLE

Our work at Reidsville for the new Conference year, seemingly, has been greatly handicapped on account of Influenza. Services were held the fourth Sunday in November, which was the first Sunday after Conference and we were not allowed to hold another service until the first Sunday in January. Our prayer is now that conditions may be such that we can hold services regular from this time on. Our plans are this year to hold services with the Reidsville church three Sunday mornings in the month and every Sunday night. The third Saturday and Sunday of each month I will preach at Happy Home Christian church.

In a business meeting of the church last Wednesday night church officers were elected for the year and plans laid for our year's work. We have gotten out our church envelopes with which to raise our church finance, and we have reasons to believe that this system is going to bring in for this year the required amount. We are planning to make this year count for the church and for the Kingdom.

Myself and family are well pleased with our new location and work. Our church people, and those of other churches, have been and are, exceedingly kind and courteous to us. They give us such a cordial welcome into their homes and we believe into their hearts; we cannot help but love them. Before Christ-

mas many of the members graciously remembered us with good things for the pantry. For almost a month they kept us supplied with fresh pork and sausages. At Christmas time one good, big-hearted man and his wife sent us one-half barrel of nice flour. Some other members sent us a nice ham, and another member presented us with a nice pig, or rather a shoat. To one and all of these generous hearted people my wife and I want to thank most kindly for these gifts and expressions of their appreciation of us. We feel obligated to render unto this church and people a better and more faithful services. Our prayer is that God may bless them both in temporal and spiritual blessings.

W. L. WELLS.

Reidsville, N. C.

GET READY

The Musical Institute as authorized by the Eastern North Carolina Sunday School Convention, will hold its annual session at Catawba Springs Christian church near McCullers, N. C., February 20-22. It is earnestly expected that all Sunday schools will be represented. The music committee is anxious to have all leaders and organists present.

GEO. M. McCULLERS, *Chairman.*
J. H. MORING,
JOHN R. BROWN,
MISS MAE STEPHENSON,
W. L. THOMAS,
Committee.

My dear Brother Riddle:

I would like to have space in our valuable paper to return thanks to Brother J. I. Branch and family of Auburn, N. C., for butter, eggs, sweet potatoes and a nice ham. May God's blessings abide with Brother Branch and his family, and may his son, Marvin, soon, be back home. He is in France in the interest of his country. We hope he will soon be back to his post of duty in his church.

J. S. CARDEN.

Durham, N. C.

SUFFOLK LETTER

Three great human achievements are working their way into fact through victory over traditional prejudice, social custom, and national ambition. These three are, Woman's Suffrage, Prohibition of the liquor traffic, and Peace. It would require too much space to trace the history of woman's suffrage in this letter. In England at an early date Benthane recognized the *injustice* of the law toward women, but considered *prejudices* too strong to be combatted; but since 1848 the agitation for equal rights with men has continued in this country, and gathered strength, till now fifteen states have conferred upon women the right to vote, and in twenty-one states they can vote for the President. No serious results in social, political, economic, or moral conditions have resulted from suffrage conferred. Their position is that, "taxation without representation is tyranny;" and that was the position of the Colonies which set the Colonies free. Her contention is just and her victory is thereby assured.

Thirty-five sovereign states have already ratified the constitutional amendment for prohibition, and it is almost certain that the six more necessary to make it apart of the Constitution, will soon ratify; and it is intimated that England will not be more than three years behind the United States in this great movement for human welfare. How did this great temperance movement start? In the temperance crusade in Ohio which culminated in the Woman's Christian Temperance Union in Cleveland, Ohio, in 1874. The Anti-Saloon League, which has done so much for prohibition, was not born in the District of Columbia till 1893. The Woman's *Christian* Temperance Union was the mother of the Anti-Saloon League—a young mother only nineteen years old. She was the virgin mother of this League of America. No wonder the statue of Liberty in New York harbor is the figure of a woman; no wonder the figure on temples of justice, holding the scales, is the figure of a woman; no wonder the pronouns applied to the great ships that plough the great seas is feminine.

Woman has been the great sufferer from the saloon and her spirit of indignation and her trust in God have inspired the states and nation to the abolition of the saloon. Social customs must yield to social justice and social welfare. Women and children are of more importance than customs founded on appetite for intoxicants. "The hand that rocks the cradle rules the world;" and the heart that bleeds under oppression will throw off the tyrant. The saloon must go!

Peace is in the air. War has done its worst. Ambition has run its course. Tyranny is dead. The honorary pall-bearers are at this very moment seated in a room in Versailles, and the monument to be erected over the grave will have written upon it: P-E-A-C-E. No more will great nations sacrifice their sons and crush the hearts of their daughters with war suffrage and prohibition enter their protest against the slaughter of men, and throw all their majestice force on the side of peace. This peace should embrace not only "freedom of the seas," but "freedom of land" as well. It will be a glad day when a passport from the United States means safety in travel throughout the world; when all nations can do business with all other nations, and when one common interest binds the whole world together as gravity binds all matter into harmonious bonds. That will be a glad time when suffrage, prohibition, and peace can be painted as the *three sisters* of a transformed world.

W. W. STALEY.

TWO ITEMS FROM BROTHER J. O. WIGGS

Dear Brother Riddle:—

You editors and preachers are always saying something about poundings. I want to tell you that you haven't so much on me. My Sunday school knows how to do the job, if it did practice it on me, simply getting their hand in for Brother Morgan at the proper time. Last Sunday morning after I had made my announcement in Sunday school and was about to ask him if he had anything to say, expecting him to say something about "Missions" he touched me on the shoulder and asked for a few moments; then brought out a handsome travelling bag and simply took me off my feet. Of course a fellow "don't know what to say," so I said it. I know how you fellows fell when you get held up in that way. Words are inadequate to express appreciation.

* *

I have noticed frequent expressions from our members about having subscribed to THE SUN or been readers from early childhood and have been impressed with the thought that someone has been derelict in duty in hiding our light under a bushel. I am like Paul "as one born out of due time." In my early life I knew nothing of the Christian denomination but as far back as I can remember I have been impressed with our Saviour's prayer in John 17:11-23, and when I learned that there was a church teaching that doctrine I determined that if I ever had an opportunity I would join it. Therefore I am a member of the Christian church and naturally a reader of THE SUN, not because of early associations nor because of the fellowship of its members but from choice because I believe in its doctrine. I believe if our teachings were more widely known we would embrace a much larger membership and I hope that we will continue to spread our teachings abroad.

J. O. WIGGS.

Norfolk, Va. L

THE TITHER

I am glad to announce that THE TITHER started last June has meet with a favorable subscrition list and nearly every week new names are being added. It is very encouraging to me that so many of our own people have subscribed to the publication.

Mr. Karl Lehmann, a member of the editorial board, contended for a publication that we could put out for fifty cents, but other members of the Board did not agree with him, feeling that such a price would not maintain the paper. Many persons have expressed themselves to the effect that they would be glad to aid in the subscription campaign if they could make it a side issue with their regular Church paper and an adjunct to it. Yielding to this demand, THE TITHER is to be fifty cents the year instead of one dollar and the number of pages reduced from sixteen to eight. This takes place with the January Number which will be mailed this week.

Those who have subscribed at the rate of $1.00 the year will be credited accordingly and the paper continued until they are notified. Those of THE SUN who desire to take THE TITHER can add fifty cents to their renewal for THE SUN and a copy of the paper will be forwarded at once.

C. B. RIDDLE, *Editor.*

We have a few more copies of Peloubet's Select Notes, and also a few copies of Tarbell's Guide on hand. Order now. The price is the same as in former years and there will be no reduced price in selling any copies that should be left on hand.

THE FORWARD MOVEMENT

Mission Boards

The Forward Movement program for the Women's Mission Boards and Societies has been worked out and adopted. Read it carefully and begin at once to work it out in your church and society. We are counting oι all our pastors to heed the instruction of the apostle, "I entreat thee also, true yokefellow, help those women which labored with me in the gospel." A church or pastor that does not have have a missionary society loses a great blessing.

Mr. Sunday School Superintendent

The Forward Movement Sunday School program has been completed and adopted by the Sunday school Board of our denomination. It will be published soon. Brother Superindtendent, we hope that you will call a Workers' Conference at once and lay it before them and ask its adoption and get at the program at once in your school. We are expecting every school in the Christian Church to be working at the Forward Movement program at the same time. It has six great outstanding items and it is the plan to major the emphasis on each point for three months. The entire program should be worked at the same time in general outline but for a definite three months the great emphasis is to be placed on a given definite part of the program. Beginning with April first all our schools should be ready to start in on the program with a vim and determination to get all the help and inspiration that comes in a united movement.

Have you ordered some of the books that the Forward Movement has recommended for your help in the several points of the campaign. The quicker you read them the more interested you will become in the Movement. Six books have been suggested on each of the following points: Devotion, Evangelism, Religious Education, Missions, Benevolence, Church Methods. They may be secured of the Christian Publishing Association in price from three cents to one dollar and thirty-five cents, postpaid. There are some very valuable books that will be of great assistance to you in your church work.

Evangelistic Program

We will soon be able to announce the Forward Movement Evangelistic program and outline of work. What a call our Forward Movement has set before us in the winning of fifty thousand to Christ in this campaign. The Forward Movement is not a call in itself alone, it is the call of God to take this world for His Son and we are to do our part in this great campaign. Every Christian should be a soul-winner, and every church should be organized for soul winning, an all-the-year evangelistic campaign. Will 1919 see a net increase of ten per cent in your church membership? Keep that aim before your soul, and before your church.

Rural Church Program

Below we give some of the things that one of our pastors, Rev. C. G. Nelson has worked out in his own church. Brother Nelson is one of our successful pastors in the rural communities and lives at Gresham, Neb., and submits this program:

Urge members to sign Prayer, Family Worship, and Forward Movement Covenants; 75 per cent of Sunday School enrollment present at Sunday services; 25 per cent increase at mid-week prayer meetings.

Evangelism—Decisions each year; observation of Decision Day in the Sunday school; occasional invitation at regular Sunday services; pastor plan a series of evangelistic sermons to be given either during a special week of service or at regular Sunday services; evangelistic campaign with evangelist either in your own church or in union meetings; personal work by the members.

Religious Education—Sunday school organized according to Sunday School Standard of the Christian Church; teacher training class to prepare new and better teachers; send delegates to religious conventions; recognize the day school, by visiting, having children to help with program, and by baccalaureate service; send students to your denominational colleges; have special religious and social programs; boost for Lyceum, Chautauqua, and Farmers Institute Courses.

Missions—Teach, preach and urge both Home and Foreign Missions; organize study classes and have special programs; take some definite mission work to do.

Benevolence—Teach and practice giving and sacrifice as set forth in the Bible; use the Budget System and every member canvass, have weekly offerings; all benevolences and bills paid up to date; make frequent reports of all money raised and expended; remember our part of the $500,000.00 goal of the Forward Movement.

Now do not say that these suggestions are all theories, for most of them are proving successful in an open country community, and every one of them are proving successful in rural communities. Do not make the mistake of adopting this whole program at once by a church that has run along for years without a program, for you would probably utterly fail. I would suggest that you try only one of the five fundamental points the first year or even less, then add more next year and so on, till you have the whole program. Thus, by careful planning of definite work to advance the Kingdom of God, in each rural church, we are expecting a great blessing through the Forward Movement of the Christian Church.

Mrs. Allen Lassiter—Find check for $4 for my church paper that I enjoy reading so much. Hope I will be able to have it in my home always.

R. N. Mitchell—I enjoy THE SUN very much and wish you very much success with your good work.

Mrs. M. F. Alphin—I am always glad to receive THE SUN and love to read its good messages.

Martyn Summerbell—Find check for $2 to help THE SUN keep on shining.

THE CHRISTIAN ORPHANAGE

SUPERINTENDENT'S LETTER

This report brings us to within $203.28 of our goal of $5,000.00 for our Thanksgiving offering. The 22nd will close this year's work and we will make our final report for the year 1918. Let us hope and pray and work that we may reach this goal. Let friends of the little orphan children make some sacrifice to help us reach the goal.

The following boxes have been received and not previously reported: Washington Street Sunday school, Norfolk, Va., two boxes of presents for the children and the Ladies' Aid Society, one box of oranges.

Urbana Woman's Missionary Society, Mrs. C. W. Johnson, President, Urbana, Ill., one box clothing for the children.

Ladies' Aid Society, Chapel Hill church, one box containing table cloths, toweling, napkins, hose, hoods, shoes, etc.

Waverly, Va., Christian church, one box containing ginghams, handkerchiefs, hose, books, soap, etc.

Travora Cotton Mills, one bolt white canton flannel containing 54 1-4 yards.

For all these contributions we are profoundly grateful. The churches have been good to us and have been very liberal in their contributions to help make the little children happy and we have tried to acknowledge each box or package sent in, and if we have overlooked anything it has been an error of the head and not of the heart. In receiving so many packages and not always present when they come in, it is right hard to keep track of each one and sometimes one will be overlooked and not reported. If we have made any mistakes we will thank you to call our attention to it and we will gladly correct any error that may have been made.

C. D. J.

REPORT FOR DECEMBER 25, 1918—(Continued)

Amount brought forward, $13,463.20.

Children's Offerings
Florence P. Holden, $1.00.

Sunday School Monthly Offerings
Berea (Norfolk), $4.00; Wakefield, Va., $1.00; Total, $5.00.

Thanksgiving Offerings
Miss Iola Sprague, $5.00; Mrs. J. A. and Ora Scott, $5.00; Ivor Christian church (Christmas), $4.16; Liberty church, $15.00; Union Grove church, $12.00; Waverly Christian church Sunday school (White Gifts), $23.30; Lanett, Ala., church, $11.66; Total, $76.12.

Special Offerings
Miss Sarah Belle, $2.00; Mrs. J. S. Kagey, $1.00; Mrs. C. B. Hall, $1.00; Mrs. Ruth B. Hall, 50 cents; Total, $4.50.
Total for the week, $86.62; Grand total, $13,549.80.

Mrs. C. O. Smith—I have been used to having THE SUN in my home, therefore I feel as if I cannot do without it.

Birdie Wilson—I am always anxious to get THE CHRISTIAN SUN. We could not do without it.

SOCIAL EVANGELISM

A church held a great meeting.
It won many, many it did not win.
It did an unheard of thing: it investigated why.
The Gospel was the power unto salvation, they said.
Yet that power had failed to reach many.
It had been powerfully preached and winsomely sung.
Evidently something was needed besides preaching.
They had talked with and prayed for many in vain.
Evidently something besides personal work was needed.
They found few men past thirty-five had been won.
They concluded the man must be saved while a boy in the Sunday school.
But they found few boys fifteen in the Sunday school.
And they found many boys in the town.
They found another town getting them with the Boy Scouts.
And another with the Junior Y. M. C. A.
And another with organized baseball.
And others in other ways that the boys liked.
And they said we will get them too—and they did.
All it needed was a man and a plan.
So they added a social service to their evangelism.
—From "Social Evangelism," a pamphlet by Alva W. Taylor, Commission on the Church and Social Service, Federal Council of Churches, 105 East 22nd Street.

QUOTED FROM THIS ISSUE

And you never cease to marvel at the humility of heroism.

Every Christian should be a soul winner, and every church should be organized for soul winning.

Teach and practice giving as set for in the Bible.

Woman has the great sufferer from the saloon and her spirit of indignation, and her trust in God, have inspireed the states and nation to abolish the saloon.

MEETING OF THE AMERICAN CHRISTIAN CONVENTION

The American Christian Convention is scheduled to meet April 29, 1919. The place is Conneaut, Ohio. It is hoped that a large representation will be present. Our Southern brethren will, we feel, do their part in helping to make the Convention useful in every way.

DR. MORRILL TO DEFIANCE

Dr. M. T. Morrill, who has served the Church efficiently as Secretary of Foreign Missions for twelve years, changes his address from Dayton to Defiance, Ohio. Dr. Morrill resigned his position some time ago to accept a position in the Theological Department of Defiance College. Success attend him in his new field of service!

J. W. Payne—I have been reading THE SUN for more than thirty-five years and am not willing to give it up. I love my church paper and all that is for the good of the Church.

NOTES

Mrs. J. O. Atkinson has been ill for the past several days, but improving, so we learn.

Dean M. H. Stacy, of the University of North Carolina, is critically ill with Influenza.

Dr. and Mrs. W. A. Harper have been sick with Influenza, but are better now, we are glad to announce.

Rev. R. S. Stephens, Dover, Delaware, was on January 13, elected Chaplain of the Senate of his State.

Solicitation from the pulpit for the Church paper is a very poor method. Personal work is the thing.

We regret to hear that Mrs. Fred Bullock is ill in a hospital in Suffolk, but trust that recovery will be soon.

We have many subscriptions that will expire February 1. They are marked on the label 2-1-9. Look at yours, and if so marked, favor this office with a remittance, please. *Thanks.*

Rev. W. B. Fuller, Y. M. C. Secretary, Camp Forest, Ga., writes: "I consider the uniting of the Conferences in North Carolina the greatest forward step in years."

The Methodist Protestant church, Burlington, has a membership of 443 and 122 copies of the Church paper go into this membership. This note is worthy of *place* and *space*. Three years ago only twelve copies of the Church paper were being taken by the congregation. The pastor is Rev. J. E. Pritchard.

Rufus Heritage, Graham, N. C., and Howard Burke of Burlington, were out auto riding at a late hour last Saturday night and ran against a telephone poll in front of the Burlington Baptist church. Heritage was killed instantly and Burke is badly wounded and may die. The young men, we are told, were drunk.

The mailing on the *Christian Annual* began last week and will be completed this week. We have printed a few extra copies and shall be glad to get orders. The price is 25 cents, postpaid. We desire, however, to call attention to friends who have an opportunity of purchasing them from their own conference. In this case orders should be placed with your conference, since the conferences appropriate the money to pay for the publication. There are those in remote places, out of the reach of their conference, and for these we printed a few extras.

Dr. Thomas C. Amick, Elon College, N. C.; head of the Department of Mathematics and a member of the Methodist Protestant Church, sends us this good letter which we appreciate: "I wish to congratulate you on your success in editing THE CHRISTIAN SUN. You are making a fine Chuch paper, and I feel that your Church appreciates both the paper and your work. I trust that every issue may bring you rich rewards in blessings from the good THE CHRISTIAN SUN is doing." Our predecessor, that prince of preachers, Dr. J. O. Atkinson, reminded us once that we must not let our modesty stand in the way of publishing a great many things. On this advice we allow the above note to appear. Dr. Amick, though not a member of the Christian Church, is a loyal friend of THE CHRISTIAN SUN.

THE HEALTH BULLETIN

To Bring Relief to Defective Children

To see that the school children of North Carolina shall be given treatment necessary to their proper physical development is the field of work that the Bureau of Medical Inspection of Schools of the State Board of Health has chosen for its future work. This Bureau, of which Dr. Geo. M. Cooper is Director, has announced that it has only one axe to grind, one hobby, one obsession, and that is that every defective child in the State shall be given the physical treatment it needs to give it an even chance in life.

Get Thoroughly Well to Avoid Tuberculosis

Get thoroughly well of "Flu" before going back to work, is the advice that the State Board of Health is giving all influenza patients. The Board feels that unless the people are made to realize the dangers that often follow influenza, that many an unsuspected case of tuberculosis will develop. Not only weeks but months are some times required for a complete recovery from influenza.

State Preparing For Soldiers' Return

To see that the returning soldier and sailor does not meet conditions that will cause his demobilization to become his demoralization, is to be the first peace responsibility of any community, says the Government. The first reconstruction work that any city, town or community undertakes after the war should be to protect the soldier from the social vices, from which he has been more or less free in the army. The War Department has announced that it is returning the soldiers to their families and to civil life uncontaminated by disease, and that it holds the community in which they live responsible for their further protection and welfare.

Better Health to Come Out of The War

One of the many good things that will come out of the war, thinks Major General William C. Gorgas, U. S. A., is that health work in this country in the future will not be the uphill business that it has been in the past. He thinks that the health training of the four million men that have been under arms during the past two years has so profoundly impressed them with the importance of keeping well to keep efficient, and with the necessity of observing various sanitary measures to maintain health, that when they get back home they will be desirous of applying these measures to their home communities as far as it is possible.

THE HIDDEN NEST

Cuddledown was a beautiful cat. She had a cold little nose and a warm little tongue and the softest, silkiest fur. When she was cross—and that never happened unless she was teased—she said "Meow!" very sharply and scratched "Meow" too with her sharp little claws. But when she was happy—and that was nearly always—she sang "Purr, purr" in the coziest way, as she cuddled down to sleep. So the children called her Cuddledown.

Now Rob and Jenny were very fond of Cuddledown. If they wanted to romp, she was ready for a game with a ball or a string. How she did run and jump! She could outbounce the ball any time. And no string could twist itself into as many knots as she could make. Besides she could untwist herself, while the string couldn't. And if Rob and Jenny preferred to curl up on the window seat with a book, Cuddledown was perfectly happy to curl down between them for a nap.

But of late something had come over Cuddledown. She said "Purr" as prettily as ever, to be sure, and she ate her food with remarkable relish, being careful to wash her paws and her face afterwards and to scrub well behind her ears. O, Cuddledown was nothing if not thorough! But when Rob and Jenny spoke to her, she seemed to be thinking about something else. And she was much too busy to play! For hours at a time she disappeared, and no calling through the house or hunting about the grounds could find where she was hidden.

One morning the children were gathering eggs. They visited all the nests and were coming back past the barn, when they saw a hen hop off the ladder that led to the loft. "Do you suppose she's made a nest in the hay?" asked Rob.

"We'd better see," said Jenny.

So the children set down their basket and climbed to the hay mow. It was quiet and sweet-smelling there, and through the high windows the light shone dimly. Rob and Jenny crawled over the hay, looking for a nest. And they found it too!

"What's that funny squeaking?" Jenny asked.

"Perhaps it's a mouse," returned Rob.

The squeaking rose suddenly in a clamor of tiny sounds. And the next minute the children were down on their knees by a cozy hollow filled with four tiny, furry, talkative kittens.

"So that's the secret Cuddledown has been keeping from us," laughed Rob.

"O, the cunning, darling things!" cried Jenny.

The babies seemed to be found. They allowed themselves to be picked up and admired. They even purred a little inside their wee little throats. And how funny it sounded!

"But I don't see why Cuddledown hid them," said

Jenny. "She ought to be proud. I should think she'd want to show them to everybody."

The babies squeaked again excitedly. There was a soft rustle in the straw, and Cuddledown appeared. She arched her back and rubbed her head against Rob and and Jenny and purred so loudly that it was almost like real talking. "Of course, I want people to see them," she probably said. "I was waiting till they were old enough. Aren't they beautiful children?"

To make them even more beautiful, she began scrubbing the babies with her pink tongue. It made a pretty rough wash cloth, but the babies enjoyed it—all but the ears. For Cuddledown was nothing if not thorough.

"We don't blame you for not wanting to play with an old string," said Rob.

"You must let us help play with your babies," added Jenny.

Cuddledown looked at Rob and Jenny purred more loudly than ever. "That will be delightful," she seemed to say. "You are right about my babies making beautiful playthings. Come as often as you like."

The playthings didn't say anything. You see, they were busy falling asleep. But they stayed awake long enough to wink at Rob and Jenny. It's fun having your playthings wink at you!

"That's the nicest nest we ever found," said Rob and Jenny.—*Abigail Burton, in Presbyterian.*

LOOMS OF TIME

Life's shuttles are shaping;
　Pray, what shall I bring
To fill out the pattern?
　And what shall I sing
As I stand at the looms
　That ceaselessly ring?

The best that I am now—
　Yes, that will I bring.
Bright hope for the better—
　Yes, that will I sing.
And I'll tend well the looms
　That ceaselessly ring.

　　　　　—*Edward A. Horton.*

Ottie Hinsley—I enclose two dollars for my renewal. I could not do without THE CHRISTIAN SUN.

O. T. Hatch—I have been taking THE SUN for forty-five years. Find enclosed $2 for my renewal.

J. R. Miles—We think there is no paper like THE SUN. Long may it shine in our home.

A. B. Taylor—We enjoy THE SUN very much and can't do without it. We appreciate the struggle you have had to keep the paper going these times.

"If you want to serve your race, go where no one else will go and do what no one else will do."

CHRISTIAN EDUCATION

(We give below two reports on Christian Education—one by the Eastern North Carolina Conference and the other by the Western North Carolina Conference. These reports are reprinted from the Christian Annual. Reports from other Conferences will follow in later issues of this paper.—Editor The Sun).

REPORT ON EDUCATION

(Eastern North Carolina Conference)

Christian Education is a dominant force in modern civilization. The world war has demonstrated that education without Christianity is a dangerous weapon, with Christianity as a guiding spirit it is an undomitble force for good. Our national leaders called upon the Christian forces of America to promote the sale of Liberty Bonds, to furnish Red Cross workers, Y. M. C. A. secretaries and chaplains to keep up the morale of the men on the battle fields and in the trenches.

When the American people began to look daily to God in prayer for the triumph of liberty and human rights, the Allies forces began a drive that never ceased until victory was won. If we, as a nation, wish to serve God in this day of large opportunity we must enlarge our interest and services and sacrifices for Christian Education.

We renew our pledge to support Elon College in all its undertakings for greater growth and usefulness to the denomination. We approve the action of the Southern Christian Convention in its purpose to increase the permanent Endowment of Elon College by raising $125,000.00 and pledge the President of the College our loyal support in this undertaking.

We pledge the College our patronage and co-operation in all its efforts in promoting the educational interests of the Church and commend its work to the favorable consideration of the general public.

Brother D. F. Carlton, a ministerial student, has been at Elon College this fall, pursuing his studies, but his physician recommends that he must stop for a while on account of his nervous condition.

Rev. B. J. Howard, a licentiate of this Conference, has been pursuing studies at the University in connection with his work as pastor of this Church and is making commendable progress. He did not think wise to undertake the full examination for ordination now but will continue his studies under the direction of your Committee.

Rev. Joseph E. McCauley is at Elon College pursuing his studies to good purpose. He has been serving one church in the Western Conference during the past year. He will serve two churches in this Conference this year. He requests a loan of $50.00 towards his expenses at College. We recommend that his request be granted.

Brothers E. H. Rainey and R. S. Rainey, members of the Biblical class who spent several years at Elon Collge have failed to report to your Committee for two years. We recommend that their names be dropped from the roll of ministerial students and that the College proceed to collect tuition for their education.

We also recommend that this Conference collect the note from R. S. Rainey due for a loan from the Educational Fund, also that all other notes due this fund be collected.

W. C. WICKER,
J. LEE JOHNSON,
R. L. WILLIAMSON,
Committee.

REPORT OF COMMITTEE ON EDUCATION

(Western North Carolina Conference)

1. This is a new day. We are living in a new age, one which is to conserve the best that the past ages have produced, and do a reconstructive work of world import for the Kingdom. Every agency of the Church must readjust itself for this larger, unified task. We think and plan no longer simply in denominational terms and interests, but in world terms and the interest of humanity. The spirit of the Master is brooding upon the chaos of a new world creation. Only that Church or institution imbued with the purpose, spirit and method of Jesus can claim immortal life and share in the glory of sacrificial achievement.

In our Church Elon College stands in the fore-front, because its aim has always been to be of the greatest service to the Church. It has been fortunate in all the presidents whom the Church has given it. It is specially so today in having a man of large, modern, consecrated vision, abounding energy, and remarkable executive ability; able to wisely direct her into this larger sphere of service. She is to be the officers training camp of the Church, the cantonment of the expeditionary forces which our Church is to send on its evangelizing mission to the uttermost parts of the earth. Loyalty to the mission of the Church means loyalty to the College.

2. That a letter of transfer be granted to Rev. J. F. Morgan to unite with the Eastern Virginia Conference, and to Rev. J. U. Newman to the North Carolina and Virginia Conference.

3. That W. J. Edwards continue his studies under the direction of the President of Conference, as outlined last year.

4. L. W. Fogleman has served two churches the past year, and we recommend that he continue his work as a licentiate.

5. W. C. Martin, a licentiate, has served two churches the past year. We recommend that he continue his work as a licentiate.

6. R. O. Smith, a member of the Biblical class and now in school at Elon College, came before the Committee and duly examined. We recommend that he be licensed.

7. That Rev. A. T. Banks be enrolled as a member of this Conference when he shall have received his letter of transfer from Eastern North Carolina Conference.

L. I. COX,
J. W. HARRELL,
D. A. LONG,
Committee.

MISSIONARY

AN OPEN LETTER

Elon College, N. C., January 11, 1919.

To the Members of the Woman's Boards in the North Carolina Christian Conferences

Dear Friends and Fellow-Workers:—

I am sure you have already learned that the three Christian Conferences in this State have united. They have left with us women the decision as to whether we will unite into one State conference or not.

I write this letter as the Secretary of the Board of the North Carolina-Virginia Christian Conference, and also as President of the Woman's Board of the Southern Christian Convention.

The Board of the North Carolina-Virginia Christian Conference met in Greensboro yesterday and requested me to issue a letter inviting the members of the three Boards in this State to meet in Greensboro on January 25 at 11:00 A. M., to consider the question of union and perfect plans. I trust that every member of each Board can be present, and I will thank you to accept this form letter as a personal one and write me at once that you will be present.

If for any reason any Board member cannot be present I request that she send me a written statement of the home work up to date, and express in her letter her opinion in regard to the question of union of our Woman's Boards.

It is particularly desired that the treasurers have an itemized statement up to date, and that the secretaries furnish a complete list of all societies and their officers.

We have not adopted our budget for next year. It is hoped that we can do this at the Greensboro meeting.

The Elon Society will be very happy to have any of the Board members who can do so to visit Elon either on the way to or from Greensboro.

Kindly let me hear from your by return mail.

Yours sincerely,

Mrs. W. A. Harper,

President of the Woman's Board of the Southern Christian Convention.

P. S. Any Society desiring may send a delegate to this meeting or express its opinion in writing.

OUR WOMAN'S MISSIONARY SOCIETIES

It is not enough to plan or organize a Woman's Missionary Society in a church. That is only half the battle and hardly that. The next thing is to keep alive and active the Society, *after it has been organized.* So many Societies, I think, make the impression that they are only organized to collect dues and raise money. This is the not primary object of a Missionary Society. A Missionary Society exists for a far holier and nobler purpose than that of raising money, as essential as this may be.

My conviction is that one great reason why so many Societies lag, or drag along and die, is because they try to make money-getting the chief, if not the sole,

object of their existence. There are at least three objects that come before that of money "raising." First, that of deepening and improving the spiritual life of the individual members of the Society.

Second, the learning and teaching of missionary facts, needs and obligations.

Third, Developing in the homes, and in the community of the members the real missionary spirit and ideals.

If these three facts are put foremost and borne in mind by individual members of each Society, the money will come all right, and the Society will be a real live and active one.

But one may wish to know how these facts may be kept foremost and in view. I have it in mind to write for THE CHRISTIAN SUN a series of five articles on *"How to Create and Keep a Live and Active Woman's Missionary Society in the Church."* I could wish for the sake of the Societies now organized that these five articles, to appear in the next five issues of THE SUN might have a careful reading by our women who really wish to improve their Societies.

We will never be a missionary people till our women, the wives, mothers and sisters, have become at heart and soul missionary. This is the center, this the foundation. We must have live, wide awake, active Woman's Missionary Societies in the churches. Let's try this good year of 1919 and see if we cannot, to a degree, reach this goal.

IS OUR GOAL TOO HIGH?

In asking for a hundred recruits in our Southern Christian Convention as ministers and missionaries the next five years, we are exceedingly modest in comparison with that which many Churches are undertaking. I see that the Methodist Episcopal Church is asking for 53,000 new recruits as ministers and as missionaries. The Dutch Reformed Church has set for its goal one candidate for the ministry from each of its congregations. As said in a previous article, when we of the Christian Church get the need of these recruits upon our hearts, the Lord will hear our petition and give us answer in abundance. This kind cometh but by prayer, but Brethren and Beloved, we shall certainly not reach the goal unless we are much in prayer for this great end. If your home, your church, or your community gave a volunteer to the war, why not now give a volunteer to the Church to become co-worker with God in helping to reach and to save this wicked world for Christ?

J. O. Atkinson,

Field Secretary of Missions.

Mrs. Annie Andrews—I like THE SUN so much and cannot do without my church paper.

Mrs. Isaac Jones—Have been reading THE SUN for so long I feel that I can't do without it.

J. W. Manning—Find my check for $2 to keep THE SUN shining for another year.

Sunday School and Christian Endeavor

HELP REFERENCES

Sunday School—Officers and Teachers Journal and Christian Bible Class Quarterly by Christian Association, Dayton, Ohio; also Tarbell's Guide or Peloubet's Select Notes from any book dealer.

For Christian Endeavor—The Christian Endeavor World, Boston, Mass., and the Dixie Endeavorer, Chattanooga, Tenn.

SUNDAY SCHOOL TOPIC, JAN. 26, '19

Israel Crossing The Read Sea

Scripture Text: Exodus 14:21-15:2.

Golden Text: Jehovah saved Irael that day out of the hand of the Egyptians.—Ex. 14:30.

Time: About April B. C. 1491.

Places: Goshen, Ttham, the Red Sea.

CHRISTIAN ENDEAVOR TOPIC FOR SUNDAY—JANUARY 26

"Books That Have Helped Me."

Scripture Text: Prov. 1-9.

A WALL OF DEFENCE

That which seems to man to be a source of ruin turns out to be in the hands of God a source of salvation. This is another way of saying that man's extremity is God's opportunity. The sea confronted the Israelites and seemed to be their immediate destruction. Under the power and blessing of God, it turned out to be their salvation and the hosts of Pharaoh were drowned in its depths while the waters were a very wall to the Israelites both on their right hand and on their left.

When Jesus was on earth, He looked upon sin and the multitudes who went in as an overwhelming flood to destroy the work He was seeking to do but as a field of unlimited opportunity. Looking one day upon the multitudes, He was not overcome by the vast amount of work to be done in the Father's name, but cried out on the other hand, "The fields are white unto the harvest."

We of the Christian Church often look upon the unconquered fields and the overwhelming floods of sin and sorrow and suffering and we wonder if our Church will ever be able to stem the tide. Trusting in God and going forward with His work the very elements which seemed to threaten us will but afford fields for service and for conquest. I never fear the Kingdoms of righteousness because the numbers and the elements in that kingdom seem few and weak in comparison with the numbers and elements in the world of sin. My only fear is that the children of light will not be as wise and as aggressive as the children of darkness and will not exercise that faith which always results in ultimate victory.

The fact that after one hundred years we have done so very little in world conquest for Christ and today see so very much to be done, should in no wise disconcert us. We have every reason to be encouraged if we will seek to do our duty and do it with our might what our hands find to do. Jehovah did not cause the sea to go back by a strong east wind nor make the sea dry and the waters divide until Moses, a human being, had stretched out his hand over the way. God commands down to this day that faithful men stretch out their hand over the sea and when they do a power becomes manifest even to the salvation of those who are crossing the sea and of those beyond whom they seek to reach. The pagan world with its untold multitudes in idolatry, in superstition, in squalor, in ignorance, seems to be the Red sea in insurmountable danger and difficulty to the forward march of God's host. This is the very reason why missions so stimulated the faith and increased the power and efficiency of the Churches and denominations are missionary. They dare to take God at His word and as Ralph Waldo Emerson says, "advance upon chaos and the dark," trusting God to guide them in the pillar of cloud by day and the pillar of fire by night. The reason why missionary peoples content quer the many obstacles at home and solve their many problems and achieve such success in growth and development at home is because they dare like Moses and the Israelites to obey the voice of God, to stretch out their hands across the sea and look for the lands that lie beyond, which hands though unseen are the promise of God. Missions have always constituted the chief challenge to the people of God and the people of God who have not been missionary having no peculiar challenge to spur them, on and no program to engage their best effort, have made little or no progress. It is inconsistent with the plan and purpose of God as taught from Genesis to Revelation and never in all the will and world of God to prosper a non-missionary people. Missionary peoples build and sustain homes for the helpless, institutions for the untaught, places of refuge for the needy, while non-missionary peoples or anti-missionary peoples have no hand or no heart for these God-given enterprises. This Christian Church will some day come to be a mighty factor in the world but before it can do so, it must stretch its hand by God's help across the seas and advance upon chaos and the dark.

J. O. ATKINSON.

FUN AND FICTION

Widower—I suppose that when you recall what a handsome man your first husband was, you wouldn't consider me for a minute?

Widow—Oh, yes, I would. But I wouldn't consider you for a second.—*Orange Peel.*

"Sam, I understand that there's a schism in your church," said the jocular man to his colored man-of-all-work. "Kain't be, less'n somebody done made us a present of it, 'cause we done spend all ouah money for a new ohgan."—*Livingstone Lance.*

"Typographical errors," said William Dean Howells, "are always amusing. When I was a boy in my father's printing office in Martin's Ferry, I once made a good typographical error. My father had written 'The showers last week, though copious, were not sufficient for the millmen.' I set it up 'milkmen.'"

"I have been thinkin' 'bout gettin' married,' said a member of his flock to Brother Williams. "You reckon I could git a marriage license for a dozen watermelons?"

"I reckon you could," replied Brother Williams. "But my whole-some advice ter you is ter eat de watermelons."—*Atlanta Constitution.*

MARRIAGES

JOHNSON-GILMORE

At the home of Mr. T. V. Wicker on December 22, 1918, Mr. H. A. Johnson and Miss Jennie Gilmore were united in marriage. Only a few of their friends were present. May their lives be long and happy.

J. S. CARDEN.

CLARK-O'BRIANT

On December 22, 1918, at my home, No. 906 Shepherd Street, Durham, N. C., at eight-thirty o'clock, Mr. Brodie Clark and Miss Ethel O'Briant both of Chapel Hill, were married in the presence of a few friend. May their lives be long and full of joy.

J. S. CARDEN.

OBITUARIES

HUGHES

Sister Hughes, the devoted wife of W. A. Hughes, died December 24, 1918. She was one of the charter members of Bethel Christian church. She was a good wife, a good mother and a good neighbor. Before her marriage she was Miss Susan Cathrine Fitch. She was born February 7, 1867. At the time of her death she was about 79 years of age. Bethel church has lost a good member. She leaves to mourn their loss: a husband, one daughter, one son and a host of friends. On the twenty-sixth we laid her body to rest in Bethel cemetery to sleep the long sleep of death. Funeral service by her pastor. May God bless and comfort the bereaved ones.

J. S. CARDEN.

WILLIAMS

Elmer P. Williams, youngest son of John J. and Elizabeth Williams, was born November 18,1890, and died in Columbia, S. C., January 8, 1919, aged twenty-eight years, one month and twenty days. He united with the Christian church at Shallow Ford when only thirteen years of age, and always loved and respected his home church. On February 8, 1917 he was married to Miss Christine Malone, who survives him, also his father, mother, one sister and two brothers.

Brother Williams had been connected with the Carolina Life Insurance Company for several years and won success. Elmer always made good, and was heldin high esteem by all who knew him. The funeral services were held from the residence of the parents by the writer, and the burial was at Shallow Ford cemetery. The floral offering was rich, beautiful, and abundant. May God comfort all the bereaved.

L. I. COX.

THOMAS

William A. Thomas, son of Benjamin and Mary Thomas, was born October 4, 1851 and died January 8, 1919, in his sixty-eighth year. He was the oldest of fourteen children. Four brother and three sisters survive him.

He was twice married. His first marriage was to Margarette M. Watson, and they had five children, four of whom are living.: Bert W., Jonesboro; Mrs. A. S Thomas, Sanford; W L. Thomas, Jonesboro, and M. C. Thomas, Cheraw, S. C. There are fourteen grandchildren. His second marriage was to Miss Francis Anna McIver, April 10, 1913.

He had been a member of Shallow Well church for forty-five years, and was faithful and devoted to his church. A good man has gone, and his splendid characteristics, kindness, devotion to family and friends, loyalty to his church and to his Christ, are very marked now that he is no more.

He was buried at Shallow Well by the masonic fraternity, he being the oldest member of his lodge.

T. E. WHITE.

A WORD TO TEACHERS

Why not have some special help on your Sunday school work? Send $1.35 to THE CHRISTIAN SUN office and get a copy of Peloubet's Select Notes.

REPORT OF THE CONDITION OF THE ELON BANKING & TRUST CO., AT ELON COLLEGE, IN THE STATE OF NORTH CAROLINA, AT THE CLOSE OF BUSINESS, DECEMBER 31, 1918:

Resources

Loans and Discounts	$22,623.95
Overdrafts, secured, $50.00; unsecured, $893.72	943.72
United States Bonds and Liberty Bonds	4,287.00
Banking Houses, $1,480.38; Furniture & Fixtures, $1,687.78	3,168.16
Demand Loans	1,700.00
Due from National Banks	16,583.09
Due from State Banks & Bankers	20.00
Cash Items held over 24 hours	1,888.65
Gold Coin	477.50
Silver Coin, including all minor coin currency	456.64
National Bank Notes and other U. S. Notes	6,945.00
Thrift Stamps	36.50
War Savings Stamps	148.05
Total	$59,278.26

Liabilities

Capital Stock paid in	5,000.00
Surplus Fund	1,000.00
Undivided Profits, less current expenses and taxes paid	653.86
Deposits subject to check	45,117.46
Time Certificates of Deposit	5,896.68
Cashier's Checks outstanding	726.79
Certified Checks	13.47
Received on Liberty Bonds	850.00
Collections	20.00
Total	$59,278.26

State of North Carolina—County of Alamance, January 15, 1919.

I, MARION C. JACKSON, Cashier of the above named Bank, do solemnly swear that the above statement is true to the best of my knowledge and belief.

MARION C. JACKSON,
Cashier.

Correct—Attest:

J. J. LAMBETH,
T. C. AMICK,
S. W. CADDELL,
Directors.

Subscribed and sworn to before me, this 15th day of January, 1919.

J. J. LAMBETH, J. P.

Help make THE SUN better, better, better. Write often, write to the point and write right now.

A colonel wanted a man-servant so he inserted an advertisement in a local weekly. One of the applicants who answered was an Irishman.

"What I want," explained the colonel, "is a useful man—one who can cook, drive a motor, look after a pair of horses, clean boots and windows, feed poultry, milk the cow, and do a little painting and paper-hanging.

"Excuse me, sor," said Murphy, "but what kind of soil have ye here?"

"Soil?" snapped the colonel. "What's that got to do with it?"

"Well, I thought if it was clay I might make bricks in me spare time." —*Everybody's.*

Scotch Sergeant: "And noo we'll try the rich tur-rn by numbers, and mind that ye don't move till ye hear the final syllable of the wor-rd tur-rn!"—*Passing Show.*

An exchange says that a lady who was looking about in a brice-a-brac shop, with a view to purchasing something odd, noticed a quaint figure, the head and shoulders of which appeared above the counter. "What is that Japanese idol over there worth?" she inquired. The salesman's reply was given in a subdued tone, "Worth about half a million, madam; it's the proprietor."

THE CHRISTIAN SUN

"IN ESSENTIALS UNITY, IN NON-ESSENTIALS LIBERTY, IN ALL THINGS CHARITY"

The Cross of Convenience

CONVENIENCE seems to be a cross on which we daily crucify afresh our Master. Our pity too often expresses itself only in tears and our passion for duty all too many times ceases with enthusiasm. A more convenient time with purse may be out of harmony with our pity, and the service to self may not accord with our passion to serve our fellowman. The crumbs from our table will not feed the needy world. The breaking of the alabaster box should not be withheld until our own heads are under it.

Volume LXXI   WEDNESDAY, JANUARY 29, 1919   Number 5

BURLINGTON · · · NORTH CAROLINA

THE CHRISTIAN SUN

Founded 1844 by Rev. Daniel W. Kerr

C. B. RIDDLE - - - Editor

Entered at the Burlington, N. C. Post Office as second class matter.

Subscription Rates

One year .... $ 2.00
Six months 1.00

In Advance

Give both your old and new postoffice when asking that your address be changed.

The change of your label is your receipt for money. Written receipts sent upon request.

Marriage and obituary notices not exceeding 150 words printed free if received within 60 days from date of event, all over this at the rate of one-half cent a word.

Original poetry not accepted for publication.

Principles of the Christian Church

(1) The Lord Jesus Christ is the only Head of the Church.
(2) Christian is a sufficient name of the Church.
(3) The Holy Bible is a sufficient rule of faith and practice.
(4) Christian character is a sufficient test of fellowship, and of church membership.
(5) The right of private judgment and the liberty of conscience is a right and a privilege that should be accorded to, and exercised by all.

EDITORIAL

THE SUN CAMPAIGN

Each year we have asked pastors and people to help in a special effort in the securing of new subscribers for THE CHRISTIAN SUN. These efforts have not been in vain, and they will never be so long as the people co-operate so beautifully as they have in the past years.

We have decided on February and March as the time for special effort for the paper. This will give pastors of country charges ample time to reach all of their churches.

There will be no special offers, reduced rates, or propositions. As printed in THE SUN each week, the price is $2.00 the year or six months for $1.00. We are trying to give our readers value received and feel that no special offers are needed.

And now brethren, we want to give you a little experience about the special offer subscriptions. Here it is: Two years ago we enrolled about 200 persons for three months at 25 cents each. Less than six of these renewed, and we are not sure that they are on the list now.

We must teach the people that THE SUN is the paper of our Southern Christian Convention; that is worth the price and should be in every home. The get "something for nothing" method will not work with a progressive paper and people. We believe that tho thing to do is to give a paper well worth the price and educate the people to it. But some one asks the question, "Why didn't the two hundred persons remain on the list, or at a larger per cent of them? The question is easily answered. They were looking for a bargain and not the Church paper. When their time was out the bargain was not renewed and neither was the subscription.

THE CHRISTIAN SUN ought to be in every home of the Church. It is not impossible to do this one thing. There was a time when some of us thought that certain drives and campaigns were impossible, but during the past two years we have seen and demonstrated things in a different light. May we not undertake for our Church paper what we have done for the Government and for the institutions behind the great war?

We call upon pastors and friends everywhere to help us. What shall our goal be? Let some one suggest this and it will be printed next week. Who will set the goal?

UNION AND UNITY

There is much ado much adoing—about union of denominations so far as the task undertake the bringing men into the Kingdom. B e may be union and not unity. The spirit of the Master is the only thing that will bring men into union and Christian unity.

EDITORIAL NOTES

"The deacons will now take the offering," says many a parson. Notice that he says "take." The word may not be wholly out of use and meaning in the sentence, for if you get money from some one you have to take it.

Ice cream suppers, oyster stews, cake raffles, tea parties and contests may develop the social side of a man, but they will never teach him how to give. These things will never cause a man to worship God with his means. Such things appeal to the stomach, but real giving (not paying) appeals to the man's heart.

One of the foremost laymen in the Presbyterian Church some weeks ago was asked to write on church finance and his experience in giving. He announced that he had tithed his income for twenty-one years. His salary when he started was less than three hundred dollars the year. Last year it passed seventy-five thousand dollars. It had grown gradually for all these years.

With much pride a man told us the other day how he had given a whole dollar to aid in the Lord's work. He took pride in speaking of his liberality (?). That man was not altogether the blame. He had farms and fields and cattle, a tenth value of which would have been a thousand times the dollar that he had given. He had never been taught to give. He had been taught to "chip in" a nickel and "help out." We must teach our children the spirit of giving. Some of the old fellows are too hard and chronic to reach now. Occasionally you can blast one and get his feet set in the right direction.

ROOSEVELT MEMORIAL DAY
Sunday, February 9th

The American people are called upon to observe Sunday, February 9th, as Roosevelt Memorial Day. This comes at the request of a committee of prominent citizens, among whom are Ex-President Taft, Cardinal Gibbons, Senator Lodge and Ex-Governor Hughes.

The churches will do well to take the lead in planning community services for the fitting observance of the day. As this is Inter-Church Campaign Sunday, a a demonstration of the united leadership of the churches in the community is especially opportune. Theodore Roosevelt was not only a great American, but he was a fearless champion of the right in many of the moral conflicts of our day.

In refutation of the report circulated by the brewers shortly before Colonel Roosevelt's death, which was so worded as to leave the impression that he sympathized with the forces opposed to national prohibition, there was published in the New York *Times* of January 20th, a letter which he wrote to Dr. Ferdinand C. Inglehart on December 19th. In this he congratulates Dr. Inglehart on the "success that is crowning your long fight against alcoholism," and goes on to say "the American saloon has been one of the most mischievous elements in our social, political and industrial life."

One feature of the Roosevelt Memorial service that every church should observe will be the singing of the Ex.President's favorite hymn, "How Firm a Foundation."

INTER-CHURCH FEDERATION IDEA GROWING IN MANY CITIES
News Items Show Progress of The Movement

The pastors and lay representatives of the churches of Rochester, N. Y., are organizing a federation of churches. The Rev. Samuel Tyler, rector of St. Luke's Protestant Episcopal Church, was chairman of the committee in charge of the preliminary meeting. A constitution was approved and a representative committee of ministers and laymen will submit it for ratification to all the churches. Secretary Guild met a group of business men at a luncheon at the Genesee Valley Club. These men guaranteed the underwriting of a budget for two years of $7,500 a year. A committee was appointed to find a secretary to be employed as soon as the federation is completed organized.

The St. Louis Federation has called Secretary Arthur H. Armstrong of the Federation at Toledo, Ohio, to be executive secretary and he has accepted this call. This federation, which has been so successful in the past, has organized its work on broader lines than ever before. To assure the financial support of the central administrative work, one hundred business men are being asked to make pledges of $100 a year for a period of years. Nearly the entire number of pledges are all ready secured.

The Federated Churches of Cleveland held a notable series of conferences in December. The different departments of the Federation had charge of the different events. Some of the best known men and women of America were present, to discuss the great after-the-war problems. A leaflet is being printed setting forth the program for the present year,as recommended by the different departments.

When the epidemic of influenza resulted in the closing of many churches throughout the country, the publicity departments of the leading federations made splendid use of the Saturday afternoon and Sunday morning issues of the daily papers, meeting the emergency by publishing Scripture Readings, prayers and short sermons for "Home Worship on Churchless Sundays."

Rev. F. G. Behner has become the executive secretary of the Akron Federation of Churches. His address is 713 Second National Bank Building, Akron, Ohio. Secretary Behner comes from St. Louis, Mo., where he was extension secretary of the St. Louis Presbytery and Chairman of the Federation Committee on Comity.

The Chicago Federation of Churches held a two days' conference for the discussion of the program for the coming year. A number of commissions prepared very strong reports containing definite recommendations which were approved and committed to the Executive Committee of the Federation. As the conference came to realize the magnitude of the program and the success of the leadership of the President, Dr. Herbert L. Willett, an enthusiastically supported recommendation was made that the Executive Committee of the Federation earnestly request that while remaining as president, Dr. Willett accept administrative charge of all the work of the Federation at least until October. It is hoped that he can give at least one-half of his time to this great task in this time of emergency.

Newark, N. J., has under consideration the organization of a Federation. Secretary Guild has been in conference with the leaders. Secretary Pearson recently gave three addresses before different audiences upon the work being done in Indianapolis.

Many cities which do not have church federations have become interested in forming such an organization. The secretary of the Commission on Inter-Church Federations has not been able to meet, personally, many of the calls for assistance made during the month of December. These calls have been met by the able assistance of Secretary M. C. Pearson, of Indianapolis, Secretary E. R. Wright, of Cleveland, and Secretary C. R. Zahniser, of Pittsburgh.

The successful launching of the State Federation of Pennsylvania is now assured. At a recent meeting in Pittsburgh one-third of the entire annual budget of $10,000 was subscribed, practically completing the balance needed to finance the organization.

PASTOR AND PEOPLE

HAPPY HOME

Last Saturday and Sunday I filled my first appointment at Happy Home' Christian church. While I was in the community I was well cared for in the home of Brother J. H. Richmond and wife. I find that this is splendid family of people who are thoroughly interested in their church.

The congregation on Saturday was small, but we feel that good was accomplished. On Sunday the congregation was fairly large and we had an interesting, and we trust, a profitable service.

At the close of the service the church voted the use of the envelope system to raise the church finance. We consider this a step forward. There is no reason why the country church could not use this system just as effectively as the town church. Give it a fair trial and it will bring in favorable results every time.

W. L. WELLS.

Reidsville, N. C.

TEN ADDITIONALS TO THE FIRST CHRISTIAN CHURCH, GREENSBORO

Yesterday, (January 19) was a great day for the First Christian church, Greensboro. The occasion was, "Go to Church Sunday." The services had been previously arranged, and a steering committee of thirty-two placed in the field to assist the pastor to work up the congregation. Large posters had been placed by the Ministerial Association of the City, announcing the special services for the day. This, together with the splendid committee of thirty-two, brought audiences to the First church that broke all records for regular service of the church for many years.

The services in addition to being largely attended, were characterized by the finest spirit of fellowship among the folks. The congregations lingered after each service in order to chat with each other before leaving. Ten members were added to the church during the day, and one decision in the evening service. My heart was made to rejoice many times during the day by expressions from men of the church—who express high hopes for the work here.

The Men's Bible Class, Ladies' Missionary Society, Philathea, Young Men's Class, and the Christian Endeavor, all are taking on new life, and from the outline of their work one would judge that great things are to be put across.

One of our greatest needs is for the people of Greensboro holding membership in other churches of our denomination to line up with the work. Again I appeal to the ministers of the Southern Christian Convention who have members in this city to send their names and addresses to me. Our Church had just as well have them as the Baptist, Methodist and Presbyterians. If you will send the names our church will do the rest.

J. VINCENT KNIGHT.

Greensboro, N. C.

RALEIGH CHURCH

Our Raleigh congregation is much rejoiced that Rev. George D. Eastes is to come to them permanently beginning the first Sunday in February. But for the Influenza epidemic and sickness in his own family the new pastor would have begun his work there some time since. In fact, he has already been present for one Sunday's service and for mapping out and planning with the officials of the church the work for the present year.

The writer was in the Sunday school and preached for this congregation twice on Sunday, the 19th inst. It was not generally known that there would be preaching services and yet there were nearly one hundred present for the eleven o'clock service and nearly that number at the evening hour.

I have nowhere found a more enthusiastic, a more determined and a more loyal congregation of worshippers than that of our Raleigh church. They certainly love their church and the cause of their Lord. I doubt if in all our Zion you will find a company of men and women more zealous for the Master's cause, and more interested in every enterprise for prayers, growth and development than you will find in the Raleigh Christian church. Brother Eastes will have him not a large, but a solid and united and faithful and true band of tried souls who will do their best to make his pastorate a success and the work a joy and a blessing.

Rev. R. L. Williamson, the former pastor, is held in highest esteem and the brethren are deeply sensible of the good work he did, and appreciate fully his life and labors amongst them.

The Sunday school is one of the livest, most wide-awake and enthusiastic I have found anywhere. Prof. L. L. Vaughan of the State College Faculty is superintendent and Deacon C. H. Stephenson is leader of choir and orchestra. They have music and they have "pep" in their school—and it counts.

Altogether Raleigh is in a prosperous and most hopeful condition and they anticipate great things the present Conference year. It was a joy to be with them in their worship.

J. O. ATKINSON.

SUFFOLK LETTER

Of all the times in the history of Christianity when Christian people should be true to Christ and faithful in service, this is *the time*. The world-war has shaken up the whole world. All nations are in a state of agitation. Autocracy is ended, but anarchy looms large in propaganda and revolution. Diplomacy is great, but it is not sufficient of itself to bring order out of chaos and to stabilize crude nations. The spirit of Jesus can remove the hostile antagonisms of races and nations and bring permanent peace and universal prosperity. There can be no universal prosperity without universal peace.

There are two methods by which peace can be established. The first is, for Christian people everywhere to *live* their religion above reproach. No milk-and-water personal piety will help the world into peace. Honesty, virtue, and good will are necessary to human welfare; and these must rest on faith in God. Business conducted on honest principles would construct a national prosperity as lasting as human needs. There is business enough for all, if fair play has its place. There are consumers enough in the world to buy all the products of field, and factory, and store; there is work enough for all who are willing to labor; and the more friendly all co-operate in the world's business the more demand for wares. Competition may be the life of trade, but dishonesty is the death of trade.

Virtue is more than innocense; it is innocense plus personal will. The child is innocent; the man is virtuous. Social impurity undermines physical health, religious character, and human values. The world can never be restored to God by impure men and women. The social world is as much a part of human progress as the business world. Rome went down in her social pollution, with Pompeii as the center of corruption. It was the Sodom of Rome. The dance hall is the school room of social impurity. It is the distinct business of Christian people to produce virtuous society; all amusements and engagements that tend toward impurity are un-Christian and negative personal religion.

God is a New Testament grace. It was a part of the Advent song of the heavenly host. It is the basis of human friendship and religious co-operation. It is the arsenal of the army of the Lord. No man can fight the good fight without good will toward men. It requires divine help to fashion the life by these elements; but the times demand honesty, virtue, and good will.

The other big thing is "Missions;" not simply a few resolutions and a few dollars, but a whole Church engaged in prayer, in service, and in systematic contributions for the evangelization of the world. It is not only the biggest task in the world, but the best task in the world. It is the only enterprise large enough to develop the whole Church and the whole Christian. The base study of one missionary field furnishes scope for great minds, and love for the people of one field would make one more like Christ. The opportunity to give is as endless as human ability. It is not the task of one generation, but of many generations. There are crude civilizations with millions of people who cannot be brought to their best in centuries. Christianity must establish itself on a personal inner basis, and then express itself on a world-wide campaign of missionary enterprise. The doors will open, as never before, when the Peace Conference completes its gigantic task, and the Church must enter in with a gospel untainted by selfish purposes and unstained by worldly alliances. And our Church must not be left out of the victorious army that is to conquer the world for Christ.

                                                W. W. STALEY.
20 *Pendelton St., Berkley, Norfolk, Va.*

THE HOME DEPARTMENT OF THE SUNDAY SCHOOL

Having been elected by the Eastern Virginia Christian Sunday School Convention as Superintendent of the Home Department I have given the subject considerable thought and am more and more convinced of the importance and possibilities of this Department. Looking at the Sunday school in its broad sense as truly a Bible school—a part of the church following specific plans of study and teaching God's word—it is obvious that each and every department is but a part of a great plan with that purpose in view, following out its own peculiar methods of reaching the untutored and presenting to them the great truths of His eternal truth. Organized primarily for the purpose of reaching those who because of circumstances could not attend the regular sessions of the Sunday school, and having them enrolled as members, considering that among that number are those most needing a knowledge of God's word—the mothers—into whose hands the first and greatest responsibility of training rests, how important it is that they be given every help and encouragement possible. The future of the Church and nation is in their hands. Truly it has been said, "The hand that rocks the cradle rules the world." Oh how important, that that hand should be guided by God's truth! But how can their hands be guided and inspired by God except they know, and how can they know except they be taught? At most the Sunday schools has the child only one hour in each week, but get the mother into the Home Department and helped to study God's word one hour at home and we more than double our influence upon the child. Add to that the father and it needs no mathematician to calculate the effect upon the future manhood and womanhood, The greatest sin of our day is not strong drink, nor is it gambling, nor other like evils but ignorance of God's word. Those evils are but a result of that ignorance. We have a slight knowledge of God historically—gathered from hastily glancing at His word—but of His love gathered from a sincere study of His truth. We know all too little. I find that many of our churches have no Sunday school. Why it it? Unable to get a leader to superintend. Unable to get teachers, and many other difficulties are offered as excuses but the real trouble, is in our lack of knowledge and "where ignorance is bliss." Some are afraid to know too much. We have not been studying and planning for the future. The Home Department offers us an opportunity to start now on a systematic plan to build for the future. Take Duet. 6:6-9 as a guide. Let God's word be emblazoned everywhere, all the time and ere long one can say, "I know not God." My appeal, therefore, is that the pastor of each church, not having one will organize a Home Department for the systematic study of God's word, designate some one to visit the home (if unable to do so himself) and encourage, instruct and help the members to a greater knowledge of His truth. To those churches who have a Home Department, redouble your efforts, pray for more enlightenment, and that God may open your eyes to your opportunities and responsibilities and increase your strength and knowledge of His truth.

Having accepted the superintendency of this Department, I am at the service of any one interested to help in any way possible in this particular field of usefulness. I would like to visit every church in the Conference and present the work personally but being unable to do so I take this method of reaching you and would like to have report from every church stating whether or not you have a Home Department if so facts concerning it—if not, will you try to organize one. "Now is the accepted time." "Study to make thyself approved unto God."

Yours in His cause,
J. O. Wiggs,
Supt. H. D. E. Va. S. S. Convention.

Notes

Note that Rev. L. E. Smith changes his address from Huntington, Indiana to 4312 Colonial Avenue, Norfolk, Va.

Attorney D. R. Fonville, who has been in France since March engaged in Y. M. C. A. work, is to return this week. Mrs. Fonville left early this week for New York City to join her husband.

Dr. J. O. Atkinson spoke to the Baracas of the Front Street M. E. church last Sunday at 10:00 o'clock and at 11:00 o'clock preached for the congregation at Burlington Christian church. He was heard gladly at both services.

THE SUN'S Editor was glad to have with him for dinner one day last week Mr. W. E. Lindsey, Chapel Hill, N. C. Brother Lindsey is one of the loyal members of our Chapel Hill church and is deeply interested in every enterprise of his denomination.

The Sunday school of the Burlington church voted last Sunday morning to send and support a missionary to Japan. The school has had this matter under consideration for some time and came to a definite conclusion about the matter last Sunday.

Mrs. J. J. Lincoln is spending some time in the home of Dr. P. H. Fleming. Mrs. Lincoln is one of the Church's splendid workers.

Rev. L. E. Smith writes: We arrived in Norfolk Tuesday of last week. The people here have certainly given us a most royal reception. The majority of the members of the Official Board met us at the station. After a hand-shake around we were then piloted to the Victoria Hotel where we were comfortably housed until our goods came on Friday. When the car arrived they took charge of us and the car and moved us bodily to our home where we will spend the winter. When we found ourselves in our new home we found our pantry simply loaded with all kinds of catables, and presently the dining table was spread for supper and a sufficiency for the coming day. It is good to be a minister and to have the privilege of administering to His people. I shall appreciate greatly your interest and prayers as we undertake the work in this most difficult field." Brother Smith's address is 4312 Colonial Avenue. Norfolk, Va.

A. T. Banks—THE SUN gets better.

JOINT MISSION BOARD MEETING

We clip the following from the *Greensboro Daily News* of January 26:

The Woman's home and foreign mission board of the North Carolina Christian conference was organized yesterday in the First Christian church, by the union of the three former boards operating in the state. These former boards were known as the North Carolina and Virginia, Western North Carolina, and the Eastern North Carolina boards, following the bounds of the three annual Christian conferences in the state. These conferences have recently united into one body, known as the North Carolina Christian conference and the action of the woman's board followed.

The personnel of the three boards party to the union, was as follows: N. C. and Virginia—Mesdames M. F. Cook, L. M. Clymer, C. B. Clark, W. A. Harper, R. J. Kernodle, J. G. Anthony, and J. H. Farmer; Eastern N. C.—Mesdames A. T. Banks, A. F. Smith, J. A. Kimball, J. Byrd Ellington, R. L. Williamson, K. B. Johnson, and Miss Alline Staley; Western N. C.—Mesdames W. H. Carroll, Edward Teague, J. D. Kernodle, W. R. Sellars, and G. R. Underwood. Each of these board members expressed herself as favoring the union, either in person or in writing and action was unanimous.

The session yesterday was called to order by Mrs. M. F. Cook, of the local society. After devotional services by Rev. J. Vincent Knight, Mrs. W. A. Harper was called to the chair and presided throughout the conference. During the afternoon session a stirring address was made by Dr. J. O. Atkinson, mission secretary of the Southern Christian convention.

Officers of the new board were elected as follows: President, Mrs. W. H. Carroll, Burlington; vice-president, Mrs. A. T. Banks, Ramseur; secretary, Mrs. W. A. Harper, Elon College; treasurer, Mrs. W. R. Sellars, Burlington; superintendent young people, Miss Bessie Holt, Burlington; superintendent cradle roll, Miss J. G. Anthony, Greensboro; superintendent literature and mite boxes, Mrs. M. F. Cook, Greensboro; superintendent boys' work, Mrs. J. W. Patton, Greensboro. These officers constitute the executive committee, with Mrs. Carroll, Mrs. Harper and Mrs. Sellars as central executive committee.

It was decided to organize 20 additional societies during the year to secure 20 new life memberships in the board and to raise $2,500 as the minimum. It was also decided to make July the rally month in the churches and the central committee is to prepare a special program. The board decided to hold its first conference on October 5-6, the place of meeting to be selected by the central committee.

The reports of. the officers of the three boards showed $1,500 was raised last year. The organizations were as follows: Women's societies 34, young people 10, willing workers 5, cradle roll 10, boys 2.

THE CHURCH PAPER AND THE CHURCH PEOPLE

Mrs. Ben T. Holden—Best wishes to you in your good work and congratulations on the improvement in the paper.

W. J. Cole—I cannot do without THE SUN. I appreciate the struggle you have had to keep the paper going. I do not see how any church member can do without his church paper. Long may THE SUN shine in our home.

Mrs. Nannie Royster—Fourteen years ago when I made a new home for myself, I made a new one for THE SUN also. I did not feel like I could do without it.

C. E. Byrd—With the very best wishes for THE SUN's success.

MISSIONARY

**HOW TO CREATE AND KEEP A LIVE AND ACTIVE WO-
MAN'S MISSIONARY SOCIETY—(IN 5 CHAPTERS).**

Chapter I. The Place of the Bible in the Missionary Society

The greatest of all missionary books is the Bible. The greatest and best of all missionary libraries is the "little library of sixty-six small books, usually bound together as one great Book, which has been the inspiration of every missionary and missionary worker since the world began."

It is presumed that every Missionary Society uses the Bible, reading a portion from the inspired page either at the opening or some time during every meeting. But too often this reading is done in the most indifferent and perfunctary manner, merely as a matter, of form and without any definite purpose or expectation of accomplishing anything. We get the idea that when the Bible is read a sort of holy service has been performed, and no matter how, the good results will surely follow.. This is a grave mistake. No part of the missionary meeting should be planned with more thought, care and consideration than that of *reading the Scripture lesson.* The fact that the Bible is inspired should cause the one who is to read it to do so most impressively, having made the selection most carefully and prayerfully, and then seek to apply most forcibly its teachings.

I read recently two instances that will each illustrate how the Bible should *not* be read in the missionary meeting. They are related in Belle M. Brain's "Holding the Ropes":

"The writer recalls a missionary meeting where the Scripture lesson, selected hastily at the last moment, was read in so perfunctary a manner that less than half an hour later, when a test was made, not a single person present was able to tell what had been read! It was one of the most striking missionary passages in the Bible, yet it had made no impression whatever.

"On another well-remembered occasion a missionary worker of no little prominence was asked to read the Scripture lesson at a missionary conference. The passage selected was obscure, with seemingly no bearing whatever on the cause of missions.. As he made no comment and drew no parallels, his hearers are still in ignorance of the lessons he intended to convey. Selecting inappropriate passages is, unfortunately, not an uncommon failing. The writer recently heard of a leader of a children's mission band who opened her meeting by reading an entire chapter from the book of Lamentations."

Not infrequently the missionary meeting, if held in the church, is opened with reading in concert, from the back of the hymn book, some short psalm in no particular sense missionary in spirit or in purpose.

The Bible deserves better treatment at the hands of any one who cares a bit about missions, and its reading at the missionary meeting may be made, and should be made, one of the most helpful, impressive and inspiring portions of the whole program.

There are several ways in which the Bible may be used most tellingly in the meeting, a few of which can only be pointed out here for want of space.

1. To be effectual the Scripture lesson should not be lengthy, but pointed, pithy and practical. On this I want to quote again from Belle M. Brain: "Sometimes a single text, just one brief verse, followed by a few pointed remarks, will make a deeper impression than a whole chapter aimlessly read. For example: *Carest thou not that we perish?* (Mark 4:38). These words of the disciples to the Master on the Sea of Galilee may well be taken as the cry of the forty million heathen who die every year in foreign lands. Forty millions will die during the ensuing year. They are passing away at the rate of one hundred thousand a day. Every tick of the watch sounds the death knell of a heathen soul. With every breath we draw four souls pass away never having heard of Christ. *Carest thou not that these perish?"*

Would not such a well chosen verse—and the Book is just packed with them—with some such brief pointed comment, be likely to have more effect in the devotional meeting than reading a whole chapter aimlessly and indifferently chosen and read?

2. Often two brief texts brought into juxtaposition may be made most helpful and impressive. This is given as a fair example: "I must be about my Father's business." (Luke 2:49). "The King's business requires haste." (I Samuel 21:8).

Such a reading would inject into the meeting some idea of a real and solemn and important business, and then would carry home the thought that there was no time to be lost about it. If we can keep the idea prominent that a missionary meeting is for business, one of the most important of all the things we will ever engage in while we are in the world; and then that it is a business of such import as to require immediate and personal and zealous care and attention, the missionary meeting will not be drag and the interest will not die.

Or another example: "Whatsoever He saith unto you, do it." (John 2:5). "See that ye refuse not Him that speaketh." (Hebrews 12:25). Now Jesus said unto us, as His most sacred and imperative command, *Go ye into all the world and preach my Gospel to all the nations.* Shall we who are here today refuse Him that speaketh these words? We, all of us can go, for Christ gave no impossible commands. We can go either in prayer, or in purse or in person.

3. Another method of Scripture reading in the missionary meeting is to use a text and then relate a missionary story connected with that text. There are several small volumes that give stories from the life and deeds of missionaries as they were especially related to certain texts of Scripture. Some of thes are: "Modern Heroes of the Mission Field;" "Modern Apostles of Missionary Byways;" New Acts of the Apostles," etc. One member could be selected to read the Scripture lesson at the meetings, say for six months or a year. Such a member could, for a few dimes, order one of these books and make the matter of leading the devotional service, particularly the Scripture reading, a matter of care, prayer and consideration.

I am fully aware that in this brief space I have only suggested a few of the ways, by no means all, in which the Bible may be made a live wire for the missionary meeting; and if this is done in any Society, a long step forward has been taken in making that Society a live and an active one for effectual missionary work.

                                                J. O. ATKINSON.

THE FOREIGN MISSIONS CONFERENCE OF NORTH AMERICA

By Warren H. Denison

The twenty-sixth annual session of this Conference will no doubt go down in history as an epoch making session. It was held at New Haven, Conn., in the beautiful Taft hotel and was presided over by Rev. Canon S. Gould, M. D., of Toronto, Canada. It is composed of the Foreign Mission Secretaries and representatives of the Foreign Mission Boards and other allied organizations doing foreign mission work.

Something over 300 representatives were present representing forty foreign mission boards, and fourteen other allied organizations such, as the American Bible Society.

The Christian Church representatives were Rev. E. K. McCord, Missionary to Japan; Miss Mary A. Rowell, Treasurer of the Woman's Board for Foreign Missions; Rev. Donald P. Hurlbert, Mission Secretary of the New England Christian Conventon, and the writer.

Among the speakers were such noted Christian statesmen as Drs. John R. Mott, Robert E. Speer, Charles R. Watson, W. I. Haven, President W. H. P. Faunce, Principal Alfred Grandier of Toronto; Miss Margaret Burton, Dr. W. E. Browning, Dr. S. M. Twemer and many other missionaries and noted workers. I have named only a few of the speakers for the meeting lasted three full days and evenings. There were 37 missionaries present. The general theme was that of the "Basis and Ideals of the New Internationalism, and the Contribution of Foreign Missions to It."

The greatness of the opportunities and the need for world-wide missions since the war have become so tremendous; the call for missionaries, funds, equipment, and literature is so imperative, that again and again we were called to our knees in prayer, and challenged to make the redoubled effort of our lives to arouse our pastors, our laymen, our churches, to hear and heed, to pray and give and go as never before. Will you, friends, of our Christian Church, listen to this feeble appeal of one who is unable in any adequate way in this short space to bring before you the view of the world as we have seen it in picture, in vivid description of scores from the fields, and of the Board Secretaries?

The great action of the Conference and which was often referred to as one of the greatest religious actions of modern times was the unanimous action approving "The Interchurch World Movement of North America." In December at a general call one hundred and thirty-five representatives of the Home and Foreign Mission Boards and allied agencies met to consider the advisability and feasability of a united campaign. A committee of twenty was named to outline a plan and submit it to the Foreign Missions Conference of North America, the Home Missions Council, the Council of Church Boards of Education, the Sunday School Council, the Federation of Woman's Boards of Foreign Missions and the Council of Women for Home Missions.

There is to be a General Committee of one hundred representing all foreign mission agencies, with state and local community organizations of all the Christian forces in interchurch committees.

It is to be a united Home and Foreign Mission campaign including all benevolent interests outside of the local church.

A survey of the home and foreign fields is to be made to find what ought to be done by the combined churches to meet the needs for at least the next five years. There is to be a strong educational and publicity campaign to carry the facts down to every Protestant church consisting of regional conferences, conventions and training conferences to appeal for the sources of spiritual power, life and money to meet the opportunities of this new era. There will be a united financial campaign probably in the spring of 1920 to secure funds to carry out this world program.

Think of what it will mean for all the foreign mission boards and agencies of North America all united under one leadership making a united campaign for a world program of missions. There was not one dissenting voice or vote, but hearty approval. All persons present were asked to make nominations of persons from whom one hundred suitable persons might be selected to form the General Committee. Let us hail the great step, let our Mission Board and Forward Movement and all our churches be heartily in this united move. Let us begin now, for it is confidently expected that every board and agency will give hearty approval.

THE POLICY BEING REALIZED

It is more and more evident that the foreign missionary policy adopted by the Mission Board more than a year ago was well considered and wise, for it is working out splendidly. At the Board meeting held in December three new missionaries were placed under appointment—Rev. and Mrs. W. Q. McKnight, to go to Porto Rico; Miss Martha R. Stacy to go to Japan.

At the present time, therefore, the Board is undertaking the following enlargement of our foreign work:

Sending a new missionary family to Porto Rico.

Sending a new woman missionary to Japan.

Building a new mission home in Tokyo, Japan.

Building a new school building for kindergarten and similar purposes in Dogenzaka, Tokyo.

Building a chapel at Kannari, Japan.

Building a chapel at Santa Isabel, Porto Rico.

Repairing our buildings damaged by earthquake in Porto Rico, and there were three of them.

Now, this is a large program for our people, as you will realize if you will follow this article patiently for a few minutes. Owing to the enormous rise in prices, it has been necessary to increase missionary salaries to a minimum of $1300. The sending of a family to Porto Rico will require, besides the salary, travel ex-

pense, some outfit allowance, house rent, some equipment to work with, travel expense on the field, and
probably a good many unforeseen items.

Sending a missionary to Japan will require expenditures similar to the above.

The land and building for the new mission home in
Tokyo will cost us not less than $10,000. If it were to
be in a small city, the story might be different; but this
is at the headquarters of our work and the capital of
the empire, where the location will be strategic and
property will continually enhance in value.

We have land, and must now erect building at Dogenzaka for the kindergarten and other activities the Gar-
mans are inaugurating. We have a good start toward
the building, which will likely cost more than $6,000,
and will be a bee-hive of Christian work.

For many years the people at Kannari, Japan, have
waited for a chapel. There is a nucleus for the building; a good sister has promised $500 soon, and when
there is $600 in hand the mission is to proceed with
the building. Two or three hundred more will be required.

Under the leadership of Miss Carrie Robison the
Young People's Department of the Woman's Boards is
raising money to build a chapel in Santa Isabel. About
half the money is already in hand, leaving a little more
than $1,500 still to be raised. The building will cost
not less than $3,000.

We are proceeding at once to repair the damage done
to our mission home and the Ponce church and Salinas
chapel by the recent earthquake. The amount of that
bill can only be conjectured now, but it is estimated
at not less than $1,500. This work must be done im-
mediately because property deteriorates so rapidly in
the tropics unless it is properly cared for.

Thus it will be seen that the Mission Board is pushing the matter of equipment and enlargement of missionary force as much as our resources will admit of.
For a number of years we have been equipping our
missions, and that was a work that made no great show
or appeal to the public; hence a good many of our
people grew restive and imagined that we were at a
standstill, or worse, were retrograding. The facts are.
we have been progressing all the time. Within a few
years the ideals of foreign missionary work have been
greatly expanded and changed in emphasis, and we
have been working as far as possible in harmony with
these changes. Both our equipment and means have
now reached the point where we can make larger ven-
tures.

One practical aspect of the work should be brought
to the attention of all our people. To make the new
program a success we must have larger missionary
revenues. The past year enables us to hope and dare
to believe that the coming year will witness hearty backing up of the Board's plans, more funds placed in the
mission treasury, and more work done for the Kingdom.

*The Christian Church is going to be a missionary
Church,* and of course you are going to help it become
such.

.   M. T. MORRILL.

Defiance, Ohio

THE CHRISTIAN AND HIS MONEY

By Rev. G. Campbell Morgan

The Christian belongs to God—spirit, soul, and body
—in all powers and possibilities.

All that the Christian has is to be used with an eye
single to the glory of God in the accomplishment of
his purposes.

These things being granted, the method of getting
will be safeguarded. No person devoted to Christ will
be able to follow any calling, or take up any business
which is harmful to himself, or to others, merely for
the sake of obtaining money. The method being thus
conditioned within the sphere of loyalty to the will of
God, the use of money will also be so conditioned. It
is at this point that so many mistakes are made. Very
much money that is properly made is improperly spent.
The purpose of spending is too often that of ministering first to the desires of the self-life, then occasionally
—and alas too often meanly—gifts are made to God.
This is wholly wrong.

Applying these principles, how should a Christian
deal with his money? Of whatever income he obtains,
he should say, "This belongs to the Master. I am to
discover by honest calculation how much I need for the
proper maintenance of my life and home, that both may
continue to glorify God. All the rest is to be devoted,
as he shall direct, for the extension of his kingdom
among men." Upon the receipt of the income the following items should be carefully and prayerfully considered:

1. Necessary for food to the glory of God.
2. Necessary for clothing to the glory of God.
3. Necessary for shelter to the glory of God.
4. Necessary for mental culture to the glory of God.
5. Necessary for recreation to the glory of God.
6. Necessary to minister to the poorer members of
my household to the glory of God.
7. All that remains for God's work.

Such a distribution of income would make a great
difference in eating and dressing, in home, in mental
culture, in recreative indulgence, in sympathetic ministry, and the church would not have to beg for assistance for its missionary enterprises from those who are
living in rebellion against the kingship of Christ. Spasmodic giving would be impossible, and the high and
glorious ideal of partnership with God would become
an every-day reality. This method, moreover, would
maintain the ideal of stewardship, and would demand
a periodic readjustment of expenditure, according to
the rise or fall of income. Here, as everywhere, no outside interference must be permitted, but there must be
a constant and unceasing submission to the direction
of the King. This will be carried out or not, according to the power which rules by love in the heart. If
the love of the Lord be dominant, the delight of devotion will be permanent. If the love of money holds
sway, the shameful meanness of giving will continue.

Don't say *collection.* Call it an *offering.* Giving of
our means to the support of the Kingdom should be too
sacred to call it a collection.

THE WAY OF A MAN WITH HIS MONEY
By Leon Wood

ONE is tempted to say, with uplifted hands, "It is too wonderful for me; I cannot understand it." For men seem to have ways with money as various and vagarious as they have with women, and nobody knows what will be the course of events whenever there is a man with money any more than whenever there is "a man with a maid." The outcome may be either poverty or riches, a happy home or a summer ·scandal.

In either case, possibly, possession for a time leads to the presumption on the man's part that he *owns* the money or the maiden, and then he proceeds to "do what he will with his own."

He himself is a personality, created to have a dominion; the money is stored personal value, and the maiden is regnant personality. Personality inheres in all three factors. Let us observe closely, for we surely may expect something to happen wherever personality is present.

In "doing as he pleases" there naturally follows profit in the form of increase. He accumulates a fortune or a family. And these are in "his own." So he says in his exultation, "See what I have gotten!" He forgets the potent power stored within the money, and he overlooks the sovereign soul of the maiden.

One day his friend says: "Come on, Jim; let's go fishing"—and Financial ·Affairs flings back, in spite of his longing for relaxation: "Can't do it, Bill; business before pleasure."

That night he tosses sleeplessly, for somehow he knows he is not "his own man." How can he "own" his money? or "manage" his business? It galls him to feel the goad—just as though he had not been called a "captain of finance," and a "master of the money market." ·

In the deepest part of his conscious soul, where he has never heretofore ventured, he knows that his money owns him. It compels him, regardless of health, home, friends and larger self-expression, to do service for *its* enlargement, not for his own development. And he has not even been aware of his shameful servitude. A sense of disappointment and defeat oppresses Him. His self-respecting spirit revolts.

Sleep finally smooths from his face the lines of a grim determination.

Next morning he feels lank and looks lean-faced. "James, we're going to the woods for a week. Can't you come along with us?" wistfully said his wife. "You need a vacation."

"I wish I could, wifey, but I guess I'll have to gather some big dollars to pay for the fun. Business won't run itself," he says grimly, finality in tone and manner.

"Yes, but you don't run the business; it runs you," she flashes back.

He is silent. The night's wrestling is on again with redoubled violence. Is he a majestic spirit, or merely the servant of .time and place and things?

Now he feels his midnight's·resolution gathering for a supreme decision, and presently he nears himself saying:
"All right; I'm yours for a week.".

Up in the woods he sleeps and reads and thinks. Often when apparently reading, he is gazing into the shifting shadows and away into the hazy distances—slowly thinking—thinking of Big Business that is eternal, ever-changing, but not quoted on 'change.

The sixth day, after a long walk through the thickets and among the trees, he and his old sweetheart sit dreamily luxuriating in every comfort of indulgent nature.

"I'll do it," he said, without preliminaries.
"Do what, Jimmy?" she inquired ·softly.
"Acknowledge Him in all my ways'!" very slowly.
"Which means—?"
"Money first. Money always has been first with me, and I guess it will have to go before me into the Kingdom. This week has made some things clear that our pastor has been saying, 'It's been a glorious week!' "

* * * *

They whispered in the market place that James Conroy Pennoyer was slipping a cog or two in his driving power—in his "efficiency." What cared he? He·had made his declaration of independence.

THE WAY TO SUCCESS

Just two men can, if they will, revolutionize the finances of any church; one a live, up-to-date pastor who believes in, practices, preaches and teaches tithing; the other a live, up-to-date layman who, in a congregation of 100 families, will be responsible for the purchase of an average of about $10.00 worth of tithing literature within.a period of six months.

Multiplying these two men in each church by an equal number in all the churches in the United States and continuing the tithing propaganda would, within two years at least, substitute affluence for mendicancy in all our missionary treasuries. Better than all, the gain would be both permanent and increasing. So much for the money side of tithing.

And Yet

If I could have the privilege of inducing 100 young people between the ages of ten and twenty, all without regular income, or.100 adults between the ages of thirty and forty, all with regular income, to adopt tithing as a rule of life, I would without a moment's hesitation select the young people.

Why? Because the primary object of tithing is distinctly not to get money; it is to build character, and youth is the time for that.

The cornerstone of all character building worthy of the name is a deeply implanted sense of responsibility to God. Teaching that responsibility in theory only may be, and very often is, evanescent. Reducing it to practice by tithing which can be done by the youngest makes it permanent. The money, while later in coming into the missionary treasuries, would be in very much larger amounts when the young people reach the age of thirty and over. But that is a secondary consideration; character comes first. ·   LAYMAN.

THE CHRISTIAN ORPHANAGE

AN ANNOUNCEMENT

Dear Friends:

This report is the final report for the year 1918 and closes our year's work. We are happy to say that we have reached each goal set for the year and have gone over the top.

The first of the year we set our goal for the Thanksgiving offering at $5,000. You made it $5,402.40.

We set for our total amount for the year at $11,000.00, you made it $14,173.12.

While we have labored under some difficulties we have been happy in the work because you stood by us so loyally and have given us your hearty co-operation. You have seen to it that we reached each goal set. And while it becomes necessary that we close our books for the year this week, it will not bar any church from taking the Thanksgiving offering and mailing it in now as we will have a place for it and would be glad to see each church make this offering.

I want to thank each pastor, each Sunday school superintendent, each teacher and each individual for the hearty co-operation you have given me during the past year. I only wish I could see you personally and tell you face to face how much I appreciate it. By your loyalty and hearty co-operation you have made the success of the work here, this year, possible. I pray that God will richly bless each one who had a part.

We are glad our Church is beginning to realize that it can do things.

I believe I promised you I would tell you a secret in this letter if you would see to it that we reached the goal of $5,000.00 for our Thanksgiving offering. You have been so good to see that I got over the top I am happy to tell you. Here it is:

The Christian Orphanage is Out of Debt.

CHAS. D. JOHNSTON, *Supt.*

FINAL REPORT FOR DECEMBER 25, 1918

Amount brought forward, $13,549.80.

Sunday School Monthly Offerings

Burton's Grove, October, November and December, $3.00; Lebanon, December and January, $4.54.

Thanksgiving Offerings

Bethlehem church, $12.80; New Center church, $15.00; Bethel, $30.35; Burton's Grove, $20.00; Pleasant Grove church, (N. C.)—additional, $1.10; Mt. Bethel church, (Additional), $2.00; New Lebanon (Additional), $2.25; Rock Stand, $7.90; Rock Spring, $5.23; Union, (Va.), $47.00; Lebanon, $101.86; Wake Chapel, $63.15; Pleasant Ridge, $10.00; Bethel Church, $3.75; Dinglers Chapel, $3.00; Reidsville, N. C., $27.80; Intermediate Class No. 5, Pleasant Hill, $7.14.

Individuals

John R. Foster, $20.00; A. L. Jolly, $10.00; A Loyal Friend, $10.00; Willis J. Lee, $10.00; J. R. Seawell, $5.00; J. O. Atkinson, $5.00; E. B. Bailey, $5.00; J. H. Overby, $5.00; Mrs. Willis J. Lee, $10.00; Mrs. Fred Holland, $1.00; Mrs. J. J. Summerbell, $5.00.

The Following Ladies $1.00 Each:

Mrs. E. W. Nevill, Mrs. Maggie Franklin, Mrs. W. C. Pierce; Blanche Pierce, Mrs. C. E. Joyner, Mrs. A. L. Jolly, Mrs. G. W. Truitt, Mrs. J. H. Massey, Asa Harrell, Mrs. Irvin Pierce, Mrs. J. W. Fulton, Mrs. J. W. Stewart, Miss Lizzie Harrell, Miss Hattie Harrell, A Friend, (one of the 79); Mrs. W. C. Whitaker, Mrs. A. B. Walker, Mrs. C. H. Buchaman, Mrs. B. W. Mitchell, Mrs. W. A. Newman, Mrs. Ida Thomas, Mrs. T. E. Green, Mrs. E. B. Bailey, Mrs. I. W. Johnson, Mrs. B. D. Crocker, Mrs. A. T. Grissom, Lillie Grissom, Miss Jennie Atkinson.

Thos. E. Green, 50c; Anna M. Green, 50c; Martin K. Green, 50c; W. S. Briggs, Henderson, N. C., $5.00; William R. Marshall, Salem Chapel church, $2.00; Primary Class, High Point S. S., $5.00; Rev. Herbert Scholz, $3.50; W. T. Foushee, Ramseur, N. C., $2.00.

From Ivor, Va.

Miss Nina Bradshaw, $1.00; Mrs. L. H. Brantley, $1.00; Mrs. B. H. Lane, $1.00; Mrs. J. E. Padgett, $1.00; H. E. Branch, $1.00; E. N. Johnson, $2.50; Mrs. E. R. Bryant, 50c; F. P. Crumpler, 50c; R. A. Hart, 50c; James Murphy, 50c; Harry Murphy, 50c; Mildred Brantley, 25c; Dorothy Brantley, 25c; Ashby Brantley, 25c; Stanley Brantley, 25c; Collection, 50c; Miss Cora Davis, 50c; Big Oak Church, N. C., $3.45; A Friend, $100.00. Total for the week, $623.32; Grand total for the year 1918, $14,173.12.

REPORT FOR JANUARY 1919

Children's Offerings

Oliver E. Young, Jr., 25c; Willie Staylor, 10c; Mills Wellons Staylor, 10c; Raymond Sharpe, 30c; Total, 75c.

Monthly Sunday School Offerings

(North Carolina and Virginia Conference)

Ingram, $3.00; New Lebanon, $1.00; New Lebanon Baraca Class, $1.00; Third Avenue, Danville, Va., $3.17.

(Eastern North Carolina Conference)

Catawba Springs, $3.15; Mt. Auburn, $15.30; Chapel. Hill, $3.75.

(Western North Carolina Conference)

Ramseur, $1.65; Baraca Class, $1.65.

(Eastern Virginia Conference)

Berea (Nansemond), $10.00; Franklin, Va., $5.00; Union (Southampton), $1.75; Suffolk, $25.00; Washington St., Portsmouth, $8.00; Old Zion, $2.00.

(Virginia Valley Conference)

Linville, $1.00; Dry Run, $3.50; Wood's Chapel, $3.00.

(Alabama Conference)

Beulah, 70c.

First Christian Church, Huntington, Ind., $15.10; M. G. Woodell for S. S., $2.50; Total $106.22.

New Year Special Offerings

Mrs. J. E. Franks, $2.00; Miss Bettie Franks, $2.00; Miss Noma Franks, $2.00; Numia Franks, $1.00; Total, $7.00. Total for the month of January, $113.97.

LETTERS

Dear Uncle Charley:—When I put on short dresses, I was promoted to Corporal and was known to my little friends as "Corporal Jr." I expect to be made Sergeant soon, for I have two little teeth almost through. My cousins, Ralph and Leon Newman, would be truly jealous if they could see Grandpa Newman teaching me to dance when his graphophone plays "Dance-a-Baby-Diddy."—*Oliver E. Young, Jr.*

Your father will feel very proud of his soldier boy when he returns home:—"*Uncle Charley.*"

Dear Uncle Charley:—I, am writing you the first letter in this year. I hope the little cousins will have a good time this year. I like your picture very well and would like you better. Enclosed find 10 cents for January.—*Mills Wellons Staylor.*

You sent in the second letter this year. Oliver E. Young got ahead just a little. I hope you will write often this year.—"*Uncle Charley.*"

Dear Uncle Charley:—We have had a wet time with snow. Sunday the snow fell fast and everything was covered with snow several inches thick. I have snowballed some since the snow fell. I hope the little children are having a good time. Enclosed find 10 cents. —*Willie Staylor.*

I can beat you snow-balling. You will have to come to see me when it snows.—"*Uncle Charley.*"

Dear Uncle Charley:—I am sending my dues for December, January and February. Santa Claus came to see me Christmas and I hope he went to see all the Orphanage, too.—*Raymond Sharpe.*

Yes, "Old Santa" came and made all the little children happy.—"*Uncle Charley.*"

CHRISTIAN EDUCATION

REPORT OF COMMITTEE ON EDUCATION

(Virginia Valley Conference)

There is danger in the excitement and busy activities of the war, of us neglecting to "keep the home fires burning," and thus losing at home as much or more than we have gained abroad.

The school and college is having a struggle for existence. Many have been forced to close their doors. We are glad to note that our own Elon College has been able to maintain its maximum enrollment of, 400 during the past year.

The young people of this generation wil need an education to meet the demands of the times. Elon College offers all the advantages of the regular denominational college. It maintains a high standard of Christian ideals, and is well worthy the support of our people.

We recommend that Rev. W. C. Hook be ordained at this session of Conference.

We recommend that Brother J. B. Shiflet be admitted to the Biblical class, and enter Elon College this fall as a ministerial student.

W. T. WALTERS,
A. W. ANDES,
B. J. EARP,
- *Committee.*

REPORT ON EDUCATION

(Alabama Conference)

The educational sentiment of the Church of today is that real, true education does not consist in colleges and universities. No life can be deep and full that is not religious. Hence the paramount idea, not to depend upon our God-given principles to make of us a mighty people, but with those Heaven-born principles we must have for their propagation a well-trained and fully equipped leadership to make them effectively known to the world. If our Conference would desire for herself a larger place in the great work of the future, she must look well to the education of her leaders. There is to be a general revolution of the educational system of our land. The state institutions have failed in the past to provide further than for the mental and physical development. The church can better care for the spiritual with the educational of the mind and body. While the heart is far more important than the head, yet the one cannot work so successfully without the best possible training of the other. Then our own Conferences of the South need a school. We need to come face to face with the issue, and provide for the education of the finest and best asset of the Church—its young people.

We offer the following recommendations:

That, we endorse the Truitt School for patronage until we can locate permanently.

That, in compliance with the request of the Southern Christian Convention, we observe the third Sunday in February or the nearest day to that on which regular service is to be held as "Life Work Recruit Day," in the interest of Christian Education. No collection.

That, no one shall be ordained to the full work of the Gospel ministry until he shall have completed the seventh grade work of the public school. And then he shall take the prescribed Theological Reading Course as adopted at the Dinglers Chapel session of this Conference, 1916. If there be a reasonable chance for a collegiate education, the ordination shall be deferred until such a course shall have been completed.

That, we assess $25.00 for Ministerial Education next year, and $100.00 for Elon College.

That, the license of C. D. Dunlap, which was granted him, March the thirtieth of this year, be discontinued, and that he surrender them to the Committee. Also that of J. M. Clifton.

That, the license of A. H. Sheppard, S. R. Waldrop and J. C. Knight be continued for another year.

That, E. T. Strickland be licensed as a probationor to. preach the Gospel.

That, of the funds now in the hands of the Treasurer, we buy one hundred dollars worth of War Savings Stamps.

E. M. CARTER, *Chairman.*

The world is talking reconstruction, and there is something to it. It cannot be denied. Let us hope that there will be a reconstruction in giving. We have played the hapzard methods long enough. Let us get down to business and the Bible and give as we are taught.

THE FORWARD MOVEMENT

"LORD, TEACH US TO PRAY"

You say you are busy this morning,
In the maelstrom of family cares,
And husband must rush to the office,
So there isn't a moment for .prayers.

Then children are sent to the school-room,
And the grind of the day thus begins,
With no word from God's Book to remember,
Nor the echo of strengthening hymns.

What wonder the burdens are heavy,
And the hours seem irksomely long;
What wonder that rash words are spoken,
And that life seems discordant and wrong.

Pause for a little each morning,
And again at the close of the day,
To talk with the Master who loves you—
Remember, He taught us to pray. .
　　　　　—*Christian Workers' Magazine.*

MAKING THE HOUSE OF GOD ATTRACTIVE

Rev. M. J. Honsberger, Newton, N. H., has done a splendid piece of work in making the buildings and grounds of his church attractive. In this brief way he describes it for our readers. Do not think that Brother Honsberger is not alive to the work of the church, too. While the church, it is right out in the country and has only about eighty members, it has full time preaching, a Sunday school, Christian Endeavor, Junior Endeavor, Ladies' Aid Society, Missionary Society, and contributes to all the calls of the church. So while he is beautifying landscape he is also beautifying souls. He speaks not of his work in the church but this is just to show what can be done in the country to make the church house and grounds attractive. How about the lawns, paint, window panes, doors, equipment of your church? Read what he says:

Making the Church Grounds Inviting

It is our aim to make the grounds around the church buildings ideal and inviting. This idea may be called an innovation in decorating; for it is usually all done with in the buildings and the grounds left uncared for and in an uninviting condition. We worked on the theory that the exterior of the church property should have a voice so that it might speak through trees, shrubs, vines, flowers, bird life and song, every day to those who passed along the highway of commerce burdened with the responsibilities of life.

To begin with the buildings were well located, on rising ground, with ample room on the front for lawns. They were also well separated, so this gave us a splendid opportunity for carrying out what we had been thinking of for years. On our arrival here eleven years ago we at once began to make our ream a living reality. Walks were laid and built, loose stones were removed,

the grounds fertilized, the lawn mower freely used, trees, shrubs, vines, and flowering plants set out. These were procured in the valleys and mountains of New Hampshire, Vermont, Maine, and Massachusetts. Now after eleven years of hard work a beautiful green lawn, with flowering shrubs, vines, perennial plants, and bulbs are blooming from early spring till late fall to greet the eye and gladden the heart, and the old gravel bank is a thing of the past. Bird houses were built and placed here and there on the buildings, telegraph poles and trees, and they were soon occupied by the feathered songsters and they assist the minister in proclaiming the gospel of hope and gladness. More than fifty blue-birds alone were brought up on the grounds last year and we suppose that somewhere in the South-land they are helping ministers this winter with their Newton song. A splendid lawn tennis court was built back of the parsonage and vestry with a twelve foot wire fence around it and the soil was used for grading purposes on the front lawns and has greatly beautified the property The tennis court gives the young people of the parish an opportunity for recreation midst beautiful surroundings, and it also helps to keep the pastor young. It is hoped that these material things will lead both old and young to see what Jesus saw in birds and flowers, and help them to surrender themselves to the service of the Master, and to mankind.

THINK IT OVER

When things look blue,
　As they sometimes do;
When you hit Fate's line and you can't break through;
When the dark is deep
　Where the shadows creep,
And ghosts of trouble break up your sleep—

How would you like to trade your hand,
　Facing the German host,
With the fellow Out There in No Man's Land,
　Hooked to the Listening Post?
How would you like to trade your job,
　Swapping it wrench for wrench,
With the fellow feeling the big gun's throb
　Out in the first line trench?

When things get tough,
　Where the break is rough,
And you slip and skid as they call your bluff;
When you're out of gear
　Where the world looks drear
And you curse your luck with a sigh or tear—

How would you like to make a trade,
　Swapping your troubles dire,
With the fellow storming a barricade,
　Raked with machine gun's fire?
How would you like to trade your turn,
　Making an even swap,
With the fellow watching the rockets burn
　At the last call—"Over the Top"?

　　　　　—*Grantland Rice.*

Sunday School and Christian Endeavor

HELP REFERENCES

Sunday School—Officers and Teachers Journal and Christian Bible Class Quarterly by Christian Association, Dayton, Ohio; also Tarbell's Guide or Peloubet's Select Notes from any book dealer.

For Christian Endeavor—The Christian Endeavor World, Boston, Mass., and the Dixie Endeavorer, Chattanooga, Tenn.

SUNDAY SCHOOL TOPIC FOR SUNDAY, FEBRUARY 2

The Giving of The Manna

Scripture Text for study, Exodus 16:1-36.

Golden Text: Give us this day our daily bread. Matt. 6:11.

Time: About May 1 B. C. 1491.

Place: Elim, the wilderness of Sin, east of the Gulf of Suez.

CHRISTIAN ENDEAVOR TOPIC FOR SUNDAY, FEBRUARY 2

The Best Things in Christian Endeavor. Titus 2:11-14; 3:8. (Christian Endeavor Day).

AS MUCH FOR OTHERS AS FOR SELF

One of our Sunday schools sent me through its Treasurer last week $2.83 for "Missions," saying: "This was our Sunday school collection last Sunday." This school has decided to take me at my word and put the matter to the test. I stated in print, also in public speech that if any of our Sunday schools would give one Sunday a month collection to the Orphanage, and one Sunday a month collection to Missions, and then did not as easily raise enough money on the other Sundays to pay its own literature and pay its own current expenses as it did before, I would personally at the end of the year pay the deficit. I wish other schools would put my word and this matter to the test. I believe that both in our church work and in our Sunday school work we should do as much for others for ourselves. When we simply raise enough money in Sunday school to pay our own literature we haven't really given anything. We have put our mites together to buy something for ourselves cheaper than we could have bought it had we paid for it separately.

It seems to me to be the finest and best sort of program for any Sunday school to adopt—as much for others as for ourselves. Let the collection, First Sunday of the month say, go to the Orphanage. Let the collection second Sunday of the month, go to Missions. Then let the other two Sunday collections go toward purchasing the Sunday school supplies. That puts the school in the right attitude toward others and towards God in the matter of entering into His program and coming to be co-workers together with Him. I believe any school trying this will find current expenses paid more easily with two Sundays per month collection than with four Sunday per month. Let other schools try—and then see what happens.

J. O. ATKINSON.

MARRIAGES

CRAVEN-YORK

A quite, but very pretty marriage took place in the pastor's study of the First Christian church, Greensboro, Saturday, January 18, at 8:00 P. M., when Miss Golda Craven, became the bride of Mr. Claude W. York of this city. The marriage took place in the company of a few invited friends of the marriage parties. Mrs. York is a very popular young lady of this city. Mrs. York is a member of the First Christian church and has many friends here. The many friends of both bride and groom will be glad to learn that they are to make their home at 1260 Gregory Street. Congratulation and best wishes to them.

J. VINCENT KNIGHT.

OBITUARIES

WALTON

Nannie Willie Walton was born March 24, 1892 an died December 8, 1918, at her home near Ingram, Va. Although she came of Presbyterian parentage, she joined the Ingram Christian Church in her childhood and remained until her death one of its most loyal members. On November 22, 1911 she was married to Robert Henry Walton. To this union a daughter, Hattie, who is now a most charming little girl about five years old, was born. For several years Mrs. Walton served on many of the committees of her church and engaged actively in all of its enterprises. Naturally she had a charming personality and with her Christian graces succeeded in almost everything she undertook. She is survived by her husband, her daughter, three sister, Mrs. Fitzgerald Bass, Mrs. J. M. Rawlings, and Mrs. Geo. W. Penton; two brothers, P. W., and J. D. Olds, and her mother, Mrs. PhH Olds. She was laid to rest by her pastor and sorrowing friends, assisted by Dr. T. S. Wilson, pastor of Oak Level Presbyterian church; and Rev. R. W. Grant, pastor of Mt. Zion Baptist church. May the Master's love abide with the bereaved.

JOHN G. TRUITT.

RESOLUTION OF RESPECT—WALTON

Whereas, it has pleased the Almighty God to remove from our midst, by death, our esteemed friend and co-worker, Mrs. R. H. Walton, who has been a faithful worker in the Ladies' Missionary Society since its organization; Therefore be it Resolved:

First, That we bow in humble submission to our Father's will, knowing that He doeth all things well and that our loss is Heaven's gain.

Second, That we try to follow her example by always giving our best service to this work which she loved.

Third, That we offer her bereaved family and mourning friends, over whom sorrow has hung her sable mantle, our heartfelt sympathy and pray that infinite goodness may bring speedy relief to their burdened hearts and inspire them with the consolation that hope in futurity and faith in God given even in the shadow of the tomb.

Fourth, That a copy of these resolutions be sent to the bereaved family, a copy to The Christian Sun for publication and a copy spread on the minutes of the Ladies' Missionary Society of Ingram Christian church.

MRS. C. V. DUNN,
MRS. W. W. HAWKINS,
MRS. I. W. BOYD,
MISS PATTIE ADAMS,
Committee.

RESOLUTIONS OF RESPECT—ODOM

Whereas, we have been informed that W. Frank Odom, a young man of sterling quality and earnest Christian character, was wounded during the closing days of the cruel world war on the battlefields of France, and died from these wounds in a hospital, December 14, 1918, and,

Whereas Brother Odom was a faithful and consistent member of Berea, Nansemond, Christian church, therefore be it Resolved:

1. That we express our gratitude for his splendid Christian life, and for his willingness to volunteer his service and offer himself a living sacrifice for the cause of freedom and human liberty; and commend his example to other young men.

2. That Berea church has lost, by his death, a young man who was highly esteemed, and whose life was full of promise for great things in character and in service.

3. That we bow in submission, in this sad bereavement, and pray for the comfort of the Holy Spirit to abide with the bereaved family in this trying hour; and extend to them our heartfelt sympathy.

4. That a copy of these resolutions be entered upon our church record, a copy sent to the family, and a copy sent to The Christian Sun for publication.

Done by order of Berea church, this eleventh day of January, 1919, in regular quarterly conference.

E. W. SMITH,
S. C. BOND,
PAUL S. BLANDFORD,
Committee.

RESOLUTIONS OF RESPECT—JONES

Whereas, it hath pleased our Heavenly Father to remove from our midst our beloved sister, Mrs. Mary L. Jones, wife of Deacon Thomas A. Jones of Norfolk, Va., and,

Whereas, by her death Berea, Nansemond, Christian church has sustained the loss of a true, loyal, faithful and consecrated Christian worker who was always willing to be of service in the kingdom, therefore be it Resolved:

1. That we bow in humble submission to the will of Him who doeth all things well; rejoicing that our sister was abiding in Him and awaiting His coming with a confident hope of eternal life.

2. That we record our gratitude for her loyalty to the church, and her faithful service in the kingdom of God.

3. That we extend our heartfelt sympathy to the bereaved family, in their sad bereavement, and commend to them the Word of God and the presence of the Holy Spirit for comfort and consolation.

4. That a copy of these resolutions be entered upon our church record, a copy sent to the family, and a copy sent to The Christian Sun for publication.

done this the eleventh day of January, 1919, by order of Berea church, in regular quarterly conference.

MRS. E. W. SMITH,
MRS. A. S. HARGROVES,
MRS. J. W. BRINKLEY,
Committee.

RESOLUTIONS OF RESPECT—CLENDENNIN

Whereas, God in His infinite wisdom, has seen fit to call from our midst our dear friend and co-worker, Mrs. J. N. H. Clendennin, we, the Ladies' Aid and Missionary Societies of the Graham Christian church, desire to express our love and esteem in the following resolutions:

1. We profoundly feel the loss of our oldest member, who always contributed willingly and liberally of her means to help in all good causes, and who was always truly loyal and true to her church and her Societies.

2. That the removal of such a useful life from our midst will leave a vacancy that cannot be filled; but we, realizing that our loss is but her eternal reward and gain, we bow in humble submission of His Divine will.

3. Though gone from us, she will not be forgotten and her life will go on among us to eternity through the encouragement to us and the influence upon our lives of such a noble life as hers.

4. That a copy of these resolutions be published in The Christian Sun and be spread upon the minutes of our Society.

MRS. J. D. KERNODLE,
Secretary.

JONES

Mrs. Mamie Savage Jones, beloved wife of T. A. Jones, Norfolk, Va., was born near the present village of Driver, Nansemond County, Virginia, October 9, 1855, and departed this life January 1, 1919, after a brief illness. She leaves to mourn their loss a devoted husband, three sons, A. Lynton, Norfolk, Va.; Ralph, an officer in the United States Navy; Carlton, a captain in the regular army now in France, and Louise, wife of Lieutenant-Colonel Williams, U. S. A., also in France.

Deceased was the daughter of the late lamented Col. A. Savage, a distinguished soldier of the Confederacy, and wife Sarah Lee; sister of the late lamented Capt. P. H. Lee, Nansemond County, Virginia. She came of courageous and heroic stock and in her career of more than sixty-three years not only lived up to the splendid family traditions but reflected honor upon the name she bore.

In early girlhood days she joined the Christian church and to her dying day was loyal, faithful and true not only to her church, but to all its interests, enterprises and undertakings for good. She was a charter member of Memorial Temple, Norfolk, though in her last years held her membership in the church of her girlhood days, Berea, Driver, Va. In her going away one of the most amiable and generous Christian characters I have ever known has been transplanted from earth to heaven. Her friends and loved ones are numbered by the hundreds. She simply lived, labored, loved and thought in terms of others. Her home was a joy to all who went to share its charming hospitality, and her presence in any circle was a blessing and a benediction. The spirit of the Master, that unselfish, and sublime spirit of love to God and deep concern for the welfare of others, was manifest in all her conduct and attitude. I recall that the writer of Acts said of Dorcas: ''This woman was full of good works and alms—deeds which she did.'' And these words are as true of Mrs. T. A. Jones as they are of the Bible character.

She has forever inshrined her noble life in the hearts not only of her broken hearted husband and bereaved daughter and sons, but in the hearts of hundreds of others who loved her for the true and beautiful life she lived, and for the triumphant death she died. Her benevolences and charity led in many directions. The Christian Orphanage had no more interested or devoted helper; The Christian Sun no more loyal and enthusiastic reader, and supporter; and Elon College no worthier or warmer friend and advocate. In fact every worthy and Christian enterprise and movement had her sympathy, interest, support and prayers. She believed heartily in missions and was a liberal contributor to the Christly work of sending the Gospel to those who had it not. Her city, her church, and the various charitable and benevolent enterprises which she loved and liberally supported are the richer for her years of sympathetic interest and devotion, and are the poorer for her going.

God comfort the sorely bereaved ones who mourn her going. but will forever cherish her sweet, sacred and hallowed memory. Her wearied body has fallen on sleep, but her splendid and beautiful life gives her loved ones and friends the blessed assurance that God now rests her noble soul.

J. O. ATKINSON.

BOLAND

James A. Boland of Burlington, N. C., was born March 18, 1852 and died January 9, 1919 from influenza followed by pneumonia. He was first a member of Union Christian church, but after moving to Burlington he transferred his membership to the Burlington Christian church. He leaves to mourn their loss a devoted companion, one son, one brother and two sisters. The funeral services was conducted from the house and interment made in the city cemetery.

J. W. HARRELL.

SAUNDERS

Mrs. Josephine Saunders died at the home of her daughter, Mrs. J. H. Freeland, Burlington, N. C., January 1, 1919 aged 76 years, 8 months and 25 days. The end came suddenly as the result of a stroke of paralysis. She was a member of the Christian church, but on account of afflictions she was denied the privilege of attending the service during her last few years. She leaves to mourn their loss an only daughter, three grandchildren and one grand child. The funeral service was conducted from the home and the body was shipped to Goldsboro, N. C., for interment.

J. W. HARRELL.

BLALOCK

Mrs. Dora Booker Blalock, wife of J. M. Blalock, McCullers, N. C., R. F. D., died Monday, January 20, 1919, from pneumonia following Spanish Influenza. She was fifty-seven years old. A husband and eight children—three sons and five daughters—survive her. The deceased was a faithful member of Plymouth Christian church and lived a consistent Christian life. A few minutes before her spirit took its departure, she told some one that she was hovering between life and death; but she did not know why she clung to life, for she was going to a "far sweeter place." Her remains were buried in the Blalock family bury-

ing ground, Tuesday. The funeral conducted at the grave by the writer, her pastor.

R. P. CRUMPLER.

WARD

John L. Ward, the four-months-old son of Sister Poly Ward of Haw River Christian church, died January 16, 1919 and was laid to rest in the Haw River cemetery the day following. Services were held in the home by the writer. Comfort be to those who mourn.

F. C. LESTER.

HERITAGE

Between eleven and twelve o'clock on the night of January 18, 1919, Rufus B. Heritage, the youngest son of Brother A. R. Heritage, Graham, North Carolina, was instantly killed in an auto wreck in Burlington. He and a friend were going into Burlington at a very rapid rate when the car struck a post. The other fellow narrowly escaped death. Brother Heritage was only a little over twenty-three years old. Burial services were held by the writer in the home where a large number of friends had gathered to "weep with those who weep." The body was laid in New Providence cemetery by the side of his only brother, who died last fall with influenza. A father, mother, five sisters, and a number of friends remain to weep. May the Comforter be very real to those who feel most keenly their loss.

F. C. LESTER.

A WORD TO TEACHERS

Why not have some special help on your Sunday school work? Send $1.35 to THE CHRISTIAN SUN office and get a copy of Peloubet's Select Notes.

CANCER TREATED SUCCESSFULLY AT THE KELLAM HOSPITAL

The record of the Kellam Hospital is without parallel in history, having restored, without the use of the knife, Acids, X-Ray or Radium, over ninety per cent of the many hundreds of sufferers from cancers which it has treated during the past twenty-two years. We want every man and woman in the United States to know what we are doing.—KELLAM HOSPITAL, 1617 W. Main St., Richmond, Va.

THE CHRISTIAN SUN

"IN ESSENTIALS UNITY, IN NON-ESSENTIALS LIBERTY, IN ALL THINGS CHARITY"

Bearing The Cross

BEARING the Cross, we believe, is an idea that has been misrepresented. Somewhere we have seen a picture of a man bearing the Cross. He was burdened and the road on which he was traveling was rugged. Indeed it was a *cross*, and not very inviting to the sinner if that be the kind of work that bearing the Cross of Christ meant. Bearing the Cross is not a burden to the Christian. *Bearing* does not necessarily mean heaviness. "My yoke is easy and my burden is light," says the Master. Then let us teach and preach that doctrine.

Volume LXXI   WEDNESDAY, FEBRUARY 5, 1919   Number 6

BURLINGTON   ·   ·   ·   NORTH CAROLINA

THE CHRISTIAN SUN

Founded 1844 by Rev. Daniel W. Kerr

C. B. RIDDLE - - - Editor

Entered at the Burlington, N. C. Post Office as second class matter.

Subscription Rates

One year .... $ 2.00
Six months 1.00

In Advance

Give both your old and new postoffice when asking that your address be changed.

The change of your label is your receipt for money. Written receipts sent upon request.

Marriage and obituary notices not exceeding 150 words printed free if received within 60 days from date of event, all over this at the rate of one-half cent a word.

Original poetry not accepted for publication.

Principles of the Christian Church

(1) The Lord Jesus Christ is the only Head of the Church.
(2) Christian is a sufficient name of the Church.
(3) The Holy Bible is a sufficient rule of faith and practice.
(4) Christian character is a sufficient test of fellowship, and of church membership.
(5) The right of private judgment and the liberty of conscience is a right and a privilege that should be accorded to, and exercised by all.

EDITORIAL

OUR ORPHANAGE AND ITS ACHIEVEMENT

The announcement in last week's CHRISTIAN SUN that the Christian Orphanage is out of debt has no doubt brought joy to the entire Church. It is the fortune or misfortune of all such institutions to be in debt at times. But in any way that the matter is reviewed such is usually the case. For such an institution to be in debt certainly welds itself to the hearts of the people. The people have an interest in things which they have *interest* in.

The pennies, dimes, and dollars that the people have contributed to help feed the children of the Orphanage and meet the institution's indebtedness have been the means that united the people and the institution. "Where your treasure is there will your heart be also."

In this week's issue Brother Johnston explains far better than we can why there should be no slacking in the giving to the Orphanage. Read his message on another page. The institution has not been able to go forward because of its financial handicaps. Let us now give the Orphanage an opportunity to meet the demands upon it and go forward.

THE CHRISTIAN SUN CAMPAIGN

As stated in last week's issue February and March are to be months of special effort and interest for THE CHRISTIAN SUN. We asked some one to name the goal. Brother W. D. Harward does that. He places the number at 500—a very conservative figure. That is less than ten subscriptions for each pastor in the Convention. You have about the right idea, Brother Harward, and we hope that all the brethren will bear you out in the goal and decision.

Last week we mailed to pastors a letter, and enclosed therein a stamped envelope for reply, and asked each one to say how many new subscribers that he would endeavor to get. Brother L. I. Cox is the first to reply. He says: "I believe THE SUN worthy of the best effort on the part of each pastor. It is truly his helper. I pledge my best efforts and hope to secure at *least* ten new subscribers." This is not only the first, but the only reply that we have received at this writing (Monday morning). Of course all will reply and rally to the cause.

We have been talking and adopting about THE CHRISTIAN SUN. We have said that it ought to be in the homes of the entire Church, but saying that it ought to be there, just voting on some conference report, will never put it there. It will take a little going *out* and going *in;* it will take a little personal work, a little effort and energy. May we not do this thing *now!* Truly the pastor's work is lighter and better when the Church paper goes into the homes of his membership. His calls do not fall upon deaf ears because his members have read and informed themselves. All together! All together now!

"HOW TO KEEP A MISSIONARY SOCIETY ALIVE AND ACTIVE"

We publish this week the second of a series of articles by Field Secretary Atkinson on "How to Keep a Missionary Society Alive and Active." These articles, we sincerely trust, will be read by every subscriber of THE CHRISTIAN SUN. The go to the heart of the matter, as we see it; and if followed, will bring a new day for the missionary interests of the local churches.

We are glad that Dr. Atkinson added "and active" as a part of his topic, for some missionary societies may be alive and not active. So far as the Kingdom's good is concerned, there is little to be gained if a society is alive and not active. This is not only a day of real living, but a day of action. We plead and pray that these articles will have a wide reading. And suppose that you are not a member of some missionary society, why not read them anyway? Try one and see how you like it.

CHRISTIAN EDUCATIONAL DAY

As a reminder to pastors and people, the third Sunday in February was designated by the recent session of the Convention to "Christian Education Day" or "Life Work Recruit Day." Full information of this can be found by turning to page 12 of the *Christian Annual.* We make this note as a reminder and will write on the subject next week.

SISTERS, BUT LIVED APART

The other day we were talking to a Methodist Protestant minister about the similarity between the Christian Church and the Methodist Protestant Church. In the course of our conversation we remarked to him that the two Churches reminded us of two sisters who, from birth, had lived in different households. The two children of the Methodist Episcopal Church, the Christian Church being the older of the two children. The Christian Church was founded and formed in 1792 and the Methodist Protestant Church had its beginning in 1824.

We have hoped for years that these two bodies might unite. As we see it the union would be a most fitting one. These Churches occupy different territory, with a few exceptions. And where both denominations do exist the equipment, if united, would not lapse. We believe that the Kingdom's work would prosper more effectively by the union of the Churches.

Methodist Protestant Herald, please print.

INTERESTED IN MISSIONS

Our people are undoubtedly getting interested in *missions*. We give this week more than the usual space to that subject. Last week this topic took two and one-half pages of THE SUN, and yet all the material in this week's paper was carried over from last week. We are today (January 31) preparing "copy" for our issue of February 12 and have on hand four articles on the subject of *missions*. And this is nearly two weeks before that issue will reach the public. We rejoice because of the awakening and trust that we shall always have plenty of material on the subject.

INFLUENZA ON THE DECREASE

That influenza is on the decrease in the State, despite the fact that outbreaks continue to occur in different localities, is seen from a recent report of the Vital Statistics Department of the State Board of Health. According to this report, there were 3,923 deaths less in November than in October and 533 deaths less in December than in November. In other words, the number of deaths decrease from 6,055 in October to 2,133 in November, and to about 1,600 in December. This steady decline is thought to be due partly to the fact that people are becoming more informed as to the ways and means by which the disease is spread, and are perhaps more careful in their practices of personal hygiene which, after all, is a great factor in preventing the disease.

A SERMON BY A FARMER

A writer—"E. J. K."—in the *Kansas Industrialist*, preaches a splendid sermon in twelve small paragraphs. The article is worthy of place on this page and we gladly reprint it:

A Farmer's Creed

1. I believe in red clover, in white clover, in sweet clover, in cowpeas, in soybeans, and above all, I believe in alfalfa, the queen of forage plants.

2. I believe in a permanent agriculture, in a soil that grows richer rather than poorer from year to year.

3. I believe in 60 bushel corn and 40 bushel wheat and shall not be satisfied with less.

4. I believe that the only good weed is a dead weed,

and that a clean farm is as important as a clean conscience.

5. I believe in the farm boy and the farm girl, the farmer's best crop and the future's best hope.

6. I believe in the farm woman, and will do all in my power to make her life easier and happier.

7. I believe in the country school that prepares for county life, and in a country church that teaches its people to love deeply and live honorably.

8. I believe in community spirit, a pride in the home and neighbors, and I will do my part to make my own community the best in the state to live in.

9. I believe in better roads, and I will use the road drag whenever the roads are ready for it.

10. I believe in happiness. I believe in the power of a smile, and will use mine on every possible occasion.

11. I believe in the farmer. I believe in the farm life. I believe in the inspiration of the open country.

12. I am proud to be a farmer, I am proud to be a farm bureau, and I will try earnestly to uphold the worthy name.

HEALTH SUNDAY SET FOR FEBRUARY 23

Letter From Surgeon General Blue to The Churches

The observance of Health Sunday in the churches has been again postponed on account of Sunday, February 9th, being selected as Roosevelt Memorial Day. The Bureau of the Public Health Service is now asking the churches to set aside Sunday, February 23, for a presentation of the campaign which has been begun by the Federal authorities against venereal disease.

In this the Government again appeals directly to the churches as such, in the following message from the Surgeon General:

"The Government of the United States is asking the churches of the country to take an active part in meeting a great national emergency.

"The War made it necessary for the nation to face frankly and courageously the menace of venereal diseases. Now the war is over and the period of demobilization has begun. Drastic measures must be taken to prevent during this period those conditions in civilian life which made these diseases the greatest cause of disability in the Army.

"In the Army and Navy a program of law enforcement, medical measures, education, and provision for wholesome recreation, was adopted. This program brought results. The venereal rate was lowered below that of any army of any nation in the history of the modern world.

"Now that the war is over, the cities and towns through which the soldiers and sailors will go and to which they will return upon demobilization must be made as safe as the camps from which they came. The fight against this menace to our national vitality and to our homes must be vigorously continued.

"It is the social responsibility of the communities, of which the churches of every denomination are a part, to continue the work carried on in time of war in order that the world may be made safe not only for democracy, but for posterity.

"It is suggested that the above communication be read from the various pulpits on Health Sunday, February 23, 1919.

"RUPERT BLUE,
"Surgeon General, U. S. Public Health Service."

Literature concerning the observance of the day has been sent to all of the clergymen of the country with a return card to the Public Health Service for ordering all literature under six appropriate groupings, viz.: pamphlets for young men, for the general public, for boys, for parents of children, for girls and young women and for educators. The ordering and circulating of this informational literature is one of the vital features of the day and should be carefully attended to in each congregation.

RANDOM PARAGRAPHS

"What is the price of THE CHRISTIAN SUN," said a man the other day as we met in a store door way. "I am a Methodist Protestant," he continued, "but the Christian Church seems near to me." And said I to him, "I feel close akin to the Methodist Protestant Church.

* *

Put in a word for the Church paper even if you do not get immediate results, for the fruits of such were clear to me the other day when a man flagged me down on the street with a two dollar bill and subscribed for THE SUN.. It had been two years since I talked with him about it.

* *

Democracy has before it the reducing of the percentage of illiterates in the United States. If democracy is for the individual he should be trained so as to be a citizen who will reflect the spirit of democracy.

* *

There are a great many fellows big as a bushel who do a lot of pint-cup thinking.

* *

I have been reading about a book, "The Living Pulpit." I wonder why the author desired to call it a "living pulpit?" He must have had in mind that some pulpits are dead.

* *

I see in my exchanges that some fellow is always hammering on some editor about something.. I frequently have this experience, but never lose sleep over it. I do my best and know that I do, and so take a good laugh and say: "If they were in my place, and I in theirs, I wonder which place would be placed and which place would be replaced."

* *

North Carolina pays eight cents per capita for university education, Virginia four cents, Georgia seven cents, and Alabama two cents. No wonder we have so many illiterates in the South.

* *

The brightest face that I have seen today was a man whose church—a country church—was considering the matter of having preaching every Sunday.

C. B. R.

NOTES

How do you pronounce Bolsheviki? Here it is; Bol-she-ve-ke. Look for an editorial on the subject next week if space permits.

Rev. D. F. Parsons has returned to Vanderbilt University to resume his studies. For a year or more he has been engaged in Y. M. C. A. work.

President Harper is to be in Dover, Delaware, at the People's Christian church on the fourth Sunday in February and the first Sunday in March.

The Burlington church has invited the first session of the North Carolina Conference to meet with it next November. It is understood that the invitation will be accepted.

Brother G. R. Maynard, Watson, N. C., called at THE SUN office last Saturday and contributed $2.00 to the Worthy Aid Fund to be used in sending the paper to worthy people.

Rev. L. I. Cox, Elon College, in sending four renewals for THE SUN says: "My work is starting off nicely this Conference year and I am happy in my new field of labor."

Brother A. A. Lynch, Mebane, N. C., a dear and devoted friend to THE CHRISTIAN SUN, came in last week to leave his "best wishes." We are always glad to have our friends call.

Brother F. C. Lester, pastor of the Graham and Haw River churches, was a caller at THE SUN office last week. He says that he is going to back up the campaign for new subscriptions for THE SUN.

We are informed that Rev. C. E. Gerringer, Jonesville, Virginia, anticipates taking regular church work when his school closes in May. Churches needing a pastor at that time have the opportunity of his services.

Beginning next week we will write editorially on the "Peace Conference." So far we have said little because we had to have time to make a study of it from a source more reliable than the secular press.

The Sunday school and Christian Endeavor matter did not reach us this week. We do not know why. We trust that the Board of Religious Education of the Convention will see that we have something for SUN readers each week.

Rev. W. B. Fuller, Y. M. C. A. Secretary, Camp Forrest, Ga., expects to return to regular ministerial work at an early date. He has not decided upon his field, and churches without a pastor can get in touch with Brother Fuller at the above given address.

The North Carolina Christian Conference was duly chartered January 27. The first meetng of the officers of the new Conference wll be held on February 6, and soon thereafter history and minutes of new body will be issued giving in full the plans and work to date.

Rev. W. D. Harward, Dendron, Va., writes: "I think that at least five hundred new subscriptions should be secured during the time of THE SUN campaign. You may count on me to bring this matter to the attention of my people." Thank you, Brother Harward, thank you.

We are indebted to Brother J. A. Fogleman, Liberty, Route 3, for a nice sack of flour. We are not so fortunate as Brother Williamson and wife and Brother Harward who tell of poundings in this week's paper but we are just as grateful for remembrances from our subscribers.

Rev. L. I. Cox held services at Hopedale, a mill town in Alamance county, last Sunday afternoon and began the organization of a church at that place. At night he preached at the Burlington church,. presenting the claims of the Missionary Association of the Western North Carolina Conference.

Under "Book Feview" this week will be found some splendid things about Dr. J. G. Bishop's book, "A Biblical View of the Church." We have read a part of this good book and find its contents well worth time and price. We need in this age, of all times, to see the Church from a Bible standpoint. Later we will give a thorough review of the publication.

Brother John R. Foster, superintendent of the Burlington Sunday school, said in his talk last Sunday that a young man, a member of the Christian Church but not a member of the Burlington church, called on him last week and left $5.00 to be used in defraying the expenses of Miss Stacey, whom the Burlington Sunday school has decided to send as a missionary to Japan. We mention this to show what an abiding interest people take in things of that kind.

COST OF THE ANNUAL

The total cost of issuing and delivering the 1919 *Christian Annual* amounted to $614.24. The total income amounted to $571.54—a gain of $42.69. Three-fourths of this gain went back to the credit of the Convention in the account of the Publishing Agent and one-fourth, or $10.69 went to me for editing and looking after the mailing of the publication.

C. B. RIDDLE, *Editor and Publisher.*
February 1, 1919.

Mrs. J. F. Renn—THE SUN is very dear to me as it has been in our home for many years.

Mrs. W. B. Bagwell—Find check for renewal to THE SUN. Its weekly visits are so inspiring and helpful.

PASTOR AND PEOPLE

SUFFOLK LETTER

A sexton is more than a janitor. A janitor is a door-keeper, a room-keeper; a sexton is an under officer of a church. In England he has a life-job; in America a term-contract-job. The sexton has charge of the buildings, furniture, utensils, and keeps all in order. He cares for heat, ventilation, opening and closing of doors, and cleaning up the premises. He provides for the physical comfort of the congregation. In some cases he digs graves and attends funerals. He may seem to the thoughtless to occupy a low position; but rightly understood and rightly performing his duty he is an important factor in worship. He has the best opportunity to make friends by making people comfortable. I offer felicitations to all faithful sextons in city and country churches, and I may be pardoned if I offer a few suggestions to those sextons who have not thought of the high position to which choice, necessity, or circumstances may have exalted them.

It is said that "cleanliness is next godliness," and a clean church may be counted as a good example of cleanliness. The sexton who keeps his church clean sets a good example for housekeepers and Christians. "The blood of Jesus Christ his Son cleanseth us from all sin;" and the broom and duster of the sexton cleanse the house of God from all dust. It is no small matter to keep a house clean. That has been the task of the housekeepers through all the centuries. We live in an atmosphere of invisible dust that creeps into home and church; and we live in an atmosphere of evil that creeps into our lives. A clean church suggests a clean congregation, and worshippers should not complain at the neglect of the sextons while their lives are more defiled than the church. The congregation can help the sexton keep the church house clean, and the sexton can help the congregation to keep their clothes and their lives clean. "Help us to help each other, Lord,' might be a good prayer for sexton and people.

Heat is very important to comfort in winter and ventilation very important to comfort in summer. This requires special attention for funerals. It is so often the case, in country churches especially, that church fires are started on a cold, wet, winter day, just before the people enter the church. This makes the most uncomfortable atmosphere, as it releases the moisture in the stagnant air, and is worse than no fire at all. Fires should be started a sufficient length of time before the service to release the moisture and dry it out of the rooms, so that the church will be a place of comfort. It is sad indeed to sit in a cold church at a funeral. It is worse than out of doors in the fresh atmosphere, no matter what the temperature is. If any sexton reads this, I hope that he will count it a Christian privilege to keep his church comfortable for funerals as well as for Sunday worship. Building fires for invited guests was always inhospitable; and it is no less so in the house of the Lord. Hospitailty is a good characteristic of a good sexton.

A church yard is a part of the church premises and should receive attention as well as the house itself. A home is judged by the outside and so is a church and religious life. The psalmist says: "I had rather be a door-keeper in the house of my God; than to dwell in the tents of wickedness;" but a sexton is more than a door-keeper; he is a church-keeper, a comfort-keeper, a health-keeper, and one might say, a soul-keeper. He opens the house of the Lord, he closes the house of the Lord, and he deserves a place in the upper temple.

W. W. STALEY.

GOLDEN DEEDS

One of the great blessings that God has given to man, is the power to do golden deeds—deeds that bless humanity, that cheer the saddended heart, and thrill the soul with joy. I find myself thanking God very often these days for the many golden deeds of which I have been the unworthy recipient; deeds that have meant more to my life than can ever be expressed, and deeds without which, my life would have been different. However, whatever good there may be in me, or the small amount of good I may have done, I attribute to the great kindness of God, and the inspiration that has come to me through the golden deeds of my friends.

When but a boy, I had gone forward to the altar of prayer to endeavor to find the Christ. I was struggling to know Him, and as I waited and prayed mother came and performed one of the many of her life of golden deeds, she put her arms around my neck, and spoke in words similar to these: "Frank, can't you trust Jesus, and we will go home and tell papa what God has done for you?" My heart answered Jesus and mother, "yes," and I became a new boy, and father knew.

I went away to school, and one day father wrote me a letter in which he said: "I want you and all my children to be better than I have been; I want you to make a man of yourself." I had always wanted to be like father; I knew he was the greatest man in the world to me, and had never dreamed I could ever be the man he was, and then came his letter. What an ideal! It was one of the golden deeds of his that has meant much to my life, for it taught me that every boy, with the training his father gives him, plus that which he may secure himself, ought to be a more useful man than his father had been, because of the greater opportunities that the boy has.

While in school I was constantly being blessed by deeds that were golden. Once my money gave out, and it looked as if I would have to leave school, and Rev. J. W. Patton, one of my most esteemed friends, gave me a month's board, and under his leadership, a number of others did the same. I remained in college, and I thank God for these men.

During the "Flu" epidemic in Norfolk I was among the first of its victims. For nine days I was confined to my room, with none of my relatives in the city I felt sorry that I was seemingly about to be a trouble to some one, but there was one who was anxious to bless my life by her deeds that to me were golden. Her name is Mrs. J. W. Mercer, in whose home I was rooming. For nine days she nursed me as tenderly as my own mother, and when I offered to pay her, she said, "No, you do not owe me a cent." Then I knew again that golden deeds are not to be purchased with money.

These are only a few of the golden deeds that have blessed my life, and I have given them with the hope that they may inspire all who may chance to read of them, to not forget to do the golden deed of kindness, which blesses both the person helped and the person who does the deed of love, and make the world a better place in which to live, by bringing sunshine into lives that are dark; joy into hearts that are sad, and a thrill that lifts mankind into a state of sublime happiness, and fills the life with the spirit of gratitude and helpfulness.

J. F. MORGAN.

Norfolk, Va.

PASTOR AND WIFE POUNDED

We had been reading about other preachers getting pounded, and had heard slight threats for ourselves, but we thought that perhaps we might escape, but it was not to be. When these good people begin thinking about doing anything they soon put their thought into action. We have found that they had been thinking.

While we were sitting quietly enjoying the peace of the fire side Tuesday, Jan. 21, suddenly the quietness was broken by a stir at the front door which was occasioned by a crowd of about forty people who had come to "besiege" the parsonage; and entering with boxes, packages, and other "weapons" of peaceful siege, they marched without resistance to the dining room which they captured. When we could summon sufficient courage to follow we found them standing around a table filled with good things to eat, with many things lying around. Then we realized that we were the "victims" of an old fashioned pounding.

To mention only a part of the good things brought would make a list too long for this article. Suffice it to say that there was enough to supply most of our culinary needs for many weeks. Words could not express (if indeed they could have been spoken which was impossible, as we did not regain our speech for some time) the feelings of gratitude and appreciation that filled our hearts.

We mention some of the thoughts that strove for utterance. First, there was a feeling of our unworthiness of such thoughtfulness and kindness. Then there was a sense of our gratitude that we can never express. We made some resolutions, too, which we hope and pray may be kept. We resolved to try to do more for the Master and for these dear, good people and to be truer to the trust imposed in us. May the Lord bless them in things temporal and may He give them the riches of His grace in their hearts and lives.

REV. & MRS. R. L. WILLIAMSON.

Henderson, N. C.

JUST A HUNDRED VOLUNTEERS

Just a few weeks past this writer received a letter from our Mission Secretary, Dr. J. O. Atkinson, concerning the hundred volunteers for the ministry and mission fields. I did not place it in the waste basket, nor use it to kindle fire, but I have read it twice. I have the letter in my office, and the contents on my heart. I am going to keep it.

When I read that letter I made a short prayer. Here it is: I said, "Lord, send me after at least one of these volunteers, and I'll do my very best to bring him in for the work." I am still on the lookout, and I know Christ will help me to find him. Our Church in the South needs at least two hundred to go from this field. How I wish the Church as a whole would come together and pray mightily for them!

Here is a thought that came to me while praying over the matter. We have a goodly number of Woman's Missionary and Christian Endeavor Societies in the bounds of the Southern Christian Convention The main object of these Societies is training Christian workers; and somehow I think each Society, with the assistance of its pastor, ought to lay the matter upon the hearts of its members and expect definite results. I believe a step in that direction would add greatly to our list of workers. How about trying it out?

Our people in the South are beginning to awake to the mission cause, and we are badly in need of additional workers in every Conference. I believe every church in the Convention with a membership of as much as two hundred ought to follow the recent step of the Burlington church. The churches ought to support a missionary, and how great it would be to have that missionary come from the local church! Suppose we try out the above plan? How about it, Missionary Societies? What say you Christian Endeavorers? Are you willing to lay this matter before your Societies? It you are Jesus will be there to assist you.

J. VINCENT KNIGHT.

Greensboro, N. C.

UNION (N. C.)

Notwithstanding muddy roads and swollen streams we had a nice congregation at Union last Sunday. We had a good service and much interest was manifested in the forward step that is being considered, which if carried out, will mean much to church and pastor. A committee of eleven was named to consider among other things the advisability of having services every Sunday. The committe was asked to consult with the membership as to wish and ascertain what could be done and report to the quarterly meeting on Saturday before the second Sunday in February. The committee is to meet at the church at one o'clock p. m., on Saturday before the second Sunday and get its report ready for the quarterly meeting which convenes at two o'clock that afternoon. Union is one of our best churches in this section. It is composed of excellent people who are capable of great things for Christ and the Church.

Services every Sunday would mean great things for the Sunday school, the Missionary Society, and the general growth and uplift of the church. It would bring the community and the church into a closer fellowship of service and worship. It would be a great thing for our young people in developing and training them in

service for Christ and humanity. The church has a great many young people in its fold and congregation and in them there are great capacibilities and possibilities for the church if the church will only undertake great things for Christ and give the young people of the church and community a chance to do great things for Christ and His cause.

Let each member make the matter a subject of earnest prayer and do in the matter as he believes God would have him do. I pray God to guide us; and I ask that His will be done. It is earnestly desired that every member who can possibly do so attend the quarterly meeting on Saturday and the Communion service on Sunday. To friends who have shown me special kindness, I return sincere thanks.

P. H. FLEMING.

Burlington, N. C.

NOTICE

On account of Influenza the Musical Institute of the Eastern North Carolina Sunday School Convention published to be held at Catawba Springs church February 20-22, will not meet until further notice.

GEO. M. McCULLERS.

PAGE VALLEY LETTER

There is very little to report from this pastorate. No revivals have been conducted since conference. All churches in the pastorate have been closed because of Influenza. Most of the county and high schools have been closed. The fact is Page county has suffered much because of this epidemic. Many churches and schools are closed at this writing.

A new church has been built in this pastorate, and is now nearing completion. The new church (Mt. Lebanon) is not one of fancy, but is built plain and substantial. The best lumber that could be secured has been put into the building. The outside work is all completed, the doors and windows in, and the inisde work is being done slowly, but carefully. We have secured two new members for the new church since conference, which makes a total of thirty-two that have been received during the sixteen months we have been pastor. We are hoping and praying that the Influenza will soon blow over so that we may get back to our post of duty. We intreat the prayers of the Brotherhood.

B. J. EARP.

Shenandoah, Va.

WINCHESTER, (VA.) LETTER

With the coming of the year, there seemed to come new life into our church work. The epidemic of Influenza was a great hindrance to our labors during the fall. We had quite a number of cases among our church people but no deaths.

On New Year's night we called a meeting of our members at the parsonage and in an informal way called for suggestions for the betterment of the church, and the laying of plans for the coming year. Notwithstanding the fact that the weather was inclement, there was a good attendance and a great deal of interest. I feel that the meeting is going to prove a decided help to the church. There were a number of advanced steps planned, some of which I will explain later. Two I want to mention here: The members decided to assist the pastor in visiting and trying to interest the members who seldom come to the services; steps were taken to pay off all the notes held by the banks against the church. There are three, one for $42.50 which the Ever Ready Society, composed of young people, will pay; the second for $120.00 which the Ladies' Aid Society will pay and the third for $870.00. We have $200.00 of this on hand and $200.00 more subscribed, leaving a balance of $470.00 to raise. We want to pay this before our Conference meets in August. We will appreciate an early settlement of all unpaid subscriptions and any help that our friends can give us in the way of contributions toward liquidating our debt at this time.

We have raised over $800.00 on the debt since our report to the Conference in August. Four new members have been received into the fellowship of the church this month. Rev. Gypsy Smith, Jr., is to hold a union revival in Winchester, February 5 to March 2. Our Sunday school rendered a splendid program at its Christmas entertainment.

Upon returning from an evening meeting, on January 9, which was the writer's birthday, the pastor and his wife found that the members and friends of the church had come in and taken possession of the parsonage and had brought with them a generous donation; in fact a big pounding, which we are still enjoying and which we shall ever remember. In addition to this friends in the Winchester, Timber Mountain, New Hope and one from Woods Chapel, whose names are too numerous to mention, have been supplying us with good things for our table which we have eaten gladly and appreciated greatly. The Lord has been good to us through these friends and we pray for strength to render a larger service to Him and the churches and that we may make ourselves more worthy of such tokens of friendship.

In addition to the work at Winchester, the writer is holding services this year at Timber Mountain, New Hope and Beulah. The people seem interested in the services at all these places but sickness has hindered the work greatly during the year. Brothers N. M. Hasler and J. E. W. Bryant have been ordained as Deacons since beginning our work there. The work is pleasant at all our churches and we find it a pleasure to labor with the good members in them.

The following amounts have been contributed on the debt of the Winchester Church:

Previously reported, $11,127.41.

Mrs. W. T. Walters, $4.00; I. N. Painter, $5.00; Ever Ready Society, $5.87; Alva C. Richards, $125.00; Rev. J. O. Atkinson, $20.00; Ladies' Aid Society, $21.52; Rev. A. W. Andes, $10.00; C. M. A. E. Va. Conference, $100.00.

Subscriptions paid on One Cent a day:

C. H. Barr, $3.65; Mrs. C. H. Barr, $3.65; Mrs. Joanna Yeakley, $3.65; W. T. Walters, $3.65; Mrs. W. T. Walters, $3.65; Arthur S. Anderson, $3.65; E. W. Cather, $3.65; Mrs. E. W. Cather, $3.65; Mrs. B. R. Richards, $3.30; Miss Goldie Edwards, $3.25; Total, $11,455.05.

In behalf of the church, I thank all who have had part in these contributions.   W. T. WALTERS.

A MESSAGE FROM REV. B. F. BLACK

A friend sends THE CHRISTIAN SUN the following paragraphs selected from a letter from Chaplain B. F. Black which we are sure SUN readers will enjoy:

The glad news of the 11th of November swept the world as no other news or message has done in all the centuries—save one—for all seemed to have been swept from the even tenor of their daily lives by the fiery tail of the mad comet, war. The predictions by the great and near-great of the possible calamities that awaited our little world when Halley's comet seemed to be coming our way were left to the devil-deluded Kaiser to hand to a world gass and hellish mixtures, falling meteors red hot with death-laden breath. On land and in sea, in air, man made for fellow a man molted liquid hell for men to wade through and swim out of. If not these, then hunger, separation, hearthunger, anxiety, with pangs more deadly than the vipers sting.

Why not rejoice? Rachel is being reconciled. The mother of nations has paid the price. They have stood afar off. The sayings are kept in their hearts.

Poor France is one vast new sepulcher, while Belgium, Flanders, Alsace-Loraine, are but blood-stained altars where human sacrifice has been made the god of war with all of the cruelty that human genius and hellish aptitude could conceive.

Skeletons now, once the flower of the allied world, stagger from the confines of prison cells. From a country, too, blooming as a rose garden where no blight of vandalism has swept—yet where passion and the spirit of rapine, double-dyed vandalism and quadrupled by baser passion, incarnate has assumed the form of human kind. They, the prison warders of our murdered dead. And living skeletons defy the heavens by calling upon God and the Kaiser to stand by them until the world should bow to the Lord of the Fatherland and call them blessed. Is it possible that this herd is made in the image of a righteous God?

           B. F. BLACK.

PLEASANT HILL AND LIBERTY

I preached at Pleasant Hill last Saturday afternoon and Sunday morning and at Liberty that night. Good congregations at both churches. The "Flu" is abating and the Sunday schools are going on in their regular work.

           D. A. LONG.

OUR CONVENTION, THE WAR, THE WORK, AND THE WORKERS

The Southern Convention in session last May felt sorely the need of workers—ministers and missionaries. It voiced that need in this vote: "That we set as our objective for which to labor and to pray 100 recruits as ministers and missionaries giving all their time and strength to Christian service for the home and foreign work."

The war is over. It is now up to the Christian forces of this world to so preach and spread the Gospel of the Prince of Peace that there can never come another bloody and cruel war. Will we do it? It is a task that requires men and women, brave, heroic, God-fearing and God-serving men and women. Are we to have them? Well, it *depends upon us*. If we feel the need and lay that need before God, He will give the workers. Here is our commission and the ground for it: "The harvest truly is plenteous, but the laborers are few; pray ye therefore the Lord of the harvest that he will send forth laborers into his harvest." (Mat. 9:37, 28).

J. O. ATKINSON.

POUNDED

I was in Wakefield, Va., on New Year's night to attend the union prayer meeting, held at the Christian church. At the close of the service, deacon J. H. Harris instructed me to drive my car to the rear of Mr. J. S. White's store, where he had been serving as salesman.

For several minutes three men were kept busy loading the car with the good things that the members of the Wakefield church had brought together for their pastor and his family.

We wish in this public way to express our sincere thanks to all of these good people and desire that we may render a more efficient service as we labor together with them. Members from the other churches in this field have also remembered us with many good things to eat. We are thankful to all of them.

W. D. HARWARD.

Dendron, Va.

THE CHRISTIAN ORPHANAGE

THE PAST AND FUTURE

Dear Friends:—The year 1918 was the best year the Orphanage has ever had, financially, and we hope it has been the best in many other ways. You have made it possible for us to meet the high prices and pay all our bills and pay off the entire indebtedness. You have also made it possible for us to reach each goal set since we have had charge of the work. Since we have had charge of the work one of our chief aims has been to get our beloved Institution out of debt and on a sound financial basis. You have been so loyal and so generous that you have let us accomplish this aim.

During the past two years, having one object in view, we have not said much to you about our many needs in the Institution. While we have paid off the indebtedness, we as a Church, ought not think for a moment that our work is done and that we are at a resting place. We are just ready to begin work and to do greater things than we have in the past. We ought to make the year 1919 our best year.

I asked you to make the year 1917 "Our Banner Year" and you did. Then I asked you to make the year 1918 "The Best Yet Year" and you did. Now I am going to ask you to make the year 1919 "Our Best Year" and you will.

Let us get an idea of what we want to accomplish during the year 1919;

First. One of our great needs is a home for small children. We already have the house and by spending some where about two hundred dollars in putting in bath, etc., and papering we can get it in condition for a home for the small children.

We have a number of applications now on hand for children less than five years of age, and it is necessary, if we take them, to put them in a home to themselves with a matron to have charge and look after their many needs. Shall we refuse these little helpless children a home or shall we open our hearts and make it possible for them to have a home and a kind matron to be a mother to them?

Second. Our buildings need repairs. It will take several hundred dollars to make such repairs as is badly needed and ought to have been made sometime ago. Painting is to be done, sleeping porch to be finished so it can be used and give more children room, and a number of other things to do.

Third. Our rooms need refurnishing. Much of the furniture put in when the Orphanage was first opened has become very much impaired and ought to be replaced with new where it is absolutely needed. Our mattresses are worn and soiled and we will be compelled to replace many of them this year.

The springs on the beds that have been used since the Orphanage was first opened have become almost useless and are uncomfortable for the little folks to sleep on.

These are some of our needs for this year. I assure you that we will be as economical as possible and will not spend a dollar where we can get along without it.

We have fifty-two children in the Institution now with eight more pleading for a home and I hardly see how we can refuse them under the circumstances. Let us all pull together during the year 1919 and see how much we can do for the Master's Kingdom in lending a helping hand to our little orphan children.

Next week I will set the goals that we will try to reach during the year 1919. Look out for next week's letter and make up your mind to do your very best to reach each goal set.

C. D. JOHNSTON, *Supt.*

REPORT FOR FEBRUARY 5, 1919

Amount brought forward, $113.97.

Children's Offerings

James Henry Craven, (Thanksgiving), $1.00; Lester B. Frank, 20 cents; T. D. Mathews, Jr., 30 cents; Total, $1.50.

(Eastern Virginia Conference)

Holland, $6.00; Antioch, $2.00; Holy Neck, $5.00; Bethlehem, $14.00; First Christian, Norfolk, $3.89.

(Virginia Valley Conference)

New Hope, $1.35; New Hope, $1.00.

(North Carolina and Virginia Conference)

Bethlehem, $1.00; Shallow Ford, $1.00; Haw River, $1.00; Reidsville, $2.00.

(Eastern North Carolina Conference)

Morrisville, $2.00; Henderson, $5.45; Sanford, $5.29; Christian Light, $1.14.

(Western North Carolina Conference)

Shiloh, $1.93.

(Georgia and Alabama Conference)

Rose Hill, (Ga.), $4.25; Total, $58.30.

Special Offerings

The O'Kelley Bible Class, Greensboro Christian Sunday school, $40.00.

Miscellaneous

Mrs. C. C. Peel, $13.32; J. H. Jones, on support of children, $30.00; Mrs. Ella J. Hughes, Elon College, N. C., $1.00; Total, $44.32.

Thanksgiving Offerings

R. T. Kernodle, $100.00; Shady Grove church, (Ala.), $7.35; Miss Annie Staley, $2.00; New Providence church, $22.00; A Friend, Graham, N. C., $1.00; Union (Surry), $11.50; Bethlehem church (Eastern Virginia), $11.00; Mrs. L. M. Rountree, $2.50; New Hope Christian church, $16.50; U. H. Deaton, Ether, N. C., $2.37; Mrs. C. B. Thomas, $1.75; Total $177.97 Total for the week, $322.09; Grand total, $436.06.

LETTERS

Dear Uncle Charley: Hope this finds you and all the children well. I am sick today. Am sending thirty cents, my dues for December, January and February.—T. D. Matthews, Jr.

Sorry you are sick. Trust you will soon be well. You must be one of the faithful cousins this year.—"Uncle Charley."

Dear Uncle Charley: I am a little boy fifteen months old and my grandpa Albright has been showing me your picture and some of the little orphans that were sent to him. My auntie has been telling me I must send a little mite to help the dear little ones who had no mamma and papa, and she is doing this for me. When I get to be a big boy I can write you then. Find enclosed $1.00 for the Thanksgiving offering.—James Henry Craven.

You are a splendid little boy. It was so kind of you to think of the little orphans and give some of your money to help care for them. You must write often.—"Uncle Charley."

Dear Uncle Charley: Enclose find twenty cents for January and February. I am a year and a half old today and weigh twenty and a half pounds. Do you think I'll be as big a man as you? With best wishes for all the little orphans.—Lester B. Frank.

If you are one year and a half old and weigh twenty and a half pounds I feel sure you will be as big as I am when you get as old. You are a fine little man anyway.—"Uncle Charley."

JUST AS THE PRESS STARTS

Mr. D. R. Fonville has arrived from overseas.

Rev. J. W. Patton writes: "I will present the claims of THE SUN to my people. Had a delightful day at Hines Chapel Sunday."

Dr. Kemp P. Battle, Sr., ex-president of the University of North Carolina, is seriously ill.

The allied troops are likely to be removed from Russia at an early date.

Five vessels are on the way bringing soldiers home.

The pressman says: "All aboard."

MISSIONARY

HOW TO KEEP A WOMAN'S MISSIONARY SOCIETY ALIVE AND ACTIVE

Chapter II—Prayer in the Society

In the previous paper the use of the Bible in the Society was discussed. In this let us consider the place of Prayer in the Society. To one looking for something novel and untried for the Society, any discussions of the Bible and prayer will seem trite and commonplace; yet it is by proper use of the commonplace that solidity is secured and sound growth is assured. No building is safe, and no Society is secure, until a sure and sound foundation is laid. The Bible and prayer are the sure foundations of any Missionary Organization, and by proper use of these the vitality and vigor of the Society is assured.

That prayer is essential to the life and power of the Society is evident from the four following quotations:

"Of all the forces God has placed at our disposal for winning the world to Christ the greatest is that of prayer."—Belle M. Brain.

"Every step in the progress of missions is directly traceable to prayer. It has been the preparation of every new triumph and the secret of all success."—Arthur T. Pierson.

"Everything vital in the missionary enterprise hinges upon prayer."—John R. Mott.

"Every element of the missionary problem depends for its solution upon prayer."—Robert E. Speer.

But to say that prayer is essential in no manner indicates that "offering a few words of prayer," or "repeating together" the Lord's Prayer, at the opening or closing of the Missionary Society, insures the life or guarantees the power of the Society. Such a "prayer" may, and often does, hinder the growth and help to kill rather than make alive the Society. I agree with one writer on the subject who declares that the Society is often opened or closed with prayer not with any special or definite purpose or object in mind, but with a sort of feeling that it is the proper thing to do, and not to do so would offend both God and the members.

"An almost superstitious feeling seems to prevail, that if the heads are bowed for a few moments while a brief petition is offered, or the Lord's Prayer is 'repeated in concert,' all will be well, and the Society may safely proceed to other business.'" Prayer offered under such conditions is not praying at all; it is the rather yielding to the demands of a refined superstition.

On the other hand the writer recalls having attended a session of a missionary meeting some time since in which the prayer was the most potent feature of the whole program. The one who led the prayer, led it, and led all the rest of us into a praying frame of mind. Every woman in the audience prayed. She had to. The whole atmosphere was charged with the spirit of prayer, devotion and supplication. The leader with reverently bowed head prayed for definite, named, and specific objects, and then told us what, and for whom, to pray.

The writer felt then and has felt ever since that no Missionary Society could lag or die, it mattered not whatever else it might do or leave undone, if it prayed like that Society did it would live and grow and flourish like the green bay tree. Such a praying society can no more lag, "dry up," or die, than can the "river of water of life" that proceeds out of the throne of God and the Lamb and whose waters are for the healing of the nations.

I mention only a few of the many ways that prayer will help, and powerfully, in the Society.

First—Be Definite in Prayer

One reason why many timid souls in the Society will not, and feel that they cannot, lead in prayer is because there is a thought in mind that one who leads a prayer or prays in public must pray for everything in general and the whole world in particular.

Praying is, and should be, as natural and as definite as a hungry child's petition to the mother for a piece of bread. If any one can ask a parent or a neighbor for a favor why can such an one not ask the finest Friend she will ever have on earth or in heaven for that which is needed and desired?

Pray for specific things, or for a specific thing. Any Missionary Society whose members believe the promises of God may "pray workers into the field, money in to empty treasuries, and heathen souls into the Kingdom of God." Else why did Lord Christ say: "The harvest truly is plenteous, but the laborers are few; *pray ye therefore the Lord of the harvest that he will send forth laborers into his harvest?*" (Mat. 9:38).

Be definite in prayer. The dying prayer of John Hunt is a model of this sort, "O let me pray once more for Fiji! Lord, for Christ's sake bless Fiji! Save Fiji; save the heathen in Fiji." Not much logical arrangement or rhetorical flourish about that prayer; but it was the expressed desire of a hungry heart and a yearning soul—and that prayer was heard and answered to a remarkable degree.

Second—Have Agreement in Prayer

Let the Society decide before the close of a meeting what it will pray for at the next meeting. Remember the promise of the Master: "If two of you shall agree on earth as touching anything that they shall ask, it shall be done for them of my Father." (Mat. 18:19). It the members of the Society actually believe that promise of our Lord let them put it to the test. In this way it may be done: Let the Society select certain definite objects to pray for, enter into a covenant to pray for these both publicly and at home, and speak to one another about the desirability of achieving these objects. Under such conditions the power of prayer in the Society would be increased a hundred fold.

Third—Pray in Faith

It is the prayer of faith and expectancy which prevails. We are to "undertake great things for God, and expect great things of God." Pouring out the soul in a whole mixed multitude of petitions is not prevailing prayer. If you do not know what you desire, it will frighten you if God were to hear or undertake to answer your prayer. First form in your own mind that which you very much desire of your heavenly Father, and

then tell the Father of that desire, with the expectation that He will give "thee the desires of thine heart."

Remember that in prayer we are dealing not with man but with God. It may seem incredible to you that a prayer offered in your Society, your town, your home, may be instantly answered in Tokio, Hong Kong or Santa Isabel; but the God to Whom we pray is Omniscient and Omnipresent, and distance is no hindrance.

"Through the divine telegraphy of prayer" writes Belle M. Brain, "which needs neither wire nor key, but simply a heart in tune with God, the remotest soul may be reached in an instant time."

Real, zealous, fervent, soul-yearning prayer in any Society will go a very long way in making the Society a live one in the Church and a power for God and righteousness in the community.

J. O. ATKINSON.

MT. AUBURN—MISSIONARY REPORT

The Woman's Missionary Society of Mt. Auburn adopted the plan of systematic study of our Church and Mission Fields two years ago. Our text-book this year has been "The African Trail," by Jean Mackensie. Our meetings have been held regularly on Thursday before the second Sunday in each month. With the help of the monthly programs in the *Christian Missionary* we have had some very interesting meetings. Our average attendance has not been very large but we have enjoyed the meetings and have learned more about the work. We hope as time goes on more of the women will come.

Our active membership numbers seventeen. Our Home Department members number forty-three, (an increase over last year of eight). These are interested in the work but can't attend regularly. Most of them pay $1.00 a year, while some pay more.

The Cradle Roll with Mrs. J. B. Ellington as Superintendent, has done well the past year. With only a membership of eight or ten, They have raised $6.24.

The Willing Workers number twenty-five. At the beginning of the year, they, with the Cradle Roll undertook to buy one hundred cement blocks for the Santa Isabel church in Porto Rico. At their four Mite Box Openings this year they have paid in $23.90. They have paid for one hundred and twenty blocks.

There is one point we always try to emphasize, and that is *cheerful giving to Christ*—not to the Society—not because we must— but because we love Jesus and want to show a little of our love for Him in this way.

Here are the figures for the past year:

Cradle Roll for Santa Isabel	$ 6.24
Willing Workers for Santa Isabel	23.90
Home Department for Barrett Home	36.30
Woman's Missionary Society for Barrett Home	32.05
Dues of W. M. S.	16.95
Literature Fund	2.01
Franklinton Church	10.00
Total	$127.45

As half of our dues are paid to Home Missions and half to Foreign Missions that makes our total to Foreign Missions $106.97. We ask God's blessings on what has been accomplished and will try to moe forward to do more for our Lord and Master who gave the command, ''Go ye into all the world and preach the Gospel to every creature.''

SUSIE SPAIN, *Sec'y.*

FIRST QUARTERLY REPORT OF W. H. AND P. M. SOCIETIES OF EASTERN VIRGINIA CHRISTIAN CONFERENCE FOR QUARTER ENDING DECEMBER 30, 1918

Woman's Societies

Amount received:—

Berea, (Nansemond), $81.45; Cypress Chapel, $11.55; Damascus, $10.00; Dendron, $21.00; Franklin, $43.75; Holland, $4.20; Liberty Spring. $5.40; Memorial Temple, $44.70; Mt Carmel, $5.80; Newport News, $14.55, Portsmouth, $29.80; Rosemont, $64.52; Suffolk, $56.85; Third Church, Norfolk, $17.05; Wakefield, $10.55; Waverly, $19.80; Total, $389.97.

It is noticeable that the Rosemont Society sent the largest amount this quarter and besides this amount has sent $20.00 to Dr. Atkinson on his Mission Fund.

These Amounts Were For

Dues, $151.98, Thank Offering, Barrett Home, $139.75; Life Membership, Mrs. Seawell, $10.00; Sunday School in Japan, $12.50; Literature Fund, $1.00; Mrs. Watanabei's salary, $52.85; Support of Coy Franklin at Orphanage, $9.89; Miss Hamaguchi's salary, $12.50; Total, $389.97.

Young Peoples' Societies

Amount received:—

Berkley, $4.00; Burton's Grove; Franklin, $3.70; Portsmouth Junior C. E., $3.00; Tide-Water C. S. S. Asso, Norfolk, $25.00; Portsmouth Sunday school, $29.00; Total $68.40.

Amount to be used for:—

Santa Isabel pastor, $12.90; Santa Isabel building block, $54.00; Support of Coy Franklin, $1.50; Total, $68.40.

Willing Workers

Amount received:—

Berea, $1.64; Franklin, $2.00; Suff lk, $3.60; Holy Neck, $7.25; Waverly, $1.50; Total, $15.99.

To be used for:—

Santa Isabel pastor, $8.74; Santa Isabel building blocks, $7.25; Total, $15.99.

Totals

Woman's Society, $389.97; Young Peoples, $68.40; Willing Workers, $15.99; Total, $474.36.

MRS. M. L. BRYANT, Treasurer.

41 Poplar Ave., Norfolk, Va.

WAR SAVINGS CERTIFICATES PAYABLE ONLY TO TO FIRST OWNERS

That war savings certificates are payable only to the first owners and that stamps are not to be offered or accepted in trade, is a recent notice given by Secretary Glass of the Treasury Department.

In pursuance of this notice, postmasters have been directed by the Post Office Department not to cash war savings certificates on which the names of the owners have not been entered or have been erased or changed except in case of death or disability. Postmasters have been further instructed not to pay war savings certificates presented by persons or firms known to be buying or publicly offering to buy war savings stamps from the owners, unless positive evidence is submitted that the certificates were originally issued to the person or firms presenting them for payment. This is in keeping with the law that makes war savings stamps nontransferable.

WHAT OTHERS THINK OF BISHOP'S ''BIBLICAL VIEW OF THE CHURCH''

Second Edition

Rev. J. O. Atkinson, of Elon College, N. C., Mission Field Secretary, writes:

''Dear Brother Bishop:—I have read with growing interest and appreciation on the second edition of your *Biblical View of the Church.* Every student in the Christian Church preparing for the ministry should read this book. Its plan is well laid and its execution is admirable. It goes to the very heart of problems vital to Bible and ministerial students, students in particular. I enjoyed the first edition which was worthy of its great and good author, but the last edition is a very improvement of the first. It should have wide reading and close study. It will result in great good in years to come. I enclose a dollar for the copy you send me, and also thank you for same.''

Rev. D. M. Helfenstein, D. D., of Orient, Iowa, Former President of Palmer College, writes:

''Dear Brother Bishop:—Your book, *A Biblical View of the Church,* places the Christian Church under obligation to you for this excellent contribution to their literature. It is true you speak your convictions of truth, as an individual, but as a church we will be glad to count this in with our 'Church Literature.'

''Personally I want to thank you for this gift to the Church and to the world. I hope that every school of the Christian Church will adopt it as a text book. I hope all our ministers will secure and read it, especially our young ministers.''

Rev. L. F. Johnson, pastor of our Vanderveer Park Christian Church; Brooklyn, New York, writes:

''I am making splendid use of your book entitled *Biblical View of the Church.* Several of my men have read it already, and have expressed words of appreciation and praise for the Book. I am going to start the book gonig among the Ladies of the Congregation soon. I hope they will appreciate it as the men do.''

Price $1.00, postpaid. Mail orders may be addressed to the author, J. G. Bishop, 1231 West 5th Street, Dayton, Ohio, or to the Christian Publishing Association, C. P. Bldg., Dayton, Ohio.

Elbert A. Herndon—I cannot get along without THE CHRISTIAN SUN. It has been a welcome visitor in our home since before I could remember, and I am now nearly 76 years old. Have been taking it myself more or less ever since the surrender in 1865. I feel that I haven't so many more years to read this valued paper but may God's choicest blessings ever abide on its Editors, present and future, and may God's children be made stronger for having read it through the years.

"THE VICTORY CAR"

The above cut shows the car load of good things recently sent the Christian Orphanage through the efforts of Brother J. M. Darden, Suffolk, Va. This scene is enough to make happy all the churches and individuals who contributed to its capacity. The children are happy—all with an apple. Brother Johnston has his, too. We doubt if Southern car No. 34640 will ever be loaded again with such a variety and representing so many hearts.

Lee Jan 1, 1919, p. 11.

NOTES

Littleton Female College, Littleton, N. C., had a $50,000 fire last week.

What layman in the Church will set out to secure as many subscriptions to THE SUN as some minister? What layman will make the challenge and what minister will accept it?

The question has been asked, "What churches will the North Carolina Conference include?" The Conference will include all the churches now within the bounds of the Western, Eastern and North Carolina and Virginia Conferences.

See that the Annuals of your Conference get into the homes and not behind the pulpit, as we frequently see in visiting the churches.

E. M. Gunn—We enjoy reading THE SUN.

We have a splendid article in type—The Peril of Ecclesiasticism—which awaits our readers. Be on the lookout for it as soon as space permits.

Dr. J. O. Atkinson is in Eastern Virginia at the home of Mr. and Mrs. W. J. Lee. Mr. Lee is feeble at this writing.

In the passing of Prof. M. H. Stacey, Dean of the Faculty and acting president of the University of North Carolina, the State loses one of its finest educators.

Mrs. E. T. Alford—I wish you could know how much my three little folks enjoy reading and hearing THE SUN *read.*

Mrs. E. W. Wilkins—May THE SUN ever remain true to its name—a shining light for the Christian—and may it continue to shine brighter and brighter, until every home in the whole Brotherhood realizes the value of its light.

THE FORWARD MOVEMENT OF THE CHRISTIAN CHURCH

Rev. Warren H. Denison, Superintendent

The Superintendent has been in the field meeting the pastors and speaking to the churches and workers in groups on the Forward Movement. He visited the Vanderveer Park church, and the Hungarian Sunday school in the church of the Evangel in Brooklyn. Those are two of our home mission points and they are fields of large opportunity. Our Vanderveer Park church of which Rev. L. F. Johnson, D. D., is the successful pastor, is in one of the best fields that the writer knows for a large work. It is in a needy field, well built homes and we are in on the ground floor. Those who invest in Forward Movement funds will be doing a great work for that is one of the great needs of the $125,000 which is to be raised for home missions, in the Forward Movement campaign.

In the same way the Hungarian Sunday school is well worth while and one need not be present long to see the good work that is being done for those bright boys and girls. That is another of our worthy home mission works. Every dollar invested in that work will do great good. We held a conference with eight ministers and eight laymen from the New Jersey Conference and the Forward Movement was heartily approved and the workers pledged each other to go back to their churches and work it out thoroughly. This group of workers began at this meeting to plan for a Field Secretary in their conference to help strengthen the work there and plan for larger things in the Kingdom. In those three meetings were represented three distinct types of necessary home mission effort; the planting of a strong city church in an unchurched, growing, desirable community; the development of a work that is of large importance among the foreigners in our country; the strengthening and the encouraging of the weak churches that have had loses and difficulties but are very much needed to meet the needs of the community. The need of just such a field secretary is very urgent in several of our conferences and will

be one of the most practical, sensible, and effective ways that we may do Christian work that will count. The $125,000 of the Forward Movement campaign for $500,000 is an absolute necessity, and it is needed now. That is the share that the Home Mission work will get.

It was a great pleasure to visit the Irvington, N. J., church of which Dr. W. H. Hainer has been the pastor for more than thirty years. Publicly and privately the strength of that great congregation was pledged to the Forward Movement. Dr. Hainer is the President of the New Jersey conference and will do all in his power to bring the message to all the churches and urge them to enlist in the Movement at once.

It was our pleasure to visit in New England the following churches: Providence, R. I., where Dr. W. G. Sargent is the strong pastor, the Assonet church where Rev. D. P. Hurlburt, the Mission Secretary of the New England Convention, is the successful pastor, and the Fall River (Franklin Street) church which is at present without a pastor since the resignation of Rev. C. E. Fockler. At the Fall River church there was a union meeting of several of our churches to hear the plans of the Forward Movement and a fine congregation was present. They will need a strong pastor in that important city in that field of large service. How great is the need of strong, trained, well equipped pastors to man our strategic centers and build large programs for the advancement of the Kingdom. At Fall River we had a conference with seven of our ministers and a number of laymen from the Rhode Island and Massachusetts conference. A strong resolution of co-operation was passed and a loyal pledge for pushing the Forward Movement was adopted. Plans of work were considered and the carnestness shown was indicative of large results in that conference for the growth of the work. We also visited three churches in the New York Eastern Conference, Albany where the President of the American Christian Convention and the chairman of the Forward Movement, Dr. F. G. Coffin, is the beloved pastor; Ravena where Rev. A. B. Kendall, D. D., is the successful pastor, and the

church at Hunter's Land in which the writer spent his childhood days where Rev. C. W. Cook has been the pastor for quite a number fo years. It was a delight to be with the membership and pastors of these churches and bring the message of the Forward Movement.

At the Home Church

It was my glad privilege to spend Sunday the 26th at the little home church. It is few in numbers, out in the open country, in a thinly settled community. It has sent out at least five ministers into our work: Revs. G. R. Hammond, E. D. Hammond, M. W. Borthwick, B. S. Crosby, W. H. Denison. It has among its few members some who are devoted and loyal. The writer spoke on the Forward Movement at 10:30 and at 1:30 and the people enjoyed a lunch and social hour between. We suggested to the people that during the noon hour that they would have the opportunity to make pledges for the $500,000 fund and that it would be our delight to have the church from which the Superintendent had gone out to make generous gifts for the work, in the beginning of the campaign. Without any begging, but voluntarily $715 in cash and pledges were received. Some how we believe that the amount will yet come up to an even thousand dollars by some who have not given and some who will increase their gifts. If all our churches will do in the same proportion according to their ability there will come a new day to the Christian Church which has a special and divine mission in the world.

In addition to the visitation of these three conferences and speaking in nine of their churches and attending conferences of workers in two of the conferences we attended the Missionary Education banquet in New York and the three days session of the Foreign Missions Conference at New Haven, Connecticut. Those were great days with great issues but we will have to speak of them at another time.

"How would you like to sign up with me for a life game?" was the way a baseball fan proposed.

"I'm agreeable," replied the girl, "where's your diamond?"—*Indianapolis Star.*

MARRIAGES

OBITUARIES

WEATHERLY-NEVILLE

A quiet but pretty marriage was solemnized at the home of Rev. W. G. Clements, Morrisville, N. C., January 27, 1919 when Miss Myrtle Angier Neville became the bride of Mr. William Burke Weatherly. Only a few witnessed the ceremony. The couple motored down from Durham and returned immediately after the ceremony where they will make their home. May God's blessings rest upon this union.   W. G. C.

JACOBY-HOLT

Amid the soft glow of myriads of candles and artistic decoration of white and green, Cecil Grady Holt of Burlington, N. C., and Cornelius Jacoby of Washington, D. C., plighted their troth on Saturday evening January 18, 1919, at the Burlington Christian church. The wedding music was rendered by Mrs. Robert Barnwell, pianist, and Misses Malone and Boyd violinists. Miss Rawlins sang sweetly "Because" and "O Perfect Love."

There were four maids, becomingly attired in pink and yellow messaline with chiffon draperies, carrying shower bouquets of Narcissus and ferns. These were followed by four groomsmen in full dress suits. The dames of honor were gowned in white georgette and carried pink carnations. The maid of honor, Miss Bessie Holt wore blue crepe de chine with silver lace. She carried Killiarnary roses. The ring was carried in the heart of a rose by little Mary Robertson.

The bride wore a gown of white crepe de chine with satin and pearl trimmings. Her veil was caught with orange blossoms. She carried bride's roses. Immediately after the ceremony the happy couple left for an extensive southern trip. Upon their return they will make their home in Washington, D. C., where Mr. Jacoby holds a position as construction engineer for the Southern Railway. The bride is an accomplished young woman and leaves many friends here who will follow her with all good wishes.   J. W. HARRELL.

BURCH

Alma Gladys Burch, daughter of the late Charlie Burch, passed from labor to reward January 27, 1919, aged twenty-three years, seven months and thirteen days. At the time of her death she was teaching school at McLeansville, N. C. Her home was at Troy, N. C. She was stricken with Spanish Influenza a week previous to her death and this later developed into pneumonia. Burial services were at Bethel Presbyterian church, Guilford County, N. C., conducted by the pastor, Rev. G. L. Whiteley assisted by Rev. Charles Whiteley of West Durham. Deceased leaves a mother, two sisters, one brother and many friends to mourn their loss. She lived a sweet Christian life and was loved by all who knew her. May God comfort the bereaved ones. Our loss is her heavenly gain.

    J. R. MILES.

MORAN

Mrs. Sarah E. Moran, widow of the late Samuel Moran, departed this life January 5, 1919, aged seventy-seven years, seven months and seven days. She leaves to mourn their loss one son, P. E. Moran, Burlington, N. C., three daughters, Mrs. Z. H. Cotner, Clemmons, N. C., Mrs. A. F. Cotner, Siler City, N. C., and Miss Swannie Moran, Burlington, N. C., also two brothers, Henry and John Whitehead, two sisters, Mrs. Henry Fogleman, Siler City, N. C., and Mrs. Jasper Clapp, Greensboro, N. C., and a host of friends. She gave her heart to God in early life and joined the Methodist church at Flint Ridge. She lived the life of a consistent Christian and we bow in humble submission to the will of God for our loss in her gain. Funeral services were conducted at the church by Rev. W. M. Pike.

    Z. H. COTNER.

LAST MOMENT EVENTS

North Carolina is to undertake a state wide road construction.

Congress is to hold night sessions with the hope of avoiding extra session.

The former emperor of Austria is to apply for a divorce. Such is the luck of the crown heads—and some who have no crowns on their heads.

The papers state that President Wilson is pounding his own typewriter in France. A very good way to get it done. That is the way that these lines are being written—our own *pounding*.

The amount of France's reparation will be about 66 billion francs and Belguim's 15 billion.

BOOK NOTES

Story Books For The Children

We now have on hand a very fine story book for the children. "Redmond of the Seventh," by Mrs. Frank Lee. The book is handsomely bound, lettered in gold and contains 290 pages. The story is wholesome—a school story. The price is within the reach of all—75 cents postpaid, or two for $1.25.

Christian Hymnaries

We have the Christian Hymnary at 75 cents the copy. How many copies?

Tarbell's Guide

How about a copy of Tarbell's Guide for the 1919 Sunday school lessons? Our supply of Peloubet's Notes has exhausted, but this year Tarbell's Guide has been very popular. It contains 464 pages, handsomely bound and will please you. Price, $1.35 delivered, or $1.25 when delivered at our office.

Bibles

Red Letter Teachers Bible, $2.65; a child's Bible $1.50; Scofield References Bible from $2.00 upwards; write us your needs and get prices.

Testaments

Khaki, 30 cents postpaid. (This is one-half the former price); Red Letter Testaments, 75 cents; leather pocket Testaments 50 cents.

Address

C. B. RIDDLE, *Publishing Agent*, Burlington, N. C.

THE TITHER

An interdenominational publication devoted to Tithing and Christian Stewardship.

Editors

C. B. RIDDLE
KARL LEHMANN
BERT WILSON
HUGH S. McCORD
FRED G. THOMAS

8 pages; issued monthly; 50c the year

Address

THE TITHER   Burlington, N. C.

TICKLES

A glue factory stands near a certain railway. Its charms are not for the nose, and therefore a lady often carried with her a bottle of lavender salts. One morning an old farmer took the seat beside her. As the train neared the factory the lady opened her bottle of salts. Soon the whole car was filled with the horrible odor. The farmer put up with it as long as he could, then shouted, "Madam, would you mind puttin' the cork in that ere bottle?"— New York Tribune.

In Tennessee they tell of a judge, well versed in law, but self-educated, who had to contend with the difficulty of orthography all his life. He lived in Knoxville, and used to spell it "Noxville." He was educated to the point of prefixing a K; so thoroughly, in fact, was the lesson learned that a few years later, when he moved to Nashville, nothing could prevent him from spelling it "Knashville."—Congregationalist.

"Umbrellas Recovered," reads a sign in a Fulton street window. Any one recovering the last three of ours may keep one for his pains.—New York Evening Post.

"I see they are going to put conscientious objectors to work on the farms."

"Gee whiz," replied the farmer, "We've had enough of that sort of help hanging around our farms already."

| 1919 FEBRUARY 1919 |||||||
Su	Mo	Tu	We	Th	Fr	Sa
						1
2	3	4	5	6	7	8
9	10	11	12	13	14	15
16	17	18	19	20	21	22
23	24	25	26	27	28	

A School of Morals

 THE home is the first and best school of morals. This *school* is not being given a fair chance. The hurry, hurry, American spirit is robbing it of its teaching forces. Long hours, the quest of riches, and the strain of our economic system all have a tendency to shorten our moments by the fireside and lessen our opportunities for companionship and meditation. Christian forces pay little attention to the remedying of the situation, but endeavor to heal the wounds of its victims.

Volume LXXI	WEDNESDAY, FEBRUARY 12, 1919	Number 7
BURLINGTON	• : •	**NORTH CAROLINA**

THE CHRISTIAN SUN

Founded 1844 by Rev. Daniel W. Kerr

C. B. RIDDLE   -   -   - Editor

Entered at the Burlington, N. C. Post Office as second class matter.

Subscription Rates

One year .... $ 2.00
Six months 1.00

In Advance

Give both your old and new postoffice when asking that your address be changed.

The change of your label is your receipt for money. Written receipts sent upon request.

Marriage and obituary notices not exceeding 150 words printed free if received within 60 days from date of event, all over this at the rate of one-half cent a word.

Original poetry not accepted for publication.

Principles of the Christian Church

(1) The Lord Jesus Christ is the only Head of the Church.
(2) Christian is a sufficient name of the Church.
(3) The Holy Bible is a sufficient rule of faith and practice.
(4) Christian character is a sufficient test of fellowship, and of church membership.
(5) The right of private judgment and the liberty of conscience is a right and a privilege that should be accorded to, and exercised by all.

EDITORIAL

SENDING LABORERS INTO THE HARVEST

In all denominations there has been a falling off of ministers and missionaries during the last few years. Church leaders have been diagnosing the problem. They do not all agree as to what the cause or causes are, neither do they agree as to methods and means of recruiting ministerial ranks. In our own communion there are differences of opinion. Some believe that the man is called of God without concern upon the part of any individual or individuals. There are those who contend that we must pray them into the work.

God does not call all men in the same way. No one theory as to getting men into the ministry will suffice. It is noticeable that our opinions on this subject follow along the line that we have experienced. Not every minister can relate the same experience—in fact very few are alike. We believe that we have a right and a privilege to counsel with, and suggest to, men concerning the ministry, but we do not, as we now see it, have the right and privilege to advise young men to enter the ministry, unless they feel impressed.

The Convention has set aside Sunday, February 16, as a time when our ministers and Christian workers should place the matter of recruiting of ministerial and missionary forces. The ministers, we are sure, will call attention to the need of new recruits and lay the mat-

ter of the Kingdom's interest upon the hearts of the young people.

No young man or young woman should be influenced to take up active Christian work under pressure or overdrawn enthusiasm. The work is a vital issue and not a thing for today only. We should be very careful to explain the importance of adequate preparation. So many enter the ministry and find the task of preparation too great, and so either give up the work or go out unprepared, which means a check in the progress of the Church.

In this connection we deem it wise to reproduce on this page an article by President W. A. Harper which appeared in print something over a year ago. It is the situation viewed from the standpoint of a layman. Read it:

A CALL TO THE MINISTRY

The Real Question of Issue

Our Educational Board is right in its plea that our young men should consider the Christian ministry as a life-work. Emphasis needs ot be placed on the claim God rightfully has on every man for his services, and too great emphasis cannot be placed here. But while this is the duty of the Board and of the churches, it should be remembered that the paramount question in each individual man's mind should be, not Shall I enter the ministry? but Can I keep out of it? No man should enter the ministry if he can get the consent of his heart to do anything else. It is not quantity, but quality, that is needed, and the attitude I have suggested as leading to an ultimate decision will yield just that very result.

God Calls His Own Prophets

It is, then, not the selection of the ministry as a life-work, but the understanding of God's will respecting life-work for the individual that is most vital concern. As a Church we ought to hold up the claims of the ministry, but God must select His own prophets. We must not make the mistake of selecting a Matthias, when God needs a Paul. He calls men into the ministry, not we, and this must never be lost sight of, even momentarily. The proper attitude for each individual is to be open-minded, ready to be convinced of his duty, and submissively anxious to be of service in advancing the Kingdom of God. The real duty of the Church is to bring home to each soul of its membership the clarion call of God to His ministry and to secure from each a reverent consideration of his personal response to such a call, knowing that the call, if valid, can proceed only from the great white Throne.

The Place of Friendship in the Call

The question immediately arises as to what constitutes a call to the ministry and what are the indicators that can assist the individual to arrive at certainty in respect to his call. One very strong indication in this direction, it seems to me, would be the voluntary advice and counsel to a man's associates. They know him thoroughly and their desire, based on his life with them, should cause any man to ponder well his duty to enter the ministry. The minister will have his place in this advice and counsel, but he should consult others before advising too surely in any case.

The Life's Influence an Indication

A second indication would be the influence a man's life is exerting in religious circles. If he is put forward as a leader and looked to with confidence, that would in itself suggest a larger sphere of service, especially, if these marks of trust and confidence came unsought and in early life.

The Life's Vital Interest Should Have Weight

One's own taste and temperament will be another pointer. Do I love the worship of the sanctuary? Do I rejoice in the things of the spirit? Is my vital concern in spiritual rather than material issues? These questions will help wonderfully in settling the matter.

But the Spirit's Witness Necessary

But the final consideration must be in every case the witness of God's Spirit in my own heart that it is His will for me through preaching to point men to the way of salvation. The writer is a layman and is so because he has never felt that witness. He is glad to serve in a layman's place the great interests of the Kingdom, but happy is that man whom God has chosen to stand in holy places and proclaim the unsearchable riches of His Grace! There is no higher happiness! In the face of such a call, every other interest must yield. "Woe is me if I preach not the Gospel," and joy, joy, joy unspeakable if I follow my Father's call and do His will! May every young man who reads these lines place himself in God's hands and trustingly await His guidance!

The Preparation It Will Require

A call to the ministry will require not only such witness as we have just suggested, but also thorough preparation. There are cases where the preparation must be limited, as when the call comes late in life. I have known such men to be of great service without the thorough preparation I suggest. But a young man ought not to be content to begin his ministry without adequate preparation. If God has called him early, it is that he may fill a large place by having opportunity to prepare for it. The times demand a superior type of spiritual leadership, and that too should encourage special effort. If a man is not willing to pay the price of his call, he may well consider whether he has really been called.

The Reward That Will Crown The Life

One final thought shall conclude this brief discussion.—the thought as to the reward awaiting the called and prepared minister. I said minister rather than ministry purposely, for the ministry, as such does not appeal to men particularly, but the individual minister does. The deference, the reverence, accorded the minister, due to his place of leadership and the vital interests he faithfully represents, will surely compensate any sacrifice exacted in his accepting the call and making the preparation. But greater than any deference, deeper than any reverence, will be the satisfaction in his own heart of having been enabled to be to men and women the gateway into the Kingdom, the everlasting Kingdom of the Christ.

W. A. HARPER.

ELON AND HER ENDOWMENT

In this week's issue we present from the view point of many members of the Church words of commendation concerning Elon's endowment fund of $125,000.00. These men and women speak for the whole Church. They voice the sentiment of every true and loyal member of the denomination. On page twelve will be found an address to the churches by the President of the Convention and members of he Board of Trustees. They state specifically and definitely why Elon should have an additional endowment of $125,000.00. The Southern Christian Convention in session at Burlington in 1916 approved of the idea, and in the Franklin Convention last May the plan was adopted by unanimous vote of that body.

A few years ago the College raised a special fund of $50,000. This fund was a result of special effort and initiative on the part of the College. The raising of $125,000 as an additional endowment of our College differs from the $50,000 fund in that it is approved and undertaken by the Church at large.

It would be futile for us to point out why this fund is needed; that is told again and again on pages 4, 5, 6 and 7 of this issue. The Church has never undertaken such a fund in the interest of education. That alone ought to be a sufficient impulse to encourage every member of the denomination. This is a day of big things, big undertakings, larger responsibilities. The problem of education is weighing heavily and mightily upon the leaders of the Church and upon every home. From millions of homes the cry for a larger and better opportunity is going up from sons and daughters. We must meet their call and their cry; we must give them a chance to meet the problems of their day. We can best give them an education by endowing and equipping our college above financial reproach.

By turning to pages 12, 13 and 14 readers will find suggested goals for the various churches in the interest of this endowment fund. Note that these goals are only suggested and are based on the Elon College Fund as apportioned by the annual conferences. They are not apportionments or assessments but what the committee feels that each church ought to give in the interest of the cause. The amounts indicated are to be paid in five years. For example: A church that is asked to contribute $500 can contribute the sum of $100 per year and raise this money in any manner and method that it so desires.

Let us keep in mind the following facts:

1. Elon College needs this money to carry forward the educational work of the Church.

2. The Church needs the educational influence and force of the College.

3. Let us pray for larger things and then pray that these larger things may come.

4. We have placed the burden of raising this sum of money upon the heart of President Harper. He needs our prayers as well as our financial support.

The raising of this fund will mark a new day for Elon College, a new day for the cause of Christian education in the Christian Church. Prayerfully and with earnest hearts let us go to the task.

CHRISTIAN EDUCATION

ONE HUNDRED AND TWENTY-FIVE THOUSAND DOLLARS

A campaign to raise *one hundred and twenty-five thousand dollars*, in addition to the present-Endowment Fund, for Elon College, has been duly authorized by the Southern Christian Convention, sole owner of the College, and the Board of Trustees of the College. The reason for this Fund is a double one. It is a necessity for the maintenance of the Institution, and the requirement for a standard college of two hundred thousand dollars endowment makes the necessity imperative.

The usefulness of Elon College in Christian Education is a moral reason for this forward step in placing the Institution on a sound financial basis and keeping it on a par with other colleges. Its reputation must be maintained and its services strengthened. A Church without a college would be like a state without a public school or a university.

The atmosphere of a Christian denomination is created by its schools, and this campaign not only deserves the endorsement of a few but the substantial support of the whole Church. Every member of the Church with means and good earning capacity should subscribe liberally to this Fund as soon as the opportunity is given. Hesitation weakens effort and success is attained by wholehearted and prompt response to conviction. This is no small matter as to importance or undertaking. It has my hearty endorsement and will have my best subscription.

W. W. STALEY, *President;*
Southern Christian Convention.

THE COLLEGE DESERVES AND NEEDS THE HELP

I notice that there is a movement on foot to secure an endowment fund for Elon College. I am very much interested in this enterprise and hope that it will succeed. Would be glad if you would insert in your paper an announcement to that effect, stating my position in the matter, viz: As a member of the Christian Church, former student of the College, and a citizen of Alamance County I give my endorsement to Elon's campaign to raise one hundred and twenty-five thousand dollars as additional endowment. I hope the movement will succeed; the college deserves as well as needs the help.

W. J. GRAHAM.
House of Representatives,
Raleigh, N. C.

HEARTY ENDOSEMENT

There was a plan that was called to the attention of the Southern Christian Convention at Franklin, Va., to raise endowment fund for Elon College I hearty endorse the plan to begin active arrangements early this spring to raise the required endowment fund for Elon College.

T. J. HOLLAND.
Wray, Ga.

A TIME TO ACT

We are in the midst of a great educational awakening. The hour is pregnant with the spirit.

Large sums of money are being poured into the endowment funds of our colleges and universities. The spirit of the times is to give where great need manifests itself.

The Methodist Church concluded a campaign for $35,000,000 for educational enterprises last June. Other Churches are doing likewise.

The Southern Christian Convention, in a recent session, voted to increase the Endowment of Elon College by raising the $125,000.00. Shall we show our approval of this most worthy undertaking and pledge our support?

Elon, in a very definite sense, is the child of the Church, and has made a most valuable contribution to the Church. She has supplied our pulpits and furnished us leaders in every department of church activity. To her we shall look for recruits for the ministry, missionaries and leaders for the future. If we would maintain our supply of workers we must support and maintain our college, and if we would have workers of the greatest efficiency and power, such as the times demands, we must maintain a high standard for our institution of learning.

Elon College is the centre of Christian Education for the Southern Christian Convention. It is an indispensible factor in the work of the Church. Elon is looking to the Church for financial support. If the Church fails, the College fails, but we believe the Church will not fail in this undertaking.

Elon has grown and developed in its short history, but funds are needed to continue its growth and development. The institution demands greater accommodations to meet the increased enrollment. With the increase in students comes the demand for enlarged equipment and more instructors. We of the Christian Church should feel the obligation resting upon us to equip and man our college to meet the demands of the times.

The $125,000.00 additional Endowment is greatly needed and the people of the Christian Church should count it a privilege to furnish it. If we as a Church would render a great service, in this day of enlarged opportunity, if we would occupy a great place in the Church of the future, we must look well to our schools. The hope of any Church as it faces the future lies in her educational institutions.

Money invested in Elon College will be a permanent investment, and will continue to work for God after we have passed to our reward. The opportunity is now being given to the people of the Christian Church to make an investment which will gladden hearts and strengthen the cause which is dear to our hearts.

MRS. J. W. HARRELL.
Burlington, N. C.

ELON STANARDIZATION ENDOWMENT

If those who go to college had to pay the cost of their keep and teaching while there, only the very rich could go. Tuition and other college charges are but a fraction of the actual cost of higher education. The State, as well as the Church, recognizes this and appropriates tens of thousands of dollars annually from the public treasury for the higher education of her sons and daughters. And this is not counted waste nor loss because every one in Church or State who receives the benefits of a college education becomes an asset, and if at all worthy, pays back more to the public than it has cost the public to help educate him.

It has cost the Christian Church several thousand dollars good money to help pay the tuition and upkeep of men and women attending Elon College; but who will say that the Church as such has not received back either more in enchanced valuation of intelligent, educated manhood and womanhood than it has ever paid out in dollars? The value of one well educated man or woman in Church, community, or pulpit, cannot be estimated in dollars.

The Christians of the Southern Christian Convention are as worthy of a well equipped college as any other people, for we need the assets and benefits of such an institution. And the only hope of maintaining and developing our College is constantly increased funds.

I favor the Standardization Endowment fund of $125,000 for three specific reasons, among many others that might be mentioned:

First, the young men and the young women in the homes of our membership both need and deserve the added advantages that such an endowment will bring.

Second, The College, to go *forward on the great mission we have appointed it, and to keep pace with the best, *must have the* Standardization Endowment.

Third, the largeness and the scope of our activities, our influence and our undertakings as a Church are broadening every day, and the bigger, better Elon as the training camp for our forces is a pressing necessity.

We can if we will, and God helping us we will do this great and needful thing.

J. O. ATKINSON.
Elon College, N. C.

NOW IS THE TIME

I heartly endorse the campaign to raise the $125,000 endowment for Elon. We need a larger endowment to keep our College abreast with other denominational colleges. We need it to enable us to enlarge our equipment so we will be able to meet the increasing demand on our College and give the student body service equal to any college and I feel now is the time to start the campaign.

D. S. FARMER.
News Ferry, Va.

NECESSARY FOR A HIGH STANDARD

In response to letter from President Harper relative to the $125,000.00 endowment fund for Elon College, from my view point this fund is necessary to carry forward the great educational work undertaken and to maintain the high standard already attained. It has always been a source of pleasure to me to contribute what I could to Elon, and I have never regretted the

$1,000.00 contributed to the Special Fund. I hope that this present fund will prove a great blessing to the institution, and I know that it has already proved a blessing to me by having made the contribution mentioned.

While we have no children to be educated, yet I know that this institution will prove of untold blessings to generations unborn.

W. Q. PEEL.
Holland, Va.

LET US DO OUR BEST

I do very heartily endorse the campaign for $125,000. It is just the little difference between the good and the best that makes the difference between the artist and the artisan. We have done well in the past, now let us do our best in this campaign.

May God's blessings rest on the launching of this great work.

MRS. S. A. CAVENESS.
Greensboro, N. C.

LET US HELP COMING GENERATIONS

Elon College is the educational center of the Christian Church in the South. The people of the Christian Church have built it and made it what it is. But because it is what it is does not mean it is what it should be. It has done and is doing a great part in the Christian Church, but with the whole-hearted support of the brotherhood, Elon is destined to do "greater things than these." Now to do greater things, it must have our sympathy our love and our hearty co-operation in a financial way.

No college that we know is self-supporting. Elon is as near or nearer than any college in the State. Other denominational institutions have a large endowment fund to take care of the growth of the institution Shall we not have as much love for our own college? The Trustees of Elon have asked Dr. Harper to raise $125,000, for Elon's future usefulness. Let us help the coming generations.

J. LEE JOHNSON.
Holly Springs, N. C.

DUTY AND EXHALTED PRIVILEGE

As one of the patrons of Elon, and also one of her greatest admirers, I want to congratulate the Board of Trustees on the big step forward in the endowment fund. It is the duty and exhalted privilege of every church in the North Carolina Christian Conference to win the flag for "over the top" subscriptions. My earnest wish is that the Ramseur church shall not fail to reach the goal.

MRS. T. A. MOFFITT.
Ramseur, N. C.

MUST GET BEHIND IT WITH OUR DOLLARS

Everywhere it has been our privilege to go, we have found men who knew something of Elon College. They talk about it, and speak highly of what it is, what it has done, and what it is destined to do in the coming years. There is no man who is loyal to his Church but what likes to hear someone who is a stranger speak highly of some auxiliary of the work that has been a blessing to humanity. That Elon has been a great success no one will deny, for thousands have been blessed by the great work of the Institution. Millions will be blessed.

Now the question of our love for the College is before us. Its President tells us that additional endowment is needed. The Southern Christian Convention voiced this sentiment, and said raise an additional endowment of $125,000, but what says the Church? The endowment is not only needed, but must be raised, before our work can go forward as it should in the future years.

One of the greatest needs of the College is a Chair of Theology for those looking forward to the ministry and mission field. Our Convention last May instructed our Mission Secretary to call for one hundred volunteers for the ministry and mission fields. These must be educated and there is no better place to do it than at Elon College. The Convention also provided that the additional endowment take care of this work. The cry for a course of this kind has been heard for many years, and now we are given an opportunity to make the work possible.

If the rapid growth of Elon is to be continued, we must get behind it with our hard earned dollars, and prove our loyalty to it by permitting our love to express itself in dollars and cents. Let us think of the 5,585 students who have been blessed by the influence of the College, and the great blessing the Institution is bringing to the now unnumbered thousands; and then we will forget that it takes money to run the College, and this endowment will be easily raised.

J. VINCENT KNIGHT.

Greensboro, N. C.

PREPARE FOR THE FUTURE

I heartily endorse the Endowment Fund for Elon College. Studying the future of the College as compared with the results of the past twenty years, we as members of the denomination ought to do so now, while money is the cheapest commodity we have to encounter with, make the future secure, and from the great value of a Christian education to young men and women, we should make a greater sacrifice at this time.

We who have had the fruits of Elon College put before us know what it has done in the beginning. The future can be made brighter year by year, if our prayers are honest and our faith by works are put in it.

L. M. CLYMER.

Greensboro, N. C.

A LARGER PROGRAM AND EQUIPMENT

In a recent *Red Cross Magazine*, there is a cartoon of Uncle Sam, laying aside his fighting clothes and trying to don his "before the war" outfit. But it is no fit. He has outgrown them. Things that once pleased his fancy, have taken second place. "Our own little affairs" have shrunk and something bigger, better must take their place.

Now can our institutions of learning and uplift set-

tle back to where they were a year or so ago? Larger interests, enlarged vision call for a larger program and equipment and if they do not arise to these demands they will be forced to drop back for shame and lack of self-respect.

So Elon College, the guiding spirit of our own Southern Christian Convention, must be filled up for further and larger service. The thought is not to be entertained that our people will not furnish her with the equipment necessary to maintain her position and standing among the colleges of the South. The hour has struck. We must not fail her.

MRS. C. H. ROWLAND.

Franklin, Va.

THAT $125,000 FOR ELON COLLEGE

The close of the war and the days of reconstruction are going to mean the launching of an era in which there will be almost unlimited opportunities for the young people of this generation. These openings will call for trained men and women. School and colleges should flourish for the next ten years as never before. The opportunity of the denominational college, will be better than ever.

To meet this condition and supply the needs of those who come our college must have a full faculty of a high standard and be well equipped in every way for its work. At the present high cost of living, and of all material used in connection with the college, we shall need more funds.

Our people have learned to give during the war and we should have no trouble in raising the $125,000 additional endowment for our college. Elon College is A-1 college now and we need this amount to keep it so. Let there be a hearty response to Dr. Harper's appeal when he opens the campaign for this fund.

W. T. WALTERS.

Winchester, Va.

DESERVES OUR BEST EFFORTS

I heartily endorse the raising of $125,000.00 additional Endowment Fund for Elon College.

It is certainly a worthy institution and deserves our best efforts to contribute everything possible towards its success.

ALVA C. RICHARDS.

Winchester, Va.

THE ELON COLLEGE ENDOWMENT FUND

According to the report of the Board of Education submitted at the last session of the Southern Christian Convention the Endowment of Elon College is $88,216.98. To meet the requirements of the departments of Education of the United States and of many individual states, Elon must have an endowment of $200,000.00, or it cannot be rated as a college. The present endowment, therefore, needs to be increased; and the amount now to be asked is $125,000.00. It is to be hoped and expected that every church shall have a part in this most worthy and, thus far, our greatest endeavor for Elon ollege.

The announcement of a campaign to raise the additional endowment does not come to us as a surprise, for the Board of Trustees at the Burlington Convention in 1916 were authorized to undertake the campaign. The reason it was postponed is due to the campaign of the $100,000.00 for missions, which to our great joy has already been raised. The Board of Trustees and the enthusiastic advocates of the additional endowment willingly and unselfishly acquiesced in the request of the Convention's leaders not to launch the campaign till the $100,000.00 for missions had been raised.

The additional endowment of $125,000.00 ought to be a willing gift, it seems to me, to our College. She not only *needs* it, *she deserves* it. It is unreasonable and selfish to expect our College to do the work we require her to do and not heed the reasonable and unselfish requests she may make. She has returned with good interest every dollar she has received, and in every enterprise of the Church is found in her influence and help. She has been, and is, the good Samaritan to the churches of the Southern Christian Convention, taking our young people from farm, factory, and shop, tenderly caring for them and fitting them for usefulness in life. These, and there are thousands of them, will ever arise up and call her blessed. And these, with a greater number still, who, while never coming directly under her care, have felt her influence for good, will, I believe, rally to her support and make this her greatest request easily and quickly realized.

T. E. WHITE.

Sanford, N. C.

THE CHRISTIAN ORPHANAGE

GOALS FOR 1919

Last year was the best year financially for the Orphanage that we have had in the history of the Institution; and during the entire year our people were called on to contribute to many different causes to help win the war. I am glad to say that our people were as loyal as any people could be to the calls of our government and contributed as never before that we might win in that mighty struggle and have a world that would be a fit place in which to live. But with the many calls and demands upon our people I am truly glad to say that the little orphan children were not forgotten but were kindly remembered in many ways. I am informed that the other Orphanages in the State had a good year, too.

It does seem to me that as the war is over and our people will not be called upon during the year 1919 for so many things, that the contributions for the little orphans should be greater than ever. Should we not do greater things for their benefit this year than last? The year 1917, we set for our goal ten thousand dollars, ($10,000.00), and we went over it. The year 1918, we set our goal eleven thousand dollars, ($11,000.00), and we reached more than fourteen thousand dollars. We ought to do more this year than last and really ought to set the goal for the total amount for this year $15,-

000. But we would rather run over the goal set than to fail to reach it. It always takes away the "pep" to fail to reach a goal and makes us feel discouraged. So we want to keep within the bounds which we feel sure we can reach and will set the goals for this year two thousand dollars ($2,000.00), more than last year and then you can run as far over as you feel that you want to go. We have three goals for the year 1919:

We want to raise for our Easter Offerings, $2,500.00
We want to raise for our Thanksgiving
    Offerings,   5,500.00
We want to raise from Sunday school
    and Special Offerings,   5,000.00

Total to be raised for the year 1919, $13,000.00

This is just two thousand dollars more than the goal set last year and it seems to me that we ought to reach each goal set without any trouble. Now let us begin to plan to do our best for this year and see that our Orphanage grows in its work and many more little children who are now knocking at its doors for admittance be not turned away.

Get your Sunday school on the list of monthly contributors and don't be satisfied until you see that this is done. We are going to make a hard fight this year to get each one on the list. We hope and trust that the pastors and Sunday school superintendents will see that this one thing is accomplished.

It will do your Sunday school a great service if you will get it on this list. The way to have a live Sunday school or a live church is to have a working one. A busy one. Doing something, accomplishing something. Rendering a service to the poor and needy, the widows and orphans.

Let our motto for this year be: "Our Best Year" for the Orphanage cause.

Our good friends still remember us. The Ladies' Aid Society of the Haw River Christian church sent to us a beautiful quilt for the comfort of the little fellows.

Miss Lena Workman, Mebane, N. C., one dozen jars can fruit; Miss Lizzie Holt, Mebane, N. C., eight quarts can fruit; Mr. W. G. Woodell, Corinth, N. C., six half gallon cans tomatoes.

REPORT FOR FEBRUARY 12, 1919

Amount brought forward, $436.06.

Sunday School Monthly Offerings

Asheboro, $2.51; Catawba Springs, $10.00; Pleasant Ridge, $3.25; Oak Level, $1.00.

(Virginia Valley Conference)

Linville, $1.00; Timber Ridge, $1.20.

(Georgia and Alabama Conference)

North Highlands, $2.00.

(Eastern Virginia Conference)

Rosemont, $5.00.

(Western North Carolina Conference)

New Providence Baraca Class, Graham, N. C., $3.30; Total, $29.26.

Special Offerings

Mrs. L. W. Paynther, Ludoniei, Ga., $2.00; Mr. A. P. Thompson, $17.00; Southern Railway Company, Error in freight, $1.42 Dr. G. S. Watson, Cash items, $2.00; Mrs. S. C. E. Beamon, Sunbury, N. C., $6.00; J. H. Jones, $5.50; Total, $33.92. Total for the week, $63.18; Grand total, $499.24.

PASTOR AND PEOPLE

THIRD CHRISTIAN CHURCH, NORFOLK, VA

My dear Bro. Riddle and Christian Sun Readers:

It has been some time since you heard very much of me. For about seven years, I believe, we have been located out of your section, but now that we are back near I am in hopes that we may see and hear more of each other. We have been on the field now about three weeks, just beginning to get acquainted and an intelligent introduction to the situation. There is certainly no question about the Third church having a great opportunity. In fact the opportunity here is much greater than I thought before coming. This means as a matter, of course, that there is a hard piece of work in store for somebody. It will mean lots of faith, lots of grace, lots of prayer, and lots of sacrifice. If you can find time to think of us when you pray we shall greatly appreciate it and shall be blessed.

The former pastors have no doubt planned wisely and worked faithfully. I happen to know two of them personally—the Rev. A. M. Hanson and Rev. G. D. Eastes. Finer spirits or more consecrated hands never gave themselves to the Gospel ministry. And no doubt but through their prayers and efforts together with the complete co-operation of the good people, this church has been made what it is today and in the beginning of my pastorate I wish to acknowledge their work and worth here. May God richly bless them daily in their respective fields.

I find a fine spirit of co-operation among the people, a willingness to forge ahead, and a consecrated determination to make the Third church take its proper place in the city and in the Kingdom. With such co-operation and assistance, obstacles move easily, tasks are completed without delay and the future opens to us. There is a joy in service and a blessing in sacrifice.

Special services have been arranged for the coming Sabbath. A missionary service at 11:00 o'clock in honor of our missionary to Porto Rico, Miss Olive G. Williams. The formal installation service comes at 2:30 P. M. A number of our own ministers and some of other denominations will take part on the program. All friends of the church are cordially invited to be present.

Yours in Christ,
L. E. SMITH.

4312 *Colonial Ave.,*
Norfolk, Va.

SUFFOLK LETTER

The February-March campaign to increase the circulation of THE CHRISTIAN SUN is a wise endeavor and should receive the co-operation of the people. Few church members stop to consider the value of the Church paper. It is called the "organ" of the Conventions, that is it is the mouthpiece of the denomination. Without such "organ" it would be a dumb church. It is larger than the greatest preacher, the greatest educator, or the greatest Institution. The splendid report of Superintendent Chas. D. Johnston

for 1918, that it was the best year of the Christian Orphanage would have been impossible without THE CHRISTIAN SUN. The Institution *calls* through THE SUN, *thanks* through THE SUN, *plans* through THE SUN. The same is true of Elon College, the Missionary enterprise, the Women's Societies, and even Conferences in their meetings and work. *It must live, if the Church is to live.*

The subscription should be increased by full-year permanent subscribers. A thousand new subscriptions ought to be added to the permanent list. That number would put THE SUN on a basis to pay expenses, and it ought not to pull all the time against a deficit, as it has been doing for a year. An average of *five new* subscriptions to a church would assured a clean thousand. It would be an easy matter to get *three months*, *six months*, and *yearly* subscribers, and *donations* to make up the balance; but these have been secured heretofore; but they are temporary; the only thing that really counts is personal subscriptions by the full-year, paid in advance. Advance payments are the most satisfactory not only to the paper, but to the subscriber. It is nothing more than cash payment; and any one knows that it is easier to pay for a pair of shoes when they are new than after they are worn out.

The constituency of the Convention represents *five thousand* families on the basis of *five* to family, but for church membership it is more than that number. Four thousand subscribers would not be too many to expect from a membership; and that number would place THE SUN on a firm financial basis and double its usefulness. Your two dollars and your prayers will help to reach the goal. Are you willing to pay the *two dollars* to place THE SUN *fifty-two* times a year in your home? You cannot spend *two dollars* in any other way that will do as much good.

I read somewhere that "great men are hospitable to ideas from whatever source they come," and a church paper is the cleanest sheet from the press. It is the rarest thing that THE SUN contains anything that is not pure and uplifting. When you read THE SUN next week, ask your neighbor to subscribe for a year. The pastor cannot see all the members, but the readers of THE SUN can. Here is a chance for *you* to help THE SUN and some member of the church. Somebody will come into your mind as you read these lines; that is the person you can win to THE SUN family.

W. W. STALEY.

A SOURCE OF HOPE AND INSPIRATION

The decision of our Burlington Sunday school on Sunday, January 26 will be far reaching in its scope and influence. It was no spasmodic movement, nor the doings of momentary impulse. For years the missionary spirit has been cultivated, and has been growing in the minds and hearts of members of this school and congregation. The school has had for years a superintendent of missions whose chief business it is to keep the school advised in missionary matters and lecture for five minutes before the school every Sunday on missions. Brother John R. Foster, one of our Orphanage trustees, brother of Jas. L. Foster and a successful business man of Burlington, held this position for years and had much to do with bringing the school to its present missionary interest, zeal and enthusiasm. For the past few months Mr. W. M. Brown, a graduate of Elon College, former Principal of Lexington schools, now a resident of Burlington, has filled to great joy and acceptance the position of Lecturer on Missions before the school, and the verdict in Burlington is that no school has a lecturer who can say more on missions in few words than Brother Brown. And my recollection is that since the early days of the pastorate of Dr. P. H. Fleming the congregation has been supporting a native Bible woman in Japan, and succeeding pastors have aided in keeping alive the missionary spirit planted years ago. The present pastor, Rev. J. W. Harrell, D. D., is noted for his missionary zeal and his vision of world-wide evangelization. His whole heart was in the movement which culminated on January 2 in the school's voting practically unanimously to support a missionary in Japan, at an annual salary of $750.00. For a Sunday school to vote upon itself a task of that magnitude, when it, with the church, was in the building program that is taxing the membership to most unusual proportion, required zeal for the cause, faith in God, and a courage worthy of the heroic souls who have labored and prayed that this very thing might come to pass. This example of our Burlington school will be followed by other schools, and in a few years, if God wills, we shall have Sunday schools and churches all over our Convention supporting one or more missionaries in the foreign field. May God hasten this glorious day with its holy achievement. One whose heart is rejoiced beyond words at the great deed of the Burlington Sunday school,

J. O. ATKINSON.

TREASURER EMERITUS

Brother D. S. Farmer has resigned his position as treasurer of Pleasant Grove church. He regretted very much to have to do this, but on account of his rather poor health and the many responsibilities devolved upon him he found it necessary. The church reluctantly granted him his request and accepted his resignation. By unanimous consent of the church he was made treasurer emeritus for life. For eighteen years he had held this most responsible position and paid in behalf of his church several thousand dollars to the five pastors that have served during that time.

May God richly bless Brother Farmer for his record is an enviable one! His brother, Pleasant W. Farmer, is his successor.

J. G. TRUITT.

News Ferry, Va.

THE PERIL OF ECCLESIASTICISM

Professional in Church Leadership Has Wrought Havoc Abroad—Why The Prussian Church Failed

(William T. Ellis in The Religious Rambler)

Professionalism in religion is a peril like unto Prussianism in statecraft. Both have their roots in the same principle. Both are doomed by the present world upheaval.

To approach this delicate and difficult subject as it exists in America, and as it is related to general religious conditions as affected by the war, one may discreetly begin as far away as Russia. All the world is totaling up its account with poor Russia, since we are now about the slow business of salvaging so much as possible of the remnants of that pitiable nation. While Russia has failed in all departments of her national life, her most culpable collapse has been within the realm of religion. If the Russian church has functioned, the people of the land would not be in their present sorry plight; and the allies would not have had to pay so heavy a toll for Russia's recreancy.

What Ailed the Russian Church

Ecclesiastical politics paralyzed the Russian church. Her people are innately religious. No other land, unless it be India, can compare with Russia in spiritual questing and devotion. From it, before the war, came more pilgrims to Palestine than from all other nations combined. Muscovite mysticism is famous. Outside of a small revolutionary and "intellectual" group, irreligion was scarcely known among the millions of the czar's subjects. When revolution befell, no hand of violence was laid on the church.

But the priesthood as a whole stood apart from the popular movement. They had been a part of the ramifications of the autocracy. Politics was the breath of life to the higher ecclesiastics. Court favor controlled the important offices. The church was a tool of the state; and a tool often used for nefarious purposes. The masses had a long bill of grievances against the clergy, who had done police work, had fostered superstition, had condoned ignorance, had blessed injustice, had been silent upon moral questions, and had themselves been crafty and avaricious.

The Church Missed Her Chance

Still, with incredible patience, the people bore with the church. They looked to it for comradeship and leadership in the new search after liberty. It was hoped that at the great Moscow conference the church would establish herself upon a democratic basis, and enter upon a new era of ministry and enlightment. At the time of the conference, the people were like harried sheep, bleeding and with their fleece torn off. All the impulses of religion would seem to operate to send the church out to the masses, in a mighty ministry and shepherding.

Nothing of the sort happened. The church was blind to the crisis, except as her own dignities and prequisites and rights were concerned. She revealed herself as ruled by a company of church politicians to whom emoluments meant more than ministry or message. Today the Russian church stands discredited, a tragic exhibition of the baneful effects of professional ecclesiasticism. The deep religious instincts of the people still continue, and may be utilized for the saving of Russia; but that is another story. The important fact for present consideration is that when war's testing blast came, the church collapsed because her leaders were ecclesiastics instead of shepherds and prophets. Some day a new Tolstoi will tell the story, in all its ghastliness.

Ecclesiasticism in the New-Old East

Less intensified and dramatic than the case of the Russian church, but likewise illustratie of the palsying effect of ecclesiasticism, is the plight of the ancient Armenian and Nestorian churches whose centers are in the neighborhood of Mt. Ararat. These bodies have had a continuous history for fifteen hundred years. The second of them once was the most glorious exponent of missionary Christianity, its outposts reaching to Pekin. Now, however, both churches are bodies so dominated by the spirit of professionalism and church politics, that they admittedly can be saved only by a revolution or a revival. Already they show signs of feeling the breeze of vitality that is sweeping the world.

Prussia's Perversion of Piety

If the Russian church was complaisant and self-seeking and despiritualized, what shall we say of the Prussian State church, the degenerate child which boasts Luther as an ancestor? Arid scholasticism, which had seriously infected the entire Christian world, and formal ecclesiasticism, have for decades characterized the church in Germany. All the world has seen how servile it has been to the impious claims of the kaiser.

Introspection and self-condemnation have marked the course of British churchmen; but this note has not echoed from Germany. Instead, the ecclesiastic-ridden state church has found apologists for every German deed of evil, from the violation of Belgium to the sinking of the Lusitania and the rape of Russia. No ecclesiastical sensibilities have been hurt by the kaiser's mad claims to special partnership with God. Blasphemy is an unknown sin to these lick-spittle ecclesiastics, who outrival their imperial master in their distortion of the most elemental teachings of religion, for pan-German purposes. The land of Luther has gone far from the days when he hurled defiance at kings and electors.

As It Is In America

Perhaps a rough definition of ecclesiasticism is in order, as we come to look upon the type in America. The ecclesiastic is the professional proponent of churchism, sectarianism, or denominationalism. He makes his living and finds his career within the real realms of church politics and activities. Usually, he is a clergyman; but all clergymen are not ecclesiastic. Most who become such are unconscious of their own deterioration. Indeed, very few are. The tendency to become an ecclesiastic is strongest among the higher officers of the religious bodies. Men whose own salaried positions and personal power are made secure by their ecclesiastical activities are the commonest recruiting ground for the type. By no means all bishops and board secretaries are ecclesiastics; those who escape this fate, however, must possess a vital religion.

Ecclesiasticism intentionally or instinctively, puts personal or denominational advantage above the larger interests of Christianity. It makes a business of religion. Ceaselessly, it is bent upon building up an institution. Craft is a familiar tool to its hand. It has the wisdom of the serpent, if not the harmlessness of the harmlessness of the dove. So it cultivates the rich and powerful, since it desires to be rich and powerful itself.

It delights in closed doors and whispered conferences; and it is so "practical" that it prefers to settle affairs by private consultation, rather than open discussion. Doctrines and forms and institutions are dear to it; and if it could, it would endow everything religious than now exists, for ecclesiasticism is the high priest of "things as they are."

Smooth, sophisticated, subtle, ecclesiasticism is worldly wisdom in vestments: it is the world within the church. There is no very great difference between the ecclesiasticism of 1918, which penalized the progressive and reforming young preacher, and the ecclesiasticism of 30 A. D., which condemned a certain radical young Nazarene. Both represent prudence and self-interest gone to seed.

War's Swift Jolt

If I have at all understood the new tides of the times that are sweeping around the world, and the fresh, fearless facing of facts which characterizes the soldier, then it is perfectly clear to me that ecclesiasticism and all that it connotes is due to receive some startling jolts in the coming months and years. For ecclesiasticism represents a ruling class, a privileged group, a cast of professionalism verging upon autocracy. It smacks of aristocracy, and not of democracy.

Soldiers who have sloughed off without an effort the conventional accessories of religion, but who have entered into a new and deep appreciation of what is vital in faith, may make short shrift of that professional ruling class in the churches which is an obstruction to progress and to the simpler expressions of Christianity which the soldiers love. If the men who come back from the trenches take any part in church affairs it will be to promote simplicity and sincerity and essential unity. They care nothing about historic bodies. Most of them would be content to see one comprehensive, elastic organization, like the Y. M. C. A., represent all religion —though this is neither likely nor desirable. A return to first principles, with an uncomplicated organization, an elemental creed, and a great and helpful fraternity, would satisfy the soldiers. They believe in a church of human brotherhood, with Christ at its head; and its "leading members" the busiest and humblest servants of all.

Many notes, editorials and items of interest crowded out this week.

Be patient friends—we had enough matter this week for two issues and did the best we could.

Several contributions concerning the Elon College Endowment Fund reached us too late for this issue. They will appear next week.

Mr. Edward Teague, known to many SUN readers, died at his home in Burlington on February 8. He was in his 86th year and a member of the Friends' Church. A good man has gone to his reward.

THE FORWARD MOVEMENT

THE FORWARD MOVEMENT

Headquarters, 27 C. P. A. Building, Dayton, Ohio

Four-Minute-Men

During the War, the Four-Minute Men appointed by the government, did a wonderful service. They brought the needs of the government directly to the people in a most forceful way at every public gathering with a freshness and earnestness that intensely interested the people and caused their hearty response to the call of the government.

The various Forward Movements that are now in progress in the several denominations, in the same way, are using strong men and women to bring to each congregation the direct news of their denominational movements from Sunday to Sunday.

Our Forward Movement desires a corps of Four-Minute Men. We ask that every church, through its pastor, or otherwise, appoint a Four-Minute Man for its congregation. The man, or woman, should be one of the strongest and best workers and an influential speaker, and it will be his duty to bring, each Sunday, a four-minute message to the people concerning the Forward Moement work of the Christian Church. The pastor should grant him or her no more than four minutes of the time when the announcements are made to present, in the most forceful and interesting and concise way, the latest and best Forward Movement information and items that it is possible for him or her to secure. He will keep the congregation informed of the progress of the Movement. His name is to be sent to the headquarters office, where it will be placed on file, so that all the literature issued by the Movement will be mailed to him.

The work of the Four-Minute Men will be most important, and the pastor or official board should exercise good judgment in the selection of such a person.

The Pastor's Place in The Forward Movement

The Forward Movement of our Church is designed to inspire, strengthen, help and lead our pastors in the wonderful days upon which the world has already entered. The Forward Movement seeks to put at the disposal of all our pastors, the most practical and helpful information concerning the whole task of the Church, including the best and most suggestive methods of work involving the activities of the local church and reaching out to the whole program of the Kingdom of the entire Church of Jesus Christ.

The Movement seeks to put a premium upon pastoral initiative. In the Christian Church it is especially clear that the pastor is the center of all the church life. His experience which he develops in the work of his own church, when put at the disposal of others, constitutes the most valuable asset of our Forward Movement.

The Forward Movement, therefore, asks every pastor to share his experiences and plans and victories with his brethren through the church papers, institutes, conferences and with other groups of our church workers. The Forward Movement suggests and often urges upon every pastor a full and hearty compliance with certain principles, methods and forms of activity. It does, however, recognize and most thoroughly appreciate his individual leadership and power of initiative.

The Forward Movement asks every pastor to re-organize his church for practical purposes and build his church program around the five fundamentals of the Movement, as they are the fundamentals of the Christian life and fundamentals of the Church life. But that request is only in order that he may distribute his responsibilities among the congregation of which he is the leader.

We believe that our pastors, practically without exception, are in hearty sympathy with the Forward Movement of our church in these wonderful days. Their loyalty and interest and initiative are most highly appreciated.

League to Solicit Life Recruits

One of our College Presidents has suggested that in the Forward Movement Department of our Church papers, we open a column for the names of those who volunteer to become members of the "League to Solicit Life Recruits." We gladly accept his suggestion and shall be glad to enroll in our office any volunteers for such efforts and report through our Church papers as securing life recruits is one of the great points of our Forward Movement.

From a recent survey of our Church, it has been established that we need at least fifty Life Recruits, educated and trained, coming out from the top of our schools; this aside from those who enter and only partially prepare themselves for life Christian service. It is a very good service to try to win the strongest, noblest and best young lives in our homes, Sunday schools and churches to enter upon lives wholly given to Christian service. We are hoping that a large number of volunteers, both ministers and laymen, will enter upon such work in their fields.

Easter Additions to The Church

On Monday, April 21, the day after Easter Sunday, we ask every pastor in the denomination to report the number of persons received into his church on Easter Sunday. We ask the number and the conference to which the church belongs, as we wish to gather an accurate statement of the number of members received into each church and each conference on Easter Sunday.

We ask that there be no delay, but on the next day after Easter we be given the definite information, and this we want if there is only one member received into your church. More and more Easter is coming to be a day of large in-gathering into the church. In many, both city and country, a special effort is made to make this a day of great in-gathering into the church.

Please bear the importance of this request in mind and let us hear from you without further delay, the number of members received into the church of which you are pastor on Easter Sunday. We do not wish the names, only the number, the church and conference of which it is a member.

WARREN H. DENISON, *Supt.*

THE
ELON STANDARDIZATION FUND
An
Address To The Churches

Dear Brethren in Christ:

It had been the plan of the Board of Trustees of Elon College, acting upon the recommendation of the Southern Christian Convention, to launch the Campaign for $125,000 additional endowment in October 1917, and everything was in readiness for the beginning when it was thought in many quarters that we ought not to divide interest in our first great campaign for missions by conducting a parallel drive for funds for another cause, however worthy or necessary.

In response to that sentiment entertained by many of our leaders, Elon postponed her campaign till the $100,000 for missions was raised. That was done early in the fall of 1918, but conditions of health in the country have impelled us to wait until the third Sunday in February to begin our Campaign for a larger and better Elon as "the Officers' Training Camp of the Church, the Cantonment of the expeditionary force which our Church is to send on its evangelizing mission to the uttermost parts of the earth," to use the fine phrase of the Committee on Education of the Western North Carolina Conference.

We have selected the third Sunday in February to begin our drive, because the Southern Christian Convention has set that day aside as CHRISTIAN EDUCATION DAY in our Churches, and it is fitting that we should initiate its advent by a memorable undertaking. On this day also let every minister preach on "CHRISTIAN EDUCATION and THE CALL TO THE MINISTRY." Let us pray that God will give us not only a clarified vision of the needs of our College on this day, but the twenty splendid young Life Recruits so sorely needed in the opinion of our Convention in our program for the advancing Kingdom.

With confidence we address this message to our people, with confidence emboldened because of their generous response to the call of missions so magnificently crowned with success as well as because of the deserts of our College and its thrilling record of achievements. "Few Colleges," says the Report on Education of the 1918 session of Eastern Virginia Conference, "have such a reputation as Elon, won in so short a time and under such a financial strain,"

In the twenty-nine years of her history our College has justified every confidence and realized every hope of our people. She has supplied our pulpits with a trained and consecrated ministry and

our pews with devout and earnest lay-workers, "Her Alumni," to quote the Eastern Virginia Conference report again, "have proved themselves in school, in business, in Church, and in war." Elon's future is bright, brilliant, radiant with prophecy of enlarging service to the Kingdom, provided proper support is granted by our people, her founders and stay.

With confidence, let us say again, we therefore address this appeal to our Brotherhood, feeling assured that every Church, minister, layman, lay-woman will respond nobly to our call, which we do not hesitate to assert is imperative in its necessity at this time. The day is past for small things and paltry gifts to our College. It has in poverty achieved recognition, but larger income from permanent funds are unconditionally necessary now in order to retain the standards already won. We feel satisfied that our people will receive President Harper and those associated with him with open hands and glad hearts, ready to respond cheerfully to the necessities of our prosperous and progressive College. We commission him and them to this work of the Lord among us. It is His work and ours, not theirs. They are to be our agents in this forward step. Let us in the speedy conclusion of this drive take the "sting out of stingy," by a generosity worthy of our great Church and her liberal principles. Let us rejoice and be glad in this challenge to our faith and our vital Christian character.

We have carefully fixed the minimum goal which each Church should reach in order for this campaign to succeed (and succeed it must, under the blessing of God). Churches should aim to go "over the top" in their subscriptions, because there will inevitably be shrinkages, and the whole sum is needed. Our plan is to issue a proper recognition flag to every church that goes "over the top," with stars added every time the quota is doubled. Appropriate recognition also will be granted individuals whose gifts by reason of their liberality or sacrifice merit them, but announcement of these will be made later. Our people have become accustomed to such recognitions in the Liberty Loan, Red Cross, United War Work Fund and other drives during the war, and will readily endorse the inclusion of them in our "Elon Standardization Fund."

Just a word in conclusion as to the name of the fund. We call it "THE STANDARDIZATION FUND" because the departments of Education of the United States and of many individual states, with the concurrence of such educational organizations as the National

Educational Association and the Association of American Colleges have said no institution of higher learning can longer be rated as a College that does not have a paid in endowment of $200,000 at the very least. It will require $125,000 additional endowment for our College to meet this requirement and so we call this "THE ELON STANDARDIZATION FUND." To the work: let us erect our standards high and make our College safe in the esteem and recognition it has attained.

Praying God's rich blessings in abundance on every subscriber to the Fund and on the College that God may continue to direct it into becoming emphasis on its worthy and inspiring motto: "Christian Character first and always at Elon," we bid the campaign God-speed and summon every man to do his full duty, confident victory shall perch on our advancing standards.

J. E. WEST,
K. B. JOHNSON,
R. M. MORROW,
For the Board of Trustees of Elon College;
Approved: W. W. STALEY,
President Southern Christian Convention.

*If for any reason service is not held on the third Sunday, the pastor is requested to preach on CHRISTIAN EDUCATION and THE CALL TO THE MINISTRY at the next service held thereafter. The value of this united preaching campaign cannot be overestimated.

SUGGESTED GOALS
For
ELON COLLEGE
$125,000 Endowment Fund
(The Elon Standardization Fund)
By
COL. J. E. WEST,
HON. K. B. JOHNSON,
DR. R. M. MORROW,
Representing the Trustees
And
DR. W. W. STALEY,
President of the Convention.

We can do it, if we will!
We can do it, and WE WILL!

It is confidently expected that every church will go "over the top."

EASTERN VIRGINIA CONFERENCE	
Church	Goal
Antioch	$2,250
Barrett's	750
Berea (Nansemond)	3,700
Berea (Norfolk)	1,750
Berkley	1,500
Bethlehem	3,400
Burton's Grove	400
Cypress Chapel	2,250

Centerville 400
Damascus 1,900
Dendron 750
Eure's 1,500
Franklin 1,500
Holland 2,250
Hobson 400
Holy Neck 5,250
Isle of Wight 1,150
Ivor 400
Johnson's Grove 750
Liberty Springs 1,500
Lambert's Point 600
Mt. Carmel 1,650
Mt. Zion 300
Memorial Temple 4,150
New Lebanon 1,150
Newport News 750
Oakland 1,150
Oak Grove 750
Portsmouth 1,150
Rosemont 500
Sarem 250
South Norfolk 750
Spring Hill 400
Suffolk 18,750
Third Church 1,500
Union (South) 750
Union (Surry) 750
Wakefield 550
Waverly 2,250
Windsor 750

Delmarvia Churches

Dover .... $ 2,000
Holden's 100
Kitt's Hammock 100
St. Paul's 100
Temperville 100
Moore's Church 100

EASTERN NORTH CAROLINA CONFERENCE

Church	Goal
Amelia	$ 650
Antioch	300
Auburn	1,000
Bethel	200
Bethlehem	200
Beulah	600
Catawba Springs	2,000
Chapel Hill	500
Christian Chapel	500
Christian Light	300
Damascus	1,200
Ebenezer	700
Franklinton	150
Fullers	600
Good Hope	400
Hayes Chapel	400
Henderson	1,000
Lee's Chapel	150
Liberty	3,000
Martha's Chapel	600
Mebane	150
Morrisville	600
Moore Union	200
Mount Carmel	600
Mount Auburn	3,000

Mount Hermon 300
Mount Gilead 600
New Elam 1,500
New Hill 350
New Hope 1,200
Oak Level 4,500
O'Kelley's Chapel 600
Piney Plains 600
Pleasant Hill 400
Pleasant Union 500
Plymouth 200
Pope's Chapel 2,000
Raleigh 3,000
Sanford 700
Shallow Well 2,000
Six Forks 750
Turner's Chapel 200
Wake Chapel 3,000
Wentworth 1,000
Youngsville 700

WESTERN NORTH CAROLINA CONFERENCE

Church	Goal
Antioch (C)	$ 600
Antioch (R)	300
Asheboro	600
Big Oak	1,000
Brown's Chapel	750
Burlington	5,000
Bennett	500
Christian Union	300
Center Grove	500
Ether	500
Graham	1,000
Grace's Chapel	600
Hank's Chapel	1,250
High Point	500
Keyser	500
Liberty	500
Mt. Pleasant	500
New Center	1,000
New Providence	1,000
Needham's Grove	250
Parks Cross Roads	1,500
Patterson Grove	500
Pleasant Cross	500
Pleasant Grove	1,500
Pleasant Hill	1,000
Pleasant Ridge	1,000
Pleasant Union	500
Poplar Branch	400
Ramseur	1,250
Shady Grove	500
Shiloh	1,000
Smithwood	600
Spoon's Chapel	250
St. John's	600
Seagrove	500
Union Grove	750
Zion	750

NORTH CAROLINA AND VIRGINIA CONFERENCE

Church	Goal
Apple's Chapel	$ 1,900
Belew Creek	1,500
Berea	850

Bethel 600
Bethlehem 2,250
Concord 400
Danville 300
Durham 2,350
Elon College 3,750
Goshen Chapel 150
Greensboro 1st Church 4,500
Greensboro Palm Street 900
Happy Home 1,150
Haw River 1,500
Hebron 1,900
Hines Chapel 2,250
Howard's Chapel 550
Ingram 1,900
Kallam Grove 150
Lebanon 2,800
Liberty 550
Long's Chapel 550
Monticello 550
Mt. Bethel 750
Mt. Zion 400
New Hope 300
New Lebanon 1,350
Pleasant Grove 3,750
Pleasant Ridge 750
Reidsville 400
Salem Chapel 450
Shallow Ford 900
Union (N. C.) 3,000
Union (Va.) 2,700

ALABAMA CONFERENCE

Church	Goal
Antioch	$ 750
Beulah	850
Bethany	600
Corinth	650
Christiana	500
Cragford	1,000
Dingler's Chapel	400
Forest Home	300
Lowell	400
Macedonia	400
McGuire's Chapel	650
Mt. Zion	850
Noon Day	500
New Home	300
New Harmony	450
New Hope	1,500
Pleasant Grove	500
Rock Springs	750
Rockstand	650
Sand Hill	250
Spring Hill	400
Shady Grove	200
Wadley	1,000

GEORGIA & ALABAMA CONFERENCE

Church	Goal
Ambrose	$ 750
Beulah	750
Brown Springs	200
Enigma	300
Kite	500
La Grange	800
Lanett	1,500
North Highlands	1,350

Oak Grove 2,000
Providence Chapel 750
Richland 600
Rose Hill 650
Union 300
Vancev1lle ....\.. 300

VIRGINIA VALLEY CENTRAL CONFERENCE

Church	Goal
Antioch ....\......	$ 1,750
Bethel	400
Bethlehem	1,400
Beulah	200
Christian Chapel	200
Concord ....,......	400
Dry Run	500
East Liberty	150
High Point	150
Island Ford	150
Joppa	200
Leaksville	1,500
Linville	1,500
Mayland	300
Mt. Lebanon	500
Mt. Olivet (G)	800
Mt. Olivet (R) ....,...	300
New Hope	1,000
Newport	1,000
Palmyra	350
St. Peter's	150
Timber Mountain	350
Timber Ridge	1,500
Whistler's Chapel	240
Winchester ....,...........	1,400
Wood's Chapel ....?......	400

*These goals are based on the Elon College Fund as apportioned by the annual Conferences and accepted by the churches as equitable for many years. They are in no sense to be taken as assessments, but rather as the minimum which each Church ought gladly to accept as its part in this greatest drive of our denominational history. We can do it, if we will. We can do it, and WE WILL.

SUNDAY SCHOOL TOPIC FOR SUNDAY, FEBRUARY 16, 1919

The Ten Commandments
Scripture Text: Exodus 2:1-17.
Golden Text: Thou shalt love the Lord thy God with all thy heart, and with all thy soul, and with all thy strength, and with all thy mind; and thy neighbor as thyself. Luke 10:27.
Time—May B. C. 1491.
Place—Mount Sinai.

CHRISTIAN ENDEAVOR TOPIC FOR SUNDAY, FEBRUARY 16, 1919

"Our Relation to God, II, Trusting."
Scripture Text: Psalm 91:1-16.

HELP REFERENCES

Sunday School—Officers and Teachers Journal and Christian Bible Class Quarter-

ly by Christian Association, Dayton, Ohio; also Tarbell's Guide or Peloubet's Select Notes from any book dealer.

For Christian Endeavor—The Christian Endeavor World, Boston, Mass., and the Dixie Endeavorer, Chattanooga, Tenn.

WHAT IS YOUR SUNDAY SCHOOL DOING?

I wish all our Sunday schools would catch, and get the meaning of this great message from that prince of Sunday school workers, Marion Lawrence: "No Sunday school can live within four square walls. To attempt it is suicidal. The Church, Sunday school, or individual, for that matter, whose Christian life is self-centered, has already started on a fatal decline. There is absolutely no exception to this rule."

It is doubtful if Marion Lawrence ever spoke truer words. Yet there are hundreds of schools attempting this impossible thing—trying to live within four square walls. They meet from Sunday to Sunday. Go through the lesson, take the "penny" collection, adjourn and go home. Just so there is enough from the penny collection to buy the literature for the school all are satisfied.

Such a school is a drag. It has a hard time "holding its own." Its attendance, this year is about, or hardly as great as that of a year ago. Now get Marion Lawrence's further declaration: "That Church, Sunday school or individual, with a world view of the Kingdom of Jesus Christ and which recognizes responsibility thereto, will grow in spirituality and power. We have forgotten all too long that the way to have plenty at home is to 'make a little cake' for God first. The more our Sunday schools know about missions, the more they will desire to help the cause. The more they help, the greater will be their interest in their home work."

In brief, as we catch a vision of the far need yonder, we catch a vision of the deep need here. The chief reason why many of our schools mean such very little to their own church and community is because they are doing so very little, and caring so very little for the churches and communities —far removed from their own.

I want to give one other statement from the greatest of our Sunday

school teachers and leaders: "It is my candid judgment that twenty-five years of sane, systematic missionary instruction in our Sunday schools will forever do away with the great debts carried by our missionary boards, multiply by millions the money poured into their treasuries, and increase ten-fold the number of missionaries who are carrying the Gospel to those who need it in the homeland and foreign countries."

What is your Sunday school doing? What is it undertaking to do? Trying to live within its four walls? Trying to live and take care only of itself? Well, according to Marion Lawrence that is a suicidal policy.

J. O. ATKINSON.

MARRIAGES

SMITH-BRASDEN

On Sunday afternoon, (January 19, 1919), Mr. James Smith and Miss Annie Brasden motored to the parsonage of the Durham Christian church and were united in marriage by the writer. There were only a few people present to witness the mutual vows. Mrs. Smith is a member of the Durham Christian church. The happy couple have the best wishes of their many friends.

R. F. BROWN.

OBITUARIES

BROWN

Mrs. Nannie J., wife of Mr. Henry Monroe Brown, departed this life January 30, 1919, being 82 years, 7 months and 23 days of age.

She married Mr. W. E. Heath in 1877. He lived about 2 years thereafter. There was one daughter, Mrs. Ella Heath Wyrick, now living.

In 1886, she, Mrs. Nannie Isley Heath, married Mr. H. M. Brown. He died two years ago, November 2," ult.

There are of these children, two girls and three boys. The girls and one of the boys, William Brown, married. They are all living.

Mrs. Nannie Isley Heath Brown was a daughter of the late Lewis Isley, of near McLeansville, N. C., who was an active

and prominent member of Hine's Chapel
Christian church. He died some fifteen
years ago. His wife preceded him some
thirty years.

Mrs. Brown was the tenth of a group
of brothers and sisters, to depart this life.
There is one left, Mr. Thomas Isley, to
mourn his loss. A noble band of men
and women, who by their Godly parents,
were taught to love the church; live for
God, and be a blessing to man. A better
woman than Sister Brown is hard to find.
Her body was quietly laid to rest in
the cemetery at Hine's Chapel. Funeral
conducted by the writer, her pastor.
                          J. W. PATTON.

GLASGOW

Mrs. Sallie K. Glasgow, wife of Mr.
G. Ollie Glasgow of North Danville, died
early Sunday morning, February 2, at the
Hilltop Sanatorium after a lingering illness of four months. Death was due to
tuberculosis of the throat.

Mrs. Glasgow was born in Halifax
county where she spent her early childhood. At the age of ten she came to
Danville where she has lived ever since.
By her sweet spirit and Godly life she
became endeared to all who knew her and
her death has caused deep gloom throughout the entire community. During her
illness and especially during the last few
days of her life she suffered greatly, but
she always maintained an uncomplaining
attitude, and showed a regard for others
which was an inspiration to those who
ministered unto her.

Mrs. Glasgow was a member of the
Third Avenue Christian church of Danville and, up until the time of her illness
was a regular attendant at the services
of the church and Sunday school. She
was our humble disciple of the Master, and
her holy influence exerted much weight
on those among whom she lived. She
was also a devoted mother and her family was always her chief concern.

She is survived by her husband, G.
Ollie Glasgow and four children, Elmer,
Kathleen, Adelaide, and Emmitt. She is
also survived by five sisters and one broth-
er, as follows: Mrs. J. S. Siveter, Mrs.
S. J. Cole, and Mrs. J. C Elliott, all of
Danville; Mrs T. J. Landrum of South
Boston; Mrs. L. J. Allen of Richmond,
and Mrs. M. W. Hart of Hopewell.

Funeral services were held in the
Christian church, the writer and Rev. O.
A. Guinn officiating. The services were
simple but impressive. The church was
crowded with loved ones and friends and

the floral designs were numerous and
handsome. Interment was made at Lee
Mount cemetery.

May God bless and strengthen the
members of the family and may the Holy
Spirit comfort them in their loss.
                      H. S. HARDCASTLE.

LIBBY

Died January 27, 1919, Mrs. Lena Libby,
daughter of the late J. C. Thomas of
Isle of Wight, after nearly three weeks
of intense suffering. On Wednesday, January 10, her clothes were ignited by contact with a hot stove and before the flames
were extinguished she was burned from
head to foot. She leaves two daughters,
two sisters and a brother. She was a
devoted member of Isle of Wight Christian church.
                          D. J. MOOD.

RESOLUTIONS OF RESPECT—LIBBY

Whereas, through the kind providence
of our Heavenly Father the soul of our
sister and classmate, Mrs. Lena Libby
was on January 29, 1919, mercifully released from her poor suffering body and
wafted to that Home above, and

Whereas, in her departure this class
loses a faithful student, her church a consistent and faithful member and her children a loving mother,

Be it Resolved, That we bow in humble
submission to our Father's will.

That we strive to follow her example
in her devotion to her church, her faithfulness to this class and her love for her
children and friends.

That we offer her bereaved children
and family who mourn, the sympathy of
our hearts, and pray that they, and we
may have a firmer faith in the love of
our Father who was so merciful to her
in her hour of sore distress.

That we forget not the orphans when
we commune with God and ever bear them
up on the wings of our faith.

That a copy of these resolutions be sent
to the bereaved children, and a copy to
The Christian Sun for publication.

Adopted by LADIES' BIBLE CLASS,
Trinity Methodist Church, Smithfield, Va.
February 2, 1919.

HOBBS

Infant of Mr. and Mrs. Ernest L. Hobbs
of Greensboro, N. C., died January 30.
The little flower bloomed only for a short
time until God took it back home. It
was seventeen days old. The remains
were laid to rest in the city cemetery

after a short service at the home of Mr.
Hobbs, conducted by the writer. God
bless the bereaved parents, who have lost
two of their children within a period of
three months.
                      J. VINCENT KNIGHT.

BROWN

Mattie Lee Craven Brown was born
January 10, 1886 and died January 18,
1919. She joined the M. E. Church while
yet young. Afterwards she joined the
Friends' Church of Asheboro, North Carolina, where she remained a member until
death. Sister Brown gave assurance of
dying with peace in Christ.

She was married to John M. Brown
March 15, 1908. Three children survive
Funeral was conducted by the writer.
                      L. W. FOGLEMAN.

FREEMAN

Augustus Burpee Freeman, son of Man-
ley Freeman, departed this life February
3, 1919. The deceased was 31 years old.
His health had been somewhat delicate
from a child. A few years ago he contracted tuberculosis, which caused his
death.

Burpee professed faith in Christ at the
age of seventeen years and united with
the Christian church at Shady Grove.
When the church was organized at Ether
he moved his membership there.

He was a faithful son, a devoted husband, a loving and compassionate father
and a consecrated Christian. While living he was not only thinking of making
his own life happy, but his great ambition
was to make others happy. He was anxious to finish his course of study in the
Theological Seminary that he might enter
a broader field of Christian service. His
spirit has returned to God who gave it.
Though we cannot have him with us again
on earth, his example will live long in
the hearts of those with whom he was
acquainted. The influence his quiet, peaceful and consecrated life has had upon
others can only be revealed in the judgment.

The remains were laid to rest in the
cemetery at the Christian church at Ether.
Rev. J. R. Comer conducted the funeral
services. A father, mother, brother, sister, his wife, who was the daughter of
Mr. J. A. McLeod of Vass and a little
son are left to mourn their loss together
with a host of friends.

May God's choice blessings rest upon
the bereaved ones.
                      W. H. FREEMAN.

Christian Education Day
February 16, 1919

Every Pastor is requested to preach on

"The Call to the Ministry"

Our Convention has said

We must have One hundred new ministers during the next five years.

Let us pray

That God will give us twenty of them on FEBRUARY 16. He is willing. Are we? God grant it.

The Gospel Ministry

Is the noblest work in the world. Its opportunities of service are accentuated now as never before. Strong men and true are needed. Let every Christian prayerfully examine himself to see if God will excuse him from this service.

Report all decisions

At once to President W. A. Harper, Elon College, North Carolina, where these candidates will be educated to serve the Kingdom through our brotherhood.

On this day also

The Elon Standardization Fund for $125,000 additional Endowment is to be launched in every church. God expects every one of us to do full duty. Let us not disappoint God. We call the Church to her knees that God may dedicate us to the recruiting of our ministry and the strengthening of our College.

J. E. WEST

K. B. JOHNSON

R. M. MORROW

For the Board of Trustees of Elon College

W. W. STALEY, President, the Southern Christian Convention

February 16, 1919—What blessing it holds.   We shall enter in.

Days of Reconstruction

 HE days of reconstruction are laden with
opportunities that fling themselves to the
door of every man, woman, and child. The
world program has been torn asunder and is
now in the re-making. Soon it will begin
to crystallize and changes will be more difficult to make. Now is the time to begin whether it be
in material or spiritual development. A man can be
a better servant if he is in tune with his time and not
ahead of it. Renounce, renew, and reconstruct now and
become a part of your own civilization.

Volume LXXI	WEDNESDAY, FEBRUARY 19, 1919	Number 8
BURLINGTON		NORTH CAROLINA

THE CHRISTIAN SUN

Founded 1844 by Rev. Daniel W. Kerr

C. B. RIDDLE - - - Editor

Entered at the Burlington, N. C. Post Office as second class matter.

Subscription Rates

One year ....$ 2.00
Six months 1.00

In Advance

Give both your old and new postoffice when asking that your address be changed.

The change of your label is your receipt for money. Written receipts sent upon request.

Marriage and obituary notices not exceeding 150 words printed free if received within 60 days from date of event, all over this at the rate of one-half cent a word.

Original poetry not accepted for publication.

Principles of the Christian Church

(1) The Lord Jesus Christ is the only Head of the Church.
(2) Christian is a sufficient name of the Church.
(3) The Holy Bible is a sufficient rule of faith and practice.
(4) Christian character is a sufficient test of fellowship, and of church membership.
(5) The right of private judgment and the liberty of conscience is a right and a privilege that should be accorded to, and exercised by all.

EDITORIAL

THE RESPONSE OF THE BRETHREN

Some days ago we asked the ministers to help us undertake a special effort in connection with THE SUN for February and March. We do not have room to quote all these letters, not even a part of them. They were liberal in every way save one, which was without explanation. Many, very many, pledged a definite number and the others pledged their heartiest co-operation and best efforts for the securing of the largest possible number. It is indeed gratifying for such a splendid co-operation and it certainly does bring cheer to this sanctum, for we are endeavoring to edit THE SUN and at the same time finance it.

The reason why we are calling upon the ministers first is because they are coming in direct contact with the people and are best situated to present the claims of THE SUN. However, this does not mean that we do not ask and invite every member of THE SUN household to take a part in this worthy undertaking. (And now if the ministers will close their eyes we will write this: Wouldn't it be fine if the laymen, during these two months, were to send in more subscriptions than the ministers?) We earnestly request all friends of THE SUN to help us out. We need, and the paper deserves, a larger circulation. But most of all the members of

the Church need the paper. It does not make any difference how many papers a man takes he ought to take his Church paper first. We trust that those engaged in the work with us will make this a definite point. Then too, we shall be glad if the people are informed that $2.00 does not pay the total expense of the publication. This means that the Convention pays a part of each subscription. The deficit on THE CHRISTIAN SUN since last May has amounted to about the same as the Editor's commission. Two dollars the year would about meet the expense of THE SUN if the Editor could do his work for nothing.

Brother Harward says we ought to get 500 and Dr. Staley said in last week's Suffolk Letter that we ought to make it a thousand. How many of this number will you get? How many?

A TRIBUTE WELL BESTOWED

We have always been a believer that many young men pick out some fellow as a model and follow his example. How examplary we should be! And most certainly we believe that "the good men do is not interred with their bones," to us a thought of Shakespeare.

The other day a good and great man died—Dean M. H. Stacy, Chapel Hill, N. C., and Prof. Francis P. Venable, an ex-president of the University, paid this fitting and well worded tribute to the deceased:

In the death of Marvin Hendrix Stacy the University has suffered one of its greatest losses. I was his teacher in his student days. I appreciated his high manly qualities, admired his strong character, and in the later days of friendship grew to love him. Mentally he was highly endowed. He grasped a subject readily, thought deeply, made his decision after careful weighing, and then was firm as a rock though just and sympathetically considerate to those who differed with him. It is not strange that such a man was a force for all that is best in the life of the University from his college days through the years of his apprenticeship to those of mature accomplishment and gathering honrs. He was one of the best teachers in the faculty, sparing himself in no detail of pains and time and repetition, getting the best work out of his students. And they appreciated the labor spent upon them, the unrugled patience, the even-handed justice and the insight into their difficulties.

He was admirable as an administrator, clear, convincing and eloquent as a speaker, a man of few words but they were well weighed, to the point and not to be misunderstood. Quiet, simple, unaffected, a thoroughbred gentleman in the highest sense, I never found in him the trait of self-seeking, rather I had to argue him out of a sort of self-depreciation. He sought no new honors nor advancement, telling me once that the thought of present duty was enough for him and I realized that duty had for him the one clear call unmarred by thought of self, unstained by pride of achievement. Such sweet, gentle, true natures are rare. They constitute the finest, the highest among men though not always so applauded. Such are the salt of the world.

We gladly print this that it may help some one. We print it that some young man may decide what kind of a tribute that he would like to be written of his life and works. The question is with you, young man, as what your friends will say about you when you are gone. Begin now to make your life count for something.

NO CONFLICT

There is no conflict between the drive for Elon College and the drive for THE CHRISTIAN SUN. The more people you get to read THE CHRISTIAN SUN, the easier it will be to get people enlisted in every enterprise of the Church. Information is the true forerunner of every undertaking, and that is what THE SUN is endeavoring to do—be a forerunner for the Church.

WHAT TO DO WITH THE ANNUALS

During the last few days we have had several inquiries about what to do with the *Annuals* on hand. This matter ought to be made uniform. Some years some of the conferences authorize the *Annuals* to be sold and again there is nothing said about it. Last year there was returned to this office a number of *Annuals* accompanied by a letter to the effect that they could not be sold. In some cases they were to be given away. If you are in doubt about the matter, turn to the proceedings of your conference and see what it says about the matter. You can find it, for it is there. Look the matter up. By all means get the *Annuals* into the hands of the people, especially in the conferences where they are given gratis. Attend to this matter now.

SOME CORRESPONDENCE

Dear Brother Riddle:—

I am in receipt of the *Annual* you sent me and in looking over same I am surprised to find no report from Ambrose, Ga. Our letter was sent to Brother H. W. Elder and he told me he instructed the Secretary to send same to you. This makes two years that no report has been printed from our church while we have sent each year our church letter to the Conference. We have always raised all Conference assessments, and more. Two years ago we paid $25.00 more than asked for. Our Sunday schools last year raised $100 and contributed $65.00 to the foreign home and $35.00 to other Sunday school causes. I regret to know that our church letters have been so carelessly handled and misplaced. You can say that Ambrose church raised all Conference requirements for the past year. We raised last year $600.00 for all purposes. With best wishes.

Yours sincerely,

T. J. HOLLAND.

Ambrose, Ga.

     • •

February 13, 1919.

Mr. T. J. Holland,

   Ambrose, Ga.

My dear Brother:—

I have your letter regarding the omission of the Ambrose church from the records of the *Annual*. I assure you that all matter received from your Conference was printed. Of course the original church letters did not reach me, but were, by your Conference secretary, condensed to table form. I regret the omission but it was not within my power to have it included.

With cordial good wishes, I am

Yours very sincerely,

C. B. RIDDLE.

NOTES

Brother W. J. Edwards changes his address from Cole's Store to Coleridge, N. C.

Rev. J. W. Holt was kindly remembered recently by many members and former members by supplies of meat, money and provisions.

We note from the Ledger-Dispatch, Norfolk, Va., that the Third church has adopted resolutions against the open Sunday in Norfolk. A commendable stand!

Brother J. F. Coghill, Henderson, N. C., sends two new subscriptions to THE SUN. He writes: "I wish that members of the Church would take THE SUN. I am going to do all I can for the cause."

Rev. R. F. Brown, Durham, N. C., writes that he is endeavoring to get fifty new subscribers to THE CHRISTIAN SUN. A splendid goal! May many others follow his example.

Rev. George D. Eastes changes his address from Portsmouth, Va. to 10 North East Street, Raleigh, N. C. Our best wishes go with him in his new undertaking at the Capital city.

Rev. L. I. Cox, on February 12, sent us five renewals and five new subscriptions. He also included $11.00 for Bibles sold and entered an order for more to the amount of $29.00.

Rev. J. V. Knight writes: "I have planned an evangelistic campaign for April. I will do my own preaching. I have secured the services of the Berge Sisters of Baltimore from April 20 to May 9 if we decide to hold that long. SUN readers are requested to pray for this meeting."

Rev. F. H. Peters, Greenville, Ohio, sends $2.00 for a year's subscription to THE SUN and says: "THE SUN came to my father when I was a very small boy and I have been reading it ever since, and have been a subscriber myself for past thirty-eight years, if I remember correctly. It was one of the means of my conversion; and coming into the Christian ministry."

Rev. M. W. Butler, Conshohocken, Pa., writes congratulatory regarding THE CHRISTIAN SUN among other things says: "THE SUN came to my father when I was—

☞ For additional notes and comments see page fifteen.

CHRISTIAN EDUCATION

FROM ONE OF ELON'S FORMER PRESIDENTS

February the sixteenth, nineteen hundred and nineteen will, for all future time, be a memorable day in the history of Elon College, and of the Christian Church. And knowing our people as I do, I feel sure that it is to be made memorable in a most delightful and gratifying way. It is to mark the launching of a campaign that is to add *one hundred and twenty-five thousand dollars* to the invested funds of Elon College. I say that it "is to," and not "ought to."

1. Because Elon College is very close to the hearts of our people—and that means easy access to our purses.

2. Because our people are progressive, and we know that there can be little progress without sufficient means for expansion.

3. Because we realize that Elon cannot longer be classed as a "standard college" without a productive endowment of at least $200.000.00—and our people will not be satisfied with anything short of the required "standard."

4. Because we realize that every dollar invested in Elon College in the past has yielded rich returns to our people of the Christian Church, to our country, and to the Kingdom.

5. Because we have confidence in those who are to have charge of the campaign, under the splendid, enthusiastic leadership of President Harper. They don't know how to do anything but succeed.

Of course, the $125,000.00 will be raised, but it ought to be done quickly; and to do this, every loyal member of the Christian Church must do his part, and do it now.

The need is great, the time opportune, the cause worthy, the promise large. May the response be ready and full-measured.

E. L. MOFFITT.

Ashboro, N. C.

ENCOURAGED BY DR. LIGHTBOURNE'S LIFE

The deep interest of the late Dr. A. W. Lightbourne, founder of the Peoples' church of Dover, in Elon College, encourages me to believe that the campaign to raise $125,000.00 additional endowment for that institution is a worthy cause. I sincerely trust that the Church will respond liberally to the call.

WESLEY WEBB,
Secretary State Board of Agriculture.
Dover, Delaware.

DUTY OF EVERY LOYAL MEMBER OF THE CHURCH

As our Convention, and all our Conferences have voted their endorsement of the Elon College campaign for $125,000.00 additional endowment, (the amount required to rate said college as a "Standard College"); and feeling sure that these bodies would not have acted favorably in this unanimous fashion, unless the occasion warranted such action, I am therefore, inclined to the opinion that it is the duty of every loyal member of our Church, whether pastor or layman, to heartily support this campaign. I give it my hearty approval and trust that the President of this growing institution, and training school of our Church, will have no trouble in "going over the top" with flying colors.

C. H. STEPHENSON.
Raleigh, N. C.

WILL GIVE IT NOBLY AND GLADLY

No lover of the Christian Church of the South can ever estimate the value of Elon College. She is in reality a central power house from which flows to all parts of our church trained talent.

She has met the demand upon her nobly in the past; but a growing Church must enlarge its source of power. No denominational College can do its best work without some financial backing besides its current income. Elon needs the increased endowment and the Church will nobly and gladly give it.

H. W. ELDER.
Richland, Ga.

WE MUST REACH THE STANDARD

What the Christian Church is today is, almost wholly, due to education. Without education, as I see it, is to remain non-progressive. We of the Southern Christian Convention want to make progress in Christian work. Therefore, we want to hold our college second to none. In order to do this, as set forth by the Department of Education of the United States, we must reach the standard and raise Elon's required endowment.

E. M. CARTER.
Wadley, Ala.

FOR THE WHOLE CHURCH

I learn through Dr. Harper that there is soon to be launched a united campaign in interest of Elon. I write to give my whole hearted endorsement to this campaign. As I write I find myself trying to imagine what would be the present condition of our Church, North, South, East and West, had it not been for the invaluable and heroic service rendered by our institutions of learning together with their sacrificing faculties. Elon has rendered a peculiar service to the Southern Convention. She has raised her ideals, trained her ministry, inspired her laymen and nerved her to the tremendous task of the Kingdom. Dr. Atkinson is doing a most wonderful work, giving our people a chance to express themselves in the larger things of the Kingdom, work that would have been practically impossible without Elon in the field as a preparing and a steering force. Elon is the willing servant of the Church. She has no doubt made possible the efficiency and the continuance of that that she serves. She now needs a more hearty support of the Church that she may be enabled to render a much larger service to the Kingdom.

This campaign was to be launched in the churches February 16. Its purpose is to increase the permanent endowment of the College $125,000.00. Elon now has an educational standard, fully recognized by the standard educational institutions of the country but she must lose this recognition unless her endowment is increased to the above figure. I know that when our people realize this fact, what it means to us and to the future of our Church, that they will rally to Elon and give and continue to give until Elon's high standard and efficient service is guaranteed. I wish for you, Dr. Harper, the most phenomenal success of your life in your endeavors to raise this fund.

— L. E. SMITH.

Norfolk, Va.

THE ELON STANDARDIZATION FUND
What My Mail Reveals

The gratitude of my heart will never adequately be expressed for the encouraging words that have come to me on the eve of launching the campaign for $125,000 additional endowment. The chorus of unanimous approval stoutens the heart and quickens the zeal for the active pushing of the campaign.

In addition to the splendid array of endorsements which Editor Riddle received and has printed or will print in THE CHRISTIAN SUN, thirty-one (up to Wednesday the 12th) dear friends have written me they will pray for the cause, and one of them significantly adds: "When the Brotherhood really gets to praying, the task for you will be easy, for true prayer means action."

A layman, living in a distinctly rural community, writes: "I am heartily in favor of keeping Elon abreast with the leading Colleges."

A city pastor writes: "I trust the drive for the endowment fund may be a great success."

A Civil War veteran and former member of his State's General Assembly writes: "I think the plan a good one and you will raise the fund if the people unite."

A veteran country preacher writes: "I hope the drive will be a success in every particular."

A licentiate says: "I am anxious to do all in my power to help forward the Kingdom."

A retired minister says: "Let me assure you of my hearty co-operation, so far as opportunity presents itself."

A layman in a country church without pastor says: "We are ready to do our part."

A Christian Woman Speaks Her Heart

But the finest of the fine is this inspiring letter from one of our Christian women, wife of one of our most generous laymen, written voluntarily out of a heart of love and loyalty, the type of a host in our Church.

She says: "Elon has for a long time had my prayers and tears, quite a few prayers and many, many tears. I have surely seen for two years that the war would deplete her students and finances. The first installment of the S. A. T. C. at Elon nearly broke my heart. I really felt that a public dance or a Sunday ball game in her sacred precincts, would cause the brick in the walls to cry out. I know now that either was impossible, and I am truly glad that the College is back again on her old footing with the spirit of the former Elon still presiding. As to the Standardization Fund, you will

get the required amount. There are thousands of members of the Christian Church that are willing to back up their prayers with their money and the endowment is sure. The Lord is still leading; and for our beloved Elon there shall be another Red Sea crossing and the springing up of the blessed wells of Elim and the Palm Trees. You have our sympathy and prayers in this wonderful undertaking. You have only to speak that we go forward."

The Church has spoken, the Brotherhood has approved, and under God's blessing we do go forward, forward to a larger and better Elon.

But do not forget, dear friends, that the initial item in our drive is for those twenty life-recruits, twenty strong young lives for Jesus and the service of His Church. Shall we not be earnest in our prayers and willing in our efforts to find them during the month February. 16—March 16?

Beginning at Jerusalem

Elon's College pastor, Dr. N. G. Newman, believing earnestly in the Scriptural way of doing things, has decided to put on the drive for funds here for the $125,0000 campaign on Sunday, the 16th and the week following. It is right and proper that the beginning should be made at headquarters. Let the Brotherhood pray earnestly for divine blessing on the campaign here.

Finally

Brother Riddle editorially said a great thing last week—that the Church has laid this drive on me. Any man is honored to have anything laid on him by so splendid a body as the Christian Church. These letters out of the hearts of our people show they are sharing the responsibility with me. It is the cause of our Church and of our College that is being presented, and with our people behind it as they are, God can but grant us the rich success our hearts so earnestly seek from Him.

I am grateful to one and all.

W. A. HARPER.

PASTOR AND PEOPLE

VALLEY LETTER

Our revival meeting at Timber Ridge was greatly interferred with by the presence of Spanish Influenza in the community. However, there was some interest manifested, and seven conversions and nine additions to the church. At my last appointment there another young man gave his heart to the Lord and united with the church, making ten additions to the church there since Conference. I have been much encouraged with the work at Timber Ridge since taking charge there a year and a half ago. I have received only the very best of treatment from every one. The prospect for the growth of the church there looks good. Some of the members seem to be getting a larger vision of the things pertaining to the Kingdom. To be sure there are others who need an awakening.

What a great thing if would be for all our churches

if only all our people would wake up to the responsibilities and opportunities that are theirs. During the past few months people have shown much loyalty to country, and have willingly made sacrifices they never thought before that they could be induced to make. Now, why should we not be just as loyal to the church and to God? And why should we not be just as willing to make sacrifices for them as we have been to sacrifice and give and talk for our country? Oh, that we might wake up, and let all that is within us bless His holy name!

A. W. ANDES.

Harrisonburg, Va.

PROGRAM DISTRICT MEETING, MT. ZION CHRISTIAN CHURCH, RANDOLPH COUNTY, ALABAMA, MARCH 29, 30, 1919

SATURDAY—10:00 A. M.
Devotional, by Rev. J. D. Dollar.
Organization.
Christian Endeavor Work, by Rev. E. M. Carter.
11:00—Preaching, by Rev. C. M. Dollar.
12:00—Refreshments.

AFTERNOON SESSION
1:00—Our Needs for a Church School,
by Rev. J. H. Hughes.
1:30—Forward Movement of the Christian Church,
by Rev. C. W. Carter.
2:00—Why Group our Churches?, by Rev. G. D. Hunt.
2:00—Mission Study Classes, by Rev. J. Taylor.
3:00—Why take and read *The Christian Sun?*,
by Rev. A. H. Shepherd.

SUNDAY—9:30 A. M.
Devotional, by W. T. Meacham.
10:00—The Adult Bible Class, by J. W. Payne.
10:00—Why a Cradle Roll?, by J. J. Carter.
11:00—Preaching, by Rev. G. D. Hunt.

J. H. HUGHES, *Chairman.*

HIGH POINT CHRISTIAN CHURCH

On Saturday night, February 1, 1919, a small portion of the membership met in the first quarterly meeting at 7:30 o'clock. Those present manifested much interest in the progress of the church and gave expression of their desire to see it go forward. One of the things passed upon was to have a "Go to Church" Sunday. The day was not appointed but a committee was selected to set a date and notify and solicit the delinquent members living in the city. We are hoping this will be a good day and trust that each member will help to make it so.

This is my first time to try to serve this church, and as pastor I desire the co-operation of each member. The Spanish Influenza was very prevalent when I took charge. The congregation was small but has increased some since the epidemic abated.

May the Lord bless and inspire the faithful, arouse the delinquent and cause them to enter the front ranks for Christ and the church, is our prayer.

L. L. WYRICK.

Elon College, N. C.

Lieutenant J. N. H. Clendenin served in the cavalry with honor, during the entire four years of the Civil War. He was married to Bettie C. Long, daughter of Jacob and Jane Long, July 31, 1862. Her maternal grandfather, John Stockard, represented Orange County in the North Carolina legislature for seventeen consecutive terms. Her father was a sturdy Piedmont farmer with a peerless wife, devoted to religion and education. Mrs. Clendenin had seven brothers, John H., who died on his farm in Missouri; Dr. W. S., the founder of Elon College; Joseph who was killed in the battle of Chancellorsville; Dr. D. A., scholar and educator; Hon. J. A., lawyer and member of North Carolina legislature; Dr. George W., eminent physician, deceased; B. F., superior court judge. Her life in the paternal home was reflected in the manners and aspirations of her brothers. A teacher herself the spirit of learning took deep root in the family.

Mrs. Clendenin was the mother of seven children: Mrs. J. F. Peterson; Mollie, deceased; Mrs. N. G. Newman; J. Frank; Mrs. Charles M. Lance, deceased; Mrs. C. C. Thompson; and George L. The family tree has, also, nineteen grandchildren and two great grandchildren.

I lived in the home with Lieutenant Clendenin and his wife on a farm in 1866. Upon his return from the surrender of Lee to Grant, at Appomattox in April 1865, he took his hand from the handle of the sword and put his hands upon the handles of the plow; and he has served his country and his God in peace as he did in war. That was one of hard work and great pleasure, a year that developed the blood-relationship into life-friendship.

This faithful husband and wife celebrated their golden wedding on July 31, 1912, an occasion as sweet as their bridal day, enriched by the good wishes and gifts of family and friends. But December 11, 1918, Mrs. Clendenin entered into rest, and on the thirteenth we said: "earth to earth; ashes to ashes; dust to dust," and laid the flowers on the grave while their fragrance mingled with the sweet songs sung by loving and sympathetic friends. More than eighty years had imprinted her life-service on many hearts. Her spirit still lingered in Graham and the Christian church. Modesty, sincerity, refinement, and purity characterized her long and useful life. Her neighbors praise her. One of her last acts was to have her husband take her to see an old lady more shut-in than herself. Her thought was of others, and her labors for others. She had the spirit of Him who came not to be "ministered unto, but to minister." Christian mothers, it seems to me, will be in the number "when I make up my jewels." Jesus seemed to have that idea on the Cross, when He said to John: "Behold thy mother!"

No mortal has such opportunity for leading the world to Christ as a Christian mother. She has the first opportunity. That is all important. "As the twig is bent, the tree in inclined." She has the longest opportunity. The years of childhood in the home are the longest years in one circle of formative conditions. It is a soul-calamity for mothers to neglect these years. She has the most *responsive* opportunity. Childhood is the most impressionable period of life and should be used to implant character in the young life. Mrs. Clendenin used her opportunity with spiritual skill and set it with deep affection. The family and the community are richer and better because she devoted her life to God and to others. No society allurements diverted her motherly heart from training her children in the nurture and admonition of the Lord. All scientific rules for rearing children drop into oblivion compared with the genuine *example* of a devoted Christian mother.

W. W. STALEY.

THE FORWARD MOVEMENT

THE FORWARD MOVEMENT

Superintendent—Rev. W. H. Denison, D. D., Dayton, Ohio.
Religious Education Secretary—Hermon Eldredge, Erie, Pa.

What Our Workers in the Field are Doing

Rev. F. E. Rockwell, Madrid, Iowa: "The Forward Movement program will be pushed by me both in my own church, and with all the vigor and influence I may have in the conferences of the Western Christian Convention. It is a comprehensive program that embraces the five essentials to permancy, power and progress for the Christian Church."

Rev. F. H. Peters, Greenville, Ohio: "We are starting the Forward Movement here. The official board has voted to make it the basis of work and is making plans for carrying this out. I am preaching a series of sermons on its five features."

Rev. Nomen McClain, Swayzee, Ind.: "I want to join you in what I hope to be an army of ministers and laymen in a general campaign for the Forward Movement."

Rev. E. D. Hammond, Lebanon, Ohio: "The first fruits from the trip by fourteen laymen took to the Dayton Forward Movement rally is a series of sermons on the Forward Movement and a new home and foreign missionary society with thirty-one members, and plans for a rally of the three churches of my pastorate February 18."

Rev. W. H. Martin, Mellott, Ind.: "I am enclosing prayer covenants. I am preaching a series of Forward Movement sermons. Dr. Hershey will preach on the Forward Movement for me two Sundays."

Rev. H. A. Smith, Warren, Ind.: "I am sending you the names of the chairmen of my special committees on the Forward Movement. I have a special committee in our church on each of the five points of the Movement."

Rev. G. O. Lankford, Berkley, Va.: "The Forward Movement program idea is already beginning to tell in our Church. This month we are having four simultaneous cottage prayer meeting on Wednesday night instead of the usual meeting at the church. In one meeting alone last night we had forty or more persons present. I have not yet heard from the other three. We are having a great experience this month as we emphasize religion in the home."

The Pastor's Place in the Forward Movement

The Forward Movement is presenting to every pastor, through his own church committee, a Church program of activity culminating in a series of spiritual achievements and financial achievements, worthy of our Church in the light of this new day.

All the five fundamentals have been carefully studied and wrought out by a strong committee of twenty-four. The Forward Movement has been officially launched in respect to a general and united feeling of our brotherhood and in response to the action of our Church boards, by the American Christian Convention.

The program is the result of the united experience of the large committee. The program and the methods have been arrived at, after most careful study of the needs of the Church, and in the light of the challenge that God is giving to His people. Every pastor is therefore, asked to join heartily in the detailed suggestions offered by the committee, in the light of general loyalty to the church of which he is a part.

We have a loyal body of ministers, whom we believe will enter heartily into the program. Each pastor is asked to adapt his individual church program to that part of the Forward Movement, during the period of the campaign.

One has said: "What the cylinders are to a gas engine, organization is to the church; organization alone, means cylinders without gas and engine without power, dead and useless. Gas without cylinders means explosion without power."

Our Forward Movement pastors are asked to adjust the cylinders of the church life to the larger load which the church must carry. We, therefore, suggest that our pastors regard the Forward Movement divine in its inspiration and purpose and that they give themselves to its full promotion in church, conference, and convention. That they get a clear realization of its spiritual objectives of lifting our church to its rightful place of vision as to opportunities and responsibilities.

Another List of Preachers

Rev. A. W. Sparks, Argos, Indiana; Rev. F. C. Lester, Graham, North Carolina; Rev. Nomen McLain, Swayzee, Indiana; Rev. E. D. Hammond, Lebanon, Ohio; Rev. John A. Dillon, Rush, New York; Rev. L. E. Dull, Mansfield, Illinois; Rev. J. J. Beisiegal, Bluffton, Indiana; Rev. S. L. Beougher, Hartwick, New York; Rev. J. E. Fry, Merom, Indiana.

This is the third list, so far, that we have published showing the loyalty and co-operation of our pastors with our suggested program. They are all preaching series of sermons on the Forward Movement.

Have you begun to tithe yet? Thousands and tens of thousands in all denominations are beginning it this year.

Have you started your mission study yet? Now is the time to begin it.

Please do not forget to send in the names and address of the *Four-Minute Man,* appointed in your church:

Mrs. Chas. H. Isley—Here's hoping for this to be the best year yet for our beloved church paper.

MISSIONARY

**HOW TO CREATE AND KEEP A LIVE AND ACTIVE WO-
MAN'S MISSIONARY SOCIETY IN THE CHURCH
(IN FIVE CHAPTERS)
Chapter 3. Music in the Missionary Meeting**

There are certain essentials to the life, growth and power of any Missionary Society. Two of these have been treated in previous papers, namely, the Bible and Prayer. The writer now names another element - as fundamental and is essential to the life of the Missionary Society as either of those already presented, namely, Music.

Will the reader bear in mind that the writer does not contend that any sort of Bible reading, because it happens to be Bible reading, or any sort of prayer, because it happens to be in the name, form and attitude of prayer, or any sort of music, because it happens to be some form of hymn, psalm or song, are essential to the life of a Society, or will guarantee to keep the Society on its feet and going. The writer does mean to contend, however, that the proper sort of Bible reading, the right motive and conduct in prayer, and sufficient care for the singing will certainly hold the Society together with a grip, and start the Society off in its meetings with a power and momentum, that will prevent paralysis in the proceedings, and produce a warmth of feeling and fellowship that even an unconcerned and indifferent membership cannot chill. There are three reasons, amongst others, why at every meeting of the Society there should be music.

First. No medium has been found among mortals, through which courage is so thoroughly awakened, and the heroic in the heart is so appealed to, as through Music. This is why war regiment has its band of musicians, and after the last words of the general in command have been spoken, before going into battle, the music starts up. Even cowardly hearts become courageous, and brave souls heroic, under the impulse and inspiration of music.

Now, I submit that the very thing which causes many a Missionary Society to lag and die, is a lack of courage, a want of the heroic that makes one dare to go and do against all odds, and difficulties, even the odds and difficulties of a chilling indifference and a killing unconcernedness.

Every Missionary Society when it meets for a session, whether in the home, in the open or in the Church should select and use in a manner herewith described some of the grand old missionary and heroic hymns. This should be done whether three members are present or thirty. The smaller the number the greater the need of inspiration, courage and uplift.

Second. The second reason why every missionary meeting should have music is that *music is the language of love.* When Moses could no longer hold the wayward Israelites in unison by law, he taught them the "Song of Moses and the Lamb." He who writes a nation's songs is mightier than he who writes a nation's laws, philosophies tell us. That which knits a

nation's heart together is not the national constitution, but the national airs and anthems, we are assured.

Now, this one grand and sublime object must ever be kept to the fore in the minds and hearts of all members of any missionary Society, namely, that since God loved the world we too must learn to love a world. It is the language and lesson of love we are trying most of all to learn in a missionary meeting. Music stirs the deepest emotions of the heart, and awakens to highest and holiest impulses. Such emotions and such impulses are needed in the missionary meeting, if it is to be a live and active one.

Third. The third reason for giving heed to the music in the Missionary Society is, music is not only a medium through which the human heart is stirred to deeds of daring, and of universal fellowship, but also to *high and holy aspirations.* How many are the souls who have been led not only to do something for missionaries, but even to become missionaries, through the singing of a hymn! The writer read recently of how a young man in the choir, possessed with a fine voice, and serving his church and community indifferently, until one evening in singing with the choir the closing hymn, and with a joy that she had never known before the words of the song the voice of God calling him to the mission field. That young man never slept that night till he had fully resolved, "God permitting, I will be a foreign missionary." And he was one. His holy aspiration found expression and bold resolution through song.

I read also another instance. A young lady had thought of being a missionary, but had not made the full surrender. The hymn, "I Surrender All," was announced in the missionary meeting. She could not sing it. Her soul was in agony while others sang the words, *which she knew she could not truthfully utter.* But shortly she won the victory, and in quiet found that peace with God that man cannot give nor take away. Then in a few days she returned to the meeting and with a joy that she had never known before said, "I surrender, I surrender, I surrender all." The service of song had brought her to face life's crisis, and she faced it.

Now, the writer does not argue that any sort of songs or singing will do for the meetings of the Society. Only the *best* that can be done in song and through song should be had at the meeting.

In attempting practical suggestions for music in the he thinks fully the limitations and difficulties under he thinks full, the limitations and difficulties under which societies frequently have to meet. Nevertheless he hazards what seems to him three practical suggestions, one or the other or all of which any Society that really cares and will try, may adopt.

First. If there are too few at the meeting, or if the voices are not strong enough, for congregational singing, let a member read the words, or better, let the few present read responsively or in unison, the word of some stirring, familiar missionary hymn. Even the words of a familiar song will often set the tune to singing in the heart if the voice is silent.

Second. Prof. Amos R. Wells, the greatest Endeavor man and missionary propagandist, makes this suggestion: "Choose a missionary hymn that shall be sung at all the missionary meetings for the year—not some flippant song, but some grand old hymn of faith. It should be committed to memory, and at the beginning of every missionary meeting the entire company should rise and sing it with fervor." Any Society with a little care may follow that, it seems to me.

Third. Connecting the hymn to be used at the meeting either with the passage of Scripture out of which it grew, or better still, with some great missionary event, as nearly all the grand old missionary hymns now are so connected will help the singing and give it zest and flavor. The writer wishes space permitted here to tell some of the missionary incidents that hinge about such hymns as "From Greenland's Icy Mountains," or "I Gave My Life For Thee," or "Christ for The World We Sing," or "A Mighty Fortress is Our God," or "All Hail The Power of Jesus' Name." But any member who will interest herself in the music of the Society, and one should be appointed in every Society for this one purpose, may easily secure a book for a pittance which will give stories about missionary songs and singing that will interest the whole Society and through the music do much to keep the whole lump leavened and every meeting of the Society an inspiration and a joy.

J. O. ATKINSON.

P. S. Suggestions on questions from members of Missionary Societies are urgently requested by the writer.

J. O. A.

PLANS OF THE WOMAN'S BOARD OF THE NORTH CAROLINA CONFERENCE

The Central Executive Committee of the Woman's Board of the North Carolina Conference met in Burlington on the 30th and definitely planned the work for the present year.

The organization of twenty new societies was assigned to the President, Mrs. W. H. Carroll. She will put forth special effort aided by the pastors to organize in the following churches: Happy Home, Salem Chapel, Auburn, Catawba Springs, Damascus, Ebenezer, Liberty (Vance), Morrisville, Oak Level, Raleigh, Shallow Well, Wentworth, Youngsville, Asheboro, Bennett, Grace's Chapel, Hanks Chapel, High Point, Liberty, (Randolph), New Providence, Parks Cross Roads, Pleasant Hill, Seagrove, and Six Forks.

The securing of twenty additional Life Memberships of $10 each was made the special duty of Mrs. W. R. Sellars, Treasurer, and a selected list was tentatively made of her prospects.

The Secretary was asked to notify the present Societies of their apportionments and make preliminary preparations for the July Rally Day program.

It was decided to meet at Elon College for the first Convention, October 5-6, 1919.

The apportionments as fixed by the Greensboro session recently are as follows:

Woman's Societies

First Church, Greensboro, $100; Pleasant Grove, (Va.), $100; Palm Street, Greensboro, $10; Ingram, $40; Elon College $100; Durham, $50; Reidsville, $10; Union (Va.), $75; Long's Chapel, $10; Shallow Ford, $10; Hines' Chapel, $15; Howard's Chapel, $10; Mt. Zion, $15; Mt. Bethel, $15; New Lebanon, $15; Liberty, (Va.), $15; Lebanon, $10; Monticello, $15; Haw River, $15; Apple's Chapel, $20; Berea, $10; Danville, $15; Hebron, $50; Union (Alamance), $25; Bethlehem, $25; Concord, $15; Mt. Auburn, $200; Henderson, $60; Wake Chapel, $75; Sanford, $30; Chapel Hill, $25; Burlington, $300; Graham, $40; Ramseur, $25.

Young People's Societies

First Church, Greensboro, $10; Elon College, $35; Pleasant Grove, (Va.), $25; Durham, $20; Union, (Va.), $20; Reidsville, $10; Burlington, $100; Sanford, $10; Asheboro, $10.

Willing Workers' Societies

Durham, $20; Elon College, $20; Union, (Va.), $20; Pleasant Grove, (Va.), $20; Burlington, $20.

Cradle Roll Societies

Burlington, $10; Graham, $10; Mt. Auburn, $10; New Providence, $10; Ramseur, $10; Henderson, $10; Elon College, $10; Greensboro, First Church, $10; Pleasant Grove, (Va.), $10; Durham, $10.

Boys' Societies

Greensboro, First Church, $25; Elon College, $25.

With these apportionments and the $1,000 we expect to raise during our rally month in July, we expect to raise a minimum of $2,500 for the following purposes:

Objects

Santa Isabel, $750.00; Barrett Home, $500.00; Japan Work, $500.00; Donna Delfina, $100.00; Mrs. Frye's School, $100.00; Bible Women, (Japan), $50.00; General Purposes, $500.00; Total, $2,500.00.

Let every woman anxiously pray and busily work that we may attain our goals.

MRS. W. A. HARPER, Sec'y.

REPORTS OF WOMAN'S HOME AND FOREIGN MISSIONARY SOCIETIES OF THE NORTH CAROLINA AND VIRGINIA, WESTERN NORTH CAROLINA, EASTERN NORTH CAROLINA AND VIRGINIA VALLEY CHRISTIAN CONFERENCES FOR THE CONFERENCE YEAR, 1917-18

(North Carolina and Virginia Conference)

Elon College—Regular dues, $24.30; Y. P. Work, $3.75; Willing Workers, $1.19; Cradle Roll, 81 cents; Special, $60.00; Life Membership, $10; Printing, $5.00; Paid Treasurer, $99.05. Total, $104.05.

Greensboro—Regular dues, $20.30; Y. P. Work, $3.75; Willing Workers, $12.80; Cradle Roll, 75 cents; Special, $36.59; Isabella, $6.50; Literature, $2.00; Life Membership, $10.00; Printing, $5.00; Paid Treasurer, $92.69. Total, $97.69.

Hebron—Regular dues, $16.39; Special, $24.00; Printing, $5.00; Paid Treasurer, $40.39. Total, $45.09.

Pleasant Grove—Regular dues, $31.30; Y. P. Work, $6.25; Willing Workers, $10.50; Cradle Roll, $1.31; Mite Boxes, 59 cents; Special, $70.00; Orphanage, $15.00; Life Membership, $5.00; Printing, $5.75; Paid Treasurer, $139.85. Total, $145.60.

Ingram—Regular dues, $11.50; Special, $3.00; Printing, $5.00; Paid Treasurer, $14.50. Total, $19.50.

Durham—Regular dues, $24.55; Willing Workers, $7.35; Cradle Roll, $2.50; Special $25.00; Literature, $1.50; Printing, $3.00; Paid Treasurer, $60.90. Total, $63.90.

Monticello—Regular dues, $12.96; Paid Treasurer, $12.96. Total, $12.96.

Haw River—Regular dues, $6.35; Paid Treasurer, $6.35. Total, $6.35.

Reidsville—Regular dues, $1.15; Paid Treasurer, $1.15. Total, $1.15.

Union (Va.)—Printing, $5.00. Total, $5.00.

Apple's Chapel—Regular dues, $9.50; Special, $8.50; Life Membership, $10.00; Printing, $1.00; Paid Treasurer, $23.00. Total, $24.00.

Berea—Regular dues, $2.50; Paid Treasurer, $2.50. Total, $2.50.

Union (N. C.)—Regular dues, $11.65; Special, $10.00; Printing, $3.00; Paid Treasurer, $24.65. Total, $24.65.

New Lebanon—Regular dues, $7.15; Special, $6.16; Paid Treasurer, $13.31. Total, $19.31.

Mt. Bethel—Regular dues, $5.20; Paid Treasurer, $5.20. Total, $5.20.

Bethlehem—Regular dues, $2.25; Paid Treasurer, $2.25. Total, $2.25.

Liberty, (Va.)—Printing, $5.00. Total, $5.00.
Shallow Ford—Printing, $2.75. Total, $2.75.

MRS. L. M. CLYMER, Treasurer.

(Western North Carolina Conference)
Woman's Societies

Burlington, $290.50; Graham, $36.55; Ramseur, $16.60; Collection taken for Barrett Home in Conference, $20.23. Total, $363.86.

Young People's Societies

Burlington, $99.45; New Providence, $12.50; New Center, $5.00; Willing Workers of Burlington, $4.25. Total, $121.20; Grand total, $485.08.

Amounts Collected and Paid Out For Year 1917-1918

Regular Dues, $85.67; Bible Woman, $50.00; Mrs. Fry's School, $30.00; Barrett Home, $58.08; Literature Fund, $1.50; Miss Olive Williams, $16.71; Dr. Atkinson, $15.00; Cradle Roll, $2.87. Total, $359.85.

Young People

Regular Dues, $21.00; Mrs. Fry's School, $30.00; Santa Isabel, $74.25. Total, $125.25. Grand Total, $485.08.

MRS. W. R. SELLARS, Treasurer.

(Eastern North Carolina Conference)

Amount received from November 8, 1917 to December 4, 1918, (our last Conference year):

Mt. Auburn, $127.41; Henderson, $57.28; Wake Chapel, $57.50; Sanford, $24.67; Chapel Hill, $12.00; Total received during the year, $278.86.

(Sanford sent $26.00 direct to Mrs. Walters, amount received from a rally for Santa Isabel blocks. This was included in report to Conference of what had been raised during the year, making a total of $306.86).

Received since Conference:

Henderson, $1.40; Mt. Auburn, $23.20; Total, $24.60.

Amount on hand November 8, 1917, $35.74; Received since, $303.46; Total, $339.20.

Forwarded to Mrs. Walters, $320.47; Balance on hand, $18.73.

MRS. A. F. SMITH, Treasurer.

(Virginia Valley Conference)

Winchester dues, $3.50; Winchester church offering, $2.62; Winchester Young People, $1.52; Winchester, Christian Endeavor, $1.26; Mrs. W. T. Walters, $1.00; Mrs. A. M. Spitzer, $1.00; Mrs. J. M. Lohr, $1.00; Timber Mt. Cradle Roll, 50 cents; Total $12.51.

Specials For Barrett Home

Miss Hazel Hook, $1.00; Mrs. Dottie Armentrout, $1.00; Miss Olive Showalter, $5.00; Mrs. Barbara Andes, 50 cents; Mrs. Fannie Zirkle, $1.00; Mrs. W. C. Wampler, $3.25; Mrs. Frank Showalter, $1.00; Total, $11.75.

Specials For Santa Isabel Chapel

Mrs. T. H. Showalter, $3.25; Mrs. Earl Showalter, $1.00; Master Billy Andes, 25 cents; Miss Pauline Armentrout, 25 cents; Collected by Pauline Armentrout, $3.00. Total, $7.75.

Total for Quarter, $32.01.

Disbursements

January 17, to Mrs. W. T. Walters, $32.01.

A VANISHING OPPORTUNITY

(By Rev. F. G. Coffin, D. D., Albany, N. Y.)

It is altogether patent that the war has brought, and is still bringing, an array of opportunities and obligations for which the Church, motived and equipped as at present, is unequal. Things have been moving at a frightful momentum. The Church, if it were so disposed, could not dodge the rush of events released by the war, nor overtake them when once passed. An age has been compressed into a day, while a single hour has encompassed activities as far reaching as those of some former generation. The demands for a keen insight into the meaning of events, a hair-trigger conscience for their moral impositions, a ready diplomacy, a statesmanship in administration and a boundless sacrifice have been, and are, an absolute necessity of the Church's function in these war days.

The supreme test of purely military ability was on three months since. The supreme test of the readiness, strength and adaptability of the spiritual force of the Church is on at this moment. Until the signing of the armistice, the objectives of the war set by patriotism, national loyalty and the appeal of the great task aided the war purposes of the Church. Motives of patriotism and Christianity have a common solicitude for growth. Since the armistice, there is a very noticeable weakening of the force of these considerations. Morale is sustained among our troops at home and abroad with greater difficulty. Discipline is less severe. The moral welfare of the soldier is less guarded by municipalities and volunteer community service. While programs of helpfulness are still employed, it is with a decreased insistance. The soldier is left more to his own devices and the lure of lucre-mad, commercialized vice appears at a time when he is less strong. He is "killing time," chafing under restriction, eager for diversion and reckless from ennui now that the big job "over there" is done. There is also a hegira of religious workers from among the soldiers from the same considerations. It is now less spectacular and more plodding to be a religious worker in a military camp. The thing which inspired in the beginning is receding to the rear. Only the strongest impulsions from contact with the Christ will keep camp workers pursuing their tasks with the same tirelessness as formerly. On the whole, there is the threat of a serious slump in the persistence of present conditions.

What opportunities are offered and what obligations are imposed in this period of transition from war to peace! These soldier boys, as no other single group, will determine our future American life. Their spirit and motive will be registered in community life far beyond numerical warrant. Their sacrifices will be credentials unquestioned; their scars will be badges of authority. None will grudge them this prestige —it will be willingly accorded. We are only anxious that such rights shall be exercised with holy purpose. The Church with more than ordinary urgency should be preparing both them and itself for this new responsibility. This can be more easily and effectually done while the men are together in camp than later. An esprit de corps of national application can be created. Religious workers in the camps and adjoining the camps, as well as correspondence with boys in service, can all assist in this preparation. Who does not sense such an obligation at this crisal time is not reading the mission of the church into the opportunity of the day.

The Young Men's Christian Association realizes this opportunity and the danger of its non-use and is putting this motto conspicuously about the camps:

"When you go back home, tie
Up to the church; you need it
And it needs you."

There is another great matter to enter the consideration by the Church. We have long been lamenting the paucity of workers. This condition has become more aggravating with the progress of time until at the present the situation is actually acute. Through the war some changes have come in the lives of those who have been in the thick of it. They may have had personal experiences with God or a contact with men which has given them a new sense of the stewardship of their own lives. Their old ante-war occupations, in many instances, will not be open to them. They face the necessity of making a new choice of life work. Certainly, under these conditions, God will be calling some of them to a life of purely Christian service. May He not call through us, or may we not at least be the Elis to these Samuels to say at the psychological moment, "If He call thee, thou shalt say, 'Speak, Lord, for Thy servant heareth.'" Circumstances have never combined to make opportunity more favorable for impressions toward life service for God than now. Should not the Church be flooding the camps with literature along these lines, not permitting the men to escape decision concerning them? A day lost now may be an opportunity lost forever.

An unfortunate fact stands beside this great opportunity and that is this—while the opportunity has been enlarging, the inclination of the church has been apparently decreasing. We did great things for the boys while they were going out in preparation for the eventualities of the war. We should be no less active for their influence and welfare in the days of peace. Too often our greatest desire now seems to be to get them back to our homes, just to have them with us. The deeper meanings of the hour are escaping attention from very many who ought to be regarding this as the great day of opportunity for both the future of the men and the Church.

May we not each accept these many obligations as personal duties from which there is no release until they are faithfully performed.

THE CHRISTIAN ORPHANAGE

SOME TITHING TALK

If we can have $194.00 to report in our next letter we will reach our first thousand dollars in the month of February. That would be fine. I hope we can do it.

Mr. and Mrs. M. E. Godwin, Stuart, Iowa, sent us a check this week for $78.01. These good friends tithe and this is the tithe money. What if all our people would tithe their income? How easy it would be to run our colleges, churches and orphanages. I feel sure our income would be so liberal that we would be able to establish our home for little children in the next few months and have our Orphanage grounds dotted over with the sweet little tots who are in need of a home.

Who would not be interested in the little tots? When you visited Elon it would be one of the places you would want to visit.

I received a letter this week from a kind friend of the Orphanage in which she said: "I am glad to see the stone start to rolling which will open the doors of the Christian Orphanage to the small children. There is nothing that appeals to my sympathy more than a small child without a mother." A check was enclosed to back up the sympathy. I had to refuse to take a small child last week because we are not prepared to care for children under four years of age. Our people ought to open their hearts and see to it that a home is prepared for the admittance of these little children. How many of our people who love the little helpless babies who have been left without a mother, and often the case without a father, will contribute toward a home for them? "He that hath pity upon the poor lendeth unto the Lord; and that which he hath given will He repay him again." Where is the person who was ever made poorer by lending a helping hand to the poor and needy? Why can't we lend unto the Lord one-tenth of our income? Why can't we trust His promise? Let us try it and see if we are not blessed in many ways.

I had the pleasure of visiting the First Christian church in Norfolk some time ago, and while talking to one of the good members of that church he made this suggestion which I think is a good one, and would have mentioned it before this date but for the fact that we wanted to close up our year's work first and mention this idea at this time. His suggestion was that our Orphanage had no endowment and why not start one by asking our people to contribute "Liberty Bonds"

to start an endowment for our beloved Institution? Now, I think this a splendid idea and I know our people within the bounds of the Christian Church could donate enough Liberty Bonds, and be the happier for the doing, to make a nice endowment for the Orphanage. I noticed in the papers sometime ago where one man in North Carolina donated to one Orphanage in this State Liberty Bonds amounting to $5,000.00. I wonder how many members in the Christian Church would like to make a contribution of this kind?

CHAS. D. JOHNSTON, Supt.

REPORT FOR FEBRUARY 19, 1919

Amount brought forward, $499.24.

Children's Offerings

Naoma Carden, 10 cents; Argene Harris, 10 cents; Total, 20 cents.

Sunday School Monthly Offerings

(North Carolina Conference)

Ingram, Va., $3.00; Danville, Va., $6.00; Chapel Hill, N. C., $2.12; Ramseur, N. C., $2.14; Ramseur Baraca Class, $3.00; Amelia, $5.00; Pleasant Hill, $2.25; New Providence, $1.64; Christian Chapel, $3.40; Durham, N. C., $5.00; Sanford, N. C., $6.79.

(Eastern Virginia Conference)

Windsor, $4.74; Berea, (Nansemond), $10.00; Antioch, $5.50; Washington Street, Norfolk, $3.00; Suffolk, $25.00.

(Virginia Valley Conference)

Antioch, $4.00; Dry Run, $2.00.

(Georgia and Alabama Conference)

Beulah, 50 cents. Total $95.08.

Thanksgiving Offerings

Greensboro, N. C., $102.70; Mt. Zion church, (Ala.), $7.00; Ebenezer church, $13.80; Total, $123.50.

Special Offerings

American Christian Convention Office, $2.00; Mrs. L. V. Bason, 50 cents; Mr. and Mrs. M. E. Godwin, Stuart, Iowa, $78.01; T. L. Chandler, Durham, N. C., $5.00; Ella Chandler, Durham, N. C., $2.00; Minnie Chandler, Durham, N. C., $1.00; Total $88.51.

Total for the week, $307.29; Grand total, $806.53.

LETTERS

Dear Uncle Charley:—I am a little girl eight years old. I want to join the band of cousins. My papa, sister, and I have had Influenza since Christmas. Papa has missed some of his appointments. You will find ten cents enclosed for February. Your little cousin, Naoma Carden, Durham, N. C.

We are glad to welcome you to our little band of cousins. You must write often this year and help keep our corner full.—"Uncle Charley."

Dear Uncle Charley:—I am sending you a dime for the little children. I want to join your little circle of writing letters. I am writing for my first time. I hope the little children are having happy a Happy New Year. I am eight years old. I have two little sisters younger than I am.—Argene Harris, Danville, Va.

We are glad to have you as a member of our little band. You are the first to join from Danville church. Write often.—"Uncle Charley."

E. K. Freeman—I like THE CHRISTIAN SUN and would be at loss without it.

The Standard Christian College

Depicting the Basis of the

Elon Standardization Fund

By

President W. A. Harper

"Few Colleges have such a reputation as Elon, won in so short a time and under such financial strain."— Eastern Virginia Conference. •

THE STANDARD CHRISTIAN COLLEGE

Standardization a Modern Characteristic

Ours is the day of standards. Railroads long since were standardized, with greater efficiency and economy for themselves and the public. The coinage of the nations when standardized wrought a notable advance over the previous confusion and injustice. Big business is standardized, and that is why it is big. We adopt standards for our Sunday Schools, our Christian Endeavor Societies, our Churches. We are perhaps approaching the day when the food each man can legally consume will be reduced to a standard—a day hard on the fats, but glorious for the leans and the in-betweens.

It Is Not An Unmixed Blessing

Standards have advantages and disadvantages. It is a well known fact that railroads are slow to adopt improvements for safety or service. The law has frequently compelled them to inaugurate changes in the line of their own efficiency. Many a patent improving a commodity, or a process of manufacturing, has been bought up and then shelved, in the interest of immediate returns. Big business, standardized business, is conservative and many times averse to innovations. Standards often fossilize. They more often tyrannize. Salvation for standardized institutions is to be sought through the employment of a body of experts giving their entire time to evolving improvements and then only with a Board of Directors looking to long-time rather than short-time profit. The Carnegie Steel Corporation has practiced this plan. A premium was set on initiative by the wily head of this amalgamated business giant. The Armour and Co. experts take rank with the great scientists of the world. John D. was wise in the same direction. That is why the by-products of the packing and oil industries are more valuable than the meat or the oil. These experts have made it possible for John D., if he chose to do so (but he won't, my word for it), to pay you five cents a gallon to use his oil, if you would not take it on other conditions, and yet to grow fabulously rich on gasoline, acetylene, and the thirty other different "enes" of the oil industry's by-products. These experts have made it possible for beef and mutton and pork to sell for less today, in war times, in the wholesale market than a half-century ago, because they have taught the packers how to save every vestige of the animals slaughtered, even to the squeal, which is safely preserved in phonograph records and sold to a gullible public.

Some Things Cannot Be Standardized

We standardize our professional men by requiring them to have a State license. Our ministers are standardized by being first admitted as candidates, then licensed as probationers, and finally ordained to the full gospel ministry. There is even talk among the eugenists of standardizing husbands—a proposition strenuously opposed by the stronger sex, and with good reason. The unmarried ones say it isn't fair to subject them to tests their fathers could not have passed. It will be a good thing not to make this standardization business retro-active—a good thing for the American home, which in spite of the lack of standardization is the noblest institution of our social order. So far there has been no suggestion of the standard woman. Her style changes so often it would be useless, say those who regard the militant suffragette and the society belle as the true representatives of the gentler sex. But those of us who know the loving heart of noble womanhood assign a different reason. We know that some things are too precious to be pared down to uniformity. Personality, individuality, difference in their engaging charm. And such is woman, the last of the Creator's handiwork and His masterpiece.

A Multiplicity of Standards For Colleges

Colleges too are being standardized, rated, and praised or condemned as they attain or fall below the standards set. Each State has its standards. The U. S. Government has also embarked in the College classification business. Denominational Colleges are rated by their controlling bodies. The Carnegie Foundation for the Advancement of Teaching and The Rockefeller General Education Board have other standards still. Each individual College has its own traditions and its own ideals. In the multitude of such conflicting wisdom surely there is safety. But where shall we find it? What is a College?

The Vital Worth of The American College

The word "College" is used about as indiscriminately as the word "professor." A group of young men were frequently in a crowded train heard to refer to a certain professor, as a great and noble leader. "And what does this professor teach?" queried a sitter-by. "He is the head professor of the College of Barbers in ———————— town," came the instant reply. We have colleges and professors of dentistry, of manicuring, of horse-shoeing, of business, of palmistry, of dress-making, of ———, of ———, ad infinitum, and also ad nauseam. What then is a College? The College is, in its true significance, an American development in the realm of higher education. In England, the Colleges group themselves into a university, but in our country the College is or should be a separate institution, standing like a noble arch over the entrance from high school into the busy work of the world or through a winding path to this same work by the way of the university or professional school, following the completion of the College curriculum. It is our country's noblest contribution to the progress of human development and the liberalization of the human mind. The late Professor Hugo Munsterberg, of Harvard, born and educated in Germany, but a remarkably appreciative man of every promising institution, in speaking of the American College said: "I believe in its mission and, in spite of the pressure from the high schools below and from the professional schools above, I believe in its essentially unchanged future. I see in the College the most characteristic expression of the American genius, the most important condition for the healthy development of the national life,..........the College is the soul of the American nation."

Its Important Place In Our Educational System

The College, of which this keen German student of our life and institutions speaks this eloquent and deserved praise, stands in the educational system as the crown of the high school and is the door-way to complete professional equipment. It is the guardian of the liberal arts. Its business is not specialization nor the practical ability so clamorously demanded by this materially obsessed day. Its function is to give those who resort to it fellowship with all and a splendid individuality peculiarly their own, to vouchsafe to them wisdom with self-masterly, to add to their days by "hastened living" as has been said, by which is meant to place at their disposal the rich and helpful experience of the race, in its upward progress, so that they may be saved the high tuition rate of that relentless school, to enable them to realize the best possibilities of our human nature, the equip them with the foundation-principles and inspire them with the spirit of that unselfish leadership so lamentably lacking in the war-ridden world of this inhuman time, to teach them vigorously to apply first to themselves and then to others, including society and its institutions, the sublime principles of the obligation of the privileged and talented to serve altruistically the interests of those whose lot is hard by reason of the lack of privilege or talent, to discipline themselves, to be joyous in honest and honorable work, high in ideals, enthusiastic in the service of human progress, with emphasis on social rather than personal gain.

Our Democratic Life Cannot Dispense With Its Service

Such is the high and holy calling of the true College. Such an institution democracy must have, since in a society so constituted there is no imperial autocrat to call men from selfish pursuit to altruistic endeavor. Democracy must fail with the spirit of individualism unrestrained by an institution somewhere in its social organization giving its future leaders the impulse to sacrificial service. No institution has yet been devised that can in any real sense offer itself as the competitor of the College in this realm. The complete and unanswerable verification of this position can be demonstrated in every community, where College graduates and men of large intellectual achievement elsewhere educated live and work side by side. The College man's unselfish service is the College's unimpeachable justification. True it costs money to erect and maintain Colleges; true it takes time to master the curriculum before university or professional training. But it is also true, in the experience of mankind, that the College is worth all its costs in money and time, that its dividends far outweigh its cost from every standpoint. Ill-advised and low-visioned is the tendency therefore to exalt the high schools into Junior Colleges and to debase the universities to the point of accepting the graduates of such schools to full standing in their graduate and professional departments. And greatly in error is that mad haste of American youth to find a short-cut from high school to specialization by eliminating from its life-equipment the American College, which is the soul of the nation, and the liberalizer and energizer with noblest ideals of every youth earnestly seeking for truth at her shrine.

The College Must be True to Its Place And Ideals

This brings me to say that the College must remain a College. No inordinate desire for mere bigness, no insatiate ambition for matching the universities and

special schools with multiplicity of schools and departments must for one moment becloud the issue. The College must be prepared to justify itself as such and content to remain such. It will absolutely divest itself of all tendencies toward spread-eagleism. Let it keep true to its place, and the nation's soul will be saved from the canker of materialism as well as from the dry-rot of mere intellectualism, the Scylla and Charybdis these of higher education in this twentieth century. The true College will leave graduate work and professional specialization to the universities and special schools. It will give itself to the teaching of language, literature, sciences natural and social, philosophy and history, with the ideal constantly before it to produce men and women of character, (and so it must teach the Bible), able to think independently and initiatively, to discern the laws of life and society, to see things in proportion and in that beautiful symmetry so abundant in God's world, to be considerate, appreciative of the great intellectual and spiritual achievements of the race and zealous to share them with all men, testing things by the scientific method, viewing them in the historical spirit, equipped with the philosophic mind and the aesthetic appreciation, crowned and glorified by the presence in all the texture of their life and in its every attitude of that most needed item of our American life—the social consciousness, the identification of the self with the race, the recognition of man's brotherhood, of humanity's oneness in essence and aim.

Its Inner Soul Cannot Be Standardized.

Can such an institution be standardized? Shall we inaugurate slavish uniformity for our Colleges and render their faculties and administrators mere puppets in the ceaseless grind of an imperious system? Remember the College is dealing with life, the priceless gift of God. Life cannot be standardized. It is never possible to fossilize the living. There is individuality, and there must continue to be. In a sense, our Colleges therefore cannot be standardized. But in another sense they can be. Their spirit is their own. It moulds their students and is the splendid heritage of a noble past plus the cherished aspirations of a hopeful future operative in unison in the fateful present, fashioning the soft clay of the impressionable life for time and for eternity. What a frightful responsibility rests on our Colleges! These things are too sacred, too tender, too elemental for standardization. They are truth and they are life.

But In Other Respects It May be Standardized—Some Instances

But sympathetic students of our educa-

tional system are convinced that Colleges can be standardized in other directions. With reference to entrance requirements, students with less than fifteen units will not be accepted, and only three conditions should be granted, the same to be removed before the beginning of the Sophomore year. Four years of two semesters each, with one hundred twenty semester hours of hour-recitation work, should be required for a degree. The minimum College to be able to do efficient work should enroll one hundred students, have a president, a librarian, and eight professors, have invested in its plant $350,000, with a productive endowment of $432,000, and an annual budget of $32,000. As the enrollment increases all other items will increase in a proportion that may be described as geometric progression or as resembling an inverted pyramid, for it is a well-known fact that higher education becomes increasingly costly per student as the institution giving it increases in numbers. A college of five hundred students, for example, according to the Association of American Colleges, should have a faculty of fifty, a budget of $166,750, a plant valued at $985,000, and a productive endowment of $2,215,000. According to this same authority, a college of 1,000 students should have a faculty of ninety-seven, a budget of $442,500, a plant worth $2,400,000, and a productive endowment of $6,250,000. The number of students in a class should also be standardized. The number of recitations a student may take is also a proper item for standardization as well as the number of hours a professor shall teach per week. The minimum salary for a College professor is regarded by the standardization specialists as $1,500 a year. Colleges should also be standardized according to the professional equipment and teaching experience of the faculty members. Several states have refused to grant recognition to any College lacking less than $200,000 of productive endowment, with a plant valued at less than $300,000, and with fewer than six full time College teachers. This minimum is the basis of the present campaign to raise $125,000 additional endowment for Elon. This is explanation of the name given the fund, THE STANDARDIZATION FUND.

The Consequence of Such Standardization

The Colleges should welcome such sympathetic study of their needs and their constituents should gladly supply them their lacks. It is safe to predict that in the next generation we shall have fewer Colleges and better ones. The standardization propaganda is making mighty strides in the realm of higher education. The fierce light of publicity is to be turned on in all its brilliancy. Every weak spot in every College will be revealed, and mercilessly held up to public scrutiny. Those Colleges whose friends refuse to supply the funds necessary for minimum efficiency according to the standardization tests will for a few years lead a precarious life, wilter, and die. Sad is the thought, because many Colleges not meeting these tests in former generations, by dint of sacrifice on the part of their administrators and faculties, have wrought a noble work in manhood and womanhood. But new conditions arise. The standardization hour has come. A discriminating public will diligently compare the College seeking patronage to the standards set for its enrollment and by the judgment of that guage will grant or without support. The hand-writing is on the wall. "**Mene, Mene, Tekel, Upharsin,**" which being interpreted and applied will read to many a noble College in our land, "**The Standards have been set. Your friends withheld their support. You have been found wanting. You must die.**" But there is also a ray of hope, bright and promising, in this standardization issue, the hope that seeing the needs and realizing the deserts of their College in view of the standardization tests, many an institution now fighting in a life and death grapple with threatening bankruptcy will be rallied to by generous hearts and so enabled to go forward to larger achievement and nobler service. Many a College in that trying hour will no doubt have sensed in the normal round of things the annunciation of its own speedy dissolution, a dissolution sure and inevitable but for the spiritual rulership of God in the world. In that hour for many such a College, men of God, trained for service at their shrines owing their all to these noble institutions, will be powerful with God as Isaiah was in his intercession for Hezekiah, and in answer to their petitions in agony of heart to the Great White Throne, fountains of generosity will open, length of days be granted, larger usefulness guaranteed, and the College itself brought into a new spiritual experience because in its weakness it learned to lean on the Everlasting Arms. Who doubts that Elon shall be among the number so blessed? No man who trusts God and loves his Church can hesitate for a moment. Elon shall be made safe in this crisal hour.

But The College Must be Distinctively Christian

And this brings me to the third remark of this paper—that the Standard College must be Christian. Note that I said, must be. The task before the College, briefly summarized concretely in the phrase "the making of a complete man" or abstractly conceived as the production

of character, requires that the things of the spirit shall be given due recognition. Education and religion cannot be divorced without direst consequence to the individual man and to the nation. Religion is essential to the adequate fulfillment of the cherished ideals of the standard College. Christian education—it is our hope, and without it there is no hope. Christian education has so far saved our American civilization from utter ruin—Christian education, whose atmosphere is a healing, nurturing spiritual balm, whose breath is prayer, whose life is faith, whose rule is love, whose inspiration is service, whose joy is willing sacrifice. Four years spent in such a College can but fulfill in the soul the purpose of the Master when he said: "I have come that they might have life, and that they might have it more abundantly."

Times may change. New standards may arise. But God is still God, and man is His child. The education which ignores that fundamental relationship is fundamentally defective. "Education that trains men without religion," to borrow the expressive sentiment of the Duke of Wellington, the man of iron who yet knew God, "but makes them clever devils." Better ignorance and Christian trust, better no Colleges and a due appreciation of God in His world, than all the wealth of the Rockefellers and the Carnegies collected in a place of learning and the spiritual essence of life left out.

For Such a College The Need is Urgent

But for the College that is standard in its equipment and personnel, and that is Christian in its inner heart, spiritual in its attitudes and in its aspirations—for this sort of College there is an abiding need, a never-ending necessity. Such an institution will make a nobler contribution to humanity than President Wilson sought for our nation to make the world by its entrance into the recent holocaust of bloodshed and slaughter. That noble statesman wishes the world made safe for democracy. The Standard Christian College will have before it as the goal of its hope and aspiration, to keep the forces and leadership of life safe for Christ and so fundamentally and truly to render the world a fit place for the unfolding of true democracy, recognizing each man as a brother and God as the Father of all. Any man can well be glad to serve with his life or his means an institution presaging such salvation for society and its organized activities. The educational need of our day and also its prophetic hope is—the Standard Christian College.

The Standardization Fund is now fundamental in the life of Elon. The Christian Church has never yet failed to do her

duty by her institutions in any crisis of life. God will not let the spring of her liberality fail now. "We can do it, and WE WILL."

MARRIAGES

MARCOM-STONE

Miss Victoria Stone, Cary, N. C., and Mr. Rex Marcom, Morrisville, N. C., were married by Rev. W. G. Clements at his residence in Morrisville. Only a few friends and relatives witnessed the ceremony. Misses Emma and Viola Stone, sisters of the bride; Mrs. Sorrell and Mr. F. H. Marcom, sister and brother of the groom, were present.

            W. G. C.

SUNDAY SCHOOL TOPIC FOR SUNDAY, FEBRUARY 23

"*Moses Praying For Israel.*"
Lesson Text: Exodus 32:1-34.
Golden Text: The supplication of a righteous man availeth much in its workings. James 5:16.
For explanation and comment see Bible Class Quarterly; also Officers and Teachers Journal, published by Christian Publishing Association, Dayton, Ohio.

CHRISTIAN ENDEAVOR TOPIC FOR SUNDAY, FEBRUARY 23

Christianity and the Toilers of Japan. (Missionary Meeting).
Scripture Text: Matt. 28:16-20. ("The Great Commission").
For explanation and suggestions see Christian Endeavor World, Boston, Mass.

THE SUNDAY SCHOOL'S BIGGEST PROBLEM

According to W. C. Pearce, Field Superintendent for the International Sunday School Association, the Sunday schools' biggest problem just now is how to regain in attendance what they lost the past year. One denomination lost from its schools in one year 125,000 pupils; another lost 70,000; and the schools of Illinois alone, according to the State's Sunday School Association, lost 17,902 members in the year 1918. Mr. Pearce says if the present rate of decrease continues the Sunday school will be extinct in one generation. The total loss of all schools in America in 1918 is put down at between 300,-000 and 400,000.

It is significant that with this decrease in attendance at Sunday school has come a very marked increased in juvenile crime. The city of Chicago handled over 30 per cent more cases of delinquent boys and girls last year than the year before. To quote Mr. Pearce again, "The religious forces of the world face their most serious crisis, just as governments are doing. From the church standpoint it is a matter of whether the Bolshevism of unbelief lack of restraint and atheism shall sweep the world. Religious indifference is always accompanied by social decay."

One of the causes of the great slump in Sunday school attendance is the abnormal condition brought on by the world-war.

But there is another cause. Sunday schools, like day schools, and like individuals, need new visions, new tasks, new duties, new experience, new undertakings.

Today there is no greater task before this Christian brotherhood than that of reaching this whole wide world for Christ. If wars in future are to be prevented then the evils that produce war must be uprooted and destroyed. Why should not the youth in the Sunday school study, at least one Sunday school period of each month, the great and vital question and problem of missions?

Throw a little "pep" into the slow life of your present Sunday school by proposing that every class in the school study missions one lesson each month—and see what happens. Let the young and the old learn something of the heroes who are out on the firing line, and the needs and possibilities of taking this wide world for Christ.

— J. O. ATKINSON.

We will pay a straight salary of $35.00 per week for man or woman with rig to introduce Eureka Poultry Mixture. Six months' contract. Eureka Mfg. Co., East St. Louis, Ill.

DR. J. H. BROOKS

DENTIST

Foster Building   Burlington, N. C.

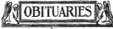

OBITUARIES

RESOLUTIONS OF RESPECT—DOWDY

Whereas, an all-wise Father has seen fit to take from "death unto life" our beloved friend and co-worker, I. L. Dowdy, one of the leading members of our church and Sunday school:

Therefore be it Resolved:

First. That we bow in humble submission to the will of our loving heavenly Father, who doeth all things for the best, knowing that our loss is Heaven's gain.

Second. That the church and Sunday school have lost a faithful member and the Baraca Class a loyal president, the family a true husband, a loving and devoted father.

Third. That we offer our heartfelt sympathy and prayers to his loved ones.

Fourth. That a copy of these resolutions be sent to the family, a copy sent to The Christian Sun for publication and a copy be spread on the minutes of the Durham Christian church.

G. VANCE MASSEY,
W. LEE HESSEE,
R. J. KERNODLE,
Committee.

PUTNAM

Mrs. Nancy Putnam died at her home at Newport News, Va., January 8, 1919, aged seventy-eight years. She was a dear Christian mother and will be greatly missed in her home, community and church. She leaves two daughters, Mrs. Mary E. Robinson and Mrs. Annie Caruthers, nine grandchildren, one great grandchild and many relatives and friends. Funeral services conducted by the writer and the remains were laid to rest in the cemetery at Newport News.

H. H. BUTLER.

JONES

Richard Alonzo Jones died at his home at Corapeake, N. C., January 5. 1919 at the age of twenty-four years, eleven months and fourteen days. He was a good man and greatly beloved by all who knew him. He was a faithful member of Parker's M. E. Church and will be missed in his church and community. He was a member of Holy Grove Lodge I. O. O. F.; also a member of the Rebecca Lodge of the I. O. O. F. He leaves a devoted father and mother, four brothers, eight sisters and many friends. Funeral ser-

---

vices were conducted by the writer at his church and his remains were laid to rest in the church cemetery. The Lord bless and comfort the bereaved ones.

H. H. BUTLER.

BOYETT

Mrs. Mary E. Boyett, widow of the late James Boyett, died at her home, Suffolk, Va., January 7, 1919 at the age of sixty-four years, four months and seven days. She leaves five children, fifteen grandchildren. She was a member of Holy Neck Christian church. Funeral services were conducted at the grave in Cedar Hill cemetery by the writer. She was a good Christian mother and will be missed in her home and community. May the Lord bless the bereaved ones.

H. H. BUTLER.

BRIEF MENTION

Last week we went to press with enough matter on hand for this issue. Most of that is in this paper, but some had to wait again for the regular weekly matter. Half of this issue was printed on February 15 and the remainder of it in type on that date save the notes in this column. Next week will about get us caught up with matter on hand. Let it continue to come.

Mr. D. R. Fonville spoke at the Burlington church last Sunday night on the recent war and his experiences in France. The house could not seat the people comfortably.

President Wilson is on his way back to the United States.

An extra session of Congress seems to be certain.

We have recently sold Berea and Mt. Zion churches in the North Carolina Conference individual Communion sets.

Billy Sunday spoke in Greensboro Monday night.

CHARLES W. McPHERSON, M. D.

Eye, Ear, Nose, Throat

OFFICE OVER CITY DRUG STORE

Office Hours: 9:00 a. m. to 1:00 p. m.
and 2:00 to 5:00 p. m.

Phones: Residence 153; Office 65J

BURLINGTON, NORTH CAROLINA

Christian Education Month

February 16--March 16, 1919

Every Pastor is requested to preach on

"The Call to the Ministry"

Our Convention has said

We must have One hundred new ministers during the next five years,

Let us pray

That God will give us twenty of them during this month. He is willing. Are we? God grant it.

The Gospel Ministry

Is the noblest work in the world. Its opportunities of service are accentuated now as never before. Strong men and true are needed. Let every Christian prayerfully examine himself to see if God will excuse him from this service.

Report all decisions

At once to President W. A. Harper, Elon College, North Carolina, where these candidates will be educated to serve the Kingdom through our brotherhood.

During this month also

The Elon Standardization Fund for $125,000 additional Endowment is to be launched in every church. God expects every one of us to do full duty. Let us not disappoint God.
We call the Church to her knees that God may dedicate us to the recruiting of our ministry and the strengthening of our College.

J. E. WEST

K. B. JOHNSON   }   —For the Board of Trustees of Elon College

R. M. MORROW

W.-W. STALEY, President, the Southern Christian Convention

Christian Education Month--What blessing it holds! We shall enter in. Pray the Lord of the harvest that He send forth laborers into His harvest.

𝔄 Call

For a Larger Circulation

of

THE CHRISTIAN SUN

Goes beyond the paltry dollar

and

The Hum of the Printing Press

. . . . . *It is a call for a larger Church*
and a more intelligent membership.

Volume LXXI	WEDNESDAY, FEBRUARY 26, 1919	Number 9
BURLINGTON	. . .	**NORTH CAROLINA**

THE CHRISTIAN SUN

Founded 1844 by Rev. Daniel W. Kerr.

C. B. RIDDLE   -   -   -   Editor

Entered at the Burlington, N. C. Post Office as second class matter.

Subscription Rates

One year .... $ 2.00
Six months 1.00

In Advance

Give both your old and new postoffice when asking that your address be changed.

The change of your label is your receipt for money. Written receipts sent upon request.

Marriage and obituary notices not exceeding 150 words printed free if received within 60 days from date of event, all over this at the rate of one-half cent a word.

Original poetry not accepted for publication.

Principles of the Christian Church

(1) The Lord Jesus Christ is the only Head of the Church.
(2) Christian is a sufficient name of the Church.
(3) The Holy Bible is a sufficient rule of faith and practice.
(4) Christian character is a sufficient test of fellowship, and of church membership.
(5) The right of private judgment and the liberty of conscience is a right and a privilege that should be accorded to, and exercised by all.

EDITORIAL

BOLSHEVISM

During the past several weeks we have heard no little about Bolshevism. The secular press has been full and aflame with all kind of reports and rumors. We say *rumors* because some of the reports have been untrue, while in many instances enough has not been told.

We have gathered our information from sources that are reliable, sane and sober and not from any hurried newspaper note.

1. *What is Bolshevism?* The frame comes from the Bolsheviki of Russia. The Bolsheviki is a great movement to get control of national affairs. It is autocracy in an enraged state; it is autocracy gone wild.

2. *What is their Platform?* We quote the "planks" in the platform of the Bolshevist movement:

"1. The church is separated from the state.

"2. Within the limits of the Republic, it is prohibited to pass any local laws or regulations which would restrict or limit the freedom, of conscience or establish any kind of privileges or advantages on the ground of the religious affiliation of citizens.

"3. Every citizen may profess any religion or none at all. Any legal disabilities connected with the profession of any religion or none are abolished.

"4. The proceedings of state and other public legal institutions are not to be accompanied by any religious customs or ceremonies.

"5. The free observance of religious customs is guaranteed in so far as the same do not disturb the public order and are not accompanied by attempts upon the rights of the citizens of the Soviet Republic. The local authorities have the right to take all necessary measures for the preservation, in such cases, of public order and security.

"6. No one may decline to perform his civil duties, giving as a reason his religious views. Exemptions from this law, conditioned upon the substitution of one civil duty for another, are permitted by decisions of the people's court in each individual case.

"7. Religious or judicial oaths are abolished. In necessary cases a solemn promise only is given.

"8. Acts of a civil nature are performed exclusively by civil authorities, such as the departments of registration of marriages and births.

"9. The school is separated from the church. The teaching of all religious doctrines in all state and public, as well as private, educational institutions in which general subjects are taught, is forbidden. Citizens may teach and study religion privately.

"10. All church and religious societies are subject to general regulations governing private associations and unions, and do not enjoy any privileges or subsides either from the state or from its local autonomous and self-governing institutions.

"11. Compulsory collection of payments and assessments for the benefit of church or religious societies, or as a means of compulsion or punishment of their co-members on the part of these societies, is not allowed.

"12. No church or religious society has the right to own property. They have no rights of a juridical person.

"13. All the properties of the existing church and religious societies in Russia are declared national property. Buildings and articles specially designated for religious services are, by special decisions of the local or central state authorities, given for free use by corresponding religious societies."

A second reading and careful study of this manifesto will aid the reader in forming a more accurate opinion of what it means and for what it stands. There are several clauses that look liberal, but screened behind the seemingly liberal policies the daggers to stab religious bodies are found. The oath is abolished, the teaching of religious subjects forbidden in any kind of school or institution. Churches cannot own property, thus making them subjects of the State or of some individual.

The name *Bolsheviki* means the *majority*, but not *majority* in the sense that Americans term it. By majority with this class is meant the ruling class, which excludes the peasants, the poor class of Russia. Eighty-four per cent of the Russian people belong to this class which one can immediately see would give the power to a few, thus forming an autocracy.

We notice that Mr. Ford's new paper, "The Dearborn Independent", exhibits a cartoon which suggests a "cure for Bolshevism." A table is loaded with good things to eat with the words "three times a day," written across it.

Now, we admire Mr. Ford as an automobile manufacturer, though we do not own one of his "famous" machines, but Brother Henry is in the wrong if that cartoon represents his individual opinion about the aim of the Bolshevist movement. Joy and happiness are not the fruits of a well filled table. The spirit of Bolshevism is the heart and not the stomach.

Next week we shall write of crimes of this movement and its dangers.

THE PEACE CONFERENCE

It is known to the reading world that the Peace Conference has been in session for some weeks. The city in which it is being held is Paris, the capital of France.

We must not think of this assembly's mission is to finally and formally accept Germany's surrender. Its work may finally embrace this, but that is not the real mission of the Peace Conference. The Conference is not only to arrange for final *peace* from the recent war, but endeavor to keep peace and avoid future wars. It would be a great relief to human hearts if we really knew that no other wars would ever be waged.

Let our opinions be what they may about the world issues of the recent war. One can easily see the hand of Providence as it has stretched itself across the horizon of time. The Y. M. and W. C. A. reached their best state of efficiency when their services were most needed to alleviate the suffering millions on war-torn battle-fields. It looks as if these things were born and fostered to meet and aid a world struggle.

The League of Nations was talked about and advocated long before our conflict with Germany. Many eminent men a few years ago thought that such a step was worthless, out of reason and of no necessity. It now seems that its need has been seen.

The Peace Conference is one thing and the League is another, though the Peace Conference is to work out the plans and approve the League. The League of Nations is to be the result of the Peace Conference.

Never in the history of the world has such a Conference met. It will no doubt be the destiny of many world movements. Christian people ought to pray earnestly that right may prevail, and that those in charge of the Conference may be divinely guided.

In brief the covenant of the League is that all nations joining shall submit to certain rules and regulations, thus bringing the nations of the earth together on a definite ground and to carry out a unified program.

In the next issue we shall write on the Articles in the covenant of the League of Nations.

THE PASSING OF KINGS

There is in sight the end of all earthly rule by kings. If memory and history serve us correctly, the first king of earth was Enshagsagana; and if the sign posts of history do not mislead us, the falling of the Kaiser will be the last "fall" of any kingly ruler. True it is that others of the land are occupying positions as "kings," but theirs will not be a "fall," but a *replacement* by condition and time. We believe that the last "king" has been dethroned.

The nations have outgrown the need of kings, emperors, czars and sultans. No nation has really prospered under the rule of overlords. Communities suffer when an individual tries to have all things his way. An institution of any kind will ultimately suffer if one man is dictatory over all its plans and programs. And this may happen when a good man is doing the ruling, for it destroys fellow feeling, obligation, initiative, for one man assume control and causes the masses—the people —to be "hands off."

A country or an institution with an imperial government finds itself hard pushed to succeed, and when it falls—for fall it must—its subjects are without power and training to act because they have been denied the capacity of these things. This is why uprisings, riots, and disturbances follow the falling of an imperial government. The people are left at the mercy of unsettled minds. What they need is leadership to take the situation in hand.

Autocratic power is against the teachings of Jesus. Power in the spirit of Christianity is service and obligation. Autocracy wants to be served; democracy, the spirit of Christianity, wants to serve. It wants to lift up the meek and the lowly.

The Peace Conference, let us hope, will forever abolish the things that tend to give power to one man to make millions helpless and keep them in a subjective state.

GENERAL PARAGRAPHS

By a vote of 55 to 29 the North Carolina Senate defeated woman suffrage.

Kurt Eisner, Prime Minister of Bavaria, and also Herr Auer, Minister of the Interior, were shot on February 21.

The University of North Carolina is undertaking to raise a fund of $150,000 to erect a building memory of the late President Graham.

A bill is before Congress to raise six billion dollars revenue this year and four billion next year, also to reduce letter postage to its former place.

President Wilson is in this country on important business, but will sail for France in a few days to take up the work at the Peace Conference.

Freidrich Ebert has been chosen president of the German state. He is from the lowly walks of life which gives some assurance of doing away with autocracy.

Premier Clemenceau of France, president of the Peace Conference, was wounded last week by a bullet of an anarchist. Mr. Clemenceau is doing well, the wound being only slight.

A FINAL CALL TO SUNDAY SCHOOLS REGARDING ARMENIAN AND SYRIAN RELIEF

The schools of our churches have been co-operating with the American Committee for Armenian & Syrian Relief in the effort to raise $2,000,000 from the Sunday schools of North America to help the starving orphans in Bible Lands. The money is now coming into headquarters in New York in a steady stream, but it will take the full help of every school to reach the quota that has been set.

A. S. Dunn—I have taken THE SUN for nearly twenty years and I don't want to miss a single copy.

NOTES

See special book and Bible prices on page thirteen.

We regret to learn of the passing of Dr. J. H. Wilson, Dover, Delaware.

President Harper of Elon College is in Dover, Delaware, for a week's stay.

Rev. E. T. Cotten sends a list of new subscribers and adds that he is going to give some one a race for the largest number.

If your label indicates 3-1-9 that means your subscription will expire March 1 and you should renew this week or early next week.

We are receiving many encouraging letters from pastors and other workers for THE SUN. Many new subscriptions are being received.

The initial offering at the Burlington Sunday school on February 16 for the support of Miss Martha Stacy, Haverhill, Mass., as a missionary, amounted to $65.67.

We are informed that the subscriptions to the Elon Standardization Fund received on the hill at Elon has amounted to $14,650 and the canvass not completed.

We have on hand two nice pulpit Bibles. One sells for $12.00 and the other for $10.00. For acceptance by March 10 we offer these Bibles at a discount of 10 per cent.

We shall be glad to have your subscription to The Tither. The price is only fifty cents the year. Last week we enrolled over 125 new subscribers from all parts of the country.

Continue to let us have good articles for publication, but do not get impatient if they do not appear in the next issue after you send them in. Few readers realize that we are today (February 21) preparing "copy" for the issue of March 5. And yet we have material on hand now that will not get in until the issue of March 12. This is written as an explanation only.

Rev. H. E. Rountree, now stationed at Portsmouth, N. H., as Chaplain in the Navy, will soon be relieved of his duties owing to demobilization of national forces and will be open for an engagement. Brother Rountree is a graduate of Elon College, has served some of our best churches. His experiences in the Navy, together with several years' experience as pastor, fully qualifies him for a responsible place.

Editors were once called "quill drivers."—This was because they wrote with pens made of goose quills. These lines are written with a quill made and furnished THE SUN's Editor by Dr. Daniel Albright Long, who once used this kind of writing implement. In the new age Editors are called "pen pushers." In the ages to come they will be "drivers" and "pushers," provided—

On February 2 Rev. L. I. Cox was instrumental in organizing a church at Hopedale Cotton Mills, Alamance County, with thirteen charter members. The organization is planning to build a house of worship at an early date. The members have pledged something over $500.00 and about $150.00 of this has been paid. The community needs the church. Brother A. H. McIver, formerly of our Durham church, is treasurer of the organization. Any friend or friends desiring to give aid to this church can send the same to Brother McIver, Burlington, N. C., in care of Hopedale Cotton Mills. We trust that many will send Brother McIver a check.

PASTOR AND PEOPLE

THE POUNDINGS CONTINUE

Recently we were given one of those great surprises about which other ministers have been writing to THE SUN. It was the kind of shocking surprise that leaves a pastor and wife speechless for a while.

We have been working in this field only eight months, and during these months the members of three churches —Isle of Wight, Mt. Carmel, and Windsor, especially the last—have been trying to obtain a house for us in Windsor. But with all of their efforts no house has been obtained, so we have been living in Suffolk, the first and only place which we were fortunate enough to find a house.

But in the face of such a difficult situation the Windsor people desired to give us another sign of their good will toward us; so on one of our visits to Windsor, we were invited into a room containing lots of packages of various sorts and sizes. When we were told that all of them were for us, our feelings were too big for expression, our surprise too great for utterance. Such a pounding filled our hearts with gratitude too deep for words. We were compelled to make two trips with our little Ford to convey all of those good eatables home.

We feel our appreciation to the people who pounded us and gratitude to God, the giver of every good and perfect gift, such that we resolve to show our thankfulness in more efficient service rendered for the Lord.

E. T. COTTEN.

INGRAM

We are hoping that the second Sunday in March will be a good day with the Ingram church. Dr. J. O. Atkinson is expecting to be present to bring his wonderful message on missions at that time. Dr. Atkinson began his campaign at Pleasant Grove now more than a year ago and was very happy in the results. I am praying that he may have a good hearing and a full and ready response to his appeals. When the whole denomination gets behind the great cause of missions it will be doing its duty and making good its most glorious privilege. When the roll of churches are called; when the larger results and the better harvests are beginning to be reaped will Ingram, or any other church, have to remain behind? Let the answer for one and all be *Never!* If I did not believe our blessed Master's commands were as fresh and imperative as they were in the days of Paul I could not believe His love to be as abiding as it was when He said: ''Come unto me...and I will give you rest.'' Believing as I do that He is the same Savior today I am impelled by His love to give the best hours of my life and the first and choicest fruits to Him.

J. G. TRUITT.

SUFFOLK LETTER

After all, life is a compound of experience, history, and hope; and one might add, service. These are interwoven with family groups and make up much of human joys and sorrows. The atmosphere of home ministers to the moral health or sickness of most mortals. There is no good reason why family life should not carry with it permanent relations and affiliations.— It is a sad picture when outside parties determine the course of children which should be determined by parental influence. A *Christian* home is the garden of the Lord in which tender life is cultivated and trained for the King and His children. No portrait is so important on the wall of home as that of ancestors whose character was worthy and has its reproduction in the new generation.

On the thirteenth day of September, nineteen eighteen a beautiful Christian spirit passed out of a long-afflicted body which had been tenderly cared for in a Christian family. On that day Miss Nellie Chapman, eighth daughter of Cornelius and Hammel A. Chapman, joined her only brother, Charles Hammel, in the better home. The home of this family is near Isle of Wight Court House, Virginia. When I first visited that home, it consisted of father, mother, one son and ten daughters. Two links have been taken out of that golden chain since then, and the chain of two links started in heaven. I witnessed the profession of the father and some of the children and their entrance into the Christian church at Isle of Wight Court House.

Nellie was a rare spirit with a charming alto voice. Her voice in songs of praise made many hearts happy and many tears of joy steal down the cheeks of worshippers. In the Sunday school and church she was dearly loved. Back and forth between home and church, like a shuttle, she wove a web of influence that will not fade or wear out. Her works do follow her.

Her bodily affliction was long and trying; but quietly she waited in patience till the end came. Her last months were spent in Lakeview Hospital in Suffolk with some member of the family always at her side. When the end came she was carried back to her church for the last rites of love. The large congregation felt the community loss and the heart of the church throbbled with deep emotion as the choir sang the songs she loved to sing. Then the loved form was laid to rest in Central Hill cemetery, and the bereaved ones went to their homes. Everybody said she was a dear, sweet girl, so useful in Sunday school and church. Such is life, love, and home. The whole gamult of the soul is touched by life, love, and home. The closest institution to heaven is the Christian home; and the nearest institution to hell is a wicked home. The sweetest memory of a departed one is that she was a Christian and the bitterest memory of a departed one is that she died without hope. The summit of all summits is the mound over a Christian grave; and the crown of all crowns is the flowers that cover such a grave. Such was the grave of Nellie Chapman. Giddy people may waste their time and energy on the varieties of the world, but wiser spirits will seek to make their calling and election sure.

W. W. STALEY.

NORFOLK CHURCHES AND FRIENDS

Saturday, February 8, found the writer with the Woman's Board for Missions of the Eastern Virginia Conference in session at Franklin, Va. What a splendid day it was! Great and good plans were laid for the future, and there will be fruits from that day's session. Among the items on the program adopted was that the Board would raise $1,200.00 a year beginning with the present year, with which to support a missionary; this to be in addition to the regular work the Board is now doing. Owing to the influenza epidemic last fall, the women of this Conference did not hold their annual session, but it was decided to hold a session early in April to lay plans for the remainder of the year.

Sunday found the writer, with Brother J. F. Morgan, pastor First church, Berkley, Norfolk, Va.. Brother Wiggs, the long time and wide awake superintendent, was in charge of the Sunday school. It was suggested that the school study missions one Sunday per month, at the regular Sunday school recitation period and the school may adopt this.

There was a splendid audience present for the eleven o'clock preaching service. It was easy, and a privilege also, to speak on missions to that congregation. Brother Morgan has the missionary vision and his fervor is contagious. His evening congregation was even larger than that of the morning, and attentive to the missionary message. In canvassing, next day, for missionary funds not a member seen declined to donate or subscribe and the pledges soon mounted up to $1,775. Since then Brother Morgan has sent in other subscriptions of $200.00 and he hopes to reach $2,000.00—only lacking one $25.00 subscription now. The writer has not anywhere found a people more ready, willing and anxious to give to our growing and needy missionary fund than these of our good Berkley church.

Sunday afternoon Brother L. E. Smith was installed as pastor of our Third church. Both Brother Morgan and the writer were present and had some part in the delightful exercises. It is needless to say that our Third church people are more than delighted with their new pastor and his amiable wife. Both people and pastor's family are happy. There is a great task ahead of this church and the feeling is everywhere prevalent that Brother Smith is capable of grappling with the great problem and solving it. The writer expects to see the Third church, Norfolk, honored before many months in one of the handsomest and most inviting buildings anywhere to be found in our Convention. The Third church deserves it; they are anxious; and by God's good help they are willing and able.

It was a day of delight in Norfolk. Our Christian cause goes well and is in capable hands there.

J. O. ATKINSON.

CHRISTIAN EDUCATION

THE SECRETARY OF THE NAVY
WASHINGTON

February 11, 1919.

My dear Mr. President:—

I am gratified to know that the friends of Elon College, and it has friends wherever its large contribution of service is known, are planning a campaign to increase its endowment fund.

I have been in intimate touch with your institution since it was founded and know the character of its work and the worth of its product. It has been one of the light-houses in the educational life of our part of the country and I know that a dollar invested in larger provision for the education of the youth who may enjoy its advantages will bring large dividends and dividends which will not terminate with any period, but endure for all time.

Sincerely yours,
JOSEPHUS DANIELS.

Dr. W. A. Harper,
President Elon College,
Elon College, North Carolina.

UNITED STATES SENATE, COMMITTEE ON FINANCE

Washington, D. C.
February 15, 1919

Dr. W. A. Harper,
President, Elon College,
Elon College, N. C.

My dear Dr. Harper:—

I have heard with much interest of your plan to launch your campaign for $125,000 additional endowment for Elon College. I have no doubt that you will succeed in raising the required sum. I regard Elon College as among the best and most useful educational institutions anywhere, and I am sure that this is the feeling among all of the people of North Carolina. I wish you to know how much I am interested in the future of your institution and to express my faith that our people, of all denominations, who are so much interested in the cause of education, will give you earnest and cordial support in your plans for even larger and wider usefulness.

With feelings of high personal esteem, and with every good wish, I am,

Sincerely yours,
F. M. SIMMONS.

HOUSE OF REPRESENTATIVES, U. S.

Washington, D. C.,
February 15, 1919.

Dr. W. A. Harper, President,
Elon College, N. C.

Dear Sir:—It has come to my attention that you are conducting a campaign to further enlarge the endowment of your college. In this matter I trust you will be entirely successful, as I feel that your institution is doing a most excellent work along educational lines.

I consider Elon College one of the most potent forces of the South in Christian education, and wish you that unlimited measure of success, which the high ideals of your institution so richly deserves.

Yours very sincerely,
R. L. DOUGHTON.

(Congressman Doughton is not a member of the Christian Church, but he selected Elon as the college for his son.—*Editor.*)

A FORWARD STEP DEMANDED

I note with pleasure and interest that it has been decided to make the campaign and raise the funds necessary to increase the permanent endowment of Elon College. This is a step forward absolutely demanded by the best interests of the College and the Christian Church.

The record of achievement of Elon College and the position she has gained in the educational world is such as to arouse our pride and demand our support. Much of this has been done in spite of the serious difficulties of inadequate means to take full advantage of its enlarging field of usefulness. It deserves to be relieved of the embarrassment of the lack of or uncertainty of an income sufficient to maintain and advance its standards in keeping with the standards of our best colleges. And the call now made to the constituency which it serves we are sure will meet with gratifying response.

D. R. FONVILLE.

Burlington, N. C.

IMPORTANT ANNOUNCEMENT

I am pleased to announce the election of Miss Helen R. Steward, A. B.; A. M., of Bryn Mawr College, as teacher of history and Dean of Women in Elon College.

Miss Steward has had four years experience in Illinois Woman's College, Jacksonville, Ill. Her testimonials are excellent. They describe her a scholar of large attainment, of pleasing personality, and deep interest in the best things of life.

Miss Helen Taft, daughter of the former president, says of her: "I remember Miss Steward myself well. When she was at Bryn Mawr she was president of the Graduate Club and one of the most attractive and agreeable of the graduate women. I think you will find her admirably fitted in every way to be your Dean of Women."

Miss Steward began her work at Elon on February seventeen.

W. A. HARPER, *Pres.*

THE OPPORTUNITIES OF THE MINISTRY

Much is being said in this time about the call to the ministry. Much also is being said about the rewards of the minstry. I would for this once rather that the young men and women of the Church should look steadfastly at its opportunities.

I do not hesitate to say that no profession offers such opportunities as the ministry. When taken in the large and ultimate sense, the ministry embraces all that is good in the other professions less the self-interest that necessarily invades them. The minister is physician, lawyer, business man, teacher—all for his people. They go to him when they can go to no one else, and his advice is without money and without price.

But in our day the opportunities of the ministry are accentuated because of the circumstances of our life. The problems that cry for solution, the minister alone can solve. How will labor and capital ever become reconciled except a prophet sent from God speaks the message, prefaced with "Thus saith the Lord?" How will the nations live together in peace unless spiritual guidance be furnished and whence shall this guidance come? How shall the disunion of Christian forces answer their Lord's prayer in the one-ness of His people unless the ministry point the way? Science and religion are arrayed against each other. Who can make science the handmaid of religion, an asset and not a liability, unless it be God's elect? How shall the religion of Jesus Christ be wrested from ecclesiasticism and made the servant of the everyday life of man? How shall men learn the pervasiveness, the immanence of spirituality and forget the now too prevalent notion that it is a matter of times, places, and seasons? They will never know unless they are taught, and they will never be taught without a preacher.

The ministry is the salt of the earth. It is the light of the world. It will not only save men, but it will brighten their lives with the illumination of Heaven's brilliancy come to earth. God bless the ministry and fill it with strong, true prophets rightly dividing His word of truth.

W. A. HARPER.

MISSIONARY

HOW TO CREATE AND KEEP A LIVE AND ACTIVE WOMAN'S MISSIONARY SOCIETY IN THE CHURCH
Chapter IV—Have An Objective

In three former chapters the fundamentals of every Missionary Society that would live and be active have been treated, namely, Prayer, the Bible, Music.

We shall bear in mind now that these are fundamentals, and on that account are essential. But foundations, however well laid, are not enough of themselves, if we are to have a complete structure. Every building requires frame work and covering, and these are no whit less essential than is the foundation.

Now the writer conceives that the frame work every well organized Woman's Missionary Society is that of having a given, and a very definite, objective—*an end in view, some thing or things to be accomplished.*

In one of his inimitable stories Rudyard Kipling describes a very beautiful and noble ship which his vivid imagination constructed and sent to sea. But sea-worthy and comely as the great ship was, it had a hard time and rough sailing on the billows until every part of that ship one day discovered just what its function was, and what its designer intended it should do and be. Then that ship settled down to business, defied the waves, and rode bravely and proudly to its intended haven. In each part's discovering what it was there for, and what it meant to all the other parts to be just where it was and perform its function, that ship, says Kipling, *found itself.* No Missionary Society has safe and sure sailing, and is certanly very tame, rather doubtful and hesitating, and never defiant of dangers and difficulties *till it finds itself*—till each member discovers what she is there for, *and what it means to the other members for her to be there.* And no aimless Society, nor any members therof, can find themselves until an objective has been specifically fixed and agreed upon.

A Missionary Society is a mighty good thing to have in the church, home and community, but just to have a Missionary Society for the sake of having one, and because others are having one, is not sufficient. In fact it is short-sighted, not to say silly policy to have a Society on that account. Even as good a thing as a Woman's Missionary Society may be a very poor sort of a thing to have, indeed a selfish sort of thing to have. If a Society is to live and to grow it must have something to live and to grow for—it must ever have some objective in view.

As briefly as possible the following may be safely posited as objectives, or as making toward an objective.

First. *To interest those not interested in world-wide missions.* This, it seems to the writer, is the supreme objective, and should not be lost sight of by any members of the Society. In every community, in every church, in every Society and in well-nigh every home there are those who are not yet interested in reaching this wide world, and saving this ruined race, for and through the blessed Christ. In your attempt, however weak, to interest others in missions you will yourself become more deeply interested in this the biggest business that God or man has ever undertaken.

"Believers in Christ," says Belle M. Brain, "are not, as a rule, won *in masse*; neither are believers in missions. In both cases they are best 'hand-picked' Christians are frequently urged to keep prayer—lists of those they hope to win to Christ. Missionary workers would do well to keep similar lists of those they hope to interest in missions. If each worker would win one other worker to the cause each year, the evangelization of the world would soon be an accomplished fact."

It may be the one you seek to interest is a possible member of the Society, or a possible contributor to your Society, or best of all, a possible life recruit, a real missionary. In either case you are following the very best line of self-education, namely that of learning church doing.

It is not a bad idea, now and then, for every Society

to resolve itself into "A win one Society"—each member going out to get some one else to become a member. Remember that our *growing* depends often upon our going.

Second. To increase our own knowledge about the needs in mission lands.

We never can do much for any cause until the need is laid upon our hearts. God had the power to evangelize China, India and Africa a hundred years before Morrison, Cary, or Livingstone were born, but He did not release that saving and evangelizing power until these human beings felt the sore need of the great task, and from the depth of their knowing minds and anxious heart cried out, "Lord carest thou not that we perish?" Felt and expressed human need is the one essential medium of communication between God's power and man's dependence. When we acquaint ourselves with human needs we open up the avenue, all the way from heaven to earth, from God to man, for the relief of that need. Let the Society learn missionary needs if it would be a power in God's hands as a missionary force.

Third. To have some goal for our giving. Each Society should by all means seek to get and to give for something. Where our treasure goes there will our heart go also. One reason why some Societies have such little heart in their work and for their task is because they put such very little of their treasure into it. Have a goal to achieve in the giving.

J. O. ATKINSON.

OTHER HEROES ALSO

All honor to the brave and fearless sons who have fallen on the fields of France to make the world safe for democracy. They have gone to their death like men and have made the supreme sacrifice for their country.

And then there are other heroes. We shall not forget them either. The ages on ages to come will not forget them. I was reading today the resolve that held one such to his heroic cause, and the motive that prompted his brave life. It was a missionary who laid down his life on the Congo, and this was his resolve:

"In this enterprise of winning Africa for Christ there must be, I know, much of what the world calls loss and sacrifice, and it may be that many will fall in the blessed work of foundation building only; but what of that? To have any share in this noblest of all toil, however humble or obscure, be it only hewing wood or drawing water, is, surely, honor and privilege any servant of Christ must count and long for. I desire to go to this work feeling yet more intensely day by day, as the days pass on, that to live is Christ, and to die is gain; and if He should ordain for me early death, after a few years of humble, obscure, pioneering work only—well, it must be right; for it means early and complete satisfaction. Then shall I be satisfied, when I awake in Thy likeness."

J. O. ATKINSON.

E. W. Clements—I need THE SUN and do not want to miss a copy.

REPORT OF THE TREASURER OF THE WOMEN'S HOME AND FOREIGN MISSION BOARD OF THE SOUTHERN CHRISTIAN CONVENTION, FOR QUARTER ENDING FEBRUARY 1, 1919
Regular Funds

Receipts—
Nov. 26, 1918, W. N. C. Conference, $20.20; Jan. 24, 1919, Va. Valley Central Conference, $9.42; Jan. 24, 1919, E. Va. Conference, $151.98; Jan. 25, 1919, E. N. C. Conference, $8.18; Jan. 25, 1919, E. N. C. Conf. (Special F. M.), $36.67; Total, $226.45.

Disbursements—
Jan. 2, 1919, Mrs. W. A. Harper, (Postage), $3.00; Jan. 2, 1919, C. B. Riddle (Printing), $54.50; Feb. 1, 1919, Mrs. W. A. Harper, (Postage), $9.02; Feb. 1, 1919, Rev. W. C. Wicker, Treas., (H. M.), $62.13; Feb. 1, 1919, Rev. W. C. Wicker, Treas., (F. M.), $98.80; Total, $226.45.

Santa Isabel
Receipts—
Nov. 26, 1918, W. N. C. Conference, $6.85; Jan. 24, 1919, Va. Val. C. Conference, $2.79; Total $9.64.
Disbursements—
Feb. 1, 1919, Rev. W. C. Wicker, Treas., $9.64.

Christian Orphanage
Receipts—
Jan. 24, 1919, Va. Val. C. Conference, 15 cents; Jan. 24, 1919, E. Va. Conference, (Coy Franklin), $11.39; Jan. 25, 1919, E. N. Conference, $10.79; Total, $22.33.
Disbursements—
Feb. 1, 1919, Rev. W. C. Wicker, Treas., $22.33.

Sendai Orphanage
Receipts—
Jan. 24, 1919, Va. Val. C. Conference, 15 cents; Cash on hand, 15 cents.

Bible Women
Receipts—
Jan. 24, 1919, E. Va. Conf. (Mrs. Watanabe), $52.35; Jan. 24, 1919, E. Va. Conf. (Miss. Hamaguchi), $12.50; Total, $64.85.
Disbursements—
Feb. 1, 1919, Rev. W. C. Wicker, Treas., $64.85.

Japan Sunday School
Receipts—
Jan. 24, 1919, E Va. Conference, $12.50.
Disbursements—
Feb. 1, 1919, Rev. W. C. Wicker, Treas., $12.50.

Mrs. Fry's School
Receipts—
Nov. 26, 1918, W. N. C. Conference, $15.00.
Disbursements—
Feb. 1, 1919, Rev. W. C. Wicker, $15.00.
Cash on hand, $35.12; Jan. 24, 1919, E. Va. Conference, $1.00; Feb. 1, 1919, Cash on hand, $36.12.

Barrett Home
Receipts—
Nov. 26, 1918, W. N. C. Conference, $81.15; Jan. 24, 1919, Va. Val. C. Conference, $11.75, Jan. 24, 1919, E. Va. Conference, $149.75; Jan. 25, 1919, E. N. C. Conference, $19.50; Total, $262.15.
Disbursements—
Feb. 1, 1919, Rev. W. C. Wicker, Treas., $262.15.

Santa Isabel Building Fund
Receipts—
Jan. 24, 1919, Va V. C. Conference, $7.75; Jan. 24, 1919 E. Va. Conference, $61.25; Jan. 25, 1919, E. N. C. Conference, $8.30; Total, $77.30.
Disbursements—
Feb. 1, 1919, Rev. W. C Wicker, Treas., $77.30.

Rev. Martines
Receipts—
Nov. 1, 1919, Cash on hand, $512.61; Jan. 24, 1919, E. Va. Conference, $21.64; Feb. 1, 1919, Cash on hand, $534.25.

MRS. W. T. WALTERS, Treas.
Winchester, Va.

Samuel Boggs—Find enclosed my renewal. I just can't get along without THE CHRISTIAN SUN.

THE CHRISTIAN ORPHANAGE

A CHALLENGE

We did not reach our first thousand in February as we had hoped to do, but we did not lack much.

Our good ladies are taking an interest in re-furnishing our building and it is real good of them. We can always count on the ladies. We received a letter last week from a good sister who said that the Ladies' Aid Society in her church would furnish one room. We have Ladies' Aid Societies enough in our Church to refurnish our building and they would be the better for it. If the ladies will furnish the building I will see to it that the men do the painting, that is much needed, and the repairs on the building.

Let us get busy and see who the next will be to take a room. Our Orphanage work ought to grow and our people ought to begin to see the great work that is to be done for the Master through this Institution.

I had the pleasure last year of visiting some of the large Orphanages of the South, and as one superintendent was showing me around the premises he would come to a splendid building and tell me that a good sister had given that as a memorial to her little daughter who died a few years ago, or that some man had given it as a monument to some member of his family.

I remember at one of these institutions I was carried through a hospital building handsomely equipped with everything needed in a building of that kind with a trained nurse to care for the sick, and the superintendent told me that one person gave that as a donation to the institution.

I wondered how many persons in our Church would like to build a monument of this kind? A monument that would give the little helpless children a kindly hand to train them to be useful in life. A kind and sympathetic mother to lay her hand upon their fever brow when sick and nurse them back to health again. Where is the man or woman who has been greatly blessed in this life with plenty and to spare, who would like to build a monument of this kind?

Last fall when we had such a scourge of the "flu" and thirty-four in bed at one time what a blessing it would have been if we had only had a hospital where they could have been cared for.

I met a man on the train a few days ago and our conversation drifted to the subject of tithing and as he was a tither and it was real interesting to hear him tell of his experience in tithing. How he had been blessed and in many unexpected ways! He was a man of great faith and believed fully that God would always carry out his contract to the letter, provided we carried out our part. If we could get our people to tithing and lend some of their income to the Lord how our work would grow in all its branches!

CHAS. D. JOHNSTON, Supt.

REPORT FOR FEBRUARY 26, 1919

Amount brought forward, $806.53.

Children's Offerings

Oliver E. Young, Jr., 25 cents; Edward Jones, 50 cents; Elizabeth Jones, 50 cents; Eula, Estelle and Viola Brady, $1.00; Total, $2.25.

Sunday School Monthly Offerings

Burlington, N. C., $39.74; Rosemont, $5.00; Wakefield, Va., $1.00; Dendron, Va., $5.37; Shiloh, $2.00; New Lebanon, $1.00; New Lebanon Baraca Class, $1.00; Wake Chapel, $5.00; Total, $60.11.

Thanksgiving Offerings

Auburn Church, N. C., $7.00.

Special Offerings

Mrs. Peter Strickland, $10.00; Mrs. G. W. Suits, $1.00; Fullers church, $29.00; Bertha Foushee, $1.00; Mrs. Ella Holt, $11.00; Mrs. Sallie Moore, $1.30; Dr. D. M. Helfenstein, $2.00; W. H. and F. M. Bd., S. C. C., $22.33; Total, $77.63.

Total for the week, $146.99; Grand total, $953.52.

LETTERS FROM THE KIDDIES

Dear Uncle Charley:—I am a little boy seven years old. I want to join the band of cousins. Enclosed you will find twenty cents for January and February.—*Edward Jones.*

Dear Uncle Charley:—I am a little girl three years old. I want to join the band with my brother, too. Enclosed find twenty cents for January and February.—*Elizabeth Jones.*

We are delighted to have you join the band of cousins. We hope many little boys and girls will join often this year.—*"Uncle Charley."*

Dear Uncle Charley:—We are three little girls who want to be your nieces and we are sending you one dollar for the little orphans. We hope the little children enjoyed Thanksgiving and Christmas. Best wishes.—*Eula, Estelle and Viola Brady.*

We give you a hearty welcome to our corner and trust you will fill your spare time with sunshine. Write often this year.—*"Uncle Charley."*

Dear Uncle Charley:—We are so glad the Christian Orphanage is out of debt. I will soon be big enough to "run away," and I will promise to make the Orphanage my first visiting place. Best wishes.—*Oliver E. Young., Jr.*

We will be delighted to have you pay us a visit. You will be royally entertained while here. I feel sure all our little girls will be crazy about you.—*"Uncle Charley."*

"IS TITHING WORTH WHILE?"

Ross Avenue Baptist Church, Dallas, Texas, Chas. D. Fine, S. S. Supt.—Organized 1908 by 62 poor working folks. Have administered $75,000; never had a collection in the church, nor a pay social, nor any schemes to raise money; just completed handsome building. Teaches tithe as standard, but not a "law" in sense of test for communion.

Methodist Bible Woman's Training School, Miss Mildred M. Blakely.—Deaconesses and Bible Women taught tithing from beginning. Acknowledging the Lord with the tithe laying foundation for self support.

FOREIGN MISSIONS AND RECONSTRUCTION

(A paper read before the Annual Session of the Eastern Virginia Conference at Eure's church, November 21, 1919, by Rev. W. M. Jay, and ordered published in The Christian Sun by vote of conference).)

Now that the great world war proper may be said to have come to an end, all minds and hearts that are at all interested in the results and effects of the war are turned to the even more momentous problems of the days and months and perhaps years of the reconstruction.

For the period of reconstruction upon which we are just entering is frought with a great perplexities, as great possibilities and as great responsibilities as the period of the conflict now just ended.

The chief responsibility of the war was to see that the war once begun was won on the side of right and that victory should come to those who were the real victors. This largely depended upon the factors of strategy and strength both physical and spiritual.

But the responsibility of the work of reconstruction is to determine now not only what is best for the present new order of affairs but what shall be a glorious and fitting inheritance for future generations.

We are charged with establishing such a peace as will make wars impossible and render needless great political upheavals, yet leave every possibility for a healthy progress and development along all avenues of life. This process of reconstruction will be many sided. It will be political, economic, social, racial ethical and religious.

It is just a phase of the spiritual or religious process of the reconstruction that we are chiefly concerned with in this discussion. The work of Foreign Missions as it may be influenced by the reconstructive processes.

It is not our intention to speak in any prophetic or visionary sense but from the point of view of what appears to us as a great need and possibility viewed partly from the religious work and accomplishments during the period of the war, and still in vogue, and also from the point of view of the extention of this work to a program covering the whole broad field of church work.

Since the scope of the present war has extended to nearly every part of the non-Christian world, and since the principal nations in this war have been nations whose religious faith is Christianity, it is of interest to note not only to what extent these non-Christian peoples shall be influenced in their religious life but in what direction shall they be influenced; whether it shall be an inspiration of a new hope in Christianity with an unselfish motive, or a reaction against Christianity as a warring faith with a selfish motive, as was certainly evidenced by some of the so-called Christian nations in the war.

As we view the situation the Church has an Herculean task before her in carrying out the great commission of the Master, "Ge ye therefore and make disciples of all nations," but with never so great and favorable an opportunity to accomplish its task as now presents itself.

In 1910 when Dr. Mott wrote his book, "The Decisive Hour of Christian Missions," he said in his last chapter on the "Possibilities of the Situation": It is indeed the decisive hour of Christian Missions. It is the time of all times for Christians of every name to unite and with quickened loyalty and with reliance upon the living God to undertake to make Christ known to all men and to bring his power to bear upon all nations. Doors open and doors shut again. The nations are still plastic. Shall they set in pagan or Christian moulds?"

If that was the visions of Dr. Mott in 1910 that desive hour has grown a hundred times more decisive and critical at this present time.

The nations of Europe and Asia and Africa are far more plastic now than in 1910. In some cases the social economic and political orders have not only weakened but have crumbled and given away.

Is Christianity ready with its new forms to receive the costs that shall be made out of the chaos of the present world situation? The war has been won on a Christian basis. The aims and motives as repeatedly expressed have been of the highest ethical order. In every Conference, commission or tribunal these same lofty ideals should be carried out regardless of the past.

The Church should be ready or immediately get ready to launch the greatest missionary movement to reach the ultimate parts of the non-Christian world it has ever undertaken and not only the greatest it has ever undertaken but a movement sufficiently great to accomplish the task.

The war despite its torments, its horrors and bloodshed has been replete with its lessons and morals.

The Church has not been unmindful of some of these. When called upon to create a spiritual atmosphere and to supply the spiritual needs of a vast army in its making, both in the cantonments and foreign camps, the Church and all its auxiliary organizations rose up a mighty army in themselves to supply this vital need of the army.

Religious lines were not entirely obliterated but they were so completely dimmed that they stood but little in the way of the religious forces operating in the army and navy. Ministers resigned their pastorates or secured leave of absences from their churches, laymen gave up important business and professional occupations to give their services to the Y. M. C. A., and kindred organizations in the camps.

Even Protestant, Catholic and Jewish distinctions, which perhaps were left most distinct, did not stand in the way of at least a co-ordination of the work of these bodies and to a very large degree a hearty co-operation to the same end.

You did not see in the camps and cantonments Y. M. C. A., Y. M. H. A. and K of C huts built side by side and close to each other competing with each other in the work they were doing; proselyting and aggravating old religious sores, but they were so placed where they could serve the greatest number and render the greatest service with no discriminations allowed except as the boys themselves made their preferences.

But what has this to do with Foreign Missions and Reconstruction? It means that if ever the task of winning the world for Christ in this or any other generation is accomplished, it must be done in this same harmonious, co-operative spirit as manifested by the Church in meeting the war work needs.

The Church of Jesus Christ must present a united front in order best to accomplish this great Foreign Mission task.

We have seen how the Churches in a united effort have been able to command all the millions of dollars that it has asked for and the people have responded nearly every time with a fifty percent over-subscription.

This meant a great effort and lots of work, but the results were well worth all the effort.

I believe that the Christian people would be just as enthusiastic under the leadership of a united Church to go "over the top" in providing the necessary millions of dollars for the execution of a world-wide program of Christian missions.

Local option has served well its day and just as the prohibition question has become nationalized and internationalized so must the Mission effort of the church be nationalized and internationalized in its program of work.

Denominational and Federated Missionary movements have so cultivated the soil of both Home and Foreign Missions as to give ample evidence of the success of the work, and to show that the fields are already white unto harvest. Will the Church rise unitedly to its supreme task in this grand hour of opportunity and reap the harvest for the Master? The doors stand wide open now to Christian missions.

Already splendid prospect of this unifying effort are manifesting themselves. The great Presbyterian church has issued a call to all the Protestant churches of America to send representatives to a meeting to be held in Philadelphia December 3-6 for the purposes of considering the proposal of organic union. Fourteen denominations have already accepted the invitation.

On November 15 three separate Lutheran bodies were united and incorporated in the United Lutheran Church of America.

Other steps in organic union have been consumated in the recent past.

At the present time the Most Rev. Meletios Hetaxikis archbishop of Athens and Primate of Greece, is in this country to learn as much as possible about Protestant Church institutions.

He told the Administrative Committee of the Federal Council of Churches that the Greek people felt very sympathetic toward the Protestant churches;—that co-operative movements seemed possible; and that the Greek Church and Protestant Church had many things in common.

He expressed a warm sympathy for Protestant Missions in the East, especially among the Mohammedan element and believe, that in the main the Greek church would welcome a conference with Protestant Christians while any such conference with Roman Catholic bodies was very much in doubt.

Some one has said that W. C. T. U. and the Anti-Saloon League are the Church in action. This is at least a very practical view of the matter and surely no discredit to the Church.

On the very day that this Annual Session of Conference was convened (November 19), there was also assembled in the city of Columbus, Ohio, delegates from all over the world for the purpose of launching a movement for world-wide prohibition. It was also in Columbus, Ohio, five years ago that this same organization launched the movement for nation wide prohibition in the United States. This has been practically accomplished and a dry nation by 1920 is practically assured.

Perhaps no more important step could now be taken in the interest of Foreign Missions than the world-wide overthrow of liquor traffic. No one knows, better than the Missionary on the field, the destructive work and influence of this evil among the natives whom he is trying to help and uplift. For while he is preaching the Gospel of Jesus Christ and its saving power, some one else, and perhaps one of his own countrymen, is following in his wake, by setting up a saloon with its damning power.

There are a great many other vices and evils contributed by our Western civilization to these non-Christian nations which have not only hindred the progress of Christian missions but have counteracted much of its work.

A writer in the "Church Missionary Review" has this to say of the modern education given the youth of India. Quoting Herbert Spencer, the writer says: "The growth of intellectualization in advance of moralization has done enormous mischief." This writer contributes most of the unrest and discontent in India to our purely secular educational systems given to them. "For be it remembered," he continues, "that while there is no moral or religious teaching in the Government schools of India there is none in the home either."

As Pandili Ramabi puts it as stated in Dr. Mott's book, "The majority of the higher classes are getting Western secular education which is undermining their faith in their ancestral religion but they are not getting anything better to take the place of the old religion in their hearts and are therefore without God, without hope, without Christ, going down socially and morally and becoming very irreligious."

It would seem that a system of education such as characterizes our Western civilization, has the power to uproot the faith of the old ancestral worship, if it were tempered with the moral and spiritual teachings of the Christian religion these people would not only be intellectualized, thus being influenced to give up their old religions, but would be supplied with a knowledge of the immortal hope and a faith in Jesus Christ that would fill that aching void in their religious life.

With a united front at home and all Christian forces harmoniously co-operating, many of these obstacles in the past can be overcome and a united effort on the foreign field will be the result and no longer will the challenge come back to us from those we are trying to convert, that the reason Christianity makes such slow progress among them is because we are not like our Christ.

THE FORWARD MOVEMENT

Headquarters, 27 C. P. A. Building, Dayton, Ohio

The Pastor's Place in the Forward Movement

No one has greater responsibilities nor larger opportunities in the Forward Movement than the pastor. He can hinder a great blessing from coming to his church or he may be the channel through which his church may be the recipient of great power.

Our strong preachers and men of vision have already seen what possibilities the Forward Movement has for them, and the blessings for their church if they give themselves heartily to the spirit and purpose of the Forward Movement.

The pastor is asked to organize his church on the Forward Movement basis and to appoint a *four-minute man*, and send his name at once to headquarters. It will be a fine thing if this Four-Minute Man can be formally set apart at a Sunday morning service. It would greatly add to the effectiveness of his work. This Four-Minute Man with the pastor will be the key men in each congregation and they should get to every family and member of the church with the detailed information concerning the Movement.

Literature and information may be secured from the Headquarters, also from the Herald of Gospel Liberty, THE CHRISTIAN SUN, the Christian Vanguard, the Christian Missionary, the Sunday School Herald, the Teachers and Officers' Journal, the Sunday School Quarterly and the special leaflet literature.

We are depending on the pastors and the Four-Minute Men to thoroughly inform the congregation of the Movement, their part in the Movement and the opportunities given them, and to urge it and push it as men do in the great drives for the Government, and as enthusiastically as the men are doing in the other denominations.

The pastor and the Four-Minute Man should enlist the Superintendent of the Sunday school, the President of the Missionary Society, President of the Christian Endeavor Society and the most able, active and consecrated men and women of the congregation in the Forward Movement. The Four-Minute Man at each service should speak right to the point, full of information and enthusiasm and carry the conviction of the Movement. In this way he will be able to lead the people of any congregation to a realization of their obligation and duty, and would enlighten the people as to the Forward Movement program and the realization of its fulfillment.

A Rural Church Program

We are glad to give this week a Rural Church Program, offered by one of our strong pastors, who has given his life to the rural church work and when he speaks on rural church programs, it is well worth listening to.

Rev. W. P. Fletcher is President of the Ontario Conference and Rural Superintendent of the Ontario Sunday School Association and a member of our Mission board.

We are glad to offer his Forward Movement Program for a Rural Church, hoping it will be suggestive to many of our rural churches.

Forward Movement Program for a Rural Church

First of all let the pastor call a meeting of the Sunday school superintendent, the church clerk, the president of the Christian Endeavor, indeed his whole church cabinet, and then make a careful survey of their church field. Every rural church should actually know the field it seeks to cultivate. Let us know who in our territory are going to church and who are not. Who are going to Sunday school and who are not, and probably we shall find to our horror that we are not cultivating one-quarter of our farm. When you have the facts, and be sure that they are facts, then call a meeting of the full church and lay bare to them the need of going forward.

1. DEVOTION—Start a campaign of prayer and Bible study. Establish a Home Department in your Sunday school and seek to get every family studying the Bible. Then seek to get them to take the next step and establish a family altar in every home. Arrange for a Go-To-Church Day, get other churches to join with you if you can. Do not play on this job; put it across and that means more prayer and organization. Then get back into prayer meeting, a real meeting for prayer where the people really agree together as touching that which they desire.

2. EVANGELISM—There is still a place for the old fashioned revival. Methods, of course may change, but the old plan of every one in the church seeking to save the lost. But do not depend too much on the public appeal. Go to your neighbor, your friend, your scholar, your child during the day with a personal appeal, and then make the evening rally the place for registering decisions. But also seek to get the Sunday school teachers to see that they have been a failure unless their teaching leads to decision for Christ.

3. RELIGIOUS EDUCATION—Seek to get your present staff of Sunday school teachers and officers to as far as possible become experts in their work. But that is but one side and the least important of Teacher-Training. Get the young men and women of your Senior Department of the Sunday school to begin at the age of seventeen the great process of equipping themselves for future success in the church and Sunday school. Get your Endeavorers to take up the expert course in their work. If it be at least equal importance to train the heart as the head, let us put ourselves to this job, or the head is going to run away with the heart as in the case of Germany.

4. MISSIONS—A missionary superintendent in the Sunday school. Missionary five-minutes in each session of the school, or a complete missionary program at least once a quarter. A study class for the Juniors. For instance, take them "Around the World with Jack and Janet." A study class for the Young People and the Adults. Adopt the Duplex and Every-Member CanVass System. Adopt some definite appealing missionary policy for the whole church and see that you carry it across every year.

5. BENEVOLENCE—Preach giving. Warn against the sin of covetousness or stinginess, the sin of all sins condemned in the Bible. The missionary of the past has fearfully failed here. Nothing but sacrificial giving will save many a soul from callousness, materialism and death. Teach stewardship, tithing, systematic giving. Pay up every church debt. Equip the rural church and support with at least as much thought and cost as you support the secular system, or improve the grain growing stock raising facilities upon the farm. Surely to save the soul and life is a worth-while job.

The Forward Movement Sunday School Program

Are you already planning to start your Forward Movement Sunday School Program, beginning April first? Start the first item of the program and make your Sunday school a standard school according to your denomination and the International Association.

Each school is expected to work at the whole Sun-

day school program and to specialize in part, upon the different items for three months each. For instance, if you lack one or more parts to make your school a Standard School work to this point between April first and June thirtieth.

By June 30, we should have a large number of standard Sunday schools throughout our brotherhood.

Write to headquarters for Sunday school programs if you have not yet received any.

WARREN H. DENISON, Supt.

OBLIGATION VERSUS ACCOMMODATION

"Doth he thank that servant because he did the things that were commanded him? I trow not: So likewise ye when ye shall have done all these things that were commanded you; say: We are unprofitable servants: We have done that which was our duty to do." (Luke 17:9-10).

THIS is but one of many passages of New Testament scripture which teach that stewardship is matter of *obligation* and not a matter of *accommodation*. This moral and spiritual obligation applies to finance as well as to prayer and personal work. The law of God permits no man to stand as a benefactor to his heavenly Father, and he who takes that position is condemned by the above passage of scripture.

Since God owns everything which He has created, including man and his money, he has a right to all the benefits which we are to bestow. "Whether therefore ye eat or drink or whatsoever ye do, do all to the glory of God." (I Cor. 10:31). We all come short of this ideal stewardship, therefore instead of being entitled to a vote of thanks from heaven, our best gifts and service should be offered in the spirit of apology, because God is not getting his dues.

Stewardship is a *debt* and not a *donation*, and any system of Church finance which reverses this divine plan is not scriptural. The free-will-offering system of Church finance is a tradition of man which makes the Word of God of none affect. Our offerings should be paid as *dues* rather than *donations* to God, lest we pose as benefactors to our heavenly Father and make Christ and his Bride objects of charity.

Christ reproved that old Jewish tradition known as the "Corban" theory of stewardship which taught that it was a gift whenever the father was profited by the son. It dishonored the parent to have a child pose as his benefactor. (Mark 7:10-13). Most Churches today have adopted the "Corban" system of financiering the kingdom of Christ.

We make the word of God of none affect by a financial tradition which says; "It is a gift by whatsoever thou mightest be profited by me." The tithe system does away with that tradition, for the sacred tenth is paid as a debt and not as a donation. Tithing is a matter of obligation and not a matter of accommodation. It is an acknowledgment of God's claims upon us and our subtance.

After his financial claims have been honored in tithing, then free-will offerings may be added for good measure without subscribing to the Corban tradition, but to make *donations* the foundation of Church finance is to make the Word of God of none affect. Children must not pay their father's bills. (II Cor. 12:14). Christ must support his own Bride with his own tithe money, and not be indebted to charitable men.

"He that provideth not for his own is worse than an infidel." (I Tim. 5:8). Benevolences are scriptural and serve a noble purpose in getting those who are fortunate to aid the unfortunate, but Christ and his Bride are not unfortunates and must not be treated as objects of benevolence. Children do not donate money to their well-to-do parents. Christian stewards should not donate funds to the Landlord of whole earth.

Our give-what-you-please system of Church finance has placed a wrong construction upon the fundamental law of stewardship. It has placed the money-giver in the position of a philanthropist toward God when he should have taken the attitude of servant of Christ. The average money-donator in the church has so lost sight of the meaning of stewardship that he feels that his own financial rights are superior to any of the claims of Christ upon his income.

God has ordained that offering money to Christ shall constitute an act of worship by setting forth God's ownership and philanthropy. The payment of tithe rental sets forth God's ownership, and his giving us the use of the nine-tenths sets forth his philanthropy. On the other hand the donation system divides the worship of God's house by offerings which bestows credit and praise upon the contributers.

True tithing is offering the first tenth or the first fruit of all our increase, thus making God first and self secondary in our business life. Any act which honors the God-first principle is an act of true worship, for the God-first principle is the first law of heaven. Our "give-what-you-please" tradition or custom is a self-first law of finance and is self-worship.

Cain started this system of finance by an offering which made self-first and God last. His offering was a donation given as a matter of accommodation. Abel had the eye of faith to see that the owner of the earth had a right to the first and best and so he offered the first fruit of his increase which was acceptable unto God. Abel's offering was that of a faithful steward who realized his financial obligation to his heavenly Landlord. Blood was not required in such stewardship offerings, but God required that the gifts of men be offered in the spirit of worship.

JUSTIN PRESCOTT.

Waterloo, Iowa.

Henry D. Gilliam—I simply can't do without my church paper. Much success to you in your work.

J. S. Peel—I have been taking THE SUN for fifty years and I want it as long as I live.

R. T. Brittle—We are all with you for the five hundred new subscriptions and you may count on us to do our share.

BOOKS, BIBLES, TESTAMENTS

In order to reduce certain stocks of books, Bibles and Testaments on hand, the following prices are made and will hold good until March 31, 1919:

Bibles

No. 312X. **Holman Self-Pronouncing Teachers' Bible.** Printed on fine white paper from good, clear type, and contains references, concordance, four thousand questions and answers and fifteen prepared maps. Size 4 3-8X6 1-2 inches. Egyptian Morocco, divinity circuit, head bands and marker, round corners, red under gold edges. Regular selling price......$4.65
Price to March 31 .... 3.90

No. 71. **Scofield Reference Bible.** Handsome binding, French Morocco limp, new and improved edition. "The neatest Scofield Bible made.", It will please you. Regular selling price $4.50
Price to March 31 .... 3.90

No. 215. **Child's Self-Pronouncing Pictorial Bible with Helps.** Bound in French seal leather, round corners, silk bands, gold titles,—handsomely made. Regular selling price $2.50
Price to March 31 .... 2.00

No. 1113 **Ideal Bible for Children.** Printed on fine white paper from the newest and clearest type of the size made. Size 3 1-2X5 3-8 inches. This Bible will please you. Regular price $1.75
Price to March 31 .... 1.40

Testaments

No. 3913 R. L. (Red Letter). Large print Morocco binding. Regular price $2.00
Price to March 31 .... 1.75

No. 2902 Cloth binding, large print. Regular price.... .90
Price to March 31 .... .75

No. 2502 P. Cloth binding, black faced type. Regular price .... .75
Price to March 31 .... .55

No. 2113. Pocket size, Morocco binding. Regular price .60
Price to March 31 .... .45

No. 0133. Pocket size, Morocco binding, overlapping edges. Regular Price .... .75
Price to March 31 .... .55

(A Testament in Modern Speech)

Cloth, $1.25; cloth, indexed, $1.75; cloth, India paper, $1.75; leather, $2.35; leather, indexed, $2.75; leather, India paper, $2.75; Persian Morocco, Divinity Circuit, $3.75; Turkey Morocco, $1.25. Pocket Edition (without notes): Cloth, $1.00; cloth, India paper, $1.25; leather, India paper, $1.85. State definitely style wanted.

The above prices are regular. Make your choice and deduct 10 per cent. State definitely Testament wanted.

Books

Pastor's Ideal Funeral, $1.15—Regular price, $1.25.

(Books for the Children)

We have several copies "Silver Rags," "Patty's Grand Uncle," "Johnny Two Boys," "A Rescued Madonna"—Your choice, 20 cents per copy. We will substitute if the book ordered is sold before the order reaches us.

Special

"Redmond of the Seventh," by Mrs. Frank Lee is a book with a fine story taken from school life, 290 pages, handsomely bound, 50 cents the copy.

Special Note: One of these books will be sent free with each order for $3.00 worth of books, Bibles or Testaments.

Address

C. B. RIDDLE ....Publishing Agent
Burlington, N. C.

Sunday School and Christian Endeavor

SUNDAY SCHOOL TOPIC FOR SUN-
DAY, MARCH 2
The Report of the Spies

Scripture Lesson, Numbers 14:1-10. Golden Text: This is the victory that hath overcome the world, even our faith. I John 5:4.

For explanation and comment, see Christian Bible Class Quarterly, or Officers and Teachers Journal, Christian Publishing Association, Dayton, Ohio.

CHRISTIAN ENDEAVOR TOPIC FOR
SUNDAY, MARCH 2

"Our Relation to God:" III Obeying. John 15:12-17. (Consecration meeting).

For explanation and comment, see Christian Endeavor World, Boston, Mass.

MISSION STUDY IN SUNDAY SCHOOLS

There are several ways in which the school, or any class in the school, may study missions, and yet keep up with the regular lesson. The writer's opinion, from the experience of many schools, is that the best and most practical method of coming at it is, for the school to have one Sunday in each month as "Mission Study Sunday." On that Sunday let the school proceed as on other Sundays in all the opening exercises, reading the lesson in concert, or in class, as on other Sundays. As soon, however, as this is over, class roll is called and the class is ready for recitation then for the whole study period of thirty minutes, let each class of the school, or as many classes as have decided to do so, take up the missionary lesson for the day that was assigned the month previously. A book may be had for 35 or 40 cents that will do for a class for six months or a year, and adapted to any class of the school.

In answer to an appeal sent out recently to all our Sunday school secretaries, many of our schools are adopting this method, and many others will do so, we are assured. No people can become a real missionary force and factor in the world until they *know* something from actual study of missionary needs and op-

portunities. And there is no better place to teach and learn missions than in the Sunday school.

It is certainly a joy to learn that so many of our schools are beginning to study missions. It means greater and better things for us in future.

A Happy Sunday School

A month ago our Burlington Sunday school voted to support a missionary at a salary of $720.00 a year. This meant that the school must contribute as a special missionary offering of $60.00 per month. The third Sunday morning of each month was decided upon as the time to take the offering. There was a feeling that the school would hardly contribute the full $60.00 on the first Sunday of the experiment; but there was hope, and there was prayer that it would come after a few months to do so. But God always does better by us than we expect when we pray earnestly and trust Him. Now read this from Pastor Harrell's letter, written on Monday, February 17: "We had a great day Sunday. The best I have seen since we came to Burlington. There was a new note in the Sunday school and church services. When we had the results of the voluntary offering for the support of our missionary our hearts were made glad indeed. Our fondest expectations were surpassed. A smile of gladness passed over the entire school when the Secretary read out $65.67 for our missionary. We believe this is an indication of what may be expected from month to month. The third Sunday has been designated as mission day in our school and upon that day the offering will be taken each month."

Surely this was a cause of gladness and a source of joy to our good Burlington people.

The resources of God are available only to those who undertake the program of God.

J. O. ATKINSON.

CHRISTIAN ENDEAVOR A BLESSING TO THE HOME

Among the many beautiful testimonies as to what Christian Endeavor had meant to the various members

of the Society in the church of which I have the honor of being pastor, which testimonies were given in the society prayer service on February 2, as we were celebrating the birthday of Christian Endeavor, one has so impressed me that I want to pass it on.

It was the testimony of a man of very few words, but a man who loves his church, his home, and his Savior. A man who never misses a service at his church, if it is possible for him to be present. His testimony was that he was grateful for Christian Endeavor because it had been such a blessing to his family, in that it had brought the members closer together, made them love each other better, and the home had been brightened, and sweetened through the influence of our Christian Endeavor society.

The man who gave this glowing tribute to the work of our Christian Endeavor Society was Brother Jackson Harris, one of the loyal members of our Society, and a staunch member of the First Christian church. If parents would, like Mr. Harris, attend a Christian Endeavor Society with their children, my prediction is that there would be many more happy homes than there are at present. Then for what Christian Endeavor means to our home, and to our individual lives, and to the cause of our Christ, let us give it our hearty support in every way possible, and in this way we will be able to brighten so many lives and homes that may now be groping in the fog and gloom of a misdirected, or misguided life.

J. F. MORGAN.

THE TITHER

An interdenominational publication devoted to Tithing and Christian Stewardship.

Editors

C. B. RIDDLE
KARL LEHMANN
BERT WILSON
HUGH S. McCORD
FRED G. THOMAS

8 pages; issued monthly; 50c the year
Address

THE TITHER   Burlington, N. C.

MARRIAGES

BURGESS-STRANGE

Joe Burgess and Mary Strange were united in the holy state of matrimony at Oak Level high school in the presence of about one hundred and forty students and the six members of the faculty, by the writer on the 12th of February, 1919.

J. G. TRUITT.

HUGHES- MARTIN

At the home of Mrs. E. O. C. Ragland, February 13, 1919, Rev. William: C. Hughes and Miss Mary E. Martin, were united into marriage by the writer. Both are teaching in the Halifax county schools, and they are also former Elon students.

J. G. TRUITT.

SMITH

Mrs. Mary Catherine Smith, beloved wife of E. R. Smith, Nansemond County, Virginia, departed this life at a local hospital, Suffolk, Va., January 14, 1919, aged forty-eight years, ten months and twenty-eight days. She was faithful in the various duties of life and will be greatly missed in her home, community and church. Surviving her are a devoted husband, three children, two grandchildren, one brother, three sisters, many relatives and friends. She will be missed very much but we hope to meet her where sorrow and separation can come no more. The bereaved ones have the sympathy of their many friends. Funeral services at Bethlehem Christian church and the remains laid to rest in the church cemetery.

H. H. BUTLER.

LIBBY

Whereas, our Heavenly Father has seen fit to take from our midst our beloved sister and co-worker, Mrs. Lena Libby. Therefore the Ladies' Aid Society of Isle of Wight Court- House Christian church offer the following resolutions:

1. That we bow in humble submission to the will of our Father who doeth all things well.

2. That our Society has lost a faithful and consistent member, always ready and willing to lend a hand in every good work that led to the upbuilding of her church.

3. That we offer our heartfelt sympathy and prayers to her loved ones.

4. That a copy of these resolutions be sent to The Christian Sun for publication, one be sent to her bereaved family and one be spread upon the minutes of our Society.

MRS. M. TURPIN WHITLEY,
MRS. MATTIE EDWARDS,
MRS. J. E. WHITE,
Committee.

RAGLAND

Brother E. O. C. Ragland departed this life January 16, 1919. He was born in Halifax county, Virginia, December 23, 1847, and resided near News Ferry, Va., during his entire life. He is survived by one sister, Miss Ellen Ragland, his wife, and two sons, Lorenzo and Comer.

Brother Ragland joined the Pleasant Grove Christian church while Rev. W. S. Long was pastor more than thirty years ago. Before his health failed him he attended Sunday school and church regularly and gave liberally of his means to their support. He was one of the best farmers in this section. May the Master's love attend his widow and the two sons.

J. G. TRUITT.

LEWIS

Mrs. Annie Frances Lewis, wife of J. J. Lewis, Newport News, Va., departed this life January 15, 1919, aged seventy-nine years, five months and six days. She was a member of Antioch Christian church from childhood. She leaves a husband, six children, fourteen grandchildren, twenty-three great grandchildren, two great, great grandchildren, one brother, R. E. Turner, Walters, Va. Her funeral services were conducted at Antioch Christian church by her pastor and her remains laid to rest in the church cemetery. The bereaved have the sympathy of the entire community.

H. H. BUTLER.

ASTON

Ocie Linwood Aston, son of Mr. and Mrs. J. M. Aston of Buckhorn, Va, departed this life January 16, 1919, aged fifteen years, three months and twenty-nine days. He was a good boy who will be missed in the community and Sunday school. He leaves a devoted father, mother, one sister, four brothers and a host of friends to mourn their loss. Funeral services were held at Mt. Carmel church and interment made in church cemetery. The Lord comfort the bereaved ones with the hope of meeting again.

H. H. BUTLER.

JOHNSON

At her home, near Windsor, Va., Mrs. Eudora Ann Johnson departed this life January 29, 1919, aged eighty-two years, nine months and sixteen days. She was one of the faithful church members at Antioch Christian church, having been a member since her girlhood. She leaves five children, three sons and two daughters, fifteen grandchildren, nine . great grandchildren, two brothers, and one sister. The funeral services were conducted at the church by her pastor and her remains laid to rest in the church cemetery. She was a good mother and we hope to meet her again.

H. H. BUTLER.

UNDERWOOD

Mrs. Mary Underwood, beloved wife of David Underwood, Suffolk, Virginia, died January 30, 1919, being twenty-four years of age. She leaves a devoted husband, one little boy, a loving mother, Mrs. Mary E. Roach Nurney, Va., two brothers and many friends. Funeral services conducted at the grave at Cypress Chapel, Va. The bereaved have the sympathy of their many friends.

H. H. BUTLER.

Twenty Strong Men Needed Immediately

That is what our Convention said

Why?

That the Christian Church may have ministers to do its part of the Kingdom's work.

For several years now the number of candidates for the ministry has been gradually decreasing. Elon is anxious to train the men, but cannot unless they be sent.

How?

We must pray the Lord of the harvest and He will give us the men.

Let us do it.

STRONG, FORWARD LOOKING YOUNG MAN, have you considered the opportunities of the Ministry? GOD NEEDS YOUR LIFE.

1. To save men from sin.
2. To evangelize the non-Christian lands.
3. To harmonize labor and capital.
4. To bring universal peace to the world.
5. To reconcile science to religion.
6. To break down ecclesiasticism.
7. To help answer Jesus' prayer for the oneness of His followers.
8. To help Christianize all the relations of life, including the social order
9. To be the interpreter of God in His world.

Great and exalted work—this!

Is the spirit stirring your your heart to action? Quench not the Holy Spirit.

Let the Church

Be much in prayer that God may find us worthy of the needed laborers and send them to us.

Report all decisions

To Pres. W. A. Harper, Elon College, N. C., who will do all in his power to arrange for the training of the men.

J. E. WEST,
K. B. JOHNSON
R. M. MORROW

{ Committee of
The Board of
Trustees of
Elon College

W. W. STALEY, President Southern Christian Convention.

Christian Education Month, February 16, to March 16, 1919.

Every minister is urged during this month to present to his people the claims of the Christian ministry.

THE CHRISTIAN SUN

"IN ESSENTIALS UNITY, IN NON-ESSENTIALS LIBERTY, IN ALL THINGS CHARITY"

Faults---Perfection

GREAT and good men have through all ages severed their connection with parties, organizations, and religious bodies because of faults and failures of such. A man ought to have a right to his convictions about things. It does not become any man to keep himself connected with things that are not right, but few of us would belong to anything if we waited for perfection. And leaving an organization of any kind is no way to remedy its faults. Strive to place something better where faults abound. Condemn not the whole on account of any one defective part.

Volume LXXI	WEDNESDAY, MARCH 5, 1919	Number 10
BURLINGTON	. . .	NORTH CAROLINA

THE CHRISTIAN SUN

Founded 1844 by Rev. Daniel W. Kerr

C. B. RIDDLE - - - **Editor**

Entered at the Burlington, N. C. Post Office as second class matter.

Subscription Rates

One year .... $ 2.00
Six months 1.00

In Advance

Give both your old and new postoffice when asking that your address be changed.

The change of your label is your receipt for money. Written receipts sent upon request.

Marriage and obituary notices not exceeding 150 words printed free if received within 60 days from date of event, all over this at the rate of one-half cent a word.

Original poetry not accepted for publication.

Principles of the Christian Church

(1) The Lord Jesus Christ is the only Head of the Church.
(2) Christian is a sufficient name of the Church.
(3) The Holy Bible is a sufficient rule of faith and practice.
(4) Christian character is a sufficient test of fellowship, and of church membership.
(5) The right of private judgment and the liberty of conscience is a right and a privilege that should be accorded to, and exercised by all.

EDITORIAL

THE LEAGUE OF NATIONS—THE COVENANT

There is no political prompting which impels us to discuss the League of Nations. The issue is world-wide, touches every group of men, every individual, and is, if properly carried out, for the safety of all mankind. The issue touches religious life and church programs on every hand. Every denomination ought to be intensely interested in the outcome of the Peace Conference and the League of Nations.

For lack of space we cannot print in full the twenty-six *Articles* that constitute the *Covenant* of the League of Nations. The following are the essential ones in an abstract form:

Freedom of the seas is promised.

All future international treaties must be registered with the society.

Old treaties inconsistent with the society will be abrogated as soon as the society comes into official life.

War or threat of war, whether between two nations members of the society or not, is declared a matter of concern to the society, and the powers reserve the right to interfere in all disputes that cannot be settled through ordinary diplomacy.

The first meeting of the society of nations shall be summoned by the President of the United States.

There shall be full and free interchanges between the nations in the society upon military and naval programs.

A permanent commission shall be appointed to advise the society on disarmament and on military and naval affairs generally.

Plans for a permanent international court of justice shall be worked out by the executive council.

The society shall consist, in addition to the delegates from the various powers, of the executive council and a permanent secretariat which shall be maintained at the seat of the society.

Each high contracting party shall have one vote, but shall not have more than three representatives at any one time.

The expenses for maintaining the secretariat shall be apportioned among the powers.

Admission to the society (outside of the signatory powers) requires the assent of two-third of the States represented.

Armaments shall be reduced to the lowest point consistent with national safety.

There shall be self-government for parts of the Turkish Empire.

There shall be freedom of religion for peoples in territories under mandatories.

Contracting parties shall "endeavor to secure and maintain fair and humane conditions of labor for men, women, and children" in all countries.

Amendments may be made to the constitution.

The day when a nation could go to war with another nation and not bring a vital issue to the whole world is past. We have come to realize that a war with one nation is a war touching *all* society. This is a growth of conscience. It is the broadening of the idea that the man who lives next door to us is not our only neighbor. It is a sign that there is being awakened in the consciences of mankind that injunction of Jesus to make disciples of all nations. It is a fulfilling of that true word of God that we are our brother's keeper, and that all are brethren.

The man who commits murder insults society at large as well as the home he saddens. The nation that takes up weapons to kill, and does kill, infringes upon the rights of other nations as well as the nation in immediate danger. This was what caused America to go to the aid of the allied nations against murderous Germany. No nation can fight with a higher motive than to liberate mankind without the desire of "a strip of land or a stretch of sea."

The compact that nations are to sign (if the League is formed) means this: That they (the nations) are to *league* themselves together to *avoid* war. All nations in the League are to be kept informed as to the impending issues, work together for international relationship that will bind themselves together, maintain and approve an international court, agree to submit their troubles to a council and counsel with each other on all national disputes.

The League of Nations is to have sufficient machin to bring a nation to justice. In short it will hav sheriff and a court, and a nation will be tried just an individual is tried. And should a nation, either member or not a member of the League, declare w upon another nation without the consent of the Leag will have a hard time.

As we see it the League of Nations is one of t greatest things the world has undertaken. Its pla now may not be infallible—it may take years to wo out its best platform, but, it deserves the support of every peace-loving citizen. Those who condemn it have not offered anything better. Their criticism stands as *destructive* until they make *constructive* by a better plan.

BOLSHEVISM—ITS CRIMES

This sentence appeared in our editorial on Bolshevism last week: "The spirit of Bolshevism is with the heart and not the stomach." See if this is true.

On February 12 Dr. George A. Simons, who returned from Russia last October, after many years of residence in Petrograd as superintendent of the Methodist Episcopal Mission, testified before a Committee of the United States Senate as to the crimes of the Bolsheviki rule. We quote direct from the records of the Senate Committee:

Murders Number Thousands

Dr. Simons told of witnessing the murder of two young men in front of his office in Petrograd, the killing taking place a few minutes before Ambassador Francis, who was his dinner guest that night, arrived at his home.

Asked to estimate the number of persons who had been murdered by the Bolsheviki Dr. Simons replied that it was in the thousands, but that no man could at this time even approximate the number of the victims.

"The Bolsheviki never investigate. They kill on the spot, as a rule," he added.

Dr. Simons cited the case of two brothers. One was wanted by the Bolsheviki to answer a certain charge. They were unable to find the brother, sought, so they killed the one against whom there was no charge or suspicion.

Blackmail and graft were everywhere recognized, said Dr. Simons. If a person could get the money, he said, it was generally possible to buy even one's life from the present regime. However, few had the money and the killings went on. He said that twelve men entered his home and tried to blackmail his sister.

"What about the criminal element in the present regime?" Senator King asked.

"There is a large criminal element in the Bolshevist regime," was the answer. "The fact that the criminal has a big part in the movement is proved by the destruction in a public bonfire of court-records, the destruction of prisons and the liberation of all criminals, who are sympathetic with the cause. We know it to be a fact that some of the worst criminal characters in all Russia hold positions under the Bolshevist government, while others are helping as agitators, while under the damnable system they call nationalization the criminal is actively co-operating."

Girl Victims of Atrocities

"What of the treatment of women and girls?" Senator King asked.

"That is a terrible question to answer. I might cite case after case in answer to it. Let me cite one of the worst.

"A few days before I left Petrograd, in October, last, a woman of the highest culture, a woman more than fifty years of age, and a teacher for years in a famous imperial institute for the education of young girls, called on me. She was in hysterics. 'Why have I lived to see all this?' she sobbed.

"Then she told the story. The institute in which she taught is one of the finest buildings in Petrograd. She said that the Bolshevist authorities had barracked hundreds of the Red Guard in one wing of the building and in doing so issued orders that all girls of and between the ages of sixteen and eighteen years were to remain in the building.

"'I wish,' the poor woman exclaimed, as she tried to tell the rest of the horrible story, 'that I had died before this thing happened.'"

"And," said Senator Wolcott, "was the result not of the act of irresponsible guards, but of the Bolshevist authorities?"

"Yes."

"In other words," said Senator King, "these poor little girls were the victims of the lust of these unspeakable creatures?"

"Yes, of the dirtiest pigs the world has ever seen. So vile no words can describe them."

We deem it our duty as a trustee or steward of the press to place such things before the people in a time like this when conditions are adjusting themselves. In our own land such movement have friends. Such a movement is liable to cause more serious trouble than it has caused. The world wants peace—lasting peace. World leaders are endeavoring to create a co-operative order in which to live and enjoy lasting peace.

Public sentiment is the strongest law in the land, and it behooves Christian men and women everywhere to create a sentiment against movements that take law and order into their own hands.

In this country we have many things that are in the first stages, and the Church has upon it a task to see that moral justice is carried into the things of the new order.

THE "CONSCIENTIOUS OBJECTORS"

In response to numerous requests, committees from the General War-Time Commission of the Churches have made a careful study of the attitude of the Government toward the "conscientious objectors." In their study of the situation, conference has been had with several groups especially concerned in the question, with the War Department, the Department of Military Morale, and various other authorities. The report as adopted by the Executive Committee of the General War-Time Commission of the Churches is as follows:

"1. It is our firm conviction that no government has made a more serious effort to deal fairly with conscientious objectors and to allow freedom in the exercise of the individual conscience than has the United States in the present war.

"2. It seems clear, however, that a considerable number of men have been treated with undue severity, in a few cases even with brutality, by certain of the military authorities. We are glad to know that the War Department has now taken steps that have relieved the situation. The cases of brutal treatment have been due, in the main, to the policy of certain army officers, who believed the conscientious objectors to be insincere and who held unreasonable and extreme views as to what is required by military discipline.

"3. The great majority of conscientious objectors were declared by the Government after investigation to be honest and sincere in their convictions. The majority also accepted non-combatant service in the army or other work of a non-military character.

"4. There are at the present time approximately 400 conscientious objectors in the military prisons in the United States, serving sentences of from five to thirty years, including both men who believe all war to be wrong and those who believe this war to have been unjustified. There are also in local jails or Federal prisons several hundred others who have been convicted under the Espionage Act for making statements contrary to the war policy of the Government.

"5. Now that hostilities have ceased, we believe that these imprisoned conscientious objectors who are beyond question sincere should be granted amnesty at the time of the signing of the Treaty of Peace. After the war is over and the danger of a division is past, the best interest of democracy will not be served by carrying out further punishments against those who honest convictions differed from the majority during the days of the war. To punish them further in times of peace would set an unwholesome precedent in a nation that has always emphasized the principle of the freedom of individual conscience.

"6. We believe further that the whole question of the treatment of political offenders in time of war should be reconsidered by Congress under conditions which make an unprejudiced judgment possible, and that a distinction should be made between those whose offense is loyalty to their own conscience, however mistaken the majority may believe that conscience to be, and those who have been guilty of criminal offences."

FOUND HERE AND THERE

The former Kaiser of Germany is appealing to his people for money on which to live.

* *

The government hospitals at Waynesville and Hot Springs, N. C., are soon to be abandoned.

* *

A gradual increase in the unemployed in this country continues. Labor is soon to be cheap, so experts think.

* *

Southern cotton manufacturers have made unsuccessful attempts to have the embargo on cotton to Austria and Germany.

* *

The Republicans in North Carolina have established a newspaper at High Point. It makes its first appearance Thursday of this week.

* *

The Peace Conference is speeding up its labors.

Mrs. J. W. Boon—I appreciate the good work you are doing to keep THE SUN up and I do not see how any church member can do without his church paper. Long may it shine in my home.

Mrs. J. W. Crabtree—THE SUN is very dear to me as it has been in my home for many years. May it ever be a shining light in my pathway.

Miss A. M. Rollings—THE SUN has been in my home many years and I would not know how to do without it. I wish it could be in many more homes than it is.

PASTOR AND PEOPLE

DURHAM LETTER

In the midst of varied and singular experience our church has enjoyed a steady advance. Although our doors were closed for more than four weeks our hearts were open and responsive to the many calls of sympathy, and our vision was clarified and we have been able to look into the most commonplace affairs of life. It is true we have done nothing worthy of special mention. Neither have we been so heroic that we are entitled to the *Croix de Guerre;* but our achievements have been satisfactory, and in some respects exceeded our high hopes.

During the year the church and all of its auxiliaries raised $3,258.06, besides the many special class offerings in the Sunday school for the poor and other purposes. We also raised in cash and subscription about $2,500.00 on the home and foreign mission fund, of which Dr. J. O. Atkinson is champion, and have a number of paid-up memberships in the Home Missionary Association. But we would not be misunderstood. Money is not a test of achievement, but it is essential. Money is a blessing when used as a servant, but a curse when hoarded and hailed as a master. It is powerful when placed on the altar of God and humanity; it is pitiful and impotent when allowed to remain in the safe unused and undedicated.

We are expecting fruitful results from the service which was held in our church last Sunday (February 16). The writer presented "The Lord's Labor Problem" and was gratified, and felt amply repaid for his efforts, when he saw eighteen people stand and say they were willing to give their lives to the ministry or the missionary work if God should call them.

R. F. BROWN.

SUFFOLK LETTER

Will and Lizzie married young. Their youthful love matured in life devotion. Three children added strength to their union. One died in infancy. Willie and Mary remain to comfort the bereaved mother. W. E. Brinkley had served as Chief of the Suffolk Police force for many years, and had won the love of his associates. His official career had been faithful and tragic. Several times he had been wounded in the discharge of his duty; but no danger deterred him from the performance of his obligation as the custodian of public order. He had the gift of a detective, the courage of a soldier, and the human feeling of a tender citizen. He gave his life to the cause of temperance, being shot by a colored man with illicit whisky. Both were carried to the same hospital and Chief Brinkley pled for good treatment of his slayer while he himself was dying. Both of them died and answered at the same judgment. That is the tragedy of the liquor business—that good men must die in the discharge of public service.

Few chiefs in any city had such loyalty among the members of the police force as he had. They all knew that he was true to the community and to them. He trusted them and they trusted him. He treated female prisoners with marked consideration. It became necessary, at times, to arrest women who were check-flashers; and he would rent a room for such prisoners at the hotel and spend the night in the lobby on guard, rather than put them in the lock-up; yet he never failed to bring to the court any who were charged with crime. He combined the elements of stern justice and tender mercy.

In his home he was affectionate and faithful. No want was neglected and no service was omitted. His home was his citadel. Here his heart found rest from crimes and criminals. His wife and children rise up and call him blessed. He assured his companion that he was not afraid to die. He was a member of the Suffolk Christian church. Often public duty required his absence from worship; but religion often expresses itself in serving the community. The policeman who tramps all night in the storm to guard the safety of life and property is not valued as he should be by those who sleep in comfort. The unseen servants of society are often forgotten by men; but they rank high on the ledger of human values. The keepers of order in a city are worthy of our prayers and our gratitude. The night-watchmen guard the mills and the shops that keep labor and markets.

Chief Brinkley's wife, who was the late Deacon Junius S. Carr's daughter, has been one of the sweet singers in our choir and has comforted many weepers by her solos at funerals. This bereavement may deepen her feelings, sweeten her tones, and enrich her songs of praises. Many lives have been made more useful by great sorrows. The crushed rose releases its fragrance.

December the third, 1918, the great throng gathered in the church—city officials, church members, citizens in large numbers; friends and family—all in one common sorrow. The whole community felt that a martyr lay under that pile of flowers. The value of his life had hardly dawned upon us till they reported that W. E. Brinkley was dead. His virtues, his value, his service loomed up with new beauty, new worth, and new importance.

W. W. STALEY.

THE NEED FOR MORE MINISTERIAL STUDENTS

Allow me to call to the attention of the readers of our church paper a paragraph taken from the "Report of the Board of Education," which was read and adopted by the Southern Christian Convention during its April 30, 1918 session:—

"A few years ago the College counted in one year forty-four ministerial students. This year we enrolled only twenty-two, and but seven of these came from our own church. We regard it a solemn duty to urge upon this Convention that it take reassures to replenish the leadership of our pulpits. Our ministry is our hope. Without ministers our noble cause must lie prostrate. No more vital question faces this session of the Convention. The College is anxious to train men, but the Churches and Conferences must send them up."

There is enough couched in that paragraph to bring every true member of our church to his or her knees. From 44 to 22, and only 7 of them from our Church!

Think of it! Meditate upon it. Pray over it. When the kingdoms of the earth wanted political liberty they mobilized armies upon armies to gain it at whatever cost. Now when the whole earth is in need of that freedom which comes by the Truth shall the Kingdom of Christ be handicapped on account of the lack of men? Brethren, we are God's recruiting officers aided by the Holy Spirit we must secure the needed army. Let fathers and mothers, brothers and sisters, ministers and laymen pray the Lord of the harvest,—let us be in earnest.

JOHN G. TRUITT.

News Ferry, Va.

HOLLAND, VA.

We gave up the work of the Y. M. C. A. in Richmond, Va., September 15, 1918, having received and accepted the call to the pastorate of the Holland and Holy Neck Christian churches in the Eastern Virginia Conference.

We arrived on the field September 17, and without formalities proceeded to occupy the parsonage. Our household goods had arrived a short time before and had been placed in the parsonage.

I have moved my family several times but this is the first time that we ever moved into a house and found a large pantry well stocked with hams, flour, lard, sugar coffee, potatoes, cornmeal, tea, rice and various other articles of diet.

Hooverizing was evidently overlooked in stocking the parsonage pantry, presumably leaving the matter of Hooverizing to the pastor and his family in the use of the stock, which was carefully done.

The work at both churches started off with bright prospects but just as suddenly were we enveloped in the scare of the Influenza which has to the present time handicapped the work very greatly. During the first attack Holland and surrounding territory were worse off from the scare than from the "Flu," there being but few cases, but in the second wave of the plague the whole field has yielded to the attack which is only now abating in an appreciable degree. Fortunately we have suffered but few deaths. Yet since coming to this work we have officiated at twelve funerals.

Holland and Holy Neck are two strong rural churches and each church is blessed with splendid lay talent and a still larger talent leadership which if brought to the front will greatly strengthen the work of each place.

Both churches may be likened the horse that does not realize its strength and hence is held in by a very small rein. The people are generous and willing to follow a leader. They have a desire to be front rank churches which gives the pastor ample work to keep something worth while before them.

As an example of the generosity of these people wa cite the instances of the World War Work Drive when Holy Neck responded to the amount of $905.00; then came the Thanksgiving Offering to the Orphanage which amounted to $197.00, a part of which was contributed through Mr. J. M. Darden, Suffolk, Va. One hundred dollars was given to the Armenian and Syrian Relief; on another Sunday a charitable offering of $32.00 was given to one of the needy members of the

Church. In like manner the Holland church gave $364.00 to the War Work Fund; $171.00 to the Orphanage; $23.00. to one of its members whose home and all contents were recently burned; and at our next regular service an offering will be taken for the Armenian and Syrian Relief Fund.

The new church at Holland to cost about $25,000 is to be a modern brick structure. It is already under roof and plastered and will be completed some time during the summer. At present the congregation is worshiping in the school auditorium.

The pastor is preaching a series of sermons on the Forward Movement and making good use of the Forward Movement literature. Splendid interest is being manifested. At Holland we have a Christian Endeavor Expert class of 12 members which has given new life to the Society.

W. M. JAY.

THE FORWARD MOVEMENT

Some of our pastors are placing the Forward Movement program and hand design on their stationery. That will be helpful.

Are you using the Forward Movement song in your church and institute work? It will help.

A number of our pastors are preaching on the five points of the Forward Movement Campaign and follow the Sunday sermon with the same one of the points at the mid-week service so that there is opportunity by the people for special prayer and discussion of the theme after the pastor has preached upon it. That is fine.

Forward Movement Rally at Lebanon, Ohio

The rally of the Bethany, Germtown, and Fellowship churches in the large hall at Lebanon Ohio was a most delightful occasion, February 18. A supper preceded the Forward Movement program. The orchestra furnished splendid music for the evening. Pastor, Rev. E. D. Hammond was in charge. Rev. McD. Howsare spoke on "The Forward Movement's Challenge to the Men of Our Churches"; Mrs. Athella M. Howsare on "Our Women Utilizing the Forward Movement in their Work"; Rev. J. F. Burnett, D. D., on "The Place of Prayer and Money in the Forward Movement; The Superintendent on "The Forward Movement and the Christian Church." The fine attendance, the intense interest, the delightful fellowship and the strong messages all made the impression most helpful and those churches are determined to be a very part of the Forward Movement. A good delegation from the Franklin church was present too. The Forward Movement song was used.

We urge our pastors and workers to arrange Forward Movement rallies in all the conferences.

W. H. DENISON, *Supt.*

Mrs. Elsie Eason—I just cannot give up THE CHRISTian Sun.

CHRISTIAN EDUCATION

ELON COLLEGE STANDARDIZATION FUND

A standard college is one that has been tried by the proper test. It is one that meets an established rule or model.

To standardize is to make to conform to a rule or standard. As to scholarship, faculty, physical equipment, and number of students, Elon College has met the established rule or model laid down for a standard college; but according to certain rules laid down by some States, a standard college must have at least $200,-000.00 endowment. To meet this financial rule as laid down by certain States, Elon needs an additional endowment of $125,000.00; hence the Board of Trustees decided to ask for $125,000.00 to met this requirement and other needs of the College; and they asked Dr. W. A. Harper, president of the College to take charge of the campaign for raising the said amount. He has wisely and cheerfully accepted the responsibility. I do not say task—let us make it a joy.

It is not for any one man or set of men or women that this $125,000.00 is to be raised; but for the College, for the Church, for humanity, for the Master Teacher—Jesus of Nazareth.

As a member of the Board of Trustees, its secretary, and as a minister and member of the Christian church, I bespeak for the representative of the College in the raising fo this Standardization Fund, a courteous reception, a prayerful hearing, and a hearty and liberal response.

P. H. FLEMING,
Secretary Board of Trustees of Elon College.
Burlington, N. C.

REPORT OF COMMITTEE ON EDUCATION

(Eastern Virginia Conference)

The world war has demonstrated the necessity for Christian education. Culture has failed in Germany as it failed in ancient Greece. True education embraces head, hand, and heart; and the principal thing is heart. Science is of the head; art is of the hand, and character is of the heart. Science deals with law, art with matter, and character with spirit. These three enter into education, but the greatest of these is spirit. Human sympathy has more value than human knowledge. Knowledge is *power*, but love is *salvation*.

The motto of Elon College, "Christian Character First and Always," challenges the faith and support of this Conference. Her alumni have proved themselves in school, in business, in church, in pulpit and in war. The four hundred stars on the service flag twinkle with patriotism, while her unit is training for war against wrong. Few colleges have such a reputation as Elon won in so short a time and under such financial strain.

We recommend to the churches of this Conference the Institution, and earnestly request that men and women subscribe liberally to the Endowment Fund of $125,000.00 which the Southern Christian Convention and the Board of Trustees have authorized President Harper to raise the coming year.

We recommend the ordination of Rev. Edward Thomas. Cotten, who has served Isle of Wight C. H., Windsor, Mt. Carmel and Mt. Zion churches during the past year, and has been recommended for ordination.

Rev. D. F. Parsons, Army Branch of Y. M. C. A., Chattanooga, Tenn., who was licensed by the last Conference, and Revs. L. L. Lassiter and J. M. Roberts have paid their indebtedness in full, and have thus set a good example for others who have been aided in their education by the Educational Fund.

The following names are on the list as Biblical students, but none of them have indicated to the Committee their plans or purposes: C. W. Rountree, G. L. Huber, Floyd D. Ballard, Wm. A. Brinkley. Such indifference discourages and retards progress in ministerial educational, but it should not lessen our effort in the good work.

The Committee recommended the licensure of Wilbur H. Baker of Newport News church, as a war measure and under the advice of the church and pastor, J. V. Knight, and Executive Committee, gave him certificate of licensure in December 1917.

W. W. STALEY,
I. W. JOHNSON,
G. D. EASTES,
Committee.

REPORT ON EDUCATION

(Georgia and Alabama Conference)

The Church is facing a splendid opportunity and a fearful responsibility. The masses are being educated and in order to hold them to the Church, we must have an educated leadership. We need this in the pulpit, Sunday school and Christian Endeavor. We need men and women not only trained in literature, but with special training for their religious work. We can not secure this in our high schools nor State schools. We must look to religious institutions for this training. We heartily recommend Elon College to our people and hope to see more of our people patronize it. We still cherish the hope that some day, not far off, we may have a school nearer our work here. We make the following recommendations:

1. That we raise $75.00 another year.
2. That Brother C. W. Hanson be ordained to the office of an Elder.
3. That the names of Elders and Licentiates who fail to report for two consecutive years be dropped from our roll.
4. That Brother W. D. Wilkerson and Miss Ophelia Miles be licensed for one year.

H. W. ELDER,
P. L. DUKE,
Committee.

CHRISTIAN EDUCATION*

"Jesus Began Both to do and to Teach." Acts 1:1.

Three questions concern us at this time.

1. What is Christian Education? Christian education is more than any course of study or curriculum. It is education based on the fundamental principles of Christianity, and these are the fundamental things in the life and teaching of Christ. Reduced to the final analysis they are two—the right relation of a man to God as Father and the right relation of a man to man as brother. It is education by Christian people in a Christian atmosphere and for a Christian purpose.

2. What Will Christian Education Do? It furnishes a foundation that makes all education worth while. It is the philosopher's stone that transmutes all baser metals into gold. All professional or technical education having as its basis the relation of man to God and his fellowman as exemplified in Christ, becomes Christian.

Christian education gives a man the right intellectual attitude—the right attitude toward truth because the right attitude toward the Author of truth. This gives inspiration to scholarship and makes possible its achievements. It gives the right moral attitude. Man's mission is to serve his brotherman. The right moral attitude alone can make possible the fulfillment of this mission. It furnishes the right spiritual attitude—the attitude of Jesus toward his Father, that is love, homage, obedience and trust. It unites man in fellowship with God and opens up the unlimited possibilities of earth and heaven.

3. Where can Christian Education be Obtained? There are three possible sources—the home, the church and the school. The home, the most potent of all institutions, has great limitation here. Many are godless or un-Christian. Others are too ignorant to impart religious instruction. There are others, both intelligent and Christian, that find any systematic instruction impracticable amid the complexity and strain of modern life.

The Church has a free hand with its own but its achievements in Christian education have not been commensurate with its opportunity. Much of its instruction has been dogmatic and denominational rather than Christian and its chief end has been to hold the young to the communion of their parents. The Sunday school is the Church's one organization devoted to religious instruction and this is usually Christian. It reaches the largest numbers, at the right age, and holds them for a long period. Its great limitation is that it has them only one hour in the week. It takes a man forty years to get as many hours instruction in Sunday school as he gets in college in four years.

The public school is more nearly universal than any other institution. It includes all children, compels attendance through the vital period, and has strong control; but law, as well as custom and tradition, forbid all religious instruction. For the same reason the higher state schools cannot become centers of propaganda for Christian education. Universal Christian education is yet an unsolved problem. Potent influences, however, are at work in the educational and religious world and the idea, like Banquo's ghost, will not down. Never to be forgotten among the influences of the past and present for Christian education is the Christian college established by Christian men on Christian principles and taught and administered by Christian men for a Christian purpose. Limited to the few and reaching them when comparatively mature it has been the great source of supply for the Kingdom's leaders. From it has come the ministers who fill our home pulpits, the missionaries in the foreign fields, our Christian educators and other Christian leaders and teachers. These are the men and women who have kept alive the idea of Christian education and whose influence has leavened American thought until the demand for Christian education is becoming universal.

This is a great hour in the history of the Christian college. At great labor and sacrifice it kept the fires of learning burning upon its altars when there were no other institutions to do it. Our present great educational system is the result. To educatiou it ever united the Christian idea till its leaven has leavened the lump. It is beginning to see of the travail of its soul. It is the day of its achievement and victory. It is no time for the Christian college to lower its flag. Let the Christian college celebrate its victory by raising its flag to the top mark as a signal for the gathering of loyal souls to its aid that it may be freed from the impediments of the past and equipped for the opportunities and responsibilities of the future.

⸺Preached by Dr. N. G. Newman at Elon College on February 16, 1919

A WORTHY UNDERTAKING

Elon College will have the good wishes of all churches and college people in its efforts to secure $125,000 additional endowment. It would be impossible to give the colleges of the State too much support. They form an indispensible part of the educational life of the State.

Elon under the aggressive administration of Dr. W. A. Harper has taken a new stride and is doing an eminently useful work. Money invested in better equipment and facilities for Elon will be money put at a vital point in the life of the people.

The denomination behind Elon College is not one of the larger denominations of the State, but its aspirations towards the higher things make it as worthy as any of the name which it takes as its mark of indentification.—*Editorial, News and Observer, February 19, 1919.*

THE CALL TO THE GOSPEL MINISTRY—AND AFTERWARD

The true minister is born, not made; he is called of God as Aaron was. This call cannot be defined with words perhaps, but who has it understands it, and feels that it is a life-long call.

God makes no mistakes in calling men to the ministry; and to every one thus called there comes much more of an impression than can possibly come from any dream or vision which simply holds up to the dreamer the letters "P. C." which, if seen, are more likely to mean "plant corn" than to "preach Christ."

The person whom God calls to His ministry feels emphatically as Paul did when he cried out, "Necessity is laid upon me; yea, woe is unto me if I preach not the gospel!"

This "necessity" does not always lead one in the direction of the finest church building, a so-called influential congregation, and a large salary; in fact, it quite often leads toward some "Jacob's-well" where there is only a very small congregation, and where the salary is barely sufficient to buy the necessary bread. But all who are fortunate enough to be led in that direction will, when they lift up their eyes, see that the fields "are white already unto the harvest."

The real Christian minister is one who has made some preparation for his work; and his work means to him—only in a higher sense—what the lawyer's, farmer's, store-keeper's means to him.

Preaching is responsible business, and it seems so

strange to me that there is such an increasing demand on the part of the churches for very young men as preachers. In all other professions ripeness and maturity are called for; but too many churches are demanding blossom instead of fruit. God bless the young men! they have done, and are still doing noble work; but what a tremendous pity it is that they have to grow old, and have matured ideas, for them, in many localities they will not be wanted. But whether a minister is old or young, preaching is responsible business.

Clearly defined ideas of God and man are necessary to success, and he who gets the largest number of his fellowmen to turn their faces Godward, and keep them in that direction, is the most successful minister. The God-called minister is a preacher; not an advertisement, not a drawing-card. His work is to preach Christ and His gospel. Sensational themes preaching simply to please the people, or to show one's self off, only reveals the shallowness of the man who does it, and his unfitness for the sacred office he occupies.

Scolding is not preaching; a scolding pastor is the worst kind of a scold; but, evidently, some ministers think that vinegar costs less than sugar; at least their sermons are seldom dipped in the sugar barrel.

The minister as a preacher will be criticized; some people want long sermons; some short; some want the fiery kind, or else they will be out of their element, not only in this life, but in the world to come; others want watery sermons; others, purely sensational; others, the opposite; some want to be yelled at, other whispered to. Criticism there will be, because there are some people in the world who are so made up that they will not do as they please if they think they will please some one else by so doing; and I am obliged to admit that these dear people are not all on the outside of our churches.

Christ's method of preaching is the method to follow. His preaching shows that *time* is as important as eternity; that men need something in this world as well as in the next. He preached so that old and young, learned and unlearned, received something helpful.

Preaching should stimulate thought; sermons should be limited as to time, but never finished. We cannot measure a real sermon by the clock; some men preach more in thirty minutes than others do in six months.

The wise preacher will work for, and become interested in, and the hard cases in his community; "they that are whole need not a physician," the Great Preacher said, and it is well to have a definite object to aim at before firing the gun.

The Christian minister must be a pastor. Calling, or visiting, is very necessary, and not always pleasant. By the time one goes into a dozen homes and listens to all the ailments which are common to man—from the heavy feeling at the base of the brain to the rheumatic stitch at the toe joint—he feels the need of grace to sustain. But to whom shall these things be told if not to the pastor? What is the pastor for?

The pastor receives secrets, and must keep them; he must be sociable; he must refrain from gossip, some of the members of his church will have a patent on that!

The minister's work, like a woman's, is never done;

the more he does, the more he will see to do, and the more anxious he will be to do it.

The Christian minister is a clean man, is not afraid of soap and water, the clothes brush, shoe blacking and kindred articles, Brown hands are no disgrace, but hands to which the soil is never a stranger are. This cleanliness means inside as well as outside; how a minister can present his "body a living sacrifice" when it is saturated with tobacco juice or tobacco smoke, is a problem I confess I have not sufficient wisdom to solve. Hence, I believe the time has fully arrived when ordination should be refused to any person who thinks more of tobacco than he does of the Christian ministry.

The minister should be clean in his speech; fun, wit, humor, rightly used, are so far removed from the low, dry-goods-box, language, that there is no comparison. The Christian minister is natural in his work; there is some little excuse for a monkey which imitates, but none for a minister. God wants and the world needs men, not imitators. How many sensible people have turned away in disgust because of the airs put on by ministers! Because a man wears a long coat, a long hat, and a face longer than either, it does not necessarily follow that God has put into his make-up the material which produces a successful minister. Sanctified common sense is just as necessary as a consecrated heart, and the minister who tries to work his heart without his head will always be unnatural, and partly, if not wholly, a failure.

The position of the Christian minister is very different from what many think; he is not his own by any means. He must be ready at all times, and under all circumstances; he must be ready to answer all calls at all times, along various lines of work and, no matter how trying the circumstances, or how much he is hurried, he is expected to do his work promptly and cheerfully. He must rejoice at the wedding—whether he is sure of a fee or not; must weep at the funeral, and say nice things over some of the worst sinners the world ever saw; must be calm and careful at the bedside of the sick; must never be late at the church services or other appointments; must never "talk back" if slandered or abused—must never manifest a dislike for the "cross-grained" of his parish; must never be discouraged—his members appropriate that privilege; must preach good sermons, whether he has time to prepare them or not; must fill all vacancies caused by the absence of others in the various meetings of the church; he must be in sympathy with all improvements of the community, and in a thousand ways make himself generally useful.

He must buy books, keep himself well clothed, also his family; must pay all bills due, whether he gets his salary or not; must have his home furnished so that his people will not be ashamed of its appearance; he must give to the various calls which are religious or otherwise; and then sometimes some well-meaning people wonder why their pastor does not have money enough to buy a farm, or build a new church, or endow a college, or why his wife and children are left destitute when he dies.

But God is calling men today to His ministry, and the men so called are responding heartily and cheerfully, for they "reckon that the sufferings of this present time are not worthy to be compared with the glory which shall be revealed in" them later. It certainly is a constant joy to know that one has been "called of God, as was Aaron," and has responded to the call.

HENRY CRAMPTON.

3000 Hamilton Avenue,
Columbus, Georgia.

THE CHRISTIAN ORPHANAGE

FIFTY CHURCHES AND SCHOOLS FAILED

We are very happy to have reached our first thousand dollar mile post for this year and have gone beyond it. Brother S. C. Hobby of Raleigh mailed us a check for $50.00 this week. Brother Hobby always remembers us each year with a check to help care for the little orphans.

We would like to get every Sunday school on our list of monthly contributors this year. I wish I could enlist every Sunday school superintendent, every teacher and every secretary as an Orphanage worker.

More than fifty churches and Sunday schools in the Southern Christian Convention did not contribute a penny, last year, toward the support of the orphan children. Still last year was our best year, financially, for the Christian Orphanage in its history. Suppose that each delinquent church and Sunday school had done its part how much more we could have done in this work?

This year we want to get this fifty on our list and we will do all we can to get them there. I would be happy and delighted to be able to report to you at the end of this year that each church and Sunday school had made contributions to help in this work.

Brother superintendent, will you see that your Sunday school makes the monthly contribution? Let us have pride enough in our church and Sunday school to want to be on the *banner list.*

Our friends still remember us. The following contributions have been sent in recently:

Mrs. M. E. Boyd and Miss Sarah Boyd, Richmond, Va., 9 yards table linen.

Mr. and Mrs. L. E. Carlton, Richmond, Va., 7 yards table linen.

Ladies of Liberty Sunday school, 4 dozen cans fruit. Junior Willing Workers, Sarem church, 1 nice quilt. Ravina Sunday school, Ravina, N. Y., 1 box containing clothing, books, dresses, etc., for the children.

For all this we are profoundly grateful.

CHAS. D. JOHNSON, *Supt.*

REPORT FOR MARCH 5, 1919

Amount brought forward, $953.52.

Children's Offerings

Willie Staylor, 10 cents; Mills Wellons Staylor, 10 cents; Richard Bost, 30 cents; Total, 50 cents.

Sunday School Monthly Offerings

(Eastern Virginia Conference)

Antioch, $2.00; Holy Neck, $4.00; Third church, $16.81;

Spring Hill, $2.00.

(North Carolina Conference)

Mt. Auburn, $9.25; Pleasant Grove, $4.25; Palm St., Greensboro, $4.00; Henderson, N. C., $8.50; Oak Level, $1.00; Christian Light, $2.27; Haw River, N. C., $2.72.

(Virginia Valley Conference)

New Hope, Va., $1.00; Total $57.80.

Thanksgiving Offerings

Holland, Va., $111.00.

Special Offerings

J. H. Jones, on support of children, $30.00; J. D. Oldham, $12.50; S. C. Hobby, Raleigh, N. C., $50.00; Total, $92.50.

Total for the week, $261.80; Grand total, $1,215.32.

THE CHILDREN WRITE

Dear Uncle Charley: Here comes a little boy who wants to join the band of cousins and help the little orphans. My Sunday school teacher has been telling us about them and we feel sorry for them. My teacher is Mrs. Glass. I attend the Christian church. We like our pastor, Rev. L. L. Wyrick. We were delighted to have Rev. L. I. Cox with us Sunday night. Enclosed find thirty cents, my dues for February, March and April.—*Richard Bost.*

We give you a hearty welcome to our corner. Hope you will write each month. Help us keep the corner full this year.—"*Uncle Charley.*"

Dear Uncle Charley: Here is my dime for February. I was twelve years old February 11. I hope the cousins are well and having a good time. It is fair here but the wind is blowing fierce around the corner of the house.—*Willie Staylor.*

You are beginning the new year all right. I am counting on you to help brighten the corner this year.—"*Uncle Charley.*"

Dear Uncle Charley: I will send my dime for February. I was promoted to the third grade and am eight years old. I hope you and all the cousins are well.—*Mills Wellons Staylor.*

You are a smart little boy. I am going to come to see you some time and tell you how proud of you I am.—"*Uncle Charley.*"

Mrs. T. W. Chandler.—THE SUN this week (February 19) is indeed inspiring and filled as it is with plans and visions of greater things for our Church, delights the heart.

Mrs. J. L. Pointer.—We all love to see our dear SUN shine in our home. It is a welcome visitor.

Miss S. R. Byrd.—I am sure you have no subscriber who wishes you more success with our dear SUN than I and if at any time I am where I don't receive its rays, I 'll subscribe at once.

Thomas Whitt.—THE SUN gets better each week and I do not want to do without it.

MISSIONARY

HOW TO CREATE AND KEEP A LIVE AND ACTIVE WOMAN'S MISSIONARY SOCIETY IN THE CHURCH

(IN FIVE CHAPTERS)

CHAPTER V. HAVE A PROGRAM

In the previous chapters it has been shown that the live, active Woman's Missionary Society will have, and must have, a proper regard for the Bible, Prayer and Music, as fundamentals; and, in order to build and grow, will set for itself an objective. These all have been likened in our thought to the foundations and frame work of a building. Carrying out further that figure the building must have also a covering. The program is the covering, the shelter, the protection. You can no more have a Society without a program than you can have a building without a covering.

Unless you have a roof and shingles on your building, it is open to all sorts of weather, and being exposed, soon begins to decay and go to pieces. A Society without a program is exposed to every temperament, disposition, caprice and mood that one or two members may happen at any time to have, and soon begins to crumble and fall apart. If a Society really means business it should make for itself a program from time to time covering several weeks, months or a year.

Now every program should be built upon two fundamental ideas, or rather upon one idea with two fundamental facts in it, namely: That a Missionary Society is a body and as such, like every other body, *must have both food and exercise.* Spiritual growth goes upon exactly the same method as physical growth, and certainly no physical body develops and flourishes upon food alone. Exercise is essential. Do not many Societies ignore this fundamental fact, and suffer its tragic consequences? I fear so.

The following is quoted from Belle M. Brain, that versatile writer of "Fifty Missionary Programs," and author of many other helpful missionary volumes: "Food of the best quality," says Miss Brain, "served in the most appetizing manner, is provided in abundance, but rarely, if ever, is there exercise enough to make it digest well. For this reason many a society that might be large and active is small and weak, and in a state of lethargy from which it seems impossible to arouse it." It is not sufficient for the Society to simply meet from time to time to study, to read, to pray, to sing. These are good; but they are food, and that only. Possibly your Society from too much food is becoming sleepy; from lack of exercise is suffering inertia, perhaps even now has indigestion.

Let me quote Miss Brain again, "In the old days God greatly blessed the work of willing hands and put a high value upon it. In the building of the tabernacle there was need not only of gold, silver, and precious stones, fragrant woods, sweet spices and anointing oils, but of the blue and purple and scarlet, the fine linen and the goat's hair which *wise hearted women spun with their own hands.* In the building of the spiritual Kingdom of our Lord today there is a place for the work of the hands as well as of the heart and brain.''

Your Society must have a program, and that program must provide for exercise as well as for food. The following order should be observed in building the program: Devotional (which includes Bible reading, prayer and music); Self-improvement and individual inspiration (which includes mission study, discussion of methods, making contributions, paying dues); Exercise, (which includes the actual doing of some missionary deed either for the home or foreign work).

If the Society will lay upon itself a program which involves those three thoughts for every meeting, there will be life, vigor and activity.

This is not as cumbersome, neither is it as impossible or as impracticable as at first it might seem. The writer imagines now he sees some anxious sister reading these lines, and hears her saying, ''Well our Society has a hard time living now, and in fact hardly can exist as it is, without trying to branch out and take on all these new and complicated notions our Field Secretary is trying to hamper us with.'' Whereas the real fact is that many a Society is dying because obsessed with complexities. The most complex and mysterious and abnormal thing in the universe is a body trying to live and grow by caprice, by hap-hazard, by unnatural processes. These we call in physiology freaks of nature, abnormal growths, unnatural bodies. The Society that is just trying to live any sort of way is having a hard time of it; it is traveling a rough and rugged path, if travelling at all. God Himself never built a body except by the best possible of well ordered programs; and even the wisdom of good women cannot improve on God's method of successful building, growth and development.

Sufficient in previous papers has been said of two parts of the program, namely, the devotional and self-improvement; commonly called the ''opening exercises'' and the mission study. Brief space is left now for the *active* part of the program. Let every program contemplate doing something.

An artist learns how to paint by painting; a musician learns music by singing; the architect designs by drawing; and we learn missions by the same process. We come to know missions by being missionary. There is no other method.

If your Missionary Society is having a hard time in just trying to exist, give it something to do and see if life does not quicken. What can it do?

First. Are there no orphans to whom your Society might send boxes?

Second. Do you know of no missionaries at home or abroad to whom you might send a fine ''pounding'' of clothing for the family, table-linen, needle work for the busy wife and mother in the missionary home?

Third. Do you know of no families in your community where some token of esteem and consideration from your Society would do good, carry cheer, hope, sunshine and help?

Fourth. Has your Sunday school a good missionary library, all the books that it needs for the children to take out and read on the stewardship of life, money, of

talents? Why not put on your Society's program of action the item of building up a missionary library for your Sunday school—giving to it the books you have studied and read in Society, and others that you know about? This writer could fill all this page with suggestions for the *doing* part of the program; and if any Society wishes something to do and can think of nothing, just let its members for once lift up their eyes unto the hills whence cometh all our help and say separately or in concert: ''Lord, what wilt thou have me to do,'' and see what happens.

Try the tonic of an active, vigorous program for your Society a while, and see if God does not breathe into it the breath of life so that it shall become a living soul.

Our Father's blessings upon our dear, noble, faithful women who are trying, God help them, in their modest way to build up and keep alive the Woman's Missionary Society. They are sowing seeds whose fruitage they themselves will never know but the generations to come after will feed thereon and live.

J. O. ATKINSON.

NOTES

What do you think of Brother Crampton's article?

Dr. Frank S. Child is at Elon College this week delivering his annual series of lectures.

Many subscriptions to THE SUN expired March 1. Let each subscriber whose label reads 3-1-9, renew promptly.

Out-of-town callers at the SUN office last week were: Rev. J. S. Carden, Durham, N. C., and Brother L. M. Clymer, Greensboro, N. C. We are always glad to have our friends call to see us.

Dr. P. H. Fleming leaves this week for Dover, Delaware to spend a month with the Peoples Christian church. His pulpit at Union will be filled next Sunday, March 9, by the SUN's Editor and on the fourth Sunday in March by President Harper.

We are grateful to the ministers who are sending us renewals and new subscriptions to THE SUN. So far the work of our campaign has not yielded very satisfactory results but we hope that the work in March will suffice for the whole period.

Sunday, March 9, is Mission Day throughout the entire Church. It is requested and hoped that the cause will be presented in all sections of the Zion. This does not conflict with any program already in use, but is only the day set apart for the whole Church to consider the mission interest of the denomination.

Mrs. J. H. Pierce.—THE SUN has been in our home for over fifty years and I want it to shine as long as I live. I cannot do without my church paper.

A RECONSTRUCTION PROGRAM FOR OUR CHURCH

My article in The Herald of February 6, "The Call to Christian Service," has been misunderstood from two sources. At least one dear friend interpreted it to mean that I desired to eliminate God from the call to the ministry. I welcome this opportunity to state again, what I have stated so many times elsewhere, that God calls all men to His service. As I see it, absolutely none is excused. Now, whether a man or woman shall become a minister of the Gospel depends on other things than this call. It depends in part on one's fellows, and they are under obligation when so impressed to present the call to the ministry to any person whom they believe to be qualified to serve God effectively there. The strongest men of this day are holding back fro mthe ministry for lack of this encouragement on the human side. They are red-blooded men, virile, forward-looking. They set great store by the ministry and feel themselves unequal to its claim. Properly approached these men will become the Samuels and Pauls of the next generation. And may I further say that many of the men who have offered themselves to the ministry without being sought out by their fellows have proven by their unfitness in service the error in their having been divinely summoned to the ministry?

An iconoclast of a few weeks ago declared that the trouble with the ministry is that it is called by the celestial suffrage and not the people whom it is to serve. He would have been Scriptural if he had said, the call to the ministry is both human and divine. One's fellowmen are one's interpreters to one of God's will. There will be exceptional cases, such as was Paul's, but they will be only for exceptional men, and what the Church needs is an increasing number of men ready to serve, though not qualified to mould the Church for centuries as did Paul. May I add finally on this point that of the men whom God has led me to approach on this theme and who became ministers not one has failed to rejoice my heart by his service?

The second source of misunderstanding is that my article is too circumscribed in its scope. "Do you think we have done enough for the men in service, when we have presented to them under God's leading the claim of His service?" queries a friend.

"Certainly not," I reply. I was in the article referred to discussing a special problem, and hoped I had made plain that our COMMISSION ON MANNING THE FIELD would give us the full program later. However, the golden days are going fast. Without thinking of exhausting the theme, I have decided briefly to outline some of the other things we should include in our reconstruction program.

We should of course co-operate with every welfare agency, governmental or voluntary, designed to promote the morals and purity of our discharged soldiers and sailors and of our own community's citizen's.

We should take part in every welcome to the returning men, but in addition no man in any congregation should return without the Church's taking public recognition of that fact. I think each Church should have its own welcome service when demobilization is over, and some sort of memorial service should be undertaken if members of the congregation have made the supreme sacrifice.

Every church should have an employment committee to help every returning man get quickly located in service upon his return. The United States Employment Bureau touches only a few large centers of population and the larger industries. The Churches might well in union provide for each county, at the county seat, a bureau, but the local church too needs its committee on this humane errand bent.

Our Chaplains, when they return, should be a chief concern. We have a Committee on Chaplains. This Committee might very well make its field of further service to bring chaplains and our churches together, and I am not so sure but that we should raise a fund to support these brethren, on condition that they lecture under the control of the Committee, until they are located in a suitable field.

We should adapt our evening service at least to meet some of the aspirations of the returning men. Would it not be well to place some of them on a committee with others to help outline the church's program locally? The Federal Council recommends motion pictures of the proper kind and the open forum for these services. One thing is certain, the old type evening services is largely doomed. A few magnetic orators can no doubt hold it to its traditional ideal, but such instances will be sporadic.

The main thing is to approach these men sympathetically and not patronizingly. Seek their service and lead them to become the friends and supporters of the Kingdom, just as they have so heroically been of the cause of human freedom.

Finally, our Church as a denomination should at its adjourned A. C. C. session this April present a welcome to our returned heroes worthy of them and of ourselves. And this welcome should perpetuate itself in enduring style, preferably by the erection of a great Church in some large city, as Washington, D. C., making the erection a denominational-wide enterprise. The different Conventions and Conferences might well too erect such memorials in their contiguous territory, subscribed to in a smaller area.

By all means, and foremost, let us not, as giving soul and ultimate purpose to all these things we may do for the men, neglect to present Christ to them as personal Savior and to hold up the Kingdom's claim as fundamental in every man's life.

                                        W. A. HARPER.

(Editorial Note: Since the Herald of Gospel Liberty is taken more or less in practically all sections of the Southern Christian Convention; also since we are crowded for space, we print the above without printing the article referred to. A copy of the original article was not furnished The Sun for publication.—C. B. R.)

RIGHT-TO-THE-POINT REMARKS

Render to God the things that are God's.

Giving a tenth is a trust—a trust in the Lord.

No honest, careful man will be financially embarrassed by tithing.

The person who gives one-tenth enjoys his nine-tenths so much more.

To spend money rightly is one of my first tasks as a Christian.

Tithing is the only God-given plan for financing the work of Christ's Kingdom.

My money is mine, only in trust. It belongs to God just as I do.

If the Lord has given you a horn of plenty don't toot it; tithe it.

Heathen nations observed the law of the tithe before the days of Abraham. We should not do less.

    Not the tithe, but the tither,
    Not the gift, but the giver,
    Not the money, but the man,
    Not the possession, but the possessor.

                            —The California Endeavorer.

THE CHURCH PAPER COMING INTO ITS OWN

According to the prophets of the present day, this war is going to turn the church upside down, give us a new brand of religion, and make the mossbacks in theology take a back seat.

Out of the wrecks of the past and the creations of the present, we hope that the church papers may secure more recognition than pastors seem disposed to give them. We have never been able to follow the line of reasoning that prompts a congregation to organize its membership into classes for the study of missions, both home and foreign, and tax themselves to support a preacher who is to teach them the Bible and train them in building up the church, yet at the same time they neglect the church paper that combines all of these various kinds of work, and that follows the members into their homes and speaks to them at all times. One would suppose that this important ally would be welcomed and used to the fullest extent. On the contrary, among the stereotyped beliefs of the past is the one that a Church paper is a luxury in a home, and not a necessity, and that even if you do take it, you need not read it. Of course the church paper is largely to be blamed for this view, because the church paper of the past was dry reading, and even now there are some that are "nearest of kin to those of the past. We claim, however, that of kin to those of the past.

We are glad to learn that in the $3,600,000 drive for benevolences the Stewardship Committee recognized what few pastors do, that a Church paper in every home would be a fine piece of constructive work, and that it would do much to establish on a firm foundation their work.

The Third Presbyterian Church of Fort Wayne, Indiana, has gone even further than our committee. They have decided to put the church paper into every home in the church, and have made provision in their annual budget to pay for the same. We do not believe that we are oversanguine when we predict that such will, in time, be the policy of every wide-awake church.— *Presbyterian Standard.*

IT IS MORE BLESSED

(A Recitation)

Give! as the morning that flows out of heaven;
Give! as the waves where their channel is riven;
Give! as the free air and sunshine are given;
Lavishly, utterly, joyfully give:—
Not the waste drops of thy cup overflowing,
Not the faint sparks of thy hearth ever glowing,
Not a pale bud from the June roses blowing;
Give, as he gave thee, who gave thee to life.

Almost the day of thy giving is over;
Ere from the grass dies the bee-haunted clover,
Thou wilt have vanished from friend and from lover;
What shall thy longing avail in the grave?
Give as the heart gives, whose fetters are breaking,
Life, love, and hope, all thy dreams and thy waking;
Soon, heaven's river thy soul-fever shaking,
Thou shalt know God and the gift that he gave.
—*Selected.*

BOOKS, BIBLES, TESTAMENTS

In order to reduce certain stocks of books, Bibles and Testaments on hand, the following prices are made and will hold good until March 31, 1919:

Bibles

No. 312X. Holman Self-Pronouncing Teachers' Bible. Printed on fine white paper from good, clear type, and contains references, concordance, four thousand questions and answers and fifteen prepared maps. Size 4 3-8X6 1-2 inches. Egyptian Morocco, divinity circuit, head bands and marker, round corners, red under gold edges. Regular selling price......$4.65
Price to March 31 .... 3.90

No. 71. Scofield Reference Bible. (Handsome binding, French Morocco limp, new and improved edition. "The neatest Scofield Bible made." It will please you. Regular selling price $4.50
Price to March 31 .... 3.90

No. 215. Child's Self-Pronouncing Pictorial Bible with Helps. Bound in French seal leather, round corners, silk bands, gold titles,—handsomely made. Regular selling price $2.50
Price to March 31 .... 2.00

No. 1113. Ideal Bible for Children. Printed on fine white paper from the newest and clearest type of the size made. Size 3 1-2X5 3-8 inches. This Bible will please you. Regular price $1.75
Price to March 31 .... 1.40

Testaments

No. 3913 R. L. (Red Letter). Large print Morocco binding. Regular price $2.00
Price to March 31 .... 1.75

No. 2902 Cloth binding, large print, Regular price.... .90
Price to March 31 .... .75

No. 2502 P. Cloth binding, black faced type. Regular price .... .75
Price to March 31 .... .55

No. 2113. Pocket size, Morocco binding. Regular price .60
Price to March 31 .... .45

No. 0133, Pocket size, Morocco binding, overlapping edges. Regular Price .... .75
Price to March 31 .... .55

(A Testament in Modern Speech)

Cloth, $1.25; cloth, indexed, $1.75; cloth, India paper, $1.75; leather, $2.35; leather, indexed, $2.75; leather, India paper, $2.75; Persian Morocco, Divinity Circuit, $3.75; Turkey Morocco, $1.25. Pocket Edition (without notes): Cloth, $1.00; cloth, India paper, $1.25; leather, India paper, $1.85. State definitely style wanted.

The above prices are regular. Make your choice and deduct 10 per cent. State definitely Testament wanted.

Books

Pastor's Ideal Funeral, $1.15—Regular price, $1.25.

(Books for the Children)

We have several copies "Silver Rags," "Patty's Grand Uncle," "Johnny Two Boys," "A Rescued Madonna"—your choice, 20 cents per copy. We will substitute if the book ordered is sold before the order reaches us.

Special

"Redmond of the Seventh," by Mrs. Frank Lee is a book with a fine story taken from school life, 290 pages, handsomely bound; 50 cents the copy.

Special Note: One of these books will be sent free with each order for $3.00 worth of books, Bibles or Testaments.
Address
C. B. RIDDLE ....Publishing Agent
Burlington, N. C.

Sunday School and Christian Endeavor

SUNDAY SCHOOL TOPIC FOR SUNDAY, MARCH 9

Joshua, Patriot and Leader

Scripture lesson: Joshua 1:1-9.

Golden Text: Joshua 1:9, "Be strong and of good courage."

Time: B. C. spring 1451.

Place: East of the Jordan, opposite Jericho.

For comment and explanation, see Bible Class Quarterlies, or Officers and Teachers Journal, C. P. A., Dayton, Ohio.

CHRISTIAN ENDEAVOR TOPIC FOR SUNDAY, MARCH 9

"Lost by Looking"

Sripture lesson: Prov. 23:29-35. (Temperance meeting).

For explanation and comment, see Christian Endeavor World, Boston, Mass.

HOW TO STUDY MISSIONS IN THE SUNDAY SCHOOL

There are four practical methods now employed in getting missions studied and taught in the Sunday school. It does seem that every school, and every class in the school could and should adopt one or the the other since the chief business of the school is to learn missions, teach missions and be missionary.

First. On one Sunday in each month let every class in the school, (after the regular scripture lesson of the day has been read in concert) devote the whole recitation period to the study of some suitable missionary book. Our Publishing Agent, Rev. C. B. Riddle, Burlington, N. C., has on hand, or will secure, books suitable to every class in the school and the books are not expensive. This should be known as "Mission Sunday" and the offering of the classes on this day should go to missions.

Second. A certain portion of each recitation—say ten minutes each Sunday—can be devoted to the study of missions. This gives some time to lesson study and some to mission study each month, and a certain part of each Sunday's offering can go to missions.

Third. Have a missionary superintendent whose business it is to lecture, say five minutes each Sunday, to the whole school on the subject of missions, and bring the missionary idea before the whole school as he may and can. He can suggest special offerings for missions.

Fourth. Have a missionary committee in the Sunday school whose business it shall be to plan missionary programs, prepare missionary days and rallies for the school; and take special offerings for missions.

The writer much prefers the First plan mentioned, that of "Mission Sunday" once per month when the whole school gives the whole recitation period to the one theme of "winning this wicked world to Christ." God knew the crying needs of a whole world and gave His Son to redeem it. We will give ourselves, our sons, our daughters, to helping save the world to Christ when we, too, shall know and understand the needs of the world for the blessed Gospel.

Then surely every school should have a missionary library. The writer will take pleasure in helping any school select books for its missionary library. Some of the very best, most thrilling, inspiring, and heroic books of the present are those telling of the wonders and miracles of the mission field; of what God is doing out there, and of the great and good and brave men and women who are being so wonderfully used of Him to win a world to a saving knowledge of our Christ. These are not dull books; they are books of action, deeds, daring, fearless courage and noble conquest.

Get a missionary library into your Sunday school, even if only a few volumes to start with.

If you wish further facts about mission study in Sunday school, how happy the mission secretary will be to help.

CHILD'S SELF-PRONOUNCING PICTORIAL BIBLE WITH HELPS

This Bible is bound in French Seal Leather, has round corners, silk head bands, gold titles, handsomely bound.

Regular selling price..........$2.50

Price till March 31............ 2.00

Call for Bible No. 215.

Address

C. B. RIDDLE, *Publishing Agent*

Burlington, North Carolina

MARRIAGES

BAILEY-PADGETT

Married, at the Christian parsonage, Waverly, Va., January 22, 1919 by Rev. Jas. L. Foster, Mr. Dillard B. Bailey and Miss Ruth Bain Padgett. Only a few of the near relatives witnessed the ceremony.

Mr. Bailey is a prosperous young farmer of near Wakefield, Va. Miss Padgett is a popular young lady of near Waverly, Va., and a member of Centerville Christian church.

The very best wishes of pastor and their many friends accompany them on life's journey.

—JAS. L. FOSTER.

OBITUARIES

BIGGS

Miss Alice Biggs was born June 18, 1891, and was taken to her eternal home February 14, 1919. When she was about 14 years of age she professed faith in Christ and united with the church. She did not long enjoy the privilege and pleasure of attending her church, however, as the hand of affliction was laid on her about ten years ago, and she had been a sufferer ever since. But it is sweet to know that her afflictions did not cause her to lose faith in her Savior nor the assurance of her salvation. Only a few days before her death she expressed her readiness to go if it should be the Lord's will. She was laid to rest at Fuller's Chapel.

She leaves one brother, Ira Biggs, and two sisters, Mrs. C. L. Taylor and Mrs. G. P. Taylor. May her good works follow her, and the influence of her life continue to lead others to her Savior.

R. L. WILLIAMSON.

HARRIS

After several years of declining health, and a few months of suffering, Brother Robert T. Harris died February 15, 1919, lacking 1 day and 5 minutes of 5 months after his wife. He had been to the hospital for treatment but found no relief. He came quietly to the end. He had lived in the same quiet manner in which he died.

Brother Harris spent his entire life in the community of Waverly, Va. He joined the church early in life. He was a charter member of the Waverly Christian church and remained a consistent member till his death.

On December 17, 1874 he married Miss Mahala Alley, and to this union 7 children were born E. Mertie, J. Kemper, John Alley, and Robert Hinton; Mrs. Mary Lillian Holloway who died 3 years ago; Mrs. Iola Graham Faison and Miss Laura Harris.

His was the quiet Christian life. He loved his home. He was faithful in church attendance till health failed. He was 65 years, 1 month and 6 days old. Thus our men and women of mature years are passing beyond. The beautiful flow-told of the high esteem in which he s held. Funeral services from the home and burial at Waverly cemetery in the presence of a large gathering of relatives and friends. Services by his pastor.

JAS. L. FOSTER.

WICKER

Mrs. Anna Belle Wicker died at her home on East Main street, Durham, N. C., February 14, 1919. She was in her 64th year. The last two years of her life were spent in Durham. She formerly lived in Lee county and was a loyal and lovable member of the Zion Christian church. She was known by a large circle of friends in her home county as well as in Durham, and hence her death brought sadness to many hearts, because all who knew her loved her.

She had been in declining health since Christmas, but her death came suddenly. Many times the writer visited her and always received a blessing by so doing. But she is gone, and a large number of friends are left to think of the loss sustained by her going. She was a devout Christian, a congenial friend, and a loving mother.

Surving her are three sons and two daughters Lacy P. and J. F. Wicker of Greensboro and Delancy D. Wicker with the A. E. F. in France and Mrs. E. D. Kelly, of Moncure, and Miss Ida Belle Wicker of Durham. A brief service was conducted from the home by the writer, after which the remains were carried to her home church for burial. May the Spirit comfort the bereaved.

R. F. BROWN.

TEAGUE

Sixty years ago a bright, industrious young carpenter came from his country home to a little village in the woods known as "The Company's Shops," of the North Carolina Central Railroad. This young man, Edward Teague, was born June 30, 1833, in Chatham County, North Carolina, near Cane Creek. His father was John Teague, and his mother Ann Hounaday Teague. He was married to Lucy Ann York, on November 1, 1858. Children of this union: John P. Teague, deceased; Miss Dora M. Teague; Banks E. Teague, of Burlington; Clarence W. Teague, of West Durham; Mrs. W. T. Williams) of Chester, South Carolina; Maurice E. Teague, of Brooklyn, New York, and Charles Howell Teague who died in infancy. Our departed brother moved to this place about sixty years ago, and lived here continuously, until he was called from labor to reward, about four o'clock Saturday morning, February 8, 1919. In 1878, he united with the Friends Church, during a revival meeting conducted by the late Elder Daniel McPherson.

Second marriage occurred August 6, 1906, to Mrs. Ada A. Isley.

In all the relations of life, Edward Teague showed himself to be a true man, a devoted husband, a loving father, and an agreeable neighbor.

As a friend, he worked and prayed for peace; yet the last letter he ever wrote, was to Roy Fonville, of Burlington commending him for his bravery and patriotism.

His mind was clear through all the days of his life. And when the golden sun of his life of service was resting sweetly, and invitingly, upon the silver mountains, and he could only speak to Dr. Page, and his own devoted wife, and loving children, in a whisper, never did a sign or word of complaint, come from this man of God. And when the mist of the Jordan gathered on his brow, he "fell on sleep" as quietly, and peacefully, as a babe folded in the arms of a loving mother. Well did the Psalmist say: "Mark the perfect man, and behold the upright; for the end of that man is peace."

In Numbers XXIII: 10 you find these words, "Let me die the death of the righteousness, and let my last end be like his." In Job 1115 17 you find these words, "There the wicked cease from troubling; and there the weary be at rest."

Our departed brother was a man who had a lambent vein of good humor running through his entire being, yet no citizen of Burlington ever heard him tell a story that could not be repeated in the presence of refined ladies.

Many exemplary men have I known within the three score and ten years of my life; but none who was more devoted, outwardly and inwardly, to the service of God, I have not known. He needs no eulogy from any one.

"Green be the grave above thee Friend of my early days, None knew thee but to love thee, None named thee but to praise."

D. A. LONG.

DICKERSON

W. H. Dickerson was laid to rest in the family burying ground near Epsom, N. C., January 19, 1919. He was forty-one years old and had been a member of Liberty (Vance) Christian church for a number of years. He leaves his wife and seven children. The church and community have sustained a considerable loss in his decease. But the family is the greatest loser after all, for no one else can take the place of father in the home. May the Lord's grace sustain them.

G. J. GREEN.

WRENN

Sallie Lou Wrenn, infant daughter of Clarence O. Wrenn and Mamie (Newman) Wrenn, deceased, was laid to rest in Liberty cemetery January 29, 1919. Left by its mother when only a few days old, like a flower it shed its fragrance on those who cared for it and then went to her. Mother and child are united in Heaven while we are left to mourn their departure. What will be sweeter than meeting these little ones on the other side! This will be the reward for our service.

G. J. GREEN.

ELLINGTON

Lucy Daniel Ellington, six-year-old daughter of Mr. and Mrs. Ed Ellington, and granddaughter of Mr. Dave Weldon, was buried in the Weldon burying ground near Epsom, N. C., January 23, 1919.

The after-effects of influenza was the cause of her death. She was a dutiful child and was greatly loved by her kin and her little friends. Though "absent from the body and present with the Lord" she still lingers on earth in the hearts of those who knew her.

G. J. GREEN.

THE CHRISTIAN SUN

"IN ESSENTIALS UNITY, IN NON-ESSENTIALS LIBERTY, IN ALL THINGS CHARITY"

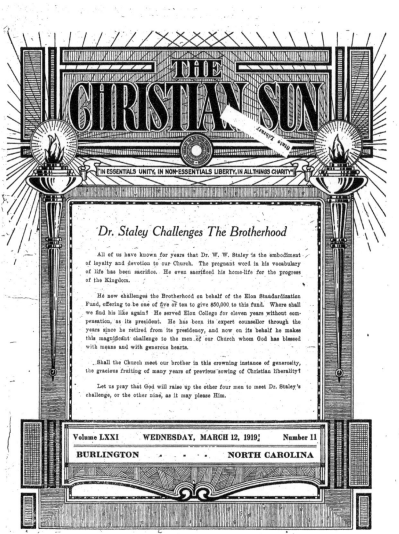

Dr. Staley Challenges The Brotherhood

All of us have known for years that Dr. W. W. Staley is the embodiment of loyalty and devotion to our Church. The pregnant word in his vocabulary of life has been sacrifice. He even sacrificed his home-life for the progress of the Kingdom.

He now challenges the Brotherhood on behalf of the Elon Standardization Fund, offering to be one of five or ten to give $50,000 to this fund. Where shall we find his like again? He served Elon College for eleven years without compensation, as its president. He has been its expert counsellor through the years since he retired from its presidency, and now on its behalf he makes this magnificent challenge to the men of our Church whom God has blessed with means and with generous hearts.

Shall the Church meet our brother in this crowning instance of generosity, the gracious fruiting of many years of previous sowing of Christian liberality?

Let us pray that God will raise up the other four men to meet Dr. Staley's challenge, or the other nine, as it may please Him.

Volume LXXI	WEDNESDAY, MARCH 12, 1919.	Number 11
BURLINGTON	. . . .	NORTH CAROLINA

THE CHRISTIAN SUN

Founded 1844 by Rev. Daniel W. Kerr

C. B. RIDDLE - - - Editor

.- Entered at the Burlington, N. C. Post Office as second class matter.

Subscription Rates

One year ....$ 2.00
Six months 1.00

In Advance

Give both your old and new postoffice when asking that your address be changed.

The change of your label is your receipt for money. Written receipts sent upon request.

Marriage and obituary notices not exceeding 150 words printed free if received within 60 days from date of event, all over this at the rate of one-half cent a word.

Original poetry not accepted for publication.

Principles of the Christian Church

(1) The Lord Jesus Christ is the only Head of the Church.
(2) Christian is a sufficient name of the Church.
(3) The Holy Bible is a sufficient rule of faith and practice.
(4) Christian character is a sufficient test of fellowship, and of church membership.
(5) The right of private judgment and the liberty of conscience is a right and a privilege that should be accorded to, and exercised by all.

EDITORIAL

AS WE WERE THINKING

'Burdens often help rather than hinder. In the winter the forest at times is usually laden with snow and ice. Every sprig is bent—and thus tested. The stormy wind is ever testing the forest. The consequences of all this is that the trees come forth with renewed energy, have their roots planted deeper into the earth. A choppy sea makes the captain see that his ship is secure.

* *

Those who claim that the Bible is a back number are those who know more about the Bible from *heresay* than they do from *experience* and the study of it. And that reminds us that all criticism of the Bible is destructive, because nothing better is offered. There is nothing better for them to offer.

* *

There is now going the rounds a soft, soupy, silly, senseless criticism of the Church by those who are looking for something "new." The strange thing to us is how a man can appreciate the "new" unless he has experienced the "old." We admit that the Church is not perfect, but its criticisms come from those who help the Church—the least.

* *

It is not more laws that we need but an execution of those we now have. In fact we have so many laws that

the dread of their conflict often defeats justice. Washington ought to be a modern city. There our President lives, the highest law-making meets, and in brief the scales of justice are supposed to be kept there. But Washington has the open Sunday and many other things to her discredit. She, as well as many other places, needs a stronger public sentiment to back up the laws already on her books.

* *

We know some local churches that have the "Changing Fever." They seek a pastoral change every year—and usually get it. They do not give their pastor time to begin any constructive work. The persons who constitute this class ought to change brands of flour, soda, lard, and other things each time they buy. They ought to carry out to the letter their logic.

* *

Elon's campaign for $125,000.00 additional endowment is an undertaking supremely great for the Church. All too long have we laid too little stress on our educational needs. Educated leadership is the supreme need of our day, and this leadership should be Christian. The Church colleges now of all times need support and the country needs them.

* *

Some time ago a good lady wrote the Editor asking what would become of those who are indifferent about the church and would not attend it. That all depends upon how long they continue to do this. A church and a community ought to make a program of service and worship sufficient to enlist the indifferent of the community. A community may scorn at some of its inhabitants and at the same time scorn at its products.

* *

We fear that many good men and women of the land do not rightly interpret the mission of the Church. So many express themselves as if the only work of the Church is to evangelize. Not by any means. The Church has for its task to nourish as well as to evangelize. Great revivals often seem like failures in a few months afterwards because the local church failed to carry on that which was started.

* *

Commencement season is approaching and schools, colleges, and seminaries are on the lookout for some one to preach the commencement sermon or deliver the address of the occasion. Remember that the minister you get does not make a charge, but don't let that keep you from doing your duty by him. Don't ask him how much his fare cost, his hotel bill, but keep in mind his time for preparing for the occasion, his extra expense, his supply in his own pulpit, if he is away over Sunday, and make him feel like you have appreciated him.

* *

It is easy to criticize the other fellow—it is a difficult thing to see his way, though he may be right. Praying for a man is much better than cataloging his faults. We are all human. Let us forgive and forget. Take it for what it is worth, criticize it if you may, but we deem Mr. Wilson's words at the opening of the

Peace Conference Christian: "I may say without straining the point that we are not representatives of Governments, but representatives of peoples. It will not suffice to satisfy governmental circles anywhere. It is necessary that we satisfy the opinion of mankind."

CONFERENCE OF RESOLVES AT THE PORTSMOUTH CHURCH

This event held last month created quite a little interest among the churches of Norfolk and Portsmouth for the reason that nothing like it had ever been heard of before. The pastor, Rev. Henry W. Dowding has withheld reports awaiting a suggestion of what the results might be.

A description of the "Conference of Resolves" follows: A Committee was asked to visit every organization of the church and request them to meet in business session, to draw up a set of resolutions pledging their loyalty and support to the church and in a special manner for a period of six months, during which period they further resolved to do special work or make some larger contribution to the work and to cause one copy of the "resolves" to be spread upon their minutes the other to be read by a duly appointed delegate at the Conference.

A Program Committee was asked to prepare a program in two parts, the first part to consist of high class vocal and instrumental music by outside talent, with an intermission of thirty minutes for refreshments, the second part—more music and three short addresses—by local pastors, the entire conference lasting three hours, from seven until ten P. M.

The outstanding features were the procession of each organization into the church, each bearing a badge and singing a verse of some familiar hymn, then all uniting with the audience in singing the stanza, "We Are Not Divided, All One Body We." The reading of the carefully prepared resolutions by a delegate from each organization (the delegates going to the front) and the salutation of the three flags—Church, National and Service—placed at different parts of the church.

As to immediate results, it did for the local church what a more general conference does for a number of churches. It brought all the organizations together and presented the combined working force in one single gathering. It called attention of the public to the many sides aspect of a city church. It impressed each society with its relation and importance to the whole and created a friendly rivalry between them. It is impossible to call attention in this article to the score or more resolutions made by the various societies. We desire, however, to say that a resolution made by two societies to have twenty-five per cent of their members present at each weekly prayer service has resulted in the attendance being nearly doubled. Another resolution by the "Loyal Helpers Bible Class" resulted in the Class asking the pastor to preach a series of sermons, which they agree to advertise, pay expenses of, and attend in a body. One taken by the "Men's Bible Class" results in increased attendance and the establishment of "a sinking fund". The Ladies' Aid Society is busy keep-

ing its pledge to visit a certain number of church members each month and increase its membership twenty-five per cent in six months. The Senior Endeavor Society has pledged to pay the printing and advertising bills of the church. The life of the church has been renewed along all lines.

One very important provision is the appointment of a General Secretary to meet with the different organizations from time to time and keep them in touch with their pledges and also to arrange for a "Conference of Results" to be held in June. The secretary is Mrs. J. C. Ellis, 510 Mt. Vernon Avenue, Portsmouth, Va., who will gladly furnish details to other churches.

NOTES

Rev. A. D. Woodworth, one of our missionaries to Japan, is in this country on a furlough.

Rev. J. W. Wellons makes a brotherly offer on page 6. Read what this veteran of the cross has to say.

Brother C. H. Stephenson has an important announcement on page 14 of this issue. Read it and heed it.

Rev. J. D. Wicker has been in Charlotte since February 24, where he is taking treatment under Dr. Crowel at the "New Charlotte Sanatorium," and will undergo an operation while there.—*Sanford Express.*

The Eastern Virginia Woman's Missionary Conference will hold a meeting April 10 with the Berkley church. This meeting is to take the place of the Conference postponed last fall.

Friends continue to send us new subscriptions to THE SUN, but we regret to say that so far the drive has been far below what it was a year ago. Many write us that conditions are not so favorable this year owing to recent disturbances in the regular services. Do your best, dear friends, and let us make good during the next three weeks.

A Sunday school institute for the benefit of the teachers of Alamance county will be held in Burlington, March 16-20. The speakers are: J. Norman Wills, Greensboro; J. M. Broughton, Jr., Raleigh,; Dr. W. C. Wicker, Elon College; E. S. Parker, Jr., Graham; Miss Martha Dozier, Greensboro; Mrs. Chas. L. Van Noppen, Greensboro; and Gilbert Stephenson, Winston-Salem.

Dr. Martyn Summerbell, Lakemont, N. Y., is at Elon College this week delivering his annual series of lectures. They are as follows:

"A Studay in Influence," "Christian Usefulness," "Personal Freedom in America," "America's Ideals," "America's Patriotic Spirit," "Making the Kaiser," "German Provocation to America," "The Collapse of Kaiserism."

PASTOR AND PEOPLE

DR. LIGHTBOURNE AND THE PEOPLE'S CHURCH

The test of real greatness is in the construction of a work that will survive you. I did not think I was mistaken in my judgment respecting my late lamented friend, Dr. A. W. Lightbourne. Now I know I was not.

I have been to his church two years and more after his translation and find it not the work of a leader merely, but of God. The People's church of Dover, Del., sustained a signal loss in Dr. Lightbourne's untimely taking off. His son, Victor, succeeded him, but he too is gone now, having heard his country's call and answering it in allying himself with the "Y" overseas religious work. Some of the men "over there" have regretted that preachers were sent out by the "Y." It is safe to say that none will regret that Brother Victor was sent. When Dover was asked to furnish a "Y" man, every eye turned toward him, and he could not resist.

His going left the People's church shepherdless. They have had supply preaching since he left, but no pastor. The "flu" epidemic has been raging and pastoral service has been especially needed. Yet in spite of all discouragements and hardships, the Church is serene and hopeful and undismayed. Had Dr. Lightbourne been just an ordinary man, the seed of his sowing could not have survived such misfortune, separated as the church is from our other work. A great man labored there and wrought an enduring monument.

But I have other reason, too, to justify my estimate of Dr. Lightbourne. Not only by the church he founded survived, but it is not localized. It has vision and outreach. For while I was in Dover, I presented the Elon Standardization Fund and this Church, apportioned $2,000, gave $4,200 and more will follow. It was fitting that they should in their generous response perpetuate the name of their great leader, and so they called the fund they raised "The Dr. A. W. Lightbourne Fund," given in his honor by the following members of the People's church: Wesley Webb, E. E. Benson, W. S. Hardcastle, Wm. J. Benson, Margarette G. Stevenson, J. R. McGonigal, E. E. Clements, W. V. Cosden, R. H. Lewis, Georgia A. Carroll, John D. Hawkins, Mary T. Smithers, James H. Hazel, E. J. Faucette, W. C. Moore, John B. Hutton, J. A. Richard, A. G. Massey, John B. Wharton, James B. Keith, John W. Caulk, Eugene Raughley, Sophia Jackson, W. J. Massey, Mrs. E. L. Jones, H. E. Lynch, J. H. Taylor, Wm. Dyer, R. E. Lewis, Mary Mills Wolcott, W. D. Clements, E. L. Hardesty, Mary Lasher, and T. V. Keith. Thus the People's church has perpetually identified itself with our College and done honor to their founder. God can but honor such a church.

For two Sundays and the intervening days I was their pastor, a new and unique experience for a layman, but rich in blessing to me. I visited the sick and aged, attended funerals in homes of sorrow, broke bread around the festive board in the quiet of happy families. My cup ran over. "My Dover pastorate" will fill a large place in memory's gallery of rich and choice experiences. Never breathed a finer people than those of Dover. God bless them!

My Sundays there were filled to the bursting with good things. Class meeting at 9:30; preaching at 10:30; Sunday school at 2:00; Brotherhood at 6:45; preaching at 7:30, and it was good for me to be in all of these. The Class meeting for the reconsecration of the leaders, with song, prayer, and testimonies, and the Brotherhood for the cleaning up of the town and the relief of need and suffering, were the two services that especially gripped my heart. The People's church has a program of service in its Brotherhood, and that program is given a spiritual basis in the Class meeting. Is that not fine? Is it not scriptural? And it is succeeding.

I noticed the fall of former leaders in the congregation there. Brothers T. J. Stephenson and Henry Ridgely, Professor J. E. Carroll, Dr. J. H. Wilson and others have gone to their reward, but God has raised up younger men worthy to be their spiritual successors.

Dr. P. H. Fleming, Burlington, N. C., has agreed to serve the church one month and the congregation anticipates rich blessing from his ministry there. He will be greeted in his new field by Brother Jacob Long and family, former parishoners of his in Burlington, now residents of Dover and affiliated with the People's church.

I shall hope to visit Dover again soon.

W. A. HARPER.

P. S. While in Dover I met Dr. R. S. Stephens and Rev. Wilson C. Moore, two of our ministers. Both of them are busy and serviceable in the Master's work. Dr. Stephens is chaplain of the Deleware Senate, Brother Moore is a prodigy in ability to work and a benediction in spiritual influence.

W. A. H.

SUFFOLK LETTER

Mother is the sweetest word in human language, and the only word of endearment that touches every human heart. It is the one sweet word husband uses when he puts the finest meaning into his soul and calls his wife, "mother." That word is the magnet that holds family units together to make home. Home can never be the same without her presence, her voice, and her love; but the memory of mother is a song in the night of sorrow and a star in the sky of hope.

Mrs. Thomas A. Jones left her sweet home in Norfolk, Virginia, on the last day of December, nineteen eighteen, and spent the first day of the New Year in heaven. She was the daughter of Col. A. Savage, and her mother was Sarah Lee, sister of Captain P. H. Lee. On both sides her ancestors were distinguished for bravery in war, success in peace, and great service in the Christian Church. Mrs. Jones combined the courage of her father, the meekness of her mother, and added the charm of her own genuine life. "Her children arise up, and call her blessed; her husband also, and he praiseth her."

The second day of January was the day we buried her from the dear home long enriched by her presence and her love. The flowers made the casket a thing of beauty, fragrant with sweet odors.

Mrs. Jones was famed by three virtues. She was an artist in home-building. Ancestral reputation for home-life flowered out in her home with a simple beauty so genuine that family and guests "felt at home." This is no mean art, and it is both ancient and modern. There is no place on earth equal to the Christian home; and one found it under the roof where she was mother.

Hospitabilty seemed natural in her life and it was Christian. The door into her heart was as wide as the door into her home. It seemed to be a luxury to her to entertain her friends, their friends, and strangers. Her table seemed to be a perennial feast. The atmosphere within that home seemed to contain the freshness of Christian hospitality. Guests breathed it, enjoyed it, and respected it. Her religious influence was felt in her summer home by the sea as really as the breezes that come in from the ocean.

Her Christian life was a genuine as her domestic life. From a child she had known nothing but to trust in Jesus, and she had crowned her years with faithful service. The Christian Church was a part of her life. Her thought, her prayer, her money, her service lay on the altar. She looked for opportunity, she found work and she did it with her whole being. All the institutions of the Church had her sympathy and her help. The beauty of the character, the strength of her purpose, and the devotion of her life, must remain in the life of her husband children as the inspiration of their faith, the service of their lives, and the hope of reunion in that house not made with hands.

She had afflictions which would have discouraged weaker souls; but nothing seemed to reduce her strong faith, her cheerful disposition, or her bright hope. Like a crushed rose, her life seemed sweeter when tribulation harrowed her soul.

Her pastor, Rev. I. W. Johnson, D. D., had an engagement the day of funeral, and I served.

W. W. STALEY.

DR. FRANK S. CHILD AT ELON COLLEGE

Dr. Frank S. Child, pastor of the First Congregational church, Fairfield, Conn., delighted the faculty and students with a visit on March 2 and 3. For reasons of health Dr. Child has not been able for some years to deliver his annual course of lectures.

Dr. Child preached on Sunday from the words, "The Children of this World are Wiser in Their Generation Than the Children of Light." He showed how Christian people fail in the very important equality of shrewdness or wisdom in their use of the Bible, the Sabbath, and also in their attitude toward the future life, etc. The sermon was strong, beautiful, and withal graced by a spirit enriched by the experiences of the passing years.

On Monday the Doctor spoke in the auditorium giving one of his unique word pictures of the quaint customs, and matchless landscape beauty of Mentone, France, and the Riviera. We were all charmed and at the close felt a strong impulse to embark for those regions.

On Monday afternoon Dr. Child visited, in company with others, the historic Guilford Battle Ground and was delighted with the many fine monuments and historical associations that gather about the place.

Dr. Child's coming to us is both a joy and blessing. Our love and prayers follow him, and we trust he can come oftener in the future.

N. G. NEWMAN.

Elon College, N. C.

POUNDING OR DONATION

In the South we would call it a pounding; but in Pennsylvania they call it a donation. It seems about as near akin to a Southern pounding as the winter is to a Southern winter, but we will just let the people call it as they like.

On the evening of February 26 the good people of Washington Valley church came to the parsonage and brought flour, meal, beef, bacon, pork, eggs, butter, maple syrup (the genuine), potatoes, cabbage, canned fruit, a nice pair of shoes for the pastor and a cash purse.

We are grateful to these kind people for the real value of the articles brought and for the spirit that prompted the action. After the people had spent a pleasant evening together, refreshments which the women had deposited on the dining room table, were served. Before we separated, Mrs. B. S. Mitchell presided at the piano and we sang together, "Praise God From Whom all Blessings Flow," and had prayers together.

While we have had many hindrances since coming here two months ago our work is moving on quietly. Our congregations have improved since the "flu" epidemic has subsided. We have spoken several times along the line of the Forward Movement and hope to adopt a specific program at both churches in the near future.

We have some loyal members in both the churches and we are hoping for a fruitful year in our church work.

R. H. PEEL.

Cambridge Springs, Penn.

A DAY IN THE CHRISTIAN ORPHANAGE

One of the most enjoyable days of my life was spent Friday, February 28, in the Christian Orphanage at Elon College, N. C. I went down in answer to an invitation from Superintendent Chas. D. Johnston, and spent most of the day in the home with the children. I came away feeling that I had never spent a more enjoyable day. Without the slightest suggestion from any one, or Brother Johnston's knowledge of it, I wish to speak of the work there, hoping the whole Church will read these lines and think much of the great work there.

That a wonderful work is being done, no one will deny. Brother Johnston is the right man in the right place. Its a great work to raise over $27,000 in less time than twenty-five months. Yet, it has been done for our Orphanage, and has been done in such a way as to educate our people to the work of giving. The Church is better, greater and richer by having had a part in this work of Christ. It is a fact that men do not mind giving when they know their money is being spent for a noble cause.

The spirit of that home was the thing that was most impressive to me. In fact it is home. I do not have words to express my own feelings concerning the spirit of the home. I tried to watch the attitude of Superintendent, helpers, and the children of the home. A more beautiful spirit of co-operation I never saw. The rule of those in authority is that of a father or mother for their child; and those children obey orders because they love to do so, and not because they are afraid. I talked with several of the children who had been there a long time, and some who were new, and in every instance they told me they were satisfied, and having a good time. The largest child in that home is Superintendent Johnston. I make this statement, because of his attitude toward the children. He loves them, and it goes without saying that they love him. I, somehow, wish I could go on into details and tell more of the home, but space will not admit, and I close with a word to anyone who might read these lines. Any money, time or energy we as a Church may spend will bring a hundred percent in the dollar returns to us. The work of our Institution is getting the very best services that the helpers there can give, and is soon to be in first-class working order, for the debt is now removed and the money will go to build new things for the Institution. Come, let us give it our very best support.

J. VINCENT KNIGHT.

Greensboro, N. C.

AN OFFER

Being much interested in old people who are unsaved, I desire to say that I shall be glad to preach for any church that has any such persons living within reach of it. I am only in my ninety-fourth year, possibly the oldest man many have ever heard preach.

J. W. WELLONS.

Elon College, N. C.

"AIDED"

Preachers have been "pounded" and "potatoed" and have had "suits" brought against them, but this preacher has to report that he and his wife have had the good fortune, recently to have been "aided." It came about in this way: One afternoon twenty members of the Ladies' Aid Society of the Dendron Christian church come to the parsonage well armed, not to do us injury but to help us, and this they did by leaving many good things to eat, too numerous to mention. I would say to any preacher who has not a Ladies' Aid Society in his church to try to get one organized. I am glad to say that ours at Dendron is running on a biblical basis, so far as finances are concerned any how, and do not have to run on lemonade, ice cream and oyster stews. We did not expect them to come to us as they did in this helpful way but as they did we want to express in this public way our sincere appreciation of their kind remembrance.

W. D. HARWARD & WIFE.

Dendron, Va.

CHRISTIAN EDUCATION

GOV. BICKETT COMMENDS ELON'S UNDERTAKING

I am much interested in the effort about to be made to raise the sum of $125,000.00 for the benefit of Elon College in North Carolina. I know something of the work of this College, and consider it a splendid asset to the intellectual and spiritual life of the State. It does clean, conscientious work, and the young men and women who attend the college go out into the world and make the very best of citizens. I commend this college to the kindly consideration of any one who may be disposed to invest a part of their means in a way that will accomplish great and permanent good.

(Signed) T. W. BICKETT.

FROM CONGRESSMAN STEDMAN

I can only say that in my opinion the campaign of Elon College and its work in behalf of education entitles it to the high consideration of the public and I sincerely trust that the campaign will be a complete success. There has been no time in the history of our country when it was more necessary to look after the education and careful training of our young men.

(Signed) CHARLES M. STEDMAN.

ENDOWMENT FOR ELON

The friends of Elon College have undertaken to raise $125,000 as an endowment fund for the college. Already the plans have been laid, and there is much enthusiasm among the workers and it is confidently believed that the fund will be raised. This campaign has been authorized by the Southern Christian Convention, and the entire Church is behind the movement.

This sum will be raised because the people of the Christian Church have a way of making a success of their undertakings, as is evidenced by the oversubscription of the big missionary fund last year.

We feel that Burlington and Alamance county should have an especial interest in this work. The college is located in our county and has been a wonderful influence for good. It is the only college within our county, and we feel a just pride in the work being done. It is almost a local institution, and we believe there is no citizen who does not feel a personal interest in its success and future.

We have been familiar with the work done by this college for 20 years. We have watched its wonderful growth during these years with a great deal of interest and have been gratified to see it grow bigger and better as the years have gone by. Its influence has been felt here, and it has been a blessing to our community.

We feel that in raising this endowment fund Burlington and Alamance county, outside of the Christian Church, should have a part and we believe that the friends of the college would appreciate very much a manifestation of our interest in a practical manner and no donation could be given to a more worthy or useful cause.

Exerting as this great institution does, a wonderful influence for good, the college has given to our community a higher standard, an elevating influence that has been felt, and in order to make it stronger and more useful this endowment should not only be raised but our local people should determine to supplement this endowment by a voluntary fund that would show our appreciation of this institution.

We hope that plans will be undertaken to the end that Burlington and our county will demonstrate how kindly we feel toward this college, and how much we appreciate its work.—*Editorial Burlington News.*

DOVER AND ELON SET THE PACE

The drive for the $125,000 Standardization Fund began at Jerusalem, that is, at Elon on February 16. It is right that it should have begun there. Scripturally that was proper. The quota at Elon was $3,750.

In the drive Jericho (which would have been Burlington or Greensboro) was temporarily skipped and the next point visited was "the uttermost parts of the earth," that is, the most outlying territory of the Convention, the People's Church of Dover, Del. How the heart rejoices to tell the story of the generous hearts and true there. The quota was $2,000. They went "over the top" with a shout and gave $4,200. Fine! Elon and Dover have set the pace for the Brotherhood. The fine words of endorsement in THE SUN had forecasted the unity of the brethren for the success of the drive, and these two vastly different congregations have amply justified every hope. God bless Elon and Dover, our pace setters, and all the other churches that shall shortly "follow in their trail."

W. A. HARPER.

THE CHRISTIAN ORPHANAGE

SUPERINTENDENT'S LETTER

Dear Friends:—Sometime ago the Lowell church, (Ala.) mailed me a check for $11.66 for its Thanksgiving offering, and by an oversight it was credited to Lanett, Ala. I am sorry this error occurred but however careful errors will sometimes be made. I am always glad to make any correction when my attention is called to it.

Our financial report this week is the smallest it has been for a long time. I truly hope that as soon as the "Flu" blows over and our Sunday schools all get in action again that our income will soon reach the point where we can feel safe in taking the little children who are crying to us for help.

I received a very encouraging letter from Sister Mary F. Roberson, Oblong, Ill., this week with check - for $10.00 to help give the little babies a home. We have two of the sweetest little girls here now—one has been with us for several weeks—the other just came and if you could hear them sing "Jesus Love Me," it would touch the tenderest places in your heart and you could not help but just open your purse and give that the others who are not much younger and perhaps just as sweet might have a place too that they could call home. Jesus loves them too and has blessed you bountifully for the past few years that you might divide and help

give these little ones a home. Will you hear their cry?

I want all the little cousins to write me a letter for the month of March and I am going to send to each one, who writes a picture of one of our little girls who sings "Jesus Loves Me."

Your Superintendent will be glad to visit any church from now on through the spring and summer. If you would like for him to visit your church please write and name the date you want him to come, and if he has no previous engagement, he will be glad to pay you a visit and tell you something of our Orphanage work. We think it best for you to name the time as you know the conditions and the time best to come for your church. Will be glad to hear from you.

I will thank each Sunday school secretary to mail me the name and address of the superintendent and secretary of your school so I may make my list complete for this year. See to this right away.

CHAS. D. JOHNSTON, *Supt.*

REPORT FOR MARCH 12, 1919

Amount brought forward, $1,215.33.

Children's Offerings

Irene Patton, High Point, N. C., 10 cents; Martha, Robert and Havanah Mitchell, $1.00; Total, $1.10.

Sunday School Monthly Offerings
(Georgia and Alabama Conference)

North Highland, Ga., $2.00.

(Eastern Virginia Conference)

Mt. Carmel, $2.10; Mt. Carmel, $1.00; Union (Southampton), $3.50; First Christian Norfolk, $5.15.

(North Carolina Conference)

Elon College, $5.00; Ebenezer, $3.26; Morrisville, $2.00; Damascus, Orange Co., $1.30; Union, (Va.), $2.00; Total, $27.40.

Special Offerings

Mrs. Effie Wicker, $2.00; American Christian Convention office, $8.38; Mrs. Mary F. Roberson, Oblong, Ill., $10.00; Total, $20.38.

Total for the week, $48.88; Grand total, $1,264.21.

CHILDREN'S LETTERS

Dear Uncle Charley:—Here comes a little girl who wants to join the band of cousins and help the little orphans. I am sorry for them. My Sunday school teacher, Mrs. Glass, has been telling us about them. I hope they are well and happy. Enclosed please find my dime for February. With lots of love to all.— *Irene Patton.*

We are real glad to have you join our band of cousins and give you a warm welcome. It is real good of your teacher (Mrs. Glass) to tell you about the little orphans. If all our Sunday school teachers would feel the same interest in our work here and hold the orphan cause before their Sunday schools it would not be long before we could take the babies who are pleading for a home here.—*"Uncle Charley."*

Mrs. W. P. Betts—I have no home church in Batesburg so I have put my letter in the Methodist church while I stay here, but I still want THE CHRISTIAN SUN.

See special Bible offer on page 13.

PROCEEDINGS

OF THE

Union of The North Carolina and Virginia, The Eastern North Carolina, and The Western North Carolina Conferences

Into

The North Carolina Christian Conference

HISTORICAL DATA

The North Carolina and Virginia Christian Conference, in 92nd annual session at Haw River, N. C., on November 22, 1917, passed the following enabling resolution, looking to the union of the Western and Eastern North Carolina Christian Conferences with itself into one body of Christians in the State of North Carolina:

"That it is the sense and desire of this Conference that, for the best interest of our cause and the Kingdom, there should be a consolidation of our Conference with the other two Christian Conferences of this State.

"That we memorialize the Southern Christian Convention at its next session to permit such consolidation, if desired by either or both of the other Conferences.

"That we petition the other two Conferences to unite with us in this movement for a consolidation.

"That the Conference elect three Commissioners to take this matter under advisement and present the same to the next session of the Southern Christian Convention, of the Eastern North Carolina, and of the Western North Carolina Christian Conferences."

The Commissioners elected were P. H. Fleming, J. O. Atkinson, and W. A. Harper.

On May 3, 1918, the Southern Christian Convention in its 23rd session at Franklin, Va., adopted the following resolution:

TO THE SOUTHERN CHRISTIAN CONVENTION:

"Brethren:—We, the undersigned Commissioners elected by the North Carolina and Virginia Christian Conference at its last session to memorialize the Southern Christian Convention now in session, and the other two Conferences in North Carolina regarding the formation of one Christian Conference in North Carolina out of the present three, or out of any two of them, do hereby petition the honorable body now assembled, permission to undertake the work; and that permission be granted the said Conferences—the North Carolina and Virginia, the Eastern North Carolina and the Western North Carolina—to unite; provided said Conferences, or any two of said Conferences shall vote to do so.

"We further ask that the aforesaid Commissioners be authorized and empowered by this Convention to take the matter of the union up with the three Conferences, and effect a union of the three, or any two of the three that shall vote to unite."

(Signed)
P. H. FLEMING,
W. A. HARPER,
J. O. ATKINSON,
Commissioners.

It was the intention of these Commissioners to present the union proposition to the Eastern and Western Conferences in their November 1918 sessions, and to report the results to the 1918 session of the North Carolina and Virginia Conference, meeting after them. But the epidemic of Spanish Influenza necessitated the postponement of these Conferences, and the North Carolina and Virginia Conference met before they did. Under the circumstances, the Commissioners submitted the following report, which was adopted and they were continued to pursue the matter further:

"We, your committee to memorialize the Eastern and Western North Carolina Christian Conferences on the question of Christian Union, report that these bodies have not met, and so we cannot now report.

"We request that this matter lie open and that this committee or another be constituted to make further report at our next session.

"We should further add that the Southern Christian Convention gave its consent to effecting the union of these three Conferences, should they desire it."

P. H. FLEMING,
W. A. HARPER,
J. O. ATKINSON,
Committee.

The Western North Carolina Conference met at Shiloh Church, Randolph County, in its 52nd annual session on November 26-28, 1918, and on November 27 passed the following order, upon recommendation of a special committee, electing Rev. T. E. White, Rev. L. I. Cox, and Dr. E. L. Moffitt as Commissioners:

"Whereas, the Southern Christian Convention in its last biennial session gave its consent to the union of the Western North Carolina, Eastern North Carolina and North Carolina and Virginia Conferences to unite into one Conference, we, your committee of the Western North Carolina Christian Conference, therefore recommend:

"That we unite with the other two forming one Conference to be known as the North Carolina Christian Conference, including all the churches in the above Conferences."

T. E. WHITE,
J. W. PATTON,
L. I. COX,
E. L. MOFFITT,
W. H. WRENN,
Committee.

The Eastern North Carolina Conference met in 25th annual session at Chapel Hill, N. C., December 4-6, and on December 4 voted to accept "the invitation of the other two Conferences to enter into the union." Dr. W. C. Wicker, Hon. K. B. Johnson, and Rev. A. T. Banks "were appointed as Commissioners to represent this Conference in organizing the new North Carolina Christian Conference," so runs the record of its printed proceedings.

PRELIMINARY COMMISSIONERS' MEETING

On December 26, 1918, the nine Commissioners named above met at Elon College and decided to apply for a charter. Hon. J. Dolph Long was present as attorney and gave valuable advice to the Commissioners. Drs. J. W. Wellons and N. G. Newman were also present as visiting brethren.

The following were appointed a special Committee to draft the charter and present it for ratification on January 23, 1919: Dr. J. O. Atkinson, Rev. L. I. Cox, and Dr. W. C. Wicker, with J. Dolph Long as attorney.

The Commissioners of the North Carolina and Virginia Conference gave notice that they would seek the approval of their Executive Committee before signing the charter.

NORTH CAROLINA AND VIRGINIA CONFERENCE EXECUTIVE COMMITTEE APPROVAL

On December 28, 1918, the Executive Committee of the North Carolina and Virginia Conference met in Graham, N. C., with a full attendance consisting of P. H. Fleming, N. G. Newman, and J. W. Holt, At this meeting permission was granted the Commissioners appointed at the Haw River and Reidsville sessions to sign the charter, merging this Conference and the Eastern and Western Conferences into the North Carolina Christian Conference. The official report follows:

"Notice is hereby given that on December 28, 1918, with all members present, the Executive Committee of the North Carolina and Virginia Christian Conference met in Graham, N. C., and gave approval to the union of the three Christian Conferences in North Carolina, authorizing its Commissioners, P. H. Fleming, W. A. Harper, and J. O. Atkinson to take such legal steps as may be necessary to make this action effective. Rev. J. W. Holt voted in the negative and desired it to be so recorded."

—(Signed).
                    N. G. NEWMAN,
          Sec. N. C. and Va. Christian
          Conference Executive Committee.

THE CHARTER GRANTED

Pursuant to adjournment, the nine Commissioners met at Elon College on January 23, 1919, and adopted the following charter:

No. 16726

CERTIFICATE OF INCORPORATION
OF
THE NORTH CAROLINA CHRISTIAN CONFERENCE, INC.

This is to certify, That, we, the undersigned, do hereby associate ourselves into a non-stock corporation under and by virtue of the laws of the State of North Carolina, as contained in Chapter 21 of the Revisal of 1905, entitled "Corporations," and the several amendments thereto, and to that end, do hereby set forth:

1. The name of this corporation is The North Carolina Christian Conference, Inc.

2. The location of the principal office of the corporation in this State is in the town of Elon College, County of Alamance.

3. The objects for which this corporation is formed are as follows:

(a) To do religious, benevolent, charitable and missionary work and promote the cause of righteousness both at home and abroad as opportunity may afford and as the corporate body herein formed may direct from time to time.

(b) The North Carolina Christian Conference, Inc., is to be the successor to the Eastern North Carolina Christian Conference, the Western North Carolina Christian Conference, and the North Carolina and Virginia Christian Conference, as per vote of these several bodies in their regular annual sessions, the two first mentioned in 1918, the last mentioned in 1917, and confirmed by vote of its executive committee and also by vote of the Southern Christian Convention in regular biennial session in May, 1918, and by these several acts all property, real and personal, heretofore owned and held by these corporations inheres in the North Carolina Christian Conference, Inc.

(c) To make such by-laws, rules and regulations and

elect such officers, representatives and agents as it may deem proper for the execution of whatever plans and purposes that it may adopt for the proper execution of its plans, and purposes not inconsistent with the Constitution and laws of North Carolina, the United States, its territories and dependencies.

And in order properly to prosecute the objects and purposes above set forth, the corporation shall have full power and authority to purchase, lease and otherwise acquire, hold, mortgage, convey and otherwise dispose of all kinds of property, both real and personal, both in this State and in all other States, territories and dependencies of the United States, and generally to perform all acts which may be deemed necessary for the proper and successful prosecution of the objects and purposes for which the corporation is created.

4. The corporation is to have no capital stock.

5. The names and postoffice addresses of the incorporators are as follows:

Name	Postoffice Address
J. O. Atkinson	Elon College, N. C.
A. T. Banks	Ramseur, N. C.
L. I. Cox	Elon College, N. C.
P. H. Fleming	Burlington, N. C.
W. A. Harper	Elon College, N. C.
K. B. Johnson	Kennebec, N. C.
E. L. Moffitt	Ashboro, N. C.
T. E. White	Sanford, N. C.
W. C. Wicker	Elon College, N. C.

6. The period of existence of this corporation is limited to 99 years.

7. Members may be admitted after organization upon the following terms: by a majority vote of the body.

In Testimony Whereof, We have hereunto set our hands and affixed our seals, this the 23rd day of January, A. D. 1919.

          J. O. ATKINSON,   (Seal)
          A. T. BANKS,   (Seal)
          L. I. COX,   (Seal)
          P. H. FLEMING   (Seal)
          W. A. HARPER   (Seal)
          K. B. JOHNSON   (Seal)
          E. L. MOFFITT   (Seal)
          T. E. WHITE   (Seal)
          W. C. WICKER   (Seal)

Signed, sealed and delivered in
the presence of Marion C. Jackson, Witness.

STATE OF NORTH CAROLINA
                                        SS.
COUNTY OF ALAMANCE.

This is to certify that on this 23rd day of January, A. D. 1919, before me, a Notary Public, personally appeared J. O. Atkinson, A. T. Banks, L. I. Cox, P. H. Fleming, W. A. Harper, K. B. Johnson, E. L. Moffitt, T. E. White and W. C. Wicker, who, I am satisfied, are the persons named in and who executed the foregoing certificate of incorporation of The North Carolina Christian Conference, Inc., and I having first made known to them the contents thereof, they did each acknowledge that they signed, sealed and delivered the same as their voluntary act and deed, for the uses and purposes therein expressed.

In testimony whereof, I have hereunto set my hand and affixed my official seal, this the 23rd day of January, A. D. 1919.
                    MARION C. JACKSON, Notary Public.
My commission expires February 18th, 1920.
(NOTARIAL SEAL)

          Filed Jan. 27, 1919.
          J. Bryan Grimes,
          Secretary of State.

After the adoption of the charter the Commissioners authorized W. A. Harper to apply for the certificate of incorporation and to call a meeting on February 14, 1919, for purposes of organization and planning the work of the new Conference.

PROCEEDINGS OF THE NORTH CAROLINA CHRISTIAN CONFERENCE

Elon College, N. C.
February 14, 1919.

The North Carolina Christian Conference, Inc., was duly chartered by the State of North Carolina on January 27, 1919 and held its initial session here today to organize and plan the work for the coming year.

Prayer by Rev. L. I. Cox.

The following officers were elected:

PRESIDENT—T. E. White.
VICE-PRESIDENT—W. C. Wicker.
SECRETARY—W. A. Harper.
TREASURER—K. B. Johnson.
EXECUTIVE SECRETARY—L. I. Cox.

On motion the following ministers were elected to membership in the Conference:

H. A. Albright, J. F. Apple, J. S. Carden, W. G. Clements, J. O. Cox, R. P. Crumpler, T. B. Dawson, H. J. Fleming, J. E. Franks, W. B. Fuller, T. J. Green, G. J. Green, H. S. Hardcastle, J. W. Harrell, W. N. Hayes, W. T. Herndon, J. W. Holt, A. F. Iseley, J. Lee Johnson, P. T. Klapp, J. Vincent Knight, J. W. Knight, F. C. Lester, W. S. Long, D. A. Long, C. E. Newman, J. U. Newman, N. G. Newman, J. W. Patton, J. W. Pinnix, C. B. Riddle, Herbert Scholtz, H. S. Smith, J. C. Stuart, J. G. Truitt, G. R. Underwood, W. L. Wells, J. D. Wicker, R. L. Williamson, J. W. Wellons, and L. L. Wyrick.

On motion the following churches were elected to membership in the Conference:

Amelia, Antioch (W), Antioch, (C), Antioch (R), Apple's Chapel, Asheboro, Auburn, Belew Creek, Bennett, Berea, Bethel (C), Bethel (Cas), Bethlehem (A), Bethlehem (W), Beulah, Big Oak, Brown's Chapel, Burlington, Catawba Springs, Center Grove, Chapel Hill, Christian Chapel, Christian Light, Christian Union, Concord, Damascus, Danville, (Va.); Durham, Ebenezer, Elon College, Ether, Franklinton, Fuller's, Good Hope, Goshen Chapel, Grace's Chapel, Graham, Greensboro First Church, Greensboro Palm Street, Hank's Chapel, Happy Home, Haw River, Hayes' Chapel, Hebron, Henderson, High Point, Hines' Chapel, Howard's Chapel, Ingram, (Va.), Kallam Grove, Keyser, Lebanon, Lee's Chapel, Liberty (R), Liberty (V), Liberty, (Va.), Long's Chapel, Martha's Chapel, Mebane, Monticello, Moore Union, Morrisville, Mt. Auburn, Mt. Bethel, Mt. Carmel, Mt. Gilead, Mt. Hermon, Mt. Pleasant, Mt. Zion, Needham's Grove, New Center, New Elam, New Hill, New Hope (F), New Hope (R), New Lebanon, New Providence, Oak Level, O'Kelley's Chapel, Parks Cross Roads, Patterson's Grove, Piney Plains, Pleasant Cross, Pleasant Grove, (NC), Pleasant Grove, (Va), Pleasant Hill (J), Pleasant Hill (A), Pleasant Ridge (R), Pleasant Ridge (G), Pleasant Union (H), Pleasant Union (R), Plymouth, Pope's Chapel, Poplar Branch, Raleigh, Ramseur, Reidsville, Salem Chapel, Sanford, Seagrove, Shady Grove, Shallow Ford, Shallow Well, Shiloh, Six Forks, Smithwood, Spoon's Chapel, Turner's Chapel, Union (N. C.), Union (Va.), Union Grove, Wake Chapel, Wentworth, Youngsville, and Zion.

On motion the Conference voted to assume responsibility for all contracts, appropriations, and obligations made by the three Conferences merged into itself, on

condition that the treasurers of the former Conferences and Boards turn their funds in hand, notes, and deeds over to the proper officers of the North Carolina Christian Conference.

On motion the amended charter of the Home Mission Board of the North Carolina and Virginia Christian Conference was accepted to read as follows:

HOME MISSION BOARD CHARTER

The General Assembly of North Carolina do enact:

Section 1. That W. P. Lawrence, P. T. Klapp, W. A. Harper, S. A. Caveness and D. L. Boone, together with such others as may become members of the board, and their successors in office, are hereby constituted and declared a body politic and corporate under the name and style of the Home Mission Board of the North Carolina Christian Conference, and by that name shall have perpetual succession; may sue and be sued, plead and be impleaded, contract and be contracted with, may acquire by purchase, donation, devise or otherwise, property, real, personal and mixed, for the purpose of carrying out its objects, which are the promotion of Home Mission work within the bounds of said conference; and may do any and all other necessary acts and things in the promotion of said objects, including the sale and disposition of any property it may acquire.

Section 2. That the officers of said corporation shall be a president, vice-president, secretary and treasurer, whose duties shall be such as may be prescribed by said board and the said conference.

Section 3. That the said association shall have power to make its own by-laws, rules and regulations for its government, subject to the Constitution and laws of this state, and such rules and regulations as may be made by said conference of which said board is a part.

Section 4. That the successors in office of the persons named above shall be chosen in the manner provided by said North Carolina Christian Conference, and when so chosen, and have accepted, such successors shall be members of this corporation instead of the persons whom they succeed.

Section 5. That the principal place of business, or office, of said corporation shall be at Elon College, Alamance county, North Carolina, but its meetings may be be held at any place designated by the board or its proper officers, and at such meetings it may transact such business as shall be prescribed by the by-laws.

Section 6. That all property owned by said corporation, shall be exempt from taxation so long as such property or the income therefrom shall be used for the promotion of the home mission work of said conference.

Section 7. That this act shall be in force from and after its ratification.

On motion all money to the credit of the Home Mission funds or Boards of the former Conferences was ordered turned over to the treasurer of the Home Mission Board.

The Secretary was ordered to secure the records of the former conferences and to preserve them safely, to provide a record book for the proceedings of the Conference, to have a seal made, and do such other things as are necessary for the proper conduct of his office, and to draw vouchers on the treasurer in payment of the same.

The fee of four dollars for incorporating the Conference was ordered paid.

On motion the churches elected to membership in this

Conference will be apportioned as printed in the *Christian Annual* for 1919.

On motion, the President and Secretary were authorized to take such steps as may be necessary to secure the title to all property of the several Conferences entering this Conference.

On motion, the officers of the Sunday School and Christian Endeavor Convention of the Eastern North Carolina Conference are hereby elected the officers of said Convention of The North Carolina Christian Conference, since they have agreed to this plan. The first session of the said Convention will be held at Shallow Well Church July 15-17, 1919.

On motion, the minutes of the Union Conference of the Women's Home and Foreign Mission Boards were ordered printed in the proceedings of the Conference, as requested by the women.

It was voted to accept the invitation of the Burlington Church to meet with them in the first session. The date of the meeting was set for November 12-15, 1919.

The following committees and boards were elected to serve until the November session 1919 or until their successors are elected or appointed:

STANDING COMMITTEES AND BOARDS

Executive

T. E. White, P. H. Fleming, L. I. Cox, G. J. Green, G. R. Underwood, N. G. Newman, J. W. Holt, J. E. Franks, and J. D. Wicker.

Education

W. C. Wicker, J. O. Atkinson, D. A. Long, J. W. Wellons, P. T. Klapp, N. G. Newman, J. W. Harrell, J. W. Patton, R. L. Williamson, J. Lee Johnson.

Sunday School

C. H. Stephenson, F. M. Wright, C. B. Riddle, D. A. Long, J. A. Kimball, J. H. Moring, A. M. Long, J. F. Apple, J. W. Knight.

Christian Endeavor

J. V. Knight, J. G. Truitt, R. C. Boyd, C. B. Riddle, Mrs. A. T. Banks, Miss Lessie Pugh, Mrs. J. B. Phipps.

Moral Reform

C. E. Newman, Mrs. W. H. Hudson, Mrs. J. Milton Banks, Mrs. H. E. Pearce, H. A. Albright, T. J. Green, Hiram Freeman, J. S. Carden, F. C. Lester.

Superannuation

K. B. Johnson, D. S. Farmer, E. L. Moffitt.

Apportionments

L. I. Cox, D. S. Farmer, K. B. Johnson, W. C. Wicker, J. Byrd Ellington, W. A. Harper, L. M. Clymer.

Woman's Board (Elected)

Mrs W. H. Carroll, Mrs. A. T. Banks, Mrs. W. A. Harper, Mrs. W. R. Sellars, Mrs. M. F. Cook, Miss Bessie Holt, Mrs. J. G. Anthony, Mrs. J. W. Patton.

Religious Literature

C. B. Riddle, W. L. Wells, G. T. Whitaker, H. J. Fleming, N. F. Brannock, E. L. Moffitt, A. T. Banks, E. M. Newman.

Foreign Missions

J. W. Harrell, J. Byrd Ellington, P. T. Klapp, H. A. Albright, W. S. Long, J. W. Holt, J. C. McAdams, S. M. Rowland, R. C. Underwood, J. O. Atkinson.

Tabulation

L. L. Wyrick, W. E. Cook, R. A. Truitt, W. C. Wicker, R. C. Boyd.

Program

T. E. White, P. H. Fleming, G. J. Green.

Home Missions (Elected)

T. E. White, President ex-officio, W. P. Lawrence, W. A. Harper, Secretary-Treasurer, K. B. Johnson, W. G. Clements, E. L. Moffitt, G. R. Underwood, J. O. Atkinson.

Historian

W. G. Clements.

The Secretary was ordered to print 1,000 copies of the minutes and circulate them in the Conference free of cost, paying for the same out of the Conference Fund.

The Treasurer was authorized to purchase a suitable book and other necessary articles for the proper conduct of his office.

The Secretary was ordered to notify the treasurers of the three former Conferences that it is their duty now to honor drafts in favor of K. B. Johnson, Treasurer, on their respective treasuries for all funds now in hand and to order them also to turn over to said K. B. Johnson, Treasurer, all notes, deeds, and other evidences of property in their possession belonging to said Conferences.

Dr. W. C. Wicker and Rev. L. I. Cox were constituted an Auditing Committee to audit the funds coming in from the various conferences and to submit their findings to the Secretary for inclusion in the printed record.

AUDITORS' REPORT

From the Western North Carolina Conference

E. L. Moffitt, Teasurer

Home Missions	$ 59.85
Ministerial Education	53.60
Superannuated Fund	231.89
Special Home and Foreign Missions	1.56
Savings Account	201.82
Total	**$548.32**
Less overdraft Conference Fund	45.29
Net balance	**$503.03**

From the Eastern North Carolina Conference

W. J. Ballentine, Treasurer

Home Missions	$219.48
Convention Missions	.50
Foreign Missions	4.02
Ministerial Education	222.12
Superannuated Fund	6.06
Conference Fund	16.33
Total	**$468.51**
Less Convention Fund overdraft	.21
Less Elon College Fund overdraft	3.92
	4.13
Net balance	**$464.38**

From the North Carolina and Virginia Conference

D. S. Farmer, Treasurer

Home Missions	$ 11.00
Ministerial Education	201.50
Superannuated Fund	125.24
Elon College Fund	.67
Convention Fund	.49

Convention Home Missions 1.14
Home Mission Board 10.72

                                    —————
                    Total $350.76
Less overdraft Conference Fund 72.10
                                    —————
                    Net balance...... $278.66

Notes

The treasurers also turned over notes as follows:
Western North Carolina Conference................ $ 691.25
Eastern North Carolina Conference 1,162.80
North Carolina and Virginia Conference............. 1,959.70
                                    —————
                    Total,......... $3,813.75

Deeds

They also turned over deeds in the following numbers:
Western North Carolina Conference 6
Eastern North Carolina Conference 1
North Carolina and Virginia Conference................. 9

Home Mission Board Funds

The Secretary-Treasurer of the Home Mission Board reported funds on hand in the Elon Banking and Trust Company amounting to $1,195.63 according to the cashier's statement under date of February 28, 1919, with two checks outstanding against the account amounting to $57.50. These funds came from The Home Mission Board of The North Carolina and Virginia Christian Conference.

We, the incorporators of The North Carolina Christian Conference, have read and signed the above records and send them forth as our official acts as Commissioners of our respective Conferences now merged into The North Carolina Christian Conference, Inc.

J. O. ATKINSON
A. T. BANKS
L. I. COX
P. H. FLEMING
W. A. HARPER
K. B. JOHNSON
E. L. MOFFITT
T. E. WHITE
W. C. WICKER

Incorporators
of
The North Carolina
Christian Conference

The minutes were read and approved.
Dismissed with prayer by Rev. P. H. Fleming.

T. E. WHITE, *President.*
W. A. HARPER, *Secretary.*

MISSIONARY

THE GOOD WOMEN GO FORWARD

The Field Secretary is in possession of the following which explains itself, and will carry joy and inspiration to many hearts:

Dr. J. O. Atkinson,
  Sec. Mission Board S. C. C.,
    Elon College, N. C.

Dear Sir and Bro.:

The Woman's Board of the Eastern Virginia Conference in annual session here today decided that the time has come when the women of this Conference should support a missionary and to this end we voted to raise the sum of $1,200.00 the present year for the first year's salary of the missionary. It was decided to defer till our annual meeting in October the naming of the missionary and the field. The Board does this in addition to its other work, and thus makes a beginning which it is our hope and expectation to continue and further develop in the coming years.

Sincerely yours,
Mrs. C. H. ROWLAND, *Chairman.*
Mrs. I. W. JOHNSON, *Secretary.*

Again and again a thousand thanks to the good women for their great work.

J. O. ATKINSON.

HIS MISSION MONEY WILL BE PAID

Leaving off names and places I have this letter from a good brother: "I regret very much that I did not send you my pledge of $20.00 last year on my pledge of $100.00 for missions. It seemed that my obligations were such that I could not get the amount. I am trying a new plan which I know will work all right. I began the first of the year to tithe my income, and in this way I feel sure I will have a plenty to meet all my church obligations and charitable causes, also enough for my last year's pledge and this year's pledge. You will be hearing from me in a month or two with check covering my pledge."

That brother's pledge will be paid. I never fear or feel uneasy for the man in meeting his church obligations if he tithes. I would give one hundred cents on the dollar for all our mission pledges, if all who gave them would accept and strictly follow the law of the tithe. It pays. J. O. ATKINSON.

MISSIONS A CHARITY OR A DEBT—WHICH?

By R. H. Glover

"*I am debter........So, as much as in me is, I am ready to preach the gospel to you.*" (Rom. 1:15, 16).

In these forcible words the great Apostle expresses his own personal missionary conviction and resolve. He confesses himself the heathen's *debtor*. He *owes* them the gospel. Even though he has already done more than any dozen other men of his time, he lays no claim to merit, nor considers that he is conferring any favor on the Romans in making an added effort to take them the gospel. It is his duty, his *debt*, and he is only seeking as an honest man to discharge it.

Now if it was for Paul a debt, can it be something less for the rest of us? Yet how few appear to treat it so! The majority of professing Christians regard missions with utter indifference. They wonder by what strange freak of nature certain pious people choose to go and live among yellow or black folk rather than stay at home. And it is to be feared that very many even of those who profess a degree of interest in this work conceive of it merely as charity.

Is there any essential difference between regarding missions as a *charity* and as a *debt?* Let us see. Here comes a ragged, unkempt creature, holding out his cap to me. I recognize him as a beggar. So I pull out a coin—a nickel, a dime, *anything*—and throw it to him. That is CHARITY. It is cheap; it is easy; it feels no responsibility; it is purely a matter of personal choice. But now another man steps up and hands me a paper. I open it and find it a bill of debt, perhaps for $100. Do I presume to deal with this man as I did with the first, by flinging him the first coin that comes handy? Not by a good deal. This is a very different matter, for it is a DEBT. I am bound to face it seriously, and do all in my power, even giving my last dollar, to wipe it out.

Applying now this illustration to missions, what have we?

Missions viewed as a Charity: Secondary, optional, little concern or prayer or effort, spasmodic, insignificant giving.

Missions viewed as a Debt: Primary, obligatory, earnest concern and prayer and effort, systematic, sacrificing giving.

Charity *foots* the list of your expenditure and claims your *spare* cash. Debt heads the list, if you are honest, and cuts out everything non-essential, *until it is fully met.* You give a little of the *interest* on your money to charity, but you dip deep down into your *principal* and give *all*, if need be, to pay your debts.

I visited a church and met a number of its leading members, all earning liberal salaries. They professed great interest in missions. On inquiry I found that the church was giving $25 a year to the cause. I went on to a Convention, and a colored washerwoman brought up her yearly missionary offering of $200. What made the difference between these two standards of giving? Simply the viewpoint. The church treated missions as a *charity*, the woman as a *debt*, and both gave accordingly. To them it was one among a score of equally important (or *unimportant!*) things; to her it was the *one supreme thing.* They *played* at missions as a sort of diversion; she *worked* at missions as the business of her life.

Christian reader, in which light have you regarded this work—as expressed, by your prayers, your gifts, your efforts to go? Has your conscience been convicted of a debt you owe the heathen, or have only your emotions been stirred at times with a weak feeling of pity for them?

Oh, let me repeat it—we OWE the heathen the gospel; we are their DEBTORS:

(1) *Out of gratitude for our own salvation,* realizing that only "by the grace of God I am what I am."

(2) *Out of loyalty to Christ,* since He commanded, "Go ye into all the world and preach the gospel to every creature."

(3) *Out of compassion* for heathen suffering and sorrow.

(4) *Out of the realization that in the gospel we have the only hope for their souls' eternal welfare.*

May God convict His children of their debts, and make them *ready, as much as in them is* to meet them! Then, at last, will there be no lack of missionaries to go, or intercessors to pray, or money to send.

Sunday School and Christian Endeavor

**SUNDAY SCHOOL TOPIC FOR SUN-
DAY, MARCH 16, 1919**

Cities of Refuge

Scripture Text: Joshua, Chapter 20.

Golden Text: ''Blessed are the merciful; for they shall obtain mercy.'' Matt.
5:7.

Time, B. C. 1444.

Place: Shiloh; center of Hebrew worship at this time and during the days
of the Judges.

For comment and explanation, see Bible
Class Quarterlies, or Officers and Teachers
Journal, C. P. A., Dayton, Ohio.

**CHRISTIAN ENDEAVOR TOPIC FOR
SUNDAY, MARCH 16, 1919**

Envy and Covetousness

Scripture Text: Luke 12:13-21.

For explanation and comment, see
Christian Endeavor World, Boston, Mass.

**TEACHING TITHING IN THE SUN-
DAY SCHOOL**

I met a very successful professional
and business man not long since who
attributed much of his success, both
in his spiritual development, and in
his financial prosperity, to the fact
that firmly believed in tithing and
scrupulously practiced it. And he
became convinced that tithing was
wise and biblical during his youthful
days in the Sunday school.

If teachers could convince their
pupils in the Sunday school that tithing was the divine law of giving, and
was the only wise law of business and
religious book-keeping, much indeed
would be accomplished both for the
business of the future, and for financing the Kingdom.

J. O. ATKINSON.

THE EXPERIENCE OF A TITHER

The Missionary Review of the
World gives this interesting item
from a tither's experience and accounts: ''I went into a mercantile
business, known as the 'five and ten
cent business,' in Browie, Texas, in
1894, and in January following my
pastor and I agreed to tithe for one
year. Before the year was out I said,
'This suits me, and I will tithe, not
for one year only, but for life.' The
business prospered from the start, although begun in a small way. Having only about $700 capital, doing a

strictly cash business, both in buying
and selling, of course our business
was limited. Yet the first year our
tenth was $100; the second year,
$154; third year, $360; fourth, $388;
fifth, $330; sixth, $662; seventh,
$556; eighth, $150; ninth, $556;
tenth, $1,040; eleventh, $650; twelfth,
$1,223; thirteenth, $1,221; fourteenth, $1,143; fifteenth, $2,742. I
have tried the Lord in this business
way, and I would no more quit tithing than I would quit providing for
my family.''

J. O. ATKINSON.

**A MESSAGE FOR EVERY SUNDAY
SCHOOL OF THE CHRISTIAN
CHURCH IN THE STATE.**

It is now ten weeks since I published through THE SUN to the Sunday schools and Christian Endeavor
Societies of the State of North Carolina the plans and purposes of the
newly elected Board of Religious
Education. As Secretary-Treasurer
of this organization I appealed to the
Christian workers of the North Carolina Conference not only to *send in
honor roll contributions*, as we are
now working on borrowed money, but
to offer suggestions as to how we may
most effectively do the thing this
Board has set out to do. Now there
are ninety-four schools in the North
Carolina Conference that have neither
sent a penny or a word of encouragement. It is evident that these schools
either have not seen the appeal or
have neglected to answer it, either of
which indicates that many of our
schools are not awake to their full
possibilities for progress and growth.
Please take this message to heart.
It is your responsibility, be you a
teacher, officer, or member, and only
in so far as you co-operate with the
Board can its work serve a good purpose, and better the Christian statues
of the State. When you, readers of
THE SUN, and workers everywhere
feel that you owe us not only interest
but support. Read this to your
school; raise a contribution for this
work, but if this is impossible write
me how you feel regarding the matter and this will be a great moral
help. With all the schools and societies pulling together we can look for

the greatest Sunday School and
Christian Endeavor Convention this
summer that this part of the country
has ever seen.

Yours for immediate service,

C. H. STEPHENSON,

Secretary-Treasurer.

Raleigh, N. C.

MARRIAGES

BEALE-WILLS

A pretty marriage was solemnized
at the home of Mr. and Mrs. Lorenza
Bailey, Windsor, Va., Thursday
evening, February 27, 1919, when
Miss Mary Estelle Wills became the
bride of Mr. Raby R. Beale, both of
Franklin, Va. The bride was attended by her cousin, Mrs. W. D. Joyner;
the bridegroom, his brother, Mr. Le-
lian Beale. The ring bearer was little Virginia Bailey.

The ceremony was performed
promptly at 6:30 o'clock by the writer in the presence of a splendid company of relatives and intimate
friends. Mrs. B. B. Herrin played
the wedding march. Mrs. E. T. Cotten sang the solo, ''I Love You
Truly.''

The bride was attired in a reindeer
coat suit with hat and gloves that
harmonized and carried a beautiful
bouquet of roses. Immediately after
the wedding Mr. and Mrs. Beale left
on the Norfolk and Western on their
bridal tour.

E. T. COTTEN.

OBITUARIES

BROWN

Oscar Brown departed this life Febru
ary 20, 1919 at the age of forty-five year
and eleven days. He joined the churcl
at Union Grove when about fourtee
years old and has ever been a faithf
and active member, having been electe
deacon in 1912.

He leaves a wife, three children (girls
an aged mother, four sisters, three br
thers, besides many other relatives a
a host of friends who lament his passi

But the life he lived and testimonies he left behind are sufficient evidence that their loss is his eternal gain.

After service by the writer and high tributes to his memory by his pastor, Rev. L. W. Fogleman, and others, his body was laid to rest in the cemetery at Union Grove February 22, 1919. He will be much missed not only in the church but in the community.

May the Comforter ever abide in the hearts of his loved ones.

                              T. J. GREEN.

KEARNEY

January 19, Mrs. Dora Kearney, wife of Robert N. Kearney, was buried at Plank Chapel Methodist church. She leaves her husband and four children. Mrs. Kearney was a faithful wife and mother. She performed to the full limit of her strength the part that fell to her lot in life. She did not profess one thing and live another, but lived more than she professed. With her life, was not a theory but an activity. She proved her faith by her works.

                              G. J. GREEN.

WHITE

Mrs. Eckie White was born December 18, 1848. She died January 26, 1919. Her husband, Lonnie White, died in 1889. She was a faithful and devoted member of Oak Level Christian church. Though too feeble in recent years to attend church, she never failed to bear her part of its financial burdens without having to be asked to do so. She was buried in the family burying ground at her home near Franklinton. A a large attendance at the service was evidence of her standing in the community. She is survived by three sisters.

                              G. J. GREEN.

PREDDY

Many have already learned with sorrow of the death of Bob Preddy, who passed from this life on February 9. He lived all his life near the town of Franklinton and was laid to rest in the family burying ground near his home. He leaves three daughters and five sons, two of whom are soldiers in France, and doubtless have not yet learned of their loss. Mr. Preddy was a highly respected citizen and leaves an impression on the community. His companion is still living.

                              G. J. GREEN.

FERGUSON

Mrs. Frances Ferguson was buried at Pope's Chapel Christian church February 26. Paralysis was the cause of her death. She was sixty-nine years old and had been a member of Youngsville Christian church for a number of years. She leaves her husband aged ninety-four, one daughter and seven sons. To see this daughter and these seven sons at the grave of their mother made one feel that her life had not been idle; and the strength of character expressed in their faces impressed one with the thought that her labors had not been in vain. Surely she has gone to receive her "crown of life."

                              G. J. GREEN.

CHILD'S SELF-PRONOUNCING PICTORIAL BIBLE WITH HELPS

This Bible is bound in French Seal Leather, has round corners, silk head bands, gold titles, handsomely bound. Regular selling price..........$2.50
Price till March 31.......... 2.00
Call for Bible No. 215.
                    Address
C. B. RIDDLE, *Publishing Agent*
Burlington, North Carolina

THE TITHER

An interdenominational publication devoted to Tithing and Christian Stewardship.
                    Editors
            C. B. RIDDLE
            KARL LEHMANN
            BERT WILSON
            HUGH S. McCORD
            FRED G. THOMAS
8 pages; issued monthly; 50c the year
                    Address
THE TITHER   Burlington, N. C.

DR. J. H. BROOKS

DENTIST

Foster Building   Burlington, N. C.

BOOK NOTES

Story Books For The Children
We now have on hand a very fine story book for the children, "Redmond of the Seventh," by Mrs. Frank Lee. The book is handsomely bound, lettered in gold and contains 290 pages. The story is wholesome —a school story. The price is within the reach of all—75 cents postpaid, or two for $1.25.

Christian Hymnaries
We have the Christian Hymnary at 50 cents the copy. How many copies?
                    Address
C. B. RIDDLE, *Publishing Agent*,
Burlington, N. C.

WE CAN'T DO IT

(Courtesy Centenary M. E. Church)

Two Big Opportunities

For Elon College

Elon College needs our prayers.
——Shall we pray for it?

Elon College needs our money.
——Shall we give it?

Elon College needs our patronage.
——Shall we patronize her?

Elon College is our property.
——Shall we neglect it?

Elon College is a child of the Church.
——Shall we allow it to suffer?

Elon College CALLS you with a loud voice.
——Shall we hear her voice?

Knock the "t" out of the Can't

For The Kingdom's Work

We need more missionaries at home.

We need more missionaries abroad.

We need more men in the ministry.

We need more trained leaders.

We need more life recruits.

We need to help lay the burden on more of our
young men.

We need to help them answer the call and the
challenge.

We need to do this NOW.

——The
question is
with
you.

Will your answer knock the "t" out of the
Can't?

THE CHRISTIAN SUN

"IN ESSENTIALS UNITY, IN NON-ESSENTIALS LIBERTY, IN ALL THINGS CHARITY"

The Revival of Giving

GENERATIONS are chapters in the history of the world. Some chapters in a book are more interesting than others. An unselfish author welcomes a better treatise on the subject that he has just finished. An unselfish citizen desires the coming generations to be better than his generation. Our own shortcomings can best be mended by planting the right kind of seed to be harvested from in the next generation. The present generation is only beginning the revival of giving for the Kingdom's progress. To live in the next generation will be to see the full fruitage of present day endeavors. A few men are preaching and teaching the gospel of stewardship. Their kind is multiplying, but it will take more missionary work along that line to answer the Lord's Prayer "......thy will be done on earth as it is in heaven......,"

Volume LXXI	WEDNESDAY, MARCH 19, 1919	Number 12
BURLINGTON	· · ·	NORTH CAROLINA

THE CHRISTIAN SUN

Founded 1844 by Rev. Daniel W. Kerr

C. B. RIDDLE' - - - Editor

Entered at the Burlington, N. C. Post Office as second class matter.

Subscription Rates

One year .... $ 2.00
Six months 1.00
In Advance

Give both your old and new postoffice when asking that your address be changed.

The change of your label is your receipt for money. Written receipts sent upon request.

Marriage and obituary notices not exceeding 150 words printed free if received within 60 days from date of event, all over this at the rate of one-half cent a word.

Original poetry not accepted for publication.

Principles of the Christian Church

(1) The Lord Jesus Christ is the only Head of the Church.
(2) Christian is a sufficient name of the Church.
(3) The Holy Bible is a sufficient rule of faith and practice.
(4) Christian character is a sufficient test of fellowship, and of church membership.
(5) The right of private judgment and the liberty of conscience is a right and a privilege that should be accorded to, and exercised by all.

EDITORIAL

OBITUARIES

We doubt if many readers of THE CHRISTIAN SUN realize what a problem it is to handle the publicity of a Church paper that is doing five or six times more than it did ten years ago, and at the same time with the same number of pages. We are conscientiously doing our very best. In order to properly divide space, a little over a year ago we were compelled to limit marriage and obituary notices to one hundred and fifty words unless paid for at the rate of one-half cent per word. Few of our exchanges are so liberal as this. A number of Church papers have the limit to fifty words, some sixty, and very few go beyond one hundred. Exceedingly few Church papers make a charge so small as one-half cent per word.

So far as the Editor is concerned, personally, it does not differ but there has been entrusted to his care and keeping the interests of the official organ of the Church. We consider it a sacred and solemn trust. If we could not feel in the preparing of each issue of the paper that the work was not as sacred and lofty as standing behind the pulpit, we would today send our resignation to the Executive Committee of the Convention. More and more we are brought face to face between decisions for the larger good and interests of the Church and the things that might please a few. We know that it is impossible to please everybody. Christ could not do that, and though the devil wanted to, he failed.

Our policy as to obituaries is the best that we can do with the space we have. Our good friend, The Biblical Recorder, Raleigh, N. C., writes to the point on this subject, and so timely are Dr. Johnson's words that the reprinting of them seems to us to be in order:

The Recorder management is greatly embarrassed to know what to do about publishing obituaries. There are many deaths in the State because of the epidemic which has prevailed, and the number of obituaries is greater than ever before. Those who have glanced at the page of obituaries for the past several weeks have observed that the notices are longer than formerly. We have now on hand obituaries that have been on file several weeks because we have not had room to publish them. We make a charge of a cent a word for every word over sixty. This is scarcely sufficient to cover the bare cost of publication. We would be glad to give space without charge if we could afford to do so.

It will be remembered that the Baptist State Convention some years ago, decided to abolish the report on obituaries for the reason that the report had grown so long it occupied too much space in the minutes, and in lieu of the obituaries, a memorial service is held at each Convention, when tributes are paid to brethren who are known throughout the State.

This is a very delicate matter, and we have hesitated to say anything about it in these columns lest we might deepen the wounds in hearts that are already bleeding. But we do not believe these notices are read by any except those who are interested in the one who has been called away. If a brother has been engaged in work which has given him a wide acquaintance, many might read a notice of his death. This is no reflection upon the one who is known only locally. Some of the purest and best saints on earth are not known beyond their own communities. Their "witness is in heaven" and their "record is on high."

May we ask in all kindness, and in deepest sympathy with those who sorrow, that the writers of obituaries will make their notices as short as possible. When the main facts can be stated in sixty words we shall greatly appreciate it.

A NEW YEAR FOR A NEW WORLD

For The Easter Week of Prayer, April 13-20, 1919

To the Churches of Christ in America and to all people throughout the Nation:

We live in a new world. Old things pass, better things appear and the nations seek light and larger growth. The team-work of the Nations for the war was superb and Christians now face open doors unsurpassed for number and worth. Compelling desires to be and to do are challenged by plans and purposes more daring than men and women ever before matured. God leads and His will must be done.

In keeping step as one body, to honor Christ and His Kingdom, we are all heartened. Victory began when the allied armies had one General, and it begins for us in city or town, in church or community the day, we unite to seek Christ's Captaincy, before we plan or move.

Quickened by the redemption of Jerusalem and the blessing of God upon the Moslem and the Eastern world, our appeal for prayer and praise widens since Jew and Gentile, Eastern and Western, are all concerned in the greater aims and hopes for humanity.

Help us our Father to do Thy will and to follow fully Thy plans and methods. Teach us to think in terms of world-need and establish in righteousness the nations now disordered and confused. Give us courage to tread unfamiliar roads and keep us free from unclean alliances. May the experiences and discipline of today make more worthy the citizenship of tomorrow. Rekindle our smouldering fires, quicken our spiritual hunger and give us holy unrest with present attainments. May our work be done with deepening desire and joy to the praise of Him who ever lives to intercede for us.

Federal Council of the Churches of Christ in America
HUBERT C. HERRING,
Acting Chairman of Executive Committee.
CHARLES S. MACFARLAND,
General Secretary.

EASTER WEEK OF PRAYER

Subjects Recommended in the Call for Prayer Issued by the Federal Council of the Churches of Christ in America

Sunday, April 13.—Sermons on a New Year for a New World. We have not passed this way before. The New Church Life. Hosannas in the Redeemed City. Isa. 65:17-18; John 3:17; Eph. 2:13-22.

Monday, April 14.—The New Discovery of Self. (Create in us clean hearts O God). In confession, thanksgiving and cleansing get new strength for tasks and temptations. Covet a richer personal religious life. Prayer and praise with faith and zeal bring manifold blessings. Seek a new sense of the worth of prayer; cultivate the habit of praying every day at noon. Psalms 51:10-17; Eph. 4:1-2; Peter 1:13-16; Jude 20-21.

Tuesday, April 15.—The New Discovery of God. (I am with you all the days.) Exult in the Fatherhood of God. Find Him anew in the grass, the lily and the sparrow, in the immigrant and the child. Crave for every day the quickened sense of God felt during war-days. Loyalty to our Leader as true as soldiers and sailors were to their leaders. Let men read as living letters of Christ. Psalms 8; Isa. 45:20-25; Matt. 5:16, 23:8-10; Heb. 2:10-11.

Wednesday, April 16.—The New Stewardship. (Stewards of the grace of God). In the Home if Jesus came what would we change? In business would His presence change employers and employees? In colleges and schools; that more men and women may give themselves to His ministry. In getting and spending and giving show that we live not unto ourselves. Add to the generous war-time gifts for the bigger fight to overcome evil with good. Num. 14:24, 31:12; I Cor. 10:31-32; II Cor. 8:7; Rom. 12:9-13.

Thursday, April 17.—The New Passion for Others. (The love of Christ constrains us). World-wide zeal to give the Gospel to every creature. Prayer for the associations of men and women that build up youth and carry Christ to the poor, the children, the immigrants and the derelict of society. Church unity and co-operation. Higher ideals for town and community made good by the Churches of Christ. To bring in better days. Move from words to work, from sentiment to strategic co-operation. Isa. 56:6-8, 56:5-7; Matt. 9:35-38; John 17:22-23; James 2:15-17.

Friday, April 18.—The New Sacrifice. (He gave Himself for us). They who are best do best, for being is the measure of doing. Emulate the men at the front. Share Christ's spirit of self-sacrifice to do the will of God. Walk with Him, not compelled as Simon, but joyously as Paul; if need be witness

as martyrs for Christ. The only fruitful thing is sacrifice; great things come chiefly through great sacrifices. Carry sympathy to wounded soldiers and sailors, to widows and orphans and to the destitute in every land. Bear others' burdens and lift the heavy end of the load. Psalms 40:7-8; Isa. 58:9-11; John 17:18-19; James 1:27.

Saturday, April 19.—The New Day for Palestine. Rejoice with Armenia and Syria and in the redemption of Jerusalem. The New Patriotism. International justice and goodwill. The partnership of nations. The commonwealth of the world. Psalms 122:147;1-3; Acts 17:26-26-28; Heb. 12:22-24; Rev. 21:1-2.

Sunday, April 20.—Sermons on the Resurrection. Jesus and the resurrection. Victory through Christ. The King of Glory. The King of Kings. Luke 1:32-33; Rev. 11:15; 12:10.

NOTES

The annual series of revival meetings are being held at Elon College this week. Pastor Newman is doing the preaching.

"The First Century Call to Twentieth Century Men," is Dr. Atkinson's topic for his lectures on missions at Elon College this week.

Brother Chas. D. Johnston calls the attention of the good ladies to an important item this week. Don't worry, Brother Johnston, they will respond.

Brother J. D. Gunter, Sanford, N. C., dropped in to see us one day last week. He is one of THE SUN'S most loyal friends and says that he cannot understand why a man will not subscribe for and support his Church paper.

We note from *The Richland News* that Rev. H. W. Elder has been pounded graciously by the Ambrose, Georgia, church. The splendid outlay of good things includes seven hams. We are writing this note before breakfast, and how the thought of that ham does make us hungry!

We chronicle with sadness the passing of Brother D. S. Farmer, News Ferry, Va., on Thursday, March 13, at 3 P. M. Brother Farmer had been in poor health for about a year, though his last sickness had not confined him to his bed but about ten days. He was in his 56th year, a loyal and devoted member of his local church, Pleasant Grove, (Va.), and a useful man in his denomination. He was a loyal supporter of every enterprise of his Church, and reared a family to follow his own footsteps. We counted him among our closest friends. He lived close in fellowship to his brethren and friends, and all who knew him called him "Brother Sam." The funeral took place at Pleasant Grove March 15, service being conducted by Pastor Truitt and Dr. J. O. Atkinson, a former pastor. A good man has answered the call to brighter clime.

David McClenny—THE SUN has been coming to our home for forty-five years and we don't want it to stop.

PASTOR AND PEOPLE

ELON COLLEGE, N. C.

Elon College has again been delighted and edified by a visit from Dr. Martyn Summerbell. He preached on Sunday the ninth, morning and evening using as his themes, "A Study in Influence," and "Christian Usefulness." These were great messages, strong in vital truth and spiritual power. The evening sermon was especially enjoyed by the audience.

Six lectures from the following themes were given, two each day: "Personal Freedom in America;" "America's Noble Ideals;" "America's Patriotic Spirit;" "Making the Kaiser;" "German Provocation to America;" and "The Collapse of Kaiserism."

To each of these great and interesting themes Dr. Summerbell had given a patient and careful study and brought us the rich results of his labors. No brief analysis could do them justice. The results speak best. We felt a greater appreciation of our personal liberty and greater admiration for America's patriotic spirit and lofty ideals. We understood more clearly the causes producing the great war and the forces bringing about the collapse of Kaiserism.

Of the many strong speakers coming to us each year none brings a riper scholarship or a richer and more varied experience. His coming is always a benediction and we await his return with eager anticipation.

Mr. J. M. Darden, a prominent and successful business man of Suffolk, Va., spoke to the Ministers Association in the dining hall of West Dormitory on the evening of the 12th inst. The speaker was introduced by Dr. J. O. Atkinson in his usual pleasing style. Mr. Darden's address was a strong and forceful appeal to the young ministers to make good in this great day of need and opportunity, declaring that with a pure heart and an energetic brain and hand man could achieve whatever society needed and God willed at his hand. The discourse was aptly illustrated by examples from current history and observation, and was marked by a spirit of earnestness and deep religious conviction.

Brief and timely remarks were made by Drs. W. A. Harper and J. U. Newman, and by Revs. G. O. Lankford, R. F. Brown and F. C. Lester.

A violin solo by Prof. Bryan and a duet by Messrs. Lindley and Sides added much to the interest of the evening. After refreshments all joined in "Blest be the Tie That Binds," and Dr. J. W. Wellons closed the service with prayer.

N. G. NEWMAN.

SUFFOLK LETTER

Believing, being, and building are three good words for Christians to ponder. Without faith it is impossible to please God;" but one must not be "carried about with every wind of doctrine." Paul says, "I know whom I have believed." He believed in a person. "Believe not every spirit, but try the spirits whether they be of God." Belief is the exercise of faith, and faith is "the gift of God." God bestows faith upon men, but men must exercise that gift and this human

exercise of faith is belief. Men must believe on the Lord Jesus Christ to be saved. God gives voice, but men must sing "He that believeth and is baptized shall be saved; but he that believeth not shall be condemned." Believing is at the base of life. Jesus not only had faith in God; but he had faith in men; and He thus set us an example. The race is hindered in its progress by lack of faith in one another. That lack of confidence interrupts peace, causes war, and keeps nations apart, when they might co-operate with advantage to all.

Being is also an essential in Christian life. Believing is not sufficient of itself. "The devils believe, and tremble." Faith must produce being. What one is in his real life determines the value of character. Good and bad are determined by what the thing is in itself. The value of an egg is determined by the egg itself. No market can make good eggs. No society or church can make good men. Men are good or bad in themselves. Men and women make the church and not the church the men and women. There were saved men and women before there was a church. The main thing is to be good by the help of Him who is good, that is God. And one can be good in bad environments. Noah was a good man in a bad age. It is a subterfuge to put one's wrong-doing on conditions. The age did not corrupt Paul. "Virtue consists in overcoming evil; we "overcome evil with good." Kindness subdues where force fails. Personal character is the mightiest force in a human society. Joseph had it. Hatred, lust, prison, had no power over him. He was like a great rock in the midst of a stream. Evil forces surged around him, but did not move him. What the world needs today is rock-like character built on Jesus Christ by a personal faith that knows Him.

Building is only another word for doing or working. Spiritual life cannot be held within the domain of believing and being. Sound faith and being good without building would die. "Faith without works is dead." The real Christian is a working Christian. A city that has faith and character will build—will grow. This is a working world. It is easy to imagine a stagnant river as an idle Christian. Jesus said: "My Father worketh hitherto and I will." And in the parable He said: "Go work in my vineyard." "Work while it is day, for the night cometh when no man can work." But what is the work to be done? The work of building the church; not the house alone but building up the congregation of believers in the Lord. It is character-building. This can be done by precept, by example, by confidence, by creating a spiritual atmosphere in the church and the community. Environment can be made so it is harder to do right or easier to do right, and the reverse of that, so that it is harder to do wrong or easier to do wrong. This is not a sermon. It is simply a letter. It is for you. It is a letter to help you. Please answer it by a better life.

W. W. STALEY.

FAMILY REUNION AND OTHER ITEMS

The "flu" has nearly disappeared from Liberty and Pleasant Hill. I preached at Liberty the fourth Sunday in February and at Pleasant Hill the first Sunday

in this month. Last Sunday I preached at the resi-
-dence of Brother Clay Teague and attended the family
reunion and dinner in honor of mother, Laura Ann
Teague, widow of Christopher Teague. She was eighty-
five years of age March 5. Her parents were Braxton
and Mary Ann York. Her parents had fourteen children, all dead but two, Mother Teague and a brother
in Indiana. The following are her children—Boys:
Dolph, Eugene, Clay and Edward. Edward is dead.
Girls: Rosetta Workman, Henrietta Solmon, Florence
Euliss and Della Fogleman.

The long table, built for the occasion, out in the yard,
was loaded with choice articles of food and surrounded
by her children, grandchildren and great grandchildren.
Neighbors and friends were there to rejoice with her
and receive her benedictions. It was a very joyous occasion.

Before I left I asked her if she still took THE CHRIST-
IAN SUN. She said, "Of course I do. I just would not
know how to keep house without THE CHRISTIAN SUN."
Then she added, "Brother Riddle is very good in sending me papers to read, in addition to THE SUN. He
knows how I love to read and is very thoughtful in
remembering me."

I have just received a telegram from the pastor of
the Christian church at Graham informing me of the
death of Brother John Longest, and requesting me to
aid at the funeral. Brother Longest leaves a wife and
nine children. Mrs. Long and I will leave on the
next train.

Judge Patterson, of this place, was taken quite sick.
one week ago. The doctor has been with him every day
day since. No improvement for the better up to this
time.

                                        D. A. LONG.
Liberty, N. C., March 10, 1919.

CHURCH UNION TAKING PLACE

"Nothing succeeds like success." While in many
quarters the pros and cons of church union are being
debated, in others church union is going on at a rapid
pace.

During the past nineteen months, twenty-two unions
and federations have taken place in Vermont. Nine
towns of that State have been left to the care and charge
of one Protestant denomination. As a result fourteen
ministers have been released for service elsewhere and
fourteen preachers are receiving better salaries. Average church attendance has increased, town and communities heretofore divided on non-essential church differences, now co-operate in Christian service; large
numbers of "out-siders" have been enlisted in Christian
service; and $1,900.00 have been released for home mis-
sion work elsewhere.

Soldiers returning to these Vermont towns will find
conditions similar to those in the army in this particular, Christians uniting their forces for the good of all.
                                        J. O. ATKINSON.

RALEIGH LETTER

In order to give CHRISTIAN SUN readers all the facts
regarding the work of the Raleigh church, it will be

necessary to go back a few months and record a little
ancient history. The purpose of this letter is to give
an account of the work already done in 1919 and the
plans that are now being shaped to continue this work
under the direction of the new pastor, Rev. George D.
Eastes.

Brother Eastes was to have commenced his work
here the first of the year, but owing to the illness of
Mrs. Eastes, he did not get started promptly. In reality, therefore, he has been with the church only during
the month of February and the two Sundays in March
which have already passed.

During even this short period, however, it is evident
that the work is going forward, and the church is planning for much greater things. The weather has kept
the attendance lower than would have ordinarily been
the case, but on Sunday evening, March 9, the first
pretty Sunday evening since Brother Eastes came to
Raleigh, the auditorium was entirely filled.

Throughout the membership there is a great increase
in interest and it will probably be helpful to other
churches, and interesting to friends of this church, to
know just what is responsible for this.

First of all, interest has been increased by the fact
that we have a new pastor. The people want to hear
him—and be it said to the credit of Brother Eastes,
they want to hear him *twice*. This means bigger and
bigger congregations as the weeks go by.

Second, we have put on an advertising campaign. A
contract has been given each of the two local newspapers for a five inch, single column space every Saturday for a year. This is used in announcing the sermon subjects for each service. In addition to this, small
posters have been typewritten and placed in the display
windows and other prominent places in the business
part of the city. Last Sunday, the moving picture
shows of the city were also provided with slides announcing service and these were shown at every performance Saturday and Saturday night. In addition
to all this, arrangements have been made for reporting
all the services to the local papers, and indications point
to the probability that they will be liberal with their
space.

At the last meeting of the Business Board, a plan of
church organization was adopted, and the pastor is to
name chairmen for the various committees which are to
be created. Among these committees will be one on
missions, one on music, one on evangelism, one on finances, and one on publicity. Others will probably be
included.

At this meeting it was also decided to set up a goal
for the work of 1919, which is as follows: First, that
we clear ourselves of debt and become self-supporting
with a pastor's salary of $1,800 a year; and second,
that we double our membership.

With these goals in view, and with the work now
seeming so encouraging, I trust that I will have great
things to report to SUN readers in the coming months.
                                        P. T. HINES.
Raleigh, N. C.

A CALL IN ORDER

It has been some time since I have written anything for THE SUN to let the people know about our work in Alabama.

Owing to the fact that our preachers are few in number, it has been a difficult matter for some of our churches to get a pastor, though I think they are all arranged for now except New Home church. I understand that they are without a regular pastor.

I think that the Convention's call for one hundred new recruits for the ministry is in order and should be heeded by evey praying man and woman in the entire Convention. It seems to me that the time has never been when the field was whiter to harvest than at the present time and as we see and feel so keenly this need in the Master's vineyard let us pray the Lord of the harvest and he will send more laborers into His vineyard. Not only do we need new recruits in the ministry, but one of our greatest needs in some of our churches in Alabama is more men and women whose lives are on the altar to take the lead in the work of the Sunday school and song services. Another great need is a consecrated church membership to follow their leader. Jesus Christ said, "I am the Way," and in another place he said, "Follow Me." His was the way of service and sacrificing for others. The Son of Man came not to be ministered but to minister and to give His life a ransom for many. So let us all be Christlike in our lives that the world may stop and take notice that we have been with Jesus.

J. D. DOLLAR.

LOSING LIFE TO FIND LIFE!

Selfishness is a big obstacle to spiritual growth and progress. "Except a grain of wheat fall in the earth and die, it cannot yield fruit." Losing in order that he might find was the great motto of Jesus Christ, "I lay down my life that I might take it up again. If I have power to lay it down I have power to take it up again." He lost the Heavenly life that he might gain it again not only for himself but for others, yea he gave, lost his own dear human life that he might save other lives.

We, his followers, must get self in the background and invest something, give life in order to receive life. Life is a process that is mysterious, none but God and Christ know exactly what it is. But we are given this much truth on the hypothesis that life is progressive. It takes life to make life.

We speak of the life of a nation. Its citizens constitute the elements of the nation. The life of a school or institution is its faculty, pupils, influence and productions. In community or town the inhabitants compose the life. A church has life or it is dead. Its active, live members is the life. Something must be invested on the part of its individuals if it counts for much. What have you or I lost for the cause of the Church of God? It is worthy of our all and can reward eternal life and blissful joy. It always pays double-fold and interest.

L. L. WYRICK.

Elon College, N. C.

BEFORE AND AFTER THE WAR

It seems to me, previous to this last war, Isaiah expresses the condition of affairs which existed throughout our so-called Christian America. (?). In chapter 53, verse 6: "All we like sheep have gone astray; we have turned every one to his own way."

Man had fallen away from his church, from his Sunday school and prayer meetings. Living after the flesh, or worldliness, which leads toward death. Romans 8-6. The real cause is the *neglected prayer*. The good women, thank the Lord, have kept up their weeks of prayer—and the poor neglected wife and mother, praying for the wayward or club-going and society seeking husband, has kept them nearer together. So many midweek prayer meetings we have attended to find a few faithful women, the pastor and maybe one or two other men.

The Civil War came on and was possibly a chastisement, as if our Father would say, "Children, you have already gone too far, won't you return to Him who has done so much for you?" You remember our great President called his people to prayer. It is very plain to those who believe that God heard and answered. We saw our need and knew to whom to go in the time of trouble. "The Lord is good, a stronghold in the day of trouble and he knoweth them that trust in Him."

There semed to be on the part of our people a casual, "I thank you," as it was on the part of the children of Israel. When God spoke to them through Moses near Mount Sindai, they said, "All thou hast said we will do." But not being a heartfelt repentance they soon returned to their worldliness and demanded of Aaron that he make them a gold calf.

The war was indeed destructive and caused much bloodshed, but it seems not to have been a sufficient lesson. Then came the great world's plague, Influenza, which has taken many more lives than the German bullets. First and second attack and in some places the third. Are our people ready to listen and heed? Do we recognize the fact that it is the great love of God, our Father of Heaven and of earth?

Now brethren and sisters, may I implore you to return to your closets and when the door is shut, tell the Lord we have sinned, and beg Him to forgive and save lest a worse calamity befall us. His promises are secure —they have never failed. Just take time to read Romans 12:1-2, "Be ye careful for nothing (over anxious) but in everything prayer and supplication and with thanksgiving. Let your requests be made known unto God. For the peace of God which passeth all understanding shall keep your hearts and minds through Christ Jesus." Then turn to your Bible and read the last words of Isaiah 53:6, not quoted in the beginning of this. "And the Lord hath laid on him the iniquity of us all." Shall we not love Him? John 15:7. "If ye abide in me and my word abide in you, ask what you will and it shall be done unto you." Isaiah 12:2—"Behold God is my salvation; I will trust and not be afraid, for the Lord Jehovah is my strength and my song and he is become my salvation." First Corinthians 15:57-58.

200 Oak St., Atlanta, Ga.   E. B. ATKINSON.

CHRISTIAN EDUCATION

FROM DR. LONG, ELON'S FOUNDER

Dr. W. A. Harper,
Elon College, N. C.

Dear Brother:—

I want to assure you that my whole heart is with you in the great and important step you are about to take. I am confident that when the matter has been properly and intelligently presented to our people that they will respond generously and meet all that is required.

The whole brotherhood has become convinced of the vital importance of the college and its value as an institution in our Church, and it should be a great pleasure and joy to have an opportunity to contribute to its permanent establishment.

I shall aid you as far as I can. May the good Lord bless you and the college.

As ever, very truly,
W. S. LONG.

THE ELON STANDARDIZATION FUND

The Plan

We are now prepared to announce our plan for the conduct of The Elon Standardization Fund campaign. We believe that the Church will endorse our judgment as wise and proper, and co-operate with us wholeheartedly in the drive. Our confidence in the method, based on experience in other churches and in the various war-fund drives, is firm, and so is our confidence in our Brotherhood. "We can do it, and we will."

We are to associate with President Harper in the field work five men of proven ability. These six brethren are to push the field work for funds as rapidly as they can until June the first. June is to be our final drive month, during which every church not already visited will be canvassed, utilizing local workers just as far as possible in the grand finish.

We have reasons for this decision. Two campaigns right together conducted in just the same way will lack the variety that produces zest and enthusiasm. A long drawn out campaign is expensive. The College needs its president on the Hill to direct its affairs, and particularly during the summer months in the campaign for students ought he to be free from other cares. The cooperative drive we suggest is free from these objections, and the team-work it will necessitate is prophetic of great good to our cause. Then it will teach us that this drive is ours, not Elon's. Remember, brethren, we own Elon College and it is our duty to care for it at whatever cost.

The churches that will by our plan be called upon to give up their pastors for a few months will we feel sure be honored in the sacrifice such generosity will entail. Our Christ teaches sacrifice, He also illustrated it, and the church that follows in His trail never loses, but gains immeasurably. Other denominations have laid such requisition on their leaders, with blessed response and gratifying results. Our people will rise to the occasion.

A Few Details

The minimum subscription is to be $100, or $20 the year for five years.

An individual who gives at least one thousand dollars may perpetuate his own name or the name of a friend in the establishment of a fund, whose interest the Trustees shall use for the general purpose of the College.

An individual, church, or organization that gives $25,000 may endow a professorship in the College Faculty.

Liberty Loan Bonds and War Savings Stamps (at their redeemable value) will be accepted in payment of subscriptions.

Any church that reaches its quota will be given a beautiful recognition card, handsomely printed in Maroon and Old Gold, the Elon colors, for display in its place of public worship. Any church that doubles its quota will have a golden star affixed in the white field of this recognition card, and additional stars will indicate still further doubling of the quota.

Let the Brotherhood be earnest in prayer that God may give us speedy and pronounced victory in this great drive to place our College on a solid financial basis.

J. E. WEST,
K. B. JOHNSON,
R. M. MORROW,
Committee Representing the Board of Trustees.
W. W. STALEY,
President of the Convention.

The Campaign Leaders

In accordance with the plan printed above, there will be associated with me in the drive as campaign leaders: President T. E. White, of The North Carolina Conference, Sanford, N. C.; Rev. G. O. Lankford, Berkley, Va.; Rev. R. F. Brown, Durham, N. C.; Rev. E. M. Carter, Wadley, Ala.; Dr. N. G. Newman, Elon College, N. C., I bespeak for these brethren the earnest prayers of our people and that ready response which has made the raising of funds for our college a proverbial joy.

We six will give ourselves to the field work as rapidly as we can loosen ourselves from our local situations. We will be assisted by many others, who cannot go into the field as such. We feel sure the sacrifices the churches are making in letting these brethren off will be met by a generous response in liberality wherever they go. Elon is ours and we shall demonstrate our devotion to her by doing this thing in great style.

One other item. I am sure you have enjoyed the final page of THE CHRISTIAN SUN. Rev. C. B. Riddle has agreed to use this page during the campaign for its benefit. He will prepare the copy and see to its display. Brother Riddle is one of the best publicity men in the country and this generosity of his will be appreciated and enjoyed by all.

Pray that this work may go forward in the Master's chosen way.

W. A. HARPER.

Mrs. R. S. Sheffield—I can't do without my church paper.

THE FORWARD MOVEMENT

(Rev. W. H. Denison, D. D., Superintendent)

The Superintendent will meet with the workers of the Northwestern Indiana Conference at the conference mid-year institute March 18-20 to consider the Forward Movement work.

He will also meet the workers of the Warren, Indiana church and the churches within reach of Warren at the Warren church, Friday afternoon and night, March 21 for conferences and for a Forward Movement rally.

He will meet another group of workers at Huntington, Indiana, March 23 and 24.

At all of the gatherings he is exceedingly anxious to meet the pastors, Sunday school superintendents, the Four-Minute Men and key workers in the churches in the interest of the Forward Movement.

The Four-Minute Men's names are coming in every day from the churches. Have you sent your name in yet? We want *four-minute men* in every church right away.

The Prayer Covenants are being signed and sent in nearly every day. Have you signed yours yet? Have you sent in any from your church? It is very important and their effect is felt in many churches. A number of pastors are reporting increased interest, double attendance at prayer meetings and a spiritual uplift in the church.

Rev. E. C. Geeding, Atwood, Ill., says: "I am enclosing names of Four-Minute Men. Next Sunday evening five of the young people will read papers or give a short address on the five points of the Movement. I have finished my series of Forward Movement sermons. My church is moving forward."

Rev. D. M. Helfenstein, D. D., Orient, Iowa: "We observed the first three weeks of February in harmony with the Forward Movement. I feel there was a quickening of the spiritual life, and a deepening of the interest in the things of the Kingdom. I am sending you the name of our Four-Minute Man."

Rev. A. O. Jacobs, Olney, Ill.: "We have adopted the Forward Movement plan here and we are making a canvass and drive for church membership from now until Easter. Our prayer meeting attendance has been doubled and all of the services have increased."

In October the Southern Indiana Wabash Conference will celebrate its one hundredth anniversary. The program will be built around the Forward Movement program. Our last session was built around the five points.

The Indiana and Illinois state conference will hold a joint session in June and the program is arranged on the Forward Movement fundamentals.

Church Programs

Many appreciative words are spoken for the list of church program that have been given for the Forward Movement. They have been very suggestive to our pastors and church officials and a goodly number of our ministers have outlined a definite church program around the Forward Movement fundamentals.

We have given a number of rural church programs.

We are pleased to give this week a city church program as has been carried out by our Durham, North Carolina church under their splendid pastor, Rev. R. F. Brown. It may be suggestive to many city churches.

DURHAM, NORTH CAROLINA, CHURCH PROGRAM

I. Devotion

OBJECTIVE—Intensify the devotional and spiritual life of the church.

METHOD—1. Increase the interest and enthusiasm in the church services and encourage larger attendance.

2. Make all church services artistic, well balanced and effectual.

3. So co-ordinate the church services as to make them adapted to the young as well as the old.

4. Service and worship by the people and not for the people.

5. Encourage every attendant to pray.

6. Enlist all of our members in a daily prayer league.

7. Enlist two hundred signers of the Forward Movement Covenant.

8. Enlist one hundred signers of the Family Altar Covenant.

9. Emphasize the work of the Holy Spirit.

10. Appoint a devotional committee.

Appoint a devotional committee.

II. Evangelism

OBJECTIVE—Encourage personal evangelistic work.

METHOD—1. Encourage the young people to attend at least one church service each Sunday.

2. Enlist the young people in some special work of the church and Sunday school.

3. Take at least six of our most promising young people and give them special training for work in the church and Sunday school.

4. Increase the interest, activity and efficiency of the various committees.

5. Reach the strangers within our gates.

6. Conduct a church community survey.

7. Provide transportation for the old people to attend the monthly communion services.

8. Emphasize the importance and the work of the publicity committee.

9. Emphasize the fact that God holds every person responsible for the way in which he hears His word.

10. Every member of the church hospitable, gentle and polite to visitors and strangers.

11. Solicit the co-operation of every member of the church in winning souls to Christ.

12. Launch a campaign on Ministerial Evangelism and increase our depleted ministerial ranks.

13. Insist on every officer and worker in the church and Sunday school being proud of his job.

14. Designate some Sunday which shall be known as "Go to Church Sunday."

15. Take a more definite interest in the physical, social, as well as the spiritual nurture of the children.

16. Designate some Sunday each month which shall be known as "Church Membership Sunday."

III. Religious Education

OBJECTIVE—Promote religious education among our people.

METHOD—1. Twenty per cent increase in Sunday school and church attendance.

2. Increase class membership.

3. Simplify our Organizations.

4. Impress the fact that the work of the Sunday school is intimately related to the work of the church.

5. Every teacher in the Sunday school a Christian in belief, —

experience and example.

6. Cultivate a fraternal spirit among the Sunday school classes.

7. Keep close watch over the social functions of the Sunday school.

8. Every officer and teacher present at every monthly meeting.

9. Every member of every class 80 per cent efficient on Sunday school lesson.

10. Urge our people to read the Bible daily; subscribe for and read the Herald of Gospel Liberty and The Christian Sun.

11. Inspire our young people to aspire for a higher education and encourage them to attend our own institutions of learning.

12. Acquaint ourselves more thoroughly with our Creed—the Bible.

13. Make known our principles in circles hitherto unreached.

IV. Missions and Benevolence

OBJECTIVE—Double our interest and work in both home and foreign missions.

METHOD—1. Launch a comprehensive study of home and foreign missions.

2. Register every member of the church as favoring home and foreign missions.

3. Make regular offerings to home and foreign missions.

4. Daily prayer for our mission work.

5. Double the present membership in the Women's Missionary Society.

6. Cultivate a willingness comparable to our wealth.

7. Perpetuate the every-member canvass.

8. Make weekly contributions for the support of the Kingdom.

9. Double our contributions to the Charity fund.

10. Tithe our income.

ABRAHAM SACRIFICING ISAAC

(Sermon by Rev. A. W. Andes, Harrisonburg, Va.)

Text: Take now thy son, thine only son Isaac, whom thou lovest, and get thee into the land of Moriah; and offer him there for a burnt offering upon one of the mountains which I will tell thee of. Gen. 22:2.

No doubt during the recent call to arms for freedom's sake, many a fond parent has had the heartbreaking experience of saying good-bye to a loving son, knowing that the enemy might slay him on foreign soil before time for his return home. How sad such a parting is some can only guess at while those who have had the experience know but cannot express. While I am sure such good-byes are sad beyond expression, I think Abraham's trial must have been still sadder. In Abraham's home is an only son whom he loves as devotedly as ever a son could be loved, and through whom he expects, according to the plain promises of God, to be a great blessing to the world. No doubt, as the days go by, and Abraham sees the unfolding of the life of rich promise in his son Isaac, his hopes grow still brighter, and the ties of affection grow stronger and stronger around the hearts of both father and son. The peace and love of this happy home are suddenly startled by the voice of the Lord that said to Abraham: "Take now thy son, thine only son Isaac, whom thou lovest, and get thee into the land of Moriah; and offer him there for a burnt offering upon one of the mountains which I will tell thee of." How the words "offer him there for

a burnt offering" must have driven the dagger into the heart and the hopes of good old father Abraham! But the Lord had spoken, and that settled it. Early next morning everything is ready for the journey, and they are off. What a sad journey it must have been for Abraham! What could have been the nature of the conversation with Isaac during those three days of traveling together? Finally the journey is ended and Abraham builds an altar, lays the wood on it, and binds Isaac his son, and tenderly taking him up lays him on the altar. Oh, how hard it must have been at that moment for Abraham to seize the huge knife and hold it aloft as he looked down into the dear face of his own son lying helpless on the altar, and think that in the next moment he must see the dying agonies and hear the dying groans of that dear boy! But love to God, and obedience to Him have gained the victory, and the hand that holds the knife is about to make the fatal plunge, when hark, an angel's voice breaks the awful silence saying, "Lay not thine hand upon the lad, neither do thou anything unto him; for now I know that thou fearest God, seeing thou hast not withheld thy son, thine only son from me."

Let us in meditation stand by Abraham's altar, lay our hand upon his shoulder, look into the calm happy face of the old patriarch and learn once for all time that God must be first always in our love, that our obedience must be perfect, and that our faith must be unshakable even in face of the severest tests that can ever come to us. Just there let us breathe a prayer that God will help us learn these lessons.

Having learned them we are now prepared to build a few altars and make some sacrifice ourselves.

On altar number one we will lay our Isaac of Love for the World. We are commanded in I John 2:15 to "Love not the world, neither the things that are in the world." But there are many worldly agencies bidding for our love. Here are the useless luxuries that afford an attraction and perhaps a momentary pleasure. Here are the prospects of getting rich and piling up a little of this world's goods to rest in ease upon after a while. If we have learned to put God first in our love and obedience we will bind this Isaac of Love for the World and lay him upon the altar. And then instead of planning only how to accumulate wealth or shine in society or live easy we will plan how we may serve the Lord best, and do the most good in the world. Living and planning thus may mean that we shall have to deny ourselves many things the earthly appetite craves; it may mean years of preparation for life's greatest duties; it may mean the expenditure of money in school before the money is earned, but what matters all that if our Life's journey is directed by a high and holy ideal, and our God with an abundant reward awaits us at the journey's end? Can you look into the face of this Isaac and proceed quickly with the sacrifice?

On altar number two we will sacrifice our Isaac of Biased Opinions. Ofttimes our opinions of Bible doctrines are moulded by our own desires. For example, some people do not believe in missions because they do not want to. If they believed in missions they might feel under obligation to give a few of their dearly beloved dollars for mission work. But if they can only shut their eyes to plain Bible teaching they can keep the dollars, and erroneously think they feel better. But if we were in heathen darkness and other nations had the gospel we would believe in missions, because the good things would then be coming our way. Likewise, some people do not believe in tithing. But if the Lord had promised an additional dime for every dollar we made it would be an easy matter to get people to believe in that kind of tithing. Common honesty should compel us to abide by plain Bible teaching, and not try to twist such teaching to suit our own carnal desires. Too often our Isaac of Biased Opinions is allowed to play an important part in our choice of a life work. We too often allow ourselves to believe that the calling that promises most from a worldly standpoint is our God-given mission, and that the vocation promising most of hardship and sacrifice is for some one else. Deciding upon our life work should be done without asking our own worldly desires or ambitions any questions; but looking to the Lord in sincere and ceaseless prayer, settle upon that course that promises to make us the greatest possible blessing to the world. Young man, before settling this matter do not fail to consider well the ministy as probably the course of greatest usefulness for you to take. Is our Isaac of Biased Opinion and Carnal Desire well bound and safely laid on the altar?

Around altar number three I see a crowd of parents. But what are they doing? Are they laying their children on God's altar? Alas, not all of them are. Some want their children to shine in society, or make plenty of money, or win worldly honor, while others are satisfied if their children simply keep out of the clutches of the law, and get along through life most any way they can. What are they preperaing their children for? Oh, simply to reach the goals just mentioned. Is it not a sad fact that these are the highest and only ambitions of many parents for their children? They have never prayed that the children might be useful in God's service; that they might some day shine as bright stars on God's great honor roll; that they might be brought up in the nurture and admonition of the Lord, and be great in God's sight, even though obscure in the estimation of the world. I believe the scarcity of efficient church workers and ministers is due more to the wrong ideals of parents for their children than to anything else. The child is usually, to a certain extent, directed by the parent into the ways the parent desires the child to go, whether to money-making, pleasure seeking, or serving the Lord. If parents could only be induced to lay their children on God's altar instead of on the world's altar, a few years would reveal to us all the good church workers, God-fearing ministers, and consecrated dollars needed for the successful prosecution of the King's business. Oh, parents, parents, upon which altar have you laid your children? If you lay them on the world's altar and they amount to nothing really good and worth while don't blame any one but yourself. And if they bring you trouble just remember where you laid them and repent of your mistake. But the sad part about it is that it may then be too late to mend matters much. Lay them on God's altar in infancy and nurture them there.

I hear some saying, we have laid our children upon God's altar. All right, that is fine. Now let us see what kind of wood you have piled around them. Here is one good father who has laid his son on God's altar, and then piled around him the daily papers, the farm papers, the lodge papers, the latest fiction, etc. No church paper there, no Bible teaching there, no religious books there, no course in his own church school there. How do you think that boy will likely turn out? I have a question for that parent: Why don't you lay close to the heart of that dear boy the Bible, your church paper, some good religious books, and a course in your own church school? Here is the common answer: "Well, we are now taking about all the papers we are able to pay for, and all we have time to read." And as for an education that takes too much time and money or there are schools closer home and cheaper than our denominational college. I don't know what to think of such a parent. Consecrate the child to the Lord and then give him everything except the things he needs to direct him in the right way. Verily, there is a great deal of gross inconsistency in many Christian homes. If money and time are limited why not provide only such reading matter for the home as will cultivate the best spiritual atmosphere possible? And in selecting a school why not select the one with the best religious influence instead of one that is almost Godless and may crush out the spiritual life? If our boys and girls are ever to be religiously inclined and become faithful servants for the Master they must be fed upon the mental and spiritual food that will cause development in that direction. So there are two sins of which parents may be guilty. One is to sacrifice the children upon the world's altar, and the other is to make a pretense of laying them on God's altar, and then not helping prepare them for lives of usefulness in His service.

Before we take our eyes off of Abraham as pictured to us in the chapter from which our text is taken may we all gather around God's altar, and lay ourselves upon that altar, and lay our children there, and our money there, and all that we have and are, there, and then our pulpits will be filled with spiritual preachers, our pews with faithful worshipers, our colleges will be supported and patronized, our missions will flourish; coming generations will rise up and call us blessed, God will be honored and pleased, and we shall rejoice in his smile of approval forever and ever.

Mrs. Tom Cobb—I trust that we may succeed in sending THE SUN in every home that doesn't take it, for I know if they once take it they would not be without it.

NOTICE

Let every Missionary Society of the Eastern Virginia Conference send representatives to the Woman's Missionary meeting at Berkley, Va., April 10. The program committee is preparing something interesting. Let every congregation in the Conference be represented.

MRS. C. H. ROWLAND, Pres.

PRIVATE ARCHIE B. PIERCE

son of Mr. and Mrs. J. J. Pierce, Youngsville, Franklin County, North Carolina, who gave his life in France October 11, 1918.

CARD OF THANKS

We desire to thank our friends and neighbors for the many kind deeds and words of comfort rendered us during the sickness and death of our loving wife and mother. May the Lord bless each one abundantly.

J. W. MORTON & CHILDREN.

ORIGINAL EXTRACTS FROM LETTERS RECEIVED FROM DRAFT BOARDS AT WASHINGTON

"I ain't got no book lurning and am writing for inflamation."

"She is staying at a dissipated house."

"Just a line to let you know I am a widow and four children."

"He was inducted into the surface."

"I have a four months old baby and he is my only support."

"I am a lone woman and parsley dependent."

"As I need his assistance to keep me enclosed."

"I did not know my husband had a middle name, and if he had one I don't believe it was none."

"Caring for my condition which I haven't walked for three months from a broken leg which is number 75."

"Kind sir or she."

"I enclose loving yours."

"I am left with a child seven months old and she is a baby and can't walk."

"Your relationship to him? Answer: I am still his beloved wife."

"And he was my best supporter."

"In the service of the U. S. Armory."

"I am his wife and only, sir."

"You asked for my allotment number. I have two boys and four girls."

"Please correct my name as I would not and could not go under a consumed name."

Extracts from a boy's letter to his mother: "I am sitting in the Y. M. C. A. writing with the piano playing in my uniform."

"Please return my marriage certificate, baby hasn't eaten any for three days."

"Date of birth: Answer: Not yet but soon."

"Both sides of my parents are old and poor."

"Please send me a wife's form."

"We have another war baby in our house now how much more do i get?"

"My Bill has been out in charge of a spittoon (platoon): Do I get any more pay?"

"You have changed my little girl to a little boy will it make any difference?"

"Please leave me know if John has put in an application for wife and child."

"I am pleating for a little more time."

CHILD'S SELF-PRONOUNCING PICTORIAL BIBLE-WITH HELPS

This Bible is bound in French Seal Leather, has round corners, silk head bands, gold titles, handsomely bound.

Regular selling price.........$2.50
Price till March 31.............2.00

Call for Bible No. 215.

Address
C. B. RIDDLE, Publishing Agent
Burlington, North Carolina.

Sunday School and Christian Endeavor

SUNDAY SCHOOL TOPIC FOR SUN-DAY, MARCH 23

Israel Warned Against Compromise.

Scripture Lesson: Joshua 23:1-13.

Golden Text: "Evil companion-ship corrupt good morals." Cor. 15:33.

For explanation and comment, see Bible Class Quarterly or Officers and Teachers Journal, Christian Publishing Association, Dayton, Ohio.

CHRISTIAN ENDEAVOR TOPIC FOR SUNDAY, MARCH 23

"The Art of Building Character." Scripture Lesson: I Cor. 3:10-17.

For explanation and comment, see Christian Endeavor World, Christian Endeavor Publishing Company, Boston, Mass.

FROM CHARLES G. TRUMBELL

(Editor Sunday School Times)

"The day is coming," writes Mr. Trumbell, "when the Sunday school that has not sent some of its members to a home or foreign mission field, while at the same time numbering still others in its membership as volunteers pledged to go, will be ashamed and self-condemned. The reason why Sunday schools generally have not yet reached this high but practicable standard is because most Sunday schools do not know what the Sunday school is, and what is the real end of its effort.

"For example, the Sunday school is often spoken of as the church of to-morrow, or the child of the church, or as a branch of the church. All of these definitions are misleading.

Again, the purpose of the Sunday school is commonly spoken of as Bible study. And the great end of the Sunday school is usually said to be soul-winning. Both of these state-ments are not only inadequate, but positively harmful in the narrowing, stultifying limitations that they im-pose.

The Sunday school is not the church of tomorrow, nor a branch of the church of today; it is the church engaged in the most important work that God commits to man. As the church teaching, the Sunday school is the church at work carrying out the Great Commission; making dis-ciples, or learners, of all men.

Bible study is, of course, only a means to the end that the Sunday school has in view. And that end is not soul-winning; the church would be a body of babes, untrained and useless, if it were true. Soul-winning is vital; but soul-winning is the first step, not the last, in Sunday school effort. Yet many a teacher really seems to think that he has done about all he needs to do for a given class if he has brought the members of that class to an open confession their Sav-ior.

What, then, is the end of Sunday school work? *Character training for service in the extension of the King-dom.* Not a selfish salvation, a sav-ing merely of our own self-centered souls; but a salvation for great purpose only; power to win others to Christ, and to train them up in Christ."

"This then," continues Mr. Trum-bell, "may fairly be said to be the *chief and sole purpose of the Sunday school, the implanting of the mission-ary spirit so as to give it control of the life of every pupil.*"

No one is better equipped for de-fining correctly the Sunday school and what its purpose is than Mr. Trumbell who has given his great talent and consecrated ability to Sun-day school work on a large scale.

J. O. ATKINSON.

MARRIAGES

HAGWOOD-HUDSON

Sunday morning, March 2, 1919, the writer united in marriage at his home in Franklinton Mr. Luther Hag-wood and Miss Aurelia Hudson, both of Youngsville, N. C. Miss Hudson is a member of Oak Level church and is very popular in that community. The marriage was a quite one, only a few of the most intimate friends of the contracting parties being present. We wish them a long, happy, and prosperous life.

G. J. GREEN.

OBITUARIES

MAY

Mrs. Lonie May, wife of Mr. K. S. May, was buried in the family burying ground near her father's home, eight miles from Louisburg, N. C., March 1. Mrs. May was an excellent woman as evidenced by the many words of appreciation uttered by her neighbors in the hearing of the writ-er. She was plain, unpretentious, sin-cere, a rare personality, and faithful to life's duties. She belonged to a family of unusually high moral serving, their word being as unquestionable in their community as if were on sacred page. Her father, J. Oliver Inscoe, and her mother, Bettie Inscoe, into whose home much sor-row has come within the last two years, still survive her. She leaves also one sis-ter and three brothers, two of whom are in the United States Army in France. One other brother died at Camp Sevier near the beginning of the recent war. Of her immediate family there still sur-vives, husband and three children.

G. J. GREEN.

McCANE

Henry Walter McCane, son of Alfred Perry and Ellen Apple McCane, Caswell County, N. C., was born July 10, 1865 and died February 28, 1919, aged 54 years, eight months and eighteen days.

The father of the deceased was a Pres-byterian Scotchman and the son followed the faith of the father. His mother was the daughter of the late Rev. Solomon Apple. When a young man he married Miss Kate McAden, Semora, N. C., and settled in Newport News, Va., where for years he held a position as a mechanic in the ship yard. A short time ago he ac-cepted the position as manager of the Warwick Company farm with the hope that his failing health would improve. In the fall he had influenza from which pul-monary heart failure developed, resulting in his death. He is survived by a wife, three sons and three daughters. The re-mains were interred in the Lebanon church cemetery, March 3, in the presence of a concourse of relatives and friends. Ser-vices conducted by the writer. May a strong faith in the personal God comfort the husbandless and fatherless.

C. E. NEWMAN.

Ramseur 25.00
Christian Light 10.00

Young People's Societies

New Center ....$ 10.00
First Church, Greensboro 10.00
Elon College 35.00
Pleasant Grove (Va.) 35.00
Durham 20.00
Union (Va.) 20.00
Reidsville 10.00
Burlington 100.00
Sanford 10.00
Asheboro 10.00

Willing Workers Societies

Mt. Auburn ....$ 20.00
Durham 20.00
Elon College 20.00
Union (Va.) 20.00
Pleasant Grove (Va.) 20.00
Burlington 20.00

Cradle Roll Societies

Burlington ....$ 10.00
Graham 10.00
Mt. Auburn 10.00
New Providence 10.00
Ramseur 10.00
Henderson 10.00
Elon College 10.00
First Church, Greensboro.......... 10.00
Pleasant Grove (Va.).............. 10.00
Durham 10.00

Boys' Societies

Elon College ....$ 25.00
Burlington 25.00
First Church, Greensboro 25.00

Signed: MRS. J. W. PATTON,
MRS. A. T. BANKS,
MRS. W. R. SELLARS,
Committee.

Dr. Atkinson gave an address on "Successful Woman's Missionary Society."

The reports of the treasurers showed the following amounts on hand:

North Carolina and Virginia Board, by Mrs. L. M. Clymer:
Women's Societies $43.23
Young People's 19.50
Willing Workers .... .72
Elon Orphanage 6.50
Santa Isabel 10.00
Thank Offering 27.65
Board Expense 41.50
Total...... $154.10

Western North Carolina Board, by Mrs. W. R. Sellars:
No balance on hand.

Eastern North Carolina Board, by Mrs. A. F. Smith:
Balance on Hand $18.73

These funds were ordered turned over to Mrs. W. R. Sellars, Treasurer, who is to receive all money from now on.

Mrs. J. G. Anthony made a verbal report on the Cradle Roll work. The minutes were read and approved.

After prayer by Dr. Atkinson the Board adjourned.

MRS. W. H. CARROLL, President.
MRS. W. A. HARPER, Secretary.

BOOKS, BIBLES, TESTAMENTS

In order to reduce certain stocks of books, Bibles and Testaments on hand, the following prices are made and will hold good until March 31, 1919:

Bibles

No. 312X. Holman Self-Pronouncing Teachers' Bible. Printed on fine white paper from good, clear type, and contains references, concordance, four thousand questions and answers and fifteen prepared maps. Size 4 3-8X6 1-2 inches. Egyptian Morocco, divinity circuit, head bands and marker, round corners, red under gold edges. Regular selling price......$4.65
Price to March 31 .... 3.90
No. 71. Scofield Reference Bible. Handsome binding, French Morocco limp, new and improved edition. "The neatest Scofield Bible made." It will please you. Regular selling price $4.50
Price to March 31 .... 3.90
No. 215. Child's Self-Pronouncing Pictorial Bible with Helps. Bound in French seal leather, round corners, silk bands, gold titles, handsomely made. Regular selling price $2.50
Price to March 31 .... 2.00
No. 1113. Ideal Bible for Children. Printed on fine white paper, from the newest and clearest type of the size made. Size 3 1-2X5 3-8 inches. This Bible will please you. Regular price $1.75
Price to March 31 .... 1.40

Testaments

No. 3913 R. L. (Red Letter). Large print Morocco binding.
Regular price $2.00
Price to March 31 .... 1.75
No. 2902 Cloth binding, large print. Regular price.... .90
Price to March 31 .... .75
No. 2502 P. Cloth binding, black faced type. Regular price .... .75
Price to March 31 .... .55
No. 2113. Pocket size, Morocco binding. Regular price .60
Price to March 31 .... .45
No. 0135. Pocket size, Morocco binding, overlapping edges.
Regular Price .... .75
Price to March 31 .... .55

(A Testament in Modern Speech)

Cloth, $1.25; cloth, indexed, $1.75; cloth, India paper, $1.75; leather, $2.35; leather, indexed, $2.75; leather, India paper, $2.75; Persian Morocco, Divinity Circuit, $3.75; Turkey Morocco, $1.25. Pocket Edition (without notes): Cloth, $1.00; cloth, India paper, $1.25; leather, India paper, $1.85. State definitely style wanted.
The above prices are regular. Make your choice and deduct 10 per cent. State definitely Testament wanted.

Books

Pastor's Ideal Funeral, $1.15—Regular price, $1.25.
(Books for the Children)
We have several copies "Silver Rags," "Patty's Grand Uncle," "Johnny Two Boys," "A Rescued Madonna"—your choice, 20 cents per copy. We will substitute if the book ordered is sold before the order reaches us.

Special

"Redmond of the Seventh," by Mrs. Frank Lee is a book with a fine story taken from school life, 290 pages, handsomely bound, 50 cents the copy.
Special Note: One of these books will be sent free with each order for $3.00 worth of books, Bibles or Testaments.

Address

C. B. RIDDLE ....Publishing Agent
Burlington, N. C.

Mrs. N. E. Smith—I always feel like I want to tell you how much I enjoy the paper.

MISSIONARY

MINUTES OF THE WOMAN'S BOARD

Greensboro, N. C., January 25, 1919.

The Woman's Boards of the North Carolina and Virgina, the Western North Carolina and the Eastern North Carolina Christian Conferences, upon invitation of the North Carolina and Virginia Board, met in the First Christian church at 11:30 A. M. today to consider the union of these three boards into one.

There were present the following members:
North Carolina and Virginia Conference: Mrs. M. F. Cook, Mrs. J. G. Anthony, Mrs. L. M. Clymer and Mrs. W. A. Harper. Mrs. Chas. R. Clark, Mrs. J. H. Farmer and Rev. H. S. Hardcastle of this Board sent their approval of the union.
Western North Carolina Conference: Mrs. W. H. Carroll and Mrs. W. R. Sellars. Mrs. G. R. Underwood sent a letter favoring the union.
Eastern North Carolina Conference: Mrs. A. T. Banks. Mrs. R. L. Williamson, Mrs. K. B. Johnson and Mrs. A. F. Smith wrote letters favoring the union.

Devotional services were conducted by Rev. J. V. Knight, after the Boards had been called to order by Mrs. M. F. Cook.

Mrs. Cook called Mrs. Harper to the chair after the devotional services and she presided throughout the session.

Mrs. Cook stated the object of the meeting.

Dr. J. O. Atkinson presented cogent reasons for the union.

Every delegate present, including Mrs. J. W. Patton of the Southern Christian Convention Board, expressed individual approval of the union idea.

It was then formally voted to unite and to call the new board The Woman's Home and Foreign Mission Board of the North Carolina Christian Conference.

The following committees were appointed:
Constitution: Mrs. Cook and Mrs. Carroll.
Nominations: Mrs. Clymer, Mrs. Anthony and Dr. Atkinson.
Goals: Mrs. Patton, Mrs. Banks, Mrs. Sellars and Dr. Harper.

Adjourned thirty minutes for luncheon.

AFTERNOON SESSION

Devotional services by Rev. J. W. Patton.

The Committee on Constitution recommended the adoption of the Eastern Virginia Conference Constitution with necessary changes in the name. The report was adopted.

The Committee on Nominations reported as follows:
President—Mrs. W. H. Carroll, Burlington, N. C.
Vice-President—Mrs. A. T. Banks, Ramseur, N. C.
Secretary—Mrs. W. A. Harper, Elon College, N. C.
Treasurer—Mrs. W. R. Sellars, Burlington, N. C.
Supt. Literature and Mite Boxes—Mrs. M. F. Cook, Greensboro, N. C.
Supt. Young People—Miss Bessie Holt, Burlington, N. C.
Supt. Cradle Roll—Mrs. J. G. Anthony, Greensboro, N. C.
Supt. Boys' Department—Mrs. J. W. Patton, Greensboro, N. C.

These officers were unanimously elected.

On motion the officers were constituted the Executive Committee, with Mrs. Carroll, Mrs. Sellars and Mrs. Harper as the Central Executive Committee.

The Committee on Goals reported as follows:
We recommend the following goals:
20 new societies by September 30.
20 Life Memberships by September 30.
$2,500 to be raised from all sources, to be appropriated as follows:

Young People	$ 250.00
Willing Workers	100.00
Cradle Roll	100.00
Boys' Societies	50.00
Women's Societies	1,000.00
July Rally Offerings	1,000.00
Total	$2,500.00

and that this money be devoted to the following objects:

Santa Isabel	$750.00
Barrett Home	500.00
Japan Work	500.00
Donna Delfina	100.00
Mrs. Fry's School	100.00
Bible Women	50.00
General Purposes	500.00
Total	$2,500.00

That the Central Executive Committee make a program for the Rally to be held in each society and church in July, 1919.

That the Board hold its Convention October 5-6, 1919, leaving the place with the Central Executive Committee. (It has since been decided to meet at Elon College).

That the money to be raised, except for the Rally Days, be apportioned as follows:

Women's Societies

First Church, Greensboro	$100.00
Pleasant Grove (Va.)	100.00
Palm Street, Greensboro	10.00
Ingram (Va.)	40.00
Elon College	100.00
Durham	50.00
Reidsville	10.00
Union (Va.)	75.00
Long's Chapel	10.00
Shallow Ford	10.00
Hines Chapel	15.00
Howard's Chapel	10.00
Mt. Zion	15.00
Mt. Bethel	15.00
New Lebanon	15.00
Liberty (Va.)	15.00
Lebanon	10.00
Monticello	15.00
Haw River	15.00
Apple's Chapel	20.00
Berea	10.00
Danville	15.00
Hebron	50.00
Union (N. C.)	25.00
Bethlehem (A)	25.00
Concord	15.00
Mt. Auburn	200.00
Henderson	60.00
Wake Chapel	75.00
Sanford	30.00
Chapel Hill	25.00
Burlington	300.00
Graham	40.00

THE CHRISTIAN ORPHANAGE

AN URGENT NEED

I suppose in orphanage life there will hardly ever be a time when we will not have a need to be supplied. We often need articles very badly and do without them and are denied the comforts they would bring. We often need some articles more than others.

We now have a need that must be supplied, and one that we cannot do without much longer; and if our friends could visit us and see for themselves they would realize that I am stating facts. We have been fighting against the high prices and have made all kinds of make-shifts to put off supplying this need till prices might be adjusted to a lower level and we have waited patiently. We need sheets, about one hundred of them, for double beds. *We need them now.* We also need one hundred counter-panes or spreads of some kind for the beds.

When we call on the good ladies to supply any need we have we always get a very liberal response. Sometime last fall we were very much in need of table linen and we asked our good ladies to supply that need and the response was beautiful. We now have a nice white cloth on each table and a reserve supply for changing. I feel sure all who had a part in supplying that need feel glad that they had the opportunity of contributing. I am going to ask the good ladies of our churches to supply the sheets and counter-panes and I feel sure they will be glad to do it. Just think how easy it would be to supply this need if just one good woman in each church would make it her business to see the women of her church and make up enough money to buy just a few sheets and counter-panes and mail to us by parcel post. How easy and quickly this need could be supplied and what a change we could make in the looks of our beds!

This is an opportunity you have to make a nice clean bed for some little orphan boys and girls where they can rest and sleep sweetly and dream of mother who one time in their sweet lives sang them to sleep and tucked the cover around their little form and placed a good night kiss on their tender cheek, and prayed that the guarding angel would watch over them during the night.

Of this sweet happiness and tender love, many of them are denied, as mother has closed her eyes in death and her tender caresses are theirs no more to enjoy but while you cannot take the place of mother in their little lives you can supply this need and bring to them the comfort and joy these blessings will bring.

You now have this opportunity and privilege to render this service and I feel sure you will be glad to make use of it. I am counting on you and feel sure in the next few weeks this need will be supplied.

CHAS. D. JOHNTSON, *Supt.*

REPORT FOR MARCH 19, 1919

Amount brought forward, $1,264.21.

Children's Offerings

Ruth Lasiter, 10 cents; Naoma Carden, 20 cents; Total, 30 cents.

Sunday School Monthly Offerings

(North Carolina Conference)

Ingram, $4.00; Asheboro, $1.49; Wentworth, $3.03; Marcellus Woodell for Sunday school, $1.80; Sanford, N. C., $22.50; Shallow Well, $2.62; Poplar Branch, $4.66; High Point, N. C., $3.88; Hine's Chapel, $3.75; Wentworth, $3.58; New Providence, $1.54; Ramseur, N. C.,$1.58; Ramseur, N. C., Baraca Class, $1.95; Raleigh, N. C., $4.00; Pleasant Ridge, $4.10; Catawba Springs, $6.59; Durham, $10.09; Parks Cross Roads, $1.00.

(Eastern Virginia Conference)

Old Zion, Norfolk, $2.00; East End, Newport News, $10.42; Isle of Wight, $3.50; Washington St., Portsmouth, $3.00; Berea, (Norfolk), $2.00.

(Virginia Valley Conference)

Dry Run, $2.50; Linville, $1.00.

(Alabama Conference)

Beulah, 80 cents; Total $107.69.

Thanksgiving Offerings

Beulah Church, (N. C.), $30.00.

Special Offerings

A. P. Thompson, on support of children, $17.00; L. I. Fields, estate, $113.28; W. H. Thomas, on support of children, $25.00; Total, $155.28.

Total for the week, $293.27; Grand total, $1,557.48.

Dear Uncle Charley: It has been some time since you heard from us but we have come again with our dues for three months, January, February and March. We had whooping cough but we are well now and have been going to school. Hope you and the little cousins have been getting on fine this winter. Enclosed find $1.00. Love to all the cousins.—*Martha, Robert and Havanah Mitchell.*

Always glad to get your letters. It is good of you little cousins to help keep the corner full.—"*Uncle Charley.*"

CHILDREN'S LETTERS

Dear Uncle Charley: I am a little girl twelve years of age. I wish to join the band of cousins. Enclosed find ten cents for which to pay for March. Hope all the little cousins are well and getting along nicely.—*Ruth Lassiter.*

We are glad to have you join the band of cousins and hope you will write often.—"*Uncle Charley.*"

Dear Uncle Charley: Here I come again with twenty cents for March and April. I wish I could see you and the little cousins. I hope you all will have a grand Easter.—*Naomi Carden.*

Would be glad to have you visit us sometimes and see all the little children. I know you would be delighted.—"*Uncle Charley.*"

Mrs. Jennie Penny.—I love THE CHRISTIAN SUN and want it regularly.

Mrs. Amanda Wright.—I am now too blind to read much, but feel like I can't be without THE CHRISTIAN SUN. My granddaughter reads it for me.

THE CHRISTIAN SUN

"IN ESSENTIALS UNITY, IN NON-ESSENTIALS LIBERTY, IN ALL THINGS CHARITY"

Lessons From The Flowers

SPRINGTIME brings us the flowers and the flowers bring us messages that are many. They call and challenge us to a higher and nobler life. They are the emblems of purity and their fragrance fills the air, which reminds us that we should fill the earth with goodness and break the alabaster box of love that it may spread in all directions. The brevity of the life of their bloom reminds man of his numbered days. Flowers grow beautifully in filthy places and this reminds us that from ours sins and selfishness God can lift us up and make our lives beautiful and sublime.

Volume LXXI   WEDNESDAY, MARCH 26, 1919   Number 13

BURLINGTON   •   •   •   NORTH CAROLINA

THE CHRISTIAN SUN

Founded 1844 by Rev. Daniel W. Kerr

C. B. RIDDLE   -   -   -   Editor

Entered at the Burlington, N. C. Post Office as second class matter.

Subscription Rates

One year .... $ 2.00
Six months 1.00

In Advance

Give both your old and new postoffice when asking that your address be changed.

The change of your label is your receipt for money. Written receipts sent upon request.

Marriage and obituary notices not exceeding 150 words printed free if received within 60 days from date of event, all over this, at the rate of one-half cent a word.

Original poetry not accepted for publication.

Principles of the Christian Church

(1) The Lord Jesus Christ is the only Head of the Church.
(2) Christian is a sufficient name of the Church.
(3) The Holy Bible is a sufficient rule of faith and practice.
(4) Christian character is a sufficient test of fellowship, and of church membership.
(5) The right of private judgment and the liberty of conscience is a right and a privilege that should be accorded to, and exercised by all.

EDITORIAL

THE CHURCH AND HER PROGRAM

(Extracts from a sermon preached, recently in the Christian Church, Burlington, N. C., by The Sun's Editor.)

The Church has always had a program—the program of Jesus Christ. Men have never differed on that point but, inhuman like, they have waged wars over the presentation and interpretation of that program. It is not law alone that brings men into conflict so much as it is the result and the interpretation of law. If the world war has been a blessing in any way it has blessed the Christian forces of the land by bringing them to see a program of unity, a program for the salvation of the world—a new program, a unified program.

The recent war was often called a religious, a righteous war, but it was not the first to be called that. Through all ages men have fought for religious freedom but in many instances men have made that freedom a prisoner in their own hearts. They have not heeded the injunction, "He that saveth his life shall lose it, and he that loses his life shall save it." Ideas shape themselves into ideals and it is the ideals that we differ from each other about. It was the ideals of Germany that came into conflict with the ideals of a Christian nation. We were as sure of which would win as we are sure that the stars are in the firmament.

Things have been shaken up very much during the last four years. Democracy has been on trial and Christianity has been tested. Democracy triumphed and Christianity has proven itself again and again. But just as we found threat-barren places in Democracy we also found weak places in the Church. Take heed that we say "weak places in the Church and not in Christianity." Out of the turmoil and upheaval the spirit of Christianity has come like a flame from a burning volcano. In every world conflict has come out a shining light in the path of men and a joy to all who have sought and practiced its teaching. We have no fear of Christianity—its application is that which concerns us.

The narrowness of the Church's program has given birth to hundreds of humanitarian organizations that are within the scope and work of the Church. The spirit of Christ will have an outlet, and if the Church, the one supreme organization by and for Christianity, fails to give it its largest expression, it will seek, an outlet through some other avenue. Christianity is a principle, and therefore, cannot be hemmed or hedged about. We hear it said that the young men back in the trenches will think more of the Red Cross and the Y. M. C. A. than they will of a Church. If they do, it will be on account of the Service that these organizations have rendered the young men.

The future Church and its program must be so vital and faithful to the life and teachings of Jesus that it will not be difficult to distinguish men of the world from men of the Kingdom's interest. All too long we have been satisfied with Sunday display of our Christianity—we must live it seven days to the week. The prayers of a man who has mistreated his employees will not lead them to a throne of grace on Sunday morning. The invitation of a fellow workman will not get his comrade into the Sunday school if that workman has been dishonest six days in the week. The pious soul on Sunday will not suffice the other six. So many of us conserve the wick and oil during the week and burn it to a smoking flame on the Sabbath.

To many who have joined the Church there has been a sad disappointment. They have been expecting to get something out of it, and they have not. The reason is simple: They have put nothing into it. They have sought to draw dividends where they have not invested; they have sought to reap where they have not sown; they have asked before they have given.

A QUESTION FOR CONSIDERATION

It is no spasmodic thing that our people are being called upon to give greatly and graciously—it is the result of growth and demands of the Kingdom. And the beauty of it is that people grow in grace and financial ways when they give. It liberates their spirit and activities. But here is the question for consideration: Has the time not arrived when we need to make a drive for a definite setting aside of a certain part of our incomes for the cause of Christ? All denominations are rapidly doing this thing. When we have raised our mission fund, our educational fund, and reached the goals set in all other lines, the start will only be made. We must teach the masses to give systematically that great results and steady growth may continue to come to the Church.

THE SUN CAMPAIGN

During the last few days the campaign for a larger subscription list for THE CHRISTIAN SUN has been moving along very nicely. So far we have not announced just what has been done. We endeavor to be optimistic all the time (and it certainly takes that to edit and finance a Church paper) but the work in February and March, unless radically changed within the next week, will fall far below our expectations. The following ministers have been active in the work, and according to their work for new subscribers they stand on the list in the following order: J. E. Franks, E. T. Cotten, L. I. Cox, R. F. Brown, T. E. White, L. L. Wyrick, J. L. Foster, W. D. Harward, J. Lee Johnson, I. T. Underwood, W. L. Wells, B. J. Howard, C. E. Newman, D. A. Long, A. W. Andes, and J. F. Morgan.

The above names are given in order from the highest number to the lowest. There are two names on the list that have the same number and then another group of three having the same number each, and still another group of six that have the same number each. We leave it to the brethren to guess who they are tied with and to work out the tie. Our report for the period will include the work done on the fifth Sunday and up to Wednesday, April 2. This will give ample time for all work done during March to reach this office.

A SUNDAY SCHOOL INSTITUTE

An experiment in the form of a Sunday School Institute was inaugurated in Alamance County last summer by the Board of Religious Education of the County Sunday School Association. The original plan was to have a regular school for one week for the benefit of officers and teachers of the Sunday schools. An able faculty was secured. All plans were ready for the execution of the work when the epidemic of Influenza struck the country. The work was postponed from time to time, always with something to conflict. It was finally decided to put on the Institute beginning with Sunday, March 16, with the same faculty except for each faculty member to lecture on his or her subject and to omit the class work. One session was held each evening for a period of one week. The members of the faculty secured were: Mr. J. Norman Wills, Greensboro, N. C.; Mr. J. M. Broughton, Jr., Raleigh, N. C.; Dr. W. C. Wicker, Elon College, N. C.; Prof. C. C. Haworth, Burlington, N. C.; Miss Martha Dozier, Greensboro, N. C.; Mrs. Chas. L. Van Noppen, Greensboro, N. C.; Mr. Gilbert T. Stephenson, Winston-Salem, N. C.

These specialists in Sunday school work brought rare messages that filled every auditor with a vision for greater things in the Sunday school work of the County. Practically all sections of the County were represented at different times.

As a result of the Institute the Board of Religious Education decided to take steps and employ an all time secretary to look after the Sunday school work of the County just as the Superintendent of Public Instruction looks after general schools. The Board, together with the County Association, is of the opinion that the time has come when such a step is necessary. It is being worked out in many counties in North Carolina and Virginia and is certainly worthy of consideration.

OF WORLD INTEREST

As we go to press the news reaches the country that Hungary has proclaimed an armed alliance with Russia and proposes war against the entente. The following notes taken from the daily press of this (Monday) morning, March 24, may be of some interest:

London, March 23.—The Budapest government is reported to be signing a proclamation acknowledging a state of war between Hungary and the entente, says a dispatch to the Exchange Telegraph from Vienna.

"The dispatch adds that the Czechoslovaks government is preparing to issue a mobilization order."

"Copenhagen, March 23.—A dispatch from Budapest dated Friday said that time order was being maintained by the troops and the national guard. The revolutionary government, it was stated had issued a prohibition against the carrying of arms, making the penalty for disobedience five years penal servitude and a fine of 50,000 kronen.

"Other dispatches announce that order prevails in the country districts around Budapest."

THE EDITOR'S SIDE LINE

If an editor could close his work when he closes his office for the day it would not be quite so bad, but his work cannot be confined within four walls. We make it a rule not to report all the services we hold and the things that engage us on the Sabbath unless they are in churches of the denomination. Last Sunday was not altogether typical of our work, but many are not far from it. On that day we met our Bible class at 10 o'clock, preached at the Webb Avenue M. E. church, Burlington, at 11 o'clock; met the Board of Religious Education of Alamance County at 2 o'clock, heard Judge Stephenson in the final session of the Alamance County Sunday School Institute at 3 o'clock, met the County Sunday School Association at 4:30, preached at the above named church again at 7:30, and at 8:45, by invitation, made a "talk" to the colored organization of the M. E. church of the city. Pen points are not the only things worn out by an editor of a religious periodical.

The coming of spring gives renewed life and vigor to every living creature. It is just another way that God changes the scene and gives rest to his children.

If you appeal to the real man to join the church on the ground that it is a *rest room* you cannot win him. Men want something to do.

PASTOR AND PEOPLE

THE CHAPEL HILL FIELD OF THE CHRISTIAN CHURCH
Chapel Hill

The work here is encouraging to say the least. We received three valuable additions to this membership at last Sunday evening's service. The Sunday school is alive with interest and is growing, under the superintendency of Brother W. E. Lindsey. One Sunday in each month is devoted to the study of missions and the offering of the day is given to the same cause. Brother E. L. Daughtry, a graduate student in the University, and teacher of our Men's Bible Class, was the interesting speaker to the school on this subject last Sunday. We are also giving (investing) one Sunday's offering to the Orphanage. Our school offers testimony for the "Give and Grow" idea. The Christian Endeavor Society is doing well. Brother D. J. Rose, a medical student in the University, is its president.

Now, dear reader, allow me a word about "pounding." The Chapel Hill and Damascus people are perpetual pounders. Instead of all coming together once or twice in a year, as is the old custom, it is every few days that we are reminded of their thoughtfulness and devotion by a load of wood being dumped on our woodpile and the driver refuses to take pay, or a sack of flour, a ham, (yes, a real Orange county ham), a bag of potatoes, eggs, chickens and other things carried to our kitchen and we have to hurry to even say "thank you." Each seems to know his "time," and the plan works like a charm.

Damascus

This church maintains its reputation as an old stand-by. Its spiritual life proves itself in its responsiveness to the many calls of the needy. They paid on pastor's salary last year $75.00 more than was promised at beginning of year, and the same amount is promised this year. A live Sunday school, under the leadership of Brother Bunnie Crabtree, survives the the "flu" and winter weather.

Martha's Chapel

This badly scattered membership is not without a majority who are loyal. Our first quarterly meeting of the year was held recently, at which time mention was made of the fact that our Church needed a new roof, and with less than a dozen male members present, more than $70.00 was raised in about five minutes. More was raised on Sunday, so the roof is assured. This church also paid its pastor more than it promised last year, and votes a $50.00 raise in salary for this year. We received one new member here at our last appointment.

O'Kelly's Chapel

We have been to this point only twice this year. The congregation at our last appointment was encouraging. We are hopeful of results at this place. Brethren, pray that among these people I may prove myself a workman that needeth not to be ashamed.

E. J. HOWARD.

"NOT WITH US"

"John answered and said, Master, we saw one casting out devils in thy name, and he followed not with us and we forbade him, because he followeth not with us." Luke 9:49. Mark reports him as saying, "We forbad him because he followed not us." Mark 9:38. Jesus said, "forbid him not." This was the same John who a little later, with James, wanted to call fire down from heaven to consume the inhabitants of a certain Samaritan village, because Jesus was not allowed to pass through on his way to Jerusalem. Jesus again gives a rebuke when he says, "Ye know not what manner of spirit ye are of."

This same John was also with James in the request that they made of Jesus, that they might sit, the one on the right hand and the other on the left, in his Kingdom." The rebuke comes again in the words, "Ye know not what ye ask."

Think of a man with this spirit going out to forbid a worker for Christ against the devil, and for the simple reason that, "he followed not with us."

But there came a time in John's life when he saw things in a different light and had a different spirit, a spirit of helpfulness. It had come when Peter and John were going up to the temple to pray, as recorded in the third chapter of Acts. That was on the other side of Pentecost. Selfishness and the Holy Ghost do not abide in the same life, at the same time. As to a man filled with the Holy Ghost there will be something of higher consideration than, "politicking" in religion.

W. D. HARWARD.

Dendron, Va.

SUFFOLK LETTER

I am thinking just now of the kitchen and the cook. These are two essentials in the home. The parlor is more prominent, where there is one, but the kitchen is more essential. The piano costs more, but the range is more useful. The pictures on the parlor wall may attract more attention than the pans on the kitchen wall; but they do not serve human necessity as well. The guests sit in the parlor, but get their dinner from the kitchen. There is too little thought given to the size, ventilation, and furniture of the kitchen. The kitchen should be large enough for comfort and convenience and the furniture should include all possible helps. It is vanity to spend a thousand dollars on drawing-room, and a hundred on a kitchen. Yea, more, the husband overlooks fair play when he has an elegant office for his business a shabby kitchen for his wife.

Think of the work of a cook. Three times a day for three hundred and sixty-five days in a year means ten hundred and ninety fires, meals must be prepared and dishes washed and pans, too. In most kitchens as many fires must be built and as many buckets of water must be brought in. In many kitchens it is too cold in winter and too hot in summer; yet the cook must prepare the meals. In addition to the work, there must be the plan for the meal first. What shall it be? How shall it be prepared? When shall it be served? How long shall it wait for thoughtless eaters? It is one round of repetitions for which few are ever thanked. As many complain as praise. It is the largest number of workers in the world. There is no other group or class of workers as large as the number of cooks in the world, and they get less pay. Most of them are housewives, mothers af families, performing their task with a devotion and fidelity more bravely than the soldiers in war. Yet little is thought, and less is said, about these millions of women who feed the world. Much is said about farmers feeding the world. The cooks feed the farmers and all the world beside the tillers of the soil. Many of them hack wood with dull axes, build fires with wet wood, draw water with poor rigs and cook in smoky kitchens; and then get good meals and keep cheerful. There is as much grace as grease in many kitchens, and more religion than in many parlors and offices. Many prayers have gone up to God over the bread tray or the frying pan, and many sacred altars are close to the kitchen stove. Here is the mint where love is coined into biscuit and steak, doughnuts and pies, pickles and preserves. Here is where mother thinks of papa at work and children at school, and plans for dinners and suppers to please both, never thinking of herself. Thus the kitchen toilers are in an endless chain of service for those they love. The kitchen chimneys are more than the factory and steamer smokestacks, with the locomotive added in; and the smoke rises from furnaces just as essential to the life of man and the business of the world.

Henry Grady went to his boyhood country home in Georgia after he had made his reputation by his great Boston speech, and requested his mother to cook him some cakes as she did when he was a boy; and then let him say his evening prayer at her knee again before he went to bed at night. No newspaper praise was as sweet to this great man as that revival of childhood in a country home. No state dinner can equal the kitchen meal on a winter day in the home where love builds the fire, cooks the dinner, and serves it with a mother's hands. All hail! to the cooks of the world.

W. W. STALEY.

INGRAM AND PLEASANT GROVE

Dr. J. O. Atkinson's visit to Ingram marked a new day in our midst and although the weather was most inclement and only a handful heard the most inspiring message which he brought us, over six hundred dollars in cash and subscriptions were added to his past achievements.

On the next Sunday afternoon President Harper met the church in a call meeting and delivered a message full of fundamental principles on "Lessons we have learned from the war." Dr. Harper impressed his audience with his clear, forceful, and forward-looking ideas making it easy for him to go "over the top" by getting $1,900.00. Brother J. H. Osborne, although he himself is a Baptist with his children members of the Christian church, established a $1,000.00 fund in memory of his deceased son, George A., who was a beloved Elon student. Ingram was glad to rally to both of the above causes.

Pleasant Grove

Within the last six months we have lost here four leading and subtantial members by death but we trust we have not been afflicted in vain. Our spiritual natures have been deepened and our forces have been turned afresh toward the Bulah Land.

Dr. Harper came along with large vision for and faith in Pleasant Grove. He transmitted a part of it to us in his fine address delivered Sunday at the eleven o'clock hour. In a few days following he was responded to by the Pleasant Grove people in terms not of $3,750.00 as was our apportionment, but in terms of $15,000.00. Brothers P. W. and A. B. Farmer gave $5,000.00 each, establishing thereby a $10,000.00 Farmer Fund in memory of their beloved brother, D. S. Farmer. May God bless each one who so nobly gave.

J. G. TRUITT.

News Ferry, Va.

ELON COLLEGE

Dr. J. O. Atkinson delivered a series of lectures on missions here 16-19 inst. The general theme was "The New Internationalism," or "World-wide Evangelism." The separate themes were "The Problem Stated," "Separation," "The Task Worthwhile," and "Service." The doctor poured into these all the eloquence and enthusiasm of his ardent soul and both delighted and inspired his hearers. May their fruits be seen in the days to come.

A play, "The Dream That Came True," by Miss Flowers' expression class on the 19th inst. brought together a large crowd and gave them a delightful evening. The play had a fine moral and was well rendered throughout.

The revival services have begun with large attendance and fine spirit. Rev. J. V. Knight is leading the singing this week. Rev. O. D. Poythress will lead next week. The pastor is doing the preaching.

N. G. NEWMAN.

RALEIGH, N. C.

Rev. George D. Eastes was formally installed as pastor of our Raleigh church last night. The service was well attended, was solemn and impressive. The new pastor was welcomed to the city in an impressive address by Mayor Jas. I. Johnson; to the ministerial association by Rev. J. L. Morgan, president; to the church by Prof. L. L. Vaughan of A. and E. College. Rev. J. Lee Johnson gave a most impressive charge to the church and the writer gave the charge to the pastor. The orchestra of the church furnished splendid selections, and several selections by the choir were impressive. The closing prayer and benediction was by Rev. J. E. Franks. Raleigh people are already in love with their new pastor and are rallying to his call to service.

J. O. ATKINSON,

March 20.

E. B. Bailey.—It gives me lots of pleasure to have THE SUN visit in my home. I wish it could shine in every home.

A TALE OF INSPIRATION

Trustee D. S. Farmer of the College; after a lingering illness, crowned by a triumphant transition to the home of the soul, was laid to rest on Saturday, March 15. With many another sorrowing friend I was present at the impressive funeral service. Dr. Atkinson preached a rare sermon, one that stirred every heart with desire to meet the larger days ahead in the becoming and liberal spirit. Brother Sam was worthy of the large concourse that assembled under threatening weather conditions to do him honor, of the beautiful floral offerings that graced his grave, of the words of praise that fell from every lip, of the tears that stole down the cheeks, expressing the sympathy of all with the bereaved family. He was characterized by large faith, rare humility and generous sacrifice for the Kingdom's sake. His kindness to the colored people on his farms was eloquently attested by their tears, as they looked for the last time upon his mortal remains. Their tears are a sacrament to us all. It is great satisfaction to have known and loved this man of God.

And now for the tale of inspiration. On Sunday morning his family expressed the desire that I proceed at once with the raising of the endowment fund in Pleasant Grove church. The deacons, of whom Brother Farmer had been one, held a meeting and voted to raise $5,000 in the church aside from what Brother Farmer's family would give. This was readily done, and then in honor of their brother, Brothers A. B. and P. W. Farmer each duplicated the church's donation, giving $5,000 each, making the church's total $15,000 and entitling Pleasant Grove to three seals of gold on her recognition card. In addition Brother Farmer himself left a bequest to the College he loved. The pastor, Rev. J. G. Truitt, is one happy man, and so is Dr. Atkinson, the former pastor. This rare liberality is challenge to the whole Church. It is tribute to Trustee Farmer that his people have thus honored his memory.

Another tale of inspiration is that related to Ingram's drive. The Mission Secretary was there Sunday before and was given a hearty subscription and gracious welcome. They oversubscribed their quota to the Elon Fund, too, evidence that missions do not hurt Christian Education nor vice versa. This little band of the faithful have made it forever impossible for any church to say "we gave to missions; we cannot give to Christian Education." All can do it, and all will.

Two tales shall grace this paragraph. Danville and Reidsville both mission points, both in debt, both struggling heroically to establish themselves. Without the inspiration of a public service these two infants of the Kingdom by an exploit of rare sacrifice doubled their quotas and earned a golden star for their recognition banner. Sure, by now we shall be agreed that money invested in mission churches pays good dividends.

And Sanford and Turner's Chapel have subscribed their quotas under the able leadership of Rev. T. E. White, thus placing every church so far visited on the banner list and many of them far "over the top."

Finally, Dr. Staley's challenge is stirring the hearts of our people. In a private note he made the statement that his offer was not according to his *ability* but according to his *interest* in the cause with the hope of stimulating our people to drop the paltry way of supporting the Kingdom and to give till the windows of Heaven are opened with blessings too large to be received. In all the history of our brotherhood no such sacrificial offer has been made as this leap of faith on Dr. Staley's part. He has brought us to a new day freighted with enlarging possibilities for the Kingdom's growth.

Surely this is a tale of inspiration. Surely God is in this work.

W. A. HARPER.

Elon College, N. C.

NOTES

The Franklin, Virginia, church will be dedicated the fourth Sunday in April.

Many subscriptions will expire in April. If your label is marked 4-1-9 your subscription is in the list.

Dr. J. O. Atkinson is away on a trip for several days in Georgia and Alabama in interest of the mission cause.

Rev. R. L. Williamson writes that he has had Influenza and that has hindered his work for THE CHRISTIAN SUN.

Don't forget to move up your time-piece one hour Sunday morning, March 30. If you fail to do this you will be one hour late with the time over the country.

Sister M. E. Rowland, mother of Dr. C. H. Rowland, has passed her 85th birthday. She has been an invalid for thirteen years. For the last four months she has been confined to her bed. Though an invalid her life is full of sunshine. To know her is to love her.

On page 6 of this issue will be found an article by Dr. Harper that is full of inspiration. Some men die that others may live, and this has been our thought since receiving that article for publication. Brother Sam Farmer's body is dead, but he still lives. What a source of comfort and strength to his loved ones and friends! Surely the Church is entering upon great things.

Mrs. L. H. Brantley—Hoping you much success in your good work. I have been taking THE SUN so long that I would feel at a great loss without its bright pages.

Mrs. L. S. Vaughan—I have taken THE CHRISTIAN SUN many long years and cannot now do without it.

CHRISTIAN EDUCATION

MAN POWER AS A MINISTERIAL QUALIFICATION

By George C. Enders, Dean Christian Divinity School

The final means winning the great war was not the tank, nor the submarine, nor the aeroplane, nor the machine gun, nor poison gas, nor high explosive. The determining factor in deciding that great world struggle was MAN POWER. This is the verdict of those who are in a position to speak with authority.

In the present great struggle, in which our very civilization is at stake, in the contest between the evolutionary and revolutionary forces set free by the war, in the stupendous task of reconstruction, there is no force so potent as MAN POWER.

If we are to believe the great cloud of witnesses returning from the war zones, the success of the Christian work done in the armies was due not to denomination, or creed, or ritual, but to MAN POWER. And a host of these witnesses are insisting that the one thing needful, the one vital necessity, in the church work of the future will be MAN POWER.

In view of this broad and general emphasis, it would seem that a study of man power as a qualification for the minister would be of timely interest and value to the members of the Christian Church. It is for this reason that the present study is undertaken.

Just what do we mean by "man power?" Our ideas on this subject are apt to be vague, indefinite. We know there are various kinds of power in the world, such as horse power, and steam power, and electric power, and so on. But evidently by man power we mean something different. Evidently by man power we mean PERSONAL POWER.

"But," you ask, "what is personal power?" In answer, let me say, that personal power is the one thing almost universally sought. It is the philosopher's stone. It is the pearl of great price. To have it in high degree is to be highly successful; not to have it in any degree is a calamity. By personal power I mean simply PERSONAL INFLUENCE. Not the bad kind. By personal influence I do not mean that strange magnetic influence which we call prestige which bedazzles the intellect and bewilders the reason and makes us do or say things, which we afterwards learn are not in harmony with our own best interest. But I mean the good, inspiring, constructive kind. I mean the up-lifting effect of a strong and good personality.

As a qualification for the minister of the Gospel personal influence is all important. It is, broadly speaking, the sum total, or the result of all other qualifications. Without personal influence, preaching, teaching, pastoral work are of little value. Personal influence backs up the logic and eloquence of the pulpit, vitalizes the instruction of the Sunday school class, and puts genuine life into pastoral work.

If personality or personal influence is of such inestimate value, it is important that we should make, if necessary, the most pains-taking search to find its sources, and, if possible, to learn how it may be secured.

Much of what we call personality is hereditary. It is ours by inheritance. It is born with us. And it is so closely associated in our thinking with bodily form that many regard personality as inseparable from, if not identical with the physical body. A large, well-proportioned body is a valuable asset to personality. But care must be taken not to overestimate its value. The question may well be raised whether an impressive physique is an absolutely essential part of ones personality. If so, then one can not build for himself a strong personality when nature has given him an insignificant or deformed body. This question perhaps can best be answered by a study of the personal influence of two great ministers, Phillips Brooks, and Henry Van Dyke.

Bishop Brooks had a large, well-poised, well-proportioned body. He stood six feet three, inches, and weighed three hundred pounds. It goes without saying that he was an unusually strong and impressive personality. Few now can realize the very wonderful and very powerful personal influence he had upon thousands of people. And doubtless to most of these his large physique was a vitally essential means to his influence. And so it was in his case. But contrast with him the personality of a man like Henry Van Dyke, whose body is scarcely large enough to make a vest-pocket edition of Phillips Brooks. And yet who will say that the personal influence of Van Dyke, as poet, teacher, preacher, statesman, is less than that of Brooks. I once heard Professor Van Dyke deliver his great lecture on Tennyson. A week later I asked a friend how he liked the lecture. His reply was, "I can not tell yet. Van Dyke lifted me up so high I have not gotten back to earth yet."

Illustrations like these could be given without number, proving conclusively, first, that personality is not dependent upon bodily form, and, second, that the personal influence of no two persons can be analyzed into the same elements. This means that every personality is unique and that the elements of which it is composed are largely acquired. God through nature gives to each an individuality, but out of it each must make his own personality. It is the primal purpose of the college and the divinity school to aid the ministerial student in acquiring the strongest possible influence of personality.

In the educational process by which personality is acquired or developed there are three fundamental elements. These are knowledge, discipline, and personal association. There is little danger that the importance of these factors to personal influence will be overestimated. It matters not how richly the minister may be endowed with natural powers. These are the raw material only, and of little value unless properly developed.

Other things being equal a minister's personal influence will be directly proportional to the amount of his knowledge. In no other calling in life may so large use be made of learning. All knowledge has for him a practical value. There is no department of learning with which it will not be advantageous for him to be familiar. Finding it his province as a theologian to explain the ultimate meaning of things, it is necessary that, to an extent at least, he understand the things themselves. Called upon to administer to people of all occupations and professions he must at least be family with the knowledge which pertains to the work of these persons. This does not mean that he should know as much about everything as specialists know about some things, but it does mean that he should know enough about the various subjects of human knowledge to enable him to show an intelligent interest in them and to save him from making false statements in regard to them.

But while knowledge of facts is all-important to personal power it is not all-sufficient. Much of personal influence is due to discipline, whether received as the result of routine work performed in willing obedience to accepted regulations in school or in society, or whether it comes from the varied experiences of life; its joys and its sorrows, its victories and its defeats, its Mounts of Transfiguration and its Gardens of Gethsemane. Whom the Lord loveth he chasteneth. The undisciplined soul will have little personal power to lead another soul to Christ.

To these two factors of knowledge and discipline there must still be added the personal element of association. Without coming into living association with living personalities, human and divine, a strong personality is impossible. Let the minister, therefore, know man, the crown of creation, not only as he reveals himself in poetry and history, in philosophy and religion, but also and especially as he is in himself. Next to knowing God, and His Son Jesus Christ, the greatest being to know is man. He is the wonder of wonders and the miracle of miracles. Well-might Shakespeare exclaim; "What a piece of work is man. How noble in reason, how infinite in faculties, in form and moving, how express, how admirable! In action how like an angel; in apprehension how like God! The beauty of the world; the paragon of animals.'' And yet how few men do we really know. It is a sad, a melancholy fact that we are comparative strangers in this world. Our actions are often misinterpreted and our words not understood. We have a speaking acquaintance with many, but most of us can number on the fingers of one hand the persons whom we really know, and the number who know us is often smaller still. Hence our personal influence is far less than it might be. And if human association is so important as an element in personal influence, of how much more importance is association with God and His Son Jesus Christ?

Man power, or personal influence, is, therefore, a very broad ministerial qualification. It includes nearly, if not quite, all the other qualifications. It is unique in character, and largely the result of acquisition. It is more powerful than horse-power, electric power, or explosive power. In fact it is the most potent force in the universe, for it is the means chosen of Jesus Christ by which His kingdom is to be established.
Defiance, Ohio.

MISSIONARY

MINUTES OF THE WOMAN'S MISSION BOARD OF THE EASTERN VIRGINIA CONFERENCE

The Woman's Mission Board of the Eastern Virginia Christian Conference, met in the Ladies Parlor of the Christian church in Franklin, Va., on Saturday, February 8, 1919, with the following members present:

Mrs. C. H. Rowland, president, Franklin, Va.; Mrs. M. L. Bryant, corresponding secretary and treasurer, Norfolk, Va.; Mrs. W. V. Leathers, superintendent of Young People, Holland, Va.; Miss Mary Andrews, superintendent of Cradle Roll, Suffolk, Va.; Mrs. W. D. Harward, superintendent of Literature and Mite Boxes, Dendron, Va.; Mrs. I. W. Johnson, secretary, Suffolk, Va.; and two visitors, Dr. J. O. Atkinson, Field Secretary of Missions, and Dr. C. H. Rowland.

The meeting was called to order by the President, Mrs. C. H. Rowland, at 9:40 A. M.

Prayer by Dr. Atkinson.

Minutes of last meeting were read and approved.

Mrs. Rowland read the report she sent to the Annual Conference as follows:

This has been one of the most successful years of our work. We have 56 organizations in 27 churches of the Conference. Our goal for the year was $2,500.00; the amount raised for all purposes was $2,902.42. On account of the Influenza epidemic, our annual meeting which was to have been held at Portsmouth, has not convened, but the present Board expects to meet soon and formulate plans for the coming year. We are exceedingly desirous to reach the women in every church in the Conference and ask the co-operation of the pastors and leaders to this end.

It was suggested that since we did not have the annual meeting last October, on account of Influenza, we have a meeting on April 10, 1919.

Moved and carried that a spring meeting be held on the above mentioned date.

Mrs. J. L. Foster was elected second Vice-President.

Mrs. Rowland appointed Mrs. W. D. Harward, committed to find a place for the April meeting.

Mrs. Leathers reported a new young People's Society, organized at Windsor, Va.

Moved and carried that the Young People's Societies raise $500.00 to buy blocks to help build the Santa Isabel church, and that the Willing Workers raise $150.00 to support an orphan at Elon College.

Moved and carried that $4,000.00 be the minimum goal for the year from all departments of the work.

Mrs. Leathers read a letter from Mrs. Denison, asking for $500.00 for the Hungarian Mission in Brooklyn.

Moved and carried that all Societies that did not take the Thanksgiving Offering for the Barrett Home be requested to take an Easter Offering for this purpose.

The Board decided that the time has come when the women of the Eastern Virginia Conference should support a missionary, and to this end, we make as our objective $1,200.00 to be raised during this year, the missionary to be decided upon at our regular annual meeting. The Societies were apportioned as follows:

Berkley, $25.00; Bethlehem, $75.00; Berea, (Nansemond), $50.00; Damascus, $50.00; Dendron, $50.00; Franklin, $25.00; Holland, $50.00; Holy Neck, $50.00; Liberty, $50.00; Ivor, $25.00; Memorial Temple, $25.00; Mt. Carmel, $50.00; News-port News, $25.00; Oakland, $50.00; Portsmouth, $25.00; Rosemont, $25.00; Spring Hill, $10.00; Suffolk, $350.00; Third church, $25.00; Waverly, $50.00; Wakefield, $25.00; Windsor, $15.00; Union, (Southampton), $25.00; Isle of Wight, $35.00; Cypress Chapel, $25.00.

Mrs. M. L. Bryant was appointed to write to each Society and notify them of their apportionment.

The following churches having no Societies are to be written to, and asked for $10.00 each for the support of said missionary: Antioch, Barretts, Berea (Norfolk), Centerville, Eures, Hobson, Johnson's Grove, Mt. Zion, Lamberts Point, Oak Grove, Sarem, South Norfolk.

Miss Mary Andrews, Superintendent of Cradle Roll, gave the following report:

Number of children enrolled..................156
Number enrolled since last report 65
Amount of dues collected .... $ 9.55
Amount from Mite Boxes $0.97
             Total..................$46.52

Number of Rolls in Conference.............11
Number of new Rolls since last report 5
New Rolls at Berkley, Dendron, Holland, Holy Neck and Ivor. No report from the Berkley, Holland and Memorial Temple Societies.

It was decided to hold the annual meeting with the Portsmouth Society on October 23, 1919.

Adjourned to have lunch with the Young People.

          Afternoon Session

Called to order by the President at 2 P. M.

The following books were recommend for Mission Study Classes:

For Women's Societies—"The Path of Labor," and "Women Workers of the Orient."

For Young People's Societies—"The Price of Africa," "The Gospel for a Working World," "Ancient People at New Tasks."

For Willing Workers—"Jack of all Trades," and "Jack and Janet in the Philippines."

Mrs. Rowland and Mrs. Leathers were appointed on the program committee for the April meeting.

Closing prayer by Dr. Atkinson.

Adjourned to meet subject to the President's call.

MRS. C. H. ROWLAND, Pres.
MRS. I. W. JOHNSON, Sec.

WOMAN'S BOARD MEETING
North Carolina Conference

The Central Executive Committee met in Burlington on March 7, with all members present. Miss Bessie Holt, Superintendent of Young People, was also present.

Mrs. W. R. Sellars reported progress in securing life memberships. She expects to secure the full twenty shortly and to go over the top.

Mrs. W. H. Carroll reported that she had written all prospective churches and their pastors and had had only one response. We wonder why pastors and church secretaries refuse to co-operate in the missionary work.

Mrs. Harper reported on the prospect of the Missionary Rally Day Program and the printing of the minutes.

Miss Holt outlined her plans for aggressive work among the young people.

The secretary was requested to write the other officers of the Board, urging them to redoubled efforts in their departments.

MRS. W. A. HARPER, Sec'y.

SEASIDE CHAUTAUQUA AND SCHOOL OF METHODS OF THE CHRISTIAN CHURCH

The Seaside Chautauqua and School of Methods of the Christian Church will hold its sixth annual session at Virginia Beach, near Norfolk, Va., beginning Tuesday, July 29, 1919.

The strong programs of the previous sessions will be continued. The strong speakers, Christian work specialists and visions of Christian leadership will make it worth while for those who wish preparation for the great days upon which we are entering. Every church and Sunday school in the Christian denomination should have some members present.

For information write S. M. Smith, General Secretary, Chamber of Commerce Bldg., Norfolk, Va., or the undersigned.

WARREN H. DENISON, Pres.
27 C. P. A. Bldg., Dayton, Ohio.

Editor Lehmann states a very important principle. Begin with the children—that is the place.

No wonder the church is being criticized for its slow speed. The investments in it are not large enough.

THE CHRISTIAN ORPHANAGE

SOME QUESTIONS

We are at a loss to know just what to do. We have taken in as many children as we feel ought to be in the building. We have more than a dozen applications on file. All of them urgent. A number of them for small children—bright little boys and girls. We are compelled to say no to their pleadings and refuse to give them a home for the lack of room. We are willing to work still harder and make greater sacrifices in order that these children may not be denied a home. Will our people sacrifice, too, and come to our rescue that room may be provided for the helpless? Will our Church make the Easter offering large enough to enable us to provide more room? The "flu" epidemic has subsided and many little helpless orphans have been left in its wake. Many in pitiful circumstances calling to us for help. What will we do about it? Will we, as a Church, make some sacrifice that they may have help?

During our Thanksgiving offering campaign, the "flu" epidemic was raging and many of our churches were closed, and the churches that did have services had small congregations and in many instances the collections were small. May of the churches did not make an offering at all. Now the "flu" is abated and it will soon be time for our Easter offering and I wonder if we could not make a special effort and raise enough money from that offering to open up the home for the little children?

If our people will make a special effort and begin to lay their plans now and then work the plan, I feel sure we can do that thing. Then when you visit the Orphanage and see the home for little children full of bright, sweet faces how glad you will be that you had a part in giving them a home. "He who gives lives; he who does not give does not live. Let us keep on giving and keep on living."

We had the very great pleasure of spending the second Sunday with Brother T. E. White and attended services at Sanford, Shallow Well and Poplar Branch churches. We were delighted with the sweet spirit we found in these churches and the kindly sympathy they have for the Orphanage work. We presented the Orphanage work the best we could and trust the interest will still grow and that greater work will be accomplished in the future.

We were very kindly entertained in the home of Brother J. D. Gunter, Sr., and found it a great pleasure to be in his home and associate with his splendid family, and could not help but feel that a man who has such an interesting family must be one of the happiest of men.

CHAS. D. JOHNSTON, Supt.

REPORT FOR MARCH 25, 1919

Amount brought forward, $1,557.48.

Children's Offerings

Annie Aldridge, 25 cents; Oliver E. Young, Jr., 25 cents; Erma Jean Whitaker, 25 cents; Doris Whitaker, 25 cents;

Lorane Whitaker, 25 cents; Eric Whitaker, 25 cents; Ellen Gray Franklin, 30 cents; Mae Thomas, 10 cents; Hermon Thomas, 10 cents; Total $2.00.

Sunday School Monthly Offerings
(North Carolina Conference)

Bethlehem, $1.00; Shallow Ford, $2.00; Reidsville, $2.00; New Elam, $2.61; Chapel Hill, $2.58; New Providence Baraca Class, $3.00; Piney Plains, $5.49; Shiloh, $2.12; New Lebanon, $1.00; New Lebanon Baraca Class, $1.00; Union Grove, $3.00; Lebanon, $3.74.

(Eastern Virginia Conference)

Dendron, $4.72; Franklin, $5.00; New Lebanon, $3.00; Berea (Nansemond), $10.00; Wakefield, $1.00.

(Alabama Conference)

Wadley, Ala., $1.03.

(Virginia Valley Conference)

Union Memorial, $6.18; Mayland, $4.25; Total, $64.72.

Special Offerings

Chas. M. Gant, $1.00; D. J. Mood, 50 cents; Mrs. W. H. Speight, $1.00; Ellen Speight, $1.00; Edgar Speight, $1.00; Total, $4.50.

Thanksgiving Offerings
(Pleasant Union Church)

J. A. Long, $5.00; Miss Laura Green, $2.50; J. D. Long, $2.00; Miss Ora Lee Green, $2.00; Mr. and Mrs. J. C. Upchurch, $1.25; U. C. Long, $1.00; Rev. J. Lee Johnson, $1.00; Cleveland Mathews, $1.00; Miss Iola Upchurch, $1.00; Perry Raynor, $1.00; J. Add Johnson, $1.00; John Green, $1.00; Joseph Johnson, $1.00; T. J. Howington, $1.00; Carlie Johnson, $1.00; W. S. Long, 50 cents; A. M. Long, $2.00; Mrs. A. M. Long, $2.00; Buie and Louise Long, $1.00; R. B. Butts, 50 cents; Miss Caro May Green, 50 cents; Miss Mary Green, 50 cents; Milton Mathews, 50 cents; Gordon Long, 50 cents; Mrs. Perry Raymond, 50 cents; T. E. Green, 50 cents; E. V. Green, 50 cents; K. A. Stuart, 50 cents; Mrs. Mollie Dees, 60 cents; Miss Alma Green, 25 cents; J. V. Butts, 25 cents; J. A. Betts, 25 cents; W. A. Green, 25 cents; J. L. Wilder, 25 cents; Mrs. Ernest Wilder, 25 cents; General collection, $5.15; Total, $40.00.

Total for the week, $111.22; Grand total, $1,668.70.

CHILDREN'S LETTERS

Dear Uncle Charley: I am a little boy six years old. I am going to school. I like to go very much. My teacher is Mrs. R. E. Apple. Please find enclosed 10 cents for the little orphans. Love to all the cousins.—*Hermon Thomas.*

I'll bet you are a fine little boy. Study hard and learn all you can and some day you will be a smart man—*"Uncle Charley."*

Dear Uncle Charley: Here comes a little girl who wants to help the little orphans. I am nine years old and am going to school every day. My teacher is Mrs. R. E. Apple and I like her fine. Enclosed please find 10 cents for the little orphans. With lots of love to all.—*Mae Thomas.*

We are glad you want to help us. There are so many who need help and we have to turn them away for lack of room.—*"Uncle Charley."*

Dear Uncle Charley: Enclosed please find 25 cents for the little orphans. Please send me a picture of one of the little girls who sings "Jesus Loves Me." I know He loves the little orphans and I love them, too.—*Annie Aldridge.*

Glad to have your letter this week. Our little cousins are doing fine. We hope to keep the page full this year—*"Uncle Charley."*

Dear Uncle Charley: I am sending thirty cents for January, February and March. I am away out in the country going to school. I am in the third grade. My teacher is Miss Nannie Monk. I want to come to the Orphanage to see my brothers and all of you.—*Ellen Gray Franklin.*

Will be glad to have you visit us any time. You must work hard in school and beat your brothers here.—*"Uncle Charley."*

Dear Uncle Charley: Mother said you wanted all the cousins to write for March and we think that includes us. Enclosed find 25 cents each.—*Erma Jean, Doris, Lorraine and Eric Whitaker.*

You are fine little folks. You make good soldiers. You complied with my request at once. Just fine.—*"Uncle Charley."*

Dear Uncle Charley: Having teeth is not much fun, is it? I almost wish mother would buy me some false ones. Love for all the little cousins.—*Oliver E. Young, Jr.*

If you are having trouble with your teeth, you have my sympathy. But they will be real helpful to you after you get them.—*"Uncle Charley."*

SOME STRANGE CUSTOMS THAT PERSIST IN INDIA
(Related by a Methodist Missionary)

Up a winding stair we go into a tiny room. It has no outlook but courtyard of the house. It is well closed in, secluded from all outer things. Here is a young pupil—a Mohammedan girl. Must she stay within these closed doors always? Yes, until she marries. And then she will leave these closed doors, only to go behind others just as tightly closed!

Here is a little girl of eight, just taken away from one of our schools, where she was getting on so well! She has to be in "Purdah"—secluded—now. Why? Because she has reached the mature age of eight, and must no longer be seen by anyone outside! Now begins for her the closed-in life, which will go on until she dies, unless—what? Unless she should, in the providence of God, join the freed ones by and by.

We are invited to tea in a Hindu home. Suddenly our hostess gets up and leaving us, hides behind a door. Why? A man servant has brought in the tea and he must not see her face! Yet she is the mother of married sons and daughters! "This is our custom," the son says, smiling.

FORWARD FOR EVANGELISM

The time has come for a new emphasis upon the first duty of the church. We are being summoned to new activities in all directions; but first of all is the need for a more effective presentation of the claim of our Lord for an immediate decision and consecration to his service.

When the great war broke upon the world, men's hearts failed them. Religion seemed to be discredited. The church seemed to have lost her power. Men asked if, after all, Christianity was a failure, seeing it had not kept men from flying at each other's throats.

But the issues have cleared. It is becoming plain that the religion of Jesus Christ has not lost its power. Rather, has every sanction of our religion received new confirmation. The doctrine that "Might makes right" is forever discredited. Justice and righteousness are seen to be more powerful than fleets and armies. Summoned to the defense of the weak and helpless, and to the maintenance of pledged word and ideals of freedom and enlightenment, the unprepared nations developed an irresistable strength. Out of the wreck and ruin of war is rising a new world order. God is in His heaven. All will be right with the world.

Out of this new confidence there is coming a new appeal. Spiritual values are seen to be the supreme things. Never before could we so assuredly insist upon the great fundamentals of the Kingdom of God. In the sober mood induced by sacrifice and suffering, with the testimony that has been borne by men and women who have cheerfully surrendered their all for the good of all, we can call men to a like dedication of themselves. God demands our allegiance. The Cross of Christ is the symbol of the only life worth while. Surely in this hour of unequalled opportunity, the Church will not fail to make her message clear and strong and tender and insistent.

The opening months of this new year should mean much to us. We should not wait until the great motives have lost their freshness. Our hearts have been stirred to sacrifice and helpfulness and loving ministry. We have heard the call of the Christ in the opportunity to feed the hungry, clothe the naked, relieve the sick, deliver the prisoners, and help the bewildered and distressed of a half world. Now is the time to urge upon men that they recognize it as His call, and undertake the continuation of this ministry in His name. Only so will the great motives become permanent in our lives. The present impulse may pass with the first response; but the heart touched and changed by the Love of Christ will continue to manifest His spirit.

Therefore, let us press anew the claim of our Lord for surrender and confession. Let us say to our neighbors and friends, "Let us go to the house of the Lord." Let us lay the foundations of the new social order in a definite acknowledgment of Jesus Christ as Lord of our lives.

Ministers, church officers and church members can join in certain definite things, which will further these aims. Why not make these our special objectives for the next few months.

First, definite prayer for a revival of religion in the hearts of all of our members.

Second, definite plans for personal appeal to those who are not open Christians to accept and publicly acknowledge Jesus Christ.

Third, meetings of every congregation wherever possible, with especial appeal for a deeper Christian life, a public confession, and union with the church.

Fourth, prayer groups of three or more, for definite intercession on behalf of the church, and for individuals. These may be neighborhood groups, Sunday school classes, Church committees, or groups of friends. Utilize whatever organization or grouping there is at hand.

Many of our churches have suffered interruption of church services on account of sickness. Some have had their attention distracted from the regular worship by war activities. Many of the churches of our own brotherhood are without pastors. All the more is there need of this special movement. Let no one wait for some one else to lead the way.

If you love the Lord and your fellowman, you can lead in this work. Let the Evangelistic Campaign begin now, and begin with you. We need at once a strong evangelistic effort—a soul-winning campaign in all the churches. Where pastors are not available let a few laymen go together and hold meetings. Let there be much praying and planning and personal evangelism, until the whole church is aflame with soul-winning passion. It is exceedingly important that every pastor, church officer and member give heed to this message.

OLIVER W. POWERS,
Secretary for Evangelism and Social Service.
JOHN MACCALMAN,
Chairman of Commission on Evangelism.
WARREN H. DENISON,
Superintendent of the Forward Movement of the Christian Church.

THE SUN CAMPAIGN

During the last few days we have been very much encouraged by the many good reports of THE SUN workers. The list is climbing rapidly and we are grateful for the efforts of all who have given aid. Some of the pastors have not sent anything from their fields of labor. Let all put forth an effort between now and March 31.

HOW YOU CAN HELP

Order your books, Bibles and church supplies from the Convention's Publishing Agent. Seventy-five per cent of the profit made on all sales remains in the work to help support THE CHRISTIAN SUN. And also bear in mind that you can buy a book from your Publishing Agent at the same price as you can get it from the publishers.

THE TITHER

We have mailed to a number of SUN subscribers a copy of *The Tither*. This is an invitation for you to subscribe. We shall be glad to have your subscription. The price is only fifty cents.

THE GARDEN GATE

Early and late, early and late,
Little Boy swings on the garden gate.

"It isn't a gate; it's a motor car!
I'm traveling fast, and I'm traveling far.
I toot my horn, and I turn my wheel,
And nobody knows how grand I feel."

Early and late, early and late,
Little Boy swings on the garden gate.

"It isn't a gate; it's a great big ship!
I'm off to the pole on a 'sporing trip.
I'll ride a white bear, holding on by his hair.
nd I'll hurry him up with a whale-skin whip."

Early and late, early and late,
Little Boy swings on the garden gate.

"It isn't a gate; it's a big ballon!
I'm going to sail till I reach the moon·
I'll play with the man as hard as I can,
And I'll stir up the stars with a great horn spoon."

Early and late, early and late,
Little Boy swings on the garden gate.

"It's not a gate; it's"—off runs he,
His mother is calling: "Come in to tea!"
It's a wonderful gate, but it just isn't able
To turn itself into a supper table.

—*Laura E. Richards, in Woman's Home Companion.*

SNOW STORIES

There had been a November snowstorm and the woods and fields were white and still. All the summer-birds had gone, while the pine grosbeaks, the snowflakes, the cross-bills, the siskins, and the other winter-folk were yet in the far North. This morning there was not even the caw of the crow from the cold sky. As I followed the unbroken wood-road, it seemed as if all the wild-folk were gone or asleep.

The snow told another story. On its surface were records of the life which throbbed and passed and ebbed under the silent trees. Just ahead of me were long lines and traceries of footprints with a tailmark between. In and out they ran among the dry stalks of lobelia, yarrow and tansy, showing where the white-footed deer-mice had frolicked and feasted the long night through on the store of seeds left on the plant-stalks, underneath and around which their little tunnels ran beneath the snow. These are the same little rascals which swarm into my winter camp and gnaw everything in sight. One of my friends one night left

a new felt hat on the window-seat. The next morning there was a little circle of neat round holes gnawed around the crown of the hat!

Today among the mouse-tracks was a faint trail only just visible, made up of what looked like a string of exclamation marks with a tailmark showing between them. It was the track of the masked shrew, a little plush-covered animal, the fiercest fighter of all the wild-folk. If he were the size of a dog, no one's life would be safe in country districts. The large deer-mice and meadow voles, and even the gray Norwegian rat, give him a wide berth. That night, the snow said, the shrew was a most unwelcome arrival at the dinner of the Merry Mice Association. At first their trails all ran together in a maze of tracks. Where the trail of the shrew touched the circle, there shot out separate lines of deer-mice tracks like the spokes of a wheel, with the paw-marks far apart, showing that the guests had all sprung from the table at the approach of the stranger, and dashed off in different directions. The shrew-track circled faintly here and there, then started off in a lonely trail, ran for some distance and—stopped.

The sword of Damocles, which hangs winter and summer over the head of all the little wild-folk, had fallen. The shrew was gone. A tiny fleck of blood and a single track like a great X on the snow told the tale of his passing. All his fierceness availed nothing when the great talons of the flying death clampered through his soft fur. An X on the snow is the monogram of the owl-folk, just as a K is of the hawk-kind. The size of the mark in this case showed that the killer was one of the larger owls, probably the great horned owl, that fierce king of the deep night woods whose head, with its long eartufts or horns, I had seen peering from his nest of sticks on the mountainside in a high treetop, as early as February. On wings so muffled with soft downy feathers as to be absolutely noiseless, he had swooped down in the darkness and broken the tiny bubble of the shrew's life.

Now the trail wound upward toward the slope of the Cobble, a steep, sharp-pointed little hill which suddenly thrust itself up from a circle of broad meadows and flat woodlands. By the road the snow had drifted over a low patch of sweet-fern in a low hummock. As I plodded along I happened to strike this with my foot. There was a tremendous whirring noise, the snow exploded all over me, and out burst a magnificent cock-patridge and whizzed away among the laurels like a lyddite shell. When the snowstorm began, he selected a cozy spot in the lee of the sweet-fern patch, and had let himself be snowed over. The warmth of his body had made a round, warm room, and with plenty of rich fern seeds in easy reach he was prepared to stay in winter quarters a week if necessary.—*Samuel Scoville, Jr., in Sunday School Times.*

The war taught us to give. The conditions brought about by it placed us on a new basis for thinking of others. May the spirit continue!

Giving with the *getting* left out is the spirit of the Master.

THE FORWARD MOVEMENT

IN THE FIELD

The Superintendent presented the Forward Movement program at the Phillipsburg, Ohio, church March 6.

The Mt. Vernon, Ohio, Christian conference institute met at Coshocton, Ohio, March 11. The entire program was a Forward Movement program. The speakers were Rev. R. H. Long, President; Rev. H. R. Clem, Secretary, and the Superintendent. The ministers and laymen gave close attention and got a vision of the possibilities of the Movement for their conference. The executive board passed a resolution pledging co-operation in every way.

The Superintendent will present the Forward Movement work at the Northwestern Indiana Conference institute March 18-20, and will meet the workers of the Warren, Plum Tree, Majenica and Six Mile churches at Warren, Indiana, for a workers' conference and rally March 21.

He will speak on the Forward Movement at Huntington, Indiana, March 23, meet the executive board and trustees of the Eel River, Indiana, conference the 24th and hold a rally at Huntington that night.

The Executive Committee of the Forward Movement will meet at Dayton, Ohio, at the headquarters March 26.

The Superintendent will visit the Urbana, Illinois, church March 30 and conduct a campaign there.

The Quadrennial Convention

Every delegate to the American Christian Convention should be present at that convention. The work of the present quadrennium will center around the Forward Movement and every member and laymen who can possibly do so should be there to carry back to his section the inspiration, information and plans of work for the quadrennium.

This is the Way one Pastor and Church Do It

Dr. W. H. Hainer is pastor of the Irvington, New Jersey, church and president of the New Jersey conference. Dr. Hainer is pastor of the largest Sunday school enrollment of any church in the denomination. He says: "I am glad to report that our church has decided to go into the Forward Movement to the full extent. After my first sermon on the five Points of the Movement, I asked if they would express their willingness to back up the Movement and every individual in the congregation rose to his feet."

Have you read "Money the Acid Test"? Every member of the Christian Church ought to read that splendid book. It costs only sixty cents postpaid, and is worth many times that amount.

WARREN H. DENISON, Supt.

Recently we heard of a man who said that he felt better when he gave to his local church. Later we learned that he contributed five cents per month and he is able to pay one hundred times that much. If five cents would make him feel better, we wonder how he would feel if he tithed his income. He would get well.

BOOKS, BIBLES, TESTAMENTS

In order to reduce certain stocks of books, Bibles and Testaments on hand, the following prices are made and will hold good until March 31, 1919:

Bibles

No. 312X. Holman Self-Pronouncing Teachers' Bible. Printed on fine white paper from good, clear type, and contains references, concordance, four thousand questions and answers and fifteen prepared maps. Size 4 3-8X6 1-2 inches. Egyptian Morocco, divinity circuit, head bands and marker, round corners, red under gold edges. Regular selling price......$4.65
Price to March 31 .... 3.90

No. 71. Scofield Reference Bible. Handsome binding, French Morocco limp, new and improved edition. "The neatest Scofield Bible made." It will please you. Regular selling price $4.50
Price to March 31 .... 3.90

No. 215. Child's Self-Pronouncing Pictorial Bible with Helps. Bound in French seal leather, round corners, silk bands, gold titles,—handsomely made. Regular selling price $2.50
Price to March 31 .... 2.00

No. 1113. Ideal Bible for Children. Printed on fine white paper from the newest and clearest type of the size made. Size 3 1-2X5 3-8 inches. This Bible will please you. Regular price $1.75
Price to March 31 .... 1.40

Testaments

No. 3913 R. L. (Red Letter). Large print Morocco binding. Regular price $2.00
Price to March 31 .... 1.75
No. 2902 Cloth binding, large print. Regular price.... .90
Price to March 31 .... .75
No. 2502 P. Cloth binding, black faced type. Regular price .... .75
Price to March 31 .... .55
No. 2113. Pocket size, Morocco binding. Regular price .60
Price to March 31 .... .45
No. 0133. Pocket size, Morocco binding, overlapping edges. Regular Price 75
Price to March 31 .... .55

(A Testament in Modern Speech)

Cloth, $1.25; cloth, indexed, $1.75; cloth, India paper, $1.75; leather, $2.35; leather, indexed, $2.75; leather, India paper, $2.75; Persian Morocco, Divinity Circuit, $3.75; Turkey Morocco, $1.25. Pocket Edition (without notes): Cloth, $1.00; cloth, India paper, $1.25; leather, India paper, $1.85. State definitely style wanted.

The above prices are regular. Make your choice and deduct 10 per cent. State definitely Testament wanted.

Books

Pastor's Ideal Funeral, $1.15—Regular price, $1.25.

(Books for the Children)

We have several copies "Silver Rags," "Patty's Grand Uncle," "Johnny Two Boys," "A Rescued Madonna"—your choice, 20 cents per copy. We will substitute if the book ordered is sold before the order reaches us.

Special

"Redmond of the Seventh," by Mrs. Frank Lee is a book with a fine story taken from school life, 290 pages, handsomely bound, 50 cents the copy.

Special Note: One of these books will be sent free with each order for $3.00 worth of books, Bibles or Testaments.

Address

C. B. RIDDLE ....Publishing Agent
Burlington, N. C.

Mrs. Lucy Sanford—Please renew my subscription to THE SUN as it brightens a little corner in my home.

Sunday School and Christian Endeavor

SUNDAY SCHOOL TOPIC FOR SUN-
DAY, MARCH 30, 1919

God's Hand in a Nation's Life

(Review Lesson)

Scripture Lesson: Joshua 24:14-28
Golden Text: "Righteousness
exalteth a nation; but sin is a reproach to any people." Proverbs
13:34.

For explanation and comment, see
Bible Class Quarterly or Officers and
Teachers Journal, Christian Publish-
ing Association, Dayton, Ohio.

CHRISTIAN ENDEAVOR TOPIC FOR
MARCH 30, 1919

"On The Fence"

Scripture Lesson: Matthew 27:11-
26.

For explanation and comment, see
Christian Endeavor World, Christian
Endeavor Publishing Company, Bos-
ton, Mass.

THE SUNDAY SCHOOLS TAKE UP
THE WORK

In response to a letter sent recently to the secretaries of the various
Sunday schools, many schools are
beginning both to study missions and
also to take a missionary offering
once a month. Those thus far taking
the monthly offering and remitting
the same to the Mission Treasurer,
J. O. Atkinson, Elon College, N. C.,
are the following: Chapel Hill, N.
C., Reidsville, N. C., Wentworth
Sunday school; McCullers, N. C.,
Beulah Sunday school, Wadley, Ala.,
Linville, Va., and the New Providence Sunday school, Graham, N. C.

Others are writing that their
schools will fall in line. Sooner or
later we believe that every Sunday
school in the Southern Christian
Convention will be studying missions in one way or another and most
of them making a missionary offering. The writer repeats what he has
said to some schools personally that
any school which will give an offering a month to missions and fails
because of that to have sufficient
funds with which to conduct its affairs and pay the local expenses, he
himself will make up the deficit out
of his own purse at the end of the
year. His firm conviction is that any

school which will give half to others
will certainly have enough out of the
other half for self. The school which
will take up one offering per month
for the Orphanage and one for missions is in a good way to progress and
prosperity, and will have funds in its
treasury with which to buy its own
literature and to do its local work.
The writer stated in one of our
schools not long since that at least
half of our Sunday school funds
should go to other purposes than for
local Sunday schol expenses, and it
chanced that there was in the school
that day a member of a Baptist Sunday school of the community. This
member stated to the writer after
the school had adjourned that her
school did not use any of the money
it raised to purchase its own literature, but that was made up by individuals on the outside, and all
funds given by the classes and
through the regular channels of the
Sunday school went to other purposes than to the School. I think
we teach a lesson of selfishness, possibly without being aware of it,
when we raise money in the school
and spend it all on the school. A
Sunday school as well as an individual may be selfish and become self-
centered. As much for others as for
self should certainly be the slogan of
every school.

But the writer is even more anxious that our schools study missions
than he is that they now begin to
give for missions. Several secretaries have written us that their funds
are needed and they canot now begin to contribute to missions. Such
schools can certainly begin the study
of missions as the books for this purpose are well adapted and certainly cost very little. A book costing
say thirty-five or forty cents per
copy, to be studied once a month,
would last six months or a year.
There are now books prepared for
every member of the class from
primary to old people's, and it does
seem that every Sunday school could
give some time to the study of the
greatest problem that the Bible
teaches, and the greatest task ever
committed of God to man. If the

Sunday school is unwilling to give
its session once a month to the study
of some missionary book, why not
spend five minutes or ten minutes of
each Sunday in every class discussing, teaching, learning some missionary problem. If there are those unwilling to do either of these, why not
have a missionary committee, or a
missionary lecturer or a missionary
superintendent who from Sunday to
Sunday will devote five minutes of
the hour to talking about and explaining to the Sunday school items
of missionary moment and concern.
We will become a missionary people
only as we learn about the missionary
problem and there is no better place
to teach and to learn this problem
than in the Sunday school.

J. O. ATKINSON.

THOMAS

John Wesley Thomas died March 17,
1919 in his seventieth year. He was a
charter member of Center Grove Christian church and had filled the office of
deacon since the organization of the
church. Every pastor of this church, now
living, will feel a loss in his death, and
remember him as a good man and faithful to his church. His faith in Christ
was like the faith of a child. His cup
often ran over, and he shouted aloud
the praises of God. He was powerful in
prayer, and many have been the times
when congregations felt God was near.

He married Flora Elizabeth Knight,
and they had eight children. Four died
when small. Bertha, who reached womanhood and married Alexander Eddins,
died several years ago. Chas. E. lives in
Greensboro, Ira, in Elizabeth City, and
Arthur lives at the home. He was greatly afflicted in his last years. He lived
with his son, Arthur, and he with his
other brothers did all they could to make
his afflictions easy.

He was buried at Center Grove by the
side of his wife, and his funeral was conducted by the writer, who feels the loss
of a cherished brother.

T. E. WHITE.

FARMER

Brother David Samuel Farmer died at his home near News Ferry, Va., March 13, 1919, being 56 years, 8 months and 13 days old. He married Miss Mary Virginia Lovelace on December 16, 1885 from which union the following childre survive him: Joseph Pleasant, Nannie Baker, Mrs. A. C. Hall, John Lovelace, David Samuel, Jr., Emily Esther, and Archer Duncan. He is survived by three brothers Joseph H., Archer B., and Pleasant W., and one sister, Mrs. Minnie F. Cook.

—With perfect control of mind and emotions Brother Farmer announced to his family Thursday morning after breakfast that he was dying. He called each one to his bedside and gave them parting words of counsel, and endearment too sweet and sacred for public print. Although those with whom he lingered in the last moments were prostrated in grief and sorrow he made them feel as though they had accompanied him to almost within the gates of Heaven itself.

Brother Farmer was a leading spirit in his church and community and his leadership was wise, gentle, and thoroughly Christian.

Drs. J. O. Atkinson, T. S. Wilson, and the writer conducted the funeral services. Dr. Atkinson preached the sermon, which seemed inspired for the occasion, so appropriate was it May God richly bless each member of the bereaved family.

J. G. TRUITT.

CHILD'S SELF-PRONOUNCING PICTORIAL BIBLE WITH HELPS

This Bible is bound in French Seal Leather, has round corners, silk head bands, gold titles, handsomely bound. Regular selling price..........$2.50
Price till March 31.......... 2.00
Call for Bible No. 215.

Address
C. B. RIDDLE, *Publishing Agent*
Burlington, North Carolina

REPORT OF THE CONDITION OF

The Elon Banking and Trust Co., at Elon College in the State of North Carolina, at the close of business, March 4, 1919:

RESOURCES

Loans and Discounts $23,449.62	
Overdrafts, secured, $208.33; unsecured, $648.55	856.88
United States Bonds and Liberty Bonds	6,150.00
Banking Houses, $1,480.38; Furniture and Fixtures, $1,774.68	3,255.06
Demand Loans	2,290.00
Due from National Banks	9,170.97
Cash Items held over 24 hours..	2,555.96
Gold Coin	482.50
Silver Coin, including all minor coin currency	988.27
National Bank Notes and other U. S. Notes	2,045.00
Thrift Stamps	36.50
War Savings Stamps	655.65
Customers' Liability on Acceptance, Profit and Loss....	29.00

Total $51,965.37

LIABILITIES

Capital Stock paid in...\......$ 5,000.00	
Surplus Fund	1,000.00
Undivided Profits, less current expenses and taxes paid....	193.18
Bills Payable	5,000.00
Deposits subject to check....	28,852.41
Time Certificates of Deposit....	10,539.71
Cashier's Checks outstanding..	253.10
Certified Checks	14.47
Interest Reserve .'..........	328.96
Received on Liberty Bonds....	962.50
Accrued Interest due depositors	150.00

Total $51,965.37

State of North Carolina—County of Alamance, March 18, 1919.
I, Marion C. Jackson, Cashier of the above named Bank, do solemnly swear that the above statement is true to the best of my knowledge and belief.

MARION C. JACKSON,
Cashier.

Correct—Attest:
J. J. LAMBETH,
W. P. LAWRENCE,
S. W. CADDELL,
Directors.

Subscribed and sworn to before me, this 19th day of March, 1919.
J. J. LAMBETH, J. P.

BOOK NOTES

Story Books For The Children
We now have on hand a very fine story book for the children. "Redmond of the Seventh," by Mrs. Frank Lee. The book is handsomely bound, lettered in gold and contains 290 pages. The story is wholesome —a school story. The price is within the reach of all—75 cents postpaid, or two for $1.25.

Christian Hymnaries
We have the Christian Hymnary at 50 cents the copy. How many copies?

Address
C. B. RIDDLE, *Publishing Agent*,
Burlington, N. C.

A BIG TASK

—BUT WHO SAID WE COULDN'T DO IT?—

THE PLAN

Five men are to associate with President Harper in the field.

* *

The campaign is now on. The workers are at work.

* *

The minimum subscription is $100 to be paid in five years. That is *only* $20 the year—a little over $1.50 per month.

* *

An individual who gives at least one thousand dollars may perpetuate his own name or the name of a friend in the establishment of a fund, whose interest the Trustees shall use for the general purpose of the College.

* *

An individual, church, or organization that gives $25,000 may endow a professorship in the College Faculty.

* *

Any church that reaches its quota will be given a beautiful recognition card, handsomely printed in Maroon and Old Gold, the Elon colors, for display in its place of public worship. Any church that doubles its quota will have a golden star affixed in the white field of this recognition card, and additional stars will indicate still further doubling of the quota.

THE EDUCATIONAL PROGRESS

Of The

SOUTHERN CHRISTIAN CONVENTION

Depends Upon

WHAT WE DO FOR THE ELON STANDARDIZATION FUND

THE PURPOSE

To bring Elon's endowment up to the educational requirement.

* *

To help her enlarge her work for the Church.

* *

To help Elon provide for a larger faculty to take for the additional life-recruits that are to be trained there.

* *

To enlarge her opportunity of service to the coming generations.

* *

To provide ample pay for her professors who have sacrificed beautifully through many years.

* *

To educate the young men and women of the Church who have given their lives to the Gospel's cause.

* *

TO DEFEND CHRISTIAN EDUCATION—*The hope of the day.*

Ask God to lead you as to your duty in this matter.

Are You Praying That The 100 Recruits May Be Secured?

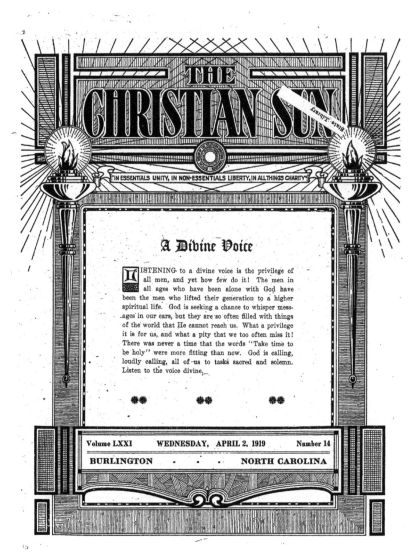

THE CHRISTIAN SUN

"IN ESSENTIALS UNITY, IN NON-ESSENTIALS LIBERTY, IN ALL THINGS CHARITY"

A Divine Voice

LISTENING to a divine voice is the privilege of all men, and yet how few do it! The men in all ages who have been alone with God have been the men who lifted their generation to a higher spiritual life. God is seeking a chance to whisper messages in our ears, but they are so often filled with things of the world that He cannot reach us. What a privilege it is for us, and what a pity that we too often miss it! There was never a time that the words "Take time to be holy" were more fitting than now. God is calling, loudly calling, all of us to tasks sacred and solemn. Listen to the voice divine.

Volume LXXI   WEDNESDAY, APRIL 2, 1919   Number 14

BURLINGTON   -   -   -   NORTH CAROLINA

THE CHRISTIAN SUN

Founded 1844 by Rev. Daniel W. Kerr

C. B. RIDDLE - - - Editor

Entered at the Burlington, N. C. Post Office as second class matter.

Subscription Rates
One year .... $ 2.00
Six months 1.00
In Advance

Give both your old and new postoffice when asking that your address be changed.

The change of your label is your receipt for money. Written receipts sent upon request.

Marriage and obituary notices not exceeding 150 words printed free. If received within 60 days from date of event, all over this at the rate of one-half cent a word.

Original poetry not accepted for publication.

Principles of the Christian Church
(1) The Lord Jesus Christ is the only Head of the Church.
(2) Christian is a sufficient name of the Church.
(3) The Holy Bible is a sufficient rule of faith and practice.
(4) Christian character is a sufficient test of fellowship, and of church membership.
(5) The right of private judgment and the liberty of conscience is a right and a privilege that should be accorded to, and exercised by all.

EDITORIAL

OUR FUTURE EDUCATION

During the last four years there have been injected into the curricula of our colleges and universities as well as high schools, certain educational reforms. We have been dealing in these changes largely with the training of mechanics. We have been in a rush to turn out a finished product ready to meet some problem caused by the world war. Military life has found its way into the educational institutions and the beat of the drum and the presence of marching orders have placed their stamp upon educational life. Efficiency has been somewhat of a watchword and we have searched the entire military vocabulary seeking expression as to the onward march of education.

Education is a slow process and while the war and world conditions have taught us many lessons about our educational work, we fully believe that we should not lose sight of the real arts in education, literature and sciences as the fundamentals. We are of the opinion that the greatest men of our land are those who have been privileged to sit at the feet of teachers who emphasized the well rounded soul. The mastering of some of the choicest selections in literature and language work makes its stamp upon a life that is telling to the world. We make a plea for the teaching of the Bible as never before in all our institutions where the law does not prohibit it.

Physical training had just made its start when the world war came. Physical training is now going to be a part of every standard educational institution. We have learned long ago that a great mind largely depends upon a great body. The laws of health are also going to be recognized and taught. It is very difficult to outstrip the man who has a healthy body, a trained heart and mind and is well grounded in the fundamentals of education. May the day of education and instruction be outstripped of fads and fancies and filled with the things that make man's life happy and helpful; and a well rounded Christian citizen.

NO HONOR

We heard a Sunday school superintendent say recently that it was no honor to hear a superintendent say that he had not missed his school in two, three, or five years. And this man who so spoke is the superintendent of a Sunday school that has a teaching and official force of 120. He knows his business. Here is the point: The man who stays at home all the time never has a chance to find out what other people are doing. Don't get it into your head that you know it all, fellow Sunday school man, for there are some up-to-date workers in the country. Get in touch with them.

RAISING THE FINANCES OF THE CHURCH

It is a common error that many local churches have dropped into of paying no special attention to the finances of the church during this season of the year. They feel that they will have ample time after the announcements begin to appear that Conference is soon at hand. This is a mistake because it robs the people of the benefit of a good system and teaches them in the wrong direction. We have always contended that the best time to begin to raise finances of the church is the first Sunday *after* Conference and not the *last* Sunday before Conference.

A NEEDED EDUCATION

While our people are growing along the line of giving there is still a needed education in this particular field of work. We sincerely believe that if we had started a campaign of education along this line of giving twenty-five or fifty years ago that our Church would be ten or fifteen years ahead of its present work. And this reminds us to say that we believe that we can do no greater work than to teach our people in every possible way the spirit and the joy of systematic giving. The Church must continue to grow and prosper. It depends entirely upon the attitude of the people as to how fast it will grow and how well it will prosper.

ELON STANDARDIZATION FUND

We are delighted to announce that the Elon Standardization Fund is meeting with splendid success. The hearts and minds of our people are rapidly opening to the joy of giving. After all, what we have and what we are does not belong to us, but to God and the dedication of these things to the service of God is our best opportunity, and our greatest privilege.

THE NORTH CAROLINA CONFERENCE

Let us all bear in mind that the three conferences in North Carolina have merged into one and it is now the North Carolina Christian Conference. Let us so speak and write it. Let us also prepare to attend the initial session of the enlarged Conference. The place for meeting is Burlington, North Carolina and the time is November, next.

SEND YOUR PASTOR

The American Christian Convention is soon to meet. What about sending your pastor? If he deserves the trip you ought to send him, and if he does not, his going may make him worthy of such consideration. Begin now to raise a budget to send him. It will help the church far more than it will help him, for he will be able to impart new ideas and plan more largely. If you want to think well of your pastor do something for him and this is a good time. Remember that the date is April 29. Begin today on the matter.

HE IS RIGHT

A man stepped into THE CHRISTIAN SUN office the other day to arm himself with a copy of some reliable Sunday school book so that he could get a more intelligent view of the lesson. "I am the teacher of an organized class," said he as he proceeded to speak of his work; "and my strong point in favor of the organized class is that the best work of any kind is done through organization. When you organize men they get interested in each other. No man was ever brought to Christ without some one getting interested in him." He is right. We must get interested in the individual before he can lead him to a better life. You cannot compel a man to get interested in you, but you can get interested in him and win his interest for you and the cause you represent.

THEN AND NOW

There was a time when the health of a family or an individual concerned the outside world but little. Such is not the case now. Health authorities are educating the people to the point that the health conditions of one family or one citizen is a thing vital to *all* the people. Business men are beginning to realize that people who do not care to keep themselves or families well are not as safe to have financial dealings with as citizens who protect their health. Wealth and happiness depend largely upon health. Being our brother's keeper has a larger significance and broader meaning than we often think.

THE CHURCH UNION PROPAGANDA

(Biblical Recorder)

We do not feel panicky about the proposed organic union of all the churches. We have no idea that such a union can be brought about upon any basis that has yet been proposed. When Christians get ready to unite on a Scriptural basis, Baptists of all people, will be most eager for it. Until then, we see no danger, if our people will hold to the New Testament as their guide. A distinguished brother who has had an un-

usual opportunity to study the views of several denominations, said this to the writer some time ago: "The approach of our people to the Word of God is more direct than that of any other denomination. There are fewer non-conductors between the Baptist mind and the Bible than is the case with any other people."

So long as we maintain this attitude toward the Bible we are on safe ground. But it is well for us to keep informed as to some of the modern movements which have as their aim the elimination of denominational distinctions, and the forcing of all the denominations into a conglomerate organization, which, in the very nature of things, can have no definite, clear cut convictions as to the teaching of God's Word.

The latest thing along this line which we have seen, came out in a rather unexpected place. Dr. W. A. Harper, president of Elon College, wrote an article for the *News and Observer* some time ago, in which he held that there should be more religious instruction given in our State schools. If we understand Dr. Harper, he favors the teaching of religion at our State colleges by the several churches in the college community. His idea, if we get it clearly, is to let the churches employ a teacher who shall teach religion according to the views of the denomination which employs him. He recognizes that, according to our form of government, the State cannot teach religion, and this is his method of having the churches do an important work from which the State is estopped.

It is not our purpose to discuss the suggestion of Dr. Harper, but to call attention to a reference he makes, we suppose with approval, to the following deliverance of the Church Council Board of Education. The Board was discussing the plan suggested by Dr. Harper, and giving several advantages that would accrue from it among which is the following:

"10. Working together at a common task is the surest and safest method of bringing about the organic union of the churches. This organized co-operation of a group of denominations to provide Christian education, training for Christian service and to develop loyalty to the organized church, will not only promote the spirit of unity in the co-operating agencies, but will train large numbers of students to propagate the same spirit and plan in their home communities. Leaving these students adrift in their religious life without personal allegiance to any denomination operates to delay the proper unity of the churches."

So here is "the cat in the meal tub." The Council of Churches would seize this opportunity to further their pet scheme of bringing about organic union of the churches. And yet there are those who seem to be totally blind to the fact that there is any movement of any kind which is trying, in the most remote degree, to bring about church union.

Let Baptists stand where they have ever stood, on the Word of God as the only basis for union which we can consider. Dr. Shakespeare, of England, may be ready to surrender, but Southern Baptists are not. Some other denominations might merge with others, but our principles are too dear and sacred to be bartered away.

Sunday school and Christian Endeavor matter failed to reach us this week.

AS AN ENGLISH WOMAN SAW IT

(This private letter from an English woman, who was in London on November 11, Armistice Day, tells rather more vividly than anything we have yet seen the reaction of the citizens upon that day of days.)

I must tell you something of the wonders of Armistice Day. November 11, at 10:56, as I was just arriving in London, I heard the guns begin!...... All the office windows round Westminster were flung up, and the cheering began (that wonderful cheering that rolled back and forth through London like the sound of waves all day afterward). I rushed into the Court Hall where some twenty men and four women were just mustered, the clerk beginning to read the minutes. "Gentlemen, do you hear the guns?" I cried. "Yes," said the chairman solemnly, does it mean the armistice?" "Listen to the cheering." "Oh, let us get on with the work," said some of the older men, but three women looked at me, and I at them (N. B. They were the three best and most active workers of the whole committee). "Come along!" I cried, and out we went down the street to Westminster, in time to watch the whole population streaming out from office and factory, faces as white as death, often, and all the flags running up like a scene in a theater.

We just saw, and cheered like mad, the flags go up on the House of Commons and St. Margaret's—cheered the little bugler lads coming out to sound "All clear," as after air raids—and then went back to our committee!........finished the work, and then raced past Buckingham Palace, where the huge impromptu procession was gathering, to fetch my daughter from her office in the Strand. It was a struggle to get there, and even greater to get back, but I had learned the massed bands of the Guards were to play, and the King and Queen come out at 1:30, but in spite of the crush and the rush I would not have missed it for worlds.

After four and a half years of oppression, anxiety and distress, to see the myriads of happy faces! Every one (even in deepest black) smiling, and all the dull dark streets waving with flags, taxis and lorrys—motors and wagons covered with soldiers, nurses, munitioneers, flags waving in every hand—bands playing—and all so spontaneous, so sudden—and so beautiful! Well! M. and I ran behind motors, dived through the American Army (so she says!), round taxis, in front of lorrys, under horses' noses. Every one laughed, every one helped us, every one was a friend and a comrade. And so we reached Buckingham Palace just as the bands struck up. At least 100,000 were there, waving flags and cheering; and then we sang, "Tipperary," "Keep the Home Fires Burning," etc, and then "Home, Sweet Home," and a good many voices choked, till only young voices rang out; then the "Old Hundredth," and then the national anthems of the Allies, while Queen Mary waved her flag and the King saluted—then a pause, as he stepped forward, and quite clearly his voice rang out: "Friends, we must all thank God for this great victory." The most wonderful hush fell on that huge shouting crowd for a couple of minutes and then all the bands struck up, "Now Thank We God Our Lord." Every one sang it and then dispersed. It was wonderful!

Now I have said very little of the last stages of the war. Certainly we all felt that America's response to Lloyd George's telegram was great, and it was wonderful to hear how your boys did fight in those last attacks. Nothing could have been finer. And all this autumn we have had the comfort of their freshness and keenness as a great asset of moral as well as physical help. Not that spirit had failed here—but I do think the last six months had brought a really terrible strain—so many homes utterly desolate, whole districts in mourning. My son trained and sent out two hundred boys of under 19 in September; 70 per cent were killed within a month! This was no uncommon story; and with poor food and many other minor hardships cumulative in effect, I think nothing could have helped us like the coming of America.

Such fierce fighters, too! The Germans certainly dreaded them, and clearly some of the new and stringent rules they brought were all to the good.—New York Christian Advocate.

MORE INSPIRATION

That is it, exactly, more inspiration. The churches continue to go over the top with a relish that is exhilarating, and optimism prevails in every quarter. Our beloved Mission Secretary taught us the larger and better way and blazed the path of this glorious time. He has always said that all we needed as a people was a chance. He gave us one. We accepted it joyously. We now have another, and it is fast becoming a twice-told tale. "Our people are folks," as Dr. Rowland has so often said, and Brother Charlie knows.

But I must not drift. Union, (N. C.), Apple's Chapel, Chapel Hill, Monticello, Belew Creek, First Church of Greensboro have the past week gladdened every heart with their lovely response. The week has been crowded with interest and joy, and the work is not yet done in any of them. Rev. L. I. Cox has greatly helped in the magnificent results.

The largest gift of the week was by Hon. R. T. Kernodle, familiarly known as Alamance County's great-hearted sheriff, who gave $5,000. The spirit in which he and his wife gave this large sum for Kingdom service was even more satisfying than the gift itself. It is good to see a man who has worked hard and been prospered show his gratitude to God in such liberal fashion. Sheriff Kernodle thus becomes the first member of our Church in North Carolina to give $5,000 to any Church enterprise but he is not the last. God has greater things in store for us and this pioneer in Christian liberality shall see the fruit of his daring for Christ bear a larger and still larger harvest of generosity among our North Carolina brethren.

The First Church of Greensboro, with a few years ago a mission point, has produced a cluster of strong young business men who presage much for the Kingdom. They more than doubled their quota, Brother S. A. Caveness and wife giving $2,500, as a thank offering that God had spared his life in his recent serious illness. When young business men urged to it by-their wives give so liberally, it promises large for the Kingdom's coming. We need more such friends. They are the future's guarantors.

Several brethren this week have given a thousand dollars each to establish funds perpetually to work for our Christ through Elon in the training of Christian ministers and workers. In Greensboro Mr. and Mrs. L. M. Cylmer in memory of their angel daughter, Rena Maude Clymer; Mrs. Cora L. Anthony of her sainted husband, so recently taken from her heart and home; and Deacon H. C. Simpson, the first student ever registered at Elon, who worked as a laborer in building the College and earned his expenses thereafter through College,—this man, prospered in his business, honors himself and family and expresses his gratitude to God in this signal style.

At Belew Creek, Brother V. O. Roberson has established the Roberson Fund; Brother Z. V. Strader, another in loving memory of his daughter, Miss Margie May, recently taken to Heaven in the joyous days of young womanhood; and Brother Allen W. Preston, a third in devoted memory of his sainted wife, Sudie Boyd Preston.

At Union, Deacons J. D. Wilkins and G. R. Maynard, two noble men of the Kingdom, with the hearty approval of their life companions, have perpetuated their names and expressed their gratitude to the Master in creating the Wilkins and Maynard Funds. It requires sacrifice for them to do this, but they are rejoiced to make it. These brethren realize that the measure of our soul is the magnitude of our sacrifice for noble causes. God multiply their kind!

Surely these are tales of inspiration. Surely God is blessing this work. Pray for it and the workers.

W. A. HARPER.

WANTED

THE CHRISTIAN SUN desires the name and address of every invalid and shut-in member of the Christian Church in the Southern Christian Convention. If you know of one man, woman, or child, report it at once. Don't take it for granted that some one else will. Let us hear from you.

Rev. W. B. Fuller writes:— "I look forward each week for THE CHRISTIAN SUN and enjoy reading about what the people are doing. I wish that THE SUN could shine in every home in the Southern Christian Convention."

President Harper was at Suffolk, Virginia, last Sunday in the interest of the Elon Standardization Fund.

If you want a good home Bible, one with large print and good binding, order No. 2014. The price is $4.00. Your money refunded if you are not pleased.

If your label reads 4-1-9 you should renew now. And a good time to do a thing is NOW.

Chaplain H. S. Smith writes us from France that he is enjoying his work very much.

PASTOR AND PEOPLE

NOTICE

The Sunday School and Christian Endeavor Convention of the North Carolina Christian Conference meets with Shallow Well Christian church July 15-17. The general theme for discussion will be "The New Sunday School for the New Time," and all talks and addresses are expected to be somewhat related to the general theme. The Sunday schools within the bounds of the Conference are requested to make an earnest effort to have themselves represented by capable delegates. It would be nothing but right that the travelling expenses of these delegates be paid by the Sunday schools.

Each Sunday school is requested to send to the Convention an amount of money equal to four cents per member of its enrollment. Churches that have been accustomed to holding their protracted meetings the week following the second Sunday in July are requested this year to arrange a different time for the protracted meeting, in order not to conflict with the Convention.

It is the purpose of the executive Committee to get out an attractive program that shall be instructive and inspiring, and to this end we solicit the co-operation of the brotherhood.

HERBERT SCHOLZ, Sec'y.

A LETTER FROM REV. J. W. WELLONS, D. D., TO D. S. FARMER'S FAMILY AND FRIENDS, AND TO THE MEMBERS OF THE CHURCH AT PLEASANT GROVE

My dear Brethren and Sisters and Friends:—

I am very sorry that I cannot attend the funeral of my dear Brother, Sam Farmer. My age and infirmity forbid my taking a trip like this at this season of the year. I am now in my 94th year and my capacity for walking is very poor, nevertheless I feel just as much for you, and my tears of sympathy shall be mingled with yours as much as if I were there.

Once I was the pastor of the church at Pleasant Grove and have always felt a deep interest in the people of the community and church. I was the pastor of Brother Farmer's father and mother, and knew Sam from a little boy, but all the older people there when I was pastor are gone. Pleasant, Archie, Willie, and Obe Farmer; John Boyd, John Herbert Boyd, Scott Boyd, Ed. Pierce, John Russell, Walter Mills, Broady Anderson, Ed. Belew, Bob and Joe Crews, James Moore, James Hankins, and Sandy Farrell were some of them. These dear brethren, though they were not all members of the Christian church, were my friends. While I was pastor there I visited them, broke bread with them, enjoyed the association with them, and they all attended regularly at my church. I knew no difference between these dear brethren than I did my own members, but they are of the past.

God! bless the dear sisters! How many of them I could mention as true to their God, true to their church, true to their family, and true to their pastor: This was a delightful congregation to serve.

As to Sam Farmer, he was a leading man in the church, in his family, in the community, in his conference and in his convention. His worth to the community and to the church is unknown. But these are things of the past. Let us deal a little with the things of the present.

The opportunities of these older brothers and sisters were limited compared with what they are now. Their means of accumulating the things of the world were limited. The many opportunities that we have at the present are giving us quite an advantage over the past. We should feel as the children and grandchildren of these dear ones that are gone that there is an unlimited field of usefulness laying before us. May we all feel that we want to make an improvement in all relations of life to do our duty to those of the past. May we feel that we are living in a progressive age, and let us feel that by the help of the Lord we shall move forward with the forward movements in our church work, in home, in community, and that it may be equal to the times. May we feel we live not looking so much to the future as it is to be prepared for the future. May we feel as we close with the earthly life that we will bring in our sheaves as reapers in the Master's vineyard.

May God bless the dear family of Brother Farmer, and the dear friends and sisters and brethren, and may this stimulate us to live nearer our God and stick to our duty. The harvest is ripe, let us go forth to labor.

This may be my last word to you dear brethren and sisters. But if we meet no more on earth may we meet our dear brothers and sisters that have gone before us! And what a happy meeting it will be to meet the dear old friends on the other shore and walk with them on the golden streets! God bless you all is my earnest prayer.

SUPPOSE

Do you ever stop to think that this is God's time; that we have no promise of tomorrow—only the present moment? Suppose we all realized this fact, how much more would we do?

Suppose you thought of your church and Sunday school as often as the cigarette smoker thinks of his smoke. Suppose you carried your Bible and referred to it as often as the cigarette smoker does his cigarette. Would you know more of the truth of the Bible? Suppose the dancer should turn his steps heavenward; suppose the gambler should direct his plans for service to his fellowmen rather than cheat them.

Habits are formed for worldly ambition and desire. Why not form them for spiritual and religious things? Religion, we say is the best thing that a person can possess. Should we not put more time and thought into it?

In forming habits, read your Bible, pray and meditate upon Biblical truths and teachings and note the difference in your life. Does it pay? The Apostle Paul says, "Finally, brethren, whatsoever things are true, whatsoever things are honest, whatsoever things are just, whatsoever things are pure, whatsoever things are lonely, whatsoever things are of good report; if

there be any virtue, and if there be any praise, think of these." Phil. 4:8. Think of the above things and note your experience and the trend of your habits.

               L. L. WYRICK.

Elon College, N. C.

SUFFOLK LETTER

The following was sent out to members of the Suffolk Christian church congregation for a meeting, May 22, 1918:

On Wednesday, the twenty-second, from eight until ten,
   Come to the Christian Church and you'll want to come again.
To get acquainted is the object of the meeting
   And you'll find awaiting you a right hearty greeting.
The pastor will be there and his charming daughter, too,
   And they will be most happy also to welcome you.
We want to get together to have a very good time,
   That's the reason we are sending you this little rhyme.

The reception was equal to "Elder Brown Donation," by Will Carlton and more; for it was not poetry, but pantry goods which one might call the poetry of generosity. It is late to write of the happy occasion, but it takes a long time to get the facts of history together to write true history. It takes a year to recover from such a surprise, and as long to test the gifts that touch the heart as well as feed the body. I am sorry for the typesetter in this case for there are so many items. Two hundred and ten registered at the reception and many came who did not register. About one hundred persons made donations; perhaps more as some made gifts without names. I must be permitted to mention, so far as I can, the gifts in kind and in cash: Cash, $8.00; 16 cakes of soap, 210 pounds of sugar, 60 pounds of flour, 9 pounds of rice, 18 pounds of coffee, 3 pounds of butter, 1 pound of cakes, 9 hams, 7½ dozens of eggs, 15 quarts of fruit, 10 quarts of vegetables, 1 bottle of plum juice, 7 quarts of pickles, 1 quart of apple butter, 1 quart of citron, 1 gallon of syrup, 5 packages of seeded raisins, 1 bottle of cherries, 3 bottles of olives, 1 can wesson oil, ½ gallon of peanuts, post toasties, 1 hen, apples, corn starch, 1 can of milk, dates, strawberry preserves, 2 boxes of baking powder, 2 cakes of chocolate, 2 cans of fine apples, a package of postum, a package of cocoa, pancake flour, cream of wheat, rolled oats, salt, 1 broom, 1 can of scouring powder, 1 can of gold dust and vegetables.

We have tested and tested these gifts, and the donors know how to select the best. There is no way to repay kindness when it breaks out in a flood as it did on that occasion. Music, conversation, and happy feelings seemed to convert the hours into minutes of joy. To me it was overwhelming and I have not fully recovered from the shock.

There is a lesson in this donation. It shows what many can do by putting their efforts together. That is the power of the Church. If all would bring something of thought, prayer, song, interest, and gifts to the regular services, and all come, it would make Sunday great in worship, and great in happiness. In all this large donation there was not a gift that was useless and not one that was small in the eyes of the recipient. It was the gift and not the size or value that we appreciated. The Lord is more appreciative than we can possibly be, because He knows the mind and heart of the donor. We are too prone to judge motives by actions; God judges actions by motives. The least child can bring a tribute of praise well-pleasing to God. What the Church needs is the presence, prayer, and praise, of all its members.

One other thing fastens itself more and more in life: and that is that I receive more than I deserve. People have always done more for me than I have done for them. The world itself has treated me better than I have treated the world; and this is doubly true of the Church; and I really believe that the Church is hungry to do more and more for ministers and the Kingdom they serve. People really look for opportunities to express their love, their liberality, and their life. I fear the energy of the world is sometimes interpreted in terms of selfishness. Because men are devoted to their business they are accused of narrowness; what they want is an opportunity and a cause worthy of their confidence, their consideration, and their contributions.

This is my thanks for the kindness of the congregation that I love.

W. W. STALEY.

FIRST CHURCH, NORFOLK

The First Christian church, Berkley, Norfolk, Va., is in the midst of her Easter evangelistic meetings. The pastor, Rev. J. F. Morgan, is doing his own preaching, and the music is being led by two splendid choirs, a Junior and a Senior. The meetings began on Sunday, March 23, and by the 26th twenty-two had united with the Church.

On Sunday, March 16, the pastor asked his congregation for $500.00 to lift the debt from the Sunday school room, and they contributed more than $780.00, thus lifting the debt, and paying some on the parsonage debt as well.

The emphasis in this Easter drive is being laid on the winning of men to Christ, and the interest seems to be increasing each night.

Brother E. T. Cotten, Suffolk, Va., one of our young pastors, writes: "I am glad to help THE SUN and also help my members by sending these few subscriptions. But there are others to be brought into our list, and I hope to get them soon. Probably I shall get a few more Sunday. I do not want this February-March Campaign to be the last time you hear from me in the way of sending new subscriptions." We appreciate this and the good work that Brother Cotten is doing for the cause. His message rings true.

The Durham church begins its revival next week. Rev. J. Lee Johnson is to do the preaching and Rev. O. D. Poythress to lead the singing.

Dr. J. W. Harrell was in Dayton, Ohio, last week attending the meeting of the Executive Board of the Forward Movement.

COMRADES IN SERVICE

Last night hundreds of the soldiers of Camp Valdahon, France, came in the "Y" hut to learn about a movement that is literally attracting thousands of the men of the A. E. F. The pent-up emotion of a great and manly ideal is seeking outlet through a fraternal organization that bids fair to play small part in American life. The growth is phenomenal when considered in the light of its short history. For the benefit of those who are at home and read the church papers I want to give a few things that may be interesting regarding your boys.

The germ of the movement was planted by the Y. M. C. A. and religious workers of the American Cantonments. The fellows felt the need of getting in close contact with each other for mutual benefits in the days ahead of them. So they became "comrades" and signed a little card that became their creed and guided them in their practical efforts to entertain and satisfy and instruct those of their ranks. Being more of a "spirit" or "mutual impulse" than an organization, it came to France with the boys and has proven such a developer of all-around manhood that it has been approved by General Headquarters as the uniform method of welfare work throughout the A. E. F.

On Monday, December 30, 1918, at Paris, the Chaplains and the various accredited representatives of the welfare organizations entered into a formal agreement to give "Comrade in Service" a wide-spread recognition and operation. A Central Council was effected as follows:

President, Bishop Charles H. Brent, Senior Chaplain G. H. Q.; Vice-Presidents, Mr. E. C. Carter, Chief Secretary, Y. M. C. A.; Mr. E. L. Hearn, Chairman Overseas Commission K. of C.; Rabbi H. G. Enelow, Director Jewish Welfare Board; Colonel W. S. Barker, Commander Salvation Army; Chairman of Executive Committee, Chaplain Edwin F. Lee, U. S. Army; Executive Secretary, Dr. O. D. Foster.

Later there have been added to the personnel of the Council additional vice-presidents consisting of one Army Officer from G. H. Q. and another officer, non-commissioned officer and one or two privates to be selected from the field. This provides representatives from every branch of the A. E. F.

The following fifteen articles of agreement subscribed to form the working basis of the movement as initiated:

1. That this movement be a means to an end and not an end in itself and as such strive to adjust itself to conditions that may serve best all concerned.

2. That the Comrades in Service be a movement of the soldier, for the soldier and by the soldier promoted and guided by a Central Council composed of the military and the auxiliary organizations of the A. E. F.

3. That the Central Council be composed of the heads of the organizations concerned, or some one designated by them.

4. That all policies governing the operation of the activities by the Comrades in Service be approved by this Council.

5. That all literature concerning the Comrades in Service be passed upon by the Council, or a smaller committee that it

may appoint, before the manuscript is sent to press.

6. That all the organizations concerned be charged with the responsibility of promoting the movement throughout the entire A. E. F.

7. That the various agencies here represented focus their attention upon the furtherance of this program in the interest of unity and efficiency in the largest service of all.

8. That all share the expenses incurred in proportion to their respective constituencies.

9. That no man be expected to compromise his faith, but rather become a more worthy respresentative of it, adopting the attitude of a genuine comrade toward men of other faiths.

10. That every member of the Council continue to share with the entire body any such perplexities as might tend to make the Comradeship here any less complete, in order that the absolute confidence and faith in each other and in the organizations represented, may be maintained.

11. That the various organizations provide as far as the demands require, personnel for the Field and Central Headquarters Staff.

12. That the means of publicity at the disposal of the agencies here represented be used freely in the furtherance of the movement.

13. That the heads of these organizations immediately instruct their respective constituencies that they are expected to give their hearty co-operation in the promotion of this movement.

14. That the Central Council meet once a month or as often as deemed advisable by the President.

15. That the Executive Secretary, in conference with members of the Central or Headquarters Staff be charged with directing the work according to the lines laid down by the Central Committee.

The aims and ideals are set forth in an Enlistment Card as follows:

"Having answered the call of my country in the defense of Liberty, Justice, and Humanity, and recognizing that on me falls the obligation of being the best man possible in continuing this struggle in every realm of life for these essentials to human welfare and happiness, to this end I unite myself with others of like mind among my "Comrades in Service" to strive to help make real throughout the world the aims and ideals of the Comradeship stated on the reverse side of this card.

Name ....

Home Address ....

Date ....Unit ....

AIMS AND IDEALS

1. To create the highest type of morale by stimulating interest in helpful activities of all kinds and by encouraging in every man self-respect, self-reliance, loyalty, the spirit of team play, pride in himself, his fellows, his organization, his calling, and above all, his country.

2. To develop the best citizenship through clean living, generous respect for the rights of others, settling differences so far as possible through mutual understanding rather than by force, giving sympathetic attention to the sick and afflicted and encouragement and an all round human development through various lines of organized endeavor; physical, social, relief, educational, and religious.

3. To bind together in lasting comradeship on the democratic platform of Service, all the forces, both military and auxiliary operating in the Army and Navy."

The initial meeting of "Comrades in Service" with President and Mrs. Wilson as distinguished guests, was held on Sunday night, January 12, 1919, at the Palais de Glace in Paris. The large pavilion was packed with five thousand men of the A. E. F., representatives of the welfare organizations being present. Men of vision and leadership, both Catholic and Protestant, delivered speeches in which they approved most heartily the movement and pledged the co-operation of their respective constituencies.

Already flying squadrons are touring France to give publicity and enthusiasm to the work of the organization. Everywhere the men are fascinated with the idea. The insignia of Comradeship is suggestive and inspiring. The emblem unites in beautiful symbolic form the forces that have made American life powerful; the double triangle in blue representing Judaism, and the binding White Cross of Christianity. These are brought together on the face of a golden world of opportunity to strive as "Comrades" for a greater America and a grander world. Symbolically, but truly, they build with their sword by their side.—Nehemiah 4:18. In the service of one's country and world building there is no difference.

Why is the movement succeeding, and why will it continue to grow? Because it is not a "cut and dried" organization foreign to the spirit and ideals of our soldiers imposed from above. It is the crystallization of an impulse that surges in the veins of every American. It is giving articulate expression to a mighty emotion that has been developed by a common cause. Men of all stations in life have fought together for our flag against a common foe. They have sacrificed and suffered together as brothers for the defense of an ideal that was the outgrowth of liberty. They sealed their brotherhood as their blood mingled in the trench. Now the hands of all will be engaged in binding up the wounds of a shattered and bleeding world. I wish the folks back home could knew how anxious our boys are to maintain the ideals for which they have fought. Numbers of men, Catholic and Protestants, are coming and inquiring how they can help the cause of humanity and right when they return home. They are "Comrades" over here. Will they have the chance to be "Comrades" when they get "Over There?"

CHAPLAIN H. SHELTON SMITH
142nd Field Artillery, A. F. O. 704
American E. F.

All Bible and book prices hold open till April 10.

Take advantage of our reduction on books and Bibles. See prices elsewhere in this issue.

THE SUN's Editor is scheduled to be at High Point next Sunday.

Chaplain B. F. Black has sent this office copies of "Star and Stripes" which we appreciate.

Job G. Holland—THE CHRISTIAN SUN has been in my father's home and mine since it was founded 1844 by Rev. Daniel W. Kerr.

THE CHRISTIAN ORPHANAGE

SUPERINTENDENT'S LETTER

When we ask the good women in our Church to help us we always get a hearty response. Sometime ago we asked for sheets and counterpanes or spreads for our beds and this week Mrs. M. E. Boyd and Miss Sarah E. Boyd, of Richmond, Va., sent us six sheets and one spread for our beds.

These good folks always come to our rescue whenever we call. Mrs. W. P. Betts, Batesburg, S. C., also mailed us check for $2.00 to buy sheets. If our good women will take hold of this proposition it will not be long till all our beds will be supplied and we will be glad.

Another Ladies' Society has decided to furnish one room in the Orphanage and are asking what it will cost to furnish a room.

I will say for the benefit of those who want to take part in this work that it will take some thing like sixty dollars to furnish a room with everything new. Of course much more could be spent in furnishing a room but we are calculating on just plain furniture, good substantial beds.

Have you been thinking about the Easter Offering in your church and Sunday school?

We must raise enough money from this offering to enable us to open up the home for the little children.

Begin to make your plans now and then work your plan. I will mail you envelopes for this offering soon and I trust you will get a splendid offering in your church.

CHAS. D. JOHNSTON, Supt.

REPORT FOR APRIL 2, 1919

Amount brought forward, $1,668.70.

Children's Offerings

Frances Horne Everett, 10 cents; Irene Patton, 10 cents; Pauline Trotter, 10 cents; Beulah and Clayborne Hodges, 50 cents; T. D. Mathews, Jr., 10 cents; Total, .90 cents.

Sunday School Monthly Offerings

Suffolk, Va., $25.00; Mt. Auburn, $5.00; Berea (Norfolk), Va., $2.00; Wake Chapel, $6.00; Mt. Carmel, (Va.), $5.00; Mt. Carmel S. S. Class No. 6, $1.00; Windsor, Va., $2.00; Morrisville, N. C., $2.00; Holy Neck Baraca Class, Va., $1.91; Liberty, (Vance County) $2.85; Holy Neck S. S., Va., $4.00; Damascus (Orange County), N. C., $1.05; New Hope S. S., (Valley Va.), $1.00; Auburn, $3.00; Total, $69.81.

Special Offerings

J. H. Jones, on support of children, $30.00; Mrs. W. P. Betts, Batesburg, S. C., $2.00; Lois C. Lawrence, Takoma Park, D. C., $6.00; H. B. Parson, Brushart, Ky, $10.00; Total, $48.00.

Total for the week, $110.71; Grand total, $1,779.41.

CHILDREN'S LETTERS

Dear Uncle Charley: Here comes a little girl only four years old who wants to join the band of cousins and help the little orphans. I go to Sunday school at the Christian church. Our teacher, Mrs. Glass, had us to sing in class last Sunday. We sang "Anything for Jesus" and the little shine song. We all like to sing. Hope all the little orphans are well and having a good time. Enclosed find my dime for March. Lots of love.—*Pauline Trotter.*

We are glad to have you join our corner and help keep it bright. We now have a little girl in the Orphanage who has pretty brown eyes. You must come to see her.—*"Uncle Charley."*

Dear Uncle Charley: Here I come with my dime for March. I am about to be late. I am so glad spring is here. The birds sing so sweetly and we have pretty flowers and fruits. Hope all the cousins are well and happy. With lots of love to you and the cousins.—*Irene Patton.*

Of course you would have to come with your dime with all this pretty weather and amid the songs of birds and the pretty flowers. All must be happy together. Glad to get your letter this week.—*"Uncle Charley."*

Dear Uncle Charley: I am four years old and mother thinks I am big enough to join the Children's Corner. I go to Sunday school and like to go very much. I belong to the Cradle Roll and like to put my money in my mite box. I am sending a dime for March. With love for all the cousins.—*Frances Horne Everett.*

Glad to have you join. Yes, you are old enough to join the Corner. You will help to brighten it.—*"Uncle Charley."*

Dear Uncle Charley: I hope this finds you and all the little cousins well. Enclosed find dime for March. With love to all.—*T. D. Mathews, Jr.*

You are as faithful as the boys who broke the Hindenburg line. You are always right on time. I will mail you a picture of our little girl who sings, "Keep the Home Fires Burning."—*"Uncle Charley."*

Dear Uncle Charley: Here comes a little girl and boy, eight and ten years of age. We have always been taught to care for the little orphans. Enclosed you will please find fifty cents.—*Beulah and Clayborne Hodges.*

I am very fond of little boys and girls and have two at my home. My little boy is seven and my little girl five. Both are sick this week, and their mother is, too. I am a trained nurse by experience and am keeping them all in bed and if I can do that, don't you think I am doing pretty well?—*"Uncle Charley."*

Ask your neighbor if he takes THE CHRISTIAN SUN, and if he does not, get him to take it.

See special offer on books and Bibles. We hold the offer open till April 10.

WORSHIP AND MEDITATION

THE REVERENT MIND

I think the immortal servants of mankind
Who from their home watch how by slow degrees
The world-soul greatens with the centuries,
Mourn most man's barren levity of mind—
The ear to no grave harmonies inclined,
The witless thirst for false wit's worthless lees,
The laugh mistimed in tragic presences,
The eye to all majestic meanings blind.

O prophets, martyrs, saviours! ye were great,
All truth being great to you; ye deemed man more
Than a dull jest, God's ennui to amuse;
The world for you held purport; life you worse
Proudly, as kings their solemn robes of state;
And humbly as the mightiest monarchs use.
—*William Watson.*

EACH MORNING A NEW EARTH

Did you ever go out of doors in the gray of the morning before the long yellow rays pushed back the heaps of black as night fled to the west? If you were up early enough to hear the voice of the first bird, you felt the sense of surprise in the strange new comradeship. Then, from one tree and another the nests yielded their chorus, until the whole air was vibrant with melody. Then, all of a sudden, a section of orange light crept across the placid water of the inland sea to make a golden pathway from the measureless depths beyond straight to you. As the light grew brighter and the rays lifted long fingers up, up toward other boundless deeps beyond man's keen, you felt a strange sense of unfitness. "Surely, this is not all for me. Can the path to heaven be as clear for me as this unbroken way, that across the deep to the rising sun?"

Involuntarily, you turned your back to the sun—perhaps the glory was too great, or was it the soul's unworthiness?

Again, the joy in life was reflected from the myriad drops of dew that caught the generous light and flashed it about in the blues, and reds, and all the rest of the rainbow tints. Land, sea and sky had awakened while you stood in wonder.

Oh soul of mine, awake; awake! A new earth is yours each morning. On waking turn your face toward Him, and the clouds of doubt and despair will be dispelled. Sorrow and sighing shall flee away. The sweet communion with Him before you break the silence of night with the tattered speech of day will set your soul in the clear light of His love, so that all day you may reflect His presence in the varied experiences that await you.

Oh soul of mine, awake! Look for the new heaven and the new earth wherein dwelleth righteousness!—*Exchange.*

LISTENING TIMES

What we need above all things in these crowded days is the setting apart of many listening times; times of quiet in which we can hear the heavenly voices that call to us unregarded in the busy day. The great clock bell of Saint Paul's is not heard even a few streets off in the roar of traffic all day long; but it can be heard over half the metropolis in the silence of the night. One reason why God so often spoke to His servants in the night was that all was quiet then.—*G. H. Knight.*

"TONED UP"

Most of the time-honored stimulants are under the ban today. Scientific investigation has proved that the old-fashioned "tonic" was really no tonic at all. The man who took a drink of whisky to prod his brain fooled nobody but himself. He merely induced in himself a fallacious *feeling* of mental speed. Most of the so-called "spring tonics" were merely whips to a tired horse; they made the victim "go" at cost of increased weariness. But there are some tonics that are safe in the taking and sure of results. There is the stimulant of a new idea, of a passionate goodness, of an exalted love. There is the touch of that presence which "disturbs us with the joy of elevated thoughts." There is the gift of a supreme forgiveness or the call of a paramount duty. Life at its best is rich in moral stimulants. Perhaps that is what we need just now; to take a tonic from the pharmacopoeia of God—*George Clarke Peck.*

TAKE THEM AS THEY COME

"The lessons as they come every day are not so hard. It is after a while, when the examinations come and bring them all at once, that the trouble comes," fretted a girl who wanted to stand high in her studies.

"Take them as they come. If you learn each one well you will find when you meet them again in examination, that they are old friends," wisely encouraged her mother.

That is the good, old rule. It smoothes away many a Hill Difficulty that seems to loom up ahead. We need not do all our life tasks at once. Take them as they come, master them thoroughly, and each conquered lesson, when we meet it again, will prove an old friend instead of a new foe.—*Selected.*

HELPING A TROUBLED HEART

There are always those about us who are in trouble of some kind. Vexations meet and greet us all. These are the times when we need a little comfort, a little cheer, or a little gentle talk. There is no consolation like a little encouragement when the hours are dark and gloomy, when the sky is out of our sight and the clouds of life lingering very near. Let us seek to help another and thus be a real brother.

MISSIONARY

A LETTER APPRECIATED

The Mission Treasurer received a few days since the following, which had no name, but which is appreciated beyond words, and which will be used as directed. It was without postmark or signature, and read as follows:

"Dear Dr. Atkinson:

"Enclosed is $10.00. I want you to please send it overseas to help feed the poor starving little children over there. It may be if they are spared to live they will be good Christians and workers for the Lord Christ."

We have no idea as to the writer, but the $10.00 reached us safely and is used in the way designated. Some heart anxious for the salvation of the unsaved thus performs a noble task without making known his or her name.

ANOTHER LETTER

The following is received and is like others which we are receiving now from time to time and manifests somewhat the spirit that is growing in our Sunday schools:

"McCullers, N. C., March 8, 1919.

"Dr. J. O. Atkinson,
    Elon College, N. C.

"Dear Sir:

"Enclosed herewith post office money order for $.78, offering from Wentworth Christian Sunday school for missions. The school has decided to give one offering each month to missions and to spend a few minutes each Sunday to the study of missions. Hope you are having much success in your great work.

"Our school is small at present. We reorganized since the first of the year. We believe we are going to have a good school.

"With best wishes, I am

"Yours very truly,
        "L. D. Stephenson, Secretary."

The following also tells what another school is doing and is appreciated beyond words:

"Graham, N. C., March 17, 1919.

"Dear Sir:

"As the New Providence Christian Sunday school has pledged to give one Sunday's collection to the foreign and home missions, the third Sunday in the month being the one accepted. So please find enclosed the collection of $3.50.

"Miss Effie Hall, Secretary."

This comes from Wadley, Alabama, and is also appreciated:

"Dear Brother:

"Enclosed find post office money order for $.70, the monthly offering of Beulah Christian Sunday school. Please send receipt.

"Yours truly,
        "Grace Kenley, Secretary."

Another letter comes from Linville, Virginia:

"Dear Brother:

"Your letter of January 28th to hand. Please pardon the delay in answering, for only today the school, by a large vote decided to send the fourth Sunday's collection for missions, as your letter indicated. As Secretary of the School, I was instructed to send this amount each month. So I ask that you write me how and to whom I am to send same. For this month I will send with this letter.

"As to the study of missions, the Superintendent failed to mention; yet I feel sure the school will want to take up this part also, and I am asking you to send samples such as you think will suit best a country school; adult, junior, intermediate and primary classes, also prices of the same and I will present this school. Money order for $1.15 is enclosed for February. Our Sunday school is sending one Sunday's offering to the Christian Orphanage.

"Cordially yours,
    "Miss Mary E. F. Kratzer,
            "Sunday School Secretary."

PROGRAM OF MID-YEAR MEETING OF THE EASTERN VIRGINIA WOMAN'S MISSIONARY CONFERENCE BERKLEY, VIRGINIA

APRIL 10, 1919—10:30 A. M.

Topic: Woman's Work in This New Time.

Motto: "Behold I Make All Things New."—Rev. 21:5.

1. Song.
2. Devotional Service, Isaiah 2:1-5, led by
            Mrs. C. H. Rowland, Franklin, Va.
3. Appointment of Committees.
4. Report of Woman's Board.
5. The Most Pressing Need of the Present Intercessors, Mrs. W. D. Warrington, Driver, Va.
6. The Most Pressing Need of our Mission Field,
    (1) Equipment; (2) Recruits,
            Mrs. W. D. Harward, Dendron, Va.
7. Music.
8. Organizing our Young People,
            Mrs. M. L. Bryant, Norfolk, Va.
9. Reaching the Young People for Life Service,
            Mrs. L. E. Smith, Norfolk, Va.
10. Prayer Service for Life Recruits, led by
            Dr. J. O. Atkinson.
11. Adjournment for Luncheon.

AFTERNOON SESSION—2:00 P. M.

1. Call to order.
2. Devotional Service, led by
            Mrs. R. B. Wood, Portsmouth, Va.
3. Address—Enlisting Women for the Larger Task,
        Dr. J. O. Atkinson, Elon College, N. C.
4. Exercise—A Missionary Clinic.
5. Miscellaneous Business.
6. Adjournment.

A good way to make *tomorrow* better is to make *today* better.

CHRISTIAN EDUCATION

THE CALL TO THE MINISTRY*
I Cor. 6:19-20. "Ye are not your own's; ye are bought with a price."

You have seen the full page announcement on The Christian Sun of the Southern Christian Convention's request that our pastors preach today on the subject, "The Call to the Ministry." The request is urgent and the need for more ministers is imperative, and therefore I shall carry out the wishes of our Convention and, I fully believe, the wishes of the Master of the harvest.

The need of men for the harvest shall be our first consideration. The need perhaps has never been more evident for the inhabited world is larger. The expansion of the territory is both local and universal—the vacant places are filling up; the unreached territory is being populated. The harvest fields are becoming fertile everywhere; populations are increasing in every country. And every soul must have Christ or be lost! In the larger world our blessed Savior sees a larger number of men with the possibility of becoming leaders and I see Him standing amongst us with up-lifted head; with out-stretched hands; with a throbbing, blood-stained breast saying, "Ye are not your own's; ye are bought with a price."

The universality of education makes the demand for true, orthodox, Christian leadership more urgent. "A little learning is a dangerous thing," so also is un-Christian learning. We could but shudder in fear for this old world and its future if we only knew the vast amount of tommy-rot that is being taught by so-called thinkers of new thought, spiritualism, higher criticism, super-manism! The old world needs true education, but what shall become of us if we allow the new tossing, tainted tide of religious infidelity to sweep so much of the good of our greater cities off of its feet? Hear me, young man of our church, God is going to call you—enough of you—to drain dry the cess pools of sin on this earth! You are needed to leaven the present great lump of education. You; because you are the sons of Christian fathers and mothers; you because your precious lives have not been tainted by the wicked and vulgar tide of which I speak; you because you have been taught from your infancy the orthodox views of Christianity! Our entire Southern Christian Convention is calling for young men and women who are not afraid to read, to love, to believe, to teach this blessed Book from the first chapter of Genesis to the last past of Revelation just as it is! It must live in the heart of education, and unless it does our fairest hopes are futile.

Never was the opportunity larger because wealth and material riches are at their zenith. "The earth is the Lord's and the fullness thereof; the world and they that dwell therein." And unless we can bring this great age to see and to know that our vast riches spring from the eternal garners of God we shall surely meet a final crisis such as war met by Greece, Athens, Carthage, and Rome. We must keep a full, grateful stream of our money flowing back—ever back—to God, for such is in keeping with his natural laws,—from the ocean abundant and copious rains pour but back to the ocean streams of water ever run. While wealth is at its crest a large army of zealous, wide-awake, brainy young men and women are needed to turn the tide toward suffering and superstitious humanity in larger areas of the earth.

And war has enlarged the opportunity. Democracy has been on trial. War has put it in this case to its supreme test. Seeing the urgent need the leaders of democracy's realm raised army after army—mobilized millions upon millions of men—

until finally the shout of victory was heard. The issue has put Christianity to the test. O, Christ, will you not raise an army equal to the need? See the wide open doors of China, India, Japan, Africa, South America and the isles of the sea. They are opened now as never before—never! And things are happening! Aetheism, agnosticism, skepticism and all the damning afore-mentioned-isms are rushing in at those doors, and now as never heretofore we are needed to hasten in. Oh! men—young men—I challenge you to a task magnanimous in size. I challenge you. Shall we good people out here in our large Christian communities evade so great a question? Nearly a score of men from this church offered their lives for democracy. Shall we do less for Christianity? Or shall we do nothing? May God bless every young person who hears that question, and may he be willing if God so directs to say—"Here am I, send me." Hear Paul as he thunders the truth of the text at you: "Ye are not your own; ye are bought with a price."

And while the opportunity has never been larger never has it been easier to miss. You honest, conscientious young people will not all miss the opportunity without some consideration but the seeming importance of other fields will lure you away. Many other professions, vocations, and callings will make their bids for your times, talents and possibilities. For instance, the teaching profession of which I have tasted will bid high and well for first place in your considerations. And indeed it is a most delightful experience to have a group of clean, talented, happy, and eager boys and girls sit about you and with never-failing faithfulness attend your every teaching. I have watched the play of intelligence upon their foreheads, the gleam of gratitude in their eyes, and known the purity of their love! But oh! pleasanter—pleasanter still it is to have each of the same group of young people say: "You have shown the Christ to me; here and now I give my heart and life to Him!" Yes, yes other important fields may lure us away!

We might miss the opportunity by being lured away by wealth. Wealth, a medium which may be transformed from a holy and heavenly thing to "the root of all evil." Oh! wealth, you will sing your choicest anthem to many a young man and young woman who is already "bought with a price" far greater than you can ever pay! "For what shall it profit a man if he gain the whole world and lose his own soul!" He is bought with things eternal which are worth more than the material wealth of the world. Listen not, young man, to the song of the wealthy siren until you have heard and heeded the voice of the Master, saying: "Seek ye first the kingdom and its righteousness, and all these things shall be added unto you." God will supply your needs and open to you the wealth of the world if you need it.

And then you might be lured away by ambition. "Caesar was ambitious, and I slew him." Saul was ambitious and did not slay king Amelek and was himself rejected as king of Israel. The word "ambition" is not so far as I know in the Bible. Beware of being ambitious. When I was first hearing the call to the ministry I desired with all my heart to be a lawyer—and eventually a statesman—if you will permit me now to express my boyish dream. I practiced law behind the plow, in the woods, with my chums and schoolmates, everywhere. I loved lawyers. I could listen at them at the bar with intense pleasure. They were my heroes. I knew some good ones; I loved them then; I love them now. But all the time there was something teaching me that there is a Law higher than the law man. I heard the Voice calling—the old desire began to go slipping and I yielded. To myself I said, "I will plead at the bar of God's mercy; I will practice a Law that will never be repealed; I shall be an ambasador for Christ and do business for and with the 'King of kings and Lord of lords." Young men, your command is from Him—'Slay all." 'As you are you are prince with an opportunity. You stand head and shoulders above some of your fellows,—and "you are not your own, you are bought with a price." Miss not your opportunity by any of the three, afore mentioned allurements. "The path of duty leads but to glory."

How may I know I'm called to so responsible a position? I feel sure that by the time we have reached this point in the discussion some of you are beginning to want an answer to this question. Oftimes Christ answered a question with a question. May I ask this one, Are you sure you are a Christian? Are you a citizen in the kingdom of Christ? Are you on the altar of God? Oh, Savior, help us first to answer these questions steadily and faithfully before our God! Help us to answer them now! It is no time for trifles! Life is too serious; responsibility too great for any quibbling or vacillating. It is the time for men, true men, to answer this great question in a great way, Am I really a Christian with all that that implies? Oh! for scores upon scores of young men and women in our beloved Christian church who will answer that question rightly. With that one answered let us take a few more. What were you saved for? Ornament? Never—except as you shall glorify Christ in active service for Him. The world is the field—the harvest is ripe—why, is it possible that the ungarnered grain shall fall to the earth and decay? I believe that if every person Christ chooses would answer the call there would be men to do the harvesting. Not more than enough, but enough. Christ has said plainly. "Go ye into all the world and preach the gospel to every creature." Can you be sure that does not mean you? You cannot, unless you bring the matter to most serious prayer and consideration. When He says, "Thou shalt love thy neighbor as thyself," you say "That's to me, you and everybody." But have you diligently considered the former commandment which I have just quoted?

My friends listen to this: "Now Samuel did not yet know the Lord, neither was the word of the Lord yet revealed unto him. And the Lord called Samuel again the third time. And he arose and went to Eli, and said, 'Here am I; for thou didst called me.' And Eli perceived that the Lord had called the child. Therefore Eli said unto Samuel, Go, lie down; and it shall be if he call thee, that thou shalt say, 'Speak, Lord, for thy servant heareth.' So Samuel went and lay down in his place. And the Lord came and called as at other times: 'Samuel, Samuel.' Then Samuel answered, 'Speak, Lord, for thy servant heareth.' " Did Samuel ever regret that night, or the answer he made his Lord? Oh! my friends, you know the beautiful story of Samuel's long and glorious career! Suppose he had not answered as he did, unto oblivion a useful life would have gone. If he had said, "I fear my chums will call me sissy," he would never have crowned kings, nor nursed a nation. Not just any pious young man can be a minister, but a God-called, level-headed, consecrated man who is not afraid, will become a power in the world.

Do you want a large place, or would you fill a small corner well? Do you want to serve your day and generation? Do you want to be a blessing to humanity? Then if God calls say, "Speak, Lord, for thy servant heareth."

In conclusion allow me to say you will not all be called to preach, but each of you are called to do service in the harvest field. Some of you, I sincerely believe, will hear the call. I pray the Lord of harvest to help you to realize that "ye are not your own; ye are bought with a price." Amen.

*Sermon preached by Rev. J. G. Truitt, Sunday, February 16, 1919, Pleasant Grove(Va.) church.

BOOKS, BIBLES, TESTAMENTS

In order to reduce certain stocks of books, Bibles and Testaments on hand, the following prices are made and will hold good until April 10, 1919.

Bibles

No. 312X. Holman Self-Pronouncing Teachers' Bible. Printed on fine white paper from good, clear type, and contains references, concordance, four thousand questions and answers and fifteen prepared maps. Size 4 3-8X6 1-2 inches. Egyptian Morocco, divinity circuit, head bands and marker, round corners, red under gold edges. Regular selling price......$4.65
Price to March 31 .... 3.90
No. 71. Scofield Reference Bible. Handsome binding, French Morocco limp, new and improved edition. "The neatest Scofield Bible made." It will please you. Regular selling price $4.50
Price to March 31 .... 3.90
No. 215. Child's Self-Pronouncing Pictorial Bible with Helps. Bound in French seal leather, round corners, silk bands, gold titles,—handsomely made. Regular selling price $2.50
Price to March 31 .... 2.00
No. 1113. Ideal Bible for Children. Printed on fine white paper from the newest and clearest type of the size made. Size 3 1-2X5 3-8 inches. This Bible will please you. Regular price $1.75
Price to March 31 .... 1.40

Testaments

No. 3913 R. L. (Red Letter). Large print Morocco binding. Regular price $2.00
Price to March 31 .... 1.75
No. 2902 Cloth binding, large print. Regular price.... .90
Price to March 31 .... .75
No. 2502 P. Cloth binding, black faced type. Regular price .... .75
Price to March 31 .... .55
No. 2113. Pocket size, Morocco binding. Regular price .60
Price to March 31 .... .45
No. 0133. Pocket size, Morocco binding, overlapping edges. Regular Price 75
Price to March 31 .... .55

(A Testament in Modern Speech)

Cloth, $1.25; cloth, indexed, $1.75; cloth, India paper, $1.75; leather, $2.55; leather, indexed, $2.75; leather, India paper, $2.75; Persian Morocco, Divinity Circuit, $3.75; Turkey Morocco, $4.25. Pocket Edition (without notes): Cloth, $1.00; cloth, India paper, $1.25; leather, India paper, $1.85. State definitely style wanted.

The above prices are regular. Make your choice and deduct 10 per cent. State definitely Testament wanted.

Books

Pastor's Ideal Funeral, $1.15—Regular price, $1.25.

(Books for the Children)

We have several copies "Silver Rags," "Patty's Grand Uncle," "Johnny Two Boys," "A Rescued Madonna"—your choice, 20 cents per copy. We will substitute if the book ordered is sold before the order reaches us.

Special

"Redmond of the Seventh," by Mrs. Frank Lee is a book with a fine story taken from school life, 290 pages, handsomely bound, 50 cents the copy.
Special Note: One of these books will be sent free with each order for $3.00 worth of books, Bibles or Testaments.

Address

C. B. RIDDLE ....Publishing Agent
Burlington, N. C.

MARRIAGES

SAVEDGE-SPRATLEY

On the afternoon of March 11, 1919, at the Christian parsonage, Dendron, Va., then was a quiet marriage, when Mr. Beverly Allen Savedge led to the marriage altar Miss Ruth Atkinson Spratley. Immediately after the ceremony, which was said by the writer, the happy couple motored to Wakefield, Va., where they took the train for Washington. They will make their home in Dendron, Va., and they have the best wishes of their many friends.

W. D. HARWARD.

BROWER-SHEFIELD

On March 16, 1919, 311 Chestnut Street, High Point, North Carolina Mr. Oscar Floyd Brower and Miss Ethel Shefield were united in the holy estate of matrimony. They both live in High Point where they plan to continue their home

The ceremony was performed at 4:00 P. M., in a quiet manner with only a few intimate friends present. Immediately after the ceremony they motored to the home of the bridegroom's parents.

May theirs be a life, long, peaceful, prosperous and happy.

L. L. WYRICK.

MORTON

Mrs. Mamie McKinney Morton, wife of J. W. Morton of Burlington, N. C., was born December 22, 1876 and died March 8, 1919. She was married to J. W. Morton June 17, 1894. To this union ten children were born, nine of which survive. She is also survived by two sisters and two brothers. She was a faithful wife and a kind and loving mother. She professed faith in Christ when but a girl and united with Bethlehem Christian church and later transferred to Burlington Christian church. She was a faithful member to the end. For several years prior to her death she was a patient sufferer. She was patiently waiting for the summons to her heavenly home. God bless the husband

and children in their great loss. The funeral service was conducted by her pastor from Bethlehem Christian church and the interment made in the church cemetery.

J. W. HARRELL.

MORELAND

Lemuel Herbert Moreland was born December 28, 1862, and departed this life March 6, 1919. His age was 56 years, 2 months and 8 days. Brother Moreland was a faithful member of the Timber Ridge Christian church and was held in high esteem by all who knew him. He will be greatly missed. Surviving him are his wife, his mother, one brother, and three sisters. Funeral services were held at Timber Ridge March 8. A large congregation attended the services, thus showing the esteem in which Brother Moreland was held by the entire community.

A. W. ANDES.

KAGEY

On March 8, 1919 Ida Permelia Kagey, wife of Erasmus Kagey, departed this life at the age of 47 years, 6 months, and 18 days. Deceased was a member of the Methodist church at Quicksburg for about 20 years. She was regarded by all who knew her as a good Christian woman. There are left to mourn her death, her husband, two daughters, her parents, and three brothers. The funeral service was held at Cedar Grove church of the Brethren near New Market, March 11, and the remains laid to rest in the cemetery near by.

A. W. ANDES.

STRADER

John Wellon Strader, son of J. Wellons and Maude Strader, died March 10, 1919, at the tender age of one year, ten months and twenty-eight days. This bright little boy was sick only a few days, but lived long enough to win a strong hold upon the hearts of many friends. The parents, four sisters and one brother are in deep sorrow because of his early death. Funeral and interment at Below's Creek, conducted by the writer. May God comfort the bereaved.

J. W. HOLT.

HURDLE

Charles Wesley Hurdle, of Greensboro, N. C., was born March 24, 1873 and died March 12, 1919. He was married December 23, 1915 to Miss Annie Danieley of Danville, Va. He leaves three brothers and four sisters to mourn their loss.

His was the fourth death out of a family of eleven children. He was a great sufferer for several years prior to his death. He was reared in the neighborhood of Union Ridge, N. C., hence was buried in the church cemetery. The funeral service was conducted by the writer from Union Christian church. The blessings of our heavenly Father be upon the bereaved wife and loved ones.

J. W. HARRELL.

LONGEST

At eight o'clock Sunday morning, March 2, 1919, the soul of Brother John Longest quietly slipped from the suffering body into the eternal freedom of God's presence. He had reached the age of sixty-three years. Only a few years ago he professed faith in Christ and united with the Christian church of Graham, North Carolina. His final testimony gives such comfort to those who mourn that they "sorrow not as others." Perhaps the wife and children feel most keenly the loss, but a brother, two sisters and a host of relatives and friends join them in their grief. Dr. D. A. Long assisted the writer in the funeral services which were held in Graham Christian church. Interment was in Graham cemetery.

F. C. LESTER.

GODFREY

Lucy Kate Watson, daughter of R L. Watson and wife, and the beloved wife of J. W. Godfrey was born November 30, 1897 and died March 22, 1919. She was a member of the Christian church at Shallow Well, and has left for the consolation of her loved ones a beautiful life and testimony. She leaves to mourn her departure her husband, father, mother, three sisters, and four brothers. She was buried at Shallow Well, and a large congregation gathered to sympathize with the bereaved. Her funeral was conducted by her pastor, assisted by Rev. T. E. Witche of the M. E. church.

T. E. WHITE.

SLOAN

Leon Ellington, infant son of A. H. and Cassie Sloan, died March 23, 1919 at the age of four months. It had been seriously ill for several weeks, and the doctor and loving parents did all they could to save its life. We buried it at Shallow Well and felt that it is now free from pain and safe in the arms of Jesus.

T. E. WHITE.

WISE AND OTHERWISE
A Reform School

I wish that I could make a rule
That every moth must go to school,
And learn from some experienced
　mole-
To make a less conspicuous hole.
　—R. R. K., in Harper's Magazine.

English Howlers

The following quotations from
British examination papers and
themes, ridiculous as they are, might
be matched from many an American
teacher's experience:

Queen Elizabeth was tall and thin,
but she was a stout Protestant.

During the interdict in John's
reign births, marriages and deaths
were not allowed to take place:

Henry VIII gained the title Fidei
Defensor because he was so faithful
to his queen.

Cave Canem.—Beware lest I sing.

A vacuum is an empty space with
nothing in it; the Pope lives in one.

A vacuum is an empty space full
of nothing but Germans (germs?).

A Conservative is a sort of green-
house where you look at the moon.

Parliament assembled in September and dissembled in January.

Wolfe gained fame by storming
the heights of Abraham Lincoln.

Where was Magna Charta signed?
At the bottom.

Where was Mary Queen of Scots
born and why was she born there?
Mary was born at Linlithgow be-

cause her mother happened to be
there at the time.

What is the object of distillation?
Describe the process and the apparatus used. Answer: The object
of distillation is the making of
whisky. You have a box and a glass
tube at one end and another at the
other end; and if you pour water in
at the one end it comes out whisky
at the other.—The Independent.

Oiling the Cylinder

The motorist emerged from beneath the car and struggled for
breath. His helpful friend, holding
an oil can, beamed on him:

"I've just given the cylinder a
thorough oiling, Dick."

"Cylinder?" howled the motorist.
"That wasn't the cylinder. It was
my ear!"

Mother's Ologies

Daughter—Yes, I've graduated,
but now I must inform myself in
psychology, philology, bibli—

Practical Mother—Stop! I have
arranged for you a thorough course
in roastology, bakeology, stitchology,
darnology, patchology and general
domestic hustleology.

Advanced Methods

A sign in a window near a railroad station out West reads: "Suits
pressed between trains." Novel, we
think, but hardly practical.—Lutheran.

Agnes, aged three, had just heard
a graphophone for the first time.
She described it thus to her mother:
"It was the funniest thing; there
was an old man sitting behind a
table, where we couldn't see him
singing for us; and the woman was
feeding him with tin plates."—
Watchman-Examiner.

"Papa, how can guns kick when
they have no legs?" asked Willie.

"Don't ask absurd questions."

"Guns haven't any legs, have
they, papa?"

"Certainly not!"

"Well, then, what's the use of
their having breeches?"—Boston
Evening Transcript.

A—Time flies.

B.—I can't. They're too quick for
me.—Christian Register.

CHILD'S SELF-PRONOUNCING PIC-
TORIAL BIBLE WITH HELPS

This Bible is bound in French Seal
Leather, has round corners, silk head
bands, gold titles, handsomely bound.
Regular selling price.......... $2.50
Price till April 10............ 2.00
Call for Bible No. 215.

Address

C. B. RIDDLE, Publishing Agent
Burlington, North Carolina

BOOK NOTES

Story Books For The Children

We now have on hand a very fine
story book for the children. "Redmond of the Seventh," by Mrs.
Frank Lee. The book is handsomely
bound, lettered in gold and contains
290 pages. The story is wholesome
—a school story. The price is within the reach of all—75 cents postpaid or two for $1.25.

Christian Hymnaries

We have the Christian Hymnary
at 50 cents the copy. How many
copies?

Address

C. B. RIDDLE, Publishing Agent,
Burlington, N. C.

CHARLES W McPHERSON, M. D.

Eye, Ear, Nose, Throat

OFFICE OVER CITY DRUG STORE

Office Hours: 9:00 a. m. to 1:00 p. m.
and 2:00 to 5:00 p. m.

Phones: Residence 153; Office 65J

BURLINGTON, NORTH CAROLINA

CANCER TREATED SUCCESSFULLY
AT THE KELLAM HOSPITAL

The record of the Kellam Hospital is
without parallel in history, having restored, without the use of the knife, Acids, X-
Ray or Radium, over ninety per cent of
the many hundreds of sufferers from cancers which it has treated during the past
twenty-two years. We want every man
and woman in the United States to know
what we are doing.—KELLAM HOS-
PITAL, 1617 W. Main St., Richmond, Va.

INDIVIDUAL COMMUNION SERVICE

THE BEST WAY
to serve Communion.
It is reverent, sani-
tary, and increases attendance at the
Lord's Supper. Our services are chaste
and beautiful. Made of finest materials
and best workmanship.

Send for illustrated price list

C. B. RIDDLE, Publishing Agent,
Burlington, North Carolina.

DR. J. H. BROOKS

DENTIST

Foster Building　　　Burlington, N. C.

THE CHRISTIAN SUN

"IN ESSENTIALS UNITY, IN NON-ESSENTIALS LIBERTY, IN ALL THINGS CHARITY"

The Spirit of Larger Things

THERE is a spirit of larger things brooding in the minds of our people. In every home and in every church the spirit of giving is finding its way. The people are accepting the great challenge before them and taking God at His word. The result is that a new day is dawning for the Christian Church. Littleness is being pushed into the corners and will soon be a thing of the past. Our people are getting richer in wealth, sweeter in spirit, greater in soul. The windows of heaven are being opened and the blessings of the Kingdom are being poured out upon them.

Volume LXXI   WEDNESDAY, APRIL 9, 1919   Number 15

BURLINGTON · · NORTH CAROLINA

THE CHRISTIAN SUN

Founded 1844 by Rev. Daniel W. Kerr

C. B. RIDDLE   - - -   Editor

Entered at the Burlington, N. C. Post Office as second class matter.

Subscription Rates

One year .... $ 2.00
Six months 1.00

In Advance

Give both your old and new postoffice when asking that your address be changed.

The change of your label is your receipt for money. Written receipts sent upon request.

Marriage and obituary notices not exceeding 150 words printed free if received within 60 days from date of event, all over this at the rate of one-half cent a word.

Original poetry not accepted for publication.

Principles of the Christian Church

(1) The Lord Jesus Christ is the only Head of the Church.
(2) Christian is a sufficient name of the Church.
(3) The Holy Bible is a sufficient rule of faith and practice.
(4) Christian character is a sufficient test of fellowship, and of church membership.
(5) The right of private judgment and the liberty of conscience is a right and a privilege that should be accorded to, and exercised by all.

EDITORIAL

SOME REFLECTIONS

An editor is supposed to write editorials but he may write articles that are not classed as editorials. A definition for an editorial might not cover this article, and so we do not claim it to be an editorial, but a little testimony to a feeling within that is finding sanction without.

For several weeks

we have been sharing a feeling of larger things for the Kingdom. Our work along this line, aside from editing THE CHRISTIAN SUN has recently been challenged and the outcome of it will surely be seed sown in fertile soil to bloom into the fullness of the Kingdom's cause. The public will learn further as the matter develops.

Going after the mail

after supper is a set custom of ours. We enjoy the many good things that friends write us. These letters, together with our splendid exchanges, make the evenings all too short and the call of the bed time too soon. Last Friday evening we went for our mail and then on to THE SUN office. Among the many good things in our mail were three articles from President Harper. These articles are printed in full in this week's issue of THE SUN and need no comment. When we read these letters they lifted our soul to a feeling that we

rarely ever experienced. It was a feeling like unto that which we had been feeling for months—that the time was at hand for larger things and larger tasks for our Church and for all Churches. Suffolk's challenge made our heart glad, and almost before we knew it, we were on our knees by the side of the desk, where the routine of business is hammered out, praying to God that the good work might be continued and the people of the Church enter into the wide open door of opportunity. We returned to our home and told the "assistant editor" of what had happened and how we felt. Turning to an exchange we found the following article, which seemed to be in accord with what we had experienced and felt:

Money can be converted into happiness, and that makes it much more worth possessing. It has, in fact, usually been sought for that reason and the additional one that it gives power.

Money can secure power much easier than it can secure happiness. It cannot buy happiness as a cross-counter transaction. Happiness is not so cheap as that.

Money cannot buy happiness, but it can be changed into it. This can only be done through some intermediate object or person. Money consecrated to Jesus Christ breaks out into the great golden flower of happiness both for the giver and for many others whom the gift reaches.

The very act of consecrating money to Jesus Christ makes it a kind of sacrament, and it washes the heart of unselfishness and awakens in it urges of kindness. There is no way to consecrate money to Christ except by giving it to the needy ones of earth.

Up to this time the matter of $125,000 had looked large but not impossible. It now looked small and our mind immediately began to think of the $250,000 margin. A big task but one not impossible. And then we thought of all the churches that would not be given a chance if we stopped at $125,000; we thought of the good men and women in this generation whose only opportunity this was to contribute to Elon's endowment, for the endowment of a college rarely ever challenges the people but once in a generation; and so

here is the point

that we make—a thing that almost staggers us, but with a clear conscience and a feeling of duty to say it: Let us make it TWO HUNDRED AND FIFTY THOUSAND DOLLARS. We can do it and do it easily. And thank God we can do it without calling it "begging" for money. Beggars beg, but Christian men and women who represent the cause of the Kingdom do not beg but give opportunities. It would put the privilege and the pleasure into the hearts of a few churches and individuals were we to stop at $125,000. It is our College— the College of the people and for the people and so let us give all the people a chance. A part of Elon's present endowment is in the form of a note and it has been learned that it cannot be counted as strictly endowment. This with the fact that the college is to have under its care 80 young men and women to train as ministers and missionaries during the next four years makes it imperative that we double the quota of each church and make the amount $250,000.00.

This good feeling

continued throughout the day Saturday and remained with us. Saturday night we went to High Point to be with the good people of that congregation on Sunday. We were met at the train by Brothers R. C. Boyd, J. E. Bost, and Rev. L. L. Wyrick, the pastor, and then carried to the home of Brother Vuncannon where we met more than twenty-five young people of the church and community who had gathered for singing. Their first song was "Strengthen your Hold upon Jesus," and how they did sing it! We listened to it with interest and rapt attention and reviewed time after time the things that we had been thinking about for weeks, for they were things that would cause us to get a greater hold upon Jesus and let Him get a greater hold upon us. Other selections followed and in all of them there was a beautiful revelation of our feelings.

The evening soon passed away. Brother R. C. Boyd made a splendid talk of how community singings were bringing the young people of the church into Christian fellowship. THE SUN's Editor led in prayer and all went to their homes feeling happy—and they were happy. We were carried to the home of Brother Whitt and found there a bed fit for a king and a room set in order by the hands of a splendid Christian woman. We asked Brother Wyrick if we should not undertake to raise High Point's goal of $500 for Elon's Standardization Fund. He said that he would leave it to us, and so we prayed over it that the coming day might break clear and the homes be opened to us for this work. We spent a pleasant night. Our sleep was as sweet as that of a baby and our dreams as charming as fancy ever dared to make them. We were out early next morning and began to call on the people. We had just one hour and thirty minutes before Sunday school, and in this time raised High Point's quota with $200 over.

We went to Sunday school

and there Superintendent Boyd had everything in fine running condition. Life was put into the songs, variety into the opening and enthusiasm into the work. The school is flourishing and meeting a long felt need in a splendid community. The school gives a Sunday's offering to the Orphanage and one to missions.

Preparation had been made

for the regular services. Hand bills had been scattered over the city, and by the kindness of the *High Point Enterprise*, the services had special mention and space on Saturday afternoon. The attendance was good. By the advertising, many old friends of the Editor who were in the city, (though their whereabouts unknown to us) were in attendance. We endeavored to speak at the appointed time and had the co-operation of good attention. At the close of the service we announced that the High Point church had suberibed her quota to the Elon Standardization Fund and that we wanted to see the church double it. *No soliciting was done from the pulpit.* After the service the required amount of $300.00 was soon subscribed rounding out

one thousand dollars for High Point

and again demonstrating that a mission church can do

things if it will—and they all will if given a chance. We were hastened to Brother L. R. Gibson's hospitable home, given one of the best dinners ever spread, and then rushed to the train at 1:40 and began our journey back home.

We stopped in Greensboro

between trains for two hours and met up with pastor J. V. Knight of the First church. He carried us to his study and we talked over things worth while. He too, like, Brother Wyrick at High Point, is doing a good work and bringing things to pass. The special meeting is to begin April 20 and already much work is being done to make it count for the Kingdom's growth. And now for

a summary of the situation

and a few facts worth stating: THE CHRISTIAN SUN had paved the way for the work at High Point. There is no question about it. The people had been reading THE SUN on the back page, too. No details were necessary. They knew it all. Oh, how long will it be when all the pastors will begin to see that the Church paper is needed to help them carry out their work! May the day hasten! The people who gave the $1,000,- 00- were, with two exceptions, tithers and readers of *The Tither*. One man said: "All right, I want to help and can do it for I am tithing my account," and with his pen signed the pledge with delight. God's plan of financing His work is coming, coming, and it will be a good day when it comes.

Hats off

to High Point and her band of loyal workers. She is talking about all-time service, and one of these days it will be more than talk. It's a joy to be with such good people; it's a joy to work when there is work to do; it's a joy to write when you have something to write about. There is a better day, a brighter day, for the Kingdom's work and that day is here and is challenging all of us for LARGER things.

At the close of this writing when we are due to make up THE SUN forms we have received nothing on the Sunday School and Christian Endeavor topics. We carried nothing last week. This work was generously taken over by the Sunday School and Christian Endeavor Board of the Southern Christian Convention. The work has been very irregular for some time. Complaints have been coming to us about it. The fault is not our, dear friends. We put the matter up to the Committee to do the work or otherwise advise us so that arrangements can be made for regular weekly contributions for these two important topics.

Brother J. F. Morgan sends this note, March 31: "Our meeting is still interesting—33 received into the church to date."

Look for our report on THE SUN campaign next week. Did not have room this week.

President Wilson is reported ill in France. His condition is not serious, however.

CHURCH PAPER WISDOM

Brother T. N. Ivey, Editor of the *Christian Advocate*, Nashville, Tenn., has the following timely things to say in his paper of March 28:

It is a question whether the great public has yet become fully awake to the fact that without the newspapers of the country the great war could not have been won by the United States and the Allies. If it had not been for the newspapers, public sentiment could never have been worked up to the point of strength necessary to our entering the war. If 't had not been for the newspapers, the great Liberty Loans and other helpful enterprises could not have been floated. If the secular newspaper is so necessary to a country in carrying on successfully a war and other important enterprises, can there be any exception to the rule in the case of the Church? Should we not see that for the Church to neglect the matter of publicity in carrying on the war against evil is to meet defeat?

Lately we received from one of our subscribers, evidently a lady of culture, a request for the discontinuation of this paper. She said that nothing could be said against the paper, but that she was already taking more papers than she could read. This plea is very familiar to every editor in the land. In nine cases out of ten it is equivalent to the declaration that in the cutting down of the number of periodicals the work must begin with the newspaper representative of Jesus Christ. Such a plea more often betrays a greater lack of consecration than of time to read. "Seek ye first the kingdom of God and his righteousness" applies as much to the reading of newspapers as to going to preaching and to praying. Many professing Christ, who expect daily visits of Jesus Christ in the shape of material blessings, draw the line at spiritual blessings brought by the weekly religious newspaper.

Early in the Editor's newspaper experience he received a rude jar. He heard a worthy pastor offer one of his members an apologetic explanation of the fact that he had approached her with the Editor to solicit a subscription for the Church newspaper. The Editor could not understand it. During his pastoral life he had been in the habit of presenting frequently to his congregations the claims of the connectional and the Conference organ. The idea never occurred to him that he was doing anything unusual or irregular or prejudicial to himself as pastor of a flock. On the contrary, he felt thankful for the opportunity of doing something that would be so helpful to his people and his work. And to this day he is puzzled over the fact that some preachers have the idea that a sermon or a talk on the circulation of Christian literature, or even a canvass of the congregation for subscribers, is an innovation to be justified only by an apology to the congregation. Why apologize for doing that part of pastoral work which keeps solid and sound the very foundation on which real Christian service rests—that is, knowledge of God and his Church? Surely the dignity which prompts such feeling of apology is that dignity which is but the "starch of the shroud."

WORLD'S CHRISTIAN CITIZENSHIP CONFERENCE STRONG PROGRAM

The Third World's Christian Citizenship Conference which was to have been held in Pittsburgh, Pa., last summer but which was postponed on account of the war, will be held in Pittsburgh, Victory Week, November 9-16, 1919, under the auspices of the National Reform Association.

An exceptionally strong program is already assured. Among the Americans who have agreed to speak at the Conference are the Hon. Charles Evans Hughes, formerly governor of New York, justice of the United States Supreme Court and nominee for the presidency of the United States; P. P. Claxton, U. S. Commissioner of Public Education; Frank J. Cannon, formerly U. S. Senator from the Utah and the greatest living authority on Mormonism; Arthur Capper, Senator from Kansas; Henry M. Temple, U. S. Congressman; Henry Van Dyke, author, poet, ambassador to Holland; Gifford Pinchot, statesman and authority on conservation; Drs. James A. Francis, Charles F. Jefferson, Charles L. Stelzle, Samuel Zane Batten, Edwin C. Dinwiddie, Charles L. Godell and B. S. Steadwell, well known reformers, and Mrs. Ella A. Boole, first vice-president of the W. C. T. U.

The purpose of the conference is to gather together representatives from various nations to compare views as to the moral interests of mankind and to aid in conserving the moral gains and repairing and the moral damage of the war.

This conference is not an experiment. The first of the kind was held in Philadelphia in 1910 with an attendance of 1,500 and seven countries represented on its program. The second met in Portland, Oregon, in 1913 with 15,000 people in attendance at some sessions and seventeen countries represented on the program. It is proposed to make this third conference much larger and more representative in every way, particularly in view of the world's need in this period of reconstruction.

GROWTH OF WOMAN SUFFRAGE

Woman Suffrage has had a gradual growth for several years. The following are the countries that have adopted it, also the years of their adoption:

New Zealand, 1893; Australia, 1902; Finland, 1906; Norway, 1907; Iceland, 1913; Denmark, 1915; Great Britain for England, Scotland, Ireland, Wales, 1918; Canada, 1918; Sweden, 1918; Germany, 1919; Holland, 1919.

PLACING THE VALUE

It is a significant fact that the laws of the State of North Carolina afford better protection to the live stock of the State than is provided for the citizens. Mr. M. W. Wall, Farm Demonstration Agent for Northampton County, has just returned from Ohio with a carload of thoroughbred milk cows. Before being allowed to bring these cattle into the State Mr. Wall had to have them tested for tuberculosis. The State law prohibits any cattle with tuberculosis or any hogs with cholera from being brought into the State, requiring examinations to be made to prove that the live stock are free from these diseases. People suffering from tuberculosis and other infectious diseases, however, may come and go at will. Does this mean that North Carolina places a higher value on its stock than upon its citizens? Or is a lack of appreciation of the worth of human life the cause?

PASTOR AND PEOPLE

GREENSBORO LETTER

Our work here goes good at present. Services, both morning and evening, are still on the increase in interest and attendance. The "Efficiency Contest" in the Sunday school has aroused much interest, and installation of the double envelope is bringing the double interest in missions we expected. By means of the efficiency work over 90 per cent of the classes in the school have registered 95 per cent on preparation for the last three Sundays.

It is wonderful to see how our people are lining up for our evangelistic campaign which begins April 20. Seventy-six have pledged themselves to pray every day for the meeting. Thirty have joined the personal work group, and fifteen have joined the personal workers' class and will make special preparation for their work. I am predicting a great meeting for the First church because the work needs it; the folks are praying for it, expecting it and I know God is always mindful of our needs. Then I have secured the service of two of the leading evangelistic workers of our country. Those of us who are acquainted with the work of the Berge Sisters know what a treat our people have in store awaiting them. Another evidence of the progress of our work is seen in the matter of the Elon Standardization campaign. Our church was apportioned $4,500, and we are now rounding out $10,000 and the work is not yet done.

The writer did the preaching for the Palm Street meeting which closed last night (March 30). Rev. John W. Knight of Stokesdale is their pastor. We had a great meeting, which he will probably speak of at a later date. The people there love Brother Knight, and it is a great pity that he cannot give his whole time to that field. The great need of that church is full time preaching, and a pastor on the field all the time. The church is able to do it, and I believe with a little encouragement from the Conference Board of Missions, they would undertake it. Our Greensboro work as a whole needs the service of two men all the time. As I see it, the time is ripe for the establishment of an all time pastorate at the Palm Street church. I hope the people will pray for it, and lend their aid in bringing it about.

J. VINCENT KNIGHT.

Greensboro, N. C.

GEORGIA AND ALABAMA CHURCHES

Sunday, March 23, was spent by the writer with Rev. E. M. Carter at Lanett, Ala. Brother Carter has been pastor of our church here "off and on" for several years. He enjoys the utmost confidence and esteem of his people, and is in turn devoted to their moral and spiritual welfare. He can now only give them one Sunday a month appointments and he and they much desire at least two Sundays of each month. A pastor should by all means be located here, and give the other two Sundays of the month to the very promising near-

by points of Langdale and Fairfax. There is a wonderful opportunity for the Christians at these latter two points, as well as at Lanett, and we certainly losing a fruitful field of service by not so locating a pastor. Our Lanett brethren need a new house of worship, and they are seriously considering rebuilding. If they had, a resident pastor it is likely they would have on a building program at an early date. We have some splendid people at Lanett; none better any where. A visit in their homes was a great joy.

Early Monday morning the writer left for Lumber City, Ga., where he met Rev. H. W. Elder, our Georgia miracle of church builders. Brother Elder has long felt we should have a Christian church in Lumber City. He has built churches in the last few years at Kite, Ambrose, Enigma, and Vanceville, and now wishes to build the most costly and permanent of all at Lumber City. All these towns are in South Georgia, and in a few years we should have a thriving Conference here. We found some most delightful, amiable and loyal people there, and they can and will have a permanent and handsome church home if they really desire it, and decide to undertake to build. There are three families of Elders there, relatives of our beloved and hustling H. W., and they are aggressive builders in the business and financial world as their cousin is in the church world. If they build at all—and the writer thinks they will—they will have a house of worship of which the Christians from any quarter will not be ashamed.

In fact our people are determined to build better and more handsome houses of worship whenever they build in future. This sentiment prevails wherever the Mission Secretary has been. We have already put up too many cheap, shoddy, indifferent church buildings. You simply cannot have a wide awake, active congregation in an indifferent, inadequate house of worship, for long at a time at best.

Our stay at Lumber City was a great joy, being inhanced by the opportunity of preaching at night of Tuesday in the M. E. Church. We trust to know more of the good people of Lumber City.

J. O. ATKINSON.

SUFFOLK LETTER

There is a feeling in these times that the people of God ought to be more spiritual by making religion more real. There is not so much a demand for emotion as for devotion, and that not a devotion separate from daily life but permeating daily life.

"They who seek the throne of grace
Find that throne in every place;
If we live a life of prayer,
God is present ev'rywhere."

The growing thought is not that the world's work should be brought into the Kingdom, but that the Kingdom should go into the world's work. "I pray not that thou shouldest take them out of the world, but that thou shouldest keep them from the evil." The sunlight is not contaminated by the earth, but it blesses the world. It is the function of the Christian to go into the farm, the shop, the school, the store, the lodge, the political meeting, and to manifest the spirit of Jesus by doing all to the glory of God. The sparks from a 'Christian blacksmith's anvil may help to enlighten the world. The yardstick has its place as well as the hymn book. The ledger may honor the Bible, and the bookkeeper may serve God. It is this larger Christian life that the present time demands·

It must nowhere be taught that any human service, apart from God, is a substitute for religion. There is no human service a substitute for divine grace; but divine grace may work in all human service. The Christian religion has expressed itself in the prohibition of the liquor traffic, the abolition of slavery, the removal of the lottery, and the prohibition of vile literature from the mails. A labor union in Mississippi has elected a chaplain for the first time, and there is no reason why labor organizations may not become agencies for saving men. That will be a great day when railroads and steamboats are Christianized and carry no evil thing. That day may come. They require sober men to operate them, and they should refuse to transport what unfits men to do their work. The time is within the memory of men now living when railroad officials had liquors on the table in their private cars; but that day is gone. The day is near when it will not be in the freight cars. The spirit of Christ has entered the train.

The time is near when the farmer's religion will not be in the church only but in the field as well. He will not only treat his neighbor right, but his mule. I caught a hired man taking corn from the trough of mules to feed his hog and he was a member of the church. I said to him: "It would have been bad enough if you had stolen corn from my crib; but it is mean to steal from a mule. Those mules have worked hard all day and will have to work tomorrow. You have stolen from them and they cannot tell their loss." He said: "Fore God I never thought of that;" and many people wrong dumb beasts without thought. The time will come, and is already here when religion will be determined by how men treat mules·

     W. W. STALEY.

WHY WAS THE CHRISTIAN ENDEAVOR LEFT OUT?

In THE CHRISTIAN SUN for April 2 appears a notice concerning the *so-called*, "Sunday School and Christian Endeavor Convention of the North Carolina Christian Conference." Before reading that notice I had thought there was such a convention in existance, but now I have another "think" coming. Note the general theme of the Convention: "The new Sunday School for the New Time," and quoting the notice further, "all addresses and talks expected to be in line with the general theme," and still further, "let all Sunday schools have themselves represented by capable delegates—and raise four cents per member for the Convention." Then why not call it the *North Carolina Sunday School Convention of the Christian Church* and be done with it, since the Christian Endeavor is left out? Rest assured brethren, that your Christian

Endeavor Committee will *never* ask the Societies to raise funds for a Convention that does not recognize its work in the bounds of the Convention. Be it far from us to even dream of such methods of proceedure.

True, the Christian Endeavor in our Southern churches has never done very much, but that is neither the fault of Christian Endeavor nor of Christian Endeavor principles. As I see it, this part of our Church life is sorely neglected. I have no criticism to offer on the general work, but the Sunday school has never and never will do the work of the Christian Endeavor. It is not supposed to do it. The primary aim of the Christian Endeavor is to "train Christian workers," and for that reason it ought to be given a place in all our Conference and Convention program. The reason our Societies have never done much is because they have never been given any encouragement to do it. Give it a chance in the Convention and Conference work, or publicly place the stamp of disapproval on that line of work and let it die decently.

     J. VINCENT KNIGHT, Chm.
     Committee on Christian Endeavor.
Greensboro, N. C.

AN ANNOUNCEMENT

I will preach at the Masonic Home in Greensboro, N. C., Sunday, April 13, 1919, to all the old people and particularly to the unsaved. All the old people who desire to do so, may attend· I am very much interested in persons who have reached old age that are unsaved.

On Sunday, April 20, 1919, I will preach at Bethlehem, six miles north of Elon College, to old people. All persons are invited to be present but I desire especially that all old people of that community, who are unsaved, attend. I am now in my ninety-four year, perhaps the oldest minister that many have heard preach, and I trust that much good may be accomplished.

Other churches or places desiring my services will please write or call me.

     J. W. WELLONS.
Elon College, N. C.

REVIVAL AT ELON COLLEGE

Revival services were held here beginning March 20 and closing March 30. Revs. J. V. Knight, Greensboro, N. C., O. D. Poythress, South Norfolk, Va., and P. E. Lindley, Elon College, N. C., led the singing and conducted the preliminary services. They rendered valuable service and it was highly appreciated by pastor and audience. The preaching was done by the pastor. All services were well attended, and a quiet and serious spirit of interest prevailed. There were eighteen decisions for Christ and seven reconsecrations. Eight united with the church and were baptized. Others have signified their intention to unite at the next service.

     N. G. NEWMAN, *Pastor.*

Rev. B. J. Earp changes his address from Shenandoah to Stanley, Va.

CHRISTIAN EDUCATION

"THE GREATEST EVENT IN OUR HISTORY."

That was Colonel J. E. West's animated statement. The scene was enacted on Friday morning, April 4 at 9 o'clock in the pastor's study of the Suffolk Christian church, where for more than a generation a modest leader of men and self-forgetful man of God, has wrought out sermons that have changed men's lives and initiated plans that have advanced the interests of the Kingdom in our Christian Church. Present were that man, Colonel J. E. West, Mr. C. A. Shoop, Dr. I. W. Johnson, and the writer.

The writer announced that Col. J. E. West would be the first speaker. He spoke as the Chairman of the Drive Committee on the Elon Standardization Fund. He stated that this Committee had agreed that any Church which should give $50,000 in this drive could designate some one in whose honor the chair of the presidency in Elon College should be named.

Mr. C. A. Shoop, as Chairman of the Finance Committee of the Suffolk Church, was next heard, stating that Suffolk had met this condition and had designated Dr. W. W. Staley as the man in whose honor the chair should be named, in view of his signal service as pastor during 37 years of the Church in Suffolk; as Elon's president for eleven years of unpaid labor, and in the leadership of the Southern Christian Convention for a generation.

Dr. Staley was visibly affected. Who could but be under such circumstances? It is worth while to have lived and labored and toiled for a life-time for a moment like that. True to his characteristic modesty, he began to beg to be excused. Others were more worthy. His interest was safe and nothing could alienate it. The bestowal of the honor in another place would win friends for the cause. Thus the great man pleaded. But the Committee was unyielding. They would have nothing but his acceptance, and they won.

Then Dr. Johnson led in a beautiful prayer of gratitude to God for Dr. Staley, for the college, for the generous friends of Suffolk—a prayer tense with sweet sentiment and simple as the language of the child, because God was being addressed directly and no garnishment of words could enrich the occasion. It was a tender moment.

The writer then congratulated Dr. Staley on being thus honored, expressed his satisfaction at being the first occupant of the W. W. Staley Chair of the presidency, and voiced the prayer that God would spare the honoree for many long years yet of service in the Church.

Then it was that Col. West declared what all present felt, that "this is the greatest event in the history of our Church." We are sure every reader will agree with us.

The raising of this magnificent sum was easy. Nine men gave five thousand dollars each: W. W. Staley, C. A. Shoop, Holland and Beamon Co., J. E. West, E. E. Holland, Lakeview Hospital, S. E. Everett, A. T. Holland, and G. W. Truitt. There were four gifts of $1,000 each by Ballard and Smith, J. T. Williams, Mrs. H. M. Phillips, and R. C. Harrell. Mrs. W. H. Jones, Jr., Miss Dorris Jones, and Lyman R. Brothers each gave $500. The other donors were H. Woodward, Sr., H. M. Holland, J. P. Lee, W. E. MacClenny, E. H. Rawles, J. D. Rawles, Philathea Class, Fred Bullock, and J. D. Luke.

Colonel West and Mr. Shoop are a continuation Committee to bring the total up to at least $50,000 in addition to Dr. Staley's subscription, and it will be readily done. Mr. J. M. Darden, who recently gave $5,000 to missions, is expecting to give $5,000 to this good work too, and will announce his decision shortly.

Dr. Staley was kept absolutely in the dark as to the plan to honor him, and only learned of it when officially notified. God bless him and multiply his kind. God bless the Christians of Suffolk and multiply their kind.

THE VICTORY AT SUFFOLK AND PRAYER

Something always happens when God's people pray. The overwhelming flood of generosity in Suffolk, which consecrated more than $50,000 to the cause of Christian Education in our Church, is attributable to prayer as its fountain source.

On Sunday morning just before going to the service there, when I was to speak on "The Church in the New Time," I received the following telegram: "At request of the pastor the faculty met in prayer tonight (Saturday) for God's blessing on you and His service while in Suffolk. We further covenanted to pray individually for you daily that you may acceptably represent Him and that those you approach there may do His will. (Signed) W. P. Lawrence, Dean." I handed it to Dr. Staley after reading. No comment was necessary. Sunday, morning and evening, went well, and seed were sown soon to fruit gloriously.

On Monday morning after Dr. Staley had subscribed $5,000, we walked to the postoffice to find this letter from the professor who has served Elon longest and who is giving $1,000 in this drive: "We are watching the canvass with increasing anxiety and joy, believing that God is blessing your labor because you fully realize this is His work and you have consecrated yourself to His service in it. This trip to Suffolk is a crucial point in the campaign. What Suffolk does means so much to the brethren there, to the college and to the Kingdom. A response worthy of them will be a new day for the larger spiritual life of the local Church and larger effort in the other Churches will ensue. We follow you with our sympathies and our prayers. God will prosper you."

Seven other letters of similar import came to me, being so timed in their arrival as to revive any depression from the nervous tension inescapable in such a drive and cheering my heart to new effort.

But all the prayer was not on the part of the dear ones at Elon. The pastor of the Suffolk church held me up constantly to the Throne. In his homely way, and yet so forceful, when the goal had been reached, he likened himself during the week to a sitting hen, busy in prayer for God's blessing, and occasionally looking around to see what was happening. Prayer did it. That is all. To Him be the praise.

FIVE HOURS AND $6,100

On Thursday afternoon of the Suffolk drive week Dr. Johnson thinking a little ride would be helpful, a party consisting of himself and wife, Dr. Staley and Miss Annie and the writer, forded it down to that genial center of Christian hospitality, the home of Trustee and Mrs. Willis J. Lee. Brother Lee has been quite feeble, but was up and able to greet us in his usual happy style. Mrs. Lee was in bed, but her welcome was equally cordial and happy. Two dearer friends Elon never had. While in their home they volunteered to give $5,000 to the drive, and Mrs. Lee called on Dr. Staley to give thanks that they could do it. How precious the moment!

On this little outing we called upon Mr. and Mrs. R. B. Odom, dear friends whose hearts bleed because of the death of their eldest son of his wounds in France. Sergeant W. F. Odom was an Elon student when the war broke out. On the following day he volunteered in the service of his country and on December 12, 1918, he died in France of his wounds received in the desperate fighting two months before. His friends called him "Happy," and happy he is now in his Master's presence. His grief-stricken parents desiring to perpetuate his name have decided to build Sunday school rooms to his home church, Berea, and to establish in his honor the W. F. Odom Fund of $1,000 in his Alma Mater. This is the first instance where loving parents have thus honored a fallen hero son; but it will not be the last. How could parents do a finer thing than this?

On the way back we stopped to see Mr. and Mrs. John E. Benton and these loyal alumni of the college gave $100, making $6,100 for our five hours of outing. Some outing,—eh?

I should say that later I return to Berea and give the other friends there their anticipated opportunity to help the cause of Christ through Elon.

             W. A. HARPER.

Dear Dr. Harper:

I just want you to know that I am sure we shall succeed in the drive for $125,000.00. I do not feel that this is merely an educational move, but more to fit our College, therefore our denomination in order that it may hold its own with the other churches. We *must* succeed in this.

         Very sincerely,

            MRS. W. C. WHITAKER.

Kittrell, N. C.

Don't forget the Easter offering for the Orphanage. See Brother Johnston's letter on this page.

Are you going to attend the American Christian Convention? Remember the date, April 29.

THE CHRISTIAN ORPHANAGE

EASTER OFFERING APPEAL

My dear Sunday School Workers and Friends:

Since our last Easter offering our country has been visited by one of the worst epidemics of flu that this country has ever experienced. It has been no respecter of persons, but has taken fathers and mothers, as well as younger people, and has left many little helpless orphans in its wake.

In all my experience in this work, I have never had so many urgent applications to take little helpless orphan children, as we have had in the last month. We have filled our Institution to the limit of its capacity and now have fifty-seven in our care. Bright and happy little boys and girls.

One of the Many Little Outstretched Hands to Receive the Easter Offering

We have fifteen urgent applications on file in our office pleading to us for a home. Helpless and in destitute circumstances and no where to go—pitiful in the extreme.

One of the heaviest crosses we have to bear in this work is to be compelled to say NO to the cry of little orphans who so much need a home of this kind, because we have no more room. What can we do to relieve the situation at present? Let us open up another home for the small children and that will make ample room at present to take care of the situation.

We want to raise for our Easter Offering this year the sum of $3,000.00 to enable us to open this home for the small children. We want your Sunday school to have a liberal offering in this task. If you could but read the pitiful letters that come to me, or come in touch with the pitiful cases that I do, it would make your heart ache and melt your eyes to tears. You would be glad to divide the last dollar you have and freely give that a home might be provided for these children.

I plead with you in behalf of the children who have been left alone in the world, to make an offering on or near Easter Sunday to help in making a home available for them. Give as you have never given before. Give because the need is urgent. Give because the cry of the little helpless orphan child is ringing in your ears. Give because you will be the better and the happier. Give as God has prospered you. Remember "He that hath pity upon the poor lendeth unto the Lord; and that which he hath given will He repay him again."

Make your offering liberal to meet the need.

Yours in the work for the Master,
CHAS. D. JOHNSTON, Supt.

REPORT FOR APRIL 9, 1919

Amount brought forward, $1,779.41.

Children's Offerings

Raymond Sharpe, 30 cents; Lizzie Lawrence, 10 cents; Maple Lawrence, 10 cents; John B. Taylor, 25 cents; Total, 75 cents.

Sunday School Monthly Offerings

(Eastern Virginia Conference)

Third Christian church, Norfolk, January, February, March and Birthday Offerings, $27.69; Rosemont, $5.00; Spring Hill, $1.00; Centerville, $1.00.

(North Carolina Conference)

Grace's Chapel, $3.00; Pleasant Hill, $4.00; Henderson, $8.85; Pleasant Union, $6.00; Shallow Well, $1.39.

(Virginia Valley Conference)

Antioch, $2.00.

(Georgia and Alabama Conference)

Lanett, $10.35; Rose Hill, $4.00; Total, $74.28.

(Thanksgiving Offerings)

Suffolk church, Suffolk, Va., $100.00.

Special Offerings

Mr. H. B. Parsons, Brashart, Ky., $100.00; Mrs. E. W. Graham, Burlington, N. C., $1.00; Mrs. James Huffine, $2.50; Total, $103.50.

Miscellaneous

Cash Item, $3.00; Cash Item, $15.00; Total, $18.00.
Total for the week, $296.53; Grand total, $2,075.94.

LETTERS FROM THE COUSINS

Dear Uncle Charley: I am sending you 25 cents for the orphans. I am one year and eight months old. Aunt Jennie thinks I am the sweetest thing on earth. Best wishes.—*John B. Taylor.*

You are just at age when all little boys are sweet—one time in life. You must keep sweet. Laugh and grow fat—*"Uncle Charley."*

Dear Uncle Charley: How are all the children getting on these pretty spring days? Would like to go to see them some of these times. Our Sunday school starts tomorrow. Guess I will go, too. Here are my dues for March, April and May.—*Raymond Sharpe.*

Would be glad to have you visit us and see all our little folks. You would enjoy it.—*"Uncle Charley."*

Dear Uncle Charley: We are each sending a dime for the orphans. We hope they are all well. Our school was out three weeks ago. Since it was out we have been helping father and mother. We would be delighted to visit the Orphanage and see the little cousins. Wishing you all a happy Easter.—*Lizzie and Maple Lawrence.*

We would be delighted to have you come to see us and see all our little children together. I am sure you would be delighted.—*"Uncle Charley."*

WANTED

THE CHRISTIAN SUN desires the name and address of every invalid and shut-in member of the Christian Church in the Southern Christian Convention. If you know of one, man, woman, or child, report it at once. Don't take it for granted that some one else will. Let us hear from you.

NOTICE

The Sunday School and Christian Endeavor Convention of the North Carolina Christian Conference meets with Shallow Well Christian church July 15-17. The general theme for discussion will be "The New Sunday School for the New Time," and all talks and addresses are expected to be somewhat related to the general theme. The Sunday schools within the bounds of the Conference are requested to make an earnest effort to have themselves represented by capable delegates. It would be nothing but right that the travelling expenses of these delegates be paid by the Sunday schools.

Each Sunday school is requested to send to the Convention an amount of money equal to four cents per member of its enrollment. Churches that have been accustomed to holding their protracted meetings the week following the second Sunday in July are requested this year to arrange a different time for the protracted meeting, in order not to conflict with the Convention.

It is the purpose of the executive Committee to get out an attractive program that shall be instructive and inspiring, and to this end we solicit the co-operation of the brotherhood.

HERBERT SCHOLZ, Sec'y.

"Dr. Harper spoke here yesterday and I will report if he succeeds here as we hope he will. I am hoping for a quarter of a million for Elon in the campaign when all the churches have had a chance to go over the top as all have so far," so writes Dr. Staley to the Editor under date of March 31.

WORSHIP AND MEDITATION

THE VINDICATED HOPE

(Rev. S. Parker Cadman, D. D., in The Christian Work)

St. Paul was an optimist from principle, not from sentiment. He wrote his letters to the churches as a Christian Jew who was thoroughly acquainted with the varied fortunes of the human race and of his own people. He knew the historic epochs of triumph and disaster; the anticipations of patriarchs and the predictions of seers were familiar to him. Many of their efforts seemed futile. Civilization in his day was apparently decadent; the richest promise of Judaism had been tragically negatived by the Scribe and the Pharisee.

Nevertheless, this stupendous breakdown of faith and morals did not breed despair in the apostle. Neither could the fierce persecution to which his new religion was subjected cause him to waver for a moment. His tribulations worked for that patience which is no cheap nor common virtue. His golden age persisted in au invironment of hurricane and disaster. It was born of his conscious acceptance with God; fostered by his intimacy with his Risen Lord. These divine relationships created in St. Paul the ardent expectation of better things beyond which was too reasonable and inspiring to be thwarted by outward circumstances. Every Christian is the heir of God's love shed abroad in the believing heart by the Holy Spirit. And out of that love arises the hope that cannot be frustrated nor put to shame. We have to wait for its regal fulfilment which forecasts the future as the supreme opportunity for all righteousness.

In the meantime, those who do not share the love have not the hope. They mock its radiant prospectus and deem us dreamers of the impossible, peddlers of illusions, who have utterly miscalculated human destiny. How chimerical to speak of the approaching reign of peace and fraternity in a world where wickedness is rampant and the old feuds persist! There are good sincere individuals who yield to this accusation of our hope. Discouraged by the delay of their Deliverer, they are tempted to cast away the confidence which has "great recompense of reward," or to mention it cautiously and with rigid reserve. Such a timid attitude is not very serviceable against those patronizing tendencies of modern literature which insists that religious ideas are only a product of egotism, in which the living atom man persuades himself that he is infinitely more honorable than the rest of the universe, and upon terms of peculiar friendship with its Maker. Nor are we sure that the insistence would be altogether groundless but for one indisputable fact of Christian experience. None who has really felt the love of God, not our love for Him, but His overwhelming and boundless love for us, can doubt the security of life and of its every noble cause, or succumb to the demoralizing skepticism that we are helpless puppets manipulated by blind insenate powers. The transfiguring truth that

the Father's love is already ours; that we do not have to win it, but accept what He bestows, who loves us even in our sins to save us from our sins, unites us with the Deity of life and might. His delight is with the sons of men, with all His children, with the sailor on the sea, the soldier on the field, the husbandman tilling the soil, the miner delving in the rocks. He is as Martineau has said—"the dear God of the home," upon whose loving kindness we can draw and not be disappointed. He underprops our hope so that it is no flattering guess-work, and gives us here now the earnest of its long-lost achievement to come.

The routine we must follow teems with tokens of His accompanying presence. The fevered dusty atmosphere of ordinary existence is purified by celestial breezes. We could not testify of these things so dogmatically had we not seen them demonstrated to the hilt. The wayfarers of our youth were not socially fortunate. The majority were colliers and ironworkers, men of strong elementary passions and vigorous physical equipment. But once they knew the Love Divine they were transferred into new beings, a literal miracle of grace which we have seen repeated in numbers instances. There they ceased to speculate, and were possessed by the gladdening reality of an inward witness which enabled them to sing—

"Thrice blessed bliss-inspiring hope,
It lifts the fainting spirit up.
It brings to life the dead.
Our trials here will soon be past,
And you and I ascend at last
In triumph with our Head."

In this frame of mind they were nearer to the apostle's type than are many erudite and eloquent divines and teachers who bid on the future out of the resources of the earth and are worsted. Let the man who has lost hope seek first a renewal of his apprehension of the love of God, forever full and free, and he will not remain in darkness.

———————

Brother L. I. Cox writes under dater March 31: "I had a good day Sunday at New Center and Seagrove. The people are becoming interested in larger things for the Kingdom, and are responding more than ever for the call of Missions and Christian Education."

Dr. P. H. Fleming, now at Dover, Del., writes that he will fill his regular appointment at Union (N. C.) on the second Sunday.

Abe Mulky, one of the great evangelists of the M. E. Church, is dead.

Brother J. W. Wellons came down from the College one day last week and paid us a brief visit. He is in his usual good health.

MISSIONARY

SOME MORE GOOD SUNDAY SCHOOL LETTERS

In reply to the letter recently sent to our Sunday school secretaries, asking them to take up the matter of mission study and a missionary offering, one or the other, or both, for their Sunday school one Sunday a month, many responses are coming in for which we are profoundly grateful. As our Sunday schools take up this matter, we feel that the beginning is being made at the right place. Many schools are discussing either taking the offering or, that which is even better, studying missions once per month and for this the Mission Secretary is profoundly grateful. Here are three letters by recent mail:

"Durham, N. C., March 29, 1919.

"Dear Sir and Brother:

"Enclosed I herewith hand you check for $11.02, Sunday school collection for the third Sunday in March. The Durham Christian Sunday school has voted to give the collection on the third Sunday of every month to missions. Trust our collections will be good on this Sunday.

"Yours truly,

"R. J. KERNODLE, Treasurer."

"News Ferry, Va., March 31, 1919.

"Dear Sir and Brother:

"The Pleasant Grove Sunday school has decided to give the collection of one Sunday per month to missions. Enclosed please find check for $2.15, the one Sunday's collection for missions.

"With best wishes, I am

"Yours sincerely,

"P. W. FARMER, Acting Secretary."

"Raleigh, N. C., R. 3, March 23, 1919.

"Dear Sir and Brother:

"I am glad to tell you that our Sunday school (Catawba Springs) has adopted one of the three points mentioned in your letter. We have decided to give one Sunday's collection to missions and I hope that as our people become more interested in the work, we will take up the other two.

"With all good wishes for your success,

"B. F. BRANCH, Superintendent."

PLEASANT GROVE SETS THE PACE

Dr. Harper's report of the liberality of the dear Pleasant Grove people in the Elon Standardization campaign must have sent a thrill of joy to all who love our Elon, and have a care for our cause. It was at Pleasant Grove the writer began his active campaign for our missionary drive, and when the great and good people of that congregation pledged $3,000.00 for missions, the writer knew then that victory was sure, and that the day of our missionary awakening had come.

And now that the same generous people have pledged $15,000.00 to our beloved College the writer feels our denominational awakening is assured, and that the hour of our great opportunity and unlimited service has

struck. God cannot prosper a non-missionary people and keep His word. Nor conversely can He fail to prosper a missionary people and not keep His word. "Lo I am with you unto the end," is conditioned on "Go ye." What the Christian Church needs most of all is "Christ with us." And we have Him with us when we undertake His program.

God bless our dear, loyal, faithful, generous Pleasant Grove people. They have set the standard high in the Elon Standardization drive as they did in the *hundred thousand dollars* missionary drive, and as other churches and congregations not only flocked to that standard but helped to raise it even higher and higher, so will it be in the Elon drive.

Elon is our very own. Her needs have from the beginning been close to our Christian heart, and between now and July first, by our Father's great wisdom and indulgent hand, we shall witness the outpouring of our love and our dollars such as we have not witnessed heretofore.

No one can know how every report of success and victory in this great work rejoices the Mission Secretary's heart. It is all but the confirmation and the glad realization of his hopes, his dreams and his desires for as he has even contended. We will freely take care and provide for our own when we become willing to do our best to carry out the great commission.

J. O. ATKINSON.

TWO GENEROUS WOMEN

This was found in an exchange the other day and because it represents the spirit, character and conduct of many of the good women I have met since I became Mission Secretary, I pass it on through these columns:

Two Generous Women

Their name is legion, but two instances will suffice. They do not live on Fifth Avenue or own limousines. One is a professor in college, drawing a small salary, upon which she supports herself besides helping out her family. She met the secretary of her Foreign Board on the street one day and asked if it were true that the Board had turned down the offer of the officials in a certain province in China looking to the Mission taking over the conduct of the public schools. She was informed that such was the case, as there was no money in the treasury for the support of the educational supervisors who would need to be sent out. After expressing her sorrowful surprise that such an opportunity could be allowed to pass, she said, "I cannot be content until I will have done my own little part to make possible such a strategic move as it proposed. I was about to purchase a new gown which I have greatly needed, not having had a new one for a year, and I have set apart $50 for that purpose. I will try to get along for another year, and let you have this amount."

The secretary was so impressed by her self-denial that he took the matter up in one of the Board's publications, mentioning what this woman had done, and asking if others would not like to join in the movement. Without any further reference or pushing, within two weeks $15,000 had been secured from givers all over the country, mostly women, and the Board cabled to

China its acceptance of the offer. The two educational supervisors are now on the ground and a work of splendid promise has been launched by which the Chinese officials and the missionaries are working hand in hand in the promotion of Christian education.

The other case is that of a young lady who is obliged to support herself and her mother by taking boarders. In addition she was receiving an income of $100 a year from a mortgage investment, and for a number of years she had been devoting this sum to the support of two native preachers in Africa. The last time she brought in her check the secretary, who knew her circumstances, expressed his surprise that she was able to maintain her gift from year to year. She replied, "I had a terrible scare. A few weeks ago I learned that the interest on my mortgage had failed, and that I would have to get along without that help. It looked for a time as if I would have to give up this work in Africa!" "How then," asked the secretary, "have you been able to secure the money?" "Oh," she replied, "I at once went to work and earned $100 by a special enterprise in which I engaged."

That evening the secretary mentioned this incident to his wife, whereupon she remarked, "That explains why Miss W. has been going around the neighborhood taking orders for silk stockings. I wondered that she should do this, but knowing she must have some good reason I thought I ordered a pair, although I felt I really did not need them."

How many persons situated as this young lady was, would have taken such pains to keep up her missionary giving, and how many would have let the thing drop?

"THANK YOU": A TRUE STORY

Inga is a little Swedish girl, only eight years old, whose home is in the country, many miles from town.

Swedish parents teach their children to be very polite. Every little favor or gift meets with a prompt "Thank you." It sounds very sincere, and if they are especially grateful the "Thank you" is apt to be emphasized by a hand-shake. When the Swedish children eat a meal at a friend's home, upon arising from the table, they smile and say, "Thank you very much for the meal." It is a very pretty custom.

Now, Inga is very fond of something all boys and girls enjoy, though she seldom has it—only at Christmas. It is candy.

One day an aunt came to visit Inga's parents, and she brought a box of candy and gave it to Inga. Immediately Inga treated the entire family. Finally the box was put away, so as to save the candy as long as possible; but when it was brought forth the family once more was treated and the box again put away. Inga had just put the pretty candy box on the table and was about to take a piece when her mother entered the room.

There were only three pieces left, and she had been very generous. Mother was busy and had not noticed the box. Inga could easily hide it away, but no! she would be selfish were she to do that, so she called: "Come, mother, have some candy."

"Yes, dear," mother responded, but when she looked in the big box and saw only three pieces of candy left her mother-heart made her exclaim: "No, mother doesn't want any. Keep it yourself; you have been so generous to all."

Back came the reply of her small daughter with such a sincere ring of thankfulness as almost made her gasp in surprise, for Inga wildly shook her mother's hand, exclaiming: "Thank you, mother; thank you very much, for not taking any!"—M. E. G.

HOW A SEAL GETS AIR THROUGH THE ICE

When the Artic Ocean is entirely covered with many feet of ice the seal has to find some way of obtaining air to breathe. So he selects a spot and begins to drill a hole to the surface by pressing his warm nose against the ice. No one knows how many hours it takes him to accomplish his task, but he manages it; and although he is obliged to work most of the time, because the surface of the hole is continually freezing, he keeps it open all winter and obtains air.

Seals have been known to drill in this manner through 50 feet of solid ice. Whether or not they take turns in the slow drilling is not positively known.

It is at these "seal holes" that the polar bear seeks food in the winter, and there the Eskimo waits, spear in hand, for his weekly supply of meat.—Apples of Gold.

"What's all that noise over at the minister's house?"
"Oh, he's memorizing his sermon; he always has to practice what he preaches."—Judge.

Papa—"Bobby, if you had a little more spunk, you would stand better in your class. Now, do you know what spunk is?"
Bobby—"Yes, sir. It's the past participle of spank."

"Well, after all," remarked Tommy, who had lost a leg in the war, "there's one advantage in having a wooden leg."
"What's that?" asked his friend.
"You can hold up your sock with a tintack!" chuckled the hero.—Boys' Life.

We must succeed with the drive for $125,000 for Elon College. Of course we will.

What about an individual Communion set for your church? Will ship on 60 days' time. Write for prices.

J. H. Carter—I want THE SUN to keep coming to my home.

E. A. Brady—Wishing you much success and hoping that THE SUN may shine long in our home.

THE FORWARD MOVEMENT

WARREN H. DENISON, Superintendent

The Forward Movement Executive Committee spent a day planning the work and in counsel with the Superintendent, President W. A. Harper asked Rev. J. W. Harrell to represent him at the meeting. The whole Church seems to be awakening to the fact that this is our day of opportunity to serve. The time has come for the Christian Church to come to her own.

The Forward Movement representatives are meeting with groups of workers, conference officials, pastors, and representative laymen in strategic centers. Many more calls are coming than the present force of workers can answer.

The Northwestern India mid-year institute raised several hundreds of dollars more for missions than ever in its history. The Forward Movement vision caught the people and the Woman's Mission Board benefitted. The Deer Creek, Indiana, church which is a rural church was greatly blessed. Five persons subscribed $1,400 for the Forward Movement. The mission offering of the night before did not hinder giving to the Forward Movement. Again it is demonstrated that giving to one benevolent cause does not hinder but helps another. The Superintendent will soon return to see others of that congregation and receive their gifts.

The Superintendent has already secured $6,394 in cash and subscriptions while conducting a preliminary publicity campaign. The Executive Committee reports that $10,000 have been subscribed to the initial promotion fund to inaugurate the campaign.

Every pastor in the denomination is asked to appoint a *four-minute* man or woman for his congregation to keep them informed of the Movement.

Easter results for membership additions from all the churches will be gathered. Our pastors are requested to report on Easter Monday the number of members received, church, conference, and pastor.

Forward Movement speakers are at Urbana, Ill., in a Forward Movement drive, also at Antioch church near Frankfort, Ind., and at the Joint Convention of the Western, Indiana, Conference.

Scores of our pastors are working out and working at definite church programs and they are built upon the points of the Forward Movement.

Our pastors and conference officers in nearly every case are showing the heartiest co-operation, and spirit of working together in the large program of our church for the Kingdom.

Rallies have been held in the last few days at Warren, Ind., Huntington, Ind.

Many decision days in the Sunday schools are now being planned at this Easter time.

BOOKS, BIBLES, TESTAMENTS

In order to reduce certain stocks of books, Bibles and Testaments on hand, the following prices are made and will hold good until April 10, 1919.

Bibles

No. 312X. Holman Self-Pronouncing Teachers' Bible. Printed on fine white paper from good, clear type, and contains references, concordance, four thousand questions and answers and fifteen prepared maps. Size 4 3-8X6 1-2 inches. Egyptian Morocco, divinity circuit, head bands and marker, round corners, red under gold edges. Regular selling price......$4.65
Price to March 31 ....: 3.90
No. 71. Scofield Reference Bible. Handsome binding, French Morocco limp, new and improved edition. "The neatest Scofield Bible made." It will please you. Regular selling price $4.50
Price to March 31 .... 3.90
No. 215. Child's Self-Pronouncing Pictorial Bible with Helps. Bound in French seal leather, round corners, silk bands, gold titles,—handsomely made. Regular selling price $2.50
Price to March 31 .... 2.00
No. 1113. Ideal Bible for Children. Printed on fine white paper from the newest and clearest type of the size made. Size 3 1-2X5 3-8 inches. This Bible will please you. Regular price $1.75
Price to March 31 .... 1.40

Testaments

No. 3913 R. L. (Red Letter). Large print Morocco binding. Regular price $2.00
Price to March 31 .... 1.75
No. 2902 Cloth binding, large print. Regular price.... .90
Price to March 31 .... .75
No. 2502 P. Cloth binding, black faced type. Regular price .... .75
Price to March 31 .... .55
No. 2113. Pocket size, Morocco binding. Regular price .60
Price to March 31 ....: .... .45
No. 0133. Pocket size, Morocco binding, overlapping edges. Regular Price 75
Price to March 31 .... .55

(A Testament in Modern Speech)

Cloth, $1.25; cloth, indexed, $1.75; cloth, India paper, $1.75; leather, $2.35; leather, indexed, $2.75; leather, India paper, $3.75; Persian Morocco, Divinity Circuit, $3.75; Turkey Morocco, $1.25. Pocket Edition (without notes): Cloth, $1.00; cloth, India paper, $1.25; leather, India paper, $1.85. State definitely style wanted.

The above prices are regular. Make your choice and deduct 10 per cent. State definitely Testament wanted.

Books

Pastor's Ideal Funeral, $1.15—Regular price, $1.25.

(Books for the Children)

We have several copies "Silver Rags," "Patty's Grand Uncle," "Johnny Two Boys," "A Rescued Madonna"—your choice, 20 cents per copy. We will substitute if the book ordered is sold before the order reaches us.

Special

"Redmond of the Seventh," by Mrs. Frank Lee is a book with a love story taken from school life, 290 pages, handsomely bound, 50 cents the copy.

Special Note: One of these books will be sent free with each order from $3.00 worth of books, Bibles or Testaments.

Address

C. B. RIDDLE ......,....................Publishing Agent
Burlington, N. C.

Sunday School and Christian Endeavor

The North Carolina Christian Conference, chartered by the State of North Carolina, January 27, 1919, held its initial session at Elon College, February 14, and among other things, transacted this item of business: "On motion the officers of the Sunday School and Christian Endeavor Convention of the Eastern North Carolina Conference are hereby elected the officers of said Convention of the North Carolina Christian Conference, since they have agreed to this plan." The first session of said Convention will be held at Shallow Well church, July 15-17, 1919.

Pursuant to above the Executive Committee of said North Carolina Sunday School and Christian Endeavor Convention, met in a called session March 19, in Raleigh, N. C., and decided the following:

First, that the first annual session of the North Carolina Sunday School and Christian Endeavor Convention be held at Shallow Well Christian church (near Jonesboro, N. C.), Tuesday evening, Wednesday, Wednesday evening and Thursday, July 15-17, and that the general theme of this Convention shall be "The New Sunday School For The New Time."

Second, that the apportionments, or Convention dues from the schools and Societies, be 4 cents per member for the enrollment of each school and society, not having a fixed apportionment by its convention last year.

The above are facts that I want you to get firmly fixed in your mind. Read again, and memorize, and don't forget; and in view of the fact that this is now a *State Convention* embodying all the Sunday schools and Christian Endeavor Societies, in what was formerly the Eastern North Carolina Christian Conference, the Western North Carolina Christian Conference, and the North Carolina and Virginia Christian Conference, the call is greater now than ever before to put through the *greater work* God has intrusted to our care. To live up to this new challenge in the coming Convention, we must have the full support of every Sunday school and Christian Endeavor Society

within the bounds of the *new Conference*. We cannot afford to do anything less than this. Therefore, I am asking you to read these facts before your school; begin now, and boost the Convention until it comes off. Your school and Society are entitled to one delegate for every twenty-five members, and fractions thereof. Elect a live, wide-awake delegation, that is really interested in the work of the Church and Convention. Choose the delegates who are most interested and capable, and see that they are there for the first session, and remain throughout the Convention. We are preparing the best program yet, and propose to give you at the Convention that which will help your school or Society practically. The rest remains with you and your delegation.

Hoping that you will catch the spirit of the new undertaking to "consolidate our forces and broaden our fields of service in the Master's Kingdom," I am

Yours for a greater Convention,

C. H. STEPHENSON, *Pres.*
State S. S. and C. E. Convention.
Raleigh, N. C.

MARRIAGES

KERNODLE-KECK

At the residence of Rev. J. W. Holt, March 26, 1919, Mr. Ralph C. Kernodle and Miss Geneva Keck were married in the presence of a few friends, the writer officiating. May good wishes go with these young people for joy and happiness.

J. W. HOLT.

WALKER-TEER

Mr. George Lacy Walker, Watson, N. C. and Miss Clarice Teer were married March 23, 1919 at the home of the writer. Daniel E. Louder, Braxton Perry, Miss Mamie Walker and Miss Lou Eva Pritchette came with the bridal party. A number of the friends of the bride and groom came over to witness the marriage ceremony.

J. W. HOLT.

OBITUARIES

WICKER

Mrs. Anna Belle McFarland Wicker was born November 10, 1854, and departed this life February 14, 1919, aged 64 years, 3 months and 4 days. She was married to Thomas L. Wicker March 4, 1877. To this union were born six children: Lacy Wicker, Norfolk, Va.; DeLaney D. Wicker, A. E. F. in France; Mrs. E. D. Kelly, Moncure, N. C.; Miss Ida Belle Wicker, Durham, N. C.; and Miss White Wicker. Besides the children there are nine grandchildren and scores of other near relatives and friends left to mourn their loss.

For some time the deceased has lived in Durham, having moved here about two years ago from Lee county. She was a member of the Zion Christian church at the time of her death and had been for many years. Her husband, Thomas L. Wicker, preceded her to the grave and to God twelve years ago.

Mrs. Wicker's funeral was conducted in Durham from her home on East Main street. The body was then carried to her old home in Lee county and the interment was made at her home church cemetery Sunday, February 16, 1919. To all who knew her death brought sorrow. She was a good mother, a congenial friend and a faithful Christian, and she will be missed in her home, in her community and in her church. To all of her relatives and friends we offer our deepest condolence and urge them to turn to God for solace.

A FRIEND.

GRIFFITH

Mrs. Mary Griffith was born in 1843 in Wake county, North Carolina and died at her home in Petersburg, Va., March 9, 1919. She was 76 years old. In 1868 she married Robert Griffith of Cumberland, Maryland, where she made her home for a number of years. She then came to Durham and resided till a few months ago when she left and went to Petersburg to live with her son, Henry.

About three years ago she lost her eyesight and since then she has been an invalid. She is survived by one brother,

Dock Sanderford of Wake county, two sons, Henry Griffith of Petersburg, Va., and Samuel Griffith of Richmond, Va.; three daughters, Mrs. Henry Beach of Raleigh, N. C.; Mrs. Lonnie Glosson of Durham, N. C., and Mrs. William Ferrell of Durham county.

The funeral was conducted by the writer and the interment was made in the Maplewood cemetery. May the Holy Spirit comfort the bereaved.

R. F. BROWN.

CHILD'S SELF-PRONOUNCING PICTORIAL BIBLE WITH HELPS

This Bible is bound in French Seal Leather, has round corners, silk head bands, gold titles, handsomely bound. Price till April 10............ 2.00
Call for Bible No. 215.
Address
G. B. RIDDLE, *Publishing Agent*
Burlington, North Carolina

THE TITHER

An interdenominational publication devoted to Tithing and Christian Stewardship.

Editors
C. B. RIDDLE
KARL LEHMANN
BERT WILSON
HUGH S. McCORD
FRED G. THOMAS
8 pages; issued monthly; 50c the year
Address
THE TITHER   Burlington, N. C.

CANCER TREATED SUCCESSFULLY AT THE KELLAM HOSPITAL

The record of the Kellam Hospital is without parallel in history, having restored, without the use of the knife, Acids, X-Ray or Radium, over ninety per cent of the many hundreds of sufferers from cancers which it has treated during the past twenty-two years. We want every man and woman in the United States to know what we are doing.—KELLAM HOSPITAL, 1617 W. Main St., Richmond, Va.

BOOK NOTES

Story Books For The Children

We now have on hand a very fine story book for the children. "Redmond of the Seventh," by Mrs. Frank Lee. The book is handsomely bound, lettered in gold and contains 290 pages. The story is wholesome —a school story. The price is within the reach of all—75 cents postpaid, or two for $1.25.

Christian Hymnaries

We have the Christian Hymnary at 50 cents the copy. How many copies?

Address
C. B. RIDDLE, *Publishing Agent,*
Burlington, N. C.

BIBLES! BIBLES!! BIBLES!!!

The Christian Sun
Burlington, N. C.

INDIVIDUAL COMMUNION SERVICE
THE BEST WAY
to serve Communion.
It is reverent, sanitary, and increases attendance at the Lord's Supper. Our services are chaste and beautiful. Made of finest materials and best workmanship.
Send for illustrated price list
C. B. RIDDLE, Publishing Agent,
Burlington, North Carolina.

ELON COLLEGE NOTES

The annual Freshman-Sophomore debate occurred on April 4. Harold W. Johnson presided and made the introductory address. Miss Mary Miller was secretary. The marshals were: Sam Cozart, Chief; Misses Margarite Corbitt, Esther Chandler, Janice Fugham and Nettie Tuck. The query was: "Resolved that the railroads of the United States should be owned and operated by the Federal Government."

The affirmative was represented by J. Horton Doughton, Miss Lula Cannon and William R. Thomas; the negative by Lawrence M. Cannon, Miss Maude Sharpe and Joseph E. McCauley. The affirmative contended, among other things, that private ownership had been marked by discrimination in freight rates, rebates to great concerns, over capitalization of stock, corrupting of legislatures and opposition to measures of public safety. The recent war had demonstrated their incompetency in a time of stress. Germany and other great nations have made government ownership a success and we could do the same. The Post Office Department showed the cheapness and efficiency of government operation.

The negative declared government ownership economically impracticable and politically impossible. It would hoist an enormous debt on the country. The government is generous in wages and improvements and would increase the cost of operation. The people are opposed and would never vote for government ownership, which would mean political control. Under private ownership our railroads have made the greatest development, paid the highest wages and given the lowest freight rates and the most efficient service. Private ownership, under Inter-state Commerce Commission with enlarged powers, was in accord with American ideals and would be the solution of the problem. The negative won.

N. G. NEWMAN.

THE CHRISTIAN SUN

Easter Rapture

PHOTO BY FRANK FOURNIER

"Which hope we have as an anchor of the soul both sure and steadfast."—Hebrews 6:19.

Vol. LXXI }   BURLINGTON, N. C.   { No. 16
WEDNESDAY, APRIL 16, 1919

THE CHRISTIAN SUN

Founded 1844 by Rev. Daniel W. Kerr

C. B. RIDDLE   -   -   -   Editor

Entered at the Burlington, N. C. Post Office as second class matter.

Subscription Rates

One year .... $ 2.00
Six months 1.00

In Advance

Give both your old and new postoffice when asking that your address be changed.

The change of your label is your receipt for money. Written receipts sent upon request.

Marriage and obituary notices not exceeding 150 words printed free if received within 60 days from date of event, all over this at the rate of one-half cent a word.

Original poetry not accepted for publication.

Principles of the Christian Church

(1) The Lord Jesus Christ is the only Head of the Church.
(2) Christian is a sufficient name of the Church.
(3) The Holy Bible is a sufficient rule of faith and practice.
(4) Christian character is a sufficient test of fellowship, and of church membership.
(5) The right of private judgment and the liberty of conscience is a right and a privilege that should be accorded to, and exercised by all.

EDITORIAL

EASTER THOUGHTS

Easter is a symbol of new life, life of freedom.

* *

Easter is a reminder of the open tomb. We go *into* it, but we come *out* of it. Christ showed us the way.

* *

The Resurrection put a new life into all society and a new meaning into death.

* *

The grave has no victory over the spiritual life.

* *

He rose from the grave and so we shall come forth in His *likeness* if we are *like* Him.

* *

The New Life has overcome the victory of the grave.

* *

The Easter lilies remind us of a pure and undefiled life—a Christ life.

* *

The stone was rolled away. Have you rolled the stone away from the door of your heart and let Him in?

* *

How happy is the thought that Christ is living and not dead!

* *

Easter has a new meaning to us this year because of our hero dead who lie beneath the lilies of France.

* *

Everything about Easter time means a new face. This reflects the resurrected life.

* *

"The powers of death have done their worst,
But Christ their legions hath dispersed."

* *

We cannot lose our dead. They are but for a time out of our sight.

* *

There is hope and joy in the thought that, though we die in body, we shall live again.

* *

Live not for self, but for Him Who came forth from the tomb.

THE DUTY OF THE LOCAL CHURCH TO THE STANDARDIZATION FUND

We are of the opinion that in many local churches the question has come up as to its duty toward the Standardization Fund for Elon College. For example, some church says that it has never sent a student to the College and does not know of one to go from the community. We deem such a case would be rare but the first thing that such a church should remember is that it gets the benefit of every trained leader of the College who goes into that community and renders any service to that church. It must also remember that our duty is not to live solely for the benefit and pleasures of our own days, but to help build well the foundation safe and secure for the coming generations. From such a community God will some day call some young man or young woman to teach or to preach in this or in the foreign lands. The local church that has provided something of the building and enlarging of our educational interests will only be preparing to do a duty by the coming generations of its own neighborhood.

We challenge any church in the Southern Christian Convention to intelligently point out where it has derived no benefit from Elon College. The other day we were at a mission point and pointed out to the people that every pastor who had filled the pulpit at that place was an Elon product and that they had been benefitted almost directly because of the work of the College they agreed with us, even to the extent, of subscribing liberally to the Standardization Fund.

The time has come when no local church can clam like draw itself apart from every activity of the denomination. The hour has struck for united effort in education, in missions and in every progressive enterprise of the denomination to carry out the program of Jesus and obey the command, "Go ye into all the world."

THE SUN CAMPAIGN

The February-March SUN campaign brought the following results worth noting: 162 new subscribers were added in addition to a large number of renewals. 111 of these were for one year and the remainder for less than one year.

The ministers participating in this special effort were as follows: (The figures in parentheses after each name indicating the number of new subscriptions secured.)

Revs. J. E. Franks, (31); E. T. Cotten, (19); Jas. L. Foster, (14); L. I. Cox, (12); L. L. Wyrick, (12); W. W. Staley, (12); R. F. Brown, (8); T. E. White, (5), W. D. Harward, (4); I. T. Underwood, (3); J. Lee Johnson, (2); A. W. Andes, (2); J. O. Atkinson, (1); J. F. Morgan, (1); C. E. Newman, (1); B. J. Howard, (1); B. J. Earp, (1); D. A. Long, (1); J. O. Atkinson, (1); W. L. Wells, (1).

It would be justice to state that 12 credited to Brother Franks, 7 to Brother E. T. Cotten, 7 to Brother Wyrick and 3 to Brother I. T. Underwood were for less than one year.

The pastor sending the largest amount of money for new subscriptions and renewals was Brother J. E. Franks and the next following was Pastor J. L. Foster and then Brother E. T. Cotten stood third.

Notes

By adding the figures given after each name the total will not be 162 as given above. This is because several friends sent one or two each, the enumeration of which would be too numerous. We are, however, grateful to all and appreciate the good work done by those who aided.

Several of the ministers have written us that they expect to do their part this month or next. Among this number we recall the names of Rev. R. L. Williamson, Henderson, N. C. and Rev. G. D. Eastes, Raleigh, N. C.

Rev. J. W. Harrell of Burlington does not have credit for any work but this was the Editor's fault, he working the Burlington field himself.

After closing our books for April Rev. L. I. Cox sent in three subscriptions for six months each to be credited to his number. We are glad to make this mention though unable to technically include it since the books had been closed.

We are grateful to the large number of persons who bought books, Bibles and Testaments during February and March and know that their number will increase. If we have left out any credit, or failed to make any mention that is due anyone, we trust that our attention will be brought to it.

It was on January 31 that we wrote the ministers asking if they would help us in this special effort: Below is a condensed report taken from each reply received:

L. I. Cox—Favors campaign. Hopes to secure at least 10 new subscribers.

W. D. Harward—Will bring the matter to attention of the people. Thinks 500 new subscriptions should be secured during the campaign.

J. W. Patton—Will present the claims to his people.

G. D. Hunt—Will do what he can for THE SUN.

N. G. Newman—Will canvass the situation.

T. J. Green—Will present the cause of THE SUN to congregation.

J. S. Carden—Will do all he can. Pledges 5 subscriptions.

Jas. L. Foster—Thinks plan wise. Pledges 8 new ones. Desires 4 or 5 copies for samples each week.

R. F. Brown—Favors idea. Pledges 50 new names.

T. E. White—Pledges 5, and promises to do more if he can.

G. J. Green—Does not care to pledge definitely.

J. E. Franks—Anxious to increase circulation. Pledges 20 new ones. Desires 6 copies for samples each week.

L. L. Wyrick—Pledges 5.

J. F. Morgan—Is presenting the matter, does not pledge certain number.

R. L. Williamson—Pledges 10 new ones.

W. T. Walters—Will make effort to secure 5 subscribers.

E. T. Cotten—Intends to give someone a race for the largest number.

A QUESTION

A Brother raises the question as to whether a man should serve as superintendent of a Sunday school that will not take the offering for the Orphanage. We feel that this question is based on conditions, and before we would answer such a question we would have to know the reason why the school would not make the offering. So far as we can see there should be no reason why any school of the Church should not take an offering for the benefit of our Orphanage. It is possible, however, that ignorance and prejudice would so blind the majority of a Sunday school that they would refuse to give. In a case like this it would be a man's duty as well as a Christian privilege to serve such a people that might be lead into the light. We, however, pass the question along and open the columns of this paper to any one who desires to speak on it.

READS THE SUN

A. B. Chandler, a rural letter carrier on Route No. 2, Nelson, Va., writes: "I am a Baptist, but read THE CHRISTIAN SUN on my R. F. D. route each week and enjoy it a great deal. I notice that you want the names of your "shut-in" members. Mrs. O. L. Keen, who is old, blind and unable to walk, is a member of Hebron church. Her husband was a deacon. I think that she is pitiful sitting by the side of the window wishing to see the beautiful flowers and birds as they spring forth these warm days." Thank you, Brother Chandler, we are going to give our readers an opportunity to bring a bit of sunshine to these unfortunate ones. Our announcement later.

REV. JOHN BLOOD DEAD

We learn of the passing of Rev. John Blood last week. Brother Blood was known to many readers of THE SUN who will mourn his going. He was very much interested in Franklinton College and a loyal supporter of the Church's every enterprise. He lived at Riegelsville, N. J. Mrs. Blood died some months ago.

The Church should be able to meet every human need (not want).

Pastor and People

AN UNUSUAL QUARTERLY CONFERENCE

During the fall and winter months the Influenza epidemic decreased church attendance, and, even closed some churches for a while, thus retarded greatly the progress of the churches. Saturday, March 15, was the regular time for Quarterly Conference of the Isle of Wight Christian church. It was a rainy time; not many were expected to attend. The pastor, however, found a good attendance. For the reason stated above, not much was expected financially; but an unusual amount was paid into the treasury. After many matters had been attended to, and much business was ended successfully, the pastor was asked into the men's class-room, on business, he supposed. On opening the door, to his amazement he realized a pounding was being given. Those present can tell of his excited countenance, and unplaced words uttered. But none can realize the momentum of the heart's beating and the fluttering feelings of the pastor, but the pastor himself. There before us were: Eggs, butter, lard, ham, shoulder, sausages, coffee, sugar, dried apples, soap, meal, sweet potatoes, Irish potatoes, cans of fruit from the store, and home-put-up cans of fruit; preserves, pickles, etc.

On account of the long distance to all my appointments of the Third Sunday with rainy weather, my wife was not present. But no one was desired more than my wife, for I wanted her to share the excitement and help give thanks to the people for their kindness. Several members did not write their names on their gifts, and so we must express our great appreciation to the church all together and not individually.

The pounding was left at Isle of Wight in care of Mr. and Mrs. Clarence Edwards, while I drove to Mt. Carmel to spend the night. Sunday morning I preached on "The Call to the Ministry," at Mt. Carmel; drove 14 miles and preached at Isle of Wight Sunday afternoon on "The Call to the Ministry." After the service, by the help of friends we managed to pack all of the pounding in the back of the car, in the foot, and on the seat beside me, in bags, and a big basket. Then I drove to Mt. Zion, a distance of 18 miles and preached at eight o'clock on the same subject. I felt that I had a most appropriate sermon for that day. On leaving Mt. Zion church for home, I was given some oysters, and a nice shad. With such a pounding, most any man would feel rejoiced.

One of the thoughts that I gained from this unusual conference was that, although the minister may, like Samuel the prophet, sometimes deliver an unpleasant message, one that goes straight home to the soul, that convicts and converts, if he has yielded to the call to the ministry and is trying to serve God and save souls, he will be blessed by God and helped by men. May all those who showed the desire of their hearts to give, receive the blessings of God, and may our service to the church ever grow greater and more efficient for the Master's sake.

Suffolk, Va.   E. T. COTTEN.

A MORE EXCELLENT WAY

It is an excellent way, that of having a revival i the church, some time during the year. This is bette than not having one at all. The records seem to shov that most people who come into the church have don so as a result of some special meeting. So we believ in special meetings and plan to have them. People ge blessed in these times of refreshing from the presenc of the Lord.

But I am thinking of a more excellent way, that o having the evangelistic spirit so in evidence, at the regular services, during the year, that we should be led to expect, and have the joy of seeing the people come out and take a stand for Christ at these services.

With the membership on fire with the love of God and a desire to see souls saved, such an atmosphere would be created as to appeal to those out of Christ and to make it more favorable for them when they come into the church. This would lend great hopefulness to the work of the church.

A soul winning campaign in our churches, beginning, now, growing out of a love to God and for souls, with a consciousness of an acceptance with God and of accountability to God, and not limited to a week or ten days, but continuing, would bring us to a blessed sense of what the church was founded for.

In the pamphlet, "Forward for Evangelism, A Call to the Churches," there is a plea for some definite things, which are very fitting: Definite prayer for a revival of religion, definite plans for personal appeal to those who are not Christians, definite meetings for the deepening of the Christian life, prayer groups of three or more for definite intercession for individuals.

I am impressed with the importance of having a personal workers' band in our churches. I am hoping to have one in each one of my churches in the near future.

         W. D. HARWARD.

Dendron, Va·

DISTRICT MEETING

We had a great meeting at Mt. Zion last Saturday and Sunday, (March 29 and 30). The brethren seemed very anxious to have the meeting and did their best to make it a success. The good people of Mt. Zion cannot be beaten when it comes to hospitality. We had with us Dr. J. O. Atkinson, our mission secretary, who is always a great help and inspiration in a meeting of this kind. He gave us a great sermon Saturday.

A few subjects of special importance were discussed: "A School in our Conference," by Rev. E. M. Carter. Brother Carter made a very able speech, and while he spoke of Elon College in highest terms, pointing out the great work that she has done, he also pointed out clearly the needs of a church school in this section of the country. The other subject under consideration was "Grouping our Churches," by Rev. G. D. Hunt. Brother Hunt made a splendid speech. He made us see the wisdom of grouping our churches.

I failed to get to the meeting on Sunday but understand that the Mission Board had a meeting and made arrangements to resume the mission work in northern Alabama.

After another able sermon by Dr. Atkinson the meeting adjourned. As the brethren turned their faces homeward ho doubt they had a feeling in their hearts akin to that feeling which David had when he wrote: "Behold how good and how pleasant it is for brethren to dwell together in unity."

J. H. HUGHES.

R. 4, Roanoke, Ala.

MOTION AND EMOTION

The age of emotion is not passed. God forbid that it ever should pass. Emotions are some times fundamental, and when stirred action and motion become possible. The time has come when emotion that does not result in motion is counted of little worth or merit. We have at last learned that creeds must be translated into deeds. What you believe must be proven by what you do, that our emotions are very shallow unless they produce motion, and that praying does not count much unless backed up by paying. Holding a service without doing a service is folly. "Show us your faith by your works," is the cry of the hour.

The men of letters tried long ago to bring this truth home. I scissored this from a Christian Herald recently and it is worth while.:

Ruskin said, "Life without industry is sin." Carlyle said, "The end of man is an action, not a thought." When Cavour died Mrs. Browning wrote, "That noble soul who meditated and made Italy has gone to a diviner country." The words "meditated" and "made" are significant Creed without deed is useless. Emotion without motion is null and void. To hold a service and not do a service is folly. The Word must become flesh. Doctrines must be incarnated. The tree must be vindicated by its fruit.

All this is being demonstrated by the various movements, evangelistic, aggressive, extensive and intensive, that are now showering manifold blessings along the Jericho road of life. They are the practical demonstration of the parable of the Good Samaritan. They are the recovery of the first-century passion impelled through twentieth-century channels. It is a return to the Christian fundamentals. It is presenting the world with the Rose of Christ rather than the botany of Christ. It is a return to Christ, who did much preaching but who also did more good. The Church is now singing all of Wesley's hymn, for it realizes that it has not alone "a never-dying soul to save," but the God-given task "to serve the present age."

All this is as it should be. It is the Church taking itself seriously. It is "Stressing the Great Commission." It is heeding the things that matter most, and it is following the gleam instead of the glitter. It is thinking in world terms, looking beyond sectarian fences and over denominational retaining walls. It is abandoning forever the petty and picayune policy of "you in your corner, and I in mine." The practical result will be not the making of more members for some communion in particular, but the making of more and better Christians in general.

J. O. ATKINSON.

COURTESIES TOWARD THE MINISTER

Ministers need not read this—it is for the laity. There is no penalty, however, if a minister does read it. The sole object in writing it is to enable our church members to see more things from the pastor's viewpoint.

1. Remember that your pastor is human, and can make some mistakes.

2. Attend all the service possible, and be on time.

3. Invite others to go with you to hear your minister. Be proud of him—if you can.

4. Pray for him and his daily work; he does that for you and yours.

5. Watch your life, so that he will have no *unnecessary* mortification because you belong to his flock.

6. Pay promptly what you owe him; see that his salary is paid promptly.

7. After he receives his salary, remember that it is *his* to do as he pleases.

8. Don't buy his clothes, nor his wife a hat; if you have a liberal streak, give him the extra money. Let him choose his own clothes, and give his wife the same privilege about her hat.

9. When you are ill, send word to your pastor as well as to your physician. How can he know unless he is told?

10. When you die, have it arranged so that the minister will be notified in time to re-arrange his plans to meet yours, if necessary. (A few days ago I was asked over the phone at 1:30 if I could conduct a funeral at 2:00, more than one mile away. It was short notice, but I was there on time).

11. If you wish to die happy, stand by your minister in all *needed* improvements. Give him all possible opportunity to build up God's Kingdom.

12. Be courteous by hearty *appreciation;* plan little surprises for him by suggesting the omission of a service if you know he would like to be elsewhere for something special; or a vacation, or tickets to a lecture. If his sermons help you, tell him so; if they strike you rather hard, thank him heartily. Make his work as easy as possible, for it is hard enough then.

13. Always remember that his wife and family are his own; they belong to his home, and are for his comfort. You only hire *him*, not his family. His wife has household cares as well as the lady members of the church, and it takes time and strength to keep her home as you wish it to be kept.

HENRY CRAMPTON.

3000 *Hamilton Avenue,*
Columbus, Georgia.

P. S. When your minister is new to you—just arrived on the field—don't eat him up—you may wish afterward that you had—but go easy with him; strike a pace that you can keep up. You will feel better and so will he.

H. C.

ANSWERING A CALL

"I want to help some one now," said a Sunday school teacher a few weeks ago. Though this statement made by a young lady may display some of the enthusiasm of youth, yet I believe it to be prompted by a sincere desire to be of service to humanity and the Master.

This young girl proposes to go down among the sick

and suffering and there minister to their needs and offer a word of hope and cheer. She says, ''I can hear their voices calling me, many of them, and I feel I have in my heart a message for them.'' Truly this is a beautiful expression of sacrifice and service, of loyalty and devotion to the Master.

What if all our young people should express such a desire and then put it into practice? What if our young people who are to be the future leaders of the Church, and the human agency through which the world must be brought to Christ, would hear the call for service ''in the Army of the Lord?''

The call for young men to prepare for the ministry would be answered, as well as the ever present call for workers in the foreign field. But this is not all. Though we can not all enter this, the most noble field of all human endeavor, we can let our light ''shine for Jesus where we are.'' There is abundant opportunity for service, for Christian living in our churches, Sunday schools and homes. May we answer the call.

ROY W. BARNETTE.

Mebane, N. C.

RALEIGH LETTER

When our Sunday school contest was begun, the goal was set for 150 members. This goal has now been reached, and a new one set at 200. The contest will close Easter Sunday and all indications point toward reaching the new goal by that time.

At the last Board meeting, the report of the Music Committee was adopted and this included the employment of a competent music director for the choir. The Music Committee was also given authority to purchase new song books.

The Publicity Committee reported that sign boards for placing on each side of the church door had been arranged for at a cost of $25. These boards will include the name of the church, the date of organization, the hours of service, the name of the pastor, and the principles of the Christian Church. The Board also decided that moving picture slides were not suitable for church advertising.

A committee on constitution and by-laws was also appointed. Heretofore, the church has had no concrete local church organization, and the duty of this committee is to draft suitable rules of procedure and organization.

Several people have been added to the church roll by letter recently, the record number for one Sunday being four on March 31.

P. T. HINES.

Raleigh, N. C.

An engine gains steam by stopping as well as the boiler taking on more fuel. Stopping to pray is the Christian's privilege and opportunity for a life more abundant.

Dr. P. H. Fleming is in Waverly, Virginia, assisting Rev. J. L. Foster in a meeting.

Don't forget the Easter offering for the Orphanage.

NOTES

We understand that Dr. P. H. Fleming is planning to engage himself during the summer in evangelist work by aiding the pastors who secure outside help for their work. Dr. Fleming has many friends in all sections of the brotherhood and this decision of his will place him in touch with them again. Pastors desiring to secure Dr. Fleming's services will do well to write him the date or dates of their meetings and get in touch with him before all his time is taken up. Dr. Fleming is a sound preacher and his services will be appreciated.

The Young People's Missionary Society of the Burlington church on last Sunday night had under its auspices the services of Dr. J. O. Atkinson and Miss Toshio Sato of Elon College. Miss Sato told about the educational work in Miss Fry's school and Dr. Atkinson spoke concerning the work at Santa Isabel. The service was enjoyed by all present and the spirit of it was uplifting.

Rev. J. E. Franks was the first to respond to our call for the names and addresses of all invalids in the churches of our denomination. Do not overlook this matter. We will tell you a little later what we want with them.

Next Sunday is the time for the Easter offering for the Orphanage. Of course, the churches will respond in the usual liberal way and manner. The institution needs the offering, and our people need to give it for their spiritual benefit. Let all the churches take the offering.

Mrs. J. J. Lincoln, who has been spending some time with her sister, Mrs. P. H. Fleming, Burlington, N. C., is now making her home at Williamsburg, Va., with her son.

Dr. C. M. Walters of the Union Ridge church, has sold his country home and moved to Burlington where he will pursue his practice. We are glad to have Dr. Walters and family in our city.

Rev. H. Jennings Fleming is at home from Vanderbilt University.

''The Church paper in every home,'' should be the goal of every pastor.

''The mills of the gods grind slowly, but they grind exceeding fine.''

Help to make THE SUN better and brighter.

Brother Crampton's article is worth your reading.

PRIZES FOR BOOK MANUSCRIPTS

Aiming to secure volumes treating important questions of the day, yet possessing permanent value, the American Sunday School Union, under the provisions of the John C. Green Fund, offers the following prizes:

1. A prize of ONE THOUSAND DOLLARS for the best book manuscript on the subject, "Christianity and Modern Industry": How to apply Christian principles to the relations of employer, employee, and consumer.

This work should deal with actual achievements, as well as with principles and methods. It should include the rural as well as the urban situation.

2. A prize of ONE THOUSAND DOLLARS, in two parts, six hundred dollars for the best manuscript and four hundred dollars for the next best, on the subject, "Everyday Heroism;" The challenge to the heroic presented by the common tasks of life. The "moral equivalent for war" found in self-sacrificing service in peace.

This work should have special application and appeal to young people. It should emphasize present-day calls to community service, and world-wide brotherhood. It should be freely illustrated by examples from real life.

Instructions to Writers

Each writer shall give an appropriate original title to his work and may choose his own method of treatment, using such literary form—discussion, story, or other—as he may prefer. It is desired that the books shall be of a practical, instructive, and popular sort, containing from 40,000 to 70,000 words each.

The manuscripts shall be typewritten, or in plain, legible handwriting. They must reach the Union, to be submitted to the judges, on or before December 1, 1919.

Each manuscript shall have a designating mark or number, and the name and address of the author shall be sent at the same time in a sealed envelope (not to be opened before the award) bearing the same designating mark or number. Both are to be addressed, post or express prepaid, to the *American Sunday School Union*, 1816 Chestnut Street, Philadelphia, Pa.

The manuscripts winning the prizes are to become the exclusive property of the American Sunday School Union; the prizes to be paid as soon the copyrights are so secured to and by the Union.

The Union reserves the right to decline any and all manuscripts not suitable for its purpose.

The manuscripts not winning prizes will be returned to the writers, at their request and expense, within ninety days after the award. All manuscripts will be at the risk of the writer.

Conditions of the Fund

These prizes are offered under the conditions of the John C. Green Income Fund, which was created "for the purpose of aiding in securing a Sunday school literature of the highest order of merit," and germane to the objects of the American Sunday School Union.

The Deed of Declaration of Trust of this Fund provides that a certain portion of its income shall be used in securing such works, either

1. By arranging to have them written by authors of established reputation and known ability. In this case $1,000 is to be paid the writer for the copyright of the work, which then becomes the exclusive property of the American Sunday School Union. The sum thus paid is intended to reduce the selling price of the book and thus increase its circulation and usefulness; or

2. By the prize plan as announced in this circular. It is required that this prize plan be followed for one thousand out of every three thousand dollars of income provided by the Fund.

Additional copies of this announcement may be had upon application.

AMERICAN SUNDAY SCHOOL UNION
1816 Chestnut Street
Philadelphia, Pa.

March 15, 1919.

PERTINENT FACTS ABOUT THE AMERICAN SUNDAY SCHOOL UNION

The American Sunday School Union is undenominational in its form, and interdenominational and cooperative in its work.

Organized 1817 under the title of "Sunday and Adult School Union." Name changed in 1824 to "American Sunday School Union."

Object: To establish and maintain Sunday schools, and to publish and circulate moral and religious publications.

It has organized 131,814 Sunday school (an average of over 3 schools for each day in 100 years). Into these schools have been gathered 699,034 teachers and 5,179,570 scholars.

It has published a literature for these schools on the basis of the truths of Christianity held in common by all evangelical denominations. By avoiding sectarian differences and teachings, this literature has united the people of rural communities throughout the United States in active religious study and work.

It has published 21 papers and magazines between 1861 and 1917.

These papers and magazines had a total circulation of 174,013,400 copies, or an average circulation of 3,163,880 copies a year.

Its publications cover nearly every phase of Sunday school work.

It has distributed by sale and by gift over ten million dollars ($10,000,000) worth of morally sound and instructive literature.

It aims to extend its work into every unorganized and undeveloped community of the country, for intellectual, social, moral, and spiritual development.

NOTICE

At present it is my intention to move back to my home at Morrisville in the fall. If any churches within reach of that place desire my services as pastor for next Conference year I shall be glad to communicate with them.

Franklinton, N. C.　　　　　　　　G. J. GREEN.

Dr. P. H. Fleming has returned from Dover, Delaware, where he has spent some time with the Dover church. He speaks well of the work there and of the fine prospects for the congregation.

CHRISTIAN EDUCATION

A COUNTRY PARSON AND SIX CHURCHES

This week my lines were cast in pleasant places—with Rev. J. Lee Johnson and his six country churches. It has been a week of victory and at the same time of spiritual feast.

Brother Lee took me in his Ford and we stuck strenuously to our text—"to place his field on the map of the Elon Standardization Fund"—until God had blessed us abundantly. These people love their pastor and his presence with me demonstrated his interest in the cause and so insured its success. Every one of his churches gave its quota and five of them went over the top. It has been a blessed week, replete with inspiration and uplift.

Brother Lee's presence, however, was not his only contribution. He gave himself $250 and at every moment of crisis threw his weight to the side of a favorable response. He based his remarks always on Scripture and urged his people to give because the Bible teaches it. No man suggested that he would rather give to the preacher who did not hear his preacher urge him to do this good thing and have no fear for the preacher. This man of God with his one arm is unique. Lacking all the tricks of the orator, called to preach somewhat late and for a long time unresponsive to the call, he yet wields such an influence in his community as no minister ever had there, and people of all faiths and Communions hang on his words. Why? Because he has a message from God. I thank Him for such a man.

Catawba Springs and Wake Chapel each more than doubled the quota and so each earned a star on its recognition card. Wentworth, Christian Light, and Pleasant Union went over the top. Piney Plains may yet do so. contingent upon the subscription of another brother, but its quota is safe. What a tribute this to the shepherd of this flock—the Rev. J. Lee Johnson, the country parson of this fortunate people!

Hon. K. B. Johnson gave $5,000 for Wake Chapel. Brother Kemp is Elon's loyal trustee and member of the Drive Committee. No man enjoys religion more than he does. "THE CHRISTIAN SUN and Puck, Circuses and protracted meetings, Elon and Wake Chapel" —these are his specialties. Here is one of the Kingdom's noble men.

Five friends each gave a thousand dollars this week, and so perpetuated their good names in a fund that will work the works of the Lord when they shall have gone home. They were: Deacons John Murray and T. M. Franks, Rev. J. E. Franks, and Brothers E. B. Utley and J. Beale Johnson. May our Master multiply their kind!

There is not space to detail each donor, but their names are written on the Lamb's Book of Life, where their generosity is recorded as a memorial to them.

A Thousand Dollar Letter

Just as I was leaving my country parson's field, a letter was handed me, stating that in my absence from the office Mr. W. F. Corwith, of New York City, but wintering, though it seems like summering as I scribble away, in Southern Pines, had volunteered through the mails to give $1,000. Not a word of solicitation had been spoken or sent. He had learned of our campaign and wanted to help. He is brother-in-law to Dr. Martyn Summerbell and a member of The Francis Asbury Palmer Fund Board, in which position he has helped Elon before. The Lord multiply his kind.

A Thousand Dollar Editorial

I am sure you read Brother Riddle's editorial last week, telling of the thousand dollar mission Church at High Point. Well, that was a thousand dollar editorial, I call it, and if you didn't read it you are out a thousand dollars. Brother Riddle not only fills the back page of THE SUN with "punchy stuff," but he goes out and puts the regular field men to shame by a stunt in demonstration of his major thesis—that we can make it $250,000, doubling it if we will, by inducing a poor, struggling mission church to do the thing he advocates. Some Riddle— eh?

Surely the lines have fallen for me in pleasant places. Surely God is in this work.

                    W. A. HARPER.

CHRISTIAN EDUCATION*

Matt. 28:19—"Go ye therefore, and teach all nations;" or make disciples of all nations;" or "make Christians of all nations." Three translations: perhaps the last is the best.

The Century Dictionary gives no definition of Christian Education. It names Physical Education, Intellectual Education, Aethetic Education, Moral Education, and Technical Education; but Christian Education is a new term in the field of human development. Jesus made this the *first* and *last* word in His program for the church. They were commanded to *teach all* nations. The middle wall fell before His word, as the walls of Jericho before the shout of Israel. All education is missionary in motive and object. The public school undertakes the education of *all* children. Christian education includes the *whole man* and the *whole race*.

P. P. Claxton, Commissioner of Education for the United States, sounds the tocsin of danger of the more than five million illiterates in this country; but mass-ignorance is not as dangerous as un-Christian education. The world suffers today from culture without character. The chemistry of this age is the devil of destruction; and every human invention has been perverted to human injury.

Christian education develops the spirit of man into the likeness of Him who was stronger than the strongest, wiser than the wisest, and better than the best. Nicodemus called Jesus "a teacher come from God"; and the church is a teacher of truth. A teacher is one who shows others how to do or how to live. Precept must be sustained by example; teaching is essentially personal, and its quality will vary with the character of the teacher. The reason why Christianity has produced the best nations is because Jesus is a better teacher than Confucius or Mohammed. His disciples imbibe His spirit and are moulded into His likeness. There are three places where Christian education may flourish:

I. *The Home.*—The Christian home is the greatest institution on earth. The Christian home has Christian parents. It trains the children in the nurture and admonition of the Lord." Nurture is a great word and includes food for body, mind, and spirit; "but if any provide not for his *own*, and specially for those of his *own house*, he hath denied the faith and is worse than an infidel." I Tim. 5:8. "Train up a child in the way he should go; and when he is old, he will not depart from it." Prov. 22:6. Great responsibilities rest on parents, and great happiness rewards faithful precept and example. The surprise, in many cases, is not why children do so bad, but why they do so good. Christian education has its essential beginnings in the Christian home. Foundation principles are imbedded in the plastic life that world-influences cannot destroy. The wrecks of the world are reflections upon the home.

II. *The Church.*—This is first and always a school of Christian education. The Sunday school co-operates with the home in training the young. The history of the Sunday school challenges the reason of men as to its good work. It is the rarest thing that young people go astray while they are true to home and Sunday school. The break comes when they break away from the Sunday school and church. The education here is Christian in its teachers, its subjects, and its objects. Its text book is the oldest, the wisest, and the purest of all books. It is a character-builder, a home-builder, and a state-builder. Character rooted in the Bible is Christian character, and Christian character is the only character that fears no foe and does no harm. Christian character is the gold-standard of all character, without which all other character is worthless. The base character of the world rests on the character of Christian education. The Christian home and the Christian church create an atmosphere in which life and property are safe.

III. *The School.*—The church school is the only Christian school. State schools have never claimed to be Christian. Great universities profess to teach *higher learning.* Technical and professional schools lay no claim to Christian teaching. It remains for church institutions to furnish Christian training. Here is the school to develop Christian leaders in all departments of Christian activity. Where do you get ministers, missionaries, Christian authors, and workers? From church colleges.

Elon College makes "Christian character *first* and always. *It* is the exponent of our Convention, the training-ground for our young people, the source of our leaders, the conservatory of our traditions, the interpreter of our purposes. It nourishes our church-life, inspires our activities, relates us to other denominations, and gives us place in public consideration. It embodies our ideals, emphasises our position, and illumines our horizon. It reflects our loyalty, develops our liberality, needs our support, and rewards our help. It is the child of our faith, the pride of our hearts, and the test of our fidelity.

Christian education binds home, church, and school together with indisoluble bonds and develops character that is rock-like in its strength and stability. And all this looks beyond self-interest to the salvation of others, even all nations.

The church college is the heart of church intelligence, of church usefulness, and church influence.

Sermon delivered by Dr. W. W. Staley, Suffolk, Va., on Sunday morning, February 23, 1919.

THE CHRISTIAN ORPHANAGE

MRS. CHAS. D. JOHNSTON

Superintendent Johnston has no report this week. For several days he has been at the bedside of his sick wife whose spirit took its flight to the home eternal on Friday morning, April 11, at their home in Graham, N. C. The funeral was conducted from the home at 11 o'clock, Saturday morning where sorrowing friends gathered in a large number to pay their respect to a beloved wife and mother.

Mrs. Johnston had been afflicted for some time with Bright's disease. Her passing will be mourned by the entire Church. The public knows very little of the great heroic sacrifice her life played in the work of our Orphanage. She sacrificed the presence of her husband from their home that he might give his time to the Orphanage and live there almost exclusively. Her part was that of unseen sacrifice but nobly given by a noble heart that the Kingdom's work might prosper through the efforts of her devoted husband.

Brother Johnston has been twice married. He now fathers a family of eight motherless children—three by his first wife and five by the second. No man among us has a heart more sympathetic for the fatherless and motherless than Brother Johnston. He is a great father to the household made up from a number of homes. His grief will bring him to see a new meaning in his work. The Church will pray that his grief may be translated in the Kingdom's service.

C. B. R.

One of the most surprising facts discovered during the examination of our men for army service is that rural people are more susceptible to infectious diseases and succumb to them much more readily than do urban people. During the war the Federal Government by a uniform method of examination applied to something like ten million men, from all walks of American life and from the healthiest age group—from 21 to 31 years of age—pronounced 38 per cent of those examined unfit for military service. It is from the records of these examinations that it has been found that a large majority of those rejected were from the country districts.

Brother J. L. Jones of the Pleasant Hill church, in the Southern part of Alamance county, was a caller at THE SUN office last week. Brother Jones is one of THE SUN's faithful subscribers.

WORSHIP AND MEDITATION

THE WAY, THE TRUTH, THE LIFE

The world is weary of new tracts of thought
    That lead to naught;
Sick of quack remedies prescribed in vain
    For mortal pain;
Yet still above them all One Figure stands
    With outstretched hands.

Man's ears are deafened with conflicting cries;
    "Here wisdom lies!"
"Here rest and peace are found!" Lo here, lo there,
    Are all things fair!
Yet still One Voice repeats the tender plea:
    "Come unto me!"

Fools stumble on strange paths their fathers trod
    In search of God,
But found Him not, and in the defeat died
    Unsatisfied;
Yet now, as then, One ceases not to say:
    "I am the Way."

Would-be philosophers make blind our eyes
    With sophistries,
And bid our faith by science stand appalled
    (Falsely so called);
Yet still ring out those words of tender truth:
    "I am the Truth."

Men seek in vain some charm whereby to flee
    Mortality—
Some magic potion which to them shall give
    The power to live;
Yet still One Message sounds above the strife:
    "I am the Life."
      —*Ellen Thorneycroft Fowler.*

TRANSPLANTING

The minister's wife was transferring some plants from one pot to another and remarked that she did not see why some plants were so hard to get to take root and grow when good soil was offered them in the new pots. With some she had no trouble at all, while with others it was a very difficult task and really endangered the life of the plant.

Not long since an article appeared in one of our papers under the question: "Will your religion stand transplanting?" The thought of the writer was that so many, when they leave the old home church, find it easy to drift in the new field and do not get into the church whither they have gone. Even those who have been active at home often become inactive and even fail to attend the house of God by reason of this moving about. The writer seemed to have in mind those who have changed their residence from the East to West, but the same thing obtains among those who go from the open country into the city.

There is nothing which gives the pastor more concern than this matter of getting hold of those coming into his community as professed Christians and who are yet refusing to line up with the Master's forces. There is no question of the need, and their reception would be of the heartiest. Still they persist in holding aloof upon one pretext or another. Many schemes have been proposed to meet this difficulty, but none have been found altogether effective. The result must depend largely upon the one who is being transplanted. Even when the pastor writes to the minister in the new home, as he certainly should do, and the minister goes immediately after the newcomer, as he is almost sure to do, the plant may persist in withering. The church letter is too often left in the old home church until the session feels compelled to place the name on the reserve roll, or it is dropped into the trunk and allowed to stay there until its owner has become like a withered plant which has died for want of the nourishment which the soil should gladly have supplied.

It is to be hoped that all pastors will immediately inform their fellow ministers of any one removing into the other's parish, and also follow the member by letter and counsel to get him into the garden where he belongs as early as possible. The new era and the new year and the changing conditions may be occasions of getting such transplanted with safety. There can be no doubt of the need of a revival just here. If only all those whose Church letters are elsewhere would come forward and be planted in the local garden and take root and grow as they might, how the Lord's gardens would flourish!—*Exchange.*

TURNING THE NEXT CORNER

It sometimes happens that the court jester is a philosopher and that his merry quips contain bits of good advice and suggestions of practical value and importance. As, for example, this from a supposedly humorous column in a daily paper: "My friend, Jerry, who is the pilot of a taxi, told me the other night that the hardest thing to learn about drivin' was to realize that you did not have to go the way you had planned. If you decide that you are goin' to turn at Herkimer Street into Main, and you get there and there are four trucks, a street car, and an ash wagon in your way, it is best to keep right on down the street and turn at the next corner, or your friends will be apt to be talkin' of what a nice fellow you was when you was still among us."

There is a good deal more than a joke in that. Perhaps one of the hardest things in life is to learn that it is not necessary that all our plans shall be carried out in every particular as we have framed them; that there may be other ways to a given destination than that which we have decided upon; that a goal is of more consequence than the manner of going to it. We are in danger of becoming enslaved to plans and methods. We are used to certain ways; our judgment approves the wisdom of certain lines of approach to the desired objective; history, observation, and experience set their seal upon the advisability of certain things as related to the end we have in view; we cannot see how the end proposed can be reached in any other way so easily, if at all. And when we come to Herkimer Street and would turn the auto of our endeavor down it, we find it blocked by all sorts of things that make going impossible. Very well; that settles it! We cannot reach our destination! The thing that we desired — to do cannot be done! We will give it up and own ourselves beaten! Too often that is the story when we encounter obstacles in the course that we have mapped out as the one in which we are to go.

But perhaps the clogging of traffic at the predetermined corner does not mean "no thoroughfare," after all. It may simply mean "Try the next corner." It may simply suggest the recasting of plans and the making over of methods, or the discarding of them entirely and the trying of new ones. It is not of superlative consequence that a given plan be followed or a certain method be employed. What is of consequence is that the end sought be attained. The "how" of doing a thing is subordinate to the doing of it. Success in any line is usually achieved through a series of experiments, many of which have necessarily been modified or have failed altogether. There is greatly needed in the Christian Church the breaking of the shackles of methods, the release from the thrall of the things that have always been done in the same way, and the cultivation of the grace of spiritual initiative and ingenuity. It is impossible always to go on in the same old way and to turn at the same old corner.

In these days it is especially important that we realize this. We shall make a lamentable failure in many of the tasks which changing conditions are thrusting upon us if we persist in limiting endeavor to the ways that we have always known and the methods by which we have always worked. When the four men of the Gospel story sought to bring their friend to Jesus, they could not do it in the usual manner. The door was blocked, and the passageway was jammed. So they simply climbed up the outside staircase, tore up a portion of the roof, and let the sufferer down through the hole to the Master's feet. Nobody ever did anything of that sort in that way before. It is not declared that it was the best way of doing it. Certainly it was not the easiest way. But it happened to be the only way in which it could be done just then, and therefore it was the right way. It was getting to the destination by turning at the next corner. The significant thing about it, and the only thing that we need to remember, is that they reached their destination and did the thing they set out to do. There is a difference between not being able to do a certain thing and not being able to do it in the way that we had expected. Harking back to our taxi philosopher, it is a great lesson to learn that we do not have to go the way we have planned. —*Watchman-Examiner.*

SAVING THE RED HILL DAM

"Let's fire our signal so that Mr. Hill will know that we are here again," said Walter Lenox, turning to his companion, Lawrence Graham, who was standing at his side.

The two were standing on the right bank of Fresh Water River, just above the Red Hill Diversion Dam, which supplied one of Arizona's most fertile valleys with irrigation water by means of long canals leading across the desert. On the opposite bank from which they stood was a small house, the home of Mr. Hill, who had charge of the dam.

"You might as well," replied Lawrence to his friend's question; "for if the river continues to rise, he probably won't be able to cross to this side before long, as the water will overflow on the spillway."

Picking up the repeating shotgun which lay at his side, Walter fired three shots into the air; then, after a moment, two more. In a short time a man appeared through the door of the house on the opposite bank of the river. He hurried across on the spillway of the dam, which was yet half a foot above the water being diverted into the great main canal.

"Well, boys, out hunting again!" Mr. Hill called as he approached the spot on which the two boys were putting up their tent preparatory to their nights encampment.

"How do you do, Mr. Hill!" cried Walter. "Yes," we came out for a week this time. School has been closed on account of the State Fair being held, you know. Looks as if the water were rising some from last nights rain."

"I should say it is," replied Mr. Hill. "I just received a report from the government station above here that a two-foot wall of water was coming down the river. It will be a sight for you boys to see. I notice that you have your camp high and dry so that you are in no danger. If there is anything you need, you had better let me know so that I can bring it over right away, for that water will be here in a half hour or less, and it will be impossible to cross the river after that hits us."

The boys assured him that they were amply supplied with all that they needed. For a few minutes they discussed the hunting possibilities, and then Mr. Hill rose to go. "I'll have to be going now," he said, "or that water will be here before long. O, by the way, you remember that Mexican, Carlos Montijo, I had working for me? I had some trouble with him yesterday and had to discharge him. If you should see him over here, I wish you'd keep your eyes on him, as he vowed he'd get revenge— not that I pay much attention to that sort of thing, but it will do no harm to watch out."

A few minutes after he had crossed safely to the other

side the boys heard a low, deep roar, for all the world like a great gale of wind, approaching them from up the river.

"The water's coming!" cried Lawrence, and both boys jumped up and rushed to a safe vantage point from which they could watch the approach of the flood.

It was but a few seconds before they saw it— a great angry wall of muddy water full of brush and the limbs and trunks of trees bearing down upon the dam with the speed of an express train. With a reverberating roar that shook the ground beneath their feet, the mighty wave struck the spillway of the dam and surged over, the trunks of great trees crashing and booming down the torrent. With unabated force, though with a lessened roar, the flood of water rushed on, fully a foot and a half over the top of the dam's broad spillway.

"It'll keep that up all the rest of the day and all night," said Walter, "but the dam is strong enough to hold. A lucky thing, too; for if it should give way, the whole valley would be flooded and dozens of people drowned. There must have been a terrible cloudburst up in the mountains to cause the water to rise like that."

The next morning when they awoke they found that the flood had subsided until there were but a few inches of water running over the spillway. All over the top of the spillway and along its upper edge the brush and tree trunks washed down by the flood had formed a small barricade through which the water rustled.

"It'll take a gang of Mexicans to clear that brush away," said Lawrence, sweeping his eyes up the muddy river.

"Say, what's that?" he asked a moment later, pointing to something floating on the stream. "It looks like a small raft or something. Maybe it's some kid's toy submarine, as it seems to have a conning tower made out of a tin can on top."

Walter picked up a pair of field glasses and focused them on the object which was rapidly approaching on the current. "That's funny," he said after a while; "it looks like a baking powder tin fastened to a dynamite can, and the whole thing is tied tightly to a little raft. I wonder what it can be." As he handed the glasses to Lawrence the little raft, struck by some cross current, veered around.

"Walt!" gasped Lawrence as he put the glasses to his eyes; "there is a burning time fuse hanging out of that baking powder tin! Do you suppose that Carlos"—

Snatching the glasses from his hands, Walter gave a quick look. Sure enough, he could distinguish a piece of time fuse hanging from the baking powder tin and a red spark halfway up its length. "What can we do?" he said. "That raft will just swing down into that brush and stuff that has accumulated on the spillway and hang there until the thing goes off! And then—we've got to do something, Larry!"

Suddenly, just before the tiny raft came abreast of them, he rushed to their improvished gun rack in the fork of a tree and seized his automatic rifle. Throwing it to his shoulder, he took careful aim and pressed his finger hard against the trigger. A stream of lead crashed from the mouth of the gun straight into the dynamite can. And then, suddenly, it seemed as if a great hole appeared in the water while a deafening crash echoed and re-echoed from shore to shore. The flotsam which had accumulated on the spillway, loosened by the terriffic jar, plunged over and on down the river. Then, except for the steady roar of the river, all was silent again.

Though they immediately patrolled the bank of the river for several miles, they could find no trace of Carlos, although they were sure that he had been the author of the crime. It was not until next day that Mr. Hill was able to cross the river to give them his hearty thanks for what they had done. He told them that Carlos had been captured on the opposite bank by a cowboy just after he had launched by the deadly raft.

"I certainly appreciate what you have done," said Mr. Hill; "and I think that the city of Aqua Frio will appreciate it just as much when they learn what you have done." And as subsequent events proved, Aqua Frio did appreciate it.—*Joseph Thalheimer, Jr., in the Junior Herald.*

MISSIONARY

IN THE ALABAMA CONFERENCE

The fifth Sunday (and Saturday) District Meeting in this Conference is almost as largely attended, and as deeply interesting and worth while as the annual sessions of the Conference. At any rate this was the case of the meeting at Mt. Zion, near Roanoke, Ala., Saturday and Sunday, March 29 and 30. A majority of the churches were represented by delegates, and about all of the preachers on the Conference answered to the roll call. Rev. E. M. Carter was elected Chairman and Rev. J. H. Hughes Secretary of the session. The body is deliberative and the object of the meeting is to discuss topics of vital interest to church and Sunday school. Few votes are taken, but all subjects introduced are open to discussion, and the discussions are generally lively and interesting.

One of the topics was The Mission Study Class. After discussion every delegate present voted to try to introduce the study of missions in the Sunday school, and every woman delegate present voted to undertake to organize, or get organized, a Woman's Missionary Society in every church of the Conference. We know that quite a number of the good women present went home determined to use their utmost endeavor to plant a Woman's Missionary Society in their church. It is the writer's firm belief that in a few years the women of this Conference will take rank along side the best and most aggressive in our other Conferences in the number and strength of their Societies. This is the great hope of the Conference. No people can come to be a great missionary factor and force until the women are aroused to their duties and opportunities in missionary work.

This Conference finds itself greatly in need of ministers. We have no Conference in which there are more and better fields of usefulness and service than this. But the work cannot be done because of the great lack of workers. Right now they should have one of their number in Northern Alabama and another in Northern Louisiana. Some of the ministers have visited both of these fields and find members of our Church there who would help build, and want churches and Christian preachers. But the preachers are lacking. They cannot be spared from the field at home. Great indeed is the pity. From all reports if we had a good, live, consecrated, active man in northern Alabama and one in Northern Louisiana we would in a few years have ample churches in these districts for a Conference. But where are the workers? Surely the harvest is white, but the laborers are indeed few. Funds are available for the work, but the workmen are not at hand.

Rev. E. M. Carter represented the Elon Standardization Endowment at the meeting, and not only made a telling and powerful plea for the fund, but did personal work among the members and delegates present. The people of this Conference are loyal to Elon and have given it liberal patronage through the years. And four of our bright, big, best ministers now in other Conferences have come from this Conference, or rather from the churches composing it: L. E. Smith; G. O. Lankford, R. F. Brown, J. V. Knight. A Conference that can give to the Church at large such men in a few brief years has push and power worth reckoning with. Some of the most devoted and loyal members of the Christian Church to be found any where are in our Alabama Conference. From such members and the homes they make will come other ministers, and other benefits to our whole Convention in the years to come. It is a joy to be with them in their homes and in their Conferences.

J. O. ATKINSON.

SOME INSPIRING LETTERS

Egg an Chicken Money

One year ago, I recall that a lady who had promised five dollars a year to our Mission Fund, handed me the $3.00 for the first payment and stated that that was "egg money," and the hens had never seemed to do quite so well as during the month set aside to make this $5.00 for missions. Today the Secretary is in receipt of a letter from the same person enclosing $5.00, as a second payment on the original subscription and $5.00 as a first payment on a new subscription equaling the one previously given with this fine statement:

"This is more chicken money. It was "egg money" last year. So you see that a woman's chickens or whatever she decides upon as a place to get results will in some way always bring the desired results when she becomes interested and really wants these results, for something worth while. Particularly is this so when it is to be used for the Master's work. Truly 'where there's a will, there's a way.'"

With hundreds of our good women feeling that way about this mission work and their number seems to in-

crease constantly, what may we expect through the agency of our dear Church in the years that are to come in furthering the cause of our Master in the world? God bless the good women of such noble sentiment and such untiring effort to help win the wicked world to Christ. They are a source of joy and inspiration to all who are trying to carry out the great commission of our Lord.

Another Letter

I am just in receipt of a very helpful and cheering letter which I think I will be pardoned for publishing in this department and which I think some readers will enjoy. The persons writing the letter subscribed, the husband $100.00, the wife $50.00 making a payment of one-fifth when the pledges were given. I am profoundly grateful to these noble hearts and appreciate immensely the motive that prompted them in their liberality. Their letter reads as follows:

"Dear Friend:

"In reply to your letter, enclosed you will find a check for myself and wife, $80.00 for myself, and $40.00 for my wife, total $120.00. Will you please send us our receipts. We are sending the whole amount. We have lived nearly three score years, and we may not live to pay it yearly. Wishing you success in all your works.

"Respectfully yours,
"J. B. BLAND & WIFE, Walters, Va."

Still Another

The following letter, like many others reaching the Secretary these days, is exceedingly encouraging and makes him very grateful for the friends who are taking interest in the great work of trying to reach an unreached world for Christ:

"Dear Brother:—

"The Sunday school at Lebanon has decided to give one Sunday's collection each month to missions, so I am enclosing $4.75 for two months.

"Yours sincerely,
"M. M. TAYLOR, Secretary, Semora, N. C."

And Finally

Brother J. M. Crabtree of our Damascus church, Chapel Hill, N. C., R. F. D. No. 1, writes: "We received your letter asking us to give one Sunday in every month to missions, both in teaching and in the collection. I brought it before the school last Sunday and all were in favor of it. So we have decided to try it the first Sunday in every month. Please give us full information. With yours for much success."

There is no better place to begin the study of missions than in the Sunday school and we are rejoiced that so many of our schools are beginning to see it this way.

J. O. ATKINSON.

The work of the Peace Conference is speeding up and many are hoping for an early settlement of world conditions.

Sunday School and Christian Endeavor

SUNDAY SCHOOL LESSON FOR
APRIL 20

Our Risen Lord (Easter Lesson)
Matthew 28:1-10

Golden Text: He is risen, even as He said. Matt. 28:6.

Thoughts for Teachers: "The resurrection of Jesus is more capable of proof than the death of Napoleon or of George Washington."

If the body of Jesus was not raised, why did not the Jews bring it out and exhibit it? They were powerful enough to find it, no matter where a few frightened men might have hidden it.

If Jesus did not rise, explain what caused the change in Peter who faced, unhesitatingly, thousands of men and women and proclaimed the facts while but a scant six weeks before he had lied in fright of the words of a maid servant.

A roll of linen and a hundred pounds of spices, make a thick and bulky roll when wound around a body. It was from out this roll, like a chrysalis from its shell that Jesus rose. So when John saw the linen clothes lying wrapped just as they had left the body, the head cloth a neck's length away, he immediately believed.

The Easter Story in Our Sunday Schools

Easter is a time of new birth. But who would be satisfied with just being born? How soon we commence to fret if the infant does not grow? What shall we do for the little new souls in the Kingdom? Are we content to have them remain in swaddling clothes? Do we ever give them a chance to stretch their spiritual muscles and grow?

"The Sunday school is the church at work, winning souls for Christ and *training them in His service*." The reason we have so many paralyzed Christians is because we have never given them a chance to grow and their spiritual bodies have atrophied.

Plan for "Children's Week" that the children may come early to their Savior and grow up in service for Him.

John A. Alexander had a class of boys recruited from the barges along the Hudson River. These boys formed an organization with pins, mottoes, etc. Their badge was a button with a lily, and the letters "F. B. L." "To those who questioned, the boys replied it meant "brave, live fellows," but each fellow understood that its secret meaning was "Flower of a Blameless Life." So the Easter message is a message of Life from Death, a flowering of the plant, a fruiting of the tree, a growth and development, until we all attain unto the perfect man, unto the measure of the stature of the fulness of Christ.

CHRISTIAN ENDEAVOR TOPIC FOR
APRIL 20

Eternal Life and How to Live It
John 5:24; Eph. 2:1-10

This is not a *heaven* topic, but an *earth* topic. "He that hath the Son hath eternal life. What are you doing with it now?"

A boy goes away to school, but he comes home to begin to live. So God has sent us here to school, but when we are ready, He will bring us home to fullness of life.

If we are living the eternal life, can we live it as does the one who is living the world life, whose days are as grass, as a flower of the field, so he flourisheth?

SUNDAY SCHOOL LESSON FOR
APRIL 27

The Holy Spirit Our Helper
John 16:7-15; Acts 2:1-18

Golden Text: If ye then, being evil, know how to give good gifts unto your children, how much more shall your Heavenly Father give the Holy Spirit unto them that ask Him? Luke 11:13 Devotional Reading: Rom. 9:9-17, 26, 27.

Thoughts For The Teachers

"The Greek word *paraclete* is not adequately translated Comforter; it means a helper, particularly a legal helper, an advocate or counsellor in a court of justice. In this character the Holy Spirit suggests true reasoning to our mind, and true courses of action for our lives, convicts our adversary, the world, of wrong, and pleads our cause before God our Father."—*Peloubet's Notes*.

The Holy Spirit could not come until Jesus went and opened the way. Nor can it come now to the world, unless we, too, go and open the way.

"I would like to do right, but it is so hard to know what is right," how many say that. If you cannot decide which of two courses is right, then it is because you have not accepted the Spirit as your Helper, for "He shall guide you into *truth*."

Make the Spirit, the Comforter, Guide and Friend, a reality in your thought and life, and you will have no trouble in making Him real to your pupils.

CHRISTIAN ENDEAVOR TOPIC FOR
APRIL 27

Christianity and the Toilers of America
Matt. 19:35-38 (Missionary Meeting)

It was the weak-kneed, the spineless, the down-and-outer, the no-count for whom Christ *died*. What are *you* doing for them?

A Sunday school superintendent told me recently. "Our greatest difficulty is the floating population; the renters who only stay a year; the lumber mill folks who stay a year—or a month—and are gone again we cannot depend on them for anything." But can they depend upon us for anything? Does the Christian Church owe a duty to the renter? Ought the Church to be interested in soil conservation, in better understanding between renter and rentee? Ought it to undertake to aid men in deciding to buy, rather than to rent? Are the home-making people or the attitude of mind that makes home-makers the concern of the church? Ours is largely a rural population; let us consider these questions.

What about the mill people? Shall we permit the children to grow up, but little above the beast that a few may become rich? Has the Church any duty to them?

What about the negro? He is a foreigner, a heathen sometimes. As a purely selfish proposition because the ignorant negro in our midst, the ignorant or vicious negro in our homes is a positive menace, we are taking cognizance of them.

OBITUARIES

ROBERTS

Mrs. Sallie A. Roberts was born August 13, 1834, and died March 17, 1919. Sister Roberts, formerly a Miss Butler from Carrsville, was married to Mills W. Roberts, who passed to that great beyond December 9, 1893. To that union eight children were born, two of which survive. She leaves twelve grandchildren—one in the service in France, eighteen great-grandchildren, other relatives and friends to mourn their great loss. May God bless the bereaved ones. She was a faithful Christian from youth, a member of Hebron church near Holland in childhood days, after marriage she joined Antioch Christian church, and later moved to Windsor and joined the Windsor Christian church, of which she was a faithful member till death. She was active unto her last days, was planning to help cook supper when the paralytic stroke came upon her Saturday evening about 6 o'clock. The funeral service was conducted by the writer, assisted by Rev. L. T. Lewis, at the Windsor Christian church, and interment was made in the cemetery. A large congregation attended the services, thus showing the esteem in which Sister Roberts was held by the entire community.

E. T. COTTEN.

THE TITHER

An interdenominational publication devoted to Tithing and Christian Stewardship.

Editors

C. B. RIDDLE
KARL LEHMANN
BERT WILSON
HUGH S. McCORD
FRED G. THOMAS

8 pages; issued monthly; 50c the year

Address

THE TITHER   Burlington, N. C.

BIBLES! BIBLES!! BIBLES!!!
The Christian Sun
Burlington, N. C.

CHARLES W. McPHERSON, M. D.

Eye, Ear, Nose, Throat

OFFICE OVER CITY DRUG STORE

Office Hours: 9:00 a. m. to 1:00 p. m. and 2:00 to 5:00 p. m.

Phones: Residence 153; Office 65J

BURLINGTON, NORTH CAROLINA

BOOK NOTES

Story Books For The Children

We now have on hand a very fine story book for the children. "Redmond of the Seventh," by Mrs. Frank Lee. The book is handsomely bound, lettered in gold and contains 290 pages. The story is wholesome —a school story. The price is within the reach of all—75 cents postpaid, or two for $1.25.

Christian Hymnaries

We have the Christian Hymnary at 50 cents the copy, How many copies?

Address

C. B. RIDDLE, *Publishing Agent*, Burlington, N. C.

CANCER TREATED SUCCESSFULLY AT THE KELLAM HOSPITAL

The record of the Kellam Hospital is without parallel in history, having restored, without the use of the knife, Acids, X-Ray or Radium, ever ninety per cent of the many hundreds of sufferers from cancers which it has treated during the past twenty-two years. We want every man and woman in the United States to know what we are doing.—KELLAM HOSPITAL, 1617 W. Main St., Richmond, Va.

HITS AND HAPPENINGS

Senatorial Brethren

Senator Spencer tells the story that recently when Hiram Johnson had finished a certain speech another senator sent across to him a penciled note reading: "Johnson, you're an ass." Johnson wrote back immediately, "Thank you for the information. Fraternally yours."

* * *

Experimental Religion

One of our prominent authors and clergymen was attending a dinner recently when the conversation turned to charity, whereupon the distinguished guest remarked:

"Speaking of charity reminds me of the millionaire who was dying. He had lived a life of which, as he now looked back on it, he felt none too proud. To the minister at his bedside he muttered weakly:

"'If I leave a hundred thousand dollars or so to the church, will my salvation be assured?'"

"The minister answered cautiously, 'I wouldn't like to be positive, but it's well worth trying.'"

* * *

All Things to All Men

In a speech at New Bedford, President of the New Haven Railroad told this story, according to the Truth Seeker:

I well remember, when a little boy, hearing my father tell a story that his father told him about the great Lafayette, who was such a warm friend of the United States, then in the making, when Lafayette came back to this country on a visit. My grandfather met him at a reception, and as an evidence of his tact and humor, to one man to whom he was introduced Lafayette said.

"How do you do? Are you a married man?" The man replied, "Yes, sir."

And Lafayette said, "Happy man! Happy man!"

The next man to whom Lafayette was introduced was asked, "Are you a married man?' and replied, "No, sir."

Whereupon Lafayette said, "Lucky dog! Lucky dog!"

E LON
A LWAYS
S TANDS
T RUE
AND
E VER
R EADY
TO HELP
U

R U
READY TO
HELP HER?

$250,000
140,000
☞ $110,000

That is the Balance to Double the Original Goal

Didn't Know It, Did You? Yes, the Amount Raised to Date is $140,000, and Yet

BROTHER DOUBTER

Stroked His Beard and Said, "No, We Can't Raise One-half of the $125,000"

R U CAMPING IN THE CAMPAIGN?

THE CHRISTIAN SUN

"IN ESSENTIALS UNITY, IN NON-ESSENTIALS LIBERTY, IN ALL THINGS CHARITY"

BERGE SISTERS, SINGING EVANGELISTS
who are assisting in the revival meeting now
in progress in the First Christian church,
Greensboro, North Carolina.

Volume LXXI	WEDNESDAY, APRIL 23, 1919	Number 17

BURLINGTON · · · NORTH CAROLINA

THE CHRISTIAN SUN

Founded 1844 by Rev. Daniel W. Kerr

C. B. RIDDLE - - - Editor

Entered at the Burlington, N. C. Post Office as second class matter.

Subscription Rates

One year .... $ 2.00
Six months 1.00

In Advance

Give both your old and new postoffice when asking that your address be changed.

The change of your label is your receipt for money. Written receipts sent upon request.

Marriage and obituary notices not exceeding 150 words printed free if received within 60 days from date of event, all over this at the rate of one-half cent a word.

Original poetry not accepted for publication.

Principles of the Christian Church

(1) The Lord Jesus Christ is the only Head of the Church.
(2) Christian is a sufficient name of the Church.
(3) The Holy Bible is a sufficient rule of faith and practice.
(4) Christian character is a sufficient test of fellowship, and of church membership.
(5) The right of private judgment and the liberty of conscience is a right and a privilege that should be accorded to, and exercised by all.

EDITORIAL

ANOTHER CHALLENGE TO THE BROTHERHOOD

For some time Superintendent Johnston of our Orphanage has been reminding us of a great need of a home for the small children. He tells us on his Easter Offering envelopes that he has fifteen applications on file. The demands on the institution are becoming greater and we must go one way or the other.

In a personal letter to THE SUN's Editor under date of April, Brother Johnston informs us that his sainted wife decided to tithe her account some time ago and had $200 of the Lord's money, which she instructed, just before she became unconscious, to be placed as a part of the building fund of the baby home at the Orphanage, in memory of her. As will be seen from the report this week, one man offers to be one of the twenty to give $500 to meet this need. We are permitted to say that Brother Johnston will place $300 with the $200 of his wife's, making $500 in memory of Mrs. Johnston, whose noble sacrifice in behalf of the Institution has been a silent working force in the Master's Kingdom.

Brother Johnston suggests—which suggestion seems to us well and wise—that each person contributing $500 do so in the memory of someone, and that in the building be placed a memorial tablet indicating the giver and the person whose memory is perpetuated. A fine

thought, and we believe that the Church will meet this challenge of the good Brother who has given $500 to start the work. What will you do for this cause?

OUR NEW READERS

We are glad to welcome to THE CHRISTIAN SUN list the many new subscribers that have been placed on during the past few weeks. Many of these probably never read THE SUN before. We welcome them and trust that the mission and message of the paper will always find a reception in their hearts and homes. It is a good day for any denomination when its membership begins to read of what that denomination is doing. May our new readers remain with us from year to year and become permanent members of THE CHRISTIAN SUN household.

THE PRESENT POSTAL SYSTEM

The present postal system under the direction of Mr. Burleson has been getting some very sharp criticism of late, and it seems that some of it is justifiable. We are aware of the fact that the conditions brought about by the war have imposed added burdens on the system and probably disorganized a part of it, but many who have made a study of the present situation do not let this come in to be the sole excuse for the poor services that the public is getting. From the platform, on the street and in practically all leading papers, are voices, regardless of political party, that can be heard denouncing our present postal system. Here is a case that we cite:

On April 10 the Woman's Missionary Convention of the Eastern Virginia Conference was to meet with the church at Berkley. Four days before that time we mailed the programs. They should have reached the party, Mrs. M. L. Bryant, 41 Poplar Ave., Berkley, Norfolk, Va., on the next day after leaving this office. We are informed that this package was delivered six days after the Convention was held, or ten days after mailing from this office. This seems to us to be inexcusable. We could cite many other cases.

OYSTER STEWS AND ICE CREAM SUPPERS

We are aware of the fact that all of us do not agree as to oyster stews and ice cream suppers for financing the church. There are good men and women who engage in these things and by them many a struggling church has been *financially* benefitted. We have always felt that there is a better and safer plan of financing the Kingdom. These things are only substitutes for the Bible standard of giving and support of the church.

We have often wondered where the actual profit came in after the preparation of many such functions. There could really be but little profit if the church itself had to buy the material out of which to make that which was sold. Such methods will never develop the spiritual interests of the church. There are local churches that have depended on quilt parties, cake raffles and the like until they have taught their membership that that is the only way to raise money. The real joy of giving will never come to the individual by such a process. We cannot honor God with our money by such a method. The Lord says to bring an offering into His courts. We are not commanded to come into His courts and buy as we do in the market.

THEY MEAN BUSINESS

The Drive Committee of the Elon Standardization Fund meant business when the work was begun. The Committee outlined what it wanted to do and meant to do. The members of the Committee have set an example to prove their earnestness in the matter, two of them have already subscribed $5,000.00 each—Col. J. E. West and Hon. K. B. Johnson; also Dr. Staley, President the Convention, and *ex-officio* of the Committee, has subscribed $5,000.00. This is *practicing* and not *prating;* demonstrating and not illustrating.

A LETTER FROM DR. LONG

Editor The Christian Sun:

Dr. Fleming will fill, or cause to be filled, all of my appointments at the churches of which I am pastor. I think you, Mrs. Riddle and Ruth, would certainly enjoy a visit to Florida. Why, some of these days when the press is going smoothly and the number of subscribers has doubled, and the fishing is good, and the orange and grape fruit trees are bending, and the limbs are low enough for Ruth to climb easily, I'll edit THE SUN for a month and let C. B. take his bunch to the land of the mocking bird and golden apples. Fine! Fine!

Billy Sunday closed a great revival in this city last night. I heard him many times last week—repeated some sermons I heard him preach, in part, years ago—greatly improved. Much slang eliminated—not so much time taken up telling how he once served the devil. Thousands "hit the trail." The tin pans gave up $14,144. At the written request of President Wilson, Sunday started today on a whirlwind campaign for the Liberty Loan, to wind up at San Francisco, and then go to his ranch at Hood River, Oregon, and take a rest with "Ma" Sunday and his four children.

I received a letter from Mrs. Long today, telling of the departure of the wife of the Superintendent of our Orphanage. A good woman has gone home to glory, a good man left to mourn and care for motherless children. Such visitations serve to remind us all of the words of that One who said, "Be ye also ready."

DANIEL ALBRIGHT LONG.

Tampa, Fla., April 14,

GOVERNOR BICKETT'S LETTER

Governor Bickett, North Carolina's eloquent and working governor, whose heart and hand seem to be in every good thing, sent out this letter to many citizens of the State last week:

Dear Sir:—

Our soldiers and sailors are now returning home in great numbers. We are receiving them with open arms and it is eminently fitting for their return to be celebrated with great

outbursts of patriotic enthusiasm. But these men cannot live on cheers and music and flowers and kisses. The fairest and finest thing we can do for them is to see to it that every man of them at once gets a good job.

I want every town and county in North Carolina to highly resolve that no soldier or sailor shall be denied a chance to make a decent living. Please lay this matter on the hearts of your people. Make it a matter of community pride and patriotism. Let each community be very sensitive on this point. Let no community be willing for another community to provide jobs for its heroes.

These men are neither afraid nor ashamed to work. They seek no charity—they scorn it. They want a job, and they must not be denied.

Very truly yours,
T. W. BICKETT, Governor.

NOTES

Are you going to the A. C. C.? Remember the date, April 29.

See Brother Chas. D. Johnston's letter on another page. Read it.

Rev. J. F. Minnis, a Senior at Elon and a ministerial student in the Methodist Protestant Church, preached at Salem Chapel last Sunday.

We mourn the loss of our good friend, Brother J. B. Rogers of Long's Chapel church, who died last Saturday night. A good man gone.

The State Christian Endeavor Convention meets in Burlington, N. C., June 6 and will be in session until June 8. Karl Lehmann and others of C. E. fame will be speakers of the occasion.

Rev. H. Jennings Fleming left last week for Newport News, Va., to accept the pastorate of the Christian church at that place. Our prayers go with our young brother in his new responsibilities.

Rev. J. W. Pinnix, Kernersville, N. C., in renewing his subscription says: "I am very feeble and in bed most of the time. I have been feeble for two years, though long to be able to do some service again."

Brother J. W. Wellons preached at Bethlehem in Alamance county last Sunday. Brother J. W. Holt, the pastor, reports a fine service and a large audience. The church remembered the Orphanage in good style. Friends also sent THE SUN office money for renewals.

The revival meeting is in progress in the First Christian church, Greensboro, Rev. J. V. Knight, pastor, doing the preaching. Brother Knight says of the Berge Sisters of Baltimore: "They are among the leading evangelistic workers of today and any ministers in our Church needing the services of evangelistic will find these among the best."

PASTOR AND PEOPLE

BROTHER BUTLER WRITES
Newport News

The work at Newport News is progressing very well. We have some fine workers there... It is pleasant to work with people who are earnestly engaged in the Master's work. I was with the people of this church from Saturday, April 5, until the following Thursday morning. I preached for them on Sunday morning and night, also Monday, Tuesday and Wednesday nights and held their church meeting. The reports from the different committees of the church were fine. They all showed much progress.

While in Newport News I visited some forty or fifty homes; some old friends whom I had not seen for several years. There are a good many of our members there from other places who should unite with that church. This we are trying to get them to do.

The people were very kind in taking me around to see the friends and members. I had a good time and believe that many were built up and made stronger in the Master's work. Brother C. D. West's wife was sick and he could not be with us much of the time. We trust that she is much improved.

Union

On the second Sunday my appointment is at Union or Joyner's church. We are few in number there but they are good workers and are doing well. God bless our little band of workers at old Joyner's church.

Antioch

Owing to sickness and the influenza our work has been thrown back some at Antioch. We are now doing well. We have good workers at this place. Brother Elisha Bradshaw, our good Sunday school superintendent, and one of the deacons of the church, remembered the pastor with a bag of fine Irish potatoes some days ago, which we appreciated very much. God bless him and his dear family. May the pastor live worthy of his love and prayers.

Oak Grove

The writer served as pastor of this church five years and found it a good church to serve. Rev. J. M. Roberts is now pastor and is doing fine work. These people are workers for the Master.

On Thursday, April 10, that good man, that hard and earnest worker for the Master's cause, Deacon W. C. Beamon, came to my home while I was away, and left with my family a real good pounding which he and his little church gave. God bless Brother Beamon and the good people at Oak Grove. We appreciate their love and kindness more than we can express in words. May their old pastor and his family live worthy of their love and kindness.

H. H. BUTLER.

A GREAT CAMPAIGN WITH GREAT RESULTS

The Elon Standardization Campaign first for $125,-000, now for $250,000 by July 1, because the first named amount was exceeded in six weeks from the time the campaign began, is showing us what we may do for the Kingdom when a great need is felt, and is brought home to our hearts. President Harper and his co-workers in the campaign are making us all rejoice as our faith is enlarged and we see visions of a brighter, bigger, better day for our dear church, our Elon, and all the interest committed to our care. Surely a greater day dawns for us, and we thank God for the liberality of our great people, and take courage.

J. O. ATKINSON.

POUNDED

This time I might report it as being a cross between being "aided" and "pounded," and it was a very happy cross (for the pastor and his wife) for the pounding was like those we have heard about, years ago, before provisions were so high.

The Ladies' Aid Society, of Burton's Grove church, in session, suggested that they lead off in a movement to pound their pastor and his wife. The suggestion worked substantial results, as we have now learned, the members of the church, as well as the Ladies' Aid, taking part.

We were for the first time apprised of the fact, at the close of our last service at the church. On going to the machine to start for home, we found it well loaded with the good and useful things that these kind and appreciative people had gotten together. Many were still on the grounds, watching us as we made our happy discovery. If they enjoyed it anything like as well as we did, they were feeling mighty good.

We would like to mention the many good things that we found, as we unloaded the car, but will not take the space, suffice to say there were five splendid old Virginia hams (not Smithfield but just as good), flour, butter, eggs, potatoes, canned goods, etc.

We wish to express our sincere thanks to all who took part in getting together these good things for the body and we hope to be instrumental in bringing them to a larger enjoyment of things spiritual.

W. D. HARWARD.

Dendron, Va.

ADDED TO THE CHURCH

We read in Acts 2: 47: "And the Lord added to the church, daily, such as should be saved," those who were being saved. This was when the pentecostal fervor was upon the people. Believers, "were together." They regarded what they had in their possession as something which they might use to help supply the needs of the people who might lack. They frequented the temple for worship, broke bread from house to house and did eat their meat with gladness and singleness of heart, praising God and having favor with all the people.

Through a people, so unselfish, sincere and devoted, God could work and did work, to add to the church, the body of called out ones, daily such as were being saved.

The atmosphere was charged with the power of God, conviction took hold of the sinner and through faith he was saved. The church was alive and on fire with holy zeal, and thrilled by beholding the power of the risen Christ drawing, "all men to himself," after his being "lifted up."

I am more and more impressed that our conception of the value of the soul, the uncertainty of life, the sacrifice of Christ, and our desire to, "win for the Lamb that was slain the reward of his sufferings" should lead us to sincere personal work and to expect to see souls added to the church, if not daily, at least at the times of our regular services.

My last Sunday services, three in number, were an encouragement to this larger hope for a continuous evangelistic spirit among the churches. At the close of the service Sunday morning, at Wakefield, I gave an invitation to come forward in decision for Christ. One strong man, head of a family came and made the good confession. He united with the church, also his wife who joined by transfer, together with a young man who made a profession in our service, two weeks before, and a bright young boy who had recently made profession during a revival held at the Methodist church.

Sunday afternoon at Burton's Grove there were several who came forward to reconsecrate their lives to the Lord and his service. There was one addition to the church by letter.

At the night service at Dendron we had a large congregation and a good service. There were several requests for prayer. Some one remarked that things looked favorable for a revival. We want it to start this time before the protracted meeting begins and to continue after it closes.

W. D. HARWARD.

Dendron, Va.

ANOTHER PREACHER POUNDED

This time it is the pastor of the Ashboro Christian church. On April 10 our people and their friends gave us a complete surprise by entering our home and placing upon our dining room table many good things too numerous to mention. Dr. E. L. Moffitt, master of ceremonies, introduced Mrs. S. S. Hayworth who in a very tender and appropriate speech, presented the many good things that tend to make a preacher's heart glad. Among them was a beautiful silk dress from the Ladies' Aid Society for Mrs. Underwood.

These acts of friendship form another link in the golden chain that binds our hearts together in service for the Master.

May the good Lord bless all who took part in this very pleasant surprise.

G. R. UNDERWOOD.

ROSEMONT—BEREA, VA

The work on this pastorate goes well. In fact, it is moving forward now in a way that has not been witnessed before during the two years the present pastor has been on the field.

At Berea congregations have greatly increased, and the Sunday school attendance is much better now. Interest is encouraging. On a recent Sunday morning

an offering was taken for the St. Isabel Chapel in Porto Rico. This offer unted to a little more than $125.00. A good member was received on profession of faith on the fifth Sunday in March.

Rosemont has just closed a gracious revival that continued for two weeks. The attendance at these services was good throughout the two weeks and on two Sunday nights during the revival, the house was crowded to the doors. The pastor did the preaching. The church was deeply revived and strengthened. Thirty-three members were received into the church.

The Rosemont Sunday school also recently made an offering to aid in building the St. Isabel Chapel in Porto Rico. The offering from this school was $86.00.

This church rejoices also that it will soon be free from debt. A little more than two years ago the church owed on the property $3,500.00. This amount had been "whittled down" until we owed only $850.00 more. The second Sunday in March was fixed as the day for lifting the debt. Success crowned the efforts of the day. We "went over the top," and raised $1,005.00 in cash and pledges. Within a few weeks now the pledges will all be in hand and the late note will be paid in full.

G. O. LANKFORD,

Berkley, Va.

A QUESTION

I have been thinking that in many churches and Sunday schools there is need of improvement in the singing. I believe readers of THE SUN will agree with me in this, and that steps should be taken to improve same. Though there are in every community some who devote themselves to this work, they should be aided by a competent organization and thus be enabled to do more efficient work in this branch of church work.

Cannot the Department of Christian Education solve the problem by employing a teacher capable of organizing and training a choir in each church and Sunday school? Or could not this work be taken up by the organized Sunday school forces in each county and thus make the work inter-denominational?

I believe the people can be interested and their co-operation secured, if an organized campaign were made in this way. And will the results not be worth the efforts?

ROY W. BARNETTE.

Mebane, N. C.

GREAT REVIVAL IN FIRST CHRISTIAN CHURCH, NORFOLK, VA.

We have just closed the greatest revival in the First Christian church that we have ever had. The meeting began Sunday, March 23, and closed on April 6. Every service was good, and each service was well attended At several services chairs were used to accommodate the large audience, and the annex rooms had to be thrown open. Both of them were filled every Sunday evening. As a result of the meeting there were fifty additions to the church, and the church was very much revived.

The preaching was done by our pastor, Rev. J. F. Morgan. He was at his best all through the meeting, and everybody seemed to enjoy every sermon. Mr. Morgan also led the music during the meeting. He was assisted in the music by two fine choirs, a junior and a senior. Miss Lula Bell, one of our most consecrated young ladies, presided at the piano in the absence of our organist, Mrs. W. J. Spence, who was kept away from the meeting on account of sickness in her home. Miss Bell also had charge of the junior choir, and met with this choir fifteen minutes early each evening for prayer and devotion, before the hour for preaching.

We feel that the meeting has done a wonderful amount of good, and we are grateful for every blessing that has come to us.

We are expecting a number of others to unite with our church by Easter, as our pastor has announced that all our services from now until then are to be evangelistic. We hope to make Easter Sunday a great day in our church, and we crave the prayers of the brotherhood in our behalf.

MRS. J. A. LEWIS.

SUFFOLK LETTER

"Just as good" might be taken as a modern phrase substituting for real things. There are so many artificial products on the market that take the place of natural and real products, that one hardly knows when he is getting what he buys. There is butter that is not butter, silk that is not silk, diamonds that are not diamonds, wool that is not wool, linen that is not linen, and medicine that is not medicine. This is the artificial age. It is artificial in thought, in literature, in inventions, in manufactures, in social life, and in character.

What is the use of demanding the real, when the artificial is "just as good?" Why examine shoes to see whether the soles are leather, when you cannot tell the difference? Why question theology or religious character, when new ideas and practices take the place of the old? Why be so rigid in to "remember the Sabbath day to keep it holy," when people are so busy during the week that they need recreation on Sunday? The idea of office and shop people going to church on Sunday, when they have been housed up for six days! They need the park, the woods, the stream, the ride, the baseball game, anything for recreation. It is "just as good" for the soul as poor sermons. They talk of God's "out-of-doors," His "sunshine," His "temple of nature."

It is not strange that the artificial age should run into religious life. There is a sort of tendency in human society that affects everything, even conduct and character; and the substitutes in material, commercial, and social life, evidently affect religious life. The people at Berea "searched the scriptures daily" to find out whether what Paul and Silas had preached were so. "These were more noble than those of Thessalonica." It seems, from this, that the more noble are those who are looking for the real in religion. It is evident that religion is always colored by the age in which it develops; but it should not yield to the age to the extent of losing its reality; it should be the potter rather than the clay. This age is full of amusement, entertainment, and that of the lighter kinds. Everything is lighter in these days. Machinery is lighter, literature is lighter, music is lighter, pictures are lighter, dress is lighter, life is lighter. This tendency calls for lighter religious services; something attractive, something that will appeal to the young people. Shorter hours for work lead to shorter religious services. Even higher schools are dropping out Greek and Latin and substituting lighter studies as electives for degrees. The word films expresses the idea: It is thin, transient, requiring little reflection or discrimination.

I raise this question for thoughtful readers and earnest Christians. Is it not a good time, when the world is working for re-adjustment, to undertake to make the Church the one real institution? Can international peace and universal welfare be achieved without genuine spiritual character? I would not rob the earth of its flowers, but its pines and oaks but furnish material for homes and ships, and tower above the world of beauty. The Church is more than an institution to touch and please the lighter nature; it must vitalize the spiritual life and prepare the soul for eternity. Of all the values that should be kept real and genuine, it is character.

W. W. STALEY.

BURLINGTON LETTER

Work on the new church is going forward. However, there is much to be done before the building will be completed. We are expecting it will be ready for occupancy in the early fall. To date we have expended about $29,000 on the building. A pipe organ fund is being raised and we are about ready to place the order. The purpose is to open with complete equipment.

The public meeting of the Young People's Missionary Society Sunday evening, April 13, was a very helpful one. Miss Toshio Sato, a Japanese student of Elon College, told of her high school experience in Mrs. Fry's school. The large congregation present followed her with intense interest. All of her difficulties were overcome one by one and it was interesting to hear her tell how and to look upon her as a living product of Christian teaching and influence. In a short time she will graduate from Elon and go back to tell her people about the Christ who has done so much for her. Dr. Atkinson spoke on the needs of the work at Santa Isabel, Porto Rico, and made us feel that the new building for which money is being raised ought to be erected at once. The offering was nearly $50.00.

April 15 was a delightful day at the home of Mr. and Mrs. W. M. Walters, near Burlington, N. C. It was their golden wedding anniversary. Children and grandchildren gathered to enjoy the occasion. The writer and his wife counted it a privilege to meet with them. This home was established fifty years ago. What is more beautiful than a Christian home? Brother and Sister Walters have walked together half a century and have bravely fought life's battles. They have shared life's joys and sorrows. God has blessed this union with three sons and two daughters—Rev. W. T. Walters, D. D., Winchester, Va.; Dr. C. M. Walters, Burlington, N. C.; George W. Walters, Spencer, N. C.; Mrs. Martha Piper, Burlington, N. C., and Mrs. Mary Blanton, Lee, Fla. There are sixteen grandchildren.

The writer, on behalf of the children, presented the couple a gift of golden coin amounting to $50.00.

J. W. HARRELL.

ABOUT THE OFFICE

Friends interested in making a better Sunday school will do well to read "Marion Lawrance Answers the Question" on page fifteen of this issue.

Since closing our books for the February-March campaign, Rev. A. W. Andes favors this office with 4 more new subscribers. Thank you, Brother.

Do you need a good Bible Dictionary? This office can supply you at the following prices: Cloth binding, $2.40; sheep binding, $3.00. This is the Smith International and will please you.

In the report last week of THE SUN Campaign Rev. E. T. Cotten should have been credited with twenty-four new subscriptions instead of nineteen, as printed. Twelve of this number were for less than one year. The five extra added to the number of new subscriptions sent in by Brother Cotten, were last week credited as *renewals*. Thus, the amount of money sent in by him remains the same and his standing is as reported in last week's SUN. Rev. J. L. Foster should have been credited with 15 instead of 14. We are glad to make these corrections.

MISSIONARY

SHALL WE ACCUMULATE OR DISTRIBUTE?

If the writer were to answer that question his testimony would not be worth much. He has very little to distribute. He has been distributing all his life. But when a man of great wealth is asked the question, his testimony should have weight. Recently Mr. A. A. Hyde, President of the Mentholatum Company, of Wichita, Kansas, was asked the question and his answer, as it appears in *The Missionary Review*, is worth while and will have weight: "Sherwood Eddy told us of talking with a millionaire once over his financial responsibilities to the Kingdom of God until the man was really in agony. Finally this Dives turned to his son and said: "John, commence giving away money. I have reached the point where I can't." (There are men who would really like to give but they neglect to cultivate the grace and virtue of giving till they can't give). "We sincerely believe that it is not vision which people want, but consecration; not light, but love; not knowledge, but power.

"Shall we accumulate the wealth of the world and lose the souls of the world, as well as our own? Surely no one who has a right vision of the life, death and teachings of Christ can answer in favor of accumulation. No one who has studied the unmeasurable relief from human suffering, which men and money have accomplished in this war, can justify themselves hereafter in failing to distribute. In addition, no one who has experienced the depth and lasting joy of giving beyond the shallow temporal joy of receiving will hereafter hoard wealth to shrivel his own soul and handicap his children."

Mr. Hyde goes to the heart of the matter. For well may the increasing number of men of wealth of our day inquire, "What shall it profit a man if he shall gain the whole world, and lose his own soul?"

J. O. ATKINSON.

THE NEW "ACTS OF THE APOSTLES"

In the first "Acts of the Apostles," says a recent writer in *The Missionary Review*, three thousand were baptized in a day, but in India's "New Acts of the Apostles," three thousand are baptized every two weeks. What is known as the "Mass Movement" in India is one of the most remarkable scenes and triumphs of all missionary history. Some days as a result of preaching or teaching by the missionaries, whole villages become Christian and ask for baptism. They are pressing with violence into the Kingdom. And yet not many years ago there were those who declared that India with its caste system and its ancient superstitions could not be reached for Christ. Verily we are living in the days of miracles.

J. O. ATKINSON.

MISSIONARY SOCIETY, CHAPEL HILL CHURCH

The Ladies' Aid Society of the Chapel Hill Christian church at its second meeting this year, discussed the advisability of changing the Society from an Aid Society to a Missionary Society. After discussion, the Society voted unanimously for the change.

The Society voted to give $50.00 to the work in Porto Rico, the money to be used for repairing and building places of worship.

The Society also took a Life Membership in the Building Fund. This was $10.00.

One of our members, Mrs. E. W. Neville, is also a Life Member of this Fund.

Our Society will use as a text-book for the year, "Women Workers of the Orient."

Funds

Our Society is a Larkin Club. We accept no premiums, but let all premium money go into the Society treasury. In this way we keep our treasury replenished and are not confronted with the necessity of giving suppers, teas, etc. We also raise money by special offerings and through our Mite Boxes.

The above is written in the hope that it may give some other Society an idea as to how they may solve the problem of finances.

(MISS) LILLIAN LONG, Sec.

According to an estimate made based on last census, about thirty-eight per cent of the people in North Carolina are non-church members.

CHRISTIAN EDUCATION

MT. AUBURN AND ELSEWHERE

The Southern Christian Convention was organized at Mt. Auburn, Warren County, North Carolina. That fact marks it with distinction, but it has other marks too. It has always prided itself on meeting every obligation to the general enterprises of the Church, and Southern hospitality and graciousness abound in its homes. No finer people breathe than they who worship at this holy place. It is always a joy to go there, but never more so than on this occasion.

An all-day service had been provided. Rev. J. W. Patton is pastor of these people, and is greatly beloved by them. At the morning service he preached a most magnificent sermon. I hope it will be printed. During the noon hour he gave a subscription of $250 for himself, his wife having previously done the same. At the afternoon hour I spoke to a good audience and Brother Patton urged his people to do their part nobly. He had set them the example and they gladly followed his lead.

On Monday morning Mr. J. A. Kimball laid aside everything, though his farm is without labor, and took me in his automobile to see the brethren. He started the subscription that day with $1,000 and urged his brethren to come and do likewise. Well, they did, and when we finished at noon Tuesday the church had doubled its quota. The recognition card with the golden star on it was placed in his hands and how proud he was of it.

Two of Brother Kimball's brothers also gave a thousand dollars each. These men, like their brethren at Mt. Auburn, love the Kingdom's work and rejoice to help it forward. There are many tithers in the church, and tithing makes the Lord's treasury full and gladdens all hearts. I must specifically mention one tither, —the thirteen year-old son of Brother W. W. Kimball, my young friend, Master Charles Lewis. He had his first crop this year. It netted him $550 and $55 of it went to the tithe box. I read the items to which he had devoted it, and missions led the way. How beautiful thus to train up the children in the way of the Lord!

At the home of Brother Allie G. Hayes on Saturday night I met for the first time "Aunt" Ellen Tunstall. She was the first Mt. Auburn member in 1889 to make a subscription to the Building Fund for Elon. She led the way again this time, in her sunset period of life subscribing $100. All honor to her generous heart. The subscription there was closed by Deacon G. W. Ellington, now living on borrowed time, a veteran in Christian devotion, and in between these two silver-haired saints flowed the generous contributions of stalwart Christians of younger years, whose future presages much for this grand old church.

And Elsewhere

From Mt. Auburn I went to Macon and in company with Rev. Herbert Scholz, visited our border churches in Warren county, Antioch and Bethlehem. Both these churches are on the map, and Pastor Scholz is happy. A pastor has a right to be happy when his people do their Christian duty.

Thence to Youngsville, where Deacon W. T. Young lived and died the noble Christian man that he was. He is followed there by a cohort of the faithful, and his works do follow him. This church, too, did its part, and received a star on its card of recognition.

Rev. L. I. Cox in Rockingham county and Rev. T. E. White in Wake and Chatham, rendered valiant service for the cause during the week, and the goal of $250,000 seems in sight, under God's blessing, by June 30, 1919. May it please Him that it should be so!

Funds This Week

Five funds were established this week, of one thousand dollars each, as follows: Brother W. E. Lindsay, Chapel Hill; Brother J. A. Kimball and Brother W. W. Kimball, Manson; Brother J. E. Kimball, Townsville; and Deacon and Mrs. J. L. Brown, Youngsville. The establishment of these funds means sacrifice, but our sacrifice is the measure of our Christian growth. How the Heavens rejoice when Christians grow!

A Letter That Cheers

The first Elon Alumnus to give Alma Mater $5,000 was the Honorable S. E. Everett, Suffolk, Va. Some men repent of a generous deed, but not so with this beloved and honored son of the College. Read this letter to the writer, marked personal but too good to be kept: "I feel that you will be glad to know that not only do I not regret the pledge I made to the College, but that it makes me happy every time I think of it. I am sure I have never in my life enjoyed giving anything so much as I have enjoyed this gift. I am convinced that the money given to the College will mean many fine young lives enriched and blessed and given back to the country and the Kingdom for enlarged usefulness." The cheerful giver the Lord loves and this kind of lawyer not only do clients seek out, but Jesus owns and blesses. This letter has cheered my heart. It will also cheer yours.

W. A. HARPER.

THE MAN WHO OVERCAME

By Herman Hagedorn, Author of The Boys' Life of Theodore Roosevelt

Roosevelt was frail. He became a tower of strength. Roosevelt was timid. His name became the synonym for courage. Roosevelt was a dreamer, dreaming of ancient heroes. He became one of the great doers of all time and when he died joined the company of those magnificent spirits he once worshiped from afar.

Two lines which he ran across one day as a boy in Brownin's "The Flight of the Duchess" exercised a decisive influence on his life. These were the lines, recounting the ambition of a poor sprig of an honorable family:

All that the old dukes had been without knowing it, This duke would fain know he was, without being it.

The young duke, it seemed, wanted to appear to be like his famous ancestors without taking the trouble necessary to make himself their equal.

Roosevelt, thirteen years old, felt that those lines were aimed straight at him. He resolved then and there to be that which he wanted with all his heart to *appear*.

He was made of the stuff of heroes. From his birth he was encompassed "by the terror that walketh by night." For years he was racked by the agonies of asthma, and night after night in summer his father would drive him in the buggy through the countryside, so he might breathe. For weeks on end he lay in bed. But he was indomitable, even then, reading and writing and gathering his sisters and his brothers and their friends about him and, between fits of coughing, telling them wonderful stories of adventures that never came to an end.

He determined to conquer the weakness of his body, and after twenty years of struggle he did conquer it. On the plains of Dakota he finally put the asthma under his heel, so that it never showed itself again. The rough life brought its own perils. He was bucked off a horse during a round-up, and finished the round-up with the point of a shoulder blade broken; at another time he rode after cattle from dawn until dark with a fractured rib.

It was so when he was twenty-five it was so when he was fifty; it was so all the days of his life. In the spring of 1910 he was hunting hippopotamus at Lake Naivasha, in Central Africa, when he was laid low by an attack of the Cuban fever, to which he had been subject at intervals ever since the Santiago campaign. And these were the entries in his journal during the days he was prostrate:

> July 16. Fever; wrote.
> July 17. Fever; wrote.
> July 18. Feeling better.
> July 20. Five hippos.

Three years later he was in the jungles of Brazil. He and his men were in grave peril. They faced the alternative of death by drowning in one of the countless rapids which impeded their journey, if they hurried, and death by starvation, if they did not. Roosevelt was taken ill with malignant fever, and for two days lay at death's door. He pleaded with his men to proceed without him, to leave him to die, rather than to sacrifice the whole expedition. His loyal companions refused. By the force of his will he pulled himself up from his sick bed and went on with his journey, succumbing to the fever at last only when they had reached civilization and all danger to the expedition was over.

History will speak of Theodore Roosevelt as a great statesman and as one of the world's greatest leaders. But men and women who are encompassed with difficulties will remember him with tenderness and gratitude as a man who overcame. Men with weak eyes will remember that Theodore Roosevelt had weak eyes all his life and became a successful hunter, an omnivorous

reader and a keen naturalist. Men with defective hearing will remember that Theodore Roosevelt lost the use of one of his ears and could still distinguish the calls of birds and lead a people magnificently. Men stricken with pain will remember that once Theodore Roosevelt worked at his correspondence until he fainted and the couch on which he lay was drenched with blood. Cripples will hear the word that Theodore Roosevelt spoke when a physician told him in the last month of his life that he might be confined to his chair the rest of his days: "All right! I can live that way too!"

The millions will remember the inspiring leader, but a few with terrors to face will always cherish most the man who overcame.—*Carry On.*

TWO FRIENDS

"In-a-minute" is a bad friend. He makes you put off what you ought to do at once, and so he gets you into a great deal of trouble.

"Right-away" is a good friend. He helps you to do pleasant and quickly what you are asked to do, and he never gets you into trouble.—*Our Little Ones.*

Little four-year-old Harold met with a very serious accident, having both a broken arm and a broken leg in consequence. When he was able to talk his father questioned him as to how it happened. "O," he said, "I went upstairs and there was a window open. I looked out, then I hollered out, and then I jest followed the holler."—*Selected.*

Nothing in the universe is so enslaving as sin. It shackles body, mind and soul. Without it, the Eternal Prison would be empty.—*Baptist Boys and Girls.*

BIRD SONGS

The robin sings: "Cheer up! cheer up!"
  The bluebird: "Tru-al-ly!"
The meadowlark: "Spring o' the year!"
  Goldfinch: "Per-chic-o-ree!"
The crow sends forth his: "Caw! caw! caw!"
  Redwing his: "O-ka-lee!"
And we all know the blithesome song
  Of merry chickadee.

And then who has not heard bobwhite
  His name call o'er and o'er,
From fence rail or an old stone wall
  Where he has perched before?
"Chewink! chewink!" ground robin says,
  "Teacher!" the oven bird;
And I suppose there're many notes
  That I have never heard.
     —*Helen M. Richardson, in Our Dumb Animals.*

K. C. Rountree—I enjoy reading THE SUN. I think it gets better all the time.

    • •

Mrs. A. F. Meeler—Find enclosed my renewal to THE SUN which I enjoy reading every week.

WORSHIP AND MEDITATION

O HELP US PRAY
By J. C. Cason

To thee all praise, almighty Love,
Who dost attend us from above,
And spirit's cry wilt yet inspire
With utmost of divine desire.

Hear with us, Lord of tender care;
On each bestow the heart of prayer.
No ampler gift may man receive;
Without, what might our want relieve?

Kind helper of the blind and weak,
We are most strong when thee we seek;
Thou canst not strive in us in vain,
While we thy purpose would attain.

O help us pray, we humbly call,
And still would know 'tis asking all;
Thy will our joy—our sorrows blessed,
Rich, being poor, thy burden rest.

CHRISTIAN STEWARDSHIP
By Hon. James M. Robertson
(Reprinted from the Christian Advocate)

The subject of Christian stewardship is one of vital importance from the subjective as well as the objective standpoint. What we really believe and daily practice in our lives affects our character. It also determines whether the Church shall be adequately or inadequately supported and sustained. It is a commonplace in theology and in current thought that God is not only over all, but the owner of all. No one would question the Psalmist that the "earth is the Lord's, and the fullness thereof; the world, and they that dwell therein." To his proposition there is almost universal agreement, but few of us put into practice the deep and far-reaching principles involved. One has said that "An honest man is the noblest work of God." Whether we accept this statement as true or repudiate it as false will depend upon our definition of the word "honest." If this statement has reference to business relations between men only, then it is false; but if used in a larger and more extended sense, then we accept it. It is easy to find men who are strictly honest, judged by the world, who are nevertheless dishonest in the larger relations of life toward God. Our trouble is not that we over-emphasize honesty as between man and man, but that we overlook or ignore the possibility of our dishonesty in our relations to God, the creator and owner of all of us. Are we really honest, or are we really honest in the lower sense of man to man? That a man should, if possible, pay his honest debts is a truth universally accepted. Men attempt to justify almost every act and crime known to the law except that of dishonesty among men. Men have defended the liquor business, gambling, the red-light district, Sabbath desecration, and almost every other wrong known to frail humanity; but have you ever heard one say that an honest debt should not be paid where payment is possible? So our trouble is and has been that we have failed to recognize obligations which were and are upon us—why we owe God and why we should meet this obligation.

No man owns anything. He merely holds what he has in trust from God for the purposes of the kingdom; and yet, unfortunately for us, many of us still adhere to the heathen conception instead of that taught by the Bible. In contradistinction to any other man, you own your home; as against him and all others it is yours, and the terms of ownership are absolute in that limited as between man and man; but as between God and yourself, it is he who owns the house deeded in earthly courts to you. It is his, intrusted to you as a steward. This law of God's ownership, or stewardship, if you please, is universal. A man who deliberately violates a trust, takes for his own use that which has been intrusted to him by another, is worse than the highwayman. An honest man cannot afford to violate a trust. What we have we hold in fee simple as against all other men, but it is always in trust from God.

We have been blind to the great fundamental truth of God's ownership and our stewardship. But the time has come when, as individuals and as a Church, we must face the facts as they are and become either faithful stewards or deliberate defaulters in the sight of God. Our accountability to God for every dollar we handle and spend, for all we have and are, cannot be escaped by denial upon the one hand or by ignoring it upon the other. An honest obligation is not paid by a mere denial, and ignoring a debt does not pay it. We have acted as the absolute owners of everything we have and everything we control; but God is calling us through the widespread stewardship to the great and higher truth so plainly taught us by Jesus Christ. Every one is under this law, rich and poor, in or out of the Church, he who by denial attempts to escape and he who by acceptance finds in it the place of peace and power.

We must give to this great fact of stewardship more than mere assent. It must be incorporated into our thinking and become the principle governing our daily life. What we do regarding the principle of stewardship declares what we are and determines what we shall be. What we commonly call the Jewish law of the tithe existed and was practiced by various peoples before Abraham ever left the shelter of his father's house to go forth to an unknown land. His meeting with Melchizedek, king of Salem, is an illustration of this fact. It did not originate with the children of Israel. Many devout and scholarly men hold that the law of the tithe and all other laws passed away with the coming of Christ. Whether we accept or reject this view, there is one point at which we can all meet and one fact upon which we can all agree—namely, that God does not set for us, who are the heirs of all the ages and who have all of the blessings of the gospel of the Son and who face the open doors of the twentieth century, a lower standard of liberality than was set for the Jews three thousand years ago. Whatever conclusions we may reach concerning the tithes, we certainly cannot think of paying less than ancient Israel paid before gifts and freewill offerings were made. Avarice is an evil so great and insidious, so destructive, that Christ gave warning again and again concerning it. We must not approach the practice of tithing from any narrow or legalistic standpoint, but surely we should dedicate to the service of God at least one-tenth of our income as an acknowledgment of his ownership of all. Paying the tithe for religious purposes does not release us from the law of stewardship concerning that which is left, neither does it represent what many should pay for the purpose of the kingdom. It is an acknowledgment of God's ownership, of all, not the settlement of any account he may have against us. It is the beginning and not the end of Christian liberality.

Meridian, Texas.

THE CHRISTIAN ORPHANAGE

A CALL IN SEASON

This week brings in the first Easter offerings. We trust each church in the entire denomination will make this special offering because the need is great and the cause is worthy. Let us give and let us build a home for the little tots. Do you know of anything for which you could make a sacrifice for, that you would receive more joy from the giving, than to see a beautiful modern building filled with little orphan children at the Christian Orphanage?

I have a letter in my hands written a few days ago making this challenge to the church. This brother has this to say: "I will be one of twenty to give $500.00 each, making a total of $10,000, to build a new building for the children."

It seems to me that we ought to have nineteen others who would meet this challenge in the next few weeks. Now, dear friends, when you read this letter and read the challenge contained in it, and the Lord has wonderfully blessed you in the past, will you not make up your mind to invest this amount in the home for the little helpless boys and girls who need the home so much? How much interest would you feel, when you visit the Orphanage, in the home for the little children.

The happiest part of your visit would be the time you spent in the baby home. A little child always appeals to our sympathies and reaches the tenderest places in our hearts.

Who will be the next to subscribe $500.00 to this fund? Let me hear from nineteen others in the next thirty days, if possible.

The response to the call for sheets has been beautiful and our hearts have been made to rejoice in the sweet spirit in which they have been given. The following have contributed:

Mrs. M. E. Boyd and Miss Sarah Boyd, 6 sheets, 1 counterpane; Mrs. Fred Holland, 2 sheets, 1 counterpane; Mrs. R. C. Cotten, 2 sheets, 1 counterpane; Mrs. W. C. Pierce, 2 sheets; Mr. and Mrs. L. E. Carlton, 6 sheets, 1 counterpane; Mr. Jas. P. Montgomery, 20 sheets; Mrs. C. D. Ives, 2 sheets; Mrs. J. H. Alford, 2 sheets; Mrs. G. M. Spain, 2 sheets; Ladies' Aid Society, Berea, (Nansemond), 18 sheets, 2 towels; Mrs. W. C. Wampler, 2 sheets, 1 counterpane; Miss Daisy Wyatt, 1 sheet; The Ladies, Union Church, Virgilina, Va., 13 yards of sheeting, 2½ yards of towling; The Ladies, Pleasant Hill church, N. C., 12 sheets, 1 counterpane; Ladies' Aid Society, Graham Christian church, 6 sheets: One bolt of sheeting, (No name given); Mrs. J. W. Page, Burlington, N. C., 6 gallon cans of tomatoes; Lakeside Mills, Burlington, N. C., 51¾ yards of heavy goods; Mrs. A. J. Cotten, one spread for bed; Mrs. Nancy Ann Baynes, one quilt; Miss Dora Edwards, and other ladies, 49 cans of fruit.

CHAS. D. JOHNSTON, *Supt.*

REPORT FOR APRIL 16 AND 23, 1919
Amount brought forward, $2,075.94.

Children's Offerings
Edward M. Albright, Jr., $3.00; Lois Sout, 10 cents; Leon Newman, 10 cents; Ralph Newman, 10 cents; Lester B. Frank, 20 cents; May Emma Adkins, 60 cents; Herman Thomas, 10 cents; Mae Thomas, 10 cents; Oliver E. Young, Jr., 10 cents; T. D. Mathews, Jr., 10 cents; Total, $4.50.

(Special Offering for Furnishing Rooms)
T. E. Brickhouse, Norfolk, Va., $60.00.

(Special For Children's Home)
Rev. W. B. Fuller, $10.00; Mrs. F. E. Sellars, $25.00; Mr. and Mrs. B. F. Gwaltney, $4.00; Total, $39.00.

(Special Offerings)
W. C. Massey, Raleigh, N. C., $1.56; Mrs. J. W. Boone, $1.00; T. E. Milloway, $1.00; Mrs. Lula F. Brickhouse, $6.00; Ladies of Liberty church, (Va.), $10.00; Ladies New Center church, $3.00; W. H. Thomas, on support of children, $25.00; Total $47.56.

(Special Easter Offerings)
Bethel church, (N. C.), $11.33; Plymouth church, $6.75; Miss Annie Staley, $5.00; Sanford Sunday school, $20.87; T. D. Mathews, Jr., $1.00; Good Hope Sunday school, (N. C.), $6.00; Bethany Sunday school, (Ala.), $4.00; Mt. Zion church, (N. C.), $22.60; Mrs. Pattie White, $5.00; Rev. J. P. Apple, $5.00; Howard's Chapel church, $8.10; Total, $95.65.

(Sunday School Monthly Offerings)
New Providence, $2.98; New Providence Barnca Class, $1.85; Oak Level, $1.00; Christian Light, $3.00; Hines' Chapel, $1.92; Durham, N. C., $5.00; Pleasant Hill, $5.13; Catawba Springs, $10.38; Raleigh, N. C., $4.00; Burlington, N. C., $72.49; Wentworth, N. C., $7.25; Ingram, Va., $3.00; Shiloh, N. C., $3.60; Palm Street, Greensboro, $4.00; Howard's Chapel, N. C., $1.00; High Point, N. C., $7.61.

(Eastern Virginia Conference)
Third Avenue S. S., Danville, Va., $6.00; Wakefield, Va., $1.00; Isle of Wight, $1.50; Portsmouth, Va., $3.00; Union, (Southampton), Va., $2.25; Rosemont, $5.00; Berea, $10.00;

(Virginia Valley Conference)

Dry Run, Va., $3.52; Linville, Va., $1.00.

(Georgia and Alabama Conference)

North Highlands, Ga., $2.00; Beulah, Ala., $1.13; First Christian church, Huntington, Ind., $4.87; Total $175.48. Total for the week, $422.19; Grand total, $2,498.13.

CHILDREN'S LETTERS

Dear Uncle Charley: I am three years old now and just begging for pants. Mother says she will make me some. Uncle Charley, wasn't the Golden Text hard last Sunday? I could not learn it. I told mother I would rather say "Tom, Tom, the piper's son, etc." I send a dime. Your little boy.—*Leon Newman.*

All little boys want pants and think they are little men when they get them on. My little boy begs to go barefooted.—*"Uncle Charley."*

Dear Uncle Charley: Mother has just read the letters in the Corner to us. Leon said, "Write a letter for me and give them a penny." I will give a dime. Aunt Anna gave me a quarter for my birthday. I will give a dime of that. I was five years old last Friday. I had a cake with five candles.—*Ralph Newman.*

You are a fine little boy and have a great big heart full of love. I hope you will live to have many more birthdays and have a nice cake for each one.—*"Uncle Charley."*

Dear Uncle Charley: This is my first letter but not the last. I live in Norfolk, Va., but my daddy is in France. He has charge of the Financial Division of the Y. M. C. A. Headquarters in Paris, so mamma and I are spending the winter with my aunt, in Maryland. I am two and a half years old, so owe you for dues, $3.00. Enclosed please find check.—*Edward M. Albright, Jr.*

You must be a good boy till "daddy" gets home. I know he will be glad to take his little boy in his arms again.—*"Uncle Charley."*

Dear Uncle Charley: Here comes a little girl who wants to join the band of cousins. I am most five years old. Will soon be old enough to go to school. I go to Sunday school at the Christian church. You ought to see my big doll. I think a lot of it and have the nicest time playing. Hope all the orphans are having a good time this fine spring weather. Enclosed find dime for April.—*Lois Stout.*

We are glad to have you join the Corner and be one of the little cousins. I am mailing you a picture of the little girl who sings, "Jesus Loves Me."—*"Uncle Charley."*

Dear Uncle Charley: I hope you have nursed your little boy and girl and their mother back to good health. I have been sick, too, but am well now and hungry nearly all the time. Enclosed find twenty cents for

March and April. With lots of love to the dear little orphans.—*Lester B. Frank.*

The little boy and girl have gotten well but the Angels came and took their mother to live in Heaven. Her vacant chair in our home brings sorrow to each heart.—*"Uncle Charley."*

Dear Uncle Charley: I am sending 60 cents for January, February, March, April, May and June. I send my love to the little orphans.—*Mary Emma Adkins.*

You are a splendid little girl. You are paying ahead this time. I hope Easter will bring you much happiness.—*"Uncle Charley."*

Dear Uncle Charley: I am sending you a dime for April. I am going to join the Sunday school. I want to go very much. Love to all.—*Hermon Thomas.*

You are making a good step when you join the Sunday school. I remember the first day I went to Sunday school and I have always been proud of it.—*"Uncle Charley."*

Dear Uncle Charley: I am daily expecting my picture of the little girl who sings, "Keep the Home Fires Burning." Am sending my dime for April, also a little offering for Easter. Wishing you a happy Easter.—*T. D. Matthews, Jr.*

I am mailing the picture of the little girl. Let me know how you like her.—*"Uncle Charley."*

Dear Uncle Charley: I have decided not to be a lawyer like daddy, but a farmer like Grandfather Newman. I think his corn and chickens the most interesting of anything I have yet seen. Love for all.—*Oliver E. Young, Jr.*

If you are as good a worker as Grandfather Newman, you will make a splendid success.—*"Uncle Charley."*

Dear Uncle Charley: I am sending the little orphans ten cents for April. I have a little brother a month old. I am going to join the Sunday school. I want to go every Sunday. Love to all the orphans.—*Mae Thomas.*

You must take good care of that little brother. Brothers are real nice to have around.—*"Uncle Charley."*

Mrs. L. H. Brantley—Enclosed find money order for a new subscription. Hope to be able to send more new subscriptions. Best wishes for the advancement of our Church paper.

R. U. Laine—It is a pleasure to help in my humble way in helping the publication of my church paper. It was the first paper I ever remember reading.

THE FORWARD MOVEMENT

Rev. Warren H. Denison, D. D., Superintendent

Urbana, Illinois, church—Rev. Roy C. Helfenstein, D. D., pastor, Central Illinois Conference has given over $4,000 in cash and pledges for the half-million dollar fund for the Forward Movement.

Deer Creek church near Galveston, Indiana—Rev. Roy E. Lucas, pastor, in the Northwestern Indiana Conference has given in cash and pledges $3,120 for the Forward Movement Fund.

Antioch church, near Frankfort, Indiana—Rev. Clarence Defur, D. D., pastor, in the Western Indiana Conference has just given in cash and pledges $4,105 for the Forward Movement Fund.

The pastors of all these churches are in hearty sympathy with the Forward Movement, and gave it their loyal support. Leading laymen helped in the canvass and counted it a privilege to leave their work for the work of the Kingdom. These pastors and laymen believe that the Forward Movement is a blessing to their local churches and will help their local enterprises. It is not true that large giving to the work of the Kingdom hurts the local work of the church.

The Antioch church has sent to the headquarters fifty signed Prayer Covenants. How many have you sent in?

The Urbana church has a large number of tithers among its leading laymen and they bear happy testimony of the blessing both temporal and spiritual. Do you tithe? How many tithers in your church?

All delegates and visitors from the bounds of the Southern Christian Convention will have a Forward Movement meeting at Conneaut, Ohio, at the American Christian Convention, Thursday night at 7 o'clock for thirty minutes.

The Forward Movement hopes that every church will have a splendid ingathering on Easter Sunday. Each pastor is requested to report the day after Easter the number of members received into the church on Easter Sunday, the name of the church, the conference, and the pastor's name.

The Forward Movement Committee of Twenty-Four will have a meeting at an early time during the week of the American Christian Convention at Conneaut, Ohio. The committee consists of Revs. F. G. Coffin, M. T. Morrill, O. S. Thomas, J. O. Atkinson, D. B. Atkinson, J. P. Barrett, J. F. Burnett, W. H. Denison, W. P. Fletcher, J. W. Harrell, C. B. Hershey, C. B. Kershner, F. H. Peters, W. G. Sargent, H. A. Smith, W. W. Staley, J. A. Stover, E. A. Watkins, W. C. Wicker, and laymen W. A. Harper, Hermon Eldredge, Netum Rathbun, J. O. Winters, O. W. Whitelock.

The names of the *Four-Minute Men* from the churches are coming in rapidly and we are asking that every church appoint such person to keep the church informed concerning the Forward Movement work and message. Have you sent in the name from your church yet? *Do it now.*

Are you working to have your Sunday school a Standard Sunday school according to your own denomination and the International Sunday School Association by the end of June? If you lack any of the ten points now is the time to bring them up and join the ranks of a Standard school. The ten points are: 1. A Cradle Roll and Home Department; 2. At least one organized class in both the Young People's and Adult Divisions; 3. A Teacher Training Class; 4. Your school graded both in Organization and in Instruction; 5. Missionary instruction and offering; 6. Temperance instruction and Pledge signing; 7. Definite decision for Christ urged; 8. A Workers' Conference held regularly; 9. Annual reports and an annual offering to the Sunday school work of the Christian denomination; 10. Delegates, reports, offering to the Sunday School Association work.

FROM OVER THE SEAS

To the Editor of The Christian Sun

Dear Brother:—

"I remember my faults this day," as I think of the kindness you have shown in sending the paper to me for nearly three years, I believe, and the scanty measure of appreciation that I have shown. I certainly have been glad to receive its messages and especially have rejoiced in the progress of foreign mission work of which it tells. I trust that many of THE SUN's subscribers are also readers of the *Christian Missionary.* Almost everything I write for print is sent to the editor of that magazine,—and the total is so small as to seem indivisible. Yet, not to seem even in my own eyes too ungrateful a critter, I want to write you at least a little of a letter.

A forward movement has been launched here by your Japanese brethren of the Christian Church, similar to the one in America. Your success there will encourage toward like advance here. "We be brethren."

Here at Utsunomiya our latitude is not far from yours, being about 36.30. This province of 1,000,000 population is still largely vacant of Christian work, and there is much prejudice, and what is worse, much sheer indifference to the things of the spirit, but there are also souls hungering for the bread of life. I have known a man so stirred by receiving a tract while traveling, as to walk to the nearest church, eight miles away, a few days later, to make further inquiries into the matter.

While this is a personal letter, you may print any parts of it that you wish.

Yours in Christ,
E. C. FRY.

Utsunomiya, Japan, March 21, 1919.

Mrs. W. C. Whitaker—We often hear comments on the improvement of THE SUN.

Sunday School and Christian Endeavor

S. S. TOPIC FOR MAY 4, 1919

Man made in the image of God.— Gen. 1:26-28; 2:7-9; Eph. 4:20-24.

Golden Text: God created man in his own image. Gen. 1:27.

Devotional Reading: Ps. 8:1-9.

Thoughts For Teachers

"The breath of God unchanged became the breath of man; man received life of the life of God. With this divine life he was a living soul. At that moment religion became possible. For the first time there was in the earth a person whom God could love. It was God-like to make a man—*Peloubet.*

Sometimes the image of God is so defaced, so covered up, that it is almost impossible of detection, but it is there. It needs the sunlight of God's love, the washing of the blood of Christ, and the work of His servants to bring it forth.

Many old manuscripts were blotted out by monks that they might rewrite on the pages some of their own imaginings. So much precious material was apparently lost. But science has discovered how to bring to light the original writing. So Satan writes over the precious manuscript his superscription. But like the solution of the scientist, the blood of Christ will bring to light the original handwriting of God.

Children's Week

Did you observe Children's Week? Did you make a special plea for the babies to have their names on the Cradle Roll? Did you invite every parent to join some department of your school? Did you plan for a bigger, brighter, better Beginners and Primary Department? If not, it is not too late to do it now. The need of the child must be our basis of service. Let us help the parents to answer the question of Manoah, "How shall we order the child, and what shall we do unto him?" Let us help the child, so that he, too, out of a full heart shall say, "I was glad when they said unto me, 'Let us go into the house of the Lord.'"

MRS. FRED BULLOCK.

CHRISTIAN ENDEAVOR TOPIC FOR MAY 4, 1919

Our Relation to God—Serving. Matt. 2:20-28; (consecration meeting).

"Trusting in the Lord Jesus Christ for strength I promise Him"—what? Are you giving Him a soul, or a life? Have you consecrated yourself to His service? Dan Crawford says about the verse "How beautiful upon the mountains are feet of those who bring good tidings, "It's not your talk, it's your walk that counts."

Jesus did not say, "He who becomes a famous physician" but "he who visits the sick;" not he who becomes a prison reformer" but "he who visits the prisoner;" not "he who feeds the world" but "he who gives a cup of cold water." Does this mean that we should give only little services? No, it means that we are to give the best we have and all we have, whether it be large as the world or small as a glass or water, just so it be done "In His Name."

MRS. FRED BULLOCK.

AN APPEAL TO OUR PASTORS

Please begin now to make your arrangements to attend the first annual session of the State Sunday School and Christian Endeavor Convention which meets at Shallow Well Christian church July 15-17. It is generally conceded that there is no more important organization in the Church than the Sunday school—and I am inclined to think that the Christian Endeavor Society should have the same consideration—as this strong right arm of the Church. I believe that the pastors of our churches will agree with me when I say that these two organizations furnish the great dynamic force of the Church. If this be true, and these organizations are necessary in the advancement of Christ's kingdom on earth; then isn't it the duty of every pastor in the State to stand by these organizations, and lend them all the encouragement in their power? We want you at the Convention, and you can be there too, if you want to, and will plan your work to this end. Please don't plan your *summer*

outing, *lodge meetings*, or *revival meetings* for this one week. You have fifty-one other weeks, and it does seem to me that you can give three days in the whole year, to *your* convention. Have you ever stopped to think that if you hold a revival meeting at any one of our churches during this week, that you not only stay away from the Convention yourself —but you actually *keep others away* who would be glad to attend. A good brother said to me a few days ago: "I wish you would get after our pastor and ask him not to hold protracted meeting this year during the week of the Convention." He said further, "I want to attend the Convention, but we have a protracted meeting every year, the second week in July." Now Brother Pastor, won't you please let this good brother attend the Convention this year and feel that he is loyal to his church too. Won't you help us to make this the very best Convention possible, not only by your presence at the Convention but by talking it, and boosting it from now on until it is over?

C. H. STEPHENSON,
Pres. S. S. & C. E. Convention.
Raleigh, N. C.

THE CHRISTIAN ENDEAVOR WAS NOT LEFT OUT

Judging from his article in THE SUN'S issue of April 9, Rev. J. Vincent Knight seems to have buckled on his armor, unsheathed his sword and declared war on the Executive Committee of the Sunday School and Christian Endeavor Convention of the North Carolina Conference. Brother Knight seemingly has little faith in the Committee, in that he allows himself to doubt their sincerity, or to think that any member of this Committee would discriminate in any manner.

I was present at the meeting of the Executive Committee in Raleigh on March 19, and can assure Brother Knight that if any error has been made in choosing a theme for the Convention, it was an error of oversight; there was certainly no such thought as that of leaving out the Christian Endeavor work.

It has been my privilege to attend the sessions of every Convention for the past four or five years, and from observation and reference to the minutes can show that the Christian Endeavor has always had its place on the program.

The Christian Endeavor is a great Auxiliary, it is wonderful in its field of training young people to become Christian workers, it is a part of the Convention, has been in the past, will be in the future. Let us all pull together for a great Convention at Shallow Well in July, united action, concerted effort and the prayers of the people will accomplish great results.

J. BYRD ELLINGTON.

Manson, N. C.

MARION LAWRANCE ANSWERS THE QUESTION

For the three years that I have been handling books for the Southern Christian Convention, I have so many times had this question put to me: "Can you get me a little book that will help to improve conditions in the small Sunday school?" The persons who have asked me this question have gone on to state that they have been unable to get a book that will apply to the Sunday school in the country church where there are few class rooms and no modern equipment.

The other day I was in Greensboro to hear Marion Lawrance, the Sunday-school specialist of the world, speak, and after the session, I went to Mr. Lawrance and asked him the question that so many have asked me. He replied: "Get the little book, HOW TO RUN A LITTLE SUNDAY SCHOOL, written by E. Morris Fergusson." He told me where to get it and I got it. It is fine, has 128 pages, cloth binding, neatly bound. The author sticks to his text with commendable consistency, having continually in mind the needs of a small school with its circumscribed facilities, and furnishes suggestions of especial benefit to such an organization. I quote from the preface these words: "This book is written for the man or woman in the little Sunday school to show how such a school may lift itself out of the ruts of custom and tradition, gain the vision of a better day and take its rightful place among the progressive, graded, efficient and spiritually-successful Sunday school of its field."

The price is 75 cents, delivered. Send for a copy today.

C. B. RIDDLE, *Publishing Agent*
Burlington, N. C.

If you are not an officer in your Sunday school, show this to some interested party. Thank you.

DR. J. H. BROOKS

DENTIST

Foster Building   **Burlington, N. C.**

GYPSY SMITH, JR.

who is to begin a union revival-meeting in Burlington, N. C., May 11. Prayer meetings are now being held in all parts of the city in preparation for his work.

OBITUARIES

BECKHAM

On March 6, 1919 death entered the home of Mr. C. L. Beckham, and bore away the spirit of his beloved companion, Mrs. Effie Harton Beckham. She was born August 28, 1886. At an early age she gave her heart to Christ, and to the last lived a consistent Christian life. She was devoted to the work of the church and attended its services regularly. In her devotion to her home and church she has left an example worthy of emulation. Besides her husband she leaves two children, Elizabeth and Edwin; father and mother, Mr. and Mrs. C. D. Harton; four brothers, William, Leonard, Marvin and Wayland Harton; four sisters, Mrs. B. H. Nelson, Mrs. O. C. Ham, Mrs. Pearl Renn, and Mrs. W. J. Holmes. Services were conducted by the writer, and what was mortal was laid to rest in Elmwood cemetery May the Comforter speak peace to the bereaved.

R. L. WILLIAMSON.

ROSS

Mrs. Elizabeth Ross passed from this life March 16, 1919. Had she lived till June 10 she would have been 100 years old. She leaves a large number of descendants. She was buried at Mt. Carmel church of which she was a member. She had outlived her generation and had almost become a stranger. Although her community and even the nation had quadrupled its population in her life time and steam and electricity had transformed the world as by magic, her life had not been swerved by these things, but had continued to move and to think in terms of former times. There had been a "parting of the ways." How the world outgrows us! Worn out with years and toil the end was not unwelcome. "Even death is yours," said the great apostle, and many times instead of being dreaded it comes as a welcome relief.

G. J. GREEN.

LANGSTON

Another home was saddened when Mrs. Annie Gupton-Langston answered the call of the great "reaper" on March 8, 1919, leaving her husband, Mrs. Jesse Langston; four children, Herbert, Oscar, Louise and Charlie; father and mother, Mr. and Mrs. W. T. Gupton; four brothers, Joe, Alfred, Charlie and George; five sisters, Mrs. D. J. Langston, Mrs. William Range, Mrs. William Crabtree, Mrs. Henry Faulkner and Mrs. William Medlin. She was born August 31, 1886. Early in life she joined the Baptist church, and soon became an active worker. She was devoted to her home, and left a vacant place in heart and home that cannot be filled. Services were conducted by the writer, assisted by Rev. S. W. Taylor, pastor of the M. P. Church of Henderson. May the Lord comfort the bereaved husband and children.

R. L. WILLIAMSON.

RESOLUTIONS OF RESPECT— RAGLAND

Whereas, it has pleased Almighty God to call from among us our Brother, E. O. C. Ragland, Be it Resolved:

First, That we bow in humble submission to His holy will, and that we remember his widow and children at the Throne of Grace;

Second, That we have lost a capable and honored member of our church, and that although his afflictions kept him from church he will be greatly missed, and

Third, That a copy of these resolutions be spread upon our church record, a copy sent to the bereaved family and the same be published in The Christian Sun, our church paper.

R. D. THOMPSON, Sr.,
O. S. BOYD,
P. P. JONES,
C. D. S. FARMER,

Committee.

THE CHRISTIAN SUN

"IN ESSENTIALS UNITY, IN NON-ESSENTIALS LIBERTY, IN ALL THINGS CHARITY"

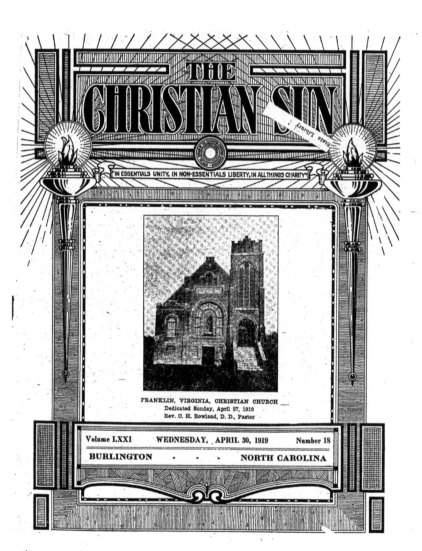

FRANKLIN, VIRGINIA, CHRISTIAN CHURCH
Dedicated Sunday, April 27, 1919
Rev. C. H. Rowland, D. D., Pastor

Volume LXXI	WEDNESDAY, APRIL 30, 1919	Number 18
BURLINGTON	· · ·	NORTH CAROLINA

THE CHRISTIAN SUN

Founded 1844 by Rev. Daniel W. Kerr

C. B. RIDDLE - - - Editor

Entered at the Burlington, N. C. Post Office as second class matter.

Subscription Rates

One year .... $ 2.00
Six months 1.00

In Advance

Give both your old and new postoffice when asking that your address be changed.

The change of your label is your receipt for money. Written receipts sent upon request.

Marriage and obituary notices not exceeding 150 words printed free if received within 60 days from date of event, all over this at the rate of one-half cent a word.

Original poetry not accepted for publication.

Principles of the Christian Church

(1) The Lord Jesus Christ is the only Head of the Church.
(2) Christian is a sufficient name of the Church.
(3) The Holy Bible is a sufficient rule of faith and practice.
(4) Christian character is a sufficient test of fellowship, and of church membership.
(5) The right of private judgment and the liberty of conscience is a right and a privilege that should be accorded to, and exercised by all.

EDITORIAL

A WORD TO CONTRIBUTORS

We appreciate the good articles that the brethren send THE SUN from time to time. We welcome them. However, a few of our contributors make a copy of what they send THE SUN and send it to other papers. This is all right in many cases, but so often we are crowded and cannot use the article immediately upon arrival, and when it is used, some reader informs us that such an article appeared in *The Herald of Gospel Liberty* or some other paper. The fact is that, though we print the article after it has been printed in *The Herald of Gospel Liberty*, there is no credit given that paper. When the article is sent us we are not informed that a copy of it had been sent to some other paper.

We are endeavoring to make THE CHRISTIAN SUN original in every way so far as possible, and it is a matter of justice to our readers that we publish articles that they do not get in other papers taken by readers of THE SUN. If a man takes *The Herald of Gospel Liberty*, he expects to get something from it which he cannot find in THE CHRISTIAN SUN, and *vice versa*.

This does not concern official notices of the Church. We do not feel obligated to publish articles after a copy of them has been submitted to another paper for publication that is widely circulated in our own constituency. The papers that become popular and great are those you have to read in order to get what they print.

One Church publication of our reading has been hindered and handicapped by this method until it has adopted the policy of paying a small sum for each article submitted and accepted for publication, except regular field news. Our problem is our problem and we trust that all readers and lovers of THE SUN will help us to continue to make a popular paper.

The Church can take a tip on this from the big metropolitan papers that have a circulation which runs into thousands. They demand original matter. (And 'v the way the Church paper is seeing a hard time because of their influence in the home. They have catered to business and the Church paper has catered to sentiment).

When the Church paper becomes as original as the magazines, and the "funny sheet" it will become more popular.

DEDICATION OF FRANKLIN, VIRGINIA, CHURCH

The Franklin, Virginia, Christian church was dedicated last Sunday, April 27. We present on the front page of this week's issue a cut of the church and glean the following items from the program used on the occasion:

A Word of Appreciation

To All Those to Whom This Message May Come:

It is with a large degree of satisfaction that the building committee is enabled to declare this building ready to be dedicated to the service and worship of Almighty God.

We wish to record our appreciation for the hearty co-operation of our people, which under the blessing of Heaven has enabled us to carry to completion so large and important an undertaking.

We desire to express our appreciation to Mr. E. C. Smith, the contractor. Much credit is due him, and this building will long stand as a monument to his good workmanship and honest service.

To the various builders and artisans who have labored upon this building and to all who have assisted in a financial way we express our gratitude.

It is one of the most delightful experiences of a lifetime to present such a structure as this to the congregation, to the community, and to God for the worship of His Son through the Holy Spirit. This church is yours, if you will have it so.

C. H. ROWLAND,
E. L. BEALE,
L. R. JONES,
J. A. WILLIAMS,
J. L. MOREL,
W. J. M. HOLLAND,
Building Committee.

Morning Service, 11 O'clock A. M.

Organ.
Doxology.
Invocation.
Hymn, "The Church's One Foundation," 506.
Responsive Reading No. 30.
Quartette, "In The Beautiful Land Over There," Brown.

Scripture Lessons.

Prayer.

Anthem, "Hark! The Song of Jubile," Edwards.

Offering.

Solo, Mrs. E. T. Cotten, Suffolk, Va.

Historic Sketch of Church, W. A. Daughtrey.

Sermon, Rev. J. O. Atkinson, D. D., Elon College, N. C.

Prayer of Dedication.

Hymn, "I Love Thy Kingdom, Lord," 499.

Benediction.

Organ.

Evening Service, 8 O'clock P. M.

Some Facts About The Church

The Franklin Christian church was organized April 22, 1883, in the Masonic Hall, with eleven charter members.

The pastors who have served the congregation: Revs. M. L. Hurley, R. A. Ricks, J. Pressley Barrett, J. W. Barrett, J. T. Kitchen, J. W. Rawls, W. S. Long, N. G. Newman and C. H. Rowland, the present pastor.

The new church is of hard brick with pressed brick front, and is constructed of first class material throughout. It has twelve separate rooms suitable for class and committee purposes, and a pastor's study. The building enterprise has cost more than $20,000.00.

MAY FOURTH—EMPLOYMENT SUNDAY

Sunday, May 4 will be observed as "Employment Sunday" in nearly every Protestant and Catholic church in the land. On that day ministers from their pulpits will urge their members to co-operate with the United States Employment Service by calling upon employers to register their needs for help, with the Service or its Bureaus for returning soldiers and sailors. They also will urge that every effort be made, individually and collectively, to find jobs for the men who have offered themselves for the supreme sacrifice for their country, thus making May 4 a day for a great country-wide drive for employment, in which the co-operation of labor will prove an all important factor.

The War Emergency and Reconstruction Joint Centenary Committee of the Methodist Church, has arranged to have 60,000 five-minute men address meetings and congregations on the subject.

The General Wartime Commission of Churches, which includes all of the Protestant churches, is co-operating with the U. S. Employment Service to the extent of appropriating five thousand dollars for spreading propaganda for the employment of the returning men, and to promote the observance of May 4 as "Employment Sunday," when clergymen, Bible class teachers and special speakers will appeal for support of the work of the U. S. Employment Service and urge employers to keep all employment openings listed with the local offices of this Service and its Bureaus. It has, by direct appeal, enlisted the co-operation of more than 150,000 ministers of America.

Not alone the churches, but welfare organizations, chambers of commerce, organized labor and private individuals, are co-operating with the U. S. Employment Service in assisting men to jobs.

It is a matter of record that 35 per cent of all the men discharged from the Army and Navy, leave the Service without prospects of positions. Of these, the United States Employment Service is placing 80 per cent in good jobs through its 400 regular offices and about 2,000 Bureaus for returning soldiers and sailors. In many instances, labor unions are supporting and continuing the employment offices for the U. S. Employment Service, temporarily abandoned, owing to the failure of Congress to appropriate funds, recognizing the vital necessity for continuing this work, not only in the present emergency, but as a permanent organization following the completion of demobilization.

With returns from the 14 largest states not yet tabulated, the U. S. Employment Service in 34 states, for the week ending March 29, received 43,512 applications for jobs. Of this number 41,972 were referred, 31,600 reporting back to the Service as placed. Returns from the 14 missing states undoubtedly will more than double the placement record for that week. Placement figures from 16 of the 30 demobilization camps in which the U. S. Employment Service has offices, for the same week, show that of the 8,470 men discharged who applied for jobs, 8,042 were referred to positions, and that of this number, 5,429 are known to have been placed immediately.

Among the industries and individuals who have come to the assistance of the U. S. Employment Service in carrying on this work, is the firm of J. P. Morgan and Co., who have contributed $100,000 to the Service for the purpose of tiding it over until Congress in extra session provides the necessary funds for a continuance of the work, this fund being devoted to finding suitable jobs for the discharged men.

PRESIDENT WILSON APPEALS FOR UNIVERSAL OBSERVANCE OF SUNDAY, MAY 4, AS EMPLOYMENT SUNDAY

President Wilson has cabled from Paris to the White House, Washington, D. C., (April 17, 1919), the following public statement on "Employment Sunday," May 4:

"The church organizations of the country having generously united in an effort to assist the Employment Service of the United States in finding work for returning soldiers and sailors and war workers, and having designated Sunday, May 4, as 'Employment Sunday,' I am happy to add my voice to others in an appeal to our fellow countrymen to give their earnest and united support to this and every similar movement.

"I hope that the people of the country will universally observe 'Employment Sunday' as a day of fresh dedication to the mutual helpfulness which will serve to work out in the months to come the difficult problems of employment and industrial reorganization. In these days of victory we can make no better offering than that of service to the men and women who have won the victory.

"WOODROW WILSON."

FAMOUS MUSICIAN ·TO BE AT ELON COLLEGE MAY 6

The people of Alamance and Guilford counties will have a rare treat offered them on Tuesday evening, May 6, when Mrs. Crosby Adams, a world famous teacher and composer in piano, will give a lecture recital in the Elon College auditorium.

Mrs. Adams for many years now has been giving her summers to teaching music teachers at Montreat, North Carolina and each year the number of such teachers who resort to that mountain retreat for her instruction grows perceptively larger. She has the rare faculty not only to compose great music but to those who study under her direction to interpret it.

In her lecture recital at the College 'she ·will demonstrate how great music composition grows in the soul of the musician and she will at the same time demonstrate her own rare talent 'as a performer.

The Y. W. C. A. of the College is presenting her for this event and they have placed the admission charge at 25 cents. They have no thought of making money but to give all those who love music in this section an opportunity to hear a real artist and we feel confident that the confidence that the young women have in the musical taste of the people in the community will be rewarded with a large audience at this great event.

Following Mrs. Adams' public appearance there will be a reception given in her honor by President and Mrs. Harper at their home.

Do not forget the date, May 6, nor the hour, 8:30 P. M.

EDITORIAL NOTES

There is no sin in making money, provided it is by honest methods.

The Church has no right to glory in its · poverty. Christ did not teach that we should remain poor.

So long as selfish hands hold God's money, the Church cannot prosper.

An *offering* comes after we have paid our debts—our debts to God.

You say that tithing puts the Church on a cash basis. Good! She has been on a credit system long enough.

. Giving is a growth. When a man has money and fails to let God have His part, the usual reason is because the man has not been taught to give.

When a man considers that he is a steward of what he has, he will take more thought as to how he will administer it.

Let there be ·a crusade everywhere to say *offering* instead of *collection*.

It may be a thing with which you cannot very well reckon, but the man who *really* dedicates 'a part of his money to the Lord dedicates his life also to the Lord.

PASTOR AND PEOPLE

POUNDED AGAIN

Brother Editor:

If you have never been pounded—oh; I mean in the good way—then you don't know just how it makes one feel. To see the people interested in the Master's business, to see souls getting blessed in your services, and to get a good pounding occasionally, well it is delightful and encouraging.

This time the New Lebanon folks did the pounding and they knew how. This makes three Ford loads we have brought in this year. In this last list of useful things we found: money, meat, meal, flour, sugar, coffee, eggs, potatoes, canned fruit, etc. We wish in this way to express our sincere thanks to these thoughtful people, for this gracious remembrance.

W. D. HARWARD.

Dendron, Va.

Editor's Note: Yes, Brother Harward, it must be great to be pounded. Editors never have such good luck. Their joy is to read first what has happened to the other fellow. The next time you think there is a pounding in the air for you, let me know, or better still, send the Ford after me, so that I can see the "thing" and know better what to say about poundings. If this office should get such a pounding as you have been getting of late readers of THE SUN would certainly miss a copy.—C. B. R.

RAMSEUR PASTORATE

The work of the Ramseur pastorate is doing fine as a whole but I shall not speak in this letter with reference to only two of the churches in charge, the others need to be mentioned as well as the two I am going to write about but for lack of space I shall speak of them later. I am writing this time of Ramseur and Parks X Roads.

We began a revival with the Ramseur church the fifth Sunday in March and closed Wednesday night after the first Sunday in April. We had no outside help either to sing or preach. The meeting was good from the beginning. We had a packed house the first service and the congregations were large throughout the meeting. There was a deep work of the Spirit at every service. There were a number of professions and reclamations and six united with the church at the closing service. I think others will join later. The whole church was revived and a good work done.

The activities of the church are good. The envelope system is working wonders in the finances. The church is up to date with all finances—a thing that was never known before here at this season of the year.

The Ladies' Aid Society is doing fine work. The Society has about $100.00 in cash and is going to make some needed improvements on the inside of the church soon. They have presented the church, since Christmas, with a handsome Individual Communion service.

The Woman's Missionary Society is growing in interest. The Society has adopted for present study at each meeting the five points in the Forward Movement program. A Cradle Roll has been organized which is rapidly growing. We are going to do something extra for missions this year.

The church has gone on record as endorsing the Elon Standardization Fund and the campaign for missions. You will hear more from Ramseur later.

Park's X Roads

I feel encouraged with the work at Park's X Roads. If these good people could only see the possibilities for them by opening their almost unlimited means to the Lord, what a blessing it would be!

We have been greatly hindered here this year, but last Sunday we had a fine day. A large congregation and good interest. We raised $35.65 as an Easter offering for the Orphanage. The Sunday school is giving one Sunday's offering to the Orphanage. The Sunday school is also giving one Sunday's offering to missions. This means an advance step for them. I feel that they are beginning to see things in a larger way. This church and Ramseur ought by all means to give a man full time to preach to them. It would mean so much for them.

We are planning for the annual memorial service the third Sunday in May. This is the annual house coming day for the church. We hope and pray that it may be a great day for the church. I am looking for larger things from these people this year. Pray for us, brethren.

—Yours in His service,

A. T. BANKS.

DURHAM LETTER

On April 13 the Durham church began a series of evangelistic meetings which closed last night, (April 24). Rev. J. Lee Johnson did the preaching. It seems easy for him to preach. The only explanation of this that I can give is that he is a *preacher* and has something to *preach*—the Bible. He uses the Word of God frequently and freely and quotes it at will, and his interpretation of the Bible was entirely satisfactory to all.

The singing was another great feature in the services. Rev. O. D. Poythress, pastor of the South Norfolk church, led the choir. He not only preaches the Gospel but sings it. He is possessed with a talent that few men have. The people here fell in love with Brother Poythress, while with Brother Johnson it was a case of renewing their former love. He was here three years ago in a meeting.

The services were attended by large crowds. At almost all the services the house was well filled, chairs being frequently used, while the Sunday school rooms were resorted to two or three times. Men who have a message will always have somebody to hear it.

During the services there were forty-one professions and twenty-six additions to the church. There are several others who will join later. We hope that a similar series of meetings can be held in the near future with greater results.

R. F. BROWN.

HIGH POINT

Some one said this was the first time it had happened that Easter came on the Sunday of the regular preaching day at High Point Christian church. It was an ideal day in weather conditions. Quite a number were out for Sunday school and preaching; several whom the pastor had never met.

It was a good day for me and greatly enjoyed, especially when the Easter offering for the Christian Orphanage was taken. Brother R. C. Boyd, the superintendent, announced the time to take it and the writer suggested the method. The Bible was placed on a chair convenient for the little folks, because some had taken envelopes and also solicited for their respective classes. How beautiful it was to see the children bring their offerings for the helpless ones. It was an inspiration to me. Practically all present took a part and all looked happy over it. Look for Brother Johnston's report for the amount. May the Lord abundantly bless all in this noble deed.

Our evangelistic services begin on Wednesday, April 30, 1919, at 8:00 P. M. Rev. J. W. Knight of Stokesdale, N. C., will assist in the preaching. A good man and a great Gospel man is he. It is good to hear him and to associate with him in the Master's work. Let all who are interested in the Lord's work here pray for the success of the meeting and that the Lord's will may be done in and through us. We want all who attend to feel at home. The meeting will continue for about ten days.

One and all are welcome to attend and help in this specified time and all other preaching days.

L. L. WYRICK.

Elon College, N. C.

UNION, SURRY COUNTY

We had a good service here last Sunday morning, April 20. Brother T. S. Wrenn was ordained to the office of deacon.

There was one profession of faith in Christ, and one reconsecration at the close of the service.

W. D. HARWARD.

NEW LEBANON

At the close of our service here in the afternoon there were two professions of faith in Christ, two young boys, the father of one of the boys came forward and professed to have been reclaimed from a backslidden condition. Prayer meeting services have recently been started in the church, being held each Thursday evening. The meetings are well attended and there is a good interest.

W. D. HARWARD.

SUFFOLK LETTER

One of the least thought of and most useful workers is the faithful Sunday school teacher. Parents *send* their children to Sunday school and expect the teacher to be there and to give them the help of their example and their instruction. Often parents do not know the name of the teacher. They take the teacher as a matter of course, and find relief when the children are off to the school. That hour in the Sunday school is the most important hour in the one hundred and twenty-eight hours of the week. The three essentials for a teacher are: Christian character, punctuality, and interest in the members of the class. Expert knowledge is valuable, aptness to teach is important; but nothing takes the place of the above essentials. Love for God, love for the Bible and love for human souls, will make a triangle by which all other problems can be solved. "Love never faileth." It must not be inferred that this position is in opposition to teacher training, expert knowledge, parallel study, pedagochical experience, or any modern requirement. Any addition that can be made to the essential qualifications is to be approved and recommended.

It may be set forth as a self-evident proposition that the *majority* of workers in all spheres must do their work without expert training; and, further, that much useful knowledge is acquired by experience. This opens a field of usefulness for untrained Sunday school teachers who are willing t oconsecrate themselves to this noble service. It, also, is an encouragement to those who have not had the opportunity for expert training. Some of the best cooks never read a cook book; and some of the best farmers never read an agricultural paper; and this says nothing against cook books or agricultural journals; it simply recites a great fact in the world's work. All the learning in the world cannot substitute for inherent, God-given, capacity to do good work; and the Sunday school teacher is no exception. If the teacher loves the Lord, the Bible, and the children, punctuality will follow. To be present on time, to be patient with scholars, to be earnest in teaching, to win their friendship by being friendly, will make success with any grade and in any school. There is no higher service in the church than to teach a class faithfully. The position is inconspicuous, without material renumeration, requiring personal sacrifice, carrying with it great responsibility, and, sometimes, without appreciation. It imposes self-denial, the faithful observance of the Sabbath, real consecration, and loyalty to church institutions. The Sunday school teacher is a model Christian, a real worker, a home-helper, a soul-saver, and an invaluable citizen. Parents should love them. The community should appreciate them. The church should pray for them. The children should praise them. Heaven should bless them. There are a million of these good people in the United States. They are the captains of an army twenty millions strong. They carry no weapon but the sword of the Spirit, which is the *Word of God.* They are encamped in every part of these forty-eight States. Their songs reach the throne of the King of Kings. The tramp of their feet is greater than Roman legions or Hun minions. When they pray, Heaven answers; and when they sing, Heaven rejoices. All hail to Sunday school teachers!   W. W. STALEY.

———————

There is no Christian satisfaction in being a miser. *Miser* seems very much akin to *miserable.*

———————

Those who begin to tithe keep at it. There seems to be no disappointment about it.

MISSIONARY

A CLARION CALL TO ACTION

"The way to keep up is to keep on." Only those are keeping up who keep on trying by prayer, purse or person, to make known the gospel of our blessed Lord to a sin cursed and needy world.

The church today is seeing the world as it never saw it before. "And the world sees the Church as it never saw it before." The Church sees a whole world —not one section, race, tongue or nation, but the whole of it—in the tight grip of sin.

The missionary movement in all the churches means the awakening of the Church to grapple with the monster evils that stalk abroad and at mid-day and never sleep at night. "Emotion without motion is null and void." And in the movements for mission and for righteousness now there is something for everybody to do.

A TRAGEDY UNSPEAKABLE

The Northern Baptist Laymen have issued this manifesto:

"It would be a tragedy unspeakable if we should win the war and after all fail to achieve the purpose for which we are fighting. To what end shall we have spent millions of treasure and the far more precious lives of our sons if we fail to take a long step toward the creation between nations and races of those relations of good will and helpfulness that are in accord with the principles of Christ and are necessary to the welfare of the human race?"

The only way we are to avoid this unspeakable tragedy is to stress the Great Commission. Brave men, strong men, willing men, prepared men, are needed today in the Army of the Lord as they were never needed before. Brave men and devout women won this world war for democracy. It will now require brave men and devout women to win the world to the only true democracy there is, namely the democracy of the Man of Galilee. We will never have permanent peace in this world till the Prince of Peace shall have won His way into the lives and hearts of enough men and women to control this world for Him.

TAKING THE KINGDOM BY VIOLENCE

"And from the days of John the Baptist until now the Kingdom of heaven—suffereth violence, and men of violence take it by force." (Matt. 11:12). Taking the Kingdom of heaven by force is no puny job or puerile task. It requires stalwart manhood, dauntless womanhood, fearless courage to go out on the firing line in the bloody battle of the Cross, and there teach and live and proclaim the gospel of righteousness in its conflict against iniquity. The call, the challenge, the need now is for strong, courageous, invincible souls who are willing even to make the Kingdom itself suffer violence in their onslaught for truth and conquest in the name of the Prince of peace.

     J. O. ATKINSON.

SECOND QUARTERLY REPORT OF WOMAN'S H. & F. MISSIONARY SOCIETIES OF EASTERN VA. CHRISTIAN CONFERENCE, QUARTER ENDING MARCH 31, 1919

Woman's Societies

Amounts received:

Berea, Nansemond ....$ 17.25
Bethlehem, Mite Boxes 14.00
Berkley 10.00
Cypress Chapel 7.05
Damascus 16.70
Dendron 20.20
Franklin 15.75
Holland 8.95
Holy Neck 22.95
Liberty Spring 10.60
Memorial Temple 7.30
Mt. Carmel 8.40
Newport News 5.90
Portsmouth 17.05
Rosemont 14.90
Spring Hill 10.00
Suffolk 75.95
Third Church 43.85
Waverly 15.50
Wakefield 7.01
Windsor 15.90
Union Southampton 7.80
New Lebanon 6.30
	$374.31

Young Peoples

Amounts received:

Berkley ....$ 10.00
Burton's Grove 5.75
Dendron 7.50
Disputanta 10.00
Franklin 6.30
Memorial Temple 25.00
Portsmouth 3.00
Suffolk 23.10
Spring Hill 10.00
Third Church 1.00
Rosemont Congregation 84.00
	$185.65

Willing Workers

Amounts received:

Berea, Nansemond ....$ 2.25
Franklin .... .80
Holy Neck 8.77
Waverly 1.50
Wakefield 1.34
Windsor 3.19
	$17.85

Totals

Woman's Societies ....$ 374.31
Young People's Societies 185.65
Willing Workers 17.85
	$577.81
Collection at meeting, April 10 .... 23.86
	$601.67

MRS. M. L. BRYANT, Treasurer.

CHRISTIAN EDUCATION

THE SECOND MILE

No principle is more fundamental in the Christian program of life and none less fully comprehended than that of the second mile. Jesus urged His disciples to go two miles with the man who would compel us to go one. Love always outdoes necessity, and the Christian religion is love. "Now abideth faith, hope and love." When love prompts hope, faith says "I can and I will," and the second mile becomes sweeter than the first. Some of us have known this a long time. Many more of us are happily learning it these good days.

It is certainly so in our Christian Church these happy times. Our beloved Mission Secretary set out to raise $50,000 and the Brotherhood went with him the second mile. Our College sent forth the call for $125,000, and the brethren began to demonstrate the joy of the second mile and are making it $250,000. The churches are individually with a remarkably generous stride going the second and often times the third and fourth mile with their quotas, and everybody is happy.

The explanation is easy. Elon has proven to the Church her worth and in the hour of her crisis the Church is willing to go the second mile to render her safe in her place of primal service to the Kingdom. It is heartening to those who labor at Elon that the Church is expressing its devotion to her in this gracious manner. With city church, town or village church, with the church in the open country, with the strong and the weak, with the pastored and the pastorless, the story is one unbroken tale of triumphant liberality. Surely God can but bless a people so cheerfully willing to go the second mile for His cause.

I am indebted for this thought to Superintendent R. B. Wood of our Portsmouth Sunday school, a real statesman in Christian service. He took me around in his city and aided me in ways unnumbered, and stoutened my heart by expressing the hope in the outset that Portsmouth would go the second mile. Well, she went the third. Isn't that fine for a church not yet entirely out of debt!

Berea (Alamance) went the third mile too this week and so did Berea (Nansemond), and more is yet to be done at the second Berea. A third Berea, that of Norfolk, has made a noble start. One member only has been seen, and she gave $1,000. God bless the Bereas! Surely there is something in a name. We read in Acts 17:11 that the Bereans of Bible times were a noble people "in that they received the word with all readiness of mind, and searched the scripture daily." The churches of our brotherhood who are named for them have imbibed the spirit of their nobility and perpetuated it in noble deeds. We need more Bereas.

The churches at Graham, (N. C.), and the grand old Memorial Temple, Norfolk, have this week gone over the top. They both deserve special mention. Graham has this year doubled the pastor's salary and is engaged in paying for a parsonage for the man who ministers to them to live in, and yet she oversubscribed. And the Temple is without pastoral care. A beloved minister of the Congregational Church, executive secretary of the Norfolk Church Federation, a big job for any man, preaches for them, and is doing fine work, but Dr. Ekins cannot pastor the people. Besides many members have left the church recently. In spite of all this, this monument to the union of our Northern and Southern churches after the Civil War has maintained her long-established record and gone over the top. A princely people have done the princely deed.

Funds This Week

Funds this week have been established by Deacon Thos. A. Jones, Norfolk, in memory of his wife in the sum of $2,500; and in sums of $1,000 each by Mr. and Mrs. H. C. Pollard, Elon College; Mr. and Mrs. J. H. Farmer, Elon College; Attorney John M. Cook, Burlington, (a good Methodist Sunday school teacher) in memory of his mother, Mrs. Melissa Staley Cook; Mr. and Mrs. R. B. Wood, Portsmouth; Mr. J. F. Brothers, Jr., Portsmouth; Mr. Walter C. Rawles, Norfolk; Mr. B. L. Nichols, Norfolk, in memory of his daughter, Mrs. Lillie Nichols Wright; Deacon James H. Craig, Norfolk; Mr. Logan McCloud and wife, Norfolk; Hon. I. W. Pritchard, Chapel Hill; and Mrs. J. E. Hall, Norfolk county, in memory of her late husband. Veritably do the righteous rest from their labors and their good deeds follow them in the loving sacrifices of their loved ones.

The chorus of generous response remains without an unbroken note, and the second mile has become the prevailing style, for which we thank God and take courage.

Let the Church continue in intercession for God's continued blessing on this work and that the churches yet to be visited may learn in happy experience the joy of the second mile.

W. A. HARPER.

More Cheer Yet

Upon my return to the office for a few hours, a letter was awaiting me from Brother W. F. Corwith, New York. He had previously given $1,000. He now makes it $5,000. May the Lord multiply his kind.

W. A. H.

THE CALL TO THE MINISTRY*

I Cor. 1:1, "Paul called to be an apostle of Jesus Christ through the will of God."

There are three classes of ministers:

1. *Apostles* and *Prophets* who *founded* the church. "Ye are no more strangers and foreigners, but fellow-citizens with the saints, and of the household of God; and are built upon the *foundation of the apostles and prophets*, Jesus Christ Himself being the chief corner stone." Eph. 2:19, 20.

2. *Evangelists* who *extend* the church by preaching the gospel *where* it has not been preached or *to whom* it has not been preached, and winning souls to Christ and the church. Missionaries are evangelists.

3. *Pastors* and *teachers* who have the *care* of churches and edify congregations. These all work in harmony toward one common end.

Apostles and prophets did their work in *founding* the Church as an institution. Having performed their task, they passed on to their reward and had no successors. Missionaries are evangelists to extend the Church into all lands and among all peoples; pastors and teachers must care for churches in their development.

Ministers are called to their work, and Paul says he was called by the *will* of God. His call was divine. Samuel was called when a *child*. He was the last of Judges and the first of the regular succession of prophets. Elisha was called when a *man*. God directed Elijah in the cave at Horeb to anoint Elisha a prophet in his room. He found Elisha plowing in the field with twelve yoke of oxen and cast his mantle upon him; and it fell upon him again as he ascended in a chariot of fire. God never called an *idle* man nor an *immoral* man into the ministry in early times.

The call of the minister is,

I *To a New Life*

Jesus called men from secular occupations to spiritual occupations. He said to the fishermen: "Follow me and they followed Him"; to Matthew at the Receipt of Custom, and "he followed Him." This was to them a *new life*. He trained them first as disciples in this new life. This new life was more than separation from wrong world-ways; it was separation from right world-ways. It was a separation from secular occupations. It was the first step into the ministry—separation from secular life, no matter how good it might be. Fishing and official service are both necessary and good in the world's business; but Jesus called them away from *their* business to follow Him in *His* business. "The ministry requires the whole man," and the man's whole life.

II *To a New Office*

"When it was day, He called unto Him His disciples; and of them He chose twelve, whom He also named apostles." Luke 6:13. Matthew says, "He gave them power against unclean spirits, to cast them out, and to heal all manner of sickness and all manner of disease." Saul was already a church man when he was called into the office of an apostle.

In Matthew nine thirty-eight Jesus said to His disciples "Pray ye therefore the Lord of the harvest, that He will send forth laborers into His harvest." The ministry is not a self-chosen office, but one into which God *calls* men; and there is a double danger: (1). That of entering the ministry without a divine call. Think of the man at the wedding without a wedding garment. (2). That of not yielding to a divine call. In that case, it means failure in the world. Paul was very much impressed by his call: "Woe is me if I preach not the gospel." Aptitude for work may help the individual to decide. A person without a musical soul would hardly be chosen leader of a band or choir. The presumption is that God will choose wisely no matter what men may think.

III *To a New Work*

There is work for all in the vineyard, but special work for ministers who give up secular employment and devote their whole time to religious work by the *will* of the Lord. Paul says: "This one thing I do," and that is the essential thing in the work of the minister. The soldier commits himself, without reserve, to his country, and depends upon his country for support. The minister must commit himself and his life to God, and depend upon God for support. "The laborer is worthy of his hire;" and "they that preach the gospel shall live of the gospel;" and Paul says again: "I count all things but loss for Christ." God calls untaught men into the ministry, as the fishermen; but it is their business to prepare for the great task. The hardest thing in his experience is the self-denial necessary in his preparation. No matter how much time is required in preparation, it should be given to that herculean task.

The ministry is a most trying and delightful service. It tries human faith and human patience; but "this is the victory that overcometh the world even your faith;" and "let patience have her perfect work." The beauty of the ministry is its satisfaction. Nothing is more satisfying than a good conscience, and that cannot be enjoyed when deep conviction is not obeyed. This question of conviction as to a call, and obedience to the call, must have a personal and individual answer; and it must be the *will of God*. "To him that knoweth to do good, and doeth it not, to him it is sin;" for "whatsoever is not of faith is sin." The call to the ministry roots itself in conviction and faith, and gets its answer in the obedience of the will to the *will of God*.

*Delivered by Dr. W. W. Staley, Suffolk, Va., February 23, 1919.

A VILLAGE 4,000 YEARS OLD

Dr. John H. Finley, who visited the Holy Land for the Red Cross, tells in the Asia Magazine about the old town of Halhul one of hundreds of villages in Palestine which have not changed in 4,000 years.

"I have visited today a village that is four thousand years old, but that is without certain facilities which the newest town in Oklahoma would insist upon having in as many hours as this village has known years. It stands upon a hill almost bare of trees and looks at the left between the mountains to the Mediterranean sea, and at the right across the Dead sea. This village was doubtless sitting in the same place where Abraham left Lot and journeyed from the plains of the Jordan down into Hebron, which is only four miles away. David often passed by it when he was fleeing into the wilderness from Saul or during his seven and a half years' reign in Hebron. A little way off soldiers of the new crusades are encamped in a fold of the hills and, in the valley of Caleb's lower springs, close by one of the springs, new refugees from the plain of Jordan are pitching their black tents. This village,

Halhul, is more like one of our Indian adobe towns than any other communities in the States, except that the huts are of stone. There are no streets, only winding, labyrinthine paths round and about, up and down, sometimes over the roofs of the huts—paths made by the feet of men, women, children and donkeys through the centuries. There are no vehicles, wagons, motors, street cars. There is no postoffice, for never a letter comes to the village, I suppose. There are no newspapers, no schools, no places of amusement (there is one man, at least, who plays a primitive pipe), no running water, no signs, no stores so far as I could see, no libraries nor books, no women's clubs, no telephones—there was nothing to give the inhabitants communication with the world beyond the sight of their eyes or the reach of their feet. And few, I suppose, had journeyed beyond Hebron to the south, or Jerusalem at the north.

"Halhul! What a new life would come into your old stone body if the children of a typical American village would come to sing and play with your children. Halhul! How many summers will you sleep in the sun, how many winters will you shiver in your windowless huts, before the civilization which has come up to your gates, across the seas and up from the ports of Egypt, shall not only pass like the automobile at your feet or fly like the aeroplane over your head, but will enter your heart with its joys, its higher joys and its deeper sorrows. Halhul! Will not the new Joshua give you an inheritance not merely to some particular tribe or nation, but to the world, that it may add its comic gifts in this Tele-Victorian age to those which you have gathered out of your long past with its narrow horizon—a horizon whose edge is not cut by the sky-scrapers of your coast, dear America!

"Halhul! I should like to come to you in the year of our Lord 2000."

PRIZE FOR SCHOOL GIRLS AND BOYS OFFERED BY STATE BOARD OF HEALTH

2,626 children die in North Carolina each year under the age of two from diarrheal disease, this one disease causing the largest number of deaths in the 33,914 which occur yearly.

With a desire of calling the attention of school children in North Carolina to the large number of children under five who die annually in the State and to those conditions which contribute to their death, and with the hope of attracting through the school children the attention of mothers and fathers to these facts and conditions, the Bureau of Infant Hygiene of the State Board of Health offers a prize of $10 for the best composition giving ten contributing factors to diarrheal diseases of infants under two years of age, and the best methods of removing these conditions.

This composition is to be sent in to the Bureau of Infant Hygiene, State Board of Health, by May 10th and must contain a statement that said composition was composed and written without assistance.

Information regarding the cause of disease can be obtained by applying to the State Board of Health, in case local teachers are not prepared to furnish it.

WORSHIP AND MEDITATION

LIFE'S SAMENESS AND FRESHNESS

(By Rev. Arthur Pringle)

Reprinted from The Christian Work

This, we say, is a "new" age, the events through which we are passing are "unprecedented," and, of course, this has its strong element of truth. Perhaps, however, it would make for our strength and wisdom if we allowed the other side of the case to take firmer grip of us, remembering that history repeats itself, and that so many of the things that are now disconcerting us with their freshness have in reality traveled through long ages to reach us. For all their novelty and surprise, they bear, on close inspection, the marks of their journeying, making us understand how a wise man could once say that there is no new thing under the sun. It is in this connection that Mr. Havelock Ellis makes the acute observation, "He who would advance can never cling too closely to the past . . . . You may spare yourself some unhappiness if, beforehand, you slip the Book of Ecclesiastes beneath your arm." Here we are, for example, in the midst of international and social and industrial upheavals and readjustments, and our proper demand is for alert, enterprising leaders in touch with our own time. But they cannot be this unless they are in touch with all other times. They must bring out of their treasure things new and old, or they will land us on the rocks. War, for example, has come to us with a literally terrifying newness, and we see how, without check, it will become newer and newer until it means the end of all things. But, nevertheless, there is a weird antiquity stamped on its panoply and horror; it is essentially the same war that has ravaged the ages, the same in its root causes and accompaniments and results. Our social problem, too, is, from one point of view, intricate with incalculable factors; but, stripped to reality's bone, it rehearses the ancient lesson that Nemesis must overtake any community which acquiesces in the jostling of senseless luxury and hopeless need, and in complacent about evils that would yield to resolute attack. Epochs and centuries have their individuality, just as persons have, and in this our time it is our business to be ourselves, to see with our own eyes our specific task and vision. Each generation ought so to put its distinctive stamp on history as to hand it on fresher and finer than it has ever been before. But under the stamp there will ever be the unalterable factors and the unimprovable lessons; and the age intent on solving its peculiar problems would be wise to steady itself with much preliminary reflection on the riddles and guessers that have gone before.

This combination of sameness and freshness is also the key to a right estimate of individual experience. At first blush we appear so painfully or gladly new to ourselves, as the case may be; painfully, in the awful uniqueness that sorrow has a way of assuming, so that it seems as though no one could ever have had to face such a trial as ours; gladly, in the wonderful sense that comes even to the moderately fortunate that life is whispering to them a separate, intimate secret. Without a doubt, all youth should hear before and behind and on every side the heartening challenge, "Behold, I make all things new," and should feel, with something like rapture, that its life has never been lived before. In that sort of spring and mid-summer madness there is a sanity that may keep life warm to the winter's end.

But in and by itself this is no use; it is even dangerous, for it makes people act as though the great thing were to be "new" and "up to date" and superior to convention—phrases which, isolated from wholesome qualification, are danger signals rather than goals. When people declare their intention of living "their own life," it may mean the best or the worst. If they propose following the healthy bent of their individuality, thinking for themselves, opening all the windows of their soul and drinking in all the winds of God—what more legitimate? But if they intend the careless defying of accepted codes and rash moral adventuring—what more disastrous? In such a day as ours it is worth while insisting that conventions have only had time to become conventions because they have somehow justified themselves, and the wise will respect them accordingly. Religion holds no brief for hidebound staleness, and the magic phrase about "having life abundantly" as final warrant behind it. But here again our treasure is new and old. We are, in essence and at heart, what others have been before us. In Sir Thomas Browne's quaint words, men are "lived over again." The drama of humanity is like the drama of the playhouse; the scenery becomes more elaborate, the actors appear in garb that alters with the times, all manner of ingenious changes are rung upon the plot—but the plot, in all its comedy and tragedy, remains the same. So, when all is said and done, we are not lonely in our sorrows or peculiar in our joys; they are shared by an unnumbered host who did our laughing and crying, our fearing and hoping, before ever we were thought of. We are, then, as new as this very minute; we are, also, as old as Adam, and it all makes life very wonderful.

Should we be so liable to panic about modern problems of faith if we remembered this mingling of the old and the new in human experience? It is the fashion to talk of the religious difficulties "created" by the war, but, if put to it, could you name one? Providence, prayer, free will and "fatalism," the death of the good and the frequent immunity of the vile: what age has not known, in whatever form, these familiar offshoots of the ancient riddle? Each successive period discusses philosophy in its own jargon, but in the stuff of our philosophical perplexities and conjectures is there not more redressing of the old than manufacture of the new? No people are the people with whom wisdom was born or with whom it shall die, and all the ages are concluded under one impenetrable mystery. Is there any speculation or problem whereof men say, "See, this is new;" it hath been already of old time, which was before us.

Out of which spring two practical suggestions. One is specially the concern of preachers and all people who care or the pulpits fair name. Do we not see by this time the absurdity of dividing theology into "old" and "new," and its exponents into "orthodox" and "progressive"? The theology that was only "new" would be a plant without root, a house without a foundation, and that which was *merely* "old" would be the equally futile reverse. The "progressive" preacher who fails to gather the essence of his message from the rich stores of the ages—the man who forgets that temptation and sorrow and immortal longing spell the same hunger in all time: what a figure he cuts, what short vogue the need of humanity gives him! Yet, as he brings the old out of his treasure, it is his to ensure that, even as the mercies of God, it is new every morning. Old, the truth is paralyzed; new, it is the whim of a moment; old *and* new, it is the meat and drink of every generation. So in the true pulpit the conservative weds the adventurous, and when this happens there is fine progeny of helpfulness.

The other suggestion is for the general run of work-a-day people. Do what we will, every life must have a big element of sameness, and for many monotony is the great enemy. Whoever we are, we must needs do the same thing day after day, year in and year out. Name what you will, from what is called menial drudgery to what seem the dazzlingly attractive professions, there is not much promise of happiness or success to the man who will not squarely face up to routine repetition, demands that, having been put to bed tonight, rise up with aggravating renewal of insistence tomorrow. To this we must make up our minds, but it need not take the heart out of us, for when a man catches the spirit of Christ he may sometimes be tired, but *he does not easily become stale*. Out of the heart of God, triumphantly meeting all lifes flatness and sameness, his faith and courage receive the answering promise, "Behold, I make all things new."

BOLSHEVISM

The Bolsheviki of Russia have issued a decree abolishing Sunday, and a pronouncement forbidding weddings or funerals to be held in any of the churches. They have also issued a decree that lessons in Atheism shall be given in the schools, and all religious instruction is forbidden.

This is not the first time in history that a nation has tried to abolish God and the Sabbath and sacred things by decree. But all such decrees have failed, and with them has gone the failure of the nation making such mad decrees. This godless decree of the Bolsheviki may result in blood-shed, death and destruction of property but it at the same time seals the fate and pronounces the doom of this uprising of anarchists.

J. O. ATKINSON.

NOTES

Rev. L. E. Smith sends this note: "Special meetings closed Sunday evening, (April 20) with 101 new members since I arrived January 15, 1919. The Lord has wonderfully blessed us. The building has been enlarged to accommodate the people. The possibilities here are certainly unlimited. I covet the prayers of the Brotherhood. More later."

Rev. J. W. Wellons writes: "I preached at the Masonic Home in Greensboro, N. C., the second Sunday and administered the Sacrament. I enjoyed the day very much. I will preach at Shiloh, Randolph County, the second Sunday in May."

We have received from Chaplain H. S. Smith a copy of *The Soldier-Student*—the official organ of the American students at the University of Montpellier. A readable sheet, it is.

At this season of the year the income of THE SUN falls off considerably and remains so until fall. We suppose that the nature of the crops in the rural sections accounts for this. Such a condition means that the summer months are hard on us, financially. There are many who can renew just as well at one time of the year as another, and so we call the attention of our friends to our needs. If your subscription is due, renew now. We must meet our bills promptly and have no means of so doing except as the people pay.

Y. M. C. A. FOR BURLINGTON

Burlington, N. C., is to have a Young Men's Christian Association building that will cost about one hundred thousand dollars. It is to be a gift to the city by a prominent family.

THE AMERICAN CHRISTIAN CONVENTION

The American Christian Convention is in session at Conneaut, Ohio, this week. Many of our Southern brethren are in attendance. We hope to give some of the main items from the Convention in next week's issue of THE SUN.

LATEST NEWS FROM THE SECULAR WORLD

The revised covenant of the League of Nations has been adopted without amendment. The amendments by the French and Japanese have been withdrawn. The outlook is hopeful for an early peace.

The Council of Four to present a provision to try the ex-Kaiser has made provision for his trial by five judges. He is to be tried for: "A supreme offense against international morality and the sanctity of treaties."

Postmaster General Burleson says that all cables will be turned back to private owners.

THE CHRISTIAN ORPHANAGE

SUPERINTENDENT'S LETTER

Our financial report this week is encouraging to us. Our churches and Sunday schools are responding splendidly. This week runs our Easter Offerings to a little more than one thousand dollars. So the first thousand has been reached and passed. Now for the second thousand right quick. Let us all pull together and at the same time and just keep on pulling till the three thousand dollar mark for the Easter Offering is reached.

Two churches were placed on the honor roll this week as their contribution was more than $100. One other church just lacked a small amount reaching the $100 mark.

How many will we have on the honor roll when the Easter offering is all in? I trust a number will be there.

It has been suggested that we build a new home modern and up-to-date for the little children. One that the Church will be proud of. Why not raise enough money in the next two months to build this home? A home of this kind would cost something like ten thousand dollars. Twenty persons giving $500 each would built it. Forty persons giving $250.00 each would build it. One hundred persons giving $100 each would build it.

How easy it could be done if our people would just stop and think. Who will be the first to mail us a check for either of the above mentioned amounts to raise this fund and give the little children a home, home?

         CHAS. D. JOHNSTON, Supt.

REPORT FOR APRIL 30, 1919

Amount brought forward, $2,498.13.

Sunday School Monthly Offerings
(North Carolina Conference)

Poplar Branch, 93 cents; Ramseur, $2.20; Ramseur Baraca Class, $3.35; New Lebanon, $1.00; New Lebanon Baraca Class, $1.00; G. W. McDonaldson, for Sunday school, $1.51; Long's Chapel, $1.00; Reidsville, $1.00; Pleasant Grove, (Va) $4.00.

     (Eastern Virginia Conference)

Liberty Spring, $5.00; Suffolk, $25.00; Windsor, $5.90; New Hope, $2.45; First Church, Norfolk, Va., $10.18; Timber Ridge, (Va. Valley), $2.55.

     (Georgia and Alabama Conference)

Richland, Ga., $2.00; Total, $69.07.

Children's Home

Mamie Cambell, Luray, Va., $3.00,

Special Offerings

A. P. Thompson, on support of children, $17.00.

     (Long's Chapel Church)

General Collection, $2.09; Mrs. M. E. Fitch, 25 cents; Alice Blanche Steel, 25 cents; B. W. Johnston, 25 cents; J. P. Pace, 25 cents; M. T. Garrison, $1.00; Jas. W. Wall, $1.00; G. L. King, $1.00; Harvey A. Jeffreys, $1.00; Luna Pritchett, $1.00; Mrs. J. Walter Johnston, $1.00; J. W. Noah, $1.00; A. N. Johnston, $1.00; C. H. Roney, $1.00; Mrs. G. L. King, $1.00; H. C. King, $1.00; Ernest Tillman, $1.00; N. L. King, $1.00; C. G. Jeffreys, $2.00; Myra Anderson, 11 cents; Eva Wyatt,

5 cents; Lacy B. Hurdle, 50 cents; Sam Weldon, 25 cents; H. C. Roney, 50 cents; Ida Jeffreys, 50 cents; Total, $20.00.

     (High Point Church and Sunday School)

Primary Class, $1.00; Junior Class, $1.20; Miss Louis Albright, $1.40; Jas. R. Clodfelter, 25 cents; M. L. Boswell, 50 cents; R. F. Brown, 50 cents; Nova Brown, 50 cents; Athaleen Keneday, 50 cents; Mrs. L. R. Gibson, $1.00; Mrs. R. C. Boyd, $1.00; J. C. Henderson, $1.00; J. E. Clodfelter, $1.00; Mrs. A. E. Lunsdon, $1.00; Mrs. and Mrs. J. A. Lee, $1.00; Mrs. Hattie Glass, $1.00; O. L. Brady, $1.00; R. C. Boyd, $1.00; Mrs. W. A. Henderson, $1.00; Miss Flossie Manning, $1.00; Miss Minnie Shelton, $1.00; Miss Flora E. Elmore, $1.00; L. L. Wyrick, $1.00; Miss Mary Gibson, $1.00; Blanche Leonard, $1.00; Treva Ward, $1.00; Mrs. J. W. Whitt, $1.00; Miss Dora Vuncannon, $1.00; W. A. Henderson, $1.00; Total, $25.85.

     (Bethlehem (N. C) Ladies' Aid Society)

Mrs. J. M. Story, $1.00; Mrs. Lillie Sutton, $1.00; Mrs. Mamie Simpson, $1.00; Mrs. Margaret Wilkins, $1.00; Mrs. J. W. Holt, $2.50; Mrs. W. A. Paschal, 25 cents; Mrs. Loma Gilliam, 50 cents; Almeta Kernodle, 25 cents; Mrs. C. E. Kernodle, $2.00; Mrs. A. C. Madren, 50 cents; L. L. Troxler, $1.00; Mrs. L. F. Troxler, $1.00; Mrs. Many Garrison, 50 cents; Mrs. Eliza J. Cook, $1.00; Mrs. Sadie Ross, 50 cents; Bethlehem church and S. S., $39.40; Total, $53.40.

General

Mrs. Sue Brooks Siler, $5.00; Glencoe Union Sunday school, $10.55; Virgalee Chrisman, 15 cents; Mrs. Alfred Apple, 25 cents; Miss Irene Pritchett, 25 cents; Miss Ethel Pritchett, 10 cents; Miss Mildred Pritchett, 10 cents; Mrs. John D. Pritchett, 35 cents; Claude Pritchett, 10 cents; Mildred Pritchett, 10 cents; John D. Pritchett, 15; Mrs. J. L. Barksdale, $1.00; Lois C. Lawrance, $10.00; Blanche Penny, $5.00; Piney Plains church, $15.05; Oakland Sunday school, $17.51; Henderson Sunday school, $100.56; Damascus S. S., $13.12; Mt. Carmel S. S., $12.00; Burlington Sunday school, $103.05; St. Johns Sunday school, $6.40; Grandmother Stephenson, $2.00; Hank's Chapel Church, $23.00; Mt. Bethel Church and Sunday school, $18.10; Miss Stella Sharpe, $2.25; Miss Luna Sharpe, $2.00; Lanett Christian S. S., $17.77; Beatrice Mason, $5.00; Mrs. M. A. Atkinson, $2.00; Vanceville S. S., Va., $12.01; J. Godley, Trenton, N. J., $10.00; Mt. Auburn Sunday school, $23.00; Mrs. Lucy Vanderhoof, Parker, Kans., $3.00; E. B. Bailey, $4.50; Mr. Henry Hatch, $5.00; Mrs. N. P. Hatch, $5.00; Brown's Chapel church, $5.36; Pleasant Grove church, (VA.), $55.00; Timber Ridge, Va., $91.58; Beulah Sunday school, (Ga.) $5.00; Reidsville Church and S. S., $15.25; Beulah S. S. (Ala.), $4.40; Mayland Sunday school, $7.55; Liberty church, (Vance), $21.20; New Hope Sunday school, (Va.), $24.00; Parks Cross Roads, $35.65; Pleasant Ridge church, $9.38; New Lebanon S. S., $3.45; New Lebanon Baraca Class, $3.00; Hope-Dale S. S., $3.79; O'Kelley's Chapel church, $3.05; Enigma church, $5.26; Salem Chapel church, $10.44; M. C. Jackson, $5.00; Mt. Hermon church, $8.65; Miss Carrie McGray, $1.00.

     (Antioch Church, Valley Va.)

Frank H. Showalter, $20.00; T. L. Deavers, $5.00; Mrs. T. L. Deavers, $5.00; W. C. Wampler and Wife, $5.00; Owen Andes, $5.00; E. Floyd Showalter, $3.00; Mrs. E. Floyd Showalter, $2.00; Virdie Showalter, $1.50; Barba Andes, $3.00; Fannie J. Zirkle, $1.00; B. Frank Zirkle, $1.00; W. P. Showalter, $1.00; Benjamin Deavers, $1.00; Mrs. E. A. Showalter, $1.00; Mrs. Frank Showalter, $1.00; Sarah A. Tate, $1.00; Carl Showalter, $1.00; Nellie Deavers, $1.00; Eula C. Wampler, $1.00; Myrtle Showalter, $1.00; Carlton Wampler, 25 cents; Harold B. Wampler, 25 cents; Lura Green, 25 cents; Grace Berry, 25 cents; Carrie Berry, 25 cents; Alma Berry, 25 cents;

C. D. Broadrap, 12 cents; Woodrow Wampler, 5 cents; Bertie F. Argenbright, 50 cents; William Tate, 25 cents; Dillie M. Broadrap, 10 cents; Essie Tate, 25 cents; Jennings Wampler, 25 cents; L. C. Broadrap, 10 cents; Emma S. Fulk, 25 cents; Willie Grady, 25 cents; Mrs. Ed Ritchie, 10 cents; Ella Green, 25 cents; Elsie Green, 25 cents; Ethel Green, 25 cents; Edna Green, 25 cents; May Niwander, 25 cents; R. A. Hinton, 50 cents; Mrs. R. A. Hinton, 50 cents; E. L. Deavers, $1.00; Friends, $2.85; Total, $69.57.

Total for the week, $1,011.32; Grand total, $3,509.45.

THE FORWARD MOVEMENT

(Rev. Warren H. Denison, D. D., Superintendent)

Notes From The Field

Rev. George D. Eastes, Raleigh, N. C., is intensely interested in the Forward Movement, and says that we may count on him in every possible way. One of the finest things in this Movement is to notice the loyalty of our pastors.

President W. A. Harper, Elon College, has the hearty congratulations of the Forward Movement in his splendid success for Elon's endowment fund. Dr. Harper is a member of the Forward Movement Executive Committee.

The New England Christian Convention is building a strong Forward Movement program for its annual meeting in June. All the points of the Movement will be strongly emphasized.

Professor J. N. Dales, editor of the *Christian Vanguard* in Ontario, hopes that every one of our Canada churches may enlist in the Forward Movement.

The Forward Movement requests that every conference in the Southern Christian Convention appoint a Forward Movement committee, and report the names of said committee to the Superintendent. Let the executive committee of the conferences take up this matter soon.

The latest word from Urbana, Illinois is, that they have pledges for $625 more to be added to their former pledges of $4,000.

Rev. J. E. Etter, D. D., Troy, Ohio, reports 55 new members received into his church in the pre-Easter evangelistic campaign.

Rev. W. H. Hendershot, Towanda, Kansas, says "I believe the Forward Movement plan is born of God. The Towanda church, Sunday school, Mission society, are all working on the Forward Movement plan."

Rev. Frank H. Peters, D. D., Greenville, Ohio, says, "In response to the leaders of the Christian Church in the United States and Canada, our Greenville Christian church has adopted the five-point program of the Forward Movement as the basis of its work. Devotion, Evangelism, Religious Education, Missions and Benevolence will be made the center of our activity. Special committees have been appointed. The committee on evangelism has districted the city and appointed assistants for active, continued work throughout the year."

Mr. Claude Norfleet, Holland, Virginia, is the Four-Minute man of the Holy Neck church.

We are expecting some splendid reports from the churches of the Southern Christian Convention immediately following Easter, for a number of the churches are expecting to receive a goodly number of members on Easter Sunday. We ask all pastors to report to the Forward Movement their Easter ingatherings.

The Virginia Valley Central Conference is planning a Forward Movement program for its Sunday School and Christian Endeavor Convention, in May.

Rev. G. W. Shepherd, Summer, Illinois, has appointed a laymen's evangelistic campaign team of sixteen men, as one of the Forward Movement items of his church.

Miss Letha McGuire is pushing the Forward Movement work in the Sunday schools of the Des Moines Conference.

INCREASE

The nineteenth century witnessed an increase of professed Christians in the world from 200,000,000 to about 500,000,000. This represents an increase of 2 to 1 to the world's increase in population in the same period. There are now nearly 50,000,000 Christians in the United States and church property in the United States is estimated at over a thousand million dollars. "And of the increase of His government there shall be no end forever."

J. O. ATKINSON.

Forty-six doctors were killed in the recent war, twenty-two died of wounds, twelve of accident and one hundred and one of disease. Four were lost at sea and seven were missing in action. Thirty-eight were taken prisoners and two hundred and twelve were wounded in action, according to an exchange.

* *

Samuel T. Dutton, formerly head of the teachers' college of Columbia University, died recently. At the time of his death he was one of the editors of *The Christian Work*, printed in New York.

* *

The students and president of the A. and E. College at Raleigh have been in mental conflict concerning certain regulations and government of the institution.

* *

One-tenth is not all that one should give—that should be the minimum amount.

* *

Civilization is not secured by poverty but by property. Society would be better off if we had less poor —and we would have less poor if more men would give God a square deal.

* *

W. N. Pierce—I will be eighty on my next birthday. Most of the time since the Civil War I have had THE SUN to shine in my home and I can't now do without it.

J. W. Elder—Find enclosed $4.00 to renew my subscription. I appreciate your sending the paper on with its sunshine.

Sunday School and Christian Endeavor

SUNDAY SCHOOL LESSON FOR MAY 11

Sin And Its Consequences.—Gen. 3:1-24; Romans 1:18-23; James 1:15.

Golden Text: The wages of. sin is death; but the free gift of God is eternal life in Christ Jesus our Lord. Rom. 6:23.

Devotional Reading. Ps. 51:1-13.

Thoughts For Teachers

The devil has found no new arguments through all the years, "It won't hurt you;" "You are strong enough to know when to quit;" "A man has got to see life." These are the devils stock arguments. And our excuses have not changed much either. "I was led into it;" "I was overpersuaded;" "It is hard to know just what is right." The great trouble is that we, like Adam have a "guide who shall lead us into all truth" but we think we are strong enough to cope with evil. Adam and Eve had no need to debate the question with the Serpent at all. God had spoken, and His word was sufficient. It is only when we begin to debate with evil that we are in trouble, for he is more subtile than we when we are depending upon human strength and wisdom alone.

No death till Sin entered, and then a long obituary column, as long as the birth list, with but two exceptions. All sicknesses are caused by broken laws, directly or indirectly; all death is caused by Sin. The last *Enemy* that shall be destroyed is *death.*

            MRS. FRED BULLOCK.

CHRISTIAN ENDEAVOR TOPIC FOR MAY 11

The Lure of The World.—II Tim. 4:10; I John 2:15-17.

Vice is a monster of such hateful mein
That to be hated needs but to be seen,
But seen too oft, familiar with his face,
We first endure, then pity, then embrace. (Pope).

You've heard of the snake in the grass, my lad;
Of the viper concealed in the grass;
But now you must know,

Man's deadliest foe
Is a snake of a different class;
Alas!—
'Tis the viper that lurks in the glass. (Saxe).

VACATION CARDS

Some of your pupils are going away for the summer. Are they going away from the Sunday school—some Sunday school—as well? Why not arrange now to have some vacation cards, either printed for your individual school, or buy the regular cards from the Publishing House, and see that each vacationer is provided with a card to have signed by the superintendent or teacher of the Sunday school or schools he attends while absent from home? Then when they return and these cards are turned in, their record will be clear and clean, and the goodly habit of church and Sunday school attendance will not have been broken into because "we were away all summer." It is evident that Satan works while summer weather brings fruit to the trees. Shall we be more slothful?

            MRS. FRED BULLOCK.

CHILDREN'S DAY

The Sunday School and Christian Endeavor Board of the Southern Christian Convention, through its Executive Committee, is preparing a program for Children's Day. These programs will come from the press in a few days and it is believed the exercises are adapted to the needs and conditions of the largest as well as the least of our schools. The programs are for free distribution, to a limited number, and can be had by addressing a request to the undersigned. It is planned by the Board for every school in the Convention to have Children's Day on some Sunday of June. This should be a great and good day not only for the children, but for the whole school and the community. By all means let every school have Children's Day in June. Make it a rally day for the school, as well as a glad day, and through it seek to increase attendance and interest.

         J. O. ATKINSON, *Sec.,*
Elon College, N. C.

MARRIAGES

MORGAN-WILLIAMS

At the home of the bride's parents on Easter Sunday Mr. Elder V. Morgan and Miss Cora Ida Williams were united in marriage by the writer. None but homefolks were present except Eddie Morgan, the twin brother of the groom, and his wife. The bride is a daughter of Mr. and Mrs. Baxter Williams of Eagle Springs, N. C., and the groom is a son of Mr. and Mrs. Joseph P. Morgan, Spies, N. C. Both are popular young people.

May happiness and prosperity be theirs through life.

            T. J. GREEN.

OBITUARIES

CARR

S. Livy Carr was born March 18, 1874, and died April 6, 1919. He had been enjoying the best of health for twenty years, and was seemingly in perfect health Saturday night. He was found sleeping the eternal sleep Sunday morning, the cause being heart-trouble. His wife, Marthia E. Carr, departed this life six years ago. Five children survive, the oldest being nineteen years of age, and the youngest nine. Besides these our Brother leaves three brothers, relatives, and a host of friends to follow the Savior to whom our deceased Brother was ever a faithful servant. He made a profession of Christ at the age of fifteen, united with the Mt. Carmel Christian church, and throughout the thirty years of his church membership he was a willing and ready helper in all good causes. He was a member of the "Woodmen of the World." Neighbors and friends wanted it remembered that there was "never a better neighbor, nor better citizen, nor more faithful husband, nor more devoted father, nor more earnest and energetic farmer" than Livy Carr. Funeral services were conducted by the writer, assisted by Dr. C. H. Rowland. Interment was made in the cemetery. The crowded congregation not being able to find seats shows the high esteem in which the community held Brother Carr. May the Heavenly Father comfort and bless the bereaved ones.

E. T. COTTEN.

RESOLUTIONS OF RESPECT— COVINGTON

Whereas, it has pleased our Heavenly Father to call from our midst Sister Covington, wife of Brother Henry T. Covington, and a member of Pleasant Grove Christian church, be it Resolved:

First, That we have lost a long time friend and devotee of our church;

Second, That we emulate the Christian graces in her character;

Third, That we commend the Savior as a Comfort and Guide for her children;

Fourth, That we send a copy of these resolutions to the bereaved family, spread a copy on our minutes, and have the same published in our church paper, The Christian Sun.

R. D. THOMPSON, Sr.,
O. S. BOYD,
P. P. JONES,
C. D. S. FARMER,
Committee.

COCKES

Benjamin William Cockes was born October 11, 1865, and died at his home in Surry county, Virginia, April 5, 1919, aged 54 years, 5 months and 4 days. He leaves two brothers, James E. and Obie L. Cockes, the latter of Emporia, Va., and one sister, Mrs. M. A. Valentine, Montrose, Pa. Burial services conducted by the writer. Interment in the family burying ground.

W. D. HARWARD.

RESOLUTIONS OF RESPECT— FARMER

Whereas, it has pleased our Heavenly Father to call Brother Sam Farmer, our fellow deacon and honored Brother from our midst, and whereas we are bowed in sorrow and grief, be it Resolved:

First, That one of our foremost men, both in church and community, is at rest from his extensive and fruitful labors;

Second, That his widow and children have sustained an irreparable loss, while his memory and example is a priceless heritage.

Third, That our church and its every auxiliary has lost a large factor and great asset;

Fourth, That we, the Board of Deacons, have lost a beloved friend, fellow-worker, and counsellor, and

Fifth, That a copy of these resolutions be placed upon our minutes, a copy sent to the bereaved family, and that the same be published in our church paper, The Christian Sun.

R. D. THOMPSON, Sr.,
O. S. BOYD,
P. P. JONES,
C. D. S. FARMER,
Committee.

SEATE

Mrs. Sallie Susan Seate was born in Halifax County, Virginia, January 4, 1870 and died Sunday, March 30, 1919, aged forty-nine years, two months and twenty-six days. Her parents were Captain Ned and Julia Overby Tuck.

At the age of seventeen she united with Union Christian church where she held her membership till death. In 1887 she married Robert Lipscomb Seate, who died October 19, 1909, leaving her with the responsibility of a large family of children. No widow ever labored more heroically and showed a more loyal, sacrificing spirit in her home than she.

She is survived by her mother, two brothers, five sons and five daughters, and one granddaughter. Two sons have served in the army. Russell received his discharge in time to spend a few weeks at the bedside of his mother. Corporal Ned Seate, at the time of his mother's death, was being treated in a hospital in New Jersey for a shattered bone from a wound in the right arm received last October near Verdun. He arrived on a furlough about one hour before the funeral. The highest tribute to the life of Sister Seate was given publicly at the funeral by a prominent neighbor when he spoke of her excellent children, having known them from early childhood.

The funeral was conducted from the home near High Hill, Va., on Monday, March 31, at 4:30 P. M., by the writer and the burial was in the family burying ground nearby.

A splendid Christian woman has gone to her reward. Her influence for good will live on in the lives of others and serve as an impelling force to duty and right.

C. E. NEWMAN.

WALKER

Died, April 13, 1919 in his 71st year, John Calvin Walker of Watson, Alamance County, N. C. He leaves two sisters, Mrs. E. A. Trolinger of Watson, N. C., and Mrs. J. W. Smith of Durham, N. C.,

one brother, James Monroe Walker of Safford, Arizona. He was a good citizen, friend, and neighbor. He was a successful business man, kind and courteous. He will be greatly missed in his community. The funeral service was conducted by the writer in the presence of a large audience at Union Christian church and his body laid to rest in the church cemetery.

P. H. FLEMING.

1 8 8 9   **1 9 1 9**

30 Years of World Building
IS ELON'S CONTRIBUTION TO CIVILIZATION

For thirty years Elon College has been doing, in a noble way, her part toward building a world—a civilized world where happiness is assured and where peace is soon to be maintained as a safety to mankind.

A MINISTER

in practically every pulpit, teachers in our schools, lawyers at the bar; judges on the bench, statesmen in the Capitol, business men in every walk of life, to say nothing of the trained men in other professions and the women who make *houses* into *homes* and strengthen the pillars of civilization by their lives, is only a *part* of Elon's contribution to the work of the Christian Church.

THESE YEARS OF SERVICE

have been years of *sacrificial* service, rendered by competent men and women whose first thought is to build character—*Christian character*.

AND THESE YEARS

must be multiplied many times in their service to meet a larger program for the Church and the Kingdom. To do this the College is, with hands that are outstretched, calling us to this challenge. We are meeting it and will continue to do so until we "go over the top."——all together.

PRAY FOR THE WORK AND THE WORKERS
—OURS IS THE BUSINESS OF THE KING—

Let Us Pray and Let Us Pay and Open the Way—For Elon

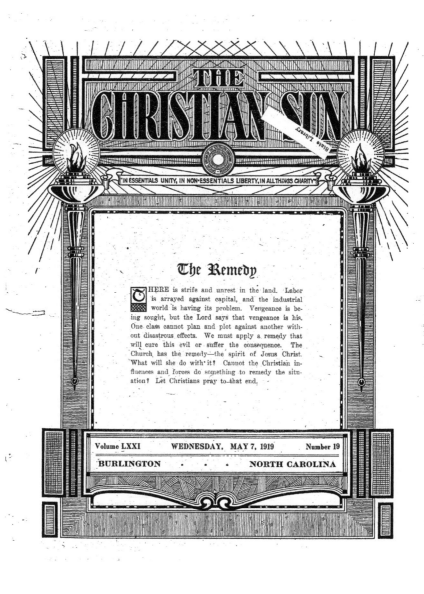

THE CHRISTIAN SUN

"IN ESSENTIALS UNITY, IN NON-ESSENTIALS LIBERTY, IN ALL THINGS CHARITY"

The Remedy

THERE is strife and unrest in the land. Labor is arrayed against capital, and the industrial world is having its problem. Vengeance is being sought, but the Lord says that vengeance is his. One class cannot plan and plot against another without disastrous effects. We must apply a remedy that will cure this evil or suffer the consequence. The Church has the remedy—the spirit of Jesus Christ. What will she do with it? Cannot the Christian influences and forces do something to remedy the situation? Let Christians pray to that end.

Volume LXXI   WEDNESDAY, MAY 7, 1919   Number 19

BURLINGTON   .   .   .   NORTH CAROLINA

THE CHRISTIAN SUN

Founded 1844 by Rev. Daniel W. Kerr

C. B. RIDDLE   -   -   -   **Editor**

Entered at the Burlington, N. C. Post Office as second class matter.

Subscription Rates

One year .... $ 2.00
Six months 1.00

In Advance

Give both your old and new postoffice when asking that your address be changed.

The change of your label is your receipt for money. Written receipts sent upon request.

Marriage and obituary notices not exceeding 150 words printed free if received within 60 days from date of event, all over this at the rate of one-half cent a word.

Original poetry not accepted for publication.

Principles of the Christian Church

(1) The Lord Jesus Christ is the only Head of the Church.
(2) Christian is a sufficient name of the Church.
(3) The Holy Bible is a sufficient rule of faith and practice.
(4) Christian character is a sufficient test of fellowship, and of church membership.
(5) The right of private judgment and the liberty of conscience is a right and a privilege that should be accorded to, and exercised by all.

EDITORIAL

"FINISHED"

There are a great many things on the market today that are labeled "finished." Not only are there things on the market so labeled but there are individuals who are labeled "finished" by schools and colleges. The "finished" product is found everywhere these days. It seems to be the outgrowth of specialization. For nearly twenty-five years specialization has been stressed by individuals and institutions. We agree that conditions have made it imperative that specialization be made in a number of lines, but like many other things, it has gone to the extreme and we feel that the time has come, especially in this period of reconstruction, when the matter should be amended.

We take one case for illustration: The other day we needed some extra help and advertised for a stenographer. More than a dozen applications were received. Many of these applications were from students in business colleges, or had just left some business college, and all of them said that they had "finished." We recall one letter in particular, which letter was brief, and the young lady said that she had "finished" her course and was waiting for a position. Although the letter was short, more than a dozen errors could be pointed out as to the arrangement, punctuation, paragraphing and other details. The worst part of the application, however, was that this young lady who had "finished"

did not seem to know where to end a sentence or how to begin a new sentence.

We take advantage of this instance to point out the danger there is in many so called business and technical schools that claim to give a complete course in a certain number of weeks. It is possible for them to do it, provided they have the necessary material, and so the question now goes back to the literary schools.

So many of the high schools fail to thoroughly prepare their students, and so when they leave the school and enter the business college they are not able to master the principles of shorthand and bookkeeping. When they begin their work they find that such principles and literary qualifications are so united that they cannot separate one from the other. A person may know shorthand and be able to take dictation rapidly but the putting of that dictation into good English form is another proposition. Large corporations everywhere will tell you that they seek out the men who not only have the business training but the literary qualifications as well.

Young man, young woman, don't let some small business college deceive you by making you believe that it can turn you out as a "finished" product in a few weeks capable of holding some responsible position. Know well that your literary foundation is secure and on this build your knowledge of business and your specialization. If specialization comes first, it is like the pyramid turned upside down, but if you make your preparation first, the pyramid of your life will be properly prepared and it will take something more than a mere push to turn you over.

MEMORIALS

At this season of the year the various country churches are planning and holding their annual memorials. We have always felt that these occasions were helpful and uplifting in many ways. They keep us in touch with the deeds of our fellowmen—deeds we seldom appreciate until our loved ones have been taken.

This year these occasions bring to us another phase for meditation. Since last year many of our friends have fallen in the foreign fields and in the home lands. Some of our brave young men lie beneath the wooden cross in sunny France. Their place is vacant in the home, in the church, and in the community. We trust that a fitting part will be given in all memorial services to these young men who have sacrificed their lives for freedom's sake. But their grave is not in the home cemetery, and we cannot place on their resting place flowers, but there are other ways that we can show our appreciation and pay our tributes of respect. May no church fail in the highest tribute to these young men!

WHERE THE TROUBLE IS

For some time our good Baptist brethren have been pouring "hot shot" into the church union idea. The *Biblical Recorder*, Raleigh, N. C., has had more or less to say about the uniting of churches, and a few weeks tgo it carried a cartoon called the "Union Hen." The cartoonist spread before the eyes of the public a very large pile of eggs with each labeled showing what the result would be from union. The cartoonist had in mind this idea: That when churches united, it meant the breeding of more sects.

Mr. Gordon Poteat, a son of Dr. E. M. Poteat, the former President of Furman University, Greenville, S. C., writes an article for the *Biblical Recorder*, which, it seems to us, brings a strong indictment against his own denomination. The article speaks for itself and far better than we could state his position. We print it in full and would like very much for Editor Johnson of the *Recorder* to tell us how he can get around Mr. Poteat's position.

HOW TO OPPOSE THE UNION MOVEMENT

Gordon Poteat.

(Reprinted from the Biblical Recorder)

Southern Baptist papers have of late been full of articles and editorials on the Union Movement. These articles bespeak an agitation of mind because of a situation which seems fast getting beyond control, because what is being done is more or less in the dark and there is no way of resisting the hidden opponent. Some feel that the Movement is quite sinister; that its purpose is the disintegration and destruction of the Baptist denomination and the truth for which Baptists stand. As we have observed the Movement, however, its impetus has been directed rather to a task which its leaders have conceived on broad lines—a conception which takes in the whole world, home and foreign. Baptists generally do not believe in their methods, and see in their effort to integrate without regard to the general belief of some bodies a danger something like that of Catholic ecclesiastical conformity. But, rather than setting their forces to overcome or overwhelm Baptist opposition, they are sweeping on to the accomplishment of the task they have set themselves, and are leaving us behind. In one article it is said that the movement "bears much resemblance to certain phases of politics, socialistic in spirit; which develop a type of thinkers and talkers who know how to do everything, from financing and running the Government down and out to all the small particulars of social life, but never do anything but talk!" Far from doing nothing but talk, they are acting in extensive and statesmanlike ways, whatever we may think of their ruling ideas.

May I give one or two illustrations from the mission field? We shall probably all agree that one of the most strategic places for mission work is in the capital of the nation. The Unionizers have combined in the capital of China, Peking, for a great Christian university, with the strength of several smaller faculties, Chinese and foreign, uniting in the one institution, and the various participating denominations, combining financial resources to build a plant and run an institution in no sense inferior to the best American educational institutions. However we may dissent from their plan, as far as it might involve our interests, we cannot blink facts like these: (a) that the institution will include in its faculty some of the most able and well trained men in North China; (b) that its equipment will be standard and adequate, costing hundreds of thousands; (c) that it will be a model for the Chinese, and without a shadow of a doubt gain their respect and admiration and support. The same thing may be said of the new medical work in Peking, which by combination has made available large resources of men and modern equipment. Baptists have no work in the capital of China, nor in but one or two provincial capitals.

In contrast with the situation just pictured, much of our work is in out-of-the-way places, where we are little calculated to affect the life of the nation as a whole, though, of course, we shall do good in the various forms of service. As one who has visited already many of our nations in China, as one who believes deeply in the Baptist message and its adaptability for China and its assured welcome where it is widely proclaimed, I have to confess with shame the inadequacy of our program and our present contribution to the needs of China. Proud of our faith, we stand abashed because of our conspicuous lack of works. One of our most strategically located stations is the capital of Honan, the center of the government, educational and commercial life of thirty millions of people. An indescribable opportunity there, made possible by a location in the heart of the city far superior to all the other missions, and a present missionary force more numerous than the other missions, is discounted and defeated by buildings not only greatly inferior to all the other missions, but to the neighboring Chinese buildings which border us on the street. Yet, appeals for equipment have resulted in nothing, so far, from the denomination—only a few personally solicited subscriptions secured by an interested mother's earnest effort, naturally far short of the amount necessary.

The shoe is on the other foot. It is we who are doing the talking; it is the Unionizers who are at their work. We talk of our great numbers, and boast that we are more numerous than any other denomination, but in comparison with their deeds we cannot claim a high place in the ranks. Our name is scarcely known in great sections of more or less evangelized territory in China. Others are producing already many trained leaders in their churches; while we are having difficulty in getting pastors or teachers for our most important places. Are we really serious in our mission as a denomination, after all? Can we play dog in the manger very long?

The only practical opposition to the ideas of the Union Movement is a revolution in our own ideas of our responsibility for mission work, an enlargement of our program, and an elevation of the standard of support ten to fifteen times as great as the present more or less insignificant million and a half from three million Baptists. Our articles of criticism of the Movement serve only to excite ourselves. They are read by almost no one else. We are spending our newspaper space talking of the danger of Unionism; they are raising their tens of millions to carry out their plans. Our talk is futile; their actions are sure of success. And the opportunities which we might well seize today will be gone from our hands soon, unless our Convention rises to totally new standards of giving.

Not every one who saith unto me, "Lord, Lord," shall enter the kingdom, but he who doeth the will of my Father.

Kaifeng, China.

NORTH CAROLINA STATE CHRISTIAN ENDEAVOR CONVENTION

The North Carolina Christian Endeavor Convention will convene in Burlington, June 6 and will remain in session until June 8. A strong program is being prepared and a great convention is expected. The following constitute some of the personnel of the program:

Karl Lehmann, Southern States Secretary United Society of Christian Endeavor; Lieut. Duncan B. Curry, of 312 Trench Motor Battery, just returned from France; Dr. Chas. F. Myers, one of the ablest pastors of Southern Presbyterian Churches, Greensboro; H. Galt Braxton, Vice-President World's Christian Endeavor Union, Kinston; Dr. W. A. Harper, President Elon College, Elon College; a National Boy Scout Speaker; Rev. A. L. Peeler, Reformed Church, Hickory; Dr. A. D. McClure, Presyterian church, Wilmington; G. M. Beaty, War. Y. M. C. A. Secretary, Charlotte; Rev. O. G. Jones, Greensboro; Mrs. L. W. McFarland, State Junior Superintendent, High Point; Rev. C. D. Whiteley, West Durham; J. D. Foster, Tarboro; Rev. Chas. G. Lynch, Charlotte; Miss Ruth Vogler, Publication Superintendent, Winston-Salem; H. S. Hardcastle, Elon College; J. E. Franklin, formerly President Roanoke Christian Endeavor Union, Leaksville; Dr. N. G. Newman, College Pastor of Elon College; William M. Brown, one of Virginia's greatest Christian Endeavor leaders, Danville, Va.

CHANGE IN LUTHERAN PUBLICATIONS

The Lutheran of Philadelphia and *The Lutheran Church Work and Observer*, of Harrisburg, Pa., two very readable and well edited papers of the Lutheran denomination ceased their publication last week, and to take their place will be *The Lutheran*, published in Philadelphia. These two papers have been in existence for a number of years, but the recent uniting of three Synods of the Lutheran Church, brought about a new issue in that it needed only one publication and a stronger publication to circulate in its enlarged territory without competition. *The Lutheran* and *The Lutheran Church Work and Observer* have been welcome visitors to this office and we look forward to the arrival of the new *Lutheran* and shall welcome it to this sanctum.

We have praised the soldier for his work, and so now let us give him work at home. See that all discharged men in your community find employment.

Have you subscribed to the Elon Standardization Fund? Don't miss the opportunity of having a part in the work.

MISSIONARY

MESSENGERS OF MERCY

"And Jesus answered and said unto them, Go and tell John the things which ye hear and see: the blind receive their sight, and the lame walk, the lepers are cleansed, and the deaf hear, and the dead are raised up, and the poor have the gospel preached to them." (Matt 11:4, 5). These are the word Jesus chose to cheer a man in prison. And those who bore these words, and the faithful ones who go out into the world to hear them today to those who are in the prison of sin are veritable messengers of mercy.

The missionary challenge today is for messengers of mercy.

The missionary movement today means the sending out of messengers of mercy.

SOMETHING GREATER THAN DEMOCRACY

What a fight has been made, and what treasure has been poured out, that the world might be made safe for democracy. How many of our gallant sons went out from our homes and our churches to enlist in the army of their country to fight in that momenteous cause?

But great as it is, there is something yet greater than democracy to fight for. I quote from Bishop Brent: "While ago the bugle called men to be led to lay down their lives in order that the world might be made safe for democracy. We counted democracy such a precious thing that we were led to give our lives for it. But there is something still greater than democracy to give life to. There is the Kingdom of God that must be spread throughout this world, and, until it covers the world as waters cover the sea, even a league of nations, however wisely organized, cannot hope to maintain stable and righteous peace. The missionary, the despised missionary, is the greatest candlestick of God in the whole world at this present time, as he has been in the past and must be in the future." The army of missionaries out on the firing line is engaged in a war that means more for democracy, for righteousness, for peace in the world than any other army that ever engaged in battle. Other brave men and true, other noble women and faithful, are needed there.

Are we doing our part to send them out, and support them after they are sent out?

PLEASE DO NOT COME

"Please do not come here for the next two weeks. We like to have you come, but you see, the next two weeks is our special time for thriving and your message of Jesus creates in us a desire to be honest and righteous. If you continue to come we will not have the courage or desire to steal." This was the message of people in Ballia, India, sent to a Christian missionary. What a tribute to our Lord Christ and His message!

J. O. ATKINSON.

PASTOR AND PEOPLE

FAVORABLE RECEPTION

The members and friends of the East End Christian church, Newport News, Va., gave me a very cordial reception when I came to them as pastor on the twentieth of April. Due to the kind and generous reception which was given me I feel very much at home.

Easter Sunday the children of the Sunday school gave an excellent exercise which took the place of the morning service. That night I preached my first sermon to a large and appreciative audience.

This past Sunday morning the theme for discussion was, "The Great Commission," and at night, "St. Paul's Answer to the Commission." At both these services a good audience was in attendance and we had fine meetings.

The people of the church are very much interested in the work and a good work is being done by them for the cause of Christ in this part of the Kingdom. The prayers of all members of our denomination are asked in order that the pastor may faithfully and effectively serve this people.

H. J. FLEMING, Pastor.

1023—25th St., Newport News, Va.

FOUNDED!

There is hardly a more pleasant little church to serve anywhere than Christian Light, and a few days ago they made it all the more pleasant by piling good things to eat all over my Ford. Sausage, eggs, cereals, canned stuff, etc., that were fit for the whole family young and old. It is hardly to be said that all the goodies were engaged by our little family.

But the most enjoyable thing about a pounding after all is not simply the eating, but the feeling of love and friendship which prompted the gifts.

May the heavenly Father, who is rich in mercy, repay a thousand fold, those whose hearts were so generous and make the receiver more worthy by every good word and work.

J. LEE JOHNSON.

A VISIT TO MY CHILDHOOD NURSE

One beautiful morning in April, I passed over the busy highway of life through the most enchanting scenery, when spring was putting on her summer dress, and looking her best in decorated splendor. I was invited to visit the home of my dear old nurse, who lives at Story, on the Southern road in Southampton County, Virginia. She lived in my home and cared for me so tenderly when my life was new. She loved me very truly and I loved her so devotedly that time nor distance have not diminished my love for, and a deep interest in her. Her lovely white, wavy hair—bleached in spotless purity with drifting snows of ninety-six winters—looked extremely beautiful to me. She appeared like an angel, while her honest, sweet, pure, calm, face seemed to be resplendent with a heavenly smile. Her mind is clear and active and she talked with me so brightly about many things which occurred in my childhood days, until emotions too deep to tell, pervaded my whole being.

What momentous thoughts trembled in my heart as she so vividly and tenderly recounted the eternal past! My feelings at meeting her were mingled with both joy and sadness. So glad was I to meet her after a long separation. I was glad that the dear old Christian woman has lived so long and spent such a useful, Godly life. This in itself caused me to love her more and better. I was glad to be entertained so nicely and sumptuously in her quiet and pleasant home. Among the many pleasant visits to other homes, none of them surpassed the visit to this one. The sad part came when we thought of the fact that we two were the only ones left to tell the eventful story of a happy past. She and I are the only living ones of a large family. Father and mother, four brothers and two sisters are sleeping in the long dreamless night in old Virginia's soil. The silent echoes of their voices came whispering over the hills of time as we sat and talked together of their living, as we hoped, in a more beautiful and happy world. Her pure, true character is reflected as perfectly as a still, clear pond of water mirrors the flower that sleeps on its rim.

After spending a few days with this nurse of mine, the time came for us to part again. As I took her soft tender hand in mine, the other arm being entwined about my neck, she said in a sweet voice, "John, be a good boy and meet me in Heaven." I responded through tears with visible emotion, "We are both standing in the lonely glimmering twilight of the evening of life, awaiting and watching for the dawning of the morning, the cloudless morning of eternal day."

J. T. KITCHEN.

Windsor, Va.

SACRIFICIAL SERVICE

Men judge by outward appearances; God by inward motives. Men often misjudge; God never. Bounties that men receive are often accepted as being in the natural course of things, while God knows that they come because of sacrificial service. Could men but realize the amount of sacrificial service done for their benefit they would be more appreciative. It is Christ's sacrifice that draws all men to Him. We Americans eat Chinese rice by the forkful or spoonful never thinking that some human sufferer picked that same rice grain by grain. We wear our nice clothes never dreaming that some poor boy or girl sacrificed an education and spent the very vitality of youth in manufacturing the goods; or for that, perchance, a widowed mother worked long, weary hours in a mill when health demanded that she be out doors and her children cried for her motherly care, yet she worked that we might enjoy the comforts. Sacrificial service is the highest form of human endeavor.

Not all heroic souls fought on Flander's field or in any part of the recent bloody conflict. (All glory to those who did!) There are in our midst women and men doing just as heroic tasks. I shall be pardoned for a personal reference, I am sure, for why should all the flowers be saved until one cannot see them?

We have all been delighted to know of the great and good work that has been done at the Christian Orphanage. It is a joy to know that the Institution is free from debt and the needed improvements are being made. Yet I dare say that but few know of the heroic sacrifice of our excellent Superintendent, Brother Chas. D. Johnston. He knows how to refuse other work that offers more money, fewer hours, less worry, and more time with his family and for personal enjoyment. Only a great heart could refuse. More than once he has done it. The Christian Church will never know how willingly and how freely this man of God has sacrificed all the things that men call dear in order that he might serve his Church and his God by being a father to the fatherless. In this sacrifice his good wife joined heartily up till the last day of her earthly life—her last provision being for the Orphanage.

As you have seen in THE SUN she gave $200, and out of his meager salary he gives $300 with it. This is not all these good people give by any means. This is a special free-will offering in order that the Orphanage may do a greater work, and it means sacrifice. Surely none of us will make a greater sacrifice than our Superintendent is doing. It is no easy matter for him to be away from his own motherless children all the day and travel twelve miles each day that he may be with them at night. Thi Christian Church should never allow any call from this man and this Institution to go unheeded.

Remember, fathers and mothers, that when you have given a dime or a dollar you have made no sacrifice. You still live with your darling babies and they have plenty. Think, will you, of other babies just as innocent and helpless as yours pleading for a home in our Orphanage where they may have bread to eat and clothes to wear. No less than twenty of them are now pleading for shelter. It is no fault of theirs that they are homeless. If the Church refuses them a home where shall they go? The answer is with you. Are you willing to sacrifice in order to serve?

F. C. LESTER.

Graham, N. C.

EASTER SUNDAY

This is the day when the whole Christian world commemorates the resurrection of the Savior. It dates back to the earliest Christian times and is participated in by Greek and Roman, Catholic and Protestant. At first, there was much confusion as to the exact date. The Roman Emperor Constantine called the Council of Nice in 325 A. D. This body fixed upon the first Sunday after the full moon following the vernal equinox.

Many curious customs grew up with the observance, such as the lighting of great candles in the cathedrals of the old world. These were called paschal candles, and one in Durham, England, was with its candlestick, seventy feet high. Many of the old customs were done away with at the time of the reformation, but others, notably the part played by colored eggs, have survived.

The rolling of eggs on the White House lawn, by the children of Washington, is one of our American customs.

In this country too many make it an occasion for the display of new hats, toothpick heels, and fine clothing. Surely this is a curious way to commemorate the memory of Him who had no where to lay His head.

D. A. LONG.

Tampa, Fla., April 20, 1919.

LAST MOMENT EVENTS

The United States is to furnish Latin America 14 ships for trade purposes.

The peace questions are near a settlement so a communication fixed.

Greensboro has just suffered a disastrous explosion thought to be the plot of enemies. The Texas Oil Company's plant was blown up. One life was lost, several injured and the damage was many thousand dollars.

French Government has denied the German delegation of a sight seeing tour, fearing that such would cause a great disturbance.

AT RANDOM

Teacher—"If a farmer sold 1470 bushels of wheat at $3.17 a bushel what would he get?"
Boy—"An automobile."—*American Boy.*

For Sale.—Baker's business; good trade; large oven; present owner's been in it for seven years; best reasons for leaving.—*Herald and Presbyter.*

"Are you going to have a garden this year?"
"No, it isn't my turn to make a garden. I'm going to keep chickens this year and let my neighbors make the garden."—*Exchange.*

Specialist—You are suffering from nerve exhaustion. I can cure you for the small sum of $2,000.
Patient—And will my nerve be as good as yours then?—*Montreal Star.*

Sandy (newly arrived in Canadian forest land)—Whatna beast's yon?
Native—A young moose.
Sandy—Och, haud yer tongue! if that's a young moose, I'd like to see ane o' yer auld rats!—*Punch.*

THE COOK KNOWS

"How late shall you remain at your summer cottage this year?"
"Ask the cook."—*Boston Transcript.*

Mrs. Mary L. Sockwell.—Am wishing you much success with THE CHRISTIAN SUN. I enjoy it so much.

Help us to make THE SUN better. There many ways in which you can help.

THE CHRISTIAN ORPHANAGE

ENCOURAGING REPORT

: The response to the call for the Easter Offering has been beautiful. We just lack a small amount this week being two-thirds of the way to the goal. Eighty-nine churches have responded to the call. One hundred and thirty to hear from.

/We trust that all will join in this great work and make this offering and mail it in. We are hoping to go over the top in this offering and go far enough to make the home for the little children look near in the future. We have received, some very encouraging letters in regard to the "Little Children's Home" and we feel sure our people will see that it is built in the near future. The good ladies have been very kind to us in responding to the call for sheets. The following have been sent in since our last report:

Mrs. E. A. Floyd, Abanda, Ala., two sheets; Mrs. Ella Hall, Great Bridge, Va., three spreads; Adna Thomas Williamson, Great Bridge, Va., one dress for little girl; Mrs. R. A. Thompson, Altamahaw, N. C., two sheets; Annie Rippy, one pillow case and one table scarf; Mrs. W. A. Paschal, one pair of pillow cases; Mary Peel McCray, one pair of pillow cases; Lottie McRay, one pair of pillow cases; Mrs. C. W. Isley, one pair of pillow cases; Miss Ida Keck, one sheet; Mrs. A. C. Madren, four yards of goods; Fannie Paschal, one pair of pillow cases; Mrs. H. R. Lowe, one sheet; Ladies' Aid Society Isle of Wight C. H. Christian church, four sheets, one counterpane; Ladies of New Hope Christian church, eight sheets, pair pillow cases; Mrs. Speight, Sunbury, N. C., two sheets; Mrs. J. H. Massey, Durham, N. C., two sheets, two pair towels; Ladies' New Lebanon church, 16 cans of fruit; Rountree-Holland Co., Norfolk, two crates of oranges for Easter.

The fertilizer people are good to us, too, and the following have contributed five bags of fertilizer each for our spring crops: F. S. Royster Guano Company, Swift & Co., American Fertilizer Co., Navassa Guano Co., Baugh & Sons Co., Old Buck Guano Co., Pamlico Guano Co., Virginia-Carolina Chemical Co., Careleigh Chemical Co., and Union Guano Co.

CHAS. D. JOHNSTON, *Supt.*

REPORT FOR MAY 7, 1919

Amount brought forward, $3,509.45.

Children's Offerings

Willie Staylor, 80 cents; Milla Wellons Staylor, 80 cents; Pauline Trotter, 10 cents; Ethel Leigh Joyner, 50 cents; Total, $2.20.

Monthly Sunday School Offerings
(Eastern Virginia Conference)

Holy Neck, $4.00; Antioch, $2.00.

(North Carolina Conference)

Pope's Chapel, N. C., $5.00; Apple's Chapel, $1.00; Morrisville, $2.00.

(Alabama Conference)

Mt. Zion, $2.65; Wadley, $1.49, Total $18.14.

Special

Ladies' Aid Society, Holy Neck church, $25.00; J. H. Jones, one support of children, $30.00; Dr. J. F. Burnett, Sec. A. C. C., $1.00; Total $56.00.

Easter Offerings

Linville, S. S., (Va.), $21.50; Christian Chapel church, $20.00; Mrs. Helen B. Phelps, Powell, Pa., $5.00; Lebanon, S. S., $4.00; New Center S. S., $7.75; Liberty church, (Vance Co.), $16.00; Spring Hill, (Ala.), $5.20; New Hope church, (N. C.), $9.15; Wake Chapel church, $43.12; Belew's Creek church, $1.50; South Norfolk church, $77.00; Mrs. W. H. Speight, $1.00; Edgar Speight, $1.00; Ellen Speight, $1.00; Holy Neck church and S. S., $105.50; Union Grove S. S., $13.20; Members Mt. Auburn church, $68.00; Liberty church, $4.50; Kellam Grove S. S., $5.00; New Hope S. S., $6.60; Locktown Christian S. S., Locktown, N. J., $5.00; Union S. S., Virgilina, Va., $12.50; Big Oak church, $9.68; R. E. Warren, for Sunday school, $1.67; Dr. R. S. Stephenson, Dover, Del., $2.00; Vaughnsville Christian church, Vaughnsville, Ohio, $9.75; Pleasant Ridge church, (Additional), $1.23; North Highlands S. S., $51.25; Shady Grove S. S. (Ala.), $6.00; Mrs. N. A. Whitman, Warren, Ind., $1.00; Durham S. S., $52.25; Pope's Chapel S. S., $2.75; Pleasant Ridge, $6.10; Mrs. Kate Ives, Norfolk, Va., $3.00; Christian Light, $14.65; New Elam S. S. and church, $50.60; Grace's Chapel S. S., $8.50; Monticello church and S. S., $7.20; Apple's Chapel S. S. and church, $9.40; Third Ave. S. S., Danville, Va., $14.05; Morrisville, S. S., $11.50; Berea church and Sunday school, $50.00; Spring Hill church, $17.39; Cypress Chapel S. S., $32.10; Damascus, S. S., $18.00.

(Barretts Sunday School)

W. F. Richardson, 75 cents; A. G. Barnes, $1.00; R. U. Lane, $2.00; James W. Rollins, $1.00; Cosco Spivey, $1.00; E. T. Rollins and Sister, $1.00; P. A. Hines, 50 cents; P. H. Barrett, $1.00; Mrs. Esta Jones, $1.00; J. F. Wellons, $5.00; W. G. Rollins, $1.00; E. F. Kitchen, $1.00; Thomas Spivey, 5 cents; R. H. Rollins, 10 cents; Total, $16.40.

Pleasant Hill church, $17.06; New Hope S. S., (Ala.), $18.25; Wadley S. S., $5.62; Palm Street S. S., $7.50; Auburn church, $15.00; Antioch church, (Chatham), $10.00; Ambrose church, $15.60; Spoon's Chapel, $3.30; Antioch S. S., Frankfort, Ind., $20.00; Concord church, $8.89; Mt. Oliyet Sunday school, $5.00; Total, $956.21.

Total for the week, $1,032.55; Grand total, $4,542.00.

CHILDREN'S LETTER

Dear Uncle Charley: Here is 50 cents for Easter, and 30 cents for March, April and May. I hope all the cousins got along fine Easter.—*Mills Wellons Staylor.*

You are a fine little boy, and pay for one month in advance.—*"Uncle Charley."*

Dear Uncle Charley: I hope the cousins had a good time Easter. We had an Easter egg hunt. I found two eggs. We went about two miles out in the country and had to walk. We had some ice cream on the lawn of Mrs. Powell. Since we have been in Edenton we go to the Baptist church. There is not a Christian church in Edenton. Aren't we the only ones who take THE CHRISTIAN SUN here? Enclosed find 30 cents for March, April and May and 50 cents for Easter, even if it has already passed.—*Willie Staylor.*

Our little folks had an Easter egg hunt, too. One little girl found one dozen. She was an expert on finding, wasn't she?—"Uncle Charley."

Dear Uncle Charley: Since writing my last letter, we have moved to Asheboro. Uncle Charley, I have lots of dolls, and I love them all, but the one I love best is "George Henry." I would like to visit the Orphanage and see the cousins. I am sending my dues for April. Much love and best wishes.—Pauline Trotter.

You ought to have my little girl to play dolls with you. She is very fond of them.—"Uncle Charley."

Dear Uncle Charley: I have not written you for the past two weeks. I have had pneumonia but am able to be up now, although not strong enough to go back to school. Enclosed find 50 cents for my dues. I hope you and the cousins are well.—Ethel Leigh Joyner.

Well Ethel, I am glad you are better and will soon be well again. Pneumonia is dangerous. I am always uneasy when any one has it, till they get better.—"Uncle Charley."

THE LITTLE COOK

By Florence Jones Hadley

Sometimes when mamma goes away
And leaves the work for me,
I quickly tidy all the house,
Then hurry to get tea.

I try and try so hard to think
Of something good to eat,
And everything that I like best
Somehow seems to be sweet.

I get some cookies and some tarts,
A cake all frosted white,
A jar of jam, a jelly mold,
Then tea is ready quite.

And when my papa hurries home
As hungry as can be,
He laughs and says he's very glad
He has a cook like me.
—From Child's Gem.

MY RACER

Some people have buggies and horses to ride
And autos with just lots of room.
But the racer that pleases me best of them all
Is my mother's old-fashioned broom.
—L. Æ. W., in Our Boys and Girls.

THE GOLDEN RULE OF OUT-OF-

There's a Golden Rule to govern our visits to the woods,
The pastures, fields and meadows of country neighborhoods
Where we go for flowers and berries and other treasures wild,
'Tis a rule that should be memorized and kept by every child.

The sign "No Trespassing" is placed for those who take no pains
To put up bars and fasten gates when leaving fields and lanes,
And for those who break the branches off and tear the fences down—
Who left their manners far behind when they tramped in from town,

The little signs along the road were also meant for those
Who "hook" the farmer's apples from beneath his very nose;
For those who tease his watch dog and rob the phoebe's nest;
Most farmers think such folks are worse than a caterpillar pest.

Should we be always welcome in the country, you and I
Must never be ill-mannered nor always try
To keep Dame Nature's golden rule, which should be widely known—
Treat woods and field and all therein as if they were thine own.
—Annie Balcomb Wheeler, in Christian Work.

A TRUTHFUL BOY

How people do trust a truthful boy! We never worry about him when he is out of sight. We never say, "I wonder where he is; I wish I knew what he is doing." We know that he is all right, and that when he comes home we will know all about it and get it straight. We don't have to ask him where he is going, or how long he will be gone every time he leaves the house. We don't have to call him back and make him "solemnly promise!" the same thing over and over. When he says, "Yes, I will," or "No, I won't," just once, that settles it.—Robert Burdette.

THE OTHER ROBIN

Montreal, as most people know, is blessed with long, cold winters. The snow covers the ground for about five months, while the thermometer is often down below zero. Consequently all the song-birds leave early in the autumn and do not return till toward the end of April or the beginning of May. Of course the English sparrow stays, for the sparrow can live, it seems, in any climate. The crow and the flicker also stay, but they cannot be classed as "song-birds."

This winter it was a surprise for one to see a robin feeding on the dried berries which still hang on the Virginia creeper which covers part of our house. We wondered at first what had kept him from flying off with all the other robins last October, at which time we often see large flocks making their annual migration South, but we soon found that one of his wings had been injured, and this had no doubt been the reason for his enforced stay.

He must have found some very warm shelter in which to spend the nights (and I assure you we have had one or two very cold ones), although the winter, on the whole, has been very mild—for Montreal. We could not but pity our robin, for we knew he must be very lonely, with only the sparrows, who are his "sworn enemies," for company. The robins and the sparrow, it is sad to relate, fight all summer long. One morning about Christmas-time we saw for the first time the injured robin's mate! The two were having a very substantial breakfast of berries. Since the return of the "other robin" we often see them feeding together.

Now the most interesting part of my story is the fact that the "other robin" came all the way back from the South. Heretofore we always thought that robins did not remain mated after the young birds had been fledged. We knew that the old nest was never reoccupied, and it seemed natural that a new mate might be chosen to make the new nest in the far South after the long flight. (Our robins never build a second nest in the season.) And then also, as the flocks going South number hundreds, it would seem likely that mates might get separated by miles and miles, and never find each other again. We know now, however, that robins remain mated, and we also know that mated robins will seek each other, even going hundreds of miles to do so.

At Christmas the long-separated one having appeared for the first time, I have no doubt that last October, when the time came for the long Southern journey, and hundreds of robins congregated, the "other robin" flew off with the great flock, and did not miss her mate till the end of the long journey had been reached. When she could not find her mate, she must have started North, probably flying over exactly the same ground, searching every corner, covering hundreds of miles. How far she flew may be roughly estimated by the time it took to get back here. It was about three months.—*Lewis Skaife, in The Christian Register.*

A Canadian named Casey was appointed to a government place. Technically it had to be held by a lawyer, which Casey was not. The benchers of the Law Society, however, undertook to obviate the technicality. "Well, Casey," said the examiner, "what do you know about law, anyway?" "To tell the truth," replied the candidate, "I don't know a single thing." The examiner reported in his affidavit "that he had examined Mr. Casey as to his knowledge of the law, and, to the best of his information and belief he had answered the questions that he had put to him correctly." The aspirant was admitted.—*Law Notes.*

CHRISTIAN EDUCATION

CHRISTIAN EDUCATION AND THE CALL OF THE MINISTRY*

Text: Study to show thyself approved unto God a workman that needeth not to be ashamed rightly dividing the word of truth. II Tim. 2:15.

Our subject today, which is one that has been assigned for the occasion, is of a two-fold nature but I think that both phases of the subject have their basis in the words of our text.

When Paul said to Timothy, "Study to show thyself approved unto God a workman that needeth not to be ashamed," he proclaimed what is fundamentally the soundest principle of our present day system of education; that it should be God approved and therefore Christian in character.

When Paul said to Timothy that such a presentation before God was necessary for handling aright (R. V.) the word of truth he was explicitly stating the qualifications accompanying the call to the ministry. Timothy himself had heard the call to the ministry and had already been vested with its special prerogatives by the Apostle Paul.

At the time Timothy received these inspiring words from the Apostle, he was actively engaged in the ministry somewhere in the Northwestern part of Asia Minor while Paul was spending the last days of his final imprisonment in a Roman prison.

His friends were fast deserting him, and knowing the perilous times through which the church would have to pass because of persecution, the strange doctrines that would arise to deceive even the very elect, and momentarily expecting his fateful end, with the sword of the executioner almost ready to be unsheathed, he hastily dispatched this letter to Timothy, his son in the gospel, requesting him if possible to come shortly to him, but nevertheless "to hold fast the form of sound words," "to be strong in the grace that is in Christ Jesus," "to suffer hardship with me as a good soldier of Jesus Christ," and finally in the words of our text the Apostle as a last council to his faithful friend if he could not come to him, exhorts Timothy to equip himself for the great work that was before him by giving "diligence to present thyself approved unto God, a workman that needeth not to be ashamed handling aright the word of truth." (R. V.)

He made it plain to Timothy that it was not the work of the minister to strive or be contentious, but to be apt to teach and patient; in meekness correcting those who were of an opposite opinion.

I submit to you brethren, that herein do we have set up a splendid standard of preparation for the gospel ministry. It could well be translated into what we today are pleased to call our standard of Christian Education.

If a Christian Education may justly be required in preparation for the gospel ministry, and since a considerable portion of the period of preparation is the same for all professions as for the ministry then the logical inference is that the best kind of preparation with which the youth of our country should be equipped for whatever calling in life, is a Christian Education.

Among the many institutions of learning the college may be said to be the chief exponent of Christian Education. Aside from the home it is a college life that Christian character gets its greatest pronouncement.

If the College is the soul of the American nation as the

(Continued on Page 12)

WORSHIP AND MEDITATION

BITS OF CHEER

Catherine of Siena, whatever her sufferings, was always jocun, "ever laughing in the Lord." The blind Madame du Deffand rejoiced that her affliction was not rheumatism; Spurgeon's receipt for content- ment was never to chew pills, but to swallow the dis- agreeable and have done with it; Darwin's comfort was that he had never consciously done anything to gain applause; and Jecerson never ceased affirming his belief in the satisfying powers of common day- light, common pleasures, and all the common relation of life. Essipoff, when commiserated on the smallness of her hands, insisted that longer ones would be cum- bersome. Robert Schauffler's specific for a blue Mon- day is to whistle all the Brahms tunes he can remem- ber. Dr. Cuyler, when very ill, replied to a relative's suggestion of the glorious company waiting him above: "I've got all eternity to visit with those old fellows; I am in no hurry to go;" and old Aunt Mandy, when asked why she was so constantly cheerful, replied, "Lor', chile, I jes' wear this world like a loose gar- ment."—*Lucy Elliot Keeler.*

ENVIRONMENT

God puts His own with the people who and in the place which will tend most to develop the spiritual graces.

He puts one who is quick with one who is slow, and one who is quiet with one who is talkative; that the one who is quiet may be patient with the one who is talkative.

He puts one who is orderly with one who is untidy, that both may learn lessons. Often our environment is but an answer to our prayers.

We pray for patience, and God sends those who tax us to the utmost; for "tribulation worketh pa- tience" (Rom. 5:3).

We pray for submission, and God sends suffering, for we learn obedience by the things we suffer. (Heb. 5:8).

We pray for unselfishness, and God gives opportuni- ties to sacrifice ourselves by thinking on the "things of others" (Phil. 2:4).

We pray for victory, and the things of the world sweep down upon us in a storm of temptation; for "this is the victory that overcometh the world, even our faith", (I John 5:4; 4:4).

We pray for humility and strength, and some mes- senger of Satan torments us until we lie in the dust, crying to God for its removal (2 Cor. 12:7, 8).

We pray for union with Jesus, and God severs na- tural ties and lets our best friends misunderstand or become indifferent to us (John 15:2).

We pray for more love and God sends peculiar suffering, and puts us with apparently unlovely per- sons and lets them say things to rasp nerves, lacerate

the heart, and sting the conscience; for "love suffers long and is kind; love is not impolite, love is not pro- voked, love bears, love believes, hopes, and endures; love never faileth" (1 Cor. 13:4-8; John 15:9, 10).

We ask to follow Jesus, and He separates us from home and hindred, for He himself said: "Whosoever he be of you that forsaketh not all that he hath, he cannot be My disciple." (Luke 14:33).

We pray for the Lamb life, and are given a portion of lowly service, or we are injured and must seek no redress; for He was led as a lamb to the slaughter, and opened not His mouth (Isa. 53:7).

We pray for gentleness and there comes a perfect storm of temptation to yield to harshness and irrit- ability.

We pray for quietness, and everything within and around us increases, that we may learn when He giveth quietness no one can make trouble (Job 24:29).—*Miss Hulda Stumpf, Kijabe, B. E. A., in "Africa Inland Mission."*

OVERLOOKED RICHES

But in spite of God's continual revelation in star and ower, in conscience and human love, we have struggled in the dark. Insufficient the wisdom of Plato, the art of Phidias, the genius of Homer! After centuries of research humanity bowed to "the un- known God." Insufficient, too, our own philosophy, with its Kants and Schopenhauers, its Ibsens and Omar Khayyams! So thickly our souls are encrusted in sin! So utterly blinded our vision!

What else is there that God might do to make Him- self known? The voice of mountain and sea and sky has left no echo in our hearts. Even conscience speaks with stammering lips. On the height of the centuries stands that master of scientists, Du Bois Reymond, re- peating in his own words the confession of Pilate, "We know nothing and we shall know nothing."

Clearly there is but one thing left. God may descend from His height into our depth. He may become one of us. He may assume a human voice. He may live among us and speak with our own tongue.—*Andrew Bard.*

THE WALLS ARE BREAKING DOWN

If one doubts that the walls around ancient China are not breaking down, read this: "Three thousand big bricks from the Wall around the forbidden city of Chington, West China, have been contributed by the Government for the foundation of a Methodist church in the city."

J. O. ATKINSON.

"Come unto me all ye that are laden and I will give you rest."

NOTES

Rev. J, V. Knight writes that the Greensboro church is experiencing a great meeting.

Mr. Z. H. Cotner, Clemmons, N. C., a dear friend of THE SUN, was a caller at THE SUN office last Monday.

Rev. W. B. Fuller has been discharged from the Y. M. C. A. work and is now at his home near Henderson, N. C.

Rev. E. M. Carter has helped us to increase THE SUN's circulation and financial budget during the past few days. Thanks!

We are grateful to the many kind friends who are responding to our call that their subscriptions be paid now so as to help us during the summer months. Many thanks, dear friends.

Rev. J. E. Franks, Cary, N. C., does not cease his work for THE SUN when a campaign is over. He just keeps on sending us new subscribers and renewals. Last year we called on Brother Franks to tell us how he did all of this but he never answered directly, but a few days after we wrote him, he sent us another list. If he does not have any patent on the principle we will appreciate it if he will tell the brethren how he does it.

We have received the following communication from Dr. P. H. Fleming written from Conneaut, Ohio: "Please announce on that there will be all day services at Union on the second Sunday in May. Preaching at 11 A. M., and also at 2 P. M. There will be quarterly meeting at 2 P. M. on Saturday before. The Deacons are called to meet in the church at 1:30 P. M., (Saturday). The Lord's Supper will be administered at the close of the morning service Sunday. Two visiting ministers are expected to be with us "

Just as we go to press, we are in receipt of three copies of The Conneaut News Herald giving splendid write-ups concerning the American Christian Convention. The papers received are dated April 28, 29, 30 and May 1. They do not contain any definite accounts of the Convention, and so we have no special news for our constituency this week from the Convention.

There is to be a lecture in the city auditorium at Raleigh Monday night, May 12, in which all CHRISTIAN SUN readers will be interested and which they will do well to attend, if possible. This lecture will be "The Life Story of Gypsy Smith," as told by his son and will be given under the auspices of the Raleigh church. This lecture will not only tell the inspiring story of the life of that great evangelist, Gypsy Smith, but it will also tell about many of the customs and ideals of the Gypsy race. Admission will be free.

THE FORWARD MOVEMENT

(Rev. Warren H. Denison, D. D., Superintendent)

Splendid Easter Results

A splendid harvest seems to have been reaped in all sections of our Brotherhood and the Forward Movement rejoices to hear the first reports of the Easter ingathering and they come from every section. The Forward Movement is laying much emphasis upon its evangelistic program, and we are expecting all our churches to lay much emphasis upon an all-the-year evangelistic spirit. Easter, we hope, was only the first fruits of a new and enlarged evangelistic effort to reach the 50,000 set as our Forward Movement goal to be added to the churches.

Early Reports

Lima, Ohio—28 members received, Rev. E. A. Watkins, pastor; Rosemont, Va.—39 members received, Rev. G. O. Lankford, pastor; Conneaut, O.—20 members received, Rev. A. E. Kemp, pastor; Columbus, O.—6 members received, Rev. A. M. Hainer, pastor; Versailles, O.—28 members received, Rev. D. G. Pleasant, pastor; Newton, Ill.—8 members received, Rev. A. H. Bennett, pastor; Warren, Ind.—4 members received, Rev. Hugh A. Smith, pastor; Assonet, Mass.—2 members received, Rev. Donald P. Hulburt, Pastor; Greenville, O.—28 members received, Rev. F. H. Peters, pastor; Argos, Ind.—50 members received, Rev. A. W. Sparks, pastor; Eaton, O.—91 since February 9, Rev. Hiley Baker, pastor; West Liberty, O.—12 members received, Rev. T. C. House, pastor; Amesbury, Mass.—8 members received, Rev. R. G. English, pastor; Oshawa, Ont. —10 members received, Rev. Calvin J. Felton, pastor; Ravena, N. Y.—15 members received, Rev. A. B. Kendall, pastor; Hartwick, N. Y.—14 members received, Rev. S. L. Beougher, pastor; Haubstadt, Ind.—2 members received, Rev. C. C. Tarr, pastor; Dayton, O.— First Church, 25 members received, Rev. McD. Howsare, pastor; Vanderneer Park, Brooklyn, N. Y.—10 members received, Rev. L. E. Johnson, pastor; Vaughnsville, O.—19 members received, Rev. Rufus Emmert, pastor; Urbana, Ill.—Membership certificates were given Easter Sunday to all who united with the church during the year and we had a 14 per cent net gain in membership during the year, Rev. R. C. Helfenstein, pastor.

By next week's issue of THE SUN we hope to hear from every pastor in the Convention who received any members into his church at the close of his Easter campaign.

If your church has not yet appointed a four-minute man, please attend to the matter very soon and report the name and address to the Forward Movement headquarters, C. P. A. Building, Dayton, Ohio. This four-minute man will be able to render large service to your church and to the Forward Movement.

Did you get a letter from this office last week calling attention to our needs for the summer? Let us hear from you if you did.

CHRISTIAN EDUCATION

(Continued from Page 9)

late Professor Munsterberg of Harvard has said it must be because that here Christian Character is not only fostered, but encouraged and made to function in all student activities.

The test for the continued existence of all college activities is: are they productive of the elements of Christian character? If not, such activities find but little place in the student life in college.

The first requisite of a Christian college is that its faculty be not only well trained for their respective duties but that the personnel of that faculty shall be distinctively Christian in character.

It is a Christian teaching force that gives the first tinge of Christian color to college life. This is supplemented by the additional hues of a Christian student body and the result is a beautiful reflection of the life of the Great Master Teacher of us all.

Under such environment and in such an atmosphere college is a safe place to send our boys and girls for the development and training of their powers and faculties.

One who is just trained to think and act without regard to a proper direction of his thinking and acting is a dangerous person to society. There are many such persons now, who instead of going by name, go by number in some of our State institutions.

To get a one sided education may be to get a dangerous thing. The danger, however, is not so much in the getting as in the forgetting. To forget God; to forget the deeper things of the spiritual life; to fail to get the understanding heart in the process of getting an education, is what the wise man pronounced "vanity of vanities."

Solomon tried his wisdom without God; he sought every human pleasure and folly that was under the sun and when he had tried all he summed it up in these words: "All was vanity and a vexation of spirit. "Let us hear the conclusion of the whole matter, fear God and keep his commandments for this is the whole duty of man."

A Christian education will bring one to this same conclusion without the marks of a prodigal life. It prepares the individual not only to face his task but to face the environment surrounding his task. Many a person has succeeded at his task but went down to defeat before the evils of his environment.

Education prepares one for his task. Christian education prepares him for a life.

Education is no mystical process; it is simply the unfolding of the possibilities of life as a scroll.

Religion is a part of life and Christian character is the vital product of religion. If, therefore, Christian character is not shown on the unfolded scroll of life, that education was incomplete, onesided and will be barren of the best and most permanent results.

Christian education is obtained in the institutions where Christ is in the curriculum and where Christian character is held in par excellence with the best that the institution has to offer.

I am glad that we have an institution of our own in our midst that emphasizes just such preparation for a life work.

Elon College has done and is still doing a work in the Southland that is having its telling effect in the churches perhaps as no where else. A large number of the churches of the Southern Christian Convention are now being served by her graduates, or men who have received Christian training within her walls; and her ambitions are far beyond present attainments.

But Elon's future is now in the crucible. Shall she take her rightful place among the standardized colleges of the land and thus maintain the splendid standard of work she has already been doing, as well as her bright and hopeful future. Whether she shall enjoy this splendid prestige all depends upon whether Elon's friends are her friends in time of need. The standardization fund of $125,000 must be met and it will be met.

Elon's friends will not see her lose her rank and place among the colleges of the country and ultimately her student body, when the raising of the above sum will insure her future.

The Southern Christian Convention has issued the call for twenty recruits for the ministry, annually, for the next five years, and Elon's share in this work is not only to furnish her quota, but to provide Christian training for these recruits.

Shall we not earnestly pray that the Lord shall move upon the hearts of at least twenty of the best young men of our churches to answer this great and important summons this year?

It seems to me that no church has risen to its highest duty until it has furnished at least one recruit for the gospel ministry.

Must we continue to look to the little old church in the wildwood for recruits to the ministry? I know that upholstered pews and stained glass windows do not produce preachers, but a Christian atmosphere, and prayer and Christian admnition from parents and friends and pastors does create a productive environment for the recruiting of the ministry.

If the home and school and the church were sufficiently permeated by the spirit of the Master, the ministry and other Christian callings would not go wanting for recruits.

Young men and women have no right to discriminate against the call to definite Christian work, without giving it any consideration, just because the call to the commercial life may permit of more luxury, more salary, a looser life religiously. Perhaps due consideration of the work of the ministry or other Christian work may be all that is necessary to show the need and to prepare the heart to hear that still small voice calling to this particular work.

I think that God would be greatly pleased if more young men of the surrendered life type, would offer their services to Him in the gospel ministry instead of waiting for some voice to speak to them, or some peculiar demonstration of power to come over them.

Let there first be the surrendered life, a consciousness of the need, a fitness for the work, and a willingness to go, and surely the Lord will bid you enter in.

*A sermon preached by Rev. W. M. Jay, Holland, Va.

TWICE FIVE TRIUMPHS

The old Roman generals used to affix to their names the number of times they had marched in regal procession over the broken walls of the city of Rome. They called these processions triumphs. A general could triumph in Rome only after he had won victory elsewhere. To show her great confidence in her conquering hero's ability to preserve her at any cost, Rome would tear down her own protecting wall to let him ride in.

No such triumph as this are those to which reference is here made. We are getting away, forever I hope, from the celebration of one nation's victory over another. I write now of the triumph of generosity over self-interest, of the upward and outward look for Christian workers, and of a new day just dawning. Twice five triumphs the Lord has granted us this week, and two preachers wear smiles that will not come off, since they irradiate from happy souls within.

On last Saturday I landed in Waverly, Va., and was greeted by Rev. Jas. L. Foster, the ministerial outpost westward of the Eastern Virginia Conference, a sentryman worth while, believe me. That afternoon and Sunday morning Barrett's church, by the generosity of a promising group of her younger men and devout women not a few, went on the map. Sunday afternoon old Spring Hill, one of the landmarks of Christian history, a tower of strength even now in her old age, went the second mile. Monday Centerville executed the same rare, no prevailing, stunt for the Kingdom, and Waverly gave more than four times her quota, and is not done yet, thus taking her place with Elon and Pleasant Grove by achieving three stars on her recognition card. Uncle Jim was a whole menagerie of smiles, a full nursery of blossoming loveliness. His rainbow countenance was something to behold when the grand climax was reached.

To Raleigh next the journey lay. At mid-week prayer meeting Pastor Eastes presented me to a fine body of the Lord's elect. The next day we went at it, rain to the contrary notwithstanding. Here again a group of young men put the thing across, and what the wise ones said was impossible is a sweet achievement. Raleigh is on the map, and Brother Eastes, the proud father of a fine son, is the pastor of a people who have lifted up their eyes from the hard grind of a severe local struggle to see the stars of the Kingdom's glory and to discover that it is good, blessed, more blessed to give than to receive. Keep your eye on Raleigh. Her young men have seen visions, and Raleigh is destined not only to become self-supporting, but to do large things for others these days ahead.

Five More Funds

Brother J. D. Gray, Waverly, Va., this week gave $5,000. He is number 16, sweet sixteen, in this galaxy of the great-souled of our Church in this new time.

Also at Waverly, Brother J. W. West founded a fund of $1,000. Judge J. F. West, member of Elon's Provisional Board of Trustees, did the same, and Rev. Jas. L. Foster likewise in loving memory of his sainted parents, Deacon James Henderson and Lucinda Fitch Foster.

At Raleigh, Brother P. T. Hines, in his twenty-fourth year, the youngest man yet to do so, gave $1,000, in memory of his father, Deacon E. D. Hines. Brother Hines is a tither, but to make this large gift he had to add to his tithe "an offering to the Lord." He is learning the blessing of the second mile personally. God multiply his kind.

And so this week I have had twice five triumphs. Five churches have gone over the top and five noble souls, the Lord's anointed for this good time, have founded funds for the Kingdom's advance in our Brotherhood. Of such is the Kingdom of Heaven.

Such are the salt of the earth. Such are the light of the world.

I like these Christian triumphs better than those of the Roman conquerors. Don't you?

Pray that God may continue to own and bless His work and this cause.

W. A. HARPER.

MORE TRIUMPHS YET

I reached home Friday night and found three more triumphs in store.

Deacon W. W. Tuck, Virgilina, upon the solicitation of Dr. W. C. Wicker, had founded a fund of $1,000.

Brother J. M. Darden, Suffolk, Va., had sent in $1,000 to found the L. H. Whitley Fund, Brother Whitley being one of Elon's noblest friends and father-in-law of Brother Darden.

Brother B. W. Card, Raleigh, upon the solicitation of Pastor Eastes, had founded a fund of $1,100 in memory of his sainted mother, whose sweet life he thus perpetuates in a tender manner.

And so the cause of our Master continues to triumph. To Him be the praise and thanks.

W. A. H.

GLEANINGS FROM THE SECULAR WORLD

The German delegation to the peace conference arrived last week. The speaker of the delegation was soon overcome by emotion and the first session of the meeting with the peace council lasted only five minutes.

Last week there was unearthed in New York a plot that was scheduled to kill a number of prominent citizens. Sixteen bombs found securely wrapped and mailed to prominent people in the various parts of the country. One of the bombs was addressed to Senator Lee S. Overman at his home in Salisbury, N. C.

Three giant hydroplanes of the American Navy started a flight across the Atlantic last week.

Americans seem to object to the International Court to try the ex-Kaiser. The American delegates are unwilling to punish the Kaiser if he did not order atrocities. Others were implicated with him, it seems.

The Belgian Government seems somewhat dissatisfied with the peace terms offered it.

Secretary Daniels, who is now in Europe, is expected to sail on next week.

Parts of California suffered an earthquake last week.

Repeating the Lord's Prayer is not living it. It is not enough to report it.

If you attend the American Christian Convention, let THE SUN have a note from your pen.

Are all the boys and girls in your community in the Sunday school?

Sunday School and Christian Endeavor

SUNDAY SCHOOL LESSON FOR MAY 18

The Grace of God.—Gen. 6:8; Ex. 34:6-7.; II Cor. 12:9; Eph. 2:4-10; Titus 2:11-14.

Golden Text:. We shall be saved through the grace of the Lord Jesus. —Acts 15:11.

Devotional Reading: Ps. 32:1-11.

. *Thought for Teachers*

God's grace is a sufficient grace. He supplies all our needs. How? Not out of his riches; nor even according to my needs or my petitions, but *according to His riches* in glory through Christ Jesus our Lord. Can you measure the riches of God? Then you can measure His grace. .

He kept Noah from the flood of waters; He kept Lot from the flood of fire; He kept Abram from being overwhelmed by a godless generation in Ur. Is He less able to keep you today in the flood of worldliness? But you say your faith is and you are not able to lay hold on Him? Thank God, you don't have to lay hold. His strength is made perfect in *weakness* for as long as you trust in yourself, you don't trust Him entirely. Don't try to hang on to God; let God hang on to you. *Underneath* are the everlasting arms. "Just let go, and—let God."

MRS. FRED BULLOCK.

CHRISTIAN ENDEAVOR TOPIC FOR MAY 18

Life, the School of God and its Lessons.—Ps. 119:1-8; 33-40.

What do you learn in school? Well, the three "R's" must be learned in the very first grades. Reading! Have you learned to read intelligently? "Understandest thou what thou readest?" Do you study a lesson every day until you can spell your way through the Book? Or do you take a lesson once a week —or less often—and then cry because it is hard? Writing! No other tablet in the world like the human heart. You can write on it over and over and across and across, and all that you write is graven there for eternity. Have you learned to form your letters with care? Are you writing what you will enjoy in reading? Arithmetic! Can you count

with but one figure?. The first lesson in Arithmetic is Addition. Do you think God's arithmetic is any different? His first lesson is addition —"Add to your faith," and "come with me." I may be only a cipher but if I put *one* in front of me, and follow Him, I am ten, but if He is before me, I am *going* somewhere, someway. He never said "I am with you, to the stay-at-home in heart and body. (Matt. 28:19-20.) But if I go, I am out of the primer Class, for I am learning History "Thus far the Lord hath led us on," and Geography "all the world," and Grammar "speak forth the words of truth and soberness and some day I shall graduate, and receive 'the laurel wreath which the Lord the righteous Judge shall give to me at that day, and not to me only but to all those who love His appearing."

. MRS. FRED BULLOCK. .

THE LIST INCREASES

Continued reports from our Sunday schools are exceedingly encouraging. They show that the schools *want* to grow and go forward. Marion Lawrance points out the fact to our consternation that the Sunday school has been losing out very rapidly the past year or two, and that during the same time juvenile crime has been on the increase. He says if the Sunday school continues to lose in the next decade as it has the past two years, it will be extricate as at that the Sunday school must get to doing things for others. If the school just lives for itself, it has no right to live and no claim to life. It may be selfish, as well as the individual may be. Why not seek to get out of the old idea of living for self, just going on in the same old way, and begin to think, study, teach, and do for others? The Sunday school has fallen into a grove, into a well-worn rut. It needs to fall in with the spirit of this new time, and do something outside its own for the salvation of this wicked and sin-cursed world.

If any school thinks it cannot yet spare the offering of once per month to help reach and save the world,

why not spend some time once per month at least in trying to find out the distress, the misery, the poverty, the want, the need of the two-thirds of the human family today who are without the Gospel and without hope either in this world, or in that to come? Why not let the Sunday school. understand that two out of the three infants born into this world look up into the faces of mothers who can never tell them anything about the blessed Christ, because those mothers themselves never heard that Name which is above every name and the One whereby we must be saved, if we are saved?. If children in the Sunday school can learn such facts as these they will have pity, even if the grown-ups will not.

J. O. ATKINSON.

KINDERGARTEN HELPS FOR PARENT

By Mary E. Dozier

A child of fours years who was in the habit of pinching her neighbors, was asked by her kindergarten teacher, "Would you like to have Alice pinch you?" "No." "She doesn't like it either, Dorothy, and will not care to sit by you if you continue."

But the talk did no good, for the little tot went on repeating her offense. Then the teacher quietly took her handkerchief and, wrapping it around the offending member, said: "Suppose we cover up this little hand, and not let it be seen until it can remember not to pinch."

After a few minutes the child came over to the teacher to say that the hand could take care of itself now. Smilingly the teacher unwrapped it and said; "I am so glad."

A mother for a similar offense, was seen to slap her child's hand and jerk his arm. Which do you think the better method to follow?

In a kindergarten room of forty children, the story hour was in progress. The room was small, hence the attention of all was a necessity. Two boys, half listening, half playing, were continually rocking their chairs. The teacher's efforts to gain their complete attention proved fruitless. She stopped long enough to say: "Those who cannot sit quietly on their chairs must sit on the floor.' One of the boys immediately gave perfect attention, but the other continued his noise. When the teacher reached over to take his chair, he resisted, then went off by himself in a distant corner.

Knowing the disposition of the boy, the teacher let the matter pass until the next day when he asked for some work which he specially liked to do. The she replied: "I will be glad to let you have it John, after you have obeyed about sitting on the floor."

For three days the boy rebelled, and for three days this teacher of forty children did not forget the individual problem, refusing all of John's requests for the things he desired—always, however, in a pleasant manner.

The fourth day a dramatized story was on the program and the boy longed to be "the old troll." "May I be?" in his enthusiasm he asked. "I am sure you would make a fine troll if you would first obey your teacher." He looked at her, smiled and slid down onto the floor.

Too much attention devoted to such a simple act? Not when a child learns thereby that disobedience is not worth the price of forfeited companionship, and that to be an active and desired member of the school group he must comply with its necessary laws.

In some cases a child may be talked with and his sense of honor and dependableness aroused, while another child for the same offense must be dealt with more severely to awaken him to better action.

Study the nature of the child with whom you have to deal, and although it may take many months of patient study, and perhaps much experimenting, work out the best approach for a permanent lesson with him.

OBITUARIES

RESOLUTIONS OF RESPECT— JOHNSTON

Whereas, Mrs. Charles D. Johnston, one of our best loved members departed this life on April 11, 1919, for an eternal and celestial home with her Heavenly Father: Be it Resolved:

That as she had dedicated her life to the extension of the Kingdom of God on earth, so may we more fully dedicate our powers of body and mind to the same purpose;

That we extend to her bereaved husband and children our deepest sympathy, and that a copy of these resolutions be sent to The Christian Sun and Alamance Gleaner for publication, and a copy be sent to her husband and children and that a copy be spread upon our minutes.

LUTA HARDEN, Pres.,
MATTIE LONGEST, Secy',
Philathea Class, Graham Christian church.

ROGERS

Joseph Braxton Rogers was born January 9, 1859, and died Saturday, April 19, 1919. He was buried Sunday afternoon at Long's Chapel Christian church of which he was a member and a deacon. The funeral was conducted by the pastor, assisted by Rev. L. I. Cox.

Brother Rogers was married to Miss Jennie Allen November 9, 1888. She died February 11, 1902. Four children, one brother and two sisters survive him. He joined the church at Long's Chapel January 5, 1890, and was elected deacon May 6, 1911. A good man is gone. The church will miss him.

May God bless and comfort the bereaved ones.

J. F. APPLE.

CHRISMON

Miss Mamie Chrismon passed to her reward on Saturday evening, March 29, 1919, after a short period of serious illness. She had been a sufferer from tuberculosis for several years and spent a few months at the State Sanatorium where she apparently improved and looked well until a few days before her death. Funeral services were conducted by Rev. D. W. Overby, a Baptist minister, at Apple's Chapel where she was a member. The family could not secure a Christian min-

ister to assist. A large concourse of people gathered to pay their tribute of respect to the deceased. One brother is in France in the service of our country. May God bless and comfort the bereaved.

L. L. WYRICK.

CARR

Little Johnnie Carr died at his home at New Hill, N. C., April 19, 1919, aged thirteen years and one month. He was the son of Fen and Mary Carr. He is survived by two brothers and two sisters: George Fen, Edwards, Eula and Janice Carr. Burial was at New Elam Christian church, conducted by Rev. J. E. Franks.

Johnnie was a good boy and loved by all who knew him. His health began to fail about five years ago, but he never complained. We can never know the suffering that he bore, but we feel that his suffering is over and now he is singing with the angels, awaiting and watching for his dear ones to come. May the Lord bless and comfort the dear family in their sad bereavement.

A FRIEND.

TATUM

Harvey F. Tatum, youngest son of Allen and Mary Elizabeth Tatum (deceased) was born February 2, 1896 in Sussex County, Virginia, and united with Centerville Christian church August, 1913. He volunteered in the United States army May 14, 1917, in Company B, 4 Infantry, Newport News, Va. In September, 1917, he was sent to Camp McClellan, Anniston, Ala., for further training.

He was sent overseas June 15, 1918, for active service. He was immediately put into active service, and followed closely in battle, and was killed in action about November 2, 1918, in Company E, 116 Infantry, 29 Division.

The family have been unable to get full details of the death of this splendid soldier. He was a popular young man in his community and had bright future before him. He gave all for humanity. May God bless the memory of so splendid a sacrifice as was his.

JAS. L. FOSTER.

MOTHERS' DAY

NEXT SUNDAY

is Mothers' Day—ah, all days are theirs! Why just one day? But this is a particular day on which we make amends for all the days that we have failed to think of them. MOTHERS' DAY—beautiful thought. All of us know what it means, even those who know not the love of mother, for they, most of all, miss her.

THERE IS ANOTHER MOTHER

but she cannot *speak*, and yet she speaks; she cannot *sing* and yet she sings; she cannot *walk*, and yet she walks; she cannot *love*, and yet she loves; she cannot call her children to her, and yet they come. She is a mother made of earth and stone and personalities. She is

"ELON, DEAR ELON"

to use part of a song that her every child can sing with the familiarty of "My Country 'Tis of Thee." This Elon College is the mother who speaks through others, who sings through others, and who is the foster mother of a large family that calls her *blessed*.

LIFE

seems to even things up. When you were helpless she took care of you; now you should take care of her. She was patient with you; now you have an opportunity of showing your appreciation. She fed you mentally; it is your privilege to now feed her financially. You were re-born of her intellectual life—a thing that you cannot lose. She watched you while you grew into a capable man or woman. It is your privilege to now help her to continue that watch. She is watching on the Rhine—and everywhere. Beautiful mother, faithful, patient, GOOD, ready, willing, anxious.

HER FINANCIAL CALL

is challenging every soul that ever came under her watch-care. Today is a day of appreciation of what she has done for us, fellow former students.

COME TO THE FRONT, FELLOW ALUMNI, AND LET'S ALL HAIL TO THIS GOOD MOTHER OF OURS

THE CHRISTIAN SUN

"IN ESSENTIALS UNITY, IN NON-ESSENTIALS LIBERTY, IN ALL THINGS CHARITY"

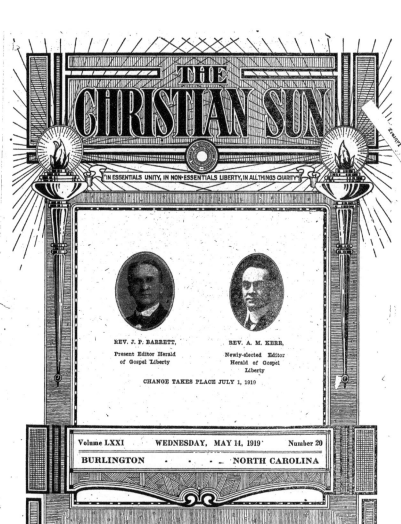

REV. J. P. BARRETT,
Present Editor Herald
of Gospel Liberty

REV. A. M. KERR,
Newly-elected Editor
Herald of Gospel
Liberty

CHANGE TAKES PLACE JULY 1, 1919

Volume LXXI   WEDNESDAY, MAY 14, 1919   Number 20

BURLINGTON   •   •   •   •   NORTH CAROLINA

THE CHRISTIAN SUN

Founded 1844 by Rev. Daniel W. Kerr

C. B. RIDDLE   -   -   Editor

Entered at the Burlington, N. C. Post Office as second class matter.

Subscription Rates

One year .... $ 2.00
Six months 1.00

In Advance

Give both your old and new postoffice when asking that your address be changed.

The change of your label is your receipt for money. Written receipts sent upon request.

Marriage and obituary notices not exceeding 150 words printed free if received within 60 days from date of event, all over this at the rate of one-half cent a word.

Original poetry not accepted for publication.

Principles of the Christian Church

(1) The Lord Jesus Christ is the only Head of the Church.
(2) Christian is a sufficient name of the Church.
(3) The Holy Bible is a sufficient rule of faith and practice.
(4) Christian character is a sufficient test of fellowship, and of church membership.
(5) The right of private judgment and the liberty of conscience is a right and a privilege that should be accorded to, and exercised by all.

EDITORIAL

THE AMERICAN CHRISTIAN CONVENTION

(Abstracts taken from the Conneaut, Ohio, News-Herald)

April 28

The First Christian church of this city, Conneaut's oldest church and the church having the largest membership in the Erie Christian Conference, will be the scene of this year's American Christian Convention. The opening date of the Convention is tomorrow afternoon. Thereafter three sessions daily will be held until next Tuesday, May 6. The Convention was brought to Conneaut for October 15-22, 1918, but was twice postponed and then called off until this spring because of influenza regulations.

April 29

M. R. Smith, mayor of Conneaut, today issued the following message, welcoming to Conneaut on behalf of the administration the 400 delegates of the American Christian Convention:

"As mayor of the city of Conneaut, I wish to extend to the delegates of the American Christian Convention the welcome which I am sure the whole community accords and which I believe our visitors will feel are their departure.

"It is indeed unusual that a city of the size of ours finds itself host to the distinguished assemblage of men and women who are now our guests. In full realization of this and trusting it may not be regretted our city was chosen for this honor, we bid our guests a sincere welcome from the depths of our hearts.

"M. R. SMITH, Mayor."

Scores of delegates have been arriving hourly since Sunday from all parts of the country to attend the big American Christian Convention which opened in the First Christian church of this city at two o'clock this afternoon.

This afternoon's session will be chiefly a business affair taken up for the most part with appointments of committees and presentation of reports. The time up until the opening of the afternoon session was spent in getting acquainted and learning the location of various departmental headquarters, etc.

Tonight Rev. F. G. Coffin, of Albany, N. Y., president of the Convention, will give his message. An address will also be given tonight by Rev. Warren H. Denison, of Dayton, superintendent of the famous Forward Movement.

The Chamber of Commerce at its meeting last night passed a resolution extending a welcome to the American Christian Convention and offering the services of the Chamber in any way they might be acceptable to the Convention. The Chamber offered, if it may be arranged, to conduct an automobile tour for the delegates during their sojourn in the city.

President Dunn was named chairman of a committee of five members he was asked to select to carry out the plans of the Chamber. The committee includes Charles Marcy, Wm. Fortune, M. R. Smith, G. M. Whitney and C. L. Whitney.

April 30

The fourth session of the American Christian Convention was in session here this afternoon and owing to radical changes made in the previously arranged program some of the most important business of the entire Convention, in fact business characterized by one delegate as "the most important in our church history if we adopt it" was under consideration.

May 1

With over three hundred delegates now in attendance the sessions of the American Christian Convention are already beyond expectancy in the enthusiasm, interest and importance. Two of the most instructive and most entertaining addresses Conneaut has been privileged to hear were given at the sessions yesterday afternoon and evening.

May 2

Three more sessions of the Christian Convention, attended by about three hundred delegates, were held Thursday afternoon and evening and this morning. The tour of the city conducted by the Chamber of Commerce was held yesterday afternoon and attended by practically all the delegates. Several more interesting addresses and many important reports were made with committee sessions continuing. The committee on nominations is to report late this afternoon and election of officers is to be held.

Thursday afternoon the Christian Publishing Association was in session. The Board of Trustees of the Association reported through its Secretary, which was followed by reports of the editors of the various publications issued by the Association.

Rev. J. P. Barrett, D. D., editor of the Herald of

Gospel Liberty, the oldest religious newspaper in the county, devoted himself to a statement of his editorial ideals and the general conditions affecting religious journalism in the country.

Rev. S. Q. Helfenstein, D. D., editor of all the Sun day-school papers and quarterlies of the denomination (except the Teachers' and Officers' Journal) reported in similar vein concerning his work, and behalf of the Armenian and Syrian refugees.

Mr. Netum Rathbun, popular Manager of the Association's publishing house and business located in Dayton, Ohio, was called to the platform for a short speech.

Rev. Martyn Summerbell, D. D., Lakemont, N. Y., conducted a memorial service for ministers who have fallen by death during the past four years. Rev. W. W. Staley, D. D., Suffolk, Va., offered prayer. Dr. Summerbell then read a long list of deaths and commented on the note-worthy lives of several of these men, including Revs. C. H. Hainer of Ontario; O. J. Hancock, of Maine; A. W. Lightbourne, of Delaware; H. J. Rhodes, of New York; G. D. Lawrence, of Illinois; Henry Brown, of New York; Albert Dunlap, of Ohio; N. Del McReynolds, of Ohio; P. W. McReynolds, of Ohio; David E. Millard, of Michigan; Elisha Mudge, of Michigan; R. O. Allen, of New York; S. S. Newhouse, of Ohio; John Blood, of New Jersey.

The Convention then adjourned for the auto ride to the harbor, generously provided by the Conneaut Chamber of Commerce.

May 3—An Appreciation

The News-Herald today received from the American Christian Convention in session in the First Christian church of this city a resolution of appreciation for the efforts of the paper to give publicity through its news columns to the events of the Convention. The resolution follows:

"The American Christian Convention wishes to express by resolution its grateful appreciation of the fine courtesies which have been extended to it by the Conneaut News-Herald.

"At no other Convention in many years has any paper been so generous in the space given to our publicity, and so anxious to print in full all matter which our reportorial committee has prepared for it. Its editors have been anxious to do everything possible to serve us and have admirably succeeded in doing so. We wish to express our thanks for the splendid service which they have rendered us.

"The Convention votes that in connection with the efforts of the Conneaut News-Herald to give our Convention due recognition, we should also record the untiring efforts of the chairman of the reportorial committee of this Convention, Rev. Alva Martin Kerr, who personally wrote a large part of the copy for the press."

May 4—Officers Elected

The following officers were elected for the American Christian Convention:

President, Rev. F. G. Coffin, D. D., Albany, N. Y.; vice-president, Rev. D. B. Atkinson, D. D., Defiance, Ohio; secretary, Rev. J. F. Burnett, D. D., Dayton, Ohio; secretary for the department of finance, Mr. S. O. Albaugh, Dayton, Ohio; secretary for the department of publishing, Judge O. W. Whitelock, Huntington, Ind.; secretary for the department of education,

Rev. W. G. Sargent, D. D., Providence, R. I.; secretary for the department of Sunday schools, Mr. Hermon Eldredge, Erie, Penn.; secretary for the department of home missions, Rev. Omer S. Thomas, Dayton, Ohio; secretary for the department of foreign missions, Rev. W. P. Minton, Defiance, Ohio; secretary for the department of Christian Endeavor, Rev. A. B. Kendall, Ravena, N. Y.

Home Mission Board: Rev. Carlyle Summerbell, D. D., chaplain in A. E. F.; Mr. M. S. Campbell, Collison, Ill.; Rev. C. B. Kershner, Frankfort, Ind.; Rev. J. W. Harrell, Burlington, N. C.; Mrs. Athella Howsare, Dayton, Ohio.

Foreign Mission Board: Rev. Warren H. Denison, D. D., Dayton, Ohio; Rev. W. P. Fletcher, Toronto, Ont.; Rev. L. E. Smith, Norfolk. Va.; Mr. J. O. Winters, Greenville, Ohio; Mrs. Alice V. Morrill, Defiance, Ohio.

Board of Education: Rev. R. C. Helfenstein, D. D., Urbana, Ill.; Rev. W. T. Walters, Winchester, Va.; Rev. John MacCalman, D. D., Lakemont, N. Y.; Rev. H. A. Smith, D. D., Warren, Ind.

The following officers were elected for the Christian, Publishing Association:

President, Judge O. W. Whitelock, Huntington, Ind.; vice president, Rev. J. O. Atkinson, D. D., Elon College, N. C.; secretary, Rev. R. H. Clem, Springfield, Ohio; treasurer, Mr. D. M. McCollough, Troy, Ohio.

Trustees: Rev. Frank H. Peters, D. D., Greenville, Ohio; Rev. C. G. Nelson, Gresham, Neb.; Mr. J. N. Dales, Toronto, Canada; Rev. W. W. Staley, D. D., Suffolk, Va.; Mr. J. B. Pease, Gassport, N. Y.; Mr. E. L. Goodwin, Boston, Mass.; Rev. C. B. Hershey, Merom, Indiana.

Editor of the Herald of Gospel Liberty, Rev. Alva Martin Kerr, Pleasant Hill, Ohio; editor of Sunday School Literature, Rev. S. Q. Helfenstein, D. D., Dayton, Ohio.

May 5

Eminently satisfied with the achievements of their seven days' stay in this city, members of the Christian Convention left last night and today for their homes or for the Inter-Church World meeting in Cleveland, after having concluded the quadrennial church session here.

The church board of polity, a new institution in the church, will be formed at a meeting of the various department boards to be held in Dayton, May 27. This is following up a decision made on the floor of the Convention just closed to have a board to decide matters of polity in the future and carry out the program of the Convention so that resolutions and movements brought up might not die with the Convention.

Editorial Staff

The following is the editorial staff of the American Christian Convention for the next four years:

Herald of Gospel Liberty—Rev. A. M. Kerr.

Sunday School Literature—S. Q. Helfenstein.

___

EDITORIAL NOTE

The Sun's Editor was deprived of the privilege of attending the American Convention. The foregoing is the best information that we have at this time as to the work of the Convention. Readers will note that little is said as to the actual happenings of the Convention as to plans and policies, but presume that we will be furnished this for publication at later date.

GREAT COMMENCEMENT PLAN FOR ELON

The Elon College commencements have become gala occasions in Alamance County history each year, and the approaching commencement, which begins on Sunday, May 18, and continues through Tuesday the 20th, promises to surpass its predecessors in items of general interest to our people. It is the purpose of the College always to adhere to the spirit of the times and this thought has been kept in mind in the present program. The people of Alamance and Guilford Counties will recall the great event of the closing day of the 1918 commencement when after a splendid address by Governor Bickett the giant service flag of the College, representing the hundreds of Elon men who had gone into the service, was unfurled amid thunderous applause. That was a dramatic moment in the history of Alamance County. This year it is highly appropriate that the College should observe memorial exercises for its sons who have fallen in the cause of human freedom. It is appropriate also that the orator of this occasion should be Col. Albert Cox of the 113th Artillery, a unit of the 30th Division which broke the famous Hindenburg line. Col. Cox was an outstanding lawyer of the North Carolina Bar before he entered the service of his country and he may be depended upon to speak forth words of soberness and inspiration when on May 20 at 2:00 o'clock in the afternoon he is to speak to the leading citizens of this county and of Guilford County in a memorial celebration, which we have said is so highly appropriate for the College to observe at its present commencement.

Hon. E. S. Parker is to preside at this celebration, and will introduce Col. Cox.

The Commencement will begin on Sunday morning at 10:30 o'clock when the baccalaureate sermon is to be given by Rev. Peter Ainslie of Baltimore. Dr. Ainslie is one of the first men in the American pulpit today. He has constructed a magnificent piece of Christian statesmanship during his thirty-five years of service in Baltimore. The theme that is nearest his heart is that of Christian union, and for this cause he has travelled the earth around and held conferences with Christian leaders in every land. He is a man of devotion to life and his message will be looked forward to with rare pleasure. It is expected that a great audience will hear him.

Sunday evening the baccalaureate address will be given by the President of the College. His theme will be: "The New Task For the College."

On Monday, May 19, at 10:30 o'clock in the morning the class day exercises will occur, and that afternoon at 3:00 o'clock the society representatives will speak. The annual celebration of the College Choral Union will occur Monday evening at 8:30 P. M., when

the famous oratorio, "The Triumph of the Cross," will be rendered with Prof. E. M. Betts as director.

The final day of commencement will be May 20, as has been said, and the exercises will begin at 10:00 o'clock in the morning when the class of 1919 will read their essays, deliver their orations, and receive their diplomas. At 2:00 P. M. in the afternoon Col. Albert Cox will speak. The closing item of the commencement will be the alumni address, which will be given by Mrs. W. A. Harper, '99. Her subject will be: "Shoulder to Shoulder, a Study in Human Equality."

The College authorities wish us to say that the people of Alamance and Guilford Counties are cordially invited to attend all these exercises, and we feel sure they will avail themselves of the opportunity.

NOTES

Rev. H. J. Fleming writes: "THE SUN came this morning and I never knew the value of it until I got into regular work of the Church."

The annual memorial service held at New Providence church, Graham, N. C., will be held this year on the first Sunday in June. A program has been prepared which indicates that a good day may be expected. Dr. W. W. Staley, Suffolk, Va., is to preach the annual sermon.

We mourn with Pastor C. H. Rowland in the loss of his mother on May 3. Mrs. Rowland was one of THE SUN's many devoted friends. She was truly a saint. Though helpless, her life was sunny. A great and good mother gone. See obituary on page 15.

Many of the preachers have been "pounded," some have been "suited," some "coated," some "aided," some "watched." None of these things have happened to the Editor, but he is one ahead of the other brethren as to what has been done to him. He has been "billed." A good Brother—who has been taking THE SUN for 60 years, and began before joining the church—presented us the other day with a five dollar bill. No bad gift, sir, and we are grateful.

Gypsy Smith, Jr., began a meeting in Burlington on Sunday evening, May 11. His tent is within twenty-five yards of this office. At this writing he has preached only one sermon, but the verdict of those who heard him is that it was a sermon. Every available seat was taken at the first meeting with possibly one thousand persons left without seats. The people heard him gladly. If all his sermons come up to the first, our decision is that he is a great preacher.

The Editor was due to be with Brother J. F. Apple at Mt. Zion last Sunday. Brother Apple told us on Saturday that if the weather was very unfavorable on Sunday morning not to come. This was the case, and it looked as if it might rain any minute. In a short time after the train passed the clouds cleared away and the most of the day was favorable. We regret losing the trip, but have charged it to the weather man. Two years ago we started to this church, but through some misunderstanding no one met us at the train. We were unable to get any one by phone and had to take the next train back home. If for any reason that our failure to appear last Sunday was a disappointment, the church will have to break even with us for their failure before.

AN ANNOUNCEMENT

Mrs. William Thomas Fryer announces the marriage of her daughter, Violette Hope and Dr. Jennings Sipe Lincoln, Captain United States Army, on Tuesday, the twenty-ninth of April, nineteen hundred and nineteen, Baltimore, Maryland.

THE HERALD OF GOSPEL LIBERTY CHANGES EDITORS

The American Christian Convention in session at Conneaut, Ohio, last week elected Rev. Alva M. Kerr, Pleasant Hill, Ohio, to the editorship of The Herald of Gospel Liberty. The present Editor, Rev. J. P. Barrett, D. D., has been Editor of The Herald twelve years. Dr. Barrett was Editor of THE CHRISTIAN SUN from 1881 to 1894. Thus he has served the Christian Church for nearly a quarter of a century in an editorial capacity, As Editor of THE SUN he was able and efficient, and his training on this publication well qualified him for the work on The Herald of Gospel Liberty. As Editor of THE SUN he gave the people a good paper and as Editor of The Herald he maintained the same good standard. He is a man of conviction, and carries at the masthead of his paper, "Earnestly contend for the faith which was once delivered unto the Saints." To this text he sticks unflinchingly. He has his views and expresses them. Dr. Barrett is an able writer, and as an evidence of this, it is common to see in many of our exchanges quotations taken from his pen. He gives up his work on July 1 and expects to return to some part of the Southern Christian Convention. His coming to the pastoral ranks will be a blessing to the Church. His experiences as pastor and editor fit him in every way for a successful work in some field.

Brother Kerr, the new Editor, is a young man full of promise, and has done his work well in every task of the Church committed to his care. We welcome him to the editorial tripod. We speak for him a loyal support from the Brotherhood at large, and especially from the South. May the blessing of God follow the work of these brethren and continue to bless the mission of The Herald of Gospel Liberty.

FROM RECENT MAILS

W. H. Ligon.—Wishing for THE CHRISTIAN SUN a large circulation.

J. J. Rountree.—Wishing you every success and that all will help in the work.

P. P. Jones.—When I get so I can't take THE SUN I will not take any other paper.

G. C. Brown.—My wife does not see how she can get along without our Church paper.

Mr. and Mrs. B. P. Sale.—We enjoy reading THE SUN more each week.

Mrs. H. L. Jones.—I want THE SUN to continue for I can't do without it.

Mrs. S. V. Holt.—I pray that this will be the best year that you have ever had.

PASTOR AND PEOPLE

THE KEY-WORD OF THE TEN COMMANDMENTS

The key-word of the Ten Commandments is Love. The life of the ancient Mosaic laws is not to be found in exacting, rigid justice according to the popular idea of justice. Often the time before Christ is spoken of as a dispensation of law, as being somewhat different from the present dispensation which is spoken of as a dispensation of love. The Pharisees gathered about Christ and asked Him the great commandment of the law, He replied, "Thou shalt love the Lord thy God with all thy heart, and with all thy soul, and with all thy mind," and he added a second which He said was like unto it, "Thou shalt love thy neighbor as thyself." The soul, the spirit, the life of each of these commandments is Love. "On these two commandments," He said, "hang all the law and the prophets."

J. G. TRUITT.

News Ferry, Va.

NORTHERN ALABAMA

Rev. J. D. Dollar, of the Alabama Christian Conference, was with us the fourth Saturday and Sunday in April. Brother Dollar did some good preaching and we were glad to have him with us. We hope to have Brother C. W. Carter the fourth Sunday in this month, Rev. G. D. Hunt in June and Rev. E. M. Carter in July. We are glad that the Alabama Conference has taken hold of the work here and we are glad to welcome the ministers.

We have an organized church of but a few members. We have no church building yet, but expect to begin one soon and trust that by the help of the Lord we may have a building for our ministers to preach in before another year. The Methodist people have been kind in permitting us to hold services in their building and we appreciate their help very much.

Brethren and sisters, pray for this little band and especially the work at this place.

MRS. LELA JEAN.

A VISIT

On Saturday, May 3, memorial services were held at Mt. Zion Christian church. Through the courtesy of Rev. J. D. Dollar, the pastor, the writer had the pleasure of attending. The weather was fine and the congregation large and attentive. The dinner served could not be beat. One of the best programs that has ever been my privilege to witness was rendered.

Brother Dollar has served as pastor for these people a number of years and is doing a great work here. He is much beloved by his people.

The next day, Sunday, by request of Rev. E. M. Carter, I went to New Harmony to fill his appointment. This was a great pleasure because I had once been pastor for these people. It was a pleasure to meet and shake hands with these old friends again. Brother Carter is doing a good work at this place, as the newly painted house of worship, a live Sunday school and a large congregation attest.

The service at this time was good, five new members were received into fellowship of the church.

I had the pleasure of visiting a number of homes while at this place, one of which deserves special mention. On Sunday night I stayed at the home of a good old friend, Rev. J. C. Knight. Brother Knight is an invalid and cannot walk without help, yet his faith seems to be strong in God and his hopes bright for an eternal home around His throne.

The work seems to move well in the Alabama Conference.

J. H. HUGHES.

Roanoke, Ala., Route 4.

SUFFOLK LETTER

(The American Christian Convention)

The postponed meeting of the quadrennial session of the American Christian Convention opened in this city on Tuesday, April 29, 1919, and will close May 5th.

The church is a splendid edifice, with modern apartments, well furnished, in the best part of the city, and will seat, in the main auditorium, more than five hundred, and the membership is more than seven hundred. Rev. A. E. Kemp, the pastor, is a well-balanced minister, a beloved pastor, and a successful preacher.

By the kindness of the Congregational church, the dining hall, in that church, was tendered for use during the Convention. The room seats about two hundred and it was crowded every meal. Meals cost forty cents and tickets were sold outside the door of the dining room. The ladies of the church served the meals in a manner that deserves praise and grateful thanks.

More than three hundred delegates registered and the attendance has been good and the interest has been at tension most of the time.

The Forward Movement has been prominent throughout the Convention. Attractive banners around the gallery and the platform have kept it before the eye, frequent reference to it has kept it in the air, and the committee of *twenty-four* has changed the goal from *half a million* to *two million* and this was approved, heartily and unanimously, by the Convention. All Mission money, Endowment funds, and Benevolences are to be counted in the *two million* during the *five-year* period, starting with 1918.

I think there are seven from North Carolina and twelve from Virginia present and they are representing the Southern Christian Convention with credit.

Many distinguished visitors have added to the interest by great addresses. Daniel Couve, a French chaplain, gave a splendid address. Rev. Dr. Worth M. Tippy, representing the Inter-Church World Movement and Dr. Bruner, also, gave splendid addresses.

Dr. H. C. Armstrong of Baltimore, representing the Disciples of Christ, pleased the Convention by an address on the relation of our body and theirs, and left the audience feeling that we ought to be united.

Drs. J. O. Atkinson and L. E. Smith made great addresses and the feeling is that the South furnishes orators; but they must not take our best for all.

Ministers, by request, were sent to the other churches in the city and adjacent villages, even to the Episcopal on the same street with our own. It does seem that the Protestant churches are getting closer together. Christian unity is in the air—yea, in the heart of the denominations. The difficulty is in getting the heads together.

The Missionary Pageant on Sunday, which was a report to the eye of the woman's work for four years and it made a vivid and hopeful impression upon the great congregation. It introduced placards, ribbons, recitations, women and children, and all was led by Mrs. M. T. Morrill. It was one of the most impressive lessons of the Convention, not only in the matter of statistics, but it was intensely spiritual.

The Chamber of Commerce carried the entire Convention in more than fifty automobiles out to the docks on Lake Erie—the greatest *ore docks* in the United States.

W. W. STALEY.

(Written from Conneaut, Ohio.)

THE CHRISTIAN ORPHANAGE

SUPERINTENDENT'S LETTER

Dear Friends:—

Our Easter offerings have been coming in splendidly and this week's report runs us up to $2,535. We just lack $465 reaching the goal. Shall we reach it in our next report? I trust we will. Since I have been in this work I have never made a campaign to reach a goal under such trying circumstances. Let each church that has not taken this offering take it and mail it in so you will have a part in this great work and happy task. Make some sacrifice for the little orphans and help give them a home.

We have several contributions this week on our home for the little folks and as the interest increases I hope to see this fund climb upward at a rapid rate.

I know you want to have a part in this the most sympathetic work connected with our Orphanage. Who is it that has a heart that a little child left helpless, fatherless and motherless, cannot touch?

My heart goes out to those little ones. You should open your heart to them too. Let us all sacrifice to the end that a home will be built in the near future for their comfort and happiness.

Last week we gave Berea church, Altamahaw, N. C. credit for $50.00 on the Easter Offering which was an error. It should have been credited to The Young Ladies' Sunday school class of that church.

CHAS. D. JOHNSTON, *Supt.*

REPORT FOR MAY 14, 1919

Amount brought forward, $4,542.00.

Children's Offerings

Helen Newman, 10 cents; Geo. Newman, 10 cents, Total, 20 cents.

Sunday School Monthly Offerings

(North Carolina Conference)

Haw River, $3.26; Oak Level, $1.00; Long's Chapel, $1.00; Chapel Hill, $2.96; Hine's Chapel, $2.08; Parks Cross Roads; 61 cents.

(Eastern Virginia Conference)

Centerville, $1.00; Holland, $12.00; Isle of Wight, $2.50; Dendron, $4.00.

Miscellaneous

Dry Run, Va., $3.24; Beulah, Ala., 72 cents; Total, $34.37.

Special Offerings

Marion N. Beall, Holland, Va., $5.00; Mrs. Nannie Royster, $1.00; Cash Items, $9.00; Total, $15.00.

Special Offerings For Baby Home

J. L. Scott, Jr., Graham, N. C., $25.00; Mrs. W. P. Betts, Batesburg, S. C., $5.00; Mrs. Waymon, Yohey, Ind., $2.00; Mrs. G. S. Watson, Elon College, N. C., $25.00; Mr. H. J. Pritchett, Elon College, N. C., $5.00; Total, $62.00.

Special Easter Offerings

Union church, (N. C.), $21.05; Antioch church, (Ala.), $10.50; Pleasant Grove church, (Ala.), $5.00; Hebron Christian church, $6.61; Machias church, (N. Y.), $44.39; Zion church, $10.10; Haw River church, $12.20; Jeff Shelley, Crawfordsville, Ind., $5.00; Amanda Shelley, Crawfordsville, Ind., $5.00; Nole and Ada Shelley, Crawfordsville, Ind., $3.00; Moore Union church, $7.50; Mt. Carmel, Sunday school, $6.00; Mt. Carmel Sunday school class, No. 6, $1.00; Mrs. Margaret Myers, $10.00; Mr. and Mrs. J. W. Nicholas, $5.00; Cypress Chapel Sunday school, $21.00; Wakefield Christian church, $20.50; Rock Island Sunday school, $1.65; Union (Surry) church, $7.50; Union (Surry) Sunday school, $6.00; Pleasant Union Sunday school, $6.00; Wm. L. Coryell, Pine Castle, Fla., $5.00; Beginners and Primary Department, Lincoln, Kans., $1.30; Centerville church, $7.15; T. H. Crocker, Middleberg, N. C., $10.00; Amelia, (N. C.) Sunday school, $31.95; Carey Welch, for Sunday school, (No name given), $20.00; Fiatt Christian church, Fiatt, Ill., $7.00; Lee's Chapel church, $2.05; New Providence Sunday school, Graham, N. C., $13.51; New Providence Sunday school Senior Philathea Class, $13.54; Ivor Christian church, Va., $6.91; Chapel Hill Sunday school, $13.49; Leaksville church, $14.23; New Port church, $8.25; Mt. Lebanon, $8.41; East Liberty, $3.81; Bethel church, $7.42; St. Peters, $1.08; Miss Jessie Wample, Harrisonburg, Va., $5.00; Dendron Sunday school, (Va.), viz.: Class No. 1, $1.90; Class No. 2, $2.70; Class No. 3, $2.70; Class No. 4, $2.06; Class No. 5, $1.88; Class No. 6, $1.66; Bible Class, $7.25; 1910 Bible Class, $3.35; Ebenezer church, $10.05; Six Forks church, $5.01.

(Members of Ingram Church who live in Richmond, Va.)

Mrs. L. E. Carlton, $10.00; Mr. H. A. Carlton, $5.00; Mr. P. J. Carlton, $10.00; Mr. J. W. Carlton, $2.00; Mrs. L. E. Carlton, $10.00; Mrs. M. E. Boyd, $10.00; Miss Sarah E. Boyd, $10.00; Total, $57.00.

Waverly Christian church, $40.75; W. C. Pierce, $2.00; Mrs. W. C. Pierce, $2.00; Miss Blanche Pierce, $1.00; Hine's Chapel Sunday school, $10.00; Memorial Temple, $50.00; Catawba Springs, $15.50; Mrs. A. G. Hayes, $1.00; Mr. A. H. Hayes, $2.00; Total, $611.61.

Total for the week, $723.18; Grand total, $5,264.95.

A LETTER

Dear Uncle Charley: I found a dime. Mother says I may send it to the Orphanage. She gave George one to send, too. I am eight years old and George is six. I hope I shall come to Elon this summer and if I do I shall visit the Orphanage.—*Helen Newman.*

You are a nice little girl to give the money found to the little orphans.—*Uncle Charley.*

ITEMS FROM THE OFFICE

We are grateful to the many friends who have renewed their subscription accounts during the past week.

Don't forget about the little book, "How to Run a Little Sunday School." The price is only 75 cents. It is practical. Send for a copy.

We have on hand a nice supply of Bibles and Testaments. If you want something to read send for Bible No. 2014—large print. The price is only $4.00. We also have large print Testaments, the prices being 85c, $1.00, and $2.00. The $2.00 Testament is morocco binding and is a beauty. Your money back if you are not pleased.

Do you know how to reach the Sunday school lesson? Yes, you say that you know. Well, then, perhaps you want to know how to teach it better. Send 75 cents for a copy of "How to Teach The Sunday School Lesson."

Sixty cents sent to this office will bring you a copy of "The Sunday School Teacher at His Best." Are you at your best in teaching? Get the book and apply the standard.

If you like THE SUN, tell your neighbor, and if you do not like it, tell us—also tell us how to make it better. We want criticism but only the constructive kind. kind.

ODDS AND ENDS

When should the service flag be taken down? According to the War Department, the Service Flag should be taken down when the one for whom it was displayed is discharged from the service.

* *

President Wilson will be back in this country about June fifteenth, so a report says.

* *

The Fifth Liberty Loan has been oversubscribed according to press reports.

* *

The Dutch are not willing to surrender the ex-Kaiser. So far as we are concerned, this suits us if they will agree to keep him until 1999.

MISSIONARY

ON BEING BENEVOLENT

God did not build this planet on an economic, but on a benevolent basis. And His method of procedure from beginning till now has not been materialistic, but moral. His laws are not the laws of matter, but of spirit. Hence the writer of Hebrews declares, "By faith we understand the world was made by the word of God." We cannot understand it any other way than by faith; how things we call material grew out of that which is immaterial, and that which is seen grew out of that which does not appear. Verily, we walk in all this world, as Paul declares, by faith and not by sight.

Economy then is of man: benevolence is of God. Matter is due to man's limitation, for in the realm of the Infinite all is spirit. I once read a book called "Natural Law in the Spiritual World." It was a misnomer and you never hear anything of it now. It should have been "Spiritual Law in the Natural World." There is no natural law. All law is spiritual. We call it natural because of our finite limitations. Natural law is our human reading of the mind and spirit of God seeking to break in upon us through the crust and shadow of things called material.

This universe is a moral universe, and all its creation, its government and its destiny are benevolent, are spiritual. If the universe had been economic, constructed and developed according to the laws of saving; its Creator would not have dug the seas so deep, made its oceans so wide, nor piled its mountains so high. What do the infinite depths of the seas and the towering peaks of mountains declare, save that God who made the earth and the sea had plenty and to spare, and the Hand that created was outstretched, open and abundant. We have talked economy and preached economy and practiced economy until we have almost forgotten that the God who made us did not have to practice economy but was abundant, resourceful, benevolent, and that His reservoirs were, and are now, and ever will be unlimited, inexhaustible, infinite.

This is why it is that men, communities or states when they become benevolent do not get poorer but richer. The Secretary of State for North Carolina just after the second Liberty Loan issued statistics showing that before North Carolina began to give for Red Cross, Y. M. C. A., Y. W. C. A., Missions, and to buy thrift stamps and Liberty Bonds, it had $22,000,000.00 in the Savings Banks to their credit; but within a year's time after they had manifested their benevolence, they had $73,000,000.00 in Savings Banks to their credit. God constructed this universe on a benevolent basis and when men and States become benevolent they tap the sources of His abundance, and the streams of wealth gush forth. This is why Malachi cried forth in the days of the waning strength and increasing poverty of Israel and said: "Return unto me and I will return unto you, saith the Lord of hosts, But ye said, Where-

in shall we return? Will a man rob God? Yet ye have robbed me. But ye say, wherein have we robbed thee? In tithes and offerings, is the sure and quick reply. Prove me herewith saith the Lord, if I will not open the windows of heaven and pour you out a blessing, that there shall not be room to contain it." You will note that it is not to be handed out, counted out nor doled out! It is to be "poured out." When God gets ready to bless He does not have to measure out or keep accounts, for His supply is inexhaustible, and He just pours it out.

Oh! my brethren, how we have pauperized the Kingdom of our Lord. We have sometimes made God a pauper by going out begging for Him. Think of it! Begging for Him. God is no pauper. All the gold and all the silver and the cattle upon a thousand hills are His. Sometime since I asked a man to make a contribution to missions. "Not a dollar," said he. "Why?" was my query. "Because," said he, "God does not need my money." I said, "My Brother, you are right. God does not need your money. For by the breath of His nostrils every trembling leaf on every bending bough of all the forests could be changed in an instant into hundred dollar notes. By the word of His mouth, every sparkling blade of grass beneath the sun would turn to gems and pearls and diamonds; and every grain of sand would be changed to silver dollars or golden eagles. No sir, God does not need your money. But, sir, because He is God and is benevolent, He wants you, made in His image, to be benevolent, and so be like Him. You cannot be like God and not be benevolent. For God is benevolent."

When the Word declares that God made man in His own image, that is what He meant. He meant that man should be, and if he is to be like God, he must be benevolent. This explains why you cannot find in the Bible, or in any other book, the beginning of the law of the tithe. That law did not begin. Like God it had no beginning. It was one with the creation. I have heard people who ought to have known better call the law of the tithe a Jewish or a Mosaic law. The law of the tithe already was before the beginning of Jewry and before the ancestors of Moses to the tenth generation had been born. Abraham, the father of the faithful, did not enact the law; he practiced it as an accepted statue, and Melchizedec, king of righteousness, priest of the Most High God, having neither beginning of days nor end of life, sanctioned the law and received with his blessings its bounty. And now historians tell us that all nations, pagan, heathen, barbarian, Greek, Jew and Gentile, practiced the law of the tithe from their earliest records. This act of benevolence, this law of God, this much of the nature and character of God were wrapped up in the very nature and make up of man; until man crowds it out of his nature with his short-sighted and ruinous policy of what he calls economy, but what God knows is wickedness, folly, madness.

We are told that the love of money is the root of evil (or of all kinds of evils), and it is. For a man can love money till the last spark of benevolence dies out of his heart and of his nature.

But the love of the good money can do is also the root, stem and branch of all kinds of righteousness, truth, justice and mercy in this earth.

We Christians have been, for the past few months, talking about the Forward Movement, and writing about it and wondering about it, praying over it. We wonder where that paltry $500,000.00 is to come from and how it is to come. And it is safe to say that even while we have been talking and writing and paying and wondering, those self-same Christians have worse than wasted far more than that amount. I hazard here and now the statement, and fling it forth as a challenge for any to prove the contrary that before we raise that $500,000.00 and pay it into the Lord's treasury, the very peoples who are to pay it will fling away twice that much in trifles and spend four times that much for that which neither buys bread nor keeps alive. "Try me," saith the Lord God, "Become benevolent as I am benevolent," saith the Lord God, "and see if I do not open the windows of heaven and pour you out a blessing such as you cannot contain."

Brethren, the resources of God are evermore available to those who undertake the program of God. Let us get right with God, set ourselves to the sure purpose of executing the program of God, and I declare to you that before five years, we will not have a half million, but a million and more of God's good dollars going through our treasury with which to do the work of God. There are no limits to the resources of God, to those who undertake and do the will and work of God. When we invest our money in the Kingdom we are laying up treasures in heaven and in the act are becoming benevolent as He Himself is benevolent.

J. O. ATKINSON.

CHRISTIAN EDUCATION

DURHAM AND HINES' CHAPEL

On Sunday, last, it was my pleasure to speak twice to our Durham congregation and once at O'Kelly's Chapel, where the great founder of our Brotherhood spent his latter days and near which his body now rests, marked by a simple, yet appropriate shaft of granite. I reached Durham in time for the closing exercises of the Sunday school. Superintendent D. L. Boone is doing a splendid work and is very popular with his people. So is Pastor R. F. Brown.

This Church went over the top and so did Hines' Chapel this week under the leadership of Dr. W. C. Wicker. O'Kelly's Chapel was left to be canvassed later by Rev. R. F. Brown, who did the work well. Rev. B. J. Howard is pastor at O'Kelley's Chapel. He is a very promising leader in our ministry. He has agreed to help the drive in his old home church, Moore Union, and that means that church does her duty, especially since her pastor, Rev. P. T. Klapp, has started the subscription there.

Funds This Week

Funds of $1,000 each have been established this week by Deacon Brooks Wyrick, Mrs. J. P. Avent,

on the annuity plan; Mr. and Mrs. J. H. McNeil in loving memory of their daughter, Mrs. Frankie McNeil Cooke, and by Dr. W. H. Boone and Deacon D. L. Boone in memory of their sainted parents, Rev. and Mrs. C. A. Boone. What satisfaction of heart it is to be able to place a portion of the means God so graciously bestows on us to do the work of Christian Education, the hope of the world, perpetually!

Commencement and The Final Plunge

The College Commencement is rapidly approaching. Everything must be in readiness for its arrival. That means curtailment of time in the field and longer hours in the office at home. But with the first Sunday in June, we shall have our plans matured to reach every church not so far on the map for this greatest drive of our history. A good man said to me recently, "God has great blessings ahead for the Christian Church." Even so, as He always does when Christians do full duty and cheerfully meet their privileges in sacrificing for His cause.

Let the brethren continue in prayers, and our good sisters too, that God may continue to bless this work.

W. A. HARPER.

WELCOME HOME!

A Welcome Service to the Returning Soldiers, Prepared by the War Work Commission of the Christian Church

SUGGESTIONS TO THE DIRECTORS OF PROGRAM

1. True Patriotism and Vital Religion should be blended in this service, in such a way that the service may be attractive and inspirational to both the soldier and the civilian:

2. The Double Objective of the service should be constantly before the mind of the leader; first, to give the soldier a whole-hearted welcome home which will show our appreciation of his service and sacrifice and, second, to enlist both soldier and civilian to "Carry On," these ideals of Service and Sacrifice in the life of the Church, the Community, the Nation and the World.

3. The Decorations should be in keeping with the occasion and it is suggested that the National colors of Red, White and Blue are most appropriate and should be used lavishly with the National Flag and the Christian Flag as a prominent part of the decorations

PROGRAM

I. "THE STAR SPANGLED BANNER"—Sung by Congregation.

Oh, say, can you see by the dawn's early light,
What so proudly we hailed at the twilight's last gleaming,
Whose broad stripes and bright stars, thro' the perilous fight,
O'er the ramparts we watched, were so gallantly streaming?
Oh, thus be it ever when freemen shall stand
Between their loved home and wild war's desolation;
Blest with vict'ry and peace, may the heav'n-rescued land
Praise the Pow'r that hath made and preserv'd us a nation!

II. INVOCATION—Pastor.

III. "THE BATTLE HYMN OF THE REPUBLIC."

Mine eyes have seen the glory of the coming of the Lord;
He is trampling out the vintage where the grapes of wrath are stored;
He hath loosed the fateful lightning of His terrible, swift sword!
His truth is marching on.
I have seen Him in the watch-fires of a hundred circling camps;

(Continued on page 12)

WORSHIP AND MEDITATION

THE STATE OF BEATITUDE OR SOME FUNDAMENTALS IN PURE RELIGION

(Rev. J. W. Patton, Greensboro, N. C.)

Text, Mat. V; 2 and 3: "And He Opened His Mouth, and Taught Them, Saying, Blessed."

The incarnate and immaculate Son of God was the greatest Teacher the world has ever known, but He could learn for no man.

The benediction of Jesus Christ, is the richest legacy in the universe of God. Its source is obedience; its effect is happiness; its result is marvelous. The heart craves it, the Devil hates it but few possess it.

All have the natural birth; some are born spiritually, and the world today is unhappy.

Every true Christian has four perfect points of entering the Kingdom of God: (1) Repentance; (2) Faith; (3) Regeneration, and (4) Obedience.

Repentance produces reformation; Faith seeks for God; Regeneration produces a new creature, and Obedience clings on to Jehovah.

Note With Me

I. "Blessed," is Beatitude in the Reach of Every One. God's commands are both reasonable and possible; crucifixion to the flesh, but life to the soul. . . . . (Gal. 2:20), "I am crucified with Christ: nevertheless I live; yet not I, but Christ liveth in me: and the life which I now live in the flesh I live by the faith of the Son of God, Who loved me, and gave Himself for Me."

"Blessed" represents the beatitudes spoken of by Jesus Christ, comprehending the introduction and fundamental statements in His marvelous and memorable Sermon on the Mount.

These Beatitudes are natural, logical, and essential. No soul can reach Heaven without them. God is no respector of persons.

These nine states of blessedness, lead those who are exercised thereby, from poverty of Spirit to a pure heart, making of them peace-makers, enabling them to endure persecution for righteousness sake; and when revilings and persecutions and all manner of evil speaking are against them, they can and should rejoice with exceeding gladness because Jesus said: "Great is their reward in Heaven."

(a) The first Beatitude, poverty of spirit, is the initial step in, and toward complete salvation. It represents a condition that must be realized before any person will rightly seek God. God appeals to every man through (1) Nature, (2) Dealings and (3) Revelation, reinforced by aid of the Holy Ghost.

(b) The second Beatitude, or mourning, takes up the essential doctrine of repentance. Its purpose is, a change of heart and faith in God.

When a sinner sees and realizes his lost estate and miserable condition, he will mourn and seek God.

This doctrine of "mourning," in the great plan of Salvation, has, to a large degree, been modified, and in many cases nullified by the human made machine that appeal to the emotion, finding expression in the hand-shake and large numbers reported by the preacher, with a small percent holding out faithfully to their profession; rather than appealing to the trinity that is in man, viz: the emotion, the judgment and the will.

"Marvel not that I said unto thee, Ye must be born again."

(c) The third Beatitude, meek, is the first evidence of a changed heart. Meekness is greatly a lost art.

The fourth and fifth Beatitudes are additions to the third, producing the finished product, viz: A pure heart.

The pure in heart are blessed, for Jesus Christ said: "They shall see God."

The logical steps, in regeneration, as enumerated by Christ, are (1) Poverty of Spirit, (2) Mourning, (3) Meekness, (4) Hungering and thirsting after righteousness and (5) Merciful, thus producing God's ideal, a pure heart, and a spirit-filled life.

This is all internal work, producing a condition and an absolutely necessary qualification to be prepared for, and able successfully to meet external demands.

The pure heart is a diploma from the university of God, in which the Holy Spirit is the Great Teacher and the Holy Bible the text book. With this pure heart, man is ready to commence real and true and happy life. He then becomes a positive factor in religious life. That is, he becomes:

(1) A peace-maker. This is an external evidence of an internal change and condition of heart, making him a powerful asset in the Church of Christ and for the Kingdom of God.

(2) He will have persecution. He must be tested. He must be tried by the furnace of fire.

Jesus Christ could create the universe, but He could not save a lost soul until He was perfected by trials and temptations and persecutions of the incarnate life. Heb. V, 9: "And being made perfect, He became the author of eternal salvation."

(3) The Pure in Heart will be reviled. But they can overcome, and demonstrate to the man of sin, the power of the believed gospel of our resurrected Lord, over all forms and conditions of satanic temptations. Such are the salt of the earth and the light of the world.

II. The Beatitude of Blessed May Be Lost. Because a man has accumulated much of this world's goods is no positive proof that he will die rich. Because a person has a finished education does not necessarily carry that such an one will be a blessing in life. Because any person has lived a moral life, professed faith in Christianity and is even an active member of the church, having many opportunities thereafter to "do good, is no absolute proof that he will reach heaven at last.

(Gal. V; 1): "Stand fast therefore in the liberty wherewith Christ hath made us free, and be not entangled again with the yoke of bondage." (Gal. V; 7): "Ye did run well, who did hinder you that ye should not obey the truth?" (Mat. VII; 21): "Not every one that saith unto me, Lord, Lord, shall enter into the kingdom of heaven; but he that doeth the will of My Father which is in heaven."

The word of God is full of warnings along this line.

(Eze. III; 20): "Again, when a righteous man doth turn from his righteousness, and commit iniquity, and I lay a stumbling block before him, he shall die: because thou has not given him warning, he shall die in his sins, and his righteousness which he hath done shall not be remembered; but his blood will I require at thine hand." (21), "Nevertheless if thou warn the righteous man, that the righteous sin not, and he doth not sin, he shall surely live, because he is warned; also thou has delivered thy soul."

So the way to hold the state of beatitude, is not to sin. Some of the most dangerous people in the world are the educated. Educated in head and hand—e. g. the Hun. Their literary attainments are wonderful and their manual productions marvelous, yet they prepared for, and precipitated the most barbarous war the world has ever known. And Mr. Frederick Boyd Stephenson says of this war: ''In balancing the books against William Hohenzollern and Co., on the New Year, not one dollar, not one good deed during the four and one-half years of murder, pillage, incendiarism and rapine can be placed on the credit side of the ledger.''

There is a trinity in education, without which no man can be his best. Educate properly, the head to think, the heart to feel, and the hand to do, then you have the ideal character. Some of the most wicked people in the world are members, in name, of the Church of Jesus Christ. Judas was one of this class. The heart must be regenerated or the life will be a failure and a liability upon the world.

A good way to re-enforce a profession of religion and church membership is, to apply to life, the warning usually placed at a railroad crossing: Stop! Look!! and Listen!!!

(1) Stop.—Stop to consider what your church membership represents; what kind of a life you are living—whether or not your conduct is an exponent of the teachings of the great Christ.

(2) Look.—Look to see which way you are really going. See if there is danger ahead; see if your feet are in that straight and narrow way that leads to the haven of rest.

(3) Listen.—Listen to hear God's message to you. His words of warning, of admonition, of love; the Spirit's leading, the call of suffering humanity. Be a neighbor living in a house by the roadside and be a friend to man.

III It Requires the Supreme Effort of God and Man to Save a Soul. I submit, reverently, that God has exhausted His ways and means, in the installation of a supreme plan to save rebellious man.

God's part has been so amply, lovingly and lastingly provided, that no one can have a single excuse, so far as God's provision for man's eternal salvation is concerned. Man must do his part because every one of God's promises are based upon conditions.

God's Part

(1) Giving His Word by Inspiration. The Holy Bible, the message from heaven, has stood the acid test of the ages and even the Teutonic war of this decade, has made its sacred page appear more sublime.

(2) Sending His Son to Die in Our Stead. The love of God our Father, as demonstrated in the gift of His Son, is incomparable. The belief of this love, stops man, and saves him from his sins.

(3) Establishing His Church Militant. The Militant Church of God, is the mobilized armies of the Christian religion on earth, to help each sinner to overcome the great enemy of man, as existing in his flesh, the world and the devil.

(4) Calling and Sending Men to Preach the Gospel. Some times God has a hard task to get a man to preach the gospel; but after He allows him to go his way, until a limb of his body is lost, a failure in his business comes, or some great calamity overtakes him, he then, sometimes, reconsiders his way, listens to the divine call, turns to the profession of preaching the gospel and becomes an efficient teacher in the church of God.

Millions have heard their country's call to arms, thousands have died upon the European battlefields; but many pulpits are vacant, few heed the call of God to preach, men are turning away from the church and the world is facing toward

hell. If some thing is not speedily done for the purity of the peoples of earth, if those whom God calls to sacred ministry will not heed, God almighty may uncork perdition and pour out from the ''bottomless pit'' upon the nations of earth, fumes a thousand-fold more deadly than the mustard gas from the laboratories of the Hun, or the liquid fire upon the Allies on the devastated battlefields of Northern France, or the destructive torpedo from the hellish Teutonic submarine.

(5) Sending His Holy Spirit to Call and Teach Man. (Jno. XIV; 26): ''But the Comforter, which is the Holy Ghost, Whom the Father will send in My name, He shall teach you all things, and bring all things to your remembrance, whatsoever I have said unto you.''

God, our Father, in doing, in amplified form, His part for the salvation of men. And yet men are wicked, and multitudes are sinful, and countless hosts are being eternally lost.

Man's Part

(1) Repentance. This is a Godly sorrow for sin and a turning away therefrom. Jesus Christ came to save man ''from'' and not ''in'' sin. Even from the (a) Guilt, (b) Practice and (c) Power of sin.

(2) Faith (Romans I; 16): ''For I am not ashamed of the gospel of Christ: for it is the power of God unto salvation to every one that believeth; to the Jew first and also to the Greek.''

(3) Regeneration This produces a new creature. A new creation. New as to: (a) Heart, (b) Disposition, (c) Love, (d) Deportment. Regeneration is a fundamental doctrine in the gospel of Christ and the Christian religion.

(4) Obedience The great trouble in the world has ever been, the misappropriation of power.

If the church of Christ would obey God, conserve her power for His glory, and use energy, divinely directed, to evangelize the world, as men do to advance their own selfish purposes; then the world would soon be Christianized, the nations of the earth indissolubly united, a league of nations formed upon the basis of the Fatherhood of God and Brotherhood of man, with peace on earth and good will toward men pervading.

May the church of God awake to her pristine valor, may the doctrines of repentance, faith, regeneration and obedience be more constantly and thoroughly emphasized from the purity of the pulpit; may the members of the church be taught, by actual experience, that they cannot remain members and live in open rebellion to God's holy commands though they may pay their thousands; then the pulpit and pew will be reinstated, then the world will have confidence restored, then the unbeliever and the sinner and the ungodly will seek, by a new humanity, to be fitted for and admitted into the association of the pure in heart.

MR. FONVILLE HONORED

Mr. D. R. Fonville, of this city, who served as Secretary of the Y. M. C. A. in France for several months, has been honored by receiving the *Croix de Guerre*. Mr. Fonville will leave May 15 for Washington, D. C., where he will be officially awarded this medal.

Be a friend to some one. Human sympathy is always needed.

A man may be a great sinner, but Christ is a great Savior.

When the Lord begins to get a man's money, He soon gets the man.

WELCOME HOME

(Continued from page 9)

They have builded Him an altar in the evening dews and
   damps;
I have read His righteous sentence by the dim and flaring
   lamps:
His truth is marching on.
In the beauty of the lilies Christ was born across the sea,
With a glory in His bosom that transfigures you and me;
As He died to make men holy, let us die to make men free,
   While God is marching on.

IV. THE SALUTE TO THE FLAG.

"I pledge allegiance to the Flag and to the Republic for
which it stands; one Nation, indivisible, with liberty and
justice for all."

V. RESPONSIVE SCRIPTURE READING.

The Lord is my light and my salvation; whom shall I fear?
The Lord is the strength of my life; of whom shall I be
afraid?

When the wicked, even mine enemies and my foes, came
upon me to eat up my flesh, they stumbled and fell.

Though an host should encamp against me, my heart shall
not fear: though war should rise against me, in this will I be
confident.

One thing have I desired of the Lord, that will I seek after;
that I may dwell in the house of the Lord all the days of my
life, to behold the beauty of the Lord, and to enquire in His
temple.

He that dwelleth in the secret place of the most High shall
abide under the shadow of the Almighty.

I will say of the Lord, He is my refuge and my fortress:
my God; in Him will I trust.

Surely He shall deliver thee from the snare of the fowler,
and from the noisome pestilence.

He shall cover thee with His feathers, and under His wings
shalt thou trust: His truth shall be thy shield and buckler.

Thou shalt not be afraid for the terror by night; nor for
the arrow that flieth by day;

Nor for the pestilence that walketh in darkness; nor for
the detruction that wasteth at noonday.

And whosoever will be chief among you, let him be your
servant:

Even as the Son of man came not to be ministered unto, but
to minister, and to give His life a ransom for many.

Know ye not, that to whom ye yield yourselves servants to
obey, his servants ye are to whom ye obey; whether of sin
unto death, or of obedience unto righteousness?

For he that is called in the Lord, being a servant, is the
Lord's freeman: likewise also he that is called, being free, is
Christ's servant.

Ye are bought with a price; be not ye the servants of men.

Brethren, let every man, wherein he is called, therein abide
with God.

No man can serve two masters: for either he will hate the
one, and love the other; or else he will hold to the one, and
despise the other. You cannot serve God and mammon.

And whatsoever ye do, do it heartily, as to the Lord, and
not unto men;

Knowing that of the Lord ye shall receive the reward of
the inheritance: for ye serve the Lord Christ.

For, brethren, ye have been called unto liberty; only use
not liberty for an occasion to the flesh, but by love serve one
another.

For all the law is fulfilled in one word, even in this: Thou
shalt love thy neighbor as thyself.

I beseech you, therefore, brethren, by the mercies of God,
that ye present your bodies in a living sacrifice, holy, acceptable unto God, which is your reasonable service.

How firm a foundation, ye saints of the Lord!
How firm a fondation, ye saints of the Lord!
Is laid for your faith in His excellent word!
What more can He say, than to you He hath said;
To you, who for refuge to Jesus have fled?
To you, who for refuge to Jesus have fled?

When through the deep waters I call thee to go,
The rivers of sorrow shall not overflow;
For I will be with thee thy trouble to bless,
And sanctify to thee thy deepest distress,
And sanctify to thee thy deepest distress,

The soul that on Jesus hath leaned for repose,
I will not, I will not desert to his foes;
That soul, tho' all hell should endeavor to shake,
I'll never, no never, no never forsake!
I'll never, no never, no never forsake!

VII. PRAYER—By Pastor.

Followed by Announcements and Offering.

VIII. "THE WELCOME."

(1) Why we are glad to welcome you, by a Layman or
Pastor. (Five minutes).

(2) Why we are glad to get home, by a returned soldier.
(Five minutes).

IX. SONG, "ONWARD CHRISTIAN SOLDIERS."

Onward Christian soldiers!
  Marching as to war,
With the cross of Jesus
  Going on before;
Christ, the royal Master,
  Leads against the foe;
Forward into battle,
  See His banners go!

CHORUS—
  Onward Christian soldiers!
    Marching as to war,
  With the cross of Jesus
    Going on before.

Like a mighty army
  Moves the Church of God;
Brothers, we are treading
  Where the saints have trod;
We are not divided,
  All one body we;
One in hope and doctrine,
  One in charity.

Crowns and thrones may perish,
  Kingdoms rise and wane,
But the Church of Jesus
  Constant will remain;
Gates of hell can never
  'Gainst the Church prevail;
We have Christ's own promise,
  And that cannot fail.

X. "CARRY ON."

(1) In the Church. (3 minutes)—By a Layman.
(2) In the Community. (3 minutes)—By a Soldier.
(3) In the Nation. (3 minutes)—By a Soldier.
(4) In the World. (3 minutes)—By the Pastor.

XI. THE ENLISTMENT COVENANT—of the
"Carry-On Group."

, Every true man and woman has had his or her part in this war. It may have been in the Front Line Trench, in the Training Camp, on the Sea, or saving, giving, praying and working at home. America stood together in all this struggle or we would have been like Russia today.

The object of the "Carry-On Group" is to carry on the ideals of Christian Democracy for which we fought, labored and prayed during the war into every department of life.

The "Carry-On Group" shall consist of all who sign the "Enlistment Covenant." (See last page). They shall hold a C. O. G. "Review" as often as once a month which shall be socially attractive but whose main object shall be to re-view the work of the Church, Community, Nation and the World and to plan future constructive activities. (See "Carry-On Group" Notes for further details).

XII. SONG, "TO THE WORK."

To the work! To the work! We are servants of God,
Let us follow the path that our Master has trod;
With the balm of His counsel our strength to renew,
Let us do with our might what our hands find to do.

Chorus—

Toiling on, toiling on, toiling on, toiling on;
Let us hope, let us watch, and labor till the Master comes.

To the work! To the work! Let the hungry be fed;
To the fountain of Life let the weary be led;
In the cross and its banner our glory shall be,
While we herald the tidings, "Salvation is free!"

Chorus—

XIII. ANNOUNCEMENT OF THE MEETING OF THE FIRST "CARRY-ON GROUP REVIEW."

XIV. CLOSING PRAYER AND BENEDICTION.

"CARRY-ON GROUP"

Enlistment Covenant

I hereby covenant, with God's help, to enter or to extend my activities along the lines I have checked below and thus help, "Carry On", the best things of life in the Church, the Community, the Nation and the World.

(1) In the Church:
By joining the Church.
By service in the Church program as assigned by the pastor.
By some special service in the Sunday School.
By some special service in the Christian Endeavor Society.
By rendering some special service not above noted.

(2) In the Community:
To help make this Community a good place in which men, women and little children may live.
To help plan and promote a program for Civic Betterment.

(3) In the Nation:
To lend aid in the promotion of a true democracy—a government of the people, by the people and for the people—guaranteeing a square deal to every man, woman and child under the flag, rich and poor, high and low, without regard to race, creed or condition of life; and to place the weight of my influence against all erratic movements which endanger our civic institutions.

(4) In the World:
To promote International friendship by an effort to know the differences of environment and view-point of my fellowmen and to find ways of bridging those differences.
To give of my substance to aid those lands and peoples who are not so favorably situated as my own and to thus minister to their physical and spiritual needs in the Spirit of Him who gave His life that they might have eternal life with Him and with us all.

To make it the rule of my life to pray daily for those in every land who do not know Christ or who have mis-understood or not accepted His life of sacrifice and service.

Trusting in the Lord Jesus Christ for help and direction, I hereby willingly give myself to Him and to what-ever special life-work of Christian Service He may open to me.

If it is His will, I will gladly go as a missionary to a Foreign Field or be a religious worker in the Homeland as He may open the way, and I hereby pledge to do all in my power to bring this to pass.

I hereby solemnly but willingly enter into the above covenant with God and all others who may sign this pledge of service. I agree to the best of my ability and with God's help to fulfill this my vow.

(Signed)

Name ....

Address ....

NOTES ON THE "CARRY-ON GROUP"

1. The lessons of the war must not be lost. The sooner they are appreciated and built upon, the more certain will be the response. Do not wait until all the boys come home. Hold more than one Welcoming Service and let the boys you first welcomed help welcome those who come later.

2. The "Carry-On Group" should be assembled for its first "Review" as soon after the Welcome Service as it can be ar-ranged and an evening given to organizing and vitalizing the Group. It is not designed that it should be composed of sol-diers only, though all soldiers should be in it.

3. The Group should have at least the following officers and committee:
A president. (He may be called the captain.)
A vice-president. (He may be called the lieutenant.)
A secretary. (He may be called the field clerk.)
A treasurer. (He may be called the paymaster.)
The Pastor should be the Chaplain of the Group.

Committees:
THE TRAINING CADRE. (The Church Group.)
THE WELFARE WORKERS. (The Community Group.)
THE DEPARTMENT OF MORALE. (The National Group.)
THE AMERICAN EXPEDITIONARY FORCES. (The World Group.)

he pastor and official should plan world-while jobs for these groups. Each "Carry-On Group" should, if advisable, have a "Carry-On" Bible Class in the Sunday School.

The Church should:
(1) Welcome the Returning Soldier by (a) A Committee to meet him when he comes. (b) A Welcome Service. (c) Making him continue to feel Welcome.
(2) Get the Soldier a Place where necessary by (a) A Com-mittee of three active members of the church. (b) Looking for him; consulting him! suggesting to him; securing for him his old job or a better one.
(3) Enlistment in a Life of Service by The Carry-On Group and in every other possible way.

NOTE—Copies of this service can be secured by addressing War Work Commission of the Christian Church, Room 45, C. P. A. Build-ing, Dayton, Ohio. Sufficient should be ordered to enable each per-son present at the Welcome Service to have an individual copy in order that each may have an opportunity to enlist in the "Carry On Group," which is the climax and objective of the service after the Welcome to the Soldiers.

Sunday School and Christian Endeavor

SUNDAY SCHOOL LESSON FOR MAY 25, 1919

Repentance

Jonah 3:1-10; Luke 13:1-5; Acts 2:37, 38.

Golden Text: Repent ye, and believe in the gospel. Mark 1:15.

Devotional Reading: Luke 15:11-24.

Thoughts For Teachers

Have you gotten discouraged with that bad boy or careless girl? The Lord had to speak to Jonah a second time. The Lord said "Go" to Jonah and he went—in the wrong direction. The Lord has said "Go" to you; which way are you going?

God had thought for the 120,000 children in Nineveh who would be lost if the city was destroyed; have you thought that we have 25,-000,000 boys and girls in America who are not connected with church or Sunday school? I have recently heard a stirring address on "Saving the Loss" those who go out from our Sunday schools, and form the continual loss which accounts for the fact that with all the numbers in our Sunday school, our churches increase so slowly. Except our nation repents, we shall perish as did all the civilizations of old. Shall we pray "Thy will be done" unless we are doing it, and helping others to learn it that they, too, may do it?

MRS. FRED BULLOCK.

CHRISTIAN ENDEAVOR TOPIC FOR MAY 25, 1919

Kings 8:54-61; II Peter 1:1-4

(Union Meeting with Juniors and Intermediates. A memorial meeting).

Sing some of the Promise Songs, and plan a meeting which shall be a future promise for the younger, a past promise for the older ones, and also a future of which we are sure, based upon the past. A splendid Christian woman went as a missionary. While upon a furlough home, she went to a doctor concerning a spot upon her face and learned to her horror that she had contracted leprosy. She said nothing to her parents or friends that her furlough time with them might not be spoiled, but when she returned, she went to a leper colony as missionary. Eventually she was cured, but she chose to stay and labor there. Years later a friend came to see her. As she went away, she turned back to wave a final farewell, and word of encouragement. Her word was "Hitherto," and the brave missionary returned the wave, and shouted back "Henceforth." If we are surely doing the work of God then so surely as "Hitherto' He hath helped us, has He 'Henceforth' a crown of Righteousness laid up for us.

MRS. FRED BULLOCK.

CHILDREN'S DAY

Are you planning for Children's Day in your school? Let us have a special day in June when the flowers are blooming and the birds are singing to have a very special day for the children and invite the fathers and mothers to come. There are splendid programs prepared. You can secure them from the publishing houses, or from the publishers of almost any Sunday school song book. If you want a missionary program, write "The Missionary Education Movement, 156 Fifth Ave., New York City." Some people object to Children's Day on the plea that every day is a children's day in Sunday school, but this objection is not well founded. The older people should be found in the Sunday school, and if they are not there, something is radically wrong. "Train up the child in the way he should go"—and go that way yourself.

MRS. FRED BULLOCK.

CHILDREN'S DAY PROGRAM

June has been decided upon as the month in which every Sunday school of our Southern Christian Convention should have Children's Day, some Sunday in June. Let's make it unanimous. The children deserve the day and the occasion, and will make both memorable, if given a chance. Give the children a chance. Give them the joy, and the wholesome service of Children's Day.

The Sunday School Board of the Convention, with the invaluable aid of Mrs. J. W. Harrell, of Burlington, N. C., and Mrs. Fred Bullock of Suf-

folk, Va., have done their best on a program. We have every reason to believe the program is suitable to all our schools, and will satisfy. A copy has been sent by mail this week to every Sunday school secretary and to every pastor of the Southern Christian Convention. The programs are for free distribution. By copying the parts as needed no school need require many copies. But to a limited number additional programs will be sent on request.

Some trouble to have Children's Day? Some effort? Some work? Well, what is there on this earth that is worth while which does not require trouble, effort, work? Announce your Children's Day. Send request for programs. Get ready for the glad day. You want a bigger, better Sunday school? Well, we think Children's Day will inject new life—and will help. Try it. Let all the schools try it. Let's make it unanimous.

Your request to the undersigned for programs will have immediate response.

Yours for a great Children's Day.

J. O. ATKINSON,
Sec. S. S. Board S. C. Convention.

THE TITHER

An interdenominational publication devoted to Tithing and Christian Stewardship.

Editors

C. B. RIDDLE
KARL LEHMANN
BERT WILSON
HUGH S. McCORD
FRED G. THOMAS

8 pages; issued monthly; 50c the year

Address

THE TITHER Burlington, N. C.

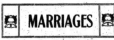

MARRIAGES

COLEMAN-KIMBRO

Mr. George R. Coleman and Miss Ava Kathleen Kimbro of Union Ridge, N. C., were married at the home of the writer, May 5, 1919. Only a few friends of the bride and groom witnessed the ceremony.

J. W. HOLT.

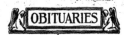

OBITUARIES

SCOTT

Mrs. Lottie M. Scott, wife of Franklin Scott, died April 22, 1919, at the age of nearly forty-four years. She was married to Brother Franklin Scott May 2, 1902, who, with a number of friends and relatives, are left to mourn their loss. Funeral services were at Needham's Grove, conducted by the writer. May God bless the husband and may he be ready to meet her in the glory land where there will be no parting.

W. J. EDWARDS.

ROWLAND

Mrs. Margaret E. Rowland, widow of the late Elmond Rowland, was born January 20, 1834 and departed this life at the home of her son, Rev. C. H. Rowland, Franklin, Va., on May 3, 1919, aged eighty-five years, three months and thirteen days.

Mother Rowland had been an invalid for thirteen years and five months during which time she was a great sufferer, but through it all she was very patient and never lost her keen interest in Christ's Kingdom. For many years, though not able to be out of bed, she listened, by means of a telephone, to her son preach the riches of Christ's Gospel. Her sweet Christian life during the years of her suffering was a constant inspiration to all who knew her. She was affectionately known by all in the community as "Mother Rowland" and no one ever left her bedside without a blessing. She was a member of the Plymouth Christian church.

Her husband and five children preceded her in death. Surviving are two sons: Dr. C. H. Rowland, Franklin, Va., and J. T. Rowland, Raleigh, N. C.; seven grandchildren and five great grandchil-

dren; three sisters and one brother, Beside these relatives, a host of friends will greatly miss her.

A large concourse of people gathered at the Pleasant Grove church near Raleigh where the funeral was conducted by Revs. J. Lee Johnson, R. P. Crumpler and the undersigned on Sunday afternoon, May 4.

GEO. D. EASTES.

DR. J. H. BROOKS

DENTIST

Foster Building . . . . Burlington, N. C.

CHARLES W. McPHERSON, M. D.
Eye, Ear, Nose, Throat

OFFICE OVER CITY DRUG STORE

Office Hours: 9:00 a. m. to 1:00 p. m. and 2:00 to 5:00 p. m.

Phones: Residence 153; Office 65J

BURLINGTON, NORTH CAROLINA

CANCER TREATED SUCCESSFULLY AT THE KELLAM HOSPITAL

The record of the Kellam Hospital is without parallel in history, having restored, without the use of the knife, Acids, X-Ray or Radium, over ninety per cent of the many hundreds of sufferers from cancers which it has treated during the past twenty-two years. We want every man and woman in the United States to know what we are doing.—KELLAM HOSPITAL, 1617 W. Main St., Richmond, Va.

JUST A LITTLE FUN

Equipped

The polar bear again we note
With jealousy 'intense.
He's born with a fur overcoat,
Which saves him much expense.
　　　—Washington Star.

Just Bragging

"A man betrays hisse'f by braggin'," said Uncle Eben. "When I hears a man tellin' 'bout how easy he kin drive a mule, I knows right off he ain't no reg'lar mule-driver."

How Natural!

Visitor (to facetious farmer): "I'd like to know why on earth you call that white pig 'Ink.'"

Facetious Farmer: "Because he's always running from the pen."

He Was Rude to Follow

"Oh, madam," said Jane to her mistress on returning from an errand. "There's been a young man following me!"

"Indeed!" replied her mistress.

"Yes, madam, I know he was a-following me, because he kept looking round to see if I was a-coming!"
　　　—Pittsburgh Press.

Might Have Happened Here

It is in Wichita they are telling the story of a woman who called at the police station and asked help in locating her husband, who had been missing several days. When asked why she waited so long before reporting his disappearance, she replied: "For the first three days I supposed he was just down at the corner waiting for a street-car."

Perhaps Reinforced, Too

There had been a painful scene the night before when Bertie had asked "papa" for Beatrice, and now the lovers were talking over the future.

"I am shocked," said Beatrice, "at the way father treated you. I always worshipped papa, but it seems my idol has feet of clay."

"Clay?" exclaimed Bertie. "Clay? Concrete, more likely!"

LAST MINUTE ITEMS

Dr. P. H. Fleming reports a good day at Union last Sunday. The attendance was perhaps the largest ever known.

Brother Eastes writes encouragingly of the Raleigh work. Here is every good wish for that church.

President Harper spoke at Holland, Virginia, last Sunday and is in that section this week in interest of the College.

Rev. J. L. Foster, Waverly, Va., has just paid this office a visit.

Broke a part of our press just now and so THE SUN may reach you a day late.

This office is in mourning. Some fellow sends us word to stop his paper.

ONCE UPON A TIME

(Written for the historian fifty years from now)

But this is not the story. I said once upon a time. Yes, it was in the year
1919—fifty years ago—that this institution needed an endowment fund of
people in giving this $250,000 called it going over the top, employing a military

Once upon a time an institution—Elon College by name—needed financial help. This educational institution was founded eighty years ago. Its founders have passed away. This college to which I refer is located in North Carolina institution. Time went by and he saw the splendid work of Elon College, saw and felt her influence on every hand and there was continual ringing in his ears, his Lord's money and regretted it.

And, lo and behold, this writer forgot that he was in the year 1969 and thought that he was in the year 1919—and looking over this story to correct it, the fellow who would not, and so it was the case. There was a man, a certain man—Oh, his name is forgotten—who could, but would ~~not~~, help this deserving
$125,000. The promoters of the work began to give the people an opportunity
had not sinned—he had just missed an opportunity of spending well some of
to $250,000. This was just after the great world war closed and a great ex-
to give to this fund, and so hearty was the response that the amount was raised
"I didn't help do it." He would have given a hundred times that which he
lamp to every quarter of the earth.
owning and controlling the institution) many great men and the world many
term to express their willingness.
of a need, nurtured in love, and has given to the Christians (the denomination
Staley, D. D.; Dr. E. L. Moffitt and Dr. W. A. Harper. This College was born
pression in that day was "Over the Top," because the American boys had gone "over the top" and hammered back the hordes of Huns that were hurrying
was asked to do it he could only have recalled the opportunity to give the small
down the hills of France with their heavy heels in a hellish way. And so the
Raleigh. Its first four presidents were: Rev. W. S. Long, D. D.; Rev. W. W.
Alamance County, seventeen miles East of Greensboro and sixty miles West of

Yes, the people gave willingly, but like many other things there had to be screamed out in wild imagination, WHO WILL THIS MAN BE?

amount asked of him. He died with this expression of regret upon his lips. H
valuable citizens. Missionaries trained there have carried the Gospel to a
heathen world, and its almost unnumbered teachers are carrying learning's

---

The printer had a mix-up, didn't he? Not exactly that way this time. The *scribe* of this page instructed that the type be mixed up—to be made into a "pi," to use a printer's term. But what for? Here is what for: We want you to write it out in correct form. You will find the story complete—no part of it has been omitted. To each person sending a correct copy of the story by May 20 a neat prize will be given. The contest is open to all subscribers of THE CHRISTIAN SUN and their families. Get your pencil and begin now. Send your answer to C. B. Riddle, Burlington, N. C.

ELON'S COMMENCEMENT MAY 18-20

If a quitter had a quota
Just and fair and right,
Would e'en a quitter quit a quota
And leave us in a flight?

ELON'S COMMENCEMENT MAY 18-20

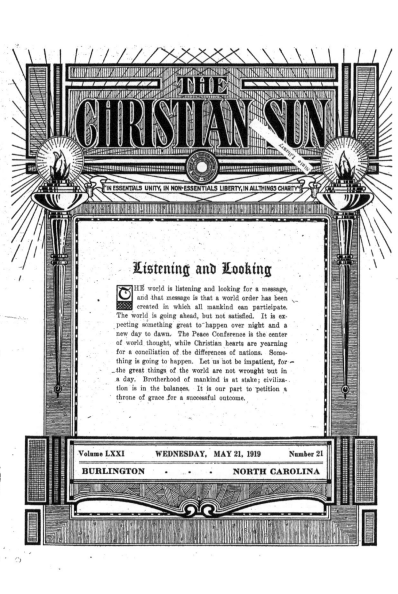

THE CHRISTIAN SUN

"IN ESSENTIALS UNITY, IN NON-ESSENTIALS LIBERTY, IN ALL THINGS CHARITY"

Listening and Looking

THE world is listening and looking for a message, and that message is that a world order has been created in which all mankind can participate. The world is going ahead, but not satisfied. It is expecting something great to happen over night and a new day to dawn. The Peace Conference is the center of world thought, while Christian hearts are yearning for a conciliation of the differences of nations. Something is going to happen. Let us not be impatient, for the great things of the world are not wrought out in a day. Brotherhood of mankind is at stake; civilization is in the balances. It is our part to petition a throne of grace for a successful outcome.

Volume LXXI	WEDNESDAY, MAY 21, 1919	Number 21
BURLINGTON	· · ·	NORTH CAROLINA

THE CHRISTIAN SUN
Founded 1844 by Rev. Daniel W. Kerr

C. B. RIDDLE - - - Editor

Entered at the Burlington, N. C. Post Office as second class matter.

Subscription Rates)

One year .... $ 2.00
Six months 1.00

In Advance

Give both your old and new postoffice when asking that your address be changed.

The change of your label is your receipt for money. Written receipts sent upon request.

Marriage and obituary notices not exceeding 150 words printed free if received within 60 days from date of event, all over this at the rate of one-half cent a word.

Original poetry not accepted for publication.

Principles of the Christian Church

(1) The Lord Jesus Christ is the only Head of the Church.
(2) Christian is a sufficient name of the Church.
(3) The Holy Bible is a sufficient rule of faith and practice.
(4) Christian character is a sufficient test of fellowship, and of church membership.
(5) The right of private judgment and the liberty of conscience is a right and a privilege that should be accorded to, and exercised by all.

EDITORIAL

KEEPING THE CEMETERY CLEAN

In going about over the country at this season of the year, you can see cemeteries, especially in the country, raked and scraped very clean. This is the annual memorial season; and by custom, we clean the cemetery as a part of the preparation for these occasions. This is well and good and it ought to be done. But we want to make a further suggestion about cleaning the cemeteries.

In the first place, they ought to be kept clean and free from trash and weeds all the year, and, in the second place, we feel that it is a mistake to scrape all the grass from the ground. Our cemeteries ought to be seeded with some suitable grass and the land enriched instead of scraping the soil off once a year and hauling it out as we often see. It is a common thing to pass a cemetery and see all the soil raked up in piles with the grass and packed in some remote corner or heaped over the fence. The consequence is that the cemetery looks barren all the time and the heavy rains, especially if the ground is sloping, washes away still more soil and often does damage to the graves. Let us begin to enrich the soil in the cemetery and get the land covered in a lawn grass and then the flowers will look so much better with a back ground of grass, the cemetery more beautiful and our lands preserved, and the burying place of our dead made attractive. Let us change some of our ways of doing things.

THE DIFFERENCE

Something less than one hundred years ago, we went to a certain country church. It was our first visit there. Upon arriving, the first thing that greeted the eye was an ordinary structure free from paint and resembling some forsaken farm building. The yard was poorly kept and there were few suitable hitching places. We had never met the people before and we knew nothing of their hospitality. We were treated all right and treated in a kind manner, but there was a feeling that was present, akin to the way the house and the yard were kept. There was a kind of "don't care" spirit in the air. Not many children gathered there that Sunday and we wondered why. We believe that we know why now.

Another occasion carried us to a country church and it was our first visit there. A beautiful little church building could be seen for some distance before we reached the spot. It had paint upon it, and as we drew closer to the place, there was something of a smile upon the grounds that gave us a welcome that made a glad heart. The ground about the church was neatly kept, the building was well cared for, and there was a feeling of progressiveness there that was not experienced at the other place. The children were there in great numbers and they seemed to be at home on the two acres of land swept clean for the patter of little feet. It was easy to preach that Sunday because there was a spirit that embraced us.

The country church ought to be the place of attraction, the building should be kept in the best condition, well painted, care given to the inside looks and arrangement. The yard or grove about the church should always be kept in the very best condition for these things have their bearing upon the children as well as the older ones. Few of us have a desire to visit a lonely, forsaken place once every week or once a month, but all of us delight in going daily to the places about the farm that are beautiful and about the woodside where beauty abounds and where we find the things that we appreciate and love and adore. Why not make the church yard attractive by shrubbery? Why not plant flowers there just as we plant at home? And why not have a cultivation committee to look after these things? Such a work is worth while and we need to give it our attention.

Just one other word on the subject: The reason that we do not have the church grounds more attractive, than we do is because many churches are poorly located. They are located on some barren hill that is fit for nothing else except a building. We express the hope that people will quit this kind of a thing and locate the house of worship where the grounds can be beautified as well as the building. We must remember that it is the house of God and that it deserves the best location, and the best of our ability to make it beautiful and attractive.

CHILDREN'S DAY IN OUR SUNDAY SCHOOLS

The Board of Religious Education sent out last week a suggested program to be used for Children's Day exercises in our Sunday schools, and the Board urges that some Sunday in June be set aside for this day of special exercises by the children. This move upon the part of the Board is commendable and is certainly a step in the direction of better Sunday schools and better training for children. The children take a delight in doing these little tasks, and their recitations certainly bring joy to the hearts of those who hear them.

We earnestly hope and urge that every Sunday school in the Southern Christian Convention have a Children's Day exercise some Sunday during June. It will take time, but why have a Sunday school if you are not going to invest some of your time and talent in it. Why advocate the *instruction* of children if you are not going to *instruct* them? Why have a school for the children if it does not *school* them? There is enough talent in every Sunday school to train the children for this day and for these exercises. Of course, some will say that they do not have time but let us learn that what we do for the children, we must do for them now. Very soon they will be grown-ups and we will miss the chance of bringing them under the influences of these good things; we will miss the chance of instructing them early in the great lessons of Christian life.

Let no Sunday school fall short of its duty—its whole duty by the child. Let there be a universal move upon the part of our people to carry the program into effect for the Church and for the Kingdom—and for the children.

WE CONDEMN IT

We have in our possession a secular paper containing a large advertisement of the Methodist Centenary Fund, the advertisement being contributed by the Cocoa-Cola Company, Atlanta, Georgia. We believe that the Cocoa-Cola bottle fascination leads to the beer bottle, the beer bottle to the wine bottle, and the wine bottle to the whisky bottle. The Church needs to condemn these slop factories, and it seems to us that when the Church resorts to them for free advertising that it is giving them its approval. We believe in the Methodist Centenary Fund, but condemn the promotion of it through Cocoa-Cola agencies.

CONFIDENCE OF THE ALLIES

Confirmation of the abiding confidence of our Allies of the Old World in the energy and generosity of America is given by Major Pierre Blommaert Protestant Chaplain in Chief of the Belgian Army who has just arrived in this country. The Major, who is a Chevalier of the order of Leopold, has been officially delegated by the Belgian government to spend three months in America for the purpose of making known the actual situation of the Belgian people at present and their needs in the work of reconstruction. But he is also an unofficial ambassador from the Belgian Protestant Churches to the Churches of America, and is confident that Americans, who gave so freely to Belgium in her darkest days will not allow Protestantism to go under for want of timely assistance at a critical hour.

He admits frankly the disadvantages of Protestants in Belgium; "we are few in number," he declares. "We are not united as we should be. We are new comers. Although Protestantism first appeared in Belgium at the time of the Reformation, it was nearly stamped out by persecution, and for almost two centuries only one or two churches remained to keep alive the fire of the Huguenot faith. My own parish of Maria Hoorebeke is the sole Belgian parish which remained constantly Protestant from the Reformation until 1830."

THE CHRISTIAN SUN IN EVERY HOME

Our leaders are appealing to the people in behalf of Missions, Education, the Forward Movement, the Orphanage and the various other enterprises of the Church. All these things have the fullest endorsement from this office and we stand ready and willing to help in any way. These leaders are making some valuable discoveries, and one of these is that their work is easier where THE CHRISTIAN SUN is read.

Our great need is THE SUN in every home, and in behalf of the Board of Publication of the Convention, we make application now for time and approval to line up the whole Convention to visit every home where THE SUN does not go and make an extra effort to put it there. To this end a large card has been prepared for display in every church. It reads:

OUR ONE GREAT NEED

THE CHRISTIAN SUN

IN EVERY HOME

This card is soon to be mailed to every church and we seek the co-operation of the pastors to see that this card is displayed. We have also had these same words placed on a small gum label to be used on correspondence, packages, programs, hand bags, and other such places as they can be used. Let us pull together with this in mind—THE SUN in every home—until we get the thing to a practical issue. First, we must feel that it ought to be done and then do it. When our financial leaders tell us that those who read THE SUN contribute more liberally and willingly, is it not time for the Church to wake up to see that it must get the Church paper into the homes? If the denomination can benefit one hundred dollars, or five hundred dollars at the expense of a year's subscription as a medium of information and inspiration, we suggest that some of the money being raised be used in this way as part of the advertising of the work. If the departments of the Church cannot live without THE SUN, and depend upon it weekly, they ought to feel free to help support their best medium of communication with the people. We leave it to their good judgment.

STATE CHRISTIAN ENDEAVOR CONVENTION

The Christian Endeavor Convention in North Carolina meets in Burlington June 6-8. A great time is being planned for and the outlook for it is hopeful.

AMONG OUR BRETHREN

Church Members Need an Explosion

The statement is made that the gas shells used in the late war really contained no gas. They held two or three liquids that united to form gas only after an explosion. With no desire to carry the figure out to its last analysis, we stop to remark that there are many Church members who need an explosion to make them effectual. The elements are there which, if stirred together under due pressure, would work wonders. They need to be jarred into usefulness. The transfer of the Church's potentiality into dynamics is the problem of the age. We beg leave to draw a good, long breath before attempting a solution.—*Northwestern Christian Advocate.*

Religious Opportunity in New York

Greater New York is now said to be the largest city in the world, with a population of nearly six million. From the Church standpoint it presents the greatest field for mission work that can be found probably on any like area in the world. Of all that vast population, it is said that in all the Protestant Churches there are only 330,000 contributing members. There are registered in the public schools 1,750,000 children. Besides these, there are vast numbers of school age who are not in school. In Protestant Sunday schools there are only 185,000, and in Roman Catholic Sunday schools there are 158,000. This leaves in that great city 1,410,000 children who are not touched by the Sunday school. What an opportunity that presents to the Churches!—*Presbyterian.*

Horrible Crimes of Bolshevists

The most horrible crimes in the history of the world are now taking place in Russia. There have been as many people killed by Asiatic hordes which have swept down on civilization in past ages; but never has there been so deliberate, never so brutal a selection of the best people of massacre in large numbers. The case of the Bolsheviki massacring two thousand of the best citizens of a small city, selecting all of any education, is only typical. It would be as if the I. W. W. here should get control of a small town, line up and shoot all persons who had received a common school education. Last week the Bolsheviki troops got into Riga with the avowed intention of killing all the middle-class people. Bolshevism is war on intelligence, on all above the lowest classes of a nation.—*Journal and Messenger.*

CLASSIFIED ADVERTISEMENTS
(Northwestern Christian Advocate)

Wanted—A few ravens of the Elijah type that know how to feed preachers when salaries are slightly under par. Well-trained birds are required for this service, as it is emergent.

Change of Time—Morning services as announced for 10:30 o'clock will hereafter begin at 10:30 sharp. No more waiting until the last straggler presents himself or even until the choir shows up. Kindly take notice. The preacher means business. This train starts on time.

Wanted—Church members to fill empty pews near the altar rail. Best seats in the house. Must be filled if the preacher does his best. Move out from the back seats. First come first served.

Wanted—A working official board, one that will not only attend meetings upon call, but will work between times. Apply at any pastor's study.

Lost—A loud, sonorous "amen." When last heard it was in the "amen corner." It suddenly vanished and has never been heard from since. If found, deliver at next morning service sometime during the opening prayer or the preacher's sermon.

No Dumping Here—Please do not dump your rubbish in this church. Thoughtless ones have used the church vestibule and aisles to gossip and complain in. Please unload your troubles somewhere else. This is no dump.

Business Change—I wish to announce that I have closed up my business of knocking the preacher and obstructing the progress of the Church. Found it didn't pay. Am doing business for the Lord at the new stand, corner of Service Street and Faith Avenue. Sign of the Illuminated Cross.

Wanted—Fifty-three thousand young men and women to volunteer for kingdom-building. A score of lines are offered. Openings on all hands. Must have that number to keep pace with the Centenary. Apply to any pastor or Sunday school superintendent.

Investments Solicited—Splendid investments solicited by the Bank of Centenary. We take deposits of money, prayer, or service. Fine opportunity. Big returns. No risk. Inquire of your pastor or unit leader.

Found—A Methodist without a church home. We saw him wandering about in aimless fashion, not knowing where to go. We are detaining him temporarily by talking Centenary. Any one losing a member recently can secure the same upon application.

Lost—The spirit of testimony. It was once at home in every church and the possession of most Christians. But of late it has vanished. Its recovery is generally desired. Finder will be generously rewarded.

Agents Wanted—Wanted, a score or more of canvassers to introduce a brand-new article called the "Centenary," in every community. Short hours. Selling points unsurpassed. Home territory. Must be put on the market immediately. Splendid commissions. Inquire immediately of any pastor.

THE BOOKKEEPER SAYS

Blessed is the subscriber who pays his subscription when due.

Blessed is the subscriber who frets not when he gets a "love letter" from this office.

Blessed is the pastor who continues to send subscriptions for it brightens the corner where I am—and makes the Editor SMILE.

Blessed is the subscriber who when he desires his address changed, gives the old as well as the new.

"WHAT'S THE LAW?"

That the readers of THE CHRISTIAN SUN and especially those in North Carolina may have in detail some of the principal laws recently enacted in North Carolina we are submitting, in brief, a few of them and others will appear next week:

1. An Act to amend the Constitution of North Carolina in regard to the taxation of homestead notes and mortgages, which provides that "notes, mortgages and all other evidence of indebtedness given in good faith for the purchase price of a home when said purchase price does not exceed $3,000, and said notes, mortgages and other evidences of indebtedness shall be made to run for not less than five nor more than twenty years, shall be exempt from taxation of every kind, provided that the interest carried by such notes and mortgages shall not exceed 5½ per cent." Chap. 119, Public Laws 1917.

2. An Act to provide for the teaching of agriculture, manual training and home economics in the public schools of North Carolina. Chap. 190, Public Laws 1917.

3. An Act to relieve the crop lien evil which provides that landlords and other persons advancing supplies to tenants shall not charge for such supplies a price or prices of more than ten per cent over the retail cash price or prices of the article or articles advanced. Chap. 134, Public Laws 1917.

4. An Act to provide for assisting rural communities in the utilization of small water powers, which authorizes the State Highway Commission to advise and assist in providing a water supply and electric power and electric lights for such communities, and provides $5,000 annually for the purpose of carrying out the provisions of the act. Chap. 267, Public Laws 1917.

5. An Act providing for installation of rural telephone lines and the formation of rural mutual telephone system. Chap. 267, Public Laws 1917.

6. An Act to improve the social and educational conditions in rural communities, which makes it the duty of the State Superintendent of Public Instruction to provide for a series of rural entertainments consisting of moving pictures given in rural school houses, the cost of same to be borne one-third by the State, and two-thirds by the County Board of Education or the rural school community desiring the entertainment; and appropriate $25,000 per year to carry out the provisions of the act. Chap. 186, Public Laws 1919.

7. An Act making it mandatory upon the county commissioners to levy an annual tax for upkeep of roads, the amount of said tax to be in proportion to the amount spent on the construction of roads. Public Laws 1919.

8. An Act to amend the Constitution of North Carolina so as to insure a six months school term. Chap. 192, Public Laws 1917.

9. An Act to provide for the incorporation of rural communities. Chap. 128, Public Laws 1917.

10. A Resolution directing a commission to make an extensive investigation of the subject of taxation, said commission to be appointed by the Governor. Resolution No. 46, Public Laws 1917.

11. An Act to provide for the physical examination of the school children of the State at regular intervals, and appropriating for the purpose of aiding in the treatment of children found to be defective a sum not to exceed $10,000 per annum. Chap. 244, Public Laws 1917.

(Continued next week).

SLIPPED IN BY THE BOOKKEEPER

Dear Brother Riddle:—

I am sorry that I let my subscription expire before renewing. It was a case of pure neglect and I appreciate the fact that you did not stop the paper from shining in my home. Your editorials and Dr. Staley's letters are worth the price of the paper, to say nothing of the many other good things. I have been taking THE CHRISTIAN SUN for thirty years and want it to ever shine in my home. I enclose check to renew my subscription.

Yours very sincerely,

....

Greensboro, N. C.

FROM TWO LETTERS

"I feel that I am not doing my duty as a church member if I do not encourage and urge our members to take THE SUN. I am glad that the paper has improved, and feel that we should not be satisfied until it is in every home in the Christian Church. * * THE SUN is a necessity. Why subscribe for another paper because it is cheaper? Why compare it with other denominational papers? Does a farmer buy a hoe when he needs a plow? Does a carpenter buy a hammer when needs a hatchet? * * * I am interested in my Church paper.   E. B.

I believe in tithing and missions * * * I don't understand why people cannot understand the Bible. * * * I cannot do without THE SUN, and I never expect to be behind with my subscription account.

N. L. H.

QUOTATIONS FROM THE SHOP FORCE

"One side is ready—let her shine."

• •

"She is O. K.—let her roll." , "Here she goes."

• •

"Second side ready. Lock her up and let her go."

• •

"That will get 'em. That's the thing."

• •

"On time is the word here. Let her go to the P. O."

NEW HERALD EDITOR NOT MARRIED

We made a blunder some days ago and it is too good to keep. This office sent Brother A. M. Kerr, the newly elected editor of *The Herald of Gospel Liberty*, a little present. The present had a place in it for his name, and also for his wife's, and so we filled in the names before sending. He sends thanks and gives us the information that he is not married. We gladly apologize for the error, but advise Brother Kerr to let the name stand for a while yet. Brother Kerr is not married. Keep it in mind and don't send his wife any presents.

Don't strike your horse until you are ready for him to go. Don't insist upon your people to do something without giving them something to do.

PASTOR AND PEOPLE

FROM A PASTOR AT LARGE

I left home Saturday morning, May 10, and that afternoon found myself in the neighborhood of Shiloh, Randolph County. I preached at this place over sixty years ago and since that time there have been many changes. Practically all the old people are gone and their children and grandchildren are taking their places. I went out to Shiloh church on Sunday morning and memorial services were held. A large crowd was in attndance and I shook hands with many dear friends. I preached a sermon to the old unsaved people in the afternoon and we had a delightful service. Brother Banks is doing a great work here and all seem to like him and he enjoys his work among them. I spent the next three days in the community. I went to the homes of Rev. H. A. Albright, Brother William Craven and several of the Moffitts, the names of whom I cannot separate. I came home exhausted, but after having rested a little I am ready for the next work.

I enjoy talking to the old people, and particularly to the unsaved. The fourth Sunday I expect to be at Barrett's church, in Southampton County, Virginia. This is my natural and spiritual birthplace. It has been over eighty years since I was spiritually born at that place. If able to get there I am anticipating a delightful time.

J. W. WELLONS.

Elon College, N. C.

GREENSBORO REVIVAL

What has been called the greatest meeting in the history of the First Christian church, came to a close last night, (May 8), with 119 professions and reclaimations. The pastor did the preaching and was ably assisted by the Berge Sisters, singing evangelists of Baltimore, Maryland. From the first service, Sunday, April 20, the power of the Spirit was in evidence, and much interest, in spite of the difficulties and opposition a man has trying to hold a meeting in Greensboro.

One of the greatest features of the meeting was the work of the Berge Sisters. To say they are great expresses it in a very mild form. They sing the Gospel in the most effective manner of any workers I have ever met. They sing with the spirit and the understanding which makes an audience sit up and listen. In addition to their musical qualities, both are great in personal evangelism—entirely free from sensational devices and methods. They depend upon the Lord for the revival, and it comes. Both persons are filled with the spirit of enthusiasm, and the power of the Holy Spirit.

One great blessing of the meeting was the awakening on the part of the church. We had a revival in the church. It was great to see strong men and women who had lost the joy of salvation, and numbers who were unsaved, rush into the altar and pray through, for the altar was used from the very beginning, and every profession was made at the altar of prayer. We have great reason to believe that the work is going to accomplish something as a result of the great revival it has has just witnessed.

Another great feature of the meeting was the noon hour shop meetings. The writer has always loved these services, and found his helpers in the same frame of mind, and ready at all times for the services. The men and women in the shops gave us a warm reception, and gladly gave of their time for the noon hour meetings.

During the meeting a number of distinguished visitors called. Among them were Drs. W. A. Harper and W. P. Lawrence, Mrs. Lawrence, Mrs. N. G. Newman, Mrs. J. O. Atkinson, and Mrs. C. C. Johnson from Elon, and a number from this city. We were glad to have them, and welcome them back to see us again.

On the last Wednesday of the meeting we were given a delightful surprise by two of our best and most loyal friends, Messrs. L. S. Thompson, and W. L. Rilee, from Newport News, Va., who came down to spend a day or so in the meeting with us. We were overjoyed to have these men come to see us. Both united with the Newport News church during our ministry there, and have always been among our very best friends, as well as the leaders in that church. God bless and multiply their kind in the Christian denomination. We were glad to have all the visitors with us and hope one day to have them call again. Pray for our work.

J. VINCENT KNIGHT.

Greensboro, N. C.

FROM W. D. HAWARD'S NOTE BOOK

First Sunday.—Preaching at New Lebanon at 11:00 A. M. One member received on confession. Attended Young People's Missionary Society at the same church at 3:00 P. M. From there we drove to Union and attended a meeting of Young People's Missionary Society. From there we drove home and had not been in the parsonage very long before a young couple came in to be married. They were Mr. Clyde Clifton Hart and Miss Edna Atkinson, both prominent young people of Dendron. The groom has recently returned from France where he saw service in several hard fought battles. In the evening we attended service at the Methodist church. A full day.

Second Sunday.—Preaching at Wakefield at 11:00 A. M. A good service. Mothers' Day was observed here and at Burton's Grove in the afternoon. At the last named place there were four reconsecrations and one member received on confession into the church. The evening service at Dendron was called in on account of a protracted meeting at the Baptist church. That meeting closed last night, May 14, with several additions to the church. There will be some to join the other churches. The movie man is here with a big tent but was kind enough not to run his show while the meeting was going on. He will have a crowd tonight. Many feel, perhaps, as I heard a good sister once remark: "I enjoy everything that comes along."

W. D. HAWARD.

Dendron, Va.

WELL (WELLS) SUITED

Sometimes people are "well suited" with their surroundings and sometimes they are not. What will suit some people will not suit others. The writer was "well suited" a few weeks ago when he was instructed by some of our most loyal and faithful members of our Reidsville church to go to the dry goods store and select himself a nice hat and have his measure taken for a new suit of clothes not to cost less than $50.00 and they would see that the bill was paid. Their instructions were immediately carried out, not reluctantly, but gladly and cheerfully. The selections were made at a cost of $51.00 and I am now wearing my hat and suit with a very high degree of satisfaction and appreciation. It is a real joy to the pastor's heart to be so generously remembered in such a way by the people whom he serves. I appreciate these gifts not only for their money value, but more for the love that these big liberal hearted people have for their pastor that prompted the giving. As one of the members said to me: "Brother Wells, we are not presenting you with this suit and hat because we feel that you are not able to buy them yourself, but we are doing this as an expression of our love and appreciation of you as our faithful pastor." Words like these are words worth while. They make me feel like I want to keep going; to strive harder to be worthy of such expressions of appreciations and to live a better life and be a better pastor. I have never served a people more appreciative than the people of our Reidsville church, and I want to say, "God bless and prosper them."

W. L. WELLS.

Reidsville, N. C.

UNION, ALAMANCE

On the second Sunday in May we had a very large audience and delightful services at Union, Alamance. It was Mother's Day and the writer spoke on that theme at the morning hour and Rev. J. W. Holt administered the Lord's Supper at the close of the morning service. Rev. D. A. Long preached at the afternoon hour. It was a pleasure to have Brothers Holt and Long present and to hear them. They are men of ripe experience and their words of wisdom doeth the heart good.

Dinner was served on the ground and a more bountiful one it has not been my privilege to see. This is a fine community and they have large opportunities for service in the Master's work.

The Sunday school has decided to give one Sunday's offering to the Orphanage and one Sunday to Missions each month. It has also decided to take up the study of Missions in the Sunday school.

P. H. FLEMING.

Burlington, N. C.

SUFFOLK LETTER

The American Christian Convention was a very busy one. Commissions on many subjects consumed much time, provoked discussion, interested the majority, and made voluminous matter for future reference.

The recommendation, by the joint Committee of the Executive Board and the Commission on organization, to make out of the Executive Board of 10 of the Convention and the Board of nine Trustees of the Christian Publishing Association, a Board of Polity to work out the policy for the next four years and, at the same time, to clothe said Board of Polity with power to elect all editors, provoked spirited discussion. It was finally passed with the provision that it go into effect at the close of the present session. Hence editors were elected at the Conneaut session; but the joint Board of Polity will meet in Dayton, Ohio, May 27, and hereafter that Board will elect editors.

Two new District Conventions were provided for, but none of them are to be units of the Convention except the Southern Convention. There will be the New England Convention, the Southern Convention, the Western Convention, and the two others to be formed, making five in all. It looks as if such Conventions would, eventually, become units in the American Christian Convention; and, if they do, this would look to some real constructive work in organization. They seem to think, in the north and west, that the Southern Convention is doing progressive work; but I tell them, it is not our *men*, but our *organization*. There is nothing the American Christian Convention needs so much as organization. She has a host of capable men, but they are too far from the center of the organization. Conventions in smaller groups, and meeting biennially, as units, would develop system, leaders, activities, and furnish material for reports to the Quadrennials.

The new goal of $2,000,000.00 for the Forward Movement, created more enthusiasm and received greater applause, than any financial announcement ever made in open Convention; and this impressed me with the feeling that the people are pleased when we undertake big things. Small propositions do not stir men and women. Leaders must plan larger things for the Church, if they want to secure enthusiastic co-operation. We must make our goal in the Southern Convention for the five years, $500,000.00; $250,000.00 for Elon Endowment, $150,000.00 for Missions, and $100,000.00 for other purposes. When that is done we can go up to the next Quadrennial feeling that we have some right to work in a great Convention. The beauty of doing great things is that many doing little things can have part in the great work. Our God is a great God above all gods, and we belittle Him when we plan on a small scale. We do not work in our own name, but in His name; and He will help us to accomplish great tasks, if we lay out great plans. The Convention wants to come South in 1922 and no doubt the choice will lie between Suffolk and Burlington. It has never met in the South but once and that was in Norfolk.

Altogether the Convention was earnest, forward-looking, seeking to advance the Kingdom-interests; and the entertainment was ample, hospitable, and enjoyable.

W. W. STALEY.

We are grateful to the many friends who have renewed their subscriptions since May 1.

CHRISTIAN EDUCATION

A BUSY AND HAPPY EXPERIENCE

On Saturday, last, I landed at Carrsville, where Brother Howard Luke met me and delivered me safely at his father's home in Holland soon after. I was not feeling very well physically and so I sought the advice of Dr. John G. Holland, one of the Kingdom's noble men, and he soon set me right.

Sunday morning I rode over to Holy Neck with Brother Dick Butler, who is a Sunday school teacher worth while. The Sunday school there is a remarkable one. In the open country where it is supposed things cannot be done in business-like, modern manner this school is thoroughly up-to-date. The more I travel around, the more I am convinced that it is folks and not the place that causes the Kingdom to flourish. Holy Neck flourishes, though more than a century old, and will continue to flourish. We need more such country churches.

That afternoon I attend a Sunday school Convention at Berea (Nansemond). My host, Deacon I. A. Luke, was president and not only presided well, but delivered a splendid address on Evangelism in the Sunday School. "Saint Luke," he is called, and I wish we had more such saints, not the saint of the cloister he, but the busy business man who yet has large time for Kingdom service.

Sunday night I was worshipping with our beloved Holland congregation. They meet in the town school building, while their new church, an edifice that would do honor to our cause in a great city, moves on toward completion. If ever a church had excuse for withholding from our Elon drive, these people did. Their church is really a tremendous undertaking for them. And yet it happened with them as always with God's true servants: the more they do, the more they can do, and so Holland joins Elon, Pleasant Grove (Va.), and Waverly in winning three stars for her card of recognition, giving thus four times her quota, with a magnificent church in course of construction and local conditions, from the world's standpoint quite unfavorable, for any undertaking at this time.

I returned to Holy Neck Tuesday for the drive. It was their memorial day, and Rev. L. E. Smith delivered the sermon, a fine effort and greatly appreciated. On Sunday, I neglected to say, Mrs. Fred Bullock gave an excellent Sunday school address at Holy Neck and Commonwealth's Attorney S. E. Everette, reared in the church, rejoiced every heart with one of his inimitable addresses. Monday night I attended a Sunday school class social at the home of Mrs. Job G. Holland, where I met as fine a company of young people as my experience numbers. So that I have feasted on the fat these days.

But back to Holy Neck. Her quota was the largest of any country church in the Convention and next to the great church at Suffolk among all the churches, and she came. "Over the top" she went and everybody is glad.

Two things have made the victory in this field possible—the people love the Kingdom in reality, that is, they are willing to sacrifice for it, and their pastor gave his unqualified support. Rev. W. M. Jay took me in his car and for three days and nights nobly seconded my appeals to the friends, and whenever I would reach my limit, he would come with a solar plexus blow that would put the thing across. He is a loyal son of Defiance College and as such must contribute to her necessities, and yet he volunteered a subscription to our drive, dividing it between his two churches. His people love him, and they have every reason to do so.

Funds This Week

Brother I. A. Luke gave $5,000 this week in memory of his father, Rev. J. M. C. Luke, a minister of the Baptist church, and of Rev. R. H. Holland, his wife's father, and one of the pillars of strength in our own Brotherhood.

Deacon R. H. Riedel gave $1,000 in memory of his daughter, Mary Natalia, who with his four other children, would have come to Elon, had God not called her. In her memory in Elon the tuition cost of a Christian minister is thus perpetually provided.

Mr. and Mrs. J. J. Gomer lost a most lovely and promising son, James Hallie, in the cause of freedom; and in his memory they have provided a fund of $1,000. At Holy Neck the memorial service in his honor, tributes were paid his Christian character by Deacons B. D. Jones and E. T. Holland, and then Pastor Jay announced the gift of his devoted parents in his name. It was a tender moment.

Other funds of $1,000 each this week were founded by Brother Wilson J. Holland, Dr. Job G. Holland, Brother W. Q. Peele, Brother R. C. Norfleet, Brother E. T. Holland, Mrs. Willie E. Lee in memory of Capt. P. H. Lee, one of Elon's noblest friends; Brother A. L. Jolly, Brother B. D. Jones, and Brother W. H. Riddle of Shallow Well church. May God multiply their kind!

Commencement

I write this on the train homeward bound. Two days are left to get ready for commencement. Next week we shall be busy with that great annual event in the Elon calendar, and then to the field again till this campaign has been gloriously crowned with victory and every heart shall rejoice.

Let our friends pray earnestly that God may continue to bless this cause.

W. A. HARPER

And Then More

Good things never cease—and that is why there is always more. Under the leadership of Dr. W. C. Wicker, Shallow Well church has gone over the top, and through the efforts of Rev. G. O. Lankford, Rosemont has doubled its quota.

People are always ready for something that will stir them to do something.

Are you on the band wagon helping your church do something, or walking behind?

THE CHRISTIAN ORPHANAGE

AND OVER THE TOP WE GO

Dear Friends:—

You remember in the beginning of the Easter campaign I asked you to make the Easter offering $3,000.00. I am glad to inform you in this letter that the financial report for this week carries us over the top with twenty cents to spare.

The response to the call for the Easter offering has been beautiful, indeed, and makes us very grateful to our churches and Sunday schools that have been so loyal to us in this work. We have quite a number of churches to hear from yet. We truly hope that each church will make this offering as we want to get each church and Sunday school interested in our little orphans and lend us a helping hand in caring for them.

One hundred and forty churches and Sunday schools have joined hands with us in reaching this goal of three thousand dollars for the Easter offering. Eighty-two churches and Sunday schools have not yet answered the call. How many more little helpless children we could help if all our churches would help us! I truly hope that sometime all our churches and Sunday schools will join in the work and get interested in helping the fatherless and motherless children.

If God has been so kind to you, as to see fit to spare you to be with your little children and to train them, don't you think you ought to be so grateful to Him, in His great love, to make some sacrifice to care for the little helpless children who have been deprived of the loving and tender care of a mother or the strong arm of a father to lean upon?

No mother upon whose knee to climb. No mother's sweet lips to kiss. No mother's neck to put their little arms around. No mother to listen to their little prayers at night. No mother to lay her hand upon their fevered brow while sick.

No mother to lay her gentle hand upon their little head and impart to them that mother's love no other can give. Left alone to go all through life deprived of this great blessing. Do you love them? Do you pity them? How much?

In a recent report we gave Liberty church, Vance county, credit for $21.20 when it should have been credited to the Sunday school.

In our last report we gave Cary Welch credit for $20.00 and it should have been credited to New Hill Christian church.

We are glad to make these corrections.

CHAS. D. JOHNSTON, *Supt.*

REPORT FOR MAY 21, 1919

Amount brought forward, $5,264.98.

Monthly Sunday School Offerings

(North Carolina Conference)

Mebane Sunday school, $3.00; Ramseur, $6.17; Christian Chapel, $3.40; Pleasant Hill, $3.57; Piney Plains, $6.36; Graham, N. C., $5.00.

(Eastern Virginia Conference)

Suffolk, $25.00; Third Avenue S. S., Danville, $10.60; East End Christian S. S., Newport News, $9.69; Washington St., Norfolk, $3.00; Berea (Nansemond), $10.00.

(Virginia Valley Conference)

Linville, $1.00; Timber Ridge, $1.91; Total, $88.70.

(Special Offerings)

Star Class, Suffolk Sunday school, $2.00; W. H. Thomas, $25.00; Lebanon church(for sheets), $15.00; Mrs. George McNeal, (Sunday eggs), $10.00; The O'Kelley Bible Class, Greensboro church, $25.00; A. P. Thompson, $17.00; Total, $94.00.

Special for Children's Home

R. L. Holmes and R. Dewey Farrell, Graham, N. C., $25.00.

Easter Offerings

Oak Level Sunday school, $8.58; Oak Level church, $2.42; Wentworth Sunday school, $12.45; Hayes Chapel church, $19.00; Dr. Anna Helfenstein, Miles City, Montana, $5.00; Hobson Sunday school, $10.00; East End Christian church, Newport News, $31.85; First Christian church, Raleigh, $74.00; First Christian church Sunday school, Raleigh, $18.05; New Hope church, $21.11; Mt. Zion church, (Ala.), $3.34; Winchester, Va., church, $6.25; Antioch church, (Va.), $51.80; Bethlehem Sunday school, (Va.), $13.35; Smithwood Sunday school, $6.70; Happy Home church, $15.00; Martha's Chapel church, $17.25; Graham Christian church and S. S., $25.25; First Church Sunday school, Norfolk, $19.30; First Church, Norfolk, $42.30; Burlington church, $31.00; Ingram Church, Va., $15.00; Isle of Wight, C. H. Sunday school (Va.), $6.00; Lagrange church, $8.50; A Friend, $2.00; Total $465.20.

Total for the week, $672.90; Grand total, $5,937.88.

DREAMINGS FROM THE FIRESIDE

There is no place like home. The patter of the rain on the outside presses the heart closer to the thought of a household where the footsteps of a baby make music that is sweeter than the playing of an artist.

No greater joy could come to us now than to have the whole SUN Family if it were possible come and greet each other in this little home. Their handshakes would make a melody in our heart.

Our highest hope is that THE CHRISTIAN SUN may bring some joy to a discouraged heart tonight.

We had a letter today—a real "God bless you letter" and greatly enjoyed it. As we read it we wondered why people did not write their friends letters more often. We appreciate the letters that come to this place and regret that time and expense forbid us from answering each.

There is a pleasure in serving a people who are good and kind and pleasant—such as we have as friends. God bless them all—all of them and multiply their kind in great numbers.

There is no rest in our work. It is one continual grind. There is little to break the routine feeling and "over and over" happenings. But there is that sense of pleasure that it will help some one—and that alone is joy.

WORSHIP AND MEDITATION

WHY MOST MINISTERS SHOULD PREACH SHORT SERMONS

By E. C. Ferguson, Ph.D.

(Reprinted from The Christian Advocate)

It is said of Francis Bacon that so entrancing was his eloquence the only fear of his audience when once he began to speak was that he would stop. The opposite fear too often pervades many a long-suffering congregation, but the preacher never will stop.

In his rules for a preacher, as contained in the Discipline, John Wesley says: "Take care not to ramble, but keep to your text, and make out what you take in hand." An additional advice might well be added, that after you have made out what you took in hand, bring the sermon to a conclusion. It is better to leave one saint wondering why the preacher stopped so soon, than ten wondering why in the world he did not stop sooner.

It is not because the people are worldly, wicked, unspiritual that short sermons are more popular than long ones. The spirit is willing but the flesh is weak, was Christ's apology for the shortcomings of His disciples on a critical occasion, and so, while the poet, in an ecstatic mood, may long for the state where

     Congregations ne'er break up
         And Sabbath has no end,

it is certain that the average congregation is in no humor for such protracted services.

It is said that Bishop Morris, after preaching about twenty minutes, used sometimes to surprise his audiences by closing the book and sitting down, making no other explanation afterwards than that he stopped because he was through. But such brevity in a bishop would scarcely meet the popular demand, as people expect longer sermons on such special occasions. On circuits, where people have preaching only once a month, it would seem desirable that the sermons should be longer; but in stations where there are two sermons on Sunday the preacher should cultivate brevity.

The teacher adapts the length of his lessons to the average members of his class; not to the bright ones, and the preacher should time the length of his sermons not to the saints in the Amen-corner, but to the average member of his congregation.

Unhappily for their own good, preachers do not hear all the comments which the people in the pews make on their sermons, otherwise there would be a speedy reform in some quarters.

Awhile ago I spent a Sunday in a station in a certain Conference. The good woman at whose house I was staying remarked to me: "Our preacher will preach us to death." Of course she did not tell him that, and so he goes on all ignorant of the death-dealing properties of his sermons. The brother who, with glowing face, grasps the pastor's hand as he comes down from the pulpit, exclaiming, "O, how much I enjoyed your

sermon! Why did you not continue longer?" is not followed by the ten dissidents remarking, "If you had only stopped when you got through what a fine impression you would have left."

When I have seen preachers, especially in revival meetings, preach the congregation into the spirit, and then by hanging on so long preach them out of it, I have thought of no more apt comparison, to use a homely illustration, than a cow giving a brimming pail of milk and then kicking it all over.

Brevity is the one merit in a sermon that is in the power of everyone. Every minister cannot be eloquent, learned, profound, logical, impassioned, poetic and interesting, but he may be brief.

Though, strange to say, this seems, judging from their talk, to be the one thing beyond the preacher's power: "I did not intend to preach so long, but then I did not find any place where I could stop without marring the symmetry of my sermon."

But edification, and not symmetry, is the end of the sermon, and if one of the two has to be sacrificed, one would better sacrifice symmetry.

It is curious how different symmetry looks from the standpoint of the pulpit and the pew. While the pulpit says, "I would like to close now and I know I ought to, but I cannot see any proper place," the pew can see plenty of places where the sermon could be brought to a close with good effect.

An anecdote has been going the rounds of the papers illustrating this point. Dr. Thomas A. Hoyt, the pastor of the Chambers-Wylie Memorial Church, of Philadelphia, was entertaining President Patton, of Princeton, General John B. Gordon, and other eminent men at dinner. The guests were speaking in strong praise of a sermon the minister had just preached, and those who were versed in theology were discussing the doctrinal points he had just brought out. Dr. Hoyt's young son was sitting at the table, and President Patton, turning to him, said: "My boy, what did you think of your father's sermon? I saw you listening intently to it," at which praise Mrs. Hoyt smiled cordially, and all listened to hear what sort of reply the lad would make. "I guess it was very good," said the boy, "but there were three mighty fine places where he could have stopped."

The difficulty of stopping is not half as great as many preachers imagine. In the times when the resumption of specie payments was being discussed and the difficulties and even impossibilities of such resumption were being learnedly presented, John Sherman cut the knot by declaring, "The way to resume is to resume." So the way for the preacher to stop is to stop.

Germany must accept or reject the peace terms as they are.

NOTES

Rev. F. H. Peters, Greenville, Ohio, writes: "Congratulations on the fine things that the South is doing."

Rev. J. G. Truitt will be assisted by Rev. L. E. Smith at the meeting at Pleasant Grove in August.

If THE SUN is any better than usual this week it is because our mother-in-law gave us a ham the other day.

Rev. W. B. Fuller, recently discharged from the Y. M. C. A. work, was in to see us the other day. He is open for church work now.

Mrs. W. S. Hardcastle and daughter, Mary, Dover, Delaware, called to see us a few minutes Monday morning. They are attending the commencement at Elon this week.

Rev. L. L. Wyrick and Miss Annie Brown were married last Wednesday, May 14. Rev. J. F. Apple officiated. Congratulations and best wishes. A long and happy life be to them.

Brother J. T. Cox, Lanett, Alabama, writes: "Our home was made dark some time ago by the loss of our son in France. North Carolina is my native State and I enjoy THE SUN."

The Elon commencement is on this week. Dr. Peter Ainslie, Baltimore, Md., delivered the baccalaureate sermon yesterday (Sunday) and Dr. W. A. Harper delivered the baccalaureate address. Owing to sickness we were deprived of attending. Following our custom, a full announcement of the commencement will be given next week. Look for it.

The annual memorial service was held at Bethlehem last Sunday. Dr. W. C. Wicker spoke at the eleven o'clock service and Dr. P. H. Fleming in the afternoon. Pastor J. W. Holt had the service in charge: This church has installed new pews and five dozen folding chairs. Brother Holt goes to Belew Creek next Sunday to hold memorial service there, he being pastor.

DR. BARRETT TO COME SOUTH

Dr. J. P. Barrett, Editor of The Herald of Gospel Liberty plans to move South about July 1 when his term of office expires. He is open for work in the Southern Convention. He is too well known to our people to need any introduction. Any Church needing a pastor of ripe experience and well qualified will do well to get in touch with Dr. Barrett.

CONGRATULATIONS TO BROTHER HARDCASTLE

Rev. Howard S. Hardcastle, Dover, Delaware, is the valedictorian of the Senior class at Elon College this year. Brother Hardcastle was a Freshman when the Editor was a Senior and we had the privilege of rooming with him that year. Of course our association did not help him to win the honor—in fact we have sent him word that it was for his good that he did not have but one year's experience with us, or else he would not have won.

MEETING OF THE NATIONAL CONVENTION OF THE ANTI-SALOON LEAGUE

The National Convention of the Anti-Saloon League of America will be held in Washington City, June 3-6, followed on Sunday 8th by a Field Day for the presentation of the prohibition situation to the churches of the Capitol City. Therefore, as the most convincing proof that the better citizenship of the country, which is the overwhelming majority, not only wants the enforcement of prohibition, but intends to see that it is accomplished, the Anti-Saloon League of America suggests and earnestly requests that the pastors of the churches in favor of prohibition throughout the country shall on June 8th bring the issue involved to the attention of their respective congregations to the end that Congress may be advised that not only has there been no reaction against prohibition but that on the contrary, the overwhelming majority of the people not directly interested in the liquor traffic want it fully and faithfully enforced, and desire the immediate enactment of the permanent code to carry into effect both war-time prohibition and the 18th Amendment to the Constitution.

LAST MOMENT WORLD NEWS

The American troops in Russia are to be withdrawn June 1.

Germany is divided over what action to take about signing the peace terms.

Congress convened May 19. The Republicans have the majority.

A great strike is on at Concord, N. C. One man has been killed. The feeling is becoming strong on both sides.

The boiler of a big Seaboard engine exploded one day last week near Raleigh, killing three men. One man killed, Carl D. Buie, was a former school mate of THE SUN'S Editor.

300 Turks and 100 Greeks have just been killed in Constantinople.

China is considering a boycott against Japan. The boycott deals with bank notes, shipping and general trade.

Last Saturday airships started across the Atlantic ocean and have made a successful trip.

This is where we close this week, and before you read this, next week's issue will be well under way. Help us to make THE SUN better all the while. We are endeavoring to make every inch of space count for the Church.

FROM OVER THE SEAS

THE JEWISH PASSOVER, 5679-1919, AND THE COMMUNION SERVICE

(Chaplain C. Summerbell, 318 Field Artillery, A. E. F., France)

"This is as the bread of affliction which our ancestors ate in the land of. Egypt; let all who are hungry, enter and eat thereof; and all who are needy, come and celebrate the Passover! This year we celebrate it here, but in the year to come, we hope to celebrate it in the land of Israel. This year we are as slaves; next year we shall be as freemen in the land of Israel."

Thus spoke Rabbi David Goldstein as he held up the "dish," at the Feast of the Passover, held in Chatillion-sur-Seine, on the evening of April 14, 1919. It was a unique occasion, for here were gathered five or six hundred Jewish soldiers, with a few of us Gentiles as invited guests, to celebrate the Passover an army gathering, held in a great Y. M. C. A. hut; it typified the New Day dawning on the world, when Knights of Columbus Orthodox and Liberal Jews, Y. M. C. A. men, and Army Chaplains of Christian and Jewish faiths, united in the Seder service.

Generally this is a home service, where families are gathered, but any poor Jew can knock on the door of the home of a fellow Jew, and has a right to enter and partake of the feast. After the second cup of wine is filled, the child, usually the youngest, asks, "Why is this night distinguished from all other nights?" and the parent answers in Hebrew:

"Slaves were we unto Pharaoh in the land of Egypt, and the Eternal, our God! brought us forth from thence with a mighty hand and an outstretched arm; and if the Holy One, blessed be He! had not brought forth our ancestors from Egypt, we and our children, and our children's children, had still continued in bondage to the Paraohs in Egypt; therefore, even if we were all learned, all men of understanding, all of us having knowledge of the Law, it nevertheless would be incumbent upon us to recount the departure from Egypt; and it is accounted praiseworthy to discourse at length thereon."

It was a great privilege to attend this Feast of the Passover, and as I looked down the long tables where sat hundreds of soldiers, all dressed in the same uniform, with similar faces, answering in Hebrew, there came to me a new meaning to the Lord's Supper.

Invariably men brought up under the influence of Christian traditions and atmosphere, like myself, look upon the Passover as a sad celebration, because our hearts are filled with sorrow as we read of the "Last Supper" that Jesus ate with his beloved disciples. To them, that Passover feast was a time of farewell and tragedy. But to the Jew, it is an occasion when religion

and patriotism are united, and he feels his nearness to Jehovah, and what the Lord has done for him; and he rejoices at this Feast, remembering that his condition of freedom came only through the mercy of God to the Jewish race, of which he is one. All his family love, all his patriotism, all his appreciation of religious ties, are aroused and strengthened.

To this Feast, the greatest Jew of all, looked with expectation of sweet communion, having loved his own that were in the world, he loved them unto the end. And as the death shadows began to darken the joy of living, when the hour was come, he sat down and the apostles with him, and he said unto them, "With desire, I have desired to eat this Passover with you before I suffer; for I say unto you, I shall not eat it until it be fulfilled in the Kingdom of God."

The Fourth of July to America lacks the family and religious association, but patriotically it has something of the national joy of the Passover, for the Passover is a feast.

Modern religious movements are coming back to the feast idea of this ancient celebration. In New England, the Parish supper, in the West, the Men's Club of the church, where eating is abundant, many forward movements are launched; a favorite approach to the business man that the Y. M. C. A. has successfully adopted, is a supper, after which religious plans are enthusiastically outlined. And Jesus himself asked to be remembered by an act of eating and drinking.

Again we are reminded that true religion is life, abundant life. After they had sung a hymn—one of the Passover psalms, they went out to the Mount of Olives. How many times these inspiring psalms help us to be brave and heroic! The hymn that Jesus and his chosen brethren sang must have been sad, but it was full of the strength that supports men's souls in deep anguish. After this, the Captain of our Salvation, was prepared for the Garden of Gethsemane.

At this crisis in the history of the world, many have gone, lonely, to a Garden of Gethsemane, without knowing that angels of God are ever by their side to strengthen in time of sorrow. Alas! too often, humanity neglects a spiritual preparedness. It becomes arrogant and proud, taking pride in a national God who has spoken in the past, but not desiring to catch the "accents of the Holy Ghost" concerning the every-day world of the Now.

"In these days," said Rabbi Goldstein, in an after dinner speech, "the world is looking for deliverance." "President Wilson," he affirmed, "is the modern Moses, and the men who hold up his hands are General Pershing and Admiral Sims."

To Americans, who are accustomed to hear their political leaders spoken of as the worst men out of state's prison, these words seemed extravagant. Yet we are surely living in grand and awful times.

This Passover, the Seder service, was entered into in the responsive exercises, not only by the Jews present, but by the Gentiles, and the Senior Chaplain of our First Army; and the Division Chaplain led in the English reading by invitation of the Ruler of the

Feast, who considered this the largest Seder Service in the world in which Christians and Jews jointly participated.

And yet to me this Seder service seemed to lack the atmosphere engendered by the awe inspiring truth of a Jesus or the missionary zeal of a Paul. At one time we were asked to eat, the Jew in honor of Hilel who the Rabbi claimed originated the movement, eventuating in the Christian religion; the *Christian*, to eat to the worship of Christ. As I try to worship, not Christ, but God alone, and consider Christ, the originator of Christianity, I was probably by myself in the large company. Nevertheless, I was thankful that Providence put it in my way to attend the Passover in France. The Heavenly Father is better to us than we can understand. And as I went out unto the heavy rain to find my side car which was to convey me back to my billet, I was happy in the consciousness of greater truths. I hope I understand a little better the real inner truth of the communion, in having partaken of the Passover with the fellow countrymen of Jesus. The Last Supper which artists have made immortal, and his disciples have made sublime, was a family gathering. He, as the head of the family, would not leave them comfortless, he would come to them that where he was, there they might be also, for he was going to prepare a place for them in the Heavenly Father's Home.

The Communion is not a time of division, or a separation, or critical self analysis, but simply a remembrance of *Jesus*, and how He sacrificed in life and death, wooing us to the same life of gentle sweetness, until we shall see him face to face.

AT RANDOM

No Tick Under The Pillow.—Small Scout—"Dad, what are the silent watches of the night?"

Indulgent Father—"They are the ones which their owners forgot to wind, my son."—*Boys' Life*.

Jimmie Knew.—A teacher was instructing a class in English and called a small boy named Jimmy Brown.

"James," she said, "write on the board, 'Richard can ride the mule if he wants to.'"

"Now," continued the teacher when Jimmy had finished writing, "can you find a better form for that sentence?"

"Yes, ma'am, I think I can," was the prompt answer. "Richard can ride the mule if the mule wants him to."—*Boys' Life*.

In The Neck.—Patrol Leader (In charge of camp of Scouts, to Tenderfoot who is trying to dive into two feet of water)—"Hey, Scout, if you break your neck diving into that water, I'll be the one that'll suffer for it."—*Boys' Life*.

A HINT TO DOUSE THE GLIM OR GO

"That young man stayed very late again, Edith."

"Yes, papa; I was showing him my picture postcards."

"Well, the next time he wants to stay late, you show him some of my electric light bills."—*Boston Transcript*.

MISSIONARY

THE BURDEN OF MISSIONS

No pastor is effectual, for the cause of missions, with his congregation, until he himself feels the burden of the missionary need. Rev. J. Campbell White who has likely stirred more people to missionary activity than any other man now in the public eye relates that recently he heard one of the most prominent missionary secretaries in this country make a speech, and a very fine speech, before a national convention; and then he heard a layman say after it was over "that speeches of that kind would not lay any burden of missions upon the Church in a thousand years." Dr. White's comment on this episode was, "We must feel this burden before we communicate it; and if we give the impression, the idea, that the Church is doing very well by giving seventy cents a year for the redemption of the world, it will go on sleeping until we all sleep in death."

The writer wonders what Dr. White could say of a Church that instead of giving seventy cents a year for the redemption of the world, gives less than a third of that amount. Will it go on sleeping until we all sleep in death?" The writer wonders how long our own dear Church is going to keep on sleeping the sleep of indifference to the one great object of the Church.

Are our pastors burdened with the missionary needs of the world? If so, are they crying out to their congregations from hearts that ache and agonize for the salvation of a lost and sin-cursed world? We cannot communicate a burden until we feel that burden ourselves.

False Education

Dr. White warns us as to a false sort of education. "We are not doing the thing (the missionary work)," declares Dr. White, "and that is the first thing we ought to realize; and when church boards give the impression that we are doing our duty, I am very much afraid that they are educating the people in falsity unless we ask for many times what we have asked them for yet."

It is easy to believe with Dr. White that we are today confronting the biggest responsibility that ever rested upon mortals, and the greatest opportunity, if we can only see it, and if alongside of the responsibility we can see our Lord with His resources and take the whole task in His name "In the presence of standing armies of 25,000,000 of men today, we ought not to be afraid to ask for 100,000 missionaries if we really believe they are necessary in order to carry on Christ's world campaign."

We are not feeling the heavy burden of a world's need, and so we are not asking with intense earnestness for the life recruits we now so much need.

J. O. Atkinson.

Is your Sunday school *schooling*, or just *meeting*?

Let your articles to this paper boost something, tell of something done, or how to do something.

Sunday School and Christian Endeavor

SUNDAY SCHOOL LESSON FOR JUNE 1, 1919

Faith: What it is and what it does Heb. 11:1-40; 12:1-2.

Golden Text: Believe in God, believe also in me. John 14:1.

Devotional Reading: Ps. 27:1-40.

Thoughts For Teachers

"According to thy faith," is God's rule. Archaelogists have found that the Greek word translated "substance" here in Heb. 11:1, is the same word they used for a title deed for property. So what the writer really says to us is this, "Now faith is your title deed to the things you hope for; the evidence of your ownership in things not yet seen." Is your faith small? Then so is your Heavenly property. Have you faith to remove mountains? Then they will be removed and your inheritance will be a land flowing with milk and honey, a Heavenly plane. If you hope for a large inheritance in Heaven, then get ready here to care for it there. The shirker here will never be a worker There, and there is a work there, for "His servants shall serve Him." MRS. F. BULLOCK.

CHRISTIAN ENDEAVOR TOPIC FOR JUNE 1, 1919

Our Relation to God. VI Reverence and Public Worship. Ps. 33:1-11, John 4:19-26.

Keep thy feet when thou goest into the house of the Lord. Are our feet kept when we go in loudly and boisterously? What about the times when we discuss "peanuts" and "cotton" and "house-cleaning" and a multitude of other things in the house of God? Are we reverent if we are talking of school or home or work until the very minute when the meeting is called to order, or even finish a sentence afterwards? What about the churches where spittoons are still kept as in a smokers club for those who cannot leave their tobacco outside the house of God? Are we showing reverence and respect to God when we allow trivial things to keep us away from His house on His Day? Would we break solemn engagements with anyone else as we break them with our Father? Think of these questions, and find the answers. MRS. FRED BULLOCK.

FORWARD MOVEMENT IN THE SUNDAY SCHOOL

What are you doing toward adopting and aiding the Forward Movement as it relates to the Sunday school? Have you a class in your school that is praying for a definite object? Is your school praying for any specific thing? Jesus said: "Whatsoever ye shall ask in my name," and our prayers, if they were analyzed, would often be like the oft-told tale of the aged lady's prayer for a husband, "Anything, O Lord, anything." What does your school need? What does it *want*? For what is it working? For what is it praying? MRS. FRED BULLOCK.

WHY WAS THE CHRISTIAN ENDEAVOR LEFT OUT?

"Why was the Christian Endeavor left out?" asks Brother J. V. Knight, of Greensboro, N. C., in THE SUN of April 9, as he proceeds to play the promoters of the "So-called Sunday school and Christian Endeavor Society Convention." I deem it neither necessary, or called for, to answer this question for Brother Scholz But for Brother Knight's information, be it known that with all our efforts in previous Conventions both by addresses and a half session devoted entirely to the interest of Christian Endeavor, there have not been more than three Christian Endeavor Societies represented at any time in the past five years. This would seem to indicate that Brother Scholz's omission springs not from "sore neglect" on the part of the Convention, but rather from something that is akin to neglect within the Christian Endeavor Societies themselves. We admit freely that the Sunday school cannot do the work of the Christian Endeavor Society. It does not pretend to. Brother Scholz rather included the two under the one head, as is commonly done in the Convention, than omitted one in favor of the other one. As for funds, the Convention has not, nor shall at any time solicit a cent from Christian Endeavorers, without first doing in all its power, both for the improvement of individual Societies, and for the promotion of general Christian Endeavor activity throughout the State. We challenge Brother Knight to hurl his energy expended in flaring Brother Scholz omission *into* spreading Christian Endeavor at the so-called Sunday School and Christian Endeavor Convention in July, "for Christ and the Church."

C. H. STEPHENSON, *Pres.*

Raleigh, N. C.

CHILDREN'S DAY

Programs for Children's Day in our Sunday schools were mailed last week to the Superintendent or Secretary of every Sunday school of the Southern Christian Convention, and two copies of the program to every pastor. Also a letter with each showing and urging the helpfulness of Children's Day. We have ample programs on hand. Address a request to the undersigned and program will be sent gratis.

And on Children's Day urge that the offering be liberal and large. This will all go for Sunday school missions. We can never do much in building up weak schools and in planting new ones until we have a fund with which to do this needed work. The Board should have a thousand dollars this year with which to plan its work for next year. Have a great Children's Day and take a good free-will offering, remitting same to the writer. Thanks.

J. O. ATKINSON.

A FEW NOTES—READ THEM

Is your Sunday school planning to have Children's Day in June? If not, why not?

Give the children a chance. A Children's Day will help to interest them in the work of the Sunday school, and will inspire the grown-ups also.

If you need Children's Day programs, address request to J. O. Atkinson, Secretary, Elon College, N. C., and same will be sent.

The Board of Religious Education of the Southern Convention have prepared a suitable program for Children's day and are now anxious to supply every school in the Convention that desires to have Children's Day—and that should mean all the schools.

MARRIAGES

OVERMAN-FOX

Mr. W. E. Overman and Miss Lizzie Fox, of Liberty, N. C., were married at the residence of the writer, Burlington, N. C., May 15, 1919. May their wedded pathway be a long and happy one.

P. H. FLEMING.

HOLWELL-HELMER

Mr. Warner Holowell and Miss Harie Helmer were united in marriage by the writer at the home of Mr. J. R. Osborne, 1023-25th St., Newport News, May 13, 1919. The bride is the attractive daughter of Mr. and Mrs. George Helmer of Newport News and the groom holds a responsible position in this city. May the blessings of God rest upon this new home and may their wedded life be long and happy.

H. J. FLEMING.

BEALE-ELDER

Mr. William James Beale, a former merchant of Elon College, but now a successful traveling salesman of Burlington, N. C., was happily married to Mis Una Mae Elder of Burlington, at the residence of the writer, Elon College, N. C., on the evening of May 15, 1919.

Two or three invited friends witnessed the ceremony and immediately after solemn vows were said the happy pair left for the North on an extended bridal tour. A host of friends will join in wishing them a long and happy married life. Officiating minister,

J. O. ATKINSON.

DR. J. H. BROOKS

DENTIST

Foster Building   Burlington, N. C.

CHARLES W. McPHERSON, M. D.
Eye, Ear, Nose, Throat
OFFICE OVER CITY DRUG STORE
Office Hours: 9:00 a. m. to 1:00 p. m.
and 2:00 to 5:00 p. m.
Phones: Residence 153; Office 65J
BURLINGTON, NORTH CAROLINA

OBITUARIES

KOSTYAL

The funeral service of Mrs. J. O. Kostyal was conducted by the writer on May 5, 1919, at the home of her father, Mr. Netles, on Maple Avenue, Newport News, Virginia.

Mrs. Kostyal was a faithful member of the Christian Church, a devoted wife and mother. A bereft husband, mother, father and eleven children mourn her death. Interment was in Green Lawn cemetery. May God's richest blessings be upon those who mourn for her.

H. J. FLEMING.

RESOLUTIONS OF RESPECT—JOHNSTON

Since God has, in His infinite wisdom, seen fit to take from us one of our best beloved members, Mrs. C. D. Johnston, we The Ladies' Aid Society of Graham Christian church wish to put on record the following:

Resolved, That deeply deploring her death, we will ever keep fresh in our hearts the fragrant memory of her life and virtues.

Resolved, That we tender to her stricken family our loving sympathy, commending them to that One who alone can give strength and comfort in the hour of bereavement.

LADIES' AID SOCIETY,
of Graham Christian Church.

INDIVIDUAL COMMUNION SERVICE
THE BEST WAY
to serve Communion. It is reverent, sanitary, and increases attendance at the Lord's Supper. Our services are chaste and beautiful. Made of finest materials and best workmanship.
Send for illustrated price list
C. B. RIDDLE, Publishing Agent,
Burlington, North Carolina.

CANCER TREATED SUCCESSFULLY
AT THE KELLAM HOSPITAL
The record of the Kellam Hospital is without parallel in history, having restored, without the use of the knife, Acids, X-Ray or Radium, over ninety per cent of the many hundreds of sufferers from cancers which it has treated during the past twenty-two years. We want every man and woman in the United States to know what we are doing.—KELLAM HOSPITAL, 1617 W. Main St., Richmond, Va.

HITS AND HAPPENINGS

A Contrary Youngster

Mrs. O'Flanagan—"Come here, ye obstinate young Irish raskil, an' put yer hat on! Shure, if ye hadn't got one ye'd always be wearin' it, ye're that contrairy!"

* * *

Willing to Take a Chance

"Here, hold my horse a minute, will you?"

"Sir! I'm a Member of Congress!"

"Never mind. You look honest. I'll take a chance."

Inside Dope

If you ever get a case of love at first sight on your hands, just take her to a cafe some night, and let her watch you eat corn on the cob. If she speaks to you the next day, you may rest assured that it is the real stuff.

* * *

His Financial Measure

Lady (entering bank, very business-like)—"I wish to get a Liberty Loan Bond for my husband."

Clerk—"What size, please?"

Lady—"Why, I don't believe I know exactly, but he wears a fifteen shirt."

ONCE UPON A TIME

(Written for the historian fifty years from now)

Once upon a time an institution—Elon College by name—needed financial help. This educational institution was founded eighty years ago. Its founders have passed away. This college to which I refer is located in North Carolina. Alamance County, seventeen miles East of Greensboro and sixty miles West of Raleigh. Its first four presidents were: Rev. W. S. Long, D. D.; Rev. W. W. Staley, D. D.; Dr. E. L. Moffitt and Dr. W. A. Harper. This College was born of a need, nurtured in love, and has given to the Christians (the denomination owning and controlling the institution) many great men and the world many valuable citizens. Missionaries trained there have carried the Gospel to a heathen world, and its almost unnumbered teachers are carrying learning's lamp to every quarter of the earth.

But this is not the story. I said once upon a time. Yes, it was in the year 1919—fifty years ago—that this institution needed an endowment fund of $125,000. The promoters of the work began to give the people an opportunity to give to this fund; and so hearty was the response that the amount was raised to $250,000. This was just after the great world war closed and a great expression in that day was "Over the Top," because the American boys had gone "over the top" and hammered back the hordes of Huns that were hurrying down the hills of France with their heavy heels in a hellish way. And so the people in giving this $250,000 called it going over the top, employing a military term to express their willingness.

Yes, the people gave willingly, but like many other things there had to be the fellow who would not, and so it was the case. There was a man, a certain man—Oh, his name is forgotten—who could, but would not, help this deserving institution. Time went by and he saw the splendid work of Elon College, saw and felt her influence on every hand and there was continual ringing in his ears, "I didn't help do it." He would have given a hundred times that which he was asked to do if he could only have recalled the opportunity to give the small amount asked of him. He died with this expression of regret upon his lips. He had not sinned—he had just missed an opportunity of spending well some of his Lord's money and regretted it.

And, lo and behold, this writer forgot that he was in the year 1969 and thought that he was in the year 1919—and looking over this story to correct it, screamed out in wild imagination, WHO WILL THIS MAN BE?

NOTICE

Several have requested that we print the above story in correct form. We are glad to do so. A number of answers have been received. Full Announcement next week.

SEE THAT YOUR CHURCH DOES ITS WHOLE DUTY

ELON'S NEED IS YOUR OPPORTUNITY	Pray God's blessing upon the graduates this year and help to secure others to take their places.	ELON'S SUCCESS IS YOUR GAIN

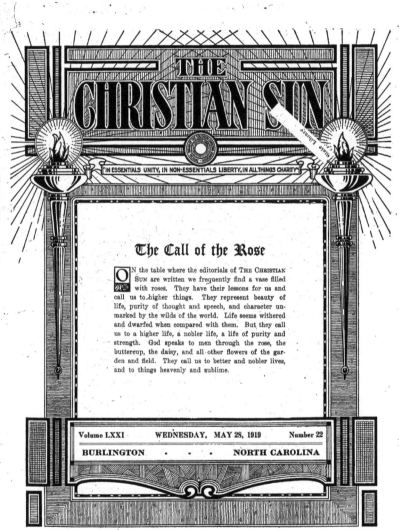

THE CHRISTIAN SUN

"IN ESSENTIALS UNITY, IN NON-ESSENTIALS LIBERTY, IN ALL THINGS CHARITY"

The Call of the Rose

ON the table where the editorials of THE CHRISTIAN SUN are written we frequently find a vase filled with roses. They have their lessons for us and call us to higher things. They represent beauty of life, purity of thought and speech, and character unmarked by the wilds of the world. Life seems withered and dwarfed when compared with them. But they call us to a higher life, a nobler life, a life of purity and strength. God speaks to men through the rose, the buttercup, the daisy, and all other flowers of the garden and field. They call us to better and nobler lives, and to things heavenly and sublime.

Volume LXXI	WEDNESDAY, MAY 28, 1919	Number 22
BURLINGTON	• • •	NORTH CAROLINA

THE CHRISTIAN SUN

Founded 1844 by Rev. Daniel W. Kerr.

C. B. RIDDLE - - - Editor

Entered at the Burlington, N. C. Post Office as second class matter.

Subscription Rates

One year .... $ 2.00
Six months 1.00

In Advance

Give both your old and new postoffice when asking that your address be changed.

The change of your label is your receipt for money. Written receipts sent upon request.

Marriage and obituary notices not exceeding 150 words printed free if received within 60 days from date of event, all over this at the rate of one-half cent a word.

Original poetry not accepted for publication.

Principles of the Christian Church

(1) The Lord Jesus Christ is the only Head of the Church.
(2) Christian is a sufficient name of the Church.
(3) The Holy Bible is a sufficient rule of faith and practice.
(4) Christian character is a sufficient test of fellowship, and of church membership.
(5) The right of private judgment and the liberty of conscience is a right and a privilege that should be accorded to, and exercised by all.

EDITORIAL

AN EXPLANATION

Having more matter than we can handle this week, we are giving over the editorial space to the happenings at Elon during commencement week. We feel that the friends and former students of the College are more interested this week in the commencement items than in the usual editorials.

ELON'S 29th COMMENCEMENT

(Reported by C. M. Cannon)

MAY 18

The Elon College commencement opened with the baccalaureate sermon this morning by Dr. Peter Ainslie of Baltimore, Md. Dr. Ainslie brought a vital message, and was heard with appreciation by a large audience. His subject was: "Is God Here?" The message was timely and inspiring. The following is a resume of the sermon:

"The greatest fact in the world is God. You cannot look into the face of a blooming dahlia or newly opened buttercup without having the thought to arise in your mind, who made this? You cannot stand out under the skies at night or on the beach of the rolling ocean without the same interrogation arising in your mind. Men can get away from each other by moving to different parts of the city or different parts of the country, but we cannot get away from God. Every day is a reminder that He is alive and alive in tenderness and love.

"We are accustomed to think that things cannot be except they have a purpose. We may not have discovered the purpose of some things, but when man looks in upon his own heart he cannot come to any other conclusion but that the purpose of his existence is immortality with the Almighty Father. Our minds are clouded and we think in error. We blame God for our sins and accuse Him of being the source of our sickness and our disasters and sometimes such criminal transactions as the great war, but God is not a part of man's unholiness. The roots of our sins and our crimes are in ourselves and God gives to us the right of self-mastery which can only come by toil and overcoming every adversary until we shall stand with Him in the morning when the world of God's adjustment shall displace the world of man's injustice. Nature, history, philosophy, science, conscience and experience prove man's obligations both to himself and to God and opportunities are around us like open doors, inviting us to leave our meaner selves for the self that is most like God.

"We have sought to define God and try to find satisfaction there as though it bore some evidences of piety. We have chafed under His moral government as though we knew better what we needed than God. We have said, in our hearts what we would do for others rather than what is being done. We have spent more time on the wrong road than we have in our attempt to discover the road in which alone walks Jesus whose paths are those mysterious paths of peace and light that satisfy the soul beyond any experience known to mortal man.

"Let us study the art of friendship, the art of manliness, the art of interpreting the Spirit of Christ to others as He interpreted the Spirit of God to us. Then all other occupations and all other tasks become but nursery games by the side of this the greatest task for the soul of man."

Dr. Ainslie is well known here, as well as all through the South, and his presence on the Hill this year is a source of pleasure to his many friends here. He arrived Saturday morning and has been entertained in the home of President and Mrs. Harper. On account of other engagements it was necessary for him to leave immediately after the sermon, but his presence here will be remembered for a long time by the student body.

Following the baccalaureate sermon this morning by Dr. Peter Ainslie the baccalaureate address was delivered this evening by President W. A. Harper of the college, to the graduating class. His message was, "The New Task of The College," the text being from Rev. 21:5. "And He that sat upon the throne said, behold, I make all things new." Dr. Harper brought to the students a message from his heart, and during the address he discussed the great need of religious education in the colleges, and the permeation of the spirit of Christ in the lives of all college students; that the colleges had failed in their duty to truly educate until they had instilled into the minds and hearts of the individuals some definite religious program for their life.

"Jesus Christ was the true," said Dr. Harper, "the real, the original progressive in Kingdom affairs. Forward is the only direction suitable to His teachings. The age in which we live is highly favored by its revelations of spiritual principles and its opportunities to apply them to new situations. There is no doubt the Gospel of Jesus Christ has a message for this hour, in the interpretation of which the college must play a large role. Colleges shall never be the same again as in the days before the world war, they will seek to equip themselves for life-direction with some essentially new ideals for the guidance of their attitude and conduct of life in the unfolding years.

"Central among these ideals we shall find a new and enlarged conception of Brotherhood's place in determining the relations of men. But the college cannot do this unless it makes Christ central in its curriculum. We must devise some plan by which religion may be taught in tax-supported institutions of higher learning.

"Democracy is not an end in itself and the college must give direction to democracy in terms of service. Too often the church has mistaken Christian activity for Christian service. The scope of service touches every realm of our life. But lest men should serve selfishly, with their eyes on the reward that ever blesses him who serves, the college must equip the leaders of men with the spirit of sacrifice.

"And finally, "for others," Class of 1919, let this be your motto as you pass out into the stirring realities of our troubled and uncertain time. "For others," this shibboleth shall admit you to the realm of the genuine servants of the race. It may bring you to the judgment seal of a Pilate, it may nail you to the Cross, it may send you into the tomb, even as it did our Lord. But why should you fear or falter?

"Such is the new task of the college. Such is Elon's task. May she be true in this crisal time."

MAY 19

Following the baccalaureate sermon and address Sunday of the college commencement the Class Day Exercises were held this morning. The college auditorium was full to overflowing with the many friends of the graduating members, and visitors of the college. The Class Day exercises is always an event of great interest in the commencement and proved to be no exception this year. The history of the class was rendered by Mr. Floyd, and the Class Prophecy, the Last Will and Testament, and the delivery of trophies to the members of the Class of '19 furnished merriment to all who were present; and the program was thoroughly enjoyed by all. The following program was rendered:

Devotional Exercises ....J. F. Minnis
Welcome...........................Annie Lindsay Raper
Class History..............................Henry T. Floyd
Class Poem ....Pearle Frances Teter
Class Prophecy ....Leo D. Martin
Last Will and Testament ....Ida Viola Wilkins
Delivery of Trophies ....H. S. Hardcastle

At 3:00 P. M. the society representatives delivered their orations and essays; two members from each of the three societies participating. The representatives were as follows:

Thelma Guldmar Burton ....Psiphelian
                The Woman of Tomorrow
Hobart M. Lynch ....Clio
                America's Mission
Percy E. Lindley ....Philologian
                Laborat Qui Vincit
Benjamin Bunn Snipes ....Philologian
                Democracy and Reconstruction
Toshio Sato ....Psiphelian
                Your Opportunity in the Land of Morning.

Immediately following the program of the Society representatives the Society reunions occurred in their respective halls.

At 5:00 P. M. the Art Exhibit was held in the Art Gallery of the West Dormitory, where the paintings and works of art of the students of the Department of Fine Arts were displayed.

At 6:00 P. M., the College Band gave a concert on the campus and rendered many pleasing numbers.

The last item of today's program was the Oratorio in the evening, "The Triumph of The Cross." This Oratorio was a decided success and was well received by all the music lovers. Under the supervision of Professor E. M. Betts of the Music Department the students composing the Oratorio have practiced faithfully, and made a fine show of talent this evening. The musical number of the commencement program is always enjoyed, and was looked forward to on this year's program.

MAY 20

The climax of the Elon College commencement occurred today, this being the final day of the commencement. At ten o'clock this morning the Graduation Exercises took place, the following program being rendered:

Salutatory by ....Leo DeWitte Martin, Salutatorian
The Art of Failure ....Hattie Edna Brown
Patriotism Purified ....Henry Terrie Floyd
Woman's Place in Social Service........Bessie Lee Baldwin
"Carry On" ....Leo DeWitte Martin
The Star of Hope ....Minnie Atkinson
Social Education for Peace ....William Carson King

Following the literary items of the program each member of the graduating class, twenty-four in number, were presented with a Bible by the President of the College, after which degrees were conferred and diplomas and certificates awarded.

The concluding item of the Graduating Exercises was the Valedictory Address by Howard Scott Hardcastle, Valedictorian.

The memorial service in the afternoon was an event that will long be remembered in the history of Alamance County. Last year it will be remembered by the citizens of Alamance and Guilford Counties at the commencement a giant service flag was unfurled for the men in the service after an address by Governor T. W. Bickett. It was therefore very fitting that the College should hold a memorial service at its commencement this year in honor of the men that made the supreme sacrifice during the war. Col. Albert Cox of the 113th Artillery, which played an important part in the breaking of the Hindenburg line, was the orator.

Col. Cox in civilian life was a lawyer, and did full justice to the occasion by his oratory.

At the conclusion of the address a silk banner bearing gold stars representing the Elon men who died for the cause of freedom was unfurled. The President of the College read the names of those represented by the gold stars, and announced the memorial funds that had been established in the College by their parents and loved ones.

Also a service flag was unfurled bearing the letters "S. A. T. C." and carrying 112 stars, representing the men of the Elon S. A. T. C.

The giant service flag of the college was again unfurled bearing its full numbers of stars, over 800.

At this occasion many prominent men of Alamance County were seated on the stage and in reserved seats. The College chapel would not hold the crowds that thronged to hear Col. Cox.

At 5:00 P. M. the Art Exhibit occurred in the annex —2nd floor, of the West Dormitory, where the works of the diploma and certificate pupils in the Art Department were displayed.

This evening the concluding number of the commencement program occurred. The Alumni Address, by Mrs. W. A. Harper, followed by the Alumni Banquet in the College Dining Hall was the final item. Mrs. Harper graduated with the Class of '99. Her subject was, "Shoulder to Shoulder."

"Woman," said Mrs. Harper, "is by nature intended to obey, but not to be regarded as the inferiors of man. All through history men have ever placed women under guardianship and perpetually violated the trust committed to their tutelage. The religions of the world are man-made. Women are naturally religious and religion has been deftly fashioned to overlast and submerge them.

"As we women view the intricacies of the mental operativeness of men to perpetuate and untenable conception as to the relations of the male and female created in God's image, we would lose heart and conclude with Lady Somerville, 'the more we see of men, the better we like dogs,' but for the teaching of our Master. Progress, we recognize, to be a painful process, tedious, but sure, and in the long run self-interest will surrender to simple right and elemental justice, and when that day has come, as come it will, the epic of woman's patient suffering will crown the racial accomplishment with a glory never to be dimmed.

"Women, with their wonderful intuition and love for service, when given an equal chance, will become evangels of light. We shall transform the world in that day of equality marching "shoulder to shoulder" with men by deeds of mercy and love."

MAY 21

Commencement closed officially here Tuesday night but the Board of Trustees did not conclude its session until a late hour last night, and many things of a constructive character were passed upon by the Board, which have since been announced.

From the students' point of view the two most important items which the Board of Trustees passed were the fencing and grading of the athletic grounds and the erection of a grandstand, and permission for the college to engage in foot ball, which for twenty-nine years has been strenuously opposed. The grounds on which the Board of Trustees finally yielded on the foot ball question was that the sport was not the inhuman thing it once was and that it would bring opportunity for a larger number of the students to be engaged in athletics. The alumni were heartily in favor of it as well as the student body, and the permission to engage in this sport for the future was passed without a dissenting vote.

The alumni association with the approval of the Board has decided to employ a secretary whose residence shall be at the College and whose duties shall be to stimulate the alumni in methods of loyalty and support to Alma Mater. Next year is to be the official home-coming year and a committee of seven was appointed with C. C. Forville as chairman, and instructions were given to secure a large tent and provide cots to take care of the inflow of alumni at the 1920 commencement. The alumni orator for next year is Hon. S. E. Everett, Suffolk, Va., with Hon. G. E. Whitley, Smithfield, as alternate. The Alumni scholarship was awarded to Miss Zula Patterson, Franklinville, N. C.

The Summerbell scholarship was won by Miss Bertha Paschal, Manson, N. C. The Standford Orator's medal was won by L. D. Martin, Suffolk, Va. Miss Minnie Atkinson, Mullins, S. C., won the Moffitt essayist medal, and He S. Hardcastle, of Dover, Del., won both the Morrow Thesis medal and the Wellons scholarship medal.

Rev. L. E. Smith, pastor of the Third Christian church, Norfolk, Va., was given the honorary degree of Doctor of Divinity.

The Board of Trustees appointed a special committee to outline a system of accrediting college hours and official positions. This committee will report to the Executive Board their findings. The design is to prevent college offices accumulating to the hurt of the individual student, too many on one man. The investigation will cover the practices of the colleges throughout the country.

It was also voted that beginning with the summer of 1920 an Institute of Religious Education will be held for a six weeks' term, and the President is authorized to plan for this school, select the faculty for it, and bring it to the attention of the Christian leaders. It is the purpose of the college through this Institute to do for the teachers in Sunday school and other Christian works what the summer schools for professional teachers are doing in the secular branches.

The Board of Trustees unanimously voted to confer the degree of A. B. upon John Carl Miller of the Class of '19 and upon Charles Nottingham Whitelock of the Class of '18 and the degree of Ph. B. upon William Frank Odom of the Class of '18. These men gave up their courses to enter the world war and gave up their lives in the cause of freedom. These diplomas will be mailed to their parents and they will be included in the list of graduates of their respective classes. Twelve other Elon men are definitely known to have lost their lives, but they had completed their courses here before they entered the war. Should it develop when the official casualty list has been finally passed upon that other men who left their college course to enter the service have given up their lives they too will be decorated with their degrees.

RESOLUTIONS OF RESPECT—FARMER

Whereas, God in His wisdom has seen fit to take from our number, by death on the 13th day of March, 1919, our esteemed Brother, David Samuel Farmer, who, for years has been a member of the Board of Trustees of Elon College, be it Resolved:

1. That while we are deeply sensible of the great loss that has come to us in the death of this loyal and always faithful member, we bow in humble submission to the will of our Heavenly Father.

2. That we commend to the members of this Board and to our successors the beautiful spirit of devotion and sacrifice that has ever characterized the life of our consecrated, modest Christian brother in the discharge of every duty he has been called upon to perform for the College—he loved so well, as well as for every other enterprise of his Church.

3. That we extend to the bereaved wife and children our profound sympathy in this hour of supreme distress, commending them to the mercies of a kind Heavenly Father who can heal every wound and dispel every sorrow.

4. That a copy of these resolutions be sent to Mrs. Farmer, a copy spread upon the minutes or this Board, and a copy be sent to The Christian Sun for publication.

I. W. JOHNSON,
E. L. MOFFITT,
W. T. WALTERS,
Committee.

The above Resolutions of respect and esteem were unanimously passed by the Board of Trustees of Elon College, assembled in session, May 20, 1919.

P. H. FLEMING,
Secretary to Board.

RESOLUTIONS OF RESPECT—ROWLAND

Whereas, Mrs. Margaret Rowland, mother of Trustee, Dr. C. H. Rowland, has recently passed from labor to reward, and whereas, she was always deeply interested in the College and the cause of Christ, therefore, be it Resolved:

1. That we express our sincere appreciation of her long and faithful Christian service. She was a mother in Israel and had an abiding interest in the progress of the kingdom.

2. That we express our deepest sympathy to Trustee, Dr. C. H. Rowland and his family in their recent bereavement, and commend them to the Heavenly Father who can comfort them at all times.

3. That a copy of these resolutions be entered upon the records of this Board, a copy sent to the family, and a copy sent to The Christian Sun for publication.

I. W. JOHNSON,
E. L. MOFFITT,
W. T. WALTERS,
Committee.

The above Resolutions of respect and esteem were unanimously passed by the Board of Trustees of Elon College, assembled in session, May 20, 1919.

P. H. FLEMING,
Secretary to Board.

RESOLUTIONS OF RESPECT—LEE

Whereas, Trustee Willis J. Lee, of Nansemond County, Virginia, came to his death suddenly today, and whereas, he was for thirty years a faithful trustee and loyal friend of the College, therefore be it Resolved:

1. That we record our sincere appreciation of his Christian character and faithful service to the College and the cause of Christ. No man among us has been more generous and faithful. He was modest and humble yet brave and strong in every field where duty called him. His counsel was wise, his example worthy of emulation.

2. That we bow in humble submission to the will of God who doeth all things well. We thank our Heavenly Father for extending his life well beyond three score and ten years, and we devoutly pray that God may raise up some worthy successor in our beloved Zion.

3. That we extend to Mrs. W. J. Lee and the family our sincere sympathy in their great bereavement and pray that His divine grace may be sufficient in this dark hour.

4. That a copy of these resolutions be entered upon the records of the College, a copy sent to Mrs. Lee, and a copy sent to The Christian Sun for publication.

I. W. JOHNSON,
E. L. MOFFITT,
W. T. WALTERS,
Committee.

The above Resolutions of respect and esteem were unanimously passed by the Board of Trustees of Elon College, assembled in session, May 20, 1919.

P. H. FLEMING,
Secretary to Board.

PASTOR AND PEOPLE

HERE AND THERE

I preached at Martha's Chapel second Sunday in April at 11 o'clock and administered the Communion, the pastor, Rev. B. J. Howard not being ordained. At 3 o'clock P. M., I preached at O'Kelleys Chapel and after the service enjoyed a privilege that I had long desired—that of visiting the resting place of the Christian hero, the founder of the Christian Church, Rev. James O'Kelly. When I preached at the grave where his remains lay, I must confess, I was humiliated. The grave was covered with vines and surrounded by bushes and briers. And again, when I looked at the simple square stone that marks his resting place, and found almost nothing on it, I said in my heart that we as a people had failed to show our appreciation for this great man who fought the battle and gained freedom and liberty for the Christians. Mr. Upchurch, whose wife is the nearest relative to James O'Kelly, went with me to the grave.

The fourth Sunday I preached at Chapel Hill—morning and evening, and administered the emblems of the body and blood of Christ to a large number of communicants. Rev. B. J. Howard is pastor of these churches, and is highly spoken of by his people.

The first Sunday this month I preached to a large congregation in the First Presbyterian church in the city of Richmond, Va. Here I found a spiritually minded people. Dr. McFaden, the pastor of this church, is a grand and noble man. This church edifice has been standing for 107 years and Dr. McFaden is the seventh pastor. When I was through preaching I was met by a number of our own people, who have moved into this city, and have no church home. Some of our people, for the lack of having no church of our own denomination, have placed their membership with other branches of the Church, and have gone to work. The longer we wait, the more we will lose. Richmond is a beautiful city, and why not take our place there along with the other branches of God's Church?

Yesterday, (May 11), I preached at home, Elon College, to a very appreciative congregation. And now for all these blessed gospel privilege to witness for my Master, I give Him all the praise.

Next Sunday, (May 18), I go to Moore Union, where I began my first pastoral charge forty-four years ago. This is my fourth term with them. The condition here is not what we would like to see it, but from what they tell me there is some indications for improvement. We are praying daily for a great revival at this place. Pray with us.

                                        P. T. KLAPP.
Elon College, N. C.

A SUNDAY IN NORFOLK, VA.

The writer was invited to supply for Memorial Temple in Norfolk the second Sunday in May. A very beautiful exercise for Mothers' Day was held in the Sunday school. Lovely flowers, carefully and tastfully arranged about the pulpit and other places, were very inviting and added much to the service.

I listened with delight and helpfulness to Dr. Baird as he taught the Men's Bible Class in a very impressive manner. He seemed to put his best thoughts and energy into the teaching of the lesson. He is kept busy as a physician to the City Home and is doing a great work there as well as in his church work and city practice. He and his wife lived in Windsor some years ago when I was pastor there. They were popular and had many friends. I dined with him on Sunday and was entertained in his home in a delightful way by Brother Baird and his wife, who is a splendid Christian woman. They have a quiet and pleasant home and are consecrated workers for the Lord.

I was glad to preach for these people and greatly enjoyed the kindness shown me.
                                      J. T. KITCHEN.
Windsor, Va.

A VISIT TO NORTHERN ALABAMA

The writer reached Cullman County on Friday afternoon before the fourth Sunday in April and preached at the home of Brother J. E. Almon that evening. Saturday at 11:00 A. M., I preached in the Methodist church and Saturday evening at Brother J. C. Brown's. Sunday morning at 11:00 o'clock I again preached at the church. We have a small organization in this vicinity and it seems to me that we might soon have a strong church. We need to put our hearts and hands to the task and erect a building of our own. There are a number of heads of families in this community

who have never made a profession of religion, and as they learn of the Christian Church they speak favorably of its principles, and we would be glad for them to unite with us.

From the above named place I went to Brother J. G. Bryan's, a distance of fifteen miles, and preached in a Baptist church. This is in the corner of Blunt County and is a fine section for farming and there are good homes, too. We think that there is an opening here for our church.

The things that the Christian denomination need in North Alabama are men and money. I trust that God will call men from some part of the Southern Convention soon, in order that the work may go forward. Brother Hughes worked faithfully in this field for two years during the period of the war. I feel that we need one or two men in the field, not to plow five or six days in the week, but to represent the Christian Church and he will find enough to do that will pay us. Brother Carter, let us hear from you when you return from Northern Alabama.
                                        J. D. DOLLAR.
Roanoke, Ala.

ALABAMA LETTER

Dear Brother Riddle:—

I am at Lagrange, Ga., for a few days, in a meeting with Rev. C. W. Hanson. Prospects are good for a fine meeting. I am seeing a number of my old friends and quite a few of my new ones.

A few years ago I was pastor here, and I am glad to be among the flock once more. But a goodly number have crossed over and are at rest, and I am glad to say that I find many others who seem to be ready.

It seems that the work here is in fairly good condition. Brother Hanson is here for two Sundays in each month and the people have the utmost confidence in him. In fact his home is here which makes it so much better for the church.

Our work in this country is suffering for the lack of service, the cause generally is suffering for more men. We need some good, strong, young men in these two Conferences, and especially in South Georgia.

I am just from Enigma and Vanceville. These little churches are trying to co-operate, and are in need of a man to locate in their midst. I am trying to preach there this year, and the prospects are encouraging; and if some good man can be induced to locate in their midst a great work can be done. Who will step out on the Altar and say: "Here am I, send me"?

The work at Enigma, Vanceville and Ambrose, which are some thirty miles away, will support a man and keep him on the field. Can it be done? Who will answer the question?
                                        G. D. HUNT.
Wadley, Ala.

SUFFOLK LETTER

At the close of the Suffolk Sunday school on April 27, 1919, a photograph of Captain Robert B. Brinkley was presented to the school by his neice, Miss Margaret

A. Brinkley. Captain Brinkley was one of the twenty-five charter members. His parents lived near the mill, now the pumping station of the water works. He and his sisters were members of the choir and sang at the dedication the second Sunday in March 1861. In April of that year the church met to organize a Sunday school and elected Captain Robert B. Brinkley and Captain James A. Turrentine superintendents; but war had been declared, both volunteered and the school was not conducted. Brinkley was Captain of Company I., Va. Infantry, Mahones Brigade and, "after faithful and distinguished service, was killed at Hanover Junction, in May 1864." His body was taken to Petersburg, Va., and forwarded to Suffolk by Rev. W. B. Wellons, and carried to the family burying - ground near Cypress Chapel. Peter Duke, a nephew of Col. A. Savage, and a colored man conveyed the body from Suffolk to the country in a wagon at night; and Peter used to say "that he was scared almost to death." He was a boy of eighteen years old. The portrait is an enlarged copy of a Civil War photograph, in his uniform, and is placed on the wall of the Sunday school *fifty-five years* after his death.

Captain James A. Turrentine, Burlington, N. C., is the only surviving charter member of this church, and his picture graces the main Sunday school room, back of the platform. The old clock on the wall is between them. Captain Turrentine says he skinned the pine poles for the scaffolding in the erection of the old church. The pulpit Bible in the Sunday school here was given by Captain and Mrs. Turrentine; and the old pulpit Bible in New Providence church was also given by them. I was impressed by that fact when I came from Graham to Suffolk, that both pulpits had Bibles given by the same devoted Christians. It seems from the records that Captains Brinkley and Turrentine were elected joint superintendents or superintendent and assistant superintendent. When the Brinkley portrait was presented, W. T. Beamon, the present superintendent, responded in fitting words of acceptance and thanks to Miss Brinkley for this gift to the school. Their pictures now face us every Sunday and remind us of the beginning of a Sunday school in this church.

The Sunday school was a small institution in this country before the Civil War. It has grown to twenty millions with a million officers and teachers, and a literature that is immense in its quantity, and splendid in its quality. No mind can estimate the full value of the Sunday school. Many are wanting to change the name and call it "The Bible School," "The Church School," or by some other name. I enter my protest against any change of name. It puts emphasis on *Sunday*, and we need that emphasis because so many things tend to ignore *Sunday*. It is more than a Bible school; it is more than a church school; you can have either of those schools on secular days; it is a SUNDAY school. It helps men to remember the day to keep it holy.

W. W. STALEY.

Suffolk, Va.

NEWPORT NEWS, VA.

The work of the East End Christian church continues to progress nicely. The Sunday school is well attended and a good and great work is being done by it for the rising generation. The regular church and prayer meeting services are well attended and a lively interest is being shown by the people.

On May 16 The Christian Endeavor Society was reorganized and a contest for new members was put on. This contest is to last a month at the close of which time a social will be given and a business meeting held. This past Monday night was the first meeting and at the opening service the pastor led the meeting. There were fifty-five in attendance, the majority being young folks. We aim to have one of the best Endeavor Societies anywhere in this section before long.

Last week Rev. J. V. Knight of Greensboro, N. C., and Rev. G. O. Lankford of Berkley, Va., were our visitors in the interest of the Elon Standardization Fund. We were glad to have them and we folks of the East End Christian church will do our part on this endowment.

With best wishes for the work of our beloved Church and earnest prayers for the men and women of all communions who are in the great work of building a New World and training the New Humanity for the most possible service to the world and their fellow man:

H. J. FLEMING, *Pastor.*

Newport News, Va.

MEMORIAL DAY AT BETHLEHEM

May 18 was our annual memorial day at Bethlehem. The weather was pleasant and the people came in large numbers until the church was more than filled. At eleven o'clock Rev. W. C. Wicker preached the memorial sermon. It was a discourse filled with good thoughts and inspiring truths. At the close the children marched into the cemetery bearing flowers which they placed upon the graves of departed loved ones.

In the afternoon dedicatory services were conducted by the pastor, after which Rev. P. H. Fleming preached for us. We were glad to have these visiting brethren with us and hope they will come again.

J. W. HOLT.

DEDICATORY SERVICE AT BETHLEHEM CHURCH
MAY 18, 1919

(Delivered by Pastor Rev. J. W. Holt)

More than one hundred years ago when the hills that overlook Haw River which flows between them, and when dense forests of oak covered nearly the whole land, the people who lived in this section established a place for the worship of Almighty God in a building made of hewed logs furnished with simple benches for seats. As the years went by and population increased better houses and seats took the place of the first ones, and today finds us enjoying more comfortable and modern pews.

This result has been brought about by a proposition made to the church a little over one year ago by Brother Daniel Davis Sutton in which he generously proposed to pay $800.00 towards the cost of new seats in honor of his father if the church would raise the balance. His proposition was accepted by the church and the result is that we have new seats, and have them paid for, and in addition we have five dozen folding chairs to be used when crowded. This addition is made as a memorial in honor of Brother Rily Sutton who was for many years collector, treasurer, and deacon of Bethlehem Christian church. Other improvements have been made recently to the appearance and comfort of the church.

In grateful appreciation of the liberal contributions of all who have helped in this matter, and in recognition of the blessings of our Heavenly Father by which alone it could be done, and further as expression of our desire and purpose to honor Him and to advance His kingdom among men, we wish now to solemnly and unitedly consecrate this addition to our house of worship to the service of God, and to present the same as an offering to his divine goodness.

The audience will stand while we solemnly present these things to God in behalf of the church and congregation.

The Prayer

Almighty God, the Father of our Lord Jesus Christ, we present the pews and chairs and other improvements which we have placed in this church as an offering unto Thee, to be dedicated to Thy divine service and to the upbuilding of Thy kingdom on earth.

We dedicate them to be used by devout worshipers to holy meditation, and to earnest inquiry after the truth by all who may occupy them from time to time in coming years.

We dedicate them to the free use of all who are seeking to know the truth, to find the way of life, and to do thy service.

We dedicate them to the glory of God our Father, to Jesus Christ our Redeemer, and to the Holy Spirit our Comforter, now and forever. Amen and Amen.

LADIES' AID BETHLEHEM CHURCH

The Ladies' Aid Society of Bethlehem Christian church was organized in the year 1890 by Rev. J. W. Holt with ten charter members.

The object of this society is to raise funds for the benefit of Bethlehem church, and other good causes.

The first meeting was held February 16, 1890, with the following officiating members:

President, Miss Addie Rippy, now Mrs. O. P. Shelton and an active member in the Ladies' Aid Society of the Christian church of Burlington. Vice President, Miss Octavia Ireland, who is now a member of Berea Christian church. Treasurer, Mrs. L. D. Rippy, formerly Miss Sudie Waynick, and still a member of this Society. Secretary, Miss Iola Hall Simpson, deceased.

This Society has continually grown and at the present time we have 71 members.

During this time the Society has collected the sum of $684.71. This money has been used for the benefit of the Church, the Christian Orphanage at Elon College, and other causes.

Since the organization of the Society, there are several who have withdrawn their names to join other churches. Several active members have died. They are: Nancy Isley, Ida I. Kernodle, Georgiana Kern-

odle, Rachael Sutton, Madison Smith, Mary Kernodle, Margaret McCray, Daisy Shepherd, Sally Isley, Hepsy Barber, Esther Rippy, Malinda Sutton, Elizabeth Simpson, Bettie Holt, Isabella Smith, Annie Faucette, Lena Wagoner, Iola Simpson, Minnie Smith.

The following are the officiating members: Miss Fannie Paschal, president; Miss Lottie McCray, secretary.

HIGH POINT

On Wednesday evening, April 30, 1919, at 8:00 P. M., the evangelistic services began at High Point and continued for ten days. The ministerial help became sick and was not able to be with me any during the meeting, so the pastor had to do all of the preaching. It seemed that the Lord was putting me to the test. The task was large but the Lord gave strength. It seemed the largest task that I had ever undertaken but the Lord gave victory.

The church was greatly revived. Pastor and people were drawn closer in purpose and effort. Cottage prayer meeting groups were held a few weeks previous to the beginning of the meeting which was a great power for the success of the revival. I never have had a finer spirit of co-operation on the part of the militant church in my previous experience. This is a good and progressive people to serve which is a pastor's joy.

The visible results were not as much as we had hoped to see. There were five professions of faith in Christ, several for prayer and four united with the church. There are more to come in yet.

During the meeting on Saturday night before the first Sunday in May was the regular time for quarterly Conference. The church met at an appointed hour. Besides regular reports, one thing was accomplished which all had worked and prayed to see done. The note of indebtedness was covered and all went home feeling good. No other important business claimed the attention of the church, the meeting adjourned for three months hence.

Dr. J. O. Atkinson, Field Mission Secretary of the Southern Christian Convention, Elon College, N. C., has promised to preach the dedicatory reunion which is to take place the first Sunday in June at eleven o'clock. Every one interested is cordially invited to attend.

The Sunday school and church are going to observe Children's Day in June. The Sunday school is giving one offering each month to the Christian Orphanage and one to Missions.

For all of the above blessings and accomplishments we are grateful and to God be all the glory.

L. L. WYRICK.

Elon College, N. C.

Last Sunday the Editor was scheduled to be at Concord in Caswell county, eighteen miles from Burlington, with Rev. L. L. Wyrick in an all day service. A down pour of rain from early morning till about 2 P. M., prevented any one coming for us, and so far as we know, prevented the services.

MISSIONARY

PUSHING SPIRITULITY ASIDE

I found this very significant utterance in *The Ohio State Journal* of April 29th and I very much wish CHRISTIAN SUN readers could and would all see, read and carefully weigh it. Are its statements true? Read and answer:

"In an address by John Galsworthy at Columbia University, last Wednesday, the renowned author spoke of the tendency of the times, and said, "if America should get that purse and power proud fever, which comes from national success, we are all destined to another flare-up." We go about bragging of our tons of pig iron, bushels of wheat, and balances in the bank, without understanding that all these material things are simply millstones about the neck unless we grace them with much spiritual purpose. A man with simply materialistic power is not worthy of honor or praise. He is nothing; worse than nothing. Mr. Galsworthy says:

"We were rattling into a new species of barbarism when the war came, and unless we check ourselves, shall continue to rattle, now it is over. The underlying cause in every country is the increase of herd-life, based on machines, money-getting, and the dread of being dull.

"But power for real light and leading in America will depend, not so much on her material wealth, or her armed force, as on what her attitude towards life, and what the ideals of her citizens are going to be.'

"We are spending billions and billions in making the world better and really how much better is it? How much less is there of selfishness vice, overreaching, prejudice, distrust than a few centuries ago? Indifference and vice are more respectable than they were a few centuries ago. But their hold on human life is nearly as strong. Why?' Because we are pushing spirituality and religion aside and putting on style and frivolity, which unrestrained, are as hurtful to a nation as espionage.' "

Are we pushing spirituality aside? Long, long ago One asked very candidly and very seriously, "What shall it profit a man if he gain the whole world and lose his own soul?" And what will it profit a nation if it get all the riches of earth, and push spirituality aside?

J. O. ATKINSON.

FLASHLIGHTS

"Christianity is very particularly to be considered as *trust*, deposited with us in behalf of others, in behalf of mankind, as well as for our own instruction."— *Bishop Butler.*

"Moderator, rax me that Bible!"—*Dr. Erskine, when, in an assembly of the Church of Scotland, the duty of sending the Gospel to the heathen was questioned.*

"Should he (a voyager) be shipwrecked on an unknown coast, he will devoutly pray that the missionary may have preceded him."—*Charles Darwin.*

"The work of missions is nothing else than the One Church of God in motion."—*Wilkelm Loche.*

"Christianity is more than 'let us sing Hymn 297.' "—*Dan Crawford, twenty-two years' missionary in Central Africa.*

"Show at what rate you prize your own blessings, pardon of your sins, peace with God, the hope of heaven, by your eagerness to impart the same to others.'—*Archbishop Trench.*

"I will place no value on anything I have or may possess, except in relation to the kingdom of Christ."—*David Livingstone.*

NEW NORTH CAROLINA LAWS

(Continued from last week)

12. An Act to prevent the sale, offering for sale or advertising certain proprietary or patent medicines. Chap. 27, Public Laws 1917.

13. An Act to allow absent electors to vote, or better known as the Absentee Voters Law. Chap. 23, Public Laws 1917.

14. An Act to amend Chap. 97 of the Revisal of 1905, relating to hospitals for the insane, to provide for the appointment of consolidated board of directors for such hospitals, and to create a co-operative purchasing committee for said institutions, and for the school for the Deaf, the School for the Blind, and the Caswell Training school. Chap. 150, Public Laws 1917.

15. An Act to issue bonds of the State for the permanent enlargement and improvement of the State's educational and charitable institutions to an amount not to exceed three million dollars. Chap. 154' Public Laws 1917.

16. An Act to provide for the preparation and review of estimates for expenditures and revenue, and to establish a budget system for all State expenditures. Public Laws, 1919.

17. A memorial endorsing the proposed League of Nations. Public Laws 1919.

18. An Act to prevent incurable mental defetives from perpetuating their species. Public Laws, 1919.

19. An Act to provide for the removal of physical defects of indigent children at the expense of the State, and appropriating $50,000 to carry out the provisions of said act. Public Laws 1919.

20. An Act to provide machinery and raise revenue for a minimum school term for six months in every school district in North Carolina. Public Laws 1919.

21. An Act raising the minimum salary of school teachers from $45 to $65 per month. Public Laws, 1919.

22. An Act requiring children under the age of 14 to attend school during the entire school term. Public Laws 1919.

23. An Act to prevent children under the age of 14 from working in mills or other industries. Public Laws 1919.

24. An Act to enable the State to secure the benefit of the Federal appropriation for good roads without issuing State bonds, and providing that the county may put up one-fourth, the State one-fourth and the Federal government one-half for the construction of a State system of highways. Public Laws 1919.

(Continued next week)

WORSHIP AND MEDITATION

THE RIGHT KIND OF A MAN

While pastor of our church, at Newport News, Va., I went over town, from the East End, one Sunday afternoon, and listened to an address by a man by the name of Williams. His subject was that given above. I still have the impression that the address was a good one, though I am not able to reproduce it. This reminds me of a young lady who was questioned, on returning from a preaching service. She said the sermon was fine and that she enjoyed it but she did not remember the text nor anything the minister said.

In regard to the address of which I speak, I do remember the outline and have carried it with me for these years, although not being able to recall the body of the address. The speaker said that the right kind of a man must be right—First, in conscience; second, in conduct; third, in companionship; fourth, in competency; fifth, in character, positive, sympathetic, tolerant, stable; sixth, in consolation; seventh, in consecration; eighth, he must be right with Jesus Christ.

These are the eight points of the address as I remember them, but as it occurs to me now, they all might be summed up under the last, that of being right with Jesus Christ. If a man is right with Him, he is all right but if he is not right with Christ, he may have many good qualities but he still lacks the essential as held up in the above named points.

We cannot be right with Jesus Christ by accepting his words yet denying his works. We cannot accept his ethical teachings and deny the Virgin birth, his blood atonement, his resurrection and miracles.

If we cannot remember the many points that are characteristic of the right kind of a life, and a life that is well pleasing to God. We can be right with Jesus Christ and thus have them all, "For to me, to live is Christ." "I live, yet not I, but Christ liveth in me, and the life which I now live in the flesh I live by the faith of the Son of God who loved me and gave himself for me."   W. D. HARWARD.
Dendron, Va.

LOOK UNTO ME

When we can put our minds and eyes upon the wonderful, the beautiful and the sublime things of creation, how much better we feel and how much better we appear with such delightful and profitable exercise! And while thus beholding the great and wonderful things of God the impressions are deep and profound. Some things are very attractive while others are repulsive, but the most attractive things are not always the safest and best for our good. You have seen many beautiful and attractive flowers, but it was not safe to gather them because they were poison, so, you had to leave them alone. Some other rare flowers you have seen which you ardently desired to take but they were imbedded in thickly set thorns which would pierce and

hurt the fingers in the effort to pluck them. And much, very much to your regret you had to leave them, but in the end it was far better that you did. It seemed so hard to resist them, for above everything else you wanted them the most. But after a while you saw it was better that you did not gather those flowers.

In like manner many of the sins of life invite us to engage in them; they are so alluring, so attractive, so beautiful, as you think, that there is a constant and earnest desire to engage in them. The most sinful, the most beautiful and attractive things are often dressed in the most winsome and inviting way; so very much so that it even becomes difficult to resist their powerful influence. You have seen beautiful colored serpents, but you would not dare to touch them with even one of your fingers, because they would bite you. You admired and loved the color, but you hated the snake. You admire and love many sinful pleasures but you hate the terrible, the awful effects of those pleasures.

Experience and observation enable us to understand and appreciate more fully the true, the pure and the good, and help greatly in a right discrimination of their character. After the terrific grandeur of the thunderstorm we appreciate more fully the calm. The dashing waves tossed over the deep sea fringed with white foamed beauty are admirable to behold, even in the midst of the storm, but how delightful to look at the water when the waves are at rest upon the placid bosom of the deep water! Yes, after the storm is over, how delightful, pleasant to rest in the calm hours of repose!

After a long time of sickness it makes you so very happy to be restored to health again, and to engage into the activities of life. And you enjoy and appreciate health better because you understand what it is to be well. Rest is also enjoyed more after labor. The labor enables you to rest well, and you realize what rest means. And in a like manner you greatly enjoy life after trouble and much anxiety.

It is not always best to have all we want although the heart craves for it.   J. T. KITCHEN.
Windsor, Va.

A PRAYER

O great Lord of the harvest, send forth, we beseech Thee, laborers into the harvest of the world, that the grain which is even now ripe may not fall and perish through our neglect. Pour forth Thy sanctifying Spirit on our fellow-Christian abroad, and Thy converting grace on those who are living in darkness. Raise up, we beseech Thee, a devout ministry among the native believers, that, all Thy people being knit together in one body, in love, Thy Church may grow up into the measure of the stature of the fulness of Christ; through Him who died, and rose again for us all, the same Jesus Christ our Lord. Amen.—*Bishop Milman.*

NOTES

-Remember that the State Christian Endeavor Convention meets in Burlington, June 6-8.

Rev. J. O. Cox changes his address from Asheville, N. C., to Flat Rock, N. C.

We regret to note the death of Rev. R. L. Williamson's mother-in-law; also the sickness of his wife's father.

Rev. H. S. Hardcastle preached in our Raleigh church last Sunday in the absence of the pastor, Rev. Geo. D. Eastes.

Brother B. J. Howard has offered his resignation of the work at Chapel Hill to take effect August 1. He is open for work elsewhere.

Persons desiring copies of Children's Day programs will be furnished same gratis by Rev. J. O. Atkinson, Secretary, Elon College, N. C.

The Board of Trustees of Elon College, in session last week, conferred the degree of D. D. upon Rev. Leon Smith, Norfolk, Virginia. An honor well bestowed and will be worn with credit to the Church.

Brother O. D. Poythress writes that the church at South Norfolk is now in the third week of a most successful meeting. More than seventy professions and forty-eight additions to the church. Brother Poythress is doing the preaching and is conducting the singing.

Tuesday afternoon, May 20, Mr. Willis J. Lee, Bennett Creek, Virginia, passed to his reward. His passing means the loss of one of the Church's most devout members. Brother Lee was a warm friend to every enterprise of the Church. The Orphanage, the College, THE CHRISTIAN SUN, the Missionary enterprises, all had a place in his heart and purse. He was a man of God and lived a life that portrayed the spirit of Christ. At the time of his death preparations were being made in his home for the celebration of the Golden Wedding of Brother and Sister Lee. We are not in possession of facts concerning his age and other details of his life. To his widow and many friends we extend sympathy.

Mr. L. C. March, a member of Elon's 1916 Class, entered the service of his country shortly after his graduation. Several months ago he was reported missing in action, and not being found, was reported dead by the information authorities of the Government on October 8, 1918. His name appeared in the regular casualty list, and a special note was made of it in THE CHRISTIAN SUN of November 6, 1918. Some weeks ago he reached this country and is now at home near Holland, Va. He is a member of Holy Neck church. We rejoice with his parents and friends that he is still alive. The Editor having been reported dead twice

himself a few years ago knows how to appreciate with his classmate what it means to still be alive, and to receive the congratulations of his friends.

COLLEGE ADVERTISING CONTEST

The "puzzle type" that appeared on the back page of THE CHRISTIAN SUN May 14 created no little amount of interest. We were pleased to hear expressions concerning it from various parts of the Brotherhood, and while only thirteen sent papers to enter the contest, we are grateful for the many others who spoke of it and manifested an interest in its solution.

We received five correct papers, and eight papers that were not correct. We take pleasure in printing below the names of all persons who participated, and list them in order received indicating after each name the per cent made:

Rev. L. I. Cox, Elon College, N. C.	98
Dr. W. A. Harper, Elon College, N. C.	100
Rev. B. J. Earp, Luray, Va.	100
J. Maryon Saunders, Durham, N. C.	100
Leslie Knight, Cragford, Ala.	100
Rev. E. T. Cotten, Suffolk, Va.	99
L. W. Vaughan, Elon College, N. C.	98
Mrs. Julia Holt, Chapel Hill, N. C.	98
E. K. Freeman, Eagle Springs, N. C.	99
Mrs. W. A. Newman, Henderson, N. C.	97
Mrs. J. P. Moss, Keats, Va.	95
Mary Addie White, Sanford, N. C.	100
Bettie Franks, Cary, N. C.	95

Each of the successful participants have been sent a valuable prize.

BROTHER FRANKS REPLIES

In a recent issue of THE SUN we asked Brother J. E. Franks to tell us how he managed to get so many new subscriptions. He replies and we deem his letter worthy of a place in this paper. Here it is:

No, Brother Riddle, I haven't any patent on getting subscriptions for The Sun. If there is a possibility of helping others, I will try to tell first why I get subscriptions and second, how I get them.

Why Get Subscriptions

You are giving us a first class religious paper. I consider it good, clean, and wholesome. The Sun is free from secular advertisements, and well edited. It represents the general interest of our Church, and is vigorously pushing forward its enterprises.

Every member of our Church should have the information and inspiration that The Sun gives. We do a good deed when we get The Sun into a home. As we extend The Sun's circulation we enable you, Brother Editor, to devote more time and secure additional talent that should give us a bigger and better paper, and consequently be a greater blessing to our cause.

How to Get Subscriptions

Earnestly go after them, realizing that duty and fidelity demand that you do your best. Exemplify some of the tact and determination of successful business salesman. Don't be shamed to speak of The Sun in public. Though you may be able to tell the public, eloquently, of its worth and great good, don't stop there and depend on that alone. Personal solicitation with the belief that "I can if I will, and I will if I can," will generally get them.

J. E. FRANKS.

THE FORWARD MOVEMENT

(Warren H. H. Denison, D. D., Superintendent)

$2,000,000 Is Our Goal

The Forward Movement Committee had several meetings and enlarged the scope of the Forward Movement. It was decided to include all the regular benevolences of the whole Church from January 1, 1918 to January 1, 1923. This will include, not only the Forward Movement financial drive in five year subscriptions but all the general Home and Foreign Mission, Education, Convention, and all other benevolent offerings of the Convention, the college drives, gifts to benevolent institutions, conference, state, and district convention offerings in so far as they pass through the hands of treasurers. Thus they placed the goal of the Forward Movement at $2,000,000. It will be seen at once that this is a much larger financial program than the Movement had anticipated. It is made necessary by the great needs of the Church that she may do her share in meeting the world's needs. It challenges us to much larger service and giving than we have ever undertaken before.

It was decided that the canvass for the financial goal in our five point program should be made within the next eighteen months; that the Movement should finance itself after the initial promotion fund has been expended; the endowment and active funds were made more elastic, giving to the donor a chance to express his wish to which fund they should go; and in case no expression is given, the recipient church boards are to use their judgment in placing the funds in either of these two funds.

Three persons were added to the Forward Movement committee of twenty-four, thus making a committee of twenty-seven. The committee is limited to thirty. The new persons are President A. G. Caris, Defiance, Ohio; Rev. W. J. Hall, Franklin, N. H.; Rev. Roy C. Helfenstein, D. D., Urbana, Illinois.

The Convention Expresses Itself

The Convention unanimously and enthusiasticly adopted the following resolution, as well as the above recommendations of the Forward Movement committee: "Resolved, That this Convention, in quadrennial session, hereby gives its hearty and strongest endorsement to the Forward Movement of the Christian Church, as our denomination's answer to Christ's call and challenge for these wonderful days, and pledge ourselves sacredly as officials, ministers, delegates, both in our representative and individual capacity, to aggressively carry out this five-point program, recognizing that these five points are fundamentals in Christian and church activity. We express the conviction that this Movement is divine in inspiration and purpose. We believe that our brethren were led of God to present such a program for our Church. We believe that it will help us to fill our place and do our part in these days of reconstruction. We offer our allegiance to The Forward Movement of the Christian Church and pledge our co-operation to those who are called to direct its activities."

Mrs. A. E. Hines.—I enjoy reading THE SUN and trust that you will have much success in your work.

THE CHRISTIAN ORPHANAGE

SUPERINTENDENT'S LETTER

The financial report this week takes us past the sixth mile post or the six thousand dollar mark. We have been reaching thousand dollar mile posts right along since the Easter offering has been coming in. The response to the Easter offering has been beautiful and we are glad. We now number fifty-seven children and our expense is much more than it was when we had a smaller number. We have used the last barrel of flour, we had on hand, and from now till our wheat crop is garnered, we will have to buy flour. Flour, meat and lard are three big items in our expense account.

It was a great pleasure for us to have the Board of Trustees with us on Tuesday, May 20, and a number of visitors who were attending the Commencement at Elon College.

Our little folks are always happy to have the Board meet with us for on that day we always set them up to ice cream and they enjoy it.

We are glad to have visitors because we find that the more we can get people to come to see us and look into the faces of the children and see the opportunity the Church has for doing a great work for the Master through this Institution, the more they become interested.

The following contributions have come in since our last report:

L. C. Huffines, two suits and collars; Berea Christian church, Norfolk, 25 yards sheeting; Rosemont Christian church, South Norfolk, 25 yards sheeting and one counterpane; Mrs. J. L. Pointer, two sheets; Intermediate Class-Pleasant Grove church, (Va.), two sheets; The Ladies' of Catawba Springs church and friends of the Orphanage, two counterpanes, one sheet, 35 yards double sheeting; Ladies' Aid Society, Berea church, (Nansemond County), Va., one counterpane and three towels; T. E. Brickhouse, two boxes of oranges for Easter, (overlooked in previous report); Ladies' Aid Society, Shallow Well church, six sheets and one pair of pillow cases; Mrs. J. P. Sharpe, Cumnock, N. C., 12 sheets and one pair of pillow cases for the Ladies' Aid Society.

CHAS. D. JOHNSTON, Supt.

REPORT FOR MAY 28, 1919

Amount brought forward, $5,937.88.

Children's Offerings

Mary, John and Fleeta Harrell, $1.00; Philipps Harrell, 25 cents; Total, $1.25.

Monthly Sunday School Offerings
(North Carolina Conference)

Howard's Chapel, $1.00; Sanford, $6.60; Shiloh, $2.00; Bethlehem, $1.00; Mt. Auburn, $16.13; Shallow Ford, $2.50; New Lebanon, $1.00; New Lebanon Baraca Class, $1.00; Liberty, (Vance County), $5.12; Durham, $5.00; Wake Chapel, $6.25.

(Eastern Virginia Conference)

Johnson's Grove, $8.00; Berea, (Norfolk), $4.00; Needham Grove, $2.00; New Hope, Va., $2.31; Kite, Ga., $2.00; Total, $66.16.

Special Offerings

J. R. Seawell, Elon College, $5.00; G. G. Anderson, Altamahaw, N. C., $1.75; Total $6.75.

Easter Offerings

Howard's Chapel (Additional), $1.95; R. L. George, High Point, N. C., $1.00; Woods Chapel church, $5.08; Lois C. Lawrence, Takoma Park, D. C., $10.00; Berea Church, (Nansemond County), Va., $30.00; M. W. Hollowell, $5.00; Bethel Church, $31.50; Oak Grove church, $6.02; Berea, (Norfolk), Va., $32.50; Mt. Zion church, (Va.), $15.00; Wayland Christian church, Nebraska, $43.25; Sarem church, (N. C.), $7.50; Fuller's church, $20.00; Ebenezer church, (Additional), $2.25; Rev. E. T. Cotton, $2.00; Mrs. E. T. Cotton, $2.00; Macedonia, Forest Home and Corinth, Ala., $17.00; Union, Southampton, Va., $5.55; Elon College, S. S. and church, $24.87; Greensboro church, $20.00; Total $282.47.

Total for the week, $356.63; Grand total, $6,394.51.

CHILDREN'S LETTER

Dear Uncle Charley: Enclosed please find 25 cents as my Easter offering. Mamma gave this to me for feeding her little chickens and turkeys. I am a little boy two years old and think that I am a little man when feeding the little biddies. I hope all the little cousins had an enjoyable Easter. Found several Easter eggs.—*Phillip Harrell.*

I wonder if I can beat you raising chickens. I took off a hen the other day with eighteen little biddies. I like to feed little biddies, too.—*'Uncle Charley.'*

Dear Uncle Charley: Enclosed please find check for $1.00 as our Easter offering. Papa paid us to pop his peanuts so we are sending a part of our money to the little orphans. Love to all the cousins.—*Mary, John and Fleeta Harrell.*

You were smart to pop peanuts for papa. It was good to send the money to the Orphanage.—*'Uncle Charley.'*

GLEANINGS FROM OUR MAIL

E. A. Johnson.—May God's blessing be with each reader of our Church paper.

* * *

I. A. Lloyd.—I certainly enjoy reading THE CHRISTIAN SUN and hope that I will not miss a copy.

* * *

Mrs. R. A. Butler.—THE CHRISTIAN SUN is a welcome visitor in our home. Long may it shine.

* * *

Mrs. J. J. Harrell.—I just don't feel like I want to be without my Church paper.

* * *

Mrs. L. W. Paynter.—I enjoy THE SUN so much each week.

* * *

D. A. Ritenour.—Please renew my paper. I enjoy reading its columns.

WHAT GERMANY FACES

At this writing, (May 23), Germany has not signed the Peace Treaty. Here are some of the *main* things to which she must submit when she signs:

The League of nations made a part of the treaty to be signed.

Internationalization of the Saar Basin for a number of years.

Permanent internationalization of Danzig.

Territorial changes in Belgium and in East Prussia.

Cession of Upper Silesia to Poland.

Creation of international labor body.

Creation of commissions for holding various plebicites.

Leaving disposition of former German colonies to Allies.

Cession by Germany to Belgium of 382 square miles; to Poland, of 27,686 square miles; to France (Alsace-Lorraine), 5,600 square miles.

Seizure by France without payment of all Hohenzollern property in Alsace-Lorraine.

Abrogation of the Brest-Litovsk treaty.

Renunciation to China by Germany of the remainder of the Boxer indemnities.

Recognition of British protectorate over Egypt.

Cession to Japan of all right in the Shantung peninsula.

Demobilization by Germany within two months after the signing of peace.

Closing of all German munition works within three months after signing of peace.

Renunciation by Germany of all her territorial and political rights outside of Europe.

Recognition of the total independence of German Austria, Czecho-Slovakia, and Poland.

Reduction of German army to 100,000 men.

Abolition of conscription within German territories.

Razing of German forts for fifty kilometers east of the Rhine.

Continued allied occupation of part of Germany.

Reduction of German navy to six battleships, six light cruisers, twelve torpedo boats, and no submarines.

Destruction by Germany herself of all Helgoland fortifications.

Surrender of naval and military air service by October 1, 1919.

Acceptance by Germany of the principle of the League of Nations.

Retention by Allies of German hostages until persons accused of war crimes shall be surrendered.

Determination of German indemnities by an interallied commission before May 1, 1921.

Initial payment of twenty billion marks for civilian damages, with subsequent payments to be secured by bonds.

Replacement by Germany, ton for ton, of all shipping destroyed.

Trial of former Emperor William by an international court. Abrogation of all treaties and agreements with Bolshevik Russia.

Opening of Kiel Canal to all nations.

Interest on Germany's debt to be five per cent unless otherwise determined.

Payment by Germany of the total cost of the armies of occupation from the date of the armistice.

Mrs. Chas. R. Clark.—Please find check for renewal to THE SUN. I think that everyone should be interested enough in their Church to take the paper.

Sunday School and Christian Endeavor

Obedience. Gen. 12:1-4; Matt. 7:16-29; John 15:21-24.

Golden Text: Ye are my friends, if ye do the things which I commend you. John 15:14.

Thoughts For Teachers

"Wherefore seeing we are compassed about with so great a cloud of witness," says the writer of Hebrews, speaking of the faithful. Is it not equally true of the obedient? Has one a real faith if it is not a working faith? If you tell me you have placed a thousand dollars to my credit, have I real faith, no matter what I say, if I never draw or use a cent of the money?

"The Lord said unto Abram" or Isaac, or Jacob or Moses. Whenever they spoke, He answered, and told them what they desired to know. We are apt to say, it was easy to do right in those days. But we have the Word of God for the statement that God Who in times past spoke to and through His prophets, hath in these latter days spoken unto us through His own Son. They did not know, in the olden days, half so well as we, for the revelation was only a partial one; no matter how clear the voice of God might be, its applications and implications were necessarily limited by the ear of flesh which heard. But when His Son spoke, piercing, as it were that earthly veil, and permitting us to speak directly to our Father, the entire truth was given once for all. There remains only its direct application to our particular case, an application made by the Holy Spirit, who guides into all truth, and our obedience to the Heavenly vision.

MRS. FRED BULLOCK.

CHRISTIAN ENDEAVOR TOPIC FOR JUNE 8, 1919

Conditions necessary for world peace. Micah 4:1-15.

For peace as for everything else of value, other foundation can no man lay than that is laid, even Jesus Christ. Men cry peace, peace today, and there is no peace. The world is in turmoil and trouble and perplexity. A veritable fire of trouble seems to be consuming parts of it. We are told that the League of Nations no. where mention the name of God. If this be true, certainly it is that it will not accomplish the things designed by its founders. It may be, in a measure a success, but neither a righteous nor a lasting success. The Lord must build the house of the nation as well as the individual if it is to be founded on a rock.

MRS. FRED BULLOCK.

GIVE THE SUNDAY SCHOOLS A CHANCE

Continued reports from our Sunday schools are exceedingly encouraging. They show that the schools want to grow and go forward. Marion Lawrance points out the fact to our consternation that the Sunday school has been losing out very rapidly the past year or two, and that during the same time juvenile crime has been on the increase. He says if the Sunday school continues to lose in the next decade as it has in the past two years, it will be extinct as an institution. The plain remedy is that the Sunday school *must get to doing things for others.* If the school lives just for itself, it has no right to live, and no claim to life. It may be selfish, as well as the individual may be. Why not seek to get out of the old idea of just living for self, just going on in the same old way, and begin to think, study, teach and do for others? The Sunday school has fallen into a groove, into a well-born rut. It needs to fall in with the spirit of this new time, and do something outside its own for the salvation of this wicked and sin-cursed world.

If any school thinks it cannot yet spare an offering once per month to help reach and save this wicked world, why not spend some time once per month at least in trying to find out the distress, the misery, the poverty, the want, the need of two-thirds of the human family today who are without the Gospel and without hope either in this world, or in that to come? Why not let the Sunday school understand that two out of three infants born into this world look up into the faces of mothers who can never tell them anything about the Blessed Christ, because those mothers themselves never heard that Name which is above every name and the One whereby we must be saved, if we are saved? If the children in the Sunday school can learn such facts as these they will have pity, even if the grown-ups do not. Let's give our children in the Sunday school a chance to know and to understand. Is it not high time we were teaching missions in our Sunday schools, and teaching the pupils there to give of their means for missions? Give the Sunday schools a chance and see if they do not take on new life.

J. O. ATKINSON,
Sec. Miss. S. C. C.

ANNOUNCEMENT No. 1

The First Annual Session of the new North Carolina Sunday School and Christian Endeavor Convention will be held at Shallow Well church, (near Jonesboro, N. C.), Tuesday evening, Wednesday, Wednesday evening, and Thursday, July 15-17. This Convention embodies all the Sunday schools and Christian Endeavor Societies in what was formerly the Eastern North Carolina, the Western North Carolina, and the North Carolina and Virginia Christian Conferences.

So if you were related in any way to either of the above named Conferences, this notice is for you and we want you to get it fixed firmly in your mind that the success of the coming Convention depends largely on you. The Convention wants your presence and you should want all the inspiration, information and other fine things that the Convention can give you.

We have done our utmost to prepare the best program possible which will be ready for the press in a few days. We want you to enjoy it. Keep the time and place of meeting before your friends, your church, Sunday school and your Society, and let's all begin now the big drive for the victory Convention at Shallow Well.

C. H. STEPHENSON, *Pres.*
Raleigh, N. C.

MARRIAGES

HATFIELD-RICHARDSON

Mr. Paul Carr Hatfield and Miss Marion Richardson, of Norfolk, Va., were married at my residence, 207 Chestnut Street, Suffolk, Va., May 17, 1919.

H. H. BUTLER.

GULLEN-ODEM

On May 20, 1919, at 4:00 oclock P. M., Mr. Lewis Gullen and Miss Josie Odem, daughter of Mr. and Mrs. B. J. Odem of Suffolk, Va., were married at the home of the writer. After the marriage the happy couple left for Washington, D. C.

H. H. BUTLER.

WYRICK-BROWN

On May 14, 1919, at 6:30 oclock, Rev. Lonnie Lee Wyrick and Miss Annie Ethel Brown were united in marriage at my home, Elon College, N. C. The marriage was a quiet affair, being witnessed by a few friends and relatives. They are making their home at Elon College, N. C. Mr. Wyrick is a minister of the Christian Church of which both parties are members. The writer officiated. We wish for them a successful and happy life together.

J. F. APPLE.

INDIVIDUAL COMMUNION SERVICE
THE BEST WAY
to serve Communion. It is reverent, sanitary, and increases attendance at the Lord's Supper. Our services are chaste and beautiful. Made of finest materials and best workmanship.

Send for illustrated price list

C. B. RIDDLE, Publishing Agent, Burlington, North Carolina.

CANCER TREATED SUCCESSFULLY AT THE KELLAM HOSPITAL

The record of the Kellam Hospital is without parallel in history, having restored, without the use of the knife, Acids, X-Ray or Radium, over ninety per cent of the many hundreds of sufferers from cancers which it has treated during the past twenty-two years. We want every man and woman in the United States to know what we are doing.—KELLAM HOSPITAL, 1617 W. Main St., Richmond, Va.

THE TITHER

An interdenominational publication devoted to Tithing and Christian Stewardship.

Editors

C. B. RIDDLE
KARL LEHMANN
BERT WILSON
HUGH S. McCORD
FRED G. THOMAS

8 pages; issued monthly; 50c the year

Address

THE TITHER   Burlington, N. C.

THE FINAL LAP

Get Ready for the Final Lap

June Is To Be the Closing Month

A Big Job, But Easy to Handle

The Campaign Leaders Underestimated the People and the Esteem in Which Elon is Held

SEE THAT YOUR CHURCH GOES ON RECORD FOR ITS FULL QUOTA

SEE PAGE ELEVEN OF THIS ISSUE

SEE THAT YOUR CHURCH DOES ITS WHOLE DUTY

ELON'S NEED IS YOUR OPPORTUNITY	R U Giving —or— R U Getting	ELON'S SUCCESS IS YOUR GAIN

THE CHRISTIAN SUN

"IN ESSENTIALS UNITY, IN NON-ESSENTIALS LIBERTY, IN ALL THINGS CHARITY"

Slang

SLANG is mockery of our mother tongue, depreciates the fine elements of expression and cheapens our communication. It is a sign that the speaker's vocabulary is limited and that he takes his auditors to be on the same level. Slang in the mouth of the child takes from the home some of the sweets and is an inducement to be irreverent. Slang in the pulpit debases the Word of God and undervalues the Story of the Savior. Literature is too rich with choice words—words that convey thought—for the minister to resort to slang in order to lead men and women to a richer life.

Volume LXXI   WEDNESDAY, JUNE 4, 1919   Number 23

BURLINGTON   ·   ·   ·   NORTH CAROLINA

THE CHRISTIAN SUN

Founded 1844 by Rev. Daniel W. Kerr

C. B. RIDDLE   -   -   -   Editor

Entered at the Burlington, N. C. Post Office as second class matter.

Subscription Rates

One year ....$ 2.00
Six months 1.00

In Advance   -

Give both your old and new postoffice when asking that your address be changed.

The change of your label is your receipt for money. Written receipts sent upon request.

Marriage and obituary notices not exceeding 150 words printed free if received within 60 days from date of event, all over this at the rate of one-half cent a word.

Original poetry not accepted for publication.

Principles of the Christian Church

(1) The Lord Jesus Christ is the only Head of the Church.
(2) Christian is a sufficient name of the Church.
(3) The Holy Bible is a sufficient rule of faith and practice.
(4) Christian character is a sufficient test of fellowship, and of church membership.
(5) The right of private judgment and the liberty of conscience is a right and a privilege that should be accorded to, and exercised by all.

EDITORIAL

CHURCH ADVERTISING

The topic for this article embraces too much territory for us to discuss all of it at one time. We are, therefore, undertaking to mention only one phase of church advertising.

It is custom of ours, and we presume a custom of many others, to look over the church notices in the Sunday paper. It is true that we do not read all of them, but usually look for the announcement of certain churches, and especially of our own denomination.

The church notices in the Sunday paper seem to be taking the place in the city of the time-honored bell. The church notices in the Sunday paper meet our approval in every way, but the topics sometimes announced are not in accord with our way of thinking. We ask the question: What is the object of the church notice if it is not to give information? Some of the sermon topics given in these church notices. are vague and convey no information whatever to the reader. Let us quote a few of them which we take from the papers before us: "A complaint and a challenge;" "Seeing the invisible;" "On the Gaza Road;" "When the wife wishes she were single;" "The telling of it;" "A forgotten secret."

What reader of this article can tell what is to be discussed by reading these announced topics? What information do they convey? Or suppose that you are looking for a certain article, and wanting to know some-

thing about the article, a placard with words on it as vague as these was hung on the article, what information would you have about it?

The need of church publicity through the Sunday paper seems to be universally recognized, but we are wondering if we ar not making some of these Sunday church notices about as interesting as a list of real estate transfers? Why should we desire to announce some subject in order to decoy the reader and get him to church? Is it not time that we begin to think about such tendencies and give the people the information that they need?

THE INDIVIDUAL CHURCH AND THE ELON ENDOWMENT

Just now there is a great responsibility resting upon the individual church in regard to the Elon Endowment of $250,000. Especially is this true of the church if it has not raised its quota. Every enterprise of the Church is united by a bond that is strong. Every enterprise of the Church needs the co-operation of every other enterprise. The local churches cannot live without linking themselves up to every enterprise of the Convention. No church in the Southern Christian Convention can afford to withhold its support from our College. It is a duty, a privilege and an opportunity.

The various churches have been asked to raise through their members a certain amount to apply on the endowment fund of our College. It ought to be the pride of each local church to see that its part of this fund is raised. What church desires to come up blank in the final report? What member of any local church will not be humiliated at such a statement? What pastor will not be humiliated to know that his church failed to do its duty and to grasp its opportunity?

EVADING THE LAW

The Siler City Grit, Siler City, N. C., an independent newspaper, has been writing editorially of late on a very important subject—the subject of punishing the guilty who continue to deal in the whisky traffic. The Grit points out that in its own county and in other sections the offenders of the law are often apprehended and brought to face their crime, but due to some spasmodic effort the question is settled and the offender goes free.

This paper continues: "The question is, shall a few law-defying blockaders and whisky dealers set aside the will and the law of the majority of the honest, thrifty, law-abiding people of this country?" This is the question important and not until penalties are dealt out sufficient will the whisky business be finally overcome. At the present price of this hellish fluid, a man can soon pay a small fine and will be glad to do so. We have prohibition in this country and why not unite and let it prohibit?

THE METHODIST AND BIG THINGS

Our Methodist brethren and sisters are showing us how to do big things for the Kingdom. The Southern Methodist went over the top in their drive for $35,000,000. The Methodist Episcopal church went over the top in its drive for $80,000.000. Of course they did. They were celebrating the one hundred anniversary of their missionary endeavor. It was in 1819 that Methodist missionary work began, though not till several years later did they send out their first foreign missionary.

When the Christian Church has for one hundred years been seriously engaged in the matter of missions, and has carried on a real missionary propaganda for a century, then it too can celebrate a centenary of missions and raise $105,000,000.00. But when are we to begin seriously that one hundred years? There is one reason and only one today why we are driving for $2,000,000 instead of fifty times that sum and that is because we have not been an active, aggressive missionary force. That is all.

"PRAY AND FAINT NOT".

Jesus taught His disciples that they should pray and not faint. This does not mean fainting in the ordinary term.

Many persons do not pray unless they have a particular desire to do so. They want to be prompted to pray. So often we pray when we do not feel in a prayerful attitude, but we believe that the reason for this is because of the lack of prayer. When we talk daily with the Lord, the association becomes pleasant and interesting.

It is only the snare of Satan to make us feel inclined to pray only when we feel like it. A very good time to pray is when we do not feel like it because that is the time when we need strength that is divine. Cultivate the habit of daily prayer.

TONING DOWN

We believe that Editor Johnson of the *Biblical Recorder*, Raleigh, N. C., is toning down somewhat as to the position of his paper on the union idea. Read the following editorial from his pen:

For quite awhile several of our papers have been warning their readers against the danger of being swept away by the union propaganda. These papers have urged our people to stand firmly by their convictions and for the integrity of our denomination. This paper has no apology to make for having used what influence it may possess, in behalf of denominational integrity. It believed there was real danger, and that a warning note needed to be sounded. The Convention in Atlanta puts itself on record so overwhelmingly and emphatically as opposed to union, or federation, of any kind that little more space will be needed for the publication of defensive matter.

There are two things, however, which, at this juncture, we should do. One is to cultivate a fraternal spirit, and the other is to leave the trenches and launch out in a great offensive movement. We must be very careful not to allow our opposition to union to engender a feeling of bitterness toward those with whom we think it best not to unite. They are our brethren, and they love the Lord, "whose we are and whom we serve." They are as anxious to extend His Kingdom as we are, and many of them are making greater sacrifices than we, for the spread of His glorious gospel. While we differ as to the methods to be used for accomplishing the great task, we are one in wanting the thing done, and while

we believe that each denomination should maintain its separate organization, we can, and should, have unity of spirit, and each division in the army should rejoice in every victory gained by any of the others. We should show to others that we are willing to co-operate with them whenever and wherever we can do so without a sacrifice of principle. We should make them to understand that it is conscience, and not a lack of fraternal feeling, which prevents us from going as far in the work of co-operation as they think we should go.

While we believe that our position as to union is the only consistent one and, therefore, the one that we must take, we should give those who differ from us credit for honesty of opinion. They, no doubt, are conscientious in the belief that by some sort of interdenominational movement the world can be more speedily evangelized. When the disciples told Christ that they had forbidden a man who was casting out devils in His name, Christ said, "Forbid him not, for no man can do a mighty work in my name, and straightway speak evil of me."

We Baptists certainly cannot afford to spend all our time defending our position, while others are engaged in a great offensive. If the principles which we hold are worth so much to us, surely we should make every sacrifice within our power to give them to the world. A well-known Baptist brother, who is in thorough accord with the position taken by the Southern Baptist Convention on the subject of union, said this to the writer the other day: "We Baptists profess to 'stand by the Book,' and we are true to our profession, we 'stand by the Book,' but the time has come when we should take the Book to the millions who have never seen it.".

With compassion for a lost world, loyalty to Christ and His Word, and love to all who love our Lord, we must launch out in a great offensive, and do our full part in this agressive warfare.

Brother Johnson's last paragraph says it all; there he admits the need of unity of the forces of Christ.

The ministers can help us materially this summer by sending short articles. Let them come along.

Watch your label, but not too long.

"A man may be down, but he is never out," says a motto of the Salvation Army.

If you need a nice Bible or Testament, write this office. We can supply you.

SMILE

He (silly with the season): "Really, I'm so fond of strawberries that I'd like to be straw-buried."
She: "Well, I'd prefer to be ice-cremated."—*Boston Transcript.*

    • • •

"I never saw such a man as you are. I really believe you hate yourself."
"Well, why shouldn't I? My mother is English and my father is a German."—*Puck.*

    • •

"What dirty hands you have, Johnny," said his teacher. "What would you say if I came to school that way?"
"I wouldn't say nothin'," replied Johnny. "I'd be too polite."

PASTOR AND PEOPLE

BETTER THINGS FOR THE CHRISTIAN DENOMINATION

The spirit of a forward movement is in the air. Perhaps no small denomination in the United States has given more time, thought and energy during the past year to devise and perfect plans for aggressive effective work. Especially in our missionary and educational work largeness of vision, a buoyant spirit, a hopefulness, an earnestness and a consecration of purpose everywhere manifest that it is full of promise for the future.

Here in the South all eyes are naturally turned to THE CHRISTIAN SUN, Dr. Atkinson for Missions and President Harper for Christian Education. Others are just as loyal and liberal, but certain names and personalities are inseparably connected with any great movement as spokesmen and leaders.

Some are too old and too poor to do and give very much but no loyal member of the Christian Church can or will withhold his prayers and benedictions as the campaign for an Every Member Canvass is being planned and carried out.

Yes, yes, they are after money, and they are getting it, too. But listen—it is something more. Combined with getting money and "back of it as a motive power, should be the effort to deepen the conservation of our people, and to quicken into newness of life a sense of the joy of service," in the vineyard of our Lord.

D. A. LONG.

SUFFOLK LETTER

The "city of the dead" lies close by the "city of the living" and the two are joined by invisible bonds as well as beaten roads. The obliteration of human life is impossible. Life is linked up to events in such a way as to make them inseparable. Immortality is written in the universal thought and experience of mankind. What we call death is only the separation of spirit and body and not the death of spirit. The body is animated by the spirit, and the return of the spirit into the body re-animates it. The twelve-year-old daughter of Jairus proves this: "Her spirit returned, and she arose immediately." Jesus Christ re-entered His buried body and arose from the dead. All who believe in Him shall, also, arise from the dead. Resurrection includes the body and is without meaning, if the body is left out.

Mrs. Ella Milteer Norfleet was born August 15, 1872, and passed out of the body March 16, 1919, in her 47th year. She was married to A. T. Norfleet April 19, 1899. She leaves her husband and one daughter, Cecil, besides a brother, John A. Milteer, and two sisters, Mrs. R. L. Wilkinson and Mrs. M. F. Martin.

Mrs. Norfleet had been long afflicted but of such a cheerful and hopeful disposition as to dispel the gloom that usually settles down upon a sick woman. She made her friends almost ashamed of themselves when they visited her. They found her so happy and so cheerful in spite of a fatal disease. People in health

are often rebuked by the life of the afflicted. "It is not all of life to live, nor all of death to die." More is in the spirit of man, and the hope of the heart.

Mrs. Norfleet was a faithful member of the church, of the Philathea Class, and lived in a large circle of friends who enjoyed her fine spirit and her brave life. The end found her ready for the change, and left a glow like the setting sun that relieved the darkness that flooded the home. She will rise again on a new day and shine like a star in the firmament. Jesus made the tomb the hope of the world, and the cemetery the place of flowers and of sweetest memory for the living. Sickness and death develop patience, service, love, and sympathy. If the world had no trouble sympathy would die. Adversity binds the human family together; prosperity separates men and nations. The wild animals of the west have been known to huddle on the shore of the Great Lakes in perfect peace when driven from the jungle by great forest fires. When safe in the woods they were enemies; when in danger of life, they were friends. Pain is a great friend because it warns us of danger, sends for the doctor, takes the bitter medicine, and saves life. The rent earth and the broken heart keep us tender, sympathetic, humble, prayerful, and useful in life; but the darkened chamber, the vacant chair, the silent voice, the absent spirit, the face that is gone, all fill the soul with griefs that God alone can assuage; but His grace is "sufficient" and His promises are "sure."

W. W. STALEY.

Suffolk, Va.

A SUNDAY EVENING MEDITATION

Reading so as to communicate intelligently to hearers is an art. Not everyone who reads has acquired this art.

Many attempt the reading of the Holy Scripture from the sacred desk and utterly fail. They have not failed to read, of course, but they have failed to communicate God's message in that particular Scripture to the listeners and worshippers. Thus the latter has lost the heart of the message and the devotions of the hour.

This is very disappointing to the earnest seeker of God. He who goes to the sanctuary because to him it is the "Courts of the Lord" and because there he wants to hear God's voice and the message from the altar, cannot leave the sanctuary satisfied, because he has failed in one particular thing for which he is looking. If he is satisfied the greater is the loss, for then he is content to be without due contemplation of the Holy Writ. The greater, too, is the loss if the *messenger* is content to read without conveying the meaning, for he is indifferent to results with his audience. He may be dissatisfied but the fact that he is not satisfied with this does not alter the case for the result is the same and the omission is a little less than a calamity.

Public reading of God's word should always be with understanding both on the part of him who reads and of him who hears. If the worshipper hears without understanding he has not missed it all, of course, but he has missed much which is of primary importance.

There is another reason why such care should be given the reading of the Scriptures. The congregation nearly always consists of promiscuous intellects such as the educated and the illiterate, the cultured and the uncultured, the devout and the indifferent, the Christian and the sinner, and perhaps fifty or more other characteristic minds. Many of the worshippers in almost any congregation have almost everything else in mind but a concentration of thought on the Scriptures. Perhaps many of them are not able to comprehend the language read so monotonously, or perhaps they have not time nor the ability to read just misplaced emphasis given by the reader; and there are others who are not disposed to do so. Therefore, it is the task of the reader to so read as to engage the attention of all and to convey the truth of his message.

The meaning of the Scripture may be interpreted and conveyed in the flexibility of the voice and in properly placed emphasis. To do this it may often be necessary for the reader to pause to put the message into everyday parlance.

It is thus the truth engages attention by becoming the living truth, and living truth is that in which living people are interested. Every public reader of God's word should study to show himself approved of God in the reading of His message and the interpretation thereof just as much as he seeks to show himself approved, "A workman who needeth not to be ashamed."

H. E. ROUNTREE.

Portsmouth, N. H.

DENOMINATIONAL DAY

April 28, 1919, was set apart as "Denominational Day," when every Baptist minister was asked to preach on "How Baptists Differ From Other Denominations." The *Watchman-Examiner* perhaps the ablest Baptist paper in America, commenting on this subject, among other things said: "Christian co-operation and Christian union have been in the limelight of discussion so long that Baptists are wondering whether the time has not come to preach our distinctive principles without running counter to the spirit that is abroad and without appearing to the narrow and unfraternal." Again in the alarmed and faithful Baptist *Watchman* on the walls of denomination ramparts says, "It is manifestly our duty to safeguard our principles and to continue their advocacy. If in such a day we abandon our distinctive principles or turn aside from their advocacy, we shall prove traitors to our trust." He then tells us about a few of these "distinctive principles." They are: "Toleration in Religion," "Absolute Soul Liberty." As Church and State are not united in the United States this distinctive principle is not clear. The second "distinctive principle is this: "Baptists protest against "Sacramentarianism." This big word is understood to imply a sort of superstitious belief that baptism saves men by some mysterious *ex-opere operato* magic.

The third distinctive principle mentioned is the belief that "the Bible is the only and all sufficient rule of faith and practice." Protestants generally agree on this principle.

Would it not be a good idea to set apart a day for all denominations to try to find out how many principles they can, and do agree upon? Most of the principles are about things non-essential to salvation, and concerning which good men and women can think differently, in Christian love. Magnify the agreement and disagreement.

D. A. LONG.

POUNDING PREACHERS

I feel impressed to write on the subject of "Pounding Preachers." I believe that we should pound them, but I do not think that we should wait for a definite time to do so. It should be a regular habit with us. The preachers come once a month, and perhaps oftener, to bring us a soul feast and we should treat them in a way that will show them that we appreciate their efforts on our behalf. I do not mean that we should get up a regular pounding, but some could give one time and some another and in so doing our preachers would not go away in need at any time.

Also concerning tithing, the tenth part, or tithe, belongs to the Lord and if we give only that we have only done our duty, Let us give that and add thereto a free-will offering so we will have something to our credit if we expect the Lord's blessing upon us.

MRS. A. D. BAKER.

Route 1, Kipling, N. C.

SALEM CHAPEL, N. C.

One service there last Saturday. My friends went and cleaned off the cemetery. Basket dinner and two services Sunday. The Communion in the afternoon.

LIBERTY, N. C.

Expect to preach here at 11 A. M. tomorrow. Immediately after preaching I must go ten or twelve miles into the country and preach at the residence of Mr. Sylvester Spoon. Many of his relatives and friends will be there on account of Mr. Spoon's ninety-second birthday.

D. A. LONG.

May 24, 1919.

THE MOST PRECIOUS THING ON EARTH

While trying to explain the nature and fruits of repentance as set forth in the Sunday school lesson for May 25, my attention was called to what Thomas Moore tells in his poem, "Paradise and the Cari," a story of the most precious thing on earth. It is a story which comes from Arabia, and relates how a woman was refused admittance to Paradise until she should bring as an offering the most precious thing on earth. She returned to earth and searched in all parts for what might prove to be earth's most precious treasure. Passing a battlefield, she saw a patriot dying on the field, and she caught up the last drop of his life-blood given for his country and bore it up to the gates of Paradise. But they were not opened for her, and she was sent back for something more precious still. She found a mother giving her life for the child, and caught up her last sigh of self-sacrifice and took that to heaven, but even that did not gain her admittance. Coming to earth again, she saw an old man and a little child as the call to prayer was sounded. The little child spread his prayer rug on the ground, and as the man looked at the child at prayer in his innocence and purity and then remembered his own innocent youth and his evil life since, hot tears of repentance fell to the ground The woman caught one of these tears of the old man's repentance and swiftly carried it up to the gate of heaven. This time she was admitted.

D. A. LONG.

NEW NORTH CAROLINA LAWS

(Continued from last week)

25. An Act providing for the erection of a new building for the Agricultural Department, the cost of same not to exceed $250,000. Public Laws 1919.

26. An Act to provide for the transfer of the State Prison from Raleigh to the State Farm, and to convert the present prison into a hospital for the insane. Public Laws 1919.

27. An Act to protect sheep better known as the Dog Law, which meets the Governor's urgent recommendation that dogs be kept up at night. Public Laws 1919.

28. An Act ratifying the Federal prohibition amendment. Public Laws 1919.

29. An Act submitting a constitutional amendment to the voters of the State at the next general election to reduce the poll tax to $2.00. Public Laws 1919.

30. An Act submitting a constitutional amendment abolishing the requirement of the payment of poll tax as a prerequisite to voting. Public Laws 1919.

31. An Act submitting a constitutional amendment to reduce the time of residence in the State for voting from two years to one year. Public Laws 1919.

32. An Act increasing the exemption from taxation of household and kitchen furniture tools of farmers and mechanics and books scientific instruments from $25 to $300. Public Laws 1919.

33. An Act submitting a constitutional amendment to provide for taxation of income although derived from property that is taxed. Publi Laws 1919.

34. An Act to provide for the listing and valuing of all property real, personal and mixed at its real value money, better known as the re-valuation act. Public Laws 1919.

35. An Act to provide for sanitary closets. Public Laws 1919.

(The end)

FROM OUR SUBSCRIBERS

Mrs. Sallie McCauley—I enjoy reading THE SUN more each week. I hope it will find a place in every home in the Christian Church this year.

Mrs. Joseph Liskey—May this be the best year yet.

Mrs. A. D. Baker—I just love THE SUN and am so glad it is shining in my home. I expect to do all I can to keep it shining as long as I live.

Mrs. B. F. Frank—THE SUN is a welcome visitor in our home. It seems like an old acquaintance coming in every week to cheer our lonliness as we are so far removed from our home church.

WITH THE POETS

A LITTLE WALK AROUND YOURSELF

When you're criticising others and are finding here
  and there
A fault or two to speak of or a weakness you can tear;
When you're blaming someone's meanness or accusing
  some of pelf—
It's time that you went out to take a walk around
  yourself.

There's lots of human failures in the average of us all,
And lots of grave shortcomings in the short ones and
  the tall;
But when we think of evils men should lay upon the
  shelves,
It's time we all went out to take a walk around ourselves.

We need so often in this life this balancing of scales,
This seeing how much in us wins and how much in us
  fails;
But before you judge another—just to lay him on the
  shelf—
It would be a splendid plan to take a walk around
  yourself.   —*Exchange.*

TRUST

The thunder roared; the lightning fell
  And crashed the chimney to a heap;
And darling screamed as if she dreamed
  Some dreadful dream in her first sleep.

"Hush," said the nurse. "You're not afraid;
  See, all the house in safety stands.
Nothing can happen us, indeed,
  For, darling, we are in God's hands."

And on the morrow darling said:
  "I was mos' scared to deff. That's so!
But now I'm not afraid at all,
  For I am in God's hands, you know."

Sweet confidence of childhood that
  Believes hands always there at call,
Oh, as the rainbowed years fleet by,
  May that sweet trust remain to all!
     —*Harriet Prescott Spofford.*

THE DAY'S NEED

Each day I pray, God give me strength anew
To do the task I do not wish to do,
To yield obedience, not asking why,
To love and own the truth and scorn the lie,
To look a cold world bravely in the face,
To cheer for those that pass me in the race,
To bear my burdens gaily, unafraid,
To lend a hand to those that need my aid,
To measure what I am by what I give—
God give me strength that I may rightly live!
     —*The Youth's Companion.*

THE SECRET

Who's that by the garden rim,
  Head a-bobbin'?—
Scarlet vest and jacket trim;
  Mr. Robin!

Now he whistles, loud and clear,
  Eyes a-glisten;
Runs a bit, then stops to peer,
  Look, and listen.

Crocus lifts her waxen cup,
  Brimming measure;
Jonquil's golden lamp lights up
  For his pleasure.

There's a secret glad and gay
  In his keeping;
Can he keep it for a day
  Without peeping?

Nay! he's whispered it about;
  Heads are noddin';
Spring is here! your secret's out,
  Mr. Robin.
          —*Pauline Francis Camp.*

LIFT A LITTLE

Lift a little, lift a little.
  Neighbor, lend a helping hand
To that heavy-laden brother
  Who from weakness scarce can stand.
What to thee, with thy strong muscles,
  Seems a light and easy load,
Is to him a heavy burden
  Cumbering his pilgrim road.

Lift a little, lift a little.
  Effort gives thee added strength.
That which staggers him when rising
  Thou canst hold at arms' full-length.
Not his fault that he is feeble,
  Not thy praise that thou are strong;
It is God makes lives to differ,
  Some through wailing, some through song.

Lift a little, lift a little.
  Many are they that need aid;
Many lying by the roadside
  'Neath misfortune's dreary shade.
Pass not by like priest and Levite,
  Heedless of thy fellow-man,
But with heart and arm extended
  Be the good Samaritan.   —*Watchman.*

"GOD BLESS MY MOTHER!"

A little child with flaxen hair,
And sunlit eyes so sweet and fair,
Who kneels when twilight darkens all,
And from those loving lips there fall
The accents of this simple prayer:
"God bless—God bless my mother!"

A youth upon life's threshold wide,
Who leaves a gentle mother's side,
Yet keeps enshrined within his breast
Her words of warning—still the best;
And whispers when temptation tries:
"God bless—God bless my mother!"

A white-haired man who gazes back
Along life's weary, furrowed track,
And sees one face—an angel now!—
Hears words of light that led aright,
And prays with reverential brow:
"God bless—God bless my mother!"
          —*Ladies' Home Journal.*

OUR PLACE

We cannot fill another's place,
  Our own we scarce aright can fill:
No strength have we for other's work,
  Nor yet have we the needed skill.

If faithful to our trust we prove,
  Our place will ever wider grow;
Yet still 'tis ours, by God assigned;
  Beyond its bounds we cannot go.

If other hands in needful toil
  At length too tired and weak have grown,
And we have strength that work to do,
  It is not theirs, but just our own.

The soul enlarges in its sphere,
  The place expands to give it room;
For ev'ry day God gives the strength
  Its varied duties to assume.
          —*Exchange.*

MISSIONARY NOTES

Our Holland, Va., Sunday school has decided to devote five minutes each Sunday morning to missions, and Mrs. Chas. Daughtry has been elected superintendent of the work. If we mistake not our Burlington, N. C., school followed this plan for years, and the result has been that this school has decided to support a missionary and take an offering once a month for this purpose, the offering amounting to at least $60.00 monthly. Every Sunday school can, if it will, study missions in some manner. And any school studying missions will become missionary in spirit, power and activity. No human being with a mind to think and a hart to love can know missions and not be interested in missions. When you see a person's indifference to missions you may know that person does not know missions.

          J. O. ATKINSON.

Mrs. Hattie Glass—I enjoy THE SUN. Let it keep shining.

What has your church done for the Elon Standardization Fund? Will it do its part, or fall behind?

CHRISTIAN EDUCATION

SADNESS AND JOY COMMINGLED

1. Sadness

Elon's 29th commencement closed on May 20, the anniversary day, the 30th in sucession, of the laying of the first brick of the college plant. That glad day was saddened for two reasons this year—it being in the first instance the day on which honor was done in the memory of the fifteen gallant sons of the college who died in the cause of freedom and in the second instance it was the day of the death of that beloved man, Trustee Willis Lee, the only word properly characterizing his interest in Elon being devotion.

"Uncle Willis," for such he was affectionately called at Elon, fell on sleep at 1:15 p. m., on May 20. He went to his Heavenly home as he had lived on earth, gently as a babe. Truly a prince of the Kingdom and a great man has left us. To know him was to respect and love him. Three great soul qualities constitute in memory's gallery his Trinity of life—considerateness, generosity, spiritual-mindedness. The courtesy, the deference, which true men accord their mothers, sisters, and wives this splendid man accorded to everyone. His generosity knew no limitation. Tithes and offerings, and especially offerings were his delight. But the crown of his Christian manhood was the deep undercurrent of a vital spirituality. The Kingdom and its interests were his first consideration. "He was the most useful Christian man from every standpoint I ever knew," declared a life-long friend, Senator J. E. West. I attended Brother Lee's funeral in a representative way, as the special envoy of the Board of Trustees of Elon College. My real place was with his stricken family, for truly has Elon lost a loved one whose place cannot be filled. This must not be taken as his obituary. Other and worthier pens will garland his life. I have no language in which to express my sorrow over his leaving us nor my sympathy for his loved ones in this sore affliction. Let me finally add for their comfort and for inspiration to all who would emulate him, that you cannot coffin the life of such a man as Willis J. Lee. He lives and he will continue to live in the gracious deeds of his gracious life.

2. Joy

I turned from the grave-side of my beloved friend, to take up with Rev. E. T. Cotten the Standardization Drive in his field. We began at Mt. Zion church, where a few men and "devout women not a few," gave nearly four times the church's quota. With such a splendid start, despite unfavorable weather conditions, we could but achieve a notable victory for the Christ. Mt. Carmel next opened up her heart and purse and wreathed Brother Cotten's face with smiles. At Bethlehem Deacon-elect Fred C. Holland was my pilot, tired and true. That grand old church, named for the birth-place of the Savior, despite many predictions to the contrary, went "over the top." May God richly bless the noble souls that did it! Isle of Wight, C. H. then joined the procession, by the generous hearts of a group of young men and widows. Why is it that a widow never fails to be generous? I sometimes think it might be spiritual economy for God to make all women widows, and especially is this so when I indulge in self-examination. There is something in the state of widowhood that brings a keen sense of dependence on God and that means generous support for the Kingdom. Blessings on the widows! To Windsor next and finally we went, and the same story is told. This town was first in Virginia in every drive during the war, and it went safely over for this cause. God has greater things in store for Windsor. He has greater things in store also for Isle of Wight C. H., Bethlehem, Mt. Carmel, Mt. Zion, and Pastor Cotten.

Brother Cotten is one of our young ministers. He is a faithful worker, has the sermonizing sense, is vitally spiritual, puts the Kingdom first, loves his work and his wife, who is a genuine minister's help-meet. I expect God to make a real leader in our Brotherhood out of this devoted young preacher. My fellowship with him was sweet and satisfying. His people are devoted to him. He is their devotee also. We need more such Cotten in our harvest field.

Three Funds

Out of Brother Cotten's field came three funds. They were established by Deacon J. W. Folk and Deacon-elect W. Ermotte White, of the Bethlehem church, and by Mrs. Nannie V. Bradshaw of the Mt. Carmel church.

Mrs. Bradshaw is the only surviving child of the late Major I. W. Duck, one of the Kingdom's noble men of our Church. His delight was to help educate Christian ministers and to entertain them in his home. His daughter's home now is the preacher's home. She is a queen in the fine and happy art of making you feel that you are not visiting at all. And she has his joy too in helping to educate ministers. She founded her fund to pay the tuition cost of instructing perpetually a minister of the Gospel in loving memory of her father. How sweet, how heavenly the deed, and the fine spirit in which she did it, that is one of life's oases, green and refreshing through all time and through eternity, too!

Finally

Such is life. Sorrow and joy commingled make up its busy activity, but why should we spurn the one or too eagerly grasp the other? It is our Heavenly Father Who directs, and joy or sorrow, all is well.

                    W. A. HARPER.

The other day Henry J. Heinz, the Pickle King," passed away. His "57 varities" are known all over the world, and what possibly made them known as well as their flavor, was that Henry Heinz was a man of God and did much for the Kingdom's growth.

Last week the General Assembly of the Presbyterian Church elected a layman as moderator, the first instance of its kind in that body for 130 years. John Willis Baer was the chosen one.

MISSIONARY

AN ENCOURAGING LETTER

Buffalo, Ala., May 19, 1919.

Dear Dr. Atkinson:

As you suggested we invited the ladies to stay after services at Pleasant Grove last Saturday for the purpose of organizing a Woman's Missionary Society. The pastor suggested that we organize before the benediction. We organized Saturday P. M., with eight members, but before service was over Sunday, (May 18), we had enrolled twenty-one members. So we are now twenty-one strong and hope to grow stronger. We need literature and suggestions for our program when we have our next meeting. Please send us this if possible by return mail. Thanking you in advance.

Yours for service,

Minnie L. Edge.

As far as we know, this is the first Society to be organized in our Alabama Conference, though we believe at an early date every church in this Conference will have a Woman's Society. This will add greatly to the strength, power and growth of the Conference.

WOMEN AND MISSIONS

No wonder women are interested in missions especially when they know what missions have done for women. Buddha who today has more followers and adherents than any other religious teacher that ever came to this earth, our own Christ not excepted, rejoiced that he had escaped three curses: one was that he was not born in hell; second that he was not born a vermin; and third that he was not born a woman. Yet, I say, the man who held woman in far lower esteem than he did a cow or a horse, and cursed woman throughout his teachings, has more human beings worshiping him and following him today than any other religious teacher or founder that ever visited this planet.

And Mohammed was even worse than Buddha in his curses upon woman. This religious teacher with untold millions of worshippers made Heaven itself contingent upon the eternal degradation of woman. Thus Mohammed was not content with woman's enslavement and inferiority in this world, but declared that Heaven could not be a place of happiness unless women were kept eternally in a state of shame and degradation.

I want to quote a few sentences from the Code of Mann, that book far older than the Law of Moses, and which is the Bible today that rules nearly 300,000,000 of the earth's population in India. "Though destitute of every virtue, or seeking pleasure elsewhere, or devoid of good qualities, a husband must be constantly worshipped as a god by a faithful wife." (Mann V, section 154). "Sinful woman must be a fool as falsehood itself. This is a fixed law." (Mann IX.) "He is a fool who considers his wife as his friend. Educating a woman is like putting a knife in the hands of a monkey."

All Hindus, of every sect, name and creed, are agreed upon two points: The sanctity of the cow and the depravity of woman. Every Brahman suspends reading his Vida (Bible), if a woman approaches because her ear is too impure to hear what he reads, no matter how vile he is. The law of Manchu declares: "A woman is not allowed to go out of the house without the consent of her husband; she may not laugh without a veil over her face or look out of a door or a window."

On the other hand our Bible with its Christian civilization has made of woman a person and a comrade for man while heathen civilization everywhere has made her a slave and a thing contemptible. The only reason why all our women are not missionary in spirit and in activity is because they do not know, and will not learn.

J. O. ATKINSON.

REPORT FOR THIRD QUARTER OF THE VIRGINIA VALLEY CENTRAL CONFERENCE WOMAN'S BOARD

New Hope Society	$ 2.60
New Hope C. E.	7.07
Leaksville Cradle Roll	.75
Leaksville for Orphanage	1.75
Winchester Dues	.90
Winchester Willing Workers	.76
Winchester Young People	1.12
Winchester Christian Endeavor	.52

Personal Contributions

New Hope Special	15.79
Mrs. J. E. W. Bryant	1.00
Mrs. Tom Myers	1.00
Mrs. W. J. Fleming	1.00
Mrs. B. F. Frank	1.00
Mr. Levi Rhodes	5.00
Mr. G. W. Rothgeb	7.00

Special for Santa Isabel

Mr. John Oats	1.00
Leaksville	3.25

Specials for Winchester

Mrs. T. H. Showalter	15.00
Miss Virdie Showalter	10.00
Miss Olive Showalter	10.00
Mr. and Mrs. Floyd Showalter	5.00
Leaksville	3.25
Mrs. Willis Baylor	3.00
Antioch Young People Society	25.00
Mr. P. H. Swope	.25

Total	$123.01

MISS VIRDIE SHOWALTER, Treas.

Harrisonburg, Va.

Mrs. Elsie Eason.—Please renew my subscription to "The Dear Old SUN."

"Make him a Christian, and make him a missionary."
—*Daily prayer of Dr. John Scudder for his son.*

"I cared not where or how I lived, or what hardships I went through, so that I could but gain souls to Christ."—*David Brainard.*

WORSHIP AND MEDITATION

THE MOUNTAINS OF JEHOVAH

By William C. Allen

A few years ago when in Korea I several times enjoyed fellowship with one of the best interpreters I have ever had. He was a native Korean a devout Christian and a pastor. The spiritual needs of his distraught country rested heavily upon him and often he would go up into the mountains adjacent to Seoul and pass the nights in prayer. There under the stars or in the storm he would hold communion with his Lord.

Did not this Korean when thus sacrificing his body also lift up his eyes to the eternal hills of God from whence all help comes? Is Jehovah not found by all of us when nothing intervenes between Him and ourselves—when in the silence of our inmost souls we pour out our thoughts and entreaty to, Him? How vital is the prayer! How vibrant is the answer! The hills of God are holy ground, yet all of us may daily tread them if we will, and lay our temptations, our weaknesses, our burdens at His feet. Then, after such a period of communion and we perforce return to the valley of commonplace existence, to its enjoyments, its sordidness and its carking cares, we jealously exclaim with that grand old Hebrew prophet, "He maketh my feet like hinds feet and will make me to walk on my high places!" Even in the somber lowlands of life we may live on the spiritual hills of God.

Those glorious elevations are beautiful to look at from a distance—they seem like exquisite amethyst in our quiet moments, like transparent amber in hours of questioning, like massive battlements in days of fear. But it is infinitely better to arise and go to them than to simply view them from afar. Every sinuous canyon within them leads upward, every rugged rock is of immutable strength, every towering peak points to the Son of God. Every flower is refreshed with the dew of heaven, every shrub is redolent with the fragrance of love. The rills of divine goodness pour down their rugged slopes—we satisfy our thirst for Jehovah in their refreshing pools. I ask my readers to set their feet toward those beautiful mountains where they may commune with the Holy One and find strength and rest for their weary souls.

The sacred charm of the unchangeable mountains of God is found in the fact that they are all around us. We do not always know this—our eyes are sometimes holden that we do not see God; how unprotected at times we feel ourselves to be! How the swirl of apparently uncontrollable events threatens to engulf us! How frequently we gaze on the clouds big with darkness and are filled with dread lest the rage of the tempest sweeps us away! Then we remember the everlasting hills—we again look up to them because from them cometh our help. We behold them behind the menace of the storm and its furry is stayed by their sheltering sides. Over their lofty tops is arched the bow of promise and renewed confidence in the Eternal Goodness speeds us on our way. We know that God is all about us and we understand the sweetness of the glory of the peace of the prophet who declared:

> As the mountains are round about Jerusalem
> So Jehovah is round about His people
> From this time forth and for ever more,

NEXT TO GODLINESS

Three wash basins, a number of towels and a few cakes of carbolic soap form a part of the equipment of the evangelistic parties engaged in our present campaign. These articles are used in one of the "stunts" in the Boys' Club work. After first day or two of one of our campaigns the ticket of admission for a boy to the hall where the club meetings are held is clean hands and face.

It is the carbolic soap that makes this stunt so popular. Water is not a curiosity and enamel wash basins are becoming a familiar sight in these regions. But the soap is wonderful. Out in front of the hall where hot water is provided the lads scramble over each other to get hold of the soap. They fairly revel in the lather it produces. After the towel they walk toward the hall putting their hands frequently to their faces and inhaling deep breath of air. The carbolicky fragrance delights them. Women crowd around with their babies and ask the Boy Club workers to wash them.

A little boy on being asked if he had washed replied in the affirmative and at once lifted his hands to his face. Turning to another lad standing near he said, "How fragrant!" The disappointed look in the second boy's eyes as well as the condition of his hands and face showed that he had missed something. The next day he was in line pushing his way for a chance at that wonderfully scented soap.—*Grace Darling Carson, Hinghwa, China.*

It is impossible for us to expect too much from his generosity, or to trust too implicitly to the bounties of his providence and the aids of his Spirit. It is equally easy for God to supply our greatest as our smallest wants; to carry our heartiest, as our lightest burdens.—*Thomas Guthrie.*

Thine anxious desire, thy prayerfulness, thy longing for God, are but the shadows of the divine will upon thine own will! Imagine not that thou canst get the start of God in the race of mercy.—*C. H. Spurgeon.*

A man's willingness to give is not measured by his pocket book.

When you take your vacation this summer, don't forget to attend church.

NOTES

Dr. P. H. Fleming filled pastor Eastes' pulpit in Raleigh last Sunday.

Dr. W. W. Staley was in Dayton, Ohio, last week. On his return home he preached the annual memorial sermon at New Providence last Sunday. He was a caller at this office today, (Monday).

Dr. W. D. Harward writes under date of May 29: "I received nine members into the Dendron church Sunday morning on confession. Rev. L. I. Cox has been with me this week in behalf of the Elon Standardization Fund. All the churches went over the top. Wakefield and Burton's Grove doubled their quotas. We all feel good."

President Harper is with Brother Banks in the Ramseur pastorate this week in the interest of the College.

On Friday, May 30, about 25,000 people assembled in Burlington for the greatest celebration that Alamance county ever witnessed. The occasion was unique in every way. We were glad to see many old friends in the city that day.

Rev. Henry Crampton has resigned his charge at Columbus, Georgia, and takes up work at Mt. Sterling, Ohio, at an early date.

Mr. W. S. Sutton, Cooleemee, N. C., was a caller at THE SUN office this week. Though Brother Sutton has changed his church membership on account of being out of reach of any Christian church, he still takes THE CHRISTIAN SUN.

Dr. D. A. Long is this week in Florence, South Carolina.

A very severe electrical, hail, rain and wind storm visited Burlington Sunday night about 8:15 o'clock. The wind blew at almost hurricane speed, vivid flashes of lightning and long, roaring peals of thunder were nearly continuous, while hail stones the size of cherries preceded the torrents of rain. Services were being held in the Gypsy Smith tent which was well filled with people, when suddenly it collapsed and crashed down over the congregation. Fortunately only a very few were injured and none seriously. Among those hurt the worst were Mrs. E. S. W. Dameron, Miss Ella Robertson and Mr. H. W. Trollinger. Several others were slightly injured. When the tent fell there was a wild scramble to get from under, women screamed, and men greatly excited, tried to help one another to safety.

The Allies have presented their terms of peace to Austria and it follows in about the same manner as the terms presented to Germany.

SEASIDE CHAUTAUQUA AND SCHOOL OF METHODS

Virginia Beach, July 29—August 5

One of the strong features of this year's session of the Chautauqua will be the discussion of some real church problem. Especially qualified men will each day discuss some such problem as is of vital interest to the church in these reconstruction days. For example, "The Community Church," "The Merger Service." It is especially important that every church and conference officer and pastor be present to get the benefit from these messages. The discussion during one period of some one of these problems may be of untold value to you and your church.

There will be a Christian Endeavor period daily and all Christian Endeavorers are invited to participate in this important theme. Are you interested in Christian Endeavor work? Three Christian Endeavor workers will present messages on Christian Endeavor lines. They will be practical and vital to every Christian Endeavorer.

In these days after the war there is no theme that is engaging the attention of more people than that of Christian leadership. There will be a daily message to young people on Christian leadership and it is expected that many a young life will get a vision of Christ's call to him for real Christian leadership. It is important that pastors and parents see that the young people of their churches are present at these daily inspirational messages.

It is the aim of the Chautauqua management to offer instructors who are especially fitted for the special themes which they present. It is our aim to arrange the program each year so as to meet new conditions and emphasize calls that come to the Church.

Do you hear the ocean waves calling you to a delightful dip? Do you recall the fine fellowship of the past years? Have you counted up the new Christian acquaintances formed at the ocean side? If so, you are planning now to be at the opening session.

WARREN H. DENISON, *President.*
27 C. P. A. Bldg., Dayton, Ohio.

THE CHRISTIAN CHURCH

On page 59 of *The Lutheran,* official organ of the United Lutheran Church in America, of May 15, 1919, you may find the following: "Mr. George Eddy, who has just returned from China, states that the Chinese have little sympathy or enthusiasm for our denominational differences and that Nanking is the first city in the world to unite all the church forces under the title, "The Christian Church." Good for "Nanking" but what about "Antioch" where the disciples were first called Christians and where one organization appeared to exclude no follower of Christ?

D. A. LONG.

A woman was delivery a suffrage lecture when a man in the audience thought he would be funny. "Say, madam," he called out to her, 'would you like to be a man?" "Yes," she replied. "I should. Wouldn't you?"

THE CHRISTIAN ORPHANAGE

SUPERINTENDENT'S LETTER

The income from June to November in the past has always been much less than the expense account. So it makes the work for these months discouraging because when our income is not enough to meet our expense bills at the end of the month, and we have to cut down our bank account to meet this deficit, it is like our bills at home running more than our salary check.

To help us to keep in good spirits this summer while everything is so high, I want to appeal to the Sunday school superintendents and teachers to see that the Sunday schools make the monthly offering. Let us make a big effort to get each Sunday school on the list of monthly contributors. If each superintendent will make himself a committee of one to see to this I feel sure in the near future each Sunday school will be credited on the list. You may think this a small matter and think the Orphanage can run without your help, but suppose all the Sunday schools should think the same way, what would be the consequence?

We cannot reach as many children without your help as we can with your help. We want your school to have a part in this great work. We must have you on our list. We are going to look for your contribution in the month of June. We will be greatly disappointed if you fail us.

While I was writing this letter I received a letter from a poor widow who has three little children who wants to get a place for them in our Orphanage. Are you willing to give of your money that these little helpless children may have a home? We have twenty-seven other applications on file and we must say "No." to them unless we can get more room and our income up to the point where we can support them. What are you going to do about it?

CHAS. D. JOHNSTON, Supt.

REPORT FOR JUNE 4, 1919

Amount brought forward, $6,294.51.

Children's Offerings

Manrine Wilson Isley, 50 cents; Oliver E. Young, Jr., 10 cents; Total, 60 cents.

Sunday School Monthly Offerings

(Eastern Virginia Conference)

B. E. Worrel, for Sunday school, $4 cents; Holy Neck, $4.00; Antioch, $2.00; Union (Surry), $1.00; Burton's Grove, $5.00; Mt. Carmel, $3.11.

(North Carolina Conference)

Damascus, Orange Co., $1.80; Salem Chapel, $1.15; Poplar Branch, 50 cents; Lebanon, $7.65; High Point, $2.20; Henderson, $6.50; Asheboro, $2.50.

Antioch, Valley Va. Conference, $4.00; Total, $41.95.

(Easter Offerings)

Burton's Grove church, $12.70.

Special Offerings

J. H. Jones, on support of children, $30.00; Mrs. G. R. Sutton, $1.00; Total, $31.00.

Children's Home

Mr. and Mrs. C. A. High, $10.00.

Total for the week, $96.25; Grand total, $6,390.76.

LETTERS FROM THE COUSINS

Dear Uncle Charley: We are expecting daddy home from Germany in June, and I am such a happy little boy. I am trying to walk and talk and do everything at one time. Even grandfather Newman is kept on the jump watching after me.—*Oliver E. Young, Jr.*

I know you are happy that papa will soon be with his boy. I am looking for my boy home most any day as he landed in Newport News on the 24th.—*"Uncle Charley."*

Dear Uncle Charley: I am sending fifty cents for an Easter offering; it is rather late but mother was sick at the proper time and since she just neglected it. I earned it myself. I put up mother's little chickens every night so she gave me a quarter. Because I so seldom get quiet, grandpa said he would give me fifty cents if I would sit perfectly still for five minutes. Mother said if she were in my place she would give half of it to the orphans because she thought the gifts that gave us the most pleasure were those that cost us a great deal; and she knew that was hard earned money. I had a birthday party on the fifteenth of February. My cake had five pink candles on it. I hope you will get enough for the new building.—*Manrine Wilson Isley.*

I guess the fifty cents grandpa gave you was hard earned money. I am glad your mother is well and you have her to love you and to care for you. I have a little girl five years old, but her mamma has gone to live with the angels.—*"Uncle Charley."*

BORN FEBRUARY 30!

"For such a beastly month as February, 28 days are as a rule sufficient," as the late Sir W. S. Gilbert once remarked. But nevertheless it is actually possible for there to be a February 30th.

Every one knows that in voyaging round the world a day has to be added or "heaved overboard," according to the direction travelled. The adjustment is invariably made when crossing the 180th meridian, almost midway between Japan and California, so a vessel on that spot on February 29 in leap year must according have a February 30. Indeed February 30 does, in fact, appear on the ship menu.

But it is hard lines on any baby born abroad that day, for it can never have another birthday, even if it lives to be a centenarian.—*London Chronicle.*

We put every part of our work on a systematic basis and let the Lord have the fragments. It is unfair. Put God on the pay roll, too.

Men who are leading great financial movements in all denominations tell us that their work is easier among tithers.

Germany virtually refuses to sign the peace treaty. She claims that it is too severe.

THE NEWSBOY'S MOTHER

He was a ragged little newsboy who lived with his mother. They were all in all to each other. Tenderly he cared for her, bringing to her small earnings and doing his best to help her in the household tasks.

One day the tired mother, weary of her hard struggle, closed her eyes to the scenes of earth. The lad was inconsolable. How could he live without her? After a few days of giving way to the bitterness of his grief, he began to wonder what he could do to show his love for her.

The picture of the unmarked grave came before his eyes. Other graves were marked by stones; why not hers? Of course, stones cost a great deal, and his earnings were small.

But love found a way. At a cutter's yard he found that even the cheaper stones were far too expensive for him. He was turning sorrowfully away when he saw a broken shaft of marble, part of the debris from an accident in the yard. Eagerly he asked the price of the irregular piece. The low price named by the proprietor came within his means. But he knew he would be unable to pay for cutting the inscription. The brave little chap made up his mind to do his best to prepare the marble himself.

The next day he carried the stone away on a little four-wheeled cart, and managed to have it put in position. One who was curious to know the last of the stone made a visit to the cemetery one afternoon. On his return he thus described in an article what he saw and learned:

"There was our monument at the head of one of the newer graves. I knew it at once. Just as it was when it left our yard. I was going to say, until I got a little nearer to it and saw what the little chap had done. I tell you, when I saw it there was something blurred my eyes so's I couldn't read it at first. The little man had tried to keep the lines straight, and evidently thought the capitals would make it look better and bigger, for nearly every letter was a capital. I copied it and here it is. But you want to see it on the stone to appreciate it:

    "'MY MOTHER
    SHEE DIED LAST WEEK.
    SHEE WAS ALL I HAD.
    SHEE SED SHEAD BE
      WAITING FUR——'.

And here the lettering stopped. After a while I went back to the man in charge and asked him what further he knew of the little fellow who bought the stone.

"'Not much,' he said, 'not much. Didn't you notice a fresh little grave near the one with the stone? Well, that's where he is. He came here every afternoon for some time, working away at that stone, and one day I missed him, and then for several days. Then

the man came out from the church that buried the mother, and ordered the grave dug by her side. I asked if it was for the little chap. He said it was. The boy had sold all his papers one day, and was hurrying along the street out this way. There was a runaway team just above the crossing, and—well, he was run over, and lived but a day or two. He had in his hand when he was picked up, an old file sharpened down to a point that he did all the lettering with. They said he seemed to be thinking only of that until he died, for he kept saying: "I didn't get it done; but she'll know I meant to finish it, won't she? I'll tell her so, for she'll be waiting for me.' And he died with those words on his lips.'"

When the men in the cutter's yard heard the story the next day, they clubbed together, got a good stone, inscribed upon it the name of the newsboy, and underneath it the words: "He loved his mother."—*Baptist Commonwealth.*

MOTHER

The noblest thoughts my soul can claim,
   The holiest words my tongue can frame,
Unworthy are to praise the name
   More sacred than all other,
An infant, when her love first came—
   A man, I find it just the same;
Reverently I breathe her name,
   The blessed name of mother.

        —*George Griffith Petter.*

THE SEASIDE CHAUTAUQUA

The sixth annual session of the Sea Side Chautauqua and School of Methods of the Christian Church will be held at Virginia Beach, beginning Tuesday evening, July 29, closing the following Tuesday. A strong program is being prepared. Several new speakers will be on the program. It is now time for all those who have ever been at the Chautauqua to urge upon those of their acquaintances the importance and the real value of this valuable institution of the Christian Church. We know of no place where our workers may get so much benefit within a week as at Virginia Beach. We offer a strong program, a most delightful fellowship, a practical presentation of church problems and bring to the Chautauqua those who have been eminently successful in their chosen lines. In the five years past many hundreds of our workers have gone back to their churches with vision, consecration and methods that have helped to mold the life of the home church and make it more able to do the work of the Lord. The recreation, the bathing, the fellowship, the opportunity for rest, are worth all it costs to go there if there were no classes, lectures and sermons at all. Plan now to come and have a good time. Let every pastor come himself and bring other workers from his church. Write the secretary, S. M. Smith, Chamber of Commerce Building, Norfolk, Va., for any information concerning rates, rooms, routes and general information and the undersigned concerning the program.

        WARREN H. DENISON, *Pres.*

Sunday School and Christian Endeavor

SUNDAY SCHOOL LESSON FOR JUNE 15, 1919

Prayer. Matt. 6:5-15; Luke 18:1-14.

Golden Text: In nothing be anxious; but in everything by prayer and supplication with thanksgiving let your requests be made known unto God. Phil. 4:6.

Thought For Teachers

How are you teaching prayer? Do you have prayer in your class? Do you repeat the Lord's Prayer in your school, and consider that is all that is necessary? Are you willing that the next generation in our church and Sunday school should be as tongue-tied as we are of the present generation have been? Are you praying for your pupils, for your school, for your church? One of the most successful Sunday schools I know asks all the teachers to come together for fifteen minutes before the opening of the Sunday school. This time is their "upper room" period when they are all with one accord in one place.

"All of God's large promises regarding prayer, however, are defined and conditioned: we must believe, we must abide in Him, we must ask in His name, His spirit. It is morally impossible to have a real confidence that the things we are asking for shall certainly be received, unless our petitions are grounded on some real knowledge of the mind and method of God; otherwise asking would be crying for the moon. But observing these conditions, we have a right to perfect confidence. Christ's signature is at every promise, his name perfumes each one." (Peloubet's Notes.)

MRS. FRED BULLOCK.

CHRISTIAN ENDEAVOR TOPIC FOR JUNE 15, 1919

What We Owe and How to Pay It. II Cor. 8:1-15, (Tenth Legion Application).

Can we give anything until we have paid our debts? If Jesus said, speaking of tithing: "This ought ye to have done," have we paid our debts until we have paid our tithes? What about our offering? When we

"make an offering unto the Lord," how shall we make it? This is, as we understand it, something over and above the tithe, perhaps a thank-offering for restoration to health, or for some good news, for a specially good crop or a good business year. Many States had a "war chest" and persons regularly pledged a certain amount to the fund. Then when a special call was made for any particular purpose, they agreed upon amount was taken from the war chest, instead of making a desperate last minutes canvass for it. Would this plan work in the church? Is this what Paul meant by "laying by you each week—that there be no gathering when I come" to make a special plea for the Jerusalem needy?

MRS. FRED BULLOCK.

FOR CHRISTIAN ENDEAVORERS IN THE NORTH CAROLINA CHRISTIAN CONFERENCE

No doubt you read my note of April 9, relative to the Christian Endeavor being left out of the Convention notice, and the two replies that have been made. Hope you have, and that you will see the situation as it is. The purpose of my note was not to critizice the Committee but to get an explanation, and a reason before the public. My note brought the desired results, and I am glad. Thank you Brother Stephenson, for setting forth the reason for the omission of the Christian Endeavor from the Convention notice.

Now Christian Endeavor workers, note that Brother Stephenson says, "With all our efforts in previous Conventions,—there have not been more than three Societies represented at any Convention within the past five years." Well, that does look discouraging to the Committee and to the work, but you need not give up, for Brother Stephenson is now President of a Convention three times as large, as the one of last year and we hope to have at least nine represented this time. The writer gladly accepts any challenge the Committee throws, on condition, however, that he be furnished a list of all Societies, and their officers in the State work

before June 15. I have written twenty letters since I came to the State last November, trying to get this information, and not a single reply has been received.

Let every Society that reads this note have at least one delegate at the State Convention, June 6-8, in Burlington. Then, raise the same amount that your Sunday school does per member, and have at least one delegate at the coming Convention at Shallow Well next July. Let each Society pay the expense of its delegate, and see to it that the delegate stays through the Convention. Also, have a representative at the Seaside Chautauqua at Virginia Beach, July 29 to August 3. You could not spend your vacation at a better place.

J. VINCENT KNIGHT,
Chm. Christian Endeavor Com. Greensboro, N. C.

P. S. When you read this note, stop right there and send the name of your Society, the name and address of your president and corresponding secretary to the Chairman of this Committee.

J. V. K.

MISSION OFFERING IN THE SUNDAY-SCHOOL

I visited a Sunday school recently which has a Duplex envelope for each class. Some years ago, when I made my first visit, they told me they had hard work to collect enough to keep up their expenses, that people did not give. I wondered how their treasury was standing the strain of a double offering. I found they had about thirty dollars in their treasury, that they were giving once a month to the Orphanage, and on the Sunday of my visit, the benevolence side of the envelope contained more than the Sunday-school side. "Bring ye all the tithes—and prove me now—if I will not open the windows of Heaven and pour out such a blessing that there will not be room to contain it." Is it possible it means Sunday schools, as well as folks? Why not?

MRS. FRED BULLOCK,
Field Secretary, Eastern Virginia Sunday School Convention,

MARRIAGES

YOUNG-WEATHERS

The writer united in holy estate of matrimony Miss Glads Weathers of Youngsville and Mr. Kenneth Young of Wake Forest on April 21, 1919. The ceremony was performed at the home of Mr. June Johnson, Franklinton, in the presence of a few friends of the contracting parties. That they enjoy a long and prosperous life is our wish.

G. J. GREEN.

OBITUARIES

DUDLEY

Miss Martha Dudley died at the home of her brother, Mr. Edward L. Powell, Savage, Gates County, N. C., May 6, 1919, aged seventy-one years. She was a member of the M. E. church, Norfolk, Va. She was a good Christian woman and will be greatly missed by all who knew her. She was an aunt of Mrs. W. C. Beamon, Savage, N. C. She leaves four brothers: E. L. Powell, Richard Powell, George Powell and Isaac Powell, and many relatives and friends. Funeral services were conducted at her home by the writer and her remains were laid to rest in the family cemetery. May the Lord comfort the bereaved ones.

H. H. BUTLER.

GRAVES

Little Curtis Elkanah Graves was born March 29, 1917, and died May 13, 1919, aged two years, one month and fifteen days. He was the son of Mr. and Mrs. Floyd Graves of Seagrove, N. C., Route 1. His grave is the first at New Center Christian church where his mother holds her membership.

The floral offering which was abundant shows how quickly he had won the love of many hearts; but Jesus took him and by this taking we are reminded of His saying: "Suffer little children to come unto me and forbid them not for of such is the kingdom of heaven."

May the Master comfort the hearts of the parents and loved ones.

T. J. GREEN.

TUCKER

Saturday, May 17, Benjamine Tucker, aged 26 years, was laid to rest in the family burying ground near his home about eight miles east of Louisburg, N. C. He was a member of Mt. Gilead Christian church. He leaves one brother and one sister, the remainder of the family having preceded him. May the Holy Spirit comfort the bereft.

G. J. GREEN.

RESOLUTIONS OF SYMPATHY—
NORFLEET

Because we mourn an empty chair when we meet, and because we have benefited in the past by her presence, we are participants in the sorrow that has come to the home of Mrs. A. T. Norfleet because she has passed to her Father's House, therefore, be it Resolved:

That we thank our Heavenly Father for her life with us; that we shall bear in remembrance the example she has left us of steadfast fulfillment of duty, and patience in bearing whatever befell her, and that we join her family in thanksgiving for her life here with us;

That we extend to them our sincerest sympathy in their sorrow and loneliness, yet we know and believe that her love is theirs now in even fuller measure than when bounded by the limitations of earth.

Resolved further, that a copy of these resolutions be spread upon the minutes of the Philathea Class and Woman's Missionary Society of the Suffolk Christian Church, a copy sent to The Christian Sun, and another copy sent to the bereaved family that they may know we share their grief, while reminding them, and our selves, that we sorrow not as those who have no hope, but look forward with confident joy to the glorious day of His coming when we shall be ever with the Lord.

MRS. Mm. R. MITCHELL,
MRS. FRED. BULLOCK,
MRS. B. D. CROCKER,
    for the Philathea Class.
MRS. W. C. CROCKER,
MRS. A. D. BRINKLEY,
MRS. I. W. JOHNSON,
for the Woman's Missionary Society.
Suffolk, Va.

If you enjoy THE SUN, tell others —if you do not, tell us—and also tell how to make it better.

REPORT OF THE CONDITION OF

The Elon Banking and Trust Company, at Elon College, in the State of North Carolina, at the close of business, May 12, 1919:

RESOURCES

Loans and Discounts	$21,955.31
Overdrafts, secured, $467.72;	
unsecured, $104.10	571.82
United States Bonds and Liberty Bonds	4,850.00
Banking Houses, $1,480.38;	
Furniture and Fixtures,	
$1,776.26	3,256.64
Demand Loans	1,835.00
Due from National Banks	9,856.14
Due from State Banks and Bankers	973.77
Cash Items held over 24 hours	4,674.56
Gold Coin	477.50
Silver Coin, including all minor coin currency	1,250.70
National Bank Notes and other U. S. Notes	1,393.00
Thrift Stamps	37.25
War Savings Stamps	655.63
Total	$51,787.34

LIABILITIES

Capital Stock paid in	$ 5,000.00
Surplus Fund	1,000.00
Undivided Profits, less current expenses and taxes paid	146.87
Deposits subject to check	31,097.18
Time Certificates of Deposit	12,489.09
Cashier's Checks outstanding	127.57
Received on Liberty Bonds	624.00
Interest Received	103.86
Accrued Interest due depositors	225.00
Collection Items	973.77
Total	$51,787.34

State of North Carolina—County of Alamance, May 23, 1919.

I, Marion C. Jackson, Cashier of the above named Bank, do solemnly swear that the above statement is true to the best of my knowledge and belief.

MARION C. JACKSON, Cashier.

Subscribed and sworn to before me, this 23 day of May, 1919.

J. J. LAMBETH, J. P.

Correct—Attest:

J. J. LAMBETH,
S. W. CADDELL,
W. P. LAWRENCE,
    Directors.

WHY I GAVE TO
Elon's Standardization Fund

(By one of the givers)

I thought of the little wooden crosses that decorated the graves in France. The sight of a little home came to me, and in the door-way, while the evening shadows fell, a silent figure stood. Around the door played a little boy and a little girl. A gold star hung on the wall, it appeared to me. . That silent figure was a mother—the mother of the children—and her silence was broken only by her sobs as she thought of her husband who slept in sunny France. Out in the unknown and untried future that mother tried to see the pathway of her children. She could not. She wondered if they would be educated, if she could not do it, and if not, what reflection would they, untried in Christian's way, bring upon the dead hero of their home.

The curtain of night grew darker and the smiles of heaven were shut out by the untouchable thing we call night. I saw it all, and the home was here in my midst. Unable to comfort, to soothe, to speak a word of cheer, unable to carry out my heart's desire, I turned, with tear-dimmed eyes, and lifted my voice and heart to heaven.

There was a joy, I thought, that could in a very large measure, compensate for the gloom of that home—and that was the proper education and training of that sweet little girl and sunny-faced boy. Then I thought of how my own body would perhaps be moulding in mother earth before they were ready for college. Ah! no worry there, I thought, for the money called *mine* is *His*, and I shall dedicate a part of it to make the future safe for that mother's companions that her heart may rejoice, and a world blessed. I signed it—that pledge, five of them, and now I am happy, thrice happy.

How Will the Record of Your Church Look When the Published Account of the Campaign is Issued?

Your Church is Receiving the Benefit of Elon College. How Much Are You Grateful for This? Your pledge Will Register the Answer.

We Have Made the World Safe For Democracy

Are We Willing to Make It Safe For the Child?

Your Answer May Determine the Destiny of Some One

The
CHRISTIAN SUN

"IN ESSENTIALS UNITY, IN NON-ESSENTIALS LIBERTY, IN ALL THINGS CHARITY"

Personality

PERSONALITY can be defined and it cannot be defined. Philosophers can satisfy *themselves* as to what personality is, and their definitions are plausible. But personality is so close to us, is so much of us, that we do not know what it is because we do not know ourselves. Men know us better than we do— hence they know more about our personality. With our personality we change minds, hearts and destinies. Then it must be an influence that is sacred. God gives us our personality and when we use it for evil we rob God of the fruit of His gift. Personality used for the Kingdom's growth is rendering unto God that which is His.

Volume LXXI   WEDNESDAY, JUNE 11, 1919   Number 24

BURLINGTON   ·   ·   ·   NORTH CAROLINA

THE CHRISTIAN SUN

Founded 1844 by Rev. Daniel W. Kerr

C. B. RIDDLE   -   -   -   Editor

Entered at the Burlington, N. C. Post Office as second class matter.

Subscription Rates

One year .... $ 2.00
Six months 1.00

In Advance

Give both your old and new postoffice when asking that your address be changed.

The change of your label is your receipt for money. Written receipts sent upon request.

Marriage and obituary notices not exceeding 150 words printed free if received within 60 days from date of event, all over this at the rate of one-half cent a word.

Original poetry not accepted for publication.

Principles of the Christian Church

(1) The Lord Jesus Christ is the only Head of the Church.
(2) Christian is a sufficient name of the Church.
(3) The Holy Bible is a sufficient rule of faith and practice.
(4) Christian character is a sufficient test of fellowship, and of church membership.
(5) The right of private judgment and the liberty of conscience is a right and a privilege that should be accorded to, and exercised by all.

EDITORIAL

THE PASTOR'S VACATION

The summer months are here and those of us who are accustomed to, or in a position to, take a vacation are thinking of that time when we can leave our worries at home and go to some place for rest (unfortunately we are forced to speak from observation and not experience).

Your pastor needs a vacation. You may not believe that, but you should not say so until you had some opportunity of experiencing the duties and obligations of a pastor. The pastor needs a vacation that he may get away from the daily grind of things that absorb his energy, and thought and make his work one continuous grind. The pastor needs a vacation that he may have time to meditate and think on obligations that are new and conditions that are perplexing. Vacations do not come without their price; and since the average preacher is not paid a decent salary, there is something else to consider as well as granting him a vacation; he needs the expenses of a trip and we certainly hope that no church voting its pastor a vacation will overlook this very important item. Your pastor will come back rested in body and mind and equipped and prepared to do a larger and greater work than before. Give your pastor a fair deal and give him a vacation. Do something for him that you have not been doing and you will love him better than you have ever loved him and

appreciate his messages more than you have ever appreciated them.

And now a word as to the pastor's duty when he takes his vacation: the pastor owes it to his church when he takes his vacation to take a genuine rest and not go elsewhere and engage in a revival meeting or some other work, for this kills the opportunity of a vacation and defeats the purpose.

LYNCHING

The matter of lynching continues to grow and the protests against it also increase. Within the last two weeks, not less than three very disgraceful lynchings have taken place in the United States. If memory serves us right, about 100 persons were lynched in the United States last year despite what the law could do. This unfair method of taking life seems to continue in its death-dealing sweep. Such crimes are a disgrace upon the state in which they are committed, and for that matter, upon the civilized world.

Very drastic steps have been taken in a number of states to prohibit lynching, and we are of the opinion that steps still more drastic will have to be taken before this evil is abolished. The lynch law is dangerous to society, breeds unlimited trouble, and creates an opportunity of revenge that a century cannot wipe out.

There are many things that we could suggest in order that public sentiment be crystalized against lynching, but none possibly would be better than this: To see that the offenders of the law are brought to a speedy justice. The fear of the mob is that justice will not be done. It is the duty of all good citizens to lend their influence in every possible way to see if this curse cannot be removed from our land.

THE IGNORANT WHO ARE TO BE PITIED

An ignorant man is to be pitied. We do not mean by this that a man without an education is to be pitied, because the lack of education does not always make a man ignorant. There are persons who are educated that live in gross ignorance because of their surroundings and the way in which they have been taught to think. The man who is pitiful is he who has lived to himself and depended upon the thinking of other people until his horizon of life is but an inch before his eyes. He cannot see that the world is depending upon him, neither can he see that he is depending upon the world. He has ignored. "that no man liveth to himself and no man dieth to himself." He has never explored the beauties of life because he has not launched out far enough to break the shackles from his own soul. We pity the man who is so limited in vision, so shallow in thinking that he feels that the world is trying to rob him of his possessions when it is only seeking his co-operation and offering him the finest opportunity to develop into a Christian citizen in everyway.

FOR BETTER COMMUNITY LIFE

The American nation was startled first and then dismayed and disheartened when the selective draft showed that our young men were fast becoming weaklings. The great per cent of young men who were found to be either physically or mentally unfit for military duty was like a fire alarm at night. The utter change that the customs of the country had undergone in the last twenty-five years, the lack of sports, the absence of physical exercise, the ravages of disease, the cigarette, soda fountain, picture show, hot house lives, and the absence of everything calculated to produce manly vigor, have so devitalized the young manhood of the country that serious alarm has been raised. Not only has this been felt upon the condition of the population, but like a canker it has eaten into the moral and mental stamina of the young. Now there is a great cry, led by the national government itself, for better health, better sports, better recreation, better physical habits, better eating and drinking habits, more clean living, more out-of-door exercise, and in short, more of everything that is likely to produce normal and happy and strong and efficient human beings. This work will begin with the infants in arms, nay with the mothers before the infants are born, and go all the way up through the schools, through young manhood and womanhood, middle age and old age, before we shall have succeeded in producing the vigorous and healthy manhood and womanhood that we once had. The coming era is to be the era of sane and happy living. The patent medicine habit and the dope habit and the ease habit must go the way of the liquor habit.

We hail with joy any proposition that tends to develop the spirit of out-door sports. Games should be encouraged in every community. We need hospitals, but we also need playgrounds and sane living and clean exercise to keep the population from falling prey to all the modern diseases that have developed as a result of wrong living. Every community should have ball grounds, tennis grounds, volley ball grounds, and all other kinds of grounds that will encourage the population to use them. What indeed shall it profit a man if he gain the whole world and lose his own soul? And what indeed shall it profit us if we have the means of living comfortable and happy lives if we let the inducement to languor and disease and physical laziness sap the vitality of life generally and cut down the three score and ten years of a man's life to two score, which is becoming almost the dead line for the business and professional man, and the period of decay, ugliness, and weakness of the women? Cosmetics cannot take the place of physical and joyous exercise in women any more than soft drinks and tea parties can make children grow up strong and manly and beautiful. The human body is a thing of marvelous beauty and efficiency when given a chance to be. Modern habits might well be defined as a conspiracy to enrich the medicine fakirs, the doctors and the sanitariums, and to sap and devitalize the physical, moral, and mental efficiency of mankind.

"THE LORD GAVE AND THE LORD TAKETH AWAY"

In practically every funeral service that one attends, if not every service, you will hear this quotation: "The Lord gave and the Lord taketh away; blessed be the name of the Lord. Now, we believe that the Lord does

give and we believe the Lord does take away, but He does not take away every time we think He does.

The thing in our mind now is this: So often people neglect their children through ignorance and carelessness, and the result is that they die. The question with us is: Does the Lord take away in every such case? For example: A child is given improper food, is not given sufficient baths and is compelled to sleep in a place without sufficient air, and takes some disease; and then possibly not given proper medical attention when it becomes sick. The child grows worse and dies. Now, the Lord gave, but did the Lord take away? Was it the Lord Who took away or was it careless hands? Can we bless the name of the Lord every time a loved one dies?

A man may engage in some habit, such as drinking, or smoking, and bring a disease upon his body that will take his life. Does the Lord take away in such a case, and can we bless His name?

We believe that thousands of persons are going to their graves every year through sin and ignorance and yet our ministers stand up and say at the funeral, "The Lord gave and the Lord taketh away; blessed be the name of the Lord." Surely our conscience will never condemn us as long as we are taught to believe that it is the hand of the Lord and the Lord is blessing.

Since writing the above paragraphs, we find the following in the North Carolina Health Bulletin: "The time is not far distant when local health authorities will be held responsible for an epidemic of typhoid fever. The responsibility for individual cases is going to be fixed also by the courts of the states, as is clearly indicated from a decision handed down by the Supreme Court of Wisconsin in the case of Vennen V. Dells Lumber Company, 154 N. W. Rep. 640 (October 26, 1915). The Supreme Court of Wisconsin decided that the death of an employee caused by typhoid fever, which was contracted by drinking impure water furnished by the employer, was the result of an accident under the terms of the Workmen's Compensation Law, and the person responsible for the impure water was liable for damage resulting there from."

When the Supreme Court decided on such a case as above quoted, it is an indication that individuals are thinking seriously that the responsibility of many lives lie with them and not with the Lord. When we fail to provide pure drinking water or wholesome food for our families, or let some one go to bad through drinking or some other abusive habit, we place a responsibility upon ourselves; and though the Lord gave, we are the ones who take away, and we ought to, in many cases say: "The Lord gave but we took away; cursed be our name."

Minds may run in the same channel, and so even after quoting the above, we have, by accident, in reading a health bulletin, found the following which we quote, and which seems to be in accord with what we have written:

Two Towns

Mr. Billy Jolly of Bumtown, dropped an orange peel on the sidewalk. His fellow-citizen, Mr. Bob Ernest, stepped on it, broke his leg, and was laid up for three months with no accident insurance policy to help out. Neither Billy nor Bob knew that it was Billy's fault; in fact, Billy did not remember he had dropped an orange peel. He never thought about such things. He was a good-hearted fellow at bottom, fond of Bob, and both put the whole blame on the orange peel. If Billy had known the truth, it would have been a terrible lesson for him, and Bob would have been obliged in his heart of hearts to blame Billy for doing such a fool trick. Of course, no one blames those who did not kick the orange peel off the sidewalk before it got in its work.

Mrs. Ownway, also of Bumtown, let little Jack play on the sidewalk when his sister, Ethel, had the diphtheria; little Jenny Lovejoy, from the other side of town, stopped to speak to Jack, and now little Jenny is dead. Mrs. Ownway said she really hadn't the heart to keep Jack so closely confined when he was perfectly well, and that this foolish quarantine was so perfectly unnecessary. Of course, Mrs. Ownway really killed little Jenny; but she didn't know it, and Mrs. Lovejoy didn't know it. Mrs. Ownway was terribly distressed, wrote Mrs. Lovejoy a sweet letter of condolence, and sent a bunch of lilies of the valley for the little coffin. The two mothers agreed that these germ diseases were awful and that the blame was on the germ. Mrs. Lovejoy did not blame anybody and Mrs. Ownway felt no personal responsibility.

Bumtown was inhabited by some of the best people in the State, kindly, accommodating and easy-going. They had excellent sanitary regulations all printed out in plain English on paper, and most of them could read. They would not have hurt a fly, and, in fact, they seldom did. It was the business of the town government and the health officers, armed with these nice laws, to bring health to Bumtown. The citizens felt no responsibility individually or collectively. But the city government was composed of good, kindly, fairly intelligent, average citizens, who were elected to give a nice, quiet, neighborly government to Bumtown, and who honestly tried to do so. "Laws were not to be taken too seriously; to enforce these sanitary laws strictly might offend some of our best citizens. We are getting on very well." So said they all.

No citizen, meanwhile, complained of the lack of law enforcement, or saw in it a cause of the high death rate. If any one was shot, the shooter was promptly punished. The shootee knew he was hurt and who hurt him, and immediately got busy. The government and the citizens were opposed to open crimes of violence that endanger the lives of innocent people. But, when it came to sanitary matters, nobody made any fuss. It would not be nice or popular. As to the death rate, they were sure there was some mistake about it. They said they liked a quiet life. But, as they continued to die, it rather looked as though many of them preferred death and an early one. Still, if one looked carefully, he would have observed that the very best citizens spit on the sidewalks, that food was sold under most unsanitary conditions (even candy was handled with dirty hands and soda fountains were vile), that the sections

in which the servants lived who served the food were refused proper water and sewerage facilities, that flies were bred in stables permitted to be run under conditions contrary to law, that for the servants a vile surface privy on the lot was considered good enough, and above and beyond all, that press and pulpit were silent on the moral responsibility of each man for the health of his neighbor.

The story of Goodtown is less eventful, because nothing happened. Mr. Bob Jolly went there on a visit, to be sure, and dropped an orange peel on the sidewalk, but Mr. Aristides Faithful came along and kicked it off. Nobody was hurt. Nobody felt grateful for not being hurt. Mr. Faithful did not know whether he had saved any one or not, and, if he thought he had, there was the whole town to chose from.

Mrs. Ownway, who had not developed diphtheria but who proved to be a carrier, also visited Goodtown as soon as little Ethel was discharged. Strange to say, a child in the house she visited soon had diphtheria. But they at once administered the proper treatment, gave every one in the house the antitoxin, and observed the strictest quarantine in spite of the inconvenience. Therefore, no one else got it and the invalid was soon well.

So it was with sporadic cases of several other communicable diseases. They seldom got beyond the first case. Everybody cheerfully obeyed the laws and backed up the doctors and health officers. Goodtown people did not have typhoid. They knew that, in plain language, it came from swallowing the excrement of other people, and they did not think it was nice. Besides, it was so unnecessary. They actually insisted on the strictest enforcement of the sanitary regulations (which Bumtown had adopted word for word) and, besides, they all took the anti-typhoid vaccination every few years. They insisted on this for all who handled food, raw or cooked food, in public or in private houses. Any one who had typhoid in Goodtown brought it with him; in fact, this is what worried Goodtown. Being a delightful, healthy town, it attracted many visitors from the best people in many of the finest cities of the State, and soon after arriving, some of them had typhoid. They blamed Goodtown. Goodtown loathed them and doubted their intelligence, their Christianity, and their patriotism. They nursed them carefully and pulled most of them through. Some of them died, and for these they wrote nice obituaries and tried to respect their memories.

The city government of Goodtown had no easy time. They had to fight some of the oldest citizens, but they well knew that that was what they were elected for, and that failure to enforce the law strictly on every one would surely prevent their re-election. The press fearlessly told the whole truth about health conditions and violations of law. The pulpit joined with the press in preaching that any one was a fool who did not look out for the health of others for his own sake, and no Christian if he did not do so for the sake of others. Hence, every one felt a conscientious responsibility for the life and health of every one else, everybody loved everybody, and the life insurance companies just loved the town.

PASTOR AND PEOPLE

CHURCH DEDICATIONS

It is a most wholesome sign to see so many of our churches clearing themselves of indebtedness now, and dedicating the houses cleared of all encumbrances, to the service of the Lord. A dollar now is worth in purchasing value about what fifty cents was when most of these church debts were incurred, and so it is in keeping with the best sort of economy to clear up the debts while money is cheap and abundant. If you cannot get money for church and charity now it is likely you never will, or certainly not with as little effort and sacrifice as now.

Franklin

Franklin, Va. church, Rev. C. H. Rowland, D. D., pastor was dedicated on the fourth Sunday in April. The day was ideal, the audience large, the fellowship was sweet, and the free-will offering wonderful. Our membership at Franklin has wrought so well and worthily that it has won the respect, confidence and admiration of all who are acquainted with the situation, and so-it is easy to get assistance there. Just before the sermon on the day of dedication the pastor simply announced that a free-will offering would be taken, and whatever was given would be properly used and appreciated. The ushers began passing the plates, but they were quickly filled, refilled and filled again, till more than $4,700.00 had been placed on the plates. The church had been cleared of indebtedness by agreement, and assuming of all obligations by individuals, the week before.

It was a happy day, and the audience that taxed the capacity of the building seemed to enter heartily into the joy and solemnity of the occasion. The decorations were appropriate and comely, and the music for the occasion was inspiring and beautiful. Dr. Rowland and his faithful wife are much beloved by the congregation and have the hearty support of a most joyal and devoted membership. They have built a splendid house of worship with a large basement for dining room and kitchen service, ample room for Sunday school classes, pastor's study and social gathering, and a main auditorium easy to speak in, happily ventilated and substantially furnished. An elegant pipe organ and a well trained choir furnish soul stirring music. It is a beautiful temple of worship worthy of the great preacher and liberal souls who, as co-workers together with God, have conducted it.

High Point

Last Sunday, June 1, the writer was again in a dedicatory service. The High Point Christians had a few days before paid off the last dollar of indebtedness on their church. Rev. L. L. Wyrick, Elon College, N. C., is the pastor. The church was organized by Rev. J. F. Morgan, now of Berkley Ward, Norfolk, Va., with fourteen charter members. There are now seventy-one members. Other pastors have been Rev. H. Shelton Smith, now an Army Chaplain in France and Rev. H.

S. Hardcastle, who graduated from Elon College recently. There is a flourishing Sunday school under the aggressive leadership of Brother R. C. Boyd, and the school gives the offering of one Sunday each month to missions, and that of another Sunday each month to the Orphanage. The church and school are alive to all the interests of the Kingdom, loyal to all the calls of Convention and Conference. There are faithful and active members in this church who have sacrificed nobly to build a house of worship and they are now happy in having their building paid for and their house consecrated and dedicated to the worship of God. Brother Wyrick is a faithful pastor, deeply interested in his work, and is laboring earnestly to build up the congregation to which he has been called. They are soon to repaint their building and Brother W. E. Lowe, of Elon College, N. C., who kindly used his car Sunday to carry the writer to the dedication, gave the first dollar, unsolicited, with which to begin the work of painting. It is a faithful band of workers and when they put on a new coat of paint, as they soon will do, they will have a neat, comfortable and attractive house of worship.

Rosemont

On the fourth Sunday of this month Rev. G. O. Lankford and his good people of Rosemont are to dedicate their beautiful house of worship, the debt having already been paid and the preparations are now being made for the great and glad day soon to come. The writer anticipates a day of joy and sweet fellowship with the faithful and beloved at Rosemont, for in all our Communion it is doubtful if we have a people more imbued with the spirit of devotion and of self-sacrifice than the saints at Rosemont. But of this dedication after the event.

Besides dedications several points are on the eve of purchasing lots and erecting buildings; and this is well. For now is the time to secure funds with which to do the Lord's work.

J. O. ATKINSON.

SUFFOLK LETTER

By invitation of "The Memorial Association," I delivered the memorial sermon at New Providence church, Graham, N. C., on the first Sunday in June. The church was planted there before the county was created, before the railroad was built, and before the town was even dreamed of. It was, in its earliest years, what is called, in modern phrase, a "community church." School was taught there by one who was, afterward, Governor Worth. It was the meeting place for people interested in the community welfare. The community was composed of good people, was prosperous, intelligent, and religious.

Later came the new county of Alamance, the North Carolina railroad, the towns of Graham, Haw River, Burlington, cotton mills, electric cars, and all the modern movements. These new communities built school houses, churches, homes, making new centers of business, social, and religious life; but during those early years the people buried their dead near the old church. This has kept alive an interest in the place. and the Association keeps the cemetery, provides for a great service on the first Sunday in June of each year, and thus revives memories of loved ones and cultivates a community social and religious spirit, and decorates the graves with summer flowers. The music is rendered by the joint choirs of Graham churches, dinner is provided without cost to the large audience, and the day is enjoyed by old and young. In the afternoon of this occasion Captain James A. Turrentine made an interesting talk reminiscent in character in which he recited incidents of unusual interest.

Mr. E. S. Parker, Jr., President, presided over the services. Vice-President, McBride Holt, made a brief talk. Pastor F. C. Lester read the scripture lesson, and Rev. W. S. Long, D. D., who was pastor and built the present edifice in the sixties, offered prayer.

It was a revival of memories, a quickening of affection, a brightening of hope, and a reminder of mortality and immortality. Christianity rests upon death and the empty tomb. "Except a grain of wheat fall into the ground and die, it abideth alone." The harvest that feeds the world depends upon the empty tomb where the seed died. Christianity could not survive without the empty tomb. The fowls of the barnyard and the birds in the forests can all be traced back to the empty shell. Our hope of reunion is derived from the empty tomb. Jesus robbed death of its sting and the grave of its victory. The grave is the hope of the world. Every church should hold a memorial service once a year. It is so sweet to see age placing flowers on the grave of childhood, and the young placing flowers on the graves of ancestors. The flowers represent fading life and the beauty of life as well. Flowers speak of feelings and loves that cannot be expressed in words; and that is the reason Jesus gave His Son for us, because He could not tell us His love in the Bible of words; and hence He calls His Son His "Word," "The Word was made flesh, and dwelt among us."

                   W. W. STALEY.

EARTH'S DEAREST SPOT—THE GRAVE

"This day shall be unto you for a memorial."—Ex. 12:14.

"Thy prayers and thine alms are come up as a memorial before God."—Acts 10:4.

Memorials are memory helps. They may be tablets, monuments, feasts, or services; but they all revive memories and remind us of other days, other persons, and other events. A Confederate monument reminds us of the Civil War. The Washington monument reminds us of George Washington and the infant Republic, now so great. The Passover reminded the Hebrews of deliverance from Egypt; and the Lord's Supper reminds us of the death and sufferings of Jesus Christ. Memorial services remind us of loved ones gone from us, and they are more affectionate than monuments, because flowers appeal to the heart more than cold marble. "This day shall be unto you for a memorial," as the Passover feast was to the Jew; and there were quali-

ties in Cornelius that reminded God of his worth. Cornelius embodies four essential elements of a good man: 1. He was devout. 2. He feared God with all his house. 3. He gave alms. 4. He was a praying man. One is surprised to find such a man in such a position. He was an alien, a Gentile, a Roman centurion; but he had made religious use of what he had learned of the Jewish faith. Good people are found everywhere. Under a bunch of wild flowers, on Memorial Day, may rest the remains of one as noble as Abraham Lincoln or Robert E. Lee. The Passover reminded the Hebrews of deliverance from bondage, the centurion's life reminded God of his good life, and this day reminds us of loved ones as sweet to us as the flowers you place on their graves today.

I. Angel Visits.

Angels visit good people. They visited Abraham, Lot, Mary, Joseph and Mary, and Cornelius. "The angel of the Lord encampeth round about them that fear Him." Angels were at the tomb when the women went, "early in the morning," with sweet spices to embalm the body of their dear Lord. Angels enlarge life's outlook and hopes and reveal the path of duty. The angel visit to Cornelius opened a new world to him, and a new day for mankind.

II. Memory a Fine Artist

Memory selects and preserves the best in men, the best in history, the best in literature, the best in painting, the best in music, the best in family life, and the best in religion. You never hear the worst of men at a funeral; you never hear the evils of men at a memorial service. Epitaphs tell the best of the dead. Memory puts in the best colors as artists do. Nothing smoothes out the wrinkles of experience so much as memory.

III. The Good Recognized by God.

It takes the world a long time to appreciate the ordinary. It took the Jews two thousand years to see any good in the Gentiles. Jesus had to teach that lesson; and Peter's experience made him realize it. It took the world sixty centuries to appreciate the common people. The great world-war has opened the eyes of mankind to the value of democracy. We are just beginning to appreciate good folks and trees. The barren earth reminds us of devastated forests and makes a tree seem almost human in value.

Graves speak to us. That cemetery is a library full of messages, reminding us of home and love. Libraries are the cemeteries of human achievement; they are as silent as graves and as eloquent as living speech. Mount Vernon speaks of Washington and the birth of a nation that seems to have come forth to serve the world in such a time as this. The Holy Sepulcher is the open mouth of a new era, a new faith, and the proof of a new life. The empty tomb announces the resurrection of Jesus Christ and assures the Christian of the resurrection of his beloved dead. Dust once animated by spirit is imperishable. It may be sown in weakness, but it is raised in power. Memorial services are memory services. This day reminds us of a congregation that used to sing, pray, and rejoice in the pews you occupy today. They help to make this occasion and to bring you to this place. You would not be here, if there were no graves here. We bring the flowers to decorate the graves of dear ones, not for what we can do for them, but for what they have done for us. This sacred day would be unknown but for sacred graves. Christianity would die without the empty tomb. We stand between the living and the dead—between the past and the future—between the rising and the setting sun. Families, churches, nations become great as they pay honor to the noble dead—the *good* dead are the *great* dead, and Jesus is the great example. He was the *best* and therefore the *greatest*—the most loved and the most honored. The women brought sweet spices to the tomb sweet spices to the tomb of their departed Lord; you of their departed Lord; you bring sweet flowers to lay upon the graves of those you still love, moved by the hope His tomb inspires.

The Hebrews carried the bones of Joseph into the Promised Land; we carry the memory of our dead in our hearts, and baptize their graves with tears.

This war has added a new chapter to Memorial Day; beyond the graves of the Civil War are the graves of the world-war where white crosses mark the spot where heroes sleep in the fields of France. We will not forget them this sacred day. Men and women love to visit the graves where true men rest. If in Brussels, you would want to go out ten miles to Waterloo where the Allied armies of the British, Dutch, and Germans, under Wellington, defeated Napoleon and the French Army, June 15, 1815. The battle commenced at 11:30 a. m., by a French charge and was defeated; renewed in the evening by the last charge of the Old Guard and this failed and was followed by an advance of the combined armies. The Allies lost 22,000 of their 67,000 and French 35,000 of their 72,000. At change in the tide Blucher came up with 50,000 Prussians and joined in the pursuit. That was a great day and people love to visit the spot. Then British and Germans were allied against France; in the last victory British and French allied against Germany; such is the course of human history. Those great historic spots have multiplied until every grave has become sacred and every little child's grave is honored by a flower and a prayer.

*Abstract of the Annual Memorial Sermon, preached at New Providence Church, June 1, 1919, by W. W. Staley, D. D.

CONFERENCE RESOLUTIONS

It is not an easy task—writing resolutions is not. And yet it is easy compared with the keeping of them. I have just been reading the *Christian Annual*, and I find it full of most interesting facts—facts worth knowing; facts that ought to be known and treasured by the members of the Christian Church. There are resolutions there, too—resolutions of all shapes, kinds and sizes; resolutions written hurriedly and perhaps on the back of an old envelope and handed in hastily to some Conference official; resolutions written by a special resolution committee; resolutions of praise to men, some of praise to God; some to be kept in the hearts of men and women; some to be kept only in the Conference records.

"Daniel purposed in his heart. ..." The heart is the seat of good resolutions. To stand they must be supported by the personality and character of the maker,—and that personality must be linked up with the personality of God. Such was Daniel's. And some such we have had recently in our own denomination. For instance, two good women in the Virginia Valley Central Christian Conference formulated a plan by which three of their churches were canvassed for THE CHRISTIAN SUN under the direction of the Conference. That resolution is found on page 18 of the 1918 *Annual*. On page 43 of the 1919 *Annual* they reported 26 subscriptions from those three churches. That is certainly to be commended, not because of the great showing made for the percentage of subscriptions is small considering the number of homes reported, but because it was a resolution with a history—a resolution with *something* done about it.

This study will be continued next week.

J. G. TRUITT.

LA GRANGE, GA.

We have just closed a ten days' meeting at the La Grange Christian church. Brother G. D. Hunt was with us one week and was a great help. He is a man that the people are always glad to see and hear.

Twenty new members were added to the church and everything is looking good. There is a great work to be done here. We have planned to run another week's meeting about the first of September. We hope that Brother Hunt will remember us and come again, also Brother Elder, who spent a week with us in April and got things started off for a meeting.

C. W. HANSON.

BROTHER CLEMENTS WRITES

I am writing a few lines because I am happy. I want my friends to rejoice with me in being able to take three steps yesterday, (June 2), without my crutches. That may look like a very little thing but it was a mighty big thing to me. God has been good to me.

W. G. CLEMENTS.

Morrisville, N. C.

DESPOTIC GODS

Such were the duties of the Egyptians, the Canaanites, Greeks and Romans. Their Gods courted, married, swore and lied. The ignorant people, in superstitious fear, tried to keep their gods good natured by sacrificing regularly to them—ofttimes offering their own flesh and blood.

Now do not be shocked when we say that the belief of the Jews, in the beginning, was a little better than their heathen neighbors. The idea that Jehovah was the only God developed gradually. At last they learned that the punishments which came upon them were not due to the whim of God, but to the sin and disobedience of man. Gradually the morning light broke in. David swept his fingers over his harp and sang, "Like as a father pitieth his children, so the Lord pitieth them that fear him." At last, Deity, embodied in human form, smiled in a manger, wept at a grave, died on a cross, robbed death of its sting, the grave of victory. Soon after this, the prejudice of the Academy, the pride of the portico, and the fasces of the lictors were humbled in the dust. The light of the knowledge of God, through the gift of the Holy Spirit, reached, rested at noon, in Christ, the Redeemer of Jew and Gentile, yea, of all who trust and obey the One who died, that we might live.

D. A. LONG.

A FEW PARAGRAPHERS

No, indeed brother, we have not outgrown Christianity; we had, to some extent, forsaken it or never really understood it. It never can be outgrown. Its author is "the same yesterday, today, and forever."

Listen, you chattering critics of the old, and you glibbed tongued prophets of the new, do not forget that while you are calling upon the editors and preachers for a clearer and more vigorous message, that the challenge that comes to them comes to you—yes, to all.

The protracted meeting season is at hand. Beloved, we may not be able to distinguish, every time what is essential, and what is non-essential. We know that never was the world in greater need of the loving truth of the Christian religion. We should not indulge in any foolish talk, or fritter away our time quibling over trifles. Let us, by pen and tongue, by giving and praying, do what we can to evangelize the world, feed the hungry, the body and spirit, to open the eyes of the physically and spiritually blind, to proclaim the good news that Christ is able and willing to save from sin to eternal life, all who, with broken hearts and contrite spirits, come to Him.

D. A. L.

A LETTER OF INTEREST

It is a pleasure to have the opportunity of writing to THE CHRISTIAN SUN. I have been a member of the Christian Church for about fourteen years and love it better each day that I live. My husband is a member of the Christian Church also, having joined with me. We have tried to live Christian lives. We now have six children living—one girl and five boys. We are trying to rear our children the right way. They go to Sunday school regularly and they enjoy going.

We all love our pastor, Rev. T. E. White, and wish him much success in life and his work. Our two oldest boys are members of Sanford Christian church.

We enjoy reading THE CHRISTIAN SUN and no other paper can fill its place in this home. My mother and father were members of the Christian Church and of course it is natural for me to love the denomination. My mother is dead and it is my desire to meet her and all our loved ones when the Lord calls.

We desire the prayers of the Christian people that we may live the way that we should live in order that our children may be loved and respected by all.

MRS. W. M. DOWDY.

Sanford, N. C.

IN LURAY, VA.

Those who were reared in and are still living, can tell you much more than I can about these incomparable valleys—Page and Shenandoah. Soon the long, wide fields of waving wheat will be ready for the binders, and the extensive hills and plains of thrifty growing clover, timothy and other grass will invite the mowers to give them needed attention. The click and clatter of these machines drawn by fine teams will be a scene of great interest and profit.

The fine orchards of apples, peaches, cherries and other kinds of fruit are loaded with delicious and valuable fruit. Truly this is a land full of greatness, and plenty. Natural scenery of superlative, stupendous and inexpressible beauty invites us to look, praise and admire until we exclaim: What hath God wrought! If I had the pen of a ready writer—the skillful touch of a painter or sculptor, the eloquence of the most gifted orator, the spiritual energy and power combined with the zeal and zest of Paul, I could not tell what I want to say about the matchless and thrilling caves, mountains and valleys. But I am inspired on the way with the precious and entertaining thought, that all of these things are the works of my Father, and that He is nearer and dearer to me.

J. T. KITCHEN.

DISABLED SOLDIERS

In his work throughout the country in behalf of discharged service men Colonel Arthur Woods, Assistant to the Secretary of War in charge of finding employment for demobilized soldiers, sailors and marines, has learned that in many sections people generally do not know just what the Government is doing to enable men disabled in the line of duty to re-establish themselves in civil life.

Inasmuch as the Government took these men out of civil life and placed them in camps and in the trenches where their disabilities were incurred, the obligation upon the Government to re-establish them in civil life is clear. And it should be understood that those injured in France are not the only ones entitled to assistance, for all disabled service men, whether injured in the United States or abroad, are provided for equally.

For re-establishing the disabled in civil life, the authorized agency of the Government is the Federal Board for Vocational Education, which is charged by Congress with the "vocational training of disabled soldiers and the placement of rehabilitated persons in suitable and gainful occupations," after their discharge from the army.

The Government, it will be noted, not only trains the disabled man, thus enabling him to assume again with unimpaired efficiency, the responsibilities of civil life, but also assists him in securing employment at the end of his period of training.

In some large cities crippled men in uniform are seen on the street engaged in "panhandling" kindly disposed persons. It has been found that in nearly every case these men were just plain ordinary fakirs in the guise of soldiers, who took this method of enlisting unmerited sympathy from the public. There is no excuse for these fakirs. No man disabled in the service need engage in any sort of hold-up game on the streets nor need he engage in any occupation whatever which is not becoming to him. Anyone seeing men in uniform so engaged should inform of provision made for their training and placement by the Government. If any man after being informed what his opportunities are continues his game, a favor will be done the great body of self-respecting disabled men who are trying to make something of themselves, if every case of this character is reported to the nearest branch office of the Federal Board for Vocational Education.

MISSIONARY

ABOUT THE CHURCHES AND SUNDAY SCHOOLS

Rev. O. D. Poythress, pastor of our South Norfolk, Va., church has enjoyed recently a very gracious revival season. Under date of May 21 he writes: "You will be interested to know that our work here has the most promising outlook in its history. We are in the third week of the most successful revival ever held in our church here. More than seventy professions and fifty additions to the church. The pastor is doing the preaching and also led the singing the first two weeks. Rev. J. F. Morgan has assisted with the music two nights this week." Nothing rejoices a pastor's heart more, or helps a church more, than a spirit filled revival.

Sister T. Upton Savage, Suffolk, Va., writes: "I think the Children's Day programs are the very best, and as I have been training the children at Bethlehem for many years, that means right much." Many words of commendation for the programs have come, and we are grateful. If other schools desire copies, send request at once, as the supply is limited. And all schools should have their Children's Day in June.

SUNDAY SCHOOLS AND MISSIONS

The number of our schools that are contributing one Sunday's offering each month to missions constantly increases. Our Durham school is among the most liberal, its check being about $10.00 each month. No school loses anything, no more than does an individual, by dividing liberally for missions and world-wide evangelization. When a school spends all its offerings upon itself, it is in that act as selfish as an individual who does the same. The writer had a letter from a Sunday school secretary the other day who said that the school could not give one Sunday a month's collection for missions or for the Orphanage, as it barely got enough to buy its literature, maintain current expenses. That school is having a hard time living, and it should have. It is just living for itself. It spends on itself all it gets. It thinks and acts in terms of self. "He that loses his life shall save it," says the Word. Some schools need to lose sight of themselves in order to save themselves.

OUR CHAPEL HILL CHURCH

It is doubtful if any church amongst us deserves more credit and has from the beginning been more loyal than our Chapel Hill church. It has responded to every call, and is awake to every interest and progressive step of the Church. In the Elon Standardization drive Chapel Hill was apportioned $500. It responded with $1,500. In our special missionary drive it gave about $1,000. It gives one Sunday school offering each month to missions and one to the Orphanage. It has been, and is one of the most liberal congregations, despite the fact that it is a mission point and still owes heavily on its building indebtedness, and only has preaching one or two Sundays each month. All have a right to feel proud of what our Chapel Hill church has done, and what it gives promise of doing in the future. Located as it is at the State University it should be one of our strongest and most aggressive churches, and here is hoping that it will be before many years.

J. O. ATKINSON.

BUYING HEALTH

America's determination to eradicate venereal diseases is best demonstrated by the action of the legislatures in thirty-one states which have appropriated large sums of money to be used for this purpose exclusively. In each of the states the Federal government augmented the appropriation and the United States Public Health Service officers are co-operating with state health officers.

Most of the states not included in the following list are confidently expected to make appropriations as soon as their legislatures meet:

Arizon	$ 4,500
Arkansas	34,237
California	201,600
Colorado	17,000
Connecticut	24,000
Delaware	2,500
Indiana	29,360
Iowa	15,000
Kansas	105,550
Maine	8,000
Michigan	300,000
Minnesota	60,000
Montana	8,177
Nebraska	25,925
New Hampshire	9,363
New Jersey	27,586
New York	100,000
North Carolina	23,988
North Dakota	12,548
Ohio	25,000
Oklahoma	86,000
Oregon	25,000
South Carolina	10,000
Texas	45,000
Utah	8,000
Washington	175,000
West Virginia	7,000
Wisconsin	50,000
Wyoming	4,000

WORSHIP AND MEDITATION

WINNING OTHERS

No, it is not the business of the minister and the evangelist only to ask individuals to accept Jesus Christ, nor of some central committee which sends out literature suggesting ways and means. It is everybody's task. The injunction, "Go ye and make disciples," is just as binding upon the man sensitive to his Christian obligations as "Come unto me" or "Learn of me."

Really, now, how long is it since we tried to induce some one else to walk the Christian way? When did we speak or write a note with this in view? When was the last time we prayed that a certain person might be converted from the self-centered life and enter the Christ life?

O, yes, one's first reaction toward the idea is quite understandable: "I'm not built that way; it doesn't come as easily to me as it does to some persons. I try to live a decent and useful life; I am supporting the Church and missions, but this business of approaching another person goes against my grain. At heart he may be as good as I and perhaps better. I don't like to interfere with another man's private affairs or invade his personality."

Ah, but on this last point you remember the story about Father Taylor, famous as a preacher to sailors? He sometimes included in his round of visitations the wealthier section of the city. One evening when a prosperous merchant came home to dinner, his wife informed him that Father Taylor had called on her that afternoon and had inquired about her soul. "I should think you would have told him to go about his business," grumbled the man just back from downtown. "If you had heard him, husband," said the wife, "I guess you would have thought that he was about his business."

Going out after the other man reacts on the man who goes: Nothing so quickly and so thoroughly rouses us steady-going, conventional Christians as the effort to help some one else see the glory of the Christian life. It sets us to thinking and planning. It leads us to ask how much of a Teacher, Master, and Saviour Christ is to us, anyway. It impels us to clean up our lives. It defines more sharply the contents of our religion. It burnishes the weapons of our warfare. We may fail or we may bungle the matter, but our spiritual assets will increase through the effort to share them.

But we shall not fail. The person addressed will not be offended if, without fuss or sanctimoniousness we say: "Come and live the Christian life with me. I make poor work of it at times, but I know that I possess an urge, a recourse, an ideal of priceless worth, and I know they all proceed from Christ. Won't you settle once for all the question of your personal attitude to him?"

Be an Andrew. Be an Andrew under your own roof. Be an Andrew in the factory, the store, the club, the community. You don't have to make a fool of yourself or become a bore in order to fulfill Andrew's role and bring some one else to the Master.

The world needs many more disciples and followers of Jesus Christ. They and not external arrangements in the way of treaties and covenants will be the salt and leaven of society. Who are to help Christianize this distressed and turbulent world and all who dwell in it if not just such everyday Christians as we?—*H. A. B., in the Congregationalist and Advance.*

THINGS BROKEN

God uses most for his glory those people and things which are most perfectly broken. The sacrifices he accepts are broken and contrite hearts. It was through the breaking down of Jacob's natural strength at Peniel that got him where God could clothe him with spiritual power.

It was when the three hundred elect soldiers under Gideon broke their pitchers, a type of breaking themselves, that the hidden lights shone forth to the consternation of their adversaries.

It was when Esther risked her life and broke through the rigid etiquette of a heathen court, that she obtained favor to rescue her people from death.

It was when Jesus took the five loaves and broke them that the bread was multiplied in the very act of breaking sufficient to feed five thousand.

It was when Mary broke her beautiful alabaster box, rendering it thenceforth useless, that the pent-up perfume filled the whole house.

It was when Jesus allowed his precious body to be broken to pieces by thorns and nails and a spear that his inner life was poured out like a crystal ocean for thirsty sinners to drink and live.

It is when a beautiful grain of corn is broken up in the earth by death that its inner heart sprouts forth and bears hundreds of other grains.

And thus on and on through all history and all biography and all vegetation and all spiritual life. God must have broken things.

Those who are broken in wealth and broken in self-will and broken in their ambitions and broken in their beautiful ideals and broken in worldly reputation, broken oftentimes in health and those who are despised and seem utterly helpless and forlorn, the Holy Spirit is seizing upon and using for God's glory. It is the "lame that take the prey," Isaiah tells us. It is the weak that overcome the devil. God is waiting to take hold of our failures and nothingness and shine through them.—*British Evangelist.*

NOTES

The Rose Hill Christian church, Columbus, Georgia, is in need of a pastor. Any one interested may write See, Houghton, 642-25th Street, Columbus, Ga.

Some days ago Mr. Basil S. Cox, son of Rev. L. I. Cox, met with a painful accident at High Point by getting part of his toes cut off by a moving car. He is in the hospital at High Point and is dong well. We sympathze with him in his accident.

We cannot refrain from calling attention to Mrs. Dowdy's letter on another page. So often we call upon people to write for THE SUN, and the reply is that they cannot because they cannot discuss some topic. Mrs. Dowdy's letter is a good testimony, an example of what many could write, and would certainly be helpful to readers. Let us have more such letters.

The North Carolina Christian Endeavor Convention was in session in Burlington, N. C., June 6, 7, and 8. The attendance was the largest in the history of the work in the State, the reports registering the highest degree of work done, and the fellowship could not be surpassed. We cannot undertake to tell of the splendid work. Officers for the coming year were elected as follows:

Rev. J. V. Knight, president, Greensboro; Eli P. Barker, vice-president, Greensboro; Miss Eunice Long, secretary, Greensboro; W. P. Smith, treasurer, Graham; Rev. L. A. Peeler, vice-president and superintendent of western district, Newton; Eddie Shepherd, vice-president of northwestern district, Winston-Salem; Rev. C. D. Whiteley, superintendent central district, Durham; J. D. Foster, vice-president and superintendent northwestern district, Tarboro; Rev. Charles G. Lynch, vice-president and superintendent southern district, Charlotte; James Wells, vice-president and superintendent southeastern district, Wilmington; H. Galt Braxton, vice-president World's Christian Endeavor union, Kinston; Rev. C. B. Riddle, superintendent tenth legion, Burlington; F. M. Harward; superintendent Quiet-Hour, Henderson; Mrs. W. H. Howell, superintendent junior work, Wilmington; Miss Ruth Vogler, C. E. World and Dixie Endeavor representative, Winston-Salem; C. B. Way, press superintendent, Burlington; Rev. Douglas Wright, missionary superintendent, Winston-Salem; T. G. Finley, superintendent floating work, Wilmington; Mrs. J. W. Beaty, superintendent intermediate work, Charlotte; Miss Annie Wilson, superintendent prison work, Greensboro.

THRIFT SUNDAY

The churches of the country have been asked by the Treasury Department to make Sunday, June 22, Thrift Sunday and to devote it to the aid of the savings movement which is sweeping the country. A direct message from Secretary Glass to the Treasury Department, to be read to congregations from the pulpit, will set forth the personal and patriotic reasons for seeking to perpetuate the lessons of thrift learned by the people through the struggles and self-sacrifices of the war period.

The moral value of thrift to the individual and to the community make the savings movement a particularly appropriate subject for church activity. The great services rendered by the churches to all public causes during the war period have demonstrated the value of church co-operation in great public movements.

Rev. W. B. Fuller has accepted a call to Damascus church, near Sunbury, N. C. His address, until further notice, will be Sunbury, N. C.

Dr. W. A. Harper spoke in the Burlington church last Sunday. : His message was heard gladly.

Rev. H. J. Fleming of Newport News, Virginia, came in to see us the other day.

We rejoice to know that Brother W. G. Clements is improving. See his letter on another page.

We are unable to give the names of all our subscribers who called last week during the Christian Endeavor Convention. We are always glad to see our friends. Come again.

President Wilson is to sail from France in a few days.

Uncle Wellons writes interestingly of his trip to Eastern Virginia. His letter will appear next week.

6-1-9 on your label means that your subscription expired June 1. Look and see if these figures are on yours.

Remember the Sunday school and Christian Endeavor Convention that is to be held at Shallow Well, July 15-17.

Your pastor may need a great many things that cannot be bought with money. He may need a word of cheer and encouragement.

If there is anything about this paper that you do not approve, let us know it.

Let us have your renewal during this month.

Do you need a nice Bible or Testament? We have a full line of each.

Last week we completed the mailing of a handsome card to each church in the Convention to be placed on the wall. Has your church received its card? If not, let us know. Every church is due to have this card calling attention to THE SUN.

Let us have short articles for publication. We need them and welcome anything that you may send.

CHRISTIAN EDUCATION

A WEEK IN RANDOLPH COUNTY, NORTH CAROLINA

Rarely have I enjoyed a season of fellowship so well as the five days I spent with Pastor A. T. Banks and the group of churches he serves in Randolph county. Brother Banks was graduated in the class of 1913, the class which promulgated the Alumni Building Fund and published the first issue of the Phipscili, the College Annual. You would expect such a man to be a progressive and he does not disappoint your expectation. In his work he is ably and sympathetically assisted by his consecrated wife, also an Elon graduate with three diplomas at that.

I reached Ramseur on Saturday afternoon and was soon discussing the Standardization Drive with Deacon T. A. Moffitt and wife. They gave us a good start, subscribing $1,000, being the first subscription for that large an amount given for any purpose in the Christian church by a member of the Western North Carolina Conference. With that start, following a tender prayer by Brother Banks, we were ready for victory all along the line.

Sunday morning found us at Park's Cross Roads, one of the strong country churches of our entire Brotherhood. God has greater things in store for this grand old church. It doubled its quota in the drive.

Sunday afternoon we met a small band of the faithful at Shiloh. Shiloh is a Scriptural word, and means salvation, deliverance. Here have been born many leaders in the Christian Church. The best days are ahead, for this church has learned the blessed joy of helping the Lords work. "Over the top," she went, Deacon J. C. Cox giving one-half the original quota to make it possible.

Sunday evening we were to have held a service at Pleasant Ridge, but a terrific storm prevented. Pleasant Ridge, however, on Wednesday night, too went over the top, and a new day of rich blessing awaits the noble band who worship there.

Ramseur, of course, went over, and in as happy a mood as any church I have visited. I left Pastor Banks smiling, and why should he not smile in such a case? It must greatly grieve a pastor's heart when his field does not do its part generously for the great enterprises of the Kingdom. It is natural therefore for his heart to rejoice when they step out with firm tread for these causes. Keep your eye on Brother Banks. He is one of the coming men of our ministry.

Funds This Week

Deacon and Mrs. T. A. Moffitt named their fund in loving memory of their deceased daughter, Virginia Lehman, who would have entered Elon as a Freshman this fall, as her brother and sister had done, but God claimed her. What sweeter thing than for her devoted parents thus to preserve her memory in the College they love and of which she would have been an Alumna! Brother B. F. Craven and wife, of Park's Cross Roads church, lost a noble son in the World War. He

was killed in action on November 9 at Menhaulles Meuse, France. In his honor in the old home church they have provided a beautiful memorial window, to be unveiled on June 29 by Rev. T. E. White, a former pastor, assisted by Revs. A. T. Banks and T. J. Green. In addition these devoted parents have perpetuated his memory forever by founding a fund of $1,000 in Elon to be used to pay the tuition cost of educating a Christian minister. "Though dead, he speaketh." What a precious tribute this to Floyd Craven, their hero son!

A Thought For The Week

Two things are had in remembrance in the sight of God, according to Acts 10:31—our prayers and our alms. Prayers without alms are hypocrisy in His sight. Alms without prayers are a mockery to Him. It takes both to make the Christian man or woman full orbed in His sight. Our Christian brethren and sisters are, by their generosity and their prayers in this drive to make our College standard, causing many things to be done on earth that will be remembered "over there," when this life is ended. God has rich blessings in store for our people and our cause. He can not fail to bless with every joy those who thus do His will.

W. A. HARPER.

P. S. Brother Riddle, I have urged the other brethren who are in the field with us in this final lap to write each week of their experiences. They are too busy to do so, but I can assure you and the interested friends that they are hitting the trail hard and faithfully. Pray for us all. W. A. H.

THE CHRISTIAN ORPHANAGE

SUPERINTENDENT'S LETTER

It is a busy time with the Orphanage boys now. We have had so much rain for the past fifteen days that we have not been able to get our work in the condition we would like to have it. We had planned to get our corn all worked the second time and ten acres of beans sowed before harvest. Our wheat is nearly ripe and there is much work to be done before we go into the harvest, but we have a crowd of faithful boys who like to work and who work like men when they are at it.

We have three Easter Offerings reported this week—two churches and one friend. I had hoped that each church would make the offering this spring and help swell the amount but it seems that quite a number did not avail themselves of the great privilege of helping the little orphans in this way.

We have one letter for the Corner this week. Lester B. Frank is a faithful little cousin and always gets his letter in on time, though he lives in a distant state. He wants to help keep the Corner bright and cheerful. I would like for all the cousins to write through the summer months and keep our page full.

We trust the Sunday schools will lend us a helping hand from now till the Thanksgiving offering comes in. Through the summer months our income is not large enough to meet expenses. While we do all in our power to keep the expense account as low as possible it will run up at the end of the month when we get all our accounts in. Everything that we have to buy is so high and the children wear as much and eat as hearty as they do when everything is cheaper.

I truly hope that the day is not far distant when each family in the Christian Church will take THE CHRISTIAN SUN so they may be able to keep up with the different departments of the Church and the Orphanage. If each family in the Church were a subscriber to THE CHRISTIAN SUN, then I could reach each family weekly through the paper. My only way of keeping this work before our people is through my report in THE SUN, by personal letters and visits to the churches and Sunday schools. If you are not a subscriber, subscribe now and when I tell you of our need for the comfort of our little folks open your heart and send a contribution to help supply the need.

　　　　　　　　　　　　CHAS. D. JOHNSTON, Supt.

A LETTER

Dear Uncle Charley:—Your sad letter came some days ago. We have a sympathy too deep for words for you and your little boys and girls. It was so sweet and dear of Mrs. Johnston to think of starting a fund for a baby home at the Orphanage. I hope I may visit the home and play with the babies some day. I thank you for the pictures of the little orphan girls. Enclosed find twenty cents for May and June.—Lester B. Frank, Lindsay, Okla.

Glad to have your letter this week. It is the only one to brighten the corner. I hope you will have the pleasure of visiting the Orphanage sometime and see our little boys and girls. They will give you a good time playing ball and jumping the rope.—"Uncle Charley."

REPORT FOR JUNE 11, 1919

Amount brought forward, $6,390.76.

Children's Offerings

Lester B. Frank, Lindsay, Okla., 20 cents.

Sunday School Monthly Offerings

(Eastern Virginia Conference)

Portsmouth, $3.00; Wakefield, $3.60; First Christian church, Norfolk, $5.47.

(Virginia Valley Conference)

Dry Run, $3.00; Linville, $1.00; Wood's Chapel, $1.00.

(Georgia and Alabama Conference)

Kite, Ga., $3.00; Kite, Ga., $5.00; North Highlands, Ga., $3.25.

(North Carolina Conference)

Pleasant Hill, $2.75; Catawba Springs, $8.60; Union, (Va.), $4.00; Amelia, $4.80; Long's Chapel, $1.00; Morrisville, $2.00; Christian Light, $2.00; Total $56.47.

Special Offerings

Whistlers' Chapel, $14.00; Dry Run S. S., $19.35; W. H. Mills, Raleigh, N. C., $5.00; Mrs Mary H. Whelless of New Hope church, $10.00; A Friend, Erlanger, N. C., $5.00; New Harmony church, (Ala.), $5.60.

Total for the week, $118.62; Grand total, $6,506.31.

Renew your subscription to THE SUN now. We need your check.

THE TALE OF A DOG
By W. H. Burgwin

When Gypsy came to our house she was a bit of a pup, a dark-brown, short-haired, kindly-eyed, tail-wagging, fun-loving bundle of cheerfulness. Her business, among other things, was to grow and to learn good dog manners in the house and out. These she did in her happy way, and very quickly, too.

She was the property of our boys, but she soon adopted our baby girl as her special charge. Wherever that baby went Gyp was. The baby carriage with its precious cargo was to go down town. A small brown doggie tagged along, as proud as any prize-winner could ever be. The carriage was left outside the store while grandma or mamma did the shopping. Whereupon without orders, Gyp mounted guard, and the carriage was always safe. When a new baby girl came along, there was no jealousy on Gypsy's part. She was delighted and at once added the new baby to her responsibilities. One day that baby had been asleep in her carriage in a grove by the seashore. Mamma was on the beach a short distance away. Baby wakened. A friend near at hand was about to lift the child from the carriage, but Gyp was on guard. The friend thought it best to call mamma, saying that he was about to bring the baby, but the dog objected, and he thought it prudent to desist.

On another occasion papa took the older child to the city to see her doctor. It was convenient to push her to the station in her carriage. The travelers returned some six hours later to claim the carriage left in charge of the express agent. He asked if we had brought a little brown dog with us. We did not know. But Gyp was there and had watched that baby carriage in a strange place and would not be driven off during the whole of a long summer afternoon. How glad she was to see us!

At another time a minister friend who knew our children met them on the sidewalk and stopped to talk with them, patting the baby, then two years old, on the cheek. Gyp was puzzled. She was kind in her act, but very insistent as she walked up and put her nose between the baby's cheek and the minister's hand, pushing the hand away. The minister told us the story, so we know it's true.

We call ourselves a Christian nation, but we can learn some valuable lessons—from the heathen. In the Japanese language it is impossible for a man to use profanity, as there are no profane words in their vocabulary. What a pity that this useless and degrading form of speech was ever introduced into our Language.—Biblical Recorder.

Subscribe to THE SUN and get your friends to do so, too.

Sunday School and Christian Endeavor

SUNDAY SCHOOL LESSON FOR JUNE 22, 1919

Love. I Cor. 13

Golden Text: Now abideth faith, hope, love, these three; and the greatest of these is love. I Cor. 13:13.

Thoughts For Teachers

Love is the fulfilling of the law. It is the law of teaching, the law of the home maker. No parent will have obedience, no teacher will secure results through fear. "If ye love Me," said the Master Teacher, "ye *will* keep my commandments." Oh, yes, if we love Him, we shall desire to keep His commandments. The unloving, no matter what he thinks, has no part in God, for God Himself is love. What about our neighbor? "If a man say "I love God, and hateth his brother, he is a liar." Who is my brother? Answer this for yourselves. If Christ *died* for the weaker brother, can we not live with Him in peace? Suppose he does not do our way, what then?

God so loved ....
That He gave ....
How much do you love?........
What do you give?............
MRS. FRED BULLOCK.

CHRISTIAN ENDEAVOR TOPIC FOR JUNE 22, 1919

Christianity and The Toilers of India. Isa. 40:18-31. (Missionary Meeting).

Let us know something of India; its needs and its conditions. Do you know of the sickness which comes every year from unsanitary conditions? Of the thousands who drink the poisoned waters of the Ganges every year, waters poisoned by dead bodies, and filth? Do you know of the tens of thousands of child widows of India? What about the little lads of ten and eleven deprived of childhood to become heads of families? What of the coolie class, without hope of ever having enough to eat or enough to wear? What hope for these in the native religions? What hope for them in Christ? What have we done, what can we do to send His Word to a people two and a half times as numerous as the population of the United States?
MRS. FRED BULLOCK.

THE LARGER PATRIOTISM

We are coming close to the Fourth of July. How will you celebrate it in your school? What will you do with it, pass it by, and ignore it, or make such a use of it that your boys and girls will begin to be fitted for world citizenship? They need to learn the larger patriotism of the world, to learn that "all ye are brethren," that "God hath made of one blood all the peoples of the earth," and that no member can sin against another without causing suffering to all. And, when you teach the Brotherhood of Man, remember there can be no common brotherhood, without a common Fatherhood. Have a patriotic program, a program which, if possible, shall include a speech by some soldier, either of this or the preceding wars. Have all soldiers on the platform, make a strong appeal for patriotism, love of country, reverence for the flag and all for which it stands, and then; as the closing number, have the pastor or some one in his place, to make an appeal for the Christian flag and the things for which it stands, an appeal for loyalty to the King and the Kingdom.
MRS. FRED BULLOCK.

ANNOUNCEMENT NO. 2

The first annual session of the State Sunday School and Christian Endeavor Convention of the North Carolina Conference will be held at Shallow Well Christian church, July 15-17. This church is located near Jonesboro and Sanford, N. C. Delegates coming on trains will be met at Sanford. Arrangements are being made to accommodate all who will attend—*and this means you.* Every Sunday school and Christian Endeavor Society in the State should be represented—*and this evidently includes yours.*

Will you take this to heart and see to it *that you and yours* are in the front ranks where love, loyalty and duty calls you? I believe you will.
C. H. STEPHENSON, *Pres.*

SUNDAY SCHOOL SKEDADDLERS
By S. J. Porter

Skedaddle comes from the Greek word skedannumi. It means to run away, to scamper, to spill, to retreat disorderly. According to the findings of the Commission for the Adolescent Period appointed by the International Sunday School Association, the proportion of boys and girls between thirteen and sixteen years of age, who dropped out of Sunday school was sixty-two per cent; and from seventeen to nineteen years of age, seventy-seven per cent. In other words, sixty-two of every 100 younger boys and girls, and seventy-seven out of every 100 older pupils "skedaddle" from the Sunday school at the time when they need its training and anchorage most. Something ought to be done to stop this "spilling," this disorderly retreat. It is said on good authority that in eight years 11,000,000 scholars passed through the Sunday schools of the United States without manifesting any definite decision for the Christian life. We are of course accomplishing much in the Sunday school, but are we not also losing a great opportunity? Some one once asked, "How shall we keep our older boys in the Sunday school?" "Build a wall of men between them and the door," is the reply. And if this be made up of the fathers, it will be all the stronger. Instead of "skedaddling" in the opposite direction, let parents blaze the way to the Sunday school and it will be easier to win and hold the young people.—*Baptist Messenger.*

MARRIAGES

FALLIN-MICHAEL

Mr. Willie T. Fallin and Miss Sallie Michael were married at the home of the late Alfred Michael, Washington Township, Guilford County, N. C., May 28, 1919. After a sumptuous dinner the bridal party left for a trip to Washington. The ceremony was performed by Rev. J. W. Holt, Burlington, N. C.

Many good wishes go with these young people. They will reside in Guilford county.   J. W. HOLT.

BEAN-YOW

At the home of the officiating minister (Rev.) T. J. Green, in Asheboro, N. C., May 28, 1919, Mr. Harrison Bean and Miss Dewie Yow were united in marriage.

The groom is a son of Mr. and and Mrs. Calvin Bean and the bride is a daughter of Mr. and Mrs. Martin Yow, all of Seagrove, N. C. They were accompanied by the bride's sister, Miss Dena Yow, and brother of the groom, Mr. Eli Bean.

The young couple will make their home at Bynum, N. C., where Mr. Bean is engaged in the saw milling business. May happiness be theirs.
    T. J. GREEN.

TUCK-WHITT

At my residence, Virgilina, Va., on April 30, 1919, at 1 o'clock P. M., I married Mr. John Tuck and Miss Janie Whitt, of Nathalie, Va. In the wedding party that motored across the country that morning were Messrs. Rasser and Charlie Tuck, brothers of the groom and Miss Mary Bray and Mr. Silas Bray, cousin of the bride.

Mr. Tuck is an industrious farmer and for the past year has been serving as a member of the Coast Guards. His wife is a daughter of Mr. James Whitt of Northern Halifax and a charter member of Liberty Christian church. She is active in Sunday school, Christian Endeavor and the Ladies' Missionary Society.

They are an excellent young couple and may their marriage add to the happiness and usefulness of each.
    C. E. NEWMAN.

SHARPE- LAWRENCE

Luther A. Sharpe and Myrtie A. Lawrence were united in the bonds of holy matrimony on June 4, 1919, at the home of Mr. and Mrs. E. M. Cheek, Church Street, Burlington, N. C. The ceremony was performed at 7:30 A. M.—at the beginning of a new day in the world and a new day in their lives. Several invited friends were present to witness the occasion and to wish them well. The ring ceremony was used. May it always be a symbol of an endless bond of love and fellowship!

Mr. Sharpe is a number of one of Alamance county's best families. Mrs. Sharpe is the daughter of Mr. and Mrs. T. W. Lawrence of Randolph county, and represents another good family. Their home ought to be, and will be a model one.

The writer officiated.
    C. B. RIDDLE.

OBITUARIES

WOLFORD

John Lawrence Wolford, infant son of Charles and Nora Wolford, was born July 14, 1917, and died April 11, 1919, aged 1 year, 8 months and 27 days. Two little sisters yet remain in the home. Funeral services were conducted at Palmyra, April 12, 1919.
    A. W. ANDES.

HUFFINES

Mrs. Annie Wakefield Huffines was born in Canada, January 3, 1861, and died at her home near Pleasant Ridge Christian church, Guilford county, North Carolina, April 26, 1919, aged 58 years, 3 months and 23 days. When she was 11 years old her parents removed to Friendship, Guilford county, N. C., there she grew into womanhood.

While in school at New Garden, (now Guilford College), she professed faith in Christ and joined the Friends church at that place:

Thirty-one years ago she was happily married to L. C. Huffines. To this union was born seven children: Mrs. L. A. Beeson of Friendship; Mrs. E. G. Farlow of Teachey, N. C., Allen Huffines, Charlotte, N. C.; Mrs. L. B. Farlow of Greensboro, N. C.; Mrs. L. L. Isley and Craven at home. One son, Henry, a noble young man, died last fall.

Her husband being a member of the Christian church at Pleasant Ridge, after her marriage, she transferred her membership to Pleasant Ridge of which church she remained a consistant helpful member, always gladly and faithfully performing all tasks assigned her. She was a model wife, mother and neighbor. She walked the path of life with her husband for thirty-one years. "Her children rise up, and call her blessed; her husband also and he praiseth her." She was ever ready to help the needy.

In the absence of her pastor the funeral was conducted by the Rev. Edgar Williams, pastor of the Friends church at Guilford College, assisted by the writer.
    S. STARR HIGGINS.

MOORE

Mary R. Moore was born October 15, 1847, and died April 21, 1919, at the age of 71 years, 6 months, and 6 days. Sister Moore united with the Christian church at Union, Southampton County, Va., at an early age, and lived the life of a faithful Christian until death. On October 21, 1868 she was united in marriage to Rev. H. C. Moore. She was a devoted wife and mother. Sister Moore was well known and highly esteemed in all parts of the Virginia Conference where Brother Moore has been pastor of several churches in recent years. At the time of her death they were living in Charlottesville, Va. Death, however, occurred while on a visit to her son, John, near Beaverdam, Va. In addition to her husband, she is survived by six sons and two daughters, one being the wife of Rev. R. L. Williamson of Henderson, N. C. Funeral services were conducted by the writer at Charlottesville, Va., April 22.
    A. W. ANDES.

THE TITHER

An interdenominational publication devoted to Tithing and Christian Stewardship.

Editors

C. B. RIDDLE /
KARL LEHMANN
BERT WILSON
HUGH S. McCORD
FRED G. THOMAS

8 pages; issued monthly; 50c the year

Address

THE TITHER   Burlington, N. C.

Why We Should Give to The Church College

For Our College
For Our Church

For Our Girls
For Our Boys

"The Missionary Review of the World has gathered some interesting statistics relative to the influence of small church schools. It says: "A small Christian College in New England, which recently celebrated the centennial of its birth, has never had, in the one hundred years of its existence, an attendance that exceeded one hundred students, yet its record of graduates show 542 clergymen, 70 foreign missionaries, 102 college professors, 32 college presidents, 9 governors of states and 15 members of Congress.

De Pauw University, a Methodist institution in Indiana, numbers among its graduates 448 ministers and missionaries, 107 editors and journalists, 146 college professors, 57 college presidents, 5 governors, 15 members of Congress, 2 cabinet officers, and a host of other public servants and useful citizens.

Much of the same evidence comes from other denominations. In 1915 Presbyterian colleges in America reported 28,445 graduates, of whom 5,830 were in the Christian ministry. 714 were foreign missionaries and 1,385 were in other Christian work. There were on the list 727 college professors and 4,762 teachers. The law claimed 4,064; medicine, 3,796, and other professions, 1,733. Forty per cent. of the graduates were in altruistic work. The Presbyterian Board of Foreign Missions reports that 70 per cent. of their missionaries prepared in Christian institutions.

Our own Elon College stands for "Christian Character first and Always." Its ministers, missionaries, teachers and trained workers everywhere claim for it our unstinted support. Shall we give or shall we withhold from the Church college? Her brightest day is before her. Shall we dim her lamp or aid her in the radiation of a greater light?

Will YOUR Church Go Over The Top?
Your Figures On The Dotted Line Will Answer
THE QUESTION

THE CHRISTIAN SUN

"IN ESSENTIALS UNITY, IN NON-ESSENTIALS LIBERTY, IN ALL THINGS CHARITY"

The Message

NEW themes, new thoughts, new things—all these call and challenge us. They are worthy of consideration, but mistakes are being made by isolating them from the Great Message of the Book. The message of Christ and Him crucified preached by a spirit-filled soul will draw the crowd. Men never tire of it—they love to hear it and to support it. There is no substitute for the Gospel and no theme so dear to the hearts of men. Teach it, preach it, for it is the message of all ages—and for this age.

Volume LXXI   WEDNESDAY, JUNE 18, 1919   Number 25

BURLINGTON   ·   ·   ·   NORTH CAROLINA

THE CHRISTIAN SUN

Founded 1844 by Rev. Daniel W. Kerr

C. B. RIDDLE   -   -   -   Editor

Entered at the Burlington, N. C. Post Office as second class matter.

Subscription Rates

One year ....$ 2.00
Six months 1.00

In Advance

Give both your old and new postoffice when asking that your address be changed.

The change of your label is your receipt for money. Written receipts sent upon request.

Marriage and obituary notices not exceeding 150 words printed free if received within 60 days from date of event, all over this at the rate of one-half cent a word.

Original poetry not accepted for publication.

Principles of the Christian Church

(1) The Lord Jesus Christ is the only Head of the Church.
(2) Christian is a sufficient name of the Church.
(3) The Holy Bible is a sufficient rule of faith and practice.
(4) Christian character is a sufficient test of fellowship, and of church membership.
(5) The right of private judgment and the liberty of conscience is a right and a privilege that should be accorded to, and exercised by all.

EDITORIAL

BRIEFS

Cheerfulness is a child of kindness and a cousin to religion.

It is not enough to hope for a thing—translating our hope into help is the practical method.

Sorrows may have in them great blessings. It is said that "every cloud has a silver lining." Often the hand of God seems hard, but He is leading, and it is faith only that will enable us to follow.

Doing a good deed gives a blessing in two ways: It helps the one doing the deed and also the one to whom it is done. That is why selfishness is not Christ-like—it is void of that mutual spirit.

The Church is due the retired minister an honor and consideration. The Church should set a far better example than a corporation in such matters. The government often retires men on a pension. Let us not forget those who have been faithful in the Lord's work.

We note that a sister denomination in another State is raising a fund to send the Church paper to all its ministers. A good thing to do, but a bad thing that all of them have not beek taking the official organ of their Church.

The Church cannot afford to suffer any relax from its present position in giving. The urgent needs are too many and the call of the Kingdom too loud for any backward step.

These are days when we need to keep close to God. Things are unsettled, temptations abound, and sin is lurking. This is a day of impatience when the nervous strain is hard upon us. So let us guard ourselves physically as well as spiritually.

There is a certain satisfaction in all States of their wealth. A thing to rejoice in to be sure. A State has a right to feel proud when its wealth is great. God is the Giver, and in our boastings of State wealth, God should be praised—and honored by it.

There are hundreds of young men and women in the Church who should be induced to attend college this fall. The educational activities of our denomination need very much to enlist more of the young men and women for future leaders.

The other day we heard W. J. Bryan speak on prohibition, and among the things he said, he told of the start against whisky in his own State—Nebraska. He opened the campaign himself, but so unpopular was the issue that he could not find a man who would sit on the platform with him. Today old Nebraska is dry. It takes courage to fight some things, and you often have public sentiment against you. Right will win.

OFFERINGS AND COLLECTIONS

The other day we had the pleasure of being in a community and speaking in a Church not of our own denomination. In that church not less than twenty families worship. The average family is worth not less than five thousand dollars in material things. Acres of waving grain and growing corn greeted the eye, while fine horses and automobiles filled the church yard. The occasion spread a dinner worth $250.00. That church pays its pastor $350.00 per year, and in the last six months its Sunday school has contributed the sum of $13.50 for all purposes. (No error in these figures). The *collection* plates were passed for a *collection*, and we had the audacity to remind the people that the plates were for the *offering* and not for a collection. Collections are made in churches that do not *give*.

"ASLEEP"

The most of us dread death, and perhaps all of us, if we could really know ourselves. It is the passing into that unknown that we dread. It is the separating from this life that we fear.

The other day we read of a missionary who died about three weeks ago in Brazil. His associates sent a cablegram and said: "Dr. Butler Asleep." How happy that thought! It rang in our ears again and again. Asleep! Not dead!! His work was finished, his task completed and then he went to sleep. Precious thought that one can go to that eternal sleep where only the touch of an angel can wake us.

We get so busy living that we forget about dying. We make it a rule not to talk too much about dying, but. rather to be so busy living and endeavoring to do right that death will take care of itself. However, all of us need to be reminded that death is certain and that it comes to all of us. We know not the day nor the hour. It is our part and privilege to be ready.

Going to sleep! What a good feeling after a hard day's work! It is delightful. Let us, all of us, pray and prepare that our going will be "just going to sleep," peaceful sleep to wake no more here; but on that shore where there is no night, no pain, no sorrow, no trials, no partings, no cares, and where rest is assured to the children of the Lord.

CONCERNING A GOOD AND GREAT MAN

Dr. J. P. Barrett, Editor of *The Herald of Gospel Liberty*, speaking of the late Willis J. Lee says:

Death of Willis J. Lee

In the early days of our ministry we found a friend in the person of Willis J. Lee, of Nansemond County, Va. Till the day of his death, we always counted him among our dear friends. It was Tuesday afternoon, May 20, 1919, that our dear brother made the great surrender of his life and went back to God who gave it. During the morning of that day he had been busy on his truck farm. At noon he took dinner with his wife as usual, and then lay down to take a little rest. Mrs. Lee discovered that he was breathing hard, and undertook to minister to him, but it was too late, for in the space of a few moments he had quietly slipped away from earth and gone to be with Jesus. He was a warm friend to the Christian Church and to the cause of Christ. He was a man of means and was liberal toward the great enterprises of the denomination. He was especially interested in the Orphanage at Elon College, in the great missionary work of the Church, and also in our educational enterprises. Especially was he a great friend to Elon College. Then, too, he took great interest in the local church at Berea, Nansemond County, Va., where he held his membership for perhaps fifty years. When he died he was within five days of the fiftieth anniversary of his marriage to Miss Jennie Jones, who remained with him through all of his long and useful life, a faithful and devoted companion. Through his long journey in business and in church affairs, we cannot recall having seen him excited, or out of an even frame of mind even once. He was as gentle as a woman and true and faithful to his Lord and to His friends. His life among men was a blessing. He had been for the last few years in poor health, and yet he kept along most of the time and looked after his business affairs. It was only a few days before his sudden going that he gave $5,000.00 to Elon College, and he did it so quietly that you would have thought that it was nothing more in the way of an event in his life than the eating of a regular meal, but that was characteristic of the man. Memories of his life will long remain as the fragrance of sweet flowers to give comfort and joy to loved ones left behind. Good-bye, beloved brother, till we meet in the morning in the Father's house on high!

A LETTER

Ether, N. C., June 12, 1919.
Dear Brother Riddle:—

I injured my back by falling and carrying a heavy piece of wood last March. Later Myleitis developed and I have not been able to do any work since. I have been slowly but surely growing worse since.

I am interested very much in the work of the Kingdom. I trust you will pray for me that God may restore me back to health. I am sure that He is abundantly able to restore me.

I am sending you a few odds and ends which came to my mind while lying on my bed of affliction. You may use them if you think they are worth while.

W. H. FREEMAN.

Brother Freeman is a member of our Ether church and has been active in the Master's service in teaching and doing good work for his local church. Let the Brotherhood pray for Brother Freeman that he may be restored to health.

THIRD CHRISTIAN CHURCH BUYS PROPERTY

The Third Christian church has purchased the lots on the northwest corner of Thirty-third street and Llewellyn avenue, from C. Elmo Billups and Captain Francis for $3,500. This property is 100 by 110 and is adjoining the property now owned by the church.

The official board of the church made this purchase as a preliminary step towards the erection of a church for the congregation. A campaign towards this end is planned for the fall. The congregation has for some time been using a small wooden structure which was erected on their first property near the corner of Thirty-fourth and Llewellyn.—*Norfolk Ledger-Dispatch, Wednesday, June 11, 1919.*

DR. CHASE NEW HEAD OF NORTH CAROLINA'S UNIVERSITY

Dr. H. W. Chase, chairman of the faculty of the University of North Carolina, has been elected to the presidency of that institution to succeed the late Edward Kidder Graham.

Dr. Chase was born in Groveland, Mass., April 11, 1883, took his A. B. at Dartmouth in 1904, his A. M. in 1908 and his Ph. D. at Clark University in 1910. He has been connected with the University of North Carolina as Professor of Psychology about five years. He comes from a family of teachers and is expected to reflect greatly upon his newly elected position.

Miss Martha Stacy, Haverhill, Mass., the young lady chosen by the Burlington Sunday school as a missionary, is in Burlington this week. She conducted the Christian Endeavor meeting last Sunday evening, also spoke to the congregation of the church at the regular preaching hour. She made a good impression.

Last Sunday night lightning struck the Sellars Hosiery Mill, Burlington, N. C., and set the building on fire. The damage is about $40,000.00 with $25,000.00 insurance. The mill is owned by D. E. and C. V. Sellars of our Burlington church and we sympathize with them in their loss.

PASTOR AND PEOPLE

NOTICE

The Sunday School Convention of the Eastern Virginia Christian Conference will meet with Oakland Christian church, near Suffolk, Va., at 10 A. M., on Wednesday, July 23. By vote it was decided by the last session of the Convention to hold only a two days' session this year. The program, therefore, has been arranged accordingly. Let each superintendent keep this in mind in planning for the Convention. For information as to trains, see the pastor, Dr. I. W. Johnson's announcement in THE SUN. All together for a successful session. Meet us at Oakland on July 23 and 24.

G. O. LANKFORD,
Gen. Secretary.

Berkley, Va., Route 3.

(We have not received announcement from Brother Johnson.—*Editor.*)

MUSICIANS—TAKE NOTICE

The North Carolina Sunday School and Christian Endeavor Convention will meet with the Shallow Well Christian church near Jonesboro, N. C., July 15, 16, 17. Our president and secretary are planning for the very biggest and best Convention we have ever held. The music committee is anxious that the musical part of the Convention be "steadily on the job." Leaders of music in our Sunday schools are earnestly requested to be with us and to use their best efforts to have their singing classes represented. We especially ask that all who can play an instrument of any kind to be there to take part with our Convention orchestra. Bring your violin, your horns, or whatever instrument you play and tell us who you are. We want to know you and have you join us in our work. We will use our regular convention song book, "Joyful Praise," published by the A. J. Showalter Co., for sale by Alfred Williams and Co., Raleigh, N. C.

Any members of our Committee will gladly give information concerning the work to any one interested. Get ready, come and help us.

GEORGE M. McCULLERS, Chairman,
PROF. J. H. MORING,
JOHN R. BROWN, .
MISS MAY STEPHENSON,
W. L. THOMAS,
Committee.

A SERMONETTE

(G. C. Crutchfield)

Henceforth there is laid up for me a crown of righteousness, which the Lord, the righteous Judge shall give me at that day; and not me only, but unto all them also that love His appearing. II Timothy 4:8.

These are the words of a man who had given his life for the Lord's cause since he was stricken to the ground on his way to Damascus. We find that from that day

until his death he followed the Lord, and gave his life for his Master's service. We also find that his life was spent in helping others to find Christ. This should be the object of every man and every woman.

When we read of the life and work that this man did we should not become discouraged, but when we have persecutions and hardships to bear we should only be drawn closer unto Christ.

Hebrews 12:1, 2, we find these words of Paul: "Wherefore seeing we also are compassed about with so great a cloud of witnesses, let us lay aside every weight, and the sin which doth so easily beset us and let us run with patience the race that is set before us, looking unto Jesus the Author and Finisher of our faith." If a man who had been caught and imprisoned could have such hope and courage, why can't the Christians of today who have no such trials as those to overcome? Because we are not living as close to God as we should or could. We undertake to run the race and we do not lay aside all that hinders us we cannot make it to the end. So let us get everything out of the way and make a sure race for Christ, and let our light so shine that the world may see our good works and glorify our Father in Heaven. When we do this we can say as Paul has said, "There is a crown of righteousness laid up for me."

Elon College, N. C.

WHY DON'T THEY DO SOMETHING?

While reading the proceedings of the Southern Christian Convention my attention was arrested by the following resolutions:

Report of Committee on Evangelism

Resolved:

1. That the Southern Christian Convention, through its Home Mission Board, employ an evangelist to take the field at the earliest day possible for the purpose of aiding our people, as far as possible, in evangelizing those who have not been brought to Christ.

2. That said evangelist aid in securing services for all pastorless churches within the bounds of said Convention.

I think the following question is in order: Why has the evangelist not been employed by the Home Mission Board? I have been trying to answer this question for myself. At first I tried to satisfy my mind with the thought that perhaps the man was not available. But when I began to reason I found that I had no foundation for such an argument. Then I thought that this delinquency on the part of the Board might be due to inadequate means. But my reasoning broke down when I thought of the money that is now available.

Some of our leaders complain because our denomination has not grown as rapidly as some other denominations that are not so old. The answer is not far to seek. The theoretical eloquence that we so often hear in our Conferences and Conventions must give place to practical methods and practical applications. The above resolution, no doubt, was prompted by an evangelistic motive, but it has not been backed up by an evangelistic drive and push. Are we afraid to undertake new and bigger things? The above resolution calls for one evangelist. The Baptist Convention called for and employed one hundred evangelists and their slogan is, "one hundred thousand souls for Christ and the church this year." Are we not willing to undertake one hundredth part of what the Baptist people are undertaking?

I want it distinctly understood that I am not writing this article to criticize, but to stimulate action. Evangelism is a thing that we content ourselves to talk about, and not a thing that we really do. Evangelism is no commonplace thing. It is a big thing—that of winning men to Christ. It calls, not for comfort and complacency, but for concentration and consecration. People must be won to Christ before they can be trained for Christ, and not until we feel, and feel deeply, the impulse of evangelism will Christ be enthroned in the hearts of men.

                                R. F. Brown.
Durham, N. C.

ADOPTING AND ADAPTING

In the 1917 *Annual,* on page 121, a recommendation is made against "ice cream and oyster suppers to raise money for church purposes"—and certainly not to raise money for any other purpose. What do you think of that? It was adopted in solemn council by one of our Conferences, and it should have been, but was it carefully and prayerfully observed by the churches whose representatives helped to place it upon our records? You will find the writer's name subscribed to that recommendation and yet the thing has been done at one of my charges since its adoption. If it had been properly laid before my good people I feel sure they would have gladly abided by it, consequently I have no one to blame but myself. Therefore, brother pastor, and delegates, we are not doing our duty unless we carry the actions of our Conferences back to those who committed to us the responsibility and privilege of representing them.

In conclusion permit me to summarize by saying we should be very careful in adopting resolutions; we should be just as careful in seeing them given a proper charge; in taking an inventory of what they have meant during the past year, or years; and in making them affirmative rather than negative. Our Conferences and Conventions are great, good times. Resolutions thrive, but unless they come up out of a soil well filled with prayer and meditation, nurtured throughout the year with abundant rains of toil, and unless they be kissed daily by the sunshine of faith they will wither and die. Prayer, toil, and faith like that bestowed upon the resolutions which contain the first actual launchings of our great missions, and college endowment campaigns will make resolutions worthwhile and the hours of resolving memorable and sacred.

                                J. G. Truitt.

SUFFOLK LETTER

Paul says, "the fashion of this world passeth away," and Isaiah says, "the flower fadeth; but the word of our God shall stand forever." The best things are the most permanent things. Change is a mark of the transient and evanescent. The value of things is measured by their permanence or capacity for repetition. Good things grow better by repetition, while bad things grow worse by repetition. A good piece of music grows better by repetition, while poor music soon wears out. God's great creations repeat themselves without loss of interest or value. The motion of the heavenly bodies, the rising and setting sun, the four seasons, the flow of rivers, the ebb and flood of the tide, the pole star; all these repeat themselves without change and without loss of interest or value to mankind.

"The Athenians and strangers there spent their time in nothing else, but either to tell, or to hear some new thing;" but all that passed away, while their great orations and poems, great architecture, great sculpture and great paintings remain as models. These all repeat themselves in all the centuries since their day. Mendelssohn's "Wedding March," and his "Elijah" and "St. Paul," two great oratorios, require repetition to be appreciated. Light music is at its best when first heard; but great music grows upon the mind by repetition. As a rule the "taking things" are light and will not bear repetition. Moving pictures make a great contrast with great paintings. Human conduct can be measured in its social and moral worth by the merit of its repetition. Good conduct may be repeated with personal satisfaction and public approbation. Good sermons, good music, good stories, may all be repeated with profit; in fact the test is whether they will bear repetition. The poor books are read, pass out of print, and are forgotten, while great books remain on the shelf and are re-read, and are recommended to other readers. The Bible is the *One Book* that remains in print, is reprinted in larger numbers than any other book, and is printed in more languages. It is gaining in favor all the time. Its pages do not exhaust by reading. There is a depth, a divine-human quality in its message, and a response in the soul to its teaching, that makes it the *The Book* for the home, the church, and the world.

In the smallest details of life truth and falsehood can be tested by repetition. Truth can be repeated, even under oath in a court of justice; while falsehood can be overthrown by evidence. Gossip does its mischief by repetition; but it dies of its own shallowness. All the delicacies of life are tiresome when oft repeated. Bread never surfeits the appetite; but delicacies do. The plain foods may be repeated with delight and physical benefit; the luxuries break down health and enjoyment by constant use. All attempts at satisfying the appetite with special dishes, all tempting drinks, and all artificial tonics, weaken the system and rob it of the pleasure which belongs to sane eating and drinking. God has so made man and the world that all service and all eating should be a pleasure. All devices for entertaining men break down by excesses or artificial methods. Plain food, honest work, pure religion, and commonsense manners will furnish the average man with a lifetime of usefulness and happiness. A good rule is to do what you can afford to repeat without injury to self or offense to others.

                                W. W. Staley.

PROGRAM
THE MISSIONARY ASSOCIATION TO BE HELD AT NOON DAY, JUNE 28, 29, 1919

Saturday—10:00 *O'clock A. M.*

Devotional Services ....Rev. C. M. Dollar
10:20—Enrollment of Ministers and Delegates
10:40—Opening address by the President
11:00—Preaching ....Rev. G. D. Hunt
12:00—Dinner.

Afternoon Session—1:30 *O'clock*

Devotional Services ....A. H. Shephard
1:45—The Missionary Outlook ....Rev. J. D. Dollar
2:15—Address ....Dr. J. O. Atkinson
3:15—Address ....Rev. J. H. Hughes
4:00—Business Session

Evening Session—8:00 *O'clock*

Sermon by Rev. E. M. Carter

Sunday—9:00 *O'clock A. M.*

Sunday School conducted by Superintendent
9:45—Sunday Schools and Missions..Rev. G. D. Hunt
What can be accomplished by our women
in Mission work?........Rev. E. M. Carter
11:00—Preaching by Dr. J. O. Atkinson
Adjournment.

J. T. CLACK,
J. J. CARTER,
J. M. WELCH, *Committee.*

TO THE CHURCHES AND PASTORS OF THE ALABAMA CHRISTIAN CONFERENCE

Dear Brethren:—You remember that the 1917 session of the body appointed a committee to investigate the field and make some recommendation, with reference to grouping the churches of this conference, into groups or pastorates. This committee was not ready to report at last session of the conference, and was continued.

We have carefully and prayerfully looked into the situation as best we can and have decided to recommend the following groups, to the next session of the conference. We are publishing them that you may be considering them, and if you think advisable, plan your work for next year accordingly. We will recommend the following groups:

Group No. 1—Noon Day, Rock Stand, Rock Springs and Mt. Zion.

Group No. 2—Lowell, Antioch, Forest Home and Bethany.

Group No. 3—New Hope, Pleasant Grove and Christiana.

Group No. 4—McGuire's Chapel, Beulah, Wadley and Corinth.

Group No. 5—Cragford, New Harmony and Spring Hill.

Group No. 6—Shady Grove, Dingler's Chapel, New Home and Macedonia.

Now you will note that two of the groups recommended have only three churches, but you will see if you study the situation, that in the territory occupied by these churches, or right near them, there is a fine field for missionary work, and it is territory that we should occupy, and the pastors of these groups could

do the work, to the better advantage than any one else. Let us consider the above groups, having the good of the cause in our hearts, and not look at the matter from a selfish stand point. Let us not say, ''Will it suit me best,'' but let's ask the Living God to show us what is best for His cause and we will make a safe decision.

COMMITTEE.

DR. LONG WRITES FROM SOUTH CAROLINA

Florence, S. C., June 5, 1919.

Editor Christian Sun:—I am spending some time with Mrs. Long on a visit to my only son, Joseph, and his friend in this city. Joseph graduated from Union Christian College with the class of 1912. His wife, nee Lenora Vinson, of Muncie, Ill., also from Union Christian College.

I came via Raleigh and spent one night with Mr. and Mrs. Chas. H. Belvin. I learned, through my daughter, Mrs. Belvin, that our good brother, W. B. Mann, had been too feeble to attend any business at his store for several days.

Mrs. Long and I have had a delightful time here, attending the State Sunday School Convention. The 42nd annual Convention of the South Carolina Sunday School Association closed here tonight, after having completed the greatest program, according to the delegates attending from nearly every county in the State, that the Association has ever known. E. O. Excell led the singing and many of the State's ablest educators took part in the exercises. Also speakers from other States.

As South Carolina,—with the exception of Louisiana, has more illiterates in proportion to the population, her leading men and women are putting forth a mighty effort to have every one, of all races, educated. Hundreds of boys and girls, just home from college, will give their services, free to teach night schools, during the summer vacation.

When the late Kemp P. Battle was called to the head of the University of North Carolina, I was, on his motion, chosen agent to canvass South Carolina for students for the University of North Carolina, as the University of South Carolina had not sufficiently recovered from Conby rule, and carpet bag government, to open its doors. A mighty change has taken place in South Carolina. Then she was poor and discouraged: No factories to speak of, now manufactures about as much cotton as North Carolina, or Massachusetts. Her farmers are prosperous and happy, and as for patriotism, one of her Governors furnished more boys for the United States army, in the last war, than any Governor in the United States, and as for liberality in giving to the cause of Christian Education, only ask Jew and Catholic, Baptist, Presbyterian and Methodist. The Methodists requested the village of Bennettsville, S. C., to give $12,000 as a centenary offering. The village Methodists responded with a little over $132,000. Mark you, South Carolina will not be ''next to foot'' many years in anything ''worth while.'' The Governor of North Carolina will have to introduce another subject to the Governor of South Carolina, outside of ''drinks.''

D. A. LONG.

UNCLE WELLONS GOES VISITING

He Finds Suitable Husbands and Wives. He asks Questions And Offers Advice to Companion Seekers

I left home May 23, 1919, for Waverly, Va., and on to Barrett's church to attend an annual home coming. I stopped at Waverly with R. E. West. The next day Rev. J. L. Foster took me into the neighborhood of the church. We spent the night with Mr. H. E. Rollins. Here he and his sister have long lived together at the old homestead, and some man has missed a good wife, and some woman a good husband.

That night a heavy rain came but we went to the church the next morning, and through the mud and water the crowd began to assemble until we had the house full. We had a pleasant service. Brother Foster gave them a fine sermon, and after dinner I did the talking. After we got through with the services I sat there and shook the hands of all the congregation, asking: "Who are your father and mother?" and more particularly, "Who were your grandparents?" Then I could identify them. They left a kind remembrance on the table as they passed.

I told them I was naturally born in this vicinity, January 1, 1826, the first day of the week, the first day of the month, and the first day of the year. But that was a matter of record. In ten or fifteen feet of where I then sat, Monday after the fourth Sunday of August, 1837, I was spiritually born. I got a little spark of grace that has gone with me through life this far.

Brother J. W. White took me to the home of J. F. Wellons and sister, the old Wellons homestead of my grandfather where I saw the graves of Grandfather Wellons and wife as I had never seen before. Here the neighbors came in and we had a pleasant evening. Here were the two bachelors again and my cousin, Olive who is small in stature, but fine in appearance. I can't see why some bachelor hasn't long since taken her away from her bachelor brother, leaving him to seek an associate.

We took dinner on Monday with Brother R. M. Jones, whose wife was a Wellons. We went, that afternoon, to Hebron church and heard Rev. Mr. Roane preach an extra good sermon, and then we spent the night with R. C. Hines and family, another cousin. Tuesday evening we went out to the cemetery that contained the bodies of my mother and father and grandfather and grandmother Stephenson. Here I spent a good while with friends, in pleasant interview and prayer. Brother J. W. White and R. C. Hines promised to see that a wire fence is placed around my parents' graves.

I spent the night with Brother J. W. White and family and visited Mrs. A. E. Hines the next morning and that evening Brother White took me to Windsor, and I don't know how to say enough thanks to Brother White for his kindness in taking me everywhere I wanted to go.

Stopping at Brother R. E. Hines, P. M. Hines, T. H. Harris, I met my old friend, R. C. Richardson. Here I visited different families and had so many callers. I visited the daughters of my old friend, Frank Baines.

I found Misses Sally and Poke and other friends there. I, yet, can't see why some bachelors or widowers don't sweep them right off and break up that old maid's home. Their father and I were reared together, and if he had been living and there, I would have heard him say, "Howdy, Jim!" and I would have replied, "Howdy Frank!"

I spent two nights with the dear little family of my cousin, T. H. Harris. Friday evening Brother R. C. Richardson took me to Spring Hill, to the Memorial Day services where I used to go to church eighty years ago and saw the same old spring gushing forth. Here I saw so many old friends and visited the graves of so many friends that had long since passed across the Jordan

As Brother Richardson told me of the old homes that I used to know, I couldn't recognize any of the places as new houses had all been built.

While in this section I spent every hour so pleasantly with children and grandchildren of my old friends of the days past and nearly everybody were cousins; and how pleasant it was to be there! On Saturday morning I "ran" down to Suffolk, where Col. J. E. West and Rev. E. T. Cotten met me at the station. We hurried away to the Seaboard road, meeting with obstructions and freight trains. The Colonel succeeded in getting me on the train, turning me over to the captain to take me to a seat in the car. Here I met Dr. J. O. Atkinson and Miss Mary D. Atkinson, who secured me a ticket and arranged my trip to Henderson. Here I went to the home of Miss Ayscue where a number of friends came in to see me, and I spent the night so pleasantly, but it would be dangerous for a widower to go around there if he wanted to go without sore shins. Sunday I attended the church with Rev. R. L. Williamson and we had a pleasant service. I talked for the people and assisted in administering the sacrament. I attended the service again at night and Brother Williamson gave us a fine sermon. I spent the night with W. N. Newman, who kindly took me to see a few friends on Monday morning, and safely put me on the train for Durham.

At Durham I spent two or three hours looking after a little matter of clothing, and spent the remainder of the time in shaking hands and speaking words of greeting to old friends. I promised to return in a few days to visit a friend older than I am. I boarded the train for Elon College. On my arrival, when I entered my room, how things were changed! The most of men have one hen to peck at them but as I have five or six you may guess the hair was pretty thin on the top of my head. But some of them had dispersed. I went into my room, and everything was turned around. Hot water and soap were exhausted on the floor. My room was calcimined. Some pieces of furniture were taken away with others in their places, everything turned around. But as I have so many hens pecking at me, I let them fix it to suit themselves, and make myself quite contented.

J. W. WELLONS.

Elon College, N. C.

THE CHRISTIAN ORPHANAGE

SUPERINTENDENT'S LETTER

We have received several letters this week containing checks for monthly offerings for the Orphanage from Sunday schools and telling us that the school had decided to give one collection each month toward the support of the Orphanage cause. We truly hope that each Sunday school that has not been making this monthly contribution will begin now. I am real anxious to get each school on the list this year. Work is made lighter when all pull together. It puts "pep" in the spirit of the work and all become more interested.

From now until the Thanksgiving offering comes in our income depends largely upon the Sunday school monthly offerings for support. Our schools should bear in mind that we have fifty-seven children and all we have to buy is very high. It costs us three times as much to live now as it did four years ago. Yet we have failed to get many of our Sunday schools to realize this fact and many of the schools that have been contributing one dollar per month for the last ten years still contribute one dollar. While everything the farmer has to sell is much higher in price and those who work for a salary get much larger salaries than a few years ago.

Some of our Sunday schools have increased their monthly offerings to help us meet the high prices we have to pay and they find it just as easy to raise the amount they now contribute each month as it was to raise the amount they contributed several years ago. Why can't all our schools take on the new spirit and see how much they can do? I believe each school could double its monthly offerings and find it just as easy to raise. The more we do, the more we find that we can do.

The home for small children should be and must be built. We will build this home as soon as we have the funds in hand to build it. I want to say that all contributions made for this building will be kept in a separate fund for this purpose and those who contribute may rest assured that it will not be spent for any other purpose. I am anxious to know how many persons in our denomination are interested in this undertaking and will show how much they are interested by their contributions for this home for the little children who are so much in need of a home of this kind.

How many would like to give us $100, $500, or $1,000 toward this building? Or have we one man or woman in our church who would like to give $10,000 to build the building?

I visited an orphanage in another state last year and several modern buildings were pointed out to me where one individual had contributed a building for the cause of the orphan children. What a beautiful monument it was, given in memory of some loved one to be a blessing for all time to come to the little helpless orphan children?

CHAS. D. JOHNSTON, Supt.

REPORT FOR JUNE 18, 1919

Amount brought forward, $6,506.31.

Children's Offerings

Freeman Horne Everett, 30 cents; Pauline Trotter, 20 cents; Lois Stout, 20 cents; Richard Bost, 20 cents; Irene Patton, 20 cents; Total, $1.10.

Sunday School Monthly Offerings

(Eastern Virginia Conference)

Isle of Wight C. H., $2.50; Franklin, $10.00; Rosemont. $5.00; Old Zion, $3.00; Windsor, $6.08; Berea, Nansemond, $10.00.

(North Carolina Conference)

Beulah, $1.50; Christian Chapel, $4.50; Ramseur, $2.45; Sanford, $8.68; Wentworth, $3.77; Shallow Well, $1.67; Youngsville, $5.00; Shiloh, $2.40; Hines' Chapel, $2.00; Durham, $5.00.

(Virginia Valley Conference)

Timber Ridge, $2.28; Concord, $3.79.

(Georgia Conference)

Rose Hill, $4.00.

(Alabama Conference)

Beulah, $1.26; Mt. Zion, $1.00; Total, $85.88.

Special Easter Offerings

Beulah Sunday school, (N. C.), $2.00; Palmyra Sunday school, $26.53; Joppa Sunday school, $3.92; Third Christian church, Norfolk, Va., $44.01; Total, $94.46.

Special Offerings

A. C. C. Office, Dr. J. F. Burnett, Sec., $34.50; Primary Department, Suffolk Christian S. S., $40.00; Willing Workers Society, Asheboro S. S., $3.75; Total, $78.25.

Total for the week, $282.04; Grand total, $6,788.35.

LETTERS FROM THE COUSINS

Dear Uncle Charley:—I am sorry I failed to write last month. I will try not to do so again. Hope all the little orphans are well and having a good time. Enclosed please find twenty cents, my dues for May and June. Lots of love.—*Irene Patton.*

I am glad to have your letter this week. We will forgive you for not writing last month if you will promise to be real good in the future.—"*Uncle Charley.*"

Dear Uncle Charley:—Here I come again. School is out and I am having a fine time playing. I guess all boys do if they like play as well as I do and especially ball game. Hope all the cousins are well and having a fine time. Enclosed find twenty cents, my dues for May and June. Love to all.—*Richard Bost.*

Our little boys like to play ball, too. If you could visit them you would have a good time.—"*Uncle Charley.*"

Dear Uncle Charley:—Here I come with my letter. Mother has been real sick. I am so glad she is better and hope she will soon be well again. I will be glad for the orphans to come to see us when Children's Day comes. Hope they are having a good time. Enclosed find twenty cents, my dues for May and June. Love to all.—*Lois Stout.*

I am glad your mother is better and hope she will

soon be entirely well. Your mother is your best friend. You must always be kind to her.—*"Uncle Charley."*

Dear Uncle Charley:—I am the only cousin that I know of in Asheboro. I have a nice time playing with my dolls as I am not large enough to help mother yet. I have no brother or sister so I play with my dollies. Enclosed find twenty cents, my dues for May and June. Love to you and the cousins.—*Pauline Trotter.*

I know you have a good time playing with your dolls. One good quality about the doll is that they don't cry.—*"Uncle Charley."*

Dear Uncle Charley:—I am sending my dues for April, May and June. I should have written before now and shall try to be more prompt hereafter. I was so anxious for a picture of the little girl who sings "Jesus Loves Me," but one never reached me. Love to all.—*Frances Horne Everett.*

I am sorry you did not get the picture of the little girl I mailed you sometime ago. I am mailing you another today. If you do not get it, let me know.— *"Uncle Charley."*

MISSIONARY

THE SUNDAY SCHOOLS AND MISSIONS

The following of our Sunday schools have voted to give one offering per month to missions and sent the amounts named during the month of April:

Durham, $11.02; Pleasant Grove, $2.15; Holy Neck, $2.90; Parks' Cross Roads, $1.50; Wentworth, 95c; Reidsville, $5.00; Haw River, $3.60; Pleasant Union, $2.50; Wadley, Ala., $1.04; New Elam, $2.56; Burlington, $176.74, (for three months); Ingram, $4.00; High Point, $3.77; Catawba Springs, $1.50; Parks' Cross Roads, $1.39; New Providence, $2.50; Spring Hill, $1.58; Holy Neck, 91c; Wadley, Ala., 86c; Lanett, Ala., $5.00; Linville, Va., $1.77; Total, $233.20.

The following sent in during May: Durham, $8.30; Chapel Hill, $3.00; Roanoke, Ala., $1.14; Isle of Wight C. H., $2.50; Reidsville, $3.69; Wentworth, $1.12; New Lebanon, $3.19; Beulah, Ala., $1.12; Lebanon, (Semora), N. C., $2.81; Salem Chapel, $1.03; Union (Alamance), 65c; New Providence, $1.25; Durham, $10.00; Ingram, Va., $3.00; Catawba Springs, $1.54; Lanett, Ala., $3.50; Roanoke, Ala., (J. L. Liles, Sec.), $1.05; Pleasant Grove, Va., $2.85; Linville, Va., $2.35; Lebanon, (Semora, N. C.), $2.63; Pleasant Union, $1.50; Parks' Cross Roads, $1.40; High Point, $3.20; Total, $63.00.

These schools are trying out the plan, "as much for others as for ourselves," and give one Sunday's offering each month to missions, one to the Orphanage, the other two Sundays to their local expenses. The writer's firm conviction is that any school adopting this plan will as easily secure the funds with which to buy its own literature and pay its own local expenses as it will

by spending all its money on itself. In fact a Sunday school that spends all its money on itself is like a person who does the same thing, namely, always hard-up. It is just as easy for a Sunday school to be self-centered as it is for an individual to be so. And isn't it a pity to teach and train a Sunday school to be selfish?

A good Baptist lady told the writer not long since that the school of which she was a member never spend any part of its regular Sunday collections upon itself, but gave all to missions, and then individual members of the school made up the money with which to buy literature—that they wanted their school to think, act, give in terms of others.

Mission Study in the Schools

But along with the giving for the Orphanage and for missions, many of our schools are adopting the plan of studying missions either the whole period once per month, or say five minutes of the lesson period every Sunday. This is splendid. The writer wishes all our schools would in some way study missions, give our young people the opportunity of understanding the needs, the pressing, crying needs of this sin-cursed world for the Good News of our Lord and His power to save. If our children knew the needs, they would have pity, even if the grown-ups will not. How many children in our Sunday schools know anything of factory conditions, say in China or Japan, and of the mothers and the children there who toil from twelve to sixteen hours a day, seven days in the week the year round?

After his recent visit to China, Robert E. Speer said, "It is heart-breaking to go into the great cotton factories and see the men and women and children, chiefly women and children, eight years old and upward, working in long twelve-hour shifts, seven days in the week, and every week of the year."

In Japan the industrial system is working ruin to hundreds of thousands of poor innocent before they have known what life really is. Dr. Gulick in his "Working Women of Japan," says: "As a rule the girls are apprenticed for from two to three years immediately on leaving the primary school, at an age therefore of twelve to thirteen. They barely earn their living, although they work from day-break to ten or eleven at night—from fifteen to eighteen hours a day. The hygiene and moral conditions are about as bad as they can be. It is estimated that one-half of the girls are ruined before the close of their apprenticeship." This sentence is quoted from "Women Workers of the Orient": "In another city in Northern Japan, where fifteen hundred girls between the ages of twelve to twenty-eight are working in 130 factories, the hours are reported to be from five in the morning until ten at night, with an hour off at noon. There is, of course, no Sunday rest day, but two holidays a month are granted. The girls are given food and clothing and from fifteen to forty cents a month in money."

What Japan must have to make child-life bearable and worth while is Christianity. Millions are perishing before their day for no other reason than that they know not our Christ, Him who said: "It is not your Father's will that one of these little ones should perish.'' And Who also said, ''Suffer the little children to come unto me and forbid them not for of such is the Kingdom of Heaven.'' But the little ones are not permitted to come unto Him, for neither they themselves nor their parents know anything of Him. Give the Sunday school a chance to learn the real needs of this world for Christ.

J. O. ATKINSON.

CHRISTIAN EDUCATION

BURLINGTON OVERSTEPS THE MARK

We have two congregations that are deeply engrossed in building plants for themselves at this time—Holland, (Va.), and Burlington, (N. C.) I was at Holland the second Sunday in May and that band of noble Christians added three stars to the card of recognition. I was at Burlington the second Sunday in June, and this grand old Church more than doubled its quota.

It is no use to say that sacrifice for a local situation hinders the general enterprises of the Church. Both these Churches did splendidly in the mission drive and Burlington has also during her building operation undertaken the support of a missionary in the foreign field. God somehow enables people who do to keep on doing. Have you also noticed that the growing Churches are the giving ones? Have you ever heard of a Church that grew and did not give? Have you ever known of a generous man's not prospering? Can you conceive of God's giving back on His promise? And has, He not promised if we prove Him to open us the windows of Heaven and pour us out blessings such that we cannot receive them?

At Burlington I had good help. Trustee D. R. Fonville and Editor C. B. Riddle hit the trail with me and that meant success. The Fonville family gave a thousand dollars and Rev. C. B. Riddle, Mrs. Riddle and little Miss Ruth Teague Riddle are the first one hundred per cent family we have. Each of them made a subscription, and Miss Ruth is the youngest contributor to the fund, nineteen months old, and the fund is being being raised in the year nineteen nineteen. Her parents said: ''We desire that her first gift should be to our Alma Mater, one day to be hers we hope.'' Is that not fine? How do they do it? Brother Riddle not only edits THE CHRISTIAN SUN, but also The Tither, and he practices what he preaches.

Funds This Week

Seven funds of $1,000 each were founded this week. They follow:

John R. Foster, joining his brother, Rev. Jas. L., in a fund of $2,000 in memory of their sainted parents.

Jas. P. Montgomery for himself and wife; Charles A. Walker for himself and wife; Capt. W. H. Turrentine for himself and wife; John W. Fonville in memory of his parents; L. J. Fonville for himself and family; and Dr R. M. Morrow for himself and wife.

Two More Weeks

We have but two more weeks now to complete the campaign. I have faith that we shall overtop the mark. I have never doubted that we would. I know these people of the Christian Church. I know their generous hearts. I know their love for Elon. I am gratified, but not surprised at their magnificent generosity in this drive, and God has great things in store for them in the days ahead.

These two weeks are great weeks for the field men. Pray for us that we may be fit representatives of our Master and of His cause in these closing days of our greatest denominational drive.

W. A. HARPER.

THE LORD'S LABOR PROBLEM*

(Text: ''The harvest truly is plenteous, but the laborers are few: pray ye therefore the Lord of the harvest that he will send forth laborers into his harvest.'') Matt. 9:37-38.

The Minister and His Call

These were unusual days in which Christ and His disciples were living. But as unusual as they were, they were no different from the present hour, especially in regard to the needs of humanity. Since Christ is gone He is depending upon the minister to supply this need, being aided by the Holy Spirit. The present-day need of mankind is great and no ordinary person can supply this need.

That these are unusual times no one needs to be told. About four years ago the fire was kindled around the melting pot of the age, and new things have been continually springing forth. History is being made. Nations are being born. We have never lived in a time like this. God is doing and seeking to do great things. Yea, I may say God is about to do a great thing. This new thing will not be an act of creation. God's creative acts were all completed centuries ago. But this new act will express itself in the form of a ''re-making.'' God is about to remake the marred world. He has been trying to accomplish this momenteous task since the day when man just became marred; but the task is great and the work has been hindered on account of the labor problem. God has never ceased to honor men and women by calling them to preach His Word and make disciples of all nations.

The world's war-time experiences have prepared it for spiritual leadership. New calls are heard, new problems are here. Problems not so much of rebuilding roads, reconstructing bridges, clearing the debres from the overrun soil, rehabilitating the shattered territory, rebuilding the devastated cities; but problems of remaking and remolding the devastated souls of men. This particular need was not caused by war conditions so much as by the pre-war conditions.

The work of the minister is negative as well as positive. He must defeat the designs of the evil one and build up the crumbling walls of devastated souls. His work is great and no ordinary man can do it. An architect with ordinary ability can build a house or a ship but God wants specialists in His harvest field. The minister is such a specialist. May his kind increase! The Lord is encountering and has ever encountered very serious handicaps for lack of laborers. The situation is appalling. Shall we not aid in mobilizing this man-power adequate to the demands of the hour?

This is a great undertaking, but the call of Christ is imperative. The harvest is ready. The laborers are few. Pray ye. If we fail to respond to this command we thrust the burden of a keen disappointment upon the heart of our Lord. Let us not be guilty of this. The Master is counting on us, not to *make* ministers, but to pray the Lord to send them forth.

It may be that some of us will have to help God answer this prayer for more laborers. It may be that He cannot answer your prayer by sending some one else. He may want you as a laborer. Is the sacrifice too great? No. God never makes a demand that is too great, or calls for a sacrifice that we cannot meet. To enter the ministry is no sacrifice. It is a joy.. It is a privilege, an honor, that all men do not receive. The Gospel ministry has a charm that is unprecedented..

The Minister and His Equipment

While we are mindful of the urgency of the King's business and the need of more ministers we should not overlook the call for special equipment. The first duty of every minister is to prepare himself for his work if it is within the range of possibility. This he must do if he is to meet God's expectations and demands of him in these days of thoroughness in which we are living. In order to fulfill his high calling in the salvation of souls, building Christian character, and drawing men closer to God and the things of His Kingdom the minister should spare no time in his preparation. The minister should not secure this preparation in order that he may look wise and walk with an exalted gaze. There are too many star-gazers in the world already. What the world needs and what Christ wants is not the Priest or Levite but "Good Samaritans"—men who can look down and see the oppressed. God needs men who can reach out their arms and hearts and help men. The minister must be a man who can read human nature, interpret life, discover values, and direct the course of every religious energy, just as the compass directs the ship with her cargo of values to the port where the values may express themselves.

Thus realizing the vast field of labor and the varied problems confronting him, the minister should not content himself with less than four years of college training. This goal is not too high for any ambitious person who is blessed with good health and possessed with a will to work.

The minister must have heart training as well as head training. His true business is the enlargement of life. To this end he must bend every fiber of his being. His most effective weapon is the Holy Spirit, his strong hold is the proclamation of the good news; he must illustrate with his own life the prize which is within reach of every man who will lay aside every weight and run with patience the race that is set before him.

The Minister and His Reward

What is the minister's reward? This question, no doubt, is one of the first questions the prospective minister asks. But why should he ask this question? Why not proceed without inquiry? There is a reason. None of us would accept employment with an individual, a company, or a corporation without definite assurance of adequate compensation. You do not only demand *something* for your labor, but you must know just how *much* you are to have and *when* you are to get it. This is a right and a privilege that belongs to every person. Men must have a living. The minister is a man, therefore, he is no exception.

By turning to the *Christian Annual* for 1918, I find that we have about seventy-five active ministers in the Southern Christian Convention. I have further discovered that the 235 churches which have a membership of 22,886 paid these ministers last year $46,714.08—an average salary of $622.85. The average truck driver or bank janitor makes more money than that. And yet the minister with all his preparation is called upon to serve in a more important capacity for less compensation. Shame! He must be the most active man in his community. He must make as many calls as the busiest and most popular doctor. He must do as much walking as an industrial insurance agent. He must rival the best banker as a financier. He must know how to raise money and keep folks in a good humor. He must do as much talking as a politician, and three times a week bring to his people a message from God. Should the minister have pay for this? Some people think not. The average amount paid per member on pastor's salaries for 1918 was $2.04. It does seem to me that we ought to pray for ourselves before we pray the Lord of harvest for more laborers.

*Abstract of a sermon preached by Rev. R. F. Brown recently before a congregation of the Durham Christian church.

ODDS AND ENDS

We should not seek honor but strive to do right; then honor will come unsought. If you would really be happy, seek to make others happy. You will become happy in doing so.

Why not all unite for the common cause of righteousness? Certainly we are all striving for the same heaven. Our daily lives are sermons to those around us. Brother, what sort of sermons are you preaching?

We should do right not simply because there is a hell to shun and a heaven to gain, but because it is right. We should be careful what we say. A word carelessly spoken may cause some heart to become broken.

W. H. FREEMAN.

Teacher—What is an alibi?
Bright Boy—Being somewhere where you aint.—*Life*.

* *

"Is your son ambitious?"
"Very. He wants some day to pitch a no-hit, no-run game."—*Detroit Free Press*.

* *

The fly lays four times each summer, and eighty eggs each time. The descendants of one female fly in a single season may number 2,080,320.

THE BY-AND-BY BOY

He lives in the house of things-never-done,
The by-and-by boy I know—
The lights of the windows are broken and out,
And they let in the rain and snow.

In-a-minute's the schedule he works on, you see,
And duty waits on a side track;
His intentions are good—there's no fault found
with them—
The *doing's* the thing that they lack!

"And what happens," you say, "to the by-and-by
boy?"
Let anyone answer who can—
Unless he soon changes his name, he becomes,
'Tis certain, a *Too-Late Man!*
—*Adelbert F. Caldwell, in Child's Gem.*

SCOTLAND SAVED BY A THISTLE

Billy, a bright-eyed boy, in his eagerness after bow-
ers, had wounded his hand on the sharp, prickly thistle.
"I do wish there was no such thing in the world as a
thistle," he said in hot temper.

But his father said calmly: "And yet the Scottish
nation think so much of it that they engrave the thistle
on the national arms."

"It is the last bower I should pick out," said Billy.
"I am sure they could have found a great many nicer
ones even among the weeds."

"But once this thistle did them such good service,"
said the father, "that they learned to esteem it very
highly. One time the Danes invaded Scotland, and
they prepared to make an attack upon a sleeping garrison. So the Danes crept along barefooted, as still as
possible, until they were almost on the spot. Just at
that moment a barefooted Dane stepped on a great
thistle, and the hurt made him utter a sharp, shrill cry
of pain. The sound in the still night awoke the sleeping Scotch soldiers, and each man sprang to arms. They
fought with very great bravery, and the invaders were
driven back with great slaughter. So you see this
thistle saved Scotland, and ever since it has been placed
of their seals and emblems as their national flower."

"Well," said Billy, "I would never suspect that so
small and ugly a thing could save a nation."—*Exchange.*

A STRONG FAMILY

"You just ought to feel my muscle, papa," said
Johnny; "ain't it big and hard!"

The blue blouse and the flannel shirt were pushed up
into wrinkles at the shoulder, and a very soft and pink
arm presented itself proudly for the father's inspection.

"Pretty good for seven years," said papa, smiling.
"I hope some day to see you as strong as a family 1
know, who carry the world on their shoulders."

"What's their name?" asked Johnny, forgetting his
muscle at this first hint of a story.

"Their name is Never," answered the father with a
queer little wrinkle at each eye corner, as if a smile
was curled up there.

"Never! What a funny name!" exclaimed Johnny.
What are their other names?"

"Oh, there are a lot of them. There is Mr. Never-
drink; he has such clear eyes and such a steady step,
you'd know him anywhere; a strong fellow is Mr.
Never-drink. He is always ready to lift his end of the
log.

"Another is Mr. Never-swear; you will know him by
the company he keeps, and I suppose he grows strong
by not wasting his breath. Then there's Mr. Never-lie,
everybody trusts him; and Mr. Never-forget, who loses
nothing; and Mr. Never-be-idle, who does the world's
work; and Mr Never-be-discouraged—"

Papa stopped and laughed aloud, for Johnny was in
the midst of a big yawn. "You don't seem to care
much about my strong young people, Jack," he said.

"I like stories about sho-nuff people," owned Johnny.

"All right. Once there was a little boy who wanted
to be very strong—oh, as strong as Samson. So he went
to the strongest man on N. Street, and asked him how
he got so strong and hardy. 'By never touching strong
drink,' said the man on N. Street. He asked another
steady fellow. 'Never swear,' said the man; 'it takes
you into low company, where God and men are dishonored.' Another said 'Never lie.' A single lie takes
away a man's courage.—"

"Who was that little boy, papa?" interrupted
Johnny.

"He was that little boy that I want my little boy to
be," answered the father. "I want him to make
friends with the Nevers, because they are the friends
of God, and their family motto is, 'Thus saith the Lord,
Thou shalt not.'"—*Exchange.*

Why She Wanted a New One—Ethel, who has lately
been blessed with a baby sister, said to her mother one
day:

"I wish I had a new doll!".

"A new doll?" said her mother. "Why, your old
doll is as good as ever."

"Well," answered Ethel, "so am I just as good as
ever; but the angels gave you a new baby."—*Cleveland
Plain Dealer.*

* *

Enough State Legislatures have responded to the
poetic appeal of the Prohibitionists: Drink to me only
with thine eyes.—*New York Evening Sun.*

* *

Even the Prohibitionists would like to see food prices
take a drop or two.—*Boston Transcript.*

* *

A dog is to be appreciated because he does not pretend to be anything except a dog.

WORSHIP AND MEDITATION

SUNDAY EVENING MEDITATION

"It is The Spirit That Quickeneth."

Everything we look upon has its message for us. "The heavens declare the glory of God and the firmanent showeth His handiwork. Day unto day uttereth speech and night unto night showeth knowledge." "There is no speech or language where their voice is not heard."

In the rising sun and the setting thereof He has set the tabernacle for His voice. In every budding tree and blossoming flower, He has set a throne from which issues His infinite love. Great is the Lord and greater to be praised.

When we sit in the sanctuary all that our eyes behold speaks to us. Everything in the construction and furnishing thereof is placed there to speak to us. If this is not so it should be so.

The church is the one institution given us for the specific purpose of imparting the inspiring word and the Holy Spirit of God. We behold the Cross. It is the supreme symbol of all the church represents. It is therefore the supreme symbol of the quickening spirit of all things, and nowhere should we be without its presence. Everywhere should the Cross appear before us to convey to us the inspiring message of Christ's sacrifice. Of course it brings to us a very sad story and yet it was the most joyous event which ever transpired. For the death of our Lord is most far-reaching in its significance for the good of humanity. It set in motion life which can never die. It sent into the world this spirit of our Lord which quickeneth.

But it matters not how forceful and beautiful the messages of things; it matters not how clarion the voices we hear; it matters not how inspired the church; it matters not how inspired the Word; we ourselves must be inspired to appreciate any of it. We ourselves when standing before a primrose must be inspired if we would behold therein the throne of God. We ourselves when opening the Bible must be inspired or else its messages will be meaningless. Every day the Bible should be new and gripping to us and it can be this only through our own inspiration and hungerings for it. The *church* cannot impart its divine message to us if we are not inspired to its life. "It is the spirit that quickeneth," and by it the church must be and is new to us every week.

Thus, the Holy Spirit indwells the church because He indwells the believer. Thus, the Holy Spirit is fruitful in the believer only as the believer appropriates Him. The fruit of the Spirit is love, joy, peace, long suffering, gentleness, meekness," etc. These are the manifest fruits of an inspired believer. Thus, the Holy Spirit is of use to us only when we accept Him and appreciate Him and apply Him to the issues of our lives.

Portsmouth, N. H.   H. E. ROUNTREE.

MORAL ADVANTAGES OF PHYSICAL POWER

Many who are weak physically are strong intellectually, and have made a success of their work. Living and dead examples could be given if necessary. Some who are strong physically are weak intellectually and there are different causes for this condition, which need not be stated, as the reflective mind can see them. And it is a self-evident fact which needs no proof. Have seen some appear delicate, but they were charged with a full amount of electricity. Touch them at any point in their physical and intellectual departments and they have power. Their magnetic influence attracts and holds. Then, too, their work is such as to impel and compel them to do it on time, and in a right way. This has much to do with their efficiency and power.

One who has nothing to do does nothing because he has nothing to make or cause him to do things. But when physical, will and intellectual powers are combined, and properly regulated, then he who has them, possesses a power at once beautiful and forceful.

Let everybody train himself physically and intellectually as much as he can for best results. I saw a young man the other day just coming into the beginning of the prime of life. He had been fettered, and hindered by disease. "O," said he, "I want to get well, and be a man in the world. If I had the health, power and gladness you seem to enjoy, how happy I would be. I feel like this world is some pleasure to you." The reply was: "Live in the sunshine and air all you can; be prudent, prayerful and hopeful, following Him who said, 'I am the way....and the life.'"

America talks much about her millions of people, and her unlimited means—riches and honor, but sin in public and private places has ruined a great part of the beauty and strength of the American people by taking away much of their physical power and leaving them invalids and poor.

Very much of our weaknesses has come from sin and ignorance. Hear, O, hear the voice of nature, repeating to you these friend words: *Know thyself.* Then listen with earnest delight to these helpful words: Jesus Christ, the same, yesterday, today and forever.

J. T. KITCHEN.

Windsor, Va.

Mrs. W. M. Dowdy—I enjoy reading THE CHRISTIAN SUN and no other paper can fill its place in our home.

* *

Mrs. J. T. Hopper—Enclosed find renewal to THE SUN. I like the paper fine.

* *

We have passed through the "penny age" and let us never return to it. Pennies have been so faithful to the church that they are due a rest.

Sunday School and Christian Endeavor

SUNDAY SCHOOL LESSON FOR JUNE 29, 1919

Review—Response to God's Love. Selection for Reading. Phil 3:7-14. *Golden Text*: I will praise thee, O Lord my God with my whole heart. Ps. 86:12.

Thoughts For Teachers

Do not be content with a review of the title, golden text, and principal truth. Make this lesson a real review of the things you have studied together through the quarter. Review for yourself what you have learned. What do you know more of the Fatherhood of God, the saving power of Christ, the guiding power of the Spirit? What have you done to bring back the image of God in some one, or to preserve it unmarred in some other? Have you kept away from sin, or relied more in the grace of God and less on yourself? Have you repented of your past sins of unbelief, and is your faith stronger in itself and in its working power? Have you learned to obey more readily? Have you taken more joy in your prayer life? Above all, have you learned to love? Answer these questions, earnestly and sincerely, then and only then are you ready to teach these things to the pupils committed to your care.

What response are you making to God's love? What response have you asked from your class? What response is being made in your family life, or in your church life? "If ye love me," said Jesus, "ye will keep my commandments." Have you responded to God's perfect love by a full surrender of self, and an ardent desire for service? Have you heard the call of God for workers, and responded, "Here am I, send me to the place where thou dost need me most"? If not, how can you claim the love of God, when you have no love to offer? MRS. FRED BULLOCK.

CHRISTIAN ENDEAVOR TOPIC FOR JUNE 29, 1919

What does loyalty to our Church and country call for? Matt. 22:15.22.

We have a different conception of loyalty today than we had two years ago. We know it is not enough to rise when the band plays, "The Star Spangled Banner," if our physical habits have been such that we are unfit when called to the colors. We have learned that a man's patriotism may be shown by the care of his teeth or his feet, or his eyes. We know that the sins committed in secret stand out, when the test comes, as a real treason against his country as though he had sided with her enemies.

What, then, about the church? Is the same thing true? Do we owe a physical fitness to the church? (I Cor. 6:19,20). Do we owe a mental fitness to the church? Above all, do we owe a spiritual fitness? Have we any right to remain unfit spiritually? How shall we avoid this? (II Tim. 2:15). See "The Makers of the Flag" in. *Teachers and Officers Journal* for Second Quarter. This will make a splendid reading to use in this service.

MRS. FRED BULLOCK.

FIRST STATE SUNDAY SCHOOL AND CHRISTIAN CONVENTION

I am wondering as I sit here meditating on things that should be done, *and done well* at the coming Convention, just how many of the men, women, boys and girls belonging to the Christian Church in North Carolina will read these lines, and consider that they are a part of the Convention, and what the Convention is for anyway.

Too few of our people read their Church paper, and when they do accidentally see an article of this nature, they seem to think that it is for the other fellow. I wish that I had the writing capacity to say something that would cause each one of us to realize *our individual duty to the Church we represent.* Don't get it in your mind that we are not going to have a good Convention July 15, 16, 17 at Shallow Well Christian Church, because you don't feel inclined to attend, and take a part in making it a success yourself. Don't think for a minute that you are so important that we cannot get along without you, and the church work will stop in its entirely, BUT THINK SERIOUSLY what you are missing, and will continue to miss as you go along the journey of life, if you keep on neglecting to do your bit in the Master's kingdom. The Conventions that are to be held during the summer should have our first consideration a this time. We should do all we can to make each one a great success, and at these Conventions get full fledged behind the work of the Sunday School and Christian Endeavor Board, (or The Board of Religious Education), in such a manner as to make this organization also, a success in every detail. Whether you are on the program or not, if you live in the State and are interested in Sunday school and Christian Endeavor work, we want you to attend the Convention that meets at Shallow Well Christian church next July.

C. H. STEPHENSON,
President.

NOTICE

We want every Sunday school in the Christian denomination to have Children's Day in June, but if you find that it will have to be in July, make it the first Sunday, and be sure that you report the results to Dr. J. O. Atkinson, Elon College, N. C., promptly.

We want a report from him at the different Conventions, and you doubtless know that the first North Carolina Convention meets Tuesday, Wednesday, and Thursday after the second Sunday in July, (15, 16, 17), at Shallow Well church, near Jonesboro. I am hoping that we can get the Sunday School and Christian Endeavor Board, (The Board of Religious Education), before our people at the Convention, in such a manner that its future will be assured, and it will mean much in the field of progress, among our Sunday school and Christian Endeavor workers. I have not received any report from your Sunday school. What is the trouble? If you have just simply put it off, or through the rush of other things neglected it, take a few minutes to discuss this Board and its mission in your school, and be ready to give us your honest opinion regarding its future at your Sunday School and Christian Endeavor Convention.

C. H. STEPHENSON,
Sec'y. & Treas.

CLARDY

Brother James David Clardy was born in April, 1859 and died at his home near Houston, Va., May 22, 1919. He joined Pleasant Grove, (Va.), Christian church when he was twelve years old. While he was a young man he went to Lexington, N. C., to school. He was never married, but bought a home near his church and induced his sister, Miss Sallie, and brother, Charles H., to make their home with him. The three lived faithfully and lovingly together until his death.

James David Clardy was the youngest of a family of eight children—four boys and four girls. They all survive him. Brother Clardy was a good man. In his church work he was teacher, singer and Sunday school superintendent, all of which places he filled well. He was laid to rest in the church cemetery by his pastor and friends.

J. G. TRUITT.

RESOLUTIONS OF RESPECT—LEE

Whereas; it hath pleased our Heavenly Father on Tuesday, May 20, 1919, to call from labor to reward Deacon Willis John Lee; and, whereas Deacon Lee has always done more than his duty as a member and a deacon of Berea Christian church; and, whereas, his life of humility, gentleness and service has been of such unbounded benefit to his church, his denomination and to Christianity at large, therefore, be it resolved:

1. That while we do deeply grieve over our loss and sadly miss him from his place among us yet we humbly bow to the will of him who doeth all things well, Who has called him to become a member of that Church not made with hands eternal in the Heavens.

2. That we thus record our deep feeling of gratitude for his life among us and the noble Christian example of word and deed he has given us to follow.

3. That we express in these resolutions, inadequate though they be, our love for him as a man and a follower of Christ, a man who neither spoke nor thought evil of his fellow man nor did naught but good for all mankind. As a man who ever thought and ever deported himself as a true follower of Christ spreading the spirit of Christianity both at home and abroad. As a man whose time and means were ever at the service of Christ or those of his creatures whose necessity required it. As a Christian gentleman whose courage, patriotism and Christian zeal will ever be an example worthy of commendation and imitation.

4. That we strive to emulate the glorious example of Christian manhood he has given us, keeping the memory of him ever before us that we may be enabled to live better lives and die as sure of a heavenly reward.

5. That we express our most sincere sympathy to his widow and to the other members of his family, their loss is in some small degree our loss, we mourn with them. May the Comforter of man be with them in this their great bereavement.

6. That a copy of these resolutions be entered upon the records of the church, a copy sent to The Christian Sun for publication and a copy sent to the family.

PAUL S. BLANDFORD,
R. B. ODOM,
W. H. BRINKLEY,
JESSE W. BRINKLEY,
A. S. HARGROVE,
Committee.

WATKINS

May 5, 1919, Gladys Elizabeth Watkins came for a brief stay in the home of her parents, Mr. and Mrs. R. A. Watkins. On May 24, 1919, her spirit was called from her earthly home to her home above. Though the stay was brief, yet ties of affection and love were twined about the hearts of parents and child that death cannot part asunder. As they weep for their dear child may they ever remember that their loss is Heaven's gain, and their own treasure has been made richer and sweeter by her going.

Funeral services were conducted from Liberty church.

R. L. WILLIAMSON.

RESOLUTIONS OF RESPECT—TATE

Whereas, our Heavenly Father in His infinite wisdom, has seen fit to call our dear sister, Luna C. Tate, to that home where pain and suffering are no more; and

Whereas, we feel that we have lost a friend whose place cannot be filled, yet we realize that our loss is her gain, and she who was so patient, and cheerful through years of affliction, is now at rest; and

Whereas, the Christian church and the Willing Workers' Sunday school Class have lost a loyal member;

Therefore, be it resolved by the Christian Church at Antioch:

First, That we extend to the family our heartfelt sympathy, with the prayer that God will comfort and bless them.

Second, That a copy of these resolutions be sent to the family, a copy to The Christian Sun for publication, and a copy be spread upon our church record.

VIRDIE SHOWALTER,
GRACE BERRY,
JESSIE WAMPLER,
Committee.

WEMBLEY

Mr. Peter Wembley, well known citizen of New Hill, N. C., departed this life May 14, 1919, after an illness of a few days. He was about sixty-three years of age. His remains were laid to rest in the family burying ground near his home the following day. A good neighbor, father and husband has gone. May God's blessings comfort the hearts of the bereaved ones is the prayer of a former pastor. Funeral services conducted by the writer.

J. S. CARDEN.

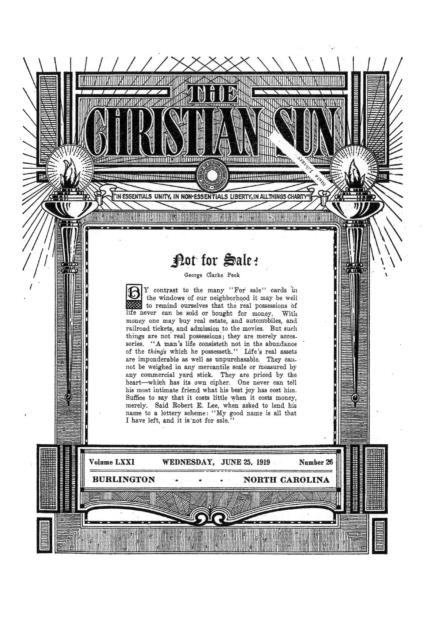

THE CHRISTIAN SUN

"IN ESSENTIALS UNITY, IN NON-ESSENTIALS LIBERTY, IN ALL THINGS CHARITY"

Not for Sale:

George Clarke Peck

BY contrast to the many "For sale" cards in the windows of our neighborhood it may be well to remind ourselves that the real possessions of life never can be sold or bought for money. With money one may buy real estate, and automobiles, and railroad tickets, and admission to the movies. But such things are not real possessions; they are merely accessories. "A man's life consisteth not in the abundance of the *things* which he possesseth." Life's real assets are imponderable as well as unpurchasable. They cannot be weighed in any mercantile scale or measured by any commercial yard stick. They are priced by the heart—which has its own cipher. One never can tell his most intimate friend what his best joy has cost him. Suffice to say that it costs little when it costs money, merely. Said Robert E. Lee, when asked to lend his name to a lottery scheme: "My good name is all that I have left, and it is not for sale."

Volume LXXI   WEDNESDAY, JUNE 25, 1919   Number 26

BURLINGTON   •   •   •   NORTH CAROLINA

THE CHRISTIAN SUN

Founded 1844 by Rev. Daniel W. Kerr

C. B. RIDDLE - - - Editor

Entered at the Burlington, N. C. Post Office as second class matter.

Subscription Rates

One year .... $ 2.00
Six months 1.00

In Advance

Give both your old and new postoffice when asking that your address be changed.

The change of your label is your receipt for money. Written receipts sent upon request.

Marriage and obituary notices not exceeding 150 words printed free if received within 60 days from date of event, all over this at the rate of one-half cent a word.

Original poetry not accepted for publication.

Principles of the Christian Church

(1) The Lord Jesus Christ is the only Head of the Church.
(2) Christian is a sufficient name of the Church.
(3) The Holy Bible is a sufficient rule of faith and practice.
(4) Christian character is a sufficient test of fellowship, and of church membership.
(5) The right of private judgment and the liberty of conscience is a right and a privilege that should be accorded to, and exercised by all.

EDITORIAL

DOING OUR PART THIS SUMMER IN THE EDUCATIONAL FIELD

There are three hundred and sixty-five days in the year in which we have opportunity to do work along the lines of education. But the summer months seem to be a time most opportune. This is true because it is vacation period. It is also true because of the new students who will make their plans during the summer to enter college in the early fall. During the next 3 months many young men and women within our reach will be planning to go away to college. There are those who will not be planning to go to college, but who could go, and who would go, if they but had a little encouragement. It is our part and portion to congratulate those who have decided to go to college and encourage those who have not decided to go. Many a life has been changed by some word of encouragement, some suggestion, some inspiration along an educational way. A brotherly talk to a man has often kindled in his soul an ambition to rise up and dare and do. This is true of many a young woman, and we ought to seize these opportunities and to inquire diligently concerning the young people of our community.

This is a day in which we ought to encourage college attendance as much as possible. The world is calling for leaders, yea, it is needing them. The world is calling for leaders who are trained in heart, in head, and in hand; the world is calling for that type of leadership that can weather the storm of stress and strain through years of devotion and sacrifice. Such a leadership cannot be had and cannot be developed from minds and hearts untrained in the great fundamentals of life.

Four years of preparation is a very short period. Let us go forth into the highways and hedges seeking out the young men and women of our country and encourage them to endeavor for an education. It is our privilege, our opportunity, and our Christian duty to thus act.

CONCERNING OUR CIRCULATION AGAIN

We have written in these columns so often about the circulation of THE CHRISTIAN SUN that we feel at times that it is useless to say anything more about it. We are glad to state that the circulation has grown slowly during the past three years climbing from 1,650 on May 1, 1916, to 2,150 on May 1, 1919. However, this gain is not what it should have been and what it should be for the good of the Church. Five thousand subscribers to THE SUN woud be a very modest number for our constituency in the Southern Christian Convention. We have something over 25,000 members in this section of the Church and 2,150 subscribers to the official organ of the Church is far from what should be expected.

In every church community there are homes where THE SUN does not go. Many of our pastors have done well and many have done very little.

When it is possible for us to raise large sums for various enterprises of the Church, it does not seem possible to induce a man to take his Church paper at the small sum of $2.00 a year. When you get a man to take his Church paper, you are giving him more than value received; you are not asking him for a gift.

THE SUN needs a larger circulation from a financial standpoint, and also from the standpoint of the good that it can do. If our pastors will not help to get THE SUN into every home on account of the financial condition of the paper, we do beg them in the name of missionary work to help extend the circulation.

We have often wondered why certain pastors have done so little for THE SUN. There are churches with only one or two families taking THE SUN. There are a few churches where THE SUN does not go into a single family. Just how a pastor can be contented to serve under such condition is beyond our comprehension.

Can we not, in some way, get THE SUN into the homes of our people? If it is worth while, let us do it, and if it is not, let us say so.

PERISHING CHURCHES AND TITHING CHURCHES

There are churches that perish and there are churches that tithe. Here is an example between a perishing church and a tithing church which we glean from "Men and Money":

When Dr. Potter went to the First Methodist Episcopal church of Anderson, Indiana, the church was $2,100 behind on its current budget and no fairy god-mother in sight. Dr. Potter thought and prayed and finally warned his official board that he was going to put the tithing stewardship proposition up to the church; that it was for them to vote yea or nay, with nobody excused on account of a cold. Seventeen men on the board voted in favor of this action, while, in spite of warnings, several asked to be excused.

On the following Sunday after a stewardship sermon 79 people signed as tithing stewards, and at the present date more than 180 are enrolled from that church. Moreover the church is not only out of debt, but the benevolences, both home and foreign, are greatly increased.

TWO INSTANCES

We recall two instances that are only typical of the many that we have witnessed during the past three years. We think of these instances because of the impression they made upon us. The first instance was our visit to a home where every comfort and convenience that farm life could afford, was there. There were several hundred acres of beautiful farming land with every acre growing a splendid crop. We learned that there were no debts upon that home and upon that farm. The dwelling was worth about $10,000.00 with barns and out houses in proportion. We were assured by the pastor that this family was one of the most loyal families in the church—and we have learned since that his statement was correct.

THE CHRISTIAN SUN did not go into this home. We made inquiry as to why it did not go and we found that no effort had been made by the pastor to get it there. Just why we cannot understand. That family was placed on THE CHRISTAIN SUN list and is faithful to the paper.

And now the instance. Not over one hundred years ago we were in the field of a pastor who has done good work for THE SUN, and yet we found in his pastorate a family living in comfort, with conveniences, a productive farm, all interested and good workers in the church. We asked members of the family if they had ever seen a copy of THE CHRISTIAN SUN and they replied that they had not. This ends the story. We leave it to our readers to guess what happened.

All of us can see things that the other fellow does not do, and we can tell the other man things to do that we cannot do. Beloved pastors, you will never convince this scribe that if he ever assumes the *responsibility* of being a pastor to a people, that he will not soon personally visit every home for one purpose only—and that is to know if THE CHRISTIAN SUN is going into that home. That will be the first approach. There will be no talking about the weather, the crops, the church, the school or anything else. Our message will be first about THE CHRISTIAN SUN, and they will have no difficulty understanding that THE SUN's interest is our chief business on that trip.

TWO METHODIST PAPERS MERGE

The Raleigh Christian Advocate, Raleigh, N. C., and *The North Carolina Christian Advocate*, Greensboro, N. C., merged themselves last week. Dr. L. S. Massey, Editor of *The Raleigh Christian Advocate* joins Dr. H. M. Blair, Editor of *The North Carolina Christian Advocate* in making one strong paper for the Methodist in North Carolina. The paper is published in Greens-

boro under the name of "The North Carolina Christian Advocate," the Raleigh office being discontinued. The Methodist people did not own their printing place in Raleigh, but the. paper was published on contract. They own their own publishing house in Greensboro which is estimated to be worth about $40,000. The move seems to be one of wisdom since the two papers were published in the same State, and we predict for the united efforts of these two good editors great success. May the blessings of God continue to rest upon their work.

NUMBER TWENTY-SIX

By referring to the front page of this issue of THE SUN, you will notice that it is number twenty-six of the present volume. One-half the year is gone—twenty-six more numbers and the volume for Nineteen Hundred and Nineteen will be completed. How time does fly! It seems only yesterday when we placed on the shelf the volume for Nineteen Hundred and Eighteen and marked No. 1 on the front page. Let us all unite to make the remaining twenty-six numbers of this year the very best possible.

MISS MARTHA STACEY AT BURLINGTON

Miss Martha Stacey, Haverhill, Massachusetts, who is to sail in September as a missionary to Japan to be supported by the Sunday school of the First Christian church of Burlington, N. C., visited the Burlington church last week. As stated in THE SUN last week she conducted the Christian Endeavor meeting on Sunday evening and made a talk after the usual preaching hour.

On Tuesday evening at 8:30, the church and its organizations gave a reception to Miss Stacey. The different organizations of the church extended greetings and a most happy and joyful program was rendered. Miss Stacey was presented with a gold watch, and also a fountain pen.

On Wednesday evening a beautiful installation service was held. Brother John R. Foster, Superintendent of the Sunday school, presided. Dr. P. H. Fleming made a talk on "The Gift of Life;" THE SUN's Editor made a talk on "The Gift of Money," and the Pastor, J. W. Harrell, made a talk on "The Gift of Prayer."

At the close of Brother Harrell's talk, Miss Stacey came forward, and after being asked questions, accepted the work in the name of the Sunday school and then the Sunday school accepted her by unanimous vote. She made a very impressive and beautiful talk expressing her appreciation to the Sunday school for making it possible for her to go and do the work that she had chosen to do.

The Third church, Norfolk, Va., last week gave a reception to the more than one hundred new members received since January 15 when Brother L. E. Smith assumed charge as pastor.

Brother M. J. W. White, Norfolk, Va., called by to see us last week. He is one of THE SUN's most faithful friends and we are always glad to shake his hand.

PASTOR AND PEOPLE

PLEASANT GROVE, VA.

The writer had the privilege and pleasure of being with Brother J. G. Truitt the first Sunday in June. It was memorial day. A sermon was preached and a short memorial address delivered, after which Brother Thompson, superintendent of the Sunday school, took charge and directed the distribution of the flowers. The flowers were in abundance and some were placed upon every grave. This was a happy day for me as I was pastor of this church some twenty-five years ago, for a period of seven years. Many that were active members of the church then were missing—they had gone to their reward. My visit here brought to mind many sweet and pleasant remembrances.

Brother J. G. Truitt is the beloved pastor of this church and his people love him dearly and regret that he is going to leave them this fall. He intends to enter some Bible school. God bless the pastor and people.

The third Sunday I met our congregation at Moore Union. It was a day that will not be forgotten soon, because the presence of the Lord was so wonderfully manifested. Many souls were filled with joy and made happy. We are praying for and expecting a great meeting at this place. Pray for us. Here comes six subscribers to THE CHRISTIAN SUN from this church.

P. T. KLAPP.

P. S. I think that THE SUN needs an endowment fund, for it is the hand maid of missions and all other enterprises of the Church.

SOUTH NORFOLK REVIVAL

Our revival which began on Sunday May 4 and closed on Sunday night, May 25, has proven to be the greatest meeting ever held in the South Norfolk Christian church. The pastor did the preaching throughout the meeting and led the singing most of the time. He was loyally supported both in attendance and in prayers by the membership of the church. The power of the Holy Spirit was in evidence from the very first service. The attendance and interest were good throughout the meeting, and the church could not accommodate the crowds that sought admission to many of the services.

It was the idea and plan of the church to carry the meeting fifteen days but at the end of the first two weeks the meeting had grown in such proportion that it was unanimously voted to carry it on another week, which proved to be the crowning days of the meeting. During the revival over one hundred persons professed faith in Christ, and sixty-four of these united with our church. A number joined other churches of the community. One of the greatest blessings of the meeting was the revival that was experienced in the church. We have always believed in the "good old fashioned way" of praying at the altar. This method was used throughout the meeting. When penitents would come and kneel at the altar, it was inspiring to see the church members come and kneel by them and

pray as I have never heard them pray, and would not let go, "except He bless them." The Lord heard and answered.

Rev. J. F. Morgan and Rev. G. O. Lankford were present a number of times during the meeting and assisted in the song services. Brother J. S. Carden of Durham, N. C., paid us a visit while in Norfolk. The pastor and people were delighted to have these brethren with us and invite them to come again.

At the close of the meeting the pastor was given a delightful surprise when the superintendent of the Sunday school, Mr. B. F. Meginley, stated he wished to say something. He came forward and proceeded to present the pastor with a purse of $66.00, stating: "This is a little gift of the church and Sunday school we wish to make to you as an expression of love and appreciation we have for you as our faithful and untiring pastor." Words and deeds like these fill my heart with joy. They make me want to strive harder and harder to prove worthy of such expressions of appreciation, to live a life more like Jesus, and be a better pastor to these good people.

As a result of the great revival which we have just witnessed, we are beginning to see marked improvement of the work. Our Sunday school has increased in numbers until we have nowhere to put the people. But praise the Lord a movement has been started to have our present building enlarged at the earliest possible date. At the mid-week prayer service Wednesday evening eighty-five people were present, and a large number gave personal testimonials of the religion of the Lord and Savior Jesus Christ. God is wonderfully blessing us in our feeble efforts at South Norfolk. To Him be all the praise and glory. Brethren, continue to pray for us.

O. D. POYTRESS.

South Norfolk, Va.

DANVILLE, VIRGINIA

The evangelistic services which had been in progress during the past twelve days at the Third Avenue Christian church came to a close last night when a number of persons made professions or re-consecrated their lives to Jesus Christ, while eight united with the church on profession of faith. It was an inspiring service and God is to be praised for the wonderful way in which He blessed us. To Him be all the glory. In all there ware about thirty professions and re-consecrations and the church was greatly revived.

Rev. F. C. Lester did the preaching and he brought some splendid messages. He dealt with fundamentals and always appealed to the reason as well as to the feelings. It was the beauty of holiness and the love of a dying Savior that formed the central theme of all his messages, and they were delivered with a simplicity and yet, withal, an earnestness that won his hearers. We also enjoyed the wholesome fellowship of this genial and consecrated man.

There is a great field of service at Danville and I am planning to spend my entire summer with my folks there. They are loyal and earnest, and they show a spirit of service that is an inspiration to anyone who witnesses their work. They need a pastor on the ground all the time and I hope and pray that God may thrust forth some laborer into this rich field. I am planning to enter Yale in the fall to complete my preparation for the mission field, or otherwise I would be glad to serve these people as pastor. It is with keen feelings of regret that I leave them, and I pray God's richest blessing on the work. May it grow and may the church become a real factor in the community life.

Elon College, N. C.   H. S. HARDCASTLE.
June 14, 1919.

SUFFOLK LETTER

Sunday, June 15, 1919, was red letter day at Oakland Christian church, ten miles from Suffolk. It was the twenty-first anniversary of the pastorate of Rev. Dr. I. W Johnson. The day was ideal, the grove was full of automobiles, the house and yard full of people—the community was there and many from cities and other neighborhoods. At least *twelve hundred* enjoyed the great dinner. The tables accommodated two hundred and fifty at a time and I saw the tables crowded four times, to say nothing of those who ate inside and as a final few outside. The dinner was a real dinner, with meats, vegetables, breads, cakes, pickles, *et cetera*, all well prepared and enough to have fed as many more. Many were there who had never seen an all-day meeting with dinner on the ground at a country church; and they enjoyed it, too.

The exercises in the church began at noon, and were resumed at four in the afternoon. Dinner and social intercourse filled up the recess. A big choir and Chandler's orchestra furnished music. Dr. W. A. Harper delivered a great address at the first service. At the afternoon service Leo DeWitte Martin, a recent graduate of Elon College, and a member of Oakland, pastor I. W. Johnson, and this pencil pusher, made brief addresses. The choir and orchestra enlivened both services with splendid music.

Dr. Johnson entered upon his work as pastor in June 1898. At that time the membership was *one hundred and thirty-four.* *Two hundred and fifty-two* members have been received during his incumbency, and the present membership is *two hundred* and *eighty.* The sum raised for *benevolences* the first year of his pastorate was $20.20; the sum raised last year for *benevolences* was $500.00. The result of these years has been a source of gratification to pastor and congregation; and the address of L. D. Martin expressed, in words of which the people were proud, the appreciation of the congregation for their pastor. A liberal offering was made for benevolences, and the day celebrated an event of great significance to the people, and, no doubt, the beginning of great usefulness in the service of the Master. If the increase in benevolences were to be as much during the next *twenty-one years*, as during the past *twenty-one years* Oakland would be giving in *nineteen forty* $12,500.00 per year. It is safe to hope that the future will increase all the activities and gifts of the congregation. We used to sing, "Shout, Shout, We're Gaining Ground," "Glory Hallelujah," and now, we add to that song, that we are paying as well

as singing, and doing as well as believing, remembering that "faith without works is dead."

Great days mark great achievements. July the fourth celebrates a great victory. The Passover celebrated a great deliverance. Such days as Oakland had, celebrate a relation between pastor and people that touches deeper things than years and numbers. That day was the flower of spiritual births, Christian burials, marriage altars, growth in grace, community betterment, and the promise of fruits yet to be harvested. "By their fruits ye shall know them."

Monday followed Sunday by subscription to the Elon Endowment Fund, and Dr. Harper moves on toward *three hundred thousand.*   W. W. STALEY.

ANOTHER RECOMMENDATION

There are many splendid resolutions and recommendations introduced in our Conferences and Conventions, the majority of which are *adopted,* and many of which are *adapted.* If wisdom *adopts* resolutions, energy augmented by wisdom should *adapt* them.

The following recommendation was adopted by one of our progressive Conferences during its last session:

"We recommend to each church and Sunday school to have at least one splendid representative at the Seaside Chautauqua and School of Methods of the Christian Church at Virginia Beach, Va., paying at least a part of said representative's expenses, that he may bring back much of the valuable work of that summer Conference to our Churches."

This recommendation should not only be adapted by the churches composing said Conference, but by all the churches of our denomination. Our churches and Sunday schools will grow no faster than the leaders; the leaders will grow only as their vision is expanded. Proper expansion, a splendid vision, and adequate enthusiasm may be obtained by attending the Chautauqua. Let every Sunday school superintendent see that the above recommendation is *adopted* by his school. Send at least one representative, that he may bring back to your school the best and most practicable thoughts of the summer Conference.

Durham, N. C.   R. F. BROWN.

NOTICE

The Sunday School Convention of the Eastern Virginia Christian Conference will meet with Oakland Christian church, near Suffolk, Va., at 10 A. M., on Wednesday, July 23. By vote it was decided by the last session of the Convention to hold only a two days' session this year. The program, therefore, has been arranged accordingly. Let each superintendent keep this in mind in planning for the Convention. For information as to trains, see the pastor, Dr. I. W. Johnson's announcement in THE SUN. All together for a successful session. Meet us at Oakland on July 23 and 24.

G. O. LANKFORD,
Gen. Secretary.

Berkley, Va., Route 3.

(We have not received announcement from Brother Johnson.—*Editor.*)

CHRISTIAN EDUCATION

TWENTY-ONE YEARS A CHRISTIAN MINISTER

On the third Sunday in June Rev. I. W. Johnson, D. D., concluded his 21st year as a Christian minister and as pastor of the church at Oakland. It was a great and good day. His people celebrated in his honor, as only Eastern Virginia people can celebrate. Tables were built to accommodate 400 people at one time and four times they were filled. There was ample to have fed as many more. On few occasions have so many people ever assembled at a country church in any section. It was good to be there. The people love this man of God and they came to do him honor.

In the morning Dr. Johnson insisted that I speak and at the conclusion he expressed the hope that his church, apportioned $1,100, would give $2,100, making it $100 a year for each of his 21. These people would do any reasonable thing for their beloved pastor. and they did this. In the afternoon Dr. Staley brought a great message on the four-square church member. He squared him perfectly and instructed every listener. He was preceded by Mr. L. D. Martin, who graduated from Elon in May of this year, and who brought not only a message of appreciation from the local church to Dr. Johnson, but a challenge also to Oakland to become a real community centre. Dr. Johnson told some of his experiences during a 21 years pastorate and wittily remarked that a good preacher gets promotion. His people felt he had been promoted by remaining with them. It is lovely to see how these people love their pastor.

I must not forget to mention the splendid music at the anniversary celebration. Dr. Johnson's wife was accompanist during the day and her wifely heart must have swelled with pardonable pride in the esteem in which all could see her husband is so universally held.

But the best part of it all comes now. When I was in Suffolk in March Dr. Johnson did not make a gift. He had a reason. He was to be 21 years of age in the ministry on the third Sunday in June and he had decided on that day to make his gift. So at noon at Oakland he walked up to me and said he and his wife had decided to give $1,000 on his anniversary day. Is that not fine?

Dr. Johnson's other churches, Hobson, Liberty Spring and Berea have also gone over the top. His churches will give double his salary to general enterprises of the church for the next five years. Is that not something for a preacher to be happy over? And Dr. Johnson is happy. May he preach for 21 more years, twice over.

Other Places

I have also this week visited Union, (South.), Antioch, and Franklin.

Rev. H. H. Butler is pastor at Union and Antioch. He is a banner pastor, both his churches going over the top. I have rarely found two more promising churches than these. Antioch is a deeply spiritual church. It has been the seminary of preachers, and

others yet are destined to come forth from her. Seven of her deacons, all we could see, subscribed to the fund, and a church with seven such deacons is highly blessed. Brother L. W. Vaughan at Union gave the drive a good start by subscribing very liberally.

Rev. C. H. Rowland and his wife preside at Franklin. They have been there since 1900 and have wrought a splendid work . Their new house of worship was dedicated on the fourth Sunday in May, when $13,000 was raised to wipe out the indebtedness. The people there are especially generous to their pastors, (plural properly), and they were generous to the fund too. Not a person canvassed refused to subscribe, and over the top the church went. Franklin is further proof that generous support to local enterprises does not hinder large giving to general enterprises. Has a church any more right to be selfish and self-centered than an individual? Can it be so and expect the blessing of God? Franklin says "No."

More From Suffolk

Suffolk originally gave $52,800. It is now $55,000. This makes it possible to say the church itself gave the $50,000 to endow the chair of the presidency in Dr. Staley's honor and leaves the $5,000 he gave to found a fund in memory of Mrs. Staley. Suffolk may do more yet. There is no end to what Suffolk may not do. Mr. B. D. Crocker and Mr. John King made the $55,000 possible for Suffolk.

Funds This Week

By Rev. and Mrs. I. W. Johnson on Dr. Johnson's 21st anniversary in the Christian ministry, in memory of their deceased parents, Mrs. Georgiana Johnson and Mr. F. R. Ellenor.

Mr. B. D. Crocker in memory of his Wife, Mrs. Adona Brinkley Crocker and his son, Marvin Franklin Crocker.

Mr. John King out of his deep affection for Dr. W. W. Staley.

Deacon Elisha Bradshaw for himself and wife, a real help-meet in his Christian life. Brother Bradshaw is a deacon that really "deaks."

Deacon W. C. Moore for himself and wife and because of his deep devotion to Dr. I. W. Johnson.

Finally, Brethren

Before another issue of THE SUN is printed, the Elon Standardization Fund drive will be history. The field force are earnestly engaged these latter days to put the fund safely over the top. Bear us up in your prayers that God may use us to do His will and that His cause through Elon may prosper.

W. A. HARPER.

Rev. O. B. Williams, Seattle, Washington, a member of the M. P. Church, is one of the several subscribers to THE CHRISTIAN SUN who are not members of the Christian Church. He writes that he cannot do without THE SUN and we assure Brother Williams that we are glad to have him on the list.

Rev. D. F. Parsons changes his address from Nashville, Tenn., to Brownsville, Tenn., for the summer.

THE CHRISTIAN ORPHANAGE

SUPERINTENDENT'S LETTER

We had hoped to reach the seven thousand dollar mile post in this report as our next report will be dated for July, but we fell just below that amount. I wish we could have reached it. We always feel happy when we reach the goal we set and try not to be discouraged when we do not reach our mark.

The summer months are always discouraging in this work as our financial income generally runs below our expense account and when we have to cut our bank account down to live it always hurts.

We do everything we can to keep the expenses as low as possible and try to raise as much on the farm as we can to help feed the children, and this spring we have been blessed with nice vegetables from the garden and now have plenty of Irish potatoes, snap beans and cabbage. But the things we have to buy are the items that cost us money and come at a high price.

Mrs. Wicker, our efficient kitchen and dining room matron, and the girls have had their first lesson in canning for this season. They were very industrious one day last week and put up thirty-six gallons of snap beans. They were so industrious that they conscripted all the boys and girls to help pick the beans and made the Superintendent help, too, and made us stay on the job till ten-thirty that night, till all the strings were pulled off and the beans snapped.

Two of our larger girls have reached the age limit in the last few weeks and have gone out. One took a place in the New Bern General Hospital, New Bern, N. C., and the other went to the Lakeview Hospital, Suffolk, Va., to take training to nurse. Both are highly pleased with their new homes and the work, and I believe they will make good. It gives us much pleasure to secure for them, when they reach the age limit, places in institutions of this kind where they can be trained for usefulness in life.

Mrs. Wicker carried four of our little girls to visit the High Point church and to sing for them on their Children's Day, Sunday, June 15, and were highly pleased with their trip and the kindness shown them while there. Our High Point people are a great people.

CHAS. D. JOHNSTON, *Supt.*

REPORT FOR JUNE 24, 1919

Amount brought forward, $6,788.35.

Children's Offerings

John B. Taylor, Jr., 25 cents; T. D. Mathews, Jr., 30 cents; Oliver E. Young, Jr., 10 cents; Total, 65 cents.

Sunday School Monthly Offerings

(North Carolina Conference)

Liberty, (Vance Co.), $3.40; New Lebanon, $1.00; New Lebanon Baraca Class, $1.00; Mt. Auburn, $8.16; Union, (N. C.), $1.20; New Elam, $4.04; Howard's Chapel, $1.00; High Point, $11.00; Haw River, $3.55; Bethlehem, $1.00; Lebanon, $5.00; Wake Chapel, $5.72.

(Eastern Virginia Conference)

Holy Neck, Young Men's Baraca Class, $1.98; Suffolk, $25.00; Centerville, $1.00.

New Hope, $2.15.   Va. Val. Conf.

(Alabama Conference)

Wadley, Ala., $2.40; Mt. Joy Christian church, Otway, Ohio, $5.00; Total, $83.60.

Easter Offerings

Liberty church, Randolph Co., Va., $7.20; Asbury Wheeler, 10 cents; Total $7.30.

Special Offerings

W. H. Thomas, on support of children, $25.00; W. H. Freeman, Ether, N. C., 50 cents; B. C. Vuncannon, $1.00; R. S. Caudle, Elon College, N. C., $10.00; Total, $36.50.

Total for the week, $128.05; Grand total, $6,916.40.

LETTERS FROM THE COUSINS

Dear Uncle Charley: I wish to thank you for the picture you sent me. I think she is a very sweet looking little girl and I would like to hear her sing. Am sending thirty cents for May, June and July. Hope you and all the cousins are well.—*T. D. Mathews, Jr.*

I am glad you liked the picture of our little girl. She is a very sweet little girl. "Uncle Charley."

Dear Charley: I am slow but I am coming with twenty-five cents for the orphans. I have been sick a long time and they won't give me anything to eat but malted milk. I just cry for chicken soup. I have a little sister seven days old. Thank you for the lovely pictures you sent me.—*John B. Taylor.*

I am sorry you have been sick. Glad you are better. You must be good to that little sister.—'*Uncle Charley.*'

Dear Uncle Charley: I am almost one year old and I feel my importance, too. Grandfather Newman has gone to Asheville and I miss him so much. Love to all.—*Oliver E. Young, Jr.*

"I see you are a very energetic young man. I know you miss grandfather.—'*Uncle Charley.*'

HOUSEKEEPING HINTS

Put a little saltpeter in the water you use for your bouquets and the flowers will last for a fortnight.

To remove water spots on a dress dampen in lukewarm water. Place a blotter over warm spots on the wrong side and press with a warm iron.

When roast is small it is best to start it on top of the stove. Heat the pan very hot, put the roast in and turn it frequently. The quick searing holds the juices.

French Toast With Berries.—Cut stale bread into small, regular slices about one-half inch in thickness. Beat two eggs until light, add one-quarter teaspoonful of salt and one and one-half cupfuls of milk. Mix, dip the slices into this mixture, allow them to become thoroughly saturated, then fry in a shallow pan in hot melted butter. Or, if you have a gas range, place the slices on a pan or on the broiler, and toast on each side to a golden brown, and spread, while hot, with fresh butter. This is the more wholesome way. In either case, when the toast is made, sprinkle it thickly with powdered sugar to which just a little ground cinnamon has been added. Arrange the toast on a platter and heap the berries on top.

"SHOULDER TO SHOULDER"

"That woman is by nature intended to obey, is shown by the fact that every woman who is placed in the unnatural position of absolute independence at once attaches herself to some kind of man, by whom she is controlled or governed; that is because she requires a master. If she is young, the man is a lover; if she is old, a priest." These are the sentiments of Schopenhauer, a typical Prussian. A nation founded on such misconception of woman as this was destined to curse mankind, and it did. We know the sad story, written in blood, and in the interest of man we women earnestly pray that the earth may be spared a repetition of the horrors through which it has been called upon the pass in our day. Autocracy has been done away, we say, but all autocracy, all over-lordship, all injustice in not political and governmental. We must go down to the roots of things. We must examine with fearless and sympathetic scrutiny the foundations of all the superstructure of our life, individual and organic. But not only among the Huns have women been regarded as the inferiors, not to say the vassals of men. Sad is the picture as we look down the vistas of recorded history to the earliest groups of human beings whose customs we can know. The most primitive, nomadic tribes, with no settled habitation, in company with their civilized brothers in the centuries since, regarded their women as weaker than themselves, and yet imposed on them the heavy routine work of the hut which they dignified with the name home. The first farmers, the first wood-hewers and drawers of water, were the women, the weaker half of these Bedouin tribes. And all through recorded history since the same rare inconsistency glares us stolidly and shamelessly in the face. The imperial Persian, the philosophic Syrian, the learned Egyptian, the cultured Greek, the lordly Roman, the pious Hebrew, the scornful Hun, the autocratic Churchman each and all agree in the divinely appointed limitations of women and in their laws as well as in their social customs modesly claim for their stronger selves advantages over the weaker sex. The disabilities of women legally to control their property or their children constitute a record of shame in the annals of mankind, while the monstrous age of consent legislation beggars appropriate description. It is a case of the strong legislating to perpetuate their strength, a glaring instance of the "CAT AND MOUSE" philosophy. Men have ever placed women under guardianship and as perpetually violated the trust committed to their tutelage.

Let us look at the picture of the ideal woman from the viewpoint of the religious Hebrew. We find it in Proverbs 31, and it reads as follows: "Who can find a virtuous woman? for her price is far above rubies. The heart of her husband doth safely trust in her, so that he shall have no need of spoil. She will do him good and not evil all the days of her life. She seeketh wool and flax, and worketh willingly with her hands. She is like the merchant-ships; she bringeth food from afar. She riseth while it is yet night, and giveth meat to her household, and a portion to her maidens. She considereth a field and buyeth it: with the fruit of her hands she planteth a vineyard. She girdeth her loins with strength, and strengtheneth her arms. She perceiveth that her merchandise is good; her candle goeth not out by night.

"She layeth her hands to the spindle, and her hands hold the distaff. She stretcheth out her hand to the poor; yea, she reacheth forth her hand to the needy. She is not afraid of the snow for her household: for all her household are clothed in scarlet. She maketh herself coverings of tapestry; her clothing is silk and purple. Her husband is known in the gates, when he sitteth among the elders of the land. She maketh him fine linen and selleth it; and delivereth girdles unto the merchants.

"Strength and honor are her clothing; and she shall rejoice in time to come. She openeth her mouth with wisdom, and her tongue is the law of kindness. She looketh well to the ways of her household and eateth not the bread of idleness. Her children rise up, and call her blessed; her husband also, and praiseth her. Many daughters have done virtuously, but thou excellest them all. Favor is deceitful and beauty vain: but a woman that feareth the Lord, she shall be praised. Give her of the fruits of her hands; and let her own work praise her in the gates."

Does this picture satisfy the heart? Is it woman's sole duty to look well to her household cares, working till late at night, rising before day to prepare for family, saving from her extra sewing sufficient money to purchase additional land for her husband and sire, to fear God and be proud that her master is known among the town elders? Is this an inspiring challenge to the heart of woman? Yet the Hebrew women were taught to regard the realization of this scene as the highest life-expression for them, and the teaching was based on religion than which no stronger appeal can be made to the heart of woman. Have you noticed that the religions of the world are man-made? Have you also noticed that they are for the most part woman-obeyed? Women are naturally religious and religions has been deftly fashioned to terrorize and submerge them.

But let us examine the writings of the Apostles and the church Fathers. We expect the writings of these men to be flavored with the Hebrew conception of woman's place and our expectation is not misplaced. These venerable saints exhort to personal and social purity and condemn divorce, as their Master did, but they cannot free their minds of the teaching of Genesis that a woman is the cause of all the woes of mankind nor of that in Ecclesiasticus that the badness of men is better than the goodness of women. Wives, therefore, are to be in subjection to their husbands, daughters to their fathers, sisters to their brothers or other male kinsman, and such failing to some guardian of the virile sex. "Let the wife see that she fears her husband," says the Apostle Paul. Peter declares woman to be the weaker vessel. She is, therefore, to be silent in the church and if she desires to learn anything, she is to ask her husband at home. Paul writes his spiritual son Timothy some real philosophy on Christian equality of the sexes. "I permit not woman to teach, nor to have dominion over man, but to be in quietness. For Adam was first formed, then Eve; and Adam was not beguiled, but the woman being beguiled hath fallen into transgression," asserts this doughty champion of men's rights. The Apostles also legislated against certain apparel of the women, forbidding jewels, precious stones, and costly garments unbecoming a modest woman. Women were required by the same religious men to pray with their heads veiled, "for the man is not of the woman, but the woman for the man," they said.

Coming to the Church Fathers, we shall see these same ideas elaborated with all the zeal of religious intolerance. Jerome proves that all evils spring from women and considers marriage a lottery rendered because of their vices too risky to be tried by a real saint. The great Augustine logically proves that woman is not created in the image of God. Here is the proof: "The Apostles command that a man should not veil his head because he is the image of God; but the woman must veil hers according to the same Apostle; therefore the woman is not the image of God." These same spiritual leaders of the Church regarded marriage as a necessary evil, an indulgence to the weakness of the flesh, the view to this day of the Catholic Church, which teaches as Ambrose did the "Celibacy is the life of Angels" and with Optatus that "Celibacy is a spiritual kind of marriage." When the leaders of the Church entertained such notions of marriage, it is not strange that some of them like Tertullian and Paul ran away from their wives after marriage. A favorite theme with some men has ever been the style of women's dress. The Church Fathers are severe in their castigations of the gentler sex in respect to their dress. Tertullian would make them wear black or white and reaches his conclusions by a rare demonstration of logical power. "Inasmuch as God has not made crimson or green sheep, it does not behoove women to wear colors that He has not produced in animals naturally." And Augustine forbids nuns to bathe more than once a month surrounding them with other restrictions lest they become too attractive to their stronger brothers and divert their minds from the ways of sobriety and holy living.

As we women view the intricacies of the mental operations of men to perpetuate an untenable conception as to the relations of the male and female created in God's image, we would lose heart and conclude with Lady Somerville" the more we see of men, the better we like dogs," but for the teaching of our Master, who came to seek and to save the lost, to exalt the abased, to give full freedom to all. His loving tenderness to women and His insistency on every courtesy to them has been our Magna Charta through the Christian centuries. We, therefore, are not heartless, but hopeful. Progress we recognize to be a painful process, tedious, but sure, and in the long run self-interest will surrender to simple right and elemental justice, and when that day has come,

as come it will the epic of woman's patient suffering will crown the racial accomplishments with a glory never to be dimmed. We women shall wait and love, we shall labor and hope, till the Shiloh-hour of our deliverance has struck, content with Jesus to endure humiliation in the interest of a cause that deserves our best, even the salvation from selfishness and self-interest of the stronger sex of the race and their consecration to a complete self-investment for others.

Jesus revealed to men their brotherhood, He taught us women too that we are endowed with personality. With him there is no respect of persons nor sexes. One-half of the race is not to be enslaved because weak. Men will see, men are now seeing, they have been seeing for a long time and now with increasing clarity, that the true goal of mankind is equality of men and women marching "shoulder to shoulder" in heroic spirit to subdue the world into a loving allegiance to the program of the Man of Galilee. I would not be misunderstood. All true men have ever loved women individually, in the concrete relations of life, so to speak. It is when we look at woman in the abstract that the inequality stands forth is glaring inconsistency. In the days ahead equality is to emerge in all their relations, concrete and abstract, personal and social, domestic and industrial. For a long time I have dreaded the thought of woman suffrage. Like every true soul when facing a great responsibility, I have shrunk from pleading for it. So have other thoughtful, true women, many of them. But "it is useless to kick against the pricks." Woman suffrage is bound to come or the program of our Master cannot be fully realized, and when it comes, we women, will be found as faithful and conscientious in the discharge of our duty as voters as we have been in the realms heretofore to which social customs and the wills of fathers, husbands and brothers have permitted us access. I know there has been a frantic over-working of the "woman's sphere" argument. But woman has a divine right to go wherever her father, husband, or brother may go, and if they are not willing that she should do so, they ought not resort to such a place or prerogative themselves. "A woman's place," says the sage Hennessy, "is in the home, darning her husband's childher, I mean ......" "I know what ye mean," says Mr. Dooley. "'Tis a favorite argument iv mine whin I can't think iv inything to say." And Mr. Dooley is right. Woman has no sphere. Every sphere is hers, as created in the image of God, as the help-meet, the complement, the equal of man, and while men may stay the speedy coming of the logical consequences of the hand-writing of the All-Father in the act of creation, they cannot permanently delay its glorious consumation, the dawning of the era for which the noblest and best and devoutest of the race, men and women alike, have looked and longed and prayed and to which He, even the Christ, gave the charter of everlasting truth when he said, "With God there is no respect of persons."

It is true, we women have not furnished half the leaders of the world. How could we? Education underlies leadership, and the denial of education to woman is a rank injustice. Our right to be educated is distinctly a movement of the last half of the nineteenth century. Queen's College for women in England, was incorporated by royal charter in 1853. Eight of the ten men's universities of Great Britain now allow examinations and degrees to women, but Oxford and Cambridge do not. In the United States, the first school of college rank for women was Mt. Holyoke, founded in 1836. Vassar came in 1865. Radcliffe, the much abused "Harvard Annex" began in 1879. Antioch in 1826 and Oberlin in 1833 were the first instances of co-education in the sense of equal education for men and women. The allegations against equal education have been exploded by the stern argument of fact, and the day will come when woman's unfitness to profit by higher education on equal terms with man will take its place in the intellectual museum of mankind's upward progress with the Copernician theory of the earth's flatness.

. Yet despite the denial to us for a long centuries of the foundation stone of leadership, education, we women have in every generation produced our Miriams, our Deborahs, our Faustinas, our Susanna Wesleys, our Mary Lyons, our Jane Addamses, our Alice Freeman Palmers, our Frances Willards, our George Elliotts, our Louisa May Alcotts, our Susan B. Anthonys, our Hettie Greens, our Helen Goulds, our Olympia Moratas, our Lady Jane Greys, our Queens Elizabeth and Victoria, our Marys and Marthas. We are proud of our women leaders. They are an earnest of our larger accomplishment when equality of privilege shall have fully dawned. Women, with their wonderful intuition and love for service, when given an equal chance, will become evangels of light, angels of mercy, servants in joy of our fellow-men. Through our faith in Him we will assist our brothers in subduing the Kingdoms of evil, in doing the work of righteousness throughout the earth. And with our brothers we shall obtain the promises eternal because we shall stop the mouths of the lions of selfishness and greed, exterminate the social vultures that now prey on the vitals of our life, waxing valiant in our equal fight for truth and complete salvation, bringing in the blessed benedictions of the life that is hid, for both men and women, with Christ in God. We shall transform the world in that day of equality marching "shoulder to shoulder" with our brothers by deeds of mercy and love. We shall subdue it to the Christ.

Am I speaking in a dream? Or do I speak forth the words of truth and soberness? Eventually, without the shadow of doubt, the latter. But I may be dreaming for this present generation.

Then the women who have matched the sacrifice of the men in the world war, whose hearts have ached as their fingers have toiled in their homes that the soldier boys might have comfort and protection, who have died as nurses in the camps here and in the hospitals there,—these women, true to the resigned heart of women in every age, will dream on and in their dreams they will catch luminous glimpses of the face of Him who came to make all free and equal. We women of this day have gladly suffered our part to banish autocracy from the governments of the earth. We shall hopefully trust the gallantry of manhood to break the bands of the autocracy that confines us in limits too narrow for the fullest ripening of our souls, and if they do not, God will give us the grace to love on and, in a happier and juster day ahead, He will raise up a generation of men who will be real democrats, ready to remove every obstacle fettering the full and complete expression of the womanly spirit for the uplift and betterment of the race.

We women do not want rights. We want the opportunity of service. We do not wish to lessen our sacrifices. Sacrifice is the keynote, the major cord, the melodious theme of our symphony of life. But we know our Master's program of life cannot be fully achieved till we shall climb the long ascent up to equality with men, enabling us when we have scaled it to march "shoulder to shoulder" with them on the unending plateau of God's infinite purpose for the race's achievement. And when the summit is attained, "shoulder to shoulder," as God planned and as Jesus taught, together we shall do the work of our humankind.

"The woman's cause is man's; they rise or sink together, dwarf'd or God-like, bond or free; If she be small, slight-natured, miserable, how shall man grow?"

"For woman is not undeveloped man,
But diverse. Could we make her as the man,
Sweet love were slain: his dearest bond is this,—
Not like to like, but like in difference.
Yet in the long years liker must they grow;
The man be more of woman, she of man; .
He gain in sweetness and moral height,
Nor lose the wrestling thews that throw the world;
She, mental breadth, nor fail in childward care,
Nor lose the childlike in the larger mind,
Till at the last she set herself to man
Like perfect music unto noble words;
And so these twain, upon the skirts of time,
Sit side by side, full-summed in all their powers,
Dispensing harvest, sowing the to-be.
Self-reverent each and reverencing each,
Distinct in individualities,
But like each other even as those who love.
Then comes the statelier Eden back to men;
Then reign the world's great bridals, chaste and calm;
Then springs the crowning race of human-kind."

*Alumni Address, given by Mrs. W. A. Harper, '99, on the evening of May 20, 1919.

WOMAN SUFFRAGE WINS

The United States Senate on June 4 adopted the Woman Suffrage Amendment by a vote of 56 to 25. The House voted 304 to 89 on May 21. Three-fourths of the Legislature will have to ratify the amendment before it is incorporated into the Federal Constitution. This movement was started in 1875 by Susan B. Anthony, and after more than a quarter of a century, seems to be on the eve of victory.

MISSIONARY

MADE READY FOR FURTHER ADVANCE

This sentence from a well known writer caught my eye recently, "Now is the time for the greatest missionary program of the greatest financial advance the women of America have ever made. Instead of being exhausted by sacrifice we have been made ready by sacrifice for further advance." And then the same writer asks this question which is as pertinent to men as to women, "Shall we American women maintain the standard of simplified living and sacrificial giving that has helped to win a war in order that a world may be led to Jesus Christ?"

Are the American people willing to do as much to make the world safe religiously as it has done during the war to make it safe politically? If we did great things, and rendered great service, and made great sacrifices to win a war for our country, ought we not now to do as great things to win a war for our Christ? One woman in North Carolina, of whom the writer has account took about the right view of the situation when she said, "When money was asked for War Savings Stamps I felt that I must help. Somehow I have managed to put $50 in Savings Stamps. Now when I get to thinking about the matter, I am determined that I can give as much to my Lord as I have invested in my country."

This woman had been a dollar a year woman in her Missionary Society. When this thought came to her she readily gave $50.00 for missions in Japan. A very wealthy woman in Philadelphia recently said, "Why should I not maintain the standard of sacrifice for the Lord's work that I set for patriotism during the days of war?" To ask the question was to answer it with far larger gifts than she had ever made before to missions.

We have released billions in money to be used in saving the world politically. Are we now willing to release as much to redeem the world through Christ our Lord? The sacrifices we have made have not exhausted our resources. They have made us richer. Are we ready now for further advance, or are we to recoil, and begin to lavish upon ourselves the rapidly accumulating wealth which our Creator is making us stewards of for the time being?

We shall have to bear in mind that it is not poverty but wealth that destroys a people, corrupts government and overthrows principalities. No nation has yet gone to ruin because of poverty. In the abundance of earthly possessions men forget God, indulge their passions, develop abnormal appetites, and create destructive lusts. The safety value of our civilization, and of our American people, is a rapidly increasing spirit of benevolence, and a growing sense of our responsibility for the salvation of others not favored as we are. This war with all its sacrificial offerings of men and money will have been fought in vain unless these sacrifices shall have made us ready for further advance.

J. O. Atkinson.

"I HEARD THE CHILDREN SINGING"

By John Leonard Cole, in The Christian Advocate

The minister sat in his study, in solemn meditation. Perhaps it was a knotty theological question which engrossed him, but whatever it was, it escaped him completely when he heard from below, apparently from the front steps, a song of two small sopranos—Virginia, aged six, and Barbara, aged five. The song which they raised to the top of their little voices was:

> Jesus loves me, this I know,
> For the Bible tells me so.

Now, there was no reason why such a perfectly proper religious song, sung by little people to whom he had himself taught it, should so startle a minister, even though he were in the midst of a critical "thirdly." But still the sound of those piping, girlish voices, issuing from his front steps at the hour of noon, seemed to be something out of place. The first thought was: "Why does not some one keep those girls still? There are people in numbers passing, and what will they think of two children, sitting right on the front steps, singing 'Jesus loves me, this I know'? They should be brought inside and stood beside the piano, if they are to sing so heartily at the hour of noon."

But, then, as the enthusiastic voices continued warbling "For the Bible tells me so," the minister began to wonder whether, after all, they were out of place or whether his ideas of propriety were? After all, why should not little girls sing on the front piazza? After all, were not Virginia and Barbara doing the very natural and proper thing? that is, they were voicing the emotion of their own small hearts, right where they happened to be. Yes; the girls had the right of it. There was nothing that they were ashamed to have passersby hear in that sweet song of theirs and, as the minister meditated, he began to wish that more people had such a spontaneous and natural emotion of delight over Jesus' love that would set them a-singing just where they happened to be. The poor convention-bound grown-ups must have a special place, some retired spot lit with "dim religious light," before they would dare to sing out loud a song of holy joy. The minister was almost ashamed of his first impulse to quiet the little singers, and he felt like praying that he himself and others, who had grown up, and ought to prize more this wondrous love, might have the "holy boldness" to sing about it—to tell about it, wherever they were. He felt such an object lesson as this was much needed by many stolid professors of religion, who would sing in a prayer-meeting room:

> I love to tell the story
> Of Jesus and His love,

and then, when the song had ceased and the time was come for testimony, would all with one accord sit silent, glum, and wonder why some one did not testify.

A Singing Lesson

Once again the minister was taught a practical lesson by the singing of his six-year-old. They were walking, he and she, during the height of the holiday season, along the street in front of Mr. Woolworth's five and ten-cent store. The crowd was thick. People were hurried and harried. Women with their bundles jostled one another and little holiday gladness was discernible on their faces. While they threaded their way along, the minister and his Virginia (she had gotten a step or two behind), he heard of a sudden a sweet girlish voice singing, most naturally and happily, "Brighten the corner where you are." The first impulse, again, was to say: "Be still, dear; somebody will hear you." At home, in the music room, or over at the church, in Sunday school, he would have thought nothing of it, but somehow on the street, in such a crowd of hurried people, it seemed such a very conventional thing to sing about "Brighten the corner." But the little singer was undisturbed by any doubt about propriety or convention. Whether it was the holly that decorated the nearby window, or the jolly Santa Claus that looked out from the shop window, or just the general anticipation of Christmas coming, something within her had made her feel like singing at just that time and spot, and "Brighten the corner" was the song that came to her lips. Therefore she sang it.

As far as one could judge, the effect was not unpleasant on the passer-by. Everyone who was within the sound of that song looked up and smiled and went their way with more peace and good will written on their faces than had been there before. And as the singer and song continued down the sidewalk it appeared that the corner where she was was certainly being brightened.

Again the man beside the song was taught a lesson. Why should not a heart full of light and joy express itself in song, even in so "secular" a place as by a five and ten-cent store? Or why not sing on the street and in a crowd if one's heart was full at just that time and place? Why should not a believer sing at work as well as at his worship, or whistle and hum the melodies that are in his soul while he buys a beefsteak or drives an auto down the street? One invariable effect of a revival in a city is to set the people singing. It may be Alexander's "I will hold Thee fast," or it may be Rodeheaver's "Brighten the corner." But whatever be the popular song of the revival meetings the whole community is set to singing and whistling. And why not, all the year, have this mark of the glowing, happy experience of Christ? Why not sing and whistle after special meetings are over? Cannot the ordinary, everyday experience of Christ keep one in a tuneful mood? Do we indeed need a special pianist or trombonist to set our hearts aglow or make us bold enough to sing and speak of the joy of the Lord before men?

In Playtime, Too

And once again he "heard the children singing." This time it was the little three-year-old, trying to imitate a song of Rodeheaver's that she had heard the big folks sing, in which there is a strain:

> He walks with me and He talks with me,
> And He tells me I am His child,

But, to this little miss of three, "talking with" was not nearly so interesting as "playing with." So the version Gwendolyn surprised the minister with was:

> He walks with me and He p'ays with me.

"P'ays" was the nearest that her small mouth could get to "plays." Plainly, what she sang the Lord did for her was to walk and to play with her. And under her ludicrous attempt to echo the grown-up's song there is a precious lesson. Why should not our Lord play with us as well as walk and talk with us and do the more solemn things? If He be indeed so real and natural to us we will find our Lord accompanying us not simply to church and to prayer meeting and Sunday school, but we will have the delightful sense of His going with us to our games and recreations. Our amusements and our "good times" will be all the better times because "He plays with us." It may be, too, that if we thought of Jesus as desiring to enter into our pleasures and amusements we would omit some forms of our amusements and diversions because they would not seem to be just the sort of things that He would care to indulge in.

What tremendous lessons these little ones can teach us in their songs and playing, in their laughter and their games! He was a wise Teacher, indeed, who, when He desired to convey a supreme truth to grown-ups, set a little child in their midst. "A little child" has "led us" all the time. How very natural it was, then, that, as a part of His triumphant entry to the Holy City, Jesus heard the children "crying in the temple and saying, Hosanna to the son of David." The children's song pleased Jesus so that He refused to quiet them and said to the complaining scribes and priests: "Did ye not learn that out of the mouths of babes and sucklings thou hast perfected praise?" Jesus plainly liked the singing of children, and that seer who endeavored to picture the New Jerusalem surely used a most accurate and descriptive phrase when he said:

> I heard the children singing,
> And ever as they sang
> Methought the voice of angels
> From heaven in answer rang.

Plattsburg, N. Y.

There is considerable disturbance in Congress over the political classes concerning the League of Nations.

* *

It is expected that President Wilson will appoint E. Y. Webb of Shelby, N. C., as an additional Judge for the Western North Carolina district.

* *

Preparations are being made by the Allied troops to invade Germany if she should fail to sign the peace treaty. We have divisions now in Europe ordered home several weeks ago that are being held for that purpose.

* *

The Legislature of Ohio goes on record as being against prize fighting and adopts resolutions requesting Governor Cox to prevent the Willard-Dempsey match. Good for Ohio!

WORSHIP AND MEDITATION

THINGS WE ALL KNOW

That millions of men have been killed, and billions of dollars wasted by cruel wars.

Force may conquer men into submission for a time, but the enmity out of which future wars may spring will still be in the heart.

The world never stood in such desperate need of something which can unify men and nations in harmonious co-operation.

Jesus taught men to pray, "Thy will be done on earth as it is in heaven." The truth of the Fatherhood of God is the only permanent and sure foundation of the brotherhood of man. Only the power of love will transform the hearts of those who now survive the terrific wars, and form a sure basis of peace.

What shallow hypocrisy to quote about the "Fatherhood of God" and the "Brotherhood of Man," and yet to go on glorifying war and trying to widen the chasm between nations and fan the fires of hatred, and array the rich against the poor, and the poor against the rich!

Once the Jew despised the Greek because he did not "observe the laws of Moses." The Greek despised the Jew as a "barbarian." When the love of God came into their hearts a few of them had sense enough to see in each other the brothers for whom Christ died.

Once the boys of this land flew at each others' throats. Now they march to the music of the union. When Jesus comes into the hearts of Japanese, Chinese, Russians and Germans, French and English, Italians and Belgians, Turks and Spaniards, they will all take up the angel chant that shook Bethlehem, "Glory to God in the highest, on earth peace and good will to men."

D. A. LONG.

WHY STUDY THEOLOGY?

There are those who sneer at the suggestion of making a study of theology—especially by two classes of well meaning people. First, those who do not know what theology is, and second, by those who get what little knowledge of the Bible they have from going to church services occasionally, when some well advertised evangelist preaches, who tells his hearers that he knows nothing and cares less about theology.

"Theology is just as necessary in religion as botany is to the man who would not only see and smell flowers but also understand them." If religion is to become effective we must think out what lies back of its great experiences, and theology is just the ordered statement of these fundamental truths. Read the story of the blind man in the ninth chapter of John. The healed man exclaimed: "Well, herein is a momentous thing that ye know not whence he is. If this man were not from God, he could do nothing." When he thus reasoned "he passed from fact to its interpretation," from

"experience to theology," and his healing was a different thing to him because he had grasped the meaning of the power that had cured him." A great writer has said: "Theology for Paul was the root which drew moisture and strength from the soil of truth, in order that the flower of life might be fully developed, beautiful and attractive."

D. A. LONG.

VALLEY OF VISION

Isaiah speaks of the "valley of vision." The phrase is very suggestive and presents an unusual idea. It is to the mountain top and other high eminences that men think they must go in order to see. The valley hinders vision and narrows the horizon. Distances are cut off by the surrounding hills. So men climb to the heights to see.

But we sometimes forget that mountain-top vision, too, is limited—quite as much so as valley vision. While great distances may be swept by the eye, things appear in outline only, indistinct and blurred. Detail and individuality are lacking. In the valley we see things close at hand. The forest is not now a confused group of trees, but each stands out distinctly and is known by its family name. The river is no longer a mere silvery seam drawn carelessly across the land, but a living, bubbling, edifying artery, carrying life and verdure wherever its winding course lies. Beautiful flowers smile up from the most unexpected places; they never could have been seen from the mountain-top. The birds in their gayety of color are seen flitting to and fro, while they fill the air with their melody. And we become conscious of a thousand things we never could have known had we never come down from the lofty eminence. We are learning this more and more. The telescope must share honor with the microscope. There is more to be seen in the valley than on the mountain.

All of this is equally true in the spiritual realm. Mountain-top experiences, of course, are needed, too; but let us thank God for the "vision in the valley." Ah, what visions of truth have come to such as have walked there! Many a man has said that no price could buy from him what his soul saw and experienced when walking through the valley of sickness and bereavement and disappointment and trial. New glory has come into his life, and God is more real.—*Evangelical Messenger.*

President and Mrs. Wilson visited Belgium last week and were given a great welcome by the officials and people of that country.

Major Chas. M. Stedman, it is said, will be a candidate to succeed himself in the Fifth District as Congressman in the 1920 campaign.

Sunday School and Christian Endeavor

AN EXPLANATION

No Sunday school and Christian Endeavor matter this week. We had not received any material at the time this page had to be made up.—*Editor.*

ANNOUNCEMENT NO. 3

No Sunday school or Christian Endeavor Society can hope to make much progress without good music, *and plenty of it.* Now this is one of the features of our Sunday School and Christian Endeavor Convention that is to be held at Shallow Well Christian church July 15, 16, 17. It is our purpose to make it this year a "BIG FEATURE." Do you believe in good music? Do you think it is essential to a live, wide, awake and progressive Sunday school, or Christian Endeavor Society? Do you believe in having an orchestra to lead your singing in your Sunday school? Yes, I believe that *you* believe in all this; and enjoy good music just as much as any of us, and so I am going to ask that you give this matter just a few minutes of your time now.

If you have in your school or Society an orchestra, or any part of one, I want you to see that we have same in full force at the Convention. We can use violins, cornets, clarionets, trombones, or any instrument that goes to make up a first class orchestra. If you have such in your possession, and will join ourt State orchestra, please let me know a once, and bring it with you to the Convention.

I am counting on you. Write me, or Brother George M. McCullers, McCullers, N. C., at once and let us know that you are with us. If you cannot play, or sing, come on to the Convention anyway.

C. H. STEPHENSON, *Pres.*

ATTEND THE CHAUTAUQUA

The time for holding the next session of the Seaside Chautauqua and School of Methods is near at hand. The session this year will begin on Tuesday, July 29, continuing for one full week. The program for the coming session is in the hands of the President, Dr. Warren H. Denison, and will soon be ready for publica-

tion. The faculty this year consists of some of the strongest men and women of our own denomination with several from the outside. While it is impossible at this writing to forecast the attendance, we can say that if our people accept conditions this year as against those of last, we should have a much larger attendance. Last year the railroads made no concession in the way of reduced rates. This year summer rates to Norfolk will be on from almost every point of the Mississippi river. Those who have never attended before should by all means be present this year. The rates at the hotels and cottages at Virginia Beach will be about the same as heretofore. Considering the high cost of everything the rates last year were lower than we expected. We hope to be able to make special arrangements for those who desire still cheaper accommodations.

We shall urge this year more than ever a large attendance of our people in Eastern Virginia. Those desiring special information should write to,

S. M. SMITH, *General Secretary.* 604.5 *Bank of Commerce Bldg., Norfolk, Virginia.*

THE TITHER

An interdenominational publication devoted to Tithing and Christian Stewardship.

Editors

C. B. RIDDLE
KARL LEHMANN
BERT WILSON
HUGH S. McCORD
FRED G. THOMAS

8 pages; issued monthly; 50c the year.

Address

THE TITHER   Burlington, N. C.

MARRIAGES

FULLER-BROWN

Mr. Aaron Y. Fuller and Miss Josephine Brown were married at the home of Mr. J. D. Huffines, May 11, 1919, at 3:00 o'clock P. M. The occasion was a very quiet one, only one sister of the bride being present.

These young people are very popular in their community. They will make their home in Greensboro. Their friends wish for them long, happy and prosperous lives. The writer officiated.

L. L. WYRICK.

MARTIN-HUFFMAN

Married, June 18, 1919, at the home of the bride near Burlington, N. C., Mr. F. H. Martin and Miss Lula B. Huffman The writer officiated.

It was a beautiful home wedding, witnessed by friends who vied with each other in good wishes for the happy couple.

The bride is a daughter of Mr. and Mrs. A. O. Huffman, and is very popular. Mr. Martin is a Southern Railway conductor and lives in Charlotte, N. C.

After an excellent wedding supper the bridal party motored to Burlington, N. C., where the bride and groom took the north bound train for Washington, D. C., and other northern cities.

May the blessing of God attend their wedded pathway.

P. H. FLEMING.

GERMANY ACCEPTS

Germany has accepted the peace terms and will sign tomorrow (Tuesday), or a day or so thereafter. It is likely that she will insist that the terms will be again modified when her representatives assemble to sign, but such will not be granted, so it is stated.

A MEMORIAL—MRS. ELISHA HOWELL

Our Heavenly Father has in His infinite wisdom taken from our circle and from all pain and suffering our dear friend and sister, Mrs. Elisha Howell. She has been transplanted to that beautiful home beyond where joy, peace and happiness reigneth forever. Amid all her suffering and sickness she was cheerful and hopeful and her faith in God was unshaken. Her religious life was one of deep conviction, great faith and fervent zeal. Her interest in the Church was great and responsive to its needs and she attended every service whenever she was able.

Therefore, the Ladies' Aid Society of Holland Christian church, of which she was a charter member and one of its most faithful workers, would express its love and esteem in the following resolutions:

First, That such a life from our midst leaves a vacancy and a shadow that will be deeply realized by all the members of the society and will prove a great loss to her immediate relatives and friends.

Second, That we extend our heartfelt sympathy to the bereaved family and commend to them the Word of God and the presence of the Holy Spirit for comfort and consolation.

Third, That a copy of these resolutions be entered upon our minutes, a copy be sent to the family and a copy be sent to The Christian Sun for publication.

By order of the Ladies' Aid Society.

MRS. W. M. JAY,
MRS. JOB HOLLAND,
MRS. P. A. HOWELL,
Committee.

WILKINS

Annie Laura, infant twin daughter of Brother and Sister W. P. Wilkins of Liberty Christian church, died May 24, 1919, aged one year, seven months and twenty-eight days. The burial was at Liberty cemetery Sunday afternoon, May 25. The parents are sad to lose one of their bright little daughters but they sorrow with the hope of the promises of God's word concerning the resurrection of the body and the immortality of the soul.

C. E. NEWMAN.

CHANDLER

Thomas Edwin Chandler, infant son of Mr. and Mrs. T. W. Chandler of Virgilina, Va., was born November 1, 1918 and died June 1, 1919, aged seven months. The absence of the bright, interesting little boy from the home brings deep sorrow. Yet there is a comfort for Christian parents in the words of the Savior, "That in heaven their angels do always behold the face of my Father which is in Heaven."

The funeral was conducted from the home by the writer on the afternoon of June 2 and the burial in Union cemetery.

C. E. NEWMAN.

STEPHENS

William M. Stephens was born February 11, 1865, and died May 30, 1919, a few weeks after submitting to an operation in the hospital. The death came in his home near Isle of Wight Courthouse. He was for many years a faithful member of the Isle of Wight Christian church, which church he served as deacon for quite a while. He was a quiet and devoted servant of the Lord, and a man ready and willing to do his part for the uplift and betterment of the church and community. He will be greatly missed by his church.

He leaves to mourn their loss a devoted wife, ten children, four grandchildren, one brother and two sisters, and a host of relatives and friends. The funeral was conducted at Isle of Wight Christian church by the writer. Interment was made in the family cemetery at his home. The floral tributes were many and beautiful.

E. T. COTTEN.

PERRY

Carlton C. Perry, the son of Mr. and Mrs. W. W. Perry of Myrtle Avenue, North Danville, was drowned while swimming in an old rock quarry pond about two miles north of town on Monday afternoon, June 8. It was a tragic death and it cast a deep gloom over the entire community where young Perry was known and loved by all. He was but a little over fifteen years of age, having passed his fifteenth birthday on May 19, 1919.

He was a young man of splendid character, obedient and devoted to his parents, a genial companion, and an ambitious and aspiring young fellow. He commanded the respect and admiration of all who knew him.

Funeral services were held at his home on Wednesday afternoon. The writer had charge of the service, assisted by Rev. F. C. Lester. Interment was made at Leemont cemetery.

May God bless and comfort the bereaved parents and loved ones.

H. S. HARDCASTLE.

JOHNSON

Frank Eldridge Johnson, infant son of Mr. and Mrs. Frank Johnson, was born January 7, 1919, and departed this life June 12, 1919, at 6:30 A. M. He is survived by a devoted father and mother, one sister, two grandfathers, one grandmother, one great grandfather, and three great grandmothers, several uncles and aunts, and other relatives and friends. The remains were laid to rest in the Mt. Carmel cemetery after a short service in the church, conducted by the writer.

E. T. COTTEN.

WALL

George C. Wall, son of Mr. and Mrs. W. Paul Wall, Virgilina, Va., was born March 6, 1884 and died June 9, 1919 at his home near Averett, Va., aged thirty-five years, three months and three days. He was twice married. After the death of his first wife, who was Miss Millie Ford, he married Miss Hallie Tuck, who survives him, together with three children. Two years ago he united with Hebron church where he remained a consistent member till death. Brother Wall was a painter by trade and in recent years did some farming. He was of a pleasant disposition, kind and generous to those about him. A year ago his health gave away. He spent a while at Catawba Springs sanatorium but continued to decline until tuberculosis brought an end to his earthly career. The funeral and burial was at Hebron church in the presence of a crowd of relatives and friends on the afternoon of June 10.

C. E. NEWMAN.

HAD YOU NOTICED?

Had you noticed that THE SUN is now being printed on better paper? With a little more cost we are enabled to get THE SUN back to its standard quality of paper. Our supply of the former stock having exhausted, and there being so little difference in the price, we decided in favor of better paper. A better paper all the time is our aim. Help us!

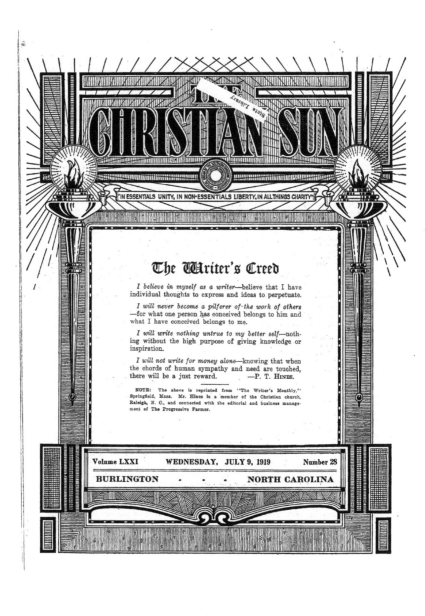

CHRISTIAN SUN

"IN ESSENTIALS UNITY, IN NON-ESSENTIALS LIBERTY, IN ALL THINGS CHARITY"

The Writer's Creed

I believe in myself as a writer—believe that I have individual thoughts to express and ideas to perpetuate.

I will never become a pilferer of the work of others —for what one person has conceived belongs to him and what I have conceived belongs to me.

I will write nothing untrue to my better self—nothing without the high purpose of giving knowledge or inspiration.

I will not write for money alone—knowing that when the chords of human sympathy and need are touched, there will be a just reward.   —P. T. HINES.

NOTE: The above is reprinted from "The Writer's Monthly," Springfield, Mass. Mr. Hines is a member of the Christian church, Raleigh, N. C., and connected with the editorial and business management of The Progressive Farmer.

Volume LXXI	WEDNESDAY, JULY 9, 1919	Number 28
BURLINGTON	- - -	NORTH CAROLINA

THE CHRISTIAN SUN

Founded 1844 by Rev. Daniel W. Kerr

C. B. RIDDLE - - - Editor

Entered at the Burlington, N. C. Post Office as second class matter.

Subscription Rates

One year .... $ 2.00
Six months 1.00

In Advance

Give both your old and new postoffice when asking that your address be changed.

The change of your label is your receipt for money. Written receipts sent upon request.

Marriage and obituary notices not exceeding 150 words printed free if received within 60 days from date of event, all over this at the rate of one-half cent a word.

Original poetry not accepted for publication.

Principles of the Christian Church

(1) The Lord Jesus Christ is the only Head of the Church.
(2) Christian is a sufficient name of the Church.
(3) The Holy Bible is a sufficient rule of faith and practice.
(4) Christian character is a sufficient test of fellowship, and of church membership.
(5) The right of private judgment and the liberty of conscience is a right and a privilege that should be accorded to, and exercised by all.

EDITORIAL

RALEIGH CHURCH GOES FORWARD

The church at Raleigh, N. C. seems to be taking on new life under the leadership of Pastor Eastes. Under recent date Brother Eastes writes: "The outlook for our work is very gratifying at present. Raleigh church was to have raised $3,000 for the Elon Standardization Fund and to our people the amount seemed large but the church gave $4,750. Immediately following this campaign the church put on a drive to liquidate a debt of $500 which had been borrowed to keep things running in the past, while the remainder of a thousand dollars was to pay for interior for Sunday school equipment, such as chairs, tables, etc. The canvass resulted in securing $2,000 instead of $1,000. This amount is to be paid in by the first of August. It is half in cash now. In addition to these things a piano has been purchased at a cost of $350, which makes a total of $2,350 for special local work."

In addition to these things above mentioned by Brother Eastes the church has organized from the ground floor and added to its organization a Woman's Missionary Society. Twenty-three adult members and two children have been added to the church in recent months. Several conversions have been during the regular services. The average attendance at mid-week prayer meeting during the last four months has been sixty and sometimes going over the one hundred mark.

PRESIDENT WILSON ADDRESSES HIS COUNTRYMEN

Immediately upon the signing of the peace treaty last week President Wilson delivered a very timely and significant message to his fellow countrymen. To us it seems worthy of consideration upon the part of every citizen and we are glad to reproduce it for the benefit of some subscribers who have not had an opportunity to see it. It is as follows:

"My fellow countrymen:

"The treaty of peace has been signed. If it is ratified and acted upon in full and sincere execution of its terms it will furnish the charter for a new order of affairs in the world. It is a severe treaty in the duties and penalties it imposes upon Germany, but it is severe only because great wrongs done by Germany are to be righted and repaired; it imposes nothing that Germany cannot do; and she can regain her rightful standing in the world by the prompt and honorable fulfillment of its terms.

"And it is much more than a treaty of peace with Germany. It liberates great peoples who have never before been able to find the way to liberty. It ends, once for all, an old and intolerable order under which small groups of selfish men could use the peoples of great empires to serve their ambition for power and dominion. It associates the free governments of the world in a permanent league in which they are pledged to use their united power to maintain peace by maintaining right and justice. It makes international law a reality supported by imperative sanctions. It does away with the right of conquest and rejects the policy of annexation and substitutes a new order under which backward nations—populations which have not yet come to political consciousness and peoples who are ready for independence but not quite prepared to dispense with protection and guidance—shall no more be subjected to the domination and exploitation of a stronger nation, but shall be put under the friendly direction and afforded the helpful assistance of governments which undertake to be responsible to the opinion of mankind in the execution of their task by accepting the direction of the league of nations. It recognizes the inalienable rights of nationality; the rights of minorities and the sanctity of religious belief and practice. It lays the basis for conventions which shall free the commercial intercourse of the world from unjust and vexatious restrictions and for every sort of international co-operation that will serve to cleanse the life of the world and facilitate its common action in beneficient service of every kind. It furnishes guarantees such as were never given or even contemplated for the fair treatment of all who labor at the daily tasks of the world.

"It is for this reason that I have spoken of it as a great charter for a new order of affairs. There is ground here for deep satisfaction universal reassurance and confident hope.

(Signed) "WOODROW WILSON."

A PLEA FOR THE SUNDAY SCHOOL

In these days of unrest and days when transportation and travel are in such an efficient way, we cannot too strongly urge the people to guard well against non-attendance of Sunday school. One Judge in the United States has sentenced 2,500 boys in five years and in keeping a record of them he finds that not on-of that number were members of the Sunday school.

This alone is a sufficient argument that we should lay special emphasis upon the Sabbath schools. Boys and girls are going to go somewhere and unless we give them a live and wide-awake Sunday school to attend, they will congregate together for other purposes. But the argument comes that boys will go elsewhere after Sunday school. This they will do and let them do it. It is the inculcation of the principles taught in the Sunday school that will guard them against entering into evil things upon the wholly and sacred day.

We were reminded of the little boy who was caught fishing on the Sabbath and after being scolded for it, replied that he was not fishing but just teaching the worms how to swim. That often is the case but it is breaking the law of the Sabbath and we know nothing that will help our boys to guard against such practices as the principles taught them in the Sunday school.

THE SUNDAY SCHOOL AND CHRISTIAN ENDEAVOR CONVENTION OF THE NORTH CAROLINA CONFERENCE

The Sunday School and Christian Endeavor Convention of the North Carolina Conference is to convene at Shallow Well church, near Jonesboro, N. C., next week. On page 14 and 15 of this issue will be found announcements concerning this Convention that are far better than we can write, but we take the space and pleasure of adding our hopes that the Convention will be well attended and that each school in the bounds of the Convention will strive to make a good report. For several years there has been considerable lack of interest and enthusiasm upon the part of the Sunday schools in North Carolina. It seems to us that the day has come when definite and progressive action is needed and should be taken. The work now seems to be thoroughly organized and under the direction of capable directors. The work has no occasion to lack in interest or lag in activity.

Should there be any school or Christian Endeavor Society that has not planned to send a delegate and a report to the Convention, let that school or Society take steps today to be represented.

SCIENTIFIC EXPERIMENT

Dr. J. F. McCulloch, Editor of the *Methodist Protestant Herald*, Greensboro, N. C., visited his son in Pittsburgh, Pa., a few days ago, and so interesting is a part of his write-up of the trip we reproduce it, feeling that it will be a bit of information:

While the editor was in Pittsburgh he visited the plant (one of them) of the Westinghouse Electric Company. First he visited the research laboratory. This stands on an eminence reached by a stairway of 110 steps. The building, several stories high, is divided up into rooms, each of which is equipped with apparatus for chemical or physical experiment, and has its own force of men engaged in the study of some practical problems arising in the processes of manufacture. The editor's older son is one of the workers there. His work just now is to discover why metals rust and how to prevent it. He had been given the problem of dis-

covering why brass castings contain "air holes." He had solved that, proving that the holes are caused by hydrogen gas generated in the furnace. The problem of preventing this generation of hydrogen was then given to another set of men. This illustrates the plan of operation. A general problem is divided into parts and assigned to different groups of men. Every few weeks they meet in conference and discuss their problems and report progress made and help each other. We then visited the great shops where things are made. These shops cover many acres. The buildings are said to extend for a mile in one direction. The employes number many hundreds, perhaps a few thousands,—men, women, and girls. Many electrical devices are made, motors being the principal ones, we believe. One requires a pass to get in, and note is made of what time he enters and what time he leaves. During the war visitors were not admitted, and the engine rooms where power is generated were guarded by men with guns to keep any German or pro-German from wrecking the power plant and stopping the works.

While in the research laboratory we were shown some liquid air. It looked like water, but on being poured into the room, it immediately evaporated in a dense vapor and disappeared. A stream was poured out through a rubber tube. The end of the tube became hard and brittle like glass. On being struck with a hammer, it broke into fragments. We picked one of them up cautiously. It felt like a piece of ice. A drop of liquid air striking the hand would probably cause a blister as does hot water. We were also shown the texture of different metals through a microscope.

These are interesting places to visit and to work in, for those that have the requisite tastes. The research is important work that a few men must do and that all mankind profit by.

This office is just in receipt of a letter from Chaplain B. F. Black telling us that he hopes to arrive in this country within the next two or three weeks. Brother Black will be open for work and will also be glad to visit churches or speak concerning his work and experiences in Europe. Address him at Elon College, N. C., and your letter will have proper attention by his splendid co-pastor and assistant, Mrs. B. F. Black.

Just as we go to press we have before us the initial copy of *The Herald of Gospel Liberty* under the editorship of Dr. A. M. Kerr. It glows with new life, presents a changed appearance and sounds a note of progressiveness. Success to Brother Kerr's labors and continued prosperity to *The Herald*, the oldest religious newspaper in the world.

Dr. Anna Howard Shaw honorary president of the National American Woman Suffrage Association, died at her home at Moylan, Pa., on July 2. Dr. Shaw came to this country from England, an unknown pioneer girl of four years. She was known the world over and her name will go into history as one of the country's great leaders.

We see the statement that Harvard University has never graduated a student with honor that was addicted to the tobacco habit.

PASTOR AND PEOPLE

VALLEY LETTER

On account of the epidemic of influenza during the fall and winter I am about two months behind schedule time with my revival meetings. Since beginning meetings in the early spring I have held at Wood's Chapel, Palmyra, Bethlehem, Concord and Mayland. At Woods' Chapel we had ten conversions and ten additions to the church. At Palmyra we had eleven conversions and eleven additions to the church, and another one has been received since.

The meeting at Bethlehem did not bring forth any visible results, but we hope the result of the seed sowing will be seen later.

At Concord six publicly confessed faith in Christ and united with the church. The work at Concord looks more encouraging than at any time since I have been pastor there.

At Mayland we were gladdened with fifteen public confessions and sixteen additions to the church. This church enjoys a steady growth from year to year, and the outlook is promising, although for several years after the establishment of the church there it looked very discouraging. Dr. W. C. Wicker, at that time representing the Elon College Standardization Fund in the Valley, preached for me several nights at Mayland. Aside from this I have had no ministerial help in my meetings.

I have not held my meetings at Joppa and Dry Run yet, and as it is such a busy time with the farmers now and will likely be for some time, I do not know whether I shall be able to wedge these meetings in before Conference or not.

We held our annual memorial service at Timber Ridge third Sunday in June. As is always the case, a large congregation gathered for the occasion. Dr. W. C. Wicker did the preaching which was very much enjoyed by all.

Our Sunday School Convention at Newport was an excellent one, and we trust will do much to inspire interest and activity in Sunday school and Christian Endeavor work throughout the Conference. Dr. N. G. Newman, of Elon College, added very much to the Convention by his addresses on Religious Education, and in other ways as opportunity afforded.

The next station of importance to us is New Hope where the Conference will be held, August 14-16. Those coming by rail will be met at Harrisonburg, which is only about three and a half miles from the church. Come and let us have the best Conference we have ever had yet.

A. W. ANDES.

Harrisonburg, Va., July 2, 1919.

UNION, N. C.

The Sunday school is arranging for Children's Day at an early date.

On the second Sunday in July Brother C. D. Johnston, Superintendent of our Orphanage with a class of children will be with us. Brother Johnston will present the needs and the claims of the Orphanage and the children will sing.

Our revival services are to begin on the fourth Sunday in July. Rev. George D. Eastes is to be with us. We are planning for a good meeting.

The young men of the church and congregation are called to meet at the church on the second Sunday in July at 10:30 A. M. for the purpose of organizing a young men's Bible class. The plan is to organize an up-to-date, progressive young men's class, elect officers, appoint committees, and get ready to do great things for Christ, the church, and the community. Let every young man who can possibly do so be present.

P. H. FLEMING.

Burlington, N. C.

PROGRAM OF THE FIRST ANNUAL SUNDAY SCHOOL AND CHRISTIAN ENDEAVOR CONVENTION OF THE NORTH CAROLINA CONFERENCE

July 15-16-17, 1919, at Shallow Well Christian Church, Jonesboro, N. C.

Tuesday Evening

Musical and Devotional Exercises, directed by the President
Address of Welcome ....W. H. Lane
Response ....Herbert Scholz
Business Session
Assignments of Homes
Announcements
Benediction

Wednesday Morning

Song Service—Congregation and Orchestra
Devotional Exercises ....T. E. White
Business Session
Annual Address ....C. H. Stephenson, Pres.
Reports
Organization and Expansion ....J. E. Franks, Chm.
Address, "A Great Motive for a Great Mission,"
R. L. Williamson
Teacher Training ....R. L. Williamson, Chm.
Special Featres: "In My Sunday School and C. E. Society"
Discussion led by ....L. L. Vaughn
Home Department ....Miss Mary Green, Chm.
Address, "The Sunday School That's Different,"
J. W. Harrell
S. S. and C. E. Literature ....A. T. Banks, Chm.
Address, "The Sunday School and Missions".....L. I. Cox
Recess

Wednesday Afternoon

Song Service ....Congregation and Orchestra
Devotional Service ....J. O. Atkinson
Business Session
Report—Primary Department ....Miss May Stephenson, Chm.
Address, "The S. S., a Spiritual Force
in Reconstruction"..................R. F. Brown
Report—Intermediate Department ......W. L. Thomas, Chm.
Address, "The Importance of You and Me".....P. T. Hines
Report—Adult Department ....Geo. T. Whitaker, Chm.
Address, "A Tithing Sunday School For
the New Time"...................J. E. Franks
Announcements
Benediction

Wednesday Evening

Musical Concert, directed by........Geo. M. McCullers, Chm.
Address, "The Sunday School and the

Orphanage'' ....Chas. D. Johnston, Supt.
Music .... Special Selections
Address, ''The Sunday School, An Evangelistic
          Force'' ....Geo. D. Eastes
Announcements
Benediction

Thursday Morning

Song Service—Congregation and Orchestra
Devotional Service ....N. G. Newman
Business Session
Report—Christian Endeavor:
    Senior Society ....Miss Lessie Pugh, Chm.
    Junior Society ....W. H. Stephenson, Chrn.
Address, ''The Challenge of The New
          Time'' ....J. V. Knight
Address, ''What Will We Do With
          Victory'' ....W. H. Stephenson
Report—Music Committee ....,Geo. M. McCullers, Chm.
Address, ''Spiritual Life in The Sunday
          School'' ..../....W. G. Clements
Report—Cradle Roll ....Mrs. Harriet McCullers, Chm.
Address, ''Missions in the Sunday School''.....J. O. Atkinson
Announcements
Recess

Thursday Afternoon

Song Service
Devotional Service ....Geo. D. Eastes
Report Nominating Committee
Business Session
Address, ''The Sunday School as a Servant''....W. A. Harper
Experience Meeting—General Topic
''What Good Has This Convention Done For
          Me,'' by ....All Present
Address, ''The Sunday School, a Factor in
          Religious Education''..............N. G. Newman
Odds and Ends
Unfinished Business
Adjournment

NOTICE

To all members, delegates and visitors who expect to
attend the Sunday School Convention, North Carolina Conference to be held at Shallow Well July
15-17:

You will please notify me as soon as you are elected
or appointed in order that entertainment may be provided, also state whether you will come by rail or private conveyance.

We prefer as many as can to come by private conveyance.

Your failure to comply with the above might result
in homes not being provided for you.

L. M. FOUSHEE,
Chm. Entertainment Com.
Jonesboro, N. C.

SEASIDE CHAUTAUQUA

**Virginia Beach, near Norfolk, Virginia on the Atlantic
July 29-August 5**

Dr. L. E. Smith, of Norfolk, will preach the series of
Chautauqua sermons this year. Dr. Smith is a great
preacher and it will be a treat to hear him on great
themes of ''Man and His Relationships.''

Dr. J. F. Burnett, Dayton, Ohio, will preach the
Sunday night sermon.

Mr. Hermon Eldredge will speak Sunday at 4:30 on
''Lessons Learned in the Camps.''

Dr. E. K. McCord, missionary to Japan for seventeen years, will conduct a daily mission class on the
great themes ''The Missionary Task,'' ''The Missionary
Church,'' ''The Missionary Process,'' ''Heathenism's
Response,'' ''Our Own Missions.''

The Forward Movement messages will be given daily
by Drs. R. C. Helfenstein, F. H. Peters, W. H. Denison,
and Mr. Hermon Eldredge.

The Christian Endeavor study hour will be conducted by Revs. J. V. Knight and R. F. Brown.

Some of the themes to be treated by that Sunday
school specialist, Rev. H. G. Rowe just home from ''Y''
work in France, will be: ''Sunday School Publicity,''
''Discovering and Training Sunday School Leaders,''
''The Workers Meeting,'' ''The School in Session,''
''Building an Adult Class from 5 to 100.''

Rev. W. P. Minton, Defiance, Ohio, will conduct the
music for the Chautauqua sessions and Mrs. E. T. Cotten will preside at the piano.

The Chautauqua lectures will be given by W. C.
Pearce of Chicago; Dr. Peter Ainslie, Baltimore; Dr.
R. C. Helfenstein, Urbana, Illinois; Rev. G. H. Ekins,
Norfolk.

Special Days

Wednesday—Norfolk and Tidewater day.
Thursday—Sunday School day.
Friday—Christian Union Day.
Saturday—Enlisted men from our churches and Sun-
day schools.
Monday—College day. Boost your college.

Write S. M. Smith, Norfolk, Va., General Secretary,
for rates and accommodations, Chamber of Commerce
Bldg.

WARREN H. DENISON, *Pres.*

SUFFOLK LETTER

The fourth day of July was Suffolk's biggest, brightest, and best day in her history; and she has had many
great days. It was the *Home Coming Day*, the welcome
to the boys from Suffolk and Nansemond county. Senator J. E. West was county chairman, and Congressman E. E. Holland was the chief speaker. J. M. Darden
had charge of the great dinner. Many faithful and efficient helpers aided Chairman West and Chairman
Darden in their plans and the execution of them to a
wonderful success. To tell the whole story and give
all the names in this great day and its work would
fill a paper; only bare mention can be made of the
chief parts in this spontaneous welcome to the boys
who have returned from the world-war, and who have
done their part in the fight for human liberty.

The business of the city was closed for the day. The
entire population abandoned itself to the spirit of a
new celebration; not simply the celebration of Independence Day for our nation, but the celebration of a
welcome that contains the germ of international Independence. That will be a great day when the whole world
celebrates some fixed day as the Independence Day of

the world. The stars and stripes would make a good flag for such independence—a star for every free nation under the sun; that will be a greater day when the Banner, with one star, waves over a redeemed race, "when every knee shall bow, and every tongue shall confess that Jesus Christ is Lord to the glory of God the Father."

The day was a typical "fourth of July"—clear, hot, and long. The parade started from the City Hall at 12:30, and consisted of returned soldiers and sailors, Confederate Veterans, Home Guards, Firemen, Marshals, floats, automobiles with Red Cross ladies, city officials, clergymen, bands, autos, fire engines, and the streets lined on both sides with people of the city and from the good county of Nansemond. About three hundred men were in the procession on foot, and more than two hundred of them were young men who had returned from service in this war to make the world a safe place in which to live.

At the close of the parade at the starting point in front of the City Hall, Chairman J. E. West introduced Mayor Stallings who made a brief speech, after which Senator West introduced Congressman E. E. Holland who made a splendid address, full of good words for the boys, praise for their heroic service, and sound advice as to the duties of citizenship. His final exhortation was beautiful, wise, and inspiring, that loyalty to government, fidelity to church, and the maintenance of social order require the same kind of courage that they had displayed on the field of battle.

The soldiers, sailors, veterans, and invited guests repaired to the Armory where three hundred Spartans sat down to a sumptuous dinner served by an army of young ladies. Movies and base ball free to the boys for the day, and the management throughout is worthy of praise for the success of Suffolk's biggest, brightest and best day.

W. W. STALEY.

RECONSTRUCTION POLICY OF THE CHRISTIAN CHURCH

The Executive Board of The American Christian Convention on December 19, 1918, requested the Commission on "Workers for the Field" to consider and report on a Reconstruction Policy for the Christian denomination for these days after the war, these wonderful days, pregnant with possibility and responsibility, as we face a new world order, an order that calls for workers as at no time in our history, and with a vision of the bigness of the Kingdom's program.

In response to the above request and instruction, the Commission on Workers for the Field begs leave to offer the following supplemental report:

I. That this Convention, in quadrennial session, hereby gives its hearty and strongest endorsement to The Forward Movement of the Christian Church, as our denomination's answer to Christ's call and challenge for these wonderful days, and pledge ourselves sacredly as officials, ministers, delegates, both in our representative and individual capacity, to aggressively carry out this five-point program, recognizing that these five points are fundamentals in Christian and church activity. We express the conviction that this Movement is

divine in inspiration and purpose. We believe that our brethren were led of God to present such a program for our Church. We believe that it will help us to fill our place and do our part in these days of reconstruction. We offer our allegiance to The Forward Movement of the Christian Church and pledge our co-operation to those who are called to direct its activities.

II. We are of the opinion that Christian Unity must have a large place in these days of reconstruction. The Federal Council of the Churches of Christ, the Interchurch World Movement, the Foreign Missions Conference, and many other Christian bodies, the great interdenominational religious papers like *The Christian Herald*, the secular press, are all placing a new emphasis on Christian Unity. We believe that there is no good reason why the Christian Church, in convention assembled, pioneers in the movement for Christian union, should not, in a very definite and positive manner, issue a challenge to the Christian forces of America to come together on a common platform, and send it forth in such a way that it will challenge the attention of the great bodies of the Church, and that we back up such a pronouncement with all the energies of our Church, that we commit ourselves definitely to all movement looking to the closer co-operation of Christian forces, and that we and our churches show the spirit of Christian unity in our own denominational enterprises. Therefore, we recommend that our Commission on Christian Unity be asked to offer such a manifesto, and that it be carried forth until Christ's prayer is answered. (The Commission on Christian Unity offered such a report and it was adopted).

III. After a careful survey of the field it is our judgment that we need at least fifty additional educated, trained workers, each year, or two hundred for the next quadrennium. As all who begin preparation do not complete their preparation, and as the number estimated is fifty thoroughly trained workers, it will therefore be necessary to have a much larger number begin such preparation in order to allow natural shrinkage. These would be pastors to take our present vacant churches, pastors to take the churches that need now to be brought to full time service, new home missionaries, new foreign missionaries, field secretaries, denominational specialists in education, rural life, social service, pastor's assistants and secretaries, and to supply the wastage that comes by death and old age. This is a conservative number and means that we actually need that number of well equipped, prepared Christian workers. We hereby call upon our Christian Divinity School, our colleges, our Educatonal Board, our conferences, and our homes to furnish annually this number of life recruits for Christian service, the same to be educated and thoroughly trained.

IV. We would urge individual and group study of the outstanding and immediate problems of reconstruction. We would suggest as a guide some such work as the "Study Outline in the Problems of the Reconstruction Period," prepared by experts and published by the Association Press and which may be secured from The Christian Publishing Association. One or more study groups of this kind in each of our churches would be a most effective means in aiding that church to solve its local problems of reconstruction. We further urge that adequate provision be made in our conference, institute, convention, Seaside Chautauqua, Craigville, Winona Lake programs, for the consideration of specific phases of those problems of reconstruction, such as the problem of the Community Church; the Sunday Evening Service; the Sunday Morning Merger Service of Church and Sunday-school; the Mid-week Prayer-meeting; the Returning Soldiers, Sailors, and Aviators; the Broken Family.; Mobilizing the Churches for Community Service; Adequate Church Programs; and others of vital importance.

V. We suggest to the editors of our denominational papers to arrange a plan whereby they may take up constructively the great vital themes of the Church, perhaps stressing great themes of the Church's need for a month each. If it were planned well in advance, with editorials on the theme, and by the strongest articles by our own men who are especially fitted to write on the theme to be considered, and these special themes fitted to most appropriate seasons of the year as to church work, and in harmony with the announced denominational plans, great good would result. The Herald of Gospel Liberty and THE CHRISTIAN SUN took up most effectively the theme of Life Recruits, for the third week in February, at the suggestion of the Board of Education. Were such issues put out on such a theme for a longer period of time, say a month, it would make a deep impression on our people. Some of the themes might be: Evangelism, Life Recruits, Christian Stewardship, Christian Unity, Church Attendance, Religious Education, Missionary Responsibility, Rural Church, Community Service, Interdenominational Movements, Young People's Work, Mid-week Prayer-meeting. There are many others.

VI. It is the judgment of your Commission that in these days of reconstruction we must enter in a larger way, through delegates, representatives, and in our church literature, the many great co-operative Christian movements. The Federal Council of Churches, the laymen's Missionary Movement, the Interchurch World Movement, the Missionary Education Movement, International Sunday School Association, Christian Endeavor Conventions, and similar agencies of the Kingdom should have our best and fullest representation, and the largest possible publicity of their messages and conclusions.

VII. The return of our enlisted men is now revealing to our churches their opportunity and responsibility. The war has emphasized the need that they and others had before the war, viz., that the Church should reach after them in the strongest possible way to win them to Christ and enlist them in the work of the Church for the Kingdom. The Church should give to them tasks that are worth while, that they may put into Christian activity the splendid principles of sacrifice, service, unity, which they have learned and used Parents, Sunday school teachers, pastors, should place before the men returning to our churches the world call for Christian service. The view-point of life of our enlisted men has enlarged, their knowledge of the responsibilities of human relationships has increased, service to their fellowmen has become a habit; courage, loyalty, friendliness, sympathy, have become realities. The Church has the solemn duty of capitalizing in the most practical way this new, God-given power and turn it into channels which will advance the Kingdom of God. The Church must spare no effort to bring the returning soldier into relationships—business, social, and religious—which will be most helpful to him.

VIII. Again we express the conviction that one of the greatest needs of our people is that we get a church vision, and plan by systematic effort to enlist the people of the community with a church program—some organized system of church activity. It is believed that our people have the means and qualifications, let them but once get the vision of what ought to be done and how to do it. To this duty we challenge our church officials and our pastors. From our Forward Movement, our Seaside Chautauqua, our Craigville, and other summer conferences we expect large visions to be given, new inspiration imparted; thus we urge our people, the rank and file of our churches, a part of their reconstruction program, to avail themselves of these means of religious education. We suggest also that each church embody the outline of the Forward Movement program in a church program that will enlist all the members in active Christian work.

IX. We regard it important that we place greater emphasis on the social side of the gospel, on a present life religion essential to right living and serving, salvation from sin here and now, and for service to our fellowmen, not merely a form of words, but a living, loving power in and behind the words.

Respectfully submitted,
THE COM. ON WORKERS FOR THE FIELD,
WARREN H. DENISON, Chairman,
N. G. NEWMAN,
GEO. C. ENDERS,
WILLOE J. HALL,
J. J. DOUGLASS,
C. B. HERSHEY,
J. PRESSLEY BARRETT,
J. C. DEREMER,
E. F. SAUNDERS.

Adopted by American Christian Convention.

MONEY, THE LEAST OF HIS EXPENSES

Harry T. Hartwell of Mobile, Ala., was defeated in his race for Congressman in the First District. According to his statement filed with the Secretary of State, his expenditure of money was the least of all as his statement shows:

"I lost six months and ten days canvassing, lost 1,000 hours' sleep worrying over the results of the election, lost 20 pounds of flesh, kissed 500 babies, kindled 100 kitchen fires, put up 10 stoves, cut 11 cords of wood, carried 50 buckets of water, pulled 400 bundles of fodder, walked 1,100 miles, shook hands 20,000 times, and talked enough to fill one month's issue of the New York World, baptized four different times, made love to nine grass widows, got dog bit nine times, then got defeated."

THE CHRISTIAN ORPHANAGE

A PLEA FOR THE CHRISTIAN SUN

We have just four methods of reaching our people and keeping them in touch with the Orphanage work.

First: By making personal visits to churches and Sunday schools and telling them about the work here.

Second: By writing personal letters to the churches and Sunday schools and also to individuals.

Third: By friends of the Orphanage making personal visits to the Institution and seeing at first hand the building and the children.

Fourth: Letters in THE CHRISTIAN SUN. THE CHRISTIAN SUN is really the strongest medium by which we can keep all our people in constant touch with the work. I am truly sorry that all families in our Church do not take our Church paper. Every family ought to have THE SUN in the home and read it. Then our people would keep posted as to the different institutions of the Church and would be more interested in the success of the Church.

People, generally, are not so much interested in things they know nothing about. If we could get each family in our Church to take THE CHRISTIAN SUN and read it, I feel sure that all departments of our Church would grow as never before.

Our people ought to take THE CHRISTIAN SUN, not because THE SUN needs subscribers so much, but because our people are so much in need of THE SUN to be able to keep up with the workings of the Church and know what each department is doing.

THE SUN has never been more ably edited and we should show our appreciation for the efforts our Editor is making to give us a Church paper, as good as the best, by getting it in each home.

I am informed that we lack eight hundred subscribers having it on a paying basis. If we could place it in eight hundred homes not now taking THE CHRISTIAN SUN it would take care of itself and the Editor would get salary enough to make a living.

We have 226 churches in the Southern Christian Convention with a membership of 25,750. To raise the eight hundred subscriptions needed to place THE SUN on a paying basis it will be about four subscriptions to each church. How easy it ought to be raise four subscriptions in each church! If the pastors and superintendents of the Sunday schools, and also individuals who are interested in this, would make an urgent campaign for the month of July I know it could be done. I will see that four goes from my church. Let us raise the eight hundred. Then you will see our mission fund grow, our college grow, and the contributions to the Christian Orphanage will double.

CHAS. D. JOHNSTON, Supt.

REPORT FOR JULY 9, 1919

Amount brought forward, $7,037.91.

Children's Offerings

Mae Thomas, 10 cents; Herman Thomas, 10 cents; Total, 20 cents.

Sunday School Monthly Offerings

(Eastern Virginia Conference)

Wakefield, $4.59; Mt. Carmel, $4.50; Mt. Carmel Sunday school class No. 6, $1.00.

(North Carolina Conference)

Pleasant Grove, (Va.), $4.00; Six Forks, $3.15; Ebenezer, $6.95; Damascus, (Orange County), $1.07; Oak Level, $1.00; Eure, $5.00.

(Georgia and Alabama Conference)

Kite, Ga., $2.00; North Highlands, Ga., $3.25; Total, $36.51.

Special Offerings

A. P. Thompson, on support of children, $34.00; G. L. B. Penny, Guardian, $139.52; E. L. Aldridge, $1.75; Mrs. E. L. Aldridge, 75 cents; Bethel Sunday School Rally, $23.00; Total, $204.02.

Total for the week, $240.73; Grand total, $7,278.64.

LETTERS FROM THE COUSINS

Dear Uncle Charley:—I am sending a dime for the orphans. I am proud of my little picture you sent me. I would like to hear the little girl sing.—*Herman Thomas.*

I am glad you like the little girl's picture. I hope to have the opportunity of bringing her to Bethlehem to sing some Sunday.—*"Uncle Charley."*

Dear Uncle Charley:—I am sending the orphans a dime for June. I did not have time to write last week. I was so busy attending to my little brother. He is three months old.—*Mae Thomas.*

You have a splendid job attending to your brother. You must be good to him and he will soon grow up and be a big brother to you.—*"Uncle Charley."*

DOCTOR SUNSHINE

"Course I'm going to be a doctor when I grow up," declared Tom. "I guess my Uncle Robert's a doctor, and I'm going to be just every bit like him when I grow up."

"Then if you're going to be a doctor," broke in his Uncle Roberts, "you're just the little boy I'm looking for."

He took an orange from his overcoat pocket. "Put that in your case," he said, "and then put on your hat and go down the street till you come to a small gray house with green shutters. A little boys lives there who has a broken leg. Give him the orange and see if you can make him laugh."

Tom trudged off in great delight. It was a long time before he came back; but when he did he was so happy that his eyes shone.

"Well, Dr. Sunshine, how do you like it?" asked his uncle.

"O, I'm going every day till he is well," Tom cried.

"I shall put Tom under the seat of my automobile," laughed the doctor, "and when my patients are cross I will bring Dr. Sunshine in."—*Exchange.*

Churches are now making their plans for another year. If you keep your same pastor, show your appreciation by raising his salary, and if you change pastors, be sure to give the new pastor more money.

CHRISTIAN EDUCATION

IN UNBROKEN SUCCESSION

On the fifth Sunday in June I was at Damascus church, Sunbury, N. C., and that church too went safely over the top. It was the 80th church I had the pleasure to visit in person in the drive and personally it was a genuine satisfaction for this final church like the 79 preceding to go over the top. Rev. W. B. Fuller is the pastor of the Damascus people and is meeting with excellent success. He has a noble band to serve and will serve them effectually. He took the field like a hero and helped valiantly to put the thing over.

As I think over the days from February 16 to June 30, I am overcome with gratitude to God for His unmerited blessings. I have worked in four states, interviewed more than a thousand individuals, been entertained in more than 100 homes, and everywhere the courtesies that have been thrust upon have filled me with the sense of my unworthiness . I have accepted them as the representative of a great people in a great cause. My heart wells up in gratitude to every one.

The Elon drive has succeeded far beyond our expectations. It has done so because of wise and statesmanlike direction and a wonderful display of team-work on the part of the people. The Drive Committee, consisting of Col. J. E. West, Hon. K. B. Johnson, and Dr. R. M. Morrow, with Dr. W. W. Staley, ex-officio, as president of the Southern Christian Convention, directed the work in a spirit of sympathy and a determination that knew no defeat. I take off my hat to them. They will long be remembered in Elon annals for their brilliant guidance in this forward-moving event.

The field men did splendid work and were ready to do all in their power, consistent with other obligations in their time, to put the drive across. For varying portions of time outside their own churches the field men associated with me were; Rev. T. E. White, Rev. W. C. Wicker, Rev. L. I. Cox, Rev. J. V. Knight, Rev. A. T. Banks, Rev. R. F. Brown, Rev. C. B. Riddle, Rev. W. W. Staley, Rev. G. O. Lankford, Rev. E. M. Carter, Rev. H. S. Hardcastle, Rev. N. G. Newman, Mr. L. W. Vaughan, and Prof. C. C. Johnson. These brethren were busy pastors, editors, and college professors and officers, but each of them gave such time as he could and did it in beautiful spirit. My heart-felt thanks are due them.

I must particularly thank Rev. C. B. Riddle, our Editor. He not only helped in the field work, but he supplied the publicity matter for the back page of THE CHRISTIAN SUN, and this matter was largely read by our people, thus making the presentation to individuals easy. The generous space accorded the drive in the reading columns of the paper is deeply appreciated. The college could not have asked for more than was willingly accorded in this instance. I am grateful.

Our pastors too without exception have received me open-heartedly. They opened up their pulpits and their homes. They arranged for my transit in their fields. They personally accompanied me and when I would get weak they would come with renewed vigor to cheer. God bless our pastors and multiply their kind!

And the laymen and lay-women of our churches—they are the light of the world, they are the salt of the earth. They have responded to the appeals we made in the spirit of a liberality as genuine as the principles of our beloved Church are generous. More than a thousand of them gave subscriptions from $100 to $5,000, and gave with smiling countenances. God loveth the cheerful giver. He has many in our Church that He loves. God has great things in store for the Christian Church. He must greatly bless her in this wave of splendid generosity.

But my chief thanks are to my Heavenly Father. He gave the health and strength for the tremendous strain of such a drive and He blessed the simple appeal for a great cause with willing responses from consecrated hearts. Through four states I traveled thousands of miles on automobile, with only one puncture. He knew we did not have time for punctures and prevented. There are numerous instances in the drive when I was conscious in a peculiar sense of His intervention and provision, but these things are too sacred for a printed page. He has been good to us. Blessed be His name!

We had hoped this week to give a verified statement, but some of the field-men have been delayed in getting their reports to the office. We shall certainly hope to have the statement final by the next issue. We are far beyond the $300,000 mark, and at this every heart will rejoice. It means not only enlarged resources, but multiplied friendships and amplified opportunity for service on Elon's part. May Elon be faithful and true to these friends and to this opportunity for service.

Funds This Week

The only full graduate of Elon to be killed in the world war was Herbert Harper Barber, '18. In his memory his brothers have founded a fund of $1,000. How sweet and appropriate! God bless these brothers.

Deacon M. J. W. White, Norfolk, Va., lost by death a splendid son in the person of Charles Nyack White, a Y. M. C. A. secretary. He perpetuates his beautiful life in a fund of $1,000. How fine a deed!

A few years ago a splendid son of Mr. and Mrs. W. S. Johnson, Gilmerton, Va., was prepared to enter Elon, but by accidental drowning his precious young life went out. His parents have founded a fund in his memory.

Mr. Boyd Richards, Winchester, Va., the first man of the Virginia Valley Central Conference to give $1,000 to any church enterprise, founds a fund. May he be the first of a long line of spiritual successors!

There may be other funds to report next week.

Let every heart give thanks to God for His wonderful blessings to us in this campaign.

W. A. HARPER,

WHY EDUCATE

It will soon be time to pack valise and trunk and start off to school. "Shall I send my son or daughter, and if so, where?" is being asked by many anxious parents. The same question "shall I go to college, and if so, where?" is being asked by many anxious young men and women who have to map out their own way and pay their own bills.

Shall I go to college? The business world is calling for just such young people who have seen a vision of larger things and are desirous of entering some college or university.

The immediate remuneration seems enticing with a bright future; and the expense of an education is no small item. And besides the thought of getting out of the usual college or university with a degree and nothing to do and a big debt is not very prepossessing to those who have to foot their own bills. And yet it is those of this class who go usually make good.

But shall I go to college? In what way will it help me? Is it worth while? These are not idle questions. They need to be pondered well and answered wisely. The answer depends somewhat upon your idea of an education, your purpose, and the use you make of an education. It is will to go to college; it will help you; it is worth while, if you will make it so. Decide what you want to be and do and work it out in the school of life using all the means at your command for the accomplishment of your purpose.

I came across some striking figures in the "World Call" the other day that interested me. Let us study them:

"The child with no schooling has only one chance in 150,000 of performing distinguished service. With an elementary education he has four times the chance. With high school education he has eighty-seven times the chance. With a college education he has 800 times the chance."

To this general education, and Christian education and the chances are wonderfully increased for performing distinguished service. There is a distinctive need and place for the Christian college in the educational world. Every educational institution of our land ought to be permeated by the principles and teachings of our Lord and Savior Jesus Christ.

Again I noticed in the same magazine these significant figures:

"Less than one per cent of American men are college graduates. Yet this one per cent of college graduates has furnished fifty-five per cent of our presidents; thirty-six per cent of our members of Congress; forty-seven per cent of the Speakers of the House; fifty-four per cent of Vice-President; sixty-two per cent of the Secretaries of State; fifty per cent of the Secretaries of the Treasury; sixty nine per cent of the Attorney General; sixty-nine per cent of the Justices of the Supreme Court."

These figures speak for themselves and need no comment. Does it pay to go to college if you want to render distinguished service to your land and country? Does it pay to have an education if you wish to broaden your opportunities for advancement and useful service to God and man? It certainly does.

Where shall I go to college? Go where you want to go. Go where you can get that training you wish; and where the training will fit you for the best possible service for "God, home and native land." Go where with all your getting you will get an education plus *Christian*, and not doubt and unbelief.

A Christian college of your own Church that rings true to true educational principles and Christian teaching and that will fit for service in the home church, and in the great world field for Christ, the Church, and Humanity, is a good place to go.

Denominational colleges ought to look out for their young people and ever seek to fit them for service in their chosen field, so that when they have completed their college course, they may go forth trained men and women. It is a good thing for their Alma Mater to ever lend a helping hand to those she sends out into the battle fields of life. Let us think of our college and see what we can do for it.

Adoniram Judson is quoted as having said, "If I had a thousand dollars to give away, I would put it into a Christian school in America, because in building Christian schools and in filling them with boys and girls we are raising the seed corn of the world."

We needed money for our college and the Church responded largely; now let the Church respond with her boys and girls; for money is naught without them.

P. H. FLEMING.

Burlington, N. C.

MISSIONARY

CASUS GRATIAE

President Harper's wonderful campaign and glorious achievement for Elon bring us to our knees in gratitude and praise to the Giver of all good. Raising in a period of four months more than three hundred thousand dollars for our college shows that our people are both able and willing. And it has not yet begun to appear what we can do, and what by our Father's help, we shall do to advance His Kingdom.

The College began the campaign four months ago to raise $125,000.00. It was seen within a month after the campaign began that we had all of us underestimated the desire and the ability of our people to give to a worthy cause. Then the amount had to be doubled; the goal was fixed at $250,000.00. But long before the four months were out it was seen that we still were wanting in faith, and were still underestimating the strength and the willingness of our people to give.

How this wonderful work should inspire all of us! We are getting to be a missionary people. And a missionary people are always able, and always willing to give. We shall now have to fix our missionary goal at half a million, and when that is raised and paid in and used to the glory of God and to the advancement of His Kingdom, the President of our College after that will not have to ·start out for a quarter of a million—he may start .out for a million—and get it. Ours is a benevolent God. He showers His bounties and His abundance upon those who undertake His program. Ours is a cause of rejoicing, for the people who have given $300,000. for a Christian cause will not be poorer but richer when they shall have paid it.

THE SPIRIT OF SACRIFICE

One of the benefits accruing from the war was the increased spirit of sacrifice. It was thought that there would be loss to the Mission Boards during the war. The opposite was true, as the following figures show. Putting it in round numbers contributions to foreign missions from the United States were as follows:

For 1915, $16,000,000. For 1916, $17,000,000. For 1917, $19,000,000. For 1918, $20,700,000.

Now if to this constant increase could be added as much the next four years to the cause of missions as we spent on the war, this whole world would be evangelized with this generation. .

Are we ready for this spirit of self-sacrifice? Are we ready to do as much to redeem and save our fellow-man as we were to help kill and destroy?

MISSIONS IN HOLLAND SUNDAY SCHOOL

Mrs. Chas. H. Daughtrey, Holland, Va., has been elected Superintendent of Missions in our Holland, Va. Sunday school. On Sunday, June 29, she gave her first public missionary exercise by the children of the school. A splendid audience assembled in the High School building. The writer has never attended a more impressive and inspiring and suggestive missionary exercise. The Superintendent brought out on the stage in epitome that which is actually taking place on a world-wide scale in reality. The millions of unsaved who wait and weep in heathen darkness, the need of funds and more funds with which to send missionaries, and then the compelling need of more missionary volunteers were all represented in a most impressive manner. Holland Sunday school has made a great move in the right direction.

THIS LOOKS GOOD TO ME

I have in hand a letter, dated June 23, 1919 from one of our best business laymen, in which are these lines: "I am very glad to see the success that Dr. Harper is having raising the Elon College Endowment. Our people have always been to conservative. We have never tried to do anything for our Church (till recently). I feel like you should raise five hundred thousand dollars in five years for missions. Our Church needs it. We need several new churches now (in the home field). I believe you can raise half a million dollars for missions if you will keep hot on the trail."

I wonder if there are others amongst us who really have the growth of our dear Church at heart who feel as does this hustling, wide-awake, successful business man?

J. O. ATKINSON.

NOTES

Rev. J. S. Carden, Durham, N. C., called at THE SUN office last Saturday, and as usual, brought a new sub scriber. Come again.

Rev. R. F. Brown, Durham, N. C., is doing the preaching in a series of evangelistic services now being held in Providence Christian church, Graham, N. C.

On June 30 Rev. J. O. Cox and wife, Flat Rock, N. C., had the misfortune of losing an infant child. Their friends will sympathize with them in the loss of their loved one.

We see in the *Granite State News*, Wolfeboro, N. H., a neat advertisement of the Christian church at that place, announcing the service on June 30 which was held by Chaplain H. E. Rountree.

Rev. A. H. Morrill, Newton, N. H., writes: "You people in the South are doing splendidly in rallying to the support of missions and in increasing the endowment of your college."

Mrs. E. W. Wilkins, Route 2, Burlington, N. C., sends this office five pounds of nice honey with her compliments and best wishes. Many thanks, Sister Wilkins. We are enjoying it very much.

This office has been assured by Rev. E. K. McCord, Dayton, Ohio, that he will write a monthly letter for our Southern people. We appreciate this on Brother McCord's part and know that our people will much enjoy what he has to say.

We have before us a well planned and prepared program of the fiftieth annual session of the Eastern Virginia Sunday School Convention. The Convention is to be held at Oakland Christian church near Suffolk, Va., on Wednesday and Thursday, July 23 and 24. We trust that two goods days will be spent for the Master's cause through the Sunday school work.

We chronicle with sorrow the passing of Mrs. S. C. E. Beamon, Sunbury, N. C. She was one of our friends whom we knew only by correspondence. She was a loyal and devoted worker and always interested herself in increasing THE SUN's circulation. She made it a rule to keep her subscription paid more than two years in advance. Her passing was on July 1. She was in her eighty-sixth year.

"Uncle" Wellons informs us that he overlooked one thing from his article of June 25 that he meant to say. He writes: "On one of the trains passing here (Varina, N. C.) the engineer whistled at all the stations, 'O, Happy Day, O, Happy Day, When Jesus Washed my Sins Away.' He whistled it just as if he meant it—and I think that he did.'"

WORSHIP AND MEDITATION

WORSHIP

By Charles L. Brooks, in Christian Advocate, Nashville, Tenn.

The word "worship" is a compound of the Anglo-Saxon *weorth*, worth, and *scipe*, ship. Worth signifies "deserving of" and ship, "reward." Hence worship literally means "deserving of reward." The Greek word is *proskuneo* from *pros*, toward, and *kuneo*, to kiss the hand; and literally means "to kiss the hand toward," in token of reverence. In the New Testament sense it is homage paid to God. Worship, then, is the act of paying to the Supreme Being what is his due; the homage and reverence that belong to him; adoration.

The Roman Catholics distinguish three kinds of worship: (1) *Latria*, the worship that belongs to God; (2) *hyperdulia*, the worship that is due to the Virgin; and (3) *dulia*, the worship that belongs to the saints. The influence of these distinctions in worship is seen in the titles of honor applied to magistrates in some places, "Your worship." But in the light of divine revelation such distinctions are seen to be false. Only God is entitled to be worshiped; only he is worthy of worship. The messenger from heaven, whom John was about to worship on the isle of Patmos, commanded: "See thou do it not: for I am thy fellow servant, and of thy brethren that have the testimony of Jesus; worship God."

But how is one to worship—pay to God what is his due? The Book tells us: (1) *En pneumati*, in spirit, with that reverence which the Spirit begets. Otherwise one can have no reverence at all; only the cringing fear of devils. God is a spirit and demands above all that one's inner nature, or spirit, unfettered by any hindrances, shall be distinctively, consciously related to him. But (2) also *en aletheia*, in truth, reality as opposed to mere appearance, that which ought to be and alone has a right to be as opposed to the specious, the normal as opposed to the abnormal, the formula as embodied in the religion of Jesus Christ, opposed alike to the inventions of the Jews, the superstitions of the Gentiles, the speculations of corrupt men, and the precepts of the false teachers even among the Christians themselves. It is a categorical, imperative *dei*, must. Those who worship at all must worship after that fashion. Otherwise there is no worship. Everything is solemn mockery.

The worship of God, then, springs out of a heart of love. And love to God, as taught by the Master in the parable given at Luke VII, 41-47, is in proportion to man's sense of God's forgiveness. The poor woman who stood weeping at the feet of Jesus and washed them with her tears and wiped them with her hair and kissed them and anointed them with the ointment in the alabaster box did so because she had an acute sense of having been forgiven much. So she loved him much and worshiped him in proportion to her love. Worship is sometimes also an expression of faith preparatory to supplication. The poor leper, who came to him as he descended from the mount, worshiped him, saying: "Lord, if thou wilt, thou canst make me clean."

The ideal of Christianity can only be made actual through worship. The reasoned idea without worship is theology; worship without the reasoned idea is superstition. Worship is the means of cultivating reverence and inculcating piety and obedience. It is both individual and social, not possible to the individual without the influences that make men devout, nor to society without organization and control. The influences that make men devout are the consciousness that they are related to God and God is related to them; that they can talk to God and God is able to hear and answer them; and that if their hearts are wounded and sore from trial and affliction, God is both willing and able to heal them. Christianity (whose heart and center are Christ) through the agency of the Church organizes and controls worship.

All true service to God springs out of the worship of God. He who does not worship does not serve. The critical Pharisee, in the parable already cited, did not worship the Master, and so did not serve him, even in the matter of common courtesies, water for his feet, the customary kiss and oil for his head. The character of one's worship types his service. If one is inattentive, listless, lazy, and sloven in worship, he is likewise inattentive, indifferent, lazy, and sloven in service. Where the pews are vacant on Sunday, the house of God is very apt to be dirty (unless the preacher sweeps it), the music a scream, the elements absent from the Lord's table on communion days, and the pastor's salary unpaid. Furthermore, the man who goes to church on Sunday and reads a few verses of scripture and says a prayer and sings a psalm and lets that end his program is neither worshiping not serving God; he is camouflaging. The worshiper goes out from his holy communion with God into the great needy world to minister unto the bodies and souls of men in an effort to do God's will and work and build up his Kingdom.

On account of the failure to worship and so the failure to serve, effort is often made to substitute service for worship. This always results in rites and ceremonies; the less Christianity there is, the more rites and ceremonies there are. In some places it is all rites and ceremonies. The mighty choir does not want the plebeian multitude to break the harmony by joining in the song, so congregational singing is dead. The sermon is crowded out altogether or is reduced to a thin, skimmed-milk affair, in which floats one little idea vainly seeking, like Noah's dove, to find a place to rest its feet.

Religion without worship is nothing but a philosophy. The true end of our religion is to induce men to worship God. Then they will faithfully serve God. Whatever hinders worship hinders services. Out of the hindrances of worship commonly given I note two:

1. *Mental Emptiness.* There are minds that can pass through divine worship and never know what happened, unless there was something novel or strange about it. This makes a berth for a clown in the pulpit, and a clown is always popular with the empty-headed. A stick can travel around the world, but it is still a stick. So an empty mind may go to church and be just as empty when it leaves, no matter how profound the discourse. I don't know what is ever to become of such souls, unless God in his pity has provided for them in the same provision he has made for infants and idiots. Meditation and prayer are closely related. The Psalmist said: "While I was musing the fire burned: then spake I with my tongue, Lord, make me to know mine end."

2. *Disorder.* The thing that does more to destroy worship in a modern congregation than anything else is disorder. If the cackling of geese could save souls as it saved Rome, then would we all get to glory. The modern babel just before and at the close of our Sunday worship is nothing short of sacrilege. The fact is that many of us have never learned to properly appreciate God's house. The humble Mexican, commonly called "greaser" by us, will lift his hat and pass the house of God with uncovered head, just as a patriot will uncover before the flag of the nation; but our modern American, who looks down upon this humble soul, as the ancient Pharisee did upon the wretched publican, will carry on his twitter and gossip and 'gabble and giggle even in the house of God itself, as though that place were no more hallowed than the market place or a common dance hall.

Instead of taking our cue from newspaper correspondents, let us learn with Habakkuk: "The Lord is in his temple: let all the earth keep silent before him." So shall we learn how to worship God and go out from his presence with our souls strengthened for life's tasks.

Lord, teach us to worship!

McAlester, Okla.

THE LION

By Dr. William C. Herman

There are more than forty species of the cats, and of all that number but one is entirely domesticated; that is Thomas, the housecat. Nearly all of this noisy family are marked by stripes or spots. All live and prey upon other animals, usually weaker than themselves.

The lion is the recognized head of the entire cat family. For a long time he has been called the "King of Beasts." He is the monarch of all that he surveys. This well-known animal is found both in Africa and Asia, wherever sufficient game exists. When his natural quarry is wanting, this noble beast will not hesitate to attack man himself or more frequently the domestic animals.

The lion is a most powerful animal. A single blow of his mighty paw will fell an ox. His voice is a mighty roar; no other animal, with the exception of the hippopotamus, can surpass the fullness of the roar of the lion. This mighty cat preys on the deer, zebra, antelope, and other grass-eating animals. He is the terror of the natives and very frequently makes a meal off of a man.

A man-eating lion is usually an old one, who, being unable to capture his usual prey, must capture such as he can by his stealth and cunning, and he does not have much trouble in killing and carrying off a sleeping native. Several years ago two man-eating lions in Africa actually stopped the building of a railroad, because of their man-eating character. A large number of Indian coolies were employed in the building of this line and were housed in rough shacks and cabins. The man-eaters discovered how easy it was to break in and seize a sleeping man. Each night the lions would come there would be a loud cry from the victim, and the beasts were off. This occurred each night until twenty-eight coolies and an unknown number of natives were carried off and eaten by the man-eaters. Finally the men refused to work while they were in such danger, so all work stopped, and a search for the lions was begun. They were finally shot by one of the engineers, and the building of the line proceeded.—*In Boy Life.*

WILL EAT OUT OF YOUR HAND

The chickadee will eat out of your hand if you show him that you have something good to eat and he is not already pretty well satisfied; for he is a social, fearless, and responsive little fellow, says the American Forestry Association, Washington, which is conducting the national bird house-building contest that school children are entering into with great interest and enthusiasm. Another thing is that if you whistle to the chickadee he will invariably respond, which is more than can be said of most other birds. The chickadee braves the winter cold and remains even when the snow makes it hard for him to find much food. The top and back of his head are jet black, and there is a big black spot on his throat, while the rest of the bird is shaded from white to gray and buffish.—*Exchange.*

THE SPEED LIMIT

Uncle Sam Hodge came down from the Kentucky mountains with his yearly produce to market. His team of oxen was somewhat weary with a two days' pull. But when Sam reached the city limits he was confronted with the sign: "Speed limit, fifteen miles an hour."

He pulled his whiskers a moment in silent meditation, and then drawled out to his oxen, "Well, I know darn well we'll never make it, but we'll do our doggone best."—*Everybody's Magazine.*

Sunday School and Christian Endeavor

SUNDAY SCHOOL LESSON FOR JULY 20, 1919

The Lord's Supper. Matt. 26:26-30; I Cor. 11:20-34.

Golden Text: For as often as ye eat this bread and drink the cup, ye proclaim the Lord's death till he come.

This is another great lesson on the Sacraments of the church. You will remember, of course, that we are in the midst of a six months' study of the great fundamental truths of the Bible beginning with the first of April and to be concluded the last of September. This lesson is not to be a disquisition on the last night of the life of Christ, but a lesson on the observance and the meaning of the Lord's Supper. This is a memorial rite for us, of which the Lord said "as oft" and "do this in remembrance of Me." How often should we observe this Sacrament? How often should we remember our Lord by the rite which He Himself instituted? We know something of what broken bodies mean nowadays; something more than we used to know. We shall never forget those broken bodies, and all we can do for them and theirs we will feel to be all too small a remembrance. The body of our Lord was so marred that there was "no comeliness." His visage was "so marred from the form of man that his appearance was not that of a son of man," (literal rendering Isa. 52:14). All this was to happen within the next few hours, and with wistful tenderness and love He said, "Do this in remembrance of Me." His body was bread—that best of all foods for man, a food made of many small grains broken and blended for our food. His blood was our drink, like the fruit of the grape, strengthening, renewing, rejuvenating. "Don't forget me," He says. How long shall we remember Him? Till he comes. Do you pray, "Thy Kingdom come?" Do you earnestly look for His coming? Do you say, each time you commemorate His death, "Even so, come Lord Jesus"? What a supper that glad reunion feast will be, when we sit down with Him to drink of the new fruit of the vine in His Father's Kingdom! MRS. FRED BULLOCK.

CHRISTIAN ENDEAVOR TOPIC FOR JULY 20, 1919

Crusading Against Intemperance. Eph. 6:10-20.

Last night I read two articles in *McClure's Magazine* for July. One by a woman, "Why I Am Against Prohibition;" one by a man, "Why I Am For It." Such articles cause us to remember and proclaim that this is no sudden spurt of feeling, no "few fanatics" as Mrs. Atherton says, who have forced their will on the majority. This is the sober thought of a nation reached through almost a century of effort and crusade. It has been a *majority, not a minority* vote that has made township, districts, counties, states, and finally a nation dry. Do not let any one make you believe this is a sudden impulse. It is not even religious or moral, on the part of thousands, possibly millions, who have voted for it. It was distinctly a matter of business. Business men found their outgo being lowered, their accident list lengthened, and they decreed against it. Life Insurance men found drinkers lived shorter lives, and they decreed against it. Railroads grew alarmed at the lengthening list of accidents and they decreed against it. And so it grew. The church, and the prohibition societies set the people to thinking, and their God-given commonsense has done the rest. Do not believe that nonsense about the results being different were the soldier's home. Hundreds of thousands had already cast their vote to make their own country or State dry before they went. As a matter of fact, the great majority of those who would have voted wet were right here in America, rejected for physical unfitness, either altogether from the army or held for selective service. This is not to say all who were rejected were rejected for these reasons, but a great majority were rejected for that cause, or for evils arising from it.

MRS. FRED BULLOCK.

ANNOUNCEMENT NO. 4

The program for the Big Convention is ready and you will find same elsewhere in this issue of THE SUN. So far as the efforts of your Executive Committee are concerned, we have done our best and hope that *you* will like the program, *and do your part* toward making the Convention a *Victory Convention* indeed and in truth.

Don't forget that we want every Sunday school and Christian Endeavor Society in the State represented, and this evidently means *your school and society*. It is now only a few days before the Convention convenes, and when you elect your delegates, read the program over carefully, and assign to each delegate, one or more subjects to report to your school, and insist that these reports be made in writing. In this way you will be able to boost the Convention before it meets, and your school after the Convention adjourns.

Let's line up now for the *Big Victory Convention* and after that, the *best year* in our Sunday school and Christian Endeavor work, not only in our individual school, but in the entire State. Lest you forget—the Convention meets at Shallow Well Christian church, July 15-17, 1919.

C. H. STEPHENSON,
President.

A BETTER SUNDAY SCHOOL CONVENTION

We are now preparing to attend the Eastern Virginia Christian Sunday School Convention, which convenes Wednesday and Thursday, July 23 and 24, at Oakland. We should be making better preparations to accomplish more during this session than we did last, and we should accomplish more, easily so, because we have known one whole year in advance both the place and the time for the coming session, neither of which did we know for the last session until shortly before the Convention was to convene. And we shall convene two days instead of one this year.

May we call attention to a few things, some of which were not done last year, which must be done this year, if we shall go forward.

In the first place, the Recording Secretary should be at the very opening of the Convention and on time to the minute. He should from then to the close make the closest copy of all the proceedings, and be ready to read the minutes, before the close of the Convention, for corrections, and lastly, have the minutes published and distributed to each and every Sunday school in a few weeks after the close of the Convention.

Next, each and every secretary of a Sunday school should fill out the Annual Report, that all the statistics be given for his school, and mail it to the General Secretary, Rev. G. O. Lankford, before July 20, or be sure it gets to him at the opening of the Convention.

Let each and every · Department Superintendent make a written report to hand the Secretary of the Convention. This will not prevent a lengthy speech, but give the Recording Secretary something definite to place in the minutes for publication.

Last but not least, let each and every Sunday school have at least one delegate, if not the whole number permitted, present to the whole session. The best needs of the whole 39 schools cannot be planned and worked out unless every school is represented. If the individual school has a matter to place before the Convention, let that delegate speak for the school and be prepared to vote for same.

E. T. COTTEN,
Recording Secretary.
Suffolk, Va.

THAT INTERNATIONAL CHRISTIAN ENDEAVOR CONFERENCE

Two great gatherings our Young People ought to be interested in for the summer months are:

First, the Seaside Chautauqua and School of Methods of the Christian Church to be held at Virginia Beach, July 29-August 5, at which time Christian Endeavor work will be given one of the most prominent places on the program. Our young people who go away for their summer vacation could not find a more desirable place than to spend one week of it at Virginia Beach. Those who have been there know it to be true.

The second is the International Christian Endeavor Conference to be held in Buffalo, N. Y., August 5-10. The writer has an outline of the program of that Conference before him. It is one of the finest roster of speakers I have ever seen. Some of the world's greatest speakers are on that program. I am sending a copy of it to our good Editor hoping that he will find space to give a list of some of these speakers and special features.

The railroads are giving reduced rates. *One plus one-third fare.* The fare one way from Greensboro is $23.25, plus war tax. Here's hoping some more of our people will line up with the Greensboro delegation. It will do both you and your Church much good.

J. VINCENT KNIGHT.

ALL SUNDAY SCHOOL AND ENDEAVOR OR WORKERS, TAKE HEED!

The stage is now set for the greatest Conference of Sunday school and Christian Endeavor workers ever held in the State. Never before was there such a good and fruitful period for Christian work as now. A year ago our energies were tied up with a great national strife. Today we turn to building Sunday schools and Christian Endeavor Societies in our land. They must be built right. That is why we urge you ot attend the Sunday school and Christian Endeavor Convention at Shallow Well Christian church July 15-17 without fail. Not only will there be new ideas and methods there for you, but the hospitable people of the community have promised us entertainment, that will cause all delegates to remember the occasion forever and aye.

A program and train schedule elsewhere in THE SUN will give you an idea of the work of the Convention, and also show you how to get to Shallow Well. *Meet me there.*

C. H. STEPHENSON,
President.

ANNOUNCEMENT NO. 5

Tuesday evening at 8:00 o'clock, July 15, rain or shine, the first State Sunday School and Christian Endeavor Convention, convenes at Shallow Well Christian church, located near Jonesboro, N. C. If you are going via Raleigh, notice the following train schedule—*and don't get left:*

Trains leave Raleigh at 8:45, 3:57, 4:45 A. M.; 6:47, 4:20 P. M. and arrive at Sanford 10:16, 5:12, 6:10 A. M.; 8:00, 5:56 P. M. *All dele-*gates *will be met at Sanford.*

For further information, write Mr. L. M. Foushee, Jonesboro, N. C., who is chairman of the Entertainment Committee, and at your service. *Get busy and be there.*

C. H. STEPHENSON,
President.

CHILDREN'S DAY

Many of our Sunday schools are having, and are planning to have Children's Day. But many are not. Programs are prepared, are in print and are for full distribution. A request to the writer will bring as many programs as needed and without price to the one requesting. Having prepared the programs we are anxious for the schools to use them. So if your school has not prepared, send fo rthe programs, as many as you need, and they will be sent gratis at once. Let all our schools this year have Children's Day.

J. O. ATKINSON,
S. S. and C. E. Board.
Elon College, N. C.

OUR SUNDAY SCHOOL AND CHRISTIAN ENDEAVOR CONVENTION

The Eastern North Carolina Sunday School and Christian Endeavor Convention, the Western North Carolina Sunday School and Christian Endeavor, and the North Carolina and Virginia Sunday School and Christian Endeavor Convention having been consolidated into one we certainly ought to have this year the greatest and best of all our Conventions. Chairman C. H. Stephenson, Raleigh, N. C., who has been so efficient in the Eastern Convention is Chairman of the consolidated body, and is working commendably and enthusiastically to make our first all State Convention a great success. His efforts should be applauded and enthusiastically supported by Sunday school superintendents and pastors in all the churches of the consolidated Conferences. The Convention is to be held at Shallow Well church, Jonesboro, N. C., July 15, 16 and 17 and every school and Endeavor Society should be represented. An excellent program has been arranged and the Convention should mark an epoch in our work.

J. O. ATKINSON.

OBITUARIES

WHITE

Mrs. Mary E. White was 81 years old when she departed this life on the evening of June 26, 1919. She was the wife of William White who preceded her to his reward several years ago. To this union were born three children, two of whom are dead. Mr. E. L. White, the only living relative of the White generation, resides in Norfolk, Va.

The funeral was conducted from the Christian church of which Mrs. White has been a faithful member for a number of years. Rev. J. S. Carden assisted the writer in the funeral services. The interment was made at Mount Hermon church. May the Lord bless the lonely son and the many friends who have sustained the loss of her friendship.

R. F. BROWN.

WILLIAMS

Sister Martha Jane Williams passed away to her home in the spirit land June 22, 1919, at the age of eighty-two years, one month and twenty-five days. She was the mother of eight children. She had twenty-five grandchildren and twenty-five great grandchildren. She connected herself with the Christian church at Damascus, Orange County, early n life. May God bless the bereaved. Funeral and service conducted by the writer.

P. T. KLAPP.

RUSH

Jessie May Rush was born August 9, 1894, and died June 11, 1919. Her age was, therefore, 24 years, 10 months and 2 days. Miss Jessie had suffered many afflictions during her life, but she bore them patiently.

She was a member of Palmyra Christian church from childhood, though for several years prior to her death she had been absent from the community most of the time. She is survived by her mother, and other relatives and friends who mourn her departure. Funeral services at Palmyra, June 13.

A. W. ANDES.

SHOMO

Mary Catherine Shomo was born January 19, 1837, and departed this life June 21, 1919, aged 82 years, 5 months, and 2 days. She was left a widow by the death of her husband about 13 years ago. Sur-viving are five daughters, eleven grandchildren, and eleven great grandchildren, two sisters and one brother.

Sister Shomo united with the Christian church at Bethlehem more than forty years ago, and lived a consistent Christian life. The place she filled for so long on earth is vacant but Heaven is richer. Funeral services were held at the Lutheran church in New Market, June 23, conducted by the writer, assisted by Rev. Mr. Derrick, pastor of the church where the burial took place.

A. W. ANDES.

ANDERSON

June 6, 1919 closed the earthly career of Mary Frances Anderson, wife of Deacon A. S. Anderson of Timber Ridge Christian church. Sister Anderson was born June 2, 1844, and was, therefore, 75 years, and 4 days old when death came. Her life was full of good deeds and good service to humanity, to church, and to God. Since childhood she was a faithful member of the Timber Ridge church.

Surviving are the sorrow-stricken husband, four daughters, one son, and many other relatives and friends who deeply mourn her death. But in our sorrow we have the assurance that she is happy with other loved ones who have gone before. Funeral services at Timber Ridge, June 8, in which the writer was assisted by Rev. W. T. Walters, a former pastor.

A. W. ANDES.

SMITH

Departed this life at her home near Hopedale, N. C., Mrs. Margarett C. Smith, July 2, 1919, in her 86th year.

Mrs. Smith was a daughter of Henry Trolinger and was twice married. Her first husband, Willie Harder, died a number of years ago. Her second husband, John W. Smith, and three children, John R. Harder, Willie Harder, and Miss Corna Smith, survive her.

She was a member of New Providence Christian church and had been for a number of years. She had been sick for some time and death came not as a surprise. She fell asleep trusting Him who saved her.

The funeral services were conducted from Haw River Christian church by the writer and the interment was in the old Trolinger cemetery at that place. May the Healer of broken hearts comfort those who mourn.

P. H. FLEMING.

FROM OTHER SANCTUMS

Must Divide With Them.—Some one, writing of the perishing people of the Near East, whom he had seen and was trying to rescue, said: "It is wicked to let them starve." How can we excuse ourselves, if in our own abundance, we let others die for want of food? How can we excuse ourselves, either, if, knowing the gospel of God's grace, we permit those in heathen lands to perish without the knowledge of the way of life?— *Herald and Presbyter.*

Who Am I?—Last leap year I did not wish to embarrass my best girl by letting her propose to me, says the editor of the "Orangeville Sun," so I asked her to be my wife, but she said she would much rather be excused, so I foolishly excused her; but I got even with her because I married her mother and when the girl became my daughter, and when my father married my daughter he became my son. When my father married her she became my mother. If my father is my son and my daughter is my mother, then who am I? My mother-in-law, who is my wife, must be my grandmother, and I, being my grandmother's husband must be my own grandfather.—*Afton Free Press, (Canada).*

THE CHRISTIAN SUN

"IN ESSENTIALS UNITY, IN NON-ESSENTIALS LIBERTY, IN ALL THINGS CHARITY"

July Fourth

THE FLAG is the center of attraction on July fourth. It is a symbol of what the nation is and what it has for its ideals. We float the flag because we have freed it from tyranny and are willing to protect it at the cost of blood. July fourth, nineteen hundred and nineteen, will have a deeper meaning than it has ever had. It means not only *independence* but *inter-dependence*. We have learned that our glory is not in maintaining our country alone, but in the protection of all mankind. It is in giving moral, social, economic and spiritual justice to the peoples of the world that we glory in and not in self-preservation alone. The occasion this year is sublime because of the larger freedom it signifies and the cost in blood of that freedom.

Volume LXXI	WEDNESDAY, JULY 2, 1919	Number 27
BURLINGTON	· · ·	NORTH CAROLINA

THE CHRISTIAN SUN

Founded 1844 by Rev. Daniel W. Kerr

C. B. RIDDLE   -   -   -   Editor

Entered at the Burlington, N. C. Post Office as second class matter.

Subscription Rates

One year .... $ 2.00
Six months 1.00

In Advance

Give both your old and new postoffice when asking that your address be changed.

The change of your label is your receipt for money. Written receipts sent upon request.

Marriage and obituary notices not exceeding 150 words printed free if received within 60 days from date of event, all over this at the rate of one-half cent a word.

Original poetry not accepted for publication.

Principles of the Christian Church

(1) The Lord Jesus Christ is the only Head of the Church.
(2) Christian is a sufficient name of the Church.
(3) The Holy Bible is a sufficient rule of faith and practice.
(4) Christian character is a sufficient test of fellowship, and of church membership.
(5) The right of private judgment and the liberty of conscience is a right and a privilege that should be accorded to, and exercised by all.

EDITORIAL

CROSSING THE ATLANTIC

Some days ago the first successful attempt to cross the Atlantic in a seaplane happened. The *London Daily Mail* offered a prize of $50,000 for the first non-stop trans-Atlantic flight. The world is proud that the flight was a success. It is the revelation of the continued advance of civilization. May such progress continue, but may it not continue if the Lord is to be left out of all our daring and doing in this day of high accomplishment. Every modern invention and convenience should be used for the carrying on of the Gospel of Jesus Christ that all the world may have the privilege of the Gospel.

THE PRESIDENT AND PROHIBITION

There is being a hard fight made in Washington to get the war-time prohibition act repealed. The opponents of prohibition think that Mr. Wilson will do something for them whenever he returns. We believe that he will do something, but we believe that he will do the same thing that he did before—sign in favor of prohibition. Mr. Wilson is considered a war leader and admired by all parties, but if he signs the bill giving the whisky elements a longer chance to deal out their soul-killing stuff, he will undoubtedly lower his standing in the minds of thousands of people.

PEACE TERMS WITH GERMANY

This note is written Friday morning, June 27, while the world is anxiously waiting to know the outcome of the terms with Germany. The final terms have been issued and it is said that no change will be made. Before this note is read, these terms will likely be signed. There is a feeling of satisfaction that the world will hasten to its normal condition. But the signing of the peace terms will be of no avail unless it is the good will of the Germans to keep these terms. Just what per cent of the American people can trust Germany we do not know, but we are of the opinion that the number is small. We claim to be an optimist but fear that there is danger ahead. Let the nation pray that the world may become a community of friendship.

FLEETING YEARS

As we look upon the men and women about us we see those who are on the shady side of fifty; those who are soon to count their three-fourths of a century, and those who have already counted these three stages. There was a time when we considered old age as being unpleasant and being a day of sadness and sorrow. Such is not our thought now, but as we see our aged friends slowly walking down the sunset valley, there comes a thought that is hallowed and a pleasure of mind that these veterans have seen this world long enough to begin to yearn for a habitat elsewhere. The only regret and sorrow that comes to us in seeing these pilgrims living out the last half of their days is to think of those who know not God and whose lives are not in accord with the principles of Jesus.

> The years on quiet sandals go
> So softly we are not aware
> Until summer's singing vales
> We find the snow is everywhere.

MENDED MEXICO

The trouble in Mexico has started again and it points to the same grave danger that Mexico will one day do harm to us if we do not do something to her, or for her. Mexico's problem is unique and most complicated. The people who live there have ideals far different from ours. There seems to be little chance of co-operation with them. Mexico's problem is economic, social and religious. These are the three things that must develop in any nation before it can gain the respect of the best civilization. In these three, Mexico is behind. In some parts of this land of confusion, developments are going forward. But in other parts the situation is exceedingly difficult. We believe that it is America's duty for America's sake, and for Mexico's good, to take over Mexico and point her people to the way of safety and satisfaction.

THE COWARDICE OF THE BREWERS

We have always known that there was a streak of cowardice in the man who makes whisky and beer for the detriment of his fellowman. The brewers have found that they can no longer operate in the United States, and so they are trying to shift their business into Japan and China, where they can hide behind ignorance and superstition. This undertaking is twice cowardly because they know that they can take advantage of the educational conditions and sow tares in the ignorant minds of the people. But thank God there are a few Christians in these countries who have backbone enough to put a fight against their coming; and if this country is in earnest about its missionary work, they will join hands with these benighted lands and the whisky business will be dumped into the Atlantic ocean when it starts its transfer from the shores of America to the shores of the Orient.

A PASTORAL VISIT AND A———

The other day I was on my way from............ to ..:............... The curtain of night was beginning to shut out the light of the day as I viewed a little house on the top of the hill. Having heard that a member of the Christian Church lived there, I stopped and knocked upon the door. A saintly soul came to greet me. Her form was bent by the toil of years and time had written wrinkles across her brow. In that house, cozy and comfortable, she had lived alone for ten long years. That many years ago her husband answered the summons of heaven. In my new friend's hand was held a bundle of papers that were being re-read because she wanted something to help her pass away the time. I told her that my first object was to meet her and to see if I could interest in her taking THE CHISTIAN SUN. "I shall be glad to take it, Brother Riddle," she replied as she reached into her apron pocket for a ten dollar bill. She expressed a desire, a very earnest desire, to see the first copy.

No fiction! The story is too sad! For ten years THE SUN would have been a comfort to that lonely widow. Some pastor failed to *pastor*. I hurried home amid the shadows of night rejoicing that one more of the three thousand homes in the Southern Christian Convention without THE CHRISTIAN SUN was to have it. A glad rejoicing it was, and it would be yet if my heart was not bleeding over the thought of the 2,999 other homes without the official organ of our work; homes with a pastoral visit about once a year and the privilege of hearing preaching possibly once a month.

I stretched myself upon the resting couch to restore energy from the day's toil and dreamed of a new day, a new time, a new era, in which the ministry and the laity would give of their time *just one* whole day to visiting their fellow church members in interest of THE CHRISTIAN SUN. How peaceful that sleep would have been had it not been disturbed by the break of the morning and the facing of another day of strenuous effort to make a great task go!

Utinam modo agatur aliquid!

           C. B. R.

AN UNUSUAL OFFER

THE CHRISTIAN SUN office has decided to offer a reward of $25 in gold to the pastor sending on or before August 1 the largest list of persons who *do not* take THE CHRISTIAN SUN. The conditions are as follows:

1. The list must be made up of members of the Christian Church.

2. The list must be members of the church or churches of the pastor sending the same.

3. The names composing the list must be heads of families, or what you would consider the logical person of the family to subscribe to the Church organ.

4. Only one name from the family can be given, unless some member is making his or her home permanently elsewhere.

5. The pastor must make up the list himself and get no information from this office.

In addition to the prize of $25 in gold, each pastor falling below the regular prize will be rewarded for his work.

☞ Three thousand families in the Southern Christian Convention without THE CHRISTIAN SUN. How many, dear brother pastor, of this number in your field! It will be a good day's work for the cause for you to get the facts. Will you do it?

SUFFOLK LETTER

The Church paper fills a place in Christian society that no other publication can fill. It is the organ of the denomination it represents, and is supposed to express the beliefs and doings of the body. It is the medium of communication between the scattered constituency, and the advocate of all its enterprises. No department of the Church could live, much less prosper, without the help of the church paper.

The Christian Church made an invaluable and permanent contribution to the progress of Christianity when, in September 1808 at Portsmouth, New Hampshire, through Elias Smith, it published *The Herald of Gospel Liberty*, the first religious newspaper in the world. It was a necessity for the Church separate from the State. From that day till this day Christian agencies have multiplied in all denominations with increasing efficiency.

The epistles of the New Testament were the first hints of a Church paper. They were letters written to the churches and individuals touching the vital interests of the life of the Church and the activities of the people. These letters gave the idea of personal touch and spiritual interest and remain as evidences of the wisdom and zeal of the apostles. The Church paper really copies this personal and Christian interest in the churches; and there is hardly an enterprise of the denomination that could live and prosper without this medium of inter-communication. The Orphanage lives because THE CHRISTIAN SUN is all the time speaking of its work, its needs, and its purposes. The little letters of children, the great words of the Superintendent, Chas. D. Johnston, and the reports of things accomplished all tell the same story of a great purpose. Through THE SUN one can hear the heart-beats of the liberal souls that give of their means, their prayers, and their thought to this one great charity of helping orphans. The cry of the orphan is also heard through this same organ, so that the work goes on, hopefully. The Institution would be impossible without such organ. The same is true of the College, the missionary enterprise, the woman's work, and all the general work of Christianity.

The Church paper does even more than propagate the teachings and work of the Church; it enters the field of public education and fashions many of the moral ideas that determine human welfare. It challenges the attention and moral consideration of society on many questions and wins its way into the confidence and approbation of the people. National prohibition would have been impossible without the religious press. The secular press with its paid advertisements would not have initiated a campaign against the saloon business. The Anti-Saloon League would have been powerless alone in such an undertaking.. The religious press has a field of usefulness all its own, and no one can make a contribution of so great value for so small a sum of money as to subscribe for his Church paper.

THE CHRISTIAN SUN costs $2.00 a year. It speaks to 2,000 homes every week. It should speak to 3,000 homes every week. If you could *know* what it is doing for you, your family, and your business, you would subscribe at once and send Rev. C. B. Riddle a $2.00 check.

W. W. STALEY.

Some weeks ago we made a request for the names of invalids of the Church. To that request we received responses that gave us a list of fourteen who are invalids or shut-ins. We have always endeavored to let this office be the largest possible service to the people, and so we are mailing these fourteen invalid friends our exchanges. Our exchange list contains about twenty-five of the leading Church papers throughout the country. These papers are valuable, well edited, and many of them very beautiful in their make-up. We have enough copies to send these persons papers practically every week, and we are glad to do so. The only cost is postage. Only two of this list of fourteen take THE CHRISTIAN SUN, and so if there are friends who would like to contribute something to help send THE SUN to these persons, it will be gladly received and used for that purpose.

THE WAR'S GREATEST HERO

The war's greatest hero is Sergeant Alvin C. York, who killed twenty-five Germans and captured one hundred and thirty-two. Young York is from Pall Mall. Tenn. On June 7, 1919, he himself was captured by Miss Grace Williams and the marriage ceremony was performed by Governor Roberts of Tennessee. Congress has voted young York a medal for his bravery in the war.

Miss Sarah Nall—I do not see how I could do without my church paper. I hope THE SUN will continue to shine in my home.

PASTOR AND PEOPLE

BURLINGTON LETTER

Since the Burlington Sunday school decided to support Miss Martha R. Stacey we have been looking forward to the time when she should visit us. By the courtesy of the Mission Board she was with us June 15 to 19. In this brief time we came to know each other in a measure at least. The fellowship of those days was much enjoyed and will prove very profitable. A bond has been created between us. She will go to Japan as the representative of our school and congregation. There is a mutual gladness about the privilege to go and to send. Miss Stacey came before the Mission Board in its last session and sought the privilege to go and later the Burlington Sunday school asked the privilege to send her. When the life was offered the support was soon provided. God will provide support for His workers. Men and women ready to go out is the need of the hour. Let there be more offering of life and support will be provided.

Miss Stacey while here impressed us with the fact of her love for mission cause. She has been contemplating the matter for a number of years. In fact she was consecrated to mission work by her mother. She has been in city mission work for several years in connection with her work as a public school teacher. She is a graduate of the Gordon Mission Training School and has since April first been taking special work in a Boston Kindergarten school. She is well equipped for her work and has natural gifts which promise great usefulness. Best of all she is promised the prayerful, sympathetic and loving support of the people who are sending her out. The few days with us developed beautiful touches of interest and called forth the expression of consecrated purpose.

The messages brought to us by Miss Stacey were much enjoyed and filled with helpful suggestions. She spoke to the Sunday school, the church, the Young People's Missionary Society and also spoke at the midweek service and the reception given in her honor. The Sunday school presented her with a fountain pen and the Ladies' Societies presented her with a wrist watch. She is expecting to sail about September 5.

The work on the new church is being pushed. We are fully expecting to have it ready for the meeting of the new State Conference in November. However, considerable work remains to be done.

J. W. HARRELL.

NOTICE

The Sunday School Convention of the Eastern Virginia Christian Conference will meet with Oakland Christian church, near Suffolk, Va., at 10 A. M., on Wednesday, July 23. By vote it was decided by the last session of the Convention to hold only a two days' session this year. The program, therefore, has been arranged accordingly. Let each superintendent keep this in mind in planning for the Convention. For information as to trains, see the pastor, Dr. I. W. Johnson's announcement in THE SUN. All together for a successful session. Meet us at Oakland on July 23 and 24.

G. O. LANKFORD,
Berkley, Va., Route 3.   Gen. Secretary.

NOTICE

The Eastern Virginia Christian Sunday School Convention will meet at Oakland Christian church, near Chuckatuck, Nansemond County, Virginia, Wednesday and Thursday, July 23 and 24, 1919. All persons coming by railroad will come to Suffolk, Va., and, if possible, should try to reach Suffolk not later than 10 o'clock Wednesday morning. All coming by railroad will please notify the undersigned at once, and state just when you desire to secure transportation from Suffolk to Oakland. It is nine miles from Suffolk to Oakland. There are about 24 trains coming into Suffolk daily. It is impossible to meet all these trains. Please be prompt and let us know the train you wish to have met, and we will do our best to accommodate you. It is desired that all who can do so, come by private conveyance.

I. W. JOHNSON, *Pastor.*
Suffolk, Va.

NOTICE

To all members, delegates and visitors who expect to attend the Sunday School Convention, North Carolina Conference to be held at Shallow Well July 15-17:

You will please notify me as soon as you are elected or appointed in order that entertainment may be provided, also state whether you will come by rail or private conveyance.

We prefer as many as can to come by private conveyance.

Your failure to comply with the above might result in homes not being provided for you.

L. M. FOUSHEE,
, *Chm. Entertainment Com.*
Jonesboro, N. C.

NOTICE

The first annual Sunday School and Christian Endeavor Convention will be held at Shallow Well Christian church, July 15-17. All parties attending this Convention who wish homes provided, will please notify Mr. L. M. Foushee, Jonesboro, N. C., who is chairman of the entertainment committee. Don't wait until the day before you start, but write him at once, as soon as you are elected to go; and advise him what train you will go on, or if you intend going by private conveyance. This is important, and if you will heed the request it will be so much better for the committee.

S. A. L. trains from the north arrive at Sanford at 10:00 A. M., and 6:00 and 7:00 P. M. S. A. L. trains from the South arrive at Sanford at 3:00 and 10:00 P. M. All delegates coming on trains will be met at Sanford. If you wish any further information, write the Chairman, or write to me. We are at your service.

C. H. STEPHENSON, *President.*

SPRING HILL

This is a mother church. Many good men and women have found the Kingdom of God at her altar. She has been the spiritual birth place where the men and women were born who have organized, and built up Waverly, Wakefield, and Dendron Christian churches, to say nothing of the members she has given other churches. We hope in her age that there may yet come strength and multiplication in her membership. The attendance in Sunday school and church services the past year has been larger than in preceding years. There are some loyal and faithful members as well as some who are indifferent but these conditions exist in all churches. The church has recently been recovered with tin and a splendid metal ceiling put up, and one of the best picket fences built and painted that is to be found in the community; also nice cement walk in front of the church. This is not all. A Ladies' Aid Society is kept up. This Society does many things useful as well as some things ornamental. They are largely responsible for much of the improvements done —then I forgot—a number one organ has also been placed in the church.

And the pastor has been pounded. Recently this Ladies' Aid Society met at the parsonage in Waverly, and the pastor noticed that the good women carried bundles, but that is nothing new when women go to town but when they were through with the meeting and ready to go home they left all their bundles. There it was that the pastor and his family found some of the best country eatables. The many articles donated formed a splendid "pounding" and pastor and family felt deeply grateful for these substantial gifts at this day of "high cost of living." We are praying for a good meeting on the second Sunday in August.

JAS. L. FOSTER.
Waverly, Va.

A MESSAGE FROM THE PORTSMOUTH CHURCH

Since the "Conference of Resolves" held in this church five months ago renewed activity has marked the work of every organization. In no part of the work is the interest better manifested than in the Sunday school where Brother R. B. Wood, superintendent with his officers and teachers are maintaining a high grade of efficiency, where the missionary spirit of giving and interest in other benevolences is constantly kept before the school and out of which recruits are being secured for church membership. A young people's class alone having raised $200 in six months for various purposes.

The Ladies' Aid and Missionary Societies have done excellent work with increased finances, which has enabled the church to contribute substantially to the various causes of city and State.

During the winter and fall congregations have been large. Up-to-date advertising and popular themes have made Washington Street church known all over the city as a good place to visit.

In common with other churches we feel the pressure of modern modes of life, especially in a city near a still larger one surrounded by so many attractions which even church people seem unable to resist and which the war period had had a tendency to increase. We are looking forward to a larger spiritual awakening in the fall.

H. W. DOWDING.

Portsmouth, Va.

DEDICATION DAY AT ROSEMONT CHURCH

Last Sunday was a day long to be remembered by the members and friends of Rosemont Christian church, the occasion being the dedication of the church building.

The day itself was ideal. Although the sun shone forth from an almost cloudless sky, his rays were so tempered by the breezes from the ocean that we hardly knew summer was on. The very beauty of the day spoke to us of the goodness and the glory of God.

But what was better than the day was the sweet spirit of fellowship that entered into it. Not all days are the same. Into some days may come the fruit of experiences of months and even of years. This must have happened with us on the last Lord's day. What was once toil and labor was experienced again as the fruit thereof, what was once prayer was translated into its answer, what was once hope was realized in its actuality, and what was one day faith was lost in sight —all of which entered into the day making fellowship sweet and worship a delight and an inspiration.

Rev. J. O. Atkinson, D. D., was the visiting speaker for the day. In the morning he gave a strong message on "Christian Courage." At the evening hour, at which time came the crowning service of the day, the dedicatory program, the speaker was at his best and from his heart he delivered a soul-stirred and a soul-stirring message on "The Significance of the Sanctuary," after which he dedicated the church to the worship and service of God.

As a part of the dedicatory exercises Brother T. O. Morrison, a charter member of the church, read the following sketch:

Historical Sketch

With the building of communities and the coming together of groups of families in neighborhood life arises the need for new enterprises for the public good, chief among which is the Church of Christ. Not many years ago the sections of land about us were devoted almost entirely to agricultural activities, but natural conditions were such as to determine that these fields should no longer be laid off by the plowman's measure, but by the surveyor's line and compass, and that industry must take the place of agriculture. So this community came into being and with the birth of the community was born the religious needs and responsibilities thereof.

It was out of this need and responsibility that this church came to be. So on August 14, 1902, almost seventeen years ago, Rosemont Christian church was organized, Rev. J. Pressley Barrett, D. D., being the organizer. The organization was very small at the beginning, there being only thirteen charter members, most of whom are still with us, the absent ones having finished their earthly task and are now in the experience of their reward.

The church has been served by the following pastors: Revs. J. W. Harrell, J. W. Barrett, W. D. Harward, C. C. Ryan,

McDaniel Howsare, D. A. Keys, W. H. Denison, and the present pastor since March 1917.

The land on which the church now stands was given by Mr. John L. Gibson, now of sacred and sainted memory.

Upon this plat of ground two structures have been erected, the two being now as one. The first was built in the year 1900, or thereabout, and the second in 1915, and was opened for worship on the second Sunday in January 1916.

The history of the churches has often been a history of struggle. This church has been no exception in that case. Periods of sunshine and shadow have come and gone. At times failure has seemed almost inevitable, but out of the clouds the sun would shine again, and out of these alternating experiences has come at last a day of growth and progress. A spirit of earnestness, enthusiasm, and optimism at present so pervades the membership that a still larger and a better day in the future in the Master's service is assured.

After some years of toil and sacrifice mingled with a measure of faith and prayer, it now gives us pleasure to present this building with its furniture and fixtures unto Him Who is the Author of every good gift to be dedicated in the honor of His name and to the cause of truth and righteousness in the earth.

All in all the day was one of joy and gladness, of victory and inspiration, out of which comes to the church a forward and an upward look.

G. O. LANKFORD.

A VISIT TO WAKE COUNTY

On Friday, June 13, I left for Fuquay Springs, going by way of Raleigh. I arrived at the home of Brother K. B. Johnson, Varina, N. C., in the afternoon and spent the night pleasantly, seeing many old friends. On Saturday I visited the Springs and Wake Chapel church where I met a number of friends. We had a pleasant service. Rev. J. Lee Johnson, the pastor, is doing a great work at Wake Chapel. On Sunday we attended services at this dear old church where I commenced working in 1857. They have an excellent church, well furnished and a good organ of which Miss Ruth Johnson, a former Elon student, is organist. It is indeed a delightful place to worship.

What a change in the community since I organized the church at Wake Chapel! The Springs then had but three or four cabins where a few families would gather for the improvement of their health. Not a railroad was near, but now two roads are located near. Varina depot is in sight and a quantity of tobacco is sold in these two places. They have a fine school building with good teachers and prosperity seems to be in everything. At Varina I met many old friends and preached to a crowded house on Sunday. We had a delightful service and I saw many dear friends, among them being K. B. Johnson, Beale Johnson, J. Lee Johnson, the Ballentines, Smiths, Dr. Judd and family, and many others that I cannot recall. I spent nearly a week in the community. I saw Rev. R. P. Crumpler, who was once a student at Elon, and family. I never spent a more pleasant week than I did with these dear people. May God bless them.

J. W. WELLONS.

Elon College, N. C.

CONCORD

On Saturday, May 24, 1919, at four o'clock, a few members of the Concord church assembled. After preaching by the pastor the second quarterly business was called. Some improvements have been made among which was the putting of a new fence around the graveyard. There was a special effort to get started on finishing some formerly started improvements. We hope to see it done by the revival meeting which will begin the fourth Sunday in July. Rev. J. F. Apple of Elon College has promised to assist in the preaching. Brother Apple is well known to this congregation.

The fourth Sunday in May was designated as Memorial Day which has been a custom of the church to observe for many years. Rev. C. B. Riddle was to be with us under the auspices of the Woman's Missionary Society. On account of a heavy rain that Sunday we were unable to have services.

A very large crowd assembled the fourth Sunday in June. The church has met its quota for Elon Standardization Fund, for which I am grateful.

L. L. WYRICK.

Elon College, N. C.

CHAPLAIN BLACK RETURNING

The many friends of Rev. B. F. Black will be delighted to know that he is expecting to return from France about August 1. Brother Black has entered very heartily into his work across the seas and gathered therefrom much valuable experience. He is anxious to be back in the pastorate and will be glad to correspond with any churches needing a pastor. In the meantime he will be glad to assist brethren needing his services in their protracted meetings, or speak on his "Experiences Over the Sea." Address him at Elon College, N. C.

N. G. NEWMAN.

MOORE UNION

On Sunday, June 22, I had the pleasure of preaching, and presenting the call of the Elon Standardization Fund to a large congregation at my old home church, Moore Union. With only a few minutes on the grounds after the services, (on account of sickness in my family, I was compelled to make the round trip from Chapel Hill in the same day), the church's allotment to the Fund was subscribed.

Rev. P. T. Klapp is the beloved pastor at this place and under his leadership Moore Union can and will do things.

B. J. HOWARD.

Chapel Hill, N. C.

GRAHAM-HAW RIVER CHARGE

Perhaps the friends of Graham and Haw River would be interested to know something of the work that is being done on this field. I have spent a little more than a half year on this field as resident pastor and find it to be a good place to live and work. The people are very responsive and are willing to work when directed. There is need for two pastors on this field, if not three. Last fall the churches were having preaching services and Sunday school and the ladies of Graham and Haw River were doing good work in the Ladies' Aid Society and Woman's Missionary Society. Now there is a mid-week prayer meeting in these churches and a thriving Christian Endeavor Society in all three churches. The New Providence Society has been publishing a little paper each week for some time and is installing a printing press so it can do its own printing. The young people are very much interested in the Endeavor work and I prophesy great things for these churches if this work is continued.

From a financial stand point the churches have far exceeded previous records. They have increased the pastor's salary and at the same time bought a parsonage and made improvements on the churches . The first half of this year Graham alone raised more than three thousand dollars. This is a small amount for a big church of wealthy people but a large amount for a small church with limited means. Haw River has bought song books and a pipe tone organ and is preparing the basement of the church for Sunday school rooms. The Sunday school has more than doubled its membership during the last few months. More room is necessary at once.

This field has not been without its sorrows, however. My record of funerals reads as follows: December 13, Mrs. J. N. H. Clendennin, members of Graham; Dec. 24, Mrs. Malinda Whitsell of Haw River; January 17, Jno L. Ward, infant, of Haw River; January 20, Rufus B. Heritage, son of Treasurer Heritage of New Providence, killed in auto wreck; March 10, John G. Longest, member of Graham; April 11, Mrs. C. D. Johnston, wife of the Orphanage Superintendent, supporter of Graham though a member of Howard's Chapel; May 26, Mrs. Annie Albright, oldest daughter of Brother W. H. Holt, member of New Providence. There are several others who are not members of the Christian church. Many vacant chairs are in our midst, but we look to the better home where we all hope to be soon.

Revival services begin tomorrow, June 29, at New Providence and July 17 at Haw River. Rev. R. F. Brown is to preach for us at New Providence and Rev. H. S. Hardcastle at Haw River. Each series will last ten days or more. We invite all who can attend and all to pray for the success of the services.

F. C. LESTER.

Graham, N. C., June 28.

The country is advised by Mr. Wilson that he has no authority to make null and void the prohibition measure enacted for the duration of the war. A part of the measure reads: "* * * until the conclusion of the present war and thereafter until the termination of the demobilization, the date of which shall be determined and proclaimed by the President * * ." The war is over, but the demobilization is not. Bad for the beerites and liquorites, but good for the country. They close July 1.

Many articles left out this week. Continue to send them and be patient.

MISSIONARY

THE SPIRIT OF SERVICE AND OF SACRIFICE

Perhaps our most apparent gain through the war is the most marvelous development of a spirit of service and even of sacrifice. The spirit of unselfish service became the law of common life. On his first return from Europe after the war began, Dr. Mott reported how this spirit had swept Europe so that a distinguished government leader said to him on one occasion when Dr. Mott was questioning our right to claim of certain men certain great service, "Dr. Mott, you will not find a selfish man in Europe today." Discount as we may the permanency or the depth of this spirit of service, the fact remains that with the advent of the war, suddenly, as by magic, the law of unselfishness for which the missionary enterprise had so long borne witness, became the common practice of the world. Where once it was irritating to business circles to have philanthropic proposals leave the rather small worlds in which they had been given birth, and the brazen statement that "business is business" was supposed to set the money-earning powers of men free from all claims to generosity, the war somehow changed all that: Dollar-a-year appointments became respectable, almost popular; corporations found it quite business-like to vote contributions to the Red Cross and the Y. M. C. A.; firms readjusted the work of their staffs to set some major members and numerous minor members of the firm free for unremunerative war service while the rest "carried on" each man with a double load; Congress found it constitutional to vote $100,000,000 to relief work; the public rallied to appeal after appeal for all the varied forms of war service until an aggregate of a thousand million dollars is estimated to have been freely contributed to such causes. As did men stop with money; life itself was poured out like water. The Allied dead number well over five million of the cream of these nations; and this takes no reckoning of lives laid down in like spirit and often much more sacrificingly by those who belonged to civilian classes, a yet greater number of women and a host of children, too—whose measure of courage in carrying increasing burdens, and of sacrifice in making constant self-denial, yielded to them also the crown of death. So, as some one has put it, we have come to realize "the undreamed of resources and splendor of even ordinary human nature, when touched by sacrifice into fire. And so we have discovered, too, our own past mistake—the common mistake of the majority of modern Christians,—that of asking of men, in Christ's Name, not too much, but too little."

FOURTH QUARTERLY REPORT OF THE WOMAN'S HOME AND FOREIGN MISSION BOARD OF THE SOUTHERN CHRISTIAN CONVENTION

REGULAR FUNDS

Receipts

1919
April 4—N. C. Conference ....$ 95.16
April 23—Eastern Va. Conference 182.80

May 1—Virginia Valley Central Conference.......... 19.50
May 1—Special Home Missons 15.79

                   $313.25

Disbursements

May 1—W. C. Wicker, Treas., Foreign Missions......$148.73
May 1—W. C. Wicker, Treas., Home Missions......... 164.52

                   $313.25

SANTA ISABEL

Receipts

April 4—North Carolina Conference ....$ 46.23
May 1—Virginia Valley Central Conference.......... 13.72

                   $59.95

Disbursements

May 1—W. C. Wicker, Treasurer ....$ 59.95

CHRISTIAN ORPHANAGE

Receipts

April 4—North Carolina Conference ....$ 9.93
April 23—Eulice Bradshaw 15.00
April 23—Coy Franklin 10.25
May 1—Virginia Valley Central Conference.......... .37

                   $35.55

Disbursements

May 1—W. C. Wicker, Treasurer......................$35.55

SENDAI ORPHANAGE

Receipts

Cash on hand ....$ .15
April 4—North Carolina Conference .... .75
May 1—Virginia Valley Central .... .38

                   $1.28

Disbursements

May 1—W. C. Wicker, Treasurer ....$ 1.28

BIBLE WOMEN

Receipts

April 23—Eastern Va. Conf. (Mrs. Watanabe)........$ 24.75
April 23—Eastern Va. Conf. (Miss Hamaguchi)....... 12.50

Disbursements

May 1—W. C. Wicker, Treasurer ....$ 37.25

JAPAN SUNDAY SCHOOL

Receipts

April 23—Eastern Va. Conference ....$ 12.50

Disbursements

May 1—W. C. Wicker, Treasurer ....$ 12.50

MRS. FRY'S SCHOOL

Receipts

April 19—North Carolina Conference ....$ 30.00

Disbursements

May 1—W. C. Wicker, Treasurer....................$ 30.00

BARRETT HOME

Receipts

April 19—North Carolina Conference $130.25
April 23—Eastern Virginia Conference 70.80

                   $191.05

Disbursements

May 1—W. C. Wicker, Treasurer $191.05

        MRS. W. T. WALTERS, Treasurer.

Winchester, Va.

THE FORWARD MOVEMENT

Warren H. Denison, Superintendent

The Superintendent spent June 15-17 with Hannas Creek church in the Eastern Indiana Conference. Rev. Fred Stovenour, eighty-five years of age, has been preaching at this church for twenty-one years. There are eighty members on the church roll and the gifts for the Forward Movement work were $6,535.00 with the promise of more pledges. The men of the church left their work in the absence of their pastor and gave their hearty co-operation. Mrs. Olive Lafuse did a splendid thing in giving $1,000 to the Forward Movement as a memorial to her husband, William Henry Lafuze, who was an active Christian worker, both in his church and in the Conference. There is no more beautiful act that one can do than to give a fund of money to some Christian agency such as the Forward Movement, or as several have done, for Elon College in its present financial canvass.

The Indiana State Christian Conference and the Illinois State Christian Conference held splendid joint session at Merom, Indiana, June 10 and 11. The heartiest kind of endorsement was given to the Forward Movement. Nearly a third of the membership of the denomination is located within these two states and large opportunity and responsibility rests upon the workers and the leadership of these Conferences.

The American Christian Convention at its last session adopted a reconstruction policy for the Christian Church and ordered that it should be issued from the Forward Movement office. The program has been printed and is now ready for use by all pastors and church workers. Sufficient copies for your church workers may be had for the asking. It will be suggestive to pastors and other church workers and should be in their hands. Please write to the Forward Movement office for as many copies as you need.

All Sunday schools are asked during July, August, and September to lay special emphasis upon such matters as will deepen the devotional and worship spirit of the Sunday school. A goodly number of churches during April and June came to the place of a Standard Sunday school. We hope that others will report by the end of June that they too have reached a Standard school. There are many things that will help the worship in the Sunday school; among them, we suggest that the officers and teachers read some book especially prepared for such help. Some of those books are: "The Training of the Devotional Life"—Kennedy & Myers, "The Devotional Life of the Sunday School Workers" —Prewbaker, "The Spiritual Life of the Sunday School"—Chapman; to encourage and secure pledges for observance of the Quiet Hour; carry and use your Bibles at church and Sunday school; encourage the Pocket Testament League; emphasize definite prayer for definite causes and persons.

Rev. J. W. Wellons will preach at Good Hope, Granville County, the second Sunday in July and at Antioch, Chatham County, the third Sunday in July.

THE CHRISTIAN ORPHANAGE

REMEMBER THE ORPHANAGE IN YOUR WILL

I sometimes wonder how many friends of the Christian Orphanage who have money and property to give to charitable purposes have made provision in their wills for a part of it to go to the Orphanage?

Suppose in writing that document—that is, to make the final distribution of your worldly possessions after you are gone—that you remember the Christian Orphanage and leave a portion of it to care for some worthy child, and from this portion of your estate a child is taken care of, trained and educated, and goes out into the world as a teacher to train the young to live and do right and be honest and upright citizens; or suppose that this child grows up to be a preacher to carry the message of the gospel to the unsaved; or perhaps the child becomes a trained nurse to administer to the sick and nurse them back to health, what a lasting monument you have built for yourself! You have built one that will last throughout the years of eternity, the value of which cannot be estimated. Could you help a more worthy cause than that of the little helpless children who have been unfortunate, and who are worthy of your love, your sympathy and your sacrifice?

If you have already written this final document and have left the Orphanage out, I appeal to you to add another clause and make provision for the fatherless. If you have not written it, then when you do, remember the little helpless ones who need your help and sacrifice.

Our friends still remember us and th following contributions have been received: J. Walter Johnston, 1 bushel seed corn; Mrs. J. T. Williams, one counterpane, two sheets, one pair pillow cases; Hon. C. D. West, one bag of peanuts.

CHAS. D. JOHNSTON, *Supt.*

REPORT FOR JULY 2, 1919

Amount brought forward, $6,916.40.

Children's Offerings

Ethelene Strader, 10 cents.

Sunday School Monthly Offerings

(Eastern Virginia Conference)

Franklin, $5.00; Antioch, $2.00; Centerville, Va., $1.00.

(North Carolina Conference)

Morrisville, $2.00; Pleasant Ridge, $10.00; Good Hope, $4.45; Apple's Chapel, $1.00; Zion, $3.05; Henderson, $8.81; Happy Home, $3.00; Pine Forest, (Union Sunday School), $2.40; Auburn, $3.00; Spring Hill, $2.00; Total, $47.91.

Special Offerings

Clone Christian church, N. Y., $5.00; J. H. Jones, on support of children, $30.00; Graham Christian church (Special Offerings), $25.00; Interest, $10.00; Total, $70.00.

Miscellaneous

Rev. L. I. Cox, for cutting rye, $3.50.

Total for the week, $121.51; Grand total, $7,037.91.

L. W. Vaughan—I feel that I could not do without THE SUN.

A LETTER

·Dear Unce Charley:—I am a little girl ten years old. I want to join the band of cousins. Grandma Preston promised me a dime each month to send to the little orphans. I hope they are well and having a good time. Enclosed find my dime for June.—*Ethelene Strader*.

We give you a warm welcome and trust that you will write each month. I wish many of the little children would write for the corner.—*"Uncle Charley."*

SEASIDE CHAUTAUQUA

Virginia Beach, July 29-August 5

Mr. W. C. Pearce, one of the best known Sunday school men of this country, will be at the Chautauqua and give two Chautauqua lectures and two class messages on different phases of Christian leadership. The Chautauqua management counts itself fortunate to secure this great field secretary of the International Sunday School Association. Mr. Pearce will give the opening message to the Chautauqua on Tuesday night, July 29. Every one who expects to attend the Chautauqua should be present.

Church Problems

Almost every church has some particular church problem. One period a day will be given to the discussion of church problems under the leadership of persons capable of speaking on those problems. Some of the problems to be considered are, "The Community Church," "The Church for the New Time," "The Merger Church and Sunday School Service," "Christian Stewardship," "The Sunday Evening Service." It will be very valuable for ministers and church workers.

The Commissions on Christian Unity from the Christian Church and from the Disciples of Christ will hold their meeting at the Seaside Chautauqua this year. The members of the Christian Church Commission are: Rev. F. G. Coffin, Rev. J. F. Burnett, Rev. W. H. Denison, Mr. Hermon Eldredge, Rev. John MacCalman, Rev. O. B. Whitaker, President W. A. Harper and Rev. P. S. Sailor. The Disciples of Christ Commission is headed by Rev. Peter Ainslie.

Rev. H. G. Rowe has arrived hom from "Y" service over seas and will speak daily on Sunday school organization. Rev. J. V. Knight, Greensboro, N. C., and Rev. R. F. Brown, Durham, N. C., will conduct the Christian Endeavor work. The Sunday morning service will be a merger service illustrating the merging of the morning church and Sunday school services. The sermon will be by Dr. Roy C. Helfenstein, Urbana, Ill. Mr. Hermon Eldredge will be the superintendent. Now is the time to plan to be at the greatest Chautauqua session we have yet had and carry back to your church the best methods and plans for these reconstruction days. Write S. M. Smith, Chamber of Commerce Building, Norfolk, Virginia for information concerning rooms, rates and time tables.

WARREN H. DENISON, *Pres.*
27 *C. P. A. Building, Dayton, Ohio.*

ODDS AND ENDS

Smile when you can. Heaven alone can reveal its worth. Live up to all the light you have and trust the rest to God.

God loveth a cheerful liver. Christians should be the happiest people in the world. There is no reason why we should put on a long face when Jesus takes up his abode in our hearts.

God pity that man whose mind is so narrow that he believes his Church contains all the good people in the world.

It is not all of life to live. If we fail to properly use the talent which God has intrusted to our care, we have failed to accomplish God's purpose in creating us. Therefore we have lost all.

Why are we so unthankful, unhappy, miserable! Certainly we should not be thus. God created us in his own image and has placed all things at our disposal which can contribute to our happiness in this life.

W. H. FREEMAN.
Ether, N. C.

CHRISTIAN EDUCATION

IN OLD VIRGINIA AND NORTH CAROLINA

The week just closing has been spent almost entirely in the field of Rev. J. M. Roberts, in Eastern Virginia and Gates County, North Carolina. Brother Jesse was with me at Oak Grove and Cypress Chapel. Monday evening we separated to meet Wednesday morning at Ivor to canvass that loyal people and Johnson's Grove.

Brother Roberts had gone home to see his two sick children. They were taken worse and I have not seen his smiling face since. Wednesday morning came a brief telegram telling the sad news, and Thursday a letter overtook me, as follows: "Children are worse. Charlotte has pneumonia in both lungs and J. M. Jr., we fear, has typhoid fever. He had two hemorrhages yesterday afternoon and last night at eleven. We are very anxious about him. Tomorrow will be the 21st day since he was first taken sick." I am sure all hearts will deeply sympathize with Brother Roberts and family in this sad hour and that many prayers will be offered up in their behalf.

Rev. J. L. Foster, "Uncle Jim," we call him, came to my rescue for Johnson's Grove, Brother L. H. Brantley and Brother B. H. Lane helping me through at Ivor. I then headed it to Gates and the Lord had one of the Kingdom's noble men waiting for me in the person of Brother Sam Harrell, who gave me a subscription and delivered safely despite rain and "tough" roads to Brother Dempsey Harrell's, who subscribed, took care of me, decided to send his daughter to Elon this fall, and conveyed me from place to place, rain or no rain, with mud all the time. His church, Sarem, went on over.

I next found myself in the home of my friend of many

years, Deacon T. A. Eure. His beloved wife is now in Heaven, but his two daughters make his heart glad and did mine too. We are now -at work in Eure's church and hope for good results.

When Eure's and Damascus are through, the churches I was to visit in the drive are canvassed and then I can wend my way home where work in plenty in the beloved atmosphere of home awaits me.

Funds This Week

Brother R. S. Holland, Cypress Chapel church in loving memory of his brother, I. C. Holland, a student of Elon in my college days.

Brother Leteher Gay, upon solicitation by Dr. W. W. Staley, in memory of his wife.

Mrs. E. J. Brickhouse, Norfolk, Va., in memory of her sainted husband.

Finally, Brethren

Give our Heavenly Father thanks for His blessings upon our Brotherhood in the success of this drive. To Him be all the praise.

W. A. HARPER.

Editorial Note:—Since receiving the above we are informed by President Harper that every church in Bro. Robert's field, including Eure, has done her part. We have also been advised by 'phone from the College office that two other ·funds have been established—A. B. Hartz and wife, and Dr. and Mrs. S. W. Caddell.

C. B. R.

NOTES

President Wilson is on his way home from Europe.

Rev. J. F. Apple preached for the Christian (Disciples) at Pinetown, Beaufort County, two nights last week.

No Sunday school and Christian Endeavor notes this week. The matter reached us too late to be included in this issue.

Germany signed the Peace Treaty on Saturday, June 28. She said that she wouldn't sign, couldn't sign, but she did sign. China, at the last moment, failed to sign, but no great significance is attached to that.

Brother F. C. Lester figures that four additional subscriptions to THE SUN from each church in the Convention would bring the list up to 3,000 and says that he is going after the four from each of his churches. Good! Next?

Dr. E. Oscar Randolph, one of THE SUN's loyal subscribers, who for the past . year has been teacher of Geology in the A. and M. College, Bryan, Texas, changes his address to Chapel Hill, N. C., where he will be located during the summer, teaching in the Department of Geology.

We have before us the last issue of *The Herald of Gospel Liberty*, under Dr. J. P. Barrett's editorship. He bids his brethren farewell in the editorial field, thanks the friends and foes and asks that support be given to his successor, Rev. A. M. Kerr, D. D., and we speak for this section of the Brotherhood a loyal support to the new editor.

For some time great dissatisfaction has been growing out of the work of Postmaster General Burleson. The American Federation of Labor, in its annual session at Atlantic City, New Jersey, the other day, demanded that the present Postmaster General be removed. The probability is that he will be asked to leave the service.

Brother W. E. Cook, Mebane, N. C., called at this office last last week for the purpose of subscribing to the Elon Endowment Fund. Some days ago the Editor was in Brother Cook's church community in the interest of the College, but Brother Cook was away from home. He said that he wanted to have a part. We can think and feel it, but we have no words to express our appreciation of such acts. Steward of the Kingdom he is.

Just as we started to press this (Monday) morning, the telegram shown on page 16, was received. It reached Burlington at 10:34 as shown on the message. It reached this office at 10:50. The messenger boy brought us the message while we were standing on the outside of THE SUN office talking with Hon. R. T. Kernodle, the only man who has given $5,000.00 in cash toward the Elon Standardization Fund. Others have given that amount, but Brother Kernodle is the only man to make his subscription in cash. Next to the Editor, he was the first man to read the telegram. How fitting! Better still: How he rejoiced! He said, "good" and that is what say us all.

Pounded! Of course so—yes "cashed," "checked" and "honeyed," (who can beat that!), Mt. Auburn church, a place where THE SUN is popular, remembered the Editor the other day with a check for $26.60, while Brother T. H. Crocker, Middleburg, N. C., a member of Mt. Auburn, remembered us with a check for $20.00. Brother Crocker is a shoe salesman. He is not only interested in *soles*, but *souls*. "A friend" recently made us a gift of $5.00 (in cash), while Mrs. W. G. Teague, Route 2, Siler City, N. C., sent us recently a fine jar of honey, the finest that we have ever seen. So you see how we have been "cashed," "checked," and "honeyed" and all this happened in June. Of course we feel like a June bride. Thank you, kind friends, and God bless and multiply your kind is our wish.

Brother Irving Hitchcock, 801 Allison Street, Washington, D. C., is interested in locating all members of the Christian Church who live at the Nation's capitol. Let any interested write him. If you have friends in Washington give Brother Hitchcock their names and their location.

THE BOY THAT LAUGHS

I know a funny little boy—
 The happiest ever born;
His face is like a beam of joy,
 Although his clothes are torn.

I saw him tumble on his nose,
 And waited for a groan—
But how he laughed! Do you suppose
 He struck his funny bone?

There's sunshine in each word he speaks,
 His laugh is something grand;
Its ripples overrun his cheeks,
 Like waves on snowy sand.

He laughs the moment he awakes,
 And till the day is done;
The schoolroom for a joke he takes;
 His lessons are but fun.

No matter how the day may go,
 You cannot make him cry;
He's worth a dozen boys I know
 Who pout and mope and sigh.

     —*Exchange.*

PLAIN WHITE

Mary June caught sight of the tired little figure by the big range as soon as she reached the kitchen door. "I'll dish up the potatoes, mother," she called out, cheerily.

Mother turned. She was a little frail woman, with soft brown eyes.

"That you, dear?" she said, with a relieved sigh. "Run in, please, and see if the table is all right. Mrs. Jackson is bringing a friend to dinner today and I do want everything to be nice."

"Poor little mother!" she whispered. "She's forgotten to give Mr. Snodgrass a napkin and Mrs. Willets hasn't any fork. It's just a shame she has to work so hard. Boarders are no fun and she has had them so long. If father had just lived," and then Mary June, supplying the missing napkin, sighed a little.

Father had *not* lived and mother had been obliged to work, and work very hard, to keep food in their mouths and a roof over their heads and Mary June in school.

After seeing that the table lacked nothing Mary June went back to the kitchen, and for the next few minutes both were so busy that neither spoke. It was just after dinner that the opportunity came.

"Marjory Mills has invited me to her party," said Mary June, suddenly.

"She has?" answered mother, and then just a little

shadow crept over the sweet, tired face, for Mary June would have to have a new dress if she went to the party, and with the high cost of living, how was she to give it to her?

When her bills were met there was scarcely anything left. For boarders, to be permanent, must be well fed, and Mary June's mother could not economize at *their* expense.

Mary June saw the look, and when she came back from the pantry she put her arms about her. "Now, mother," she said, fondly, "if that party is going to worry you, I won't go."

"But your dress," protested mother, faintly.

"Well," replied Mary June, with a practical air, "I've about figured out the dress. What the other girls wear must not influence me. Wasn't it grandma who used to say that we must not 'measure our oats in other people's half bushels'? In other words, what the rest of the world has need not concern us."

"And I thought," added Mary June, in her sweet young voice, "that if you could get me a few yards of plain white goods I could make it myself after school."

Mother looked at Mary June. "Plain white" she repeated.

Mary June nodded. "Plain white and nothing else. The goods won't cost much and the making nothing. And I can go to the party after all.

"You remember the little rhyme of the 'Birds' Ball' you used to tell me about, and what Jenny Wren said? The other birds were all going to dress up, but Jenny Wren said:

> "'I must wear my brown gown,
> And never look too fine.'

"I'm Jenny Wren and my mother keeps boarders, but when I get to teaching after I have my diploma, *she's* going to rest. We can both have better clothes then, but just now it has to be plain white. Why, mother, I don't care a bit, really. That Alice will wear pink chiffon and Edith blue messaline and Mildred lace does not matter to me. If my mother is willing I will be happy to go in the plain white."

For a moment mother did not reply. She could not. Mary June was such a help, and so unselfish, asking for so little always.

And then she saw Mary June in the plain white, with her sweet, glowing young face and her brown curls, and she knew that even in a plain white dress Mary June would still be Mary June—the sweetest little daughter in the world. It was worth all her struggles to feel that. A tear ran down the pale cheek, but there was joy in her heart.

"We will get the plain white, dear," she said, huskily.—*Susan Hubbard Martin, in Baptist Boys and Girls.*

Mrs. E. J. Hicks—Please renew my subscription to THE SUN which I enjoy reading so much.

   * *

S. B. Lea—I cannot do without THE SUN. I want it to shine in my home as long as I live.

WORSHIP AND MEDITATION

By Cleora H. Read

O God, I thank Thee that I can see:
The blue of the ocean; the green of the hills against the sunset sky; the moon-lit world; the autumn-tinted forests; the eager smile of youth; the love-light in a mother's eyes; the courage in a father's face; the wonders, the glories all around. For these I thank Thee.

I thank Thee that I can hear:
The singing of birds; the murmur of the tide against the shore; the soughing of the wind among the trees, the laughter of little children; the crooning of a lullaby; the many harmonies throughout this world of Thine. For these I thank Thee.

I thank Thee that I can feel:
The balmy air; the winter's chill; the rushing wind; the love of friends; my baby's kiss; the comforts of home; the manifold blessings of the life that Thou hast given me. For these I thank Thee.

I pray Thee that my eyes be closed, my hearing dulled, my feeling lost to envy, hate, maliciousness and shame, for these are not of Thee.

But may my heart know loving sympathy and cheerful ministry and my spoken words bring comfort. May I show truth and steadfastness when all the way is bright and peaceful faith when all my life seems dark. Thus only may I strive to make myself as Thou wouldst have Thy children. Amen.

WHAT IS MY CROSS?

As the shadow of the Cross begins to darken the road along which, in reverent retrospect, we are following the Master, are we fallen low indeed if we do not feel the reproach of the passion of our Lord, lending new and searching significance to the threshold command of Jesus, "If any man will come after me......let him take up his Cross......"

> Thou sayest, Take up thy cross,
> O man, and follow me.
> Thy Voice comes strange o'er years of change,
> How can we follow Thee?

What are our crosses? The little sacrifices and self-denials to which sometimes we are compelled, to which sometimes we compel ourselves, seem too inadequate Is there no middle way between trivialities which do not deserve that august and hallowed name and self crucifixions whose barrenness does but mock their austerity?

What was Jesus' Cross? It was, in those aspects which we are called upon to imitate, no more assumption of sorrow, fate or penalty. It grew out of the main purpose of his life. It was what He had come to do and to be, followed clean through to the end. The hostility of the leaders of His people set up the post of it; His courage spread the arms of it. He began by teaching, whosoever would hear, healing whosoever

would be restored, cleansing whosoever would be made clean. That was His central essential service, the great continuing thing for which He was commissioned.

Our own Crosses are like His. They are not austerities and limitations which we have searched out; they are holy tasks which search us out, lifted to splendid and fruitful conclusions. A man's Cross is the thing he was meant to do, done as Christ would have him do it, his own distinctive task in which he spends and expresses himself, his contribution to the kingdom of God. The Cross of the teacher is his teaching, of the doctor his healing, of the minister his preaching, of the business man the administration of his business, all carried, in the spirit of the Lord Christ, to those fulfillments which crown them with fruitfulness and power, by men who are halted by no barriers of pain or fear, but, true to themselves and their Master, find in the completion of their tasks the consummation of their discipleship.

The sorrow and pain of the Cross are its accidents; the joy of it is eternal. There are men to whom it has been given again and again to render the last full measure of devotion to holy and accepted causes who through it all have walked in ever increasing fullness of life and in ways seemingly remote from the bitterness of Golgotha. None the less they bore their Crosses and were comrades of the Christ. Nay, they were prophets of what Christ meant cross-bearing should be in those diviner and ampler days which He died to make possible.

Most men who follow great causes to grave and consistent ends find themselves, at least once, called to those roads of loneliness which lead across the slopes of the hill of crucifixion or even to its crest. The world is not yet so constituted that we can be wholly true to the ideal without paying the price. Yet even then the Cross is not merely the lonely, tragic culmination of hostility between far-seeing love and short-sighted hate. Even then our Crosses are the supreme tasks of our life, the great work of love and service to which we have long been committed. Whether on ways of light or hills of pain, to have served, is to have borne the Cross, to have been true to holy love is to have shared the secret of the Master —*The Congregationalist.*

A good word is just as easily spoken as an evil one. Kind speech is as easy as profane language and is often invaluable, while profanity is absolutely useless and vile.—*Young People.*

LAND ABOVE SEA LEVEL

The amount of land above sea level in the world would make a crust 600 feet thick if evenly distributed all over the globe.—*Kind Words.*

Mrs. W. H. Williams—I love to read THE SUN. I get inspiration therefrom.

Sunday School and Christian Endeavor

NORTH CAROLINA SUNDAY SCHOOL AND CHRISTIAN ENDEAVOR CONVENTION

Every Sunday school and Christian Endeavor Society of the North Carolina Christian Conference should be represented at the first Convention in the new State Conference. The place is Shallow Well Christian church and the time is July 15-17.

Has your school appointed delegates? See that it is done next Sunday. Appoint delegates who will attend and help to make a great Convention. It is of importance that your school shall be represented. The Convention needs you and you need the Convention. This is the day of great Conventions. All causes are using them and finding them helpful. Will our Sunday schools and Christian Endeavor Societies use the coming Convention and become a blessing to themselves and others?

A splendid program has been prepared. There is help for all in its execution. The Convention will suggest to you how you may have a better Sunday school or Christian Endeavor Society. Attend the Convention with a prepared heart and mind. Take in all you can and carry back home to your work the largest inspiration possible.

Another thing of great importance is a well prepared report. Let secretaries and superintendents see that reports are properly prepared before they are sent to the Convention. Give your school or Society credit for all it is doing. Report on all vital matters and let us know what you are doing. Your school may be an example to others. Exert the best influence possible. Let your light shine. Do not put it under a bushel by means of a poorly prepared report. Have the report from your school in good shape and bring it to the Convention with lots of good cheer. Let's realize we are in big business—business that is abundantly worth while.

The Convention has a live, wide-awake president in Brother C. H. Stephenson of Raleigh. He is doing his best for a great Convention. He is vitally interested in Sunday school work. He is enthusiastic about it.

Let us rally about him. Let's help him. Let's heed his calls.

The Board of Religious Education of the Southern Christian Convention of which the writer is Chairman, is back of the Convention in the strongest way possible. We are expecting a great Convention.

             J. W. HARRELL,
                   Chairman.
Burlington, N. C.

A CHALLENGE TO CHRISTIAN ENDEAVORERS

All denominations in the State having Christian Endeavor Societies are planning great things for their work during the next Christian Endeavor Convention year, and are coming to the next State Convention in Greensboro June 11-13, 1920, with a great work done. Ours must not be behind the times, and it is for the purpose of stirring interest that this challenge to the Christian Endeavorers in our churches in North Carolina is given. What will you do about it, Christian Endeavorers? Here it is:

What do you say about having a rally day at some central point, at a date not later than September 25, for the purpose of getting our Christian Endeavor workers together, laying plans, stirring up enthusiasm, making a drive for the organization of new Societies, reviving the dead ones, and placing before our people a definite program of work?

It seems to me that a rally day of this kind would be one of the most helpful meetings our work could have, and it would help to stimulate the work in such a manner as to make Christian Endeavor one of the most interesting topics of our coming Conference next fall. What about it, Christian Endeavor officers, committees and Societies? This work is recognized by the State Christian Endeavor Union, and will be given recognition in the Convention work, provided the plans are worked.

In the interest of the State work, and the work of the Christian Church in North Carolina I make this appeal to you in behalf of Christian Endeavor.

       J. VINCENT KNIGHT, *Pres.*
Greensboro, N. C.

THE BOOKS OF THE BIBLE

Do you know many books are in the Bible? You once knew, but have forgotten? Let me tell you one good way to remember, so as never to forget. First, write down the words "Old Testament."

Now, how many letters are in the word "old"? Three. How many in the word "Testament?" Nine. Put three and nine together and you have 39—the number of books in the Old Testament.

Next, write down the words "New Testament."

There are also in "New" and "Testament" 3 and 9 letters. Now, multiply 3 and 9 and you have 27—the number of books in the New Testament.

Of course by adding 39 and 27, you have 66 —the number of books in the Bible.

Any boy or girl who will read this over twice will never forget how many books are in the Bible.—*Select: ed.*

MARRIAGES

JANKOVSKY-THOMPSON

Married, June 18, 1919 at the residence of the bride's mother, Mrs. Anna Jankovsky, near Waverly, Va., Miss Anna E. Jankovsky and Mr. George M. Thompson of Robinson County, Kentucky, at 2:30 P. M., in the presence of the family and a few friends.

Miss Jankovsky is one of Virginia's splendid daughters who loved home and mother and is the last of five sisters to leave and go out set up a new home.

Mr. Thompson is one of Kentucky's substantial farmers and with so splendid a wife the friends wish them a happy home and long, useful life. The ceremony was performed by the pastor of Waverly Christian church.

       JAS. L. FOSTER.

OBITUARIES

HOBBY

Mrs. Virginia Atkinson Hobby departed this life June 18, 1919. She was the daughter of George Atkinson, deceased, and Alice Atkinson, living. She married T. C. Hobby, son of S. M. Hobby, Raleigh, N. C., and to them were born six children, all living. The youngest child is only about two months old. Besides her husband and children she leaves behind three sisters, Mrs. Sadie Jones, Mrs. Vivian Stephenson and Mrs. Ethel Smith and three half brothers, J. O. Atkinson, Moses Atkinson and C. H. Stephenson.

Mrs. Hobby had for several years been a member of Wentworth Christian church. Her body was laid to rest at the family burying ground at Mr. S. M. Hobby's country home. Services were conducted by Rev. George D. Eastes, Raleigh, and the writer. May God's richest blessing rest upon the bereaved.

J. LEE JOHNSON.

WELLONS

Virginia Murdur Wellons was born November 10, 1833. On February 14, 1860 she was married to M. M. English, and after his death on August 23, she was married to Z. W. Wellons. She died June 20, 1919, aged 85 years, 7 months and 10 days. She is survived by three children, Mrs. M. L. Williams of Petersburg, Va.; Mrs. J. E. Barrett, and J. W. Wellons of Wakefield, Va., 5 grandchildren and one great grandchild.

She was converted and joined Barrett's Christian church when about 18 years old, and remained a member till death. Burial on the fourth Sunday in June at 2 o'clock in the family burying ground on the English farm, by the pastor. She selected text for her funeral occasion: Rev. 14:13.

JAS. L. FOSTER.

LEE

Willis John Lee, son of Capt. P. H. Lee and Mrs. Joanna Lee, was born in Nansemond County, Virginia, January 12, 1846, and died at his home, near Bennett's Creek, Nansemond County, Virginia, May 20, 1919, at the age of 73 years, 4 months and 8 days. On May 25, 1869, he married Miss Mary Jennet Jones, daughter of the late William Henry Jones, Sr. This was a happy marriage. Their devotion was tender and beautiful. Bro-

ther Lee fell asleep just five days before the fiftieth anniversary of his marriage.

Brother Lee united with Holy Neck Christian church when a young man, and after his marriage, united with Berea, Nansemond, church. He was truly devoted to his church. Punctual and faithful in attendance, active and loyal in supporting the work of the church and the Kingdom. He was generous in his contributions and personal interest in the organization of Memorial Temple, Newport News, Portsmouth and many other Christian churches of the Eastern Virginia Christian Conference. He helped many churches throughout the Southern Christian Convention. He was an honored and faithful trustee of Elon College from the founding of that institution till his death. He was also a trustee of the Christian Orphanage, and was one of a committee of three who located the institution at Elon College, N. C. He was a veteran of the Civil War, serving in the Confederate forces, Co. I, 13th Va. Regiment-Cavalry. He was a brave and honored soldier. It would be difficult to give even a synopsis of this useful life. He was industrious and successful as a business man; in the forefront as a progressive farmer; true and faithful as a friend; generous, consecrated Christian gentleman. His was a great, good life. He was modest, humble and deeply spiritual. He is not dead but sleepeth. How beautiful to fall asleep at the end of such a worthy life. He walked with God. His funeral service was conducted at Berea church by the pastor, assisted by Revs. W. W. Staley, C. H. Rowland, W. V. Savage, G. O. Lankford, W. M. Jay and Dr. W. A. Harper. His body was laid to rest in Cedar Hill, Suffolk, Va. His dear, devoted wife and all the other members of his family have the prayers and sympathy of many friends.

. I. W. JOHNSON.

RESOLUTION OF RESPECT— STEPHENSON

Whereas, it has pleased our Heavenly Father to call from labor to reward, Deacon William M. Stephenson, on May 30, 1919; and whereas, Deacon Stephenson has always done his duty as a member and deacon of Isle of Wight Christian church; and whereas, his life of humility and service has been of great benefit to his church and to Christianity, therefore, BE IT RESOLVED:

1. That while we realize our loss and sadly miss him from his place among us,

yet we humbly bow to the will of Him Who doeth all things well.

2. That we thus record our deep feeling of gratitude for his life among us, and the Christian example of word and deed he has left for us to follow.

3. That we express our most sincere sympathy to his widow, and to the other members of his family. May the Comforter of man be with them in this, their bereavement.

4. That a copy of these resolutions be entered upon the records of the church, a copy sent to The Christian Sun for publication, and a copy sent to the family.

C. H. ATKINS,
R. T. WHITLEY,
C. H. CHAPMAN,
MRS. L. H. WHITLEY,
MRS. W. T. PORTER,
Committee.

WESTERN UNION TELEGRAM

Form 1204

GEORGE W. E. ATKINS, First Vice President

NEWCOMB CARLTON, President

State Library

RECEIVED AT

9 D N 59 Ble

Suffolk Va 935 Am June 30th 1919

C B Riddle

Care The Christian Sun

City

Our Elon drive has closed and we are far over the top. We are not far from three hundred thousand. We give thanks to every field man, every contributor, every one who prayed for or wished the drive well, and especially to God for his rich blessing upon the work. Next week we hope to furnish a verified statement.

J E West

K B Johnson

R M Morrow

Representing Bd Trustees

W W Staley

President S C C

1034 A

THE CHRISTIAN SUN

"IN ESSENTIALS UNITY, IN NON-ESSENTIALS LIBERTY, IN ALL THINGS CHARITY"

Deal Directly With Christ

Bishop J. C. Ryle

E that thirsts and wants relief must come to Christ himself. He must not be content with coming to his church and his ordinances or to the assemblies of his people for prayer and praise. He must not stop short even at his holy table. He that is content with only drinking these waters shall "thirst again." He must go higher, farther, much farther than this. He must have personal dealings with Christ himself; all else in religion is worthless without him. The King's palace, the attendant servants, the richly furnished banqueting house, the very banquet itself—all are nothing unless we speak with the King. His hand alone can take the burden off our backs and make us feel free. The hand of man may take the stone from the grave and show the dead, but none but Jesus can say to the dead: "Come forth and live." We must deal directly with Christ.

| Volume LXXI | WEDNESDAY, JULY 16, 1919 | Number 29 |

BURLINGTON   •   •   •   NORTH CAROLINA

THE CHRISTIAN SUN

Founded 1844 by Rev. Daniel W. Kerr

C. B. RIDDLE - - - Editor

Entered at the Burlington, N. C. Post Office as second class matter.

Subscription Rates

One year	$ 2.00
Six months	1.00

In Advance

Give both your old and new postoffice when asking that your address be changed.

The change of your label is your receipt for money. Written receipts sent upon request.

Many persons subscribe for friends, intending that the paper be stopped at the end of the year. If instructions are given to this effect, they will receive attention at the proper time.

Marriage and obituary notices not exceeding 150 words printed free if received within 60 days from date of event, all over this at the rate of one-half cent a word.

Original poetry not accepted for publication.

Principles of the Christian Church

(1) The Lord Jesus Christ is the only Head of the Church.
(2) Christian is a sufficient name of the Church.
(3) The Holy Bible is a sufficient rule of faith and practice.
(4) Christian character is a sufficient test of fellowship, and of church membership.
(5) The right of private judgment and the liberty of conscience is a right and a privilege that should be accorded to, and exercised by all.

EDITORIAL

ODDS AND ENDS FROM THE EDITOR'S NOTE BOOK

On July 2, Rev. J. E. Franks, the pastor who has never claimed to have finished canvassing his field in the interest of THE CHRISTIAN SUN, sent this office five new subscribers. On July 7, he started another list of eleven in our direction, which makes a total of sixteen to his credit since July 1. Brother Franks has secured fifty-three subscribers for THE SUN since January 1 of this year.

Some of our ministers write that they are unable to get any new subscribers. These letters come from pastors, where, according to our mailing list, the least number of copies of THE SUN go. So far as we are able to say there are more copies of THE CHRISTIAN SUN being mailed to the field of Rev. J. E. Franks than any other pastor in the Southern Christian Convention, no church, city or rural, excepted. This proves to us beyond a shadow of a doubt that there are families in every church that ought to have THE SUN and would take it if the proposition was put up to them.

Let us repeat what we have said before that the way to get subscribers to THE CHRISTIAN SUN (and the pastors who are the most successful tell us that this is their way) is to go to see the people for that purpose only, tell them that it is your only mission on that day, your only business and that you have come in the interest of the Kingdom through the Church paper.

We believe that if each minister in the Convention would give one day's work wholly, without any reservation, in the interest of THE SUN that the list would climb from 2,200 to 3,000. How many will do it?

Prohibition has now become a part of our basic law. That it should fail of enforcement through apathy, or in consequence of the influence of special interests, is inconceivable in a democratic country. Whatever vigilance is necessary to make the law effective will surely not be lacking.

The passing of the saloon which with all its pernicious influences, was yet a social center to a multitude of men, creates a new obligation to replace it with wholesome equivalents. Community centers, the church as a social center, fraternal orders and private clubs, public recreation, education in the use of leisure time,—all these should be developed rapidly and with great power and attractiveness. Especially should our churches be opened seven days in the week, with helpful religious, educational and social activities. But let us remember that the best equivalent is the home, and that whatever makes homes possible and renders them beautiful surpasses every other method.

Possibly the greatest question before the public today is the League of Nations. There are those who oppose it and those who approve it. From an impartial viewpoint, we have reached the conclusion that the main differences center around political parties and principles. We had hoped that the uniting of all forces to win the war would mean the uniting of all forces to preserve peace and protect mankind. We do not say that the present arrangement will guarantee this, for we are not wise enough for that, but as we see it, there is no particular united effort upon the part of our leaders to find the best principle. We are aware of our ground when we speak as we do. Principle is always bigger than a party and the Church will have to show her heroism one of these days to get what the world needs. Differences between men should not become oppressions for all mankind.

Attention is being called to our Chautauqua that is soon to meet at Virginia Beach, Virginia. The Chautauqua is more than a meeting place; it is a place where practical things are talked over and talked about; a place where workers of the Church come together for fellowship, information and inspiration. Such meetings ought to be attended by many more than usually attend. So many of us are so busy with our work that we forget our fellow-workers. And too, we are often in need of new ideas and fresh inspiration that we cannot get from work and books. Human association is the finest in the world, and we entertain the hope that this summer may be signal season for our Chautauqua.

This is the usual revival season and we pray that thousands may be born again and taste of that happiness at heart that only a Christian knows. There are some fundamentals that we ought to remember in connection with those who take upon themselves this new privilege and obligation. It is unfair to the new convert to teach him that he must fight against the world, the flesh and the devil and then not give him something with which to make that fight. It is unfair to him to point out the road to happiness without showing him how to find some unfortunate who is traveling from Jerusalem to Jericho and how to heal the wounds of the traveler. We feel that many have given up the fight for the lack of a job. Goodness alone will not save a world. Happiness is born in work and not idleness. Christianity is active and seeks to do something and the new convert should be given something to do.

Wherever you go during the summer months you find young people who are talking of their educational plans next fall. It is a common scene to visit a home and find a college catalogue on the summer benches in the front porch where young men and women have been reading it. Some young people have their minds made up as to what school they will attend while others debate this question for several weeks. In our own denomination there should be no question as to the best place to go. Our people should attend our own college —Elon. That college is maintained by our own people, fosters the principles of the Church, but above all other things stands for Christian character first and always. Our ministers, we are sure, will lose no time this summer in bringing to the attention of our people the interest of Elon College.

Brother B. D. Jones, Holland, Virginia, sends this message: "I see in THE CHRISTIAN SUN that Brother Chas. D. Johnston offers to raise four subscriptions for THE SUN from his church. I will double that at Holy Neck and make it eight. Any church ought to raise eight new subscribers." Here is a challenge from a layman to a layman. Who will challenge Brother Jones and offer to double his number? Who will undertake to equal what Brother Jones is to do—and what he will do? It would be fine to have a move upon the part of laymen in the direction of what Brother Johnston and Brother Jones have offered to do. Let us hear from others.

A paper in a sister denomination announces that it has lost $48,000.00 in six years—eight thousand dollars a year. Why the loss? This paper goes on to state that in six years it has booked $48,000.00 in accounts that it has failed to collect. Think of Christian people owing that much money—honest debts so far as we know —and then will not pay it! But such is the cry with all Church papers. Week after week we see where some editor has been forced to call attention to just this sort of a thing.

Dr. W. W. Staley never forgets the cooks and those who do the drugery work of the home. His article on page 12 is a gem and should be read by every reader of THE SUN. We hope that every tired mother will read it, and we especially recommend it to a certain class of husbands. When the world is brought to Christ it will be through efforts and bits of love from the many duties of life. In the kitchen, behind the plow, behind the counter, the desk, at the loom, and in all walks of life the Christian can sing the spirit of the Master and worship Him.

The Commission on the Church and Social Service is projecting the largest mailing in its history. Every Protestant minister in the United States will receive during July a pamphlet containing the Commission's statement on social reconstruction, its Labor Sunday message to the churches, and abstracts of significant social documents. The Labor Sunday message this year is concerned with the principle of industrial democracy. It contains information concerning new and vital tendencies in the industrial world. The churches should plan well in advance for the observance of Labor Sunday which this year comes on August 31.

In Sad Remembrance of
JOHN BARLEY CORN
who passed away, officially, June 30, 1919,
and left behind no *real* friends to mourn his going
Peace to his ashes and *no* return of his spirit

In one afternoon last week three persons came to THE CHRISTIAN SUN office and subscribed to THE CHRISTIAN SUN. These persons were from different pastorates. Their subscriptions made us rejoice, but the thing that bothers us is how these three persons who really wanted to take THE SUN, escaped the solicitation of their pastors. If some one can set us straight as to how these persons escaped it will give us relief of mind. Who will send the solution?

A man is not always wrong when his views fail to coincide with yours. So many of us get into the habit of under-rating our fellow-man just as soon as he fails to go in the direction that we want him to go or do the things we would have him do. Every man is free to act for himself. It is unfair to pass judgment upon our fellowman because his views do not agree with ours. It is not only unfair, but it is un-Christian and is void of the Master's way of doing things.

Brother C. D. Johnston, our enterprising Orphanage Superintendent, is still calling for help to build a home for small children. Let us remember that his pleadings are for the Church and the Kingdom's interest and not for his alone. He is sacrificing in many instances to carry on the work which we have placed upon his shoulders and the Church has no right to ask that his pleadings go unheard. The Church can build that home.

PASTOR AND PEOPLE

LETTER FROM OVER THE BORDER

Liberty

Children's Day was observed first Sunday in July. The exercises were very creditable. Miss Elsie Bray and other ladies had well rehearsed the children. The program was used as supplied by our Mission Secretary. An offering was made for missions. The pastor made a short address on "The Duty of the Church to the Child," and the Comunion was administered. The Sunday school, Christian Endeavor Society and Woman's Missionary Society are organizations of this church. Dr. W. C. Wicker was in this congregation recently in the interest of the Elon Standardization Fund. He was taken through the community by Deacon J. A. Bray, who is eighty-eight years of age. The people responded in a substantial way.

Lebanon

Children's Day was observed here the third Sunday in June. A large crowd was present and a very interesting and instructive program rendered under the direction of Mrs. John Pointer and others. There was a special offering for missions and an address, Lebanon has a very live Sunday school under the management of Deacon W. L. Taylor, a former Elon student. This is not a wealthy congregation, but very liberal. Besides looking well to the needs at home, these people have contributed in cash and subscriptions, since December 15, 1918, $4,500 to the general enterprises of the church.

Hebron

For several years the church building has needed remodeling. This work was planned but postponed on account of the war. Recently about $1,000 in improvements has been made. This is the congregation that the late Rev. C. C. Peel served for eleven years, and here, if I mistake not, he preached his last sermon. His memory is very dear to this people and it has been discussed to perpetuate the same by a memorial of some kind. The ladies have had a prosperous missionary society and all obligations are promptly met.

Union (Virgilina)

I am serving this church for the twelfth year. The Sunday school under the leadership of Deacon Alfred Hayes is growing. The ladies have a missionary society. Children's Day was observed the fifth Sunday in June. The program was very interesting. The children were well trained by Missess Lucy Gregory and Pearl Tuck. A special offering was made for missions. Brother Nick Oakley of Goshen Chapel united with us some time ago. A citizen of the town is to join next Sunday, July 13.

Dr. P. H. Fleming will be with us in a series of meetings the second wek in August. Plans for enlarging our work are being discussed and will be made public later.

C. E. NEWMAN.

Virgilina, Va.

NOTICE TO THE ALABAMA CHRISTIAN CONFERENCE

My dear Brethren:—

I see in THE SUN a suggestive report of the Committee, that was appointed to consider the question of grouping our churches into pastorates, and as this is only suggestive, I feel at liberty to write not as a dictator but as a servant.

My suggestion is that the churches in the several groups correspond with each other immediately and begin to co-operate now, in order that you may have the business in hand by the time Conference meets. I feel that we can make this system a success by prayerful consideration. Let each church appoint a committee, and let that committee meet at some convenient place and discuss the matter, lay your plans and pray that God may bless you in the effort.

We surely must do something to better provide for our ministry and the support of our dear old Church or else we will still suffer more and more. Remember, my brethren, there is nothing compelling in this move, but only a suggestion.

G. D. HUNT.

HOLLAND AND HOLY NECK

The fifth Sunday was a splendid day with the Holland Christian church as it marked the beginning of the study of missions in the Sunday school as a definite aim. The introduction took the form of a missionary rally with a splendid program.

The principal feature of the program was a missionary episode entitled, "In as Much" which indeed was a very impressive presentation of the need of missionary work on the foreign field and the support of missions at home; also the splendid and stirring address on missions by Dr. J. O. Atkinson.

His subject was the theorem: "If I had all the children of the church before me what would I like most to tell them?" Dr. Atkinson then recited an array of facts, figures and incidents which held the attention of the children and grown folks as well.

The Woman's Missionary Society rendered splendid assistance to the Superintendent of Missions in arranging the program.

The Children's Day services at this place will be held in the new church on the second Sunday night of July.

The first regular services in the new building will be on the morning of the second Sunday and will consist of preaching services, reception of new members, and Communion.

The Sunday school and Christian Endeavor Society met in the basement of the church last Sunday and both services report splendid sessions. A record attendance in the Sabbath school was established. The pastor could not be present at the first session of the Sunday school in the new church as he had to be at his other charge, at Holy Neck.

The service last Sunday at Holy Neck was the annual Children's Day service. It was a hot day and required much fanning but a splendid program had been prepared and it goes without saying that when others fail the children can hold your attention, and you forget all about the weather being hot. The children were well trained and rendered their part on scheduled time and in good order, which reflects much credit upon those who had in charge the training of the children.

Again we were rejoiced to have with us on this occasion Dr. J. O. Atkinson who spoke on the subject of missions, and closed his remarks by introducing a member of the Home Mission Board, Mr. J. M. Darden who had accompanied Dr. Atkinson to Holy Neck. Brother Darden, with his winsome smile, his pleasant look and an earnestness of heart and conviction, succeeded in holding the attention of the vast audience after an extended program and told the people how the Home Missions Board was going to spend the money contributed by the churches.

To the pastor the most impressive scene of the program was the taking of the offering which was handled by four small boys while a little girl stood on the platform, while the offering was being taken, received the offering plates from the boys and gave the offertory prayer.

W. M. JAY.

Holland, Va., July 7, 1919.

CENTERVILLE

Centerville Christian church is on the Western border of the Eastern Virginia Christian Conference within 18 miles of Petersburg. During the present pastorate there has been no large number of additions to membership but quite a number of heads of families have joined the church. A gradual growth has been the outcome of regular attendance, and reasonable co-operation among the church families and community interest. This is an easy church to preach to, there is but little criticism of the minister's way of preaching. If the member is hit, he takes it for his part, the *real truth is* that many members of this little church and congregation love *plain, practical* gospel truth. It is one of the most prompt country churches to pay pastor's salary which the writer has ever served. They have but one collector and he is the church treasurer—Deacon W. T. Gordon is on the job. Our plans for protracted meeting first Sunday have just been broken up and meeting postponed.

JAS. L. FOSTER.

Waverly, Va.

DANVILLE CHRISTIAN CHURCH

The Children's Day exercises of the Danville Christian Sunday school were held in the church on the first Sunday night in July and the affair was a great success. The writer has never attended a program of like kind that surpassed it in general excellence. Every member on the program, whether drill work, song, or recitation was presented in a way that would reflect credit on adults, and the children deserve the highest praise for their splendid work. The members of the Committee also deserve special mention in recognition of their faithful and efficient services in training the children, and much of the success of the occasion was

due to their efforts. It was a gala night and long to be remembered.

But it is in keeping with the spirit of the Sunday school and the good people of this community for they make good in whatever they set out to do for the Master and His Kingdom. The Sunday school is a live organization and is reaching and gripping both old and young. But there is a large field of opportunity and the school is striving to broaden its activities. Four delegates were elected to the great Sunday school and Christian Endeavor Convention to be held at Shallow Well and they are expected to bring back methods and inspiration that will prepare us for greater undertakings. The church has engaged the writer for three Sundays a month during the summer and there will be regular preaching services on the first, second, and fourth Sundays of each month, which the writer will also remain in Danville so that he may be at the service of his people.

Brethren, pray for the work at this strategic point.

H. S. HARDCASTLE.

Danville, Va., July 8, 1919.

FROM THE FAR SOUTH

I am taking a few moments of this patriotic day to write to THE SUN. I am with Rev. H. W. Elder in a meeting at Ambrose, Ga., this week. We are having a good meeting with fairly good attendance, considering the busy season with the farmers.

We are planning for and expecting some great meetings in the Southland this year. It is true that we have only a few laborers, and those we have are very busy, all this assures me that a great revival is in store for us. The busy pastor and the busy church can always be depended upon to bring things to pass.

I pray that God may bless abundantly every effort to the glory of His name.

G. D. HUNT.

July 4, 1919.

THE LAW OF SUBSTITUTION

The law of substitution is difficult to understand. It is the central thought in the idea of atonement, and the word *atonement* is used through with propitiatory sacrifices. It means to cover up. We may not know why Christ should die to cover up our sins, but the Word says, "It was expedient that one man should die for the people." This wonderful philosophy gathers all history into one sentence; the tragedy of life in one palpitating line. How could Christ die for all people and for all ages? Christ has quality enough to die for all the world. This mystery we may not be able to fathom, but its results can be felt, its work can be seen, and the eyes of the soul can behold it. There are many things too grand, too sublime, too satisfying for explanation. "Great is the mystery of godliness." Men are not saved because they can explain the mysterious process by which they are saved, but because they believe it. The recipients of this grand vicariousness have a hint of the marvelous work of God, by which His own death in the person of His Son is equal to the death of all who have sinned.

Man's sin created the necessity for the tragical death of Christ. Vice is overwhelmed by virtuous sacrifice. The cleansing of the heart is a heavenly work, wrought through the mysterious process of blood. If man's sin had been trivial and shallow, a trivial and shallow remedy would have been found for him, but man's sin was deep; it penetrated his soul, it collapsed the inner sanctuary of his being, and polluted his heart, therefore nothing can supply man's need but God through the sacrifice of His Son. The body of Christ was merely the symbol of the blood. The sinner is saved by the blood, for without the shedding of blood there is no remission of sin. This is God's compassion expressed through the law of substitution.

In the material world too many claims are placed upon substitutes and panaceas, while in the spiritual world the air is not burdened with these claims. Men reject work and accept leisure, reject comfort and accept pain, reject sound doctrine and accept false teaching. But if a happier life through salvation is the object of the soul's adventure, it will find no substitute for Christ. This is the unchangeable law of God. He inaugurated this law to save the world. This was the only way by which God could fully express Himself to the world. God revealed His infiniteness in nature, His wisdom in law, His likeness in man, and His heart in Christ, God stained the Cross with the blood of Christ for all men, and the only way to know God is to know Christ. For, "Herein is love: not that we loved God, but that he loved us, and sent his Son to be the propitiation for our sins." This world was marred by sin, and God used this remedy to heal it. This was God's law, and this law was not a fetter upon God, but an expression of His love.

Sin is not an offence against the judge, against the law, against some standard, but against the very heart of God, the tragedy of which we shall not know this side of eternity. Nothing but a heart of love could reach the depths of degradation and bring man to repentance and to a new life in Christ.

It is difficult to see how One could die for all, how the atoning blood of Christ is sufficient to "renew a right spirit within" a man. We may not understand why "He was a man sorrows and acquainted with grief." We may not know why "He was wounded for our transgressions, He was bruised for our iniquities, the chastisement of our peace was upon Him," but we know this is true, and the sinner who calls upon Him can be saved, and his song will be, "Safe in the Arms of Jesus."

                                        R. F. BROWN.

A CARD OF THANKS

To the good women of Ambrose, Georgia, Christian church, and their friends: I desire to express my sincere thanks for the donation sent me for the service rendered you by my husband in your revival. Perhaps you will never know how glad you make hearts at home feel by your thoughtfulness. "It is more blessed to give than to receive." May God abundantly bless all who took part.

                                        MRS. G. D. HUNT.

CHILDREN'S DAY

During the month of June Children's Day exercises were held at Wakefield, Dendron and New Lebanon churches. The committees had access to the program issued by the Sunday School and Christian Endeavor Board. It takes time and persevering effort on the part of those who train the children for these exercises but it is worth while and more of our schools might profit by such exercises. They have an educational value for the children and also for the congregation. An offering for missions was made at the close of each of the aboved named exercises.

The Young People's Missionary Society of the Wakefield church gave an instructive and impressive program the fifth Sunday night. An offering was taken for missions.

                                        W. D. HARWARD.

WHAT PROMINENT MEN THINK OF THE PEACE COVENANT

B. A. Abbott, Editor, The Christian-Evangelist, St. Louis, Mo.: I do not know of a single argument against the Covenant for a League of Nations adopted by the Paris Peace Conference which I consider good. I look upon it as the organization of international good will, and believe that when it is sufficiently emphasized it will change the hearts of the nations of the earth towards one another. In the past different nations thought of each other as enemies, and this led them to act in education, politics and economies in a selfish manner. But the League of Nations will reveal to us the benefits of international co-operation instead of international antagonism, and we shall find that every good thing in international and individual life will be quickened by it. As a churchman, I consider it the most important step yet made toward the organization of the Kingdom of God on earth.

* *

Grant K. Lewis, Secretary, American Christian Missionary Society: The church ought to favor the Paris Covenant because it seems to present the best practical remedy of the world's unrest. America should not hesitate to sign at this stage of the proceedings. She crossed the Rubicon when war was declared. The Paris Covenant is the fruit of victory won by our men in battle. To refuse to receive it would seem the height of folly.

* *

Thomas E. Cramblet, President, Bethany College, Bethany, W. Va.: I am very greatly interested in the Covenant for the League of Nations, as set forth in the amended form recently adopted by the Paris Peace Conference. From my viewpoint, the principles adopted by the Conference of the League of Nations safeguards, in every way, the highest interests of our own Government and at the same time places the American people where they will be able to render a world-wide service for humanity. The adoption of this League gives every promise of lessening the danger of future wars.

Editorial Note: President Cramblet since writing the above has passed to his reward.—C. B. R.

CHRISTIAN EDUCATION

AND THE END IS NOT YET

On February 16 the drive for the Elon Standardization Fund in our beloved Church began and it was scheduled to close on June 30, 1919. Well, it did, so far as solicitation is concerned, but the end is not yet. Almost every mail has brought us welcome accretions to the magnificent total, which now soars far beyond the $300,000 mark. A few more have sent us word to withhold the final report till they can be heard from and so we cheerfully refrain. When we do make our final announcement, we are confident a shout of praise will ascend from 25,000 grateful voices, giving thanks to God for His blessings.

I have never for a moment doubted that we should attain our objective in this campaign, nor even the doubled goal, and in this confidence the Drive Committee fully shared. Here is what they said in their initial address to the Church on the eve of the campaign's launching:

"With confidence we therefore address this appeal to our Brotherhood, feeling assured that every Church, minister, layman, lay-woman will respond nobly to our call, which we do not hesitate to assert is imperative in its necessity at this time, The day is past for small things and paltry gifts to our College. It has in poverty achieved recognition, but larger income from permanent funds are unconditionally necessary now in order to retain the standards already won. We feel satisfied that our people will receive President Harper and those associated with him with open hands and glad hearts, ready to respond cheerfully to the necessities of our prosperous and progressive College. We commission him and them to this work of the Lord among us. It is His work and ours, not theirs. They are to be our agents in this forward step. Let us in the speedy conclusion of this drive take the sting out of stingy, by a generosity worthy of our great Church and her liberal principles. Let us rejoice and be glad in this challenge to our faith and our vital Christian character."

This confidence, the fruitful days of February 16-June 30, have abundantly justified and we can all rejoice and be glad in the good hour that our Convention put this challenge up to our faith and by it proved the genuineness and vitality of our Christian character. Never has a people bent its energies spiritually more generously to a task than our Christian Brotherhood did to the raising of this magnificent fund to stabilize our College and guarantee its usefulness in perpetuity. God bless them, every one. They took the "sting out of stingy" all right and with open-hearted liberality went "over the top for Elon" to the tune of more than $300,000.

Suffolk, The Largest Giver

Suffolk, of course, was the largest giver. She always is. The chairman of the Drive Committee was there, and so was Dr. Staley, ex-officio, a member of the Committee and these men guaranteed success there. Suffolk totaled $56,600, which is slightly more than three times her quota.

But Waverly Gets The Crown

But Waverly outdistanced all the churches. Her quota was $2,250 and she gave $10,300, that is four times her quota and $1,300 besides. Elon was a close competitor. She gave four times her quota and $1,100 more. Pleasant Grove, (Va.), and Holland, (Va.) each quadrupled their quotas. Many doubled, but of these a final list will be given in the Drive Committee's official bulletin next spring.

The Finest Fund Yet

The First Church of Norfolk, Va., the church of my childhood days, has done a most splendid deed. Rev. M. L. Bryant burnt out his useful life in arduous service in that church. The church in business session established a fund of $1,000 in his memory, authorizing the treasurer, Brother J. O. Wiggs, to sign it officially for the congregation. This was in addition to what individuals gave to the fund. Is that not fine?

The Only Banner Conference

Every church in the Eastern Virginia Conference gave its quota or more in the drive. $153,000 is officially credited to that Conference alone. It is the only banner Conference. I am glad I was born in the Eastern Virginia Conference. Hats off, beloved, to the Eastern Conference, and breathe a little prayer of thanks to God that we have such a Conference.

More Yet

I hope next week to bring you more yet of good cheer in the final report on our campaign. For all of which let us thank God and take courage. Pray that Elon may be true to her beautiful motto—"Christian character, first and always, at Elon."

W. A. HARPER.

We glean the following note from *The Herald of Gospel Liberty*: "Rev. O. W. Powers, D. D., who for so many years has been connected with the work in and about Dayton, and who has served so well in so many capacities in the Christian Church, has accepted the pastorate of the church at Lynn, Mass., and will leave in a few days for that place. Dr. Powers has for so long been such a helpful friend to so many of us in this part of the country, as well as a tireless worker and a man of great scholarship, whose knowledge and council was always an inspiration, that his going comes as a real personal loss to many of us. Mrs. Powers has for many years had charge of the literature for the Woman's Boards, and the workers in that department feel most keenly the fact that she will not be able to remain near here and in close touch with them, for she has made a wonderful development of that class of literature and extension of its use in their work. Their daughter, Miss Florence Powers, has been the private secretary of Dr. Burnett and rendered commendable service in that office. The entire family has been putting their lives and hearts into the work here in such a way that they will be greatly missed. We are sure they will soon find a place of equally large worth in their new field."

The New Task of the College*

And He that sat upon the throne said, Behold, I make all things new.—Rev. 21:5.

Jesus was no reactionary. The religious stand-patters of His day, the Scribes, the Pharisees, the Sadducees, the Herodians received small courtesy and scant sympathy at His hands. He denounced them with an invective unmatched in any other recorded utterance of man. Jesus was the true, the real, the original progressive in Kingdom affairs. The preg-nant word of His thought-conception is progress. Forward is the only direction suitable to His teach-ings. Change, newness, freshness—these are the en-gaging charm of His unfolding program for men and society. Every age since His advent has made new, rich discoveries of His deeper meanings and brought forth brilliant nuggets of His ever-advancing truth.

The age in which we live is highly favored by its revelations of spiritual principles and in its oppor-tunities to apply them to new situations. For all time to come men will look back to this day as one richly endowed with spiritual possibility for the Kingdom's growth. There is no doubt the Gospel of Jesus has a message for this hour. Equally there is no doubt that this hour challenges the gospel expositors to re-veal to it its inner meaning, to interpret to it its spiritual significance. The church dares not in an hour like this to refuse to adjust herself to the cherish-ed expectations of the times.

In this interpretation of our age to its inner self, the college, the seminary of leadership, the shrine where ideals are forged affecting for good or ill all the life of men,—in this interpretation the college must play a large and important role. Colleges shall never be the same again, as in the days before the World War. Their purpose in the ultimate may be the same, but their whole inner life must be readjusted to meet the crying need of the hour with a leadership adequate to satisfy men's heart-hunger for a full, free, complete self-expression. And in generous, whole-hearted response to that cry the college worthy the confidence of the new day will seek to equip those who resort to it for life-direction with some essentially new ideals for the guidance of their attitude and conduct of life in the unfolding years.

I. The New Brotherhood

And central among these ideals we shall find a new and an enlarged conception of Brotherhood's place in determining the relations of men. This splendid word must become more than a word in the days ahead. Jesus came to teach the Brotherhood of Man. We have said it, over and over again. But we have not acted on it. We have not even lived up to the demands of neighborliness. The Good Samaritan is yet an exalted ideal of the true Christian to most of us. But the good Samaritan, good as he was, is as

far beneath the standard of genuine Christian Bro-therhood as the priest and Levite were beneath Him in all the essentials of true manhood. A neighbor may content himself to go to the rescue of a fellow who has fallen among thieves, and thereafter minister to him tenderly, with never a thought that he is respon-sible for the thieves who assaulted him, and with never a thought of bringing the thieves to the bar of justice. Brotherhood can never be satisfied with neighborli-ness. The Christian man in this new time must be more than a Good Samaritan.

Never can I forget the thrill of horror that surged through my soul when I read President Wilson's Philadelphia speech, in which he said in the event of a future World War no nation could remain neutral. He had just been returned to the highest office in the gift of our people on a peace platform, and yet even before his inauguration he was preparing the nation to take its place in the conflict then raging. My heart sank within me. "What can our President mean?" I said again and again to myself. And then these Scriptures came to me with a new and subtler mean-ing: "Ye are members one of another," "Bear ye one another's burdens and so fulfill the law of Christ," "Am I my brother's keeper?", and then I comprehended as never before that Brotherhood is more than an American doctrine, that it has universal application, and that I dare not undertake to enjoy any good thing for myself, that all must be shared with my brother-men. From that time on I was sure America would enter the war, that she ought to enter the war, that she would be cursed of God if she did not.

It remains for the college now to interpret to the bright young lives that seek ideals in her borders this spirit of Brotherhood in terms of personal living, so that the young people who go from her walls shall go conscious of the solidarity of the human race and pulsing with desire to invest themselves in speedily realizing it.

II. A New Appreciation of Christian Education

But the college cannot do this unless it makes Christ central in its curriculum. Christian education is the hope of the hour, as Brotherhood is its chal-lenge. Education that essays to leave Christ out of its teaching is fundamentally defective. It will eventually curse the earth. It will not do merely to train men's minds and cultivate their social graces. Germany did that, and behold! the devastation Ger-many has wrought. No mighty nation has ever fallen so mightily, as has this giant of our day. Germany was the most intellectual nation of the world. Her universities furnished the ideas of the race. It was impossible to be accepted for an advanced degree in any university of America, England, or France unless you could read and understand the works of German authorities in the original. Germany was the intel-lectual leader of the world. And her culture surpass-ed that of the other nations in like degree. It is said that of trained scientists per thousand of population the United States had eight, England eleven, France slightly above thirteen, but Germany thirty-four. She was the most cultured nation of our time. And Germany the intellectual, Germany the cultured has cursed mankind as no other nation ever did, crucifying them with inhuman horror upon the cruel cross of her intellectualism and of her Kultur. Why? Because Germany dared neglect the cultivation of the spiritual faculties in her educational program.

Shall America escape Germany's doom? The American college shall answer. We fought in the World War to make the world safe for democracy. Shall democracy degenerate into Bolshevism, into Sovietism, into Anarchy? It shall undoubtedly, if we neglect the heart in our college curriculum. All that we Christian educators have pleaded for since the days of the Rennaissance has been justified, vindicated in the sad experiences of our day. We have spilt the sacred flood of our heroes in vain if we fail to make our educational system Christian in its inner life and purpose. Christian character is to be the first and foremost product of our educational system, or democracy will be mankind's undoing.

And this brings me to say that we must devise some plan by which religion may be taught in tax-supported institutions of higher learning. The American principle of the separation of Church and State must be respected, and this makes it impossible for public money to be used to teach religion. Even in wartime the religious welfare of our fighting men was turned over to voluntary organizations. Voluntary assistance in teaching religion must be granted our State Colleges and Universities that they may help us make democracy safe for the world. I do not hesitate to say that the finest mission field in our country for recruiting the Kingdom's leadership is not to be found among the millions of immigrants that flock to our shores nor among the negroes nor among the mountain whites, but on the campuses of our tax-supported institutions of higher learning, where young men and young women are congregated in thousands during the ideal-forming period of their lives. If we fail to reach these promising lives with the Kingdom message, America is to do her part at making democracy safe for the world, if she does it at all, at tremendous odds. The colleges of the Christian type must not only look well to their own curricula, but they must render real assistance to the state institutions, which are handicapped by the fundamental law of the land. We must adjust ourselves to the demands of the hour and find how we can Christianize the American system of higher education in all its departments, for Christian education is democracy's only hope of permanent blessing to men.

III. An Enlarged Conception of Service

But democracy is not an end in itself, and this leads us to declare in the third place that the college must give direction to democracy in terms of service. What does it mean to serve? And what is its scope? We cannot divorce service from religion, for the thought is foreign to any other realm of life. Does the Christian ideal of service need re-interpretation in our day? No, but that of the church does. Too often the church has mistaken Christian activity for Christian service. Too often leaders in the church have busied themselves in maintaining public worship and keeping the local organization's machinery in working order, and thought they had in that completed the circle of Christian duty. Has a church a right to be self-centered and narrow-visioned? Can such a church please God? Can it do the work of the Kingdom? I know a Church with five deacons and three other church officials whose horizon of service is limited to keeping the local work alive. That Church would be blessed to have eight funerals in rapid succession. God cannot let a selfish church live, and conversely He will ever keep alive and in flourishing condition any church that forgets itself in a program of service for the Kingdom's advance.

But what is the scope of service? It must touch every realm of our life. God made man, all of man, and all of him is sacred to God. No one part of our nature can be truly said to be lower than another, and if it should be, that part should receive the greater consideration at the hands of Christian leaders. Colleges must teach the future leaders of the church that all of life is religious, that all of life is spiritual, and that all of life is consequently to be ministered to by a full-orbed church. Men must see that God is present everywhere and they must learn in all the experience of life to sense the fellowship of His presence. We must consciously realize Him in our every department of life. We must recognize that we serve Him in our daily toil, in our public worship, in our private devotions, in our moments of leisure and recreation as well as in the tense and busy activity of our application to our life-work. Such a spirit of service will make democracy safe for Heaven as well as for the earth and is its own rich and fruitful reward.

IV. A New Recognition of Sacrifice's Place

But lest men should serve selfishly, with their eyes on the reward that ever blesses him who serves, the college must equip the leaders of men with the spirit of sacrifice. We must not forget the lesson of sacrifice we have learned in the World War. We learned that lesson in anguish of heart and in bitterness of tears, but we needed to learn it. The magnitude of our sacrifice is the measure of our soul growth. America's soul has been graciously enlarged during the past two years. We have as a nation learned to sacrifice. We entered the war with no ulterior motive. We desired no reward for our sacrifices, not even any indemnity. We were willing to sacrifice our all for the good we could bless our brothermen with, with no thought of reward. It is the sublimest instance of sacrifice on the national scale in human history, and behold! America has become central in the thoughts and affections of mankind. Her voice was the voice of hope for a crushed and bleeding humanity. Her voice is now the voice of authority and leadership in the council-chamber of the nations. From being the most hated of nations, America has become the most beloved, because America has been willing to give herself, her all, for others, without stint or thought of self. It is ever-so. The only service worthy the name is based on sacrifice, and selfish service is an auto-poisoning process for which there is no cure but a new birth into the Kingdom of sacrifice, joyous, full, free,—sacrifice that knows no limit.

Why is Jesus the best loved man who ever lived? Is it because he amassed for Himself a great fortune? The Son of Man had not where to lay His head. Is it because He left great works of literature to perpetuate His name among His fellows? Our Master wrote only one line. He wrote it on the ground, with ed woman taken in an awful sin, and the rains of Heaven washed it away. Is it because He came to great preferment by the suffrage and approval of His fellow-men? He was crucified by their suffrage and with their loud approval. Why is Jesus the best loved man who ever lived? It is because as no other man He absolutely gave Himself for others.

And Finally

"For others," Class of 1919, let this be your motto as you pass out into the stirring realities of our troubled and uncertain time. "For others," this shibboleth shall admit you to the realm of the genuine servants of the race. It may bring you to the judgment seat of a Pilate, it may nail you to the Cross, it may send you into the tomb, even as it did our Lord. But why should you fear or falter? For with us as with Him, when we have died "for others" we shall arise in His likeness to a new and rich eternity.

"And He that sat upon the throne said, Behold, I make all things new." He has been doing it for nineteen centuries. He is doing it now in accelerated manner. Shall we discern His handiwork, constituting, interpreting anew the fundamental concepts by His finger. It was a sentence of pardon to a wretch-which our life is to be ordered? Do we see His pregnant meaning for Brotherhood, for a true Democracy rendered safe by Christian Education, for a Service that shall embrace all of life and quicken it with spiritual force, for a Sacrifice that shall match His own in its willingness to give all "for others"? Let us be earnest in our sincerity to discern the signs of the times aright. Let us pray that we ourselves as we pass out into active life may be animated by these foundation principles of the new time and let us also pray that our Alma Mater may be crowned with Heavenly blessing in her efforts to instill into those who shall take our places here these same splendid criteria of the Kingdom for men's lives. Such is the new task of the college. Such is Elon's task. May she be true in this crisal time.

*President Harper's baccalaureate address to the Class of 1919, given May 18, 1919, at 8.30 P. M.

MISSIONARY

GROWING MISSIONARIES

We of the Christian Church, since we cannot and *must* not *make* missionaries, must by God's help grow them. And where is there a finer field for this growth than our Sunday schools? Our good Doctor J. G. Bishop in a recent cheering letter to the writer says: "I am much interested in your work with missions in our Sunday schools. Surely the Sunday school is a *great* field that needs larger and closer cultivation, and gives hope of a larger harvest of missionary zeal and power for Christ and the Kingdom. We hope and pray that your successful effort along this line may become contagious." Every Sunday school should have an objective worthy of its pains, its plans and its efforts. What higher objective could it have than that of growing men and women who will go "and teach all nations" the blessed story of our Christ, and of His power to redeem and save?

OUR GREATEST WEALTH

"A nation to be truly great and to be sure of its future development and success must realize that its greatest wealth lies in its children; its highest possibilities are wrapped up in all its little ones; its one hope of the future is in the childhood of the nation." We see such a truth frequently reiterated and emphasized. And what is true of a nation is certainly true of a church. Children are not wealth, but well-being, and writers who emphasize the above truth really mean well-being where they employ the term *wealth*. So in fact our greatest well-being in the future lies in our childhood.

If this Christian Church of ours is to grow in future, and come into its own, it must now give heed to the right sort of childhood. The older ones, the grown-ups, and the fixed-in their habits cannot be expected to change appreciably. But the childhood of the Church is its one hope of a successful future. And so we can never be a missionary people, that is to say a growing and progressive people, until we shall have taught our children to be missionary in spirit and in activity. We must carry home to the child-mind the real facts of a world that is in need of Christ. We must imbed in the child-mind of the church the necessity of carrying out the Great Commission of our Lord, and of what it means to them, and also to those who sit in darkness without Him, to try to carry out this Commission.

I know of one Sunday school teacher from whose class have gone out fifteen missionaries. That teacher had the care of a sin-cursed world upon her heart, and the care for the children who were entrusted to her to teach from Sunday to Sunday. We grown-ups may not have pity, but the children will have pity if they can but know conditions as they are in the world to-day. It is indeed a pity not to let the children know.

- J. O. ATKINSON.

THE CHRISTIAN ORPHANAGE

FARMING

This spring has been one adverse to farming in this section. I hardly think I have ever tried to farm under more discouraging circumstances. We have had much rain and the ground has been too wet to work for ten days at a time; and when it would clear up, the ground would get so hard we could not plough it with horses. But in our distress last week when we were trying with all our might to get our ground ploughed and our Soja Beans in the ground to make feed for our cattle this winter, and the ground so hard we could not make much time, our old friend, Chas. P. Harden, of Graham, N. C., came to our rescue and gladly sent his farm tractor and plough and gave us three days of its use. This helped us wonderfully and we shall always appreciate his big sympathetic heart and are grateful indeed for the help when we needed it so much.

We also had a letter from a warm friend of the Orphanage who lives in the State of California, telling me he wanted to be one of the twenty to give five hundred dollars for the Children's Home. Letters like this one make me glad.

I wonder who will be the next one to join the twenty to make the amount needed to build the Children's Home?

CHAS. D. JOHNSTON, *Supt.*

FINANCIAL REPORT FOR JULY 16, 1919

Amount brought forward, $7,278.64.

Sunday School Monthly Offerings

(North Carolina Conference)

Amelia, $4.11; New Providence, $2.41; Pleasant Hill, $3.06; Catawba Spring, $10.00; Pleasant Ridge, $2.55; Chapel Hill, $4.71; Glencoe (Union Sunday school), $10.00; Popes Chapel, $2.60.

(Eastern Virginia Conference)

Berea, (Norfolk), $4.00; Holy Neck, $4.00; Union, (Southampton), $4.25.

(Valley of Virginia Conference)

Concord, $3.90; Linville, $4.90; Huntington, Ind, First Christian Church, $7.55; Total, $64.14.

Special Offerings

New Providence Baraca Class, on support of little girl, 25 cents; Philathea Class, Liberty, (Vance County, N. C.), $37.50; Woman's Board S. C. C., $35.55; Rev. B. J. Howard and Wife, $2.00; American C. C. Office, Dr. J. F. Burnett, Sec., $10.00; Total, $85.30.

Children's Home

The Fidelity Class, Durham Christian Church, $5.00; Mrs. D. S. Welch, Graham, N. C., $5.00; Total, $10.00.

Total for the week, $159.44; Grand Total, $7,433.08.

Congress began the consideration of the Peace Treaty and League of Nations Monday, July 14.

President Wilson has vetoed the Daylight Savings Bill. That means no change in your watch for the present.

Swat the fly. B. good. N. joy life.

NOTES

Dr. J. U. Newman is spending the summer in Asheville, N. C., where he is engaged in that favorite occupation of his—teaching.

We have had several callers during the past several days from Alamance and adjoining counties. Come again, brethren. We are always glad to see you.

Prof. A. L. Hook is at Cornell University this summer, and writes that he cannot do without THE SUN while away from home. His address is 308 Eddy St., Ithaca, N. Y.

Brother T. J. Holland, Wray, Georgia, is interested in increasing the circulation of THE SUN and says that he is going to see that THE SUN has a larger circulation in his church.

Practically all this issue was set up and ready for the press by noon, July 10, and that will explain why your article did not appear. We take the "copy" as it comes, unless circumstances demand it otherwise.

THE CHRISTIAN SUN is being represented this week at the Sunday School and Christian Endeavor Convention of the North Carolina Conference by Miss Bessie Holt, who so efficiently represented THE SUN at several Conferences last fall.

Mr. Ira R. Gunn, Wentworth, N. C., a former linotype operator on THE CHRISTIAN SUN, called to see us one day last week. We are always glad to see Gunn. He is a member of Elon's class '17, and has just returned from service.

Mr. V. P. Heatwole, Dayton, Va., who graduated at Elon College with the Class of '17, and who was once the pressman on THE CHRISTIAN SUN, is serving in that capacity this summer. Heatwole returned from service a few weeks ago.

Just as we go to press a letter is received from Brother T. J. Simpson, Stokesdale, N. C., sending us seven new subscribers to THE SUN and the cash for all. Another layman demonstrating that the thing can be done. Of course it can be done, brethren, and so we wait for the next report.

We note that many pastors write very little for THE SUN during the summer months. This is a privilege all their own. However, our side of the case is that it takes the same work (and a little more it seems in hot weather) each week in the year to produce the paper. We desire to make each issue as original as possible. Let the notes come along, and if the weather is too hot for a long article a short one will do. And what we say to the ministers applies to the laymen. We have too few letters from the laymen of the Church.

WORSHIP AND MEDITATION

GET READY TO ASCEND UNKNOWN HEIGHTS

There is yet very much to learn in the schools of Nature and Revelation. Ever learning and yet never able to come to the knowledge of the truth. Present attainments do not, and ought not to satisfy. We are learners, but if we fail to study, not much will be learned. There are great models in Revelation as well as in nature and it is such a delight to think the thoughts of God after Him. So many things demand your life, your care, your all.

Michael Angelo once visited the study of young Raphael. The junior artist was not in, and Angelo departed without leaving his name, but before he left he took a piece of chalk and drew on the canvass beneath the poor and meagre design of Raphael, a bold, sweeping line, and added the word, Amplius. When Raphael came in and saw this he knew at a glance who had been there and at once his style was changed and he became the painter the world calls divine. Let us believe that Jesus comes to us and looking at our imperfect aims and meagre work, He writes beneath our hearts: "Amplius, Amplius—wider and further; more and still more."

In the natural world there is a limitation to growth and development; but in the spiritual the growth or development is illimitable. The clothes I wore when a child would not fit me now. They were discarded piece by piece and year after year for larger garments. This had to be repeated until I was grown, physically. I have lost all the fondness for the toys and playthings of my childhood sunny days. They do not interest me now. But there is still room for improvement of my mind and soul, and I am hoping to ascend even to higher heights in the Christian life. The natural strength will fail, but the soul can grow stronger until the perfect day. It is cultivatable and must be cultivated for the best and happiest results.

We believe that the unknown state will be supremely glorious. If God has made this and other worlds so attractive and useful, how much more lovely and infinitely beautiful must be the heavenly world in which the children of God expect to live!

The soul now blunted and stunted by so many adverse conditions will there be immortalized with continual happiness. The imagination is drawn on very largely for future events and changes, and in our present condition there is nothing better to do.

We look upon life as the most real and profound thing in the kingdom of nature. Oh, how we like life and love to live it! In any and every condition we try hard to hold on to it. Mysterious as it is, it is, nevertheless, sweet and dear to all. When sudden and extreme causes surround us nothing is so helpful as the word live. Even amid the cloudy days of the cold gray, cheerless winter, while trembling or shivering in the cold, you were still looking for sun's healthful rays to shine through the parting clouds to give a thrill of gladness.

Today I heard a despondent one say: "I wish I could get more out of life and enjoy it more fully that I might understand the words, 'Make me to hear joy and gladness'" Joy and gladness may be heard all about you. Are you listening to hear them? Tune your harp. Sing praises to God, and listen, wait, expecting joy and gladness to come. Will you try at once?

J. T. KITCHEN.

Windsor, Va.

SUFFOLK LETTER

"Sweet Peace........God's Love"

I passed a residence one day in July and heard a lame woman singing in the kitchen, "Sweet Peace, the Gift of God's Love." I listened as I walked and I heard her sing: "There comes to my heart one sweet strain, a glad and a joyous refrain, I sing it again and again, sweet peace, the gift of God's love." It seemed to come from the heart of the afflicted woman who is shut in, though she loved to go to church. No choir could render more acceptable praise; no soloist could render finer tones. It was not sung for human ears, but it mingled with the songs of angels in the temple where the blood-washed spirits render praises day and night to the Lord of hosts. I felt like stopping and peeping into that kitchen, but I really felt like my presence would be an intrusion. The glory of it was its sincerity. The marvel of it was the happy heart on crutches, and working in the kitchen, and that in July. All of the outward conditions spoke of suffering, of confinement, of labor; but within, there was "peace, sweet peace, the gift of God's love." This the "peace which the world can neither give nor take away," the "peace that passeth understanding."

Peace is the gift of God's love. Environment cannot produce it; education cannot bring it; wealth cannot buy it; nations cannot force it; alliances cannot guarantee it; it is God's gift. Moreover, it is in the heart. It is not in the intellect, but in the seat of the affections, and, therefore, within the reach of all individuals who will enthrone Jesus Christ in their souls. It is, indeed, a "sweet strain" and must be sung "again and again" to fill the heart with "sweet peace." As many beautiful flowers bloom at the base of the mountain, in some nook under a great bowlder where cool water oozes out from hidden fissures, so sweet souls sing joyous songs in hidden places, and the kitchen is one of those places. The seat may be hard, the air may not be clean, the odors may not smell like sweet incense, but through the smoky windows, a light shines, and in the room joy sings its song of praise.

Religion is not for the market place only, but for the obscure routine of life. "When thou prayest, be not as the hypocrites; for they love to pray standing in the synagouges and in the corner of the streets, that they may be seen of men.'' Praise should not be rendered unto men, but unto God; and it may be done in the kitcheff as well as in the temple. Kitchen religion is the finest type of religion, because it sweetens the entire home. The cooks represent the largest army in the world. No other like of workers embraces such a large percentage of human race. At least ten percent of the human family is engaged in this necessary occupation; and that means that a hundred and fifty millions of people, mostly women, kindle the fires, scrub the pots, rub the pans, fry the eggs, make the coffee, do the rest, and then wash the dishes; and this three times a day. 450,000,000 of meals are served each day and little thanks from those who eat. No wonder so many people eat their meals without asking a blessing; they do not even thank the cooks. How many women sit down to meals too tired to eat and are happy to see their families enjoy what they have prepared with love for them and love for God. Nothing could take care of the kitchen and prepare our food but love. The incense of the kitchen fills the world with peace; and no sacrifice on battlefields can be compared with the courage of song-filled cooks who make the bread of earth while they eat the bread of heaven. I can see my own mother now flop down at the table when dinner is finished and the family is tempted by odors from smoking dishes which her dear hands prepared. There she sits, tired but happy, because her family enjoys the meal. She rests from her good labors now and sings with the angels the praises which she sang in the kitchen when she was there.

W. W. STALEY.

THE FORWARD MOVEMENT

Warren H. Denison, D. D., Superintendent

We rejoice to see the splendid success of President Harper as he sweeps on to the $250,000 additional endowment fund. President Hershey and the trustees of Union Christian College have voted to raise an additional $100,000 for Union Christian College. President Caris and the trustees of Defiance College are now raising an additional endowment fund of $200,000 from the Defiance territory in addition to the $100,000 recently raised by the citizens of Defiance county. The Forward Movement bids these great institutions of ours the heartiest Godspeed. We hope all our people will heartily support these institutions with prayer, money, kind words and by sending their sons and daughters this fall to our worthy institutions.

The Eastern Indiana Conference held a very profitable Quarterly June 25 and 26, in Beaver Chapel and the pastors and laymen at that Conference have pledged their heartiest co-operation. Many of the pastors have already taken up a church program built upon the basis of the Forward Movement outline.

Some two thousand, five hundred people from the twenty Christian churches of three counties of the Northwestern Ohio Conference met at the fair grounds at Lima, Ohio June 29 in a Forward Movement rally, and the Superintendent and Dr. O. S. Thomas spoke on the Movement. Great interest was shown. The Superintendent spoke at the Lima church at night.

Rev. E. A. Watkins, D. D., Lima, Ohio; Rev. C. F. Baldwin, Darlington, Ind.; Rev. R. C. Helfenstein, D. D., Urbana, Ill., have been placing great emphasis upon Christian stewardship and tithing. recently with large results, for large numbers of their congregation have become tithers.

The time is here for most of our Conferences in the Southern Convention to begin to plan their Conference program. We urge all committees to keep in mind the importance of making the programs in harmony with the Forward Movement. These programs should be built around the five fundamentals of our denominational Forward Movement. This means much more than an address or two and carries with it the idea of building these fundamental ideas of the Movement into the life and plans of every church in the Conferences. The Convention contemplates making these principles a very part of the fiber and life of the church in all its departments. We ask the Conferences to so plan the programs as to help the churches in a most practical way to get the spirit and method of the Movement. The Conferences should lay upon the churches and pastors the importance of making a very definite church program.

In one of our canvasses recently in Indiana a Jew came and of his own accord offered a pledge of ten dollars per year, saying that he was interested in such work as he had heard we were doing and would be pleased to have some part in it. During another canvass in Illinois a man riding along the road saw our committee canvassing and asked if we would accept as small an offering as ten dollars per year from an outsider, and if so he would be glad to give such a contribution of fifty dollars. As we came in from the field the other day where we had been securing pledges there came to our desk a check for five hundred dollars from a party in New York state who had not been solicited.

TWO FRIENDS

''In-a-Minute'' is a bad friend. He makes you put off what you ought to do at once, and so he gets you into a great deal of trouble.

''Right-Away'' is a good friend. He helps you to do pleasantly and quickly what you are asked to do, and he never gets you into trouble. —Our Little Ones.

HIS CORRECT ADDRESS

A certain man, who had been invited to speak at a lodge meeting, was placed on the list of speakers. However, the chairman introduced several speakers whose names were not on the program, and the audience was tired out when he eventually introduced the last speaker.

''Mr. Bones will now give his address.''

''My address,'' said Mr. Bones, rising, ''is No. 551 Park Villa, and I wish you all good night.''

Sunday School and Christian Endeavor

**SUNDAY SCHOOL LESSON FOR
JULY 27, 1919**

Christian Fellowship . Acts 2:42, 46, 47; Philippians 4:10-20.

Golden Text : "If we walk in the light, as he is in the light, we have fellowship one with another."

Devotional Reading: I John 1:1-9.

"If we walk in the light, we have fellowship." If, then we insist that we will have no fellowship, by that same token we have no light. People say: "I keep myself to myself. I am a Christian, but I do not care to mix with the other people in the church. I do not find anyone in the community who is my social equal, and I do not mix with them." Then you are walking in darkness. There is no such thing as walking with Christ and walking alone—that is, without effort to bring another with you. "Where two or three are gathered together," said Christ. A Christian alone is only possible on the mission field where none as yet know the Lord Christ, and then, they should be so surrounded with an aurea of love from those back home who think of them and pray for them, that they should never need to feel alone. The war has taught us many things about fellowship. The man who has fought side by side with the French, the British, the Italian, the Indian, the African, the negro, who has seen their splendid service, will find it hard, and should find it impossible, to go back to the place where he put a fence between them and himself in his daily life. "One is your Master, even Christ and all ye are brethren."

MRS. FRED BULLOCK.

**CHRISTIAN ENDEAVOR TOPIC FOR
JULY 27, 1919**

"How do men confess Christ and how deny him? Luke 22:55-61.

The story is told of a young man, a member of the church who was going for six months into the lumber woods of Michigan. "You will have to be careful up there," said his friends, "for those people are heathen. They have no regard for God, and you will have a hard time when they find you are a Christian." Six months later the young man re-

turned, and his friends asked him: "What did they do when they found you were a Christian?" "Oh," said he, "they never found it out." Did this young man deny Christ? If we never ask another to meet our Lord, never talk of Him or about Him, are we confessing Him? Let us read a well-known verse in this way: "He that introduces me to men, the same will I introduce to my Father and the holy angels." Can you see the implication? Heaven will be a new place for all of us. Shall we be strangers there, or will our Lord Himself introduce us to His Father, and the angels, so that we shall at once be at home? Yes, if we have introduced Him to those we met here. "Meet my friend," says the young man as he meets another on the street, with a third person beside him. When you meet a friend of yours who is not acquainted with Jesus, do you say to him: "Meet my Friend?" We confess Christ by our lives, or we deny Him by them, quite as much, more perhaps, than by our words.

MRS. FRED BULLOCK.

English Church Agitated.—The leaders of the English Church are greatly agitated over the proposal of the Bishop of Winchester for the exchange of pulpits with ministers of other Churches. The proposition was not to exchange or unite with them in the regular religious services, but upon special occasions outside the regular appointed service of the church. Several convocations have been held, and the matter has been laid on the table indefinitely. Serious objection was made to asking the ministers of other denominations to pray in their consecrated buildings. Isn't t about time that our Episcopalian brethren would move away from the darkness of the Middle Ages?—*United Presbyterian.*

There are two kinds of dollars—one that is never worth more than a hundred cents, and one that grows in value. When you put your money in War Savings Stamps you change your hundred-cent dollars into the kind that grow.

SHALLOW WELL CHRISTIAN CHURCH

where the first session of the Sunday School and Christian Endeavor Convention of the North Carolina Conference is being held this week.

MARRIAGES

POLLARD-AMOS

In the parlor of the writer, on July 3, 1919, John I. Pollard, Greensboro, N. C., and Miss Iva Lee Amos, Altamahaw, N. C., were married in the presence of a few friends. Mrs. Pollard is a former student of Elon College. Immediately after the ceremony they left for Richmond, Va. May happiness and usefulness be theirs to enjoy all through the journey of life.

P. T. KLAPP.

EDWARDS-ALBRIGHT

Mr. Robert Edwards and Miss Laura Albright were married July 6, 1919 at 5.30 P. M. at the home of the bride, 110 Bradshaw Street, High Point, N. C. The groom has recently been discharged from service in the United States army where he has been in service for eleven years. Both persons are popular with their associates. They will reside in High Point. May theirs be a happy married life. The writer officiated.

L. L. WYRICK.

BRITTLE-PADGETT

Married at the Christian parsonage, Waverly, Va., in the presence of a large number of relatives and friends, July 3, 1919, 5 o'clock P. M., Mr. John Burgess Brittle to Miss Lucy Padgett. The attendants were Miss Minnie Goodrich with Mr. Alfred J. Brittle, Miss Rebecca Moss with Mr. Percy Carroll.

Mr. Brittle has just returned from the war in which he is credited with going over the top seven times. He goes back to the farm near Wakefield, Va. Miss Padgett is from near Waverly, Va. Thus two farm lives are united.

Ceremony by the writer who always appreciates, and doubly so when both bride and groom seem delighted to begin a new home on the farm. The many friends follow them with all good wishes.

JAS. L. FOSTER.

Saving is not a dull duty. It is a ticket to the land of prosperity. Buy W. S. S.

GLOVER-CHANDLER

At the residence of Mr. Thomas Chandler, Virgilina, Va., at 2 o'clock P. M., June 29, 1919, Mr. Henry Raymond Glover and Miss Emmie Chandler were united in marriage. The ring ceremony was read by the writer and interpreted in the sign language by Miss Robina Tillinghast, of Spartanburg, S. C.

Just before the ceremony Miss Lucy Gregory sang, "Somewhere a Voice is Calling." Mrs. Thomas Chandler played Mendelssohn's wedding march as the bride and groom entered the tastely decorated parlor of the Chandler home. Little Louise Elam, neice of the bride, acted as ring bearer.

The out-of-town guests were: Miss Elmer Glover of Washington, D. C., and Miss Lillian Glover of Columbia, S. C., sisters of the groom; Miss Cora Byrd of Morganton, N. C.; Miss Robina Tillinghast of Spartanburg, S. C., and Mr. Vernal Glover, brother of the groom, Greenville, S. C.

Immediately after the ceremony Mr. and Mrs. Glover with his sister, Miss Elmer Glover, left for Washington, D. C. They will be at home in Columbia, S. C. after July 7, where Mr. Glover holds a position as a printer.

The bride is the eldest daughter of Mrs. Rosa Chandler and a young lady of splendid attainments and a lovely disposition. Mr. Glover is fortunate indeed to win for a companion one so nearly ideal in her every manner.

The writer joins a host of friends wishing and bespeaking for them a useful and happy career.

C. E. NEWMAN.

DR. J. H. BROOKS

DENTIST

Foster Building   Burlington, N. C.

CHARLES W McPHERSON, M. D.

Eye, Ear, Nose, Throat

OFFICE OVER CITY DRUG STORE

Office Hours: 9:00 a. m. to 1:00 p. m. and 2:00 to 5:00 p. m.

Phones: Residence 153; Office 65J

BURLINGTON, NORTH CAROLINA

OBITUARIES

BEAMON

Sallie Caroline Edosia Costen was born in Gates County, North Carolina, March 24, 1833; Married William Beamon December 1856; was the mother of William W., Norfolk, Va.; Mrs. J. H. Seawell, Mrs. J. E. Smith, Sunbury, N. C., and James H., deceased; and died July 1, 1919. Her husband died in 1882 and she remained a widow thirty-seven years. Mrs. Smith and her husband resided in the old homestead where she passed away. She was a sister of the late George Costen.

Mrs. Beamon gave her heart to Jesus Christ in early girlhood, united with Damascus Christian church, and spent her life in useful, exemplary, influential service for seventy years. She was musical, spiritual, and full of good works. Her home was the center of social and religious influence and "her children rise up and call her blessed." She leaves eleven grandchildren and seven great grandchildren.

The funeral service was conducted at the family residence on July 2, Revs. W. B. Fuller, I. W. Johnson, and W. W. Staley taking part. "Asleep in Jesus as a Dream," "Abide With Me," by a quartette, were sung, and Dr. Johnson sang, "No Burdens Yonder," and the remains were laid to rest in the family graveyard. "I Need Thee Every Hour," was sung at the grave.

The old homestead, the great oaks in the yard, the old neighbors, the old colored people, the memories of childhood, the family re-unions, the silence of the parlor where mother lies in her casket, and speaks through mute lips to the very soul of all, is a message from God to mourning and grief-stricken loved ones. Seventy years of service in the home, the neighborhood, and the church, deserve rest, crowned with flowers and a good name.

W. W. STALEY.

HOLLOWAY

Richmond Washington Holloway was born May 30, 1893, and died at hospital No. 52 of pneumonia contracted in line of duty. He was buried at Grande Cunhere, Le Mans, Sorthe, France. His grave is numbered 66, in Lot 4, Section 20, plainly marked with a cross bearing military organization. Burial services were held by Chaplain Ross Miller. It was a regular military burial with escort of both French and American soldiers. The band played, "Nearer My God to Thee." The band may not have known it but that grand old hymn was appropriate for Brother Holloway was a good young man. He was a member of Waverly Christian church. The call to the ministry bore heavily upon his mind and heart before he left Waverly, Va., for the war. His wife died about three years ago, and since then his wife's father and mother, Brother and Sister R. T. Harris, with whom he lived for a number of years, have also died —4 deaths in one family! He leaves six brothers and sisters to mourn their loss. A splendid man, a Christian soldier has gone to his reward. Peace to his dust in beautiful France till the resurrection morning.

JAS. L. FOSTER.

DREWERY

Gilbert Augustus Drewery was born in Southampton County, Virginia, April 26, 1849, and died June 29, 1919. He spent his life in his native county and Sussex county, where he had resided a long time when death claimed him.

February 15, 1871 he married Miss Martha L. West. To this union three boys and three girls were born. His wife died quite a number of years ago. Miss Mattie E. Drewery died about six years ago. He is survived by the following children: Messrs. Emmett T., James A., and William H. Drewery and Mrs. Annie Sue Cooper, and Miss Fannie May Drewery. James A. and Fannie May still resided with their father. He has been in declining health for two years, but for the past five months he has gradually failed till the end came as the sun was lowering in the West so this story may come down to his grave at 6 p. m., fifth Sunday in June. He was a good neighbor, kind hearted and friendly; lived largely at home. The burial was at Spring Hill in the family plot. The beautiful flowers told the tale of love for the deceased Burial services by the pastor and writer.

JAS. L. FOSTER.

EVERHART

Mrs. Luola May Everhart was born May 14, 1898 and died July 4, 1919, aged twenty-one years, one month and twenty days. She was married to Mr. Percy Everhart may 18, 1918. She leaves to mourn their loss a beloved husband, one child, father, three brothers, five sisters and a host of friends. Her mother and

one brother preceded her to the Glory land. She was a loyal member of the High Point Christian church, where the funeral services were conducted by the pastor on July 6, 1919. A large concourse of friends assembled to pay their last tribute of respect. Interment was made in Pleasant Grove cemetery. May God bless and comfort the bereaved ones.

L. L. WYRICK.

WILLIAMS

Sister Martha Jane Williams passed to her spirit home June 22, 1919, aged eighty-two years, one month and twenty-six days. She had been a member of the Christian church at Damascus since early childhood. She was the mother of eight children, four of whom survive her. At the time of her death she was living with her daughter, Mrs. William Noe, Gibsonville, N. C. Her scripture motto was: "She looked well to the map of her household and eateth not the bread of idleness." — Prov. 31:27. Interment was in the cemetery at Shallow Ford church June 23. Service conducted by the writer.

P. T. KLAPP.

"Waste is worse than loss. The time is coming when every person who lays claim to ability will keep the question of waste before him constantly." (Thomas Edison.) Edison *buys* War Savings Stamps.

Eat Less, Live Longer.—The New York Life Insurance Company has issued a statement that the mortality of the company in Germany during the four years of the war was twelve per cent less than for the eleven years of peace immediately preceding. The company's chief actuary gives as the explanation that it is the result of restriction in eating and in the drinking of alcoholic beverages and the enforced exercise the insured were compelled to take. The actuary gives a prescription for prolonging life: "Restricted diet, total abstinence, and proper exercise." Good.— *Richmond Christian Advocate.*

Save first; then invest— For this, War Savings Stamps are best.

Give the graduate a good start in life with War Savings Stamps.

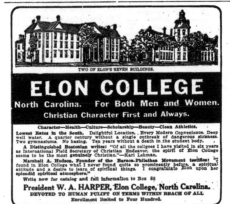

THE CHRISTIAN SUN

"IN ESSENTIALS UNITY, IN NON-ESSENTIALS LIBERTY, IN ALL THINGS CHARITY"

A Call From The Watchtower!

YOU do not appreciate the religious press. You are not using it to the extent you ought to. The result is the enemy are gaining ground on you, for they are sending their sheets broadcast. There is not a form of error in this age that hasn't its printing press, and putting thousands of dollars into it to send forth a propaganda if possible into every heart. Your children are reading it when you do not know it. You ministers have people reading this error when you are not aware of it, and you find them losing interest in your work and in the cause, and you do not know what did it. It is a false press that did it, and if you are to get the work out of the press that you would like, you must come to the support of the evangelical press, that comes to back you up and help to do a work you cannot do, and to spread the influence which you are intensifying and establishing.

—David S. Kennedy, D. D., in the Presbyterian, Philadelphia.

Volume LXXI   WEDNESDAY, JULY 23, 1919   Number 30

BURLINGTON   -   -   -   NORTH CAROLINA

THE CHRISTIAN SUN

Founded 1844 by Rev. Daniel W. Kerr

C. B. RIDDLE   - - -   Editor

Entered at the Burlington, N. C. Post Office as second class matter.

Subscription Rates

One year .... $ 2.00
Six months 1.00

In Advance

Give both your old and new postoffice when asking that your address be changed.

The change of your label is your receipt for money. Written receipts sent upon request.

Many persons subscribe for friends, intending that the paper be stopped at the end of the year. If instructions are given to this effect, they will receive attention at the proper time.

Marriage and obituary notices not exceeding 150 words printed free if received within 60 days from date of event, all over this at the rate of one-half cent a word.

Original poetry not accepted for publication.

Principles of the Christian Church

(1) The Lord Jesus Christ is the only Head of the Church.
(2) Christian is a sufficient name of the Church.
(3) The Holy Bible is a sufficient rule of faith and practice.
(4) Christian character is a sufficient test of fellowship, and of church membership.
(5) The right of private judgment and the liberty of conscience is a right and a privilege that should be accorded to, and exercised by all.

EDITORIAL

ODDS AND ENDS FROM THE EDITOR'S NOTE BOOK

This is the heading under which the Editor's contributions appeared in last week's issue. It is not our desire to make these notes too brief to be void of interest but trust that they may be helpful and contain some suggestion that will find root. We are of the opinion that suggestions are the greatest producers. Sign boards indicate the way and few get lost who travel in that direction.

"How do you like your work?", we are frequently asked. We have only one answer, and that is: "Just fine." Our work is exacting and never ending, going over practically the same things every day and a job that you must care for each day to avoid accumulation. It is like having a bear by the tail and going around a tree—if you turn loose you are caught. We are writing these notes on Tuesday night, July 15, for the issue of July 23. This week's issue was mailed this afternoon. This explains the bear theory—the printer will catch us in the morning if we are not ready for him.

Teachers and ministers are the guardians of the highest and holiest things in life and yet they receive less pay than the man who guards convicts at a prison camp. The average minister receives less pay for his work than the man who polices the streets of your city. Here is a good query: Resolved, That it is more business like to pay a higher salary to guard the moral interest of the community than it is to guard men after they have gone astray.

The *idea* of the newspaper has greatly changed in recent years; the *ideal* of the newspaper has also changed. Twenty-five or fifty years ago the newspaper that could furnish the strongest and ablest editorials was counted the strongest and ablest paper in the country. Papers sold largely for their editorial value. Such is not the case today. A newspaper sells because of its medium of news. The paper that can furnish the most reliable news, and the most of it, is the popular newspaper of today and soon gains prestige in the financial world. We deplore this modern tendency and find very little in the average country weekly except local news items of visiting, accidents, happenings, parties, etc. The community newspaper should be a builder of thought, of principle and should at all times champion the progressive interest of its community and state, regardless of its criticism.

President Wilson's estimate of the church is found in the following quotation uttered by him the other day: "To my thinking, the Christian church stands not only at the center of philanthropy but at the center of science, at the center of philosophy, at the center of politics—in short, at the center of sentiment and thinking life; and the business of the Christian church, and the Christian minister is to show the spiritual relation of men to the great world processes, whether they be physical or spiritual. It is nothing less than to show the plan of life. I wonder if any of you realize how hungry men's minds are for a complete satisfactory explanation of life."

When we attend Conferences and Conventions it is a very easy matter to make a resolution and fail to carry out that resolution. We don't make the failure because we mean to but because we get absorbed in many other things and neglect it. The Sunday School and Christian Endeavor Convention of the North Carolina Conference, which closed last week, went on record for many good things, and no doubt there will be an honest effort

Read The Front Page

made to carry out the resolutions and suggestions of that body. Next Sunday will be a good time to begin to carry out these things, if you did not make the start last Sunday. We need better Sunday schools, bigger Sunday schools and brighter Sunday schools. The only way to achieve these three points is to work for them and we express the confidence of the schools of the North Carolina Conference that the Convention ideas be put into practical experience.

In THE CHRISTIAN SUN for July 16 we gave the information that Rev. J. E. Franks had secured 53 new subscribers to THE CHRISTIAN SUN since the first of July, 16 of which he had sent during the last few days. The ink was scarcely dry on THE SUN when another letter from Brother Franks arrived with 13 new subscribers (let 13 be lucky or unlucky, we consider it lucky) and one renewal and a check enclosed for $28.00. Brother Franks made no comment except writing at the bottom of the list, "More to follow." Had he thought of the matter a whole day no message from his pen could have been more interesting or cheerful than the three words, "more to follow." Think of it, more to follow. How many others have more to follow?

Here is a fine estimate of the religious journal which is given out by the advertising clubs of the world: "It has the highest political ideals; it is foremost in promoting good citizenship, education; first, in establishing and supporting philanthropy. Equally true is it that the most worth-while portion of the religious element anywhere is that which subscribes to the religious press."

There is a general criticism that the Church is a poorly organized piece of machinery. We have noticed that those who say this are those who know the least about the Church as an organization. They speak from observation and re-say what some other misinformed and prejudiced persons have said. The Church has always been ready and willing to prove her ability as an organization, though she has never been called upon for just that thing. Every agency for doing good is today depending upon the Church as an organization. And the Church press, why bless your life, dear reader, if you could spend one day in some Church paper office you would be amazed at the requests from every conceivable agency asking for public support in some way. The most useful thing about our desk is the waste basket. We are compelled to use it, not because these calls are unworthy, but because we do not have the space for them.

Upon a hill that overlooks the Holy City, the Mount of Olives, the mountains of Moab, and the hills back of Bethlehem, is the home for children orphaned by the war. The Mount Zion Home was founded several months ago by the American Red Cross Commission for Palestine, but has since been entrusted to the Juniors to maintain. They have adopted the home fully equipped with orphans. The running expenses are to be provided for by the school children of America out of the million 'dollar fund which they have pledged to carry on their works of relief this year for children throughout the world. Their little proteges have seen months, even years of hardship, cruelty and fear. But their future will be one of rosy promises, as the dream of their proud American sponsors, the Juniors, gradu-

ally unfolds. First, there is the home where they have care and love and laughter that they may become physically normal girls and boys again; secondly, a school and a church where they may study to become powers for good in the world.

Everywhere we hear the cry that the young people are not interested in the Church and its workings. Why? Many of our churches have Children's Day once a year, (some not even this) beyond this there is nothing except the regular Sunday school and preaching services. Is this fair to the children who demand some new activity almost every hour, three hundred and sixty-five days in the year? From some country churches we hear there will be no Children's Day for lack of time to train the children. When children are put off a few times like that, will there be a progressive church in that place twenty years hence? There are other churches in which all the programs, plans, etc., for special occasions are prepared by the older members, even the choir is composed practically of such members. These are conditions that progressive pastors and superintendents should not allow to exist. All should take part, and the young people especially should be given a part.

The attitude of church organizations toward the movement for thrift and savings is well exemplified in a resolution adopted by the Christian Endeavor Union of California, in convention at Long Beach, Calif. recently. The Christian Endeavor organization endorsed the encouragement of thrift as a public policy, and authorized its Citizenship Department to co-operate with the California savings officials to make the 1919 thrift movement a success. The resolution adopted by the convention reads: "Be it recommended by the California Christian Endeavor Union that it fully endorse and urge that, as essential to character formation, to the welfare of the American people, and to the promotion of a national habit, the practice of the national program of thrift instruction, the organization of Savings Societies and the sale of thrift stamps and Savings Stamps become a part of public procedure; and that the Citizenship department of the California Christian Endeavor Union be named to co-operate with each state division of the War Savings Organization for California toward making the government plan of 1919 a success"

The Baptist denomination has set out to raise seventy-five million dollars. Startling! Can they do it? Of course they can—and will. This is a day of big things. We are rising upon our dear selves to things that are higher. The shame upon the Church is that it has not done more in days gone by. We mean all denominations. As an organization the Church has not taught its members to give. We are only in the beginning state of giving. Better days ahead. We are realizing that our business is the Lord's business and what we have is His, and that we are only trustees for it. Of course our Baptist brethren will raise the $75,000,000, and here is every good wish for them.

NEW COMERS TO THE SUN FAMILY
(New Subscribers Added Since July 1, 1919)

L. M. Truelove ....Holly Spring, N. C.
W. G. Woodell ....New Hill, N. C.
J. W. Womble ....New Hill, N. C.
Sarah F. Carpenter ....New Hill, N. C.
Mrs. L. C. Upchurch ....Apex, N. C.
Jacob Golladay ....Timberville, Va.
E. J. Norfleet ....Holland, Va.
T. C. Pounds ....Clayton, N. C.
Mildred Stephenson ....Clayton, N. C.
M. B. Mooneyham ....Clayton, N. C.
W. O. Bundy ....Clayton, N. C.
K. B. Jones ....Clayton, N. C.
J. Q. Stephenson ....Clayton, N. C.
J. B. Harrison ....Clayton, N. C.
J. O. Stuart ....Clayton, N. C.
W. D. Eatman ....Clayton, N. C.
C. P. Hill ....Clayton, N. C.
W. C. Carroll ....Garner, N. C.
R. T. Slaughter ....Berea, N. C.
Mrs. A. A. Riddle ....Burlington, N. C.
R. A. Truitt ....Elon College, N. C.
Mrs. W. N. Huff ....Gibsonville, N. C.
Mrs. R. T. Holland ....New Hill, N. C.
J. Arthur Middleton ....Stokesdale, N. C.
Mrs. J. J. White ....Stokesdale, N. C.
Maude Middleton ....Stokesdale, N. C.
F. Collins ....Stokesdale, N. C.
John Matthews ....Raleigh, N. C.
A. L. Horton ....Raleigh, N. C.
E. R. Cotten ....New Hill, N. C.
L. M. Holt ....New Hill, N. C.
G. L. Stone ....New Hill, N. C.
Sallie Carpenter ....New Hill, N. C.
W. H. Sloan ....New Hill, N. C.
R. A. Ansley ....New Hill, N. C.
B. M. Dickens ....Merry Oaks, N. C.
Mrs. A. G. Ellis ....Merry Oaks, N. C.
R. M. Cotten ....Merry Oaks, N. C.
W. H. Woodell ....Merry Oaks, N. C.
O. C. Cotten ....Merry Oaks, N. C.
A. M. Pollard ....Corinth, N. C.
R. H. Yarbrough.............................Corinth, N. C.
Mrs. J. L. Hall ....News Ferry, Va.
Clinton V. Williams ....Quicksburg, Va.
Mrs. Cobel Murry ....Virgilina, Va.
C. C. Brown ....Asheboro, N. C.
L. R. Townsend ....Riverdale, Md.

(Record to July 18)

TO THE PUBLIC

While the horror of the latest bomb outrage is still fresh in the minds of Americans, we would call attention to the menace of the growth of the spirit of violence, bitterness and unreason among our people. We sincerely trust that the criminals responsible for these outrages will be discovered and punished by due process of law. Terrorism must be given no room in our land. But to eliminate this menace it is not enough merely to join in the hue and cry against anarchy and Bolshevism; we must also study the economic and mental factors which make the background for this half-insane type of terrorism. A common resolve to abide by our time-honored principles of free discussion and the reg-

ular processes of constitutional government is the need of the hour.

Unhappily violence, recently employed in the name of patriotism has been allowed to go unpunished by the authorities, and has even been praised by leaders in government and in the press. In New York on May Day peaceful meetings were attacked, The Call building was raided, and innocent men and women suffered serious injuries. Many voices openly praised such treatment of "the Reds." But condonations of violence lead to contempt of law and strengthen those who counsel revolution.

To meet the situation we urge:

1. That all men and women of good will set themselves to influence public opinion through every available medium against lawless measures by whomsoever they may be employed.

2. That they resolve to see that fair hearings and just trials are given to men, irrespective of their political or economic opinions, so that it may be said that in America no man's case, be he an I. W. W. or a Bolshevist or the most reactionary conservative, is prejudged by an appeal to popular feeling; and in particular that they set themselves against the counsels of hate, whose effect upon the rising generation can be only to pile up future disaster for mankind.

3. Since, in the judgment of the Attorney General of the United States, existing laws against criminal terrorism are adequate, and since free discussion is essential for the exposure of economic and political errors, that the attempt be abandoned to coerce minority opinion so long as it does not promote disorder, or to defeat social change by repressive legislation.

As ministers of the Christian Church and as citizens of this liberty-honoring Republic we plead for faith in reason, good-will and fairness to oppose the forces of bitterness and violence in our national life.

(Signed):

REV. GEORGE ALEXANDER,
    First Presbyterian Church, N. Y.

REV. CHARLES R. BROWN,
    Dean of the School of Religion, Yale University.

REV. HENRY E. COBB,
    West End Collegiate Reform Church, N. Y.

REV. HENRY SLOANE COFFIN,
    Madison Ave., Presbyterian Church, N. Y., Assistant Prof. Union Theological Seminary.

REV. HARRY E. FOSDICK,
    Minister in First Presbyterian Church, Prof. Union Theological Seminary N. Y.

REV. WILLIAM P. MERRILL,
    Brick Presbyterian Church, N. Y.

REV. HOWARD C. ROBBINS,
    Dean of Cathedral of St. John the Divine, N. Y.

REV. WILLIAM AUSTIN SMITH,
    Editor of Churchman.

REV. RALPH W. SOCKMAN,
    Mad. Ave. Meth. Episcopal Church, N. Y.

REV. FRANK MASON NORTH,
    Secy. Bd. of Foreign Missions of the Methodist Episcopal Church, President Federal Council of the Church of Christ in America.

PASTOR AND PEOPLE

NOTICE

To the Church in the South:

Those interested in the building of a church in Richmond, Va., to be known as the Haggard Memorial in honor of one of the pioneers of our Church and denomination will please write to H. J. Fleming, 2314 Roanoke Avenue, Newport News, Va. There are about two hundred members of our Church in the city and they are desirous that the Church at large place in the capital city of the Old Dominion a church named as above. The Rev. Rice Haggard who suggested the name *Christian* for the denomination once held a pastorate in Richmond and it is no more than right that as a church in the South and the United States see that the movement initiated by the members of our church to secure a building in the city of Richmond, be supported by our financial and moral influence as well. I hope that a great number may become interested in the matter and that before long we shall have the necessary means to push this movement to a glorious culmination. With best wishes for the work.

H. J. FLEMING.

SOME INTERESTING HISTORY

The Eastern Virginia Sunday School Convention embracing the Sunday schools of the Christian Church in this section will meet with the Oakland Christian church on July 23 and 24. This church is nine miles from Suffolk and about one mile from the village of Chuckatuck, Va., and is in one of the most historic spots of Nansemond County. In the same vicinity the powerful tribe of Nansemond Indians had their headquarters when Captain John Smith sailed up the Nansemond on his first exploring expedition, and found that Indian corn was raised by those Indians in abundance, so that when starvation was facing the Jamestown colonies it was to this place that he repaired and procured food to relieve the situation. In the neck below is thought to have been the first land or farm granted to an individual, and from him it took its name Barrett's Neck. Near here the first settlement in the county was started by John Martin and his associates in 1609.

By 1672 this section had become thickly settled by colonists, and Rev. George Fox of the Friends Church visited Chuckatuck and a Friends church was founded, and was in existence for a great many years. Their record of their meetings is now the oldest records of the county, and is of great interest to the historian.

St. John's P. E. church near here is one of the oldest colonial churches in this section, having a history that goes back beyond 1702. On the establishment of this church the Quakers began to leave the community and a good number settled in the Eastern part of North Carolina, especially in Perquimans County, where the denomination still has churches.

From tradition and contempory records the County court house was located near here in the early days, and the first mail route in this section passed here.

The first stage route from Norfolk to Richmond, as well as the first telegram line also passed this section. News of the Battle of Lexington passed here on its way South either the last of April or the first of May 1775. General Tarleton's British troops were defeated near here by the American Militia in the closing years of the Revolution, and Lord Cornwallis marched his army through here on his way to Portsmouth, before going to Yorktown in 1781.

The Methodist missionaries began work here about 1774, and the Baptists near here in 1779 or 1780. Revs. Mintz and Barrow, the first Baptist ministers to visit the section, were dipped in the river until they were nearly drowned at Sleepy Hole, yet they soon established churches on both sides of the river. The Masonic Lodge here dates back to 1797.

The Christian Church had an organization near here known as Wills Chapel early in the last century, it taking its name from the Hon. John Scarborough Wills who had been an officer in the American army in the Revolution, and who also represented Isle of Wight County in the General Assembly of Virginia for a great many years. This church had as many as 130 members at one time, but it gradually declined being represented the last time in the Eastern Virginia Christian Conference at the session of 1840 by Stephen Smith. From that time until 1872 there was no regular organization of the Christians in the community. At that time Oakland was organized, and has grown until it now reports 272 members, to the annual Conference.

The surrounding country is progressive, some views not being surpassed by any in this section of the State. The community is progressive and up-to-date, and everything bids fair for this to be one of the best Conventions ever held.

Suffolk, Va.   W. E. MacCLENNY.

NOTICE

The Virginia Valley Central Christian Conference will meet with the New Hope Christian church, August 14-17, 1919. Those who expect to attend as delegates or visitors should write N. M. Hasler, Harrisonburg, Va., and state when they will arrive and how they will travel. Those going on the train will be met at Harrisonburg.

Following a good year's work by the churches, this promises to be the best and most largely attended conference ever held in the Valley. The following brethren are expected to attend and take part in the proceedings: Rev. W. W. Staley, President of the Southern Christian Convention; Rev. J. O. Atkinson, Mission Secretary of the Southern Christian Convention; Dr. W. A. Harper, President of Elon College; Rev. L. F. Johnson, Mission Pastor, Brooklyn, N. Y.; Mr. C. D. Johnston, Superintendent Christian Orphanage; Mr. W. R. Daniels, President Rays Hill and Southern Pennsylvania Christian Conference, and probably one speaker from headquarters at Dayton, Ohio.

All churches are requested to send complete reports and full delegations.

W. T. WALTERS, *President.*

A. W. ANDES, *Secretary.*

FROM BROTHER FOGLEMAN'S FIELD
Union Grove

Union Grove sustained a great loss early this year in the death of two of her deacons. Brothers C. A. Byrd and C. C. Brown were elected to fill the vacancy and were ordained by Rev. L. I. Cox.

The Sunday school, under the leadership of C. A. Byrd, is making an effort to increase attendance and improve the singing. We have a growing Sunday school already as a result of the efforts. July 6 was Children's Day here. We are expecting Rev. J. F. Apple to assist in our meeting the third week in August.

Antioch

Services at this place were conducted by Revs. H. A. Albright and W. N. Hayes twice this year. At my last appointment here the township Sunday school Convention was held in the afternoon.

We do not have a very large membership at this church but we usually have a large number of earnest hearers. Rev. J. F. Apple is to help in our meeting the fourth week in September.

Spoon's Chapel

The congregation at this place is usually small; but a few earnest people are always faithful. We are planning to hold our revival meeting here the fourth week in August.

We find it very agreeable to be near all of our churches and to be able to mingle with our people. Our trying to farm has robbed us of needed time in which to visit our members.

L. W. FOGLEMAN.

Seagrove, N. C.

DISTRICT OF COLUMBIA

The notice of Brother I. W. Hitchcock recently published in THE SUN concerning the organization of a Christian church in this, the Nation's capitol city, and requesting the Brotherhood to send him names and addresses of any of our people residing here, resulted in the first meeting for prayer and worship being held last Sunday, July 13, at the home of Brother and Sister T. J. Lawrence, 114 Carroll Ave., Takoma Park.

Brother Hitchcock led the meeting and Miss Louise Lawrence read the scripture lesson. Gospel songs were sung and earnest, fervent prayers offered to Almighty God for the success of the enterprise. The spirit of the meeting was excellent and we were indeed grateful for the privilege of being one of the number in attendance.

Definite plans were outlined looking toward the erection of a temporary building for public worship in a splendid, rapidly growing, section of the city in the near future. However, we need the names and addresses of a larger number of our people that we may get in touch with them and hope every reader of this item will appreciate the great assistance they might render at this time by furnishing this information. Simply drop Brother Hitchcock a card addressed to 801 Allison Street, Washington, D. C., giving name and street address of any persons whom you know were formerly members of our church.

Riverdale, Md.   L. R. TOWNSEND.

SUFFOLK LETTER

Reconstruction is a familiar word in the Southern states, and it is a work that is going on all the time in the world. At the close of the Civil War Congress passed two acts by which the Confederate states might be restored to the rights inherent in the Union. Each state must frame a new Constitution; this Constitution must be ratified by popular vote and approved by Congress; the new State legislature must ratify the fourteenth amendment; when the requisite number ratified this amendment, any state which had fulfilled *all* requirements should be re-admitted to the Union and entitled to Congressional representation. By 1870 all the Southern states had been re-admitted to the Union; but not till 1871 were all of them represented in Congress. It thus appears that it took five years from 1865 to 1870 to complete this work of reconstruction; and one more year to get full representation in Congress. Jefferson Davis was arrested near Irwinsville, Ga., May 10, 1865, and imprisoned in Fortress Monroe, Va., 1865-67, and was pardoned in 1868. Those were times that tried the souls of men; but out of it all came a *new South*—a better and a richer South.

The Kaiser's crime is greater than that of Jefferson Davis. Davis was contending for the rights of States; the Kaiser invaded such rights. We are in the midst of reconstruction for the *world*. Blunders will be made, injuries will be inflicted, rights will be invaded, and individuals will suffer injustly; but out of it will come a better and more brotherly world. War always multiplies wrongs, blunts consciences, degrades virtue, increases greed, convulses society, generates lawlessness, and leaves religion in a state of chaos. The state and the church must perform the task of integration and this requires time and patience.

The fact is plain that the work of reconstruction is an unfinished task. The work of road-building, of city building, of machinery, of farming, is one endless chain of reconstruction. The salvation of men is a work of reconstruction. "Therefore if any man be in Christ, he is a new creature; old things are passed away; behold, all things are become new." John wrote: "I saw a new heaven and a new earth"; and He that sat upon the throne said: "Behold, I make all things new." The whole process of salvation is a process of reconstruction, of making man over, changing him from a rebel to a son. And this great work is often accomplished through suffering. "Before I was afflicted I went astray; but now have I kept thy word." In the language of the poet:

"Afflictions, though they seem severe,
Are oft in mercy sent;
They stopp'd the prodigal's career,
And caus'd him to repent."

The world was saved by the sufferings of Jesus and "He shall see of the travail of His soul and shall be satisfied." Even pain is a friend, for, without pain, we would not take medicine, consult a doctor, or destroy evil. World-travail may mean world-release from world-wrongs. Of course there will be crimination and re-crimination, oppressions and social evils, but out of the tragedy of war and sin will emerge a new world and a new spirit that will set mankind forward in all the departments and interests of the race.

W. W. STALEY.

CHRISTIAN EDUCATION

AND STILL THE VOLUNTEERS CONTINUE

Last week I felt sure I could in this letter announce the final result of our Standardization Drive, but I cannot. I did not know our people's deep and abiding concern for the College. I shall, I trust, be able next week to announce what will be the sum raised.

When I tell our beloved friends that two brethren this week volunteered to give $1,000 each and that another wrote he had been earnestly considering it, but could send only $250, I believe they will patiently wait till one or two others who are considering prayerfully have been spiritually lead to do or not to do their part.

The first fund this week came from Brother Alva C. Richards, Winchester, Va., one of the promising young business men of the Valley Conference. Three weeks ago I announced that Brother Boyd Richards was the first man in that Conference to give $1,000 to any of our Church enterprises. I prophetically said he would not be the last. I did not know who the next man would be, but I am so happy it is his younger brother. Is it not fine for two brothers thus to honor God with their substance? Brother Alva says he hopes later to do more. He will do it all right.

The second fund came from far away Florida. Many years ago one of the leading laymen of Holy Neck church went to the far South. That man was C. A. Howell. He is true to the Church yet and always will be. One of Elon's most talented alumni is his son, C. C. Howell, a leading lawyer of Florida, with offices in Jacksonville. Brother Howell is one of the Kingdom's noble men.

The two hundred and fifty dollar gift came from J. Pettaway Johnson, recently moved to Newport News. Va., from New York City. He is the son of the sainted. J. W. Johnson of Johnson's Grove church. His letter expressing his love for the Christian Church is worth more than his generous gift.

First Convention

Last week I attended the first session of the Sunday School and Christian Endeavor Convention of the North Carolina Christian Conference. It met with the Shallow Well church and was gloriously entertained. I have attended many such Conventions, but none excell this. Forty-four schools were represented and twenty preachers were there. Brother C. H. Stephenson presided and would have been re-elected president, had he not said he preferred some one else be chosen. He was made General Secretary and Hon. S. T. A. Kent elected as President. The Convention next year meets at Elon College. I have but one regret over the Convention. The great speech I had prepared is still in my system. There was no time for it. The people are to be congratulated however.

Twenty-One Years Ago

My heart yearns to go to the Eastern Virginia Convention this week. I may go yet. Twenty-one years ago I attended my first gathering of the Christian church in a representative capacity. It was the Eastern Virginia Convention and it met at Oakland church, where it meets this week. How I yearn in heart to be there! God has been good to me these twenty-one years and so have the brethren. I have no language in which to express my appreciation. I am grateful, but I have not deserved it.

W. A. HARPER.

NOTES

Dr. J. P. Barrett's address to August 10 will be 1315 First Avenue, Columbus, Ga.

Prof. Arnold Hall has been elected Welfare Supervisor for Scotland County. Scotland is wise.

The Virginia Valley Conference meets August 14. The meeting place is New Hope church.

Brother J. W. Winfree, Virgilina, Va., has helped us to increase THE SUN's circulation during the last few days. Many thanks.

We are glad to learn that Mrs. J. O. Atkinson, who has been taking treatment in a Suffolk, Virginia, hospital, is improving.

Brother W. C. Hook and wife, Mt. Jackson, Va., we understand, are to return to Elon this fall to pursue their studies. It will be Brother Hook's senior year,

We trust that readers of THE SUN will turn to the notice written by Rev. H. J. Fleming. It seems to us that the undertaking is timely and worthy of consideration.

Wymer W. Manning, son of Dr. J. W. Manning, Norfolk, Va., passed the State Board of Dentistry some days ago and will enter the profession of his father. Young Manning graduated at the Medical College of Virginia, June 16, 1919. Success to his career.

N. C. Riddle, son of Mr. W. H. Riddle, of Shallow Well church, graduated some weeks ago from the Jefferson Medical College of Philadelphia, and last week passed the State Board, ranking second in the class. Young Riddle is a cousin to the Editor.

Mrs. J. B. Vaughan—The SUN has been coming to my home for thirty-six years, so here is another lifetime member.

R. H. Barrett, Sr.—I love THE SUN and want it to come to my home as long as it is as good as it is now.

MISSIONARY

THE SUPPORT OF ANOTHER MISSIONARY

It was the writer's privilege to attend, last Sunday afternoon, the quarterly meeting of the Tidewater Christian Sunday School Association. The Association is composed of the Sunday schools of our Christian churches in and about Norfolk and the meeting last Sunday was in our Portsmouth church. The several schools were well represented both by the pastors of the churches, superintendents, officers and delegates. Rev. G. O. Lankford is president of the Association. The body is intensely interested in the work of the Kingdom, and besides doing much to promote the interests of its several schools, is thoroughly missionary in spirit and vision. It was voted unanimously last Sunday to support a missionary on the foreign field, each school agreeing to do its part, after excepting Third Church and Memorial Temple because these two schools with their churches have their pastors each on the foreign field. With such a vision as this, and such a task before it, the Association has promise of great things and its influence for good will be mighty in the future.

THE IMPERATIVE NEED OF WORKERS

The salvation of Christian America, and of other Christian countries, depends not upon their material resources or financial prosperity, but solely upon what these Christian lands shall do to help save the non-Christian peoples of the world. Our Heavenly Father gives superior advantages, wealth, blessings, benefits not because He loves some lands better than other lands, or would be better to some people than He would to others. Nay verily. Our God is no respector of persons, peoples or nationalities. If He seems for a reason to favor any people above their unfortunate brothers, it is only that the more favored may be of service to the less favored. Our country with all its wondrous wealth today is being weighed in the balances to see whether it is itself worthy of being saved. And it is to prove its worthiness in no other manner than by what it gives of its own life and resources for the saving of others. The very salvation of America hangs in the balances today. Will it save itself by losing itself that others may be saved? That alone is the Biblical and the Christian standard of measurement.

After a hundred years of modern missions we have not yet sent to China, India, Africa, Japan, and the other non-Christian lands as many missionaries as would be needed to evangelize and redeem a great city like New York. We Americans are spending more money on Coca-Cola and "soft drinks" than we are to reach the non-Christian lands for Christ. Nothing weighs the character of a people or indicates the love of a people as does the manner in which it spends its money.

If Christian America would in the next ten years spend as much to send the Gospel to those who have it

not as it spends for cigarettes, the whole world within that time would hear and know of Christ. As a student of missions I want to assert that the greatest need of our Church today is workers—I mean by that volunteers to go as missionaries to the foreign field.

The Church Missionary Society of England has made it a rule since 1887 never to refuse a properly qualified

Read The Front Page

missionary candidate. "*They have never failed to find the money after they have found the man.* After what we have seen the past two years will we ever again doubt our ability to get money when young life is involved? Let us find the workers for this great cause and the money will surely come."

I was quoting these the words of a great writer, but the sentiment is thoroughly my own. If twenty men and women were to offer for the foreign field here in our Southern Christian churches within the next six months, the writer believes with all his heart that the money would be immediately forthcoming to support them and to supply their equipment on the field. Brethren and beloved, where are the men and women who will go for us?

J. O. ATKINSON.

HELP TRAIN THE BOY FOR MISSIONS
By Mrs. J. W. Patton

Everything that we learn of young people shows us that they are very near to God. They easily believe in Him and recognize His rightful rule over them.

The energy of youth will spend itself in some direction. Why not direct it toward the greatest of all good works, that of bringing the whole world to Christ? Many of the greatest missionaries of all time, and many of the most liberal givers to missions, received their most potent and lasting impressions in youth.

Our boys must be reached for the missionary cause. They are organized into various other clubs, why not the Missionary Club? It can be called by any name you may choose—Christian Knights or Missionary Scouts.

There is a need for leaders in this work. Men and women must be asked to devote a serious part of life's unpaid effort to this phase of the mission cause. If any are hesitant about their call thereto, let them remember the words of the Master, "Lift up your eyes and look on the fields."

The Church must speak with the power of a great conviction, with the message of a mighty mission. If the boys are trained for missions we will have a Church trained for missions. The need is great. May we have the power to meet that need.

FROM OVER THE SEAS

A LETTER FROM MISS WILLIAMS

This is a rainy Sunday afternoon, and rain in the tropics means that one stays in doors, for in a very few moments so much rain will fall that the streets resemble rivers, but in equally as short a time the water will all run into the sea, the sun comes out brightly and the next day there will be little, if any, mud. So this being an afternoon-free from interruptions I have been enjoying the luxury of visiting again, through THE CHRISTIAN SUN, my friends in Virginia and North Carolina. How often as I read THE SUN do I recall the many friends I met at the Southern Christian Convention which met at Franklin, in April of last year, and of the delightful visits I had with the churches in Norfolk, and vicinity, of the evening spent at Suffolk, and later in the day there attending a Sunday-school Convention, of my Sunday in Holland, Va., and then of the many friends I made at the Seaside Chautauqua, and my trip from there to Pleasant Grove, Greensboro, Elon College, Graham, and Burlington. Each of these places has a corner in my heart as I eagerly scan the pages of THE SUN for news from them, and more than once I have longed to write a personal letter of sympathy when I read of the sorrow that has come to some, and of congratulation over the joy of others. To me THE SUN has been like a nice newsy letter from these kind friends, who did so much to make my furlough a happy visit to the States and I thank the Editor for his invitation to tell you something of our work in Porto Rico.

First, we have a very especial interest just now in Elon College, because one of our own boys, Victor Rivera has gone there. Oh, if you could have read that young man's letter back to Mrs. Barrett, describing a picnic he had attended, his first picnic in the States, and the enthusiastic manner in which he writes of everything, you would feel more than repaid for your kindness.

Slowly the buildings damaged by the earthquake last October are being repaired. Slowly, because so much material has to be brought by boat; that work cannot proceed rapidly here as in the home land. The repairs upon the church at Salinas have been completed, the interior of the church freshly decorated, electric lights installed and the wood work of the outside painted, so that church presents the neatest appearance of any of our buildings in Christian missions. Last week special services were held in Salinas. Monday evening Mr. Barrett took all of the workers over in the automobile, Mrs. Barrett, Dona Delfina, Pedro Romana, the pastor at Artiz; Mr. Martinez, pastor at Santa Isabel, and myself, and after an hour spent in prayer in the church

we went to the home of the native pastor, Rev. San Doval, where his wife had an excellent supper prepared. They are living in the same house that was the home of Rev. T. E. White, and as we sat at the table with the view of the mountains facing us, and the fresh breeze from the sea blowing into the room we felt sure that the thoughts of Mr. White often turned to Porto Rico and that there was a place in his affections for Salinas.

After supper Mrs. Barrett proposed that we all walk around the old corner where the first Christian services had been held and then going on a square further down the street Mr. Barrett stopped and gave out a hymn. The little band of workers formed a circle, a larger circle of people gathered, attracted by the music, and another hymn was sung, a prayer offered and a cordial invitation given to all to attend the services at the church, and a third hymn was sung. I stood facing the setting sun, and I never witnessed a more glorious sunset any where than that one. The purple mountains, the dark green leaves of the palms and the golden glow of the sky, made a picture never to be forgotten, while all around stood the children attracted by the music. We passed on to the hotel and stopping in the street there, another hymn was given out and soon we had a large audience, this time of men, and older boys, and we stayed even after it was too dark to read the words of the hymns, singing songs that might draw some to Jesus until the sound of our church bell called us to service. *Our church bell!* Oh, how sweet it fell upon the evening air, and only those of us who had witnessed conditions here transformed by the power of the Gospel could realize just what the sound of the church-bell means.

Dona Delfina spent the week in Salinas. The second evening Mr. and Mrs. Barrett took over a number of the young men of our Ponce church to assist in the service. One of them Juan Rodriguez, has just recently returned from six months stay in Santo Domingo in government service, and so Tuesday evening was a missionary evening, telling of the need of the Gospel in Santo Domingo.

On other evenings Mr. Barrett went over taking with him different workers of our Ponce church, and the week was not without its results as there were a number of professions of faith.

Returning to Ponce, we passed through Santa Isabel where our new church is so badly needed. The children in the states have already given about $2,000 but fully $3,000 must be in the hands of the Mission Board for the building of that church. I spoke so often in the States of the need of a church at Santa Isabel that I am going to make just one more plea to the children through THE SUN for blocks for this church. Your pastors and Sunday school teachers know all about the block plan and can explain it to you.

Work is to begin tomorrow upon the repairs of our church here in Ponce. The towers fell at the time of the earthquake, and when this work is completed we hope the contractor can start on the church at Santa Isabel.   OLIVE G. WILLIAMS.

Ponce, Porto Rico, July 6, 1919.

SEASIDE CHAUTAUQUA—SCHOOL OF METHODS
VIRGINIA BEACH, NORFOLK, VA., JULY 29-AUGUST 5
A Glimpse of the Good Things

Mr. W. C. Pearce, Chicago, Ill., International Sunday School Association Field Secretary, wll speak four times: 1. Two messages on young people on Christian Leadership. 2. Chautauqua lectures: (a) Religious Education and Democracy; (b) Religious Education and Reconstruction.

Dr. Geo. C. Enders, Defiance, Ohio: 1. A message each day on the Bible. It will be a rich hour of spiritual uplift and Vision.

Mrs. Isaac Sewell, Nashville, Tenn., will give the Elementary lesson each day. Mrs. Sewell comes highly recommended by Miss Lewis who has conducted this department two years. also by Dr. Beauchamp, formerly of Portsmouth, Va. She is the Elementary specialist of the Southern Methodist church.

Mr. Hermon Eldredge, Camp Upton, N. Y., will give three messages on Christian Leadership: 1. The Builder; 2. The Call to Service; 3. An Open Door. Also he will give a discussion on "The Merger Service of the Sunday School and Morning Church Service." He will give an address on "Lessons Learned at the Camp," conduct the Sunday school part of the Sunday morning service, and speak once on the Forward Movement.

Dr. I. E. Smith, Norfolk, Va., will be the Chautauqua preacher and will speak on the following great themes: 1. Man and His God; 2. Man and His Man; 3. Man and His Money; 4. Man and His Master; 5. Man and His Mission; 6. Man and His Destiny.

Dr. Roy C. Helfenstein, Urbana, Ill., will preach the Sunday morning sermon at the Merger service. He will also speak on the Forward Movement, and deliver one of the Chautauqua lectures on "The Quest of an Ideal." He will

---

Read The Front Page

---

discuss two of the Church's great problems: 1. The Church for the New Time; 2. The Sunday Evening Service.

Rev. Wilson P. Minton, Defiance, Ohio, will conduct the singing during the Chautauqua and speak at one of the Vesper services.

Rev. J. Vincent Knight, Greensboro, N. C., will conduct three Christian Endeavor periods: 1. Christian Endeavor's New Day; 2. Christian Endeavor and the Forward Movement; 3. Our Christian Endeavor Task.

Rev. H. G. Rowe, Merom, Indiana, will conduct a daily class on Sunday School Organization. His themes are: 1. Sunday School Publicity; 2. Discovering and Training Sunday School Leaders; 3. Workers' Meetings; 4. The Sunday School in Session; 5. Building and Adult Class from 5 to 100.

Rev. R. F. Brown, Durham, N. C., will discuss Christian Endeavor principles in two session as follows: 1. The Ultimate Objectives of Christian Endeavor Principles; 2. The Remaking Power of Christian Endeavor Principles.

Rev. E. K. McCord, D. D., Missionary to Japan, home on furlough will conduct the daily mission class. His themes for discussion are: 1. The Missionary Task; 2. The Missionary Church; 3. The Missionary Process; 4. Heathenism's Response; 5. Our Own Missions.

Rev. G. Herbert Ekins, Norfolk, Va., City Church Federation Secretary, will discuss the problem of the Community

Church; and will also give one of the Chautauqua lectures on "The New Emergence of Woman as Seen by a Mere Man."

Rev. Peter Ainslie, D. D., Baltimore, Md., will give one of the Chautauqua lectures on: "Is Christian Union Desirable?" He is one of the greatest leaders in America on that vital theme.

Rev. J. P. Burnett, D. D., Dayton, Ohio, will preach the Sunday night sermon.

Rev. Wm. Mason Jay, Holland, Va., will discuss the important theme of "Christian Stewardship," one of the great Church problems. The daily discussion of a very practical "Church Problem" will be one of the most helpful themes of the Chautauqua.

Vesper services each evening at the side of the Ocean is a distinctive feature of our Chautauqua. The different speakers will be Rev. B. F. Black, just back from France as Chaplain; Rev. W. P. Minton, the song leader and Foreign Mission Secretary-Elect; Mr. J. J. Pitt, just back from overseas "Y" service; Rev. H. G. Rowe, just returned from overseas "Y" service; Rev. H. J. Fleming, a worker with enlisted men at Hampton Roads.

The Forward Movement Message each day will be given by the Superintendent, Rev. W. H. Denison, D. D.; Rev. Dr. R. C. Helfenstein; Rev. F. H. Peters, and Mr Hermon Eldredge, the Religious Education Secretary of the Movement.

Mrs. E. T. Cotten, Suffolk, Va., will be the pianist for the Chautauqua.

Christian Union Commissions

The Disciples of Christ Commission on Christian Union and the Commission on Christian Union of the Christian Church will hold a joint session on Thursday and Friday of the Chautauqua. Speakers from these two Commissions will furnish the program Friday from 10 A. M. until 12:40 P. M. The following will likely be the program for that period:

1. "The World-field Demands for Christian Unity"—Rev. Finis Idleman, D. D., New York City.

2. "City and Rural Community Demands for Christian Unity"—Rev. P. S. Sailor, Westerly, R. I.

3. "Christian Union and the Conservation Program of the Church"—Rev. F. H. Peters, D. D., Greenville, Ohio.

4. "Necessary Steps to Christian Unity"—Rev. B. H. Melton, D. D., Baltimore, Md.

5. "Danger Points to be Avoided"—President W. A. Harper, LL. D., Elon College, N. C.

6. "Progress of Christian Unity to Date"—Rev. H. C. Armstrong, D. D., Baltimore, Md.

7. "How Near may Disciples and Christians Come Together with Assurance of the Endorsement of Their Constituency"—Rev. E. B. Bagby, D. D., Washington, D. C.; Rev. J. F. Burnett, D. D., Dayton, Ohio.

The School of Methods of the Christian Church is worth your while You need it and it needs you. It trains you and the workers and officers of your church. It gives Vision, uplift, inspiration. It combines recreation and study. It gives power and fellowship.

The ocean beach is fine, and the bathing is a delight to all who go to Virginia Beach. Let Mr. S. M. Smith, General Secretary, help find your accommodations. Write him at Norfolk, Va., Chamber of Commerce Building. Remember that Mr. W. C. Pearce, a great man with a great message will open the Chautauqua Tuesday night, July 29, at 8 o'clock.

WARREN H. DENISON, President.

Mrs. J. C. McAdams—I don't want to be without THE SUN. Dr. Staley's letter in last week's issue is a comfort to me, more so because I am sick in bed.

THE CHRISTIAN ORPHANAGE

THE CHILDREN GO VISITING

Our singing class, composed of ten little girls, was invited to give a song service at Union Christian church, Union Ridge, N. C. on the second Sunday. Brother Fleming, the pastor, gave us a very warm welcome and the little girls enjoyed the service very much. It was a treat for them to get out from home and sing for those who are aiding in giving them a home here at the Orphanage. The people were very kind to them and the good ladies served lunch on the grounds after the service, and Mr. C. P. Aldridge treated to lemonade which was very refreshing on a hot summer day. A free-will offering was taken and about thirty-one dollars was raised.

If the people enjoyed having the little girls with them as much as they enjoyed being there it was a very happy occasion for both. We hope to go to other churches in the near future. We find that the more we can get this work before the people and the better acquainted they become with its possibilities, the more interested they become in its success.

When you give money for this work it is not thrown away by you so that you will never hear from it again. Perhaps in a few years it may come back to you in the personal form of a trained nurse, a teacher, a doctor, a lawyer or some other professional person. So if by investing a part of your income in this work you help to train a little helpless boy or girl to be useful and of service to mankind and be a blessing to the community and an asset to society have you not invested your money wisely?

A good lady in the State of Ohio mailed us a check for $25.00 some days ago. I am told that this lady makes her money by running a truck farm and is a hard worker, but she believes in giving a part of her income to the Lord. She has never seen the Orphanage or any of the children. She gives this contribution because she has love and tender sympathy for the little orphans of our Church. We thank God for such noble women.

We have lots of glass fruit jars but no fruit. If any of our good ladies who have fruit will be so kind as to fill some for us, we will be glad to ship any number of cans you want.

CHAS. D. JOHNSTON, *Supt.*

REPORT FOR JULY 23, 1919

Amount brought forward, $7,443.08.

Sunday School Monthly Offerings

(North Carolina Conference)

Reidsville, $3.00; Long's Chapel, $1.50; Shady Grove, $2.00; Raleigh, $2.00; Pleasant Cross, $9.00; Union Ridge, $1.37; Wentworth, $6.54; Durham, $5.55; Ramseur, $3.83; Ingram, (Va.), $3.00.

(Eastern Virginia Conference)

Isle of Wight, $2.60; Suffolk, $25.00; Berea, (Nansemond County), $10.00; Washington St., Portsmouth, $3.00.

(Valley Virginia Conference)

Wood's Chapel, $1.00; Timber Ridge, $4.25; Dry Run, $3.00.

(Alabama Conference)

Mount Zion, $1.70; Lanett, $5.00; Total, $92.34.

Special Offerings

Mrs. C. H. Coles, Portsmouth, Va., $10.00; W. H. Thomas, Durham, N. C., $25.00; Lula C. Helfenstein, Utica, N. Y., $1.00; Mrs. Minnie Andrews, Burlington, N. C., $5.00; Mrs. R. A. Garrett, Danville, Va., $2.00; Mrs. Elmer Jenkins, Dayton, Ohio, $25.00; Mr. Hersey Woodard, Jr., Suffolk, Va., $5.00; Union Ridge church, N. C., $31.63; Total, $104.63.

Total for the week, $196.97; Grand total, $7,640.05.

HOUSEKEEPING HINTS

Sandwiches and Tea.—Just a hurried sandwich that you can make in a jiffy and then turn to your books again. Simply white bread, nice and moist, the edges trimmed and thrown to the crumb jar for breadings at some other time. Butter the bread after cutting in strips and fill with cream cheese blended with a little peanut butter. Have a tiny bowl of pinmoney pickles to nibble. Orange Pekoe tea, plenty of sugar and a slice of lemon.

During damp weather salt shakers will clog on the inner side of the holes. If a few kernels of rice are placed in each cellar with the salt, it will sift better. Cornstarch mixed with the salt will prevent its absorbing dampness. When it is possible during the damp season the salt cellars should be cleaned and freshly filled every day. The latest salt cellar has a glass perforated top, which has two glass prongs, extending down into the bowl. These can be revolved by turning the top.

AT RANDOM

"Say, Pat, phwat is dis ting dey call a chafing dish?" asked Tim.

"Why, man, don't ye know? It's a frying pan dat's broke into society."—*Pleasant Hours.*

"How are you gettin' on wid yer 'rithmetic, Lou?"

"Well, I done learned to add up de oughts, but dem nggers bodder me."—*The American Boy.*

Friend—"How's your boy getting on in the army, Mr. Johnson?"

Johnson—"Wonderfully! I feel a sense of great security. An army that can make my boy get up early, work hard all day, and go to bed early, can do anything."

The twins had gone in swimming without their mother's permission, and they anticipated trouble.

"Well," said Tommy philosophically, "we're both in the same boat, anyhow."

"Yes," returned Ray, "but I'm afraid it's going to be a whaleboat."—*The Boys Magazine.*

The power of love—God's greatest gift!
Forget it not, dear heart. 'Twill lift
The weight of burdens heaviest.
When thou rememb'rest that the best
He gives is thine—thou still canst love!

WORSHIP AND MEDITATION

TO PRAY

To pray—not ask an alms of fate,
Nor beg, nor placate, but to bring
An offering, to give myself,
For this is prayer.

To pray—not toward the earth or sky,
But to that Friend within my soul,
To that strong Life I feel so near,
The God in me.

To pray—not for the gain of it,
But for the joy of it. To laugh,
To weep with God, to learn His call,
And answer back.

To pray—to hope, to fear, to fail;
And then when all is lost, save prayer,
O, soul of mine, to pray again,
And then be strong l.
          —Hugh Robert Orr.

THE PEACE THAT CLINGS

The prophet speaks of the perfect peace that comes to the man "whose mind is stayed on thee." It is not the man whose mind is contented or stationary. That mind may be a stagnant mind. It is like the boulder in the open field. If the rock had eyes it might see; it might admire the field and the sky and the song of birds, but it is a rock without blessing, a rock without helpfulness, a rock without a soul. Winter and summer and cold and heat and day and night it is still a rock, always a rock, and nothing but a rock. The prophet is talking about another sort of peace; the peace of mind stayed upon God. It is that sort of a mind that rejoices in God. To be stayed on Him is conscious strength and constant strength; the consciousness of the strength that has Jesus at the heart of it and also at the circumference of it. It is the one way to be blest, and the one way to be a blessing. The mind that is not "stayed," lacks reliability; it lacks centralization; it lacks unity of action and definiteness of Christlik': purpose.

Dr. Matheson once said that peace comes by the thing to which it is fastened, something that is constantly moving. Said he: "What would be the difference between a soul bound to a rock and a soul bound to a star? The soul bound to the rock would be stationary; the soul bound to the star would be ever on the wing. The world's peace is standing still; God's is moving on. The world's peace is silence; God's is a living voice." The inference is therefore plain that "the peace of God descends on every man as it descended on Jesus—in the midst of the waters." When he is resting in Jesus he is doing his best for Jesus. The peace that comes by "staying" is the peace that manifests itself by acting. Lean hard and you will work hard.—*United Presbyterian.*

IRREVERENCE AND PROFANITY

There is no great gap between the two. The one is the vestibule, the other the room into which it leads. We have more than once called attention to the tendency among clergymen to touch things holy with unwashen hands, and we do so again. We have just returned from a Bible Conference and seen how much levity is mixed up with an otherwise earnest handling of the Scriptures. The ease with which the American mind switches from the sublime to the ridiculous, from the sacred to the frivolous, from the serious to the comical, is directly responsible for the growing spirit of profanity. Who is shocked when boys and girls on the streets use vulgar or profane speech? Who teaches them that some things are holy and other things profane? When they can quote teachers and clergymen as damning things and persons, and consigning them to hell, why should they have reverence and respect for the name of God and for the things made sacred because of that name?

It has come to be the fashion to exploit wit at the expense of the Scriptures. Many a passage is wrenched from its sacredness and made the carrier, not of the truth of God, but of the foolishness of man. Men handle the Bible with a freedom and familiarity that borders on profanity, and it is not to be wondered at that it has been robbed of its power of appeal as the Word of God. We deplore this irreverent handling of the Scriptures, this playing fast and loose with sanctities holy as God Himself and pure and clean as heaven. It is

Read The Front Page

coming to be the bane of pulpit speech. Preachers seem to think that if they would be heard they must descend to street-corner slang, if not downright profanity. Lutheran pulpits are not altogether free of it and that is why we speak of it here. If we wish to lend encouragement to a tendency to abolish the distinction between the sacred and the profane, all that is needed is to excuse or condone such breaches of our Lord's simple and plain command, "Let your communication be, Yea, yea; Nay, nay; for whatsoever is more than these cometh of evil." We challenge any Christian to show that those words have become obsolete.—*The Lutheran.*

Have not you and I the power to live more unselfishly today because of the unselfishness of the great, monumental lives of devotion?—*Phillips Brooks.*

THE NORTH CAROLINA CHRISTIAN SUNDAY SCHOOL AND CHRISTIAN ENDEAVOR CONVENTION

The Convention met in first annual session at Shallow Well church, Jonesboro, Tuesday P. M., July 15. President C. H. Stephenson of Raleigh called the Convention to order and after stirring and soul-inspiring music by the orchestra of the Raleigh Sunday school Brother W. H. Lane of the Shallow Well school gave cordial words of welcome and Rev. H. Scholz responded. The business session followed, program for the session was adopted, delegates, pastors and superintendents were enrolled. The enrollment and attendance from the various schools were excellent, I think between forty and fifty schools being represented and possibly two dozen pastors and superintendents were present. Exercises opened at 9:15 sharp Wednesday morning with a concert by the orchestra. Here let it be said that the orchestra was the feature of the Convention and gave life, vivacity, "pep," enthusiasm to all the proceedings. It rendered invaluable assistance and made us have pity for those Conventions that are held without the help and glory of an orchestra.

In the absence of the pastor, Rev. T. E. White, J. O. Atkinson conducted the devotional services.

A business session followed in which many delegates were enrolled and a motion prevailed that the Convention proceed under the rules and regulations previously governing the Eastern North Carolina Convention until the Committee on Constitution and By-Laws should have time to report.

The President's annual address was delivered, subject: League. The points of the address were "L"—League; "E"—Earnestness; "A"—Action; "G"—God; "U"—Unity; "E"—Eternity. It was a superior and timely and comprehensive address, impressively and eloquently delivered. The Convention decided to make the address a part of its minutes, to print it in The Christian Sun and also in tract form and send out a copy with each copy of the printed minutes.

Rev. J. E. Franks moved the Convention to enthusiasm and action on the subject of "Organization and Expansion." He recommended that a thousand dollars be raised for Sunday school missions and that a Sunday school missionary be put in the field. A committee was at once appointed who recommended that $1,500 be raised the coming year by every school's taking one offering each month for missions and that a Sunday school missionary be put in the field for half his time. Rev. J. E. Franks was the man recommended by the Convention and the Committee has every reason to believe that because of his great interest in the work, and his feeling of great need for expansion, he will make the sacrifice and accept.

This was one of the many great forward steps of the Convention. It means that a man is to be sent out who is to find places where Sunday schools are needed and where if planted there will be prospects for churches.

In the absence of Rev. R. L. Williamson, Dr. W. A. Harper was appointed to make report on Teacher Training which he did at a later hour.

Prof. L. L. Vaughan, of Raleigh, most ably led a helpful discussion on "Special Features in My Sunday School and Christian Endeavor Society." This discussion gave insight into many novel features in the schools and resulted in Dr. Lawrence's wise plea to every school present to try to excel in some one feature during the coming year.

Rev. J. W. Harrell, D. D., delivered a most wholesome and practical address on "The Sunday School That is Different." This address was one of the features of the Convention and should by all means have a wider hearing and permanent form.

Rev. L. I. Cox delivered a very practical, pointed and powerful address on "The Sunday School and Missions" and on the last day the writer spoke on "Missions In The Sunday School." The missionary note was struck often in the Convention and many are seeing and are saying that we must become a missionary people in school and in church before we can grow and achieve as is our privilege.

Miss May Stephenson presented the report on the "Primary Department," Miss Mary Green that on the "Home Department," Brother George T. Whitaker on the "Adult Department," Mrs. George M. McCullers on the "Cradle Roll," and Brother W. L. Thomas on the "Intermediate Department." All of these reports showed interest and gave valuable suggestions for the good of the work.

Addresses were delivered Wednesday afternoon by Rev. R. F. Brown on "The Sunday School, a Spiritual Force in Reconstruction," Brother P. T. Hines on "The Importance of You and Me," and Rev. J. E. Franks on "A Tithing Sunday-School for the New Times." These were all reported to be excellent and helpful addresses, the writer not being privileged to hear them, having committee work at the hour.

Wednesday night Rev. George D. Eastes, the wide-awake and beloved pastor of our Raleigh church, delivered a great and spirited address on, "The Sunday School, An Evangelistic Force," and Ensign W. H. Stephenson spoke eloquently on "What Will We Do With Victory."

Thursday was a busy day and much was accomplished. In a testimony meeting almost every school represented decided to go home and start something that it hadn't had, and try to excel in some one thing. Among the splendid, eloquent and moving addresses of the closing session were: "The Challenge of the New Times to Christian Endeavor" by Rev. J. V. Knight; and "The Sunday School and The Orphanage" by Superintendent Chas. D. Johnston. An offering was made for the Orphanage of $160.00.

The Shallow Well people entertained the Convention with cordial hospitality. Elon College is to have the joy of being host to the Convention next year. Dr. S. T. A. Kent was chosen President; Dr. E. L. Moffitt, Vice-President; Rev. H. Scholz, Recording Secretary; J. Byrd Ellington, Treasurer, and C. H. Stephenson, General Secretary. Brother Stephenson is a live wire in planning and creating a Sunday School Convention and as General Secretary he will give us next year the biggest and best yet.   J. O. ATKINSON.

Sunday School and Christian Endeavor

SUNDAY SCHOOL LESSON FOR
AUGUST 3, 1919

Christian Worship. Matt. 6:5, 6; John 4:1-10, 19-24; Heb. 10:19-25.

Golden Text: God is a Spirit, and they that worship him must worship in spirit and in truth. John 4:24.

Additional Material for Teachers. Exodus. 34:5-8; II Chron. 29:29, 30; Ps. 84 and 122; Matt. 4:10.

"I was glad when they said unto me, Let us go into the house of the Lord." Do we have such service that every child can say that? Only recently I went into a Sunday school which is using the Graded Lessons. There is objection, it seems to the children going to their own rooms for opening service, and so they stood there absolutely without a thing to do, except join in the singing. Why? Because the same form of opening exercise was being used, the reading of the opening service in front of the quarterly, which they did not have, and the reading in concert of a lesson which was not theirs. Why not plan to buy some of the splendid books of opening exercises, and have one in which the entire school can join if for any reason it is not considered advisable to let the younger children have their exercises by themselves? Personally, I advocate the latter way, for just teaching the Sunday school lesson is not all that should be taught in Sunday school. We should teach worship. No child should leave our Sunday schools who has not been taught to pray; who has not learned that worship means to do something as well as to be done for? The person who will lead in prayer in a public place is few and far between in any or all of our churches. Why? Because they did not learn to pray when they were children. They are afraid to speak, or testify, because they never learned how, and so our prayermeetings and Christian Endeavor Societies in all too many places, yes and our Sunday school classes, too, resemble old fashioned Quaker meetings. Is this worship?

MRS. FRED BULLOCK.

There, little brewery, don't you cry; you'll grind sausages by and by. —*Memphis Commercial Appeal.*

CHRISTIAN ENDEAVOR TOPIC FOR
AUGUST 3, 1919

Our Relation to Others—Toward Parents and Others in the Home Exod. 20:12; Eph. 6:1-9. (Consecration).

The last Consecration meeting, we discussed our relation toward our enemies. If we were to listen to the manner in which some of our young people talk to and about their parents, we would have to assume that enemies and homefolks were one and the same. "Oh, Ma's always fussing. She don't want us to have any fun. But we slip out whenever we can," says the girl gleefully, not realizing that when she "slips out" she almost inevitably "slips down" as well. "Pa's old fashioned. He thinks anything he didn't do as a boy is all wrong for us," says the boys, and so he drives the car twenty or thirty miles from home, meets with others whom he would not wish his parents to know, and—is on a road that leads—away from home forever. "Old folks are such a bother. They think they ought to have a word in everything, and they are too old to know anything about our ways today," says a thoughtless grandchild, and grandfather or grandmother goes away with their hearts breaking, and praying for death because they are no longer needed. Jesus was obedient unto His parents until He was thirty years old. His last thought for any human being was for His mother. His last conscious cry was to His Father. Can you better His example? Can you imagine Him cross or ungrateful, or disobedient in His home? If you will read carefully, you will find that this oldest Son knew many of the cares of housekeeping; He knew about dishwashing and floor sweeping and bread making, and fire kindling, and He did not consider it beneath Him, nor did He hide His knowledge for fear some one would discover it. Jesus forever ennobled the Home.

MRS. FRED BULLOCK.

No beer, no work. No work, no wife. No wife, no home. No home —tramp, tramp, tramp, the bums are marching!—*Toledo Blade.*

APPRECIATES HIS PAPER

Don't stop my paper, printer;
Don't strike my name off yet;
You know the times are stringent
And dollars hard to get;
But tug a little harder
Is what I mean to do,
And scrape enough together—
Enough for me and you.

I can't afford to drop it,
And I find it doesn't pay
To do without a paper,
However others may.
I hate to ask my neighbors
To give me theirs on loan;
They don't just say, but mean it,
"Why don't you have your own?"

You can't tell how we miss it
If it, by any fate,
Should happen not to reach us
Or come a little late;
Then all is in a hubbub
And things go all awry;
And, printer, if you're married
You'll know the reason why.

The children want those stories,
And wife is anxious, too,
At first to glance it over
And then to read it through;
And I read the editorials
And scan the local views,
And read the correspondence
And every bit of news.
—*Exchange.*

A little girl wrote the following composition on men:

"Men are what women marry. They are more logical than women, also more zoological. Both men and women sprang from monkeys, but the women sprang farther than the men."

A French learning English said to his tutor: "English is a queer language. What does this sentence mean: 'Should Mr. Noble, who sits for this constituency, consent to stand again and run he will in all probability have a walkover'?"

MARRIAGES

WILLS-PORTER

The home of Mr. and Mrs. W. S. Porter of Isle of Wight was the scene of a very pretty wedding Thursday evening, June 26, 1919, at six oclock, when Miss Emily Kay Porter became the bride of Mr. William Edward Wills.

The bride wore a gown of white Georgette and Crepe de Chine and carried bride's roses and sweet peas. Mary Latimer, a cousin of the bride, acted as maid-of-honor, and the groom had as his best man, his brother, Dudley Wills.

Miss Elma Hedgepeth played Lohengrin's wedding march as the couple entered after which the ceremony was read by the writer.

After many congratulations and showers of rice from the relatives and friends who witnessed the pretty occasion, Mr. and Mrs. Wills motored to Windsor and took the train to Norfolk. On their return they will make their home in Suffolk where the groom is engaged in business.

E. T. COTTEN.

OBITUARIES

WHITMORE

Ashby D. Whitmore, a son of Mr. and Mrs. J. P. Whitmore, died at Riverside Hospital, Newport News, Va., June 24, 1919, aged 24 years, 10 months and 23 days. On November 23, 1917, he was married to Miss Iola Hargrave. He leaves a wife, one child, Ashby Dee, Jr., parents, one brother, Philip, and one sister, Ivin, all of Newport News, Va., the family having moved from Dendron, Va., last September.

The deceased was a member of the Dendron Christian church also of the Junior Order of American Mechanics. The body was brought to Union Christian church where funeral service was held. Interment was in the church cemetery.

W. D. HARWARD.

ANDREWS

Miss Adlina Andrews was born December 14, 1869, in Surry county, Virginia, and died at her home in Dendron, Va., June 17, 1919.

On January 12, 1887, she was married to P. E. Slade of Surry county. To this union were born three children: W. O. Slade, Mrs. Grace Leadbetter and Mrs. Lillian Hargrave. There are four grandchildren. She also leaves three sisters: Mrs. S. W. Carroll, Wakefield, Va.; Mrs. A. B. Taylor and Mrs T. F. Spencer, Newport News, Va. She was a faithful member of the Dendron Christian church.

The funeral service was conducted in the home after which the remains were taken to Wakefield, Va., and laid beside her husband who departed this life March 7, 1913.

W. D. HARWARD.

FULGHUM

Sunday afternoon, June 30, 1919, death entered the home of Mr. Charles Fulghum, and bore away the spirit of his beloved companion, Mrs. Fulghum who died at the age of 66 years, one month and one day. At an early age she gave her heart to Christ, and to the last lived a consistent Christian life. She was a member of Antioch Christian church, then moved her membership to Windsor Christian church where she remained till the departure of her life. She was devoted to the work of the church and attended the services regularly, until the paralytic stroke came upon her a few days before her death. In her devotion to her home and church she has left an example worthy of praise. Besides her husband she leaves three sons, one daughter, one step-son, one step-daughter, one half-sister, besides other relatives and friends who mourn their loss. Services were conducted by the writer, assisted by Rev. J. T. Kitchen, and Rev. N. L. Lewis. Interment was made in the cemetery at Antioch.

E. T. COTTEN.

LUKE

The funeral services of Mr. L. R. Luke were held at the East End Christian church on July 9, 1919. The deceased was married, having married Mrs. Sherwood of Concord, N. C., February 20, 1919. A wife and three children mourn the loss of father and husband. Five sisters are left to go through this life minus one who was dear to them and to whom they were devoted. The writer was assisted in the service by Rev. W. L. Murphy of the Chestnut Avenue M. E. church. The interment was at Providence M. E. church, five miles from Suffolk, Va. May the blessings of God rest upon those who are now separated from one whom they loved

and cherished and may those of his relatives and friends who are left behind prepare to meet their kinsman in the better world.

H. J. FLEMING.

BEAMON

The soul of Mrs. Sarah Carolina Eudosia Beamon passed from labor to reward July 2, 1919. Mrs. Beamon was in the eighty-seventh year of her age. She was the daughter of James and Mary Costen and was born January 24, 1833. In early life she married Mr. William Beamon. To this union four children were born—W. W. Beamon, Mrs. James Seawell, Mrs. Joe Smith and Mrs. Pallie Hodges. All except Mrs. Hodges survive her. The funeral services were conducted from the home and the interment made in the home cemetery. Rev. W. W. Staley, assisted by Revs. I. W Johnson and W. B. Fuller, conducted the service.

Mrs. Beamon was one of the charter members of Damascus church, having been a member more than seventy years. She was as true to its interests as she was to her own people. With her prayers, her purse, and her presence she rendered constant aid. A most beautiful Christian spirit actuated and adorned her conduct in all her relations of life. Meek and unassuming in manner, gentle and lovable in disposition, patient, kind and ever considerate of the welfare of others. Her pastor knew that he could depend on her to support any church institution to the extent of her ability and that a hearty welcome ever greeted him. She kept her face to the future and would not look back. When one administers with a tender hand for the healing of a sufferer, or speaks a word to cheer the heart, such acts live. Like the good Samaritan, who poured oil on the broken body, hers has become a living name. She was greatly beloved by all who knew her. She was especially fond of music. Her home was the musical center of the community. She was a faithful, cheerful laborer in the Lord's vineyard.

ONE WHO LOVED HER.

IN MEMORIAM—PAYNE

Whereas, the great and supreme Ruler of the universe has in His infinite wisdom removed from among us a worthy brother, James Asbury Payne; and whereas, the long and intimate relation held with him in the discharge of his duties this church makes it eminently befitting that we record our appreciation of him.

Therefore, Resolved:

That the wisdom which he exercised in the aid of our church by service and counsel will be held in grateful remembrance;

That the removal of such a member among our midst leaves a vacancy that will be realized by the members of this church;

That with deep sympathy with the bereaved relatives of the deceased we express our hope that our loss may be overruled for good by Him who doeth all things well; for,

"Many days he suffered,
And now it is at an end,
And while his body sleeps in death
In Christ he has a friend;"

That a copy of these resolutions be placed upon the church record, a copy sent to the family, and that they be printed in The Christian Sun.

    MRS. EDGAR CHAPMAN,
    R. ROY HOSAFLOOK,
    JOSEPH TAYLOR,
        Committee.

A detective asked an office boy if it was Mr. Jones or his partner who reached the office first as a rule.

"Well," said the boy, turning very red, "Mr. Jones at first was always last, but later he began to get earlier, till at last he was first, though before he had always been behind. He soon got later again, though of late he has been sooner, and at last he got behind as before. But I expect he'll be getting earlier sooner or later."

REPORT OF THE CONDITION OF

the Elon Banking and Trust Company, at Elon College in the State of North Carolina, at the close of business, June 30, 1919:

Resources

Loans and Discounts	$26,842.15
Demand Loans	1,925.49
Overdrafts, secured, $342.20;	
unsecured, $388.10	730.30
United States Bonds and	
Liberty Bonds	4,850.00
Banking Houses, $1,480.38;	
Furniture and Fixtures,	
$1,776.26	3,256.64
Cash in vault and net amounts	
due from Banks, Bankers	
and Trust Companies	9,576.66
Cash Items held over 24 hours	3,729.82
Thrift Stamps	37.25
War Savings Stamps	655.65
	———
Total	$51,603.96

Liabilities

Capital Stock paid in	$ 5,000.00
Surplus Fund	1,000.00
Undivided Profits, less current	
expenses and taxes paid	432.06
Bills Payable	8,000.00
Deposits subject to check	20,467.41
Time Certificates of Deposit	15,186.34
Cashiers Checks outstanding	426.32
Certified Checks	30.00
Received on Bonds	781.00
Accrued Interest due depositors	277.83
	———
Total	$51,603.96

State of North Carolina—County of Alamance, July 14, 1919:

I, MARION C. JACKSON, Cashier of the above named Bank, do solemnly swear that the above statement is true to the best of my knowledge and belief.

    MARION C. JACKSON, Cashier.

Correct—Attest:
    W. P. LAWRENCE,
    J. J. LAMBETH,
    G. S. WATSON,
        Directors.

Subscribed and sworn to before me, this 14 day of July, 1919.

    J. J. LAMBETH, J. P.

The person who doesn't save goes without worth-while things today, and will go without them tomorrow. The person who saves has everything he needs today, and will have still more tomorrow. Buy W. S. S.

Mrs. Smith hired a Chinese servant and tried to teach him how to receive calling cards. She let herself out the front door and when the new servant answered her ring she gave him her card. The next day two ladies came to call. When they presented their cards the alert Chinaman hastily compared them with Mrs. Smith's cards and remarked, as he closed the door: "Tickets no good; can't come in."

The blind man—I picked up a hammer—and saw.

The dumb man—I picked up a wheel—and spoke.—The Oteen.

A barrister, not so discreet as he might have been in the expression of his ideas, was engaged on a case concerning some pigs.

"Gentlemen of the jury," he began, "there were twenty-four pigs in the drove, just twenty-four; exactly twice as many as there are in that jury box."

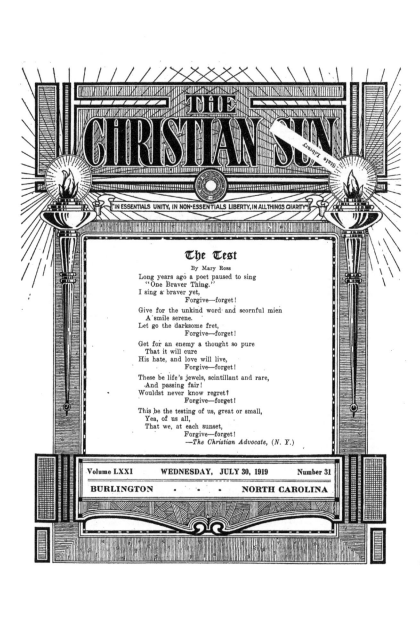

THE CHRISTIAN SUN

"IN ESSENTIALS UNITY, IN NON-ESSENTIALS LIBERTY, IN ALL THINGS CHARITY"

The Test

By Mary Ross

Long years ago a poet paused to sing
"One Braver Thing."
I sing a braver yet,
    Forgive—forget!

Give for the unkind word and scornful mien
A smile serene.
Let go the darksome fret,
    Forgive—forget!

Get for an enemy a thought so pure
That it will cure
His hate, and love will live,
    Forgive—forget!

These be life's jewels, scintillant and rare,
And passing fair!
Wouldst never know regret?
    Forgive—forget!

This be the testing of us, great or small,
Yea, of us all,
That we, at each sunset,
    Forgive—forget!
         —The Christian Advocate, (N. Y.)

Volume LXXI   WEDNESDAY, JULY 30, 1919   Number 31

BURLINGTON · · · NORTH CAROLINA

THE CHRISTIAN SUN

Founded 1844 by Rev. Daniel W. Kerr

C. B. RIDDLE - - - Editor

Entered at the Burlington, N. C. Post Office as second class matter.

Subscription Rates

One year .... $ 2.00
Six months 1.00

In Advance

Give both your old and new postoffice when asking that your ad dress be changed.

The change of your label is your receipt for money. Written receipts sent upon request.

Many persons subscribe for friends, intending that the paper be stopped at the end of the year. If instructions are given to this effect, they will receive attention at the proper time.

Marriage and obituary notices not exceeding 150 words printed free if received within 60 days from date of event, all over this at the rate of one-half cent a word.

Original poetry not accepted for publication.

Principles of the Christian Church

(1) The Lord Jesus Christ is the only Head of the Church.

(2) Christian is a sufficient name of the Church.

(3) The Holy Bible is a sufficient rule of faith and practice.

(4) Christian character is a sufficient test of fellowship, and of church membership.

(5) The right of private judgment and the liberty of conscience is a right and a privilege that should be accorded to, and exercised by all.

EDITORIAL

MORE ODDS AND ENDS

This is vacation season, and among those who cannot afford such a luxury, is the Editor of this weekly periodical. "The Editor's Easy Chair" is usually the name applied to general paragraphs in the editorial world. The idea comes from moments of time picked up between regular duties when the editor can write *short* notes while he would not have the time to write long ones. Hot weather is not very inducive to study as some of our preacher brethren will testify. The presence of these notes on the editorial pages instead of long articles means that the Editor is either fanning between times or watching a shower.

Speaking of education, there are some things about it that have changed along with many other things. During the last few years it has been our pleasure to interview possibly more than a thousand young men and women concerning the matter of a college education. One argument that we have always placed before them is this: That the college trained man has a better chance in life to earn money than the man without a college training. This is only one of the *minor* reasons for a college education, but it can no longer stand.

The college man is in the rear today so far as earning more money is concerned, unless he ranks in profession either as a general laborer or a professional man of more than average standing. These are abnormal times, and arts, the children of education, suffer in such times. Few men want to serve as an apprentice today because they can go into the ordinary work shop and earn large salaries. Hundreds of young men and women are being deceived by just this sort of a thing and turning aside their educational work for immediate money. A

"All lines of useful service fall within the center of gravity of every life and the center of gravity is never found to lie within the small circle of selfish gain or glory."

few years from now many of them will be in the non-professional class and too old to begin a solid foundation. Not only that but circumstances and obligations will not permit. The consequence will be that they will have to take the situation as it comes and fight hard on the bread line. Then it will be for the wise young men and women of today who attend college to surpass them—and they will.

After two thousand years of healing sick souls, the church is again stressing its opportunities for furthering the gospel of public health. In the wake of the great war came national and world scourges that were more frightful than the battles themselves. Preventable disease and infant mortality are among the world's greatest enemies. Six million people succumbed to influenza; two out of every seven babies die during their first year. The complications of living in the present age have made specialists of us all. Each organization has worked more or less apart from other organizations, but that scheme of things is passing away. We do not cease to be specialists, but by co-operating we can the more readily and satisfactorily carry out our works for the betterment of the race—mentally, morally and physically.

A custom that seems to us to be unfair is the matter of placing a person's name on a program without consulting the person. We have seen this done many times but have never approved of it. It is unfair to the person and to the cause to be represented. Many times we receive information in this office from some persons that only through THE SUN did they know that they were on a certain program. We have a letter on file now from a good woman who, several months ago, was placed on a program for a very important meeting. Her first knowledge of this was to see her name in print. She told us confidently that she had to sit up practically all of three nights in order to get up the work assigned to her. Such methods are not business-like; and while it is kind and charitable for persons to accept a place on the program after their names have been placed there without their knowledge, we doubt the wisdom of it and would never censure a person for not accepting.

It was noticed in these columns two weeks ago that Brother B. D. Jones, Holland, Virginia, had challenged Brother Chas. D. Johnston that he would double the number of subscriptions secured by Brother Johnston. On July 21 Brother Johnston sends this note: "I am enclosing five new subscribers for THE SUN from the Graham Christian church, (my church). I have other prospects and hope to send you another list soon. It was very easy to secure these subscribers, and I think when I turn the Orphanage work over to some other person I will apply to you for a job to work for THE SUN. If some one would become interested in this matter in each church I fully believe the desired number of subscribers could be obtained in the next two months. Now, I know that Brother Brock Jones is a hustler, but you may tell him that I have sent in one more than I agreed to and he will have to come across with ten instead of eight." We have written Brother Jones the substance of this letter and know that he will not fall short of Brother Johnston's expectations.

On page 6 of this issue will be found an interesting letter from Chaplain B. F. Black. Brother Black is a man mature in years and habits and has gained a wonderful experience from his work overseas. Black was born with the habit of collecting historical specimens and curiosities. His work for the Elon College

---

"The great offerings of this day, if accompanied with grace, will be a great blessing; without grace they will sink the church."

---

museum speaks for that fact. He now offers himself for a few weeks to our churches. He should have calls for as much time as he can devote to this. His message is first missionary, because it gives first-hand information of a country that must be reconstructed, rebuilt and redeemed. In the second place his message is the most accurate history, because what he tells is what he has seen with his own eyes and heard with his own ears. In the third place his message is inspirational, because it is the experienced giving an experience. It is worth while to hear him. He spoke at Elon College last Sunday morning and at Greensboro that night and brought a message to each place that was interesting, and those who heard him counted themselves fortunate. Brother Black offers to go for his expenses and we believe that those pastors and churches that secure him will be doing a thing helpful in many ways for their people.

It ought to be encouragement to the whole denomination to know that Rev. J. E. Franks is to become Sunday School Secretary of the North Carolina Conference. We understand that he is to give only half of his time for the first year, but even this will be a forward step in our Sunday school and Christian Endeavor work. We know that it will soon be followed by an all time secretary. The choice of the Convention in selecting a man is a wise one. Brother Franks is in every sense a Sunday school pastor, a Sunday school worker and a Sunday school booster, and fruit will spring up

in his footsteps. The step is a forward one, and the only regret that we have is that such a step was not taken many years ago. Here is every good wish to you, Brother Franks, not only our good wishes shall attend you in your labors, but our prayers shall follow you while you labor.

Speaking of secretaries for different departments of our Church work, we deem the time opportune to say a thing which we have felt for several years: We need a Secretary of Education whose business it would be to visit the churches and speak in the interest of Christian education. Our pastors discuss this theme and our worthy president of Elon College never loses an opportunity to appeal to the youth of our Church. These things are well and good, but our pastors, with a multitude of other things to do cannot devote more than one or two sermons a year to the theme, and our president is the first an executive, whose time, every minute of it, is needed for the guidance of affairs at the College. We have already overworked him. He has been instrumental in raising the largest fund ever given for any enterprise of our denomination. The next need of the College is students, students from our own Church that they may be trained and go back to the Brotherhood as leaders in the several walks of life. We need a man whose heart is burdened with the education of

---

"Our prison-trained men outnumber our college trained men more than two to one, as do the men from the jails those from the high schools."

---

our young men and women and will go out with that burden and speak from every pulpit an inspiring message to create in the hearts of our young men and women a desire for a college education.

Our dollars given for the cause of Christian education will be in vain if these gifts of ours are not translated into great and living souls for the Church and the Kingdom. The biggest difficulty is over with a young man when a desire comes into his heart for an education, and the same is true of a young woman. The greatest asset to the Church is our young people and we must inspire them to build greater than we have.

If we had a Secretary of Education giving all his time to inspiring and appealing to our people in the matter of giving our sons and our daughters a better education, our College would overflow with students without solicitation. The money that our College has to spend for advertising purposes would be used at home in making a beautiful campus and other needed additions to our College. Is such a move worthy of our consideration, and are we ready for it?

The S. A. T. C. would not mix with the schools, especially the Church schools. Here is the reason: Christian education makes the approach through the soul and not by external force. The best discipline is influence and not force, and two principles of government cannot be worked out in one institution.

PASTOR AND PEOPLE

CHRISTIAN ENDEAVOR REPORT

Patronize Elon College

One of the many fine things in the Sunday School and Christian Endeavor Convention at Shallow Well was the report showing the work done in Christian Endeavor. In the absence of the committe on Christian Endeavor, that Christian Endeavor enthusiast who has two Societies in each church in his pastorate, Rev. F. C. Lester, of Graham, made up the report. He did it in the right way to bring out the facts, and to get the work before the people in the right way. He is on that Committee for next year.

But this article is to call the attention of churches and pastors to another part of that report, and that is to the effect that the Christian Endeavor Committee will double the present number of Societies in our Convention during the next year or "BURST." Now, Mr. Preacher man, which had you rather the Committee would do? Mr. Sunday School Superintendent, and Mr. church member, what do you say? The Christian Church in the Southern Christian Convention not only needs the Christian Endeavor work, but is *suffering* for the lack of it.

The Committee was not satisfied to *resolve, adopt,* and *recommend,* but it went further and asked the Convention for a Steering Committee on Organization—each member located in a different part of the State—to look after this work. The Committee is: Miss May Stephenson, Raleigh; Rev. F. C. Lester, Graham; and Mr. A. E. Pye, Greensboro. This Committee will work in conjunction with the three Secretaries of Christian Endeavor in this Convention.

Now brother pastor and Mr. Superintendent, you can greatly help us in this work by writing to the undersigned, or any member of the above committee, stating definitely what you wish in this connection. If you do not have a Society in your church, tell us so and let us help you to get one organized. Immediately after my return from the International Christian Endeavor Convention, I shall place in the hands of this Committee all the information needed, for the organization of a new Society—together with a complete outline of the work. *Write to me* if I can aid you in any way.

J. VINCENT KNIGHT.

Greensboro, N. C.

NEWPORT NEWS, VA.

The work of the East End Christian church is progressing nicely. A good interest in being shown in the work and I believe that God is blessing our efforts to help further His Kingdom.

A few days ago the Senior Christian Endeavor Society gave a social at the home of Miss Minnie Cole. There were about twenty-five present and a pleasant evening was spent. Officers for the next six months were elected and $10.00 of the State Christian Endeavor pledge of $15.00 was raised and paid in cash.

The Junior Christian Endeavor has been running for nearly a month and the little folks show an interest which is fine and speaks of better things for the coming generation, if they stick to their way of doing things.

A bulletin board with movable letters has been donated to the church by Mrs. R. L. Stringfield's class of young girls who believe in working. Not long since they gave to the church a set of offering plates which were appreciated by the members. We hope to have our new bulletin board up in a few days.

Some much needed sanitary conveniences have been put in at the church thus increasing the efficiency of the plant.

We are trying to do a great work for the Lord at this place and the interest of friends is appreciated. The prayers of God's people are needed for this field as well as others, for the harvest is great but the laborers are not sufficient to meet the demand of a fast growing populace, which to a certain extent everywhere, are not as much interested in things Christian as they could be.

H. J. FLEMING.

UNCLE WELLONS MAKES A TRIP

To be missionary is supreme purpose of the Church

I started to Creedmoor, N. C., July 12, going by way of Durham. From Creedmoor I went to Good Hope in Granville County. I was met in Creedmoor by Brother Catlett who carried me to his home. Here I met many old friends. On Sunday morning I went to Good Hope, where I began preaching the second Sunday in February, 1863 and continued for fifteen years, after which I was absent for ten years and returned and served five more. A few brethren met at this church in 1847, representing the North Carolina and Virginia Conference and the Eastern Virginia Conference. They organized an association bringing these conferences together in their operations. From that association the Southern Christian Convention was finally organized, resulting in the building of Graham Christian College, afterwards Elon College.

At the close of the Civil War the church building at Good Hope was so delapidated that it became necessary to build a new one. This being just after the war, labor was scarce and the people were unaccustomed to giving to religious purposes. It caused one to have to work hard to accomplish the task of building the church. My recent visit to this church showed marked improvements. There has been an addition to the building and the inside and outside shows a neat appearance.

The agricultural conditions in the community are much improved. New buildings have been established, making the farming interests much greater than formerly. Most of the older people have passed away and their places filled by their children and grandchildren. I met some persons whom I received into the church. The service here was splendid. I administered the Sacrement to the congregation at the close of the preaching service. I spent a few days in the neighborhood with these dear friends. Brother R. P. Crumpler, the pastor, is looking forward to a great meeting there in August. This is his first year as pastor of this church.

On my return from Good Hope I passed through Morrisville where I inquired of a party as to how Brother W. G. Clements' health is at present. I was informed that he has been able to walk down town a few times, by the aid of his crutches. He is recovering from a fall that he had last year.

The trip was a delightful one and I trust that I may be permitted to have this pleasure at some future time.

J. W. WELLONS.

IS THIS THE SOLUTION?

I see that Brother Riddle is asking for some one to tell him why some recent subscribers to THE CHRISTIAN SUN, who called at his office, missed the solicitation of their pastors. I thought I would give one answer that perhaps will solve the problem.

Recently at preaching after the sermon and the announcement of the date of the coming revival, our pastor opened a bundle of CHRISTIAN SUNS saying, Brother Riddle asked him to hand them out, and if there was any one present who wished to subscribe to THE CHRISTIAN SUN he would take their subscription, and closed his remarks by saying: "I'm not selling papers though, understand, I'm looking forward to that meeting in _____."

As long as our pastors take no more interest in their Church paper than that, we will not only have sleepy churches and a small circulation of THE CHRISTIAN SUN but we as a denomination will make slow progress. A favorite maxim of *The Progressive Farmer* is, "The man who leads is the man who reads," and it is no less applicable to our churches. And it is principally up to the pastors to tell their people how badly they need their Church paper.

Now, we love our pastors and will stand behind them and hold up their hands; but please wake up to the needs and possibilities of our people and don't let our beloved Christian Church suffer for lack of knowledge when only two dollars a year will carry us forward.

ONE WHO READS AND LOVES THE CHRISTIAN SUN.

SUFFOLK LETTER

The Christian Sun is your friend

Pure religion is an unchangeable reality, but the interpretation and expression of religion change continually. Light is unchangeable, but the manifestation of light has changed many times. At one time it expressed itself through fire; at another, through grease and wicks; again through gas; and last through wires and globes. It remains for the reader to decide whether light is more universal and more useful today than it was thirty years ago. The great light is the sun and it does not change its manifestation or its quality. Religion has passed through as many forms of manifestation as light. At one time it expressed itself in dogmatic theology; at another time through the persecu-

tion of heretics; at another period through great buildings and display in worship; again it took the form of explosive emotion; the worshippers shouted aloud in meetings. Some people look to those seasons when religion expressed itself through emotion as the high tide of spirituality in the church. But it should be kept in mind that religion expresses itself in terms of the dominant idea of the age. When feeling controlled human society, religion was expressed in shouting. At the present time electricity is the dominant force in the world of power, and light expresses itself in terms of kilowatts of electricity. The dominant idea in the world today is business or its equivalent money; and religion is beginning to express itself through money. Money is the great power and religion is beginning to use it.

A glance at what the denominations are undertaking to do in the raising of money within the next five years to advance the Kingdom interests will show that religion is expressing itself through this medium. It is hardly fair to say that the church is losing its spirituality because it is expressing its faith and its purpose through a new medium. It would be a travesty on religion for a millionaire or its equivalent money, get happy, shout in meeting, and then go home. God has given him more than feeling, and the world needs blessings that money can furnish. The world needs missionaries, teachers, Bibles, medicines, doctors, and the rich man's money can help to send all these and more to the ends of the earth. See what Christian literature, hospitals, orphanages, charities have done for the ignorant, the sick, the fatherless, the destitute, and then consider what a shouting church would be worth in the Kingdom at this day. This says nothing against emotion, feeling expressing its faith and joy through a happy shout; it is trying to say that religion is not confined to any one mode of expression; but the emphasis of religious expression is determined by the dominant idea in any one generation. The world is thinking in terms of commerce, of trade, of business, and religion must enter that great idea and spiritualize it; and it can do this no better than by laying out great educational and missionary plans that require large funds and then call upon the people of God to give! give! ! To give cheerfully, liberally, religiously, and thereby win the respect of the world in its thought of great enterprises. Benefactors poured into the treasury of benevolences last year millions upon millions and that means that Christians are now giving their money as they once gave their feelings.

W. W. STALEY.

THE UNION OF THE FOLLOWERS OF CHRIST

The secret of progress of the early church lies revealed in the exclamation of the pagans: "Behold how these Christians love one another." Nowadays we have much gush about "love for humanity." It is all right to be "winning victories for humanity," but it is well to remember that it is not love for the community, or love for humanity, but love for one's fellow-Christian by which the door of the world's heart is to be opened. The teaching was plain and the early

Christians caught and understood the lesson.

The brotherhood of man, and not the brotherhood of Christians, is the doctrine which our century is ready to hear.

The air is full of talk about brotherhood. New societies are being formed. Badges are worn, grips are given, but real Christian brotherhood does not come by poetic quotations and rhapsodical orating. Brotherhood is a spiritual creation, the work of men who have been re-created in Christ. It is a fellowship of souls based upon fellowship with God's only begotten Son. The redemption of the world is carried onward by the "building of Christian hearts and lives together."

"Blest be the tie that binds."

D. A. LONG.

A WORD FROM CHAPLAIN BLACK

The man who prays is the man who pays

My dear Brethren:—Waiting for a boat in France is some task. We entered the confines of the ancient city, St. Nazaire, on June 23, having evacuated Base Hospital No. 136, Vannes; 50,000 waiting at the gate. Some nerve racking. Sunday, June 29, at 10 o'clock A. M., I talked for the Salvation Army; 300 men present. Many testimonies, many requests for prayer. At 7:30 P. M. a band concert was given in the auditorium, which seats 3,000. At the close of the concert, I spoke to 1,500 men.

My last report to Headquarters shows my meetings averaged 630. Memorial Day, I spoke to 1,800. We put lovely flowers on 105 graves; took pictures of many graves and sent to inquiring loved ones.

I was on my job from the start in 1918 until June 9, 1919, with but 48 hours leave from my work. Had hoped to get a trip to Rome, Venice, Naples and Southern France, but the sick by the Italians on the peace terms cut me out of that trip. All things come to those who wait (?).

On June 8 word came to my hospital to break up The next day found me on my way to England on my, five months overdue, leave. I took in London, saw the country by rail; went to Scotland, then back to France. From Boulogne I went to Calais, on the English Channel; then to Ypres, back to Calais; then to Lille, from there down to Amies; then to Paris.

London, Edinburg and Paris are some towns. Add to these the coast towns, Brest, Lorient, Quiberon, Vannes and St. Nazaire and Oray, and the inland towns where my work called me often, Reims, Nantes, Angers, Savanery, Tours and Le Mans and you will realize that I have seen some of France. While in Paris, I went to Versailles where the Peace Commission was in session.

President Wilson and the King and Queen of Belgium heard, I suppose, that I was to be in Ypres, so they "blew" in about 2:30 P. M. while I was looking over the once-beautiful city. I rode trains at night and "saw things" at day.

I made notes of all my traveling and have a wonderful collection of post cards and pictures. So think I have a story worth while to tell. I have planned twenty-five distinct lectures for my own Church, when I get one. You see it should be easy for me to entertain and instruct as well, as any crowd for one evening at least.

I will not make public property or merchandise out of the sea accident, which I was in, but will tell the story to my many personal friends. I feel richer in an experience that money could not buy. This experience has given me a new vision of service.

Now that I am home again, having arrived July 23, just one month from the time we broke camp, I feel that my family is due a vacation and real recreation. I hope to be in Eastern Virginia by the middle of August for a month's real joy.

Any pastor or church wishing to hear my story, drop me a line and we will arrange a get-to-gether.

I must have work. Any church needing a pastor and preacher, write me at once. Will be glad to correspond or visit you in person.

Here and now, I desire to thank our many friends for their thoughtfulness as shown in many acts of kindness to my family during my long absence. My daily prayer was that God would give them friends. He did. I am billed to speak for Dr. N. G. Newman's good people at Elon, Sunday at 11 A. M., July 27, and to Rev. J. Vincent Knight's congregation at 8 P. M., and at Franklinton, N. C., August 3.

B. F. BLACK.

Elon College, N. C.

SWEDEN TAKES IN SUFFERING CHILDREN

At the solicitation of the Swedish Red Cross, four hundred Swedish households have opened their doors to the sick and undernourished children of Germany, Austria, Belgium, Poland and the Baltic provinces. The Red Cross has entered into negotiations with the respective governments and Germany and Austria have already accepted the generous offer of their northerly neighbor. Five hundred children from those countries arrived in Stockholm May 6.

The Swedish railroads lend their heartiest co-operation to the idea, in running special boat trains to meet the children, who are accompanied to their various destinations by Red Cross representatives.

Rev. A. T. Banks, Ramseur, N. C., called by to see us the other day. He had been to Long's Chapel to assist Rev. J. F. Apple in a meeting. Owing to excessive rains, the meeting was postponed until September.

Rev. J. W. Harrell is in Rainey Hospital, Burlington, N. C., for two slight operations. He is doing nicely and will soon be out.

Hats off to President Harper and his Committee. Read his article on page seven for the *why*.

CHRISTIAN EDUCATION

$350,000 FOR CHRISTIAN EDUCATION IN THE CHRISTIAN CHURCH

Three weeks ago I predicted that when final announcement had been made concerning the unparalleled generosity of our people toward the endowment campaign for our College, every heart would rejoice and those who had sacrificed to make the grand achievement possible would shout for sheer delight. We then lacked a few thousand dollars of what our leaders felt the Church wanted the grand total to be, and so we just waited and expected and received in answer to our prayers.

I am now prepared to state that *the Church has given three hundred and fifty thousand dollars* in cash and subscriptions for the cause of Christian Education in our Brotherhood as Elon represents that hopeful guarantee of a democracy that shall be safe for the world. I am glad God has permitted me to live to see this day and to be privileged to make this announcement. I can hear in anticipation the prayers of gratitude to God that will go up from hundreds of sacrificing hearts that this great blessing has come to our College. And as the president of our College, speaking for the Trustees, the Faculty, the Alumni, and the students, I promise under the blessing of Heaven to put forth every effort to collect these pledges and to see that the money is so invested as to produce an income perpetually for the work of Christian Education in our Church. No man's usefulness to the Kingdom, who has given to this cause, shall ever perish from the earth. The fruit of his good deeds joined to the fruit of others shall through the ages ahead yield a harvest perpetually in Christian service.

I call on our people everywhere to pray for Elon, that she may be true and faithful to her great trust.

Who Made It Possible

The man who put it across is one of Elon's splendid sons, living in Tampa, Florida. After two terms at Elon, making 97 on Latin, (for which I am deeply grateful), and 90 on Bookkeeping, S. B. Denton turned his face Southward and began his work in Florida. Being a man of splendid Christian integrity, abounding energy, affable, and of sound judgment, he soon, though poor, won his way into the confidence of men of means. He is now one of Florida's most prosperous lumber manufacturers, with a direct shipping line to Cuba and the West Indies. He has connections too in Chicago, New York, and Philadelphia. I journeyed to Philadelphia to see him, and have never enjoyed a happier fellowship. His gift of $5,000 made up the magnificent total. Elon is proud of her son, and he loves Elon.

Other Funds This Week

. A business man whose name I cannot use this week, who is connected with two Alamance county churches,
volunteered to give $1,350 to put them on the map. This makes every church in Alamance county, the home of the College, a banner church. Not one of them has fallen short of its quota. How proud we are of Alamance and of this generous business man. May the Lord multiply his kind.

Dr. E. H. Bowling, one of Elon's tried and true friends, volunteered a thousand dollar gift, and Miss Helen R. Steward, our Dean of Women, did the same. Mr. T. W. Chandler, Virgilina, Va., son-in-law of Elon and loyal patron, also did likewise.

James Truitt and his Brother, W. B. Truitt, founded a fund in memory of their father, one of the pillars of strength in the First Christian church, Greensboro, N. C. To each of these and the hundreds of others who have made the $350,000 possible, we express devoted thanks and upon each and every one we pray the rich blessing of our Heavenly Father.

This is the final announcement of the Church's generosity toward Elon in this drive. May Church and College and the Kingdom be blessed in the ultimate results!　　　　　　　　W. A. HARPER.

WHY PATRONIZE ELON?

Because it is our own college and cannot exist without our support.

Because the courses of instruction are adequate to the needs of our people.

Because the members of the faculty are well equipped for their work and their instruction thorough.

Because the morals of the students are safeguarded as thoroughly as it is possible to safeguard them.

Because the expenses are as moderate as can be found anywhere else in an institution of similar grade.

Because it is our duty and privilege to support our own institutions.

Because it is co-educational, where young men and young women meet on equal footing and thus preserve the natural order of the Divine scheme.

Because Elon graduates are making good everywhere and are a safe index to the character of the college.

　　　　　　　　　　　　　　HERBERT SCHOLZ.

Macon, N. C.

COLLEGE TRAINING VS. EXPERIENCE

The passing of a boy from his father's protective care into a free man means new dangers as well as opportunities. A dreamer tears down, remodels, and refixes all that his mind is capable of doing. His success is limited to his natural ability and experience. It may take a life-time to gain what may be had in a few years from the printed page. Colleges form the best channels to the best and richest experiences. Professors are more able to help than even the printed page, and the two together form an ideal place for receiving the best instruction. The college undertakes to point out and show the young man the best things in life. The school experience is to be sought after training and not before.

Seagrove, N. C.,　　　　　　L. W. FOGLEMAN.

MISSIONARY

MY PREACHER FRIEND

A book may be as great as a battle

It is not essential for my letter that I tell you my friend's name. None of the subscribers to THE CHRISTIAN SUN have ever met him. So I shall just call him "my preacher friend" and go on with my story. I first met him early in the year of 1902 when he had just returned from America to Japan and was conducting a small independent mission in the city of Tokyo. A few weeks later he became a member of our Church and settled as pastor of one of our churches. A year later Mrs. McCord and myself were deputed to the same city as that in which he had settled, and ever since that time he and I have been yoke-fellows for Jesus Christ The purpose of my letter is to show something of the sterling qualities of our Japanese pastors, and I have chosen this friend as my illustration. I shall not tell you all about his life—it is too large and rich and full, but I shall hope to lead you into a bond of sympathy and Christian love toward our co-laborers across the sea.

He is, first of all, filled with sympathy and kindliness for every unfortunate being about him. Again and again as I have watched him I have thought of the reply which Jesus sent back to John: "The blind receive their sight, and the deaf hear; the lame walk; the lepers are cleansed; dead are raised up, and the poor have the Gospel preached unto them." For my friend and his wife, who is as tenderly in earnest about these things as he is, never deny themselves to the unfortunate. I have seen their home so filled with children from th famine district that there was not room enough to move about without stepping over the sleeping bodies that literally covered all the floors. I have seen him standing at the prison gate with a package of clothing in his arms which his wife had gathered together, waiting for a prisoner who was to be released at that time, ready to change his prison garb that he might appear as a normal citizen and have a chance to rehabilitate himself. I have seen their home the abiding place of prisoner after prisoner who had been released, until they could find work by which to maintain themselves. Indeed so good a friend to ex-prisoners has he become that on several occasions the judge of the local court has called him to the court house and bound some offender over to him instead of committing the offender to prison. I have seen him traveling dangerous mountain paths, deep hidden beneath the snow, with a pack upon his back filled with succor for the unfortunates of the mountain districts. I have stood with him in the presence of the civil authorities and heard him plead the cause of the unfortunates. I have sat with him in the sick room and listened to his gentle pleading with the Father for the sick one's comfort. And I have traveled with him over hundreds of miles of country roads and mountain paths, through mud and slush and bridgeless streams, in order to carry the Gospel message to sin-sick souls. *But I have never seen him turn away from a call of need.*

I have called him my preacher friend, and I have said nothing about a sermon, as we usually speak of sermons. But his life is a living sermon—a living picture of the love and compassion of Jesus. And one of the many rich compensations of my missionary life has been the fellowship of such a friend as this.

Dayton, Ohio. E. K. McCORD.

THIRD QUARTERLY REPORT OF W. H. AND F. MISSIONARY SOCIETIES OF E. VA. CHRISTIAN CONFERENCE

Woman's Societies

Amount sent:

Berea, Nansemond	$ 19.35
Bethlehem	7.75
Cypress Chapel	4.20
Damascus	26.77
Dendron	40.65
Franklin	24 45
Holland	6.30
Holy Neck	70.82
Liberty Springs	10.70
Memorial Temple	33.50
Mt. Carmel	9.45
Newport News	6.10
New Lebanon	4.10
Portsmouth	15.10
Rosemont	15.10
Suffolk	51.60
Third Church, Norfolk	17.44
Waverly	15.50
Wakefield	13.00
Windsor	5.95

Total $397.33

Young People

Berea, Nansemond	$ 25.75
Berkley	7.00
Bethlehem	15.35
Burton's Grove	17.00
Dendron	6.10
Portsmouth	3.00
Suffolk	82.90
Wakefield	28.70
Holland	50.00

Total $235.80

Willing Workers

Berea, Nansemond	$ 4.74
Holy Neck	6.70
Suffolk	14.53
Waverly	1.50
Franklin	1.10

Total $28.57

Grand Total

Woman's Societies	$397.33
Young People's	235.80
Willing Workers	28.57

Total $661.70

MRS. M. L. BRYANT, Treas.

THE CHRISTIAN ORPHANAGE

SUPERINTENDENT'S LETTER

Not only wear the cross but bear it

The writer had a very pleasant trip to the Sunday School and Christian Endeavor Convention held at Shallow Well church. The Convention remembered the little orphans very kindly by making a contribution of $72.92 in cash and $89.58 in subscriptions. I was delighted to have the pleasure of attending this Convention and am very grateful for the liberal contribution received.

We are glad that the Convention will meet next year at Elon College when all the members can visit the Orphanage and see our big family. We trust we will get a place on the program for the children to give an entertainment for the benefit of the Convention.

We enjoy having people to visit the Christian Orphanage. We find the more we can get people to visit us, the more interested they become in the work.

We will be glad to have the Sunday schools to bring their picnics here this summer. We will do all we can to give them a good time and will furnish cool water for the occasion.

It is a very happy occasion for the children here when a Sunday school brings its picnic here because they are very fond of chicken and cake.

Don't forget we have lots of glass fruit jars and will be glad to ship them to any one who can fill some of them.

CHAS. D. JOHNSTON, *Supt.*

REPORT FOR JULY 30, 1919

Amount brought forward, $7,640.05.

Children's Offerings

Francis Everett, 10 cents; Willie Staylor, 10 cents; Mills Wellons Staylor, 10 cents; Total, 30 cents.

Sunday School Monthly Offerings
(North Carolina Conference)

Bethlehem, $1.00; Sanford, $13.02; New Lebanon, $1.00; New Lebanon Baraca Class, $1.00; Burlington, $101.47; Christian Light, $2.64; Ebenezer, $6.07; Piney Plains, $5.60; Shiloh, $1.50; Hine's Chapel, $1.80; Shallow Well, $1.05; Christian Chapel, $4.00.

(Eastern Virginia Conference)

Young Men's Baraca Class, Holy Neck, $1.53; First Christian church, Norfolk, $14.00; Dendron, $5.71; Rosemont, $5.00.

(Virginia Valley Conference)

Hubert E. Liskey for Sunday school, $1.47; Hubert E. Liskey for Special Offering, $7.30.

(Alabama Conference)

Beulah, Ala., $1.09; Total, $176.25.

Special Offerings

Rev. and Mrs. R. G. English, $2.00; Mr. P. C. Harnish, Waynesville, Ohio, $50.00; Wellons Baraca Class, Liberty S. S., Vance, $37.50; J. H. Jones, on support of children, $30.00; Total, $119.50.

Children's Home

Sunday School and Christian Endeavor Convention, $72.92.

week, $368.97; Grand total, $8,009.02.

Dear Uncle Charley: I will send my dime for July. I hope the cousins are getting alone fine. I will be promoted to the fourth grade. I am glad school has closed. —*Mills Wellons Staylor.*

I guess you are having a good time since school has closed.—*"Uncle Charley."*

Dear Uncle Charley: I will send you my dime for July. I have some little chickens that are eight days old. I have a fine little garden. We have snaps, tomatoes, corn, beets and butter beans in it.—*Willie Staylor.*

You seem to be a good trucker. I will have to get you to come up and farm for me.—*"Uncle Charley."*

Dear Uncle Charley: I am a little late, but mother and I have been very busy. I thank you so much for the picture. I hope the little girl may be a nurse if she wants to be. Wish I could see her and all the other little girls and boys. Enclosed find my dime for July. Love to the cousins.—*Frances Everett.*

You are a good little girl to help mother. You must be good to her; you are more fortunate than many other little girls who have lost their mother.—*"Uncle Charley."*

HOW CAN PASTORS AND OTHER LEADERS HELP YOUNG PEOPLE TO FIND THEIR LIFE-WORK?

By J. Campbell White

1. *By making clear to them that God has a perfect plan for every life.* Many young people grow to maturity without realizing this. Is it any wonder that there are so many misfits and failures and so much unhappiness in view of the spirit and method in which many life-plans are made?

2. *By remembering that all young people need help in this realm.* Not only those who are to give their lives to Christian work, but also those who are to go into business or professional life need guidance. There is no other matter in which young people generally are more deeply interested than in finding their life-work. Approaching them from this vantage-point of interest, many other helpful influences can be brought to bear upon them. They can also be led in this most natural way to an understanding of many of the deepest facts and principles of life. Can anything be more important than helping young people to find what they can do best and can do with largest measure of personal development and happiness? Surely all of this is in the will of God for every life.

3. *By recalling the fact that life-choices are often made at a very early age.* Though not then made known, very many of them are arrived at between twelve and eighteen years of age. This emphasizes the great importance of bringing proper influences to bear upon young people during this period, as well as throughout the later years of preparation.

4. *By providing adequate public and private instruc-tion in the fundamental principles underlying all right choices in life, and by making very clear and emphatic the spiritual conditions under which God's guidance may be expected and secured.* This instruction should include an occasional series of sermons, systematic in-struction in the Sunday school, periodic discussion in Young People's Societies and Mission Study Classes, the circulation of carefully selected literature among young people and a vast amount of personal conference with individuals.

5. *By arranging for systematic, comprehensive and thorough processes of education upon the total task of the Church in this world of need.* These should show the wonderful opportunity for the Christian solution to be applied to all problems in our own land and among all the nations of the world, and also the way God uses individuals in expanding His Kingdom.

6. *By persuading many bright boys and girls to go forward with their education in a College with a healthy and vigorous Christian atmosphere.* This is one of the greatest services that can be rendered both to the young people themselves and to the Kingdom of Christ. One of the chief aims of Christian Colleges is to train an adequate supply of leaders for all kinds of Christian callings.

7. *By placing definite responsibility upon some care-fully selected individuals in each congregation, who will give special and sustained attention to this matter of helping young people to find God's plan and will for their life-work.* These individuals should then be brought together occasionally in District Conferences to share their best experiences with others and thus multiply the number of recruiting specialists and voca-tional counselors. The Inter-Church World Movement will arrange for such conferences.

8. *By following up carefully those who show special interest.* This may be done with suitable literature, Bible Classes, Personal Workers Groups, Mission Study Classes, and other forms of Christian education and activity, so that the interest that is once awakened may be fed and developed. Most of this follow-up work can be done by local leadership, either by the pastor or others working closely with him in these matters.

9. *By practicing the habit of prayer for laborers to be thrust out into the harvest fields, and by laying this burden of prayer upon others.*

10. *By making plain to parents the folly and sin of interfering with God's plan being realized in the lives of their children.*

11. *By promoting vital religious faith and life in the homes of the people.* This may be done in such a way that, from childhood, the young people shall be living in an atmosphere which breathes the habitual prayer: "Thy Kingdom come; Thy will be done on earth as it is in heaven."

J. H. Smiley—I enjoy reading the dear old SUN and hope that it will shine in many more homes.

THE FORWARD MOVEMENT

Headquarters 27 C. P. A. Bldg., Dayton, Ohio

You and your Church paper are partners

Prairieville, Indiana, church in the Western Indiana Conference, Rev. U. S. Johnson, pastor, responds to the Forward Movement canvass with $3,091. The church has a small membership with only seventy on the roll and the actual membership is even much smaller.

Six Mile church, near Bluffton, Indiana, Rev. J. J. Beiseigle, pastor, located in the Eel River Conference, responds with $4,275. This church has a roll of about 139 members and is located as in the Prairieville church in the open country.

Rev. D. G. Pleasant, pastor at Versailles, Ohio, sends in additional pledges to the amount of $150, making the amount from that church at this date $5,105.

In all the canvasses so far made by the Superinten-dent a committee of strong laymen has accom-panied the pastor and the Superintendent and if has been a joy to them to be in the canvass. Every committee of laymen, we believe, would be glad to go again on a similar errand for the Kingdom. We have some fine laymen in these Christian churches and our field men who represent the cause will all bear witness to the fact.

Every Conference and Convention of our people that we have heard of which is now preparing its program for its annual session is planning a Forward Movement program in harmony with the Convention's request.

The Superintendent, Rev. W. H. Denison, will be at Virginia Beach, Va., from July 29 to August 5 and mail addressed there will reach him.

The Superintendent will attend the New York East-ern Quarterly Conference at Otego, N. Y., August 8-10.

W. H. DENISON, *Supt.*

NEW COMERS TO THE SUN FAMILY

Miss Una McIntyre	Burlington, N. C.
J. D. Newman	Henderson, N. C.
Mrs. J. M. Brannon	Jonesboro, N. C.
Dr. S. T. A. Kent	Ingram, Va.
Mrs. J. G. Longest	Graham, N. C.
Ray Harden	Graham, N. C.
Robert Roberson	Graham, N. C.
Mary Ruth Johnston	Graham, N. C.
Joanna Jones	Graham, N. C.
W. H. Blanchard	Kipling, N. C.
Rogerlee Avent	Kipling, N. C.

(Record to July 26)

Have you, brother pastor, sent in the list of names of your members who *do not take* THE SUN? Get them in by August 1.

Rev. W. M. Jay, Holland, Va., sends us four new subscribers and says "more to follow."

Sarah Nall—I don't see how I could do without my church paper.

TITHE GIVING

Mrs. Lois Reed Dunn

The command is that a tenth shall be the Lord's and how few of us heed it! In the olden times, when the people lived closer to their God than our nations do today, they set aside one-tenth of all their money and one-tenth of their crops to go to the glory of the Lord. And the people prospered and were blessed accordingly.

Today, when the world is engaged in the throes of this horrible war, the people seem to be too hurried and too busy to think seriously of their duty and debt to God. The Bible tells us plainly that if we give one-tenth of our earnings we will reap our reward; and it is not as though we were calmly making the gift from ourselves, but one-tenth that we have rightfully belongs to God, and not to give it means a taking for ourselves of something that belongs to another.

You wouldn't think of calmly taking a tenth of your neighbor's corn crop and feeding it to your stock; still, when you refuse to give a tenth of your earnings to God you are stealing from Him. We should consider this tithe as an investment—one that is surer of returns than any first mortgage or stocks or bonds ever given. It is an investment for your soul and a security for your after life. The best way to teach it in the home is through the children—and if there are no children, begin with yourself.

Some people think tithe giving a bit old fashioned. It isn't old fashioned at all—it's merely a forsaken duty. Can you think of any more certain way to support your church, your mission, or your religious obligations than by a definite saving and giving of a tenth? If the passing world is too hurried to pay attention to the tithe giving custom, suppose you work out a plan of your own, and reserve a tenth for Him who has given so much to you.

THE WAR AND STEWARDSHIP

By W. H. P. Faunce, D. D., President of Brown University

The willingness to sacrifice for a brother's need, a brother forever to be unseen and unknown, the cheerful yielding to restrictions inconceivable in days of peace, is a revelation to us all. Food and light and heat, meat and sugar and coal, and a score of things that we have regarded as private property are now seen as part of the common stock of civilization, as physical means to ideal ends. The ton of coal, or the pound of sugar belongs to humanity's great storehouse; it is the possession of all liberty-loving men; and a passage in the New Testament which we have always explained away now suddenly becomes the expression of the national ideal: "Neither said any of them that aught which he possessed was his own; but they had all things common."

What changes shall come to the social order out of the universal reorganization forced by war, no man can tell. We have watched the Russian Revolution with hope and yet with fear. Those who struggle for democracy may get more of it than they want. But they cannot get more than Christianity wants. Already a change of temper, a new scale of values, has permeated civilization. Never again can we return to the old petty individualism and *laissefaire*. The new world will be newly organized. The only welcome man will be the man qualified for team-work. "Me" and "Mine" will be small words in a new world which has learned to say the great word "Our."—*From "Religion and War."*

INTERNATIONAL CHRISTIAN ENDEAVOR CONFERENCE—BUFFALO, N. C., AUGUST 5-10, 1919

Support your church first; your party second

For the first time in four years Christian Endeavor will hold one of its great gatherings for the inspiration and guidance of the aggressive, enterprising young people who are enlisted for Christ and the church.

Two years ago the Convention that was to have been held in New York was postponed on account of war conditions. This year for local reasons New York could not entertain the Convention.

The Place

When the plan for an International Christian Endeavor Conference was outlined, the Christian Endeavorers of Buffalo, N. Y., extended a unanimous and enthusiastic invitation to hold the Conference in Buffalo. The invitation was accepted by the United Society of Christian Endeavor in the same spirit, and the announcement has brought letters of heartiest approval from all parts of the United States and from Canada and foreign lands. A large and representative attendance is assured. On the border line between Canada and the States, Buffalo is an ideal place for an International Conference. The Conference headquarters will be at the spacious First Baptist Church, corner of North and North Pearl Streets, and the evening and Sunday platform meetings in the Elmwood Music Hall, one of Buffalo's largest auditoriums.

The Date

The date selected is August 5-10, 1919, in order to avoid so far as possible conflicting with State conventions and summer institutes. Buffalo by the lake is an ideal place for a Conference in August. The journey will make a fine vacation trip, including Niagara Falls and other places of interest.

The Programme

The mornings are devoted to practical conferences under expert leaders, closing with an inspirational address; the afternoons are given to business sessions of the trustees of the United Society and the field-workers, and the evenings to great platform meetings. New problems that have grown out of the world war and that are now challenging the Christian forces will be considered. Plans for our 1919-1921 Christian Endeavor campaign will be presented and adopted.

Mrs. J. L. Hall—I received the first copy of THE CHRISTIAN SUN today. I don't think I will ever let my subscription expire.

WORSHIP AND MEDITATION

SOLDIERS OF THE WOODEN CROSS

Address Delivered at the Memorial Services Held With the
305th, 306th and 307th Infantry Regiments, at Chateau
Villain, on January 5, 1919

(By Charles H. Brent, Senior Staff Chaplain of the A. E. F.)

The lips of a British war poet, before they were
hushed in death by the battle's stern lullaby, were
stung into song in an immortal sonnet:

> If I should die, think only this of me:
> There is some corner of a foreign field
> That is forever England.

Rupert Brooke here gives the keynote of the soldiers
who have earned by the supreme sacrifice the highest
and proudest of all decorations, the Wooden Cross.
Medals that adorn the uniform of courage and endurance and heroism that braved the worst for the cause.
Their wearers live to hear the acclaim of their comrades.
But there is another decoration, the commonest even
though the most distinguished—the Wooden Cross—
that is awarded only to the men who have done the
greatest thing that man—yes, even God—can do.
"Greater love hath no man than this, that he lay down
his life for his friends."

Now that "grim-visaged war has smoothed his wrinkled front," we gather to pay simple homage to our
comrades who have the supreme distinguishment of the
Wooden Cross. Yonder they lie, along that front
where, with face to the foe, they counted not their lives
dear unto themselves but bore the standard of liberty
onward. Above their graves rise the Wooden Cross—
of the roughhewn Cross than which no fitter monument
ever reared its form over mortal remains.

Our comrades they were. Our comrades they are.
Death was powerless in the face of their bold daring
to rob us of them or them of us. They are separated
now from us, not by the gaping gulf of time but by a
veil so thin that at times we almost see their figures
through its waving folds. They live—live gloriously in
the land of far distances. Death stripped them of nothing essential. In the permanent society of the world beyond this they think and speak and see and love. They
are what they were, except so far as the river of death
has washed away the dust of earth and left them cleaner
and better by reason of this, their last great adventure.
They keep pace with us and we must keep pace with
them.

> One Army of the living God,
>   To His command we bow;
> Part of the host has crossed the flood,
>   And part is crossing now.

We cannot rehearse the story of each one's going as
he went over the top to meet the foe and found his
rendezvous with death on shell-scarred slope or battered hill, or in some flaming town or maze of tangled
wire. The same dauntless spirit moved them, one and
all. There was something dearer than life. To it they
gave themselves and their all, and won the decoration
of the Wooden Cross. Here, for instance, is a chaplain
whose unstudied cry, as the finger of death touched
him, was: "Father, I thank Thee for this affliction."
Not that he courted pain as in itself a blessing, but as
an opportunity to show God and men that he was able
in all things to be a super-victor. Now it is not a
chaplain. but a doughboy that is smitten. "Buddy,"
says his comrade who holds him while his life rushes
out in a crimson flood, "Buddy, have you any message
for the folks at home?" "Yes," is the prompt reply
of the dying Galahad. "Tell them I went as clean as
I came." Again, look at that stiff, silent body, much
of the glory of its splendid manhood still lingering behind as though loath to abandon the well-knit form.
Death in him is not ugly nor repulsive. His left hand
still clutches the bosom of his shirt, which he tore aside
in order that his right hand might hold through death
his crucifix, the symbol of his faith. He, though dead,
speaketh:

> Nothing in my hand I bring,
> Simply to Thy cross I cling.

These men and a myriad more are calling to us, calling to us and bidding us to carry on. If we would still
hold to their comradeship we must display in life the
spirit they displayed in death. We must live for the
things for which they died. They "went West" beyond the sun. Soon in another sense shall we, please
God, go West— west across the sea—to that dear land,
America, that is impatient for the pressure of our feet.
We must make ourselves fit to meet, with unshamed
brow, wife, sweetheart, sister, mother. Our going may
not be to lower our sense of service and look for any
reward except opportunity to serve again and better.
Patriotism finds in war only a starting point for peace.
That which we have achieved by victory we must weave
into the fabric of the new world and the new age. The
Wooden Cross of our dead comrades is for them a
glorious decoration. For us it is the banner of our
life that is to be. It challenges us to hold more precious than mortal life ideals of honor, justice and righteousness. After all, the Cross that redeemed the world
was a wooden cross, too, was it not? It was no toy nor
pretty bauble, but a thing of nails and pain and death
—and yet a thing of glory. According to its pattern
we shape our own cross.—*In Christian Advocate, New
York.*

When you have once carefully decided that a certain
thing is right or wrong, let your decision stand as a
rule of conduct. Do not reargue the matter every time
you come to it.—*Queens' Gardens.*

A LIVE SOUVENIR FROM VERDUN

By Julian Wadsworth

Help support the Christian Orphanage

While others were bringing away with them bits of shrapnel, helmets and rusted bayonets and buttons and rags of uniforms, and in some grim instances human bones, as souvenirs of the battlefields, may I let you see one that to my mind is far more interesting? It is only a broken bit and the awful marks of warfare are fresh upon it. But it is yet alive and can be restored and again made beautiful.

I refer to a little lad whom I found; so far as I know, the only surviving member of his family. His home village, near Verdun, was completely destroyed. The lad does not even know if another one of its inhabitants remains alive.

The story of Robert Michaud is only one of many which might be told of these orphans, now being picked up all over war-ruined France and being placed in our *Foyer Retrouvee* (home recovered).

I wish you might have seen the little lad as Private Bateman, of Bakery Co. 311, found him one morning in March on the edge of the camp, alone and friendless, but for the company of a big brown dog, "Un bou camarade," the lad explained. How long the two had been together it was not known, or from whence they had come. The lad was hobbling on one leg and smiling up into the face of the American soldier in a way that wins friends wherever he goes. The dog was not so friendly, feeling his responsibility and showing such jealousy of the Americans that he could not be kept in the camp. Soon the lad had crept into the hearts of the entire company, and the lads would have been glad to keep him, but for the order from headquarters that in preparation for their movement home the camps must let all French children, dogs and other mascots go. "For a time," the captain said, "we allowed the boy to stay, by simply not seeing him. He was so unusually bright and likable." But at last little crippled Robert must be sent again into the world to make for himself a new place and other friends.

Captain West told me his story: In the summer of 1916, when he was then just past eleven, the Germans entered his village. An officer insulted his mother. The father was sick in bed. The lad managed to get a pistol and shot the officer. Whereupon others burst into the room and shielded both the father and his mother, and with an axe cut off the boy's right leg. What became of his only sister, who was seventeen, Robert does not know, as he was unconscious, and only remembers being taken in an ambulance and later finding himself

in a French hospital. After several months, with others, he was discharged and fell into the friendly hands of the A. E. F. Bakery Company at Saint Florentin. It is supposed that when this company received its orders to move, he and the big brown dog must have been left behind, for they were thus found on the edge of the Bakery Camp at Is-sur-Tille.

Having a feeling that there is exceptional promise in this boy, I was anxious to save him from another chance of being lost, and if possible get him into our Foyer Retrouvee orphanage at Charvieu.

As a secretary of the Y. M. C. A. I had an opportunity to make a four days' visit to the old battle front around Verdun. I took Robert with me, in the hope of finding some persons in the village of Posatdin who might know the fate of his sister, and if possible bring them together. But it was impossible to find a single person who had returned to the village, as yet, so completely was it demolished and the few remaining refugees scattered. Though disappointed in locating his friends, it was a pleasure to have the little fellow with me on this trip. He seemed a part of the whole scene. He "wore well" in the close companionship of the trip. From some source he had gained a refinement of manner that showed good parentage and careful training, as when, at night, without a word of comment from either of us, he quietly knelt by the bed for his evening prayer. He would also positively refuse to receive gifts of money, which was a bit unusual in a boy of his age. But having a 50-centime piece (10 cents), he bought a small book, which he read on the journey.

At length the order came for the camp at Is-sur-Tille to break up, and in due course I brought the boy to Lyons and to the Foyer Retrouvee at Charvieu.

Here we are at the Methodist home at last! I am glad I did not wait for word from the Reception Committee, for it might have been a refusal, since Robert makes the *fifty-first* child in the family and it seems now the home is full, even beyond its capacity. Being here, they will not turn him out. "Surely we will make room for another bed," they said, "and take him in, though we are so full." Mrs. Haden, the directress, is surely the person in the right place, with her long experience as a missionary in China. Her husband was lost on one of the last passenger steamers that the Germans sunk before we entered the war. She is now about to be transferred to the Methodist house at Chateau-Thierry, where she is absolutely required. At the Foyer one finds himself in the atmosphere of a Christian home, and the more he sees of this splendid plant, with its infinite possibilities, the more he is impressed with the value of the investment in the lives of these boys, made orphans by the war. I feel so thankful for the providence of God that spared the life of Robert Michaud from the hand of the enemy and that, having led out people to provide such a shelter as this for him and others like him.—*In New York Christian Advocate.*

Sunday School and Christian Endeavor

SUNDAY SCHOOL LESSON FOR AUGUST 10, 1919

Winning Others to Christ. Acts 16:9-15; James 5:19-20.

Golden Text: Ye shall be my witnesses both, in Jerusalem, and in all Judea, and in Samaria, and unto the uttermost parts of the earth.

"Where there is no vision, the people perish." Have you ever seen a vision of the needs of the world? "Oh, they are satisfied," says someone. "We concern ourselves unduly about the heathen." So were the men of Macedonia satisfied. It is noteworthy that no man, only a few women, were even praying, and Paul met no man who cried, "Come over and help us." What then? God saw their need better than they it themselves, and it was He who sent Paul, just as it is He who sends you. You owe a duty to the unconverted one of your own household; the one across the street; the neighbor down the road. But your duty does not stop there. These are your *Jerusalem* folks. But how about the *Samaritans?*—the ones who live down in the hollow; that "tough" family back in the grove; those no-count folks along the railroads? What about your *Judea* people?—those perfectly good and respectable people, who are moral, and self-righteous, and don't need to belong to church because they are better now than many of the church people. But shall you stop there? What about the "uttermost parts of the earth?" Did the disciples win all of Jerusalem and Judea and Samaria, before they went further? Nay, they even tarried too long trying to do it, and God sent, or permitted persecution to come that scattered them abroad. If our local church, our denomination, nay if our nation, does not willingly *witness* we, too, shall be scattered abroad. Will we, as did the disciples, go everywhere preaching the word?

MRS. FRED BULLOCK.

CHRISTIAN ENDEAVOR TOPIC FOR AUGUST 10, 1919

Speech Wise and Unwise. James 3:1-18.

"Behold how great a matter a little fire kindleth." This is as true of the wise as of the unwise speech.

A passing stranger's little talk with a shoeman in a store kindled a fire in the heart of D. L. Moody which set the world on fire. A little fire kindled in the heart of a ball player, and America throbs with the words of Billy Sunday. A little fire kindled in the heart of a lad who was laughed at for his club foot, and a fire of hatred grew in the heart of a man who because the South's most bitter enemy during the reconstruction period. A jeering word, turned Byron from a clean living, clean hearted boy to a hater of respectability and a hurter of himself and many others. If your heart is filled with trivial things, bitterness, or malice, those things will come out of your lips. If your heart is full of clean, high thoughts, of love of God, of purity and high resolve and love your tongue will betray that too.

MRS. FRED BULLOCK.

WHY IS THE BIBLE THE BEST SELLER?

In the special Bible number of the World Outlook, March, 1918, appeared the following concise but excellent statement by Dr. Frank Crane in answer to the question, "Why is the Bible the Best Seller?" A careful perusal of the article will strengthen the faith and fire the zeal of God's people for a more careful study of the Bible and for its dissemination throughout the world:

Why is the Bible the best seller? Because it is the most universal in its appeal—it knows no class, race, sect or cult; it is humanity's book.

It is the common reservoir from which all men draw their supplies.

It is the community power house of the spiritual world.

It is read by the white man and the negro, the Oriental and the Occidental, the proletariat and the aristocrat, the college professor and the hodcarrier, the ruddy-cheeked boy in the Sunday school and the pale and wasted old man on his dying bed.

Nobody, no group, no organization has been able to box it or fence it or own it as exclusive property.

Churches are founded upon it, rise, increase, and in time decay; theologies are constructed from its texts,

and they flourish and dissolve; it abides as the mountains abide whence flow the inexhaustible springs - of human hope.

It is a book that reaches back into gray antiquity, forward to the golden age.

It is like the great tree Yggdrasill, whose roots are in the past and whose branches wave in the sky of the future.

It contains the only program of civilization.

Its principles constitute the only practical basis of commerce; it is the cornerstone of business.

Only by its teachings can we come to the parliament of man, the federation of the world.

It is not the Jew's book, nor the Catholic's, nor the Protestant's, nor the orthodox's nor the heretic's; it is man's book; and wherever a soul is born into the world this book is for him.

It contains the rarest traditions, the noblest poetry, the most convincing preachment; it is the world's greatest literary masterpiece.

It portrays for mankind the Hero of history, the majestic, baffling alluring Jesus, rightly called Wonderful.

A myriad of Magdalenes have wept away their shame at his feet; myriad soldiers have lisped his name with their last breath upon the shotted field.

The Bible utters the soul of man. It is mysterious, as he is full of mystery. To its commands he responds with an instinctive "Amen." To its vision of holiness his heart turns, as a flower to the sun. Its appeal to conscience lays upon him a ghostly, compelling hand.

It restrains crime more than all the police. It solves more problems than all the philosophies. It wins more wars than all the armies. It promotes progress more than all the reformers. It is the terror of the oppressor, the liberator of the slave, the solace of the disillusioned, the morning star to them that overcome, and the cup of comfort to them that fall by the way.

It is the pledge and program of the millennium.

It is the secret source of the world's optimism.

And in that final hour that comes to all men, when the spirit shudders forth into the unknown, this book alone brings the word, like a bell in the fog, of Him who says: "I am the resurrection and the life."

HITS AND HAPPENINGS

Details

"Richard," said the teacher in the language class, "you may write a sentence illustrating the use of the word details."

After some study, he produced the following:

"Details of peacocks are very vain."

* *

Her Unreasonable Request

"Look here," said the indignant mistress of the house to the small peddler, "do you call these safety matches? Why they won't light at all!"

"Well, Ma'am," said the peddler snavely, "wot could you 'ave safer?"

* *

What He Lived On

It was in the poor section of the city and the school examination question was:

"On what continent do you live?"

Little Joseph wrote down his answer very carefully:

"I live on bread, coffee, and potatoes—sometimes beef."

* *

Why He Couldn't Do It

"You claim that you love me," said Gladys.

"And so I do," responded Clarence fervently.

"Do you love me enough to die for me?" she continued.

"Well, hardlly that," said Clarence, "because mine, you see, is undying love."

* *

A Proof of True Love

Little Edna one day turned to her mother, who was a widow, and said:

"Mamma, do you really and truly love me?"

"Why, of course, my dear. Why do you ask?"

"And will you prove it to me?"

"Yes, if I can."

"Then go marry the man around the corner who keeps the candy store."

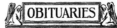

OBITUARIES

POWELL

Margarete LeVister Powell, wife of the late K. S. Powell, was laid to rest on May 25, 1919, in the family burying ground near the LeVister home. Though it was an unfavorable day there was a considerable number present at the burying. She was not a member of the church, though she had professed faith in Christ several years ago and just before her death she stated to a friend that she was ready to go. She leaves one sister and three brothers, besides a large number of more distant kin. Service was conducted by the writer.   G. J. GREEN.

WILLIAMS

Dorsey R. Williams, son of the late Martin B. Williams, Franklin County, N. C., departed this life June 8, 1919. He was born July 21, 1889. He leaves his mother and three sisters, and a host of friends and distant relatives. The writer heard, at the burying, many words of warm appreciation spoken of him by his acquaintances. The family with whom he boarded at Henderson, spoke in highest terms of his noble purpose and ideals. Evidently he was a man who formed close friendship which is an evidence of trustworthiness and large-heartedness. He was buried at Pope's Chapel Christian church where a large congregation, by their presence, showed their respect for him and their sympathy for the family.
G. J. GREEN.

ROWE

Celesta Rowe, wife of C. H. Rowe, was born June 2, 1849 and died June 26, 1919, being a few days past seventy. She leaves her husband and one daughter, another daughter having died about a year ago. The body was laid to rest in the cemetery at Mt. Gilead Christian church where she was a member. She bore a good name in her community which, we are told, is better than great riches. A large audience was present at the burial service which was conducted by Rev. Mr. Morton of Louisburg, and the writer.
G. J. GREEN.

JONES

The death angel entered the home of Mr. S. A. Jones, Raleigh, N. C., June 19, 1919, and took the soul of Edna Lee, aged

thirteen years. She was sick with pneumonia only five days. She was a true little Christian and loved by all her friends and schoolmates. She gave her heart to Jesus one year before He called her home, and was an active member of the Sunday school and B. Y. P. U. She was the oldest of three children and the pet of the family. Father and mother do not see how they can do without her but they know that God never makes a mistake and they are looking forward to that bright home where all is peace and love and there is no more separation. They have the sympathy and prayers of their many friends in this sad hour of bereavement.

MRS. J. L. HALL.

WINDOM

Thomas Windom departed this life June 27, 1919, at the ripe age of seventy-one years. Brother Windom married the widow Julia Davis Patrick about fifty years ago, who survives him, also their only child Ronnie, the wife of James Reynolds. The deceased was converted some forty years ago under the pastoral charge of Rev. W. G. Clements and joined Christian Chapel church. He ever remained a faithful member and expressed himself a few weeks before the end as being prepared and ready to meet his Savior in peace.   J. E. FRANKS.

RESOLUTION OF RESPECT—EVER-HEART

Whereas, our Heavenly Father has seen fit to take from our midst our beloved classmate and co-worker, Mrs. Ola Ever-heart, Therefore the Philathea Class of the High Point Christian church offer the following resolutions:

1. That we bow in humble submission to the will of our Father Who doeth all things well.

2. That our class has lost a faithful member, one who was always ready to lend a helping hand to all work that led to the upbuilding of her class.

3. That we offer our heartfelt sympathy and prayers to her loved ones, and ask God's richest blessings to rest upon them all.

4. That a copy of these resolutions be sent to The Christian Sun for publication, one to her bereaved family, and one spread upon the minutes of our class.

MRS. A. E. LUMSDEN,
MISS FLOSSIE MANNING,
MRS. J. W. WHITT,
Committee.

AYSCUE

Sallie Ann (Rudd) Ayscue, wife of the late Thos. L. Ayscue, was born November 10, 1848 and died July 7, 1919, being 70 years, 8 months and 27 days old. She was laid to rest by the side of her husband in the cemetery at Liberty Christian church where she had been a faithful and attentive member for a number of years. She was modestly disposed but always ready to do her part both in the home and in the community. She was married in early life and reared a large family of children, eight of whom are still living, four dead. She leaves 23 grandchildren and 5 great grandchildren. Both the community and the church have sustained a considerable loss in her death.

G. J. GREEN.

JONES

Mrs. Hattie M. Jones was born March 22, 1840 and died June 29, 1919. She was married in 1864 to Mr. Robert Beale, and to this union there was one son, Mr. R. E. Beale, Franklin, Va. Mr. Beale was killed at the battle of Spottsylvania, C. H., and in 1869 she was united in marriage to Mr. Isaac Jones. There were three Jones children, Baker, deceased; Thomas S., Norfolk, Va.; and Isaac J., Franklin, Va.

Mrs. Jones made a profession of religion at the age of thirteen, and was ever a faithful Christian. She was a charter member of Bethany church, and after Bethany discontinued services she transferred her membership to the Franklin Christian church.

She was a woman of great strength of character, and was loved by all who knew her. She was a great sufferer for many months before her death, but she bore with patience her affliction, and was resigned to the Lord's will, and wanted to go and be at rest.

The funeral services were conducted at the old home at George's Bend, by her pastor, assisted by Rev. Wm. M. Jay, Holland, Va., and the interment was in the family burying ground. A good woman has gone to her reward. The blessings of our Father be upon the loved ones.

C. H. ROWLAND.

HAND

The church at Vanceville, South Georgia, has been sorely bereaved in the death of Brother W. M. Hand, which occurred at his home, Brookfield, Ga., July 13, 1919. Funeral the following day.

Brother Hand became ill at the church two weeks prior to his death. He had gone to assist in cleaning off the church yard and improving the ground, looking forward to the revival meeting which was to have been held this week. He was much concerned about this meeting, speaking frequently to family and friends about it, but he was denied the privilege of attending, but no doubt he is attending a more glorious one in the church triumphant.

Brother Hand was more than sixty years of age. He had been married thirty-six years and had served as deacon of his church for thirty-five years. He leaves to mourn his departure a wife, nine children, two half brothers and a host of friends. His going is much lamented by his church but we bow in humble submission to our Master's will, knowing that he is able to fill the vacancy with his presence.

G. D. HUNT.

HOLMES

Priscilla Margarette Holmes was born September, 1849 and died July 17, 1919, being nearly seventy years old. She was born, and lived all her life, near Pope's Chapel Christian church of which she was for many years a consistent and faithful member. She was never married. There were ten of the family of children, she being the youngest. Two sisters and one brother still survive her. She was laid to rest in the Pope's burying ground where a large congregation met to pay their final respects, and to see the body returned to the dust, conscious that the spirit had already returned to God who gave it.

G. J. GREEN.

Democracy

A multimillionaire, as he climbed into his limousine, snarled at a newsboy:

"No, I don't want any paper! Get out."

"Well, keep your shirt on, boss," the newsboy answered. "The only difference between you and me is that you're makin' your second million, while I'm still workin' on my first."
—*Washington Post*.

Loose quarters may become lost quarters. Thrift Stamps tighten your hold on them.

It is not what you make,
It is not what you spend,
It is what you save
That counts in the end.
Buy W. S. S.

Make your money "work or fight." If it is not fighting for you in the industrial field, put it to work in War Savings Stamps.

THE CHRISTIAN SUN

"IN ESSENTIALS UNITY, IN NON-ESSENTIALS LIBERTY, IN ALL THINGS CHARITY"

C. H. STEPHENSON

Retiring President Sunday School and Christian Endeavor Convention of the North Carolina
Christian Conference. He becomes General Secretary of the work

| Volume LXXI | WEDNESDAY, AUGUST 6, 1919 | Number 32 |

BURLINGTON · · · NORTH CAROLINA

THE CHRISTIAN SUN
Founded 1844 by Rev. Daniel W. Kerr

C. B. RIDDLE   -   -   -   Editor

Entered at the Burlington, N. C. Post Office as second class matter.

Subscription Rates

One year ....$ 2.00
Six months 1.00

In Advance

Give both your old and new postoffice when asking that your address be changed.

The change of your label is your receipt for money. Written receipts sent upon request.

Many persons subscribe for friends, intending that the paper be stopped at the end of the year. If instructions are given to this effect, they will receive attention at the proper time.

Marriage and obituary notices not exceeding 150 words printed free if received within 60 days from date of event, all over this at the rate of one-half cent a word.

Original poetry not accepted for publication.

Principles of the Christian Church

(1) The Lord Jesus Christ is the only Head of the Church.
(2) Christian is a sufficient name of the Church.
(3) The Holy Bible is a sufficient rule of faith and practice.
(4) Christian character is a sufficient test of fellowship, and of church membership.
(5) The right of private judgment and the liberty of conscience is a right and a privilege that should be accorded to, and exercised by all.

EDITORIAL

ARE YOU GUILTY OF THE HABIT?

The Lutheran gives its readers a little sermon on a subject that is timely; so timely that we deem it worthy of reprinting. Here it is:

In one of our up-state towns a harpist had the instrument keyed to a perfect pitch for a special performance. A couple of meddlesome boys, at the last moment, stealthily unstrung it. The result was that when she gave the strings her most magical touch they failed to respond, except with a series of harrowing tones that set everybody's nerves on edge. And they all said, "What a failure!"

There is a parallel case, with a sequel most sad. A minister has heart and mind keyed up for the church service. He has spent an hour or two in prayer and meditation and the thoughtful study of his subject. His soul is filled with sweetest harmonies. But just before he enters the pulpit half a dozen persons thrust themselves upon his notice, each with a tale of woe. Something has gone wrong in one of the church societies; one of the neighbors hasn't acted very nice; the pastor himself has failed in one of his duties; there is

trouble in one of the homes. And the minister must know it at once; it won't keep! And so they will station themselves where he cannot escape. And then and there they will pour the unwelcome news in his ears and send him into the pulpit with unstrung nerves. His heart is heavy; his soul has lost its music; the melody has gone out of his voice, and his sermon is a series of discordant thuds, with neither spirit nor life. And, of course, he gets the blame for a lifeless pulpit performance.

The wreckage of the work of thoughtless people —people who even think they are doing God service. If there are things that the preacher should know, there are times and places when he will lend a willing ear to all complaints. But to cut all the music out of his heart just when he has tuned it to the sweetest harmonies, is a cruel performance. As a rule, there are only a few people who do it; but there are enough in every congregation to spoil every sermon, however well the pastor's spirit may be turned to present it. Dear church member, don't touch the strings of the harp when it is tuned to give forth heavenly melodies.

A MISSION FIELD

The University News Letter, a one page weekly sheet issued by the University of North Carolina, always contains some interesting things. It takes a pride in boosting North Carolina when she does deserve it; it speaks the facts. Last week *The News Letter* carried the following information that was interesting to us, and we believe will be interesting to many others:

A Home-Land Liberia

We have in North Carolina at least three liberias that call for help quite as appealingly as the Liberia across the seas in far away Africa.

Our attention has recently been called to one of these benighted areas by an inquiry from Mr. I. C. Wright of Wilmington. In hunting down the information he wanted, we ran across some astounding facts.

For instance: The negroes in seven counties of the Lower Cape Fear—Brunswick, Columbus, Duplin, New Hanover, Onslow, Pender, and Sampson—number 59 thousand in round numbers. They are a little more than one-third the total population of this area. The negroes of responsible ages, ten years old and over, are 43 thousand, and 33 thousand or 78 percent of these are not on the rolls of any colored church of any sort whatsoever.

Which is to say, seven of every nine negroes of responsible ages are members of no church. It is hard to see how the negro churches of any area could have less influence and exist at all, even in Liberia.

Arranged in the order of negro non-church membership, these counties are as follows:

	Percent
Duplin	94
Sampson	91
Columbus	85

Pender 84
Onslow 83
Brunswick 73
New Hanover 76

As we have said, the *University News Letter* gives facts let them be favorable or unfavorable. The above is a serious charge against any State. We have no reason to doubt the statement given. · It is time that something be done to better conditions in Eastern North Carolina. We used to hear of the Western North Carolina. If we have that section in good condition let us turn our faces to the shores.

The Government is making an attempt to reduce the hight cost of living. Here is every good wish to such a move.

Mexico is still giving trouble to the border sections of the United States.

Cole Blease, the whisky friend in South Carolina, is to make a race for Congress on his own initiative. His party is not backing him—and we think that it will not be long before Mr. Blease will find out that the populace will not support him.

Rev. G. D. Eastes, Raleigh, N. C., was with Dr. P. H. Fleming in a meeting at Union Ridge last week. At this time we have not been apprised with the results.

Brother J. W. Wellons came over from Elon last. Saturday and paid us a short visit. He has been busy for some time visiting his· friends and preaching. He left an article with us that will appear next week.

Rev. J. V. Knight writes: "Our church conference took up the matter of THE SUN and made arrangements whereby we might canvass the whole field for subscriptions." Good news!

At this hour (Noon Saturday) when we are forced to close the main part of the paper, we have not received the Suffolk Letter and Dr. Harper's letter on Education. We suppose that these brethren have found the waves at Virginia Beach not in accord with the wielding of their pens—and we don't blame them a bit.

Brother Chas. D. Johnston sends other new subscribers and says that he finds the work easy. Brother B. D. Jones, his champion, sends us word that he will stick to his original agreement to send eight new subscribers from Holy Neck. All right, Brother Jones, we shall look forward for their coming.

There was never a time when conditions between employer and employee were so serious. On every ·hand great strikes are being called, men wounded and killed and strife made more bitter. Something will have to be done. It ·is far from democracy. We have helped to make a democracy for the world, and now it is a democracy for home rule that we need.

Here is a little story that brings out a fine illustration: A preacher had served a church about a year and had received nothing. One Sunday morning he stated that he was in need of money clothing and food, and the church owed him and had not paid him. One old hypocritical deacon arose in reply and said, "Go on pastor, and preach the gospel; and Paul says, 'They that preach the gospel shall live of the gospel.' The Lord will give you souls for your hire.'" "Yes," said the pastor, "I know God will give me souls for my hire, and comfort my heart; but I can't eat souls. My family and my hire can't feed on souls and if we could it would take about seventy-five souls of your size to make us a breakfast." The stingy old molecule took his seat, and the brethren paid the debt. How. many of these little covetous, stingy hypocrites infest the churches, like moths that eat through the hive, destroy the honey, and kill the bees.

The school for your daughter is Elon College
Send your son to Elon College this fall

Crossing the ocean in the air seems to be practical, and no doubt regular lines of travel will be established by air crafts.

Levi P. Morton, ex-President of the United States, is critically ill at his home in New York State. He is 96 years old.

It would be interesting to know the number of names who do not take THE SUN sent in by pastors. These names, according to the agreement, are heads of families or represent one family. Several pastors have been unable to work up their list in the time alloted, and so we have notified them that the time has been extended to August 10. We trust that all will respond by that time. We shall use the names to advantage, so send them on.

A few days ago Washington experienced a .race riot. Several persons were killed and many injured. Just as the thing was about to be written as permanent history, another riot broke out in Chicago, which meant the loss of more than thirty lives and several hundred injured.

Rev. G. D. Hunt and Brother L. M. Veazey, of the church at Vanceville, Ga., send us $2.00 as a gift, or to be used as best we see fit. In almost the same mail we received a letter from a crippled girl saying that her paper would have to be stopped (some friends had donated her subscription last year) though she is fond of THE SUN. We have used the $2.00 to send THE SUN to this shut-in and know that it will meet the approval of these good hearted brethren.

Pastors will do us a favor by sending a report of their meetings shortly after they are held. Let us have the *news* while it is *news*. Then too, by reporting each meeting *now* it will not crowd us so later.

A GREAT WORLD CONFERENCE

By Larimore C. Denise

The Third World's Christian Citizenship Conference which will be held in Pittsburgh, Pa., armistice week, November 9-16, 1919, will be in every sense a world assembly and promises to do much to aid in advancing the moral welfare of mankind and in bringing to the attention of the governments of the world the necessity for basing national laws upon Christian principles.

Dr. James S. Martin, the General Superintendent of the National Reform Association, Pittsburgh, Pa., under whose auspices the Conference is to be held, has just returned from abroad where he was successful in obtaining representatives to the Third World's Christian Citizenship Conference to the number of eighty-seven from forty-seven allied and neutral countries. Of these thirty-seven, fifty-nine are government officials.

Among those definitely secured are M. Pierre Choteh, Minister of Justice and also of Public Education in Montenegro; Dr. C. Telford Erickson, Alabania; Bishop Nickolay Velemirovich, until recently ambassador of Serbia in London, England; Captain N. M. Bachman, native of Russia, and special envoy of the American peace delegation to Russia for data to be used by the peace conference; Senator Ruffini, Rome, Italy; Dr. Henry Anet, Brussels, Belgium; Bishop Stoelyn and wife, Christiansand, Norway; Dr. J. L. Pierson, Groningen, Holland; Dr. William Thomas, Vaud, Switzerland; Mr. W. J. Hanna, of Australia, for forty years a member of the Public Service Commission of New South, Wales; Paul Bellany, mayor of Nantes, Eugene Reveillaud, serving his ninth year in the French Senate, the distinguished Madame Avril de Sainte-Croix, of national and international fame, and Dr. Andre Monod, Secretary of the European Protestant Committee—all of France; Dr. and Mrs. Danjo Ebina, Tokio, Japan, both of whom are recognized leaders of the new movement in Japan in favor of industrialism, democratization and internationalism; Ping-Wen Kuo, Ph. D., Nanking, China, President of the National Higher Normal School and also chairman of the Educational Commission, consisting of twenty presidents of Chinese universities, colleges and normal schools to visit European and American educational institutions; Mrs. Theodore Cory, London, England, the distinguished writer under the cognomen, "Winifred Graham," and also a recognized authority on Mormonism; Dr. A. C. Dixon, for the past eight years pastor of the Metropolitan (Spurgeo Tabernacle church), London; Henry Peel, Liverpool, England, authority on Mormonism in Europe; Rev. Norman McLean, D. D., Edinboro, Scotland, a noted Scottish Highland orator thoroughly versed on all moral reforms and especially interested in subjects relating to the family; Joaquin Mendez, Uruguay; Policarpo Bonilla, formerly president of Honduras; Antonio Burgos, Minister Plenipotentiary to Spain from Panama and a noted international attorney, who had to do chiefly with the drafting of the constitution of Panama, and whose opinion on international law prevailed on more than one occasion in disputed questions in the peace conference in Paris;

Alexander Hume Ford, of Honolulu, editor of Mid-Pacific Magazine, and an authority on the problems of the peoples of the Pan-Pacific countries.

More than two hundred of the statesmen, Christian thinkers and moral leaders of the world were interviewed by Dr. Martin, who worked chiefly through the peace delegation at Paris. He was met cordially and assured of co-operation by practically all.

This Conference, by the blessing of God, seems destined to be a mighty factor in creating and strengthening throughout the world the Christian moral sentiment so much needed in this hour of world reconstruction. A cordial invitation is extended to all Christian laymen and ministers to attend it. Further information can be obtained from the National Reform Association, Pittsburgh, Pa.

PASTOR AND PEOPLE

THE FIRST CHRISTIAN CHURCH, WASHINGTON, D. C.

The work in Washington is organized. At a meeting Sunday, July 28, 1919, a little group of interested members of the Christian Church gathered and organized and chose the name at the head of this article.

Several weeks ago the movement was started and in the home of T. J. Lawrence, those who had been formerly members of the Christian Church in other parts of the country gathered, and held an informal meeting; since then we have met at the home of the writer, adding a few interested persons at each assemblage.

Out here in the northwestern section of the city are the homes of those who have come from different states of the Union to work for the Government and to make their homes in the National City. Perhaps there is nowhere a more cosmopolitan assemblage, Americans all, with the interests and hopes and aspirations of their government constantly before them, with the spirit of America, with the outlook for a bigger and better, and more enlightened nation, in the making of which they are a part.

They want their children to learn something of the principles of Christian living, they themselves want to take positions of responsibility where they can serve their fellowman. They come from all denominations, from all methods and forms of doctrine and belief, and we think because of the absolute freedom to worship God according to the dictates of their conscience they will come to the Christian Church, they will respond to the invitation to cast in their lot with us, their opportunity to work for the cause they love will be at hand and they will embrace it.

The prospects for a church in this section are very good. It is seven squares from the location selected to the nearest church, and the streets are all built up solid in every direction. It is not some outlying district in the woods, but on the main artery of travel from the city to the suburbs, the homes around sell from seven thousand upwards and all the occupants of these houses own them, so they will be permanent, and once-reached will become a stronghold for the development of the church here. The city is growing very rapidly, there is a new section opening immediately adjoining the location of our church, so when it is completed we will be entirely surrounded with the finest homes and the finest people America can produce.

Many of you have friends in this city. Perhaps some of them would be interested to come and unite with us. All the urging necessary might be a line from you to your friends, or if you will send me the name and address we will see what they think about the matter.

When you come to Washington, come out to see us.

At the meeting last Sunday the following officers were elected to take office until the first of October, when we hope to effect a permanent organization:

President, L. R. Townsend; Executive Secretary-Treasurer, Irving W. Hitchcock; Trustees, T. J. Lawrence, R. Lee Klapp, Mrs. Bessie Staley Cheatham; President of Christian Endeavor, Miss Virginia Lawrence.

Those in attendance were: Mr. L. R. Townsend, Mr. R. Lee Klapp, Mr. T. J. Lawrence, Mrs. Lawrence, Miss Virginia Lawrence, Miss Lois Lawrence, Miss Nina Clendenin, Mrs. Bessie Staley Cheatham, Mrs. Hitchcock, Miss Virginia Hitchcock, and the writer.

Miss Clendenin took the minutes of the meeting. A very helpful prayer meeting was held in which most everyone took part, Miss Lawrence and Mr. Townsend favoring with musical selections.

　　　　　　　　　　　IRVING W. HITCHCOCK.

Washington, D. C.
　801 Allison Street.

MISSIONARY

ELON CRADLE ROLL ENTERTAINED

The babies of the Missionary Cradle Roll and their mothers enjoyed a delightful afternoon Friday evening, July 24, when the Superintendent, Mrs. N. G. Newman, entertained them at her home. After a splendid program by the little tots the mite boxes were opened and it was found they contained $8.58. Out of the twenty-six babies enrolled, twenty-three were present, when the program was over and the mite boxes opened.

Mrs. Newman, assisted by her daughters, Blanche and Marion Lee, served delicious ice course to the babies and their mothers. Mrs. Newman is doing splendid work with the Cradle Roll.

　　　　　　　　　　　MRS. W. A. HARPER.

THE BIG AND THE LITTLE PUSHES

The historian Greene says, "The world is not so much advanced by the gigantic pushes of its mighty heroes as by the little pushes of the multitude of lesser folk." I wonder if that principle is true and will hold? If so, the little pushes of the multitude are needed, and must be made to count now. The heroes on the field of blood and death have made some gigantic pushes lately. Millions of brave men have gone to their graves in the carnage of battle, and billions of money have been consumed in a mighty attempt at world-advancement. Shall we measure up to this gigantic push? Or shall

the fruits of a great victory be taken from us? Unless we are now brave for the bigger battle, that battle for morality and spirituality, we shall not be worthy of our boys and brothers who have died before their day "to make the world safe for democracy."

INCREASING THE PASTOR'S SALARY

I have one sure and safe remedy for increasing every pastor's salary in the Christian Church. It is the same remedy that Bishop Phillips Brooks gave the poor country pastor with a meager salary and a big church debt years ago. Mrs. Cronk gives it from a pastor who applied the remedy and tells about it in his own words: "I know of one small congregation in a cotton mill suburb of a Southern city. The members had been given little missionary information. The pastor's salary was far below the 'living wage,' and it was necessary for him to supplement it in many ways. It seemed very evident to the non-missionary contingent that charity should begin at home. However, home charity persistently delayed its beginning until a missionary campaign was begun in the church, during which literature was distributed, addresses were made, and an Every Member Canvass was conducted. The missionary offerings were increased from $39.66 to $183.00 and with the broader outlook the congregation saw their pastor's work in a new light and increased his salary 66 per cent."

When a pastor and his people catch the missionary vision something always happens, and things worth while take place for the Kingdom.

　　　　　　　　　　　J. O. ATKINSON.

BECOMES INTERESTED IN MISSIONS

I have been a member of the church for twenty-nine years and regret to say that I have never been interested in missions and have never contributed to the cause but very little until recently.

I was awakened to the need of this work by a sermon which I heard in a neighboring church last Easter. It was one that I shall never forget. Never before did I realize what missions really meant. A picture was drawn in words by the minister in which he pointed out how the mothers would look into the faces of their little ones and see them die without hope in their hearts of ever seeing these dear ones again. They could not teach their children about Jesus because they themselves did not know of Him, and of how He died for them to make it possible for them to be with their loved ones again. Oh, the pity of it! It makes my heart ache for them for they do not have the comfort and help that Christ can give to sorrowing hearts, especially when a dear child is taken.

I have often been bereaved and I do not feel that I could bear it without God's help. Dear Christian mothers of America, let us lift our hearts to God in prayer and thankfulness that we live in a Christian land and can teach our own children about Jesus and can contribute of our means to help those in foreign lands learn of Jesus and His great love to his followers

I am poor and cannot give much but I made a solemn

promise to God the day I heard that sermon that I would from that time give all that I possibly could. I have made a few small offerings and have been happier for the last few months than ever before for having done so. Imagine what this world would be without Christ and we can sympathize with our friends in foreign lands. I sometimes wonder if each of us will be held responsible for some poor soul that we could have helped to have some knowledge of Jesus. I pray that God will cause us all to feel our responsibility and that we may help more than we ever have in spreading the Gospel to the heathen lands. I trust that these few lines may cause somebody to make a liberal offering for foreign missions and I would feel that at last I had done something for my Savior.

MRS. J. L. HALL.

News Ferry, Va.

CHRISTIAN EDUCATION

OUR YOUNG PEOPLE—THEIR DECISION

Many an American youth will be concerned with serious thoughts as the hot days become fewer and the finger of father time points to the approach of autumn. Each year this season means a crisis to many boys and girls. This is a time when a choice must be made as to whether or not "Will" or "Annie" will enter college. Thousands are going to make their decision in favor of the negative, and as a result will not make of themselves the men and women that otherwise they might have been. Later in life they will see their mistake when too late, and would gladly give all their fortunes for a college course.

Among the many who decide this question in the affirmative and go to college, a question more serious will confront their mind. "To what college shall I go?" This question is as serious as any that occupies the mind of parent or child. The mere studying text books and reciting lessons is not education. When time and money are to be spent for education the individual should be wise enough to select an institution that will help him in his preparation for two worlds. The youth who prepares for this life only is unwise. The average life here is less than fifty years. The college or institution that fails to throw about its students the pure and wholesome atmosphere of Christian character is a failure. "The wisdom of this world is foolishness with God." "Education can furnish you headlight but only the grace of God can help you make steam." Greece of old, believed in education, Rome believed in law, and the Germans are the best (worldy) educated people of our day, but unless Christ is connected to the word educate, and made a part of the life of the individual seeking knowledge, the end will be like Solomon tells us that "Vanity of vanities, saith the preacher all is vanity."

If there is a young person, who, by chance, should read these lines, I want to recommend an institution that stands *greatest* in the preparation of young people for this life and another. That institution is Elon College. The reason she has had 29 years of such

illuminating success, and that her sons and daughters everywhere are in such demand, is that Godly men and women are keeping that college saturated with an influence that is found only through prayer and humility.

B. J. EARP.

AN IDEAL COLLEGE

1. It should be co-educational for the best symmetrical development of the young of both sexes.

2. In location it should be insular. A small city with modern conveniences and without modern vices is to be preferred for the sake of the community life and interest among the students.

3. Its numbers should not exceed three hundred to five hundred students, making possible democratic conditions and intimate acquaintance between faculty and students.

4. Its faculty must be men of scholarly training, with a teaching instinct, and with distinctly Christian character.

5. Its curriculum should combine the time-tried cultural courses in language, literature, history, mathematics, and philosophy, with a thoroughly modern study of the fundamental elementary science. A temperate indulgence in electives should allow for individual taste and intellectual capacity.

6. Its social life should be simple and democratically American, void of snob-breeding cliques, extravagant functions, and silly dissipations.

7. Its physical training should provide for the largest number of students. Its athletics should be sanely regulated and free from even the suspicion of trickery or professionalism.

8. Its literary spirit and religious atmosphere should permeate the entire range of student activities.

9. Its physical plant should be modern and complete in every detail with well-equipped laboratories, with well-selected library, with complete gymnasium, furnished with all modern apparatus, for the development of the physical man, with attractive class rooms and beautiful campus.—*Western Christian Advocate.*

HEALTH CERTIFICATES FOR TEACHERS

Every teacher in North Carolina schools this year must hold a certificate from a reputable physician stating that he or she has not an open or active infectious stage of tuberculosis, or any other contagious disease. This is in accordance with an act of the General Assembly of 1919 that was fathered by Representative Turner of Mitchell county. The law provides that the teacher must secure such certificate each year before assuming his or her duties, the examination to be made without charge by the county physician.

Congress is not to have a recess now as planned some weeks ago. Too many problems to be solved and settled to take a vacation, thinks President Wilson.

INSPECTING HOTELS

In the endeavor to better safeguard the health of summer vacationists inspectors of the North Carolina State Board of Health this week are making official inspections of resort hotels in the western portion of the State. The effort will be made to reach all points in the mountains, and to carefully examine all places catering to summer tourists.

MISS BEATRICE MASON TO WED

Many SUN readers, and especially many former Elon students, will be interested in the following invitation:

Mr. and Mrs. Henry Columbus Mason request the honor of your presence at the marriage of their daughter, Charlotte Beatrice, to Mr. Samuel Rufus Gay, on Wednesday evening, August the twentieth, Nineteen hundred and nineteen, at nine-thirty o'clock, Methodist Episcopal church, Nashville, North Carolina.

At home after September first, Cumberland, Maryland.

CHILDREN OF THE ORPHANAGE TO ENTERTAIN

The children of the Christian Orphanage have prepared a special play and will render it at Haw River, Dixie Theatre, Wednesday night, August 6; Graham, Thursday night, August 7; Burlington, Municipal Theatre, Friday night, August 8. The Graham date has not been definitely settled at this time (Monday morning) but the date given is very likely.

NEW COMERS TO THE SUN FAMILY

Rural Hedgebeth ....Holland Va.
Mrs. F. D. Carr ....Holland, Va.
Mrs. G. E. Worrell ....Holland, Va.
Sarah A Hedgebeth ....Holland, Va.
Luta Harden ....Graham, N. C.
W. A. Johnson ....Fayetteville, N. C.
Mrs. John A. Dillion ....Rush, N. Y.
Irving W. Hitchcock ....Washington, D. C.
Laura Green ....Lillington, N. C.

(Report to August 2)

Supt. Denison of the Forward Movement, says: "Dr. I. W. Johnson, Suffolk, Va., has a pastorate of four churches which he has served successfully for years. The membership of these churches is about 625. These churches of this pastorate are undertaking to give for benevolent purposes for the next five years $5,600 per year or $28,000 for the five years. That is giving several times "as much for others as for ourselves." We congratulate pastor and people on this splendid Forward Movement financial program. We are anxious to hear from other churches and their programs of giving and of work. We have felt for some time that our people would do worth-while things and they are proving it."

The railroad companies are suffering much on account of strikes among their shop workers throughout the country. They are asking for a raise in their wages. Many of the workmen are receiving 68 cents an hour, but demand 85 cents.

WE MUST DOUBLE TEACHERS' AND PREACHERS' SALARIES

(The Progressive Farmer)

There is not much hope for developing a really satisfactory rural civilization in our time unless we actually double teachers' and preachers' salaries.

We say double and we mean what we say. Little piddling advances will not suffice. We might as well face the fact that these salaries must be actually doubled—and the communities that get and keep the best teachers and preachers will be those that have the grit and grace to act first in this matter. And these, too, will be the neighborhoods which will most easily attract settlers and laborers and renters, and where land values will advance most. People worth while will go where they find good schools and churches, good teachers and live preachers. And people will move away from communities where their children must go to school to scrub teachers and where churches and other civilizing agencies are most poorly supported.

In every part of the South our farmers are better able to support school and church than ever before. Yet, as a matter of fact, the average farmer is not giving as much support to these agencies, if reckoned in quantities of cotton, tobacco, peanuts or pork, as he gave ten years ago. We could easily double our present contributions and not feel it, so small is the percentage of total earnings that we now spend for school and church.

In this connection, too, we should like to urge that every man who owns land in a community no matter whether he lives there or not, should be asked to give something for the support of the neighboring church as well as the neighboring school. Even if a landowner thinks of everything in terms of dollars and cents, a contribution to church or school is still worth while. If these agencies of civilization are not properly supported in a community, land values as quickly as anything else, feel the depressing effects.

THE SUN'S Editor will be at Mt. Zion next Sunday to supply for pastor, Rev. J. F. Apple.

We were glad to see Brother J. M. Lambeth of Reidsville in our town the other day.

Dr. P. H. Fleming reports a successful revival at Union. Many additions to the church.

Fan, keep cool and watch your label.

President's Annual Address

C. H. STEPHENSON

Before the Sunday School and Christian Endeavor Convention of the North Carolina Christian Conference

July 16, 1919

THEME: LEAGUE

My friends, since last we met in a Sunday School and Christian Endeavor Convention vast changes have been wrought in the world. A year ago today the world was anxious and troubled—torn by the strain of a terrible war. Today this strain has been lifted, and we are privileged, my friends, to live once more in a world of peace.

At a heavy sacrifice of manhood and wealth we have throttled a criminal nation, which in 1914 got loose in the world, and threatened to scotch forever the wheels of progress—until America intervened. And now the nations who made the fight have felt that it was not enough to overcome this enemy of justice. They have foreseen a need for a common arrangement whereby it will forever be impossible again to commit against the people of the earth such a crime as was attempted by the rulers of the German nation. And so a League of Nations has been formed by the Big Four,—has been ratified by Germany and is now pending the action of the United States,—which puts right, and not material force in command of the future.

And these great world movements, since last we met in this Convention, have not been without their effect in the Church, Christian Endeavor Society, and the Sunday School. These organizations have sent their representatives through the Y. M. C. A., K. of C. and kindred organizations into the thick of the fight where they have found a more vital, active Christianity than we have known before.

And in my analysis of this new awakening in the Sunday school, I have chosen the word LEAGUE as a central theme. Today is a day of leaguing the forces of progress together to assure a better future. There is a movement on foot in this country and in England, to establish a World Church Union which shall extend its organization over all the civilized world. The denominations of America have many times been unusually active during the last few months in the attempt to league up their scattered units in a more centralized Church system. And in this state the same tendency was manifested when the Christian denomination consolidated the Conventions of the North Carolina and Virginia Conference, the Western North Carolina Conference and the Eastern North Carolina Conference into this first State Sunday School and Christian Endeavor Convention. But the tendency to league together all our agencies of right has but begun. It falls our lot to extend it so that Sunday schools and Christian Endeavor Societies not only in every county, but in every community in North Carolina shall be leagued up for the new work that lies ahead of us.

And as the letter L stands for the "League" that we must extend to every community where Christ is worshipped; so the second letter of our theme word stands for "Earnestness" which is the first step toward bringing it about. Earnestness has to do with attitude. And you will agree that the way we go about anything, such as planting a crop, or running a business, largely determines its success. We must have serious intentions before we can raise a good crop, or establish a good business. Just so in the Sunday school,—what we need first of all is seriousness of purpose. This serious, determined attitude as suggested by the second letter of the word league, is but another name for "Earnestness."

Earnestness has been the keystone to all the great world movements of the past. Before our time many treaties and alliances were drawn up between peoples, but none ever proved strong enough to absolutely prevent war. Today the major nations in the world family; after being driven to it by the pain of war, have set about the task with such unprecedented earnestness that it has been a success, and we trust that it is to last for all time. Then will you not take a lesson from this fact, and carry away with you a renewed spirit of Earnestness for the Sunday School and Christian Endeavor work, you are doing in your respective communities?

As I have said, earnestness for the right is the strongest single current in the world today; but it has not yet completely won. For there is loose in the world a spirit which is the opposite of earnestness. In government it has cropped out in bomb plots, in politics its expression is the I. W. W. and Bolsheviki element, in the Sunday school it takes the form of sectarian emphasis and factional wrangle. Members of this Convention: we have failed if we drive the Hun out of Europe, and do not drive his spirit out of our schools and lives. In the many distractions that flourish in the post-war relaxation of our day, it will be easy enough to swerve from the straight and narrow path, if we do not first fortify our Sunday schools, our Christian Endeavor Societies, and our individual lives with sufficient earnestness to withstand any attack.

You Superintendents, have you not too often let personal inconveniences, and petty obstacles keep you from your obvious duty,—just because you were not earnest enough for the welfare of your school? And, you delegates, how many times have you missed Sunday school, or failed to meet a Christian Endeavor obligation, all because you were not charged with enough of the spirit —I call Earnestness? Then let us take from this Convention, first of all, earnestness of purpose for our individual task, whatever or wherever it may be.

But my friends, we need more than earnestness. We have many times resolved on New Year's day to do things that never materialized. Righteous intentions merely, avail nothing if they are not followed with prompt execution. And so my second step toward a new league in the Sunday school, as suggested by the third letter of the word "League" is: Action. We may be serious about our Sunday school and Christian Endeavor work. We may have a definite purpose in view, but unless this purpose be translated into carrying it out, and seeing it through, we might as well never have purposed at all.

One of the most permanent lessons of the war has been the development of a new active religion by Christian workers, who have carried their standards through an actual "baptism of fire." And you will find no finer illustration of this than the activity of the Salvation Army. Under the gruelling test of war, it demonstrated that religion is an active thing, springing from God, whether expressed in sermons and hymns in our churches or coffee and doughnuts for our soldiers on the battle fields of France. And this was possible because these Christian workers, rising above sectarianism, were guided solely by the light of active service. Delegates of this Convention, look for the light yourselves! Our boys who fought in France felt the power of a more vitally active religion than they had known before. This it was that increased, more than anything else, their love and respect for Jesus Christ. The support of religion by the young manhood of this nation is stronger today than it ever was before, and it rests with us, you and me, my friends, to keep it so. And this is best done by putting our young manhood to work. The business world has urged its men to create jobs for returning soldiers, not merely meaningless clerkships, but real jobs, which are the direct result of business expansion. How much more necessary is it that you superintendents, officers and teachers create jobs for returning soldiers in the Sunday school. A soldier is the most active of individuals, and once you have him in action, you will find that he is not only a good worker, but will bring other men to work for Christ. And I want especially, to emphasize the need of reaching the young people. It was the late Theodore Roosevelt who said: "If you are going to do anything permanent for the average man, you have got to begin before he is a man." The chance of success lies in working with the boy, and not the man. Therefore we must spread the activity of our school to include, and utilize all young people, if we would hold them to the highest standard of Christian respect, and allegiance.

But in religious activity, tremendously increased by the stress of war, and now, I hope, maintained by home service, we must never forget to temper our every act with God—my fourth step toward a new league in the Sunday school. The old adage "Trust in God and keep your powder dry" is just as true now as it ever was. In war however, with its accompanying rush and strain, the tendency was to put more emphasis on keeping the powder dry than trusting in God. Still it was the grace of God that brought us victory. It is the grace of God that has brought good crops, and material prosperity. It is the grace of God that has given us life.

Careful investigation has revealed the fact, that there are in the South today something over four million young people between the ages of ten and twenty, who are not identified with God through any Church, Sunday school or Christian Endeavor Society. And yet the church of tomorrow walks in the boys and girls of today, and never before were the conditions for spreading God's influence so propitious as now. Then let us

realize the immediate seriousness of the task before us. The late Edward K. Graham, while President of the University of North Carolina, said: "One great lesson, bitterly hard to learn, but holding the infinite secret of individual and national freedom that we seek, and the great lesson that we learn, is that these streets and stores, fields and banks, factories, school houses, churches and all the rest, are but folds across the face of God," and that Thy will for which we daily pray will be done here and now, or nowhere; and that banking, agriculture, education, freedom, and life itself, are but instruments for finding the common God in the common good, and making through our daily task, His will prevail. God is love, and Jesus Christ was the great Lover. His life shows how self-forgetful, and self-giving one becomes who gives supremacy to God. "Give my love to the world" gasped dying Whittier, who had loved so wisely and so well, that nothing less than the whole world could measure his love's breadth. Then let us not try to build a class, a Christian Endeavor Society, or a Sunday school without God as a serious member of the firm. His resources are infinite—His security is perfect. No human corporation can exclude God and hope to compete for honor in the stock market of Heaven: Listen to the words of the sainted Paul, "For every house is builded by some man, but He that built all things is God."

But after we have earnestly set about with a more active Christianity, to serve God more acceptably we still need to co-ordinate our forces so as to bring them together in a more perfect unity. And by "union" I mean co-ordination. It has been a great fault, not only with our Sunday schools of the past, but with all religious organizations that they inclined too much to carry on their work as separate units; busy among themselves, but having no relation to their sister organizations engaged in similar work. The result is that Christian work has progressed more in some communities than in others according to the effort put forth. The same practice obtained in industry and business before the war, but unusual needs and demands forced business men and government officials to see the necessity of correlating their activity, so as to allow the many to profit by the lessons of the few.

And now in the Sunday schools of the South we are working for precisely the same thing. It is indeed the master purpose of this Convention, namely, so to unite our schools and societies in every part of the State, that they will all profit by the ingenuity of the leaders, so that they will co-operate in the transfer of members who are changing their address, so that they will exchange ideas and experiences, for the mutual benefit of all concerned. For once this correlated union is set up throughout the bounds of the Convention, our Eastern Sunday schools and Societies may have the benefit of new ideas and schemes that originate in the West, and vica versa. In this manner, new methods such as vocational Sunday school classes, special day features, and the solving of reconstruction problems, will rapidly spread to all of our schools and Societies, wherever they may have sprung up. This alone, my friends, is enough to impel us to a stronger centralized union, and especially since this Convention has extended its organization to cover the entire State.

And now, finally, my friends, as the first five points of my theme word have had to do with achieving a new league in the Sunday school and Christian Endeavor Society, just so, the last is the reward that follows, once it is achieved. If you only league your Christian forces under the banner of Earnestness, Action, God and Union, then yours is the final glory that rewards every good fight, Eternity,—The Home of The Soul. Be thou, not faithful alone unto death,—but earnest, active, God-like and united, and thou shalt receive the Crown of Life. And how glorious it is to feel that our efforts are not in vain, that our hardships are not without their reward. Without the hope of Eternity, mankind could not persevere the trials of life. Without faith in Eternity he could not persist in the world. Then let us turn our faces toward the beacon light of Eternity as we work. And, in the confidence of eternal life, let us so charge our Sunday schools and Christian Endeavor Societies all over the State, with such Earnestness, Activity, Godliness, and Unity that they will continue to grow, to flourish and accomplish good, so long as God shall rule the minds, and hearts, and deeds of men.

THE CHRISTIAN ORPHANAGE

WHAT THE CHURCHES ARE DOING

Sometimes it puts us to thinking to know just what we are really doing. So in this letter I want to give you a list of the Conferences with the number of Sunday schools giving toward the support of the Christian Orphanage. I am making this list from the Conferences as they were arranged last year:

Name of Conference	No. Churches	Gave Easter Offering	Gave Month- ly Offerings	Do Not give
Valley Va. Central ..	26	16	10	16
Alabama	24	9	4	20
N. C. and Va.	35	32	21	14
Eastern Virginia	41	26	27	14
Western N. C.	38	18	18	20
Eastern N. C.	45	32	27	18
Ga. and Ala.	14	6	6	8
Total	223	139	113	110

You see from the above list that we have 223 churches. 139 churches gave an Easter Offering. 113 are making the monthly offering. 110 out of the 233 churches have not made an offering this year.

Now my dear friends, if you are a member of one of the 110 churches that are not doing anything toward the support of our little orphans who are crying to you for help, do you feel down in your heart that you have done your full duty? If you have just, rest easy. If you do not, then don't you think it is time to get busy and see that your church gets a little more life in it, that your Sunday school gets more enthusiasm in it and that

you begin to render some service for the Master's Kingdom? We need your sympathy. We need your prayers. Your sympathy and your prayers are all right so far as they are backed up with your works. But suppose you pray for us the balance of your life and give us your warmest sympathy and never give a penny toward helping to feed and clothe a little child in the Institution, then pray tell me how much you have helped in this great work? The Bible teaches us that faith without works is dead.

We have in the Southern Christian Convention 139 churches that have stood by us loyally as can be and we have a warm place in our hearts for them and only wish we could visit each one and express to them our appreciation in words. Now we have a very great love for the 110 that have not helped us this year. We wish we could visit each one of these churches and tell them of our great need. The golden opportunity they are losing in not lending us a helping hand; of the great pleasure they are denying the little boys and girls in their schools by not giving them an opportunity to give something toward the support of the little children who have been so unfortunate as to lose father and mother. And they will give their nickels and dimes toward the support of the work if they are given the opportunity. I have mailed a letter to all churches not now on my list of monthly contributors asking them to make an offering and get on the list at once. I am real anxious that each church shall have a part.

CHAS. D. JOHNSTON, *Supt.*

REPORT FOR AUGUST 6, 1919

Amount brought forward, $8,009.02.

Children's Offerings

Ethlene Strader Belew Creek, N. C., 10 cents.

Sunday School Monthly Offerings

(North Carolina Conference)

Fuller's Chapel, $8.00; Morrisville, $2.00; Grace's Chapel, $3.00; Mt. Auburn, $12.66; Asheboro, $2.37; High Point, $2.60; Pope's Chapel, $1.80; Henderson, $6.77.

(Eastern Virginia Conference)

Union (Southampton), $2.50; Antioch, $2.00; Ivor, $1.89; Spring Hill, $2.66; Holy Neck, $3.60.

(Virginia Valley Central Conference)

Bethlehem, $4.58.

(Alabama Conference)

Wadley, Ala., $1.59; Wadley, Ala., $1.90; Total, $59.92.

Special Offerings

First Christian Sunday school, Rush, N. Y., $10.00; Dr. T. Edwin Baird, Norfolk, Va., $30.00; Ladies' Aid Society, Eure's Christian church, $5.00; Washington Grove Christian church, Ashton, Ill., $5.00; American Christian Convention Office, $12.50; Allie L. Thompson, Haw River, N. C., $5.00; Chas. M. Gant, Graham, N. C., $6.00; Total, $73.50.

Total for the week, $133.52; Grand total, $8,142.54.

A LETTER

Dear Uncle Charley:—I am late in sending my dime for this month, but hope that it will get there in time. I have been so busy that I have not had time to write. Hope you and the children are well.—*Ethelene Strader.*

Glad to have your letter this week—the only one to brighten the corner.—"*Uncle Charley.*"

TEN MISSING PRESIDENTS

Fill the spaces with names of ex-Presidents:

Before the summer sun begins to————the
  morning —————,
The camp cook lights the breakfast fire and cooks
  above the blaze.
And when with shout and poke he calls the boys their
  fast to break,
He finds how ————— of earth can be when
  half awake.
No more sleep can he ————— boys, for night is
  growing paler;
Soon dandy Dick is neatly dressed, a credit to his
  —————,
They sit on carpet gree, more fair than —————
  hardwood floor;
And, as when good King ————— ruled, much
  food should be in store.
They —————plates with flapjacks hot, and
  sausage, ————— link,
And when the coffee brown gives out, there's—————
  ————ale to drink.

—*The Continent.*

A CURE FOR SLANG
By Flora Huntley

The boy, a lad of ten, was quick to learn and particularly good in "language," as his report card showed. His vocabulary was not so choice as varied, and the slang of the street was irresistible.

"By heck, I'm cold!" he would exclaim as he came in, and at a request from his mother would inquire, "Who do you think I am?"

She explained to him that these phrases were not used by well-educated people, but he was unconvinced.

"All the fellows talk that way, but I can cut it out if you say so."

But he continued to use the expressions; and, while his mother did not wish to "nag," she felt that she ought to show in some way that she disapproved and that the language was undesirable, even though it was not profane.

One evening, as she was reading aloud from Swiss Family Robinson and noting its formal, precise sentences, a sudden thought came to her. She acted on it instantly, and continued to read.

"'It seems absolutely necessary, my dear wife,' I began, 'to return at once to the wreck while it is yet calm, that we may save the poor animals left there, and bring on shore many articles of infinite value to us. which, if we do not now recover, by heck, we may finally lose entirely. On the other hand, I feel there is an immense deal to be done on shore, and that I ought not to leave you in such an insecure shelter as this tent.' "

The boy raised his eyes in startled surprise, but the mother continued her reading:

"'Cut it out. Return to the wreck by all means,' replied my wife, cheerfully. 'Who do you think I am? Patience, order and perseverance will help us through all our work, by heck; and I agree with you that a visit to the wreck is without doubt our first duty. Come, let us wake the children and set to work without delay.' "

The boy's face was red with embarrassment, which changed to anger as his sister giggled.

"That isn't there," declared, rather impatiently, but the mother continued her reading, with no comment at all, but she inserted no more slang. She had shown him for once just how the words sounded to her.

He sulked a little during the evening, but was himself at breakfast. And, when his mother asked whether he wished another dish of oatmeal, he cried, "Yes, it's good, by —Yes, mother." He did not overcome the habit at once, but he had become conscious of how the words sounded and in time he succeeded. His mother saw he was trying, and they never spoke of that peculiar page in Swiss Family Robinson.—*Christian Endeavor World.*

LIGHTNING CALCULATION

The following "short cut" in addition is much used by expert accountants and auditors, also by bank and insurance clerks. The following example practically explains itself:

```
          6,487,35
          3,514,62
          2,398,27
          7,143,65
          8,343,79
          1,085,64
          2,007,39
          4,586,72
          5,888,27
          9,847,23

         51,302,93
               53
               44
               58
               54
               37
               47

         51,302,93
```

Instead of "carrying" from one column to another, set down the sum of each column by itself, as shown above. The sum of these smaller amounts will be the total of the whole. The recommendation of this method, where one has to work rapidly, is that if the figurer's attention is distracted in any way, thus causing an error, only the column then being added would be affected, and the mistake could be corrected in a fraction of time.—*The Presbyterian.*

WORSHIP AND MEDITATION

FAMILY ALTAR

We can never be in error in giving our children their religious training at the family altar. We may not, as families, be able to spend as much time together in the sacred work as might be desirable, but we can at least habituate the young people to the practice of recognizing the Lord's hand in all the details of life. Seldom will a boy or girl forget or reject the principles of God's Word as taught at the altar of the hearth.

A young British officer now on service in France, where he has been for two years, in writing to his parents, indicates that years of education and transition had produced a surface disregard for the vital things, but he writes, "underneath all I have never forgotten the things I learned at ———," the reference being to the place of his plastic years. How comforting to a mother's heart to get such a message from the shell swept fields of Europe, for that message came before the war ended.—*Rev. Joseph W. Kemp.*

HOW OLD ARE YOU?

Time may have plowed long and deep furrows on your face, and with his chisel may have cut up and down across and above your brow, but try to make the best use of yourself in the sunset and twilight hours, and embrace every opportunity to do good. There can yet be many spare moments to improve, and in helping somebody along the way. You will greatly benefit yourself.

Improve the present, and it will help you on to the attainment of greater and better things. Use the advantages that surround you and make life more beautiful by looking at the helpful and beautiful things which God has given us. He supplies our needs and has promised not to forsake us, and never to leave us. Yes, down to the evening time of this earthly pilgrimage He will abide with us. Many a tired one often feels like saying: "Being tired and weary with the journey of life, I want to get home and rest." But don't be in a hurry to go—stay here as long as you can before taking the final flight. Look out and get the abundant life in your soul. Think of and live the abounding, abundant life until you feel like exclaiming: "My wings are plumed, and I am willing and ready to soar in the splendors and happiness of immortality."

Let those who have children to help and bless their homes pray that our sons may be as plants grown up in their youth; and our daughters as cornerstones polished after the similitude of a palace.

It will help the older people to keep in touch with the children all they can, not that they should not associate with their old friends and help them in every needed way, but when opportunity offers be patient, helpful, encouraging to the children. Some children don't like old people because they are too serious, sour and grum. Show a spirit of kindness, love, tenderness and sympathy for them. The old people neglect the children in their Sunday school and church work. They go through the Sunday school lessons, and that is the last of it until next Sunday. They ought to have a short, interesting talk or sermon, at least, some of the time, by some suitable one, and not to let them run out and away so soon from the services.

The old people will have to guard against being too sensitive. They must remember that they have had their time, and that they cannot fill many places in human affairs as once they could. Then too there is a tendency to stop and retire too soon. Of course, infirmity and other causes often prevent them, but let them try to hold on to duty as long as possible, and try very hard to live in the present, in the future too, and not in the past so much. Some of us as we grow old dwell too much on the past, and tell our friends too often that we are worn out.

No matter how much time you have thrown away, begin now to accomplish something. Try not to think that you are too old. Age may mean glasses and stiff joints, but not a dimming of the wind or the capacity for doing good and being happy.

J. T. KITCHEN.

Windsor, Va.

WHICH WAY ARE YOU LOOKING?

Dear reader, pause just long enough to ask yourself this very important question, "*Which way am I looking?*", then at the bar of your own conscience, assisted by the divine Word, get the answer. Then use the answer in the way that will bring to you the greatest good in this life; then you need not trouble yourself one moment about the other—the eternal life. Upon this answer, and the way you use it, depends your present and future real and abiding happiness.

A man goes the way he looks—the way he faces. If he is looking toward the world, that is all he sees; it is all to him, and it is all he will get. Men of the world who have their portion in this life. He not only loses the best and most satisfying portion in this life, but will have neither lot nor share in the immortal life.

What a man has constantly before him, that which takes his time and attention, fills his heart so that there is no room nor space for any other thing, is what makes him what he is and what he will be. He cannot be anything else while his mind is preoccupied. We grow to be like our ideals. You never knew a worldly man to be anything other than worldly; he has no place for anything else. He can never make his own the best this life can give until he faces about and turns away from the world, and toward the heavenly.

The difference in looking world-ward and God-ward, is just the difference between success and failure, safety and danger, peace and unrest, eternal life and eternal death.

. Father's finger-board, His word, not only admonishes, exhorts; it points way—the only one to life eternal: "Looking unto Jesus the author and finisher of our faith;" "There is none other name under heaven given among men whereby we must be saved;" "Looking for that blessed hope, and the glorious appearing of the great God and our Saviour Jesus Christ;" "Look unto me, and be ye saved, all the ends of the earth; for I am God, and there is none else;" "Turn ye, turn ye from your evil ways; for why will ye die, O house of Israel?".

Benhadad, king of Syria, looked world-ward, trusted in its power, and he lost; Elisha, the prophet of Israel, looked to God for wisdom and power, and he won not only victory, but peace.

But we need not look to the Bible alone, or wait until the day of judgment for similar instances, we have them here now.

I knew two brothers, young men of more than ordinary ability, with apparently equal chances for a successful life. The older, not forty years old, is dead; he died a drunkard. He leaves a sorrowing widowed mother—a lovely wife, broken-hearted. She could not live with him because of ill treatment. He looked to the world for his portion; he got just what and all the world has to give—*death!* The younger brother, early in life, like David, faced God-ward. He is a faithful member of the church; has a lucrative position on a city paper; a nice home, a lovely wife and three beautiful children, and a hope that reaches into the life-land. He wins. Here we see success and failure; and the reason why. These are not isolated cases, they are duplicated every day. Dear reader, you are certainly looking—but *which way?*

                      D. I. PUTNAM.

Schenectady, N. Y., 28 James St.

THE FORWARD MOVEMENT

Warren H. Denison, Superintendent

Headquarters—27 C. P. A. Bldg., Dayton, Ohio

Bismarck, Illinois, $5,475.00

Pleasant View church at Bismarck, Central Illinois Conference, gives $5,475.00 to the Forward Movement and there is a keen interest in the work both on the part of the pastor, Rev. Rue Burnell, and people. It rained but that did not stop the canvass and the strong laymen of the church enjoyed the canvass heartily.

Rev. Pleasant, Versailles, Ohio, sends in $150 additional for their Forward Movement fund, making it $5,105.00. He speaks of the value of the campaign in his church and urges all pastors to put on the Forward Movement program and to prepare the church for the larger giving when the canvass is made.

Four superintendents conducted the dedicatory services for the new North Star, Ohio, church on July 20. The former church house burned in February, 1918, and they have built a new building costing $15,000. There

was something over $5,000 needed to be raised and some $6,000 were pledged. The day was very rainy but the people were happy in their new building. A splendid spirit prevailed all day.

Special Church Architect

It would be a fine thing if some one in the Christian Church would make a speciality of church architecture. Our people are building many new churches these days and the number will increase as we go forward. Others are rebuilding and remodeling. A real church architect who understands Sunday school departmental work and modern needs in church work could render invaluable service and we believe he would be in demand by our churches. Many of our nice, new, good churches that are being erected are so inadequate to meet the needs of the children and youth of the church. Under the direction of a church architect the thousands of dollars now being spent could count for much more for the Kingdom and for Christian workers. Such an architect, especially fitted, who knows our needs would, in our judgment, make a real contribution to our work.

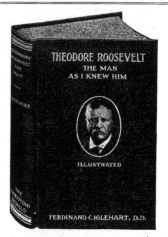

Sunday School and Christian Endeavor

SUNDAY SCHOOL LESSON FOR
AUGUST 17, 1919

Christian Missions. Act 1:8; 13:1-14:28.

Golden Text: "Go ye into all the world, and preach the gospel to the whole creation." Mark 16:15.

Devotional Reading. Isa. 6:1-8.

"Ye shall receive power—and ye shall be witnesses." Have you received power, and are not witnessing? Then you are like a man with legs who will not walk. Have you not received the power? Then you have not yet put yourself in condition of mind and spirit so that the Holy Ghost may come upon you. A man said concerning a woman who is possessed with one of the new religious fads: "She never goes out without a bundle of literature, which she hands out to everyone." How many of us witness for the old, old story in that way? How many of us have realized that it was for the *weaker* brother that Christ Jesus gave His life, and it is for the weaker brother that we as a denomination have been giving something like $1.00 a year per member? I have come to doubt whether the Christian was sent to "preach the gospel" primarily for the sake of others. Our Lord wishes you and me to be the best that we can, to have the fullest, richest life it is possible for a human being to have. So He said to the woman at the well, "The water that I shall give you shall be as a well—springing up." Our Christianity must be an overflowing, everflowing stream. Such a stream *must have an overflow.* If you would have the richest Christian life, it must be an overflowing life, and the whole creation is not too large a place for the overflow. The little spring which runs away in your pasture lot or by the roadside, joins the creek, the creek joins the river, and the river flows into the ocean. So your overflowing life, and mine, expended in service, will join with the lives of thousands of others, until all alike shall reach the boundless ocean, and touch all shores, and they shall say no more, 'know the Lord' for the earth shall be full of the knowledge of the Lord, as the waters cover the sea."

MRS. FRED BULLOCK.

CHRISTIAN ENDEAVOR TOPIC FOR
AUGUST 17, 1919

How do men sell their heritage. Gen. 25:27-34.

The same heritage, and the same environment, were around these two brothers, and to the average eye, we may believe that Esau was apparently the better favored of the two. He was "hail-fellow-wellmet", always ready to go somewhere or to do something. Jacob was the stingy, quiet, stay-at-home. We are not concerned today, however, with the sin of the man who buys his brother's birthright, (a sin for which Jacob paid dearly enough) but we are thinking of those who sell their birthrights as lightly as did Esau. A mess of pottage, the gratification of the senses! Men step down lightly from the pedestal of absolute honesty, and before they know it, their birthright is gone. "A good name is rather to be chosen than great riches," because it is worth more, but men sell the birthright of a good name for a very few of the paltry dollars, at times. "There is no place like home," but how lightly boys and girls leave home, or older people blast its joys and happiness for the gratification of appetite. Anything which takes away from us the power to be developing into the perfect man, "the measure of the stature of the fulness of Christ" is taking away from us our birthright by just so much as we fail to measure up.

MRS. FRED BULLOCK.

MISSIONS IN THE SUNDAY SCHOOL

It has been told in these columns how every Sunday school that cares to do so may have missions studied and taught in one way and another. The approval and workable methods are four:

1. Let the whole school once a month devote the whole recitation period (after the regular Scripture lesson of the morning has been read in class or in concert) to the study of missions.

2. Let every class in school be a missionary class and give, say, ten minutes of each lesson period to mission study and discussions. the school who will now and then

3. Have a missionary committee in put on missionary programs, secure for the school missionary maps, charts and books, and seek in various ways to increase interest in missions on the part of the school.

4. Have a mission superintendent in the school who will be given at least five minutes each Sunday morning to the missionary stories to the school, make a talk on missions and bring missionary facts and needs to the attention of the school.

The writer is much pleased to note that two of ur very earnest and wide-awake schools, Holland and Holy Neck, have recently elected mission superintendents, and they are doing great work for the most worthy of our causes. Mrs. Chas. Daughtry is the mission superintendent of the Holland school, and Mrs. B. D. Jones of the Holy Neck school. We have already had the strongest sort of evidence that both of these schools chose most wisely, and that the missionary part of the Sunday school program is going to be the most wholesome and helpful of all.

We cannot understand why every school of all our number should not decide to teach and learn something about missions in one of the four ways mentioned. If we are not willing that the school as a whole study missions, secure some one in the school to teach missions in a five minutes talk each Sunday morning.

J. O. ATKINSON.

HENRY YOUTSEY PAYS TRIBUTE TO CHRISTIAN ENDEAVOR

"If it had not been for the practical help, spiritual inspiration and the sunshine of genuine Christian friendship of Christian Endeavor these last nineteen years would have been unbearable," said Henry Youtsey, who was recently pardoned after serving nearly twenty years in the State prison at Frankfort, Ky., on a sentence imposed in connection with the assassination of Governor Goebel of Kentucky, nearly a quarter of a century ago.

For the past several years Henry Youtsey has been in charge of the night school in the prison and has taught more than 1,000 men to read and write, 125 men have been personally led to Christ as their Saviour by Mr. Youtsey during his prison term.

Instead of whining and grumbling about his hard sentence as so many prisoners do, Henry Youtsey determined to make his life helpful to the men about him while he served what he felt was an unjust sentence. He gave every hour away from assigned duties to the building of Christian character in the men about him. He served six years as Secretary and President of the Christian Endeavor Society in the Prison at Frankfort.

The Christian Endeavorers of the South are doing a magnificent work for the men and women in prisons, prison farms, reformatories, jails and convict camps, bringing sunshine and cheer to unfortunate folks and giving them a start when they come out to take their places in society once more after their term of imprisonment is ended.

MARRIAGES

ELLIS-OLIVE

On July 19, 1919, Miss Maude Annie Olive was married to Mr. Paul Clayton Ellis at the home of the writer. Both persons are from Morrisville, N. C. May God's blessing be with them in their married life. The writer officiated.

W. G. CLEMENTS.

KERNODLE-ROSS

Miss Lemma L. Ross became the bride of Mr. Robert Kernodle July 20, 1919. They went to the home of Rev. J. W. Holt, accompanied by a few friends, and were quietly united by the bonds of matrimony. They will reside in Morton's Township, Alamance County.

J. W. HOLT.

APPLE-WRAY

A quite but very pretty marriage took place at the home of Mr. and Mrs. J. Wray, 218 East Gaston Street, Greensboro, N. C., Sunday, July 6, 1919, when their daughter, Miss Lottie Wray, became the bride of Mr. Linwood W. Apple, of Win-

ston-Salem. The marriage was attended by close relatives and friends of the bride and groom. Immediately after the ceremony by the writer the young couple left for Winston-Salem where they will make their home.

Both parties once lived in Greensboro, and have many friends in and around the city, who wish for them a long and happy life.

J. VINCENT KNIGHT.

COCHRANE-NEEDHAM

Mr. H. J. Cochrane and Miss Pearl Needham of Martin's Mill, N. C., were married July 19, 1919 at the home of the writer, Asheboro, N. C.

Mr. Cochrane is superintendent of the Sunday school at Shady Grove, and is one of Montgomery County's best teachers. These are popular people in their community and give promise to be a valuable asset to the place in which they may locate. Congratulations and best wishes accompany them.

G. R. UNDERWOOD.

MARTIN-JOHNSON

On June 29, 1919, Rev. W. C. Martin, of Martin's Mill, N. C., a former student of Elon College and Miss Ruth Johnson of Jackson Springs, N. C., accompanied by a few intimate friends, motored to Asheboro and were happily married by the writer at his home. The best wishes of their many friends accompany them.

G. R. UNDERWOOD.

FARMERS, SHIP US YOUR BUTTER FAT!

We will pay the highest market price, stand all express charges, and pay cash for all shipments. Why not try us out?

CATAWBA CREAMERY CO.,
Hickory, N. C.

OBITUARIES

MASSEY

Rufus Massey died at Watt's Hospital, Durham, N. C., June 21, 1919. Funeral service was conducted at the home of his brother, Superintendent Massey of Durham County schools, by Rev. W. G. Clements and Rev. Mr. Johnson of the Baptist church. For a number of years he had been a member of Durham Trinity Methodist church. He was regarded by the business men as honest and truthful. The congregation at the funeral was very large. He was buried at the old home of his father, John Massey, about seven miles South of Durham. Surviving him are four brothers and three sisters. May God bless them all.

W. G. CLEMENTS.

THOMAS

J. W. Thomas, a well known resident of Greensboro, and father of the Thomas Brothers, widely known all over the South in real estate circles, died at his home in Glennwood, July 18, 1919, at 11:45 P. M.

Mr. Thomas was one of the oldest residing citizens of Greensboro, and had a host of friends in the city. He was a Confederate Veteran, and his stories of the war were always interesting. He leaves to mourn their loss: his wife, R. T., C. E., J. C., 1. R., and J. B. Thomas, and Mrs. T. L. McLean of the city, and Mrs. Ed Brockman of Asheville, N. C.

Funeral services were held from the home of C. E. Thomas by the writer, assisted by Revs. J. G. Walker, A. W. Plyler. A mixed quartette from the First Christian church, and Mineota tribe 52, Red Men, and the remains laid to rest in Green Hill cemetery. Blessings upon those that mourn their earthly loss.

J. VINCENT KNIGHT.

TROLLINGER

Benjamin Franklin Trollinger of Graham, North Carolina, died at his home, July 23, 1919, and was buried in the village cemetery, July 24. His funeral services took place from the Presbyterian church, of which he was a member. He was married to Miss Pattie Whittemore in 1881. He left his wife and three children, two daughters and one son. His son is a non-commissioned officer in the United States army. A large number of relatives and friends followed his re-

mains to the grave. There were many
beautiful flowers, and sincere tears. All
of the children were present except the
son. He reached the three score.
"Ben," as he was familiarly called, was
an honest, industrious man, and he will
be greatly missed in the village where
he labored and lived so long.

D. A. LONG.

RESOLUTIONS OR RESPECT—SIMP-SON

Whereas, Deacon Haywood H. Simpson,
who was born September 25, 1852, came
suddenly to the end of his earthly life
at his home in Haw River, North Carolina on July 24, 1919 in the sixty-seventh
year of his age; and

Whereas, for nineteen years as a member, and for about seventeen years as
a deacon of Haw River Christian church
he has proved loyal, faithful and true to
his Church and God; Therefore, be it Resolved:

First. That in Deacon Simpson God has
given us a noble example of a devoted
husband, faithful father, Christian brother, patient sufferer, and loyal soldier of
our Lord Christ.

Second. That wherein he was worthy
we emulate his example.

Third. That to his grief-stricken family
we offer our sincere sympathy and commend them to God and the word of His
grace—the only source of strength in
such a sad hour.

Fourth. That a copy of these resolutions be sent to the family, a copy sent
to The Christian Sun for publication, and
a copy be spread on the minutes of our
church for permanent keeping.

Ratified by the church and signed by
the Deacons:

J. H. McCLURE,
W. E. COOK,
HUGH GILLISPIE,
A. Q. HAILEY,
JNO. B. SHARP.

RESOLUTIONS OF RESPECT—BEAMON

Whereas, Mrs. S. C. E. Beamon has recently passed from labor to reward and

Whereas she has always done her duty
as a devoted member of Damascus Christian church, Therefore be it Resolved:

1. That, we record our sincere appreciation of her Christian character and
faithful service to the church and the
cause of Christ. No woman among us
has been more generous and faithful.
Her counsel was wise, and her example worthy
of emulation.

2. That we bow in humble submission
to the will of God who doeth all things
well. We thank our Heavenly Father for
extending her life well beyond three score
and ten years and we pray that God
may raise up some worthy successor.

3. That we extend to the family our
sincere sympathy and pray that His divine
grace may be sufficient in this dark hour.

4. That a copy of these resolutions be
entered upon the church records and Missionary Society and also a copy be sent
to The Christian Sun for publication.

MRS. R. L. CORBITT,
MRS. E. S. PIERCE,
MRS. J. E. CORBITT,
Committee.

YORK

Henry Garfield, second and infant son
of Mr. and Mrs. Ernest C. York, of 1250
Gregory Street, Greensboro, N. C., died
July 8, 1919, at the age of 11 months
and 6 days. Garfield was a fine picture
of health until within five days of his
death, the angels carried him home to
glory, and has left a vacancy in the home
that the world can never fill. A short
service in the home was held by Rev. W.
R. Cox, following which the remains were
carried to Parks Cross Roads where the
funeral services were held by the writer
and the remains laid to rest in the church
cemetery. May God's richest blessing be
upon the sorrowing family.

J. VINCENT KNIGHT.

DR. J. H. BROOKS

DENTIST

Foster Building   Burlington, N. C.

Don't save for a "rainy day."
Save, and there will be no "rainy
days. Buy W. S. S.

Think in interest—your own interest—save and invest. War Savings Stamps pay 4 per cent interest,
compounded quarterly.

LAUGHS

Safe Business

"I'm a very busy man, sir. What
is your proposition?"

"I want to make you rich."

"Well, leave your recipe with me
and I'll look it over later. Just now
I'm engaged in closing up a little
deal by which I expect to make three
dollars and a half real money."—
Brooklyn Citizen.

Proof of Heredity

If you do not believe in heredity,
read this story that emanates from
a public school, and be convinced
that there is omething in it after
all.

A new boy from a neighboring
State and just joined the class, and
though he was bright, and there was
nothing the matter with him physically, still it was almost impossible
to understand him.

"Why don't you speak up? Why
don't you articulate?" pleaded the
exasperated teacher. "Didn't any
one ever try to teach you to speak
up so that you and could be understood?"

"They used to," mumbled the boy,
"but they gave it up when they
found my father was a train an-
nouncer and my mother a telephone
girl. They said it was born in me."
—Times-Star.

Would Leave

"If me mistress don't take back
what she say to me this mornin', I'll
leave!" exclaimed the irate Bridget
to the ice man.

"What'd she say?" he asked.

"Sure, she told me to leave," said
Bridget.

It Was Not Auntie

A little girl went to the drug store
and asked for some pills.

"Anti-bilious?" asked the clerk.

"No, auntie's all right. It's my
uncle," replied the little girl.—Sel.

Tender Hearted

Mr. Miller—My wife is so tender-
hearted, she won't whip the cream.

Mr. Smith—That's nothing; my
wife won't beat the carpets, and tears
come to her eyes when the onions
are skinned.—Tit-Bits.

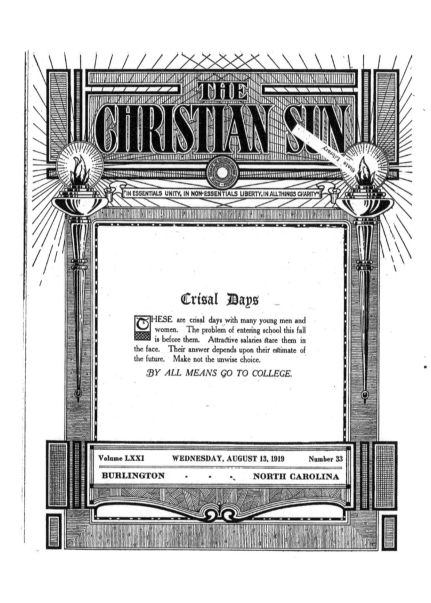

THE CHRISTIAN SUN

"IN ESSENTIALS UNITY, IN NON-ESSENTIALS LIBERTY, IN ALL THINGS CHARITY"

Crisal Days

THESE are crisal days with many young men and women. The problem of entering school this fall is before them. Attractive salaries stare them in the face. Their answer depends upon their estimate of the future. Make not the unwise choice.

BY ALL MEANS GO TO COLLEGE.

Volume LXXI   WEDNESDAY, AUGUST 13, 1919   Number 33

BURLINGTON   · · ·   NORTH CAROLINA

THE CHRISTIAN SUN

Founded 1844 by Rev. Daniel W. Kerr

C. B. RIDDLE   -   -   -   Editor

Entered at the Burlington, N. C. Post Office as second class matter.

Subscription Rates

One year ....$ 2.00
Six months ....,................ 1.00
In Advance

Give both your old and new postoffice when asking that your address be changed.

The change of your label is your receipt for money. Written receipts sent upon request.

Many persons subscribe for friends, intending that the paper be stopped at the end of the year. If instructions are given to this effect, they will receive attention at the proper time.

Marriage and obituary notices not exceeding 150 words printed free if received within 60 days from date of event, all over this at the rate of one-half cent a word.

Original poetry not accepted for publication.

Principles of the Christian Church

(1) The Lord Jesus Christ is the only Head of the Church.
(2) Christian is a sufficient name of the Church.
(3) The Holy Bible is a sufficient rule of faith and practice.
(4) Christian character is a sufficient test of fellowship, and of church membership.
(5) The right of private judgment and the liberty of conscience is a right and a privilege that should be accorded to, and exercised by all.

EDITORIAL

LIFE AND LITERATURE

There is a life in literature that all of us recognize. The Bible, the greatest masterpiece in literature, speaks to us in a way that makes us recognize that it contains a certain element of life that grips us. To read the writings of Moses is to hear that great law giver speak; to read the songs of David is to hear the harpist sing; to read of Paul and his initiative work for Christianity is to feel that thrill of life that makes us want to conquer and to overcome.

Aside from the Bible, great mountain peaks of literature stand as beacon lights to guide us. The weary and worn and tired find consolation and comfort in reading "Pilgrim's Progress;" the prophetic in mind turn to Shakespeare to point out the history of the times; the life soon to enter the sunset valley finds joy in reading "In Memoriam" by Tennyson.

The great pieces of literature are those that are filled with life, portray life, and point out things to make life sweeter and happier. The brains of all ages are reflected in thought expressions, and noble emotions have always endeavored to express themselves in printed form.

The thought in every world event finds itself crystallized in art and literature. Flags, guns, and emblems of war have been the foremost things in art and literature during the past four years. The close of the war brought our thoughts to the dead who sacrificed their lives that we might live. In turn we have written into literature and woven into art words and symbols to express our appreciation of them and to console those who mourn. Those who mourn the loss of loved ones have turned to song and other forms of literature and art to find comfort and consolation. Theirs is the quest of satisfaction that their loved ones rest in that eternal resting place.

There is life in literature. A book may be as great as a battle; a picture may change a life, and that life may change a nation, and that nation may change the world. Let the Bible be the standard of all art and literature and your choice will be wise.

We are endeavoring to breathe the spirit of the age and point to the sign board of the future.

TWO METHODS

There are just two methods for industrial conciliation: The rapid reformers, socialistic and pessimistic class, endeavor to bring conditions to a normal state by demanding, rioting, and overthrowing. This class is not represented by the Church. The second method is fostered by Church leaders who endeavor to reconcile normal conditions by the terms of peace, arbitration and reason.

These two methods have almost reached their climax in the present age. Social unrest and individual anxiety are foremost in the activity of the world's forum. They are presenting problems that are world-wide in scope and touch the life of individuals everywhere. There is impatience, unrest, disturbances in all sections of the country. Men are demanding a change and are demanding that change now. Strikes are prevalent and point to the fact that organizations are becoming supreme. The flash-light of the Church is not throwing its rays of activity in the foreground so vividly as these labor unions and other industrial line-ups. But that does not argue that the Church is not alive and active in in the pushing of its own program—the program of conciliation by reason and thought and deliberation.

No man among us can fail to see the near approach of these two methods of world readjustment. One is working as hard as the other. One is receiving more publicity than the other, but if we sense the trend of things correctly, they are about on an equilibrium. We are bold enough to assert that the time is not far distant when a readjustment will come. Just which method is to win out we cannot say—we wish we could. The successful outcome of either method will doubtless bring satisfaction to the disturbed hearts and minds of the people, but it ought to be the hope and prayer of every Christian that the method of the Church should win. There is a reason: If the method of arbitration should win it would strengthen the arm of the Church, but if the method of force wins the influence of the Church may be hindered. It ought to be the hope and the prayer of the Christian people that the Church should win because of the conditions to follow after such a winning. When force and might win out it digs a deep chasm between two classes of people and it may take many, many years to abolish this line of separation. The method of the Church heals as it goes, and unites by the tie of brotherly love.

. It is the duty and the privilege of every American pulpit to sound the note for cool heads, honest and sincere hearts and deliberation upon the part of our people. It is the duty and the privilege of every American pulpit to lead the people into the right paths in these days of social unrest and industrial activity when a strife is abroad in the land. Will the greatest institution in the world, the Church, fail to measure up to its obligations?

— — — — — — — — — — — — — — — — —

New impulses lead to new thoughts; new thoughts to new actions, and these to service, if properly guided

— — — — — — — — — — — — — — — — —

CHURCH AND STATE

It furnishes amusing reading to scan the articles of many present day writers because of their estimate of the Church. There are, in every community, those who are stirred "to do something" because of new impulses brought on by changed conditions. There are many classes of these people, but we confine this note to one class only.

The class to which we refer is that group of men who have not identified themselves with the Church sufficiently to know its latitude and and the strength of its work. Constantly, earnestly, and sincerely forces of Christianity have gone forward. World movements and world conditions spring up as if by magic. Those who have been the least concerned about the Church and its work are ready in a moment to point out that the Church ought to line herself up *with* certain present day problems. They forget that the greatest influence of the Church can be obtained only through and by absolute divorce from the State. The method of the Church to purify is not to engage *with* but to go *against*. The best illustration that we have of this is the Church in the European countries. The ministers of England own 8 per cent of the stock in breweries of that country. This alone is sufficient proof that the conscience of such leadership is blunted until it loses that fine appeal, and earnest condemnation that causes reaction against immoral tendencies. Two powers cannot unite without a common absorbing influence.

The Church is the searchlight in the lighthouses along the shores of time, carefully inspecting every incoming ship of immorality. When these on-rushing things come she is aloof from their interest and is ready in a moment's time, without condemnation of her conscience and her interest, to summons her forces to ward off the on-slaughts of immorality that impeach the character and lives of her devotees.

Three cheers for America and her Protestant Churches! They are free from the connection of State politics. Our Constitution makers saw the danger and said that the Church and State should forever be separated. If the American Churches should ever find themselves willing to live up as commercial industries the fate of America would be the fate that came to the European countries—the fate of disorder and ungovernable outrage.

Let those who see the Church and State too far apart review the ruins of nations that rose to the zenith of their power and crumbled to dust because their moral fibre gave away.

— — — — — — — — — — — — — — — — —

New duties, new dangerous—these are the outposts of civilizations. Our effort is to point them out for the Kingdom's good.

— — — — — — — — — — — — — — — — —

CLEAN SPEECH

The Christian Endeavor topic for August 10 was "*Speech: Wise and Unwise.*" This reminds us of the great tendency towards cheap talk, slang and profanity in this age. Slang seems to be common coin. Slang cheapens the expression, obstructs thought, clouds accurate thinking, and closes avenues to a larger approach on any subject. There is no excuse for slang. We will admit that the English language is not perfect in every respect, but there is a sufficiency of it to aid a man in expressing himself without using slang.

Slang has come into the pulpit, and we believe that every time slang enters it that that much of the true Gospel goes out. We pity the man who has to resort to slang in order to preach the unsearchable riches of Christ. Slang in the pulpit will never convey to the minds and hearts of the people the richest expressions and sentiments of the Christian life. Slang words are not rich; they are poverty stricken, and will never be able to tap the fountains of life.

Cursing and swearing is another uncalled for, unfit, unclean and dirty habit that mortals enter into. God save our youth from such unclean talk! We have driven the bar-room out of our land. Public sentiment has been the prosecuting attorney in this move. We believe that public sentiment will exert itself again some good day and say to slang and profanity that they, too, shall go. When we passed the bar-room unnoticed, and approved of the drunkard by our smile, they were in our midst. When we became deeply concerned about these things the condition changed, and so when we as Christian people become deeply concerned over the sayings of our people, these things, too, will change.

"A word fitly spoken is like apples of gold in pictures of silver."—*Proverbs* 25:11.

OUR PROGRAM

With such a limited number of pages, and with the constant growth of the Church with which to encounter, it is no little problem to figure out a division of space for the proper allotment of each call and need. It is almost impossible for us to get out special editions, or editions that feature special themes. We had hoped to bring out an Educational Number this summer, but we do not see our way clear because these special numbers paralyze our weekly plans for more than a month. We are, however, stressing the theme of education during the summer months, as has already been noticed. We have also invited a number of contributors to THE SUN to let their articles stress education's interest from now until the first of September. Several contributions on education have already appeared and others are to follow. By this method we are endeavoring to emphasize during the vacation season the importance of education. After the first of September we hope to stress more fully the matter of pastors' salaries because we feel that more pastoral changes will be made during September, October and November, and certainly no church will offer to call its pastor for another year, or extend a call to any other pastor without some increase in salary.

During the winter months, when the evenings are long, we hope to be able to stress the devotional side of life, and so on during the various seasons. We solicit the co-operation of the Brotherhood in our program.

Bigness may not be greatness. Deliberation may not be decision. We endeavor to create an impulse to distinguish the difference.

THE WISDOM OF OUR BRETHREN

(_Chrisian Observer_):

The denominational college is the great fort of the Church where the freedom of religion will be maintained with the same courage as the freedom of science will be defended in the State institutions.

(_Western Christian Advocate_):

Unless the salaries of teachers are generally raised, our children will soon be placed under inferior instructors. This vacation is offering to many double what they can get for teaching during the winter.

(_The Christian Evangelist_):

The public schools are not godless. Morality is taught in them. Honesty, truthfulness, helpfulness, friendship, honor, justice, patriotism, liberty and intelligence are the fundamental considerations in the public schools, and surely these are bed-rock moralities.

(_The Herald of Gospel Liberty_):

In many a home the future destiny of some boy or girl will be decided within the next few weeks. We cannot believe that any father or mother will permit such a vital decision to rest solely upon the matter of money alone.

PASTOR AND PEOPLE

DR. W. J. McGLOTHLIN

I listened to his course of lectures at Tampa, Florida and learned, in part, the secret of his great power among the Baptist ministers who attended the Southern Theological Seminary. He is justly regarded, by educators of all denominations who know him, as one of the finest scholars and sweetest spirited Christians in our country. No two denominations in the United States hold more divergent opinions about baptism than the Baptists and Lutherans. Yet, _The Lutheran_, official organ of the United Lutheran Church in America, for July 24, 1919, contains the following able article which is applicable to all the Christian colleges in America:

"The _Watchman-Examiner_ reports the resignation of one of the most distinguished professors of the Southern Theological Seminary, Dr. W. J. McGlothlin. He leaves the seminary to engage in Christian college education. He is deeply impressed with the necessity of this kind of education, and believes firmly that the maintenance of Christian colleges is the only thing that will save us from traversing the road that led to the downfall of Germany. State education must be supplemented by the work of Christian institutions. As President of Furman University, Dr. McGlothlin will have a chance to put his deep faith in the Christian college to active test. In a recent article he said: 'In a large measure education made this war, and education must help mightily to create an international mind that will eliminate war. Ignorance is inefficiency and unimportance; education is power, beneficent or dangerous according to the character of the education. We must neither leave our people uneducated nor suffer them to be wrongly educated. The Christian Church, strong and efficient is a necessity of the future. And now it is the supreme time to endow and equip them worthily. It ought to be done and finished within the next fifteen years. To lose the opportunity that is now open to us will be to doom ourselves to long and painful efforts and long-continued inefficiency.'"

Dr. McGlothlin is in no way prejudiced against the Germans. After graduating, with _magna cum laude_, from American universities, he studied at German universities and was greatly appreciated and honored. He knows whereof he speaks. Mere intellectual culture never did, and never can, elevate either an individual or a nation, morally or religiously. Greece reached her highest mark in plastic art, under Pericles, yet it was her most corrupt period. Intellectual training in Rome was highest under Caesar Augustus and it was her most degraded, morally. England showed her highest intellectual period under Elizabeth and it was a period of her lowest morals. If we are too poor to aid in giving money we can use what influence we have to heed the bugle calls from Elon College and THE CHRISTIAN SUN office.

D. A. LONG.

Be good for something and not good for nothing

The Sixth Annual Session of the Seaside Chautauqua and School of Methods closed on August 5, 1919. It was not *largely* attended, but it was *faithfully* attended. The work, taken all together, was the best of any year and the weather was ideal. The guarantors have stood by the benevolent work, and financially, it has been a success. But plans were started that may transfer the responsibility of the Chautauqua to some official body of the Church in order to make it a permanent Church institution; but for the next year it will be conducted as heretofore, financed by the guarantors. Some of those who have supported the Chautauqua by their presence and their money went to Virginia Beach discouraged this year, and returned to their homes with renewed interest and hope.

The program was so full, so completely carried out, so varied and of such high order, that a feeling was created that the attendance *must* be larger next year; and it will. I cannot give the program nor the names of all the speakers and teachers. It would require too much space; but I may say that the Bible Study, Sunday School in all its Departments, Missions, Christian Leadership, Church Problems, Christian Endeavor, the Forward Movement, Sermons, Chautauquqa Lectures, Vesper Services, Intercession, Music, and recreation filled each day to overflowing with the cream of modern progress in the things of the Kingdom. Each day was as long and as full as the above sentence. The faculty consisted of seventeen persons, many of them specialists in the department which they filled.

Dr. Geo. C. Enders of Defiance College, Ohio, full series of morning Bible Studies; Dr. L. E. Smith, Norfolk, Va., series of sermons; Rev. E. K. McCord, series of lectures on Missions; Mrs. Isaac Sewell, Nashville, Tenn., series on Elementary Work in Sunday School; W. C. Pearce, See'y International Sunday School Association; Hermon Eldredge, series on Christian Leadership; Dr. R. C. Helfenstien, Rev. G. H. Ekins and Rev. Wm. M. Jay, series on Church Problems; and thus the reader will see that it was a *real school of methods.* Dr. Enders took occasion to say in the closing meeting, when President Denison requested any present who desired to say what impressions they had received from the Chautauqua, that the Christian Church had produced the *Big·Four* in Sunday school and Christian Endeavor work: Marion Lawrence, W. C. Pearce, Amos R. Wells, and Hermon Eldredge.

In addition to the regular work of the Chautauqua, Commissions from the Disciples and Christians held meetings of interest on church unity and Drs. Peter Ainlie of Baltimore and Finis S. Idleman of New York, delivered Chautauqua lectures. From 10:000 A. M. to 12:45 P. M. of Friday was given over to a meeting and discussion of Christian union by leaders of the Disciples of Christ and the Christian Church. Drs. Armstrong, Miller, and Idleman spoke for the Disciples; Drs. Peters, Harper, and Burnett for the Christians. It was a great meeting and if *all of both* Churches could have been present union between the two bodies could have been consumated.

The only change in the official Chautauqua is that C. H. Rowland, D. D., becomes President and W. H. Denison, Vice-President. They exchange paces as Dr. Denison is so far away from the center. Prof. S. M. Smith remains General Secretary and W. C. Rawles was elected Treasurer.

W. W. STALEY.

THE FUQUAY SPRINGS BIBLE CONFERENCE, AUGUST 31 TO SEPTEMBER 7, 1919

Rev. George E. Guille

Rev. George E. Guille, Extension Worker of Moody Bible Institute, will deliver daily lectures at the Conference. Some of his subjects will be: "The Exaltation and Present Service of Christ," "The Coming of Christ," "The Judgment Seat of Christ," "The Times of the Gentiles and the Predicted End of the Age," "The Holy Spirit," etc.

Mr. Guille is one of the greatest teachers of the Bible in this country, and a rare treat awaits those who will hear him.

Rev. R. V. Miller

Rev. R. V. Miller, Bible teacher, evangelist, and lecturer of wide reputation and of deep scriptural insight, will alternate with Mr. Guille in delivering addresses and lectures on Bible subjects, such as "The Teaching of the Epistles," "Christ in Prophecy, His Coming and Kingdom," "Teaching Concerning Salvation and the Christ Life," etc.

Of him Rev. F. W. Troy, Field Secretary Fulton Street Bible and Evangelistic Movement, New York City, says: "I consider Brother Miller the clearest, sweetest and strongest teacher on prophetic subjects I have ever had the privilege of listening to."

The singing will be in charge of Rev. Charles Butler, whose sweet voice and pleasing personality need no recommendation or introduction to the people of this section. Indeed, such is his own reputation, that but little, if any, additional luster is cast upon his name to say that he sang for Billy Sunday and Doctor Torrey for several years. Everybody knows and loves him here, and the fact that he will have charge of the singing insures a treat for all who attend these daily conferences.

We cordially invite every one to attend every conference.

J. S. FARMER,
J. LEE JOHNSON,
F. B. LYERLY,
V. A. ROYAL,
Pastors of Fuquay Spring Churches.

Finally, brethren, pray for us, that the Word of the Lord may have free course and be glorified. II Thes. 3:1.

It is easy to criticize; therefore many do it

Are you moving with the Forward Movement?

ANTIOCH, CHATHAM COUNTY, NORTH CAROLINA.

In 1857 I had a church—or rather a school house—in which to preach, and which is now Antioch. In December of that year I attempted to find the school house one Sunday, but it being located in a large body of woods, I failed to find it until about 1:00 o'clock. A few brethren were patiently awaiting my arrival. I told these brethren that I could not accomplish anything with such a building and location. I went to dinner with a very congenial family; and after we had eaten, the good sister of the house felt it her duty to inform me that the people in that community did not need another church. But in good faith I convinced her that there was a large field of usefulness for another church, a Christian church. I took great pleasure in defending my denomination.

In the afternoon I visited some of my little flock and told them that I did not feel that we could accomplish anything in a school house, but that I would visit them during the winter, hold prayer meetings, and look after a location on which to build a church in the spring.

In this community I made many friends and acquaintances of other denominations. There was a good neighborhood where the old church had been, about 300 yards from the public road. I decided upon this place. In March I had an appointment there, and with scarcely any preparation, we assembled. When I arrived Sunday morning the thick woods about the old spot were filled with horses, vehicles and people and we had a splendid service. I preached in the afternoon and a Methodist minister and his congregation went with us, making an immense crowd. I told them that we must have a church at once and steps were taken for its beginning. Many of the brethren had lumber and other material and could commence at once. A month later I arrived to dedicate the church building. Of course we didn't have any painting, ceiling or plastering done, I preached for these people three years, and in the meantime gathered together a fine congregation. Many were members of other churches but assisted me in my work and opened their homes to me. I found Brother Dorsett and his little family pleasantly located in a cottage with plenty of room and comforts. Mrs. Dorsett is a most excellent woman, good church and Sabbath school worker. Their daughter, about fourteen years old, is much interested in Sunday school work.

Next morning we started to the church, a distance of two and one-half miles. We had a good Sunday school of about 100 members. They were engaged in preparing for Children's Day the next Sunday. A Mr.

Alexander lives in the community, who recently purchased a farm and brought his children to the country in preference to rearing them in the city. They are members of the Presbyterian Church, but there being no church of their denomination close by, are doing active work with us. I preached especially to the unsaved and I think that I reached the hearts and minds of many. Due to excessive rains and bad roads, none of the old people could get to the church. Not even an automobile could make the trip, and so I failed to have the pleasure of shaking the hands of many old friends. The ground was too wet for me to visit the cemetery.

I returned to Brother Dorsett's. Rev. R. P. Crumpler, the pastor of the church, spent the night with me at Brother Dorsett's. Brother Crumpler was sick and hardly able to attend church. Monday afternoon I returned to the station, Brother Dorsett carrying me in his surry. We reached the station just in time to catch the train. I made the entire trip without being caught in the rain, except as I left the depot on Saturday. I made my way home, having traveled possibly 200 miles, tired but not sick. I enjoyed my trip so much, but regret that the weather was such that I could not see more of my dear friends at Antioch.

I cannot recall names and consequently cannot mention many friends I would like to.

J. W. WELLONS.

Elon College, N. C.

CONCORD

The revival meeting began here the fourth Sunday in July 1919, at eleven o'clock. The weather was fair and a large crowd was present. The church was much revived and was brought closer in fellowship by coming together. The visible results were eleven professions of faith in Christ and four additions to the church. I think there will be more to join later.

Rev. J. F. Apple of Elon College did all the preaching. He brought plain Gospel messages which were inspiring and uplifting. The people were glad to have him again.

On Saturday before the fourth Sunday in August, at 4:00 P. M., the church is to meet for a business meeting and the calling of pastor for another. May the Lord lead in all that shall be done. Communion and baptizing of the candidates on Sunday following.

I was with Rev. J. W. Knight at Smithwood in a very successful revival this week.

L. L. WYRICK.

Elon College, N. C.

NEW COMERS TO THE SUN FAMILY

Miss Iola Upchurch............................Lillington, N. C.
Mrs. Martha Cotner...............................Liberty, N. C.
E. L. Beale ....South Norfolk, Va.
J. T. Jones ....Holland, Va.
D. R. Butler ....Holland, Va.
Walter A. Spitser ....Broadway, Va.
J. F. Cook ....Akron, Ohio

(Report to August 9)

NOTES

The Virginia Valley Conference is in session this week.

Rev. J. W. Holt has been called to serve Bethlehem for another year.

Dr. P. H. Fleming is assisting Rev. C. E. Newman in his revival meetings this summer.

We sympathize with Brother T. H. Crocker, Middleburg, N. C., in the loss of his mother, August 4, 1919.

Rev. P. T. Klapp sent this office a list of new subscribers the other day. Brother Klapp has always been faithful to THE SUN.

Rev. H. J. Fleming, Newport News, Va., called in to see us the other day. He goes back to Newport News for another year,

Rev. C. H. Rowland, D. D., has been elected president of the Chautauqua and School of Methods. Dr. Rowland will fill the place well.

Rev. J. O. Cox changes his address to Lee, N. C., Madison County, near Hot Springs. He is in charge of Spring Creek State High School.

If you are in favor of Christian union, you should read Dr. W. A. Harper's address in this issue. If you are opposed to union, then by all means read it.

Dr. J. W. Harrell is at home from the hospital much improved. He expects to leave this week for Eastern Virginia to spend some time with his father.

Congratulations and best wishes to our good friends, Rev. J. F. Morgan, and wife, who was Miss Lula Bell until July 31. Happiness and long life be theirs!

Rev. B. F. Black went to Camp last week to get his discharge, but failed to get it owing to infected tonsils. He has had an operation and hopes to soon be at home.

Rev. J. L. Foster advertises in this issue a valuable piece of property at Elon College. A good chance to secure a home in the College community and educate your children.

Dr. L. E. Smith is at News Ferry, Va., where he is taking a rest. He will return to Norfolk about September 1. He is to put on a campaign for THE SUN in his church in the early fall.

Misses Edith Walker, Nonie Moore, Sadie Fonville and Nellie Fleming, of our Burlington church, attended the International Christian Endeavor Convention in Buffalo, New York, last week.

The office of publication of *The Missionary Herald and Christian Star,* the official organ of the Afro-Christian Convention, has been moved from Franklinton, N. C., to Raleigh, N. C.

Dr. J. U. Newman writes from Chicago, Ill., under date of August 4: "This Elon crowd of eight never enjoyed THE SUN so much. Thought it was a good paper when at home. It seems better now."

Last Sunday afternoon the Editor preached for the congregation at Mebane. The attendance was not large, but those present manifested a spirit of loyalty and are deeply interested in the work at that place. We believe that the Mission Board of the North Carolina Conference ought to give this work personal attention and decide the future policy of the undertaking.

The children of the Christian Orphanage gave an entertainment at the Municipal Theatre, Burlington, N. C., Friday evening, August 8. The play was of a high order, well presented and those present counted themselves fortunate. Brother Johnston and co-workers are to be congratulated. If the Orphanage children could go to every church in the Convention and present themselves in the same way as they did in Burlington, the financial problem of the Orphanage would be solved.

We had the privilege of being at Mt. Zion in Orange County last Sunday to fill an appointment for Brother J. F. Apple. The weather was clear, the attendance good, and the occasion much enjoyed. Our welcome was all that could be asked; the hospitality, well, it was 100 per cent. The Lord's Supper was administered after preaching. Many more families in that community are this week to receive THE SUN and we welcome them to the list. We are indebted to Brother Julius Pace for his kindness in "fording" us to and from the station, also to his good wife for a good old Southern country dinner.

The time for the contest for names of non-subscribers has closed. Many have responded. We have not had the time to check up the list and will not for several days. Suffice to say that four pastors furnished a total of more than one thousand names. They certify that these are heads of families or logical persons in the family to take THE SUN. Much work has been done in securing these names. Each list received shows that time was given to it. Just how much service this list will be to this office is yet to be determined, but it substantiates one fact, that when four pastors can marshal a list of their members totaling more than a thousand who do not take THE SUN, there is yet work to be done.

(*For additional notes, see page 15*)

ANNOUNCEMENT

There will be a call meeting of the members of Liberty (Vance) Christian church Saturday, August 16, at 2:30 P. M. Important business. The presence of every member is desired.

G. J. GREEN, *Pastor.*

CHRISTIAN EDUCATION

THE CHURCH COLLEGE

It sets the standard of American education and has maintained it.

It is the mother of college presidents and America's most prominent educators.

It is the college which has furnished the church with its ministry.

Its American patriotism has been tested by two wars, and not found wanting.

Its form of government is truly American and free from politics.

It is thoroughly Christian, yet free from bigotry.

Its scientific departments are manned by scholarly, Christian men.

It is free from that irreligious sectarianism which denies a place to the Bible in the curriculum of study.

It believes in a philosophy which holds to a personal God, a divine Christ, an immortal soul, and an imperative duty. It is free from agnosticism and pantheism, the greatest foes to Christian truth.

Fundamentals in its curriculum is love for all truth. It does not prejudice the student against the truth by refusing it a place in the curriculum.

It believes that the formative element in history is Christianity, and that any curriculum is defective which fails to reach it.

It believes that the words of Jesus and Paul should be studied as well as those of Socrates and Plato.

It believes that teachers of youth should know the truth.

It is an institution born of sound doctrine and fostered by those who have a vital faith.

Its educational work has been done for less money than that of any other agency. It is the greatest tax-saving institution in the State.

It gives the greatest return to the country of any philanthropic investment known to Christian men and women.

It is the safest investment of Christian money known to the church.

Its students, coming from the best Christian homes, help to create a clean, strong collegiate life. Its students are taught to live economically, to think rightly, and to act nobly.—*Indiana Farmer's Guide.*

Come, my way, my truth, my life;
    Such a way as gives us breath;
Such a truth as ends all strife;
    Such a life as killeth death.

Come, my joy, my love, my heart;
    Such a joy as none can move;
Such a love as none can part;
    Such a heart as joys in love.

               —*George Herbert.*

THE CHRISTIAN ORPHANAGE

PAINTING!

The Christian Orphanage is dressing out in a new dress. The painters are painting the outside and it makes our building have a much better appearance. This should have been done some time ago but we wanted to wait till we got the Institution out of debt before we began to make improvements. We expect to paint the inside of the building as fast as our bank account will permit. We wish we could spare the money now to go over the entire building and make it all look fresh and new.

Our Singing Class had quite a pleasant trip on July 31. We were invited to attend the Masonic Picnic at Baynes Store and to give an entertainment there. Our children have been very kindly invited out there on several occasions before.

The Singing Class from the Oxford Orphanage attends this picnic when they can make it convenient and gives entertainments for the picnic, and when it is not convenient for them to come, the managers very kindly extend to our children an invitation to go out there and give an entertainment which we are always glad to do. It is a treat our Class looks forward to with much pleasure and enjoy the dinner and the many kindnesses shown them.

             CHAS. D. JOHNSTON, *Supt.*

FINANCIAL EXHIBIT FOR THE WEEK

Report For August 13, 1919

Amount brought forward, $8,142.54.

Sunday School Monthly Offerings
(North Carolina Conference)

Lebanon, $3.52; Haw River, $2.20; Beulah, $12.25; Ebenezer, $3.69; Christian Light, $1.52; New Providence, $2.00; Mt. Pleasant, $2.05; New Providence, $1.90; Catwaba Springs, $8.46; Ramseur, $3.54; Wake Chapel, $5.00; Plymouth, $3.89; Pleasant Hill, $2.94.

(Eastern Virginia Conference)

Hebron, $2.82; Mt. Carmel, $3.30; Mt. Carmel, $1.00; Centerville, $1.00.

(Valley Virginia Conference)

Wood's Chapel, $1.00; Linville, $1.00.

(Georgia and Alabama Conference)

North Highlands, $5.00; New Hope, $2.00; Total, $70.08.

Special Offerings

Millwood Christian church, (Ind.), $3.50; Bethlehem Sunday school, Va., (on pledge), $16.00; Miss Ellen Speight, $1.00; Total $20.50.

Special Easter Offerings

Bethlehem Christian church, Va. (Nansemond Co.), $18.52.

Children's Home

W. L. Thomas, $5.00.

Total for the week, $114.10; Grand total, $8,256.64.

Annie Atkinson—I enjoy reading THE SUN and want want it to continue to come to my home.

        * *

C. A. High—Please renew my subscription to THE SUN as we cannot do without it.

MISSIONARY

PASTORS "CARRY ON"

I wonder if the faithful pastors in our Christian churches have fallen into ruts and are preaching in the same old way they did before the war; or are they awake and alive to the wonderful opportunities of this new time, and are athrob with vigor and bigness of this world-wide life into whose vortex we have been whirled in the last few months? I heard of a minister the other day who burned up every sermon-note and manuscript he had made in the past twenty-five years. Trade and commerce and politics and state-craft and thought and feeling and endeavor had all taken on world-wide scope of late months, and the provincial, restricted message of the past could have no meaning, and get no results, in this large and growing time. God loved a whole world from the beginning, loved it all so supremely, so devotedly that He gave the best He had to reach, redeem and save it all.

Recently Mrs. E. C. Cronk, of Richmond, Va., that woman of a most fertile and tireless brain who conducts each month "Best Methods" in the *Missionary Review* of the world, sent this question to a number of pastors who "carry on" and who have done things, and are doing things on a large scale for the Master, "What Are Your Best Methods?" Many of the replies are printed in July *Review*. They are worth reading, and are suggestive indeed to those who would like to carry on, and undertake things.

One pastor of a small congregation of about two hundred and fifty people who with his Bible classes gave $83,722.00 for missions alone in 1918, says: "*Never ask people, but ask God and tell people*. We make no appeals, and do not solicit funds, but at church and classes we state the needs, present the opportunities, and leave it to Him whose we are and whom we serve to accomplish His pleasure. Like Manoah and his wife, we look on while He doeth wondrously (Judges 13:19) for He is surely the Doer of it all. The results of this method have been gifts of $1,045,598.65 for missionary work in thirty years."

That pastor has been thinking, acting and "carrying on" in the spirit of this new and world-wide time for thirty years.

WHEN GOD PLEASES TO CONVERT THE HEATHEN

You know some people believe that God will convert the heathen "when He plans to convert them." Also some believe He will convert them "in His own good time and way." This writer is among the number who believe in both the above propositions.

Yes, God will convert the heathen when He pleases to convert them. There is no sort of doubt about that. But in the name of His mercy, goodness and love I declare that He pleases to convert them *now—just now*—forthwith and immediately as soon as those of His children, whom He has converted, are willing to obey His imperative command and carry the message of His saving love and power to His children who have not yet heard about that love and power. "How shall they believe in Him of whom they have not heard? And how shall they hear without a preacher? And how shall they preach except they be sent?" Our Father who pleases to save *now* gave those stinging questions to us long ago through the inspiration of Holy Writ. (Rom. 10:15, 16.)

"And in His own good time and way." Of course, God will only save the heathen in His own good time and way. When is that time and how is that way? The time is now, when His messengers are ready; and the way is through the "foolishness of the preaching" of those messengers. God was ready in 1791 to do the work of redeeming and saving India. (He had been ready more than a thousand years before that) But in 1791 one of His servants over in England—and he just an ordinary shoe cobbler—became willing to obey his Master's command, "Go." William Carey arose in a company of Christians and said he wanted to go and be used of God in converting the heathen. Then it was that a Mr. Ryland bawled out, as many another weak and ignorant professed Christian has cried out since, "Young man, sit down! When God pleases to convert the heathen He will do it without your help or mine." But William Carey did not sit down. By the help of a few of the faithful the shoe cobbler set out on his great task of "helping God convert the heathen," and God has been converting the heathen ever since. And He will keep on converting them, as He keeps on converting men and women, boys and girls in the homeland, by using human and mortal messengers to tell the plain, simple story of the Cross.

God puts tyrants under His feet, abolishes human slavery, overthrows soul-less militarism, and closes up death-dealing saloons only when human beings who believe in Him are willing to do these needed things. There is just one reason why the God of heaven and earth did not shut up the deadly saloon a thousand years ago, and left that hell-trap open to catch millions of men before their time, and make millions of weeping widows where there should have been as many happy homes with husbands, and that reason is that God committed this work to mortal men, human beings who professed to love, serve and honor Him. And when these men and women, His human agents, His sole dependents were ready then He was ready. He had been ready all these centuries. But we rebellious subjects stood in His way.

"Wherefore it is not your Father's will that one of these little ones should perish." And yet they do perish, are perishing by the millions without hope in this life or in that to come. God is ready, willing and able to save them—to save the whole heathen world. But we to whom His mercy and wisdom have committed this task are not ready or willing to obey His superlative and supreme command. How long, dear Christian church, before we are ready to do His bidding and enter into His joy through service?

J. O. ATKINSON.

CHRISTIAN UNION*

Dangers to be Avoided

It is said that fools rush in where angels fear to tread. I have never been an angel. I have frequently been a fool. All college presidents are fools. It is said that a man cannot have brains and hair at the same time. I once saw four hundred college presidents in a room together, and no bald heads were there. College presidents have hair, and plenty of it.

I have never carried a red flag before. When President Coffin asked me to speak on this theme, I demurred. He charged it up to modesty. I had deeper reasons. The reds are not popular in America. A red flag shaken in a bull's face provokes a fight. Fat men ought not to shake such emblems in hot weather.

But I believe in Christian Union and even though I do have hair and am a college president and may provoke a fight, and though I am fat and it is hot, I shall lift aloft my red bandana and give the brethren some spiritual advice. I will do anything for Christian union, any where, any time, any how. I have been a party to a union, a minor member of the firm I admit, for twenty years and it has been so gratifying I should like to get married once more and on a larger scale, and so I am going to tell the dangers to be avoided if this second marriage I hope to be party to is to succeed.

And first of all we must avoid the discussion of our pedigree. I was once written to in a delicately tinted and much-perfumed envelope by a lady whose husband's name was the same as my last one to send her my pedigree that we might establish our kinship. I told her I was too busy to climb my ancestral tree, and further I was afraid to because I feared I would shortly encounter a baboon or a monkey. Pedigrees are all right for hogs, horses, and poodles, but we are all children of the King and as such are brothers and sisters, and that ought to be sufficient.

Seriously, beloved, we must avoid historical discussion if we are to get together, as Jesus wants us to do. Recently a minister entertained me for about three hours on the injustices that had been done him. I listened patiently. When he had finished, I told him I was sure he was a very much maligned and persecuted man, and then I asked: "Brother, do you believe in forgiveness?" "Yes," he instantly replied. "And are you ready to practice it?" I asked. He then did what he had argued he could not do because of the injustices he had suffered. When we have forgiven each other, we can answer Christ's prayer for the oneness of His followers and not before.

It is useless to try to unite on the basis of our historical integrity. For nearly a hundred years the two bodies whose commissioners are here courting today (and I regret to say that there are no ladies present in either commission. You can't do much courting without a lady)—well as I started to say, these two bodies of Christian workers have crossed each other's paths a good many times in the past century, and some unpleasant things have happened, some un-Christian things, some horrid injustices have been perpetrated. Brethren, if we do not "let the dead past bury its dead," we shall never answer Christ's prayer for the union of His followers. Any discussion or rehearsal of these old scores will take us back to the old days when public debates, bitterness, strife, and suspicion were the marks of true Christian Knighthood. But thank God! a new chivalry has come to the Church of Christ— a chivalry that essays to excell in forgiving and not in laying claim to its rights—a chivalry based on love and not on ascendancy—a chivalry that is willing to sacrifice all that Christ's prayer may be answered in our day and that we may have part in its answering. If history is keeping the household of God divided, let us burn all our records and pray God to paralyze our historical brain cell that there may be no recollection among men of the things that once were, but that are no more useful.

The second danger is insistence on the distinctive things for which we stand. I crave no distinction for myself, exept the distinction of being a child of God. Our Heavenly Father made us different, just as the trees are different from each other. Yet they make one forest. "The things that we peculiarly stand for" we must forget. We must make Christian character the test of genuineness in the individual life. If a belief or practice sets us off from some one else, we may be sure the peculiar thing is not universal and that it is not essential to salvation. If it is not essential, we should not insist on it for our brother and he should not insist that we are wrong in fondling it closely to our bosom. If we are to set out to write a creed that all men must subscribe to in order to enjoy our united fellowship, we have met in vain. There is but one source of all the creeds in Christendom, the Bible. Every bit of truth it teaches is for every man, but not every man can appropriate it all. Let each man interpret it for himself, as the Spirit shall lead, and let no man say "nay" to a brother who seeks fellowship by a different method than the one he has decided on for himself.

What I am trying to say in that we must avoid the theological pitfall. Theology is a voluminous science, but not always luminous. All the good that has ever come of theologic controversy has been to drive the participants farther apart spiritually, and today when men's hearts yearn within them for the oneness of Christ's people, we are kept in divided camps because distinctive differences—God's divine order—have been magnified into underlying characteristics—contrary to God's divine order. God teaches by all the physical universe about us, a beautiful unity amid an endless variety. The universe is one. The Church of the living God is chaos, and the Spirit of the Lord must move over the face of this deep disaster and bring order out of confusion, and crown the spiritual forces of the Kingdom with victory.

---

*Address delivered by President W. A. Harper, Elon College, North Carolina, before the Commission on Christian Union, Seaside Chautauqua, Virginia Beach, Virginia, August 1, 1919. Printed in The Christian Sun by request of the Editor.

Let the subject of Christian union for any two churches be breached and the result is a thousand little voices begin to croak out how the two bodies seeking union differ. You would never settle a difficulty between two brethren in that style. Once upon a time two brethren had a falling out. After some months the preacher got them together to settle it. The reverend brother knew both sides. He first related one side. Then he related the other. Then he asked them to shake hands, but they were enraged at each other and the meeting broke up in a furor. Two days later, they met and without a reference to the past, took each other by the hand, knelt in prayer, and are good friends to this day. You can never get married by telling each other how you differ. You expect some difference, if a marriage is to take place. Else why should there be a marriage at all?

And then in the third place we must avoid all reference to the attempts that have been made at Christian union heretofore and which have failed, or been, costly to us. Every good thing costs us something. Men love their wives most who spend most on them. Where your money is there will your heart be also. Lovers have quarrels, but they refuse to discuss them. They make up by focusing attention on other themes. We have in the Protestant Churches made several abortive attempts to mend our differences in the past, and we have failed. We are still rebellious in our attitude toward our Lord's prayer for the oneness of His people. We are like the man and his wife who had quarrelled. He was a high-tempered man, but of loving disposition. His wife was slow to wrath and equally slow to forgive. She always reminded him of his shortcomings when the fit of his passion had subsided. One day she sought advice of her pastor. He listened patiently and counselled heaping hot coals of fire on his head. "It won't work," she replied. "Why, have you tried it?" he inquired. "No, but I have tried hot water many a time," she said. We must try the hot coals method, since to our sorrow hot water will not work. Let us not despair of success. Marvels have been wrought in our day. The American Republic has participated in a World War. A League of Nations has been provided. Men everywhere else are willing to forget the past and to look to the future. Shall the Churches of God not go and do likewise?

One other danger we must avoid—and that is all thought of property rights and of official positions. Churches need property, but only as a means to insure population for the mansions in the sky. Earthly property is a poor thing at best. It is temporal, but riches eternal are ours in the new Jerusalem. Yet property rights and official positions are doing more to prevent Christian union today than any other causes. But one man went away from Jesus sorrowful, and he was a rich young ruler—he had property and held an office. Property and office-holders ever since, when they have met the demand for self-sacrifice in the call to give up all and to follow Christ, have many times gone away sorrowful.

We preach sacrifice for the individual. Why not preach it for the Church as an organization? Why not preach it for our officers? Why not practice it too? And just as the individual who sacrifices most will be most blessed in his Christian life, just so will the Church which gives and sacrifices most, in order that Christian union may come. Brethren, we can do it if we will. I am one who says, we can do it and we will, and I say so because God's Word teaches me it must be done before Christ's program of world evangelization can be accomplished.

The hour of Christian union has struck. I have said it before. I must say it again. The hour of Christian union has struck. The professing Christian who wilfully and knowingly opposes its realization is a traitor to the cause of Jesus Christ. I pity him. May God forgive him! The man who ignorantly opposes it needs enlightenment. Pray for him. Instruct him. Guide him aright. But the men and women who have sensed the spirit of the times and who have dedicated themselves to the realization of the Master's prayer in the union of His children—of such is the Kingdom of Heaven. Such are the salt of the earth. Such are the light of the world. May God multiply their kind.

A LITTLE PRAYER

Where'er thou be　　　　　　God keep thee ever,
On land or sea,　　　　　　　Heart's delight!
Or in the air,　　　　　　　And guard thee whole.
This little prayer　　　　　Sweet body, soul,
I pray for thee—　　　　　　And spirit high;
God keep thee ever,　　　　That, live or die,
Day and night—　　　　　　　Thou glorify
Face to the light—　　　　His Majesty;
Thine armor bright—　　　　And ever be,
Thy 'scutcheon white—　　Within His sight,
That no despite—　　　　　His true and upright,
Thine honor smite!　　　　Sweet and stainless,
With infinite　　　　　　　Pure and sinless,
Sweet oversight,　　　　　Perfect knight!
　　　　　　　　　　　　　　　—*John Oxenham.*

THE KEY TO SUCCESS

George Stevenson was a man who accomplished very much during his lifetime. The motto which he had adopted and followed is credited with having had much to do with it. This motto was, "Make the best of everything, think the best of everybody, hope the best for yourself." Such a motto means optimism, charity, and ambition—all of those in their highest character and in their smallest manifestation. It is a motto well worth copying.—*Exchange.*

Beholding Jesus as the Lamb of God gives us sight with which we may ever afterwards see Him in all the perfection of His character, and "seeing Him as He is" is the means by which the Holy Spirit transforms us into His likeness. Such a vision is the privilege of every Christian and the secret of perpetual joy, and victory is translating the vision into daily experience.—*A. C. Dixon.*

WORSHIP AND MEDITATION

A TRIBUTE TO MOTHER*

Who is the most sparkling jewel in the world's wondrous crown? It's mother. She is humanity's gem. It's our mothers who instill into our hearts the best principles of our lives. It was at mother's knee where we used to rest our weary heads and receive the gentle touch of her loving hands and the benedictions of her kisses and prayers, the worldly wise, the wayward, the business ridden and the prodigal, find the love of. mother awaken in their hearts If God is love, we know mother loves most of any earthly creature. She is the holiest thing alive. She will sacrifice most freely. She will deny herself most cheerfully. She will endure most patiently, labor most resolutely and forgive most fully. She does most for less, hopes even against hope. She toils and struggles, when all others have given up in despair. It matters not how disobedient her child may be, or how deep her son may be sunken in. drink, or in disease, she does not see it, for she sees only that which is good. No matter how deep in sin her son or daughter may be, or how many times they may trample the loving words of her advice under their feet, mother is still ready to love and claim them as hers. The secret of her love is fortitude and forbearance, patience and tenderness. The depth, sweetness, holiness and beauty of mother love has been recognized and glorified all down the ages. We all know that her words are comforting, her touch tender, and her sympathy helpful. Thank God that no valley is so deep, no burdens too great and no grief too burdensome to cause her to stop to count the cost of her sacrifices.

Mother is the first word on infant's lips; all the perfumes in the world could not add sweetness to that name; all the gems on earth and in ocean could not adequately crown her; all the angels forget-me-nots in heaven could not brighten her being. ''The bravest battle ever fought—shall I tell you where and when? On the map of the world you will find it not, it was fought by the mothers of men.'' The task of painting the lily's petals or brightening the golden sun, or whitening the untrodden mountain snow, would be easy compared with the task of improving the Golden Rule and yet there is one that improves on the Golden Rule every day. Her name is mother. The best woman in the world is your mother and mine. She's founded an empire in the homes and hearts of our great nation. She's the full blown flower of creation. She who clasped our hands in childhood and guided us over life's stormy way; always giving us good counsel, advice and cheer. She gently smooths the pillow of death; she is the greatest of God's pearls and her love is eternal. A mother's love—it's meaning who can measure? Or who such depths of hallowed mystery sound? Outside the heart of God so rich a treasure, has never yet been found. A mother's face all radiant and resplendent, where memory guards the shrine with watchful care, what master hand o'er wrought with touch transcendent, a thing so wondrous fair. A mother's kiss—oh, it's impress lingers, through all the changes that o'er one's soul may creep; it thrills me now as these poor trembling fingers, the chords of memory sweep. We have reached the point in our civilization where motherhood is enshrined in the hearts of the human race, as in no other sentiment. We have arrived at a destiny which reveals to us the divinity of mother. We have come to appreciate so far as the finite mind can appreciate the blessed sacrifices which she makes, the patience which is hers, the saintliness which she possesses.

The best that is in us we owe it to her. Our dads may have been all right; in fact, as men go most of them were, but they did not cuddle us or soothe our businesses, or pillow our weary little heads on loving hearts to sob away our griefs of the day, or make us forget the fears of the stormy nights.

Poets have sung of it, painters and sculptors have sought unceasingly to transfix its inspiring spirit upon canvass or in wondrous carvings of stone; religion has tried by aid of it to build a ladder to the stars, and yet the divinity of it surpasses our power to express and almost our capacity to understand. What transforms in a few fleeting years the shy and gawky girl of the early teens into that marble of patience, devotion, sympathetic understanding and surpassing courage which unfolds with maternity? Isn't it God once more sending His Spirit to abide among the sons of men? If we are fortunate to have mother with us, let us tell her we love her and in some manner express our appreciation of her. Maybe her mile stones are numbered, the battles almost over, the goals almost reached, her journey nigh ended. She is now bending low, her face is pinched, her forehead is wrinkled, and her head is snowy white,—but her gentle, loving voice and her pleasant smiles are the same today as yesterday. If we are away, let us write her a letter of tender rememberance; though we are grown, we are always little children to her. But alas, if mother is gone, let us meditate upon her teachings. Maybe she has placed some of her curly-headed jewels in God's care to blossom and bloom in the spring time of eternity. Though she be sleeping some where beneath the cold clods and the mossy tomb. We know that we shall see mother again, for we feel that Jesus and the holy angels would not bar the pearly gates of heaven against so precious a jewel. Though her dear form be lying beneath the daisies, we know that spirit is one of God's most beautiful angels. God grant that her going was as the rod, softly fading through lesser lights of beauty into night universal, or as the morning star swallowed up into white floods of light, or as the dew upon the grass kissed by the morning sun, or as the perfume of flowers wafted fro mthe vase, or the sound of the harp moving and perishing among listening souls.

Her pale withered hands that more than four score years have wrought for others, soothed the hurt of tears, dropped balm of love in many an aching heart, now lies stirless folded like wan rose leaves pressed; above the snow and silence of her breast, in mute appeal they toil of labor done, and well earned rest that came at set of sun.

What is that wonderful, soul-inspiring, joy-compelling, love abiding sacred place of love and sweetness which is a child's refuge, a maiden's dream, and a man's inspiration? It's home,—but what is home without mother?

---

* Sent for publication by Miss Sallie Poor, Roanoke, Alabama. R. F. D. No. 5.

Mrs. J. W. Whitt—May THE SUN shine forever. I could not get along without it in my home.

FOLLOW THE LEAD OF THE DOUGHBOY!

Wanted: An orphan. Must be a little girl about eight years old with red hair.

"Does that order suit you fellows? Do you consider it specific enough?" asked a doughboy who hailed from Kansas—and, according to the legendary idea concerning Kansas men, he was over six feet tall, had auburn hair, freckles, and smiling eyes.

"Exactly right, I can fairly picture her now—a dainty little French maiden with quaint clothes and a seriously droll expression, but when she smiles—she is the light of the earth!"

"Some poet you are getting to be, Pard."

The four companions of the Westerner assented to his order. It was during the big Orphan Drive in France during the fall of 1918, when soldiers individually and collectively became foster parents of many of the children there. This particular group of five men, belonging to one of our famous divisions, had pooled their contributions for the highly pleasing purpose of sharing an orphan between them.

The order was sent at once to the "Stars and Stripes," the official newspaper for the men of the A. E. F. in France, which in turn gave over all the funds to the A. R. C. for disbursement. This task involved finding orphans to fill orders, and finding orders to fit orphans.

Now the five men are home again, and though widely separated by distance they find their common interest, little Renee Marquard, keeps them in close touch with each other. They have a treasurer and secretary, to whom letters are sent monthly by the A. R. C. concerning Renee's health, her progress at school, and the conditions prevailing in her home. They each possess her picture, and one of them even painted his copy in order to make the red hair more realistic. Best of all are the letters from Renee herself, which are laboriously written and are eagerly answered by every one of her five god-fathers. For Renee, of course, lives in France with her mother, and her small brother. She is learning to speak English, so she proudly reports.

Orphans are in great demand these days. To be up to the minute you must own one. And now the Juniors of the A. R. C. have absorbed this idea so thoroughly that *they* are adopting orphans by the orphanageful, from Palestine to Antwerp and from Le Havre to the Balkans.

THE SACRIFICE

"She died that we might live," is the epitaph of a little Russian girl, Feodora Hurtat, who saved her younger sister and brother, but in so doing sacrificed her own life. Down through the ages, the supreme sacrifice is repeated again and again. It is, however, for the child heroes and heroines that the heart beats in its greatest sympathy.

A little dark-haired girl with black eyes serious from premature cares, yet retaining their natural fun-loving look, was taking a walk with her brother and sister in town. She became so interested in gathering the pretty flowers along the way that she forgot that danger lurked for the small kiddies strolling on the track. Suddenly looking up, she saw the train approaching; it was nearly upon them. With lightning speed, she raced to save them. She reached them in time and hurled them off the tracks, but could not get away herself from in front of the onrushing train; and was dragged beneath the wheels of the engine. When she was lifted from the track, terribly injured, she was still living, but quite unconscious. The Red Cross ambulance at Vdladivostok was rushed to the scene of the disaster, and the little heroine was carried to a white bed in the American Red Cross hospital.

Everyone at the hospital was interested in her case. A special nurse looked after her day and night; her mother was with her constantly; doctors, nurses, orderlies were eager to see her open her eyes and live again. Everything humanly possible was done in her behalf but to no avail. For five days she lay thus, and then slept the eternal sleep.

Sunday School and Christian Endeavor

SUNDAY SCHOOL LESSON. FOR AUGUST 24, 1919

Social Responsibility. Luke 10:25-27; Gal. 6:2, 9, 10; James 2:14-16.

Golden Text: "As we have opportunity, let us work that which is good toward all men." Gal. 6:10.

(For Teaching Points, see Teachers and Officers Journal)

This lawyer was trying to tempt Jesus by asking an answer to an impossible question. There is nothing one can do to inherit for that is a matter of birth. So Jesus said, "Ye must be born again." P. Whitwell Wilson, the author of "The Christ We Forget" has written a little book called "Two Ancient Red Cross Tales." I am sure you will enjoy reading the version there given of this old, ever new story of the Good Samaritan. What is the social duty of the Christian today? What, if any, duty does he owe to his community? Do you think, as you men folks cast your votes of your responsibility before God for those votes? "Oh,' you say, "we must not mix politics and religion," but I say to you that if "the powers that be are ordained of God," they are mixed, and the trouble has come because you have tried to separate them. This is not a mixing of Church and State, but it is a putting of your religion into your politics. What about the social life of your town? "Satan finds some mischief still for idle hands to do." Have you tried to be as clever for God as Satan's agents are for him in finding some good thing for the idle times? Any one with a pair of heels and an instrument to make music can dance. It requires neither brains nor ability. Yet in many communities that is absolutely the only form of amusement open to the young life. If we really believe that God made them, we must believe He implanted in them their love of fun, their desire for a good time. Shall we sit supinely by, and allow Satan to turn their good times into bad times? Shall we not be as wise in our generation? Who, then, is my neighbor? He who needs my help of any kind whatsoever.

MRS. FRED BULLOCK.

WE GO FORWARD

The Sunday schools of one of our great Conventions have decided in annual session assembled, and unanimously, to "go forward." Look: Resolved, "That the Sunday schools of this Convention set as their goal the coming year $1,500.00, one-half for Home, one-half for Foreign Missions, and that to raise this amount every school in the Convention give one offering a month." So voted the North Carolina State Christian Sunday School and Christian Endeavor or Convention in annual session at Shallow Well church, July 15-17. Will they do it? Well, just watch them put it over.

Already one school—Durham—is sending in $10.00 a month. If twelve other schools of the Convention were to do as well the goal would be reached, and more. And we have other schools as able and as liberal as Durham. Several other live schools of the Convention have already voted to give one offering a month to missions—Reidsville, Lebanon (Semora), Pleasant Grove and Ingram, Va., Graham, New Providence, Haw River, Catawba Springs, Wentworth, New Elam, Chapel Hill, and maybe others of this Convention, have already voted and the number increases constantly.

We believe that every school in the Convention will ultimately come in, and the funds will grow, as will interest in the one thing for which every school and church exists, namely, missions. If a Sunday school is not to have a part in world-wide evangelization, have a hand in helping reach this world for Christ, why should the school exist at all?

And then the Convention did another great and good thing for itself. It decided that it must have a Sunday school missionary in the field, planting and organizing Sunday schools where there are not any and where there should be both schools and churches. In short the North Carolina Sunday School and Christian Endeavor Convention has decided to grow—to start something, to "carry on."

J. O. ATKINSON.

CHRISTIAN ENDEAVOR TOPIC FOR AUGUST 24, 1919

The Folly of Pride. Prov. 16:1-19.

A poor man watched the funeral carried out, and then turning to a bystander said, "Well, yesterday, I didn't have a dollar and that man had a million. Today he has not a cent, and I have a dollar." You own nothing that can be taken away from you. You say you own an automobile, but a collision occurs, and all you have is a scrap pile. You own a house, but there is a fire, and all you have is a pile of ashes. You own your land, but who owned it a few years ago and who will own it by and by when you are gone? How foolish then, the pride which rejoices in vanishing possessions. Some have pride in their learning, but this simply shows how much that one has yet to learn. The one who is really knows enough to see how much is still unknown. "My soul shall make her boast in the Lord." That is the only true pride. All other is the kind that goeth before destruction."

MRS. FRED BULLOCK.

912 NEW CHRISTIAN ENDEAVOR SOCIETIES ORGANIZED IN SOUTH

"In spite of the war, the Kaiser, the Flu and the sleeping sickness we have organized 912 new Christian Endeavor Societies in the South during the last two years," said Karl Lehmann of Chattanooga, Tenn., Southern States Secretary of the United Society of Christian Endeavor in his report at the International Christian Endeavor Conference in Buffalo, N. Y., August 5-10.

Secretary Lehmann told of the great gains made in Christian Endeavor in the Southern States with the addition of 75,000 new members to the ranks of the organization in the past two years. Four employed Field Workers have been constantly traveling and at work under the direction of the Endeavorers in the South. Karl Lehmann of Chattanooga, Tenn., is the executive in charge of the work and edits the monthly paper, *The Dixie Endeavorer*, Charles F. Evans of Lexington, Ky., as Field Secretary has brought great blessing and inspiration to the young people of the churches of the South. W. Roy Breg of Dallas, Texas, has been serving as General Secretary of the Texas Union and has just been put in charge of the new Southwestern Christian Endeavor Federation to direct the work in Texas, Oklahoma, Colorado, New Mexico and Arizona, and Chien Tsai of Shanghai, China, a native Secretary in China whose salary and expenses are paid by the Christian Endeavorers of the South.

An additional Field Worker will be added to the forces in the South in September.

MARRIAGES

MORGAN-BELL

One of the prettiest weddings of the season was solemnized Thursday afternoon, July 31, 1919, at the First Christian church, Berkley, Norfolk, Va., when Miss Lula Wilmath Bell became the bride of Rev. Joseph Frank Morgan. The bride is the beautiful and accomplished daughter of Mr. and Mrs. K. R. Bell of Berkley, and a loyal member of the First Christian church. The bridegroom is the son of Mr. and Mrs. Joseph P. Morgan of Spies, N. C. He is a loyal minister of the Christian Church, and enjoys the esteem of the Brotherhood. He is the popular pastor of the First Christian church, Berkley, where he is loved by all the members.

The church was decorated with ferns and cut flowers. Just before the ceremony Mrs. Edward T. Jones sang, "O Promise Me," accompanied by Mrs. W. J. Spence, who also rendered the wedding march from Lohengrin.

The ushers were Mr. Silas Morgan, brother of the bridegroom, and Mr. W. J. Lewis. The ring bearer was little Miss Katherine Morgan. The bride entered with her sister, Miss Sarah Bell, who was maid of honor. She was dressed in white organdie and carried pink killarney roses. The bride was attired in a blue traveling suit, with hat and gloves to match, and carried an arm bouquet of brides' roses. The bridegroom entered with his best man, Rev. J. V. Knight, pastor of the First Christian

church, Greensboro, N. C., and met the bride at the altar. The ceremony was performed by the writer, in the presence of an audience that filled the church, using the beautiful ring ceremony. Immediately after the ceremony, the happy couple left by boat for Washington, D. C., New York, Niagara Falls, and other points North, on an extended bridal tour. After August 15 Rev. and Mrs. Morgan will be at home to friends at 15 Hough Ave., Berkley, Va.

The bride was the reception of many beautiful and useful presents. May happiness and prosperity be theirs through life.

O. D. POYTHRESS.

NOTES

Congress has taken up the matter of the high cost of living and relief is being sought throught the various government agencies.

Miss Hester Stuart, the efficient bookkeeper and assistant in THE CHRISTIAN SUN office, is spending this week in Randolph County. Readers of THE SUN reap many benefits from the labors of those whose names never appear in the paper.

Rev. J. E. McCauley writes: "My meeting at Ebenezer closed August 1. Six professions made and several reconsecrations. Rev. B. J. Howard did the preaching and Brother J. H. Moring conducted the singing. Both did splendid work. The church is much revived."

The governor of North Carolina, T. W. Bickett, paid Burlington a visit the other day. He exceeded the speed limit and was halted by the traffic police and cited to the mayor's court. The officer informed him that the city traffic laws had no reservation for governors.

Recently we stated that Rev. J. E. Franks had been elected Sunday School Secretary of the Sunday School and Christian Endeavor Convention of the North Carolina Conference. A member of the Convention informs us that Brother Franks is to give one-half of his time as Sunday School Missionary. We are glad to make the correction. After all our work is first missionary.

The railroad shopmen over the country struck last week for an increase in pay. They put it up to the administration that their action is due to the high cost of living and that they want the cost of necessities of life reduced. At this writing many of the shopmen have returned to work. President Wilson advised them through Director Hines that nothing could be done until they returned to their jobs. The matter will soon be settled, it is thought.

Mrs. Mary Bradley, a member of Mt. Zion church, is a cheerful cripple. She is one of the fifteen whom we remember with our Exchanges after reading them. We visited her last Sunday and enjoyed a few moments in her home. She is a loyal and faithful reader of THE SUN. She said that she had imagined for a long time that the Editor was a middle aged man with black mustache and was surprised to see a "boy."

Dr. D. A. Long gives us this information in a personal letter dated at Liberty, N. C., July 30: "While at Salem Chapel the third Sunday I was cared for by Brother Will Strader on Saturday and by Brother J. G. Fynt on Sunday. While at Winston-Salem I called to see Dr. W. T. Herndon. Although feeble, he was able to sit up and converse about old times..........Brothers Hatch and Trogden are some better, though too feeble to look after their usual work. Two services here last Sunday; good prayer meeting Wednesday night ....I expect to preach at Pleasant Hill once next Saturday and twice on Sunday."

For lack of space, many notes had to be left out this week. They will appear later.

A Terror

"Bertie," said mother, sorrowfully, "every time you are naughty I get another gray hair."

"My word!" replied Bertie, "you must have been a terror. Look at grandpa;"—*Tit-Bits.*

Some Run

Mose was telling of a battle he was in—how terrifying it was. Some one asked, "Didn't you run, Mose?"

"No," said Mose, "I didn't run, but I passed some niggers what was running."—*Selected.*

Up to The Undertaker

Mayor Mitchell, of New York, was talking at a dinner about office-seekers.

"A good man had just died," he said, "and with unseemly haste, an office-seeker came after his job.

"Yes, sir, though the dead man hadn't been buried, yet this office-seeker came to me and said breathlessly: 'Mr. Mayor, do you see any objection to my being put in put in poor Tom Smith's place?'

" 'Why, no,' said I. 'Why, no; I see no objection if the undertaker doesn't.' "

Those Wonderful French

A Chicago boy, who had the good fortune to return in good shape from his thrilling experience with the marines at Chateau Thierry, was prevailed upon by some girl friends to relate his experiences there.

Quite differently he recounted what he remembered of the fighting at the point where he was stationed. "We were having a terrible time," he said, until the French brought up their 75,s."

Whereupon one of the girls exclaimed: "I think it is so splendid for men of that age to be fighting, don't you?"—*Cartoons Magazine.*

Days of The Future

Friend of the Family—Where's everybody, Bennett?

The Butler—Well, sir, the missus and the young ladies is up in the sky, learning to fly, and the master's in his submarine in the hornamental lake. It's very seldom you catches them on terry firmy these days.—*London Opinion.*

FOR THE DIGESTION

What is the Color of Blue Grass?

Overheard in a seed and grain house:

Young Matron—We are starting a new lawn. What can you advise me about the seeding.

Proprietor—Well, clover, and blue grass is a good mixture.

Young Matron—But—oh, I don't want blue grass; I want green grass.

Located The Money

First undergraduate: "Have you telegraphed for money?"

Second Undergraduate: "Yes; I telegraphed yesterday."

First Undergraduate: "Got any answer?"

Second Undergraduate: "Yes, I telegraphed the governor. 'Where is that money I wrote for?' And his answer reads: 'In my pocket.' "—*Baltimore Sun.*

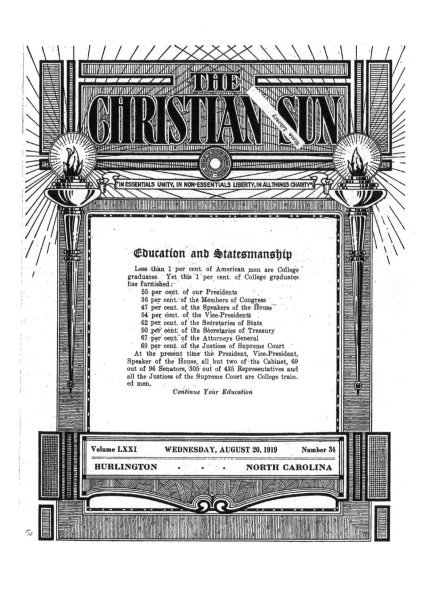

THE CHRISTIAN SUN

"IN ESSENTIALS UNITY, IN NON-ESSENTIALS LIBERTY, IN ALL THINGS CHARITY"

Education and Statesmanship

Less than 1 per cent. of American men are College graduates. Yet this 1 per cent. of College graduates has furnished:

55 per cent. of our Presidents
36 per cent. of the Members of Congress
47 per cent. of the Speakers of the House
54 per cent. of the Vice-Presidents
62 per cent. of the Secretaries of State
50 per cent. of the Secretaries of Treasury
67 per cent. of the Attorneys General
69 per cent. of the Justices of Supreme Court

At the present time the President, Vice-President, Speaker of the House, all but two of the Cabinet, 69 out of 96 Senators, 305 out of 435 Representatives and all the Justices of the Supreme Court are College trained men.

Continue Your Education

Volume LXXI	WEDNESDAY, AUGUST 20, 1919	Number 34
BURLINGTON	· · ·	NORTH CAROLINA

FOR THE DIGESTION

What is the Color of Blue Grass?

Overheard in a seed and grain house:

Young Matron—We are starting a new lawn. What can you advise me about the seeding.

Proprietor—Well, clover, and blue grass is a good mixture.

Young Matron—But—oh, I don't want blue grass; I want green grass.

Located The Money

First undergraduate: "Have you telegraphed for money?"

Second Undergraduate: "Yes; I telegraphed yesterday."

First undergraduate: "Got any answer?"

Second Undergraduate: "Yes, I telegraphed the governor. 'Where is that money I wrote for?' And his answer reads: 'In my pocket.'"—*Baltimore Sun.*

A Terror

"Bertie," said mother, sorrowfully, "every time you are naughty I get another gray hair."

"My word!" replied Bertie, "you must have been a terror. Look at grandpa;"—*Tit-Bits.*

Some Run

Mose was telling of a battle he was in—how terrifying it was. Some one asked, "Didn't you run, Mose?"

"No," said Mose, "I didn't run, but I passed some niggers what was running."—*Selected.*

Up to The Undertaker

Mayor Mitchell, of New York, was talking at a dinner about office-seekers.

"A good man had just died," he said, "and with unseemly haste, an office-seeker came after his job.

"Yes, sir, though the dead man hadn't been buried, yet this office-seeker came to me and said breathlessly: 'Mr. Mayor, do you see any objection to my being put in put in poor Tom Smith's place?'

"'Why, no,' said I. 'Why, no; I see no objection if the undertaker doesn't.'"

Those Wonderful French

A Chicago boy, who had the good fortune to return in good shape from his thrilling experience with the marines at Chateau Thierry, was prevailed upon by some girl friends to relate his experiences there.

Quite differently he recounted what he remembered of the fighting at the point where he was stationed. "We were having a terrible time," he said, until the French brought up their 75,s."

Whereupon one of the girls exclaimed: "I think it is so splendid for men of that age to be fighting, don't you?"—*Cartoons Magazine.*

Days of The Future

Friend of the Family—Where's everybody, Bennett?

The Butler—Well, sir, the missus and the young ladies is up in the sky, learning to fly, and the master's in his submarine in the hornamental lake. It's very seldom you catches them on terry firmy these days—*London Opinion.*

THE CHRISTIAN SUN

"IN ESSENTIALS UNITY, IN NON-ESSENTIALS LIBERTY, IN ALL THINGS CHARITY"

Education and Statesmanship

Less than 1 per cent. of American men are College graduates. Yet this 1 per cent. of College graduates has furnished:

  55 per cent. of our Presidents
  36 per cent. of the Members of Congress
  47 per cent. of the Speakers of the House
  54 per cent. of the Vice-Presidents
  62 per cent. of the Secretaries of State
  50 per cent. of the Secretaries of Treasury
  67 per cent. of the Attorneys General
  69 per cent. of the Justices of Supreme Court

At the present time the President, Vice-President, Speaker of the House, all but two of the Cabinet, 69 out of 96 Senators, 305 out of 435 Representatives and all the Justices of the Supreme Court are College trained men.

Continue Your Education

Volume LXXI	WEDNESDAY, AUGUST 20, 1919	Number 34

BURLINGTON   ·   ·   ·   NORTH CAROLINA

THE CHRISTIAN SUN

Founded 1844 by Rev. Daniel W. Kerr

C. B. RIDDLE   -   -   -   Editor

Entered at the Burlington, N. C. Post Office as second class matter.

Subscription Rates

One year .... $ 2.00
Six months 1.00

In Advance

Give both your old and new postoffice when asking that your address be changed.

The change of your label is your receipt for money. Written receipts sent upon request.

Many persons subscribe for friends, intending that the paper be stopped at the end of the year. If instructions are given to this effect, they will receive attention at the proper time.

Marriage and obituary notices not exceeding 150 words printed free if received within 60 days from date of event, all over this at the rate of one-half cent a word.

Original poetry not accepted for publication.

Principles of the Christian Church

(1) The Lord Jesus Christ is the only Head of the Church.
(2) Christian is a sufficient name of the Church.
(3) The Holy Bible is a sufficient rule of faith and practice.
(4) Christian character is a sufficient test of fellowship, and of church membership.
(5) The right of private judgment and the liberty of conscience is a right and a privilege that should be accorded to, and exercised by all.

EDITORIAL

WILL THE CHANGE BE?

Hon. P. P. Claxton, United States Commissioner of Education, has pointed out to college and university presidents the great possibility that this country has in making it take Germany's place in the realm of education. Our people have gone to Europe for advanced study. German universities have been great centers of educational work. But Germany's theory of education has proven futile. Will America become the educational country, and will the day come when the scholars of Europe will come to us for study? The answer is with us.

BEATING THEM TO IT

General Julian S. Carr, and his son, J. S. Carr, Jr., Durham, N. C., are working out a plan of democratic control over the eleven hosiery mills in which they have controlling stock. The plan is to be modeled after the Federal Government—the employees to constitute the house of representatives, the managers the senate, and the owners the cabinet. The experiment is unique and will be watched and studied with interest. This is beating the strikers to it.

WHERE THE POPULACE AGREE

Some of us are Democrats and some of us are Republicans—and perhaps some of us are of some other political faith. We differ in *name* and disagree on *certain* principles. We are not so far apart—just enough to keep each other careful while in power—that's all. But while we differ on points, we are all agreed upon one thing: That our law-making bodies lose too much time while the people suffer. The people want relief and they should have it. The cost of living is outrageous. Some one is profiteering and the people want Congress to find the man. That is what the people want most just now.

LEVELING DOWN OR LEVELING UP

Talking about leveling things, it is better to level *up* than it is to level *down*. Education levels *up*, and that is the reason that the "privileged class" is no longer found. The people are becoming an educated people, and education is leveling them *up*. When the people are leveled *down*, a few are able to stand above the others, but when all are leveled up, the difference is not so great. Go to school this fall, young man, young woman, and help to level your generation *up*. Education levels *up*; ignorance levels *down*.

HIS EARNESTNESS

"He is not such a great preacher," said a man the other day in speaking of his pastor, "but he is earnest," he continued. So this member puts *earnestness* before *greatness*. A good estimation, for we cannot become great unless we are earnest in our task. Sincerity is the key that unlocks the hidden treasure to those who desire to be masters of their work. We must mean well and put forth the right endeavor to win others and win our way. In all things be true. "Truth crushed to earth shall rise again—the eternal years of God are hers."

BANKRUPT CHRISTIANS

A man never becomes bankrupt until his assets become less than his liabilities. A Christian may also become bankrupt in his life by allowing the assets of his Christian life to get too low. He ceases to draw from the fountain of life and the liabilities soon overcome the assets. The Christian life is too free and plentiful for any man to perish his soul and place it upon the bankrupt market.

A LITTLE REASONING

There are a few (very few) readers of THE SUN who do not fully comprehend the situation between the columns of THE SUN and the work of the Church. They expect *as much* publicity, as much space, as was given five or ten years ago. That long ago we had the same number of pages that we have now. But the Church has grown, more departments have been created, more work undertaken and more work being done. When a business develops it would seem that its publicity should become larger—and it should. But unless the publicity medium becomes larger, such cannot be. On the other hand, it must be less for the amount of space must be divided by a larger number.

PROFITS

Profits is the bone of contention and discussion now in connection with the high cost of living. Congress is endeavoring to regulate profits, and it seems that such a step is about the only way to handle the situation. There are many who have stopped figuring on what is a fair profit, but how much they can get for the article, or how much the customer will stand. If we can get the profiteers—the ones who are able to corner and hold the products—there is much hope in reducing the cost of living. It is a matter in which all of us are concerned.

SUNDAY SCHOOLS AND CEMETERIES

There are many Sunday schools that are not far from the cemetery. In fact the question with us is: How they have kept out of the burying place these many years? These schools to which we refer are stale, static and stupid. They open the same way they did after the war—the war of '62 to '65 and close—well, some of them don't close; they just quit and go home, announcing that there will be "school next Sunday morning at 10 o'clock." Our problem in the Sunday school work is to make the indifferent school different. What are you going to do with yours?

THIS WEEK AND NEXT

This week and next many decisions will be made by young people about going to college. Numbers of young men and women have already made up their minds as to where they will go and made arrangements therefor. Many have not. Some during these weeks will take the step not to go and such will be a fatal blunder to their life's career. Living is high and many may not feel that they can attend college, but we cannot afford to measure a college training by the yard stick of dollars and cents. Go to college, go this fall —and go to your own college—Elon.

METHODS versus ENTHUSIASM

We believe in enthusiasm, but we believe more in methods. We have heard many great and stirring addresses that set our hearts to a desire to act, but when we went to act we were without a plan and a method. Such is very true in many Sunday school addresses we hear nowadays. They enthuse us to do, but fail to show us how to do. What the religious activities of the Church need is plans—practical plans—and demonstrations. It is unfair and unbusiness-like to stir a man to do a thing, and not tell him how to do it. In one case he may be able to do it, but in another he may not be able. An idea ought to be backed up by a plan, and a program. It is not enough to just to speak—we need to outline something in the speech.

FIFTEEN MILLION DOLLARS

The State of North Carolina estimates that it loses fifteen million dollars annually because of the unsanitary habits of the people. The Board points out that if modes of living, and means of sanitation could be brought up to a certain standard that the State's saving each year would amount to this enormous amount of money. There is said to be about four thousand

deaths each year in the State, due directly to preventable diseases. From the same source of sickness there is estimated to be thirty-five thousand cases of sickness, the total cost of which, together with the deaths caused by this sickness, cost the State of North Carolina fifteen million dollars. The Church is the one great educational factor in each community and ought to unite with the State Board of Health in preventing this waste of manhood and wealth.

FIFTY THOUSAND NEW C. E. MEMBERS IN DIXIE

Fifty thousand new members to be added to the Christian Endeavor societies of the South this fall is the aim of a great membership increase campaign to be conducted in October for which plans were announced from the Southern Christian Endeavor Headquarters in Chattanooga this week.

Christian Endeavor has made some great advances during the past four years in the South and the leaders are confident that this goal will be passed also.

The Christian Endeavor movement now has 4,000,000 members in 80,000 societies found in churches of 87 different denominations and in every country of the world. The Methodists lead throughout the world, though in this country many of their churches have a denominational society known as the Epworth League.

ANDREW CARNEGIE

Andrew Carnegie, the great steel magnate, passed away at his summer home at Lenox, Mass., Monday morning, August 11. Carnegie had passed his eightieth mile post. He was a great and good man. He came to America when a mere boy, and began his first work in the railroad industry as a telegraph operator. He applied himself well and had a great genius for mechanical inventions. He accumulated a fortune of many millions of dollars. In his late years he used most of this in establishing libraries, endowing colleges and doing general benevolent work. He was a great idealist and was a great advocate of the idea of universal brotherhood among men. He was not a great business man, but a good writer and enriched the world's literature by his pen. His life was simple and his habits few. He was not buried amid pomp and splendor, but in the same simple way in which he had lived. Carnegie had the idea that riches did not constitute greatness, but that he was a steward of his wealth, and proved that stewardship in later years by Christian use of his money.

EDUCATING OUR OWN PEOPLE

It takes leadership to build a denomination and keep it going and growing. Our first effort ought to be to get our own people to attend our own colleges. Elon, the college of our Southern work, ought to be filled to its capacity each year with young men and women of the Christian Church. However, because no larger per cent of our people graduate from Elon is not the fault of the College but of the people. Our people are first in attendance and have the largest per cent of graduates, but the point we make it that it could be made larger and in so doing would be to the interest of Church and its growth.

PASTOR AND PEOPLE

WINCHESTER LETTER

We have come to the close of another conference year. We have had a good year from the standpoint of finances, but not a large increase in membership. Eight members have been received during the year and all church organizations are actively at work. The salary and conference apportionments have been paid in full and $1,679.50 raised on the church debt. We shall have regular service next year and we are laying our plans for a larger and more aggressive work.

The writer has tried to serve the churches at New Hope, Timber Mountain and Beulah during the year We have had very little time for these churches and but little progress has been made. They will all meet all financial obligations and New Hope has installed a new lighting plant. We received two members at Beulah at our last appointment.

It was our privilege to spend ten days with Brother W. C. Hook in a meeting at Mt. Olivet, Greene County. It was a pleasure to be with those good people and the Lord richly blessed us in the service. Brother Hook is held in the highest esteem both by the church and the community. I spent one day very pleasant with Rev. Killis Roach at the High Point church. They are planning for new churches at both these points during the year.

The following is a list of contributions to the Winchester church:

Previously reported, $11,455.05; W. A. Crawford, $5.00; Rev. G. D. Eastes, $25.00; Rev. J. O. Atkinson, $10.00; Ever Ready Society, $42.77; Rev. W. C. Hook, $10.00; W. A. Larrick, $2.00; Col. Robert F. Leedy, $3.00; Ladies Aid Society, $100.00; C. H. Barr, $5.00; 1. A. Loyd, $5.00; Alva C. Richards, $110.00; Mrs. Alva C. Richards, $100.00; W. F. Recherd, $10.00; Women's H. and F. Board, Val. Conf., $148.25; A. D. Larrick, $5.00; M. S. Loy, $5.00; Rev. L. F. Johnson, $1.00; C. J. Sibert, $5.00; F. L. Oates, $25.00; Mrs. W. A. McCurdy, $5.00; E. W. Cather, $100.00; Mrs. W. T. Walters, $3.00; A. B. Richards, $100.00; Total, $12,289.07.

We are thankful for this good report.

W. T. WALTERS.

Winchester, Va.
August 12, 1919.

FROM A CHAPLAIN ON THE GO:

There is an old saying that is true: "You can't always, sometime tell."

Why should we worry? After a whole Sunday in the town of Franklinton, N. C., anyone would forget the worry.

By invitation I spoke to a full house at the M. E. church in Franklinton, N. C., on August 3, at 11:15 A. M., and also at 8:15 P. M. I was privileged to be in the home of Brother Geo. T. Whitaker, also the homes of Brother Allen and Brother Utley. It was good to meet Pastor G. J. Green and his family, where we broke bread and renewed an acquaintance of fourteen years of absolute separation.

Brother Green will teach school the coming year, which leaves a splendid field for someone who is willing to be a pastor and a preacher. If you are interested, write Brother Geo. T. Whitaker, Burlington, N. C.

Franklington is a coming town. Will the church keep up? Good water, lights, streets and lovely homes. Splendid people live there and the town is backed by a good farming section.

Here I am wandering from the subject. Go back to the first of this letter. I am at Camp Lee, Base Hospital, Petersburg, Va. I came here Monday afternoon, August 4. When I left Elon College, I assured my family and friends that I would return about August 6 or 7. I hope to be back about August 13 or 14. Uncle Sam has a way of looking a fellow over before he says: "Go, my son and live ever happy."

I suffered just a little from the "Flu" but kept "mum" (as good soldiers should do).

The tonsils are now out. I feel sure my big uncle will soon turn me loose. It is a hot sight here. Living on milk is no fun.

B. F. BLACK.

August 8.

FROM THE HOSPITAL WARD

I am thinking not only of my family at dear old Elon; not only of that old mother of mine in her little village home in the valley of old Virginia—that mother of mine waiting for her boy to return and tell her of the second war she has passed through; not only of my many friends in Virginia and North Carolina, but I am also thinking of the world about me. I have met the boys from every clime. Here before me in a little book are their names and addresses. The Indian Captain from out West; the French Canadian lad and all the rest, for we were pals. I am thinking of the Jap, of the boy from the Phillipines, from Porto Rico and Cuba. I am thinking of the English Tommy; of the Scotch and many others.

If I could get in an airship and visit a dozen countries in Europe there I would find a glad hand and hear the welcome: "Hello Padre." "Ah! there Chaplain! Come right in, not as you were but as you like." There are my friends indeed. They are numbered by the thousands and are in far away France. They paid the price, their hands are motionless and their tongues forever silent; yet louder than all the tongues on earth they speak to me and to you. Their offering calls to me to help garner the harvest from the soil enriched by their royal red blood. Oh: I know, for I held their hands in that last moment. I wrote that last letter to the dear ones at home. Some of these letters went around the world. Today these hands I cannot touch, because they were given to the world, and today lie beneath the wooden crosses in "Sunny France" where I was privileged to place the stars and stripes upon their caskets, flowers on their little graves and to place a cross to mark the head of their resting place. I was privileged to give them a Christian burial. Today as I look back it seems like an awful dream, yet my soul is flooded by some mighty tidal wave, some holy desire and some unexplainable inspiration calling me to a greater service. Not in doing the big things, but in doing the little things.

I am trying to think in constructive terms. The challenge of my friends, living and dead, is a call to me; and is some how pleading for an awakening in my own heart. Through the long nights and by the electric light and the candle, I have been thinking of these boys. I have been thinking of the little bundled cot, the Bible in my hand and how we turned to sacred pages from the first Chapter of Genesis through Jeremiah. I am trying to catch the great idea of a constructive program. For two months now I have been a globe trotter. I am trying to pull my own self together. The Holy Christ tells me of the constructive man. The man who built a house upon the rock, where the winds and the storm were defeated in their vandal effort. But there is the beckoning hand of destruction. A man built a house upon the sand, the waves came and the house fell. The Master also spoke of another constructive element—good fruit and evil fruit. What shall our program be? Shall it be constructive or destructive?

There are two classes in the world. One looks into the pit, and the other gazes into the sky. In the quiet of this holy and beautiful Sabbath day on which I write, there comes that call to me: "Look unto the hills from whence cometh my strength." The call of this day and generation is great.

Sure there must come something to us out of the great noise of the battle—empires have fallen and the cry of the unrest is heard. To one it is the sound of thunder; while to another it is a voice from Heaven. What is our view point of life? Where do we receive help and strength? What are our plans?

We have the privilege of drawing from that fountain which never runs dry. Why feed from crumbs under feet that are unholy, when we can draw from the fountain in our Father's house?

B. F. BLACK.
Base Hospital, Camp Lee, Va.

CHRISTIAN EDUCATION

ADVOCATES A TEACHERAGE
(An article written for The Burlington News by C. B. Riddle.)

I notice in *The Burlington News* of August 6 that a committee has been appointed to look after homes for the teachers who are to teach in the city schools. This brings to mind several things that are of interest and vital concern.

A few years ago there was bidding for the teachers in any community. Many homes counted themselves fortunate to secure for board the teachers in the community school. This was true in city as well as in rural localities.

Why has such a change come? Changes in the mode of living have come. The automobile is now ready for the members of the family to take a ride after supper and we no longer care to have boarders in our home to hinder us from going at our leisure. Possibly this reason alone counts to a large extent for the reason that teachers find it more difficult to secure boarding places than they once did. The servant problem is another factor, and it would also be unfair to the question not to mention the unsettled conditions of the markets. Today we may accept a boarder at one price basing that price upon the market of today, and tomorrow you have lost. You also know that the teacher's salary remains the same, and it would be your embarrassment as well as hers to constantly increase the amount of her board account.

I believe that the board problem of the school teachers of the country will continue to be a difficult one and become more acute. I have pointed out the problem, now for the solution.

The progressive churches in every city have parsonages and manses for their pastors. These are the property of the churches and the churches could not do without them. Following this idea, why not have a teacherage? By this I mean a building owned by the city and used for the purpose of the teachers of the city schools. This home or building would be occupied by the superintendent and his family, and part of his consideration for his services would be the use of this building for his domicile. The building could have ample rooms for the teachers of the school and also provision for the lady members to do light-house keeping, in case they prefer to do. Or the idea could be carried a step further and the school system of the city provide a manager and servants and board the entire teaching corps, letting this consideration become a part of their fixed salary.

We seek the best teachers and are not content without them, but it is unfair to demand the best equipment and not give them the best in comfort and entertainment. We demand of them the best service and yet we ought not to do this unless we are willing that they demand of us a suitable place to live without canvassing the entire city for a place to board while they are engaged in the most important work of the land.

I wonder if some man, or group of men, would not be interested in fathering such a move in behalf of the school system of our progressive city? I send this message forth for consideration because of my interest in education.

C. H. Stephenson—I hope to be able to keep THE SUN shining in our home as long as I live. I wish we could get more of our church people to read their Church paper. (This is our Roanoke, Ala., C. H.—*Editor*).

• •

Get the reading habit—it is hard to beat

• •

Pray for the missionaries—they need it

• •

Get your neighbors to read the Christian Sun

EDUCATION FROM DIFFERENT VIEWPOINTS
Does Education Pay?

The title of a little pamphlet issued by the Department of Education of Tennessee, is "Does It Pay?" which proves by statistics that education is a paying investment, even from the standpoint of dollars and cents.

After comparing the nations of the world and showing that education determines the wealth and power of peoples, figures are cited to prove that in the countries having the best educational systems the per capita production of the population is much higher than in those with poor school facilities.

For instance, the annual earning capacity per inhabitant of England, France and Germany, where the educational systems are efficient, is $180, $155 and $125 respectively, while in Sain, Greece and Russia, nations with "inadequate educational systems," it is only $80, $65 and $50 respectively.

The author of the pamphlet then draws the comparison between states of the United States, showing how it pays the state to educate, and cites statistics to prove that the earning capacity per inhabitant is large in proportion to the amount the state spends for education.

As an example, in comparison between Massachusetts and South Carolina the returns upon investment in education are brought out in a convincing manner. Massachusetts gives her citizens 7.4 years schooling and spent last year $26 per pupil or a total of $16,013,000. South Carolina gives 3.18 years schooling and spent last year $1,678,000 on education, or $6.95 per pupil.

The Massachusetts citizen produced $466 per year, while the South Carolina citizen produced only $171 per year.

The statistics on the per capita production in Texas are not available, but the per capita production of this state is doubtless below that of the states spending more for education than does Texas. This state is at the head of the list among Southern states, in amount spent per capita of total population for education, but it is far below some of the Northern states, for instance, spent $7.35 per capita in 1916, while Texas spent only $4.76. Mississippi with its large negro population, spent only $1.48 per capita.

It is time that there be a general recognition of the fact that the money put into schools is not charity, nor yet simply for broadening the culture of the citizen, however desirable that may be, but that it is a business proposition for the citizen and the state. The money put into education represents an investment that pays big dividends in money. The returns in other ways can not be estimated.—*Houston (Texas) Post.*

Are You Educated?

A professor of the University of Chicago has evolved a series of test questions for the educated which he avows, are the best evidences of a real education. If you can answer yes to all the questions are truly educated the professor says. Here are the questions:

Has education given you any sympathy with all the good causes and made you espouse them?

Has it made you public-spirited?
Has it made you a brother to the weak?
Have you learned how to make friends and keep them?
Do you know what it is to be a friend yourself?
Can you look an honest man or a pure woman in the eye?
Do you see anything to love in a little child?
Will a lonely dog follow you in the street?
Can you be high-minded and happy in the drudgeries of life?
Do you think that washing dishes and hoeing corn is just as compatible with high thinking as playing piano or golf?
Are you good for anything yourself?
Can you be happy alone?
Can you look out on the world and see anything but dollars and cents?
Can you look into a mud puddle by the wayside and see a clear sky?
Can you see anything in the puddle but mud?—*The Christian News Letter.*

What About The Church Colleges?

The Disciples of Christ have recently completed their Men and Millions campaign for millions with which to finance enlarged work at home and abroad. But money will not save this world. We must match our dollars with men and women—Christian men and women of great faith, trained minds, and broad vision, else will our program fail at the most crucial point. The church is calling for one thousand trained workers. What is the source of supply for these workers? It must be our own church school.

One of our great educators recently said: "The success of the Church of Christ itself is dependent upon the Christian college." That is a challenging statement and worthy of serious thought. We believe that to a very large degree it is true. A large majority of our ministers and nearly all of our missionaries have come from our own colleges. State institutions and other colleges are not giving to the Disciples of Christ any number of workers. In its history, Hiram College has sent forth 1,000 ministers of the gospel to serve our churches and nearly 100 missionaries to carry the gospel message to the ends of the earth. Without the support of our churches the colleges will fail.—*Christian, Springfield, Ohio.*

THIS THING OF GIVING

How few people understand it. The writer knows no more about it than do others. But there is something about giving that benefits us. No one can give, even a cup of cold water, without feeling the benefit of it. We can never give to the point of exhaustion. Those who give most, have most left. No man has ever died of giving away too much. He who gives bread to another never goes hungry himself.

What a spendthrift the American nation has been during the World War! We have been lavishing billions of money in charity, and many billions more for war supplies, and yet we are the richer for it. Of all the people in the world we are in a position to feed the hungry and clothe the naked of the world. We are able to do abundantly above all that a needy world may demand of us.

And is there any reward in this thing of giving? Yes, no one can do a favor to another without receiving a blessing. You give a dollar, and you will get back another, if not in kind at least in richer value. There is no richer privilege than the art of giving.

"Giving—and in the giving live the life a human being is entitled to enjoy. Give—and let no thought of sorrow abide with you, because you did not give. Give—and somewhere, from out the clods, or from the sacred depths of human hearts, a melody divine will rich your ears, and gladden all your days upon the earth."—*The Outlook of Missions.*

OBITUARY OF JOHN BARLEYCORN

(By E. F. Leake, in The Christian-Evangelist)

The deceased, Mr. John Barleycorn, was born in the City of Appetite, in the County of Lust and in the State of Degradation. He came to America with the forefathers and did a very profitable business for himself in all the colonies. He has been at one time or another the lawful resident of every state and practically every city and hamlet of the nation.

The subject of this sketch was in many respects the most remarkable man of his age; remarkable in his views, in his attitudes and in his character. The things which decent people naturally love and reverence, these he hated and sought with all his tremendous power to destroy.

He was always to be counted upon to exert his great influence to the utmost against all honest and decent government, though it is due the departed to say that he always claimed to be a patriot and particularly devoted to "personal liberty." His Fourth of July speeches were always upon this favorite theme of "personal liberty." However it should be said that Mr. Barleycorn carried the idea a great deal further than other people. With him it meant the right to do anything he saw fit which might contribute to the success of his own business. It is but just to the departed to say that in respect to this view he always practiced what he preached. With terrible consistency he degraded womanhood; deprived childhood of even the right to be decently born; he robbed the poor without mercy, in numberless instances depriving them of all the ordinary comforts of life; he corrupted courts and legislatures and often made the politics of our cities and states a stench in the nostrils of all decency; filled almshouses, asylums, orphanages and penitentiaries to overflowing. Numberless other mentionable and unmentionable crimes did he commit because they contributed tremendously to his wealth.

In all this, Mr. Barleycorn simply followed out to their logical conclusions his life-long conceptions of "personal liberty," his notion being that in this "land of the free and home of the brave" "personal liberty" under the Stars and Stripes is identical with unbridled license to seek in any and all ways the prosperity of one's own business and the enhancement of one's own wealth. Mr. Barleycorn, because of the unparalleled patience and long-suffering of the American people was permitted to accumulate incalculable wealth. He is reported to have enjoyed an annual income, during the last decade, of something like two billions of dollars. This vast income was no doubt due in part to the fact that Mr. Barleycorn never relinquished any of his money for the support of any of the benevolences and philanthropies of the day as Mr. Rockefeller, Mr. Carnegie and other of our very rich men have done. The license money which he gave, no matter how it was used, whether for school-fund, road-fund or otherwise, was always charged to "operating expenses," and Mr. Barleycorn himself never thought of the matter in any other way, though some of his friends always insisted it was pure benevolence on the part of their rich and powerful friend.

The departed enjoyed a large and more or less intimate acquaintance with many men of eminence throughout the world. Many famous men, in practically all lines of human endeavor, have pathetically acknowledged Mr. Barleycorn's superiority. One of Napoleon's chief concerns in exile was to have "John" with him on lonely St. Helena. "John" seemed to possess a sort of magic power in enabling great historic butchers to temporarily forget their slaughteries. Even Alexander the Great died with his hand in the hand of his old friend "John." But why multiply examples? Everybody knows that such was the marvelous power of the departed in this life that until recent years only the most optimistic souls dared to imagine that old John Barleycorn could ever taste of death. But God is no respecter of persons. His mills grind slowly but they grind exceedingly fine. It was written in the good book of a growing American and world conscience that despite his marvelous wealth and power the great and bloated John Barleycorn must die.

And so, in spite of all the shrewdness and skill, defense and protection accorded him by many powerful friends the deceased gradually gave way under the advancing power of right and decency until the end came at twelve-one a. m., July 1, 1919, amid the revelries of some of his drunken devotees the sound of which revelry was soon drowned by the joyful hallelujahs of all lovers of God and home and native land.

Final interment will be made January 16, 1920. The body of the deceased will be placed in a bottomless vault in the great Cemetery of Oblivion. There will be no resurrection. "So mote it be."

Springfield, Mo.

AT RANDOM

As a pleasant-faced woman passed the corner, Jones touched his hat to her, and remarked feelingly to his companion, "Ah, my boy, I owe a great deal to that woman."

"Your mother?" was the query.

"No, my landlady."

EASY.—Astronomers are making an attempt to weigh light. Some grocers have been doing it for years,—*London Opinion.*

THE CHRISTIAN ORPHANAGE

SUPERINTENDENT'S LETTER

Had you noticed that our financial report still climbs upward. and that we just lack a small amount being to the nine thousand dollar mile post since January first, this year? We are happy that our people are taking so much more interest in *"our Orphanage work."* It enables us to pay all our bills at the end of the month and keep ourselves in good standing with those from whom we buy. It also enables us to help more little children and give them a home here. We are now taking care of ten more than we did eighteen months ago. I truly hope that our income will still increase so we can add ten more to the list we already have. Of course the less number of children we have, the easier it is on the superintendent and the matrons. But our desire is to help as many little children as we possibly can. Nothing gives me more pleasure than to give some little worthy helpless orphan child a home and give it an opportunity to make good in life.

In this work we have our little worries and problems to meet, but after a child spends a number of years here in the Institution and reaches the age limit and goes out in·life·and makes good, we forget all the little worries it gave us while here and only pray that its life may be crowned with success.

Our Singing Class has had good success so far·and the people have complimented very much. We are very proud of our little boys and girls in taking a great interest in playing their part. We gave our concert in Burlington on the night of the eighth, and my heart was made glad the next day when one of the citizens of Burlington called me over the phono and asked us if we would come to see him that evening. I went and had a heart to heart talk with him and he asked me a number of questions about our work here and how we handled it and said to me that he saw the concert the children rendered and was well pleased with it and wanted to give the Orphanage $500.00 to help us along in this great work for humanity. This Christian gentleman is not a member of our Church, but is in deep sympathy with our work and wants to help us. I thank God for such big hearted men and men who have such a warm place in theirs hearts for the little helpless orphans of our land.

CHAS. D. JOHNSTON, *Supt.*

REPORT FOR AUGUST 20, 1919

Amount brought forward, $8,256.64.

Children's Offerings

Lester B. Frank, Lindsay, Okla., 20 cents.

Sunday School Monthly Offerings

(North Carolina Conference)

Oak Grove, $2.00; Union, (Va.), $2.00; Zion, $4.10.

(Eastern Virginia Conference)

Third Christian church, $32.04; Washington Street, Portsmouth, Va., $3.00; Isle of Wight, $2.50.

(Georgia and Alabama Conference)

Mt. Zion, $2.65; Kite, $2.00; Beulah, $1.83.

(Valley Virginia Conference)

Dry Run, $3.31; Beginners and Primary Dept., First church, Lincoln, Kans., $2.50; Total, $57.93.

Singing Class Receipts

Haw River, N. C., $35.00; Burlington, N. C., $43.50; Total, $78.50.

Special

Mr. Lawrence S. Holt, Sr., Burlington, N. C., $500.00; Mr. C. L. Stroud, South Norfolk, Va., $25.00; W. H. Thomas, Durham, N. C., $25.00; Total $550.00.

Total for the week, $686.43; Grand total, $8,943.07.

A LETTER

Dear Uncle Charley: We are having some very warm and dry weather in Oklahoma now. Wish the little boys and girls at the Orphanage could enjoy melons and peaches with us. Enclosed please find twenty cents for July and August. Best wishes to all the little cousins.—*Lester B. Frank.*

If you could see our little fellows eat melons, it would make your heart glad. We hope to have some ripe next week.—*"Uncle Charley."*

THE DENOMINATIONAL COLLEGE NECESSARY

The denominational college fills a vital and necessary need in our modern life. President W. O. Thompson, of the Ohio State University, has expressed the deep conviction that the Church will make a mistake if it loosens its hold on its colleges, or weakens the control which conserves the thing for which these institutions were founded, which assures their loyalty to moral and religious ideals. Dr. Thompson points out that the State starts from the doctrine of duty, growing out of a child's right to an education. On the other hand the Church starts from the Christian impulse—the love of God and of man. To the Church the spiritual ideals are supreme in the busiest and best of worlds. The denominational college is the great fort of the Church where the freedom of religion will be maintained with the same courage as the freedom of science will be defended in the state institutions.—*Christian Observer.*

ANOTHER SCORE FOR THE CHURCH COLLEGE

Medical schools are poor places for the training of Christian doctors, according to a statement credited to Dr. Salmans in these columns. The Interchurch World Movement is planning an immense advance in the Christian hospital field. Really pious physicians and surgeons will be needed in larger numbers. The Centenary's provision for new medical missions abroad points in the same direction. But a good Christian young man entering the average medical school runs the risk of losing his spiritual life. Unless he is a Daniel, he will come out wise in mind, skillful of hand, but unbelieving in heart. He may have picked up other worse things. The attention of our church leaders should be called to this weak link in the chain of Christian service. There is no real reason why medical schools should not be as much a training for Jesus' work as any other school, for healing was a part of his ministry.—*Western Christian Advocate.*

MISSIONARY

A QUESTION AND ANSWER

In this morning's mail came this word from the Treasurer of our Woman's Foreign Board: "Our receipts now stand at $8,000. Can we make it $10,000 by September 15?" About five minutes ago the afternoon mail brought the answer—*seventy-five* signed Intercessor's Covenants from the Greenville, Ohio, Missionary Society, the largest number yet received from one church.

Our Young People's Superintendent is asking, "Will our young people of the South reach $1,000 to finish the Santa Isabel Chapel Fund, and the young people of the North $1,000 for its equipment by September 15?"

With these seventy-five women and the other seven hundred and fifty who have signed this Covenant claiming the promise, "Whatsoever ye shall ask the Father in my name, that *will I do*, that the Father may be glorified in the Son," who can doubt that we shall reach our goals by the time the books close?

Dear Intercessors, if I had a stenographer I should write a personal letter to each one of you; but will you not accept this message as just for you? For the next six week will you not pray daily for this definite result—that our Woman's Boards may reach their financial goals by September 15?

"If we only had the money
That belongeth to our King,
If the reapers of God's bounties
Would their tithes and offerings bring,
Then the windows of heavens
Would open wide at His command,
And He'd pour us out a blessing
That would overflow the land.

"If we only had the money,
It would give redemption's song
To weary hearts now crying out,
'How long, O Lord, how long?'
And the thirsty land would blossom,
And the waiting isles would sing,
If—we only had the money
That belongeth to our King.

"O ye stewards, get ye ready,
Soon will come the reckoning
When we will answer for the money
Which belongeth to our King."

ALICE V. MORRILL.

NORTH CAROLINA WOMAN'S BOARD MEETING

The Executive Board of the North Carolina Women's Convention met in Burlington August 11 annd planned the program for the Convention this fall. The time of the meeting was set for November 8 and 9 at Elon College.

The speakers outside the Conference will be Rev. E. K. McCord, Missionary in Japan on furlough at home; Victor M. Rivera of our Porto Rico work; and Toshio Sato San of Japan. A great Convention is expected.

Between now and September 30, the women are to round out their year's quota of $2,000 and raise $350 special to finish paying for the Santa Isabel chapel in Porto Rico. Be sure to hold Rally Day in each church, says the Board.   MRS. W. A. HARPER.

SOUTHERN CHRISTIAN CONVENTION MISSION BOARD MEETING

Col. J. E. West, Chairman, has called the annual meeting of the Mission Board at Suffolk, Va., Wednesday, September 17, 1919, at 10 o'clock A. M. Following are the members of the Board:

J. E. West, Suffolk, Va., Chairman; J. M. Darden, Suffolk, Va.; J. A. Williams, Franklin, Va.; Rev. C. H. Rowland, Franklin, Va.; Rev. G. O. Lankford, Berkley, Va.; K. B. Johnson, Kennebec, N. C; Rev. J. Lee Johnson, Holly Springs, N. C.; Mrs. W. A. Harper, Elon College, N. C.; W. P. Lawrence, Elon College, N. C.; Rev. H. W. Elder, Richland, Ga.

As the Board undertakes to complete its work in one day written facts, data and applications are preferred to personal pleas and representation. Therefore all applications for help the coming year with salient facts and data should be in the hands of the undersigned not later than September 10.

By order of J. E. West, Chairman.

J. O. ATKINSON,
Executive Secretary.

Elon College, N. C., August 11, 1919.

IN WASHINGTON

By invitation of a representative those of our household of faith in Washington, D. C., I came her Saturday night to learn what I might be able to learn about the prospects and possibilities of organizing and building a Christian church in our National capitol. By urgent request, Brother J. M. Darden, member of our Mission Board and one who is always ready to be of service, came with me. We were carried over the section in which the proposed church is to be organized and later met with a few of the faithful in the home of Brother Irving Hitchcock, 801 Allison St., Washington, D. C. There for two hours we discussed the situation. Shall we undertake to build, or not build, in Washington? That is the question. And none are wise enough to answer that question off hand. Our Mission Board meets September 17 and will have such facts and data before it as will, we trust, enable it to decide wisely and well. There are great opportunities here in this thriving and growing National capitol. Should the Christians, along with the other denominations, do their bit in trying to Christianize this center or not? Have we the money, the faith and the men to help in this great task; or shall we leave the task wholly to others who have money, faith and men? It is a problem. It requires thought, wisdom and prayer—much and earnest prayer.

J. O. ATKINSON, *Sec.*

A GENERAL VIEW OF THE CENTRAL SECTION OF ELON'S CAMPUS. STATELY OAKS AND A WIDE
SPREAD CAMPUS GIVE THEIR HELP TO BROADEN LIFE'S IDEALS AND PLACE BEFORE
THE PLASTIC MIND A LARGER AVENUE OF USEFULNESS

NOTES

Elon opens September 10. Remember the date and have your patronage there.

At the time of going to press we have not received a report from the Virginia Valley Conference.

Two airmen, Davis and Peterson, are said to be held in Mexico at the demand of a ransom of $15,000.00.

Friends interested in building a church in Richmond, Va., should write to Rev. H. J. Fleming, Newport News, Va., who is collecting information as to the outlook for a house of worship in the capitol of the Old Dominion.

We understand that Union, Alamance, has increased the pastor's salary for the coming year $150.00, making the salary $500.00. Good for Union! It is no surprise, however, because we know that the membership of that church know how to spell *progress* and *justice*.

The work at South Norfolk, Va., under the leadership of Brother O. D. Poythress, seems to be progressing. This church's quota of the College Endowment Fund was $750.00 and it subscribed $2,025.00, with over fifty per cent of the membership contributing.

At the present the church is planning a building program to extend over a period of five or seven years, looking in the direction of building a $40,000.00 church in the near future. The present pastor has been called to serve another year with an increased salary.

The emphasis of this issue is on *Education*. The time is now at hand for the final stroke to be made before the opening of the schools and colleges. Let every pastor, every friend of education, and all who are interested in the cause interest some young person in a higher education.

Mrs. Sarah Fix, one of THE SUN's life-long and faithful friends, died at Winston-Salem, N. C., August 13, and was buried in Pine Hill cemetery, Burlington, N. C., on the following day, the funeral being conducted by her pastor, Dr. J. W. Harrell. Mrs. Fix was a model mother, symbol of patience and love, and her friends were numbered by the thousand. She lived a life consecrated to the Master's cause and impressed upon her neighbors the piety of a true and devoted life. She was a sister to Brothers J. A. and W. H. Turrentine and the mother of Messrs. J. M. and W. J. Fix. An extended obituary will appear later.

NEW COMERS TO THE SUN FAMILY

D. V. Carter ....Liberty, N. C.
Mrs. B. A. Meadows ....Columbus, Ga.
Jas. N. Morris ....Pirkey, Va.

AN INSPIRING SCENE OF AN ELON GRADUATING CLASS. FROM MANY SEC-
TIONS OF THE COUNTRY YOUNG MEN AND WOMEN GATHER TO PREPARE
AND TO RECEIVE THEIR BENEDICTION FOR A LIFE CAREER

Mrs. G. A. Knight .... Pirkey, Va.
Mrs. J. G. Faulkner .... Henderson, N. C.
Florence Holt .... New Hill, N. C.
D. A. Jones .... New Hill, N. C.
J E. Barnett .... Louisburg, N. C.
Lee Wilks .... Youngsville, N. C.
Lessie Lambert .... Clayton, N. C.
C. H. Dupree .... Raleigh, N. C.
W. B. Jones .... Raleigh, N. C.
C. B. Franks .... Cary, N. C.
Levi R. McAdams .... Efland, N. C.
Mrs. J. B. Richmond .... Mebane, N. C.
Mrs. C. J. Vincent .... Mebane, N. C.
L. W. Compler .... Rock Creek, S. C.
Zeb. H. Lynch .... Efland, N. C.
Miss Texie Penticost .... Cedar Grove, N. C.
Miss Rosa Sharpe .... Efland, N. C.
J. R. Daughtry .... Norfolk, Va.
J. J. Hall .... Graham, N. C.

(Report to August 16)

THE STRANGER

You may not know his name,
  And you may not know his face;
But go to him just the same,
  He's a stranger in the place.
Go and stretch your hand to him,
  Have a cheerful word to say;
For his struggle may be grim,
  And 'twill help him on his way.

There's no need to ask him what
  Is his claim upon your smile,
Has he ancestry or not
  That will make him worth your while,
What he's done or hopes to do,
  Is he famous or unknown?
Speak a cheerful word or two,
  Make him feel he's not alone.

To be strange is not a crime,
  To be lonely no disgrace;
You yourself may yearn some time
  To hold a smiling face.
You some day may stand alone
  And know what it is to sigh,
When with strangers you are thrown,
  And you see them hurry by.

We're too formal. Let us go
  To the stranger who is near,
And a friendly feeling show;
  Let us speak a word of cheer.
Let us stretch a kindly hand
  To the brother who's unknown;
We can make him understand
  That he doesn't dwell alone,

WORSHIP AND MEDITATION

SUFFOLK LETTER

Lines of demarkation are growing less distinct in almost all relations. Universal education has broken down the middle wall of partition between literate and illiterate. The wider distribution of wealth has removed the lines that separated the rich and the poor. The interstate and international commerce has reduced the geography that kept states and nations apart. Oceans are not as wide as lakes and rivers once were. "Who is my neighbor," is no longer a question that requires a parable for an answer. We communicate under seas, trade over seas, and the lead the news of the world every day. Lines of demarkation that once were plain have faded from the map of human relations until religion itself has lost itself in a thousand fields of fertile soil. Once a Christian was a conspicuous figure over against profane and godless man. The line that separated the church from the world was as plain as the line marked by a surveyor's axe or stones.

The present day intermingling of the church and the world, the cross-currents of pleasure that obscure pure and undefiled religion baffle the wisest men and the devoutest women. Things once condemned as wrong and un-Christian are tolerated by the church. Evil seems to be subtler, religion seems to be laxer, and the line between churchman and non-churchman seems to be like other lines more difficult to trace. The question of supreme importance is to discover whether religion is making inroads upon the world-life or whether the world-life is making inroads upon religion. The blending of all other institutions and relations would seem to argue that society is passing the grosser forms of evil and that a hopeful friendliness between the church and the world prophesies the permeation of society by spiritual forces. It can hardly be proven that the world is growing worse. Too many great evils are being removed and too many welfare plans are being projected at great cost of money and service to leave any doubt that Christianity is taking root in the thought, life and activities of the world. The abolition of the liquor traffic from this Republic, and the campaign for world-prohibition alone indicates the power of religion not only in church, but in business, and government. Religion is doing pioneer work in felling the forests of evil and pulling up the stumps; the wire-grass and crab-grass work must be done as the spiritual machinery is improved for clearing the field of sin and producing a finer type of Christian manhood and womanhood. The time will come when the dance-hall will pass away as surely as the saloon has passed away. Human feet were never given to sport on the brink of social ruin and a better way will be found for the young. Malaria meets the clean, pure breath of the sea, but it can never contaminate the life of old ocean; the world can never destroy the saving atmosphere of religion, but must some sweet day itself be healed of its sin and shame. Jesus will reveal Himself to the world as He did to the woman of Samaria at Jacob's well and cleanse the world of its old life of shame. The only requisite for the church is to keep itself pure in the midst of a world that is unclean.

W. W. STALEY.

FIRST THINGS FIRST

Suffer me first to go and......" It is not that you desire wrong things; it is not that you desire to avoid right things; but you say, "Suffer me first to do the inferior, and then I shall be ready for the superior. Suffer me first to take care of myself. Suffer me first to take care of my household. Suffer me first to take care of my business. Suffer me first to look after this enterprise and then——" No! This constant habit of humbling the higher, and making it subordinate to the lower; this constant preference of the inferior to the superior, works demoralization. A man does not need to throw away his Bible, nor defy his God, nor sell his soul voluntarily. He needs only to say, "Suffer me first to do this lesser thing." The moment that is done, there begins the wrong emphasis and proportions in life which bring defeat. If we put the inferior duties in the place of higher duties, we will fail at last.— *Selected.*

GENIUSES AT EARLY AGE

Handel had produced an opera before he was fifteen. Corneille had planned a tragedy before he was ten. Auber wrote an operetta for the stage before he was fourteen. Pitt was chancellor of the exchequer before he was twenty-five. Schiller was widely known as a poet before the age of twenty. Kant began his philosophical and metaphysical speculations before the age of eighteen. Goethe had produced a considerable number of poems and several dramas before he was twenty. Raphael showed his artistic abilities at the early age of twelve, when he was widely known as an artist in oil.—*Kind Words.*

We reap what we sow; but nature has love over and above that justice, and gives us shadow and blossom and fruit that spring from no planting of ours.— *George Eliot.*

The truth is pure, and purifying, yet can it not of itself purify the soul, but by the obeying or believing of it.—*Robert Leighton.*

Delight thyself also in the Lord; and He shall give thee the desires of thine heart.—*Psalm* 37:4.

Goodness and mercy—do you possess them?

THE NEW ERA

Tables and chairs, chairs and tables. They inevitably travel together. So even in their journey to the home of our French brothers, they will be tied together—three chairs to every table: The great army of boy workers in the schools throughout the land are endeavoring in their own way to alleviate the needs of the destitute refugees across the sea. When the Red Cross offered to assist the French Government in its work of reconstruction, it turned at once to its Junior organization for the fulfillment of the furniture part of the order. And it is with no small amount of enthusiasm that they undertook this seemingly gigantic task of making ten thousand tables and thirty thousand chairs.

When questioned as to whether they preferred to continue their pre-war work in the manual training classes, the boys were, in the great majority, eager to undertake the furniture making. They work exactly according to specifications, without any variations, but even this requires a great deal of ingenuity. The furniture is shipped knocked down, but can be readily put together by anyone who follows the simple directions which accompany each set. Approximately fifteen thousand homes will be supplied by this means with a good start toward home life once more. Many of the schools completed their allotments of furniture before the close of the school year in June but the beginning of work in the fall will start anew the enthusiasm of these eager young world citizens to fulfill their allotments and, then clamor for more. Manual training instructors like the work because it brings hearty and enthusiastic response from the students. Every Junior Red Cross boy can aid in the work. Schools can obtain full information and directions from the A. R. C. Headquarters in Washington.

To accompany each table and its three chairs is a letter written in French by a high school French class. This is to convey to the recipients the good will and fellowship which we in America have for them over there.

During the war, nearly ten per cent of the timber in France was destroyed, besides furniture valued at several millions of dollars. France has neither furniture, nor wood to make it with. So in this task of making furniture for France, the Junior Red Cross is putting its energies into a field that will truly aid the French people and will give to the Juniors the great satisfaction of a worthy purpose well done.

ALL WISHES COME TRUE NOWADAYS

"Don't you wish that some of those orphans in Europe could come over here and go to school with us?" asked Joe.

But the practical David was very careful about making wishes. He always considered a question carefully first, thinking it over and over in his mind before discussing it rashly. He looked at Joe thoughtfully as he said, "Joe, those orphans *are* going to go to school with us after awhile."

"They are? Who told you so? I can hardly wait! How soon will they come?" And Joe fairly jumped up and down in his excitement.

But again the slow David thought awhile before he spoke. "Of course they are going to school with us—*in a way*. First of all they are to be given a home right in their own town, and it will be furnished by the very furniture that our Junior Red Cross sent over for them. They are going to learn all about us, what we do and how we do it. And then, we are to learn all about them, too. Because they are beginning life all over again since the war left them homeless, it will be all the more interesting to follow their development, I think. My Dad says it's the best League of Nations there is—this getting the school children of the world to know each other in spirit."

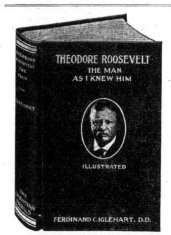

This book is printed on fine book paper and includes 16 pages of illustrations on plate paper. There are nearly 400 pages, in 31 chapters. The binding is made of fine cloth embossed in gold. Size 5x7 inches.

The price is only $1.50 a copy post-paid.

C. B. RIDDLE, Pub. Agt.,..................Burlington, N. C.

Sunday School and Christian Endeavor

SUNDAY SCHOOL LESSON FOR
AUGUST 31, 1919

Temperance. Dan. 1:8-20; Rom. 14:21; I Cor. 9:24-27.

Golden Text: "Every man that striveth in the games exerciseth self control in all things."

If ever there was a good cause for going with the crowd, or when in Rome, do as Rome does, Daniel had it. Can you imagine the little lonely lad, far away from home and friends, a slave, at the mercy of other slaves? Can you imagine him as he approaches the great city with its lofty walls on which six chariots could drive abreast?; its wonderful palaces, its huge halls, and can you then imagine the strength of purpose which nerved one little lad to stand his ground, and purpose in his heart? We give way and do that which we know to be wrong, many times, because of some one, or two or three who may laugh if we do not, or because we will be lonely and have no fun if we don't go with the crowd. In such times, think of the courage of that little prince of Israel, a prince in heart no matter where he was, who purposed, and kept his purpose.

What can we do for temperance today? If liquor is a medicine, should it be used indiscriminately? Would we think of keeping any other deadly drug in quantities, and using it without a doctor's prescription? Why do people look so lightly upon the breaking of prohibition laws? A story is told of a Spanish priest who wished for money to build a new monastery. Finally the devil appeared to him according to the legend, and offered him the money if the priest would consent to commit just one crime. The priest consented, and then the question arose what the crime should be. "Kill your father," said the tempter, but the priest recoiled horrors stricken. "Strike the abbot of your order," but this was even worse, if possible. "Steal from the baron," but again the priest refused. "Then get drunk," said the tempter. This was an easy sin, and a small one, so the priest consented. He found his money exhausted ere he had full gratified his appetite, and opportunity serving, he stole from

the baron to buy more wine. The abbot, indignant at his condition, remonstrated with him, whereupon the priest in drunken frenzy struck him. Turned out of the monastery for this crime, he returned home, and enraged by his father's reproaches in a sudden temptest of wrath, he killed his father. The moral is clear: Alcohol, "Spirit of Evil," as the old Persian word means, still leads to all other crimes.

MRS. FRED BULLOCK.

CHRISTIAN ENDEAVOR TOPIC FOR
AUGUST 31, 1919

The Christian Challenge For Life Service: Matt. 4:18-22. (Missionary vocational meeting. Life work recruits).

One of the posters which was most effective in winning recruits to the British army, was one which said: "Your King needs you." That is the slogan for every Endeavor Society, and the thought which should come home to every young Endeavorer. "Your King needs you." Perhaps you say, "I have no talent to make me fit for service." Read again the call of Jesus to the fishers "Come with me and I will make you—." Never mind what you are; you can become whatever God wants you to be when He has made you. You are just in the process of being made now. Do you want to be great? Then be good. No evil living person is ever great; they may become notorious they are never famous. The call of God is always for great tasks and high positions "ambassadors" for Christ; "kings" and "priests" unto God.

MRS. FRED BULLOCK.

BOARD MEETING

As per adjournment, and by order of the Chairman, Rev. J. W. Harrell, D. D., the Board of Religious Education, Inc. (which Board was created by the last session of our Southern Christian Convention to have the general oversight of our Sunday School and Christian Endeavor work), is called to meet at Raleigh, N. C., in regular annual session on Thursday, September 11, at 8 P. M. The members of the Board are:

Rev. J. W. Harrell, Chairman, Burlington, N. C.; Mrs. Fred Bullock, Suffolk, Va.; Brother I. A. Luke, Holland, Va.; Brother C. H. Stephenson, Corresponding Secretary and Treasurer, Raleigh, N. C.; Rev. J. V. Knight, and Hon. C. A. Hines, Greensboro, N. C.; Rev. A. T. Banks, Ramseur, N. C.; Rev. W. T. Walters, D. D., Winchester, Va.; J. O. Atkinson, Recording Secretary, Elon College, N. C.

This is to be a most important session. Any suggestions for progress and development in our Sunday school and Christian Endeavor work will be glad'y received.

J. O. ATKINSON, Sec.

Elon College. N. C.

DIXIE WELL REPRESENTED AT INTERNATIONAL C. E. CONFERENCE

There were more than 200 delegates representing the Southern States at the International Christian Endeavor Conference in Buffalo, N. Y., August 5-10.

Secretary of War, Newton D. Baker and William Jennings Bryan were among the speakers who addressed this great gathering. There were delegates and speakers from Canada, England, Ireland, France, Italy, Belgium, Africa, India, China, Japan, Korea and South America, besides the thousands from all parts of North America.

Among the Southerners to address the Convention were: Lieut. Duncan B. Curry of Jacksonville, Fla.; Karl Lehmann, Chattanooga, Tenn.; Chas. F. Evans, Lexington, Ky.; L. C. Little Winnfield, La.; W. Roy Breg, Dallas, Texas; A. Clinton Decker, Birmingham, Ala.; Miss Mary Bullock, Russellville, Ark.; George M. Rusk, Atlanta, Ga.; Rev. W. H. Hopper; Louisville, Ky.; Jas. L. Webster, Shreveport, La.; Rev. John A. Wood, Canton, Miss.; Rev. J. V. Knight, Greensboro, N. C.; Wyatt A. Taylor, Columbia, S. C.; Warren Newsum, Memphis, Tenn.; Rev. J. B. Gonzales, Dallas, Texas; G. E. Miley, Richmond, Va.; Rev. Gilbert Glass, Richmond, Va.; Dr. Jas. Lewis Howe, Lexington, Va.

"HOW TO INTEREST YOUR SUNDAY SCHOOL IN MISSIONS"

The above is the title of a book by Mrs. Sue R. Staley, and I wish that some one person in each one of our Sunday schools would buy and read that book—and then get busy, as Mrs. Staley tells them how to get busy, in interesting the Sunday school in missions. The book has 140 pages, is substantially bound in cloth and can be had of THE CHRISTIAN SUN, Burlington, N. C., for 75 cents. Take this word from the "Introduction," "Men cannot be enlisted in a cause of which they know nothing. Most men do not know even the primary facts and principles of missions. The young people and the children will not grow up to be missionaries or to support missions, while they know nothing of the great enterprise."

Or take this from the first page of Chapter I: "The Sunday school has an army of fifteen million scholars, from whose ranks we may well seek to organize a world-wide missionary campaign. If every member were trained to give at least two cents a week to missions, it would produce a missionary income of fifteen million dollars annually, and if only one out of every thousand of the members would go as a missionary, we would have fifteen thousand additional missionaries—enough, we are told, with native helpers and the present force, to evangelize the entire non-Christian world."

The writer is of opinion that if one person in a Sunday school will read and carry out the suggestions of Mrs. Staley, the whole Sunday school will become interested in missions.

J. O. ATKINSON.

CHARLES W. McPHERSON, M. D.

Eye, Ear, Nose, Throat

OFFICE OVER CITY DRUG STORE

Office Hours: 9:00 a. m. to 1:00 p. m.

and 2:00 to 5:00 p. m.

Phones: Residence 153; Office 65J

BURLINGTON, NORTH CAROLINA

OBITUARIES

DINGES

John Henry Dinges was born April 17, 1851, and died July 28, 1919, aged 68 years, 3 months, and 11 days. He is survived by his widow, three sons, three daughters, and two brothers. For about 15 years prior to his death he was a member of the Methodist Church. Funeral services were conducted at his late home in Powell's Fort, July 29.

A. W. ANDES.

HOOK

Lycurgus C. Hook was born August 23, 1847, and died at his home at Hook's Mill, W. Va., July 3, 1919, aged 71 years, 10 months, and 10 days. He is survived by one son; his wife having died in April, 1909. He was a member of the Christian Church for many years, holding his membership at Timber Ridge. He was a man of prominence and held in high esteem by all who knew him, and will be greatly missed in his community. A large congregation of friends and neighbors gathered at Timber Ridge for the funeral, July 5, 1919.

A. W. ANDES.

CROCKER

Another good woman has fallen. Early on the morning of August 4, 1919, in the home of her son, Mr. T. H. Crocker of Middleburg, Vance County, North Carolina, Mrs. Martha Greene Crocker passed away suddenly and most unexpectedly. She was spared sickness and suffering, being called while apparently in her usual health. Her son, T. H. Crocker, was at her side in death, as he had ever been in life, sustaining her with an unfailing devotion.

Mrs. Crocker was the daughter of the late Stephen H. Turner, a well known and highly esteemed citizen of Warren County. Her mother departed this life when Mrs. Crocker was but a girl.

She professed religion in early life and joined Mt. Auburn Christian church of which she was a most faithful member to the time of her death.

September. 29, 1863 she was married to Luther R. Crocker of Franklin County, North Carolina, who preceded her to the Great Beyond by three years. To this union were born four sons: E. L., T. H., S. L., and J. T. Crocker, all of whom

survive their mother. Besides these, she leaves to mourn their loss one brother, Mr. Z. T. Turner, a well known and popular citizen of Vance County; one sister, Mrs. Sue Jones of Durham, N. C.; a host of relatives and loving friends.

Mrs. Crocker was a most excellent woman, always bright and cheerful, and never more happy than when surrounded by her four sons in whom her heart delighted and of whom she was proud. She was a devoted wife a kind and affectionate mother, a loyal friend, charitable to those in need, and just to all.

God in His goodness granted her a long life, her eightieth birthday being only two months distant.

She was laid to rest in the Middleburg cemetery beside her lamented husband. Her popularity was attested by a large attendance and beautiful floral offerings.

The burial service was conducted by Rev. W. C. Merritt of the Methodist Episcopal church.

A LIFE-LONG FRIEND.

RESOLUTIONS OF RESPECT—WELLONS

Whereas, it has pleased Almighty God in His infinite wisdom to call from our midst our beloved sister, Mrs. Virginia Murder Wellons; and whereas, by her death Barrett's Christian church has sustained the loss of one of its oldest members. Her life and service has been of great benefit to her church and to Christianity, therefore, be it Resolved:

1. That we bow in humble submission to the will of Him Who doeth all things well, rejoicing that our sister was awaiting His coming with a confident hope of eternal life.

2. That the wisdom which she exercised in the aid of our church by service and counsel will be held in grateful remembrance.

3. That we offer her bereaved family, and mourning friends our heart-felt sympathy, and commend the Savior as a comfort and guide for them.

4. That a copy of these resolutions be entered upon our church record, a copy sent to the bereaved family, and a copy sent to The Christian Sun for publication.

Done, by order of Barrett's church, this the twenty-six day of July, 1919, in regular quarterly conference.

O. R. CORNWALL,
HAZEL HINES,
GLADYS KITCHEN,
Committee.

A LINE OR TWO O' SENSE

Each small duty is a tiny, steady lamp which the Christian must fill with the oil of steadfast obedience. How the Light of Financial Freedom shines with each War Savings Stamp added to the Thrift Flame!

A silver bell, even when carelessly touched, sends out sweet sounds. A Christian life, to all who meet and touch it, should ring the praise of God sweetly and clearly.

Suspicion is like a fog in which no one can see things clearly. Get rid of the Fog of Waste, Want, sickness, and Old Age by the penetrating Light of Thrift.

Every life teaches something to the onlooker, either of good or evil. Make your life an example of Thriftiness to your neighbor.

You never miss the water till the well runs dry. A financial drought will never come if you keep on buying War Savings Stamps.

Four out of five men when they die leave no estate. Buy War Savings Stamps and be a No. 5.

WHEN DEBTS DON'T COUNT

Having made his payments for Liberty Bonds, war chest, rent, coal, gas, and groceries the poor man was broke. But he needed winter clothes, so he compromised by digging through a closet and unearthing a heavy vest that belonged to a winter suit he had worn last year. He brushed the vest off and felt in the pockets.

Eureka! A discovery!

In the inside pocket of the waistcoat was a war savings stamp certificate with 15 squares filled with savings stamps. Safe to say he bought his winter suit—and then some.

FOR RENT OR SALE

Five-room cottage, electric lights, good well water, small barn, fruits, about 1 acre lot. One block south of depot, Elon College, N. C. Rent $10 per month. For sale cash or terms at bargain. Address

JAS. L. FOSTER,
Waverly, Va.

"Wust" of the Bargain

Ezra Winrow—I hear you swapped automobiles with Si Skinner yesterday. Who got the wust of the bargain, Hi?"

Hi Huskins—W-a-ll, the one I got thrust on me is sufferin' horribly from. ague, an' balks quite a lot 'count uv missin' on each and every mornin' that Si is huntin' fer the justice uv the peace in order to swear out a warrant fer somebody.—*Buffalo Express.*

To be a Lasting Lesson

This old story is again going the rounds of the papers: "Rastus," said the sheriff, "have you anything to say before the sentence of death is carried into execution?" No boss, I ain't no speechifier but I suttenly believes this am gwine to be a lesson to me."

THE CHRISTIAN SUN

"IN ESSENTIALS UNITY, IN NON-ESSENTIALS LIBERTY, IN ALL THINGS CHARITY"

Go To College

THESE are decision days with the young people. Entering college is before them; the time is short, and many have not decided as to their course. Life's future hangs in a balance. These young people are at the place where one road becomes two. Which one will they take? The answer may be with you. Help them to take the right road—the one that leads to college. It may not glisten with shining shekels and be spread with roses, but its course leads to a larger life, to leadership, better citizenship, and to the expansion of the latent powers. Go to college!

Volume LXXI   WEDNESDAY, AUGUST 27, 1919   Number 35

BURLINGTON   .   .   .   NORTH CAROLINA

THE CHRISTIAN SUN

Founded 1844 by Rev. Daniel W. Kerr

C. B. RIDDLE   -   -   -   Editor

Entered at the Burlington, N. C. Post Office as second class matter.

Subscription Rates

One year ....$ 2.00
Six months 1.00

In Advance

'Give both your old and new postoffice when asking that your address be changed.

The change of your label is your receipt for money. Written receipts sent upon request.

Many persons subscribe for friends, intending that the paper be stopped at the end of the year. If instructions are given to this effect, they will receive attention at the proper time.

Marriage and obituary notices not exceeding 150 words printed free if received within 60 days from date of event, all over this at the rate of one-half cent a word.

Original poetry not accepted for publication.

Principles of the Christian Church

(1) The Lord Jesus Christ is the only Head of the Church.
(2) Christian is a sufficient name of the Church.
(3) The Holy Bible is a sufficient rule of faith and practice.
(4) Christian character is a sufficient test of fellowship, and of church membership.
(5) The right of private judgment and the liberty of conscience is a right and a privilege that should be accorded to, and exercised by all.

EDITORIAL

THE "BEST YET" IN BUFFALO

Christian Endeavor's First International Conference Proves to be The Best Convention of all Its History—A Summary of Its Inspiring Features and Results

(*Press Bulletin from the United Society of Christian Endeavor, used as an Editorial by request*).

Sessions that crowded Buffalo's great Music Hall, the most enthusiastic crowds that Christian Endeavor has ever brought together, a series of meetings unequalled for power, new Christian Endeavor plans unequalled for promise—all this makes the First International Christian Endeavor Conference, held at Buffalo on August 5-10, in reality Christian Endeavor's "best-yet" Convention.

Buffalo the Beautiful

The beautiful city itself with its embowered and superbly paved streets, its palatial homes, and its noble churches, filled us all with admiration. The weather was clear and remarkably cool. The Endeavorers are all ready to recommend Buffalo as a summer resort.

A Conference-Convention

The Conference, with its more than two thousand registered delegates, was much larger than the officers had expected, and crowded the biggest auditoriums in Buffalo. Christian Endeavor could not undertake one of its usual vast Conventions in this year of reconstruction and turmoil; but the Conference that was undertaken, though not in our Convention series, really belongs there in numbers as well as in power and influence.

The Conference Vim

It was a youthful crowd, alert and jovial, sparkling with all of youth's enthusiasm, responsive to all fine impulses, fired with eager resolves, a most lovable and hopeful assembly. The singing, both of the choir and the audience, was superb. The cheers and impromptu songs, of which so much has been made in recent State conventions, burst out irrepressibly whenever a good opportunity was afforded. No one could be in Buffalo and have any doubt of Christian Endeavor's abounding vitality and undying zeal.

They Meant Business

It was a faithful crowd. The Endeavorers did not go to Buffalo to see the sights; though there were many sights well worth seeing, and they came from distant parts of the country. They went there to attend the Christian Endeavor Conference, and this they did with constant and glad fidelity. Not only were the evening mass-meetings all crowded, but so also were the more practical and less inspirational conferences of the daytime. Nor were the Endeavorers satisfied with the crowded Conference programme, but they packed the time between sessions with impromptu conferences on all sorts of helpful themes, till we wondered when they ate and slept.

Leaders That Lead

The Buffalo Conference also brought out in splendid fashion the quality of Christian Endeavor's leadership. It showed for the first time the new personnel of the nation officers, the able and winsome young men and young women who have been drafted during the past two years into the forces of the United Society from the State unions. It also made evident the vigorous and delightful personalities of the State officers, including the constantly enlarging number of field-secretaries. Christian Endeavor has never before been so well manned—and womanned.

The General Secretary Resigns

One of the national leaders, however, presented his resignation, and with reasons which made its acceptance necessary. Dr. William Shaw, after twenty-six years of conspicuously faithful and successful service of the United Society, as publication manager, treasurer, and general secretary, found it necessary, in view of his physical condition, to withdraw from the office of general secretary, the resignation to take effect on the first of next January, by which time, it is hoped, an efficient successor will be found, though no one can take the unique place which he has so long filled. Dr. Shaw, however, is not at all resigning from Christian Endeavor. He has been made a life trustee of the United Society, he will continue to be treasurer of the World's Christian Endeavor Union, and will keep right on in his immensely important work as publisher of *The Christian Endeavor World.*

Expectant Denominations

The attitude of the denominations toward Christian Endeavor was also well illustrated at Buffalo. An unusual number of denominational leaders were there, especially the denominational secretaries of young people's work. The denominations are trusting Christian Endeavor. They are looking to it for inspiration and help. They are ready in turn to help Christian Endeavor.

A New Commission

To an extent greater than ever before the denominational leaders are willing to enter Christian Endeavor councils and guide the movement,—something for which Christian Endeavor leaders have always been eager. The denominational young people's secretaries are by virtue of their offices trustees of the United Society of Christian Endeavor and at Buffalo the United Society took a long step in advance by forming a Standards and Programme Commission to be made up of the denominational secretaries of young people's work and the executive officers of the United Society an expert body whose task it will be henceforth to determine all lines of work in which Christian Endeavor and the denominations are expected to co-operate.

The New Programme

In the meantime, while this new commission is getting to work, the trustees, executive officers, and field-secretaries outlined with care a simple but aggressive and inspiring programme for the next two years. It deals with fundamentals in regard to which all denominations will wish their Endeavorers to advance, and it presents in a strong way some of the most important principles of Christian service. The "goals" of 1920-21 will be more popular and will prove more profitable than any other proposals ever placed before Christian Endeavor.

Standards

Along this same line, the Conference devoted two important simultaneous sessions to consider, under the guidance of experts, the relation between State Christian Endeavor standards, national Christian Endeavor standards, and denominational standards for young people's work. These sessions were clarifying and illuminating.

The Boy Scouts

A formal and definite alliance between the Boy Scouts and Christian Endeavor was proposed at Buffalo, and the first steps toward it were authoritatively taken. The arrangement will be free and flexible, and will be of decided advantage to both bodies.

"C. E. E."

Buffalo made evident, in its Experts' banquet and in many other ways, the strong hold that the course of study leading to the degree of "C. E. E." has upon the affections of the Endeavorers. The Efficiency Charts, and the entire line of varied work which they tabulate, are continued in full force and with new energy. The Conference also gave fresh impetus to the important

Junior and Intermediate work, as proved by the largely attended and finely effective Junior and Intermediate conferences, rallies, and banquets.

Not Forgetting Our Work

None of the standard and well-recognized lines of Christian Endeavor activity were forgotten, but all were recognized, stimulated, and developed at Buffalo. The Tenth Legion had a rousing banquet, with a glorious conference on stewardship. The Quiet Hour had constant mention in the meetings, and was illustrated in many devotional addresses, in one of the best open-air sunrise prayer meetings ever held, and in the Conference Quiet Hours. The citizenship and temperance rally was a rouser. Union work was promoted a many ways, but especially by a new feature, Challenge meetings, in which the various State and local unions "dared" each other to many large undertakings and initiated many contests that will fill the next two years with pep and point.

Old and New

The Christian Endeavor committees, the prayer meetings and socials, were by no means forgotten, but were discussed with zest which proved that the Endeavorers are anything but weary of time-honored methods Missions were to the fore, as always in Christian Endeavor meetings, and both home and foreign missions were illustrated forcibly in pageant, in stereopticon pictures, and in noble addresses. An entire session, and one of the best, was devoted to the new Interchurch World Movement. The enrollment of Life-Work Recruits was promoted quietly but effectively. Not one of our great Christian Endeavor aims and ideals was omitted from the comprehensive programme.

A Neighborly Visit

The Conference, of course, visited Niagara Falls, and we held an inspiring outdoor meeting on the Canadian side. In many other ways the International aspects of Christian Endeavor were kept to the fore throughout the Conference.

Great Speeches

Virtually every session was distinguished by at least one great address. President Wilson sent a cordial message. Secretary of War Baker made a remarkable presentation of the war aims and achievements of the nation and of the ideals of the League of Nations. William Jennings Bryan, kept from the Conference by the serious illness of his wife, wrote and sent a noble sermon, which was read by Dr. Poling. Dr. J. Stanley Brown, of the United States Treasury Department, gave a wise address on Christian Endeavor Thrift Clubs. Ira Landrith gave two of his inimitable talks, absolutely unreportable in their wit, force, and fire. Two eminent missionaries, Dr. Hume of India and Dr. Pettee of Japan, illuminated the situation in those empires, and Mr. S. R. Vinton gave us a great treat in his world survey with the stereopticon. The quaintly and wisely humorous Dr. J. B. Baker, the statesmanlike Dr. J. Campbell White and S. Guy Inman, the manly and inspiring Dr. John Timothy Stone and Dr. J. T. McCrory—these are only samples of the quality of the programme.

In 1921

Much interest was shown as always, in the friendly struggle of cities desiring to entertain the next Convention. New York, St. Louis, and Des Moines were in the field, all eager for the honorable service. The trustees were grateful for these three cordial invitations, and hope some day to go to all three cities, but felt in honor bound to go to New York City in 1921, since that city had already made so much preparation for the Convention which was to have been held there in 1917, but could not be held on account of the Great War.

Enter; the Alumni

But if we were asked to name any one outstanding feature of the Buffalo Conference, we should say, the Alumni banquet. The Alumni idea was proved o have such a hold on the interest and affection of the Endeavorers as ensures its permanence, and with it the continued devotion of the old-time members of our society. Thus a strong backing for Christian Endeavor is made certain, a backing of influence as well as of money. The gift of more than $10,000 made by the 800 Alumni at their banquet is an indication of the way in which this Alumni plan will place Christian Endeavor on an adequate financial basis. The moral support of these old-time Endeavorers is equally important and equally prized. In return, their continued association with the ever-youthful Christian Endeavor society will keep them young, and add indefinitely to the joy and power of their Christian life.

NEW COMERS TO THE SUN FAMILY

Miss Lessie Stanfield ....Durham, N. C.
T. W. Morgan ....Holland, Va.
Miss Sallie Britton ....Holland, Va.
Eddie Worrell ....Holland, Va.
Jobie Harrell ....Holland, Va.
John Luther ....Holland, Va.
Mrs. W. L. Jones .... Holland, Va.
C. T. Parker ....Holland, Va.
Joe Smith ....Holland, Va.
Mrs. R. W. Duke ....Holland, Va.
J. M. Jones ....Berkley, Va.
W. H. Wiggins ....Holland, Va.
J. E. Foster ....Luray, Va.
J. E. Eaton ....Trone, Va.
E. M. Spitzer ....Harrisonburg, Va.
Edward Herring ....Elkton, Va.
J. N. Shiflet ....Mt. Jackson, Va.
Mrs. Lydia A. Pickering ....Broadway, Va.
Mrs. Nettie Derrow ....Broadway, Va.
Mrs B. S. Royal ....Ambrose, Ga.
A. P. Liskey ....Elkton, Va.

(Report to August 23)

REV. J. G. TRUITT ILL

We have just learned that Rev. J. G. Truitt is seriously ill in a local hospital at South Boston, Va., though it is thought that he is past the danger point. He had to undergo an operation for appendicitis and complications set in. The Brotherhood will pray that this useful and talented young man may be restored to health and strength again. Let us pray to that end.

PASTOR AND PEOPLE

SUFFOLK LETTER

The Valley Virginia Central Conference convened in New Hope church August 14 and closed with all-day meeting on Sunday, seventeenth.

E. K. McCord, Nettum Rothbun, J. O. Atkinson, W. A. Harper, C. D. Johnston, and W. W. Staley were among the visitors who took an active part in addresses and discussions. W. G. Shipley, Presbyterian and Dr. W. H. Weekley, United Brethren, were also present.

The Conference was well attended and the hospitality was unbounded. The work of the Conference year was encouraging and plans were greatly enlarged for the year to come.

Fifteen Women's Societies had raised $492.39 and their plans provide for much larger sum the coming year. How could it be otherwise with Mrs. Walters leading the good women of the Valley? During the woman's public meeting Acting Missionary Secretary, McCord, gave a fine demonstration of what the women of the Church are doing in Japan. Mrs. Walters and McCord representing the missionary and his wife; five preachers representing the five pastors supported; women to represent Bible women; girls the Girl's school; children the Christian Orphanage. When these were all seated near the pulpit, McCord explained as the groups were called, the work being done. In this concrete way we saw the work from the Missionary's home to the Sendai Orphanage, clearly and impressively.

The Conference decided by vote without a negative to comply, fully, with Convention request for increase in apportionments; and, in addition to this, the Conference adopted, after consideration by a committee, a suggestion made by President Walters for a "Bigger and Better Conference;" namely, to put on a *five-year campaign* to raise $15,000.00, in addition to regular means, for Home Missions and church extension within the Conference. The object is to assist local congregations in erecting churches and parsonages, and a committee was appointed to work out a plan and put it into operation. Throughout the Conference there was a disposition to formulate larger plans and to execute them.

The Conference, through individuals, had already surpassed itself in subscribing $12,500.00 to the Elon Endowment Fund, and a remarkable experience was developed in raising that fund. Edward Herring, a man passed middle life, made a subscription of $225, went to church the same day, made a profession of religion and joined Mt. Olivet church, which was started by Dr. W. T. Herndon, and is now enthusiastic over building a new house of worship and reviving a cold and disheartened congregation; and they are going to do it. New spirit, new hope, and new purpose have entered into that work. This should be a joy to our dear Dr. Herndon, in his feeble state, to know that the little church which he helped to plant in the mountain is springing into new life; and that a man who was not a Christian at that time, but who loved Dr. Herndon and wanted me to convey his best wishes to him and that he is now in that Mt. Olivet church with his heart, his money, and his life.

All the active pastors in this Conference are Elon College men, and their salaries the past year averaged more than $1,100.00 each. They have put new service, new visions, new faith, and new liberality into the Conference. As ministers raise more money for the Lord's work, the people raise more money for the ministers. Pastors who do not bring up Conference calls always get poor salaries. Investigate and test this statement. In this Conference the outlook brightens and every prospect pleases.

All the Conference officers were re-elected except Treasurer, Samuel Earman, who was succeeded by his son, Frank Earman.

Delegates to the Southern Christian Convention were chosen as follows: *Ministers*—W. T. Walters, A. W. Andes, B. J. Earp; *Laymen*—R. A. Larrick, C. W. Louderback, and J. E. W. Bryant.

Looking backward the Conference can give thanks and looking forward take courage.

Good country, good folks, good roads, good crops, and a good Conference.

W. W. STALEY.

THE VIRGINIA VALLEY CENTRAL CONFERENCE

The Virginia Valley Central Christian Conference held its seventy-first annual session at New Hope Christian church, August 14 to 17. The attendance was large and the reports from the churches were good, showing a substantial increase in membership and an advance of over 30 per cent in contributions. Drs. W. W. Staley, J. O. Atkinson, W. A. Harper, L. F. Johnson and E. K. McCord and Superintendent C. D. Johnston were with us and contributed much to the Conference by their splendid addresses and wise counsel.

There is a great need in this Conference for more ministers, for a grouping of the churches and for parsonage. To meet this need the Conference adopted a "Bigger, Better Conference" program, which has as its aim the raising of $15,000 for Conference work during the next five years; the sum raised to be equally divided between Home Missions and Church Extension. The Conference also decided to lay an apportionment on the churches to meet the apportionment of the Southern Christian Convention. This required an increase of 57 per cent. We may not raise it all the first year but the most of our churches will make the effort and I am sure that we shall raise much more for these funds than heretofore.

The work of liquidating the Winchester church debt was discussed and steps were taken that we feel will mean the clearing of the church debt this year.

The Women's Home and Foreign Mission Board set a goal of $300 last year. They found upon coming to the Conference that they had raised about $500. They set the goal at $700 for this year. The organization is doing a splendid work. We believe that our Conference is going to go forward as never before.

- W. T. WALTERS.

The seventy-first session of the Virginia Valley Central Conference met August 14-16 with the church at New Hope. The following ministers of the Conference were present: W. T. Walters, W. C. Hook, A. W. Andes, B. J. Earp. Killis Roach was absent. The following churches were represented by one or more delegates: Antioch, Bethel, Bethlehem, Beulah, Concord, Dry Run, Joppa, Leaksville, Linville, Mayland, Mt. Olivet, (R.), New Hope, Newport Palmyra, St. Peter's, Timber Ridge, Whistler's Chapel, Winchester, Woods' Chapel, thus leaving seven which were not thus represented, although five of these sent in their reports.

Rev. L. F. Johnson, D. D., of Brooklyn, N. Y., conducted the devotional services throughout the entire Conference, giving a series of studies in the book of Acts. These services were very helpful and enjoyable, and the Conference people are under many obligations to Dr. Johnson for his splendid service.

Rev. W. T. Walters, D. D., the President of the Conference, delivered the President's Address, in which he outlined a plan and proposed a campaign to raise $15,000.00 within the bounds of the Conference to be used in making out a bigger and a better Conference. Following out his suggestions a committee of five was appointed to manage the campaign. Those appointed on the committee were Dr. W. T. Walters Samuel Earman, R. A. Larrick, C. W. Louderback, and Roy Hosaflook. This campaign, which will be an every-member canvass on a large scale, will be launched as soon as the Winchester church debt shall have been paid.

The Annual Address was delivered by Rev. A. W. Andes.

C. D. Johnston, Superintendent of the Christian Orphanage, made two addresses in behalf of the Orphanage. An offering was taken for the Orphanage amounting to $41.51.

The Woman's Mission Board occupied a part of one afternoon, and showed by their reports that they were making rapid progress in the Conference. They raised nearly $500 during the year.

The Conference Missionary Association also made a splendid report showing $253 raised during the year.

Dr. W. A. Harper was elected to deliver the annual address next year, with Rev. W. C. Hook as alternate.

The Conference, by vote, instructed the Apportionment Committee to make the apportionments sufficiently large to cover all the requirements made upon us by the Southern Christian Convention, which means an increase in our apportionments for this year of $625. The Conference Fund was also increased $5.00 to cover necessary expenses. This increase of $630 means and an increase of about 57 per cent to the apportionments of every church in the Conference.

The following visiting brethren were present at the Conference and were helpful to it: Dr. L. F. Johnson, Dr. W. W. Staley, Dr. J. O. Atkinson, Dr. W. A. Harper, Dr. E. K. McCord, Superintendent C. D. Johnston, and Netum Rathbun. Dr. Staley flavored the Conference with wit and wisdom; Dr. Atkinson thrilled us with the missionary spirit; Dr. Harper enlightened us on educational matters; and Dr. McCord interested and instructed us about mission work in Japan.

The following are enrolled as banner churches by reason of their having paid at least the amount asked for by Conference: Antioch, Bethlehem, Beulah, Christian Chapel, Concord, Dry Run, High Point, Joppa, Leaksville, Linville, Mayland, Mt. Olivet (G.), New Hope, Palmyra, Timber Mountain, Timber Ridge without an apportionment sent up $71.70, Whistler's Chapel, Winchester, Woods' Chapel.

The attendance throughout the session was exceptionally good, and much of the time the house was filled to overflowing. The Conference was live, busy, and interesting from start to finish, and we believe can truly be said to be one of the best sessions we have ever had. There is growth all along the line, and, it appears, especially along financially lines. We shall need to do more in a financial way this year than ever, and I hope we shall more than keep pace along spiritual lines. The discouragement that faces us is that the laborers are so few, but we are spurred on by the fact that the harvest truly is great.

                                        A. W. ANDES.

PERSONAL FROM CHICAGO

I arrived here about 5 o'clock on the afternoon of July 21. About the same hour a great disaster occurred, when an airship sailing over the city exploded and crashed a thousand feet or more through the roof of a big bank, killing eleven persons and wounding many others. A few days later a street car strike and a race riot struck the city the same night. You, perhaps, know the rest in the papers you have read. But the papers likely did not give all deaths occurring from the riots. Suffice it to say that the great body of people, both white and colored, who are the responsible citizenship here, deplore such viciousness and the damaging reputation abroad on the good name of Chicago.

There has been a regular colony of the Elon faculty here this summer preparing to give better service in Art Music and in the academic subjects. There were eight of the last year teachers here, viz: Miss Jenkins, in Art; Mr. Betts, in Piano; Mr. Alexander, in Voice; and Messrs. J. U. Newman, Wyrick, Cotten, and also the Dean of Women—all doing academic work. Besides this number, Professor J. M. Barra, who is a graduate student here, has been added to the Elon faculty. Mr. Barra is a native of Piedmont, Italy. He is, from reputation and personal acquaintance, a man of excellent Christian character. He was educated in an Episcopal college in his native land. He has done missionary work among his own people in America until last year, when he taught modern languages in an American college. He speaks fluently, Italian, Spanish, and French. He speaks English so as to be understood. His addition to our faculty brings opportunity as Elon has never offered for our young people to learn the Roman languages, i. e. French, Spanish and Italian

I have, in recent years, heard the theology of this university denounced. Whatever one's objection may be, I have never before heard such high exaltation given

to Jesus Christ as the Son of God, as I have heard here. One of these great sermons was by Dean Willett of the Theological Department.

                                        W. P. LAWRENCE.
University of Chicago
August 17, 1919.

TWO PICTURES

I see two pictures in the twenty-fifth chapter of Matthew—one is sad and the other is glad. There are ten virgins spoken of. Five are wise and are the true children of God. They have their vessels full of oil and their lamps burning and are ready for service at any time. They are always willing to speak, sing, pray, lead, teach, help to lead souls to Christ. In fact they are not ashamed nor afraid to follow anywhere the Lord leads. This represents the glad picture, or the wise virgins. The Holy Spirit dwells here.

The sad picture, or the foolish virgins may be spoken of as church members who want to do the will of God but are afraid to speak and work in church and are ashamed to talk to sinners. They can't lose sight of self, are weak spiritually, and can't see how to walk the narrow way because their lamps are not burning and they have no oil. The Holy Spirit cannot dwell here.

Which of these pictures represents you?
                                        MRS. A. D. BAKER.
Kipling, N. C.

DAMASCUS

The church at Damascus has been without a pastor since last September until I was called the first Sunday in June, to serve until conference, preaching twice a month.

I have never seen a more loyal or better people than those at Damascus. Everything has been done to make my stay with them pleasant.

I found the church with a live Woman's Missionary Society that has been doing a great work. A Young People's Society and a Junior Christian Endeavor Society have been organized with thirty and twenty-two members each, respectively.

Last week we held our revival meeting. Dr. C. H. Rowland, Franklin, Va., did the preaching and won the hearts of the people. His sermons were filled with the spirit of Christ and, as a result of his preaching, between thirty-five and forty professed faith in Christ. Twenty-two united with the church and twenty of that number were baptized Sunday, August 17.

                                        W. B. FULLER, Pastor.
Sunbury, N. C.

PROGRAM COMMITTEE OF THE NORTH CAROLINA CONFERENCE MEETS

The program committee of the North Carolina Conference met in Burlington August 22. The members of the committee are: Revs. G. J. Green, T. E. White, and P. H. Fleming. Brother Green could not be present. Dr. W. A. Harper, Rev. L. I. Cox, and THE SUN's Editor were invited to sit with the committee. We feel sure that the members of the Conference will be pleased with the program. Later we shall have something to say concerning its plan and purpose.

THE FORWARD MOVEMENT

(Warren H. Denison, Superintendent)

The Conferences and the Forward Movement

1. Each Conference should build its program upon the five points of the Forward Movement and provide time for Conferences and informal discussion.

2. The Conference officials should see that the five year program of intensive work is fully explained.

3. All the details of the two million dollar goal should be made perfectly clear to all.

4. It should be made the specific duty of some official to see that each pastor and church work out and put into effect a definite church program in harmony with the general Forward Movement program. The church and pastor failing to do this is the one that needs it most.

5. A strong co-operating and promotion committee should be appointed to encourage and develop the work of the Movement and assist its officials when the special million dollar drive is made.

6. Plans should be made for a strong stewardship educational program in the churches so that when the financial campaign is made by the Forward Movement the people will have been thoroughly informed as to its great need.

Seaside Chautauqua

The sixth successful session of the Chautauqua has closed. By many it was said to be the best yet held. I presume we will never be satisfied until other hundreds of our people realize its importance and avail themselves of its value. It is one of the most far reaching institutions among us. It is permanently fixed in spirit and place among our people. The management has suggested to the Executive Committee of the American Christian Convention the idea of further developing the School of Methods idea and encouraging the establishment of several in various sections of our brotherhood.

Officers For 1920

President .... Rev. C. H. Rowland
Vice-President .... Rev. W. H. Denison
General Secretary .... S. M. Smith
Assistant General Secretary .... Rev. L. E. Smith
Recording Secretary .... Rev. W. W. Staley
Treasurer .... Walter C. Rawles
Director of Publicity .... Hermon Eldredge

Central Executive Committee

The above named officers and Mr. I. A. Luke.

Program Committee

Rev. W. H. Denison, Chairman; Mr. Hermon Eldredge, President W. A. Harper, Mr. S. M. Smith, Rev. C. H. Rowland.

The Woman's Mission Board of the Southern Christian Convention held its meeting at the Chautauqua.

The Association for the Promotion of Christian Unity of the Disciples of Christ Church and the Commission on Christian Unity of the Christian Church held joint sessions during the Chautauqua. Some strong messages were given by speakers from both Commissions and a most delightful fellowship was manifested. Our representatives were Revs. F. G. Coffin, J. F. Burnett, F. H. Peters, P. S. Sailer, W. H. Denison and President W. A. Harper.

Plan now to attend the seventh session of the Chautauqua at Virginia Beach next year; and more, plan to see that some representatives are present from your church.

Otego, N. Y., $2,106

The Otego church is a rural church in the hills of Eastern New York Conference and with a roll of seventy-six names and quite a number of them not available but they are interested in the Forward Movement and go over the top and make a splendid record of $2,106. This is the first church in the Conference to make a full canvass and it will be an inspiration to all the other churches.

NOTES

Get ready to attend Conference this fall. See that your church is represented.

The church at Union Ridge had excellent exercises by the children last Sunday night.

The Burlington Sunday-school enjoyed a picnic at the Christian Orphanage one afternoon last week.

Rev. J. W. Harrell is recuperating from his recent operations and will resume his duties next Sunday.

It seemed expedient that we leave out our editorial this week and give the room to a matter of news that should interest our people.

Brother B. D. Jones, Holland, Virginia, favored this office with eleven new subscribers last week. Thank you, Brother Jones, thank you.

Brother A. M. Kerr, editor of *The Herald of Gospel Liberty* is making a most excellent paper. He is due the congratulations of the Church in his splendid beginning.

If there is a church in the North Carolina Conference needing a pastor for the third Sunday during the coming year, a letter addressed to this office will probably be the means of getting that church in touch with a pastor for that Sunday.

Dr. J. P. Barrett is now in Beloit, Wis., 932 Eighth Avenue. Several calls have been extended to Dr. Barrett, but so far as we know he has not accepted any of them. He is desirous of locating where he can be of the largest possible service. Dr. Barrett is a scholar, and a capable preacher and pastor.

MISSIONARY

MINUTES OF THE WOMAN'S MISSION BOARD OF THE
SOUTHERN CHRISTIAN CONVENTION IN SESSION
AT VIRGINIA BEACH, JULY 31, 1919

Devotional service was conducted by Dr. W. A. Harper. The text of his discourse was Matt V: "Ye are the salt of the earth."

The minutes of the Woman's Board meeting and Convention at Franklin, Va., 1918, were read as a matter of information. The following officers gave reports which were of great interest:

Mrs. W. A. Harper, President, read a fine paper which appears elsewhere in this issue of THE SUN. Also Mrs. A. T. Banks, Corresponding Secretary. The Treasurer's report showed an increase in funds over the last year's report. Contributions by Conferences:

Eastern North Carolina	$ 255.75
Eastern Virginia	2,713.01
Georgia and Alabama	5.00
North Carolina	302.32
North Carolina and Virginia	428.00
Virginia Valley Central	360.08
Western North Carolina	294.22
Southern Christian Convention Offering	16.00
Total	$4,374.38

Mrs. W. V. Leathers reported that the challenge made to the young people of the Southern Convention by the Northern Woman's Mission Board to furnish the interior of the Santa Isabel Chapel provided the Young People's Societies of the Southern Convention raise the $1,000 still lacking on the building fund, had been accepted and that the various Conferences be apportioned sufficient amounts to complete the Santa Isabel building fund. Mrs. Leathers' report was approved and the following apportionment made:

Eastern Va. Young People's Societies	$ 600.00
North Carolina Young People's Societies	350.00
Va. Valley Central Y. P. Societies	50.00
Total	$1,000.00

This amount to be raised by the October Conferences.

Dr. J. O. Atkinson was present and lent inspiration and enthusiasm to the meeting by his wise counsel.

Dr. E. K. McCord, returned missionary from Japan, spoke briefly upon the outlook of the work being done by the Southern Boards, congratulating those churches that have recently arranged to put missionaries in the field.

Dr. Chas. Rowland made interesting remarks emphasizing the spiritual side of missions.

Rev. W. P. Minton, the newly elected Mission Secretary, was introduced, and set forth the thought that before our people can be really missionary in spirit they must get right with God.

The Board adjourned to meet in the spring of 1920.

MRS. W. A. HARPER, President.
MRS. W. H. CARROLL, Secretary.

President's Address
Mrs. W. A. Harper

It is a real pleasure to greet my colleagues, of the Woman's Board in the first session since I was so unexpectedly and unworthily honored with its presidency.

The days since our biennial Convention session in Franklin have been momentous and testing for our work as well as for the world. The epidemic of influenza in the fall necessitated the postponement of our fall Conference Conventions and the closing of the churches to worship hindered the local work. Yet despite these two handicaps, so solidly had our work established itself that we have raised more money than in any previous year and we have met here enthusiastic for larger undertakings. My prediction is that we have but begun the great work we are in the future sure to accomplish.

You have heard the reports of the various officers and of the Conferences affiliated with our Board and have heard the recommendations. This report was written before coming here and it may in places duplicate what has already been said, but does it matter? When we love our work it is sweeter to croon over it again and again.

High Spots of the Year

Aside from the evidence of general advance during the year, we have occasion to rejoice in the sending out of an additional missionary by the Burlington Sunday school in which our women there are foremost leaders, in provision for a further missionary by the Eastern Virginia young people to complete the raising of the fund for the Santa Isabel work, and in the union of the three boards of North Carolina into one, so making for efficiency. The budget of the North Carolina women for their first year calls for $2,000 in money, besides the Rally Day offerings, for twenty new societies, and for twenty life-members. The prospect is that they will arrive at their objective.

Rally Days

Last summer and again this summer, I have prepared a Rally Day program for July and August rallies in all our churches. These have been sent to the societies and, where no society exists to some prominent local leader in each church, and to ministers. In this way we have not only raised money but we have sown seeds that will render the organization work later easier. The last thing I did before leaving home was to send to a church that has no society a second installment of Rally Day literature the first being lost. I prophesy this church will give the program and there organize a society.

I recommend that the money which comes in through these rallies, be retained to the credit of each Conference treasury to pay the expenses of the Conference Board in its regular and special work. One handicap of our work has been expense money when officers go out to boost our present work or organize new work. This fund will release for the Southern Christian Convention Woman's Treasury all money coming in from societies for dues and other special and supply a basis for internal growth and expansion.

Literature

One of our great needs in the work is literature. I recommend that the President be authorized to have twelve pamphlets written and published the coming year for free distribution and that $500 be appropriated for printing and circulating these pamphlets.

I recommend that we print in THE CHRISTIAN SUN the program from the Christian Missionary every month, so that more of our women may see it.

I recommend that we set our goal to secure 500 additional subscribers to the *Christian Missionary* before the next session of the Southern Christian Convention and that our Superintendent of Literature be made the captain to make the recommendation effective.

Final Budget

I recommend that we set our goal financially for the period since May 1919 to May 1920 at $8,000 actually sent to Mrs. W. T. Walters, Treasurer, and that it be apportioned as follows:

Georgia and Alabama	250.00
Eastern Virginia	$ 4,500.00
Valley Virginia	500.00
North Carolina	2,500.00
Alabama	250.00

And that each Conference Board apportion its allotment to the departments as it may deem best.

Our Relation to Special Missionary Movements

I recommend that where our societies as such subscribe to any special movement of a financial character, whether primarily for missionary or for other purposes, such money or any part of it, to Mrs. W. T. Walters, Treasurer, and by her paid to the proper authorities, so that our women may secure proper credit for all money raised in the societies.

Recommendations as to Officers

I recommend that our officers be urged before the Southern Christian Convention session of May 1920 to do the following things:

Vice-President, assist the president in her work.

Secretary, collect and print in permanent form the minutes of the next Conference Conventions.

Corresponding Secretary, collect and tabulate on cards all societies, their officers, and other vital facts connected with them, and by installments print them in THE CHRISTIAN SUN. They should also appear in the minutes to be printed by our Secretary.

Treasurer, to get a full financial statement from each Conference treasurer, and to exhibit for the biennium not only all money sent to her, but raised from other sources as well by the societies, and to have a chart prepared for the Convention Hall showing the financial growth of our Women's work.

Superintendent Young People, organize twenty new societies in addition to the work now being done.

Superintendent Cradle Roll, organize thirty new societies and get full report by the Convention's meeting.

Superintendent Boys' Work, organize thirty new societies.

Superintendent Literature and Mite Boxes, send out the pamphlets to be written, the minutes to be printed, and furnish monthly in THE CHRISTIAN SUN a list of good books for all grades of missionary society, as well as a list of literature for full distribution.

Mission Secretary, Dr. J. O. Atkinson, help our officers in the many ways that shall occur to them and to his fertile resourcefulness, but particularly as a Rally Day speaker, society organizer, and pamphlet writer.

I recommend our societies use the regular books for mission study which are for the women, "A Crusade of Compassion for the Healing of the Nations" (Foreign), and "Christian Americanization" (Home).

Report of Corresponding Secretary

Mrs. A. T. Banks

In this time of fast development when nothing seems too great for the mind of man to use as he determines, we find missions fast developing into the church spirit, not because we feel it only a Christian duty to support, but because we are more interested in the welfare of our brother.

The more distant human being has become our neighbor. We have long dreamed of the needs of the sin perishing souls.

The vision is no longer afar off, but so near it seems that daily we feel ourselves in contact with the hungering souls who want the help of the Christian world.

In our Southern Christian Convention the work has gone forward, and yet we must still be busy organizing and getting people to study missions. Without study a society loses interest, and we find, too, that our women are hungry for such literature as our mission literature offers. A number of societies have been organized since the last sitting of our Board. But our aim is to organize where it is possible to reach and to ask pastors to co-operate and ask their wives to organize.

The Cradle Roll is an important feature and there should be one connected with every missionary society. Willing Workers and boys societies should be more emphasized and the Home Department is of no less importance. I report as follows:

Woman's Missionary Societies	65
Willing Workers	24
Cradle Rolls	25
Home Departments	1

Increase of 4 Woman's Societies in North Carolina Conference and 1 Cradle Roll.

Virginia Valley Central Conference, 4 Woman's Societies.

MEANS TO AN END

The Greensboro Daily News of August 13, reports Rev. M. E. Melvin, D. D., to have delivered at Montreat "one of the ablest addresses here before the Conference on Christian education and ministerial relief that has been heard at Montreat on this subject." "Evangelism and education are inseparable," declared Dr. Melvin, "and the church must reach the point of realizing that foreign missions is the end and that home missions and Christian education are the means of leading to the ends as expressed in the great commission, 'Go ye into all the world and preach the gospel to every creature.' ''

Dr. Melvin's idea, shared so universally by the membership of the great Presbyterian church, of which he is a part, accounts in a large measure for the fact that his church has gone forward with much leaps and bounds the past few years in winning the world to Christ. The church that makes missions an end, and every other agency, institution and organizations in the church a means to that end cannot help but grow. From the time our Savior gave His great commission till now, God has never prospered a church that would not undertake an adequate missionary program, and He never will. God loved a whole world, He does now love a whole world, and is undertaking to reach and redeem a whole world. That church that does not love a whole world, does not undertake to help reach and save a whole world is neither God-like, nor can it expect the power of God and the presence of God in its tasks and undertakings. The fact that Christ said, ''Go ye into all the world'' is an evidence that we can go if we will, and the fact that we don't go shows our obstinacy and rebellion instead of our trust and faith.

J. O. ATKINSON.

CATCHING MEN AND KEEPING THEM

I was much interested in a statement from one of our best men and deepest thinkers recently: ''The Christian Church has produced the *Big Four* in Sunday school and Christian Endeavor work: Marion Lawrence, W. C. Pearce, Amos R .Wells, and Hermon Eldredge.'' It is glory for a Church to be able to produce such men. A Church that can produce such men must have somewhat in it that is holy, sacred, worth while. But, why can't the Church that produces such men, keep them? Only one of the *Four* is now, so far as I know, in any way connected with the Christian Church, and the one left, I believe, makes his living in some other way than as an official or an employee of the Church. I wonder if our glory is to be our shame. These men are all linked up for life service with other organizations than our Church. There must be a reason.

Before we condemn these men for seeking active fellowship and their life's work elsewhere, three of them wholly, would we not for the sake of the future, do well to inquire if the fact, if there be any, is not elsewhere than with them—in past at least.

Why can't a Church that can produce such men, keep such men? If these three were all the question might not be so serious. But there are others, scores and hundreds.

I am wondering if there is not something lacking in our program. Jesus our Lord gave a program great enough for the greatest men we could produce. But somehow we have not seen fit to adopt that program even to the extent of our ability or capacity. We have made that program a side issue a secondary matter a thing to be tampered and played with, as children might a useless toy. We have never taken that program seriously. We have never laid the burden of it on our hearts; we have never brought the binding force of it to our hearts and to our consciences. Until we do that we are going to keep on producing men whom we can't hope to keep, nor to employ, because as they grow in vision and in strength they discover that our program is inadequate. The Christian Church has fundamental principles to make giants. But its program has not been adequate to challenge their strength, develop their loyalty, and grip their faith.

Lord Christ, Whose name we wear, gave the program which we are so reluctant to adopt, ''Go ye into all the world.'' And we who bear that name and share its joy have not been willing, even to a tithe of our ability, to make known the name or proclaim its joy to the millions who have never heard the name nor known the joy.

J. O. ATKINSON.

ODDS AND ENDS

Smile when you can. Heaven alone can reveal its worth. Live up to all the light you have and trust the rest to God.

God loveth a cheerful giver. Christians should be the happiest people in the world. There is no reason why we should put on a long face when Jesus takes up his abode in our hearts.

God pity that man who believes his church contains all the good people in the world.

It is not all of life to live. If we fail to properly use the talent which God has intrusted to our care, we have failed to accomplish God's purpose in creating us. Therefore, we have lost all. Why are we so unthoughtful, so unhappy, so miserable? Certainly, we should not be thus. God created us in His own image and has placed all things at our disposal.

O God, I thank Thee that I can see the blue of the ocean, the green of the hills against the sunset sky, the moonlit world, the autumn tinted forests, the courage in a Father's face, the wonders and the glories all around.

I thank Thee that I can hear the singing of birds, the murmur of the tide against the shore, the sighing of the wind among the trees, the laughs of little children.

I thank Thee that I can feel the balmy air, the winter's chill, the rushing wind, the love of my friends, my baby's kisses, the comforts of home, the manifold blessings of life that thou has given me.

I pray Thee that my eyes be closed, my hearing dulled, my feeling lost to enemy, hate, maliciousness, and shame for these are not of Thee. May I show truth and steadfastness when all the way is bright and peaceful and faith when all my life seems dark. Thus may I strive to make myself as thou wouldst have thy children to be.

MRS. ANNIE SMITH.

Route 1, New Hill, N. C.

CHRISTIAN EDUCATION

SOME LATE NEWS FROM ELON

Elon begins her thirtieth year on September 10. The office force has done its best to insure its being a creditable opening, and despite handicaps of various sorts the prospect looks good. One thing that greatly grieves us is that for many years almost half of our students have come from other Churches than our own. It should not be so. Our young people belong here, and their going elsewhere impoverishes the College and our local churches as well. It is not the case with young people of other churches that come here. The Christians are not proselyters and Elon returns them prepared to be loyal to their own in their home communities.

Our ministers, alumni, church leaders, and students have a fine opportunity in the few days that remain to bring many an undecided young person to Elon. The Church has liberally given of its money to make Elon bigger and better. This is evidence that the College has firmly justified itself in the minds of the adults of our Brotherhood. But our young men and young women are unable to form their judgment on the College's worth unless these same adult friends shall direct and guide. Money is good, but life is better. Elon can never serve our Church 100 per cent till 100 per cent of our young people come here for life direction and impress. I am calling on the generous friends who made the Standardization Drive successful to rally to her now and fill her halls with buoyant young lives from our Christian homes, the hope and promise of our beloved Church.

Beloved friends of the cause of Christ as the Christian Church represents that cause, *this means you*.

I call upon our people in their public worship and their private devotions to pray that Elon may constructively serve our Master's cause.

Faculty Additions

Miss Celia Smith, of the New England Conservatory, becomes assistant in piano, voice, and theoretical work.

Miss Anna Mary Landis, of Columbia University, becomes head of the Department of Domestic Science and Household Arts.

Miss Katherine L. Sturm, of the Cincinnati Conservatory and the Northwestern University School of Music, becomes head of the Violin Department and Director of the Orchestra.

Miss Ruth Hawk, of the King's School of Oratory, Pittsburgh, Pa., where for two years she has been a member of the Faculty, becomes head of the Department of Expression and Physical Culture.

Professor J. M. Barra, a native of Piedmont, Italy, and graduate student of the University of Chicago, becomes head of the new Department of Romance Languages. Professor Barra speaks Italian, French, Spanish, and English fluently.

Senor Victor M. Rivera, of our Porto Rico Church, becomes assistant in Spanish to Professor Barra.

Mr. T. E. Powell, Elon '19 and of the Summer School of Cornell University, becomes instructor in Geology and Biology.

Mrs. J. J. Lincoln, so favorably known to all our people, is added to the administrative force and becomes librarian-in-chief. She will be assisted by three young ladies of the student body.

Mr. L. W. Vaughan, Elon '17, becomes College Bursar and will be assisted by Miss Lillie Mae Johnson.

The Staff and The Summer

During the summer two members of the Faculty have taught in Summer Schools of other Colleges, and sixteen have studied in the Summer Schools of the Northern and Western Universities. Soon after the opening we will have a Faculty night and each member will tell his or her Summer School experience. We feel that new life will come to us this year as a result of this migration to the great centers of learning and culture.

Finally

Beloved, remember the days ahead are critical days for many young people, and you may be the one to start some one of them on the road to a larger usefulness in life. Will you endeavor to be?

W. A. HARPER, *President.*

GO TO COLLEGE

These are critical days for many young people. Just now they are considering the matter of going to college and securing additional training for the work of life. Perhaps there are hindrances, yea even formidable difficulties to be overcome before the wise decision can be reached. Nothing should be allowed to keep a young man or woman from college. The greatest difficulties can be overcome where there is sufficient purpose and effort. That which the heart is set upon can be achieved. All who really desire a college education today can have it. Decide to go to college and you will find the difficulties vanishing one by one and the way opening to larger and better things. There are those who are standing ready to help all who put forth an honest effort. Young man, young woman, be full of courage!

A college education greatly increases a young person's chance for success in life, for doing good, for usefulness and for the living of a life that shall really count. A college education is cheap at almost any price. You can afford to go in debt in order to obtain it. Many of our greatest men left college with debts upon them and not one of them today would tell you that such a debt was a bad thing. They are glad they had the courage to make a debt for such a purpose. It pays to obtain the best training possible for the work of life. The best is none too good for the only life we will have a chance to live upon the earth.

The writer is profoundly grateful that he decided to go to Elon College when he was a young man and obtain training for the work of life. The debt incurred has long since been paid off and the time spent in college was abundantly worth while. The four years spent in Elon College were the best years of his life. The sense of his indebtedness to the institution grows with the passing years.   J. W. HARRELL.

WORSHIP AND MEDITATION

I THANK THEE, LORD

I thank Thee, Lord, at break of day,
 When all the east is red with sun,
For health and hope and heart to say,
"I would be part of any way
 In which the will of God is done.'

And though the task that I have sought
 Transcends my hands' unaided skill,
I thank Thee for this mighty thought—
That all the wonders to be wrought
 Lie hidden in Thy perfect will.

I thank Thee, at the time of rest,
 For strength that held the long day through,
Footsore and worn, yet peace-possessed,
I know the honest toil is best
 Of him who strives Thy will to do.
—Author Unknown.

DOING TOO MUCH

To do too much is to do less than we ought. Most of us are doing too much; therefore most of us could do more if we would do less. Most of us are giving too much time to activities of various sorts—good activities, of course: doing things that the Lord wants to have done by some body, very likely. But we are giving too much time to such activities, with result that we are not giving time enough to being alone with God in prayer and in feeling on His Word. So our activities are failing to have anything like the effectiveness and the results that they should have. The leader of a great Christian work said, concerning a certain active Christian man: "We need a man, but we hesitate to employ him because he is becoming so busy with such a multitude of things that we fear his time for private intercession and prayer is being crowded out." Evidently that man was doing so much that these leaders feared that he could not do enough in this position of Christian responsibility. It takes *courage*, and *surrender*, and *faith*, deliberately to lay aside some, perhaps many, of our activities in order to have the time alone with God that He says is vital. But would it not be worth while to enter upon a new experience of Spirit-energized service.—*Sunday School Times.*

HOUSES AND HOMES

When we get down to the consideration of those things which are fundamental to welfare and happiness, we must always find that there is nothing so essential, either for this life or for the life to come, as the establishing and maintenance of Christian homes. No fundamental fact has been more widely disregarded in recent times than this one, and no other disregard for a fundamental fact has resulted in greater misery and greater loss of realities than this one. We invite our readers, therefore, to pause in the midst of their serious considerations of many other problems, which are generally supposed to be more important and more pressing, to hear what Dr. Jowett has said on the difference between a house and a home: "Any one can build an altar; it requires God to provide the flame. Anybody can build a house; we need the Lord for the creation of a home. A house is an agglomeration of brick and stones, with an assorted collection of manufactured goods; a home is the abiding place of ardent affection, of fervent hope, of genial trust. There is many a homeless man who lives in a richly furnished house. There is many a fifteen-pound house in the crowded street which is an illuminated and beautiful house. The sumptuously furnished house may be the very hearthstone of the eternal God. Now the Christian religion claims to be able to convert houses into homes, to supply the missing fire, and to bring an inspiring flame to the cold and chilling heap. The New Testament does not say very much about homes; it says a great deal about the things that make them. It speaks about life and love and joy and peace and rest. If we get a house and put these into it, we shall have secured a home. Here, then, are two houses. In both of them there is no love, no joy, no peace, no rest. There is no flame of genial and radiant hope. Let us bring the Christian religion into one of the houses, and do as you please with the other. In one house the tenants all kneel before King Jesus. They shall be one in common purpose, and they shall strive together with common mind and will. What will assuredly happen? With absolute certainty the house will become a home! That is a glorious commonplace in the history of the Christian faith. When Christ has been enthroned and every member of the family becomes a worshipper, there steals into the common life a warmth of affection which converts even trivial relationships into radiant kinship. What shall we do with the other house? Sin reigns! Passion reigns! Estrangement reigns; There is continued tumult and unrest. What shall we do? Call upon Baal! Call upon 'the god of this world!' It would be a fruitless quest. There is nothing for it but the grace of Christ."—*Lutheran Survey.*

The book of Jeremiah has the words, "Dwell deep!" What a motto for a life!
"'Dwell deep' the little things that chafe and fret,
 O waste not golden hours to give them heed!
The slight, the thoughtless wrong, do thou forget;
 Be self-forgot serving others' need.
Thou faith in God through love for man shalt keep—
 Dwell deep, my soul, dwell deep!"
—Exchange.

A free forum is the demand of this age. Love (rather even than truth) is the real ground of unity.
—DeVore.

THE CHRISTIAN ORPHANAGE

SUPERINTENDENT ATTENDS VALLEY CONFERENCE

The writer had a very pleasant visit to the Virginia Central Valley Conference, August 14-16 and had the pleasure of telling the people in that section something of the work being done for the Church through the Christian Orphanage.

This Conference has come to the front in the Orphanage work rapidly in the last three years. Three years ago just a few of the Sunday schools (three I think) were making monthly offerings to help support the Orphanage. Now all the churches except eight have made contributions this year.

If we could get in closer touch with the good people in the Valley I feel sure that the response would be greatly enlarged. If it could be possible for the people in the Valley to visit the Institution and see the boys and girls they would get a greater vision of the work and would do larger things for the Orphanage.

As I was traveling through that beautiful section of our great country and looking at the apple trees full of fruit, I thought that if twenty-five persons who have apples would ship us 1 bbl. each, what a small sacrifice it would be to them. But just think what a blessing twenty-five barrels of apples would be to us in this work and how the children would enjoy them!

The people in the Valley are a great people and are able to do great things.

We enjoy each visit to the Conferences in the Valley and hope to be able to attend again next year.

CHAS. D. JOHNSTON, *Supt.*

REPORT FOR AUGUST 27, 1919

Amount brought forward, $8,943.07.

Children's Offerings

Jewel Way, $1.00.

Sunday School Monthly Offerings

(North Carolina Conference)

High Point, $2.91; Wentworth, $7.47; Piney Plains, $6.90; Shady Grove, $2.00; Shiloh, $1.00; Asheboro, $1.21; Haw River, $1.75; Hines Chapel, $1.95; Christian Chapel, $4.50; Reidsville, $1.00; Liberty, (Vance County), $6.50.

(Eastern Virginia Conference)

Franklin, $10.00; Wakefield, $3.49; Waverly, $40.00; Suffolk, $25.00; East End, Newport News, $9.22; Berea (Nansemond), $10.00; Union, (Surry), $1.00.

(Virginia Valley Conference)

Palmyra, $3.08; Leaksville, $3.14; Liberty, $2.00; Timber Ridge, $2.20; Concord, $3.47; Antioch, $6.00; New Hope, $18.00; Winchester, $12.00; Leaksville, $2.50; Newport, Va, $1.50; Rev. W. C. Hook, for Sunday school, $1.00.

(Alabama Conference)

Rock Stand, $1.01; Wadley, $1.45; Total, $168.80.

Special Offerings

Va. Valley Conference, New Hope church, $40.51; E. M. Spitzer, $10.00; First Christian church, Higginsport, Ohio, $11.00; Mrs. D. W. Gilliam, McIver, N. C., $40.00; The Union Vocal service, New Hope, ch. N. C., $8.35; J. Pressley Crawford, Morgantown,. W. Va., $7.00; LakeView Christian church, $2.60; C. C. Way, $5.00; Rev. J. L. Foster, on pledge, $25.00;

Mrs. Nannie Hawkins, Hurdles Mills, N. C., $2.00; J. A. Long, Haw River, N. C., $1.00; C. R. McCauley, expenses in conveying the children to picnic, $13.00; M. Orhau, Jr., Whittier, Cal., $100.00; Total $266.46.

Special Offerings For Furnishing Rooms

Linville S. S. (Val. Va.), $60.00.

Singing Class

Caswell Lodge No. 529 A. F. and A. M., $50.00.

Total for the week, $570.71; Grand total, $9,513.78.

NEEDLES

Needles are of ancient date. Harriette Martineau tells of seeing a piece of darning that had come out of an Egyptian tomb and had the threaded needle still sticking in it after 1,000 years. This one remaining needle of the world of 5,000 years ago of wood.

Before the reign of Queen Elizabeth steel needles were entirely unknown and only bone, wood and bronze ones were used.—*Ex.*

• •

IT DEPRECIATES RAPIDLY.—We've often thought what a pity it is that a man can't dispose of his experience for as much as it cost him —*Elkridge Independent.*

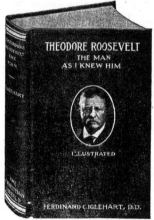

This book is printed on fine book paper and includes 16 pages of illustrations on plate paper. There are nearly 400 pages, in 31 chapters. The binding is made of fine cloth embossed in gold. Size 5x7 inches.

The price is only $1.50 a copy post-paid.

C. B. RIDDLE, Pub. Agt.,..................Burlington, N. C.

Sunday School and Christian Endeavor

SUNDAY SCHOOL LESSON FOR SEPTEMBER 7, 1919

The Kingdom of God. Matt 6:10; 13:31-33; 44-50; 18:2-3; Luke 17:20-21; II Cor. 10:3-5.

Golden Text: "Seek ye first his kingdom and his righteousness."

What is the Kingdom of God? It is not meat and drink; it is not riches in this world "My Kingdom is not of this world." Jesus is not the lord of this world nor its prince. "The prince of this world" is the enemy of our Lord Christ. So, He bids us keep ourselves unspotted from the world. But the day will come when the kingdoms of this world shall become the Kingdoms of our God. What can we do to aid? What do we do to hinder His coming Kingdom? Do we let Him reign in our lives and hearts? Does He reign in our home? Does He, so far as we have the power, reign in our community? D. L. Moody heard a man say it was impossible to tell what God could do with a man whose life was wholly dedicated to Him, and then and there decided that God should have his life with which to demonstrate what could be done. And God did show what He could do when He took an ignorant, untrained shoe-salesman, and made of him a true Ambassador for Christ. The "Sermon on the Mount" is the enunciation of the laws of the Kingdom delivered by the King, "I say unto you." What has He said unto you? Have you ever listened to hear? What can we do to prepare for the coming Kingdom and the coming King? Are you looking for the coming of the Lord Jesus? Are you doing your best to prepare for His coming? Do you, too, say: "Even so, Lord Jesus, come quickly?" Do you mean it, with all your heart and soul, with all your strength of purpose, of mind and of body, when you kneel and pray, "Thy Kingdom Come?"

MRS. FRED BULLOCK.

CHRISTIAN ENDEAVOR TOPIC FOR SEPTEMBER 7, 1919

Our Relation to Others (Towards Neighbors and Friends). Phil. 2:1-11. (Consecration meeting).

A story went the rounds some time ago, which ran something like this: "What do you think of my new dress?" asked Maud of her friend, Belle. "Well, to tell you the truth, my dear," began Belle, when Maud said sharply, 'Stop right there; if you are going to be disagreeable, I don't want to hear it.'" Why is it that it is only disagreeable truths that we are fond of telling? Is it not strange that we so often forget the truthful nice things we could say of our neighbors and friends? Were they dead, what splendid tributes we would pay to their memory, but "a rose to the living is more than bountiful wreaths to the dead." Who are our neighbors? Are they only the good folks in the neighborhood, the ones we like best, who have the best manners, or an auto in which they invite us to ride in? What about the poor neighbor on the back streets whose back yard is neighbor to ours? The Bible laid down rules for those who make a feast, that it should be the poor, those not able to return the kindnesses who should be invited. How about applying the same rule for neighborly kindnesses? Such kind deeds is like bread cast upon the waters, which returns after many days. Deacon West of the Spring Hill Sunday school used to send two carts or wagons to church every Sunday, one for his own family, one down another road to gather up those who had no means of conveyance of their own. His four sons are all splendid Christian workers in our church today. Can you see any connection?

MRS. FRED BULLOCK.

ORIGIN OF THE AMERICAN SUNDAY SCHOOL

Some years ago. the Ohio Sunday School Association instructed an investigator to find out if possible the earliest attempts at the establishment of Sunday schools in America, and after due investigation the following facts were found:

The town records of New Town, Long Island, show that Rev. Morgan Jones established a Sunday school there February 28, 1683, fifty years before Robert Raikes was born. But

it is not certain that even this was the first Sunday school in America. A writer in the *Historical Magazine*, says that in 1674 the Puritans had a Sunday school in Roxbury, Mass. There seems to be, however, no authority for this beyond the mere statement; but the town records of New Town, Long Island, are copied in full in *Thompson's History*, a very rare book at this day, so there can be no doubt as to the date of the establishment of Morgan Jones' Sunday school.

There is some doubt as to the exact date on which Robert Raikes started his Sunday school in Gloucester, England, but assuming that it was in 1781, then there were certainly five and perhaps more Sunday schools in America before that date, viz.: At Roxbury, Mass., 1674; at New Town, Long Island, 1683; Christ Church, Savannah, Ga., 1736, (started by John Wesley while priest there); at Ephrata, Penn., 1740; at Bethlehem, Conn., 1740; and at Philadelphia, Penn., 1744. The Ephrata school was interrupted after the battle of Brandywine, September 11, 1777 in order that the school room might be used as a hospital for the wounded American soldiers.

The date of the Sunday school in Savannah, Ga., is shown on a bronze tablet which reads as follows: "To the glory of God in memory of John Wesley, Priest of the Church of England, minister to Savannah 1736-1737. Founder of the Sunday school. Erected by the Diocese of Georgia."

The official records of the church show that Rev. John Wesley assumed charge in 1736 and started a Sunday school. Under him Mr. De La Motta, instructed the "children of the church." Every Sunday afternoon it was Wesley's custom to meet the children of the congregation before service and hear them recite the catechism, question them as to what they had heard from the pulpit in the morning, instruct them still further in the Bible, endeavoring to fix the truth in their understandings as well as their memories.

This Sunday school was established nearly fifty years before Robert

Raikes originated his scheme of Sunday instruction in Gloucester, England. The Christ church Sunday school is still going on.

In order to teach his household regularly, William Elliott organized a Sunday school house in his home in 1785, and this was kept up until Burton Oak Grove church was built when it was carried to the church, and has been in continuous existence since that time. This locality is where Watchaprague now stands in Accomac County, Virginia.. William Elliott's Bible containing a history of the organization of this Sunday school is still in the possession of Mrs. Wessie E. Neck Eason, a great-great-granddaughter of William Elliott The history of the school is preserved in a pamphlet by Mr. L. James Hyslop of Keller, Virginia, Historical Bulletin No. 1, Virginia State Sunday School Association.

In 1786 Rev. Francis Asbury established a Sunday school in the house of Thomas Crenshaw, Hanover County, Virginia, and this became noted in that section.

We can see from the above that there were several Sunday schools in different parts of America long before Robert Raikes took his walk in the suburbs of Gloucester, England, in 1780 or 1781, and saw the wretches in the streets, and employed four women to teach the children on Sundays, . It would appear that Rev. Morgan Jones was the originator of the idea long before Robert Raikes, the printer was born, and that America and not England should have the honor of starting this great institution,. that now extends over a large part of the earth.

W. E. MacCLENNY.
Suffolk, Va.

CHARLES W McPHERSON, M. D.

Eye, Ear, Nose, Throat

OFFICE OVER CITY DRUG STORE

Office Hours: 9:00 a. m. to 1:00 p m

and 2:00 to 5:00 p. m.

Phones: Residence 153; Office 65J

BURLINGTON, NORTH CAROLINA

OBITUARIES

FIX

Mrs. Sarah Fix, the daughter of John S. Turrentine, was born September 18, 1838 and died August 13, 1919, aged 80 years, 10 months and 25 days. She was married to Joseph Fix of Burlington, N. C., October 5, 1857 To this union were born ten children She is survived by two sons, two daughters and also two brothers. There are thirteen grandchildren and sixteen great-grandchildren.

A mother in Israel has fallen. She was a great and good woman, highly honored and respected by all who knew her. She was the friend of all and the servant of all, ever ready to minister. Her joy was found in helping the needy. For a long while she was President of the King's Daughters and faithfully served in that capacity. She met Christ's test for greatness in a marked manner. She will be remembered by the good she has done. Many will rise up and call her blessed.

The secret of this beautiful life is to be found in the fact that she was ever hungering and thirsting after righteousness. Her soul hunger was intense. The more she knew of God, the more she wanted to know. When a girl she united with Providence Christian church and after the organization of the Burlington church transfered her membership. She was faithful to her church and present at all of its services whenever possible. She will be greatly missed. She faithfully cultivated, the religious life and kept the fires of God's love burning upon the altar of her heart.

The funeral service was largely attended and the floral offering very beautiful and large. The service was conducted by her pastor assisted by Dr. Wellons.

J. W. HARRELL.

WHITWORTH

George B. Whitworth passed away at his home, 1344 North Main Street, Danville, Virginia, on Saturday night, August 9, after a lingering illness of three months. Death was due to an affection of the throat and lungs. Mr. Whitworth had been a sufferer for several years but his condition became serious a few months ago and since that time he became gradually weaker and weaker. He was very patient during all his suffering.

He is survived by a wife one son, and three step-sons, and also two brothers and a sister in addition to other relatives.

Funeral services were held at the home. Interment at Leemont cemetery. The writer had charge of the services.

H. S. HARDCASTLE.

GASKINS

Sallie Grant Gaskins, relict of Walter B. Gaskins, died July 28, 19 9, at the home of W. S. Long, in Chapel Hill, N. C. Her husband died about two years previous. Her only child, Vernon, died in December 1918, and a brother Vernon Grant, who had lived in her home, died in January 1919. Thus in a brief period the entire family passed away from the cares, the joys, and the sorrows of this world. With bowed heads and sad hearts relatives and friends placed their bodies side by side in the cemetery in Norfolk, Va. Our sister was a member of the Presbyterian Church, and a devout Christian.

W. S. LONG.

BOYD

About fifteen years ago Brother T. A. S. Boyd died, and August 3, 1919, his widow died in Richmond, Va., and her burial took place in the cemetery of Pleasant Grove church, Va., the church of her youth and of her father's people. Many relatives and friends gathered to show their love and respect. Three of her former pastors attended her funeral: J. W. Wellons P. T. Klapp and the write.. She was the youngest daughter of Archibald Farmer, one of the most useful and substantial citizens of that section, and a sister of Mrs. William Dunn, Mrs. E. T. Pierce, and Mrs. Edward Carlton, all of whom preceded her to the grave. Sister Boyd leaves several children, and many relatives and friends who sorrow on account of the loss they have sustained, but not as those who have no hope for the life and testimony bequeathed them assures them of the rest and blessedness of a dear mother.

It was my good fortune to begin my ministry with the church at Pleasant Grove Va., in the fall of 1860. The next year I baptized two sisters, Ellen and Annie Farmer, and two other sister, Lou and Charlotte Boyd. This was my first service of this kind. They were all good women, and adorned the homes in which they lived and have all died leaving a good record behind them.

W. S. LONG.

IN MEMORIAM—LEE

Whereas, the great and supreme Ruler has in His infinite wisdom called from labor to reward Mr. Willis J. Lee, who from the organization of both the Woman's Home and Foreign Missionary and our Ladies' Aid Societies of Berea (Nansemond) Christian church, has always done his duty as a faithful and devoted member. Therefore be it Resolved:

First, that we record our sincere appreciation of his Christian character and faithful service to the Societies and the cause of Christ. No man among us has been more generous and faithful, his example is worthy of emulation.

Second, that we bow in humble submission to the will of God Who doeth all things well. We thank our Heavenly Father for extending his life well beyond three score years and we pray that God may raise up some worthy successor.

Third, that we extend to his dear wife and family our sincere sympathy and pray God to sustain them in this dark hour.

Fourth, that a copy of these resolutions be spread upon the records of our Woman's Missionary and Ladies' Aid Societies, a copy sent to the family and a copy sent to The Christian Sun for publication.

MRS. J. W. BRINKLEY,
MRS. R. B. ODOM,
MRS. A. E. RAMSEY,
MISS HELEN BRINKLEY,
Committee.

FOR RENT OR SALE

Five-room cottage, electric lights, good well water, small barn, fruits, about 1 acre lot. One block south of depot, Elon College, N. C. Rent $10 per month. For sale cash or terms at bargain. Address
JAS. L. FOSTER,
Waverly, Va.

Birds of a Feather

"A scientist, eh?"

"Yes."

"What's his specialty?"

"He's trying to find a substitute for gasoline."

"I have an eccentric friend he ought to meet."

"What is your friend working on?"

"Perpetual motion."—*Birmingham Age Herald.*

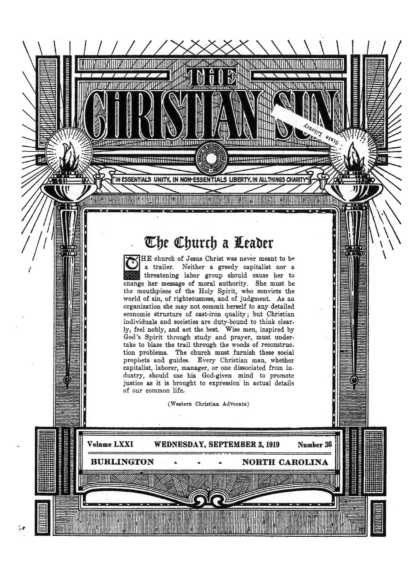

THE CHRISTIAN SUN

"IN ESSENTIALS UNITY, IN NON-ESSENTIALS LIBERTY, IN ALL THINGS CHARITY"

The Church a Leader

THE church of Jesus Christ was never meant to be a trailer. Neither a greedy capitalist nor a threatening labor group should cause her to change her message of moral authority. She must be the mouthpiece of the Holy Spirit, who convicts the world of sin, of righteousness, and of judgment. As an organization she may not commit herself to any detailed economic structure of cast-iron quality; but Christian individuals and societies are duty-bound to think clearly, feel nobly, and act the best. Wise men, inspired by God's Spirit through study and prayer, must undertake to blaze the trail through the woods of reconstruction problems. The church must furnish these social prophets and guides. Every Christian man, whether capitalist, laborer, manager, or one dissociated from industry, should use his God-given mind to promote justice as it is brought to expression in actual details of our common life.

(Western Christian Advocate)

Volume LXXI   WEDNESDAY, SEPTEMBER 3, 1919   Number 36

BURLINGTON   -   -   -   NORTH CAROLINA

THE CHRISTIAN SUN

Founded 1844 by Rev. Daniel W. Kerr

C. B. RIDDLE   -   -   -   Editor

Entered at the Burlington, N. C. Post Office as second class matter.

Subscription Rates

One year .... $ 2.00
Six months 1.00

In Advance

Give both your old and new postoffice when asking that your address be changed.

The change of your label is your receipt for money. Written receipts sent upon request.

Many persons subscribe for friends, intending that the paper be stopped at the end of the year. If instructions are given to this effect, they will receive attention at the proper time.

Marriage and obituary notices not exceeding 150 words printed free if received within 60 days from date of event, all over this at the rate of one-half cent a word.

Original poetry not accepted for publication.

Principles of the Christian Church

(1) The Lord Jesus Christ is the only Head of the Church.
(2) Christian is a sufficient name of the Church.
(3) The Holy Bible is a sufficient rule of faith and practice.
(4) Christian character is a sufficient test of fellowship, and of church membership.
(5) The right of private judgment and the liberty of conscience is a right and a privilege that should be accorded to, and exercised by all.

EDITORIAL

THE TRUE SPIRIT

Did you ever see a person whose conduct, language and ideals were below what they should be? How did you feel when you were in his or her presence? Did you want to get away? Did you have a feeling never to see the person again? If this is the way you felt you did not have the right spirit. Did you long for just the power to lift that person up out of his or her low ideals and place such a one on a plane of higher living? Did you have a desire and wish that you were able to point out to such a person the beauties of a clean and undefiled life, and just long to lift them up to something better and nobler? If this is the spirit you had, it is the right one, and is the spirit of the Master.

CHURCHES AND CRIMINALS

Judges, jurors, attorneys, and solicitors of courts know as few other men the value of moral training. They see and hear things to convince them that the Church has a great influence over life—and we regret that every participant of the law is not a Christian

Last week we received a letter from a friend, Mrs. S. W. Summers, a court stenographer. It was written from Durham and while the Durham County court was in session. It is part of a personal note, but it would be unjust to the public not to reprint a few paragraphs. Here they are:

"In our court this week no less than eight or ten young boys, white and colored, ages ranging from sixteen to nineteen have been tried and convicted of larceny of automobiles, clothing, jewelry and car breaking,—all of whom stated they did not go to church and Sunday school—and two boys (white) 19 years of age, their parents stated that they had gotten beyond their control—and after Judge Stacey questioned the parents, it was found that they did not send them to Sunday school regularly.

"But such a condition does not exist alone among the boys. Out of a special venire of twenty-two jurors seven of them were not church members and professed no religion. Four of whom were unmarried and the judge stated that they ought to marry and perhaps their wives could convert them."

It is very evident from the above that Judge Stacey takes into consideration a man's connection with the Church. It is interesting to note that he would ask questions of that nature. They are pertinent and to the point. Some of these days a man will have to be a qualified Christian to be a qualified juror. And he should be.

DATE OF THE ALABAMA CONFERENCE

The Alabama Christian Conference meets with the church at Antioch, Tuesday after the second Sunday in October at 10 o'clock. Rev. J. D. Dollar is president and Rev. E. M. Carter is secretary. Their post office is Wadley, Alabama. Get ready to attend and see that your church is represented.

GEORGIA AND ALABAMA CONFERENCE

The Georgia and Alabama Conference adjourned last year to meet in its annual session at Lanett, Alabama, on Tuesday after the third Sunday in October, which is October 21. Rev. H. W. Elder, Richland, Georgia, is the president of the session and Brother S. H. Abel is acting secretary. J. F. Hill is the treasurer whose address is Phoenix, Alabama, Box 96. Get ready for this Conference. Be on time, stay through the session—and add something to it.

EASTERN VIRGINIA CONFERENCE

The Eastern Virginia Conference held its session at Eure's church last year and this year goes to the other side of the territory and meets with the Waverly Christian church. The time of the meeting is Tuesday before the first Sunday in November, which will be October 28. Rev. I. W. Johnson, D. D., Suffolk, Va., is the efficient secretary while Rev. O. D. Poythress, South Norfolk, Va., is his assistant. Dr. C. H. Rowland, Franklin, Va., is president and Dr. W. W. Staley, Suffolk, Va., is vice-chairman. Plans are being formulated for a great meeting and the churches within the bounds of this Conference are urged to make preparation for the coming event.

NORTH CAROLINA CONFERENCE

The North Carolina Christian Conference meets with the church at Burlington, N. C., on November 11, next, and will be in session to November 14, inclusive. This is the first session of the united Conferences, which embraces the Western North Carolina, Eastern North Carolina, and North Carolina and Virginia Conferences. Rev. T. E. White, Sanford, N. C., is the president, while the record-keeper is Dr. W. A. Harper, Elon College, N. C. A tentative program is now in circulation and every church, minister and member of this Conference is urged to begin now to make it a star session.

MISSION BOARD TO MEET

The Mission Board of the Southern Christian Convention is to meet on September 17. The place of meeting is Suffolk, Virginia, and the hour set for the initial session is 10 o'clock A. M. Col. J. E. West is chairman while Brothers J. M. Darden, J. A. Williams, C. H. Rowland, G. O. Lankford, K. B. Johnson, J. Lee Johnson, W. P. Lawrence, H. W. Elder and Mrs. W. A Harper are the members. Dr. J. O. Atkinson is the Executive Secretary. If you have any matter with the Board attend to it now and place it in the hands of the Executive Secretary, or the chairman. Send your requests in written form because it is the desire of the Board that personal representation be eliminated.

BOARD OF RELIGIOUS EDUCATION TO MEET

On Thursday, September 11, at 8 o'clock P. M., the Board of Religious Education of the Southern Christian Convention is to meet. The Board is to meet in Raleigh, N. C., and the session is the regular annual. The members of the Board are: Rev. J. W. Harrell, Chairman, Burlington, N. C.; Mrs. Fred Bullock, Va.; Brother I. A. Luke, Holland, Va.; Brother C. H. Stephenson, Corresponding Secretary and Treasurer, Raleigh, N. C.; Rev. J. V. Knight and Hon. C. A. Hines, Greensboro, N. C.; Rev. A. T. Banks, Ramseur, N. C.; Rev. W. T. Walter, D. D., Winchester, Va.; J. O. Atkinson, Recording Secretary, Elon College, N. C.

A CONSIDERATION AND AN APPRECIATION

Many persons who enjoy food and clothing forget those whose hands make these things possible. A suit of clothes may be worn and appreciated and the one who wears it perhaps never thinks of the dozen hands that went to make the fabric possible. From the raw material to the finished product faithful souls worked diligently that every part of the suit might be right and acceptable.

Those who read and enjoy papers so often forget those who make them possible. The name of the editor may be at the masthead of the paper and his name may become a household word, and yet those who labor with him to make possible the publication may never be known to the reading public.

THE CHRISTIAN SUN passes through a half dozen hands before it reaches the post office. Next to the Editor is the faithful linotype operator who sets the type on the most modern and up-to-date type composing machine. The servant of THE SUN in this capacity is Mr. James Marvin Vestal, who has been the linotype operator for this paper practically ever since the present Editor has been in charge. Mr. Vestal is a deaf man but does his work to a great degree of efficiency and satisfaction. He is a good machinist and operator, and is well acquainted with the linotype. The Editor had the privilege of seeing him put the machine up without the aid of an inspector or any other machinist. He was educated at the State School for the Deaf, Morganton, N. C. His education is thorough and practical. He is faithful in his service and untiring in his effort to bring THE SUN up to the standard every week. This week he is at Morganton attending the twenty-fifth anniversary of his *Alma Mater*. He was chosen to deliver the response to the welcome address. We have had the privilege of reading the message which he delivered to his former teachers and friends. Without his consent or knowledge we kept his response, and in consideration of his services to this paper, and appreciation of our esteem for him, we print below his message in full. We believe that it is worthy for we feel that it will reveal to others what it revealed to us—that optimistic look that our unfortunate (?) fellow citizens have:

Response To Address of Welcome

J. M. Vestal, Burlington, N. C.

Former Students, Friends and Associates:

Great and good is this occasion on which I have the honor of thanking you on behalf of your guests, for the kind words of welcome accorded us. We assure you that we are glad to be here—glad to be where we have not been for so long. This is no strange place to us. It has been out of our eye-sight, but not out of our hearts and interest. We are glad to find all the doors wide open to us. We feel very much at home and why should we not?

At this moment, I take great pleasure in telling you that we rejoice to have the privilege of helping you to celebrate the twenty-fifth anniversary of the founding of this school. Our school is among the youngest of its kind, but not the smallest. It is the special pride of the founder, but it is an institution that we all love. And to be here today makes us love her still better. She is nearer to our hearts now than she was yesterday.

We are glad that North Carolina has a school where the Deaf can prepare themselves for useful life. Without this school we do not know where we would be. We are too proud to be pitied. We regret to say that we have heard of persons pitying us, because we are deaf. Very often we find ourselves glad because we are deaf, and while we are deaf we are not dead. Again we have heard persons praise us for doing certain deeds on no other grounds than that we are deaf. We do not want to be praised for that reason, but we want to be praised for the things that we do. And still we have heard persons say that we cannot do certain things, because we are deaf. How mistaken they are! They have forgotten that the tongue and ear do not represent the ability of a man. The trouble is that we have never been given the chance. In most cases we can do nine out of ten things as well, and very often better, than our hearing brothers. So we have reason to be proud of our school and those connected with it. We are happy because our school is rapidly showing the world that the day of the impossible things has passed.

To Superintendent Goodwin is due much credit for his hard and loyal work in building up the school. He has pulled through many hard places where others would have failed. He has reason to be proud of what he has done. His work speaks for him. To the members of the Board we are grateful for their loyal and faithful support. We are sure they acted to the best of their knowledge. To North Carolina and her citizens we are grateful for the purse. She is among the poorest States, but has a big heart for the good causes.

So let me say that this day is a great day, and it is good to live in this generation. The incoming generations will not find themselves wanting. They will look upon the founders with great pride because the way has been prepared for them to have good standing in the elevating forces of life and society.

So accept Sir, our hearty appreciation for your kind words of welcome. We assure you that it is good to be here.

THE LEAGUE OF NATIONS—SIX REASONS WHY IT SHOULD BE RATIFIED

Dr. Frederick Lynch, Editor of *The Christian Work*, gives the following six reasons why the League of Nations should be ratified by the United State Senate:

1. It would delight Germany beyond all measure and encourage the reactionary group to such bold steps as now they dare not dream of. For it would mean to Germany that the Allies had hopelessly disagreed among themselves as to the aims and ends of the war, and it would also establish that belief which evidently is now being deeply grounded in Germany that after all the United States is more sympathetic in the long run with Germany than with England.

2. It might mean that the whole of Europe would soon be plunged into anarchy and chaos. For it is to the United States that Europe is looking for the steadying hand. We are the youthful nation and have great resources. Furthermore, we are trusted by the nations of Europe. With us beside them England and France feel that they can handle the chaotic conditions of Europe. With us in the group the numerous nations and races now in turbulent and seething state, with vague aspirations hardly capable of expression except in restlessness, would feel a confidence in the great powers which they will never feel with us outside, snugly sitting at home, having washed our hands of the burden of the world beyond our shores.

3. It will mean that our boys fought in vain. We went into this war "to make the world safe for democracy," to secure lasting peace, to guarantee the rights of small nations, to make it impossible for big powers to do what they pleased in the world. If we withdraw from the community of nations *now* not one of these things will have been attained. France is powerless to do much for a long time. If we withdraw it leaves only England. But England cannot alone keep the world safe for democracy, cannot alone make permanent peace, cannot alone guarantee the rights of small nations, cannot alone prevent nations from doing again what Germany did, that is, acting as they please.

4. It will mean that everybody in Europe will lose faith forever in the United States. We have been in Europe for three months and most of every day was spent in talking with Frenchmen, Englishmen, Italians, Poles and members of every race in Europe. President Wilson was absolutely right when he said that if the United States fails to ratify the League it will break the heart of the world. It was the United States that put idealism into the war. It was the United States that said the great end of the war was a community of free, liberty-loving, peace,loving nations pledged to live together in peaceful co-operation and maintain such law and order in the world as should make it a safe world for all peoples. The war has merely prepared the way to do this. The League of Nations has been set up purposedly to fulfill this task. It is simply the Allies staying together, inviting other nations of like ideals to co-operate with them, to accomplish this task. If the United States leaves the Allies now, refuses to remain in the League, all Europe will look upon her as a deserter, as a nation that puts her hand to the plough and then turns back, as a nation of spent enthusiasm, one which promises big things and then backs out.

5. It would mean not only that all the Tory, Junker, Chauvenist, militarist groups of Europe would rejoice, but that all the Bolshevist, anarchistic revolutionary groups of Europe would rejoice with them. No one can have failed to notice the bitter hostility of the radical groups, even in our own country, to the League. It is intense in the Bolshevist countries of Europe. Why? Because the League is the only promise of law and order in Europe, and law and order are their most hated things, unless it be democracy. But the League is the one guarantee of democracy in Europe. It looks as if the only two choices that confront Europe are these two—democracy and anarchy.

6. Finally, it would mean that the United States threw away its high place of leadership in the world. We had been a provincial nation, living for ourselves alone except that we had touched the world superbly through our foreign missions. When we were suddenly summoned to take our place among the liberty-loving nations in a great, common world cause we acted at once on an international scale, putting our armies in Europe beside those of England and France. We began to think in international world terms. Soon we became the recognized voice of the aspirations of the

whole world. The Allies looked to us to state the ideals of the war. We sprang as by miracle.into world leadership. That leadership we did not lose at the Peace Conference in spite of what the carpers say. (We dread to think of what might have come out of the Peace Conference had America not been there). That leadership we can still exercise if we will. It is a wonderful opportunity But if we refuse to enter in this the New Community of Nations, pledged to establish justice in the world, to care for the oppressed of all lands, and to settle all disputes as neighbors cherishing good-will, then we resign our place of world leadership; we have no more voice in *world* affairs, the great, new world, born out of the war, stumbles gropingly and haltingly on its upward path and we have neither share nor leadership in its holiest aspirations.

PASTOR AND PEOPLE

BURLINGTON LETTER

The work on the new church is being pushed to completion as rapidly as possible. If there are no unforeseen delays it will be in readiness for the State Conference in November. We are hoping to occupy the building before that time. We would like to begin our fall work in the new building. Private class rooms are being provided for each class in the Sunday school and there is ample provision for other class rooms as the school may grow. Each of the departments will be properly provided for. If desired the building is so planned, as to take care of a full departmental school.

As is the custom of the church, the pastor was given a month's vacation, which he is now enjoying. The first two weeks were spent in the Rainey Hospital of Burlington, undergoing minor operations. This was not a pleasant way to begin a vacation but we trust it will prove profitable. We are finding it so, only two weeks after leaving the hospital. The latter end of our vacation we are spending at our old home in Nansemond County, Virginia. It is good to go back home and visit the scenes of childhood and cheer the hearts of loved ones. There is no place like home. God established a great institution when He established the home. It antidates all other institutions and in it is wrapped up the destiny of individuals and nations. All that tends to destroy the home is an enemy of human society.

We need in this day a new sense of the value of the Church and its services. The vacation season should help to awaken this sense. The fact that we are deprived of the privilege of public worship in the accustomed place, should awaken in us a new appreciation of its value and its importance. The church service helps us in a way that no other public service can. In the church service we are brought face to face with the eternal verities; we come face to face with God, we worship Him together, we face our common duty and are toned up spiritually and thus better prepared for coming tasks. The vacation season will prove a great blessing to the cause of Christ, if pastors and peoples will now take up the work with greater zeal. Let there be a real purpose to do more and to be more faithful

than ever before. There is room for improvement in all of us. We can render better service, if we set our hearts upon it. Greater faithfulness will gladden the hearts of pastors and inspire them for larger service. Every congregation has the power to make or mar the work of its pastor. Be faithful to the mid-week service, the Sunday school, the preaching service and in all the little duties that can be performed by a member. These who are faithful in small things will not be unfaithful in great things.

Let there be an expression of the new sense of value that has come to us during the vacation season, concerning things spiritual.

                                                J. W. HARRELL.
August 22, 1919.

A new age of giving, this is, and the hope of a new day for the Church is here. We have made the Church a "poor house" long enough. God is beginning to get His share of the world's money that the Kingdom's work may go forward.

SUFFOLK LETTER

The odds and ends of vacation make a sort of crazy quilt in one's life. There is nothing as coherent as honest work. When out of regular service everything is disjointed, aimless, and heterogenous. But summer letters are not supposed to be deep, heavy, or of much value. Yet recreation is as necessary as work; for "all work and no play makes Jack a dull boy;" and one might coin an expression of his own and say that "all play and no work makes Jack a useless boy."

I have been at "Fuquay Springs" for a week and will leave next Monday, stop over in Louisburg to see the Holdens and resume work in Suffolk the first Sunday in September. Annie Staley, William Staley Cheatham, and Dr. C. H. Rowland and family were here, but they have all gone. Dr. Rowland and I had two fine days on Mr. J. Beale Johnson's pond, with "good luck" as fishermen call it. His kindness and that of his wife linger with us through a whole year. The abandon of a day on a pond is the completest recreation to those who have the spirit of Isaac Walton.

We attended Sunday school at Wake Chapel on Sunday where Dr. Rowland had preached a great sermon the third Sunday. In addition to the regular exercises, they had a missionary program of interest in which nineteen children took part; and at the close, blocks were taken for the Santa Isabel church. The Woman's Board had allotted $25.00 to this church and they had forty-two names at twenty-five cents each, making $10.50. This is a good start and they will get the sum allotted.

Among other incidents in this quiet corner I had a pleasant interview with "Swizzell." Now "Swizzell" is an old bachelor, a local wit, a genuine tar heel, and a good jolly fellow. Dr. Rowland introduced us and we enjoyed his bright sayings. It is impossible to report wit or even to repeat it as the chief thing is "personality" and "spontaneity." The first thing that attracted my attention was while he was seated in front of a store. It is restful to sit in front of a store

for conversation, though that good old feature of store
life is fast passing away. Well, a young fellow drove
up in a buggy, hopped out and handed "Swizzell" his
buggy reins and said, "Hold this for me till I go in
the store." "Swizzell" took the lines and said to the
boy: "Have you got a nickel?" When the boy returned and took the reins he said, "Thank you,"
"Swizzell" handed over the reins and replied: "That
won't buy anything." I asked him if he were a member of the church. He said: "I am like the drunken
man who was standing against a church and a man
asked him the same question, and he said: "I am
leaning that way."

A man asked him one day why he kept his mouth
open and he replied: "The main spring is broken and
I can't shut it." On another occasion after a long
rainy spell, some one asked him why he kept his mouth
open and he said: "I am sunning my teeth for fear
they will mill dew."

One day he was driving a cart and an old woman
said, "What are you doing, Dick?" and he said: "I
am raising nothing and hauling it off as fast as I can."
These are a few of his original witticisms.

Soon after the interview I saw him leaving the mill
with a sack of meal around his neck. "Dick Smith" is
a very clever fellow, full of sunshine and good cheer,
harmless and undefiled and the world would be happier
if it had more of the real and less of the artificial in
life.

In passing I will remark that one mystery remains
to me unsolved. Why does every neighborhood produce a leader of music for the church, a wit, a first
class person for every department of life? The distribution of the human race over the whole earth, the
distribution of talent where it is needed, and the distribution of the products by nature and their re-distribu-
tion by man, equalizes God's blessings and man's use
of them so that all men and all ages are on a par. The
ratio of human condition is fixed quantity, and the differences are accidental and artificial. When all the
subjective and objective human relations are analyzed
it will be found human differences are imaginary. The
story of the tramp who was refused food at the rich
man's door on the theory that the tramp had "appetite
and no food," while the rich man had "food but no
appetite" illustrates the point. Capital and labor are
on the same basis whether they knew it or not.

The Masonic Lodge 614 had a barbecue on the night
of the twenty-sixth to which I was invited and I made
successful test of what they say of Fuquay Springs,
that you can eat all the barbecue they
drink Fuquay water and suffer no harm. There was
a large company of men and women at the banquet,
the provision was super-abundant, and seventeen members came out from Raleigh to help in giving the
third degree.   W. W. STALEY.

President Wilson leaves this week on an extended
tour in behalf of the League of Nations, the Peace
Treaty and his party. A number of newspaper men
will follow his trail and undertake to get the crystallized opinion in regard to the present administration.

FROM THE FAR SOUTH
Dingler's Chapel

My first meeting was held with the church at Dingler's Chapel. It began Saturday before the third Sunday in July and continued the following week. Rev.
A. H. Shepherd was with us here and assisted in the
preaching. Our meeting was not what we had hoped
for it to be but we trust much good was accomplished.

Mt. Zion

Our meeting began here Saturday before the first
Sunday in August and closed the following Friday.
There were seven new members received into the church
and it was much revived. Rev. J. H. Hughes was with
us here and did some strong, forceful preaching. Mt.
Zion is a pleasant place to work and the people are a
willing people. We have been with them seven years
and have enjoyed our whole stay with them.

Rock Springs

Our next meeting was with our home church at Rock
Springs. This was the week following the second Sunday in August. Rev. A. H. Shepphard was with us
here and did some good work. His sermons were plain
and full of Gospel truths. Our meeting closed here
Thursday afternoon with eight additions to the church
and the church greatly revived.

Shady Grove

The meeting began at Shady Grove Saturday before
the third Sunday in August and closed the following
Thursday night. There were twenty-three additions to
the church. Brother Shepherd was with us here and
did some good work. This is our first year with these
good people and we find them pleasant to work with.
They are a consecrated people and willing to do things.
On the last night of our meeting here we just merely mentioned the fact that we had some obligations to
meet with our Conference in October and in five minutes we had raised our apportionments and a little
over. We are predicting great things for the church
and people at Shady Grove.

                                    J. D. DOLLAR.
Roanoke, Ala.

NOTICE

To the churches of the Alabama Christian Conference:
For several years some of our pastors have been overworked and for that reason churches and pastors have
suffered. We now have in our Conference a splendid
young minister who is making good as a preacher and
we feel he will make good as a pastor. We feel sure
that some of our churches will do well to secure his
services as a pastor.

                                    J. D. DOLLAR,
                                    J. H. HUGHES.

Mrs. C. H. Wells—It is not our privilege to attend
a Christian church, so THE SUN is like a message from
home every week—something we do not like to do without.

UNION, (N. C.)

We began our protracted meeting at Union, Alamance, on the fourth Sunday in July. Brother George D. Eastes of Raleigh, N. C., came on Monday and remained with us till the close of the meeting on Friday afternoon. Brother J. W. Holt of Burlington, a former pastor, was with us one day. Brother Eastes did the preaching after his arrival. He is a strong preacher and is especially adapted to revival work. We had a good meeting. The church was much revived, several professed Christ and eight united with the church at the close of the service and were baptized.

Our audiences are growing and the outlook for good progressive work is encouraging. Thanks to members of the church and congregation for kindness shown and special donations made during the year.

P. H. FLEMING.

CONCORD

On Saturday, August 23, 1919, at 4:00 P. M., a number of members met at Concord, Caswell county, for the third business meeting of the year. Since last preaching day a new recess for the pulpit has been constructed. As pastor, I am very grateful it is done. The house looks much better and gives more room inside. It is much more pleasant for the preacher now. A motion was passed in the business transaction to put on the rostrum of the pulpit at once.

In the business meeting the church gave the present pastor a unanimous call for next year and was approved by the congregation on Sunday.

Sunday afternoon, at 3:00 P. M., a large crowd gathered to witness the baptism of the candidates who joined the church during the revival meeting. This took place in the "Old High Mill Pond."

There will be, the Lord willing, all day service the fourth Sunday in September. Come, bring dinner, something is in store for all.

L. L. WYRICK.

Elon College, N. C.

The street car employees in Charlotte last week went on a strike and some of them got struck. The general public and transportation men came in conflict. The State had to send special troops to quiet the situation. Many were wounded while several were killed. Charlotte is called the "Queen City" of North Carolina and queens are supposed to be of a quiet nature, but she rose up in her indignation one time and placed a blot upon her history that a thousand years will fail to erase.

The matter of strikes and riots seems to be an epidemic. Last Sunday in Knoxville, Tenn., a scene of rioting and bloodshed was witnessed. Fifteen persons were killed and a number wounded. A negro was accused of murdering a white woman. The mob battered down parts of the jail, turned out all the prisoners, and looted the sheriff's home. It took eleven hundred of the State's National guard to patrol the streets. The mob spirit is dangerous and all of us are hoping that something may be done to relieve the country of such uprisings.

IN HONOR OF THE RED CROSS NURSES

Among all the service flags flown in America in the past two years, one flag is unique. Upon it burns a single star of blue; the others are all gold, 198 of them.

This flag hangs in the marble building of the American Red Cross national headquarters in Washington. The single blue star represents the 19,877 Red Cross nurses in active duty with the army and navy nurse corps and the Red Cross during the war. The gold stars represents the Red Cross dead.

The first two were sewn on the flag in memory of Mrs. Edith B. Ayres and Miss Helen Burnett Wood, of Chicago, both of whom were killed by the explosion of a defective shell on the Steamship Mongolia in May, 1917, while on their way to France.

The last star on the flag is for Jane A. Delano, the "Florence Nightingale of the war," who directed the American Red Cross Nursing Service and sleeps today with the American dead in the military cemetery at Savenay, France.

The other 195 stand for nurses who rest today in the soils of many lands—America, England, Belgium, France, even Germany, where a white cross marks the grave of Jessie Baldwin, Summerville, Pa., who was cited for extraordinary heroism when her hospital was shelled and later, going with the Army of Occupation, died at Coblenz.

Wednesday, September 17, will be celebrated throughout the nation as "Constitution Day," in commemoration of the Birthday of the Constitution of the United States. This movement is promoted by the National Security League, in association with the other leading patriotic societies of the country, with the purpose of strengthening the people's faith in our form of government and thus combating atheistic Bolshevism.

The Christian Orphanage received a handsome gift last week from the hands and heart of Mr. Lawrence S. Holt, Sr., Burlington, N. C. The gift was a complete office outfit consisting of one $75.00 desk, one desk chair, twelve chairs costing $150.00, one new Underwood typewriter, one typewriter desk, one typewriter table, one sectional book-case, one stationery cabinet, one filing case and one filing-card case, and many other valuable office attachments.

Dr. J. P. Barrett has received and accepted a call to the Columbus, Georgia, church and expects to take charge about the first of October. Dr. Barrett is spending some time with old friends and relatives in Eastern Virginia. His address till October 1 will be Zuni, Virginia.

Dr. J. W. Wellons will preach at High Point, N. C., on Sunday, September 7, at 11 A. M. The church has had posters printed announcing the coming of the oldest minister in the Christian denomination, and possibly in any other denomination.

Elon College opens September 10. Remember the date.

CHRISTIAN EDUCATION

EDUCATION AND CHARACTER

By W. A. Harper LL.D., President Elon College

Character shall mean in this brief article, character of proper type, Christian character. Does education assist in producing it?

A great many well-intentional saints think it does not. A few years ago a progressive business man said to me he admired the saints of his acquaintance, but regretted their ignorance. He was convinced that ignorance and saintliness are related as cause and effect. He specifically asserted that educated preachers are not consecrated and referred to the twelve apostles as "little ones" and as "ignorant and unlearned."

Were they? They had spent more than three years in the greatest university of history with the Son of God as president and sole professor. With Him they had searched the Scriptures, just as He urged is ecclesiastical high-brow enemies to do and with Him they had tested His wonderful teachings in terms of life. He sent them out in two occasions alone to do reputation work, and marvellous success had attended their ministry. On one occasion nine of them were in dire straits because they had not profited by His prayer-life in the effort to meet a crisis in His absence.

Were these men "ignorant and unlearned?" Their enemies said so but they did not know the standards in the university from which they had graduated. It was not in the list of standard synagogue or rabbinical schools of that day and they held no academic degrees. We must not accept their charge as substantiated unless the work-years of these men warrant and justify their assertion. Did they?

Peter was an alumnus of which any university might boast. He was a man of action impetuous, making mistakes, but this cursing fisherman demeaned himself well on the day of Pentecost and throughout his eventful career in the infant Church. His trainings gave him Christian stability. He became a rock and his impetuousness made him the initiator of the growing Kingdom. To transform a weakness into an excellency shows the value of education, but only Christian education could do that.

It is sometimes said that education develops what is in a man. If that were all it could do, Peter would have been the arch curser of the ages and a veritable dynamite mine as to temper. Secular education would have done that for him. But Christian education transforms the man till he becomes a mighty force for righteousness in the very line of his former weakness. That is why there is more hope of a spendthrift for generosity after a man becomes a Christian than there is for a miser. Peter was more hopeful from the beginning than Judas though Judas was promising enough to become the Bursar of the First Christian University.

John was the real scholar of the school. The philosophy of his gospel and epistles surpasses anything in the history of human thought. Not all students in a college become scholars. John was a scholar. He like

Peter had a weakness. He loved. He loved himself and his brother and his own family. Now love and selfishness are very close akin. It is the object loved that marks the difference. John was a self-lover. His course in the university of Jesus did not eliminate his passionate love. It transformed, redirected that passion so as to make his brothermen the center of his affection, and we find this splendid fellow in his gospel telling of the love of God (Jno. 3:16) and in his epistle (I Jno. 3:16-17) declaring that we cannot love God unless we love our brothermen, and yet he wanted the chief places in Christ's Kingdom for his brother and himself his mother approving, when he first entered the university. Here is a man of scholarly tastes essentially selfish, after graduation, forgetting self in his love for others and devoting his scholarship to an age-long service to the spiritual life of the race.

James was an organizer and administrator. He would have been a billionaire in this day had he gone into business. He would have been rich in any day. Like his brother he was self-centered. Most business men are. They have an idea business and selfishness are twins. They need a new birth into the spirit of Brotherhood. Business men must learn that labor and capital are partners, not competitors. James did not have this notion. He wanted to organize the Kingdom of Jesus in advance. He wanted John to be prime minister and he would be chancellor of the exchequer. He came out of the university an organizer and administrator still, but he had lost his selfishness. He is now loyal to a cause, and not to himself, and that cause is the spread of the Good News to the ends of the earth, with all the give and take, with all the adaptability that would require. Jews and Gentiles were in the early Church. Then Jews wanted the Gentiles to become Jews. They could not distinguish between the essentials and the non-essentials in religion. The situation was critical when the fathers heard the commissioners from the Gentile Church at Antioch make their report at Jerusalem. James took in the situation at a glance. All born administrators have this talent. A new field is to be entered by the business. New methods must be instituted, yet the new field must not split the business into the businesses. He spoke the words of wisdom—this chairman of the Board of Directors of the early church did—calling for concessions, for sacrifices, for unselfishness on both sides, and the day was saved. This man was so prominent as an organizer in the Church that its enemies honored him with the first martyrdom among the apostles. In his Christian education wrought a gracious work.

Matthew was another honored graduate of the University of Jesus. He was a self-server. He sought the office of collecting taxes that he might gain riches for himself and influence with the alien government that oppressed his people. After his graduation he writes the finest account of the finest life ever lived and in its 25th chapter gives us the finest encomium of service as central in the Christian life ever penned. The gospel, according to Matthew, is the Magna Charta of the social program of the Church of our day. In it he is still a server, but his weakness has become his strength.

His impulse to serve is socialized, and he delights to paint his Master as servant of all. Only Christian education could have so transformed this publican.

But even Christian schools fail in some cases. Not all who graduate from Christian Colleges have the spirit of Christ. Jesus had twelve to graduate, while seventy went through the sophomore class, and a great company matriculated only to drop the course. These things are recorded here to comfort the aching hearts of the teachers and administrators of Christian Colleges. One of the twelve failed. He failed in the line of his weakness. The love of money was his undoing. It will ruin any Church. The university had given him a thorough course not only in the dangers of this weakness of his life, but in the proper use of the thing he loved. He simply would not yield and be transformed. Jesus failed to reach him. So Christian Colleges fail today. Judas might just as well have attended a rabbinical school as the University of Jesus, so far as character is concerned.

We have not the time to consider the other seven men. They were marvellously helped by their education. The leadership of the world is now being helped by it. The danger is that the education men get may be the Juda type—such as to develop their inborn qualities, strengths and weaknesses alike, and not have the transforming power which we find in Peter, John, James, Matthew, and other men who became everything else than "ignorant and unlearned" and for whom the phrase "little ones" had no significance, as their powers ripened under the matcheless Teacher of Nazareth.

Christian education, the education that puts character first and always, such education is the hope of the world. Without it we perish. Without it, there would have been no Church of Christ in the world today. Without it, the Church we have will lose her spiritual leadership for the race. Without it, the Kingdom cannot come.

The Church must see to it that education and character go hand in hand increasingly. So shall the Kingdom dawn in its radiant glory. In the spiritual realm, education and character are one and inseparable, now and forever.

MISSIONARY

MY FRIEND, THE BIBLE WOMAN

In writing these few letters about certain types of Japanese Christians whom I rejoice to call my friends I am not simply seeking to acquaint the readers of THE CHRISTIAN SUN with the individuals mentioned, nor even merely with the types produced, but, rather, to place emphasis upon the fact that the Oriental mind and heart are quite as ready in their response to the impact of the Gospel as is the case with the Occidental; and that the impress of the Gospel upon the Oriental lip is as wide and deep and rich as it becomes upon the Occidental lip; and that in consequence of these facts, the evangelization of the Oriental world finds its hindering problems, not so much in the Orient as in the hesitancy of the church at home to carry forward a vigorous program for reaching the whole world with the life saving truth.

Mrs. Watanabe Toki is the widow of one of our earlier Japanese pastors who fell a victim to that dread disease, tuberculosis, about fifteen years ago. During his illness she not only tenderly nursed him and cared for her three small children, but continued much of his work as pastor, even to the extent of going regularly to the surrounding villages to teach the women and children whom he had been wont to gather for Christian instruction. After his death she continued his Christian work, teaching the Sunday school, holding meetings for women, calling on women in their homes, using her own house as a place where the Christians and inquirers of both sexes might meet for worship and prayer; in fact doing practically every item of a pastor's work except actual preaching, and even doing much of that under the more simple terminology of "leading" meetings, etc.

Thus she has continued for fifteen years, and now, with her children grown and away from home, she is living and laboring, as above outlined, in a town in Northeast Japan, somewhat isolated geographically, alone in her home, quite destitute of Christian fellowship save for the little handful of believers who have been won mostly by her own faithful efforts.

In the village lives a half crazed man who has made three unsuccessful attempts to murder her, on account of which we have feared for her safety and have on different occasions urged her to remove to a nearby city she would have a greater abundance of Christian fellowship, be in perfect safety from bodily harm, and at the same time have as large a field of Christian service, nothing would be lost in the sum total of service, and much would be gained in the way of personal safety. Would she go? Not a step! "If I go who will come to this village to teach these people about Jesus?" That was her cry; and there she stays to this day. I wonder if Heaven has an especially bright assortment of crowns for such loyalty and devotion as that? Oh, God! Help us to love that. Help us to see the world's need of Thee as Mrs. Watanabe sees the Inogawa people's need of Thee and help us to respond with the loyalty and devotion and heart love with which she gives her very life to satisfy their great need!　—

E. K. McCORD.

Dayton, Ohio.

PROGRAM FOR SUNDAY EVENING OR MID-WEEK SERVICE

General Subject—"Power of the Published Word."

Hymn—"Sound, Sound the Truth Abroad," 583 Christian Hymnary.

Scripture lesson—Esther 3:1-15.

Hymn—"Ye Christian Heralds, Go Proclaim," 507 Christian Hymnary.

Prayer.

History of *The Christian Missionary*, given briefly by one speaker.

Song by Choir—"We've a Story to Tell," 96 in Missionary Hymnal.

Sermon or address—"Printing Press Evangelism." Distribution of *Christian Missionary* subscription envelopes.

Hymn—"Thy Kingdom Come," 577 Christian Hymnary.

Benediction.

Suggested Sermon Outlines

I. The increase of knowledge:
1. Through school instruction.
2. Through journalism and ephemeral literature.
3. Through books and lasting literature.

II. The application of knowledge:
1. To produce better living and higher standards.
2. To win men to Christ.
3. To extend the kingdom of God.

Reaching the World With the Word

1. How foreign missionaries must reduce spoken languages to writing, and create readers and Christian literature—necessity, and value.

2. Bible translations and circulation.

3. Religious journalism—denominational and undenominational papers and magazines.

4. Christian text-books and school literature (for Sunday schools and others).

5. How the printing press has thus aided in spreading Christianity—God seems to have blessed the agency.

Materials may be found in the following books: Social Aspects of Foreign Missions, by Faunce; Modern Missions in the East, Lawrence; Educational Conquest of the Far East, Lewis; Rex Christus, Smith; Christian Literature in the Mission Field, Ritson; The Christian Movement in the Japanese Empire. All books can be obtained of C. B. RIDDLE, *Publishing Agent*, Burlington, North Carolina.

Mrs. A. A. Terrell—I pray that our people may be awakened to a sense of duty to see the need of our Church paper.

We have limped along trying to carry on God's work by *taking collections*. If we are to win the world to Christ and for Christ we must *make offerings*. Think of the difference in *taking* and *making*, also of the difference between *collection* and *offering*. Call it an offering.

High Point, N. C. suffered the shame and disgrace of a strike and rioting last week. Labor and capital seem to have been arrayed against each other and the outcome was rather bitter. Many were wounded and possibly a few were killed. Too bad for High Point. A few more things like this and it will have to change its name to Low Point.

This is a day of service, not only in deeds but in dollars. Dedicate all to humanity's good.

LITTLE FOLKS DEPARTMENT

FOR THE BENEFIT OF EVERY CHILD IN THE COMMUNITY

(Burdette B. Brown)

A Program

The following program emphasizes the stress points in the church work of conserving the life and best development, of the children.

I. CONSERVATION OF HEALTH BY MEDICAL EXAMINATION AND NECESSARY TREATMENT. This means that every child shall receive a complete examination by a physician at least once each year and if any defects or weaknesses are discovered, that they shall receive prompt treatment until corrected. Sixty to eighty per cent of the child population is physically handicapped. They have breathing defects, enlarged tonsils and carious teeth which have a direct effect upon the eyes, the heart and the nutrition. Neglect of such conditions often results in diseases that kill in adult life. It is a mistake to neglect a child that has some remediable defect until it is seriously ill, the effects of which may be life-long injury. Preventive measures and prompt treatment will usually avoid the illness and save unnecessary expense.

A primary cause of Infant Mortality can be removed if expectant parents are instructed in the proper care of the baby. Community Health Stations and Hospital Clinics are agencies that can make the plan effective. The influence of the church can do much to create right sentiment for their establishment and maintenance.

II. ADEQUATE NOURISHMENT TENDS TO INSURE STRONG VITALITY. Food must be selected that is wholesome in quality and sufficient in quantity and variety, and it must be properly prepared in order to nourish the body. Thirty-three per cent of the children of the United States are estimated to be underweight. In New York City in the third and fourth school grades 120,000 are undernourished. These partly starved bodies cannot support either strong mentality or strong spiritual sensibility and they easily become the prey of disease. The Nutrition Class, Calculation of Food Values and Record of the Children's Diet will interest parents and supply them with instruction which they ought to have.

III. SYSTEMATIC RELIGIOUS INSTRUCTION IS ESSENTIAL TO THE HAPPINESS OF MANKIND. In the best sense religious instruction should keep pace with grade work and be reported to parents with equal punctilio. When half our child population is without religious instruction, efforts to provide it should be redoubled. Justice, love, truth, faith in God, in personality and in the spiritual realities are the very foundations of government and order.

IV. ENROLLMENT IN PUBLIC OR PRIVATE SCHOOLS WITH PROVISION FOR REGULAR INSTRUCTION MAKES EDUCATED CITIZENS. The percentage of illiteracy in the

United States is discreditably high and constitutes an element of weakness that need not exist. In New York, Chicago and other large cities tens of thousands of children are crowded out, placed on part time or absent themselves from school. Most of these are from homes of poverty or misfortune and need the benefits of the school much more than those who have an uplifting environment. Whether the school be in a fine building or on a park bench is minor in importance to having a teacher and a lesson with regularity throughout the school year.

Personal Hygiene, by which is meant cleanliness and proper care of the body, should be included with play activities in the regular course of instruction.

V. THE HANDICAPPED CHILD SHOULD HAVE AN OPPORTUNITY TO BECOME TRAINED. Those unfortunates

whose physical or mental capacity limits their field of accomplishment and who as a result are backward in school, should be taught simple vocations that they may become self-supporting, and those recognized as afflicted with amentia should have protecting supervision in institutional homes.

If the Church Committee is informed how to place children in private and institutional homes when emergencies arise, it will supply a much to be desired service and save embarrassments.

The supervision of delinquent children, after dismissal from institutions where they have been well cared for, can be rendered by a competent probation officer who may also be a factor in securing enforcement of the Child Labor law.

VI. CO-OPERATION OF ALL COMMUNITY AGENCIES INSURES SUCCESS. The public conscience should be thoroughly awakened to the importance of this work and a general, whole-hearted co-operation in making the program effective should be secured. Private agencies must demonstrate its worth and sustain it for a time, but it is a community responsibility, and full success will be attained when the entire community undertakes the program.

New York City
150 *Fifth Avenue.*

JOINING THE OLD WORLD WITH THE NEW

The children of the world are to know more truly the meaning of brotherhood than has been possible since the beginning of creation. Seas and old landmarks do not have their former prestige in forming barriers; languages, creed and opinions take second place to this newer idealism that is possessing the hearts and minds and works of the school children of America in their solicitude for the children of Europe who have been ruthlessly deprived of all that they really should have. They need everything that makes up the list of the physical necessities of man, but most of all, they need a friend. The Junior Red Cross with the characteristic friendliness of youth has offered its hand, its heart and its activities in assisting the needy ones to a normal plane of living in order that they may have homes wherein is retained that sweet intimacy of family life, its protected seclusion, its playtimes, its chores, its chumminess—and in knowing the joys of all these things, that they in turn may radiate happiness to the whole world.

Rev. B. F. Black has accepted a call to the Franklinton, North Carolina, pastorate. Brother Black says that he wants it written "*Franklinton Parish.*"

We trust that Dr. Harper's article in this issue will have a wide reading, for it deserves such.

Rev. B. F. Black and family are in Eastern Virginia. Brother Black is preaching and lecturing in old territory. He is this week at Oakland in a meeting with Brother I. W. Johnson, and on the first Sunday in September will be a meeting with Brother Johnson at Liberty Spring.

The final call: Elon is *our* college, built with *our* money, maintained by *our* means—and it deserves *our* support in sending *our* sons and daughters. All aboard for Elon. That is the next stop, and the date is September 10.

Rev. J. T. Kitchen, Windsor, Va., has very ably contributed articles to our "Worship and Meditation" page. His two articles this week will be read with interest and delight. Brother Kitchen is a sweet spirited man. May he continue these articles.

We have no further news from Rev. J. G. Truitt, but presume that he is recovering slowly.

WORSHIP AND MEDITATION

SOME BRIEF PASSING REFLECTIONS

Do not publish the sad, unpleasant things which occur in your experience, but tell the glad, good things that spring into your life, and it may not be best to write and talk too much about gray hairs and the deeply cut furrows on your cheeks and brows, but think about the beautiful and wonderful things of God, and it will help you to look more lovely, refreshed and happy.

If you have not already done so cultivate the practice of speaking kind, tender, helpful, loving words to one another in the midst of discouragement, trouble, cares and great responsibilities. Sweet and inspiring words are a great help to them who are in any adverse condition, and will give a charming influence to every depressed or discouraged heart.

Try to be as happy as you can with present surroundings, and if you have not as much as you desire, do not worry and cause your wife, your husband, your children, and your friends to feel unhappy, but listen to what a great man said about learning to be contented in any condition. He said: "I have learned." Let us try to learn it. Do not fret and blame some one for the present circumstances over which you have no control. Parties have been known to censure one another in times of need and destitution for their unfortunate conditions, when, in truth, they were not blamable, but needed that sympathy and encouragment which the occasion greatly demanded. "Keep a watch on your words, my darling, for they are sweet as the fresh, new honey or like the bee's terrible sting."

By all means try to save the feelings of the depressed and the oppressed ones, and help them to have more self reliance that they may, if possible, rise to better and greater success. It is not always easy to consider the poor and needy when one is possessed with plenty. He often has not the time nor the inclination to consider the condition of the destitute ones.

The one who is healthy, strong and active cannot fully realize the position of the other one who is sick, weak and disabled. But when the reverse condition takes place and the once strong and active body is weakened by disease how marked the change and how different the feelings. Many things have to be learned by experience and observation, and the bitter must some time be taken after much sweetness and luxury have been indulged. And the bitter is more unpleasant after a long time of sweet indulgence. In other words when you have lost what you once had you feel it more keenly and look at things with less hope and more discouragement. When you are gaining and making something you feel happy, but when losing, anxiety and trouble take hold of you and bind you with a terrible grip. Prosperity elates the heart and fills it with gladness, while adversity depresses the spirits and binders

the rise of progressive ambition; but this may be necessary to develop the latent powers of capacity and ability in the individual. Necessity has done much to lift from a lower to a higher place in human activity, as many incidents in life have a history in them showing that it is true.

New, fresh, truthful, honest thought is what the current of passing events needs to satisfy the minds of them who have to meet the demands of the times, and to inspire more confidence in them who are afraid of being deceived by those with whom they come in contact. For in some places, so many are being deceived, that others fear to act even when the way before them appears to be inviting. It will take much care, prudence and prayer to steer clear of the breakers of indulgence temptation and sin. Our safe and only hope is in Christ the friend of sinners and the Savior of the world. And if He were to strictly mark iniquity against us, but very few would be saved. But Jesus loves us tenderly and is willing to forgive the humble penitent one who is seeking the joy of His salvation. Every doubting, sinful, polluted one ought to look into Him with new hope and a stronger faith, expecting greater strength and a better development in the Christian life.

J. T. KITCHEN.

DO YOU SMOKE?

Yes or *no* may be the answer. What I want to say is intended for those who answer *yes*.

Yonder goes down the avenue of life toward the long, lonely valley of death the pale-faced youth, with hacking cough and hectic fever, the cigarette smoker, with trembling hands and yellow stained nervous fingers, trying to grasp and hold the duties and responsibilities that demand his attention. With haggard looks and faltering steps, caused partly by smoking, and some other causes, he finds himself nearing the verge of nervous destruction. To him the habit, often repeated, is a most pleasant time, but an expensive one to himself and an offensive one to others who inhale the odor of his pleasant perfume.

Look at him in the steel grasp of this useless habit, wanting to be free from it, but feels bound more firmly by repeated practice. Is there no way by which he can come out of this condition? Yes, there is a way to stop its use, consider its effect, and refrain from it entirely before you are in the strong grip of the iron hand of destruction.

But the practicing party may say: "I have a right to smoke if I want to, and it is no one's business to object." Well, the reflecting mind will see that it is a right business to object when a person meets you, or sits near you when he is soaked from head to foot with the essence of tobacco. Some are known who have a pipe, cigar, or some smoking machine in their mouths every time you see them. You can smell their odor several feet away, and it is not as pleasant to inhale as some other perfumes.

I was in a large gathering recently, and on the next seat sat a man whose clothes were saturated with that objectionable oder from his lovable perfume. If there are habits which are offensive to other people, the guilty party ought to get clear of them. Let us try, at least, to be attractive, neat and clean, for a clean body is essential as well as a clean soul. There are many good (?) people who smoke, but it takes their time, retards their energy, dethrones their ambition, quickens the excited action of the heart. numbs the sensibilities, and is a useless, unnatural habit. It will be a good helpful, healthful thing to stop right now. Stop it now. It will be so much better for you.

J. T. KITCHEN.

Windsor, Va.

THE CHRISTIAN ORPHANAGE

SUPERINTENDENT'S LETTER

There are four days in the year that our children very greatly enjoy: Christmas, when they look for something from Santa Claus; the day of the Board of Trustees meets, when we serve them ice cream; the day on which the Burlington and Reidsville Sunday schools come for their picnics.

This year the Burlington school came on the afternoon of August 21. The time was a joyful one and the occasion a delight to us. We had in advance prepared a long table on which to spread the splendid supper which was so small item in the event.

The Reidsville school held its picnic on the twenty-seventh and spent the day with us. It was a delightful crowd of children and our little folks greatly enjoyed being with them as they did with the children from Burlington. The table was filled with good things to eat and it was a beautiful sight to see how it was enjoyed by all present. After the meal talks were made by Uncle Wellons, and Revs. L. I. Cox and L. L. Wyrick, also Mr. Lambert, Superintendent of the Reidsville Sunday school.

It is a delight to have these Sunday schools come here for their picnics each year. We trust that they greatly enjoy them. We are certainly glad to have them. We welcome any and all Sunday schools to picnic with us. When you bring the children of your school here they mingle with our children and it brings us in closer touch with each other. We have a beautiful lawn and plenty of house room for shelter. The children join me in extending a hearty welcome to all Sunday schools.

Donations

Mebane Bedding Company, two mattresses; Senior Philathea Class, Durham Sunday school, furnishings for one room, consisting of mattress, springs, bed linen and curtains. A Friend, Burlington, N. C., who has a big heart full of sympathy for little orphans, and as has been truly said of him, "A man who scatters his flowers as he goes along," made us a contribution of

twenty books, by O. S. Marden. We find these books full of good thought and knowledge that will be elevating to our children. We are grateful for all these contributions.

CHAS. D. JOHNSTON, *Supt.*

FINANCIAL REPORT FOR SEPTEMBER 3 1919

Amount brought forward, $9,513.78.

Children's Offerings

Ruth Lassiter, 50 cents; Pauline Trotter, 40 cents; Richard Bost, 20 cents; Total $1.10.

Sunday School Monthly Offerings
(North Carolina Conference)

First Christian S. S., Greensboro, (Jan. to May), $38.23; Morrisville, $2.00; Six Forks, $2.75; Sanford, $7.84; Bethlehem, $1.00, Wake Chapel, $5.51; Mt. Auburn, $16.76; New Lebanon, $1.00; New Lebanon Baraca Class, $1.00; Pleasant Union, $7.80; Apple's Chapel, $1.00; Mt. Bethel, $3.00; Henderson, $7.42.

(Eastern Virginia Conference)

Holy Neck, $4.00; Rosemont; $5.00; Windsor, $4.47; Total, $110.78.

Miscellaneous

Mrs. C. C. Peel, $7.00; J. H. Jones, on support of children, $30.00; total, $37.00.

Total for the week, $148.88; Grand total, $9,662.66.

CHILDREN'S LETTERS

Dear Uncle Charley: I am sorry I failed to write but will try to do better in the future. I was glad to receive the pictures you sent me. I am sending my dimes for five months. I hope all the orphans are well. —*Ruth Lassiter.*

Glad to have your letter this week. It will make the Corner look good, as this makes the fourth letter.—*"Uncle Charley."*

Dear Uncle Charley: I failed to write last month so I will send twenty cents, my dues for July and August. I have moved back to High Point. I can go to Sunday school at the Christian church again. Hope all the cousins are having a good time. Lots of love. —*Pauline Trotter.*

Glad you moved back to High Point. It is a nice town to live in. I am glad you go to the Christian Sunday school and write for the Corner.—*"Uncle Charley."*

Dear Uncle Charley: I am sending my dues for July and August. Hope all the cousins are enjoying life fine. It will soon be time for us to go to school again.—*Richard Bost.*

I know you like to go to school. You must study hard and make a fine young man.—*"Uncle Charley."*

Dear Uncle Charley: Here I come with my dues for July and August. Hope all the cousins are well and having a good time. Enclosed pleased find twenty cents. With much love to you and the cousins.—*Lois Stout.*

I am glad so many of our little cousins have a letter for the Corner this week. It is more encouraging.—*"Uncle Charley."*

Sunday School and Christian Endeavor

SUNDAY SCHOOL LESSON FOR SEPTEMBER 14, 1919

The Future Life. Matt. 25:31-46; John 14:2, 3; II Cor. 5:10; I Peter 1:3-5.

Golden Text: "For we must all be made manifest before the judgment seat of Christ." II Cor. 5:10.

We must all wish we knew more of the future life than we do, and yet we have been told a very great deal. We know the conditions for entrance; we know it is our Father's House. We know that Jesus is there. We know that He rose from the dead, and "became the first fruits of them that slept," and we know that because He lives, we shall live also. Phillips Brooks is reported to have said: "Some things I hope, some things I belive, but this I *knew*," "I *know* that my Redeemer liveth," said Job. "We *know*—we have a house not made with hands eternal in the heavens," says the Gospel writer. "I *know* in whom I have believed." Oh, yes, there are many things we know. We may feel assured, also, that we shall know each other there. If Moses and Elijah, who died nearly five hundred years apart, knew each other; if the rich man recognized Lazarus, may we not feel sure that we, too, shall know each other there. "For whom the whole family in Heaven and in earth is named,' says Paul, speaking on another matter, but giving to many a joyful assurance that the family is still *whole*, only that part are here and part are there. How shall eternity be spent? Not in idleness, we may be sure. "His servants shall serve him," but it will be a work without weariness, a serving that is not labor; a rejoicing without tiring. And best of all, Jesus will be there. We shall see Him as He is. But this is the preparatory place. There are no wedding garments in Heaven, no oil for lamps, no invitations to the feast. These things we secure here, or not at all. A story is told of a driver of a stage coach in the old days, who cursed and swore at his horses, was surly to his passengers, and drank at each public house he passed. A godly gentleman said to him one day, "I cannot think what you will do in

Heaven. There are no horses there; no cursing or swearing or drinking will be allowed. No one could speak in Heaven as you speak here. I cannot think what you would do there." Are our occupations such that they are fitting us for Heaven, and its work and rest, its prayer and praise?

MRS. FRED BULLOCK.

CHRISTIAN ENDEAVOR TOPIC FOR SEPTEMBER 14, 1919

The Great Companion and How to Live With Him. Luke 24:13-32.

Some suggestions for this topic will be found in the Sunday school lesson for this week. If we do not live with Him here, we shall not do so hereafter. He would be a stranger to us, and we strangers to Him. "Closer is He than breathing; nearer than hands or feet." Do we ever think when we do or leave undone certain things whether our Unseen Companion likes them? A young man will ask a young lady if she objects to his smoking; do Christian young men ever think to ask their Fellow Traveler that question? When you invite Him into your house, do you think whether the house is fit for His occupancy, as you would think if you invited some friend home with you? Are you as courteous to Jesus in consideration of Him in every-day matters as you are to your friends? Think of these things.

MRS. FRED BULLOCK.

HOW TO ORGANIZE A C. E. SOCIETY

Are you interested in a Christian Endeavor Society for your church? If so, look out for the most interested young person you have in the church; one who will be interested in the work enough to push it. Make that young man, or young lady, chairman of the crowd so you can organize the Society. Do not give it up because you do not have a large crowd to start with. Remember some of the most important things are done up in small packages. By all means start the work, if you have only a half dozen. If you need further aid, write Miss Mae Stephenson, Raleigh, N. C.; Mr. A. E. Pye, Greensboro, N. C.; Rev. F. C. Lester, Graham, N. C.,

or the writer. Any of us will gladly help you solve the problem and organize the work.

Organize with president, vice-president, recording and corresponding secretaries, treasurer, and music director. The following committees will be needed to start the work: Prayer meeting, Lookout, Social, Music, and Information. Send to *The Dixie Endeavorer*, 5 Ferger Building, Chattanooga, Tenn., for any information needed. Work up a club of subscriptions for the paper, and get at least one copy of the *Christian Endeavor World*. Remember that all officers of your Society should come from the young people of the church. When you have completed the organization, report it to me if you are in North Carolina giving full names and addresses of your president and correspondent secretary; also, to Miss Eunice Long, Greensboro, N. C., State Christian Endeavor Secretary giving the same information.

Our Christian Endeavor work in Dixie, is booming, and our aim is for 50,000 new members during our fall drive. Large number? Yes, large but we are going over the top. North Carolina must have 3,000 of this number; Virginia, 5,000; Georgia, 2,000; Alabama, 1,000. Will our churches and pastor's in these States see to it that a Christian Endeavor Society is organized in each church in their fields? We must put this program across. We can do it, and we will. Remember the goals set by the Board of Religious Education for the Southern Christian Convention calls for a Society in every church. Let us get busy, and do the work. Who will be first to organize a Society and report it to the Committee? Special recognition will be given. "Come on! Let's Go! !"

J. VINCENT KNIGHT.

Greensboro, N. C.

P. S.—How about a Christian Endeavor Missionary for the Southern Christian Convention? In the last Christian Convention of the North Carolina Union, the young people of the Christian Church pledged themselves to raise $1,000 for special missions during the year. Our young people in Virginia matched it with another thousand. That means $2,000 will be raised for missions between now and next June. This is a part of no fund, but is special. Why not support at least a native worker and give our young people credit for the work? The money is in sight. Who answers this challenge?

L. C. LITTLE OF LOUISIANA NEW C. E. FIELD SECRETARY

The work of the Christian Endeavor Society in the South is growing so fast that it has been found necessary to employ an additional Field Secretary to cover this territory for the great movement.

L. C. Little of Winnfield, La., a school teacher and outstanding leader in the Young People's work in the South in the Methodist Protestant Church is the new Field Secretary and will begin his work on September 1.

The five Field workers employed by the Southern Christian Endeavorers typify the Interdenominational aspect of Christian Endeavor work by their own church affiliation, as each of them represents a different church, one is a member of the Presbyterian Church in China, one of the Southern Presbyterian, one of the Christian (Disciples), one Congregational and the fifth is in the Methodist Protestant Church.

Mr. Little begins his field work in the Mississippi State Christian Endeavor Convention in Canton, August 30 to September 1, and on September 2, begins a tour of the State of Kentucky.

MARRIAGES

HOPKINS-TYREE

At the home of Mrs. Carrie V. Coombs, 1253-24th Street, Newport News, Va., on Wednesday afternoon, August 20, 1919, at 5:30 o'clock, Mr. Grover Chandler Hopkins and Miss Margaret Lee Tyree were united in marriage, Rev. H. J. Fleming of the East End Christian Church officiating. The ceremony was performed in the presence of a number of friends and relatives of both parties.

The bride has a pleasing disposition, is attractive and much respected and loved by those who know her. The groom is a trusted employee of the Shackleford Auto Company, and is a man who knows the value of a friend.

They left a short while after the ceremony, accompanied by friends, for Old Point where they took the boat for Baltimore, going from there to New York and points of interest in the East.

The best wishes of all their friends are extended to Mr. and Mrs. Hopkins, trusting they will have a happy and joyous wedded life.

H. J. FLEMING.

OBITUARIES

WALKER

Mary Anderson Walker died at the home of her husband, Levi H. Walker, deceased, near Anderson's store, July 18, 1919, at the age of seventy-one years, one month and ten days. She was married to Levi H. Walker October 16, 1884. To them were born three children: Dr. J. B. Walker, Gibsonville, N. C., Rosa Walker and W. B. Walker, Union Ridge, N. C.

Mrs. Walker was the daughter of Rev. A. G. Anderson of the Christian Church. She was one of the charter members of Bethel church. A large number of friends and relatives attended the funeral service which was conducted by the writer, and interment was made at Bethel. A good woman, loved and respected by all who knew her, has fallen asleep.

"Asleep in Jesus, blessed sleep."

. . J. W. HOLT.

MOORE

We wish to express our appreciation of the life, character, and labors of our co-laborer in the ministry, Rev. H. C. Moore. During the years of his active ministry he served to good acceptance several churches in the Virginia Valley Central Conference.

On July 21, 1919, the death angel came to his home in Charlottesville, Va., and called him from labor to reward. We bow in humble submission to this dispensation of Providence, and, knowing that the Lord doeth all things well, we would endeavor to say, in our grief, not our wills, but thine, O Lord, be done. Brother Moore loved the Christian Church devotedly, and stood firmly for Bible truth, and was an able advocate and defender of the same. Though we say he is dead yet we know his influence for good still lives in many lives, and many may strike glad hands with him in the New Jerusalem because of the good he has done them here in the world below.

In giving this feeble expression of our love and appreciation for our dear brother we would not forget to mention also his faithful wife who during a long married life was a comfort, a joy, and an inspiration to him in his work, and who preceded him to the glory land just three months.

We would comfort ourselves . and all who mourn the departure of these two servants of the Lord, by calling to remembrance the scripture which says, "Blessed are the dead which die in the Lord; * * * that they may rest from their labors; and their works do follow them."

A. W. ANDES,
B. J. EARP,
W. T. WALTERS,
Committee appointed by Va. Valley Central Conference.

BOYD

This tribute is to the memory of Sister Ann Boyd who passed to her reward July 23, 1919. At the time of her death she was living at Richmond, Virginia. On July 26 her body was placed in the cemetery at Pleasant Grove Christian church, Halifax County, Virginia. This is where Sister Boyd was born and reared. Her body was borne from the church to the grave by her sons and neighbors, assisted by friends.

Sister Boyd was a woman of fine character and had been a faithful wife to her husband, who preceded her to the spirit

world a few years before. She was a
sweet and loving mother, of amiable disposition and was loved by all who knew
her. She had been a faithful member of
the Christian Church from her youth. She
was about eighty-two years old. Two sons
and two daughters are left to mourn their
loss. The love and respect for her was
beautifully demonstrated by her relatives
and friends in the floral offering.

The writer knew her intimately for
nine years, as her pastor. To know her
was to love her as one of God's dear
children. I hope that the memory of her
amiable Christian disposition like a guardian angel may hover around her dear
children and as they think of her in their
hearts they may say:

"Mother, you have left us.
Here your loss we deeply feel.
But 'tis God that hath bereft us.
He can all our sorrows heal."

The funeral and burial service were
conducted by Revs. W. S. Long, J. W.
Wellons and the writer.

                                        P. T KLAPP.

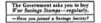
GREEK TO FATHER

Son: Father, I passed Cicero today.

Father: Did he speak?
                        —Boys Life for August.

PURSUIT OF KNOWLEDGE

Son, why are you always behind in
your studies?

So that I may pursue them, father.
                        —Boys Life for August.

THE BEE'S ADVANTAGE

"The busy bee is much better off
Than the busy man," said McGuirk.
"For the bee has a sting,
A most helpful thing,
When a loafer butts in on its work."
                        —Boston Transcript.

THE BURNING QUESTION

Gerald Draper of Royers: Arkansas wants to know if Ann Thracite
is any relations to Old King Cole.
                        Boys Life for August.

FOR RENT OR SALE

Five-room cottage, electric lights,
good well water, small barn, fruits,
about 1 acre lot. One block south of
depot, Elon College, N. C. Rent $10
per month. For sale cash or terms
at bargain. Address
                        JAS. L. FOSTER,
                        Waverly, Va.

REV. L. I. COX
Born November 20 1868
Died September 5, 1919

Volume LXXI	WEDNESDAY, SEPTEMBER 10, 1919	Number 37
BURLINGTON	· · ·	NORTH CAROLINA

THE CHRISTIAN SUN

Founded 1844 by Rev. Daniel W. Kerr

C. B. RIDDLE   -   -   -   Editor

Entered at the Burlington, N. C. Post Office as second class matter.

Subscription Rates

One year .... $ 2.00
Six months 1.00

In Advance

Give both your old and new postoffice when asking that your address be changed.

The change of your label is your receipt for money. Written receipts sent upon request.

Many persons subscribe for friends, intending that the paper be stopped at the end of the year. If instructions are given to this effect, they will receive attention at the proper time.

Marriage and obituary notices not exceeding 150 words printed free if received within 60 days from date of event, all over this at the rate of one-half cent a word.

Original poetry not accepted for publication.

Principles of the Christian Church

(1) The Lord Jesus Christ is the only Head of the Church.
(2) Christian is a sufficient name of the Church.
(3) The Holy Bible is a sufficient rule of faith and practice.
(4) Christian character is a sufficient test of fellowship, and of church membership.
(5) The right of private judgment and the liberty of conscience is a right and a privilege that should be accorded to, and exercised by all.

EDITORIAL

REV. LENNEOUS ISAAC COX

Many who take the first glance at THE CHRISTIAN SUN this week will be grief-stricken because of the announcement on the front page. "Rev. L. I. Cox is dead," was the message sounded in our ears at ten o'clock on Friday morning, September 5, 1919, he having passed away two hours earlier at his home in Elon College.

Brother Cox was in his usual health. He went to Raleigh, N. C., on the day before his death, returning home late in the evening, retiring as usual and died almost suddenly the next morning about eight o'clock. For some time he had been suffering with high blood pressure and that seems to have been the means that brought on his untimely death.

Brother Cox was in his fifty-first year, having been born November 20, 1968. He united with Pleasant Ridge Christian church in Randolph County at the age of thirteen. At the time of his death he held his membership with the church at Elon College where he has made his home since 1894. He was a student in Elon College during the sessions of 1894-1896. He was licensed by the Western North Carolina Conference November 12, 1896 and ordained an Elder by the same body November 17, 1898.

He was married to Mattie H. Craven March 27, 1894. He leaves the following family: A widow, one brother, Stanley C. Cox, and one sister, Mrs. Romelia Yow, both of Asheboro, N. C.; six sons, Basil S., Elon College, Newman C., U. S. Navy, Lenneous R., Washington, D. C., Walter Eugene, Woodrow Wilson and William Osborne, Elon College; five daughters, Mrs. Stella C. Huffine, Elon College, N. C., Mrs. Myrtie L. Sutton, Lillington, N. C., and Fleta Lawrence, Alta C. and Mattie Moffitt of Elon College and one grandchild, Martha Sutton.

The funeral took place in the College chapel on Sunday, September 7, at 11 o'clock, the pastor, Dr. N. G. Newman having the service in charge, who read a brief history of the life of the deceased. Dr. P. H. Fleming read the Scripture and Dr. J. U. Newman offered prayer. Dr. J. O. Atkinson delivered the funeral oration, which was based on II Samuel 3:38, "Know ye not that there is a prince and a great man fallen in this day in Israel?" His message was timely and paid a fitting tribute to the life of Brother Cox.

The large College auditorium could not begin to seat the people. The rostrum, aisles and stairways were filled with weeping friends who had come to pay a tribute to the man of God who had fallen in the midst of his great work. One hundred and thirty-four automobiles, some twenty-five carriages and wagons and other means of transportation brought Brother Cox's friends from several counties. Large delegations were there from Reidsville, Apple's Chapel, Monticello, Greensboro, New Lebanon, Pleasant Hill, Mt. Bethel and other near by churches where he had been pastor in former years. At the time of his death he was pastor of New Lebanon, Mt. Bethel and Apple's Chapel churches, also Executive Secretary of the North Carolina Christian Conference and Treasurer of Elon College. The following churches were organized and built by him: New Lebanon, First Church, Greensboro, Reidsville, Monticello and Hopedale.

The interment took place in the Elon College cemetery. The abundance of flowers laid on the mound in the presence of a large assembly of sorrowing friends attested the high esteem in which Brother Cox was held.

For a quarter of a century Brother Cox has been a leading spirit in his denomination. He was a born executive, a man of keen insight and deliberative judgment. His counsel was always worth considering. His heart was a throb with the love of the Master and his energy was unbounded. He was a worker that never tired, a friend that never turned his back upon you. He was a preacher of the first magnitude, a business man of rare ability. He guided the affairs of his household, of his churches, and the things of his community entrusted to him, with a judicious mind and a steady hand. He began life a poor boy and was a great admirer of the man who didn't mind work. He encouraged young men and women to get an education and inspired them first to get wisdom of the Lord. He was intensely interested in the educational work of his town, both the College and the local school. He was a neighbor who neighbored, and a friend who befriended. This we can speak from experience, because for two years we could chat with each other from our porches.

It takes feeling to describe some things, and so here our words fail. If only the reader could have been present at the funeral and have witnessed the hundreds of men and women in a long line, who viewed for the last time the remains of their former pastor, it could have only in a small way expressed the things which we cannot find words to express. Hundreds who had been converted under his ministry came to join each other in paying a final tribute to the great preacher man, while hundreds in other sections could not come but sorrowed in the hour when the final tributes were being paid.

Rev. L. I. Cox was a man of conviction of purpose that was definite and ever had his heart set upon a goal that was high. His community loses a wise counsellor, his home a devoted and diligent husband, his local church a loyal member, his Conference a deliberative and wise adviser, THE CHRISTIAN SUN a most loyal friend, his denomination a preacher of the Word, a real watchman who stood brave and strong and true upon the walls of Zion in the interest of the Master's work. Brother Cox was a man with the constructive mind, having always in mind the matter of building and building well. He was a champion of missions, a disciple of giving, a friend of education, a lover of that which is true and right and honorable and just.

We mourn with his family because of his untimely going, but to them and all his friends we point to that resurrection morn when the dead in Christ shall rise and tears shall be no more; we point them to that fountain of Truth where our beloved Brother drank and was satisfied. May his going be our gain in that our resolves shall be for greater and nobler things, thus carrying out his aim in life.

I am the resurrection and the life; he that believeth in me, though he were dead, yet shall he live; and whosoever liveth, and believeth in me, shall never die.—John 11:25, 26.

REV. OLIVER WORDEN POWERS, D. D.

Rev. Oliver Worden Powers, M. A., D. D., was born May 9, 1856 and was promoted to a higher life on Sunday evening, August 31, 1919. Dr. Powers began his ministry in 1877 and was ordained in 1878. December 24, 1824, he was united in marriage to Miss Florence Davis, of Edinboro, Pa., and graduated from Antioch College in 1890. In 1893 he taught in Demorest Normal School in the state of Georgia. He was a successful pastor at Yellow Springs, Conneaut and Columbus, Ohio. At each of these places he served with great acceptance and did a great work for his denomination

and the Kingdom. He has also served other churches in New York, Pennsylvania and Ohio. For two terms he was honored with the presidency of the American Christian Convention. For eight years—1906 to 1914 —he was Home Mission Secretary, which office he filled with great acceptance and wrought many commendable changes in the administration of his work. Dr. Powers was twice married, his second wife being Miss Emma C. Southward, Yellow Springs, Ohio.

Dr. Powers had been in declining health for some weeks before his passing, but his actual physical condition was known to only a few of his intimate friends. For a number of years he has made his home in Dayton, Ohio, but death took him at Circleville, Ohio, where he had gone for medical treatment. The funeral took place in the College Chapel at Antioch College where he was buried. Rev. McD. Howshare, pastor of the First Church, Dayton, Ohio, preached the funeral, Dr. F. H. Peters read the Scripture, Dr. Warren H. Denison offered prayer and Rev. Alva M. Kerr read an appreciation of his life. Dr. M. T. Morrill took part in the service at the grave.

Dr. Powers was a man of more than ordinary ability. He was a great reader and was in every sense of the word a student. He had made a specialty of more than one subject and kept abreast with the issues of his day, both in the nation and in his denomination. He was deeply interested in education and the upbuilding of his denomination in both spiritual and educational matters.

The Christian Church loses a good and a great man in the passing of Dr. Powers. It is a great challenge to some young man to aspire to fill his worthy footsteps. His faith in God was strong and his loyalty to the Christian Church was unquestioned.

It was our privilege to personally know Dr. Powers and we feel that we speak the sentiment of all who came in contact with him that his leaving is a keen loss to his friends, to his denomination, to his State and to the Nation.

May the Lord comfort his bereaved ones and be their Companion, their God and their Guide.

I know that my redeemer liveth, and that he shall stand at the latter day upon the earth; and though, after my skin, worms destroy this body, yet in my flesh shall I see God; whom I shall see for myself, and mine eyes shall behold, and not another.—Job 19:25-27.

REV. HENRY ALEXANDER ALBRIGHT

Below Rev. A. T. Banks gives us the news that Rev. Henry Alexander Albright was translated August 31, 1919. This item reached us after last week's paper had been mailed. The announcement of Brother Albright's passing will be read with sad hearts by all who knew him—and that is a great host of friends.

We look back and recall our first visit to the Western
(Continued on Page 6).

PASTOR AND PEOPLE

NEWS ITEMS FROM FIRST CHURCH, NORFOLK, VA.

The First Christian church is putting on new life as her members who have been on their vacation return to the city, and to their post of duty in their church. The pastor and his wife were away only two Sundays, and since their return the services have been fairly well attended. Brother J. O. Wiggs, our lay leader, having had his vacation earlier, was in charge of the services in the absence of the pastor, thus making it possible to keep the church open all the summer. A splendid number of our members have rested in the mountains, others have traveled as far as Niagara Falls, and others have rested at the sea shore, and still others have visited in the homes of their friends in the good old country sections, and when they all return, we feel sure that interest in all our work will be fine.

Three members have been received since the pastor's return, and we are looking for others to join soon. The Sunday evening services of September 7 and 14 will be given over to the young people, and the pastor will discuss "The Ideal Girl," and the "Ideal Boy." A rally will be held in the Sunday school in the near future, and it is hoped to make it one of the greatest rally days our school has ever held.

Mrs. M. E. Nichols, our Deaconess, Brothers J. W. Mercer, and Deacon G. H. Frey, and Miss Elizabeth Brothers, one of our faithful Sunday school teachers, have all been quite ill here of late, but all seem to be on the road to health again now, and it will be a joy to see them back in our services again.

J. F. MORGAN, *Pastor.*

HENDERSON

During the months of July and August the churches of Henderson united in holding evening services on the Court Square, the pastors of the various churches preaching alternately. These services have been enjoyed very much. They have given an opportunity for the members of the various congregations to worship together and deepen the spirit of fraternity among the denominations.

Our work here seems to be in good condition, though there is at present no distinctively aggressive or progressive movement. Our attendance both at preaching services and Sunday school is slightly larger than it has been. The Christian Endeavor Society, under the leadership of Mr. F. M. Harward, president, is doing good work, and the other auxiliaries are trying to perform the duties pertaining to them. In all of these we have a loyal and earnest band of workers.

Following the Christian Endeavor prayer service last Wednesday evening, a social was given on the lawn, under the auspices of the Social Committee. Refreshments were served and social intercourse enjoyed by a goodly number of invited guests. It was a pleasant occasion; and we hope thereby new interest has been added to our work.

Fuller's Chapel

The second Sunday in July we began our meeting here. Rev. P. H. Fleming, D. D., came Tuesday, and thereafter did the preaching; and he did it well. All his sermons revealed Brother Fleming's characteristics of deep thinking, beautiful and forceful diction, spirituality and earnestness. We think much good was accomplished. Many, we are sure, would gladly welcome Doctor Fleming back in a similar service, or at any time. The Fuller's people are good people to serve, and while the inconvenience of access has prevented us from spending as much time among them as we had desired to do, we have thoroughly enjoyed our service with them. We hope to spend more time with these good people soon.

R. L. WILLIAMSON.

MOORE UNION

We began our meeting at Moore Union Saturday before the fourth Sunday in August and continued for nine days. I quote the words of some of the oldest men of the community who said: "It was the greatest revival that we have seen in twenty years." I know it was the greatest revival that I have seen for a long while. In fact it was a glorious revival, not only for the members of Moore Union church but for the members of other churches. God only knows the results of this meeting. According to the count that some made there were between thirty and fifty who professed faith in Christ, including those who professed reclaimation. Several united with the church.

The congregations were very large from the beginning until the close of the meeting and for all this we give God the glory and honor.

If the Lord permits, we expect to conduct a series of meetings South of this church, a distance of ten or fifteen miles, between now and Conference.

R. T. KLAPP, *Pastor.*

Elon College, N. C.

WHAT A PITY

A young minister who has been in the service of the Christian Church for only a few years tells me that he will be compelled to resign his work and enter some other field of employment. He says it takes about two-thirds of his meager salary to pay his car fare.

I am reliably informed of another who has been in the ministerial work for several years, and who is a very successful minister, who says he is getting about enough to pay his car fare. He had a bank account when he began the ministerial work. From this he has been obliged to draw from time to time to pay his bills. He too, says he will have to give up his work and engage in some business to support his family.

These two brethren are fair examples of the average minister of the rural church . What a pity it is that during these prosperous times when money is more plentiful than ever before, wages higher, and everything we farmers have to sell more than doubled in price, we seem to have forgotten our pastors. We are driving them out into the world to make a support.

It is time for us to awake. If our services are worth one hundred per cent more than in normal times, and everything we grow on the farm more than doubled in value, certainly our pastors' salaries should be increased also. They must pay higher prices for the necessaries of life, and if we do not pay them a living salary it is up to them to engage in other work or starve. (Read Malachi 3:8-12).

Brethren, let us get busy and see that our pastors get a substantial increase in this year's salary.

. A LAYMAN.

REV. R. F. BROWN TO LEAVE DURHAM

Rev. R. F. Brown is to leave Durham and accept the Chapel Hill charge, so we are informed from the following taken from a letter from Brother Brown under date of September :

"I have been called to this pastorate again for another year with an increase in salary, but have declined the call to accept a call to the Chapel Hill church. I am making this change because I am so profoundly impressed with the needs of the Chapel Hill church. I will give my full time to this church, if the Mission Boards stand by the work, which I am sure they will do. This is one of the most strategic points in our denomination and I earnestly solicit the prayers of the brotherhood as I undertake this work."

SALARIES OF PREACHERS AND TEACHERS

(Editorial in Biblical Recorder)

We are publishing in this issue two articles from laymen urging the necessity of increasing the salaries of preachers, and one of them includes teachers. One of the articles is clipped from the *Progressive Farmer* and was written by Dr. Clarence Poe, Editor. The other is an article written for the Recorder by Dr. J T. Henderson, Secretary of the Laymen's Movement of the Southern Baptist Convention.

Dr. Poe insists that the salaries of preachers and teachers should be doubled. He shows that the little increases which have been made in salaries do not begin to keep pace with the increase in the cost of living. We commend these articles to the earnest and prayerful consideration of our churches and school committees.

Our attention has just been called to an article in the September number of the *American* in which Dr. Hibben, President of Princeton University, gives some stunning facts in regard to the salaries paid teachers. One of the most startling examples of the niggardly salaries comes from our own state. Here it is:

"Two advertisements were set side by side in the Raleigh News and Observer of January 13, 1919. One of them read: "Wanted—Colored barber for white trade in camp town; permanent position. We guarantee $25 per week. Right man can make $35 per week. Let us hear from you at once. Fleming and Elliott, 6 Market Square, Fayetteville, N. C.'

"The second advertisement wasted no words: "Wanted—Teacher of Latin for Lumberton High School, Lumberton, N. C. Salary $70 per month. W. H. Cale, Superintendent.

"Here was a guarantee to a negro barber that he would be paid $1,300 a year, with a good prospect of $1,820, while the Latin teacher, drawing his salary for nine months, would receive $630—less than half of the negro barber's assured minimum.'"

Two years ago Brother Middleton made a careful investigation and arrived at the conclusion that the average salary of the Baptist pastors in North Carolina was $750. The small increases that have been made since then would, perhaps, run the average up to $840, which would be the same per month as was offered the teacher in the high school. Is further comment necessary? Are our churches and schools satisfied to have colored barbers paid twice as much for trimming hair as is paid our teachers for training the minds of our children, and our preachers for caring for the spiritual interests of those to whom they minister?

We appeal to our business laymen in behalf of the under-paid preachers. If some layman in each church would call the attention of the church to these two advertisements, we believe that many churches would determine to do a better part by the men who minister to them in spiritual things.

BARBER'S SALARY, $1,300!
. PREACHER'S SALARY, $840!

THE TEST OF A MAN

Franklin K. Lane

The test is to be in peace what it was in the time of war. Are you fitted for the fight? The man who knew how knowledge could be converted into power was the man for whom there was unlimited call. So it is increasingly to be.

To be useful is to be the test that society will put Each man's rights are to be measured, not by what he has, but by what he does with what he has. The honors—the Croix de Paix—the richest rewards will go to the capables those who are not standardized into "men machines," those who dare to venture and learn to lead.

But all must work, and this duty to work and respect for work should be the earliest lesson learned. And it should be taught in the school, not as an homily, but in a living way, by tying work with instruction, making the thing learned apply to something done.

I should like to see the day when every child learned a trade while at school, trained his mind and his hand together, lifted labor into art by the application of thought. To be useful is the essence of Americanism, and against the undeveloped resource, whether it be land of man, the spirit of this country makes protest.

The nearer we get to Jesus Christ, the more will our consciences be enlightened as to the particulars in which we are still distant from Him. A speck on a polished shield will show plain that would never have been seen on a rusty one. The saint who is nearest God will think more of his sins than the man who is farthest from Him. So new work of purifying will open before us as we grow more pure, and this will last as long as life itself.—*Alexander Maclaren*.

EDITORIAL

(Continued from Page 3).

North Carolina Conference, and among those who gave the glad hand to a boy who desired one day to become a preacher, was our dear departed friend, Rev. H. A. Albright. That year, and practically all the years thereafter, we were privileged to meet this great man of God at the annual Conference. We look back to those times and feel anew that cordial handshake and hear again that clear voice as it gave words of wisdom and counsel and consolation.

Brother Albright was one of the pioneer ministers of his Conference. He was a man of rare ability and was a citizen with most exceptional qualities. For a number of years he was county surveyor of Randolph County. As an officer he filled well his position and carried the scales of justice in all his work. In the pulpit he was earnest and sincere and gave counsel out of the deep of his heart and the wide experience of his Bible reading and acquaintance with God. His messages were not carried on the wings of polished oratory, but sprang out of a devoted soul for a devoted cause. As a pastor he was a faithful and attentive, ever taking sufficient time to think and visit and care for those under his ministry.

Brother Banks states that Brother Albright was a champion for the cause of prohibition. As we write, there comes to us in a very vivid manner, how he always championed the cause of prohibition, clean speech and clean habits in his address on Moral Reform at the annual Conferences. He was a man who preached these things and practiced them.

Many are the men and women who have been converted under his ministry, influenced by his Godly life and walk daily in life's narrow way because of contact with this rare character whose heart was set upon building up the Kingdom. He is gone; he is not forgotten. May his spirit continue to live amongst us, and may his God call some one to fill his place.

Verily, verily I say unto you, The hour is coming, and now is, when the dead shall hear the voice of the Son of God; and they that hear shall live.—John 5:25.

REV. H. A. ALBRIGHT

After an illness of three weeks Rev. Henry Alexander Albright departed this life, at his home, August 31, 1919. He was born October 22, 1836, and was eighty-two years, ten months and nine days old. On September 23, 1866 he was married to Miss Margaret E. Farrell, who preceded him to the home beyond more than two years ago. To this union were born five children: Mrs. Sallie A. Hatten, Seagrove, N. C.; Rufus Lee Albright, Seagrove, N. C.; Joseph Walter Albright, Haleyville, Ala.; William Henry Albright, Thomasville, Ga., and Mrs. Ida Mair Craven Seagrove N. C., and ten grandchildren.

When a young man Brother Albright entered the ministry in the Christian Church and was ordained by Conference when about thirty-two years old. Revs. J.

N. Farrell and J. W. Holt signed the Certificate of Ordination. He was an active pastor until age and health failed him.

As a man he was gentle and kind to all who knew him. He was a devoted husband and father. A man of strong convictions but well balanced in attitude. The cause of prohibition has lost one of its strongest friends and advocates. Conference has lost one of its best and most reliable ministers. As to committee work he is considered one of the most conservative and well balanced men of the Conference and yet willing to undertake and work new plans.

I have been his pastor since last November and I found him true and devoted to his church and denomination. I have never heard any man speak ought against him as a citizen, a minister or Christian. His character was absolutely above reproach. Everything good and nothing bad could be said of him.

His funeral was conducted from Shiloh Christian church, in the midst of a throng of people, by the writer, assisted by Revs. G. R. Underwood, W. N .Hayes, T. J. Green and W. J. Edwards.

May the bereaved ones be comforted by the Holy Spirit is the prayer of pastor and friends.

A. T. BANKS.

And I heard a voice from heaven saying unto me, Write, Blessed are the dead which die in the Lord from henceforth: Yea, saith the Spirit, that they may rest from their labours; and their works do follow them.—Rev. 14:13.

WILLIS J. LEE—AN APPRECIATION

From time to time, Brother Editor, have appeared in your columns words of esteem, appreciation and admiration for the life, love and labors of Willis J. Lee as seen by friends and associates in church, in community, and in business. I am wondering if a line, by one of his house, will be pardoned and printed, referring to that life as it was lived out in the home and spent in the family circle?

I am constrained the more to offer such a line because only those who knew his family life, that life of the family board and fire-side, could properly appreciate his worth or discover his merits. He was a modest man. That is another way of saying that his great mind expressed itself in deeds rather than in words, and his busy, tireless hands wrought for his loved ones that which his great heart felt, but which weak words could not say. The public called him a timid man; his family knew that he was trusted, tried and true in every circumstance, ordeal and condition of life. Those who met and mingled with him said he was courteous; the loved ones of his house knew he was as constant as the needle to the north star, as courageous as a lion, as kindly and as considerate as the mother to her first born and as the Master, Whose he was and Whom he served, when he called the little ones, set them in the midst and said: "Of such is the Kingdom of heaven."

They say he was liberal to charity, to church, to community; his family knew that his love for these was large because his love for his home and dear ones was beyond expression and knew no metes nor bounds. Unless one knew the gentle spirit of the house, the considerate heart of the home, the loving hand of the hearth and family circle, one could not appreciate nor begin to estimate the real worth and value of such a life.

The depth of his heart was revealed in friendship; the breadth of his spirit was manifest in the family circle; the real meaning of his great and good life was only discovered by and known to those who lived with him under the same roof, and shared with him the comforts and joys of his household.

This writer knows that his was one of the loftiest spirits that has graced this day and time; and his one of the noblest and most unselfish souls that has ever wrought and labored and loved. This rich, rare, noble life, so suddenly taken from us, on May 20, 1919, has dug deep a wound that is hard to heal; but has wielded an influence and brought a joy that will abide all the time and bear fruit through the endless ages. This then is greatness, to have lived well, wrought nobly, won the undying and ever increasing love of those who knew him best, and having invested his substance and his influence generously and lavishly in the work of the Kingdom, and for the glory of God, sweetly and peacefully falls on sleep.

J. O. ATKINSON.

NOTES

Let the pastors send us a write-up of their meetings. Don't put it off too long.

More good articles next week. We have something in store for you. Look for it.

By the way, don't forget to send that $2.00 for your renewal. It will be WELCOME.

Do you believe in superstition in any form? If so, turn to page 12 and read "Superstition Kills." Read it, for it will greatly repay you.

We regret that we are not able to present the pictures of Brothers Albright and Powers in connection with a note of their life, labors and death.

We mourn with Brother J. G. Flynt, Winston-Salem, N. C., in the untimely death of his six-year-old son, Clarence, who was killed by an automobile last week.

A PERSONAL LETTER

Dear Brother Riddle:—

Many thanks for your favors.

I have been home two weeks but am still in bed. I have had a trained nurse nearly all the time and she is with me yet. I am improving at present, it seems for which I praise the Lord.

I thank you again.

Sincerely,
J. G. TRUITT.

News Ferry, Va., Sept. 6, 1919.

FOUR AND MORE

Four and more is the record of *The Dixie Endeavor*. This splendid little sixteen page Christian Endeavor monthly bristles with good things every month. It has just completed its fourth volume and starts on its fifth. The indications are that its circulation will soon reach ten thousand. Our friend, Karl Lehmann, is the editor and publisher, and this explains the very large success of this publication.

Live on, *Dixie Endeavorer*, live on! You are a welcome visitor to this sanctum. The only fault we find of you is that your visits seem too far apart.

WRITE IT RIGHT

We find the following in *The Methodist Protestant Herald*, to which we add our approval:

"We often hear the expression, "the past year." But there are a great many "past" years. What is meant is "the last year."

"Again, we frequently read in marriage notices: "The bride is the accomplished daughter of Mr. A. B. Jones," when Mr. A. B. Jones has other daughters just as accomplished as the one referred to. When there are other daughters or other sons, we should say "a daughter" or "a son."

"Think before you speak and before you write whether you are following fact or mere habit or fancy, and you will be better able to speak or write correctly.'"

Let us add this, not on the marriage note, but in the obituary: So often we find it in the manuscript written in this manner: "He leaves a host of friends to mourn *his loss*," when it should be to mourn *their loss*. There is a difference.

NEW COMERS TO THE SUN FAMILY

V. T. Huffman ....Timberville, Va.
Mrs Ada Hillyard ....Broadway, Va.
Erwin E. Layman ....Daphna, Va.
Edward F. Spitzer ....Broadway, Va.
Sidney L. Layman ....Broadway, Va.
W. B. Holsinger ....Timberville, Va.
J. C. Gerringer ....Brown Summit, N. C.
T. W. Price ....Summerfield, N. C.

(Report to September 8).

For, behold, the day cometh, that shall burn as an oven; and all the proud, yea, and all that do wickedly, shall be stubble; and the day that cometh shall burn them up, saith the Lord of hosts, that it shall leave them neither root nor branch.—*Malachi* 4:1.

(Selected and sent for publication by Mrs. Annie Smith, Route 1, New Hill, N. C.)

REMINDERS

Conferences will soon be here. Get ready for them.

Pay your pastor a larger salary. He needs it and you need the joy of giving it.

Watch your label and renew promptly.

MISSIONARY

ANNUAL REPORT OF THE TREASURER OF THE WOMAN'S HOME AND FOREIGN MISSION BOARD OF THE SOUTHERN CHRISTIAN CONVENTION—1918-1919

Regular Funds

1918		
April 27 to E. N. C. Conference.............. $	7.40	$
May 15 to W. N. C. Conference..............	4.05	
July 4 to Ga. and Ala. Conference..........	5.00	
July 8 by Mrs. J. W. Patton................		11.96
July 9 to N. C. and Va. Conference.........	55.20	
July 11 by Mrs. W. A. Harper...............		9.50
July 11 by C. B. Biddle, Pub. Agt..........		4.75
July 15 by Mrs. W. T. Walters.............		21.25
July 24 to E. Va. Conference..............	140.77	
July 26 to E. N. C. Conference............	22.28	
July 27 by Mrs. M. F. Cook...............		11.96
August 1 to N. C. Conference..............	15.90	
August 1 to Va. Val. Conference...........	23.50	
August 1 by C. B. Biddle, Pub. Agt........		31.15
August 1 by W. C. Wicker, Treas., (H. M.)..		88.04
August 1 by W. C. Wicker, Treas., (F. M.)..		88.03
August 21 to Va. Val. C. Conference........	4.60	
August 25 to W. N. C. Conference..........	2.05	
September 20 by Mrs. W. H. Carroll.........		9.58
October 3 to W. N. C. Conference..........	6.50	
October 18 to N. C. and Va. Conference.....	71.21	
October 23 to Va. Val. C. Conference.......	32.35	
November 1 to E. N. C. Conference.........	17.04	
November 1 to E. Va. Conference..........	187.28	
November 1 by W. C. Wicker, Treas., (H. M.)..		180.53
November 1 by W. C. Wicker, Treas., (F. M.)..		180.52
November 26 to W. N. C. Conference.......	20.20	
1919		
January 2 by Mrs. W. A. Harper............		2.00
January 2 by C. B. Biddle, Pub. Agt........		54.50
January 24 to Va. Val. C. Conference.......	9.42	
January 24 to E. Va. Conference..........	151.98	
January 25 to E. N. C. Conference........	8.18	
January 25 to E. N. C. Conf. (Special F. M.)..	36.07	
February 1 By Mrs. W. A. Harper...........		9.02
February 1 by W. C. Wicker, Treas., (H. M.)..		62.18
February 1 by W. C. Wicker, Treas., (F. M.)..		98.80
April 19 to N. C. Conference..............	95.16	
April 23 to E. Va. Conference............	182.80	
May 1 to Va. Val. C. Conference..........	19.50	
May 1 to Va. Val. C. Conf. (Special H. M.)..	15.79	
May 1 by W. C. Wicker, Treas., (H. M.).....		164.52
May 1 by W. C. Wicker, Treas., (F. M.).....		148.73
Total..............	**$1,177.03**	**$1,177.03**

Santa Isabel

1918		
May 1 to W. N. C. Conference..............	20.95	
July 9 to N. C. and Va. Conference.........	4.83	
July 26 to E. N. C. Conference...........	6.95	
August 1 to Va. Val. C. Conference........	17.30	
August 1 by W. C. Wicker, Treasurer......		29.08
August 21 to Va. Val. C. Conference.......	8.51	
September 20 to W. N. C. Conference.......	9.35	
October 3 to W. N. C. Conference.........	18.17	
October 12 to N. C. and Va. Conference....	39.49	
October 12 to W. N. C. Conference........	20.88	
November 1 to E. N. C. Conference........	8.75	
November by W. C. Wicker, Treasurer......		106.05
November 26 to W. N. C. Conference.......	6.85	
1919		
January 24 to Va. Val. C. Conference......	2.79	
February 1 by W. C. Wicker, Treasurer.....		9.64
April 19 to N. C. Conference.............	46.23	
May 1 to Va. Val. C. Conference..........	13.72	
May 1 by W. C. Wicker, Treasurer........		59.95
Total........	**$204.72**	**$204 72**

Christian Orphanage

1918		
April 27 to E. N. C. Conference..............	9.39	
May 15 to W. N. C. Conference.............	.53	
July 9 to N. C. and Va. Conference.........	1.00	
July 24 to E. Va. Conference.............	27.41	
July 26 to E. N. C. Conference...........	7.76	
August 1 to W. N. C. Conference..........	1.43	
August 1 to Va. Val. C. Conference........	1.73	
August 1 by W. C. Wicker................		59.88
August 21 to Va. Val. C. Conference.......	1.95	
October 12 to N. C. and Va. Conference....	14.80	
November 1 to E. N. C. Conference........	2.78	
November 1 to E. Va. Conference..........	166.74	
November 1 by W. C. Wicker, Treasurer.....		197.16
1919		
January 24 to Va. Val. C. Conference......	.15	
January 24 to E. Va. Conference..........	11.39	
January 25 to E. N. C. Conference........	10.79	
February 1 by W. C. Wicker, Treasurer.....		22.33
April 19 to N. C. Conference.............	9.93	
April 23 to E. Va. Conference............	25.25	
May 1 to Va. Val. C. Conference..........	.37	
May 1 by W. C. Wicker, Treasurer........		35.55
Total..........	**$294.92**	**$294.92**

Sendai Orphanage

1918		
May 15 to W. N. C. Conference.............	.53	
July 9 to N. C. and Va. Conference.........	1.03	
July 24 to E. Va. Conference.............	14.41	
August 1 to W. N. C. Conference..........	1.44	
August 1 to Va. Val. C. Conference........	1.72	
August 1 by W. C. Wicker, Treasurer......		19.13
August 21 to Va. Val. C. Conference.......	1.95	
October 12 to N. C. and Va. Conference....	1.90	
November 1 to E. N. C. Conference........	2.77	
November 1 to E. Va. Conference..........	5.88	
November 1 by W. C. Wicker............		11.90
1919		
January 24 to Va. Val. C. Conference......	.15	
April 19 to E. Va. Conference............	.75	
May 1 to Va. Val. C Conference..........	.38	
May 1 by W. C. Wicker...............		1.28
Total............	**$32.31**	**$32.31**

Bible Women

1918		
July 6 to W. N. C. Conf., Mrs. Takahashi....	25.00	
July 9 to N. C. and Va. Conf., Dona Delfina..	18.54	
July 25 to E. Va. Conf., Mrs. Watanabe.....	23.25	
July 25 to E. Va. Conf., Miss Hamaguchi....	12.50	
August 1 by W. C. Wicker, Treasurer......		79.39
October 12 to N. C. & Va. Conf., Dona Delfina..	10.72	
November 1 to E. Va. Conf., Mrs. Watanabe..	26.35	
November 1 to E. Va. Conf., Miss Hamaguchi..	12.50	
November by W. C. Wicker, Treasurer.....		50.07
1919		
January 24 to E Va. Conf., Mrs. Watanabe...	52.35	
January 24 to E. Va. Conf., Miss Hamaguchi..	12.50	
February 1 by W. C. Wicker, Treasurer......		64.85
April 23 to E. Va. Conf., Mrs. Watanabe....	24.75	
April 23 to E. Va. Conf., Miss Hamaguchi....	12.50	
May 1 by W. C. Wicker, Treasurer.........		37.25
Total......	**$231.46**	**$231.46**

Japan Sunday School

1918		
July 24 to E. Va. Conference..............	12.50	
August 1 by W. C. Wicker, Treasurer......		12.50
November 1 to E. Va. Conference.........	12.50	
November 1 by W. C. Wicker, Treasurer....		12.50
1919		
January 24 to E. Va. Conference..........	12.50	
February 1 by W. C. Wicker, Treasurer.....		12.50
April 23 to E. Va. Conference............	12.50	
May 1 by W. C. Wicker, Treasurer........		12.50
Total............	**$50.00**	**$50.00**

Literature Fund

1918		
May 1 balance on hand................	16.87	
July 9 to N. C. and Va. Conference........	.59	
July 24 to E. N. C. Conference...........	2.36	
September 20 by W. N. C. Conference.....	1.50	
October 12 N. C. and Va. Conference......	3.50	
November 1 to E. Va. Conference.........	10.30	
1919		
January 24 to E. Va. onference..........	1.00	
Total............	**$36.12**	**$36.12**
May 1 by cash balance................		5.56

Santa Isabel Building Fund (Blocks)

1918		
April 27 to E. N. C. Conference	8.15	
May 1 to E. C. Convention (Collection).....	16.00	
July 8 to W. N. C. Conference..........	.59	
July 24 to E. Va. Conference..........	135.70	
August 1 to Va. Val. C. Conference.......	18.25	
August 1 to E. Va. Conference.........	7.50	
August 1 by W. C. Wicker, Treasurer......		167.60
August 21 to Va. Val. C. Conference......	5.00	
August 25 to W. N. C. Conference.......	5.00	
November 1 to E. Va. Conference.........	283.29	
November 1 by W. C. Wicker, Treasurer....		317.44
1919		
January 24 to Va. Val. C. Conference......	7.75	
January 24 to E Va. Conference.........	61.25	
January 25 to E. N. C. Conference........	8.30	
February 1 by W. C. Wicker, Treasurer.....		77.30
April 23 to E Va. Conference............	119.90	
May 1 by W. C. Wicker, Treasurer........		119.90
May 1 to overdraft...................	5.56	
Total............	**$682.34**	**$682.34**
May 1 by overdraft		5.56

Barrett Home

1918		
April 27 to E. N. C. Conference............	16.85	
May 15 to W. N. C. Conference...........	2.70	
July 9 to N. C. and Va. Conference........	15.00	
July 9 to N. C. and Va. Conference........	5.00	
July 24 to E. Va. Conference............	62.74	
July 26 to E. N. C. Conference..........	31.88	
August 1 to Va. Val. C. Conference.......	12.00	
August 1 by W. C. Wicker, Treasurer......		114.82
August to Va. Val. C. Conference........	10.00	
August 23 to E. Va. Conference.........	10.00	
September 20 to W. N. C. Conference.....	21.00	
October 3 to W. N. C. Conference.......	5.00	

October 12 to N. C. and Va. Conference...... 165.00
October 28 to Va. Val C. Conference......... 20.00
November 1 to E. N. C. Conference.......... 13.05
November 1 to E. Va. Conference........... 146.68
November 26 by W. C. Wicker, Treasurer......   422.58
November 26 to W. N. C. Conference......... 81.15
1919
January 24 to Va. Val C. Conference......... 11.75
January 24 to E. Va. Conference........... 149.75
January 25 to E N C. Conference.......... 19.50
February 1 by W. C. Wicker, Treasurer 262.15
April 19 to N. C. Conference............. 120.25
April 23 to E. Va. Conference............. 70.80
May 1 by W. C. Wicker Treasurer...........   191.05

       Total $990.10 $990.10

South Boston
1918
July 9 to N. C. and Va. Conference......... 18 54
August 1 by W. C. Wicker, Treasurer.......   18.54
October 12 to N. C. and Va. Conference...... 10 72
November 1 by W. C. Wicker, Treasurer.....   10.72

       Total...........$29.26 $29.26

Rev. Martinez
1918
May 1 to cash on hand.............. 128.11
July 24 to Va. Conference............. 213.17
November 1 to E. Va. Conference......... 171.83
1919
January 24 to E. Va. Conference.......... 21.64
April 23 to E. Va. Conference............ 73.85
May 1 by W. C. Wicker, Treasurer.........   500.00
May 1 by balance 107.60

       Total $607.60 $607.60
May 1 to cash balance 107.60

Mrs. Fry's School
1918
October 12 to W. N. C. Conference......... 15.00
November 1 by W. C. Wicker, Treasurer.....   15.00
November 26 to W. N. C. Conference........ 15.00
1919
February 1 by W. C. Wicker, Treasurer.....   15.00
April 19 to N. C. Conference.........*. 30.00
May 1 by W. C. Wicker, Treasurer.........   30.00

       Total $60.00 $60.00

Franklinton Church
April 27 to E. N. C. Conference............ 10.00
November 1 by W. C. Wicker, Treasurer......   10.00

       Total.............$10.00 $10.00

Sendai Station
1918
November 1 to E. N. C. Conference.......... 4.90
November 1 by W. C. Wicker..............   4.90

       Total.............$4.90 $4.90

Dr. Atkinson Mission Fund
1918
November 1 to E. Va. Conference........... 50.00
November 1 by W. C. Wicker, Treasurer......   50.00

       Total.............$50.00 $50.00

Orphanage Room
1919
May 1 to Va. Val. C. Conference............ 1.75
May 1 by cash balance...................   1.75

       Total $1.75 $1.75
May 1 to cash balance................... 1.75

Winchester Church Debt
1919
May 1 to Va. Val. C. Conference...........,. 71 50
May 1 by W. C. Wicker, Treasurer.........   71.50

       Total.............$71 50 $71.50

Literature Fund 26.12
Rev. Martinez 107.60
Orphanage Room 1.75

       Total.......... ..$145.47
Less overdraft Santa Isabel Bldg. Fund...... 5.55

       Total cash on hand..$139.92

Contributions by Conferences

Eastern North Carolina 255.75
Eastern Virginia 2,713.01
Georgia and Alabama 5.00
North Carolina 202.32
North Carolina and Virginia 428.00
Virginia Valley Central 360.08
Western North Carolina 294.22
Southern Christian Convention (Offering).... 16.00

       Total............$4,374.38

           MRS. W. T. WALTERS, Treasurer.

PETS MY CHILDREN HAVE HAD

By Jess Sweitzer Sheaffer

The child on the farm has many opportunities to own pets and to live close to Nature which a child in the city lacks. Nevertheless, there are a number of gentle and very interesting pets which a child in the congested city districts may have.

My children have taken a great deal of pleasure in caring for their different pets—of which they have had quite a variety. The first was a canary. Birds are always a joy, especially the canary, which is quite at home in a cage, and is content with a vessel of pure water and fresh seed each day. His cheery song gives pleasure to the grown-ups as well as to the children.

Then, too, goldfish are a never-ending source of wonder and interest to children. The fact that their environment is so different from our own, and that they live constantly under water will start the child to thinking and asking innumerable questions. The fish need very little care and two or three of them flashing about in a glass bowl are an attractive addition to any room. A small piece of especially prepared fish food broken and dropped into the bowl every other day and fresh water once or twice a week, and that is all that is necessary for their comfort. Little shells or pebbles which the children may have gathered along the beach in summer can be put into the bowl although they are not essential. A few water plants are also desirable, and help to purify the water. Our goldfish have thrived for more than two years with very little care.

Our family of guinea pigs were more unusual, and were the cleanest little animals one could find. "Jack and Jill" were the original couple, but the children were delighted, upon going out to feed them one morning, to find three little baby guineas snuggled down in the hay! They were the tiniest, furriest little babies with the pinkest of pink ears, and just as lively as could be! They varied widely in color, so the children immediately claimed certain ones as their particular property and watched their growth, from day to day, with great glee. Their house in the back yard was a small wooden box, about three feet by four. It was partitioned off and covered with wire netting and one-half of it was sheltered from the storms with a piece of oil cloth. Their snug bed of hay was frequently replenished, for they not only slept and burrowed in it but nibbled at it constantly. They liked cabbage leaves, lettuce, clover and plantain and also relished a cake made of corn meal, salt and bran mixed with water, and baked in the oven till dry.

My children enjoy kittens and Bantam chickens, too, but their favorite pet is a big Scotch collie. He is noble and intelligent, and is their constant companion. A dog not only needs food and water, but also craves kindness and companionship to a greater degree than almost any other animal, and, when he becomes attached to his master, is the most dependable sort of friend.

Help to reach all the parents of the country by cutting this out and passing it on to a friend.

CONSISTENCY
By Sarah G. Simpson

Consistency is one of the fundamental qualities of discipline, and from my own experience I have found it to be most important. It should always be accompanied by kindness. More mothers have trouble with their children because of their own inconsistency than for any other one reason.

Johnnie comes home from school and asks, "Mother, may I go over to Billy Baker's to play?" and Mother, knowing that Billy's influence is not good, refuses. Johnnie displays more or less temper, but Mother is firm, and Johnnie stays at home. A few days later, however, Johnnie makes the same request, and Mother, who is entertaining a caller, lets him go for a little while. This is case of inconsistency, and, in order to save one scene, Mother is laying a good foundation for many more. The probability is that had she replied, "Mother has told you before." The matter would have ended there, or even if he had cried a little and "made a scence," the son would have had a valuable lesson and learned that Mother meant what she said. His love for the moment might have been shaken, but eventually Johnnie would have been a happier boy and his love and respect for his mother would have been greater.

The value of consistency cannot be over-estimated. The tiniest baby should be dealt with kindly, but firmly. A mother can develop the teasing habit in her child while he is still in his cradle if she lack this quality of consistency. At one time when her baby cries she does not pick him up for she says, "It is not good for him and he is forming bad habits." But the next day if she is nervous and unwilling to endure his noise, she yields "just for once." The result is that she gives in to her child more or less through his later childhood.

Again, with an older child, the mother will partially concede, a sort of compromise, and the child is keen enough to know that he has gained his point and each time he will seek to gain a little more, until the mother realizes when it is too late that her problem is great and her word really has very little weight.

My advice is: Be considerate in your requirements of a child and then be consistent in seeing that these requirements are carried out. Irritable, nagging mothers and unattractive, nervous children would be almost unknown if the former could realize the importance of kindness and consistency. Lack of sympathy and strained relations between parents and their older children often spring from habitual inconsistency.

Perhaps the most important thing of all is this. When you make a legitimate request you must know within yourself that you expect it to be carried out. Then if you are disobeyed you must calmly, but definitely and emphatically, see to it that your request is complied

with. This method cannot be practiced today and neglected tomorrow, but must be consistently followed.

The future happiness, character and well-being of your little one depends entirely upon firm, wise and consistent guidance. It is these fundamental qualities of mother-discipline that train the strong-willed little sons and daughters into splendid men and women.

Help to reach all the parents of the country by cutting this out and passing it on to a friend.

THE CHRISTIAN ORPHANAGE

THE CHILDREN'S HOME

There are fifty-seven children in the Christian Orphanage, six more accepted and thirty-five on the waiting list to be admitted and pleading to come at an early date.

How shall we meet the need? Build the home for the smaller children is the answer. Shall we as a Church let thirty-five children stand and knock at our doors pleading for a home and something to eat and to wear; pleading for a chance to make good in life, and refuse to help them?

We are now asking for twenty men to give us $500 each to build this home. We are asking for smaller subscriptions to equip this building when completed. We want every member of our Church and all friends of the little children to have a part in this home. So to enable one rich or poor to have a part we will take subscriptions for smaller amounts so you may get on the list and have the pleasure of having a part in this work.

All who give as much as $500.00 can give it in memory of some loved one as a memorial.

If you want to give $500.00 and don't feel able to pay it all in one year, let us have your subscription and pay $100.00 each year for five years. If you want to give a lesser amount you may pay it the same way if it will be more convenient to you. We want you to have a part in this undertaking.

If a church or a Sunday school wants to give $500.00 in memory of some faithful beloved member who has gone to the better world we will be glad to have subscriptions of that nature. We ought to raise enough money by November first to build this home or have it in subscriptions.

The Board of Trustees has authorized us to commence this building as soon as the money is in sight. Let us have your subscriptions right away. You want a part in this work of love and sweet sacrifice.

The heart of the Superintendent was made to rejoice last week when a citizen of Burlington who has a big heart of sympathy for the fatherless ones asked us to come to see him, and we went. He very kindly gave the Orphanage an outfit of furniture for the office consisting of a full office equipment in quartered oak with typewriter and all equipments for same.

This outfit consisted of twelve office chairs, one large desk, one typewriter desk, typewriter chair, one office desk chair, nice drugget and rug, book case, filing cabinet and number of other articles. This donation is very highly appreciated as we were very poorly equipped in this line and I know of no present that would have been more useful to us.

We are very grateful indeed and thank God that He has made such big hearted men who have a heart full of sympathy for His little ones and who are glad of the opportunity to lend them a helping hand.

CHAS. D. JOHNSTON, *Supt.*

REPORT FOR SEPTEMBER 10, 1919

Amount brought forward, $9,662.66.

Children's Offerings

Oliver E. Young, Jr., 20 cents.

Sunday School Monthly Offerings

(North Carolina Conference)

Christian Light, $4.63; Union Grove, $3.00; Pleasant Grove, $4.00; Ebenezer, $5.30.

(Eastern Virginia Conference)

Centerville, $1.00; Oakland, $5.30; Holy Neck, Young Men's Baracca Class, $1.73; Ivor, $2.61; Holland, $12.00; Mt. Carmel, $3.70.

(Virginia Valley Conference)

Wood's Chapel, $1.00; Wakefield, $5.14.

(Georgia and Alabama Conference)

Kite, Ga., $3.30; Corinth, Ala., $1.00; Spring Hill, Ala., $2.65; Total, $56.36.

Special Offerings

Mrs. Mary Griffith, Reidsville, N. C., $5.00; Mrs. May High, $1.00; A Friend, Snow Camp, N. C., $10.00; Total, $16.00.

Total for the week, $72.36; Grand total, $9,735.02.

A LETTER

Dear Uncle Charley: Daddy is back from Germany and we are now in Alabama. I like it, but I miss you all very much. Love and best wishes.—*Oliver E. Young, Jr.*

Glad your "daddy" is back from Germany, but sorry he carried you so far away. We miss you very much. You must work for the Orphanage in Alabama. —*"Uncle Charley."*

STIR US TO PRAY

Stir me, oh! stir me, Lord—I care not how,
  But stir my heart in passion for the world;
Stir me to give to go, but most to pray,
  Stir till the blood-red banner is unfurled
O'er lands that still in heathen darkness lie,
O'er deserts where no Cross is lifted high.

Stir me, oh; stir me, Lord, till prayer is pain,
  Till prayer is joy—till prayer turns into praise;
Stir me till heart and will and mind, yea, all
  Is wholly thine to use through all the days;
Stir, till I learn to pray "exceedingly,"
Stir, till I learn to wait expectantly.

—*Alliance Weekly.*

The difference between the regenerate and the unregenerate man is that the unregenerate man lives in sin, and he loves it; but the regenerate man lapses into sin, and he loathes it.—*A. J. Gordon.*

THE FORWARD MOVEMENT

(By Warren H. Denison, Superintendent)

The superintendent has had the privilege of meeting many of our church-workers and denominational leaders in a number of Conferences in various states, and has had a hearty welcome at all of the Conference sessions. The Conferences are all alive to the privileges that are offered to the churches through the Forward Movement program and the Conference officers are making every effort to carry the Forward Movement message into the most remote churches in the Conference.

The Western Indiana Conference, the Miami Ohio Conference and others are naming special committees or appointing definite officers whose duty it shall be to see that the work is begun and carried on in the several churches of the Conference. It seems to be in every section their honest effort to place the Forward Movement program in the heart and center of the Conference work and a determination on the part of the officers to see that the work is inaugurated in all of the churches.

The Forward Movement campaign will begin in New England about September 10 and the brethren there are enthusiastic. Our New England church realize the importance of the Forward Movement and are giving themselves whole heartedly to its plans and work.

Nearly all our colleges are now making a canvass for necessary endowment funds. Elon has just closed her campaign with three hundred and seventy-five thousand dollars pledged. Defiance is in the midst of a three hundred thousand dollar campaign. Palmer college has begun a two hundred and fifty thousand dollar campaign. Union Christian College has a one hundred thousand dollar campaign. Our educational institutions and are deserving of the money and of the young people from the homes of our church.

We hope that all the Conferences of the Southern Christian Convention which will soon begin their annual meetings, will join with the other Conferences in a strong Forward Movement program consisting of addresses round tables and a definite action, making it the duty of some person or persons to see that every church within the bounds of the Conference is reached with its message.

Have you secured "Money, the Acid Test"? If not, we hope you will do soon soon. We wish that book might be in the home of each family in the church. We hope our pastors will call attention to it.

Have you been developing your Sunday school in *Worship* and *Devotion* during the months of July, August and September? Many Sunday schools have been laying emphasize upon that particular, in accordance with the Forward Movement program of the denomination. A number of Sunday schools have placed books in their libraries, others have had talks each Sunday on some theme that would help develope devotion in worship. These three months of study and effort on the part of our Sunday school to develope worship and devotion, will bring about an enlarged spirit of worship in our whole church,

WORSHIP AND MEDITATION

SUPERSTITION KILLS

(An Editorial in The Christian Herald)

A girl in Kalamazoo read her future in cards and, having turned up a direful black ace killed herself.

It is not the sort of suicide that comes of superstition. Superstition kills. something in all of us. It kills something of faith reason, courage and right impulse in each of us.

Who can guess how many possibly great enterprises have aborted because people have feared to begin on a Friday and never found opportunity again?

- Who can estimate all the brave hearts that have turned faint, the good purposes that have been blasted, at some "sign" which seemed to foretell disaster?

We may laugh at the simple folks who are thus deluded, but we are apt to forget that superstition in innumerable forms lies at the very base of our moral being, as the blighting worm lies at the root of the rose.

Who knows to what heights, now undreamed of, courage and faith and hope might have lifted the world ere this, had not superstition, through all the ages, shackled mankind with fear and doubt and despair?

Superstition has formed the first filled man with fear and cowardice. It has taken iron out of the blood and fire out of the brain, and curdled in the heart the milk of human kindness.

Superstition has covered the seas with terrors and filled the forests with fearful things before which mankind has cowered, and exploration and discovery and development have been delayed for centuries.

Superstition, like the blackness of night, has hidden from the truths of physical science, of religion, of social ethics; and for what little trace he has got of them he has had to grope in doubt and fear.

Superstition caused the world to force the fatal poison on a Socrates, to put a Galileo to the rack, and to crucify the Christ. And just so has it killed out of the human heart much that is good and pure and sweet.

Superstition has been, through all time, the chief weapon of tyrants; it has ever afforded the chief hold for quacks and charlatans of all sorts and all degrees; it has ever made man a slave to the worst within himself and victim to the worst without.

Superstition has made the heart of man a cesspool of evil passions and has filled the world with malice, murders, wars, persecutions, poverty and endless woe and wrong, and has made history a hideous record of cruelties and crimes.

As the youth out in the night whistles and sings to make himself believe he is not afraid, but still starts and trembles at sight of every bush and post, so has mankind come whistling up the ages, but doubting shrinking, trembling, at every mile-post of progress.

Little wonder that these devil's whisperings, which have swayed the world, should prove too much for the reasoning and resistance of a simple girl in Kalamazoo.

There are superstitions also that lead to good?

No!

Nothing that does this is a superstition, but is a part of the eternal verities, a ray of the vital light divine.

Whatever makes the soul of man braver, more hopeful, more cheerful and kindlier has in it a gleam of heaven and the heart of truth, however distorted it may be in form.

LESSONS IN THE SCHOOL OF EXPERIENCE

Formerly Chaplain 133d and 318th Field Artillery, American Expeditionary Forces

(Carlyle Summerbell)

To those of us who have not completed our education, and to whom this world is an increasing revelation of divine wisdom, service in the American army in the great war, especially when we had the privilege of being chaplains, has been of immense advantage. Some of the things which impressed me and, I believe, many others, were the following:

1. A real appreciation of America and of American institutions as never before.

2. Recognizing without the help of the harsh tutorship of death, the great place in our life held by the home folks and the home.

3. The basal unity of the different phases of religion. At my last service with the 318th Field Artillery, Judaism, Christian Science, Catholicism, Protestantism, were represented, and we worked in harmony, as well as worshiped together, I myself have preached in a Roman Catholic church at the invitation of the priest.

4. The feeling that we were a part in the national machinery, and not simply a separate machine.

5. Disgust with men who assume the title of king, prince, kaiser, emperor, or potentate, by birth, and with men who give consideration to artificial titled nobility, who themselves are citizens of a republic. The world should be wise enough to leave princelings and kinglings alone.

6. The joy of being willing if necessary to give all.

7. The comradeship of the great souls who aspire to the highest and best.

8. To understand the truth that he that would save his life shall lose it, and he that would spend his life shall save it.

9. To find the pity of the great God for men in pain, in the delusion of lust, in the false or fool's paradise of drink, and the innate goodness of men in every condition and walk of life in the American army.

And after all, how can you tell which act is small, which great? These measurements are human, not divine. God's standard is very different from ours.—
G. H. Morrison.

CHRISTIAN EDUCATION

SUFFOLK LETTER

The *public* schools are opening all over this great country. They can no longer be called *free* schools. The cost of books, tablets, pencils, and other expenses make the *public* school a burden on the poor. The publishers of books are largely responsible for the too-frequent changes in text books. Books used by older children no longer pass down for use into the hands of younger brothers and sisters. The change requires *new* books. This creates an immense revenue for book-makers. It should not be so. The *public* school should teach fewer subjects, use books longer, and be a real boon to the poor. The *public* school is an overgrown institution and undertakes to do too much for the young. The tendency is toward the *State* doing *all* and the *individual* doing little. The truth is, that these capable of higher education should be under necessity of individual effort. Classics should not be taught in the public school.

Statistics show that there are 24,000,000 pupils in the *public* schools of the United States. That is nearly one-fourth of the population. There are 700,000 public school teachers engaged in the work of instructing the children and 500,000 of these teachers are females Only two sevenths of the teachers are males. The question of Woman Suffrage will be settled in the *public* schools. In this formative period of citizenship women control. The matter of feminine control is inevitable. In the home and in the school woman already has control. Her power is greater than the power of Congress. She bends the twig. She has changed the atmosphere of the *public* school-room. It is cleaner, it has more flowers, behavior has improved, improvement in manners, and a charm and dignity pervade the whole institution. Man is the fighting human; woman is the refining human. He legislates; she controls. She mothered the world's Redeemer; but He had no human father. Bethlehem set the standard of human supremacy. It was transferred from man to woman; and it will remain in her hands, unless she forgets her Lord. The all-important matter is for the young women, who teach in the public schools, to be genuine followers of the meek and lowly Jesus. Religious character in the public school teachers is a power greater than the Army and Navy; and that army of twenty-four million children may be the conquering army of the world some day. It is easy to see that the women and children hold the future destiny of this nation in their hands; but if God could trust His only Son and the hope of the world to the love and care of a woman, we may congratulate the future upon the great majority of public school teachers being women. There is no higher service, no greater opportunity, and no greater honor, than to be a good young woman engaged in public school work. That position represents more value and gets less pay than any other service.

W. W. STALEY.

PUBLIC WELFARE

The meaning of public welfare needs an immense enlargement in the public mind.

The stupidest man among us must be brought to see that it concerns the curse of illiteracy and near-illiteracy, commercial amusements and wholesome community recreation, preventable disease and postponable death, feeble-mindedness and its causes, insanity, poverty and its manifold relationships, orphan children in poor homes whose fathers are dead and orphan children in unsafe homes whose fathers and mothers are alive, the placing-out of children and their guardianship, wayward children, children maimed and lame in body and brain, the families of convicts in prison, returned convicts, prisoners on parole, men wanting jobs and jobs wanting men; that it concerns jail and chain-gang conditions, poor house and pauper conditions, juvenile courts and the oversight of juvenile probationers, fallen men and fallen women alike, and the whole subject of social hygiene; that it concerns the conditions, causes, consequences, and cure of social ills, of every sort; that it sweeps the whole immense field of social science, theoretic and applied.

To build a meaning of this adequate and needful sort in the public mind, to stir the consciences and wills of men and women into activity and to erect suitable institutions in North Carolina, county by county, is an exceedingly difficult but an exceedingly necessary task.
—*E. C. Branson, address before the N. C. Social Service Conference.*

A PATHETIC DEATH

Sic Transit Gloria Mundi.—What a pathetic description is that of Cardinal Mazarin, rousing himself from his dying bed at Vincennes to take a last look at the treasures which his long ascendency in the councils of the French Monarchy had enabled him to accumulate. When his nurses and doctors were away he rose from his couch, and with his tall figure, pale and wasted, closely wrapped in his fur-lined dressing-gown, he stole into the gallery; and the Count de Brienne, who reports the scene, hearing the shuffling sound of his slippers as he dragged his limbs feebly and wearily along, hid himself behind the curtains. As, in his extreme weakness, the Cardinal had to halt almost at each step, he feebly murmured, "I must leave all this." He crawled on, however, clinging, so as to support himself, first on one object and then on another, and as at each pause, exhausted by pain and weakness, he looked around the splendid room, he said again, with a deep sigh, "I must leave all this." Then, at last, he caught sight of Brienne. "Give me your hand," he said, "I am very weak and helpless, yet I like to walk, and I have something to do in the library." And then, leaning on the count's arm, he again pointed to the pictures. "Look at that beautiful Correggio, and this 'Venus' of Titian, and this incomparable 'Deluge' of Antonio Caracci. Ah! my poor friend, I must leave all this. Good-bye; dear pictures, which I have loved so well!"—*Dean Liddon.*

Sunday School and Christian Endeavor

SUNDAY SCHOOL LESSON FOR
SEPTEMBER 21, 1919

The Holy Scriptures. Ps. 19:7-14:
119:9-16, 97, 165; Acts 17:10-12; II
Tim. 3:14-17.

Devotional Reading: Ps. 1.

Golden Text: "Thy word is a
lamp unto my feet and a light unto
my path." Ps. 119:105.

(For Teaching Points, see Teachers and Officers Journal).

One of the saddest mistakes in life
is made when we lead children to
believe that the Word of God· is a
stiff, solemn book, full of "don'ts".
It is in reality the most wonderful
story book in the world, filled with
the most charming stories, the most
enthralling romances.   It contains
some of the best sanitary laws ever
written, some of the finest legal advice, and some of the best suggestions on every phase of human life.
Recently I read an article on "The
most exciting book in the world."
One would hardly think that of the
Bible, but a young man in a hospital
in Paris who had never before seen
a Bible, was handed a New Testament by the nurse one morning. He
accepted it, with some reluctance, but
she had nothing else.   The next day
she brought him a book of fiction.
"Take it away," he said impatiently, "I haven't got through with this
yet, and I want to see how it turns
out." There is nothing so dear to
us when we are away as a letter from
home. How we read it for news of
the homefolks, of the neighborhood
doings. We read thoughtfully and
carefully the bits of advice tucked
in by the dear homefolks. Perhaps
mother or sister has clipped a bit of
poetry and added it. But best of
all, would be the news tucked in at
the end that father or mother or
brother was coming to visit us by
and by, and that plans were on foot
for our own homecoming to which
all looked forward so eagerly. The
Bible is my Father's letter to me.
He has told me of all the "home·
folks" and all the neighborhood news
and we call that history.   He has
tucked in so many bits of advice and
loving counsel as He went along. He
has remembered to clip some bits of
wonderful poetry and insert for us.

And then, best of all, most wonderful of all, He has told us of the plans
He is making for our homecoming;
He tells us our room is ready and
waiting, and that we will be met by
friends and relatives when we arrive.
He tells us that our Elder Brother
is coming soon to visit us, and take
us back with Him when He goes, and
that never, never again will we be
separated. Surely our Father's Letter is worth a careful reading, and
a loving acceptance.

MRS. FRED BULLOCK.

**CHRISTIAN ENDEAVOR TOPIC FOR
SEPTEMBER 21, 1919**

Truthfulness. Eph: 4:25; 11 Kings
5:20-2.

"I believe in telling the truth, and
nothing but the truth, but not· the
whole truth," was a laughing remark
made lately. But is that not often
the feeling we have about the matter? Why do we take it for granted
that the truth must be unpleasant?
"To tell you the truth" is a common
beginning for an unpleasant statement. But truth is beautiful,' and
there are few things so disagreeable
that some fine thing can not be said
for it,—or them. If the truth is
necessary, its disagreeableness, however, ought not to keep us from telling it. "He never knowingly spoke
or acted a lie," was the high tribute
paid to a general in the army by one
who knew him well. "Acted a lie"! !
Many who would not speak a lie,
will act one, or evade the truth.
"Speak every man truth with his
neighbor." How many unfair advantages would be lost; how many
unfair bargains would never take
place. How much better a world
this would be in which to live if all
obeyed this first elementary law.

MRS. FRED BULLOCK.

MARRIAGES

RITENHOUR-FUNK

Mr. Wesley G. Ritenhour and Miss
Isabelle Funk were united in marriage on August 16, 1919, at the home
of Ernest Spitzer near New Hope
church, where the Virginia Valley
Central Conference was then in session. These two happy and fortunate young people journeyed from
Dry Run church in Powell's Fort to
New Hope for the double· purpose
of attending the Conference and having their pastor tie the knot while
there. They are a splendid couple,·
both are members of the Dry Run
church, and have the best wishes of
a host of friends. May their wedded
life be both happy and useful.

A. W. ANDES.

GAY-MASON

Prof. Samuel Rufus Gay of Cumberland, Md., and Miss Charlotte
Beatrice Mason of Nashville, N, C.,
were united in marriage Wednesday
P. M., August 20, 1919. It was a
double marriage. Mr. Jake W.
Batchelor and Miss Sallie Ricks Boddie, both of Nashville, being married
at the same time and at the same
altar. The Methodist church of Nashville which had been most beautifully
decorated with rare potted plants,
ferns and flowers, illuminated with
hundreds of candles, was packed
from chancel to gallery with admiring friends and neighbors gathered
to show the esteem in which the happy couples were held. Eighteen of
Nashville's most gifted singers rendered a becoming and appropriate
musical program just prior to the
ceremony. Mrs. M. W. Linche presided at the pipe organ and rendered thrilling instrumental selections;
Mrs. M. A. Ross sang an inspiring
solo, and the choir sang "The Bridal
Chorus." To the strains of Mendelssohn's Wedding March the bridal party entered the church. First
the ushers in opposite aisles and in
single file, Messrs. D. W. Perry, W.
C. Ferrell, M. C. Gulley and Arthur
S. Vick. These were followed with
bride's maid and groom's man. Mr.

Kenneth E. Bane with Miss Gladys Holleman of Smithfield, Va., followed by the dames of honor, Mesdames W. G. Dozier of Nashville, and C. C. Johnson of Elon College. The two ring bearers, little Rebecca Brooks Dozier of Nashville, and Mildred Taylor of Richmond, Va., were followed by the flower bearers, little Misses Iris Boddie and Erline Kent who scattered roses in the pathway of the bridal party from church entrance to altar. From the right vestibule door came Miss Sallie Ricks Boddie on the arm of her cousin, Mr. R. T. Vick, and from the left door Miss Beatrice Mason on the arm of her sister, Miss Gertrude Mason, her maid of honor. Near the chancel they were met by Mr. J. W. Batchelor attended by his brother as best man, Mr. Lewis Batchelor, and by Mr. S. R. Gay attended by his best man, Prof. W. C. Whitlock of Charlottesville, Va. Reaching the altar Mr. Batchelor stood beside his bride-to-be, Miss Sallie Ricks Boddie, and Mr. Samuel Rufus Gay stood beside his bride-to-be, Miss Charlotte Beatrice Mason. Revs. L. B. Jones and Oscar Creech of Nashville, and the writer, used the ring and souvenir ceremonies of the Methodist and Christian churches which united the two happy and popular couples. The brides' maids wore pink Georgette and carried white asters; the dames of honor wore white Georgette and carried asters; the maid of honor wore pink Georgette and carried white asters; the brides wore white Georgette and veil of tulle arranged with orange blossoms and carried shower bouquets of brides roses. The gentlemen were in full dress evening suits with white vests and white gloves. Immediately after the ceremony Prof. and Mrs. Gay left on an extended bridal tour to New York and other Northern cities. Prof. Gay is principal of Cumberland, Md. City High School. The bride is an Elon College graduate with host of friends and is herself a popular and successful teacher.

J. O. ATKINSON.

OBITUARIES

SIMMERS

Mrs. Hattie L. Simmers, wife of John Simmers, was born December 14, 1879, and died August 18, 1919, at the age of 39 years, 8 months, and 4 days. Surviving are two sisters, two brothers, her aged father, husband, and an infant son. Sister Simmers was a faithful member of the Linville Christian church. She was a general favorite among a large circle of friends, who deeply mourn her untimely death. This breaking up of a happy home calls forth the deepest sympathy for the husband and little motherless babe. Funeral services were conducted at Linville, August 20, by the writer, assisted by Rev. I. W. Miller of the Church of the Brethren. May the Lord comfort and bless the sorrowing, and prepare us all for a happy home in eternity.

A. W. ANDES.

MOORE

Rev. H. C. Moore was born March 13, 1851, and died July 20, 1919. His age was 68 years, 4 months, and 7 days. He was married to Miss Mary R. Davis in 1869. Was licensed to preach by the Eastern Virginia Conference at Spring Hill, Nansemond County, Virginia, August 6, 1881. He preached at various places in Eastern Virginia, and for several years was pastor of churches in the Virginia Valley Conference. He had about retired from the active ministry, and was living in Charlottesville, Virginia, when death called him from labor to reward. Brother Moore was an honest, conscientious preacher of the Word, and wielded quite and influence for good. His many friends where he lived and labored during his life will mourn his death. His wife's death occurred just three months prior to his. Six sons and two daughters survive. Funeral services were held at the home in Charlottesville, Va., July 22.

A. W. ANDES.

LEWIS

On August 21, 1919 Mr. J. D. Lewis died at Riverside Hospital, Newport News, Va. Prior to his death Brother Lewis had not been well and went to the hospital for an operation and complications arose which caused his death.

He was a member of Antioch Christian church, near Windsor, Va. He was a man of sterling qualities and thoroughly devoted to his wife and two daughters, who mourn the loss of their father and husband. May God's richest blessing rest upon them and may Christ the great Healer be comfort in this time of sorrow.

The funeral was conducted by the writer at the home on Sunday afternoon, August 24, 1919. The interment was in Green Lawn Cemetery,

H. J. FLEMING.

LAWRENCE

Mrs. E. B. Lawrence died at her home in Brickhaven, Chatham County, N. C., July 4, 1919. She was educated at Elon College in the business department and was assistant postmaster at Morrisville, N. C., for about three years. She made friends wherever she went. She leaves to mourn their loss a father, and mother, Mr. and Mrs. H. T. Johnson, Morrisville, N. C., a husband, two children, the youngest being only five days old, four sisters and three brothers. She was buried at the home cemetery. May God bless those who are left to mourn their loss.

W. G. CLEMENTS.

Irish beggar: "Please give a poor old blind man a dime."

Citizen: "Why, you can see out of one eye."

Irish beggar: "Well, then, give me a nickel."—Exchange.

ANTI-DISMALS

"Nellie is just like cider, so sweet until she starts to work."—*Michigan Gargoyle.*

* *

Sign in theater lobby: ."Crying children must be immediately taken out or we will refuse to admit them."

* *

"I understand your neighbor keeps chickens."

"Not exactly. He owns chickens, but my garden furnishes their keep."

* *

"Wilbur, dear, you mustn't eat your jelly with your spoon."

"I have to, mother. I put it on my bread, but it wouldn't stay there; it's too nervous."—*The Delineator.*

* *

"Is that young lady I saw you with the other day your wife or sister?"

"Er—I haven't asked her yet."—*Judge.*

* *

"Are you troubled much in your neighborhood with borrowing?"

"Yes, a good deal. My neighbors never seem to have a thing I want."—*The Bulletin.*

* *

Bobby was saying his prayer in a very low voice. "I can't hear you dear," whispered his mother.

"I wasn't talking to you," replied Bobbly firmly.

* *

Polly: "What's Freddy crying for?"

Dolly: "Because he dug a big hole in the garden, and mamma won't let him bring it into the house."

* *

Scout (to an old farmer): "Will you take my coat to town?"

Farmer: "Sure I will. But how are you going to get it?"

Scout: "Oh, I intend to remain in it."—*Exchange.*

* *

The Dentist: "Thought you said this tooth hadn't been filled before?"

The Patient (feebly): "No, it hasn't."

The Dentist: "Well, there are traces of gold on my instrument."

The Patient (more feebly): "Perhaps you've struck my back collar stud!"—*The Passing Show.*

The street-car conductor examined the transfer thoughtfully and said meekly, "This here transfer expired an hour ago, lady."

The lady, digging into her purse after a coin, replied, "No wonder, with not a single ventilator open in the whole car!"—*Exchange.*

* *

"You say your laundry woman reminds you of a good preacher?"

"Yes; she's always bringing things home to me that I never saw before."
—*Boston Transcript.*

"What has become of your niece, Miss Murphy, Mrs. O'Rafferty?"

"Och, sure, an' she's done well wid herself. She married a lord."

"Why, you don't tell me! An English lord?"

"No, I don't think he's an English lord. He's a landlord. He kapes a hotel out in Indiana."—*Exchange.*

* *

Head: "Well, O'Brien, what are you doing out of bed?"

O'Brien: "I just got out to tuck myself in."

THE CHRISTIAN SUN

"IN ESSENTIALS UNITY, IN NON-ESSENTIALS LIBERTY, IN ALL THINGS CHARITY"

LET US BE RIGHT

(By Clarence B. Flynn, in The Christian Life Magazine)

Let us be right, though all the world may follow
  The broken fabric of some failing dream.
As sounds upon our ears its outcry hollow,
  And men lose all for some deceiving scheme,
Let us forsake the gold and tinsel masking,
  And live for things enduring and secure.
Whate'er the prize the idle crowd is asking,
  Let us be right. The path of truth is sure.

Let us be right, whatever seem our losing,
  Some day the tide will turn, and men will know
The thing abiding. Then the common choosing
  Will be the substance, not the empty show.
Let us be right. When self's poor plans are shattered
  And all the castles lifted mountain high
By evil hand, are broken down and shattered,
  The right shall stand beneath the mighty sky.

Volume LXXI	WEDNESDAY, SEPTEMBER 17, 1919	Number 38
BURLINGTON	· · ·	NORTH CAROLINA

THE CHRISTIAN SUN
Founded 1844 by Rev. Daniel W. Kerr

C. B. RIDDLE   -   -   -   **Editor**

Entered at the Burlington, N. C. Post Office as second class matter.

Subscription Rates

One year .... $ 2.00
Six months 1.00

In Advance

Give both your old and new postoffice when asking that your address be changed.

The change of your label is your receipt for money. Written receipts sent upon request.

Many persons subscribe for friends, intending that the paper be stopped at the end of the year. If instructions are given to this effect, they will receive attention at the proper time.

Marriage and obituary notices not exceeding 150 words printed free if received within 60 days from date of event, all over this at the rate of one-half cent a word.

Original poetry not accepted for publication.

Principles of the Christian Church

(1) The Lord Jesus Christ is the only Head of the Church.

(2) Christian is a sufficient name of the Church.

(3) The Holy Bible is a sufficient rule of faith and practice.

(4) Christian character is a sufficient test of fellowship, and of church membership.

(5) The right of private judgment and the liberty of conscience is a right and a privilege that should be accorded to, and exercised by all.

EDITORIAL

FACING THE ISSUE

We are facing the issue—that issue of ministerial help. There is no getting around it. Many churches are without pastors, and many of those who have pastors should have more and better services. This is especially true of the churches in the rural districts. We are in a position to know. This office is reminded of it practically every day and the issue is getting more acute. There must be something done.

We are not criticizing, and if this article is so taken, then, dear reader, give us the credit of offering constructive criticism, for we hope to point out a partial remedy.

The whole system of dealing with candidates for the ministry in the Conferences must be changed. We have taken young men at their word, let them join the Biblical Class, stay in college or out just as they desired. If they wanted to drop out and take churches, all well and good. The Conferences have lowered the standard, or rather they have never put it high enough. We have never favored giving young men churches until they reached the middle of their college course. It may seem cruel, it may seem wrong, but the facts are

against such a system. The young men have meant well, the Conferences have meant well, and so have the churches, but the fruit is how you tell about the sowing.

Today we tried to think of the many young men whom we have known in Conference and college during the last half dozen years, and only the smaller per cent can we place. Where are they? We do not know. Their names are not on the subscription records in this office; and most certainly if they are doing anything worth while, they would support the Church paper. We turn through the *Annual* of a few years ago and find many names recorded, and then return to the records of the last two or three years, and these names are not found. Turn to the records at Elon College and make a list of the men of our Church who have matriculated as ministerial students, then check that with the ministerial roll in the last *Annual*. It will be a discovery worth while.

What has the result been? Young men have taken church work in order to supply the churches without a pastor. By this method they meant well, but there are still more churches without pastors and the number is increasing. Why? With limited education, short experience, and not knowing how to overcome some of the pastoral problems, they have become discouraged and dropped out. They do not represent that type of leadership so necessary for the progress of the work. Their messages have not given that impulse for larger things; their personality has not been strong enough to turn the tide of the "ruts" in the local church and transform a community. They have shouldered a burden too heavy for their experience, while the churches that they have served have gone backward for the lack of a vision.

Is this all? Not quite. The dropping out of the ministerial students, their failure to make good, and their type of work, all have discouraged those who would enter the work and carry it to a successful completion. Men like great and heroic tasks and are always willing to do the thing that the other fellow has succeeded in, regardless of the difficulties.

The Conferences have been looking out that no conscience would be hurt; they have been very careful that no young man would be turned down and "humiliated." Thoughtful, considerate, great. But churches have been "humiliated," the denomination has been retarded and the growth of the Kingdom hindered. The issue is this: The larger or the smaller thing under consideration. The churches, the denomination, or the man? Which is greater?

You say that we must pray the young men into the work. True. And it is also true that we must not be so prayerful as to pray them out. Any real man is ready to prove himself, and that is just what the Conferences need to have these young men do. By permitting a young man to preach his way through college may be the most expensive way after all. It might be better for his Conference to *give* him the money for his education, and say to him that he must make good during the years of his preparation. He needs the practice, we will grant, but our experience is that practice is easier obtained than training. We have seen the young men side by side in this very thing, and our observation is this: In most cases the young men who preach during their college days preach better for a while after graduation than their comrades, but in a few years the men who placed emphasis on preparation while in college and gave less attention to church work, are those who become the strongest men. There are of course, exceptions to all rules.

No young man should be admitted to the Biblical Class until he has reached his Freshman year in college. (Some of the Conferences are requiring this).

No young man should be given church work until he has completed his Sophomore year, and then not more than one church.

No young man should be ordained until he has completed his Junior year.

No young man should shoulder full time church work until he has completed his Senior year.

These are the remedies that will add to the efficiency of the Church, add to her power, add to her leadership, challenge the young men and help to solve the problem of ministerial supply. We have made the job too little. By so doing we have driven from the ranks some of the best men and wisest heads, the noblest hearts, and we are now face to face with the issue. Can we meet it? Will we meet it? We leave the answer with the Committee on Education in the various Conferences.

The Church of God is still the Church of God, and when we use it otherwise it ceases to be the dedicated temple of the Lord.

"MARY HAS GONE TO COLLEGE"

You have heard of Mary and her little lamb in all its forms, feats and fashions. Mary is popular. The name "Mary" is a household word everywhere. History tells us about one Mary in the Savior's day, and so it is Mary that we want to talk about.

Yes, Mary has gone to college! We don't know whose Mary, but Mary has gone. She packed her trunk one afternoon last week, slept only a few hours that night and hurried away next morning to take the train for college. Station after station she passed, and then the porter called out the college station. What a thrill went through Mary's heart! She sighed deeply, arose from her seat, and soon landed among the talkingest, strangest, laughiest and most gleeful crowd she was ever in. Such names! Why Mary had never heard such names before. And there were so many to help her with her baggage, tell her about the college, about what a good time she was going to have and how glad that they were to see her!

Up to this place Mary has had a good time. She is now settled in her work and has received a letter from home and the homefolks have received one from her. She has told them about the things that she likes and the things that she dislikes. It's a wonderful subject to write on, and it is no trouble to close the letter at a mid-night hour. It is a wonderful world into which Mary has been cast and her experiences are varied.

We are not uneasy about Mary, for she is all right and will soon gain her independence, know how to associate with other girls, and it will not be long before she will fall in love with all the college and surroundings.

Our fears come here: That mother—just that sympathizing mother—will write Mary and agree with her on the things she dislikes, and encourage her to come home if everything doesn't suit Mary. A big hearted mother she is. God bless her and all her kind. But Mary, her only daughter, is trying life alone for the first time and that good mother forgets that Mary cannot always be at home, and so she writes her a letter that is discouraging. She tells Mary all about the young folks and what a good time they have had at the community school, and at the country church. She tells Mary how many young men have called her over the telephone and the papers and other pieces of mail that she has at home that cannot be forwarded; she tells Mary all about the loaded scuppernong vine and how bushels are going to waste. Now, Mary has always had a good time under that vine and her mother's letter makes her feel that something great will happen if she misses the fruit of this season.

Mary gets this letter and she reads it, and she reads it, and she reads it. She tells her room-mate that she believes that she will go home, and the next day on class she doesn't know a thing about the lesson, and she decides that the professor does not know a thing about the subject. The next meal is anything but ideal. Mary hears the sound of a train, and though she was tired from the trip getting to college, and felt that she would never care to ride on the train again, she decides that she wants to go home at once. The president of the college is consulted and matrons are confused. Her friends persuade her but all of no avail. Mary goes home.

Alas, we have called this person Mary, but it can be a Johnny or a Jimmy or a Charley, and too, it can be a father to write such a letter. Too bad!

Next week we will write on what happened after Mary got home and the years thereafter.

Giving is the first essential of getting, and yet we proceed in the capacity of getting and ignore this fundamental thing in life.

"HE CAN LIVE UPON IT"

These are the words spoken by a friend one day when we were talking to him about his pastor's salary. Oh, yes, we agree that he may be able to live upon it, but can he die upon it? That is the question.

In business? Why, then are you just making enough to live upon and laying nothing aside for the family? How about the "rainy day"? How about those children now at your knee, but one day will, or should be, in college? How about the old age when churches will seek younger men? How about the time when you are disabled to preach?

A farmer? Yes, and just meeting expenses and laying aside nothing for the poor crop years? Are you not paying for that piece of land? And if you are, then what for? Of course it is providing for the day when your earning capacity will be less. Do you own your farm, and yet say that the pastor can live upon his usual salary? Then sell the farm and get on a basis with your pastor. Provide not for the days to come.

Come and let us reason together: Poor encouragement it is for the pastor to have nothing left over at the end of the month, or at the end of the year. Poor indeed is the encouragement. One day he must die, and perhaps he will die before his wife does, and is he to leave her with just a week's provision? Is he to leave nothing for the education of his children? Is he to go to his death-bed with the thought that he has advocated peace, prosperity, happiness and the reasonable things in life, and yet leave his family to the cold world. Ah! The thought is too fearful. What a dread it has!

Yes, the pastor lives on his salary, but can he die upon it? If a man who does not provide for his own household is worse than a thief, in the name of heaven tell us how those are classed who force their pastor to be a thief? Pretty plain? Well and good, for that is the way we mean it.

A genuine sacrifice precedes our best joys. Giving of bread to the poor when we have plenty left is far from giving when we have little or none left.

THE BALANCED MIND

This is a time when the balanced mind is in demand. So many things are now before the people that are the fruit of radicalism and extremity that it is so easy to be lead astray by some mind that thinks only on one side of a question. No one thing alone is the cause of social unrest, labor troubles and the general tendency of the present day, and it is unfair to so see the situation. No one remedy alone can cure these evils, and again it is unfair to say that your idea is *it* above all others.

Study both sides of any question. Be liberal and well balanced in your opinions. Do not let feeling and prejudice interfere with justice. Be balanced in mind, for this age needs you.

A principle is greater and bigger than a creed. A creed is an *attempt* to circumscribe a principle. A principle enlarges itself to give justice.

RACE RIOTS DISCUSSED

For the purpose of discussing the inter-racial situation in the country as manifested in the Chicago race riots, a representative group of leaders of the Christian Church of all denominations both North and South met in the office of the Home Missions Council, New York City, September 4. Representatives of several philanthropic and sociological organizations were present, the purpose being to secure the widest possible activity in a nation-wide movement for the bettering of relations between the white people and the Negroes and for the development of a satisfactory program to meet the present Negro situation. A committee on pronouncement will report through the Federal Council of Churches of Christ in America. Bishop Wilbur P. Thirkield of New Orleans, Chairman of the Committee of Negro Churches of the Federal Council of Churches of Christ in America, presided. Dr. Alfred Williams Anthony, Secretary of the Home Missions Council, was secretary of the Committee. It was the unanious opinion of those present that the Negro situation in both North and South is critical; that it is no longer a sectional but a national problem and that it is the immediate duty of the churches and of all earnest, patriotic men and women throughout the land courageously to meet the issue.

The present generation brought up on cake raffles, tea parties, toy shows, oyster stews, and the hundred other man-made methods of financing the Kingdom, will produce a generation of church starvers.

INDIAN CONFERENCE

The Central Committee on Indian Affairs announces that the place of the conference on Indian affairs called for September 24-26 has been changed from Oklahoma City to the Hotel Lassen, Wichita, Kansas. The Hon. Cato Sells, Commissioner of Indian Affairs, and others from the Department of the Interior will be present and take part in the conference, which is one of the resent-day evidence of co-operation on the part of the Christian Church.

BIBLE SUNDAY—DECEMBER SEVENTH
Let All Unite to Magnify the Word of God

Have you ever tried to imagine a world without a Bible? Suppose, for instance, that by some miraculous means, the Bible and its influence could be erased from the history man. Instantly thousands upon thousands of beautiful churches and cathedrals would become senseless edifices, and the sacred ideals for which they stand, meaningless nonsense. You and I would not know from whence we came, nor whither we were bound, or for what purpose we lived, and death we would regard with a sickening sensation of horror. Much of our finest literature would be no more. The world's most famous paintings would fade from their canvasses, and a great deal of its best music be silenced forever. This may seem like a startling statement, but it takes something of the sort to make us stop and think how much we owe to our Bible.

"Oh," I hear you say, "of course I know how much we owe to the Bible." That is just the point; you stated it yourself in those two words, *of course*. That is just how a great many of us think of the Bible, as a matter *of course*. Just as a great many families love mother. Of course they love her, but mother has to go away for a visit before sister realizes that the dust does not stay out of the parlor of its own accord. Father finds that the buttons are not irrevocably attached to his clothes, and brother discovers that his shirts do not go to the laundry unless they are sent *Then* they begin to appreciate mother, not as a matter of course, but as a real, vital, necessary part of their lives. Is that the way you appreciate your Bible?

You honor your flag, don't you? On Flag Day everyone mentions the fact that this is the day set apart to do honor to the flag, and nearly all of us hang one in the window or wear a bit of flag ribbon on our coats. What do you do on *Bible Sunday?* Do you mention the fact that this is Bible Sunday at the breakfast table? Do you suggest to your pastor that some special recognition of the fact he made in the morning service? Do you give a special Bible talk to your Sunday school class? Or do you just let it slide by as a matter of course? Is it to you the Book of books, the Companion of your daily life, or is it just something that gives a solid respectable look to the parlor table, and helps to furnish the family pew?

December the seventh, the third Sunday before Christmas, is Bible Sunday. The idea of Bible Sunday is that one and the same day all Christians everywhere shall unite to exalt the Word of God. The necessity for the observance of one special Sunday when the Book of Life shall be the theme of prayer and teaching, the wider circulation of which shall become the zeal of the church, is at once apparent and commendable. There is special value that all unite on one day. An individualistic and scattered cheer would not make much impression compared with the cheer from a thousand throats shouted simultaneously. The Anglican and Episcopal church has for centuries emphasized the Bible on this day. The New York Bible Society, taking this Sunday which is near to December 4, the day on which the Society was organized 110 years ago, has enlisted the endorsement of official bodies of the Presbyterian, Reformed, Methodist and Baptist Churches The International Sunday School Association has recommended that every Sunday school observe this Sunday as Bible Sunday. The annual observance of this day must result in an intensity of purpose, and a fraternal spirit that will tend to magnify Jesus Christ through the honoring of the Word. The Bible is the Book of Life and power, and there is greater need of emphasizing its value today than ever before. We suggest that you start now to plan in what way you will observe it. Find out what is going to be done in the church service and in the Sunday school. Remind your pastor so he will have time to prepare an appropriate sermon. If more church members asked their pastors to preach on the Bible, fewer of the men in the pulpit would be wandering so far afield. The church that loves the Bible the most is invariably the strongest church.

Literature giving suggestions and information regarding Bible Sunday and its observance can be obtained by writing the New York Bible Society, 675 Madison Ave., New York. John C. West is President; James H Schmelzel, Treasurer and Rev. George William Carter, Ph.D., the General Secretary.

CORRESPONDENCE

The following letter was received by Captain James A. Turrentine from Dr. W. W. Staley. We have asked permission from Captain Turrentine to publish it, feeling that its message will be received with sincere appreciation by the large number of friends of Mrs. Fix:

APPRECIATES THE LIFE OF MRS. JOSEPH FIX

Capt. Jas. A. Turrentine,
    Burlington, N. C.
My dear Brother:

I am writing you, as the representative of the family, to whom I desire to express my appreciation of the character and life of your sister, Mrs. Joseph Fix. I can see them, now, in New Providence church when that church housed the worshippers from Company Shops, Haw River, Graham and a large scope of country besides. She filled out her four score years and then went to rest. "Gathering Homeward, one by one" was a sweet little song we used to sing in Providence Sunday school and is real in human experience.

If you have opportunity extend my sympathy to other members of the family, and believe me to be one of your true friends.
                                    W. W. STALEY.
Suffolk, Va.
September 8, 1919.

The letter printed below was sent to THE SUN office by a member of the mechanical force, Mr. J. M. Vestal, and we deem it worthy of publication. Mr. Vestal is a member of the Baptist Church, but possibly knows more about the details of the Christian Church than many of our members who are considered church leaders. His privilege of reading in detail every item of news printed in THE CHRISTIAN SUN and the *Christian Annual* gives him opportunity for constant study of our Church and its work:

APPRECIATES RECOGNITION

Rev. C. B. Riddle,
    Burlington, N. C.
My dear Mr. Riddle:—

In your issue of September 3, I was surprised, but very glad, to find an article under the caption of "A Consideration and an Appreciation," which speaks of me and my work as a linotype operator, and which also carried my response to the address of welcome delivered to my former teachers and friends at Morganton, N. C.

Through the columns of your excellent Church paper I am trying to express my appreciation for the good and kind words spoken of me, and to say that I appreciate it so much is only putting it mildly. Perhaps our English language is below par for I find myself in the same position as the poet who rarely, if ever, can put on paper that which he feels.

I am so glad that you thought my address worthy for public reading and it has greatly encouraged me. With some more such public sentiments, we deaf people would feel that we are crawling out of the harness of pity which has held us for so long.

You may not know it, but I have learned a great deal from your good paper. Your editorials, along with a good many other articles, never fail to give me light on many subjects. I am violating no confidence when I say that you are among the leading editors of this country, and your Church is fortunate in having you at the head of its paper. Your linotype operator knows whereof he speaks for he knows what it takes to turn out a good paper.

Again thanking you for your favors in words and deeds, and whenever I can be of service to you, command me.

Very Sincerely yours,

J. M. VESTAL.

September 11, 1919.

PASTOR AND PEOPLE

AMONG MY CHURCHES
(Plymouth)

When, on last Saturday afternoon, I started into the pulpit to preach at Plymouth church, I found the pulpit partially filled with packages of various sizes and shapes. On inquiring as to what that meant, I was informed that it was a "pounding" for the pastor. However, when I reached my home Monday morning with Mr. B. N. Ferrell's Dodge car almost loaded down, a visiting lady at my home remarked that she thought it was a "busheling" instead of a pounding.

There was something like sixty pounds of flour, one and one-half bushels of sweet potatoes, more than five pecks of apples and pears, three young chickens, about three pecks of corn meal, as well as Irish potatoes, bacon, coffee, oatmeal, preserves, jelly, molasses, dried apples, laundry soap, baking soda, lard, canned tomatoes, salmon, sausage meat, and some cloth. Little Miss Evelyn Partin also give me a dime as her part in the pounding. I was filled too full of the sense of gratitude and a feeling of my unworthiness to express, in words, my thanks and appreciation to these good people as I wished to.

This is my second year as pastor of Plymouth church; these good and appreciative people have long been very dear and sweet to me. I am much encouraged about the work here.

We held our annual memorial services the first Sunday in May of this year.

We held our revival, here, during the week following the first Sunday in August. Rev. W. L. Wells did the preaching, during this revival, from Monday afternoon until Thursday night. His preaching was able and effective; and our people were simply "carried away with him." Brother Wells is not only a good preacher, but is an exceptionally good personal worker. As direct result of this revival, there were three additions to the church at the close of the meeting. Three more united with the church last Sunday as a direct result of revivals in M. E. churches in the community. One of these new members is a wife and mother. The other five are grown young people—or, practically grown.

We are planning to repair and remodel our house of worship at Plymouth this fall. The work of raising the necessary funds and of deciding on the changes to be made is already under way.

Last Sunday this church extended me a call to serve another year. While the matter of acceptance is still under consideration, I should feel loathe to say "No" to them. I have long since learned to love the members very much; and feel that I can never do enough for them. My family joins me in thanking them for the very liberal "pounding" in a time of need.

R. P. CRUMPLER.

Varina, N. C.

SUFFOLK LETTER

A man said to me the other day: "I do not measure a Christian man's honesty by his meeting his commercial obligations, but by his payment of his church obligations;" for, said he, "if he pays his church obligations regularly, he will meet his commercial obligations." If that view is correct, one can see that the systematic habit of paying church dues, and more, the habit of all church members paying regularly their church dues would save much commercial trouble with little accounts which so often are unpaid. It may seem a small matter, at first thought of it, but a more thoughtful consideration of the subject will make it clear that church obligations include commercial obligations because our first duty is to God and our second duty is to man.

The apostolic rule was, "upon the first day of the week let every one of you lay by him in store, as God has prospered him, that there be no gatherings when I come." I Cor. 16:2. There are four things included in this rule: 1. Weekly system—first day of week. 2. *Every one* of you. Every member should make a separate contribution *every week* or *every month* as the meetings may be held; but it should be laid by in store *every week*. This habit is educational and begets thoughtfulness. 3. According to prosperity—"as God has prospered him." When people earn more, they should give more. To maintain that habit would fill the Lord's treasury, and develop his followers. This rule, if obeyed, would make the poor give more than they do, and the rich give abundantly. 4. To prevent the day of worship from being a day for *trying* to raise money. It should be already in hand and ready for the treasury. The cultivation of this four-fold rule would keep money in the treasury, so that the church would not have to devise means for raising money, but the committee would simply have to appropriate money; and that would be a delightful service. As it is, in most congregations, the task is to raise money. It should not be so.

Such a system, wrought into a fixed habit, would develop such a spirit of religious and commercial honesty, that commercial obligations would be met without trouble or criticism. The outsider usually gets his idea that church people do not pay their bills any better than non-church people from those church people who make no systematic contributions to their church. Consider church members who make weekly and liberal contributions to their church and find out whether they pay their grocery and other bills. By this standard judge the church on the financial line. *System* is the word for church finance. The Postal Department if Government may illustrate system. Each letter costs only two cents; but every person who uses the mail pays the two cents. Every person who is a member of the church should make regular offerings; five cents a week would probably be the smallest offering; then ten cents, fifteen cents, twenty cents, twenty-five cents, fifty cents, one dollar, and on up according to personal property. Some rich people prefer to wait for months and then give check; but they lose the benefit of *thinking* of it weekly, and others lose the benefit of their example putting in the envelope every Sunday.

I overlooked, somehow, Rev. L. F. Johnson, D. D., of Brooklyn, N. Y., who delivered a very helpful and delightful course of lectures on the Acts of the Apostles at the Valley Virginia Central Conference, and thereby made a spiritual contribution to the excellent business session of that body.

W. W. STALEY.

NOTES

Rev. J. L. Foster was in this section last week for a few days rest and in the interest of some property.

Rev. W. G. Clements, Morrisville, N. C., sends greetings to all the brethren and sisters. We miss Brother Clements' occasional visits since his impaired health.

We are informed that Dr. D. A. Long will not return to his present field another year. He is serving Pleasant Hill (Alamance County), Liberty, N. C., and Salem Chapel.

The church at Burlington is nearing completion. The total spent to date is a little over thirty-five thousand dollars, and the estimate to complete it is about ten or twelve thousand more.

The Board of Religious Education of the Southern Christian Convention was in session at Raleigh, N. C., on Thursday night, September 11. At this writing we have no report as to what was done, but presume that a full report will be furnished for next week's paper.

Brother E. L. Aldridge, Altamahaw, N. C., R. F. D. No. 2, and a member of Concord church, was in to see us the other day. Brother Aldridge says that he once thought that he was not able to pay for his Church paper, but now since he wants it, that such an idea seems foolish.

Rev. Stanley C. Harrell has recently received his discharge as a Chaplain and is now in a position to consider a call to some church or groups of churches. Brother Harrell is a young man, well educated, having served as pastor several years. Some church in need of
(Continued on Page 10)

MISSIONARY

HELPING WIN THE WORLD FOR CHRIST

July 8 to August 1 the Methodist Episcopal Church held a training Conference at Evanston, Ill., for its newly appointed missionaries. Over one hundred were present, and immediately after the Conference the entire number left for their appointed fields, in various parts of the world. Happy indeed is that Church which can send out at one time over one hundred new recruits to help win this world to Christ in those regions where our blessed Gospel has never been known, and so has had no chance. A people who have for more than fifty years turned every Sunday school class into a missionary class may expect to raise over one hundred million dollars for missions in a few months and then may expect men and women to volunteer by the hundreds to go into all parts of the world for Christ.

The Presbyterians who are also busy raising a new era fund of millions are sending out one hundred and ten new recruits to various foreign fields and the Reformed Church is sending out twenty-two new missionaries. Our Father in Heaven, in His wisdom and discretion, has never yet let a church grow at home and become powerful in winning souls here until that church has become willing to send missionaries abroad, and seek to enter into His program of winning the whole wide world for Him.

Our dear Christian Church will grow and become powerful in the world one day; but under God's wisdom that day will never dawn until we become worldwide in vision and give our supreme effort to helping win a whole world through and by a whole Gospel.

CRADLE ROLL DAY

Quite a number of our women are making the children happy by having a "Missionary Cradle Roll Day." Mrs. A. T. Banks writes of such a day, in her church: "The Missionary Cradle Roll Day was observed in Ramseur Christian church first Sunday in July. An interesting program was carried out by the children. The offering received was $7.79. Mrs. I. H. Foust is the efficient superintendent of this work. The following Wednesday the mothers and babies were invited by the Woman's Missionary Society to its regular meeting at the home of Mrs. Foust, after which an afternoon of social pleasure was enjoyed. Ice cream, cake, lemonade and fruit were served by the Society in honor of the visiting guests. The mothers were delighted and the babies had a good time. I believe the meeting will mean much for our mission work here." Of course, it will mean much. That which is done in the Master's name to help kindle interest in the souls of the unsaved millions in pagan lands who have no opportunity of knowing of our Christ and His blessed Gospel always means much. If we had women like Sister Banks in every church and congregation, it would not be long before our dear Church would be awake to our duty and privileges in the mission field. May the good work continue.

J. O. ATKINSON.

OUR RESPONSIBILITY AS A MISSIONARY PEOPLE*

Since time began there has never been anything to compare to the position which America now holds in the world. For the first time in all history one nation is looked upon by all other nations as the unselfish and universal friend of all, leading out into a new day of international brotherhood.

Will it be possible now for America to transform that patriotism to a larger morn until its loyalty and its fervor shall be as intense and unselfish for the flag of the Cross in world dominion in the days of peace as it was for "Old Glory" in time of war? Will men and women continue to pour out their money with generous prodigality for the weak and defenseless, and for the finer services of humanity? Will our young men and young women be as ready to put something big and fine and wonderful into the world life by their living and giving day by day as they were ready to die for these things on the field of battle? In this new and more difficult undertaking, whatever may be the tasks of the Government and of industry, the larger responsibility will fall upon the Church of Christ.

The conflict is ours. We of the Christian Church must shoulder our part of this great responsibility and obey the Master's call: "Go ye into all the world and preach the Gospel," which was not spoken in a faraway sense alone. It included the land of Jesus' own sacred presence as well as the uttermost ends of the earth. Home Missions are building the base behind Foreign Missions. We now have Home Mission churches in twenty-four towns and cities in the United States and Canada and mission work is being done in Northern Alabama, Eastern New York and Eastern Wyoming. There are fifty million people in America unaffiliated with any religion. There are said to be one and a half million Latin Americans (most of whom are illiterate) in the Southwestern part of the United States. More than half the population of El Paso, Texas (a city of 60,000 people) is made up of refugees from Mexico.

There is a call of the West today, by Rev. W. S. Alexander, for workers. The majority of the "Loggers," as they are called in the West, were of a rough class. But gradually a better class began to come, more stable in character and purpose. They bought homes; saw the danger lurking in the cities and began to "clean up;" they closed the bar-rooms and dance halls, and in 1912 the loggers and the women united forces and have voted the coast countries dry. The "logger" has good roads, cleaner camps, reads more, work eight hours a day, where before he worked from day light until dark, Sunday included. Yet with all his material advancement, he has not been drawn to church. He needs to have Jesus Christ taken to him, in his camp, on week days as well as on Sundays; he needs wholesome Christian literature, for he now has time for reading. The West's greatest need, says Mr. Alexander, is religion, and no other organization has anything better than the Christian Church. The ringing call sounds forth. We are responsible to the degree of our power. Great changes are taking place. Characteristic qualities necessary to win are: A clear vision of future possibilities; willingness to assume our full share of responsibility; wisdom to embrace our opportunity; persistence; moral courage; self-sacrifice and endurance to push to a successful conclusion the work needed. The fight is on, whose will be the victory? All things are possible with God.

*Paper read before the Durham Sunday school on Mission Sunday, July 20, 1919, by Mrs. J. P. Avent.

MISSIONARY INTEREST

Dear Friends:

You all know from a previous article in THE CHRISTIAN SUN that working and pleading for missions is new to me, and that probably it would not last long, but the missionary spirit has not died out in my heart yet, and if anything it gets stronger every day. I feel like I want to divide every dollar I have, and would if I could. I feel like the best part of my life has been spent, or at least the most number of years. But with God's help not the best years, for I expect to help in the Lord's work all I can from now on.

Let me tell you about a sermon I heard the first Sunday in March in a church in this neighborhood. The text was Ephesians 6 chapter, and a part of the 20th verse: "An ambassador in bonds." When I heard the text I wondered what kind of a sermon could be preached from that text. It was just splendid, and so plain and helpful. The minister explained what an ambassador means—that it means to be a messenger for Christ. It was a most earnest and touching sermon. He defended our Savior with such force and power as I never heard before. Anyone hearing him could say that truly Jesus was his Lord and Savior. When the minister portrays his Master it is not the word painting, the beautiful coloring or the wonderful power of the speaker that thrills you, but the perfect image of the Lord Jesus Christ. That will ever remain engraved on the memory imprinted on the heart. A God of love of mercy of forgiveness sheds His kindly light for all and steadily leads to the higher life, and makes us want to sing. "Oh for a thousand tongues to sing my dear Redeemer's praise."

Now all of us cannot be preachers; cannot be messengers for Christ in this country nor missionaries in foreign lands, but we can give of our means to help send the message to those who do not know about Jesus. I want to ask all who read this article, for my sake, who is new in the experience, and for the sake of the One who died for you, to make a contribution to missions. If you are a regular contributor, or have never given anything before and if you cannot give more than ten or twenty-five cents, that will count greatly, for I guess THE CHRISTIAN SUN has many readers. You will experience more joy and pleasure than from anything else you ever did.

We can be His messenger in many ways. If we do not have the courage to speak about the best friend we have in the world we can write to our friends. There is power in the written word sometimes, and above all, try to live as Christ would have you live in your homes. Religion in the home is what counts most with the unsaved.   MRS. J. L. HALL.

News Ferry, Va.

CHRISTIAN EDUCATION

ELON OPENING

The thirtieth annual opening of Elon College on September 10 was the largest in the history of the institution, excepting the abnormal conditions produced by the S. A. T. C. last autumn. Both the ladies' dormitories are crowded and the Board is called to meet Tuesday, September 16, to consider the enlarging of facilities.

The spirit of the campus, always fine, is unusually inspiring. The strenuous and successful campaign for the Standardization Fund, the special courses of summer study by sixteen of the professors, together with the addition of new members to the faculty, have created a new spirit of optimism and enthusiasm. We are confidently expecting the best session in our history.

A feature of the opening day was an assembly of the students, faculty and citizens in the auditorium at which time President Harper called on the professors who had been at the different universities to relate some of their experiences. This brought forth sufficient jokes and general fun to enliven the weary and dispel all home sickness.

N. G. NEWMAN.

ADDITIONAL ITEMS

A most pleasing feature of the opening days of the college in the way of social activity was a reception at the home of President and Mrs. Harper Friday evening for the new members of the faculty. The new members were greeted by the old members of the faculty and their wives, and an enjoyable evening was spent by all. Mrs. Harper was assisted in the serving of refreshment by Mesdames W. P. Lawrence, J. O. Atkinson, J. R. McNally, and Misses Susie Riddick, Lila Newman, Annie Watson, Mary D. Atkinson, and Marion Lee Newman.

Another pleasing feature was the annual opening reception given by the faculty to the students, which occurred on Saturday night in the parlors and halls of the West Dormitory.

It has been recently announced on the Hill that the college has acquired a thirty-four acre tract of land just south of the college, and convenient to the college campus, on which is to be constructed a modern athletic field. This addition to the equipment of the college will mean much in the development of the athletic life here.

C. M. CANNON, *Correspondent.*

SUNDAY EVENING SERVICES AT ELON THIS YEAR

The Sunday evening services at the College this year will consist of a varied type of message. Experts in many fields of life activity will be invited to give the messages closest to their hearts. The speakers and their subjects will be announced for a month in advance.

The speakers for the remainder of September will be Dr. N. G. Newman for the second Sunday whose subject is "The Changing Time and the Unchangeable Christ." Dr. J. O. Atkinson will speak on the third

Sunday on "Christian Service as a Life Vocation." Chaplain Black will speak of his war experiences on the fourth Sunday. Dr. N. G. Newman will preach each Sunday morning and is Chairman of the Committee to arrange for the evening services.

W. A. HARPER.

CONCERNING OUR SOLIDARITY

Referring to the call issued by certain brethren to come to the rescue of the Restoration Movement for which we do not tremble in the slightest degree, our good friend, *The Word and Way*, Baptist, Kansas City, Mo., among other comments, makes the following:

There is, perhaps, no religious body that has less solidarity, coherience, consistency and harmony than the Disciples denomination. These people are famous for their contention for union, and they promise to be quite as famous for contention, discord and division. * * *

The transformation, disintegration and decay of the Disciples denomination are a proof of the folly, inconsistency and futility of their "plea" for union.

To which we reply: Dear Friend, you do not understand. We hereby extend you a sincere and cordial invitation to come to our convention in Cincinnati, October 13-20, and see for yourself. We will welcome you as a fraternal delegate and extend you the privileges of the floor. We will let you hear and read our reports and we promise you a season of the warmest fellowship you have ever experienced. You will be among fifteen thousand delegates and never in your life have you witnessed as much good nature, "joyful visiting," and glad handshaking as you will see there. You will note that there has been growth in every department of the work and big growth at that.

We do not blame you for being mistaken about our "divisions." From the first we have discussed in the open and we are free to take up any question we please. The truth is, we rather like to "discuss." But dividing is another question. We refuse to do that. If you come do not wait around hoping to gather up the fragments. "There ain't goin' to be any." We have always welcomed differences in opinions. It keeps off crystallization and steers us clear of the dead line. And we thrive on it, for we have been that way from the first and yet we have grown into the millions and planted churches all over the earth. We have always held that we had a right to differ, but not to divide—and that very idea is a big contribution to the Christian union problem.

Come over to our convention, Brother *Word and Way*, and we pledge you beforehand that you will not have to become unclean by touching a corpse.

NOTE: The above was found in The Christian Evangelist, and we believe it will interest our people in view of the fact that union negotiations are on foot between the Disciples and our people.—Editor.

Rev. L. L. Wyrick, Elon College, N. C., has the second Sunday open for the coming year if any church is in need of a pastor for that Sunday.

NOTES
(Continued from Page 7)

a pastor will do well to communicate with Brother Harrell. His address is Suffolk, Virginia.

The trustees of the Burlington Church have been instructed to offer the old building and real estate for sale. The location of the property is ideal and in a few hundred yards of the very business of the city. Only the street divides it from the new church lot and building. Brother D. R. Fonville is chairman of the trustees.

Sunday schools and churches should elect superintendents, secretaries and other officers now so that their names can be included in *The Annual*. So often names of officers are reported to Conferences, and immediately after that time these officers go out and new ones come in. In this way the departments of the Church do not have a correct list of these officers. The list included in *The Annual* should be the officers for the coming year so that when some one desires to write some Sunday school superintendent or church secretary that it will be no trouble in getting the letter into the hands of the right party.

One of or very able *Exchanges* has discontinued the use of the Sunday school comments so that the space may be given to other matters. We quote this from the announcement: "* * * Then we cannot close our eyes to the fact that literature upon the Sunday school lesson is abundant and easily accessible. We do not presume to think that we can improve on that which is already furnished by the Church." We pass this along for what it is worth, and ask these questions: Is the Sunday school lessons furnished THE SUN an improvement upon our regular literature? When we are asked to see the *Officers and Teachers' Journal*, what good does it do if the reader does not have that *Journal*? If he had the *Journal*, would he not use it anyway without being cited to it? For what other purpose would he have it? These same questions apply to the Christian Endeavor helps, for instance, if a man takes *The Christian Endeavor World*, would he have to be reminded that such a paper would be a good place to find help on the topic? If he didn't have this paper, would the reference help him?

Last week the Board of Religious Education met in a commercial hotel at Raleigh, N. C. We were just wondering how much better it would have been if the Convention had some official headquarters for this meeting. Last year the Mission Board of the Southern Christian Convention met at Elon College, and this week it is in session at Suffolk, Virginia. We were just wondering that if the Convention had some regular headquarters that the satisfaction and dissatisfaction about the better place to meet would not be settled. The Field Secretary has his office located in his own home, sacrificing the room of his library for it. We were just wondering how long the Convention would be satisfied in keeping the office under such an arrangement. The Mission Board of the Southern Christian Convention is incorporated, and each corporation is required to hang out a sign indicating the official location of its office. We notice there is no sign in the front of the home of our Mission Secretary. We were just wondering how embarrassing it would be to him if he should be forced to carry out that requirement. In the meeting of the Board of Religious Education last week steps were taken looking forward to employing a man for all his time for the work of Sunday school and Christian Endeavor. We were just wondering where this man would be located. One of these days we are not only going to have a Secretary of Missions, but we are going to have *Secretaries*—one for the home work and one for the work abroad. We were just wondering how nice it would be to have these offices located at the same place. One of these days we are going to have a Secretary of Education, whose business it will be to travel throughout the length and breadth of our Convention and speak to the young people about their educational career. We were just wondering if the office of this man would be isolated from the other Convention offices. The Editor of THE SUN owns a little stock in a printing plant, and because of his connection he has mutual arrangements to have an office in the same building, and therefore, saves the Convention a monthly expense of not less than $25.00. We were just wondering that if the Editor should sever his present connection with the printing business what effect it would have on the THE CHRISTIAN SUN, since THE SUN has no home of its own. In the stock room section of the Burlington Printing Company the files of THE CHRISTIAN SUN during its entire history, are lying in a pile in the form of junk. The building is protected by insurance but not a penny of the insurance would go to THE SUN in case of a fire, and certainly the records could never be duplicated. We were just wondering if the Church has enough of interest and pride to inquire into this and make some provision for these records to be placed in a safety vault. The first volume of THE CHRISTIAN SUN, the entire *monthly* issue (for then it was a monthly) of 1844, is locked up in a fire proof safe, but that safe is not the property of the Church. We are just wondering that if for any reason this accommodation could not be longer continued where this valuable volume could be kept. So often some important item is known by the officers of the Convention and should get in the *next* issue of THE SUN, but for the lack of proximity of THE SUN to these places of activity the paper often goes to press without a knowledge of these items that should not wait. We were just wondering when the light breaks upon the Convention to do these business-like things and establish Convention headquarters, where such headquarters would be.

Well, we were just wondering, that's all.

The manufacturers and employees in the city of High Point have been at variance for several weeks. Governor Bickett was called in last Saturday and continued a conference through part of Sunday, which succeeded in getting the two factions together. Work in the High Point shops will be resumed September 17.

THE CHRISTIAN ORPHANAGE

SUPERINTENDENT'S LETTER

We are very happy to pass the $10,000.00 mile post in our financial report for this week. The churches and Sunday schools have been very loyal this year and have made it possible to reach this amount at this time. If we have no "Flu" this fall and our churches do as well as they should do in the Thanksgiving Offering, this year should far surpass any year yet in the history of the Orphanage.

The writer had a very pleasant visit to Catawba Springs on the second Sunday. Brother B. F. Branch met me at the station and carried me to the church, entertained me for dinner and delivered me at the station in time to catch the evening train for home. While Brother Branch could not get his "black mule" to go as fast as our Ford, yet I enjoyed the ride splendidly. It reminded me of days gone by when I was a boy on the farm and had the pleasure of driving a black mule, and on some occasions I persuaded the mule to go as slow as possible as we wanted to say all the nice little things we knew how to say.

Brother J. Lee Johnson kindly gave me an opportunity to make a talk in behalf of the Orphanage work and an offering was taken. We also received several subscriptions for the Children's Home. Brother Johnson preached a splendid sermon, and we thought it well worth our trip to Catawba Springs just to get to hear him preach again. The Catawba people are very loyal supporters of the Orphanage and we expect a number of subscriptions from that church yet for the Children's Home.

Some of our Sunday schools have not gotten on the list of monthly contributors for this year. I want to insist that if your school is not on this list that you see to it that a contribution is made in your school and mailed in. If you read this letter and know your school is on the delinquent list, get busy and don't rest or let your school rest till it gets on the "banner" list. I am anxious to have each school on the list by Conference. It will do your school good to get on this list, it will make your little children more interested to help the little orphans. Let us hear from your school in the next few weeks. You must help others if you want to grow. You will find the more you give for the support of the Orphanage and for missions, or for any other cause for the Church's good, the more you will want to give.

Get in the habit of giving and you will enjoy it. When you lend a helping hand to the helpless it makes you better. Did you ever do a kind deed that helped some one else that you did not feel better by the doing?

CHAS. D. JOHNSTON, *Supt.*

FINANCIAL REPORT FOR SEPTEMBER 17, 1919

Amount brought forward, $7,935.02.

Children's Offerings

T. D. Mathews, Jr., 40 cents; Lee Hilliard, 15 cents; Rozelle Hilliard, 10 cents; Thomas Hilliard, 5 cents; Norman Hilliard, 5 cents; Total, 75 cents.

Sunday School Monthly Offerings

(North Carolina Conference)

Burlington, two months, $61.25; Oak Level, $2.00; Long's Chapel, $3.46; High Point, $2.45; Catawba Springs, $10.50; Shallow Ford, $3.00; Mt. Pleasant, $1.75; Plymouth, $2.80; New Lebanon, $6.60; Amelia, N. C., $5.77; Christian Light, $3.75; New Providence, $1.45; New Providence Baracca Class, $2.15.

(Eastern Virginia Conference)

Washington St., Portsmouth, $3.00; Union, $2.00.

(Virginia Valley Conference)

Concord, $2.76; Dry Run, $3.27; Linville, $1.00.

(Georgia and Alabama Conference)

Lanett, Ala., $4.70; Total, $123.59.

Special

R. S. Chandler, $10.00; Reidsville Sunday school Bible Class, $12.00; Chas. D. Johnston, Guardian, $115.32; Mr. Hilliard, $2.25; Mr. Hilliard, 25 cents; Total, $139.82.

Children's Home

Eden Christian Sunday School, Swanson, Sask, Can., $10.00. Total for the week, $274.16; Grand total, $10,009.18.

FROM THE COUSINS

Dear Uncle Charley: We are a little band of four. We send our mite and hope it will help the little orphan children some. Best wishes to all the cousins.—*Lee, Rozelle, Thomas, and Norman Hilliard.*

P. S.: Papa joins us with $2.25 and Grandpapa with 25 cents.

We give you the good hand of welcome. Trust you will come often.—*"Uncle Charley."*

Dear Uncle Charley: I am sending my dues for June, July, August and September. Hope this finds you and the cousins well.—*T. D. Mathews, Jr.*

I hope you have had a good time this summer. I am glad you have not forgotten the corner."—*"Uncle Charley."*

CALEB COOKSTOVE'S COUNSEL

(By Marian Churchill Graves)

"O dear, O dear!" sighed Billy Broom. "Will this spring housecleaning never end? I've swept and I've swept all day long until I'm so tired I can't sleep a wink."

"You can't be any more in need of a rest than I am," rattled Delia Dishpan from her hook by the sink. "I'm so tired of dishes that I'm planning to spring a leak so I can be thrown on the ash heap. At least that would be a change from dishes three or four times a day."

"I think it's change I need, too," crackled Billy Broom. "If I could have Felicia Feather Duster's place and dust now and then, I'm sure I shouldn't get so tired of life."

(Continued on Page 13)

WORSHIP AND MEDITATION

MEMORY

(Rev. J. T. Kitchen)

Do not let memory linger too long lamenting over the days which are gone. The unpleasant things will do you no good to recall, and the pleasant ones will only give transient joy. Imitate much as possible one who expressed himself in so many admirable, beautiful ways. One of which is: "Brethren, ..., but this one thing I do, forgetting those things which are behind, and reaching forth unto those things which are before, I press toward the mark for the prize of the high calling of God in Christ Jesus."

The real, living, active present surrounds us. Let us grasp it with a steady purpose looking with confidence for the best results. We can take a bundle of arrows from the quiver of truth and have them ready to speed their way to the mark. Many, too many, never say much except in the past tense, and the flight of years has a special charm for them which the present and future do not give. It is very hard to prevent the mind from running backward and dwelling upon the eventful past. Very many delight in telling what they did, where they went and how they felt, but it is better to tell where they are from—what they are doing, and how much gladness they get out of life. The happiness is in us, and we can and must bring it out and give it to others.

The pleasure which memory gives cannot be told—it is to be felt, but too profoundly great to tell, and the heart which feels knows better than tongue or pen can express or describe. Some of you as you meditate upon a long, long past will have many mingled remembrances of it. Some will have sad remembrance of an unhappy past, while a few others will have glad remembrance of a happy past. What intense feelings and great emotions tremble in the heart and quiver on the lips for deliverance and utterance as they feel like saying: "Bring back to me the simple joy and youthful glee that once pervaded the entire being, and sent a thrill of transport to the heart. Give them back to me for a while, and let me live over my life again in its fading twilight before the curtain is rolled down and the dark night surrounds me."

But do not linger too long on the dim, distant past. Only this very time is yours—use it then in the very best way, for tomorrow, yes, tomorrow may never come to you. Today is yours; today, today. To grasp the present situation, rightly, rise and improve it is the duty of all.

The seams of years may be deeply impressed on your carded, honest face, but the remembrance of honesty and truthfulness in your character will give a hopeful inspiration to your looks and a touch of polish and brightness to your whole being which wealth, prestage and honor without them could never impart.

All these subjects have been thought, talked and written over and over so many times; every phase of thought has been produced and expressed in the most lucid, beautiful and logical way, but when memory, precious memory surveys the past, it is forever new, bright and fresh, and still lands a pleasing charm to the imagination.

Up and down the ways of life, it has traveled with untold, unmeasured, and unknown swiftness over life's eventful ways, and is still ready to scale the heights of time in searching for and contemplating the great and the good.

Do you remember? Yes, you remember pleasantly when you did right, and you also remember sadly when you did wrong. There was a continual conflict in your life between right and wrong—each wanting to gain the victory over the other. With tear-dimmed eyes and tear-bathed cheeks there are so many regrets to remember. So many remember how they grieved that dear mother who had been the support and joy of their life, and since she parted with them for a clime when they never change nor get old they can almost hear her sweet voice saying: "Come, and live with me for it is so peaceful, lovely and beautiful up here." That home is fairer than day with no clouds and no night.

Memory, precious memory, we love to think of its boundless ways, and recall with much delight its pleasant, happy past. That sweet dream of life is a bright star in memory's fadeless crown and we will wear it proudly and gladly as the imagination ascends and brings back to us beautiful and pleasant thoughts.

It would be a blank, dark existence if we had no memory. If it could not survey the places and things of early and later times how terrible would be the condition. But memory still retentive and active like a bright star of hope gleams over the way and gives inexpressible pleasure to the mind. The pleasant events of life would not be appreciated so much if we did not remember the unpleasant ones with which to compare them. After many days of suffering in untold ways, one bright, glad, sweet day of happiness may more than compensate for all of the adverse conditions, when memory shall be so full, that the soul will be overflowing with supreme gladness.

Windsor, Va.

NOT THAT

The call of the tithe is not a call for relief to some struggling church. A rich church should tithe as well as the poor church. The poor man should pay his tithe as well as the rich man, for it identifies man with God. Money getting is not the object; man getting and soul getting—these are the things that grow out of partnership with God.

LITTLE FOLKS DEPARTMENT

(Continued from Page 11)

"And I've always felt that I'd like to be Eva Egg Beater," confided Delia Dishpan. "She doesn't work all the time, but what a lively time she has when she does work, hopping and dancing about and singing at the top of her lungs."

"Miss Egg Beater is too noisy for me," remarked Billy, "I like quiet folks better. That's why I should choose Miss Feather Duster's lot. But of course I'd prefer to be myself some of the time. It would grow just as tiresome to do nothing but dust forever and ever as it does to sweep, sweep, sweep, until I feel as if every bristle I have is loose."

"You speak the truth, Billy," agreed Delia Dishpan. "I believe that no one who does the same thing day in and day out can ever get far ahead in the world."

Caleb Cookstove creaked and groaned in an effort to make himself heard: "See here, see here, what do you young folks think of me!" he rumbled. "I'm the oldest inhabitant of this kitchen, and I've done the same thing day after day for thirty days. The only rest I ever have is during the hottest weather of the summer, and then I'm not expected to move from my place."

"Yes, and where has work put you?" snapped Billy Broom. "Are you any better off in the world for doing the same thing over and over?"

"Don't lose your temper, my friend. I'm the one who should get hot," answered Mr. Cookstove. "I am growing old now, but I know that I am of more use to the lady of the house than I was when I first came here, for I've tried to do my work better each day and she has found that she can depend on me. She wouldn't trade me for a new stove, and it's all because I've learned to do my work well by doing it over and over. But if I had felt as you do, Miss Dishpan, and tried to make myself useless, I should now be sold for old iron and be of not much use to any one. Why don't you brace up and learn how to do your work better? And when you prove that you are worth it and are not likely to spring a leak at any minute, the lady of the house may use you to hold her embroidered napkins while she boils them. And you, Billy, should be ashamed of what every one says about you: 'A new broom sweeps clean.' Get a little ambition and show that you can do better as you grow older. I tell you, my friends, the folks that amount to the most in the world are those who do about the same thing day after day and do it better each time."

"Perhaps you are right, Mr. Cookstove," said Delia Dishpan. "I believe I'll try your way, anyhow."

"And so shall I," said Billy Broom. "You make me feel ashamed of my complaining."

"That sounds more hopeful," said Mr. Cookstove. "I must settle down for my night's rest now, or I won't be ready to make up when the master shakes me down in the morning. Good-night, my friends."

"Good-night," rattled Delia Dishpan.

"Good-night," crackled Billy Broom.—*In Child's Hour.*

THE COW'S CONTRIBUTION TO ART

"Why do you clip the cow's ears?" asked an interested observer of an employee in a large meat packing establishment. The plant was a model of cleanliness and great care was exercised in handling the meat, but in what way the clipping of a cow's ears could aid in maintaining sanitary conditions was a mystery to the onlooker.

"That," said the worker as he snipped the hair from the inside of an ear, "is the cow's contribution to art. Until recently when some one discovered that the hair in a cow's ear is the most delicate, yet strong and soft hair known, it was believed that the best substance for the making of high-grade brushes for water-color painting was camel's hair."

"And so," said the man as he passed on with his shears, "practically all the 'camel's hair' brushes are now made from the hair of cows' ears, and they are said to be better than those made of real camel's hair."

The scarcity of camel's hair, due to the difficulty of importing it, brings to mind the fact that shortly before the Civil War an attempt was made to introduce the raising of camels in the southwestern section of the United States and using them for transportation purposes in the deserts of Arizona and New Mexico.

Jefferson Davis, then Secretary of War, secured an appropriation of funds for this purpose and two herds of camels, numbering about sixty animals, were brought here from Algeria, but, after having proved their usefulness during the period of unrest at the time of the Civil War, they were allowed to perish at the hands of Indians and Mexicans or became the victims of wolves, cougars and rattlesnakes.

It is possible that a few wild survivors of the two herds still exist in northern Mexico, but the belief is based on nothing more definite than the tales of prospectors who, in their search for gold, frequently are rendered somewhat visionary through suffering for the want of water.

Besides supplying a substitute for camel's hair brushes, other "waste" portions of slaughtered cattle furnish material for many useful articles. It is, of course, well known that cowhide makes a very durable leather. The hair which is shaved from the hide is used in wall plaster. Some portions of the bones and horns are used in the manufacture of buttons and the remainder is ground and used as a fertilizer, as is also the blood after it has been dried.—*A. H. Dreher, in Kind Words.*

———

Necessity is not only "the mother of invention," but it is the father of industry and the grandfather of prosperity.—*Exchange.*

———

We have had occasion to talk with many persons who have been connected with large financial campaigns for churches and schools, and are informed that those who tithe can always be counted upon to do their part in such campaigns.

Sunday School and Christian Endeavor

SUNDAY SCHOOL LESSON FOR SEPTEMBER 28, 1919

Review: Jesus our Savior and King.

Selection for Reading: Matt. 21:1-9, 15, 16.

Golden Text: "Hosanna to the Son of David. Blessed is he that cometh in the name of the Lord; Hosanna in the highest."—Matt. 21:9.

The Church of Jesus Christ (Lesson I). Has our local church, our denomination, performed the duties God has given it to do? Are we willing to inquire of the Lord "what wilt thou have me to do?" in our church, or do we say: "What does Mr. Biggest Payer want done?" or "What will Mrs. Church Worker say about that?" "The trouble with most of our churches," says Rev. B. B. Sutchliffe, "is that so many are *church workers*, not Christ workers. Church workers are always looking for reward, and are always in trouble. Christ workers know that their reward is in Heaven, and they strive to please their Lord." Baptism—the "answer of a good conscience toward God," the act by which we announce to the world that we 'have put on Christ" is a sacrament of the church instituted by the words of Jesus Himself (Lesson II), while the Lord's Supper (Lesson III) is the time when those who love their Lord join with their brethren in closest communion with Him, and in this and other acts of Christian Fellowship (Lesson IV) we prove that. "we know that we have passed from death unto life because we love the brethren." Who would not worship the Lord in the beauty of holiness, He who has done so much for us? If we would worship more in our churches, we would not have so much time for criticizing the preacher, and we would prove to the world that the statement made in a comic journal lately that "A Christian is one who goes to church on Sunday to obtain forgiveness for the sins he committed on Saturday and expects to commit on Monday" is a lie and no truth. (Lesson V). Could we but so live, there would be no question of our winning others to Christ (Lesson VI), and instead of a pitiful bit of money once a year to

Christian Missions. (Lesson VII), we would give of our best to the Master, our sons and our daughters, and His share of our increase. What responsibility has the church for the young, and for their amusements? Whose fault if "politics are rotten?" Who is to blame if things are wrong? Who is the neighbor to whom we are to show mercy? Who is he not? (Lesson VIII). What shall we do about the temperance laws? Do we owe any duty to our neighbor here? If we can keep liquor in the house without over indulgence, or use it to flavor cooking, shall we lay a stumbling block in the way of our neighbor, and cause him to stumble? (Lesson IX). "Thy Kingdom Come. (Lesson X). It has not come yet; this is the period of grace, not of rule, but should not we love Him, pray for the time when He shall reign? (Lesson VI). If—and when —His Kingdom comes, what part shall we have in it? It is only the Scriptures which tell us of the way to the City and the welcome which awaits us there. (Lesson XII), but if we study them they are able to make us wise to salvation, if we are willing to accept Jesus as our Savior and King. (Lesson XIII).

MRS. FRED BULLOCK.

CHRISTIAN ENDEAVOR TOPIC FOR SEPTEMBER 28, 1919

The Christian Athlete and His Training. I Cor. 9:19-27.

"Training for service," "He that striveth in the games." Have you ever noticed how many words there are in the Bible that signify effort. "Striveth," "exerciseth," "fervent" —red-hot glowing; "fight;" "compel." This is no passive war of nonresistance. It is a 'contest between trained gladiators, fit in body mind and soul, one to work the works of evil, the other "the works of Him that sent me." "I am not here to dream, to drift," but to keep myself in condition in every sense, and "having done all—to *stand*, not supine, but alert, thoroughly armed for an offensive as well as defensive warfare, "against pricipalities, and powers and against spiritual wickedness in the heavenly places."

MRS. FRED BULLOCK.

SUNDAY SCHOOLS "CARRY ON"

One of our good Sunday school superintendents writes: "Our Sunday school has started something." Now isn't that fine? So many of our schools are willing just to keep on in the same old way from year to year. If a farmer were to farm that way, or a merchant were to merchandise that way, both would be out of date and go broke in a few years. Truly the Word says: "The children of this world are wiser in their day than the children of light." Some of the hardest things you can say about some people, and some Sunday schools, and some churches, is to tell the naked truth about them. That was what the Bible was doing in the above declaration about how stupidly unwise the children of light are. They know better, for they have the light; but they are then not as wise as the children of this wicked world. What if the church and the Sunday school were to become as wise and shrewd and active and vigorous for the Kingdom as are the people of the world in business and professions and politics! My! how soon this whole wicked world would be won for Christ.

But we are content to drag on in the same old way. The world is forever starting something. Why not the Sunday school? The world all around us has decided to "carry on." Why not the church and Sunday school?

This particular school decided to take one offering each month for missions. (It was already taking one offering a month for the Orphanage). Any Sunday school that hasn't the faith to give as much to others as it spends on itself hasn't enough faith to achieve anything worth while, and is selfish rather than unselfish in its conduct. It requires faith to achieve things worth while in this world; and if some of our schools will exercise more faith they will do more work both for themselves and for others. Get your Sunday school to "carry on," *start something*, and see if a new source of life does not spring up within it.

Our mission church at Danville, Va., has started the monthly missionary offering and sends $10.86 the first Sunday's offering. How is that for a struggling mission point? Ebenezer Sunday school (Wake Co.) decides to send a missionary offering once a month, and sends $4.00 as a starter. Here are the schools, with amounts. sent in, for missions from these schools in August: Lebanou (Semora), $1.88; Durham, $10.00; Holy Neck (a class), $1.66; Isle of Wight C. H., $2.50; Ivor, $2.00; Pleasant Grove (Va.), $3.00; Wentworth, $1.38; New Lebanon, $1.81; Wadley (Ala.), $2.00; High Point (Va. Valley), $2.00; Holy Neck S. S., $20.30; Pleasant Union, $1.20; New Providence, $1.91; Beulah (Ala.), 98 cents; Reidsville, $2.29; Parks Cross Roads, $1.50; Ingram, $3.00; High Point (N. C.), $3.72; Sanford, $5.78; Linville, $2.00; Lanett, $2.30; Catawba Springs, 95 cents; Ebenezer, $4.00; Mt. Zion. (Ala.), $1.05; Danville, $10.86.

Other schools than these are contributing but some send in once in two or three months. These are the offerings sent to the Secretary in August; and the number increases. Here is hoping and praying that all our schools will before long have a care for the unsaved millions if they would and will make an offering for their salvation.

J. O. ATKINSON, Sec.

PELOUBET'S SELECT NOTES

Send your order for Peloubet's Select Notes on the Sunday school lesson along with your renewal to THE CHRISTIAN SUN. The books will be ready for delivery December 1. You need not send the money now, unless you want to. Just indicate for us to send you a copy December 1 and that will be all right. The price is $1.50.

MARRIAGES

STOUT-BEAN

At the home of the bride's parents, Mr. and Mrs. D. E. Bean of Seagrove, N. C., Route 1, at noon, Friday, August 26, 1919, Mr. Walter J. Stout and Miss Isa Bean were united in marriage in the presence of a number of friends and relatives.

Mr. Stout is a son of Mr. and Mrs. J. E. Stout of Moffitt, N. C., and has served overseas. Both are popular young people and their many friends wish for them a prosperous and happy wedded life. Ceremony by the writer.

T. J. GREEN.

WARD-BOST

Miss Myrtle Ward, the daughter of W. S. Ward of High Point, N. C., was married to Charles A. Bost of Salisbury, N. C., on Wednesday evening, August 27, 1919, at the home of Rev. P. D. Brown, on English St., High Point, N. C., at 7:30 P. M.

Mr. and Mrs. Bost will make their home in Salisbury, N. C. Mrs. Ward is a member of the Christian Church and her many friends wish her and her companion a very happy life.

R. C. BOYD.

OBITUARIES

BROWN

Sister Minnie Brown, wife of W. W. Brown, was born October 16, 1881, died August 21, 1919.

Sister Brown had been a member of Union Grove Christian church for about fifteen years, and a model Christian she was, loved by all who knew her.

She leaves to mourn their loss a husband, three little girls: Allie, Ruth and Lois, a father and mother, four brothers and four sisters, besides a host of relatives and friends.

May they be comforted at the thought of meeting again to part no more.

T. J. GREEN.

BOONE

Henry Milton Boone departed this life at the Old Soldier's Home, Raleigh, N. C., September 3, 1919, aged seventy-seven

years, eleven months and three days. He was one of a family of fifteen. He came to Alamance County from Guilford about forty years ago. He served as a soldier in the Civil War with the Guilford greys of the 47th Regiment. He was a good soldier, a good citizen and a kind husband and father. Three children survive him: Mrs. E. M. McDade, Memphis, Tenn.; Mrs. J. U. Faucette and Mrs. R. C. Hall, Burlington, N. C. He leaves six grandchildren. He was a member of Union Christian church in Alamance County where the funeral service was held, followed by interment in the cemetery at that place. The service was conducted by the writer.

J. W. HOLT.

BOSWELL

Mrs. Margaret Frances Boswell died at her home, 940 Adams Street, High Point, N. C., at 11:00 P. M., Tuesday night, September 2, 1919. She was fifty-seven years old. She leaves to mourn their loss a devoted husband, five children, two sisters, two brothers and a host of friends.

Mrs. Boswell was a woman of excellent traits and was loved by all who knew her. She was an invalid for nineteen months, which affliction she bore most patiently. She was a member of Hillsdale Baptist Church for fourteen years. She was loyal to her Christ and Church.

Funeral services were conducted from her home on Thursday morning and interment took place in Hillsdale cemetery.

May the Lord comfort the bereaved.

L. L. WYRICK.

RESOLUTIONS OF RESPECT—COX.

Whereas, the late Rev. L. I. Cox of Elon College, N. C., was called from labor to reward on September 5, 1919, and whereas, he was a faithful minister and pastor of this church for eight years; Therefore, be it Resolved:

First, That we request our present pastor, Rev. Daniel Albright Long, to preach a sermon in memory of Brother Cox at this place tomorrow at the same hour of his funeral service at Elon College;

Second, That our sympathy and prayers be extended his family and a copy of these resolutions be sent to his widow and a copy to The Christian Sun for publication.

Pleasant Hill Christian Church,

PAUL E. COBLE,
JAMES L. JONES,
MISS WILLIE ANDREWS,
Committee.

September 6, 1919.

TUCK

Little Edith Tuck, the bright and interesting little girl of Brother and Sister Hosea Tuck of Virgilina, Va., was accidently scalded on August 7, 1919 and died from the effects of the same on August 9.

The little one's body was laid to rest in Union cemetery on Sunday afternoon, August 10. Edith had been in the home just twenty-two months. The parents are deeply grieved but find comfort in the promise of seeing their child again.

C. E. NEWMAN.

TUCK

Riley Dunberry Tuck was born in December, 1856 and died July 19, 1919, aged 62 years and seven months. In 1884 he married Miss Flora Tuck who survives him together with seven sons and one daughter.

Brother Tuck was a most energetic farmer and thought well of by all who knew him. The burial services were conducted at the grave in Union church cemetery, near Virgilina, Va., on Sunday afternoon, July 20.

May a strong faith in God's providence comfort the bereaved widow and guide the fatherless in all the affairs of life.

C. E. NEWMAN.

TAYLOR

Mrs. Sennora Stella Taylor, daughter of James M. and Caroline McAden, was born March 20, 1871, and died August 18, 1919, aged 48 years, four months and twenty-nine days. When a young girl Sister Taylor professed faith in Christ and united with Lebanon Christian church where her membership remained till her death.

On December 13, 1893 she married Mr. W. Scott Taylor of Semora, N. C. The husband, two sons, Scottie and Morris one daughter, Mrs. Clyde Allen and one grandson survive her; also three sisters and one brother. The sisters are: Mrs. J. H. Yarboro and Mrs. Bettie Wells of Semora and Mrs. Kate McKane of Newport News, Va. The deceased was the sister of J. H. McAden of Semora.

Sister Taylor was an excellent Christian woman, a faithful wife and mother. She loved her church and all its enterprises. She bore her sufferings during months with a submissive and resigned spirit. All that medical skill could do was done for her recovery, but the summons came and she entered the rest of the faithful.

C. E. NEWMAN.

RESOLUTIONS OF RESPECT—FIX

Whereas, it hath pleased our Heavenly Father to remove from our midst one of our best loved members, Mrs. Sarah Fix and

Whereas, by her death the Christian Church, Burlington, N. C., has sustained the loss of a consecrated, faithful, loyal member, one who was ever ready to lend a helping hand, contributing liberally of her means, her time and energy to the church and the advancement of Christ's Kingdom, Therefore, we, the members of the Woman's Missionary Society, desire to express our love and esteem in the following resolutions:

1. That we bow in humble submission to the will of Him Who doeth all things well, realizing that our loss is Heaven's gain.

2. That we seek to emulate her example by rendering our best service to the work she loved. We are grateful for her beautiful Christian life and we do feel keenly the loss of this most loyal and faithful worker.

3. That we extend our sincerest sympathy to her bereaved family, assuring them of our prayer that His grace may be sufficient in this hour of sorrow.

4. That a copy of these resolutions be sent to The Christian Sun and the Burlington News for publication, that a copy be sent to the family of the deceased and that a copy be spread upon the minutes of our Society.

MRS. J. W. PAGE,
MRS. J. W. HARRELL,
MRS. W. R. SELLARS,
Committee.

THE TITHER

An interdenominational publication devoted to Tithing and Christian Stewardship.

Editors

C. B. RIDDLE
KARL LEHMANN
BERT WILSON
HUGH S. McCORD
FRED G. THOMAS

8 pages; issued monthly; 50c the year

Address

THE TITHER Burlington, N. C.

SEPTEMBER SMILES

A resident of Nahant tells this one on a new servant his wife took down from Boston:

"Did you sleep well, Mary?" the girl was asked the following morning.

"Sure, I did not, ma'am," was the reply; "the snorin' of the ocean kept me awake all night."—*Fitchburg Sentinel*.

* * *

Heydon, the six-year-old son of Heydon W. Buchanan, accompanied his mother to the office of Dr. (Captain) S. O. Leak, recently discharged from military service. Observing the doctor re-enter his private office after giving counsel, the boy inquired:
"Mother, why do you call him 'captain'? Don't you see it says 'private' on the door?"—*Indianapolis News*.

* * *

"In writing a short story," said the ambitious young woman author to the editor, "one should strive only for the telling points, the high lights, so to speak, making the narrative crisp, bright, and with a punch to it. It is often not so much what one puts in as what one leaves out that counts."

"Same with a magazine," replied the editor, handing back her manuscript with a crisp to-the-point rejection slip."—*New York Evening Post*.

* * *

Willis: "What is the crowd doing around Hardupp's house?"
Gillis: "Waiting for the contest."
Willis: "Contest?"
Gillis: "Yes. Grocer Bump is coming up to collect a bill. He has just taken a course in collecting, and Hardupp has just finished a course in the development of will-power."
—*Judge*.

𝔒ur 𝔄nnual 𝔆onferences

1. Should be attended by those who are interested in the progressive work of the Kingdom and are praying and living "Thy Kingdom come."

2. Should do away with some of the time-worn methods of procedure, finance, discussion, and strike a new chord that will vibrate with the new day.

3. Should distribute the responsibility of the Church's work, laying hands upon new leaders that they and the Church may go forward.

4. Should pass only those resolutions and programs that can, and will be, carried out for the largest possible interest of the work everywhere.

5. Should fully recognize that the future leadership of the Church must come from the best blood of the race, and that the work of the Kingdom is a *job* and not a *problem*.

Volume LXXI	WEDNESDAY, SEPTEMBER 24, 1919	Number 39
BURLINGTON · · ·		**NORTH CAROLINA**

THE CHRISTIAN SUN

Founded 1844 by Rev. Daniel W. Kerr

C. B. RIDDLE   -   -   -   Editor

Entered at the Burlington, N. C. Post Office as second class matter.

Subscription Rates

One year ....$ 2.00
Six months 1.00

In Advance

Give both your old and new postoffice when asking that your ad dress be changed.

The change of your label is your receipt for money. Written receipts sent upon request.

Many persons subscribe for friends, intending that the paper be stopped at the end of the year. If instructions are given to this effect, they will receive attention at the proper time.

Marriage and obituary notices not exceeding 150 words printed free if received within 60 days from date of event, all over this at the rate of one-half cent a word.

Original poetry not accepted for publication.

Principles of the Christian Church

(1) The Lord Jesus Christ is the only Head of the Church.
(2) Christian is a sufficient name of the Church.
(3) The Holy Bible is a sufficient rule of faith and practice.
(4) Christian character is a sufficient test of fellowship, and of church membership.
(5) The right of private judgment and the liberty of conscience is a right and a privilege that should be accorded to, and exercised by all.

EDITORIAL

THE CONFERENCE YEAR

Since this scribe has been attending Conference a lax method in regard to the Conference year has prevailed. Some church letters date from one time and some from another. Not only this, but many pastors date their reports from different points on the calendar. A rather unbusiness-like arrangement, it seems to us.

With the average local church, the Sunday before Conference is usually the end of the Conference year. This means at least four different dates used in all the churches. Each local church is a *unit* of the Conference in which it is located. The records of all the churches in one Conference constitute the records of the Conference; and it is the Conference and not the local church that is looked to for final reports.

The Convention has the power to set a date for the official year of the churches; but it has never done this. We presume that on account of the Conferences meeting at different times, that the Convention has had a hesitancy in doing this. Each Conference should set its own date to close the official year

and each church in that Conference should conform to this. Such a date should be set well ahead of the Conference date so as to give ample time for any church liable to miss a service to close up its work.

Put this in your hat, Brother Delegate, and if it is worth while, bring it before your Conference.

"MARY HAS GONE TO COLLEGE"

Part II

Now, Mary got home all right and was just as happy as a lark. If you could have heard her telling father and mother about the things at college that were not just up to the standard (in her estimation) it would have been a charming story, indeed. Of course father and mother agreed with her, petted their only daughter, and assured her that she could stay at home the remainder of her days. At that time Mary thought that she wanted to stay at home the remainder of her days, but a day came when she could not stay at home because father and mother passed away and Mary had to look out for herself.

Mary thought that the girls at college were having a hard time and that hers was an easy one—and it was for a while. The girls left at college continued their studies, returned to their homes better equipped for life, and in all the days to come had every advantage over Mary. For a long time Mary could not see this, but others could, and one day Mary realized it, too.

Not a long story, you say. Well, the story is longer than here told. Go on in your mind and compare Mary with her lost opportunities and with the girls who seized theirs. You have seen it, and are now seeing it every day.

Keep Mary in College. Every crown has its thorn. Mary is your girl, and so love her to the extent of obedience and do not stop with her childish desires, for they are but for a day.

BE PATIENT

Again we ask our friends to be patient. We are writing this note on Wednesday afternoon, September 17, and most of THE SUN for September 24 is in type and enough copy on hand to finish the issue and part of the issue for October 1. Your article will appear. Write often, be brief, say what you have to say with preliminaries, and stop when you have finished. Each week our problem becomes more difficult—the problem of serving a Church, doing three times the work that it once did with the same number of pages in the official organ. Be patient, or give us the means for a larger paper. The latter will suit us better.

THE CALL OF OUR ORPHANAGE

Our Orphanage is calling for a very special help and the Church should, and will, respond to the call. That call is for funds to build and equip a building for the small children who seek admittance to that institution. The call is worthy, deserves our every consideration and the Church will meet the call and meet it gladly. Send a contribution today to Superintendent Chas. D. Johnston. . It will give him a glad heart, cheer him in his endeavors and help you in a way that will bring joy and gladness to your own heart.

A GOOD SIGN

We see in the press notes that all schools and colleges have had a good opening. A good sign that the people are acting wisely regardless of high prices for provisions and attractive wages. We understand that Elon is taxed to its capacity. We are delighted and wish for her and her sister institutions a most successful year.

HAS YOUR CHURCH ADVANCED ITS PASTOR'S SALARY?

.The Editor of *The Herald of Gospel Liberty* is endeavoring to get the name of each church in the denomination that has advanced its pastor's salary during the past year. We fully believe that a very large per cent of the churches has advanced the pastor's salary, but the failure to report this gives *The Herald* in its efforts, a very poor showing. We note that less than fifty have reported and we know that this is only a very few of the churches that have added to the pastor's salary during the past year. In behalf.of *The Herald* we call upon our people to make report at a very early date. Just drop Brother Kerr a postal card and tell him how much advance you have received, Brother Pastor, and give him the name of your church. Do this and do it today.

WHY AND HOW MISSIONARIES ARE BORN

We have just finished reading a somewhat personal editorial in *The Watchword*, a publication of the United Brethren Church. We quote from this editorial the following note that will be of interest to many and presents a point worthy, we think, of the heading that we have seen fit to place above:

One-day, during the Christian Endeavor Conference at Buffalo, Secretary O. T. Deever and the editor had the inspiring privilege of spending the lunch hour at the table with two big-minded veteran missionaries. One of the helpful privileges of the International Christian Endeavor conventions is fellowship with strong men among the kingdom builders.

On this day we sat with Dr. Robert A. Hume, of Abmednager, India, and Dr. James H. Pettee, of Japan.

The conversation ranged from the care of babies to the League of Nations. I do not know just how the first topic was introduced. But Doctor Hume said that he had been a foreign missionary for seventy-two years—at least, he said, he had first raised his voice in India seventy-two years ago. Doctor Pette has been a missionary for forty-five years.

The robust Doctor Hume was born in India; that is how he came to lift his voice in a foreign land so long ago. His father was taken ill and it became

necessary to return to America. As the vessel was passing through the Indian Ocean, the spirit of his father took its flight and his body was buried in the sea. He did not know it at the time, but among the last prayers of his father was one that baby Robert might be a missionary. The boy knew nothing of this prayer, but after receiving his college education, the call of God seemed clear to him, and he has spent many years in India as a missionary of the American Board of Foreign Missions. To add to his joy and his usefulness, five of his seven children are missionaries, the last of the five now under appointment to go out to India in the near future.

Doctor Pette's call to the mission field came simply and naturally during the process of his course in education and during his college course. He was a classmate of Dr. Francis E. Clark, the two graduating fifty years ago.

Do not mistake personal *convenience* for personal *guidance*. So often we are inclined to let convenience suit our giving. We should seek guidance of the Holy Spirit and not convenience from self.

* *

The Methodist Church lays great stress upon stewardship. Recently it completed its largest financial undertaking. Stewardship was given much attention, while about 35,000 tithers were enrolled. Plans give strength. God's plans give aid to worthy causes.

* *

Some claim that they do not know what one-tenth of their income is, because of the miscellaneous incomes. To those who think so we ask them if they have ever rightly endeavored to figure their tenth out?—and we further ask: Do they really want to find out?

NOTES

Rev. G. J. Green changes his address from Franklinton, N. C., to Stem, N. C.

Rev. J. G. Truitt writes that he is now able to be up. His friends will rejoice to hear this.

As usual Elon has had a great opening. Congratulations to friends and the administration.

We have received from Secretary E. T. Cotten the proceedings of the fiftieth annual session of the Eastern Virginia Sunay School Convention.

Rev. A. Victor Lightbourne has returned from overseas where he served as Religious Divisional Director at Chaumont, the headquarters of General Pershing. Brother Lightbourne sends, through this office, greetings to the Brotherhood. He is open for evangelistic engagements.

Let us have your co-operation at all times.

Building a Church, or Churches

(An editorial in The Herald of Gospel Liberty)

There is no more important question, apart from those touching the spiritual life, for the ministers and laymen of the Christian Church to ask themselves just now than whether or not we all together are building a church, or whether we are simply building churches—here a little group and there a little group making the largest object of their Christian activity to bring their own church in its own little field up to its largest local effectiveness. For the question is fundamental and primary. It touches the very life-sources of our denominational existence. It embraces the very possibility of there being any real organic usefulness and leadership for the Christian Church as a whole at all. Upon its answer will depend our future as a people, even as the way in which it has been answered shaped the history of our past. For it is simply impossible to build up any large and potent force out of separate church units which think of themselves as the real end of their endeavor.

As we interpret the history of the Christian Church, we feel sure that the greatest weakness of its past was that its pastors and people were busy building churches, and that they had little real consciousness of being engaged together in creating a great church, the united power of which should become a mighty force for the Kingdom of God in His world. As we have read of those days, and especially as from the lips of our older men we have learned that more personal and intimate story of the past which never finds its way into the printed page, we have been impressed with the patent fact that they were days of splendid achievement, and many of them of romantic interest, so far as individual preachers were concerned; but there was an absolute dearth of organic accomplishment to stir our admiration and applause.

They were days of great preachers, men who were vibrant with the spirit of freedom and who dared at the cost of persecution and ridicule to be pioneers in the way of religious liberty. They went everywhere preaching their new gospel, and at a cost to themselves of financial remuneration and personal comforts that bordered on the heroic. But as we look back over those years, it is hard for us to place our finger on any specific and definite fruit of their labor. They were busy, slavishly busy, preaching to churches—sometimes making it a point of satisfaction that the number to which they preached were so many; but there is little to indicate that those great preachers gave any real and purposeful thought to the building up of the Christian Church as a whole. The consequence was that there was no vessel, as it were, to receive and conserve their

efforts; there was no organization with clear objective and determined purpose ready to pick up their work and carry it on when they must lay it down. So all of their tireless labor and their touching sacrifice slowly disappeared with the dropping out of their converts, and there is scarcely a thing that is tangible now to show for all of their strenuous personal endeavor.

Every young preacher in the Christian Church today should be keenly conscious of the fact that he stands to have his life-work evaporated like that if he is simply touching folks, and is not interweaving much of his toil and energy into the fabric of some great organization. For organizations of men and women are the only permanent things in this world. And even organizations must be of greater than neighborhood significance in order to be permanent. Your individual converts will die, the homes to which you minister will soon be gone, and with the passing of a generation the influence which you have left in the world will have dwindled down to such homeopathic measure that it is invisible and uncertain—if you have been satisfied to wear your life out simply in serving folks. You have a duty to make your ministry more permanent than that. You owe it to yourself and you owe it to your Christ to so build it into His church that even through the centuries much that you have done shall remain.

Those days of the past were days of great churches as well as of great ministers. From our older men we have learned of many churches, some of them in the cities, but most of them in towns or the open country, which two score of years ago or more were crowded with communicants and apparently filled with a spirituality and power which must endure. Yet to us, those churches are mostly only names and a memory. In large part, they have passed away entirely. A few remain, but with old and dingy buildings and a little handful of people who compose a struggling and discouraged congregation. Almost without exception, we think, wherever any of those local churches are at present a strong and vigorous and admirably going concern, it is the result of more recent renewal and reinvigoration by some of our present preachers—and not the accumulated power and glory of the past handed as a rich heritage to our present generation. It all seems a pathetic and dreadful loss—a loss that would discourage Christian service and sacrifice if we were not wise enough to analyze its history and learn the reason. No man or woman would want to give large sums for the erection of a church building in their community, if such is to be the inevitable, or even the likely, result. No real Christians would be satisfied to wear their lives out

We ask a most studious reading of this long editorial only because we feel that the subject is primary to all that the Christian Church can ever hope to be or to do as an organization. Too few of our pastors have seemed to realize that it is basic, and vital to their future as well as to that of the Christian Church.

to build up their church and Sunday school if they felt that these were to be of such short duration—and that a single generation might see them become only a shadow of their former usefulness, or even disappear altogether. No preacher who has in his heart any real concept of his commission as a minister of the gospel of Christ could for a moment be content to spend any part of his life in an effort so transient and evanescent.

Yet it is to this very gloomy outlook that every minister and every layman is doomed as they meditate upon the final outcome of their Christian service, if they are engaged in simply building up local churches. If the object of their endeavor is only the particular church of which they happen just now to be the pastor, if their time and thought and energy are lavished upon it as an end within itself or even as the instrument of Christian ministry in that local community, then there is nothing in the history of such churches to warrant a pastor in expecting anything really permanent either for that community or for the world to come out of his ministry. The experience of every denomination has been just to the contrary; for it has shown how vain and unprofitable a thing local church ambition and selfishness. is. Every man and woman who is a member of a congregation ought to be made to realize this. They should understand from the very first that any church that lives just for itself and for its own community will afterwhile die—that there is no power of finance and no amount of spiritual ardor that can preserve its glory for any long number of years. They should be made keenly to feel that all of their gifts and all of their sacrifices and all of their labor for its upbuilding are very transient things, the fruits of which may pass away with their own generation. How true this is, we every one know if we stop to think. Many a person who has given liberally to the church in his own community in the days of its vigor has lived to see it go out of existence, or to become a decadent and ineffective institution. For it is an eternal law of God that individual churches cannot long be self-sustaining and continue an independent existence. They must either be an organic part of some larger and more permanent organization, or they will perish.

Yes, those were days of great churches—but they were not the days of a great church. Those local units had no impelling aspiration larger than their own community existence and success. It was very rare that any of their pastors even tried to make those churches feel that they had a ministry just as definite and just as imperative to perform for the Christian Church at large as they did for their own home neighborhoods. Indeed as we know the history of these men, and as we know the men of our ministry today, we doubt very much if those pastors felt that they themselves had any definite and binding obligation to the denomination. They were absorbed in their little local church work, and gave little time or thought to the building up of the Christian Church. They and their membership were trying to build churches, and not to build a church.

The result was inevitable. After while that strong pastor left that strong church, and slowly through the years it disintegrated. The conferences were too loosely builded together to conserve and care for that which its great preachers left behind. But worse than that: The strong churches really competed with each other and with the weak churches to secure the few able preachers. The struggling mission points, which might have been nurtured by the combined effort of the churches into great city organizations, were left to struggle along the best they could with the weak and indifferent type of preacher which was the only kind they had money enough of their own to hire. It did not take many years of such a process for the larger part of the conference to die out. This left the big church or two isolated and alone. Such isolation means extinction for a church—and in every case it proved so. Thus have whole conferences gone out of existence. Hence these local congregations defeated their own selfish purposes. Trying to get for themselves the best obtainable preachers—regardless of how much those men were needed at the strategic points or in the general work of the denomination—they came afterwhile to stand so isolated and alone that no strong man cared to minister to them. The whole condition was also conducive to an inefficient type of minister. There was nothing in it to challenge the best blood of youth—and scores of young men of finest caliber in the membership of our churches in those days found nothing in such a condition to win them to the ministry as a life-work.

If the churches defeated their purpose, even so did the pastors who devoted their lives to building up these local fields instead of the Christian Church. As they grew older, there was no advancement for them—and some of them passed away in obscurity and poverty whose old age would have been fruitful and glorious if they had labored to larger and more permanent purpose. Nothing else could have been expected. And nothing else can be expected now if our preachers and our laymen are busying themselves with building churches. If their thought and their motive and their interests and gifts are circumscribed to their own local community, the Christian Church as a whole and in its parts is doomed.

It is not a principle which can be fulfilled by tacking on the conference and denominational interests as a subsidiary and after-thought. It is a law of life which is far more primary than that. It requires that the church at large shall come first and be the real object of our endeavor. The aim and ambition and purpose of the preacher and of the layman must come to be that larger ministry to the world which can be given only as our local churches are builded into the organization that is spending itself for these broader interests of the Kingdom.

When you have thought it through, you will agree with me that it is primary, and that the whole tenor and impress of our lives will be decided by whether or not we are endeavoring to build a church, or whether we are frittering our lives away on building churches!

If you have a neighbor to whom you would like to have a few sample copies of THE SUN sent, send us the name.

PASTOR AND PEOPLE

SUFFOLK LETTER

There are two classes of human beings that are to be pitied rather than blamed: they are myopes and hypermetropes, near-sighted and far-sighted people. . The myopic person sees the things near, close at hands; the hypermetropic sees the things that are far away. This, so far, has reference to physical vision, seeing material objects; but there are mental myopes and mental hypermetropes; persons who are questions in one or the other of these two extremes. Such persons are in society, in business, in the State, and in the church. In the church there are some who see nothing beyond their local congregation and its work at home. They might be called near-sighted Christians. Their spiritual world is a single neighborhood, a few neighbors, a small Sunday school, and Saturday and Sunday preaching once a month. They do not attend the Saturday service; but "we pay him to preach on Saturday, and we expect him to do it." Now "Saturday preaching" was useful in by-gone years; but that day has passed away with the pitcher of water on pulpit and the spittoon on the floor of the church, and *in* the pulpit. The congregation, in these days, should spend Saturday in closing up the work of the week and preparing to give Sunday to the work of the church.

These myopic or near-sighted Christians believe in home missions only, if they see far away, to believe in missions at all. They believe in saving the "heathen at home." Tears of sympathy for people who live close to the church, but never attend, flow from myopic eyes; but they have not seen their duty in trying to save those near by their own door. They are so narrow in their vision that they see only their own officers and even the "home church" gets very little of their thought, their presence, their money, or their prayers. I saw the limb of a Spanish oak once that grew out and then back into the trunk, but it grew no leaves and no fruit. Myopic people see very little beyond themselves and then turn their eyes back into their own little world of self-interest.

The hypermetropic people are of the opposite type; they see things far away. They see just what others should do in their homes, and neglect their own. They believe in foreign missions, in great schemes, in world-reforms, in public sanitation and good roads. They read great books and neglect small duties. They tell you how to farm, but neglect to plow; they lecture on sanitation and fail to remove rubbish from their back yards. They plead for woman's rights while their children cry for maternal attention. Public welfare is in their broad vision, while home suffers for the use of the broom. The club rises above the kitchen, and the public meeting fares better than the husband at home. They tell us how to bring up children while they neglect their own. Visions of great things loom up before them while small duties lie at their door crying for help, "If the prophet had bid thee do some great thing, wouldst thou not have done it? how much rather then, when he saith to thee wash, and be clean." Jesus made

Himself the world's great example by serving in small things while He planned for great things.

Choosing between the near-sighted Christian and the far-sighted Christian, between the myopic and the hypermetropic, I would choose the far-sighted as he might give others a vision of something worthy to be done; but there is a normal vision that sees little things and great things in right relation, and embraces Home Mission and Foreign Missions, local needs and benevolent obligations on a large scale.

W. W. STALEY.

NEWS FROM REV. G. D. HUNT

I am at Lanett, Alabama, assisting Rev. E. M. Carter in a meeting. We are having good attendance and expect a good meeting. I have had good meetings at all my churches and some have been *very* fine but no great ingathering.

I have been in revival meetings since the last of June, with the exception of a few days. There remains only a little more than five weeks before conference meets and we will now bestir ourselves to get ready for that occasion. The writer expects a great meeting and hopes to be ready when the time comes. Our conference will meet at Antioch, three and one-half miles South of Roanoke, Alabama, Tuesday after the second Sunday in October. Let all who desire to come take notice. There are some very grave questions that will present themselves at this session of our body, and therefore I beg of you to send a full delegation of the best you have, and let us do business for God on a larger scale than before. By the help of the Lord we must provide for our work. Our ministry needs to be better cared for, our local churches need to be better provided for and our general missionary work needs provision in some substantial manner. Let us not be in such a hurry but come determined to attend the Lord's business in a business way.

September 5, 1919. G. D. HUNT.

UNION (SOUTHAMPTON), VA.

The second Sunday in September was appointed for the protracted meeting at this church. I went over Saturday before, and remained a few days. Brother H. H. Butler, the pastor, filled his appointment Sunday but had to return home the same day on account of illness in his family. He secured the service of Brother W. W. Staley to conduct the meeting in his absence. He came Monday and did the preaching the remainder of the week. Everything seemed to be favorable for a good meeting.

While there I stayed at the pleasant home of Brother E. L. Joyner who is one of the oldest members of the church. He has been a faithful and useful member. He, his helpful wife, the kind, polite entertaining boys and girls did everything to make me pleasant and at home. Indeed, I have been in this delightful home so much that I feel at ease and happy whenever I am there. I hope I will never forget them for their many acts of kindness to me. May our Father bless them greatly, and give them the victory through Jesus.

J. T. KITCHEN.

AMONG MY CHURCHES
(Good Hope)

I took charge, as pastor, of this church last January. Bad weather and Spanish Influenza caused our congregations to be small the first three appointments. We had a large congregation the second Sunday in April, however; and the congregations have been still larger ever since. A cemetery having been started on the church grounds in April, we held the first memorial services at Good Hope church on the second Sunday in May. The building would scarcely hold all of the people who attended the services.

We held our Children's Day exercises here, the second Sunday in June. There were more people on hand for this occasion than the church could seat; but many of those who saw and heard the exercises, told me afterward that they thoroughly enjoyed them. This was the first Children's Day exercises that Good Hope Christian church ever held.

The second Sunday in July was another gala day for Good Hope; for it was on that day that "Uncle" Wellons preached so ably and so timely a sermon to one of the largest congregations that have attended this church in many a day.

Our revival here this year began on the second Sunday in August, and closed on Friday of the same week. Rev. B. J. Howard came to our assistance on Tuesday, and did the preaching the remainder of the time. We received three members into the church as a result of this meeting. Not only our own people, but also our Baptist brethren of the community were very highly pleased with Brother Howard and with his preaching. Several voluntarily told me that they thought I got the right man to assist me in this meeting. Brother Howard is a good preacher. The Spirit was certainly with him during the entire series of meetings. We feel that the spiritual condition of the church was considerably bettered by his preaching and other efforts.

Our people here, as well as at Plymouth, are planning to make some necessary repairs on the building this fall, and to put better furniture into it, (seats and pulpit chairs). Furthermore, our wide-awake Sunday school here, as well as the one at Plymouth, has voted to give the offering of one Sunday in each month to the Orphanage, and one Sunday's offering in each month to Sunday school missions. We have a flourishing Sunday school here.

This church has called me to serve as its pastor for another year. Thus far, three of my churches have called me back for another year: Youngsville, Plymouth, and Good Hope. My definite reply to these calls must be given very soon. I am very thankful to God for the privilege of serving, feebly though it has been, all four of my churches this year.

R. P. CRUMPLER.

Varina, N. C.

UNCLE WELLONS VISITS HIGH POINT

On Saturday, September 6, in company with Rev. L. L. Wyrick and wife, I started on a trip to High Point. We arrived there that afternoon and the night was pleasantly spent with Brother J. G. Albright, the grandson of Rev. Joseph Albright, of my early association. Brother Albright has a pleasant family and is living with his third wife.

Next morning, Sunday, I went to the church where they had a splendid Sunday school under the direction of the faithful superintendent, Brother R. C. Boyd. At 11:00 o'clock a very large congregation gathered and the children remained for preaching. I preached, using as a text, "Prepare to Meet Thy God." I addressed myself mainly to the old and unsaved, and at the close of the service several old people, by invitation, came expressing a desire for prayer. It was a great pleasure to see these aged persons coming forward asking for prayer.

It was a great joy indeed to spend this day with High Point church. I took dinner with Brother M. L. Boswell and had a pleasant rest there. Brother L. R. Gibson took me to Brother H. T. Moffitt's, where I spent the night. I met Alpheus and Hugh, the two sons of Rev. H. T. Moffitt, deceased. Sunday night I attended the Methodist Protestant revival. The service that night was conducted in the Methodist Episcopal church in order to hold the large congregation made up of the two churches that were worshipping together at this service. Monday morning I visited the Methodist Protestant Orphanage near High Point. Superintendent Garrett and his wife made my visit pleasant and profitable, gave me a good dinner and an opportunity to speak to the children. I reached home in the afternoon, after seeing and shaking the hands of so many dear friends.

As the weather grows cooler it will be a pleasure to visit some other churches that have in their congregations old and unsaved persons, if they will command me.

J. W. WELLONS.

THE EMPTY HOTEL

A traveller drew up at a country inn. But when he asked for oats for his horse he was told by the landlord that he "didn't keep oats." When he asked for hay the reply was that he "didn't keep hay." It was the same when he asked for ham and eggs for himself. The landlord didn't keep ham and eggs.

"But, landlord," cried the exasperated tourist, "what do you keep?" "Well, sir, I want you to know I keep this Hotel!"

A writer in the *Philadelphia Presbyterian* uses this story to illustrate his own experience when he listened to the "constitutional questions" put to a young candidate for Presbyterian ordination.

The young man didn't hold to the inspiration of the Scriptures, the Fall of Man, the Virgin Birth of Jesus, or His bodily Resurrection; but still he insisted he "kept the fundamental doctrines of Presbyterianism." He kept "this Hotel" all right but the trouble was that he kept nothing in its cellar, its pantry or its barn.

It is a sad experience when hungry travellers come on Sunday to the church inn, one of its resting places on life's way, and are sent away hungry.—*Presbyterian Record.*

CHRISTIAN EDUCATION

OUR PUBLIC SCHOOLS

A Bird's-eve View of One of the Greatest of American Institutions

One of the biggest tasks that the United States has on her hands is the work of educating the nation. In public and private schools and colleges in 1915 (and the figures of today do not materially differ) there were 23,113,931 scholars. Of this immense number 19,990,316 were in elementary schools,—kindergarten, primary, and grammar; 14,841,028 were enrolled in high schools and academies; 80,944 in primary departments of higher institutions; 237,168 in universities and colleges; 66,065 in professional schools; and 100,325 in normal schools. The task of providing equipment and teachers for this great army of youth is truly gigantic.

Every State in the Union has on its statue-books some kind of compulsory attendance law, but there is no uniformity either in the laws themselves or in their enforcement. There are multitudes of children in the United States who somehow escape going to school. This is shown by the fact that of children between 14 and 16 years of age to whom Federal certificates are issued under the Federal Child-Labor Law of 1916 one-fourth were unable to sign their names legibly. A yet greater number do not take the full course even in the grammar school, only 13 per cent of those in the primary school succeeding in passing the eighth grade.

The matter of educating the children of the country is left to the States, although the Federal Bureau of Education is working hard to raise the standard. There are some States (few, to be sure) that have no standard at all and present no education requirement. New York, which has a high standard, calls for schooling for nine years, and insists that illiterates between 16 and 21 years old shall attend night school. Children of 14 may leave school if they have an eighth grade certificate; or a sixth grade certificate if they are 15, and then they must attend continuation classes.

There are States, on the other hand, whose standard is very low. The period of school attendance required in Mississippi is only 60 days a year, and the minimum session required in Arkansas, Oklahoma, and South Carolina, is three months, or 60 school days, a year. A Federal standard for school attendance should be fixed, probably at least eight months in the year.

From tables published by the Bureau of Education it is made plain that only 117 out of every 1,000 pupils who enter the first grade in school graduate from high school.

Almost 58 per cent of the school population in the United States is found in rural communities—a rural community being defined in government tables as the population outside cities of 5,000 inhabitants.

The total number of common school teachers in 1916 was 622,371, and this number is probably slightly higher today. In 1870 there were only 200,515 common school teachers engaged in the various States. In 1890 there were 363,922; in 1910 there were 528,210; and

in 1915 there were 604,301. Of the 622,371 teachers employed in 1916 no fewer than 499,333 were women.

In 1916 there were 1,229 cities of more than 5,000 inhabitants in the United States. There cities had a combined enrollment of 7,173,112 pupils and an average attendance of 5,762,197. They had 194,449 teachers and 13,269 supervising officers. The cost of running the schools in these cities was $256,941,963, not counting more than $58,000,000 for new buildings and equipment. Of public school teachers 33 per cent are in the cities, and they receive about 51 per cent of the salaries paid to teachers; the running expenses of the city educational systems amount to about 48 per cent of such expenses for the whole of the United States and their outlays for buildings, sites, equipment, and so on, reach 57 per cent.

The average monthly salary of male teachers is only $85.36, and of female teachers $66.88, the annual average salary of all teachers, male and female, being $63.08. Of course the rate of pay varies greatly in the different States. Taking the pay for male teachers, the average in New Hampshire is $116.39 a month; in Maine, $83.26; in Vermont, $90.39; in Rhode Island, $142.03; in Connecticut, $127.03; in Pennsylvania, $68.63. Salaries are lowest in Delaware, where the average for men is $57.06.

It is evident that public schools will do little good if the children are not kept in them. In view of the fact that nearly sixty per cent of the school children live in rural communities, it is strange that one-third of the States actually exempt from school attendance children who live at a distance from school of from two to ten miles, unless transportation is furnished them, the same time only a half a dozen States actualy furnish the necessary transportation.

When some of our States passed child-labor laws they evidently forgot that they had compulsory education laws on the statute-books. At least, no attempt was made to reconcile the two classes of laws. The Oklahoma public school law, for instance, exempts, for employment purposes, no children under 16 years of age, but the child-labor law permits them to go to work at 14. Minnesota has a school law that exempts children of 1 from school duty4 between April 1 and November 1, if they work at home; but the child labor law permits the boys and girls of this age to work all the year round in factories. In Texas children must go to school until they are 14 but they cannot go to work until they are 15. In Montana they may leave school at fourteen, but may not work until 16. What a paradise for youth!

The Federal Bureau of Education is working toward better educational facilities in all States, and progress is being made. Many States supply free textbooks to the scholars, and a few Sstates supply even clothing to poor children.—*Christian Endeavor World.*

Large salaries are making great inroads upon the minds of the young people, and in many cases causing them to leave school. No thoughtful parent will permit this.

WHAT NATURE TEACHES ABOUT GOD
A Campus Address to Elon Girls

(Mrs. W. A. Harper)

The subject which you have chosen for this occasion, assembled as we are around the arching doom of the sky is, it seems to me, most appropriate; for here on this campus unembellished by the art of man, rich in native splendor and simplicity, God and nature have met.

We want to consider together the characteristics of God which our campus teaches us. And first among these I think we should observe that he is a God of beauty, for not only has he furnished us with beautiful trees and undulating surface, but he covers every barren spot of that surface with a shining coat of green, by unanimous consent, the color most pleasing to the esthetic sense unless it be brown, in which he gloriously robes the autumn leaves and all nature in the wintry months.

But our God is a God also of generous loving heart, and this too is taught by the natural aspect of our campus. For on this campus God has lavishly provided large trees for our shade and comfort, and glorious birds for our delight and challenged us to sweet meditation.

He is in the third place the God of life. With each recurring spring nature gives abundant proof of the quickening into newness of life of all things in accordance with the life loving program of our Creator. It seems to me that this campus has become a special object of His life-loving nature. We read in the papers where death has invaded the sacred precints of student life on other campuses round about us, but for thirteen years the hand of Providence has granted immunity from death to every student* of this our Alma Mater. So that when I say our God is a God of life, how grateful we should be of the abundant evidence of it in our own midst!

But I would go a step further and would add that God is not only the God of life but of everlasting life. He has not made us tenants for a day nor even for the three score years, and ten said to mark the limit of the normal man's pilgrimage, but he has provided for us "through the Resurrection and the salvation of Jesus that for which the human heart has always longed, the sure possession of everlasting life."

And now may I not also have a little heart to heart talk with you in this connection in regard to your relation to college, because the God of nature through his kind providences has made possible for you the splendid privilege you now enjoy of being college girls?

The college drill you are getting will be a means, a method of force through which you will be given a vision of the possibilities that lie within you. It will open the windows of your soul, and the air of human life will sweep in to make you a sturdy and fine character if you arise to your opportunity. Then, too; I would have you look beyond the college walls. A college education is not the all, the be-all and end-all of life, but always a means for a larger vision, a method for better service and a force for greater power. Then, too, your parents sent you to college that you might be prepared to live at home. They would have you become wise and larger minded in order that you may bring a new strength and an earnest appreciation into the home which shall be loyal, rich and fine; that you may become great in heart and strong in will in order to bring into the home a gentleness which is sympathetic, loving and true.

I would have you lay a great deal of stress on the value of your health. Physical soundness gives great aid in getting hold of and holding sound views of life. Life is a mirror. One smiles into it and it smiles back, one frowns into it and it frowns back. If one is sick all life is sick. What ails you ails most folks in this world. Now all life is not well, sound and vigorous but if you yourself are, you can help to transmit that vigor and life into some one else. If we would only open the doors and windows of our hearts and souls in the presence of a strong, vigorous, happy person, we would just as surely catch that disease as we would smallpox from one infected with that disease.

At the age of thirty-two Robert Browning fell in love with Elizabeth Barrett. At that same period his headaches began. Up to that time he had been free from such symptoms. The relation between the head and heart may be close. The college girl should keep herself free from suffering and incapacities. She should not be plagued by headaches, heartaches, nervousness and indigestion. Therefore, I would caution you to be careful—very careful of your health.

Then I want to say get the very best for yourself from college. That may sound a little selfish but wait a bit and let me emphasize for yourself. For do you know what may be good for one may not be good for another? Try to find in college the supplies for your dire and direct wants. No gardener tries to raise cabbage from cucumber seed. You might wish you had more and better stuff in you, but you are what you are and education must educate that individual and individuality which God in nature out of all his material made you. In getting the best for yourself, let one element of that best be appreciation. In other words a love for the best. I want you to be able to know, just what is best, then love that best and then make that best a part of yourself. Perhaps you have already found that your teachers are nearer perfection in some lines than others. What I would have you do is to take each at his best and think as little as possible about his not best.

Cultivate an appreciation of the best books. Perhaps books have been so common a part of your furniture and homes that you may not know that some books are good, some better and some best. Be able to know the best books and make them a part of your life. I would like to say the same about music, hear the best music. Also about art, study the best pictures and paintings you can. By studying the best in nature, the God in nature and in art, you will know the best. By knowing the best, you will love the best. By knowing and loving the best you will become a part of the best.

This same rule holds good in forming friendship. Do you know the way for getting the very best friendship? Of course you do. It is to give the best of yourself. And do you know the surest way of giving the best of yourself? Of course you do. It is to find the best in the other girl. She has her best and not best just as you do. Find her best and help make it better. By so doing you will find yourself lifted, enlarged and inspired and the best of friendship formed.

I want to say one thing more, perhaps it is most important of all. Get the best and most out of your religion. The relation one bears to the Supreme Being is the most important. Many people do not get much out of their religion and certainly religion does not get much out of them. Emerson says somewhere every man must pray. The mood of prayer and the act of prayer belong to the devout soul. Keep up your church life. If the church is poor and the preaching uninteresting make the service of the church worship even if you cannot make it instruction and inspiration. Many girls and boys think they have to study on Sunday. It is very foolish. Use Sunday for a time of interpretation, reflection and inspiration. Make each day, too, like George Herbert's Sunday, "The bridal of the earth and sky," then your own intuitive good judgment will make you the real women of your mother's aspirations and prayers.

*This address was given before the influenza epidemic of 1918 took away three Elon students.

MISSIONARY

THE ONE FOLLOWS THE OTHER

The Methodist Episcopal church set out to raise $85,000,000.00 for missions throughout the world and easily went over the top and raised $112,000,000.00. That is testimony to the material possibilities of the Methodist church, and means service and sacrifice. Now the Committee on Findings for that church has adopted the following: "We recommend that we have a campaign of evangelism that shall occupy the pre-eminent place in the conservation program of the Church, and that the goal shall be at least one million souls won for Christ by June 1920."

This will call for an awakening of spiritual fervor and will no doubt result in winning hundreds of thousands, let us hope, even a full million souls to the blessed Christ within a year. They are ripe and ready for spiritual zeal and fervor who have been brought to the point of sacrificing material resources on the altar. The church that undertakes great things for Christ may expect great things of Christ. Any adequate program for a working church must be big, must be built on faith, and must challenge to sacrifice and evoke earnest effort and much prayer. We congratulate our Methodist brethren on a big program and a great vision for Christian service and conquest. God speed them.

WHEREIN IS POWER?

Are you surprised that students, teachers and workers of the Moody Bible Institute, Chicago, Ill., won 7,600 souls to Christ last year through personal effort and evangelistic endeavor? This writer is not. That Institution trained and last year sent out to foreign fields in various corners of the earth 120 missionaries. When an Institution, like a Church, catches a vision of world conquest for Christ, and undertakes to live up to that vision miracles take place and marvelous things happen.

J. O. ATKINSON.

IMPORTANT NEWS FOR ALL WOMEN OF THE CHRISTIAN CHURCH, THE NORTH CAROLINA CONFERENCE

1. Our Convention

We women are to hold our first Missionary Convention for the three former North Carolina Conferences at Elon College, November 8 and 9. You will find the program printed below—a great one I am sure you will agree with us.

We want every missionary organization in the Conference to send at least two delegates. We want every church not having a missionary organization to send at least two women delegates. The Elon women will give the best entertainment they can and will not be satisfied unless full delegations come. They are preparing for them. Send names of delegates to Mrs. J. O. Atkinson, Elon College, N. C.

We want you to make it impossible for your pastor to fail to be present. Some of us women feel our pastors

do not aid us as they might. Get yours to come and it will help matters.

2. Santa Isabel Chapel Fund

Our Conference is asked to raise over and above its regular apportionment $350 to complete the Santa Isabel Chapel. Your are requested to raise ten dollars at least and forward to Mrs. W. R. Sellars, Burlington, N. C., at once and to state it is for this purpose. We must have this at once for our Porto Rico work.

3. Dues and Regular Apportionments

All the regular societies have been asked to raise a certain apportionment besides dues. We urge that this matter be attended to immediately and the money forwarded to Mrs. W. R. Sellars, Burlington, N. C., stating clearly what society is to be credited and what goes to dues and what to the apportionment. We lack $1,500 now of raising our quota for this year, and must raise it by September 30.

Churches that have no missionary society have been asked to send at least ten dollars as an offering to the women's work. We want this in addition to the special offering asked for Santa Isabel.

4. Rally Days

All money raised in July and August Rally Days is to be kept separate from dues and apportionments. It will be used for literature. We expect to publish 12 pamphlets the coming year and will send them out free. Send your Rally Day money, properly marked, to Mrs. W. R. Sellars, Burlington, N. C. immediately.

5. Finally

Finally, won't you pray for the Women's Missionary Work of our Church? More things are accomplished by prayer than this world knows of. Won't you pray for the work?

MRS. W. A. HARPER,
Secretary N. C. Women's Missionary Board.

THE CHRISTIAN ORPHANAGE

A TRIP WE ALL HIGHLY ENJOYED

Some time ago we were invited to take our Singing Class to Liberty church, Vance County, N. C., and give a song service. We gladly accepted the invitation and also made arrangements to visit Fuller's Chapel and our friends at Henderson on the same trip. On Saturday, the thirteenth, of this month we bought tickets to Henderson, N. C., and were met there by friends from Henderson and Liberty churches who gave us a warm welcome. We were entertained Saturday night by the good people of Liberty church and gave our song service there Sunday morning at eleven o'clock. We were met there after service by our good friends of Fuller's church and entertained for dinner by them and gave the song service at Fuller's at three o'clock in the afternoon. At the close of the service we were then carried to Henderson where we were entertained Sunday night and gave our service there.

We have never enjoyed a trip more anywhere than on this occasion. The people at all the churches did all they could to make our visit pleasant and showed us every courtesy possible. The warm welcome we received inspired the children to do their best in rendering the song service and we trust that they, through this service of song, carried the gospel message to those who were present.

Mrs. Effie Wicker, the teacher, who has trained the Class and has it in charge and plays for them, joins me in expressing our sincere appreciation of the warm welcome extended to us and the class and the many kindnesses shown us while on this trip.

The free-will offering at Liberty church was $50.61 and the subscription for the Children's Home, $405.00.

The free-will offering at Fuller's church was $27.22 and the subscriptions for the Children's Home, $230.00.

The free-will offering at Henderson was $123.28 and the subscription for the Children's Home, $525.00.

CHAS. D. JOHNSTON, *Supt.*

FINANCIAL REPORT FOR SEPTEMBER 24, 1919

Amount brought forward, $10,009.18.

Sunday School Monthly Offerings

(North Carolina Conference)

Hine's Chapel, $2.00; Pleasant Hill, $3.50; Durham, $8.50; Shady Grove, $2.00; Sanford, $7.83; Lebanon, $5.69; Ramseur, $3.24; Wentworth, $6.71; New Lebanon, $1.00; New Lebanon Baraca Class, $1.00; Piney Plains, $4.70; Ashboro, $1.34; Christian Chapel, $4.50; Reidsville, $1.00; O'Kelley Bible Class, First Church, Greensboro, $25.00; Ingram, Va., $3.00.

(Valley Virginia Conference)

Timber Ridge, Va., $3.24.

(Eastern Virginia Conference)

Isle of Wight, Va., $2.50; Berea, (Nansemond), $10.00.

(Alabama Conference)

Rockstand, Ala., $1.26; Beulah, Ala., 98 cents; North Highlands, Ga., $2.30; Roanoke, Ala., $1.57; Wadley, Ala., $1.01; Total, $103.92.

Children's Home

Willis J. Lee (will), $500.00; Mrs. D. I. Langston, $5.00; Total, $505.00.

Singing Class

Liberty Church, (Vance County), $50.61; Fuller's Chapel, (Vance County), $27.22; Henderson Church, $123.28; Total, $201.11.

Special

W. H. Thomas, on support of children, $25.00; A. P. Thompson, on support of children, $25.00; Woman's Missionary Society, Memorial Temple, Norfolk, Va., $6.00; J. H. Jones, for children, $7.10; Masonic Lodge, near Liberty church, $8.30; Total, $71.40.

Total for the week, $881.43; Grand total, $10,890.61.

CORRESPONDENCE

AGED BIBLE WOMAN DIES

To the Editor of The Christian Sun:

I certainly appreciate the privilege you offer me of getting more directly into touch with the readers of THE SUN through its columns.

The most recent event with us here in Japan was the very sad one of the sudden death of Miss Hamaguchi, our oldest Bible woman, at the comparatively early age of 50. As the funds for her support were for quite a while specially provided by people in the Southland, there are no doubt those among your readers to whom

notification should be sent. Will they kindly accept this as such?

While of a quiet disposition, Miss Hamaguchi was a great force for good, and she will be sorely missed. Entering our work from what was very nearly its start, at one time and another she has been quite closely connected with all of our lady missionaries.

The workers die, but the work remains and institutions persist. In every way we give thanks to God for the advance which is making toward the building up of Japanese Christian Churches to continue the work of the Lord here after all the present workers have passed on.

We are looking forward to the World's Sunday School Convention which meets in Japan next year, as destined in the good providence of God to be one of the great landmarks of progress. I trust that many, both there and here, are already praying much for its success.

E. C. FRY.

Utsunomiya, Japan, Aug. 21, 1919.

A TROUBLED MOTHER

I have the following question from a heart-broken mother: "I am writing you about something that has grieved me because I cannot fully understand. It is about God answering prayer. I thought possibly you could explain in a way that would ease my poor aching heart. I love my Savior, and am trying to live nearer Him every day. I had two sons to go into the war. The younger went in May, 1919, the older in June, 1918. My older son was wounded on November 4, and died November 8. My younger one was spared. They both were in the last hard battles. My younger did not get a scratch, and is home now. I am thankful, Oh so thankful, that he was spared to come back, but my heart aches for the one "over there." I can hardly bear the thought that I shall never see him again on this earth. I used to bow my head before their pictures every morning and plead with my Heavenly Father to spare them and let their poor mother see them once more, but that if it were His will that they would be killed that they might be prepared for death. When the older sailed for France, he wrote a letter telling me that he was going to live a better life and sent a card signed pledging his allegiance to Christ, and the card allied him with Y. M. C. A. Now, my question is: Have I the right to believe that God did answer my prayer in behalf of the one that was killed as much so as did He in behalf of the one that returned safely?"

I am of the conviction that this mother has every right to believe that her prayers were answered in both instances. Our prayers are often answered for us far better than we ask or at the time can know. The fact that the older son did not return is no evidence whatever of our Father's cruelty or unkindness to Him any more than to the other. Time will reveal all things and some day we shall understand but this we may know and be assured of; at all times, namely; that God hears and answers prayer. He is too wise to err, and too kind and loving to do any cruel thing. Blessings upon this broken-hearted mother. J. O. ATKINSON.

WORSHIP AND MEDITATION

THE PHILOSOPHY OF CRUCIFIXION
(Rev. R. F. Brown)

Religion must be established before the religionist, crucifixion before philosophy, the birth before the birthday. Every great movement has its birthday. It must undergo the trying ordeals of incarnation. And, what is more, it cannot get into the world without a great man—a great leader. There is no such thing as painless birth; but associated with every great movement worthy of acceptance there is found one who has paid the price for its existance. With this price is associated the fact of crucifixion. There is no adequate expansion without proper nourishment, safe and sane management, and devout loyalty. Neither is there perpetuity without true and tried principles.

Crucifion is the result of loyalty to principle. This is not a new doctrine. Its origin runs back to the days of ancient thought and finds favorable comment in the modern world. It has been preached and practiced by individuals of varying conception and personality. The road is no new one. It has been beaten and blazed by other travelers in order that they might give expression to their profound feeling of love and devotion to a principle that was near and dear to their hearts. To crucify self was the noblest act, the highest embodiment of a desire to reach and end, which end would be the culmination of their glory, the final goal of their weary struggle. Abraham is an example of this same principle. He was willing to crucify his son that he might prove his loyalty to God, his willingness to put God first, since he loved God supremely. This was not only an act of sacrifice, but an act of service. Abraham crucified his own will, his personal desires, his selfish motives, and his fatherly ambitions in order that God's demands might be accomplished.

The Hindoo supported this same doctrine of crucifixion. In their "Doctrine of Progress," they laid peculiar stress on the fact that there must be a definite restraint of the senses in order to experience the joys of temporal and spiritual blessing and achievement. To them the senses proved to be mysterious and molesting tyrants. They seemed to think that if they were to depend upon their senses that the eye might guide them in the wrong direction, the ear might convey the wrong message, the feeling might prove to be a traitor and thus upset and forever hinder their peace of mind and banish their hopes of the future. Therefore they found great satisfaction in crucifying these senses. In every life there are deep feelings of devotion and reverence, keen desires for better things to satisfy the longing of the subjective man.

Gautoma, the Buddha, tried to find satisfaction in crucifixion. But to him this proved to be a false philosophy. It was his notion that man could secure peace only in practical oblivion. He thought that the final extinction of all desire aspiration and effort, and even of personality itself, was the only worthy goal of the faithful. This course of action by Gautoma was caused by the suggestion of the priest. The priest insisted on Buddha crucifying his whole physical being in order that he might obtain salvation. But after he had gone through with all the processes and experienced all the excruciating pain, the weakness of the theory was evidenced by the absence of the thing for which he was striving. He and Luther had a similar experience in this respect, so they worked out a new theory, and set about the task of accentuating the doctrine of the new philosophy, which with some it was received with favor, while with others it met with stern opposition.

Men ignored and opposed the ideal for which Christ died. But He never could have taught the world in things of life and eternity had He not had grace to look over and rise above the things of the world. If crucifixion is to become a reality there must be grace, resignation and obedience. Thus adhering to these three things, devotion to principle and loyalty to truth are displayed to the admiration or utter dismay of men and angels.

Crucifixion is a terrible thing, but it may be, and frequently is, the best policy and the best adopted course for obtaining the blessing for one's self, or another. This was certainly the best plan for God to reveal Himself to the world, and shows the infiniteness of His love. No other act could have borne testimony to the love of God so completely as the act of crucifixion. This is not only true with God, but it is equally true with reference to man. It is evident that the efforts of man are well nigh exhausted when he appeals to the transaction of crucifixion to bring to pass the results which his feelings so crave.

It is obvious that no one would resort to crucifixion in order to obtain certain results unless there is a dislike for present situations and a hatred of the subsequent responses. It was because Christ hated the existing conditions of the world that He allowed Himself to be subjected to such an act of self-denial and shameless death. Buddha was seeking to better his OWN conditions and thus give the world the benefits of said betterment through the form and medium of thought. Luther was seized by the same thought when he searched for satisfaction through the act of crucifixion.

The events of Christ's crucifixion serve as an illustration to all the world. By this act our sins and innumerable transgressions have been expiated, by this act the reconciliation of hand, head and heart is derpetrated. It is on the cross of crucifixion that peace of conscience is obtained. On the Cross the handwriting of other days is cancelled. On this same Cross we ascend the other heights, and experience the joys of promotion into other environments, in Kingly company, where the soul finds refuge and repose.

Durham, N. C.

If the getting of money alone was all the benefit that would come to the Church by the method of tithing, it would be a failure. But when a man recognizes God by paying his tithe, he acknowledges God in other ways and God will soon have his life. A man's treasure and his heart are inseparable and where you find one you will find the other.

Some men pray that God may send some one to do a thing, while perhaps what God wants is for them to go. Others pray that some way may be opened, while the way may be in their purses. Take out your pocket book and pray for the Lord to its contents. We must open our purses as well as our mouths.

Trust in God as well as in gold.

A MODEL LIFE

When you think, when you speak, when you read,
　when you write,
When you sing, when you walk, when you seek for
　delight,
To be kept from all harm when at home or abroad,
Live always as under the eyes of the Lord.

Whatever you think, never think what you feel
You would blush in the presence of God to reveal;
Whatever you say in a whisper or clear,
Say nothing you would not like Jesus to hear.

Whatever you read, though the page may allure,
Read nothing of which you are perfectly sure
Consternation at once would be seen in your look
If God should say solemnly, Show me that book.

Whatever you write, though with haste or with heed,
Write nothing you would not like Jesus to read;
Whatever you sing in the midst of your glee,
Sing nothing that His listening ears would displease.

Wherever you go, never go where you fear,
Lest the great God should say, How camest thou here?
Turn away from each pleasure you would shrink from
　pursuing
If God should look down and say, What are you doing?
　　　　　　　　　　　—Selected.

OUR ALL THE YEAR ROUND GARDEN

By Ellen Eddy Shaw, Brooklyn Botanic Garden

The best behaved fall garden child I know is Daffodil, and next to her, her little brother Jonquil. Sometimes great big fat Hyacinth behaves, but small, brown-coated, smooth-looking, long-nosed Daffodil is quite the nicest. So buy a few daffodil and jonquil bulbs and get acquainted with these two good children.

I would let our new friends stay on the table for several days before I planted them, so that we might get to know them by sight and by name, as we learn to know real flesh-and-blood children. But I would be very careful to place these little comrades so that the rounded part or base was down and the pointed face sticking up, and I would never squeeze their noses!

By and by the day will come when Jonquil and Daffodil must be planted. There are several ways of doing this. Suppose we use a glass jar first. It may be a little fern bowl, like the one in which patridge berries are sometimes planted. We fill the bowl almost full of fine white sand and if we have no sand we take some baskets or our little carts and go to a house that is being built and ask the builder if he will give us just a little sand for our garden. Into this bowl full of sand we plant our daffodil or our jonquil bulbs. They must

nestle down so that only a little bit of their noses stick 'out. Two bulbs must never touch each other. They would not be comfortable that way. Two little girls would not like to sit so close to each other at the breakfast table that neither one could move.

Next, give the bulbs a big enough drink to soak the sand thoroughly, but not enough to have water standing on the surface. Now put the bowl away in the dark. The place need not be cool, but every little while the sand should be moistened.

In about ten days or two weeks, lo and behold, you will notice long white roots struggling all around and through the sand close to the glass where you can see them, and the noses have put forth some white leaflike shoots. It is now time to bring our little garden to the light. Then in just a few days a miracle takes place. The roots have shot back into the sand; they do not like the light, and want always to remain cool and covered. The noses have turned green. And within about three weeks Daffodil and Jonquil blossom!

Sometimes instead of using the sand, place some small stones in a low, pretty bowl and arrange the bulbs on top of them. This bowl should be put away in the dark for about ten days or two weeks and then brought out into the light. There should always be enough water to touch the base of the bulbs, but never to come around them. This, you see, is just the way we start Chinese lily bulbs, but Daffodil behaves better than the Chinese lilies because her blossoms rarely blast.

If you like, Daffodil and Jonquil may also be planted in a pot or soil. Even so, leave their noses sticking out and you must put them in a dark, cold place for five or six weeks. It is better, I think, to use the sand or the stones with Daffodil and Jonquil because then you don't have to wait so long for them.

After you have planted your first two or three daffodils and find out just how long it takes in your home for them to blossom, you could start some for Father's birthday, timing them just right. Of course, it is understood that Father will be kind enough to have a birthday this fall. If he will not, then Mother or Grandmother or Baby surely will. I cannot imagine a family without at least one birthday in the fall or early winter.

To the parents: Just what does a child get out of this little garden? One lesson is a lesson of observation, and another is one of care; careful watering. The greatest lesson is the lesson of life: how out of something apparently lifeless there springs into being something living, beautiful and sweet. It is a great revelation to anyone, young or old, to handle life and to be able to produce something living, to care for it, and to make it comfortable and happy. And then, you can have such fun planting bulbs.

Of course, there are other bulbs one may plant, but I am choosing two perfectly satisfactory, absolutely responsible ones. I believe that in work with children one should rarely choose what may be a failure. So, in our all-the-year-round garden we pick out successes. Do not forget the names of our fall children, Daffodil and her little brother, Jonquil.—In The Christian Advocate (New York).

Sunday School and Christian Endeavor

Editorial Note: At this writing (Wednesday, September 17) when we are called upon to supply the matter for this page, the Sunday school and Christian Endeavor topics have not reached us.

MEETING OF THE BOARD OF RELIGIOUS EDUCATION

This Board which has charge of the Sunday School and Christian Endeavor work for the Southern Christian Convention met in annual session at Raleigh N. C., September 11. Members present: Rev. J. W. Harrell, *Chairman*, Burlington, N. C.; Rev. A. T. Banks, Ramseur, N. C.; R. C. Boyd, High Point, N. C.; Rev. J. V. Knight, Greensboro, N. C.; C. H. Stephenson, Raleigh, N. C., Secretary-Treasurer; Rev. W. T. Walters, Winchester, Va.; Mrs. Fred Bullock, Suffolk, Va.; I. A. Luke, Vice President, Holland, Va.; J. O. Atkinson, Recording Secretary, Elon College, N. C. Absent: Hon. C. A. Hines, Greensboro, N. C.

A Committee from the Eastern Virginia Sunday School Convention, under appointment of its recent session was present, consisting of Drs. W. W. Staley, Suffolk, Va.; C. H. Rowland, Franklin, Va.; L. E. Smith, Norfolk, Va.; and these brethren were invited to sit and to counsel with the Committee.

The meeting was opened with prayer led by Rev. W. W. Staley. Treasurer C. H. Stephenson reported expenditures for the year of $108.21, also a loan to the Board from the Mission Board of $200.00 and a check from the Recording Secretary, J. O. Atkinson of $116.54 by offerings on Children's Day.

It was decided that Children's Day be observed annually hereafter in all our schools on some Sunday in June and that on that day an offering be asked by the Board for the promotion of Sunday school and Christian Endeavor work.

It was voted unanimously that all our Sunday schools and Christian Endeavor Societies be asked to make a monthly offering to the mission cause, one-half for home missions, one-half for foreign missions, and that it be the sense of this Board

that the half for home missions be turned into the Board, and the half for foreign missions to the Mission Board of the Southern Christian Convention, and that the same rule be applied to Christian Endeavor Societies.

After such discussion and consideration it was moved and carried that a Field Secretary for Sunday school and Christian Endeavor work be employed for full time provided that the Mission Board of the Southern Christian Convention turns the Sunday school home mission funds and home mission offerings into the hands of the Field Secretary be left to the Executive Committee.

The request from the North Carolina Sunday School and Christian Endeavor Convention that Rev. J. E. Franks be put in the field for half time in the coming year to do work as Sunday school missionary was unanimously approved, and the Home Mission Board of the North Carolina Christian Conference to whom properly this work belongs was asked to finance and have oversight of the same.

It was voted that the Southern Convention at its next session be asked to revise its church letter blank and that a member of the Board be placed on the Revision Committee so that there shall be ample space for getting essential Sunday school statistics. Mrs. Fred Bullock of our Board was elected to represent us on the proposed Revision Committee.

A sub-committee of three was selected to shape the policy of the Board, and submit the same to the members thereof for ratification and the same when ratified be presented to the next session of the Convention. Revs. Harrell, Knight and Atkinson were named on this sub-committee.

It was voted that Mrs. Bullock be elected to furnish the Sunday school matter for THE CHRISTIAN SUN the coming year and that Rev. J. V. Knight be elected to furnish the Christian Endeavor matter, and that one-half of the space allowed be given to the treatment of the topic and the other half to Sunday school

and Christian Endeavor matters.

The meeting time of the next annual session is Thursday after the first Sunday in September, 1920, and the place, Raleigh, N. C.

It was voted that we approve the Seaside Chautauqua and School of Methods and the proposed Religious Institute to be held at Elon College next summer, and that we co-operate in any way we can for the success of both.

The counsel and presence of Dr. Staley, Dr. Rowland and Dr. Smith added much to the interest of the meeting and the Board was greatly aided in its work by their wise counsel.

The feeling prevails that we are continually working toward a policy which shall vitally effect the Sunday School and Christian Endeavor work throughout the Convention.

J. O. ATKINSON,
Recording Secretary.
Elon College, N. C.

JUST COUNT ON HOLY NECK

It is a principle of missions, as it is of the Kingdom, that where you have just one person with zeal for a good work others catch fire and the flame spreads. Holy Neck Sunday school has such a person in Sister B. D. Jones. And things are taking place in the Kingdom there. She is Missionary Superintendent in the Sunday school. I received this morning this letter from Sunday school Treasurer C. A. Piland: "Holland, Va., September 12. Dear Brother Atkinson: Enclosed you will find check for $13.55. Mrs. B. D. Jones raised $11.50 on the fifth Sunday in August. They had a real nice missionary program that day and everybody enjoyed it. The Sunday school sends $2.55, its regular missionary offering."

(A former Missionary Day netted $20.30 which Brother Piland sent in August).

Somebody told the writer not long since that some of Sister Jones' five minutes Missionary stories and talks to the school on Sunday mornings were wonderful, in fact the feature of the Sunday school. Here is prophesying, on a basis of past facts, that if this work is kept up in a few years Holy Neck Sunday school and church will not only have their missionary in the field, but some of their sons and daughters volunteering to go as missionaries to carry the message of our blessed Christ where that message is needed most. Just count on Holy Neck. Our Father's blessings upon Sister B. D. Jones and the good work she is doing there.

J. O. ATKINSON.

ONE BY ONE

The Sunday schools are falling in line one by one in the matter of teaching and studying missions and giving one offering a month to missions. The North Carolina Christian Sunday School and Christian Endeavor Convention unanimously voted in annual session at Shallow Well last summer that all its schools should do this good thing, and the schools are proving their loyalty by doing so. This week comes a check of $3.36 from Treasurer W. S. Ayscue of Liberty (Vance County, North Carolina) stating the school had begun the missionary offering first Sunday of September. Good! The list of missionary Sunday schools is beautifully enlarging itself. Our schools are deciding to start something, to "carry on."

J. O. ATKINSON.

THE TRUE HOME
(John Ruskin)

This is the true nature of home—it is the place of Peace; the shelter, not only from all injury, but from all terror, doubt and division. In so far as it is not this, it is not home. So far as the anxieties of the outer life penetrate into it, and the inconsistently minded, unknown, unloved, or hostile society of the outer world is allowed by either husband or wife to cross the threshold, it ceases to be home; it is then only a part of that outer world which you have roofed over, and lighted fire in. But so far as it is a sacred place, a vestal temple, a temple of the hearth watched by household gods, before whose face none may come, but those whom they can receive with love—so far as it is this, and roof and fire are types only of a nobler shade and light,—shade as of the rock in a weary land, and light as of the Pharos in the stormy sea;—so far it vindicates the name and fulfills the praise of home.

And wherever a true wife comes, this home is always round her. The stars only may be over her head; the glow-worm in the night-cold grass may be the only fire at her feet; but home is yet wherever she is; and for a noble woman it stretches far around her, better than ceiled with cedar, or painted with vermillion, shedding its quiet light far, for those who else were homeless.

INDIVIDUAL COMMUNION SERVICE

THE BEST WAY to serve Communion. It is reverent, sanitary, and increases attendance at the Lord's Supper. Our services are chaste and beautiful. Made of finest materials and best workmanship.

Send for illustrated price list

C. B. RIDDLE, Publishing Agent, Burlington, North Carolina.

PELOUBET'S SELECT NOTES

Send your order for Peloubet's Select Notes on the Sunday school lesson along with your renewal to THE CHRISTIAN SUN. The books will be ready for delivery December 1. You need not send the money now, unless you want to. Just indicate for us to send you a copy December 1 and that will be all right. The price is $1.50.

CHARLES W. McPHERSON, M. D.

Eye, Ear, Nose, Throat

OFFICE OVER CITY DRUG STORE

Office Hours: 9:00 a. m. to 1:00 p. m.

and 2:00 to 5:00 p. m.

Phones: Residence 153; Office 65J

BURLINGTON, NORTH CAROLINA

OBITUARIES

BROWN

Mrs. Minnie Brown, wife of W. W. Brown, was born October 16, 1881 and died August 21, 1919, at the age 37 years. Surviving are four sisters, four brothers, father and mother, husband and three daughters.

Sister Brown was a faithful member of Union Grove Christian church. She was a general favorite among a host of friends who deeply mourn her untimely death. This breaking up of a happy home calls forth the deepest sympathy for the husband and motherless children.

Funeral services were conducted at Union Grove, August 23, by Rev. T. J. Green, assisted by L. W. Fogleman and R. O. Smith. May the Lord comfort and bless the sorrowing and prepare us all for a happy home in eternity.

MRS. C. C. BROWN.

SMITH

Joseph Eldredge Smith was born January 29, 1864 and died August 23, 1919, aged fifty-four years, six months and twenty-five days. He is survived by his wife and daughter, Mary Elizabeth, Sunbury, N. C., and two brothers, R. B. Smith, Meldrin, Ga., and J. A. Smith, Dendron, Va.

Brother Smith had been away from home about six weeks, working as a sawyer at Jacksonville, N. C. It was at this place that he was instantly killed, the carriage passing over him. It was a great shock to his family and many friends.

The deceased was a member of Damascus Christian church. He was a devoted husband and an affectionate father. Many grief-stricken friends gathered at his home on Sunday afternoon, August 25, 1919, to pay their last tribute of respect. Funeral service was conducted by the writer and interment was made in the family burying grounds, being in charge of the Masonic Order.

May God comfort the grief-stricken hearts.

W. B. FULLER.

DR. J. H. BROOKS

DENTIST

Foster Building   Burlington, N. C.

MORE SEPTEMBER SMILES

Reliable Firms

A pretty good firm is Watch & Waite.
Another is Attit, Early & Layte;
And still another is Doo & Dairet;
But the best is probably Grinn &
Barrett.
—*Woman's Home Companion.*

A Man of Parts

A celebrated vocalist was in a motor car accident one day. A paper, after reading the accident, added, "We are happy to state that he was able to appear the following evening in three pieces."—*Selected.*

Preferred Light Cream Color

Photographer.—Is there any particular way in which you would like to be taken?
Mr. Johnsing.—Yes, sah, if dere's no dejection, I'd like to be taken a light cream color.—*Boys' Life.*

Missed, But Not as Often

"I see they have taken the 7 a. m. train off this line. Do you miss it?" asked one suburbanite of another.
"I miss it, certainly; but not so often as I used to when it was on."
—*Selected.*

A Wonderful Memory

Elsie—"Mamma, George Washington must have had an awful good memory, didn't he?
Mother—"Why, my dear?"
Elsie—"Because everywhere I go I see monuments to his memory."

Changed The Tune

"Say, Eph, what's all the crowd hanging around Doolittle's emporium for?"
"Why he's got hold of a curiosity down thar," chuckled the village constable.
"What kind of curiosity?"
"Why, that old Jersey cow of his'n. T'other night she had colic, and he went down with his lantern to give her a dose of cow medicine. He made a mistake and fetched around a bottle of gasoline instead and give it to the cow!"
"Did it kill her, Eph?"
"No, but now, instead of going 'moo, moo,' like any ordinary, sensible critter, she goes 'Honk! Honk!' like a auttymobile.'"

Easily Explained

"Why does a woman value pearls and diamonds so highly?"
"I dunno," replied Farmer Corntossel. "I guess maybe it's for somethin' of the same reason these summer-girls think more of a four-leaf clover than they do of a whole load of hay,"—*Washington Star.*

Law!

"You'll plaize lave your umbreller or cane at the dure, sor," said the new Irish attendant at the picture gallery.
"Very proper regulation," said the visitor. "But it happens I have neither."
"Then go and get one. No one is allowed to enter unless he leaves his umbrella or cane at the dure. You may read the card yourself, sor."

Just 'Hollers

"What did your husband think of the ball game?"
"Oh, he doesn't go there to think. He just hollers."

Whoppers

"Are you aware, Lemuel, that alligator's eggs are so big that it only takes nine of them to make a dozen?"
—*The Independent.*

Do you know.

that saving three nickels a day with interest will come to $1,500 in about fifteen years.

THE TITHER

An interdenominational publication devoted to Tithing and Christian Stewardship.

Editors

C. B. RIDDLE
KARL LEHMANN
BERT WILSON
HUGH S. McCORD
FRED G. THOMAS

8 pages; issued monthly; 50c the year

Address

THE TITHER   Burlington, N. C.

THE CHRISTIAN SUN

OUR MOTTO: "ON TIME"	RELIEF AND BUSINESS NUMBER	OUR AIM: "SERVICE"

VOLUME LXXI   NUMBER 39½

To

the on-time and faithful

Subscribers

who pay in advance

*thus saving us time and expense of sending statements
and making collections*

this issue of

The Christian Sun

is dedicated

*that the number may increase and by so doing give us that
cooperation for a larger service*

BURLINGTON, NORTH CAROLINA
WEDNESDAY, SEPTEMBER TWENTY-FOURTH, NINETEEN AND NINETEEN

THE CHRISTIAN SUN

Founded 1844 by Rev. Daniel W. Kerr

C. B. RIDDLE - - - Editor

Entered at the Burlington, N. C. Post Office as second class matter.

Subscription Rates

One year ....$ 2.00
Six months 1.00

In Advance

Give both your old and new postoffice when asking that your address be changed.

The change of your label is your receipt for money. Written receipts sent upon request.

Many persons subscribe for friends, intending that the paper be stopped at the end of the year. If instructions are given to this effect, they will receive attention at the proper time.

Marriage and obituary notices not exceeding 150 words printed free if received within 60 days from date of event, all over this at the rate of one-half cent a word.

Original poetry not accepted for publication.

Principles of the Christian Church

(1) The Lord Jesus Christ is the only Head of the Church.

(2) Christian is a sufficient name of the Church.

(3) The Holy Bible is a sufficient rule of faith and practice.

(4) Christian character is a sufficient test of fellowship, and of church membership.

(5) The right of private judgment and the liberty of conscience is a right and a privilege that should be accorded to, and exercised by all.

EDITORIAL

AN EXPLANATION

For several weeks we have been overrun with "copy" and we have hoped that each week's issue would give us relief, but instead of finding relief we have found more and more accumulated matter awaiting publication. When the issue of September 10 went to press we had enough matter on hand that we were forced to carry over to make practically all the issue of September 17; and before the issue of that date was in the post office, pratically all the regular issue for this week was in the form. When the issue for this week was ready to mail we had twelve pages left over for the issue of October 1, and enough manuscript on hand to more than make out the sixteen pages.

By turning to the front page you will find that you have in your hand a "Relief and Business Number," and we hope that this extra issue will serve our purpose in three ways: (1) Help us to catch up with our accumulated copy. (2) To educate our readers a little more fully along the lines of the business end of the publication and thus seek their further co-operation. (3) To set forth the accommodation of the office in regard to books, Bibles and church supplies. The second and third items we had hoped to feature in some edition during the latter part of this month or the early part of October, but with the constant accumulation of articles we foresaw the impossibility of being able to do these things. We have, therefore, condensed what we had hoped to say in combining the two ideas in this issue, and in the meantime, publish along with it a reasonable amount of matter we have on hand, the most of it being crowded out material of the last two editions of the paper.

So far as we know, we are breaking a precedent in issuing this extra edition of THE SUN, but it is a day of precedent breaking and there just as well to be something new in a church journalism as in other things. The thing which we are seemingly forced to do this week is another strong indication that we are unable to serve the Church as it should be served with our limited number of pages.

We send this issue forth to our readers with our usual prayer that it may bless, benefit and brighten as it goes. If we are co-operated with as we suggest and ask, this extra work will be worth its cost, otherwise it will not. We trust its future into the hands of our kind and good and generous friends.

ON THE FIRST DAY OF SOME MONTH

Readers of THE SUN will note that the middle figure on the label is always 1. This means that the subscription expires on the first day of the month. All subscription accounts of THE SUN are placed on the first of some month. There is no expiring of a paper on the tenth, thirteenth, twentieth or twenty-fifth of the month but always on the first day of some month. By this method our accounts are divided into twelve divisions and in the meantime saves considerable amount of time in posting and crediting subscriptions. It has been one of the most satisfactory changes that we have made and seems to be universally approved.

If we receive a subscription between the first and tenth of the month we begin the account on the first of that month, provided we can supply any numbers of the paper that have been issued during the month. If we cannot do this the account is run up until the first of the next month and the remainder of that month sent without charge. If the subscription reaches this office after the fifteenth of the month the account is placed on the first of the next month, unless we are otherwise instructed and can supply numbers so as to date back to the first of the month on which the subscription is entered.

The first figure or figures, on the label indicates the month in which the subscription expires—that is, 1 means the first month, or January; 5 means the fifth month, or May, and so on. The last figure, or figures, indicates the year—that is, 9 means 1919, 20 means 1920 and 21 means 1921.

We admit that this is a simple matter to be writing about and yet our experience leads us to know that a very large number of subscribers do not seem to know how to reckon their time.

TYPEWRITERS NEEDED

An editor appreciates the man who has a typewriter and can use it. Our predecessor, Dr. J. O. Atkinson, if we correctly recall, offered to raise a fund once for the benefit of a few of his contributors. We recall that in the list Rev. C. E. Newman was to have a machine. Now, we would like to renew that good work and not only add Brother Newman to the list but also Dr. Atkinson. Dr. W. A. Harper's friends used to insist that he use his typewriter more. We are not exactly including the Doctor in the list of those who need to use one, but perhaps it is because of our several years of experience in reading his handwriting. At any rate, the typewriter helps the work of an editor. We commend the use of this modern piece of machinery to our brethren who do not have one and have never taken lessons in writing.

OUR SUBSCRIBERS WHO ARE NOT MEMBERS OF THE CHRISTIAN CHURCH

THE CHRISTIAN SUN appreciates the fact that it has a number of subscribers who are not members of the Christian Church. Just how many we are unable to say because of constant discovery of different ones who are not members of the Christian denomination. We heartily and sincerely appreciate this recognition and assure them that we are glad to have them.

ERRORS IN A PRINT SHOP

Errors in a print shop are almost unavoidable. Perhaps we should say *unavoidable* and leave out *almost*. We make this statement because we find errors every week in every exchange that we read. For instance, we have just noticed an error in *The Herald of Gospel Liberty* which was caused by two corrections having to be made in one paragraph, and the corrected lines being put in the wrong paragraph. By the mix-up the editor of THE CHRISTIAN SUN is credited as one of the trustees of the Christian Publishing Association, has undergone a successful operation in a Western hospital—supposedly in Toronto, Canda—and possibly a few other things, all unknown to us. We can readily understand it. But of course something must happen so that the editors will get an extra number of "blessing outs."

EDITORS OF THE CHRISTIAN SUN

The editors of THE CHRISTIAN SUN since its beginning have been as follows: D. W. Kerr, H. B. Hayes, W. B. Wellons, J. T. Whitley, W. T. Walker, D. T. Dunbar, J. P. Barrett, W. G. Clements, E. L. Moffitt, J. O. Atkinson, C. B. Riddle.

A PRINT SHOP "PI"

Occasionally some contributor gets worried because his article is "pied." We shall explain what a "pi" is. The type is cast in lines on a linotype, and should these lines get mixed up by some disorder, the mix-up is called a "pi." One of our exchanges recently pied an article and from it we quote the following items:

"Mr. Hinman Smith, a soldier just back from France, was disposed at public auction last Sunday by Penny Brothers, world's original twin auctioneers, to Miss Carrie Huggins, on my farm, one mile East of Fairplain, rain or shine, in the presence of seventy guests, including the following to wit: Two mules; thirteen pigs, one feed grinder, * * * etc.

"Just before the ceremony was pronounced Mendelssohn's inspiring wedding march was softly rendered by Live Wire Band, carrying a bunch of flowers in her hand and looking charming in a gown made of a light spring wagon, a box of apples, six stacks of hay, one grind-stone."

Sometimes we make errors but not as gross as the above. We dedicate these quoted paragraphs to any contributor who might become incensed of any mix-up that we might have with his or her article.

HOW LONG HAVE YOU BEEN TAKING THE SUN?

We are anxious to secure the names and addresses of all those who have been taking THE SUN twenty-five years or more. Drop us a card today. Mention this to your friends as a reminder. Don't forget it. We want the list.

SHE WANTED THE SUN A WEEK

A former editor of THE CHRISTIAN SUN tells a rich thing that happened in this way: Some one was pleading for THE SUN from the pulpit, and calling attention to the fact that three cents a week would pay for it. (It was $1.50 the year then) and after the service an old lady came up and said she had decided to subscribe for it a week.

OUR JOKES

We are of the opinion that the average man enjoys a good joke and that the "Smiles" we print on the back page furnish material for many good laughs. A family quarrel is often averted by something to laugh about; a sad mood is often banished by a real joke; a laugh is good for the digestion. We believe in laughing. Don't you.

Miss Hester Stuart, THE SUN's efficient book-keeper and stenographer supplies the material for our "Jokes." She gives credit whenever the origin is known. She also endeavors to see that no "Joke" is repeated; and if she ever repeats one, don't think it is an oversight, for you know some things are worth telling twice.

A WORD ON ADVERTISING

Some good friend of THE SUN is constantly reminding us that we need more advertising and that it will pay. We always appreciate these suggestions, but to be kind and candid about the matter, our experience, as well as the experience of other church papers of a small circulation, is that these friends mean well and will probably hold their present opinion until they have been through the "mill" and found out otherwise. A church paper with a small circulation cannot even attract large advertisers. Practically all reputable advertising is handled through advertising agencies, and by the time these agencies substract a big commission for their work there is nothing left for the paper with a small circulation. Not only is this true but there was a time when you could get a man to set and distribute advertisements on a paper for $12 or $15 a week, whereas now a good man will cost about $30 a week. There is also another reason why THE SUN cannot carry so much advertising, even if it had a circulation large enough to demand a high rate, and that is this: The first function of a Church paper is to serve the Church and we do not have room enough now to render the service that we need to render.

OUR EXCHANGES

This office is favored with a very excellent list of Exchanges which we read with a great deal of pleasure and profit. If we have not overlooked any, the following is a complete list of the papers that we read and enjoy each week:

Herald of Gospel Liberty, Dayton, Ohio.
North Carolina Christian Advocate, Greensboro, N. C.
Methodist Protestant Herald, Greensboro, N. C.
Christian Missionary, Dayton, Ohio.
American Friend, Richmond, Ind.
Biblical Recorder, Raleigh, N. C.
Christian Advocate, Nashville, Tenn.
The Lutheran, Philadelphia, Pa.
Dixie Endeavorer, Chattanooga, Tenn.
Missionary Herald and Christian Star, Franklinton, N. C.
Christian Endeavor World, Boston, Mass.
Wesleyan Methodist, Syracuse, N. Y.
Christian Evangelist, St. Louis, Mo.
Progressive Farmer, Raleigh, N. C.
Sandhill Citizen, Southern Pines, N. C.
The Expositor, Cleveland, Ohio.
The Falcon, Burlington, N. C.
The Vanguard, New Market, Ontario.
The Burlington News, Burlington, N. C.
New Era Magazine, New York.
Siler City Grit, Siler City, N. C.
Epworth Era, Nashville, Tenn.
Methodist Protestant, Baltimore, Md.
Sanford Express, Sanford, N. C.
The Watchword, Dayton, Ohio.
News Letter, Chapel Hill, N. C.
Christian Index, Atlanta, Ga.
Men and Money, New York.
Western Christian Advocate, Cincinnati, Ohio.
Christian Observer, Louisville, Ky.
Christian Herald, New York.

OUR NEIGHBORS

Our neighbors in the newspaper craft are *The Burlington News* and *The Burlington Falcon*. *The Burlington News* is under the editorship of our friend, O. F. Crowson, who furnishes the public a good weekly paper. This paper appears every Wednesday in the form of from eight to twenty pages. It is possibly one of the largest weekly papers in the State. *The Burlington Falcon* is under the editorship and direction of Mr. S. F. White. *The Falcon* is a six column, eight page weekly. Our friend White is a newspaper man by birth and experience and furnishes his readers a very worthy publication.

WHAT YOUR LABEL MEANS

(Told in the Language of a Child)

1-1-9 means that your subscription expires January 1, 1919.
2-1-9 means that your subscription expires February 1, 1919.
3-1-9 means that your subscription expires March 1, 1919.
4-1-9 means that your subscription expires April 1, 1919.
5-1-9 means that your subscription expires May 1, 1919.
6-1-9 means that your subscription expires June 1, 1919.
7-1-9 means that your subscription expires July 1, 1919.
8-1-9 means that your subscription expires August 1, 1919.
9-1-9 means that your subscription expires September 1, 1919.
10-1-9 means that your subscription expires October 1, 1919.
11-1-9 means that your subscription expires November 1, 1919.
12-1-9 means that your subscription expires December 1, 1919.

OUR OFFICE ACCOMMODATION

We want to assure SUN readers again of the office accommodation which they have. Our office is open from 7:30 A. M. to 6:00 P. M. Our office is never closed at the noon hour. Mail is promptly received after the arrival of each train, and such as requires answering, is given prompt attention. All subscription money is carefully and accurately handled. Our bookkeeper is accurate and is a master of details and it is a rare exception when anything escapes her attention. Do not be uneasy about your remittance, for if it reaches this office it is safe. Labels are changed just before each issue goes to the press. We invite our attention being called to any error or oversight that we may make.

HOW THE EDITOR SPENT THE SUMMER

You hear much talk about vacations and read what others say about some vacation that they have had. The Editor has had no vacation this summer, in fact he has never had such a treat. His work this summer has been more exacting than any summer in his life. He has spoken once or twice practically every Sunday since last March. This service has not all been rendered to congregations of his own denomination but other denominations, community Sunday school work, rally day assemblies and many other occasions. If any reader has made up his or her mind that the Editor has an easy job just let such a person drop into this sanctum and stay awhile. The Editor's office hours are from 8:00 A. M. to 1:00 P. M., and from 2:00 P. M. to 6:00 P. M. These hours added to his public service on Sundays, together with many other duties that must be performed each day, make him a *fairly* good week's work. He seems to be thriving on it and weighs fifteen pounds more than he has ever weighed, bringing his avoirdupois up to 160.

REV. A. W. ANDES WINS THE PRIZE

Some time ago The Sun offered a prize of $25.00 in gold to the pastor sending the largest list of persons (members of the Christian church and heads of families, or logical persons to take the paper) who do not take The Sun. We have been delayed in announcing this prize owing to pressure of work in the office. We have checked up all the lists sent in and find that Rev. A. W. Andes has a total of 401 names to his credit. Rev. T. J. Green stands second; Rev. B. J. Earp third, and Rev. J. L. Foster fourth. These constitute the pastors whose lists totaled more than 100 each. For lack of space we are not giving the remainder of the list but suffice to say that the total number received is so alarming that we are ashamed to announce it. Only a small per cent of the pastors participated. Had all complied with the request it would have given us a list running into many, many thousands.

ADDITIONAL PERSONAL MENTION

Dr. D. A. Long and Rev. J. V. Knight are holding a revival at Salem Chapel this week.

We learn that Rev. G. D. Eastes, Raleigh, N. C., is sick and that the revival in progress in the Raleigh church had to close on account of the pastor's illness.

Rev. T. J. Green was a caller at The Sun office Monday. He was in company with Brother J. F. Apple and they were on their way to Long's Chapel to begin a revival meeting. Brother Green is pastor of five country churches and is doing a splendid work. He is a consecrated man of God and is appreciated and loved by his people. He tells us that his salary for three years has been far below what it has cost him to live, and that he does not feel that he can continue to make the sacrifice. He has a good farm a few miles from Ashboro, but for the benefit of his churches in the way of a convenience, moved to Ashboro a year or two ago and rented a home. He has been able to meet the sacrifice by the products of his farm but finds that a continuation of such a sacrifice would some day be more than he could continue. He is giving up his churches and will move back to the farm. This is only another case of which the Church must deal. The minister is worthy of his hire and cannot be expected to work for less than it costs to live.

ENDOWMENT OF CHURCH PAPERS

(Editorial in North Carolina Christian Advocate)

Among the institutions of the church there is nothing now subject to more serious peril and sore trial than the Church paper. The periodical must appear just as often and must maintain just as attractive form in its dress of paper and type as when conditions were normal. This, of course, cannot be done unless the income can be increased. To expect it would be to expect ordinary mortals to perform miracles. A paper has but two sources of income, subscriptions and advertising. It is exceedingly difficult to increase the former; the

latter is a constantly decreasing item for the reason that public opinion demands a more and more careful censorship. There is now a very small field for the advertiser in the religious press. The scent for fraud is altogether too keen now in the church to tolerate even the moderately extravagant language used by the average vender of wares or remedies.

The time has come when the Church must consider how this important and essential arm of our educational work is to be maintained. It can not be dispensed with, and it must be made even more attractive and efficient than ever before, for the reason that we have an ever-increasing constituency of intelligence. They will not be satisfied and can not be benefited by a sleazy and slip-shod periodical literature.

It will do no good to heap ridicule and contempt upon the press that we have. Men who have been required to make brick without straw deserve at least the sympathy of their fellows, unless it be clear that they have shown too great eagerness to rush into a hapless enterprise. The attitude of the Church at large must be changed from a contemptous indifference or mere tolerance to that of intelligent and sympathetic co-operation in the effort to make periodicals that will appeal, both because of their literary merit and of the attractive style of the printer's art in which their menu is served.

Our schools are no longer housed in log cabins or old barns, nor are they served by faculties whose support comes from the income from tuition. They must either have an income from endowment or they must have a conference subsidy. This subsidy may not be continued as a settled policy, but it will have to be continued till the schools have sufficient endowment to meet the demands or else many of our educational institutions will have to be abandoned. It is a fortunate thing that our people are beginning to realize that our schools must not be commercialized. Why should they expect us to commercialize our press? The answer to this question is that heretofore our people have not classed the church paper with the educational institutions of the church. We will all get right on this subject when we awake to the fact that the church paper is vitally related to both our educational and missionary work.

One of our Northern religious exchanges, in a recent issue, has the following on the subject:

"Religious journalism' has been passing through its Gethsemane, and in every denomination, as I meet and converse with some of the recognized leaders, Baptist, Congregational, Lutheran, Presbyterian, and Protestant Episcopal, they do not hesitate to speak of the difficulties of the editor and the publisher, in these days of increasing costs and ofttimes decreasing receipts. If the Rockefeller Foundation feels justified—as it certainly does—in augmenting the endowment of colleges and universities of all denominations, why should it not consider the wisdom of setting apart from its princely principal, equally generous amounts for the endowment of some of our great religious weeklies which cannot look to any church funds to supply deficits or to supplement salaries in such trying times as these? Cannot some layman be found who will endow the editorial chair?

PASTOR AND PEOPLE

PLEASANT HILL CHRISTIAN CHURCH

The protracted services began on Saturday before the first Sunday in September, 1919, and continued until Thursday afternoon, following. There were six accessions to the church. There will be baptisms, in some stream, near the church, immediately after preaching, 11:00 o'clock A. M., the first Sunday in October.

Brother L. W. Fogleman preached a very helpful sermon on Monday.

Brother J. W. Holt, a former beloved pastor at Pleasant Hill, came to our assistance and preached to attentive congregations with marked ability, and to the delight of his old friends. Brother Holt will remain a student to the end of life's journey.

The church gave me a unanimous call for another year. I regret that I cannot see my way clear to accept. I want to aid Pleasant Hill, Liberty and Salem Chapel to find pastors. No man ever served a kinder people.

I preached a sermon in memory of Brother L. I. Cox, at 11:00 A. M., the first Sunday in this month. He preceded me as pastor at this place. Zion mourns her heroes fallen. Henry Albright was my cousin. Boarded at my father's sixty years ago, when he attended Graham Institute. Oliver Worden Powers and wife were students at Antioch College. I handed him his diploma. I officiated at his marriage. My pen drags heavily as I write about Albright, Cox and Powers. I drop a tear at their graves. I take fresh courage from the inspiration of their lives.

DANIEL ALBRIGHT LONG.
September 17, 1919.

JUST A THOUGHT

It has been said:

"If you would be an author sage,
Think a volume write a page,
And frame every page of thine
Publish but a single line."

We cannot, or do not, avoid speaking the thoughts of some one else. Being, mainly, copyists. All our knowledge has been acquired from the production of others. If we were not taught by others, competent to give instruction we would know comparatively little. What some of us do undertake to speak or write is full of redundancy and tautology that we are almost ashamed to see it in print. Perhaps every writer sometimes sees his mistakes or faults. Often he does not see them but others, better informed, and having a critical eye, see them plainly. Our educational acquirement and our environment have very much to do with what we think and say. Therefore, we ought to get all the education we possibly can, and be surrounded by the very best conditions which will enable us to be more careful and correct in our department, whether it be active or silent. Some of us are very wordy speakers and writers have more words than extra, fine logical thoughts.

But Paul, the great missionary, teacher and preacher, made some mistakes in style and composition. He very

often turned from one subject to another without thoroughly discussing it, because he had so much to say, and said it with such impassioned zeal, that he lost sight of some minor points. When before Agrippe and Festus in his masterly defense, Agrippe answered him cordially: "Almost thou persuadest me to be a Christian." If we can persuade somebody to be a Christian we will have accomplished great good.

J. T. KITCHEN.

FROM DR. D. A. LONG

The Christians (Disciples) at Farmville, N. C., gave me a special invitation to preach for them last Sunday, September 14. Mrs. Long and myself enjoyed the kind hospitality of Brother and Sister A. J. Moye.

I find that the Christians in Eastern North Carolina confidently expect President Harper to attend their meeting at Columbus, Ohio, that is soon to meet.

The beloved pastor of the First Christian church, Raleigh, N. C., is conducting a protracted meeting at that place. The Lord appears to be with him and his people in power. I attended two very impressive services.

D. A. LONG.

IMPORTANT NOTICE

To Pastors Particularly and Others Generally:

Will any one who reads this, and all who read it, do the writer a favor and the church a real service? Very well. If you know of any one in Richmond, Va., belonging to the Christian church, or who was a member before going to Richmond and still resides there, will you please send his or her name and address to the undersigned? Please do. We want to organize and build a Christian church in Richmond. Your compliance with this request now will help determine whether we shall undertake such a work, or keep on deferring the matter. Let every SUN reader who knows a Christian church member in Richmond, Va., send me, please, the name and address at once. Thank you, dear friends.

Yours to serve,
J. O. ATKINSON.

Elon College, N. C.

NEW COMERS TO THE SUN FAMILY

Mrs. Sarah M. Brown ....Bennett, N. C.
Rev. J. Clyde Auman ....Whitakers, N. C.
Mrs. M. J. Ward ....Cedar Grove, N. C.
T. W. Woodlief ....Youngsville, N. C.
E. H. Rainey ....Elon College, N. C.
Mrs. S. R. Gay ....Cumberland, Md.

One man has given one hundred thousand dollars to the Baptist 75 Million Campaign, and another man, a full blooded Creek Indian, has given two hundred thousand dollars.

We call attention to the advertisement of the Burlington Church in this issue. The trustees are offering a valuable piece of property for sale.

MISSIONARY

PROGRAM OF THE WOMAN'S MISSIONARY CONVENTION OF THE NORTH CAROLINA CHRISTIAN CONFERENCE, ELON COLLEGE, N. C., NOVEMBER 8-9, 1919

Saturday, November 8—10:00 A. M.

Devotional exercises ....Mrs. A. F. Smith
Address of Welcome ....Dr. N. G. Newman
President's Address ....Mrs. W. H. Carroll
Reports of Officers:
    (a) Secretary
    (b) Treasurer
    (c) Superintendent Young People
    (d) Superintendent Literature and Mite Boxes
    (e) Superintendent Boys' Work
    (f) Superintendent Cradle Roll
A Word from the Southern Convention Board by
                  Mrs. W. A. Harper
Address ....Rev. E. K. McCord,
                  Returned Missionary from Japan

2:00 P. M.

Devotional services ....Mrs. W. J. Pierce
Round Table conducted ....Mrs. L. L. Vaughan
    ("The best thing my society has done during the
    year" by representatives of the societies).
Christian Work in Porto Rico........Senor Victor M. Rivera
Christian Work in Japan ....Toshio Sato Saa
Women and the Kingdom................Rev. Geo. D. Eastes

8:00 P. M.

Devotional services ....Mrs. A. T. Banks
Music Program ....the College Choir
Pageant by the Burlington Young People's Missionary Society

Sunday, November 9

Missionary Sermon ....Dr. J. O. Atkinson

3:00 P. M.

Devotional services ....Mrs. Charles R. Clark
Question Box ....Mrs. T. A. Moffitt
Our Women and The Future.................Rev. L. I. Cox
Business session.

8:00 P. M.

Mission Sermon ....Rev. E. K. McCord

REPORT FOR FOURTH QUARTER OF THE VIRGINIA VALLEY CHRISTIAN CONFERENCE MISSIONARY WOMAN'S BOARD

Dues

New Hope Woman's Society, $4.53; New Hope Christian Endeavor, $6.25; Winchester, 90 cents; Winchester Christian Endeavor, 55 cents; Winchester Young People, $1.24; Winchester Cradle Roll, $2.25; Antioch Cradle Roll, $2.10; Concord Cradle Roll, $1.95.

For Orphanage Room

Mrs. W. E. Bowman, $1.00; Mrs. Cora Huffman, $1.25; Bethlehem Young People, $5.00; New Port, $5.00; New Hope, $7.95; Antioch Young People, $5.00; Winchester, $15.20; Timber Ridge, $9.25; Dry Run Willing Workers, $10.00.

For Winchester

Mr. and Mrs. Frank Showalter, $5.00; Mrs. W. J. Fleming, $1.00; Mrs. Martha Driver, $1.00; Mrs. Cora Huffman, $1.25; Bethlehem Young People, $5.50; Mrs. A. W. Andes, $5.00; New Port, $10.00; Mrs. Roy Hosaflook, $5.00; Mrs. N. M. Hasler, $10.00; Mrs. Barbara Andes, $10.00; Miss Tracy Liskey, $5.00; Mrs. John Vanpelt, $1.00; Mrs. Cora Bryant, $1.00; Mrs. E. M. Spitzer, $1.00; Mrs. Clarence Dovel, $1.00; Mrs. Reuben Fultz, $1.00; Mrs. D. J. Driver, $5.00; Mrs. Robert Sellers, $3.00; Mr. J. B. Shifflett, $5.00; Dry Run Willing Workers, $10.00; Mr. Loy Hook, $1.75.

For Santa Isabel

New Port, $10.00.

Regular Funds

Miss Mamie Summers, $2.40; Mrs. J. E. Foster, 50 cents; Dr. W. T. Walters, $1.00; Mrs. W. C. Wampler, $1.00; Mr. J. E. W. Bryant, $5.00; Mrs. J. E. W. Bryant, $2.00; Mrs. W. T. Walters, $4.00; Mrs. W. C. Hook, $1.00; Mrs. A. B. Richards, $1.00; Mrs. James Wotring, $1.00; Mr. James Wotring, $1.00; Mr. John Wotring, $1.00; Mr. C. A. Henton, $5.00; Leaksville Society, $30.00.

Total for quarter, $233.82.

Disbursements

To Mrs. W. T. Walters, $233.13; To Virdie Showalter for Postage, 69 cents; Total, $233.82.

              VIRDIE SHOWALTER, Treasurer.

Harrisonburg, Va.

OFFICE NOTES

Start a Teacher-Training Class in your Sunday school. Write us for suggestions, book recommendations and price.

We are now ready to furnish prices and samples of offering envelopes. Write us your needs and get full information. Correspondence solicited.

What kind of a Bible are you looking for? Describe to us in a letter, and if we do not have it on hand, we can get it for you if it can be had.

The season of the year is now at hand when we try to collect as much money on the paper as possible. Will you, dear subscriber, send your renewal without having us to send statement? It will save time and money. Just look at your label, and if your time is out, remit promptly. It will be appreciated.

The trade house that furnishes Communion sets has just issued us a beautiful descriptive catalogue, a copy of which we shall be glad to send to any Church thinking of making a purchase.

We are informed from two or three sections that THE SUN issue of September 3 failed to arrive. We cannot account for the trouble and trust that only a few missed the paper that week.

The new mission study books are the "Crusade of Compassion" (foreign) and "Christian Americanization" (home) and can be secured from THE SUN office. State in ordering whether you desire cloth or paper binding.

CHRISTIAN EDUCATION

THE SIGNS OF THE TIMES*

Matt. 16:3—Can you not discern the signs of the times?

In a sense, a real sense too, every age is new. But a period following a world war may be justly said to be new in a vitally different sense. We need only to look out upon the life of our day to realize that we have made great strides in social and political progress during the past five years. Who could have dreamed of a League of Nations five years ago? Who could have dreamed of organized labor issuing an ultimatum to the American people five years ago? And what shall we say of Woman Suffrage and National Prohibition? Of World Prohibition? Ours is a new day.

I regret to see that many Christian leaders have not discovered this. In this respect they are unlike the Master. He was expert in discerning the signs of the times and found fault with the religious leaders of His day for being adept in reading the weather signs in the sky, while they were blind to the vocal signs of spiritual change all around them. They were ritualists. He was not. They were legalists. He was not. They were traditionalists. He was not. They were reactionaries. He was the original progressive. They dubbed Him a devil and a blasphemer. He replied by styling them whited sepulchers, ravening wolves, hypocrites. They would not understand Him and so He had to reject them.

Let us pray that those who lead in the Kingdom in our day may not be so blind to the new spirit of the times and that with open-mindedness they may discern the signs that redden the sky of our day with radiant hope, that beckon with inviting charm to a larger service. Out of the upheaval of the world cataclysm we have acquired a new interpretation of spiritual values, a new fulfillment fo Kingdom hopes, a coterieo of new conceptions for the Christian life. It is at these we should look with that enthusiasm which has through the ages characterized the prophetic spirit of youth.

I. A New Loyalty

And first among these new conceptions let us place that noblest element of the moral life—loyalty. We have learned the new and deeper meaning, the full meaning of loyalty in our day. We have always been proud we are American citizens. We have loved our country in a way, and we fancied we were truly loyal to it. But we have learned in the service and sacrifice of war what loyalty is. When the call of country came, as one man our nation arose in her majestic might to the demands of loyalty. The Selective Draft Act called our noblest young men from professional offices, from business and industry, from farm and college. They answered like the heroes they were and forever broke the power of autocracy. And those of us who stayed at home were loyal too. We did our best to quicken industry, even though our best workers were gone on a stern task. And our women, God bless them, by their tireless fingers and countless deeds of mercy and sacrifice, added a new halo of glory to the diadem that has ever crowned the loving heart of womanhood. There has never been enacted in human history such a magnificent pageant of loyalty, and out of it and in consequence of it, America has been exalted to world-leadership.

Shall we who love the Kingdom not profit by this display of loyalty to our country? Shall we be content to give more and do more in response to country's call through her Selective Draft Act than we shall undertake to do in response to our Master's Universal Service Act? Let us not forget that nearly two thousand years ago Jesus enunciated this act. "Go ye into all the world," He said, "and preach the Gospel to every creature." This act has never been repealed. It never will be, and yet after these twenty centuries barely one-third the earth's population has been reached by us Christians and those who have been reached are far from the representatives of Him they ought to be.

Churches floated their service flags proudly during the war, with stars for each noble son who had gone to the colors. But how many of these churches can duplicate that flag with Christian workers dedicated to Kingdom service? Are churches founded to win wars or to win a world for Jesus? Ought not our churches to institute methods of recruiting the army of the Kingdom? Ought they not see to it that the fields white unto the harvest are supplied with workers, even as they threw the weight of their influence to the winning of the war?

And no banners floated more gloriously in our colleges then the service flags showing the number who had gone to the redemption of the race from the iron heel of Prussianism. Elon counts it a splendid distinction to have sent 601 to this grand crusade, fifteen of whom paid the supreme sacrifice. But Elon is a Christian college, at least in purpose and hope, and she owes a duty to the Kingdom in this hour. She owes it to herself and to the splendid young men and women who have entrusted their lives to her to hold up the first claim of the Kingdom on every life. It has been said: "Do not give yourself to the ministry or to other Christian service if you can help it." This is not the teaching of Scripture. We must put the Kingdom first. We are all priests unto God. We must all give ourselves to Kingdom service definitely, unless we can satisfy God in those moments when we have been deeply conscious of His presence that He can not use us in His work. We dare not choose our own career. We must seek His will and win his approval to the designs and purposes of our hearts for our life-work. And in this opening service of the college year, I call upon every young life here to face this issue honestly, squarely, reverently, and then to act as God directs. The Kingdom, young friends, must have recruits and Elon must not fail to furnish her quota. Let her answer this call with a loyalty as genuine and as sincere as she did the call of country in the World War.

II. A New Meaning of Salvation

The second sign that reddens the horizon of our day spiritually is a new meaning for salvation. We must be born again, all right. But spiritual birth is but the beginning of salvation. Salvation is a constant process, a constant growth, an unending development. It is not a once-for-all affair. It is a daily ration. It is to the soul of men as the manna of the Wilderness. We get a sufficiency for the day only and we cannot store it, or it will putrify. It is a life-principle, a ripening experience, a passport not into a finished city, but into a vast forest, where trees are to be felled, roads laid out, farms cultivated, homes constructed, cities builded, and the work of the Kingdom wrought out. How happy we should be to have part through the blood of Jesus in a work like this!

Salvation is personal? Yes, but it is also social. Jesus did not come to save me. That is a partial statement of a great truth. Jesus came to save me that I might be the means of saving others. That is the whole truth. We are brothers whether we wish it or not. The social fact of salvation confronts us on every hand. We may shut our eyes to its call and deafen our ears, but that cannot change the fact. We may erect us a mansion and equip it with every convenience and elegance, and in our snug security disdain to do a broth-

* Address of President W. A. Harper, Elon College, N. C., before the new student body, Sunday, September 14, 1919.

er's part by our poorer neighbors. With what result? With the result that direful diseases will germinate in his unsanitary quarters and be wafted on the wings of the common air we breathe with him to our palatial residence, and we shall die. Whether we wish it or not, we must recognize the social obligation of salvation. But if we have become thoroughly saturated with the spirit of salvation, we shall rejoice that it is social and that we can bring its comforts and inspirations to our brothers. For myself, I have reached the point in my Christian life, where if I am to be the only person saved, I would rather go to Hell with the rest of the folks. And does not the doctrine of the Holy Trinity teach me that my heart is right in its feelings? Even God is social.

Salvation is personal? Yes. Salvation is social? Yes. But it is also societal. It cannot content itself with reaching the lives of the individual men and women of the race with its message and words of purification, cleansing and uplift. It must regenerate the institutions and organizations that minister to the life of men. "The Christianization of the Social Order"—the dream of an idealist? Not so, but the unyielding purpose of the saved life on fire to rescue the world. We cannot save men out of society. Monasticism and asceticism and cynicism have taught us that. Men must be saved in society, and the only way to make their salvation sure and effective is to save society too. It is useless to call men from a life of sin and dissipation, if all around them when they leave the altar for their homes the red flags of Vice flaunt themselves shamelessly in their faces. We have removed the saloon and the brothel. Every cesspool of vice must likewise go, and in their places institutions that minister helpfully and wholesomely to the Christian life must be erected, so that righteousness with its beauty shall gladden the heart even more than sin with its siren deadened the nobler impulses of the soul. Even more, we must Christianize the institutions we do not and cannot supplant. We are Christianizing the governments of men by the League of Nations, to oppose which is to advertise you are a pagan and not a Christian, and we must do the same for every industry by which men live, for every college in which men learn to aspire, for every amusement that delights their leisure, for every institution everywhere that even most remotely touches their life. Such is the new conception of salvation that has come to us in the new day in which we live.

III. The Necessity For Christian Union

But we shall not be able to meet the demands of Christian loyalty nor appropriate the blessings of the full salvation Jesus taught unless we shall be able to discern a third sign written large in the spiritual horizon of these times. This is Brotherhood's day. Fraternity is in the very atmosphere we breathe and the hour of the Christian Union has struck. A divided Church, a Church hampered by denominationalism can no more meet the responsibilities or discharge the obligations of spiritual ministry in our day than a world cursed with nationalism could serve its economic and political interests. The shame is that we who love Jesus and profess to be willing to do His will have permitted the nations to anticipate us in reacting favorably and constructively to the tide in men's hearts that runs towards Brotherhood. The League of Nations is not only a rebuke to a divided Christendom. It is the handwriting on the wall announcing the speedy dissolution of a caste that has belittled Christ and condemned His Kingdom to defeat all too long. It is high time that we who hope to dwell together in eternal bliss in the future life should begin to practice living together in this present life and especially so since our 183 divisions of "sects and insects" spell failure for the cause so dear to our hearts.

Let us learn the lesson of union from the World War. The horror and dread of those fateful days in the spring and summer of 1918 hang like a frightful nightmare in memory's gallery now. The Hun was making his last desperate drive for Paris and the channel ports. The Allies on four different fronts were doing their best to stem the onrolling tide of death and destruction to all the things free men have ever cherished. But the Hun kept plunging on. The Italian supreme command, the English supreme command, the French supreme command, and the Americans under General Pershing were resisting titanically but steadily onward rolled the frightful Hun. It looked as if God had deserted us and that victory would come, if at all, only after many years of long-drawn-out struggle. In this dramatic and tragic moment, something happened. It should have happened before, but it took impending defeat to bring it to pass. What happened? The Allies got together and made Marshal Foch supreme, commander for the allied nations, and from that day till November 11, the day of the armistice, the Hun never advanced another inch on any battle front except in the direction of Berlin. And in that united victory, there was victory for Englishman, there was victory for Frenchman, there was victory for American, there was victory for Italian, there was victory for the cause of right, which had come so near to defeat. In union there was strength and there was victory.

Let the divided household of the Christ practice a similar strategy. Let each of the competing bands bring its quota of fighters and its ammunition of truth, and a glorious victory will crown the Kingdom in our day. And in that crown of victory, there will be glory and victory for Methodists and Baptists and Presbyterians and Episcopalians and Catholics and Disciples of Christ and Christians and all the rest, and best of all there will be glory and victory for Christ.

All the more should the churches unite because our Master prayed that we should do it. "That they may all be one," He prayed to His Father and ours on the eve of His crucifixion, "even as we are one." And then he foretold the doom of denominationalism, its inadequacy, its failure, when He gave as the reason for the oneness of His followers, "that the world may believe that thou hast sent me." We are Christians. We love Jesus. We desire, we pray, we labor that His cause may triumph in the earth, and yet we tolerate the petty divisions of His cohorts which make all our hopes impossible of realization. Was ever there such tragic folly in a cause affecting the salvation of the race of men and the fruition of the Kingdom of God?

Let each of us give heed to these heartening signs of the times. Let us face in the moment of conscious fellowship with our Father the requirements of loyalty to His Kingdom upon our lives. Let us consider what salvation involves and be ready to render becoming response to its every claim upon or challenge to us. And let us not disappoint the hopes of men in this splendid hour, clamant with the thrilling appeal of Brotherhood's claims and privileges, and prophetic of hope and salvation for the race through the coming fully of the spiritual Kingdom Jesus came to found, delayed in its fruition by the disunion of His followers, for whose union He devoutly prayed. And let us looking to Him for wisdom and strength devote ourselves and all we hope to be in these splendid behalfs.

Mrs. Sallie A. Hattman—I have read THE SUN all my life and want to keep it always.

Mrs. J. W. Freeman—I wish you all success with the work of our dear Church paper.

LIFE, THE SCHOOL OF GOD

(A Story)

Long ago there came into the world two little babes whose names were Patience and Impatience. The mother, with eyes full of love, looked into their innocent faces and wondered what they would be or what good they would do. Mother's care and watchfulness often kept the children from falling, but when they did she kissed the bruises. The children have great faith in mother's love.

There came a big day in their lives, the first day at school. Mother went with them but left them in the teacher's care, and the teacher, how kind and gentle, how loving and patient, and yet how firm and unyielding towards the wrong-doer but how forgiving when asked! Patience and Impatience learn quickly because mother helps them with the difficult tasks and they loved their teacher.

Now, what is wrong? Teacher has given a lesson a little harder than usual. Patience listened closely and tried cheerfully to do her best. But Impatience! Her book is thrown aside and a frown had chased the sunshine from her face. She had not listened closely but the teacher patiently helped her over the difficulty.

A holiday came and teacher went with them for a walk. Impatience ran ahead to pick the pretty flowers. Patience walked by the teacher's side and listened while he told her how the birds were protected and provided for and why they never complained when compelled to work in sunshine or rain, and how the flowers get their sustenanma from the earth yet they never fail to send their fragrance or praise heavenward. When they reached home Impatience chided Patience because she didn't have outward tokens of her trip but Patience smilingly reminded her that her flowers had faded already. Teacher smiled as he left the sisters.

They left primary school and their greatest joy in grammar school was that teacher went with them. When he gave them a task Impatience was sure to claim the reward and just as sure to deserve it as little as possible. Patience was thorough, and if she could not finish or did not understand her work, she went to her teacher for help. By so doing she made her final tests easier. Impatience hurried over her task or asked some one to finish it for her, thereby losing golden opportunities. She was too much occupied with her own pleasures to care.

One Sunday morning teacher went with them to church, as the church was strange. Impatience was concerned about her personal appearance, wondering if she looked well. Patience thought how kind her teacher was to have time to go, but she wondered if she would hear or see anything that would help her. They left the city before they came to the church. With wonder and surprise the girls were led by their teacher into God's great cathedral. The pillars at the door were giant oaks, the carpet soft green grass, the organ the great trees, the musicians, the wind playing upon the leaves, the choir, the birds flitting through the leaves or resting upon the branches, the congregation, whoever wanted to go, the minister, God Himself. The sermon that day was: "Strength and Trust." This is the sermon: Look at the mighty oak. The wind tosses its branches, bows them, bends them to its will and the tree raises it arms to Heaven for protection. Never so strong that we do not need God's care. The little vine springs up, trustingly puts out its tiny little tendrils which catch a cling to whatever they touch. It seldom clings to the underbushes but constantly climbs upward. Now it has dared to climb upon the mighty oak. With trust and faith we may dare to do great things for God. How did the girls like the

service? Impatience tossed her head and thought her time had been wasted. No one saw how carefully she had been dressed, but Patience went home happy with a new light in her eyes and joy and thankfulness in her heart.

Are they happy girls? Yes. Are they ever punished? Yes, their teacher would not be just to them when he saw them doing wrong and did not tell them of it. Patience took her punishment humbly and thankfully because she knew that teacher did it for her good. But Impatience used angry words and acted very ugly indeed to her teacher, although she knew all the time that he loved her even when the punishments were most severe. Her heart grew harder instead of kinder. Impatience always had to have the prettiest clothes, she teased her father to give her jewels, all that valued peace had to do as she said. She was always too busy to help with the household duties. She was the happiest when going to some social function. Did Patience ever wish for these pleasures? Yes, but father told her that she would have them by and by. To her lot fell the duties of helping at home, but these were love tasks and not duties. She had a smile or a kind word for all.

But when discouraged or blue she went to her teacher for comfort and cheer. She was not complaining to him. He talked to her of the wonderful country that he had spoken of to his pupils. It was a place where no tears are ever shed, no aches, no pain, no sickness, no deceit, no parting from loved ones or friends because there are no good-byes ever spoken, all sing and praise the King. The inhabitants of that country are dressed in wonderful clothes that show the beautiful soul as well as the beautiful face. What need did she have for Impatience's poor worthless things when she had the promise of such joys? Not so with Impatience. She thought these promises well enough, but she wanted her joys now.

Examinations came, they passed from grammar to high school. Their examinations were upon Kindness, Humility, Truthfulness, Forbearance and Godliness. Both passed, Patience with honor and Impatience just making the mark. She did not care as long as the world did not know the truth but teacher with a wounded heart understood.

They are very happy in High School. True their tasks were harder but they were prepared. Mother was proud of her girls but hurt that the social world had such strong attractions for Impatience. True the world threw attractions and temptations into Patience's way but she had some task to do for mother or an errand to run for father, or a broken toy to mend for little sister, or some task for others outside of home. Besides she had her own lessons to learn. Does Impatience have time to mend little brother's or sister's toy? No, she has an engagement with the social world and wants some one to help her get ready. Her time is spent in selfishly letting others do for her and neglecting her lessons.

Time passed all unheeded and testing time came. Impatience began to be uneasy. Her teacher's face has been very grave and this was the cause of her uneasiness. No one could help her now, she had spent her time in worldly amusements and had little or no time to get her lessons. But look at Patience! Joy radiating from her face kindled hope, joy and love in other hearts. She was ready and willing for her tests.

The tests were given and they received their diplomas. The teacher arose and with a wonderful, heavenly smile upon his face, held out his arms to Patience. She rose, having a wondering smile upon her face at receiving so much honor. The teacher said, "Take your diploma, it entitles you to a home forever in that beautiful country." She thanked him and still wondering read, "Well done, thou good and faithful student, you have been faithful in little things, now be ruler over great.'' Was not that a diploma well worth working for? Impatience turned to receive her diploma. The teacher turned to her and with a wounded, grieved look said, ''You were given a fair chance, yet you thought more of your pleasures than you did of your lessons. Now you stand alone, pleasures, jewels, friends are all gone. You have failed to do the things worth while and to take the joys that do not fade away. Here is your diploma;'' and with a stern look he left her to read: ''Depart from me thou faithless one, into the land prepared for those who have failed. Your pleasures and joys were worthless because they were not the curing of the sin-sick souls or ministering to my perishing children.''

The school that those girls attended is Life. The primary school is childhood when mother is greatly responsible for our lessons. Grammar school is the early matured years. High school is the full matured years. Our teacher is Jesus. The tests are the afflictions God sends. The final test is death. Our diploma, if faithful, is a home in Heaven. This is a school that all attend and the success depends upon us. Are we learning our lessons faithfully? Are we grieving our Teacher because we fail in our tests? Are our joys, the joys that last? Are we wasting our time or spending it ministering to the million perishing sin-sick souls? Do we receive our punishments with cheerfulness or wonder why God is so cruel? The Teacher punishes children because He loves them and wants them to do right. Which diploma do you want to receive? It is in our power to receive the one which is a pass to the beautiful country or the other. When the test comes which will we receive?

                              ELIZABETH BROTHERS.
Hickory, Va.

CHRISTIAN ENDEAVOR, A SPIRITUAL FORCE IN RECONSTRUCTION*

No one needs to be told that Christian Endeavor is a mighty spiritual force in reconstruction. We are of one mind when we say that life is not four-square in its finality until it is spiritual; that force is a positive power that must be reckoned with; and that the challenge of peace brings its responsibilities. These terms are vital to life and organization. Christian Endeavor is organized man-power, consciously co-operating for a single objective, which is the formation and development of Christian character. Spirituality is the whole human structure in close relation to God, consciously co-operating toward a single objective, that of enriching the inner sanctuary of man. Force is positive and active power, consciously or unconsciously co-operating by means of artificial devices, toward a single objective, that of changing the position, purpose, and plans of things that be. Reconstruction is the organized physical, social, political, and practical efforts of men consciously co-operating toward a single objective, that of directing the motives and conduct of men, so that their lives may become normal and happy. If these terms are adequately applied and properly heeded, nations will be born in a day and the ideas of Jesus will become sacred to all men. As Prof. Barton puts it: ''When these ideals control the peoples of the world, wars, oppression, crimes, and international injustice will vanish from the earth and there will be an era of international, industrial, and social peace.''

''Those who have caught the spirit of Jesus and would strive to lift the world to His ideals are faced in both fields with appalling difficulties. The difficulties are, however, no excuse for not making the attempt. That transformation which

---

*Delivered at the Chautauqua at Virginia Beach, Va., August 5, 1919, by R. F. Brown.

is bringing in the Kingdom of God will not come by miracle or magic, it will come only by the process of spiritual regeneration and evolution social and international.'' There is not much in the way of transformation that a man can effect with his fist. Men as well as nations will not submit to being held by the throat any longer than they can prepare to take revenge. Transformation through physical force is not of an enduring kind. Such conquests of force often end in failure. But that there is force somewhere and of some kind that controls and limits us, that expends and readjusts, that refinds and elevates, is undeniable. This force is God. His chief weapon is the Spirit which calmly works, and waits.

To say that Christian Endeavor is a might force in the formation and development of Christian character is saying something that we have all taken for granted, but because we have taken it for granted it is my purpose to call our attention to that phase today.

The Jews were a chosen people, but they were chosen that they might be the messengers of God to the rest of the world. There was a time in their history when they looked to God for everything, even food and water were given, one day's allowance at a time. But when the Prophet Jeremiah lived they had become a mighty people and were forgetting God. Jeremiah is sent with a message to his people, the message is one calling them away from the world back to the God whom they had forgotten.

''Thus saith the Lord, let not the wise man glory in his wisdom, neither let the mighty man glory in his might, let not the rich man glory in his riches, but let him that glorith, glory in this that he understandeth and knoweth me that I am the Lord.'' Likewise it seems that Christian Endeavor is an organization born in due time to be a messenger of God to the nations of the earth. The influence and power of Christian Endeavor principles has radiated from the Williston church to the four corners of the earth. It has increased in numbers. Instead of counting its force with two numbers one must employ seven. These millions of men and women, boys and girls are emphasizing anew the message of the prophet. This message is timely and appliable in our own day. The Endeavor Society is mighty, rich, and wise in peace as well as in war. It is based on democracy and the American democracy is altruistic. The people of every land are saying that it was the might of the American forces that brought the war to such a successful end and did it so quickly. The world has come to see that with resources almost inexhaustable, with the advantage of two oceans, and a canal to connect them, and a strong, freedom, loving people, we are a force to be reckoned with. We could glory in that and I sometimes fear that we are doing so. Although the Hon. Franklin K. Lane, Secretary of the Interior, said in his address at the State University, June 18, 1919, that the wine of military glory had not gone to our heads. Perhaps he was right, but I fear it has gone to our hearts.

We are not only powerful but we are a rich people. New York has become the banking center of the world. The nations of Europe are looking to us for credit to rebuild. We speak in terms of billions as if we know just what that means. The Government can raise six billions in a very few days.

Even our wisdom would come in for a shower of the glory if changing the center of learning from German to American universities means anything. The delegates at the Peace Table in Paris seemed to wait for the American statesman to speak first. But if we do have priority in might, riches, wisdom, and the confidence of the whole world, splendid as these things are, our powers as a nation does not lie in these things. You will recall Burns' poem, ''Cobbler's Saturday Night,'' it is the picture of a very simple home, the wants of the family are few, the living is marked by simplicity, but the members of this family are in love with each other and they love God supremely. Before they retire a part of God's Word is read and prayer and thanksgiving are offered. Then the closing lines, "Its scenes like these old spotters grandeur lies!" We will well remember that in scenes like these the foundation is laid for all the things in our nation that are to abide.

It is Christian Endeavor, however, that we have in mind today, and it too is mighty, rich and wise. In a very telling sense Christian Endeavor is felt as it spreads its pinions to persue its appointed mission and reach the objective for which it was designed. For example, is there anything in your community that the adherants to Christian Endeavor could not do? With Christian Endeavor working as a unit you can carry an election for anything you want. How many of the biggest, the brightest and best men, women, boys and girls in your community who are not affiliated with Christian Endeavor in some way? Might is good used right, but we cannot depend upon that.

One can make liquor laws with mighty teeth, but no law will make a man sober. We can drive out the harlot with law, but that will not make virtuous men. A snake in the flower garden is no less a snake because of his environment. I am out and out for any program that makes for increased knowledge of God, rehabilitation of devastated lands, the elimination of decorated debauchery and the betterment of man, provided first things come first. If what we have in mind is only to better the conditions of men, then I agree they may play a cleaner game in the Christian Endeavor rooms of our churches than in the dirty smoke shop. They might even dance with less bad effect under the direction of a Christian Endeavor (?) dance master. But the Gospel that is taught, practiced and treasured in the Christian Endeavor Society warns people against wrong doing and ultimately makes new creatures of men, and that is not alone by might, riches, or wisdom, but by the power of Almighty God. "For the Gospel of our Lord Jesus Christ is the power of God unto salvation to every one that believeth."

Then the Christian Endeavor is rich. The time was when we could plead poverty, but that time is gone. The Christian Church through its prayers and gifts has effective Christian Endeavor Societies in Japan and Porto Rico, that are teaching the principles of Christianity and moulding Christian character. It is doing a fundamental work, and its influence is being felt by tens of thousand. Our own Church is looking to the raising of two million dollars within the next few years. The most optimistic and far-seeing among us did not dream a few years ago of these great amounts for which we are asking. We are coming to our own as a denomination. We are rich as Endeavorers. The Christian Endeavor, through its leaders, is adding the pluck and push to the campaigns which have worked such wonders among us and which hold out such hope for the future. How could it be otherwise when these very principles are taught in our Christian Endeavor? We should not forget nor allow our people to forget that we may be as rich as the church at Leodicea, as mighty in strength as Sampson, and as wise as Solomon at the same time be wretched miserable, blind and naked. We shall be much poorer with these large sums of money if in the getting them we impoverish our spiritual life and glory in our financial achievements.

There are many evils which have been encouraged by the war and our modern times, and which have made great progress in recent months. God's day has been almost entirely disregarded in army life, and many of our war-time activities seemed to demand seven days of the week for their successful prosecution, and Sabbath desecration has become so common as to become well nigh universal. Many of our soldiers are coming home from the army with new ideas of religion, "The Atonement of the Trenches" as it is called, having taken strong hold upon them. On every hand they have been hearing the false teaching that if a man is brave and heroic, and gives himself for the salvation of the oppressed, he thereby atones for his sins, however many and great they may have been. Thus they have been taught to depend upon themselves and their own suffering and sacrifices rather than the blood of God's own Son for their sins.

The word tells us that, "the blood of Jesus Christ cleanseth from all sin," that with the heart man believeth unto righteousness and with mouth confession is made unto salvation; and "except ye repent ye shall likewise perish." Jesus is the way of salvation and not by the way of the trenches, noble and splendid as the sacrifice is. I know the advocates of "The Atoning Blood of the Trenches," will tell you that Jesus died to save men. This I grant, but it was not a physical salvation, which He wrought, but a spiritual salvation. He did not die to save their lives but to save their souls. But your advocate would say that the Book says, "Greater love hath no man than this that a man lay down his life for his friend," and this too refers to the physical salvation of man. When a man dies for another he indicates his love for humanity, and he goes to the length of his life to save his friend. This is all he can do. But this sacrifice of man for man does not effect the soul of either, "For the gift of God is eternal life through Jesus Christ our Lord."

Many of our boys will have new ideas of Christian Endeavor and of what it ought to do and what it ought to be. It is for the Christian Endeavor to so plan its program as to be able to tell the boys what they ought to be and what they ought to do. It must hold out for them a new objective.

Christian Endeavor must not only strive to reconstruct lives and lands, perfect programs in training boys and girls, but it must work out the problems which go with a recruiting station. Christian Endeavor needs more men of vision. A vision is an architectual design of God given to man. It is the lens through which man looks into the future and reads the actions of peoples and things. Such men are useful. The world wants their message. A crusade of righteousness is now in order since peace has come. England wants prohibition. I heard an eminent Londoner say recently in a speech: "Send some of your most pious, your most religious, your most thoroughly trained men to England that they may teach us the value of prohibition." France wants us to come to her land and help heal her sores and soothe her sorrows. Belgium also needs comfort. This awful war has cost the struggling nations of the world 221 billions of dollars, has slain 8 million men in battles, besides the other millions mamed for life, and it has orphaned 20 million children. It has paralized industry and trade, and devastated and turned into desert or a wilderness millions of acres of once fertile farm lands. France alone has lost two and one-half million of her heroes dead or maimed for life, one fifteenth of her effective population. The widowed mothers and millions of fatherless children must be cared for. Hundred of hamlets, towns and cities are to be rebuilt and equipped for every kind provided. Ten thousand square miles of devastated farm lands must be cleared of debris, leveled, plowed and prepared for cultivation again. France, the land of LaFayette, lies in ruin and cries to us for help. She has fallen among the thieves who have robbed, stricken, wounded and stripped her beyond expression. What can man who has been trained in Christian Endeavor do?

If our churches and Christian Endeavors are to spend millions of dollars on reconstruction and missionary programs then hundreds of young men must lay their lives on the altar of service to spend this money. In the Christian Endeavor room is a good place to secure these recruits. There is one method of getting these recruits and that is to pray th Lord of the harvest that He send forth the laborers in His harvest. In an address by a missionary secretary of the northern Presbyterian church some months ago this statement was made: ''I have five men who have asked me to get them a missionary of their own. I have the money ready but have not found the men.'' There are some things, thank God, that even money cannot do.

Christian Endeavor is wise as men count wisdom. It has ever stood for training, progress and education. Many of our great leaders in church and nations are men who have been taught in Christian Endeavor principles. It is a splendid place to get a knowledge of God to learn the Bible. We have learned the Bible until we can, or at least we think we can analyze it like a school boy would a simple sentence. Our education is even accused of having put God in practical eclipse so that He has no practical significance, for a large part of the modern world. ''The wealthy think Him unnecessary and the poor think Him useless; scholars have put Him out of their thinking, and the ignorant out of their lives. Thus among the learned the substance of things hoped for have passed off into notions, for the unlearned the notions of things have become the substance.''

No matter how wise men become they cannot by wisdom find God. True knowledge of God is by revelation, and revelations are only made to listening spirits. Christian Endeavor ought to be an authority here and if we as Christian Endeavorers cannot speak with authority here, we speak with false authority on every other subject. Instead of being conformed to the world about us, we as Endeavorers must be agents in God's hands to transform the world. Our ability to do this will not depend upon our might our riches, or our wisdom, but upon our knowledge of Almighty God. The secret of Paul's power, Bushnell's power, Philip Brooks' power, was in the fact that they knew God rather than they knew anything else. Everything depends upon this. You remember Amos said there would come a famine in the land, not a famine of bread nor of thirst for water, but of hearing the words of the Lord. That time cannot come until men cease to know God, and they will not cease to know God until they cease to attend His word. To me this is the peril of our time.

If I am to judge the church auxiliaries by some I know best, then the first test in carrying out any constructive program is to get our people filled with a knowledge of God and a love for men. I presume it is no secret with us that the only time we count some of our people is when we give the number on roll. When there is a work to do that calls for consecration and sacrifice that can only be done by men of God we are forced to count out a large percent of our people.

One thing is sure and that is there are enough men and money to do the work that God wants done if we can command them. No amount of schemes or movements or devices will get our people to make the sacrifices that are necessary until they see the glory of the Lord fill the Temple and in that hour hear the call, ''Who will go for us.'' Dr. George Adams Smith while traveling in the Alps reached a very high peak and the guide cried: ''To your knees, to your knees; it is very dangerous to stand up at this height.'' Christian Endeavor is today standing at the very highest peak of opportunity, and it seems to me that we can best stand here upon our knees.

NOTES

Rev. A. B. Kendall is to take up the work in Washington, D. C., under the direction of the Mission Board.

The Editor was in Lee county last week, and while it was not his privilege to conveniently visit any of Brother White's churches, we heard only good things about the work in that part of Zion.

Brother D. E. Michael, of Apple's Chapel church, called to see us a few days ago. Brother Michael is one of THE SUN's best friends and we appreciate him and his kind.

Rev. G. R. Underwood has given up the work at Ashboro, N. C., sold his home there and bought a small farm in the Pleasant Grove community near Bennett, N. C., and will move there within the next few weks.

Dr. J. O. Atkinson's note elsewhere in this issue is worthy of the attention of all who may be able to assist him in the matter of information. Turn to another page and read what he says, and if you can assist him, do so, and do so now.

Superintendent H. A. Garrett of the Methodist Protestant Children's Home, High Point, N. C., was a pleasant caller at THE SUN office this week. Brother Garrett is to speak before the North Carolina Conference this fall. Our people will be pleased with him.

Mr. G. C. Crutchfield, a second year student in Elon College, and a ministerial student under the direction of the North Carolina Conference, offers himself to any church or churches needing a pastor for next year.

Mr. G. D. Lambeth, a son of Brother J. M. Lambeth, Reidsville, N. C., but who makes his home in Burlington, had the misfortune a few days ago of breaking his leg by falling while playing with one of his children. Brother Lambeth is now in Rainey Hospital, Burlington, and is resting well. His father was over to see him a few days ago, and while here called at THE SUN office. We are always glad to see Brother Lambeth.

NOTICE!

On October 15, 1919—at 7:30 P. M.

The Board of Trustees of the First Christian Church of Burlington, N. C., will receive sealed bids for purchase of old church building and lot on the southeast corner of West Davis and Church Streets, Burlington, N. C.

Said lot fronts 70 feet on West Davis Street and 100 feet on Church Street.

The right to reject any or all bids is reserved. Terms of sale: Cash.

D. R. FONVILLE, Chairman.

J. M. FIX, Secretary.

Burlington, N. C.

Sunday School and Christian Endeavor

THOSE CONFERENCE CHALLENGES

One of the new ideas brought forth at the Buffalo Conference was the plan of *challenges* issued by one State or one union to another State or union to a contest along different lines. For instance, one state union might challenge another to a contest along three different lines of increase. First. The largest net increase in membership. Second. The largest increase in the number of tithers. Third. The largest increase in mission study classses. The challenge might have been along the line of increase in comrades of the Quiet Hour; new Alumni Associations; Life-Recruits gained; new societies formed; money raised for missions; or Christian Endeavor Experts.

At our denominational rally it was the unanimous opinion that it would be a good plan for our Conferences to issue challenges to other Conferences along these lines. It would not be necessary to confine the challenge to our Conference alone. For instance, one Conference might be challenged to a contest for increase in Tenth Legioners, another to increase in Comrades of the Quiet Hour, another to increase in Christian Endeavor Expert, etc.

To carry out this plan it would be necessary to set the date when you were to begin the contest; then having received an acceptance to the challenge, notify all societies in the Conference of the contest and urge them to do their part to help win.

Write me telling the terms of the contest and who the contest is between and then have each of the contestants inform me of their gains each quarter and I will publish the standing of the contestants in *The Herald of Gospel Liberty, The Vanguard* and THE CHRISTIAN SUN.

Make the contest for at least two years closing, say the first of October or November.

It would be the duty of the Christian Endeavor Conference Secretaries of the different Conferences to obtain the facts with regard to the progress of the contest at the close of each quarter and report to me. To illustrate, if the New York Eastern Conference should challenge the Eel River, Indiana Conference to a contest along the line of increase in Christian Endeavor Experts and the Erie Conference to a contest for new members it would be the business of the Christian Endeavor Secretaries for these different Conferences to inform the different societies in their Conference of the contest and obtain from them their report at the end of each quarter as to gains made and then report to your A. C. C. Secretary of C. E., your humble servant.

I would like to hear of a challenge from every Conference or Convention.

A. B. KENDALL.

Ravena, N. Y.

ABOUT THINGS THAT MAY INTEREST YOU

Are you one of those to whom this issue is dedicated? We hope so.

* *

Read the article on page 5 about endowing Church papers and see what you think of it.

* *

Did you ever see a Scofield Reference Bible? Send to this office for a descriptive circular telling you all about it.

* *

We will gladly send any book, Bible or Testament on approval. You will be under no obligation to buy. Let us serve you.

* *

Look at your label and if your subscription has expired renew promptly. We need the money and you need the pleasure of having your account paid.

* *

How about a Communion Set for your church? Send for latest price list and our handsome 24-page descriptive booklet. It is yours for the asking.

* *

We have a number of nice khaki Testaments that we are closing out at the small sum of twenty-five cents each, postpaid. Add this amount to your renewal and let us send you one.

* *

Do you need a Bible or Testament of any description? THE SUN office can supply you. If you fail to find what you want in this line, write us a letter and describe the kind of book you want.

* *

Place your order now for a copy of Tarbell's Teachers' Guide or a copy of Peloubet's Select Notes. The price for each book is $1.60, postpaid. The delivery will be made about December 1, at which time we will send your bill.

* *

Brother preacher keep on hand one or two copies of "Merrill's Marriage Ceremony." It is a suitable souvenir. Seventy cents, if sent to this office, will bring you a copy. Your money refunded if it doesn't increase your marriage fees.

* *

We are going to do it. Yes, we are. Going to do what? A few of our subscribers are getting a little behind with their subscription account. Those who desire to catch up and get a little ahead by sending as much as $4.00, on or before October 10, will be given a useful present.

* *

If you want to give a friend a nice Bible and want his or her name on in gold letters, we can have it done for you at an extra cost of only 35 cents. It takes about ten days extra time to fill an order like this. This is because we must have the order made up by the manufacturers instead of shipping from stock.

* *

Just as we go to press Rev. J. E. Franks sends nine new subscribers to THE CHRISTIAN SUN. This means a new song in the Editor's heart, a smile on the face of the office help and an extra hum in the press.

"SUFFOLK LETTER"

Every Week   - - - -   Every Year

SMILES
Business Egotist
"We need brains in this business, sir."

"I know you do. The business shows it."—*Baltimore American.*

Difficulties of Family Discipline
"This hurts me more than it hurts you," the fond parent remarked sadly to his punishment-suffering son. "Then," said the bad lad, gritting his teeth, "keep on with it, dad. I can stand it."—*Boston Post.*

Not Yet
Maud: "Your friend, Miss Blank, going to be married? Why, I had the impression that she was a woman in her declining years."

Ethel: "Oh, dear no. She's in her accepting ones."—*Boston Transcript.*

He Had It
Customer: "I want a machine that isn't expensive as to gasoline or upkeep and one that I needn't worry about in the way of punctures."

Automobile Agent: "All right. I can sell you either a wheel barrow or a baby carriage."—*Judge.*

PELOUBET'S SELECT NOTES

Send your order for Peloubet's Select Notes on the Sunday school lesson along with your renewal to THE CHRISTIAN SUN. The books will be ready for delivery December 1. You need not send the money now, unless you want to. Just indicate for us to send you a copy December 1 and that will be all right. The price is $1.60, postpaid.

If we have not mentioned what you want, let us know, and if we do not have, and it can be had, we will get it for you.

An illustration of one of our khaki Testaments that are offering for 25 cents, postpaid.

Write for prices and samples of church offering envelopes.

GENERAL MENTION

A Marvin Carr, son of General Julian S. Carr, died on September 21.

General Pershing returned to the United States the other day and was received by a great reception.

The manufacturing plants at Albemarle, N. C., are continuing to have trouble with the labor unions.

Many carpenters in Charlotte, N. C., are on a strike demanding more pay and less hours.

Thirteen divorces were granted by the court in Guilford County, North Carolina, last week.

President Wilson is continuing his tour through the country in the interest of the League of Nations and the Peace Covenant.

Court is in session at Albemarle. N. C., and twenty-nine men are on trial for taking part in a riot in connection with a strike there a few days ago.

One of the biggest strikes in the country is one with the steel workers in Pittsburgh, Pa. Thousands of men are affected by the strike. Guards are on duty. Several persons have been killed and many wounded.

Eight men were carried from Guilford County to the State penitentary last week. Five of them are to serve 10 years each for holding up and robbing some citizens from Gibsonville, N. C., about two months ago.

Specimen of Type Holman Home Bible

AND it came to pass, that when Isaac was old, and his eyes were dim, so that

Flexible Binding

Specimen of type of the Holman Home Bible as shown on this page. It is a Bible that will please you.

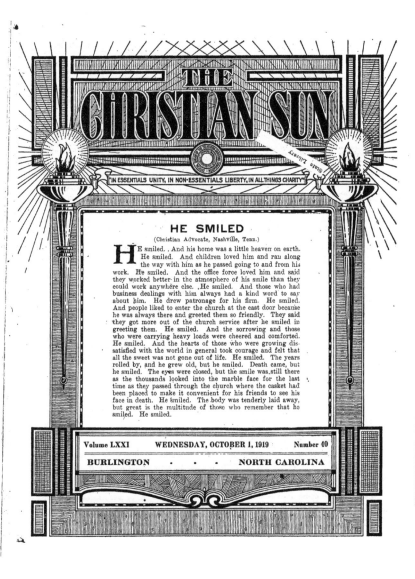

THE CHRISTIAN SUN

"IN ESSENTIALS UNITY, IN NON-ESSENTIALS LIBERTY, IN ALL THINGS CHARITY"

HE SMILED

(Christian Advocate, Nashville, Tenn.)

HE smiled. . And his home was a little heaven on earth. He smiled. And children loved him and ran along the way with him as he passed going to and from his work. He smiled. And the office force loved him and said they worked better in the atmosphere of his smile than they could work anywhere else. He smiled. And those who had business dealings with him always had a kind word to say about him. He drew patronage for his firm. He smiled. And people liked to enter the church at the east door because he was always there and greeted them so friendly. They said they got more out of the church service after he smiled in greeting them. He smiled. And the sorrowing and those who were carrying heavy loads were cheered and comforted. He smiled. And the hearts of those who were growing dissatisfied with the world in general took courage and felt that all the sweet was not gone out of life. He smiled. The years rolled by, and he grew old, but he smiled. Death came, but he smiled. The eyes were closed, but the smile was still there as the thousands looked into the marble face for the last time as they passed through the church where the casket had been placed to make it convenient for his friends to see his face in death. He smiled. The body was tenderly laid away, but great is the multitude of those who remember that he smiled. He smiled.

Volume LXXI	WEDNESDAY, OCTOBER 1, 1919	Number 40
BURLINGTON	. . .	NORTH CAROLINA

THE CHRISTIAN SUN

Founded 1844 by Rev. Daniel W. Kerr

C. B. RIDDLE - - - Editor·

Entered at the Burlington, N. C. Post Office as second class matter.

Subscription Rates

One year ....$ 2.00
Six months 1.00

In Advance

Give both your old and new postoffice when asking that your address be changed.

The change of your label is your receipt for money. Written receipts sent upon request.

Many persons subscribe for friends, intending that the paper be stopped at the end of the year. If instructions are given to this effect, they will receive attention at the proper time.

Marriage and obituary notices not exceeding 150 words printed free if received within 60 days from date of event, all over this at the rate of one-half cent a word.

Original poetry not accepted for publication.

Principles of the Christian Church

(1) The Lord Jesus Christ is the only Head of the Church.
(2) Christian is a sufficient name of the Church.
(3) The Holy Bible is a sufficient rule of faith and practice.
(4) Christian character is a sufficient test of fellowship, and of church membership.
(5) The right of private judgment and the liberty of conscience is a right and a privilege that should be accorded to, and exercised by all.

EDITORIAL

AN ADVERTISEMENT

We have just finished a study of an advertisement issued by the General Board of Education of the Presbyterian Church in the United States. The advertisement is headed: "Wanted more and Better Trained Ministers." We note the following significant facts:

(a) 54 fewer ministers were licensed last year.
(b) 35 fewer licentiates were enrolled last year.
(c) 192 fewer candidates were enrolled last year.
(This comparison is based on figures six years ago).

Such conditions are not only true with the Presbyterian Church, but with other Churches. From all denominational headquarters similiar statements are being issued. There must be a cause for this condition, and if the cause can be found, a cure should also be found. Let us consider the case for a few moments, first taking into consideration the cause:

1. Material progress during recent years has eclipsed the larger callings in life. Literature of a very light nature has crowded out the masterpieces that stir men's souls to a fervor ·for larger and holier tasks. Secular schools have played a large part in forming character, and too many times not inducive to the the Gospel ministry. Lighter subjects have been offered in many schools, and in so doing, some of the fundamentals have been omitted. The Bible has been debarred from the public schools in many states, and this alone is having its effect upon the young mind. These are only a few of the things that have directed the minds of the young away from the ministry.

2. The remunerative side comes in for a serious consideration and is to be reckoned with in changing the situation. The minister has too long been the object of charity. In literature, in the movie, and on every-hand the minister has come in as to the man of charity in the many cases. This has fastened itself firmly upon the plastic mind; and it is not American-like to aspire to positions of that kind and character. Gifts are always in place, but where we have made the mistake is considering these gifts as a part of the pastor's salary. Gifts should not be so considered, and so long as they are, the minister will be held up as an object of charity. Aside from this the business world has placed a premium on preparation and has rewarded accordingly. The pew has always had a premium on preparation, but with few exceptions, has not rewarded accordingly. The keen mind has sensed the difference—a difference in health, happiness, comfort, and respect—and acted upon its judgment. The pulpit and pew have suffered; the business world has prospered.

With these things as suggestions only, the remedy can be very easily seen and applied. The remedy is too plain to point out, Is this not true?

It would be unjust to the subject not to point out the deeper spirituality that must come into the American homes that preaches may be born. The home is the base. There we must begin, but what of the beginning, if we fail to care for the growth and the harvest? The answer to this is also too simple to state. Do you say that we must pray that the Lord of the harvest may send helpers? Let us ask this question: Have we cared for all those whom He has sent? We must pray and we must provide.

————

"Evil is the exception and not the rule and attracts more attention simply because it is unusual and not the general fact. Let one man beat his wife and the whole neighborhood will quickly resound with the sensational tale, while no notice will be taken of the hundred exemplary husbands that treat their wives with most praise-worthy propriety. A spot on the sun will attract thousands of observers, while its steady shining occasions no remark."

————

"BUILDING A CHURCH, OR CHURCHES"

Under the above heading Editor Kerr of The Herald of Gospel Liberty in a recent issue wrote editorially along a line that is pertinent to the whole Church. We have not read an editorial in any paper that sounds the keynote like the one we have referred to. We consider it GREAT, and so great do we consider it that last week we gave two pages to reproducing it. If there is a minister in the Southern Christian Convention who has not taken the time to read that editorial, or will not take the time, we feel that he is unfair to his calling and the denomination he represents. We ask for it a careful reading by all CHRISTIAN SUN readers.

But now to the object of this article. There must be an answer, or rather a cause, why we have been building churches and not a Church. All this is read between the lines in Brother Kerr's editorial, and yet, we must seek to find the way to building a Church—a denomination—and not churches—local churches alone. The editorial referred to has opened up the way, in thought, for us to say that which has been our conviction for a long time.

In a recent editorial on "Facing the Issue," which article brought many favorable comments, we endeavored to point out some of the weaknesses in our educational work as it is related to the candidates for the ministry. We believe that a change will come in all parts of the Convention, and we look forward for such a change, at least in part, this fall. We make this statement not because of what has been said in these columns, but because others have seen the issue just as we have seen it, and so see it. A strong ministry cannot be developed when the educational bars are too low; and without a strong ministry a strong denomination cannot be built.

We have been wondering why it is that the masses of the people are not more fully educated along denominational lines than they are. Is it for the lack of interest upon the part of the people? We think not. Is the matter altogether with the ministry? We think not. Is the matter with our system? We think so. And now why? Let us consider for a few moments.

We hold our Conferences. We adopt and seldom adapt. We resolve and rest; we make motions and stop the motion. We go back to our fields to carry out the plans. Are they carried out? Most of them. Then where is the trouble? As we see it, here it is: Our plans are all too local. They concern themselves with churches and not a CHURCH. They concern themselves with the Conference and not enough with the larger things of the Kingdom. And when we center our work upon ourselves, thus making it selfish, the measure of our progress is then taken. We have concerned ourselves too long with affairs that are local and have not gone out to the larger things. We are, however, slowly emerging from this state of affairs through missions, education, and other enterprises of the Church, but where we are going forward there can be found plans that are large and take in a situation not local.

The pastor is too busy with local affairs to educate his people very largely upon things of his denomination (unless he is able to get them to read the Church papers) and so the responsibility goes beyond the pastor and is a matter with the larger bodies of the Church.

In each Conference there should be an Executive Secretary whose business it would be to line up the people with the larger things such as denominational enterprises, state and world movements, etc. He should

be the custodian officer of the Conference's plans. There is no use trying to carry out plans, except local ones, with each pastor responsible for his part. It will not be done in any creditable manner. Other denominations have found out just this thing and they have acted as we have suggested and have their field men, each man for a special work. We, too, must come to it. Don't have the money? Why bless your life, we do have it. Our problem is getting it turned loose.

And what about the Convention? Who goes down from the Convention to the local churches to carry the plans and actions of that body? How far does the work of the Convention's Secretary reach? Just as far as we have commissioned him, and that is to keep the records, call the roll, be on time, have the minutes printed, and be at the next session? How about the President of our Convention? The office is practically honorary, with an emolument of fifty dollars a year for stamps and stationery. Does he do what we require of him? Certainly and more. He is a part of our system, is on time, presides well, and does exactly what we ask of him. He is a man of affairs, a preacher entrusted with a large and growing city church, and so he cannot reach the local churches, except through a few members at the Conference that he is privileged to attend. But this is speaking of the present President, while what we mean to say is about the office and not the officer.

Has the time not come when either the Secretary or the President of our Convention should be a salaried man and give all his time to the field in building a great system through which the Kingdom may go forward more rapidly? Is it not time? From the Convention should go out a representative to keep before the local churches the larger things of that body. The pastors have jobs of their own. Our Mission Secretary has a job. All others who go into the field have jobs, and so each man is doing his work; each man is representing a branch, but we are allowing the tree to die. We are building the branches, the local churches, but not the main tree, the denomination. It is through the denomination that we must function. This does not mean denominationalism—far from it, for those denominations that do the largest amount of inter-denominational work are the ones that have a strong base of supplies, and that base is their coherent denomination.

Will our Convention continue to be a body to meet and turn the general plans over to all? What is every man's job is no man's job. Is is worth while? Shall we build locally only and not organically? Shall we continue to exercise "liberty" until liberty will keep us from becoming great. Liberty is not license and we should not expect liberty to do all things.

The hour has struck for larger things and we must meet the demands of the hour. Our principles are great; some of our practices are poor. Our willingness is all right; our ways we must change.

"Humanity does not march with steady onward steps; at times it halts, breaks and falls back; but we should measure its movement not by its slips and falls but by its forward strides."

ARE YOU SATISFIED?

Are the readers of THE SUN satisfied with the paper that we are giving them? When you go to a hotel and make no complaint of the service, the proprietor takes it for granted that you are pleased. When you buy a pair shoes, and the next time you need a pair, buy from the same store, the dealer understands that you like his brand of shoes. We hear no complaint, and yet we may have readers who do not like the paper. We are honestly and earnestly doing all we can to make it the real mouthpiece of the Convention and to reflect the work and undertakings of that body. We seek no praise; we dislike it. If we should fail at any place or point, we have the confidence in the leaders of the Church to think that they will tell us where we fail. Their silence gives us courage, and upon this we press forward. THE SUN is the paper of the people and we ask that they speak when they do not approve of the work we are doing. A pastor can tell by the look upon the faces of his auditors whether his messages are sanctioned or not. The editor cannot; his work is without public inspiration. Four walls, a telephone, desk, chairs, papers, books, the hum of an electric fan, Ah! these constitute our visible congregation. Tell us when we are wrong; we are brothers.

"The chief line of progress in the Church and Christianity of our day is that it has shifted its chief emphasis from DOCTRINE to SERVICE. Doctrine has not been discarded or even depreciated, for it is still and ever will be the necessary root of all duties and deeds. Yet doctrine is no longer simply proved as an abstract theological proposition, but is planted as a living root to sprout and blossom and bear fruit."

INCENTIVES FOR GIVING

By Rev. W. B. Gray, D. D.

1. Because God demands that every one should give. Deut. 16:16-17.
2. Because our ownership of what we call our own is not absolute, only relative. We are stewards, and the word means, "Keeper of the sty." I Peter 4:10.
3. Because we will be called upon to give an account of this stewardship. Luke 16:1-2.
4. Because money given to God is seed of a glorious and bountiful fruitage. II Cor. 9:6; Mark 10:29-30.
5. Because all that we have comes from God, and by using it for Him we become workers together with Him. I Chron. 29:14-17.
6. Because we can thereby share in the glory of sending the light to those who are in darkness. Romans 10:15.
7. Because by giving we can send treasure on ahead and thus be rich after the period of our stewardship is over. Matthew 6:19-21.
8. Because by giving we may best be able to save ourselves from drifting into currents that have drowned so many. I Tim. 6:9.
9. Because God's fierce denunciation awaits all those who spend money in selfish gratification. James 5:1-5.
10. Because our Lord and Master is concerned about what we do with the money we hold. Mark 12:41.

NOTES

The Mission Board of the North Carolina Conference meets at Elon College today, Tuesday.

We understand that Rev. George D. Eastes is still quite sick and is unable to meet his appointments.

Rev. J. W. Holt, Burlington, N. C., has the first and second Sundays open for the coming year if there are churches desiring his services on these dates.

Just as we go to press a letter is received from Rev. J. V. Knight—and it is more than a letter. Ten new subscribers to THE SUN and the cash for all. Thank you, Brother Knight. Who will be next?

We have received the Sunday school notes for this issue, but no Christian Endeavor topic. *Wanted*: A Board that will see that we get this material on time. Reasonable appreciation for the right party.

Dr. J. O. Atkinson furnishes for this week's issue the proceedings of the Mission Board meeting recently held. It reveals several interesting items. Note that the goal has been set at $500,000. Of course it will be reached. The greatly increased work of our Mission Board is due largely to the fact that the Convention put a man in the field. This ought to be a great example for other departments of the Church. There is no use trying to do things by old methods. The work of our denomination must be carried to the people by representatives for the different branches of the work.

We understand that a religious census was taken at Elon College last week. We trust that President Harper, or someone, will furnish THE SUN an article giving the facts concerning this census. We would be particularly interested in the following items: (1) Per cent of student members of the church. (2) Per cent of our own denomination. (3) Number of ministerial students. (4) Number of ministerial students in each Conference in the Southern Christian Convention. (5) Number of ministerial students to graduate in 1920, 1921, 1922, 1923 and 1924. We believe that these facts would be of great interest to the Brotherhood and trust that they will be furnished for publication.

Mr. H. M. Neese, well known to many SUN readers and former Elon students, was instally killed on his farm, five miles South of Burlington, Friday afternoon, September 26. He was engaged in operating a hay rake when his team became frightened, threw him from his machine and inflicted two fatal wounds upon his head, this causing instant death. He was familiarly known as "Mac" Neese, was a licentiate in the Methodist Protestant Church, and intensely interested in the moral welfare of his community. He was never married and lived with his mother and two sisters. To them he was devoted and lived in the hearts of all who knew him. The funeral took place from Belmont Methodist Protestant church on Sunday, September 28. His pastor, Rev. J. A. Burgess, conducted the service, which had to be held in the church yard to accommodate the more than 2,000 people who assembled to pay their respects to a man who was a friend of all. Tributes to the life of the deceased were paid by Dr. W. A. Harper, Dr. T. C. Amick and THE SUN'S Editor.

NEW COMERS TO THE SUN FAMILY

G. T. Holt ....New Hill, N. C.
N. A. Gardner ....New Hill, N. C.
J. A. Mann ....New Hill, N. C.
W. A. Drake ....New Hill, N. C.
K. B. Riddle ....New Hill, N. C.
L. G. Gunter ....New Hill, N. C.
D. S. Sauls ....Merry Oaks, N. C.
Charley Hearn ....Merry Oaks, N. C.
J. E. Massey ....Elon College, N. C.
B. A. Barber ....Burlington, N. C.
J. W. Johnson ....Brown Summit, N. C.
B. A. Busick ....Brown Summit, N. C.
J. E. Cook ....Brown Summit, N. C.
(Report to September 29)

PASTOR AND PEOPLE

PROGRAM
of the
TWENTY-FIRST SESSION ALABAMA CHRISTIAN CONFERENCE WHICH MEETS WITH ANTIOCH CHRISTIAN CHURCH, CHAMBER COUNTY, ALABAMA, OCTOBER 14, 15, 16, 1919

Tuesday, October 14—10:00 A. M.
Devotional Services ....President
Organization
11:00—Annual Address ....Rev. J. H. Hughes
12:00—Refreshments

Afternoon Session
1:00—Prayer ....Rev. J. Taylor
1:20—Reading Ministerial and Church Reports
Miscellaneous Business
Adjournment

Wednesday, October 15—9:00 A. M.
Devotional Services ....Rev. A. H. Shepherd
9:20—Report of Executive Committee
9:35—Report of Committee on Grouping Churches
Discussion, led by J. W. Payne
10:30—Report on Sunday Schools
11:00—Preaching ....Rev. H. W. Elder
12:00—Refreshments

Afternoon Session—1:00 P. M.
Devotional Services ....W. R. Knight
1:20—Report of Home Mission Board, led by Rev. J. D. Dollar
2:20—Report of Committee on Education
Address ....Rev. E. M. Carter
3:00—Report of Committee on Moral Reform,
Rev. C. W. Carter
Miscellaneous Business
Adjournment

Thursday, October 16—9:00 A. M.
Report of Committee on Foreign Missions

Address ....Rev. G. D. Hunt
9:45—Report of Committee on Religious Literature
Address ....Rev. J. H. Hughes
10:30—Report of Committee on Christian Endeavor
Address ....J. J. Carter
11:00—Preaching ....Rev. C. M. Dollar
12:00—Adjournment

J. D. DOLLAR, Chairman.
Executive Committee.

IN BROTHER CARDEN'S FIELD
Auburn

We began our revival meeting at Auburn the second Sunday in August and closed the following Thusday evening. We experienced a great revival with several conversions.

Bethel (Caswell Co., N. C.)

Our meeting was held here the first week in August. God gave us a good revival. Several professed faith in Christ and two joined the church. The church was greatly revived.

Pleasant Ridge

The meeting at Pleasant Ridge began the third Sunday in August. This was a great revival with several professions. Revs. L. L. Wyrick and S. S. Higgins assisted me in this meeting and preached very fine sermons. The writer was unable to aid much in the meeting on account of sickness. I was not able to fill my appointment the fourth Sunday in August but was able to go to Lee's Chapel the fifth Sunday. We had a successful meeting, several professing faith in Christ.

ZION

Brother Neal Roland assisted me in the meeting at Zion, which was held the first week in August. God gave us a great meeting at this place. Ten new members were received into the church.

J. S. CARDEN.

Durham, N. C.

FROM THE FAR SOUTH

We began a tent meeting at Lowell Sunday, September 7, and closed it Thursday night, September 18. We had a great meeting. The meeting was a union meeting of three denominations, Methodist, Baptist and Christian. There were about forty-five additions to the three churches.

The thing that the Christian church needs in Roanoke is a house of worship—a place we can call our own. When we get a building of our own we can build up a strong work. We want to undertake to build soon, and desire to ask the good people of the Southern Convention to help us. We want this building to be a credit to our denomination.

J. D. DOLLAR.

Roanoke, Ala.

"IN GREEN PASTURES"

On the fourth Sunday in July I was hurried off to the Halcyon hospital in South Boston, Va., to undergo an operation for appendicitis. At eleven o'clock, surrounded by nurses and physicians, I faced an ordeal entirely new to me. The operation was very successful and after ten days I was beginning to think of re-

turning to my field of work when suddenly one morning I was overcome in a complete faint to awake with
an acute pain in my right shoulder which finally reached the lung and proved to be pneumonia and pleursy.
For several days I was critically ill.

But why "In Green Pastures"? For two years I
had been principal of a high school with a nine-months
session, and pastor of two rather large country churches.
I was going at full speed. I was scarcely taking inventory. My tasks were so exacting I was missing some
of the finer things of life, but in the midst of it "He
made me to lie down in green pastures," for scores of
friends came to bring their love, their most heart-felt
sympathy, and their tenderest words in that quiet time.
Mother, father, sister, and a brother sat by that bedside
and a new interpretation of the light in their eyes
flooded my soul. The untiring, never-ceasing, and sympathetic attention of Mr. and Mrs. D. Jennings Sipe,
and Miss Lydia Dunn is—"a thing of beauty" in the
green pasture in which I was lying,—morsels of fragrant grasses never to be forgotten. Indeed I was up-
lifted spiritually by the devotion and anxiety of my
churches; the prayers of the sister churches of other
denominations and their pastors; the service rendered
by Rev. L. E. Smith in conducting the Pleasant Grove
series of meetings; the kindness of my surgeon, Dr. H.
S. Belt, and my physician, Dr. S. T. A. Kent; my special nurses and many others. And the Shepherd, the
blessed Christ was there to Whom he all praise forever!
JOHN G. TRUITT.

News Ferry, Va., Sept. 23, 1919.

AMONG MY CHURCHES

(Antioch, Chatham County)

I began serving as pastor of this church in July of
1918, completing the unexpired term of R. S. Stephens.
At the conclusion of that term, the church extended to
me a call for the present year. The work here is rather
encouraging to us. There are a large number of children in the community; and all these attend our Sunday school at Antioch regularly. The Sunday school
at this place is very promising indeed.

The annual memorial services were held at Antioch,
this year, on the third Sunday in May. A large congregation attended both services—in the forenoon and in
the afternoon. "Uncle" Wellons was with us and
preached for us the third Sunday in July. Owing to
the very rainy weather at time, however, as he stated
in his letter, the congregation was rather small.

The Antioch people held their Children's Day exercises, this year, on the fourth Sunday in July. These
exercises were pronounced the best of the kind this
church has ever had.

Our protracted meeting at this church began, this
year, the third Sunday in August and closed on Thursday afternoon following. Rev. Geo. D. Eastes of Raleigh, N. C., did the preaching for us after Sunday.
Some able preachers have conducted revivals at Antioch in former years; but the people, up there, pronounce Brother Eastes the best yet. All of us are very
proud to know that the Christian Church, South, has

such an able preacher and revivalist. He did some excellent work at Antioch; but, just as a real interest in
salvation began to be manifested, we had to close in
order to commence our revival at Youngsville the following Sunday.

I have greatly enjoyed my work here the past year.
R. P. CRUMPLER.

Varina, N. C.

SUFFOLK LETTER

There is so much spoken and written in these days
about the rearing and training of children that one
wonders how they came to manhood and womanhood in
past years. It seems to be in the minds of many gifted
and good people that the whole matter of human up-
bringing can be accomplished through social activities.
It seems to me that the main question lies back of all
this widespread teachings in the home.

The original method among religious peoples was to
train children in the home. It was so among the Jews;
and whatever else may be said about the Jews, they
have maintained their religious characteristics and race
identity better than any other people. No climatic,
governmental, or social conditions have changed the
Jew. In all lands, among all conditions the Jew remains a Jew. He did not learn his lesson in the school,
but in the home. More than fourteen hundred years
before Christ the Jews were commanded to teach the
words that were to be in their hearts: "Thou shalt
teach them diligently unto thy children, and shalt talk
of them when thou sittest in thine house, and when
thou walkest by the way, and when thou liest down,
and when thou risest up." That was a home school in
which the best instruction was given by the best teacher.
Instruction that comes from the heart is the best lesson
ever learned; and no teacher loves the child as mother
loves. Love is always a good teacher, because love
is wiser than intellect. To say that "God is love" is to
include all the attributes of wisdom, goodness, holiness,
justice, mercy, and truth that belong to God's moral
nature. The safest thing on earth is real love. The
child is safer in the care of mother-love than in any
school in the State or the Church.

I have a letter only three days old telling of a family
of eleven, the last one dying, as the letter was written,
at ninety-four; and all of them consecrated Christians,
and, as the letter said, thankfully, "all left the assurance that they were going home—a family re-united."
It was the daughter of Rev. H. A. Albright, who died
August 31, 1919, with visions of angels before him,
that wrote the above. No modern school could improve
on such a family record. The father of that large family was Rev. Joseph Albright, a Christian preacher.
His greatest sermon was his life in the home.

The danger in these times is the surrender of this
God-given obligation and privilege to the Sunday school
and the day school. These are fine institutions, but
they cannot substitute for the home-school. The home
is the essential human institution for the church and
the State. It is the oldest, purest, wisest, the best. If
the home were to die it would wreck the world. If vir-

tue fade from the *home*, the world would be a Sodom. If wisdom were to perish in the *home*, schools could not save the race. If *home* were to become a bad place, there would be no need of hell. The sweetest thing that can be said of heaven is that it is a *"home."* It is a house with *"many mansions"* and that *home* is a "temple" where Jesus dwells. "Hear thou from thy dwelling-place, even from heaven" is repeated in Solomon's prayer at the dedication of the temple. As so much is written on "Back to Christ," may it not be well to write "Back to the Home."

W. W. STALEY.

FROM THE RAMSEUR PASTORATE

We began our meeting at Shiloh the second Sunday in August. Rev. J. F. Apple assisted and did all the preaching. His sermons were of a high order and well delivered. The congregations were large at all the services.

There was considerable interest on the part of both the church people and unsaved, but there were only a few unsaved who attended the meeting. As a result of the meeting three united with the church.

The work here has been a pleasure this year. There are some evidences of progress. The church has made the every member canvass to install the envelope system next year. I feel sure that Shiloh will send up to Conference a full report this year. I am looking for better things next year.

Park's Cross Roads

We began our revival meeting here the third Sunday in August. Rev. I. W. Johnson, D. D., came to our assistance Monday afternoon and did the remainder of the preaching to large and appreciative congregations. The meeting continued until Friday afternoon with an increase both in interest and congregation. The services reached a climax Friday afternoon when there were more than a score of professions and reclamations. It was as fine a service as I was ever in. I have seen services with as many professions but the character of it was just a little different from anything I had seen. It was a joy to be there. At the close of the service sixteen united with the church.

We have also made the every member canvass here to install the envelopes next year. There are also signs of progress here and you may expect some great things from the Cross Roads next year.

Pleasant Ridge

We began our meeting here the fourth Sunday in August. Dr. Johnson remained with us and did all the preaching here, and did it with acceptance. While there were large congregations all the week and a number of unsaved yet it seemed impossible to reach them, save three young girls. I do not understand the conditions here. There is no friction in the church and the church seems interested but we failed to reach a number of fine young men. However I trust that much and lasting good may have been accomplished.

We have also made the every member canvass here to install the envelope system. I believe it will mean much for the progress of the church. There are signs of progress in all my work. I am expecting to go to

Conference with a full sheet. The help that I had in these meetings was all that I could wish for I am sure the churches would be glad to have these brethren with them again.

A. T. BANKS.

ELON NEWS

The Executive Board of Trustees met on Wednesday of last week, and spent a busy afternoon. The spirit was fine and many important measures were disposed of. The Board of Trustees evidently have it enshrined in their purpose as a sacred trust to make Elon College a truly Christian institution. It is a great inspiration to be associated with such a capable body of men.

The overcrowded condition of the ladies' dormitories led them to add the residence erected here several years ago by Prof. P. J. Kernodle and which the College acquired two years ago to the dormitory system permanently. It will be steam-heated, have a matron, and accommodate 28 young ladies. It will undoubtedly become a very popular dormitory.

The death of Rev. L. I. Cox, Treasurer, gave the Board a serious problem in locating the right person as his successor. Rev. L. I. Cox did everything he undertook with such thoroughness and satisfaction that the College would suffer unless the right man should be found. The selection of Dr. Thomas C. Amick has commended itself to all here and will to all who know his sterling worth and tireless energy.

Dr. Amick's acceptance of the treasurership vacated the office of Dean of Men. This too is a position requiring rare tact, modern spirit, and sympathy with young life as well as devotion to the ideals of the College. The selection of Dr. W. C. Wicker to this high responsibility will command itself to all.

The College farm is to be equipped with a barn and cattle for a dairy and Brother W. M. McCauley and his family will take charge of it. This ought to be an important asset to the College Boarding Department. We feel that Brother McCauley will make it a success.

The Summerbell Lectures

Dr. Martyn Summerbell will reach the College Sunday morning, October 5 and will preach twice that day and lecture twice for Monday, Tuesday, and Wednesday following. We trust many friends can attend these lectures.

The subjects announced are:

Sermons
Sunday Morning—The Victory of Democracy.
Sunday Evening—The Sacrifices of Love.

Lectures
Monday Morning—The Dark Ages.
Monday Evening—The Middle Age and Feudalism.
Tuesday Morning—The Rise and Influence of Chivalry.
Tuesday Evening—Peter Preaching the Crusade.
Wednesday Morning—The First Crusade.
Wednesday Evening—Godfrey and the Kingdom of Jerusalem.

First Recital of Year

The Expression and Violin Departments gave the initial recital of the year on Friday evening, last. Miss Hawk as reader and Mrs. Sturm as violinist were happy in their respective numbers and competent judges considered the College had been wisely guided in their

choice as the heads of these departments.
The program rendered was as follows:
Program

The Cabin is Empty Again...........................Lloyd
MISS HAWK
Fantasia Appassionata
Allegro Moderato ....Vieuxtemps
MRS. STURM
The Bride at the Butcher's.............................Fiske
My Mother's Song ....Byron W. King
MISS HAWK
Romance .... Svendsen
Mazurka (Obertass) .... Wieniawski
MRS. STURM
Musical Readings
The Usual Way ....Anonymous
What's the Good O' That, Huh?..................Crawford
I've Got the Mumps ....Franklin
MISS HAWK
Mr. Betts at Piano.

W. A. HARPER.

POUNDED

On Monday night, September 15, I responded to the call of the door bell, and when I did I was informed by one of the faithful members of the Christian church that they had come over to give me a pounding and they certainly did, for they were soon in the act of unloading the truck and filling up our pantry. After they were gone, Mrs. Wells and myself began to take an inventory of what was left us, and we found flour, meat, lard, coffee, sugar, oatmeal, corn-flakes, jelly, honey, tomatoes, corn, and money. And we are still being remembered by others who did not have a part in the bountiful supply on the night of the fifteenth. To be remembered in this way by the good people whom we are trying to serve helps wonderfully in a temporal way in these days when the cost of living is high, and it helps us to feel our obligation to serve better those who have remembered us so bountifully. Mrs. Wells and myself cannot find words to express our sincere thanks and appreciation for being so kindly remembered. The members of our Reidsville church know how to make their pastor's heart feel glad, and may God bless and prosper them all, is my prayer.
W. L. WELLS.

DATE OF THE ALABAMA CONFERENCE

The Alabama Christian Conference meets with the church at Antioch, Tuesday after the second Sunday in October at 10 o'clock. Rev. J. D. Dollar is president and Rev. E. M. Carter is secretary. Their post office is Wadley, Alabama. Get ready to attend and see that your church is represented.

GEORGIA AND ALABAMA CONFERENCE

The Georgia and Alabama Conference adjourned last year to meet in its annual session at Lanett, Alabama, on Tuesday after the third Sunday in October, which is October 21. Rev. H. W. Elder, Richland, Georgia, is the president of the session and Brother S. H. Abel is acting secretary. J. F. Hill is the treasurer

whose address is Phoenix, Alabama, Box 96. Get ready for this Conference. Be on time, stay through the session—and add something to it.

EASTERN VIRGINIA CONFERENCE

The Eastern Virginia Conference held its session at Eure's church last year and this year goes to the other side of the territory and meets with the Waverly Christian church. The time of the meeting is Tuesday before the first Sunday in November, which will be October 28. Rev. I. W. Johnson, D. D., Suffolk, Va., is the efficient secretary while Rev. O. D. Poythress, South Norfolk, Va., is his assistant. Dr. C. H. Rowland, Franklin, Va., is president and Dr. W. W. Staley, Suffolk, Va., is vice-chairman. Plans are being formulated for a great meeting and the churches within the bounds of this Conference are urged to make preparation for the coming event.

NORTH CAROLINA CONFERENCE

The North Carolina Christian Conference meets with the church at Burlington, N. C., on November 11, next, and will be in session to November 14, inclusive. This is the first session of the united Conferences, which embraces the Western North Carolina, Eastern North Carolina, and North Carolina and Virginia Conferences. Rev. T. E. White, Sanford, N. C., is the president, while the record-keeper is Dr. W. A. Harper, Elon College, N. C. A tentative program is now in circulation and every church, minister and member of this Conference is urged to begin now to make it a star session.

NOTICE!

On October 15, 1919—at 7:30 P. M.
The Board of Trustees of the First Christian Church of Burlington, N. C., will receive sealed bids for purchase of old church building and lot on the southeast corner of West Davis and Church Streets, Burlington, N. C.
Said lot fronts 70 feet on West Davis Street and 100 feet on Church Street.
The right to reject any or all bids is reserved. Terms of sale: Cash.

D. R. FONVILLE, Chairman.
J. M. FIX, Secretary.
Burlington, N. C.

WHAT YOUR LABEL MEANS
(Told in the Language of a Child)

1-1-9 means that your subscription expires January 1, 1919.
2-1-9 means that your subscription expires February 1, 1919.
3-1-9 means that your subscription expires March 1, 1919.
4-1-9 means that your subscription expires April 1, 1919.
5-1-9 means that your subscription expires May 1, 1919.
6-1-9 means that your subscription expires June 1, 1919.
7-1-9 means that your subscription expires July 1, 1919.
8-1-9 means that your subscription expires August 1, 1919.
9-1-9 means that your subscription expires September 1, 1919.
10-1-9 means that your subscription expires October 1, 1919.
11-1-9 means that your subscription expires November 1, 1919.
12-1-9 means that your subscription expires December 1, 1910.

MISSIONARY

NOTICE

The Eastern Virginia Woman's Missionary Conference meets with the Portsmouth Christian church, October 23, 1919. We are anxious to have a full attendance and all of our churches represented. An interesting program has been prepared; we want to make this our best meeting. We are asking that all societies which have not yet sent in apportionments on the fund for the support of a misssionary, send them to Mrs. M. L. Bryant, not later than October 15. We want to have the full amount in hand when we meet.

MRS. C. H. ROWLAND, Pres.

MISSION BOARD MEETS

The Mission Board of the Southern Christian Convention met in regular annual session at Suffolk, Va., Wednesday, September 17, at 10:00 a. m. Members present: Col. J. E. West, Chairman; J. M. Darden, J. A. Williams, W. P. Lawrence, K. B. Johnson, Revs. H. W. Elder, G. O. Lankford and C. H. Rowland. Absent: Rev. J. Lee Johnson.

Chairman West called the meeting to order and Rev. H. W. Elder led the devotional exercises. Minutes of last session, also minutes of intervening executive sessions were read and approved. The report of the Secretary and Treasurer was read. Dr. J. W. Harrell of Burlington, N. C., was invited to sit with the Board as a deliberative member.

A delegation from Third church, Norfolk, Va., asked to be heard for fifteen minutes and the request was granted; Dr. L. E. Smith spoke for the delegation and was followed by Dr. J. W. Manning and Brother Walter Rawls. The delegation was willing to labor under the auspices of the Board and build as directed by the Board. Three months ago it was thought a suitable church building could be erected for $125,000.00, but prices had advanced and such a building as was needed and desired would cost $150,000.00. The delegation was of opinion that the church membership would give $85,000.00 on such a building; that $25,000.00 could be secured from friends of the church in and outside of Norfolk, and it was desired that the Board donate $40,000.00 Dr. Smith was of the opinion that this would not be a donation, but an investment. Dr. Manning speaking for the church declared that if they could get proper help they could build large, if not, they would have to build small; and that the appropriation asked of the Board would amount to more than its face value would indicate, because it would inspire the church to do more than it would if it had to go alone in the matter. Dr. Smith was of the opinion if this Board would appropriate $40,000.00 the church and its friends outside would put up $110,000.00, and would more likely put up $125,000.00 before the task was complete. Later in the proceeding the matter was discussed by the Board and the request was granted practically as made. Third church is in a growing and

rapidly developing section of the city, and there is great opportunity for our work. The church has some of the most active and loyal and consecrated members to be found anywhere in all our Zion.

Miss Iola Hedgepeth, a member of Barrett's church, was present by request of the Secretary and was requested to tell of her work the past summer in the mountains of Virginia. Her work of a volunteer character was done last summer in Franklin and Patrick counties, the latter supposed to be the poorest in the State. She told a remarkable story of ignorance, immorality and irreligion in many districts far back in the mountains. She made an appeal for the Southern Christian Convention to establish a training school to help educate and Christianize these people who have not had advantage of schools and churches.

A motion was made and after discussion was unanimously adopted that the mission funds raised by the various missionary units and organizations be correlated, and that our goal be set at $500,000.00, including what has been subscribed and collected, by September 1, 1922. The Board first set its goal at $50,000. This was later fixed at $100,000; then later at $125,000. We had not sufficient faith in the task and in the people. Our people have been more willing and anxious than any had anticipated. It was the unanimous opinion of the Board that a half million dollars for the five years beginning September 1, 1917 is not too much to expect of our people who are anxious to undertake great things for the Kingdom.

Among the appropriations made by the Board were $700.00 to Columbus, Ga., work (Rose Hill church.) Dr. J. P. Barrett is to be the pastor and is to begin his pastorate October 1. Lanett, Ala., was given $200.00 to enable the pastor to live there and give two Sundays of the month to this church. The church at Vanceville, in South Georgia, was given $100.00 to help pay off its indebtedness. Winchester, Va., was voted $550.00 on salary and an appropriation of $2,000.00 provided the church liquidate its indebtedness. Chapel Hill, N. C., was given $600.00 on condition that the pastor reside there and give all his time to the building up of this work, he being allowed to serve Damascus on third Sundays. Reidsville, N. C., was given $600.00; Lamberts Point $250.00 to liquidate its indebtedness and $100.00 on salary; South Norfolk, Va., $300.00; Franklinton, N. C., to join with the Mission Board of the North Carolina Conference mutually in giving $5,000.00, provided Franklinton church and town people give $5,000.00; and $5,000.00 is given by friends outside—on a building to cost $15,000.00. Portsmouth, Va. church was voted an appropriation of $200.00. The Field Secretary is to visit and investigate prospects for beginning a work in Richmond, Va., and report his findings to the Executive Committee who has power to act. Lumber City, South, Ga., is given $2,000.00 on their contemplated $6,000.00 building, or one-third of total cost not to exceed $7,000.00, provided this clears same of debt.

A work in Washington is to be begun, the Board paying the pastor's salary, but ask the Woman's Con-

(Continued on page 13)

CHRISTIAN EDUCATION

WHEN THE GIRLIE GOES TO COLLEGE

By Mrs. W. A. Harper

You have often heard it said that a woman without a child call tell you better how to rear one than a mother of six can. Whether or not this is the reason that I am writing out what I should tell a daughter of mine going to college I do not know. I haven't a daughter, but if I did these are a few of the things I should tell her.

Any way the first thing I should do would be to try to impress upon her mind what a college education means. I should want her to value her college course in the fullest and not consider it of slight consequence, a mere incident, or accident. The college will be a means, a method or force through which she will be given a vision of the possibilities that lie within her. It will open the windows of her soul and the air of human life will sweep in to make her a sturdy and fine character if she arises to her opportunity. Then too I would have her look beyond the college walls, a college education is not the all, the be-all and end-all of life, but always a *means* for a larger vision, a method for better service and a force for greater power. All this I would tell her.

I should tell her also to remember home; that we were sending her to college in order that she might be prepared to live at home; that I desired her to become wise and large minded in order that she might bring a new strength and an earnest appreciation into the home which shall be loyal, rich and fine; that she was to become great in heart and strong in will in order to bring into the home a gentleness, which is sympathetic, loving, and true.

Then I should lay a great deal of stress on the value of the girlie's health. Physical soundness gives great aid in getting hold of and holding sound views of life. Life is a mirror. One smiles into it and it smiles back. One frowns and it frowns. If one is sick, all life is sick. What ails you ails most folks in this world. Now all life is not well, sound and vigorous, but if you yourself are, you can help to transmute that vigor and life into someone else. If we would only open the doors and windows of our hearts and souls in the presence of a strong, vigorous, happy person we would just as surely catch that disease as we would smallpox from one infected with that incubus.

At the age of 32 Robert Browning fell in love with Elizabeth Barrett. At the same period his head-aches began. Up to that time he had been free from such symptoms. The relation between the head and heart may be close. The College girl should keep herself free from sufferings and incapacities. She should not be plagued by headaches, heartaches, nervousness, and indigestion. I would caution her to be careful, very careful, of her health.

I would in perfect privacy put my arms around her and say: "I want to say to you, my daughter, as you go away from home, get the very best for yourself from college. That may sound a little selfish, but wait a and let me emphasize *for yourself*. For do you know what may be good for one may not be good for another Try to find in the college the supplies for your dire a direct wants. No gardener tries to raise cabbages from cucumber seed. We might wish you had more and be ter stuff in you, but you are what you are and educa tion must educate that individual and that indivi uality which nature out of all her material made yo In getting the best for yourself, let one element of th best be appreciation. In other words, a love for tl best. I want you to know what is best. I want you then, to love this best and then want you to make th best a part of yourself. Now you will find your teach ers in college like teachers in schools everywhere, an like all other folks, having a great variety of abilitie. Perhaps you will have the idea that each professor i pretty near perfection. Well, go on thinking so unt you have to think otherwise. But you will soon fin they are a bit nearer perfection in some lines tha others. What I want you to do is this: take each a his best and think as little as possible about his *not best*

"I want you to have an appreciation of the bes books. Books have been so common a part of you furniture and of your home, you may not know tha some books are good, some better and some best. Wha I want you to do is to be able to know the best book and make them a part of your life.

"I would like to say the same about music. Hear the best music. Also about art. Study the best pictures and paintings. By studying the best in nature and in art, you will know the best. By knowing the best, you will love the best. By knowing and loving the best, you will become a part of the best.

"Apply this same rule in forming your friendships. Do you know the way for getting the very best friendship? Of course you do. It is to give the best of yourself. And do you know the surest way of giving the best of yourself? Of course you do. It is to find the best in the other girl. She has her best and not best just as you. Find her best and help make it better. By so doing you will find yourself lifted, enlarged and inspired and the best of friendships formed.

"I want to say one thing more. It is perhaps the most important of all. Get the best and most out of your religion. The relation one bears to the Supreme Being is the most important. Many people do not get much out of their religion and certainly religion can not on that account get much out of them. Emerson says somewhere that every man must pray. The mood of prayer and the tact of prayer belong to the devout soul. Keep up your Church life. If the church is poor and the preaching uninteresting make the service of the church worship, even if you cannot make it instruction and inspiration. Many girls and boys think they have to study on Sunday. It is very foolish. Use Sunday for a time of interpretation, reflection and inspiration. Make each day too like George Herbert's Sunday, 'The bridal of the earth and sky.' If you will follow these simple principles, your own intuitive good judgment will make of you the real woman of your mother's aspirations and prayers."

And now as to her relations to the opposite sex I know of nothing to tell her that would convey to her my feelings more than the story of that young girl whose mother told her to always keep her person sacred, never to allow a young man to touch her more than to catch hold of her arm to assist her when assistance was needed and if she ever did contemplate doing otherwise to first take a knife and cut her throat from ear to ear that she might die believing in her innocence rather than live and know she was guilty.

ADDITIONAL NOTES

Roger M. White, a former Elon student and known to many Sun readers, died September 22.

Miss Annie Simpson and Miss Minnie Gibson of the First Church, Greensboro, N. C., are due the thanks of this office for securing the new subscribers mailed us by Rev. J. V. Knight. We are deeply indebted to these young ladies for this splendid work.

Rev. T. E. White, Sanford, N. C., has organized a Christian Endeavor Society in the Sandford Church with twenty-one active members. We also understand that Brother White has organized a Teacher-Training Class.

We have the mission study books on hand. The book for the home study is "Christian Americanization," and the foreign study is "Crusade of Compassion." Send your order early. Bill will be sent with books.

For the many kind and appreciative expressions of our "Business and Relief Edition" of The Sun we are grateful. We also record our thanks for the new life that it has put into the financial side of our work.

OF GENERAL INTEREST

England is suffering the result of a railroad strike.

All high schools and colleges report crowded conditions.

The great steel strike in parts of Pennsylvania is reported to be somewhat quieted.

Omaha, Nebraska, was the scene of a riot and lynching Monday. The city jail was partially destroyed by fire.

Editor Bok, of The Ladies' Home Journal, has resigned to take effect January 1, next. On that date he will complete his thirtieth year as editor of that paper.

President Wilson has had to abandon his trip on account of a break-down in health. He has been compelled to return to Washington. President Wilson has stood the hard fight for a long time and a collapse in his health is no great shock to the people.

EDITORIAL NOTES

The Methodist Centenary enrolled 193,210 persons in its Tithers' League.

Those who tithe their income should be careful how they spend the tenth. Remember that it is the Lord's and that we are to administer it for Him. Seek the guidance of the Holy Spirit, and where you are in doubt, let the doubt rule. Make a discrimination.

The Sunday school is a good place to teach tithing. Get the children interested in the subject, and encourage them to begin. They will grow up to regard it sacred, and will in the meantime form the habit. Begin early, begin in the Sunday school.

There is a decided difference between *tithing* and *Stewardship*. *Tithing* is the principle of paying to God what we owe. *Stewardship* embraces the principle that we are only stewards of what we have, and that we are trustees only and not owners.

GIVING AND HAVING MORE

Giving and yet having more. Isn't that strange? That is what the Bible teaches and again and again men have proved it.

> "A man there was, some called him mad
> The more he gave away, the more he had"

says Bunyan, and that spoken years ago. Some men today will tell you that so and so is foolish because he gives his money freely. The critics of such persons have not understood how it is that a man may sow and reap not; how a man may scatter and fail to gather—if the sowing and scattering is not of God.

WHAT THE LATE CARNEGIE HAD TO SAY ABOUT STEWARDSHIP

"The duty of the man of wealth is to set an example of modest, unostentatious living, shunning display or extravagance; to provide modestly for the legitimate wants of those dependent upon him, and after doing so to consider all surplus wealth which comes to him simply as trust funds which he is called upon to administer in the manner which in his judgment is best calculated to produce the most beneficial results for the community. There is no mode of disposing of surplus wealth creditable to thoughtful and earnest men save by using it year by year for the general good * * * The man who dies leaving behind him millions of available wealth which was free for him to administer during life, * * * dies disgraced. Such, in my opinion, is the true Gospel of Wealth."—*Andrew Carnegie.*

The Burlington Sunday school had a rally day last Sunday.

We are indebted to Rev. J. F. Apple for a list of new subscribers.

We are making October pay-up month. If your subscription is out, please let us have remittance. The Sun needs the money to meet its accounts.

THE CHRISTIAN ORPHANAGE

SUPERINTENDENT'S LETTER

In the Orphanage work we have many things to make us happy and the work pleasant. We received a little package this week that brought with it a pleasure that was a joy. The Sunbeam Workers Society of the Graham Christian church sent to us a package of stockings for the children.

I have been informed that the good lady who is teacher of that class of little girls asked them some time ago not to go to the "Movies" for a certain length of time, and keep the money that they would spend in going to the "Movies" and buy something for the little orphan children.

The package of stockings was the result. This brings us a sweet pleasure because we know if there is anything that is a sacrifice to a little girl, or at least many of them, it is to refrain from going to the "Movies." They enjoy it. It is a great pleasure to them. Now, if little children are willing to make a sacrifice that is so great to them, how much more ought we grown-up folks be willing to make?

Then too, we have something to come along sometimes that is really discouraging. It makes our heart ache and we cannot see just why people can feel so little interested in this work realizing that more than forty children are knocking at our doors pleading for a home—little children who are worthy of the love and sacrifice of our people. I have this instance in mind: I remember sometime in the past that a church sent us a check for less than one dollar for a monthly contribution. I happened to know a large percent of the membership of that church. I know that church has more than two hundred members. The wealth of the membership is, in my opinion, not less than one half million dollars. I know, too, that there are at least thirty members in that church who could give as much as $100 per month, or $5.00 per month each, and be the richer.

No better community exists anywhere. No better people live than these dear people. Have splendid houses; fine horses and cattle; costly automobiles. Sixty little orphans in the Christian Orphanage to feed, clothe, train and educate. Forty little homeless boys and girls with bright minds and strong bodies knocking at our doors pleading for an opportunity to make good citizens and are denied this opportunity and are turned away because our Church has not made provisions for their care. Turned away to drift, oh where! Turned away to be subject to all the temptations the world has to offer. It is not the small amount of the offering that hurts. We would be grateful if it had been only a dime. But it is the lack of interest in God's work, and in lending a helping hand to the helpless, that made our heart ache.

The following has been sent in since our last report: B. A. Sellars & Sons, Burlington, N. C., one box containing dresses, coat suits, etc; Ladies Aid Society, Dendron church, Va., one counterpane, one pair pillow

cases; Mrs. Fannie Brickhouse, Norfolk, Va., two packages books, one package of games for the children, one quilt.

CHAS. D. JOHNSTON, *Supt.*

REPORT FOR OCTOBER 1, 1919

Amount brought forward, $10,890.61.

Children's Offerings

Oliver E. Young, Jr., 20 cents.

Sunday School Monthly Offerings

(North Carolina Conference)

Shiloh, $1.40; New Hope, $10.00; Oak Grove, $1.87; Shallow Well, $2.33; Union, 77 cents; Mt. Auburn, $10.65; Chapel Hill, $11.17; Bethlehem, $2.00; New Elam, $4.81; Pleasant Cross, $4.25.

(Eastern Virginia Conference)

Dendron, $4.50; Hobson, $1.30.

(Alabama Conference)

Linville, $3.50; Total, $58.45.

Special Offerings

J. H. Jones, on support of children, $30.00; Women's Missionary Society, Locktown Christian Church, N. J., $10.00; Miss Mabel Eaton's Class, Lakemont, N. Y., $7.75; Miss Ida Belle Wicker, on pledge, $5.00; Total, $52.75.

Children's Home

Mrs. E. J. Gunter, Atlanta, Ga., $5.00.

Total for the week, $116.40; Grand total, $11,007.01.

A LETTER

Dear Uncle Charley: It's so hot in Alabama that I would enjoy being at Elon today where it must be cool. I am walking now, and find it a better way to gain my wants, although I have many a tumble and fall. Love for all.—*Oliver E. Young, Jr.*

No, my little man, it has been very warm up here. We were thinking perhaps it was cooler in Alabama. Glad to have your letter this week. It keeps the "Home Fires" burning in our corner.—*"Uncle Charley."*

"I believe that every man is entitled to an opportunity to earn a living, to fair wages, to reasonable hours of work and proper working conditions, to a decent home, to the opportunity to play, to learn, to worship and to love, as well as to toil, and that the responsibility rests as heavily upon industry as upon government or society, to see that these conditions and opportunities prevail."

"I believe that the application of right principles never fails to effect right relations; that 'the letter killeth but the spirit giveth life,' * * * and that only as the parties in industry are animated by the spirit of fair play, justice to all and brotherhood, will any plan which they may mutually work out succeed."
—*Jno. D. Rockefeller, Jr.*

"The brotherhood of mankind must no longer be a fair but empty phrase; it must be given a structure of force and reality. The nations must realize their common life, and effect a workable partnersip to secure that life against the aggressions of autocratic and self-pleasing power."—*President Wilson.*

WORSHIP AND MEDITATION

A STARLESS CROWN

This world is so full of beauty for every one who will look, listen and admire. Even the least observer admires its lovely and wonderful things. The starry realms of unknown worlds glittering with star light splendor form a crown of surpassing grandeur to beautify and adorn our world. With glad hearts and delighted vision we look upon this crown of beauty with almost perfect delight. When the sun is set and its departing rays flame against and paint with matchless coloring the golden draped curtains of the east which are rolled down for the return of night the light of the stars is like candles blazing in the sky. All these lights turned on from the great power and lighthouse of God flash in quick succession from star to star until uncounted worlds praise Him with their light and brightness.

There is a great difference between a starless and a fadeless crown. A crown without stars is not so beautiful nor attractive as one which is well decked with them. There was a person who once dreamed he went to heaven to wear a crown but there were no stars on it, and his expectation was disappointed at receiving a starless crown, so that it troubled his waking thoughts. How very much we love to sing and hear sung the words: "Will there be any stars in my crown?" We want to wear the brilliant star-decked crown of righteousness in the kingdom of our Father, and many will be greatly and sadly disappointed if they do not. The more stars a crown has to adorn it, the more lovely and admirable it is. To wear a star spangled crown in heaven is surely worth contending for—is worth laboring for. Jesus the judge the worlds with His own cross-scarred hands will give a fadeless crown to every faithful one, and it is to be worn all through the realms of infinite day.

Surpassingly beautiful will be that life of rapture and endless joy. With white robes, palms of victory and starry crowns glittering with the brightness of heaven, how beautiful will be the scene and how glorious the enjoyment for the saints of the Lord!

Gaze upon this astronomical scene which crowns this world with a cap of superlative beauty and look at it a thousand times, and it appears more wonderful and attractive each time you turn your eyes upon the scene. It is always new, inspiring and interesting, and the eye never tires looking upon such elevating scenes. What a wonderful crown is the canopy of the sky! And as it is admired by millions in every age and in every clime under the sun, so will the heavenly crowns be admired by the great throng of the tribes and nations of the congregated worlds who will be permitted to wear them in the saints everlasting rest. There in that state of life, light, love and liberty they will lose their national or worldly idenity and be the heirs of God to the heavenly inheritance and wear as victors over sin, crowns of glory.

No literal crown is meant or expected but a crown of glory and spiritual blessings to adorn and beautify the soul through eternity; and to be crowned with immortal life, with a deathless life is great and grand to contemplate. How we look for the happy day of eternal rest. Oh, may we reach the prize and wear the crown!

                                        J. T. KITCHEN.
Windsor, Va.

MISSIONARY

(Continued from page 9)

ferences to make this salary their Home Mission special. Rev. A. B. Kendall was unanimously chosen pastor to begin the work, and all moneys raised by him from the local membership is to be applied to paying for lot.

Rev. T. E. White, Sanford, N. C., has visited Sanatorium, N. C., the state tuberculosis institution, and held religious services there once per month, the Board bearing his expenses for the same. This is to be continued another year if Brother White can do the work. The Board voted $300.00 to help finance the Board of Religious Education till Convention meets, and a definite policy has been worked out by and for that Board.

After paying expenses and appropriations the past year the Treasurer's report showed total assets on hand of $25,170.68 for both Home and Foreign Missions.

When the Board began aggressive work two years ago there was available in the Convention about $1,200.00 for each Home and Foreign Missions. In next week's SUN the vital matters attended to by the Foreign Board and the appropriations made will be given.

                                        J. O. ATKINSON, Sec.

MR. GLADSTONE ON GIVING

Mr. William Gladstone is quoted by his biographer as follows:

"In regard to money as well as to time, there is a great advantage in its methodical use. Especially it is wise to dedicate a certain portion of our means to purpose of charity and religion, and this is more easily begun in youth than in after-life. The greatest advantage of making a little fund of this kind is that when we are asked to give, the competition is not between self on the one hand and charity on the other, but between the different purposes of religion and charity with one another, among which we ought to make the most careful choice. It is desirable that the fund thus devoted should not be less than one-tenth of our means; and it tends to bring a blessing on the rest."

A principle is greater and bigger than a creed. A creed is an *attempt* to circumscribe a principle. A principle enlarges itself to give justice.

Sunday School and Christian Endeavor

SUNDAY SCHOOL NOTES FOR

OCTOBER 12, 1919

Fishers of Men.—Mark 1:14-20.

Golden Text: Jesus said unto them, Come ye after me, and I will make you to become fishers of men. Mark 1:17.

Be sure to use additional material on this lesson as you study it. See for yourself the "Ways of Winning Men for Christ" (Senior and Adult Topic).. Know the "Work of a Disciple" (Intermediate Topic), and be prepared to show the Juniors how "Peter and John Became Disciples of Jesus," and teach the Primaries how they, as well as others may "Help Others to Know Jesus."

The keypoint of this Lesson is found in the Golden Text, "Come with me, and I will make you...." It does not matter how unpromising the material. Jesus can "make" us what He wishes us to be. A little booklet, costing five cents, I think, written by Ridgway, "The Iron Man," may be secured from the *Sunday School Times*, showing that practically every big business in America has among its leaders, men who are strong workers in the Kingdom. One needs not to be a minister to be "made" by God. Exodus 31:1-5 tells how God "made" artisans for His Tabernacle. 1 Chron. 4:24, in the midst of a long genealogical table, gives us a hint of how they are made. "They dwelt with the King for his work." God can make us what He wants us to be if we are willing to be made. He will put us where He wants us if we are willing to be pleased. The first Psalm tells us "and he shall be like a tree—planted." Planted trees are where the Gardener wants them. What can be finer, more joyful, more secure? "Come ye after me, fishers of fish, and I will make you to become fishers of *men*."

MRS. FRED BULLOCK.

THAT OPENING SERVICE IN YOUR

SUNDAY SCHOOL

I wonder what you do in the opening service. I think I can pretty nearly tell you. Doesn't your program run something like this?:

Song (anyone of about ten hymns).

Prayer.

Song (another one of same ten; never a new hymn; not much if any regard as to whether it fits the Lesson or not).

Reading of opening exercise in front of quarterly (both of them).

Reading of Lesson.

Teachers take charge of classes.

How much more do your children know of the Bible, or about the Bible after a year in your school? Why not take part of this time to learn some of the great Bible verses, and some of the Bible truths? There is a splendid little book "Manual of Bible Drills" I think is the name, which the Publishing Agent will secure for you. It costs 50 cents and has enough material in it to supply you for a couple of years. You would find that it would assist you in really having Bible "Scholars" in your school. Why not learn some new songs? Never mind if you cannot get the choir together to practice. Learn them right in Sunday school.

MRS. FRED BULLOCK.

CHRISTIAN ENDEAVOR AND THE

CHRISTIAN CHURCH

Ever since I learned my first lesson in Christian Endeavor work, I have wondered why the Christian denomination did not have a Society in every church. The principles of the Christian Church are open to the Christian Endeavor work and the principles of Christian Endeavor are so closely associated with the doctrine of the Church that an outsider would

"**FINEST OF FINE ARTS, OR HOW TO**

BE ALWAYS HAPPY"

By Dr. Chas. E. Barker

1. Cultivate the habit of always looking on the bright side of every experience.

2. Accept cheerfully the place in life that is yours, believing that is the best possible place for you.

3. Throw your whole soul and spirit into your work, and do it the best you know how.

4. Get into the habit of doing bits of kindness and courtesies to all those who touch your life each day.

5. Adopt and maintain a simple, childlike attitude of confidence and trust in God as your own Father.

think that the same master mind had moulded the two. Now, since I have tried to study my second lesson, I still wonder why our Church as a whole has not made Christian Endeavor a practical thing with us. Why is it that a Church as large as ours, standing as it does for Christian union, open fellowship and co-operation with all God's people, has so few Societies among us? Whose fault is it?

Christian Endeavor stands for loyalty to Christ and the Church; for training our young people for Christian service; for interdenominational work among the followers of Christ; for Christian Union among his people, and carries a program of service backed by more than thirty of the leading denominations of the world, and a score of the world's best and greatest Christian statesmen. What is the trouble with us? Is the Christian Church too conservative to put on a program big enough to save the young people of the Church?

It seems to me (and I am not knocking) that the trouble lies in the fact that no one has ever undertaken the work. Every great work must have a leader. As I see it, we need two things. One is a secretary who will give three hundred and sixty-five days in the year to this work, and line up the different Conventions in our Church for the work; and second, each of these Conventions should have a secretary who would line up the work with the State and field secretaries and the big program they carry, and help our people get some first-hand information on what Christian Endeavor really means to the Church. I am not referring to the ignorance of any one in that last sentence, but the fact that there are nine letters on my desk from young people saying they have tried to organize Societies and could not on account of opposition on the part of their pastor and church leaders, led me to write it that way. What is to be the remedy? I pray that some-how, God will lay this matter on the hearts of the leaders of our Church everywhere, and that within the next year, our Societies will double in number.

J. VINCENT KNIGHT.

TILLOTSON

Martha H. Tillotson, daughter of William and Nancy Clark, Granville county, N. C., was born May 10, 1843, and died at her home near Buffalo Junction, Va., September 14, 1919, aged seventy-six years, four months, and four days. Early in life she professed faith in Christ and united with Hibran Christian church. In 1866 she was married to William Rufus Tillotson, who preceded her to the Spirit land four years ago. There are six children: Mrs. Hurley Person, Oxford, N. C.; Mrs. James Puryear, Virgilina, Va., and Mrs. R. C. Overby, Mecklenburg County, Va. The sons are Lee and Hammet Tillotson of Buffalo Junction, Va., and Ollie Tillotson, who has served in the U. C. army for twenty-seven years. He has recently returned from oversea service and is now stationed in New York City. There are forty grandchildren and one great grandchild living.

The funeral was conducted from the Tillotson home by the writer on the afternoon of September 16, in the presence of a crowd of relatives and friends, and the burial was in the family cemetery.

A faithful mother in Israel has gone to her reward. She wrought well in her day. Many will rise up in the judgment and call her blessed.

C. E. NEWMAN.

TATUM

Mrs. Irene E. Tatum, daughter of Mr. and Mrs. John Paine, was born May 5, 1887 and died August 17, 1919, aged thirty-two years, three months and twelve days. In 1913 Sister Tatum professed faith in Christ and united with Centerville Christian church, where her membership remained until her death. On February 22, 1905 she married Mr. W. A. Tatum of Sussex County, Va., The husband, four sons, and one daughter survive her; also two sisters, four brothers and a mother.

Sister Tatum was an excellent Christian, a faithful wife and mother. She loved her Church and all its enterprises. She bore her sufferings with a submissive and resigned spirit. All that medical skill could do was done for her recovery, but the summons came and she entered the rest of the faithful. May the memory of her amiable Christian disposition like a guardian angel hover around her dear

husband, and children and as they think of her in their hearts they may say: "Wife and mother, you left us here, your loss we deeply feel, but 'tis God that hath bereft us. He can all our sorrows heal."

The funeral was conducted by Rev. W. W. Edward at the family burying ground. May God comfort the grief-stricken hearts.

MRS. G. W. BAIN.

MOFFITT

John Thomas Moffitt, the eldest son of the late E. A. and M. A. Moffitt, died September 17, 1919 at the age of fifty-two years. Although he was an intense sufferer for about twelve months he was never known to murmur or complain, but was patient and submissive to the Lord's will, and he died trusting in his Savior.

He leaves to mourn their loss a widow, two sons, Herndon Moffitt of High Point, N. C.; John T. Moffitt of Petersburg, Va., and one daughter, Miss Mary Moffitt of Ashboro; two brothers, Dr. E. L. Moffitt of Ashboro, and Herbert Moffitt of Winston-Salem, N. C.; and three sisters. Mrs. E. H. Morris of Ashboro; Mrs. J. Rankin Parks of Greensboro and Mrs. C. C. Howell of Jacksonville, Fla., and his mother, who lives in Greensboro.

The funeral was conducted from the Ashboro Presbyterian church, by the writer. The music by a selected choir was sweet, and the floral offering was beautiful.

May the Lord bless and comfort the bereaved family.

G. R. UNDERWOOD.

RESOLUTIONS OF RESPECT—COX

Resolutions of Executive Committee of Board of Trustees of Elon College adopted at a meeting September 24, 1919, are as follows:

Whereas, death has claimed our dear brother and faithful co-worker, Rev. L. I. Cox, Treasurer of Elon College, and whereas, his life was an inspiration because of its faith, its Vision and its untiring energy for those things that build wisely the cause of Christian Education and of our beloved Christian Church.

Be it Resolved, that we mourn his death and miss his counsels; that we express to the family of the deceased our sympathy and sorrow at his passing; that a copy of these resolutions be sent to the family, a copy to The Christian Sun, and a copy to be spread upon our minutes.

D. R. FONVILLE,
For the Committee.

CHARLES W. McPHERSON, M. D.

Eye, Ear, Nose, Throat

OFFICE OVER CITY DRUG STORE

Office Hours: 9:00 a. m. to 1:00 p. m.

and 2:00 to 5:00 p. m.

Phones: Residence 153; Office 65J

BURLINGTON, NORTH CAROLINA

DR. J. H. BROOKS

DENTIST

Foster Building   Burlington, N. C.

INDIVIDUAL COMMUNION SERVICE

THE BEST WAY to serve Communion. It is reverent, sanitary, and increases attendance at the Lord's Supper Our services are chaste and beautiful. Made of finest materials and best workmanship.

Send for illustrated price list

C. B. RIDDLE, Publishing Agent,
Burlington, North Carolina.

PELOUBET'S SELECT NOTES

Send your order for Peloubet's Select Notes on the Sunday school lesson along with your renewal to THE CHRISTIAN SUN. The books will be ready for delivery December 1. You need not send the money now, unless you want to. Just indicate for us to send you a copy December 1 and that will be all right. The price is $1.60, postpaid.

Write for prices and samples of church offering envelopes.

Don't put off the matter of purchasing your church envelopes too late. Remember that they must be printed after the order is received.

SMILES

Tommy (at Red Cross concert): What's that man got his eyes shut for while he's singing?

Friend: Because he can't bear to see us suffer.—*London Opinion.*

Advertisements are meant to "pull." During the war an office manager in desperation tried to get pulling power into his desire for a messenger. The advertisement he printed read: "Boy wanted—young or old—either sex."—*Nation's Business.*

On a recent church bulletin the pastor's theme for the following Sunday, "What Is the Worst Thing in the World?" was announced in large type, and following, in much the same type, "Singing by our Quartet Morning and Evening."—*The Vermont Advance.*

A Frenchman, learning English, said to his tutor:

"English is a queer language. What does this sentence mean: 'Should Mr. Noble, who sits for this constituency, consent to stand again and run, he will in all probability have a walkover'?"—*Selected.*

Motorist (blocked by load of hay): I say, there, pull out and let me by. You seemed in a hurry to let that other fellow's carriage get past.

Farmer: That's 'cause his horse wuz eatin' my hay.—*Brooklyn Eagle.*

Purchaser (who is selecting a wedding gift): Yes, I rather like that. What is the title?

Picture Dealer: "The Coming Storm"—would make a splendid wedding present.—*Blighty, London.*

Do you know.

that saving three nickels a day with interest will come to $1,500 in about fifteen years.

HOLMAN BIBLES

The Best Editions of the World's Best Book.
Durable Flexible Bindings. Will Not Break in the Back.

FOR CHILDREN PICTORIAL BIBLES WITH HELPS

The text is self-pronouncing, by the aid of which children can learn to pronounce the difficult Scripture proper names.

Specimen of Type.

AND the third day there was a marriage in Cana of Galilee; and the mother of Jesus was

With beautiful photo views of scenes in Bible lands distributed throughout the text. Also maps of Bible lands in colors. Also new Practical Helps to Bible Study, especially designed for instructing children in scriptural information.

No. 51. French Seal Leather, overlapping covers, round corners, gold edges, gold titles. Publisher's Price, $3.20.
Our Price—Postpaid **$1.85**

For Adults, Teachers and Preachers

and all who would study the Word of God intelligently this edition is unsurpassed. The type is large, clear Bourgeois, Self-Pronouncing, with liberal space between the words and lines, which makes it easy to read.

Size 8 x 5½ Inches

Specimen of Type.

¶ "From that time Je'-| to preach, and to say," F the kingdom of heaven

Containing New Copyrighted Helps by the most reliable Authorities, a Treasury of Biblical Information, Practical Comparative Concordance, Oriental Light on the Bible, Four Thousand Questions and Answers, New Colored Maps.

No. 47. Divinity Circuit Teachers' Bible, French Seal Leather, red under gold edges, Silk Head bands and Silk Marker. Publisher's Price, $4.00. Our Price—Post Paid **$3.75**

No. 81. RL Red Letter Teachers' Bible. The Words of Christ in the New Testament, Old Testament Passages Alluded to by Christ, Various Prophecies Relating to Christ in the Old Testament, etc., all PRINTED IN RED, Binding same as described above and same large Self-Pronouncing type. Publisher's Price, $5.10. Our Price—Post Paid **$4.25**

No. 73X. Holman India Paper, Genuine Morocco, Leather Lined, Silk Sewed, Divinity Circuit, round corners, carmine under gold edges, silk head bands and silk marker, same type and Helps as above. Publisher's Price $9.00.
Our Price—Post Paid **$6.50**

For Intermediate S. S. Scholars

Large Clear Black Type, Self-Pronouncing, containing Helps to Bible Study, 4000 Questions and Answers, Maps in Colors, and Presentation Page. A Beautiful Gift Bible.

Specimen of Type.

28 And the prophet Ěl'ī-ä, and said unto thyself, and mark, and for at the return of t

Size 7 x 5 inches.
No. 21. Divinity Circuit Style, Bound in French Seal Leather, round corners, red under gold edges, silk head bands and purple silk marker, gold titles, etc. Publisher's Price, $2.80. Our Price—Post Paid **$2.35**

For OLD FOLKS and The HOME

Specimen of Type. Holman Home Bible

AND it came to pass, that when Isaac was old, and his eyes were dim, so that

The exact size of Bible when closed is 6⅛ x 9 inches

Flexible Binding

Printed from large Clear Pica Type, with Marginal References, Family Record and Maps. This HOME BIBLE is new and very desirable for every day use, containing all the advantages of a Family Bible in a compact size that can be easily handled; with Record for Births, Marriages and Deaths. The best Bible obtainable for old folks who need extra large clear print and a light-weight book.

No. 2014. Durably Bound in French Seal Leather, full flexible covers, round corners, red under gold edges, gold titles Publisher's Price, $5.00. Our Price—Post Paid **$4.15**

WE HAVE THE ABOVE BIBLES IN STOCK AND CAN SHIP PROMPTLY. SEND YOUR ORDER NOW. HOLMAN BIBLES SATISFY.

THE CHRISTIAN SUN

"IN ESSENTIALS UNITY, IN NON-ESSENTIALS LIBERTY, IN ALL THINGS CHARITY"

A New Song

Christian Guardian

THE Psalmist tells us that the Lord had put a new song into his mouth, even praise unto our God. Probably that would be a new song to many of us too. We are interested in patriotic songs, in sentimental songs, some of us even have a fancy of comic songs, but that song of praise unto our God is not quite as popular as it might be. Suppose we cultivate it a little; or perhaps some of us would have the Lord do for us, what He did for the Psalmist, teach us the song from the beginning. There are many reasons why we should sing it. He has been very good to us in very many ways and life has had very many blessings that must have come from His gracious and loving hands. Yes, even though we may not make much of a hand of it at first, we ought to try to sing that song a great deal more than we do. And trying to sing it there is no doubt that He will help us until it will grow into a hymn of joy and praise that will fill our own souls with rapture past anything we have ever known.

Volume LXXI	WEDNESDAY, OCTOBER 8, 1919	Number 41
BURLINGTON	· · ·	NORTH CAROLINA

THE CHRISTIAN SUN

Founded 1844 by Rev. Daniel W. Kerr

C. B. RIDDLE   -   -   -   Editor

Entered at the Burlington, N. C. Post Office as second class matter.

Subscription Rates

One year ....$ 2.00
Six months 1.00

In Advance

Give both your old and new postoffice when asking that your address be changed.

The change of your label is your receipt for money. Written receipts sent upon request.

Many persons subscribe for friends, intending that the paper be stopped at the end of the year. If instructions are given to this effect, they will receive attention at the proper time.

Marriage and obituary notices not exceeding 150 words printed free if received within 60 days from date of event, all over this at the rate of one-half cent a word.

Original poetry not accepted for publication.

Principles of the Christian Church

(1) The Lord Jesus Christ is the only Head of the Church.
(2) Christian is a sufficient name of the Church.
(3) The Holy Bible is a sufficient rule of faith and practice.
(4) Christian character is a sufficient test of fellowship, and of church membership.
(5) The right of private judgment and the liberty of conscience is a right and a privilege that should be accorded to, and exercised by all.

EDITORIAL

OVERLOOKED

There is no end to the social service organizations these days, and to all we send best wishes and congratulations. They are doing a long needed and neglected work. Possibly the late war had much to do with bringing this situation to pass; arousing the public conscience. So far as we can, these organizations will have our support so long as they undertake to make society a better place in which to live. Our only criticism is this: Some of these organizations are hurling stones against the Church and saying that it has been asleep and should have undertaken such a work years ago. We will not enter into the reasons for or against, but stop to remind those who bring such an accusation that had it not been for the Church the way would have never been opened up to such a work as social welfare. Social welfare work is just a big part of the program of the Church, and for centuries the Church has been educating the public conscience to do what it is now trying to do. These social organizations outside of the Church are just co-operating with the Churches. To the Church they are due their thanks for making such a work possible. They have overlooked this; here is a reminder of it.

PASTORLESS CHURCHES

We have in our possession a list of twenty churches, so far as we know, without a pastor for the coming Conference year. It may be possible that such a shifting can be made so that these churches can be supplied. However, we know that some of them have been making efforts to secure a pastor and has so far failed. The question is vital and concerns the whole Church. As it looks to us, some of the Conferences have some big problems on their hands this fall, and one of the problems is to see that all churches get some kind of service for another year.

ONE ON THE LEADERS

That is just an everyday way of expressing it, but for years some of our leaders have been saying that if, the people would do so and so that such and such could be done. The problem has been this: That the leaders in church activity have not made the task big enough. A real man wants a man's job. The average fellow is not willing to undertake a child's play, and so our work has been too often held back for the lack of plans large enough to challenge the best in our people. Is this not/true? The leaders are learning all right—and learning that they had not discovered all.

OVERBALANCED

There is great danger in a time like this when *organization* seems to be foremost and *expansion* the goal that men may lose their religious equilibrium and become overbalanced, thus failing to enjoy some of the finer things in life. The present methods of living make a great drain upon one's time for devotion and meditation, and yet we should do more of it now than ever before. There is a danger zone which so many of us reach. We should be careful and see that our devotional life is well cared for and not overbalanced by the business or commercial activities.

A CHANCE TO HELP

Brother Johnston in his report for the Orphanage this week opens up to us an opportunity to be of real help to that institution just now. Note that he is very much in need of clothing for the boys and girls. It would be great indeed if Sunday schools, Christian Endeavor Societies, churches, and individuals would come to the rescue of our Orphanage Superintendent just now and help him meet the situation. This is not the best part of it. It would help those who help. If you want some real joy to come to you, do something for some one else.

DELEGATES TO CONFERENCE

There is a custom in many churches to elect the delegates to Conference the Sunday before the Conference meets. We trust that no church will be that slow this year. Elect your delegates as far in advance as possible. Remember that people have plans, and often short notice is not sufficient to change some plans. It is, too, business to look after a matter so important well ahead of time. After you elect your delegates see that they attend. Once more. Insist that they stay until Conference adjourns.

As Seen by Fellow Editors

SELF- DETERMINATION OF COLLEGES

(The. Presbyterian)

The mandamus action of the Norristown, Pa., court asking the re-instatement of a student at Bryn Mawr College, is attracting attention. Miss Taft, acting president of this college, is away, and for this reason the trial has been postponed. In the meantime, opinion is being freely expressed. There seems to be a general consent to the conclusion that, generally speaking, the question of admission and demission should be left to the faculty, acting on common principles and rules, without arbitrariness and without partiality. It will also be conceded that faculties . are human, and there may be some disposition to regard theirs as the "infallible profession," yet they must submit to law and right as well as all others. If a faculty or majority thereof, or an officer thereof, passes unjust judgment, or does injury to the rights of a student, there should be the means of appeal from such judgment as much as there is an appeal from the judgment of a lower court to a superior court or supreme court. Arbitrariness and the profession of infallibility anywhere is undemocratic, and must lead to demagogy and injustice. There are records of marked discriminations and some injustice upon the part of faculties or their agents, and these should no more be tolerated or sustained than would like actions be approved in any other connection. We pass no judgment upon the particular case, but only upon the general principles involved.

AN ANGLICAN NOTE

(Northwestern Christian Advocate)

One hundred and thirty Anglicans of high standing in England, including two bishops-designate and nine deans, have signed a memorandum to the archbishops and bishops on "the sin and folly of the present disunion among Christian people," and urging unity. The signatories state:

"While we are convinced that espiscopacy is demanded both by history and by needs of ultimate unity, we recognize that the main communions of non-espiscopal Christians are true parts of the one church of Jesus Christ and their ministry, in and for their own communions, is a true ministry of the Word and sacraments. We believe, therefore, that the issues which divide us are questions rather of order than of grace; in other words, that the ministry and sacraments of non-episcopal churches are not inoperative as means of grace, but irregular from the point of view of historic Catholic order."

The foregoing statement gives clearly the seemingly insurmountable difficulty in the way of union. But there is a strong party of Anglicans, the prevailing party, who insist that the question of order is primary. Not until the Anglican Church of England and the Protestant Episcopal leaders on this side of the water recognize the order of the humblest Wesleyan or Methodist minister, will any discussion of the subject of church union bring forth fruit.

LEAVING THE PULPIT TO ENTER THE MINISTRY

(United Presbyterian)

"A prominent clergyman of New York recently surprised his congregation by notifying it that he was "leaving the pulpit in order to enter the ministry." He was going into humanitarian work. We were startled at the announcement until we discovered that he was a Unitarian. He had no gospel to preach. He who has not a gospel that can meet the problems that men are thinking about and give power to overcome sin and rise into a higher life, should to some other line of service. The gospel that saves is more than one that presents merely an ideal to be attained. It must carry with it the power to reach the ideal proclaimed. He who has such a gospel has not to leave the pulpit in order to enter the ministry.

METHODIST UNION IN GREAT BRITAIN

(New York Christian Advocate)

While Methodist union or unification—whatever the difference may be—halts upon its thigh in America it seems thus far to have run well in Great Britain. The Primitive Methodist Conference, the first of the three major bodies to receive the report of the joint committee on union, has adopted the resolutions with unanimity and enthusiasm. Should the conferences of the Wesleyans and United Methodists concur as heartily, the measure will proceed to the constitution making stage. We have been too close to similar proceedings in America to be absolutely sanguine of success until the pact is signed, but those who prophesy in such matters are foretelling that when the next (fifth) Ecumenical Conference convenes in England, in October, 1921, the divided Methodism of America will find but one solidly united body of Methodists in England.

WAGES AND WITS

(Collier's Weekly)

The curious part of it all is that in most discussions of wages, what the man does for a wage is seldom considered, while page after page of testimony is taken as to how much it costs to live, although it must be self evident that as long as we work under a wage system, if production be not returned for wages, then a living wage can never exist. Inevitably a wage paid which is not wholly earned must be added into the price of fin ished product and eventually raise the price of all products, so that when the wage earner goes to buy he is bound to find his money insufficient.

NEW PARTY

(Herald and Presbyter)

The liquor element is announcing that it will start a political party to devoted to the task of getting the saloon back into its old place. What a rare collection of worthless and abject material might be gathered together for this detestable purpose! Having tried to degrade each of the existing political parties to their use for these many years, and now, being offcast and outcast, the old longing for power through politics still clings to the vicious crowd. No political party thus formed could thrive or even live. Vice can conspire.

PASTOR AND PEOPLE

YOUNGSVILLE

I suppose the work of the Youngsville Christian church this year is progressing "about as well as can be expected under the circumstances." Our membership there is small. Practically everybody in Youngsville belongs to some church with the exception of a few middle-aged and old people of the case-hardened kind. Our Sunday school there is small, also—having an enrollment of twenty-two. This Sunday school voted, the fourth Sunday in September, to give one Sunday's offering in each month to Sunday school missions. It has, for sometime, been sending one Sunday's contribution in each month to the Orphanage.

Our series of meetings at Youngsville began, this year, the fourth Sunday in August and closed on the fifth. Rev. George D. Eastes of Raleigh, N. C., did the preaching for us, with the exception of a mighty good sermon that Dr. C. H. Rowland preached to us on Wednesday night. Brother Eastes delivered thirteen as able and as timely sermons as we have ever heard. Prof. C. O. Lehmann of Berne, Indiana, conducted the singing for us. This energetic young man has rare ability as a soloist; and is an exceptionally good choir leader. He got the Youngsville people to singing as we have not heard them sing before. Yet, with all of Brother Eastes' good preaching and all the good singing, as was the case in my other meetings, our meeting at Youngsville closed just as a real interest in salvation was beginning to be in evidence.

As has been mentioned in a previous letter, the Youngsville brethren have called me to serve them as their pastor for another year.

R. P. CRUMPLER.

THE BIG BRANCH MEETING

This meeting began the third Sunday in September and continued until the fourth Sunday evening. We were invited by the Methodists, Baptists and Presbyterians to conduct this series of meetings. The congregations were large throughout the meeting. Quite a number professed faith in Christ and more than a hundred said that they had been greatly benefitted by the meeting, and promised to live more useful lives. It was considered by all as being a good meeting, and to God be all the praise, honor and glory. During the meeting we had at our services two Baptist brethren, Revs. Baxley and Walker.

The meeting was held in a large academy in Harnett County, near the line. The interest of the meeting was such that ungodly men ask if it could be continued another week, but I had to leave.

P. T. KLAPP.

HOLY NECK

Sunday, September 21, was a great day at Holy Neck. The pastor preached on the subject of Christian Stewardship and at the close of the service asked all who desired to take the Lord into full partnership and return to the Lord his Biblical share, to come to the front and give their hand in token of their pledge to do this. As a result six deacons, three deacons' wives and two others came forward and took the pledge.

After the service two young ladies added their names to the list, the one having been a tither for some time.

This service was as impressive to the pastor as extending the right hand of fellowship, receiving so many into the church.

The last Quarterly Conference had adopted the budget system for the coming year. This was explained in detail to the whole church and on Monday, September 29, the canvass to raise the funds began, although some work had been done at odd times the week previous.

The church area is divided into four districts and one or two influential laymen in each district were selected to go with the pastor to make the canvass. While this meant from one to two days work for each man it meant five solid days riding for the pastor but it paid wonderfully. It gave the pastor an opportunity to visit more homes and talk personally to more of his members about the work of the church and their Christian duty in supporting it than he could have done otherwise in many months.

It was hard work but it was a pleasure. We found the folks usually busy with their cotton and peanut crops but we were everywhere cordially received and given hearty response. Hearts that heretofore were almost closed to the spirit of giving to the Lord's work opened wide and gave liberally. Many are deserving of personal mention but that would not be wise here. A few will share this word of praise and appreciation who deserve it not, but that number is few when you think of a membership of 500 to be reckoned with.

We can now say, with a few distantly located members yet to be heard from, the budget is assured and provision is thereby made for every worthy cause the church has in the past supported with a liberal amount provided to take care of unexpected calls and expenses. This is understood to eliminate all public appeals for money at church services except emergency cases, which are becoming a bore to many of our churches.

I am fully persuaded that our people are willing and ready to liberally support all our church enterprises when approached in the right manner. This has been amply demonstrated by the recent campaigns of Drs. Harper and Atkinson and other campaigns now in progress.

I am also of the opinion that constant and frequent appeals for funds in small amounts and for divers causes, have a tendency to chill and check the giving spirit of the average church member, and the results obtained in this way are far less than when you present the task of supporting the church in a business way as one of the greatest obligations and responsibilities resting upon the people of God.

W. M. JAY.

Holland, Va.

PAGE VALLEY, VIRGINIA

Our annual conference closed the third Sunday in August. It was the general sentiment that this session was the "best yet." Since this time the pen of this scribe has been idle but his tongue not silent, as we have held a revival campaign in three of the churches of this pastorate.

The first meeting was at Mt. Lebanon and lasted a week, resulting in one member being received into fellowship. I feel like there is a brilliant future for this church. We have just completed a nice new church in the same spot where the old one stood. Thirty-six members have been received at this place since we have been pastor.

The next campaign for members was at East Liberty church. This revival lasted a week and resulted in the addition of three members.

Last week we conducted a revival at St. Peters church and as a result two members were added. .

In the other three churches of the pastorate the work is going along nicely. No special features have taken place.

B. J. EARP.

ARE CHURCHES DISHONEST?

I pass this sentence on to SUN readers for what it may be worth from a page in Dr. Cortland Myers "Money Mad." If churches are dishonest, maybe that accounts for the fact that so few young men are entering the ministry. At any rate read what Dr. Myers has to say: "A great many churches are dishonest while they think they are honest. They are dishonest with the minister sometimes and dishonest churches are cursing this land by keeping the minister on starvation wages and some of them do not even pay the small salary they pretend to pay. A church ought to give the minister a large salary, the larger the better. If any man in this world ought to have money to give away it is the minister of Christ. I tell you a church can pay a large salary a good deal easier than it can pay a small one. That never fails in church or business. Let a church try to be miserly and mean with all its methods and that church goes rapidly down and God marks it the same as He would mark a business man who is dishonest. I am writing for the young men and women growing up in the church. Just as sure as you are dishonest, your young men will not go into the ministry and your churches are going to fail. The real crisis in the churches is that which they have brought upon themselves because they have been niggardly with the ministers and in reality dishonest.

"I can hardly believe this is true that the average minister's salary in America now, with the high cost of living, with his good clothes that he must have, with his family, with his books, the average salary is only $600.00 a year. And yet we expect young men to go into the ministry. Every hod carrier, mason, ditch digger and everybody else gets more than that. I am speaking of something which is of tremendous importance, for this great principle of real honesty goes to the bottom of human life and human society and the church of Jesus Christ is in it and ought to be the real example and not try to get the best of everybody and not pay its minister what he is worth."

Dr. Myers makes a hard claim against the church. Is he right?

. J. O. ATKINSON.

SUFFOLK LETTER

Judge Richard Henry Rawles died in Suffolk on September 26, 1919, after a lingering illness of several months. He was the son of Henry A. and Annie Eley Rawles of Holy Neck, Nansemond County, Virginia, and was born September 15, 1850. He united with the Suffolk Christian church on March 5, 1875, the year he began the practice of law. On January 7, 1880, he was married to Miss Mary Woodward who survives him.

From 1879 to 1883 he represented this district in the Virginia Senate; and from 1883 to 1887 he was Judge of the Nansemond County Court. From 1887 to 1919 he practiced his profession of law in Suffolk and, at his death, was the senior attorney of the city and, one might say, the dean of the bar in Suffolk. He was President of the Suffolk and Nansemond County Bar Association, and held in high esteem by the profession.

Judge Rawles was local counsel for the Atlantic Coast Line and Norfolk and Western Railways, and was connected with some of the most important cases in this part of Virginia. He was the best trial lawyer in this city of seventeen men of the legal profession.

His professional life was conspicuous in the range of his attention to clients. He would give the most painstaking attention to the humblest client's small case as to the most important case where much value was involved, often rendering gratuitous service to the poor and ignorant, because it was an opportunity for helping others. In any public service he was willing to do his part without regard to remuneration. He was so thoroughly courteous to his brothers of the same profession as to win their confidence and good will. He was not jealous of young members of the Bar, but helpful to them to the extent of opportunity.

With a fine practice for more than forty years he did not leave a fortune, but was content with a competency for his own life and his companion after him. He was, in a sense, as he has told me, a protege of Rev. Dr. W. B. Wellons, who took special interest in his education and his entrance upon the practice of law. The memory of that interest which Dr. Wellons took in him as a young man was never forgotten or undervalued. So often have I met with men who had received and appreciated the kindness of others as a great factor in successful careers.

His domestic life was as thoroughly happy as his professional life was successful. His office for work; his home for rest; and he was devoted to both. His mother died when he was a little child, he had no children, and hence his wife had a double portion of his love. His affection for other members of his family was constant and sincere; one brother, J. T. Rawles of Holland, survives him.

The funeral on Sunday afternoon was simple and held at the grace. A mountain of flowers made the grave a garden of beauty and sweetness. Four nephews of his own and four of his wife bore that sacred casket to its resting place in Cedar Hill, while sixteen lawyers attended as honorary pall-bearers. His pastor was assisted by Rev. J. F. Coleman, the Episcopal Rector, who read Tennyson's "Crossing the Bar," and the Odd Fellows, also, held service at the grave.

W. W. STALEY.

INHERITED MONEY

Many of us poor, short-sighted mortals toil our days out seeking by every rigid economy to accumulate money to leave our children so they will not have to work as hard, and fast as badly as we have. On this point Dr. Cortland Myers in his 'Money Mad'' has some very pointed words to this effect, ''Remember God expects you to teach your children how to make a good living and to set them a good example but not to save money by rigid economy just to have them live in luxury and then go to ruin. Inherited money has damned more people than we can ever imagine; that is not Christinity. People are hoarding their money so as to have their children fight over it and distant relatives go to the courts after it.'' Many a man has missed the real joy of living and ruined his children under the vain delusion of trying to provide that his children shall not have to work as hard as he did—as if work were a crime and a disgrace   J. O. ATKINSON.

NOTICE

All persons who expect to attend the Eastern Virginia Christian Conference which convenes at Waverly, Virginia, on October 28, 1919, will please notify the undersigned at their earliest convenience, stating what day they expect to arrive in Waverly and whether they will come by train or private conveyance.

R. T. WEST, Secretary.

Waverly, Virginia.

A FORGED LETTER ASCRIBED TO CHRIST

(Methodist Protestant Herald)

Three persons at considerable intervals within the last fifteen years have each sent us a copy of a letter purporting to have been written by Jesus Christ, and requested us to publish it in the Herald. The last request came a few days ago.

With all respect to the person making the request, we must again decline to publish the letter. It is a fraud on the face of it, and we would feel that we were dishonoring Christ to publish this letter and ascribe it to Him.

It is said to have been written by Jesus ''just after his crucifixion,'' and signed by the angel Gabriel 99 years later and deposited under the stone at the foot of the cross.

What a collection of absurdities!

The letter contains threats against those who refuse to publish it, and promises ''good luck'' to those who keep a copy of it in their houses. We presume this explains why so many people go through the labor of copying all its eight pages. But it can appeal only to the superstitious.

It is true it encourages Sabbath observance and industry and plain living, but it contains much that in letter and spirit is very unlike the teachings of the Jesus of the Gospels.

The next time you run across the letter in your secular paper, pay as little attention to it as possible.

(We say Amen! to the above. We have had this same thing to contend with. When you see or hear of a copy, pay no attention to its statements.—*Editor*)...

BIBLE POINTS

Be kindly affectioned one to another with brotherly love.—*Romans* 12:10.

• •

Therefore thou are inexcusable, O man, whosoever thou are that judgest: for wherein thou judgest another, thou condemnest thyself; for thou that judgest doest the same things.—*Romans* 2:1.

Let us not therefore judge one another any more; but judge this rather, that no man put a stumbling block, or an occasion to fall, in his brother's way.—*Romans* 14:13.

• •

Charity envieth not, ...thinketh no evil.— I *Cor.* 13:4, 5.

• •

He that despiseth his neighbor, sinneth.—*Proverbs* 14:21.

NEWS OF INTEREST

Norway is considering the matter of national prohibition.

The candy makers of the country, it is said, have an abundance of sugar on hand.

The Turkish cabinet has resigned, and the resignation of each member accepted.

A mob lynched on October 6 two negroes near Lincolnton, Georgia.

A strike of great importance occurred in Gary, Ind., on October 4. Much fighting was done and hundreds were injured.

Continued discussion about the Peace Treaty and the League of Nations goes on in Congress, but little action seems to be in sight.

There is this week in session in Washington, D. C., a conference between representatives of capital and labor. An effort is being made to come to some agreement as to the work of each.

That which is of much concern to the country just now is the illness of President Wilson. His condition is reported to be more favorable. His physician says that a complete rest must be taken.

An item of interest is that of a trial ending this week in Christianburg, Va., in which a college hazing case was the point at stake. John Fox, a Freshman at the Virginia Polytechnic Institute last spring was hazed and it resulted into an assault. Benjamin Seigel, the leader in the hazing, was sentenced to serve one year in the penitentiary. Robert W. Ware was sentenced to six months in jail, George W. Botts, Jr., drew a sentence of 30 days in jail, and Albert G. Copeland was fined $50.00.

NOTES

Rev. B. J. Earp has organized another Teacher-Training. Class in his field.

Rev. H. S. Hardcastle changes his address to Box 1183, Yale Station, New Haven, Conn.

We understand that the revival meeting will begin in the Sanford church next Sunday, October 12.

Dr. J. P. Barrett has taken up the work at Columbus, Georgia, having started October 1. His address is 2605 Jones Street.

Miss Hazell McFarland, Greensboro, N. C., has given aid in increasing THE SUN list by personal work. Many thanks.

We are indebted to Mrs. M. S. Coles, Portsmouth, Va., for securing a list of new subscribers for THE SUN. Sister Coles is a faithful friend to THE SUN.

Rev. J. S. Carden, 906 Shepherd Street, Durham, N. C., is open for work on the fourth Sunday for the coming year.

We are pleased with the results, so far, from the "Business and Relief Number" of THE SUN. It is proving to be one of the best means that we ever used to strengthen the co-operation of THE SUN's friends.

Dr. W. W. Staley's "Suffolk Letter" this week will bring regret to many readers of THE SUN. The passing of Judge Rawles is a distinct loss to the Church and the nation. In his death this office loses a friend.

How long have you been taking THE CHRISTIAN SUN? In our extra edition we asked for the names of those who have been taking it for twenty-five years or more. Many have responded. Let us hear from you.

Miss Bessie Holt, Burlington, N. C., has accepted work as an assistant to Dr. Atkinson in raising the mission budget of $500,000.00 and has entered upon her work. Miss Holt is deeply interested in the mission work and will give valuable assistance to Dr. Atkinson.

Readers of THE SUN will note that Rev. J. V. Knight contributes the Christian Endeavor topic this week. Brother Knight will have this in charge from now on, and we feel that the people will be pleased with his comments.

Dr. Martyn Summerbell is giving his annual lectures at Elon College this week. His subjects are: The Victory of Democracy; The Sacrifices of Love; The Dark Ages; The Middle Age and Feudalism; The Rise and Influence of Chivalry; Peter Preaching the Crusade; The First Crusade; Godfrey and the Kingdom of Jerusalem.

On October 3 the business men of Burlington gave a dinner in honor Dr. P. H. Fleming, Superintendent of Public Welfare of Alamance County. The chief speaker was Mr. R. F. Beasley, Commissioner of Public Welfare in North Carolina. Short addresses were made by Mr. W. E. Sharpe, C. P. Albright, J. L. Scott, Dr. W. A. Harper, Rev. J, E. Pritchard and Dr. P. H. Fleming. Mr. D. R. Fonville was toastmaster.

A recent issue of THE SUN carried an article furnished us by the United States Government on the subject of home training for the children. "Consistency" is the article referred to. Brother W. G. Clements says that the article is one of the best things that he has seen in a long time. And so interested is Brother Clements in spreading the truths in this article that he has had 500 copies printed on card board and arranged for hanging in the home, the church, or Sunday school class room. We have them on hand and can be had for the asking. State number of copies wanted.

WILL THE EPIDEMIC RETURN?

Will the epidemic of influenza return this fall? is the question before many just now. We note that the State Boards of Health in different states say that it is probable and that proper prevention should be exercised. It seems to us that the issue is one that should have attention in a marked degree. Churches greatly suffered last year, and show ear marks of the epidemic yet. Such a scourge cost us too much in dollars and lives not to be deeply and vitally interested in every possible measure to ward off such a disaster to public good. We speak in behalf of all organizations and effort to fight the disease and trust our readers will so approve and act when opportunity is afforded.

NEW COMERS TO THE SUN FAMILY

Miss Edna Moffitt ....Greensboro, N. C.
J. E. Murray ....Greensboro, N. C.
Mrs. E. R. Cox..........................Greensboro, N. C.
J. B. Parks ....Greensboro, N. C.
J. R. Michael ....Greensboro, N. C.
J. H. Fogleman ....Greensboro, N. C.
R. S. Petty ....Greensboro, N. C.
Mrs. Martha Thompson ....Greensboro, N. C.
E. C. York ....Greensboro, N. C.
E. E. Hanner ....Greensboro, N. C.
Mrs. W. G. Neblett ....Boykin, Va.
O. G. Morris ....Phoenix, Ala.
N. E. Parratt ....Girard, Ala.
Harry Barber ....Girard, Ala.
F. L. Baukston ....Girard, Ala.
Mrs. M. A. Atkinson ....Elon College, N. C
Mrs. C. J. Heath ....Portsmouth, Va.
Miss Ruth Curling ....Portsmouth, Va.
James Powell ....Portsmouth, Va.
Mrs. C. W. McFarland ....Greensboro, N. C.
C. N. Herndon ....Greensboro, N. C.
G. S. Huber ....Dendron, Va.
Fred L. Oates ....High View, W. Va.
Miss Beatrice Foushee ....Burlington, N. C.
Miss Effie Hall ....Graham, N. C.
Mrs. Archie Long ....Haw River, N. C.
(Report to October 4, 1919)

MISSIONARY

MISSION BOARD MEETING

In last week's SUN the items relative to the home work, and appropriations therefor, were noted.

The Foreign Board, among other items, adopted the following: One of our volunteers, Miss Annie Floyd, Abanda, Ala., died during the year, and the sorrow of the Board at her untimely taking away, was expressed in resolutions to her mother.

Rev. H. Shelton Smith, now in Yale University, was enrolled as a volunteer for the foreign field. A most interesting letter containing much information and inspiration, was read from Brother Smith. Letters were also read from volunteers, Rev. H. S. Hardcastle, now also in Yale University, and Rev. F. C. Lester, Graham, N. C. These volunteers were assured of the Board's hearty support, and prayerful interest, and the Secretary was instructed to write them of our deep concern in their preparation for the important work of the foreign field.

It was voted that the Boys' Missionary Class of Greensboro, N. C., be commended for their willingness to provide for the education of a young minister in Porto Rico, the Board agreeing to stand by this Class in this worthy effort.

Voted to appropriate $3,500.00 for the purchase of the property adjoining our Ponce church in Porto Rico.

The Board decided to build a missionaries' home in Tokyo, Japan, now so much needed by the Germans. To this enterprise the Board gave $2,500.00 one year ago. It now appropriates $5,000.00 additional to go forward with this long since and very sorely needed enterprise.

A motion prevailed commending most heartily our Burlington Sunday school, the Tidewater Christian Sunday School Association and the Woman's Board of the Eastern Virginia Conference for their undertaking to provide for the support of a missionary each, each of these organizations being asked to send these funds to the Treasurer of the Southern Christian Convention Board who is hereby instructed to make disbursements of same as necessity may arise. We also commend the Young People's Missionary Societies of the Southern Christian Convention for their heroic and splendid work in completing the fund for the Santa Isabel Chapel in Porto Rico; and the Young People of Catawba Springs church, N. C. Conference, in their desire to build a chapel on the foreign field, suggesting that the details of this matter be left with the Mission Secretary. We heartily commend the women of the Virginia Valley Conference in their desire for a special in the foreign field covering a period of five years and to cost one thousand dollars. The item for this "Special" is to be suggested by our Mission Secretary.

C. H. ROWLAND, *Chm.,*
G. O. LANKFORD, *Sec.,*
Foreign Board of Missions, S. C. C.

Withal, it was the most forward looking program our Board has adopted, and there was never so much as now to encourage and inspire the Board to energy, endeavor and activity.

The raising of $500,000.00 for missions within the five year's period from the beginning, (two years ago) ought to be easy and will be if we can have the united sympathy, co-operation, prayers and support of our pastors and people.

J. O. ATKINSON.

WASHINGTON, D. C., RICHMOND, VA.

The Mission Secretary has just concluded a visit of survey and investigation of Washington and Richmond relative to beginning a work on behalf of our Church in both these important points. Twenty-two members were readily located in Washington and about thirty in Richmond. Now, if it were a matter of saving this number only to our work, and the cause we represent, we might well question the economy and propriety of beginning churches here. But that is among the minor considerations.

If our dear Christian Church is worth while, (and it is), and has a real mission in the world, (and it has), then it is equally worth while to stop, as far as possible, the leaks and drains upon its strength and its numbers. Washington and Richmond have both been constant drains upon our numbers, and perpetual leaks to our strength and resources through the past half century, and will continue so, with increasing volume, for the centuries to come, unless we proceed to prevent the drainage and the waste. These two cities, both vital to our work and growth, ought to be helps and assets to our Church; at present they are sources of increasing loss to our work and liabilities to our Church. Our people will continue to go to these points in increasing numbers. And going there, they will either find church homes elsewhere, or, that which is less desirable and more deplorable, drop out of church work altogether and lose interest in their spiritual welfare and church relationship altogether. Some of our members residing in these cities, (and the writer has no idea he located one-half, maybe not a fourth, in either place), do not now care whether we begin a church work. They have found a church home elsewhere and are content. It will be so for fity years to come, unless we act.

Others care little about a work of their own, because they belong back home and wish to be carried back there to be buried, (grave yard Christians, Dr. Archibald Johnson used to tell his Baptist brethren), and can hear good preaching in the great cities at very little cost to themselves.

But in each place there are those who believe with all their heart, soul and strength in the principles, polity and mission of our dear Christian Church; and these will form a nucleus for the planting and development of a great work. Our Board is anxious to act now and stop the leakage and the drain.

J. O. ATKINSON.

THE FORWARD MOVEMENT

Warren H. Denison, Superintendent

The New England Campaign

The New England Educational Campaign preparatory to the financial campaign is being conducted from September 4 to October 16. During this period all the New England churches are visited and the Forward Movement message, plans, and vision are presented by a chosen speaker to the congregation. All the five conferences of New England hold their annual sessions during this time and all the programs are Forward Movement programs and that is the one outstanding theme of all the Conferences. The New England men assisting in the church visitation are: Revs. W. G. Sargent, W. J. Hall, R. G. English, D. P. Hurlburt, P. S. Sailer, E. D. Gilbert, H. M. Hainer, P. W. Caswell, J. W. Reynolds, E. R. Caswell, A. H. Morrill. Those from without New England in the educational and spiritual campaign are: Hermon Eldredge, Dr. E. K. McCord, Dr. F. H. Peters and the Superintendent. During this campaign a few financial canvasses are being made at Franklin, N. H., Lubec, Me., Eastport, Me., Aroostook County, Me., Woodstock, Vt., Haverhill, Mass., Fall River, (Franklin Street), Mass., Pottersville, Mass.

The financial canvass in all the other New England churches will be made in the two weeks, October 29 to November 11. There is a New England Forward Movement Committee and this Committee helps to arrange the itenerary and select speakers. The goal for the New England churches is $100,000.00 as a minimum. It is hoped that they may exceed this. In addition to the presentation of the Forward Movement messages at the Conferences, and by the special speaker sent to each church, the pastors are all speaking and preaching on it from Sunday to Sunday so that the program may be woven into the life of the churches.

At this date, September 30, the canvass has been made in the most Eastern section of Maine, the extreme eastern points of the United States.

Eastport, Me.

This is not a strong church; indeed, for some years it was closed, but some life remained and recently it was opened and they have been holding regular services, repairing, and have received some few members. Rev. Thomas Lambert is the pastor. This church responded to the message and gave $1,610.

Lubec, Me.

has a pastor of another denomination in charge temporarily. Its extreme eastern location has prevented it from being very closely linked with our church activities and yet they responded with $3,175.00, the largest benevolent work in its history.

Aroostook County, Me.

This is the most northeastern county of Maine, a great potato country. We have some four churches there but they need leadership. One of the churches has had no services in over four years, one has but nineteen members on the roll and is is less than a year old, starting with five members. The others are ministered to by farmers who preach some on Sundays. There are large possibilities in this great territory when they can be furnished leadership out of our life recruits. This little group of pastorless churches caught the vision and responded with $2,120. If all our churches would do as well there would be great things happening in our fields.

Franklin, N. H.

The New England financial campaign opened at this church. They built a new church for $45,000.00 and some eleven thousand of it has not been paid for yet. This church gave $6,750.00 for the Movement, surpassing their fondest expectations. At the night at the close of the canvass the pastor had called a meeting of the Executive Committee of the church to look after some business matters but the whole evening was given to prayer and praise for the work of the day. The pastor says that his people were thankful for the result. Rev. W. J. Hall is the splendid pastor. He is a member of the general Forward Movement Committee.

The York and Cumberland Conference at Lowell Center, Me., after the continued presentation of the Forward Movement at its sessions broke out in its closing session in a revival meeting and twelve persons confessed faith in Christ. We are expecting that a gracious revival will result from the Forward Movement spirit in the whole brotherhood. Let us expect and pray to the end that a real revival may come to our whole Church.

Woodstock, Vt.

Rev. W. E. Baker has just sent in fourteen signed Prayer Covenants. This is one of the vital works in the Forward Movement. Have you presented the matter to the members of your church yet, Brother Pastor? Thousands of our people will thus pledge themselves to definite prayer if you will present it to them faithfully.

Our people are ready to do far beyond what our leaders have ever asked them to do in almost any phase of Christian work.

Many of our people are purchasing the book, "Money, the Acid Test." Interesting stories of its effect upon lives are constantly coming to us. We urge every family to get it. Its price is only seventy-five cents, and is for sale by your publishing agent, C. B. Riddle, Burlington, N. C.

WHAT YOUR LABEL MEANS

(Told in the Language of a Child)

1-1-9 means that your subscription expires January 1, 1919.
2-1-9 means that your subscription expires February 1, 1919.
3-1-9 means that your subscription expires March 1, 1919.
4-1-9 means that your subscription expires April 1, 1919.
5-1-9 means that your subscription expires May 1, 1919.
6-1-9 means that your subscription expires June 1, 1919.
7-1-9 means that your subscription expires July 1, 1919.
8-1-9 means that your subscription expires August 1, 1919.
9-1-9 means that your subscription expires September 1, 1919.
10-1-9 means that your subscription expires October 1, 1919.
11-1-9 means that your subscription expires November 1, 1919.
12-1-9 means that your subscription expires December 1, 1919.

IS THERE A REMEDY FOR STRIKES?

(E. Guy Talbot, in the Christian Work)

Everybody is doing it. Doing what? Striking! That is, everybody except the preachers, and even the preachers are being advised to form their unions and demand living wages. The strike method, formerly employed only by industrial employees who are manual workers, is now being used effectively by other classes of workers. For example, teachers' federations, fire fighters, policemen, actors, bank clerks and many other groups of employed people are today organized and are using strike methods to enforce their demands.

The fundamental principle in any labor organization is that of collective bargaining. This principle is recognized by the Federal Government, particularly by the Railroad Administration, and by most of the great industrial corporations. The purposes of a strike are twofold: First, the forcing of employers to recognize the right of collective bargaining, through recognition of the union of employees; second, the securing of higher wages, shorter working time and better working conditions. Then there is the sympathetic strike, which is based on the class consciousness of either all workers or of allied crafts.

Manifestly the strike is an extra-legal means on the part of labor to enforce its demands on capital. Similarly the organizations of capital use extra-legal means of throttling competition and controlling prices. Since labor union strikes and capitalistic profiteering both seriously affect the public at large even more than the groups directly concerned, is it not necessary to substitute some legal means of controlling the relations between capital and labor and of controlling their methods of enforcing their demands? The public has more at stake than either party to the industrial dispute, yet the public must suffer while strikes and profiteering go on. There is no adequate remedy for strikes unless there is at the same time a real remedy for profiteering.

Both in Europe and America many remedies have been proposed, especially since the war. But strikes continue and profits mount all the time. Responsible labor leaders and the more sensible captains of industry are both saying that the only permanent solution of the problem of constant strikes and excessive profits is to apply the principle of democracy industry. This, of course, means a fundamental change in our whole industrial system from the competitive to the co-operative basis. Any thorough-going industrial democracy means that the workers are joint owners and controllers and sharers in the industrial process. This might mean less profits to capital, but it would mean increased production and greater efficiency in the conduct of industry. It would at once eliminate strikes and profiteering.

It would eliminate strikes because the workers would have everything to lose and nothing to gain from a strike. It would tend to stabilize returns on invested capital and at the same time curtail excessive profits. Industrial democracy would mean partnership instead of partizanship in industry. The methods for bringing about industrial democracy are many and varied. Unless it can be done by legal means, that is, by appropriate legislation, then it may come as a result of concerted economic or physical pressure. Congress seems to be afraid to enact any means of bringing about even a moderate degree of industrial democracy. It seems to prefer to leave matters as they are, with strikes, profiteering and general industrial chaos.

In the interest of the entire public the extra-legal methods of both labor and capital in securing their ends ought to be brought to a stop. Chaos and disorder growing out of strikes, and discontent and extreme suffering growing out of excessive profits, tend toward revolution. Some real remedy must speedily be applied if disaster of a national character is to be averted.

TENTING BY THE CROSS

By Campbell Coyle

The times are full of theories, full of nostrums, and of
    cures,
And the times in avalanches are fast yielding to their
    lures;
Men would heaven win with goodness, and the gold of
    kindly deeds
Digged by them in mines of service, whereso'er that
    service leads;
Men would alone restore the temple, the temple of the
    soul
That God's skillful hand hath builded, and presume to
    make it whole;
But conscious of my ill-desert, my deep-seated sin and
    dross,
I have traveled back to Calv'ry and I'm tenting by the
    Cross.

Beside the Cross I'm tenting, and I feel a Presence there
That touches me with rapture, and heals all my pain
    and care.
The crimson stream flows over me, it covers all my sin,
And my soul is filled with glory that my soul and
    Christ are kin;
No gold have I of goodness stored eternal life to buy,
And to purchase at such empty price I've long since
    ceased to try.
My hope is built on better ground, for human worth
    is dross;
I have traveled back to Calv'ry, and I'm tenting by the
    Cross.

Beside the Cross I'm tenting, and aye by the Cross
    I'll bide,
And in the shelter of my Savior's love forevermore
    shall hide.
There no present storm can harm me, and no storm of
    time to come,
For His dear Presence will protect me, and bring me
    safely home.
He dwells with me on the Mountain, He whose blessed
    name is Christ;
And with Him, until He calls me, I will evermore keep
    tryst.
The times may have their nostrums—I count them all
    but dross;
I have traveled back to Calv'ry, and I'm tenting by the
    Cross.

THE CHRISTIAN ORPHANAGE

AN IMMEDIATE NEED

.·' The fall of the year is here aud winter following close on its heels. That means much to the Orphanage family and adds to the burdens of the Superintendent and the Matrons.

To see that clothes are prepared for sixty children aud to buy the material to make much of their clothing and buying shoes aud hats for the girls and boys at the present prices makes one feel that he is almost helpless.

Thirty little suits of clothes to buy for the boys. Dresses to buy for thirty girls. Sixty hats to buy for the boys and girls. Sixty pairs of shoes to buy. Oh, how would you like to have the job? Suits I could buy three years ago for five dollars now cost twelve to fourteen. Shoes I could buy three years ago for three dollars now seven. Just think of it!

Shoes, hats, caps, suits for the boys and dresses for the girls are all the go from now till all are supplied.

How easy this great need could be supplied by our. people if they could realize what a small sacrifice it would be to them and what a great blessing it would be to us. We·have four boys six years of age, four nine years, four ten years, four eleven years, two twelve years, one thirteen, three fourteen years, one fifteen, one sixteen and one seventeen years of age.

Suppose each Sunday school class, or Baracca Class, or Ladies' Aid Society should get it on its heart to lend me a helping hand to supply the many needs and just buy one boy a suit of clothes and a pair of shoes with hat and shirts; and you can buy by the ages given. How quickly all these boys could be fitted out for the winter and this great burden would roll off the shoulders of the Superintendent so easily and our bank account would still be intact to meet the increased winter expenses.

And suppose the same thing about the thirty girls. They need shoes, hats, dresses, etc., for the winter and how happy it would make you feel to know that you had contributed your part to keep .some little boy ʼʮ girl warm and comfortable through the cold winter weather! · When you are sitting in the corner this winter, when the winds are whistling around the house, just as snug and warm as you can be with every blessing to make your life happy and pleasant, remember, dear friends, that all people in the country have never been so richly blessed as you have. Remember there are unfortunate ones in your midst within the bounds of the Christian Church—your Church, the Church you love so well—whose corner is not so bright as yours, who have been denied the rich blessings you have received, whose lives are not so happy because want stares them in the face.

Remember the thirty boys and thirty girls at the Christian Orphanage, an institution of the Christian Church, the Church that is so close to your heart. These boys and girls are your boys and girls. Can you rest till you know they are comfortably provided for? Will you say to yourself that some other church will look after them and excuse yourself from the duty you have

to perform and the splendid .opportunity you have to lend a helping hand to fatherless ones?

Some time ago I wrote to nine fertilizer manufacturers and asked them to supply a need of forty bags of .fertilizer, giving five bags each, eight out of nine gladly shipped us the fertilizer we need. .I do not know that a single one of these people are members of our Church, but they gladly gave to help the fatherless ones. . Will you who are members of our Christiaⁿ Church come to my rescue so quickly and so gladly?

CHAS. D. JOHNSTON, *Supt.*

FINANCIAL REPORT FOR OCTOBER 8, 1919

Amount brought forward, $11,007.01.

Sunday School Monthly Offerings

(North Carolina Conference)

Henderson, $9.57; Liberty, (Vauce County), $7.75; Auburn, $3.00; Evely York, for Sunday school, (no name), $5.95; Morrisville, $3.27; Union, $2.00; Hope Dale, $1.45; Damascus, (Orange County), $5.00; Pleasant Union, $6.70; Six Forks, $3.10; Apple's Chapel, $1.00; Hurley Richmond, for Sunday school (no name), $4.30.

. (Valley Virginia Conference)

Centerville, $1.00; Newport, $3.19; Leaksville, $2.65.

(Eastern Virginia Conference)

Young Men's Baracca Class, Holy Neck, Sunday school, $1.17; Suffolk, $25.00; Rosemont, $5.00; Spring Hill, $2.00; Ivor, $2.32; Holy Neck, $4.00.

(Alabama Conference)

Bethany, $1.06; Antioch, $2.00; Total, $102.78.

Special Offerings

Albert Godley, $2.00; Jesse Godley, $5.00; Total, $7.00.

Total for the week, $109.78; Grand total, $11,116.79.

OBJECTIVES OF THE PRESBYTERIAN CHURCH

Here are some of the objectives of the Presbyterian Church for its new era movement:

Of Possessions:

    Preached annually in 5,000 pulpits
    Studied in 10,000 groups
    Practiced by 1,000,000 members.

Of Life:

    4,000 volunteers for the ministry
    3,500 for other whole-time Christian work
    Laymen enlisted and trained for Special Work.

A DAY OF CHRISTIAN STEWARDSHIP

This is certainly a day of Christian stewardship. We cannot live apart—we have found that out· long ago. We are our brother's keeper, and we are His trustee. God has given *all* to use and devote to the progress of His Kingdom—and that means to make all things and peoples better. We cannot live alone. We cannot die alone. A new day it is for many of us, and yet the things we are being taught to do are not new. We have been educated to them, and just now coming into a full sense and appreciation of our privilege and ·duty. We possess; we do not own. God is the *owner* of all; we are His. trustees—His stewards. What will our accounting be?

Note your label and if your subscription has expired, or is soon to expire, renew promptly.

LITTLE FOLKS DEPARTMENT

GOOD-NIGHT, MOTHER

Good-night, mother, close your eyes,
  Sleep the sleep deserving;
Finished now life's fabric lies,
  Gone the hours of serving.
Good-night, mother, though you sleep
  Love shall not forsake you;
We, who watch alone, shall weep,
  But we would not wake you.

Good-night, mother, it is night
  To the hearts that love you,
But the day eternal's light
  Marks the path above you.
Good-night, mother, in the dawn,
  Now the sky adorning,
Angel voices beckon on,
  Singing, "Soul, good-morning!"
          —*Douglas Malloch.*

CHILDREN'S SERMON

"And He arose, and rebuked the wind, and said unto the sea, Peace, be still."

"Oh, look! Look at the wind coming through the tree tops!" cried Mary, "and the Lake is all fizzing up like soda water!"

"Yes," said her father, as he quietly cast in his line again, drawing it gently over the surface of the water which a few moments before was as smooth as glass but was now covered with "fizzing" wrinkles and tiny tossing waves. "Yes, the winds come up very quickly on the lakes. See! the Storm King is chasing the sun under that big, black cloud and the white, fleecy clouds are running before him in dismay. But old Mr. Sun will win out in the end today, for the wind is due west, little daughter Mary, so we will fish on and, unless I am very much mistaken, will soon have some nice trout for dinner."

"But I don't like it out here on the water when the sun doesn't shine. Let's go in. It's cold and the water looks orful cross," said little daughter Mary anxiously. "Why, it's as black as black can be right there under the trees!" and she snuggled up close to her father, who laughed, as he put his free arm around her, saying:

"Why, little daughter Mary, the sun is there just the same even if you can't see it, and if you are cold put on your jacket, and see!" Here he stopped suddenly, drawing his arm away and beginning to reel in swiftly.

"Oh! You've got one! You've got one!" cried little daughter Mary, forgetting the wind and the clouds and the gathering shadows. "Oh, pull it in quick!"

"Not too quick," said her father, playing the fish skillfully, "or we will lose him. There—there he comes," and he leaned over with the short-handled net and scooped a shining speckled trout into the boat. When it was safely landed Mary gave a sigh of c tent, and said:

"Now we'll have one fish anyway for Mumsey's d ner, and she does like them so well. And see! the s is shining! Oh, how lovely the trees and water now with golden crinkles and smiles all over, and water is clear blue, just like the sky!"

"Yes, little daughter Mary," said her father, as cast out his line again, "the water is clear blue like sky and the trees are green and the air is warm a soft, but don't forget, little daughter Mary, that it the same woods, the same water and the same sky t you didn't like a few moments ago.. If we had g in because old Mr. Storm King covered up the sunsh for a few minutes we wouldn't have had the fish Mumsey's dinner. The world is just like that, lit daughter Mary. When the sun shines we are apt to happy and gay, but the minute the wind springs up, things don't go just as we want them, we wrap o selves up and growl and say: "Oh, I can't stand t at all!" forgetting that the sunshine of God's love always shining on us in dark and stormy weather j as on the bright days, up there beyond the clouds, a that we can forget the cold and the darkness if we ke right on doing just as we would if the clouds had i gathered; and sometimes the best things come to us the shadows, like the fish for Mumsey's dinner. you know what I mean?"

"Yes," said little daughter Mary softly, as she pa dled her hands in the water over the side of the bo "It's like Jesus saying 'Peace be still' when the stor arose—isn't it? I. s'pose if our hearts were peacef it would seem just as if the sun was shining, even if wasn't, wouldn't it?"

"You are right, little daughter Mary. The world very often like the lake—smooth and calm and beau ful to us until the wind rises and the Storm King discontent and selfishness drives away the sunshine fro our hearts; and only when we look up past the clou into the sunshine of God's love and hear His gent 'Peace be still' will we feel again content and happ Never mind the old Storm King, little daughter Mar He will come often into your life and mine, but remer ber the same sun is shining behind the clouds summ and winter; in bright days and dark days, and if y listen closely you will hear in your own heart 'Pea be still' and you will have no fear—only joy and gla ness always.—*By J. C. B., in Christian Work.*

NOTICE!

On October 15, 1919—at 7:30 P. M.

The Board of Trustees of the First Christian Church of B lington, N. C., will receive sealed bids for purchase of o church building and lot on the southeast corner of West Dav and Church Streets, Burlington, N. C.

Said lot fronts 70 feet on West Davis Street and 100 fe on Church Street.

The right to reject any or all bids is reserved. Terms sale: Cash.

          D. E. FONVILLE, Chairman.
          J. M. FIX, Secretary.

WORSHIP AND MEDITATION

HELP SOMEBODY TODAY

Some years ago there was a robust, fine looking preacher who then appeared to be in good health. He seemed to be useful and popular. A few years later he moved to a state adjoining this, having practically retired from the active work of the ministry—but was useful, now and then, as opportunity offered. He fully realized that he was in the sunset hours of his life, and that the long and eventful journey was nearly finished. His wife and other loved ones had long before passed over the way before him leaving him lonely and partly. in destitution. So he had to live single-handed and alone the later part of his earthly pilgrimage. Then disease intruded itself upon his once manly form and took from his the picturesque splendor which but a few years before adorned his manhood. He lingered for a few years trying to regain his health. While in this sick, sad, lonely condition, he wrote several short letters to his church paper telling its readers of his affliction and needs. He wanted to get medicine to heal his disease, but from what I saw through his letters but a very few responded. It is practicable to think, that the churches he had tried to serve so faithfully, would have acted at once, in his imminent condition, but so many of his former members put it off—forgot it, neglected it, and lost the last opportunity of helping him. Just a few visits, just a few kind, sympathetic words, just a few noble acts of liberality would have cheered his heart, and been a helpful blessing to the givers and to the receiver.

O, let us try to help some one before it is forever too late! Neglected opportunities, lost opportunities never to return. They have been all about us waiting to be used. "As we have opportunity let us do good toward men."

I have been sorry many times that I did not try to help this preacher about whom I have been writing—but did not; waiting for some one nearer him, and for some one more able to help him. Some sweet, kind, thoughtful, comforting, encouraging, tender loving words from his brethren in the ministry might have helped him; some short prayerful, helpful visit from them would have cheered him before he took that walk through the valley just a little way before him.

I do not remember that any one of them responded to his helpless call. A very short time after that his church paper stated "Rev ...., D. D. is dead."

Then another preacher was known who was not so old as the one mentioned above; he did not emit as many sparks from the anvil of thought as a great trio of brilliants could have sparkled, but he was a very good thinker and talker. He too, had an affliction which kept him from preaching. But he wanted to be useful in trying to help others, and he published a little book which he was trying to sell, but he had but a small income; he was anxious to help himself without being on

the charity list. He travelled mainly among the people he knew and to whom he preached in other years. He sold many copies. Some bought them through sympathy for him in his affliction, and for that reason alone helped him. He sold without molestation or objection from any one until he went to a certain town in which there lived a minister of the same denomination to which he belonged, who approached him, and said frankly: "I rather you would not sell your books among and to the members of my church, as they have money to raise for our Conference funds, education and missions, etc." That appeared to me like a very little request from one of the followers of Jesus. Help some one today.

Nor would I forget to mention John Bunyan, the immortalized writer of that splendid Christian allegory named "Pilgrim's Progress." In Bedford jail he wrote it under the most trying and adverse conditions. Put in prison, stoned, beaten for preaching the Gospel. In his day, ministers had a hard time. Today they have a good, easy time, telling people how to live, and how to slay the lions that prowl in the way. Yes, an easy time comparatively, and especially so when they are filled with the abundant life which freely gives light and liberty.

When Bunyan got out of jail he published his book, and went about selling it with some degree of success. One day he met one of those smart fellows, we sometimes see, and this man said to Bunyan: "Who are you any way? Are you a run-away, a peddler or a tinker?" Bunyan replied with this suitable and brilliant repartee: "I am all three, sir. I have run away from the devil, I am peddling upon a book I have written, and I am tinkering down upon sinners."

Many a poor, tired one struggling on the road to success, has failed in his life work, partly because he did not receive the proper encouragement. Some people like the eagle rise above the clouds of opposition, the lightning flashes vividly about them until it explodes with terrific thunder, but they soar above it in the great realm of industry. A few are like the kite which rises only above a headwind; while there are others not so brave. They are timid, and need gentle words of encouragement. They are the ones we ought to help catch up. Help form the circle and circuit by taking hold of the weak ones with willing hands, until each heart. O, for thousands of willing ones to make millions of happy souls today!

J. T. KITCHEN.

Windsor, Va.

———◆◆◆◆———

This is the day of great opportunity, and to each of us comes a call to help some one. We are our brother's keeper.

Sunday School and Christian Endeavor

SUNDAY SCHOOL LESSON FOR OCTOBER 19, 1919

Jesus in Peter's Home.—Mark 1:29-39.

Golden Text: Jesus said unto him, Today is salvation, come to this house. —Luke 19:9.

Beginning with the Primary Topic, "Things to do on Sunday;" the Junior, "A Sabbath Day in the Life of Jesus, through the Intermediate;" "Ways of Spending Sunday" and up to the Adult Topic, "Christ in the Home," this is a most helpful lesson, rich in great spiritual truths. When Jesus comes into the home, then indeed, is salvation come to that house. But first of all, He went to His father's house as his custom was. What an answer to all the cavillers who do not go to church, because they don't like the preacher, who stay away from Sunday school, because the Superintendent is no good, or the teacher is so poor. Who refuse to work with the church because there are hypocrites in it. No hypocrite today can be greater than were the Pharisees; no preacher more ignorant than the priests who refused to listen to Jesus; no man surely needs the teaching of God's word less than He who was the Word. Yet Jesus made a habit of going to church. And He went home *with those who were at church with Him.*

MRS. FRED BULLOCK.

CHRISTIAN ENDEAVOR TOPIC FOR OCTOBER 19, 1919

Our Pledge and How to Keep It. —Exodus. 19:1-8.

A pledge is a token or a surety of our willingness to do a thing. Aside from this lesson, the Old Testament presents three other passages concerning a pledge, and in each case they refer to a pledge made as a token of willingness to obey a command or an entreaty. You will find the passages in Gen. 38:17-20; Ex. 22:26; Deut. 24:10-13. In the passage from which our lesson is taken, there are two pledges and each are promises. The first is made by the Lord Himself, and the second is made by Israel.

In verse 5, God pledges to make Israel a "peculiar treasure" unto Himself, on condition that Israel keep her Covenant. Follow the work covenant and you will find back of it another covenant God had made to the same people. He had promised to make them a great people, and the pledge was based on the fact that Israel must meet conditions. So are His pledges to us. The second pledge is made by the people. "All that the Lord hath spoken will we do." Verse 8., and this was a great pledge. It was made under the fifth dispensation of law, and extended from Sinai to Cavalry. Israel smashed pledges, broke laws, sinned and committed crime while in the wilderness, but through God's pledge to them we may look far into the future and there see the Cross. He had the future of His people in mind, and kept his pledge.

Our Christian Endeavor pledge is more than great. It has stood the test of 38 years without the change of one single phrase. It is a promise made to Christ, and that on condition that He gives strength to keep it. No one has a right to break that pledge until Christ breaks His. He has pledged Himself to "hear our petitions—give when we ask of Him in faith, to keep us from temptation and to go with us always, even unto the end of the world," and in this meeting each Christian Endeavorer should resolve never to violate one part of the pledge until Christ breaks His. Keep your pledge card in your bedroom, and your pledge in your heart. Memorize every word of it, and then take up the card as a gentle reminder. Remember, making the pledge is nothing, unless we keep it. Strive to get every member to live closer to the pledge, and those who have not done so to sign one, for it's better to try and fail than never to try at all.

Suggestions For The Meeting

Have a memory meeting. Ask every member one week ahead to memorize the pledge. Divide your Society into two equal parts, and see which side has the greatest number who have memorized the pledge and will speak on some part of it. Have a testimony meeting, giving any member who will an opportunity to speak two minutes, telling what the keeping of the pledge has meant to his or her life. Select hymns that contain some pledge to Christ and the Church, such as "If Jesus Goes With Me I'll Go." Write out the pledge on the blackboard, and discuss it by phrases, asking a separate member to discuss each phrase. Ask your pastor to speak five minutes on the pledge, and if he will to give the evening hour to a special sermon on the value of a pledge. Close with a prayer by your president for strength to keep the whole pledge.

J. VINCENT KNIGHT.

HOW CAN WE TEACH THE GRADED LESSON IN A ONE-ROOM SCHOOL?

This has been the greatest objection we have had to meet in regard to the Graded Lessons. So many of us have only one room in our schools, and we feel we can have only one program. The school is not large enough to divide, and how can we arrange it? If we must all be together for the opening exercises, and the closing exercises, as we must, in a one-room school, why not plan such a program that it shall be of interest to all? As I have pointed out, even if you are using the Uniform Lesson, all the children are not reading the same text, nor learning the same Golden Text. Why not dispense with the reading of the lesson in concert and replace it a Bible drill, or endeavor to have the pupils bring their Bibles with them, such as can read, then use one of the devotional Psalms? But for the class period. Can you not plan curtains which shall divide the classes? They are not so very expensive; they need not touch either ceiling or floor; if they are three feet above the tops of the benches, and six inches below the top, that is sufficient. You would be surprised how much sound they break. And, too, most of us hear a great deal with our eyes. That is, if we do not see the speaker, or the noise maker, it does not trouble us nearly so much. A curtain which breaks our view protects our ears as well. Back of these curtains the Graded Lessons can be taught, almost as well as in a special room.

MRS. FRED BULLOCK.

CAN THE SUNDAY SCHOOL TAKE THE PLACE OF CHRISTIAN ENDEAVOR?

Now and then we find men and women who think the church is organized to death, and that we need to adjust matters by cutting out something. Naturally, the first thing to cut out is the young people's work of the church, and the result of the operation is a dead church. This spirit exists more or less in every denomination; and those who have tried it out, say they find absolutely no substitute for Christian Endeavor work in the church. The Sunday school is the mobilization station of the church, and is doing a most wonderful work along this line, as seen from the fact that 96 per cent of the church members comes through the school. And Mr. Lawrance says the only regretable thing about it is that 50 per cent of the Sunday school never joins any church. What a great work can be done in reaching those who never join the church anywhere! After considering the inefficient side of the school, we are tempted to ask the question, What would the church be without the great influence of the school? No doubt many of them would be very weak. Too much stress cannot be laid on the efficient Sunday school work.

But the Sunday school with all its organized classes, clubs and departments can never take the place of the Christian Endeavor. Why? Because Christian Endeavor is the training station of the church. Here, the boys and girls learn to express themselves, and to put into practice things learned in the Sunday school and church services. Dr. John R. Mott tells us that 98 per cent of all life work recruits come from the Young People's Societies of the church. And still, our own beloved Zion cannot supply her pulpits on any Sunday. The thing we need is to train men and women for this work, and the Christian Endeavor Society is the place to do it. I know God calls men to the Gospel ministry, but listen! Jesus said, "Pray the Lord of the harvest that he will and send laborers into his vineyard." But how can we pray for a thing we are not willing to take off our coats and help answer? It is foolish. We cannot place the young people in the ministry, mission fields and so on, but we

can train them in the societies and work of the church so they will have a mind to do that kind of work, and when we do so God will take care of the rest.

The one great outstanding need in the Christian Church, is more ministers, and mission workers. How are we to get them? Here is the way: Organize a training school in your church—go into the Sunday school and get the raw material, and train the boys and girls for service in the Kingdom, and within the next few years, you will see the answer to your prayer and our work will go forward.

J. VINCENT KNIGHT.

FROM THE STATE QUIET HOUR SUPERINTENDENT

In a recent issue of THE CHRISTIAN SUN I read a letter written by our State President, Rev. J. V. Knight. He was wondering why there was not a Christian Endeavor Society in every church of our denomination.

The writer knows of one instance where a Christian Endeavor Society was organized, flourished for a while, and soon failed to exist. Why? Because they failed to operate this Christian Endeavor Society on Christian Endeavor lines.

This Christian Endeavor Society was organized and failed in one of the leading churches of our denomination. All they needed was the right kind of leadership. They needed to plan the work, and then work the plan.

Now just a few lines to those of our denomination who are engaged in Christian Endeavor work. Every Christian Endeavor Society has its own problems to solve. Every Christian Endeavor Society at some time seems almost a failure. The question is what are you doing to better the work?

The trouble in nearly every Society is lack of knowledge on the topics which we study. The secret of successful prayer-meeting lies in having every member, or a large majority, comrades of the Quiet Hour.

A comrade of the Quiet Hour is a person who has signed the Quiet Hour pledge, agreeing to read his Bible every day, and to engage in prayer every day. The best time to engage in the Quiet Hour is early in the morning while our minds are fresh.

Now, let us all get busy. If we have not brought this important part of the Christian Endeavor work before our Society, let us do so at once. Then watch your Christian Endeavor Society grow. Kind reader, I will now appoint you as the one to see that this important matter is brought before your Society.

I wish to ask that the Secretary of each Christian Endeavor Society report to me at an early date just what has been done on this subject. If you have the Quiet Hour Covenant in your Christian Endeavor Society, please let me know just how many members you have, both in the Society and in the Quiet Hour Covenant.

F. M. HARWARD, C. E. E.
State Supt. of Quiet Hour.
Henderson, N. C.
P. O. Box 26.

A MEMORIAL—REV. L. I. COX

God in His infinite wisdom has taken from us one of the best and most dearly loved ministers of our Church, Rev. L. I. Cox, and has transplanted him near His throne in that beautiful home where joy, peace, and happiness forever reign.

Amid sorrows he was a cheerful associate, ever bringing joy and gladness to those with whom he came in contact. He was a welcome visitor into the homes of his members, always carrying a beam of sunshine to those who dearly loved him.

His interest in the church and the work of the Kingdom was done with zeal and happiness, bearing the burdens which often weighed heavily upon him with a strong and determined will.

Therefore, New Lebanon church, which Brother Cox built and has served as a faithful and consecrated pastor since its organization, would express its love and adoration in the following resolutions:

First. That in our beloved pastor God has given us a noble example of a self-sacrificing man, a patient worker, an inspiring companion and a loyal servant of our Lord Jesus Christ.

Second. That we bow in humble submission to our Heavenly Father's will, Who doeth all things well. We thank God for the privilege of having such a true, consecrated man as our pastor for twenty three years, and pray that God may raise up some man worthy to carry on the work so nobly begun.

Third. That to the bereaved family we extend our sincere sympathy and commend them to the work of God, and the divine guardian of the Holy Spirit for comfort and cheer in this sad hour.

Fourth. That a copy of these resolutions be sent to the family, a copy be recorded on our Church record, and a copy be sent to The Christian Sun for publication.

FLORENCE SHARPE,
LAURA SHARPE,
W. F. MOORE,
CARRIE SHARPE,
Committee.

DR. J. H. BROOKS

DENTIST

Foster Building   Burlington, N. C.

REPORT OF THE CONDITION OF

The Elon Banking and Trust Co., Elon College, in the State of North Carolina, at the close of business, September 12, 1919:

RESOURCES

Loans and Discounts	$32,053.63
Demand Loans	5,876.99
Overdrafts, unsecured	1,834.86
United States and Liberty Bonds	4,750.00
Banking House, $1,730.38; Furniture and Fixtures, $1,780.91	3,511.29
Cash in vault and net amounts due from Banks, Bankers and Trust Companies	13,238.37
Cash Items held over 24 hours	1,879.20
Thrift Stamps	37.25
War Savings Stamps	655.65
Total	$62,837.44

LIABILITIES

Capital Stock paid in	6,700.00
Surplus Fund	1,000.00
Undivided Profits, less current expenses and taxes paid	100.46
Bills Payable	8,000.00
Deposits subject to check	28,572.69
Time Certificates of Deposit	16,891.05
Cashier's Checks outstanding	357.74
Certified Checks	170.00
Trust Deposits, Liberty Bond Account	625.50
Accrued Interest due depositors	420.00
Total	$62,837.44

State of North Carolina—County of Alamance, September 23, 1919.

I, Marion C. Jackson, Cashier of the above named Bank, do solemnly swear that the above statement is true to the best of my knowledge and belief.

MARION C. JACKSON,
Cashier.

Correct—Attest:
G. S. WATSON,
S. W. CADDELL,
J. J. LAMBETH,
Directors.

Subscribed and sworn to before me, this 26th day of September, 1919.
J. J. LAMBETH, J. P.

Don't put off the matter of purchasing your church envelopes too late. Remember that they must be printed after the order is received.

SMILES

He Was Right.

Redd: "The doctor said he'd have me on my feet in a fortnight."

Greene: "And did he?"

Redd: "Sure. I've had to sell my automobile."—*Yonkers Statesman.*

* * *

His Special Talent

Boss (to new boy)—You're the slowest youngster we've ever had. Aren't you quick at anything?

Boy—Yes, sir; nobody can get tired as quickly as I can.—*Boys' Life.*

* * *

Would It Let a Little Thing Stand in the Way?

Gentleman: "Cabby, I'll give you $5.00 if you catch the four-thirty train."

Cabby (excited): "Jump in, guv'nor, an' I'll do it or break yer neck in the attempt!"

* * *

Some Miracle!

A Boston lady attended a funeral in a country church a short time ago. After the singing of a hymn which was strikingly melodious and appropriate, a rustic male friend who was seated beside her remarked, with an air of intense local pride:

"Beautiful hymn, isn't it? The corpse wrote it."—*The Universalist Leader.*

* * *

Teacher: "Why are the muscles in my head smaller than those in my arm?"

Pupil: "Because you don't use them so much."—*Ladies' Home Journal.*

* * *

"He's always talking. I should think he would find it hard on his voice."

"Yes; but if you listen to him you'll realize how easy it is on his mind."

* * *

"How old is your baby brother?" asked little Tommy of a playmate.

"One year old," replied Johnny.

"Ah!" exclaimed Tommy.

"I've got a dog a year old and he can walk twice as well as your brother."

"Well, so he ought to," replied Johnny; "he's got twice as many legs."—*Christian Advocate.*

THE CHRISTIAN SUN

"IN ESSENTIALS UNITY, IN NON-ESSENTIALS LIBERTY, IN ALL THINGS CHARITY"

What Harvest?

(President W. H. P. Faunce)

GREAT changes are coming either through the Church or in spite of it. We live in a moving world, and Christian men are not afraid to have it move. Either by the orderly processes of growth, by the give-and-take of reasonable men, by negotiation and concession in the presence of a common need or else by volcanic eruption and upheaval, changes must come. Alas for those—whether demagogues or Bourbons—who cry "Peace; peace!" while they sow the dragon's teeth and ignore the sure crop of armed men. America has no sympathy with anarchy. Revolution is foreign to our temperament and not to be endured in a free land which floats the stars and stripes. But we must not imagine either that the "old time religion" is good enough or that the social *status quo* is the kingdom of heaven. The things that are wrong have got to be righted by Christian men or they will be righted by anti-Christian forces. The open mind must come before the helping hand.

Volume LXXI	WEDNESDAY, OCTOBER 15, 1919	Number 42
BURLINGTON	· · ·	NORTH CAROLINA

THE CHRISTIAN SUN

Founded 1844 by Rev. Daniel W. Kerr

C. B. RIDDLE - - - Editor

Entered at the Burlington. N. C. Post Office as second class matter.

Subscription Rates

One year ....$ 2.00
Six months 1.00

In Advance

Give both your old and new postoffice when asking that your address be changed.

The change of your label is your receipt for money. Written receipts sent upon request.

*Many persons subscribe for friends, intending that the paper be stopped at the end of the year. If instructions are given to this effect, they will receive attention at the proper time.

Marriage and obituary notices not exceeding 150 words printed free if received within 60 days from date of event, all over this at the rate of one-half cent a word.

Original poetry not accepted for publication.

Principles of the Christian Church

(1) The Lord Jesus Christ is the only Head of the Church.

(2) Christian is a sufficient name of the Church.

(3) The Holy Bible is a sufficient rule of faith and practice.

(4) Christian character is a sufficient test of fellowship, and of church membership.

(5) The right of private judgment and the liberty of conscience is a right and a privilege that should be accorded to, and exercised by all.

EDITORIAL

FOR THE GLORY OF GOD

Among the new impulses that has, and will, come out of the shell-torn world is a revival of that impulse and injunction that we should do "all to the glory of God." In some way too many followers of Christ have gone through life making the Christian life a side issue. Too long, and too often, have we thought of our Father's business as something aside from our usual business, occupation or profession.

We are stewards of time, of conduct, and of possessions. Our business is our Father's business. On this same thought we find the following in The Christian Work from the pen of T. Rhondda Williams:

"Religion is not something to be practiced on a siding in the twilight hours, or on the seventh day, but on the main lines of life in the morning's activities, and in the strenuous labor of the afternoon. Justice and the spirit of common service must consecrate to God the mind and the factory, the merchant's desk and the carpenter's bench, or religion is not doing its work. It is with these ideals that the Father himself ever works to inspire His children and stands ever ready to help us all in the great achievement."

REPEATING—THAT'S ALL

The Conferences are now meeting. They have questions before them of vital interest. Will they rise to the situation and meet them? Will the leaders have vision —divine vision—and stand for its interpretation? Will the reports and resolutions be duplicates or copies of which have already been offered? Last year we read the "copy" and proof on the Christian Annual in a comparative way and found many reports as rehearsals of the Annual the year before. Some were almost word for word. Shall we keep repeating? That may be the way to get the things done—just keep on repeating. Here is the point: Let us first decide to do a thing, find out if we can do it, and then do it if we agree to. Let us repeat our work and not our resolutions.

CHRISTIAN UNION NUMBER

The Herald of Gospel Liberty last week came out as "A Christian Union Number." Dr. F. H. Peters contributed on "Christian Union and Conservation;" Rev. P. S. Sailer wrote on "Community Demands for Union;" President Harper addressed the Church on "Dangers to be Avoided;" Dr. E. B. Bagley (Disciple) and Dr. J. F. Burnett (Christian) spoke on "What Really Can Be Done," while Editor Kerr contributed on "The Disciples and the Christians." We glean the following excerpts from Brother Kerr's pen:

"The Disciple Church and the Christian Church have placed themselves on a pedestal among the other denominations long enough, and been all too free to assume to themselves a peculiar virtue above these others in the desire for union and in the freedom from guilt in the matter of sectarian division. It is time now that they be brought into the court of the world and be made to show cause why they themselves are identical in profession and separate in existence, and be given to understand that they must either live up to their profession or become silent about it. The rest of the world grows tired of hearing the Disciples and the Christians say so much about union, and they want to know now whether these Churches have in fact any more spirit and desire for union than do the Presbyterians and the Congregationalists and the rest of them. * * *

"The Disciples and the Christians can not be fair to the rest of the Church nor fair to themselves if they longer evade that question. Either there is no forgivable reason in such a day as this for them to be apart, or else they are not sincere and genuine in their basic professions. Which is it?

"They both profess to take the Bible as their only creed. It is their only written one. But there are those in both Churches who hold unwritten ones by which they individually try their fellow Christians for heresy as much as we done in the creed churches—with the added injustice of not giving the accused a public hearing and a fair trial.

"They both profess to grant the right of individual interpretation; and yet there are those in both Churches who insist on immersion for baptism, no difference how the candidate believes about his Scripture and his God

—and the Methodists and others are far more true to the principle of individual interpretation on the matter of water baptism than are the majority of the Disciples and many of the Christians.

"They both profess to have the union of all of the followers of Christ as their mission and their all-absorbing purpose—and yet there are thousands of both Churches that would rather see one of their own Churches dwindle away and die and its membership become un-Churched and un-Christian, than to see it unite with some other Church for the sake of the Kingdom in that community. * * *

"They both profess to have no other leader but Christ. But we wonder if we have not deceived ourselves in this, and if the spirit of other men have not dominated us far more than has the spirit of Christ.

"It is a day of terrible testing and crises in the life of the Church as well as in world affairs. Above everything it demands of every organization and association of men that make any pretense to being moral—let alone Christian—and that presume to offer themselves for leadership, that they be both genuine and sincere, and that they be in heart and purpose what they profess to the world that they are. It is a demand that can not be longer evaded. It is a demand that is stripping every denomination bare to the soul of it—and many of them already stand humbled and ashamed. The Disciples and the Christians can be no exception. They, too, must lay bare their soul to the light of this day. Their own young people demand it, their missionary and forward movement forces demand it, the world demands it, and the Church of Jesus Christ demands it. For either one or both of these Churches which stand on identical professions are deceiving themselves, or they are trying to deceive the rest of the Church and the world—in that they are not genuine and true to the position and the aspiration which they profess; or else there is no forgivable excuse in such a day as this for them to be two instead of one."

WHAT ABOUT THE CONFERENCE YEAR?

We called attention a few weeks ago to the matter of having a definite time for the churches in each Conference to close their work for the year. We would be pleased to have the Conferences take up this matter and at least find out how far apart the different Churches are on the matter of closing their reports for Conference. Why not have a definite date? How many ministerial reports, Brother Conference Secretary, are dated same? Is the suggestion worth while?

WAR RISK INSURANCE

The Bureau of War Risk Insurance wishes to emphasize the importance to service men of one of the provisions of the War Risk Insurance Act upon the fulfillment of which may depend the validity of their claim to compensation under the Act.

The War Risk Insurance Act provides that "No Compensation shall be payable for death or disability which does not occur prior to or within one year after discharge or resignation from the service, except that where, after a medical examination made pursuant to regulations, at the time of discharge or resignation from the service, or within such reasonable time thereafter, not exceeding one year, as may be allowed by regulations, a certificate has been obtained from the director to the effect that the injured person at the time of his discharge or resignation was suffering from injury likely to result in death or disability."

Many discharged men are not familiar with or are inclined to disregard this provision of law and are allowing their rights thereunder to lapse.

Request for the certificate mentioned above should be made to the Chief Medical Advisor, Bureau of War Risk Insurance, Washington, D. C.

WISDOM OF THE WEEK

If we indulge in sin, we invite a sorrow.—*Author Unknown.*

It is never too late to give up our prejudices.—*Author Unknown.*

A man, like his watch, is to be valued for his goings.—*The Christian.*

It is a blessed thing to sympathize with a man's successes.—*J. H. Jowett.*

You cannot dream yourself into a character; you must hammer and forge yourself one.—*The Christian.*

"We are all of us apt to play Providence in our private minds and to be very cross when our little decrees dont come off."—*Daily News.*

"The world goes stumbling on from the war to the peace, and the need of prophetic vision and the prophet's word continues urgent."—*Inquirer.*

"The world is crying out just now for a return of good humor. The world will not be saved until the good humored people organize."—*New Statesman.*

"The supreme need of the hour is for everyone to quit talking and go to work. Let us take our faith, if we cannot believe it otherwise, that you cannot get more than out of an egg than there is in it."—*Times.*

"The trains of today do not run by the time-tables of last year, and we cannot deal with the child's difficulties in the light of what former generations have thought about them, because it is only recently that anyone has really begun to think about the child at all."—*Times Educational Supplement.*

"Perhaps, when a real science of social psychology is created, it will help us to answer some questions so far left obscure. It may tell us what system best trains, braces, and fortifies the the will, calls forth latent energy, and in the long run creates the largest number of capable citizens."—*Times Literary Supplement.*

What will the laymen of the Conferences have to say this fall on the matter of ministerial support?

President Wilson is reported to be resting well and on the road to recovery.

PASTOR AND PEOPLE

HAPPY HOME

This year it has been my privilege and pleasure to serve Happy Home Christian church on the third Sunday of each month. I find the people of this congregation appreciative of their pastor, true to their Church and loyal to their God. The third Sunday in August we began revival services and continued until the following Thursday. Good interest was shown from beginning to end. We had conversions in nearly every service. On the closing day of the meeting we had quite a large number of conversions and reclaimations. During the meeting there were possibly 25 or 30 who professed faith in Christ and resolved to live a better life. It was considered by many who were there as being a most wonderful revival. Eleven united with the church at the close. These were baptized at our last appointment. The church at present is in splendid working condition. The ladies have raised enough money to purchase an individual Communion set, and it has already arrived.

Recently the members and friends of this church have very kindly and substantially remembered their pastor. It was Saturday before the fourth Sunday in September when Brother J. H. Richmond and one other of the members came to my home with a Ford car loaded with good things to eat, such as the country people have. After the car was unloaded Mrs. Wells and I. were eager to see what was left us, and we found a crate of chickens, flour, sugar, potatoes of both kinds, apples, pears, onions, money, preserves of different kinds, canned peaches, canned cherries, and canned goods of other varieties, soap, pepper, butter and other articles of usefulness. It was an old fashion pounding, just like our Editor has been talking about. To each and every one who had a part in this bountiful supply, Mrs. Wells and the children join me in extending sincere thanks. Such expressions of appreciation like this bind the pastor and people closer together, and too it makes a pastor feel good to know that he is loved and appreciated. Not only is that true of a pastor, but it is true of every life.

W. L. WELLS.

Reidsville, N. C.

DR. SUMMERBELL AT ELON

Dr. Martyn Summerbell delivered his annual course of lectures here October 6-8. The themes were: "The Dark Ages," "The Middle Age and Feudalism," "The Rise and Influence of Chivalry," "Peter Preaching the Crusade, " "The First Crusade, ' and "Godfrey and the Kingdom of Jerusalem." In addition to these the Doctor preached from the college church pulpit Sunday, October 5, both morning and evening, and was attended with the usual interest and pleasure.

The lectures were characteristic of Dr. Summerbell —not popular lectures, but scholarly ones, representing patient and faithful research. They were a feast of good things to all real students and lovers of history.

Any one who had passed through volumes in search of these facts could but feel a debt of gratitude to the Doctor who had collected in brief space and in logical order these important truths of history. These lectures have a literary finish and would make a worthy contribution to the literature on the Middle Ages. We welcome Dr. Summerbell, not only for his scholarly messages, but also for his delightful fellowship, and look w' h pleasant anticipation to his return.

N. G. NEWMAN.

SUFFOLK LETTER

.wo returned Chaplains of the Christian Church have recently spoken for us in Suffolk. Rev. B. F. Black on Sunday evening, September 7, and Rev. Stanley C. Harrell on Sunday morning, September 21. Both of them spoke out of their hearts from experience in service overseas. Their addresses were interpretations of what they had seen and felt while in France. Their messages were as distinct as their own temperaments; in fact, that illustrates personality and the coloring that evidence receives in passing through human experience. Light is composed of seven colors and these colors are separated by passing through different mediums; so truth is broken up into parts as it passes through different lives. Religion itself is not the same in form in different lives. The many religious denominations are, witnesses to this fact. No one denomination presents all of truth, but only certain phases of truth; and perhaps all of them do not present all of truth. The messages of these ministers were greatly enjoyed by the congregation and no less so by the pastor who is this scribe. We will all rejoice when these returned Chaplains are in place again, as pastors, weaving into pastoral service the larger and more real experiences of service among men in real battle for the liberty of mankind. No doubt they will put into their congregations the militant spirit against the wrongs of the world. Life to them and service to them are more serious since they have prayed with the wounded and buried the dead in a foreign land.

The Christian life is really a fight and Paul calls it "the good fight of faith." The weapons of our warfare are not carnal, but spiritual; the battle is not for temperal power, but for eternal life. Much has been said about the ruthless Hun, much more might be said about sin. It seeks the innocents for its victims and crushes out all aspirations for good. Following in the victory of temperance over the saloon as an institution is an army of law-breakers who persist in making and trading in illicit intoxicants. That army can be conquered by winning them to Christ. Fines and imprisonment may check such violations, but nothing will end it but conversion to law-abiding citizens. To conquer evil and to produce the reign of righteousness is a "good faith." It takes the whole armor of God to equip a good soldier of Jesus Christ. "Stand therefore, having your loins girt about with truth, having on the breast-plate of righteousness; your feet shod with the preparation of the gospel of peace; the shield of faith; the helmet of salvation; and the sword of the Spirit, which is the word of God; praying always with all prayer and supplication in the Spirit, and watching thereunto with all perseverance and supplication with all saints." It is no small matter to equip an army to fight for the Kingdom of God; and no half-hearted service can win the battle and the Crown. Immorality parades with brazen effrontery in these days of prosperity, rides in automobiles, sits in the boxes at theaters, bathes in the surf on summer days, surfeits in luxuries and neglects God and the heroic in life. The fight for virtue and social purity is a great fight. Its first battle is within the domain of self; that once conquered, the individual Christian is ready to join in the fight for social purity and domestic peace. Religion is no mean business, no small matter; it is the greatest work in the world. To succeed here is to win a crown of life.

W. W. STALEY.

JOHN G. AND JOHN B.

Used to live side by side—John G. and John B.—fifty years later they are separated by an impassible gulf.

John G. rides to his office in a 1919 model auto that purrs softly through the streets. John B. rides to the factory on a rattling 1908 bicycle while John G. is still asleep. When John G. takes a trip, his secretary lays his ticket and drawing room reservation in front of him along with a reply wire from the best hotel. When John B. goes on an outing he fights his way up the gang plank of a crowded excursion steamer, a baby on one arm and a lunch basket on the other. John G.'s son is at college and John B.'s son has been in the shop since he was fourteen. A wide gap? Yes. Yet they started at the little red school house with the odds in favor of John B. He used to spell John G. down and help him with his sums.

The neighbors said then that John B. would be president yet, And John B., always expecting to strike it rich put nothing by for the future. He never made that lucky strike. John G. was plodding but kept moving up the line. Part of his hard earned money was always put where it would earn more money. And finally the day came when he bought a partnership in the business. He still keeps his dollars working for him but now at sixty his income is sure whether he works or not.

Where will you be at sixty? Today is the time to find out. Can you keep a dollar? Have you the backbone to take the price of a Thrift or a War Savings Stamp out of your pay envelope according to its size? If you have there will be no lean years. If you can't save, make up your mind right now to the bitterness of a penniless old age. You don't have to guess about it, nothing added to nothing makes nothing.

Mrs. W. J. Fleming—We wait eagerly for THE SUN each week.

Occupation of Fiume by Italian regular troops is suggested by the Italian council of ministers, pending a decision by the peace conference as to the disposition of the city.

DANVILLE, VIRGINIA

I am serving this church the last three months of the year, filling the unexpired term of Rev. H. S. Hardcastle, who is at Yale University. I was here the first Sunday and the congregation at the evening service was large. After service we held a call meeting and elected delegates to Conference. In less than twenty-five minutes the Conference apportionments and several dollars over were raised. This little church has a few faithful workers.

These people are without a pastor for the coming year. I hope and pray that God will give them the pastor that they need. They have a fine Sunday school and it keeps more money in its treasury than any school that I know of, especially when we consider its financial and numerical strength. God bless this little band of workers.

P. T. KLAPP.

MOORE UNION

The writer is serving this church again this year. I intended to have taken this year off but after an urgent request consented to serve another year. Looking at this church from my view point its condition is encouraging. First, because they have had a great revival; secondly, because they received a number into church membership; thirdly, they have money on hand for Conference apportionments and their delegates to Conference have been elected. Deacon J. W. Lett has had the church painted inside. The outside was painted just after the house was finished. The pastor's salary is almost paid in full and has been increased to almost double the former salary. The church pledged more for endowment fund for Elon College than it was asked to give.

God bless this church and to Him be all the praise for what has been done.

P. T. KLAPP.

NEW COMERS TO THE SUN FAMILY

J. T. Rice	Bosley, N. C.
Mrs. S. W. Hofler	Bosley, N. C.
G. H. Lassiter	Corapeake, N. C.
E. S. Pierce	Sunbury, N. C.
J. R. Corbitt	Sunbury, N. C.
H. Shelton Smith	Fairfield, Conn.
Morris Thomas	Graham, N. C.
T. C. Elliott	News Ferry, Va.
W. S. Henderson	News Ferry, Va.
S. J. Farmer	News Ferry, Va.
Tom Jones	News Ferry, Va.
I. T. Farmer	News Ferry, Va.
J. E. Blackstock	News Ferry, Va.
E. D. Farmer	News Ferry, Va.
Walter Moore	News Ferry, Va.
O. T. Oakes	News Ferry, Va.
Willie Croxton	News Ferry, Va.
W. H. Owen	News Ferry, Va.
Morgan Farmer	News Ferry, Va.
J. D. Ross	Burlington, N. C.
William Archie Powell	Apex, N. C.

(Report to October 13)

NOTICE

All persons who expect to attend the Eastern Virginia Christian Conference which convenes at Waverly, Virginia, on October 28, 1919, will please notify the undersigned at their earliest convenience, stating what day they expect to arrive in Waverly and whether they will come by train or private conveyance.

R. T. WEST, Secretary.

Waverly, Virginia.

THE RED CROSS AT CORPUS CHRISTI

By Walter R. Brooks

When Corpus Christi, the big seaside resort on the Gulf, was wiped off the map of Texas last month by a terriffic hurricane and flood, the American Red Cross at once mobilized all its resources for disaster relief and brought them to bear on the chaotic conditions left in the wake of the storm.

For twenty hours a furious gale blew from the north, driving a ten foot tidal wave in across the low beaches to the heart of the city. The heavy surf pounded the hotels and cottages on the beach front and filled the streets of the business section with debris. During a lull in the storm the Corpus Christi Chapter of the Red Cross organized a committee and extended aid with what facilities were at hand to those who had escaped from their threatened homes and come up into the town. There was no gas, no electricity, no drinking water. Communication with the outside world was completely broken. Conditions, when the tornado had finally blown itself out and it was possible to ascertain them, were found to be frightful. Virtually every frame building on the beach front was battered to pieces, and Neuces Bay was dotted with wreckage and the bodies of those who had been washed out by the waves. The work of rescuing those who were still alive was being carried on by the few boats that were left undamaged. Five hundred people had lost their lives, 4,000 were left homeless, and it is now estimated that the property damage will run well up to $20,000,000.

Meanwhile, the whole machinery of the Red Cross has been set in motion. The manager of the Southwestern Division wired the Governor of Texas, placing his entire facilities at the disposal of the flood victims. The Director of Civilian Relief in St. Louis was ordered to the scene, and workers at Laredo and San Antonio received telegraphic instructions to accompany relief trains being made up at these points. Before wire communication with the outside was re-established these trains loaded with food, clothing and medical stores, pulled into Corpus Christi, and the Red Cross workers flung themselves immediately into the task of dispensing relief. Headquarters were established in the Presbyterian church, which had remained undamaged, and within a few hours the three canteens were feeding 4,000 people at each meal.

At Galveston the Red Cross obtained permission from the federal authorities to charter a government vessel, which lay loaded with a hundred tons of supplies, and steamed off to the relief of several small towns, completely cut off from the mainland by the high water and the lack of boats. In co-operation with army officers,

the Red Cross shipped 25 cases of clothing from Galveston, and from Houston and San Antonio and St. Louis help came pouring in.

Within a few days trains carrying refugees began to arrive in San Antonio. Red Cross workers met them at the station and served them with coffee, sandwiches and pie. Three hundred homeless Mexicans who came in on one train were housed in the nearby barracks of Camp Travis.

All Red Cross activities are being directed from St. Louis, the headquarters of the Southwestern Division, whose chapter has donated $5,000 for relief. A general committee has been formed of state and Red Cross officials, and the Director in charge of the flood swept district has completed a survey of the damage and of the most effective scheme for rehabilitation.

The story of this terrible disaster and the prompt relief which a fully organized and existing Red Cross personnel were able to concentrate immediately on a small coast town, bringing order out of chaos and saving many lives and incalculable suffering, emphasizes the importance of the work which the Red Cross has to carry on, in peace as well as in war. The desire for service, the spirit of sympathy, the sense of human brotherhood are still alive in the world. But the world is so big; they so often miss their goal. It is the aim of the Red Cross to *organize* these sentiments so that they may be practically effective—to bring them together, concentrate and focus them on a practical object. The campaign which the Red Cross has recently announced against preventable disease, for better public health condition, and for prompt and efficient service in just such disasters as this at Corpus Christi, needs and deserves the support of every loyal American who believes in extending the hand of fellowship to those who are in misery or want throughout the world.

WHAT YOUR LABEL MEANS

(Told in the Language of a Child)

1-1-9 means that your subscription expires January 1, 1919.
2-1-9 means that your subscription expires February 1, 1919.
3-1-9 means that your subscription expires March 1, 1919.
4-1-9 means that your subscription expires April 1, 1919.
5-1-9 means that your subscription expires May 1, 1919.
6-1-9 means that your subscription expires June 1, 1919.
7-1-9 means that your subscription expires July 1, 1919.
8-1-9 means that your subscription expires August 1, 1919.
9-1-9 means that your subscription expires September 1, 1919.
10-1-9 means that your subscription expires October 1, 1919.
11-1-9 means that your subscription expires November 1, 1919.
12-1-9 means that your subscription expires December 1, 1919.

Mrs. A. A. Terrell—I have been taking THE SUN for years; it wouldn't be home without it.

Germany is asking the United States for a loan amounting to 15,000,000 marks.

Dr. J. O. Atkinson, Dr. N. G. Newman and Miss Bessie Holt are this week in the far South attending the Conferences in that section.

NOTES

Rev. H. Shelton Smith is now located in Fairfield, Conn., where he is assistant pastor to Rev. F. S. Child. Brother Smith is also pursuing his studies in Yale.

We are very grateful for the continued interest that friends have in helping to increase THE SUN's circulation. New names are being added each week. Let the good work go on, kind friends.

Dr. Martyn Summerbell came over from Elon last week and gave us a pleasant call.

We are indebted to Brother W. A. McCauley of Union Ridge church for a half bushel of nice sweet potatoes. Brother McCauley is one of THE SUN's loyal friends.

The Ladies' Aid Society of the Burlington church held a memorial service Monday afternoon in memory of Mrs. Joseph Fix.

Dr. F. G. Coffin changes his address from Albany, N. Y., to Albany, Mo. He becomes president of Palmer College.

Burlington is soon to have a daily paper. Editor Crowson of The Burlington News is soon to install machinery for the new periodical.

Delegates and visitors to the Eastern Virginia Conference will take note of Brother West's notice on another page and govern themselves accordingly.

Dr. D. A. Long preached for Pastor Eastes at Raleigh, N. C., last Sunday.

We were privileged on last Sunday to hear President Harper speak to the congregation of the Burlington M. E. church. His message was timely and the people were edified by hearing it.

We now have on hand Peloubet's Select Notes on the Sunday school lesson for 1920, also Tarbell's Guide. The price of each is $1.60 postpaid, or $1.50 when delivered at this office. Send your order now. We will be in position in a few days to supply Arnold's Notes, also Torrey's Gist of the Lesson.

Brother W. A. King, a member of the Suffolk, Virginia, church and a faithful subscriber and friend of THE SUN, passed to his reward on Sunday night, October 5. Dr. Staley will give a more complete account of Brother King's life and death next week.

Rev. D. F. Parsons changes his address from Chattanooga, Tenn., to Nashville, Tenn. He is at Vanderbilt University.

Rev. P. T. Klapp has three Sundays open for the coming year. Brother Klapp is a safe man and churches without a pastor will do well to write him. His address is Elon College, N. C.

Pleasant Grove and Ingram have formed a pastorate. Pleasant Grove is to pay $800.00 and Ingram $400.00. Brother J. G. Truitt continues to serve them and will give his entire time to the work.

We quote the following from The Sanford Express of October 10: "Evangelistic services will begin at the Christian Church next Sunday evening. Rev. B. F. Black, who has seen service overseas, will conduct the meeting."

We invite the attention of church officials and committees to the price list of offering envelopes shown on page 16 of this issue. Send your order early and avoid the fall rush. Remember that the work will have to be done after your order is received; also bear in mind that other orders may be ahead of yours. Work and satisfaction guaranteed.

On September 13, Miss Margaret E. Benson, a member of the People's Church, Dover, Delaware, and Rev. James H. Lightbourne of Indiana, were married. The ceremony was performed by Rev. A. Victor Lightbourne, brother of the groom. The bride is of a beautiful Christian character, a woman of fine executive ability and a splendid musician. Her husband saw service in France as a private and recently returned to this country and took up his ministerial labors. Congratulations and best wishes.

Brother W. L. Wells, Reidsville, N. C., writes under date of October 10: "We are in the midst of a revival meeting. Rev. R. F. Brown is doing the preaching.

Rev. J. V. Knight was called to his home in Alabama on October 7 due to the critical illness of his father.

Dr. J. P. Barrett, writing under date of October 9, gives us the following information worth recording, for which we thank him: "I see you made a mistake in your note naming THE SUN's editors. Major D. B. (not T.) Dunbar was never editor of THE CHRISTIAN SUN. He was for many years foreman and for a while wrote up local items for its local department. I came in as successor to Rev. J. T. Whitley. I was succeeded by W. T. Walker and then I succeeded Brother Walker in my second term. I mention this item as to Major Dunbar simply for the sake of accuracy in history of our work as a people."

The Burlington congregation is to worship in the new church the first Sunday in November.

The North Carolina Conference meets with the Burlington church November 11-14. Mr. J. P. Montgomery, Burlington, N. C., is Chairman of the Entertainment Committee whom delegates and visitors should notify.

CHRISTIAN EDUCATION

A PLEA FOR THE KINDERGARTEN

DEPARTMENT OF THE INTERIOR
BUREAU OF EDUCATION

The great world war will be followed by years of agitation and change in which all institutions of government, including our own, will be tried and tested severely, is already evident from what is now taking place both in Europe and in America.

Intelligent democracy is the only protection against reaction toward autocracy on the one side and class rule, disintegration, and anarchy on the other.

Our American democracy, the hope of the world, demands universal education of the best type—education of all for freedom, initiative, self-restraint, co-operation, and obedience to law. In this education the kindergarten has a very important place. Its spirit is that of democracy, and tends toward freedom, initiative, self-restraint, co-operation, and obedience to law.

It is significant that the kindergarten did not receive governmental approval in Germany, because of this very fact of its spirit of democracy, and that Froebel looked to America for the attainment of his ideals in education.

For all our young children, both of native born and of foreign born parentage, and especially for the latter, kindergarten schools should be provided, either by public or by private support. Our millions of children of kindergarten age should no longer be deprived of the training which the kindergarten gives in industry, loyalty, patriotism, and the social, and industrial democracy.

I should like to urge all school officers and all citizens who are interested in the welfare of the people and in the permanency and fullest development of our democracy to use their influence for the establishment and maintenance of kindergartens for all children.

P. P. CLAXTON,
Commissioner of Education.
Washington, D. C.

THE JUVENILE COURT

By Roland F. Beasley, State Commissioner of Public Welfare.

The juvenile court is the means whereby it is found that dependent, neglected and delinquent children can best be saved from lives of failure and disaster and made to grow into useful and law-abiding citizens.

This is very good for the child; all will admit it. It is equally good for society. Paupers and criminals are liabilities to the taxpayers. Law-abiding citizens are an asset.

The juvenile court principle is now being applied all over the United States and in foreign countries. It is one of the great forward steps of the age, and the most important advance in court methods in many years. It can no more be checked than the public school. It is here to stay and to be improved.

The juvenile court can't save every child. But it has been proven that when the system is properly carried

out it will save seventy-five per cent of them. That is more than worth the money.

It costs the taxpayers ten times more to capture, try, punish, and maintain an adult criminal than it does to save a juvenile delinquent.

All the children in North Carolina under sixteen years of age who are delinquent, neglected, or dependent, are under the jurisdiction of the juvenile court.

Every juvenile court has a probation officer whose business it is to investigate every case of such children, lay the facts before the judge, and then carry out the decision of the court. This is called probation work.

The court stands in the relation of parent to such children, and will discipline, guide and control them through probation, just as a wise father would.

The court may punish a child if it is necessary, but wayward children are more in need of wise guidance and just discipline and friendly help than of punishment.

The judge is the kind and wise father, the probation officer is the big brother of the boy who is about to be lost. Both are studying ways and means to make a man of him.

Do you believe in saving boys and girls whose parents let them go astray or who have no parents?

If you are a Christian, you certainly ought to pray for and encourage this work, for it is Christ's work.

If you are a good citizen you ought to help it, for you believe in having good citizens and not bad ones.

If you are a taxpayer you ought to stand by this work, because it is cheaper to save a boy than to maintain a lifelong law-breaker.

If you are a mother you ought to help, because every wayward child is a burden to some mother-heart.

If you are a man you ought to help, because this is a practical application of the brotherhood of man.

The juvenile court is really a part of the educational system. It carries opportunity to children who otherwise would not have it.

The juvenile court does not ask what can be done to a child, but what can be done for him . . . to make a man or a woman instead of a human wreck.

The people who do not believe in human wrecks have risen in their power and wiped out the whisky traffic. They are now preparing to wipe out the other influences that make wrecks of young and helpless children.

This is a job for God's noble men and women. Such men and women are putting their hands to the plough in every community in North Carolina. They are already tasting the joy that comes from it and have no desire to look back. If these words meet your eye, you are invited to come in with us.

Write for information and literature on child-saving to The State Board of Charities and Public Welfare, Raleigh, N. C., or to your own county superintendent of public welfare.

Mrs. S. F. Coghill—I like THE CHRISTIAN SUN fine and expect to take it on from time to time.

Let us have your renewal during this month.

MISSIONARY

DR. KENDALL GOES TO WASHINGTON

The following explains itself and will be read with deep interest:

"Ravena, N. Y., Oct. 8, 1919.

"Dear Brother Atkinson:

"I will, the Lord willing, begin our work in Washington, D. C. the first or second Sunday in November. I accept the call and terms of the Mission Board of the Southern Christian Convention. I wish to say that I feel very heavily the burden of the task laid upon me and I am free to confess it is with many misgivings as to my fitness for the task that I take up the work, but as you brethren seem to feel that I am the one for this work I am willing, God helping me, to undertake it. I covet most earnestly your continued prayer for me that I may have the physical and spiritual strength needed for this work.

"Yours fraternally,
"A. B. Kendall."

I am sure our people everywhere will rejoice that we are at last taking steps to organize a church in our national capital, and that the Board was fortunate enough to secure Dr. Kendall to lead us in this important undertaking. The Lord willing we will organize and in due time build a church in Washington worthy of the great work and cause we represent.

J. O. ATKINSON,
Miss. Sec. S. C. C.

A PLEA FOR THE USE OF MORE MISSION LITERATURE

A simple definition of missions is "helping some one;" therefore, cannot we, whose hearts are aglow with the spirit of missions, seek to lead others to see the vision of a world of need and opportunity which stirs our own souls? We can do this by living Christ, teaching, Christ, and preaching Christ—all for one purpose to show the people the character and service of the blessed Master. He was always "helping some one" as He went about doing good. He came to seek and save all men of all nations, and it should be the *purpose* of *our* lives to obey His command to carry the blessed gospel to all lands and to all peoples. It is our duty to study how to carry this out most *efficiently.*

We wish to emphasize some of the goals in which our Woman's Boards have lined up with the Forward Movement. In the goal for Evangelism: (a) 100 new missionary societies; (b) 2,000 new members in the societies.

In order to accomplish this we must educate the people. How shall we go about it? By adopting and pushing forward the goal for *Religious Education*. (a) Get every society in the Southern Christian Convention to studying the Home and Foreign Mission study books each year. (b) To secure every member of every society as a subscriber to *The Christian Missionary*.

Some societies have already studied "The King's Highway" and "Western Women in Eastern Lands," "The Path of Labor" and "Women Workers of the Orient," and we know they will look forward with pleasure to the study of the new books, "A Crusade of Compassion" and "Christian Americanization."

The monthly programs in the mazagine will be based on these two books. Please don't lose a treat by failing to get them. There are many bright, helpful leaflets published that do much good, so don't fail to scatter them.

The young people will also enjoy "Around the World With Jack and Janet," "Jack and Janet in the Philippines" and "Mook." "Everyland" is a fine little magazine for Juniors of S. C. C. We will be glad to furnish leaflets and workers supplies if you will let us know your needs.

If any societies do not have a literature superintendent please appoint one right away as I should like to meet with all those of the North Carolina Conference at Elon College, November 8. Also send me a literature report before that time if possible.

MINNIE F. COOK, *Supt of*
Literature Dept. of S. C. C. and N. C. C.
Greensboro, N. C.

REPORT OF THE WOMAN'S HOME AND FOREIGN MISSIONARY SOCIETY OF THE FIRST CHRISTIAN CHURCH, BURLINGTON, N. C., FOR THE YEAR ENDING OCTOBER 1, 1919

Number of active members	69
Number of honorary members	11
Home department	8
Total	**88**
New members received this year	13
Intercessors	32
Subscribers to Christian Missionary	24
Renewals	18
Leaflets distributed by Supt	1,500
Intercessors covenant distributed	100

Receipts

Balance on hand from last year	12.87
Spring mite box opening	36.58
Fall mite box opening	62.90
Thank Offering	80.90
Received through Willing Workers	41.34
Regular dues for year	83.30
Support of Bible Woman	50.00
Ten new Life Members	100.00
Received from Cradle Roll	6.41
Total receipts	$422.90

Disbursements

For support of girl in Bible School	30.00
Pledged to J. O. Atkinson, Mission Fund	15.00
For support of Bible Woman	50.00
To Elon and Sendai Orphanages	10.00
To Literature Fund	3.00
To gifts for Miss Stacy	6.67
To floral design	2.00
To Barret home, in memory of Miss Sarah Fix	30.00
To Santa Isabel work	40.60
To Literature fund	10.00

To Santa Isabel work for Willing Workers............ 41.34
To Mission Board (regular dues) 83.30
To Mrs. W. K. Sellers, Treas. of W. B. for life members. 100.00

                    Total disbursements......$422.90
                Respectfully submitted,
                         MRS. D. E. SELLARS, Secy.
Burlington, N. C., Oct. 8, 1919.

PERSONAL MENTION ABOUT MISSIONARIES

After considerable delay in the sailing of the vessel on which she had booked passage, Miss Martha Stacy, living link missionary of the Burlington, N. C. Sunday school, sailed from Vancouver at midnight of September 29. We will next hear from her from Japan, as there are no stops by the way on that route.

When her ship reaches the one hundred and eightieth meridian she will drop a whole day out of her life in the process of "crossing the line." This will probably happen about October ninth. In all likelihood she will retire on Wednesday night, Oct. 8, and awake next morning and find it to be Friday morning, the tenth. But let us not be alarmed. She will only have been trying to catch up with the sun, which is twenty-four hours faster on the other side of that line than it is on this side, and when she returns to America a few years hence on her first furlough she will find that day patiently "hanging on the line" waiting for her, and she will pick it up again, retiring some night only to awake the next morning to find yesterday still awaiting to be lived over anew.

Dr. A. D. Woodworth and Mrs. Woodworth, who sailed for Japan, via Australia on September ninth, send back a delightful letter from Honolulu to say that God is good to them as they are out upon the great deep. They will probabably have reached Australia before this is in print, and will spend a few weeks with their daughter there before finally turning their faces toward Japan. It is a life of triangular interests which they are living. America—the land of their birth, with a multiplicity of heart interests; Australia—holding all that is nearest to them in human relationship in the person of their only child and her family, including two wonderful grandchildren whom they are now to see for the first time. What a meeting that will be! And Japan—the land of their adoption because of its heart-rending need for the Gospel.

But regardless of the heart-tuggings of human relationships Dr. and Mrs. Woodworth have never wavered from their intense loyalty to the call of God for overseas service. There have come to them peculiar difficulties and a peculiar sadness in their devotion to their chosen work in life, but they have never wavered.

Soon we will have re-enforcements on the way to our Mission in Porto Rico. Times innumerable I have thought about Rev. and Mrs. Barrett, and the frequent intervals when they have been left without co-laborers from America. Others have gone and stayed a few years, only to be called away by the force of unavoidable circumstances, and each time one of these has faced homeward there has come stealing into the hearts of the Barretts an unutterable sense of loneliness and discourage-

ment. They have not told me so—*they have not murmured*—and I have never met them, *but I know how they have felt at such times.*

Our Japan Mission has met with a very great loss to its working personnel in the death of Miss Ren Hamaguchi, a most faithful and loyal Bible woman, who had been in the service of our Mission nearly thirty years. She was a woman of extraordinary faithfulness and devotion to her task. Rev. Kitano Takaya, pastor of our church in Sendai, Japan, says in a recent letter: "I do not know whether we can ever secure so good a Bible woman as she has been or not." She had the unquestioned love and respect of all who knew her.

                              E. K. McCORD.
Dayton, Ohio.

IS OUR FAITH TOO LARGE?

One half million dollars for missions! Is that too much? The Mission Board, made up of as sensible, wise, faithful and loyal people—nine good men and one worthy, capable good woman—think that the sum is not too much to ask or expect of our people, if we want to come into our own, and see our dear Church go forward in the Kingdom's work. At first, two years ago, the goal was fixed at $50,000. Not long and it was seen that our aim was too low and the goal was set at $100,-000. Not long after the discovery was made that we had underestimated the needs of our work and the ability of our people. The goal was set at $125,000. And now all of us know that such a sum is inadequate. And the Board has fixed our goal at half a million, including what has been pledged the past two years, to be pledged by 1922—within five years from the time the work was begun.

Brethren and beloved, shall we do this great and good thing? Is the burden of world-wide salvation on our hearts heavy enough to send us to our knees for this sum, a gift of God through His devoted and willing subjects in the Christian Church here in the South, and their friends? It is a matter of burden and of need. God has never denied a people a real need, when was in keeping with His will. The Mission Board at its recent session took the most forward-looking steps yet undertaken, and mapped out for us a program of great and good things. May our heavenly Father help us to feel the need and bring us to our knees for His cause.

                              J. O. ATKINSON.

Colonel E. M. House, Confidential adviser to President Wilson, has returned from France.

A great conference was held in Washington last week between Labor and Capital.

The National Convention of the Disciples Church is in session in Cincinnati, Ohio, this week. Several thousands of people are in attendance.

Postal employes are to get a raise in salary soon.

THE CHRISTIAN ORPHANAGE

SUPERINTENDENT'S NOTES

Our little children were made happy on Saturday, October 4. The New Lebanon Sunday school, Rockingham county, N. C., came to see us on a picnic and brought dinner for all our children.

It was quite an undertaking for a Sunday school to prepare dinner for their picnic and sixty orphan children too, but those good ladies in that community know how to do things and they did a fine job too. The table was filled to the limit of its capacity and the children had a sumptuous dinner and enjoyed it very much.

We are always delighted to have the Sunday schools picnic here on our grounds. It is a delightful place, nice lawn, good water, and in case of rain, plenty of room in the building to shelter.

Don't forget that winter is close here and we have sixty children to clothe for the winter. Shoes to buy, clothes to buy. All necessaries to make them comfortable and happy. If you have had any experience lately in buying I presume that you well know that prices are high. If you have any shoes that you cannot use, and not worn too much, or any clothes too small for your children in good wearing condition, or any suits of clothes or dresses that you cannot use, put them in a bundle and ship to us. We can make use of them to good advantage. I know a great many people have garments that their children have outgrown and the garments in good wearing condition and perhaps shoes too small and are no use to the family. Send them to us by parcel post. Good second hand shoes will help us now while prices are so high.

Perhaps some of the Sunday school classes want to make a special contribution of this kind and want to buy new stuff for us. In that case we will be delighted. If all will help a little it will make the work lighter. You have been real good to us in this work and have always come to our rescue.

Don't *forget* we want to *build* a home for the *small children.* How much do you want to invest in that home? Write to us for a subscription blank. We want YOU to have a part in it. It will make you more interested.

CHAS. D. JOHNSTON, Supt.

FINANCIAL REPORT FOR OCTOBER 15, 1919

Amount brought forward, $11,110.79.

Children's Offerings

Lester B. Frank, 20 cents; John B. Taylor, 25 cents; Total, 45 cents.

Sunday School Monthly Offerings

(North Carolina Conference)

Wake Chapel, $5.70; Christian Light, $3.64; New Providence B. C. Class, $1.20; Hine's Chapel, $2.00; Long's Chapel, $2.00; High Point, $3.26; Chapel Hill, $2.26; Parks Cross Roads, 65 cents; Burlington, $37.84; Pleasant Hill, $4.64; New Providence, $1.88; Amelia, $4.84; Catawba Springs, $9.09.

(Eastern Virginia Conference)

Mt. Carmel, $4.54; Mt. Carmel, Sunday school class No. 6, $1.00; Hobson, .73 cents; Oak Level, $3.10.

(Valley Virginia Conference)

New Hope, $1.86; Linville, $1.00.

(Georgia and Alabama Conference)

Kite, Ga., $8.00; North Highland, Ga., $1.80; Total $101.03.

Special

Mrs H. C. King, (Long's Chapel), $1.00; Go. Forward Class, Vanceville, Ga., 83 cents; J. E Latham, Greensboro, N. C., $25.00; Total, $26.83.

Total for the week, $128.31; Grand total, $11,289.10.

FROM THE COUSINS

Dear Uncle Charley: September days in Oklahoma make one think of autumn, even though it has not been cool enough for frost. Enclosed please find my dues for September and October. With lots of love for the little cousins.—*Lester B. Frank.*

We have had no frost, but have lots of dry weather. We cannot plough for the ground is so hard and dry. We hope to have rain soon.—*"Uncle Charley."*

Dear Uncle Charley: Am sending 25 cents for the orphans. Don't want you to pardon me for waiting so long. I wonder why we children don't write you oftener. Best wishes.—*John B. Taylor.*

I wish the little cousins would write often. Sometimes when we are kinder blue the little letters bring sunshine to us.—*"Uncle Charley."*

CHERRIES FOR THE BOY WHO RODE

Everybody worked on the farm where Roy Anderson lived. Roy himself brought in the kindling, gathered the eggs and helped to feed the chickens and water the garden.

Now that it was cherry time Roy climbed far up in the big trees to pick the fruit that grew too high for heavier people to venture after. Of course every boy likes to climb trees; but lately Roy had got to thinking that he worked too hard, so he even grumbled about picking cherries.

This afternoon he had climbed to the top of the very tallest cherry tree on the place. Roy didn't admire the fine view or the thick clusters of luscious ripe cherries that hung all around him. He was watching a boy in a pony cart who was riding along the road.

"That boy doesn't have to pick cherries or do any other kind of work. I've seen him 'most a dozen times now," muttered the cross little cherry-picker. "He just rides and rides and rides anywhere he wants to in that cute brown pony cart with the jolly-looking black boy to drive for him. He can keep his hands clean."

Roy's own hands were brown and scratched and a little stiff now and dirty looking where they had clung to the rough bark of the cherry limbs.

"I say, Roy, can't you break off that long branch that hangs so full?" called his father. "I'd like to have you bring it down carefully and take it out to that boy in the pony cart. Stay and visit with him a while if you want to."

The jolly-looking black boy saw Roy coming and stopped the pony. He and the other boy both smiled and stared at that limb of great, black cherries.

"O, but those look good! I've seen you when you were away up in the tree. It must be great fun to pick cherries and climb about like that," said the little white boy. "My name is Donald, and this is Chester," he added.

Roy bowed shyly. "It is sort of fun to pick cherries, and they taste lots better when you eat them up in the tree. Don't you want to get out and go up there with me?"

"Yes, I want to," said Donald, with a funny, twisty smile. He jerked the dust robe from his knees, but he didn't start to climb out of the pony cart.

"Oh," was all that Roy could say, but he thought a great deal. It looked as if the queer steel box on one of those thin legs must hurt. Anyway, it didn't let a fellow climb trees or run or do any one of the dozens of things that Roy could do any minute.

"The rest of me's pretty much all right," spoke up the boy in the pony cart cheerfully. "I can do lots of things with my hands."

"That—that's good," said Roy. He couldn't make his voice sound very hearty, because even Donald's hands looked thin and weak beside his own sturdy brown fists. "You stop next time you come by, and I'll bring down another branch of cherries," he said slowly.

"Thank you, we will," promised Donald gayly. "Maybe I can stay and watch you for a while if we don't take such a long drive next time. We've been clear to the river today."

Roy hadn't been to the river for more than a month, but he felt no envy of the boy who had been there today. "He gets tired just from riding!" was what Roy thought as he clambered back to his tree-top.

That night Roy Anderson surprised his mother by something new that he put in his prayer. He said: "Dear God, I thank you for good hands and feet."

"That is a wise, true prayer, son," said his mother. "It is going to take a whole lifetime for you to learn how wonderful your hands and feet are. They ar four priceless gifts.—*Sunday School Times.*

THE UNITED STATES RAILROAD ADMINISTRATION
Announces
Reduced Round Trip Fares and Special Train Service
——Via——
SOUTHERN RAILROAD LINES
——To——
RALEIGH, N. C.
——Account——
NORTH CAROLINA
STATE FAIR AND PEACE JUBILEE
OCTOBER 20 to 25, 1919

Reduced Fare Round Trip Tickets will be on sale October 17, 18, 19, 20, 21, 22, 23, 24th, and for trains

scheduled to arrive at Raleigh before noon, October 25th. Final limit returning to reach original starting point by mid-night, October 27, 1919.

In addition to the excellent regular train service, the following special trains will be operated to Raleigh and return for this occasion:

Special Train

Greensboro to Raleigh and return, October 22 and 23

Lv. Greensboro	7:00 a. m.
McLeansburg	7:15 a. m.
Gibsonville	7:30 a. m.
Elon College	7:35 a. m,
Burlington	7:50 a. m.
Graham	7:55 a. m.
Haw River	8:00 a. m.
Mebane	8:15 a. m.
Efland	8:25 a. m.
Hillsboro	8:35 a. m.
University	8:50 a. m.
Durham	9:15 a. m.
East Durham	9:25 a. m.
Morrisville	9:45 a. m.
Cary	9:55 a. m.
Ar. Raleigh	10:15 a. m.

Returning Leave Raleigh 6:00 P. M. (Union Station)

Special Train

Oxford to Raleigh and return, October 23

Lv. Oxford	7:00 a. m.
Providence	7:15 a. m.
Stem	7:29 a. m.
Lyon	7:37 a. m.
Wilkin	7:44 a. m.
Cozart	7:50 a. m.
Gorman	8:05 a. m.
East Durham	8:35 a. m.
Brassfield	8:45 a. m.
Morrisville	8:55 a. m,
Cary	9:05 a. m.
Ar. Raleigh	9:25 a. m.

Returning Leave Raleigh 6:30 P. M. (Union Station)

Special Train

Chapel Hill Station to Raleigh and return, October 23

Lv. Chapel Hill	8:00 a. m.
University	8:40 a. m.
Durham	9:00 a.m.
Ar. Raleigh	10:00 a. m.

Returning Leave Raleigh 7:45 P. M. (Union Station)

Grand Agricultural, Industrial and Educational Displays

Uncle Sam urges you not to miss the United States Government exhibit of War Trophies. Almost every portable device used on land or sea in the World War, both allied and captured German.

For Detailed Information, Call on Local Ticket Agents.

(*Advertisement*)

Earnings of the larger railroads for August totalled $96,029,358, averaging $410 per miles of road operated, or $14 above the guaranteed rentals, according to estimates made public last week by the interstate commerce commission. The earnings for the same month last year were $548 per mile of road operated.

WORSHIP AND MEDITATION

IT IS YOURS

Not long ago I visited a fine home and a well kept farm. It was pleasing to see everything so carefully, conveniently and tastefully arranged. Gorgeous landscope views, a lovely, rich inviting valley, picturesque mountains, thrifty orchards of the best peaches and apples, all conspired to make a picture attractive and beautiful. Standing and looking at this scene with perfect delight, and perhaps with a great desire to own this home, the thought quickly and gladly came: This splendid home and all as far as can be seen, is mine. It cost me not a dollar and have no deed for it, but will when leaving here, carry it away in the mind, because it is mine. Having been impressed on the mind, it is mine, and it is there to stay. No one can prevent the possession, nor deprive the newly made owner this right of ownership. When stating this to the legal owner, he smiled and said: "You are welcome to it that way."

You don't have to buy the water, the air, and the sunshine which you use. If you had them to buy, they would cost you right much in this day when many things you have to purchase are expensive. They are all free. They are yours—all are yours. Then use freely and wisely these triple blessings, and you will be healthy, happy and strong. Use plenty of water for drinking and bathing—and use it freely for other purposes when needed, for it is yours. Don't be too stingy with it when it flows so freely from rivers and oceans, and gushes clear, sparkling and cold from the rocky glen. Come on all you thirsty ones, fatigued and worn out with the long journey, dip your cups into the water, drink and be refreshed. It is yours, and all are yours. The air, the air filled with life-breathing power. Inhale it; fill your lungs full, repeat the process often, over and over again. It will help your depressed feelings. It is free. It is yours.

The great park conservatories, and all the admirable scenery spread upon the screen of nature invites you to look, love, praise and adore Him who caused these things. Come on and in without money. Enjoy life. But use the world as not abusing it. It is yours. Given to you to study in—to learn in—to work in, and in which to prepare yourself for a more beautiful and enduring world where you can live in immortal youth, unhurt amid the war of elements, the wreck of matter and the crash of worlds. Use the means at your command—practice economy and industry, and live—live upon the great and wonderful things provided so wisely for your happiness.

Do not glory too much in men. Let there be enough of that kind of honor, namely, Christian courtesy, fellowship, friendship and love. These things ought to be cultivated more by many of us. Some great teachers of Christian ethics are deficient in their practice. "Let

no man glory in men; for all things are yours; whether * * * * the world, or life, or death, or things present, or things to come; all are yours, and ye are Christ's; and Christ is God's."

J. T. KITCHEN.

PROCRASTINATION

(V. May Dorman)

"Late, late, so late! and dark the night and chill!
Late, late, so late! but we can enter still.
Too late, too late! ye cannot enter now. . . .
Have we not heard the Bridegroom is so sweet?
O, let us in, though late, to kiss his feet!
No, no; too late! ye cannot enter now."

—*Tennyson.*

"Time there was, but it is gone;
Time there may be—who can tell?
Time there is to act upon,
Help me, Lord, to use it well."

—*Augustus J. C. Hare.*

Man is born to die, but to see him live one would think he could wheedle Death, and like Tennyson's brook go on forever. He hears with complete indifference when spoken to, or with fixed, far-off attention. One wonders at his nonchalance and dullness and unresponsiveness of soul. But to him the peril is remote, and on he goes, hoping in the tomorrow which never comes.

Why is it that the soul hearing, seeing, and knowing is unheeding? Why it that reflecting on a lost Christ, a lost heaven, and the prospect of outer darkness, we hesitate and waver and wait? We hear over and again, until we can hear no longer. We see, but "film the eyes in dreams again" until we become "too blind to have desire to see." We comprehend, but scorn the inward meaning until there is no more power to comprehend. Without the power to hear, to see, or to know; there can be no desire, and without desire, there can be no final redemption. One when dying said, "What shall I do? I am lost; I see it well." Vision came again, but it came in the hour of death. And so it will come to us, a vision of truth seen too late. That we were forewarned with Truth, pure and simple, and forearmed with the means of prevention, leaves scant evidence in favor of our defense.

Let us not become so wholly absorbed in the present, as to invite or bring upon us, a severe letting alone.—*The Christian Witness.*

The prohibition bill has been completed by Congress and is soon to be submitted to President Wilson for his signature.

* *

The 1919 Confederate Veterans Reunion was held in Atlanta, Georgia, last week. About ten thousand old soldiers attended.

Sunday School and Christian Endeavor

SUNDAY SCHOOL LESSON FOR OCTOBER 26, 1919

(Mrs. Fred Bullock)

A Lesson in Trust. Matt. 14:22-23.

Golden Text: I believe; help thou mine unbelief. Mark 9:24.

This is a wonderful story of Ever-present Help. Jesus saw them struggling. He did not need any light of moon or stars. He who can see us from Heaven could surely see through a few miles of atmosphere. Jesus said, "Be of good cheer." What a homely, cheerful phrase! "Cheer up," we say. Notice how many times, and under how many different circumstances, Jesus said, "Cheer up" to His friends. Surely when we too strive in the midst of the sea with contrary winds, and no land in sight, He is not so far away from us, but that He can see us and help us; not so far, but if we listen we can hear His tender voice saying "Be of good cheer." See how quickly help came to failing Peter. "Immediately" Jesus stretched forth his hand. Many a failing faith has felt the immediate answer of the Master when he cried "Lord, save me." An old-time saint on a stormy voyage was tossed far out to sea. "There is no help; the way is closed," cried his despairing disciples, as the waves rose above them. "The way up is always open," answered the saint.

"No storm above our heads in
    wrath shall break,
And shut the heavenward path of
    love and prayer."

Ours is a ship on a voyage, not a ship in harbor; we are going "to the other side." When He is with us, no storm can destroy, no wave overwhelm, and we shall reach our harbor safe at last. "Our hope is not in the absence of danger, but in the presence of Christ."

CHRISTIAN ENDEAVOR TOPIC FOR OCTOBER 26, 1919

(J. V. Knight)

Christianity and the Health of China. Luke 4:16-31.

China is the world's newest and largest republic. America has transported every commodity she has to this great republic—even her whisky and things detrimental to the good

of her people. Now, we must face the task of transporting the Christian religion in large enough quantities to save the Chinese people.

The population of the Chinese Empire is 435,500,000 with an area of 4,277,170. Omitting India, you find more non-Christians here than in all the rest of the world. There are at present 4,225 missionaries on that Empire, which gives 103,767 people, and a parish of more than a thousand square miles to each missionary. Compare this with figures and facts in our own country. Have we given China a square deal? Remember that of every 4,000 Christians, 3,399 of them live on American soil.

Wherever sin is found disease and death follow. China is seriously ill, and verse 18 of this lesson furnishes her only hope. But she cannot reach this Physician. A reformation and civilization may bring health of body, but China has a sin-sick soul. Her only hope is in Christ, and how shall she be healed unless the Church for which Jesus died gives the gospel to her? One of her greatest needs is physicians and nurses who are Christians and know how to minister to all her ills of life. They are waiting by the pool; the water is troubled, and who shall place them in the healing streams before it is too late?

Suggestions for Meeting

Use a black-board. Draw a map of China. On the map show the location of China's 1,850 villages and cities. Show her 108 walled cities, and note that only 26 of these cities have missionaries. Show the three large towns that have missionaries, and from it all observe that only 29 places of the 1,850 are touched by a missionary. Close with a prayer for our Chinese missions.

WHAT IS A STANDARD SCHOOL?

There appears to be considerable misapprehension about what really constitutes a Standard School. Not many of our schools have qualified, or, if qualified, they have not so notified the Sunday School Board and received their diploma of recognition. This holds our denomination back in a comparison of statistics with other

denominations, and lowers us in their eyes. "Oh," someone will say, "what difference whether we get credit or not, just so we have these points?" You might just as well say, "What difference whether we eat our meat for dinner, so long as we have bought it, we are all right." No one is stronger for uneaten meat, and no denomination is stronger when some school has the "meat", and keeps it to itself. On the back cover of the Teachers and Officers Journal, you will find a list of the Ten Points which make a Standard School. These ten points are recognized in the Christian Church, in all denominations and in the International Sunday School Association as the ten necessary points for a Standard School. We will take up the points, one at a time from week to week.

MRS. FRED BULLOCK.

DOES CHRISTIAN ENDEAVOR CONFLICT WITH THE MISSION ENTERPRISE OF THE LOCAL CHURCH?

Since Christian Endeavor begins with the Cradle Roll, and ends with the Alumni Association, one might at a glance think there would be a conflict in the work. In fact the question has been raised in some of the conference meetings. Let us see if there is: For an example of this, I use my own field. This church has a Young People's Society, a Junior Christian Endeavor, and we hope to have an Alumni fellowship soon. On the other hand it has a Woman's Missionary Society, a Young Men's Missionary Society and a Junior Missionary Society, and all of them are alive. Those who are active in one are active in the other, and there has never been the slightest conflict, or even a spirit of unfriendly rivalry. All are united in one effort for one common cause, and co-operate beautifully in their routine of work. The fact that your church has a Missionary Society does not mean that you cannot maintain a live Christian Endeavor, for one will help the other along. In the Society we are studying every phase of the mission field of service, and in addition, we are calling for life work recruits for every field of service in Christ's Kingdom. In conclusion this series of three articles on Christian Endeavor work, I am going to speak my sentiments on the question. The problem of the Church today, is the winning of its young people. The Church that fails here, must die tomorrow. And the fact that a young man or woman has made a public profession of Christ does not mean that he or she is saved. He may be saved for the present, but what about keeping saved and being saved for service? The Church that holds its young will be the Church of tomorrow. And watch that Church, if it holds the young, it will also hold the old. Our own Church is falling short of her great opportunities, because we are neglecting the young people of the Church. Too many of our young people are straying away, who ought to be in our own institutions of learning preparing for Christian leadership. What is the trouble? There is a wrong somewhere that must be righted. Where is it? Look at the machinery of the Church, and the few methods employed for the keeping of our young people in the Church work, and you will find the great trouble. Not God's fault, but ours.

My final plea, and entreaty is that every pastor and church lay plans, more plans, and bigger plans for taking care of our young people. Drop your prejudice, and biased opinions, if you have any, and line up the young folks in your field for Christian service and in the coming days you will have a strong Church that will carry the Gospel message to a lost world.

J. VINCENT KNIGHT.

THE IMPROVED UNIFORM LESSON

I trust that many of our schools are adopting the Graded Lessons. Now as you come back from vacations, and gather up the scattered Sunday schools in an earnest effort for splendid work during the fall and winter, is the time to commence them. All the Graded Series Lessons are planned to begin with the first of October, and the lessons are so arranged as to come at the proper periods of the year, Thanksgiving Lessons at Thanksgiving, Christmas Lessons at Christmas, etc. You can

secure them just as you secure your other Sunday school supplies, sending in all your orders together, as you have always done. For such as do not use the Graded Lessons, I beg to call attention to the new Improved Uniform Lesson.

MRS. FRED BULLOCK.

ENDEAVORERS, ATTENTION, PLEASE.

Will you kindly do me a *personal favor* and at the same time help on the cause of Christian Endeavor in our Christian Church? This is what I want you to do: Fill in the answer to the following questions to the best of your ability.

Questions

1. Name of church.
2. Name of C. E. President.
3. Name of C. E. Corresponding Secretary.
4. Number of members.—Active —Associate—Honorary.
5. Have you an Intermediate society?
6. Number of Intermediate members.—Active—Associate—Honorary.
7. Have you a Junior society?
8. Number of Juniors—Active— Associate—
9. Are you giving a definite sum to Home Missions?—How Much?..
10. Are you giving a definite sum to Foreign Missions?—How Much?—
11. How many C. E. Experts have you?
12. Do you have a Mission Study Class?

Will you please *do it now?* (Tune: "Glory, Glory, Hallelujah!")

Will you, will you, will you, will you,
Will you, will you, will you, will you,
Will you, will you, will you, will you, you,
Oh, will YOU DO IT NOW?

Fill in the answers, cut this out of the paper and send *at once* to A. B. Kendall, Secretary of C. E., Ravena, N. Y. THANK YOU.

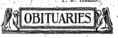

INDIVIDUAL COMMUNION SERVICE

THE BEST WAY to serve Communion. It is reverent, sanitary, and increases attendance at the Lord's Supper. Our services are chaste and beautiful. Made of finest materials and best workmanship.

Send for illustrated price list

C. B. RIDDLE, Publishing Agent, Burlington, North Carolina.

SMILES

Wanted: A boy to carry papers twelve years old.—*Advertisement in The Democrat.*

* * *

Military Commander: "Forward, march! Company, halt! Forward, march! Squads left! Squads right! On left into the line! By the right flank! Halt! Rest! Attention!"
Irish Recruit: "I'll not work for a man who changes his mind so often!"—*Exchange.*

* * *

Boy: "How much are your eggs per dozen?"
Grocer: "Fifty cents a dozen for the cracked ones and eighty cents a dozen for the good ones."
Boy: "Well, crack me a dozen of the eighty-cent kind."—*Boys' Life.*

* * *

At the Current Events Club one lady whispered to her neighbor the following: "What is the difference, if there is any difference, between Serbia and Siberia?"

DR. J. H. BROOKS

DENTIST

Foster Building   Burlington, N. C.

PELOUBET'S SELECT NOTES

Send your order for Peloubet's Select Notes on the Sunday school lesson along with your renewal to THE CHRISTIAN SUN. The books will be ready for delivery December 1. You need not send the money now, unless you want to. Just indicate for us to send you a copy December 1 and that will be all right. The price is $1.60, postpaid.

Write for prices and samples of church offering envelopes.

CHURCH OFFERING ENVELOPES

Standard Double
(Size 2½x4¼ inches—52 to Set)

White or Manila
25 to 49 sets	16 cts. a set
50 to 109 sets	14 cts. a set
110 to 209 sets	13 cts. a set
210 to 309 sets	12½ cts. a set
310 to 399 sets	12 cts. a set
400 or more sets	11 cts. a set

Minimum Charge $3.00 net.
CARTONS INCLUDED

Single Envelope System
(Size 2 5-16X3 5-8 inches. Open side. 52 to Set)

White or Manila
25 to 49 sets	14 cts. a set
50 to 99 sets	13 cts. a set
100 to 149 sets	12 cts a set
150 to 199 sets	11½ cts. a set
200 to 249 sets	11 cts. a set
250 or more sets	10 cts. a set

Minimum Charge $2.00 set.
CARTONS INCLUDED

Take Note
The following points should be taken into consideration in placing an order for church offering envelopes:

1. A set means 52 envelopes, one for each Sunday in the year.

2. When cartons are ordered the sets are arranged in their logical order, thus making it convenient for the member. We suggest the use of cartons because of the convenience.

3. If you desire monthly, double or single envelopes, without cartons, 1-3 the price of the same number of weekly sets. Cartons 3-4 cent each.

4. Semi-monthly, double or single, in cartons, 2-3 the weekly price; without cartons 3-5 the weekly price.

5. When ordering state what Sunday that your church year begins, and whether you want the dates on envelopes or not.

6. Indicate the wording that you want placed on the envelopes or leave the same with us. Samples sent upon request.

7. Allow ten to fifteen days for delivery. Order early.

C. B. RIDDLE, Publishing Agent
Burlington,   N. C.

Don't put off the matter of purchasing your church envelopes too late. Remember that they must be printed after the order is received.

Monuments and Grave Stones

Numerous Designs—Fine Georgia Granite—Satisfied Customers Our Chief Asset. Let me call and show you designs and prices.

G. A. NICHOLSON, *Representative,*
Burlington, North Carolina

R. F. D. No. 1   Phone 3804

THE CHRISTIAN SUN

"IN ESSENTIALS UNITY, IN NON-ESSENTIALS LIBERTY, IN ALL THINGS CHARITY"

OUR ONE GREAT NEED
THE CHRISTIAN SUN
IN EVERY HOME

Volume LXXI	WEDNESDAY, OCTOBER 22, 1919	Number 43
BURLINGTON	· · ·	NORTH CAROLINA

THE CHRISTIAN SUN

Founded 1844 by Rev. Daniel W. Kerr

C. B. RIDDLE - - - Editor

Entered at the Burlington, N. C. Post Office as second class matter.

Subscription Rates

One year .... $ 2.00
Six months 1.00

In Advance

Give both your old and new postoffice when asking thv your address be changed.

The change of your label is your receipt for money. P son re ceipts sent upon request.

Many persons subscribe for friends, intending that the _er be stopped at the end of the year. If instructions are given t4 tis effect, they will receive attention at the proper time.

Marriage and obituary notices not exceeding 150 words printed free if received within 60 days from date of event, all over this at the rate of one-half cent a word.

Original poetry not accepted for publication.

Principles of the Christian Church

(1) The Lord Jesus Christ is the only Head of the Church.
(2) Christian is a sufficient name of the Church.
(3) The Holy Bible is a sufficient rule of faith and practice.
(4) Christian character is a sufficient test of fellowship, and of church membership.
(5) The right of private judgment and the liberty of conscience is a right and a privilege that should be accorded to, and exercised by all.

EDITORIAL

WHERE ARE WE?

"This enlightened generation" says the orator as he sways his audience. How often have you heard it. How grateful are you for it! A great (?) civilization! Orators, poets, statesmen, historians, and artists have reminded us time and again by their products that we have trampled the wild man underfoot, left in the jungles the savage, and turned man's activities to higher and better and nobler things. All this we admit, and yet we are often reminded to ask, Where are we? How far from these ancient days are we?

Here is the point: Fourteen hundred policemen, men under oath to support the law, went on a strike and left the city to the gamblers, the hoodlums and the thieves. What happened? In fair Boston, a city of culture and refinement, where all this happened, hundreds of homes were endangered, hundreds of shops and stores were looted and robbed, men were held up in broad day light and relieved of their possessions, fronts were knocked out of beautiful stores and clerks were helpless in the face of a mob that acted like beasts from the jungles of Africa. From unsuspected corners devil-filled humans took the law in their own hands and turned a city of order to a city of disorder; turned a city of schools and churches into a city of mob rule and thievery.

What lesson does this teach us? (There are certainly many lessons to be learned from it.) Let us take this one: It shows how it is possible for churches to be built up in every section and fail to reach the hearts of the people. What a call and challenge for home mission work!

The Church paper is the one institution that must blaze the way. Its mission is Christian progress, and nothing less will justify its existence.

FOR MINISTERS ONLY

For ministers only is this note written. It is personal to our brethren in a like calling and written with the greatest respect and deepest appreciation.

We have been led to believe that only a few of our ministers are real students. And what we say of our ministers we have reason to think the same of some ministers in other denominations. There is a sort of a sameness in our Church work that leads us to make this statement; and if we are mistaken (and we hope that we are) no one shall rejoice the more than this scribe.

If you are, dear reader, in doubt as to what we mean by saying that we are led to believe that few of our ministers are real students, we pass along these questions to be answered:

1. Do you read every issue of THE CHRISTIAN SUN?
2. Do you read *The Herald of Gospel Liberty?*
3. Do you read *The Christian Missionary?*
4. Do you read other publications issued by our people?
5. What publications of other denominations do you read?
6. How many books a year do you read?
7. Do you read a daily paper?
8. What magazines do you read?

If we were called upon to draft a list of questions to ask a minister as to his study, the eight items above would be the first to be included. It is taken for granted that a minister is a student of the Bible and other biblical literature.

But are you a real student, brother pastor? Your answer to the eight questions above will about tell the tale. How wide is your horizon? Is your denomination the only household of faith known to you, except in a general way? Do you use the same sermon until it is worn into a memory speech, or do you dig deep into the issues of the day and into the depths of life and go before your people with a message of the hour? It may be that there is a reason why the church, or churches, you are serving do not go forward. How many young men and women do you lead to high school and college each year? The touch of a real student will bring young men and women flocking to college when all other persuasion fails.

The demands of the day are upon us. They challenge the best within us, and unless we are real students, these issues will baffle us and young lives, as well as old ones, will seek other sources of information and inspirations. Shall we as ministers tap the fountains of knowledge and drink daily and be refreshed, or shall we close our ears to an enlarging world of thought, dry up and let our followers perish?

These are days of conferences, plans, programs and undertakings. The highest hope of our utterances is that we shall rise to higher things and meet the challenge of the day.

GUARDING TIME

Time is money—money value, and it is just as essential to save time as it is to save money. A man who will waste time will waste money. Busy men often guard their time with greater care than they do their bank account. It is often easier to get a busy man to give five hundred dollars or a thousand dollars to a good cause than it is to get him to give a week's work. Make every hour count as the way to push your work instead of allowing your work to push you.

We wonder how many of us have a system of getting our work done. Do we break up the day into odds and ends, or have a program? The man with a system for his work will usually find more time for rest than the man without any particular plan by which he works.

If we are stewards of what we possess, we are also stewards of our time, for God gives that to us to use just as He does wealth.

Time! Time!! How we need more of it! Do we? Or do we need to know how to use that which we have? Which?

Construction and reconstruction are the foremost words around which we are endeavoring to build our editorials during these weeks when the local churches are coming together for counsel and for consideration of Kingdom interest.

A DISHONEST CHURCH

Can a church be dishonest? It certainly can, and in more than one way. We limit this note to only one of the ways in which a church may be dishonest—and that is about the matter of paying the pastor.

A church calls a pastor at a certain salary. At the end of the year all the salary is not paid. Is that church dishonest? Just as much so as the man who buys groceries on a credit and fails to settle the account. The promise of a local church to pay a certain salary should be one of the most binding obligations—and it is. If your church owes former pastors for balances on salary it is in debt in the sight of God and

man. Calling another pastor does not exempt a church from paying the former pastor what was promised him. A church that fails to meet its pastoral obligations can no more prosper than an individual who will not pay his honest debts.

Talking about revivals in the church, if some of the churches would turn to their records and settle with former pastors in full, and add interest, a revival would come all right—and it would not take so much preaching to bring it.

Pay your pastor what you owe him. If you want to change pastors, that is the business of the church, but pay your pastor, pay him in full, for the amount is small enough without deductions.

Thousands of homes in this Christian Church of ours never get a visit from a pastor, never see the Church paper, and never have the Church's ideals placed before them. "Our one great—The Christian Sun—in every home."

A LITTLE SHOP TALK

We are coming into that season of the year when we enlarge our stock of books, Bibles and church supplies. Already our fall supply of these things is arriving. Though it is nearly three months before you will need the Sunday school helps, our shelves are laden with Tarbell's Guide, Peloubet's Notes, Torrey's Gist of the Lesson and Arnold's Notes. Bibles and Testaments of most any description can be secured from this office. There was once a time when our customers had to wait to get an order filled; and while it is almost impossible to have on hand everything that calls are received for, we are usually able to ship the same day and by next mail.

Many of the local churches have purchased Communion sets and all are pleased. We can supply you with a Communion set at the same price you can get it for. The commission we get for handling the order goes back to the Church, and in so doing you help a good cause.

At this season of the year churches are thinking of their offering envelopes for another year. We invite the attention of church officials and committees to the prices indicated on page 16 of this issue. We offer an absolute guarantee that if you are not pleased, your money will be refunded without dispute.

Whatever you need in the line we carry, let us know and place your order here. All correspondence will be handled promptly and every courtesy shown.

Forty-six ministers in the Southern Christian Convention are readers of *The Herald of Gospel Liberty.* Sixteen ministers in the American Christian Convention are readers of THE CHRISTIAN SUN. Whether this is a compliment to our ministers or to *The Herald* is not for us to say. *The Herald* being the official organ of the Church does, no doubt, count for the difference to an extent. The thing that grieves us is that every minister in the Southern Christian Convention does not take *The Herald.*

PASTOR AND PEOPLE

HOLLAND, VIRGINIA

Special revival meetings were held with the Holland Christian church beginning on Sunday night of September 21 and closing on Sunday night, September 28.

Rev. J. F. Morgan, pastor of First church, Berkley, Va., did all the preaching from Monday till Saturday night inclusive; and Rev. O. D. Poythress, pastor of South Norfolk Christian church, had charge of the singing.

The pastor takes pleasure in saying, if he is any judge at all, that no two men ever consecrated themselves more to a task than did Brothers Morgan and Poythress in these meetings. The messages of Brother Morgan were deeply spiritual, thoughtful and logical; they were wide sweeping in their reach, and the familiar word was often heard that he missed no one.

Brother Poythress aside from being a preacher himself possesses rare talent in the leadership of music and solo singing. He got the folks to singing and had them in a splendid mood for the message to follow.

At first the meetings were poorly attended and the indifference of the membership was glaring. By Wednesday the crowds began to come. The rain on Tuesday, so much needed, accounted somewhat for small attendance on that day. By Thursday night the large auditorium and gallery were filled to capacity.

At first the prayer meetings were limited to the preachers but these were soon thrown open to all who would come fifteen minutes before each service and herein was a source of power.

The spiritual indifference began gradually to give away and the religion of Jesus Christ had its way. The congregations responded well to the requests of Brothers Morgan and Poythress. About twenty-five decided to accept Christ, mostly young people. There were many reconsecrations.

On Saturday afternoon Brother Morgan conducted his service of "Breaking the Alabaster Box." The request was made that all who were present who had been the recipient of any kindness or favor from another present he should go to such a one, shake hands and thank him. It was a most impressive service and very successful.

The meetings were only marred by the existence of long standing feuds among the membership. Revival meetings come and go and of course do great good, pastor preaches and prays and intercedes but the old feuds go on forever.

The every member canvass is now in progress and the budget of $2,500 for the year bids fair to be covered by pledges.

Immediately following the meetings it was decided to continue the campaign to raise the full amount of the building fund for the dedication of the church this fall. The amount yet to be raised is about $8,000.00 and already several have responded with representative gifts; other gifts are soon to be made. Nothing but the Spirit of Jesus Christ will tie a man to his Church as will a good liberal gift in its construction and their continued support afterwards.

On last Sunday afternoon baptismal services were conducted by the pastor in the church. Nine were baptized by immersion and the same number by sprinkling.

W. M. JAY.

POUNDED

On Saturday evening, October 11, at the close of our service at Wentworth Christian church, the good people of that church and other churches, began to drop packages, sacks and jars into my Ford until I was almost compelled to go home and unload rather than spend the night with some of them. The pounding contained: flour, sugar, syrup, canned fruit, soda, salmon, soap, chicken, rice, coffee, mustard, pound-cake and money. We have been fareing "sumptiously every day" since, but have endeavored to give God thanks rather than take it in the spirit of the rich man. We thank this splendid people more than we can express and only hope to prove our gratitude by more efficient service. May God's richest blessing rest upon these people and reward them for "every good word and work."

I might also state that the salary for the year was also paid in full at the same time of the pounding and a splendid purse over and above salary was given on Sunday with these words: "more to follow." Of course it makes our hearts rejoice.

Another thing of real interest at Wentworth is this: Brother S. C. Hobby of Raleigh, on last Sunday, presented the church with a beautiful individual Communion set that cost $65.00. The gift was highly appreciated by pastor and people and the first use of it made a very impressive service. May God bless the giver and make us to see more clearly the all sufficient gift of His Son for the redemption and safety of those who love Him.

J. LEE JOHNSON.

SUFFOLK LETTER

W. A. King, City Treasurer of Suffolk, Va., died at his residence on Washington street, on Sunday night, October 5, 1919, after a two months' confinement with heart-trouble. He was the son of John G. and Martha Anne King of Nansemond County, and was born February 12, 1853.

He married Etta M. Riddick, daughter of James Edward and Deborah Riddick, thirty-eight years ago. His wife and four daughters survive. The daughters are: Mrs. Finch G. Moseley, Mrs. Robert Holton, Mrs. Otis Smith, and Inez. He leaves three brothers: J. W., E. A., and F. C. King.

He was a faithful member of the Suffolk Christian church and was Secretary of the Sunday school for many years.

He was deputy Treasurer of Nansemond County for some twenty years and, when Suffolk became a city, was deputy city treasurer to N. S. Boykin, until Col. Boykin's death, when he was appointed to the office of treasurer, January 31, 1913, to fill the unexpired term.

At the regular election he was chosen treasurer which office he held in a second term up to the time of his death. His books were always adjudged by the State examiner as among the best kept books in the State.

He was a member of the Elks, Woodmen of the World, Pythians, and Masons. The Masons conducted service at the grave. These orders, and the entire city officials, were represented at the funeral. The floral tributes were many and beautiful. The service was simple, "Safe in the Arms of Jesus" and "Sometime We Will Understand" being sung by the choir, with scripture lessons and prayer by the pastor.

Human life is a link in an endless chain, and links are constantly passing out of sight, and will not appear again until we pass ourselves to the other side. Out of sight, but not out of memory, our loved ones wait for us in that house with "many mansions." "Eye hath not seen, nor ear heard, neither have entered into the heart of man, the things which God hath prepared for them that love Him." "But God hath revealed them unto us by His Spirit; for the Spirit searcheth all things, yea, the deep things of God." That is the source of comfort to Christians. God reveals to believers the hopes that inspire faith in the future life of bliss and re-union. The Christian life is nothing if it does not furnish hope for the *future;* for, "if in this life only we have hope in Christ, we are of all men most miserable."

Mr. King's life justifies this hope and this is a great comfort to his family and his friends. He was faithful in all the relations of life and his home-life was happy. He allowed nothing to interfere with his private or public duty. He will be missed in the home, the church, the office of treasurer and the city.

W. W. STALEY.

TRUTH OR OBEDIENCE?

I have read the Christian Unity Number of *The Herald of Gospel Liberty* with keen relish. I had listened to all the addresses printed therein, but it was worth while to read them again. I am particularly grateful for the Editor's great editorial. Who knows but that Dr. Kerr has come to the tripod for such a time and for such a cause as this? God knows, and the hopeful ray pray that it be so.

But I write not to praise Editor Kerr. His own utterance is his praise. I write to call attention to a point of view expressed in two of the papers printed in the issue that, to my mind needs careful examination. I refer to the papers by Drs. Bagby and Burnett. These beloved brethren refer to truth as conditioning union. Ought it?

But first hear what they say. Dr. Bagby: "Truth first, union afterwards, and union only in truth." Dr. Burnett: "Truth is more desirable than union. A union without truth would be a house of rotten straw in which would dwell all manner of impure things and crawling serpents." It is only fair to say that Dr. Bagby is speaking for the conservative element of the Disciples. Dr. Burnett speaks for our whole people.

Now it is bold for a layman to challenge the position of leading ministers in any Church, and particularly in his own Church, and yet I invite our Brotherhood to a careful scrutiny of what Secretary Burnett says, and let each reader ponder these questions as he thinks.

1. Who is the judge of truth?
2. Has division fostered truth?
3. How is the Christian to be led into the truth?
4. What is the difference between truth and "interpretation"?
5. What has divided the Church?
6. Is truth an insuperable barrier to union?
7. Is truth more likely to be attained by sectarianizing it or by a wholesome testing of it in Christian Union?
8. Since our Master prayed for the union of His followers, has the Church any right to erect barriers of truth rendering such union impossible?
9. Which is preferable—truth or obedience?

I shall not undertake to answer these questions. I shall be satisfied if our brethren will think these queries through for themselves. We should be anxious in this hour to know the mind of Christ for His Church. It is time for us to learn why our plea for Christian Union has fallen flat and to discover the method of doing the thing we have announced to be our ultimate purpose from the beginning.

Have we been searching for truth and failed to obey? Does Secretary Burnett represent our Church in this matter? Does our Church represent Christ in this issue, or must He look for another?

W. A. HARPER.

Elon College, N. C.

WITH BUSY PASTORS

It was a great pleasure, as well as privilege, to spend a Sunday recently with Brother A. W. Andes. He had three appointments for the day, Bethlehem, Concord, and Antioch, and these churches are several miles apart. Brother Andes has three appointments every Sunday. The strain on him and his Ford is immense. But both seem to not only stand up under it, but to thrive on it.

Brother Andes says, however, that such strenuous work gives him little time for his study, that he and his study have almost become strangers. It is a deplorable fact that so many of us preachers are so rushed in meeting and filling engagements that we have only the most meager allowance of time for study, meditation, reading, preparation. Dr. Staley says, in illustration of this sad fact, that you cannot continually draw water out of a pipe unless you continually pump water into the pipe, and that it is as necessary to keep water in the pipe as it is to draw it out for that which came out could not have come unless forced out by that which remained in. I recall another philosopher has somewhere said that we do not and cannot teach that which we have learned and stored up; we can only teach that which we are learning and are acquiring.

Brother Andes is a large and responsible work, and he is giving it his best strength and noblest endeavor. A day's fellowship with him and his good people was a real joy; and $650.00 was either given or pledged for our mission fund. It was indeed a regret that the writer could not remain even for a day longer and give the people a real chance at this great and good thing we are all so much interested in.

Last Sunday, October 12, was spent with Rev. W. L. Wells at Reidsville and an afternoon service with Rev. L. L. Wyrick at Howard's Chapel. Brother Wells is much loved in Reidsville and is building up a substantial and splendid congregation. He and his people are laboring to clear their house of debt and dedicate next spring. This is a great and most worthy undertaking and only by pulling together and all doing their best can the task be accomplished.

The people out at Howard's Chapel are liking Brother Wyrick, say he has improved wonderfully and is gaining in influence and in usefulness around his people. He is faithful and loyal and devoted to his work, and all that counts mightily for success. It was a real joy to be with him and his people in a service.

Our pastors are a hard working, non-complaining, self-sacrificing, hard working class of people. It is a genuine joy to be associated with them and to hear the good things their people say of them and see the real and lasting good they are doing in the world.

J. O. ATKINSON.

VIRGILINA LETTER

My excuse for sending no news from my field in such a long time is not because of a dearth of the same. Much has taken place of both local and general interest.

Hebron has undergone considerable repairs, amounting to twelve hundred dollars, and is now both neat and attractive. We had no protracted meetings here this year on account of the repairs being in progress at the appointed time.

Lebanon held a series of meetings the third week in July. Dr. P. H. Fleming did the preaching. The rainy season interfered and yet no services were missed. While there were no accessions to the church, some of the leading members pronounced it a good meeting and I trust the church is strengthened.

Liberty was also favored with the assistance of Dr. Fleming. Congregations were good. There were many professions and eight united with the church.

Union (Virgilina) had a good revival the second week in August. Immense crowds day and night came to hear the strong sermons of Brother Fleming. There were a number of professions. This church has received over a hundred members in the last five years. A campaign has been on recently for a new church building, resulting in subscriptions to the amount of over eleven thousand dollars. We have purchased six beautiful lots nearer the center of town than our present location, and will, after January first next, turn our attention to planning and erecting a handsome brick house of worship suitable to our needs and present day demands.

C. E. NEWMAN.

The rich ruleth over the poor, and the borrower is servant to the lender. Prov. 22:7. Own some W. S. S. and borrow from your own capital.

UNION GROVE

Our meeting began at Union Grove the third Sunday in August. Rev. J. F. Apple did the preaching throughout the meeting. There were twelve professions. Four joined the church and two were baptized by Brother Apple. Prayer meetings are being held on Sunday evenings since a while before our revival. Several ask for prayer at our prayer meetings and members of the meeting say they wish to keep warm all the year. Cottage prayer meetings are held in the community on Saturday evenings.

Spoon's Chapel

Rev. W. N. Hayes assisted me in the meeting here which began the fourth Sunday in August. There was no outward evidence in this meeting.

Antioch (R)

Our meeting began here the fourth Sunday in September. I was unable to secure pastoral help for this meeting. We have had good congregations throughout the year but no conversions during the revival.

The writer assisted in two meetings—one at Brown's Chapel, there being twelve conversions, and the other at a school house, within four miles of which there is no church. There were six professions here.

L. W. FOGLEMAN.

Seagrove, N. C.

GOOD HOPE

I filled my appointment at Good Hope Saturday and Sunday. Although we have one more appointment there before Conference, we elected our delegates and alternates to Conference and to the Woman's Missionary Convention, November 9 and 10, and raised our Conference apportionments in full last Sunday. We learned, last fall from the "Flu" and previous years from rainy days, not to put so important a matter off until the last moment.

By the way, how many delegates is each Church entitled to this year? We elected two to represent Good Hope.

R. P. CRUMPLER.

ANSWER

In answering Brother Crumpler's question, we quote the following from a letter sent out by the Secretary of the North Carolina Conference on October 15: "Each church may send two delegates and one additional delegate for each fifty members up to 200, but no church can sent over four delegates."

NOTICE

All persons who expect to attend the Eastern Virginia Christian Conference which convenes at Waverly, Virginia, on October 28, 1919, will please notify the undersigned at their earliest convenience, stating what day they expect to arrive in Waverly and whether they will come by train or private conveyance.

R. T. WEST, *Secretary.*

Waverly, Virginia.

Let us have your renewal during this month.

NOTES

Rev. G. R. Underwood changes his address from Ashboro to Bennett, N. C.

Rev. C. E. Gerringer has accepted work at Richland, Ga., and is now at that place.

The Georgia and Alabama Conference is in session this week with the church at Lanett, Alabama.

Brother W. B. Fuller writes that he has had a great summer. laboring in the Master's vineyard and that he has been richly blessed.

Rev. J. W. Harrell left Monday morning for Dayton, Ohio, to attend the Mission Board meeting in session this week.

Brother J. W. Lashley, Durham, N. C., paid us a visit the other day. We are always glad to see our friends.

Brother A. G. Apple, a member of Apple's Chapel church, came in Monday and renewed his subscription. He is one of the *few* in that church who take THE SUN.

Last Saturday morning we had a short, but pleasant call, by Mrs. J. P. Barrett. She was enroute to Columbus, Georgia, to join Dr. Barrett in their new field of labor.

The Woman's Missionary Conference of the Eastern Virginia. Conference will be in session at Portsmouth, Virginia, October 23. Blessings of the Father be upon the work done.

The Burlington congregation is to open its handsome fifty thousand dollar house of worship the first Sunday in November. Dr. C. H. Rowland is to be the speaker at the eleven o'clock hour and Dr. J. O. Atkinson at night.

Brother P. T. Hines, of Raleigh, N. C., called to see us the other day. Brother Hines is connected with the executive and editorial work of *The Progressive Farmer* and is making good.

No comments on the Sunday school lesson this week. We received the material on Saturday afternoon when the Sunday school and Christian Endeavor page had already been closed for the press. We have *repeatedly* reminded the contributors of this material that it must reach us by Wednesday. We are not at fault.

Speaking for the Entertainment Committee of the North Carolina Conference we want to say that homes have been secured for the delegates and that delegates and visitors are urged to comply with the notice in this week's SUN—and do so *at once*. Don't put it off till the last hour.

WORLD MOVEMENTS

On October 16 the first train from Berlin to Paris since the war made its trip.

President Wilson is reported to be steadily improving. He is, however, still confined to his room.

Dr. Lansing Burrows, aged 77, Americus, Georgia, died October 17. For thirty years he was Secretary of the Southern Baptist Convention.

The Federal Government has indicated that it will take over the coal mines and operate them in case of a strike of any duration of time.

Sunday morning, October 26, at 1 o'clock A. M. the time of the nation will be turned back one hour. Thus will end the Day Light Savings Law.

On October 16 the Senate finally took a vote on the Amendment to the Peace Treaty, which Amendment was to give Shantung to China instead of Japan. The Amendment was lost by a vote of 55 to 35.

One day last week 62 aviators started a coast to coast flight. Ten of the 62 were killed. The distance of about 5,400 miles was made in 25 hours. Lieutenant B. W. Maynard, of Sampson County, N. C., seems to be the hero of the "air birds" and has won for himself much recognition.

Action on legislation to remedy the present sugar famine is planned by the Senate Agriculture Committee, which expects to report out the bill authorizing President Wilson to continue the sugar equalization board during 1920 and giving the board power to purchase Cuban sugar.

ACCIDENT PREVENTION DRIVE

Two million railroad employes throughout the United States entered Saturday mid-night upon an intensified campaign against accidents—the National Railroad Accident Prevention. Drive. For two weeks, ending at mid-night Friday, October 31, caution and care will fight for a record clear of injuries and fatalities, which might have been avoided, on every railroad under government control.

The purpose of the drive is to eliminate so far as is humanly possible the avoidable accidents which constantly take a distressing toll of life and limb on the railroads, and thus to demonstrate what caution would mean if practiced day in and day out in the operation of the railroads. Previous campaigns conducted in regions and on individual railroads have given an idea of what can be done. The great nation-wide movement is designed to produce a more forcible demonstration, and, with the co-operation of industries along the railroads, shippers, State and municipal authorities and the public generally, to bring the lesson home to everybody.

Many thanks to our friends for many renewals.

THE LITTLE ECHO

We have an echo in our house,
An echo three years old,
With dimpled cheeks and wistful eyes
And hair of sunny gold.

This little echo, pure and sweet,
Repeats what others say,
And trots about on tireless feet
Upstairs and down all day.

It makes us very careful not
To use a naughty word,
Lest in the echo's lisping tones
It should again be heard.

Which would be such a dreadful thing,
As any one may see,
Who has an echo in their house
A little over three.

—*Selected.*

LIKE CANDY?

Willie's mother was horrified to see her son so neat. He used soap lavishly, even washing behind his ears; he shone his shoes daily; he studied his lessons most thoroughly. It is not the custom in Montenegro to use water very plentifully, even among parents. Therefore Willie was not only a puzzle, but a worry to his mother. Perhaps she feared too much cleanliness spelled saintliness, and Willie had never shown any of the known traits of a saint as the term is usually understood.

Even at the end of a week the enthusiasm had not diminished one bit, and Willie went on with his neatness in the face of violent protests from his mother, his father and his elder brother. They could not understand the docile Willie. He had suddenly developed a mind of his own, they were sure, and that is a fatal error in one so young, for Montenegrins obey their parents without a question as a rule. Willie must be subdued. But how?

It was a radiant boy who came home from school a few days later, bringing a bag of candy, a chocolate bar and several sweet cakes. When he had finally explained to his mother that he had won this as a reward for being clean she was pleased that her son could keep up with the best of them, even if he had to go so far as to digress from the faith of his father in the matter of soap, water and industriousness. It was also a matter of no small interest to the whole family that it was the American Red Cross nurse at the school who had awarded the candy. Therefore Willie's mother was eager to have him keep clean, for to her American ideas were the acme of all that is good.

FROM ME—TO YOU

"Dear American Children, I wish I could go to see you, but that can never happen. Will you come and see us next Christmas?"

Such engagingly intimate messages as this one accompany the hand made gifts which the children of Archangel have sent to the American children as an expression of their appreciation for the lunches that were given them in the schools by the American Red Cross last winter. Hundreds of little Russian children were helped through the perils of hunger by this small attention.

They show a very eager interest in the children of the new world. They have made laborious pencil drawings, colored pictures showing the land-scapes of north Russia, and sea views with blue water and bright red boats. The little children of the "Dom Trudolubia" orphanage have spent many joyous hours fashioning these gay presents and talking about the far-away children in the land that has sent the American Red Cross to them. It is natural that their thoughts should turn to the Juniors of the organization which has befriended them. They cannot let their thoughts and words suffice—their interest does not cease there. They feel that they are now personal friends of the Juniors and that they must express their friendship in a befittingly concrete form. Hence the gifts.

THE CHRISTIAN ORPHANAGE

SUPERINTENDENT'S LETTER

We were made glad on Sunday, October 12, when the clouds gathered thick and black and rain began to fall and continued throughout the night. It was the first rain we had had for weeks and the ground was dry and hard. We had begun to think we would fail to get our wheat crop in, but it was a splendid season and the ground is now in fine working condition and our teams are busy at work, and we hope, though late, that we will get all the wheat and oats in the ground that we intended to sow.

Our singing class had a splendid trip to Long's Chapel on Sunday, October 12, and gave a song service there. There was no preaching but the crowd was very good and the offering amounted to $20.05 and more than $200.00 in subscriptions for the Children's Home. Our little folks, the matron and the writer enjoyed the day very much. It was a pleasure to mingle with the good people of Long's Chapel. The Orphanage has some very strong friends in that community. It is always a pleasure to the writer to go there as it is his old home church and the community in which we spent our boyhood days. It brings back sweet memories of the past, and we often think of the many pleasant days spent in the Sunday school and church there.

We want everybody to have a part in building the Children's Home. Don't wait to be asked to help in this splendid work, but just mail me a letter stating how much you want to give and we will fill out your subscription blank and mail it to you for your signature. Every man, every woman, every boy and every girl should want to help in this undertaking. We are going to build this home and the money will be raised. The question is, Will you have a part? Of all the different calls far charity, missions, college, or any other cause, this is one that I hardily see how a member of the Christian Church can let pass without making a contribution.

"If we work upon marble, it will perish," said Webster; "If upon brass, time will efface it; if we rear temples, they will crumble into dust, but if we work upon immortal minds, we imbue them with principles, with the just fear of God and love of our fellow men; we engrave on those tablets something which will brighten through all eternity."

                              CHAS. D. JOHNSTON, *Supt.*

FINANCIAL REPORT FOR OCTOBER 22, 1919

Amount brought forward, $11,239.10.

Children's Offerings

Bennett and Allen Roberson, 10 cents; Oliver E. Young, Jr., 10 cents; Total, 20 cents.

Sunday School Monthly Offerings
(North Carolina Conference)

Piney Plains, $6.50; Pleasant Union, $10.80; Ebenezer, $4.20; Berea, by J. E. McCauley, $1.84; Bethel, $15.29; Hank's Chapel, $7.50; Sanford, $10.00; Union, (Va.), $2.00.

(Eastern Virginia Conference)

Berea, (Nansemond), $10.00; Windsor, $6.68; Isle of Wight, $2.50; Wakefield, $3.88; Ingram, $3.00.

(Virginia Valley Conference)

Dry Run, $2.22; Wood's Chapel, $1.00.

(Alabama Conference)

Mt. Zion, $1.28; New Hope, $2.75; Beulah, $1.00.

Miscellaneous

Oliver Hill church S. S., Superior, Neb., $10.00; Total, $102.44.

Singing Class

Long's Chapel church, N. C., $20.05.

Children's Home

Mrs. Lula F. Brickhouse, $100.00; Edward Brickhouse, $10.00; A. W. Norwood, $25.00; Total, $135.00.

Special Offerings

W. H. Thomas, on support of children, $25.00; The Star Class, Suffolk, Va., $4.00; J. C. McAdams, Elon College, $10.00; R. S. Caudle, Elon College, $10.00; Mrs. M. Catharine Riddick, Suffolk, Va.; $25.00; Dr. J. O. Atkinson, $47.70; Mr. A. K. Roney, Haw River, N. C., $5.00; Total, $126.70.

Total for the week, $384.39; Grand total, $11,623.49.

LETTERS FROM THE COUSINS

Dear Uncle Charley: I hope the little cousins are enjoying these fall days as much as I. I keep grandmother Young's chickens on the go all the time and prefer spending my time with the cows and pigs. Love for all.—*Oliver E. Young, Jr.*

You must be careful with grandmother's chickens. I knew a little boy one time who got among his mother's chickens with a stick and killed six at one lick. His mother then had a settlement with him.—*"Uncle Charley."*

Dear Uncle Charley: We are two little boys three and six years old, so you see papa is writing for us.

We are sending the orphans five cents apiece. Next time we will tell you about mamma going away from home for her health and about how sad we were.—*Bennette and Allen Roberson.*

You are fine little boys. I hope your mother will soon be well again. Home is not much of a home when moher is gone.—*"Uncle Charley."*

THE UNITED STATES RAILROAD ADMINISTRATION

Announces

Reduced Round Trip Fares and Special Train Service

——Via——

SOUTHERN RAILROAD LINES

——To——

RALEIGH, N. C.

——Account——

NORTH CAROLINA

STATE FAIR AND PEACE JUBILEE

OCTOBER 20 to 25, 1919

Reduced Fare Round Trip Tickets will be on sale October 17, 18, 19, 20, 21, 22, 23, 24th, and for trains scheduled to arrive at Raleigh before noon, October 25th. Final limit returning to reach original starting point by mid-night, October 27, 1919.

In addition to the excellent regular train service, the following special trains will be operated to Raleigh and return for this occasion:

Special Train

Greensboro to Raleigh and return, October 22 and 23

Lv. Greensboro	7:00 a. m.
McLeansburg	7:15 a. m.
Gibsonville	7:30 a. m.
Elon College	7:35 a. m.
Burlington	7:50 a. m.
Graham	7:55 a. m.
Haw River	8:00 a. m.
Mebane	8:15 a. m.
Efland	8:25 a. m.
Hillsboro	8:35 a. m.
University	8:50 a. m.
Durham	9:15 a. m.
East Durham	9:25 a. m.
Morrisville	9:45 a. m.
Cary	9:55 a. m.
Ar. Raleigh	10:15 a. m.

Returning Leave Raleigh 6:00 P. M. (Union Station)

Special Train

Oxford to Raleigh and return, October 23

Lv. Oxford	7:00 m.
Providence	7:15 a. m.
Stem	7:29 a. m.
Lyon	7:37 a. m.
Wilkin	7:44 a. m.
Cozart	7:50 a. m.
Gorman	8:05 a. m.
East Durham	8:35 a. m.
Brassfield	8:45 a. m.

Morrisville .... 8:55 a. m.
Cary .... 9:05 a. m.
Ar. Raleigh .... 9:25 a. m.
Returning Leave Raleigh 6:30 P. M. (Union Station)

Special Train

Chapel Hill Station to Raleigh and return, October 23
Lv. Chapel Hill .... 8:00 a. m.
University .... 8:40 a. m.
Durham .... 9:00 a.m.
Ar. Raleigh .... 10:00 a. m.
Returning Leave Raleigh 7:45 P. M. (Union Station)
Grand Agricultural, Industrial and Educational Displays

Uncle Sam urges you not to miss the United States Government exhibit of War Trophies. Almost every portable device used on land or sea in the World War, both allied and captured German.

For Detailed Information, Call on Local Ticket Agents.

(Advertisement)

PRESERVING HISTORY

The North Carolina Historical Commission is canvassing the entire State for letters, diaries, pictures, newspaper clippings—in fact, all materials of any nature that throw light on North Carolina in the World War. R. B. House, Collector of War Records for the Historical Commission, is conducting this canvass 'by going to the sources of such official records as' Red Cross Chapter Histories, Local Board reports, etc., by organizing volunteer committees to assist him in the various counties, and by going himself from community to community all over the State.

These materials canvassed for, valuable as they are, will perish very rapidly unless they are stored where fire, rats, and other destroying agencies cannot get at them. Practically the only safe depository for such things is the fire-proof Hall of History in Raleigh, built to preserve just such things as these.

Realizing the necessity of preserving these valuable records, the last General Assembly appropriated money for the work, and directed the Historical Commission not only to collect all data possible about North Carolina in the World War, but to prepare a complete history of the State's life in that great event. By this act the General Assembly placed North Carolina among the most progressive States in the Union, for North Carolina was one of the first States to inaugurate a work that all the other States are now taking up.

The General Assembly realized that history is essential to a commonwealth, and therefore placed this work on a stable foundation. The General Assembly but expressed the will of the State, and, since this will is so wisely recorded in the establishment of this work of collecting war records, it is the presumption of the Historical Commission that the people of the State are going to give the materials essential to history.

The fine success already attained by the public spirit of individual donors of material shows that North Carolinians want their State fully represented in history.

Almost every person in the State has a letter, a picture, or something that would be of value. Whatever he has, he should communicate information about it, or send it to R. B. House, Collector of War Records, North Carolina Historical Commission, Raleigh, N. C.

"FOLLOW THE GOOD IMPULSE"

A friend of both men tells me the story. Walter H. Page, our Ambassador in England, said to Edward Bok several years ago: "Do you ever write a letter to a man who does a conspicuously meritorious thing?" On the spot they entered into a comparet to try it. At a famous New York church Mr. Bok heard a sermon that stirred him. He promptly wrote to the pastor telling him so. About six months later he went to the same church again. An official met him. "Are you Mr. Bok, of Philadelphia?" "Yes." "Well, sir, I want to tell you about the letter you wrote to our pastor. As it happened, it reached him on a 'blue Monday.' He was sitting in his study discouraged. He had almost reached the conclusion that his ministry was a failure. Your letter came, and it changed not merely his day, but his decision. It gave him a new heart of grace to go on."

Said the man who told me the story: "Both Mr. Page and Mr. Bok have derived incalculable happiness from their plan. The results have more than justified it. Never frown down a good impulse. If you fail to act on it at once, it may tantalize you for months."—*Public Ledger.*

NOTICE! NOTICE!!

The Committee on Home Assignment for the North Carolina Conference, which meets with the Burlington Church November 11-14, is now ready to receive a list of delegates and visitors from each church. Give the following information when you report: 1. What church you represent; 2. On what day you will arrive; 3. How you expect to come, whether by private conveyance or train; 4. How long you will stay, unless you expect to attend the entire session, which we hope you will.

Trains arrive in Burlington as follows: Going east, 8:10 and 10:08 A. M.; also 4:55 P. M. Trains going west arrive at 5:32 and 11:20 A. M.; 6:30 and 9:23 P. M.

Everything possible will be done to give each visitor and delegate a good home, but we ask that the Committee be notified in due time. Notify the undersigned today.

J. P. MONTGOMERY, Chairman.

Burlington, N. C.

THE SUN'S ASSISTANT EDITOR

The other day THE SUN'S Editor was in his study at work when his baby, Ruth Teague, came running in with a piece of paper and pencil, saying: "I've got to work," and pushing her chair up to another to form a writing place, continued, "I am writing editorials." She will be two years old November 4 and so her editorial career looks hopeful.

We believe that this personal note will not be out of place.

WORSHIP AND MEDITATION

FAITH

(Sermon delivered in the First Christian church, Raleigh, N. C., October 12, 1919, by Rev. Daniel Albright Long, D. D.)

As I walked the streets of Jerusalem a few years ago, I thought, within myself, why is it that the land where Christ and the standard bearers of the Cross preached, should now be land for the Christian missionary? Certainly the candlestick of the Lord is a movable thing. The Union Jack now waves where the Crescent then stood. Terms of Peace and Leagues of Nations claim the attention of statesmen and lawmakers. Yet, all nations are discordant, and belligerent. The heart of humanity yearns for "peace on earth and good will to men." There can be no permanent peace in any heart, or nation, without the spirit to "do justly, love mercy, and walk humbly with God." All mobs, all wars are simply explosions of sin. The highest liberty, in any nation, is the reign of law. To live, and let live, is not Christian. It should be, to live and help to live. An organization to get the most work for the least pay is only organized selfishness. An organization to get the most pay for the least work is only organized selfishness. Faith in, and practice of, the Golden Rule would bring peace, happiness, and prosperity to all men. With all the preaching, and teaching in our land, much of our literature is tainted with rationalism, and saturated with infidelity. Unless the followers of Christ bestir themselves, the pleasant gardens of our prosperity will be uprooted by the whirlwinds of bolshevism, or iron bound by the polar frost of despotism, and these United States become land for the missionaries. For this reason, I propose to speak to you, this morning on FAITH, and the dangers of rationalism, in order that you may go away more determined, if possible, to put you trust more implicity in the world's Redeemer.

Locke defines faith as "Assent to any proposition, which is not made out by deductions of reason," "As coming from God, in some extraordinary way of communication." Paul said: "Now faith is the assurance of things hoped for, the proving of things not seen." Revelation teaches us that "things which are seen were not made of things which do appear."

Rationalism, or adherence to reason as distinct from revelation, is opposed to supernaturalism. It rejects the miraculous in Christianity, disbelieves in revelation and thinks that all the knowledge we have of true religion is derived from unassisted reason. Then the Pantheistic Rationalists, like the disciples of Hegel, resolve Christianity into a metaphysical speculation, of which the gospel history is a loose, popular, mythical equivalent.

Why should Rationalism be so much opposed to mysteries in religion? Even the boldest materialist must acknowledge that his own existance is a mystery. How often has it been imagined that the power of Christianity was to be increased by getting rid of truths that baffle the attempt at precise definition, and shade off into mystery! Drs. Channing and Gannett honestly and ably predicted that what they termed "Liberal Christianity," would prove a great bulwark against infidelity. The new era of faith has not sprung from Liberal Christianity. Never has it proven to be the solvent of unbelief.

There are those who appear to think that Rationalism must triumph and Supernaturalism must be destroyed. On the other hand the Supernaturalist appears to think that the Christian religion will be destroyed if Rationalism is not annihilated. Let us try and take and unprejudiced view of the subject and see if both Rationalism and Supernaturalism have not found that both were at least partially right and partially wrong. Look at Supernaturalism among Protestants. They held to the theory of an infallible Bible. They held the Bible to be inspired both as respects consonants and as respects vowels. It is hardly necessary to say that the number of chapters, verses and punctuation points are not looked upon as inspired by any man who deserves the name of theologian. The next mistaken phase of Supernationalism was the theory of an infallible Church. This was thought to be necessary, in order to guard against mysticism and rationalism. And what was the logical climax of this assumption but an infallible Pope. This saves time, of course, as it excludes all historical objections against the dogma. "It dispenses with the necessity for their detailed refutation by investigation and argument." Even Cardinal Newman has "offered the absolute need of such infallibility as the strongest argument for the fact of its supply." This, you see, would give the Church rest. Your faith would be settled exactly right. You would be in the majority, and you could shear off all troublesome thinkers and sing "stagnant hallelujahs." This would be false conservatism. It would make us, like the Pharisees, who would not acknowledge the "signs of the times," either in John the Baptist or Christ. It was not the men of progress, but the Conservatives, who crucified Christ. It was the Conservatives who introduced the Inquisition, burnt John Huss, and excommunicated Luther. It is true that "all change is not improvement, and all motion is not advancement." But it is equally true that continued growth and regeneration are the imperative conditions of every spiritual life, which will not succumb to death. And would you let everything remain as it is, and say you had infallible authority for so doing? To let everything remain as it is, is just not to let it remain as it is, not to preserve it as a living thing. And if, in the Conservative interest, one would keep watch by a corpse, even there all would not continue to be as it was. However, all genuine progress has its basis in a true Conservatism. According to the Rationalists, the whole Bible must be tested "by reason alone." The wonderful growth of rationalism is due to an abuse of the great Protestant right of private judgment. Having rejected the Pope and the Church in interpreting the Bible, the emancipated intellect could then proceed to reject the authority of the Bible itself. Even Luther rejected the "Epistle of St. James as a mere Epistle of Straw." Hobbes, the deist, denied that Moses wrote any part of the Pentateuch; Spinoza, the Spanish Jew, with more critical knowledge, discarded the entire Bible as inconsistant with his pantheistic views of miracle and inspiration.

The next stage of rationalism was "exegetical." It said it is our duty to save religion from Protestant mysticism, as well as the Catholic traditionalism. Semler, in his "Apparatus of Liberal Interpretation," devised the famous theory of accommodation, according to which Christ and his apostle are supposed to have adapted their religious teachings to the prejudices and superstitions of their contemporaries concerning angels, demons, the Mosaic system, the Messiah, and the judgment. Then it treated the Old Testament as Hebraic Mythology. Gradually the books of the New Testament were claimed to be largely mythical by Gabler, Sieffert and others. The first thing assailed was the birth and childhood of Jesus, then the miracles of his public ministry, resurrection and ascension. And what was left of the Savior of the world by the Rationalist? The historical Christ, with His discourses, alone remained, but without supernatural halo or divine authority. And what is the present stage of rationalism? It is dogmatic, having shown the world that the Bible miracles are myths, it demands the surrender of orthodoxy of every tongue and color. It looks upon its apostles as men of science, advanced thinkers, bold and brave. It regards every man who rejects the supremacy of rationalism, as being about eighteen hundred years behind the times, cowardly and ignorantly floundering about in the great sea of inquiry, without chart or compass. When it reaches its goal, in any community, it wholly supersedes revelation. We said the conservatives, with false notions, of improvement, crucified Christ. All violent attempts of the conservatives to defend the faith, have resulted in great injury to the faith. All the attacks made on religion itself by men of science, from Celsus to this day, have not done so much to bring religion into contempt, as a single persecution for witchcraft, or a Bartholomew massacre of seventy thousand men, women, and babes, in the name of God. What about those radicals, or men of progress, with false notions of improvement, in every age? They simple crucify Christ anew, and desire that Barabbus should be released, tread the cross under foot and set themselves up as those who look upon all men as idolators who make a Savior of Jesus Christ who was not able to save himself. The men of progress took the place of the Jesuits, but introduced the Jacobins with their bloody republic. In place of the heretics fire and stake, they set up the guillotine, and with unspeakable terrorism and fanaticism persecuted all who would not receive their mark, and fell down and worship the unclean spirit, pure reason personified by an harlot, while they wrote upon their door-posts that the Bible was a fable, Jesus Christ an impostor, and death an eternal sleep. After a sufficient amount of blood was shed, the concordat was restored, and the Nation swung to the other extreme, and caused the Emperor to bow before an infallible Pope. There is a happy medium between rationalism and supernaturalism. Revelation is largely natural and rational. In another view, revelation is a universal phinomenon. God is not revealed alone in one Book, or many books. The Creator is everywhere a revealer, and the whole creation, radiant with his intelligence. The migrating birds are moved by the Holy Ghost no less than the nomadic peoples. The bee is inspired to build her cell as well as the artist to mould the statue, or frame the temple. Whether Isaiah or Milton sings, whether Paul or Plato reasons, it is the inspiration of the Almighty which giveth them understanding. Holy Scripture itself is but the crown and compliment of the whole theophany of nature, and divine revelation only the last and highest expression of the Absolute Reason.

The pessimist regards the world, "the worst possible." This opinion is of ancient, as well as of modern growth. The Hindoo mind, for ages "looked upon existence itself as guilt, upon the universe as an illusion or abortion, and upon reabsorption in Brahma or annihilation in Nirvanna, as the only boon of mortals, to be reached after thousands of successive births and deaths." The Greek and Roman Epicureans endeavored to drown the thought of a causeless and purposeless universe in sensual pleasure. It is claimed by pessimists, that the highest wisdom of the Hebrews was expressed in the dirges of Job, and Solomon, on the misery and vanity of life; and that Christianity itself, through its doctrine of sin, had produced a breach between God and the world, requiring the destruction of the latter as vain and worthless. And though the fathers, excepting the Manicheans, had taken a more optimistic view of the origin and object of creation, yet among the scholastics and reformers, the gloomier dogmas of the Church were sometimes pushed toward that pessimistic extreme which the skeptical literature and poetry have since developed. Voltaire opened the movement with his "Satire upon the optimism of Leibnitz." Byron gave voice to the rising tendency in his "Childe Harold", and "Cain;" Shelley in his "Queen Mab" and "Prometheus;" Goethe in his "Faust." It has been echoed in "Lucretius" of Tennyson, the "Empedocles" of Matthew Arnold, the "Vanity pair" of Thackery, and consciously uttered by the Italian poet philosophor, Leopardi, in his passionate dirges upon the disappointments and miseries of existance.

The periodicals of this day are filled with the teaching of the two rival schools of the Naturalists and Supernaturalists. German naturalism explains away the supernatural element altogether. After "Edelman, Bahrdt and Basedow had championed the foreign deism with frivolity and coarseness, and Mendelssohn, Lessin and Reimarus had arrayed it in literary graces, it found more native expression in learned divines and biblical critics who sought to render it exegetically consistend with the sacred writings. Eichorn, whilst respecting the Bible as a religious and moral classic, treated the story of creation as an historical allefory; and the prophecies as poetical rhapsodies. Paulus, assuming Jesus to have been a pure theist and reformer of Judaism, explained his miracles as mere remarkable coincidences or popular illusions, DeWette, Sieffert, and Gabler found numerous traces of the ancient legend—making faculty in both the Old and New Testaments, without accusing either the apostles or the prophets of imposture. And then Strauss, massing together all previous forms of naturalism, simply voices a growing opinion of the learned world, when he expounded Christianity as mythology.

From Germany, naturalism returned to France, where Renan depicted Jesus as a romantic young Hebrew Enthusiast, defied by His followers and invested with thaumaturgic powers which modern science discredits. In England the author of Ecce Homo has revived it in the form on naturalistic Christianity and enthusiasm for humanity; Sinclair has distinguished its classic humanities from Hebraic barbarism and Pauline bigotry; Matthew Arnold opposed its literary sweetness and light to dogmatic harshness and austerity; and Mrs. Humphry Ward depicted its sentimental hero in Robert Ellsmere. In this country it was echoed in the blasphemous wit on Ingersoll. Naturalism largely pervaded our lighter literature, treating Bible stories as myths and stigmatizing reverence for a supernatural religion as ignorance and superstition. There should be no fear for results when truth and error grapple. Yet we see the disciples of Rationalism in the pulpits of our so called orthodox denominations, with cultured tongues, immaculate linen, graceful manners, telling a lost and ruined world that it is not essential for a man to either teach or believe in the physical death of Lazarus, the Virgin birth of Christ, or any of the oriental myths, called miracles, recorded in a certain old book that grandmother called "the Sacred Bible"—God bless the dear old moth eaten Saint. Her ignorant pastor gathered superstitious women about the stagnant pools of theology and taught them to sing those foolish old hymns of Watts and Wesley, but we know better now.

The waves of the coming conflict which is to convulse Christendom to her centre are "beginning to be felt." All "the old signs fail." God answers "no more by Urim and Thummin, nor by dream, nor by prophet." Thunders begin to "mutter in the distance." The winds are "moaning across the surging bosom of the deep." Everything betides the rising of that storm of divine indignation which shall sweep away "the vain refuge of lies."

When the Lord "shall cause His glorious voice to be heard," and shall show the "lighting down of his arm," with the indignation of his anger, in that day, what shall save us? For "judgment will begin at the house of God." Put your trust, neither in worldy learning, nor worldly riches. Put your trust in Him "whose eyes are as a flame of fire, on whose head are many crowns," who is "clothed with a vesture dipped in blood; his name is called the Word of God." For, "Behold, a King shall reign in righteousness, and princes shall rule in judgment. And a man shall be as an hiding place from the wind, and a covert from the tempest; as rivers of water in a dry place, as the shadow of a great rock in a weary land."

Man seeks rest for his yearning heart in something higher and better than himself. The soul can only rest in that which is at rest. The ocean, air and planets never rest.

May your careers ever be onward and upward. Cherish in your souls, these my parting words: You are children of immortality, and citizens of the universe. So live that you may never become afraid of yourselves here, and you will have no fear about meeting your records hereafter.

MISSIONARY

HALF MILLION FOR MISSIONS

The goal for the peoples of the churches composing our Southern Convention has been fixed at half million dollars for missions to be pledged within the next three years, and paid within five years from date of signing the obligation. Will our people give this amount for world wide evangelization, one-half for home, one-half for foreign missions? There is every good reason to believe they should and they will. Suppose, for instance, the people of our churches could become as eager to save men for Christ as they were to kill and be killed, in the recent war, for country and native land? Suppose we were to become as eager to save as we were anxious to destroy during the war? Suppose we were to give as much the next five years to preach the gospel of peace, truth and righteousness, as we had to give the past three years to kill and to be killed on the field of battle, blood and destruction? Then we should easily give not a half million, but several millions for missions at home and abroad.

Some one has estimated and publicly proclaimed that the recent war cost thirty-seven times as many dollars as have been contributed since Christian missions began toward teaching and spreading the gospel of peace and of Christ among men. What do you think of a world in a frenzy of madness, carnage and blood-shed spending thirty-seven times more money in three years to tear down, kill and destroy than it contributed in nineteen centuries to make known the gospel of Christ and save this world from sin?

It is not, therefore, a question of ability; it is a question of will-ability; not a question of can we, a question of will we. If we really desire to do this much for the advancement of the Kingdom, then we shall do it by our Heavenly Father's help.

The war has resulted in putting untold and increasing riches in the hands of the American people. The people have been called upon to give and give again to church, charity and benevolence. Yet they have not given even as they have received, and with all our gifts deducted we are richer by millions than we were before the war began. What are we to do with this great surplus of blood-money? Are we to spend it in waste, luxury and extravagance, or are we to use it to help advance the cause and Kingdom of our Lord?

There were never such calls, such needs, such opportunities for Christian service as today. We Christians of the South are just awakening to our obligations and needs and responsibilities. Long ago we should have had churches in Richmond, Va., Washington, D. C., Atlanta, Ga., Winston-Salem, N. C. These and other growing cities about us have been, and still are, sources of constant drainage and increasing weakness to our Christian churches elsewhere. At last we are moving to stop the loss and increase our members and our strength in two of these centers, Washington and Richmond. It is going to require increasing funds with which to build in these places. A dozen other points in the home field, to say nothing of our increasing demands and opportunities in the foreign field, are claiming our means, attention and efforts.

A long time ago, our Savior realizing that all power had been committed unto Him, all power in heaven and in earth, said, Go ye into all the earth and make disciples of all the nations. In proportion to the zeal, the willingness, the effort, on the part of any people to carry out that command, has been the growth, strength and power of that people. As a people seek to finish His unfinished task and carry on the work He began, they receive and shape that power which was given Him. Giving half million dollars within three years with which to carry on the work of our Lord will not impoverish, but will enrich us, and will not deduct from but add immeasurably to our power, prestige and influence in the world, in doing our Master's work.

And if we get beneath this task with our prayers, our fears and our faith, it will come to pass, and we shall see our dear Church go forward in its great work of helping to redeem and save this wicked and sin-cursed world.

J. O. ATKINSON.

WHAT YOUR LABEL MEANS

(Told in the Language of a Child)

1-1-9 means that your subscription expires January 1, 1919.
2-1-9 means that your subscription expires February 1, 1919.
3-1-9 means that your subscription expires March 1, 1919.
4-1-9 means that your subscription expires April 1, 1919.
5-1-9 means that your subscription expires May 1, 1919.
6-1-9 means that your subscription expires June 1, 1919.
7-1-9 means that your subscription expires July 1, 1919.
8-1-9 means that your subscription expires August 1, 1919.
9-1-9 means that your subscription expires September 1, 1919.
10-1-9 means that your subscription expires October 1, 1919.
11-1-9 means that your subscription expires November 1, 191C.
12-1-9 means that your subscription expires December 1, 1919.

Sunday School and Christian Endeavor

CHRISTIAN ENDEAVOR TOPIC FOR
NOVEMBER 2, 1919

Standing For God and the Right.
—Kings 18:17-24.

(J. V. Knight)

Too often our consecration services are meaningless. They are much like the testimony of a man who testified in a meeting that he had more ups and downs than any man in the world, and closed by asking the people to pray that he might hold out faithful. Simply holding one's own is by no means sufficient.

The Christian life is a matter of growth and development from the day of one's spiritual birth until he reaches the great climax in Christ. There can be no standstill. We are growing weaker or stronger, and that in proportion to our attitude toward God and His kingdom work. We grow strong by holding on to God's Word—the devotional life and by putting in practice the religion we claim to possess. Standing for God and the right does not always make one popular, but it does make him safe. Elijah found his strength increasing as he stood firm for the right.

To consecrate ourselves to the same thing every month is doing little to aid us in Christian development. What we need is to consecrate ourselves to some larger things we wish done, and not be afraid to do it. Let us center our minds upon one thing: Consecrate everything we have to that end. Go about it in the Spirit of Elijah, a Daniel, a Gideon, a Paul, or Christ Himself, and know that standing for God and right is better than the riches of the world and is the only thing that safeguards life.

Suggestions

Christian Endeavor in Dixie has a large task to perform. Let each Endeavorer consecrate his or her life to some of the following things:

1. Help the 8,000 churches in Dixie that have no Young People's Society of any kind.

2. Seventy-five per cent of the churches in Dixie have only one service per month. Help them by consecrating your own life to full time service for Christ.

3. Help your denominational missions. And give your own Church a chance to grow.

4. Help your own society by volunteering to be a leader, teach a Sunday school class, lead a mission study class or be a junior superintendent.

THE HONORABLE CRIMSON TREE

Suppose you had never seen a tree in all your life? Suppose a foreign woman were to give you two or three little seeds that a little boy far across the ocean sent as a gift? Suppose that the whole village united in planting the tiny tree that had grown from the seed, on a specially prepared mound, do you think you would

---

SUMMER IS DYING

Ah! 'tis a melancholy hour .
When fades . the fragrant Summer flower,
When through the woods and meadows dry
The thistle-ghosts go drifting by,
While soft and solemn winds seem sighing,
"Summer is dying."

Ah! 'tis a melancholy scene
When fields no longer smile serene
With waving grain, when .birds have flown,
And gladness seems to sadness grown,
When reminiscent winds seem sighing,
"Summer is dying."

Ah! 'tis a melancholy sound
When leaves begin to rustle round,
When crickets chirp their lonely lays .
In tune to thoughts of bygone days,
While restless, plaintive winds seem sighing,
"Summer is dying."

Ah! 'tis a melancholy air
That nips the heart with . withering care;
But bird-like, let our minds take wing
To soulful southlands, there to sing
Beyond the chill winds that seem sighing,
"Summer is dying."
—*Arcanus in New York Times.*

---

consider the tree precious enough to almost give your life for it as little Lin did in the village of the Crimson Fish, and when the little leaves turned crimson in the fall, if you had never seen a maple tree, would you fear it was going to die, and lose all desire for life yourself?

Or suppose you were a little girl and had been taught that girls could not possibly learn anything? Suppose that you were so anxious for even the tiniest bits of knowledge that you would climb up on your stilts and listen through the oil-paper windows of the school? How would you feel to hear that girls could really learn something; that a woman teacher was coming to the village, who would teach you of the Jesus religion that said even girl babies were worth while, and that little girls could go to school?

Or again if you were a little boy whose corn that he was so eagerly watching because he belonged to a Boys' Corn Club had been cut down by an angry father, do you think you would run ten miles at night to save the corn of the other boys?

All of these stories, and five others which the children will thoroughly enjoy are told in "The Honorable Crimson Tree," a book of Mission studies, especially prepared for use in Sunday school classes or Willing Workers Societies. They are stories which can be read or told to children, while the many illustrations make the book especially interesting. Get a copy now and use it alternate Sundays in your class. The cost is slight, 40 cents in paper, and 60 cents in cloth. It can be purchased of the Missionary Education Movement, Fifth Avenue, New York City. C. B. Riddle, Burlington, N. C., will secure it for you. If you want to use it with helps to make it more realistic, add ten cents for a pamphlet telling you how to do it.

MRS. FRED BULLOCK.

OBITUARIES

RESOLUTIONS OF RESPECT—HOLLAND

Since it has pleased God in His infinite wisdom to take from our midst, Mr. Joseph F. Holland we feel our Society has lost one of its loyal members. He was a good and kind man, Be it Resolved:

1. That we bow in submission to the will of God Who doeth all things well.

2. That we offer his bereaved family and friends our heart-felt sympathy and commend to them the Savior as a Comforter and guide.

3. That a copy of these resolutions be entered upon our Society records, a copy sent to the bereaved family, and a copy sent to The Christian Sun for publication.

MRS. NOVELLA HOLLAND,
MRS. E. M. TILGHMAN,
MRS. CHAS. DAUGHTRY.

SHARPE

Jesse Boon Sharpe died at his home near Haw River, N. C., October 11, 1919, aged 51 years, 4 months and 1 day. He leaves a wife and six children. His wife is a daughter of Anderson Thomas and a relative of Joe Thomas, "The White Pilgrim."

Mr. Sharpe was interested in the church and other things pertaining to the Kingdom of Christ. He was a member of the Junior Order and representatives of the Order were pall bearers and took part in the committal service at the grave.

A friend of his said to me, "A good man has gone." It was a beautiful tribute from one who knew him well.

The funeral services were conducted by the writer at Long's Chapel in the presence of a large audience. The interment was in the church cemetery. May the dear Master comfort those who mourn.

P. H. FLEMING.

BRYANT

John N. Bryant was born in Southampton County, Virginia, in 1842 and died at his home in Isle of Wight County, near Zuni, Va., October 2, 1919, being in his seventy-seventh year. The funeral service was conducted at his home by Rev. Mr. Brooks, pastor of Black Creek Baptist church, of which he was a member, and his remains were carried to Southampton for burial.

Mr. Bryant was twice married. His first marriage was to Miss Eliza J. Camp.

To this union were born seven children; four sons and three daughters. His second marriage was to Miss Anna Hatfield. To this union were born six children; three sons and three daughters, all of whom are living. "Asleep in Jesus, Blessed Sleep." We miss you father, but our miss is your gain.

M. T. BARRETT.

CANNADA

Mrs. Margaret Cannada was born in 1844 and died September 13, 1919. She leaves three step-children and five children of her own: Mrs. A. M. Culberson, Durham, N. C.; Thomas C. Cannada, Durham, N. C., Mrs. Jennie Partin, Chapel Hill, N. C., C. W. Cannada, St. Augustine, Fla., and B. C. Cannada, Durham, N. C. The step-children are: Mrs. J. W. Lashley, Durham, N. C.; Mrs. D. A. McLennan, Chapel Hill, N. C., and Mrs. Salima Morgan, Chapel Hill, N. C.

For many years Mrs. Cannada was a faithful member of the Christian Church. When the end came she expressed her readiness to meet God.

The funeral was conducted by the writer, assisted by Rev. B. J. Howard and the interment was made in the Damascus cemetery.

May the Spirit comfort the loved ones.

R. F. BROWN.

LINDSAY

William Leonard Lindsay, son of W. E. Lindsay of Chapel Hill, was born January 15, 1899 and died October 12, 1919, aged 20 years, 8 months and 27 days. He professed faith in Christ in his thirteenth year and united with the Christian Church. He lived a consistent Christian life and was loved by all who knew him. In the community, in the athletic field, on the University campus and in the Church and Sunday' schol he was very active until about a year ago when he was taken sick. Since that time he has been to a number of places trying to build up his shattered nerves which the influenza upset about a year ago. He was a brilliant young man, and but for his sickness and untimely death he would have graduated from the State University by the time he was 21 years old.

The funeral was conducted from the Chapel Hill Christian church of which the deceased was a member. The writer was assisted in the services by Rev. Mr. Baskin of the Baptist Church. The interment was made in the Chapel Hill ceme-

tery. His grave was covered with beautiful flowers, and sprinkled with the tears of many relatives and friends.

May the Holy Spirit comfort the bereaved ones.

R. F. BROWN.

IDENTIFIED BY BIBLE

Many a man has found himself through his Bible. A striking instance of the establishment of the identity of a shell shocked soldier by means of his Testament was recently disclosed by a Red Cross worker.

A letter came into the Bureau of Communication at Washington, from an anxious mother in Oklahoma begging for information regarding her son, of whom she could learn nothing except that he was in some hospital in this country. Careful searching of the records of various army hospitals did not reveal the name of the soldier. At length a Red Cross visitor was dispatched to a hospital where mental cases are treated. A man by the surname of the soldier sought was discovered, and although the first name differed the searched decided to see him.

Tall, blonde and clean cut, the youth who was ushered into the receiving room at first appeared quite normal, but upon conversing with him the visitor discovered that his mind wandered perceptibly and he could give little definite information about himself. Collecting his possessions to show his caller, the boy brought forward, among other things, a well worn Testament. On the fly leaf was a name identical with that of the soldier sought.

The Red Cross worker begged the young man to loan the Bible to her, and he willingly complied with her request. She immediately dispatched the precious packet to the mother, asking if it belonged to her son. By return mail came a letter full of thanksiving and praise of the Red Cross. The Testament was one which the Oklahoma boy had treasured from early childhood.

SMILES

Husband: "We'll have to economize, dear."

Wife: "Well, let's smoke less."

Hard-Boiled Drill Sergeant: "Straighten out that line there! Wha' d' ya think this is—the Rainbow Division?"—*Judge.*

"Truth is truth," said Uncle Ezra, "but some folks carry it out to more decimal places than others."—*Christian Endeavor World.*

"I paint what I see," an art student once said to his master, complacently.

"Well, the shock will come when you really see what you've painted," said the artist.—*Boston Transcript.*

There was once a gentleman who wired a book concern for a copy of Murray's "Seekers After God." The answering telegram said, "No 'Seekers After God' in either New York or Chicago. Try Cincinnati.'"

Johnny: "Dad, there's a girl at our school whom we call Postscript."

Dad: "Postscript? What do you call her Postscript for?"

Johnny: "Cos her name is Adeline Moore."

Johnny came home from Sunday school quite thrilled by the lesson. "It was all about the Midnights," he said.

"The what?" asked his father.

"The Midnights," repeated the boy. "The teacher told us how Gideon fought the Midnights and knocked the daylights out of 'em in no time."—*Boston Transcript.*

A leading citizen in a small town was suddenly stricken with appendicitis and an operation became necessary. The editor of the local paper heard of it and printed this note about it: "Our esteemed fellow citizen, James L. Brown, will go to the hospital tomorrow to be operated upon for the removal of his appendix by Dr. Jones. He will leave a wife and two children."—*Truth Seeker.*

Don't put off the matter of purchasing your church envelopes too late. Remember that they must be printed after the order is received.

CHURCH OFFERING ENVELOPES

Standard Double

(Size 2½X4¼ inches—52 to Set)

White or Manila

25 to 49 sets	16 cts. a set
50 to 109 sets	14 cts. a set
110 to 209 sets	13 cts. a set
210 to 309 sets	12½ cts. a set
310 to 399 sets	12 cts. a set
400 or more sets	11 cts. a set

Minimum Charge $3.00 net.

CARTONS INCLUDED

Single Envelope System

(Size 2 5-10X3 5-8 inches. Open side. 52 to Set)

White or Manila

25 to 49 sets	14 cts. a set
50 to 99 sets	13 cts. a set
100 to 149 sets	12 cts a set
150 to 199 sets	11½ cts. a set
200 to 249 sets	11 cts. a set
250 or more sets	10 cts. a set

Minimum Charge $2.00 set.

CARTONS INCLUDED

Take Note

The following points should be taken into consideration in placing an order for church offering envelopes:

1. A set means 52 envelopes, one for each Sunday in the year.

2. When cartons are ordered the sets are arranged in their logical order, thus making it convenient for the member. We suggest the use of cartons because of the convenience.

3. If you desire monthly, double or single envelopes, without cartons, 1-3 the price of the same number of weekly sets. Cartons 3-4 cent each.

4. Semi-monthly, double or single, in cartons, 2-3 the weekly price; without cartons 3-5 the weekly price,

5. When ordering state what Sunday that your church year begins, and whether you want the dates on envelopes or not.

6. Indicate the wording that you want placed on the envelopes or leave the same with us. Samples sent upon request.

7. Allow ten to fifteen days for delivery. Order early.

C. B. RIDDLE, Publishing Agent

Burlington,   N. C.

TARBELL'S TEACHERS' GUIDE

—for the—

Efficient Sunday School Teacher. $1.60 postpaid, or $1.50 when purchased at this office.

Order Early

THE CHRISTIAN SUN

IN ESSENTIALS UNITY, IN NON-ESSENTIALS LIBERTY, IN ALL THINGS CHARITY

Is Man Progressive?

PROGRESS cannot come without a *change*. A change is not forsaking the old for new, but building upon the old, enlarging the old, and making it serve greater and better. A tree is beautiful because it develops. A flower is admired because it grows into loveliness, and a child is the favorite of parents because it grows into manhood or womanhood. The physical world is admired by more people than the mental world, and there is a reason. The physical world automatically changes and the mental world is at the mercy of mankind. Then, is man progressive?

Volume LXXI   WEDNESDAY, OCTOBER 29, 1919   Number 44

BURLINGTON   •   •   •   NORTH CAROLINA

THE CHRISTIAN SUN

Founded 1844 by Rev. Daniel W. Kerr

C. B. RIDDLE - - - **Editor**

Entered at the Burlington, N. C. Post Office as second class matter.

Subscription Rates

One year .... $ 2.00
Six months 1.00

In Advance

Give both your old and new postoffice when asking that your address be changed.

The change of your label is your receipt for money. When receipts sent upon request.

Many persons subscribe for friends, intending that the paper be stopped at the end of the year. If instructions are given to this effect, they will receive attention at the proper time.

Marriage and obituary notices not exceeding 150 words printed free if received within 60 days from date of event, all over this at the rate of one-half cent a word.

Original poetry not accepted for publication.

Principles of the Christian Church

(1) The Lord Jesus Christ is the only Head of the Church.
(2) Christian is a sufficient name of the Church.
(3) The Holy Bible is a sufficient rule of faith and practice.
(4) Christian character is a sufficient test of fellowship, and of church membership.
(5) The right of private judgment and the liberty of conscience is a right and a privilege that should be accorded to, and exercised by all.

EDITORIAL

"THOSE OLD TABLES"

We quote these words because they are what we have so often heard from printers when the tables on the 'Christian Annual' had to be set (we have also heard other things not suitable to quote here—or elsewhere). We have seen the best linotype operators work for a whole day on setting the type on one page of this complicated matter. Then we have seen the hand compositor work for hours trying to get the figures to "line up"—and then when he felt sure that it was right, find that he was one line "off"—and the whole thing had to be gone over. Was this the end of the trouble with "those old tables"? No. After hours of reading and comparing, space could not be found for the changes, and then back to the linotype operator, the make-up man and back to the proof reader for more long hours of tedious reading.

Expensive? Sure, *and but few printers desire this class of work at any price.*

Can there be any substitute for this Chinese puzzle and expensive work in a time like this when labor is scarce and wages high? Let us see if a change cannot be made, and *how*, and *how* to begin.

Let us take the Apportionment Table of Eastern Virginia Conference, since we have the *Annual* open on that page. This Conference apportioned for its churches last year $7,500.00. It took the setting of 1,587 separate figures to set the type *in addition* to the names of the churches, the funds to be used for, etc. Could this table have been condensed and served the same purpose? Here is the answer to it:

APPORTIONMENTS—1918-1919

CHURCHES

Antioch	$ 232.00	Lamberts Pt.	51.00
Barrett's	87.00	Mt. Carmel	188.00
Berea (Nans.)	287.00	Mt. Zion	45.00
Berea (Norfok)	137.00	Memorial Temple ...	388.00
Berkley	170.00	New Lebanon	97.00
Bethlehem	299.00	Newport News	106.00
Burton's Grove	51.00	Oakland	177.00
Cypress Chapel	215.00	Oak Grove	61.00
Centerville	58.00	Portsmouth	327.00
Damascus	302.00	Rosemont	100.00
Dendron	110.00	Sarem	68.00
Eure'a	131.00	South Norfolk	78.00
Franklin	300.00	Spring Hill	59.00
Holland	398.00	Suffolk	1,800.00
Hobson	32.00	Third Church	154.00
Holy Neck	485.00	Union (South)	82.00
Isle of Wight	110.00	Union (Surry)	76.00
Ivor	84.00	Wakefield	68.00
Johnson's Grove	73.00	Waverly	283.00
Liberty Spring	241.00	Windsor	76.00
		Total ....$7,500.00.	

Here are forty churches listed in a space of about one-fourth the size of the original table, and set in one-fifteenth the time.

This gets by with the list of churches and the total each one is apportioned, also the total amount asked of the whole group of churches. How can we indicate to each church what its apportionment is to go for? This question will have to be answered, and so let us do it by first asking another question; Are the local churches not generous enough to let the Conference make out its budget and designate this on a percentage basis as to its use? What we mean is this: The churches above listed were asked to raise $7,500.00—*and each church told what its part was to be*; and what made matters complicated was the setting forth in tabulated form how this was to be divided with each local church. Why not, on a percentage basis, indicate the distribution of the $7,500.00 and let the local churches understand that the basis on which this is distributed would constitute about their per cent proportion to each fund? Concretely here it is:

Total Conference Apportionment—$7,500.00

Funds:	Per cent
Home Missions	15
Foreign Missions	19
Education	5
Superannuated	2
Conference	8
Convention	10
Elon College	20
Convention Missions	20
Total.................................	100%

(Note that the above percentages do not exactly tally with totals given in the *Annual*, but are approximate and indicate what we mean).

The above, together with the names of the churches and the amounts they are apportioned, is all that is required in mechanical work for the table, and at the same time simplifies the matter for the local churches.

This does not, as you have observed, provide for the general table showing what each church actually paid. If the apportionment is arranged as we have suggested, the next year will provide for that. For instance, a church is apportioned, say $233.00, as the first church in our list was apportioned, you will have:

Churches	Apportioned	Paid
Antioch	$233.00	$248.50

Your argument may be that if the local church is apportioned a fixed sum, that it should know where and how that the amount is to go. Very well, but as stated above the local churches must know this—that about the proportional percent division of the sum total will be their basis of paying to each fund; and that the Conference should be wise enough to make the proper distribution. *And does the Conference not make the division anyway when it fixes the apportionment?*

What advantages will come from this new arrangement? Here they are:

1. It will lessen the task of the Apportionment Committee.

2. It will simplify the Conference work.

3. It will take details off your Conference treasurer.

4. It will lessen and simplify the work of the treasurer of the local church. He will not have to keep separate all the funds.

5. It will save money and conserve labor, two things the Church advocates.

6. It will educate the local churches to see that they are building into a unified program, and that the Conference is their servant.

The table giving the church officers, pastors, etc., is very simple as it is, though it could be remedied. However, we will leave that for a later discussion and await the consideration of the brethren on what we have already suggested.

"The only real heretic among ministers is the man who refuses to do anything for himself. But if he thinks wider than the Church or in advance of it, nothing more is demanded of him than that he prove by his clear reasoning and his unimpeached character that his conclusions are worth while."

NOVEMBER EIGHTH-NINTH

We feel that November 8-9 will be a period of worth while history making for the women of the North Carolina Conference. This date is to be the time for the meeting of the first united session of Woman's Missionary Societies of the Eastern, Western, and North Carolina and Virginia Conferences. The Societies in the three former Conferences have had the same objectives, plans, purposes and programs. Leaders from one section have often inspired and encouraged workers in another section. They have now come together for greater encouragement, more inspiration and wiser counsel. We entertain the hope that every church embraced by the North Carolina Conference will be represented by at least one delegate. Whether your church has a Missionary Society or not, it would be a fine idea to send a representative woman to investigate and see if a Missionary Society is not worth while.

The officers have planned, prayed and sacrificed that a GREAT session may be possible, and we feel satisfied that the churches will meet this challenge by a full representation. See notices in this issue of THE SUN and heed the call. It is worthy.

"Small men are not sufficient for the Christian ministry today. The world has thrown down the challenge to the Church, and the Church must respond with men big enough to grapple with the world and subdue it to the dominion of Christ. The ministry is the big opportunity for the man who is big enough to grasp it."

A QUESTION FOR THE HERALD

Speaking for ourselves and many others, we question *The Herald of Gospel Liberty* why it does not publish the Sunday school and Christian Endeavor topics one week earlier? We presume that the majority of *Herald* subscribers get the paper in time to use the comments, but often *The Herald* does not reach this part of the Brotherhood until Saturday and sometimes Sunday. At any event the material on these topics must be used at the last moment.

We have too much "on the spur of the moment" preparation for Sunday school teaching to say nothing of those who are taught. A prepared class develops a prepared teacher.

Why not *The Herald* serve all of its constituency with its able comments on the Sunday school lesson and Christian Endeavor topic? Will Editor Kerr tell us?

THE SOUL OF THE INDIAN

In discussing "the Soul of the Indian" at the conference for Christian workers among Indians, held recently in Wichita, Kansas, under the auspices of the Joint Committee on Indian Missions of the Home Missions Council, the Right Reverend Hugh L. Burleson, D. D., Bishop of South Dakota, said: "The American Indian is a natural poet and philosopher, a mystic and dreamer. He is more naturally religious than the white man, he has a sense of the Divine Presence. He has a craving for guidance. He is not stolid; he only wants you to show that you care. He has a social concept of life; he thinks in terms of the group. Even his thriftlessness and his lust for blood revenge spring from his identifying himself and others with the group. The Indian problem is really the problem of the white man to get him to treat the Indian with due regard for the latter's soul and personality."

Seest thou a man diligent in his business? He shall stand before kings, he shall not stand before mean men. Prov. 22:29. It is the moral support of capital back of him that gives the diligent man dignity in the presence of the king.

ANOTHER INCREASE

The Christian Observer, Louisville, Ky. was once two dollars the year and then went up to two and a half. It now announces to its readers that the price will soon go to three dollars the year. We feel safe in saying that the advanced price will not much more than pay actual expenses.

This is only another reminder of the problem that is before THE SUN. It is now costing about two and one-half dollars per subscription per year to issue THE SUN and it is being sold at two dollars the year. The difference is made up by the Convention, and this means that no subscriber pays for all he gets, though two men (and one woman) have written during the last *three* years that the paper is not worth the price.

The paper on which THE SUN is printed is costing three cents more per pound than it did four months ago, and one and one-half cents more than it did sixty days ago. This means that THE SUN is to cost more each week than it did a few weeks ago and the price to remain the same. Slowly we are adding on a few more subscribers which will also increase the cost per issue, though the additional income will help to offset this.

As a matter for Conferences and the Convention members to consider is this: No man can continue to edit THE SUN on the present salary, unless the Convention can find a man who has the time to sacrifice and can live from some other source. If the work is worth placing on par with a good pastorate (and if working ten hours a day, and seven days to the week is any comparison, it is) then the extra cost is to be realized from some source. The Convention is to provide for that source, unless it can operate THE SUN without it.

This message is not out of season. It will suffice for the time to say it on Conference floors. It will be an advanced notice of some of the things that delegates elected by present Conferences will have to consider at the next Convention. *And let it be remembered that we are not speaking for the present incumbent but for the benefit of the Church.*

This one another thought: Not only will the Convention have to provide for an adequate salary, but a supplement fund to meet incidential expenses. The present plan does not provide for that, and too often must the Editor meet expense that he cannot avoid and get by with decent treatment to the public.

Of course the Convention will provide, but this note is to inform the people so that what they are called upon to do will not be foreign to them.

"God wants a man to preach the Gospel. If I am that man how can I justify myself before Him if I evade this work?"

HELP THE ORPHANAGES

We present in this issue of THE SUN an appeal from the Publicity Committee of the North Carolina Orphanage Association. The appeal is worthy of a place in this paper and the institutions of North Carolina that are doing so much for the homeless children are worthy of your consideration. These institutions depend, largely, upon the free-will offerings of the people. The money is wisely expended and goes to help those who cannot help themselves.

Set aside the earnings of one day's labor and send it to whichever orphanage you desire. You will be richly blessed by the act, a good cause helped and some child given a better opportunity. Don't forget it. Put it on your note book. Put it on your heart.

"There is hope for the world and for the Church when so many young men deliberately repudiate careers that appeal directly to self-interest and turn to careers that mean sacvifice and service."

HAVE YOUR CHURCH REPRESENTED

The North Carolina Conference is soon to meet. Will your church be represented? This is the initial session of the united Conference and it is the privilege of every church to be well represented in this session.

Whether you believe it or not, a new day of opportunity for service is upon us. Great things are in store for the churches of the North Carolina Conference. Local churches must see that the best plans are laid, the wisest steps taken and the Kingdom's work enlarged. These are the things that challenge the churches of the North Carolina Conference.

We pity that church that does not have leadership and pride enough to be represented at the annual Conference. What is the answer of your church to the call for delegates? Will the answer please the Master? See that your church is represented. See to it at once.

"World forces are struggling now to decide the destiny of all humanity for generations to come. The time has passed forever when the Gospel can be preached only in terms of local needs."

YOUR WINTER'S READING

The long winter nights are approaching and many of us will have more time for a wider reading. The time is now at hand when we should select several good papers for that purpose. It is a tragedy for the members of the family to have no more to do than to idle away time after the evening meal. Each member of the family capable of reading should have suitable pieces of reading matter. The children should have good books and papers, and the older members something to please and satisfy them.

What are you going to read this winter? How do you plan to spend the winter evening? If this paper can serve and assist, call upon us.

"The Church needs ministers, more of them and of a better sort."

PASTOR AND PEOPLE

NORTH CAROLINA CONFERENCE

The North Carolina Conference, representing the former Eastern, Western, and Carolina and Virginia Conerence, holds its initial session at Burlington, November 11-14. Each church is expected to send at least two delegates. Churches with 150 members may send three, and those with 200 or more members, four.

Church letters and the tentative program and other literature has been sent to every church and we hope for a blessed session.

Let us pray for the Conference and for a full representation.

W. A. HARPER, *Secretary.*

NOTICE! NOTICE!!

The Committee on Home Assignment for the North Carolina Conference, which meets with the Burlington Church November 11-14, is now ready to receive a list of delegates and visitors from each church. Give the following information when you report: 1. What church you represent; 2. On what day you will arrive; 3. How you expect to come, whether by private conveyance or train; 4. How long you will stay, unless you expect to attend the entire session, which we hope you will.

Trains arrive in Burlington as follows: Going east, 8:10 and 10:08 A. M.; also 4:55 P. M. Trains going west arrive at 5:32 and 11:20 A. M.; 6:30 and 9:23 P. M.

Everything possible will be done to give each visitor and delegate a good home, but we ask that the Committee be notified in due time. Notify the undersigned today.

J. P. MONTGOMERY, *Chairman.*

Burlington, N. C.

SUFFOLK LETTER

For many years I have held the opinion, and several times have written that the United States should require aliens, who come to this country to reside, to drop foreign languages and learn American English; that newspapers should not be printed in alien languages; that ministers should not preach in a foreign tongue; and that we should have "one country, one language, one flag." This conviction grows upon me in the light of current events. There can be no coherent nation without unity of language. European nations are groups of human language. People who speak the same language, think in the same terms, are united in purpose and life.

The Lord said of those who began to build a city and a "tower whose top may reach heaven," "Behold, the people is one, and they have one language; nothing will be restrained from them, which they purpose to do." "Let us confound their language, that they may not understand one another's speech." "So the Lord scattered them upon the face of all the earth; and they left off to build the city." It was the confusion of tongues that stopped the work. It will stop good work as well as evil work. A conference of many languages would reach no conclusion without an interpreter to reduce the languages to one language. They called the name of this tower "Babel," because the Lord did confound the language of all the earth. That confusion of tongues to prevent united and converted evil divided the human race; hence the division is language division. The race seems to have been united until divided language came...

In ancient Greece where learning reached the climax, the nation was divided by dialects, and those dialects were always at war with one another. So vital is the matter of language in the unity of the race and the welfare of society, that degrees of education and character separate men into groups on the principle of "birds of a feather flock together." There are intellectual groups or clubs, moral and social groups or clubs, based on the language they use in ordinary conversation. University men and illiterates do not associate on intimate terms, though they speak the *same* language; all greater difference between people who speak a different language. Men of vulgar speech and men of chaste speech do not group; the language of character keeps them apart. Language is a divider or unifier. A democracy cannot exist in safety in the midst of divided language. America must maintain her own language or lose her own freedom. It is even folly to teach modern languages in the schools. It is a vulgar truckle to another language to put social cards and hotel menu cards in French. If our language is not good enough for our use, let us make it better or move to a foreign country. Patriotism is locked up in language. The man who does not love our English does not love our flag. We have the best flag on earth. We have the best language on earth. We have the best government on earth. We have the best people on earth. But they could all be made better, if we had one language. Silence alien speech; beat out alien print; close alien schools; expel alien plots; unify the hundred million souls in the United States, then Christianize the hundred million souls, and it will be a nation invincible, a nation whose God is the Lord.

W. W. STALEY.

PLEASANT GROVE—INGRAM

Rural conditions are such that country churches can no longer hope to thrive in a passive, inactive manner. Times were when church services were a natural thing coming for country folks as regularly, irresistably, monthly as as the moon itself. That time has passed. Just as has the incandescent lights robbed the country moon of some of its glory just so has modern travel, communication and attraction won large masses away from the old type of country church. The modern newspaper makes the one time popular long "talk" by the minister before he begins his discourse unnecessary.

The printed page has changed the preacher's possibility of holding an audience for two and a half hours. The farmers' systematic book-keeping, systematic banking, and modern methods of making their crops have revolutionized their ideas of what every other institution or enterprise with which they come in contact ought to be. The farmer is no longer a "hay seed" if he has ever merited the title. His is a business. Crops no longer come inadvertently, but by thoughtful and pains-taking planning along with the laboring. The farmer is no longer ignorant of the methods of insurance and banking houses and he has now to actually cope with the industrial establishments. He demands, therefore, that his church be no longer a passive, inactive institution in his community.

The writer is fully aware of the fact that these are not entirely new ideas. It does not take a prophet to see them for the things mentioned are already material of historians.

Pleasant Grove and Ingram, striving ever to keep abreast of the times, have employed their pastor for his full time. His salary is adequate, and they expect him to be a student of the country church problem. For a country pastor to be a real pastor he must study his Bible and his particular field. In my study I have found the following books of great value: "The Challenge of the Open Country," by G. W. Fiske; "The Making of a Country Parish," by Harlowe S. Miles; "The Church of the Open Country," by W. H. Wilson; "The Country Life Movement," by L. H. Bailey; "The Country Church," by C. O. Gill and Gifford Pinchot; "Modern Methods in the Country Church," by M. B. McNutt; "The Rural Church," by Henry Wallace; "The Country Church and the Rural Problem," by K. L. Butterfield; and "The Country Church in the South," by Victor I. Masters. But for the actual study of your own parish I have found nothing better than the method and outline of a country church survey prepared by Ralph A. Felton and published by the Missionary Education Movement, 156 Fifth Ave., New York. It contains blank spaces after 47 questions concerning each individual family in a community. It is a complete and neat volume and is well bound. It is entitled "The Study of a Rural Church."

JOHN G. TRUITT.

THE CHRISTIAN ORPHANAGE

SINGING CLASS MAKES TRIP

On the third Saturday morning our singing class boarded the East bound train for Eastern Virginia with Franklin, Va. as our destination. We reached Franklin about seven o'clock P. M., and were met there by Brother B. D. Jones and two of his friends, and they carried us out to his home for supper. After supper our little folks were carried to the homes where they were to be entertained. On Sunday morning at eleven o'clock the class rendered its song service at Holy Neck church, and at four in the afternoon at Liberty Spring and at Holland at eight o'clock at night.

We had a splendid audience at each church and the interest was fine. Our little folks did their best and we trust they made a favorable impression on those who heard them.

The people did all in their power to make our visit pleasant and happy and showed us every kindness pos-

sible. There are no better people than the people of Eastern Virginia and their homes are your homes while with them.

Brother J. M. Darden, of Suffolk, Va., was with us at all three services and made very impressive talks in behalf of the Orphanage work. Brother Darden is a very warm friend of the Orphanage and the little children here have a very warm place in their hearts for him.

We want to thank each one who so kindly conveyed the children from place to place and assure them that we are very grateful for each act of kindness shown.

CHAS. D. JOHNSTON, Supt.

FINANCIAL REPORT FOR OCTOBER 29, 1919

Amount brought forward, $11,623.49.

Children's Offerings

Irene Patton, 20 cents; Pauline Trotter, 20 cents; Richard Bost, 20 cents; Lois Stout, 20 cents; Total, 80 cents.

Sunday School Monthly Offerings

(Eastern Virginia Conference).

Liberty Spring, $12.00; Suffolk, $25.00; Young Men's Bible Class, Holy Neck, $1.58; Portsmouth, $3.00; First Christian S. S., Berkley, $11.33.

(North Carolina Conference)

Damascus, (Orange Co.), $3.03; Bethlehem, $5.58; Durham, $11.00; Pleasant Ridge, $5.85; Shiloh, $1.72; Haw River, $3.82; Christian Chapel, $1.75; Reidsville, $1.00; Mt. Auburn, $18.15; Wentworth, $11.14; Shallow Well, $2.00; Pleasant Grove, (Va.), $4.00; Union, N. C., $1.25; Men's Bible Class, Reidsville, $10.00.

(Georgia and Alabama Conference)

LaGrange, Ga., $8.00; Rock Island, Ala., $1.26; Total, $142.46.

Children's Home

Mr. and Mrs. M. E. Godwin, Stuart, Iowa, $25.00.

Special Offerings

J. H. Jones, on support of Children, $30.00; Mrs. Jas. Maxon, Jamestown, Ohio, $2.25; Mrs. M. L. Bryant, $25.00; Mr. A. F. Ward, $18.00; G. L. Jones, on support of Children, $35.00; Mr. Martin, $9.20; Total, $119.48.

Total for the week, $287.74; Grand total, $11,911.23.

CHILDREN'S LETTERS

Dear Uncle Charley: I will write and send my dues for September and October. I hope all the cousins are having a jolly time. It is cold and rainy today so I can't go outside to play. I can have a good time playing with my dolls anyway. Love to all the cousins.—*Irene Patton.*

It is a smart little girl that can make herself happy all the time whether it is sunshine or rain. I love little girls like that.—*"Uncle Charley."*

Dear Uncle Charley: I will send my dues for September and October. It is not long until Thanksgiving Day. Hope the little cousins will have lots of good things to eat that day, and I hope I will too. Lots of love to you and the cousins.—*Pauline Trotter.*

One man has promised us a turkey for Thanksgiving and I know the boys will eat an opossum and will dig our potatoes by that time. We hope to have a good dinner.—*"Uncle Charley."*

Dear Uncle Charley: Here I come with my dues for

September and October. Hope all the cousins are well and having a good time. I am going to school now. With lots of love to you and the cousins.—*Richard Bost.*

You must study hard in school and make good grades and stand at the head of your class. Always set your ideal high and then strive to reach it.—*"Uncle Charley."*

Dear Uncle Charley: Here I come with my dues for September and October. It is only a short time until Christmas. I am looking for Old Santa Claus then. I hope he will find the way to the Orphanage and give each child something real nice. I hope he won't forget me. Enclosed please find twenty cents. Love to all. —*Lois Stout.*

I truly hope "Old Santa" will visit you and the orphans Christmas.—*"Uncle Charley."*

REMEMBER THE ORPHANAGES THANKSGIVING

The managements of our charitable institutions are making patriotic efforts to adjust their work to the demands of changed conditions which have added materially to and made more essential most of the normal demands upon their resources. Some of the orphan homes are finding difficulty in continuing their splendid work, even on the same or a reduced scale, with applications for admission accumulating that must, of necessity, be declined for lack of facilities to warrant reasonable expansion.

It is no small task even in normal times to secure sufficient funds for the maintenance of the orphanage work, and important departments in a number of the orphan homes have been handicapped on account of this state of affairs. The talk about the needs of these institutions may become tiresome to some, but if the people are to sustain them they must know something of existing conditions. During the present abnormal times, with increasing demands of every sort which the war has made on philanthropy, it becomes necessary to keep our orphanage work before the people. Hitherto the editors of the State have cheerfully co-operated with the committee in bringing to the attention of our charitably inclined people the imperative needs of our homes for dependent children. We again, and most respectfully, ask this favor.

The suggestion of one day's income is reasonable. Not one person in a hundred is unable to contribute of their income to that extent—and *all* can assist in bringing the matter to the attention of the people.

The Publicity Committee therefore makes its appeal—

1. To the prince of business to give out of his abundance the actual or estimated income of a day.

2. To the landlord and money-lender to give one day's rent of his houses and land, or one day's interest on his money.

3. To the professional man to give one day's earnings, specifying the day, or taking the average day.

4. To the salaried worker to give his or her salary for a day.

5. To the laborers, with only pick-up jobs, to devote some special day to this cause.

6. To the good housewife, with her ingenuity and devotion, to set apart the expenses of a day.

7. To the boys and girls, with no regular income, to find work after school hours, or on some Saturday, and give the proceeds to the orphans.

8. To everybody, old and young, rich and poor, learned and unlearned, we appeal to join heartily in this holy movement, to visit the fatherless in their adversity.

We call upon the editors of our papers, daily and weekly, secular and religious, to give the widest publicity to this movement, which is philanthropic in purpose and state-wide in extent; we call upon all church leaders of all denominations, including pastors, Sunday school superintendents, women workers, and others of influence, to urge in their respective congregations the giving of a day's income at Thanksgiving to the orphanage of their choice.

We call upon State and county officers and the officers of the various fraternal orders to bring this movement to the attention of their official families and the members of their respective organizations and enlist them in this extra offering. We admonish teachers, doctors, lawyers, merchants, manufacturers, and all others with local following and influence to induce their friends to unite with them in giving, at next Thanksgiving, a day's work, or wages of a day, to the needy orphan children of North Carolina.

Each of the twenty child-caring institutions in this State is worthy of all the encouragement a generous-hearted people may feel disposed to offer, and we will not realize the full delights of service to humanity until we provide adequate protection for those bereft of parents and denied the comforts of happy home. It was the Master who said: "Suffer little children to come unto me, and forbid them not, for of such is the kingdom of heaven."

Men and women of North Carolina, will you suffer them? Answer during the Thanksgiving season by forwarding the income of a day to the orphanage of your choice, through your church, your Sunday school, your lodge, or direct.

The call is urgent. It is our hope that few, if any, will hear it in vain, but that thousands of big-hearted North Carolinians may respond cheerfully and generously at the appointed time.

M. L. SHIPMAN,
J. R. YOUNG,
W. F. EVANS,
J. D. BERRY,
R. F. BEASLEY,
DR. LIVINGSTON JOHNSON,
MISS DAISY DENSON,

Publicity Com. N. C. Orphan Ass'n.
Raleigh, N. C., October 18, 1919.

C. E. Hanbury—We enjoy the paper.

Mrs. R. B. Williams—Our CHRISTIAN SUN, long may it shine, and let us all read every line.

CHRISTIAN EDUCATION

WHY YOUNG MEN SIDE STEP THE MINISTRY

Three Objections in the Light of the Big Challenge

By A. M. Trawick, in Epworth Era

Conferences and private interviews with young men during the past ten years have disclosed three leading objections to the Christian ministry as a life calling. They are:

First, the belief that *other forms of service* are more congenial to men who believe in the social mission of Christianity than is the ministry.

Secondly, the conviction that the ministry is so *restricted by tradition and authority* that it does not offer opportunity for the development of independent manhood.

Thirdly, a cordial *dislike of certain types of ministers and mannerisms* that seem to be invariably associated with this calling.

It is distinctly creditable to young men that in such large numbers they are moved by appeals to unselfish service. There is hope for the world and for the church when so many young men deliberately repudiate careers that appeal directly to self-interest and turn to careers that mean sacrifice and service. If any man has definitely decided that he can serve God and humanity best by entering upon the work of social settlements, charity organizations, labor adjustments, race relations, or any other useful occupation, we would not by any word of ours discourage him or seek to turn him aside from his chosen calling. But we should like a definite word with a man who is undecided and who thinks the ministry does not offer him a full opportunity for social service.

The church is not wholly lacking in a great social passion and in social effort. Witness its tremendous influence in the prohibition movement, the missionary movement, the Centenary campaign. It will soon be ready to throw the full weight of its collective conscience into other unsolved social problems, such as industrial readjustment, race relationship, and sex education. The church will ultimately have more to do in giving a correct interpretation to the Industrial Workers of the World and Bolshevism than any other agency in the world. The church will give the final guarantees of a world peace, otherwise lasting guarantees will never be found.

Many ministers and strong leaders in the church, we frankly admit, attempt to draw a sharp distinction between what they call an *individual gospel* and a *social gospel*, and discredit the one in favor of the other. All such distinctions are largely matters of *emphasis* upon different aspects of the same gospel. The church must put its emphasis upon both aspects of the gospel, and there is every indication that the church is friendly to any man who comes with a sane, all-round interpretation of the spirit of the greatest social Teacher, Jesus Christ. A Christian minister with a passion for social organization and service can do more than any other man to destroy snobbery, caste, and autocracy in the church. He can direct the group instincts of men into their highest spiritual development, and he can help the church escape the spiritual tragedy which overtakes it when it thinks more of its own life than of the broader life of the kingdom of God.

A keen social vision and social passion are not, therefore, a sufficient reason why men should turn aside from the Christian ministry. It is, on the contrary, a strong reason why they should examine the ministry in the light of its larger opportunities to do work that shall have permanent meaning for the whole of society.

A second group of men object to the ministry on the ground that it is so hedged about with *traditions and obedience to authorities* that it fails to grant the fullest freedom of self-development. The objection is expressed in such words as these: "I do not believe everything the church teaches. I am not willing to let some other man determine what I shall think and what I shall preach. My life is my own, and I must live it without arbitrary restraint and limitation." If the church undertook to limit a man's thinking to what had already been thought by the authorities, alive or dead, there would be force in this objection. But the church undertakes no such thing. The intellectual life of the ministry is embraced in the motto, "Think and let think." The only real heretic among ministers is the man who refuses to do anything for himself. But if he thinks wider than the church or in advance of it, nothing more is demanded of him than that he prove by his clear reasoning and his unimpeached character that his conclusions are worth while.

The law, medicine, politics, business—all are hedged about by tradition and inherited beliefs, yet all of them afford an opportunity for the display of independent character. The Christian ministry is not less friendly to men of aggressive leadership into new realms of thought. The ministry offers one of the best opportunities in the world to test the character-making value of a new truth. If any man has discovered a new truth or a new application of an old truth and can demonstrate its power in building up human life, the church will hear him. But it is useless to parade an old error that has already been outgrown.

The objection we are now considering is based ultimately upon a *misconception of the purpose of the ministry in the church*. The church sends out its ministers not to set up the final boundaries of human thinking, but to *keep alive the soul of man in the midst of the world*. How the spirit of men would shrivel and crumple up if some one did not continually preach the eternal word of God in the midst of human affairs! In spite of all its limitations, this is what the church wants its ministers to do. It has a message from God to the world, and this message it must deliver by the human voice into human ears. In spite of all their dullness and bewildering half light, this is what Christian ministers really want to say to the world. The spirit of man is a priceless treasure, and the ministers are God's agents in safeguarding it.

It is a trivial matter to charge that the ministry is surrounded by tradition and the opinions of dead masters. The ministry is not hampered by much excess baggage of this kind. Just enough burden of this sort is put on a man to help him keep his feet on the ground. The church leaders do not claim any inside information touching the mind of God which is not open to any honest inquirer. The ministry offers every devout man an opportunity to think to the bottom of every proposition relating to God and humanity, and a spirit of vantage from which to speak his conclusions.

Increasing numbers of young men side-step the ministry because they dislike certain manners and customs which they have seen in ministers. A catalogue of their objections would embrace the following items: The "holy tone" adopted in prayers and public speech; a peculiar style of dress; the title "Reverend"; private graft in the form of special railroad rates, reduced tuition at college, marriage fees, poundings, and the like; isolation from a real man's life in the community; the easy assumption of superiority in matters relating to the spiritual life; the preacher's terrifying solemnity when some one addresses him as "Doctor." And much more of the same sort.

There is no reason in the world why young men should not heartily dislike all these things in a minister's life. This is part of the junk which ministers have inherited and acquired, and all of it can be swept away as rubbish. But there is no reason why we should *sweep out the preacher with his rubbish.* Many preachers have already freed themselves of their junk. It is wise to think of the ministry in terms of its ideal, not in terms of its non-essentials.

None of the objections men bring against the ministry or the ministers touch the vital core of the question. It is God's will that men should preach the gospel. Some men must do it, even at the peril of their lives. If any one man has the right to dodge this solemn obligation, why has not every other man the same right? What, then, becomes of the spiritual life if a man can obey the will of God or not, just as he pleases? Young men must face this issue without flinching: "God wants a man to preach the gospel. If I am that man, how can I justify myself before him if I evade this life work?"

If a man recognizes the voice of God calling him to this work, why should he want to get away from it? It is a life work full of marvelous opportunities. Dealing with the spiritual facts of life becomes the minister's one occupation. Pointing out the ways of God to a half-blind world becomes his daily task. He is God's messenger to the sorrowing, the weak, the failing, and the strong. He deals with men and groups of men with communities, nations, races, and world-wide humanity. There is joy in a minister's life, rich compensation for all the limitation he endures, constant growth in the unfolding of ways to serve men. The attraction of the ministry is the opportunity it puts in a man's hand for multiplying himself a thousand times over to do good in the world.

The church needs ministers, more of them, and of a better sort. There are in the United States literally thousands of small towns and villages, that have no preaching in them and millions of people who have

never had the Bible taught to them. Still more millions in non-Christian lands are waiting to hear for the first time what the will of God means for them. But preaching in new and forgotten fields is only a small part of the minister's privilege today. Men need a gospel that is as big as the critical times through which they are passing. World forces are struggling now to decide the destiny of all humanity for generations to come. The time has passed forever when the gospel can be preached simply in terms of local needs or of national life. The church must have ministers who can preach a big gospel, a gospel as big as the problems of the world. Small men are not sufficient for the Christian ministry today. The world has thrown down the challenge to the church, and the church must respond with men big enough to grapple with the world and subdue it to the dominion of Christ. The ministry is the big opportunity for the man who is big enough to grasp it.

HOW GOD CALLS TO THE MINISTRY

By Rev. W. E. Snyder, D. D., in The Watchword.

Just how God calls we cannot always tell, for he deals in different ways with different personalities. But one thing is certain in every case. The individual has an inner consciousness that God is dealing with him or her, a spiritual conviction that God wants him or her to do a certain thing. That matter must be settled between the individual and God alone.

Then, "there is a human side to a divine call. God calls and man calls out. It is doubted whether there is a preacher or missionary in all the world who was not influenced by some word of some friend or loved one at the time of his surrender to God's will."

God works through individuals and agencies in fulfilling his purposes. There are three agencies which he especially uses in securing recruits for his work, and these should be as one in their relation to the kingdom.

1. The home. Ministers and missionaries almost invariably come from godly homes; seldom if ever from homes of worldliness or wealth.

2. The Christian college. Church schools must supply kingdom leaders. Not one minister or missionary in fifty is the product of a secular college. One of the best services a person can render to the cause of Christ is to support Christian colleges and turn young people to them for their education.

3. The church. To do its duty fully the church must be spiritual and evangelistic. Life Work Recruits are usually born in revivals, and invariably in a spiritual atmosphere. There is something vitally wrong in a church that is not sending its proper quota of recruits into the kingdom as well as winning souls to Christ.

Then, underlying all this, whether in the home, college, or church, is *the spirit of prayer.* Christ's formulae for securing recruits is: "Pray ye therefore the Lord of the harvest that he send forth laborers into his harvest." It was when the church at Antioch was fasting and praying that the Holy Spirit said, "Separate unto me Saul and Barnabas for the work whereunto I have called them."

WORSHIP AND MEDITATION

ROOM UP HIGHER

In cities, it often occurs, where land is valuable and much needed space is desirable, they dig down deeply, lay solid foundations and build houses many stories high to make more room above. On and on, up and up they continue to work to make more room above until structures strong, grand and imposing are completed with ample room to accommodate the increasing population.

When Daniel Webster was a young man he went to Boston to practice law, and he inquired of some of the older lawyers of the city if there was any room for a young lawyer to begin his practice. The answer from all he consulted was: "There is no room—the place is full of great lawyers already." "Well," said Webster, "there is room up higher, and I will try to go up." He rented a place, put out his sign, and went to work. Being a man of fine personal appearance, full of energy and industrious, he very soon commanded respect and attention and from the start did a prosperous business as a lawyer.

When Bunker Hill monument was dedicated, Webster was invited to deliver the address. He accepted the invitation and prepared himself for that memorable day, and when the hour came he was in place and ready to deliver it, but the great crowd of people obstructed the place set apart for the different orders to take part in the exercises, and the man who was master of ceremonies said, "It is impossible for these orders to perform their duties when all the space set apart for that purpose has been filled." Then Webster arose, saying with his magnetic look and intense earnestness, "Ladies and gentlemen, fellow citizens of Boston, please move back and give us a little more room; for there is nothing impossible with the American people." They could not refuse his eloquent request and moved back at once, making the needed room. Then Webster proceeded with his matchless oratorical ability, and delivered one of the greatest addresses of his life, which charmed and thrilled the large audience assembled to hear him. On that glad day he made room up higher for himself, and continued to go up into the upper stories of thought and action until he soared higher above some of the lawyers who tried to discourage him when he needed their encouragement and sympathy. That great ambition which he so nobly demonstrated greatly helped him to hold on to the rungs of the ladder of industry by which he climbed to almost great heights of literary distinction and eminent statesmanship.

There is room above in every department of human progress, and it matters but little where your work is, nor what it is, there is room for improvement. It will cost you time, energy and some means in many ways, but keep going, and keep right on until the tip top is reached and the cap stone put on with your work completed.

Not long ago in one of our large cities fire flamed out in a high story of a great building. All the family had escaped except a little boy. The fireman started up the ladder as a last resort to bring him down, but the smoke and fire were too much for him; the dense smoke and the long, red tongue of fire forbade his going up, but a voice in the crowd below said: "Let us cheer the fireman." Then at once came the shout from a thousand anxious ones: "Go up and in and bring down the boy." At this cheering burst of encouragement, he went up and brought him down to the admiration of all, and to the loving embrace of his dear mother.

In life there are dangerous, difficult ways to travel, and it will take a brave, true heart to pass them, but when a man of the moment steps to the front amid the cheers and encouragement of his friends he goes proudly on to success. Don't forget there is plenty of room up higher.

J. T. KITCHEN.

THESE FINE OCTOBER DAYS

During these supernal Indian summer days of gladness and etherial mildness many thoughtful ones have been drawn nearer to God in earnest contemplation of His goodness and loving kindness to the children of His creation. Our minds, in passing out beyond the sunlit blue, the star-lit blue, the moon-lit blue, beyond the far away blue searching after God, came back to us through unmeasured space with this anxious four worded question: What has God wrought? Surrounded by the constellated beauty of so many distant, mysterious shining worlds the eloquent and sublime question, so full of interest may be repeated by the angels as they wing their way, with unbroken praise, from star to star, and through still brighter, silent worlds: What has God wrought?

These lovely autumn days and scenes, admirable and delightful. Seen, felt and greatly enjoyed by so many delighted ones. Many will have something to say about this beautiful pleasant October weather, and poets will try their smooth numbers of praise. Songs, high and low, short and long will be heard as they are sweetly sounded by voice, keyed and stringed instruments and blended into lovely strains of universal admiration and praise of these incomparable days.

The sun never shone with more brightness nor its flash of light more full of boundless profusion. Yes, even in the sun-set hour, the evening twilight and the aurora of the morning light, all are worthy of our dearest admiration and profoundest love.

These mild, calm, soft autumn days when religious and love songs are sung and heard by listening and delighted multitudes while all nature, arrayed in such wonderful beauty, smiles and helps us to move on with glad hearts through dominions, empires and quick moving worlds, the imagination and the realization are greatly helped with such contemplation and scenes.

When God made the stars and suspended them in space with the tips of His fingers it was at once a work of perfection. The work of His whole creation needed no finishing touch; no repairing or remodeling. It was at once a perfect work—a product of His great wisdom and power. A most inconceivable work, yet it is true. We do not doubt it; it is before us, plainly seen and fully realized. We live, think, move and act, playing our little part each day upon this mysterious stage. Some of us know so little about even this world, our present home, that we cannot say much about it. But we can admire, praise and love this great exhibition of God's providence.

Some might be inclined to think His works would wear out, but they will last forever. The world has revolved on its invisible axis for unknown centuries, and it moves as fast, steady and noiseless today as it ever did. God's works need no patents as do the works of men. They need no touch of the artist's brush—they lack nothing. He made and gave to His world's perpetual motion, and they have been running all the time since. Science has tried hard and long to discover perpetual motion, but failed to find it. When God said, "Let there be light," He touched something connecting His extensive works and light flashed with electric swiftness and divine radiance from world to world.

As we look out upon the unbounded blue we are lost in thought, wonder, love and adoration. The forest looks somewhat like it is blazing with the fire of an October sun, and the trees which rustled in their green summer dress are changing into russet and many other attractive colors. They appear so lovely as they wave their last farewell to summer. They never attire themselves in black mourning costume, but even to the very last present a cheerful brightness to an admiring world. That is the best way for them to dress. It makes us feel better in their elegant styles with no mourners in thin black dresses to trail in sad remembrance of a glad or unhappy past.

Painter's brush and sculptor's chisel may paint and carve, pen may write; oratory, romance, and poetry may tell with amazing description, but none except the eye which sees nature can fully appreciate its beauty.

J. T. KITCHEN.

I dare not tell how high I rate humor, which is most fruitful in the highest and most solemn spirits. Dante is full of it; Shakespeare, Cervantes, and almost all the greatest have been pregnant with this glorious power. You will find it even in the gospel of Christ.—*Tennyson.*

Senator Miles Poindexter, of Washington, has announced his candidacy for the presidency in 1920.

The Conference being held in Washington between Capital and Labor of the country is making little progress.

Happy Hallowe'en to all the children.

NOTES

The Editor is this week at Waverly, Virginia, attending the Eastern Virginia Conference.

We have been calling upon the people this month to renew their accounts and the response has been beautiful. We appreciate the co-operation.

On Wednesday, October 15, Mr. Reps Williamson, Sr., Driver, Virginia, father of Mrs. J. O. Atkinson, passed to his reward. An obituary, we presume, will follow.

Brother John King, Suffolk, Virginia, surprised us one day last week by a call. He was enroute on auto from Georgia and stopped. Brother King is one of THE SUN's life-long friends. It was a genuine pleasure to see him.

Karl Lehmann and Chas. F. Evans, Christian Endeavor Specialists, paid us a short visit last Saturday. We showed Lehmann an advanced proof of the article about the tables in the *Annual*, and he said: "That's the thing." (See page 2).

W clip the following from *The Sanford Express* dated October 23: "The series of meetings which were held at the Christian church last week conducted by Rev. B. F. Black, closed Sunday night. As union services were held at the Christian church, all denominations joining in, there was no preaching at the other churches. Mr. Black delivered a most interesting lecture to an appreciative audience in the Auditorium of the West Sanford Graded School Monday night on his experience and observation while a chaplain with the Expeditionary Forces in France. He also lectured on the same subject at Shallow Well Tuesday night."

NEW COMERS TO THE SUN FAMILY

Rev. W. J. Hall ....Franklin, N. H.
Mrs. John Pease ....Wardensville, W. Va.
John Raynor ....Maurerton, Va.
J. R. Wilson ....Cragford, Ala.
J. E. Amason ....Lineville, Ala.
Iola Hunt...................................Odenville, Ala.
Dr. J. T. Clack ....Abanda, Ala.
R. L. Barfield ....Roanoke, Ala.
M. L. Hamlin ....Roanoke, Ala.
Miss Ira Strain ....Wedowee, Ala.
D. T. Pollard ....Wedowee, Ala.
Miss Minnie Huey ....Wedowee, Ala.
J. L. Huey ....Wedowee, Ala.
O. O. Mitchell ....Cragford, Ala.
Miss Ellen Ragland ....Houston, Va.
Miss Emma J. Funk....................LinVille Depot, Va.
Mrs. J. S. Bell ....Warrenton, N. C.
Rev. H. Russell Jay.........................Argos, Ind.
Mrs. Ira V. Chrisman ....Brown Summit, N. C.

(Report to October 25)

Mrs. J. W. Driver—Long may THE SUN shine.

MISSIONARY

NOTICE—IMPORTANT

The Woman's Missionary Convention of the North Carolina Christian Conference convenes at Elon College, N. C., November 8-9, 1919.

It is earnestly desired that every Missionary Society be represented at this Convention, and in churches where there are no missionary organizations the pastors are requested to appoint some one to attend.

Let us be much in prayer these last few remaining days that the presence of the Holy Spirit may be with us, to guide and direct in all our deliberations and grant success in all our plans and purposes.

MRS. W. H. CARROLL.

WOMEN'S MISSIONARY MEETING, ELON COLLEGE,

NOVEMBER 8-9, 1919

Don't forget the Women's Missionary Conference for the State of North Carolina to be held at Elon College, November 8-9. The churches in Virginia too that belonged to the North Carolina Christian Conference will please send delegates. We hope every church will send at least two women whether it has a society or not.

A splendid program has been arranged and we are confidently expecting a great and helpful Conference.

We invite our pastors too to come. We women are said to be good helpers of our pastors. We want them to show their appreciation by attending our Women's Missionary Conference.

All who can come will kindly notify Mrs. J. O. Atkinson, Elon College, N. C.

MRS. W. A. HARPER.

REQUEST RENEWED

A few weeks ago the writer asked that if any of our people or pastors knew of persons, members of the Christian Church, present or past, who are living in Washington, D. C., or Richmond, Virginia, that same be sent to him. Many have responded and the list is increasing. May I repeat this request? We are anxious to get the names of all our people who live either in Washington or Richmond, that the same may be turned over to the man who will undertake the work of organizing there. It will be a great help if the brethren will give heed to this request as every name obtained now will give inspiration to the work.

J. O. ATKINSON.

GETTING MISSIONARY IDEAS

The people of the Christian Church will do as much for missions as other people do when they learn as much about missions as other people have learned. Our people are no more averse to doing and daring and undertaking great things for the Kingdom than other people when they see and feel the need.

The writer has never desired missionary zeal beyond that required to meet missionary needs and he has always believed that missionary information of facts and conditions as they obtain leads to the safest and sanest missionary inspiration. We will get the inspiration and we will do the divine task only as we learn and realize the facts as they are, the needs as they exist and the privileges as they are presented.

It ought to be sufficient for us that Christ commanded us as the most imperative command of all His earthly teaching to be missionary, home missionary, foreign missionary, missionary in effort, missionary in vision and missionary in gifts. I say this should be sufficient because loyal soldiers always obey their Captain's command. How any Christian can stand up in the face of what Jesus Christ said namely: "Go ye into all the world," and say he does not believe in foreign missions is more than I can understand. I am persuaded that the only reason is that such a person does not stop to think and is ignorant of the facts as they exist.

As I see our people getting the vision and trying to learn the facts, it rejoices my heart. I do not wish the people swept off their feet by any sort of fervor. Neither do I desire that any sort of feeling shall lead us to do that which we should not do. But I do desire that the facts of the mission fields shall become known among our people. I am pleased on this account whenever I learn that a Sunday school has decided to study missions. I hold in my hand now a letter from the Secretary of the Rosemont Sunday school, Norfolk, Va., from which letter I take these words: "On the third Sunday of each month we devote thirty minutes entirely to a missionary program with the idea of teaching and encouraging missionary zeal. We are writing to ask you to enroll us as a missionary Sunday school." In the years to come something will take place in Rosemont Sunday school that will be a blessing and a benefit to the whole Church. I also hold in my hand a letter from Miss Bessie I. Holt, Burlington, N. C., under the date of October 8, saying: "Graham Sunday school has decided on one Sunday a month offering for missions and has also elected a Mission Superintendent. I also visited the New Providence Sunday school and find that they had just decided to give one Sunday a month offering, that they have a live Woman's Missionary Society on the way; that a Committee of three was appointed to nominate officers, and work for more members;—and I feel that we will organize with at least twelve or fifteen members." Miss Holt expects also a live Young People's Society for this church. The work is growing and should be carried into the Sunday school and to the young people so that the rising generation in the Christian Church shall have the same opportunity to know and to do for missions that the young people of other Churches have had.

J. O. ATKINSON.

We call the attention of our readers, and especially those in Alamance and adjoining counties to the advertisement of Mr. G. A. Nicholson on page 16. We know Mr. Nicholson and take pleasure in commending him and his business.

We understand that Rev. Stanley C. Harrell has accepted the Durham church.

This is NOT the Editor's picture, but just to demonstrate how proud he would look if he were privileged to visit each home that is taking THE CHRISTIAN SUN. He thinks that when he tapped on the door that he would hear a gentle voice say, "Come in" as well as a friendly greeting and a genuine old time handshake.

And this may, or may not, resemble your home, but it brings to the Editor's mind the loveliness and coziness of many homes where THE CHRISTIAN SUN goes and where he would greatly enjoy going.

But what would the Editor say if it were possible to call for only *two minutes in each home taking* THE CHRISTIAN SUN? *He would express his appreciation of the loyal and liberal support given him, and what a great pleasure it is to serve a constituency so faithful.*

The Editor would, however, in the homes where he went in which the subscription account was not paid in advance, hang a card like this on the door knob as he said *good bye.*

WHAT YOUR LABEL MEANS
(Told in the Language of a Child)

1-1-9 means that your subscription expires January 1, 1919.
2-1-9 means that your subscription expires February 1, 1919.
3-1-9 means that your subscription expires March 1, 1919.
4-1-9 means that your subscription expires April 1, 1919.
5-1-9 means that your subscription expires May 1, 1919.
6-1-9 means that your subscription expires June 1, 1919.
7-1-9 means that your subscription expires July 1, 1919.
8-1-9 means that your subscription expires August 1, 1919.
9-1-9 means that your subscription expires September 1, 1919.
10-1-9 means that your subscription expires October 1, 1919.
11-1-9 means that your subscription expires November 1, 1910.
12-1-9 means that your subscription expires December 1, 1910.

October is Pay-Up Month.   Don't let the Month Pass and Leave Your Label Unchanged---if it NEEDS Changing.

Sunday School and Christian Endeavor

CHRISTIAN ENDEAVOR TOPIC FOR
NOVEMBER 9, 1919

J. V. Knight

How To Avoid Failure.—Josh. 1:1-8.

One of the things we should fear most is failure. If you are a business or professional man you know what it will mean to you and your family if you fail in your work. The same thing should be brought out in the lives of Christians. To fail not only affects you, but those who are about you. One man fails in business and a thousand men feel it. A Christian fails in his Christian life and a thousand may suffer. We are our brother's keeper and none of us live to ourselves or die to ourselves, and this failing business is something each of us cannot watch too carefully. We hate the reproach, humiliation, and shame of failure and yet, hundreds are on the road to failure because they are content with only partial success.

How are we to avoid failure? There are many ways, but space will not permit us to enumerate but a few. First, we should have one great ideal. We cannot be master of everything. If you will notice the lives of the most successful men, you will find they have one ideal and follow it out. "This one thing I do," said Paul. He knew the only way to keep down failure was to try one thing and do it well. Second, work at it. A little girl was once asked if her mother was a Christian, to which she replied "Yes, but she is not working at it." The man who would avoid failure must work out his soul salvation with fear and trembling. If we are successful in life, we must know that an opportunity to serve comes once in a lifetime. Third, don't be a pessimist. The pessimist fails before he begins, and that because he is afraid to tackle the job. How easy it would have been for Joshua to have said, "I can't." Probably he was a bit shakey about undertaking such a task, but when God said, "Be not afraid....I am with thee ....and thou shalt have good success"—Joshua at once assumed command. The same promise is made to you and why think you can't do anything for God? Drop your pessimism or you will always be a miserable failure.

Keep up courage. An honest failure is no disgrace to one who had done his best. Columbus failed to find the route to India but he discovered a new country far more important than what he searched for. Mistakes are common, and are not always signs of failure. Never give up. "If at first you don't succeed —try again."

THE ORGANIZED CLASS AND SERVICE

How can an organized class serve? Well, there are many ways. After your organization is complete; after the officers are elected, it is wise to have an early meeting and plan some real service. One of the things an organized class can do by these business meetings is to promote the social welfare of the community. An after meeting can be held which may be given over to sociability, and thus knowing our brother or sister, as the case may be, we are better able to sympathize with him, and to rejoice with them that do rejoice and weep with them that weep. In this day, when the world offers so many social pleasures to the young, it is wise to have something of this kind where Christian youth can meet and spend a social hour.

Then an organized class can undertake some definite service that would never be carried to a successful end without an organization behind it. For instance, a number of organized classes are clothing, or partly clothing, orphans at Elon; other organized classes are helping to support missionaries or Bible women. There are yet others who undertake to send little city children into the country in the summer time; to provide a baby with clothes; a sick child with dainties; to furnish flowers to the sick. Oh, there are no ends to the ways in which an organized class can help. But the particular work your class can do, will depend upon where it is situated. A class of country boys split and corded the wood for an aged widow one winter, while a class of girls made jellies and preserves for a childrens hospital, to which another had contributed scrap books and toys. The only limit to the work of an organized class is the willingness to serve.

How is the money raised? Most classes have regular monthly dues; and in addition, it is a usual custom for such classes to give one-half of their Sunday offering to the Sunday school, retaining the other half for the special work in which they are engaged. Several classes have a "mite box" into which special offerings can be dropped; and, these are used for whatever purpose the class has decided by a general vote, is the work for which they most desire to give.

Mrs. Fred Bullock.

HYMN FOR THE WEEK

Tunes, "St. Joseph" 8.8.8.4.

Father of all, from land and sea
The nations sing, "Thine, Lord, are we,
Countless in number, but in Thee
May we be one.

O Son of God, Whose love so free
For men did make Thee man to be,
United to our God in Thee
May we be one.

Join high and low, join young and old
In love that never waxes cold;
Under one Shepherd, in one fold,
Make us all one.

A DAY

I'll tell you how the sun rose—
A ribbon at a time.
The steeples swam in amethyst,
The news like squirrels ran.

The hills united their bonnets,
The bobolinks begun,
Then I said softly to myself:
"That must have been the sun!"

But how he set I know not—
There seemed a purple stile
Which little yellow boys and girls
Were climbing all the while.

Till when they reached the other side,
A dominie in gray
Put gently up the evening bars,
And led the flock away.
—*Emily Dickinson.*

MARRIAGES

PRUITT-WOMACK

On Wednesday, October 15, 1919, Miss Nellie Pruitt became the bride of Mr. James Womack at the bride's father's home near Vernon Hill, Va. The writer officiated.

JOHN G. TRUITT.

GREENWOOD-FIRESHEETS

The beautiful country home of Mrs. Lelia Greenwood was the scene of the wedding of Mrs. Greenwood's oldest daughter, Edna, to Mr. Norman Firesheets. They were married on Wednesday, October 8, 1919, at two oclock P. M., and boarded the north-bound train at Paces, Va. The writer officiated.

JOHN G. TRUITT.

MARLETTE-BOSWELL

On October 11 1919, at 5 o'clock P. M., Mrs. Annie Marlette and Bedford Boswell were united in marriage at the Christian parsonage, Burlington, N. C. The writer officiated. They will make their home in Burlington.

Their many friends wish for them much joy and happiness.

J. W. HARRELL.

YEAMAN-WILKERSON

At South Boston, Virginia, on October 16, 1919, the writer united in marriage Mr. William M. Yeaman and Miss Mattie V. Wilkerson of Nathalie, Va.

The groom has recently received an honorable discharge from the U. S. Navy. The bride is a daughter of Mr. and Mrs. John Wilkerson and has for several years been organist in Liberty Christian church and active in all the organizations of the church.

Mr. and Mrs. Yeaman will locate near Blackstone, Va. May blessings attend them.

C. E. NEWMAN.

HAYES-DESHAZO

A quiet but pretty marriage was solemnized at the home of Dr. J. Beverly Deshazo, Ridgeway, Va., on Saturday, October 4, 1919, when Miss Blanch Deshazo became the bride of Mr. Frank Hayes of Wendell, N. C. The writer performed the ceremony in the presence of a few friends and relatives, using the souvenir ring ceremony.

The bride wore a brown traveling suit with accessories to match and carried a shower bouquet and swansonia. Mrs. Jones played Lohengrin's wedding march. Immediately after marriage the happy couple motored to Danville, Va., a distance of forty-seven miles, where they left on a North bound train for a short bridal trip.

The bride is the only daughter of Dr. and Mrs. J. B. Deshazo of Ridgeway, Va., and is a graduate of Virginia College, Roanoke, Va. The groom is the youngest son of Deacon Alfred Hayes of Virgilina, Va., and has made a splendid career in his chosen business as a tobacco auctioneer.

Mr. and Mrs. Hayes will reside at Wendell, N. C. Their many friends wish for them a happy and useful career.

C. E. NEWMAN.

MALONE-WHITE

Thursday morning, October 16, 1919, at 9 o'clock, a beautiful marriage was solemnized in the new Christian church, Burlington, N. C., when Miss Mamie Malone, daughter of Mr. and Mrs. J. N. Malone, became the bride of Mr. James I. White.

The church was lovely in its decorations of white and green. The altar was draped in white and banked with ferns.

Prior to the wedding, Miss Georgia Hatch sang "O Promise Me." Miss Hennie Malone, accompanied by Miss Allie Malone with violin, rendered the wedding music.

To the strains of the wedding march from "Lohengrin," the bridal party entered. David Curtis and Sam Bason, ushers, followed by little Miss Louise Horne, daintily dressed in white organdie, carrying the ring in the heart of a rose. Next came Miss Sallie Patterson, maid of honor. She wore taupe georgette and carried pink roses. The bride entered with her father and was met at the altar by the groom and his best man, Dunlap White. The bride wore a traveling suit of midnight blue with grey accessories and carried bride's roses. The writer officiated.

Immediately after the ceremony the couple left for a northern tour.

These are popular young people. Mrs. White is a graduate of the Woman's Hospital of Philadelphia, and Mr. White is manager of the Burlington Drug Co. They have the best wishes of a host of friends.

J. W. HARRELL.

 **OBITUARIES**

BROWN

Brother Charlie C. Brown departed this life October 16, 1919 at the age of 46 years, 8 months and 28 days. He is survived by his wife and eight children, all girls. He was a son of the late Deacon D. C. Brown of Union Grove Christian church and he himself had also been elected deacon to succeed his father. He had been a life-long Christian and beloved by all who knew him. He was a good man and will be missed much in his home and community.

God bless and comfort the loved ones.

T. J. GREEN.

AN APPRECIATION—BOYD

It is almost an undisputed fact that the meeting house which finally became to be Pleasant Grove Christian church was established about 112 years ago. In that same year was born Archer A. Farmer. From his youth until the end of his life he was a faithful member of the Christian church. In early manhood he married Lydia Carlton and established a home of piety, peace and abundant hospitality. To this home came the subject of this sketch, Mrs. Missouri Eugenia Boyd. She was the fourth and last of the children who lived to maturity, the others being Mrs. Sarah E. Dunn, Mrs. Martha E. Pierce, and Mrs. Mary Ellen Carlton. Each of these women were mothers in happy homes. Mrs. Dunn died in 1876 at the age of 40, Mrs. Carlton died in 1914 at the age of 74, Mrs. Pierce died in 1918 at the age of 80, and Mrs. Boyd died August 3, 1919 at the age of 77 years.

Missouri Eugenia married Mr. Scott Boyd and to them were born Myrtle Lydia, who is now Mrs. L. E. Carlton; Archer Wellons, Ira Willingham, and Sarah Eliza all of whom are living and are members of Ingram Christian church, of which Mrs. Boyd was a charter member.

In her youthful days she was a student of Graham Normal College in North Carolina, and although she was a woman of intellectual culture the culture of the

Christian graces was foremost in her life. She taught her own children of the Christ-child, and to love and serve the church and the ministers of God in the old time way. During her married life she read widely and yet never failed to read most devotedly the Word of God and her church paper, The Christian Sun. I loved her, as did both rich and poor, and found in her a tender and affectionate friend. She loved her church, and was a most ardent devotee of the Christian Orphanage. Never a year passed in which she did not send the Orphanage some of the gleanings from her own hand. A true mother she was and religious after the good old time type, and yet, even in her advanced years, she was the center of attraction in large groups of young merry-makers who frequented the Christian home of which she was the enthroned queen. Her sons, and daughters, and grandchildren, her relatives and all may well hallow the memory of "Cousin Ann."

JOHN G. TRUITT.

WHITE

Roger Mills White was born October 6, 1895 and died September 22, 1919, aged 23 years, 11 months and 16 days. He was the son of Eddie Mills White and Alice E. White. He was the last member of the family to die. He was preceded in death by a little sister and little brother, also father and mother. Roger was an ambitious orphan boy. He so used his time, and the strength of his mind, and the eloquence of his tongue that already he had achieved victories in speech, in debates an dih education.

He graduated at Waverly, Va. high school; spent three years at Elon College, and spent his Senior year at Washington and Lee University where he graduated in 1917. Later he volunteered to the Navy where he served till January, 1919 when permission was given him by the Navy to attend Washington and Lee University to study law. He began his law course, but soo nhad to give it up on account of sickness. He had a severe case of Influenza the last of 1918 from which he never fully recovered.

Last spring the officials of the Navy had him placed at Catawba, Va., for special treatment, where he remained till his death. He was still held under Naval authority. He professed religion and join-ed Spring Hill church when about 12 years old, and remained in the church till death.

Thus an ambitious life, a brilliant mind, and a ready tongue have passed away.

R. F. D. No. 1

May each have cast its influence on some other life. He was buried at Spring Hill cemetery in the presence of many loved ones, friends, and acquaintances. The beautiful flowers and the large number present showed the high esteem in which this young man was held.

JAS. L. FOSTER.

CHURCH OFFERING ENVELOPES

Standard Double
(Size 2½X4¼ inches—52 to Set)

White or Manila

25 to 49 sets	16 cts. a set
50 to 109 sets	14 cts. a set
110 to 209 sets	13 cts. a set
210 to 309 sets	12½ cts. a set
310 to 399 sets	12 cts. a set
400 or more sets	11 cts. a set

Minimum Charge $3.00 net.
CARTONS INCLUDED

Single Envelope System
(Size 2 5-16X3 5-8 inches. Open side. 52 to Set)

White or Manila

25 to 49 sets	14 cts. a set
50 to 99 sets	13 cts. a set
100 to 149 sets	12 cts. a set
150 to 199 sets	11½ cts. a set
200 to 249 sets	11 cts. a set
250 or more sets	10 cts. a set

Minimum Charge $2.00 set.
CARTONS INCLUDED
Take Note

The following points should be taken into consideration in placing an order for church offering envelopes:

1. A set means 52 envelopes, one for each Sunday in the year.

2. When cartons are ordered the sets are arranged in their logical order, thus making it convenient for the member. We suggest the use of cartons because of the convenience.

3. If you desire monthly, double or single envelopes, without cartons, 1-3 the price of the same number of weekly sets. Cartons 3-4 cent each.

4. Semi-monthly, double or single, in cartons, 2-3 the weekly price; without cartons 3-5 the weekly price.

5. When ordering state what Sunday that your church year begins, and whether you want the dates on envelopes or not.

6. Indicate the wording that you want placed on the envelopes or leave the same with us. Samples sent upon request.

7. Allow ten to fifteen days for delivery. Order early.

C. B. RIDDLE, Publishing Agent
Burlington, N. C.

Don't put off the matter of purchasing your church envelopes too late. Remember that they must be printed after the order is received.

"𝔅attles are not won at
headquarters; they are
won in the field."
—𝔐arshal ℱoch.

Volume LXXI	WEDNESDAY, NOVEMBER 5, 1919	Number 45
BURLINGTON	· · ·	NORTH CAROLINA

THE CHRISTIAN SUN

Founded 1844 by Rev. Daniel W. Kerr

C. B. RIDDLE   -   -   -   Editor

Entered at the Burlington, N. C. Post Office as second class matter.

Subscription Rates

One year .... $ 2.00
Six months 1.00

In Advance

Give both your old and new postoffice when asking that your address be changed.

The change of your label is your receipt for money. Written receipts sent upon request.

Many persons subscribe for friends, intending that the paper be stopped at the end of the year. If instructions are given to this effect, they will receive attention at the proper time.

Marriage and obituary notices not exceeding 150 words printed free if received within 60 days from date of event, all over this at the rate of one-half cent a word.

Original poetry not accepted for publication.

Principles of the Christian Church

(1) The Lord Jesus Christ is the only Head of the Church.
(2) Christian is a sufficient name of the Church.
(3) The Holy Bible is a sufficient rule of faith and practice.
(4) Christian character is a sufficient test of fellowship, and of church membership.
(5) The right of private judgment and the liberty of conscience is a right and a privilege that should be accorded to, and exercised by all.

EDITORIAL

RETIRING GRACEFULLY

There comes a time in the life of every man when he must begin to hand the palm of his calling or profession to some other man. This is true of the ministry as well as in other callings and professions.

There are two principal points that make their appeal in the life of the senior brother who gracefully yields his work to his junior brother. They are: Admiration of the public for the older man and appreciation of the younger comrade for his senior friend.

Ministers in declining years do not always retire gracefully to the young men. So often do we hear the young man's imperfections catalogued and his praiseworthy points go without mention. This has its effect in two ways: It causes the young man's friends to lower their estimate of the senior minister and creates a grief between the older head and the younger heart that drives away counsel.

If we expect young men to flock to the ministry, the older ministers must encourage them and retire gracefully.

And did you know, dear reader, that years of experience gives no man a monopoly upon his class of work?

"Salary and soul have a distinct relationship. It is not that the soul depends upon the salary for noble emotions, high ideals or sublime purposes. In fact it is possible for a preacher to become water-logged with too much salary. We do not remember more than two or three ministers spoiled by having too much salary."

MINISTERIAL STRIKES

Who ever heard of such a thing? A walk-out of the ministers? Not just that but this—the ministerial timber is not walking in. And that is where the ministerial strike comes in. In other strikes the men are of a trained class, but with the ministry the strike comes before they are trained.

Carpenters, masons, teamsters and other common laborers, who have but little responsibility, are getting more than the average minister. This class, as well as other classes, knows that many men in the ministry are underfed and paid, have families that must go in decent style; be educated, meet their bills and shoulder the "slams" and "bangs" of the local church, move when they are not liked, yet be a leader, and so many young men strike before they get in. You say that this class should strike, and your opinion we grant, with this rejoinder: The Gospel is a message of freedom, of comfort, of heart-ease, and it is hard to reason with a man that he can be free from financial ends that will not meet; that he can make his family comfortable without sufficient means, and that his heart can be at ease with the collector ringing the door bell. We rest the case.

"A preacher may be so limited in finances that he will be under nervous strain all the time. This eventually destroys his soul power. Again there is a terrible reaction of physical status on spiritual conditions under certain circumstances. There are literally many underfed preachers—so much so that they lack physical strength to perform the hard and exacting work of their pastorates. A man with weak legs cannot do pastoral work. Can a man with weak knees pray properly?"

WHAT MADE THE SMILE

It was late this afternoon, October 25, that our congenial Orphanage Superintendent, Brother Chas. D. Johnston, came by THE SUN office. He was wearing a smile, a happy smile; a smile that even the threatening weather could not banish. He handed out two pounds of nice honey to the Editor (think of an orphanage superintendent pounding an editor—marvelous!) and continued to smile. He told us about "taking" 67 pounds of honey today and this was our solution for the *extra* smile.

Was it? Brother Johnston reached for the crank on his Ford, and as he set the motor to a-buzzing, he said: "A man sent me $100.00 today to help buy winter clothing for the children"—and then we too, smiled an *extra*. Our faithful Orphanage Superintendent sped away while we turned to completing the odds and ends of the day, and all the while thinking how many, if only they would, could send along a little extra help for winter clothing for the children and keep Brother Johnston a-smiling.

"A meager salary may react upon the soul in the form of small ideas. The minister who is inadequately supported will not be able to take part in public movements, and the spirit of timidity will possess him until all the elements of leadership will be crushed out. He will form the habit of thinking of his soul and his work in terms and measurements of his salary."

CATCHING FLIES WITH VINEGAR

We asked a brother minister of another denomination the other day how the revival in his church was progressing, and his reply was: "Good and not good"; and then he added: "The attendance is poor and Brother ——————— (naming the evangelist doing the preaching) fusses at those who do attend about the small congregations until it is unpleasant to us."

That brings up a point—should the minister "fuss" about those who do not attend to those who do? "You can't catch flies with vinegar," our philosophy teacher used to say in discussing the philosophy of winning men—and women. You cannot force men to be good; you cannot force men to worship.

We have always had a notion that if the revivalist were to preach the riches of the Kingdom while he was scolding those who are not there, that his chances to get the non-going church man would multiply and that those present would be inspired to induce others to go.

This is our thought in theory and perhaps those who do more preaching than we do know better as to whether flies prefer vinegar to honey.

"It is increasingly necessary, in these days when large wealth abounds, and a goodly amount of it is in the church, that the preacher should know the meaning and worth of money. He ought to have ideas and experiences that will enable him to speak with confidence about the big things that consecrated money can do. How can he do this when the congregation keeps him on pin money instead of a man's salary?"

THE EASTERN VIRGINIA CONFERENCE

The Editor was privileged last week to attend the Eastern Virginia Conference which met with the Waverly, Virginia, church. We reached Waverly Tuesday night, and thus failed to get Tuesday afternoon's part of the program. In fact, we might say our work for THE CHRISTIAN SUN and the Book Depository kept us from hearing many of the splendid reports and addresses. We asked Dr. W. W. Staley, who always sits in the "Amen Corner" with a note book, to make his "Suffolk Letter" on the Conference. That is before us and appears on page 7. Dr. Staley covers in brief the whole of this great Conference. In any way you put it, you would have to be brief, for this whole issue could be used in saying much in the favor of the Conference's work.

The Conference was well attended, the spirit was fine, and the hospitality of the true Southern type. Judge West and others did all that could be asked in making the comfort of the people up to the best. Many SUN readers whom we had never seen before, their faces we were glad to see, and whose hands we were glad to grasp.

Th most of this issue was being prepared while we were away, and space forbids us to speak further. Read Dr. Staley's letter. A great Conference, we think.

"The average minister is a strong man who lives with a moral heroism that puts him above the weakness of self-pity and the worldliness of self-seeking. It may even embarrass him that we have made this plea for him, but he deserves the best the people can afford and we are persuaded that he will get it when the churches are really brought to think on these things."

BURLINGTON OPENS HER NEW CHURCH

Last Sunday was a *red letter* day for the Burlington congregation, it being the opening day for the new church. Preparation had been made for the occasion. The magnificent building's doors were thrown open Sunday morning and a great concourse of people came to worship and to witness. The music was fine and the selections timely. Pastor Harrell was master of ceremonies; Dr. P. H. Fleming, the pastor who served the church for the longest term, led the morning prayer; Rev. Jeremiah W. Holt, the founder of the church, gave an interesting talk on the organization; Attorney D. R. Fonville gave a history of the church; and Mr. W. K. Holt, Chairman of the Building Committee, gave an interesting and encouraging report of the new building. Prof. Floyd Alexander, Elon College, sang a solo, and Rev. C. H. Rowland, D. D., Franklin, Virginia, brought the people a message that inspired and electrified the attentive congregation. "I will fill this house with glory, saith the Lord of hosts" was his text. The people are still talking about the message and the messenger.

The evening service, like that of the morning, was beautiful. Special music was rendered; THE SUN's Editor led the prayer; the singing class of the Orphanage delighted the filled house with two fine selections, and Dr. J. O. Atkinson, the chosen speaker of the evening service, based his remarks on the theme "Church," and for forty minutes held the vast audience with words that edified, enlarged visions, and found their way to every heart. Dr. Atkinson was at *home* with the subject, speaking to *home* folks and *home* folks heard him gladly.

The church was organized February 16, 1884 with eighteen charter members, and the old building was dedicated in 1893. The present membership is 379. The new building will cost about $60,000.00 when the final work is done about the Sunday school rooms, basement, and the grounds beautified.

We stop the press this (Tuesday) morning to announce the sad news of Capt. Jas. A. Turrentine's passing last night at 12:15. He met with an accident some days ago by falling from a wagon and never recovered.

PASTOR AND PEOPLE

POUNDED AGAIN

Saturday night, October 25, just before bed-time, I was called from the home of one of Pleasant Union's members to to go to the church. When I went into the church what should I see but a grocery store opened up on the pulpit! But, as there were no sales going on, I did not say, "You have made my Father's house a house of merchandise." No, it was rather a gift out of the hearts of this splendid people to their unworthy pastor. I cannot describe how little I felt, and how little I felt that I deserved this kindness from them.

I mention some of the articles given and many of these were in abundance: Coffee, canned fruit, dried fruit, pickles, grapelade, lard, rice, flavoring extract, cocoanut, pineapple, pepper, salt, sugar, soap, gold dust, matches, soda, cornflakes, oatmeal, butter, cakes, starch, flour, crockery, towels, handkerchiefs, pins, garters, socks, etc.. Just one month before one of the deacons gave me one-half bushel of fine sweet potatoes. This was the largest pounding this pastor ever saw and I only hope and pray that I can prove my gratitude to the people and my Heavenly Father by more efficient service.

But that is not all. This church had promised their pastor $275.00 for this year, but they would not stop until they paid him $325.00 (lacking just a few cents). Think of it, $50.00 above salary and a pounding that amounted to half that much and more! May God's richest blessing be upon them and richly reward them for their gift. Come to see me brethren in the ministry and brother editor and friends. (Coming! C. B. R.)

J. LEE JOHNSON.

CONCORD

October 25, 1919, was the time appointed to hold the fourth quarterly meeting at this church but on account of inclement weather there was no meeting held.

After the preaching service on Sunday following, the church was called in order to transact the business of the last quarterly meeting of this Conference year. Officers were elected for the ensuing year and delegates were chosen for our Conference. The apportionments were practically paid in full. I think this church will be a banner church at Conference.

Since the third quarterly meeting a pulpit recess has been built. This is a great improvement to the church and better convenience for the preacher. A committee to raise funds for the purchase of a carpet is at work.

The present pastor has been called and has accepted the work for another year.

Howard's Chapel

The revival meeting was to have begun here the second Sunday in August but no ministerial help could be secured for that date. It was postponed until the second Sunday in October.

Rev. J. O. Atkinson, Field Mission Secretary, came out from Reidsville and preached for us on Sunday afternoon. It was a pleasant surprise to have

him with us. We heard him gladly. His message was based upon these words: "There was a man sent from God whose name was John."

Rev. J. S. Carden, Durham, N. C., came on Monday, but on account of rain no service was held that day. Brother Carden brought some simple, plain and forceful messages. The audience listened attentively and gave good response. He endeared himself very much with these people and we hope that he can come again. The church was very much revived. Several requests were made for prayer, one conversion and one addition to the church.

On Saturday afternoon before the second Sunday in November, we are to hold our last quarterly business meeting of this year. The meeting will convene about 4 o'clock.

L. L. WYRICK.

Elon College, N. C.

POUNDED

On Saturday afternoon before the first Sunday, just before sunset, the people of Park's Cross Roads church began to gather at my house. I was away from home at the time, but when I came I saw people on the porch, some in the yard and others coming, I could not imagine what was the trouble. At first I thought some one was to get married. However, I had not been in the house long before it was revealed that these good people had a big pounding for the preacher and his good wife.

Well, it was flour, sweet potatoes, apples, pears, sugar, coffee, salt, canned fruit and vegetables, honey, syrup, chickens, lard, 2 bushels of wheat and possibly some other things. All of these things were in no small quantities. It was the biggest pounding ever given to us. It is always a joy unspeakable to be remembered, but this was especially so this time when the fact that this was the first time Park's Cross Roads ever pounded their preacher. However, they did it as if they had been used to it. They laid up much goods for us for many days.

God bless these good people, that they may be the richer because of their good works. Mrs. Banks and I give thanks to all.

A. T. BANKS.

Ramseur, N. C.

HENDERSON LETTER

Following the second Sunday in September I assisted Rev. G. J. Green in a meeting at Mt. Gilead. It was my first visit to that church, and thoroughly enjoyed the stay among those good people. They treated me with every kindness and consideration. I very much appreciate their unstinted kindness and hospitality. Likely there are, as in all churches, the indifferent, but I was impressed with the number who seemed earnestly and prayerfully engaged in the Master's service. The music was good, the prayers offered earnest, and the attendance, especially at night, large. They also gave heed to the Word; at least they seemed to be attentive.

I was called home Thursday to attend a funeral, and did not get back to the meeting. The Master's blessings upon His cause there.

The Baptists and Christians of New Bethel and Liberty churches held union services beginning the third Sunday in September. The services were held in Liberty church, and the pastor of New Bethel church, Rev. John Michener, did the preaching after Sunday, the pastor of Liberty church, Rev. G. J. Green, preaching at the Sunday services. Because of his work, Brother Green could not be in the meeting after the third Sunday, so asked me to represent him in the work. Thus I had the privilege and pleasure of attending most of the services.

Brother Michener's sermons were plain and earnest presentations of sin and the sinner's doom without salvation; and Jesus the sinner's only hope of salvation and eternal life. Large congregations attended all the services, and at the evening services the church was crowded to the utmost. Many were turned away. There were many reconsecrations and renewals of vows to God, and many decided for Christ for the first time. Liberty received 21 into fellowship, and New Bethel 12; others will probably join later.

R. L. WILLIAMSON.

AN ACKNOWLEDGMENT

We would hereby express to the kind people of the Epsom community our appreciation of the kindness shown us while there. At church, in their home and wherever we saw them they seemed anxious to do everything possible for our comfort and pleasure. It was a joy to us to be among those good people. While we would not forget the kindness of any, and feel only deep appreciation for all expressions of fellowship and friendship, we would especially acknowledge the gift by Brothers E. M. and J. E. Newman of six fine Rhode Island Red chickens.

R. L. WILLIAMSON & WIFE.

AN IMPRESSIVE SCENE

One of the most beautiful and impressive scenes the writer has ever witnessed was when Rev. John Michener, pastor of New Bethel Baptist church, who had done most of the preaching during the union revival services conducted by New Bethel and Liberty churches, in company with the writer, led the candidates for baptism into the water. The ministers alternated in saying the ceremony and each baptized a candidate at the same time. This was but the carrying out of the spirit of union that had existed during the united revival effort when all were of one accord in purpose and effort for the salvation of souls and the upbuilding of the Master's kingdom, and was to me a foretaste of the blessedness of the time when all shall be gathered in the presence of the great Shepherd into one fold.

R. L. WILLIAMSON.

NEWPORT NEWS, VA.

On October 22, 1919, the series of meetings which were being held at the East End Christian church closed.

The singing was led by Mr. W. T. Baker, church chorister, who did valuable work and was of untold help to the pastor in the services. The preaching was done by the pastor and plain gospel messages were his aim, believing that the power of Christ's life is powerful enough to reach the vilest and save the most unworthy.

The attendance was good and the spirit of the folks who came was of the highest order. The church is very much revived as a result of the meeting. With few exceptions all the folks who came felt the claim Christ has upon their lives. During the services one hundred and thirty-five people consecrated their lives and their talents anew to the work of God. Sixteen young people gave their hearts to God and all of them joined the East End Christian church. There are others in the city who are members of the Christian church elsewhere whom we hope to get linked up with the local church work.

God has blessed us, we believe, but we take no credit to ourselves for He worked through us to the accomplishment of a glorious end. Without Him with us it would have been impossible to have won men and women from the ways of death and hell.

Now that the meeting is over we are going to bend every effort to have the best year in the history of the work here. Before long we are going to start a campaign to build a new building in order that we may more effectively serve the people of the town in which we are called to do the Lord's work.

H. J. FLEMING, *Pastor.*

THE ALABAMA CONFERENCE HOLDS A GOOD SESSION

The Alabama Christian Conference met with the church at Antioch on October 14. The weather was fine and every church was represented, except New Home and Sand Hill. However, the latter sent report.

Rev. J. D. Dollar was elected President; Rev. E. M. Carter, Secretary; and J. W. Payne, Treasurer. There were three items that claimed special attention: That of grouping the churches into pastorates, education, and missions. The report on grouping the churches was referred to the churches with a request that they form the groups, having respect to those mentioned in the report.

On account of conditions over which we had no control the matter of building the proposed school in our section was postponed. We feel that the churches are more interested in this cause than ever. And, that one of the objects of our prayers, this year shall be, that the Lord may send laborers into His vineyard.

Immediately after Conference adjourned the Mission Board met and employed Rev. J. W. Elder for all his time for the North Alabama work. This field is very hopeful.

While a few of the churches did not raise all their assessments, when the total for this purpose was made, it was found that just a few dollars more that was apportioned was in hand. The Apportionment Committee provided for the quota asked by the Southern Christian Convention for this year. All the pastors were better paid than ever before.

The sad features of the reports were regarding church membership, which decreased from 1771 last year to 1728; and, the total of the Sunday schools from 1233 to 964. Two of the churches a year ago reported "no school'' while five made such a report this time. It is hoped that the Sunday School Board, under the supervision of J. W. Payne, Chairman, will have the cooperation of the churches and pastors and that this condition may be much improved during the year.

We were very glad to have Drs. J. O. Atkinson, N. G. Newman and J. Pressley Barrett with us, as well as Miss Bessie I. Holt. These added inspiration to our work and we want them to come again.

E. M. CARTER.

Wadley, Ala.

NOTICE!

Educational Committee, North Carolina Christian Conference, to Meet

The Educational Committee of the North Carolina Christian Conference meets at Elon College, November 10, 1919, at 10 o'clock, to consider all matters that may claim attention of this committee preparatory to the Annual Session of the Conference, which meets at Burlington, November 11-14, 1919.

All ministerial students of the united conference should report to the Educational Committee at this session. All persons desiring examination for licensure or ordination should present themselves before this committee at the date and place named above. All educational matters coming before the annual conference should be referred to the Educational Committee.

W. C. WICKER, *Chairman,*
J. O. ATKINSON,
D. A. LONG,
J. W. WELLONS,
P. T. KLAPP,
N. G. NEWMAN,
J. W. HARRELL,
J. W. PATTON,
R. L. WILLIAMSON,
J. LEE JOHNSON,
Educational Com. N. C. Christian Conf.

RELAXATION

Some time ago the writer read a timely article on, ''What the Call of the Ministry offers to Young Men,'' and a number of reasons for the shortage of ministers were given. It is not my purpose to take issue with the writer, but simply to discuss the question from another angle.

Why the shortage of ministers in every denomination? Has the question not grown serious? Has the Church lost her charms, and attractions for the young men of today? Does it no longer appeal to broadminded young men with vigor and enthusiasm enough to do the work? These are broad questions, and I dare not claim to answer either correctly, but one thing is certain, the situation has become alarming, and especially here in the South where more than seventy-five per cent of the churches have only one preaching service per month, and not much preparation being made for more services.

It seems to me that we have come to a period of relaxation. Once upon a time the Church had men to fill her pulpits, but now no denomination in the United States, Canada, or the kingdom of Great Britain has enough ministers to supply its pulpits a single Sunday. Relaxation? Yes, we are in that state and the question has come to be more than serious. Just a few years past our colleges and seminaries had double the number of young men preparing for the ministry that they have today. What is the cause and reason for the decrease? Are we not in the relaxation period when men are at ease? But there are reasons for it, and I mention only a few.

First. The ministry as a profession, or vocation has lost its appeal. Men no longer look upon the ministry as an easy job or task. Some may, but that is caused by the lack of proper intelligence, of what the work of the minister is. Men have learned that to be pastor of many of our churches of today means to be everything from janitor down, and that the work of the minister is by no means an easy job. You may not agree, but take a look at his hours. What are they? They run from about 8:00 A. M. to 10 and 12 P. M., seven days per week for a pastor of a city church, or about ninety-eight hours per week. Of course the young man no longer expects anything but hard work in the ministry, and naturally the professional idea loses its enticing charms.

Second. His living expenses. No man can live decently on the salary of the average minister. The high cost of living makes it impossible for a man to give himself over to the gospel ministry, for where is the minister who is not carrying a heavy financial burden? And where is the preacher who has a family of as many as one besides himself, who can live on the salary he receives? I ask that question, knowing that the average salary paid by the city parish is $1,000.00, and that of the town village and country less than $600.00, which makes the average for both just a bit over $600.00 per year. Who can live and support his family on a salary like that? Is a strike in order?

Third. Disobedience to Christ's command. The greatest cause for this relaxation is disobedience to Christ's command on the part of the Church forces. Listen: ''Pray ye therefore, the Lord of the harvest, that he will send forth laborers into his harvest.''—Matt. 9:8. But what is the use? I mean what is the use to pray, unless we are willing to help the Lord to answer our prayers? Why ask for a man in the harvest, and then push him back to the farm, shop or to the office by starvation wages? Christ also said: ''The laborer is worthy of his hire.'' One of my college chums told me the other day, that he must go to the farm in order to support his family. He leaves four churches in his denomination without a pastor. Justifiable? A thousand times, yes. If we of the Church expect God to call young men into the ministry, then we must make preparation to take care of them, and the work they are to do. And, too, we must take care of those who have given their lives to the work, and have now had to cease from active service. We shall do that and more when we are willing to obey every command of the Master.

J. VINCENT KNIGHT.

Greensboro, N. C.

SUFFOLK LETTER

The ninety-ninth session of the Eastern Virginia Christian Conference, held at Waverly, Virginia, October 28-30, 1919, has now become a part of her history. The Waverly church is one of the young and growing congregations of the Conference. Rev. J. L. Foster, with a real preacher's wife, is the zealous and useful pastor.

The welcome by the Mayor, B. E. White, for the town, J. F. West, Jr., for the church, was gracious in spirit and address.

The weather was ideal, the hospitality was royal in its spirit and great dinners. The attendance was large, the work of the Conference was earnest and business dispatched by President C. H. Rowland by the clock. There was no idle or waste time in the three days of the session.

Collections reached the sum of $7,359.36 on apportionment of $7,500.00; and this deficit was caused by some churches reading the wrong table of figures. All the churches sent in their check as they had read the tables.

Three new ministers were received into the Conference: Revs. H. J. Fleming and W. B. Fuller by letter from the North Carolina Conference; and Rev. Dr. L. E. Smith from the Eel River Conference, Indiana. Dr. J. O. Atkinson, our missionary leader; C. B. Riddle, THE SUN's genial Editor; C. D. Johnston, the beloved Superintendent of the Orphanage; Dr. P. H. Fleming, the product of "Mother's Answered Prayer"; and James W. Wellons, the patriarch of the Southern Convention, all honored the Conference with their presence and their wisdom.

Two sweet fellowship meetings were held by some twenty ministers from 9 to 10 a. m., Wednesday and Thursday. Rev. A. Victor Lightbourne preached a great sermon on Tuesday night, and Rev. H. W. Dowding gave another great message on Wednesday night.

The reports this year were prepared with care and contained a Forward Movement spirit and the discussions and addresses accompanying the reports were thought-provoking and inspiring.

The report of the woman's work by Mrs. C. H. Rowland showed that they had passed their goal of $4,000.00 the past year, and had set as their goal $5,000.00 for the coming year. They have planned to carry $1,200.00 of the Washington, D. C., work for the next year. The ministers present pledged themselves to stand by the women in trying to organize a Woman's Missionary Society in every Church in the Conference.

Mr. and Mrs. W. J. Benson of the People's Church, Dover, Delaware; Rev. R. S. Stephens who has organized another church in Dover, and Rev. A. Victor Lightbourne and wife, were present to represent the Dover work. Mrs. Lightbourne sang several fine solos, and this added to the splendid musical work of the Waverly choir.

The Conference sends to W. C. Wicker, Treasurer of the Southern Christian Convention, this year, the exact sum which the Convention asks of this Conference, $5,250.00; Foreign Missions, $1,750.00; Convention Missions, $1,400.00; Convention Fund, $700.00; Elon College Fund, $1,400.00.

The delegates remained to the close of the session, this year, better than at any previous Conference. The interest was unbroken to the close and the vision of obligation broadens with the years; and the people seem to take more interest and look more to helping others. Miss Iola Hedgepeth made two touching talks about her work in the mountains of Virginia, and the women have undertaken her support in the great work which she has undertaken among the mountaineers.

The Conference goes to Holy Neck next year, and it will be the *centennial* of this Conference. Holy Neck is a historic church and the Centennial Conference will be a great occasion among us. Plans have already been started for a program to fully represent the century in ways that will be of interest and permanent historic value.

W. W. STALEY.

MONUMENT FOR REV. L. I. COX

The churches of which Rev. L. I. Cox was pastor at the time of his decease have decided to erect a tombstone at his grave. As the money is sent in, I will report the same in THE SUN.

So far New Lebanon only has sent in its money, amounting to $117 as follows:

J. T. Bason, $5.00; Jesse Comer, $5.00; S. A. Harris, $10.00; F. F. Sharpe, $10.00; Peter Strickland, $5.00; J. S. Sharpe, $10.00; H. P. Moore, $10.00; W. G. Sharpe, $5.00; C. E. Sharpe, $10.00; Laura Sharpe, $5.00; W. M. Suits, $5.00; C. C. Griffin, $1.00; J. I. Sharpe, $5.00; W. M. McCollum, $1.00; P. R. Griffin, $5.00; Mrs. Numa Comer, $2.00; W. T. Moore, $5.00; Jas. N. McCollum, $5.00; J. T. Moore, $2.00; Stella Sharpe, $1.50; Ellen Sharpe, $1.00; Mrs. J. T. Moore, $0.50; Mrs. G. C. Moore, $1.00; G. C. Moore, $1.00; Carrie Sharpe, $1.00; Clyde Sharpe, $1.00; James Sharpe, $1.00; R. E. Sharpe, $2.00; W. P. Strickland, $1.00. Total, $117.00.

As the other churches remit, report will be made, and when all is in the tomb-stone will be erected. It is beautiful for these churches to honor themselves in this way.

W. A. HARPER, *Treasurer.*

A TRIP TO DURHAM

I made an appointment to preach to the old, unsaved people at the Durham Christian church a few Sundays ago. We had a delightful service, though there were but a few old people present. The church was filled and the attention splendid.

Rev. Stanley C. Harrell delivered an interesting sermon that night, telling his experiences as a Chaplain in France. The weather was very unfavorable but a large congregation was present.

It was a great trip for me to visit the Durham church, after having served as pastor there nine years. I visited several families and enjoyed mingling with friends.

The present pastor of the Durham church is very much devoted to his work, but feels that he is called to another field.   J. W. WELLONS.

Elon College, N. C.

MISSIONARY

THEY GO FORWARD

The Woman's Missionary Conference of Eastern Virginia met in annual session at the Washington Street Christian church, Portsmouth, Va., Thursday morning, October 23· This was the best and most enthusiastic of all the sessions of this wide-awake Conference yet held. The delegation was large, almost completely filling the large auditorium of our ample church. Because of a belated train the president, Mrs. C. H. Rowland, was absent at the opening; but Mrs. R. B. Wood, acting president and Mrs. I. W. Johnson, secretary, had the Conference going almost exactly on time, and the schedule of busy activity was kept up at a rapid pace till adjournment at 5 o'clock P. M., when all business had been completed. What a day! And how our women do put us men to shame by the rapid and thorough manner in which they do things. What the women wish, they go and do. We men talk many of our best plans to death before they are well born.

Among the monumental things of the day, either already done, or planned were: The Treasurer's report by Mrs. M. L. Bryant showing the following collectivos for the year:

Woman's Societies	$2,565.02
Young People's Societies	1,462.43
Willing Workers Societies	241.55
Total raised for the year	$4,269.00

The goal for the year was $4,000.00. -
They went over the top by $269.00.
The goal was set for next year at $5,000.00.

It was decided to have a "Home Mission Special" equal in amount to the "Foreign Mission Special," and that this "special" be for the support of our Washington, D. C. pastor. The goal of the Young People was fixed at $1,000.00 and this is to be used in prosecuting our mountain work as the Mission Board may direct. The young people of Portsmouth church gave a most impressive and suggestive program in panorama of the need of foreign mission work.

Miss Toshio Sato San, our Japanese pupil at Elon, gave a very touching and beautiful and inspiring talk on "My Own Japan." The Conference was mightily moved by this stirring address. The President, Mrs. C. H. Rowland, brought a thrilling and forward looking message entitled, "That We Go Forward." Miss Jennie Willis Atkinson read a very helpful paper on "Missionary Heroes and Heroines." The reports by Mrs. W. V. Leathers for the Young People, Mrs. W. D. Harward on Literature, Miss Mary Andrews on Cradle Roll, and Mrs. I. W. Johnson for the Woman's Board were all pointed, helpful, exceedingly interesting. The writer counted it a great joy and privilege to be allowed on the program in trying to present "The Challenge of a Great Task."

The Portsmouth church ladies served a beautiful and substantial luncheon at the noon hour, and the welcome at Portsmouth was cordial and most happy. The women of Eastern Virginia are doing great things for the Kingdom. Rev. H. Shelton Smith now in Yale, is to be sent out and supported by this Conference, as soon as he is ready to go. The Conference's motto was, "Anywhere, Provided it be Forward."

J. O. ATKINSON.

INTERESTED IN HELPING OTHERS

Dear Editor:

Since I sent in the last article for THE CHRISTIAN SUN I have been very ill. I am just back from the hospital but am still in bed, wishing and praying that I could do something worth while for he Lord Who has done so much for me. Sometimes the bed of affliction reveals to us friends whom we did not know we had and proves to us a blessing.

After a life of forty-four years spent without being interested in missions, I have become deeply interested in the subject. My thoughts night and day are as to what I can do. I can neither go to Sunday school nor preaching now but will try to wait and be patient and pray that God will bless what I try to write and may I be a help to someone through writing.

When we are sick we often think of much that we have left undone and resolve to be better Christians if we are spared. I want to quote a few sentences from a book, which was loaned me by a friend, entitled "How to Interest Your Sunday School in Missions.". "An old Chinaman at the age of eighty said: 'Can it be possible that God's people have known of this wonderful Savior all these centuries and I have never heard of him till now? Why did you not come to me sooner?'" We have no words to answer that pathetic question. We cannot recall lost opportunities. The spirit of Missions is the spirit of the Master. Let me fail in trying to do something rather than to sit still and do nothing. Shall we not pray for the same Lord who anointed the eyes of the blind and gave sight to come now and anoint the eyes of our people for spiritual blindness, giving them power to see the souls that are passing out into eternity?

The following lines quoted from *The Christian Herald* have proven a blessing to me in times of trouble:

"There never were words that were sweeter,
There never was promise more dear,
Than this message God gave to His children
Bidding them trust and not fear.

'Surely I will be with thee
Yes, ever Your footsteps I'll guide,
And the storm-clouds shall not hide me from thee,
For I will be close to thy side.'"

MRS. J. L. HALL.

News Ferry, Va.

A. C. Joyce—I do not wish to do without THE CHRISTIAN SUN. Have taken it for nearly eleven years.

Ed. Smith—My family enjoys THE SUN and we don't want to miss a copy.

NOTES

Rev. B. J. Howard changes his address from Chapel Hill, N. C., to Route 2, Jonesboro, N. C.

Rev. W. S. Long changes his address from Chapel Hill, N. C. to Whiteville, N. C., Box 26.

Don't forget that the Woman's Missionary Convention of the North Carolina Conference meets at Elon College, November 8-9.

Bro. J. B. Watson, Jonesboro, N. C., writes: 'The church at Shallow Well will go over the top in all her finances this year. I say, hurrah for the pastorate system!''

A friend of ·THE SUN—a lady—renews her subscription and adds $5.00 as a "pounding" for the Editor. We are grateful and highly appreciate the gift.

The Third church, Norfolk, Va., has voted to pay the salary of a worker in Japan. This church also pays the increase made by the Mission Board in Miss Williams salary from the time it was increased.

We note that the Brotherhood Bible class,. Third church, Norfolk, Va., is doing active work among men. They are making a house to house canvass in the interest of their work.

Brother F. T. Banks, Montgomery, Ala., sends this message: "Please accept my check for the sum of $2.00. I am not a member of the Christian Church but I enjoy THE SUN. Having been a subscriber for four years, I still love my College and enjoy the Church news.

A good sister writing from Harrisonburg, Va., and signing her name "Constant Reader," sends $3.00 to be used in sending THE SUN to some worthy person. The amount will be properly applied and we thank this unnamed friend.

Mt. Bethel church, Rockingham county, North Carolina is in need of a pastor and desires to get in touch with some one who can serve them for another year. Miss Ethel Friddle, Stokesdale, N. C., is secretary and would be pleased to hear from any pastor who can serve.

Rev. John G. Truitt, News Ferry, Va., has been stirring up the brethren of late, concerning THE CHRISTIAN SUN. He has been sending renewals and new subscriptions at intervals for some time. Last week he sent sixteen new subscribers in one list, together with two renewals, enclosing a check for $36.00. Who will do likewise?

· We are informed by Brother J. P. Montgomery, Chairman of the Entertainment Committee, of the North Carolina Conference, that many churches have not as yet sent the names of their delegates. Attend to the matter now. Write J. P. Montgomery, Burlington, N. C., if you are going to attend the Conference and want a home.

As we supply the final copy for THE SUN this (Monday) morning, we hear of the passing of Dr. W. T. Herndon at his home in Winston-Salem, N. C., November 1. His body was brought to Elon this morning and the funeral will take place this afternoon from the College chapel. A good and great man has gone home. A more extended account of his life will appear next week.

THE SUN has said about ten thousand times during its history, that if you want an article published, sign your name to it. That does not mean that your name has to appear, but that it will appear unless you otherwise instruct. A letter mailed at Phoenix, Ala., telling of a meeting at Beulah church, and signed by "A Member," was received a few days ago. We cannot print this, or any other article, without the name. Sign your name, sign your name, sign your name.

We have just received a new subscriber to THE CHRISTIAN SUN that came in this way: The carrier on a R. F. D. route put a copy of THE CHRISTIAN SUN in the wrong box. The lady of the house took the paper out and read it and became so interested that she sent her subscription. This demonstrates the fact again that there are thousands of homes in our Church, that would gladly take THE CHRISTIAN SUN if only they had a fair introduction to it. If you believe in THE CHRISTIAN SUN thoroughly, do a little missionary work for us.

Many CHRISTIAN SUN readers, especially in North Carolina, will recall the name of Rev. Luther L. Folger, evangelist of the Wesleyan Methodist Church. In scanning the pages of The Wesleyan Methodist, Syracuse, New York, the other day, we found this note: "The Rev. L. L. Folger, of the Illinois Conference, has accepted a call to the pastorate of the Wesleyan Methodist church at Central, S. C., where he and his wife, Sister Anna Kirk Folger, will receive their mail from this date, as they arrived in Central the third of this month.''

We quote this from the Biblical Recorder: "We happened to be on the same train with our good friend, Dr. J. O. Atkinson, of Elon College, Mission Secretary of the Christian Church, and received some encouraging information as to the doings of the denomination which he represents. His territory covers Virginia, North Carolina, Georgia, and Alabama. They have fewer than three hundred churches, but they are doing great things. Within three months this year they raised $300,000 for Christian Education, under the leadership of Dr. W. A. Harper, president of Elon College, and Dr. Atkinson is launching a campaign for a half million for missions, and is confident that he will secure it.''

WORSHIP AND MEDITATION

LOOKING FOR SOMETHING BETTER

(Rev. J. T. Kitchen)

"I am all the time looking forward for something better—for better and happier days." These words were recently spoken to me by one who had passed in and through the depths of poverty, sorrow and suffering, and I was deeply impressed with their simplicity and beautiful sentiment as never before. To meet any one so bright, cheerful and hopeful considering their condition ought to help everybody to throw away despondency forever and to make the passing time brighter and more helpful to somebody. Little acts of kindness, loving deeds, pleasant and encouraging words have a charm to impart to every one which nothing else can. Certainly it will take time, tact and study to accomplish the best results but the happiness derived from such, helpful and pleasant exercise will fully compensate for everything spent in the accomplishment. We do not always find that for which we look, but an honest, earnest effort will often bring success. The reason why many do not succeed is because they do not try. They do not look, see, nor grasp the opportunities which present themselves. Fear, doubt, timidity and some other causes stand in the way of success; and amid the war of antagonism and conflicting elements they cringe in despair and hide in the darkness of fear.

There is so much to see and think about in the long ago that the very soul is overwhelmed in contemplation as the mind roams and strolls over eventful and familiar scenes of early days when life was fresh and new. When the mind takes such wonderful and unlimited excursions through and over vast empires and beautiful worlds, it gladly returns refreshed and invigorated by its splendid and matchless journey. Then in the stillness and quietness of reflection it lives life over again as it contemplates the illimitable height and the unknown distance it has traveled. And when moving on the verge of time looking down the gray, dim, dark vista of the future, swelling emotions of the tenderest nature pervade the whole being as you stand amazed with such hopeful aspiration. You did not—you could not, you would not listen to the silent voices of the past as pleasant memories lingered over the way and caused you to survey with inexpressible delight the pleasant emotions which trembled in the heart. Look away as much as possible from the sad things of life and fix the mind upon the scenes of immortal beauty and perpetual joy. Picture all you can an ideal life, and try to feel, that if you could prevent it your pen should never, no never, write another sad, discouraging thought, nor your tongue give utterance to another depressing, sorrowing word, but speak beautiful, encouraging, glad words and stretch them across the sky in golden letters as bright as the sun.

There are some things it would have been best not to have heard nor known them, but since you have, try to look for the good and pleasant things. Earnestly, diligently look for the beautiful, the good, and for the best things, and life will be sweeter and more attractive every day. And in contemplating and searching after the ideal life it will keep the mind from dwelling so much and so long upon the impure, imperfect and the unpleasant things.

Life is a great and wonderful thing and we are enjoying its blessings and trying to solve its rich and profound problems, which in many cases, are too deep and mysterious for us to understand. It is so strange, however, that a harp with a thousand strings should stay in tune so long, but the tunes it played were not always pleasant nor in harmony. There was some discord, and the strings were not always touched by angel fingers, but sometimes a fallen angel seemed to get hold of them. So many tunes have been played upon these harp strings that one would think they would be worn out before this time. Tunes of gladness and sadness, joy and grief come after each other in rapid succession. And they have also had to stand the strains of love and hatred and all the good and bad emotions which have swept through the soul, until tired and weary, sad and lonely has been the often repeated refrain. But in the midst of all these adverse conditions you have looked for glad, bright, better days until your harp strings have trembled with happiness which was inexpressible and full of rapture. O, the joy which clings close to the heart as it realizes these happy moments! Joy, joy is coming soon to many hearts. Let us look for and expect it to come every day. For no more important event can you look forward to than the coming of gladness. The poorest and the most humble may share in the great, rich blessings that happiness has for them. And often they enjoy it more abundantly than the rich and more fortunate ones.

Looking away from self and getting out of ourselves watching for an opportunity to help somebody, to make somebody happy is truly a grand thing to consider and to do. Living in ourselves and for self only has a great tendency to make us narrow, contracted and selfish. Yes, looking for something better is my theme, and let us practice with patience so as to perform our duties pleasantly and realize the blessings which we seek. Hold up the standard of industry, honesty and truth until they shall be seen and better understood by all who are aspiring after goodness and noble characters. To have greater and still higher ambition to reach the topmost height of success should be the constant desire of every one. So many there are who miss the prize because they fail to grasp the opportunities which are within their reach.

Windsor, Va.

THE STORY OF THE LOAF

Mary was standing by the kitchen table watching her mother deftly knead bread. "May I make a loaf all by myself some day?" she asked.

"Do you think you could make a loaf of bread all by yourself, darling?" was mother's reply.

"Why, yes, mother!" said Mary. "I've watched you so often I know just how to do it, and I am nearly nine years old, you know."

"Very well, daughter, some day you shall try to make a loaf all by yourself."

A few weeks later a letter from grandma called mother away from home for a day or two, and Mary became a proud housekeeper. "Now," said she to herself, as she hung up the tea towel after wiping the cups, "I'll make a loaf of bread and surprise father."

But when she went to scoop some flour out of the flour barrel she found it completely empty. There was nothing to do but to go to the grocer's.

"Good evening, Mr. Smith. Did mother order flour?" Mary inquired as the grocer turned to wait on her.

"I'm very sorry," replied the grocer, "but I'm just out of flour. I won't have any until the miller sends it."

Mary looked quite crestfallen as she walked up the street. She did so want to make a loaf of bread. But presently a light sprang into her eyes, and she quickened her steps, saying: "I'll go to the miller and get some flour from him."

She knew exactly where the tall mill stood on the outskirts of the village, for she had often watched the dusty millers throwing the bags of flour into the big trays or loitered to listen to the noisy machinery inside. But today the wheels were still and the usually busy miller stood with arms folded in the big doorway. "Good evening, Mr. Miller," said Mary. "I've come to see if you will sell me a little flour. The grocer has none, and I want to make a loaf of bread."

"I'm very sorry," said the miller, gazing curiously into the eager little face, "I have no flour, and I can't make any until the farmer brings me some wheat to grind."

After thinking the matter over for a few seconds Mary looked up brightly and asked: "If I get some wheat from the farmer and bring it to you, will you grind it into flour for me?"

"Indeed I will," said the miller.

But the farmer had to refuse her also. "It's too bad," he said, "I have no wheat ready to be ground." And pointing to a field near by, he added: "The wheat will be ready in a few days, but it must drink in more sunshine and rain before it will be ripe enough to cut and thresh and be ready for the miller."

Mary turned toward home, a very disappointed little girl. "What a lot of people have to work together, and how long it takes just to make a loaf of bread!" she thought.

As she was passing the miller's cottage, which stood in a pretty garden just opposite the mill, to her surprise the miller's wife appeared at the door and called out: "Are you the little girl who came to the mill to buy some flour?"

"Yes," said Mary; "I wanted some to make a loaf of bread to surprise my father."

"Well," said the kind woman, "I have a little flour left in my barrel and will give you enough to make a loaf."

NEW COMERS TO THE SUN FAMILY

Mrs. W. H. Keyser	Luray, Va.
Miss Ethel Jennings	Columbus, Ga.
W. A. Christopher	Columbia, Ga.
M. C. Upchurch	Lillington, N. C.
Mrs. Effie Baker	Haw River, N. C.
J. N. Cutchins	South Norfolk, Va.
Mrs. H. E. Roone	South Norfolk, Va.
Mrs. A. V. Allen	Norfolk, Va.
A. B. Gilliam	Reidsville, N. C.
B. D. Gilliam	Reidsville, N. C.
J. B. Little	Waverly, Va.
W. J. Benson	Dover, Del.
Mrs. John Whitlow	Ingram, Va.
Mr. R. H. Adams	Ingram, Va.
Mrs. Chas. Davis	Ingram, Va.
Mrs. Henry Osborne	Ingram, Va.
Mrs. Jeff Davis	Ingram, Va.
Mr. John Guill	Ingram, Va.
Mrs. John Chandler	Ingram, Va.
Mr. W. A. Alderson	Paces, Va.
Mr. Harry Henderson	Paces, Va.
Mrs. J. D. Moore	Paces, Va.
Mrs. L. A. Douglas	Paces, Va.
Mrs. Newton Alderson	Paces, Va.
Mr. Jim Collie	Paces, Va.
Mr. R. O. Strange	Paces, Va.
Mrs. W. C. Dunn	News Ferrry, Va.
Mrs. Leslie Alderson	Houston, Va., Route 1
Mrs. H. E. Roane	South Norfolk, Va.
Mrs. DeLacy Foust	Liberty, N. C.
M. F. Hornaday	Liberty, N. C.
Mrs. Mary McKenzie	Eagle Springs, N. C.

(Report to November 3)

Mrs. W. E. Wills, Suffolk, Va., ordered a Bible from us the other day, and upon its receipt, here is the testimony she sent: "The Bible received today. Husband and I are very much pleased with it. We thank you for the prompt attention given."

The great strike now on by the coal workers is trying to be avoided by the Government, but the outlook is not hopeful at this time.

Secretary E. M. Carter of the Alabama Conference says that the churches of that Conference raised last year, including salaries of pastors, $4,282.77 against $3,247.58 the year before. Hats off to the Alabama Conference! It is finding itself.

"O, thank you!" cried Mary. "I'll return it when we get ours." And her feet fairly danced along the road as she carried home the coveted package.

At luncheon next day when father helped himself to a slice of fresh bread and exclaimed, "Fresh bread and mother away! Where did it come from?" Mary's face was a picture. "Guess, father," she said. After mentioning several of the neighbors, "Surely you didn't make it!" he cried.

"Yes, I did," replied a joyous little voice.

"All by yourself?" questioned father.

"No-o," said Mary. "I used to think I could do it all alone, but now I know I can't. The grocer and the miller and the farmer, and O, so many more people, as well as the sunshine and the rain and the wind, have to help."

THE CHRISTIAN ORPHANAGE

THANKSGIVING OFFERING

Thanksgiving Day will soon be here. It comes at a season of the year when most of the year's work is in the past and we are gathering in the harvest from our labors. It is a time when all hearts should be filled with gratitude to God for His wonderful blessings bestowed during the year. It is a time when each and every one should want to make an offering to show their appreciation for the many blessings they have received during the year.

I hardly think there is a time more appropriate than on or near Thanksgiving Day to remember the little helpless children who have been unfortunate and have lost father and mother, and are dependent upon charity and free-will offerings from those whom God has been good to, for support. It is a time when you should open your hearts as never before and give as the Lord has prospered you, that your offering may help to give some little boy or girl a home in the Orphanage where they can be trained and cared for and given an opportunity to make good in life.

There are a great many children within the bounds of the Christian Church who, through no fault of theirs, are growing up in ignorance and sin. Children who are bright, and, if proper environments were thrown around them, would grow up to be useful citizens of our great country and for the Kingdom. Without this care on the part of the Church they will perhaps drift and yield to the many temptations the world has to offer them.

The mission of the Christian Orphanage is to reach and help this class of children, and while we may not see the results of the great work an institution of this kind may be doing now, who can tell what results the future may reveal? If the institution should only save one child—just one—who could value the worth of that one soul?

Perhaps it may never be convenient for you to make the sacrifice to be the Superintendent of the Christian Orphanage or to have charge of the work in person,

and never be able to render service of this kind, but you have a part that God has given you that you may lend a helping hand in this work. He has blessed you bountifully. He has not suffered you to be in need or want. A good home has been yours. Food and clothes to keep you comfortable. Father and mother to train you while young. Good health has been granted you; this world's goods a plenty, and to spare, and while the Christian Orphanage is now taking care of sixty little ones, you are suffering forty to be turned away from its doors for the lack of room. What part can you take in this great work for the Master's Kingdom? You can make a sacrifice of a part of that which God has given you to help in this work. Give at least the value of one day's wage.

We appeal to you from our heart to plan now what you can do for the coming Thanksgiving offering. Pray for the success of the offering, and may each of us do our full duty in regard to it. Let us perform the work and leave the great results to Him Who is good and whose mercy endureth forever.

With no "flu" and no war to hinder this fall, and no scourge of any kind to keep our people from church as we had last fall, our Thanksgiving offering should be the largest in the history of the institution. See that the offering from your church is more than last year. *Six thousand dollars* for the Thanksgiving offering is our goal and we must reach it. If you do your part we will reach it. Don't let us be disappointed because you failed to do your part. You are a link in this chain. Be a strong and worthy link. Let us do things and not dream them. I pray that God will show *you your duty* and may *you do your duty.*

CHAS. D. JOHNSTON, *Supt.*

FINANCIAL REPORT FOR NOVEMBER 5, 1919

Amount brought forward, $11,911.23.

Children's Offerings

Lenora and Lewis Welch, $1.00; Olive Daniel Poythress, Jr., 50 cents; Edgar Jones, 50 cents; Elizabeth Jones, 50 cents; Total, $2.50.

Sunday School Offerings

(Eastern Virginia Conference)

Damascus, $2.02; Antioch, $2.00; Rosemont, $5.00; New Lebanon, $6.45.

(North Carolina Conference)

Mebane, $1.00; New Lebanon, $1.00; New Lebanon Baracca Class, $1.00; Ramseur, $4.23; New Hope, $10.00.

(Virginia Valley Conference)

Timber Ridge, $3.64.

(Alabama Conference)

Wadley, $1.38; Total, $37.72.

Thanksgiving Offerings

Liberty Springs, (Eastern Va. Conference) $100.00.

Special Offerings

T. E. Brickhouse, Norfolk, Va., $100.00; Lois C. Lawrence, Washington, D. C., $15.00; Rev. and Mrs. W. G. Clements, Morrisville, N. C., $5.00; Mrs. Alonzo Bartlett, (For Woman's Missionary Society), Machais, N. Y., $5.00; Ladies' Aid Society, Ashboro, N. C., $5.00; Total, $130.00.

Total for the week, $270.22; Grand total, $12,181.45.

CHILDREN'S LETTERS

Dear Uncle Charley: I am a little boy just eight months old, weigh twenty-one pounds, and have two teeth. Now, don't you think that is fine? I am a preacher's son and my name is Olive D. Poythress, Jr. Enclosed find 50 cents for the cousins. Best wishes to all the dear little boys and girls.—*Olive Daniel Poythress, Jr.*

I am very proud of our new little cousin. We give you a warm welcome to the Corner. We hope you will write often. You are a smart boy to weigh twenty-one pounds and have two teeth at eight months of age—*"Uncle Charley."*

Dear Uncle Charley: I guess you think we are not going to write any more. Enclosed find our dues for June, July, August, September and October. We haven't paid since May. I am going to school now. When I learn to write you will hear from us more often. With love and best wishes to you and the little orphans. —*Edward and Elizabeth Jones.*

I am glad to get your letter today and to know you have not forgotten us. Always glad to have you write. —*"Uncle Charley."*

Dear Uncle Charley: We are sending you $1.00 for the orphan babies. Hope they are all well. Love to all.—*Lenora and Lewis Welch.*

You are splendid little folks. Glad to get your letter with one dollar enclosed. Write again.—*"Uncle Charley."*

LOST BAGGAGE OF RETURNED SOLDIERS

The American Red Cross notifies us that there are 150,000 pieces of lost baggage that have been stored at the Government Docks at Hoboken, N. J., made up of 20,000 trunk lockers, 15,000 bed rolls, 5,000 suitcases and 110,000 barrack bags which have come from overseas and remain unclaimed by their owners.

Most of this baggage is marked with names only and cannot be forwarded to the owners. In all cases a new shipping address is required. All owners of lost baggage should forward their claims and present addresses to the Lost Baggage Branch Pier No. 2 Hoboken, N. J., with an accurate description of the missing property.

A complete card index permits prompt identification and the baggage will be forwarded by express at the Government expense if on hand at Hoboken.

The Red Cross desires to assist each man from overseas to recover his lost property as well as to help the Government to dispose of this enormous accumulation.

He who would be no slave must be content to have no slaves. Those who deny freedom to others deserve it not themselves, and under a just God cannot long retain it.—*Abraham Lincoln.*

Billy Sunday goes to Norfolk, Va., January 4. His tabernacle there is to hold about 9,000 people.

Size 25X36 Inches

HAVE YOU HEROES?

Have you been associatel with men who have served their country, and whom you are now anxious to welcome home? Have you a friend or relative who has done Military Service of any kind, because of the War?

Have you men in your employ who have sacrificed career, prospects, income, and family ties, and risked Life itself, to Serve Their Country?

Do you want to immortalize the names of these men, that those who are to come may do them honor?

A Liberty Honor Testimonial

will hold these names in the embrace of imperishable metal—the very walls of the structure on which it is erected, will crumble to dust, while these names are still as clear as the day they were cast.

For churches, schools, lodges, banks and other institutions.

In all former Wars, it has been, with but few exceptions, the names of only the commanders, who have been honored. Through the country, there are scattered the statues of Generals, ahorse and afoot, with field-glass and with sword, but always the common soldier—the FIGHTER—has been forgotten.

It must not be so in this War—this democracy must pay its tribute to the actual men behind the guns.

For prices and particulars, address,

C. B. RIDDLE · - - - Burlington, N. C.

Sunday School and Christian Endeavor

SUNDAY SCHOOL LESSON FOR
NOVEMBER 16, 1919
(Mrs. Fred Bullock)

Witnesses of Christ's Glory.—Luke 9:28-36.

Golden Text: This is my beloved Son; hear ye him.—Mark 9:7.

Additional Material For Teachers. —Matt. 17:1-8; Mark 9:2-8; II Pet. 2:1-76.

In this lesson we go up "With Peter and John on the Mountain" (Junior Topic) to see "The Glory of Jesus Christ" (Intermediate Topic), and gain for ourselves some "Mountain Top Experiences" (Senior and Adult Topic).

And Mountain top experiences are something we all need. Our road seems to lie so level, so flat, unchanging; we can look ahead for days and weeks and months, and there is no variation, no change, and then, some way, somehow, we come to a mountain, and from the mountain we secure a new view, a new outlook, as did Pilgrim on the Delectable Mountains. We look across the hills and valleys, the sorrows and hardships, and there, at the end, we catch a glimpse of Heaven's own glory.

Had Peter and John never had this glimpse into the unsearchable riches of the glory of Christ, there might be times when they doubted the quiet man who walked in Galilee, Who "went about doing good," but never compelling the worship or obedience of men. "Whom say ye that I am?" He asked in His dusty wayside garments, and the proof that their revelations were correct was seen when He "was transfigured before them." We may not doubt that ever true believer in the Lord will have some time this experience; the soil will drop away, the grey will turn to white, the shining soul will leave visible impression on the face, and looking up, seeing Jesus only, they will be like Him, because they will see Him as He is.

It is easier to go back to the humdrum valley tasks; it is easy to cure the sick and cast out devils when we have had a mountain-top experience; God pity those who have had no "mountain-top" in their lives.

CHRISTIAN ENDEAVOR TOPIC FOR
NOVEMBER 16, 1919.
J. Vincent Knight

"*Co-operation in Christian Service.*" John 17:20-23; I Cor. 3:5-10.

One of our greatest needs is to see the importance of co-operation in Christian service, for one of our biggest blunders has been the division of our Christian forces and planning to make an individual Church grow instead of looking after the larger things of the Kingdom. It has taken the bloodshed of millions of the world's best to pay for our folly as a people, for if we had spent one-fifth of the money wasted in one year of the war, for Christian missions and Kingdom extension, we never would have heard of a world war. Yet, it has taken the most horrible war in the history of the world to convince us that we must unite our forces if we win for Christ. Our men who faced the shot and shell never stopped to ask who were Democrats, Republicans or Progressives. Humanity came first. So must we lose sight of the fact that we are Baptists, Methodists, Presbyterians, Christians, etc., for the larger interests of the Kingdom. The world will no longer recognize a divided Church, nor will it recognize the Church forces unless we join hands in the great work of the Master. United we stand, divided we fall.

Take a look at the organizations that have served as a means of bringing our Church forces together and have helped us to co-operate. The Y. M. C. A. and Y. W. C. A., the Red Cross, Church federations, and Christian Endeavor. All these have been a mighty power in pulling down the division walls, and have wielded a mighty influence for God, and the right. Through these influences the day is not far hence, when we shall have a united front for God. But externally speaking, the Church will never be united—the work must be done within, for nothing except the love of God in the heart, the greater needs of the Kingdom, and a larger vision of the great work of our Christ will make us co-operate in the work.

All Christians can co-operate in breaking down sectarianism, strife and divisions. In enforcing Sabbath observance, law enforcement, and law observance—in pushing out the liquor traffic, and other evils of the present day. One thing our young people should co-operate in is the driving from our cities and towns the public dance halls, street dances, and gambling places where our people learn to take their first chance. Then, write to your representative at Washington, and thank him for the action he has taken in pushing the whisky from our country, if he stood by the "dries," and if he did not, then cast your vote against him the first opportunity. If we win for Christ, we shall do it through the mobilizing of every force for His work.

ORGANIZED CLASS IN BOTH YOUNG PEOPLE'S AND ADULT DIVISION

This is the third point of the Standard School. What is an Organized Class? is a question asked again and again, for while we have many classes there are many, still who do not understand the work of an organized class. Briefly, an organized class is a class having a president, vice-president, secretary and treasurer. To this should be added lookout and social committees and as many more as may be needed by the size of the class. We have outgrown the idea that the teacher should do everything and be everything in the class. We are beginning to realize that we are training men and women for work in the Kingdom, not helping them to pass an hour on Sunday by delivering a lecture half an hour, or forty minutes in length. Some one has characterized such teaching as "a sermon by a layman at 10:00 A. M., and a sermon by a preacher at 11:00 A. M."; there is often too much truth in this statement. How shall our boys and girls learn to do Kingdom service unless we give them an opportunity to learn? How shall our men and women exercise their "spiritual muscles" unless somewhere, somehow, they are given something to do that will provide an outlet for their spiritual energy? "Pastor", said the deacon, "Doesn't the good Book say, 'Feed my sheep!'" "Deacon," said the pastor, "We have too many stall-fed sheep now. What you need is not more feed, but more exercise.' It is this exercise the organized class is intended to offer. A class which simply "organizes" and then does nothing with its organization is no better than an unorganized class. First of all, the class should be organized, and then it should be organized for service. People are not only *saved* when they have found Christ, they are *saved to serve*. Christ's word is, "Come" until we have found Him, but immediately after a tarrying for power, it is "GO."

MRS. FRED BULLOCK.

PROHIBITION ACTIᵥᵢITES

In a campaign conducted jointly by the Anti-Saloon League of America and the League of the state, 300 meetings in the interest of Prohibition law enforcement and world-wide drouth will be held in North Carolina, beginning November 2 and closing December 21.

Speakers in the North Carolina campaign will be M. R. Patterson, former Governor of Tennessee; Rev. J. D. McAlister, Superintendent of the Anti-Saloon League of Tennessee; George W. Morrow, former Superintendent of the Michigan League; Joseph G. Camp, Atlanta orator; Rev. David Hepburn, Superintendent of the Virginia League; Congressman W. D. Upshaw, of Georgia; Robert Lee Davis, Superintendent of the North Carolina League; Rev. Dr. Charles O. Jones, Superintendent of the Georgia League, and Wayne B. Wheeler, Washington, D. C., Attorney and Counsel for the national organization.

The Anti-Saloon League, it is announced, is pursuing the plan of holding a series of meetings in practically every state. The Prohibition Amendment and enforcement law will be explained, and the people will be urged to demand strict enforcement not only of state and local laws, but also of Federal enactments. Election of officials favorable to enforcement will be insisted upon.

World Prohibition as the next step in reform also will be brought to the attention of the people. It will be explained that the League is a constituent of the World League Against Alcoholism recently organized in Washington.

MARRIAGES

WELDON-WINN

On September 21, 1919, in the presence of a few friends, Miss Pattie Jones Winn became the bride of Mr. James D. Weldon. Mr. Weldon is a son of Mr. and Mrs. J. T. Weldon, and Mrs. Weldon is a daughter of Mr. and Mrs. R. G. Winn. They will reside near Epsom, N. C.

R. L. WILLIAMSON.

WELLS-WICKER

Mr. Willard W. Wells and Miss Helen Wicker were, by the writer, united in marriage on October 7, 1919. Mr. Wells is a son of Mr. and Mrs. E. G. Wells. Mrs. Wells is a daughter of Mr. R. B. Wicker. Their home will be in Akron, Ohio, where Mr. Wells has a position.

R. L. WILLIAMSON.

BARTHOLOMEW-WINN

On October 22, 1919, the writer united in marriage Mr. Joseph J. Bartholomew and Miss Lizzie Winn. Mr. Bartholomew is a son of Mr. and Mrs. C. T. Bartholomew. Mrs. Bartholomew is a daughter of Mr. and Mrs. R. G. Winn. Their home will be near Epsom, N. C.

The above young people are of well known and highly respected families, and their many friends join the writer in wishing for them the greatest degree of happiness and prosperity, and always the smile of the Father's blessing.

R. L. WILLIAMSON.

OBITUARIES

NEWMAN

Mrs. Lizzie Newman, wife of Mr. K. H. Newman, passed from labor to reward September 16, 1919, in her thirty-fifth year. For more than a year she had been in failing health, but hopes were entertained for her recovery until about a week before her death. She was a devoted wife and loving mother. Her home was a realm in which she reigned in wifely affection and motherly grace and love. She had been since early girlhood a consistent member of the church, and

a follower of the Lord whom she loved and served. Besides her husband, she leaves to mourn her departure her mother, Mrs. Hudson; five brothers and a sister; five children: Lizzie Bell, Pearl, Lula May, Cathreen, and William Hurley.

May our pitying Father and compassionate Savior bless and comfort the bereaved.

R. L. WILLIAMSON.

TAYLOR

A. B. Taylor was born July, 1852, and died October 20, 1919, aged 67 years. He was a faithful member of the East End Christian church, Newport News, Va., and one of the ablest men in the church. As a man he was liked by all who knew him and those who knew him as a friend valued his companionship highly. A man of sterling qualities and Godly life has passed to his reward.

Prior to his death he was confined to his bed for five weeks and four days. He was a patient sufferer and one who longed to get well, but God called and he answered.

On November 14, 1906, he was married to Miss Mary S. Andrews who is left to mourn the loss of one who was husband and companion. May God's richest blessings be with her in this hour of bereavement and may the Great Shepherd be her comfort. May God extend to the members of the family His loving kindness and may their hearts be filled with joy for Christ.

The funeral services were conducted by his pastor, assisted by the Order of Maccabees. On October 21, we laid him to rest in Greenlawn cemetery to await for the resurrection of the body. Rarely has it been my privilege to help at the funeral of one who was so well respected and loved by all who knew him.

To those who miss his companionship Christ says with outstretched arms, "Come unto me and I will give you rest."

H. J. FLEMING.

HALL

Mrs. Mary Ann Gales Hall was born in Marion County, South Carolina, June 20, 1833, and married Hanson K. Hall, January 5, 1918. Her husband preceded her to his Heavenly home, only a few months ago. Their devoted Christian lives were an inspiration to their children, grandchildren, and all who had the pleasure of knowing them.

The cure of heart trouble is faith. Christ discloses the blessed life of which the present is the vestibule. "Let not your heart be troubled." He says, "Ye believe in God, believe also in me." He discourses of the "Father's House." The Home of the soul. Home: What a magic word! As the boys lay in the trenches, the bands played, "Home, Sweet Home," and a great sob went through the army.

"Home's not merely four square walls,
Though hung with pictures nicely gilded;
Home is where affection 'calls,
And filled with shrines the heart has builded."

The best of all, in that beautiful home, to which so many happy pilgrims are going day by day, will be the Lord's presence. "Where I am, ye shall be also." Then, too, what a glorious thought, He will come "'to receive us."

D. A. LONG.

SMILES

TRY THIS RECIPE

"To give the face a good color," says an exchange, "get a pot of rouge and a rabbit's foot. Bury them two miles from home and walk out and back once a day to see if they are still there."—*Boston Transcript*.

* * *

A GLORIOUS COUNTRY

The Wild Onion school-teacher lectured on the United States a few nights ago to a large audience, reports the Frog Hollow Kentuckian. In the course of his remarks he paid a glowing tribute to our country, and it is regretted that everybody in the United States was not present. "One reason we keep so far ahead of the other nations," said he, "is because we are getting up and going to work every morning while the folks around the other side of the world are just going to bed."—*Providence Journal*.

* * *

BEGAN EARLY

A company of people were waiting in a railroad station, and fell to relating at how early an age each had chosen his vocation. A farmer had been stimulated at twelve by a plot of ground given to him to cultivate. A preacher said that at the age of seven, in church, one day, he had resolved to enter the ministry. Thus several men spoke; but a sign-painter, present, antedated them all by remarking: "I started in my business before any of you. Why, before I could talk, I made signs."

* *

"Have you seen a fellow around here with a wooden leg by the name of Murphy?"

"What's the name of his other leg?"

THE CHRISTIAN SUN

"IN ESSENTIALS UNITY, IN NON-ESSENTIALS LIBERTY, IN ALL THINGS CHARITY"

Pray!

THE North Carolina and Virginia, Western North Carolina, and the Eastern North Carolina Conferences united for larger, bigger, and better things. This week the first session of the enlarged Conference—the North Carolina Conference—is in session. Pray that the Father's blessing may be upon the Conference's every deliberation and undertaking. Pray that harmony and good will may prevail. Pray that the churches composing the Conference may have their vision of service enlarged. Pray that a new day may dawn for this part of the Zion. Pray that the Christ may be glorified. Pray! Pray!!

Volume LXXI WEDNESDAY, NOVEMBER 12, 1919 Number 46

BURLINGTON · · · NORTH CAROLINA

THE CHRISTIAN SUN

Founded 1844 by Rev. Daniel W. Kerr

C. B. RIDDLE   -   -   -   Editor

Entered at the Burlington, N. C. Post Office as second class matter.

Subscription Rates

One year .... $ 2.00
Six months 1.00

In Advance

Give both your old and new postoffice when asking tbv your address be changed.

The change of your label is your receipt for money. If not receipts sent upon request.

Many persons subscribe for friends, intending that the same be stopped at the end of the year. If instructions are given to this effect, they will receive attention at the proper time.

Marriage and obituary notices not exceeding 150 words printed free if received within 60 days from date of event, all over this at the rate of one-half cent a word.

Original poetry not accepted for publication.

Principles of the Christian Church

(1) The Lord Jesus Christ is the only Head of the Church.
(2) Christian is a sufficient name of the Church.
(3) The Holy Bible is a sufficient rule of faith and practice.
(4) Christian character is a sufficient test of fellowship, and of church membership.
(5) The right of private judgment and the liberty of conscience is a right and a privilege that should be accorded to, and exercised by all.

EDITORIAL

ON BUSINESS FOR THE KING

About two hundred delegates and visitors attended the Woman's Missionary Convention at Elon College, November 8-9. The gathering was the initial session of the united forces of the three former conferences that embraced the churches of our denomination in North Carolina. Preparation had been made upon the part of the local organization and the officials of the Convention. Business-like, to the point, to the place, and on time the Convention took up its work—its business for the King.

Mrs. W. H. Carroll, Burlington, N. C., President of the Convention, inspired the Convention by her address. Her message had to do with goals of the past and the future. The various officers of the Convention made complete and satisfactory reports, which showed progress in every department, as well as missionary interest and activity. Mrs. W. A. Harper, President of the Woman's Board of the Southern Christian Convention, brought a message that inspired and uplifted. Her theme was: "Jesus and Women." Rev. E. K. McCord, missionary to Japan, addressed the body telling of the need of investment in human life in the heathen countries.

Part of the afternoon of the first day was given over to general discussion, led by Mrs. L. L. Vaughan, Raleigh, N. C. The interest taken in this fully demonstrated that the women were on business for the King. Senor Victor M. Rivera, Toshio Sato San, students from our mission fields, spoke interestingly and entertainingly of their native lands. Prof. Barra, of the department of Romance Languages of the College, delighted the Convention by his very earnest and impressive talk, which deepened interest in the missionary enterprise. Rev. George D. Eastes, scheduled to address the Convention on "Women and the Kingdom," was unable to be present due to ill health. Dr. Atkinson took the subject and his message was heard gladly.

The Young People's Missionary Society of the Burlington church gave a pageant at the evening session, entitled "Sunlight or Candlelight," which greatly edified and enlightened.

On Sunday morning Dr. Atkinson preached a great missionary sermon from the text: "The love of Christ Constraineth Us." Mrs. E. K. McCord, in the afternoon service, spoke of the work in Japan, also the Japanese customs, and reviewed the outlook for Christianity in that country. Closing her message by allowing questions to be asked, brought forth many interesting questions, all showing that delegates really wanted to know of the mission fields. Dr. J. W. Harrell spoke on "Our Women and the Future." His message was optimistic and prophetic, prophesying great things for our women in the near future.

Sunday night, Rev. E. K. McCord, preached a special missionary sermon that enriched the thought, and added to the missionary knowledge, of those who were privileged to hear him.

Mrs. A. F. Smith, Mrs. W. J. Pierce, Mrs. A. T. Banks and Mrs. Charles R. Clark, conducted the devotional during the Convention.

Space forbids the mention of the many great things undertaken. However, it will be of special interest to state that Rev. H. S. Hardcastle was adopted as missionary of the Convention when he is ready to take up the work. Appreciation of the life and labors of the late Rev. L. I. Cox was tendered by the Convention.

Officers for the ensuing year are as follows:

President—Mrs. W. H. Carroll, Burlington, N. C.
Vice-President—Mrs. A. T. Banks, Ramseur, N. C.
Secretary—Mrs. W. A. Harper, Elon College, N. C.
Treasurer—Mrs. W. R. Sellars, Burlington, N. C.
Superintendent Literature and Mite Boxes—Mrs. M. F. Cook, Greensboro, N. C.
Superintendent Young People's Work—Miss Bessie Holt, Burlington, N. C.
Superintendent Cradle Roll—Mrs. N. G. Newman, Elon College, N. C.
Superintendent Boys' Work—Mrs. J. W. Patton, Greensboro, N. C.

The place of the 1920 meeting is to be announced later.

Mrs. C. B. R.

DR. W. T. HERNDON

Dr. William Thomas Herndon, the last grandson of James O'Kelly, fell on sleep November 1, 1919, in the seventy-ninth year of his sojourn here. This ended a useful and active life of a man who had been a modest and model character. In early life Brother Herndon was an active and successful physician, and gave up a large and increasing practice to devote his life to more direct and active ministerial work. He was a pioneer and blazed the way in many directions for his denomination that the Kingdom on earth might go forward.

In the crisal days of Elon College Dr. Herndon gave up his pastorate and devoted all his time and strength to the financial interest of that institution. He was a friend of education and a strong advocate of its every need. He was also a champion for the cause of prohibition, and in the early days of the fight against King Alcohol, Dr. Herndon was a stump speaker for the cause of prohibition. To challenge the liquor traffic in those days was an unpopular issue, but our deceased Brother stood with others and lived to see the full fruitage of his labor in this noble work.

Dr. Herndon is survived by his wife, who was Miss Clara A. Edwards. Six children were born to make the Herndon home real. Two of these also survive—Mrs. Myrtle Moffitt, Ashboro, N. C., and Mrs. Gertrude Scott, Winston-Salem, N. C. In recent years Dr. and Mrs. Herndon lived with Mrs. Scott, in whose home the summons came.

The body was brought to Elon, the funeral service being conducted from the College chapel. Dr. J. O. Atkinson preached the funeral, assisted by Drs. N. G. Newman, J. W. Harrell, J. U. Newman, and P. H. Fleming. The interment took place in the village cemetery, witnessed by a host of sorrowing friends.

C. B. R.

A GOOD MAN PASSES

In the passing of Captain James A. Turrentine, as noted in last week's issue of THE SUN, the Church loses one of its most loyal members. Captain Turrentine served well and faithfully in various capacities. He loved truth, honesty, and was a champanion for progress. THE SUN and THE SUN's Editor had no truer friend. Young and old loved and respected him. He was a Christian gentleman, rich in spirit, brotherly in conduct and noble in character. He was wise in counsel and generous of heart. No pen, page, or pages can do his life justice.

The funeral was conducted from the Burlington Christian church by Rev. P. H. Fleming, D. D., assisted by Pastor Harrell, Rev. J. W. Wellons, Rev. J. W. Holt, and Dr. W. W. Staley. Dr. Fleming's tribute to the deceased was beautiful and timely. "Know ye not that there is a prince and a great man fallen in Israel this day" (II Samuel 3:38) was the basis of Dr. Fleming's remarks.

Long live the memory of departed Brother.

C. B. R.

JAMES A TURRENTINE

James Alexander Turrentine, was born in Orange County, now Alamance, November 19, 1835 and passed from labor to reward in the early morning hour of November 4, 1919, aged 83 years, 11 months and 15 days.

Brother Turrentinue was twice married. His first wife, Miss Martissia Scott, lived only a short time—about a year. His second wife was Miss Louisiana Kilby of Suffolk, Va. To this union were born eight children, five of whom are living: Virginus L. of Kinston, N. C., Darius H. of Norfolk, Va., Mrs. J. P. Montgomery, Mrs. W. T. Stokes and Miss Mary Turrentine of Burlington; also one brother, W. H. Turrentine, Burlington, N. C.

In early life he united with the Christian church and was ever devoted to its interest. He was at one time a member of New Providence Christian church, Graham, N. C., and a charter member of the Suffolk Christian church, and at the time of his death he was a member of the Burlington Christian church, and had been for a number of years. He was senior deacon and as a member and officer he took an active interest and part in the work of the church and its progress, and, though unable to hear much that was said, he attended services. He wanted to be there.

He was treasurer of the Western North Carolina Conference for a number of years and gave up the work only when advancing years made it unwise for him to be away from home during the winter. In this office he served faithfully and efficiently and would doubtless have served on till death but for the fact of age and inclement weather which often came about conference time.

He was in the railroad service of what is now the Southern, for a number of years, first as conductor and then as agent. He represented Alamance County in the State Legislature three times—twice in the House and once in the Senate. In county affairs he has served as County Commissioner, on the Board of Charities and the Board of Pensions, and was Mayor of Burlington for several years. He was a Mason tried and true. He leaves a host of friends and relatives who mourn his death. They will miss him. His seat will be empty. He left an impression wherever he went and in every capacity he served.

P. H. FLEMING.

SOLVING THE PROBLEM OF HIGH PRICES

There are a few fundamental facts that must be reckoned with in lowering the high cost of living. Production cannot be increased by shorter hours. The law of supply and demand controls prices, and you cannot lower the cost of things until you can regulate the supply. You cannot sell an article for less than it costs and continue to do business. The labor item is the one important thing in finding the cost of an article. High labor forces the manufacturer to increase the cost of his products. Each advance in labor is an advance in the cost of the market's wares. Each hour less per day

(Editorial continued on Page 11)

PASTOR AND PEOPLE

INGRAM—PLEASANT GROVE

This pastorate is beginning to put on its program a campaign of intensive, systematic work. The pastor is visiting every home and taking a careful and thorough survey of general conditions. Within the last five weeks I have visited over a hundred families. I have talked with them face to face, and heart to heart about repentance, salvation, prayer, faith, works; about better homes, better fences, better fields, better roads; about churches, schools, and Sunday schools; and the hospitality and response have been gratifying.

Often times it is necessary for pastors to teach school, or engage in other pursuits to gain a livelihood, but such a proceeding is certainly handicapping to them in their pastoral work. I speak from experience. For two years I tried the patience of a great people. The survey which I have been making clearly reveals how great their patience was, but I trust it is henceforth impossible for a pastor to serve this pastorate with less than his full time.

There is a drought of candidates for the ministry. The crop is short. But if every minister who serves in country pastorates will but carry the love of the Christ direct to the hearts of the lads whom they have taught to love them something good and great is going to happen. The crop of candidates for the ministry must be increased, but before the crop is increased we must awaken ourselves to some fundamental changes in the methods of country church management. Country churches must be educated to the place where they will take and read THE CHRISTIAN SUN. They must be brought to the place where they will provide Sunday school rooms an up-to-date methods in their Sunday schools. They must have their minister constantly in their midst. He must himself be wide awake to the demands of his community and love it with an untiring and consecrated love. With such a love he will see the leaks and will be the better able to make his community safe for Christianity.

J. G. TRUITT.

FRANKLIN, VIRGINIA

The Franklin Christian church has experienced a revival of deep spiritual power. The special services began October 12, and continued until the 22. Rev. A. Victor Lightbourne of Dover, Delaware, was present from the first, preaching twice each day. His messages were clear, forceful and convincing and under the direction of the Holy Spirit. They had convincing and converting power. Each day for a week prior to, and during, the meetings, prayer meetings were held in homes in the town, two or three each day. There was great interest in these and they were sources of great blessings. The church was stirred and moved into a nearer spiritual relation to the Lord. This was evident in no mistakable way. Every department of our church has been made to pulsate with new life. There were over forty professions of faith, and numbers of reconsecrations. Twenty-nine have united with the church to date.

Brother Lightbourne is pleasing and attractive as a preacher, but it is the power of God working through the man that is the great secret of his success. He has felt the saving power in his own life and this has given him a love and passion for the souls of others. He is sane and safe in his methods even the most conservative could endorse. In the field of evangelism, he easily ranks first. His oversea service and his labors in the pastorate, have deepened and sweetened his experience and have tended to make him more effective and fitted him for more efficient service. Through his labors with us he has greatly endeared himself to the people of Franklin and our prayers follow him.

Mrs. Lightbourne joined Brother Lightbourne at the close of the meeting, both of whom were with us on the following Sunday evening, he preaching to an overflowing house and she delighting with the Gospel in song.

C. H. ROWLAND.

CATAWBA SPRINGS

Sunday, November 2, was a good day at Catawba Springs for several reasons. It was the first regular church service since the hot air heating system had been installed. This was planned, money raised, and installed in less than thirty days at a cost of $350.00. It works fine.

The church promised to pay the pastor $200.00, but before he left the church the collection paid him $100.00 extra, a total of $300.00. Of course, it makes a pastor feel good when such appreciation is shown. I know our Lord will reward them and I pray that He may do it through me, making me a more efficient servant.

Dr. Atkinson was there also and preached a strong sermon on missions, which I am sure the people enjoyed. We like to have him come to Catawba. He secured some pledges for the mission work and I believe more will follow. The Sunday school is giving one Sunday's offering per month to build a church in some foreign field. The new church will be also named Catawba Springs. The first offering amounted to $34.20, but they did not wait for the regular day for this offering before they added $10.00 more to it. I never had a more pleasant place to work. May God make us fruitful in every good word and work.

J. LEE JOHNSON.

NEW ELAM

The congregation of New Elam church has outgrown the present church building. At the annual revival, and on all other extra occasions, we have an overflow. A building committee was appointed in August to make plans and to decide on size of addition to the building. The Committee made its report in September and we quickly raised the required amount estimated by the Committee. The Committee proceeded to get material together, and I trust before winter the addition to the church will be completed. I offered my resignation to the church and Rev. B. J. Howard has accepted a call. At my request the church voted a raise of $100.00 in salary. The church wanted to make him feel good before he got there.

                                        J. E. FRANKS.

SOME THINGS TO BE THANKFUL FOR

Harvesting time is over and God has blessed us with plenty of this world's goods. Let us all be thankful and much in prayer and praise for His goodness, and let us not forget to render unto Him His part. We must remember that there are many who do not have bread and clothes enough to be comfortable. Of course, we can pray for those, but we ought to do even more.

Let us think of the many precious souls that ought to be saved before another harvesting time and if we are busy let us say: "Somewhere, some way, some time each day, I'll turn aside and stop and pray." I believe in much praying. I don't believe that Jesus ever made a choice without prayer. Can we afford to do so? The poverty of our prayer life is due to the poverty of our friendship with our Lord. We should read a part of God's Word daily. Let us start our day's work with prayer and praise and we will do more and better work. Remember the many young people who are starting homes of their own. Some are Christians and some are not. Let us pray that they may start with Christian homes and let Christ be the ruler. Those who welcome Jesus into their homes find that He brings many wonderful blessings with Him.

Dear friends, those of you who have Christian homes remember those who have not. Remember those who have loved ones without a Savior who are dearer to them than their own lives. I have a special request that I carry to God each day until I think He must be weary of listening to me. Sometimes I think that if He were to answer that one prayer I would not have anything else to wish for I would be so happy, but I know He will answer it in His own good time.

Let us not forget to pray for those who are sick and in trouble. I believe that if we could not go to see them and would remember them in prayer God would bless them with the consciousness that somebody cared enough for them to be praying for them while they were suffering. Prayer brings us closer together and binds our hearts in Christian love as nothing else can do. True prayer leaves all to God. It is a privilege to ask largely of God and victory comes when we can say, "Thy will, not mine, be done."

                                        MRS. J. L. HALL.
News Ferry, Va.

Serene will be our days and bright,
    And happy will our nature be,
When love is an unerring light,
    And joy its own security.
                                        —*Wadsworth.*

A PERSONAL LETTER

We have had an opportunity of seeing the following letter sent Dr. W. S. Long by Dr. W. W. Staley and take pleasure in reproducing it:

My dear Dr. Long:

Upon making an entry today, I was reminded of your birthday, and hence I write to congratulate you upon the time in which you were born, the history through which you have lived, the service you have rendered to your generation, the happy domestic relations you have enjoyed, the good children you have reared, and the parents from whom you sprang.

I also congratulate you upon your clean record, your good health, and your reputation as a man, as a Christian, and as a minister. Few men come to four score with the vigor and looks which you enjoy, and I rejoice with you and your dear wife in this greatest of blessings on earth.

        Very sincerely yours,
                                        W. W. STALEY.
Suffolk, Va., October 22, 1919.

SUFFOLK LETTER

I am thinking of those who milk the cows and those who produce the butter and cheese of this country. Government estimates the number of milch cows in the United States at 22,000,000, and the annual milk yield at 86,000,000,000 pounds, which is equal to 10,000,000,-000 gallons. The wholesale market value of milk is 30 cents per gallon, which would be $3,000,000,000.00. This sum is more than the cotton crop of the South at the present price. If one person milked ten cows it would require 2,000,000 persons to do this seven-day work. The magnitude of the dairy business is enormous in size, immense in value, and of incalculable benefit to the hundred million of people in this country. To care for these millions of cows, to provide food for them, and to milk them, and then market the milk, to say nothing of factories for producing condensed milk, cheese, cream, and other products. The manufacture of casein from skim milk and buttermilk, used in paper industry and waterproof glue, used with plywoods for aeroplane construction, extends the use of milk beyond its food value.

Think of the people who carry on dairy farms near towns and cities. They rise early, milk the cows, bottle the milk, and then hurry up and down streets to deliver the milk to customers. It is no easy service, and it is no ordinary service. It is essential to the life of the community. Children live upon it. Adults are nourished by it. Luxuries are enriched by it. The sick are fed upon it. Apart from its necessity and its usefulness, the milk-pail might be a hardship; but when one milks a cow with self-abandon and cheerfulness the work becomes a pleasure and a benevolence. The milk-man comes, no matter how cold, how hot, or how rainy the morning. He is an angel of mercy, a supporter of life, a friend of chidren, a helper to cooks, an unseen bearer of good to the household. He picks up the empties, places the white liquid at the door and passes on in a hurry. Whoever thought of thanking the milk-man

MISSIONARY

NEW MISSIONARIES URGENTLY NEEDED

The Mission Boards of the various denominations in the United States and Canada have united in sending out the following appeal, which appeal should be read and taken to heart by every member of our Christian Church, because, of all churches just now, it seems to come most appropriately from our own and apply most appropriately to our needs and conditions. The appeal is as follows:

"The need for recruits for foreign missionary service eclipses all other needs." The war is over. The battle for the ideals of righteousness, justice, and truth has been won. The victory has cost enormously in money, suffering, sorrow, and life-blood. Men have willingly sacrificed everything, including life, rather than yield their principles. They have left a legacy of heroic service that must be neither forgotten nor lost. The banner they have carried forward in war must be held high in the days of peace.

This privilege belongs peculiarly to the young man and woman of this generation. The new task will be harder than the old, for it will be shorn of the glamour, the excitement, and the pageantry of war.

The war was won with armies. It will need more than armies to keep it won. It will require men who have the power to see and follow ideals when the world has lost sight of them; men who have the capacity to draw their motives from unseen and hidden sources; men who have wills strong enough to remain faithful and patient when God is working in His ordinary and more deliberate ways.

The Christian Church must accept this challenge. Upon the ministers at home and missionaries abroad will devolve the leadership.

Our appeal is to those who have heard the call of War. The call of Peace is even more arresting. The war must be interpreted to the nations of the world. They must realize that spiritual forces are more powerful than material, that righteousness exalts a nation, that Brotherhood and not rivalry must determine international relationships, and that sacrificial service is essential to the world's well-being. These truths are at the heart of the missionary message. They must be carried to the ends of the world.

The welfare of the world will depend upon men who have incarnated these truths in their lives and are willing to live for them.

The Mission Boards of all the churches in Canada and the United States have consecrated themselves to this task. They need men and women in larger numbers than ever before. Every phase of the work needs strengthening. The strongest and finest qualities of brain, heart, and hand are required. The demand is for ministers, teachers, physicians (men and women), nurses, agriculturists, technical workers, business men. God can use every talent a man possesses. *This appeal is to you.* We are face to face with a great crisis.

It is the day of opportunity for young men and young women. Again can it be said Christ has gathered His disciples about Him and, with greater intensity than ever before is saying:

Go ye therefore to all nations, teaching them to observe all things whatsoever I have commanded you, and lo, I am with you always, even unto the end of the world.

*   *   *   *   *   *   *   *   *

I sincerely trust CHRISTIAN SUN readers will take this message seriously and consider its significance to us. Think: We are more than one hundred years old as a denomination, and so far we have not sent out one medical missionary to help heal "the open sore of the world," or stay the hand of disease so rampant and so deadly among the nations that know not God. We think it appalling that ten out of every hundred children in New York City die before they are five years old. This is because there are unsanitary conditions, a congested population, wicked, Godless, unconcerned people in that great city. But what about China where we are told that half the children, fifty out of every hundred, throughout that vast empire, die before they are two years old. "Wherefore it is not your Father's will that one of these little ones should perish." Yet they are perishing by the millions, not because it is God's will that they shall perish, but because we who are entrusted by Him with the commission and the power to go and save them will not do so. The mothers in their ignorance and superstition do not know, and often do not care, and we who do know and should care are doing almost nothing to help and to save. How much longer shall the ringing, urgent, imperative command of our Savior and Redeemer go unheeded? We often wonder. How long?

J. O. ATKINSON.

KENDALL IN WASHINGTON

Your subscription to the funds for home missions has made possible the beginning of active operations toward the establishment of our church in Washington. The little group of interested persons who have taken the initiative and started the ball a-rolling would be up against a stiff proposition but for the support which you are giving the work. In your Sunday school and church you are educating boys and girls to know and follow Jesus Christ. When in the course of human events they board a train and come here to work for the Government, or engage in some private employment, they will find ready to receive them, with a warm welcome they will understand, a small body of earnest men and women who will make it their business to see that your boy or girl finds a good home and an association with clean, upright, progressive people.

Dr. Atkinson, bumping around over the country in day coaches late into the night, getting a bite at a lunch counter here, traveling out into the country making appointments at two or three churches a Sunday, often located miles apart, eating, sleeping and being entertained in different homes, or none at all, working for the cause of Christ in trains, automobiles, by the roadside, in churches, and homes is reaching out after the foundation upon which all enterprises must rest—money.

The money you give him is not used for luxury, nor is it wasted in paying princely salaries to men who do nothing. That which your Board is spending in Washington in the employment of a pastor to give his whole time and interest in the establishment of a Christian church at the National Capital will make possible the assembling of a group of interested believers in the Gospel of Christ who will give of their means, their time, their interest upbuilding the truly great mission of the Christian Church.

This city is the common meeting ground of all Americans; they come from the South, East, North, and West to work for the Government. They come from the best homes, have had the best training the schools and churches and community interests could give them; their coming to Washington is to find a large opportunity for the development of the ideas with which giant brains are teeming. Others come hoping to connect up with the Government pay roll, a fat salary with nothing to do. These two elements of society are here. The brave, the courageous, the ambitious soul is sorely tried when he finds his opportunities thwarted by some lazy individual with more "influence." A discouraged person is easily defeated. Evil persons are looking for "easy marks," and find them among the defeated, the discouraged.

We want to establish an oasis of spiritual uplift here in this busy Capital City. A place for the lonely, the fellow who is looking for a friendly face, the girl who wants to find companions of the right sort. The money you have given to Dr. Atkinson has made this possible.

Dr. Arthur Burton Kendall is just the sort of man to fill such a place. He has had experience in the South, the West, the North, in social settlement work in Chicago, in Y. M. C. A. work, in colleges, and in the open country districts. He was born and grew as a boy among the hills of Northwestern Pennsylvania. The book of nature has opened her interesting pages to his watchful eyes, and he has made himself familiar with the technical names of flowers, birds, and trees. To take a walk with him into the country is an educational treat for those who are with him, for he sees everything, hears everything, and calls attention to the beauties and oddities of the things about him.

He is especially competent as a teacher of the Bible, which he has made his own, in which he has searched for hidden treasure and found it, and the ease with which he imparts the knowledge he has found is an inimical style peculiar to himself and pleasing to all who listen.

We have not secured a location for meeting as yet, but that will follow soon, and the church which you have given to Washington will be waiting to receive you as their guest when you come to the Government's big town.

IRVING W. HITCHCOCK.

Washington, D. C.
801 *Allison St. N. W.*

P.S.: Please send the name and address of any of your friends who have come to Washington to live.

Principles and Government of The Christian Church

(The Franklin, Virginia, session of the Southern Christian Convention ordered that the Principles and Government of the Christian Church be revised and that a committee be appointed to make the revision. The following members of the Convention were appointed to do the work: Rev. W. W. Staley, D. D., President; Rev. W. S. Long, D. D., Rev. C. H. Rowland, D. D., Rev. N. G. Newman, D. D., and W. A. Harper, LL. D. Some weeks ago the committee completed its work, and we are privileged to print, in serial form, the Principles and Government as outlined, subject to ratification by the next session of the Convention.—Editor).

CHAPTER I
THE CHURCH

The Church is composed of all who exercise repentance toward God, and faith toward our Lord Jesus Christ.

The Saviour came into the world to establish one Church, the members of which belong to various denominations, differing widely in doctrine and government, yet they form but one body, of which Christ is the head.

All the redeemed are brethren, and members of the Church. The Church is spoken of in the Scriptures as a family, of which God is the Father, and as a household, which should not be divided against itself.

All the principles, operations, and officers of the Church ought to harmonize in the administration of the Redeemer's Kingdom on earth, to the end that all the members may be brought into fellowship and communion with one another.

CHAPTER II.
THE CHRISTIAN CHURCH

The Christian Church may be composed of any or all who constitute the body, of which Christ is the Head.

But at present it embraces only a part of those who desire the reformation of the wicked, the spiritual worship of God, and the union of the great Brotherhood of Christians.

It is opposed to contentions and schisms in the body. Envying, strife, and divisions are hurtful to the Church, and antagonistic to the teachings and spirit of Christianity.

Its purpose is to propagate the fruit of the Spirit, and to cultivate brotherly love.

It fosters the essential doctrines of evangelical Christianity, by which the Church has been established, and maintained.

It remands to private judgment the peculiar doctrines and tenets which have confused and divided the Christian world, and hence they cease to be matters for debate, when such debate tends to strife.

It requires no compromise of faith on the part of any follower of Christ in order to communion or fellowship but denominational distinctions cease to exist and Christian love binds the Brotherhood together.

Its mission will be consummated in the conversion of the world, the union of all the followers of Christ, and His reign in human society.

CHAPTER III
PRINCIPLE OF THE CHRISTIAN CHURCH

The Scriptures contain an abundance of indisputable truth sufficient for the moral guidance and spiritual enlightment of man, and adapted to the comprehension of all. -The Christian Church, therefore, remands to private judgment those doctrines and tenets which divided the followers of Christ, and takes the following cardinal principles as the ground-work of organization:

(1) The Lord Jesus Christ is the only Head of the church.

(2) Christian is a sufficient name for the church.

(3) The Holy Bible is a sufficient rule of faith and practice.

(4) Christian character is a sufficient test of fellowship, and of church membership.

(5) The right of private judgment and the liberty of conscience is a right and a privilege that should be accorded to and exercised by all.

PART II
GOVERNMENT OF THE CHRISTIAN CHURCH
CHAPTER I
SECTION I
A CHRISTIAN CHURCH

A Christian Church is an autonomous body of the followers of Christ, organized for religious instruction, spiritual improvement, the worship of God, and the propagation of the Gospel.

SECTION II
ORGANIZATION OF A CHRISTIAN CHURCH

Those wishing to organize a Christian Church shall enter into the following agreement:

We, whose names are hereunto annexed, members, as we trust, of the body of Christ, having exercised repentance toward God and faith toward our Lord Jesus Christ, being desirous of associating ourselves together as a church, agree to be governed by the following principles:

(a) The Lord Jesus Christ is the only head of the church.

(b) Christian is a sufficient name for the church.

(c) The Holy Bible is a sufficient rule of faith and practice.

(d) Christian character is a sufficient test of fellowship and of church membership.

(e) The right of private judgment and the liberty of conscience is a right and privilege that should be accorded to, and exercised by all.

Those who have signed the above agreement should elect a Secretary, a Treasurer, and other officers or commitees, as may be necessary. They should also elect two, or more, Deacons. Respecting the election of Deacons time should be had for consultation, reflection

and prayer that the choice may fall upon those best suited to the office.

After organization, members may be received from any Christian Church, or other evangelical denomination, by letter, or other evidence showing their full connection therewith, or by exercising repentance and faith.

SECTION III
DUTIES OF A CHRISTIAN CHURCH

Every Christian Church should procure a pastor for full time, or associate itself with other contiguous churches in the employment of a pastor. The call should preferably be for an indefinite period, and when a change is desired by either party, three months notice should be given.

The Church should faithfully teach the duty of Scriptural giving that it may provide for the liberal support of the pastor, current expenses, and the general work of the Kingdom.

It shall be the duty of every church, as early as practicable after its organization, to unite with the conference in whose bounds it may be located, and to comply with all requests of the conference to which it may belong.

Every church should celebrate the Lord's Supper at least four times a year, and hold four conferences for the transaction of business.

The church should observe the ordinances and maintain gospel worship in its purity and simplicity.

SECTION IV
DUTIES OF MEMBERS

1. It is the duty of every member of the church to give of his substance to the support of the church and its enterprises as the Lord hath prospered him.

2. All members should attend, if possible, the stated meetings of the church, especially every church session, or quarterly conference, and identify themselves with the Sunday school.

3. They should read the Bible and engage in private devotions daily, visit the sick, and minister to the needy.

4. The members should earnestly endeavor to keep peace and unity in the church.

5. They should bear one another's burdens.

6. They should endeavor to prevent one another's stumbling.

7. They should steadfastly continue in the faith of the gospel and the worship of God.

8. They should pray for and sympathize with one another.

CHAPTER II
SECTION I
OFFICERS OF A CHRISTIAN CHURCH

The necessary officers of the church are pastor, deacons, secretary and treasurer.

SECTION II
DUTIES OF PASTOR

1. The pastoral office is the highest and most important in the church, and the person who holds this office is, in the Scripture, charged with various duties.

2. It is his duty to be a member of some Christian Church and of the Conference in which he labors.

3. It is the duty of the pastor to give himself continually to prayer and the ministry of the Word, and to study to show himself approved unto God, a workman that needeth not to be ashamed.

4. It is his duty to see that the churches to which he ministers, and also the members thereof, discharge the obligations imposed by the Holy Scriptures and by the church government.

5. It is his duty to comply with all the requests, and to execute to the best of his ability all the orders of the conference.

6. It is his duty to be present at every annual meeting of the conference and submit a written report of his labors. If prevented from attending he shall report by letter.

7. It is his duty to promote the peace and unity of the church, to study its interests, and labor for its prosperity.

(Continued next week)

EDITORIAL

(Continued from Page 3)

that man works, lessens production that much and you are thrown back on the law of supply and demand.

Legislation cannot force prices *down*, nor *up*. It may help in spots and instances, but there can be no law made, without changing the Constitution, to force a man to sell below the cost of manufacturing.

If this country is short in man-power, as it seems to be, then some sacrifice must be made and work longer hours and help to supplement for the shortage until production has been increased. It is a matter of suffering from high prices or sacrificing more time for production. This *does not* mean that man-power must work longer hours for less pay or for the same pay. The pay can be in proportion and at the same time it will increase production.

Some of the experts figured out how much time the Day Light Savings Law saved. Here is one for them: If each working man in the United States worked one hour *more* each day for sixty days, how much would it increase the nation's supply of materials?

Let the nation have a production week, or month, and let all of us get down to a little sacrifice and increase production. We had to sacrifice to win the war, so why not all get together and sacrifice to win normal conditions?

OHIO VOTES "WET"

The latest word from Ohio by telephone and telegraph indicates the defeat of the Prohibition Repeal and Two and Three Quarters Percent Beer proposals of the liquor forces by substantial majorities. The returns also show the defeat of the Crabbe Enforcement Act passed by the last Legislature and referred to the people. The endorsement of the Act of the Legislature in ratifying the National Prohibition Amendment is in doubt and conflicting claims are made. If it is carried, that of course ends the matter, for the referendum was invoked by the liquor crowd; if it is defeated, our people will na-

turally contest the validity of the whole proceeding, for we have consistently claimed from the beginning that the Federal Constitution itself specifies the mode of its amendment and no State can add to or take from the conditions specified therein.

The statement is made, however, that prohibition may be delayed if Ohio has voted against ratification, provided the Federal Courts do not decide against the applicability of the referendum to the action of State Legislatures in ratifying Federal constitutional amendments. Such delay would not result. Nebraska was the thirty-sixth State to ratify the 18th Amendment, and she did so on the sixteenth of January. Later on the same day Missouri and Wyoming also ratified the Amendment. Even if Ohio should be counted out, therefore, the Amendment was still adopted on the sixteenth of January by thirty-seven States, or one more than the constitutional requirement. Two more States ratified on the seventeenth of January and by the twenty-ninth of January—the date on which the Acting Secretary of State issued his proclamation as required by Section 205 of the Revised Statutes—forty-four States had ratified the Amendment.

DAUGHTERS OF CONFEDERACY TO ESTABLISH BED

The North Carolina Division, United Daughters of the Confederacy, is preparing to establish a bed at the State Sanatorium for the treatment of tuberculosis. A special committee for this purpose was appointed at the recent annual meeting held in High Point and the president, Mrs. C. F. Harvey, of Kinston, has officially advised Dr. L. B. McBrayer, superintendent of the State institution, that the committee is ready to begin functioning.

It costs each patient one dollar each day at the State sanatorium, with a slight addition for incidental expenses, the remainder of the cost of maintenance being bourne by an annual appropriation from the State. All told it costs the individual patient about $425 for a year, and it is understood that the Daughters of the Confederacy will make provision for an annual income that will maintain a patient.

AN INVITATION

We take pleasure in inviting delegates and visitors of the North Carolina Conference to visit THE SUN office while in Burlington. The office is in sight of the Burlington Christian church, only one block away, and on the same street. Come in and see where THE SUN is printed. We welcome you.

We lament the passing on November 8 of Miss Julia Marshall, a member of Salem Chapel church. Miss Marshall has been sick for some months. She had been contracted with to teach in the Christian Orphanage and was taken sick a few days before she was to enter upon her duties.

As we go to press the delegates of the North Carolina Conference are arriving. A great session is anticipated.

LITTLE FOLKS DEPARTMENT

THE TOUR OF A SMILE

My papa smiled this morning when
. He came downstairs, you see,
At mamma, and when he smiled, then
She turned and smiled at me;
And when she smiled at me, I went
And smiled at Mary Ann
Out in the kitchen, and she lent
. It to a hired man.

So then he smiled at some one whom
He saw when going by,
Who also smiled and ere he knew
Had twinkles in his eyes;
So he went to his office then
And smiled right at his clerk,
Who put some more ink on his pen
And smiled back from his work.

So when his clerk went home, he smiled
Right at his wife, and she
Smiled over at their little child
As happy as could be;
And then their little child she took
The smile to school, and when
She smiled at teacher from her hook
Teacher smiled back again.

And then the teacher passed on one
To little James McBride,
Who couldn't get his lesson done,
No matter how he tried;
And Jamesy took it home and told
How teacher smiled at him,
When he was tired and didn't scold
But said: "Don't worry, Jim."

And when I happened to be there
That very night at play,
His mother had a smile to spare
Which came across my way;
And then I took it after a while
Back home, and mamma said:
"Here is that very self-same smile
. Come back with us to bed."

—*Selected.*

THE REASON WHY

How Did Shaking the Head Come to Mean "No"?

The origin of this method of indicating "No" is
found in the result of the mother's efforts in the animal
kingdom of trying to feed her young. A mother animal would be trying to get her young to accept the
food she brought them and tried to put it in their
mouths. Perhaps, however, the young animal had had
sufficient food or did not fancy the kind of food offered.
The natural thing to do under the circumstances would
be to close the mouth tight and shake the head from
side to side to prevent the mother from forcing the food
into the mouth. Thus we get the closed lips and the
shaking head from side to side to mean "No." In other
words, that kind of a way of saying "No" came from
an effort to say "I don't want any."

How Did a Nod Come to Mean "Yes"?

The idea of nodding to mean "Yes" comes from the
opposite to the action which, as just described, indicates
a "No."

When the young animal was anxious to accept the
offered food, it made an effort to get at the food quickly. Hence, the pushing forward of the head and the
open mouth (always more or less opened when you nod
to indicate "Yes") and an expression of gladness.
You will notice if you see anyone nod the head to indicate "Yes" that the lips are open rather than closed,
and that there is always a smile or an indication of a
smile to accompany it. In other words, the nod to
mean "Yes" is only another way of saying "I shall be
pleased."

Why Does a Pencil Write?

You can use a pencil to write with or to make marks,
because the pencil wears off if you are scratching it on
a surface that is rough enough to make it do so. Writing, you know, is only a way of making marks in such
a manner as to make them mean something. You cannot write with a pencil on a pane of glass, because the
glass is so smooth that when you move the pencil over
its surface, the pencil will not wear off. To prove to
yourself that the tip of the pencil constantly wears off
when you write, you have only to recall that when you
write with it a pencil keeps getting shorter and shorter.
A slate pencil will wear down shortly by merely writing
with it, but a lead pencil must be sharpened—that is,
you must keep cutting away the wood in order to get
at the lead inside.

Why Can't I Write on Paper With a Slate Pencil?

You cannot do so, because it takes something with a
rougher surface than paper to wear off the point of a
slate pencil. A slate is used to write on with slate pencils, because slate wears off the end of the pencil easily,
and also because you can rub out the writing on a slate
with water. Lead pencils are used for writing on paper,
but you must have a rough surface on the paper to
write on even with a lead pencil. Some kinds of papers
have such a smooth surface that you cannot write on
them with a lead pencil.

How Does a Pen Write

Writing with a pen, however, is quite different from
writing with any kind of pencil, because in writing
with ink we do not wear off the end of the pen, but
have the ink flow from the pen. For this purpose we
must have a surface that will absorb the ink from the
pen and make it flow. A slate has no power of absorp-
tion and therefore cannot draw the ink. A piece of
blotting paper is the best kind of paper for absorbing
the ink, but it is too much so for writing purposes.

Where is the Wind When it is not Blowing?

The answer is, of course, that there isn't any wind then. To understand this perfectly we must study a little and find out what wind is. In plain words it is nothing more than moving air.

If you make a hole in the bottom of a pail of water, the water will run out slowly. If you knock the whole bottom out of the pail filled with water, the water will rush out before you know it.

That is about what happens to make the wind. The air is constantly full of air currents, like the currents you can see in a river, Down the middle of the river you may notice a softly flowing current going straight. Along the shores there will be little side currents, going in all directions, and you may find some little whirlpools. That is exactly what we should see in the air if we could see air currents.

Where Does the Wind Begin?

The movement of these currents of air leaves many pockets of space where there is no air, and when one of these is uncovered the air rushes in and creates a wind in doing so. These air currents are continually pressing against each other to get some place else. They change their direction according to the pressure that is being applied to them. Sometimes the pressure will be very light in one part of the air, many miles away, perhaps, and then the air in another part, which is under great pressure, will rush with great force into the part where the pressure is light, and thus form a big wind. When the pressure stops the wind stops.

We have probably felt the wind which comes out of the valve of the automobile tire when the cap is taken off to pump up the tire. It is a real wind that comes out. The reason is that the air in the tube of the tire is under great pressure, and when the opportunity is given to get where the pressure is light it starts for that place with a rush and comes out of the valve a real wind.—*From the Book of Wonders, Published and Copyrighted by the Bureau of Industrial Education, Inc., Washington, D. C.*

NOTES

Rev. C. E. Gerringer informs us that he will be open for work in the North Carolina Conference January 1, as it is his intention to return to North Carolina at that time. His address is now Richland, Ga.

Last week we had visits from Dr. W. W. Staley, Suffolk, Va., and Mr. J. C. Madison, Wentworth, N. C. We are always glad for the brethren passing to call in.

We have just received a new supply of "Holy Ordinances of Marriage" and can now supply the public. The price is, however, $1.00 instead of 70 cents as formerly.

We have been privileged to secure a Bible that will, we think, greatly please our trade. The print is reasonably large, the binding good, and contains all the helps, etc. The words of Christ are printed in red. This Bible is No. 830 R. L. and the price is $5.00 postpaid. Sent on approval, if so desired.

Size 25X36 Inches

HAVE YOU HEROES?

Have you been associated with men who have served their country, and whom you are now anxious to welcome home? Have you a friend or relative who has done Military Service of any kind, because of the War?

Have you men in your employ who have sacrificed career, prospects, income, and family ties, and risked Life itself, to Serve Their Country?

Do you want to immortalize the names of these men, that those who are to come may do them honor?

A Liberty Honor Testimonial

will hold these names in the embrace of imperishable metal—the very walls of the structure on which it is erected, will crumble to dust, while these names are still as clear as the day they were cast.

For churches, schools, lodges, banks and other institutions.

In all former Wars, it has been, with but few exceptions, the names of only the commanders, who have been honored. Through the country, there are scattered the statues of Generals, ahorse and afoot, with field-glass and with sword, but always the common soldier—the FIGHTER—has been forgotten.

It must not be so in this War—this democracy must pay its tribute to the actual men behind the guns.

For prices and particulars, address,

C. B. RIDDLE　　-　　-　　-　　Burlington, N. C.

Sunday School and Christian Endeavor

SUNDAY SCHOOL LESSON FOR NOVEMBER 23, 1919

Jesus Corrects John's Narrowness. —Mark 9:33-42; 10:13-16; Luke 9:46-56.

Golden Text: Grace be with them that love our Lord Jesus Christ with a love incorruptible.—Eph. 6:24.

Additional Material: Matt. 8:5-13; John 10:16; I Cor. 3:1-23; Eph. 2:11-22; 6:24; II John 2:10.

For Teaching Points, see Teachers and Officers Journal.

How easy it is to see the mote in our brother's eye; how hard to see the beam in our own! We feel that we have perfect vision because we have never seen without our own pet beam. We are sure we are right, because we have never looked at any other side than our own. So the disciples who wanted to be made rulers had not enough true greatness of character as yet to be willing for another to follow Jesus in any other way than their own "We forbade him, because he followed not us." This is different from "following not Me" whom Jesus had condemned; this is the spirit of sectarianism. "You must follow as I follow; you must believe as I believe, or you are not following after Jesus at all." See how quickly and emphatically Jesus corrects this impression. There are many to-day, outside of churches, who are doing great things for the cause of Christ and in His name; we cannot but wish they were working with us, but we dare not say they are working against us.

See, too, the latter part of the lesson, we think sometimes that James and John were disciples of peace; we forget the surname which Jesus Himself conferred on these two brothers "Sons of Thunder." Here, perhaps is one of the times when they well deserved their name. Calling down fire, is the way some good people think they can convert the world, but the judgment is for the angels, impartial messengers of God, who can do His will without bias. The longer I live, the more glad I am that God does not ask me, who can see only the outer appearance, to judge my fellow men, who can only be truly estimated by the impulses of their heart, seen by God alone.

CHRISTIAN ENDEAVOR TOPIC

We have received no Christian Endeavor topic to be used in this issue.—*Editor.*

WHEN FROST IS ON THE PUNKIN

When the frost is on the punkin and the fodder's in the shock,
And you hear the kuyouck and gobble of the struttin' turkey cock,
And the clackin' of the guineas, and the cluckin' of the hens,
And the rooster's hallylooyer as he tiptoes on the fence;
Oh it's then's the time a feller is a feelin' at his best,
With the risin' sun to greet him from a night of peaceful rest,
As he leaves the house, bare-headed and goes out to feed the stock,
When the frost is on the punkin, and the fodder's in the shock.

They's something kind o' hearty-like about the atmusphere
When the heat of summer's over, and the coolin' fall is here—
Of course we miss the flowers, and the blossoms on the trees
And the mumble of the hummin' birds and buzzin of the bees;
But the air's so appetizin'; and the landscape through the haze
Of a crisp and sunny morning of the airly autumn days
Is a pictur' that no painter has the colorin' to mock—
When the frost is on the punkin and the fodder's in the shock.

The husky, rusty russel of the tossels of the corn,
And the raspin' of the tangled leaves as golden as the morn;
The stubble in the furries—kindo' lonesomelike, but still
A preachin sermons to us of the barns they growed to fill;
The straw stack in the medder, and tho reaper in the shed;
The hosses in theyr stalls below,—the clover overhead!—
Oh, it sets my heart a-clickin' like the tickin' of a clock,
When the frost is on the punkin and the fodder's in the shock.

—James Whitcomb Riley.

MARRIAGES

RUSSELL-CAGLE

A pretty wedding was solemnized at the home of Mrs. Emma Cagle, on October 28, 1919, when her daughter, Maggie, became the bride of Mr. Ernest C. Russell.

The contracting parties were both formerly of Seagrove, N. C. Mr. Russell has of late made his home at Lecompte, La., and there they expect to make their home after spending some time on the way at Little Rock and Hot Springs, Ark., for which places they immediately left followed by the best wishes of many friends and relatives who were present to witness the marriage.

T. J. GREEN.

OBITUARIES

WILKS

Mrs. Lucinda Wilks was born July 10, 1876 and died October 19, 1919. Her maiden name was King of a large family of Kings that have been very active in New Hope church. At the age of nine years, Mrs. Wilks joined Beulah church. She married Lea Wilks in 1894 and then transferred her membership to Good Hope. A few years later she moved her membership to New Hope. Thus for thirty-four years she kept her membership with her that she might be a regular member and faithfully attend the services of her own church. A faithful husband and eight dear children are left behind. A wife's counsel and a mother's prayers will not be forgotten. Sister Wilks suffered and died from the effects of cancer. I have never seen a more patient and resigned sufferer, nor one who died a more triumphant death. Funeral services by the writer.

J. E. FRANKS.

ROGER MILLS WHITE—AN APPRECIATION

We at Elon were much grieved to learn of the untimely taking away of Roger Mills White on September 22, 1919. His pastor, the Rev. J. L. Foster, has given through The Sun the data of his all too brief history, and I am writing this line as a friend and as one who learned to love him while at Elon and now deeply mourns his going.

Roger was of an amiable disposition, big-hearted, whole souled and of a most unselfish disposition. He had high aspirations for service in life and to these aspirations gave his unstinted energy and enthusiasm of a vigorous and virile young manhood. He was marked as a public speaker and had he been permitted to live and display his talents in this direction, no one who ever heard him can doubt but that he would have arisen to eminence and fame in the world in the mastery of assemblies. He loved the combat of the forum and was an advocate of more than ordinary ability of whatever cause he championed. He was fluent of speech, vigorous in thought, enthusiastic in effort and convincing in logic. I had hoped that it would be our Father's will to call him to the ministry, for which his broad idealism seemed to fit him, and to which he seemed by nature and achievement well adapted.

His brief life was long enough in which to win friends and who will never forget him and to inspire those nearest to him to more zeal, interest and enthusiasm in efforts for achievement and success. Scarcely twenty-four years of age, cut down in the vigor of rapidly developing manhood, we mourn his going but realize that our Heavenly Father knows best and had a higher purpose for him in that better world. He knew how to be a friend and so made friends by the scores and these are the better for knowing him and in that land where friendship is complete, we shall hope to join him by and by.

J. O. ATKINSON.

RESOLUTIONS OF RESPECT
W. A. KING

Your Committee, to whom was referred the duty of drafting resolutions of respect to the memory of our friend and member, Brother W. A. King, who died October 5, 1919, begs leave to ask your approval of the following:

1. That Brother W. A. King was a Christian gentleman who merited our respect and Christian affection. His vacant seat in the church reminds us of his faithful attention upon worship.

2. That, as a member of the Union, he was loyal, faithful, and useful; always ready to assist us in worthy undertakings, and to give us the support of his sympathy and help.

3, We, therefore, recommend, that the L. B. and S. Union tender his grief-stricken and bereaved family our heart-felt sympathy in this time of sorrow, and our sincere prayers that the All-Father will prove to them that ''His grace is sufficient'' for them.

4. That, these resolutions become a part of our records, and that a copy be sent to Mrs. King and her family, and a copy sent to The Christian Sun for publication.

MRS. J. M. DARDEN,
MRS. G. W. NURNEY,
MRS. J. E. WEST,
      Committee.

CHARLES W. McPHERSON, M. D.

Eye, Ear, Nose, Throat

OFFICE OVER CITY DRUG STORE

Office Hours: 9:00 a. m. to 1:00 p. m.
    and 2:00 to 5:00 p. m.

Phones: Residence 153; Office 65J

BURLINGTON, NORTH CAROLINA

PELOUBET'S SELECT NOTES

Contains 480 pages and covers in detail the Sunday school lessons for 1920. It should be in the hands of every teacher. Primary, Intermediate, Junior and Senior topics fully treated. $1.60 postpaid. Order from this office.

Tom Thrift saw an Opening

to set up for himself. Could he swing the deal?

"We'll back you," the banker said. "Our money is safe with the man who saved his own money." That's just Tom Thrift's luck.

CHURCH OFFERING ENVELOPES

Standard Double
(Size 2½X4¼ inches—52 to Set)

White or Manila

25 to 49 sets.............16 cts. a set
50 to 109 sets............14 cts. a set
110 to 209 sets...........13 cts. a set
210 to 309 sets..........12½ cts. a set
310 to 399 sets...........12 cts. a set
400 or more sets..........11 cts. a set

Minimum Charge $3.00 net.
CARTONS INCLUDED

Single Envelope System
(Size 2 5-16X3 5-8 inches. Open side.
52 to Set)

White or Manila

25 to 49 sets.............14 cts. a set
50 to 99 sets.............13 cts. a set
100 to 149 sets...........12 cts. a set
150 to 199 sets..........11½ cts. a set
200 to 249 sets...........11 cts. a set
250 or more sets..........10 cts. a set

Minimum Charge $2.00 set.
CARTONS INCLUDED

Take Note

The following points should be taken into consideration in placing an order for church offering envelopes:

1. A set means 52 envelopes, one for each Sunday in the year.

2. When cartons are ordered the sets are arranged in their logical order, thus making it convenient for the member. We suggest the use of cartons because of the convenience.

3. If you desire monthly, double or single envelopes, without cartons, 1-3 the price of the same number of weekly sets. Cartons 3-4 cent each.

4. Semi-monthly, double or single, in cartons, 2-3 the weekly price; without cartons 3-5 the weekly price.

5. When ordering state what Sunday that your church year begins, and whether you want the dates on envelopes or not.

6. Indicate the wording that you want placed on the envelopes or leave the same with us. Samples sent upon request.

7. Allow ten to fifteen days for delivery. Order early.

C. B. RIDDLE, Publishing Agent

Burlington, ...   N. C.

WHAT CAN I DO?

What if the little rain should say,
    "So small a thing as I
Can ne'er refresh the thirsty fields,
    I'll tarry in the sky!"

What if the shining beam of noon
    Should in its fountain stay,
Because its single light alone
    Cannot create a day?

Does not each rain-drop help to form
    The cool, refreshing shower?
And every ray of light to warm
    And beautify the flower?
                    —*Anon.*

IS IT NOT BEST?

Just what awaits those who pass
    squarely through
The tests and measurements for
    souls ordained
Is the great mystery. Only One
    knew,
And almost spoke it out, but still
    refrained.

Should those who have obtained
    through death the seal
Of high approval, having won their
    quest,
Also refrain from things they might
    reveal
That we may walk by faith, is it
    not best?
                —*Alfred J. Hough.*

TARBELL'S TEACHERS' GUIDE
—for the—
Efficient Sunday School Teacher.
$1.60 postpaid, or $1.50 when purchased at this office.

Order Early

DR. J. H. BROOKS

DENTIST

Foster Building   .   Burlington, N. C.

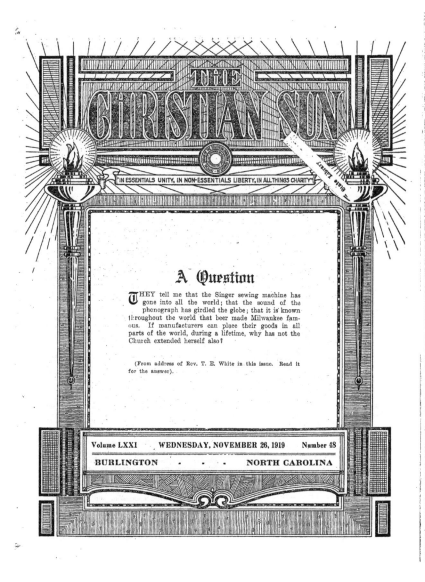

THE CHRISTIAN SUN

"IN ESSENTIALS UNITY, IN NON-ESSENTIALS LIBERTY, IN ALL THINGS CHARITY"

A Question

THEY tell me that the Singer sewing machine has gone into all the world; that the sound of the phonograph has girdled the globe; that it is known throughout the world that beer made Milwaukee famous. If manufacturers can place their goods in all parts of the world, during a lifetime, why has not the Church extended herself also?

(From address of Rev. T. E. White in this issue. Read it for the answer).

Volume LXXI   WEDNESDAY, NOVEMBER 26, 1919   Number 48

BURLINGTON   ·   ·   ·   NORTH CAROLINA

THE CHRISTIAN SUN
Founded 1844 by Rev. Daniel W. Kerr

C. B. RIDDLE - - - Editor

Entered at the Burlington N. C Post Office as second class matter.

Subscription Rates

One year .... $ 2.00
Six months 1.00

In Advance

Give both your old and new postoffice when asking tbat your address be changed.

The change of your label is your receipt for money. V.....n receipts sent upon request.

Many persons subscribe for friends, intending that the paper be stopped at the end of the year. If instructions are given to this effect, they will receive attention at the proper time.

Marriage and obituary notices not exceeding 150 words printed free if received within 60 days from date of event, all over this at the rate of one-half cent a word.

Original poetry not accepted for publication.

Principles of the Christian Church

(1) The Lord Jesus Christ is the only Head of the Church.
(2) Christian is a sufficient name of the Church.
(3) The Holy Bible is a sufficient rule of faith and practice.
(4) Christian character is a sufficient test of fellowship, and of church membership.
(5) The right of private judgment and the liberty of conscience is a right and a privilege that should be accorded to, and exercised by all.

EDITORIAL

AROUND THE THANKSGIVING FIRESIDE

How great is the nation whose chief magistrate calls the people together for a day of Thanksgiving!

——*Thanks*——

Last year we rejoiced because the world war had ended. We can rejoice this Thanksgiving because our boys are back at home—those of them who were not killed.

——*Thanks*——

"Another year of sun and rain,
Of singing birds and summer flowers,
Brings us this hallowed day again
With joy that life's great gift is ours."

——*Thanks*——

The past year has been a trying one—a year filled with uncertainties—and yet the people have wonderfully prospered. Their thanks to God on Thanksgiving Day should be a token of their appreciation.

——*Thanks*——

Shall we turn the day of Thanksgiving into a day of feasting and gluttonous eating? Let us acknowledge the providing hand and turn our thoughts upward on this day.

This scribe is thoughtful, among the many other things, for the loyal and unstinted support he has received at the hands of CHRISTIAN SUN readers during the past year. A good, great, and loyal people to serve.

——*Thanks*——

As we write we think of the lines by Francis H. Lee, and feel that they express a thought for thousands:

Our thanks go out, O God, to thee,
For all thy blessings manifold;
Then grant us, Lord, those things to see
Which finite minds oft leave untold.

Thank God for what has been denied;
Thank God for end of present ease
That sees our uses multiplied;
Thanks for th' eternal verties.

Thank God for the incentive new
That makes for work and sweeter life;
Thank God for friendships tried and true,
The ennobling toil of honest strife.

Thank God for trials and "mistakes,"
That blessings are, could we but see;
Thank Him for everything that makes
For truth and higher destiny.

——*Thanks*——

That men say the world is becoming more pagan does not make it so; and that men are less appreciative does not make that so. We believe that more people will breathe a prayer of thanks this season than ever before.

——*Thanks*——

Don't be a pessimist because the world is out of joint and fail to be thankful. Times will be better bye and bye. Life is not all smooth sailing whether with an individual or a nation.

——*Thanks*——

Be thankful that men have seen a new vision of their duty and obligation toward God and His Kingdom as it relates to wealth. Be thankful that God prospers you, and thank Him for a medium of giving.

——*Thanks*——

Be thankful for the heat, the cold, the dry seasons and the wet; for the sun and rain, the moon and the stars. Be thankful for friends and foes, and for love, for life, for hope, happiness, home, health, and most of all for the Savior Who died that you may be saved.

BEGINNING THE CONFERENCE YEAR

With many churches the Conference year is just beginning. New tasks are to be tried. New problems to be solved and new undertakings to be worked out. The attitude with which pastor and people undertake these things will depend largely upon the result at the other end of the line. No half hearted program will suffice and no half hearted undertaking will carry out the full program.

Will the pastor say to his people that the things can be done, or will he begin with a compromising attitude that they will try? Will the pastor apologize to the church for the Conference apportionment and say that it is too high? Will the churches be satisfied with what they did last year? Will pastor and people stand for growth or decide to decay?

Put life and hope into the beginning of your Conference year. Your work is the Master's work and to say that you cannot do certain things is to deny His power and strength.

A PSYCHOLOGICAL EFFECT

That reminds us, speaking about the apportionments of the Conferences that a man will never become rich as long as he is reminded that he is poor. More men go forward to greater things because they are encouraged rather than discouraged. To be continually telling a church that it cannot raise a certain sum is to help defeat the church in its own mission. When a pastor has to work as hard as grubbing in a new ground the whole Conference year to keep the lines on the church letter from being blank, something is radically wrong. Wrong with whom? *Something wrong with the pastor and the people.* They may be trying to pull the same load, but they are not pulling at the same time; they are not working at the same time; they are not *praying* at the same time, and most certainly they are not *paying* at the same time.

And one other thing, brethren: It is the big task that enlists the big things in us all. We wonder if the pitiful, puny, penurious, little sums that some of the churches are asked to raise are not too small to enlist the interest of the people.

The pastors have been writing about poundings, and it has all been dry reading to the Editor. Now, brethren, we shall read your articles with a keener sense of appreciation. The Editor pounded? Yes, sir. Brother M. L. Stancil, Raleigh, N. C., No. 3, sent us a nice supply of large potatoes by his father-in-law, Brother S. M. Rowland. That was the day before the North Carolina Conference convened. The next morning, Brother Julius Pace, a member of Mt. Zion church in Orange county, came to Conference and brought a bag of nice potatoes to THE SUN office. That day at noon Brother B. S. Moffitt arrived from his home in Randolph county and brought a large box filled with potatoes, both kinds, butter, fruit, meat and other good and valuable things. This box came from the hands of his good wife, and Mrs. M. A. Moffitt, both members of Shiloh church. The box was accompanied by this note: "We thought of you, and thought that you would like to be remembered during Conference by some of the Shiloh people. So here is a box for you. We are constant readers of THE SUN." The Lord richly bless the acts of these kind friends. Our companion joins in these thanks.

We take pleasure in presenting this week the address of President T. E. White of the North Carolina Conference. This address should have preceded in publication any other address of the Conference, but we could not get it last week in time for use and had another address already in type.

In a recent issue of THE SUN mention was made of Dr. W. T. Herndon as the last grandson of James 'O'Kelley. It should have been the last *great* grandson. We are glad to make the correction.

Dr. J. P. Barrett writes: "I sorrow because I shall not see my old friends, Rev. W. T. Herndon and Capt. J. A. Turrentine in the flesh again. Peace to their ashes and may love garland their graves."

Pastorless churches in the North Carolina Conference are requested to notify the Home Mission Board, J. A. Dickey, Executive Secretary, Elon College, N. C., giving him as full information as possible as to preaching Sundays desired, salaries paid, etc. Please do this now.

NEW COMERS TO THE SUN FAMILY

J. B. Warren ....Burlington, N. C.
J. Carl Smith ....Salem, Va.
C. L. Browning ....Tifton, Ga.
Mrs. E. J. Johnson ....Sanford, N. C.
N. B. House ....Franklinton, N. C.
Mrs. S. W. Fuller........................Louisburg, N. C.
J. W. Autry ....Cameron, N. C.
E. L. Shepherd ....Raleigh, N. C.
W. F. Watson ....Raleigh, N. C.
Robert H. W. Jones ....Mebane, N. C.
D. T. McKinney ....Lillington, N. C.
W. F. Spivey ....Jonesboro, N. C.
Miss Allene Farmer ....Morrisville, N. C.
C. E. Cagle ....Asheboro, N.
Mrs. J. S. Coleman ....Watson, N.
L. D. Stephenson ....McCullers, N. C.
Mrs. H. A. Hunt ....Littleton, N. C.
R. A. Coble ....Burlington, N. C.
J. N. Spivey ....Sunbury, N. C.
C. P. Richards ....Tifton, Ga.
J. R. Green ....LaGrange, Ga.
Miss Sarah Lawson ....High Point, N. C.
J. M. Hayes ....Burlington, N. C.
(Report to November 22)

We are indebted to Mrs. W. A. Hand, Tifton, Ga., and Mrs. W. A. Smith, LaGrange, Ga., for sending us new subscriptions to THE SUN. Many thanks to these good ladies.

Eleven States have ratified the Federal Woman Suffrage amendment. Maine was the eleventh.

President Wilson is materially improving, but his physician says that it will be some time before the President can be out.

Twenty-five women were killed as a result of a fire in a dance hall in Ville Platte, La., November 2. It is reported that among the number dead were several mothers who chaperoned their daughters to the dance.

Settle that Christmas present proposition by giving a copy of Peloubet's Select Notes or a copy of Tarbell's Guide. Either of these books will make a handsome gift to any teacher and be useful all the year. Order now.

PASTOR AND PEOPLE

We closed our Conference year at Union with the work in good shape. The church letter showed all apportionments paid and money in hand to settle all bills. We start off this conference year, not behind but a little ahead.

The church uses the Duplex envelope system and they were on hand and ready for distribution the last Sunday of the Conference year. The treasurer and the deacons have the distribution of them in hand.

The church not only paid the pastor in full, but members and friends of the church during the year very kindly remembered the pastor and family by donations, and at the close of the year gave him a nice pounding in the way of provisions and cash. On November 10, Brother W. J. Graham and wife drove up in front of our house and began unloading good things for the pantry and kitchen and handed to me a cash donation; and on the next day Brother G. R. T. Garrison called with a cash donation from some who did not get in on Monday.

We appreciate the donation and thank the donors. The spirit and the good-will which prompted such an act doeth the heart good and strengthens one for better service.

We are planning for a great year's work. I pray the Lord of the harvest for wisdom, grace and strength to sow wisely and bountifully and that the harvest may be a great and glorious one.

P. H. FLEMING.

HENDERSON MEETING

It was my privilege to assist Rev. R. L. Williamson in a meeting at Henderson, N. C., from November 3, to 9. The meeting was very good, and the only trouble was we had to close too soon on account of the North Carolina Conference which met on November 11.

It was a great joy to be with Brother Williamson, and his good wife in this meeting. I was entertained in their home while there, and no one ever made a visit more pleasant than they did mine while in Henderson. I am deeply grateful to both of them for their many kind favors while in their midst, also to the members of the Henderson church for their splendid co-operation in the meeting.

The Henderson people love Mr. and Mrs. Williamson, and they are doing a good work there. They are serving a loyal and an appreciative people, and I am expecting great things to be done there for the Master.

May the Lord richly bless both pastor and people in all their undertakings for good.

J. F. MORGAN.

BURLINGTON LETTER

The Burlington Christian church has just closed a splendid year. It was in fact a year of real achievements. The new building was opened the first Sunday in November and the State Christian Conference was entertained by the congregation the week following the second Sunday. It was a pleasure to have the first session of the united conferences in the new church. The Conference was characterized by largeness of vision, plan and purpose and was filled with inspiration. It was a great conference. It will go down into history as such.

The Sunday school decided to undertake the support of a missionary in February and has since that date been faithfully working at this new task. This has proven to be a joyful task, as well as profitable. Miss Martha R. Stacy is now in Japan as our missionary and we are glad. The Burlington Sunday school has a new and growing interest in far off Japan and will not only more largely support the work, but will more earnestly pray for the work and the workers. It is abundantly worth while to undertake definite missionary tasks for Christ in both home and foreign lands. It gives us a new sense of the value of life.

The reports from the different departments make splendid financial showing for the year. The church raised through regular channels $3,380.67; Sunday school $1,341.73; Building Fund $15,362.64; Ladies' Aid Society $379.33; Woman's Missionary Society $410.53; Young People's Missionary Society $146.52; Christian Endeavor Societies $102.10; special missions fund and Elon College $1,302.50. This makes a total of $22,426.02 raised during the conference year.

With the new and larger equipment we are trusting that this year will be the best year we have yet had in the Master's service.

J. W. HARRELL.

SOUTHERN CHRISTIAN CONVENTION

Official Announcement

Through Secretary Professor L. L. Vaughn, the Raleigh, N. C., Christian church has extended a cordial invitation to the Southern Christian Convention to meet as their guest in the next regular session. This will be the twenty-fourth regular session and will met on Tuesday evening before the first Sunday in May, 1920. Rev. George D. Eastes is pastor.

The Executive Committee is pleased to make this announcement, and will be very glad to have any suggestions for the program, which must be framed in advance of the meeting.

W. W. STALEY,
I. W. JOHNSON,
E. E. HOLLAND,
Executive Committee.

SUFFOLK LETTER

The Manufacturers Record of Baltimore, was kind enough to quote part of "Suffolk Letter" of October 29, and to make favorable comment on what was written on "One Country, One Language, One Flag." I thank this great paper for taking notice of the Letter, because the subject is of incalculable importance to this great nation.

Later I received a long pen-written letter from J. P. Holm, Editor of Collinwood Pilot, Collinwood, Tennessee, in which he says; "You made a big mistake writing as you did in The Manufacturers Record. Presume you don't know, understand from own experience much about it.'' Then he gives his idea about many things and seems to have misinterpreted what I had written.'' He says he came from Denmark and loves that country.

Still later, I received a marked copy of the *Florida Times-Union* of Jacksonville, Florida, which had copied from *The Manufacturers Record* what that paper had printed of ''Suffolk Letter,'' and then makes this comment: ''We have quoted the above from Dr. Staley, though most of what he said is pure flap doodle because a part of it is true and important and the idea pervading the whole of it—that we ought to attempt to unify our people instead of encouraging permanent divisions —is entirely right and of very great importance.'' The editor is very kind to admit that the idea is ''entirely right.''

As to his objection to the proposition to prohibit the teaching of foreign languages in schools, printing newspapers in alien language, and preaching in a foreign tongue, perhaps I should have been more explicit in ''Suffolk Letter'' in THE CHRISTIAN SUN; but I took it for granted that readers would understand that such a radical condition could not be made in a day. It would require at least a generation. Then the new generation would be speaking American English, and the gospel could be proclaimed in our own tongue. It would be a gradual process, but it ought to begin. It has been neglected too long and to the injury of the Republic.

It never occurred to me that foreign languages should not be cultivated by a few for *trade* and *diplomatic purposes;* but trade and government do not require, among the multitudes, foreign speech. It was the *schools*, not a few *universities* to which the ''Letter'' referred. Language is at the bottom of unity, and unity is the only hope of civilization and democracy. Colloquial language is one thing; literary language is another thing. The thing for which this language plea is made is that the common American citizen needs no language but his own; but unity of language can never come in this country with schools, newspapers, and pulpits perpetuated in foreign tongues. It is high time the American Republic was beginning to build a unified nation, and it can never be done with divided speech.

I have no prejudice against aliens. I could not have and be the Christian I strive to be; but I want aliens who come here to live, to grow rich, and become influential, to adopt our language, our laws, and our customs—to be Americans in peace and in war.

I hope that other pens more gifted than the pen of the ''Suffolk Letter'' will write the mind of this nation on ''One Country, One Language, One Flag,'' and that union forever will be the fruit of one language.

W. W. STALEY.

Victor L. Berger, socialist, has been denied a seat in the House. There were 309 votes cast against him and 1 vote for him.

* *

Mrs. R. A. Garrett—I trust and hope the paper will go into many new homes. I think it is such a good paper.

THE NEW PROGRAM FOR THE OLD TASK*

Out of the terrible struggle of a war in which three-fourths of the human race were involved, the Church of Jesus Christ has emerged with a clearer vision, an enlarged faith, and a stronger determination that ''the kingdoms of this world shall become the kingdoms of our Lord, and of our Christ, and that He shall reign forever and ever.''

It is our privilege to live in this new age. ''In an age upon ages telling when to be living is sublime.'' And in this new age the Church must be exalted to her true and proper place. The Church is the body of Christ. He is not only at the right hand of the Father, but He is also in the Church. He is not an absent Lord, but a present Lord. And those who are spending all their energies in looking for His return, and the establishment of a millennial reign, should give heed also to His words: ''Lo I am with you always even unto the end of the age.'' When you touch the Church, you touch Jesus. Paul verily thought it a light thing to persecute the Church, but he afterwards found that instead of persecuting the Church, he was persecuting Jesus. What strange words he heard on the road to Damascus! He thought Jesus was dead and out of the way, and that the Church by his plan and persecution would also disappear. But to his astonishment the voice which he recognized as the Voice of the Lord, responded: ''I am Jesus whom thou persecutest.'' Whether, therefore, you speak lightly or well, whether you hinder or help, whether you dishonor or honor, whether you blame or bless, whether you withhold or give, whether you condemn or commend, whether you scold or praise the Church, know this, that you are doing the same unto Jesus. Jesus needs our gifts, our praise, our love, our devotion, our service. The task of Jesus is the task of the Church. Jesus and the Church are one and inseparable. Small wonder that He said: ''Inasmuch as ye have done it unto one of these my brethren ye have done it unto me.''

The task of the Church is not new. Owing to the prevalence of evil in the world in its multiplied forms, there are new complications; but there is just one real task. The place is in all the world; and the task is making disciples of all the nations. It is a bigger job than getting men to make a mere profession of faith in Him or to receive baptism. It is to teach them to observe **all things** which He commanded. It means the feeding of the hungry, clothing the naked, giving sight to the blind, educating all children, and healing all diseases. The task which Jesus had is our task. In Nazareth He outlined His task: ''The spirit of the Lord is upon me because he hath anointed me to preach the gospel to the poor; he hath sent me to heal the broken-hearted, to preach deliverance to the captives, and recovering of sight to the blind, to set at liberty them that are bruised; and to preach the acceptable year of the Lord.'' To accomplish His task He gave Himself, and it will cost the Church her resources of men and money to save the world.

In the accomplishment of the super-human task of giving the gospel to all the world we need to keep three things constantly in mind: First, the great need of the world is Christ, and the Church is the only agent through which He may be given. Other religions, philosophies, and commerce have had a chance and have failed. Confucianism and Buddhism are older than Christianity and have had a chance. Mohammedanism has had a great political power and a large opportunity. It, like the others, failed. With all their opportunities two hundred millions are hungry and one hundred millions have no

*Annual address of the President—Rev. T. E. White—before the North Carolina Christian Conference, November 11, 1919. Printed in The Christian Sun by unanimous vote of the Conference.

shelter at night. Who can paint the picture of pain without a physician, of hunger without food, and of supersition without knowledge, existing everywhere in non-Christian lands? Yet a billion souls in non-Christian lands in all their poverty and wretchedness are human beings for whom the Christ died. Think too, of the incalculable loss of the rich harvests that might have been gathered to the enlargement and enrichment of the Church, but which, alas, have rotted and wasted to our poverty and shame, Christianity is the one panacea for all the ills of humanity and the Church is the only agent through which it can be given.

Secondly, we need to keep in mind that the task has been committed to the Church alone because of the Master's great faith and confidence in us. Jesus loves us. He has faith and confidence in us. His death not only manifested his love for a world, but also His faith in a world. When an employee receives a larger and a more responsible position in a concern it is because his employer has faith and confidence in him. A great task has been given the Church because our Christ has faith in us. Let us not disappoint Him.

A third thing we need to keep in mind is the fact that we can preach the gospel to all the world in this generation, and this for three reasons:

First, Christ, I know, wants it done; and He has all power. Did He not give the task because of this? "All power is given unto me in heaven and in earth, go ye, therefore, into all the world, etc." For the accomplishment of this task the resources of heaven and earth are at our command.

Secondly, other things both good and evil during a generation have gone into all the world. They tell me the Singer sewing machine has gone into all the world; that the sound of the phonograph has girdled the earth; that it is known throughout the world that beer made Milwaukee famous. If manufacturers can place their goods in all parts of the world, during a life time, why has not the Church extended herself also? I believe the answer is plain: The one set themselves to a world task and with a world program; the other has been content with a task embracing only Jews and a program including only Jerusalem.

Third, we can because we have the men and we have the money. In 1900 John R. Mott estimated that 200,000 men and women from the colleges and universities of Christendom would be required for a period of 20 years to evangelize the world. Now let us consider the fact that in the world war many times the number estimated by Dr. Mott were taken from the colleges and universities. Germany took more than twice the number from her universities. Twice the number went from American colleges and universities. It is further estimated that two universities, Oxford and Cambridge, contributed more men to win the war than Dr. Mott estimated; and this, mark you, in a period of a few years. Now, it has been estimated that only one in 20 of the Christian students in our country, Canada and Australia would be required to save the world in 20 years. We have the men. The question is, shall we be more loyal to the call of our country than we are to the call of our Christ?

Then, too, we have the money—plenty of it, and we are getting richer every day. Money is a great power. "It answers all things." It will feed the hungry. It saves life. It won the war; and if rightly used it will win the world We have it. Church members have it, $15,000,000,000 of it. During the war we spent $50,000,000 per day. We spent enough in a month to finance a missionary campaign for twenty years that would evangelize the whole world. The commander of the British fleet was right when he said: "If half of the zeal and passion, half of the outpouring of life and treaure or or-

ganization and efficiency that the state has put into this world war could be thrown into the cause of the Kingdom and of the eternal verities, the world would soon be won."

Big as the task may seem of winning the world it is easier for us than for any preceeding generation. Let me be content to simply name some of the reasons. (1) Inventions, (2) Opposition overcome in regard to world evangelization, (3) Missionary literature, (4) Rich missionary experience gathered from all lands and peoples, (5) Powerful missionary activities —such as Laymen's missionary movement, etc., (6) The Bible translated into 600 languages and dialects, (7) 25,000 missionaries already on the field, 109,099 native preachers and helpers, 26,210 native churches with more than two million members, (8) Many colleges and schools, orphanages and hospitals, (9) An awakened Church. An impression has already been made on the world, and the fields are white unto the harvest.

II The Program

The world war made its impression upon the world. It taught the Church valuable and needed lessons—lessons of loyalty, devotion, economy, thrift, service and unity. It compelled us to think in world terms. It revived and made real the brotherhood of man. Before we knew it an international spirit was possessing us. It greatly enlarged and multiplied our prayers. It broke the strings of our purses and made it possible for millions to be spent in relief work beyond the seas. We discovered ourselves and our ability to do big things. We saw and felt the result of a well-prepared program on the part of our enemies; and we met that program with a still better prepared and bigger program.

To elevate the program of the Church to a war basis, calling for a new scale of idealism and sacrifice of determination and energy is the need of the hour. We must do the extraordinary thing in this extraordinary time.

Our Saviour said: "The children of this world are wiser in their generation than the children of light." This has been true of the Church, but it need not be so, it should not be so; and if the Church will arise to her opportunity it will no longer be so. There is abundant evidence, too, that the Church is going to adopt and carry out a program that will mean the evangelization of the world in this generation. Great drives in many Protestant bodies where millions instead of thousands of dollars are being raised, tell the story. Better still the splendid number of Christian statesmen who are devoting their energies to the task, and the great "Inter-Church World Movement," the aim of which is to demonstrate that spiritual purpose and business efficiency can go together. It is with this end in view that the organization has been built up. Its purpose is to present a unified program of Christian service in all the evangelical Churches of North America. Great surveys are to be made. All the needs are to be discovered, and the program provides a plan for meeting those needs and to assist every Church in doing its full share of the work of world evangelization. It will enable us to know the number of men and the amount of money needed. It is a program world-wide in its scope, and promises to bring to fulfillment th prophecy of the hymn: "Like a mighty army moves the Church of God. We are not divided, all one body we." It is a splendid aim for unity. Not union of denominations, but unity in service. It will elevate the Christian forces to a war basis. And, why not? We united our forces during the war, and won. It did not make Frenchmen of Americans nor Italians of Englishmen, but it won the war. And the new program for the world task does not mean the making of Baptists of Presbyterians nor Methodists of Lutherans, but the winning of the world for Jesus. Shall we enter upon this world task with this world program? I believe we will.

Our government during the war took every precaution in carrying forward her program. Both press and speech were censored. This was necessary. We must not forget that in carrying out this new program, there will be the slacker and pessimist. We must quarantine and cure them, or they will frustrate the Kingdom of Christ. What to do with the pessimist has been a problem from time immemorial. Back yonder in the days of Moses they were a serious problem and menace to Israel. Ten pessimists in spying out the land contracted a terrible disease; for lack of a better name I have called it "cants." It is dangerous for it is deadly and contagious. They said, "we can't possess the land." And they didn't, because they said they couldn't. Unfortunately they were not quarantined when they returned to the camp, and soon the whole army was prostrated with the disease, and all said, "We can't possess the land." Now, this disease, like many others, if let alone develops into something still worse. "Can'ts is followed by "won'ts". This is exactly what happened with Israel. First, they said we can't and afterwards they said, "We won't. Let us make a captain and go back to Egypt."

Bad as is the disease, "cants," it is not incurable. It arises from a lack of faith in God and ourselves. Those afflicted need to be pitied, not blamed. Large doses of the missionary obligation, mixed with the promises of God when we undertake His program with cupfuls of the latest missionary news, is the best remedy. One of a hundred missionary books, a year's subscription to our magazine, or a visit to our woman's missionary meetings, is highly recommended. The Inter-Church World Movement will soon have sanatorium provided for all these unfortunates who will receive free treatment at the hands of specialists.

Seriously, we must be optimistic. The pessimist looks at the task and then to God, and says I can't The optimist looks first to God and then to the task and says with an inspired apostle, "I can do all things through Christ Who strengthens me."

READY TO RECEIVE YOUR OFFERING

The following orphanages in North Carolina will be glad to receive a Thanksgiving offering from you:

Orphanages Affiliated With Orphan Association

BAPTIST ORPHANAGE:
  Rev. M. L. Kesler, Superintendent, Thomasville.
METHODIST ORPHANAGE:
  Rev. A. S. Barnes, Superintendent, Raleigh.
PRESBYTERIAN ORPHANAGE:
  Rev. W. T. Walker, Superintendent, Barium Springs.
METHODIST ORPHANAGE:
  Walter Thompson, Superintendent, Winston-Salem.
THOMPSON ORPHANAGE:
  Rev. W. J. Smith, Superintendent, Charlottee.
METHODIST PROTESTANT HOME:
  H. A. Garrett, Superintendent, High Point.
CHRISTIAN ORPHANAGE:
  C. D. Johnston, Superintendent, Elon College.
OXFORD ORPHAN ASYLUM:
  R. L. Brown, Superintendent, Oxford.
ODD FELLOWS HOME:
  C. O. Baird, Superintendent, Goldsboro.
PYTHIAN HOME:
  C. W. Pender, Superintendent, Clayton.
ELEIDA ORPHANAGE:
  Rev. L. P. Compton, Superintendent, Asheville.

NAZARETH ORPHANS' HOME:
  Rev. W. B. Werner, Superintendent, Crescent.
FALCON ORPHANAGE:
  C. B. Strickland, Superintendent, Falcon.
CHILDREN'S HOME SOCIETY:
  W. L. Brewer, Superintendent, Greensboro.

Other institutions deserving of support:
MOUNTAIN ORPHANAGE:
  A. H. Temple, Superintendent, Balfour.
NAZARETH ORPHANAGE:
  Rev. George A. Woods, Superintendent, Raleigh.
ALEXANDER HOME:
  Miss Mary P. Guthrie, Sec.-Treas,, Charlotte.
ST. ANN'S ORPHANAGE:
  Sister Cecelia, Superintendent, Belmont.
COLORED ORPHANAGE HOME:
  Rev. W. J. Poindexter, Superintendent, Winston.
ORPHAN ASYLUM (colored):
  Henry R. Cheatham, Superintendent, Oxford.

"REMEMBER THE WORDS"

Saint Paul was a master in choosing material for a climax. It was a momentous event both in the life of the great missionary and in the history of the Church at Ephesus when he said his farewell words to this people. The few extracts from the sermon of the occasion that have been preserved indicate the heights which his eloquence touched. Though he was to "go bound in the spirit unto Jerusalem, not knowing what was to befall him there," he could look down from the Alpine peak of his faith and experience and say, "But none of these things move me."

While apprehensive as to his own future, his chief concern was as to the seven churches, of which the one at Ephesus was by no means the least important. The city was one of the oldest and most renowned to which Paul had carried the banner of Christianity. Here was the famous temple of Diana, one of the seven wonders of the ancient world. Several races mingled in its market places, and no doubt nearly all of them were represented in the church established there. His congregation included persons of the highest learning and attainments. The sermon just spoken of and the epistle to the church would not have been addressed to a people that was ignorant. He declares in closing his sermon that he has "showed them all things" and then dramatically concludes: "Remember the words of the Lord Jesus, how He said, 'It is more blessed to give than to receive.' "

(Acts 20:35).

From the wealth of matter that Christ had left, Paul chose these words as the message he should impress upon the memories of this congregation, and thus he concluded with them and used them so as virtually to burn them upon the hearts of a people that loved him and clung to him at the close of the discourse. It is then the message of the Great Missionary to the Gentile World.

In no other place in the Book is there an injunction to remember particular words, unless it be "to remember the commandments." Among all the words of Christ there are none save these that the Great Apostle urged upon the memories of his churches. There is a simple reason for this—the phrase epitomizes our religion. All of the New Testament characters emphasized giving; Christ, his disciples, the early missionaries and their helpers gave their all—gave their lives. "To give" is the dynamic element of Christianity. Without the gifts of lives and means that have been made from the time of Christ until this good hour the religion that the Master preached would be a forgotten story and the gift of Heaven's most precious jewel to the world an unremembered event.

The phrase that is especially urged upon our memories involves three simple and elemental ideas: (a) to give, (b) to receive, (c) blessings. It is a blessing either to give or to receive, but of the two the former is the more blessed.

No one questions the fact that the words of Christ are just as applicable to the church of today as to the band of followers at Ephesus nearly nineteen centuries ago. His words are universal—not only with regard to races and regions, but as to ages and eras. We accept, as an abstract principle, the statement Paul quotes, but in practice we do not seem to put it into practical use. This is too often our treatment of great and fundamental truths.

Giving has received a too elastic construction, or definition. It is not a synonym for contributing. The parent who puts money into a local fund for a school house or Y. M. C. A. building may expect more than his money's worth in return. The large property owner is set down for a handsome donation to some quasi-benevolence, and is given credit for being a philanthropist, when he has in his selfish mind forecasted dividends upon what he secretly regards as an investment. The industrial corporations find it to be "good business" to provide parks, playgrounds, club houses, schools and churches for their employes. While all of these are proper from a business standpoint, they are not giving in the truest sense of the word. The right hand merely lets go while the left hand is extended to receive more in return. It is very questionable whether a subscription or donation to the church in which the contributor worships is a gift. Surely one does not give to himself.

True giving—the giving for which a blessing is promised—means an offering upon the altar, for God's work, where the only return that can come to the giver is the promised blessing of the Master. It is not a gift unless the thing is given without hope or expectation of return or compensation. That is why so-called giving at Christmas time has become a sort of barter. When Livingstone went into Africa he expected nothing for himself. When Paul went into all the known world of his time he wanted nothing "but to finish his course with joy." When a man today sends a missionary to the foreign field, both the man who supports the missionary and the preacher himself are giving, in the highest sense of the term. Neither looks for aught for himself in return.

Many a man who thought he was giving—when he was merely making an investment for himself—has been disappointed because what he thought was a gift has not been blessed. Giving involves sacrifice and unselfishness. It also includes love and gladness. Those who "contribute" to all causes for which aid is asked merely to get rid of the "campaigners" have not given—they have contributed. The man who really gives does not pay money to get rid of solicitors. The true giver informs himself as to the objects of his bounty. Convinced that a thing is worthy, he gives liberally, cheerfully, ungrudgingly, uncomplainingly. The "contributor," on the other hand, has a horror of campaigns and solicitors. He does hot try to inform himself to any great extent as to what the cause is, but merely "contributes" in order to get rid of the subject. He thereafter has no interest in the cause of his contribution. How would any blessing follow? There is no promise that the Lord loves a "contributor."

These observations lead me to the point of making a few suggestions. The members of our Church should be informed as to the objects of our benevolences. We find that the Orphanage has one of the strongest appeals to our people. Our college is well supported. One can go into this Conference and raise more money for a church at some particular point—say Raleigh—than he can obtain for "Home Missions," though the latter subject might include several new church enterprises. There is more of the element of giving present when the donor is aware of the exact use of his money. Many churches that would with difficulty "raise" $250.00 for "Foreign Missions" might with comparative ease "give" $2,000.00 to support a missionary at a particular point in Japan, if sufficient evidence was kept before the church of the activities and success of the missionary.

We are moving in the direction of these suggestions. I am telling you what you already know to be cold facts. But my reminding you of them may assist in getting something of the kind actually done.

It is imperative that action be taken to prevent so many organizations outside of the church from making calls upon our people for funds to be used in enterprises of doubtful character. They not only mislead people who believe that they are "giving" when they are either "contributing" or are being imposed upon, but they cause many to question the whole system of campaigns and organized benevolences. It is also very important that the Church should so relate its work as to prevent overlapping. The calls should be reduced to as few in number as possible. Churches and individuals should have the opportunity of giving to special objects, but the local church should be given credit for such gifts. To illustrate: If ten men in the Burlington church give $10,000 to Elon College, five men give $5,000 to Foreign Missions, and fifteen give $7,500 to Home Missions this year it should be certified to the church treasurer and the reports of the latter account for it. It is a false pretense for the Conference minutes to show that a church gives $50 for Home Missions, $75 for Foreign Missions and $100 for Christian Education when probably one man has given through another channel authorized by the Conference more than these amounts. Let's get our financial system into better working order, and our records so they will speak the truth instead of belittling us. It will encourage men to give, whereas the present arrangement tends to discourage.

With these suggestions observed, one can now go to the membership of our churches and find a response to calls that could not have been found five years ago. The recent world war enlarged the heart of the American giver. You have but to show him that the object is worthy, that his money will be used in the extension of the Kingdom and that the plan and the place of its use are definite and deserving. The dollar-a-year member of the church will soon be an unknown person, let us hope.

The world is to be blessed both on account of giving and on account of receiving. Within the next few years we expect the banner of the Cross to be carried to the farthermost parts of the earth. What a great blessing it will be to many of those lands! But they will not be as fortunate as our own land and our own people, for we are to be the givers. "And remember the words of the Lord Jesus Christ, how He said: 'It is more blessed to give than to receive.'"

> "Out of the darkness of night
> The world rolls into light
> It is day-break everywhere."

*Address written by Hon. C. A. Hines, Greensboro, N. C., and delivered before the North Carolina Christian Conference, November 12, 1919.

Mr. G. G. Anderson, Altamahaw, N. C., was in to see us a few days ago. He says that he reads every issue of THE SUN,

Principles and Government
of
The Christian Church

(The Franklin, Virginia, session of the Southern Christian Convention ordered that the Principles and Government of the Christian Church be revised and that a committee be appointed to make the revision. The following members of the Convention were appointed to do the work: Rev. W. W. Staley, D. D., President; Rev. W. S. Long, D. D., Rev. C. H. Rowland, D. D., Rev. N. G. Newman, D. D., and W. A. Harper, LL. D. Some weeks ago the committee completed its work, and we are privileged to print, in serial form, the Principles and Government as outlined, subject to ratification by the next session of the Convention.—Editor.)

(Continued from last week)

SECTION IV
BUSINESS OF CONFERENCE

1. Conference shall meet annually for the transaction of such business as may advance the interest of the church and the cause of God.

2. Business shall be transacted in the order of time in which it may be presented, or in accordance with a program previously arranged under the direction of Conference, except a matter that is made the special order of the day.

3. Conference shall appoint the following standing committees: *On Education, Home Missions, Foreign Missions, Sunday Schools, Christian Endeavor, Evangelism, Social Service, Religious Literature;* and on other subjects when deemed advisable.

4. *The Committee on Education* shall be composed of Elders; all questions and matters pertaining to education shall be referred to them; all applicants for licensure or ordination shall be examined by them; and all ministers applying for admission into Conference shall be referred to them. They shall also report upon the general educational interests of the Conference

5. *The Committee on Home Missions* shall have charge of all matters pertaining to Home Missions within the bounds of the Conference.

6. *The Committee on Foreign Missions* shall keep in touch with and report upon the Foreign Missions interests of the Christian Church.

7. *The Committee on Sunday Schools* shall report the general condition of Sunday school work, and make recommendations for its development.

8. *The Committee on Christian Endeavor* shall have the general superintendence of the Christian Endeavor work in the Conference and strive to make this organization for Kingdom training effective in all the Churches.

9. *The Committee on Evangelization* shall endeavor to intensify the spiritual life of the churches, to awaken a general evangelistic spirit among them, to furnish evangelistic information, and to suggest a program.

10. *The Committee on Social Service* shall suggest service programs for the churches that the Church may be the community center in ministering to the whole life of the membership.

11. *The Committee on Religious Literature* shall assist in circulation of the Church organ, denominational publications, and recommend the best literature for the people.

12. *An Executive Committee* of three, two of whom shall be Elders, the President of Conference being Chairman, shall be appointed to transact necessary business between sessions of Conference.

13. Conference shall require every minister to make a full report in writing of his ministerial labors during the year; and, if he neglect to make such report for three consecutive years, his credentials shall be revoked.

14. Conference should provide for the support of aged and infirm ministers.

15. If deemed advisable, the above Committees, one or all, may be incorporated as Boards, in which case they should be *elected.* Such Boards are competent to transact the business specified in their charters, to which Conference must first assent.

CHAPTER V
CONVENTION

SECTION I—MEMBERSHIP

1. The Convention shall be composed of representatives from all the Christian Conferences admitted into membership, and shall bear the title of the Southern Christian Convention.

2. The Convention shall consist of an equal number of Elders and Laymen, chosen by the Conferences in annual session, in the proportion of one delegate to every two hundred members; but every regularly organized Conference shall have the right to send two delegates—one Elder and one Layman. The delegates shall be elected for two years.

SECTION II—ORGANIZATION

1. The regular meetings of the Convention shall be biennial, at which a President; a Vice-President, Secretary, Assistant Secretary, and Treasurer shall be elected, whose term of office shall continue for two years, or until their successors are elected.

2. One-third of the members of the Convention, half of whom are ministers, having met at the time and place appointed, shall constitute a quorum for the transaction of business but a smaller number shall have the power to adjourn to some future day.

3. At every biennial session each member shall furnish the Secretary with a certificate of his election, signed by the Secretary of his Conference.

5. At the opening of every regular meeting of the Convention, a sermon, or address, appropriate to the occasion, shall be delivered by the President.

6. In cases of emergency, the President may call an extra session of the Conference; and it shall be his duty to do so when requested by one-third of the members of the Convention, half of whom are ministers.

7. Three months' notice shall be given through the public press of any meeting of the Convention in extra session unless such meeting shall be agreed to by the body on adjournment.

(To be continued)

MISSIONARY

ANNUAL REPORT OF W. H. AND F. M. SOCIETIES OF EASTERN
VIRGINIA CHRISTIAN CONFERENCE FOR YEAR ENDING
SEPTEMBER 30, 1919

Our special for the year:

Woman's Societies

$1,200.00 for Foreign Missions.

Young Peoples and Willing Workers

$900.00 for Santa Isabel Chapel, $500.00 for Santa Isabel pastor,
$150.00 for Coy Franklin support.

Woman's Societies

Berea, (Nansemond)	$ 171.90
Bethlehem	43.75
Berkley	45.00
Cypress Chapel	52.00
Damascus	113.47
Dendron	99.16
Franklin	128.45
Hobson	5.00
Holland	105.95
Holy Neck	146.37
Liberty Spring	90.00
Memorial Temple	95.20
Mt. Carmel	54.70
Newport News	55.00
Oakland	50.00
Portsmouth	127.00
Rosemont	153.67
Suffolk	637.05
Spring Hill	10.00
Third Church, Norfolk	93.30
Waverly	119.30
Wakefield	67.21
Windsor	50.88
Union, Southampton	20.80
New Lebanon	10.40
Total	**$2,541.16**

Young People's Societies

Berea, (Nansemond)	$ 25.75
Berkley	90.08
Bethlehem	24.45
Burton's Grove	81.62
Dendron	36.73
Franklin	36.00
Holland	128.00
Memorial Temple	8.00
New Lebanon	13.30
Portsmouth	41.00
Suffolk Girls	606.15
Suffolk Boys	16.10
Spring Hill	13.50
Third Church, Norfolk	26.00
Waverly	12.50
Wakefield	56.30
Union, Surry	4.05
Tidewater S. S. Association	25.00
Rosemont Sunday school	84.00
Disputanta Sunday school	10.00
Berea, Norfolk, Sunday school	125.00
Total	**$1,462.43**

Willing Workers

Berea, Nansemond	$ 18.75
Damascus	2.50
Franklin	9.70
Holland	41.25
Holy Neck	39.41
Memorial Temple	56.00
Suffolk	34.13
Waverly	16.00
Wakefield	2.49
Windsor	21.84
Total	**$241.55**

Grand Totals

Woman's Societies	$2,541.16
Young People's Societies	$1,462.43
Willing Workers	241.55
Total	**$4,245.14**
Collection at Berkley	23.86
Collection at Portsmouth	27.27
Total	**$4,296.27**

MRS. M. L. BRYANT, Treasurer.
Norfolk, Va., 41 Poplar Ave.

REPORT OF TREASURER OF THE WOMEN'S HOME AND FOR-
EIGN MISSION BOARD OF THE SOUTHERN CHRISTIAN
CONVENTION, FOR QUARTER ENDING AUGUST 1, 1919

Regular Funds

Receipts:

August 1—North Carolina Christian Conference	$ 80.25
August 1—Eastern Virginia Conference	185.92
August 1—Virginia Valley Central Conference	69.89
Total	**$336.06**

Disbursements:

August 1—Mrs. W. H. Carroll, Expenses Board Meeting	13.78
August 1—Mrs. W. A. Harper, Expenses Board Meeting	13.93
August 1—Mrs. C. H. Rowland, Expenses Board Meeting	3.50
August 1—Mrs. W. T. Walters, Expenses Board Meeting	18.34
August 1—Mrs. A. T. Banks, Expenses Board Meeting	16.29
August 1—Rev. W. O. Wicker, Foreign Missions	135.11
August 1—Rev. W. C. Wicker, Foreign Missions	135.11
Total	**$336.06**

Santa Isabel

Receipts:

August 1—North Carolina Christian Conference	16.17
August 1—Virginia Valley Central Conference	18.04
Total	**$34.21**

Disbursements:

August 1—Rev. W. C. Wicker	34.21

Christian Orphanage

Receipts:

July 9—N. C. Conference, Thelma Thomas	15.00
August 1—N. C. Conference	9.01
August 1—Eastern Va. Conference	10.01
August 1—Eastern Va. Conference, Eugenia Hillyard	7.00
August 1—Eastern Va. Conference, Support of Orphan	75.00
August 1—Eastern Va. Conference, Coy Franklin	7.00
August 1—Eastern Va. Conference, Mary Thompson	2.00
August 1—Va Valley Conference	3.15
Total	**$128.17**

Disbursements:

August 1—Rev. W. C. Wicker	128.17

Christian Orphanage Room

Receipts:

May 1—Balance on Hand	1.75
August 1—Va. Valley C. Conference	50.40
Total	**$52.15**

Disbursements:

August 1—Rev. W. C. Wicker	52.15

Sendai Orphanage

Receipts:

August 1—N. C. Conference	9.01
August 1—Eastern Virginia Conference	10.01
August 1—Va. Valley C. Conference	3.15
Total	**$22.17**

Disbursements:

August 1—Rev. W. C. Wicker	22.17

Bible Women

Receipts:

August 1—N. C. Conference, Miss Takahashi	25.00
August 1—Eastern Va. Conference, Miss Hamaguchi	12.50
August 1—Eastern Va. Conference, Mrs. Watanabe	26.04
Total	**$63.54**

Disbursements:

August 1—Rev. W. C. Wicker	63.54

Japan Sunday School

Receipts:

August 1—Eastern Va. Conference	12.50

Disbursements:

August 1—Rev. W. C. Wicker	12.50

Santa Isabel Building Fund

Receipts:

August 1—N. C. Conference	10.00
August 1—Eastern Va. Conference	72.90
Total	**$82.90**

Disbursements:

May 1—Overdraft	4.45
August 1—Rev. W. C. Wicker	78.45
Total	**$82.90**

Barrett Home

Receipts:

August 1—N. C. Conference	46.71
August 1—Eastern Va. Conference	15.70
Total	**$62.41**

Disbursements:

August 1—Rev. W. C. Wicker	62.41

Rev. Martinez

Receipts:

May 1—Balance on Hand	107.60
August 1—Eastern Va. Conference	107.67
Total	**$215.27**

August 1—By Cash on Hand	215.27

Winchester Church Debt

Receipts:

August 1—Va. Valley C. Conference	88.50

Disbursements:

August 1—Rev. W. C. Wicker	88.50

MRS. W. T. WALTERS, Treasurer.
Winchester, Va.
(NOTE—This report has been delayed by late reports from Con-
ferences. Mrs. Walters.)

NORTH CAROLINA WOMEN'S PLANS

The Executive Board of the North Carolina Women's Missionary Conference met with Mrs. W. H.
Carroll, president, on November 19. The following
plans were made to accomplish the goals recently adopted by the Convention at Elon College:

Mrs. W. H. Carroll is to secure 50 Honorary Life Memberships among the men at $10.00 each.

Mrs. W. R. Sellars is to secure 50 Life Memberships among the women at $10.00 each.

Mrs. W. A. Harper is to secure 120 sustaining subscribers to the Hardcastle Fund at $10.00 each.

Miss Bessie Holt is to organize at least 20 new Women's and Young People's Societies in a selected list of churches and to re-organize and get on a working basis nine formerly active societies.

Mrs. N. G. Newman is to organize ten new Cradle Rolls.

Mrs. J. W. Patton is to organize 5 new Boys' Societies.

Mrs. M. F. Cook is to secure at least 250 new subscribers to the *Christian Missionary.*

Each new organization is to be apportioned $10.00 besides dues.

All money paid in on the Hardcastle Fund is to be placed on savings account, the certificate to be taken out in the name of Mrs. W. T. Walters, Treasurer, to the credit of this fund. The certificates are not to be cashed till ordered by the Board.

It was decided to print the goals in pamphlet form for wide distribution.

Let all our women, and pastors too, pray earnestly for these workers as they undertake these large things for the Kingdom.

We hope during 1920 to go over the top as in 1919. Prayer will put us there.

MRS. W. A. HARPER,
Secretary N. C. Woman's Board.

MISSION BOARD MEETING

The Mission Board of the North Carolina Christian Conference met in the office of the Mission Secretary of the Southern Christian Convention, First National Bank Building, Burlington, N. C., November 18, 1919. The following were present: T. E. White, J. O. Atkinson, W. K. Holt, K. B. Johnson, and W. P. Lawrence. Retiring Secretary-Treasurer, W. A. Harper, and J. A. Dickey, Executive Secretary-elect, were present. The latter accepted the position to which he had been elected, and his duties were outlined. These are, first to bring pastorless churches and churchless pastors together; secondly to aid delinquent churches in putting into effect the every-member canvass, and in otherwise marshaling their full strength in the work of the Kingdom; and thirdly, to put on the most effectual conference mission propaganda the time and means at hand will permit.

Rev. T. E. White was elected President of the Board with W. P. Lawrence Secretary-Treasurer.

The following were constituted an Executive Committee: W. P. Lawrence, J. O. Atkinson and W. K. Holt. The following members were appointed a Committee to make a tentative grouping of the churches of the Conference and report to the Executive Committee by January 1, 1920: T. E. White, W. G. Clements, E. L. Moffitt, and J. O. Atkinson.

W. P. LAWRENCE.

SHOULD MEN STUDY MISSIONS?

Rev. Stanley C. Harrell, during the recent session of the Eastern Virginia Christian Conference at Waverly, Virginia, raised the question as to whether there were any Men's Missionary Societies amongst us. Brother Harrell further inquired as to why there should not be Men's Missionary Societies since missions is the biggest business of the Church and that for which the Church exists. None present in the audience at the time seemed able to tell Brother Harrell whether a Men's Missionary Society had ever been heard of.

Now, it comes about that Brother Harrell is not the only man who is thinking along the same line. In his leading editorial entitled, "The Study of Missions," for his issue of November 6, 1919, I notice this paragraph from the versatile pen of the distinguished editor of the organ of the Methodist Church in this State:

"Why should mission study classes by confined to the women of the Church? Can anyone give a valid reason? If it has proved so advantageous for the women to get detailed information about the missionary work of the Church, will it not also be helpful for the men to get that information? To ask the question is to answer it. There is no other foundation upon which our missionary work can rest. No one can continue to give any heartfelt support to a work about which he knows nothing, or of which he has only a vague and general knowledge. And there is no miraculous way by which we can inform ourselves about mission work. We must study it. We must take the time and put forth the effort to read about the transformation our Christ brings about in the life of a Chinese, or a Japanese, or an African, or any of the rest, and the changes for the better that it brings into the communities of these people. In this truth is found the secret of missionary zeal and enthusiasm.

"You cannot beget interest apart from information. The surface emotions may be stirred for a time from without, and a temporary response may be secured; but the impulse soon passes away and the re-action comes. But when the soul is stirred by information that is imparted, when the enthusiasm is aroused by knowledge that becomes a part of himself, then you can count upon the interest being permanent. It springs from a source from within and is a healthful enthusiasm that burns and glows with the passing of the months. Shall not this Centenary movement that has so stirred the Church result in a great increase in the study of missions on the part of our people—men as well as women? Nothing less than this can make permanent the great advance that has been made. When an army makes a dash forward against the enemy, its next job generally is to fortify itself in its new position. This study of missions is the fortification of the Church in her new advanced position."

We wonder with Brother Harrell and with Dr. Massey as to why mission study classes should be confined to the women. Certainly men could give themselves to no better task than to learning of the world's needs of Christ and the opportunity of supplying this need.

J. O. ATKINSON.

THE CHRISTIAN ORPHANAGE

FINANCIAL REPORT FOR NOVEMBER 26, 1919

Brought forward, $12,719.61.

Children's Offerings

Rachel Hofler, 10 cents; Olive D. Poythress, Jr., 50 cents: Total, 60 cents.

Monthly Sunday School Offerings

(North Carolina Conference)

High Point, $6.46; Durham, $8.67; Poplar Branch, $1.50; Mt. Auburn, $9.18; Chapel Hill, $2.84.

(Eastern Virginia Conference)

Rosemont, $5.00; Suffolk, $25.00; Berea, (Norfolk), $6.(4)

(Valley Virginia Conference)

Leaksville, $3.40.

(Alabama Conference)

Mt. Zion, $2.25; Beulah, $1.00; Total, $71.30.

Special Offerings

W. H. Thomas, on support of children, $25.00; J. H. Jones, on support of children, $35.00; Mrs. Minnie Andrews, $5.00; Miss Iola Jacobs, $2.00; B. A. Sellars & Sons, to correct error, $6.15; Mrs. F. H. Pickard's Sunday school class, $3.00; Sale of calf, $9.00; Total, $85.15.

Children's Home

Miss Lillie Grissom, $10.00; Miss Lula Little, Waverly, Va., $10.00; W. H. Hudson, $10.00; Total, $30.00.

Thanksgiving Offerings

Rev. L. W. Newton, East Orange, N. J., $5.00; W. H. Ethridge, $5.00; A Friend, Olney, Ill., $5.00; Melrose Christian church, Springfield, Ohio, $10.00; Mrs. W. E. Cook, $2.00; Deep Creek Sunday school, $25.30; Rev. A. W. Hook and others, Phoneton, Ohio, $5.00; Mrs. R. H. McDaniel, South Norfolk, Va., $5.00; Rev. J. F. Apple, $5.00; J. L. Manley, $1.00; Miss Nannie Love Kimball, $5.00.

Long's Chapel Church: J. W. Squires, $1.00; G. A. Jeffreys, $1.00; H. C. Roney, $1.00; L. G. Jeffreys, $1.00; J. A. Wyatt, $1.00; Mrs. Bedford Ward, 50 cents; Mrs. G. K. King, 50 cents; J. Walter Johnston, $2.00; Sam Wellons, $1.00; Mrs. H. C. Roney, $1.00; H. C. King, $1.00; Ralph Rogers, $1.00; Lillie Jeffreys, $1.00; N. L. King, $1.00; Mrs. Nettie Squires, $1.00; G. L. King, $1.00; Mrs. C. G. Jeffreys, $1.00; Mrs. J. Walter Johnston, $5.00; Mrs. M. E. Fitch, 50 cents; Rudie Warren, $1.00; Eva Wyatt, $1.00; Hattie Rogers, $1.00; W. T. Garrison, $1.00; Blanche Steel, $2.00; C. G. Jeffreys, $2.00; General Collection, $1.28; Total, $106.08.

Total for the week, $293.13; Grand total, $13,012.74.

LITTLE ACTS OF KINDNESS

Some time ago we wrote to ten fertilizer manufacturers and asked them to donate five bags of fertilizer each for our wheat crop and all gladly donated.

Miss Vera Strader, Burlington, N. C., kindly gave one of the girls a pair of shoes. Mrs. Farrell, who lives at New Providence, Graham, N. C., contributed 30 yards of ginghams to keep our little girls looking good and happy. Miss Pearl Smith of Haw River, who is the popular millinery lady of that city, donated six nice hats for the girls. Holland & Beamon Company of Suffolk, Va., believe in keeping the little fellows warm and comfortable and for that purpose they donated a car load of coal.

The Ladies' Aid Society of Asheboro, contributed one nice quilt to make one of the beds look pretty and also comfortable.

Mrs. C. P. Harden donated clothing for some of the children. Mr. R. B. Tate and a number of others who have charge of the finishing plant at the Travora Cotton Mills, Graham, N. C., got together and donated two bolts of canton flannel to help out in the work.

Mr. N. H. Holt, Machais, N. Y., contributed one full suit for a boy.

For all these contributions we are very grateful. It helps us wonderfully in the work and saves our bank account.

Thanksgiving Offerings

The Thanksgiving offerings are beginning to come in and we trust that they will continue to come till our goal is reached. We have reached every goal set since we have been on this work and do not want to fail in this the last one we have set. *We must reach the six thousand dollar mark.*

How many churches will raise us $100.00 or more? We would like to see twenty churches send in $100.00 and we have more than that in our Southern Christian Convention that could easily raise that amount. Let all the churches put forth the biggest effort ever to make that goal.

Our Burlington Sunday school broke the record of all Sunday schools the first Sunday in November when its monthly contribution was $56.71. In fact, the Burlington school has led all the Sunday schools in the Southern Christian Convention this year in monthly contributions. The general average has been more than $36.00 per month.

Brother B. D. Jones sent in more than a $1,000.00 in subscriptions to the Children's Home this week from Holy Neck church. That is fine. Brother Jones is one of our Trustees and has a big heart full of love for the little orphans. His church is one of our loyal supporters in this work and when it comes to doing something for the Orphanage they always do something to make us happy. How many churches will do likewise?

CHAS. D. JOHNSTON, *Supt.*

CHILDREN'S LETTERS

Dear Uncle Charley: I can say "da, da" and "ma, ma" now and my gums are giving me lots of trouble, but I guess after the teeth get through I will feel lots better. Enclosed find 50 cents for the cousins for November. Hope all the girls and boys will have a glorious Thanksgiving. Love and best wishes to them all.—*Olive D. Poythress, Jr.*

Sorry your gums are giving you trouble. Be patient. The teeth will get through soon and then you will be all right.—*"Uncle Charley."*

Dear Uncle Charley: I am sending my dime for this month. I am a little girl ten years old. I am going to school and am in the third grade. I like my teacher. Her name is Miss Annie Corbett. Love to you and the cousins.—*Rachel R. Hofler.*

Glad to have your letter this week. Hope you will make your grade all right this year. I give my little girls a dollar when they get on the honor roll.—*"Uncle Charley."*

DADDY'S MONEY

Sometimes my daddy likes to tease,
  And takes me by surprise;
I cannot always tell his jokes,
  Unless I watch his eyes.

The other day he said, "My boy,
  Where did you get those clothes?
Who bought that hat that you have on?
  Who gave you shoes and hose?

"Who bought the food that gives you life?
  Who bought this house and lot?
Who paid for furniture and rugs?
  Who gave you your little cot?"

"Why you did, daddy," I answered back,
  "You bought it all—and more."
"Then—don't you love me better'n mother?"
  But I looked down at the floor.

Then I looked up at mother,
  And she looked back at me;
And, somehow, before I knew it,
  I was upon mother's knee.

And daddy's eyes just crinkled up—
  I saw he would understand—
'Cause he had a mother once, himself;
  He ain't always been a man.

Course, I don't love my mother best;
  I love them just the same.
But there's something 'bout a mother
  That a boy just can't explain.

It's something sorter tender—
  You can't tell it if you try.
It's things that mothers do for boys
  That daddy's money cannot buy!

    —Anna Kilpatrick Fain, in Presbyterian
Advance, May 1, 1919.

THE FLYING FROG OF JAVA

The Javanese frog is a creature measuring between fifteen and twenty-five inches. The skin of its back is pale blue and by night looks dark green or olive brown. The frog remains motionless during the day, with eyes sheltered from the light and with belly up, clinging to its support by adhesive cushions and by its belly, which is provided with a sticky covering, and it is hardly distinguishable from the objects that surround it. At nightfall it begins its hunt for the mammoth crickets on which it feeds, making leaps covering seven feet of ground. During the leap the play of lungs filled with air swells its body. To descend from a height it spreads wide its claws and, dropping, rests upon its feet.—*Leslie's Weekly.*

BAKING DAY

When I go down to grandma's,
  I always help her bake.
I like the best of all, though,
  When she starts to make a cake.

She beats it in the yellow bowl,
  Her spoon goes "Clop, clop, clop!"
She beats it so hard that sometimes
  I'm afraid her arm will drop.

And when she turns it in the pans,
  I watch her, and I wish
She wouldn't scrape so much out,
  'Cause I want to lick the dish.

And then she hands the bowl to me,
  And says: "Now run outdoors;
I've got to get my baking done
  And then scrub all the floors."

One time my father saw me there.
  He laughed and said: "I wish
I was a little tad again,
  A-lickin' out a dish."

        —Ellen Curtis.

THINGS THAT MAY INTEREST YOU

In 1833 a man in the United States patent office asked to be transferred to some other department. His reason was that he thought all the inventions had been made and that his department would likely close down and he would lose his position.

Prohibition is being greatly advocated in England. Good bye, John Barleycorn in England. Your opponents may be unpopular for a while, but they will win.

Many coal mines in Kansas have been taken over by the State.

Twelve negroes at Helena, Ark., have been sentenced to die in the electric chair for their conduct in a great riot in Phillips County, that State, September 30.

The Methodist Protestant Conference of North Carolina was in session at Concord last week, and at the same time the Methodist Episcopal Conference of Eastern North Carolina was in session at Wilson.

A commission is at work trying to settle the exact boundry between the United States and Mexico.

The government has discontinued coal for the use of foreign owned ships in American ports.

Sunday School and Christian Endeavor

SUNDAY SCHOOL LESSON FOR DECEMBER 7, 1919

(Mrs. Fred Bullock)

Peter and John Asleep in Gethsemane.—Mark 14:12-54, printed portion Mark 14:32-42.

Golden Text: Watch and pray that ye enter not into temptation.—Mark 14:38.

What a sad commentary on human nature in this lesson! Only a few short hours before these men had been quarrelling over who would be greatest in the Kingdom, yet now, when their Lord bids them stay awake past their usual hour, the excitement and the stress of the last few days have been too much for them, and they fall asleep. Yet they had thought themselves sufficiently strong to support the cares and burdens that fall upon officials of State. Well for us that He who made us knows us better than we know ourselves, and will not allow us to be tempted above that we are able to bear. The Intermediate Topic in this lesson, "Sleeping on Duty," suggests to our thoughts how comparatively easy it is to be drowsy-eyed in the line of duty. It is easier to sleep than to work. We must *work* out our salvation; we must bear burdens for others; we must labor in the vineyard. But the state can be lost, the church can be lost, the world can be lost, our own soul can be lost by doing—nothing. Many refuse to work because they claim to see no need. They are asleep at the post of duty, and have never lifted their eyes to look and behold the fields already white unto harvest.

"'Jesus' dependence upon His Disciples." Long ago the Psalmist cried out that when he considered the Heavens, the work of God's hands, and the earth which was His footstool, he could but stand aghast and cry "What *is* man that Thou art mindful of *him?*" And we, sensing Christ's need of us, must need question ourselves again, "What am I, all teachers of the ages, past, present, that Thou hast need of me?" Paul says, "Now are we the sons of God, and it doth not yet appear what we shall be!" What then, when Jesus asks us to watch with Him; when He shows us that He needs us, shall we refuse to answer? Shall we so strain ourselves for the things of the world that we cannot remain awake to the call of Christ? God forbid!

GRADING THE SUNDAY SCHOOL

(Mrs. Fred Bullock).

I have often been asked, "Do you believe in grading the Sunday school?" "Do you think we ought to grade our Sunday school when it is only a little one-room school?" I wish to answer: First, yes, I do believe in grading the Sunday school. Second, no, I don't think you ought to do it for you cannot, but I do think you ought to recognize what the grading God has already done for you. You know, without my telling you, that if you have children of varying ages in the home, they cannot understand the same lesson if told in the same words. You must, whether you will or not, "grade" your teaching in order to meet the intelligence graded by the divine will and word of God. It means, then, in the Sunday school, that if a teacher has a child of six and one of twelve in the same class, one or the other of these children is getting little or nothing out of the lesson, and this through no fault of the teacher, or the lesson. Why not allow God's gradings to be recognized in your Sunday school by dividing the children somewhere near to their ages, so that they may profit fully by the lessons taught them?

CHRISTIAN ENDEAVOR TOPIC FOR DECEMBER 7, 1919

(J. Vincent Knight)

"*Truths That Jesus Taught*"—Matt. 5:3-12; John 21:25. (Consecration Meeting).

In the teachings of Jesus we find every phase of life mentioned. No other teacher in the world's history ever touched the main characteristics of life as did the Master teacher. In His teachings, he set up a standard for all life, by which and on which all teachers of the ages, past, present, and to come may successfully base their doctrine. But the things He taught mean little or nothing to us unless we are willing to study His Word, and know of His doctrine. Notice some of the things He taught,

that are essential to all young lives.

First, He taught that the best time to surrender life to Him was in early youth, and that other things could come as needed. (See Matt 6:33). Second, that humility is the great cure for egotism, pride, haughtiness, self-righteousness, and leads to a life of happiness and peace (Matt. 5:3). Third, that the only life of divine contentment is found in Christian service. (John 21:15-25.) Fourth, that the ultimate objective of all Christ directed service is the salvation of the whole world. (John 3:16; 10:22-42). These four facts ought to furnish ample information for a live meeting, for each one appeals directly to the young, and these must be mobilized for Christian service.

Mentionings

The North Carolina and the Virginia Christian Endeavor Unions are formulating plans to place a Field Secretary in these two States for full time service for the next Convention year. The Virginia Union has 262 Societies. The North Carolina Union has 358 Societies, with a membership of 10,740. Pray for the development of those plans.

The last of the Christian Endeavor Institutes for this State will be held in Greensboro, N. C., Monday, December 1. You should attend this Institute. It will be conducted by Karl Lehmann, of Chattanooga, Tennessee, and Chas. F. Evans, of Lexington, Ky. The registration Committee proposes to register 800 for the Institute.

The third all-South Convention will be held in New Orleans, La., July 8-11, 1920. Send your registration fee to Karl Lehmann, Chattanooga, Tenn., and "the sooner, the quicker." (Registration fee, $1.00).

Young people of the North Carolina Christian Conference will be glad to know that the Christian Endeavor work of this Conference next year is in the hands of a Secretary who is to take up the Christian Endeavor work with all pastors and churches, organizing new Societies. His expenses will be paid by the Conference. Fine, let us back him with our best support.

MARRIAGES

MEDLIN-CARPENTER

Mr. William Medlin and Miss Lelia Carpenter, both of Morrisville, N. C., were united in marriage at my home, November 2, 1919. Best wishes.

W. G. CLEMENTS.

WHITSEL- SILER

Mr. Albert Whitsel of Burlington, N. C., and Miss Alice May Siler of Siler City, N. C., were united in marriage by the writer at the home of the bride's sister, Mrs. S. W. Caddell, Elon College, N. C., November 5, 1919. Only a few relatives and special friends were present. May happiness and success attend their wedded life.

N. G. NEWMAN.

OBITUARIES

KING

John Preston King of Burlington, N. ., departed this life, November 10, 1913, aged 69 years, 2 months and 16 days. Brother King had been twice married. His first wife was Miss Emma Graham who died about forty years ago. His last wife was Miss Lizzie Faucette who died a few years ago.

He leaves five living children. Two children preceded him to the grave.

Brother King confessed Christ about fifteen years ago and united with Union Christian church of which church he was a member when death came.

He was blessed with a good voice which he was fond of using in singing the praise of God.

The funeral service was conducted by the writer, assisted by Brothers Holt, Harrell and Kirk. The interment was in the cemetery at Union church, Alamance county, N. C.

May the dear Master bless and comfort the bereaved.

P. H. FLEMING.

OUR ONE GREAT NEED
THE CHRISTIAN SUN
IN EVERY HOME

A GREAT ACHIEVEMENT
and
WORDS OF APPRECIATION FOR IT
$375,000 Pledged For Elon College
(The Elon Standardization Fund)
by
COL. J. E. WEST
HON. K. B. JOHNSON
DR. R. M. MORROW
Representing the Trustees
and
DR. W. W. STALEY,
President of the Convention.

☞ "We said we could, if we would; We could, and so we did."

☞ The cause of Christian Education is set forward a half century in our Church by this great achievement. .

THE DRIVE COMMITTEE EXPRESSES APPRECIATION .

We wish to express our sincere appreciation of the generous response of the friends of Christian Education in the Christian Church to our appeal for funds for Elon. We had faith always in our people. We knew none are more generous, none more anxious to respond when merit claims support. We trust that every donor will consider this expression a personal word of appreciation.

WE WERE DIVINELY LED

Your Committee cannot but feel that our people were divinely led to oversubscribe the original goal we had set. We asked for a minimum of $125,000. They gave us $375,000. When our drive was launched educational authorities had set $200,000 as the minimum endowment for a Standard College and $300,000 for plant and equipment. Since it closed another basis has been arrived at and now the minimum endowment is $403,200 with a plant valued at $350,000. We can therefore, as we have said, but conclude that our people were divinely led to subscribe a sum sufficient to enable our College to meet the new requirements in advance. We give praise to Him.

INVESTMENT OF THE FUND

Every dollar of this fund is to be perpetual capital for Christian Education in the Christian Church. Its income only will be used to provide the means of instruction for Christian ministers and lay leaders, both men and women, in the Church. Even the expenses incurred in raising the fund are not to be charged against it. The College carried this item in its current expense account. We are sure our decision on this point will greatly encourage each donor to rejoice in the perpetuity of the good his money shall achieve.

A FINAL WORD

And now we call upon each subscriber to pay promptly when notified by the President of the College. Promptness will

---

add greatly to our gifts. It costs money to write letters, in postage, stationery, stenographic and other office help. We are told in Holy Writ that the Lord loveth the cheerful giver. We know also that He prospereth the prompt payer of pledges to His work.

It will be five years before all this fund will be in. If our subscribers will pay promptly in this five years our College will have saved many thousands of dollars. Are we not willing to make this larger gift to the institution we have made safe for our Christ by our great liberality? We believe we are. Let us do it.

One more word. Several have already paid their pledges in full. One five thousand dollar pledge has been paid in full; several thousand dollar ones, and a great many one hundred dollar ones. How greatly we would help our College now if those of us, who can, would strain a point and pay our subscription in full when the first payment comes due! We do not ask it, but we suggest it and we believe the same Father Who touched our hearts to liberal response in the subscription of the drive would bless us abundantly for doing even more than we promised to do. In such generosity we shall learn the blessing of "the second mile." We believe many whom God has prospered will gladly do this. Then their money will begin at once to aid our College and they can see for more years than otherwise the fruits of a generosity that shall bloom and ripen through the unfolding years.

With sincere appreciation to each and all, we are, for the Board of Trustees of Elon College and for the Southern Christian Convention.

Your grateful servants,
J. E. WEST,
K. B. JOHNSON,
R. M. MORROW,
Drive Committee.

Approved:
W. W. STALEY, President Southern Christian Convention.

☞ "Few Colleges have such a reputation as Elon won in so short a time and under such financial strain."

☞ "Her Alumni have proved themselves in school, in business, in Church, and in war."

☞ "Elon, the Officers' Training Camp of the Church, the cantonment of the expeditionary force which our Church is to send on its evangelizing mission to the uttermost parts of the earth."

☞ YOU have strengthened Elon and we are grateful. God bless you, every one.

(Reprinted from a Leaflet)

SMILES

He Was The Man

As usual, the Yankee was drawing the long bow.

"On one occasion," he said, "I shot nine hundred and ninety-nine snipe."

The Englishman looked incredulous.

"You might make it a thousand while you're about it," he sneered.

"No," answered Uncle Sam's offspring righteously, "it's not likely Im going to tell a lie for one snipe."

The Englishman determined not to be outdone and began to tell a story of a man who swam from Liverpool to Boston.

"Did you see him yourself?" inquired the Yank.

"Why, yes, of course I did. I was coming across the water and our vessel passed him a mile outside of Boston harbor."

"Well," retorted the Yankee, "I'm glad you saw him, stranger, 'cos you're a witness that I did it. I was that swimmer!"

The Englishman said no more.—*Selected.*

* *

A Perfect Gentleman

The civic car had stopped at the end of the t. Clair line and many passengers had alighted. Liza Jones was one of them, and as she walked across to take the suburban she turned towards her companion.

"Say, Bill, did you see that bloke that was sitting next to me in the car?" she asked.

"Yes," replied Bill.

"Well," he was a perfect gentleman, he was, aw I looked tired so he made his missus stand up and give me her seat."—*Selected.*

* *

Truthful at Least

A man was found by a policeman one evening investigating a Yonge Street building somewhat closely. "What are you doing?" asked the policeman. "Nothing," replied the man. "I am thinking of opening a jewelry store here and I thought I would look it over," and so he was allowed to remain. The next morning it was reported that the jewelry store had been robbed, the policeman scratched his head and finally said: "Well, that man may be a thief, but he's no liar."

His First Shave—Nearly

For some time Jones has suspected, when he stroked his chin, that there was something there, and now he was certain of it, so fearfully he hied himself to the Press barber's shop, and breathed again when he found he was the only customer. Calmly he took possession of the operating chair, and the towel had just been placed below his chin when —horrors!—the door opened, and in stalked three of his office colleagues. "Shave, sir? said Bill to the horror-stricken Jones. "N-n-no," blurted out the unfortunate youth in desperation; "f-face washed, please."—*Selected.*

* *

The Ruralite Speaks

I believe a fellow owes it to the community he lives in to keep himself slicked up good and fine. I go to the barber's myself every year or two.

Mirandy wants me to buy a motor car, but I got a kind o' notion we kin run inter debt fast enough without speedin' through life by machinery.

Whenever I come acrost a cemetery and read the epitaphs, the thing that impresses me the most ain't the epi so much as the taffy.—*Selected.*

* * *

A little girl was asked to name four kinds of sheep, and here is her reply: White sheep, black sheep, Mary's little lamb and the hydraulic ram.

PELOUBET'S SELECT NOTES

Contains 480 pages and covers in detail the Sunday school lessons for 1920. It should be in the hands of every teacher. Primary, Intermediate, Junior and Senior topics fully treated. $1.60 postpaid. Order from this office.

THE CHRISTIAN SUN

"IN ESSENTIALS UNITY, IN NON-ESSENTIALS LIBERTY, IN ALL THINGS CHARITY"

Thanksgiving!

(Abstract of Governor Bickett's Thanksgiving Proclamation).

THE Lord of the Harvest has been good to us. Our fields have yielded bountifully. Prosperity has smiled on farm, factory, bank and store...... There has been a mighty triumph of spiritual forces in our midst..........The fruits of this victory are seen in the great forward movements of all the churches, finer educational advantages enjoyed by all the children of the State........God has given to men. everywhere a bigger, broader conception of Christian service than they ever had before........We should be deeply thankful for the spirit of friendship and good will that prevails among us. Let us pray for absolute justice for all, by which alone this spirit may be strengthened and maintained.

Volume LXXI   WEDNESDAY, NOVEMBER 19, 1919   Number 47

BURLINGTON   ·   ·   ·   NORTH CAROLINA

THE CHRISTIAN SUN

Founded 1844 by Rev. Daniel W. Kerr

C. B. RIDDLE - - -   Editor

Entered at the Burlington, N. C. Post Office as second class matter.

Subscription Rates

One year $2.00
Six months 1.00

In Advance

Give both your old and new postoffice when asking this your address be changed.

The change of your label is your receipt for money. ▼ 'uttən re ceipts sent upon request.

Many persons subscribe for friends, intending that the ... , or be stopped at the end of the year. If instructions are given to us effect, they will receive attention at the proper time.

Marriage and obituary notices not exceeding 150 words printed free if received within 60 days from date of event, all over this at 'th rate of one-half cent a word.

Original poetry not accepted for publication.

Principles of the Christian Church

(1) The Lord Jesus Christ is the only Head of the Church.
(2) Christian is a sufficient name of the Church.
(3) The Holy Bible is a sufficient rule of faith and practice.
(4) Christian character is a sufficient test of fellowship, and of church membership.
(5) The right of private judgment and the liberty of conscience is a right and a privilege that should be accorded to, and exercised by all.

EDITORIAL

THE NORTH CAROLINA CONFERENCE

(Editorial Note: During the session of the North Carolina Conference last week, The Sun's Editor, was empowered with the duty and privilege of making reports to the daily press. A copy of these reports was kept and we submit a part of the same as our editorial contribution this week.—C. B. R.)

Burlington, North Carolina, November 11, 1919.— The first session of the North Carolina Christian Conference, Incorporated (being the ninety-fourth session of the North Carolina and Virginia Christian Conference; the fifty-third session of the Western North Carolina Conference, and twenty-sixth session of the Eastern North Carolina Conference uniting to make this one) met at 9:00 o'clock this morning with Rev. T. E. White presiding. Mr. W. M. Brown spoke the words of welcome and greeting, and Mr. George T. Whitaker, Franklinton, N. C., responded.

During the morning session reports were made by the Executive Committee, the program committee, and the treasurer of the Conference, Hon. K. B. Johnson, Cardenas, N. C. The treasurer's report showed that practically every church of the denomination in North Carolina had come forward in financial developments, and that the churches as well as business enterprises are going forward and that the local congregations are taking on new life and supporting in a more loyal way the local institution.

Special committees were appointed as follows to serve during the week:

Nominations—Dr. N. G. Newman, Dr. E. L. Moffitt; Rev. J Lee Johnson; *Finance*—L. M. Clymer, A. F. Smith; *Enrollment*—J. P. Montgomery, Miss Nonie Moore, Miss Bessie Holt; *Collectors*—Dr. W. P. Lawrence, Mr. L. D. Stephenson; *Press*—C. B. Riddle, President W. A. Harper, and Attorney C. A. Hines; *Resolutions*—Dr. J. W. Harrell, Rev. J. G. Truitt and Rev. J. V. Knight; *On Place of Meeting*—Rev. J. W. Patton, Rev. G. R. Underwood and Mr. J. Byrd Ellington.

President White had for the subject of his annual address, "The New Program for the Old Task." In speaking in a preliminary way concerning the united and enlarged conference, the President said: "It is not without a passing significance that the first session of our united conferences begins on the first anniversary of the signing of the Armistice. Out of the terrible struggle the Church comes with enlarged faith and vision, having learned the most valuable lessons which she will incorporate in a world program of conquest for Christ which will bring to pass the saying that is written. The Kingdoms of this world may become the Kingdom of our Lord and his Christ, and he shall reign forever and ever."

President White's message was heartily received. It was punctuated with words of wisdom. "When you touch the church, you touch Jesus," was a sample of his striking sentences that went to the hearts of those who were privileged to hear him.

At the close of the morning service the Lord's Supper was administered by four Elders of the Conference. In the afternoon Rev. J. V. Knight read the report on Christian Endeavor which embraced practical plans to be undertaken during the coming year. Mr. C. H. Stephenson of Raleigh, North Carolina, rendered a report on Sunday schools which incorporated large and progressive plans. One of the important steps taken was setting aside one week in each year to be known as "Sunday School Week" in all churches and that no other activities interfere. The Conference is looking forward to the putting on of a regular secretary to handle the work of the Sunday-School and Christian Endeavor matters in the North Carolina Conference.

Addresses on these reports were given by Rev. W. L. Wells, Pastor of the First Christian church, Reidsville, N. C.; Rev. J. V. Knight, Pastor of the First Christian church, Greensboro, N. C., and Prof. Herbert Scholtz, Macon, N. C.

The theme for the afternoon session was "Missions." Victor M. Rivera and Toshio Sato San were the two interesting speakers. Mr. Rivera is from Porto Rico and Miss Toshio is from Japan. Rev. O. S. Thomas, Dayton, Ohio, Home Mission Secretary in the American Christian Convention, and Rev. E. K. McCord, a Missionary to Japan, both addressed the evening session.

Mr. Thomas used as his theme, "The Challenge of Missions," while Mr. McCord's theme was "The Dynamic of Missions." Rev. J. O. Atkinson, D. D., Field Secretary of Missions in the Southern Christian Convention, spoke on "The Reaction of Missions."

The theme for consideration tomorrow morning will be "Stewardship," the afternoon theme will be devoted to missionary work as it is related to our helpless ones —the orphans.

Tomorrow afternon the theme for discussion will be "Training Christian Leaders."

At this time your correspondent is unable to report the number in attendance. The entertainment committee is over-run and behind with its report.

Burlington, N. C., November 12.—The second session of the North Carolina Christian Conference opened this morning promptly at 9 o'clock. The theme under discussion continued from last night was "Missions."

The report of the Home Mission Board was rendered by Rev. T. E. White, Chairman, Sanford, N. C., and was comprehensive in its scope and business-like in its program. The report lamented the fact that many churches are without pastors and urged the people not only to build churches but to support them. Rev. W. L. Wells was approved as pastor of the Reidsville church and the Board made a favorable report in behalf of the work there. Danville, Virginia, another very important mission point had due consideration. Franklinton, High Point and Mebane, New Hope (Randolph), Lucama, Hopedale, other mission points, were favorably commended of, the work ordered to go forward. The report recommended an Executive Secretary to take charge of the Home Mission work in the Conference.

Mrs. E. B. Huffines rendered a report of the late L. I. Cox, Home Mission Secretary of the Conference. Secretary Cox passed away September 5, and his office has been left open since then. Mrs. W. H. Carroll presented a report of the Woman's Board of Missions, which was favorably received and showed splendid progress in various directions. Promptly at 10:30 A. M., the theme of "Stewardship" was taken up and discussed by Rev. J. E. Franks, Cary, N. C., Dr. W. P. Lawrence, Elon College, N. C., and Attorney C. A. Hines, Greensboro, N. C. Mr. Hines was unable to be present but sent his address. All of these addresses placed a new emphasis and a new meaning upon money and the members of the Conference were greatly edified and enlightened by the splendid and scholarly addresses given by the speakers upon this theme.

The one important thing presented at the beginning of the afternoon session was a report by the Committee on Education which was read by Dr. N. G. Newman, Elon College, N. C. Robert Herbert Coble, Burlington, N. C., Route 5; Dallis Theaton McKinney, Lillington, N. C.; E, H. Rainey, Garysburg, N. C., and William Gaither Crutchfield, Guilford College, N. C., asked for licensure and the committee recommended that they be licensed. The licentiates of the Conference—R. O.

Smith, J. E. McCauley, L. W. Fogleman and B. J. Howard applied for ordination and the committee recommended that the same be granted.

Emphasis was made upon the scarcity of ministers to man the field and the Conference was asked to pray earnestly that more men might be sent into the needy fields.

The Board recommended the steps as taken by the Board of Education in the American Christian Convention, that scholarships be granted only to young men and women who declare their purpose to complete their college course and take at least one year's work in some theological seminary; also that any student preparing for the ministry in the Christian denomination, and maintaining an average grade of 80 per cent in his literary subjects during his freshman year be awarded a cash scholarship of $100.00; provided, that the student is not to take regular preaching service during the school year and that he is to carry full school work. This recommendation also carried that any ministerial student in the sophomore year of college who maintains an average of 85 per cent in his literary subjects be awarded a scholarship of $100.00 on the condition that he is not to accept regular preaching appointments during his school year, and that he is to carry full work. The ministerial students in the junior and senior years of college who maintain an average of 85 per cent in literary subjects are also to be awarded a cash scholarship of $100.00 on the condition that only half time be given to pastoral work.

These recommendations are based on a graduating scale, and so the ministerial students who graduate from college with an average grade of 85 per cent will be awarded a scholarship of $200.00 for the first year in a first class seminary.

The theme for the latter part of the afternoon service was, "Helping the Helpless." Dr. P. H. Fleming, Burlington, N. C., Superintendent; H. A. Garrett, of the Methodist Protestant Children's Home, High Point, N. C, and Chas. D. Johnston, Supt. of the Christian Orphanage, Elon College, N. C., addressed the Conference and brought messages that were gladly received.

Dr. N. G. Newman, Dr. W. C. Wicker and Dr. W. A. Harper of the Elon College Faculty, addressed the Conference tonight on the subject of "Training Christian Leaders." Dr. Newman's subject was, "Problems of Kingdom Leaders," while Dr. Wicker spoke on "The Fundamentals in Christian Education," and Dr. Harper's theme was "The New Service of the Christian College."

Burlington, N. C., November 13.—The third day of the North Carolina Christian Conference in session at this place was taken up this morning by a report on "Superannuation" by Hon. K. B. Johnson, Cardenas, N. C. The report was new in that it took forward steps looking to a larger and better support for aged ministers and the wives of deceased ministers. The report included five per cent of the Conference funds to be used for this purpose. The report was passed without a dissenting voice. Rev. C. B. Riddle, Editor of THE

CHRISTIAN SUN, rendered a report on religious literature. One of the recommendations made was that ministers not only read publications of their denomination, but of other denominations that they might keep in touch with what is being done throughout the Christian world.

Rev. J. F. Apple, Elon College, N. C., Mrs. E. K. McCord, Dayton, Ohio, and Rev. C. B. Riddle, Editor THE CHRISTIAN SUN, addressed the Conference on themes related to church publications and religious boks.

In the afternoon the spicey and important part of the Conference was on "The Best Thing my Church did this Year," by the delegates. Following this the theme was "Evangelism." Chaplain Stanley C. Harrell, Suffolk, Va., Dr. W. H. Denison, Dayton, Ohio, Rev. F. C. Lester, Graham, N. C., and Rev. J. G. Truitt, News Ferry, Va., spoke on topics relating to this subject. The addresses showed much preparation and struck a high note on the important subject of evangelism.

Tonight Dr. George J. Ramsey, Raleigh, N. C., Dr. R. M. Andrews, Greensboro, N. C., Dr. W. W. Staley, Suffolk, Va., and Dr. F. Paul Langhorn, New York City, addressed the Conference on the theme of "Christian Union." The addresses were of a very high order and were gladly received by the vast audience present to hear these specialties on a theme so important in an age like this.

Burlington, N. C., November 14, 1919.—The ninety-fourth annual session of the North Carolina Christian Conference which has been in session at this place during the past four days came to an end tonight.

During the morning session many items of business were dispensed with and the following addresses heard: "The Gospel of Comfort" by Rev. J. W. Patton; "The Gospel of Service" by Rev. A. T. Banks, and "The Church Ministering to All" by Dr. N. G. Newman.

In the opening of the afternoon session the report on apportionments brought some interesting and lively discussion. The report, however, was adopted, carrying with it 25 per cent increase. The conference also went on record favoring churches rapidly raising the salaries of the ministers. The laymen took a very active part in this, and it was very clearly seen that this matter, as well as other matters of a financial nature appealed to men when such was on a progressive scale. It was the unanimous conviction of the body that men despise small tasks, and that churches prosper when they undertake big things. The amount to be raised by many of the churches has been so small that it did not attract and call out the best in the membership.

Possibly one of the most forward addresses made during the conference was made by Mr. J. U. Gunter, Sanford, N. C., on the "The Need of Pastorates." The address was ordered printed for free distribution. Rev. R. F. Brown addressed the conference on "The Opportunities of the Ministry."

At the final closing session Dr. C. H. Armstrong, Baltimore, Md., Secretary of the Committee on Christian Union of the Disciples Church, brought a message that was gladly heard, while Rev. W. W. Staley, D. D., President of the Southern Christian Convention, preach-

ed the ordination sermon of the conference. Dr. Staley was practical in his presentation, clear in his statements and definite as to what constituted a real minister.

THINGS YOU MAY WANT TO KNOW.

The following young men were ordained as probationers to preach the Gospel: Eugene H. Rainey, Robert H. Coble, Dallas T. McKinney.

Churches making no report: Antioch (C), Bennett, Christian Union, Goshen Chapel, Hayes Chapel, Keyser, Moore Union.

Total money raised by the Conference—$7,723.00.

Apportionment for next year—$10,000.00.

Enrollment

Ministers of the Conference present.............. 36
Licentiates of the Conference Present........... 5
Delegates of the Conference present............186
Visitors (Laymen and Ministers)............... 27

Total............... 254.

Ninety-six churches had delegates present; ten churches represented by letter.

Mr. J. A. Dickey, Elon College, N. C., was elected on report of the Home Mission Board, as Executive Secretary of the Conference and is to give his entire time to the work.

Conference Year: The Conference year is run from November 1 to November 1 of each year, and churches are asked to base their financial reports on these dates.

Place of meeting next year: Park's Cross Roads.

(We have not covered all. We could not for it was impossible to be at every session and hear and see all. Bear this in mind if we have grossly failed to mention persons or items.)

THANKSGIVING PROCLAMATION
November 27, 1919

By the President of the United States of America.

The season of the year has again arrived when the people of the United States are accustomed to unite in giving thanks to Almighty God for the blessings which he has conferred upon our country during twelve months that have passed.

A year ago our people poured out their hearts in praise and thanksgiving that through divine aid the right was victorious and peace had come to the nations which had so courageously struggled in defense of human liberty and justice.

Now that the stern task is ended and the fruits of achievement are ours, we look forward with confidence to the dawn of an era where the sacrifices of the nations will find recompense in a world at peace.

But to attain the consummation of the great work to which the American people devoted their manhood and the vast resources of their country they should, as they give thanks to God, reconsecrate themselves to these principles of right which triumphed through His merciful goodness. Our gratitude can find no more perfect expression than to bulwark with loyalty and patriotism those principles for which the free peoples of the earth fought and died.

During the last year we have had much to make nagrateful. In spite of the confusion in our economic life resulting from the war we have prospered. Our harvests have been plentiful and of our abundance we have been able to render succor to less favored nations. Our democracy remains unshaken in a world torn with political and social unrest. Our traditional ideals are still our guides in the path of progress and civilization.

These are great blessings, vouchsafed to us, for which we devoutly give thanks, should arouse us to a fuller sense of our duty to ourselves and to mankind to see to it that nothing we may shall mar the completeness of the victory which we helped to win.

No selfish purpose animated us in becoming a participant in the world war, and with a like spirit of unselfishness we should strive to aid by our example and by our co-operation in realizing the enduring welfare of all peoples and in bringing into being a world ruled by friendship and good will.

Therefore, I, Woodrow Wilson, President of the United States of America, hereby designate Thursday, the twenty-seventh day of November, next, for observance as a day of thanksgiving and prayer by my fellow countrymen, inviting them to cease on that day from their ordinary tasks and to unite in their homes and in their several places of worship in ascribing praise and thanksgiving to God, the author of all blessings and the master of our destinies.

In witness whereof, I have hereunto set my hand and caused the seal of the United States to be affixed.

Done in the District of Columbia, this fifth day of November, in the year of our Lord one thousand nine hundred and nineteen, and of the independence of the United States the one hundred and forty-fourth.

WOODROW WILSON.

By the President:
ROBERT LANSING, *Secretary of State.*

PASTOR AND PEOPLE

HOLLAND, VIRGINIA

Yesterday we received one member into church by letter.

It was Ladies' Aid Day at the church service, and the Society was there in a body. The occasion was the presentation of the newly installed pipe organ by the Society to the church.

The presentation was made by Mrs. Job. G. Holland and the address of acceptance on the part of the church was made by J. P. Dalton, one of the trustees of the church. The organ was purchased and paid for by the Ladies' Aid Society at a cost of $1,800.

It was also decided by the church to proceed at once to raise the balance of the indebtedness on the church and the second Sunday in December was set for the day of dedication. The dedicatory services will be in the afternoon at three o'clock. Dr. J. O. Atkinson, Elon College, N. C., was selected by the church to preach the dedication sermon. The new building is constructed of pressed brick and stone trimmings. It has electric

lights, a water system, and hot air heat. The main auditorium and gallery will seat approximately 600 people. The pastor's study, neatly equipped, is located close by the pulpit. The Sunday school department is in the basement with a splendid auditorium, six classrooms and a kitchen. The building and enquipment has cost approximately $30,000.

A joint committee from the two churches, Holland and Holy Neck, has decided to wire the parsonage for electric lights. This generous act of the pastorate is much appreciated.

W. M. JAY.

SUFFOLK LETTER

The nation is full of clamor for the lowering of what is called the "high cost of living." From Washington down to the smallest village remedies are suggested. Even government, national, state, and municipal, would compel reduction in prices, and thus help the consumer; but the more the agitation, the less is accomplished.

The whole matter comes in as one item in the aftermath of the war, and is a necessary result of the war-spirit. When the war ends at the front, it re-acts at home. The spirit that fought in the line of battle at the front comes back home after the last battle and works among the people. That spirit operates in politics, business, social life, and even in religious organizations. Wild plans and selfish interests propose all sorts of new undertakings, and almost everything is up in the air for years.

The armistice is not an agreement for peace, but a cessation of hostilities till peace terms can be agreed upon by the belligerents. Men talk about peace, but there is no peace till the League of Nations can secure peace. The slow process of dealing with the League of Nations in our own Congress shows that *peace terms* are not so easy of adoption. While this spirit is at work over the world, with all sorts of disturbances in great centers, it is to be expected that excitement will enter the markets and financial war will rage throughout the country.

But one thing should be kept in mind that "prosperity" and "high prices" always go together; and that "low prices" and "adversity" are discouraged companions. It is true, perhaps, that prices will never reach as low a level as they did before the war; but prices will drop some day to a new normal. But when prices begin to drop business will decline, discouragement will seize investors, retailers will not be able to sell over their counters, failures may become epidemic, and the "low cost" of living may be worse than the "high cost of living. It is easy to sell while prices are rising, because customers fear prices will go higher; but when prices go downward, customers hesitate to buy hoping that prices will go lower. Then business lags, people become discouraged, and hard times begin. It would be a calamity for prices to drop suddenly. When tides are low boats cannot go up the small rivers and into the small places; but when tides are high, they go into all markets. The little business and the little people fare best when prices are high; big business and big people can stand the strain of hard times better

6

THE CHRISTIAN SUNNovember 19, 1919

and longer. People need not worry over "high prices" while general prosperity prevails throughout the land, and religious enterprises share in the spirit of liberality in the glow of the heat of widespread activity.

W. W. STALEY.

ABOUT OUR FRIENDS

Our friends came to see us last week. They came in large numbers and we are glad to have them. We dare not mention names for fear that we should have a list far from being complete. Our friends came. Come again. A welcome awaits you.

AN EXPLANATION

This issue of THE CHRISTIAN SUN was scheduled to be a regular Thanksgiving Number, but circumstances over which we have no control make it impossible for us to render that service this year. Our editorial pages are laden with messages from the North Carolina Conference, while general matter is rapidly accumulating. Recent Conferences have voted to have several papers printed and they are now coming in. To give this issue to Thanksgiving messages would make it very difficult, and so we offer this word of explanation and ask friends to bear with us.

AN APPRECIATED GIFT

When a church loves its pastor, and the pastor loves his people, there is no sigh of relief when the last dollar on salary is paid. Rather there is an appreciation that goes out of the hearts of the people as a free-will offering. Such was the case the other day with the Sanford church and its beloved pastor, Rev. T. E. White. He received a check for $75.00 as an overplus of what they had agreed to pay him. His heart was made to rejoice, but the people received the greater benefit. Now, Brother White didn't tell us to write this, neither did any member of the Sanford church, but we got the news and have told it. Some other church do likewise and send a half-paid pastor away with a smile.

AMONG THE WORKERS

This splendid word comes from Dr. L. E. Smith, Third church, Norfolk, Va.: "The way things are moving is simply wonderful. Had 502 at Rally Day Exercises Sunday morning, and at least 400 present for the evening service. The time is indeed ripe for Third church." This church under the leadership of Brother Smith is moving in such a way as to inspire all of us. Its membership is rapidly increasing. Its church Sunday school attendance multiplies, and many are eager for the building program to begin. Here is hoping that these progressive friends will build while conditions seem so favorable. A church costing not less than $150,000.00 and ample for all purposes in Park Place, Norfolk, would be a source of great inspiration to all our work in the South and we are depending on this church with its superior opportunity and privilege to lead us on to great things.

A happy Thanksgiving is the wish of the Editor to all CHRISTIAN SUN readers.

MISSIONARY

MINUTES OF THE FOREIGN MISSION DEPARTMENT OF THE CHRISTIAN CHURCH

The Foreign Mission Department of the Mission Board of the Christian Church met at Dayton, Ohio, Tuesday evening, October 21, and adjourned Thursday evening, October 23, 1919. All members were present with the exception of Rev. W. P. Fletcher, from whom a letter was read. Rev. E. K. McCord, D. D., Acting Foreign Mission Secretary, was asked to meet regularly with the Board The following visitors were present at various times: Miss Carrie Robison, Rev. E. B. Flory, Rev. and Mrs. W. Q. McKnight, Rev. W. H. Martin, Rev. William Williams, Mrs. Carrie Beaver, Mrs. E. K. McCord and Rev. J. W. Harrell, D. D.

The newly qualified board elected the following officers:
President—Rev. Warren H. Denison, D. D.
Secretary—Rev. Wilson P. Minton.
Treasurer—Rev. Omer S. Thomas, D. D.
Mission Council—Denison, Winters, and Minton.

An appropriation to the Headquarters Building expense of the Committee on Reference and Council was allowed in the sum of $50.00.

Foreign Mission Secretary Minton was named to succeed Dr. M. T. Morrill on all co-operative committees and Acting Secretary McCord was asked to place the name of the Secretary in nomination to fill such vacancies as were created by the retirement of Dr. Morrill.

The Committee on Co-operation in Latin America was voted the usual apportionment of $200.00.

It was decided to create a fund for the building of homes for our Foreign Missionaries and the Secretary was authorized to encourage gifts for this purpose.

A special committee consisting of Acting Secretary McCord, Secretary Minton and Mrs. M. T. Morrill was asked to make a thorough study of the Interchurch World Movement program for Japan and if necessary, to call the Board together to hear and act upon their recommendations.

The Secretary was requested to send suitable greetings to the Japan and Porto Rico Missions.

Japan

The request of the Japan Mission for an additional fund for the Kannari chapel was referred to the Woman's Board.

The action of the Japan Mission relative to the Narugo district was approved and the matter referred to the Woman's Board.

A year-in-grant of $250 was allowed the Garmans for the year, 1919.

A grant of $25 was allowed toward the purchase of an organ for Utsunomiya, the balance to be raised by that church.

The requested grant for the building of the Naka Shibuya church was ordered delayed owing to lack of proper funds.

A grant of $50 was allowed Miss Martha Stacy for language study.

It was voted that the money received for the temporary rental of the mission home during a short period in the summer be retained by Brother Garman.

Foreign Mission Secretary Minton was asked to visit the Japan Field as soon as possible, preferably during the year, 1920.

The matter of the unpaid balance for the Dogenzaki lot was referred to the investment committee of the Mission Board.

The Acting Secretary was authorized to call for funds to provide buildings for the Night School, Kindergarten and the pastor's and teacher's residence on the Dogenzaki lot in Toyko for which $10,000 is needed.

The Japan budget was voted in the sum of $20,675.

Porto Rico

The Porto Rico budget was thoroughly considered and voted in the sum of $9,540. .

The salary of Rev. D. P. Barrett was fixed at $1,700, including children's allowances.

Rev. and Mrs. D. P. Barrett were voted a furlough, the same to be taken next year.

It was decided to begin the erection of a chapel at Santa Isabel at the earliest possible date.

It was decided to purchase an available property for a parsonage at Arus, and that some church or individual be given the privilege of assuming that obligation, the minimum price having been set at $750.

Acting Secretary McCord was instructed to inform the Mission Board of the Southern Christian Convention . that the property in Porto Rico for which said board has appropriated $3,500 cannot be secured and that he ask the board to assist in buying another home for Miss Williams instead in an amount not to exceed $5,000.

Missionaries Appointed

Rev. W. H. Martin, Mellott, Ind., was placed under appointment as missionary to Porto Rico, the details of his sailing to be worked out by the Acting Secretary.

The privilege of undertaking the support of Brother Martin was left open for some church or Sunday school to assume.

The appointment of Rev. W. Q. McKnight was transferred from Porto Rico to Japan, with instructions to sail at the earliest moment.

Resolutions

That we commend the action of the American Christian Convention at its latest session in authorizing a deputation to visit our mission field in Japan; and we call the attention of its Executve Board to the fact that the gathering of the World's Sunday School Association in Japan will provide an opportune occasion for such a visitation.

That we express our hearty appreciation of the splendid work done by the Woman's Foreign Mission Board in exceeding their goal during the past year and that we request them to continue the support of the Sendai field.

That we learn with pleasure concerning the increasing interest in and giving for missionary work by the Southern Christian Convention as evidenced in the new and larger goal just set by our missionary workers there, viz.: $500,000 to be secured in cash and pledges within three years from this date for home and foreign missions. We hope this faith and vision may be not only blessed of God and that this goal may not only be reached, but that in so doing it shall be an inspiration to every other section of our brotherhood.

That we express our hearty appreciation of the devoted leadership of Miss Carrie Robison, and the untiring efforts of our young people in providing for the chapel at Santa Isabel.

Resolved, That it is with regret that at this session of the Mission Board we lose from our membership and official service, Rev. Milo T. Morrill, D. D.

Dr. Morrill has been a member of the Mission Board of the Christian Church for twenty years and his service has been faithfully and unselfishly rendered. Of this time he has been Foreign Mission Secretary for more than twelve years, and President of the Mission Board for several years. In all of these positions he has rendered most valuable service to the Kingdom and to our church.

We desire to express our appreciation of him as a man and a Christian and as an efficient and conscientious official. His

administration has been characterized by his splendid statesmanship.

We congratulate Defiance College and the Christian Divinity School in securing his valuable services and wish him splendid success in this new relationship.

All matters of unfinished business at the close of the session were referred to the Mission Council.

W. P. MINTON, Recording Secretary.

Members Foreign Department Board

Warren H. Denison, D. D., Mrs. M. T. Morrill, Rev. L. E. Smith, D. D., Rev. W. P. Fletcher, Mr. J. O. Winters, Rev. W. P. Minton.

THE CHRISTIAN ORPHANAGE

FINANCIAL REPORT FOR NOVEMBER 19, 1919

Brought forward, $12,398.02.

Children's Offerings

Francis Horne Everett, 50 cents.

Monthly Offerings
(North Carolina Conference)

Third Ave., Christian S. S., Danville, Va., $5.00; Reidsville, $1.00; New Providence, $2.85; Hope Dale, $2.00; Pleasant Hill, $4.40; Burlington, $56.71; Ramseur, $4.68; Ingram, $3.00; Ether, $1.70; Shiloh, $2.00; New Lebanon, $1.00; Union, Virgilina, $2.00; New Lebanon Baracca Class, $1.00.

(Eastern Virginia Conference)

Concord, $3.00; Centerville, $1.00; B. F. Meginley, for S. S., $2.00; Berea, $2.02; Union Southampton, $4.60; Isle of Wight, $2.50; Portsmouth, $3.00; Berea (Nansemond County), $10.00.

(Georgia and Alabama Conference)

North Highlands, $2.35; Richland, $2.33.

(Virginia Valley Conference)

Linville, $1.00; Dry Run, $4.55; American Christian Convention Office, $7.50; Total, $134.59.

Children's Home Fund

Rev. Joseph E. McCauley, $5.00; Nannie L. Hawkins, $1.00.

Thanksgiving Offering

Miss Vera E. Gilliam, $5.00; Frances Horne Everett, 50 cents; Nannie L. Hawkins, $1.00; Mrs. Holden, $5.00; Ben T. Holden, $2.00; Florence Holden, $2.00; Rebecca Ann Holden, $1.00; G. M. Womble, New Hill, N. C., $25.00; Dr. J. O. Atkinson, $10.00; Rev. A. F. Isley and Wife, $5.00; Total, $56.50.

Special

B. F. Meginley, $1.00; Baracca Class New Providence church, $2.00; Willing Workors, Third Ave. church, Danville, Va., $1.00; Mrs. LeRoy Adams, $1.00; Henry C. Bason, Haw River, $2.00; Special Collection N. C. Conference, $123.00; Total, $130.00.

Total for the week, $321.59; Grand total, $12,719.61.

CHILDREN'S LETTERS

Dear Uncle Charley: Today is Ben T's birthday. He is three years old. My birthday is the twentieth of this month. I will be six then. A week from my birthday is Thanksgiving and I hope all of us will have a happy time and that you will get more money for the orphans that you have asked for. I am sending our offering in this letter—$5.00 for mother, $2.00 for Ben T., $2.00 for myself and $1.00 for Rebecca Ann. Love to all the cousins.—*Florence P. Holden.*

You are a fine little girl and a good helper. I am proud of you.—'*Uncle Charley.*'

Dear Uncle Charley: I am sending $1.00. Fifty cents for the Thanksgiving offering and fifty cents for dues as I haven't sent any since last June. I enjoyed the singing so much when the girls came to Holy Neck. Hope the cousins will have a good time Thanksgiving. Love to all.—*Frances Horne Everett.*

Glad to have your letter this week. We are always glad to have the children write for the Corner.—*"Uncle Charley."*

FOR THE MASTER'S SAKE!

The mother was dead; perhaps the father might better have been. The two children were oh! so little, so little, so dirty, so world-wise, so starved for happiness, so manifestly destined to become all that Jesus Christ died to save them from becoming, that it really would have broken your heart could you have seen them.

They were children of poverty and neglect, children with but few illusions as to this world and probably with none as to the next.

The boy, in the course of time, would become an associate of criminals.

The girl—

God help us all and have mercy on our souls!

And yet there are homes for just such children as these poor castaways—these future threats to your own girl's happiness and your own boy's safety. There are homes where these forgotten bits of humanity may know what a bath means—clean clothes, abundant food, education and training for useful lives, and—greatest boon of all—where they may learn what Jesus Christ means in this world where we stay but a short while and in that other world where we shall live a long, long time.

And it requires so little—so pitifully little to take these waifs from the high road to ruin and set their little feet firmly upon a path leading to other things—to high attainment, perhaps to complete happiness and eternal salvation. So little, indeed, that hardly can there be a man or woman in North Carolina but is able to aid in saving these children from all that is vile, and in saying to God: "This I do in Thy name." Be sure the Recording Angel will note carefully the act, and on that great final day of all time will be counted to your credit.

And so you, a father or a mother with children of your own who are not in the streets, you are asked to contribute one day's income to aid in placing the waifs of the State in any one of the orphanages you may yourself select. But one day's income, mark you.

And you, a husband or a wife whose home God has not blessed with children, are asked to contribute one day's income to aid in giving a home to some unfortunate child without mother or father.

The North Carolina Orphan Association asks the business man, the professional man, the laborer and the salaried man, the farmer and the shop worker, the boys and the girls, to devote but one day's income to a cause approved by the Master, who charges you, personally, to care for the fatherless ones. There are many orphanages in North Carolina and there are countless North Carolina children without other hope of home than these orphanages.

"And what doth the Lord require of thee, but to do justly, and to love mercy, and to walk humbly with thy God?"

Are you doing justly unless you aid in saving these children who come into the world through no will of their own and who can never make a safe harbor without your aid?

Do you really love mercy unless you show mercy to these tots without homes, without friends, without food, without knowledge of God's Word?

And do you walk humbly with thy God unless you carry out His command: "Even so, it is not the will of your Father which is in heaven that one of these little ones shall perish."

And perish they surely must unless you are merciful and give of your abundance—give one day's income if you will, more if you can, less if need be. But give—give for your own children's sake, be they living or dead, and give for Jesus Christ's sake, that He may not have died in vain for such as you and I—and these street waifs.

Let this offering be given with a heart filled with gratitude, and joy, that you are privileged to serve your God and humanity in so acceptable a manner. Let it come, as is most fitting, on or near Thanksgiving Day. The need is urgent, and the cry of the orphaned child rings loud and insistent. You cannot shut your ears to that cry. Should you try and do so, should you fail to accept this opportunity of rendering service to these helpless ones most needing it, to these innocent ones most deserving, perhaps in years to come that cry will still ring in the secret chambers of your heart, and when the long journey begins you will see that inspired text written in letters of fire—*"Inasmuch as ye did it not unto one of the least of these—"*

For our Master's sake—GIVE!

M. L. SHIPMAN,
JAS. R. YOUNG,
LIVINGSTON JOHNSON,
JOHN D. BERRY,
W. F. EVANS,
Publicity Committee N. C. Orphan Assot'n.
Raleigh, N. C.
November 10, 1919.

☞ *The pastors of all churches and the superintendent of all Sunday schools are requested to direct attention to the Thanksgiving offering at their services on Sunday, November 23.*

BROTHER P. T. HINES MARRIED

"Mr. and Mrs. C. M. Pritchett announce the marriage of their daughter, Vera Marie, to Mr. Paisley T. Hines on Friday, November the fourteenth nineteen hundred and nineteen, Washington, D. C.

"At home after the first of December, 529 North Person Street, Raleigh, North Carolina."

Congratulations and best wishes.

Principles and Government
of
The Christian Church

(Continued from last week)

Section III
DUTIES OF DEACONS

1. It is the duty of the Deacons to minister to the needs of the poor, and to have charge of the temporal affairs of the church.

2. They should make suitable arrangements for, and assist the pastor in the administration of the ordinances.

3. One of the Deacons, in the absence of the pastor, should preside in all business meetings of the church, and conduct the public worship of the congregation, when desired to do so, by reading the Word of God, singing, prayer, and exhortation.

4. They should counsel with the pastor in the government and spiritual affairs of the church.

Section IV
DUTIES OF THE SECRETARY

1. The Secretary shall record all the transactions of the church, whether at stated, or called sessions or conferences thereof.

2. He shall record all admissions into the church, and state whether they be by letter or upon profession of faith; if by letter, state from what church or denomination the applicants came, always affixing the date.

3. He shall keep an account of all deaths, change of name by marriage, dismissals, suspensions, and expulsions, with marginal remarks on the church roll, and by order of the church shall issue the following letter of transfer and commendation:

CERTIFICATE OF MEMBERSHIP AND COMMENDATION

.........................19...

This certifies that ....
is a member, in good standing, of............Christian Church, ...Conference, and is, at .....
own request hereby dismissed from this church to unite with ...., church, and when
so received .... responsibility to this church will cease.

Done this the .... day of ....19...
.... Secretary. ....Pastor.

4. He shall attest all the acts and proceedings of the church.

5. He shall have in charge and carefully preserve all the records of the church, which shall be open to the inspection of the pastor and the church, and which he shall deliver to his successor in office.

Section V
DUTIES OF THE TREASURER

1. The Treasurer shall receive the dues of the members of the church, and the contributions of the friends.

He shall keep a full account of all moneys received and paid out by the order of the church, to whom paid and for what purpose. He may serve also as collector, to whom the church may appoint one or more assistants.

2. He shall report in writing, quarterly, or as often as the church may require, all receipts and disbursements.

CHAPTER III.
MINISTERS
Section I
CANDIDATES

1. A candidate for the ministry in the Christian Church shall make application to the Educational Committee of the conference to which his church belongs.

2. Such candidate shall be of approved moral character and religious experience, shall give promise of ability to make suitable preparation, and shall be recommended by the church of which he is a member.

3. The Committee on Education shall examine him as to his fitness and qualifications, and, if admitted to the class, shall have oversight of his training and preparation; and he shall report annually to the committee. Failure to report himself or to make satisfactory progress shall be sufficient ground for dismissal from the roll of candidates.

4. All applications for aid from the Conference shall be through the Committee on Education.

Section II
LICENTIATES

1. A licentiate is one authorized by the conference to preach the gospel as a probationer until he shall give proof of his ability to teach efficiently the great doctrine of salvation.

2. Special care should be taken that candidate for licensure possess the moral, religious and literary qualifications necessary to fit him for the responsible position to which he aspires.

3. He shall, therefore, be a man of unblemished Christian character, have a good English education, and be recommended by the church of which he is a member.

4. That there may be no doubt of his qualifications, he shall be carefully examined by the Committee on Education, as to:

(a) His religious experience, and his call to the ministry.

(b) His knowledge of the Principles and Government of the Christian Church.

(c) His knowledge of the Scriptures, and of the leading doctrines of Christianity.

(d) His knowledge of Arithmetic, Geography, English Grammar, History of the United States, Physiology and Elements of Rhetoric.

5. The committee shall report to the conference as to the qualifications of the applicant, and his fitness for licensure.

6. The Conference, being satisfied with his proficiency, shall provide for his licensure during the session of Conference or some subsequent time and shall issue a certificate of licensure, signed by the President and

Secretary.

7. When a licentiate shall have preached for a reasonable length of time, and his services do not appear profitable to the churches, the Conference should revoke his license, and demand the return of his credentials.

SECTION III
ELDERS

1. The importance and responsibility of the office of an Elder require that the incumbent possess an unsullied Christian character, a good education and a ready capacity to teach.

2. Every candidate for ordination shall have preached a sufficient length of time to give ample evidence of usefulness to the church, and be recommended by one or more of the congregations to which he has ministered.

3. He shall also be carefully examined by the Educational Committee of his Conference upon the following three years' course of study, the examination to be held at each successive Conference until the course is satisfactorily completed:

First Year.—(1) English and American Literature, (2) General History, (3) Church History, (4) Theology—Revealed, (5) Homiletics.

Second Year—(1) Physics, (2) Mental Science, (3) History of the Christian Church, (4) Biblical Literature, (5) Theology—Pastoral.

Third Year.—(1) Higher Rhetoric, (2) Astronomy, (3) Geology, (4) Moral Science, (5) History of the Protestant Reformation, (6) Theology—Natural.

4. Those who have certificates of satisfactory examinations on the literary studies of this course; or have a diploma from a college of recognized standing, will be required to stand examinations only on the theological studies of the course. If the candidate can stand these examinations satisfactorily in less than three years, he will be permitted to do so.

5. When the course of study shall have been completed, the Committee on Education shall report to Conference with recommendations as to ordination.

6. Conference, being satisfied with the qualifications of the candidate, shall appoint an ordaining presbytery of three elders to set him apart to the sacred office of an Elder in the church. Persons so ordained become thereby members of the Conference.

7. Ordained ministers of other evangelical denominations may be received as elders, without re-ordination, provided they pass an approved examination, and show satisfactory knowledge of the Principles and Government of the Christian Church and are recommended by the Committee on Education.

CHAPTER IV
CONFERENCE

SECTION I
MEMBERSHIP

1. A Conference shall be composed of all ordained ministers and all churches organized upon the cardinal principles of the Christian Church, within certain specified bounds.

2. Every church shall have lay representation, and

each conference shall fix its own ratio. Provided, that each church shall have at least one delegate and that no church shall have more than four.

3. One-fourth of the ministers belonging to the Conference, and as many delegates as may be present having met at the time and place appointed, shall constitute a quorum for the transaction of business.

4. Ministers and messengers from sister conferences and representatives of church institutions shall be entitled to seats as deliberative members, but may not vote. Ministers in good standing in any other evangelical church may be introduced to Conference as visiting brethren.

SECTION II
ORGANIZATION

1. Conference shall meet on its own adjournment, and be called to order by the President; or, in his absence, by the Vice President. Then shall follow religious exercises.

2. The Secretary (or, in his absence, any one invited to act pro tempore) shall then proceed to read the roll of ministers and churches belonging to Conference, and if a quorum be present the fact shall be announced and the organization completed.

3. A President, Vice-President, Secretary, Assistant Secretary and Treasurer shall then be elected in a manner approved by Conference; after which an appropriate address or sermon should be delivered by the President.

4. All officers shall be elected for a term of one year.

5. Conference shall be governed by such rules as usually govern deliberative assemblies; or it may adopt such rules and regulations as appear best suited to its needs.

SECTION III
DUTIES OF OFFICERS

1. The President shall call the Conference to order, sign all the proceedings of Conference, and perform such other duties as his office may require.

2. In the absence of the President, the Vice-President shall perform the duties of the office.

3. The Secretary shall have charge of, and preserve all the books and records of the Conference, attest all its proceedings, and see that they are duly recorded, and do whatever else may be imposed on him by the duties of his office.

4. In the absence of the Secretary the Assistant Secretary shall perform all the duties pertaining to the office.

5. The Treasurer shall have charge of, and safely keep all funds belonging to the Conference, and shall invest, dispose of, or pay out these funds only on order of Conference.

(Continued next week)

Drastic measures are being taken against the Industrial Workers of the World. It seems that the country must get rid of these I. W. W.'s.

CHRISTIAN HOME TRAINING*

The home is the storm center of God's blessings or curses. All life is in debt to the home. The beginnings of every honored institution have been in the home. Every valued form of activity may be traced to its source within these walls. Here the seed of every bit and kind of human organization has first sprung up into strong life. It is the dearest and most sacred spot on earth, a spot around which cluster the sweetest associations and the most precious memories. The home is the holy of holies of a man's life. There he withdraws from all the world, and, shutting his door is alone with those who are his own. It is the reservoir of his strength, the restorer of his energies, the resting place from his toil, the broadening place for his spirit, the inspiration of all his activities and battles.

The home was the earliest and simplest and yet most perfect form of organization. It is probably no exaggeration to say the world's life has never known such perfection of organization, and such stupendous achievements of organizations, as in our day, and it all grew up out of the home.

Christian Home Training is the most imperative need of our land. Our greatest demand of today is not upon our National Government for a better form of government, or upon our law making bodies for more laws and the enforcement of law, but our most vital need and greatest demand is for Christian training in the home, and of course before a home can give Christian training, it must first of all, itself be Christian, for Christianity begins in the home. If not there it is nowhere. We may attend meetings, and sing hymns and join devoutly in prayer, we may give money to the poor, and send missionaries and Bibles to the heathen, we may organize societies of every description for doing good, we may get up church fairs, and tea-parties and picnics, we may in short, devote all our time and all our means to doing good and yet not be true and earnest Christians as we ought to be after all. Nothing is more important than that our homes, which are as truly divine as is the church, should be saturated with the mind of Christ. The husband and father as well as the wife and mother, should possess the spirit of the Master. It is not enough that one of them have faith. A godless husband may and often does utterly nullify all the efforts of a devout wife, and a godless wife may destroy the wholesome influence of a devout husband. Co-operation is necessary, unity of heart, of hope, of aim, mutual love and companionship. The home is brightened and beautified where the members are living Christians.

Joshua declared, "As for me and my house we will serve the Lord." (Joshua, 24:14). How many parents can speak for their homes as Joshua did for his? The decision had been made in Joshua's house and he did not allow public cares or pleasures to interfere with the duties he owed to his family.

In many so called Christian homes are putrid spots, cankered lives, inflamed wounds, all because Jesus is not enthroned. Jesus is love, and He makes every home lovely where He abides, without a home Himself Christ guards the home life of the world, but if Christ is not allowed to abide in the home it is empty and meaningless.

As we study the Sacred Record we find God has His perfect plan, which if wholly carried out by the parents and children, will bring to each home a Divine benediction and blessedness. "And it shall come to pass if ye shall harken diligently to love the Lord your God, to serve Him with all your heart and all your soul, that your days may be multiplied, and the days of your children as the days of heaven upon the earth." (Deut. 11:13).

How grand and beautiful that our Heavenly Father should make an adequate provision for just such regulations in this life, placing it within the range of possibilities where the conditions are not on the human side. But we fear comparatively few take the chart of life, God's Holy Word, and go through it from Genesis to Revelation to ascertain the mind and will of God concerning the Heavenly plan for building a home and rearing children. Yet the fundamental principles are clearly defined, "But seek ye first the Kingdom of God, and His righteousness," (character) for each member of the family. This is the bed rock on which to build a beautiful, happy home. Any other foundation than this will fail when the temptations, trials, sorrows and bereavements of life come, as come they will sooner or later. The inspired writer says, "Out of the heart are the issues of life." So out of the homes are the characters of life.

As the home life is, the child life will be with but few exceptions. Make the tree good and the fruit will be good, for the tree is known by its fruit. You may bend the twig but not the tree.

Again, the church life will be as the home life is, and as we look over the church membership we find nearly, if not quite seventy per cent, are women, and the great problem is, how to save the young men. For while we have superb young men in our churches, but alas! the great masses are on the outside, drifting with the tide toward the world. How true is the Spanish proverb, "We sow a thought and reap an act; we sow an act and reap a habit; we sow a habit and reap a character; we sow a character and reap a destiny." This is done in very early life, and many parents we fear, do not seem to realize that every day they are forming character and fixing destiny for time and eternity. And is there not great cause for alarm, that Christian virtue is being lost when there is no daily recognition of God, no family altar, or teaching of Scripture, in the large majority of Christian homes. About ninety per cent of so called Christian homes have no family prayer and no direct daily teaching out of the "Book of Life."

The Word is the "Lamp" and the Holy Spirit is the "Light" and without the lamp there is no light. Where the "Lamp" has not gone is total heathen darkness and just in proportion as the lamp is hidden or obscured, to that degree do we prevent the Holy pirit from revealing Jesus as Saviour to the hearts of the children.

Oh! if we ever see the might, power and glory of God we must see it in the Word for on every page is the image of the "Man Christ Jesus." Will the parents follow out the instructions and put the Word in the hearts of their children? (Deut. 4:5; 5:29; 6:4-9; 7:9).

This is among Moses' last inspired utterances to the children of Israel and one of the most pathetic scenes in Old Testament history. He was the "grand old man" of Israel, the great leader, general-in-chief, statesman, law-giver and saint. One hundred and twenty years he had lived and toiled and suffered, yet his eye was not dimmed, nor his natural force abated. Close to heaven, yet never to pass the Jordan into the land of Canaan where his heart had been so long. About to transfer his trust to Joshua, he makes his last appeal to Israel, warning and beseeching them by every appeal that can command the reason, warm the heart, stir the conscience and fortify the will. Oh! how his great heart was stirred as he placed before them the supreme importance and necessity of teaching their children all the Words of God. And who were the teachers? Fathers and mothers. The responsibility rested upon the parents themselves. What was true then is true now. God lays this duty upon the parents and they dare not ignore it. Parents are God's appointed teachers and nothing can take' their place in reaching the heart of the child in its formation period. They have the advantage over all other teachers.

The teaching and training should begin at the altar, should develop in the Sunday school,. and blossom first in its perfection in the house of God.

The highest accomplishment in this world' for usefulness and happiness is to become intimately acquainted . with God and his Word. We know that piety cannot sanctify stupidity but we know also that piety glorifies culture. Piety without culture is robbed of her highest influence for good, and culture without piety is stripped of her noblest charm.

Having clearly seen the Divine arrangements for the home, let us ascertain His mind for the building up of the Church. And now I shall make a startling statement, but alas too true, namely: that the majority of Christian parents are by actual experience training their children directly away from the house of God. Listen, parents, God says, "Those that he planted in the house of the Lord shall flourish in the courts of our God." They shall bring forth fruit in old age; they shall be fat and flourishing (Psalm 92:13-14). We do not plant old trees, we plant the young. And God means that children while young shall be "planted" and trained up in the sanctuary. Train up a child in the way he should go, and when he is old he will not depart from it. (Prov. 22:6).

It is recorded of Jesus, the great Teacher, that "He went into the synagogue on the Sabbath day as was His custom." Indeed many children of Christian parents scarcely ever hear the gospel preached from one end of the year to another. They attend the Sunday school but not the church service. This is the most important period of the' child's life, when habits are fixed and character . formed. Oh! if there is one word that needs to be written in letters of fire over every door, if it were possible, it is the word "Habit." What is the habit of your children? Is it to attend the sanctuary on the Lord's Day? Or is it simply to go to Sunday school and then to stay away from church services? The latter is lamentably true. And especially if not early brought to Jesus and held to the church when the dangerous period of life comes. Along from fifteen, or earlier, to twenty years of age, they usually feel too big to go to Sabbath school and in their opinion have graduated from it, and as they have never cultivated the habit of going to church, it was not in the warp and woof and make-up of their being, so they are out of Sunday school and church too,

What a beautiful sight to see a whole family on the Lord's day regularly attend church and participate in Divine Worship. Oh! that God's plan might be carried out to insure His blessing on home and church, likewise the Nation; for as the home life and church is, the National will be. For the Christian homes of the Nation are the strongest forts. Undermine these homes and our Nation becomes a stranded hulk.

We look to the Christian homes to send out honest, sturdy Christian men to battle with National problems. "For righteousness exalteth a Nation, but sin is a reproach to any people." Goethe, the universal genius of Germany, and one of its greatest authors, says, "The destiny of any Nation at any one time is determined by the sentiment of the young men of that time." What is the sentiment of the young men of our time? If the Christian be taken as a standard of judgment, the young men are left out as factors, as the great multitude are drifting away from Christian virtue. If our young men are the hope of the Church and Nation, then the appalling fact stares us in the face, viz.: that not over ten per cent from sixteen to thirty-five years of age are members of our churches: Twenty per cent more occasionally attend, but some seventy per cent scarcely ever cross a church door,

A weakened home means a weakened people. It should be keenly noted that nothing else, absolutely nothing else, can take its place. A weakened home means a weakened church, a weakened Nation. It puts a greater task upon the educational institutions, and yet, however strong and able, these can never do the home's work. A father and mother living together with their children, tender in their love, pure in their lives, strong in their convictions, simple and orderly in their habits, do infinitely more than presidents and governors, legislators, educators and clergymen can do in making a strong Nation.

Susan Ann Wesley was mother of 19 children and she held them all for the church and for God. When asked how she did it, she replied, "I got a hold of their hearts when they were young, and I have never lost my grip."

Train up the children to love the Word of God, church and their God, and when they are old they will not depart from it.

*Address delivered before the North Carolina Conference, November 11, 1919, by Rev. W. L. Wells, and printed by request of that body.'

GETTING SERMONS DOWN

Dr. Staley makes the remark that most ministers talk about getting sermons "up" when they should say getting them "down." He means that a minister should get his sermon from the Father's house; should pray it *down*, and not work it *up*. We commend the thought.

Rev. O. D. Poythress, the aggressive and energetic pastor of our South Norfolk church, writes this favorable note: "Many of us feel that this is the opportune time to build a suitable and ample church at South Norfolk. Our congregations have outgrown the capacity of the present building which is quite inadequate for present purposes, to say nothing of future prospects. Our membership here favors building and we should begin to do so at no far distant date." The growth of this work since Brother Poythress went to South Norfolk has been remarkable. Col. J. E. West, Chairman of the Home Mission Board of the Southern Christian Convention, declares that the church was at a very low ebb when he urged Brother Poythress to go from Elon College to take up the work there. The prospects for a great church in South Norfolk are brightening with the passing years and we believe it will not be long before this congregation will rise and build in a way and manner becoming their increasing numbers and opportunities.

Rev. H. W. Dowding, Pastor of the Washington Street Christian church, Portsmouth, Virginia, writes November 14: "We are in the midst of a great meeting with church and Sunday school rooms crowded most of the time and a deep spiritual interest in church and community. I believe that God has a great awakening in store for us as the meetings progress." The Portsmouth church is progressive and is doing great things and in this we rejoice.

We are compelled to leave out many items of personal mention this week due to so much matter on hand.

THE ANNUAL PROTEST

Huh! What? Vacation's over with,
  I got to find my books?
W'y, ma—w'y, me an' Willie Smith
  Just' got some more fish hooks!
W'y, we'd made up to catch that bass
  Down in the willer pool!
I don't care who will head my class—
        Aw
        Pshaw,
        Ma!
  I don't wan' tuh go tuh school!

I'll bet th' teacher will be mean;
  I know just what she'll do—
She'll say my han's an' face ain't clean
  An' make me wash 'em, too!
I'd heap ruther not go.
I'll not grow up a fool!
Aw, shucks! A boy don't have no show,
        Aw
        Pshaw,
        Ma!
  I don't wan' tuh go tuh school!

What? Got to carry all them books?
  They're awful heavy, ma.
I'm sick! You'd know it by my looks.
  I don't care! Just tell pa!
I don't want to be a president—
  Ain't stubborn as a mule!
You'll whyip me! I don't care a cent.
        Aw
        Pshaw,
        Ma!
  I don't wan' tuh go tuh school!
           —Selected.

WHY THEY CALL IT PIN MONEY

This expression originally came from the allowance which a husband gave his wife to purchase pins. At one time pins were dreadfully expensive, so that only wealthy people could afford them, and they were saved so carefully that in those days you could not have looked along the pavement and found a pin which you happened to be in need of, as you can and often do today.

By a curious law the manufacturers of pins were allowed to sell them only on January 1 and 2 each year, and so when those days came around the women whose husbands could afford it secured pin money from them and went out and got their pins.

Pins have become so very cheap in these days that we are rather careless with them, but the expression has continued to live, although today when used it means any allowance of money which a husband gives a wife for her personal expenses.

Pins were known and used as long ago as 1347 A.D. They were introduced into England in 1540. In 1824 an American named Might invented a machine for making pins which enabled them to be manufactured cheaply. About 1,500 tons of iron and brass are made into pins every year in the United States.—*From "The Book of Wonders." Published and Copyrighted by the Bureau of Industrial Education, Inc., Washington, D. C.*

A VERY GOOD GOOSE

Geese are always thought to be very stupid creatures, but perhaps they are so because they never had the chance of going to school!

There are some geese that have been taught to do things, however, and they do those things in a very clever way, so that it makes me think that if every goose had the chance of going to school no one would call geese stupid any more.

Just to show you how clever a goose can be, I wi'l tell you a story of one that lived in France. Every Sunday, when an old blind woman wanted to go to church, the goose took hold of her dress in his beak and pulled her gently along the road to the door of the church. Then, when the old woman was inside, the goose spent the time in strolling about the churchyard. But when the church service was over the goose was always waiting at the door until the woman came to be taken back.

Once a gentleman said to the old woman's daughter: "Aren't you afraid to let your mother come alone?" "O no, sir," said the daughter; "we are not afraid, as the goose is with her."—*Exchange.*

Sun readers will rejoice to learn that the pastor, Rev. A. B. Kendall, D. D., has begun active work in Washington and is busy there now getting together members and friends of the Christian Church whom he hopes to organize into a band of workers and into a Christian church at an early date. The present program and try to do something with the measure at an temporary building prepared. If there are Sun readers who know of members of the Christian Church, past, present, or prospective, in Washington, D. C., will they not kindly send their names to Rev. A. B. Kendall, D. D., 801 Allison Street, Washington, D. C?

Senator Martin, of Virginia, died November 12. Carter Glass, now Secretary of the Treasury, will succeed the late Senator.

Congress has decided to limit the debate of the Peace Treaty and try to do something with the measure at an early date. Article X, it seems has been eliminated. This takes the heart out of the treaty, according to President Wilson.

The coal strike is still unsettled, both sides being hopeful for victory.

Bodies of some of the American boys who died in France are now reaching this country.

Sunday School and Christian Endeavor

SUNDAY SCHOOL LESSON FOR
NOVEMBER 30, 1919

(Mrs. Fred Bullock)

Jesus Teaches Peter True Greatness. John 13:5-16, 36-38.

Golden Text: The Son of Man came not to be ministered unto, but to minister, and to give his life for a ransom for many.—Matt. 20:28.

Additional Material: Matt. 20:20-28; 26:31-35; Mark 14:27-31; Luke 22:7-34.

For teaching points, see Teachers and Officers Journal.

We see in this lesson, "Jesus taking the part of a servant" (Junior Topic) that He might show to us, "The Dignity of Common Tasks" (Intermediate).

It is so hard for us to realize that there is real dignity in the common tasks of every day. We think if we had some big, outstanding talent, if we were rich, or great, or learned, we would be able to do great things for God. But Jesus taught greatness through little things; the grain of wheat, the mustard seed, the measure of meal, the one lost coin or lost sheep, and in this lesson, through the faithful performance of a lowly, menial duty. Longfellow tells us in a poem of a monk praying in his cell, who is rewarded by a vision of an angel. Even as he gazes in adoration, the ringing of the Convent bell reminds him that it is time for the daily dole to the poor, and it is his hand that must attend to their needs. Torn between desire and duty, he yet obeys the call of duty, and, leaving the angel, goes to his task. His joy is better imagined than described when, on his return, he finds the angel still awaiting him. "Hadst thou stayed I must have fled," says the angel, smiling at him as he once more kneels in prayer.

No matter how simple the task, if it be done "as unto the Lord", it is done right. "Who sweeps a room as unto the Lord, makes that and the action fine." God called carpenters and artisans and filled them with His spirit in order that the temple might be built. The forty thousands fighting men who "were not of doubt

hearts" and who could "keep rank" won the throne for David. These are what God asks of His workmen, spirit filled men and women, who, with singleness of purpose, keep rank in the mighty army of God. It is these alone who are truly great, and they are great, no matter what their seeming station in life may be.

TEACHER TRAINING

Have you planned for your Teacher Training Class as yet? I hope so. The Sunday School Board of the Christian Church has approved the Pilgrim Training Course for Teachers, and we are hoping that many new classes will be started during the year. Do not get old books if you are starting a new class. This is the reason: If you study Oliver's, Hurlbuts, or any of the old books, you can, it is true, secure a certificate for your one year of work, but you are not going to be content with one year of training. You will want to go on, and complete your three year course, which will alone entitle you to a diploma. certificate given for work with the old books *will not apply toward a diploma.* If your class feels as some do, that they are not getting enough Bible study. Then secure some good Bible outline work, and take fifteen minutes for Bible drill work prior to your regular lesson. But take a course of study that can be applied toward a diploma, and plan to eventually finish the three years of work, with its one year of specialization for the department in which your service is given.

CHRISTIAN ENDEAVOR TOPIC FOR
NOVEMBER 30, 1919.

(J. Vincent Knight)

Christianity and the Health of America. Missionary Lesson. (Ezek. 47:1-12).

Three main essentials to a successful life are: A strong body, an alert mind; and a fat soul. Healthy bodies and clear minds are impossible without a healthy soul. If the soul is sick, the other two members will sympathize with it, and the result will be a life whose best energy and influence is forever hampered. The world about us is sick. It is looking

toward America for a physician. Our country must furnish the cure for the ails of the world, but how can we do it unless we use the Sanitatian laws—the laws against crime, diseases of a contagious nature, and the healing resources we have at our command?

One great disease in our country that demands attention is that of "Morbus Sabaticus." Sunday sickness. It is peculiar. Those who are afflicted with it have it only on the Sabbath—they never call in a physician, nor a nurse. They are well all other days, and do not even confine themselves in bed, but go to work on Monday. It is dreadful in its results—for it destroys the soul. Christianity is the only application needed, for Christ is the one and only Physician. Our Christian Endeavorers need to watch this disease, and to fear its results for the world is dying for the great healing power of Christ, and we should always be on the alert—ready to help carry the Gospel of power to those who are ill, and need the cleansing power.

November is mission study month. Have you a missionary study class in your Christian Endeavor, Sunday school, or church? If not, get busy and organize one. If your church or school has one, get every member of your society to join.

MARRIAGES

HESTER-WYATT

Miss Daisy Wyatt became the bride of Mr. Willie Lee Hester on November 12, 1919, at the home of Rev. J. W. Holt. They went from the Christian Conference in session at Burlington, and, in the presence of a few invited friends, solemnly assumed the vows that linked them together in holy wedlock. The writer performed the ceremony.

J. W. HOLT.

REED-KERNODLE

Mr. William Lacy Reed and Miss Margaret Jane Kernodle, Altamahaw, N. C., were married at the home of Rev. J. W. Holt on the evening of November 12, 1919. Only a few friends were present to witness the ceremony. The writer officiated.

J. W. HOLT.

OBITUARIES

HORN

Mr. John Robert Horn departed this life at his home, Zuni, Va., on October 24, 1919, aged sixty-nine years, five months and nine days. He was a good man and will be greatly missed in his home and community. We have true and faithful in the duties of life and had many friends. We have sustained a great loss in his death, but our loss, we trust, has been his eternal gain. He was the father of Mr. Robert A. Horn, President of the Bank of Zuni, Va. He leaves one son and two daughters: Mr. Robert A. Horne, Mrs. J. M. Clayton and Miss Mattie Horn of Zuni, Va., two brothers: Mr. George W., and Mr. J. H. Horn of Ivor, Va., three sisters: Mrs. John R. Edwards, Mrs. J. T. Johnson and Mrs. Charlie Freeman, and a host of friends.

His funeral services were conducted by the writer, at his home and his remains were laid to rest in the old family cemetery.

H. H. BUTLER.

ELLIS

T. J. Ellis died at his home, Nurney, Va., October 26, 1919, aged sixty-six years, nine months and eighteen days. He was a most excellent Christian man, a true and faithful member of Cypress Chapel Christian church and will be missed in his home, community and church. He leaves a devoted wife and twelve children, eight daughters and four sons. Several grandchildren and a host of friends also survive him. His funeral services were conducted by the writer at his home, assisted by Rev. J. M. Roberts, Rev. W. W Staley, D. D., Rev. I. W. Johnson, D. D., and his remains were laid to rest in the old family cemetery.

God bless and comfort the dear bereaved ones.

H. H. BUTLER.

MARSHALL

One of the saddest funerals of my ministry was held at Salem Chapel church Sunday, November 9, when the remains of Miss Julia Victoria Marshall were laid to rest. The deceased was a beautiful young woman—possessed of many attractive charms, and a strong winning personality that won for her hundreds of friends who taxed the standing room of the house and yard to attend her funeral.

Miss Julia was a girl of rare ability, and whose life was marked by its deeds of kindness and service to others. She sacrificed her pleasure to make her Sunday school and church a success. She had planned to go to the Orphanage at Elon College to teach and assist Superintendent Johnston in the work there, but her illness on the first of September prevented. She was never well again, but "All is well now." Previous to her illness, she had requested her sister, Miss Lena, who is soloist for the Centenary M. E. Church, Winston, to sing, "In That Beautiful Land," at her funeral if she died first. Her request was granted, and I doubt if the soloist ever sang sweeter than she did at her sister's funeral.

Julia has gone to rest. She passed at the age of 22 years. She leaves behind her parents, Mr. and Mrs. J. A. Marshall; four sisters, Selma and Lena of Winston-Salem; Frances and Hadie, who remain in the home; three brothers, Allen of Winston-Salem; James and Edward who are in the home, and a great host of friends who will sorely miss her.

The funeral services were held in the Salem Chapel church, near Walnut Cove, N. C. by the writer, assisted by Rev. C. H. Kegorise, of Winston-Salem, using for the occasion the words of Job who said: "My purposes are broken off," for such was true with Julia. God bless the sorrowing relatives.

J. V. KNIGHT.

FRAZIER

James K. P. Frazier was born October 19, 1849 and died at his home near Elkton, October 11, 1919, at the age of 69 years, 11 months, and 22 days. He was a man of happy disposition, a good neighbor, and a kind husband and father. He leaves to mourn his departure a widow, seven children, all grown to manhood and womanhood, one brother, and one sister.

Funeral services were held at the home, October 13, 1919, and the remains laid to rest in the cemetery at East Point.

A. W. ANDES.

FULTZ

Mrs. Virginia F. Fultz was born October 17, 1854, and died November 1, 1919, making her age, therefore, 65 years and 15 days. She was the wife of Lemuel Fultz and lived near Edinburg. She is survived by her husband and many other relatives and friends. Mrs. Fultz was held in high esteem by all who knew her and will be greatly missed in her neighborhood. She was a woman of splendid character, kindhearted, and industrious. Her death breaks up a pleasant home, and leaves a vacancy there that could not well be filled. The funeral service was held at the United Brethren church at Hawkinstown, November 3, and the remains laid to rest in the adjoining cemetery. A large congregation attended the service, thus paying a tribute of respect to a departed friend and loved one.

A. W. ANDES.

CAMP RUFFIN, UNITED CONFEDERATE VETERANS

James A. Turrentine

Nature has again issued her final decree in equity. The Master Builder has invaded our field of civic righteousness and taken unto himself a knightly, gentle, saintly soul—James A. Turrentine is dead.

This entire community reverently paused in its varied activities and paid its tribute of respect, and affection for the fallen hero, distinguished citizen, and Christian leader. Camp Ruffin, United Confederate Veterans, cannot write a cenotaph that will be as beautiful and as enduring as has already been written in the hearts of all who knew Captain Turrentine, and his consecrated Christian life.

He was a soldier as we were. Was as gallant, as dashing, and courageous as the bravest. His loyalty to the Confederacy was consistent beyond doubt or criticism. After we had lost, the true test of his citizenship was exemplified in.

his devotion to another flag than the love of his young manhood. His he'rt was too tender, and his hands were too open for large accumulation; but his influence, in his daily walk and conversation, on the the people with whom he came in contact, and through them on the community at large, was far more exceeding value than all the fine gold.

Camp Ruffin reverently bows in humble submission in its great grief at his taking away.

W. A. HALL,
Adg't.

SIMPSON

B. L. Simpson, son of Lemuel Simpson, was born September 30, 1855 and died November 9, 1919, aged sixty-four years, one month and ten days. He was married to Huldah B. Iseley on May 5, 1877. To this union were born six children—three boys and three girls. Two preceded him to the great beyond. The widow and four children survive; also five grandchildren, five brothers, and one sister. Funeral services were conducted by the writer at Bethlehem Christian church. May the Lord comfort the bereaved.

J. W. HOLT.

PELOUBET'S SELECT NOTES

Contains 480 pages and covers in detail the Sunday school lessons for 1920. It should be in the hands of every teacher: Primary, Intermediate, Junior and Senior topics fully treated. $1.60 postpaid. Order from this office.

SMILES
Make Sure

If you're saddled with the notion
That you ought to have promotion
Don't mistake the mere desire, for
    ability to rise.

Give the subject more reflection;
It may take a new complexion
When you view your capabilities with
    calm, unbiased eyes.

Find out if you are returning
Value full for what you're earning.
First be sure that you've already
    done the very best you could.
P'rhaps the time you're wasting
    wishing
Takes your mind from off your fishing.
If you show a pile of sawdust, we'll
    believe you're sawing wood.
—*Selected.*

* *

Reason For Weeping

The young Shah of Persia is fond of telling the following story concerning his great-grandfather, the famous Nasr-ed-Din.

In his old age this ruler lost his good looks—a fact which troubled him greatly.

One day he studied his features in a glass attentively for some time and then dismayed by his ugliness, began to weep.

At once the Court Fool began weeping also, and even when, after lamenting for two whole hours, the Shah dried his tears the Fool continued weeping more violently than ever.

Nasr-ed-Din looked at him in astonishment, and asked him the cause of his sorrow.

"I wept with reason," he said, "at beholding my ugliness—I, the Lord of so many lands, the master of countless slaves. But I do not understand why you should thus despair."

"If you, my Lord," replied the Fool, "wept for two hours after seeing yourself in the mirror for but an instant, is it not natural that I, who see you all day long, should weep longer than you?"—*Selected.*

CHARLES W. McPHERSON, M. D.

Eye, Ear, Nose, Throat

OFFICE OVER CITY DRUG STORE

Office Hours: 9:00 a. m. to 1:00 p. m.
and 2:00 to 5:00 p m

Phones: Residence 153; Office 65J

BURLINGTON, NORTH CAROLINA

DR. J. H. BROOKS

DENTIST

Foster Building   Burlington, N. C

THE CHRISTIAN SUN

IN ESSENTIALS UNITY, IN NON-ESSENTIALS LIBERTY, IN ALL THINGS CHARITY

"Money is - - - -"

 ONEY is influence; it is power; it stands for toil and sacrifice; it is the blood of toilers changed into the permanent coin of the commonwealth. It has cursed some people, it has blessed others. But when we shall learn its Christian use, the curse will pass away. It will no longer be "filthy lucre," but a sacred instrument which may exact the soul of its possessor, increase the happiness of mankind and extend the kingdom of God on earth.—*The Christian Evangelist.*

Volume LXXI   WEDNESDAY, DECEMBER 3, 1919   Number 49

BURLINGTON   -   -   -   NORTH CAROLINA

THE CHRISTIAN SUN

Founded 1844 by Rev. Daniel .W. Kerr

C. B. RIDDLE - - - Editor

Entered at the Burlington, N. C. Post Office as second class matter.

Subscription Rates

One year .... $ 2.00
Six months 1.00

In Advance

Give both your old and new postoffice when asking tbv your address be changed.

The change of your label is your receipt for money. v when receipts sent upon request.

Many persons subscribe for friends, intending, that the per be stopped at the end of the year. If instructions are given to its effect, they will receive attention at the proper time.

Marriage and obituary notices not exceeding 150 words printed free if received within 60 days from date of event, all over it is at by rate of one-half cent a word.

Original poetry not accepted for publication.

Principles of the Christian Church

(1) The Lord Jesus Christ is the only Head of the Church.
(2) Christian is a sufficient name of the Church.
(3) The Holy Bible is a sufficient rule of faith and practice.
(4) Christian character is a sufficient test of fellowship, and of church membership.
(5) The right of private judgment and the liberty of conscience is a right and a privilege that should be accorded to, and exercised by all.

EDITORIAL

CHURCH JOURNALISM IN THE NEW ERA*

 HERE is no getting by the question that the Church is face to face with new issues, being born with new ideals and must greatly enlarge her program to meet the demands of the day and rightly function in carrying a gospel message.

Church journalism is definitely ministerial, and were it not, I could not consent to have my lot cast there and hold to my present conviction. Just as other parts and programs of the Church have had to be revised and must be revised, so must Church Journalism. The primary object of a Church paper was to give news and too long has Church Journalism been bound to tradition by that primeval idea. There was a time when the primary object of a Church paper was so give news, but not so today. The weekly newspaper established in every hamlet and city, and sandwitched with the daily press until the reading public no longer depends upon the Church paper for a medium of news. Then there must be a definite function for the Church

*Abstract from an address prepared by the Editor to be delivered before the Eastern Virginia Conference, October 31; 1919.

paper aside from giving news. The Church paper is pioneer in the field of education. It is a watchman set upon a hill who should see far and wide and hear from a distance on every side. The Church paper is constantly hearing that call "Watchman, what of the night?", and it is difficult to interpret for the people the signs of the times. Church Journalism in this new era of ours must strike, and will strike, a new chord. It is ridding itself of traditions of being merely a newspaper and must be the bulletin board for the whole Church. It must be a place, a public forum as it were, where the vital issues of the Church are laid bare for the consideration of every member and the world, at large. The editorial task of every man who stands at the tripod of the Church paper is becoming more complicated. The editor must be misunderstood at times because the questions that he is called upon to present to the people are not always settled questions. They are questions that need debating, need careful and prayerful consideration. Church Journalism in this new era of ours stands to evoke thought and not to stir up controversy. The day has passed when argument for argument's sake can be admitted to the sacred columns of the Church publications. The editor, therefore, must guard the sacredness of his columns as the minister guards the sacredness of his pulpit. With thousands of publicity bureaus in all parts of the world endeavoring by mighty strides to foster their own interests, the editor finds his mail flooded with pleas, requests, and canned editorials. To personify the situation may I say that never in the history of Church Journalism are there so many mysterious creatures that come hopping along on the editorial table. I challenge the man to say that the censorship of this conglomeration is not a difficult task.

The official organ of the Church, or a group of any Church, must in this quickened age be larger than that Church or a group of that Church. I mean by this that when the message in the columns of a Church paper extend no farther than the borders of the denomination represented by that paper, the constituency of that publication will never know anything save narrowness and littleness and stinginess. They will never know the bigness of the Kingdom's work, or the greatness and the vastness of the Master's program. Not only must a Church paper be bigger than its own denomination, but it must be bigger than any man or set of men. No editor can afford in a time like this to let the mind of a few men rule him, if indeed the heart and mind of that editor is set on the Kingdom's interest. Narrowness not only defeats its own purpose but breeds autocracy, a sample of which this world has sufficiently tasted.

A Church paper is first and last missionary. It spreads the glad tidings of the Kingdom. Advertising goodness is a part of the mission of the Church paper. The letters of Paul constituted a form of early Church journalism. They conveyed religious inspiration, set forth reports and plans and defended the teachings of the early Church. Church journalism is not only missionary in the field of Christian activity but it is missionary in social and economical conditions. It transmits plans and purposes of peoples to every part of the globe. It wings its way to every clime, and wherever the seed of the Church paper is sown the spirit of the Church will rise up to save and to satisfy.

There was once an idea that the Church paper must be a medium of advertising as well as giving news. I challenge the idea by calling upon the Church to show wherein that the object of the Church paper is to make money. And if the Church paper is not destined to make money I question the wisdom of selling space when it should be conserved for a larger program of the Church. I met the editor of a secular paper on the street the other day and he told me that he has been severely criticised by a minister of his town because his paper had admitted to its columns the advertising of a carnival. The editor said that his one and only reply was this: "The space in my paper is open to you, to your church and to the Church at large. It is open without price and yet you have not availed yourself of this opportunity. How then can you criticise me for giving space in exchange for money when you could not have received it free?" I emphatically say that it is a stigma upon any denomination that prefers to use the columns of its paper for commercial advertising rather than advertising for the Kingdom. There are thousands of men who share this thought with me, and yet they are at the head of papers filled with advertising. Why? Only because the Churches represented through and by these publications have not awakened from their primeval slumber. When all of the interests of the Kingdom have been sufficiently carried forward and need no longer to be carried before the people, thin and not until then does the Church paper have space to sell to commercial advertising.

I do not mean by these statements that some advertising is not all right. Advertisements of church bells, pews, communion sets and modern equipments for the Lord's house are all right. I am referring to the general plan of getting any kind of advertising available to make money.

Church Journalism in this new era of ours cannot go forth on its new mission on the same kind of support that it received in the days gone by; and I am happy to say that there is a new sense of appreciation prevailing in all parts of the Church paper on the same ground as they do their obligation to their pastor because the Church paper is his assistant, and I ought to say in some cases the pastor is the assistant to the Church paper. I make this last statement because the pastor in many communities makes at his best *twelve* visits a year and the Church paper *fifty-two*.

In our own Church I see a new vision for our publications. I feel a new thrill. There is to my mind the finest spirit of co-operation. We are pulling for one purpose and toward one goal. The circulation of our Church papers is steadily and gradually growing. The people are co-operating beautifully. I express the appreciation for this not only in behalf of THE CHRISTIAN SUN, but in behalf of *The Herald of Gospel Liberty*

and *The Christian Missionary*, as well as other publications of our denomination. The destiny of THE CHRISTIAN SUN, as well as other publications of our Church, rests with you. A paper is not its files and forms, its office and its equipment. A Church paper is an ideal worked into a visible form. The spirit of THE CHRISTIAN SUN cannot be destroyed with flames nor washed away with sweeping flood. Its every page so far printed could be obliterated, but in your heart and in mine there is that living ideal built up week by week; that ideal that shall live, and without copy or precedent a new paper in mechanical form could spring up but in its final analysis it would be THE CHRISTIAN SUN, born of a need and often issued under struggle and strain. There would still be with it the spirit of Daniel W. Kerr, the founder of our paper, and the pioneer of religious journalism in the Southern Christian Convention. Blessed be his memory. "Long live THE CHRISTIAN," for I quote these words from thousands of letters that come pouring into my little sanctum, where I am endeavoring to serve you and the Kingdom through the tasks you have placed upon my shoulders, which tasks I could not perform were it not for my Heavenly Father and for the prayers that go up from your hearts and your homes.

———

We have had a good year so far as THE CHRISTIAN SUN is concerned. We are pleased with the co-operation that we have had. We appreciate it more than words can tell. The year is drawing to a close and we want to round out 1919 with the biggest and best financial showing that we have ever had. Friends have responded to statements in a very loyal and liberal manner. There are a few, however, that have not given heed to past due subscriptions. Will you, if you are one of these, look after the matter today? We need the money and need it now. It has been neglect because you have not renewed. You have not meant to do it, but just kept putting it off. Don't put it off longer, dear reader, if you are behind, but remit today. We thank you in advance.

———

Third church, Norfolk, is going forward. Brother Smith writes of the work there: "Things are moving in great shape at Third church. Sunday a week ago was Rally Day; had 502 present for Sunday school. Daniel Poling spoke for us. Church was well filled for the evening service. I gave the first sermon in the series on 'The Ideal American Home.' There will be five in the series. Last Sunday we had about 370 for Sunday school and the Church was completely filled for the evening service. Our church, since it has been enlarged, will seat 512. We have that many seats. We are trying to get things ready for the Sunday Evangelistic Campaign which begins January 4, 1920.'"

———

We understand that Rev. J. E. Franks is to take up the prospective work at Lucama and West Clayton, N. C.

PASTOR AND PEOPLE

AN APPRECIATION FROM AN OLD VETERAN

I am an aged Confederate Veteran and was seventy-five years old on October 29, 1919. I served nearly four years in the army and never missed a roll call except when on duty; never was put in the guard house or never had a furlough, though I had two chances for furloughs but each time yielded to a comrade who had a family at home that he was anxious to see.

I have been a soldier of the Cross for fifty-two years. I love to read THE CHRISTIAN SUN and keep in touch with what my Church is doing for the Kingdom. THE SUN comes to my house through the kindness of my family physician, Dr. Job G. Holland.

Through the columns of THE SUN I wish to thank my friends who have been so kind to me during the period of my helplessness. They have visited me and ministered unto me in temporal and spiritual things. The Sunday school class of juniors taught by Mrs. Dr. Holland have visited me on various occasions and brought happiness and sunshine into our home by their little songs, and prayers and the errands they have done for me.

The prayer meetings held by friends and the visits of my pastor are a great delight to me.

My affliction is the result of a fall which broke my leg and hip and put my knee out of joint. It has made me practically an invalid on crutches, getting away from home only as friends come and take me.

My faithful wife, now aged and infirm also, is a dutiful companion and we together appreciate very much these kindness shown by our friends.

It is my desire to be able to attend the dedication of my church at Holland on the second Sunday of December.

J. J. FOWLER.

Holland, Va.

OLD AGE AND LIFE
An Appreciation of Drs. Wellons and Staley

Why grow old, grouchy and indifferent in this life? God has given us the best world He could make for us; has given us a happy existence, and a glorious environment, which makes it possible for us to be happy if we only use the things He gives to us. Yet, with all the good things God has given us, we can look on the dark side of life until we rob it of its best joy and most noble thoughts of human betterment, and in so doing make it one round of worries after another. In other words, it is our privilege to make it a torment or a paradise.

As I write these lines I am thinking of the many young men who are giving their lives to the ministry. We are creatures of habit, and likely to pattern after some man who is a hero in our eyes, and I see nothing wrong in that, provided we follow the lives of the very best men on the field, and let the great pattern be Jesus Christ.

I am thinking of two men who were in the recent session of the North Carolina Conference. I have no apology to offer for this note, for I know no man or men whom I admire more. They were Dr. W. W. Staley and Dr. J. W. Wellons. Both are growing *young*. They were present during the whole session, and the thing I am trying to say is this: I watched them, and every forward step the Conference proposed, these men were among the very first to express themselves in favor of it, and in every speech I heard them make they were looking forward to something greater, bigger, and better than ever before.

It is nothing less than wonderful to be growing old in years, and young in life and service. It seemed to me that the lives of these men are so absorbed in the affairs of the Kingdom, that they have forgotten self. And the best interest of the Church is the one vital thing in their lives, and that thing keeps them young. God bless and spare them for many more years of efficient service in His Kingdom, and may the sessions of many more such gatherings be graced with their timely counsel, prayers and presence.

J. VINCENT KNIGHT.

POUNDED AGAIN

We have read of different great and good poundings of the various pastors, but I believe I have them all beat. Did you ever hear of a single church giving its pastor two poundings within two months?

On Saturday night before the first Sunday in October a number of the membership of Park's Cross Roads church gave us a rich pounding which I gave account of sometime ago. On last Saturday, November 22, a number of members of the same church did the same thing. It happened so they could not get here at the first but said their time would be next. Well, it was fine that it happened that way because there was so much that we could not have taken care of it at one time. Well, they brought us, last Saturday night, two pounds of butter, several pounds of sausage, one dozen eggs, several cans of fruit, pepper, soda, baking powder, pop-corn, peanuts, jelly, cakes, one chicken, and a large quantity each of sweet potatoes, Irish potatoes, corn wheat and six dollars in money. Just think of that? Who can beat this? God bless these good people. Thanks to one and all.

A. T. BANKS.

BURGLARS (?) ENTER PARSONAGE AT NORFOLK

Last Monday evening while Mrs. Morgan and I were quietly resting in the beautiful home which our church has provided for us, we were aroused by a knock at our door. Mrs. Morgan arose, and started to the door to let the company in. The company, however, did not wait for her to open the door, but came in the house without permission. The first one that came in was little Cecil Mercer in the arms of his brother, Ashburn. Of course I had to greet this fine youngster, and when I lifted my eyes from him, I beheld Master Maxwell Jones with a half bushel of sweet potatoes. I looked again and behold the hall was full, and the parlor door was opened, and in less time than it takes to tell it our home was full of good friends who had their arms full of good things to eat for the pastor and his wife. Then Mrs.

Morgan and I realized that we were in the hands of our friends who had come to pound us. It was a great sight. In the audience were members of our Cradle Roll, members of our Junior Christian Endeavor Society, members of our choir, Official Board, Young People's Auxiliary, Ladies' Aid, Sunday school, Missionary Society, Board of Deacons, yea of every organization of our church. There were more than fifty of these good people who came to pound their pastor and his wife, and the only thing we could do was to surrender, and for the time being let them take charge of the home. They brought us everything that was good to eat. There were more than forty different kinds of articles, such as Old Virginia ham, flower, sugar, and so many other things that we will not take the space to mention.

Mrs. Morgan and I tried to tell these good friends, and members of our church, how much we appreciated their great favor, but we could not, for lack of words to express the great appreciation of our hearts. We will try to be more faithful in our service for our Master, however, and in this way continue to let the good members, and friends of the First Christian church know how much we do appreciate the great favors they confer upon us.

May the blessings of our Heavenly Father rest upon all these good friends is our prayer.

MR. & MRS. J. F. MORGAN.

A THANKSGIVING POUNDING

The members' and friends of Youngsville Christian church again manifested their love and sympathy for their pastor on Sunday, November 23, by giving him a "Thanksgiving pounding." Among the different things contributed, were: Coffee, butter, hominy grits, jelly, salt, soda, soap; and such canned goods as pineapple, corn, beans, and tomatoes; also sweet potatoes, a fine chicken, and fourteen and one-half dollars in money. Several of the brethren said they thought their pastor could carry the "cash" home with him on the trains more easily than he could flour, and such articles. Two weeks before this, Mrs. J. L. Brown gave her husband's pastor two very pretty young chickens.

For all of these things, the humble pastor and his family are indeed grateful to the dear people for giving them; and to our Heavenly Father for prompting the giving.

We are also very grateful to our Wake Chapel friends for so kindly remembering us, as they have ever since we have been living at Varina, with such things as potatoes, turnips, butter, chickens, sugar, flour, and other good things to eat.

R. P. CRUMPLER.

Varina, N. C.

PASTORLESS CHURCHES

Three churches failed to report to the North Carolina Christian Conference: Center Grove, Goshen Chapel, and Keyser. Immediately upon adjournment of Conference I wrote to these three churches, but they paid no attention to my request for information.

Also immediately after Conference I wrote to every minister whose field of labor I was not acquainted with to let me know what churches he would serve next year. Our *Annual* ought to show the pastor for the coming year in the Statistical Table, as it does the pastor of the past year in the "Abstract of Ministerial Reports." The Church Letter, however, does not ask this question. When it is revised, it ought to do so. It is therefore necessary for the Secretary to get this information from the ministers.

The following churches have not been reported so far as having pastors: Antioch (R), Asheboro, Center Grove, Christian Union, Danville, (Va.), Goshen Chapel, Hanks' Chapel, Hopedale, Keyser, Martha's Chapel, Moore Union, Morrisville, Mt. Pleasant, O'Kelly's Chapel, Pleasant Grove (N. C.), Pleasant Ridge (R), Pleasant Union (R), and Spoon's Chapel, 18 in all. If any of these churches has a pastor, I would like to know it at once. The *Annual* has already gone to press, but I will try to get the information in the proof. I have also written these churches direct for the information necessary for an accurate *Annual.*

The following ministers have not answered my letter: L. W. Fogleman, W. N. Hayes, B. J. Howard, P. T. Klapp, G. R. Underwood, W. C. Martin, D. T. McKinney. I wish they would write me at once, and if any minister who has already reported makes a change in his work, I wish too he would notify me at once.

It is true that both churches and ministers in the Christian Church are free to neglect such matters, but when they do our records are necessarily incomplete.

We face what purports to be a good new year. Let us labor and pray that it may result in decided advancement in all lines of Christian progress.

W. A. HARPER,
Sec. N. C. Conference.

SUFFOLK LETTER

On Sunday, November 23, 1919, Mr. and Mrs. J. M. Darden, Mrs. W. H. Andrews and Mrs. I. W. Johnson, all of Suffolk, went to Antioch church of which Rev. H. H. Butler is pastor, where Mrs. Andrews organized a Woman's Home and Foreign Missionary Society; Antioch is her girlhood church.

Immediately after their Sunday school Superintendent Elisha Bradshaw made an interesting introductory address, expressing how glad he was that Antioch was about to line up in the Missionary work. Mrs. Andrews presided, and made a talk, telling how glad she was to be at her old church to help them organize a Missionary Society. She took her Scripture lesson from texts that explain what the initial letters of the Society mean. With a prepared chart, she explained the Woman's Home and Foreign Missionary Society as follows:

W—Wholly Consecrated, I Tim. 4:11-16.
H—Hearers and Doers, James 1:22.
F—Fruitful Workers, Cal. 1:10.
M—Messengers of Good News, John 20:21.
S—Students of Missions, II Tim. 2:15.

Then she asked:

"As individuals, can we measure up to the standard

of our letters? We certainly can, and if we *will* our goals will be reached. God helping us, we will.''

Mrs. Andrews, also, referred to the fact that Rev. D. P. Barrett, our Missionary in Porto Rico, went from Antioch. Then Mrs. J. M. Darden sang: ''Down in Porto Rico,'' which was written by Dr. J. P. Barrett, and Mr. Darden led in a feeling prayer.

Mrs. I. W. Johnson explained the financial obligation of Christians to Kingdom interest, after which Mrs. Darden sang: ''There is a Green Hill.''

Mr. Darden made an address explaining the Washington City work in a growing section of the capitol of our nation. Mr. Darden went with Dr. J. O. Atkinson to make the survey of that field and could give a full explanation of the work.

Names were then taken for membership, and twenty-eight women and twenty-two men and boys were enrolled, making the charter membership *fifty*. The following officers were elected:

Mrs. Dana Saunders, President; Mrs. W. C. Andrews, Vice-President; Mrs. R. O. Butler, Recording Secretary; Mrs. William Garrison, Treasurer; Mrs. Cleo Clements, Organist.

It was a great day at ''Old Antioch'' and not a ''preaching day.'' Nobody dreamed when Janie Marshall, as a little country girl, professed religion and united with Antioch, that she would return some day, with such well-chosen helpers as Mr. and Mrs. Darden and Mrs. Johnson, and organize a great Missionary Society; but she did; and all of them came back to Suffolk happy because they had done a good day's work for the Master. ''If ye know these things, happy are ye, if ye *do* them.''

This is not all the good work done since the Annual Conference at Waverly. On the first Sunday after Conference, a Woman's Home and Foreign Missionary was organized at Oakland church, of which Dr. I. W. Johnson is pastor, with a membership of twenty-two women and seventeen men, a total charter membership of thirty-nine.

Then, on the second Sunday after Conference, a Woman's Home and Foreign Missionary Society was organized at Bethlehem church, of which Rev. E. T. Cotten is pastor, with seventeen charter members. Thus the good work among the women grows while the older Societies continue their work with increased efficiency and zeal. The women grow with their work, and one may doubt whether a Christian can *grow* without *working* for the Lord.

W. W. STALEY.

SPECIAL EDITORIAL NOTE

After going to press with page 6 we are informed by Dr. Harper that the following ministers and churches have been heard from since writing his article: *Churches*: Long's Chapel, Antioch (R), Morrisville, O'Kelly's Chapel, Pleasant Grove (N. C.) and Martha's Chapel. *Ministers*: L. W. Fogleman and G. R. Underwood.

CHRISTIAN EDUCATION

A CENTRAL FLAW
(Dr. Robert E. Spear)

The war has revealed to us the magnitude and gravity of our whole problem of education. A democracy is not safe with such a mass of illiteracy as the war has uncovered. But the problem is not solved simply by decreasing the percentage of illiterates to the total population. We need not simply education, but Christian education—training that issues in religious conviction and Christian personality.

Among all the things that the chaplains and others who have been in touch with the religious side of the Army have revealed to us, few are more appalling than the lack of comprehension of the meaning of Christianity and the elements of religious faith, which were found to be characteristic of great masses of our men, side by side with a widely prevalent and child-like religious instinct.

Such ignorance is a central flaw in a self-controlled and self-governed nation. Our strength lies in the intelligent religious convictions of our people.

In the more comprehensive sense of the term the whole problem of the church is now more clearly seen to be one of education. We have to bring every available resource to bear to make the pulpit, the Sunday school, the day school, the university, the theological seminary, all our educational factors, efficient in carrying out the great task of the church of training men and women in Christian character.

THANKSGIVING AT ELON

A genuine Indian Summer, a large company of friends, and good fellowship made Thanksgiving at Elon memorable for 1919.

The usual exercises took place, but not in a usual sense. On Sunday evening preceding, the Orphanage Singing Class gave a splendid exercise and our offering will, when completed, be at least $100.00, our best yet.

On Thanksgiving Day the illness of Pastor N. G. Newman was very regrettable. Dr. Atkinson, however, made a thrilling address, showing why the nation as a whole and our Church in particular should be thankful.

Two excellent college functions were staged. The Junior-Senior Debate on Wednesday night was the first, and the annual celebrating of the Philologian Society on Thursday night the second.

The Junior-Senior celebration was a debate only. The query was, ''Resolved, That the employee in the United States is more responsible than the employer for the high cost of living and the industrial strife of today.'' The seniors championed the affirmative and were represented by Messrs. J. L. Floyd and E. H. Rainey, who argued their side well. Miss Jessie Sharpe and Mr. L. B. Ezzell spoke for the Juniors and won a unanimous decision.

On Thursday evening the Philologian Society presented a more varied program indicative of the regular work of their society. Mr. C. M. Miller gave a passionate oration on "American Patriotism." Having been in the army and having lost a brother in the service, his words made a wholesome impression. Mr. J. W. Fix read an original humorous burlesque depicting the superstition and the call of the wild to the old-style darkey. Mr. L. R. Sides rendered a fine trombone solo, accompanied on piano by Mr. P. E. Lindley. Mr. R. O. Smith conducted the regular religious service, which is a part of every session of the society.

The concluding number was a debate on "Resolved, That Industrial Democracy is the best solution of the labor problem." The affirmative speakers were Messrs. E. S. Johnson and W. R. Thomas. The negative cause was maintained by Messrs. H. W. Johnson and H. G. Self. The affirmative won a hard fought battle by a unanimous decision.

It is worth while to note that both these debates concerned themselves with the labor problem. The first treated it as to cause and the second as to remedy, and in both cases the decision was unanimous in labor's favor. Surely we live in new times.

Other Items

Many of the Faculty members attended the North Carolina Teachers' Assembly in Raleigh during the Thanksgiving season.

Prof. Betts, Mrs. Sturm, Miss Fisher, and Miss Hawk gave a joint recital on November 26 at the Cary (N. C.) High School.

Prof. Alexander is scheduled to give a recital at Erskine (S. C.) College on December 5.

The new Kimball Pipe Organ is installed and will be played Sunday, November 30, for the first time. It is a rarely sweet-toned instrument.

General Julian S. Carr, Durham, N. C., is to speak on "The Democratization of Industry" at the Sunday evening service, December 7. General Carr is the apostle of Industrial Democracy in North Carolina and is always heard profitably on any theme.

The Faculty Music Recital is to be given on the evening of December 2. The public is cordially invited.

　　　　　　　　　　　　　　　W. A. HARPER.

NEW COMERS TO THE SUN FAMILY

S. E. Taylor	Elams, N. C.
Mrs. James Jernigan	Newport News, Va.
Mrs. Leslie Alderson	Houston, Va.
J. G. Brown	Kipling, N. C.
Mrs. Camillia Darden	Windsor, Va.
Miss Martha Stacy	Tokyo, Japan
Miss Bessie Miles	Fitch, N. C.
Miss Belle V. Covington	Roxboro, N. C.

If you plan to get a Bible or Testament for a Christmas present, we suggest that you place your order now. Stock is short in many numbers and labor scarce. Then, too, remember that transportation is very much torn up during the holiday season. Correspondence solicited.

　　　　　　　　　　　* *

W. H. Joyner—I enjoy every copy of my Church paper.

Negotations are now being carried on between the United States and Mexico regarding the arrest and imprisonment of citizens of the United States.

A sum of over one hundred thousand dollars has been raised by the memorial fund committee of the University of North Carolina toward the contemplated student activities building at the University in memory of the late president, Edward Kidder Graham.

The shortage of fuel seems to be a matter of great concern for the nation. People are asked to submit themselves to war-time regulations. Many offices are being closed after four o'clock P. M., and not opened till nine A. M. At this writing there seems to be no definite plan formulated.

Cotton has reached the point of nearly 39 cents the pound.

A new shipping line has been established between Norfolk and Havana, Cuba, operations to begin December 12, 1919.

Three thousand textile workers are on strike in Fall River, Mass.

Washington is still wrangling over the Peace Treaty and nothing is being done that looks toward permanent peace.

In London the infant mortality is 90 to 1,000. In New York it is about 100 to 1,000, and this is constantly being reduced,—that is to say 100 children born in New York out of every 1,000, or one in ten, die before they are five years old. We have it on the highest authority that all over China, more than half the children die before they are two years old. In Syria three-fourths of all the children die before they are two years old. And in Persia 85 per cent. And they die from two causes: First, because their parents do not know how to nourish and to care for them. Second because, particularly if girls, their parents do not care if they do die.

The Constitution of the United States requires that a census of the United States be taken every ten years. It is by this means that the apportionment of members of the House of Representatives is made as to states.

We advise those who expect to order books or Bibles for Christmas presents to do so now. Many numbers cannot be secured. We have in stock about all the available numbers that we have been carrying, but have a low stock in many instances. Order now. We also call the attention of those who want names placed on Bibles or Testaments. It takes about ten days or more to fill such orders. We would not advise such orders after December 12. We are anxious to serve, but cannot on short notice.

THE CHURCH WINNING THE YOUNG*

In our own country there are about half of the children who have no opportunity whatever of knowing the value of Christian training in the home. These must depend upon some one other than parents for a knowledge of God's Word and things pertaining to the Christian life. Two-thirds of the population of the world is outside the Sunday school, and the school loses fifty per cent of all those who enter the school from the church. They either leave the school during the intermediate period, or never join the church at all. It is in behalf of these that I am to speak today. If they are to be won to the church it must be done by some other way than the parent, or the school, or by first reaching the parent and the school for Christ.

The Bible is a Book of revelation. It reveals man, and God, and God's will concerning man. It also reveals Christ and His great commission to the world. When He gave the Commission to the Disciples, He made it broad enough in its scope to take in all humanity. He died for the world, and sent the disciples to tell the world of His death, and no tongue can tell all its meaning to the world. The commission has been extended through the centuries down to the church of today, and yet three-fourths of the world is still in sin. If the church wins the world to Christ it must win the youth of today and mould them into lifework recruits, and this will call for three definite things.

It calls for a constructive program of evangelism. A man is not saved by the simple act of professing religion. Thousands profess to know Christ every year, and yet they never mean anything to the church or to Jesus Christ. A mere profession, does not satisfy the demand—for a profession without a possession is nothing. Neither does joining the church always mean that the individual is won to Christ. For on every hand there comes the sad news from the church that it has lost some of its members, and dozens are inactive, and some never attend even a single service during the year. They are dead, and the only surprising thing about it is, they do not seem to know it. A man is won to the church and to Christ when every fiber of his life and all the energy he possesses is consecrated on the altar of service. He may claim to have the faith of Abraham, the vision of Isaiah, the love of John, and the ambition of Paul, but unless he proves his faith by his works he never recognizes the fact that he is a Christian. Jesus saves, not to keep men from going to ruin alone, but He saves men that men in turn may save others and bring them to the knowledge of the truth. He saved Andrew—and he was instrumental in saving Peter, and he in turn swayed the Multitude at Pentecost and thousands were saved.

Again, it calls for an increase of workers. There has never been a day in the history of the world when workers were needed as they are today. On every hand there comes the call for more workmen. Note the condition in our own church. A few years ago our institutions had more than a hundred students preparing for the ministry, and now they have less than forty, and still the need is greater. Why the loss? I leave you to answer the question. In our own beloved South land of which we boast so much the conditions are far from satisfactory. Look at conditions as they are. Ninety-five per cent of the churches in the South have no Society of any kind for training the young people and seventy-five per cent. of them have only one preaching service per month and not much preparation being made for more. Then, take a third look if you please, and see the great need in the world about us. Through science, and the revelation of Jesus Christ the world has grown smaller and smaller until the work is brought home to the doors of the church. Think of the need. No pen however skillful, nor tongue be it ever so eloquent can estimate the need about us, and the bigness of the call that comes. Once our churches could supply their needs but how is it now? No denomination in the United States, Canada, or the united kingdom of great Britain can supply its pulpits on a single Sunday. The queston grows more serious every day, and our only hope lies in the fact that we must pray mightily for more laborers, and then take off our coats and go after them. God's part is already done when we are ready to meet conditions. "Pray ye the Lord of the Harvest that he will send labourers into his harvest," but what is the use? I mean what is the use to pray for men and then drive them by starvation wages back to the farm and shops for support?

Finally, it calls for a program of enlargement and enlistment. When our country had a big job to do, it called upon the youth of the land and enlisted them by the millions. They responded and did a decent job for Uncle Sam, and made the world proud of them. In like manner will they respond when the church is ready to place a program large enough to interest them. Line up the young for service and stop your knocking. During all my ministry, I have never yet called upon a young man or a young woman to do something for the Church but what they tried to do it. The thing we want to do, is to place the youth of our Church in the training Societies and train for service. One can lead a hundred, but it takes a hundred to drive one. We must train, train, train and keep on training for the work of the Kingdom demands it. Let us emphasize the vast importance of our summer training schools, and chautauqua work for there are hundreds that have no other opportunity for the Christian training. Think of the twelve million girls, and the nine-million boys in the world today, who never go to college, or have a debut of their own but go to work as soon as the laws of their countries will allow. These are dependent on the Sunday school, Christian Endeavor, and the church as a whole to train them for service. Shall we leave them go until sin has ruined their lives, and Satan has destroyed their vitality and ambition for service?

Our churches must line up with the enlarged programs of the church as a whole. I am glad the day has come when we are to lose our denominational prejudice and launch out into one enlarged program for the cause and Kingdom of Jesus Christ. Our big business is to co-operate with the allied forces of the Kingdom for the salvation of the whole world, for the ultimate objective of Christ's coming to the world was to bring salvation to it. But saving one here and there is not half enough—we must save, train and serve, for if we would conserve our energy and do the work of our Christ we must make one united drive for the church of God, for through the church we shall win the world to Christ. Our money and means are nothing, as long as the energy of the youth of our church is latent. We need a thousand men to enter the field tomorrow to champion the cause of our Christ, and how shall we get them? By enlisting the youth of today, and enlarging the program of the Kingdom until we shall reach all the ends of the earth with the message of our Christ, and bring every soul under subjection to him.

*Address by J. Vincent Knight, Greensboro, N. C., delivered before the North Carolina Christian Conference in session at Burlington, N. C., November 11-14, 1919.

United States marshals acted as enumerators at the first nine decennial censuses. Each marshal had as many assistants as were necessary to properly cover his allotted territory.

THE CHRISTIAN ORPHANAGE

FINANCIAL REPORT FOR DECEMBER 3, 1919
Amount brought forward, $13,012.74.

Children's Offerings

Erma Jean, Doris, Lorraine and Eris Whitaker, $5.00; Oliver E. Young, Jr., 10 cents; James Dunn, 10 cents; Inez and Elizabeth Dunn, 20 cents; Total $5.40.

Sunday School Monthly Offerings

(North Carolina Conference)
Apple's Chapel, $1.00; Shallow Well, $2.77; Hines' Chapel, $2.00; Liberty, (Vance) $8.00; Palm Street, $14.00; Mebane, $1.00; Shallow Ford, $2.00; Wentworth, $9.59; Pleasant Ridge, $2.35; Christian Light, $9.59; Poplar Branch, $1.50.
(Eastern Virginia Conference)
Antioch, $2.00; East End, Newport News, $11.97; Young Men's Baracca Class, Holy Neck, $1.00.
(Georgia and Alabama Conference)
Rock Stand, 80 cents; Pleasant Grove, $4.75; New Hope, $2.91; Wadley, 77 cents; Total $81.97.

Special Offering

Mrs. H. C. Pollard's Sunday school class, $31.81; Dr. M. T. Morrill, Defiance, Ohio, $1.00; Seaside Chautauqua, Special Collection, $12.00; Women's Home & Foreign Board, S. C., $480.30; New Hope S. S. Ala., Birthday offerings, 76 cents; Mrs. M. C. McNeal, Hobson, Va., Sunday eggs money, $14.50; Total, $540.37.

Children's Home

Mr. E. S. Norfleet, $100.00; Mrs. Ada Teague, $50.00; S. R. A. Howell, $5.00; Total $155.00.

Thanksgiving Offering

Apple's Chapel church, $36.92; Mr. Kimery, $1.00; J. J. Douglas, Greenville, Ohio, $10.00; J. L. Barksdale, Sutherlin, Va., $2.00; Margaret Earp, $3.00; Jeff Shelley and Family, Crawfordsville, $10.00; Mr. and Mrs. B. F. Gwaltney, Disputanta, Va., $5.00; Junius Parker, New York City, $100.00; Mrs. Catherine W. Morgan, Louisburg, Pa., $100.00; Mrs. J. H. Massey, Durham, N. C., $2.00; Ladies' Aid Societies & C. E., Pinesville, S. S., N. J., $8.00; Mrs. E. J. Hicks, Ridgeway, N. C., $2.00; Mrs. S. R. Gray, Cumberland, Md., $2.50; Mrs. H. C. Mason, Nashville, N. C., $2.50; Annie & Rosa Webb, Durham, N. C., $2.00; A Friend, Comer, Ohio, $5.00; Alva H. Morrill, Haverhill, Mass., $5.00; Mrs. Nellie H. Holt, Machais, N. Y., for Sunday school, $2.00; W. L. Thomas, Jonesboro, N. C., $50.00; New Hope Sunday school, Roanoke, Ala., $16.96; Hardy Hardcastle, Dover, Del., $5.00; The Christian Endeavor Society, Darlington Christian Church, Darlington, Ind., $11.00; Mrs. C. A. Moore, Youngsville, N. C., $10.00; Ingram Church, Va., $60.00; W. C. Michael, Kenersville, N. C., $10.00; Miss Stella Sharpe, $3.00; Union Church (South Hampton) Va., $52.00; Holy Neck church, $100.00; Fred Hattman, Asheboro, N. C., $2.50; Hobson, Va., $15.50; Hobson, Va. Sunday school, $30.00; R. A. Hinton and Wife, Dayton, Va., $5.00; Sanford Christian church, $63.37; Oakland Sunday school, $11.00; W. K. Wagoner, Suffolk, Va., $5.00; Callie Bray and Sisters, $5.00; Mrs. P. L. Waller, $2.50; Mt. Pleasant Sunday school, $5.00; John Edwards, Youngsville, N. C., $5.00; Miss Eula Edwards, $1.00; Rev. and Mrs. L. L. Lassiter, Suffolk, Va., $12.00; Caswell Cotton Mills, Kinston, N. C., $25.00; Grace's Chapel Sunday school, N. C., $6.88; New Lebanon Baracca Class, $10.00; New Hope church, $3.00; First Christian church, Killery Point, Me., $39.00; Total, $863.73.

Total for the week; $1,646.47; Grand total, $14,659.21.

CHILDREN'S LETTERS

Dear Uncle Charley:—We are sending five dollars which is ten cents apiece for each month this year and five cents over because we are so late: We were glad you and Mrs. Wicker brought some of the children to our Sunday school this year and want you to be sure to come again and bring all the children you can.—*Erna Jean, Doris, Lorraine and Eris Whitaker.*

We all enjoyed our visit to your Sunday school and want to come again next year.—*"Uncle Charley."*

Dear Uncle Charley:—Here comes two little girls to join the Corner. We go to school and like our teacher fine. We are having our meeting at Ingram this week. Mr. Brown is helping Mr. Truitt and we like him very much. Enclosed find 10 cents from each of us.—*Irene and Elizabeth Dunn.*

We give you a warm welcome to the Corner. We hope you will write often.—*"Uncle Charley."*

Dear Uncle Charley:—I am a little boy twelve years old. I want to join the Corner. I go to school every day and I like my teacher very much. Enclosed find ten cents for the cousins. As ever.—*James Dunn.*

You are a splendid little man. I trust you will make good grades in school.—*"Uncle Charley."*

Dear Uncle Charley:—I hope you and the cousins will have a happy Thanksgiving. I am wishing I were big enough to eat some turkey, still Christmas comes soon and I can enjoy that.—*Oliver E. Young, Jr.*

A friend gave us a turkey and we bought one, so our little folks will have a turkey for Thanksgiving. Wish you could be with us.—*"Uncle Charley."*

Dear Uncle Charley:—I am a little girl nearly three years old, so I want to give a Thanksgiving offering to the little orphans. I am sending three dollars.—*Margaret Earp.*

I think you are the little girl I feel in love with at the Valley Conference. I know you were a good little girl. It is so good of you to remember the orphans.—*"Uncle Charley."*

ENCOURAGING REPORT

Our Thanksgiving offerings are coming in nicely and we are very happy that our loyal friends are going to make this one of the largest Thanksgiving Offerings we have had in the history of the Institution. Wake Chapel church sent us one full suit of clothing for a boy. Virginia Cotton Mills, one bolt nice dress goods. Jas. N. Williamson & Sons, 100 yards of nice outings. Proximity Manufacturing Company, 300 yards of blue Denims for overalls. Dr. W. T. Walters, two barrels of apples. Elmira Cotton Mills, 202 yards of dress ginghams. Glen Raven Cotton Mills, 128 yards of Denims for overalls. Glencoe Cotton Mills, 202 yards of nice dress outings. Lakeside Mills, 120 yards heavy goods for shirtings. E. M. Holt Plaid Mills, 87 yards of nice dress ginghams. Sidney Cotton Mills, 150 yards of plaids for aprons. Durham Hosiery Mills, 4 dozens of hose for the children. Ladies' Aid Society of the Graham Christian church, 32 cans of fruit, three bushels of potatoes, three pecks of apples, two gallons of molasses. Sunbeam Workers Society of the Graham Christian church, one cake for the little girls' Thanksgiving dinner. The Ladies'. Aid Society of the Bethlehem Christian church contributed the following: Mrs. J. W. Holt, one quilt; Mrs. John Ward, one sheet; Mrs. I. N. W. Garrison, one hat; Victora Troxler, 3 yards of gingham; Mrs. E. F. Lowe, one blouse; Mrs. W. T. Warren, 3 yards of gingham; Mrs. L. D. Rippy, 5 yards of gingham; Mr. and Mrs. R. A. Thompson, one quilt; Mr. and Mrs. N. E. A. Thompson, one quilt. Mrs. R. L. Hendrickson, Lincoln, Kans., one quilt; Mrs. L. L. Lassiter, Suffolk, Va., one quilt and one dozen cans of fruit. Rev. P. T. Klapp, one and one-half barrels of corn. The Graham Graded School, one carload (Ford car) of apples, potatoes, canned goods, coffee and many other articles too numerous to mention. The Ossipee Graded School, one barrel of apples, potatoes, canned goods, etc.

For all the above we are truly thankful and it will be lots of help to us in this work.

Our Singing Class had a very pleasant trip to Berea church near Ossipee two weeks ago and rendered its program there. The congregation was very good and gave the children splendid attention and we hope they enjoyed the program.

The Singing Class also visited the First Church, Greensboro, on the fourth Sunday and rendered its program. After the close of the service Rev. J. V. Knight, the pastor, said that Brother H. C. Simpson had something to say to the congregation and he took the floor and said that he thought after hearing the program rendered by the children that they ought to contribute $500.00 for a Thanksgiving offering. In his quiet and calm way he, in a few minutes, raised $450.00 and assured me that they would make it five hundred before they sent in the offering. Brother Simpson is small in stature, but big in heart when the cause of the little orphans is presented.

Brother J. V. Knight, the beloved pastor, of that church, kindly turned the service over to the class and we are very grateful to him for the kindness shown us on this, our first, visit to his church. Brother Knight is an untiring worker and is doing a great work in our Greensboro church and we look for greater things from that church in the future.

"Now for the *biggest* Thanksgiving offering ever." See that your church does its part in the great work. Sixty-one little fellows to love and care for.

                 CHAS. D. JOHNSTON, *Supt.*

Chief of Staff, General P. C. March, advocates a standing army of 260,000 together with universal military training.

NOTES

Rev. J. W. Holt, Burlington, N. C., tells us that he has the first and second Sundays open if churches are in need of his services for these dates.

We have received the following that will be of interest to many SUN readers:

"Mr. Samuel McPherson requests the pleasure of your company at the marriage of his daughter, Bessie Lee to Mr. Ralph Mahoney Harris, Tuesday morning, the ninth of December, at ten o'clock, at home, Liberty, North Carolina. At home after December twentieth, Oriental, North Carolina."

Best wishes and congratulations.

It will be personally appreciated by the Editor if all contributions sent THE CHRISTIAN SUN from now until December 15 be as brief as possible. Pastors will do us a great favor by keeping marriage and obituary notes below the limit. We go to press this week with enough matter on hand for the issue of December 10.

While we are able to send most any Bible ordered direct from stock, it sometimes happens that we must have a Bible sent direct from the manufacturers in Philadelphia and this takes longer to fill the order. We have on hand several orders of that kind now, and in two or three cases, the number ordered is out of stock for a few days. Be patient. You will have your order filled.

A MESSAGE FROM DR. DENISON

Dr. W. H. Denison, Superintendent of the Forward Movement of the Christian Church writes as follows about places and institutions in the Southern Christian Convention:

"It was a great pleasure for the Superintendent to be present at the North Carolina Conference and speak on one phase of the Forward Movement—Evangelism. The new united Conference promises large things for our North Carolina work. It was a pleasure to spend a few minutes at Elon College and see a few of the young people there preparing for life's larger work. The privilege of speaking at our Franklin, Va. church on the Forward Movement and greeting the splendid people of Dr. Rowland's congregation was a pleasure. We had the opportunity of preaching at the Union church also and helping in the raising of the Thanksgiving offering for the Christian Orphanage. Our stay in North Carolina and Virginia was short and very busy but a great delight. We were pleased to be present at the Women's Mission Thank-Offering services both at Franklin, Va., and at Memorial Christian Temple, Norfolk, Va. Everywhere we found our people interested in the Forward Movement program and standards."

Let us get up that Bible for that Christmas present now so as to insure your getting it.

MISSIONARY

AMONG THE WORKERS

A good sister in sending her subscription to our $500,000.00 Mission Fund, adds this note: "I have been praying every day for several years and am still praying daily that my boys may give themselves to Christ's cause and that at least one of them may be a foreign missionary. Will you pray with me for this? I am praying for you and the work you represent, and I am glad whenever I can help in any way."

The good ones of this type move forward this campaign for a half million dollars for missions and encourage the work which we are trying to do. If our mothers shall pray as this good woman is, for their own children to be missionaries, it will not be long until the volunteers will spring up from many homes. Our Saviour said, "Pray ye the Lord of the harvest that he send forth laborers into His harvest."

* *

Our Washington congregation began right. An offering was taken at the first service after the pastor, Dr. Kendall, arrived, and amounted to $29.85. That is a beginning and amounts to more than the usual offering of some of our well established congregations. Wherever the writer has been he has heard nothing but words of approval of beginning the work in Washington, and of getting Dr. Kendall to lead and develop the work there. All who know Dr. Kendall feel that he is the very man for the place so far as this writer has heard any expression.

* *

Rev. D. Clay Lilly truthfully writes, "Men (and women) cannot be enlisted in a cause of which they know nothing. Most men (and women) do not know even the primary facts and principles of Missions. The young people and children will not grow up to be missionaries, or to support missions, while they know nothing of the great enterprise."

And this by Sue Reynolds Staley, "The Methodist Episcopal Church has for fifty years had its Sunday schools organized into missionary societies, having their own scholar-officers. This method of organization has proved in no way antagonistic to the other departments of the Sunday school, but rather a source of stimulation and helpfulness. As a result of this organization, the gifts to missions of the Sunday schools of the Methodist Episcopal Church are larger than those of any other denomination."

This explains why the M. E. Church put on a Centenary Campaign for $80,000,000 for missions, and then went *over the top* with it. For fifty years they had been teaching their children missions in the Sunday school. Give the children of your schools a chance.

* *

Says Sue Reynolds Staley: "The force and strength of the Sunday school has hitherto been expended on itself. When once this giant is awakened to the world vision of missions, the entire world will receive the knowledge of Jesus Christ." George R. Trull says:

"In the hands of Sunday school superintendents and teachers lies the real solution of the missionary problem. They hold the key to the whole situation, and if they improve their opportunity, within a generation, there will be a church whose intelligence about missions and zeal for them have never been equaled in the world's history."

J. O. ATKINSON.

REPORT OF TREASURER OF THE WOMEN'S HOME AND FOREIGN MISSION BOARD OF THE SOUTHERN CHRISTIAN CONVENTION, FOR QUARTER ENDING NOVEMBER 1, 1919

Regular Funds

Receipts:
November 1—Eastern Virginia Conference	$ 199.59
November 1—Virginia Valley Central Conference	4.00
Total	$203.60

Disbursements:
November 1—Burlington Printing Co., Printing	168.50
November 1—Geo. F. Norton, Printing	4.50
November 1—Mrs. W. A. Harper, Postage	13.84
November 1—Rev. W. C. Wicker, Treas. (Home Missions)	8.38
November 1—Rev. W. C Wicker, Treas. (Foreign Missions)	8.38
Total	$203 60

Christian Orphanage

Receipts:
November 1—Eastern Virginia Conference	12.82
November 1—Eastern Va. Conference, Eulice Bradshaw	15.00
November 1—Eastern Va. Conference, Support of Orphan.	75.00
November 1—Eastern Va. Conference, Mary Thompson	2.00
November 1—Eastern Va. Conference, Eugenia Hillyard	7.00
November 1—Eastern Va. Conference, Coy Franklin	121.36
November 1—Eastern Va. Valley Central Conference	2.65
November 1—North Carolina Conference	49.15
November 1—North Carolina Conference, Thelma Thomas	15.00
Total	$299.98

Disbursements:
July 10—Rev. W. C. Wicker, Treas	15.00
November 1—Rev. W. C. Wicker, Treas	284.98
Total	$299.98

SENDAI ORPHANAGE

Receipts:
November 1—Eastern Virginia Conference	12.83
November 1—Virginia Valley Central Conference	1.23
November 1—North Carolina Conference	35.65
Total	$49.71

Disbursements:
November 1—Rev. W. C. Wicker, Treasurer	$49.71

Bible Women

Receipts:
November 1—Eastern Va. Conference, Mrs Watanabe	25.86
November 1—North Carolina Conference, Dona Delfina	100.00
Total	$125.86

Japan Sunday School

Receipts:
November 1—Eastern Virginia Conference	12.50

Disbursements:
November 1—Rev. W. C. Wicker, Treas	12.50

Mrs. Fry's School

Receipts:
November 1—North Carolina Conference	70.00

Disbursements:
November 1—Rev. W. C. Wicker, Treasurer	70.00

Rev. Martinez, Salary

Receipts:
August 1—Cash on Hand	215.27
November 1—Eastern Virginia Conference	297.34
Total	$512.61
November 1—Cash on Hand	512.61

Literature Fund

Receipts:
August 1—Cash on Hand	36.12
November 1—Eastern Virginia Conference	11.75
Total	$47.87

Disbursements:
November 1—Ida C. Bird	6.50
November 1—Cash on Hand	41.37

Barrett Home

Receipts:
November 1—Eastern Virginia Conference	52.65
November 1—North Carolina Conference	303.39
Total	$356.04

Disbursements:
November 1—Rev. W. C. Wicker, Treasurer	356.04

Santa Isabel Building Fund

Receipts:
November 1—Eastern Virginia Conference 639.02
November 1—North Carolina Conference 702.89

Total.................$1,841.91

Disbursements:
November 1—Rev. W. C. Wicker, Treas............... 1,841.91

Ellen Gustin Fund

Receipts:
November 1—Eastern Virginia Conference 4.00
Disbursements:
November 1—Rev. W. C. Wicker, Treas............... 4.00

Rev. E. K. McCord

Receipts:
August 15—Virginia Valley Central Conference.......... 5.00
Disbursements:
August 15—Rev. E. K. McCord 5.00

Special Foreign Work

Receipts:
November 1—Virginia Valley Central Conference........ 11.85
November 1—Cash on Hand 11.85

Winchester Church Debt

Receipts:
November 1—Virginia Valley Central Conference 27.06
Disbursements:
November 1—Rev. W. C. Wicker, Treas............... 27.06

Japan Work

Receipts:
November 1—North Carolina Conference 192.96
Disbursements:
November 1—Rev. W. C. Wicker, Treas.............. 192.96

Armenian and Syrian Relief

Receipts:
November 1—North Carolina Conference ....·.. 25.00
November 1—Cash on Hand 25.00
Total for quarter $3,042 85
Total half year $4,052.63

Winchester, Va.   MRS. W. T. WALTERS, Treas.

FROM OVER THE SEAS

MISSIONARY FROM BURLINGTON SUNDAY SCHOOL WRITES

Canadian Pacific Ocean Services Ltd.
R. M. S. "Empress of Japan."
Sunday, October 12, 1919.

Dear Burlington Friends:—

This is my last day on shipboard, I expect, so I am writing to mail this when I land. It has been an unusually rough voyage, so those say who have crossed several times. But these last three days have been beautiful, smooth and sunny days.

There are over fifty missionaries on board, going to Japan, China, Korea, India, and the Philippines, also a party of Y. M. C. A. men going to Russia. One night we had a missionary meeting on board, with four speakers, Mr. Reynolds of Korea, Mr. Garrison of India, Dr. Chen of China, who has been to college in our country, and Bishop Bannister of the Anglican Church who has been in China thirty-nine years. The subject of the evening was "The Progress of Christianity in Asia," and the speakers were all very good, Mr. Garrison was especially interesting. He is a member of a missionary family, third generation in India, I think, and he has with him two little boys who were born in India, and a baby born while they were home on furlough.

The long delay of this boat in Vancouver was caused by the fact that they were waiting for Chinese coolies

returning from their work behind the lines in France. There are about twelve hundred of them in the steerage, more than all the first and second class passengers together. One night last week at our dinner time a most terrifying howl arose from their quarters, and then for about five minutes such a noise as I never heard before. We learned afterwards that they are supposed to keep their own deck and sleeping quarters clean, and because they were not cleaned to pass inspection that day the poor coolies had been given no supper at night. No wonder they howled!

Another interesting party on board are some French officers going to Russia on some mission which they claim not to know all about themselves. They have with them one young man, just a boy away from home for the first time, too young to have been in the war. He is the only one among them who speaks English, and I suppose he is with them for that reason. He is a general favorite on shipboard, and the whole party in their bright blue uniforms certainly have added interest to the scenery.

Another passenger who has been very interesting to me is a Japanese lady who is returning to Kobe. She is working under the Methodist Board in a girls' school, and has been in this country (I mean America, of course) for special work in dietetics at Battle Creek, Michigan. Unfortunately she has been very seasick most of the time, so I have not been able to learn as much from her as I might have if she had been able to sit up on deck. We have also some members of the Chinese Peace Commission who are returning from Paris.

With so many missionaries on board I have been disappointed not to have more religious services than have been possible, but the boat has been so overcrowded it was hard to find a place in which to hold services, and seasickness has been so general up to the last three days that it was also hard to find anyone to conduct services. Though I have been a bit seasick, I have been very fortunate compared to some, as there has not been a day when I was not on deck part of the day, and only two days when I suffered much from the motion of the boat. One of those days, I think, was imitating a rocking horse.

I am looking forward to hearing from some of you.

Sincerely yours,
MARTHA R. STACY.

WHAT YOUR LABEL MEANS

(Told in the Language of a Child)

1-1-9 means that your subscription expires January 1, 1919.
2-1-9 means that your subscription expires February 1, 1919.
3-1-9 means that your subscription expires March 1, 1919.
4-1-9 means that your subscription expires April 1, 1919.
5-1-9 means that your subscription expires May 1, 1919.
6-1-9 means that your subscription expires June 1, 1919.
7-1-9 means that your subscription expires July 1, 1919.
8-1-9 means that your subscription expires August 1, 1919.
9-1-9 means that your subscription expires September 1, 1919.
10-1-9 means that your subscription expires October 1, 1919.
11-1-9 means that your subscription expires November 1, 1919.
12-1-9 means that your subscription expires December 1, 1919.

SOME CHRISTMAS SUGGESTIONS

CHRISTMAS BOOKS FOR CHILDREN

We list below a supply of books which we have purchased suitable for Christmas presents for the children. For the lack of space we cannot tell what each book is about, but we have exercised the very best care in the selection, to see that all stories are helpful and interesting:

The Thorn of the Fortress	50 cents
Matt of the Waterfront	50 cents
The Other Side of the Rainbow	60 cents
Lantern Stories	60 cents
Billy and Bumps	35 cents
Good Night Stories	60 cents
The Jim Family	25 cents
Little Folks of the Bible	30 cents
Sunny Hour Books	15 cents

(Little Folks of the Bible can be had in books I, II, III, and IV. Books I and II are for boys and books III and IV are for girls. We will send any four books of this title for $1.00.)

(Sunny Hour Books are made up of 14 different titles. The price is 15 cents for each title, any two for 25 cents; four for 45 cents and all over four at 10 cents per volume.)

All the above named books are suitable for children 8 to 14 except the "Sunny Hour Books" which are for little tots that cannot read or are just beginning to read. "Sunny Hour Books" contain an abundance of pictures and are bound with colored cloth and stamped with an appropriate design.

Add 4 cents per volume for postage when only one copy is ordered, and 2 cents per volume for postage in lots up to ten; all over ten volumes add 1 cent per volume for postage.

CLEARANCE SALE OF CHILDREN'S BOOKS

We make it a rule in December of each year to buy the closing out stock of several suitable books for children. By buying the closing out stock, we are enabled to get a better price and make the books within the reach of all.

We have been able this year to buy the complete stock of the following 50 cent sellers, and offer them at prices indicated:

Blazing the Way	$ .25
Bright Side and Other Side	.25
Crown Jewels	.20
From the Thames to the Toossachs	.25
Up the Susquehanna	.25

(This price is postpaid)

The following reductions will be made in lots: Any two copies, 45 cents; three copies, 60 cents; four copies, 75 cents; all over four copies at 17 cents per copy.

The supply is limited and we advise you to order early. If any title has exhausted when your order is received, we will substitute unless otherwise instructed.

These books are all well made and handsomely bound.

Make some child's life happy by presenting one or more of these books. Invest a few dollars to make the little tots of your class happy.

SUNDAY SCHOOL HELPS

We have the following Sunday school helps on the 1920 International Lesson:

Peloubet's Select Notes	$1.60
Tarbell's Teachers' Guide	1.60
Arnold's Commentary	.75
Torrey's Gist of the Lesson	.30

(These prices include postage)

ADDRESS

C. B. RIDDLE, Publisher

BURLINGTON, • • • N. C.

Sunday School and Christian Endeavor

SUNDAY SCHOOL LESSON FOR DECEMBER 14, 1919

(Mrs. Fred Bullock)

At the Trial and Crucifixion of Jesus.—John 18:15-27; 19:25-27.

Golden Text: "God so loved the world that he gave his only begotten Son, that whosoever believeth in him should not perish, but have eternal life."

How easy to falter in loyalty. How hard to remain firm. Peter, the "rockman," Peter who had declared that though all others should forsake Jesus, he would be true, to be driven from his allegiance by a servant girl! Was he afraid for his life? Perhaps. He had never learned to make a great resolve and stick to it. One day he says: "Thou art the Christ of God," the next he is ready to rebuke this Christ, and teach Him what to say and do. One day he loudly declares his loyalty, one night he cannot even stay awake. He seizes his sword, with the valiant intent to cut off a head, and—snags an ear. And now, a sneer, a laugh perhaps, from the servants gathered around the fire, and Peter is consumed with fear. One of the devil's best weapons has always been a laugh. Many a one who would have dauntlessly faced a sword has fled from a laugh. What Peter missed, and what he received He missed the nearness to His Lord, His final words, His last commission; he received a look—a look which broke his heart, and his pride, and his fire which we may believe, completed his education, hardened his rock-mass into a solid concrete, as it were, and made him fit for a stone in the Temple of God. John, quiet, dependable, loving, whose fiery temper had fused every element of his nature into a burning crucible of love for Jesus, so soon as he knew Him, John makes no boasts, but he *stands by*, too close to Jesus to meet the sneers, or to heed them. He goes with Him all the way, and when the spirit departs from the divine Body, it is into the keeping of John that Jesus bestows His dearest human possession, His mother.

CHRISTIAN ENDEAVOR TOPIC FOR DECEMBER 14, 1919

(J. Vincent Knight)

"How to Use The Bible."—Psalms 19:7-11, Matt. 4:1-4.

There are many ways in which the Bible is used. Some people use it roughly; use it as a dust pad, a relic, family record, or never at all unless the preacher comes. I know a woman who once brushed the dust from her Bible with her apron and handed it to the preacher. It opened seemingly of its own accord at the 23rd. Psalm. Why? One year previous to that time she had lost her glasses, and had searched the place for them with no avail. "O my, there are my glasses right where you left them last year," and when that was said she revealed two things. First that she had not used her Bible for the year, second, that no preacher had used it for her in a year. I know another family who lets the baby play with the Bible to keep it quiet. Fine toy! Much better is the Bible than a pack of cigarettes, or a Prince Albert box.

To use the Bible right, we should use it daily, for we need its daily message. The best time is the morning hour, before our minds are crowded with the affairs of the day. If we cannot use that hour, we should never let a day pass without using it, for when we do, God is speaking to us. Then, we should use it in a practical way. Simply reading it is not sufficient. We should practice it in ourselves and others. Then too, we should use it in cases of emergency. A man once said, "The biggest blunder America ever made was when she sent missionaries to Japan." His daughter heard his words, and quoted Jno. 3:16, and Mark 16:16, to which he never replied.

Suggestions

A fine meeting for the Comrades of the Quiet Hour. It should be lead by that Committee, and special work assigned to each. Have a contest, and call for Bible quotations, and help the members get the habit of memorizing the Scripture. Form a memory club, and let the juniors and intermediates into the club.

Some Questions

What value is Bible study in one's business or professional career? What influence does Bible study have on the student life of our own country? Why should we memorize Scriptural passages each day? Is it right to study the Bible for argument's sake?

GRADED INSTRUCTION

It is not possible to make your school a Standard School if you have no graded instruction. By graded instruction, is meant using the Graded Lessons in at least the Primary and Junior departments. It means having a lesson suited to the needs of the child. All of the Scriptures are suited for instruction, all are necessary, but all are not possible of understanding at every age. Our Father, when He wished to reveal His truth began with simple facts, with definite "Thou shalt's" and "Thou shalt not's." You will find little of explanation, or of reasoning in the early books of the Bible. You will find much of illustrative material, showing by a life, rather than by a precept, the right and the wrong way. Consequently, the early stories of God's dealing with His people, and the story of the greatest life of all, are most fitted for the comprehension of a child. It takes an adult mind to understand the teachings of Paul, which even Peter admitted were "hard to be understood." When we try to teach them to children, simplify them as we may, we find ourselves in deep waters.

The Graded Lessons, then, are simply a series of lessons prepared by those who have made a study of children of various ages, and have selected from God's Word, the parts best fitted for the comprehension of the child at various ages, and have planned for the teacher a method of telling this lesson story in such a manner as to best present it to the mind of the scholar. Why not give them a trial in your school, help the child to love the Word of God, aid the teacher in preparing her lesson, raise the standard of your school, and meet the requirements of the Sunday school department of your church?

MRS. FRED BULLOCK.

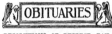

OBITUARIES

RESOLUTIONS OF RESPECT—TAYLOR

God in His infinite wisdom has seen fit to take from our midst our beloved sister, Mrs. Martha Taylor, removing her from this world of sorrow and suffering to a place of eternal joy and peace.

Her quiet fortitude in the midst of her suffering, and the calm acceptance of the Master's will, expressed a sincere devotion to her Creator. She was at all times interested in the Church and its work, and it was her earnest desire to be of help.

Therefore, we, the Ladies' Aid Society and the Home and Foreign Missionary Society of the Portsmouth, Va. Christian church do hereby offer the following resolutions:

1. That by her fortitude and courage she has set us an example by which we shall be enabled to do more and better work for the Kingdom of God.

2. That we have been blessed by having her with us, and her Christ-like life shall ever be, one of our sweetest memories.

3. That we extend our sincere sympathy to the bereaved family and commend them to the all-wise Father for comfort and consolation.

4. That a copy of these resolutions be sent to the family, a copy be spread on the records of our Societies, and a copy be sent to The Christian Sun for publication.

MRS. J. C. ELLIS,
MRS. D. P. RAWLES,
MRS. S. P. GORT,
Committee.

WILLIAMSON

Reps Williamson, Sr., son of Edward Franklin and Martha Ann Williamson, was born in Nottaway County, Va., February 22, 1855, and died at his home in Nansemond County, Va., October 15, 1919, at the age of sixty-four years, seven months, and twenty-one days. On April 29, 1874, he married Miss Adelia Jones, who survives him. Unto them were born nine children, six of whom are living: Mrs. Martha Emma Atkinson, Elon College, N. C., William Thomas Williamson of Norfolk, Reps Williamson, Jr., Norfolk County, Mrs. Mary Regina Warrington, of Driver, Va., Fred Connelly Williamson

of Georgia, and Mrs. Janet Adelia Savage of Norfolk, Va. There are six living grandchildren: Miss Jennie Willis Atkinson, Miss Mary Adelia Atkinson, James Oscar Atkinson, Jr., Emma Williamson Atkinson, John Hall Williamson, and Ada Thomas Williamson. Three sisters also survive him: Mrs. Lucy Darden, Mrs. Mattie Harrell, and Mrs. Annie Whitley.

Brother Williamson was a faithful member of Berea (Nansemond) Christian church. He served as treasurer for a long period of years. He was especially fond of music. Partial deafness gradually deprived him of this pleasure for several years. During the last few months he frequently went to church without hearing a word during the service. He was a man of many friends, and it was a great loss to him when he could not freely have conversation as in former years. He was stricken with paralysis just a few days before the end came. He regained consciousness, and talked freely about his willingness to submit to the will of God. He expressed himself as being ready for his departure. The funeral service was conducted at Berea church, and the burial made in Cedar Hill cemetery, Suffolk, Va. He was a man whose presence will be greatly missed, in many fields of civic and religious, as well as social activity. His life was a personal contribution of good cheer and uplift to many friends.

I. W. JOHNSON.

DAUGHTREY

Allen Daughtrey, son of Joshua and Priscilla Daughtrey, was born in Isle of Wight Co., Va., September 15, 1840. He was twice married, first to Miss Martha E. Norfleet, on June 13, 1867. Unto this union there are five surviving children: Mrs. Eva L. Daughtrey, Mrs. J. D. Johnson, Miss Lydia Daughtrey, W. A. Daughtrey, and J O. H. Daughtrey. His second marriage was to Miss Sarah Cornelia Rawles, on March 6, 1889. One son survives this marriage: Braxton R. Daughtrey. He leaves besides his widow and six children, fourteen grandchildren and nine great grandchildren. He volunteered and joined Barham's Cavalry in the Confederate forces during the Civil War. In 1865 he united with Hebron Christian church, in which he was elected as deacon and served as secretary for many years. He was a member of the Committee which moved the church to Holland, and remained an active member

and deacon of the Holland church until his death. He never missed but one quarterly conference of his church in a period of fifty years. He died in Franklin, Va., November 20, 1919, at the age of seventy-nine years, two months and five days. The funeral was conducted from the residence on Friday, November 21, 1919, by Rev. I. W. Johnson, assisted by Revs. J. L. Lawless, and W. M. Jay He had a large circle of friends who admired his sterling character and devoted Christian life. One sister, Mrs. Elizabeth Norfleet, and one brohter, Ely Daughtrey, also survive him. A good man has gone to his reward.

I. W. JOHNSON.

INGLE

Mrs. Elizabeth Ingle departed this life at her home near Burlington, N. C., November 25, 1919, in her eighty-fifth year.

Mrs. Ingle was twice married. Her first husband was Daniel Sharpe; her second was Mebane Ingle; both of whom preceded her to the grave.

She leaves one daughter, Mrs. E. J. Bryan, six grandchildren, and nine great-grandchildren.

She was a member of New Providence Christian church and had been for about fifty years.

The funeral services were conducted from the home of the writer and the interment was in Pine Hill cemetery, Burlington, N. C.

May the dear Master comfort those who mourn.

P. H. FLEMING.

WISE AND OTHERWISE

Just Good Enough for the Editors

A good old scout living north of town came in Saturday and handed us a dollar for his subscription. "Take it," he said, "I can't buy anything with it any more."—*From the Siloam Springs Herald.*

"Yes, they sometimes launder the soiled money at the treasury." "Can you tell me where they hang it out?"—*Louisville Courier-Journal.*

"I understand that Mrs. Sharp was not satisfied with her doctor's treatment." "No; so when he asked to see her tongue, she gave him a piece of it."—*Baltimore American.*

Mrs. Brown was at the back of the church, waiting to have her baby Christened. Baby was getting restless, so she beckoned to the verger. "Is the sermon nearly finished?" she whispered. "No, mum," replied the verger, "another half-hour of it yet. He's only on his 'lastly.'" "Bust," said Mrs. Brown, "will it take him half an hour to get through his 'lastly'?" "No, mum," was the demure reply, "but there's the one more word and I'm done,' and the 'finally,' and the 'in conclusion' to come yet. Don't be impatient."—*London Tit-Bits.*

"Come upstairs and let me wash your hands," said mother. "I don't want to go," wailed Alice, aged three. "Let her wash them down here," called grandma; "she can do it here just as well." "No," her mother said firmly, "I want her to come up with me." Alice came as slowly as she could. "O," she howled, turning a wrathfully, tearful face to her mother, "why don't you obey your mother?"—*Harper's Magazine.*

First Citizen—"You can't stop a man from thinking!" Second Ditto—"No, the difficulty is to start him!"—*Chicago News.*

"When water becomes ice," asked the teacher, "what is the great change that takes place?" "The greatest change, ma'am," said the little boy, "is the change in price."

THE CHRISTIAN SUN

"IN ESSENTIALS UNITY, IN NON-ESSENTIALS LIBERTY, IN ALL THINGS CHARITY"

REV. W. M. JAY, A. M., B. D., Pastor
Holland, Virginia, Christian Church.

Volume LXXI	WEDNESDAY, DECEMBER 10, 1919	Number 50
BURLINGTON	· · ·	NORTH CAROLINA

THE CHRISTIAN SUN

Founded 1844 by Rev. Daniel W. Kerr

C. B. RIDDLE - - - - Editor

Entered at the Burlington, N. C. Post Office as second class matter.

Subscription Rates

One year .... $ 2.00
Six months 1.00

In Advance

Give both your old and new postoffice when asking the your ad
dress be changed.

The change of your label is your receipt for money. If mails re
ceipts sent upon request.

Many persons subscribe for friends, intending that the , or be
stopped at the end of the year. If instructions are given to its effect
they will receive attention at the proper time.

Marriage and obituary notices not exceeding 150 words printed free
if received within 60 days from date of event, all over that at the
rate of one-half cent a word.

Original poetry not accepted for publication.

Principles of the Christian Church

(1) The Lord Jesus Christ is the only Head of the Church.
(2) Christian is a sufficient name of the Church.
(3) The Holy Bible is a sufficient rule of faith and practice.
(4) Christian character is a sufficient test of fellowship, and of church membership.
(5) The right of private judgment and the liberty of conscience is a right and a privilege that should be accorded to, and exercised by all.

EDITORIAL

EDITORIAL JOTTINGS

These are days when things are overflowing. Money is plentiful, work is abundant, and resources unlimited. Not often does the Editor of THE CHRISTIAN SUN have an overflow of editorials to suit his convenience, for the lack of time to prepare them. He does, however, have an inconvenient number of topics on his note book for comment. Occasionally he must have a "closing out" season and begin a new page. Such is the case with us now. We have more topics than we have space to treat them, and so we take this issue to give a few side-lights on things and jottings that we have made note of, but cannot go into detail about.

It is noticeable that certain words do not please the ear of the true worshipper. "Drive," "Campaign," "Over the Top," and such expressions have come into a very prominent place in our language through war-time measures and methods. These words have found their way into church activities and, at first, were popular. We note that deep spiritual thinkers are protesting against their usage too much, when in connection with the church.

We note in modern church architecture that the bell is being omitted. We have no definite reasons for this, but presume it is being considered that worship should be so much a part of a man's life that he should know the hour for worship just as he knows when to go to his office, place of business, or farm. If this line of thought be the right one, it seems plausible, and we endorse it. On the other hand, we like to hear the sound of the church bell. It reminds us of our privilege and duty; it reminds the non-church goer that religious services are to be held; it is a reminder that God's institution is set up in our midst. "Ding—dong." Give us the bell.

A woman has been elected to the Parliament of England, and New York is honored with a woman judge in her courts. Public opinion approves and the cause of Woman Suffrage goes on to victory. All of us do not see alike about this cause, but woman is coming into her own; and as she comes she is demonstrating her worth.

We wonder at times if it is best to always be talking about a "new age," for while we can rightly call it a "new age," it is only an advanced age. To call it a "new age" is to leave the thought that the past age is separated from the present, whereas to say advanced age leaves the idea of constant growth and not separation.

Many persons are now worried over the condition of the country and think that the devils is dragging the world to hell. As we see it, the pessimistic see the situation this way. God is ruling and things will come out all right. Don't worry.

It is fitting that the first week in each year is Prayer Week for the nation. It is a consoling thought that this nation of ours, though imperfect, is uniting for larger and greater things for Christ. When you discuss the query: "Resolved, That the world is growing better," put us down on the affirmative.

We hear much about "waking up" about things these days as if we have been "asleep" on certain things. "There is more truth than poetry" in these expressions, and we really wonder how we once got along with former methods. "Our one great need— THE CHRISTIAN SUN in every home," has behind it this fact and idea: where the largest circulation of the Church paper is found, there the Church as a whole receives its best support. The first Methodist area to raise its quota of the $80,000,000 fund was where the leading paper of that denomination had the largest circulation. If we had a pastorate and wanted to get the salary raised, we would get the Church publications into the homes; if we wanted to increase in any direction this would be the method.

Labor seems to be in the saddle these days, but we fear that it is riding too fast. Labor has an opportunity of gaining prestige, but if it keeps on it is going to bring disgust and retard its own progress many years. It is getting to be radical. We deem that a man is within his own rights to stop work, but he has no right to prevent another man from working. Labor and capital must get together—and they will.

* *

As the Christmas season draws near, the wheels of progress speed up and time is marked by the Christmas date. No event in the world's history has ever been able to have the same effect on the nations of the earth—and no event ever will, at this season of the year. We do not say so many days till the end of the month, or the end of the year, but so many days till Christmas. The date is greater than any month, year, or the beginning of any year. The way and manner in which we recognize the date is the greatest testimony of what Christ really means to the world.

* *

World events are happening so fast that it is a problem to make any definite statement for fear that the statement will be changed before you have put it into form. We have found it difficult. to write up the events of the day as they happen, because the next day's events would change what we had written. For this reason general notes have been scarce in these columns of late.

— — — — — — — — — — — — — —

Holland's New Church Building

DEDICATION OF HOLLAND CHRISTIAN CHURCH,
SUNDAY, DECEMBER 14, AT 3 P. M. .

(Reprinted from Suffolk, (Va.) Herald)

The Holland Christian Church is an outgrowth of the old Hebron church, formely located at Carrsville, in Isle of Wight county.

A committee consisting of Allen Daugherty, Eli Daugherty, Jas. H. Butler and Rev. R. H. Holland, was appointed at the September conference of the church 1890 for the purpose of choosing a suitable location.

Holland was the choice of the Committee which reported October 27, of the same year.

The building at Holland was erected out of the timbers of the old Hebron church; Mr. J. E. Daughtrey, a member of the church being the chief carpenter and builder.

The late Rev. R. H. Holland, father of Dr. Job G. Holland, now a resident of this place, was the founder and organizer of the Hebron church and served its pastor from the date of organization 1853 to 1877.

He was followed by Revs. C. J. Ralston, J. T. Kitchen, W. M. Butler, H. C. Moore, R. A. Ricks, and C. C. Peele, when Rev. R. H. Holland was again called as pastor in 1890, the year before the removal of the church to Holland. He served the church at Holland till March 1892 and was followed by the Revs. R. D. H. Demarest, J. W. Rawls, W. S. Long, D. D., W. J. Lane, I. W. Johnson, N. G. Newman, B. F. Black and W. M. Jay, the present pastor, who was called to this field September 1, 1918.

Dr. I. W. Johnson, of Suffolk, Va.; Dr. N. G. Newman, of Elon College, N. C.; and Rev. B. F. Black, of Franklinton, N. C., are the only living ex-pastors. All three are expected to be present at the dedication services. Dr. Newman will preach in the morning and. Dr. Johnson will preach at night. ·

The dedication sermon will be delivered by Dr. J. O. Atkinson, of Elon College, N. C.

The building was started under the labors of Rev. B. F. Black who resigned to go to France as an army chaplain.

R. H. Reidel, master carpenter and builder worked faithfully at his task and had the building ready to be opened for worship on the second Sunday of July, last.

The building is a credit to the town and community and in keeping with the spirit of progress and desire for the best, characteristic people of this thriving little town.

The building is of pressed brick on all sides with stone trimming. The Sunday school apartments, kitchen and furnace room are below; above are the main auditorium, seating about 500 comfortably, a gallery, pastor's study room, choir room and other modern conveniences.

The pipe organ was purchased by the Ladies' Aid Society and recently presented to the church with appropriate ceremony.

The entire indebtedness of the building has been securely underwritten.

The dedication services will be held Sunday, December 14, at 3 P. M. The public is cordially invited.

REV. A. T. BANKS MEETS WITH ACCIDENT

We learn that Rev. A. T. Banks, Ramseur, N. C., met with a painful accident December 3 by getting shot in the arm. He was out hunting when the accident occurred. We understand that no bones were broken. We hope for Brother Banks a speedy recovery.

PASTOR AND PEOPLE

FROM BROTHER H. H. BUTLER'S FIELD

Union

Owing to sickness in my home, my little granddaughter, Sarah Butler Saunders, being confined to bed for two months or more with typhoid fever during my revival work, I could not be at Union. Dr. W. W. Staley, of Suffolk, Va., who is really a great preacher as well as a great and good man, held the meeting for me, and God blessed his work. There were many conversions and fifteen united with the church. They are good working people at Union. May the Lord continue to bless those people of that dear old church.

Antioch

The work at Antioch is progressing well. I could be there only a few days during the revival meeting. We had a fine meeting, thirty or forty conversions and renewals. Thirty-two united with the church. Dr. C. H. Rowland, of Franklin, Va., who is a fine preacher, and greatly beloved by all who know him, conducted the meeting. God blessed his work abundantly and the old church was greatly strengthened. God bless Brother Rowland and may he live many years to preach the gospel of our Lord Jesus. May the Lord continue to bless us at this grand old mother church. It was there the pastor was born, and from that old church many have gone out to preach the blessed Christ. May God help the people and pastor to live nearer and to do more for the building up of the Kingdom of the blessed Christ.

H. H. BUTLER.

INGRAM—PLEASANT GROVE

We are beginning our new church year in this pastorate by giving thanks for the old year and its great blessings. The members and pastor have much for which they may give thanks. Even the errors we have made and the disappointments we have had may, by giving heed thereto, be turned into channels of blessings. Taking all things into consideration, the year's annual yield has been abundant. And each of us must realize that a full hand is often as great a test of our goodness as one that is almost empty.

The young men of Pleasant Grove have organized for the purpose of developing themselves socially, mentally, and spiritually. They are undertaking to do something worth while for themselves and for their church, to which they are all devoted. Brother P. W. Farmer has offered his parlor as a place of meeting and Mrs. D. Jennings Sipe furnished it with chairs, tables, etc. Meetings are held every Friday evening at 7:30 under supervision of the pastor.

Rev. R. F. Brown assisted the pastor and people of Ingram church and community in a series of evangelistic services. His messages were forceful, spiritual, and thoughtful. At the close of the meeting three members were received into the church. The meeting was of such a nature as to give us a good beginning for the present year.

The Thanksgiving services—at Pleasant Grove in the forenoon and at Ingram in the afternoon—were more largely attended than usual. No less than five denominations participated actively in the services at Ingram. Pleasant Grove is to have another special service tomorrow—the fifth Sunday—at which time the offering to the Orphanage will be made.

JOHN G. TRUITT.

News Ferry, Va.

A WORD FROM WASHINGTON

Rev. A. B. Kendall, D. D., the pastor of our Washington congregation, writes under date of November 25 of the work in Washington most hopefully. Among other items from Dr. Kendall are these:

"We have some very fine people here with whom I have come in contact since my arrival. If we can line them all up with the church, we shall have a corps of workers of which any man may be proud. We had twenty of our people out at our first public service, three of whom were visitors. Last Sunday we had nineteen, but some were ill and some were out of the city over Sunday, so that we felt it was a distinct gain. We have organized our Sunday school with Brother Irving Hitchcock as superintendent. At present we are holding our meetings in Perpetual Hall down town, meeting at 10:30 A. M., with the Sunday school in session and merging into the preaching service at 11:15. The leading members here seem anxious that a temporary building be erected at once. This would certainly have many advantages as we would plunge at once into a campaign in the community where we expect to do our work. We have not really organized the church as yet, as I thought it best first of all to get as many of our people as possible to sign a covenant that we might know who our members really are. We are still receiving names of our people, four having come in within a week. We have at present just sixty names of people who ought to be identified with our work here. At last I have found a place in which to live, and a very satisfactory one for the time being at least."

If any readers of THE CHRISTIAN SUN know of members of the Christian Church, past, present or prospective, living in Washington, will they not kindly send same either to this writer or to Rev. A. B. Kendall, D. D., 801 Allison Street, Washington, D. C.?

The pity is that we did not begin to work in Washington years ago but now that we have begun we shall hope, labor and pray that the Christian denomination will do the right, the good and the great thing in our national Capital. The city is growing very rapidly and it is as much the duty and the privilege of the Christian Church to have a part in the religious activity of the great center as it is that of any other evangelical Church.

J. O. ATKINSON.

HIGH POINT

Promptly at 10:00 A. M., Thursday, November 27, 1919, the congregation of the High Point church gathered for a Thanksgiving service. Everybody seemed to be happy and thankful for the blessings of the past and glad of the opportunity of assembling for a Thanksgiving service. Each one present gave some expression of gratitude to our Heavenly Father.

The envelopes for the Orphanage Offering at this appointed time had been previously distributed. During the closing part of the program this offering was taken which amounted to $34.50 and perhaps more to follow.

L. L. WYRICK, *Pastor.*

FOUNDED

After the Thanksgiving service at High Point, Brother R. C. Boyd requested everybody to go to the Sunday school room that the members wanted to see the pastor and his wife there. To our great surprise there was a large pile of packages of various sizes. Brother Boyd acting as toastmaster presented the packages in behalf of the church as a pounding for us.

In the midst of unspeakable gladness we tried to utter a few feeble words of our appreciation for this great kindness to us on Thanksgiving Day. We were overwhelmed because of joy. It was good to be there. This we shall long remember being the first "pounding" and May God bless each one who had a part.

The items were: Meat, flour, sugar, coffee, jelly and preserves, sweet potatoes, apples, meat, canned corn, syrups, kraut, raisins, candy, soda, cocoa, butter, canned tomatoes, cereal, cheese, canned fruit and many others. We are indebted to Brother J. E. Bost and wife for bringing the "pounding" and us home in his car.

This is a good people to serve. May the Lord make us more efficient for service and help me to be a better pastor. Thanks many times to one and all. To the Lord belongeth all the praise and glory.

L. L. WYRICK & WIFE.

Elon College, N. C.

SUFFOLK LETTER

The country home is the unit of the nation, the citadel of American democracy. Its individuality, its separateness, its independence, is its power. It represents government, business, society, and religion. It is simple, to be sure, but it is genuine. There is less of the conventional and artificial, and more of the real in thought, sentiment, service, and character, than anywhere else among men. There is more time for brooding over great questions, more opportunity for personal characteristics to develop than in the centers where time is lost in activity and individuality is lost in the community.

The tendency, in these days, is away from the country into the towns and cities. The soil no longer appeals to the young. The young men seem unwilling to follow the plow and the young women seem unwilling to keep a country home. This is unfortunate for the future of the state and the church. When Jesus "beheld the city He wept over it," and well He might, for it was the city that rejected Him and crucified Him. The peril of human society and civilization had always been the city. Babylon, Jerusalem, Rome, are witnesses to the tragedy of fallen civilizations. Scientists

have worked out the alarming result that the family life is unknown in the city after the fifth generation. The blood of the city, if that is true, must be supplied by the country. Whatever ministers to rural life ministers to the welfare and destiny of the nation. The hope is that good roads, good schools, good churches, good prices for garden, orchard, and farm products will preserve the love of Americans for the country, because democracy cannot thrive in great cities. The few rule in great cities, no matter what *form* of government exists. Democracy has its seat of power in the thinking people of the country. The multitudes have no time to think for themselves in great cities. In the great stores, the great factories, the great hotels, the great offices, perfect organizations locate the thousands in their places as parts of great machines. There is no necessity for individual thought—the *thinkers* think for all. In the country it is not so. Individuals *think* in the country. The leaders in the cities grew up in the country, formed habits in the country, cultivated aspirations and ambitions in the country, and then developed their places in the cities.

The relation between the city and the country should be such as to maintain justice and reciprocity between the two, and not to build up the one at the expense of the other. Cities have been too much disposed to exploit the tillers of the soil by controlling markets in the interest of traders. Rural delivery, automobiles, larger intercourse, and new conditions have corrected, in some measure, this injustice and rural population is coming more into its own. Many inventions adopted to country conveniences have also added to the comfort of rural life. The time will no doubt come when electric wires will be within reach of the average country home for lights in house and barn, with power enough to saw wood, cut feed, churn milk, iron clothes, and render work a pleasure instead of a burden. Then country life will be the luxury of society and the haven of happiness. I almost envy the farmer in the next generation going to an electric-lighted, electric-heated church, in an electric-motored machine. This and more will come, if this generation hold fast to God and maintain, with increasing interest, the cause for which Jesus died.

W. W. STALEY.

WHEN IT RAINS IT POURS, SOMETIMES AT LEAST

When I was in Columbus, Ga., last summer, I noticed that the church pulpit had only an Oxford Teacher's Bible. There was no objection to that in itself, but it seemed to me that a pulpit Bible was needed. During September I was in Virginia, and chanced to speak of the fact in the presence of some friends, when Mr. E. L. Everett of our Berea (Nansemond County) Christian church, asked me how much I wished I told him. He immediately handed me the money with which I should purchase a pulpit Bible for the Rose Hill Christian church in the City of Columbus, Ga., for which he has the thanks of both pastor and people.

A little later, I received a notice from Brother Jas. H. Blanchard of our Third Christian church, Norfolk, Va., saying that he had ordered a fine pulpit Bible to be sent to the Rose Hill Christian church from the Christian Publishing Association, Dayton, Ohio. A few days later that, too, came and it is indeed a fine Bible and also just suited to the needs of the pastor while he is in the pulpit. It is printed on India paper and handsomely bound, very light and handy. I found inscribed on the fly-leaf of this Bible the following:

Compliments of the Third Christian Church, Norfolk, Va. A Gift to the Columbus (Georgia) Christian church, as a token of esteem for their pastor, Rev. J. P. Barrett, D. D., and in recognition of the good work our brethren are trying to carry on.

Both pastor and people highly appreciate these valuable gifts and send most hearty thanks to these dear friends.

At the Rose Hill Christian church, Columbus, Ga., on the evening of November 27, 1919, we took a Thanksgiving offering for the Christian Orphanage at Elon College, N. C. Though the church is both young and poor, it gave for that good work the sum of $112.05, and it did it with such a hearty good will that every one present seemed happy over the gift for the good work in which our brother, Mr. Chas. D. Johnston, is leading so well. The Columbus church really enjoyed giving to this good work.

J. PRESSLEY BARRETT, Pastor.

MISSIONARY

MISSIONARY NOTES

China and India and Africa are poor, and their people do perish from hunger, poverty and want by the millions. All this because we have not made known to them their legacy. We keep them poor. Our Christ left a legacy that would have made them great and wonderful and rich. But we Christians withhold that legacy from them. Christ said "Go tell." But we neither go nor tell; as is our duty and our privilege.

General S. C. Armstrong once asked this pointed question: "What are Christians in the world for but to achieve the impossible by the help of God?"

Who can answer *that* question?

Missionary Sunday Schools

The number of schools entering the missionary column increases with the weeks. I am just in receipt of a letter from which this is taken:

"You may put Bethlehem (Nansemond County, Virginia) Sunday school down as a missionary Sunday school. We have decided again to give a portion of our collections for missions. I was elected Mission Leader to give a four-minute talk on missions every Sunday morning. I want you to pray that I may be able to do or say something that will make our people at dear old Bethlehem see the need of more mission work and that they will give more to send the gospel where it is needed.

"At our last Ladies' Aid, after much thought and prayer, we decided to have a Woman's Missionary Society. We have organized with eighteen members. I

beg you to pray for us to be a real Missionary Society in work and in prayer. We have started this great work and I am praying it will do great good."

This is from Sister J. E. Harris, R. F. D., Suffolk, Virginia, and it means that missionary interests will grow in the Bethlehem church. It was a man of wide observation and experience who wrote that it only required one heart aflame in a community with missionary zeal to kindle the missionary fire in any Sunday school, church or community. Sister Harris is deeply interested, as many others of our women are coming to be in the various Sunday schools, churches and communities.

Inspiration

Our General Mission Board in annual session at Dayton, Ohio, adopted the following which is very much appreciated and which ought to serve as a source of inspiration to the brotherhood of the Southern Convention:

"Resolved: "That we learn with pleasure concerning the increasing interest in and giving for missionary work by the Southern Christian Convention as evidenced in the new and larger goal just set by our missionary workers there, viz: $500,000 to be secured in cash and pledges, within three years from this date for home and foreign missions. We hope this faith and vision may be not only blessed of God and that this goal may not only be reached, but that in so doing it shall be an inspiration to every other section of our brotherhood."

J. O. ATKINSON.

SUNDAY SCHOOL MISSIONARY WORKERS

It rejoices this writer very much to learn that a number of our teachers in the Sunday schools are creating interest in missions among their pupils. We are told that the reason why the Methodist Episcopal Church was able to put on a campaign for $80,000,000.00 mostly for missions was due to the fact that that great body of religious workers resolved fifty years ago that every Sunday school should be a missionary society. This is not a bad resolution and one which it is devoutly hoped may be adopted by every Christian Sunday school in the land.

We note with pleasure that Mrs. H. E. Roane, formerly Miss Sallie Morrison, has charge of the missionary work in the adult department of the Rosemont Sunday school, and that Sister O. S. Mills has charge in the junior department of the missionary work. We predict now that the Rosemont Sunday school will be heard from as a real missionary factor in the future.

We were in Dover, Delaware, Sunday the 30th ult., and Miss Helen A. Wise was elected Superintendent of Missions for their Sunday school and we were assured that Miss Wise would do her part in making the Delaware school a real missionary factor. This school also decided to give one Sunday a month offering for the Orphanage and one Sunday a month offering for missions; a program which many schools are adopting and which seems to us most fitting indeed.

J. H. Fogleman—THE CHRISTIAN SUN is fine and I enjoy it very much.

ENFORCING PROHIBITION

To the People of North Carolina:

The undersigned having been appointed Director of North Carolina under the Act of Congress to provide for the enforcement of Prohibition, desires to make known to the people of North Carolina his purposes and plans, and to appeal to them for the co-operation, sympathy and support without which he cannot reasonably entertain hope of success in the performance of the great task that he has undertaken.

In brief my task is to bring about, in conection with others hereinafter indicated, an end to the making of and the sale of intoxicating liquors in this State. This, I realize, is a great task, but it is not impossible of achievement. We are supported by the law of this State, and by the law and the Constitution of the United States. We have the expressed will of the people to rely upon. If we fail, our failure must be interpreted as the failure of the supreme law of the land. If we lose, the victory will be the triumph of the lawless over the State, the Republic and the Constitution; of the minority over the majority. We cannot afford to fail. Regardless of our views as to intoxicating liquors, all good citizens must agree that the law must be maintained and the Constitution kept violate. If we cannot maintain the Constitution, we cannot maintain our Republic.

I realize, and the Bureau of Internal Revenue realizes, that we cannot succeed in the above by the activity of Federal Officers. We shall not undertake to do so. We shall do all we can do, but we are ready to co-operate with the State and local officers and with all good citizens; and on the other hand, we feel that we are entitled to the co-operation of the State and local officers and all good citizens. One of my first endeavors will be to effect practical co-operation between the general public, the State, county and municipal officers, and the Federal officers. The task is too great for the Federal officers alone. We shall have about forty men operating in the State, under the supervision of S. R. Brame, Supervising Federal Prohibition Agent, Richmond, Va., but these forty men will have to depend upon the police in the towns, the sheriffs, the constables and deputy sheriffs, the State authorities, the Judges, the Solicitors and the Court; and also, and in no small measure, upon the good, patriotic men and women of the State. We shall seek the co-operation of the organized opposition to liquor business, the Anti-Saloon League, the Woman's Christian Temperance Union, and other Temperance or Prohibition organization. And last, but by no means least, of the Churches, the ministers, the church members, the newspapers and of every man or woman who believes in the majesty of the law and in the duty to enforce it.

We all must recognize that the condition in North Carolina is bad; it has been growing worse rather than better for two years; but it is not hopeless. On the other hand, I am encouraged to believe that by means of active public sentiment, a wholesome regard for the law, and the earnest co-operation of the great body of law-abiding people, we can win our war against the distiller and the liquor-seller within two years. All will depend upon the earnestness with which the rank and file of our people throw themselves into this cause. I ask the people to demand that any officer, whether Federal, State or local, charged with the maintenance and the enforcement of the law shall fully perform his duty. We must catch the distillers rather than their stills. We shall tolerate no half-dealings, no slack conduct, no questionable causes by the Federal officers. They are appointed on the merit system. They must make good or be cut off the pay-roll. Their records and their conduct wil be the test by which they will stand or fall. I ask the public to judge them by their records.

Information as to sales of liquor or the operations of distillers may be sent to me, at my address given below. Or they may be sent to Mr. Mr. S. R. Brame, Supervisor for this District, Richmond, Virginia; or to the squad leaders nearest you, of whom there are four, as follows: J. F. Lifsey, Norlina; H. G. Gulley, Raleigh, P. E. Dancy, North Wilkesboro; J. H. Reed, Asheville.

But I do not want you to send for Federal men, if your local men are doing their duty. They must not be slighted or offended. I know that many of them are diligent and trustworthy. I want you to try first the men directly responsible to you—your police, constables, sheriffs, and deputy sheriffs; and let them seek Federal assistance if they think it necessary.

Finally, I shall request the Judges and Solicitors to put the heaviest penalties compatible with justice upon any offender convicted, whether in State or Federal Courts. Heavy penalties are required by the conditions —the rapid spread of distillers and their increase through the State have shown us that penalties heretofore imposed are not sufficient.

I have great confidence in the people of North Carolina. The great maority of them believe in upholding the law and the Constitution. I shall rely upon them to give unreserved support to the object of this announcement. I shall look to them for information as to violations of the law. I shall respect their confidence, divulging no names without permission: I shall expect them to demand of the Federal Deputies and of County, State, and local officers the strictest account of their responsibilities. I have labored many years in the practical work of enforcing Revenue and Prohibition laws. I am entering upon my new relation in the earnest hope that I shall live to see this State free of the blight and the stigma, the disgrace and the demolition of the distilling and the selling of intoxicating liquors. And if I have a man's part in the achievement of this end, I shall ask no more. I shall be satisfied that my life has been justified by its fruits.

Respectfully,

T. H. VANDERFORD,

Federal Prohibition Director.

Salisbury, N. C.

The second industrial congress is in session at Washington this week and it is hoped that something may be done to harmonize the situation between Capital and Labor.

THE UNSEEN, THE UNHEARD, AND THE UNKNOWN

(Rev. J. T. Kitchen)

"Eye hath not seen, nor ear heard, neither hath entered into the heart of man, the things which God hath prepared for them that love him."—I Cor. 2-9.

If some one were to give you a good home far away and you were about to move there to live, the mind would be busy and the imagination very active thinking of the place, its location and surrounding. The imagination would be induced to paint a suitable location and surpassingly beautiful scenery until you would be charmed with such delightful contemplation. Your heart would beat with glad expectation, and swell with inexpressible delight and gratitude to him who made the gift, that he would be held in loving remembrance by you. Towering mountains fertile valleys, rushing rivers, extended plains, charming landscapes, and large forests are ahead of you as you think of the way lying so beautifully before you. With these attractions you are freely and pleasantly invited onward to your new home. With all this under consideration with the imagination playing a most lovely part in the act, the fatigue and danger incident to the journey are lost in the happiness which overflows the soul.

Jesus has provided and given you a home in His Father's house, and He invites you to live with Him there when you leave this world. It is no wonder that so many sermons are preached about this home of the soul; it is not out of place to hear so many fervent prayers offered to the Lord to help you on to this new home, nor is it strange to hear so many thrilling songs about it. The home which has been so beautifully described by many in all ages of the world—that home which has been the great theme of so many anxious ones; that home which has been so tenderly and lovingly described in the Bible itself, and that home which has inspired multitudes of wandering pilgrims. All the beauty and happiness of that home has never yet been told.

Before taking a long expected journey the mind and body had been actively engaged in surveying and preparing the way, and the imagination had been playing so delightfully pleasant as it ran over the way before you. The realization of heaven will be surpassingly greater than the imagination has pictured it. To imagine a stroll through flower gardens of rare beauty is pleasing to every one who dwells on these beautiful thoughts, but when the flight, the ramble, has been made and the imagination returns to you with no real flowers to inhale and no beauty to behold it is somewhat disappointing to you, but when you enter a conservatory or garden and look with eager attention at the different colored beauties which perfume the soft morning breeze, causing feeling of peaceful delight to completely possess your whole being, the experience gives inexpressible happiness. And just somehow in this way will heaven unfold to us as we may enter to gaze upon its unfading splendor, and to enjoy the music of the new song chanted forth in strains of eternal joy. We shall be like Him and see Him as He is.

This leads us to notice that; "Eye hath not seen." The human eye, what an interesting study to the specialist, and to all who think about this great provision and helpful privilege. It has its lenses, intricate and complicated parts designed and made for us to see what God has so wonderfully made and placed before an admiring gaze. Just think for a moment what a great, happy privilege it is to use the eye at will, and it is always ready for our use. It is both microscopic and telescopic and adjusts itself in quick succession to the needs and conditions demand, contracting so as to see the very smallest things, and then expanding to take in extended views and distant worlds. That which the eye has seen has so often filled the soul with intense delight and inexpressible joy. The gift and provision for seeing, who can estimate its value? How many appreciate to its fullest extent this one of God's greatest blessings to the children of men? To gaze upon the green fields; to take a look at the majestic forests; to behold lofty mountains; to gaze upon the ocean with its rolling waves dashing themselves to pieces on a rocky shore, to scan the starry sky, and to view nature with her loveliness, beauty and attraction is a splendid thing for any one to enjoy. When you see the blind your sympathy is drawn toward them at once, and you feel, what a great pity it is they cannot see the beautiful things spread out before them. You who can see are blessed with one of the greatest privileges of life. The writer of these thoughts once dreamed that he was blind, and that dream gave him much concern while dreaming it, but he received some comfort from the experience of having committed to memory many parts of the Bible, even whole chapters, and that helped relieve the sadness of the dream.

The eye is often very active for a whole day—even into night without resting—without closing itself to sleep. The intelligent eye, the active eye and the watchful eye, are seen and much admired. So closely connected with the brain that the thoughts and emotions which tremble within sparkle and flash quickly through this wonderful means of seeing. It is important, therefore, to cultivate purity, honesty, truthfulness and every other equality that is good so as to be seen and read by others while passing over the way.

While very many things of the world have been seen, there are things "which eye hath not seen." "For the things which are seen are temporal, but the things which are not seen are eternal." While it is but natural to look at the things of earth, try to look up and see by faith the things of fadeless splendor in the immortal state. Eye has not seen the beautiful city of God; it has not seen the shining streets; it has not seen the towering walls; it has not seen the great white throne, nor looked with delight upon Him who sits upon the throne; it has not seen the twelve gates; and it has not seen the bright convoy of angels flying with cherubic and seraphic beauty through the heavenly city. In visions of rapture the soul has often been delighted. By faith and imagination it has hovered near the throne, but the natural eye has not been permitted to look upon the things of that bright home.

Age and disease dim the eye, and the keen sight is often put out by different causes. When your grandmothers' eyes were dimmed, they could not see so well to thread the needle to sew and darn for you as once they could, and some of you remember how you used to thread it for them and how it pleased you to help them in this way.

The eyes which are dim and sightless here will see perfectly clear on the other side; for they shall see with undimmed beauty and with cloudless splendor "the things which God hath prepared for them who love him." Yes, the eye which saw so much to love and admire on earth—which gazed upon so many temporal things will see with greater clearness in the eternal life. Over the extended scenes of etrnity it will forever look upon the bright mansion of light.

Now, turn your attention for a while to the listening ear. But while listening we notice that part of the text which says, "Nor ear heard." The ear has already heard much, in many places, of the music of nature, it has listened to many of its tender and loving strains. The ear is a great and wonderful blessing made by our Father for the happiness of His creatures. It is a very delicate, but a most serviceable organ—the organ of sound made so as to catch the lowest whisper as well as the loudest sound and communicate it to the brain. When hearing glad or sad news how soon it changes the looks according· to the ·nature of the message received thus touching the· emotions at once with joy or sorrow. See that drum so finely constructed and surrounding the delicate internal structure to take in and hold the sounds as they surge and roll and waft into its chambers. How the joyful sounds light up the face with inexpressible emotions which gather in the soul! When the ·air rings with harsh unpleasant sounds how it scowls the face· and perverts the· features.

Listening ones, have you heard the voices of nature speaking and singing to you in their fullness and power? An answer from millions of glad voices may roll down the ways of time saying with deep heartfelt interest: ''We have enjoyed the music of nature in a wonderful way.'' The thunder rolling quickly·through space, and from cloud to cloud, charged with electric power, and bursting with awful grandeur, is one of nature's loud voices. When ·the ground has .been so dry for a long time when no rain has fallen for weeks, how very glad our ears have made our hearts, as they heard the first distant sound. It was a welcome messenger, forerunner of refreshing showers.

The voice of nature speaks to us in· the breathing, whistling, singing wind, and even amid tis terrific power we have often been made to fear and tremble. The voice of nature speaks to us in the dashing tones of the waterfalls as it pours its water over them with ceaseless grandeur. And it is also heard in the bounding waves of lakes and oceans. The storm rocked. passengers of the ocean have heard· its voice as they moved over·the deep way. Then in fearful agony many ·minds turn. ed to the Old Book where it says: ''God is our refuge and strength, * * * though the waters thereof roar and be troubled.'' Amid many of the revolutions and evolutions of nature, in times of great distress when whirlwinds swept things in their course, and earthquakes excited, the people, the ear listened and heard the noise of these mighty forces. Then· after hearing some of these things, this part of the text tells you that ''Ear hath not heard.'' It has· not heard the names of all the things which God has prepared for His faithful, loving children. It has not heard the song of the angels nor the splendid refrain of that new song.

You have friends who are very deaf—some of them cannot hear at all—and they have your sympathy. Some of them cannot· talk—they have not had the privilege of expressing themselves in telling how glad and happy· they were with profound· emotions which filled their·lives. They have not been permitted to· hear the music of earth, nor to express the rapture it gives.

Listen now and notice that, ''Neither have entered into the heart of man, the things which God hath prepared for them that jove Him.'' The heart, the great life pump of the body, causing the life giving blood to flow through it at every throb, thus causing us to move among the scenes ·of time. It has also been called the place of the affections, for how often have expressions like these been used: ''Glad heart,'' ''Sad heart,'' ''Tender heart,'' ''Loving heart,'' ''Faint heart.'' The heart is often filled with gladness and sadness, sometime too full to tell, and the feelings can only be told by the looks as they appear on the face or in the eye. Take good care of the heart, for out of it are the issues of life. It is so often touched with many different emotions which either give it strength or weakness. The heart is a wonderful provision to give and perpetuate life. The things which God has prepared for them that love Him have not yet fully entered the heart— they are too great for it now; it must be trained, used and developed here for greater, fuller and complete blessings. O, yes, the things, the things which God has prepared for them

that love Him!· The things. What are they? The text does not tell us what they are, they have not yet been told, be. ·ause they are too many for it now, they are too large for ·t now, they are too glorious for it now, and they are too heaven. ly for it now.

No, no, it has not entered into the heart of man, the things which our Father has so abundantly prepared for them that love Him. · ''The things.'' What are these nameless things? O, I do not know, but believe they will be things of joy and blessing forever. It may be fully believed that one of them will be a beautiful, everlasting home. A home in heaven is a most joyous thing to expect. I knew a poor sufferer who was confined· to his home for twenty years. He selected the hymns and the text he wanted to be used at his funeral. The text was: ''This poor man cried, and the Lord heard him, and saved him out of all his troubles.'' In his affliction he was pleasant and patient, talking much about Jesus and his home in heaven. He lived in an humble home here, but now he has gone to his final home—a home where poverty and sickness will never come. O, the blessedness of a home, the comfort and ease and joy in a good, peaceful home! Every one who has such a home here knows what it is. It is home, home, home. To feel that you have a home in your Father's house is a great, good thing; and it is comforting experience to be an heir of God, and hope to possess and live in this home. So many homeless ones I see and hear of· in this land, our sym. pathy is drawn toward them, but when the thought of a free and permanent home dwells in the mind, it ought to be very helpful to them as they journey on the way to it.

The next best thing which God has prepared for those that love Him .will be health. This is not a healthy world. Disease, sickness and death take hold of all conditions of peace; and they all enter the homes of plenty as well as those of poverty. Over this world many sick and suffering ones may be found, and ·they are trying hard both by faith and works to get well, strong and active again. To be so is their chief desire. ·They want to get out of that pale, emaciated, bent, withering and weak state, and to come into vigorous and healthy activity. All they possess would be freely given could they just get health and strength again.. If they could get to some fountain which gave lasting health they would spare no time nor means in getting to it, and would remain drink. ing until made whole. How the encouraged face would brighten under the touch of such joy and inspiration, and what a life of hope would fill the soul every day!

Another of these things will be happiness. Happy, forever happy. You may know by a short experience what a little happiness means here—what it is to get a foretaste of its matchless feeling. How it fills you with transport and inex. pressible delight as you run up the enchanting way which in. vites you onward. All classes and conditions of people are looking for happiness in life and they expect to realize it some day, and they are very anxious for the time to come when they can·exalt in the long expected joy. Even life here would be weary without the hope of happiness. ''If in this life we only· have hope in Jesus, we would be most miserable,'' but it extends beyond the vista of time and looks over into the realms of eternity.

Those who love God are promised great things. They have not yet entered into the heart of man—those wonderful and eternal things. Do you love God? From millions of voices may be heard the joyful answer: ''We love Him now, and we will love Him forever.''

WINDSOR, VA.

Principles and Government
of
The Christian Church

(The Franklin, Virginia, session of the Southern Christian Convention ordered that the Principles and Government of the Christian Church be revised and that a committee be appointed to make the revision. The following members of the Convention were appointed to do the work: Rev. W. W. Staley, D. D., President; Rev. W. S. Long, D. D., Rev. C. H. Rowland, D. D., Rev. N. G. Newman, D. D., and W. A. Harper, LL. D. Some weeks ago the committee completed its work, and we are privileged to print, in serial form, the Prneples and Government as outlned, subject to ratification by the next session of the Convention.—Editor.)

CHAPTER V
SECTION III
DUTIES OF OFFICERS

1. The President shall preside at all the meetings of the Convention, sign all the proceedings of the body, visit annual Conferences, and confer, counsel and advise with the brethren, and perform such other duties as his office may require. The Vice-President shall perform all the duties of the President in his absence or in case of death.

2. The Secretary shall duly record all the proceedings of the Convention, attest all its acts, take proper care of all documents, records, and writings belonging to the body, countersign all drafts on the Treasurer for the payment of money, and publish the time and place of meeting when directed to do so by the President.

3. The Treasurer shall receive all moneys for the Convention, keep an accurate account of all receipts and expenditures, pay money only on orders drawn by the President and countersigned by the Secretary; and at every regular session of the body make a full report in writing of all assets, receipts and expenditures.

SECTION IV
BUSINESS OF THE CONVENTION

1. The Convention shall have the supervision of all the general enterprises of the denomination within the bounds of the Conferences of which it is composed.

2. The Convention shall appoint a Board, consisting of five, on *Publications*, whose duty shall be to provide suitable matter for reading and religious instruction, carefully examine all manuscripts and other matter designed to be published by the Convention, provide for the publication of a religious newspaper, to be issued weekly, as the organ of the Convention; provide suitable Sunday school literature, and shall be governed by such rules and regulations as the Convention may prescribe. The Board shall continue in office for two years, or until its successor is appointed; and shall make a full and complete report in writing, at each regular session of the body. The Convention should place at the disposal of the Board sufficient means to give success to the publishing interests of the Convention.

3. *A Board of Education*, consisting of five, shall be appointed, whose duty it shall be to examine all plans and projects for the establishment of schools and colleges, and to devise means and suggest ways by which the educational needs of the Convention may be supplied. This Board shall be appointed for two years, and be governed by rules and regulations prescribed by the Convention, and report in writing, at every regular session of the body.

4. A Mission Board of ten members shall be elected, five to represent Home Missions, and five to represent Foreign Missions; this Board shall have charge and control of the Home and Foreign Mission affairs of the Convention, and make a full report of their work to the Convention in its regular sessions.

5. Standing Committees shall be appointed on Evangelism, Social Service, and other subjects that require mature deliberation, with such duties as the Convention may prescribe.

6. The Convention shall elect a Board of ten members on Religious Education, five to represent the Sunday School Department and five to represent the Christian Endeavor Department; and this Board shall have charge of the Religious Education of the Convention.

7. The Convention shall have an *Executive Board,* of three, consisting of the President, who shall be Chairman, ex-officio, and two other members, elected by the Convention, to whom shall be referred all matters of business which require attention between the sessions of the body. This committee shall report in full its work biennially.

8. The Convention shall devise plans for raising funds to prosecute successfully the various enterprises under its control.

9. All difficulties arising in the local Conferences may be carried, by appeal, to the Convention, whose decision shall be final.

10. The Convention shall determine the boundaries of the local conferences.

11. For the division of existing conferences, or the formation of new ones, application shall be made to the Convention; and when the good of the cause demands the division of an old conference, a division may be ordered, or a new conference may be formed, when a number of ministers and churches, sufficient to give influence and perpetuity to the cause, are widely separated from any other Christian conference.

(To be Continued)

The fuel situation continues to be critical. Both sides are contending, while most of the mines are idle. Wartime restrictions are being put into operation for the conservation of coal. Railroads are cutting off many trains and the general public is being greatly inconvenienced.

The Department of Agriculture assisted the Census Bureau in preparing the list of questions to be asked of every farmer at the coming census.

THE CHRISTIAN ORPHANAGE

SUPERINTENDENT'S LETTER

Our good friends are very kind to us and are lending us a helping hand in the work.

Zion Sunday school, Moncure, N. C., one box containing towels, soap, ginghams, one counterpane, and one quilt. Pilot Cotton Mills, Raleigh, N. C., 64 yards of Chambrays. Mrs. Ed Smith, Clayton, N. C., 6 yards of gingham, two towels, one pair of shoes. White, Williamson & Company, 390 yards of ginghams. Mrs. L. D. Pierce, Frankfort, Ind., one box of nice clothing for the children. L. Banks Holt Manufacturing Co., 120 yards of cloth for shirts. Mildred and Kate Baldwin. one quilt. Women's Missionary Society, Ingram Christian church, (Va.), one box containing clothing, ginghams, hose, quilt, two pillows and sheets. Miss Rosa Best, Haw River, N. C., two dozen pair hose. Mrs. M. L. Bryant's Sunday school class, one box clothing for little girl.

Our Singing Class rendered a program at the College the fourth Sunday night to a large and appreciative audience and a splendid offering was made. They went to Durham on November 30, and rendered their program at the 11 o'clock service and had a splendid audience and the offering amounted, in the Sunday school and church, to about $240.00. The people were very kind to us and showed us every courtesy possible and the children were delighted with the trip.

Let all the churches do their best in this Thanksgiving offering. We need the money to feed and clothe and care for the sixty-one children in our care.

Don't forget our litle children when you are making up your Christmas presents. Remember they are just as anxious for "Old Santa" to come as any other child. They have no one to buy for them to make them happy on Christmas morn.

CHAS. D. JOHNSTON, Supt.

CHILDREN'S LETTER

Dear Uncle Charley: It has been some time since we have written to the Cousins. Hope they are all well and had a fine Thanksgiving. We have pieced a quilt for them and are sending it.—*Mildred and Kate Baldwin, Ages 9 and 12 years.*

We have received the quilt and it is very pretty indeed, and we thank you.—*"Uncle Charley."*

REPORT FOR DECEMBER 10, 1919

Amount brought forward, $14,659.21.

Sunday School Monthly Offerings

(North Carolina Conference)

Haw River, $1.50; Henderson, $11.64; Shady Grove, $3.00.

(Eastern Virginia Conference)

Wakefield, $5.23; Mt. Carmel, $4.80; Ivor, $2.30.

(Valley Virginia Conference)

New Hope, $1.65.

(Georgia and Alabama Conference)

Wadley, Ala., $6.30; Kite, Ga., $6.00; Total, $42.42.

Children's Home

Mrs. Rebecca Watkins, $10.00.

Special Offerings

Mr. Lawrence S. Holt, Sr., Burlington, N. C., $1,733.34; Glad Gleaners Christian church, N. H., $2.00; J. H. Jones, on support of children, $60.00; Bible Class, Reidsville Sunday school, $11.25; Total, $1,776.59.

Thanksgiving Offerings

Damascus church, $30.00; L. G. Gunter, New Hill, N. C., $2.00; Mrs. N. A. Whitman, Warson, Ind., $2.00; A. C. Madren, $2.15; Union Service, Merry Oakes, N. C., $14.20; Mrs. L. I. Cox, $5.00; T. C. Gillispie, $2.75; Windsor, Va. church, $139.11; Mr. Lawrence S. Holt, Sr., $100.00; Dr. S. W. Ceddell, $5.00; Christian Light Sunday school, $12.85; Mr. and Mrs. W. J. Estep, $2.00; Ivor, Va. Sunday school, $11.75; Birthday offerings, Ivor Sunday school, $4.12; L. J. Daughtry, $25.00; Carrie White's Sunday school class, $2.00.

Ingram Church Members Who Live in Richmond, Va.

Mrs. L. E. Carlton, $20.00; Mr. L. E. Carlton, $10.00; Mr. J. W. Carlton, $5.00; Mr. P. J. Carlton, $5.00; Miss Sarah E. Boyd, $10.00; Total, $50.00.

Other Donations

Mr. A. J. Daughtry, $10.00; Mrs. J. C. Goodwin, $2.00; Mr. F. L. Williamson, $25.00; Mrs. Maggie Spencer, $5.00; 20th Century Baracca Class, Suffolk, Va., $35.00; Pope's Chapel S. S., $11.00; Rev. J. W. Knight, $5.00; Kallaun Grove, S. S., $3.25; Hellem Isley, $1.00; M. Wilson Isley, $1.00; H. C. Replogle, $13.00; Christian church, Phoenix, Ala., $10.00; H. B. Parson, $25.00; Mrs. H. B. Parson, $5.00; W. A. Pierce, $2.00; Mrs. W. A. Pierce, $2.00; M. L. Pierce, $2.00; T. R. Pierce, $2.00; Mrs. E. J. Utley, $5.00; Mary Griffin, $5.00; R. L. Holt, $10.00; Mr. and Mrs. G. A. Wright, $4.00; Mr. and Mrs. Jerome Minnear, $5.00; New Hope, (Va.) Sunday school, $20.00; F. M. Carlton, $50.00; Mrs. M. B. Skeadmore, 50 cents; Class No. 4, Danville Christian church, $27.45; Joseph T. Harrell, $5.00; Mrs. Ida Williamson, $5.00; New Hope S. S. (Valley Va.), $20.00; Shady Grove S. S., $2.00; Mrs. W. H. Bales, $5.00; Ebenezer Church, $34.30; Six Forks church, $6.60; Christian Sunday school, Arthur, Ill., $5.50; Miss Annie Staley, $3.00; A Friend, $2.00; Wakefield, Va. church, $15.08; Mrs. T. E. Green, $2.00; Liberty church, $20.00; North Highlands, $12.00; J. B. Vaughan, $10.00; Ether Sunday school, $13.54; LinVille, Va., Sunday school, $32.50; Melmine Christian church, (Ill.), $6.00; Albert Godley, $1.00; Carter DeWese, $1.00; Ladies' Aid Society, Bethlehem church, Mrs. A. T. Gilliam, $1.00; Mrs. Eliza J. Cheek, $1.00; Lottie McCray, 50 cents; Mrs. R. T. Kernodle, $2.00; Mrs. W. A. Paschal, $1.00; Total, $5.50.

Hopedale Sunday school, $7.21; Concord, N. C., $10.50; Union Church, (N. C.), $87.50; Durham Sunday school, N. C., $154.40; Mr. High, Durham church, $10.00; Total, $164.40.

A Friend, $5.00; South Norfolk Sunday school, $31.43; Turner's Chapel church, $6.00; W. C. Heckok, $1.00; Willing Workers Class, Damascus Sunday school, $6.50; Morrisville church, $15.70; Morrisville Sunday school, $7.50; Total, $23.20.

M.Orban, Jr., $100.00; Shallow Well church, $36.44; Bethlehem church, (Eastern Va.), $67.00; Mt. Carmel S. S., $9.64; Union Grove Sunday school, $4.00; Jesse H. Jones, $6.00; Wake Chapel church, $125.27; Mrs. L. L. Wyrick, $1.50; Rev. L. L. Wyrick, $1.50; High Point church, $37.40; Total, $1,632.66.

Total for the week, $3,461.67; Grand total, $18,120.88.

The United States and Mexico are still at variance over diplomatic matters. President Wilson advises Congress to go slow in dealing with the situation.

THE SLEEPYTOWN EXPRESS

Just beyond the rainbow's end a river ripples down
Beneath a bridge, around a bend, and flows through
   Sleepytown—
Through Sleepytown, where goblins toil to fashion
   wondrous toys
And make up fascinating games for little girls and boys.
And automobiles, just the size for little hands to drive,
Await to whirl you all about as soon as you arrive.
But no one is ever allowed in Sleepytown, unless
He goes to bed in time to take the Sleepytown Express!

I know a foolish litle boy who always starts to whine
When he is asked to trot upstairs before it's half-past
   nine,
And often he will stamp his feet and shake his tousled
   head
And make a racket, even then, when he is sent to bed.
Of course when he has said his prayers it always is too
   late
To catch the Sleepytown Express; it starts at half-past
   eight.
And so, in all his long, long life—he's five years old
   this fall—
That little boy has never been to Sleepytown at all.

But other wiser little boys, and little girls as well,
As soon as eight o'clock has struck rush right upstairs,
   pell-mell,
Get off their clothes and say their prayers, just of their
   own accord;
And when the train comes rolling in, they're there to
   climb aboard.
Then, through a long, delightful night they wander up
   and down
And have the most exciting time in queer old Sleepy-
   town.
And not for cake or anything that children could
   possess
Would any of them ever miss the Sleepytown Express!
                              —*Kansas City Star.*

THE STORY MOTHER TOLD

   This is a true story about when grandmother was a
little girl. Her name was Carolina. It is about the Indians, too, so, of course, you will like it.
   It was the year when great-grandfather sold all his
corn and made enough money to buy a set of mahogany
chairs for the parlor, upholstered with horsehair. The
chairs had to be bought a long way from where grandmother lived, so great-grandfather hitched the pair of
grays to the farm wagon, and he said that great-
grandmother and Caroline might go, too.
   It was a pretty ride in the early morning. There was
no one out except the birds and the wild rabbits and

a fox or two. The sleepy flowers beside the long road
were just beginning to open their eyes, and Carolina
thought that she had never felt so happy in all her
life.
   They came to town at last and ate their luncheon
on the common, and then they bought the beautiful
mahogany chairs, upholstered with horsehair, for the
parlor. It surprised great-grandfather very much indeed that he had some money left over.
   "O, see, father," Carolina said as she ran to the back
of the store, where there was a little wooden rocking-
chair painted yellow. Then she sat down in it and began rocking. "It just fits me," she said. "How nice
it would be to sew my patchwork squares in it!"
   Great-grandfather smiled, and then whispered to the
shopkeeper, who smiled, too. When they started home
the six parlor chairs were in the back of the cart; and
grandmother, in her pink calico dress and sunbonnet,
was in the back of the cart. She sat and rocked in the
little rocking-chair as the cart jogged on.
   Before they reached home it began to grow dark.
The trees beside the road made long, black shadows,
and it was very still.
   "I wonder if the Indians have been seen about here
lately," great-grandmother asked.
   Great-grandfather did not answer, but he urged the
horses on. Just then a great figure in a blanket and
feathers rose in the road in front of them. Behind
him were others. They were Indians, and they wanted
the farm wagon and the horses.
   But just as the Indian chief started to lay hold of
the bridle he saw great-grandmother in the little yellow rockingchair in the back of the wagon. "How!"
he said in great fear, and then he turned and ran back
into the woods, followed by all the others. The Indians
had never seen a rocking-chair before, and it frightened them.
   So grandmother reached home safely, and she sewed
a great many patchwork squares as she sat and rocked
in her little yellow rocking-chair.—*Caroline S. Bailey,
in Mayflower.*

   If you plan to get a Bible or Testament for a Christmas present, we suggest that you place your order now.
Stock is short in many numbers and labor scarce.
Then, too, remember that transportation is very much
torn up during the holiday season. Correspondence
solicited.

   We advise those who expect to order books or Bibles
for Christmas presents to do so now. Many numbers
cannot be secured. We have in stock about all the
available numbers that we have been carrying, but have
a low stock in many instances. Order now. We also
call the attention of those who want names placed on
Bibles or Testaments. It takes about ten days or more
to fill such orders. We would not advise such orders
after December 12. We are anxious to serve, but cannot on short notice.

   Mrs. C. R. Moon—I wish for you and THE SUN great
success.

SOME CHRISTMAS SUGGESTIONS

CHRISTMAS BOOKS FOR CHILDREN

We list below a supply of books which we have purchased suitable for Christmas presents for the children. For the lack of space we cannot tell what each book is about, but we have exercised the very best care in the selection, to see that all stories are helpful and interesting:

The Thorn of the Fortress ....50 cents
Matt of the Waterfront ....50 cents
The Other Side of the Rainbow ....60 cents
Lantern Stories ....60 cents
Billy and Bumps ....35 cents
Good Night Stories ....60 cents
The Jim Family ....25 cents
Little Folks of the Bible ....30 cents
Sunny Hour Books ....15 cents

(Little Folks of the Bible can be had in books I, II, III, and IV. Books I and II are for boys and books III and IV are for girls. We will send any four books of this title for $1.00.)

(Sunny Hour Books are made up of 14 different titles. The price is 15 cents for each title, any two for 25 cents; four for 45 cents and all over four at 10 cents per volume.)

All the above named books are suitable for children 8 to 14 except the "Sunny Hour Books" which are for little tots that cannot read or are just beginning to read. "Sunny Hour Books" contain an abundance of pictures and are bound with colored cloth and stamped with an appropriate design.

Add 4 cents per volume for postage when only one copy is ordered, and 2 cents per volume for postage in lots up to ten; all over ten volumes add 1 cent per volume for postage.

CLEARANCE SALE OF CHILDREN'S BOOKS

We make it a rule in December of each year to buy the closing out stock of several suitable books for children. By buying the closing out stock, we are enabled to get a better price and make the books within the reach of all.

We have been able this year to buy the complete stock of the following 50 cent sellers, and offer them at prices indicated:

Blazing the Way ....$ .25
Bright Side and Other Side .... .25
Crown Jewels .... .20
From the Thames to the Toossachs.................... .25
Up the Susquehanna .... .25

(This price is postpaid)

The following reductions will be made in lots: Any two copies, 45 cents; three copies, 60 cents; four copies, 75 cents; all over four at 17 cents per copy.

The supply is limited and we advise you to order early. If any title has exhausted when your order is received, we will substitute unless otherwise instructed.

These books are all well made and handsomely bound.

Make some child's life happy by presenting one or more of these books. Invest a few dollars to make the little tots of your class happy.

SUNDAY SCHOOL HELPS

We have the following Sunday school helps on the 1920 International Lesson:

Peloubet's Select Notes $1.60
Tarbell's Teachers' Guide 1.60
Arnold's Commentary .... .75
Torrey's Gist of the Lesson........................... .30

(These prices include postage)

ADDRESS

C. B. RIDDLE, Publisher

BURLINGTON, · · · N. C.

Sunday School and Christian Endeavor

SUNDAY SCHOOL LESSON FOR
DECEMBER 21, 1919
(Mrs. Fred Bullock)

At the Empty Tomb and with the Risen Lord.—John 20:1-21:25.

Golden Text: "He is risen, even as he said."—Matt. 28:16.

Alternative Christmas Lesson

The Prince of Peace.—Isaiah 11:1-10; Luke 2:8-14.

Golden Text: "Thou shalt call his name Jesus: for it is he that shall save his people from their sins."—Matt. 1:21.

There are two lessons offered for today, and while the children will undoubtedly wish to study the Christmas lesson, yet it would seem to be wise for those who are following this series of studies in the lives of Peter and John to continue this study, unbroken. There is no reason why the thought of this Christmas time should not cover both the birth of our Lord and His resurrection. The one would have meant little without the other. So, in the study of these two great disciples, their birth or life would have meant nothing at all to us, had they not been born again into newness of life in Christ Jesus. The thing that makes their lives a worthwhile study for us is the fact that these lives were hid with Christ in God.

It is worthy of note that Peter, self-sufficient Peter, whom we last saw turning away to weep bitterly, is with John when the message of the Resurrection reaches them. Had he found courage and strength and promise of forgiveness in communion with the best loved disciple and the mother? We may well believe so. Younger John outruns Peter, but Peter does not hesitate at the mouth of the tomb; he goes in, and John, following, still in the shape of the body they had covered, stuffed with a hundred pounds of spices, and the napkin which had covered the face, still wrapped together the space of the neck from the rest of the wrappings saw and believed. No grave clothes here to be loosed to let Him go. No grave could hold Him. This they knew as surely as when He stood with them that later day on the shores of Galilee, and gave His last Commission.

And as the year draws to its close, we may think we hear with Peter, "Lovest thou me? Go and work for me." "Lord, what shall this man do?" "What is that to thee? Who art thou that judgest another man's servant? To his own master he standeth or falleth. It is not him that thou art to follow. Follow *Thou Me.*"

CHRISTMAS IN THE SUNDAY SCHOOL

"Putting Christ into Christmas," said a speaker some time ago, referring to the "White Gifts" Christmas; Santa Claus, and good times and first thought, but is there not a real need for this, after all? We have put so many other things into Christmas; Santa Claus, and good times and big dinners and merry making, and gift giving, all good and pleasant and proper in their places, but have we not almost forgotten that this is the birthday of the King? That we are gathering together to celebrate the birth of the Prince of Peace? Yet people often talk as though it were a wrong to the children to suggest the idea of giving to others at Christmas time. When my birthday comes, I want my presents myself, don't you? Then when Christ's birthday comes, shall we refuse Him a gift? How shall we make Him a gift? Listen to His own words, "Inasmuch as ye have done it unto the least of these, my brethren, ye have done it unto me." And listen, children, above all others, if given the opportunity, prove for themselves that it is more blessed to give than to receive. If there are poor children in your school or church, see that they are remembered, but make some plan, somewhere, so that every child may bring a birthday gift to Jesus. It is not the size of the gift, but the heart thought back of it.

MRS. FRED BULLOCK.

CHRISTIAN ENDEAVOR TOPIC FOR
DECEMBER 21, 1919
(J. V. Knight)

The Christmas Message and the Christmas . . Spirit.—Luke 2:8-14; Matt. 2:9-11. (Christmas Meeting).

It is impossible to think of Christmas without thinking of a gift, for it would be a poor Christmas with-

out a gift. Most of us expect also to receive a gift of some kind. What is a real gift? Is it not the gift we make expecting nothing in return? If we give to a friend and that friend in return gives to us, we have simply made an exchange. The Christmas message carries the idea of a real gift, for we know that God gave in order to bring it about. John 3:16.

Every year thousands of gifts are exchanged between friends, and the mail is loaded with Christmas packages until the congestion is terrible. Wonder what Jesus thinks of these costly exchanges as He looks upon the millions who stand by in need of food and raiment? Surely the great heart of God must grieve as He sees conditions as they are.

Let us exemply the Christmas spirit by looking out for those who are poor, the blind, the lame, the unfortunate and those who are unfortunate and helpless, and bestow a gift upon them that will bring a real blessing upon them and a real joy to our lives. The spirit of Christmas is the Christ-like spirit. He gave His life for others, and our lives will never find the real joy coming to them, until we have given something that will help others to a better life.

A story is told of a little boy whose parents gave him a bicycle for a Christmas present. The very next day he rode it down the street and sold his bicycle, and bought magazines, chocolates, and various things and made his way to the hospital ward where there lay hundreds of wounded soldiers, and gave each of them something to read and eat. In that way he carried out the spirit of a real Christmas for Christ. If you would have a merry Christmas, "Go thou and do likewise."

Notes

December and January are to be devoted to better prayer meeting months. December will be given to better attendance, music, and the development of the quiet hour. January to public testimony, and personal work. Get the little book, "How to Bring Men to Christ" (by Torrey) from THE CHRISTIAN SUN, or the C. P. A., it costs about twenty cents.

This is the book other Christian Endeavorers will use. Ask your pastor to give his Wednesday night messages to this work.

How about a question box for January? Do you have any problems to face in your Society? We shall attempt to answer any question you send in between now and the last week in January in the space given for the notes. Let them come. Who has the first one? The questions must be such as will be interesting to others as well as your own local society. No name will be given with the answer unless you request it for we have only so much space.

MARRIAGES

KLINE-DUSING

At the Christian Parsonage, Winchester, Virginia, on October 25, 1919, Elmer Kline and Pearl May Dusing were united in marriage by the writer. We wish them much happiness.
W. T. WALTERS.

GOOD-LARRICK

Rufus Clayton Good and Pauline Mary Larrick were quietly married at the Christian parsonage, Winchester, Virginia, November 19, 1919. The contracting parties are popular young people of Rock Enon, Virginia and we join with their host of friends in extending them our best wishes.
W. T. WALTERS.

LONAS-BROWN

A Thanksgiving wedding was celebrated at the Christian parsonage, Winchester, Va., when Isaac C. Lonas led Mrs. Mattie E. Brown to the marriage altar at 4:30 in the afternoon. The bridal couple are well known in Winchester and we join with their friends in wishing them much happiness.
W. T. WALTERS.

JOHNSON-GREEN

Miss Mary A. Green became the bride of Mr. Alton G. Johnson on November 25, 1919, at the Yarborough house in Raleigh, N. C. Mrs. Johnson is the attractive daughter of W. A. Green of Pleasant Union Christian church, near Lillington, N. C. Mr.

Johnson is the son of Archie L. Johnson of Lillington, and is also one of the United States noble soldier boys. Their home will be in Lillington and we predict for this fine couple a happy home. Only a few of their friends witnessed the ceremony which was performed by the writer.
J. LEE JOHNSON.

PARKS-BORROUGHS

November 26, 1919, Mr. June L. Parks and Miss Leta M. Borroughs were united in marriage by the writer at his home in Asheboro, N. C.

They were accompanied by Mr. Charles F. Cole and Miss Allene King of Seagrove, N. C.

Mr. Parks is a son of Mr. Lewis Parks of Seagrove and is now the popular mail deliveryman of Route 2 of that place. He has seen service overseas, being a member of the famous "Co. K.", and was twice wounded. Mrs. Parks is a daughter of Mr. and Mrs. W. E. Borroughs of Aldridge, N. C.

They left immediately for Asheville, N. C. They will make their home at Seagrove, N. C. May happiness be theirs.
T. J. GREEN.

JAMISON-PERRY

On November 26, 1919, at the home of the bride, near Youngsville, N. C., Mr. David F. Jamison of Summerville, S. C., and Miss Minnie Mable Perry were united in marriage by the writer. Mr. Jamison is a prosperous young business man and Miss Perry is the beautiful and accomplished daughter of Mr. and Mrs. J. E. Perry. The ring ceremony was used. The brother of the groom was best man and the only sister of the bride took the part of bride's maid.

Many friends were present to wish a good voyage to the happy couple. The wedding party motored to Raleigh, N. C. Mr. and Mrs. Jamison will be at home to their friends at Summerville, S. C. on their return from their honeymoon.

May their years be many on earth, filled with service and joy.
B. F. BLACK.

OBITUARIES

WOODLIEF

Deacon W. B. Woodlief of Mt. Carmel Christian church, departed this life on November 17, 1919, at the age of 90 years. Funeral services were conducted by his pastor, the writer.

For many years Brother Woodlief was a faithful officer of his church. A good man of ripe years and varied experience has gone. He leaves to mourn their loss his beloved wife, Mary G., four sons, and three daughters. Thirty-five grandchildren and thirteen great-grandchildren and a host of friends. He was laid to rest in the home burying ground.

May the Lord comfort those left behind. Surely a good man is gone to his reward.
B. F. BLACK.

HALL

Mr. Henry Hall departed this life at his home in Burlington, N. C., November 28, 1919, in his eighty-third year.

He was united in marriage to Miss Kizziah J. Jeffreys, March 14, 1867, and to them were born eight children. His wife and six children survive him.

He was a Confederate veteran. He volunteered and joined the first company that left Alamance county for the field of conflict. The Confederate veterans who followed his remains, to the grave attested his faithfulness as a soldier.

He united with Long's Chapel Christian church about thirty years ago of which church he was a loyal member till death called him from labor to reward.

The funeral services were conducted by the writer from Long's Chapel, assisted by Brothers Holt, Harrell, and Apple. The interment was in the church cemetery.

A loving husband, a kind father, good citizen, friend and neighbor has fallen asleep. The Lord bless and comfort the bereaved.
P. H. FLEMING.

CAPT. J. A. TURRENTINE—AN APPRECIATION

There is nothing grander than the home-going of one who has lived nobly and served faithfully his day and generation. We wish to express our appreciation of one whom we believe attained that distinction. In the passing of Captain James A. Turrentine the Burlington Christian church has lost a most faithful member, the town a valuable citizen, the home a kind and loving father. Perhaps no man in our city commanded greater respect, more love and admiration than our brother. His faith in God was strong, and his loyalty to his church was unquestioned. He was keenly interested in all the activities of the church and at the time of his passing he was our senior deacon.

As a man he was gentle, courteous and kind—a staunch friend, wise counselor, very energetic. He was a man of broad vision and broad sympathies. He wrought well, filling positions of honor and trust in both church and state and interested himself in many good causes. It was frequently my pleasure to listen to his narratives of the civil war. He was a good conversationalist, with a sense of humor and could relate incidents in a most interesting way.

Advancing years necessitated his giving up official duties, but his faithfulness to the end is most commendable. Of late years his hearing was very defective; many times he could not hear the sermon, but he was faithful in giving his presence, which means a great deal.

Last August we buried his sister, Mrs. Sarah Fix, a saintly character. In the home-going of these two most loyal members our church is poorer, but heaven richer. We count it a great privilege to have numbered them among our friends. To remember them will always be a pleasure. Their seats in the old church are vacant, but their influence lives on in the hearts and lives of men.

J. W. HARRELL.

REPORT OF THE CONDITION OF

the Elon Banking and Trust Company, at Elon College, in the State of North Carolina, at the close of business, November 17, 1919:

Resources:

Loans and Discounts	$ 34,823.97
Demand Loans	3,485.00
Overdrafts unsecured,	1,403.01
U. S. Bonds and Liberty Bonds	4,450.00
Banking House, $1,737.13, Furniture and Fixtures, $1,839.91	3,577.04
Cash in valut and net amounts due from Banks, Bankers and Trust Companies	25,633.80
Cash Items held over 24 hours.	2,473.10
War Savings Stamps	655.65
Thrift Stamps	37.25

Total...........$76,538.82

Liabilities:

Capital Stock paid in	7,600.00
Surplus Fund	890.00
Undivided Profits, less current expenses and taxes paid	208.90
Deposits subject to check	44,967.40
Time Certificates of Deposit	22,041.06
Cashier's Checks outstanding	244.55
Certified Checks	15.60
Rec. on Bonds	249.50
Accrued Interest due depositors	321.81

Total $76,538.82

State of North Carolina—County of Alamance, November 28, 1919.

I, Marion C. Jackson, Cashier of the above named Bank, do solemnly swear that the above statement is true to the best of my knowledge and belief.

MARION C. JACKSON, Cashier.

Subscribed and sworn to before me, this 28th day of November, 1919.

J. J. LAMBETH, J. P.

Correct—Attest:

J. J. LAMBETH,
G. S. WATSON,
W. C. WICKER,
Directors.

CHURCH OFFERING ENVELOPES

Standard Double

(Size 2½X4¼ inches—52 to Set)

White or Manila

25 to 49 sets	16 cts. a set
50 to 109 sets	14 cts. a set
110 to 209 sets	13 cts. a set
210 to 309 sets	12½ cts. a set
310 to 399 sets	12 cts. a set
400 or more sets	11 cts. a set

Minimum Charge $3.00, net.

CARTONS INCLUDED .

Single Envelope System

(Size 2 5-16X3 5-8 inches. Open side. 52 to Set)

White or Manila

25 to 49 sets	14 cts. a set
50 to 99 sets	13 cts. a set
100 to 149 sets	12 cts a set
150 to 199 sets	11½ cts. a set
200 to 249 sets	11 cts. a set
250 or more sets	10 cts. a set

Minimum Charge $2.00 set.

CARTONS INCLUDED.

Take Note

The following points should be taken into consideration in placing an order for church offering envelopes:

1. A set means 52 envelopes, one for each Sunday in the year.

2. When cartons are ordered the sets are arranged in their logical order, thus making it convenient for the member. We suggest the use of cartons because of the convenience.

3. If you desire monthly, double or single envelopes, without cartons, 1-3 the price of the same number of weekly sets. Cartons 3-4 cent each.

4. Semi-monthly, double or single, in cartons, 2-3 the weekly price; without cartons 3-5 the weekly price.

5. When ordering state what Sunday that your church year begins, and whether you want the dates on envelopes or not.

6. Indicate the wording that you want placed on the envelopes or leave the same with us. Samples sent upon request.

7. Allow ten to fifteen days for delivery. Order early.

C. B. RIDDLE, Publishing Agent

Burlington, - - - - N. C.

THE CHRISTIAN SUN

"IN ESSENTIALS UNITY, IN NON-ESSENTIALS LIBERTY, IN ALL THINGS CHARITY"

⭐ And lo, the star which they saw in the east went before them, till it came and stood over where the young child was.—*John 2:9.*

Volume LXXI	WEDNESDAY, DECEMBER 17, 1919	Number 51
BURLINGTON	· · ·	NORTH CAROLINA

THE CHRISTIAN SUN

Founded 1844 by Rev. Daniel W. Kerr.

C. B. RIDDLE - - - Editor

Entered at the Burlington, N. C. Post Office as second class matter.

Subscription Rates

One year .... $ 2.00
Six months 1.00

In Advance

Give both your old and new postoffice when asking that your address be changed.

The change of your label is your receipt for money. When receipts sent upon request.

Many persons subscribe for friends, intending that the paper be stopped at the end of the year. If instructions are given to this effect, they will receive attention at the proper time.

Marriage and obituary notices not exceeding 150 words printed free if received within 60 days from date of event, all over this at the rate of one-half cent a word.

Original poetry not accepted for publication.

Principles of the Christian Church

(1) The Lord Jesus Christ is the only Head of the Church.
(2) Christian is a sufficient name of the Church.
(3) The Holy Bible is a sufficient rule of faith and practice.
(4) Christian character is a sufficient test of fellowship, and of church membership.
(5) The right of private judgment and the liberty of conscience is a right and a privilege that should be accorded to, and exercised by all.

EDITORIAL

CHRISTMAS MESSAGES

"Christmas will soon be here," we heard a child say over two months ago. How long the time seemed to us then, but oh long it seemed, and was, to that child! Really, to us it was short and only seemed a long time because of the many things that had to be done before the coming of the good and happy day. The child was ready—and waiting for Christmas; we were not.

You cannot get away from the thought of the child when you think of Christmas—we say that you cannot. It was a *Child* who made the event, and though He grew into manhood, the world has kept the day of His coming day of His life. He himself loved childhood, held it up to His disciples as a model, and punctuated His messages with the spirit of a child.

Then we wonder how great a time we would have, what a "good" Christmas we would have, if all of us could, as children, enjoy Christmas. We *rush* and *push* to get ready for Christmas, while the child just waits (anxiously) for the day to come. The over-work breaks us down; the child's life is sweetened by the expectations.

Late trains, crowded trains, congested traffic, and a thousand other abnormal conditions remind us of how the Christmas date stands out on the calendar, and how we let that day be the greatest of the month and year. The birthday of no man has ever meant so much to the world; no man, save Jesus, could mean so much. Let skeptics speak; let those who may deny the Christ, but this great surge of traffic we hear, the tramp of millions of feet Christmas shopping tell us a story that no myth can compete and no human heart can fully appropriate to its full and final meaning. When those who do not believe in Christ, explain and do away with the Christmas, then we will take cognizance of their message and theory.

Getting and *giving* during the Christmas season are two words often used. Selfishness wants to *get*; unselfishness wants to *give*. God *gave* a Son to the world to redeem and save it. God gave His Son because He loved the world, and when we give we should do so because we *love*, and not because of custom. Give in the spirit—and let that spirit be the spirit of the child of God, Jesus the Christ.

What a beautiful scene! We imagined ourselves peeping in through the window where *all* the family had assembled on Christmas eve night. The son from afar, the married daughter from a neighboring town, and all were there. An open fire to warm the house and to light it. Happy place! The children had returned and parents were happy, happy. And such will be many scenes this year. If it is so you can, go make the old home fireside ring with childhood laughter again.

James Whitcomb Riley, the Indiana bachelor poet of sainted memory, said somethings familiar in his "The Christmas Long Ago." What a picture appears when he says:

Come, sing a halo Heigh ho
For the Christmas long ago!—
When the old log-cabin homed us
From the night of blinding snow,
Where the rarest joy held reign,
And the chimney roared amain,
With the firelight like a beacon
Through the frosty window-pane.

Ah! the revel and the din
From without and from within,
The blend of distant snow bells
With the plinking violin;
The muffled shrieks and cries—
Then the glowing cheeks and eyes—
The driving storm of greetings,
Gusts of kisses and surprise.

"One half of the world does not know how the other half lives," goes the old saying, and then let us add this: One-half the children never know how the other half spend Christmas. Today we were thinking of the poor, the destitute, and of the thousands of children who will not be visited by Santa Claus and know not the joys of toys, fruits, and other things. We were also thinking of the children whose fathers are confined in some prison, some pentitentiary, for crime. The children are not responsible for this, and yet they suffer the sadness of a lonely home. No one save the Christ could bear the heart-aches of this world.

* *

And wouldn't you like to have the names and addresses of all the children who are deprived of the Christmas, and were able to send each of them a box filled with nice things, and have it reach them early Christmas morning? Too ideal, and yet it has in it the balm of happiness. But while you cannot give to all, you can bring a little sunshine to a few, and so do that.

* *

As the big SUN family this 1919 Christmas enjoy, this scribe will be wishing for each member a happy, wholesome, and joyous good time.

NOTES

We understand that Rev. A. T. Banks is doing nicely with his wound received a few days ago by accidental shooting. Dr. D. A. Long preached for Brother Banks the first Sunday and Dr. Wicker the second.

Brother Chas. D. Johnston, Superintendent of the Christian Orphanage, informs us that he is in need of a head matron for the institution and would like to get in touch wits some suitable person. He prefers applications from members of the Christian Church.

Give THE CHRISTIAN SUN as a Christmas present. We will mail copies of all the December issues in time for Christmas, also send a letter for you. THE SUN will be a weekly reminder, for one year, of your love and esteem.

We call attention to Brother L. M. Clymer's advertisement on page 15. Brother Clymer is a member of our Greensboro church and is a mechanic of the first magnitude. His service is used by the Southern Railway and other big industries. We commend him to our readers.

We have received the following announcement: "Mr. and Mrs. J. Frank Savage announce the marriage of their daughter, Gladys Porter, to Mr. Lloyd Charles March on Saturday, November the twenty-ninth, nineteen hundred and nineteen, Norfolk, Virginia."

Long and happy life be theirs is the wish of this office.

We are glad to report that the work on the *Christian Annual* is progressing, and by the time this note reaches the public, practically all of the copy will be in type waiting for the proceedings of the Christian Missionary Association of the Eastern Virginia Conference, which met December 9. Of course, the work is not half over when the type is set, but we hope to have the *Annual* ready by the last week in December.

The *Annual* this year is to cost much more than the income. If the Conference treasurers will send check to cover the allotment of each Conference, we will endeavor to get some cash discount. Will those interested be kind enough to co-operate?

A GREAT ADVANCE IN BIBLES

Since the last issue of THE SUN went to press we have received a letter from the Bible publishers stating that great advances in prices have been made. Later we received new price list with instructions to govern ourselves accordingly. We have seen many advances in Bibles, but think that the last advance is the greatest that we have ever seen. Many numbers have advanced more than $4.00 each, whereas other advances have been from one dollar upward.

Two months ago we bought the largest line of Bibles and Testaments that we have ever purchased and have decided to sell what we have on hand at the old price. For instance: Bible No. 2014 has been selling for $4.50, and the new price is $6.50. We have about fifteen copies of this on hand and will sell for $4.50 the copy. This Bible is large type, soft binding, and very suitable for old people. A very handsome gift.

It is not practical for us to list all the numbers we have in stock, but if you plan to buy a Bible any time soon, we advise you to do so now, and we are going to make the following offer: If you want a Bible, give us the following information: 1. General description; 2. About what price; 3. For what age person; 4. For lady or gentleman. With this information we will send you as near the description as we have, and if it is the Bible you want, send us the price, otherwise return the Bible. The cost of returning will not be over ten cents. Your credit is good. Order today. The Christmas trade is rapidly taking up our stock.

We have had a good year so far as THE CHRISTIAN SUN is concerned. We are pleased with the co-operation that we have had. We appreciate it more than words can tell. The year is drawing to a close and we want to round out 1919 with the biggest and best financial showing that we have ever had. Friends have responded to statements in a very loyal and liberal manner. There are a few, however, that have not given heed to past due subscriptions. Will you, if you are one of these, look after the matter today? We need the money and need it now. It has been neglect because you have not renewed. You have not meant to do it, but just kept putting it off. Don't put it off longer, dear reader, if you are behind, but remit today. We thank you in advance.

PASTOR AND PEOPLE

MOORE UNION

We met our first appointment after Conference at this place on the fifth Sunday. The congregation was large. The first thing we did, was to tell them of the interesting session of the Conference, and of its larger plans for the future, and as a local church we must get a larger vision of our responsibilities. That we must live better, do more work, and raise more money than in former years for the extension of our Master's Kingdom. We received two members. Brother B. J. Howard was present and took part in the services, and made some timely and appropriate remarks. We are anxious for this church to go ahead of anything it has ever done in any previous year. This is the church where the first money for Foreign Missions in the Christian Church was ever given—the nest egg. With this beginning the Christian Church has grown as it never had. Since this time the Christian Church has gained nearly one hundred per cent. She has now many equipped colleges, has two foreign fields established, with a church membership of more than one thousand, with schools, and creditable church buildings.

P. T. KLAPP.

Elon College, N. C.

AN APPRECIATION

I noticed in the issue of THE CHRISTIAN SUN under date of November 12, that a pastor had been visiting the homes in his community—he said that he had visited over a hundred families in five weeks. I think that it cheers most families for the pastor to visit in their homes. It puts them on friendlier relations and when all are visited none feel neglected.

A pastor never knows how much he has helped some one by his friendly visits. I don't suppose this pastor realized that he visited one home, at least, of twenty-seven years duration, in which he was the only pastor of any denomination that had ever been in the home and read a part of God's Word and offered prayer that God might bless that family. Much sickness and several deaths have occurred in that home; yet this is true, and I think that God's blessing will surely rest on pastor and people when they meet together in the homes for a word of prayer and praise to the Father above, the Giver of all good gifts.

A FRIEND.

POUNDED

At my last appointment at Ether, N. C., for the Conference year, just before leaving on Monday morning, was notified, over the telephone, that I was wanted at the store of Brother H. Freeman. Upon reaching that place I found nearly all the ladies and a number of the men of the village, had gathered there and the next thing I knew, we were receiving a severe pounding, in the way of flour, corn, potatoes, sugar, coffee, canned goods of many kinds and other good things to eat too numerous to mention; also many pieces of wearing ap-

parel. In addition to this a nice purse was given Mrs. Underwood as her "pin-money."

This little church had already made my salary more than it promised and sent up all asked for to Conference.

Indeed it is a pleasure to serve such a people.

May the dear Lord bless them in their New Year's work.

G. R. UNDERWOOD.

Bennett, N. C.

HENDERSON LETTER

On the first Sunday in November we began revival meetings with the Henderson church. Rev. J. F. Morgan, of First Christian church, Norfolk, Va., came Monday following, and did the preaching thereafter. There was a good congregation Monday evening, and the interest and attendance increased from service to service. In his usual plain and earnest style Brother Morgan delivered strong appeals for purity of life and earnestness in service on the part of church members, and a definite decision for Christ on the part of the unsaved. His solos were an effective and pleasing feature of his work with us. He sang the gospel message with great earnestness, and we think many hearts were stirred to greater love for the Savior by these messages of song. There was a number of renewals of faith and loyalty to Christ, and several yielded for the first time to the entreaties of love and mercy. There were five additions to the church. Brother Morgan, in his short ministry with us, won the love and esteem of many who will be glad to have him come again. We believe also by his coming the cause of the Master was furthered and His name magnified among the people. We should add that because of the approaching session of Conference we closed the meeting when the interest was fine and the prospects good for great results if the work could have been continued through another week. We regretted very much the necessity of closing when we did, but we hope to continue the work at an early date.

R. L. WILLIAMSON.

PLEASANT GROVE—INGRAM

Brother George C. Talbert, the teacher of the Bible class in the Pleasant Grove Sunday school surprised me yesterday by handing me $34.00 as an expression of appreciation from the people of the community, which when added to what my parents and other persons in my pastorate have given me brings the total up to $94.00 besides many profitable gifts. Many thanks are hereby tendered all these gracious friends and may the bounty of the Father abide with them.

Just a word here to the people of this pastorate and others to whom it may apply: *Do, please, continue your attendance on church services during the winter months.*

The good old days of sumptuous dinners in country homes have not past. Being as I am the pastor of nearly five hundred country church members and living continuously with them I should be able to say whether or not the dinners of "ye olden days" have ceased. Having been to nearly a hundred special dinings in the

last twelve months I should be able to appreciate the real country dinner. On spotless linen, in bright, airy dining-rooms, dishes of turkey, turtle ', and 'possum: mutton, beef, and pork; vegetables inumerable, chickens ncalculable, eggs inestimable have graced the boards of small and great alike. Wild game, fresh fish, and delicious oysters were served in season; pies of every fruit and flavor have been in abundance; the daintiest of sweets, the sourest of pickles; and cakes the pride of an hundred cooks have been served with ices, salads, and sauces in season and out of season. The words of the hosts, the smiles of the hostesses, and the cheer of the children added to the liquid goodness of the steaming, hot coffee as the tales of merriment went around.
                                        JOHN G. TRUITT.
December 8, 1919.

NOTES FROM ELON COLLEGE

The students of Elon College have undertaken the publication of a weekly newspaper to be known as "Maroon and Gold." The first issue is to appear on Wednesday, December 10, and it will be issued each week on this date of publication. The subscription price is to be $1.00 a year. The students have rallied to the new publication with characteristic zeal and a strong appeal is to be made to the alumni also for subscriptions. It is confidently expected that the paper will be self-supporting from the beginning. The officers are: P. E. Lindley, Editor-in-Chief; L. B. Ezell, Assistant Editor; L. M. Cannon, Business Manager; C. M. Cannon, Advertising Manager; H. W. Johnson, Circulation Manager. Miss Mary D. Atkinson and Miss Lucy Eldridge with Watson D. Lambeth and the officers of the staff constitute the Board of Directors. The consultation editory representing the faculty is Prof. F. F. Myrick.

Professors Betts and Alexander of the music faculty have just returned from a trip to South Carolina where they gave a recital in voice and piano before the faculty and students of Erskine College of Due West, S. C.

The fall term recital of the faculty of music is to be given December 11 at 7:30 P. M. Professors Betts and Alexander, Mrs. Sturm, Miss Fisher, and Miss Smith will appeal in this recital.

The new pipe organ which has just been installed will be used for the first time in the faculty recital.

Elon will send five student representatives to the Student Volunteer Conference to be held at Des Moines, Iowa, during the Christmas holidays. Two young men will represent the Y. M. C. A., and three young ladies the Y. W. C. A. The Y. M. C. A. representatives are J. E. McCauley, Chapel Hill, N. C., and H. W. Johnson, Cardenas, N. C. The Y. W. C. A. representatives are Miss Juana Pinnix, Kernersville, N. C.; Miss Janie Angel, Greensboro, N. C., and Miss Maude Sharpe, Burlington, N. C.
                                        W. A. HARPER.
December 6.

Mrs. A. E. Lumsden—Please renew my subscription to the best paper that's published—THE CHRISTIAN SUN.

BROTHER EDWARDS REPORTS A GOOD YEAR

My past year's work has been a pleasant one to me. I have had several conversions at my monthly appointments. On last Sunday we had a sweet service at Randleman. Twenty, or more, young men gave their hands for prayer. One old man, sixty years old, was converted on Sunday of the revival meeting at this place. Some asked for prayer, some came to the altar weeping and confessing their sins. There has been some move on the part of the unconverted in every service since June, except five. Some were backsliders, some church members reclaimed, some were not Christians at all. The Lord has wonderfully blessed my work this year.

My churches are looking forward to greater things the coming year. Brethren pray for me that the Lord may use me in the salvation of many souls. May the Lord bless our entire Conference. May our College send out many laborers for the Master. "The harvest is ripe and the laborers are few."
                                        W. J. EDWARDS.
Coleridge, N. C.

FROM THE PORTSMOUTH CHURCH

The special services just held were marked by great success and blessing, not only to the Christian church but to the city at large. Rev. Luther B. Bridgers, a native of Portsmouth, is a man of large resources and power, not only as a preacher, but as a singer of gospel solos and a leader. Many of his sermons were masterpieces of pulpit oratory, others were clear and convincing expositions of fundamental doctrines. A mass meeting for men resulted in about five hundred men from all parts of the city coming together, fifty of whom took a stand for Christ. During the revival more than one hundred and fifty expressed a desire to live a Christian life, and have gone into different churches. Many old fashioned revival scenes were witnessed and on Sunday nights it was estimated that a thousand persons were crowded into the church and other rooms. Many others were turned away. The church is greatly refreshed and has demonstrated that there is no risk in undertaking a great revival and meeting the necessary expense without difficulty when the man who comes and the people who receive him are in the attitude of prayer and expectancy.

The Billy Sunday campaign, which is to open in Norfolk, Va., the first of the year, is receiving the co-operation of many of the churches of Portsmouth. This church has been requested to furnish twenty singers, six ushers, twenty other workers and about two hundred dollars as its share of the campaign.

Our church has suffered a great and inspeakable loss in the removal of Mr. and Mrs. R. B. Wood and family from our church. Their services to the Portsmouth church and other activities of the city cannot be estimated, their service of time, money and energy to say nothing of their personal influence, deprives us of a working force difficult to replace. Our love and best wishes go with them.
                                        HENRY W. DOWDING.

SUFFOLK LETTER

It is one thing to be ignorant; it is another thing to ignore. The former is a blessing; the latter is almost a crime. The one is a state in which the person is not informed; the other is the spirit that passes by as "unworthy of notice." They are as far apart as the poles. Without ignorance society could make no progress; with the spirit to ignore, progress would be impossible.

A state of perfect knowledge would mean a stagnant world. It is the unknown that lures men, keeps men active, and develops the race. Ignorance must remain among men as the latent resource for activity and progress. It is the ore in the mine, the power in the air, the work in electricity, the water in the earth. "God saw that everything that he had made was very good. Thus the heavens and the earth were finished, and all the host of them." There was nothing more for God to do in the physical universe. It was a finished universe, set in motion under fixed laws and moves on till this good day. If all human conditions were perfect, if all human beings knew all there is to know, the day of human development would be at an end. There would be no need for schools. There would be little need for books. There would be no need for physicians. There would be no need for lawyers and courts. The ignorance of the race makes universal and perpetual field for development and activity. If the atmosphere were always just suited to human comfort, the four hundred thousand coal miners would never strike; but the necessity for mining coal opens a great field for service, not only in mining the coal, but in determining human relations, individual and corporate rights. The ignorance of the race has created the great schools; and sickness and accident, the great doctors and surgeons. Not only so, but the great problem of the world today is not ignorance, but learning. Man knows too much to be good. His knowledge made the world-war, and all the infernal weapons used in that war. It is easier to inform the ignorant than to convert the wise. There is such a state as ignorance of God as well as ignorance of science and art, of business and law. With a generation born again, the world and the race would furnish an endless opportunity for improvement and growth. Inventors develop in the field of ignorance—in the field where men do not know. There is absolutely no end to the unknown, and in that field is the new and the better day. All finished things grow old and die. The museum is the graveyard of the mechanical world. It is the cemetery of things passed out of use. The living improvements are constantly burying the outworn and the dead that were the best in their day. The stage coach is mummy beside the automobile; if the stage coach had been the last possible in vehicle the automobile would not be. The ignorance of our forefathers makes possible the progress of the present time; and our ignorance will leave ample room for improvement in the time to come.

The field of missions is the boundless field in which Christianity can live and grow. It will die, if it remains at home. The great drives for money and spiritual life in the churches reveal a new objective in the purpose of Christianity. The pressure of great movements among the denominations bears mightily upon the thought and conscience of the followers of Christ. There is no end to this outworking of the Christian motive for the salvation and edification of the world. If I may be permitted to coin an expression in line with all the forward movements for more liberal contributions to Kingdom work, let it be that, we *put up or give up;* put up men and women, put up money, put up ourselves "in His name."

W. W. STALEY.

AMELIA

I made my first trip to Amelia the first Sunday in December. I had a very pleasant visit considering the day. After service the church held a short business meeting for the purpose of calling the pastor for the coming year. The call for me was unanimous and I am to preach two Sundays in each month. The pastor's salary was doubled.

The church seems to have the spirit of true worship. I feel that the Lord will be with us during the coming year and that we will have the best year that the church has ever had. I find the people beginning to awaken to the Master's call: "Go ye into my vineyard and work and whatsoever is right I will repay thee."

G. C. CRUTCHFIELD.

Elon Colege, N. C.

If readers of THE SUN have Bible price lists on hand from this office, they may destroy the same as prices greatly advanced last week and all former prices are withdrawn.

Next issue of THE SUN may go to press earlier than usual for special convenience of our office force.

All fuel regulations have been lifted and taken discontinued are to be restored at once.

Catawba Springs church is planning to build a church in the foreign field. A great and good thing.

A great flood swept over certain areas of Georgia last week. In the section of West Point, Ga., the water stood as high as ten feet, while much damage was done to houses.

The big coal strike was temporarily settled last week. The miners accepted President Wilson's proposal of a 14 per cent increase while the full details of the situation are being worked out.

A census of the country's manufactures was made for the first time in 1810. Under the present law a manufactures census is to be taken in connection with the Fourteenth Decennial Census and every two years thereafter.

An enumeration of the mines and quarries of the United States was made for the first time in 1840.

THE CHRISTIAN ORPHANAGE

FINANCIAL REPORT FOR DECEMBER 17, 1919

Amount brought forward, $18,120.88.

Children's Offerings

Rachel R. Hofler, 10 cents; Philip Harrell, 25 cents; Mary and Fleeta Harrell, $1.00; Total, $1.35.

Sunday School Monthly Offerings

(Eastern Virginia Conference)

First Christian S. S., Berkley, $7.62; Centerville, $1.00; Third church, Norfolk, $30.74.

(North Carolina Conference)

Pleasant Grove, (Va.), $4.00; New Providence, $1.00; Pleasant Hill, $3.88; Linville, Ala., $2.60; Total, $50.84.

Children's Home

Blanche Penny, $20.00; Mrs. A. E. Hines, $5.00; Total, $25.00.

Special Offerings

Home Mission Board, Dr. Omer S. Thomas, Treas., $123.74. Oakland church, $55.00; Miss Bernice Bland's S. S. Class, Holy Neck, $4.00; The Sunshine Band, Machais, N. Y., $12.35; The Sunday school, Machais, N. Y., $5.65; Total, $18.00. Spoon's Chapel, $5.61; Hanks' Chapel, $17.00; Christian church, Columbus, Ga., $112.05; Mr. R. H. Leonard, Mt. Airy, N. C., $1.50; Greensboro church, $500.00; Mrs. Carrie Griffin, $5.00; Assonet Christian S. S., Fall River, Mass., $3.50; Henderson church, $127.75; Elm City . Christian church, Edna, Kans., $15.55; Cypress Chapel, $25.00; Union (Va.), Sunday school, $15.00; Moore Union, $8.30; Bethlehem, $8.50; Reidsville, $22.00; Franklin Grove Union S. S., $20.00; J. B. Gay, $10.00; Washington Grove, Ashton, Ill., $6.37; Belews Creek, $6.00; Noon Day S. S., $25.00; Ramseur, $21.00; A. S. K. Burton, $1.00; Pleasant View ch., Ill., $13.50; Wadley Christian church, $15.60; Mayland S. S., $9.50; Mrs. Nash, Tithian, Ill., $1.00; Union Sunday school, Cumnock, N. C., $10.00; Memorial Christian Temple, Norfolk, $83.09—(This includes birthday offerings and check from Mrs. E. J. Brickhouse); Spring Hill church, (Ala.), $7.40; The Junior Boys and Girls, Wayland, S. S., Goshen, Nebraska, $11.48; Mrs. L. M. Rountree, $3.00; Rev. O. D. Poythress, $5.00; Lebanon church, $114.40; Centerville church, $9.30; Elizabeth Read (Mt. Auburn church), $10.00; Mrs. H. C. King, $1.00; A. E. Hailey, $1.00; Miss Edda Anderson, 25 cents; Miss Georgia Ray, $1.00; Lucile Ray, $1.00; Mrs. Broady Ray, 50 cents; Mrs. M. L. Garrison, 50 cents; Miss Eunice Rogers, $1.00; Holland, Va., $100.00; Randleman, N. C., $2.00; Pleasant Hill church, $42.50; Catawba Springs, $168.58; Nathalie, Va., $22.11; Spring Hill Sunday school, $17.00; Old Zion church, Norfolk, $42.25; Bethlehem church, Littleton, N. C., $3.75; Damascus church, Orange Co., (N. C.), $9.52; Wake Chapel (additional), $100.00; Total, $1,790.36.

Total for the week, $1,991.29; Grand total, $20,112.17.

SUPERINTENDENT'S LETTER

Our Thanksgiving offerings are coming in nicely and many of the churches have more than doubled over last year. We have already past the half way mark to our goal. We have faith enough in our Church to believe we will reach the goal and go over the top.

Let every church have a part in this the largest thank offering ever raised for the Orphanage.

Our friends are good to us and we are glad to report the following:

Mrs. Alice Kimbro, Byromville, Ga., one pair blankets, one quilt one pair towels, two sheets, two pillow cases; Ladies' Aid Society, Chapel Hill church, one box containing quilt, sheets, shoes, dresses, towels, hose, etc.; Antioch church, Valley Va., one box containing four quilts, two counterpanes, six sheets, towels, hose, etc.; Ladies' Aid Society, Franklin Christian church, Franklin, Va., one box containing clothing for the children; Foster and Caveness, Greensboro, N. C., two boxes oranges; Ladies' Aid Society, Pleasant Hill church, Albion, Ill., one box clothing for the children.

CHAS. D. JOHNSTON, *Supt.*

LETTERS FROM THE COUSINS

Dear Uncle Charley: I am a very rude little boy, about three years old. Am sending fifty cents as my Thanksgiving offering to the little cousins. Mamma gave me this money to stay home with her for company for sisters and brother to go to school. Love to all the cousins.—*Phillip Harrell.*

You ought to see my little boy. He is rude too. He likes to tease his sisters the best of all.—*"Uncle Charley."*

Dear Uncle Charley: We are sending you $1.00 as our Thanksgiving offering. We picked cotton for daddy to get this money. Love to all the cousins.—*Mary and Fleeta Harrell.*

You are smart little girls to pick cotton and give your earnings to help the orphans. I hope to see you sometime.—*"Uncle Charley."*

Dear Uncle Charley: I spent Thanksgiving with my aunt. We had lots of good things to eat, and hope the cousins did also. Enclosed you will find a dime. Hope I will be on the honor roll. I wish you all a Merry Christmas.—*Rachel R. Hofler.*

Our little folks are looking forward to Christmas with a great deal of delight.—*"Uncle Charley."*

Dear Uncle Charley: Enclosed you will find check for $2.00 as a Thanksgiving offering for Helen and me. On the sixth of October a sweet little sister came to live with us. Her name is Mildred Charline. I can hold hold her and sing to keep her from crying when mother is busy. Love to all the orphans.—*Maurine Nelson Isley and Helen Elizabeth Isley.*

You must be good to little sister. She will keep you company and play with you.—*"Uncle Charley."*

NEW COMERS TO THE SUN FAMILY

(Report to December 13)

THE SECRET CHAMBER

Into the secret chamber of my heart,
  Wherein no mortal enters, Lord, come Thou,
And make Thy dwelling-place ere day depart.

Even now the clouds are golden in the west;
  The long, slant shadows creep across the way;
The glory fades on yonder mountain crest.

It will be nightfall soon, for faint and far
  The pallid moon, a silver crescent, hangs
Above the low reach of the horizon bar.

The night is lonely and beset with fears!
  Come Thou, O Lord, come in and dwell with me
Through the long darkness till the dawn appears.

O Thou who didst create the human heart,
  Didst Thou not make one sure place for Thyself?
It is high sanctuary where Thou art!

Thou knowest, ah! Thou knowest! Words are weak!
  When the tongue falters and the lips are dumb,
Thou knowest all the yearning heart would speak!

The muttered prayer Thou hearest. Lo! the shrine
  Waits for Thy presence! Ere the day be done,
Take Thou possession, O Thou Guest Divine!
                    —*Selected.*

PAULINE'S POVERTY CHRISTMAS
Mary L. Stetson.

Three dollars! Why, that isn't enough to get what I'd planned for father himself." Sorrowfully Pauline fingered the crisp bills, her Christmas money, which father had just given her, and two big tears rolled down her cheeks. "Oh, dear me," she sighed, "if we'd ever got to be poor, I wish we'd always been poor. It wouldn't seem so hard then."

A knock sounded at the library door, a secret knock known only to Pauline and her most intimate friend.

"Come."

The door flew open, and Theda Marston danced into the room, but stopped short as she noticed the expression of dejection on Pauline's face.

"Whatever is the matter, Pollykins?" she asked.

"Draw your chair up here by the fire, and I'll tell you."

Theda obeyed and listened attentively to her chum's tale of woe. When it was finished, however, the least little twinkle lurked in her brown eyes as she exclaimed, "Oh, Pollykins, aren't you the lucky chick!"

"Lucky?"

"Yes. Why, I never had three dollars given me to spend for Christmas, never in my whole life. Last year I did manage to save two from my strawberry money, and I felt rich, I can tell you."

"Why, Theda Marston, how do you give so many presents, then?"

"Make 'em mostly," was the brief reply.

"But I can't sew."

"There isnt any such word as 'can't,' or if there is,

there ought not to be. Of course you can sew if you try. Say, have you anything on the docket for this morning?"

Pauline shook her head.

"Neither have I, as good luck would have it. I'll run over home and get my sewing, and you—Oh, Pollykins, where are those lovely pieces of silk you were showing me the other day? If you don't need them for patching, they'd make the dandiest sewing-bags," and like a flash, Theda was gone.

When, in a remarkably short time, she was back in the Varnum library she was pleased to find that Pauline had already collected, not only the pieces of silk, but also scraps of linen, laces, and the like.

"Sakes, what a lot of Christmas presents you can get out of all this!" cried Theda. "That linen will make the dinkiest little jabots, and here's a thin piece just right for a handkerchief."

Both girls were soon hard at work. By luncheon time, Pauline's plans for Christmas were nearly completed, and several of the gifts were well under way.

"Aren't those bags going to be just too dear!" exclaimed Theda. "We'll have to call in at Woolworth's the next time we're down town, for the brass rings and the ribbons. Then you can finish them in a jiffy. I think mine's the loveliest of all, and I'm glad I know beforehand that Santa is going to bring me one thing I need most awfully."

During the weeks that followed, Pauline Varnum learned the happiness that comes to those who make some real effort for their friends, a happiness that had never been hers when she could have all the spending money she wished merely for the asking.

Several days before Christmas the little gifts were wrapped in white tissue paper, tied with red ribbons, and carefully laid away in Pauline's top bureau drawer. There, too, was a pack of Christmas postals, every one of which had been selected especially for the person to whom it was addressed. Every card was stamped ready to go in the mail when the proper time should come.

And a dollar and forty-two cents still remained.

"I hardly know what to do with the rest of this money," Pauline remarked to Theda. "It seems silly to give two presents to one person, even if the presents aren't very big."

"I thought you were the girl who couldn't begin to buy your Christmas presents with only three dollars," smiled Theda. "But I'll tell you what, Pollykins. You know those Petersons that live down on French Alley, don't you?"

"Never heard of them."

"Well, anyhow, they go to our Sunday school, and they're awful poor. Let's get 'em up a Christmas box. I'll cook something, and that money of yours is enough to buy mittens for Mary and Jamie and Georgie; their hands were just purple last Sunday, poor kiddies! I shouldn't wonder if we could save enough for a doll and a book and a drum, besides."

"That's a grand idea, Theda. We'll do it. I'd like to know, though, how you come to call those children all by name, when I've been to the same Sunday school and never even heard of them."

The box for the Petersons was filled to overflowing, so that when the time arrived for the delivering of the Christmas gifts two of Theda's young brothers had to be pressed into service.

Christmas Eve father's and mother's gifts alone remained in the top bureau drawer. Pauline locked her chamber door, took out the two beribboned packages, and opened them. The collar box, covered with some of her own needlework, was hardly as fine a gift as the sectional bookcase she had planned to buy for father, nor was the soft linen handkerchief with its narrow edging of lace half as nice as the mahogany writing desk, that had long since been selected for mother.

All of a sudden, in spite of the work she had put into these gifts, they seemed so mean. Father and mother deserved so much more.

Then a happy thought came to her, and she smiled through her tears.

When, next day, Pauline's parents received the only gifts their daughter had ever made for them with her own hands, each found attached a little note. Father's read:

"I'd like to have got you, if I could,
A splendid present of glass and wood.
On a little card in the box you'll see
A picture of what my gift would be.
But since I couldn't buy that this year,
I've worked lots of love into this, daddy, dear."

And mother's read:
"This isn't the desk of mahogany fine
Which I meant to give you, dear mother mine!
In Palmer's window, that's waiting still;
You may look for yourself whenever you will.
This gift is a small one, but each stitch made for you
Brings love and best wishes from a heart that is true."

Other Christmases, father and mother had smiled and said, "Thank you, dear," when they had received Pauline's gifts, but this year they said nothing at all for as much as a minute. Meanwhile, father coughed and blew his nose very hard, and mother put her handkerchief to her eyes. It wasn't the Christmas handkerchief, though. That was too precious to be used even for tears of joy.—*Exchange.*

THE CHRISTMAS BAKING
Christmas Gingerbreads

Beat two cupfuls of molasses and a cupful of softened butter in a bowl until they are well blended. To this add a cupful of sour milk; stir in also a quarter of a cupful of hot water, in which a level tablespoonful of baking soda has been dissolved. Add the grated rind of a lemon, a tablespoonful of cloves and ginger to taste; then stir in enough flour to make a stiff dough. Roll the dough very thin on a molding-board and cut it into the desired shapes, such as toys, trees, Santa Claus, bells, stars, or stockings. Put the pieces in a well-floured dripping-pan and bake in a moderate oven. When the cakes are done, before they are altogether cold, frost lightly with pink or white frosting or add the tiny pieces of candy which are made for this purpose.—*The Mother's Magazine.*

Principles and Government *of* The Christian Church

(The Franklin, Virginia, session of the Southern Christian Convention ordered that the Principles and Government of the Christian Church be revised and that a committee be appointed to make the revision. The following members of the Convention were appointed to do the work: Rev. W. W. Staley, D. D., President; Rev. W. S. Long, D. D., Rev. C. H. Rowland, D. D., Rev. N. G. Newman, D. D., and W. A. Harper, LL. D. Some weeks ago the committee completed its work, and we are privileged to print, in serial form, the Principles and Government as outlined, subject to ratification by the next session of the Convention.—Editor.)

(Continued from last week)
CHAPTER VI
DISCIPLINE

Section 1. (a) Local churches have jurisdiction over members and should deal with offender in the light of Gal. 6:1 and Matt. 18:15-17.

(b) Caution should be exercised in receiving accusations against members, and investigations should be conducted with a view to restoration.

(c) If an accused person is unable to represent himself before a Committee of Investigation, he may request a minister or a member of his own church to represent him.

After due citation of the parties, trials shall be impartial, and in the spirit of affection.

Section 2. (a) Conferences only have jurisdiction over ministers. They are ordained by conference, amenable to conference, and from the decision of conference there is no appeal.

(b) Charges against a minister can be preferred only by two ministers, a church (I Tim. 5:19), or by common fame. Prosecutions can be made only by a minister or by a committee from the church preferring the charge. Parties prosecuting a minister should be warned that failure to sustain the charges will subject them to censure.

(c) Accused ministers shall be furnished with a copy of the charges, the names of the witnesses, and allowed twenty days to prepare for trial. The investigation shall be conducted by all the ministers present at conference, or by the Executive Committee and the ministers of the conference *ad interim;* and, in either case, the findings shall be reported to conference for final action.

(d) All trials shall be conducted in the light of Matthew 18:15-17, and the decision of conference is as final in the case of a minister, as the decision of a local church in the case of a member.

Section 3. (a) Charges against a church for neglect of duty or violation of church government may be preferred by a sister church or two ministers; and, in either case, the charges must be prosecuted in the name of the party preferring the charge. The same caution and good spirit should be exercised in the trial of a church as in the case of a minister. The investigation may be at its own place of worship, or at some other place, through a committee appointed by conference, or the Executive Committee.

(b) A church found guilty of charges may be admonished, censured, or cut off from conference; but sentence against a church should not involve members who protest against the offense with which the church is charged. A church cut off may be restored by repentance and application.

The competency of witnesses shall be determined by the court of trial in all cases.

CHAPTER VII

All amendments or changes in the Principles, Government, Directory for Worship, or official forms and ceremonies shall be authorized by the Convention; and all motions and resolutions for this purpose shall be published in the church paper three months before the session at which the subject is to be considered, and all changes may be determined by a two-thirds vote of the Convention.

PART III

CHAPTER I
OFFICIAL FORMS AND CEREMONIES

RECEPTION OF MEMBERS

1. Persons desiring to unite with the church upon profession of faith shall present themselves before the altar, while a hymn is being sung. Candidates should be previously instructed by the pastor or deacons, as to the qualifications and duties of church membership.
HYMN.

The minister shall examine the candidates in the presence of the congregation as follows:

(1) Have you sincerely and heartily repented of all your sins?

(2) Do you believe in the Lord Jesus Christ as the Savior of the world now as your personal Savior?

(3) Is it your purpose through grace to live a godly life?

These questions being answered in the affirmative, the minister shall declare the fact to the congregation; i. e., the members of the Church. The name shall here be announced, and the question asked:

You have heard the answers given by Brother (or Sister) .... to these questions. Is there any objection to receiving this brother (or sister, or brothers and sisters) into full fellowship in this church? If there is any objection on the part of any member of the church let it now be stated.

If there is an objection, the case shall be referred to a regular or special Conference of the church for investigation. If there is no objection, the minister shall proceed to receive the applicant (or applicants) into full connection with the Church, saying:

On behalf of the church, I extend to you the right hand of fellowship and welcome you into this church, and to all its privileges. May you be a blessing to the church and the church a blessing to you, I commend

to you the Holy Bible as a sufficient rule of faith and practice in the church, and enjoin upon you to study it carefully and prayerfully, and to obey its precepts according to the best of your understanding and ability.
PRAYER.

2. Applicants may be received into the church in like manner by the Deacons, when the services of no higher officer can be procured.

3. Members may be received by transfer from any evangelical denomination, and such letters of transfer shall be read before the church by the pastor or one of the deacons.

CHAPTER II
ADMINISTRATION OF BAPTISM

The mode of baptism is optional with the candidate and should be administered by an Elder.

During the singing of a suitable hymn the candidates should present themselves.

HYMN.

The minister should then read from these Scriptures or other suitable lesson:

Then the eleven disciples went away into Galilee, into a mountain where Jesus had appointed them. And when they saw him, they worshiped him: but some doubted. And Jesus came and spake unto them, saying, All power is given unto me in heaven and in earth. Go ye therefore, and teach all nations, baptizing them in the name of the Father, and of the Son, and of the Holy Ghost. Teaching them to observe all things whatsoever I have commanded you: and, lo, I am with you always, even unto the end of the world. Amen. Matt. 28:16-20.

An appropriate prayer should then be offered.

PRAYER.

After which, the minister shall proceed to administer the ordinance, saying:

In obedience to the command of my Lord and Master, and upon the profession of thy faith, I baptize thee in the name of the Father, and of the Son, and of the Holy Spirit. Amen.

The services will then proceed as usual, or close with suitable exercises and benediction.

(To be Continued)

THE CHURCH PAPER AND THE CHURCH PEOPLE

Mrs. W. A. Pierce—I have been taking THE SUN for fifteen years and enjoy reading it very much. It gets better every day and I do not want to miss a copy.

* *

John Taylor—May the subscribers to THE SUN increase during next year.

* *

C. E. Brittle—We enjoy THE SUN in our home and would not be without it for twice the money that it costs us. May it shine in every home of the Christian Church is our prayer.

* *

J. W. Michael—Let THE SUN come on as it is ever a welcome visitor.

THE STORY OF ST. NICHOLAS
Legends of the Popular Christmas Saint

Father Christmas has a strong competitor in good St. Nicholas, whose "day" falls on December 6. In some countries, Belgium, for instance, Christmas is not celebrated socially at all, except in individual cases and as a result of contact with Germany, and St. Nicholas's day is the great day of the year for the little folks. It is from him that we have borrowed some of the most memorable customs of Christmas, the stocking-hanging at the ingle, and Santa Claus, which is simply a corruption of his name.

Who was St. Nicholas? He is said to have been bishop of Myra in Lycia, Asia Minor; but his story, as it has come down to us, is purely legendary, and not a single fact of his life can be historically confirmed. If we accept the legends, he was bishop of Myra in the days of Diocletian, in whose reign he was not only persecuted but tortured. He lay in prison, like many others, until Constantine came into power. He was present, it is said, at the council of Nice; but this statement rests upon popular legend, and the presence of St. Nicholas at that council is not mentioned by the historians of the period. St. Athanasius, who knew all the bishops of his day, never once refers to St. Nicholas.

It is hard to imagine, however, that he was a purely fictitious person. Obscure he may have been, but the story of his life evidently gripped popular imagination, and legends began at a very early period to accumulate about his name. In those days, when biography passed from man to man by means of story-telling, it was natural that stories about saints should grow in wonder. It was a credulous age. Miracles seemed a part of the normal life of man, and so no one had difficulty about believing the most marvellous wonder-tales about the servants of God.

The earliest monument to the cult of St. Nicholas is the Church of St. Priscus and St. Nicholas, which was built at Constantinople by the Emperor Justinian. By the ninth century St. Nicholas appears in martyrologics in the West, and in the eleventh century churches were frequently dedicated to him. In the year 1087 the inhabitants of Bari, in southeastern Italy, organized an expedition, obtained the saint's body by means of a ruse, and carried it to their town, where they buried it in triumph. Since then pilgrimages have been steadily made to his tomb, and are made to this day.

More churches have been dedicated to St. Nicholas than to any saint except those of apostolic times. In little Belgium more than 100 churches bear his name, and in England more than 400. St. Nicholas is the patron saint of Russia, and he is the especial protector of children, scholars, merchants, and sailors.

Artists have presented St. Nicholas with three children standing in a tub by his side. This refers to a legend which tells how he miraculously restored to life three youths who had been murdered, cut up, and concealed in a salting-tub by an inn-keeper in whose house they had been lodging.

The legend, however, whose influence reaches down through the years to our own day, is one which tells of how the saint surreptitiously gave gifts of gold to three maidens who could not be married because they had no dowry, and whose father was about to sell them to a life of shame. This story was perpetuated by means of pictures which show the saint outside the house secretly casting his gifts through a window. It is said that this legend is responsible for the custom of giving presents at Christmas time, or on St. Nicholas Day, December 6; and the secrecy of the saint's act is kept up in the attitude of our own Santa Claus, who is never seen, but whose gifts nevertheless reach all good children.

St. Nicholas is often called the boy bishop. Legend has it that when the former bishop of Myra died, a certain bishop dreamed that the first person named Nicholas that came to the church doors was the person God had selected to be bishop of the church. The doors were carefully watched, and in the early morning, long before ordinary worshippers appeared, the boy Nicholas came to pray. The bishop asked him his name, and when he learned it insisted that he be made bishop. Modestly he accepted. "He woke in prayer and made his body lean," says the chronicler; "he was humble in receiving all things, profitable in speaking, joyous in admonishing, and cruel in correcting."

In parts of Europe to this day Nicholas is revered, and simple-minded peasants believe that he still gives gifts and cures disease. In Belgium and Holland he reigns supreme as Father Christmas does in other lands. It is Nicholas that rides on his ass, over the housetops, and that brings good things to the little folks. He is still a strict disciplinarian, however, for he has always with him a rod to remind the children of what to expect when they are bad.—*Christian Endeavor World.*

THE HISTORY OF THE CHRISTMAS TREE
Jane A. Stewart

The bright and beautiful Christmas tree, with its attractive gifts, is naturally looked on as an essential part of the Christmas festivities. No celebration is quite complete without it.

To whom shall we credit its institution?

To attempt to locate the original source of the idea is a fascinating bit of research.

If we look for the origin and first introduction of the Christmas tree we find it reaches far back into the night of time. Indeed, so hazy is the record back of the brightly glowing Christmas tree that it is quite impossible to tell where or by whom it was first originated. Antiquarians are prolific in suggestion on the subject. But the clues afforded immediately lead back to the dubiousness of fable and tradition.

Nearly every country has its legend claiming for its own this popular feature of modern Christmas observance. In Scandinavia the Christmas tree is said to have sprung from a "service tree" which germinated from the blood-soaked soil where two lovers met a violent death. This claim is substantiated by the statement that at the Christmas-tide inextinguishable lights gleamed from the branches.

In a French romance of the thirteenth century a great tree is described whose branches are covered with burning candles, and on whose top is a vision of a child with a halo around his curly head, the tree representing mankind, the child the Saviour, and the candles (some of which are upside down) good and bad human beings.

Some old writers would have us believe that it may be Saint Winfrith (afterward called Boniface, the name given to him when he became a missionary), who deserves the primary honor of giving the Christmas tree to the world, as narrated in a charming, suggestive story illustrative of the displacement of heathenism by Christianity.

Saint Winfrith, the story goes, leveled a majestic oak which had been worshiped by his Druidic converts, and immediately a stalwart young fir sprang up in its place.

Addressing the company of newly enlisted Christmas, Saint Winfrith said:

"This little tree, a young child of the forest, shall be your holy tree tonight. It is the wood of peace; for your houses are built of fir. It is the sign of an endless life, for its leaves are green. See how it points upward to heaven. Let this be called the tree of the Christ-child. Gather about it, not in the wild wood, but in your own homes. There it will shelter, not deeds of blood, but loving gifts and rites of kindness."

That is an interesting story which attributes to Martin Luther the inauguration of the Christmas tree. A favorite engraving represents him sitting in his family circle with a lighted Christmas tree on the table beside him.

The story goes that the idea came to Luther when he was traveling alone one Christmas eve. The snow-covered country, the trees, the sky with its gleaming points of light, made such a deep impression on him that he could neither shake it off nor express it. After he reached home he went into the garden, cut a little fir tree, brought it into the nursery, put some candles on its branches, and lighted them. Affectionate regard for the great religious leader has fostered the desire of his followers to associate his name with the popular and kindly custom. The story has wide acceptance.

There is considerable ground, too, for the suggestion that the famous tree "Igdrasil," of Norse mythology, may be the original progenitor of the modern Christmas tree. The pine trees of the Roman saturnalia have also claim to be regarded as prototypes of the Christmas tree. They were decorated, not with toys and gifts, but with images of Bacchus, as described by Virgil in the Georgics. The practice of burning Yule logs was a meiniscence of the days of those wanton winter festivals.

The Egyptians may have originated the idea in their practice of decorating their houses at the time of the winter solstice with branches of the date palm, which

they regarded not only as an emblem of immortality, but also of the star-lit firmament.

The first authentic account of the Christmas tree is dated in the seventeenth century. The manuscript is in a private collection in Friedberg, Hesse, and is dated 1608.

The world-wide adoption of the Christmas tree began at the opening of the nineteenth century. The introduction of the Christmas tree into England occurred after the marriage of Queen Victoria to a German prince, which brought German customs to England.

Holland is indebted for the Christmas tree to Queen Caroline, who introduced it in 1830. Ten years later the French were shown Christmas-tree customs by the Duches Helene at the Tuileries, and at first the tree was disliked. In France the Christmas tree, root and all, is planted in a tub and kept fresh until New Year's, when its beauty and its gifts are to be enjoyed.

The foreign immigrant who brought the Christmas tree to America did more perhaps than any other to give us the happy home festival which we now enjoy.—*Western Christian Advocate.*

CHRISTMAS QUESTIONS
E. E. Longnecker

Would you like to think, as you hurried by,
    Planning for those of your own,
That the echo of your Christmas bells
    May be a childish moan
Wrung from the heart of some little one
    Who has had no Christmas day,
Who must look on the joys of the other kids
    With a heart too sad for play?

Would you care to witness the childish grief
    And the struggle not to cry—
Then the bitter tears of some little tot
    Whom Santa Claus passed by,
Who can't understand why he was missed
    When all of his friends fared well,
Who manfully struggles to hide all trace
    Of the tell-tale tears that fell?

Have you heard the shouts of boundless joy
    Of the kids on Christmas day?
Have you ever seen the eagerness
    With which they start to play?
Have you seen their faith in Santa Claus,
    His reindeer and his sleigh?
It's seeing things with the eyes of a child
    That brightens your Christmas day.

Have you seen the light in a youngster's eyes
    When he first beholds his toys
In the early dawn of a Christmas morn?
    Then you've seen the joy of joys.
Is it worth your while to know that you,
    On whom good fortune smiled,
Have done your part to gladden the heart
    Of some unfortunate child?
                —*Toledo "Blade."*

SOME CHRISTMAS SUGGESTIONS

CHRISTMAS BOOKS FOR CHILDREN

We list below a supply of books which we have purchased suitable for Christmas presents for the children. For the lack of space we cannot tell what each book is about, but we have exercised the very best care in the selection, to see that all stories are helpful and interesting:

The Thorn of the Fortress	50 cents
Matt of the Waterfront	50 cents
The Other Side of the Rainbow	60 cents
Lantern Stories	60 cents
Billy and Bumps	35 cents
Good Night Stories	60 cents
The Jim Family	25 cents
Little Folks of the Bible	30 cents
Sunny Hour Books	15 cents

(Little Folks of the Bible can be had in books I, II, III, and IV. Books I and II are for boys and books III and IV are for girls. We will send any four books of this title for $1.00.)

(Sunny Hour Books are made up of 14 different titles. The price is 15 cents for each title, any two for 25 cents; four for 45 cents and all over four at 10 cents per volume.)

All the above named books are suitable for children 8 to 14 except the "Sunny Hour Books" which are for little tots that cannot read or are just beginning to read. "Sunny Hour Books" contain an abundance of pictures and are bound with colored cloth and stamped with an appropriate design.

Add 4 cents per volume for postage when only one copy is ordered, and 2 cents per volume for postage in lots up to ten; all over ten volumes add 1 cent per volume for postage.

CLEARANCE SALE OF CHILDREN'S BOOKS

We make it a rule in December of each year to buy the closing out stock of several suitable books for children. By buying the closing out stock, we are enabled to get a better price and make the books within the reach of all.

We have been able this year to buy the complete stock of the following 50 cent sellers, and offer them at prices indicated:

Blazing the Way	$ .25
Bright Side and Other Side	.25
Crown Jewels	.20
From the Thames to the Toossachs	.25
Up the Susquehanna	.25

(This price is postpaid)

The following reductions will be made in lots: Any two copies, 45 cents; three copies, 60 cents; four copies, 75 cents; all over four copies at 17 cents per copy.

The supply is limited and we advise you to order early. If any title has exhausted when your order is received, we will substitute unless otherwise instructed.

These books are all well made and handsomely bound.

Make some child's life happy by presenting one or more of these books. Invest a few dollars to make the little tots of your class happy.

SUNDAY SCHOOL HELPS

We have the following Sunday school helps on the 1920 International Lesson:

Peloubet's Select Notes	$1.60
Tarbell's Teachers' Guide	1.60
Arnold's Commentary	.75
Torrey's Gist of the Lesson	.30

(These prices include postage)

A FEW MORE CHRISTMAS SUGGESTIONS

Bibles

No. 71. Scofield Reference Bible. Handsome binding, French Morocco limp, new and improved edition. "The neatest Scofield Bible made." It will please you. Regular selling price $4.50

No. 215. Child's Self-Pronouncing Pictorial Bible with Helps. Bound in French seal leather, round corners, silk bands, gold titles,—handsomely made. Regular selling price $2.50

No. 1113. Ideal Bible for Children. Printed on fine white paper from the newest and clearest type of the size made. Size 3 1-2X5 3-8 inches. This Bible will please you. Regular price $1.75

Testaments

No. 6913 R. L. (Red Letter). Large print Morocco binding. Regular price $2.00
No. 2902 Cloth binding, large print. Regular price.... .90
No. 2502 P. Cloth binding, black faced type. Regular price .... .75
No. 2113. Pocket size, Morocco binding. Regular price .60
No. 0133. Pocket size, Morocco binding, overlapping edges. Regular Price .... .75

(A Testament in Modern Speech)

Cloth, $1.25; cloth, indexed, $1.75; cloth, India paper, $1.75; leather, $2.35; leather, indexed, $2.75; leather, India paper, $2.75; Persian Morocco, Divinity Circuit, $3.75; Turkey Morocco, $1.25. Pocket Edition (without notes): Cloth, $1.00; cloth, India paper, $1.25; leather, India paper, $1.85. State definitely style wanted.

Address
C. B. RIDDLE, Publishing Agent .
Burlington - - - - North Carolina

SOLVE THAT PRESENT PROBLEM

Solve that Christmas present problem by giving a copy of Tarbell's Teachers' Guide. It will be a reminder every week in the year 1920. The price is $1.60 delivered. We also have Peloubet's Select Notes at the same price.

ARNOLD'S NOTES ON THE SUNDAY SCHOOL LESSON

Arnold's Commentary on the International Sunday school will please you as a teacher. Try a copy and become a better teacher. The price is 75 cents delivered.

DID YOU EVER SEE IT?

Did you ever see a copy of Torrey's Gist of the Lesson? Vest pocket size, handy, and convenient. Send 30 cents and let us mail you a copy.

Sunday School and Christian Endeavor

The Training of Peter and John.
—Review John I 1:1-9.

Golden Text: "Ye shall be my witnesses."—Acts 1:8.

For three months we have thought and studied about these two great men. What have we learned concerning them? What do we know of them any more than we did when we began this study? Have you ever made a list of the facts concerning these two men? Perhaps such an outline will help you.

Peter: First known as Simon, surnamed Peter by Jesus. A son of Jonas, a native of Bethsaida. No mention of parents, one brother, Andrew, married, and probably having at least one child. His brother and mother-in-law appear to have lived with them. By occupation a fisherman and sailor; goes to Judea to hear John the Baptist and is there introduced to Jesus by Andrew. A rough, uncouth swearing, cursing, fisherman, unstable, hotheaded. Can you add any more?

John: A son of Zebedee, of well-to-do parentage (his father kept servants; John had his own home, and was known to the priests family). He with his brother, James, had also gone to Judea to hear John the Baptist, and there is one of the two to hear John's proclamation of the Lamb of God. He was of rather arrogant disposition, very quick tempered, so much so that Jesus surnamed him and his brother "sons of thunder." He was ready to demand the best and highest seat for himself, and to call down fire on Samaritans who refused to receive them. Probably the youngest of the disciples, and the best beloved by his Lord.

What made these men, the great men the shining lights in the gospel ministry? You will find it in the words of Jesus, "Come with me, and I will make you......" He wanted just what they had, but He wanted it put to different uses. He did not make Peter like John, or John like Peter, or either like James or Andrew. He wanted their talents, their abilities, and He wanted them

used for the Kingdom. Perhaps that is the best message of the New Year to all of us. "Just as I am" is the way Jesus wants me. He will do the refining, the changing. He wil make me what I ought to be. All I have to do is to forsake my nets, whatever those nets may be, and follow Him.

"Make Next Year Better."—Ps. 90:1-17.

Life is a busy school. We are students, and time marks the progress of every one. Year by year we advance in age, and how happy we are if we have learned to use the fleeting years well. As we develop physically and mentally, our spiritual lives should also develop into strong men and women for Christ and His Kingdom. It is our privilege to make every year better than the preceding one, and if we stop to think that we have Christ on our side we will. The young man or woman who does not make a better man or woman than father or mother, has missed the mark. Why? Because the parents' life, influence and guidance were there for an example, and what a great pity it is that so many young people never think of this until it is too late. With the influence of godly parents, and the help of Jesus Christ it is easy to do the right thing and to make a decided success. Yet, one great hindrance to the human life is the waste of time, for he who completes his work in the great school of life must use the time God has allotted to him.

This year has been great, regardless of its difficulties. True it has been marked here and there with many difficult problems, hardships, strikes, blunders in governmental affairs, restlessness on the part of capital and labor, war among ourselves over problems of no concern, and many other things too numerous to mention. Yet in spite of it all Christianity has taken a great forward step, and our people have not failed to take advantage of the opportunity to help in the work. Out of the great struggle has come an

awakening on the part of the Church, and none of the past years have been blessed with richer rewards than has 1919.

Yet, we must not be content with past or present achievements. We must make 1920 the best yet. How can we do it? We can do it by making it a year of prayer, self-sacrifice and service. Let each Endeavor resolve to concentrate all his power of purpose upon one great ideal in life, and be faithful to the trust committed to his care. The secret of the successful life is found in that attitude toward the work of the Kingdom. All the evangelical churches have had a great drive for finances, and now the one great call and need is for more men and women to do the work. Make next year better by adding hundreds of new lives to the working forces of the Kingdom. Let me challenge all who read these notes to the task before us, for nothing will put more life into your Society, school and church than for some of its members to dedicate their lives to full time service for the Kingdom. Remember our motto is: "For Christ and the Church," and we ought to make next year better by "Doubling Everything." Your church attendance, mid-week service, Sunday school and your Society needs your best service.

Suggestions For The New Year.
Start something! Better have a house party for your young people to get together than nothing. Organize a new Society. Organize a "Fill the pew Club," and fill your church with youngsters. Give your young people a chance. Don't expect a house full of folks for the first meeting. Better have a Society with three active members than one with fifty dead ones. One society in Greensboro with four active members supported an orphan, and contributed $75.00 to foreign missions last year. If they did it, (and they did) you can too. Come on, and let us place a Society in every available Christian church during 1920. What say you young people? Hands up everybody who think we can! Now, then, let us get busy and do it.

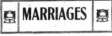

MARRIAGES

POYTHRESS-ROGERS

On November 2, 1919, Mr. Arthur H. Poythress and Miss Annie Rogers were, by the writer, united in marriage. The couple were accompanied by a few friends who witnessed the ceremony that gave the legal and religious sanction to the union of their hearts and lives. As another home is established and they begin the journey of married life together, the prayers and good wishes of many friends follow them into their new home.

R. L. WILLIAMSON.

WALLACE-ALLEN

At the home of Mrs. N. A. Allen, on the evening of November 5, 1919, at 7 o'clock P. M., Mr. E. B. Wallace and Miss Mollie Allen were united in marriage, the ceremony being performed by the writer, in the presence of a few intimate friends. Mr. Wallace is a very successful business man of Troy, N. C., and Mrs. Wallace is the accomplished daughter of Mrs. N. A. Allen of Martin's Mill, N. C. Immediately after the ceremony the young couple motored to their new home at Troy, N. C., accompanied by the best wishes of a host of friends.

G. R. UNDERWOOD.

DR. J. H. BROOKS

DENTIST

Foster Building   Burlington, N. C.

CHARLES W. McPHERSON, M. D.

Eye, Ear, Nose, Throat

OFFICE OVER CITY DRUG STORE

Office Hours: 9:00 a. m. to 1:00 p. m.
and 2:00 to 5:00 p. m.

Phones: Residence 153; Office 65J

BURLINGTON, NORTH CAROLINA

OUR ONE GREAT NEED

THE CHRISTIAN SUN

IN EVERY HOME

OBITUARIES

CAPT. JAMES A. TURRENTINE—AN APPRECIATION

Captain James A. Turrentine, the beloved senior deacon of the First Christian Church, Burlington, N. C., was translated to his rich reward November 4, 1919. To the membership of this church his life was like an autumn all aflame with crimson gold. He came to his mature life with an increasing number of friends. He grew into the sunset of life gracefully. He maintained the gallantry of a young man, the kindness of a youth, the affection of a child, and the grace and ease of middle life. To know him was to love him, and once you met him you knew him and he knew you.

Brother Turrentine's unscarred record as a member of this church stands out as a beacon light to those who travel in the direction he has gone. He was a Christian gentleman, rich in spirit, brotherly in conduct and noble in character. He loved his church and took great pride in the achievement of the church. He was ambitious for the best possible progress of his local church and for the denomination. He was wise in his counsel and generous of his means. He hated littleness and took pride in the big and progressive things of his church.

We, therefore, the members of Burlington Christian church, desire to place on record this expression of our appreciation and gratitude to God for the noble life, character and conduct of our deceased brother.

We further express our appreciation by recommending that a copy of this testimony be sent to his brother, to his sons, his daughters, to the Burlington News and The Christian Sun for publication, and a copy made a part of the permanent records of this church.

JOHN R. FOSTER,
D. E. SELLARS,
C. B. RIDDLE,
Committee.

November 8, 1919.

POWELL

Mr. Augustin Powell died November 20, 1919, at the age of fifty-seven years, seven months and eight days. He had been in declining health for some time but had been confined to his home but a few weeks. He leaves to mourn his death, a wife, eight children, three brothers, one sister, and a host of relatives and friends.

Brother Powell had been a member of Mt. Hermon church a number of years. His presence was greatly missed during his illness, and his aid will now be missed as well. He was buried at Mt. Hermon. Friday Afternoon, November 21, the funeral services being conducted by the writer. Many will miss him as a church member, a friend and neighbor, as well as in the home, but may we all be able to say like Job of old, "The Lord gave and the Lord hath taken away; blessed be the name of the Lord."

JOSEPH E. McCAULEY.

The Exception

Our personal poultry dealer said it was a good chicken, but it seems nobody has ever told our personal poultry dealer that the good die young.—*Detroit News.*

SAFES AND VAULTS

At factory prices
Expert on safes, locks and combinations
Rebuild and change combination

L. M. CLYMER,
GREENSBORO, N. C.

P. O. Box 129.

Successor to

The O. B. Barnes Safe Company.

JOKES FOR CHRISTMAS

Proving It

Lady (in party viewing stone quarry): "And which is the foreman?"

Casey (proudly): "Oi am."

Lady: "Really?"

Casey: "Oi kin prove ut. (Calls to laborer). 'Kelly, Kelly! yer foired!' "—*Judge*.

Estimating Genius

"What silly verses that woman is reciting!"

"I wrote them, sir!"

"Ah—oh, yes—to be sure—clever lines, but horribly delivered, don't you know—woman must be a fool to bungle 'em so—who is she?"

"My wife, sir!"—*Cleveland Leader*.

An Authority

Doctor (to Pat's wife, after examining Pat, who had been run down by an auto): "Madam, I fear your husband is dead."

Pat (feebly): "No, I ain't dead yet."

Pat's wife: "Hush, Pat, the gentleman knows better than you."—*Lippincott's Magazine*.

Accepting Disappointment

A correspondent of the Denver "News" writes: "Last Sunday an elder announced: 'Owing to a misunderstanding, the supply arranged for in the absence of the regular pastor has not appeared, consequently there will be no service. The congregation will rise and sing "Praise God from Whom All Blessings Flow" and be dismissed.'"

A Fatal Defeat

Hans, the ruralist, was in search of a horse.

"I've got the very thing you want," said Bill Lenox, the stableman, "a thorough-going road horse. Five years old, sound as a quail, $175 cash down and he goes ten miles without stopping."

Hans threw his hands skyward.

"Hot for me," he said, "not for me. I wouldn't gif you 5 cents for him. I live eight miles out in de country, and I'd haf to walk back two miles."

"Smart as a Philadelphia Lawyer"

The following is told of a late rail way magnate and a prominent Philadelphia lawyer:

Said the magnate to the lawyer, "I want you to show that this law is unconstitutional. Do you think you can manage it?"

"Easily," said the lawyer.

"Well, go ahead and get familiar with the case."

"Im already at home in it. I know my ground perfectly. It's the same law you had me prove was constitutional two years ago."—*Lancaster News Journal*.

An Editor's Duties

Most any man can be an editor. All the editor has to do is to sit at his desk six days a week, four weeks a month and twelve fonths in a year, and edit such stuff as this:

"Mrs. Jones of Cactus Creek let a can-opener slip last week and cut herself in the pantry. Joe Doe climbed on the roof of his house last week looking for a leak and fell, landing on his back porch. While Harold Green was ecorting Miss Violet Wise from the church social last Saturday night a savage dog attached them and bit Mr. Green on the public square. Mr. Fang, while harnessing a broncho last Saturday, was kicked just south of his corn crib."—*Yarmouth Light*.

RIDDLES

What is the longest word in the English language?

Smiles, because there is a mile between its first and last letters.

What is it that flies high, and flies low; yet has no wings?

Dust.

What word has five letters from which if you take two you have one left?

Stone.

When is it easy to read the woods?

When autumn turns the leaves.

What asks no question, yet receives many answers?

A doorbell.

What letter in the alphabet is the most useful to a deaf old woman?

"A" because it makes her hear.

When is a sailor a very small man?

When he goes to sleep on his watch.

What is a country seat?

A milking stool.

CHURCH OFFERING ENVELOPES

Standard Double

(Size 2½X4¼ inches—52 to Set)

White or Manila

25 to 49 sets	16 cts. a set
50 to 109 sets	14 cts. a set
110 to 209 sets	13 cts. a set
210 to 309 sets	12½ cts. a set
310 to 399 sets	12 cts. a set
400 or more sets	11 cts. a set

Minimum Charge $3.00 net.

CARTONS, INCLUDED

Single Envelope System

(Size 2 5-16X3 5-8 inches. Open side. 52 to Set)

White or Manila

25 to 49 sets	14 cts. a set
50 to 99 sets	13 cts. a set
100 to 149 sets	12 cts a set
150 to 199 sets	11½ cts. a set
200 to 249 sets	11 cts. a set
250 or more sets	10 cts. a set

Minimum Charge $2.00 set.

CARTONS INCLUDED

Take Note

The following points should be taken into consideration in placing an order for church offering envelopes:

1. A set means 52 envelopes, one for each Sunday in the year.

2. When cartons are ordered the sets are arranged in their logical order, thus making it convenient for the member. We suggest the use of cartons because of the convenience.

3. If you desire monthly, double or single envelopes, without cartons, 1-8 the price of the same number of weekly sets. Cartons 3-4 cent each.

4. Semi-monthly, double or single, in cartons, 2-3 the weekly price; without cartons 3-5 the weekly price.

5. When ordering state what Sunday that your church year begins, and whether you want the dates on envelopes or not.

6. Indicate the wording that you want placed on the envelopes or leave the same with us. Samples sent upon request.

7. Allow ten to fifteen days for delivery. Order early.

C. B. RIDDLE, Publishing Agent

Burlington,   N. C.

THE CHRISTIAN SUN

"IN ESSENTIALS UNITY, IN NON-ESSENTIALS LIBERTY, IN ALL THINGS CHARITY"

FOR God so loved the world, that He gave His only begotten Son, that whosoever believeth on Him should not perish, but have everlasting life. *John 3:16.*

Volume LXXI   WEDNESDAY, DECEMBER 24, 1919   Number 52

BURLINGTON   ·   ·   ·   NORTH CAROLINA

THE CHRISTIAN SUN

Founded 1844 by Rev. Daniel W. Kerr

C. B. RIDDLE - - - Editor

Entered at the Burlington, N. C. Post Office as second class matter.

Subscription Rates

One year .... $ 2.00
Six months 1.00

In Advance

Give both your old and new postoffice when asking that your address be changed.

The change of your label is your receipt for money. When received receipts sent upon request.

Many persons subscribe for friends, intending that the paper be stopped at the end of the year. If instructions are given to this effect, they will receive attention at the proper time.

Marriage and obituary notices not exceeding 150 words printed free if received within 60 days from date of event, all over this at the rate of one-half cent a word.

Original poetry not accepted for publication.

Principles of the Christian Church

(1) The Lord Jesus Christ is the only Head of the Church.
(2) Christian is a sufficient name of the Church.
(3) The Holy Bible is a sufficient rule of faith and practice.
(4) Christian character is a sufficient test of fellowship, and of church membership.
(5) The right of private judgment and the liberty of conscience is a right and a privilege that should be accorded to, and exercised by all.

EDITORIAL

THE CHURCH A LEADING FACTOR

We read with interest the other day a note written by Mr. R. W. Scott, a prosperous farmer of Alamance county, to The News Letter, a weekly publication issued by the University of North Carolina. We take pleasure in reproducing the letter here:

"The News Letter" item about the Pleasant Garden School and Community suggests to me a few words about the Hawfields Community in Alamance county. It has one of the best country brick churches in this section. Near the church is the cemetery, one of the best kept in the State. An endowment fund of $3,500 was raised and invested in Liberty Bonds. Only the interest is used for the upkeep of the cemetery. The minister lives in the manse, one of the best residences in the community. With the manse is, thirty acres of land, enough to supply wood, pasture, and garden.

The school was established in 1902 by voting a local tax. Some years later it was made a state high school, and now it offers courses in vocational agriculture.

Boys who will never go to college are being taught agriculture, and they will go back to the farms with knowledge and pride in farming. We know that few college graduates in agriculture go back to the farms.

At one time this school furnished more teachers in the public schools of the county than any other school. Students have gone direct from this school to Davidson, University of North Carolina, Elon, the A. and E. College, and North Carolina College for Women. A boy from this school went to Davidson and made the highest grade that ever was made there and then at the Union Theological Seminary made the highest average that had been made in twenty-five years. One student at the A. and E. taking the agriculture course won the Inter-College Debate medal, Oratory medal, Track medal and Loving Cup for track athletics.

Best of all, boys that are graduates are returning to their old homes to farm, one from the Mississippi Agriculture College, one from the A. and E., and one from the University. This community furnished the young man who cared for and fed the Jersey cow that made the highest record of any cow in the South.

Hawfields has not only in the past held very creditable community fairs, but this year contributed to the Mebane fair, bringing home the first prize of $100 for the best exhibit. It also made a fine display of poultry. Not only this, but the community contributed most of the county exhibit that went to the State fair.

There is no community where greater harmony, and good feeling and less jealousy exist. There never has in the history of the school been any division among the trustees, teachers, or parents.

There is much to do yet on roads, soil, and in farm-improvements. Conveniences in the homes will have to have attention in the future. Can any community in the State equal or better this? And this has all been accomplished by people in very moderate circumstances and in a community where neither tobacco nor cotton is raised.

Note that Mr. Scott begins his article by referring to the community church, which reminds us that no community can be a real place to live unless it has a church. This community of which Mr. Scott speaks can also pride itself by saying that the church was one of the first institutions to be placed there. The church is always the leading factor in the community, whether you see it this way or not. The influence of the church is the stabalizer of all good things; and all things worth while are centered around the work of the church.

There are many other communities just as good as the one about which Mr. Scott speaks, but the thing that we much hope for is that many other communities not so far advanced will note the advancement of this community and go forward. Rural life is the real life, and unless we have good churches and able pastors, good schools and other accommodations we cannot hope to hold the boys and girls. While you are lamenting the fact that the boys and girls of your community are leaving, you might also set about to investigate the why. You may find it in the absence of the things that Mr. Scott's community has.

OCCASION FOR REJOICING

We are sure that all readers of THE CHRISTIAN SUN will rejoice with the Southern Baptists in the great success of their wonderful campaign for $75,000,000.00. People who do such things are a blessing and a real asset to our civilization. For be it said that the only hope for this wonderfully prosperous and extravagant age is to increase the tide of benevolence through the channels of the Church. Unless the Church can prevail upon the people to increase, and very largely increase, their gifts and their donations to the work of the Kingdom, there can be no other destiny for our civilization than that which befell Babylon and Greece and Rome and the nations who in the past have perished, not from poverty, but from indulgence, material prosperity and greed. Our age is absorbed in the topic of money getting and money spending and unless we can imbed deep into the thought of the time, the fundamental fact that the Lord must share in our gettings, and expenditures, and that we are His stewards, a crass materialism will overtake us and we shall forget God who is the Giver of all good.

But we had started out with a word of appreciation and gratitude to the great Baptist hosts who have done such a wonderful work for the Kingdom. We wish in this connection to quote a paragraph from *The Biblical Recorder* which sets forth a truth sometimes overlooked by the casual observer:

"Perhaps the greatest blessing that has come from the Campaign is the spiritual awakening among our people. There have been many reports of conversions; and thousands have enlisted for special service. There will be recruits for the foreign field and many workers for the home land as a result of the Campaign. There is a spirit of co-operation among our people that we never knew before."

We feel that we Christians need this same benefit. We are sure that when the people are awakened to their financial obligations there will come a spiritual awakening such as we have not witnessed in years. "For where your treasure is, there will you heart be also," said our Lord. We are not surprised that the Baptists have already chartered all the space on a large Pacific liner next summer to carry missionaries to the foreign field. They are getting recruits for the foreign field by the hundreds and men are being called to the ministry and to Christian service in great numbers, which facts, of course, follows as the day the night, the great activities which were necessary to secure such a large sum for the Kingdom. Why should we Christians not undertake a similar campaign whose design shall be not to impoverish anybody in the Christian Church, but to give every individual in every church a chance to do something for the Master in these perilous and wonderful times?

SUFFOLK LETTER

The approach of Christmas suggests a world of thought and creates an atmosphere of "good will." That multitude with the angel praising God and saying, "Glory to God in the highest, and on earth peace, good will," made no mistake. There is no day in the year so full of "peace and good will" as Christmas day. It is the one day for family reunions. It is the one day that home is "sweet home." It concentrates the joys of a whole year. It reminds us of the Babe of Bethlehem, the angels' song, the visit of the shepherds, and the adoration of the wise men, with their "gifts of gold, frankincense, and myrrh. That was a "Holy Night" and its song will never die out of the human heart.

It is wonderful that the birth of a peasant changed the calendar of time. The calendar is based on great events and it has had three foundations. The first was the creation of the world. That was a great fact. God created the heavens and the earth. Men reckoned from creation: *anno mundi.* Then Rome was built and dates were reckoned from the founding of that great city and Rome became mistress of the world. But both of these yield to *anno domini,* the year of our Lord. This peasant has, also, changed the thoughts and work of the world. He made the workshop the place of honor and usefulness. The man who is ashamed to work is ashamed of Jesus. His life is an example in obedience to parents, honest work, faithful attendance upon worship, and self-sacrifice for others. He opened a new world for children, for sinners, and for the sick. And Christmas should honor Jesus because He made this joyous time for the nations.

Christmas makes business on such an immense scale as to deserve the thanks of men. The stores are crowded with shoppers. The windows are decorated with rare skill. Gifts are sent in every direction. Carriers are busy. Almost every line of trade is at high tide in and around Christmas. The markets of the world are thronged with buyers. The world is busy and hopeful. To substract Christmas trade from the world would be to impoverish business. Millions on millions are spent for Christmas. Babyhood becomes the object of thought and purchase. The toys for Christmas! Almost everybody on the street and the train has bought something for children. "A little child shall lead them." Jesus put a new spirit in the human family and it is the spirit of kindness. What would life be to the child without Christmas morning? What was life to childhood before Jesus came into the world? To recognize Christmas is to recognize Jesus, for it celebrates His birth in Bethlehem. No wonder the shepherds left their flocks to see what the Lord had made known unto them; no wonder the wise men came from the east to honor Him. Let the busy world close its stores and shops and spend the Christmas day in the home where feast and joy fill the house with gladness. "Hang up the baby's stocking," and fill it with love and good things; then await for Christmas morning. Listen at the bare-feet on the hard floor; hear the shout of infant joy as they pull out that which Santa has put into their stockings. It is worth a year of toil to see the children in their glee and to hear them tell what Christmas has brought to them. It is akin to the morning when "the morning stars sang together and all the sons of God shouted for joy." This would be a happy world all the year round, if we loved Jesus as we ought, and loved one another in Him. "Except ye be converted and become as little children, ye cannot see the kingdom of God." The child-spirit is what the world needs; the spirit that is happy with small gifts, and that loves the unseen, with a faith that is strong and beautiful.

W. W. STALEY.

For Notes and Personals, see page fifteen.

EXTRAVAGANCE NOT OF THE KINGDOM

In the old "green goods" days, the man who bought a gold brick did not usually advertise the fact and brag that he had been duped. He was trying to get something for nothing and when his efforts reacted to his own loss he usually kept his mouth shut. Now however, the American people are falling over themselves in their eagerness to spend something for nothing. And they shout the fact that they are being bilked from the housetops with pride.

The facts and figures both collective and individual showing that the high prices of necessities and non-necessities are due to reckless spending extravagance and waste speak for themselves in no uncertain terms. The Massachusetts Commission investigating the high cost of necessities recently made public some significant findings. One of the largest retail dry goods dealers in Boston told the Commission that he put on sale a lot of shirt waists at $2.50 and $3.00 but that there was no sale for them as his customers would only consider higher priced articles, and he was obliged to take the low priced goods out of his store and turn them off some other way.

A provision dealer ground up Hamburger steak. Part of it he marked twenty-eight cents a pound and the remainder forty-two cents. At the end of the day all the forty-two cent Hamburger had been sold and not a customer bought at twenty-eight cents although the meat was absolutely the same. Commissioner J. H. Sherburne said that New England people refused to buy good fresh fish caught but two days before off the New England coast at eight cents a pound but that there was a big demand for halibut caught six weeks previous in the Pacific, carried across the country and sold at forty cents a pound. Meat men report there is an unprecendented demand for the most expensive cuts and little demand for cuts for stew. Although the price of hogs in Chicago fell off at fifty percent, there was no decrease in the retail price obtained for hog in New England because of the demand at high prices for choice loins. General Sherburne said that there was a tremendous demand for four dollar silk stockings which were inferior in quality to those which formerly sold at one dollar.

Fancy shoes and expensive shoes are in tremendous demand. Manufacturers estimate that each shoe worker produces only 662 2-3 as much as in 1913. They estimate that the reduced production amounts to approximately 3,000,000 pairs of shoes per annum yet with cheap shoes urgently needed the demand for the expensive grades and freak styles keeps production devoted to those classes of goods.

Here is what London says of the buying habit in America: "America continues to be the world's great treasure chest into which is being poured millions of dollars worth of precious stones and art treasures." For the first nine months of 1919 $27,568,128 worth of precious stones passed through London for American buyers as against $12,000,000 for the same period of 1918. The value of art object sent to America through London alone for the same time exceeded $4,000,000.

America has paid a huge price in Europe for furs in the last nine months the total amount being declared as $10,354,582 or double the amount for last year. The last of the $7,000,000 worth of furs recently sold at auction in New York have just been removed from the warehouses for manufacture. These figures do not take into account the sums paid at the auction sales of furs in St. Louis and other wholesale markets.

The jeweler, the pawnbroker and the furrier have no hesitancy in saying that these luxuries are not destined for old millionaires or the new rich. They are demanded by the salaried people and wage earners who are squandering on them the savings piled up during the last few years.

One chain of drug stores alone sold $6,000,000 worth of perfumes and cosmetics during the year. It may be highly enjoyable to smell like a sweet scented geranium but the odor of $6,000,000 bearing interest in safe and profitable securities is not objectionable to the nostrils either.

It is undeniable that so long as extravagance and waste, reckless spending and dissipation of savings continues as a national habit prices will continue to remain at or above the present level.

Americans have enjoyed for over a century the reputation of being a race of hard headed, sensible, clear thinking, shrewd business men and women. They are not living up to that reputation when they fail to save at least a part of their incomes and invest it wisely.

The principles of Christianity guard against extravagance, and the saving of part of the income for the Lord's work will, as nothing else, do more to bring us to a sense of obligation that we are stewards for the Lord. Can we waste when what we have in our possession that belongs to God? Would Jesus be extravagant if He were here? Shall we dissipate our wealth or use it for the bringing of the Kingdom into the hearts of men?

"MODERN PAGANS"

"Modern Pagans," by Chas. M. Sheldon is the title of a new book which we have added to our stock. The Wallaces are a typical American family—wholesome, hearty, and honest, interested in sports and society, in politics and business. None the less, they are practically pagans, enjoying the blessings of a Christian civilization, but accepting none of its duties and responsibilities. The story of the transformation of these modern pagans into active and aggressive twentieth century Christians is told by Dr. Sheldon in picturesque and compelling fashion. How was it accomplished? That is the story. Read it and see. Price 50 cents, net.

The Bureau of the Census is a part of the Department of Commerce. It was established as a permanent Bureau in 1902. Prior to that time the census work was done by a temporary organization known as the Census Office.

The Fourteenth Decennial Census is to be taken during the month of January, 1920.

OUR "ANCIENT" CONTEMPORARIES

THE MOUNTAINEERS OF THE SOUTH

By Victor I. Masters, Baptist Home Mission Board, Atlanta, Ga.

There are about 4,000,000 mountain people in the Southern States east of the Mississippi. The mountain folks live in about 178 counties and in an area of 75,000 or 80,000 square miles, and make up a part of the population in each of the States in the Old South, except Mississippi and Florida.

Though the Southern population is more than one-fourth Negroes, only about ten per cent of the population of the Highland region of the South is black. In a number of mountain counties there are fewer than 100 Negroes. These Highlanders are pure-blooded Anglo-Saxons to a degree unequalled elsewhere in America. That needs to be remembered.

Another thing is worth putting down; the white population in the Southern Highlands, by the census of 1910, was thirty-nine per square mile, while the extra-montanic regions of the States which were partly mountains and had only twenty-seven whites per square mile. The isolation of the Highlander is conditioned by the height of the mountain and the badness of the road, and not by his lack of neighbors. The greater density per square mile of the white people in Highland regions, as compared with the lowland regions of the South, may be surprising, but it has a definite bearing. There are more native white people per square mile to be helped by missionary effort and educational effort in the mountains than there are in any other region of the South, or of the nation. And these people are less spoiled than others by some perverse currents which have conditioned modern life.

The Religious Census of 1906 showed that the religious bodies in the Southern mountain regions had the following membership: 463,200, or forty-eight per cent, were Baptists; 304,900, or thirty-one per cent, were Methodists; 56,400, or about six per cent were Presbyterians;

membership. In the 178 counties surveyed, 143 did not report on Roman Catholic. This great region is freer from Romanism than any section of America. 48,900, or five per cent were Disciples; all other religious bodies had ten per cent of the If the Romanists in the mining region of Alabama and around Chattanooga are omitted, there are only about 3,000 Roman Catholics in the entire mountain regions of the South. This survey does not include West Virginia.

The special need of the Highlanders for Christian work grows out of their quaint and primitive civilization. They have been called our "contemporary ancestors." Like the pioneers of one hundred years ago, their economic life and their social contacts are still largely confined to the community. They provide for their own simple wants, not only raising their own food but making their own clothing, candles, and many household and farming utensils. Their religious life is of the pioneer variety. Their churches are of the once-a-month order, enjoying one or two sermons on a given Sunday each month and closing up until the same Sunday in the next month. Many of these churches are without a Sunday school, and few of the preachers have had educational advantages.

The mountaineer has reverence for God. He believes his Bible and is not troubled over the imaginings of rationalistic theological professors and scientists. His religion is an individualistic matter with him, just as his life is. He does not pay much in money for the material bases of living and exhibits an equal reluctance toward paying anything to the support of his preacher. This is one thing that has fixed on him the incubus of the outworn once-a-month sermon, by which device he manages to keep only a modicum of life in his oak-embowered church by the roadside.

Many evangelical bodies, among whom Northern Presbyterians deserve the credit of priority, are now conducting systems of mission schools among the Highlanders of the South. In addition, there are some individual institutions maintained by certain benevolent organizations. Among the other denominations doing large work in the school field for mountain folks are the Southern Baptists, the Southern Presbyterians, Northern and Southern Methodists. The Disciples, Congregationalists and Episcopalians have also touched this field of effort. The Baptists have between 5,000 and 6,000 in attendance on their schools, the Presbyterians perhaps an equal number and the Methodists a smaller number.

Christian statesmanship has reached a consensus of judgment that the institution best fitted to help the mountaineer to adjust himself to twentieth century conditions is the Church, and the method by the Church must be quickened for the task is educational. It was not chance that led each Christian body which has entered this field to establish a system of secondary schools under Christian control. No other method of service has been found so full of promise.

You must vitalize the mountaineer's church through these schools. Not only are the schools now training scores of young men and women for lives of high service in the outer world, but they are sending hundreds of the mountain youth back to the coves and valleys trained to lead their communities and churches into a larger outlook on life. Vocational training is preparing them to improve living conditions in the mountains. Some are prepared to teach and others to preach and to lead people within the churches forward to larger contacts in Christian service.

The aptitude of mountain boys and girls for grasping high and worthy ideals of life deserves special emphasis. In a day of alarming materialism, these young dreamers in the quiet and immensities of the mountains are not infatuated with the glint of the dollar. In an exceptional degree they are ready to respond to the opportunity and appeal of the life of service to their fellows in some field where spiritual uplift is the frankly avowed purposes.

A large percentage of the ministers in some denominations in the South is coming out of these mountains, and an equally impressive number of the students are going into other uplift vocations. The mountain schools of the Baptist Home Mission Board during the ten years preceding 1916 sent out from its schools 350 preachers, 200 lawyers, 225 doctors, 30 trained nurses, 30 missionaries and 2,500 public teachers. More than 3,000 had returned to the farm, 900 were engaged in commercial pursuits, forty were in banks and eighteen were members of State Legislatures.

In these Highlands are vast human resources waiting the touch of Christian culture for their releasement. There is no such other field in America. But not even this field will wait long on our tardy lack of understanding. The railways are breaking through the great ramparts by which the silent giants of the Highlands seek to keep out the irreverent hand and the impertinent curiosity of modern civilization. Wherever one of these railways gets through, wherever the modern campaign for highway improvement makes another hard and safe road through the mountain sections, the primitive economic scheme of the mountainer's life has to give way to that in which everything is valued by the dollar mark.

There is pathos in it. We must either strengthen the mountaineer to play his part well under the new conditions, or the tearing up of the quaint and beautiful but outworn pioneer system of life will be his undoing. In proportion to the effort which has been put forth in this field of service by different Christian groups, the rewards have been great. They will be still greater if we shall put forth adequate effort.

There are about 200 mission schools now in the High-lands. They are probably educating 20,000 to 25,000 youths. The work should be increased five-fold or ten-fold. To do this would draw out and train more young men and women for the great tasks of constituted Christianity in the generation just ahead of us than we can hope to obtain from any other field.—*Missionary Review of the Word.*

PASTOR AND PEOPLE

CHURCH DEDICATION

I had the privilege last Sunday of rejoicing with the good people of Holland, Va., on the occasion of their church dedication. Rev. N. G. Newman, a former pastor and much beloved by all the community, preached at the 11 o'clock hour to the delight and joy of the entire congregation. In the afternoon at 3 o'clock the house was formally dedicated, with appropriate musical selections and the services fitting such an occasion. The beloved pastor, Rev. W. M. Jay, was wreathed in smiles as were also the members of the Building Committee, the members of the church and their friends and it was fitting that they should be. I feel that they have builded better than they knew. The edifice is a real temple of worship which would do honor and great credit to any people of any community. The structure is of brick, the four sides of a pressed brick with imposing colonial columns, and spacious cathedral windows on the front. The basement or first floor is ample for all Sunday school purposes with many Sunday school rooms adjoining the main auditorium and a seating capacity of 400. The floor above, or second floor, is the main auditorium and is elegantly arranged and equipped. The acoustics are well nigh perfect. The furnishings are of heavy oak. The pastor's study is to the left of the pulpit; the choir with ante-rooms to the right. The pipe organ, a gift of the Ladies' Aid Society, is a joy forever, both in appearance and in melody. The building, whose material was purchased prior to the present high prevailing prices, cost in round numbers, $30,000.00 and is equipped with its own heating and lighting plants. In three of the cathedral windows are paintings in life size from incidents of the Christ life and are exceedingly appropriate and impressive, the highest artistic taste being displayed in their selection and appointment. The main auditorium with the ample gallery has a seating capacity of 600. The house has been erected and paid for so readily and joyously that it is difficult for one to realize and certainly the Holland people themselves have not realized what a great, good and unselfish thing they had done. The church is a distinct contribution not only to the moral and spiritual life of the community but to the architectural and civic life as well. Such an imposing structure in itself is a blessing and a benefit to any community as it sets silently a noble example of the builders art and profession. The Holland people are thrifty and energetic in their daily industrial pursuits, prosperous and happy in their financial achievements, all of which they turn to good purpose, dividing up liberally with the work of the

Kingdom. It was a great day not only for the church but for the community when this house was given to the Lord and it was certainly a great privilege and joy for the writer to be present and rejoice with these good people. God's blessings upon them as they meet from time to time to worship in the splendid temple which they have so unselfishly built and dedicated to the service of their Lord.

J. O. ATKINSON.

December 15, 1919.

A FEW THINGS ACCOMPLISHED BY THE FIRST CHRISTIAN CHURCH, RALEIGH, N. C., IN THE PAST TEN MONTHS

Numerical and Spiritual

1. More than fifty adult additions to the church membership during the year.
2. Mid-week prayer services started and maintained for the ten months with average attendance of fifty-four.
3. Large permanent increase in the Sunday school.
4. One hundred per cent increase in attendance at preaching services (capacity houses frequently the case).
5. Woman's Missionary Society organized with forty-one members and maintained with average attendance of twenty-one.
6. Increased missionary interest and deepening of spiritual life in all departments.
7. Present membership 150 with about 100 prospectives.

Financial

1. Duplex Envelope System installed with 600 per cent increase in pledges for missions and benevolences. (Total pledges in first canvass approximately $600.00).
2. Congregation becomes self-supporting with increae of 92½ per cent in pastor's salary, over amount it paid the Conference year just closed. (33 1-3 per cent increase over total amount paid to pastor by both the congregation and Home Mission Board combined).
3. Approximately 100 per cent increase in current finances.
4. $4,750.00 pledged for Elon College Endowment. ($3,000.00 asked for).
5. $2,350.00 raised in cash to pay debts and purchase added necessary interior equipment.
6. More than $200.00 given the Christian Orphanage in cash.
7. $500.00 in pledges and cash to Anti-Saloon League work.
8. Purse of $100.00 presented to pastor and wife in appreciation of their services.
9. Parsonage purchased at cost of $7,000.00. (Not yet paid for but plans being worked out to pay for it.)
10. We have found it necessary to have a professional music director which we have obtained on a salary by the year.

General Statement

Everything looks encouraging. Church located at strategic center of city, and on the Capital city's best resident street. This is also, in our opinion, the logical central geographically and otherwise for denominational headquarters of the Southern Christian Convention. (Look it up and see for yourself). The Convention should have headquarters and why not make this the place?

A general feeling prevails that we must have a new and representative building to continue our growth in this, one of the most beautiful cities of the South, and one of the few Capital cities in which the Christians have a church. The building is sorely needed and must come.

The Brotherhood is asked to pray for our work here.

W. C. ADKINS,
Chairman of Committee.

UNDER THE HOLLY BOUGH

Ye who have scorned each other
Or injured friend or brother,
   In this fast-fading year;
Ye who, by word or deed,
Have made a kind heart bleed,
   Come, gather here.

Let sinned against, and sinning,
Forget their strife's beginning,
   And join in friendship now:
Be links no longer broken,
Be sweet forgiveness spoken,
   Under the Holly Bough.

Ye who have loved each other,
Sister and friend and brother,
   In this fast-fading year:
Mother and sire and child,
Young man and maiden mild,
   Come, gather here;

And let your hearts grow fonder,
As memory shall ponder
   Each past unbroken vow.
Old loves and younger wooing
Are sweet in the renewing,
   Under the Holly Bough.

Ye who have nourished sadness,
Estranged from hope and gladness,
   In this fast-fading year;
Ye, with o'erburdened mind,
Made aliens from your kind,
   Come, gather here.

Let not the useless sorrow
Pursue you night and morrow.
   If e'er you hoped, hope now—
Take heart—uncloud your faces,
And join in our embraces,
   Under the Holly Bough.

—Charles Mackay.

THE SHORTEST NAME

Among the names of $4,500,000 soldiers, sailors and marines recorded in the files of the War Risk Insurance Bureau at Washington, the shortest family name was "Ii", borne by two soldiers who were natives of Hawaii. Their name consisted of two letters, but it was pronounced in two syllables.

MISSIONARY

A CHRISTMAS GIFT FOR MISSIONS

The writer is thinking of the happy Christmas time in all Christian lands and among Christian people. It is the happiest, the most joyous of all good seasons as it should be. During these days we celebrate the greatest event since the day dawn of creation. Millions of money will be spent for gifts to make glad the members of our own homes and the friends round about us in order to make the season more happy than it otherwise would be.

But they have no Christmas in non-Christian lands and the million of children whose parents know nothing of the Christ will have no glad Christmas morning and no happy Christmas gifts nor joyous Christmas bells. They know not our Christ and the blessings he brings to hearts and homes. A good and noble Christian woman asked the other day: Why should not we Christians make Christmas gifts of our money that the gospel of our blessed Christ might be carried to non-Christian lands so that the peoples there might come to know Christ and His Christmas? (And she handed me a dollar as a Christmas gift to missions.) We are so happy ourselves on Christmas Day that it is easy for us to forget that the big majority of the human race will know nothing of the day because they know nothing of Him in whose name the day is observed. The Mission Secretary would rejoice to receive Christmas gifts for missions and would see to it that such gifts go to the right place in carrying the blessed news of Him at whose advent the angels sang: "Peace on earth; good will to men." If we of Christian countries would give half as much to spread the gospel as we spend in gifts among ourselves to celebrate the Christmas season, it would only be a few years till all nations of the earth would celebrate with us this great and happy season. Why should we not do our part to make the whole world safe for Christmas and this we can do by making known to the whole world. "Christmas gift for missions" is by no means an idle phrase, but is worth considering and would certainly be a most fitting thing to do.

BEWARE! ! A MESSAGE FOR THE DAY OF PROSPERITY

God sent us the message through His servant, Moses. It is practical, pointed and brief Read it from Deut. 8:11-14: "Beware that thou forget not the Lord thy God, in not keeping his commandments, and his judgments, and his statutes, which I command thee this day; lest when thou hast eaten and art full, and hast built goodly houses, and dwelt therein; and when thy herds and thy flocks multiply, and thy silver and thy gold is multiplied, and all that thou hast is multiplied: then thine heart be lifted up, and thou forget the Lord thy God."

AMERICA'S PART THEN AND NOW

In some carefully limited sense it is true that America won the war, the same could be said of England or Belgium or France. It was a united victory. Yet it is correct to say that, when the armies of the Allies were in dire need, it was given to America to hurl against the enemy her fresh, brave forces, and to turn the tide of conflict. Much more is it true that, while our sister churches in Protestant lands are depleted of men and of money, it is given to the American church with her unbounded resources, now to move forward with triumphant confidence, to unite the followers of Christ and to achieve the evangelization of the world, so writes Dr. C. R. Edman in the *Missionary Review of The World*. And he sounds a true note.

J. O. ATKINSON.

WEEK OF PRAYER
January 11-17, 1920

To be Observed by all Missionary Societies of the North Carolina Christian Conference

"I exhort therefore, first of all, that supplications, prayers, intercessions, thanksgiving, be made for all men."—I Tim. 2:1.

SUNDAY, January 11—Topic for Sermons and Addresses: Prayer and Missions.—Jas. 5:16; Matt. 28:18-20.

MONDAY, January 12.—Our Ministers, That they may be fully awake to missions; teaching and instructing their congregations.—Acts 13:2-4; John 15:16.

TUESDAY, January 13.—Woman's Foreign Boards and for the Work and Workers in Japan and Porto Rico—Missionaries, Native pastors, Bible women, stations and out-stations.—Matt. 25:34-40; Ps. 2:8.

WEDNESDAY, January 14—Home Boards and Home Mission Fields—Washington and Richmond specials.—Matt. 22:1-10; Matt. 10:5-8.

THURSDAY, January 15.—Young People's Work, Life Recruits for Home and Foreign Missions Fields. That many of our young men and women may hear and answer the call to definite Christian service.—Matt. 9:37-38; I Sam. 3:4.

FRIDAY, January 16.—The Church in this day of opportunity may more perfectly represent the Spirit of our Lord Jesus Christ in its life and service. That our people may be willing to learn the great lessons of stewardship. That individuals and churches may assume the support of missionaries and stations. That there may be many new signers of the Intercessor's Covenant.—Luke 4:17-19; Mal. 3:8-10; Thes. 5:17.

SATURDAY, January 17.—The Forward Movement and our Woman's Boards part in it. That all goals may be reached. The Americanization and Christianization of all races within our borders. That we may show such a spirit of love to other nationalities that have come to us that they may love and obey our Lord.—Ex. 14:15; Heb. 13:2.

SOME CHRISTMAS SUGGESTIONS

CHRISTMAS BOOKS FOR CHILDREN

We list below a supply of books which we have purchased suitable for Christmas presents for the children. For the lack of space we cannot tell what each book is about, but we have exercised the very best care in the selection, to see that all stories are helpful and interesting:

The Thorn of the Fortress	.50 cents
Matt of the Waterfront	.50 cents
The Other Side of the Rainbow	.60 cents
Lantern Stories	.60 cents
Billy and Bumps	.35 cents
Good Night Stories	.60 cents
The Jim Family	.25 cents
Little Folks of the Bible	.80 cents
Sunny Hour Books	.15 cents

(Little Folks of the Bible can be had in books I, II, III, and IV. Books I and II are for boys and books III and IV are for girls. We will send any four books of this title for $1.00.)

(Sunny Hour Books are made up of 14 different titles. The price is 15 cents for each title, any two for 25 cents; four for 45 cents and all over four at 10 cents per volume.)

All the above named books are suitable for children 8 to 14 except the "Sunny Hour Books" which are for little tots that cannot read or are just beginning to read. "Sunny Hour Books" contain an abundance of pictures and are bound with colored cloth and stamped with an appropriate design.

Add 4 cents per volume for postage when only one copy is ordered, and 2 cents per volume for postage in lots up to ten; all over ten volumes add 1 cent per volume for postage.

CLEARANCE SALE OF CHILDREN'S BOOKS

We make it a rule in December of each year to buy the closing out stock of several suitable books for children. By buying the closing out stock, we are enabled to get a better price and make the books within the reach of all.

We have been able this year to buy the complete stock of the following 50 cent sellers, and offer them at prices indicated:

Blazing the Way	$ .25
Bright Side and Other Side	.25
Crown Jewels	.20
From the Thames to the Toossachs	.25
Up the Susquehanna	.25

(This price is postpaid)

The following reductions will be made in lots: Any two copies, 45 cents; three copies, 60 cents; four copies, 75 cents; all over four copies at 17 cents per copy.

The supply is limited and we advise you to order early. If any title has exhausted when your order is received, we will substitute unless otherwise instructed.

These books are all well made and handsomely bound.

Make some child's life happy by presenting one or more of these books. Invest a few dollars to make the little tots of your class happy.

SUNDAY SCHOOL HELPS

We have the following Sunday school helps on the 1920 International Lesson:

Peloubet's Select Notes	$1.60
Tarbell's Teachers' Guide	1.60
Arnold's Commentary	.75
Torrey's Gist of the Lesson	.30

(These prices include postage)

A FEW MORE CHRISTMAS SUGGESTIONS

Bibles

No. 71. Scofield Reference Bible. Handsome binding, French Morocco limp, new and improved edition. "The neatest Scofield Bible made." It will please you. Regular selling price $4.50

No. 215. Child's Self-Pronouncing Pictorial Bible with Helps. Bound in French seal leather, round corners, silk bands, gold titles,—handsomely made. Regular selling price $2.50

No. 1113. Ideal Bible for Children. Printed on fine white paper from the newest and clearest type of the size made. Size 3 1-2X5 3-8 inches. This Bible will please you. Regular price $1.75

Testaments

No. 3913 R. L. (Red Letter). Large print Morocco binding. Regular price $2.00

No. 2902 Cloth binding, large print. Regular price.... .90

No. 2502 P. Cloth binding, black faced type. Regular price .... .75

No. 2113. Pocket size, Morocco binding. Regular price .60

No. 0133. Pocket size, Morocco binding, overlapping edges. Regular Price .... .75

(A Testament in Modern Speech)

Cloth, $1.25; cloth, indexed, $1.75; cloth, India paper, $1.75; leather, $2.35; leather, indexed, $2.75; leather, India paper, $2.75; Persian Morocco, Divinity Circuit, $3.75; Turkey Morocco, $1.25. Pocket Edition (without notes): Cloth, $1.00; cloth, India paper, $1.25; leather, India paper, $1.85. State definitely style wanted.

Address

C. B. RIDDLE, Publishing Agent

Burlington - - - - North Carolina

SOLVE THAT PRESENT PROBLEM

Solve that Christmas present problem by giving a copy of Tarbell's Teachers' Guide. It will be a reminder every week in the year 1920. The price is $1.60 delivered. We also have Peloubet's Select Notes at the same price.

ARNOLD'S NOTES ON THE SUNDAY SCHOOL LESSON

Arnold's Commentary on the International Sunday school will please you as a teacher. Try a copy and become a better teacher. The price is 75 cents delivered.

DID YOU EVER SEE IT?

Did you ever see a copy of Torrey's Gist of the Lesson? Vest pocket size, handy, and convenient. Send 30 cents and let us mail you a copy.

THE CHRISTIAN ORPHANAGE

SUPERINTENDENT'S LETTER

Our Thanksgiving offerings are very encouraging and we are now nearing the goal. The Thanksgiving offerings to date amount to $5,568.66. Let us rush it up to the goal in our next report.

We have two hundred and twenty-two churches and ninety churches have made and sent in Thanksgiving offerings to this date. We still have one hundred and thirty-two to hear from yet. I truly hope that the pastors will see that their churches make and mail in this offering. I want to have the pleasure to report to the Board of Trustees at its next meeting that each church in our Southern Christian Convention made a Thanksgiving offering to help the little orphans.

I appeal to the Sunday school superintendents to see that your Sunday schools make this offering too. Your year's work will not be complete or finished till you make this offering. If you are late that will not debar you and the door of the Orphanage will be wide open to receive your offering with a warm welcome. Let it come along.

I asked twenty churches in the beginning of this campaign to make an offering of $100.00 or more. Thirteen churches have answered this request with that amount and more. I believe that out of the other churches to report that we will get the other seven. Must have them. I know that all the churches that have contributed $100.00 are proud of the act and rejoice with us in the undertaking. If your church has not taken this offering will you make it $100.00?, or more, if you like.

Friends of the little orphans are still very kind to us and have sent in the following:

Farmers Cotton Oil Co., Wilson, N. C., 20 bags (one ton) cotton-seed meal; Farmville Oil & Fertilizer Co., Farmville, N. C., 300 pounds cotton-seed meal and 700 pounds hulls; Woman's Missionary Society, First Christian church, Urbana, Ill., one box clothing for the children; Willing Workers, First Christian church, Goshin, Ind., one box clothing; Ladies' Aid Society, Pleasant Hill church, Albion, Ind., one box clothing; Miss Alnetta Kernodle, Altamahaw, N. C., one pair pillow cases; Salisbury Cotton Mills, Salisbury, N. C., 68 3-4 yards of cloth; Miss Annie Staley and others, Suffolk, Va., one box toys for thirteen small children.

Our singing class had a very pleasant trip to Raleigh, Catawba Springs and Fuquay Springs on the first Sunday. The children rendered their program at each place and the contributions were splendid. The people were very kind to us and we enjoyed the trip more than words can express.

I want to correct an error, made in the last issue of THE CHRISTIAN SUN. The offering sent in by Shallow Well church should have been reported as Thanksgiving offering from Jonesboro Jr. O. U. A. M. Council 148. They had Thanksgiving service at Shallow Well church, and this offering was taken. I am glad to make the correction.   CHAS. D. JOHNSTON, Supt.

FINANCIAL REPORT FOR DECEMBER 24, 1919

Amount brought forward, $20,122.17.

Children's Offerings

D. B. Spivey, 10 cents; O. D. Poythress, Jr., 50 cents; Jean Simpson, $1.00; Total, $1.60.

Sunday School Monthly Offerings

(North Carolina Conference)

Burlington, $35.86; Hope Dale, $1.65; High Point, $3.56; Reidsville, $1.00; Bethel, $16.23; Shiloh, 71 cents; Sanford, $5.50; Ramseur, $3.50.

(Eastern Virginia Conference)

Franklin, $15.00; New Lebanon, $5.12; East End, Newport News, $2.57; Suffolk, $25.00; Borea (Nansemond), $10.00; Isle of Wight, $2.50; Windsor, $6.10.

(Valley Virginia Conference)

LinVille, $1.00; Timber Ridge, $5.02.

(Alabama Conference)

LinVille, $4.00; Total, $144.31.

Special Offerings

Philathea Class, Suffolk Sunday school, $25.00;—Mrs. H. C. Pollard's Sunday school class, $38.20; Mr. G. L. Gynn, Newport News, Va., $10.00; W. H. Thomas, $25.00; Progressive Bible Class, Suffolk, Va., $5.00; Total, $103.20.

Children's Home Fund

Ladies' Aid Society, Waverly Christian church, Va., $100.00.

Thanksgiving Offerings

Prarie Hope Christian church, Central, Ill., $10.00; La Grange, Ga., $16.15; Christian church, Woodstock, Vt., $8.09; Martha's Chapel, N. C., $27.50; Pope's Ave. Sunday school, Windsor, Va., $14.82; Chapel Hill Sunday school (N. C.), $40.28; T. E. Brittle, Walters, Va., $5.00; Johnson Grove Sunday school, Va., $9.00; Wood's Chapel Sunday school, Val. Va., $8.00; Bethlehem church, Val. Va., $3.70; Pleasant Grove church, Va., $111.36; Berea church, N. C., $28.72; Amelia S. S., N. C., $5.61; Oak Level church, N. C., $36.00; Borea, Norfolk, Va., $26.46; Timber Rildge, Val. Va., $44.50; Barrett's Sunday school, Va., $5.60; Pleasant Cross Sunday school, N. C., $7.35; East End Christian church, Newport News, Va., $86.63; Mrs. Maggie Myers, Col. Grove, Ohio, $5.00; Pleasant Grove, Va., church (additional) $5.00; Bethel church, N. C., $6.00; Ambrose, Ga., $20.25; Mrs. T. W. Parks, Hallison, N. C., $2.00; Burlington Christian church and S. S., $368.25; New Providence Junior Philathea class, $5.75; New Providence Junior Baracca class, $3.19; New Providence Sunday school, $25.42; Winchester, Va., $11.04; Missionary Society Christian church, Cynthiana, Ind., $9.00; Lanett, Ala., $4.00; Isle of Wight, Va., $31.00; Isle of Wight, Primary Class, $1.00; Howard's Chapel, N. C., $6.50; Dry Run, Val. Va., $12.96; Rev. J. D. Simmons, Geister, Mo., $1.00; Mr. Thomas King and wife, Geister, Mo., $1.00; Miss Bess Sparks, Geister, Mo., $5.00; Total, $1,019.33. Total for the week, $1,368.44; Grand total, $21,490.61.

CHILDREN'S LETTERS

Dear Uncle Charley:—I was ten months old yesterday. Don't you think I am getting to be quite a big boy? Daddy and mother think I am the sweetest boy in the world. Daddy bought me a nice new go-cart today. I like it fine. Guess Santa will bring me some play things, but a go-cart is the best thing for a little boy like me. Enclosed find check for 50 cents—my dues for December. Love and best wishes to all the cousins, and a merry Christmas.—Olive D. Poythress, Jr.

Of course "daddy" and "mother" think you are the sweetest boy in all the world. They could not help but think it of such a fine little fellow as you. As the one who has been telling "Santa" my needs at Christmas time is in the better world I will be lonely on Christmas morn.—"*Uncle Charley.*"

Dear Uncle Charley:—Here comes a little boy to join the Corner. I am going to school and like my teacher fine. Enclosed find 10 cents for the cousins.—*D. B. Spivey.*

We are delighted to give you a warm welcome to the Corner. Glad you joined before Christmas and hope "Old anta" will be good to you.—"*Uncle Charley.*"

Dear Uncle Charley:—Enclosed find $1.00 for my Thanksgiving offering to the little cousins. I am a little girl seven years old. I want Santa Claus to come to see me and I hope he will go to see all the little children.—*Jean Simpson.*

Our little folks are looking forward to the coming of "Old Santa" with a great deal of delight.—"*Uncle Charley.*"

LISTEN TO THE BELLS!!

What do the bells say to you, as they peal their clear, sweet music through the early, snowy dawn of the Christmas morning?

Only a few more days, and Christmas time will be here again. Christmas time; giving time; gladsome time! And when, on that early morning, you awake to the sound of pealing, joyous bell-music, lie still for a moment in the warmness of your comfy bed, and listen to those bells—listen carefully.

For they have a story to tell of little children across the ocean; little children and tiny helpless tots, fatherless, motherless, homeless; children who will know no Christmas tide; who ask no gifts of glittering tree and shining toys, such as you will find on Christmas morning. They only ask the gift of life; the gift of mothers, of homes, of clean clothes and food.

And the bells tell us a story of America; of the poor, the sick, the weak and the helpless little ones—all waiting the coming of gifts of life and hope.

That is the story of the Red Cross bells. They must be Red Cross bells, for they tell the story of service, and Red Cross means service. The Red Cross Juniors are going to answer the call of the bells. They are going to send the cheer of Christmas time to nations over the sea, and to the people of our own country. And the cheer they carry will not be the cheer of a single day —but the cheer of a whole life-time!

Listen to the bells. They have a message for every boy and girl in America. Can you hear it?

THE LAND OF TOYS

Little wooden fishes that swim right-side-up, life-sized baby elephants, bears, stags, horses and rabbits— all the animals that ever entered Noah's peak-roofed ark are there! And with them are quaint, fat little peasant women, in flaring dresses, tiny poppy-ball huntsmen, with arrows of bent twigs, green forests of cone-fashioned trees and pebble lined brooks, and cunning little villages, with real thatch-roofed huts.

The land of toys is where you will find them. And that land lies far away from here, across the sea, tucked snugly away in the heart of the Slovakian Mountains. Everyone in that far-away little country makes toys, from the wrinkled great-great-grandmother to the tiny tots of four and five years. And in the home where crippled children lie, even there small hands are busy fashioning these toys of fairy-land from cones, burrs, acorns, twigs and poppy-balls, gathered for them in the summer woods—poor little cripples of Czecho-Slovakia passing the dreary hours of patient waiting!

Santa Claus has not yet seen that wonder land. But he is going to, very soon, for the American Red Cross workers have written him a long letter telling him all about these newly discovered playthings, that would like so very much to cross the ocean and visit the nurseries and the playrooms of the boys and girls of America.

But Santa must take with him the money to pay for these toys. And it is to the Junior Red Cross members that Santa is looking for that sum. For the money that the Juniors send will make it possible for many more little girls and boys of that war-swept, out-of-the-way, mountain land to get the care and the treatment that will give health and strength to weak and crippled little bodies; that will mean food and rest for hungry, over-tired peasants.

And when Saanta comes back with his bulging pack of toy wonders, you, too, may, some Christmas morning, find tucked away in the back depths of your stocking, a quaint little peasant woman, come to you all the way from that wonderful land of toys!

AT RANDOM

A barrister, not so discreet as he might have been in the expression of his ideas, was engaged on a case concerning some pigs. "Gentlemen of the jury," he began, "there were twenty-four pigs in the drove, just twenty-four, exactly twice as many as there are in that jury box."—*Exchange.*

"It says here that blind people can be taught to distinguish colors by the sense of touch," said the Fat Man.

"Well, that isn't surprising," replied the Thin Man. "A fellow always knows when he feels blue, doesn't he?"—*Cincinnati-Enquirer.*

Edgar, aged five, was driving from the station on his first visit to Maine. His mother, noticing a troubled look on his face as he looked about, said: "Whats the matter, Edgar? Don't you like the beautiful country?"

"Yes, mother, but on my map Maine is red!"—*The Moderator.*

THE NEED OF PASTORATES

(Address delivered before the North Carolina Christian Conference, by J. U. Gunter, and ordered printed in The Christian Sun; and also published in pamphlet form for distribution.)

THE subject assigned me is the "Need of Pastorates," and while I did not confer with the program committee, I presume that it is a foregone conclusion that we need to form our rural churches into pastorates or groups. But for fear that there are some who do not recognize the proposition as a need, I shall endeavor to convince all such that it is one of the church's needs. From the tone of the addresses we have heard since we have been assembled here and the information we gather as we read expressions from the master minds of the world today, I think we will all agree that this is a new day in the church's history. It seems that there are different methods used in practically every line of industry and in every government. In other words, different methods are being used to bring about the same vital principles that have always been used in good business or good government. For instance, take the method of communication. It was the custom years ago for men to discuss important matters face to face, later it was done by written correspondence, then came the telegraphic method, then the telephone, then wireless telegraphy; but now it is entirely practical for a man just outside the city of Washington to talk with a man in Honolulu over the wireless telephone. The principle of communication is the same, but the methods employed are different and better.

When men first fought or went to war, they used as weapons, bows and arrows, the sling-shot and spears. Later they used muzzle loading guns, rifles and light artillery; but today we have the *big Betsy* which will shoot for seventy-five miles. Warfare has kept abreast of the times and has made progress.

Many years ago we walked to church, later we rode in dog carts or wagons, then came the buggy and surrey. Now we drive up in a hand-some automobile. The purpose of our going to church is the same, but the method of getting there is far different and better.

Now the great question confronting us, Have we in our churches made the same degree of progress as has been made in other lines of established business? I want to be thoroughly understood in this matter, and desire to impress upon your minds that I am not advocating any change in the well established principles of Christianity. I realize full well that I could not do this, even if I should choose to try. We worship a God, who is the same yesterday, today and forever, and whose plan for the salvation of man was first conceived in His great loving heart; it was extended to the manger, followed its course to Calvary and reached its climax at the empty tomb. We would not change these precious principles if we could. But how about the methods we are employing in letting the folks know about our Christ? Are you satisfied with our present form of Church government? Do you not think that the liberty, of which we boast, in our local church government is really detrimental to our growth and development? Can we hope to make any great degree of progress with our present system?

We are all agreed that the business of the church is the greatest business in the world today. Don't you believe this to be true? I think so, in fact, I know it is true. I know it is far larger than the little sash and blind factory that I am trying to run down in Lee County. But with all the insignificance of the little sash and blind factory, I am frank to say to you that I would not employ a man living in Elon College to take charge of the little sash and blind mill down in Jonesboro, unless he would agree to move to Jonesboro where he could give the business the attention it must have in order to be successful. What man here today would be willing to run his own business with the same methods that you are trying to run your church? How would you feel to have the superintendent of your farm live fifty or a hundred miles away, and run over and talk about the crop twelve times a year? And on the other hand, what kind of a superintendent would you expect to get for the salary you are paying your pastor? Do you think it is good business for a church up near the Virginia line to employ a preacher living in Greensboro, let him spend about 30 per cent of what you pay him for railroad transportation to and from the church, reaching there late Saturday and leaving early Monday? You do not have him on hand to Christen your babies, marry your young, or bury your dead. On the other hand, what do you think of a preacher who will accept work of this kind from a church with anywhere from 100 to 350 members and agree to serve them for $175.00 to $350.00 per year? Can we expect any progress with this kind of service? Do you think it possible for a minister to accomplish anything with that kind of encouragement? Would you expect your business to prosper under similar circumstances?

Now, brethren, it is an established fact that circumstances such as I have just enumerated are prevalent in over 50 per cent of our churches today and they have been this way for the past fifty or hundred years. Are you satisfied with the methods employed? Do you believe with our present church government, it is possible to attain the highest efficiency? I for one do not think it possible. But on the other hand, just let some fellow who has the interest of the church at heart and who wants to see it progress, stand up and insist that we group our churches and have a resident pastor, and he will meet with opposition by quite a number who will say that we are drifting back to the methods of the church we left a hundred years ago. I am persuaded that we had better get back or get somewhere to the point where our churches will be run with some degree of efficiency. And when you say to me that we are drifting back to the methods of the church we left, I find it my unpleasant duty to ask you to compare the progress of that church with that of our church today. They have it on us from nearly every point and their form of government, whether you approve it or not, has less churches, several times more members and organizations and a better paid ministry.

We are face to face with the situation. I do not lay all the blame on the founders of our church, nor the preachers nor the laymen, but I charge that all of us need to face about and get in line for action. I do not come to you with a panacea for all ailments, neither would I undertake to direct the course of the church nor dictate its policies, but I come to you today with a practical solution for a part of our short comings. It is the Pastorate Plan. It is something that has passed the experimental stage in some sections of the North Carolina Conference, and I am going to ask your indulgence for a few minutes while I give a brief history of the Christian Church Pastorate of Central Lee County. At the third quarterly meeting of the Sanford Christian church, a little over two years ago, the matter of selecting or electing a pastor for 1918 came before us. Prior to this time when the matter of selecting a pastor would come before us, sometimes a half dozen names would be presented and the church never knew whether or not any of them would consider the position if elected. Quite often we would have to hold three or four elections on account of different pastors not accepting the work. And generally before the matter was definitely settled there would come into existence factions and dissatisfactions which would require months to overcome. But at the third quarterly meeting in 1917, a proposition was made that we appoint or elect a nominating committee whose business it would be to get in touch with available pastors so that no name would go before the church unless we had some assurance that the call would be considered in the event of an election. To my great joy a motion prevailed and Mr. K. B. Way, Mr. J. W. Stout and myself were put on this committee. A few days after this some of us had talks with some of the representative members of Shallow Well, Grace's Chapel, Turner's Chapel and Poplar Branch churches, and we all agreed that we would have our churches meet and discuss the Pastorate Plan. Happily all the churches were favorably impressed with the proposition and each church elected delegates to the Pastorate

with full power to act for the churches. We formed a permanent organization, elected officers, adopted by-laws and got down to business. Now here is something that will prove that the Pastoral Plan is a success. We took an inventory of what each church could pay toward the pastor's salary and after it had been tabulated, we found that it amounted to only $725.00. Next in line was to secure a pastor who would undertake to look after the field for that pitiful sum. But the Lord had put it into the heart of one of the best men it has ever been my privilege to meet, and the honorable president of this Conference agreed to consider a call, provided it was unanimous. The name of Rev. T. E. White was the only one placed before the committee and he was unanimously elected and accepted the work. At the end of the first year, it was an easy matter to increase his salary to $1,000.00, and we have just elected him for the third year at a salary of $1,200.00, and an automobile and he has accepted the call for 1920. Now, I don't want you to think for a minute that I consider $1,200.00 a good salary, for it is not to be compared with the real worth of the pastor, but I mention it in order that you may see the substantial progress being made from year to year.

It is my firm conviction that within the next two years, we will be able to divide the pastorate and have the Shallow Well Pastorate and the Sanford Pastorate. Each of the stronger churches will take a part of the weaker and give the whole field the active services of a real pastor. You cannot estimate the value of a resident pastor. Its worth is not to be measured in dollars and cents.

I believe that the more progressive members of the Christian Church would be favorable to the Pastorate Plan, and I commend it to you as the best thing the Sanford church has ever undertaken in the way of local government. I also believe that the majority of our folks are progressive, if given a chance. I am led to this conclusion by the recent campaign conducted by Doctors Atkinson and Harper. You will recall that the committee instructed Dr. Atkinson to raise $50,000.00. He had been out for only a short while, before he was

compelled to go back and get permission to raise $100,000.00. Now, I believe the bars have been entirely lifted and he is now at liberty to raise half a million, and there will be no questions asked.

You will also recall that Dr. Harper and his able assistants started out to raise for the Standardization Fund $125,000.00. Before the field was half covered, he found that in order to give all churches a chance at the blessing, he would of necessity have to raise $375,000.00.

I am here to tell you that our people have never had a real chance. We have spent too much time discussing a well worded report on moral reform, which nine-tenths of our people never see or hear about. We make every year beautiful reports on Christian Literature, and then go home and forget to urge upon our people the value of THE CHRISTIAN SUN and Herald of Gospel Liberty. The same applies to Christian Education, we do not push our College enough when we go home from the Conference. I say, let's give the folks back home a chance.

Now in conclusion, I want to say that to organize a pastorate will require patience, prayer and work. It will necessitate the liberal spirit of give and take in non-essentials. It cannot be accomplished in a day and I think the best way to make a start is for some of the leading laymen in the churches to agitate the movement and keep it before the people; get the pastor to help you by making a talk on organized effort emphasizing the value to the whole church of the Pastorate Plan. By all means make the effort and if you are successful, and I feel sure you will be, it will be one of the greatest days in the history of your church, and your personal reward will be the eloquent expression from the inner life that you have had some part in furthering the kingdom of our Lord and His Christ.

Sunday School and Christian Endeavor

SUNDAY SCHOOL TOPIC FOR JANUARY 4, 1920

Peter Preaches at Pentecost

Lesson Text, Acts 2:14, 22-24, 32-42.

Golden Text: Whosoever shall call on the name of the Lord shall be saved.—Acts 2:21.

In this lesson we have given the outlines and salient points in one of the world's very greatest public utterances, so far as thrilling rhetoric and convincing oratory are concerned. Peter's heart was on fire, and his soul was being consumed with a passion for the unsaved of the house of Israel. His old nature of fear and denial and cursing and trembling has been washed away in his bitter tears of repentance, and here we have Peter at his best, fiery, eloquent, bold, fearless as a lion. It is a great utterance and every Sunday school pupil should study it with care.

MRS. BULLOCK RESIGNS

SUN readers will regret that Mrs. Bullock has resigned as editor of this department and the Board has accepted her resignation with reluctance. Brother C. H. Stephenson, Raleigh, N. C., Corresponding Secretary-Treasurer of the Board of Religious Education, has been elected to use the space as he may deem wise to the best interest of our Sunday schools. Brother Stephenson is a live wire in Sunday school work, and we are sure he will make this department of deep and helpful interest to our schools, and to SUN readers generally.

J. O. ATKINSON,
Secretary.

The Senate is endeavoring to revise the Peace Treaty again and the outlook is hopeful at times for its definite reconsideration.

The Government announces that bodies of American soldiers buried in France will be returned at an early date. No private conveyance of bodies will be allowed. The Government is to bear the total expense of the removal and have the same in charge.

MEDLIN-MATTHEWS

At the home of Mrs. T. I. Mawyer in Sanford, N. C., a beautiful wedding took place Thursday, December 4, when her daughter, Miss Lillian Matthews, became the bride of Mr. Haywood Medlin, of Moncure, N. C. Immediately after the marriage the bridal party motored to the home of the groom where a sumptuous supper was served.

Mr. and Mrs. Medlin will reside in Sanford. Their many friends wish for them much joy and happiness. Only a few of their friends and relatives witnessed the ceremony which was performed by the writer.

T. E. WHITE.

UPCHURCH-CHURHILL

Miss Florine Belle Churchill and Mr. Clarence Upchurch, of Morrisville, Wake County, N. C., were married at my home on December 11, 1919. The writer officiated.

W. G. CLEMENTS.

MILLER-HOOK

A beautiful wedding was solemnized at the home of the bride's mother, Mrs. R. C. Hook, December 9, 1919, at 8:00 P. M., when her youngest daughter, Miss Iva Elizabeth, became the bride of Mr. Perry Dewey Miller. The ceremony was performed by Rev. W. C. Hook, brother of the bride, assisted by the writer.

The following were the attendants: Mr. Percy Stine and Miss Mary Miller and Mr. R. O. McDonald and Miss Hazel Hook. Quite a number of guests were assembled to witness the ceremony.

The groom is a successful young farmer. The bride is a former Elon College pupil. The young people have our best wishes for a happy married life.

W. T. WALTERS.

Secretary of State, Franklin K. Lane, has resigned his position because he cannot remain in public office at his present salary.

A TRIBUTE TO A GOOD MAN

(From remarks of Dr. P. H. Fleming at the funeral of the late Capt. James A. Turrentine).

"Know ye not that there is a prince and a great man fallen in this day in Israel." II Sam. 3:38.

These are the words of king David regarding Abner, a man that he knew well, and for whom he wept and whose bier he followed to the tomb.

This man Abner for whom David wept and of whom he spoke, was not a perfect man. He had his foibles. He was human. But David knew him and he judged him to be a prince and a great man in Israel and so declared him to be.

Whatever Abner's past may have been he was doing at that time what no other man in all Israel could do to end civil war and establish the throne of David. He was on the eve of negotiating a peace when he fell with the tribes of Israel that stood aloof from David.

I come to speak to you my friends, to-day of a man who was not perfect—there has never been but one perfect man, and that was Jesus Christ whom this man of whom I speak loved and followed.

I knew the man of whom I am speaking, and I declare unto you in the language of king David, that a prince and a great man has fallen this day.

Time and words would fail me to tell of the fields wherein he wrought and the valiant deeds done in home, church, civil and military life.

In the home he was kind and loving. He was a devoted husband and a kind and considerate father.

In church he was a prince among men in his love and devotion to the cause of Christ and his duty to God and man.

In civil life he held many places of trust and honor. He was a good citizen and a friendly neighbor. He delighted to "dwell by the side of the road and be a friend to man."

In military life he was a brave and good soldier. He fought on the side of the Southern Confederacy; but when the "Stars and Bars" waned and fell at Appomattox, and the "Stars and Stripes"

with him then. Today I weep for him because I shall see him no more on this
earth; but to him and to us all behind
these clouds of sorrow the sun still shines.

To him each tomorrow held something
better than today. To him every cloud
had a "silver lining;" and thus he marched on toward the sunset hour with a firm
belief that in the evening time it would
be light and that beyond the darkness and
the blackness of death, loomed eternal
light and life.

Who did not love him and whom did he
not love? To the county home, the jail
and the convict camp together we have
often gone on mercy and love's errands.
Into the home of sickness and death together we have stood. But it mattered
not where nor on what errand bent, there
was always love in the heart and in the
deed. There was "no mourning of the
bar" when he "put out to sea."

As he grew old and feeble, I have watched his steps and I have often met him
here and there and paused for a word.
We were loth to part. I noticed that he
was bending physically before the storm,
and I knew that autumn must be near.
And as he older grew, I saw another
thing, that he grew more like a little child
in sincerity, simplicity, faith, hope and
love and trust—more like the Master—and
I said he will soon be going home—and
he has gone. Gone to be with God the
Father; gone to be with Jesus the bless-

Be patient with us, dear friends.
Because your article has not appeared does not mean that we cannot use
it but only means that the nature of
it was such that it would do to hold.
The best of things keep the longest.

The students at Elon College have
started a college publication, the title
of which is *Maroon and Gold*, the
college colors. It is a 4-column, eight
page paper and is to be issued weekly. The price is $1.00 per year. We
will have more to say about it later.

Dr. J. P. Barrett's permanent ad-
dress is 1020 Park Place, Columbus,
Ga. This is the parsonage location.
Dr. and Mrs. Barrett were pounded
December 11, the date of their oc-
cupying the parsonage.

Pastors will do us a favor by being
brief with their marriage notes during the holidays. We are crowded
for space. By the time this issue
reaches the public we will have more
matter in type and on hand than we
can possibly use in the first issue of
the New Year.

Many articles had to be left out
this week. We had more matter than
we had space, and have had for some

We covet the continued co-operation of our subscribers during 1920.

Calendar 1920